The Grove Encyclopedia of Classical Art and Architecture

The Grove Encyclopedia of

Classical Art and Architecture

Volume II

Macedonia to Zygouries

Edited by

GORDON CAMPBELL

OXFORD
UNIVERSITY PRESS

OXFORD
UNIVERSITY PRESS

Oxford University Press, Inc., publishes works that further
Oxford University's objective of excellence
in research, scholarship, and education.

Oxford New York
Auckland Cape Town Dar es Salaam Hong Kong Karachi
Kuala Lumpur Madrid Melbourne Mexico City Nairobi
New Delhi Shanghai Taipei Toronto

With offices in
Argentina Austria Brazil Chile Czech Republic France Greece
Guatemala Hungary Italy Japan Poland Portugal Singapore
South Korea Switzerland Thailand Turkey Ukraine Vietnam

Published by Oxford University Press, Inc.
198 Madison Avenue, New York, NY 10016
www.oup.com

Library of Congress Cataloging-in-Publication Data

The Grove encyclopedia of classical art and architecture / edited by Gordon Campbell.
p. cm.
Includes bibliographical references and index.
ISBN 978-0-19-530082-6 (acid-free paper)
1. Art, Classical--Encyclopedias.
2. Architecture, Classical--Encyclopedias.
I. Campbell, Gordon, 1944-
II. Title: Encyclopedia of classical art and architecture.
N5610.G76 2007
722'.8003--dc22
2007000487

1 3 5 7 9 8 6 4 2

Printed in the United States of America
on acid-free paper

Contents

The Grove Encyclopedia of Classical Art and Architecture

M

Macedonia. Region in northern Greece between the Aegean Sea and Balkan massif. Its location, climate and natural resources fostered the development of a distinctive culture but also attracted invaders and settlers. Alone of the provinces of Greece, it provides fertile, well-watered plains, cut by the great rivers Haliakmon, Axios and Strymon, and mountains rich in mineral resources, such as the gold of Mt Pangaion. The Mediterranean climate of Chalkidike encourages widespread olive production while, inland, cereals are widely cultivated and there is good grazing for cattle and sheep. From the Classical period (*c.* 480–323 BC), if not earlier, the surplus cereal production of the lowlands and the abundant shipbuilding timber of the hills were the envy of those in the south of Greece. Good harbours provide easy access to the trade routes of the eastern Mediterranean while the river valleys and mountain passes leading west, north and north-east allow good routes of communication.

Around 6000 BC a new way of life was established in Greece, based on cereal agriculture and stock raising. Villages in Macedonia such as NEA NIKOMEDIA are some of the earliest Neolithic settlements known in Europe. The pottery vessels, stone tools and clay figurines found here have parallels at early farming villages in the (former Yugoslav) Republic of Macedonia and Serbia as well as Albania—a clear indication that the new techniques were passed on to south-east Europe from Macedonia. Bronze tools first appeared around 2500 BC, but their use in Macedonia was not accompanied by the widespread economic success and social change apparent in southern Greece and the Cyclades.

A thousand years later a more sophisticated society had developed in central Macedonia. Here the landscape is dotted with small steep-sided settlement mounds which were fortified centres, each serving as the focal point for a community scattered in the surrounding landscape. At Assiros, for example, the well-planned buildings within the walls included granaries holding vast stores of wheat and barley. One room alone is estimated to have contained over 10 tons of cereals, enough to feed ten families for a year. The total of stored crops was far more than that needed for the number of people who could have lived on the summit of the mound (perhaps between 50 and 100 adults) and must have provided a reserve for the whole community. At Assiros and many other sites influence from southern Greece is shown by imported Mycenaean pottery and its local imitations, while locally made incised ware shows regular contact with the peoples living in the lower Danube valley.

At the end of the Bronze Age (*c.* 1000 BC) social and economic change occurred throughout Greece following the destruction of the Mycenaean palatial centres. In Macedonia these processes were gradual. The small mounds with tightly packed buildings were abandoned for more spacious sites, perhaps to bring the whole community within a single defensible perimeter. Although new styles of decoration were used on pottery, there is little to support theories of invasion by northern peoples, sometimes equated with the Dorians of Classical tradition.

Numerous Iron Age tombs provide further evidence of Macedonian civilization. Cemeteries near the coast at Dion and Torone have yielded many examples of southern Greek style Protogeometric pottery (in museums at DION and Polygyros) which represent the first tentative colonial movement from the south. Local forms predominated inland at Aigai (Vergina) and on the island of Thasos. Prosperity, especially from the 8th century BC onwards, is shown by bronze ornaments such as armbands, figure-of-eight brooches and cast pendants in the form of globes, vases, birds and other shapes. Such objects are commonly found in burials in Macedonia and the western Balkans but in southern Greece are only found at sanctuary sites.

By the early 7th century BC Greek colonies such as Pydna, Mende, Torone and Thasos allowed a much closer relationship to develop between Macedonia and southern Greece. These contacts are illustrated by abundant imports of pottery and other goods, even including decorated clay coffins from Klazomenai (Thessaloniki, Archaeol. Mus.) in Asia Minor. The colony on THASOS, which also controlled the neighbouring part of the mainland, exploited sources of gold on the island and on Mt Pangaion to become one of the wealthiest Greek cities in the northern Aegean. Cemeteries at Sindos, Ayia Paraskeve and Amphipolis all illustrate the wealth of Macedonia at this period. At Sindos, in particular, the gold panned from the River Gallikos enabled the inhabitants to acquire elaborate gold jewellery, probably of southern manufacture, bronze helmets, high-quality Athenian pottery vases and fine glass bottles (artefacts in Thessaloniki,

Archaeol. Mus.). They often furnished their dead with gold face masks and model tables, chairs and carts.

This wealth even attracted the interest of Darius, King of Persia (*reg* 521–486 BC). During his campaigns against the Scythians (*c.* 513 BC), Darius' commander, Megabazus, gained control of the area between the Strymon and the Axios and, according to Herodotus (*Histories* V.xvii), received the submission of the Macedonian king, Amyntas, since his son, Bubares, was married to Amyntas' daughter. About this time silver coins were minted in large numbers in central Macedonia, particularly at Liti, and found their way eastward across the Persian Empire, some as far as Afghanistan. Inland Macedonia still had a tribal organization in contrast to the colonial city-states on the coast, and the king of the Macedonians was only one of many local rulers between the Pindos mountains in the west and the River Nestos in the east. The dispute about the 'Greekness' of the Macedonians was already in existence since Amyntas' son Alexander I (*reg c.* 495–450 BC) had to prove his Argive descent when entering for the Olympic games. Their original language was probably a dialect of Greek.

The dynastic marriage between Amyntas' daughter and the Persian noble was a critical factor in the increasing domination of northern Greece by the Macedonian kings, whose traditional capital was at AIGAI (ii) (Vergina). The Thracians, who formerly had inhabited the whole area east of the Axios valley, were pushed steadily eastwards. Alexander I, however, was not slow to oppose the Persians when the time was right and to annex the areas that Xerxes abandoned when his army retreated from Greece in 478 BC. From this point on, the power of the king of Macedon was an important factor in the delicate balance between the Greek cities of the south, particularly Athens and Sparta, who sought to expand their influence amongst the colonies on the Macedonian coast.

Following the defeat of Athens at the end of the Peloponnesian War (404 BC), Olynthos in Chalkidike and Amphipolis at the mouth of the River Strymon took a leading role in opposing the ambitions of the Macedonian kings. Macedonia was no longer on the fringe of the Greek world but home to every aspect of Greek culture. At OLYNTHOS excavation has revealed the grid plan of a thriving town with spacious mosaic-floored houses, together with a host of objects that illustrate everyday life in Greece at the beginning of the 4th century BC.

With the accession of Philip II (*reg* 359–336 BC), a vigorous and talented general, as king of Macedonia, the balance of power changed. One by one the Greek city-states were brought under Philip's control. The new Macedonian capital of PELLA (ii) became a focus of political and artistic activity. Here, for a time, the philosopher Aristotle acted as tutor to Philip's son, the young Alexander the Great. Excavations have uncovered the large agora (200×180 m) and the palace on the acropolis hill as well as splendid town houses with internal porticos and superb mosaic floors.

By 336 BC Philip's generals were poised to challenge the Persians in Asia itself, but before the campaign could begin, Philip was murdered near the theatre at Aigai during the ceremonies to celebrate the marriage of his daughter. Even though he had been murdered, he received a lavish burial at Aigai. The barrel-vaulted tomb had a painted façade and contained gold burial chests, armour and weapons, as well as a profusion of bronze and silver vessels.

ALEXANDER THE GREAT first had to secure his throne, then his control of Greece, before he too was free to turn eastwards and to complete his father's plans—and to outstrip them beyond the bounds of imagination. The conquests of Asia Minor, Babylonia, Egypt and the lands of the Indus Valley followed one after the other. In 13 years he gained a vast empire and then died without securing any succession. For the next 150 years Alexander's successors fought each other to gain a larger share of this empire. The noble families built elaborate tombs which were covered with tumuli and filled with rich offerings (see MACEDONIAN TOMB and LEUKADIA). By the beginning of the 2nd century BC the Romans began to encroach on the eastern Mediterranean. When they defeated Perseus, the last King of Macedon (*reg* 179–168 BC), at Pydna in 168 BC, they carried off much of the wealth of the nobles, and Macedonia became rather a backwater in the Roman Empire.

The strategic importance of Macedonia reappeared as the Roman Empire became more oriented towards its eastern provinces. The Via Egnatia, starting at Dyrrhachion on the Adriatic coast, crossed the mountains to reach the Aegean at Thessaloniki, and thence followed the coast eastwards. In eastern Macedonia the armies of Mark Antony and Octavian (later Augustus), controlling Italy and the West, met in the plain of Philippi with those of Julius Caesar's murderers, Brutus and Cassius, who had the support of the eastern legions. For the moment, the outcome assured the supremacy of the West, but the contest was regularly replayed between rival contenders for imperial power. Three and a half centuries later the Emperor Galerius (*reg* AD 305–11) saw in the thriving city of THESSALONIKI a base for his rule over the Empire. Here he erected the great arch commemorating his victories over the Persians and built his palace and mausoleum: he persecuted Christians savagely, including the patron of Thessaloniki, St Demetrius. After his death Constantine (*reg* AD 306–37) gained sole power, Christians ceased to be persecuted, and the capital moved east to Constantinople.

N. G. L. Hammond, G. T. Griffith and F. W. Walbank: *A History of Macedonia*, 3 vols (Oxford, 1972–87)

M. B. Sakellariou, ed.: *Macedonia: 4000 Years of Greek History and Civilization* (Athens, 1983)

Sindos: Katalogos tis ekthesis [Sindos: catalogue of the exhibition] (exh. cat. by I. B. Vokotopoulou and others, Thessaloniki, Archaeol. Mus., 1985)

G. Jones and others: 'Crop Storage at Assiros', *Sci. Amer.* (March 1986), pp. 96–103

Ancient Macedonia (exh. cat., Melbourne, Mus. Victoria, 1988) [excellent plates]

R. Ginouvès: *Macedonia from Philip II to the Roman Conquest* (Athens, 1993)

I. Vokotopoulou: *Les Macédoniens: Les grecs du nord et l'époque d'Alexandre le Grand* (Athens, 1995)
P. M. Fraser: *Cities of Alexander the Great* (Oxford, 1996)
E. N. Borza: *Before Alexander: Constructing Early Macedonia* (Claremont, CA, 1999)
D. V. Grammenos: *Recent Research in the Prehistory of the Balkans* (Thessaloniki, 2003)

well as the most expensive, type of burial structure in Macedonian culture, catering for the local élite. Owing to the military organization of Macedonian society, the emphasis on military life and ideology in the tombs' decorative programmes, such the frieze from the tomb at Ayios Athanasios, is not surprising.

2. Morphology and construction. Macedonian tombs were commonly built substantially below ground, often cut into the bedrock. Often several tombs were constructed adjacent to each other, under individual tumuli, then united under a single one. A dromos (passageway) provided access to their entrance; these were often stone-built or made of sun-dried brick, covered by a flat or vaulted roof. Sometimes these passages were merely cut into the surrounding earth or bedrock.

The tombs were normally built of ashlar masonry and local limestone (very exceptionally of marble). In some cases parts of the walls were carved out of living bedrock surrounding the tomb, a practice reminiscent of the rock-cut tombs widely used in Thrace and Illyria at about the same period. Thrace has several good examples of the rock-cut type, namely those from Kazanluk and Sverhtari (both in present-day Bulgaria), while the Illyrian chamber-tombs (present-day Albania) are also similar. All visible wall surfaces, but especially the façade, were usually covered with white plaster and painted in vivid colours. The floors are paved with stone slabs, often plastered and painted (red being the colour of choice); although in some cases the floor is made of stone-packed earth, also covered with plaster and painted. The ceiling is either vaulted or flat, and is also usually covered with plaster and painted in a single colour, most commonly yellow.

Although Macedonian tombs are easily distinguishable, there is a great typological diversity among the individual examples: the burial chamber may be square or rectangular, and examples vary in size and proportions; the chamber is often preceded by a smaller antechamber, although there does not seem to have existed a consistent pattern in proportion or orientation. The embellished façades are independent aesthetic and structural elements, while the entry to the tomb, an opening on the front wall, is often furnished with double-leafed doors made of wood, stone or (normally) marble; sometimes a second door leads to the main chamber.

3. Decoration. The decoration of the façades is quite diverse, ranging from very simple to extravagantly elaborate. Some examples feature fully-fledged architectural orders, Doric (Ayios Athanasios), Ionic (Langada), or even double-tiered combinations of both (e.g. the 'Great Tomb' at Leukadia: an Ionic top storey over a Doric lower storey). The purpose of the façade is to convey for the benefit of the viewer the impression of a real building. It is often thought that these fronts mimic temple façades or porticos, or even monumental gateways to sanctuaries (*propylaia*), depending on the particular significance, funerary or otherwise, one wishes to assign to them. However, lack of further evidence renders any firmer interpretation impossible.

Macedonian tomb. A distinctively Macedonian type of monumental chamber-tomb, consisting of a built chamber roofed with a barrel-vault, sometimes also preceded by an antechamber, and covered by an earth tumulus. The type emerged some time in the 4th century BC, and was widely used in Macedonia and its sphere of influence well into the Hellenistic period (323–27 BC).

Inhumations and cremations were practised contemporaneously in Macedonia, and are often found in the same tomb; it seems that the choice was a matter of personal preference or family tradition. Cremated remains were deposited inside a chest (larnax) made of stone, metal or wood, or a metal or clay hydria (water-jug). The tombs were furnished with couches, thrones, stools, chests, tables, benches etc reproducing actual interiors. The furniture presumably had a practical as well as symbolic role as it may have been used in funerary rituals. Movable offerings were also deposited to accompany the deceased in the afterlife, offering a glimpse into a world of skilful extravagance and sophisticated luxury.

Macedonian tombs are often embellished with monumental façades, mimicking temples or propylaia (gateways). Among the best-known examples of the type are the tombs at Aigai (ii) (Vergina; Andronikos), the tomb at Ayios Athanasios, near Thessaloniki (Tsibidou-Avloniti), the Tomb of Lyson and Kallikles at Leukadia (Miller), and—the grandest of all—the Tomb of Judgement (or 'Great Tomb'), also at Leukadia (Petsas). Next to these grand examples, many more plain ones have been discovered, often embellished with nothing but some elementary ornaments.

1. Origins and chronology. 2. Morphology and construction. 3. Decoration.

1. Origins and chronology. The chronology of the Macedonian tomb as an architectural type is quite problematic, as it does not present a linear or coherent morphological development. It seems that the appearance of individual examples and their degree of architectural or decorative development or accomplishment depends on other factors. Based on the attribution of the tombs at Aigai (Vergina) to Philip II and his family (an identification that remains, however, highly debated), it seems that the type appeared slowly after the mid-4th century BC and that it remained in use for the next two centuries or so.

The origin of the type is also a matter of speculation: some scholars see the possibility of external influence, while others prefer to see it as a strictly local emergence, defined by local needs and ideologies. What remains certain, however, is that the Macedonian tomb was the most lavish and sophisticated, as

The painted decoration of the interior also presents great variety. The antechamber and the main burial chamber often reproduce the architectural embellishment of the façade, while in some examples (such as the extravagant Tomb of Eurydice at Aigai (Vergina)) the wall paintings strive to create the illusion of a three-dimensional architectural background, like a stage set, viewed 'beyond' the back wall of the tomb. After the funeral, most tombs were decorated with garlands, wreaths and items of military equipment, which were hung on pegs provided on the walls of the tomb. Several examples exist where painted substitutes for these items were created, so as to create the illusion of these items hanging on the walls. The general impression of these decorated chambers is that of a banquet hall, presumably alluding to the deceased's passing to the afterlife. The allusion to banqueting is made explicit at the Ayios Athanasios Tomb, which has a frieze of that subject above its doorway (Tsibidou-Avloniti, pl. 22–3). The frieze, 35 cm in height, depicts in its central part six symposiasts on banqueting couches surrounded by furniture and other symposiac paraphernalia; a group of three men approaching on horseback are seen on the left, and eight youthful warriors in Macedonian garb are depicted on the right. This scene is a rarity in the Macedonian context, compared to the numerous examples elsewhere (such as the Tomb of the Diver at Paestum); similar banquet scenes are featured on relief friezes on the façades of rock-cut tombs in Lycia from the 4th century BC.

M. Andronikos: *Vergina: The Royal Tombs and the Ancient City* (Athens, 1984)

M. Andronikos: 'Some Reflections on the Macedonian Tombs', *BSA,* lxxxii (1987), pp. 1–16

S. G. Miller: *The Tomb of Lyson and Kallikles: A Painted Macedonian Tomb* (Mainz, 1993)

M. Andronikos: *Vergina II: The 'Tomb of Persephone'* (Athens, 1994)

P. G. Themelis and J. P. Touratsoglou: *The Derveni Tombs* (Athens, 1997) [in Greek, with extensive summary in English, pp. 192–224]

M. Tsibidou-Avloniti: 'Excavating a Painted Macedonian Tomb near Thessaloniki: An Astonishing Discovery', *Excavating Classical Culture: Recent Archaeological Discoveries in Greece*, eds M. Stamatopoulou and M. Yeroulanou (Oxford, 2002), pp. 91–7

Macellum [Gr. makellon: 'enclosure'; Lat.: 'food market']. Type of enclosed market built in ancient Rome. Fish, meat and other perishable foods were sold there. Although the term is derived from the Greek word *makellon*, it was first used to signify this type of market by the Romans. As a building type the macellum is probably a Roman adaptation of the Greek commercial agora, although it has also been suggested that its origins are Punic. Such buildings as the 4th-century BC North Agora at Miletos, which was a rectangular space completely surrounded by porticos and shops, separated from the rest of the agora, are likely forerunners. In ancient Greece, as in Rome, such markets were designed to segregate unsightly food stalls from an increasingly monumental civic centre. In Rome the first macellum was built in the 3rd century BC, on a site in the Forum Romanum later covered by the eastern portion of the Basilica Aemilia and part of the Temple of Antoninus and Faustina. After the construction of the Basilica Aemilia (179 BC), a new macellum was built by M. Fulvius Nobilior slightly to the north, on the site later occupied by the Templum Pacis. In the later 2nd century BC macella were built at Pompeii, Morgantina and Alatri, and in the 1st century BC at other towns such as Alba Fucens and Ostia. The third macellum in Rome, the Macellum Liviae, built by Augustus (*reg* 27 BC–AD 14) on the Esquiline Hill, comprised an elongated rectangular area (80×25 m) surrounded probably on all four sides by porticos and shops. In AD 59 Nero inaugurated the largest of all macella, the Macellum Magnum, on the Caelian Hill; it measured about 93×70 m according to a fragment of the Severan marble plan of Rome. Coins show it to have been surrounded by a two-storey portico in the middle of which was a large tholos covered by a cupola. During the 2nd century AD many new macella were built in the interior of Italy, while older ones were rebuilt. The earliest macellum in North Africa was that at Leptis Magna (9–8 BC; see fig.), but the prosperity of the 2nd and 3rd centuries AD resulted in the building of many new markets in that region, such as those at Hippo Regius, Thuburbo Maius and Cuicul (Djemila).

Macella vary considerably in layout. The simplest are square in plan with shops and porticos on all four sides and a tholos in the middle. This type, which most closely resembles the Greek commercial agora, is particularly common in Anatolia, for example at Perge (2nd century AD), although the macellum at Cuicul in Algeria is also of this type. A related type has shops on only three sides, the fourth side forming the main entrance to the complex. Examples from the 2nd century AD occur at Viroconium, Thuburbo Maius and Hippo Regius. A third type of macellum is axially planned with an entrance on one side and opposite it a set of rooms of particular significance. The macellum at Pompeii follows this layout: on the side opposite the entrance are three rectangular rooms, all richly marbled, the central one built like a temple and containing an imperial statue. In some cases the central room was apsidal, as at Thugga (Dougga; AD 54, with later alterations), Paestum and Bulla Regia (both late 2nd century AD or early 3rd) and PUTEOLI (late 1st century AD). The macellum at Puteoli was an exceptionally large building (75×58 m) and may have been influenced by the Macellum Magnum of Nero. A variant of this type, frequently found in North Africa, comprised a rectangular enclosure with a hemicycle of shops at the end opposite the main entrance. This layout is found at Gigthis (mid-2nd century AD) and in the two markets at Thamugadi (both early 3rd century AD), although the central market there has two hemicycles of shops instead of one. The macellum at Leptis Magna is unusual in consisting of a rectangular peristyle enclosure surrounding two large tholoi. Finally, several towns in central Italy, such as Herdonia and Aeclanum, have a distinctive type of macellum with the shops arranged around a circular courtyard (both 2nd century AD). The macellum of Alba Fucens was rebuilt on a similar plan in the 2nd century

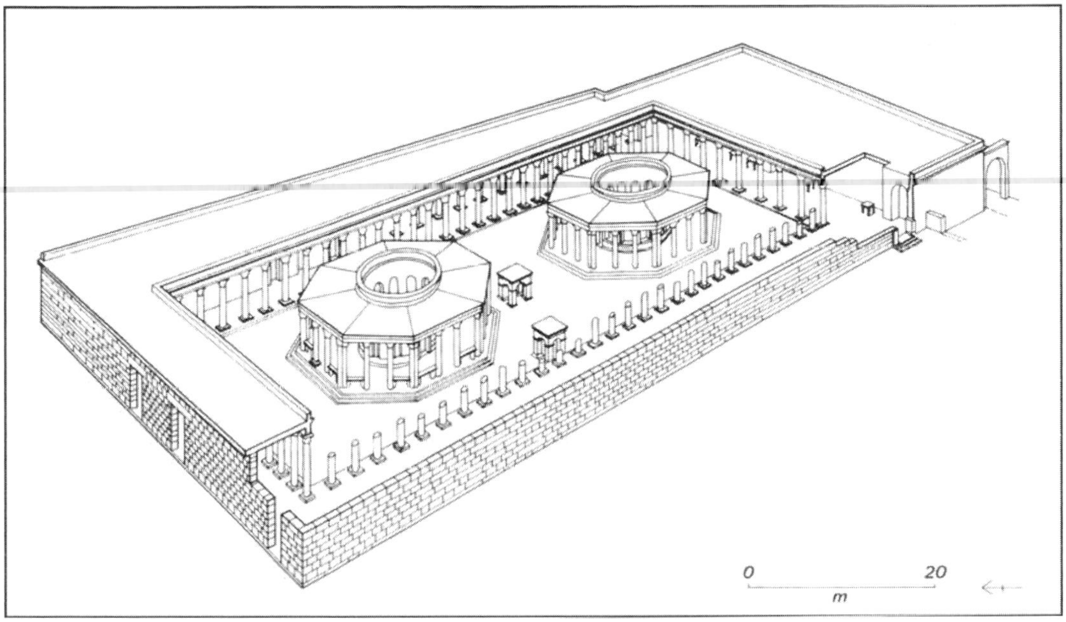

Macellum, Leptis Magna, 9–8 BC; surrounding porticos, AD 31–7; reconstruction

AD; a variant of this plan, with a hexagonal courtyard, can be seen at Saepinum (2nd century AD or later).

J. S. Rainbird, J. Sampson and F. B. Sear: 'A Possible Description of the Macellum Magnum of Nero', *Pap. Brit. Sch. Rome*, xxxix (1971), pp. 40–46

N. Nabers: 'The Architectural Variations of the Macellum', *Opuscula Romana*, ix (1973), pp. 173–6

C. De Ruyt: 'L'Importance de Pouzzoles pour l'étude du macellum romain', *Puteoli: Studi di storia antica*, i (Naples, 1977), pp. 128–39

N. Nabers: 'The Roman Macellum: The Archaeological Evidence and the Written Evidence', *J. Field Archaeol.*, iv (1977), p. 262

C. De Ruyt: *Macellum: Marché alimentaire des Romains* (Leuven, 1983) [with cat. of sites and useful bibliogs]

F. Didierjean, C. Ney and J.-L. Paillet: *Le macellum*, iii of *Belo* (Madrid, 1986)

P. Ellis: *The Roman Baths and Macellum at Wroxeter: Excavations by Graham Webster 1955–85* (London, 2000)

N. Birkle, ed.: *Macellum: Culinaria archaeologica: Robert Fleischer zum 60. Geburtstag von Kollegen, Freunden und Schülern* (Mainz, 2001)

Macmillan Painter [Chigi Painter] (*fl c.* 660–*c.* 640 BC). Greek vase painter. Active in Corinth, he is named after the aryballos found there and presented by Malcolm Macmillan in 1889 to the British Museum (see fig.). He is also known as the Chigi Painter after the Chigi Jug (Rome, Villa Giulia, 22679; see colour pl. 1:XIV, fig. 2), which was exported to Veii in Etruria. He was a leading painter in the Proto-Corinthian style (*see* POTTERY, §IV, 4(ii)), specializing in the decoration of ovoid aryballoi (containers of perfumed oil). Despite the small size of these vessels

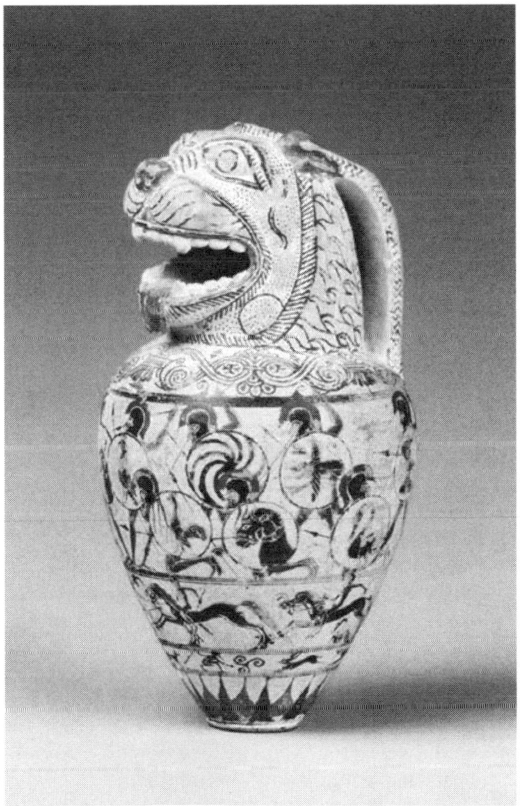

Macmillan Painter (attrib.): aryballos with lion-head mouth, Second Black-figure style, h. 68 mm, Middle Proto-Corinthian, *c.* 640 BC (London, British Museum, 1889.4-18.1)

(average h. 70 mm), there are several zones of surface decoration on the body, including an Orientalizing floral design on the shoulder, solid rays round the base, a main figured central zone and one or more subsidiary figured friezes below. The main scene exploits to the utmost the newly devised Black-figure technique of incised silhouette, which allowed the overlapping of figures in closely knit compositions without any loss of clarity (*see* POTTERY, §IV, 5). Often he varies the usual colour scheme by applying different shades of brown for human flesh and body armour, in addition to the purplish-red normally used for minor details.

This painter's aryballoi belong to the second half of the Middle Proto-Corinthian phase (mid-7th century BC), and the earliest examples bear mythical representations. On one vase, Berlin 2686 (Berlin, Antikensamml.), four centaurs collapse under a shower of arrows from Herakles' bow. Another (Boston, Mus. F.A., 95.10) shows Bellerophon with Pegasus, flying through the air to assail the fire-breathing Chimaera. The paintings on both these vases are rendered with vigour and *joie de vivre*; their backgrounds are packed with varied filling ornaments, which on the painter's more mature work are thinned out or omitted altogether. On later vases the scenes are confined to purely human conflict; tense battle scenes are wrapped round the main zones, with 18 hoplites (armed foot soldiers) on the Macmillan Aryballos and 21 on Berlin 3773 (Berlin, Antikensamml.); the warriors are equipped with the newly invented hoplite panoply. In both scenes, many different designs are emblazoned on the warriors' overlapping shields, as they endeavour to keep their ranks.

On three aryballoi the decoration breaks into the third dimension. The mouth of the Macmillan aryballos is modelled as a lion's head after the Neo-Hittite prototype: cubic, pug-like and benign. Similarly, three human heads in the Daedalic sculptural style, with Orientalizing layered wigs, surmount an aryballos in Taranto (Mus. N., 4173). Both leonine and human heads are combined on Berlin 3773, for which a tiny rampant lion serves as the handle.

The Macmillan Painter's latest work appears on a larger type of vessel, the olpe, the baggy, round-mouthed jug introduced in the Late Proto-Corinthian phase (*c.* 650–*c.* 640 BC). On the Chigi Vase, his finest work, the body carries two broad zones. Above, hoplite ranks are piped into battle by a child; the extraordinary realism of the drawing makes this scene an indispensable document for our understanding of early hoplite warfare. Below, several themes are juxtaposed: a sadly fragmentary scene of the *Judgement of Paris*, in which painted inscriptions name the figures; a double-bodied sphinx; a procession of horsemen, sometimes shown two abreast and distinguished by different colours; and a lion hunt in which the Assyrian type of lion, with heavy body, massive mane and a muzzle more pointed than in the Neo-Hittite examples, makes its first appearance in Greek vase painting.

The painter's subsidiary scenes are among his liveliest creations, showing him to be a virtuoso in miniature vase painting. Breaking away from conventional animal friezes, he specialized in horse races and hunts, brilliantly executed with a sense of rapid movement and an astonishing variety of detail, often in fields less than 10 mm high.

K. F. Johansen: *Les Vases sicyoniennes* (Paris, 1923), pp. 98–9

J. L. Benson: *Die Geschichte der korinthischen Vasen* (Basle, 1953), pp. 18–19

T. J. Dunbabin and C. M. Robertson: 'Some Protocorinthian Vase-painters', *Annu. Brit. Sch. Athens*, xlviii (1953), pp. 179–80

Macron. *See* MAKRON.

Mada'in Salih. Nabataean site in Saudi Arabia. The site, in the Hejaz *c.* 25 km north of al-'Ula, is chiefly remarkable for its funerary architecture (1st century AD). Treating the opening to the burial chamber as if it were the doorway to a building, the entrances to Nabataean tombs were decorated with both zoomorphic (e.g. lions, eagles) and architectural elements (e.g. curving pediments, architraves, rosettes, triglyphs, funerary urns, cornices, capitals). The doorway was then framed in a cleanly cut façade, flanked by engaged columns and topped by a series of cornices, often culminating in an inverted, stepped-pyramid frieze. In this way the tomb façade assumed the grandeur of a large, public building.

The rock face of Qasr al-Bint at Mada'in Salih contained twenty-three such tombs, while the smaller outcrop called Hreba contained thirteen and the Hremat outcrop contained at least four complete and one unfinished tomb. Unlike their counterparts at PETRA, the Nabataean tombs of Mada'in Salih are often characterized by the presence of a *tabula ansata*, frequently situated above the entrance to the tomb. This was a framed and recessed panel on which a Nabataean inscription was carved which, typically, named the builder of the tomb, the year of the entombed person's death and juridical conditions relating to the use of the tomb by members of the deceased's family and others.

In 1965 a stele incised with a Greek inscription was found in a well near the tombs; it was taken from Saudi Arabia but returned in 1999, and is now in the National Museum in Riyadh. The implication of the stele is that Mada'in Salih was a part of Roman Arabia. Additional evidence was found in 2003, when excavations revealed a paved courtyard with column bases, and a complete Latin inscription from the time of Marcus Aurelius (AD 161–180).

T. Barger: 'The Riddle of Meda'in Salih', *Archaeology*, xix (1966), pp. 217–19

T. Barger: 'Greek Inscription Deciphered: Seal Found in Arabia', *Archaeology*, xxiii (1969), pp. 139–40

G. Bowersock: *Roman Arabia* (Cambridge, MA, 1983)

J. F. Healey: *The Nabataean Tomb Inscriptions of Mada'in Salih* (Oxford, 1993)

P. Kesting: 'Well of Good Fortune', *Saudi Aramco World* (May–June, 2001), pp. 14–17

Magnesia on the Maeander [now Tekin]. Town in central Ionia (now western Turkey), which flourished in Hellenistic times. According to tradition, Magnesia was among the earliest Greek settlements in Anatolia and was founded by the Aeolians from Thessaly. In the 7th century BC it was captured by the Lydian king Gyges (*reg* 680–652 BC) and destroyed by the Cimmerians *c.* 650 BC. After being rebuilt with help from Miletos, it fell to the Persians *c.* 530 BC, and in 460 BC they presented it to the exiled Athenian general Themistokles. The exact location of this early city is uncertain, but in 400–398 BC the Spartan general Thibron transferred the settlement to its present site beside Mt Thorax (Gümüs Dagi), where the Archaic Sanctuary of Artemis Leukophryene stood. The reason for the transfer was to evade the silt carried down by the Maeander River. Although it retained its original name, the new settlement was not actually sited on the river but on its tributary, the Lethacus (Gümüs Çay), on an important road between Ephesos, Priene and Tralleis.

The city remained under Persian control until liberated by Alexander the Great in 334 BC. Subsequently, under Seleucid rule and later under the Attalids of Pergamon, it developed into an important centre renowned for its grain production. It was among the few Asiatic cities to side with Rome against Mithridates of Pontus in 87 BC. Consequently, in Roman times Magnesia was a free city that claimed, according to a 3rd-century AD coin, to rank seventh in Asia. From Byzantine times until the 12th century AD it was an episcopal seat. The site was first explored in 1842–3 and systematically excavated in 1891–93.

The fortified city measured 1300×1100 m, with a grid of streets precisely orientated north–south and east–west. The principal surviving monument is the Temple of Artemis (late 3rd century BC–early 2nd). According to Vitruvius (*On Architecture*, III.ii.6) this pseudo-dipteral Ionic building was designed by HERMOGENES and built on the remains of an Archaic Temple of Artemis. It faced west, like the temples at Ephesos and Sardis, and had an opisthodomos. Its 8 by 15 columns and nine stepped platform (67×41 m) made it the fourth largest temple in Asia Minor. The pronaos, with two internal columns and two *in antis*, was as big as the cella, which had six internal columns; the opisthodomos had two *in antis*. The temple's 200-m-long frieze depicting an *Amazonomachy* (Istanbul, Archaeol. Mus.; Paris, Louvre) appears to be the earliest figural frieze on the entablature of an Anatolian Ionic temple. The Attic column bases are also the earliest in Anatolia and were probably introduced by Hermogenes. In front of the temple stood a monumental altar of Pergamene type.

The replies of 70 cities invited to attend the festival of Artemis Leukophryene are recorded in inscriptions in Magnesia's agora, which covers some 26,000 sq. m, and in which stood a total of 420 columns as well as a propylon, a shrine of Athena and a fountain-house. There was also a small Ionic prostyle Temple of Zeus Sosipolis (early 2nd century BC; see fig.), also probably designed by Hermogenes.

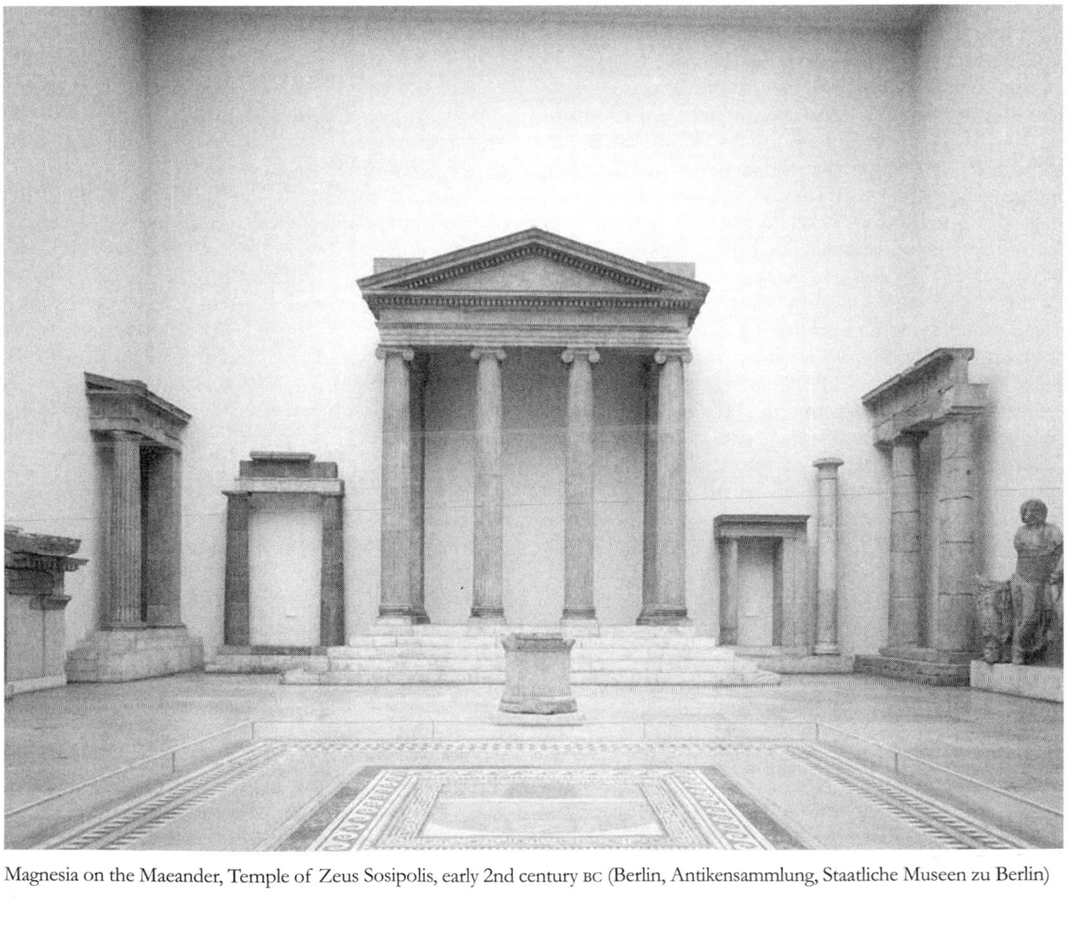

Magnesia on the Maeander, Temple of Zeus Sosipolis, early 2nd century BC (Berlin, Antikensammlung, Staatliche Museen zu Berlin)

The temple faces west and has an opisthodomos; its frieze is uncarved. Its columns have eustyle spacing, again attributed to Hermogenes (Vitruvius: III.iii. 6–8), with intercolumnar spaces of two and a quarter times the lower diameter. The agora, the Temple of Zeus and the theatre (4th century BC) are now covered by silt from the Gümüs Çay, so that only the remains of the Temple of Artemis, the Roman baths, odeion, gymnasium and stadium are visible.

C. Humann: *Magnesia am Maeander* (Berlin, 1904)

A. von Gerkan: *Der Altar des Artemis-Tempels in Magnesia am Mäander* (Berlin, 1929)

A. Yaylali: *Der Fries des Artemisions von Magnesia am Mäander* (Tübingen, 1976)

A. Davesne: *La Frise du Temple d'Artémis à Magnesie du Méandre* (Paris, 1982)

O. Bingöl: 'Zu den neueren Forschungen in Magnesia', *Hermogenes und die hochhellenistische Architektur*, ed. W. Hoepfner and Schwandner (1990), pp. 63–8

O. Bingöl: 'Vitruvische Volute am Artemis-Tempel von Hermogenes in Magnesia am Mäander', *Istanbul. Mitt.*, xliii (1993), pp. 399–415

O. Bingöl: *Menderes Magnesiasi/Magnesia ad Maeandrum* (Ankara, 1998)

O. Bingöl: *Theatron* (Istanbul, 2005) [Eng. trans. of *Magnesia ad Maeandrum* monograph]

Mahdia shipwreck. Source of a group of late 2nd-century BC Greek works of art. In 1907 an ancient shipwreck was located by sponge-divers in the waters off Mahdia on the east coast of Tunisia. The subsequent careful exploration of the ship and the lifting of its extensive cargo, carried out between 1908 and 1913, was the first operation of its kind in the Mediterranean. The principal cargo consisted of 60 marble columns, together with Ionic and Corinthian capitals, but also on board was a whole range of sculpture in both bronze and marble. The bronzes include an archaistic herm, a *Dancing Eros*, three grotesque dancing dwarfs (with suspension rings attached), statuettes of *Eros with a Lyre*, satyrs, *Hermes* and actors, two lamp holders in the form of an Eros and a Hermaphrodite, and various assorted appliqués, vessels, candelabra, lamps and couch attachments. The marbles, some badly corroded, include heads or busts of *Aphrodite*, *Artemis*, *Pan*, *Niobe* and a satyr and satyr-girl, as well as a statuette of *Artemis* and a partial torso of *Herakles*; in addition there were two marble kraters (large ornamental basins for garden furniture) with Dionysiac scenes, a candelabrum and four 4th-century BC Attic reliefs. With the exception of the last, which were being exported as 'antiques', the items were all new. The archaistic herm is signed by BOETHOS OF CHALKEDON and was probably made *c.* 130–120 BC. There are good grounds for regarding the rest of the bronzes as coming from the same workshop, probably situated in Athens, and the marbles were certainly manufactured there in a NEO-ATTIC workshop about the same time. Pottery from the Mahdia wreck indicates that the vessel sank *c.* 100 BC: it was presumably on its way from Athens to Rome when it met disaster. The extent of the craze of the upper classes in Republican Rome for collecting Greek works of art is known from excavations of villas such as the Villa of the Papyri at HERCULANEUM, as well as from literary sources such as Cicero's correspondence with Atticus, and the Mahdia shipwreck documents with especial clarity what must have been a booming industry and export trade for Greek sculptural workshops around the turn of the 2nd and 1st centuries BC. The finds are normally housed in Tunis (Mus. N. Bardo), but the bronzes were restored in the early 1990s in the Rheinisches Landesmuseum in Bonn, where they were the subject of a major temporary exhibition in 1993.

W. Fuchs: *Der Schiffsfund von Mahdia* (Tübingen, 1963)

Die bronzenen Zwergtänzer. In: Das Wrack—Der antike Schiffsfund von Mahdia (exh. cat. by S. Pfisterer-Haas; Bonn, Rhein. Landesmus., 1994)

Makron [Macron] (*fl* early 5th century BC). Greek vase painter. He has been ascribed over 350 vases, more than any other Athenian painter in the Red-figure technique. However, only one is certainly signed by him. Makron worked consistently with the potter Hieron, and of more than 30 signed works by Hieron almost all are painted by Makron. Most of the vessels are cups on tall stands, and the pictures inside these are always framed with a simple meander.

Like most vase painters, Makron may also have worked as a potter. Despite the large number of vases attributed to him, his work displays great unity. The *kalos* names correspond with those on later vases by DOURIS, suggesting that Makron worked prolifically over a short period, though a certain development can be perceived in his output.

Makron's drawing is generally less fine than Douris', but it developed rapidly, becoming richer and more decorative, more fluid and skilful, particularly in the representation of human proportions, especially in the case of women. A few pieces, mainly with mythological subjects, were thoughtfully composed and drawn in great detail. Typical features include heads with a flat skull-pan and deep eyebrows, and garments with carefully drawn and variably disposed drapery. There is sometimes a suggestion of fair hair in single locks, as well as rich figural decoration on clothing and other objects. Though Makron represented clothing with increasing virtuosity, the outlines of the body were always clearly stated—in the case of female figures in the transparently drawn *chiton*—forming the basis for the pictures. The composition of the tondi inside cups generally shows a unified conception and the outside decoration, made up of multi-figured friezes based on groups of two, has a balanced rhythm, with dancing and Dionysiac celebrations as frequent subjects. The outside and inside pictures are generally related thematically. Mythology does not feature largely in Makron's work: his preferred subjects were sport, banquets, dancing, scenes of Dionysiac revelry or worship, and erotic scenes, of which there are a great many,

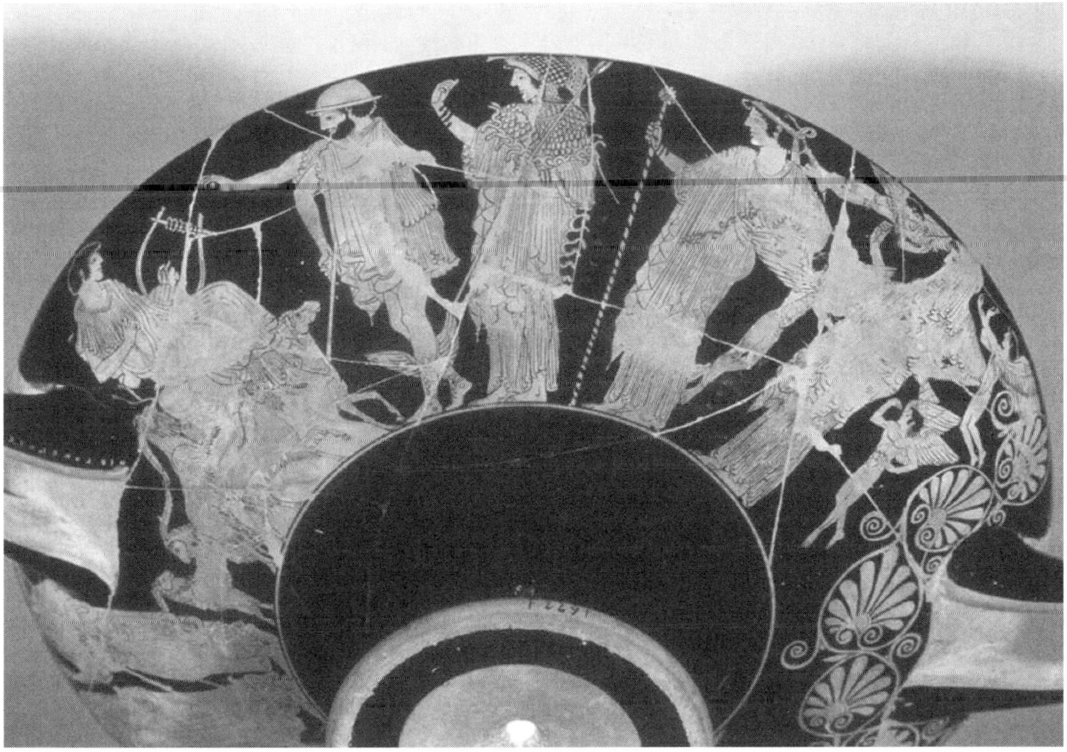

Makron: cup (detail) depicting the *Judgement of Paris,* Attic Red-figure, from Vulci, *c.* 485 BC (Berlin, Antikensammlung, Staatliche Museen zu Berlin, F 2291)

primarily rows of courting couples, more often both male than of mixed sex (see colour pl. 1:XIV, fig. 4). Among the mythological scenes, those involving the Trojans and their allies are prominent. Herakles also figures, as do Peleus and Thetis. Makron's masterpieces include a cup with the *Judgement of Paris* (Berlin, Antikensamml.; see fig.) and two exceptionally fine skyphoi, one showing *Helen with Paris* (and on the other side *Helen with Menelaus*), which carries the only unequivocal signature by Makron (Boston, MA, Mus. F.A.), and the other showing *Triptolemos among the Eleusinian Gods* (London, BM). Of the non mythological pieces, an aryballos depicting *Children with Toy Chariots* (Oxford, Ashmolean) deserves special mention.

Pupils of Makron in the second quarter of the 5th century BC probably included the Clinic Painter and the Telephos Painter. Their pictures are sometimes rather mannered, but they are more often humorous in effect than those of their teacher.

F. Leonard: *Über einige Vasen aus der Werkstatt des Hieron* (diss., U. Greifswald, 1912)

J. C. Hoppin: *A Handbook of Attic Red-figured Vases*, ii (Cambridge, MA, 1919), pp. 38–110

J. D. Beazley: *Red-figure* (1942, 2/1963), i, pp. 458–82; ii, 1654–5, 1706

L. D. Caskey and J. D. Beazley: *Attic Vase Paintings in the Museum of Fine Arts, Boston*, iii (London, 1963), pp. 30–31

J. D. Beazley: *Paralipomena* (1971), pp. 377–9

J. Boardman: *Athenian Red Figure Vases: The Archaic Period* (London, 1975), p. 140

G. Nachbaur: *Schalen des Makron aus der Werkstatt des Hieron* (diss., Graz, Karl-Franzens-U., 1978)

D. von Bothmer: 'Notes on Makron', *The Eye of Greece*, ed. J. Boardman and D. Kutz (Cambridge, 1982), pp. 13–26

L. Burn and R. Glynn: *Beazley Addenda: Additional References to* ABV, ARV2 *and* Paralipomena (Oxford, 1982, rev. T. H. Carpenter, 2/1989), pp. 243–7

M. Denouelles: 'Macron au Louvre', *Rev. Louvre*, xli (1991), no. 5–6, pp. 13–26

N. Kunisch: *Makron* (Mainz, 1997)

Mallia [Malia]. Minoan palace and town on Crete, which flourished *c.* 1900–*c.* 1425 BC. The palace stands on a small, fertile plain on the north coast of Crete, about 36 km east of Herakleion. It is relatively well preserved, and restoration has been kept to a minimum. While it is less elaborate than the Minoan palaces of Knossos and Phaistos it is nonetheless impressive. Excavations in the vicinity have revealed extensive remains of the town, while cemeteries have been found between the palace and the sea. The site was first excavated by Joseph Hazzidakis in 1915 and 1919. The French School of Archaeology in Athens took over in 1922, and by 1926 had effectively revealed the whole palace, although their programme of excavation and research has continued into the early 21st century. Important finds, including those cited below, are housed in the Archaeological Museum, Herakleion.

Evidence for Early Minoan (*c.* 3500/3000–*c.* 2050 BC) occupation at Mallia takes the form of traces of buildings beneath the palace and simple burials in the cemetery area, where natural fissures in the rock were used. The First Palace was constructed *c.* 1900 BC, but little survives, so that the visible remains belong mainly to the Second Palace, built in Middle Minoan (MM) IIIA (*c.* 1675–*c.* 1635 BC) after a major destruction. It may have followed the plan of the First Palace quite closely. The Second Palace survived until the end of Late Minoan (LM) IB (*c.* 1425 BC), when it was burnt in the wave of destructions that overwhelmed most Cretan sites.

Like the palaces of Knossos and Phaistos, the Second Palace at Mallia was constructed around an open-air central court orientated roughly north–south. It was built largely of local grey limestone and reddish sandstone, with extensive use of mud-brick. Architectural refinements common at Knossos and Phaistos, such as the use of thin gypsum slabs to cover walls and floors, are absent, giving it a more provincial air. Nonetheless, it had the state-rooms, storage areas, domestic and cult rooms typical of all the Minoan palaces, and traces of painted plaster show that some walls and floors were decorated, although no substantial wall paintings survive (see fig.).

The most carefully designed and constructed, and therefore probably the most important, group of rooms lies directly to the west of the central court. A spacious pillared hall may have had state or ceremonial functions. North of this the grand staircase led to an upper storey, which no longer survives, while further north is the so-called loggia, a room opening on to the central court, from which it is reached by four steps. The loggia is in a position analogous to that of the throne room at Knossos, and both may have had important religious functions. Finds in the room adjoining the loggia to the north-west included an elaborately carved schist axe in the form of a leopard and a bronze ceremonial sword with a rock-crystal pommel, perhaps offerings or religious paraphernalia of the Proto-Palatial (*c.* 1900–*c.* 1650 BC) or early Neo-Palatial (MM IIIA) periods.

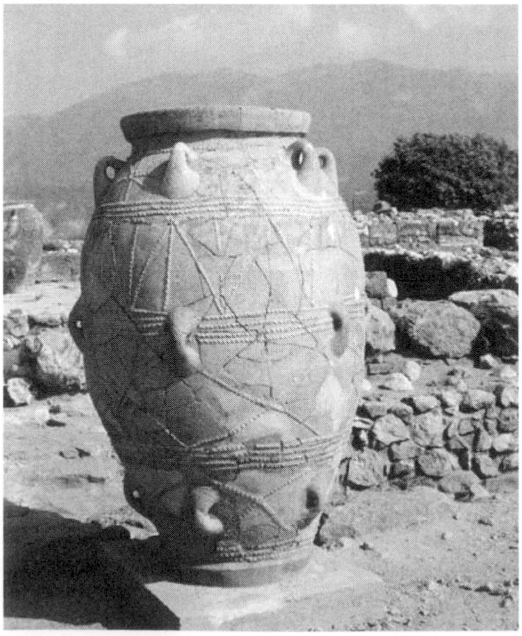

Mallia, giant storage vase from the palace, terracotta

The palace's vast stores were kept in rows of long, narrow magazines along its west and east sides and in eight circular granaries at its south-west corner. An elegant suite of apartments at the north-west has been identified as the principal residential quarters. They feature characteristic Minoan light wells to illuminate inner areas, as well as pier-and-door partitions that allowed rooms to be closed off in winter and open in summer. Two further ceremonial swords, one with the relief figure of an acrobat decorating its pommel, were found in this area (LM IA, *c.* 1600–*c.* 1480 BC).

On the north side of the central court is a large room with six square pillars, which perhaps served as a kitchen, beneath a pillared banqueting hall at first-floor level. Paved courtyards flanked the palace to the west and east, and the main approach was apparently the broad paved way leading to the central court from the south, although other entrances existed on all sides.

Impressive town houses of the Second Palace period have been found to the east, south and west of the palace, but the remains of the First Palace period town are more unusual. A series of semi-basement rooms and a large open courtyard directly to the north-west of the palace perhaps constituted a council chamber and assembly place. Extensive and elaborate mud-brick structures further to the west were probably connected in some way with the First Palace, since they contained elaborate reception rooms, large cult rooms and offices with a Linear A archive, and were adjoined by a seal-maker's workshop. Finally, to the north, in the area of the Minoan cemeteries, stands the stone-built Chrysolakkos ('pit of gold') complex, a curious structure perhaps used for funerary rituals and as an ossuary. From here came the famous gold pendant showing two bees or wasps around a granulated gold disc possibly representing a honeycomb (MM II, *c.* 1800–*c.* 1650 BC; see colour pl. 1:XII, fig. 2).

J. W. Graham: *The Palaces of Crete* (Princeton, 1962)
G. Cadogan: *Palaces of Minoan Crete* (London, 1980)
H. van Effenterre: *Le Palais de Mallia et la cité minoenne*, 2 vols (Rome, 1980)
O. Pelon and others: 'Mallia', *The Aerial Atlas of Ancient Crete*, ed. J. W. Myers, E. E. Myers and G. Cadogan (Berkeley, 1992), pp. 173–83
J.-C. Poursat and others: *Artisans Minoens: Les maisons-ateliers du Quartier Mu* (Athens, 1996)

Manastir. *See* HERAKLEIA LYNKESTIS.

Mannerist workshop (5th century BC). Greek vase painters. This group of over 15 Attic Red-figure vase painters, including the PAN PAINTER, worked throughout the 5th century BC, mainly decorating column kraters, hydriai and pelikai. Their rather affected style is characterized by tall, slender figures with small heads, and by the perpetuation of Archaic features. The latter include stacked pleats and groups of folds in garments, hanging lotus-bud chains and framed pictures on pelikai and the shoulders of hydriai, as well as subjects such as the *Draped Apollo Playing a Lyre* (e.g. on a column krater; Tarquinia, Pal. Vitelleschi, 684) and *Ajax and Achilles Playing a Board Game* (e.g. on a column krater; Berlin, Antikensamml. 3199).

The group frequently depicted revels and symposia and, later, domestic scenes. Some of their mythological scenes are unparalleled in Athenian vase painting: for example the *Madness of Salmoneus* (Chicago, IL, A. Inst., 89.16) and the *Death of Prokris* (London, BM, E 477), both on column kraters. On a pelike (Naples, Mus. Archeol. N., ex-Spinelli 2041) *Io* was depicted for the first time with a human body, under the influence of contemporary theatre.

The earliest members of the group, such as the Pig Painter and the Leningrad Painter, were taught by MYSON; it was later influenced by, among others, the NIOBID PAINTER and POLYGNOTOS and his group, the KLEOPHON PAINTER and the KADMOS PAINTER. One artist's signature survives, on an amphora (London, BM, E 284), revealing that a late group member, the Nausikaa Painter, was also called Polygnotos.

J. D. Beazley: *Red-figure* (1942, 2/1963), i, pp. 562–88, ii, pp. 1106–25

J. Boardman: *Athenian Red Figure Vases: The Archaic Period* (London, 1975)

L. Burn and R. Glynn: *Beazley Addenda: Additional References to* ABV, ARV2 *and* Paralipomena (Oxford, 1982, rev. T. H. Carpenter, 2/1989)

T. Mannack: *The Late Mannerists in Athenian Vase-Painting* (Oxford, 2001)

Marathon. Narrow coastal plain hemmed in by mountains in south-east central Greece, which was densely occupied during the entire Bronze Age, especially in the west near the mountain passes connecting it to the rest of Attica. The region contains the remains of three known Early Helladic (EH) fortified settlements situated within 3 to 5 km of each other: Kato Souli to the east, Agriliki to the west and Plassi, the only one even partially excavated, on the coast between them. At Plassi a thick wall with a gate flanked by a tower enclosed a large Middle Helladic (MH) building covering cist graves of the same period and housing a pottery kiln at one end. About 2.5 km inshore, at Tsepi, lies an extensive EH cemetery of regularly aligned family cist graves, marked off by rows of stones and poorly furnished with imported Cycladic artefacts. Further west, near the entrance to the Vrana Valley, are four low MH tumuli (*c.* 8–17 m in diameter). They consist of an earth fill held in place by a low circular wall and overlaid with stones, and cover one-, two- or three-chambered cists lined and roofed with stone slabs and containing contracted burials dating from the late 17th to the 13th century BC. One such cist held the skeleton of a mutilated horse. The two largest and earliest tumuli include an inner stone ring surrounding the main burial. Finally a tholos tomb nearby (*c.* 1400 BC) has two burial shafts, which contained a gold cup and some pottery. Two sacrificed horses were also buried in the dromos. This pattern of occupation persisted into historical times engendering many local cults and legends. Later remains in the area include the tombs of the Athenians and Plataians killed at the battle of Marathon (490 BC) and the estate of Herodes Atticus (2nd century AD).

S. Marinatos: 'Anaskaphai Marathonos' [Excavations at Marathon], *Praktika Athen. Archaiol. Etaireias* (1970), pp. 5–28

S. Marinatos: 'Further News from Marathon', *Athens An. Archaeol.*, iii (1970), pp. 153–66

S. Marinatos: 'Further Discoveries at Marathon', *Athens An. Archaeol.*, iii (1970), pp. 349–66

S. Marinatos: 'Marathon', *Athens An. Archaeol.*, iii (1970), pp. 63–8

K. P. Kontorlis: *The Battle of Marathon: And the Recent Archaeological Discoveries Made There* (Athens, 1973)

B. Petrakos: *Marathon* (Athens, 1996) [in English]

Marseille. *See* MASSALIA.

Marsyas Painter (*fl* mid-4th century BC). Greek vase painter. He is among the better known of the KERCH STYLE painters and a late but accomplished practitioner of Attic Red-figure. His tall, slender figures combine frontal with three-quarter views and other parts of the body in profile, giving an impression of three-dimensionality. This is illustrated by a pelike showing *Peleus Abducting Thetis*, which also includes a three-quarter back view of a naked nymph running into the background, creating a sense of depth that was new to vase painting at the time. He is named after the depiction on a pelike (St Petersburg, Hermitage, KEK 8) of *Marsyas Awaiting his Fate*. The characteristic crispness and plasticity of the drapery of the Marsyas Painter's clothed figures may have been inspired by sculpture. Like many of his contemporaries he used white highlighting to emphasize certain figures and objects or to focus or balance his compositions. He also occasionally employed other colours, notably blue and red, to enhance clothing and erotes' wings, with gold for jewellery, erotes' wings and any details in relief. His fine, precise drawing recalls works by such predecessors as the Jena Painter, and his stylistic innovations contributed to the final flowering of Attic Red-figure.

K. Schefold: *Untersuchungen zu den Kertscher Vasen* (Berlin, 1934), pp. 127–31

J. D. Beazley: *Red-figure* (1942, 2/1963), ii, pp. 1474–76

E. Simon: *Die griechischen Vasen* (Munich, 1976, 2/1981), pp. 157–60

A. Lebel: *The Marsyas Painter and Some of his Contemporaries* (diss., Oxford U., 1989)

Martyrium [Gr. martyrion]. Term referring to a site that bears witness to the Christian faith, such as a significant event in the life and passion of Jesus, the tomb of a saint or martyr, and his or her place of suffering or testimony. It is also used to mean the structure erected over such a site. Monumental martyria form an important category of Early Christian architecture, and were built according to a variety of plans.

Martyrion is derived from the Greek *martys*, meaning witness in the legal sense, and first appears in the Septuagint as the evidence for something. By the mid-2nd century AD *martys* or martyr came to mean someone whose testimony was sealed with suffering and death for the Christian faith, and by *c.* 350 *martyrion* or martyrium was commonly used to refer to the location of a martyr's tomb and the commemorative shrine or church constructed over it. That it had also come to mean a place revered in the scriptures is implied by Eusebios' description (*c.* 337) of the Tomb of Christ as 'the venerable and most holy martyrium of the Saviour's resurrection'.

The earliest known martyrium is probably the shrine of St Peter, which was built in a courtyard of the Vatican Hill necropolis in the late 2nd century AD (see fig. 1). The aedicula in front of the niche apparently lay above the saint's tomb and was referred to as his *tropaeum*, the monument of his victory over death and paganism. Simple, open-air martyrial precincts were also set up on the Via Appia (honouring the festival of SS Peter and Paul) and in the Christian cemeteries in Bonn, Germany, and Salona (now Marusinac), Croatia. One martyrium below ground is the so-called Chapel of the Popes in the Catacombs of St Calixtus, Rome, which was modestly decorated by 250 and provided with an altar in the 4th century. Following pagan antecedents in *heroa* (heroes' shrines) and mausolea, these martyria were equipped with a *mensa* (table) for funeral banquets or *refrigeria* in honour of the deceased. After the Edict of Milan (AD 313), these celebrations assumed increased importance.

During the 4th century open-air precincts gave way to monumental martyria, as for example the Anastasius Mausoleum in SALONA (*c.* 305–10). This two-storey, apsed building sheltered the martyr's body below the apse, and the remainder of the crypt contained the tombs of the founders. The upper level served for memorial services and banquets, apparently with an altar above the martyr's tomb, thus establishing that a martyrium's purpose could be both 'evidential' and liturgical. The combination of these two aspects can be seen in several buildings in Rome, among the most impressive of which are the so-called cemetery basilicas outside the city walls. Those of St Lawrence on the Via Tiburtina (*c.* 330), SS Peter and Marcellinus on the Via Labicana (*c.* 324–36), and St Agnes on the Via Nomentana (337–50) were built near martyrs' tombs, while the Basilica Apostolorum (*c.* 313–37), later dedicated to St Sebastian, on the Via Appia, replaced the precinct martyrium of SS Peter and Paul. The most outstanding example, however, was the huge basilica of Old St Peter's (119×64 m; *c.* 319–29) built by Constantine to house the Apostle's shrine, which was marked by a baldacchino in the middle of the transept, opposite the eastern apse. Because of its size, the building was also accessible to large crowds of pilgrims and offered space for funeral services near the Apostle's tomb.

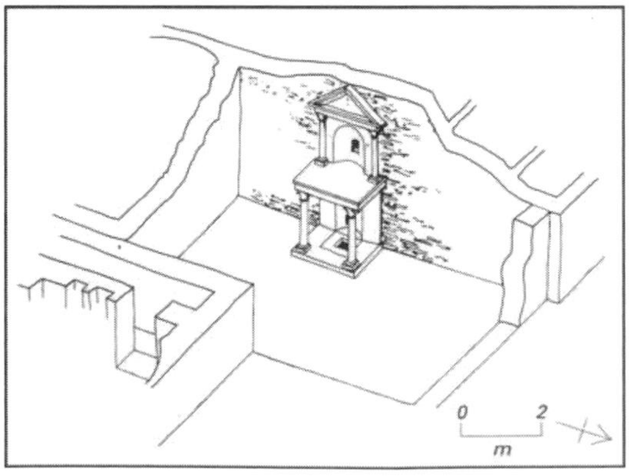

1. Martyrium, shrine of St Peter, St Peter's, Rome, late 2nd century AD; reconstruction drawing

Old St Peter's was the only one of Constantine's martyria (*see* CONSTANTINE THE GREAT) that actually enclosed a martyr's shrine. The others built by him commemorated holy places in Palestine and may be considered as the prototypes of martyria in the East. In each case the building's layout had to be adapted to the exigencies of the site. At Bethlehem (see fig. 2) the octagon enshrining the cave of the Nativity lay at the east end of a five-aisled basilica, while at Jerusalem a courtyard separated the basilica of the Holy Sepulchre (dedicated 336) from the rock of Calvary and the Anastasis (Resurrection) Rotunda, where the Sepulchre was housed. At Constantine's Eleona on the Mount of Olives, a different approach was adopted with the construction of a simple basilica above the cave where Christ taught the Apostles before the Ascension.

By the second half of the 4th century a custom had developed in the East of transporting or 'translating' relics from one place to another. The earliest recorded example is the removal of St Babylas' remains to Kaoussié, near Antioch (now Antakya), Syria, in 351–4. The bodies of SS Timothy, Andrew and Luke were brought to Constantinople in 356–7 by Emperor Constantius (*reg* 337–61) and placed in the cruciform church of the Holy Apostles, adjoining the circular mausoleum of Constantine. Thus any church, whether commemorative or parochial, could become a martyrium, and the possession of some relics became increasingly important for new foundations.

H. Leclercq: 'Martyrium', *Dictionnaire d'archéologie chrétienne et de liturgie*, ed. F. Cabrol and H. Leclercq, x/2 (Paris, 1932), pp. 2512–23

A. Grabar: *Martyrium: Recherches sur le culte des reliques et l'art chrétien antique*, 2 vols (Paris, 1943–6); review by R. Krautheimer in *A. Bull.*, xxxv (1953), pp. 57–61

R. Krautheimer: 'Mensa-Coemeterium-Martyrium', *Cah. Archéol.*, xi (1960), pp. 15–40

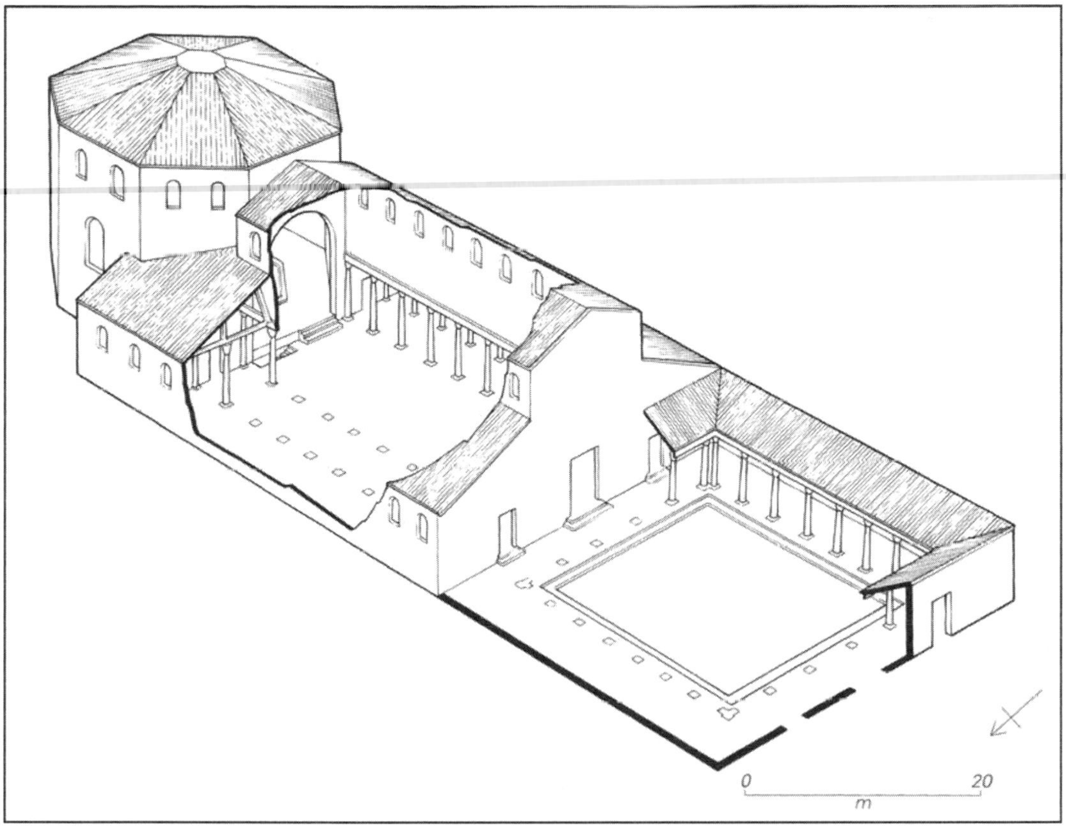

2. Martyrium, church of the Nativity, Bethlehem, AD 333; isometric reconstruction

R. Krautheimer: *Early Christian and Byzantine Architecture*, Pelican Hist. A. (Harmondsworth, 1965, rev. 4/1986)
H. Strathmann: 'Martus', *Theologisches Wörterbuch zum Neuen Testament*, ed. G. Kittel, x (Grand Rapids, 1967; Eng. trans., 1968), pp. 474–508
F. W. Deichmann: 'Martyrerbasilika, Martyrion, Memoria, und Altargrab', *Röm. Mitt.*, lxxvii (1970), pp. 144–69
T. F. Mathews: *The Early Churches of Constantinople: Architecture and Liturgy* (University Park, PA, and London, 1971)
W. E. Kleinbauer: 'The Origin and Functions of the Aisled Tetraconch Churches in Syria and Northern Mesopotamia', *Dumbarton Oaks Pap.*, xxvii (1973), pp. 89–114
J. Wilkinson: *Jerusalem Pilgrims before the Crusades* (Warminster, 1977), p. 193
P. Brown: *The Cult of the Saints: Its Rise and Function in Latin Christianity* (Chicago, 1981)
Y. Duval: *Loca sanctorum Africae*, 2 vols (Paris, 1982)
R. Ousterhout: 'The Temple, the Sepulchre, and the Martyrion of the Savior', *Gesta*, xxix (1990), pp. 44–53

Marzabotto. Modern name of an Etruscan city, the ancient name of which is unknown. Situated *c.* 50 km south of Bologna, in the central valley of the River Reno on a terrace called Pian di Misano, at the exit of the Apennine mountain passes, it was part of the Etruscan colonization of the plain around the River Po in the second half of the 6th century BC and was connected via the River Reno with Felsina (Bologna) and Spina. Marzabotto is the only Etruscan city to have been extensively excavated and studied. Its layout is based on a formal grid plan (see fig. 1), divided along orthogonal axes according to ancient rules. These axes comprise a main north–south street and three east–west streets, all of which were 15 m wide. There were also subsidiary north–south streets only 5 m wide. The precise extent of the inhabited area

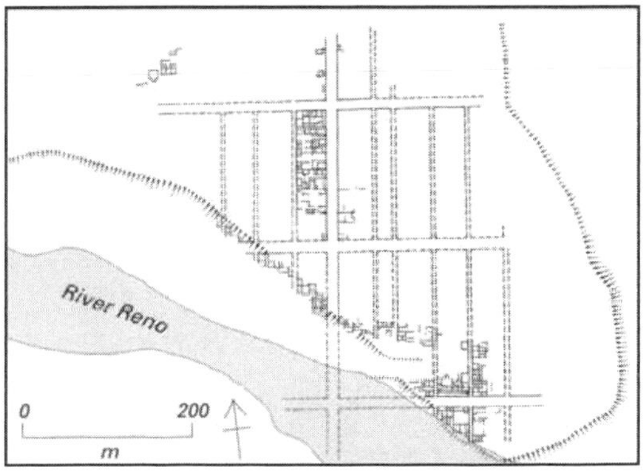

1. Marzabotto, plan of the acropolis hill and part of the town, showing a grid pattern of streets, second half of the 6th century BC

cannot be calculated because of fluvial erosion and the absence of any walls. Two monumental structures to the east and north, however, appear to have been city gates. The blocks formed by the intersection of the streets were occupied by both private dwellings and manufacturing establishments, in particular pottery and metal workshops, but nothing is known of the area given over to public buildings. The single-storey dwellings faced on to the streets, and the rooms were arranged internally around a central courtyard, open to the sky and usually containing a well. The roofs must have been ridged, since rain-water was intended to run off into collection pipes. These houses were built on foundations of river pebbles, and the walls were of compressed clay on a wooden framework (*opus craticium*; *see also* ARCHITECTURE, §V, 2 and fig. 18f). The temple area, set apart on raised ground to the north-east and dominating the city, consisted of a three-cella structure and cult altars arranged in parallel according to the astronomical orientation of the city. The necropoleis are outside the urban area, to the north and east. They include tombs both for inhumation and for cremation, though always for individuals rather than families. The earliest tombs lack identifying inscriptions, but later examples have incised river boulders, bulb-shaped stone markers and, finally, commemorative stone slabs (see fig. 2).

Archaeological evidence from Marzabotto reveals a process of colonial transplantation, with settlers arriving from central Etruria. The letter forms in inscriptions, for example, are similar to those found at Chiusi. Its geographical position and its workshops suggest that Marzabotto was a trading and industrial, rather than agricultural, centre. It was destroyed during the Gallic invasion of Italy in the mid-4th century BC, possibly before the construction of the city had been completed. It remained deserted until Imperial times, when a farm was established in what had been the north-eastern area of the Etruscan city.

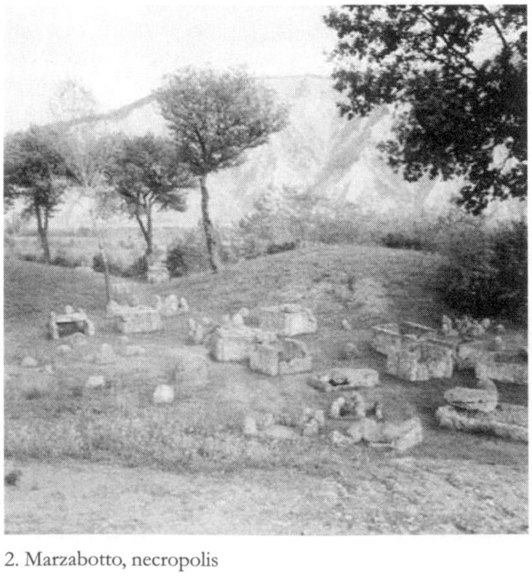

2. Marzabotto, necropolis

G. A. Mansuelli: *Guida alla città etrusca e al Museo di Marzabotto* (Bologna, 1966, 2/1978, 3/1983)

G. A. Mansuelli: 'Marzabotto: Dix années de fouilles et de recherches', *Mél. Archéol. & Hist.: Ecole Fr. Rome*, lxxxiv (1972), p. 111

G. Sassatelli: *La città etrusca di Marzabotto* (Bologna, 1989)

G. Sassatelli and A. M. Brizzolara: *I Nuovi scavi dell'Università di Bologna nella città etrusca di Marzabotto: Mostra fotografica* (Bologna, 1990)

G. Sassatelli and D. Briquel: *Iscrizioni e graffiti della città etrusca di Marzabotto* (Bologna, 1994)

F.-H. Massa-Pairault: *Marzabotto: Recherches sur l'Insula*, iii (Rome, 1997)

D. Vitali, A. M. Brizzolara and E. Lippolis: *L'acropoli della città etrusca di Marzabotto* (Imola, 2001)

Culti, forma urbana e artigianato a Marzabotto: Nuove prospettive di ricerca: Atti del convegno di studi: Bologna, 2003

Masada [Heb. Mezadah]. Fortress on a flat-topped rock on the eastern side of the Judaean Desert in Israel; to the east, the rock terminates in a sheer cliff 400 m above the Dead Sea. According to the Jewish Roman historian Josephus Flavius (AD 37–after 93), whose account of Masada is the only extant one, it was built (probably *c.* 37–31 BC) by Herod the Great. During the period of the Jewish War (AD 66–73), it was garrisoned by the Jewish Zealots, who made their last stand there against the Romans. Three years after the capture of Jerusalem, the defenders of Masada, having held the fortress during a three-year siege, destroyed themselves when it was about to fall.

Masada was encircled by a dolomite stone wall with casemates: the space between the two walls was partitioned into 70 compartments. Each of the four gates consisted of a room with an inner and an outer entrance and benches along the walls. Rising from small casemates, the 30 towers were built at unequal distances, according to the rock's topography. An elaborate water-supply system consisted of numerous cisterns linked by channels; there were also several pools, some probably associated with ritual bathing.

Eight palaces have been found in the northern and western parts of the rock. Herod's Northern palace or villa, on the northern edge of the cliff, had three storeys, the lower two with terraces; it had its own small bathhouse. Next to it was a smaller palace, the public storehouses and a large bathhouse. The Western palace, largest of the buildings, was a ceremonial and administrative centre; the main hall had a decorative mosaic floor. One group of three small palaces probably served the royal family, while a further group served as residences for high officials and as administrative buildings. The Masada palaces exhibited the basic elements of Hellenistic architecture, being characterized by a simple central court and a columned hall leading to a *triclinium*, usually in the southern part of the court.

A building believed to have served as a synagogue was added during the Zealot period. It was part of the casemate wall, with one main entrance, and measured

12.5×10.5 m, being divided by two rows of columns. It was built in two phases, in the second of which mud-plastered benches were added along the walls.

Y. Yadin: 'The Excavation of Masada, 1963/64: Preliminary Report', *Israel Explor. J.*, xv (1965), pp. 1–20

Y. Yadin: *Masada* (London and New York, 1966)

Y. Yadin: 'The Synagogue at Masada', *Ancient Synagogues Revealed*, ed. L. I. Levine (Jerusalem, 1981)

Y. Yadin and others: *Masada: The Yigael Yadin Excavations 1963–1965: Final Reports*, 7 vols (1989–)

N. Ben-Yehuda: *Sacrificing Truth: Archaeology and the Myth of Masada* (Amherst, NY, 2002)

Massalia [Lat. Massilia; now Marseille]. Greek and later Roman city founded in the south of France near the mouth of the River Rhône on the Golfe du Lion on the north coast of the Mediterranean Sea. Massalia was founded *c.* 600 BC by Greek settlers from Phokaia in Asia Minor. The area was undoubtedly found congenial because of the hot, Mediterranean landscape and climate of Provence, similar to that of areas already colonized; because of the easy defensibility of the site, on a promontory with a narrow-necked natural harbour; and because it was a convenient port for the river traffic of the Rhône and trade with the interior of Gaul. Massalia soon became one of the most powerful and prosperous Greek cities of the west; indeed, its own colonies stretched from Nikaia (Nice) to Emporion (Ampurias) in Catalonia. The city assumed a significant role in the distribution of Greek products and Greek culture in south and central Gaul, and in the early days it rivalled Carthage for the Spanish metal trade. A treasury building for the Massaliots was constructed at Delphi before the end of the 6th century BC. Its citizens chose the wrong side in the conflict between Caesar and Pompey, but Caesar spared the city when he took it in 49 BC, and it seems to have retained something of its independent status.

Unfortunately most of the ancient city has been obliterated by modern development. Destruction of parts of the city during World War II revealed the remains of a Greek theatre with circular *orchestra* just north of the old harbour; an interesting detail is the ridge or lip on the tiered stone seats to protect the backs of the spectators from the feet of those sitting behind (a feature also found in some theatres in Sicily and the eastern Mediterranean). The Musée des Docks Romains occupies part of an ancient warehouse adjacent to the Roman quayside, stretching along most of the harbourside; it preserves a large number of huge storage jars (*dolia*).

The discoveries made during the Bourse excavations are preserved in the Jardin des Vestiges (Marseille, Mus. Hist.) and include an inland extension of the harbour; a stretch of the city walls and a gateway, both built of large, carefully cut blocks of stone; part of an ancient road with grooves cut into the paving slabs to prevent horses slipping; a section of a Hellenistic (323–27 BC) aqueduct; a well-preserved merchant ship; and a very large freshwater basin or cistern with overshot water-wheel, which was evidently used for supplying ships with drinking water.

In 1994 two Greek vessels (probably 6th–5th century BC) and three Roman ships (1st–2nd century AD) were discovered next to the city hall, along with remains of docks, warehouses and a 6th-century BC Greek shipyard containing many unfinished boats.

M. Clerc: *Massalia: Histoire de Marseille dans l'antiquité, des origines à la fin de l'empire romain de l'ouest*, 2 vols (Marseille, 1927–9, R/1999)

F. Villard: *La Céramique grecque de Marseille* (Paris, 1960)

M. Escalon de Fonton, ed.: *Naissance d'une ville: Marseille* (Aix-en-Provence, 1979)

M. Euzennat: 'Ancient Marseille in the Light of Recent Excavations', *Amer. J. Archaeol.*, lxxxiv (1981), pp. 133–40

A. L. F. Rivet: *Gallia Narbonensis* (London, 1988)

A. King: *Roman Gaul and Germany* (London, 1990)

J. Bromwich: *The Roman Remains of Southern France* (London, 1993)

P. G. Bahn: 'Ancient Ships in Marseille', *Archaeology*, xlvii/3 (1994), p. 15

Phocée et la fondation de Marseille (Marseille, 1995)

J.-M. Gassend: *Les vestiges de la Bourse* (Ollioules, 1997)

M. Bonifay, M.-B. Carre and Y. Rigoir: *Fouilles à Marseille: Les mobiliers (Ier–VIIe siècles ap. J.-C.)* (Paris, 1998)

A. Hermary, A. Hesnard and H. Tréziny: *Marseille grecque: 600–49 av. J.-C., la cité phocéenne* (Paris, 1999)

A. T. Hodge: *Ancient Greek France* (Philadelphia, 1999)

L. Long, P. Pomey and J.-C. Sourisseau: *Les Etrusques en mer: Epaves d'Antibes à Marseille* (Aix-en-Provence, 2002)

Mausoleum. Monumental form of tomb. Its name is derived from one of the most famous buildings of antiquity, the funerary monument completed *c.* 350 BC at HALIKARNASSOS in Asia Minor in honour of Mausolos, Satrap of Caria (*reg* 377–352 BC), and his wife Artemisia (*d* 351 BC).

Although it has its ancestry and heritage in ancient Egypt, the mausoleum essentially evolved from the tradition of the tomb house or HEROÖN, a shrine over the tomb of a hero, which occurred in Asia Minor and in Greece itself from the Archaic to the Hellenistic periods. Early examples appeared in Lycia in the 5th century BC in the form of funeral monuments on high podia. This conception may have derived from the idea that the dead would be taken to heaven by winged creatures, as depicted on the so-called Harpy Tomb at XANTHOS (*c.* 480 BC), where a flat-roofed tomb house was hollowed out at the top of a monolithic tower. An example from Trysa, also in Lycia (first half of the 5th century BC; architectural sculpture in Vienna, Kksthist. Mus.), featured, within a walled court, a sarcophagus with a gabled top. By the end of the 5th century BC, as in the Nereid Monument at Xanthos (*c.* 425–400 BC; London, BM), which took the shape of a temple raised on a podium, the tomb house seems to have reached a characteristic form. Later, in the Lion Tomb at Knidos (3rd or 2nd century BC, sometimes dated as early as 390–370 BC; *see* TOMB, fig. 1; lion statue now in London, BM), an Egyptian-style pyramid was added to the top of these structures.

This tradition, though vastly expanded in scale, produced the Mausoleum at Halikarnassos in Caria, bordering on Lycia. This gigantic monument, which became the standard model, combined a high base, a temple-like structure and a pyramid, topped by a quadriga. This basic formula was used on a smaller scale in Asia Minor at BELEVI (3rd century BC), near Ephesos, in the Tomb of Hamrath (*c.* 75 BC) at Soada (now Es Suweidiya), Syria, and at Gümüşkesen (first half of the 2nd century AD), Mylasa. Further afield, such monuments could be found in Greece itself—that to Pythianice, erected by Harpalus (*c.* 355–323 BC) on the sacred way from Eleusis to Athens—and in Sicily—the so-called Tomb of Theron (*c.* first half of the 1st century BC) at Akragas (now Agrigento).

The mausoleum as an architectural type flourished especially in Rome, where examples in an enormous range of sizes abound from the heyday of the Republic to the collapse of the Empire. Round forms were probably the most popular type and seem to have evolved from Etruscan tumulus-type tombs (7th century BC onwards), which were earth mounds up to 48 m in diameter, sometimes resting on rock-cut or stone foundations. The Roman versions were either simple cylinders, like the Etruscan prototypes, or cylinders set on a square podium. Perhaps the most famous surviving example in the latter category, at least on a smaller scale, is the Tomb of Caecilia Metella (*c.* 20 BC) on the Via Appia; its present battlements were added in the 13th century. Others on this scale include the Mausoleum of C. Ennius Marsus (second half of the 1st century BC) at Sepino, the tombs at Gaeta of L. Sempronius Atratinus (marble facing now in Gaeta Cathedral) and L. Munatius Plancus (both *c.* 20 BC), and the so-called Tor de' Schiavi (early 4th century AD), Via Praenestina, Rome. Larger examples in Rome can be seen in the tombs of two emperors, the mausolea of Augustus (begun 28 BC; partially extant) and Hadrian (AD 130–39; now the Castel Sant'Angelo). A variant is provided by the Tomb of Romulus, also known as the Mausoleum of Maxentius (*c.* AD 307), beside the Circus of Maxentius on the Via Appia. Little survives, but reconstructions by Sebastiano Serlio (1475–1553/5) and Andrea Palladio (1508–80) in the 16th century and modern archaeological investigations suggest that it was a round, domed mausoleum but preceded by a portico, the whole set in an arcaded precinct of rectangular shape.

There were also rectangular mausolea, rather like tomb temples. In the case of that formerly assigned to Annia Regilla (*c.* AD 160), near the Via Appia, the gable-roofed temple on a low podium was articulated with four pilasters on all sides, although with the inner pair on the south side recessed into the walls as octagonal columns. Other examples include the so-called Oratory of Phalaris (*c.* 85 BC), Akragas; the Tomb of Absalom (early 1st century AD), Jerusalem; and the tomb house illustrated on a relief (Rome, Vatican, Mus. Gregoriano Profano) from the tomb of the Haterii, Centocelle. Octagonal structures were less common, but a very imposing one was the Mausoleum of Diocletian (*c.* AD 300; now Split Cathedral) at Spalatum. Recalling the familiar Egyptian format, there were also at least two pyramidal tombs in Rome itself, including the extant burial monument of Gaius Cestius (*c.* 12 BC), the proportions of which are more attenuated than those of Giza, but there is no doubt about its ancestry. Another type of Roman mausoleum took the form of a tower of multiple stages. This tendency may be seen in the Tomb of the Julii (third quarter of the 1st century BC) at Glanum (now Saint-Rémy-de-Provence; see fig.) and the so-called Conocchia (third quarter of the 1st century AD) on the Via Appia at Santa Maria Capua Vetere.

Various Roman types of mausoleum continued to be built after the triumph of Christianity, but increasingly the mausoleum came to be allied to a church. Between the 4th and 6th centuries, the traditional concept of the mausoleum became linked with the idea of the MARTYRIUM. Two of the early examples of round mausolea-cum-martyria for Christian burial are provided by the tombs in Rome of Constantine the Great's mother and daughter. The former, the Mausoleum of Helena (*d c.* 330) on the Via Casilina (now the Tor Pignattara), was a domed, circular structure, with alternating rectangular and circular niches, actually attached to the east end of the basilica built over the catacomb of SS Marcellino e Pietro. The latter, the Mausoleum of Constantia (*d* 354), was set against the south side of the church of S Agnese and featured a taller, domed, central circular section surrounded by a vaulted ambulatory; it is now the church of S Costanza.

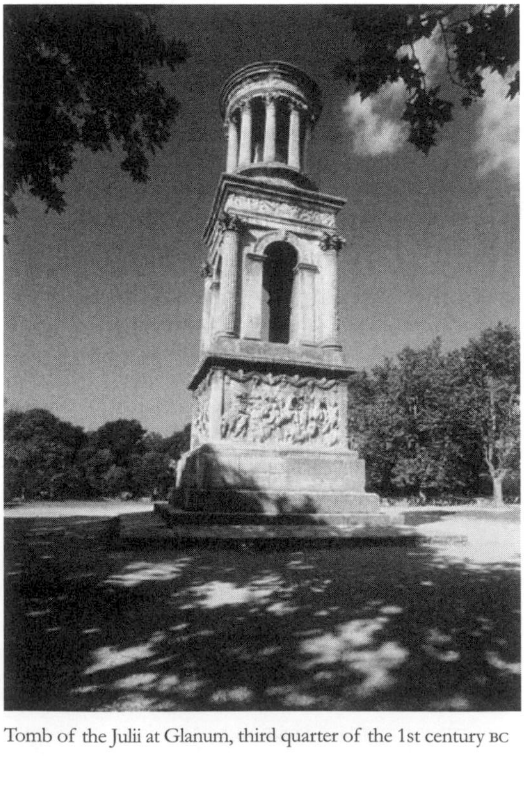

Tomb of the Julii at Glanum, third quarter of the 1st century BC

Their format was apparently related to the mausoleum of Constantine himself, a round tomb (356–7; destr. 536) that was part of the church of the Holy Apostles in Constantinople, and the Holy Sepulchre in Jerusalem, which consisted of the tomb of Christ in the garden of Joseph of Arimathea, over which Constantine had erected the Anastasis Rotunda (326–35; altered 1048), separated from a basilica by a courtyard. This conception of the Holy Sepulchre merged with the fairly common cylindrical Roman mausoleum as a model especially appropriate for a martyrium, and for a time it encouraged the erection of round mausolea–martyria.

W. B. Dinsmoor: *The Architecture of Ancient Greece and Rome* (New York, 1902); rev. as *The Architecture of Ancient Greece* (New York, 1927, rev. 3/1950)

A. Grabar: *Martyrium: Recherches sur le culte des reliques et l'art chrétien antique*, 2 vols (Paris, 1943–6)

T. Kraus: *Das römische Weltreich*, Propyläen-Kstgesch., ii (Berlin, 1967)

K. Jeppesen and others: *The Maussolleion at Halikarnassos*, 2 vols (Århus, 1981–6)

J. Rasch: *Das Maxentius-Mausoleum an der Via Appia in Rom* (Mainz, 1984)

J. J. Rasch and others: *Das Mausoleum der Kaiserin Helena in Rom und der 'Tempio della tosse' in Tivoli* (Mainz, 1988)

J. J. Rasch and H. Mielsch: *Das Mausoleum bei Tor de' Schiavi in Rom* (Mainz, 1993)

K. M. Bentz: 'Rediscovering the Licinian Tomb', *J. Walters A.G.*, lv-lvi (1997–8), pp. 63–88

M. Joly and others: 'Nouvelle Restitution du Mausolee de Faverolles', *Rev. Archéol.*, i (2003), pp. 214–16

D. Graen: '"Sepultus in villa"—Bestattet in der Villa: Drei Zentralbauten in Portugal zeugen vom Grabprunk der Spätantike', *Ant. Welt*, xxxv/3 (2004), pp. 65–74

A. Chastel and others: 'The Castle and the Angel', *F.M.R. Mag.*, vi (April–May 2005), pp. 1–26

G. Niemann and A. Conze: *Der Palast Diokletians in Spalato* (Split, 2005)

Mausolos (*reg* 377–352 BC). Ancient Greek ruler. He was the Satrap (i.e. vassal of the King of Persia) of Caria in Asia Minor, now western Turkey, and a member of the Hekatomnid dynasty. Although Carian by birth, Mausolos greatly admired Greek culture and art. He was famous for having moved his capital from Mylassa to the coastal site of HALIKARNASSOS, where there was a good harbour. He laid out the new capital in the natural hollow by the harbour, as described by Vitruvius (*On Architecture* II. 811ff), with his tomb, the Mausoleum, at the centre. He employed the most famous Greek architects and sculptors of his time to build and decorate this, but he died before it was completed. The Mausoleum was finished by his wife and half-sister, Artemisia, who reigned after him. A fine portrait statue from the Mausoleum (London, BM, 1001; *see* HALIKARNASSOS, fig. 3) has been thought to represent Mausolos, though there is no proof of this.

S. Hornblower: *Mausolus* (Oxford, 1982)

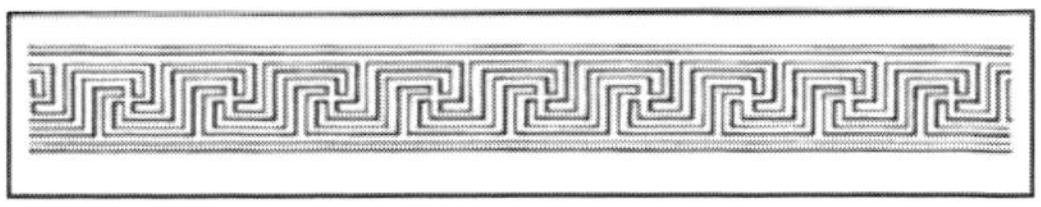

Carved meander from the entablature of the Temple of Jupiter, Baalbek, 1st century AD; reconstruction drawing

Meander [maeander; fret; Greek key design]. Decorative motif consisting of a line turned back on itself in a series of rectangular bends. There are several variations, for example involving two continuous intersecting lines (see fig.). The meander occurs on ancient Greek painted pottery from the Geometric period onwards (for example on a belly-handled amphora of the 8th century BC), and it was widely used, in painted or carved form, on flat-profile architectural mouldings in ancient Greek buildings of all periods and as a border design in floor mosaics. In Roman times it continued to occur on buildings and occasionally in mosaics, and it has remained in the decorative repertory of many art forms into modern times.

Medallion. Large medal struck normally in commemoration of an event or as a reward of merit. In the standard study of Roman medallions, J. M. C. Toynbee struggled to distinguish them from coins on the one hand and medals on the other, while admitting that medallions share features of each. She defined medallions as monetiform (coinlike) pieces that do not correspond completely to a denomination in regular use; they were 'struck by the Emperor for special or solemn commemoration' and were intended as 'individual, personal gifts, any idea of their circulation as currency being either wholly absent or, at the most, quite secondary and subordinate'. This functional definition omits mention of the high level of artistry that characterizes the pieces and constitutes the internal evidence for their status as presentation pieces. For while medallions were produced at imperial mints using the same techniques as those employed for regular coinage, they uniformly display a higher level of artistry; their larger format invited more ambitious and original compositions even when they commemorated events otherwise noted in contemporary coinage.

The first true Roman medallions stand outside the currency system, and it is this that distinguishes them from magnificent Greek coins, notable for their size and artistry, that have sometimes been called medallions. The Damareteion, the Syracusan dekadrachms made during the closing years of the 5th century BC, the dekadrachms of Alexander the Great (356–323 BC) and other heavy Greek coins all share types and weight standards with the mainstream coinage, and while a higher level of artistic expression is arguable for some of them, the principal distinction from regular coins is nothing more than their size.

Multiples of gold and silver denominations (some of dubious authenticity) exist for Augustus (*reg* 27 BC–AD 14) and Domitian (*reg* AD 81–96), and

1st-century AD coins of high style struck on unusually large flans have been called 'proto-medallions', but the continuous series of Roman medallions, in bronze or other copper-based alloys, begins with the emperor Hadrian (*reg* AD 117–38), and the objects in question are clearly not coins. Not only do they lack the letters S C, which characterize virtually all Roman base-metal coinage, but they are far less regular, in both size and weight, than the *sestertius* (around 27 grams or one Roman ounce), otherwise the heaviest coin in the Roman system.

The motifs employed were highly varied. Toynbee argued convincingly that many of them have to do with the new year and reflect the presentation of medallions as *strenae* (new year's presents); but just as commonly the themes are variations of those encountered in coinage: imperial consulships, triumphs and marriages; the birth of an heir; building or restoration of monuments at Rome; aspects of religious ritual. The urban nobility and foreign dignitaries were the principal recipients of medallions. The evidence of the surviving corpus is sufficient to show that the circulation of medallions was limited. Seldom are individual obverse/reverse combinations known in more than a few specimens, and often dies were carried over from year to year, even when this required elaborate recutting. This practice, almost unknown in Roman coinage, attests to the value placed on the work of highly skilled die-engravers, whose efforts can seldom be detected in the coinage.

Bronze medallions—what Toynbee called 'medallions proper'—continued to be produced into the 4th century AD, but even in the late 3rd century medallions began to be produced more commonly in precious metals, mainly gold. Toynbee used the term 'money medallions' to describe these objects, generally multiples of standard precious-metal denominations such as the gold *aureus* ($^1/_{60}$ Roman pound, or 5.45 grams) or *solidus* ($^1/_{72}$ pound, 4.5 grams) or the silver *siliqua* (2.6 grams). Their easy compatibility with the existing monetary system led to the inclusion of 'money medallions' in hoards, and several large hoards have included substantial numbers of medallions. The most famous of these is the 'Arras' hoard (Arras, Mus. B.-A.), discovered at Beaurains, France, in 1922, in which the medallions, like the *aurei*, correspond to imperial donatives. It is likely that medallions were included among coins distributed to high-ranking military officials on the occasions of donatives. They continued to serve as presentation pieces for foreign dignitaries and are frequently found outside the empire. There are also large numbers of imitation 4th-century medallions, mainly framed for use as jewellery, attesting to their popularity. In the 4th century the focus of medallions narrowed to the emperor and the Empire, and the typology is assimilated to that of the coinage. Common motifs include the emperor as conqueror, and gradually the Christianization of the Empire emerges as a theme: the *labarum*, for example, is decorated with a chi-rho or Christogram, and the legend TRIVMFATOR GENTIVM BARBARVM thus refers not only to the Roman conqueror of the barbarian foe but to the Christian victor over a pagan enemy.

G. Cedrenus: *Synopsis historiou*; ed. I. Becker (Bonn, 1838–9) [Gr. text]

F. Gnecchi: *I medaglioni romani* (Milan, 1912)

J. M. C. Toynbee: *Roman Medallions*, American Numismatic Studies (New York, 1944/*R* with corrections and intro. by W. E. Metcalf, New York, 1986)

L. Michelini Tocci: *I medaglioni romani e i contorniati del medagliere vaticano* (Vatican City, 1965)

H. Dressel: *Die römische Medaillone des Münzkabinetts der Staatlichen Museen zu Berlin* (Dublin and Zurich, 1972)

C. L. Clay: 'Roman Imperial Medallions: The Date and Purpose of their Issue', *Actes du 8ème congrès international de numismatique: New York and Washington, DC, 1973*, pp. 253–65

C. C. Vermeule: *Roman Medallions*, Boston, MA, Mus. F.A. cat. (Boston, 1975)

A. Alföldi and E. Alföldi: *Die Kontorniat-Medaillons*, 2 vols (Berlin, 1976/*R* 1989)

M. L. Anderson: 'The Portrait Medallions of the Imperial Villa at Boscotrecase', *Amer. J. Archaeol.*, xci (Jan 1987), pp. 127–35

A. B. Marsden: 'Between Principate and Dominate: Imperial Styles under the Severan Dynasty and the Divine Iconography of the Imperial House on Coins, Medallions, and Engraved Gemstones AD 193–235', *J. Brit. Archaeol. Assoc.*, cl (1997), pp. 1–16

Mediolanum Santonum [now Saintes]. A Gallo-Roman city in what is now the département of Charente-Maritime, western France, *c.* 35 km south-east of La Rochelle and *c.* 50 km due east of the Atlantic coast. The region has been populated since prehistory. At the time of the Roman conquest it was occupied by the Gallic tribe of the Santons. The vast Gallo-Roman city was established in 20 BC on the left bank of the Charente, at the crossing of the roads from Bordeaux to Brittany and from the Massif Central to the Atlantic. A bridge was erected, with a great double arch at its entrance; now displaced on the river bank, this 'Arch of Germanicus' is one of the significant remains of this period. Other survivals include the amphitheatre (1st century AD), aqueducts, baths and a rich collection of sculpture (Saintes, Mus. Archéol.).

Megalopolis. City in Arcadia, southern Greece, which flourished from *c.* 368 BC to the 2nd century BC. Several small and previously separate communities in south-western Arcadia united *c.* 368 BC to form a state based on a new urban centre, both of which were called Megalopolis ('Great City'). This city rapidly became a major power in the Peloponnese, and remained so despite its partial destruction by Kleomenes of Sparta (223 BC, followed by rebuilding). Under Roman rule it declined in prosperity, although it was still inhabited until the 6th or 7th century AD. Its name is now borne by a small modern town to the south. The ancient city occupied a large walled area crossed by the River Helisson. Its architecture is known chiefly from the description by Pausanias (*Guide to Greece* VIII.xxx–xxxii), who visited it around AD 170, and from the British excavations of 1890–93. Bury suggested that the public buildings of the city itself were situated north of the Helisson, while those of the Arcadian Federation lay to its south, but the location of the Thersilion constitutes the only evidence for this view.

The city's most notable remains belong to the Thersilion and the theatre. The Thersilion (4th century BC; named after its dedicator) served as a meeting place for the Arcadian Federation. It was a rectangular building (66.65×52.43 m) with its main entrance on the south side, fronted by a portico of 14 Doric columns. The single large chamber inside had a timber roof supported by an ingeniously designed grid of columns, which radiated from the speaker's platform in a way that obscured the audience's view as little as possible. The floor also rose from the speaker's platform to the outside walls, since the furthest surviving column bases are *c.* 2.5 m above those beside the platform. The Thersilion was probably destroyed in the sack of 223 BC.

Immediately to the south was the theatre, built into a hillock adapted for the purpose (see fig.). Though of the Greek standard form, with semicircular rows of seats rising around the orchestra, it has three notable features. First, according to Pausanias it was the largest in Greece; the *orchestra* has a diameter of 30.2 m and the auditorium (diam. 129.5 m) may have seated 17,000 to 21,000 spectators. Second, when the theatre was built no stage was provided, its place being occupied by the porch of the Thersilion, although by the Roman period a stone stage had been added. Finally, perhaps in the 3rd century BC, the western parodos was filled by a building for props.

Other public buildings first excavated by the British, including the great Stoa of Philip (*c.* 340–*c.* 330 BC) with its three aisles and projecting wings, are being more fully explored in current German–Greek excavations. In the south-east of the city there are well-preserved mosaics from a Roman house of the 6th century AD, depicting three Graces, animals, cupids, birds and fishes in geometric settings, although they are not first-rate works.

Some of the older settlements in the territory of Megalopolis that coexisted with the new city have been excavated. Gortys had two sanctuaries of Asklepios (one 5th–4th century BC, the other 4th century BC), and a rare example of a Greek bathhouse (4th century BC), while at Alipheira temples of Athena (late 6th century BC to early 5th) and Asklepios (*c.* 300 BC) have been found; but the most interesting of these sites is Lykosoura, where there was a Sanctuary of Despoina ('the Mistress') and a Temple of Artemis. The prostyle Doric Temple of Despoina measuring (ultimately) 21.5×12.5 m was originally built in the 4th century BC; the history of subsequent changes is not wholly clear. The colossal cult group was by the sculptor DAMOPHON of Messene (the heads in Athens, N. Archaeol. Mus.). An unusual feature of this temple is a door in the south side of the cella (similar to the side door of the Temple of Apollo at Bassai). This opened on to a flight of 10 steps nearly 29 m long that led nowhere but formed a retaining wall for the slope and may have accommodated worshippers watching ritual at the temple door.

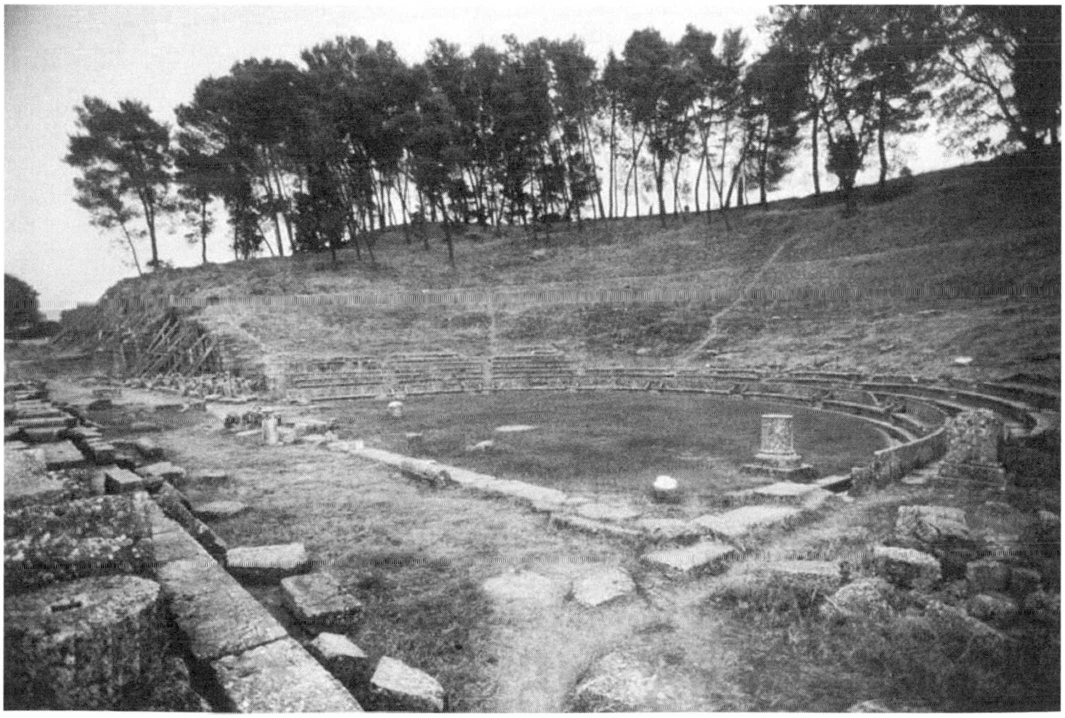

Megalopolis, theatre

E. A. Gardner and others: *Excavations at Megalopolis, 1890–1891* (London, 1892)
J. B. Bury: 'The Double City of Megalopolis', *J. Hell. Stud.*, xviii (1898), pp. 15–22
A. Petronotes: *E Megale Polis tes Arkadias* [Megale Polis in Arcadia] (Athens, 1973)
D. Leekley and R. Noyes: *Archaeological Excavations in Southern Greece* (Park Ridge, NJ, 1976)
M. Jost: *Sanctuaires et cultes d'Arcadie* (Paris, 1985)
U. W. Gans: 'Eine spatantike Terra-Sigillataschale aus Nordafrika in Megalopolis' *Archäol. Anz.*, iv (1998), pp. 499–506
H. Lauter and Th. Spyropoulos: 'Megalopolis. 3. Vorbericht 1996–7', *Archäol. Anz.* (1998), pp. 415–51
H. Lauter: '"Polybios hat es geweiht . . . ": Stiftungsinschriften des Polybios und des Philopoimen aus dem neuen Zeus-Heiligtum zu Megalopolis (Griechenland)', *Ant. Welt*, xxxiii/4 (2002), pp. 375–86

Megaron. Term used in Homeric epic for the great hall of a house or palace, and sometimes for the whole building. (In this article relative dates for the Bronze Age are being used; for discussion of chronology *see* HELLADIC, §I, 3.) The first excavators of TIRYNS and MYCENAE applied it to the main apartments of the palaces and houses there. Since then it has become the generally accepted archaeological term for an oblong structure (see fig.) entered at its narrow end and consisting of an almost square main room (*domos* (a)) with one or two vestibules (*aithousa* and *prodomos* (b)), the outer one (*aithousa* (c)) being a porch *in antis*. It is generally assumed that the megaron originated north or east of the Greek peninsula, though not from central Europe, and that it was brought south by immigrants whose ethnic identity and time of arrival remain a matter for conjecture. The Middle Neolithic square huts at Otzaki Magoula in Thessaly with their short partition walls projecting from the sides and one or two wooden columns at their entrances, which were claimed to be the archetypes, hardly qualify as such. The earliest megaron forms, however primitive, are the Late Neolithic structures at Sesklo and Dimini near Volos. The few known Early and Middle Helladic buildings are either insufficiently preserved or clearly different in plan. The first genuine Late Helladic (LH) megaron is the middle wing (LH II A–B) of Mansion I at the Menelaion, Sparta.

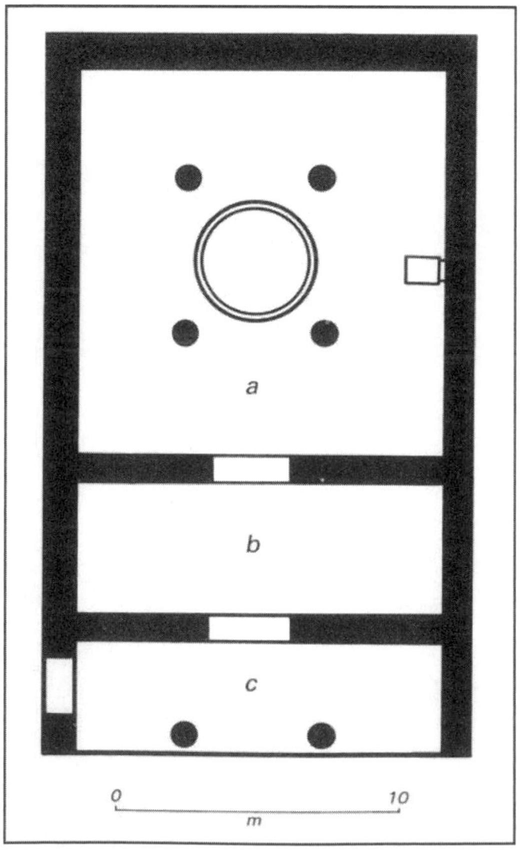

Megaron from the palace at Mycenae, Late Helladic III B, plan: (a) *domos* with hearth; (b) *prodomos*; (c) *aithousa*

In the LH palaces the megaron was the stateroom, the structure dominating the whole complex. Special materials (e.g. coloured stone, gypsum) were used in its construction, and its lime-plastered walls and floors were decorated with sculptured or painted dados and frescoes. The *domos* had a central hearth, also painted, which was surrounded by four wooden columns, fluted or sheathed in bronze. At Tiryns and PYLOS, and presumably at Mycenae, a throne stood against its side wall. Smaller megara were less elaborately constructed. Walls were coated with a lime and clay stucco, column and doorjamb bases were roughly shaped, floors were plastered but unpainted. Such megara had single (e.g. Agios Kosmas, Attica) or columnless vestibules (e.g. Korakou, Corinthia, Houses H and O; Mouriatada, Arcadia; Tiryns; Mycenae, West House and Tsountas's House; Menelaion, Sparta) or even closed vestibules, accessible from the sides (e.g. Mycenae, House of the Warrior Vase and House M; GLA, Boiotia) with no internal supports, no hearth and no throne in the *domos*.

Megara were originally isolated structures, but by the 15th century BC they were already being incorporated into larger complexes, fronting courtyards and linked by passages or party walls to other rooms. As an architectural form they occurred only in prehistoric Greece, the Aegean (e.g. Phylakopi, Melos; Poliochni, Lemnos) and Troy I, II and VI, being unknown even in contemporary Crete. But, although distinctively Helladic, the megaron is far from being ubiquitous, or even frequent, especially in Pre-Palatial Helladic settlements, where megara are not necessarily the largest structures either. The term is often used indiscriminately: true megara have been found at less than a tenth of the prehistoric sites with architectural remains, and there are about as many megaron-like buildings with some but not all the appropriate features. In historical times the term was used for sacrificial pits or caves dedicated to chthonic deities (e.g. Demeter and Persephone) and for the inner sanctums of certain temples in Greece (e.g. the Temple of Apollo, Delphi, 7th century BC;

Hekatompedon, Athens, mid-6th century BC) and Egypt. The form survived, somewhat modified, in the plans of the Greek TEMPLE.

E. B. Smith: 'The Megaron and its Roof', *Amer. J. Archaeol.*, xlvi (1942), pp. 99–118

V. Müller: 'Development of the "Megaron" in Prehistoric Greece', *Amer. J. Archaeol.*, xlviii (1944), pp. 342–8

A. Schweitzer: 'Megaron und Hofhaus in der Ägäis des 3–2 Jahrtausends v.Chr.', *Annu. Brit. Sch. Athens*, xlvi (1951), pp. 160–67

B. L. McKann: *The Development of the Megaron in the Aegean Area* (diss., Washington, DC, George Washington U., 1968)

H. L. Mace: *The Neolithic and Bronze Age megaron: A Catalogue* (diss., Chapel Hill, U. NC, 1970)

J. Warner: *The Megaron and Apsidal House in Early Bronze Age Western Anatolia: New Evidence from Karatas* (Princeton, 1979)

L. R. McCallum: *Decorative Program in the Mycenaean Palace of Pylos: The Megaron Frescoes* (Philadelphia, U. PA, 1987)

T. Schulz: 'Die Rekonstruktion des Thronpodestes im ersten grossen Megaron von Tiryns', *Mitt. Dt. Archäol. Instituts. Athen. Abt.*, ciii (1988), pp. 11–23

K. Werner: *The Megaron during the Aegean and Anatolian Bronze Age: A Study of Occurrence, Shape, Architectural Adaptation, and Function* (Jonsered, 1993)

S. P. M. Harrington: 'Cretan Shrine Discovered', *Archaeology*, liii/5 (Sept–Oct 2000), p. 17

J. Maran: 'Das Megaron im Megaron: Zur Datierung und Funktion des Antenbaus im Mykenischen Palast von Tiryns', *Archäol. Anz.*, i (2000), pp. 1–16

Meidias Painter (*fl c.* 420–*c.* 400 BC). Greek vase painter. He is named after the potter's signature on a large Red-figure hydria (London, BM; see fig.) and was one of the last great Athenian vase painters. His teacher was probably AISON, but the style and subject-matter of his work suggest that he was also influenced by the older KODROS PAINTER and ERETRIA PAINTER. The Meidias Painter himself later attracted an important following, including Aristophanes, the Painter of the Carlsruhe Paris and the Painter of the Athens Wedding. Over 250 vases are attributed to the group. Some of these artists decorated large vases, especially hydriai, but most of them favoured smaller shapes, such as choes, pyxides, squat lekythoi (see colour pl. 1:XV, fig. 1) and lekanides. The Meidian style and its iconography have a distinctive extravagance (Beazley) and evoke a sensual, leisured and luxurious world that is the visual counterpart to the poetry of the contemporary tragedian Agathon, represented in Plato's *Symposion* as a master of the flowery phrase.

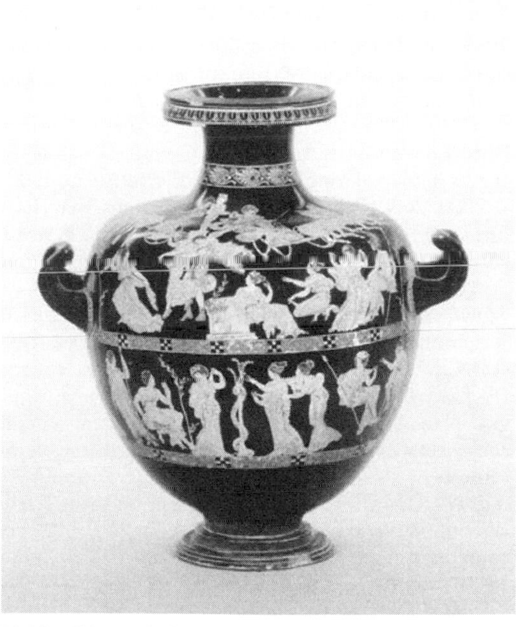

Meidias Painter: hydria depicting *Rape of the Leukippidai* and *Herakles in the Garden of the Hesperides*, h. 521 mm, *c.* 410 BC (London, British Museum, E 224)

Meidian compositions are densely packed with figures, mostly female, clustered into affectionate groups of two or three. They are generally 'Polygnotan' (*see* POLYGNOTOS OF THASOS) in having no single ground line. Instead, the figures are set at various levels and are occasionally only partly visible. White lines suggest irregularities in the terrain, while trees, shrubs and scattered flowers contribute to the outdoor effect. The Meidias Painter himself was adept at using vase shapes and compositions that complemented each other. On his name-piece, for example, the outward-facing chariot teams of the Dioskouroi lead the eye towards the projecting handles, but the focus then moves back along the horses' bodies to the central scene of the Dioskouroi and their brides, and on to Aphrodite, watching from below.

Meidian figures have distinctive faces. Noses are long and straight, eyes large, mouths small, chins heavy and rounded, and heads are often shown in three-quarter view. Women are slim and long-legged, men plump and effeminate. Both sexes have elegant hands and feet, with long, tapering fingers and toes. The women are always elaborately attired. Their often transparent, multi-pleated drapery clings tightly to the body or swirls away in exaggerated flourishes, and is sometimes decorated with stars, palmettes or wave patterns. Hair styles vary: several types of richly patterned headdress occur, but the hair sometimes hangs loose in prolific curls and ringlets. Gold earrings, necklaces, bracelets and hair ornaments are worn, while girdles are also tipped with gold.

The Meidias Painter and his associates worked during the Peloponnesian War (431–404 BC), yet their subjects were almost exclusively peaceful. Aphrodite was their favourite deity, occasionally accompanied by her consort Adonis, the dying god whose vegetation cult had recently been introduced to Athens. Thus, one of a fine pair of hydriai in Florence (Mus. Archeol., 81948) depicts Adonis lying back against Aphrodite's knees, while the other (81947) depicts his mortal counterpart Phaon, the Lesbian ferryman on whom Aphrodite bestowed eternal youth and irresistible charm. On both vases, as often elsewhere, Aphrodite is attended by a retinue of personified abstractions in the form of Eunomia (Good Order),

Eukleia (Good Repute), Eudaimonia (Happiness) and Eutychia (Good Fortune). Despite subsidiary political, religious and philosophical connotations, the main function of these figures was probably to create an atmosphere of peace, harmony and beauty, as a form of escapism from the horrors of war. Other favourite Meidian figures include the legendary musicians Mousaios and Thamyris, always attended by Muses and other women. They too occur in peaceful scenes, but even ostensibly violent subjects were generally transformed into gentle idylls. On the painter's name-piece, the *Rape of the Leukippidai* was refined into a peaceful elopement. Similarly, Herakles is depicted not battling with the Hydra or with Geryon, but contemplating the beauty of his wife, Deianeira (on a pelike, New York, Met., 37.11.23), or, as on the name vase, sitting at ease in the Garden of the Hesperides, watched by an amiable serpent and plied with golden fruit by the nymphs. Such escapist scenes were often endowed with a specifically Athenian character by the inclusion of Athenian tribal heroes. For example Akamas, Oineus, Hippothoon and Antiochos relax with Herakles in the Garden of the Hesperides, enjoying the sort of existence for which their descendants might happily have exchanged their wearisome lives. They embody the nostalgic mood of contemporary Athenian thought, as does another popular Meidian subject, the birth from the ground of Erichthonios.

H. Nicole: *Meidias et le style fleuri* (Paris, 1908)
J. D. Beazley: *Attic Red-figured Vases in American Museums* (Cambridge, MA, 1918), p. 185
W. Hahland: *Vasen um Meidias* (Berlin, 1930)
G. Becatti: *Meidias: Un manierista antico* (Florence, 1947)
W. Real: *Studien zur Entwicklung der Vasenmalerei im ausgehenden 5. Jahrhundert v. Chr.* (Münster, 1973)
U. Knigge: 'Aison, der Meidiasmaler? Zu einer rotfigurigen Oinochoe aus dem Kerameikos', *Mitt. Dt Archäol. Inst.: Athen. Abt.*, xc (1975), pp. 123–43
L. Burn: *The Meidias Painter* (Oxford, 1987)
J. Boardman: *Athenian Red Figure Vases, the Classical Period* (London, 1989), pp. 146–7
A. Schöne: 'Die Hydria des Meidias-Malers im Kerameikos: Zur Ikonographie der Bildfriese', *Mitt. Dt. Archäol. Inst.: Athen. Abt.,* cv (1990), pp. 163–78

Melanthios (*fl* later 4th century BC). Greek painter. He was a pupil of Pamphilos, a master who was said to charge extravagant fees. Apelles was a fellow pupil, and the more famous painter conceded to Melanthios superiority in composition. Pliny (*Natural History*, XXXV.50) listed him among the four-colour painters who restricted their palettes to white, yellow, red and black, but it is unlikely that Melanthios used such a limited palette in all his paintings. None of his works survives. His fame rested in part on the theoretical emphasis he placed on painting. He wrote about *symmetria* (proportion) and, in his book *On Painting*, he recommended stamping a certain wilfulness of character on works of art. When Quintilian wrote that both Pamphilos and Melanthios were renowned for *ratio* (*Principles of Oratory,* XII.x.6), he was no doubt referring to the intellectual aspect of their work. One of Melanthios' most renowned paintings, a collaboration perhaps with Apelles, was a portrait of the tyrant *Aristratos*. The tyrant was depicted standing beside a chariot driven by Victory. When Aratos of Sikyon (271–213 BC), a connoisseur who collected paintings by Melanthios, freed Sikyon from a tyrant's rule, he decreed that all portraits of tyrants should be destroyed, reluctantly including that of Aristratos. A compromise was reached when the artist Nealkes painted a palm tree over the tyrant, although the tyrant's feet remained visible below the chariot.

J. Overbeck: *Die antiken Schriftquellen zur Geschichte der bildenden Künste bei den Griechen* (Leipzig, 1868/*R* Hildesheim, 1959), nos 1748–50, 1754–9, 1895

Meletos Painter. *See* ACHILLES PAINTER.

Melos [Milos]. Greek island at the south-western extremity of the Aegean Cyclades. Its importance in the Bronze Age is evident from the finds at the main prehistoric settlement of Phylakopi, which suggest that Melian culture was influential throughout the Cyclades and beyond. This influence was probably derived from the fact that Melos was the main Aegean source of obsidian—an opaque glassy stone of volcanic origin, which was used, like flint, to provide cutting edges for tools and weapons and is found on all prehistoric sites in the Aegean, as well as farther afield. Two obsidian quarries have been located, as well as the debris of a workshop at Phylakopi. Although it is sometimes suggested that raw obsidian was collected by visitors to Melos and taken away to be worked elsewhere, it seems most unlikely that the indigenous people did not attempt to exploit this important commercial asset. The Melos Museum at Plaka contains finds excavated in 1911, a cast of the *Venus de Milo* (see below) and various Classical antiquities from the island.

Phylakopi, on the north coast of Melos, was the first major Cycladic settlement site to be excavated (British School at Athens, 1896–9, 1911, 1974–7). It was settled during Early Cycladic (EC) I (*c.* 3500–*c.* 2800/2600 BC). The earliest buildings may have been scattered and some of them flimsy. The most substantial remains of the 'First City' belong to later EC III (*c.* 2300–*c.* 2000 BC), when it seems to have grown and to have had stone-built structures. The site was then destroyed and rebuilt soon after. In the 'Second City' (Middle Cycladic (MC); *c.* 2000–*c.* 1600 BC), the houses were larger and were laid out on a rough grid plan. There may have been a fortification wall across the neck of the promontory. This phase of the settlement also ended with destruction and rebuilding. The 'Third City' is the best known. Again, it was laid out on a grid plan, the blocks separated by streets, sometimes stepped, with drains running beneath them. In its earliest stage (Late Cycladic (LC) I–II; *c.* 1600–*c.* 1390 BC) the material culture was heavily influenced by that of Crete, and there was a large administrative building with which were associated some fragments of a tablet inscribed in a Cretan script (Melos Mus.).

In LC III (*c.* 1390–*c.* 1050 BC) this was replaced by a Mycenaean-style megaron (palace)—an architectural symbol of the change in dominant power in the Aegean. Also built in the Mycenaean period was a sanctuary that has yielded many ritual objects, mostly of characteristic Mycenaean type. There was much fortification building in the time of the 'Third City'—indeed all the defences may belong to this period. The final system consisted of a thick wall with towers and casemates, though the sequence of its construction is not entirely clear. The site continued to be occupied until it was deserted in the early 12th century BC (*see also* ARCHITECTURE, §II, 3).

The importance of Phylakopi in the origination and dissemination of art styles was considerable. In late EC III the 'Geometric' style of pottery decoration apparently began there, subsequently spreading to other Cycladic islands and radically influencing the character of the Middle Helladic Matt-painted class of the Greek mainland (*see* POTTERY, §II, 1). Scientific clay analysis has supported the stylistic arguments for a Melian origin of the attractive 'Cycladic White' class of pottery of the MC period, which has many original elements and is found widely on other islands. Melian too is the fine 'Black-and-red' style. In the LC period the pottery, like the architecture, became dependent on inspiration first from Crete and then from the Greek mainland. The site has also yielded some wall paintings, including a scene of *Flying Fish* (LC I–II; Athens, N. Archaeol. Mus.; *see* PAINTING, §II, 2). A number of interesting minor objects, mostly of Mycenaean type, were found in the sanctuary: human and animal terracotta and bronze figures, pottery, sealstones and a gold mask (see fig.).

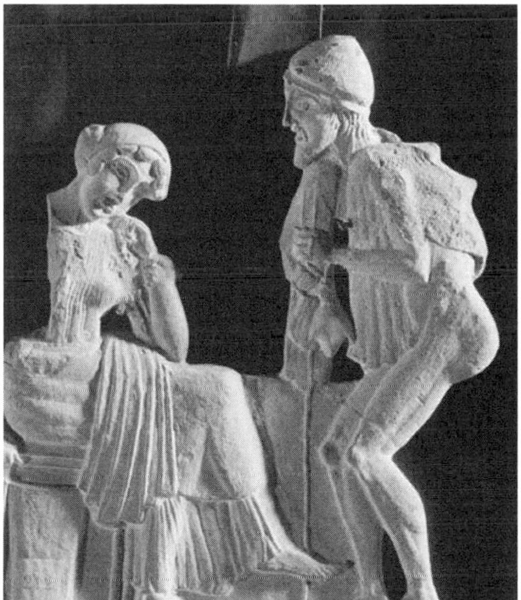

Melos, terracotta relief depicting *Odysseus and Penelope*, h. 187 mm, *c.* 460–*c.* 450 BC (Paris, Musée du Louvre)

Most of the other prehistoric sites on the island are known from surface finds, though an ECI cemetery at Pelos was excavated by the British School at Athens in 1896–7. In common with other Cycladic islands, a wide spread of settlement in the Early Bronze Age seems to have contracted sharply in the MC period. In LC I–II there was once again some expansion. The site of the later town of Melos, which flourished particularly from the Archaic to the Roman periods, lies between the present island capital of Plaka and the coastal village of Klima (the ancient harbour); little excavation has taken place. There are substantial remains of fortifications. The sites of the gymnasium, where the *Venus de Milo* (Paris, Louvre) was found, and the agora (below the hill of Ayios Ilias) have been located. There is also a Roman theatre. In the same area are impressive early Christian catacombs and a baptistery. Here and elsewhere (e.g. Provatás), Roman houses have been found with mosaic floors.

T. D. Atkinson and others: *Excavations at Phylakopi in Melos*, Society for the Promotion of Hellenic Studies Supplementary Paper 4 (London, 1904)

R. M. Dawkins and J. P. Droop: 'The Excavations at Phylakopi in Melos', *Annu. Brit. Sch. Athens*, xvii (1911), pp. 1–22

I. Khatzidhakis: *Istoria tes Melou* [History of Melos], 1927

A. Furumark: 'The Settlement at Ialyssos and Aegean History, *c.* 1500–*c.* 1400 BC', *Opuscula Archaeol.*, vi (1950), pp. 150–271

Z. A. Baos: *Naoi kai naydria tes Melou* [Shrines and temples of Melos] (1964)

R. L. N. Barber: 'Phylakopi 1911 and the History of the Later Cycladic Bronze Age', *Annu. Brit. Sch. Athens*, lxix (1974), pp. 1–53

C. Renfrew: 'The Mycenaean Sanctuary at Phylakopi', *Antiquity*, lii (1978), pp. 7–15

C. Renfrew: 'Phylakopi and the Late Bronze I Period in the Cyclades', *Thera and the Aegean World*, ed. C. Doumas, i (London, 1978), pp. 403–21

C. Renfrew and J. M. Wagstaff, eds: *An Island Polity: The Archaeology of Exploitation on Melos* (Cambridge, 1982)

C. Renfrew: *The Archaeology of Cult: The Sanctuary at Phylakopi*, British School at Athens Supplementary Volume xviii (London, 1985)

H. M. Fletcher and S. D. Kitson: 'The Churches of Melos', *Annu. Brit. Sch. Athens*, ii (1986), pp. 155–68

M. A. Seddon: *The Dark Burnished Ware from the Excavations at Phylakopi, Melos, 1896–99*, 2 vols (diss., U. Edinburgh, 1992)

A. E. McNulty: *Industrial Minerals in Antiquity: Melos in the Classical and Roman Periods* (diss., U. Glasgow, 2000)

Menon Painter. *See* PSIAX.

Mérida. *See* AUGUSTA EMERITA.

Mesara. Region in southern central Crete that flourished in the Bronze Age. One of the most fertile parts of Crete, this flat alluvial plain is about 50 km east–west, but never more than 10 km north–south, and it is surrounded on the north, east and south by foothills and mountains. It was in and around the Mesara plain in the Early Bronze Age (for discussion of Bronze Age absolute dates *see* MINOAN, §4) that a distinctive culture developed, characterized by small village communities, perhaps composed of extended family groups, who buried their dead in circular communal tombs known as the Mesara type. The wealth of attractively painted pottery, finely carved sealstones and stone bowls, well-made bronze weapons and gold jewellery from these tombs suggest that the Mesara was a prosperous area and that its people were inventive and skilled. Early in the 2nd millennium BC the whole area was presumably dominated by the Minoan palace at PHAISTOS, and much later a major Greco-Roman city was built nearby at GORTYN, which flourished until AD 670.

S. Xanthoudides: *The Vaulted Tombs of Mesará* (Liverpool, 1924/ R 1971)
K. Branigan: *The Tombs of Mesara* (London, 1970)
K. Branigan: *Dancing with Death: Life and Death in Southern Crete, c. 3000–2000* BC (Amsterdam, 1993)
L. V. Watrous and others: 'A Survey of the Western Mesara Plain in Crete: Preliminary Report of the 1984, 1986, and 1987 Field Seasons', *Hesperia*, lxii (April–June 1993), pp. 191–248
L. V. Watrous and others: *The Plain of Phaistos: Cycles of Social Complexity in the Mesara Region of Crete* (Los Angeles, 2004)

Mesembria [now Nesebăr; Nesebŭr]. Town situated on a peninsula on the Bulgarian Black Sea coast. It was founded by Greek colonists from Megara in the late 6th century BC, and it remained an important city and naval base until the Turkish conquest in the 15th century AD. Its name suggests that it had originally been a Thracian fortification (*bria*) of a local king called Mesa, but after the foundation of the Greek colony it developed, particularly in the 3rd and 2nd centuries BC, into a major port and trading centre (see fig.). As early as the 4th century BC Mesembria's coins were circulating widely throughout the Thracian interior and even beyond the Danube in Dacia. The city was at war with its neighbour Apollonia Pontica (now Sozopol in Bulgaria) during the first half of the 2nd century BC, was briefly captured by the Dacians in the second half of the 1st century BC and was included in the Roman province of Thrace from AD 46. It flourished during the 2nd century AD and was able to survive the Gothic invasions of the 4th and 5th centuries thanks to its naturally strong defensive location. The Roman and Byzantine fortifications, which command the narrow approach to the main peninsula, replaced earlier Hellenistic defences and survive, in part, to a height of 6 m.

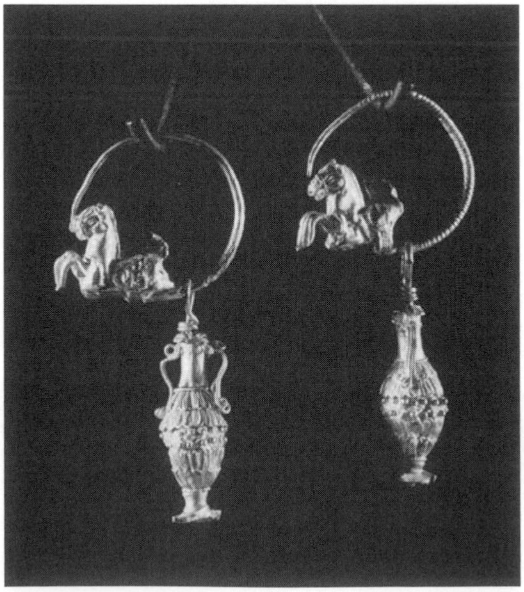

Mesembria, gold pendant earrings, 3rd century BC (Burgas, Historical District Museum)

T. Ivanov and V. Velkov, eds: *Nessèbre*, 2 vols (Sofia, 1969–80) [Ivanov (i); Velkov (ii)]
R. Hoddinott: *Bulgaria in Antiquity* (London, 1975)
L. Ognenova Marinova: 'Sull'archeologia in Tracia: Nesebar, trent'anni di ricerche di terra e subacquee', *Boll. A.*, lxxv (Jan–Feb 1990), pp. 125–9
P. Tsatsopoulou-Kaloudi: *Mesembria-Zone* (Athens, 2001)

Messene. Site on the south side of Mt Ithome in Messenia in southern Greece. The town was founded in 369 BC with the active support of the Boiotians as a permanent stronghold guaranteeing Messenian freedom from Spartan domination following the battle of Leuktra in 371 BC; it flourished into Hellenistic times. The extent of the site is considerable, with a boundary 9 km long, which included the summit of the mountain itself. This boundary was given a strong defensive wall, which, according to Pausanias (*Guide to Greece* IV.xxvii.7), was built immediately after the foundation of the city. Like the contemporary foundation of Megalopolis, which was the chief city of the Arcadians to the north, its purpose was to contain the Spartans within their own district of Lakonia. Military requirements, therefore, came first, and perhaps explain why the fortifications enclosed an area far larger than was ever occupied by the city itself, although there may have been the expectation that it would develop.

The walls (*c.* 2.5 m thick) are built of substantial quarry-faced ashlar blocks on either side of a rubble core. The technique appears identical in many parts to that of contemporary Boiotian fortifications, such as those at Siphai, and Boiotian involvement in the design and construction is virtually certain, although some have argued that they are Hellenistic. The curtain wall was punctuated at intervals by towers, of several distinct types (see fig.). All have solid, filled bases generally projecting about 6 m from the wall, and about 6 m wide. They are single storey (Hellenistic towers would have been taller). Some are rectangular, others curved to provide a better field of view from their windows. Some sections of the walls—particularly those commanding the approaches from Arcadia and the north—are more substantial than others, as they were more prone to attack. If the walls were really built in haste, it may also imply that different sections were assigned to builders from different parts of the

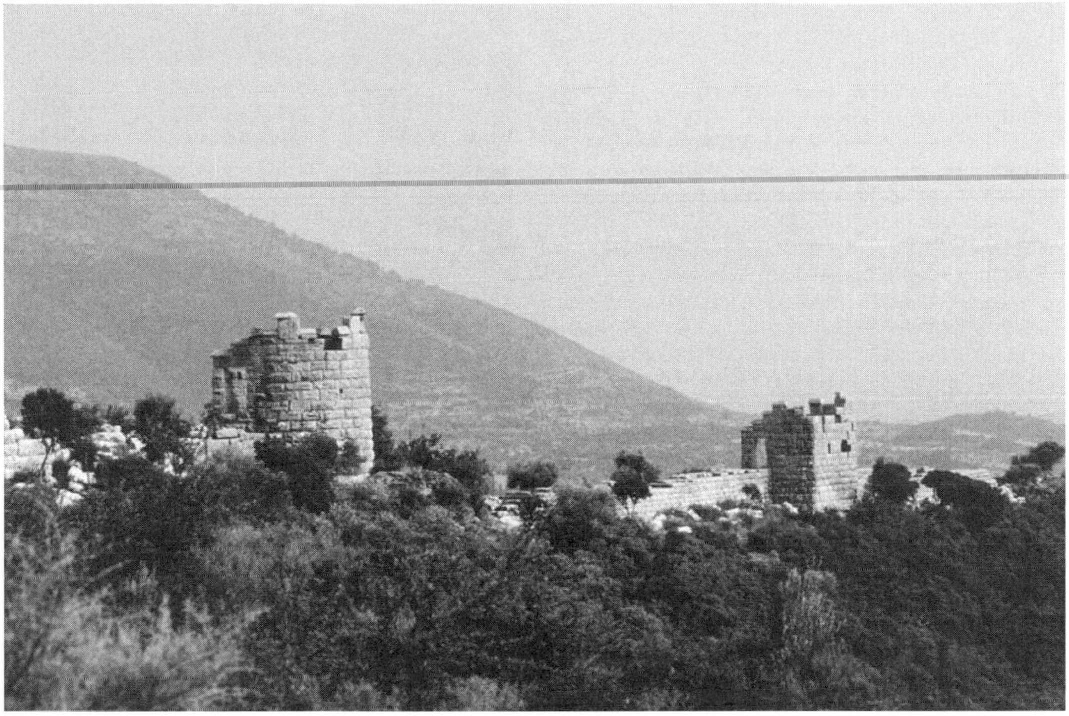

Messene, city wall

anti-Spartan alliance (it is unlikely that the Messenians themselves had the necessary skills); it is the northern sections that most closely resemble Boiotian work. The best-preserved entrance, the Arcadian gate, is in this northern section, flanked by two rectangular towers. It leads into a circular court, surrounded by massive walls of more regular ashlar masonry, with distinctively pointed facing and decorative niches. Another gateway opposite led into the city: both were surmounted by huge lintels. The whole gateway is bonded into the curtain wall and so most unlikely to be Hellenistic, as sometimes suggested.

New archaeological excavations since the 1980s have uncovered extensive areas of the ancient town, including some of its main religious and civic building complexes. The Sanctuary of Asklepios, the centre of Messenian religious and civic life, was a complex of shrines, sanctuaries and public buildings. A Hellenistic Doric temple (26.98×12.68 m with 6×12 columns), in use from the late 3rd century BC to the 3rd century AD, stood within a peristyled courtyard. A monumental propylon led to the sanctuary from the east, flanked by an enclosed theatrical structure to its north. This hall, called the ekklesiasterion (assembly house), featured a 21-m wide stage and an *orchestra* 9.7 m in diameter, and was possibly used for musical and theatrical performances as well as public meetings. A large square room, perhaps a library, stood south of the propylon, and a number of smaller rooms situated behind the western and northern colonnades of the court served as public rooms and shrines (*oikoi*).

A stadium and a gymnasium lay to the south of the Asklepieion, once decorated with votive statuary and inscriptions; a Doric Heroön (hero shrine) stood by the stadium, possibly associated with one of the distinguished founder-families of Messene. The city's theatre (built in the 3rd century BC and abandoned by the late 3rd century AD) was situated north-west of the Asklepieion, but is today largely destroyed. A further number of sanctuaries, shrines, fountain houses and civic buildings have been investigated or are currently in the process of being excavated.

The sanctuaries, shrines and other public areas of Messene were furnished with cult and votive statuary, the surviving examples of which are often heavily fragmented. *Hermes of Messene*, a 1st century BC copy of a known 4th century BC type usually dubbed the *Hermes of Andros*, and a surviving part from the torso of a Roman version of the well-known 5th century BC statue of the *Doryphoros* by Polykleitos, are good examples of both the quality and the range once attained.

Messene's only known sculptor, DAMOPHON, known to have worked between 210 and 180 BC, created, according to Pausanias, a number of individual works as well as sculptural compositions for his hometown, fragments of which have been recognized among the excavated sculpture from the site.

A. Blouet: *Expédition scientifique de Morée*, 3 vols (Paris, 1831–8)

A. K. Orlandos: 'Anaskaphe en Messene' [Excavation in Messene], *Praktika* (1957), pp. 121–5

A. K. Orlandos: 'Anaskaphai Messenes', *Praktika* (1958), pp. 177–83

A. K. Orlandos: 'Anaskaphe Messenes', *Praktika* (1959), pp. 162–73; (1963), pp. 122–9; (1964), pp. 96–101; (1969), pp. 98–120; (1970), pp. 125–41

N. Kaltsas: *Ancient Messene* (Athens, 1989)

P. Themelis: 'Damophon von Messene, sein Werk im Lichte der neuen Ausgrabungen', *Ant. Kst,* xxxvi/1 (1993), pp. 24–40

P. G. Themelis: *Ancient Messene* (Athens 1999/R 2003)

H.-A. Chlepa: *Messene: To Artemisio kai hoi oikoi tes dytikes pterygas tou Asklepieiou* (Athens, 2001)

M. Stamatopoulou and M. Yeroulanou: *Excavating Classical Culture: Recent Archaeological Discoveries in Greece* (Oxford, 2002) [contains a chapter on Messene]

P. G. Themelis: *Heroes at Ancient Messene* (Athens, 2003)

Metalwork. Metals can be defined by their properties: they are malleable, so can be shaped by hammering and bending; tough and fairly elastic, so can sustain considerable stress without breaking; and dense and highly reflective, so capable of taking a good polish. With the exception of iron, most common metals have relatively low melting-points (below 1100°C), so they can be easily melted, and on cooling they retain their molten shape. They can, therefore, be shaped by casting. Owing to their strength, metals are ideally suited for tools, weapons and machinery; they have also been used throughout history for all kinds of decorative, liturgical and utilitarian objects.

See also ARMS AND ARMOUR, COINS, JEWELLERY, MIRROR *and* SCULPTURE.

I. Minoan. II. Cycladic. III. Helladic. IV. Greek. V. Etruscan. VI. Roman.

I. Minoan.

1. Gold and silver. 2. Bronze.

1. GOLD AND SILVER. Gold and silver were first used in Crete soon after the beginning of the Early Minoan (EM) period. Gold was always more common than silver, and considerable quantities of gold jewellery have been found in EM tombs at Mochlos and in the Mesara (*see* JEWELLERY, §1). The few surviving EM precious-metal vessels and weapons were made of silver, though in later periods Minoan craftsmen used both gold and silver for such items. Unless otherwise noted, all objects are in Herakleion, Archaeological Museum.

While silver was rarely used for jewellery during the EM period, it was employed for at least two cups and two daggers, all clearly intended to bring prestige to their owners. A few silver drinking cups also survive from the Middle Minoan (MM) period, for example a kantharos with fluted rim, found at Gournia (*see* MINOAN, fig. 4). By Late Minoan (LM) times Cretan craftsmen were producing fine gold and silver vessels, and the two gold cups with scenes of bull-hunting from Vapheio in mainland Greece (MM IIIB–LM IB; Athens, N. Archaeol. Mus.; see fig. 1) were probably made either on Crete or by expatriate Cretan craftsmen.

Fine gold repoussé and openwork were used from MM times to decorate the hilts and pommels of ceremonial swords and daggers. This practice continued in LM, when gold-leaf was also used to embellish stone vases.

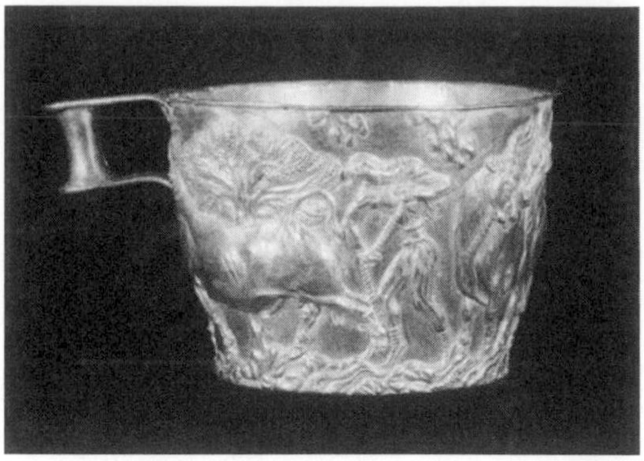

1. Minoan gold cup with peaceful scene of bull-hunting, h. 79 mm, from Vapheio, Middle Minoan IIIB–Late Minoan IB (Athens, National Archaeological Museum)

S. Hood: *The Arts of Prehistoric Greece*, Pelican Hist. A. (Harmondsworth, 1978), pp. 153–70, 173–86

P. Betancourt, ed.: *Gold in the Aegean Bronze Age: Proceedings of the Temple University Aegean Symposium, 8: Philadelphia, 1983*

C. Knappett: *Thinking through Material Culture: An Interdisciplinary Perspective* (n.p., 2005)

Y. M. Rowan and J. R. Ebeling: *New Approaches to Old Stones: Recent Studies of Ground Stone Artifacts* (London and Oakville, CT, 2006)

2. BRONZE. Minoan bronzeworking evolved in three stages. The earliest metal objects from Crete date from EM times and were of copper rather than bronze. Initially, some of the copper was probably extracted locally, but later the island increasingly depended on imported copper from the Cyclades and Attica (*see* §§II, 2 and III, 3 below). It may have been from the Cyclades that the Minoan workshops learnt how to make the arsenical bronze that many produced during EM II. This was, of course, a dangerous alloy to make and use because of the arsenical fumes given off during smelting, so, as access was opened up to tin supplies, probably from the Near East, the Cretans adopted tin bronze for tools and weapons. Copper or very low-tin bronze remained in use for jewellery, toilet implements and other delicate or ornamental items.

Most EM bronzework was devoted to the manufacture of weapons. Short, leaf-shaped daggers and long, narrow ones were the commonest items, though these were perhaps all-purpose knives rather than weapons. Carpenters' tools included various chisels, saws and awls, as well as the first axe-adzes and double axes. Toilet implements such as razors, tweezers and cosmetic scrapers also occur. Only a few other items of copper or arsenical bronze were made at this time; they include bangles, rings, pins and fish-hooks.

In MM times bronzesmiths developed their skills to produce impressive weapons, notably long-swords and spearheads. The swords, up to *c.* 800 mm long, cannot have been used in combat since they are very weakly hafted. They were, however, given gold-embellished hilts and elaborate pommels and presumably served a ceremonial function. New techniques include lost-wax casting and even an early form of 'Sheffield plating' used to silver plate the bronze heads of the rivets in some newly introduced broad, flat daggers.

Abundant supplies of copper and tin were clearly available in LM times, judging by both the quantity of material that survives and the ambitious way in which it was used. Massive cauldrons and huge two-man saws such as those from Tylissos point to a greatly increased scale of production, as does the stack of 'oxhide-type' copper ingots found at Ayia Triada. Numerous weapons, tools and bronze vessels occur in LM tombs and settlements and as many as three houses in the small town of Gournia provide evidence of bronzeworking. There must have been hundreds of bronzesmiths in Late Bronze Age Crete, though probably few were specialist craftsmen.

For bronze sculpture *see* SCULPTURE, §II.

K. Branigan: *Aegean Metalwork of the Early and Middle Bronze Age* (Oxford, 1974)

A. Matthäus: *Die Bronzegefässe der kretisch-mykenischen Kultur* (Munich, 1980)

L. Hakulin: *Bronzeworking on late Minoan Crete: A Diachronic Study* (Oxford, 2004)

II. Cycladic.

Precious metals are not common in the Cycladic Bronze Age but are most frequent in the Early Cycladic (EC) period, when Cycladic craftsmen were active in metallurgical innovation. By contrast, the islands have produced quite large numbers of bronze objects, especially of EC date, and some varieties were probably developed locally. The production of lead is closely related to that of silver, though only a few objects in lead survive: one or two figurines and some model boats from Naxos (EC II; Oxford, Ashmolean).

1. GOLD AND SILVER. Ancient mines have been located at Ayios Sostis on Siphnos, which is known to have been a source of silver and was reputed in later antiquity to possess gold. The only extant gold objects are an EC bead from Naxos (Athens, N. Archaeol. Mus.) and others from a Middle Cycladic (MC) grave on Kea (Kea, Archaeol. Col.). Silver jewellery is slightly more common, especially in EC graves. Its style is influenced by the gold jewellery produced by the people of the Troad and the Minoans. Other silver artefacts include EC shallow bowls from Amorgos (Oxford, Ashmolean) and others of unknown provenance, some with simple linear decoration (EC–MC; e.g. Athens, N. Archaeol. Mus.). Silver diadems have been found on Amorgos and Syros. One has a neat openwork rim; another, from Chalandriani on Syros, has an unusual repoussé frieze representing two collared animals (thought to be dogs), ornamental discs with elaborate sun or star patterns and a birdlike figure (possibly of a deity) with raised arms or wings. The piece is unique among extant Cycladic work and seems to imitate a series of gold diadems from Mochlos in eastern Crete. Silver bracelets and beads also occur: these are plain or decorated with simple linear designs (e.g. Oxford, Ashmolean). Pins with ornamental heads, used to secure garments at the shoulder, are much rarer in silver than in bronze. Most pinheads take the form of simple knobs, cages or spirals of wire. Some represent animals or sea birds: a silver pin from a grave on Amorgos is topped by the lively figure of a ram.

There are few surviving precious metal objects from the MC period, but the Late Cycladic (LC) tombs at Aplomata on Naxos have yielded over 80 rosettes of gold leaf (Naxos, Archaeol. Mus.), pierced for attachment to clothing, as well as some gold-leaf lions, probably made to cover figures of wood or other material. Perhaps also a covering for a figure is a tiny gold mask (diam. 40 mm) from the sanctuary at Phylakopi (Melos Mus.).

2. BRONZE. Several Cycladic islands had sources of copper, and there is evidence for mining and smelting at Siphnos, smelting on Kythnos and casting (moulds, crucibles and hearth) at Kastri on Syros and elsewhere. Tools (chisels, axe heads and a saw) and weapons (dagger or sword blades and spear heads) are the most common artefacts. Tools are prominent in the contents of two EC 'hoards': one (London, BM), long supposed to be from Kythnos, was shown by recent research to be more probably from Naxos; the other was from Kastri (Athens, N. Archaeol. Mus.; Syros Mus.). Notable examples of weapon blades and spear heads were found on Amorgos (London, BM). A number of toilet articles (tweezers) and some items of jewellery (rings, pins) are made of bronze, suggesting that it was considered precious for a long while after its introduction. Like silver pins, those in bronze have ornamental heads, with small animals, spirals etc.

As in other arts the MC period did not produce many bronze objects, but from LC I there is a fine group of bronze vessels from Akrotiri on Thera (Athens, N. Archaeol. Mus.). The shapes, and in one case the decoration, are similar to examples from Knossos and they may have been Cretan imports. Apart from numerous LC tools and weapons, Theran finds include an inlaid dagger blade (Copenhagen, Nmus.) directly comparable to those from mainland Mycenaean shaft graves (*see* §III below). Also from the LC period are a few 'Minoanizing' statuettes from Kea (Kea, Archaeol. Col.) and some of the Near Eastern Reshef type from Phylakopi (Melos Mus.).

R. A. Higgins: *Greek and Roman Jewellery* (London, 1961, rev. 2/1980), pp. 47–51

R. A. Higgins: *Minoan and Mycenaean Art* (London, 1967, rev. 2/1981)

K. Branigan: *Aegean Metalwork of the Early and Middle Bronze Age* (Oxford, 1974)

K. Branigan: 'Metal Objects and Metal Technology of the Cycladic Culture', *Art and Culture of the Cyclades*, ed. P. Getz-Preziosi (Karlsruhe, 1977), pp. 117–22 [Eng. trans. of *Kunst und Kultur der Kykladeninseln im 3. Jahrtausend v. Chr.* (exh. cat., ed. J. Thimme; Karlsruhe, Bad. Landesmus., 1976)]

E. Sapouna-Sakellarakis: 'Cycladic Jewellery', *Art and Culture of the Cyclades*, ed. P. Getz-Preziosi (Karlsruhe, 1977), pp. 123–9 [Eng. trans. of *Kunst und Kultur der Kykladeninseln im 3. Jahrtausend v. Chr.* (exh. cat., ed. J. Thimme; Karlsruhe, Bad. Landesmus., 1976)]

S. Hood: *The Arts in Prehistoric Greece*, Pelican Hist. A. (Harmondsworth, 1978), pp. 190–92

N. H. Gale and Z. A. Stos-Gale: 'Cycladic Metallurgy', *The Prehistoric Cyclades*, ed. J. A. MacGillivray and R. L. N. Barber (Edinburgh, 1984), pp. 255–76

J. L. Fitton: 'Esse quam videre: A Reconsideration of the Kythnos Hoard of Early Cycladic Tools', *Amer. J. Archaeol.*, xciii (1989), pp. 31–9

III. Helladic.

1. Gold and silver. 2. Bronze.

1. GOLD AND SILVER. A gold sauceboat (Early Helladic II; Paris, Louvre), reportedly from Heraia in Arcadia, indicates that mainland Greeks were making vessels of precious metal from an early period, and Middle Helladic (MH) Minyan ware, with its sharply angled profiles, appears to be imitating metalwork; nevertheless, what little gold and silver survives comes almost exclusively from unrobbed, high-status tombs of the Late Helladic (LH) period. The shaft graves of Grave Circle A at MYCENAE (MH III–LH IIA) contained a staggering wealth of gold and silver items, and smaller quantities have been found in graves elsewhere in the Mycenaean world. Despite grave robbing, enough has survived to demonstrate that the Mycenaeans achieved very high standards of artistry in the working of precious metals. (Unless indicated, all objects are in Athens, N. Archaeol. Mus.)

Large amounts of sheet gold were worn by those buried in Grave Circle A. Five wore death masks of thin sheet gold, each one with individual features (see fig. 2). An electrum mask, made of a natural alloy of gold and silver, was found in Grave Gamma of Grave Circle B (MH III–LH I). Gold breast-plates, either plain or decorated with spirals, were also found on some of the skeletons; these were of thin sheet gold and were probably purely for funerary use. The women wore large gold diadems and had thin gold cut-outs sewn on to their funerary clothing. A complete suit made of pieces of sheet-gold was found in Grave III of Grave Circle A; it once adorned a child.

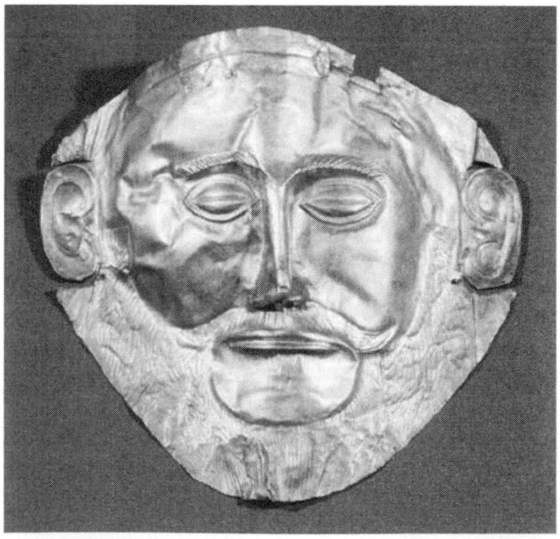

2. Helladic gold mask, the so-called Mask of Agamemnon, 260×265 mm, from Shaft Grave V, Mycenae, Late Helladic I (Athens, National Archaeological Museum)

Many gold and silver vessels were also found in Grave Circle A and Circle B at Mycenae, and some very fine examples have survived in Mycenaean tombs elsewhere in the country. These vessels fall into three broad categories: plain, decorated with repoussé technique and inlaid. They appear to have been made from the mid-LH I period to LH IIIB. The plain vessels include various forms of cups, such as the kantharos (a two-handled cup); a shallow, one-handled cup; the so-called Vapheio cup (tall and straight-sided); and the stemmed goblet. Perhaps the finest of these is the stemmed goblet from Grave Circle A known as Nestor's Cup, with a bird perched on each of two double handles. Vessels with repoussé decoration include an exceptionally beautiful, one-handled, shallow cup from the tholos tomb at DENDRA in the Argolid. Made of sheet gold, it was decorated using repoussé and incision with octopuses and dolphins (LH IIB). Two gold cups from a tholos tomb at Vapheio near Sparta (LH IIA) gave the name to the straight-sided cup already mentioned. These cups have a plain inner lining and a spool-handle, and their outer casings are exquisitely decorated in repoussé with scenes of bull-hunting, one a very turbulent scene, the other more peaceful. One of the finest of the silver vessels from the Mycenae shaft graves is the fragmentary rhyton from Grave IV of Grave Circle A. Its surviving pieces are decorated with battle scenes and the siege of a city. Two other exceptionally fine rhyta from the same grave are a silver bull-head rhyton with gilded horns and a gold rhyton in the form of a lion's head (see colour pl. 1:XV, fig. 2). Sheets of gold were also used to plate non-precious materials: from Grave V of Circle A, for example, came 12 plaques of sheet gold embossed with scenes of animals hunting.

An early example of an inlaid vessel is an electrum stemmed goblet from Grave IV of Circle A, which has a row of gold and glossy black inlaid plants around the rim. Two very similar cups, from Dendra and Enkomi on Cyprus (LH IIB; Nicosia, Cyprus Mus.), are hemispherical silver cups with one wishbone handle, decorated with bulls' heads and floral motifs in gold and a black material that may be a form of niello (an alloy of copper, silver and sulphur). A shallow cup with a ribbon handle from a chamber tomb at Mycenae (LH IIIB) is decorated with inlaid bearded profile heads. Detached heads of a very similar type (also LH IIIB) from the Palace of Nestor at Pylos must be from the same type of inlaid cup.

An inlay technique was also used to decorate the blades of what were probably ceremonial daggers (LH I–II); they are some of the finest products of the age. Several examples dating to the second half of LH I were found in Grave Circle A at Mycenae and a fragmentary blade of the same date on the island of Thera (Copenhagen, Nmus.); LH II examples have been found at the Argive Heraion, at Vapheio and in a tholos tomb at Routsi, near Pylos. The blade of these daggers is of bronze, with a strip of oxidized silver or, less commonly, gold slotted into it. This strip was then inlaid with detailed scenes using gold, silver, copper and black niello. The Mycenae daggers are decorated with such scenes as leopards hunting birds in a Nilotic landscape (see colour pl. 1:XV, fig. 3), running lions and a particularly intricate scene of warriors hunting lions. One of the inlaid daggers from Routsi has a preserved gold hilt and is decorated with leopards hunting in a forest; the other Routsi dagger depicts argonauts in a marine landscape. Sometimes a single motif was enough: on the example from the Argive Heraion there is a dolphin on one side and a flying fish on the other.

R. Higgins: *Minoan and Mycenaean Art* (London, 1967, rev. 2/1981)

E. N. Davis: *The Vapheio Cups and Aegean Gold and Silver Ware* (New York, 1977)

A. Xenaki-Sakellariou and C. Chatziliou: *'Peinture en métal' à l'époque mycénienne* (Athens, 1989)

2. Bronze. The basic functional metal of the Greek Bronze Age was, naturally, bronze. Though bronze daggers are known from Early and Middle Helladic times, most surviving remains are from the Late Helladic period. Mycenaean Greeks used bronze for making tools, weapons and armour, for vessels and for dress and cosmetic items.

Bronze weapons included swords, daggers, spearheads and arrowheads. Two types of long sword are known from the Mycenae shaft graves. The first, known as Type A, could reach almost a metre in length, with a triangular blade strengthened by a midrib. The shoulder of the blade was rounded, and a short tang affixed it to a perishable handle, sometimes made of gold or ivory. The Type B sword, marginally shorter than Type A, had a similar triangular blade with a midrib, but it had a broad, squared shoulder with flanged edges and a longer tang, to fix the blade more securely to the handle.

Much shorter swords were also part of the Mycenaean warrior's repertory, and beginning in the Late Helladic II period sturdier swords with higher midribs and thicker blades began to appear, with tangs that eventually broadened to form a true hilt cast in one piece with the blade. Bronze weapons were sometimes decorated: a beautiful butterfly with outstretched wings was engraved on a long sword (Athens, N. Archaeol. Mus.) from Grave Circle B at Mycenae, for example, and ceremonial bronze daggers were often inlaid with scenes in gold, silver and niello (*see* §1 above).

The earliest bronze spearheads appeared during the MH period and at the very beginning of the LH period; these were made in a bi-valve mould and comprised a bronze blade with a shoe-socket on each side, into which a split wooden shaft was inserted. An alternative form of spear that appeared in the Mycenae shaft graves and lasted throughout the LH period was one with a leaf-shaped blade, a medial rib and a socket for a wooden shaft. Archery was also practised: the arrows, which in the MH period were mostly made of flint and obsidian, began to be made of bronze in appreciable numbers in the MH III–LH I period.

Just as bronze was used for offensive weapons, so it was sometimes used for defensive armour. A unique set of Mycenaean armour, including a corselet with shoulder guards, skirt and greaves, was found in chamber tomb 12 at Dendra (LH IIB; Navplion, Archaeol. Mus.); pieces from similar sets of armour were found in Dendra tomb 8 and at Thebes (Thebes Mus.). In addition to those at Dendra, bronze greaves have also been found on Cyprus (Nicosia, Cyprus Mus.), in Athens (Athens, N. Archaeol. Mus.) and near Patras (Patras, Archaeol. Mus.).

Metal vessels were manufactured throughout the Mycenaean period, made of sheets of hammered bronze riveted together. Many of the surviving examples come from graves, e.g. the Mycenae shaft graves and Dendra (Athens, N. Archaeol. Mus., and Navplion, Archaeol. Mus.). Some smaller vessels have been found in excavations of settlements, such as that of Mycenae. Small bronze vessels include phiale (shallow, one-handled cups) and Vapheio cups, as well as bowls and basins; larger bronze containers include amphorae, jugs and cauldrons. As well as vessels themselves, cast tripod stands in openwork also survive. Items of personal adornment and for cosmetic use include fibulae for fastening clothing and pins, sometimes with rock-crystal heads, such as those found in Grave Omikron of Grave Circle B at Mycenae. Round bronze mirrors, originally affixed to what was probably a wooden handle, were polished until they shone. Other items of bronze for personal and domestic use include needles, tweezers and, at the very end of the Bronze Age, spatulas.

A. M. Snodgrass: *Early Greek Armour and Weapons* (Edinburgh, 1964)

J. D. Muhly: *Copper and Tin* (New Haven, 1973)

K. Branigan: *Aegean Metalwork of the Early and Middle Bronze Age* (Oxford, 1974)

H. Catling: *Cypriot Bronzework in the Mycenaean World* (Oxford, 1974)

IV. Greek.

Greek metalworkers were skilled in extracting gold, silver, copper, tin, lead and iron, and in forging, hammering and casting a wide variety of objects in these metals. There is abundant evidence for the extraction of silver, lead and iron in Greece. Siphnos was a rich source of silver, and Thasos yielded gold as well as silver and lead. The extensive ancient silver and lead mines at Laurion in Attica were in heavy use by the 6th century BC. There are remains of surface trenches, adits, galleries with lamp-blackened walls, deep shafts and abundant debris from the on-site removal of impurities. These activities included pounding, sifting, smelting and washing of the ore. Gold and silver were used primarily to make jewellery, coins and vessels. Lead was used to make various utilitarian objects, such as vessels and architectural clamps, as well as occasional votive plaques and statuettes. Ironworking was introduced to Greece from Anatolia. There were major sources of iron ore in Macedonia, Euboia, Attica, the Peloponnese, the Aegean islands and Crete. Objects such as tools, weapons, architectural clamps, pins and vessels were produced by smelting and hot-forging. There is evidence that in some places iron was worked together with bronze by the same craftsmen in the same workshops. The Greeks made a wide variety of bronze objects, including jewellery, mirrors, tripods, lamps, vessels, tools, coins, arms and armour, statuettes and figurines and large-scale statuary.

P. T. Craddock: 'The Composition of the Copper Alloys Used by the Greek, Etruscan and Roman Civilisations, 2', *J. Archaeol. Sci.* (1977), pp. 103–23

C. C. Mattusch: 'Bronze- and Ironworking in the Area of the Athenian Agora', *Hesperia*, xlvi (1977), pp. 340–79

C. E. Conophagos: *Le Laurium antique* (Athens, 1980)

A. M. Snodgrass: 'Iron and Early Metallurgy in the Mediterranean', *The Coming of the Age of Iron*, ed. T. A. Wertime and J. D. Muhly (New Haven and London, 1980), pp. 335–74

K. D. White: *Greek and Roman Technology* (Ithaca, 1984)

P. C. Bol: *Antike Bronzetechnik* (Munich, 1985)

G. Zimmer: *Antike Bronzegusswerkstätten* (Mainz, 1990)

E. Baboula: *Metalwork in Late Minoan Graves: The Social Dimensions of Depositional Practice in the Funerary Context* (diss., U. Oxford, 2003)

1. Gold and silver.

(i) Survival and evidence. Finds of hoards containing gold and silver plate, such as that discovered at Rogozen in Bulgaria (Sofia, N. Archaeol. Mus.; *see* Rogozen treasure), give some impression of the great quantities of precious metal objects that must have existed in antiquity but that no longer survive. This problem of survival has hindered attempts to understand the range and function of plate in the Greek world. Plate, unlike pottery, has an intrinsic material value and was not carelessly discarded. Instead, it was melted down to make new artefacts. Thus none of the hundreds of items known to have existed in Athens in the Classical and Hellenistic periods seems to have survived in its original form. Indeed, only two pieces from that period have been found anywhere. Much plate was stored in Greek sanctuaries, yet few pieces survive intact: one is a gold phiale from Olympia (*c.* 625–*c.* 550 BC; Boston, MA, Mus. F.A., 21.1843), dedicated by the Kypselids of Corinth after the sack of Herakleia. Thousands of other precious objects were looted during antiquity from cities, sanctuaries and even tombs. Gold and silver formed part of the booty of victorious armies, and descriptions of triumphs after Roman victories in the Greek world record waggon loads of plate. A silver phiale (Kozani, Archaeol. Col., 589), probably of the early 5th century BC but found in a 4th-century BC grave at Kozani in northern Greece, carries an inscription that shows that it had originally been dedicated to Athena at Megara, and this might indicate that her sanctuary there had been sacked.

Important sources of Greek plate are the tombs of Macedonian, Thracian and Scythian aristocrats, who were buried under large mounds with a selection of their wealth alongside them. One series of tombs at Douvanli in Bulgaria yielded several items of Greek silver (mid-5th century BC onwards; Plovdiv, Reg. Archaeol. Mus.), and another tomb group at Semibratny in south Russia contained a series of 5th-century BC silver cups (St Petersburg, Hermitage; for both *see* §(ii) below). Hoards are another important source of plate, although their survival has depended on the person who buried them never recovering the items. Some of the most important include the Rogozen hoard (probably deposited in the late 4th century BC), which seems to have consisted of two bags of damaged silver plate, both local and imported, possibly intended for melting down; the Tuch el-Karamus hoard from Egypt (*c.* 300–*c.* 250 BC; mostly in Cairo, Egyp. Mus.), which seems to have come from the ruins of a small temple and was found with coins and other gold and silver items; and the Taranto hoard (Rothschild priv. col.), which serves to illustrate the range of South Italian plate available in the Hellenistic period.

The poet Pindar considered a gold phiale to be 'the peak of all possessions' (*Olympian Odes* vii.1–4), and other sources seem to indicate that plate was used only by the social élite: during his raid on the house of Anytos, Alcibiades (*c.* 450–404 BC) found a table groaning with plate (Plutarch: *Alcibiades* iv.5), and Socrates was said to have drunk from a cup known as a 'silver well' (Athenaeus: *Deipnosophists* v.192a; Plato: *Symposium* 223c). The Athenian delegation to Segesta in Sicily before the Sicilian expedition of 415–413 BC was, however, astonished by the quantity of plate (albeit borrowed) in use in private houses (Thucydides: VI. xlvi. 3–4).

Plate was also owned by the state. Athens is known to have possessed a set of gold plate at the Olympic Games, where it was misused by Alcibiades for his own entertainment (Plutarch: *Alcibiades* xiii). A set of state plate (a krater, stand and strainer) seems to have been given to Sigeion by Phonodikos, as recorded on a stele (London, BM, 1816.6–10.107). A much larger set of plate is recorded in an inventory from the prytaneion (public hall) on Delos.

(ii) Shapes and techniques. The growing number of finds of gold and silver plate since the late 20th century has led to a reappraisal of the shapes made in precious metal. Most of the extant pieces are phialai, a shape frequently cited in temple inventories. However, as their weights often correspond to a round number of units (e.g. 100 silver drachmae or 100 gold darics; *see* §(iv) below), and phialai could easily be stacked, they probably served as a convenient source of portable wealth. Oinochoai are also relatively common. They may be plain, or ornate with elaborately worked handles.

An attractive example (New York, Met.), perhaps from Greek Asia Minor, has a handle formed by a naked youth who stands on two rams and holds the tails of two lions mounted on the rim. Alabastra are often plain, though their lugs are frequently decorated with duck's heads. One example (New York, Met.) has four incised zones depicting (from top to bottom) confronted cocks, bulls attacked by lions and lionesses, a battle and a duel, and fallow deer. Similar incised decoration is found on a 6th-century BC silver skyphos (New York, Met., 1971.118). A further shape of note is a silver incense burner (6th century BC; New York, Met., 1980.11.12) with its owner's name inscribed in Lydian. Its ridged stand has two duck's-head lugs that recall those on the alabastra, while its conical top bears a statuette of a cock.

Gold and silver rhyta and vases shaped like heads also occur frequently. The Panagyurishte treasure from Bulgaria (?late 4th century BC or early 3rd; Plovdiv, Reg. Archaeol. Mus.) contained a gold amphora–rhyton with two naked armed men attacking a man standing behind a partially open door. Other pieces include goat-, stag- and sheep-headed rhyta with relief scenes on their necks (e.g. the *Judgement of Paris*) and jugs in the form of female heads; one with griffins on the helmet may recall the chryselephantine statue of *Athena Parthenos* at Athens (*see* PHEIDIAS). A silver vase in the form of a head with two faces, perhaps from the Pithom hoard in Egypt (*c.* 400–*c.* 350 BC; London, BM, 1962. 12–12.1; see fig. 3), is also decorated with a relief scene of the *Judgement of Paris*; the figures are identified by Lycian inscriptions. Some mid-4th century BC silver rhyta from the Borovo treasure in Bulgaria (Ruse, Reg. Mus. Hist., II 357–9) are decorated with the foreparts of a galloping horse, bull or sphinx, and one from the Tuch el-Karamus hoard (Cairo, Egyp. Mus., JE 38093) is shaped like a griffin.

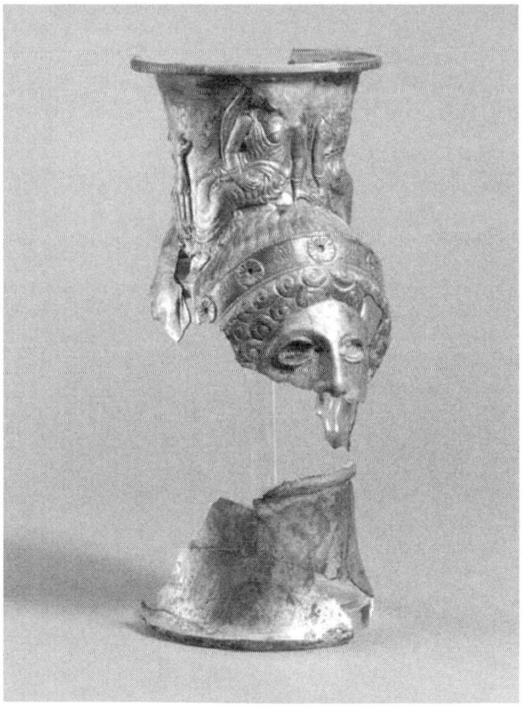

3. Ancient Greek silver double-headed kantharos depicting the *Judgement of Paris*, h. 228 mm, *c.* 350–*c.* 300 BC (London, British Museum)

Some relief scenes appear on medallions attached to pieces of plate. One inside a silver kantharos from Roscigno in Italy (Salerno, Mus. Archeol. Prov.) depicts the Amazon *Andromache*, while a gold medallion in the silver acrocup from the Chemyrev mound in Russia (once in St Petersburg, Hermitage, now lost) depicted a *Nereid on a Hippocamp*. In the gold-figure technique, gold-leaf figures were superimposed on an incised and burnished silver vessel so that the incised detail showed through. An early example of the technique is found on a silver phiale from the so-called Kourion hoard (7th century BC; New York, Met., 74.51.4554). Later examples occur on the finds from the tumuli at Semibratny and the mounds at Douvanli (*see* §i). The subjects on the silver cups from Semibratny include a *Nike*, *Maenads and Satyrs* and a scene perhaps from a Greek tragedy. The kantharos from Douvanli depicts *Maenads and Satyrs*, and the phiale a chariot race. A stemless cup that shows *Selene on a Horse* may also have been decorated in this technique, but only the incised design remains.

(iii) Craftsmen. The literary sources suggest that precious metals were used by the social élite, and it is thus little surprise to find this group owning slaves who could work in these media; in Attica the same group may have derived some of their wealth from the silver mines at Laurion. Kallias Lakkoploutos (*c.* 450–*c.* 370 BC), for instance, is said to have been worth 200 talents (or 5.2 tonnes of silver), some of which may have been obtained from his mining interests. In the confiscated property lists of the mutilators of the herms in late 5th-century BC Athens, one of the slaves is described as a goldsmith and valued at the substantial figure of 360 drachmae, while an enfranchisement decree (possibly of 404/403 BC) includes a goldsmith, which may indicate that such craftsmen were usually slaves.

A crude inscription found on a silver phiale from the Rogozen hoard shows that it belonged to Kotys from Beos and was made by Disloias. A list of metalworkers may be found in Athenaeus' discussion of objects used at a symposion (*Deipnosophists* xi.782b): in particular he noted a Herakleiot skyphos decorated in relief and bearing the epigram 'The design (*gramma*) is by Parrhasios, the work (*techna*) by Mys. I am the representation of lofty Ilium, which the sons of Aiakos captured.' The pair are known for their work on the bronze statue of *Athena Promachos* on the Athenian Acropolis, and this combination of craftsmen finds a parallel in the signatures of potters and painters on Greek pottery. The epigram implies that one craftsman worked from designs (*graphides*) prepared by the other. Pliny (*Natural History* XXXV.xxxvi.68) recorded that many of the designs of PARRHASIOS were still extant in his day (1st century AD).

A further insight into the position of metalworkers is found in the inventory lists of the Treasurers of Athena at Athens, in which objects inscribed with their makers' names are cited: particularly notable are some phialai signed by Nikokrates of Kolonos, who is known from seven inventory lists and was active for over twenty years. Some 26 vessels are linked to his name. His work seems to have included melting down dedications and reworking the precious metal: in 320/319 BC he made five hydriai from silver phialai dedicated by freedmen.

(iv) Metrology. Gold and silver plate was significant for its sheer intrinsic value. A gold phiale could be treasured precisely because it was worth its weight in gold. Temple inventories show that silver phialai regularly weighed exactly 100 drachmae, while gold objects were often equivalent to a round number of darics (though valued in silver drachmae). Many silver items in these lists were ascribed weights in Attic drachmae, though they were actually made to a weight standard based on the Persian coin called the siglos. Indeed, very little extant silver plate was made to an Attic standard, as there was a great diversity of areas that were producing plate. Some of the few pieces that do seem to have been made to an Attic standard were found at Douvanli, for example the gold-figure silver phiale weighing 100 drachmae and two silver kantharoi weighing 250 and 200 drachmae respectively. The daric seems to have been a common unit for weighing gold plate. A gold phiale (New York, Met., 62.11.1) carries the Phoenician numeral for 180 but actually weighs 90 darics, while the gold phiale from Panagyurishte (Plovdiv, Reg. Archaeol. Mus., 3204) carries two inscriptions, one giving its weight in darics (100), the other, probably, its weight in Attic drachmae.

(v) Plate and pottery. Although much ancient plate has been melted down, it is possible to obtain a glimpse of the range of objects from their pottery surrogates. It has long been noted that Greek pottery includes metallic features. Rivets adjoining handles are found on the rims of hydriai, while palmettes are painted under the handles of oinochoai in the same position as the moulded palmettes on their metal counterparts, and moulded rings emphasize different parts of the vessel. Similarly, an Attic Red-figure acrocup attributed to the Diomed Painter (Boston, MA, Mus. F.A., 00.354) is clearly derived from a silver cup such as the one found in the Chemyrev mound: their profiles are similar, and the bowls of both are decorated with vertical ribbing. The gold tondo of the Chemyrev cup showing a *Nereid on a Hippocamp* may be paralleled by the Red-figure painting of *Sparte* in the Boston cup. There are also close correspondences between two vertically ribbed mugs from the same mound at Douvanli (5th century BC; Plovdiv, Reg. Archaeol. Mus., 1518 and 1530): one was of silver and the other of Attic clay. Horizontally ribbed Thracian beakers, such as that from Boukyovtsi (4th century BC; Sofia, N. Archaeol. Mus., 6694), are directly paralleled by Attic Black-glossed beakers. Other close parallels in shape are found for Rheneia cups, skyphoi and even perfume pots.

It is possible, too, that particular colours were chosen by potters to evoke specific materials. Thus the grey slips of Etruscan pottery (*see* POTTERY, §V) were perhaps imitating 'patinated' silver, and yellow slips evoked gold. Likewise, the grey appearance of Lesbian Bucchero may have been intended to suggest silver. Similarly, the 'metallic' nature of Attic and other black-glossed pottery may reflect the taste for patinated silver in some parts of the Mediterranean. 'Patination' certainly occurs on the silverware from Dălboki in Thrace, though that found at Aigai (Vergina) in Macedonia seems to have been more highly polished. The idea that potters deliberately imitated metal prototypes is supported by Athenaeus' statement (*Deipnosophists* xi. 480e) that they 'baptized' their vases to make them appear like silver. It has also been suggested that the purple added to such features as fillets and ridges on Greek pottery might be evoking copper seams in silver vessels, and there is a clear association between the Red-figure decoration on clay vessels and the gold-figure technique found on silver ones.

D. E. Strong: *Greek and Roman Gold and Silver Plate* (London, 1966)

A. Oliver jr: *Silver for the Gods: 800 Years of Greek and Roman Silver* (Toledo, 1977)

D. von Bothmer: 'A Greek and Roman Treasury', *Bull. Met.*, xlii/1 (1984) [whole issue]

M. Vickers: 'Demus's Gold *Phiale* (Lysias 19.25)', *Amer. J. Anc. Hist.*, ix (1984), pp. 48–53

M. Vickers, ed.: *Pots and Pans: A Colloquium on Precious Metals and Ceramics in the Muslim, Chinese and Graeco-Roman Worlds: Oxford, 1985*, pp. 9–30, 71–81

M. Vickers, O. Impey and J. Allan: *From Silver to Ceramic: The Potter's Debt to Metalwork in the Graeco-Roman, Oriental and Islamic Worlds* (Oxford, 1986)

D. W. J. Gill: 'Two New Silver Shapes from Semibratny (Seven Brothers' Tumuli)', *Annu. Brit. Sch. Athens*, lxxxii (1987), pp. 47–53

D. W. J. Gill: 'Expressions of Wealth: Greek Art and Society', *Antiquity*, lxii (1988), pp. 735–43

D. Harris: 'Nikokrates of Kolonos: Metalworker to the Parthenon Treasurers', *Hesperia*, lvii (1988), pp. 329–37

M. Vickers and D. W. J. Gill: *Artful Crafts: Ancient Greek Silverware and Pottery* (Oxford, 1994)

Greek Gold: Jewellery of the Classical World (exh. cat. by D. Williams and J. Ogden; London, BM; St Petersburg, Hermitage; New York, Met.; 1994–5)

H. Mussche: *Thorikos: A Mining Town in Ancient Attika* (Ghent, 1998)

Kosmemata tes hellenikes proistorias: Ho neolithikos thesauros (exh. cat., ed. K. Demakopoulou; Athens, N. Archaeol. Mus., 1998–9)

B. Tsigarida and D. Ignatiadou: *The Gold of Macedon: Archaeological Museum of Thessaloniki* (Athens, 2000)

M. Pfrommer: *Greek Gold from Hellenistic Egypt* (Los Angeles, 2002)

Y. Kalashnik: *Greek Gold: From the Treasure Rooms of the Hermitage* (Aldershot, 2005)

2. Bronze. Our fairly extensive knowledge of ancient bronze technology is based on the evidence of ancient foundries and the bronzes themselves, as well as literary testimonia and vase paintings. Aside from the striking of coins, bronzes were hammered or cast. Analyses of bronzes from Greece reveal the use of copper–tin and copper–tin–lead alloys. Copper and tin were apparently not available in Greece itself but were imported from other parts of the Mediterranean and the Near East. Bronze-casting workshops ranging in date from the 10th century BC to the Hellenistic period have been excavated on mainland Greece and the islands; these were evidently temporary establishments. Finds from them include casting pits, simple pit and shaft furnaces and casting debris in the form of broken clay moulds, pumice for polishing the bronzes and spills or drips from the pouring of the bronze. A number of Greek vases depict metalworkers, such as the name-piece of the Foundry Painter, the outside of which shows workmen joining and polishing two bronze statues.

(i) Statuettes and figurines.

(a) Introduction. Bronze figurines were already being cast in significant numbers in the Greek world during the 9th century BC. Most served as votive gifts and were dedicated in sanctuaries. Olympia has yielded many early figurines, as well as many failed castings, proving that at least some of the bronzes were made in the region of the sanctuary. Free-standing figurines were cast solid by the direct lost-wax process: the wax was cut, rolled, pinched and tooled, and the wax body parts were stuck together; the wax model was invested with a clay mould, which was baked to burn out the wax, and bronze was then poured into the mould to replace the wax. Often the base was cast with the figurine.

The artists who made statuettes and figurines were working in a tradition that included decorative attachments for utilitarian objects, such as standing figurines made as part of mirror-handles, and reclining banqueters or cavorting satyrs, made separately as if free-standing and attached to the rims of bronze vessels.

Like the utilitarian objects and protomes that were always produced serially as a matter of course, small Greek bronzes were not necessarily unique productions. A growing body of evidence indicates that replication was an established process as early as the Archaic period. Bronzes from the same moulds could turn out looking very much alike, or the waxes could be finished so that the final appearance of the bronzes was quite varied.

Statuettes and figurines dedicated as votive offerings have been found in all the major sanctuaries. Significant numbers of small bronzes have been found in Athens, Olympia, Delphi, the Argive Sanctuary of Hera, the Kabeirion in Boiotia, Tegea, Sparta, Thasos, Samos and elsewhere. Traditionally they have been grouped according to the theory that there were various centres of production and that these turned out stylistically similar bronzes. Bronze workshops certainly existed near many sanctuaries, but small bronzes could also easily have been carried into a particular sanctuary from an entirely different locale. The use of duplicative processes complicates the question of regional styles, since this type of production meant that the master moulds taken from the original model could also be transported elsewhere for casting and finishing.

It is clear that bronze statuettes and figurines were produced long before large-scale bronzes and that their makers were working in a different technical tradition; this gave them far greater freedom than the sculptors of monumental bronzes, who were limited by types that had been established for works in marble. It was not until the Archaic period that sculptors began to make large-scale images, and these followed the formulaic types established by Archaic marble sculpture. Naturalistic statues that exploited the tensile strength of bronze seem to have first appeared in the Early Classical period. Questions still to be addressed in the field of bronze statuettes and figurines include an investigation of the nature of the connections between large- and small-scale bronzes of similar types; and a study of workshop practices, to see if artists producing large-scale bronzes might also have produced statuettes. The authenticity of certain Classical and Hellenistic bronzes collected during the 19th century has also been questioned, because of their close similarity to Renaissance and Baroque statuettes and the need at that time to satisfy an eager market.

(b) Geometric (c. 900–c. 700 BC). Geometric figurines represented birds, animals and men. Horses, cows and deer might be grouped with their young. The figurines of men had little detail beyond head, limbs, genitals and sometimes a hat or helmet, a shield and a sword. Simple standing or splay-legged figures are usually described as warriors, and early images of women can be distinguished by their long skirts. By the 8th century BC there were images of artisans and musicians (e.g. *Seated Flute-player*, Baltimore, MD, Walters A.G.), as well as chariot groups, fighting animals and even a man fighting a centaur, perhaps an early representation of Herakles and Nessos (New York, Met.).

(c) Archaic (c. 700–c. 480 BC). During the 7th century BC generic standing men became more specific representations of ram- or calf-bearers, kouroi and striding, attacking gods—all types that continued through the 6th century BC. Korai, riders and runners (see fig. 4) were also among the types of small bronzes produced during the 6th century BC. By the Archaic period bronze sculptors enjoyed great freedom to represent a wide range of poses and movements on a small scale. By contrast, large-scale cast bronze statuary was not introduced until the 6th century BC and was evidently limited, during the Archaic period, by the types and poses that were current in Archaic stone sculpture.

Archaic bronze statuettes and figurines have been found in particularly large numbers in Olympia, Athens, Delphi, Dodona and Samos. Traditionally, they have been grouped according to the theory that there were various regional centres of production, in Attica, Aigina, Corinth, Sikyon, Argos, Sparta, Arcadia, Sicily and South Italy, and East Greece. These identifications are generally based on style rather than find-spots. However, some of the most sophisticated of small Archaic bronzes have been found at the Sanctuary of Hera on Samos and were probably made in the vicinity. They complement the literary sources that ascribe legendary skills and achievements in casting techniques to the Samian bronze-workers RHOIKOS AND THEODOROS.

Hollow-cast figures could be produced by starting with a wax model on a clay core; but if the casting failed, the wax model was lost. To avoid this there

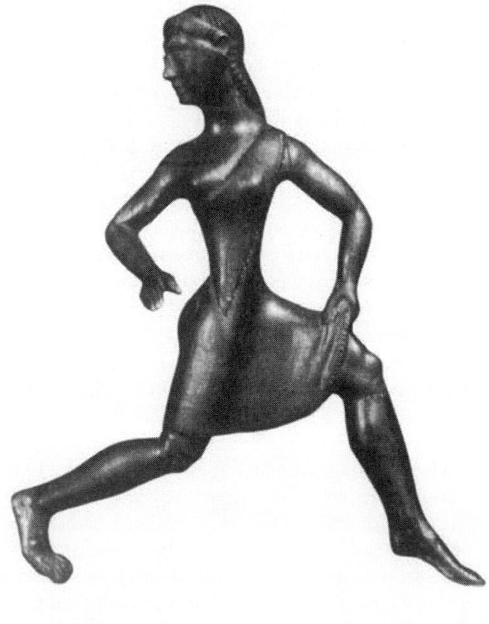

4. Ancient Greek bronze figurine of a *Running Girl,* h. 114 mm, possibly made in Sparta, *c.* 520–*c.* 500 BC (London, British Museum)

developed, as early as the Archaic period, many variations on the processes of lost-wax casting, some of which were no doubt intended to impress potential buyers, whereas others were needed to meet the growing demand for bronzes. An unusually large statuette of a kore from the Sanctuary of Hera on Samos (h. 270 mm, Samos, Archaeol. Mus., B 1441) is one of an increasing number of Archaic bronzes now known to have been hollow-cast; it originally had inlaid eyes. By the 6th century BC statuettes were being made in separately moulded sections that were either joined together before casting or cast in separate pieces and then joined. One example of this is a statuette of *Hermes Carrying a Ram*, whose left arm with ram was apparently separately cast (Boston, MA, Mus. F.A., Pierce Fund 04.6). The figure of Hermes also has black rays painted on his brimmed hat (*petasos*), an indication that colouristic effects were being sought. The use of a single model for more than one bronze is proven by the identical appearance and measurements of two Archaic bronze riders from Samos (Samos, Archaeol. Mus., B 97 and B 2608) and by two bronze kouroi, also from Samos (Berlin, Antikensamml., 31098; Samos, Archaeol. Mus., B 2605), the only real difference between the latter being that the left leg of one was inscribed by the dedicator, Smikros.

(d) Classical (c. 480–323 BC). The introduction of commemorative athletic statuary in the late 6th century BC led to an emphasis, during the Early Classical period (*c.* 480–*c.* 450 BC), on the direct imitation of the physical appearance of victors—their ages, stances, gestures and movements. The athletes that were represented might be engaged in sport or they might be shown victorious, perhaps crowning themselves or making offerings, or they were simply shown as generic standing youths in the tradition of kouroi. A concern with space, action and viewpoint is also evident in statuettes of Early Classical date. For example, a runner at Olympia tensed for the start was placed lengthwise on the base, because the anticipated action would proceed in a straight line, but a discus thrower preparing to throw was attached diagonally to the base to emphasize his pivoting movement (e.g. Athens, N. Archaeol. Mus., 6615 and 6930). The trend towards naturalism continued throughout the Classical period, in both monumental and small bronze sculpture. Copper and silver inlays were commonly used for lips and nipples, and eyes might be inset in materials that increased the illusion of realism. There is also evidence that the surfaces of some bronze statuettes were painted or patinated.

In the 5th century BC statuettes of standing athletes, heroes and generals developed from the Archaic type of the kouros. A few statuette groups from this period also survive. For example, two nude athletes of about 460 BC from Delphi (Delphi, Archaeol. Mus., 7722) stand on one plinth and turn inwards, one gesturing towards the other, who is holding jumping weights. Gaze and gesture link the two figures, not their shared base. The Classical subject of Athena

Promachos ('warlike Athena') was apparently a variation on the popular 6th-century BC type of the striding attacking god. Statuettes of Athena Promachos from Athens (e.g. Athens, N. Archaeol. Mus., 6447) may have echoed the colossal bronze *Athena* by Pheidias that stood, fully armed, on the Athenian Acropolis.

Fewer bronze statuettes survive from the Classical period than from the Archaic period, and fewer come from known contexts. As a result, scholars tend to associate them not so much with regional centres of production as with particular sculptors, such as Pythagoras of Rhegion, Myron, Kresilas, Polykleitos and Pheidias, whose most famous large-scale works the highly naturalistic and three-dimensional bronze statuettes are thought to echo. The influence of large-scale works by Praxiteles has been discerned in the statuettes of Aphrodite that began to appear in the 4th century BC. His most famous statue was the *Aphrodite of Knidos* (Roman copy; Rome, Vatican, Mus. Pio-Clementino), which showed the goddess emerging from the bath. Bronze statuettes show her thus, or with a seashell, hiding her nudity, drying her hair, crouching, binding her sandal, draped or baring one leg. Lysippos' large bronze athletes are thought to have influenced the many statuettes of athletes that survive. Lysippos was the court portraitist for Alexander the Great, and his portrait of the ruler, though based on the tradition of heroic standing figures, is a distinctive variant of that type that continued to be popular during both the Hellenistic and Roman periods. The emphasis that Lysippos is said to have placed on the turn of Alexander's head, on the gaze and on the sense of power can be seen in statuettes of this type, standing with one hand outstretched and the other raised, probably holding a spear.

(e) Hellenistic (323–27 BC). Early in the Hellenistic period significant additions were made to the types of bronze statuettes, and changes occurred in their production and distribution. The Classical stylistic tradition was still important, and some statuettes certainly still echoed large bronzes, for example one type of popular small-scale personification of Tyche (Fortune), which was presumably based upon an early 3rd-century BC statue made by Eutychides for the city of Antioch. In fact, so few original Hellenistic monumental sculptures survive that bronze statuettes are often incorrectly treated as if they were, in general, copies of large-scale works. Even for those that are, consideration must be given to reduction in scale, change in function and variations made by the new artist, who may have significantly revised the original appearance.

Small bronzes were obviously appreciated and collected for their own sake. Certain popular types, such as that of the sleeping Eros, had such a wide appeal that they were reproduced in bronze, terracotta and marble, in all sizes, and were distributed all over the Mediterranean, Europe, Egypt and Asia Minor. Genre subjects in particular proliferated, and private ownership of works of sculpture greatly increased. Deities were still represented, with new ones introduced to accommodate new cults and a wider clientele. Common subjects were Aphrodite at her toilet, Eros with his mother or on his own, hermaphrodites, Isis and Harpokrates, Hypnos, Pan, satyrs and various other Dionysiac figures. The ordinary, the exotic and the grotesque seem to have been of particular interest: besides the traditional gods, athletes and portraits, large numbers of statuettes now represented foreigners, blacks, comic actors and street-people. There were small bronzes not only of famous philosophers but also of unknown people, shown dancing, crouching, wrestling and sleeping. The human figure was shown in youth, old age, sickness and deformity. Decorative details were emphasized, patination and painting were used, and such features as eyes, teeth, lips, nipples, fillets and drapery ornaments were often inlaid in copper, silver and niello.

In addition to Greece proper, major centres of production now included Egypt, Asia Minor and Syria. During the Hellenistic period, Rome became a major market and established its own workshops, which also produced the popular types of small bronzes, in the same styles as Greek workshops. Thus an extremely widespread koine grew up, with the result that it is difficult to establish a chronology and identify regional differences among Hellenistic small bronzes. Stylistic dating is impossible: Hellenistic bronzes may be adaptations or copies of Classical or even Archaic works or types.

Because so few Hellenistic bronzes can be dated securely or placed firmly in context, much importance has been attached to the so called Mahdia shipwreck, which still contained its large cargo of marbles and bronzes when it was discovered off the coast of Tunisia in 1907. The ship is thought to have sailed from mainland Greece, perhaps Attica, during the early 1st century BC and to have been wrecked *en route* to North Africa, Rome or the western Mediterranean. Besides bronze lamps, candelabra, vessels and furniture attachments, the cargo contained a large bronze herm, a bronze statue and numerous bronze statuettes of Hermes, erotes, hermaphrodites, satyrs, dancing dwarfs, actors and a dog. Despite much scholarly speculation, it has not been possible to ascertain exactly where this cargo originated or to assign the bronzes to a particular regional workshop, and it is perhaps best to see them as exemplifying the range of marketable types and styles that were being produced throughout the Mediterranean during the late Hellenistic period.

E. Langlotz: *Frühgriechische Bildhauerschulen* (Nuremberg, 1927)
W. Lamb: *Ancient Greek and Roman Bronzes* (London, 1929/*R* Chicago, 1969)
U. Jantzen: *Bronzewerkstätten in Grossgriechenland und Sizilien* (Berlin, 1937)
J. Charbonneaux: *Les Bronzes grecs* (Paris, 1958); Eng. trans. by K. Watson as *Greek Bronzes* (London and New York, 1962)
H. G. Niemeyer: 'Attische Bronzestatuetten der spätarchaischen und frühklassischen Zeit', *Ant. Plast.*, iii (1964), pp. 7–76
D. G. Mitten and S. F. Doeringer, eds: *Master Bronzes from the Classical World* (Mainz, 1967)

C. Rolley: *Greek Minor Arts: The Bronzes* (1967), v/1 of *Monumenta Graeca et Romana*, ed. H. F. Mussche (Leiden, 1963–)
R. Thomas: *Athletenstatuetten der Spätarchaik und des strengen Stils* (Rome, 1981)
C. Rolley: *Les Bronzes grecs* (Fribourg, 1983)
K. Gschwantler and others, eds: *Guss und Form: Bronzen aus der Antikensammlung* (Vienna, 1986)
A. P. Kozloff and D. G. Mitten, eds: *The Gods Delight: The Human Figure in Classical Bronze* (Cleveland, OH, 1988)
Small Bronze Sculpture from the Ancient World, Malibu, CA, Getty Mus. (Malibu, 1990)
G. Hellenkemper Salies and others, eds: *Das Wrack: Der antike Schiffsfund von Mahdia* (Cologne, 1994)
I. Vokotopoulou: *Ellenike Techne: Argyra Kai chalkina Erga technes sten archaioteta* (Athens, 1997)
J. Maran: 'The Spreading of Objects and Ideas in the Late Bronze Age Eastern Mediterranean: Two Case Examples from the Argolid of the 13th and 12th Centuries BC', *Bull. Amer. Sch. Orient. Res.,* cccxxxvi (Nov 2004), pp. 11–30

(ii) Vessels and mirrors. During the Geometric period (*c.* 900–*c.* 700 BC), the Greeks used bronze vessels for dedications and for funerary offerings; later, bronze vessels were prizes for athletic victories. By the Classical period (*c.* 480–323 BC) they were being sold throughout the Mediterranean world as luxury items. Greek bronze vessels have been found not only in Greece, South Italy, Sicily and Asia Minor but also in northern Europe, in North Africa and at sites along the Black Sea coast. Bronze vessels were usually made by hammering discs of sheet-bronze into hollow shapes, which might then be turned on a lathe for further shaping and detailing. Occasionally, bronze vessels were cast. Handles were separately cast and mass produced, as were feet and sometimes the rims of vessels. Feet, rims and handles were soldered or riveted to the body of the vessel, which might be decorated by the addition of other cast features. Sometimes the walls of bronze vessels were given repoussé or engraved decoration.

(a) 9th–7th centuries BC. During the 9th and 8th centuries BC Geometric bronze cauldrons (round vessels with wide mouths attached to tripod bases) were standard dedications in Greek sanctuaries. Particularly large numbers of tripod cauldrons come from Olympia (Olympia, Archaeol. Mus.), but examples survive from all major Greek sanctuaries. They range in height from less than 100 mm to several metres. The smallest were fully cast, but larger tripod cauldrons were hammered vessels on to which cast legs and cast vertical ring handles were attached with rivets. The wax models made for casting the legs and handles by the lost-wax process were incised or stamped with ornaments like those on Geometric pottery: zigzags, chevrons, circles, running spirals, meanders. Sometimes small panels near the tops of the legs contain human or animal figures in Geometric style. The ring handles may be solid bronze, or they may have pierced openwork designs; three-dimensional cast birds or horses may be attached to the tops of the ring handles, or they may be cast along with them. Sometimes human figures stand on the rim of the cauldron, supporting the handles.

During the Orientalizing period of the 8th and 7th centuries BC, dedications included the phiale, a type of offering-bowl with a raised central boss and repoussé walls. Phialai were also produced in contemporary Near Eastern cultures. Also at that time a new type of tripod cauldron was introduced to Greece from the East. The legs were formed of groups of bronze rods, which were bent into arches on three sides. A bronze ring attached at the tops of these arches supported the circular base of the hammered sheet-bronze cauldron. Another support just above the feet was often used to stabilize the base. The Greeks produced such cauldrons in large numbers, with separately made decorative Orientalizing motifs attached around the rims. These motifs included bulls' heads, sirens and, most frequently, the necks and heads of griffins. Groups of four to eight griffins were attached to the rims by rivets at the bases of their long necks. The earliest of these griffin protomes were hammered bronze; by the 7th century BC they were usually cast, though some particularly large cast heads were fitted to hammered necks. Herodotus (*Histories* IV.clii) describes a huge cauldron made on Samos during the 7th century BC for a cost of six talents, a tithe of the profit made on a trading expedition to Spain. The cauldron was decorated with griffins' heads and supported by three kneeling bronze figures, which alone were seven cubits high (*c.* 3.5 m). Of the tripod cauldrons dedicated on the Acropolis at Athens during the Orientalizing period, only fragmentary sheet-bronze decorations for the tripod legs survive (Athens, Acropolis Mus.); they are embossed with both heraldic and narrative figural decoration.

(b) 6th–1st centuries BC.

Cauldrons. The popularity of cauldrons on rod-tripod bases continued throughout the 6th century BC and beyond, the tripods becoming more and more richly decorated. The legs might have feet in the form of paws, claws or hooves, and terminations above in the form of ducks' or serpents' heads. Cast ornaments, such as palmettes and, later, plaques with animal or figural decoration, were affixed to the arches at the tops of the legs. A third bronze ring was sometimes added to accommodate further ornament, such as crouching lions, striding bulls, horses' heads or snakes. Diagonal supports were sometimes needed to strengthen and stabilize the base.

Some cauldrons were colossal. One reported by Herodotus (*Histories* I.lxx) as being made for King Croesus of Lydia by the Lakedaimonians had figures around the rim and held some 2700 gallons; this, however, was only about half the capacity of a vast cauldron allegedly made for Ariantes of Scythia (*Histories* IV.lxxxi). Part of one such huge dedication survives: it is a cast bronze column in the form of three entwined snakes that supported a golden tripod cauldron set up at Delphi to commemorate the Greeks' defeat of the Persians at Plataia in 479 BC (*Histories* IX.lxxxi; Pausanias: *Guide to Greece* X.xiii.9). The column, which has been in the Hippodrome at Istanbul since the 4th century AD, is *c.* 5.35 m high; the ensemble of tripod and cauldron must have approached 6 m in height.

Other Vessels. Beginning in the 6th century BC, many of the finest bronze vessels appear to have been made in South Italy and Sicily. These workshops are often said to have been influenced by centres in mainland Greece. Both Lakonian and local workshops have been suggested for a magnificent group of six bronze hydriai and two bronze amphorae of the late 6th century BC from the underground shrine at Paestum (anc. Poseidonia) in South Italy (Paestum, Mus. Archeol. N.). When found, the vases were still filled with honey and sealed with wax.

Most extant bronze kraters range in height from *c.* 500 mm to *c.* 700 mm. However, a late 6th-century BC krater from a tomb at Vix in Burgundy, France, is unusually large, being 1.64 m high with a volume of some 315 gallons (Châtillon-sur-Seine, Mus. Archéol.). Its workmanship and its elaborate decoration are also very unusual. The body and neck of the Vix Krater were hammered from a single sheet of bronze, resulting in walls of 1.0–1.5 mm thick. The foot, evidently cast, is soldered on; the two parts of the rim, the volute handles and the strainer covering the mouth were separately cast and attached with rivets. The handles are supported by Gorgons with serpents' heads for feet. The strainer-cover, typical of large wine containers, has for a handle a cast statuette of a veiled female in a belted *peplos* (h. 190 mm). Twenty-three separately cast figures attached to the neck represent a military procession. Letters on the backs of the figures corresponding to letters on the neck indicate their proper placement. Corinth, Lakonia and a colony in South Italy have all been suggested as origins for the Vix Krater.

In addition to elaborate tripod cauldrons, other types of vessel particularly suited to manufacture in bronze included double-handled situlae, plates, and the bowls with human- and animal-figure handles known as paterae. Even some of these shapes, however, also occur in pottery. Other bronze vessels fairly closely match contemporary pottery shapes, including kraters, hydriai, amphorae, oinochoai and basins (*see* POTTERY, fig. 15). In bronze, the range of plastic decoration is vast and is generally more fully exploited than in pottery. Vertical handles may have a Gorgon's head, a palmette, a scroll, or the bust of a woman, a siren or a Silenos mask at the base. The tops of handles, too, may be decorated with floral elements, with the foreparts of horses or with busts of women. Beginning in the 6th century BC, some handles take the form of rampant lions or of youths resembling kouroi, arching over backwards (Athens, N. Archaeol. Mus.). Hands may also be used as parts of handles, either clutching a vertical handle or extending from a horizontal handle as if to clasp the body of the vessel. Handles on a type of 4th-century BC hydria known as a kalpis have relief scenes at the base of the handle relating to Eros, Dionysos, and Boreas and Oritheia.

A fragmentary late 5th-century BC cast bronze krater, found in south Russia but evidently made in Attica (original h. *c.* 420–45 mm; Berlin, Antikensamml., 30622), is decorated with an entire Dionysiac scene: maenads dance and kill animals, and heads of a bearded Dionysos adorn the bases of the handles.

Numerous bronze vessels have been found in Macedonian tombs. One of the finest is a late 4th-century BC krater from a tomb at Derveni near Thessaloniki, weighing *c.* 40 kg (Thessaloniki, Archaeol. Mus.). Its decoration is similar to that of the Berlin krater, but there is far greater detail, and the Derveni Krater was produced with a technical virtuosity that surpasses that of the Vix Krater. Because of its high tin content (*c.* 15%) and its excellent state of preservation, the Derveni Krater resembles gold. A silver inscription inlaid on the lip names the man whose ashes it contained: Asteiounios of Larisa. The body of the Derveni Krater seems to have been hammered in two parts that join halfway up the neck at a point that serves as a ground-line for an animal frieze. The base, handles and cover of the krater were cast, as were the four statuettes seated on its shoulder (Dionysos, two maenads and a satyr with a wineskin, each *c.* 300 mm high). The rich plastic ornament on the volute handles includes snakes twining along the volutes and masks of Herakles, Acheloos, Poseidon and Hades within the volutes. Below the animal frieze on the shoulder is a vine; there is another silver grapevine on the body, in appliqué. Repoussé decoration on the belly of the vase shows the marriage of Dionysos and Ariadne; a panther; and an orgiastic scene, with a wildly dancing maenad holding a child by the ankle, slung over her shoulder upside down, five more frenzied maenads, two of them holding animals, a bearded man dancing and brandishing his sword (?Pentheus or Lykourgos) and a standing Silenos. The left hand of Dionysos is solid-cast and attached to the vessel. Below the main scene, griffins tear up a stag and lions fell a bull. The decoration of the Derveni Krater has been described as chthonic, relating to resurrection and eternal revelry.

During the Hellenistic period (323–27 BC), tastes tended towards expensive and elaborate vessels, whether in bronze or silver and gold. The elegant shapes from this period include long-stemmed krateriskoi, graceful kantharoi, animal-head rhyta, fancy pyxides standing on lions' paws, and spouted situlae. On Hellenistic hydriai, oinochoai and amphorae the decoration at the base of the handle is commonly a bust or a mask, and the handle itself takes the shape of a human or animal. Inlays may be found. Decorative bosses within cups or bowls sometimes show in relief a rosette or leaf decoration, a figural scene or a three-quarter view of the head of a bejewelled woman, a drunken satyr or Silenos. Because artists travelled between cities, it is difficult to distinguish regional styles, but major centres for the production of metal vessels were apparently located in Macedonia and Thessaly, South Italy and Asia Minor.

Mirrors. Both hand mirrors and standing mirrors were cast in Greece during the 6th and 5th centuries BC (*see also* MIRROR). The disc of the hand mirror, polished on the reflecting side, terminated in either a flat handle or a tang for insertion into a wood or bone handle. The handle might be decorated with a figure in relief or with a more elaborate figural scene in openwork relief that was included between the disc and the handle. The standing mirror was particularly popular during the 5th century BC. Its handle might take the form of a column or a statuette of a kore wearing a *chiton* or *peplos*. The base of the mirror could be a stool or an animal upon which the statuette stood. Decoration included such elements as palmettes, volutes, rosettes, birds and animals, and it could encircle the mirror's polished disc. By the 4th century BC both types had been largely replaced by the more compact round box-mirror, consisting of a cast disc polished on the front and hinged to a hammered or cast lid. A repoussé decoration might be soldered on to the lid with lead. Aphrodite and Eros are among the most common subjects for lid-decoration, and there are some erotic scenes and scenes involving Dionysos or Herakles, but there are also a few examples of lids decorated with battle scenes. The inside of cast lids was sometimes decorated with incised and silvered figure scenes.

W. Lamb: *Ancient Greek and Roman Bronzes* (London, 1929/*R* Chicago, 1969)

W. Züchner: 'Der Berliner Mänadenkrater', *98. Winckelmannsprogramm der Archäologischen Gesellschaft zu Berlin* (Berlin, 1938)

J. Charbonneaux: *Les Bronzes grecs* (Paris, 1958); Eng. trans. by K. Watson as *Greek Bronzes* (London and New York, 1962)

C. Rolley: *Greek Minor Arts: The Bronzes* (1967), v/1 of *Monumenta Graeca et Romana*, ed. H. F. Mussche (Leiden, 1963–)

E. Yuri: *O krateras tou Derveniou* [The Derveni Krater] (Athens, 1978)

R. Joffroy: *Vix et ses trésors* (Paris, 1979)

B. Barr-Sharrar: 'Macedonian Metal Vases in Perspective: Some Observations on Context and Tradition', *Macedonia and Greece in Late Classical and Early Hellenistic Times*, ed. B. Barr-Sharrar and E. Borza, Studies in the History of Art, x (Washington, DC, 1982), pp. 123–39

J. R. Mertens: 'Greek Bronzes in the Metropolitan Museum of Art', *Bull. Met.*, xliii (1985), pp. 3–65

J. R. Mertens: 'The Human Figure in Classical Bronzeworking: Some Perspectives', *Small Bronze Sculpture from the Ancient World*, ed. M. True and J. Podany (Malibu, 1990), pp. 85–99

B. Borell and D. Rittig: *Orientalische und griechische Bronzereliefs aus Olympia: Der Fundcomplex aus Brunnen*, xvii (Berlin and New York, 1998)

H. Philipp and H. Born: *Archaische Silhouettenbleche und Schildzeichen in Olympia* (Berlin, 2004)

V. Etruscan.

Etruria was the primary metal-producing region in Italy, and Etruscan metalwork was of the highest quality.

1. INTRODUCTION. Literary sources refer to the extraction of iron and copper on Elba and around Populonia, and there are actual remains of open-cast workings, quarries and tunnels, although these are difficult to date precisely and some are undoubtedly not of the Etruscan period. There are also extensive traces of metalworking activities, such as the finds of slag and furnaces at Populonia, at Campiglia Marittima and on Elba, and large quantities of metal artefacts have been found at Etruscan sites. Metalwork was presumably traded abroad, along with Etruscan ore, for luxury goods such as painted vases, decorated textiles, jewellery and ivories. The main mining areas in Etruria were apparently the Monti Rognosi near Arezzo (copper and possibly iron), the regions around Velathri (Volterra; copper), Campiglia (iron, copper, tin, lead and silver) and Massa (iron, copper, lead and silver), Elba (iron and possibly copper) and the Tolfa Hills (iron, copper, lead and silver). These indigenous sources may have been supplemented by imports of tin from the 'Cassiterides' Islands off the Cornish coast and of copper from the south of France and, in the 4th and 3rd centuries BC, perhaps also from Sardinia and the Iberian peninsula.

Bronze was apparently the metal most often used. It was employed for statues and statuettes, wagons, horse-bits, urns, tools and utensils, weapons, domestic and funerary furniture, vases for both ordinary and ceremonial use, clothing accessories and coinage. Iron, too, must have had many applications. Apart from being used to make arms, utensils and fitments, it was employed in the 7th century BC as a decorative inlay for bronze objects, such as belt buckles or laminas attached to carts. Iron objects are, however, rarely found intact, since they rust away, especially in the damp conditions of Etruscan tombs. Early Etruscan lead objects are rare, but from the 6th century BC lead was sometimes used for votive figurines, sling shots and, especially at Populonia and on Elba in the 4th century BC, for imitations of some established bronze types of object, for example, plates, bowls, jugs, candelabra and grapnels. Silver was used for personal ornaments, for small urns and for plating. Like iron, it does not conserve well. Etruscan silver was probably mined locally; gold, however, did not occur naturally, though it was widely used by Etruscan craftsmen. It was almost certainly imported from Egypt, and perhaps also from central Europe.

Etruscan tombs often contained sophisticated metal objects, and these were clearly valued for their craftsmanship as well as for the intrinsic value of their metal. Pottery vases often imitated metal originals, and some surviving metal vases show signs of having been carefully repaired in antiquity. Diodorus Siculus (*Historical Library* V.xl.3) attests their function as status symbols in his description of the luxurious banquets of the Etruscan aristocracy. Similarly, the first narrative scenes in Etruscan art, depicting hunts, duels and armed dances, occurred on bronze objects such as scabbards, incense burners and cinerary urns.

These scenes allude to the power and status of an object's owner. It is also significant that innovations in the depiction of human and animal figures are invariably first evidenced on metal objects, probably because decorating metal usually requires a finer discipline than painting pottery and thus tended to attract the best craftsmen.

Most extant Etruscan metalwork comes from tombs and sanctuaries, while the little so far recovered from domestic contexts is of modest quality. Nonetheless, it is clear both from literary sources (see Diodorus Siculus quoted above and Athenaeus: *Deipnosophists* I.28 b; XV.700 c) and from evidence of usage and repair on metal objects themselves that they were not exclusively reserved for rituals or special celebrations.

2. Bronze. As engraved bronze mirrors and cists were a speciality in Etruscan art, they are accorded sections to themselves.

See also Sculpture, §V, 2.

(i) General survey. (ii) Mirrors. (iii) Cists.

(i) General survey. The great quantity of Etruscan bronzework that survives represents only a fraction of what was originally produced, much of which has been melted down. In 1546, for example, Cardinal Alessandro Farnese obtained some 6000 pounds of ancient bronzes from the inhabitants of Tarquinia (then called Corneto) to melt down for decorations for the columns of the basilica of S Giovanni in Laterano in Rome. It is also clear that bronzework from Etruria was widely distributed in the ancient world. The bronze dinner-services and candelabra used by 5th-century BC Greeks (see Athenaeus quoted above) were apparently Etruscan, and Pliny (*Natural History* XXXIV.xvi.34) spoke of Etruscan bronze statues being exported to places far away from Etruria. He also stated that when the Romans took Volsinii Veteres (Orvieto) in 264 BC they looted 2000 bronze statues. Pausanias (*Guide to Greece* V.xii.5) recorded a bronze throne at Olympia donated by Arimnestus, 'an Etruscan king, who was the first barbarian to make a votive offering to Zeus'. Archaeological evidence confirms that from the 8th century BC Etruscan bronzes, such as fibulae, razors, cauldrons, tripods, jugs and votive figurines, were exported not only around the Mediterranean but also to central Europe. The quality of Etruscan bronzework was noted by ancient writers, and Horace (*Epistles* II.ii.180) recorded that Roman connoisseurs included Etruscan bronzes among their interests.

Etruscan bronzework can be classified fairly precisely on stylistic grounds, but the frequent lack of accurate information on the original context and provenance of individual pieces imposes severe limitations on an interpretation of their cultural significance and function. Specialist study in this field tends to concentrate on questions of typology, attribution and technique, focusing on objects that demonstrate artistic achievement, such as statues, decorated utensils, laminated items and incised mirrors, rather than more mundane objects. Techniques of bronzeworking varied. Statuettes and utensils were cast solid, while larger statues are hollow. After casting, both types were smoothed and finished with scrapers and hammers, and decorative details were incised with a graver. Larger statues and complex utensils were cast in separate parts which were later soldered together. Bronzes were often clad in laminas, which could either be left smooth, or embossed or incised. Bronze products frequently demonstrate a combination of techniques, with some parts cast and others laminated, beaten or soldered together. Tripods, for example, have cast feet but beaten basins, which were sometimes made from a single sheet of bronze. From the 7th century BC, Etruscan metalworkers occasionally used the sphyrelaton technique, which involved cladding a wooden figure with bronze laminas. The cut-out lamina technique was sometimes used for figurines, notably the mass-produced votive gifts at sanctuary sites in Umbria and Latium, and it was also employed after the end of the 7th century BC for other objects in tombs, such as the series of small griffin protomes from the Montefortini tumulus at Comeana. Lastly, there is the technique of 'enriching' bronze with precious metals: gold strands were wound around the bows of fibulae, statuettes were gilded and urns laminated with silver.

The earliest Etruscan bronzework comes from the 9th-century BC tombs of the Villanovan culture. It includes fibulae, pins, razors, helmets, swords, scabbards and spearheads. During the 8th century BC, tomb contents became richer and the bronzework more varied, encompassing biconical cinerary urns, tripods, bowls, flasks, wide belts, bracelets, pins, shields and horsebits. Such objects were, however, still rare possessions and arms and armour in particular seem to have been the status symbols of a ruling warrior class.

The decoration of these Villanovan bronzes usually consists of embossed or incised geometric patterns: dots, straight and wavy lines, angles and triangles, squares and boxes, hooked crosses, meanders, circles and semicircles. Designs tend to reflect the shape of the object itself, running lengthwise along the border of a scabbard or concentrically on a shield or flask. Figures are rare and extremely schematic. Animals occur more often than humans, and distinctive features are emphasized: the beak of a duck, the horns of a deer, a boar's bristles or a dog's tail. Three-dimensional human figurines were, however, occasionally used to embellish prestige objects, for example a male and female on the scabbard of a sword from Vulci (8th century BC; Rome, Villa Giulia, 64487). Figures engaged in various activities, such as ploughing, hunting and fighting, occur on the base of an incense burner (*c.* 750–*c.* 725 BC; Rome, Villa Giulia, 57022/2) and on the shoulder and top of a biconical vase from Bisenzio (*c.* 725–*c.* 700 BC; Rome, Villa Giulia, 57066). Even though the figures probably allude to the pastimes and privileges of the aristocratic owners of the objects, they are crudely executed, with over-large heads, monkey-like features and accentuated genitals. They recall terracotta figurines from tombs in Early Iron Age Latium (9th century BC).

Nonetheless, the technical accomplishment of early Etruscan bronzeworking should not be underestimated. Several techniques had already been developed in the Bronze Age; cast pieces have been found in Manciano, in the valley of the River Fiora, and 'panels' of bronze and axes occur at various localities in Tuscany and Latium. Immigrant craftsmen probably exerted an influence: the use of incised details may have originated in the Danube area, and the figural scenes suggest Aegean antecedents. During the 8th century BC the western Mediterranean was frequented by Greek and Phoenician traders and colonists, and, while Etruria's mineral resources ensured both economic and political independence, Etruscan culture altered rapidly through foreign commercial contacts. Imports of sophisticated artefacts, not only from the Near East, but also from Greece, central Europe and Sardinia, were accompanied by foreign potters, ivory and gold workers, and bronzesmiths, who profoundly changed the techniques and repertory of Etruscan art. Geometric patterns were replaced by lively floral motifs, including palmettes, lotus buds and rosettes, real and imaginary animals, and the first identifiable mythical scenes. This Orientalizing period in Etruscan art coincided with the construction of the first great 'princely' tombs at various sites along the central Tyrrhenian coast. One of these, the Regolini-Galassi Tomb (*c.* 670–*c.* 630 BC) at Caere (Cerveteri) yielded a series of laminated bronzes, with both embossed and engraved decoration, attributed to a local workshop. From the same tomb came a cauldron, a conical stand, various discs, and laminas, decorated with typically Orientalizing felines, monsters and lotus chains (all Rome, Vatican, Mus. Gregoriano Etrus.). The lion on these bronzes, for example, with its protruding tongue, pricked-up ears and serpent-like tail, exactly matches the lions depicted on gold and silver bowls imported to Caere from some Phoenician–Cypriot source (Rome, Vatican, Mus. Gregoriano Etrus., 20207). A similar lion appears on an incised and embossed bronze skyphos from the Barberini Tomb (*c.* 675–*c.* 650 BC) at Praeneste (Rome, Villa Giulia, 13132). From the Near East, probably North Syria, came the great bronze cauldrons with laminated protomes of griffins and lions riveted to the lips of the bowls. These were imitated locally in both bronze and terracotta. Also from this period is the handle on the cover of a bronze cinerary urn from the Tomb of the Cone at Vetulonia (Florence, Mus. Archeol., 6980), made of two solid cast griffins with elongated equine ears, gaping beaks and long curving necks, executed in a fluent, almost mannerist style.

Some forms of geometric decoration survived through the Orientalizing period. Lines and circles, for example, accompany floral and animal motifs on some large bronze 7th-century BC shields. Schematized figurines continue to be used to adorn certain bronze objects. Examples include the little horsemen on the feet of Vetulonian tripods, the human figures and dogs on a tripod from the Bernardini Tomb (*c.* 675–*c.* 650 BC) at Praeneste (Rome, Villa Giulia, 61619) and the mythical beasts on a belt buckle from Massa Marittima (7th century BC). The facial details of female figures at the top of two vase stands from the 7th-century BC Tomba del Duce at Vetulonia (Florence, Mus. Archeol., 7053, 7054) are less schematic than those of their precursors, although their bodies remain geometric.

Important 6th-century BC bronzes from tombs in the Perugia area (San Valentino di Marsciano, Castel San Mariano) and Monteleone di Spoleto include chariots, tripods and thrones. The quantity, nature and artistic quality of these bronzes suggest that they belonged to 'princely' burials, which themselves imply the existence of a provincial pre-urban culture. Their place of manufacture remains uncertain, although north-east Etruria, Perusia (Perugia), Clusium (Chiusi), Vulci and Caere have all been suggested. Whatever the case, they must have originated from a region with an established tradition of metalworking. Some, at least, probably came from the same workshop; for example the Monteleone Chariot and the Loeb Tripod C (*c.* 550–*c.* 500 BC; Munich, Staatl. Antikensamml., Br SL 68), both of which feature similar versions of the *Combat of Achilles and Memnon*. Between *c.* 550 and *c.* 450 BC, workshops at Vulci produced bronzes for use at symposia and ceremonial banquets. These include jugs, rod tripods (e.g. a bronze rod tripod, from Populonia, made at Vulci, *c.* 530 BC), candelabra and incense burners, and the decoration of these pieces combines patterned motifs and mythological scenes. The latter were sometimes expanded or adapted to suit the surface available, and both their style and iconography reflect Greek influence. Vases and other high quality bronze utensils and ceremonial objects were produced in large quantities and widely exported. The long-spouted jug, for example, not only occurs throughout Etruria and in other parts of Italy, but also in north-central Europe. Some bronze objects were monumental in size and appearance. This is true of the lamp from Curtun (Cortona, Mus. Accad. Etrus.), which probably came from a workshop in central Etruria around the mid-5th century BC. This consists of a large circular basin, cast in a single block (57.72 kg; diam. 600 mm), with rich, detailed relief decoration on the outer surface, of obscure symbolic religious meaning. A central Gorgonesque mask, of Archaic type, is surrounded by a series of concentric friezes with animals fighting, dolphins leaping over waves, and sileni playing the double aulos or the syrinx alternating with sirens, with busts of Achelous behind.

Between the mid-5th century BC and the 2nd century BC the production of banquet vessels continued, including large stamnoi to contain wine, situlae with spouts in the form of lions' heads and jugs with elongated spouts. Candelabras consist of a three-footed base, a stem about 1 m tall and a top part with three or four prongs for candles and a statuette (a dancer, a musician, a satyr, an athlete, Herakles) or a pair of statuettes. The main workshops were located at Vulci, Volsinii Veteres (Orvieto), Clusium, Populonia and Spina. Incense burners stood on tables, and so were smaller than the candelabras. Their three-legged bases consist of the hind legs of animals, and they have a little pan on top where the incense burned. The workshops producing these were probably in Vulci, Tarquinia and Falerii (Civita Castellana). A painting in the 4th-century BC Golini Tomb I in Volsinii Veteres clearly shows the use of these utensils during a banquet. Kottaboi also have a base with feet and a long stem (about 2 m), but at the top there is a small disc held by a statuette. In the game of *kottabos* during the banquet, the guest had to throw the wine from a goblet at the disc; if he hit the mark he was awarded a prize that might be a young man or woman. The known examples, datable to the 3rd century BC, come from Perusia and Vetulonia.

(ii) Mirrors. The production of incised mirrors began during the second half of the 6th century BC and continued uninterrupted until the 3rd and 2nd centuries BC. Some 2000 mirrors survive. They were classified by early antiquarians and collectors of Etruscan relics as paterae (shallow dishes), then interpreted by Francesco Inghirami in 1824 as mystical mirrors and finally identified by Eduard Gerhard in 1840 as ordinary hand-mirrors. There are two main types: one with a disc and handle, the other with a hinged cover. There are far fewer examples of the second type, which were developed later, between the Late Classical era and the Hellenistic period (*see also* MIRROR).

Disc mirrors were first cast and then heated to 600–700°C and hammered into either flat or convex surfaces which were polished with emery. The reverse, non-reflective side was often decorated with engraved designs or, more rarely, reliefs, although it was also frequently left plain. The discs vary in diameter between 110 and 200 mm. The mirror handle was either made of some other material, such as bone, ivory or wood, which rarely survives, connected by means of a tang; or it could be cast in one piece with the mirror, as a baton shape ending in an animal head (a ram or a deer). Occasionally the handle takes the form of a bronze statuette. The edge of the mirror was normally folded back and decorated with motifs of beads, dentils, ovules or small tongues. The earliest examples have flat surfaces, later ones convex. On the reflective side the decoration of spirals, palmettes or other plants is restricted to the extension that connects the disc to its tang, sometimes extending to the frame of the mirror surface. On the reverse, however, it covers the whole area and is surrounded by a border of wave, meander, ropework or S-shaped patterns, floral or plant motifs or groups of animals, and divided horizontally by a lower and/or upper exergue. The whole scheme of decoration unites carefully designed devices to emphasize and enhance the form of the object itself.

Most Etruscan mirrors are of uncertain provenance and they have generally been classified on a stylistic basis. Attribution of groups or individual specimens to a particular centre of manufacture has been based largely on the sites where they were discovered, even though mirrors may well have been used far from their place of origin. It is also unclear whether the casting and engraving were carried out in a single workshop: they obviously required different skills and standard patterns were possibly used in several workshops. This inconclusive picture has been remedied to some extent through analysis of other factors. These include the shape and size of the disc; the form of its border, extension and handle; the mirror's weight; the style of decoration; the palaeographic and phonetic characteristics of any inscriptions; and the stylistic, thematic and iconographical parallels between the mirror and other figural works of art, such as painted pottery.

The few mirrors of known provenance come exclusively from tombs. This does not, however, imply that they had a purely funerary significance. On the contrary, they were almost certainly used in ordinary domestic life. Mirrors are clearly depicted in numerous Etruscan scenes of women at their toilet, while several examples show evidence of having been repaired during use. Many others bear the inscription 'suthina' (i.e. for the tomb) on the reflective surface, written in a different script with a different tool from those used for other inscriptions. This suggests that their original, daily purpose had been deliberately cancelled. Many scholars now believe that these mirrors, and the cists discussed below, were made in the first place as marriage gifts.

The circular form of the mirrors posed problems of composition for engravers, similar to those encountered by vase painters in the decoration of a plate or the tondo of a cup, and the vertical of the handle imposed a strong axial emphasis. These features caused no difficulties in the rare cases when the figural scene was modelled on some other circular composition, as in the case of a mirror portraying the *Rape of Mlacuch by Herkle* (Herakles; for illustration *see* MIRROR, fig. 2), which echoes the scenes of rape on early Attic Red-figure cups. Scenes involving only one figure were also quite straightforward, but when several figures were included the circular space proved less easy to fill. Some of the earliest engraved mirrors demonstrate the search for a satisfactory solution to this problem. A late 6th-century BC example (Paris, Bib. N., 1300) has the figures of Apollo–Helios and Artemis placed on two bases and framed by twisting vines, while the space above them is occupied by a walking panther.

Mirrors dating from the end of the 6th century BC show decorative motifs along the sides already taking the form of a frame, with the figures placed on the edge of the lower exergue. This lower section of the mirror-back later developed its own decoration. Sometimes a base or pedestal, perhaps supporting the figures in the original version of a scene, was rendered on the mirror as a decorative motif on the exergue (e.g. an Archaic example: London, BM, 543; and a 5th-century BC example: Boston, MA, Mus. F.A., 95–73).

Only two mirrors have been discovered at pre-Archaic sites in Etruria: one, from a Villanovan grave at Tarquinia, was possibly imported from Sicily or from the Aegean-Cypriot area; the other came from a late Orientalizing tomb at Populonia. Neither has any decoration. Thus large-scale production of Etruscan mirrors began only in the later 6th century BC. The development of their figural decoration follows that in other areas of Etruscan art. Successive Ionian, Attic and Italic influences are evident, with frequent archaisms, misinterpretations and adaptations by Etruscan craftsmen. The origin of incised decoration is uncertain, although it was certainly not Hellenic. Disc mirrors were widely used in Greece from the first half of the 6th century BC, but they were not ornamented in this way. According to one view they were an Etruscan innovation; another suggests that they derived from Egypt, despite the fact that few Egyptian mirrors have been discovered, none of them in Etruria.

From the period between *c.* 530 and *c.* 450 BC, a few dozen Etruscan mirrors survive. These generally have a flat disc and always end in tangs. The extension between disc and tang is either absent or in the form of a rectangle or circle. The design is of a high quality and the subjects depicted (banquets, dances, games, satyrs, maenads and Greek myths) echo those found in contemporary Etruscan tomb painting, vase painting and relief bronzes. It seems evident that the mirrors too belonged to the same wealthy members of society who commissioned the more lavish tombs. Moreover, the new popularity of mirrors in Etruria coincided with the appearance of other luxury goods, probably introduced through contacts with Greek Asia Minor. These contacts became even closer and more productive after the fall of Asia Minor to the Persians (546 BC), when East Greek craftsmen settled in Etruria. Sometimes the subjects portrayed on the mirrors provide unique insights into the development of Etruscan culture. The typically Greek satyr and maenad on a mirror in Brussels (*c.* 470 BC; Mus. A. Anc., R1270), for example, were given the Etruscan names Chelphun and Munthuch, indicating that Greek mythology was now subject to Etruscan interpretation.

In the later 5th century BC and, to an even greater extent, during the 4th century BC, there was a marked increase in the production of mirrors, which were doubtless manufactured at several centres, one of which was certainly Vulci. Mirrors of this period have an enlarged (diam. 180–200 mm) and convex reflecting surface, with a wider, trapezoidal extension and slightly longer tang. At the same time, the scenes on the reverse tend to portray more figures. These compositions were adapted so well to the circular field, through devices such as varying the figures' heights or placing curving figures at the sides, that the lower exergue was often omitted. A recurrent composition involved a central seated figure with numerous others grouped around it. This was adapted to various different subjects (e.g. *Gods Performing their Toilet, Uni Suckling Herkle*, the *Birth of Menrva* and the *Judgement of Paris*). Sometimes mirrors can be directly compared with the tondi of Etruscan Red-figure cups. Thus one (late 5th century BC–early 4th century BC; Berlin, Antikensamml., Fr. 36) depicts the naked youth Fufluns (Dionysos) being embraced from behind by the draped figure of his mother, Semla (Semele), a composition that is used on other mirrors and on cups for scenes depicting lovers.

The first mirrors to have the handle cast as one piece with the disc appeared during the second half of the 4th century BC. They are much smaller than the mirrors with tangs (sometimes only diam. 110–120 mm), their reflective sides are more markedly convex and their extensions have two tips. Their decorated sides may have an exergue or an architectural background, and the most common scenes show either four figures in conversation (two Dioscuri flanking two other figures), two Dioscuri facing each other or a Lasa (goddess of Fate). Many examples survive, but they are generally poorly executed, with repetitive subjects and layouts. Mirrors were clearly no longer the prestige objects they had been during the 6th and 5th centuries BC. Workshops were located at various centres, particularly in the hinterland of central Etruria. One group, thought to have been made at Praeneste (second half of 4th century BC–3rd century BC) and mostly found there, have pear-shaped discs with cast handles. They bear Latin inscriptions and, in both theme and style, resemble other objects made at Praeneste. Several depict the myth of Amykos which also appears on certain cists found at the site. These mirrors also include the only examples signed by their maker, and, since another engraved object found at Praeneste, the Ficoroni Cist (see colour pl. 1:XV, fig. 4), carries a similar maker's signature, that of Novios Plautios, it seems possible that Latin engravers enjoyed a higher status than their Etruscan counterparts. Despite their artistic quality Etruscan disc mirrors were apparently made almost exclusively for the local market, as only about 20 examples have been found outside Etruria, in Italy and elsewhere in Europe.

The Etruscan mirrors with hinged covers were either circular or rectangular. The circular type, of which only a few dozen examples survive, all date from the late 4th century BC and the 3rd century BC. Greek mirrors of this type, however, were already in production by the late 5th century BC. The outside of the cover was decorated with relief figures generally in mythological scenes featuring Aphrodite, Dionysos or Ganymede, or depicting *Odysseus and Penelope*, *Thetis and the Armour of Achilles*, the *Acknowledgement of Paris* and the *Death of Troilos*. The last two subjects also occur frequently in reliefs on the small funerary urns produced during Hellenistic times at Clusium (Chiusi), Perusia (Perugia) and Velathri (Volterra). Even so, the mirrors were again primarily intended for everyday use and only secondarily as funerary objects.

Rectangular covered mirrors ('book mirrors') are known only from ancient representations on the covers of small urns from Velathri of the 2nd and 1st centuries BC, which show them held by reclining female figures. There is one extant example of a circular, convex mirror, with no decoration and no handle, possibly from a tomb at Velathri of the late 2nd century BC or early 1st century BC, which may originally have been cased (London, BM, Br. 731). If so, the case was presumably made of wood or some other perishable material.

(iii) Cists. Etruscan mirrors were closely associated with the cists used for women's toilet items. The two were often depicted together and with such objects as strigils, hairpins and containers for balsam, and both have been found together. The provenance of most Etruscan cists, however, is again usually uncertain. Their chronology is based mostly on a stylistic examination of their figural decoration, cast feet and handle figurines. Since the container itself was made from a thin metal sheet, often only the feet and handle, which were cast, survive. Cast feet, however, could also come from other containers, such as situlae and cauldrons, so that attribution is problematic if they are found without other evidence.

The earliest type of Etruscan cist was cylindrical and had three feet and a slightly convex cover. The container was made by hammering metal into a sheet, bending it so that the two vertical edges overlapped, and riveting them together. It was lined with wood and sometimes had a band of pierced foliar decoration half way up. The circular base was joined to the body by folding up its edges, while the handle on the cover was formed either by a single figurine in a 'wrestler's bridge', or by a more complex group. The feet were formed as claws surmounted by a narrow moulded band, often adorned with volutes, supporting a small sculpted element. The latter was usually carved in openwork, although it was sometimes in relief, and was riveted or soldered to the outside of the cist below the main field of decoration. The earliest examples of feet to have survived have been attributed to early 5th-century BC workshops at Vulci. The small sculptures on them depict scenes from Greek myths (*Herakles and Iolaos Fighting the Hydra*, *Herakles and Apollo Fighting for the Tripod*, *Europa and the Bull*), chariot races or heads of satyrs. Other feet, decorated with individual mythological figures (demons with snake-like legs, winged figures and sirens) or with a palmette between two volutes, have been attributed to 5th-century BC workshops in northern Etruria, notably at Clusium (Chiusi). The earliest examples from a series of cists from Praeneste are also of this date. These have distinctive feet consisting of claws on a low cylindrical base surmounted by a beaded rim and supported by a four-sided plinth. The group also includes the first four-footed cists with ovoid bodies.

The greatest period of cist production at Praeneste seems to have been during the 4th and 3rd centuries BC, since more than 100 examples of this date survive. Their bodies can be cylindrical, ovoid or parallelepipedal; the decoration either pierced, engraved or executed in embossed dots, although this last method seems confined to the covers of a few ovoid examples. Engraved figural friezes are bounded at the top and bottom by borders of ornamental motifs, such as plants, waves and ropework, similar to those used in the borders of the Praeneste mirrors. The range of subject-matter is extensive, encompassing scenes of everyday life; battle scenes involving warriors, Amazons, giants and animals; Greek myths featuring Dionysos, Helen, Achilles, Peleus and Thetis, Bellerophon, Amykos, Iphigenia and other figures; and historical events. All show iconographical and stylistic resemblances to 4th-century BC Etruscan and Italic vase paintings. The appropriateness of these scenes is not always evident, and, although the numerous toilet scenes relate to the use of the cists, they normally only occupy the spaces left by the main subjects.

With the exception of a fine example from Vulci (Rome, Vatican, Mus. Gregoriano Etrus., 327) with an *Amazonomachy* in relief that shares some features with Praenestine works, most other Etruscan cists of the 4th and 3rd centuries BC are of poor quality. Their bodies are cylindrical, with bands of decoration near the base and mouth, with carrying handles in the form of quadrupeds (h. 150–180 mm, including handle). Examples occur virtually throughout central Etruria.

3. GOLD AND SILVER. The intrinsic value of precious metals such as gold and silver profoundly influenced developments in their working, especially since gold had to be imported. At the same time, it also made gold and silver objects vulnerable to looting. According to the ancient authors, about 1500 talents of gold and silver were seized during the sack of the sanctuary of Pyrgi (Santa Severa; 384 BC) and later depredations often involved the removal of all gold and silver objects from rediscovered tombs for melting down. A cardinal was sent to Tarquinia by Pope Innocent VIII (*reg* 1484–92), after news of the discovery of a rich tomb, expressly for this purpose. Although Greek writers maintained that Etruscan aristocrats had gold and silver vessels for everyday uses (see Athenaeus: *Deipnosophists* I.28b and Diodorus Siculus: *Historical Library* V.xl.3), such objects as do survive (mainly jewellery, ceremonial vases, coins and ingots) generally come from exceptional tombs and dedications at sanctuaries.

The gold used by the Etruscans was not pure, but contained some copper (0.1–10%) and some silver (15–37%). Goldworking techniques included beating, hollow or solid casting, the making of gold thread or wire and the application of thin gold leaf to other metals, ceramics or ivory. Gold objects were decorated with embossed and engraved designs, filigree, granulation or gold dust. A few were made from several pieces, soldered together with bronze. From the earliest times, Etruscan goldsmiths and silversmiths displayed considerable technical skill, although some of their products, for example fibulae, evidently reproduced objects previously made in bronze. Knowledge of the techniques of granulation, filigree and gold leaf spread throughout Etruria around the turn of the 8th and 7th centuries BC, possibly as a result either of Oriental influence or the arrival of Oriental craftsmen displaced by Assyrian expansion in the Near East. A suggestion that early Etruscan goldwork should be attributed to the Greek colony of Pithekoussai has gained little support.

In Early Iron Age times gold and silver were used only for personal ornaments: fibulae, hairgrips, discoid pendants (bullae), small rings, necklace charms, triangular and swastika-shaped plaquettes for clothes. Their decoration was geometric and they occur only in the richest tombs. With the advent of the 'princely' culture and Orientalizing styles in Etruria and Etruscan-influenced areas of Italy (Emilia, Latium, parts of Campania), exquisite imported and locally made gold and silver objects became more plentiful. Even so, extant 7th-century BC jewels and fine vases come from only a few rich tombs, including the Gesseri Tomb near Velathri (Volterra); the Tomba del Duce, the Tomb of the Lebetes and the Tomb of the Lictor, all at Vetulonia; the Perazzeta and Fibula tombs at Marsiliana d'Albegna; the Regolini-Galassi Tomb at Caere (Cerveteri); the Aureli II Tomb at Felsina (Bologna); the Bernardini, Barberini, Castellani and Galeassi Tombs at Praeneste; and tombs nos 926 and 928 at Pontecagnano. These have yielded Cypriot piriform silver jugs, which inspired local imitations in bronze and in bucchero, as well as Phoenician–Cypriot silver-gilt bowls with figural decoration that deeply influenced Etruscan Orientalizing styles and iconography.

Locally produced works reflect diverse influences. The profiles and costumes of the figures in the decorative friezes of a gilded silver bucket from Clusium (Chiusi, *c.* 650 BC; Florence, Mus. Archeol., 2594) recall Phoenician–Cypriot models, but their helmets are distinctly Corinthian. A silver kotyle (cup) from the Tomba del Duce (Florence, Mus. Archeol., 73582) displays all the incised decorative motifs typical of Phoenician–Cypriot work (files of real and fantastic animals, vegetable motifs), but is Proto–Corinthian in form. This creative eclecticism led to innovations that heralded a genuine Etruscan artistic tradition. This is apparent in the comparison of a locally made silver scabbard with an imported Phoenician–Cypriot cup, both from the Bernardini Tomb (*c.* 675–*c.* 650 BC). Both depict a deer hunt, but, where the scene on the cup (Rome, Villa Giulia, 61565) is set in a landscape, that on the scabbard (Villa Giulia, 61705) is simply framed by files of animals, a device that eliminates any impression of depth while still achieving a strong decorative effect.

Ceremonial vases in precious metals either adhered to local shapes (e.g. silver spiral amphorae) or copied Oriental imports (e.g. silver cups and plates with scale decoration) or Proto-Corinthian models (e.g. silver and gold skyphoi and kotylai). Provenance, typology and certain stylistic features seem to imply that goldsmiths were active at Caere and Vetulonia in the 7th century BC, and probably also at Tarquinia and Vulci. Their patrons were clearly local aristocrats. Silver vases from the Tomba del Duce and the Regolini-Galassi and Bernardini tombs are inscribed with their owners' names, and a gold fibula from Clusium (*c.* 630 BC; Paris, Louvre, Bj 816) was clearly a gift, since the names of both giver and recipient form part of its granular decoration.

S. Haynes: *Etruscan Bronze Utensils* (London, 1965)

I. Mayer-Prokop: *Die gravierten etruskischen Griffenspiegel archaischen Stils* (Heidelberg, 1967)

D. Rebuffat-Emmanuel: *Le Miroir étrusque* (Rome, 1973)

G. A. Foerst: *Die Gravierungen der pränestinischen Cisten* (Rome, 1978)

G. Bordenache Battaglia: *Le ciste prenestine* (Rome, 1979, rev. 1990)

U. Fischer-Graf: *Spiegelwerkstätten in Vulci* (Berlin, 1980)

R. Adam: *Recherches sur les miroirs prénestins* (Paris, 1982)

N. de Grummond, ed.: *A Guide to Etruscan Mirrors* (Tallahassee, 1982)

U. Höckmann: *Die Bronzen aus dem Fürstengrab von Castel San Mariano* (Munich, 1982)

M. Cristofani and M. Martelli: *L'oro degli Etruschi* (Novara, 1983)

A. M. Adam: *Bibliothèque Nationale: Bronzes étrusques et italiques* (Paris, 1984)

G. Camporeale, ed.: *L'Etruria mineraria* (Milan, 1985)

E. Formigli: *Tecniche dell'oreficeria etrusca e romana: Originali e falsificazioni* (Florence, 1985)

S. Haynes: *Etruscan Bronzes* (London, 1985)

E. Mangani: 'Le fabbriche di specchi nell'Etruria settentrionale', *Boll. A.*, lxx (1985), pp. 21ff

F. Jurgeit: *'Cistenfüsse': Etruskische und Praenestiner Bronzewerkstätten* (Rome, 1986)

R. D. De Puma: *Corpus speculorum Etruscorum USA* (Ames, Iowa, 1987–)

U. Höckmann: 'Die Datierung der hellenistisch-etruskischen Griffspiegel des 2. Jahrhunderts v. Chr.', *Jb. Dt. Archäol. Inst.*, cii (1987), pp. 247ff

I. Jucker: 'Bemerkungen zu einigen etruskischen Klappspiegeln', *Mitt. Dt. Archäol. Inst.: Röm. Abt.*, xcv (1988), pp. 1ff

S. Haynes: 'Muliebris Certaminis Laus: Bronze Documents of a Changing Ethos', *Secondo congresso internazionale etrusco. Atti* (Rome, 1989), pp. 1395ff

U. Höckmann: 'Zur Datierung der sogenannten Kranzspiegel', *Secondo congresso internazionale etrusco. Atti* (Rome, 1989), pp. 713ff

B. B. Shefton: 'Etruscan Bronze Stamnoi', *Secondo congresso internazionale etrusco. Atti* (Rome, 1989), pp. 729ff

A. Testa: *Candelabri e thymiateria* (Rome, 1989)

F. Catalli: *Monete etrusche* (Rome, 1990)

G. C. Cianferoni: 'I reperti metallichi', *Populonia in età ellenistica e romana. I materiali dalle necropoli* (Florence, 1992), pp. 13ff

R. V. Nicholls, J. Swaddling and T. Rasmussen: *Corpus speculorum Etruscorum: Great Britain* (London, 1993–)

A. A. Carpino: *Discs of Splendor: The Relief Mirrors of the Etruscans* (Madison, WI, 2003)

VI. Roman.

1. Gold and silver. 2. Bronze. 3. Iron.

1. Gold and silver.

(i) Introduction. (ii) Early Empire. (iii) High Empire. (iv) Late Empire.

(i) Introduction. The possession of tableware in precious metal was an indicator of wealth and status in Roman as in many later societies, and high-ranking families would have regarded it as essential. The expansion of the Roman Empire gave access to many sources of the raw materials, and the sheer quantity of plate in use was vast: though much has survived into modern times, far more must have been lost through reuse, while some remains undiscovered. But although the actual quantity of Roman silver available for study is substantial, it is seldom found in archaeological contexts, and the modern methods of archaeological research and dating can rarely be applied. Caches of silver also typically contain pieces of different date, since heirlooms were treasured in the Roman period just as they are now. In studying the products of a large area over several centuries, therefore, it is often impossible to say whether certain distinctive styles and fashions are the result of chronological development or of regional preference and manufacture. A general impression emerges, however, of supreme technical skill on the part of the craftsmen and a great variety of fashions in taste.

Silver tableware may be divided broadly into the vessels used for eating, *argentum escarium*, and those for drinking, *argentum potorium*. To these must be added the vessels that were intended only for display, some of them being virtually pictures in silver. Personal items such as cosmetic caskets were also counted among the household silver. Some hoards of buried Roman silver clearly belonged to temples rather than private households, and both religious and domestic hoards sometimes contain silver statuettes of deities, which in private possession would have been displayed in the household shrine, the *lararium*.

Literary references indicate that the wealthy sometimes also owned gold plate, but while gold jewellery survives in large quantities (*see* Jewellery, §5), few vessels or statuettes in this metal remain. In fact, too little remains for us to draw any general conclusions about style, fashion or technique, and we must simply assume that gold plate paralleled the developments that can be traced in silver. An elegant and wholly undecorated gold vase (London, BM) represents an extreme of simplicity, while the gold bowl from Rennes (3rd century AD; Paris, Bib. N., Cab. Médailles) has inset coins and elaborate relief decoration comparable with much silverware of the high and late Empire. Other famous pieces in gold are a lamp from Pompeii (1st century AD; Naples, Mus. Archeol. N.) and the bust of *Marcus Aurelius* (*reg* AD 161–80; Avenches, Mus. Romain; for further discussion *see* Sculpture, §VI, 1(iii)(a)); like larger-scale sculpture in silver, it is not cast but worked in sheet metal.

Modern scientific methods of analysis have demonstrated consistently that the purity of Roman silver matches or exceeds modern standards. Fineness of the order of 96% is quite common. This quality control can have been achieved only by official intervention, almost certainly by the same mechanisms that controlled the issue of coinage. Silver plate was a form of bullion, and we frequently find weight inscriptions punched on the undersides of vessels, apparently at the time of manufacture. In the case of matching sets of bowls or cups, the weight given on each piece is usually that of the whole set, a custom that has occasionally caused some confusion to scholars. As yet we know very little about the location of workshops in the 1st century BC to the 4th century AD, though we are probably safe in assuming that silver plate was produced at many of the major imperial mints. Workshop or manufacturer's stamps started to appear sporadically in the 4th century AD: on Byzantine silver of the 6th and 7th centuries AD they are far more common.

Overall, silver of the Roman period represents one of the greatest artistic achievements of its time. Its technical brilliance is not in question: the craft of the silversmith was already fully developed long before the rise of Rome. Artistically, it can be argued that the outstanding pieces from each of the three phases outlined below are masterpieces of the highest order. The superficial view that holds that Roman art is no more than a pale reflection of Greek forerunners is given the lie by this material. Under the Roman Empire, Greek traditions were subtly transmuted and enriched by elements from many diverse areas and cultures: the result is distinctively Roman. In the case of silverware, its finest products remain unsurpassed.

(ii) Early Empire. Three great treasures dominate any discussion of silverware of the early Imperial period, two of them concealed as a result of the eruption of Vesuvius in AD 79. These are the hoard of silver from the villa at Boscoreale (most in Paris, Louvre) and that from the House of the Menander in Pompeii itself (Naples, Mus. Archeol. N.), each collection containing more than 100 pieces. The third hoard, by contrast, is from outside the frontiers of the Empire, found at Hildesheim near Hannover in 1868 (Berlin, Antikensamml.); the reason for the burial of the Hildesheim Treasure is uncertain, as is its date, but among some 50 items it includes several of the most beautiful examples of early Roman silver. In all three groups, and in numerous other finds of this period, we see a broad range of styles, from restrained pieces with minimal decoration to exuberantly ornamented objects covered with mythological or naturalistic scenes in relief, often emphasized and enriched with parcel gilding.

At this date the display silver that was not intended for practical use as tableware takes the form of bowls with central emblemata featuring busts or full-length figures of deities or personifications worked partly in the round. The Athena dish from the Hildesheim Treasure (Berlin, Antikensamml.) is perhaps the most remarkable of these. The goddess is shown seated, with her shield tucked under her left arm. Her flesh is left unplated, as is the background, but her elaborate drapery, her hair and the rock on which she sits are all gilded. The shallow surrounding curve of the bowl's interior is chased with a complex lotus pattern, also parcel gilt. This exquisite example of the silversmith's craft reveals the Greek and Hellenistic traditions that underlie early Roman silverware, and in that sense is typical of art under Augustus. The technique is not wholly typical, however, since show plate with central motifs of this kind was normally worked in repoussé, while the Athena dish is a highly complex thin casting. Comparable vessels with medallions include the Hercules bowl in the Hildesheim Treasure and the vessel with a personification of Africa from Boscoreale (Paris, Louvre). Numerous others are known, though these are the most beautiful and ambitious examples.

Perhaps the most characteristic vessels of use in the early Empire are the drinking cups; there are many forms, but the ovoid cup with two handles and a pedestal foot is especially common. These are often decorated with naturalistic wreaths of leaves and fruit, vine, olive or myrtle. The technique (normally referred to as 'cagework') uses repoussé, with the thin outer skin of the cup attached to a plain inner liner that provides a more practical container for the wine. Early Roman silver wine cups are found as far afield as Britain, imported even before the island became a Roman province (AD 43): the comparatively plain pair from an Iron Age chieftain's burial at Welwyn, Herts (1st century BC), were found along with Roman wine amphorae. Silver mixing vessels (for diluting wine with water), jugs and ladles were also part of the appropriate equipment for the service of wine, and the finest of these were richly decorated. Complex scrolls of vine, olive, ivy, acanthus and other leaves, flowers and fruit sometimes incorporate small figures of birds, animals and putti.

Although *argentum potorium* played a major part in the silverware of the early period, there were numerous other utensils, including stands, tripods, small dishes and plates for sauces and other foods, saucepans (deep bowls with a single long handle), serving trays and spoons. A set of four little cups with everted walls and flat bases in the Boscoreale Treasure are as severely plain as other pieces in the group are ornate; form and finish rely solely on the colour and lustre of the metal for their effect. The Hildesheim Treasure includes a cup decorated only with a subtle, narrow band of delicately gilded conventional ornament below the rim, as well as a group of straight-walled pedestalled bowls, the principal decoration of which is a wreath of stylized ivy leaves and berries inlaid in niello (black silver sulphide, which forms a crisp contrast to the polished silver). This technique of decoration was to become increasingly important in later Roman times.

Large bowls shaped like fluted shells appear in early Imperial assemblages, for example in the hoard from the House of the Menander at Pompeii, and they continued as a specialized form later; they were probably intended as containers for hand-washing water to be brought to the dining table. The line between utensils for dining and 'toilet' vessels was not drawn where it would be at present, and it is important to remember that the hands were used for eating. No forks for eating are known in the Roman period, though the sharply pointed handles of Roman spoons may well have been used for spearing morsels of food. They may also have been used for picking the teeth. Certainly in the late Empire, implements that are thought to be for that purpose are incorporated in sets of table silver. We should be careful, however, not to make too many assumptions about the precise uses of specific shapes, since there may have been considerable flexibility in the way utensils were employed. Perhaps it is safe to assume that the individual vessels that look like eggcups on broad bases were in fact used for that purpose, and similarly the bowls with numerous oval depressions were very likely for serving eggs, which figured prominently in Roman cuisine.

Many other examples of silver dating to the Augustan period and the 1st century AD are known in addition to those in the large treasures discussed above—far too many to enumerate here—and they reinforce the overall impression of a highly sophisticated repertory of techniques and styles.

(iii) High Empire. By the 2nd and 3rd centuries AD the era of conquest and expansion in the Roman Empire was over. Provinces from Britain to Syria found their place in a culture that was a complex blend of native and Roman. The administration of this huge area involved much movement of senior civil and military officials, and in every sphere of the visual arts we are aware of both the homogeneity of style and the underlying local elements that were incorporated in some of its expressions. As far as silverware is concerned, there is as yet too little known from some areas to make a balanced judgement. The provinces of Gaul—France, the Rhineland and adjacent areas of the Low Countries and Switzerland—have been studied, however, and the picture that emerges is almost certainly repeated elsewhere.

Gallo-Roman silver of the 2nd and 3rd centuries AD is distinctive, and there is no doubt that there was local production as well as continuing importation of material from Italy and elsewhere in the Mediterranean area. Some of the major hoards from this period are temple treasures, which also include earlier pieces, for example that from Berthouville (nr Brionne, Eure; Paris, Bib. N., Cab. Médailles), but there are also many collections formed mainly of locally made domestic silver. Typical are the hoards from Graincourt-lès-Havrincourt (nr Marquion, Pas-de-Calais), found in 1958 (Paris, Louvre); Rethel (Ardennes), found in 1980 (Saint-Germain-en-Laye,

Mus. Ant. N.); and the Chaourse Treasure (nr Rozoy-sur-Serre, Aisne), a large assemblage found in 1883 (London, BM). Two features are immediately evident in this provincial silver of the high Empire: the forms and decoration are more subtle and restrained than those of the earlier period, and the emphasis moves away from vessels connected with drinking towards large serving dishes and bowls. Glass would have been employed increasingly for drinking vessels. Equally striking is the fact that the sophistication and technical brilliance of the work remains outstanding.

The Gallo-Roman hoards include many large round platters decorated only with a delicate bead-and-reel border and a rosette of niello-inlaid petals and arabesques in the centre. These vessels, up to *c.* 500 mm in diameter, are among the most beautiful items of silver tableware ever made. Other circular platters have small central medallions and narrow surrounding borders worked in low relief with mythological scenes or graceful, slightly stylized floral and foliate scrolls. A platter from the Graincourt Treasure has a central panel and a border featuring a marine still-life; motifs illustrating the riches of the sea and including natural and mythological sea-creatures have a long history in Roman art.

There are some other new and characteristic forms of tableware, for example a deep bowl with a decorated horizontal flange set below the upright rim, and a deep silver bucket with a handle and a border of relief decoration at the rim. A flanged bowl from the Chaourse Treasure (London, BM) is typical of the former shape; the elegant ornament on the flange epitomizes the sophisticated taste of this era. Oval serving dishes with relief decoration on the flat handles at the narrow ends often display mythological decoration, but there are many cups, bowls and jugs that are very plain indeed. One interesting form is a slender-footed cup with concave sides, a shape reminiscent of native Gallic pottery of a much earlier date, perhaps two centuries earlier; it is difficult not to suspect that Celtic sensibilities are at work in such cases.

The shell-shaped bowls continued to be made, as did the deep saucepans with decorated handles and the statuettes in silver; the saucepans were often votive gifts at shrines, and therefore tend to have overtly religious themes in the decoration. Spoons also continued to feature in collections of domestic silverware. The tiny round spoons of the 1st century AD gradually became rarer and gave way to larger forms with oval, pear-shaped or fiddle-shaped bowls. Their pointed handles began to be attached to the bowl with a vertical offset which eventually developed into an elaborate decorative feature in its own right. By the late 3rd century AD the spoon-bowls were sometimes decorated, and the offsets had occasionally started to turn into stylized animal heads.

Decoration in low relief, characteristically worked in repoussé in the earlier period, was now usually achieved by chasing, literally carving away the surface of the solid cast or raised metal. High relief was also sometimes achieved by attaching a separate cast or repoussé motif, for example on some of the saucepan handles from the votive treasure of Capheaton, Northumb. (London, BM), objects that are probably of Gallo-Roman manufacture.

The silver of this period represents the full assimilation of Greco-Roman aesthetic sensibilities to the rich cultural heritage of the native populations of the Roman provinces. It has an assurance that can be compared only with some of the finest products of the late 18th century, a technical and artistic expertise that often eschews elaboration in favour of a restrained simplicity.

(iv) Late Empire. In this period there were many changes, among them the increasing power and influence of Christianity, which were reflected in silverware as they were in other pure and applied arts. Yet in spite of the brilliant quality of earlier work, silver of the 4th century AD is in its way equally impressive. More material survives from this period than the preceding one, the burial of large hoards in many provinces of the Empire reflecting times of unrest and upheaval. The introduction of Christian elements alongside the traditional pagan iconography, sometimes blatantly using and reinterpreting those themes, is a new feature, and there is a general trend towards more complex and elaborate styles of decoration, sometimes to an extent that now appears overdone and ostentatious.

Probably the outstanding feature of late Roman silver is the survival of many large display platters covered with decoration in relief, often mythological, but sometimes reflecting the commemorative imperial purposes that were probably behind the manufacture of all of them. Large and valuable items of silver tableware were appropriate gifts between the ruling family and very senior imperial officials, and some bear inscriptions that record this function. Several 4th-century AD picture-plates are now known that are over 700 mm in diameter and weigh 10 kg or more: these are not normal serving dishes, even for the most exalted tables, but were made solely for display. One found in 1656 in the River Rhône near Avignon was christened the Shield of Scipio (Paris, Bib. N., Cab. Médailles). The partially gilded pictorial composition covering its surface is probably a scene from the life of Achilles, a traditional theme that recurs frequently on 4th-century AD display silver, for example on a superb octagonal platter in the treasure found in 1962 at Kaiseraugst, Switzerland (Augst, Römermus.), and on one of the great dishes in the 'Sevso' Treasure, first made public in 1990. The Great Dish from the MILDENHALL TREASURE, ornamented with lively Bacchic revels, is another of these flamboyantly beautiful late Roman masterpieces. Rectangular picture-plates were also made, and the Corbridge lanx, a silver tray 480 mm long found in 1735 in the River Tyne at Corbridge, Northumb. (London, BM; see fig. 5), is the outstanding example; it is decorated with a scene depicting Apollo, Diana,

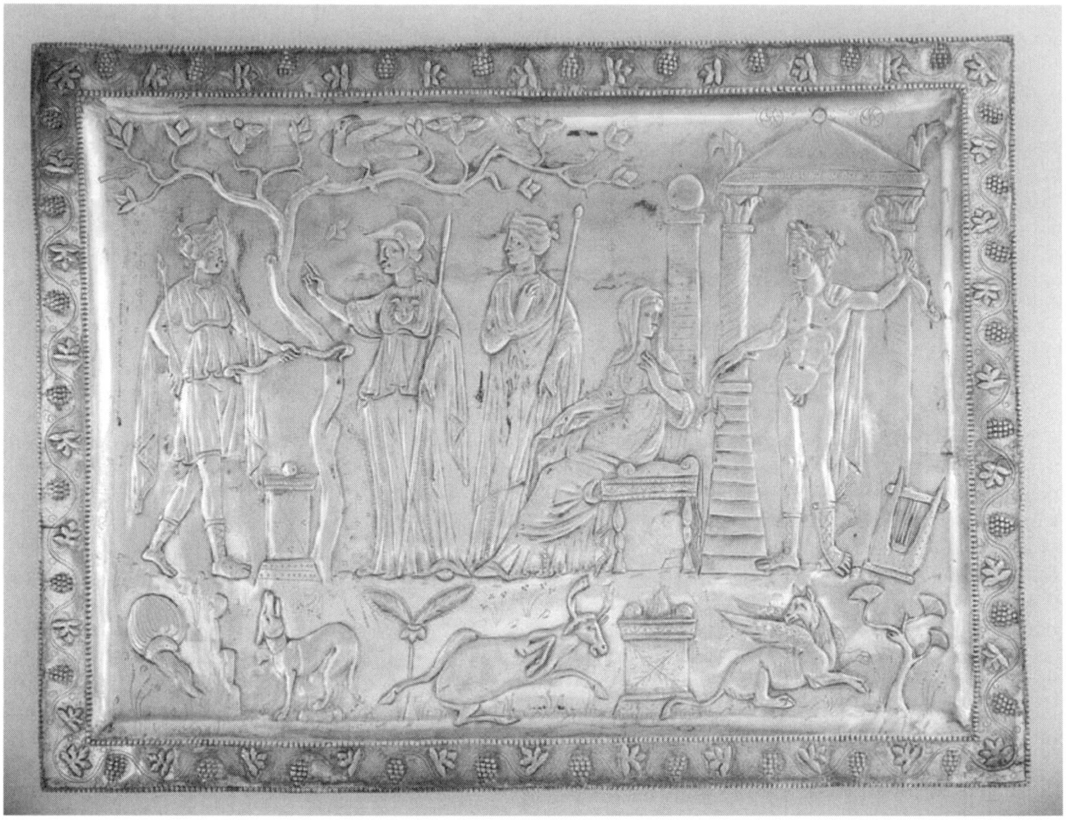

5. Corbridge lanx, silver, l. 480 mm, 4th century AD (London, British Museum)

Minerva and other deities at a shrine, and has been plausibly explained as an imperial gift made to commemorate the visit of the pagan emperor Julianus (*reg* AD 360–63) to the shrine of Apollo on Delos in AD 363.

Treasures of household silver continued to feature a variety of bowls and dishes, and as in earlier periods matching sets of four, eight or twelve vessels were often made, but in the 4th century AD spoons, likewise in matching sets, became an almost invariable feature of any important collection of silver, whereas wine cups had evidently been entirely replaced by glass. As the least expensive silver utensils, spoons were probably available to households that could not afford the more impressive pieces of plate, and hoards consisting only of silver spoons, sometimes buried together with jewellery or coins, are characteristic of this period. The typical 4th-century AD spoon has an overall length of *c.* 200 mm, an oval or pear-shaped bowl often bearing an incised inscription or decorative motif, and a slender pointed handle attached to the bowl by an offset in the form of a pierced scroll or a stylized animal head. It is on such spoons that Christian inscriptions start to appear with increasing frequency in the later 4th century AD, and it seems likely that at least some may have had liturgical uses as well as more mundane domestic functions.

A larger type of spoon also appears in some late hoards, with an oval bowl as large as a modern tablespoon and a short recurved handle terminating in a bird's head. On these, too, Christian inscriptions, including the chi-rho monogram, are a fairly frequent feature. The religious and political battle between paganism and Christianity was fought throughout the 4th century AD, and specifically pagan iconography and inscriptions still occurred in the AD 390s: a remarkable treasure from Thetford, Norfolk, found in 1979 (London, BM; *see also* JEWELLERY, §5), consists of gold jewellery and 33 spoons of both the types described above, many of them dedicated to the ancient pagan rural deity Faunus, whose name is combined with Celtic epithets. Small long-handled strainers and pointed implements identified as toothpicks also appear quite frequently in late hoards. Many of these bear Christian motifs or inscriptions, and it seems probable that we have yet to appreciate their full significance.

Fluted water-bowls, jugs and ewers of various sizes occur in many of the treasures, and as in the early hoards objects are occasionally preserved that are better classified as furniture than tableware, for example the impressive extending candelabrum in the Kaiseraugst Treasure, 1.17 m high at its fullest extent and richly ornamented with niello and gilding, or the miniature sculptures representing the tutelary deities of four great cities (Rome, Constantinople, Antioch and Alexandria) in the Esquiline Treasure

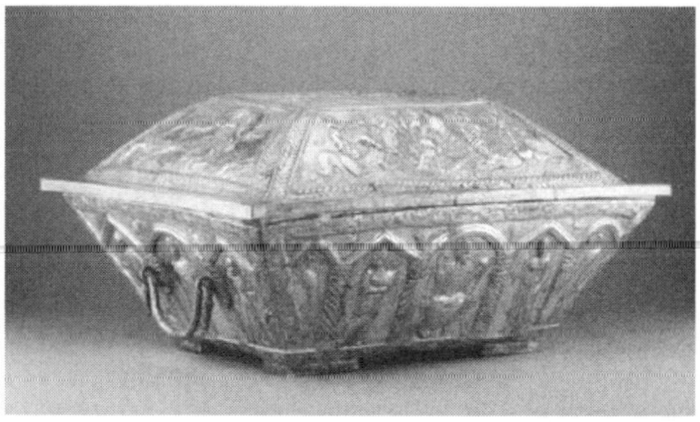

6. Projecta Casket, silver, h. 279 mm, Rome, *c.* AD 380 (London, British Museum)

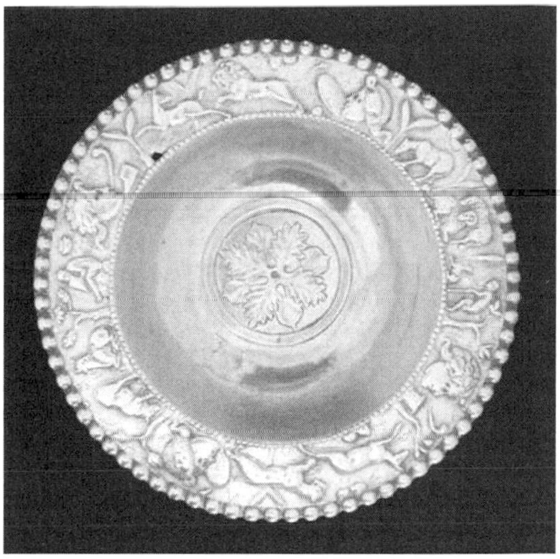

7. Roman silver bowl with relief decoration of pastoral scenes, diam. 167 mm, from the Carthage Treasure, 4th–5th century AD (London, British Museum)

(London, BM), which are probably embellishments for a throne or litter, or even a chariot. The Esquiline Treasure was found in Rome in 1793 and is another of the major hoards of the 4th century AD. The most famous piece in it is a large rectangular bridal casket with an inscription identifying it as the property of Projecta, wife of Secundus (see fig. 6); the inscription is a Christian one, but it is combined with wholly pagan pictorial motifs. A smaller relief-ornamented toilet casket in the same assemblage contains separate lidded cosmetic canisters in silver. Another casket of exactly the same type has been found in the 'Sevso' Treasure alluded to above.

Gilding and niello combined on silver to create patterns and pictures in black, silver and gold is found on many important late Roman vessels. One large platter from the Kaiseraugst Treasure has a central roundel depicting a seaside city, the buildings and harbour of which are lavishly detailed in the contrasting metallic colours: the motif is a standard one in Roman art. On the 'Sevso' plate itself, a magnificent platter 705 mm in diameter, the rim border displays hunting scenes and buildings picked out in gold and niello, while the central roundel, encircled by an inscription including the owner's name, Sevso, bears the scene of a hunt and picnic in the country that resembles those on late Roman mosaics from Piazza Armerina and elsewhere. The image vividly conveys the ideal lifestyle of the very rich in late Roman society.

Alongside these confidently ornate silver objects, the tradition of plain forms that rely on the beauty of the metal for their effect was not dead. Many of the late spoons have an elegance that comes from simple fitness for their purpose, and a set of lidded bowls in a large treasure found at Carthage (e.g. London, BM; see fig. 7) are quite remarkable for their purity of form. With high base-rings echoed on the lids, which can also be used as shallower dishes, their only decoration is a subtle faceting of the surface, and the effect is disconcertingly like that of some of the best modernist designs of the 1920s and 1930s in western Europe.

Notwithstanding the austere grace of these pieces, most people would cite the great picture-plates from the Kaiseraugst, Mildenhall and 'Sevso' Treasures, and individual objects such as the Corbridge lanx and the Missorium (dish) of Theodosios I (after AD 388; Madrid, Real Acad. Hist.) as the finest representatives of late Roman silverware. Although they lack the perfection of finish and the exquisite control of line and proportion in both abstract pattern and human and animal figures that we see in some earlier work, they are still remarkable achievements: the stylistic changes reflect wider ones that ultimately mark the development of Classical into early medieval, pagan into Christian. Just as in architecture and the other arts, the Roman tradition in silverware merges imperceptibly into the Byzantine.

A. M. Héron de Villefosse: *Le Trésor de Boscoreale* (1899), v of *Monuments et mémoires publiés par l'Académie des Inscriptions et Belles-Lettres*, Fondation Eugène Piot (Paris, 1899–1902)

J. R. Mélida y Alinari: *El disco de Teodosio* (Madrid, 1930)

A. Maiuri: *La Casa del Menandro e il suo tesoro di argenteria* (Rome, 1933)

O. Brendel: 'The Corbridge *lanx*', *J. Roman Stud.*, xxxi (1941), pp. 100–127

D. E. Strong: *Greek and Roman Gold and Silver Plate* (London, 1966)

U. Gehrig: *Hildesheimer Silberfund* (Berlin, 1967)

B. Overbeck: *Argentum Romanum* (Munich, 1973)

K. S. Painter: *The Mildenhall Treasure* (London, 1977)

K. J. Shelton: *The Esquiline Treasure* (London, 1981)

C. Johns and T. W. Potter: *The Thetford Treasure* (London, 1983)

H. A. Kahn and A. Kaufmann-Heinimann: *Der spätrömische Silberschatz von Kaiseraugst* (Derendingen, 1984)

K. S. Painter and F. Baratte: *Trésors d'orfèvrerie gallo-romains* (Paris, 1989)

C. M. Johns: 'Research on Roman Silver Plate', *J. Roman Archaeol.*, iii (1990), pp. 28–43

M. M. Mango and A. Bennett: *The Sevso Treasure: Art Historical Description and Inscriptions* (Ann Arbor, 1994)

A. Bedini: *Mistero di una fanciulla: Ori e gioielli della Roma di Marco Aurelio da una nuova scoperta archeologica* (Milan, 1995)

Roman Gold and the Development of the Early Germanic Kingdoms: Aspects of Technical, Socio-political, Socio-economic, Artistic and Intellectual Development, AD *1–550: Stockholm, 1997*

M. Bradley: 'Fool's Gold: Colour, Culture, Innovation and Madness in Nero's Golden House', *Apollo,* cdlxxxv (July 2002), pp. 35–44

L. A. Riccardi: 'Military Standards, Imagines, and the Gold and Silver Imperial Portraits from Aventicum, Plotinoupolis, and the Marengo Treasure', *Ant. Kst,* xlv (2002), pp. 86–100

B. Niemeyer: *Die silbernen Halbkugelbecher vom Typ Leuna: Fundkomplexe und Interpretationen Herstellungstechnik und Datierung* (Oxford, 2004)

P. S. W. Guest: *The Late Roman Gold and Silver Coins from the Hoxne Treasure* (London, 2005)

M. Dennis: *Silver in Late Iron Age and Early Roman East Anglia* (diss., U. Oxford, 2006)

2. Bronze. The Roman bronze industry produced over many centuries a wide range of decorative tableware and utensils, ornamental fittings for furniture, vehicles and ships, and architectural ornaments. It also produced sculpture: portraiture for imperial and private use, statuary for gardens and fountains, large images of deities for public worship and smaller-scale statuettes for lararia (household shrines). Artists and master craftsmen fashioned major works; workshops mass-produced lesser pieces with an emphasis on functional rather than aesthetic aspects (for large-scale Roman statuary and portraiture *see* Sculpture, §VI; *see also* Arms and armour, §2, and Furniture, §3).

(i) Republican. (ii) Imperial.

(i) Republican. During the early Roman Republic, the celebrated Etruscan bronzeworkers to the north (*see* §V above) and Greek craftsmen of South Italy and Sicily to the south (*see* §IV above), both relying on local sources of copper, overshadowed bronzework from Rome and Latium. Exceptions are the cists made at Praeneste, an Etruscan city that came under Roman rule in the late 5th century BC. These lidded, cylindrical boxes displayed engraved, figural scenes drawn largely from Greek mythology. The most famous, the Ficoroni Cist (*c.* 400 BC; Rome, Villa Giulia; see colour pl. 1:XV, fig. 4), shows a scene from the Argonautica and bears a Latin inscription stating that it was made in Rome (Dohrn). Whether it is Roman or Etruscan is linked ultimately to questions of national identity. Praeneste was Roman when the cist was made, and its inscription is in Latin, though most scholars classify it as Etruscan. All of Etruria came under Roman domination before the mid-3rd century BC, and Latin supplanted Etruscan by the early 1st century BC, yet whether the local inhabitants considered themselves Roman rather than Etruscan is impossible to say.

In the 2nd and 1st centuries BC the old Etruscan bronzeworking centres, famous for their 5th- and 4th-century BC products and now incorporated into the Roman Republic, continued to turn out finely decorated bronze vessels, many with figured handles, which were traded through northern Italy and exported into France and Germany and even further afield in the Mediterranean. At the same time, Capua, south of Rome, relying on Campanian sources of copper, also had workshops producing ornamental tableware. Though best-known in the early Imperial period when workshop owners put their names on their products, the industry developed as early as the 5th century BC and was flourishing in the period of the late Roman Republic, as Cato stated (*On Agriculture* cxxxv).

In the late 3rd century BC and 2nd, Roman military expeditions looted works of art from defeated cities, displaying their booty in Rome in triumphal processions. In the late 3rd century BC, art was looted from Syracuse, Capua and Tarentum (anc. Gr. Taras) in Italy and Sicily; in the early 2nd century BC, from cities in Greece and Asia Minor; and in 146 BC from Corinth in Greece. Fine bronzes must have been among these works of art. During the same period, Romans commissioned Greek-speaking artists to produce portrait statues and other bronze and marble sculptures. Wealthy Romans furnished their houses and seaside Campanian villas with works of art demonstrating Greek style and subject-matter, including marble and bronze statuary.

Little evidence exists, however, for local production of smaller-scale bronzes in Rome itself. Possible examples of late Republican bronzework are the statuettes said to have been found near Nemi, in the hills south-east of Rome (most now in London, BM). The largest, a half-life-size figure of a priestess of Diana, is in the Etruscan tradition yet anticipates the conventions of Imperial bronze images of Roman household deities.

(ii) Imperial. Most Roman bronzes have survived through two circumstances: the eruption of Vesuvius in AD 79, which buried Pompeii, Herculaneum and neighbouring villas; and the political turbulence in the northern provinces in the mid-3rd century AD, which prompted people to bury their bronzes, silver and other valuables for safe-keeping. Discoveries of hastily hidden caches in France, Germany and Switzerland, for instance, have yielded some of the finest Roman bronzes known. Although few statuettes were placed in tombs, many vessels have been recovered from burials; other bronzes were evidently lost *en route*: vessels and statuettes have been fished from rivers near Roman bridges and recovered from ancient shipwrecks.

M. C. Rolley: 'Bronzes romains', *Doss. Archéol.*, xxviii (1978) [set of illus. essays]

H. Menzel: 'Römische Bronzestatuetten und verwandte Geräte: Ein Beitrag zum Stand der Forschung', *Aufsteig und Niedergang der römischen Welt*, II/xii/3 (Berlin, 1985), pp. 127–69 [full bibliog.]

M. Barraclough: *Sovereigns and Soldiers on Horseback: Bronze Equestrian Monuments from Ancient Rome to our Times with an Epilogue about the New Leonardo Horse by Milan J. Kralik* (Ipswich, 1999)

G. Cuscito and M. Verzár Bass, eds: *Bronzi di età romana in Cisalpina: Novità e riletture* (Udine, 2002)

(a) Vessels and utensils. (b) Statuettes. (c) Fittings for wheeled vehicles.

(a) Vessels and utensils.

Techniques and distribution. Capua was the most celebrated centre for the manufacture of bronze vessels and utensils (Pliny the elder: *Natural History* XXXIX. xx.95). Many other provincial centres existed; bronzes were surely made in the valley of the Saône and in Lugdunum (now Lyon), and archaeological evidence pinpoints, for example, Alesia and Malain in Burgundy and Bliquey, Nimy and Bavay in Belgium. Metalworking centres must also have existed in Asia Minor.

Techniques of manufacture tended to respond to requirements of mass production. The bodies of the vessels were generally raised and spun on a lathe, although some were cast. The handles were cast separately and then soldered to the bodies. A collection of stone moulds said to have been found at Antaradus (now Tartus), Syria, and acquired by the Louvre in the 1890s, was used in a preliminary stage for the manufacture of handles of bronze and silver vessels. The standard copper alloy was bronze using tin, but BRASS (in which zinc replaces tin) was also employed.

Among the first Roman bronze vessels to be discovered in modern times were those from Pompeii and Herculaneum; these set the standard for modern perceptions of repertory and style. But the wealth of finds from these sites should not obscure the fact that distribution was widespread in Spain, Gaul, Britain, Germany, Switzerland, the Balkans, North Africa and the eastern Mediterranean. In the Cave of Letters overlooking the Dead Sea, for example, was found a cache of bronze vessels, some clearly of Italian manufacture: jugs, basins and a patera (Jerusalem, Israel Mus.). Bronzes from Pannonia (a region roughly corresponding with modern Hungary) were among the first to be published. Bronze vessels and utensils were exported or carried beyond the frontiers of the Empire: to Scandinavia, Poland, the Black Sea region and even Afghanistan and India. Burials in Mtskheta, Georgia, for instance, have revealed a patera and a variety of jugs (Tbilisi, Mus. Georgia).

Vessels. Among the ornamental vessels from Pompeii, Herculaneum and villas buried by the eruption of Vesuvius in AD 79 are kraters, buckets, amphorae, jugs, basins, paterae (shallow dishes) and even a type of Roman samovar (*authepsa*). The finest collection of this material is in the Museo Nazionale, Naples (Tassinari, 1993). The wall paintings of Pompeii and Herculaneum show bronze tableware of this sort both in use and in still-lifes.

Many of the shapes copy 5th- and 4th-century BC Greek metalwork. Others combine Classical forms with the native Italic heritage. A situla (bucket) with two swinging handles (Naples, Mus. Archeol. N.) is an exceptional piece, modelled on a 5th-century BC Greek bucket; it displays elaborate floral reliefs partly inlaid with silver and copper and marked with what is perhaps the owner's name, Cornelia Chelidone. Two handles of a basin or plate (Naples, Mus. Archeol. N., and London, BM) bear in relief two gorgons and two tritons derived from 5th-century BC work, but the monsters on the Roman piece are purely decorative, not functional.

Jugs from Herculaneum and Pompeii are among the best-studied shapes, with attention focused principally on the decorations of the handles. On some handles the lower attachment is merely in the form of a leaf, as on many Hellenistic jugs. More often the escutcheons on the lower attachments show the face of Bacchus or one of his retinue, a maenad, satyr, or the mask of an actor; others show the bust of a deity, or even a complete figure in relief, such as a cupid. The rim attachments are variously treated, some ending in a leaf or a thumb, the latter indicating the position of the hand grasping the handle, others sporting a female bust or the face of a lion or other animal overlooking the mouth of the jug as in earlier Greek work. The shafts of some of the handles sprout leaves or take the form of twigs.

Designers of handles drew on stock narrative scenes from the repertory of Hellenistic decorative arts. Bacchus with a satyr and a feline appear on the escutcheons of one group of jug handles. An old satyr beating a younger one is represented on three other jug handles, the shafts of which feature Bacchic symbols, arranged as vignettes in a fashion that became standard in the 2nd century AD.

Jugs dating from the 1st and 2nd century AD with decorated handles have been found elsewhere in Italy and northern Europe. An ambitious group of late 1st- and 2nd-century handles from Gaul, Britain and Germany display on the lower escutcheon a rich selection of subjects from Greek mythology, including Ajax slaughtering animals in his madness, Diana changing Actaeon into a stag, Perseus beheading Medusa, and Vulcan at his forge (Weissenburg, Römermus.). Other jug handles show one or more cupids or putti in various poses. If not completing the mythological scene, the decorative field above may be filled with bucolic devices with Bacchic cult overtones: panpipes, cymbals, altars, actors' masks or bowls of fruit. The figures are always upright, but the reliefs are arranged vertically on the handles in vignette fashion.

Jugs were often paired with paterae and were clearly used together in both domestic and religious contexts, although it is difficult to connect the subject-matter of the reliefs to any particular cult. The emblemata on several 1st-century AD paterae show figural decoration in low relief, some highlighted with silver inlay. The subjects derive from Greek mythology and other sources. The patera from the Cave of Letters in Israel shows Thetis, the mother of Achilles, on the back of a marine centaur bringing armour to her son. Another, from a villa at Boscoreale (London, BM), shows the monster Scylla attacking Odysseus' ship. Both were probably made in Campania, while a patera found at Priene in western Asia Minor and probably from an eastern workshop has an emblema showing a fisherman.

Sometimes a pictorial relief, either cast or repoussé, covers the entire body of the vessel. Pieces decorated in this fashion, most dating from the 1st century AD, must have been special orders for ceremony or presentation. A krater modelled on a Hellenistic prototype shows Orestes, Pylades and Iphigenia (Varna, Archaeol. Mus.), but with the features of the emperor Augustus, his general Agrippa and Augustus' daughter Julia, Agrippa's wife. A pitcher from a Sarmatian burial mound in the region of Rostov, east of the Sea of Asov in Russia, shows the sacrifice of Polyxena and another mythological scene from the Trojan cycle.

Inlay work in silver, copper, niello and glass brought colour to the yellow bronze of some vessels. A 1st-century AD jug and patera from Egyed in Hungary have floral inlays in gold and silver; figural scenes of an Isis cult cover the body of the jug. The handle of a saucepan from a British workshop found near Ely (London, BM) shows marine life and a scroll of vine and ivy partly inlaid with copper and niello, creating reddish and black points of contrast. A group of 2nd-century AD six-sided pyxides (small containers) from various sites in Britain and western Europe have panels of multicoloured glass inlays: red, blue, green, yellow, white and turquoise in chequerboard patterns. This technique, traditionally practised in Celtic metalwork, persisted in jewellery and metalwork in the late Roman and early medieval times, especially in northern Europe.

In the late 2nd century AD and 3rd, workshops in Germany and Gaul produced a series of brass buckets, known as the 'Hemmoor type' after the town where many have been found (Willers). These were cast, then lathe-turned on a wheel and fitted with one or two swinging handles. On some, a band of floral and figural decoration circles the body just below the rim.

In the 2nd and 3rd centuries AD small bronze containers, perhaps for perfumes or oils, appear in the form of human figures or, more usually, just the head and shoulders. Widespread through the Rhine and Danube valleys and in Egypt, many are designed as the head and shoulders of a satyr or a black African, though deities are also represented. Unique is a large flask (h. 197 mm) in the form of a tragic actor playing an Oriental king (Avenches, Mus. Romain).

Lamps and knife-handles. Portable bronze LAMPS were often of considerable artistic merit. Excavations at Pompeii and Herculaneum have yielded a great number. Single-nozzled lamps were the commonest design, with handles with a duck or horse head, a human face or an actor's mask. On one exceptional lamp a monkey is dressed as a gladiator (Pompeii, Antiqua). Double-nozzled lamps were less common: decoration includes a bat perched with outstretched wings on a handle; a boy struggling with a bird on a lid; and, on the rim of one lamp, statuettes of Sol and Luna (the sun and moon deities), appropriate images for a lamp. Lamps also took the form of grotesque heads or sandalled feet. In addition there were candelabra on rectangular bases, with multiple lamps hanging from branches extending from a pillar, column or even a tree trunk. Some lighting equipment is even more exceptional. A standing lamp from Ephesos (Vienna, Ksthist. Mus.) is of a style and design unlike anything from Italy. The shaft has an ornate capital incorporating heads of Hercules and his consort Omphale, together with relief images of Hercules reclining, and four floral stems with blossoms in the form of Hercules. The five-nozzled lamp perched on top is covered with reliefs showing plants and lion skins, the latter alluding to Hercules.

Knife-handles were often of bronze and cast in the form of gladiators or the foreparts of lions. The iron blades generally survive only as a corroded stump.

H. Willers: *Die römischen Bronzeeimer von Hemmoor* (Hannover, 1901)

L. Curtius: 'Orest und Iphigenie in Tauris zum Bronzekrater von Dionysopolis-Balčik', *Mitt. Dt. Archäol. Inst.: Röm. Abt.*, xlix (1934), pp. 247–94

A. Radnóti: *Die römischen Bronzegefässe von Pannonien* (Budapest, 1938)

A. Frova: 'Vasi bronzei romani decorati', *A. Lombarda*, viii (1963), pp. 33–43

Y. Yadin: *The Finds from the Bar Kokhba Period in the Cave of Letters* (Jerusalem, 1963), pp. 42–100

J. Balty: 'Une Anse d'aiguière d'époque romaine à incrustations d'argent', *Bull. Mus. Royaux A. & Hist.*, xxxvii (1965), pp. 13–77

R. Fleischer: *Die römischen Bronzen aus Österreich* (Mainz, 1967)

T. Dohrn: *Die ficoronische Ciste in der Villa Giulia in Rom*, Mnmt. A. Romanae, xi (Berlin, 1972)

A. Mutz: *Die Kunst des Metalldrehen bei den Römern* (Basle, 1972)

H.-U. Nuber: 'Kanne und Griffschale', *Ber. Röm.-Ger. Komm.*, liii (1972), pp. 1–233

S. Tassinari: 'Pots à anse unique: Etude du décor des anses d'un type de récipients en bronze d'Herculanum et de Pompéi', *Cron. Pompéiane*, i (1975), pp. 160–223

S. Tassinari: 'La Vaisselle de bronze romaine et provinciale au Musée des antiquités nationales', *Gallia*, suppl. 29 (1975) [whole issue]

P. T. Craddock: 'The Composition of the Copper Alloys Used by the Greek, Etruscan and Roman Civilizations: 3. The Origins and Early Use of Brass', *J. Archaeol. Sci.*, v (1978), pp. 1–16

W. Oberleitner and others: *Funde aus Ephesos und Samothrake* (1978), ii of *Katalog der Antikensammlung* (Vienna)

K. Weitzmann, ed.: *Age of Spirituality: Late Antique and Early Christian Art, Third to Seventh Century* (New York, 1979)

W. Schindler: 'Allegorie der Iulia Augusti als Iphigenie auf dem Bronze-krater in Varna', *Klio*, lxii (1980), pp. 99–109

N. Valenza Mele: *Museo Nazionale Archeologico di Napoli: Catalogo delle lucerne in bronzo* (Rome, 1981)

M. De Spagnolis and E. De Carolis: *I bronzi: Le lucerne* (1983), IV/i of *Museo Nationale Romano: Cataloghi* (Rome, 1979–85)
F. Baratte and others: *Vases antiques de métal au Musée de Chalon-sur-Saône* (Dijon, 1984)
J. Wielowiejski: 'Die spätkeltischen und römischen Bronzegefässe in Polen', *Ber. Röm.-Ger. Komm.*, lxvi (1985), pp. 123–320
M. R. Wojcik: *La villa dei papiri ad Ercolano* (Rome, 1986)
U. L. Hansen: *Römischer Import in Norden* (Copenhagen, 1987)
E. De Carolis: *Le lucerne di bronzo di Ercolano e Pompei* (Rome, 1988)
P. T. Craddock: 'Copper Alloys of the Hellenistic and Roman Worlds: New Analyses and Old Authors', *Acta of the Centenary Conference of the British School at Athens: Bangor, 1988*, pp. 55–65
T. Schäfer: 'Die Dakerkriege Trajans auf einer Bronzekanne', *Jb. Dt. Archaeol. Inst.*, civ (1989), pp. 283–317
M. Cima and L. Pirzio Biroli Stefanelli: *Il bronzo dei Romani: Arredo e suppellettile* (Rome, 1990)
M. Feugère and C. Rolley: 'La Vaisselle tardo-républicaine en bronze', *Actes de la table-ronde CNRS: Lattes, 1990*
L. Pirzio Biroli Stefanelli: *Il bronzo dei Romani* (Rome, 1990)
A. E. Riz: *Bronzegefässe in der römisch-pompejanischen Wandmalerei* (Mainz, 1990)
A. Oettel: *Bronzen aus Boscoreale in Berlin* (Berlin, 1991)
R. D. de Puma: 'The Roman Bronzes from Kolhapur', *Rome and India: The Ancient Sea Trade*, ed. R. D. de Puma and V. Begley (Madison, 1991), pp. 82–112
V. K. Gugnev and Ju. Trejster: 'Une oinochoé de bronze à scènes mythologiques', *Rev. Archéol.* (1992), no. 2, pp. 243–71
E. Künzl and others: *Die Alamannenbeute aus dem Rhein bei Neupotz: Plünderungsgut aus dem römischen Gallien*, 4 vols (Mainz, 1993)
S. Tassinari: *Il vasellame bronzeo di Pompei* (1993), v of *Soprintendenza archeologica di Pompei: Cataloghi* (Rome, 1986–)
B. Niemeyer: *Die silbernen Halbkugelbecher vom Typ Leuna: Fundkomplexe und Interpretationen Herstellungstechnik und Datierung* (Oxford, 2004)

(b) Statuettes. In the production of statuettes of deities and other figures, Roman bronzeworkers looked for inspiration to major works by earlier Greek artists, such as Polykleitos, Lysippos and Praxiteles. They appropriated poses and drapery styles, adapted attributes and combined stylistic features from different epochs. Some Roman bronzes are scaled-down versions of famous works of art; others are adaptations, eclectic in nature, often making the model difficult to trace. Certain pieces, such as garden ornaments, were purely decorative, others were votive gifts in sanctuaries or may have served as cult images. Most Roman statuettes, however, were made for display in lararia (household shrines). Statuettes were cast solid or hollow, with details often worked into the metal after casting. Frequently the left arm of a figure, particularly if it carried drapery, was cast separately and soldered to the body. This practice, first adopted in the late Hellenistic period, served to expedite the casting of figures. On better statuettes the eyes were inlaid with silver, and on male figures the lips and nipples were marked with copper.

Ornamental figures. Among the first ornamental bronzes to be found in modern times are those recovered in Herculaneum from the Villa of the Papyri in the mid-18th century (Naples, Mus. Archeol. N.). In addition to the celebrated series of portrait busts and full-size statues there is a group of smaller ornamental statues: four sileni reclining on rocks, and five pairs of cupids or putti in various mirror reverse poses.

Ornamental bronzes for the house and garden are rare outside of Vesuvian sites, but this reflects the accident of preservation. The most celebrated is the *Spinario* (Rome, Mus. Conserv.; see colour pl. 2:XII, fig. 2), a seated boy removing a thorn from his foot, known in Rome since the 12th century, much copied from the Renaissance on. This eclectic work, probably dating from the 1st century AD, derives from a Hellenistic type after which a number of marble versions, designed as garden fountains, were also made in the Roman period.

Small, table-model copies of life-size, 5th-century BC works by famous Greek sculptors were made in terracotta and bronze; the latter include the *Diadoumenos* of POLYKLEITOS, one of the wounded Amazons created for the Temple of Artemis at Ephesos (Florence, Mus. Archeol., 2293), and the *Diskobolos* of Myron of Eleutherai.

Cult images. Images of Bacchus or Liber Pater (Italian god of fertility and wine identified with the Greek Dionysos) are common in ornamental contexts in Pompeii, Herculaneum and elsewhere. The god rarely figures in lararia although images may well have been set up separately as objects of devotion. He appears in several standing poses, often with the skin of a large feline slung over the left shoulder. He wears an ivy wreath and carries a thyrsus (bacchic staff) and pours the dregs of his wine to an attendant feline, usually a leopard, at his feet. Often the attributes are missing. A good example is the 680 mm tall *Bacchus*, standing with his left foot on a leopard, found in 1961 in a lead-working shop in Herculaneum, where it may have been taken for repairs just before the eruption of Vesuvius. Lips, eyes, the berries of his wreath, the spots of the leopard at his feet and of his leopard skin are inlaid with copper. This statuette and the many others like it in various European museums must derive from life-size Hellenistic sculptures. Individual cats in several museum collections, crouching and looking up, several of superb quality, must originally have been associated with figures of Bacchus.

Bronze cult images and large-scale votive gifts rarely survive. An exception is a 360 mm tall *Hercules* (Chieti, Mus. N. Archeol. Abruzzo). Found at Sulmona in 1959, this statuette was a dedication there in the Sanctuary of Hercules Curinus by M. Attius Petricus Marsus, whose name is in silver letters on the base. The pose is a version of the well-known 'Weary Hercules' or Hercules Farnese type, leaning on a tree trunk over which his lion skin is slung, right hand behind his back. This bronze and the many other versions known, mostly in marble and some life-size, derived from a statue by Lysippos.

An exceptionally fine figure of *Jupiter* (h. 540 mm; Brussels, Musées Royaux A. & Hist.) is thought by some to be a cult image from a sanctuary. Unfortunately, its true provenance cannot be ascertained. His cloak falls off his left shoulder over his bent left arm; his right hand is lowered and once held a thunderbolt. Noteworthy are the tight corkscrew curls of the hair and beard. This and other Roman bronze versions must reflect a 5th-century BC Greek original.

Some bronzes certainly reflect major Roman cult images. A statuette of *Victory* found in the Saône in 1866 (Lyon, Mus. Civilis. Gallo-Romaine) is thought to be a portable version of the *Victory* on the famous altar of Rome and Augustus at Lyon, which is shown on coins of the emperors Augustus, Tiberius and Nero. Victory is standing at rest with her wings fully preserved; all that are missing are the palm branch and crown she once held. Other statuettes of Victory, showing her in flight alighting on a globe, may derive from the statue brought by Augustus from Tarentum to Rome after the Battle of Actium in 29 BC.

Figures for lararia: lares and Roman deities. Most smaller-scale bronze statuettes found at Pompeii, Herculaneum and elsewhere in Italy and the Empire were made for lararia. Lares, originally Etruscan divinities, became Roman household deities, shown as young men in boots and in short-sleeved, knee-length tunics that billow out as if the figures were in motion. They carry a drinking horn or sometimes a cornucopia in one hand, a libation bowl or less often a bucket in the other. They also appear carried by officials in stone reliefs showing rites of the Roman State religion. The lares were made in mirror-image pairs and flanked one or more images of the pantheon of Greco-Roman gods, of various sizes, with the general exception of Bacchus, as is known from painted versions of lararia. Specific deities represented include the Capitoline triad (Jupiter, Juno and Minerva), together with Mercury, Apollo, Venus, Hercules, a personification of Fortuna, and even such romanized Egyptian deities as Jupiter–Serapis and Isis–Fortuna. Most stand on profiled bases, cylindrical or variously angled, often ornamented with architectural mouldings and sometimes inlaid with silver designs. Bronze images were usual; more expensive ones might be of silver, cheaper ones of terracotta.

Much of the evidence comes from Pompeii and Herculaneum and from excavations and accidental finds in Britain, France, Germany and Switzerland. In the mid-1st century BC Julius Caesar (*Conquest of Gaul* VI. xvii) reported on the deities worshipped by the Gauls: ‘the god they revere most is Mercury. . . . Next to him they revere Apollo, Mars, Jupiter and Minerva.’ Mercury is indeed the god most frequently represented among bronzes from Gaul. Representations of the other four in Caesar’s list are common both singly and in groups from lararia.

Mercury is shown standing or seated in several versions, usually with wings in his hair or cap, and with his pouch (*marsupium*) and his staff (*caduceus*). The poses of the numerous standing figures derive ultimately from the *Doryphoros* of POLYKLEITOS. The seated Mercurys derive from a seated 4th-century BC statue, once thought to be the seated *Hermes* by Lysippos, now sometimes identified as a seated *Herakles*. One of the finest seated statuettes of Mercury was found with five other statuettes from a lararium in Schwarzenacker, Germany (Saarbrücken, Landesmus. Vor- & Frühgesch.). Wearing a silver hat and carrying a silver staff, he rests on a finely sculpted bronze rock, with a wild boar, a goat and a cock at his feet. In Gaul Mercury must often represent a local deity in Greco-Roman guise.

Apollo is shown as a long-haired youth in various standing poses that derive from 5th- and 4th-century BC sculptural types. Two principal types of Mars are represented in bronze. One is a youthful figure, nude except for a crested helmet, derived ultimately from Greek statues by Skopas and Bryaxis. A classicizing version of this type exists, said to have been found in Reims (Paris, Louvre). The other is a bearded figure dressed as a Roman commander in full armour, modelled after the cult statue of *Mars* created *c.* AD 90 for the Temple of Mars Ultor in Rome. A good example, said to have been found along the Rhine, is in the British Museum. Jupiter is shown both standing and seated. The seated pose derives from the statue of *Jupiter Capitolinus* in the god’s temple in Rome, a type ultimately dependent on Pheidias’ colossal *Zeus* at Olympia. Minerva is shown standing or seated, fully clothed, wearing an aegis and helmet, often crested, her right arm raised so as to rest on a spear. This imagery stems from several 5th- and 4th-century BC sculptural types.

In addition to the five gods mentioned by Caesar, there are also statuettes of Juno, Neptune, Venus, Diana, Vulcan, Somnus, Cupid and Hercules, and personifications of Abundance and Fortune (or Concordia), whose images likewise are small-scale versions of earlier Greek types.

Venus is a particular case in Syria and Egypt. Marriage contracts and other papyrus documents of the 2nd and 3rd centuries AD from Egypt record the presence in dowries of bronze statuettes of Venus (or Aphrodite, as she would have been called by the Greek-speaking population). A range of bronze Aphrodites have been found in Egypt and recovered from tombs in Syria, presumably women’s burials where they were placed after serving in some kind of household shrine. The eastern figures are plumper than their western counterparts and frequently are shown wearing elaborate headdresses.

Two collections of bronze statuettes that apparently formed lararia exemplify the quality of work and range of deities represented. The first group (London, BM) was found near Paramythia in Epiros, north-west Greece, in the 1790s. Ranging in height from 160 to 340 mm, the bronzes represent Jupiter (two versions), Mercury seated, Apollo, Venus unclothed lifting her left foot, Venus clothed (or perhaps Dione, her mother), one of the Dioscuri (?Castor), Serapis seated and a lar. These nine accomplished bronze statuettes, which were found in association with other bronzes, were originally considered Hellenistic, but since the 1930s they have been recognized as early 2nd-century AD Roman work. The two Jupiters are mirror images of one another, the stances reflecting a Lysippan original. The *Serapis*, like all statues of a seated Serapis, derives from Bryaxis' 4th-century BC cult image for the god's temple in Alexandria. The *Venus* shown lifting her foot, one of many Roman replicas, probably copies an original of *c.* 200 BC. The seated *Mercury* goes back to a 4th-century BC sculpture.

The second group of statuettes (Weissenburg, Römermus.) was found in 1979 in Weissenburg, Germany, on the site of a Roman military garrison. They apparently belonged to a temple treasury buried during barbarian incursions in the mid-3rd century AD and were associated with a substantial collection of silver votive plaques, parade helmets, bronze vessels and other objects. The figures, all standing, include the Capitoline triad (Jupiter, Juno and Minerva), two Apollos, three Mercurys, three Venuses, a pair of Cupids and three figures connected with household cult (a tutelary genius with a turreted crown, a togate genius and a lar). Some of the bronzes must once have been associated with a public sanctuary, as one of the statuettes of Venus has a slot for coin offerings in the base.

The statuettes range between 150 and 250 mm in height and stand on a variety of bases—round, square, polygonal and one semicircular with small columns. They seem to have been made in various workshops, some major, some provincial, in the 2nd century AD. The *Jupiter*, *Minerva*, *Hercules* and one *Apollo* derive from 5th-century BC prototypes; the other *Apollo*, shown with a *kithara* (lyre), relates to a Hellenistic original; the stances of the Mercurys depend ultimately on a 5th-century BC Polykleitan prototype; one of the Venuses is based on the *Aphrodite of Knidos* by Praxiteles, another on the Aphrodite Pudica type. The man dressed in a toga shown sacrificing is a standard figure in lararia. The figure with a turreted crown is the guardian spirit of a particular place.

Several such tutelary figures are known, but the places with which they were originally associated can rarely be identified. In the Roman period, the late 3rd-century BC *Tyche* (Fortune) of Antioch by the Greek sculptor EUTYCHIDES, shown as a seated woman wearing a turreted crown, was reproduced in numerous small-scale bronzes. Other cities also adopted and made statues of guardian spirits. A bronze statuette of a young man wearing a turreted crown (Paris, Bib. N., Cab. Médailles) has been convincingly identified as Aristaios, the tutelary genius of Cyrene in North Africa.

Figures for lararia: Oriental and native deities. Some customers required representations of non-Greco-Roman gods. The worship of the Asiatic goddess Magna Mater or Cybele, introduced to Rome in 204 BC, became widespread under the Empire. She is usually depicted with two lions. A 2nd-century AD bronze group, reputedly found in Rome (New York, Met.), shows Cybele seated in a cart drawn by two lions.

The cult of Cybele's consort Attis also flourished. A bronze statuette, fished out of the River Mosel in the 1960s (h. 350 mm; Trier, Rhein. Landesmus.), shows Attis as a chubby boy in distinctive dress, wearing a peaked Phrygian cap and an outlandish long-sleeved and trousered costume, buttoned down the front of the legs and body but open to reveal his stomach and genitals. Despite the unusual iconography, the sculpture is of high quality and is well-modelled in Hellenistic Greek style, front and back.

In Italy in the 1st century AD, slaves, many originally from the East, and their freed descendants worshipped the Egyptian deities Isis, Serapis and the bull god Apis. Images of Isis often show her combined with Fortuna and carrying a ship's steering oar and cornucopia, as in a bronze from Herculaneum (Naples, Mus. Archeol. N., 5313). Serapis, associated with Jupiter, appears seated, as in the statuette from Paramythia; standing (e.g. in Baltimore, MD, Mus. A., 51.256); or abbreviated with just the head and shoulders shown. Fine studies of bulls resulted from representations of Apis; they were usually shown with head turned and one foreleg raised. An Apis bull excavated from a shrine of a Vesuvian villa in Scafati, one of the finest known (Detroit, MI, Inst. A.), stands on an elaborate base with several registers of architectural mouldings.

The cults of Jupiter Sabazius from Asia Minor and Mithras from Persia also developed in Italy and Gaul in the 1st century AD. The cult of Sabazius involved bronze votive hands, and the two finest of *c.* 50 hands known are those in the Musée Romain, Avenches, and in the Antiquarium in Pompeii. The hands are upright with thumb and first two fingers open, fourth and fifth crooked, in an attitude of benediction. Covering them are creatures, emblems and images of deities, some in reference to the cult, others apotropaic in nature.

Mithras, another Near Eastern god, shown slaughtering a bull, is normally represented in stone reliefs together with images. A group of bronzes found at Angleur in 1882 (Liège, Mus. Curtius) represent some of the items shown on the marble reliefs: two dancers, heads of divinities of the winds, signs of the zodiac and other figures.

In the 2nd and 3rd centuries AD, soldiers and people of Eastern origin involved in security and trade along the Rhône and Rhine and elsewhere in Europe wanted images of these deities together with those of other imported Oriental cults, such as Jupiter Dolichenus from Syria. A bronze (Vienna, Ksthist. Mus.) of *Jupiter Dolichenus*, dedicated by one Marrius Ursinus, a veteran of the Roman army, was excavated in 1937 near the wall of the Roman castle of Mauer an der Url, near Amstetten, Austria; it depicts the deity dressed in military uniform standing on the back of a bull, circus fashion.

In Gaul the native deities Sucullus and Epona were provided with images in Greco-Roman style, many of them stone reliefs but including a few bronze statuettes. The bearded god Sucullus (sometimes called Dispater) is dressed for the misty north in trousers and a belted, long-sleeved jacket. He carries a jar and a long-handled mallet, and was loosely associated with Jupiter. The Gallic horse goddess Epona is shown riding side-saddle on a mare or seated between two horses. Well-modelled examples of Sucullus are in the Musée d'Art et d'Histoire, Geneva, and the Palais Rumine, Lausanne. One of the more classicizing versions of Epona comes from Loisia (Paris, Bib. N., Cab. Médailles).

The representation of an otherwise unknown goddess, Artio, was found in 1832 in Muri, Switzerland, where an inscription on the base indicates that it had been dedicated in a local shrine by Licinia Sabinilla (Berne, Hist. Mus.). Artio, seated with a bowl of fruit on her lap, is thought to be both a provider of the fruits of the earth and a bear goddess, not only because of the similarity of her name to the Greek word for bear (*arktos*) but also because she is confronted by a very forward yet friendly bear, its back to a tree.

Not all of the hundreds of bronzes made for the worship of these native and imported deities, let alone the Greco-Roman gods, rise to the level of art. Yet the artists responsible for some clearly aspired to high standards of style and craftsmanship, sometimes working in the neo-Classical tradition, at other times relying more on the conventions of folk art in the translation of native and imported gods to the Greco-Roman artistic idiom. Some of the native Gallic gods, such as Artio and her bear, were probably previously represented only by crude wooden images.

E. Babelon and J.-A. Blanchet: *Catalogue des bronzes antiques de la Bibliothèque nationale* (Paris, 1895)

A. de Ridder: *Bronzes antiques du Louvre*, 2 vols (Paris, 1913–15)

H. B. Walters: *Select Bronzes, Greek, Roman and Etruscan, in the Departments of Antiquities* (London, 1915)

S. Haynes: 'The Bronze Priest and Priestesses from Nemi', *Mitt. Dt. Archäol. Inst.: Röm. Abt.* (1960), pp. 34–47, pls 12–20

H. Menzel: *Trier* (1966), ii of *Die römischen Bronzen aus Deutschland* (Mainz)

T. Hölscher: *Victoria romana* (Mainz, 1967)

A. Kolling: *Die Bronzestatuetten aus dem Säulenkeller: Forschungen im römischen Schwarzenacker*, i (Einöd-Saar, 1967)

H. Blank: 'Archäologische Funde und Grabungen in Mittelitalien 1959–1969', *Archäol. Anz.* (1970), pp. 342–5, figs 95–7

S. Doeringer, D. G. Mitten and A. Steinberg, eds: *Art and Technology: A Symposium on Classical Bronzes* (Cambridge, 1970)

D. von Bothmer: 'The Babuino Bronzes', *In Memoriam Otto J. Brendel: Essays in Archaeology and the Humanities*, ed. L. Bonfante and H. von Heintze (Mainz, 1976), pp. 155–8

S. Boucher: *Recherches sur les bronzes figurés de Gaule pré-romaine et romaine* (Paris, 1976)

S. Boucher and S. Tassinari: *Inscriptions, statuaire, vaisselle* (1976), i of *Bronzes antiques du Musée de la civilisation gallo-romaine à Lyon* (Lyon, 1976)

A. Leibundgut: *Avenches* (1976), ii of *Die römischen Bronzen der Schweiz* (Mainz, 1976–80)

E. Poulsen: 'Probleme der Werkstattbestimmung gegossener römischer Figuralbronzen: Herstellungsmilieu und Materialstruktur', *Acta Archaeol.*, xlviii (1977), pp. 1–60

G. Faider-Feytmans: *Les Bronzes romains de Belgique* (Mainz, 1979)

M. Maass: *Griechische und römische Bronzewerke der Antikensammlungen* (Munich, 1979)

A. Leibundgut: *Westschweiz, Bern und Wallis* (1980), iii of *Die römischen Bronzen der Schweiz* (Mainz, 1976–80)

R. Noll: *Das Inventar des Dolichenusheiligtums von Mauer an der Url (Noricum)* (Vienna, 1980)

D. K. Hill: 'Note on the Piecing of Bronze Statuettes', *Hesperia*, li (1982), pp. 277–83

M.-O. Jentel: 'Aphrodite in peripheria orientali', *Lexicon Iconographicum Mythologiae Classicae*, ii (Zurich, 1984), pp. 154–66

E. Simon: 'Mars', *Lexicon Iconographicum Mythologiae Classicae*, ii (Zurich, 1984), pp. 505–59, esp. 512–22

E. Simon: *Augustus: Kunst und Leben in Rom um die Zeitenwende* (Munich, 1986)

I. Manfrini-Aragno: *Bacchus dans les bronzes hellénistiques et romains* (Lausanne, 1987)

J. R. Mertens, intro.: *The Metropolitan Museum of Art: Greece and Rome* (New York, 1987)

Ercolano: Legni e piccoli bronzi (exh. cat. by T. Budetta and M. Pagano, Rome, Mus. N. Castel S Angelo, 1988)

F. Burkhalter: 'Les Statuettes en bronze d'Aphrodite en Egypte romaine d'après les documents papyrologiques', *Rev. Archéol.* (1990), no. 1, pp. 51–60

E. Simon and G. Bauchhenss: 'Mercurius', *Lexicon Iconographicum Mythologiae Classicae*, ii (Zurich, 1992), pp. 500–54, esp. 507–8

H.-J. Kellner and G. Zahlhaas: *Der römische Tempelschatz von Weissenburg i. Bay* (Mainz, 1993)

(c) Fittings for wheeled vehicles. Horse-drawn carriages, chariots and other wheeled vehicles displayed sets of artistically crafted bronze fittings. Some were functional, for example the cappings on the ends of the axles or the anchors for the suspension systems; others took the form of statuettes, ornamenting the front parapet of a chariot or serving as decorative finials lining the edges of the wood frame chassis. Coins and stone reliefs show two-wheeled imperial chariots decorated with complete figures. Eighteenth-century excavations in Herculaneum revealed the remains of a complete four-horse chariot in bronze, sadly mutilated, yet still preserving five figures (h. 650–700 mm) of Apollo, Juno, Venus and two youths in armour, which are thought to have been the facing of the front of the chariot box. A set of three bronze figures (h. 330–360 mm), the personification of Roma, a goddess (?Venus) (both Malibu, CA, Getty Mus.) and a flying Victory with a cornucopia (Cleveland, OH, Mus. A.), may also once have ornamented a chariot.

The excavation of the collapsed remains of complete four-wheeled vehicles from burials in Bulgaria, Hungary, Germany and France, and from the ruins of a palace in Nicomedia in Bithynia (north-west Turkey) reveal the complete range of such bronzes. In addition, hundreds of isolated finds from sites across the Empire, including Spain and North Africa, illustrate the full range of artistic types.

Among the purely ornamental fittings are matching pairs of semicircular, curved pieces that lined forward parts of the railings of vehicles. Powerful images of lions and other big cats are common, often with copper and silver inlays to highlight their spots and stripes. Figural and narrative subjects were also attempted. The pair of curved pieces from Nicomedia (Athens, N. Archaeol. Mus.) show two women throwing dice. Another pair from a burial in eastern Bulgaria (St Petersburg, Hermitage) show Hercules and Mercury reclining. An isolated find of the early 4th century AD from Colonia Claudia Ara Agrippinensium (Cologne; Bonn, Rhein. Landesmus.) shows an excerpt from an Amazonomachy with Hercules attacking a mounted Amazon.

A decorative finial from another part of a carriage, found in Somodor, Hungary (Budapest, N. Mus.), shows Bacchus flanked by Pan and a satyr arranged as if in a chorus line beneath a huge palmette. Another finial, from a burial mound in the valley of the River Vardar (Cologne, Röm.-Ger.-Mus.), shows a similar composition. A set of relief appliqués once attached to the vehicle from Nicomedia (Athens, N. Archaeol. Mus.) show the Labours of Hercules.

Chief among the functional bronze elements that typically featured figural work are sets of four fittings that served as anchors for the suspension systems. Mounted on posts rising from the axles, these fittings have an upright finial flanked by two loops or hooks, sometimes in the form of curved fingers; the finials terminate in a knob or in the head of an animal or bird, or even in the bust of a mythological figure. In the 4th century AD some of these fittings displayed narrative scenes or an animal. One shows a Gigantomachy (Boston, MA, Mus. F.A.): snake-legged giants rise up against the towers and gate of a city defended by a god and goddess. Another from Marchena, Spain (Paris, Louvre), shows a Greek pulling an Amazon from her horse. These are among the latest bronzes that can still be called Roman.

E. Gabrici: 'La quadriga di Ercolano', *Boll. A.*, i/6 (1907), pp. 1–12

E. von Mercklin: 'Wagenschmuck aus der römischen Kaiserzeit', *Jb. Dt. Archäol. Inst.*, xlviii (1933), pp. 48–176

E. Salin: 'Le Mobilier funéraire de la Bussière-Etable près Chateauponsac (Haute Vienne)', *Mnmts Piot*, xlv (1951), pp. 89–115

A. Fernández de Aviles: 'Pasarriendas y otros bronces de carros, romanos, hallados en España', *Archv Esp. Arqueol.*, xxxi (1958), pp. 3–62

I. Venedikov: *Trakijskata kolesnica* [The Thracian Chariot] (Sofia, 1960)

M. Comstock and C. Vermeule: *Greek, Etruscan and Roman Bronzes in the Museum of Fine Arts, Boston* (Boston, MA, 1971)

C. Boube-Piccot: *Les Chars et l'attelage* (1980), iii of *Les Bronzes antiques du Maroc* (Rabat)

H. Menzel: *Bonn* (1986), iii of *Die römischen Bronzen aus Deutschland* (Mainz, 1986)

3. Iron. The Romans used iron on a scale probably unequalled before the high Middle Ages. Few parts of the Roman world were far from a source of iron ore, but as most were small, they could not cope with the demands of the major centres, so that several mining areas assumed a degree of predominance. Republican Italy was largely dependent on ore from Elba, which was smelted on the mainland at Populonia before being sent to the smiths of Puteoli, whose products were exported throughout the Mediterranean. Under the Empire this source was largely supplanted by the highly prized iron of Noricum (modern Austria), which was transported across the Alps to the industrial city of Aquileia at the head of the Adriatic. Other major sources of iron ores were in Spain, France and Britain in the West, and Turkey in the East. In some, if not all, areas, iron mines were a state monopoly. The ores were usually smelted in small shaft-furnaces that produced blooms weighing less than 10 kg. As the demand for iron rose with the expanding economy of late Republican and Imperial times it was met by increasing the number of furnaces rather than their capacity.

The raw material of the Roman blacksmith was almost always wrought iron, which contains less than 0.5% carbon and is easily shaped and welded at white heat. Carbon steel, containing between 0.5% and 1.5% carbon, was also known but was relatively uncommon. The purest form available was 'Seric iron', imported from India by way of Egypt, but its high cost limited its use to major cities on the Mediterranean. More common was case-hardened iron (wrought iron with a thin coating of steel produced by heating iron bars in a bed of burning charcoal for many hours), although even this seems to have been quite rare. That the complementary properties of wrought iron and steel were appreciated is shown by the production of pattern-welded sword blades from the late 2nd century AD. In this technique layers of iron and steel were interleaved to produce a hard but resilient material that had only to be quenched in cold water to develop its full potential. Such swords are found both inside the Empire, for example at South Shields in England (South Shields, Arbeia Roman Fort), and outside it, as in the important group from the Nydam hoard in Denmark (Copenhagen, Nmus., and Schleswig, Schloss Gottorf), so that where the technique was invented is uncertain. Other steels, made by alloying iron with metals such as manganese, were probably produced by accident during the smelting of suitable ores (e.g. those from Noricum), but their controlled production was beyond the competence of ancient technology. Cast iron was not used by the Romans.

Most smiths apparently produced a variety of items, but some specialists existed in the major cities, in particular producing knives and other edged tools, weapons and locks. An indication of the scale of production of military equipment is provided by the number and range of state-controlled armament factories in the late Empire. Most were probably created by nationalizing existing workshops, and although the majority produced a range of equipment, some specialized in a single product, such as swords or arrowheads. The range of artefacts produced by the Roman smith was immense and shows a remarkable uniformity throughout the Roman world. Such variations as exist were usually the result of cultural differences rather than any variation in smithing techniques. The vast majority of ironwork was utilitarian, encompassing a wide range of military equipment and structural fittings, tools, utensils, vehicle parts etc. Perhaps because of its ubiquity, and because of the social and artistic constraints on blacksmiths, iron was rarely used for decorative purposes, as was common in the Middle Ages. That this was not the result of any lack of skill on the part of the smiths is shown by the fine quality of many of the tools and fittings that they produced, especially in the few surviving fragments of iron furniture. Such pieces were often found at military sites, suggesting that they were designed to withstand the rigours of army life. Among the finest specimens are imitations of elaborately turned wooden bars, probably belonging to a cupboard grille (late 1st century AD; Edinburgh, National Mus. of Scotland), from Newstead, Scotland, and a folding stool from Nijmegen (Nijmegen, Rijksmus. G. M. Kam). Likewise, a series of late Roman cauldron chains from southern England (e.g. U. Cambridge, Mus. Archaeol. & Anthropol.) skilfully combine efficiency and elegance, the junction linking the main chain to the arms, which takes the form of a reef-knot, being a *tour de force* of the smith's art.

Although decoration was usually avoided on military equipment, some 1st-century AD legionary dagger sheaths were adorned with elaborate inlaid patterns in silver, copper alloy and enamel; good examples are from the fort at Hod Hill, Dorset (London, BM). Rarer but more striking are the fine parade helmets and face masks worn by some cavalry units. Although usually of bronze, or even silver, a few iron examples exist, notably one from Newstead (1st century AD; Edinburgh, N. Mus. Ant.), which testify to the Roman blacksmith's complete mastery of the difficult technique of forging sheet iron.

W. H. Manning: 'Blacksmithing', *Roman Crafts*, ed. D. E. Strong and D. Brown (London, 1976), pp. 143–54

W. Gaitzsch: *Eiserne Römische Werkzeuge*, BAR International Series 78 i & ii (Oxford, 1980)

W. H. Manning: *Catalogue of the Romano-British Iron Tools, Fittings and Weapons in the British Museum* (London, 1985)

R. F. Tylecote: *The Prehistory of Metallurgy in the British Isles* (London, 1986)

A. Künzl: *Die Alamannenbeute aus dem Rhein bei Neupotz* (Mainz, 1993)

I. Schrüfer-Kolb: *Roman Iron Production in Britain: Technological and Socio-economic Landscape Development along the Jurassic Ridge* (Oxford, 2004)

Metapontion [Lat. Metapontum; now Metaponto]. Site of ancient Greek colony in Lucania (now Basilicata), southern Italy, on a flat coastal terrace on the Gulf of Taras. The city was founded in the second half of the 7th century BC by Achaian settlers, and it flourished during the second half of the 6th century BC and the early 5th. In this period most of its public buildings were erected, and in the extensive *chora* (territory) many single-family farmsteads were established. During the later 5th century BC and the 4th Metapontion declined, though there was a revival in the second half of the 4th century BC, and its port still functioned in late Roman times. Metapontion has been the most fully studied of the western Greek colonies in terms of its architecture, owing to the excavations conducted since 1964 by the Archaeological Superintendency and the German Archaeological Institute in Rome, the extensive finds from which are on display in the Museo Archeologico Nazionale, Metaponto.

1. Architecture. Many architectural aspects of Metapontion were highly innovative. Its grid plan was among the earliest (*c.* 550 BC), its surviving 4th-century BC pattern of streets following the earlier, Archaic ones. Public and residential areas were divided by one of a series of main thoroughfares (*plateiai*) running north-west to south-east. Only the eastern third of the city has been excavated, but this includes the main sanctuary, agora, theatral/assembly buildings and industrial quarter.

The two largest temples in the urban sanctuary, Temple A (?Apollo) and Temple B (?Hera), both in the Doric order, were begun in the early 6th century BC. Their plans influenced that of the better preserved 'Basilica' at Paestum. However, in their final, elongated form of shortly after 550 BC, they in turn show Sicilian influence, and they have the same orientation as the newly laid out city. Earlier than both temples is the first phase (C1) of an *oikos* (shrine) with terracotta friezes. Terracotta revetments from Metapontion constitute the most complete available record of the evolution of temple entablatures in the 6th and 5th centuries BC, and examples discovered in 1830 (Paris, Bib. N.) provided the first clear knowledge of polychromy in ancient Greek architecture. Outside the city, the Doric Tavole Palatine or Temple of Hera (*c.* 525 BC; see fig.) has a plan that anticipates, in its system of proportions, the Temple of Athena at Paestum. It is one of the earliest Greek temples with uniform intercolumniation on façade and flank. The Ionic Temple D (*c.* 470 BC) was the last large-scale building in the urban sanctuary. Both its plan and unique decorative elements are well-preserved.

The series of structures that occupied the eastern end of the agora—two stone ekklesiasteria (assembly halls; phase I, *c.* 550 BC; II, *c.* 475 BC; these were preceded by a wooden structure of the late 7th century BC) and the theatre (second half of the 4th century BC)—was truly revolutionary. The circular stone wall of the first phase of the ekklesiasterion (h. 3.2 m, diam. 62 m) enclosed the earthen fill from which an auditorium of concentric rows was fashioned. No public meeting place of comparable size at such an early date is known elsewhere in the Greek world, and no others stand without reliance on naturally sloping ground. An *orchestra* at the centre was approached by two stone-lined dromoi (passageways; w. 7.5 m) aligned east–west along the circle's diameter. In the second phase the slope of the auditorium was increased, and the *orchestra* was enclosed by a

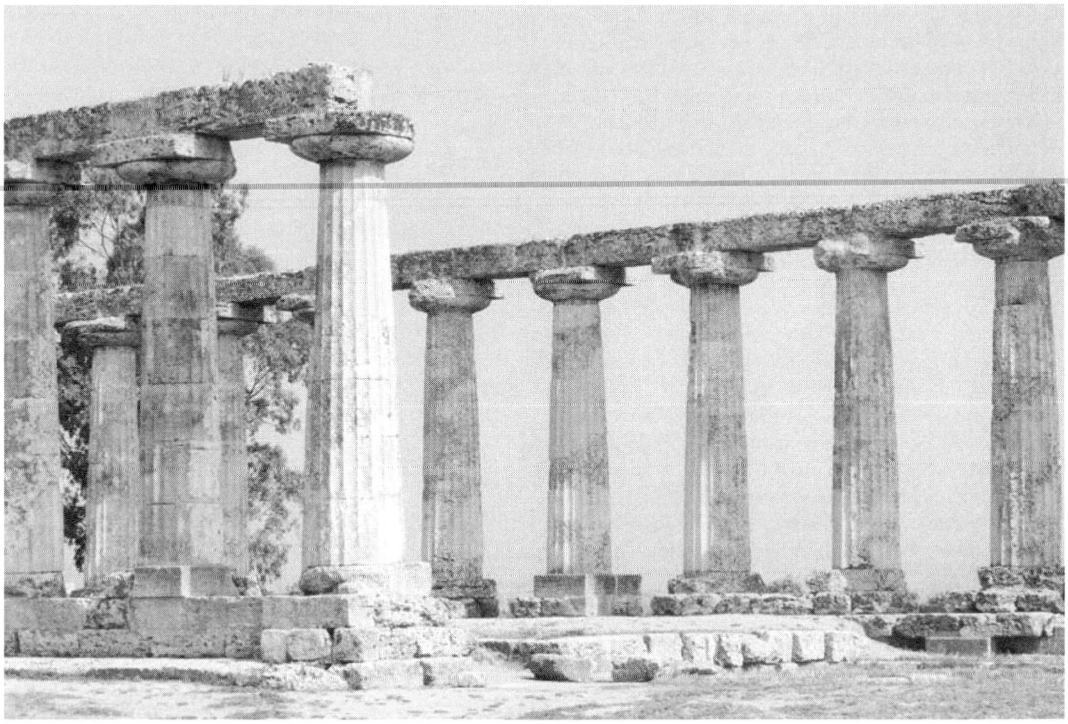

Metapontion, Tavole Palatine (Temple of Hera), *c.* 525 BC

rectangular retaining wall with a long axis corresponding to the dromoi. The building's capacity of 7500–8000 persons suggests that it was not used exclusively as a meeting-place for citizens; it may also have been used for choral performances. The building that replaced it in the 4th century BC was also free-standing but was indisputably a theatre. Its auditorium was semicircular (diam. *c.* 80 m), as in Roman theatres, and, together with a stage building, it seems to have formed a single unit, again anticipating Roman design. It was also the first theatre designed to be seen from all angles. The exterior façade of the retaining wall was articulated by an engaged Doric colonnade masking the stairs to the top of the auditorium. This is among the earliest Greek examples of purely decorative façade architecture, anticipated only by Macedonian tombs.

Extensive excavations in the *chora* have revealed the plans of farmhouses (6th century BC–4th century AD), which provide the principal evidence for the development of Greek rural domestic architecture. The standard structure from the Archaic period onwards comprises parallel rows of rooms, often on two storeys. Courtyards were introduced in the 4th century BC but were not widely used until Roman times.

2. Sculpture. The creativity of Metapontine craftsmen is evident from the long series of terracotta figurines, beginning in the late 7th century BC, and the small bronzes that have been found both within and outside the city. Only the larger-scale sculptures, however, will be considered here; and in this case, despite their outstanding quality, the question of originality is far from clear, not least because of their fragmentary condition.

Before the excavations that began in 1964, only two fragmentary marble sculptures were known: a kouros from the area of the Temple of Apollo, the only one from a southern Italian site (*c.* 500 BC; Potenza, Mus. Archeol. Prov.), and a draped female torso (?mid-5th century BC; Matera, Mus. N. Ridola) from the Temple of Hera (Tavole Palatine). The kouros has been thought to be by a Greek 'island sculptor', but, like the Grammichele Kouros from Sicily (*c.* 500 BC; Syracuse, Mus. Archeol. Reg.), which it resembles, it may have been executed in the West. The torso of a terracotta kore (original h. 1.3 m, late 6th century BC; Metaponto, Mus. Archeol. N.), found near Temple D, follows the pattern of works from mainland Greece, but the painted designs on its drapery are more ornate. Herodotus (*Histories* IV.xv) recorded the dedication of a statue of *Aristeas* next to one of *Apollo* in an oracular shrine in the agora and observed that the statues were surrounded by a grove of laurel. Gilded bronze laurel leaves were found in the excavation of this temenos. A few fragments of limestone and marble sculptures come from the main urban sanctuary and are probably architectural. The latter include an ornately coiffed female head (?*Artemis*) of extraordinary beauty and originality, a head of a youth and a male torso. All are in the Early Classical 'Severe Style' (*c.* 480–*c.* 450 BC) and resemble contemporary work from Akragas and elsewhere in southern Italy and

Sicily. The treatment of surface and the details of eyes and hair indicate the influence of bronze sculpture. The limestone fragments (*c.* 500–*c.* 480 BC) are not of the same quality. They include the torso of an *Amazon* and were perhaps attached to previously undecorated metopes of an earlier building. Terracotta architectural sculptures include the friezes from the *oikos* C1 which, with those from the sanctuary at San Biagio (*c.* 600–*c.* 575 BC; Metaponto, Mus. Archeol. N.) in the *chora*, are among the earliest of their kind and form a link between the art of Asia Minor and that of Etruria. In addition, there are two under life-size horses' heads and male torsos from the roof of a temple of *c.* 500–*c.* 475 BC. This must have resembled that of the Portonaccio Temple at Veii. Comparable large terracotta horses from roofs have been found at Gela and Lokri. A terracotta torso of an archer (?*Herakles*) was found near Temple D. From the urban sanctuary at Metapontion itself and the rural sanctuaries at San Biagio and Pantanello, there are important marble fragments of acrolithic cult statues, a form long considered characteristic of western Greek sculpture.

D. Adamesteanu: *La Basilicata antica* (Cava dei Tirreni, 1974)
Metaponto: Atti del tredicesimo convegno di studi sulla Magna Grecia: Napoli, 1974
D. Adamesteanu, D. Mertens and F. d'Andria: *Metaponto*, i (Rome, 1980)
D. Mertens and A. de Siena: 'Metaponto: Il teatro–ekklesiasteron', *Boll. A.*, vi/67 (1982), pp. 1–60
B. Chiartano and others: *Metaponto*, ii (Rome, 1983)
D. Mertens: 'Metaponto: Ein neuer Plan des Stadtzentrums', *Archäol. Anz.* (1985), pp. 645–71
J. C. Carter: 'Metapontum: Land, Wealth and Population', *Greek Colonists and Native Populations* (Oxford, 1990)
J. C. Carter: 'Sanctuaries in the *Chora* of Metaponta', *Placing the Gods: Sanctuaries and Sacred Space in Ancient Greece* (Oxford, 1994)
J. C. Carter: *The Chora of Chersonesos on the Black Sea and Metaponto in Southern Italy* (Austin, TX, 1995)
M. Prohászka: *Reflections from the Dead: The Metal Finds from the Pantanello Necropolis at Metaponto: A Comprehensive Study of Grave Goods from the 5th to the 3rd Centuries BC* (Jonsered, 1995)
J. C. Carter, J. Morter and A. P. Toxey: *The Chora of Metaponto: The Necropoleis* (Austin, TX, 1998)
J. C. Carter: *The Study of Ancient Territories: Chersonesos and Metaponto* (Austin, TX, 2000)
E. M. De Juliis: *Metaponto* (Bari, 2001)
A. De Siena and V. Cracolici: *Metaponto: Archeologia di una colonia greca* (Taranto, 2001)
J. C. Carter: *The Study of Ancient Territories: Chersonesos and Metaponto: 2003 Field Report* (Austin, TX, 2003)
V. Barberis: *Rappresentazioni di divinità e di devoti dall'area sacra urbana di Metaponto: La coroplastica votiva dalla fine del VII all'inizio del V sec. a.c.* (Florence, 2004)
M. G. Liseno: *Metaponto: Il deposito votivo Favale* (Rome, 2004)
D. Giacometti: *Metaponto: Gli dei e gli eroi nella storia di una polis di Magna Grecia* (Cosenza, 2005)
J. C. Carter: *Discovering the Greek Countryside at Metaponto* (Ann Arbor, 2006)
J. C. Carter: *The Study of Ancient Territories: Chersonesos and Metaponto: 2004 Annual Report* (Austin, TX, 2006)
M. Castoldi, S. Bruni and V. Guglielmi: *La ceramica geometrica bicroma dell'Incoronata di Metaponto: Scavi 1974–1995* (Oxford, 2006)

Mezadah. *See* MASADA.

Mieza. *See* LEUKADIA.

Mikon (*fl* earlier 5th century BC). Greek painter and sculptor. He came from Athens and although none of his work survives, paintings by Mikon and his great contemporary POLYGNOTOS OF THASOS decorated several buildings erected at the instigation of the Athenian general Kimon (*c.* 512–449 BC). An *Amazonomachy* depicting the battle between the Amazons and the Athenians, led by Theseus, which hung in the Stoa Poikile (Painted Stoa) was certainly by Mikon, and some ancient authors also ascribed to him the most famous painting in that building, depicting the *Battle of Marathon*, although it was generally attributed to PANAINOS. Pausanias (*Guide to Greece* I.xvii.2–4) saw three or four paintings in the Sanctuary of Theseus, built on the south side of the Agora after Kimon had brought Theseus' bones back from Skyros (474/3 BC): an *Amazonomachy*, a *Centauromachy*, *Theseus Recovering the Ring of Minos from the Sea* and perhaps *Theseus in the Underworld with Peirithoos*. It is possible that Mikon painted all the pictures in the sanctuary. Finally, a picture of the *Argonauts* by Mikon decorated the Sanctuary of the Dioskouroi. In it, the artist's greatest efforts were said to have been expended on the figures of Akastos and his horses. Ancient critics claimed that Mikon erroneously gave his horses lashes on their lower lids, although the mistake was sometimes attributed to Apelles or Polygnotos. An innovation associated with Mikon and Polygnotos seems to be reflected in some Attic Red-figure vases from *c.* 460 BC, which departed from a single ground line. Mikon once painted the helmet and an eye of a soldier called Butes, with the rest of the figure obscured (so that 'Faster than Butes' became a proverb for a task easily accomplished), and the motif of figures partially concealed behind hills was also taken up by Attic Red-figure vase painters. Pliny (*Natural History* XXXIV.xix.88) included Mikon in his list of bronze sculptors and said that his statues were much admired. Pausanias (VI.vi.1) saw one at Olympia, which represented the pancratiast Kallias of Athens (victor in 472 BC), and its base has been found.

J. Overbeck: *Die antiken Schriftquellen zur Geschichte der bildenden Künste bei den Griechen* (Leipzig, 1868/*R* Hildesheim, 1959), nos 1054, 1058, 1070–71, 1080–93
J. P. Barron: 'New Light on Old Walls: The Murals of the Theseion', *J. Hell. Stud.*, xcii (1972), pp. 20–45

Mildenhall Treasure. Hoard consisting of 24 items of Roman silverware (London, BM), mainly from the 4th century AD, found in 1942 by a ploughman working

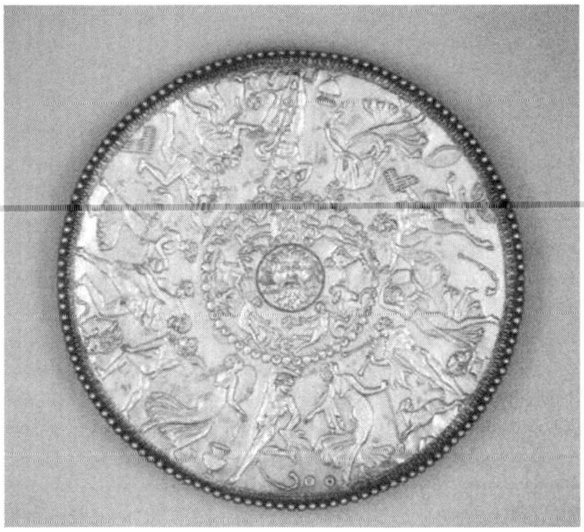

Silver *Oceanus* dish (Great Dish), diam. 605 mm, Romano-British, part of the Mildenhall Treasure from Suffolk, 4th century AD (London, British Museum)

near Mildenhall, Suffolk. The outstanding object, now known as the Mildenhall Great Dish or the Oceanus dish (diam. 605 mm; see fig.), is a shallow circular platter decorated over its whole surface with Bacchic scenes in low relief; it constitutes one of the greatest masterpieces of the Roman silversmith's art. The central motif is the head of a sea god with seaweed and dolphins in his hair and beard; surrounding it is a narrow frieze of sea nymphs riding on mythological marine creatures. The principal, outer zone of decoration depicts a Bacchic revel presided over by Bacchus himself. Several satyrs and maenads with Pan and Silenus dance and play flutes, pipes and tambourines, while Hercules, the loser in a drinking contest with Bacchus, the god of wine, is kept from drunken collapse only by the support of two companions. The entire decoration thus incorporates the sea thiasus and the land thiasus of Bacchus. As on other silverwork of the period, the figures lack the perfect proportions of their late Hellenistic and early Imperial predecessors, but the vivid, spirited rendering of movement and atmosphere compensates for their occasional awkwardness.

A pair of small platters (diam. 188 and 185 mm) in the treasure are clearly by the same artist. They depict respectively Pan and a maenad, and a satyr and maenad surrounded by animals and objects symbolic of the cult of Bacchus. The theme is repeated in the decoration of four bowls with broad horizontal rims, as well as on a deep, domed lid added in the 4th century AD to a flanged bowl, which is the earliest piece in the hoard, a Gallo-Roman product of the 3rd century AD. Another platter almost as large as the Great Dish is much more simply decorated with floral and geometric patterns inlaid in niello. Most of the bowls and dishes are bordered with a row of raised bosses, typical of 4th-century AD table silver. A deep, fluted bowl with drop handles has chased foliate ornament and a central geometric figure delineated in broad, shallow grooves. The predominantly pagan iconography is modified only by the presence of Christian inscriptions on three of the eight spoons in the hoard. Such combinations of pagan and Christian elements are common on 4th-century AD material.

The relief decoration was executed in a chasing technique that involved virtually carving the surface of the metal. Fine detail was rendered in delicately incised lines and tiny punched dots; perspective was suggested to some extent by slight variations in the height of the relief and by leaving the most distant elements in incised line only. The techniques are typical of those used on ornate display silver of the 4th century AD and exemplify the impressive level of skill attained by late-Roman silversmiths.

J. W. Brailsford: *The Mildenhall Treasure: A Handbook* (London, 1947, 2/1955)

K. S. Painter: 'The Mildenhall Treasure: A Reconsideration', *BM Q.*, xxxvii (1973), pp. 154–80

K. S. Painter: *The Mildenhall Treasure* (London, 1977)

P. Ashbee: 'Mildenhall: Memories of Mystery and Misgivings', *Antiquity*, lxxi (March 1997), pp. 74–6 [finding of the Mildenhall Treasure]

R. Hobbs: 'The Mildenhall Treasure: Roald Dahl's Ultimate Tale of the Unexpected?', *Antiquity*, lxxi (March 1997), pp. 63–73 [Dahl's account of the find]

T. C. Lethbridge: 'The Mildenhall Treasure: A First-hand Account', *Antiquity*, lxxi (Sept 1997), pp. 721–8

R. Dahl and R. Steadman: *The Mildenhall Treasure* (London, 1999)

Miletos. Site on the west coast of Turkey, near the mouth of the River Meander (now Bügük Menderes). The city flourished under the Greeks and the Romans from the 5th century BC to the 3rd century AD. A large Byzantine church was built there in the 6th century. Miletos was once a port but is now 9 km from the sea. German archaeologists have been excavating there since the late 19th century. Milesian architecture played a significant role in the development of ancient Greek architecture in general. It comprised three phases of varying importance.

1. MYCENAEAN TO ARCHAIC PERIOD (16TH CENTURY BC–EARLY 5TH). Little is known of the first settlement, established near the Theatre Bay in the late 16th century BC, except that it consisted of largish but fairly simple dwellings. Towards the end of the 13th century BC it was fortified with a strong wall, mud-brick on stone foundations, 4.3 m high and reinforced by bastions; it enclosed an oval area measuring *c.* 400×200 m. Nonetheless, the town was destroyed *c.* 1200 BC, though not totally abandoned. During the Ionian migration (11th–10th century BC) a new settlement was established and by the 8th–7th century BC this occupied *c.* 70–80 ha, stretching from Kalabaktepe in the south to the area that was later the North Agora. The southern area of the town was based on an irregular network of alleys, but the northern part near the Port of the Lions was rebuilt in the second half of the 6th century BC with a regular street plan similar to that of the later city.

Few dwellings have been uncovered; consequently no standard pattern emerges. Nearly all have courtyards, while several doubled as workplaces. Some of the few shrines from this phase (Apollo Delphinios, Dionysos) were simple courtyards, which contained a total of at least 12 largish altars, adorned with corner palmettes. Others were fairly small temples (Athena, temple on the Kalabaktepe). The principal Milesian temple, however, was that of Apollo Didymaios about 15 km away at DIDYMA, although its relation to the city proper at this early period remains unclear.

2. CLASSICAL TO HELLENISTIC PERIOD (EARLY 5TH CENTURY BC–LATE 1ST). In 494 BC Miletos was destroyed by the Persians and its population dispersed; it was resettled after the end of the Persian wars (480/79 BC) and was soon being rebuilt on a larger scale. One of the first projects was surely the reconstruction of the city walls. The first stretches were erected on earlier foundations and sometimes had mud-brick superstructures. The southern section (late 2nd–early 1st century BC) was of markedly superior design and execution, with sawtooth curtain walling and numerous towers and sallyports. The planning of the new town is attributed to HIPPODAMOS of Miletos. Its various districts were laid out on a grid pattern, with minor differences in orientation. The intention from the outset was to move the town centre to the area by the Port of the Lions, and, following the Hellenistic reconstruction of the old sanctuaries, the South (official) Agora (see fig.), the North Agora (the centre of commerce) and the most important public buildings were indeed built there: the prytaneion probably in the 4th century BC, the bouleuterion *c.* 175–*c.*150 BC and the gymnasium *c.* 150 BC.

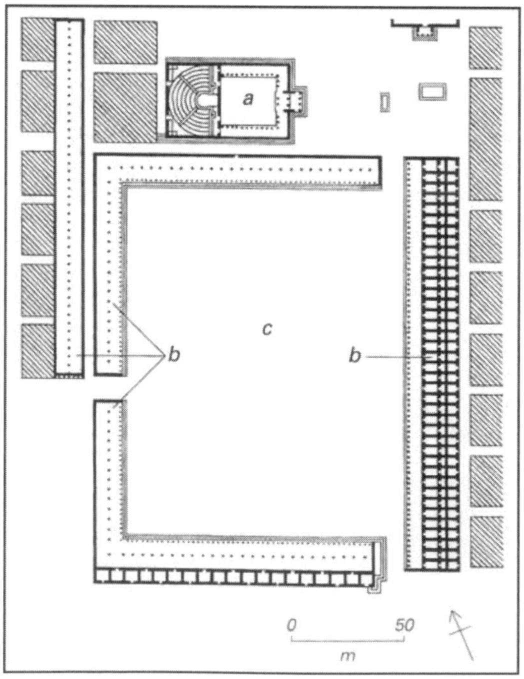

Miletos, plan of the agora, *c.* 175–*c.* 165 BC: (a) bouleuterion; (b) stoas; (c) square

A large Ionic Temple of Athena was erected *c.* 479–*c.* 450 BC, though perhaps never quite completed. It stands on a high platform, unusual for Ionia, and has an equally unusual plan (possibly pseudodipteral, i.e. without the inner row of columns). Only modest reconstructions of sanctuaries have been found from the 5th and 4th centuries BC (Apollo Delphinios, Dionysos); from the turn of the 4th century BC, however, large-scale temple building resumed, beginning with a new Temple of Apollo at Didyma. Two particularly large temples at Miletos itself were that of Dionysos (early 3rd century BC), which was unusual in combining Ionic columns with antae, and that of Demeter (late 3rd century BC), an Ionic prostyle building in a prominent position on the northern tip of the peninsula. Both were cleared away or built over in Christian times. Similarly, the remains of a large Doric building lying under the Great Basilica (6th century AD) consist only of foundations and a few architectural elements, so that its original form is uncertain. More remains of the public buildings in the area adjoining the Sacred Way. Most notable is the bouleuterion (*c.* 170 BC), a rectangular council chamber (34.84×24.28 m) with a slightly more than semicircular auditorium. Pilasters divided its inside walls into panels, some equipped with windows. Outside, the building was adorned with engaged Doric half-columns and pilasters at each corner, on a ledge well above ground. The columns' echinuses bore egg-and-dart mouldings, an Ionic feature symptomatic of the tendency to combine the orders at this period. The court in front of the chamber was lined on three sides by Doric colonnades, incorporating a Corinthian gateway with extremely elaborate column capitals opposite the chamber's entrance. At the court's centre was an altar for the cult of the Roman emperors, also with Corinthian columns. To the east is a gymnasium (*c.* 197–*c.*159 BC), with a Doric peristyle court fronted by an Ionic porch. While grey marble from local quarries on the Gulf of Latmos was the main material used for sacred and public buildings, mud-brick was widely used for houses, so that little is known of their plans.

3. ROMAN IMPERIAL PERIOD (1ST–4TH CENTURIES AD). Because Ephesos was the residence of the proconsul of Asia, Miletos was less politically and economically important at this time. Nonetheless, after regaining its autonomy in *c.* 39 BC it undertook a substantial civic building programme and maintained high building standards even until the 4th century AD. Around AD 100–150 the central area of the town was raised, the processional way linking Miletos to Didyma was extended, and an aqueduct several kilometres long was constructed. Three bath–palaestra complexes were built—Capito (*c.* AD 47–*c.* 54), Faustina (AD 161–80) and Humeïtepe (late 1st to early 2nd century AD)—as well as the great nymphaeum (late 1st century AD) and the ceremonial gateway

leading into the South Agora (*c.* AD 125; Berlin, Antikensamml.; for illustration *see* IONIA). Although it had a Hellenistic predecessor, the theatre's remains are almost entirely Roman, and its auditorium is of typically Roman form, being semicircular rather than over semicircular and largely free-standing on an arched substructure rather than completely recessed into a hillside. It has a frontage of 140 m, and it accommodated around 15,000 spectators in three tiers, each with twenty rows of seats. The lowest tier is composed of five wedges, divided by stairways, the middle one of ten and the highest of twenty. The 'royal box' in the middle of the first tier is marked by four reused columns, of which two survive. Inscriptions designate other reserved seats and also record a labour dispute that arose during the theatre's construction. Building took place in two phases: phase 1 during the reign of Nero (AD 54–68) and phase 2 around the mid-2nd century AD, when the two-storey stage building (l. 40 m) received a third level, and the *scaenae frons* was rebuilt. Several important commemorative monuments and two heroa were also erected, while the latest extant structures from this era are a large complex behind the nymphaeum with a monumental arched gateway (early 3rd century AD) and a small shrine to Serapis (mid- to late 3rd century AD).

T. Wiegand, ed.: *Milet: Ergebnisse der Ausgrabungen und Untersuchungen seit dem Jahre 1899* (Berlin, 1906-)

G. Kleiner: *Alt-Milet* (Wiesbaden, 1966)

G. Kleiner: *Die Ruinen von Milet* (Berlin, 1968)

A. Mallwitz and W. Schiering: 'Der alte Athena-Tempel von Milet', *Istanbul. Mitt.*, xviii (1968), pp. 87–160

A. Mallwitz: 'Gestalt und Geschichte des jüngeren Athenatempels von Milet', *Istanbul. Mitt.*, xxv (1975), pp. 67–90

W. Müller-Wiener, ed.: *Milet, 1899–1980: Ergebnisse, Probleme und Perspektiven einer Ausgrabung* (Tübingen, 1986)

W. Müller-Wiener: 'Milet, 1976–1986', *Ant. Welt*, xix/4 (1988), pp. 31–42

V. B. Gorman: *A History of Miletos from 500 to 432 BC* (n.p., 1993)

A. Schneider: *Die Musengruppe von Milet* (n.p., 1999)

W. Held: *Das Heiligtum der Athena in Milet* (2000), ii of *Milesische Forschungen, vol. 2* (Zabern, 1999–)

V. B. Gorman: *Miletos, the Ornament of Ionia: A History of the City to 400 BCE* (Ann Arbor, 2001)

A. M. Greaves: *Miletos: A History* (London and New York, 2002)

Military architecture and fortification. Buildings associated with warfare—usually defensive warfare—and political control.

1. Greek. 2. Roman.

1. GREEK. The citadels, gateways and wall-circuits of Bronze Age Greece and Cyprus depended for their strength not on planning but on size and adaptation to the terrain. Greek fortifications were normally defensive, aimed at providing lasting protection against current siege techniques, without being inordinately expensive. Mud-brick walls could be erected quickly and cheaply and are found in all periods; for hilltop circuits, however, stone, obtainable on the spot, was usually more convenient. Stone also needed less maintenance, and from later Classical times it was increasingly preferred. Massive rubble construction, although as effective under siege as closely fitted masonry, was generally confined to fieldworks and temporary forts. For large Hellenistic city circuits, where walls and gates were designed for visual impressiveness as well as functional efficiency, coursed masonry was normally used, being easier to assemble than irregular or polygonal blocks.

(i) Late 10th century–*c.* 490 BC. (ii) *c.* 490–2nd century BC.

(i) *Late 10th century–c. 490 BC.* In the first centuries after the fall of the Mycenaeans, Greek communities usually had neither resources nor technical skills for large-scale building and, like their predecessors, faced no threat of direct assault with siege engines. Steep-sided promontories walled across the neck, as at ZAGORA on Andros (late 9th century–*c.* 700 BC), or small hilltop circuits, as at Melie near Güzelçamı on Samsun Dağı (before 700 BC) or Emborio on Chios (*c.* 700–*c.* 600 BC), provided adequate sanctuary against attack by neighbours or pirates. These primitive defences are perhaps mirrored in the Homeric account of the Greek wall at Troy (*Iliad* VII.436–41; XII). Early walls were usually rubble or mud-brick on a rubble base. Clay mortar might be used to bind the larger facing-stones together; between the faces was a core of unworked stones and loose earth. The walls were high enough to discourage escalade and had some sort of parapet along the outer edge to protect the defenders from spears, arrows and sling-bullets. The Geometric period walls of Old Smyrna (Bayraklı Tepe) are the most imposing such structures yet discovered.

During the 7th century BC, the wealthier Eastern Greek cities increasingly attracted the attention of covetous neighbours, especially the Lydian kings, who were by then mastering siegecraft techniques learnt from the Near East. Old Smyrna, despite a great increase in area, was content with higher and thicker mud-brick walls enclosing the original peninsula; thus *c.* 600 BC Alyattes of Lydia (*reg c.* 610–560 BC) stormed the walls from the top of a great siege-mound. Yet Greek coastal cities, if provided with adequate fortifications connecting citadel and harbour, could obtain provisions by sea: during the 7th and 6th centuries BC, for instance, the Lydians were unable to take Miletos by land or to blockade it by sea and had to offer special terms. Many other Eastern Greek cities, however, accepted Lydian overlordship without struggle, and their walls, often hastily built, or rebuilt after the Achaemenid conquest of Lydia in 546 BC, were easily overcome by the mounds of the Persian general Harpagus.

Nevertheless, the advantages of both strong walls and a strong fleet, especially for island cities, were by then clear. Herodotus recounted that between *c.* 550 and 490 BC circuits linking citadel, city and harbour were built on many Greek islands, including Samos (III.liv–lvi), Thasos (VI.xxviii, xlvi–xlvii), Karystos and Eretria in Euboia (VI.xcix–ci); at Samos lower-lying sectors of wall were even protected by a rock-cut ditch. Mainland cities were evidently slower to enlarge their circuits; in 490–480 BC Athens had only an enlarged acropolis circuit, which Thucydides (I.xciii) described as being 'extended in all directions' after 479 BC. Significant for the history of Greek military architecture were such Eastern Greek strongholds as Buruncuk in Aiolis (later 6th century BC), which was probably the residence of a Persian vassal; its solidly built two-storey towers may represent Persian rather than Greek defensive theory, although the style of masonry is purely Greek.

Greek colonies overseas, for example in the Black Sea and the western Mediterranean, although not threatened by Lydian or Persian siegecraft, frequently faced hostility from dispossessed native peoples. Thus they too began, quite early, to build city (rather than acropolis) circuits, as in Sicily at Leontinoi (now Lentini) and Akragas (now Agrigento; 7th century BC–early 6th). Megara Hyblaia, in Sicily, and Poseidonia (*see* PAESTUM), on mainland Italy, even occupied completely open sites, with neither acropolis nor natural defences, surviving simply by the strength of their walls.

(ii) c. 490–2nd century BC. When in 494 BC the Persians stormed Miletos, Eastern Greeks had had considerable experience of Persian siegecraft involving mounds, as at Old Smyrna and OLD PAPHOS, Cyprus (499–498 BC); mines, as at Miletos; and rams, probably included among Herodotus' 'every known device' at Miletos (VI.xviii). The fall of Eretria and Karystos (490 BC) and of Athens (480 BC) showed the mainland Greeks also that complete and easily defensible city circuits were more important than an acropolis. Yet walls of modest height and thickness might still resist escalade, provided the curtains were enfiladed where necessary by flanking towers, and natural defensive features were used wherever possible. The Themistoklean walls of Athens were hastily built (479–478 BC) to provide a barrier 'of defensible height'. For Peiraeus, however, Themistokles planned a much more substantial rampart, but construction reached only half the intended height.

The Long Walls built by the Athenians from Megara to its port at Nisaia (461–460 BC), and the Athenian Long Walls (*c.* 457–456 BC and 440 BC), which converted Athens and Peiraeus to a single great fortress, were among the first examples of the so-called 'great circuits' that were to become common in large cities for some 150 years. Other examples included those at Thasos (*c.* 475–440 BC) and 5th-century BC Mantinea (the latter again mud-brick on a stone socle). The circuit of Eleusis was extended by Pericles, and many circuits mentioned by Thucydides during the Peloponnesian War were built earlier, such as those at Plataia (II.lxxv–lxxvi) and Amphipolis (V.ii–iii, vi–viii, x–xi). In these new systems two-storey towers became more common, especially in the exposed sectors. Some already had a hollow ground storey, for both storage and shelter for defending troops; occasionally (e.g. Megara, perhaps Athens) clay for mud-bricks was dug just outside the wall-line, the trench remaining as an additional defensive barrier.

Siege engines (rams and protective sheds) appeared in Greek warfare only in the Athenian siege of Samos (440 BC), but they were not very successful; and throughout the Peloponnesian War sieges usually ended in blockade (e.g. at Plataia, Mytilene, Melos and Syracuse). Moreover, defenders had begun to adopt a more active policy, making sallies in force against enemy works; the Athenians, for instance, built both border and coastal forts (Oinoe, Panakton, Sounion) and forts in enemy territory (e.g. at Pylos), as did the Spartans at Dekeleia in Attica.

Older Greek cities contributed little to the revolution in siegecraft during this period. 'Great circuits' continued to be built (Corinth–Lechaion system, early 4th century BC; Megalopolis and MESSENE after 371 BC). Even the Dionysian circuit of Syracuse and the Mausollan walls of Halikarnassos followed similar lines. Yet in Sicily the Carthaginian assaults on Selinus and Himera in 409 BC, and on Akragas in 406 BC, heralded a revolution in both fortifications and defensive siegecraft. Already at Akragas and Himera the defenders were making determined sallies against the Carthaginian siegeworks; in new systems greater provision for such sallies was made by greatly increasing the number of posterns, both in city circuits (Mantinea, 360s BC) and in border forts (Attic Eleutherai, second half of the 4th century BC). Towers with ground-storey chambers also became more common in the 4th century BC and later (see fig. 1), sometimes with posterns in the side wall of the chamber, as at Mantinea; and the approach of enemy engines might be further hindered by a moat or ditch (Mantinea; Athens, after 338 BC). The Persians added a ditch to the defences of Halikarnassos, against Alexander's attack; and 'great circuits' of the late 4th century BC clung more determinedly to high ground (Stratos, Kalydon).

The most influential development, however, for both attack and defence, was the development of early non-torsion catapults at Syracuse (398–397 BC) and of torsion weapons, a generation later, probably by the engineers of Philip II, King of Macedonia. When mounted in the attackers' huge, specially constructed siege-towers (*helepoleis*), originally developed by the Carthaginians and Dionysios I (*reg* 405–367 BC), advanced torsion artillery allowed the attackers to demolish protective screen walls and even damage towers with stone-throwers (*lithoboloi*, *petroboloi*) and to cripple effective defence by volleys of bolts from arrow-shooters (*oxybeleis*); rams and siege-sheds could then be brought against the rampart. Before long, however, artillery was being used defensively as well as offensively, with smaller arrow-shooters mounted on the curtains and various sizes of arrow-shooters and stone-throwers in the towers. While the engines of Philip II and Alexander

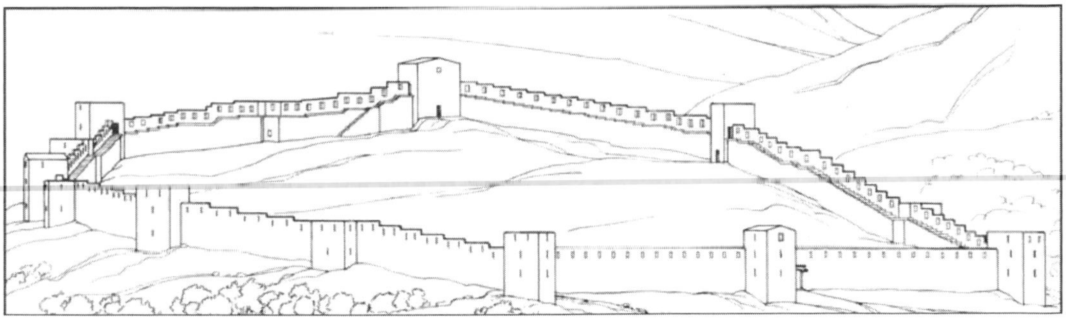

1. Ancient Greek fortification at Kydna, view from the east, late 4th century BC; reconstruction

the Great swept everything before them, Demetrios I Poliorketes (*reg* 306–283 BC) failed in 305–304 BC to capture Rhodes, despite his awe-inspiring siege-train.

Although separated by fewer than 75 years, the walls of Messene and Herakleia under Latmos belong to different worlds. The curtains at Herakleia are significantly higher; the Messenian crenellations are replaced by a high screen wall with shuttered windows; and the towers have two roofed chambers above the curtains (instead of a single chamber with an open platform above), thicker walls and some apertures clearly designed as artillery-ports. Even more intricate, though fragmentary, are the walls built at Rhodes after Demetrios' attack. One extremely thick curtain is built entirely of squared blocks, as recommended by Hellenistic theorists. Preserved elsewhere are: the ground-chamber of a huge artillery tower, standing forward from the curtain on a short spur wall; and another curtain, apparently with ground-level artillery emplacements, protected by an outwork (*proteichisma*) and perhaps also by a ditch. Similarly projecting towers are found at Hellenistic Samos. Moreover, Philo of Byzantium (*c.* late 3rd century BC) mentioned the elaborate design (presumably for installing artillery) of the curtains at Rhodes, Archimedes made similar provision at Syracuse (212 BC), and 'galleries' survive in curtains at Perge and Side (*c.* 200 BC).

Artillery, still virtually unknown in the mid 4th century BC, developed dramatically *c.* 335–*c.* 270 BC, with additional later Hellenistic and Roman improvements. The primary aim of Hellenistic defensive strategy was to destroy or disable enemy artillery and rams at a distance from the walls, either by defensive fire from walls and outworks or by trapping them in ditches. Hellenistic artillery towers sometimes exceeded 20 m in height (Perge, Sillyon and Isaura), with outworks and forward artillery emplacements of increasing complexity (North Gate, Selinus; Euryalus Fort, Syracuse, *c.* 270 BC and 214–212 BC). On level ground each curtain might be covered by a nearby tower and postern (southern crosswall, Miletos, after 100 BC) and perhaps strengthened by outworks and ditches. Intricate defences such as these largely nullified earlier progress in siegecraft, so that sieges were again likely to end in blockade. Significantly, Philip V, King of Macedonia (*reg* 221–179 BC), despite his many successes in siegecraft elsewhere, did not even attempt direct assault on Pergamon.

Nevertheless, by the end of the 3rd century BC and the beginning of the 2nd, Hellenistic theories of fortification and siegecraft had taken root far beyond the Hellenistic heartland of the eastern Mediterranean. The walls of Ai-Khanum (Afghanistan) and Vani in Colchis (Georgia), although in each case built in local style and technique, are completely Hellenistic in overall design. The gate of Vani was defended by a battery of artillery; a magazine incorporated in the thickness of the curtain yielded many stone balls of the type familiar from Pergamon, Rhodes and Goritsa in Thessaly. Hannibal's assault on Saguntum in Spain (219 BC), like those of the Romans at Syracuse (*c.* 214–212 BC), and later in Greece itself, followed a classic Hellenistic pattern (Livy: XXI.vii–viii, xi–xii). Even the Land Walls of Constantinople, laid out in the first half of the 5th century AD, are still textbook illustrations of Hellenistic theory and practice, complete with main rampart and towers, lower outer wall and large ditch.

See also ARCHITECTURE, §§II–IV, and CYPRUS, §II.

R. L. Scranton: *Greek Walls* (Cambridge, MA, 1941)

F. G. Maier: *Griechische Mauerbauinschriften*, 2 vols (Heidelberg, 1959–61)

E. W. Marsden: *Greek Artillery*, 2 vols (Oxford, 1969–71)

F. E. Winter: *Greek Fortifications* (Toronto and London, 1971)

A. Wokalek: *Griechische Stadtbefestigungen* (Bonn, 1973)

Y. Garlan: *Recherches de poliorcétique grecque* (Athens, 1974)

A. W. Lawrence: *Greek Aims in Fortification* (Oxford, 1979)

Actes du colloque international: La Fortification dans l'histoire du monde grecque: Valbonne, 1982

J.-P. Adam: *L'Architecture militaire grecque* (Paris, 1982)

J. Ober: 'Early Artillery Towers: Messenia, Boiotia, Attica, Megarid', *Amer. J. Archaeol.*, xci (1987), pp. 570–604

P. Leriche, ed.: 'Les Fortifications grecques de Mycènes à Alexandre', *Doss. Archéol.*, clxxii (June 1992)

J. Ober: 'Towards a Typology of Greek Artillery Towers: The First and Second Generation, *c.* 375–275 BC', *Fortifications Antiquae*, ed. S. van de Maele and J. M. Fossey, McGill U. Monographs Class. Archaeol. & Hist., xii (Amsterdam, 1992), pp. 147–69

P. Leriche, ed.: 'A la découverte des forteresses grecques', *Doss. Archéol.*, clxxix (Feb 1993)

A. W. McNicoll: *Hellenistic Fortifications from the Aegean to the Euphrates* (Oxford, 1997), with revisions and an additional chapter by N. P. Milner

A. E. Winter: 'The Use of Artillery in Fourth-Century and Hellenistic Towers', *Classical Views*, xvi (1997), pp. 247–92

I. Pimouguet-Pédarros and E. Geny: *Archéologie de la défense: Histoire des fortifications antiques de Carie (époques classique et hellénistique)* (Paris, 2000)

R. Sconfienza: *Fortificazioni tardo classiche e ellenistiche in Magna Grecia: I casi esemplari nell'Italia del Sud* (Oxford, 2005)

N. Fields and B. Delf: *Ancient Greek Fortifications 500–300 BC* (Oxford, 2006)

2. ROMAN. The art of fortification among the Romans began with the need to defend temporary camps set up by armies on the march, and it developed in response to changing circumstances. Alterations in shapes and plans were purely tactical and invariably the result of greater defensive needs, but the change of building material from timber and turf to stone also reflected the Romans' policy of establishing permanence. In the later Empire more naturally defensive sites were used, and walls, towers and gates were modified to accommodate developments in strategic planning and artillery.

(i) Before AD 235. (ii) The late Empire.

(i) Before AD 235. The archetypal Roman marching camp or Castra was developed to a standard plan that facilitated both the tactical deployment of troops and the maintenance of discipline (*see* CASTRUM). These marching camps were not designed to withstand a serious attack, since the Romans preferred to fight in the open, and it has been suggested that their importance was as much psychological as functional. Only later did the Romans show more concern over the siting of forts, utilizing naturally defensive positions as the Greeks had done.

The type of camp described by Polybius (*c.* 200–after 180 BC) in the mid-2nd century BC (*Histories* VI.xxvii–xlii), which could hold two legions and auxiliary forces, was to endure for centuries, as is made clear by descriptions some 300 years later in *De munitionibus castrorum*, a technical treatise attributed to Hyginus. From at least the 1st century BC temporary camps and, later, permanent establishments assumed a standard rectangular shape with rounded corners, the so-called 'playing-card' plan. There were four gateways, one in each side, with the main one facing the potential enemy; inside there were two main roads at right angles to each other, forming a junction near the centre of the fort. The two side gates were known as the *porta principalis sinistra* and the *porta principalis dextra*. The main road, the *via praetoria*, ran from the main gate (*porta praetoria*) to the headquarters complex (*principia*) and parade-ground in the centre of the fort, behind the *via principalis*, which ran across the fort from one side gate to the other. Access to the rear gate (*porta decumana*) was from the perimeter track (*via sagularis*) between the buildings and the defences. In larger camps, such as those described by Polybius and Hyginus, a second crossroad (*via quintana*) ran between the *via principalis* and the *porta praetoria*, dividing the camp into three equal parts. However, the *via principalis* normally divided the camp into two unequal parts, the *retentura* being two-thirds of the space behind the road and the *praetentura* the third in front. In the *praetentura* were the houses of the tribunes (senior officers); the *retentura* was occupied by barracks, various ancillary buildings, horse-lines and, in or near the *principia*, the PRAETORIUM (commander's quarters). Barrack accommodation in the early camps was provided in leather tents; timber buildings appeared later in semi-permanent camps.

The fortifications consisted of a ditch (*fossa*) and an earth rampart (*agger*). The ditch would be V-shaped, usually of the type known as *fastigata*, with a slot at the bottom designed as an ankle-breaker; the rampart would be reinforced with a turf facing, the top flattened and fronted by a wooden palisade. In front of the four entrances to the camp, oblique breaks in the ditch and rampart were intended to prevent a rush of the entrance and to expose the unshielded flank of an attacker. Marching camps, often occupied for a single night, could be built in a few hours, as at LAMBAESIS in North Africa, where a camp was built as a spectacle for Hadrian in AD 128. Slightly more permanent camps were built for sieges, with much more elaborate fortifications: at Numantia in Spain (133 BC) and Masada in Judaea (AD 70) the siege-camps had stone fortifications and wall-footings, although scarcity of timber was also a factor. The siege-works of 52 BC at Alesia (now Alise-Sainte-Reine, France), described by Julius Caesar (*Gallic War* VII.lxix–lxxiv), included a double line of ramparts, multiple ditches and towers. As the Roman world expanded, troops were regularly quartered in semi-permanent camps, which were essentially the old marching camps with firmer fortifications.

After the Empire was consolidated and the frontiers rationalized by Augustus at the end of the 1st century BC, more permanent forts were built, although there were no longer any serious rivals in the art of siegecraft. Legionary camps were placed at strategic sites, usually to form part of a frontier line, but they were still regarded as bases from which to engage the enemy rather than as strongholds. A typical legionary fortress, designed to hold some 6000 men, would measure *c.* 500×400 m and contain several ancillary buildings as well as barracks, usually all built of timber. These included the *principia*, *praetorium*, officers' quarters, hospital, storehouses, stables, a small training amphitheatre, baths, armoury and often a prison. Fortifications of the legionary camp varied according to the degree of local hostility anticipated, but they could be substantial, with up to three ditches, the outermost being of a type known as Punic, with a vertical outer slope to trap an enemy attracted by the shallow inner slope. Other devices included thorn hedges or concealed metal spikes (*lilia*). A flat berm separated the ditches from the ramparts, usually not more than 50 m wide, to keep the ditches within firing range. Ramparts were often up to 2.5 m high with a palisade on top; their earthen fill made them impregnable against battering-rams. They were frequently built on a corduroy of logs, laid at a right angle to the wall-line and reinforced on the inside by timbers placed at strategic points such as towers, gates and corners, especially if they carried artillery. Some, however, consisted of a wooden framework (box rampart) filled with earth, though these too were sometimes faced with clay or turf to protect them against fire. Square towers flanked the gateways, with interval towers on the walls, flush with the outer façade.

From the mid 1st century AD the timber and turf forts along the Rhine frontier began to be replaced by stone-walled forts, and by the time of Trajan (early 2nd century AD) many new forts were built entirely of stone, a material that required less maintenance and symbolized permanence. The transition was slow, however; some gateways remained in timber, and early stone fortifications, *c.* 1 m thick, still fronted an earthen rampart, the top of which formed a walkway behind a stone parapet. Although the demise of the earthen rampart was some way off, in some sites on the Rhine–Danube frontier it was replaced with a series of stone piers against and buttressing the walls and supporting a timber walkway above. This created more space within the fort and allowed the ground floors of gateway towers to be used as guard-chambers. The internal buildings were still generally of timber, although sometimes on stone foundations. The use of stone also depended on time and local availability: the legionary camp of *c.* AD 84 at Inchtuthil (Tayside, Scotland) had plain stone walls with a ditch and rampart. There is evidence that the site was only partially built and then dismantled, which has led to suggestions that a standard plan, if not prefabrication, may have been involved. A classic example of the characteristic 'playing-card' plan built in stone was the base of the 16th Legion at Novaesium (now Neuss) on the lower Rhine in Germany. An embellishment here is the monumental projecting gateway, also seen at the fortress in York, England, which reflects civilian rather than military types of gate and was perhaps the precursor of the eventual full external projection of all towers.

In the eastern provinces Roman military encampments sometimes took over earlier strongpoints, but troops were usually billeted in the larger cities and cantonments within the cities gradually evolved into specific military areas, as at DURA EUROPOS in east Syria. Evidence from north Syria, however, indicates that in the 1st century AD the Romans were also building the standard western type of fort. By the time of the Empire most urban settlements were walled. Not necessarily substantial, the walls were more a matter of civic pride and often incorporated monumental gateways.

The mid-1st-century AD push into Germany between the rivers Rhine and Danube resulted in the construction of a line of watch- or signal-towers and forts, for example at Kesselstadt. Trajan's use of auxiliaries on the frontiers, keeping his legions farther back, led to the building of smaller forts, often square but with rounded corners and an internal rampart, as at Benningen on the Rhine frontier. Hadrian abandoned the expansionist policy of his predecessor and consolidated the frontiers with spectacular linear arrangements based on small unit garrisons at the frontiers and larger fortresses in the rear, as in the Fossatum Africae in North Africa, a long ditch with forts behind it, and HADRIAN'S WALL in Britain. The latter ran for 118 km, was 2.5 m thick and 4.5 m high to the rampart walkway, with the parapet and merlons adding nearly 2 m more, and there was a series of ditches on both sides. Every 0.5 km there was a stone turret recessed into the line of the wall, and every 1.5 km a gate and small, fortified mile-castle (*c.* 21×17 m); larger forts were also built, most of which were behind the wall. They were still of the 'playing-card' shape, with towers at the four gateways and corners and an earth rampart inside the stone walls. The later, more northerly, Antonine Wall was almost entirely of turf and timber; it was not conceived as a replacement for Hadrian's Wall and was eventually abandoned.

In the unsettled conditions of the later 2nd century AD, fortress design was often severely tested. Timber was increasingly replaced by stone, walls became thicker and their foundations heavier as earthen ramparts were less widely employed. Projecting gateway towers and interval towers became more common, although the tactical value of towers projecting from rounded corners was limited. The number of ditches was also increased, except in the east where ditches were rare. Smaller outposts were increasingly used in frontier areas, such as the fort at Tisavar in North Africa, which measured only 40×30 m. It had one gateway but no other towers, and the corners were rounded. An important space-saving innovation here was the construction of the barracks around and against the walls, the roofs of which also served as a parapet.

With the accession of the Severan dynasty in AD 193 there was an unprecedented amount of fortification building, with sites more often utilizing natural defences. Interval towers projected, but rarely more than 2 m; and as square gate-towers revealed a blind spot they were quickly modified to a 'cutaway' form (see fig. 2) and later rounded. Both types were built at Gheria el-Garbia (Libya), and rounded gate-towers were built at, for example, VERULAMIUM (now St Albans) in England in the late 2nd century AD. There were few new forts in the East, but some smaller ones developed from earlier watch-towers; these were square with projecting corner towers,

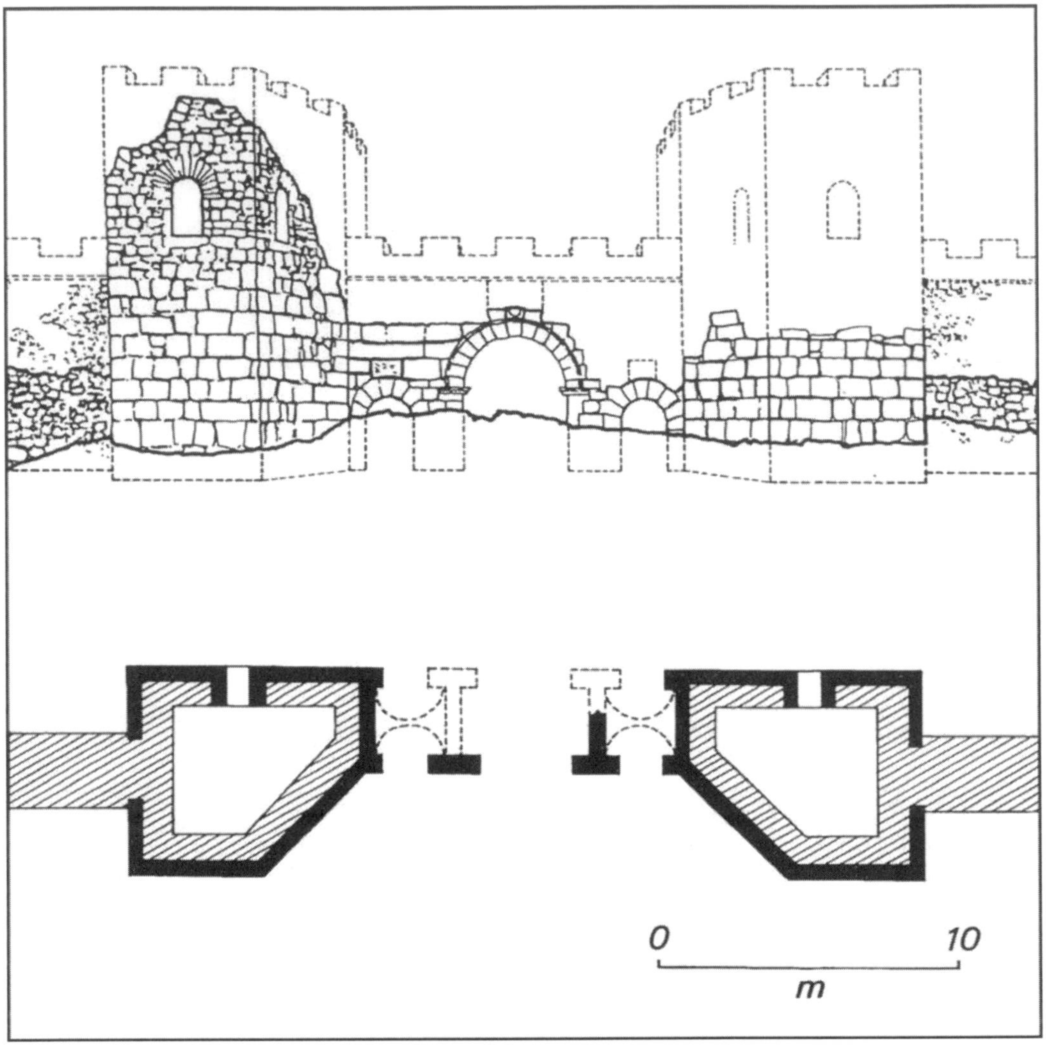

2. Roman fortification at Gheria el-Garbia, Libya, showing cutaway gate-towers, AD 198

forerunners of the Byzantine *tetrapyrgia*, as at Qas al-Hallabat (Jordan).

(ii) The late Empire. The uncertainties following the end of the Severan dynasty in AD 235 ushered in the period of late Roman fortifications, with a policy of defence in depth. With the legions pulled back from the frontiers, the old-style forts were required to stall the enemy until help arrived from the rear. Under Aurelian (*reg* AD 270–75), Rome itself was provided with a new wall that was 18 km long. It was built largely of concrete and brick, although it incorporated many existing buildings; it had 30 interval towers, nearly all rectangular or square, and rounded gateway towers, all projecting more than 3 m. Other new forts began to use rounded interval towers, either horseshoe-shaped or nearly circular, and with nearly circular corner towers.

The 3rd-century AD Saxon Shore forts on the south-east coast of Britain, built for defence against raiders from north-west Europe, developed from a plan based on the 'playing-card' pattern, such as that at Regulbium (now Reculver, Kent), to a later version with square or semicircular externally projecting towers (e.g. Portchester, Hants); most had thick masonry walls. Regional variations predominated in the late 3rd century and early 4th; the 'playing-card' shape, for example, was still preserved in new forts along Hadrian's Wall. Rounded corners and internally projecting towers gradually disappeared elsewhere, however, and existing fortifications of this type were often modified with splayed, fan-shaped towers added to the rounded corners, as at Visegrád (Hungary; early 4th century), and interval towers were now provided with external projections. Rounded towers became standard in the late 3rd century, often projecting up to 6.5 m. Owing to the unsettled conditions, old city walls were strengthened and new ones built, out of necessity rather than pride, and often with reused materials, but incorporating the latest military developments, such as projecting rounded towers (e.g. Augustomagus Sulbanectium, now Senlis, France; late 3rd century).

In the East, small square forts with massive square corner towers and barracks set against the walls, as at Han Aneybe (Syria; late 4th century AD), continued to predominate; but in larger forts an innovation seems to have been the U-shaped tower, often projecting more than 9 m. A good example of this type is the legionary fortress at Lejjun (Jordan; late 3rd century or early 4th), the small size of which (242×190 m) reflected the reduced size of the Roman legion; its square corners have large fan-shaped projecting towers and its interval towers are U-shaped. Examples of U-shaped towers also existed in the West, mostly in Lower Moesia (e.g. Iatrus on the Danube, 293–319), where the shape of the fortress accommodates the naturally defensive topography. Circular towers straddling the walls occurred in the middle Rhine region in the early 4th century, and polygonal towers also appeared, mostly in Britain, as at Eboracum (now York); although they also occur at Diocletian's palace at Spalatum (now Split), Dalmatia, Croatia, they may have been built as much for artistic purposes as military.

Although tower shapes were to some extent regional and were originally conceived as surveillance points, an increasing concern over defensibility strengthened their nature and usage. For the newer and heavier artillery the large U-shaped towers were ideal, combined with a widened outer berm and a single, wide, flat-bottomed ditch. Enemy siege capabilities were still slight, except in the East, where a number of Roman forts were successfully reduced by the Sasanians.

Roman fortification design remained basically uniform, although the increasing divergence from the marching-camp plan was a reflection of differing problems on different frontiers, resulting from a centralized strategic concern. The works of Valentinian I (*reg* AD 364–75) were the last manifestations of Roman fortifications in the West. He reintroduced the aggressive attitude of pre-emptive strikes into enemy territory, establishing surveillance posts and strongholds on high ground, and reoccupying abandoned forts. Walls were heightened, splayed fan-shaped towers were added to corners and gates were walled up. In the East some new watch-towers were built, although the continuation of a central government and a more coherent enemy necessitated a greater manpower more thinly deployed than in the previous century.

I. A. Richmond: 'Trajan's Army on Trajan's Column', *Pap. Brit. Sch. Rome*, xii (1935), pp. 1–40

H. von Petrikovits: *Die Innenbauten römischer Legionslager während der Principätszeit* (Opladen, 1975)

G. Webster: *The Roman Imperial Army* (London, 1975/*R* 1979)

E. N. Luttwak: *The Grand Strategy of the Roman Empire* (Baltimore, 1976)

A. Johnson: *Roman Forts of the 1st and 2nd centuries AD in Britain and the German Provinces* (London, 1983)

S. Johnson: *Late Roman Fortifications* (London, 1983)

J. Lander: *Roman Stone Fortifications: Variation and Change from the First Century AD to the Fourth*, Brit. Archaeol. Rep., Int. Ser., 206 (Oxford, 1984)

D. P. Davison: *The Barracks of the Roman Army from the 1st to 3rd centuries AD: A Comparative Study of the Barracks from Fortresses, Forts, and Fortlets with an Analysis of Building Types and Construction, Stabling, and Garrisons* (Oxford, 1989)

R. Brulet and others: *Forts romains de la route Bavay-Tongres: Le dispositif militaire du bas-empire: Guide publié à l'occasion du 16th International Congress of Roman Frontier Studies* (Louvain-la-Neuve, 1995)

S. Gregory: *Roman Military Architecture on the Eastern Frontier: from AD 200–600,* 3 vols (Amsterdam, 1997)

M. Konrad: 'Research on the Roman and Early Byzantine Frontier in North Syria', *J. Roman Archaeol.*, xii (1999), pp. 392–410

R. J. Brewer and G. C. Boon: *Roman Fortresses and their Legions* (London, 2000)

E. A. M. Shirley: *Building a Roman Legionary Fortress* (Stroud, 2001)

D. L. Kennedy: *The Roman Army in Jordan* (London, 2004)

I. Pagani: *Ponti fortificati del suburbio romano* (Rome, 2004)

D. B. Campbell: *Roman Legionary Fortresses, 27 BC–AD 378* (Oxford, 2006)

Milos. *See* MELOS.

al-Mina. Site at the mouth of the Orontes in northern Syria. The town functioned as a port and appears to have been both one of the earliest and the most important of the trading posts established by the Greeks in the eastern Mediterranean in the 8th century BC. Excavated by Sir Leonard Woolley in 1936–7, al-Mina yielded the earliest Greek material to have been found in the Near East. Other sites, such as Tyre, were found later to have even earlier pottery, but al-Mina retains its pre eminence in the region in terms of the quantity of Greek material recovered.

Woolley identified ten levels at the site, calling the earliest X and the latest I. Some areas had been washed away by the river, but at least part of the earliest levels remains. Levels X to VIII date from *c.* mid-9th century BC to *c.* 700 BC. The buildings were made of mud-brick on stone foundations; it appears that Level VIII reused walls from Levels X and IX and that the site was restored in Level VII. There seems to have been a native settlement at the site initially, with Green material appearing some time into the 8th century BC. Other wares at the site include Cypriot, Phoenician and North Palestinian, and the population was probably mixed. Most of the Greek material in this phase was pottery, the earliest being pendent semicircle skyphoi—cups bearing semicircles drawn with a compass—which are most likely to have originated in Euboia. Among other late 8th-century Greek Geometric pottery from this first phase at al-Mina are further types of skyphoi and straight-sided cups from Euboia, kotylai from Corinth and a few fragments of East Greek, probably Rhodian, wares. If there were Greeks in al-Mina at this time, they must have been a small body of traders.

The site was briefly abandoned *c.* 700 BC, but a new town, with the same building style as the first phase, was later set up on the ruins of the old. This phase comprised Woolley's Levels VI and V and lasted until *c.* 600 BC. In this phase Greek pottery at the site increased in quantity and appears to have been the dominant element. The evidence indicates a shift from a major Euboian element in the earlier phases to predominantly East Greek and Corinthian wares, the latter perhaps not brought directly by Corinthian traders. The East Greeks were clearly very active traders during this phase.

There is less evidence after *c.* 600 BC for continued settlement of the site, and not until the last quarter of the 6th century BC did trade with Greece pick up again. The rise of Babylonian power seems to have been responsible for the change in fortunes at al-Mina, which did not fully recover until the Persians dominated the area from 539 BC. In the second half of the 6th century BC al-Mina was thus rebuilt again (Level IV) and later in the century was trading once more, apparently as a totally Greek venture, probably still run by East Greeks. The plan and layout of Level IV was very different from what had preceded it, with large warehouses built to store the trade goods.

Al-Mina continued to flourish as a trading centre until the very end of the 4th century BC. There were further changes to its plan and the layout of its buildings as a result of destruction by fire, until the building of the city of Seleucia in 301 BC, just to the north, led to al-Mina's permanent decline.

C. L. Woolley: 'Excavations at Al Mina, Sueidia', *J. Hell. Stud.*, lviii (1938), pp. 1–30, 133–70

J. Boardman: *The Greeks Overseas* (London, 1973, rev. 1980)

J. Luke: *Ports of Trade, Al Mina, and Geometric Greek Pottery in the Levant* (Oxford, 2003)

Minoan. Civilization that flourished during the Greek Bronze Age (*c.* 3500/3000–*c.* 1050 BC) on the Aegean island of CRETE. The term was coined by ARTHUR EVANS and derived from Minos, legendary king of Knossos. The rediscovery of the Cretan Bronze Age civilization was pioneered by Evans's excavations of the great Minoan palace at KNOSSOS beginning in the year 1900. Although chance finds had been made before, these excavations were the first that systematically recovered remains from the Minoan past. Others soon followed, revealing three further palaces at PHAISTOS, MALLIA and KATO ZAKROS, as well as towns, country houses and sanctuaries throughout the island (see fig. 1). The chronological system devised by Evans remains in use, with modifications (*see* §4 below). There was much cross-fertilization between the Minoan civilization and the Bronze Age cultures of mainland Greece (*see* HELLADIC) and the CYCLADIC islands. By the middle of the 17th century BC the influence of Minoan Crete on these two cultures was especially strong. One vital factor that led to Crete's dominant position in the Aegean was the foundation, in the Middle Minoan (MM) IB period, of the Minoan palaces and the subsequent development of a palace-based administration, the system for which the Minoans are, in fact, best known. Each palace controlled its immediate area, perhaps independently at first, though eventually under the overall control of Knossos. At about the time of the foundation of the palaces writing first appeared in Crete: the unknown Minoan language was first written in the Hieroglyphic script, which was replaced by Linear A. Linear B, an early form of Greek, began to be used when it is thought that Knossos fell under Mycenaean control (*c.* 1425–*c.* 1360 BC).

See also ARCHITECTURE, §I; COLLECTION AND DISPLAY OF ART, §§II, 1 and III, 1; FAIENCE, §1; IVORY AND BONE, §1; JEWELLERY, §1; METALWORK, §I; PAINTING, §I; POTTERY, I; SCULPTURE, §I; SEALS, §1; STONE VASES, §1.

A. J. Evans: *The Palace of Minos at Knossos*, 4 vols and index (London, 1921–36, 2/1964)

J. D. S. Pendlebury: *The Archaeology of Crete* (London, 1939/*R* New York, 1963)

H. J. Kantor: *The Aegean and the Orient in the Second Millennium* BC (Bloomington, IN, 1947)

C. Zervos: *L'Art de la Crète néolithique et minoenne* (Paris, 1956)

S. Marinatos and M. Hirmer: *Crete and Mycenae* (London, 1960)

R. W. Hutchinson: *Prehistoric Crete* (Harmondsworth, 1962)

W. S. Smith: *Interconnections in the Ancient Near East* (New Haven, 1965)

R. A. Higgins: *Minoan and Mycenaean Art* (London, 1967)

S. Alexiou: *Minoan Civilization* (Herakleion, 1969)

K. Branigan: *The Foundations of Palatial Crete* (London, 1969)

R. F. Willetts: *Everyday Life in Ancient Crete* (London, 1969)

S. Hood: *The Minoans* (London, 1971)

C. Renfrew: *The Emergence of Civilization* (London, 1972)

C. Davaras: *Guide to Cretan Antiquities* (Park Ridge, NJ, 1976)

S. Hood: *The Arts in Prehistoric Greece*, Pelican Hist. A. (Harmondsworth, 1978)

P. Darcque and J.-C. Poursat, eds: *L'Iconographie minoenne: Actes de la Table Ronde d'Athènes 21–22 avril 1983, Bull. Corr. Hell.*, suppl. xi (1985)

G. Walberg: *Tradition and Innovation: Essays in Minoan Art* (Mainz, 1986)

J. W. Myers, E. E. Myers and G. Cadogan, eds: *The Aerial Atlas of Ancient Crete* (Berkeley, Los Angeles and Oxford, 1992)

R. Castleden: *Minoans: Life in Bronze Age Crete* (London and New York, 1993)

R. A. Higgins: *Minoan and Mycenaean Art* (London and New York, 1997)

J. L. Fitton: *Minoans* (London, 2002)

Y. Hamilakis: *Labyrinth Revisited: Rethinking 'Minoan' Archaeology* (Oxford, 2002)

1. GEOGRAPHY AND CLIMATE. The prosperity of the Minoan civilization and its importance in the eastern Mediterranean resulted, at least in part, from the position and natural resources of Crete itself. Some 250 km long and varying in width from *c.* 13 to *c.* 60 km, Crete is the largest and most southerly of the Aegean islands. It is situated almost midway between

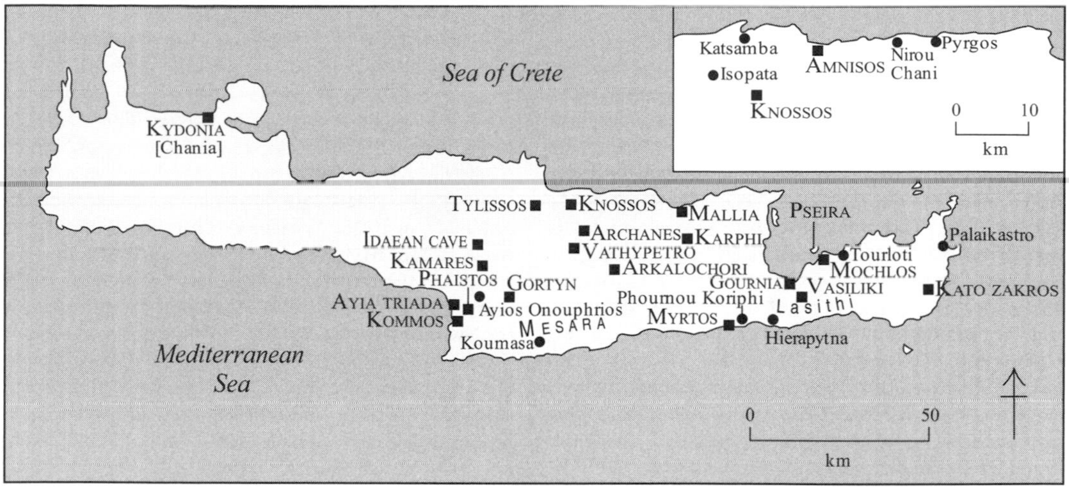

1. Map of Minoan sites in Crete; those with separate entries in this encyclopedia are distinguished by CROSS-REFERENCE TYPE

mainland Greece, Asia Minor and Africa. Further east are Egypt, Cyprus and Syria, and beyond these were the older civilizations of Mesopotamia.

While overseas contacts were always important, Crete was itself both large enough and sufficiently rich in natural resources to develop an independent and unique culture. The island has hot, dry summers with substantial rainfall in winter. Its mountainous spine shelters fertile coastal plains and inland plateaux, and the Minoan farmers grew grain, grapes and olives as well as rearing sheep, goats, pigs and some cattle. Sheep, which thrive in the mountainous terrain, were important not only for food but also for wool, and records on a series of clay tablets inscribed in the Linear B syllabary show that in Late Minoan times the palace at Knossos was an important centre of textile production. Building materials were also readily available: Crete is essentially composed of limestone, which formed the basis of most Minoan structures, while sporadic outcrops of gypsum provided the smooth slabs for covering walls and floors (*see* ARCHITECTURE, §I). Other, rarer stones were used for special architectural purposes, such as schist for paving and breccia or marble for decorative column bases, while vases were produced from various native stones, notably serpentine, though some were made from imported materials. Timber was more plentiful in antiquity than it is today, and timber-frame construction was common in Minoan buildings, a factor that increased their elasticity and made them more resistant to earthquakes. The characteristic downward taper of Minoan columns may be derived from the shape of inverted tree trunks.

2. TRADE. Long before the beginning of Minoan civilization, the inhabitants of Crete had to import certain raw materials. Initially the most important was obsidian, imported before 5000 BC from the Cyclades, especially the island of Melos. With the introduction of metalworking, Cretan dependence on raw materials from abroad increased. Reserves of copper were very limited, and Crete had virtually no supplies of gold or silver. Lead isotope analyses have revealed that soon after 3000 BC Crete began to acquire silver and lead from the Cyclades and Attica. Substantial quantities of Attic copper were also imported, and smaller quantities came perhaps from Turkey. The acquisition of these raw materials was inevitably accompanied by a smaller-scale trade in manufactured products, such as pottery and figurines. The transport of these various commodities was facilitated by the construction of larger ships, itself made possible by the new carpenters' tools manufactured from imported metals. Exactly what the people of Crete were able to offer in exchange for these imports is still not known. The few Cretan jewellery pieces, seals or metal weapons found outside Crete must have been exported with other, probably perishable goods such as foodstuffs, timber and cloth. Equally uncertain are the nature and extent of Cretan contacts with the eastern Mediterranean before *c.* 2000 BC, but the use of hippopotamus ivory for Cretan seals, the occasional use of tin bronze (tin alloyed with copper) and the importation of a few Egyptian stone vases suggest at least minor trading links with that region.

In the Middle Minoan period, around the time of the construction of the first Minoan palaces (for Minoan chronology *see* §4 below), trading contacts with the eastern Mediterranean apparently increased. Egyptian scarabs (amulets), ivory, Syrian daggers and cylinder seals were all imported in small quantities, along with greater numbers of Egyptian stone vases. The widespread adoption of tin bronze required a regular supply of tin, and the inhabitants of Crete and the Aegean in general probably obtained this via the Levant from somewhere further east. Middle Minoan painted Kamares pottery (*see* POTTERY, §I,

3(ii)) and a few elegant Minoan bronze daggers have been found in Cyprus, Syria and Egypt, and there may have been other perishable exports such as perfumes, oils and textiles. During this period, increasing amounts of Kamares ware occur both at Cycladic sites and on the Greek mainland (*see* POTTERY, §§II, 2 and III, 3). The Cretans still depended on Cycladic and Attic supplies of silver and lead, and most of the copper used in Cretan bronze production apparently still came from Attica. Trade with both the Aegean and the Near East was thus becoming increasingly important, though there is still little evidence that the authorities in the newly built palaces exercised any direct control over it.

In the 17th century BC, however, this situation may have changed. Minoan pottery and stone vases were exported in far greater quantities, and local imitations appear in large numbers. The abrupt rise in the quantity of exported goods was accompanied by the introduction to the Cyclades of Minoan writing and weighing systems, along with internal architectural features of Minoan derivation and Minoan religious artefacts and wall paintings (*see* ARCHITECTURE, §II, and PAINTING, §II). This does not necessarily imply Minoan political or commercial control over the rest of the Aegean but possibly indicates that groups of Minoans settled on several Cycladic islands (e.g. at Ayia Irini on KEA) and were active in local commerce. The role of the Minoan palace authorities in this is unclear, though they seem to have been increasingly involved in Minoan trade with the eastern Mediterranean. A few imported Egyptian artefacts of this period bear the cartouches of Egyptian pharaohs, suggesting that diplomatic exchanges of gifts between rulers took place, a common practice in the Near East. In Egypt itself, early 18th Dynasty (*c.* 1540–*c.* 1292 BC) paintings depict people called 'Keftiu' bringing tribute, or gifts, to the pharaoh. The Keftiu are almost certainly Cretans, and some of the goods they carry seem to be Minoan products.

The importance of Minoan trading connections was not simply commercial. During the 3rd millennium BC, it was the acquisition of raw metals from other parts of the Aegean that enabled the Cretans to develop many specialist crafts and technologies. At the same time, trading contacts opened up Crete to the important cultural and artistic influence of the Cyclades. In Middle Minoan times the direction of influence was perhaps reversed, and by the 17th century BC Minoan craftsmen may have been as much in demand as their products. Cretan domination of Aegean trade prompted the widespread adoption of Minoan weights and measures, writing and accounting, so creating a commercial lingua franca for the region. At the same time, increasing Minoan contacts with the great civilizations of the Near East, particularly Egypt, probably had an impact on social and political conditions on Crete itself.

R. Hagg and N. Marinatos, eds: *The Minoan Thalassocracy: Myth and Reality. Proceedings of the Third International Symposium at the Swedish Institute, Athens 1982*

N. Gale and Z. Stos-Gale: 'Bronze Age Copper Sources in the Mediterranean: A New Approach', *Science*, ccxvi (1982), pp. 11–19

3. RELIGION AND ICONOGRAPHY. The study of Minoan religion and iconography (the two are intrinsically linked) was begun by Sir Arthur Evans, excavator of the palace of Knossos, in a seminal article published in 1901. Working from an iconography derived mostly from sealstones, he concluded that the prehistoric Cretan cult was one of 'primitive' aniconic worship. His analysis was succeeded by the work of the Swedish scholar Martin Nilsson, whose *Minoan–Mycenaean Religion and its Survival in Greek Religion* (1927), while suffering from the bias evident in its title—the assumption that earlier religious beliefs can be extrapolated from later ones—still remains a basic textbook on prehistoric Aegean cult. Axel Persson's *Religion of Greece in Prehistoric Times* (1942), another essential study, possesses the same flaw. Studies produced since the mid-20th century, aided by material brought to light by 50 years of additional excavation, have tended to concentrate more on archaeological evidence and less on unsubstantiated interpretation, as Minoan religion has come to be seen as a coherent, autonomous system of belief and practice rather than merely as a precursor to Classical Greek cult.

Minoan iconography and religion are so closely related that it is impossible to discuss one without reference to the other. Certain general themes recur throughout the range of depictions on wall paintings, seals, stone-carvings and in the decoration of such materials as faience, ivory and hardstones: the idea of death and regeneration and the use of nature imagery to express this concept; scenes of a fertility goddess and a warrior-hunter god, who appear in both wild landscapes and in association with architecture, either alone, with attributes or with worshippers; and various types of hunting, procession, dancing, rites-of-passage, offering and pure landscape scenes.

Minoan cult practices and rituals were carried out in the palaces and in houses (*see* ARCHITECTURE, §I, 3), at peak sanctuaries and in caves. Obvious scenes of cult activity are depicted on seals and rings, stone vases, wall paintings and decorative objects. Cult equipment (known from actual archaeological remains as well as depictions) included libation tables and altars with incurved sides (as were painted on either side of the throne at Knossos), offering tables, sacrificial tables and libation vessels (rhyta), sometimes in the shape of animal heads. Priests, priestesses or deities might hold a double axe, which was not a weapon or instrument of sacrifice but a cult symbol, the meaning of which is unclear; it marked a sacred place or might be set up between horns of consecration, symbolic bulls' horns that are one of the more ubiquitous symbols in Minoan religion. Priests might hold a stone mace (apparently associated with sacrificial rites); other cult equipment included kernoi and tubular snake stands. Male and female votive figurines, most often with one hand to the head in devotional salute, are also common; many have been found in peak sanctuaries, where they were offered to the deity (*see* §4(ii) below). In the Post-Palatial period, terracotta sculpture was part of the cult equipment found in shrines (see below).

Whether the Minoans worshipped a single female fertility goddess under different aspects or several deities is still debated. The female goddess is most frequently depicted as the Mistress of Animals, accompanied by animals arranged heraldically—lions, griffins, birds, fish, even monkeys. Lions and griffins are her most common familiars, the griffin a composite monster whose iconography originated in the Near East, combining the features of lion and eagle, appropriate for a guardian animal (*see* PAINTING, §I, 2(v)). Griffins appear with male gods as well, but they only flank goddesses.

Where surroundings are depicted, the goddess is almost always shown in a natural, outdoor setting, often on a mountaintop. A bird-goddess occurs occasionally, perhaps the result of a merging of the goddess and her attribute in the way Egyptian deities were normally portrayed. Other variants of the Mistress of the Animals involve the goddess accompanied by dolphins, as on seals from Palaikastro and Knossos (Herakleion, Archaeol. Mus.), perhaps indicating her marine connections as the birds and quadrupeds signify her air and earth associations (*see also* PAINTING, §II, 2). The two faience statuettes of the goddess found in the Temple Repositories at Knossos (MM III; Herakleion, Archaeol. Mus.; see colour pl. 1:IX, fig. 1) depict her, as do virtually all other images, dressed in a long flounced skirt and open bodice curved around her breasts, this time with snakes wound round her arms and torso or held in her hands. Arthur Evans and Martin Nilsson after him associated the snake with a domestic house cult, serving as guardian of the palace; its association with death and rejuvenation and with cyclical fertility must also be noted, however. (For discussion of wall paintings on the theme of the Minoan nature cult and goddess *see* PAINTING, §I, 2(ii).)

The goddess is also shown attended by human figures, most frequently female. It has been argued that these adorant priestesses included in their duties of pouring libations, taking part in processions, dancing, bringing offerings of flowers or jewellery or taking part in sacrifices the function of impersonating the goddess in actual epiphany rites. The priestess who probably sat on the throne at Knossos would have been flanked by wall paintings of griffins, lilies and palm trees (a sacred tree) with, at her feet, depictions of Minoan altars with incurved sides. Priestesses and other females are often depicted wearing the so-called 'sacral knot', a bowlike arrangement of the hair at the back (*see* §4(iii) below and PAINTING, fig. 2).

Despite the predominance of women in Minoan iconography, Bronze Age Cretans also worshipped a male god, a Master of the Animals or a hunter, usually shown with lions, sometimes with bulls. He is dressed in a typical Minoan loincloth or codpiece with belt. As the goddess figure is almost always shown in her role as a nature goddess, protectress of wild things and natural places and symbol of natural cycles, so the male god may have been associated with urban centres (although he also appears in natural landscapes): a seal impression from Chania, the so-called Master Impression (Herakleion, Archaeol. Mus.), depicts the god (some would say king) standing protectively atop the architecture of a town. Male priests are distinguished by long Syrian-type robes or, in some ceremonial scenes such as a harvest procession (as on the Harvester Vase from Ayia Triada, LM I), by a type of cuirass, and by their particular hairstyle, sometimes a beard, and accoutrements: stone mace or curved axe, occasionally with a bow or pair of lances. Their role appears to have been the carrying out of sacrifices and their association with hunting and the harvest.

In addition to (and in combination with) scenes of deities, apparently secular scenes were also created, most frequently in wall paintings, though some scholars have asserted that these should also be seen as having at least an ideological purpose. Examples include painted relief scenes of bull-leaping (the bull was a potent symbol of power and virility, and its horns were associated with cult; *see* PAINTING, §I, 2(iv)); swimming dolphins, as reconstructed on the walls of the so-called Queen's Megaron at Knossos; monkeys in a flowery landscape (e.g. the *Saffron Gatherer* fresco from Knossos, showing blue monkeys in a garden gathering crocuses (Herakleion, Archaeol. Mus.; *see* §4(ii) below); dolphins and monkeys also appear in association with the goddess); and scenes of procession and court ritual (some of these in miniature paintings; *see* PAINTING, §I, 2(vi) and (iii)). Landscapes and scenes of nature were also extremely popular, the sacred lily and crocus being the most common flowers (*see* PAINTING, §I, 2(i)). Landscape scenes have been seen by some scholars as religious in nature by virtue of their suggestion of fertility and natural cycles of death and rebirth; on the other hand, the sensitive and pleasure-loving Minoans must also have appreciated them for their beauty alone.

Symbols of warfare and military prowess include the boars'-tusk helmet and the figure-of-eight shield, depicted, for example, on the walls of the Grand Staircase at Knossos (for discussion of martial arts themes in wall paintings *see* PAINTING, §I, 2(vii)). Scenes of ritual combat (e.g. the Boxer Rhyton from Ayia Triada (Herakleion, Archaeol. Mus.) and the scene of the *Boxing Boys* at Akrotiri (Thera, Archaeol. Mus.)) and puberty initiation rites (e.g. the apparently unconnected but thematically related scenes of young women and a bloody shrine on the walls of the adyton in Xeste 3 at Akrotiri) must also be ritual in nature (*see* PAINTING, §II, 1(i); for discussion of adyta *see* ARCHITECTURE, I, 3).

In the Post-Palatial period on Crete, town shrines became the place where ritual was carried out after the destruction and abandonment of the palaces. Using the example of Gournia, these were accessible from the street and usually had one room with a bench against the far wall; there might also be a niche and/or an additional platform. At Gournia were found tubular terracotta stands decorated with horns of consecration and snakes, small clay figures of birds and a clay female figurine perhaps representing the goddess. In the LM III Shrine of the Double Axes at Knossos a number of items were found *in situ* on the bench: a female votive figurine with arms folded on her chest, horns of consecration, a small steatite double axe and other female votive figurines, some with birds and one with raised arms, which may have represented the goddess. Paintings on Post-Palatial larnakes (clay coffins) frequently incorporated plant and animal motifs derived from earlier ritual art and sometimes show actual scenes of sacrifice (*see also* §4(iii) below).

See also CYCLADIC, §3; PAINTING, §II; and SCULPTURE, §I.

A. J. Evans: 'The Mycenaean Tree and Pillar Cult', *J. Hell. Stud.*, xxi (1901), pp. 99–204

M. P. Nilsson: *The Minoan–Mycenaean Religion and its Survival in Greek Religion* (Lund, 1927, rev. 1950)

A. W. Persson: *The Religion of Greece in Prehistoric Times* (Berkeley, 1942)

C. R. Long: *The Ayia Triada Sarcophagus: A Study of Late Minoan and Mycenaean Funerary Practices and Beliefs*, Stud. Medit. Archaeol., xli (Göteborg, 1974)

P. Warren: *The Aegean Civilizations: From Ancient Crete to Mycenae* (Oxford, 1975, 2/1989)

Sanctuaries and Cults in the Aegean Bronze Age. Proceedings of the First International Symposium at the Swedish Institute at Athens: Athens, 1980

Minoan Society. Proceedings of the Cambridge Colloquium: Cambridge, 1981

R. Hagg: 'Epiphany in Minoan Ritual', *Bull. Inst. Class. Stud. U. London*, xxx (1983), pp. 184–5

N. Marinatos: *Art and Religion in Thera* (Athens, 1984)

The Function of the Minoan Palaces. Proceedings of the Fourth International Symposium at the Swedish Institute at Athens: Athens, 1984

G. Gesell: *Town, Palace, and House Cult in Minoan Crete*, Stud. Medit. Archaeol., lxvii (Göteborg, 1985)

C. Renfrew: *The Archaeology of Cult: The Sanctuary at Philakopi* (London, 1985)

N. Marinatos: *Minoan Sacrificial Ritual: Cult Practice and Symbolism* (Stockholm, 1986)

B. Rutkowski: *The Cult Places in the Aegean* (New Haven and London, 1986)

Early Greek Cult Practice. Proceedings of the Fifth International Symposium at the Swedish Institute at Athens: Athens, 1986

Thanatos: Les Coutûmes funéraires en Egée à l'âge du bronze. Actes du colloque de Liège: Liège, 1986

L. Morgan: *The Miniature Wall Paintings from Thera: A Study in Aegean Culture and Iconography* (Cambridge, 1988)

Celebrations of Death and Divinity in the Bronze Age. Proceedings of the Sixth International Symposium at the Swedish Institute at Athens: Athens, 1988

P. Warren: *Minoan Religion or Ritual Action* (Göteborg, 1989)

A. A. D. Peatfield: 'Minoan Peak Sanctuaries: History and Society', *Opuscula Athen.*, xviii (1990), pp. 117–31

N. Marinatos: *Minoan Religion: Ritual, Image and Symbol* (Columbia, SC, 1993)

O. Dickinson: *The Aegean Bronze Age*, Cambridge World Archaeology (Cambridge, 1994)

E. Kyriakidis: *Ritual in the Bronze Age Aegean: The Minoan Peak Sanctuaries* (London, 2005)

4. CHRONOLOGICAL OVERVIEW. Following ARTHUR EVANS, most archaeologists divide the Minoan Bronze Age into three periods: Early, Middle and Late Minoan (EM, MM, LM). These are themselves subdivided on the basis of changing pottery styles and are broadly parallel to those adopted for the contemporary cultures of mainland Greece (*see* HELLADIC, §4) and the Cyclades (*see* CYCLADIC, §4). Although the chronological periods (see fig. 2a) are separated into discrete units, there was some overlap from one phase to the next: the inhabitants of one site might retain older pottery types for many years while another site changed to new styles. This 'regionalism' was particularly common during the Neolithic and EM periods and at the end of LM.

Late Neolithic		*c*. 4500–*c*. 3800 BC
Final Neolithic		*c*. 3800–*c*. 3500/3000 BC
Early Minoan (EM)		*c*. 3500/3000–*c*. 2050 BC
	EM I	*c*. 3500/3000–*c*. 2900/2600 BC
	EM II	*c*. 2900/2600–*c*. 2200 BC
	EM III	*c*. 2200–*c*. 2050 BC
Middle Minoan (MM)		*c*. 2050–*c*. 1600 BC
	MM IA	*c*. 2050–*c*. 1900 BC
	MM IB	*c*. 1900–*c*. 1800 BC
	MM II	*c*. 1800–*c*. 1675 BC
	MM IIIA	*c*. 1675–*c*. 1635 BC
	MM IIIB	*c*. 1635–*c*. 1600 BC
Late Minoan (LM)		*c*. 1600–*c*. 1050 BC
(a)	**LM IA**	*c*. 1600–*c*. 1480 BC
	LM IB	*c*. 1480–*c*. 1425 BC
	LM II	*c*. 1425–*c*. 1390 BC
	LM IIIA:1	*c*. 1390–*c*. 1360 BC
	LM IIIA:2	*c*. 1360–*c*. 1335 BC
	LM IIIB	*c*. 1335–*c*. 1190 BC
	LM IIIC	*c*. 1190–*c*. 1050 BC
(b)	**LM IA**	*c*. 1700–*c*. 1610 BC
	LM IB	*c*. 1610–*c*. 1475 BC
	LM II	*c*. 1475–*c*. 1440 BC
	LM IIIA:1	*c*. 1440–*c*. 1375 BC
	LM IIIA:2	*c*. 1375–*c*. 1325 BC
	LM IIIB	*c*. 1325–*c*. 1180 BC
	LM IIIC	*c*. 1180–*c*. 1050 BC
Sub-Minoan		*c*. 1050–*c*. 1000 BC

2. Chronological chart showing the major Minoan periods with their subdivisions: (a) traditional chronology; (b) alternative chronology of the Late Minoan period

Approximate absolute dates for these chronological periods are derived from radiocarbon analysis and from links with Egypt and the Near East, where relatively secure dates are based on historical dynastic sequences. Nevertheless, the field of Aegean Bronze Age chronology has been the subject of considerable scholarly controversy since the 1980s. Many archaeologists believe that dates should be higher by a century. This argument is based largely on new radiocarbon dates suggesting that the eruption of the volcanic island of THERA took place *c.* 1625 BC instead of *c.* 1525 BC, making the beginning of the Late Bronze Age approximately 100 years earlier, with concomitant effects on succeeding periods (see fig. 2b). However, not all archaeologists are convinced of the efficacy of the new scientific dating methods for the periods in question, not least because the higher chronology tends to weaken proven links with ancient Egypt. The dating system in figure 2a is the traditional chronology, although individual scholars may vary the details.

Another chronological system, preferred particularly among Italian and Greek archaeologists, is one based on developments in architecture rather than pottery: Pre-Palatial period (EM–MM IA); Proto-Palatial period (MM IB–MM III); Neo-Palatial period (MM III/LM IA–LM IB); Post-Palatial period (LM II–LM IIIC). Other systems, usually devised for a single site or period, have not been widely accepted. Even the Palatial system has lost support, because it does not permit divisions small enough to deal with brief phases. The tripartite pottery system is thus generally the most successful framework for Minoan history and art.

P. M. Warren and V. Hankey: *Aegean Bronze Age Chronology* (Bristol, 1989)

D. A. Hardy and A. C. Renfrew, eds: *Chronology*, iii of *Thera and the Aegean World III* (London, 1990)

P. M. Warren: 'The Minoan Civilisation of Crete and the Volcano of Thera', *J. Anc. Chron. Forum*, iv (1990–91), pp. 29–39 [n. 22 with previous bibliog.]

S. Manning: *The Absolute Chronology of the Aegean Early Bronze Age* (Sheffield, 1995)

(i) Early Minoan. (ii) Middle Minoan. (iii) Late Minoan.

(i) Early Minoan. The Minoan culture originated in the Final Neolithic period, a transitional phase between the Stone Age and Early Minoan (EM). Many of its distinguishing features had already appeared by this time, and EM I was a continuation of their development more than an innovative new phase. By EM I, the inhabitants of Crete were already living in large houses of stone or mud-brick on stone foundations, burying their dead in circular tombs (*see* ARCHITECTURE, §I, 5) and other communal graves and making distinctive pottery that prefigured the styles generally associated with Early Minoan. Certain artistic features, such as the use of pattern-burnished pottery, suggest Anatolian cultural influences. Even so, EM buildings were uniquely Cretan, with few close parallels discovered elsewhere (*see* ARCHITECTURE, §I). Houses were of rubble, stone or mud-brick on stone foundations, their walls already reinforced with the half-timbering characteristic of Minoan architecture throughout the Bronze Age. Good examples of EM houses have been found in eastern Crete (e.g. VASILIKI and at Phournou Koriphi near MYRTOS). Those at Phournou Koriphi cluster on an easily defensible hill, the rooms packed tightly together. No defensive wall has been found, but the house walls themselves may have formed a protective circuit. Roofs were flat, providing additional living space. Some walls were plastered and painted red or brown, but floors were of beaten earth. The community probably consisted of only a few households but was largely self-sufficient, with its own storerooms, working areas and shrine.

EM tombs varied considerably in form, suggesting that the island received settlers from different areas. Burials were usually multiple, sometimes containing several hundred bodies. The simplest burials, common in eastern Crete, consisted of rock shelters. These were simple depressions or overhangs at the side of a cliff, sometimes improved by hollowing out the bluff or by adding a wall or two for extra protection. Built tombs in eastern Crete were usually rectangular and above ground, though they were often set against a cliff to make use of the natural rock on one or more sides. Usually called house tombs, good examples were found at MOCHLOS and at GOURNIA. House tombs may have been intended to imitate natural caves, since these were often used for burial, especially in northern and western Crete. In the south the tombs were circular. Known as THOLOS TOMBS, they constitute the most monumental of EM structures. The earliest examples were built in the Final Neolithic period (e.g. at Lebena), but the type persisted into the Late Bronze Age. They had stone walls and a single doorway, but no complete example survives. Their roofs may have been flat or may have taken the form of a corbelled dome. The tombs were probably used as cult centres, since they incorporated several secondary rooms in which offerings were placed, as also occurred in the main burial chamber. Additional objects were often placed around the tombs and in small courtyards near their entrances. The EM offerings include tools and weapons, especially bronze or copper daggers, animal figurines, stone vases and implements, seals, jewellery and many types of pottery. Some of the pottery was made in unusual shapes, such as birds or animals, suggesting special productions for ceremonies associated with the dead.

Besides architecture, little monumental art survives from the EM period; assessment of Minoan tastes and styles must derive primarily from small, portable objects, chiefly from tombs. These indicate a diversity of styles and approaches, yet are recognizably Minoan. Almost all surviving EM sculpture is miniature (*see* SCULPTURE, §I). The only exception is a stylized monolithic stone figure, 675 mm high, from Samba Pediados (Herakleion, Archaeol. Mus.), consisting of a smooth pillar with a featureless oval head—an anthropomorphic shape closely resembling contemporary Cycladic figurines (*see* SCULPTURE, §II, 1). Smaller marble images of Cycladic type have been found at several sites, especially Koumasa (now in Herakleion, Archaeol. Mus.). Carved from flat pieces of marble, with simplified features and a slim, schematized body, most depict nude female figures with arms folded. As in Cycladic figurines, the sexual attributes are not prominent.

Simple clay figurines were also made, most of them of animals, especially quadrupeds. Many are hollow so that they could serve as containers, and they provide some of the wittiest and most imaginative examples of EM art. Jugs were fashioned into birds by adding wings and eyes to vessels with beak-like spouts (*see* POTTERY, fig. 1b), and shapes imitated by other vases include bulls and gourds. Hollow female figures may well represent deities. A fine example from Phournou Koriphi near Myrtos (Ayios Nikolaos, Archaeol. Mus.) holds a jug, and one from Koumasa (Herakleion, Archaeol. Mus.) handles snakes. These may be divine attributes, though they may also reflect ritual practices. Other hollow female figurines (Herakleion, Archaeol. Mus.) have pierced breasts for pouring liquid.

Among the most plentiful EM artefacts are pottery vases, and their decoration, in red, white or dark paint, is crucial to establishing the evolution of EM artistic styles (*see* POTTERY, §I, 3). Stone vases were also produced at this time, some of them highly expressive (*see* STONE VASES, §1). Examples occur throughout Crete, the finest coming from the east of the island. Two chlorite schist pyxides (boxes with lids) from Mochlos and KATO ZAKROS (Herakleion, Archaeol. Mus.) have handles in the form of reclining dogs on their lids (see fig. 3). Many of the vases were made from naturally patterned stones such as banded marble or mottled serpentinite, which could both suggest and enhance the carved designs. The range of shapes of stone vases was almost as varied as that of pottery containers.

Engraved seals (*see* SEALS, §1) survive from EM II, though the tradition is assumed to have had its origins in EM I. These were used to stamp images into clay or wax (as in Egypt), rather than for rolling (as was the custom in Mesopotamia). They were often shaped like chess pawns, though cones, discs, cubes and even animal forms were occasionally engraved as seals. The materials from which they were carved also varied but tended to be fairly soft, suitable for working with stone or bronze tools. Ivory, bone, serpentinite and probably wood were the most common. Designs, which survive as impressions as well as on the seals themselves, include geometric, floral or animal motifs and household objects. All are highly stylized, though the quality of engraving varies from accomplished to crude.

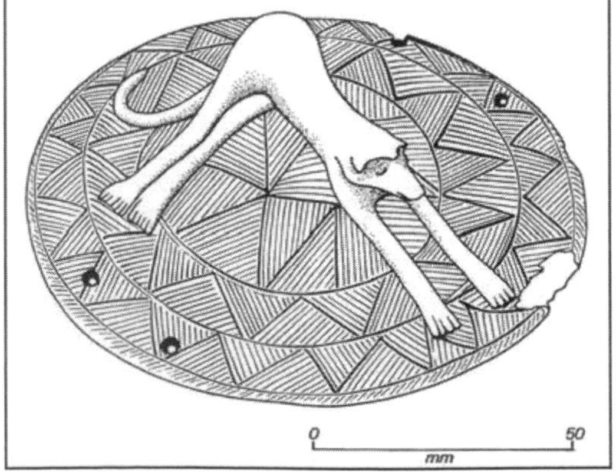

3. Early Minoan pyxis lid with handle in the shape of a reclining dog, chlorite schist, from Mochlos, EM II (Herakleion, Archaeological Museum)

Jewellery was often placed in tombs with the dead and was clearly popular, because many types survive. Beads were made of different materials, including faience and hardstones (amethyst, cornelian and rock crystal). Pendants were of stone and other materials. Bronze pins and rings may have been used in the hair. The most attractive jewellery was made of sheets of gold with embossed designs (*see* JEWELLERY, §1). The finest examples come from Mochlos (Ayios Nikolaos, Archaeol. Mus., and Herakleion, Archaeol. Mus.) and date from EM II. Some were cut into wide strips for use as diadems or for attaching to leather clothing or headdresses. Others were shaped into flowers, leaves, beads or other objects. Large diadems have dot-repoussé decorations depicting animals, geometric designs and, on one particularly striking band, a pair of human eyes (EM II; Herakleion, Archaeol. Mus.). Since the jewellery has parallels in north-west Anatolia, it may have been made by travelling craftsmen. If so, this would explain the rapid spread of new styles and techniques to distant areas. Alternatively, the jewellery may have been brought by immigrants or obtained through trade in either the objects themselves or the craftsmen who made them, or as gifts or spoils or dowry items. It is likely that several of these factors operated at the same time.

By the end of EM III, Crete enjoyed a unified artistic culture, easily distinguishable from those of its neighbours. Good communications enabled ideas to spread quickly, and foreign influences were soon incorporated into the local Minoan styles.

(ii) Middle Minoan. During the Middle Minoan (MM) period Crete achieved an ever widening sphere of both artistic and economic influence; by the end of the period it dominated the Aegean. Whether the Minoanizing settlements of the Cyclades and nearby areas were true colonies or independent towns that adopted Minoan culture as a sign of sophistication (the so-called 'Versailles effect') is a matter of controversy. But it is clear that Crete was the most advanced civilization of the Aegean; its impact was felt from Greece to Asia Minor, from Thrace to the Nile Valley.

Much of this influence seems to have derived from a new political and social organization on Crete, first evidenced by the building of the Old Palaces in MM IB. The scope of the building operations during MM I suggests a tradition of monumental architecture, though the builders eliminated almost all trace of earlier structures. Large MM palaces stood at KNOSSOS, PHAISTOS, MALLIA, KYDONIA and probably several other sites. They must have functioned as political, artistic, social, religious, commercial and economic centres. The palatial rulers seem to have organized production in the surrounding countryside, creating a period of prosperity, leisure and cultural sophistication during which the arts flourished.

MM architecture developed the EM skills and techniques, with stone, timber and mud-brick still the principal building materials. Roofs were always flat, and houses often had over a dozen rooms on different levels. Palaces were constructed around a central courtyard on a north–south axis; houses in outlying villages often had courts also. The main features of later Minoan domestic architecture were already well developed.

Tombs from the MM period also continued with established practices; in fact, many EM tombs were still in use. New developments affected details rather than basic forms. Among the few significant developments was the increasing use of burial jars and larnakes as receptacles for the dead. A larnax was a large, rectangular or oval chest or tub, usually with a lid. The earliest examples come from a burial cave at Pyrgos, in north-central Crete, and date from the EM period. Jars and larnakes were initially placed in tombs alongside more conventional burials, but by the end of MM times some cemeteries consisted of hundreds of jars buried in the soil (e.g. at Pacheia Ammos and Sphoungaras in eastern Crete). Offerings were placed in the jar or in its pit or in open areas within the cemetery. The sides of jars and larnakes provided ample scope for painted decoration, but this was not fully exploited until LM times.

The earliest Minoan wall paintings have not survived, but the tradition was fully developed by the end of the MM period (*see* PAINTING, §I). One of the earliest extant examples (Herakleion, Archaeol. Mus.) shows blue monkeys in a garden and includes the fragmentary figure often called the 'Saffron Gatherer', which was reconstructed as a boy, although it is now known to depict a monkey. The painting's white flowers on a red ground closely resemble those on contemporary painted vases. In the wall paintings the colours were applied to lime plaster, though opinion is divided on the question of whether or not the technique was true fresco (i.e. painted while the plaster was wet); mixing lime into the paint may have achieved a similar effect.

Painted pottery also flourished, especially after the introduction of the potter's wheel in MM IB (*see* POTTERY, §I, 4). Its high point is represented by the style called KAMARES ware (*see* POTTERY, fig. 1f), which used floral and geometric patterns in white, red and orange on a dark ground. This was plentiful during MM IB–II, especially at the palaces of Knossos, Mallia and Phaistos and in their vicinities. Complex schemes of interlocking curves were used to create an effect known as torsion, which draws the eye around a vase by giving an impression of balanced motion.

Sculpture continued to be made primarily in miniature, and terracotta figurines were produced in large numbers (*see* SCULPTURE, §I). They seem most often to have been used as offerings, and some 'peak sanctuaries' have yielded hundreds of examples. These sanctuaries were religious focal points placed on high hills (*see* ARCHITECTURE, fig. 1). They were the recipients of some of the most interesting art objects of the time, especially figurines. Many are of simplified human figures, the males usually dressed in the typical abbreviated costume of codpiece and belt or loincloth, with a dagger at the waist; they often clasp the chest or forehead in gestures of worship or devotion. Female figures wear long, wide skirts with short-sleeved jackets, the low bodices of which often leave the breasts exposed. Coiffures or hats are occasionally large and ornamental. Animals, especially quadrupeds, continued to be popular.

Faience figurines were also produced. This material, which probably entered Crete from Egypt originally, was made by fusing a mixture of fine sand with fluxes and copper salts in a kiln. The best selection of faience objects comes from the Temple Repositories at Knossos and dates from MM III. Besides two well-known female figures probably representing priestesses or snake-goddesses (*see* FAIENCE, colour pl. 1:IX, fig. 1), faience pieces from the Temple Repositories include cups and vases, a miniature female costume and flat plaques depicting animals. Also from Knossos are small representations of Minoan houses (*see* ARCHITECTURE, §I, 4) once set into a gaming-board or some other perishable object (all Herakleion, Archaeol. Mus.). Their naturalistic style seems likely to have been a Knossian innovation, which spread to other centres gradually, over a period of many years.

New techniques, especially the introduction of the mechanical cutting wheel used with abrasives, enabled seals to be cut from harder stones (*see* SEALS, §1). Quartzes, such as agate, chalcedony, jasper, cornelian, amethyst and crystal, were not only more durable than the substances used in EM times but also permitted crisper and more finely detailed engraving. Seals were made in several shapes, but three-sided prisms and discs with flat or rounded faces were the most common. Designs included geometric motifs, inanimate objects, human or animal figures and hieroglyphic signs. A series of seals depicting ships, some under full sail, began to be produced in MM I; the best-known large group of motifs occurs on clay sealings for jugs and other containers from Phaistos and dates from MM II (Herakleion, Archaeol. Mus.). The commonest scheme has geometric designs in a circular format, often with three or more elements radiating out from the centre. Hieroglyphic signs were first used in MM I or slightly earlier. They seem to represent an early form of the Minoan writing system that would develop by the close of the MM period into the fully formed syllabary called Linear A.

Jewellery and metalwork were also produced with greater technological sophistication during MM times (*see* JEWELLERY, §1 and METALWORK, §I). A good example is a gold pendant from a tomb at Mallia (Herakleion, Archaeol. Mus.) depicting two heraldic bees or wasps with outspread wings. The insects' bodies were cast in one piece, but some details were added in granulation, a difficult technique by which tiny gold balls were fused on to a backing without the use of solder. Several types of bronze objects, including the earliest European swords, also provide evidence of greater skill in production. Metalware vases were probably more common than the small number of surviving examples suggests. One of the finest is a silver kantharos from Gournia (Herakleion, Archaeol. Mus.), with a fluted rim and a carinated body (see fig. 4). A hoard of gold and silver vases from el-Tod in Egypt (Paris, Louvre) may include Minoan imports, since several bowls are decorated with typically Minoan spirals, and a fragment of a clay cast or mould for a similar spiral-decorated bowl has been found at Mallia. Such vessels were probably produced in copper and bronze as well.

Objects were made from many other materials. Those that survive include stone vessels, which continued to be highly regarded (*see* STONE VASES, §1). Ivory, bone and other hard substances were fashioned into useful and attractive objects, from spindle whorls and weights to pendants and pins (*see* IVORY AND BONE, §1). Casts from excavations at Mallia provide evidence for complex and attractive basketwork, with weaves rivalling the intricate patterns of Kamares ware. Textiles, rugs, leatherwork, carved wood, furniture, plasterwork and many other perishable objects must also have been produced in this rich and multi-skilled culture.

(iii) Late Minoan. The first stage of the Late Minoan (LM) period is defined by the spread of a new pottery style using glossy dark-brown to black paint on pale clay (*see* POTTERY, fig. 3). At about the same time Minoan art became more naturalistic, and new building programmes were begun at many centres. Knossos was rebuilt after its destruction by earthquake during or around the end of MM III. The town around the palace had become a prosperous metropolis, and like many smaller sites, it expanded during early LM I. Crete was a densely inhabited island, its population distributed among isolated farmhouses, comfortable villas with clusters of dependent buildings, small villages, large towns and palaces. Palaces of this period have been excavated at Kato Zakros, Mallia, Phaistos and Knossos. Other monumental LM I complexes, probably also palaces, have been found at ARCHANES, KOMMOS, Kydonia (Chania) and elsewhere, but have not yet been fully excavated. Knossos continued to be the largest and most influential centre.

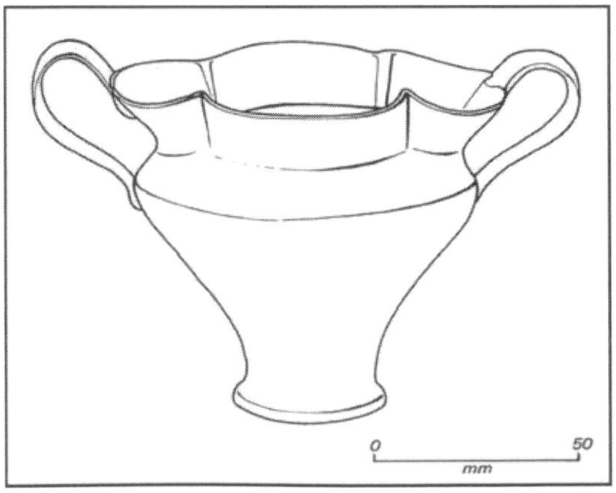

4. Middle Minoan silver kantharos with fluted rim, from Gournia, MM IB–II (Herakleion, Archaeological Museum)

By LM I, the Knossian palace was almost fully developed. Set around a north–south courtyard, it housed both the palace bureaucracy and the ruling dynasty. It provided workshops for artists and craftsmen, basement storage areas, kitchens, archives, religious shrines and private areas, including royal apartments and dining-rooms. This extensive complex exhibited a uniquely Minoan plan, at once informal and highly complex, with labyrinthine corridors linking its various elements. Minoan architecture is also characterized by other typical features: much of Cretan life must have taken place out of doors, and buildings were opened up with porticos, windows and courts. Most houses had at least one court, though some are so small that they are designated as light wells. Lustral basins, sunken rectangular chambers lined with stone, may have been used for sacred libations or (less likely) simply as baths. Pier-and-door partition walls, consisting of several doors separated by narrow jambs, allowed rooms to be completely opened up or partly or wholly closed. Columns were thicker at the top than at the bottom, like inverted tree trunks, and had spreading capitals with convex profiles. By LM I masons had become so skilled that they routinely used large square blocks, even in the walls of outlying buildings.

Controversy still surrounds the history of Knossos in the later part of the LM period. The palace was remodelled in LM II, following damage or partial destruction—perhaps by invaders from the mainland—at the end of LM IB, and it continued to be important into LM IIIA:1. It was destroyed by fire at the beginning of LM IIIA:2, and some scholars believe this marked the end of the palace-based administration. Others contend that a series of clay tablets inscribed in the Linear B syllabary date from after this destruction. Since the tablets represent the records of a palatial economy, this would imply that Knossos continued as a major centre into LM IIIA:2 or LM IIIB. Events in Crete as a whole are easier to assess. Most sites were destroyed, no doubt in the same way as Knossos, at the end of LM IB. The next phase, LM II, was much less prosperous, but by LM IIIA:1 the economy had recovered. With many new influences from the Greek mainland, the island continued to prosper until the end of the Bronze Age.

During LM I, most burials continued in the Middle Minoan tradition. Tholos tombs remained in use at sites such as Kamilari in the south, and house tombs and rock shelters were still used in the east. Pithos cemeteries also became popular in some communities. A new type of tomb, the chamber tomb, first came into widespread use in LM II, perhaps as a result of Mycenaean influence. It consisted of a long passageway (dromos) leading to an underground chamber blocked by a doorway. Many of these tombs, notably the 'warrior graves' of Knossos and its vicinity, contained swords and other weapons as well as rich burial goods in many materials. By LM IIIA:2 the chamber tomb had become the most common form of Cretan burial.

Late Minoan buildings were more often decorated with wall paintings than they had been. One of the finest, from the House of the Frescoes at Knossos, depicts monkeys and birds surrounded by rocks, flowers and streams; another, from AYIA TRIADA, features cats and birds in a similar style (both in Herakleion, Archaeol. Mus.). Details are more stylized than in MM III: some of the floral motifs (for example the 'papyrus' designs, which borrow some details from lilies) have mixed characteristics of different species, and rocks have colourful textured designs as though sawn and polished. All elements are two-dimensional, and overlapping is avoided where possible, so the compositions lack depth. Curves, particularly sinuous ones, were preferred to straight lines, producing an impression of subtle, harmonious movement. During LM I, artists began exploring a larger range of subjects. From a fine house at AMNISOS come a series of wall paintings depicting lilies against rectilinear backgrounds (Herakleion, Archaeol. Mus.). Several paintings from Knossos show human figures, including an elaborate miniature of spectators at some important event (Herakleion, Archaeol. Mus.). Sites outside Crete provide even richer examples of Minoan painting, including a seascape with flying fish from Phylakopi on Melos (Athens, N. Archaeol. Mus.), beautiful lilies from Rhodes and elsewhere, and a series of figural scenes and landscapes from Akrotiri on Thera (Athens, N. Archaeol. Mus.).

In Crete itself, the finest painting was that done on plaster relief, the only extant monumental sculpture from LM I. Large scenes of bulls and acrobats (Herakleion, Archaeol. Mus.) adorned the west and north entrances of the palace of Knossos, and it is possible that reliefs were considered more appropriate than frescoes for important rooms. A room in the civic shrine at PSEIRA, destroyed in LM IB, provides a date for the introduction of painted reliefs. Its decoration includes figures of seated women in elaborate costumes, perhaps goddesses or participants in a ceremony. One of the best-known relief figures, the so-called *Priest-King* fresco or *Lily Prince* from Knossos, is an incorrect restoration combining the upper torso of a male figure (Herakleion, Archaeol. Mus.), possibly a boxer or god, with fragments from other reliefs.

LM miniature sculpture achieved a naturalism that would not be equalled for the next millennium. Among the finest examples are the stone vessels carved with reliefs of human figures or animals. A series from Ayia Triada includes a conical rhyton (a vessel with a tiny hole in the bottom for pouring liquid) decorated with scenes of boxing and bull-leaping (the Boxer Rhyton), a cup with two youths standing in solemn poses with sword and staff (the Chieftain Cup) and a globular rhyton (the Harvester Vase) showing rows of singing men in a procession, possibly accompanying the planting or harvesting of crops. A rhyton from Kato Zakros depicts a shrine in a rural landscape with goats. Small fragments of gold found on it suggest an attempt to copy repoussé, the technique by which thin metal sheets are pressed from behind to create raised designs (all the above vases LM I; Herakleion, Archaeol. Mus.). It is likely that both of the fine repoussé gold cups from a tomb at Vapheio on the Greek mainland (probably LM IB; Athens, N. Archaeol. Mus.) were made in Crete. They are ornamented with vigorous scenes of the capturing of wild bulls in a landscape of trees and shrubs.

Bronze-casting in the lost-wax process, already in use by MM times, became increasingly popular. Most are single figures, generally men or women in attitudes of adoration, or small herd animals suitable as offerings to deities. Some of the finest LM I metalwork was discovered outside Crete, because Cretan finds are often fragmentary, and the practice of placing costly objects in graves began to decrease at the start of the LM period. The shaft graves at MYCENAE produced especially rich examples of LM I metalwork: a silver bull's-head rhyton, vessels of silver, gold and bronze, and numerous swords and other weapons (Athens, N. Archaeol. Mus.). The most elaborate weapons had blades inlaid with hunting scenes, river landscapes, animals or plants. Although the emphasis on hunting and military skills seems foreign to Minoan Crete, the iconography, style and technique of the inlaid blades leave no doubt that they were made by Cretans.

Other forms of art during LM I made use of a wide variety of materials, many imported. Ostrich eggs were cut into attractive vessels with added fittings for mouth and neck. Ivory was carved into figures and other objects, and stone vessels include a fine bull's head from Knossos and a rhyton carved from a single quartz crystal from Kato Zakros (both Herakleion, Archaeol. Mus.). Gem-cutting became a major art, and miniature designs were executed in a variety of styles, ranging from abstract symbols to naturalistic masterpieces. The best renderings of animals and humans in action have a distinctive fluidity of movement. There are suggestions from scant remains in tombs of a tradition of fine carpentry and furniture-making, and paintings show that textiles and rich embroidery were also produced. LM I was almost certainly the highpoint of Minoan artistic skill and productivity. Minoan art later became more stylized, a tendency most evident on the painted pottery and cut gems, which survive in significant quantity, though it applies equally to other fields. Carefully observed depictions of the natural world declined, and human activity, symbolism and geometric designs became more important.

In wall paintings after the LM IB destructions, landscapes were often schematized or eliminated, and figures became larger in relation to the whole picture. Good examples of later landscapes come from a large building, the so-called Caravanserai, south of the palace at Knossos. This had a room decorated with a frieze of partridges and at least one hoopoe (LM II or slightly later; Herakleion, Archaeol. Mus.). The animals were shown in a stylized setting, with artificial-looking rocks. The Throne Room at Knossos, of about the same date, has a stone throne attended by formal heraldic paintings of wingless griffins against undulating coloured bands, with only a few plants to suggest a landscape or garden. A scene of a male and two female acrobats leaping over a bull, from the Court of the Stone Spout at Knossos, is slightly later (LM II or slightly later; Herakleion, Archaeol. Mus.; *see* PAINTING, fig. 1). The style of this painting is far removed from the painstaking naturalism of LM I: the setting is not indicated, and the anatomical features are more or less eliminated, so that were it not for the convention of painting men reddish-brown and women white, even the sexes of the performers would be uncertain. The figures appear to float in suspended animation: the bull's four hooves are raised in the 'flying gallop', and none of the acrobats' feet touches the ground-line. One acrobat grasps the animal's horns, while the second does a handstand on its back and the third is painted behind it with hands upraised.

Hierarchical considerations also caused figures to be shown on different scales. The *Camp Stool* fresco (Herakleion, Archaeol. Mus.), from an upper room in the north-west corner of the palace at Knossos, included two large female figures probably presiding over a religious ceremony. One, usually called *La Parisienne* (Herakleion, Archaeol. Mus.; *see* PAINTING, fig. 2), has a sacral knot at her back and thus may be a goddess or priestess. Her curvilinear contours and ringlets of dark hair modulate the severely two-dimensional style of the painting, in which an enlarged frontal eye is combined with a face in profile.

Floors as well as walls were decorated with paintings. Marine scenes adorned a floor at Ayia Triada, and a panel of dolphins and fish from Knossos (Herakleion, Archaeol. Mus.) may have occupied a similar position. The creatures, which are shown from the side and never overlap, were painted in scattered groups, resulting in compositions with no central focus. One of the finest paintings from LM IIIA occurs on a plastered stone larnax from Ayia Triada (Herakleion, Archaeol. Mus.). On the front is a procession of men bringing gifts to a male figure standing before a building or tomb, while two women and a man playing a lyre perform a ceremony involving the pouring of liquid between two pillars surmounted by double axes. A similar ritual scene was represented on the back. Here, a sacrificial bull lies trussed up on a table, while a woman acts out a ceremony before an altar. A procession of several figures arrives from the left, and to the right stands a shrine topped by horns of consecration and a palm tree. The end panels depict figures in chariots. Although many details in the paintings are ambiguous, they clearly involve religious ceremonies, and services associated with the dead would naturally be suitable for a sarcophagus. The style of the paintings, which are dominated by human figures and give little indication of setting, is related to that of the *Bull-leapers* discussed above and other paintings from LM IIIA.

By the end of LM IIIB, artistic styles had become freer and more abstract. Pottery was often decorated with repetitive standardized patterns, many of them simple, and careful work, such as a long series of detailed octopus designs on various vessels, was exceptional. The process of stylization and simplification continued, leading to rigorously schematic compositions. The last stage of the Minoan Bronze Age, LM IIIC, is represented predominantly by small portable objects, often produced for export. Even the finest designs, for example some highly schematic octopus paintings on stirrup jars and other pottery shapes, reveal an artistic culture in decline. Yet new ideas were still being tried. Painters had long used the large spaces offered by larnakes, whose funerary function invited religious symbolism. Several individual styles can be distinguished, including that of a group based somewhere in eastern Crete, which painted horse-drawn chariots, cattle and other animals in a simple, lively manner close to caricature. Among the best work of LM IIIA–B are a group of larnakes from Armenoi near Rethymnon (Rethymnon, Archaeol. Mus.). They depict simplified, vigorous scenes of hunters, armed with spears and axes and accompanied by dogs, pursuing wild cattle and wild goats (agrimi). They suggest that the Minoan artistic tradition survived until the end of the Bronze Age, ultimately influencing the art of Classical Greece (480–323 BC).

A. Evans: *The Palace of Minos at Knossos* (London, 1921–35)
L. Pernier: *Il palazzo minoico di Festòs* (Rome, 1935)
J. D. S. Pendlebury: *The Archaeology of Crete* (London, 1939)
L. Pernier and L. Banti: *Il palazzo minoico di Festòs II* (Rome, 1951)
R. W. Hutchinson: *Prehistoric Crete* (Baltimore, 1962)
K. Branigan: *The Foundations of Palatial Crete* (London, 1970)
K. Branigan: *The Tombs of Mesara* (London, 1970)
M. S. F. Hood: *The Minoans* (London, New York and Washington, DC, 1971)
N. Platon: *Zakros* (New York, 1971)
D. Levi: *Festòs e la civiltà minoica* (Rome, 1976)
M. S. F. Hood: *The Arts in Prehistoric Europe* (London and New York, 1978)
P. P. Betancourt: *The History of Minoan Pottery* (Princeton, 1985)

Mirror. Type of reflecting surface, usually of silvered glass, metal or highly polished stone. Hand mirrors have been found at Mycenaean sites of about 1400 BC but do not reappear in Greece until *c.* 700 BC, when they are also attested in visual and written records. Of the three distinct types of metal mirror—hand mirror, stand mirror and box mirror—the earliest and most common was the hand-held mirror with a single handle. When not in use it could lie flat or be hung by a hole in its handle. The disc, made of copper or bronze, is generally circular. The handle, which was cast in one piece with the disc or made of wood or bone into which a tanged disc could be inserted, is oblong, columnar or some specific cut-out shape. The reverse of later mirror-discs are elaborately engraved with mythological subjects, while the outer borders are ornamented with vegetal, figural or patterned motifs.

The stand mirror has a reflecting disc on a support, the end of which is enlarged so that the object can stand alone. In addition to various columnar and plant shapes forming the support, human figures in the round, known as caryatids, are used (see fig. 1a). The number of pieces joined to form the caryatid mirror varies from two units, the disc and the figure-base, to as many as fifteen. Female caryatids used as supports on mirrors may be either nude or semi-nude girls standing on an animal or simple round base or women garbed in chiton (tunics) or peplos (outer robes). Male caryatids (Atlantids), either nude or wrapped in a large cloak, are also employed as supports.

By the late 5th century BC the box mirror had been invented (1b). This is a small, round disc of polished bronze without a handle, protected by a rimmed cover

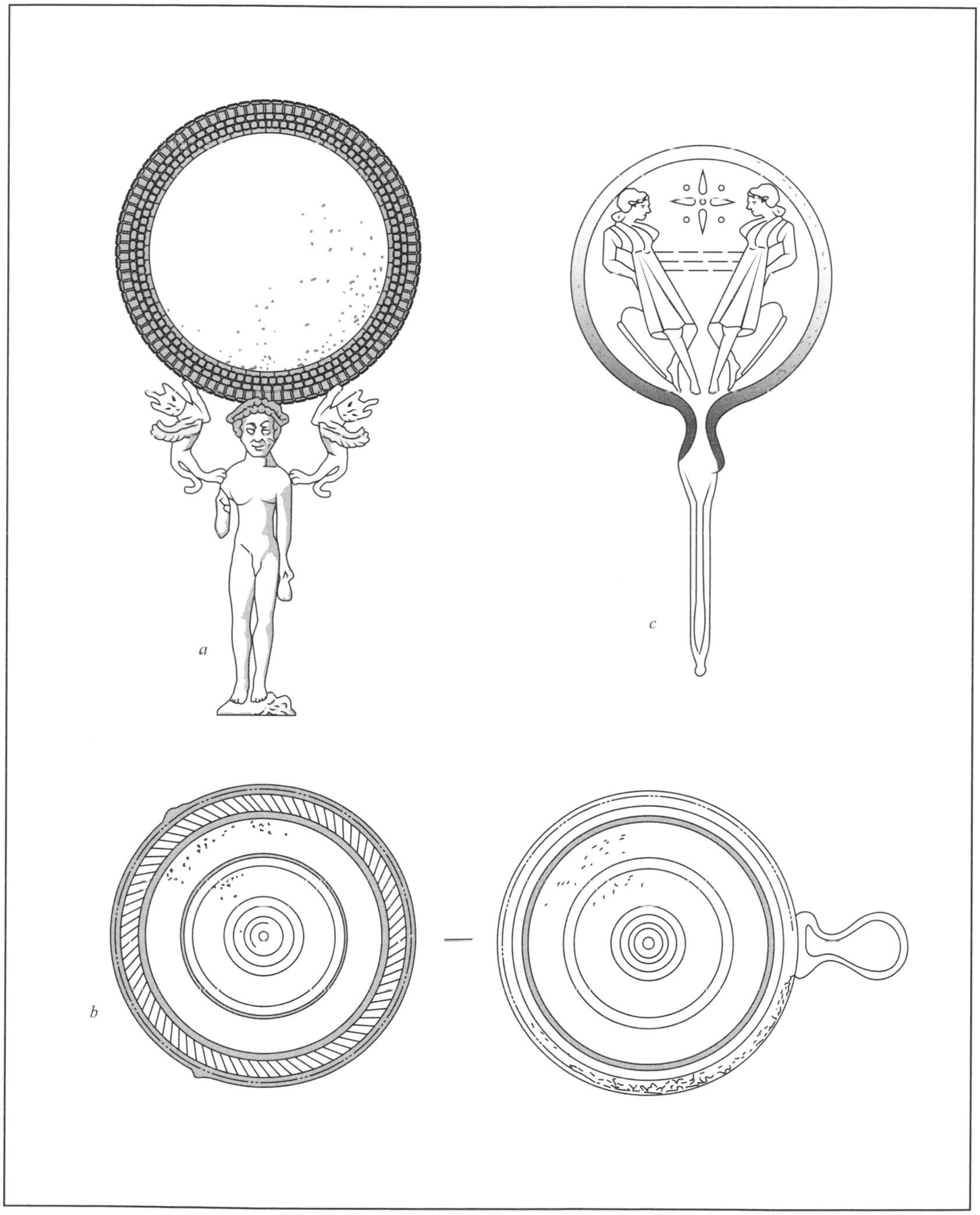

1. Mirrors: (a) caryatid stand mirror, bronze, h. 338 mm, diam. 162 mm, 550–525 BC (New York, Metropolitan Museum of Art); (b) box mirror and cover, bronze, diam. 118 mm, *c.* 400 BC (Boston, MA, Museum of Fine Arts); (c) Etruscan mirror with engraving of the Dioscuri, bronze, h. 238 mm, diam. 120 mm, 6th century BC (Bologna, Museo Civico Archeologico)

that fits over it. The lid may also be hinged to flip away, like a modern powder-compact. Lids are often decorated with relief or repoussé representations that range from profile heads and mythological scenes to the erotic and even pornographic. Decorated box mirrors continued to be produced in Roman times.

In Etruria bronze mirrors with engraved decoration are known from the end of the 6th century BC (1c). The Etruscan mirror is shaped as a circular or pear-shaped convex reflecting disc with a peg or tang to be inserted into a handle of wood or bone. The concave reverse side is engraved with a rich variety of subjects, including the cycle of a woman's life, native histories and imported Greek myths. Inscriptions often name characters in the scenes represented. Around the outer borders of the disc are ivy, vine or wave-pattern ornaments. After 480 BC mirrors decorated with reliefs were introduced: the disc is cast solid, and the reliefs are flat and resemble drawings. The preferred themes are the exploits of Herakles (e.g. 5th-century BC mirror from Atri; London, BM; see fig. 2) and romances of Greek mythology.

A type of Roman mirror that came into fashion in the 1st century BC has a baluster handle, often decorated with relief on one side; it combines the forms of the Greek box mirror and the Etruscan hand mirror. A small group of wall mirrors may belong to the same period. These consist of a bronze or bronze-alloy disc, backed with wood and framed with a border of openwork or relief in silver gilt. In the 1st century AD silver hand mirrors (e.g. Naples, Mus. N. S Martino) were widely used and commonly consist of a disc in a frame of decorated moulding with concentric circles on the reverse; a long handle is attached by arms to the disc. Metal mirrors of the 2nd to 4th centuries AD consist of plain discs, sometimes decorated with concentric circles, with either a loop or a grip handle fixed to the back. Glass mirrors were produced during the Roman period by blowing and then cutting up large glass bubbles, sections of which were backed with a dark resin or a metallic substance to create a reflective surface. Glass mirrors were generally surrounded by plaster or set in a wooden frame.

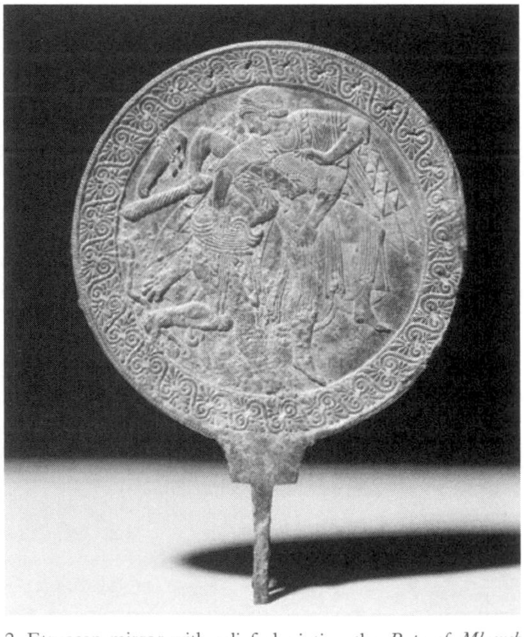

2. Etruscan mirror with relief depicting the *Rape of Mlacuch by Herkle*, bronze, diam. 180 mm, from Atri, *c.* 500–*c.* 475 BC (London, British Museum)

W. F. Petrie: *Objects of Daily Use* (London, 1927)

D. E. Strong: *Greek and Roman Gold and Silver Plate* (Ithaca, 1966)

D. Rebuffat-Emmanuel: *Le Miroir étrusque: D'après la collection du Cabinet des Médailles*, 2 vols (Rome, 1973)

G. Zahlhaas: *Römische Reliefspiegel*, Munich, Prähist. Staatssamml. cat., xvii (Munich, 1975)

C. Husson: *L'Offrande du miroir dans les temples égyptiens de l'époque gréco-romaine* (Lyon, 1977)

C. Lilyquist: *Ancient Egyptian Mirrors from the Earliest Times through the Middle Kingdom* (Munich, 1979)

R. Adam: *Recherches sur les miroirs prénestins* (Paris, 1980)

L. O. K. Congdon: *Caryatid Mirrors of Ancient Greece* (Mainz, 1981)

P. Albenda: 'Mirrors in the Ancient Near East', *Source*, iv/2–3 (1985), pp. 2–9

R. S. Bianchi: 'Reflections of the Sky's Eyes', *Source*, iv/2–3 (1985), pp. 10–18

L. O. K. Congdon: 'Greek Mirrors', *Source*, iv/2–3 (1985), pp. 19–25

N. T. de Grummond: 'The Etruscan Mirror', *Source*, iv/2–3 (1985), pp. 26–33

K. R. Nemet-Nejat: 'A Mirror Belonging to the Lady-of-Uruk', *The Tablet and the Scroll: Near Eastern Studies in Honour of William Withallo* (Bethesda, MD, 1993), pp. 163–9

L. B. van der Meer: *Interpretatio etrusca: Greek Myths on Etruscan Mirrors* (Amsterdam, 1995)

H. Wrede: 'Der Venus Felix peinvolles Schicksal im Lupercal', *Mitt. Dt. Archäol. Inst.: Röm. Abt.,* cii (1995), pp. 345–8 [2nd century Roman relief mirror]

C. Derriks: *Les miroirs cariatides égyptiens en bronze: Typologie, chronologie et symbolique* (Mainz, 2001)

A. A. Carpino: *Discs of Splendor: The Relief Mirrors of the Etruscans* (Madison, 2003)

H. Schulze: 'Der Kuss der Psyche', *Ant. Welt,* xxxvi/5 (2005), pp. 37–43

K. Zum Bahlen: *In the Eyes of the Beholder: An Analysis of Greek Caryatid Mirrors, 625 to 425 BCE* (diss., St Paul, MN, U. St Thomas, 2005)

Mnesikles (*fl* 430s BC). Greek architect. He designed the Propylaia, the monumental gateway to the Athenian Acropolis (*see* ATHENS, §II, 1(i) and fig. 7). Begun in 437 BC but never finished, probably due to the outbreak of the Peloponnesian War (431 BC), this building may have undergone several changes in design while under construction. Mnesikles showed great originality in adapting it to a restricted area on different levels. The Propylaia departs from the largely conventional character of earlier Greek architecture in giving an illusion of symmetry, housing a multiplicity of activities under abutting roofs, accommodating different ground levels and using darker stone not only for highlighting but also to create an optical illusion. The basic design, with a central structure (the gatehouse proper, consisting of porches to east and west separated by a wall with five openings) framed by projecting wings, inspired several buildings in the Athenian Agora, and probably also the *skene* (stage building) with projecting wings that became standard for Greek theatres. Though the Propylaia remained unfinished, the quality of its workmanship is exceptional. This must be attributed to Mnesikles' dual role as designer and master builder.

R. Bohn: *Die Propylaeen der Acropolis zu Athen* (Berlin, 1882)
W. B. Dinsmoor: *The Architecture of Greece and Rome* (London, 1902, rev. 2/1950 as *The Architecture of Ancient Greece*), pp. 199–205
J. A. Bundgaard: *Mnesicles* (Copenhagen, 1957)
C. Tiberi: *Mnesicle l'architetto dei Propilei* (Rome, 1964)
J. de Waele: *The Propylaia of the Akropolis in Athens: The Project of Mnesikles* (Amsterdam, 1990)

Mochlos. Tiny island off the north coast of Crete on the eastern edge of the Gulf of Mirabello. The island was almost certainly joined to the mainland by a narrow isthmus during Minoan times, when it was the site of an important settlement. The island was explored by the American archaeologist Richard Seager in 1908, but his discoveries have never been fully published. The settlement was apparently occupied from the Early to the Late Minoan period (for discussion of absolute dates *see* MINOAN, §4), but most of the information available concerns the Early Minoan (EM) and Middle Minoan (MM) tombs that Seager excavated. Some of these were simple pit graves or burials in clefts in the rock, but at least 20 were built tombs. Some were large and impressively constructed, with different types of stone apparently selected for different parts of the tomb structure. These variations in type of tombs may reflect differences of social status among their occupants, particularly since the grave goods from the larger built tombs are more numerous and of better quality than those from the other burials.

Some of the finest gold jewellery of EM Crete came from the chamber tombs of Mochlos, including gold diadems with pendant ribbons and flowers, which must have been prestigious items to own (*see* JEWELLERY, §1). Alongside them was a smaller quantity of bronze objects, mostly daggers but also toilet implements, as well as carved sealstones and a superb series of miniature vases made from a variety of coloured stones. Among the latter is a chlorite pyxis, the handle of its lid beautifully carved in the form of a sleeping dog (EM II; Herakleion, Archaeol. Mus.; *see* MINOAN, fig. 3). Certain objects from these tombs suggest that Mochlos was an important trading centre even in the Early Bronze Age. Metals used include Cycladic silver and lead, and probably imported copper too; some of the sealstones may be of ivory from the eastern Mediterranean. Connections with the East are also hinted at by the Egyptian shapes of some of the stone vases, and particularly by the discovery of a silver cylinder seal of Near Eastern type (EM II; Herakleion, Archaeol. Mus.). Mochlos may have been one of the most important settlements in pre-palatial Crete, and its location and the protected beaches on either side of its isthmus must have played a part in this. From the limited evidence available, however, its importance seems to have declined with the establishment of the palace-based civilization around MM IB.

R. B. Seager: *Explorations on the Island of Mochlos* (Boston and New York, 1912)
C. Davaras: 'Early Minoan Jewellery from Mochlos', *Annu. Brit. Sch. Athens*, lxx (1975), pp. 101–14
J. Soles: *The Prepalatial Cemeteries at Mochlos and Gournia* (Princeton, 1990)
K. Branigan: 'Mochlos: An Early Aegean "Gateway Community"?', *Aegeum*, vii (1991), pp. 97–106
J. S. Soles: 'Mochlos', *The Aerial Atlas of Ancient Crete*, ed. J. W. Myers, E. E. Myers and G. Cadogan (Berkeley, 1992), pp. 184–91
J. S. Soles and others: 'Excavations at Mochlos, 1989', *Hesperia,* lxi (Oct–Dec 1992), pp. 413–45
J. S. Soles and others: 'Excavations at Mochlos, 1990–1991', *Hesperia,* lxiii (Oct–Dec 1994), pp. 390–436
J. S. Soles and others: 'Excavations at Mochlos, 1992–1993', *Hesperia,* lxv (April–June 1996), pp. 175–230
K. A. Barnard and T. M. Brogan: *Mochlos: The Artisans' Quarter and the Farmhouse at Chalinomouri., Vol. 1B Period III, Neopalatial Settlement on the Coast: The Neopalatial Pottery* (Philadelphia, 2003)
J. S. Soles and T.M. Brogan: *Mochlos IA: Period III, Neopalatial Settlement on the Coast, the Artisans' Quarter and the Farmhouse at Chalinomouri, The Sites* (Philadelphia, 2003)
J. S. Soles: *Mochlos IC: Period III, Neopalatial Settlement on the Coast, the Artisans' Quarter and the Farmhouse at Chalinomouri: The Small Finds* (Philadelphia, 2004)

Monastir. *See* HERAKLEIA LYNKESTIS.

Monopteros. Unwalled building of ancient Greek origin with peripteral (outer) columns. Most examples were circular in plan, with conical or domed roofs, and these resembled the round buildings known as tholoi (*see* THOLOS; as distinct from tholos tomb). A few, however, had rectangular plans. Monopteroi were often dedicated to gods or deified mortals, notably Hercules, but some served merely as pavilions in markets while others housed tombs.

The first Sikyonian Treasury at Delphi (mid-6th century BC) may have been an early rectangular example. It probably had a peristyle of 4×5 Doric columns, with triglyphs over only the columns separated by elongated metopes. An early 3rd-century BC monopteros near Alexandria, supposedly built in honour of the deified Queen Arsinoe (*reg c.* 276–270 BC), wife of Ptolemy II (*reg c.* 283–246 BC), was also rectangular, with a 4×5 column peristyle; the building no longer survives. At Knidos, on the south-east coast of Asia Minor, there is a round monopteros (diam. *c.* 17.3 m) dedicated to Aphrodite Euploia. It had 18 columns, probably Corinthian, and four steps at the front, and it may have replaced a structure of the 3rd or 2nd century BC which had housed the famous *Aphrodite* by Praxiteles. This monopteros was copied in the 2nd century AD for Hadrian's Villa at Tibur (Tivoli), while a similar building (diam. 7.48 m) on the Athenian Acropolis was dedicated to Rome and Augustus. It was centred on the east front of the Parthenon, and the easternmost intercolumniation of its peristyle of nine Ionic columns was specially widened. Other monopteroi of similar date (1st century AD) include: the Mausoleum of the Julii at Glanum (Saint-Rémy-de-Provence; for illustration *see* MAUSOLEUM), raised on a high, arched platform, with ten Corinthian columns supporting a conical roof; the Mausoleum at Aquileia, in North Italy, with six Corinthian columns on a raised platform and a steep conical roof; and the monument of Babbius in Corinth, restored with eight columns.

The concrete foundations (diam 6.9 m) are all that remain of the 2nd-century AD monopteros in the Sanctuary of Poseidon at Isthmia, dedicated to Palaimon, son of Ino, who was deified after drowning. It was, however, depicted on coins and apparently had a peristyle with 11 Corinthian columns on a square platform supporting a domed roof. The easternmost intercolumniation was again widened, and the structure housed not only a statue of *Palaimon on a Dolphin* but also an underground chamber, the supposed tomb of the boy, though actually a settling basin belonging to the older stadium (6th–5th centuries BC). This was beneath the centre of the building, with a passage connecting it to the outside. Athletes were taken there in the dark and oaths administered, with threats of dire retribution for perjury (Pausanias, II.ii.1). A slightly later round building (mid-2nd century AD) in the Athenian Agora with a peristyle of eight, probably Corinthian, columns (diam. *c.* 7.17 m) and a domed roof was possibly dedicated to Aphrodite. Two small monopteroi (diam. *c.* 3.6 m), of similar date, each with eight Corinthian columns bearing a conical roof, formed part of the Nymphaion of Herodes Atticus at Olympia. By contrast, a large, 16-columned monopteros (diam. *c.* 18 m; 2nd century AD) stood in the market at Puteoli. The market at Cuicul (Djemila) housed a hexagonal pavilion, about 4 m wide with six columns. Finally, another circular monopteros (diam. 9 m; 2nd or 3rd century AD), with an eight-columned peristyle, stood in the market at Hippo Regius. The function of these market monopteroi was to provide shade.

Monopteroi were also depicted in paintings and on terracotta lamps. A lamp from Athens (Athens, Agora Mus., 751) of the 3rd century AD shows a monopteros with a domed roof and probably six columns, containing a statue, possibly of Aphrodite.

W. Binder: *Der Roma-Augustus Monopteros auf der Akropolis in Athen und sein typologischer Ort* (Karlsruhe, 1969)

W. B. Dinsmoor jr: 'The Monopteros in the Athenian Agora', *Hesperia*, xliii (1974), pp. 412–27

G. N. Szeliga: 'The Composition of the Argo Metopes from the Monopteros at Delphi', *Amer. J. Archaeol.*, xc (July 1986), pp. 297–305

H. Walter and others: 'Zum Monopteros im Heraion von Samos', *Mitt. Dt. Archäol. Inst.: Athen. Abt.*, ci (1986), pp. 137–47

S. Rambaldi: *Monopteros: Le edicole circolari nell'architettura dell'Italia romana* (Bologna, 2002)

Monument, public. Purpose-built, mainly sculptural monuments created for commemoration and addressed to the public. Further information on specific monuments can be found under the relevant city or site article, and information on types of monuments is given in the following art form articles: BUST, EQUESTRIAN MONUMENT, FOUNTAIN, MAUSOLEUM, SARCOPHAGUS, STELE, TOMB and TRIUMPHAL ARCH.

The earliest Greek monumental art was greatly influenced by contact with the East as the Orientalizing period (720–*c.* 570 BC) label suggests. Public monuments in pre-Hellenistic Greece (before 323 BC) were, however, intended to honour the city-state rather than glorify the individual. The most famous example of this is the Parthenon (447–432 BC; *see* ATHENS, fig. 6) in Athens, where Pheidias' statue of *Athena Parthenos* (446–438 BC; h. 13 m, destr.), the goddess of Athens, was displayed. The Panathenaic procession to Athena on the Parthenon frieze probably honoured victims of the Battle of Marathon (490 BC). Greek monuments proclaimed both human merit and religion; the humanist emphasis contrasts with the greater importance of the afterlife in Egyptian monuments. A new historical and archaeological consciousness of public monuments is found in the work of such Greek writers as Herodotus, Thucydides and most significantly PAUSANIAS, whose *Guide to Greece* (AD 150–80) provides detailed discussions of the public monuments he saw on his travels. His fascination with their appearance, workmanship and scale emerges in the description of Pheidias' bronze *Athena Promachos* (470–446 BC; destr.) on the Acropolis. Pausanias recorded inscriptions on the monuments and gave an account of the ceremonial rites, history and myths surrounding them. He also distinguished between dignified, predominantly artistic monuments and such utilitarian monuments as porticos, agoras and theatres.

Hellenistic public monuments were richer and more elaborate than those of Classical Greece. Due to political changes there was a movement away from commemorating the experiences of the city-state towards the Eastern tradition of grandiose glorification of individual rulers. The best-known example is the Mausoleum (370/65–*c.* 350 BC; destr.) at HALIKARNASSOS (now Bodrum) in Turkey, which commemorated Mausolos, satrap (governor) of Caria in Asia Minor. The Mausoleum was rectangular in plan with sides measuring 38.4×32.0 m and is one of the Seven Wonders of the World.

While Roman public monuments are not noted for breaking new conceptual or artistic ground, they gave late Hellenistic artists an unprecedented opportunity to exploit their talents. The distinctive qualities of Roman art—realistic portraiture, continuous narrative and three-dimensionality—culminated in monuments of the 1st and 2nd centuries AD. The most distinctively Roman monument is the triumphal arch. These usually commemorated major events, such as the *Capture of Jerusalem* depicted in narrative reliefs on the Arch of Titus (*c.* AD 81) in Rome (*see* TRIUMPHAL ARCH, fig. 1). Monumental relief sculpture was also applied in other important contexts: the Ara Pacis Augustae (13 BC, ded. 9 BC; *see* ROME, §IV, 4) commemorated, as its name suggests, the peace, stability and prosperity that Emperor Augustus attempted to establish. Trajan's Column (ded. AD 113) in the Forum of Trajan, Rome, is more grandiose in its glorification, and Trajan, Emperor of Rome, is frequently depicted in the reliefs. The column was originally intended as a look-out post, although it was dedicated as a war memorial and became the tomb of Trajan in AD 117, surmounted with a colossal bronze statue of *Trajan* (*see* ROME, §IV, 7). Portrait statues of emperors were also important public monuments, often, like that of Trajan, surmounting columns. The gilt-bronze equestrian statue of *Marcus Aurelius* (AD 166–80; Rome, Piazza del Campidoglio) typifies Roman realism and was the prototype for many later monuments.

A. Borg: *War Memorials from Antiquity to the Present* (London, 1991)

Mosaics. Wall and floor decoration formed using closely spaced polychrome or monochrome particles (tesserae) of near uniform size embedded in a binder, such as mortar or cement.

I. Materials and techniques.

The term 'mosaic' is taken from the Greek. Mosaic pieces were called *abakiskoi* by the Greeks and *abaculi*, *tesserae* or *tessellae* by the Romans. The list of artisans in Diocletian's *Edict on Prices* (AD 301) distinguishes between the *tessellarii*, who laid mosaic pavements, and the *museiarii*, the makers of wall and vault mosaics. The latter term was universally adopted to include both types of artisans in the post-Antique period.

An understanding of how mosaics were produced in antiquity is based almost entirely on the surviving physical evidence (apart from the *Edict on Prices* and some passages in Vitruvius' *On Architecture*) and on the epigraphic evidence from various mosaic projects. It is generally believed that the ancient floor mosaics were produced *in situ*, as suggested, for example, by the archaeological evidence from the 4th century AD nymphaeum at Neapolis (now Nabeul, Tunisia), where chippings and strips of the polychrome marble used in the pavement were discovered on site. A further proof of this direct method of production is found in the Late Antique relief from Ostia, which may illustrate the *in situ* production of a floor mosaic: it shows the master mosaicist directing two porters who carry sacks of mosaic material, and two mosaicists who cut tesserae on the ground. In fact, it has been suggested that corporations of mosaicists were responsible for the pavements in private buildings, as indicated by inscriptions that include such terms as *ex officina* followed by the name of the artisan.

As stone dominated the early history of mosaic production, it is not surprising that its natural colours provided the basic range of hues for the artist. The practice of using stone or marble for certain parts of a mosaic—faces, hands and feet—continued into the Middle Ages in both the East (i.e. Byzantium) and the West.

For the pebble mosaics at OLYNTHOS (*c.* 5th century BC), fairly uniform stones were selected with diameters from 10 to 20 mm. The pebble mosaics from PELLA (ii) (4th century BC) are made of natural pebbles, but in places the mosaicists found it necessary to use strips of lead to outline some of the inner markings and contours. Shaped tesserae from the 3rd century BC are found in the House of Ganymede at Morgantina, Italy, and tessellated mosaic pavements had gradually superseded pebble floors by the end of that century.

While the majority of mosaic pavements in antiquity were laid directly on site, a number of floors display emblemata, which are inset panels of images or ornamental motifs made of fine, precisely set tesserae that could be produced in another location. Emblemata were normally preset on trays of stone or terracotta, which were then embedded in the setting-bed. They are usually of very high quality, as may be seen in the 1st-century BC copy of the mosaic by Sosos of doves drinking (Rome, Mus. Capitolino).

The technique known as *opus vermiculatum* is so-called from the wormlike look of the close-set rows of undulating tesserae; it first appears in Alexandrian floor mosaics of the late 3rd–early 2nd century BC. The most famous example of this type of work is the late 2nd-century BC *Alexander* mosaic depicting the battle of Alexander and Darius at Issus found in the House of the Faun at POMPEII. Mosaics of this sort were undoubtedly luxury items.

Glass tesserae first appeared on floor and wall mosaics between the 3rd and 1st centuries BC. They brought unlimited colour possibilities to this art form, but their brittleness made them unsuitable for floor mosaics.

II. Greek.

The first figural mosaics in Western art appeared in Greece at the end of the 5th century BC or the beginning of the 4th, primarily at OLYNTHOS. They decorated floors, as did all subsequent Greek mosaics. Though earlier examples of patterned floors exist (*see* §2(i) below), the art of the mosaic, as Pliny noted (*Natural History* XXXVI.clxxxiv), was essentially a Greek development. There are three main types of Greek mosaic: pebble mosaics, which are made with unshaped natural pebbles; *opus tessellatum*, made with tesserae (small pieces of stone with squared edges); and a 'mixed' type made by combining pebbles with tesserae or with small pieces of lead or terracotta. The earliest mosaics were laid in pebbles, and this type reached a high degree of sophistication in the later 4th century BC before giving way in the decades around 100 BC to the elaborate tessellated floors of the High Hellenistic period. The time, place and exact nature of this transition are disputed; it may have been via the 'mixed' type of mosaic, though the evidence is inconclusive.

1. Introduction. 2. History and development.

1. Introduction.

(i) Uses. (ii) Materials, techniques and forms. (iii) Mosaicists. (iv) Motifs and subject-matter.

(i) Uses. Although mosaic floors, both pebble and tessellated, were used in public contexts, including temples, other sacred buildings and especially baths, most were made for private dwellings. Early pebble floors (first half of the 4th century BC) are typically found in houses of the *pastas* type (i.e. with a pillared portico opening on to a courtyard), best represented at Olynthos (*see* Architecture, §IV, 1(i)(c)). Here 12 of the more than 50 houses excavated in the 'new city' were found to contain mosaic floors. Some were in the courtyard, one was in the *pastas*, but most were in the *andron* (dining-room) and its anteroom. The *andron* normally had a flat plaster platform along the walls, on which stood couches for the reclining diners or drinkers, and a pebbled area in the centre from which they were served. When the centre had a decorative mosaic, the threshold leading to the anteroom was normally given one also. If the anteroom had a mosaic, the threshold mosaic joined the two. The two great houses at Pella (ii), which have yielded the finest pebble mosaics from the later 4th century BC, have different plans, but most of their mosaics are from *andrones*. The only large number of tessellated floors preserved in private houses is on Delos, where the houses, from the decades around 100 BC, are built around a central colonnaded court (*see* Architecture, fig. 7). Mosaics are found in courtyards and in various rooms, including fragments from collapsed upper storeys, but again most are in *andrones*. As earlier at Olynthos, however, only a small proportion of houses excavated were so adorned.

(ii) Materials, techniques and forms. In Greece and other eastern Mediterranean countries floors were generally laid by putting down plaster and packing it while wet with more or less closely set pebbles of roughly similar size, which were held firm when the plaster dried. The art of mosaic arose from arranging light and dark pebbles to make patterns in such floors (see colour pl. 2:V, fig. 1). At first naturally rounded pebbles from river-beds or beaches were used. In early mosaics they were spaced loosely, with a good deal of plaster visible between them, and they were not graded by size. Later they were more closely set and more even in size; in the most accomplished examples there is evidence of careful grading, with small pebbles used for fine detail. One early looking pebble floor at Olynthos has casual patterns that were surely put in as the craftsman or craftsmen went along, without reference to a prepared design. Most patterns and designs, however, must have followed a detailed cartoon, referred to in the Zenon Papyrus (mid-2nd century BC; Cairo, Egyp. Mus., P. Zenon 59665) as *paradeigma* ('example'). Under some of the elaborate pebble floors at Pella, traces of a *sinopia* in red were found on the lower plaster layer. This process must have been similar to that of fresco painting, with the craftsman laying only as much of the upper plaster layer as he could cover with pebbles before it dried. Basically the same methods must have been used initially for tessellated floors. For repeated patterns, instead of a *sinopia*, the craftsman of both types of mosaic probably used leaden templates, such as that for a wave-crest found on Delos. In some pebble floors, from the second half of the 4th century BC onwards, strips of terracotta or lead were introduced in figures to outline forms or emphasize details. These are also found in early tessera mosaics but later were confined to pattern borders.

Almost all pebble floors have a dark ground, with the design in lighter coloured stones, although exactly symmetrical patterns, such as wave-crests and triangles, can be read either way. A fragmentary floor of high quality from Sikyon (second quarter of the 4th century BC) has the expected light design on a dark ground for the complex floral motif that occupies the central circle, but exceptionally the ground of the surrounding square is light, and the circle has no frame but is edged with wave-crests that rise straight out of the dark ground; the light corners of the square have swimming youths set in dark pebbles. The normal scheme from which this departs is illustrated by a floor of similar design and date from Corinth, where the whole ground is dark, the central floral motif is framed by a circle of light wave-crests, and the dark corners have groups of animals in light stones. A few other contemporary examples combine light on dark figural scenes with reversed (i.e. dark on light) ornament, but only on late pebble floors are figural elements sometimes dark on light.

In Greek mosaics dark and light approximate to black and white, but the 'black' is often bluish or brownish and the 'white' an off-white of varying shades. Even in very early examples, reddish and yellowish pebbles were used discretely for enlivenment, and later these four basic colours were employed in a much subtler, more pictorial way. With the greater polychromy and pictoriality achievable with the introduction of tessera, a light ground became more common, but a dark one was still often used.

Light on dark motifs in early pebble floors produce an effect similar to that of Red-figure vases (*see* Pottery, §IV, 6). In particular, the figural groups in tondi suggest the interiors of Red-figure cups. However, the notion that vase painting influenced the mosaicists directly is doubtful. The light-on-dark principle was widespread in Greek art, notably in relief sculpture, where the backgrounds were normally uniformly painted so that the figures stood out. The mosaicists may have worked on this principle without specific reference to either sculpture or vase painting, though a shared inspiration with the latter cannot be ruled out, since Red-figure has been argued to owe something to precious metal vessels, in which gold figures were laid on silver that was then allowed to darken.

Most mosaic floors have an outer patterned frame that runs parallel to the walls of the rectangular or square room. Often most of the area is covered with a series of decreasing borders around a fairly small central feature (emblema), but in other cases virtually the whole space is occupied by a large floral or figural design. A favourite form, scarcely ever found in other branches of Greek art, is the circle within a square, whether as a small centre piece or a large circle filling most of the space. A particular feature of pebble mosaics, the form reappeared on tessellated floors of *c.* 100 BC on Delos. An emblema from Egypt (middle or third quarter of the 2nd century BC) is circular, but it may be from a circular room. Mosaics in circular rooms are known from references in the Zenon Papyrus, and a splendid pebble example has been found at Pella (end of 4th century BC). A small central circle in a square or rectangular pebble floor may have a wheel, star or flower (the Zenon Papyrus names a poppy) or a palmette design; a larger circle may contain concentric rings of animals or figures around a similar centre, or the whole area may be filled by a complex floral motif or a figural scene. Both pebble and tessellated floors sometimes have an overall geometric pattern: lozenges were favoured in both, *trompe l'oeil* cubes in tessera. Many tessellated floors have concentric frames around a central emblema, in the earlier pebble tradition, but their frames are generally sparser, with a lot of the floor left plain white. Sometimes there are several emblemata.

If figural, the emblema on an *andron* floor is designed to be viewed from the doorway, as is usually the threshold design. If there is a figural design in the anteroom, it is orientated the other way, so as to be seen from the same door. When animals, or occasionally human figures, are placed in the surrounding pattern bands, they are orientated to be viewed from the couches along the parallel wall, as in one from House B.v.1 at Olynthos (*c.* 400 BC), with its double sphinxes in a palmette band. A unique feature of this mosaic is the way the outermost pattern band, a meander, is extended to enclose the normally separate threshold design, which, unusually, is here orientated to be seen not on entering or leaving the room but obliquely from one side of the door.

(iii) Mosaicists. The only mosaicist known from literary records is SOSOS, who worked at Pergamon, almost certainly in the 2nd century BC and in tessera; none of his mosaics survives, although numerous replicas provide some sense of his achievements. Pliny recounted the artist's superior ability to create *trompe l'oeil* effects, in particular in his representations of the unswept floor (*asarotos oikos*) of a banquet hall and of doves drinking. These were widely imitated and adapted throughout Italy and elsewhere (see colour pl. 1:XVI, fig. 2).

A pebble floor at Pella from the later 4th century BC bears the name of GNOSIS as maker, and a contemporary fragment at Athens preserves the last two letters (. . . *ōn*) of another maker's name. On Hellenistic tessera mosaics the name SOPHILOS occurs at Alexandria (? *c.* 200 BC), HEPHAISTION at Pergamon (2nd century BC) and both ASKLEPIADES (*c.* 100 BC) and Antaios, son of Aischrion (*c.* 100 BC), on Delos. The name of Dioskourides of Samos appears as maker on two exquisite miniature mosaics that formed part of the decoration of the House of Cicero at Pompeii (second half of the 1st century BC). They are certainly copied from 3rd-century BC Greek paintings, and the letter forms have suggested a date of *c.* 100 BC. These pieces, however, like the mosaic of *Alexander the Great* from the House of the Faun at Pompeii (Naples, Mus. Archeol. N.), belong to the beginnings of the fashion, common in Roman art, of copying Greek masterpieces for the Roman market, often in a different medium.

On his mosaic, Gnosis wrote *epoiesen* ('made') in the past definite, as did Dioskourides. Sophilos, Hephaistion, (Askle)piades and Antaios used the imperfect tense, *epoiei*, perhaps because it was thought more appropriate for the gradual process of laying tessera. There is no way of knowing what precisely is implied in such signatures. Did the named person design the floor, execute it to another's design or, as is most likely, supply the design as well as supervise the execution? Large mosaics were probably laid by a team: this is almost certainly the case with (Askle)piades', which is composed of repeated patterns, mainly of a traditional kind. Gnosis set his signature in light pebbles on the dark ground of an elaborate and highly pictorial figural scene, and in this case the equally elaborate and individual floral border is surely an integral part of the design. The signature of '. . . *ōn*' is set within the simple circle that borders a figural scene of *Herakles Attacking a Centaur*; though at a much lower artistic level than Gnosis' work, both the design and the execution of the bird and floral motifs in the borders seem integral with the picture.

The use of terracotta and lead strips in some but not all of the floors in the two houses at Pella, known commonly as the House of Dionysos and the House of Helen but called by the excavators I 1 and I 5 (hereafter House 1 and House 5), suggests the differing practices of two workshops. One might have been responsible for the mosaics in House 1, where these other materials were used in the *Lion Hunt*, the *andron* floor and the threshold mosaic with the two centaurs and omitted only from the animal threshold. The other, to which Gnosis presumably belonged, was responsible for the *andron* mosaic in House 5, with the first workshop brought in to assist with the large floor showing the *Abduction of Helen*, where lead strips were used. Alternatively, it might be a question of different dates, with House 5 coming first and the new method introduced there at a late stage and employed regularly in House 1. However, Gnosis' lines of tiny, closely set black pebbles in the *andron* mosaic produce so nearly the same effect as the lead strips that they look like a deliberate reaction to the challenge of the other technique.

Of the mosaicists working in tessera, Sophilos signed in black tesserae on the white ground of the emblema. In this case the surround, outside the emblema frame of isometric meander, is simply a wide white area with a narrow crenellation at the edge, so that the question of whether the signature applies to the whole floor or only the emblema has little meaning. Hephaistion's case is different: his cartellino is placed at the bottom centre of an emblema surrounded by framing zones of pattern, including one with a complex floral scroll enlivened with insects and Erotes, and another that was carefully removed in antiquity but probably contained figures. Hephaistion was almost certainly signing the whole floor, though it is remotely possible that he meant only the emblem (for illustration *see* HEPHAISTION).

Since (Askle)piades' floor is a single overall design, the signature must apply to the whole. It is set in dark tesserae on a strip of white background between circling pattern bands. Antaios is a peculiar case: his mosaic occupies an exedra in the Sanctuary of the Syrian Gods on Delos and consists only of patternwork, with an area of *trompe l'oeil* cubes surrounded by a meander between two bands of wave-crest. The cubes are interrupted in the middle by a framed white panel that contains an inscription naming the man who had the exedra built and giving other details that end with the name of Antaios, son of Aischrion. His signature thus seems to be part of the very full documentation of the gift, rather than a personal artistic claim.

(iv) Motifs and subject-matter.

(a) Patternwork. (b) Figural scenes.

(a) Patternwork. The repertory of abstract patterns used on mosaic floors is generally that shared by other Greek art forms, but with its own emphases. The universal meander appears as a border on both pebble and tessellated floors. In early tessera mosaics, including Sophilos' emblema, it is found also in an 'isometric' form, giving an illusion of three dimensions. This is rare in other surviving forms of Greek art but is found earlier, on 4th-century BC South Italian vases. The chequerboard patterns evolved into a field of *trompe l'oeil* cubes in tessera mosaics (see colour pl. 2:V, fig. 1). The guilloche is not very common in pebble and always of simple form, but it was more frequent and varied in tessera. Narrow bands of black and white triangles are found sparingly in both types of mosaic. Bead and reel is rather more frequent, while other architectural patterns, such as cymation and ovolo, are used occasionally. For fields, lozenges are found in both types, scales in tessera only.

The wave-crest deserves special mention because of the frequency of its appearance in both pebble and tessera mosaics. It is found in other art forms, for instance Red-figure vase painting from the late 5th century BC or the early 4th, when pebble floors first appeared, but it is almost a hallmark of mosaic. It sometimes occurs in formalized representations of the sea, so the term is not purely arbitrary, but the Zenon Papyrus calls it *kochlos nautikos* ('spiral seashell'). Border patterns used exclusively in tessera include stepped triangles and the related crenellation, which appears, for example, on the floors signed by Sophilos, Hephaistion and (Askle)piades, where it is always an extreme outer frame.

Floral borders on early pebble mosaics are of the kind traditional in other forms of Greek art: palmette, palmette and lotus, and ivy. These continue throughout the pebble tradition but are rarely found in tessera. A floor from Alexandria showing *Three Erotes Hunting a Stag* (early 3rd century BC) has a dark-on-light ivy frame around the emblema. Complexes of palmettes or palmettes and lotuses are used for the decoration of circular or rectangular fields in pebble but not in tessera. In the 4th century BC an elaborate system of 'naturalistic' floral scrolls was developed, a phenomenon known as the Floral style (*see* §2 below). Though the same style appeared in other art forms, pebble mosaicists were apparently among its most imaginative exploiters, both for frames and to cover large fields. No surviving tessellated floor has floral motifs as field decoration, but the scroll-border on Hephaistion's floor at Pergamon is clearly a modified derivative of the earlier type, treated less calligraphically and enlivened by the introduction of insects and Erotes. This is an early example of the 'peopled scroll', which was later used to such splendid effect in Roman decorative sculpture. In tessera there also evolved a different type of garland, consisting of heavier swags of foliage, sometimes with birds and often hung with objects, in particular theatrical masks. There are fragments from Pergamon, and more complete examples are the two tall panels framing a *trompe l'oeil* cube floor in the House of the Masks on Delos. Such garlands are found in similar form in Roman mosaics; a 1st-century BC floor in the House of the Faun at Pompeii had an emblema with fish, almost certainly of Greek derivation, framed in a border that is a coarser version of Hephaistion's scroll.

(b) Figural scenes. Another type of border in pebble mosaic consists of a frieze of animals, imaginary or real, occasionally confronted over or separated by palmettes. Examples include the *Amazonomachy* pebble mosaic in House 5 at Pella and two floors dated after the mid-3rd century BC from Assos in Turkey and Olbia (Ol'viya) in southern Russia. The same scheme occurs in the two floors of mixed technique from Alexandria and in two early tessellated floors, both of the 3rd century BC, one in irregular tessera from Erythrai and the other in regular tesserae from Klazomenai in Turkey. Animal friezes are not, however, found in later tessera mosaics. Human figures are only rarely introduced in pebble borders (e.g. a *Hunter and a (?)Greek Fighting a Centaur* at Olynthos). Beasts like those found in borders are a favourite subject for *andron* thresholds in pebble, where they are shown singly or in fighting pairs or threes. Exceptionally, a threshold in House 1 at Pella has a male and female centaur with wine vessels, and one from the Villa of Good Fortune at Olynthos shows two Pans confronted over a krater. There the *andron* floor

depicts *Dionysos in a Panther-drawn Chariot with Eros and (?)Pan* (second quarter of the 4th century BC), with an unusual framing frieze, on an only slightly smaller scale, that continues the Dionysiac theme, with maenads, a satyr, a Pan and fawns.

Dionysiac subjects seem an obvious choice for the main scene in an *andron* mosaic and are found in several others, for example the *Dionysos Riding a (?)Cheetah* in pebble from House 1 at Pella. From Delos there is a beautiful emblema from an upper floor representing *Lykourgos Offending Dionysos by Attacking the Nymph Ambrosia*. This mosaic is of special interest as the first known example of a composition that was later repeated in several Roman mosaics and paintings. Subjects in a similar vein include theatrical masks, either in garlands or by themselves (e.g. in the altar room at Pergamon), and the vessels on a pebble *andron* floor from Sikyon and on a floor of mixed technique (dark-on-light) from Thasos. Wild beasts and vegetation also have a Dionysiac connotation.

Other mythological scenes appear to have been chosen arbitrarily. Those in pebble mosaics include *Herakles Attacking a Centaur* at Athens, the *Abduction of Helen* at Pella, *Bellerophon on Pegasos Attacking the Chimaera* at Olynthos and *Thetis Bringing Armour to Achilles* (second quarter of the 4th century BC) also at Olynthos. Among the subjects on tessellated floors are the *Rape of Ganymede* from Morgantina, Sicily, and from Delos an uncertain scene showing Athena and Hermes with a figure seated between them.

Mythological figures not shown in specific scenes include numerous sea creatures, which may also have Dionysiac associations, as in a floor from Sparta in irregular tesserae, where the emblema depicting a *Triton* is surrounded by a frieze of sea creatures, inside another frieze with a Pan, satyrs, centaurs and a krater. Tritons or tritonesses are found also in pebble at Rhodes, in mixed technique in the porch of the Temple of Zeus at Olympia and in tessera (apparently imitating pebble) at Delos. Scylla is depicted in pebble at Eretria, New Paphos on Cyprus and at Peiraeus in a bathhouse. Dolphins, tridents and anchors in various combinations were popular subjects in tessera on Delos. The early tessellated floor from Klazomenai has *Amphitrite Riding a Sea Monster* and, on the *andron* threshold, *Eros and Psyche*.

Eros appears in several of these scenes, and on the pebble floor of a circular bath at Ambrakia (now Arta), Erotes are shown playing with water-birds and fish. He is depicted alone in a central tondo on a pebble floor at Chalkis, which also shows a dolphin (dark-on-light). The most remarkable scene of this type is that on the pebble floor from Assos, showing *Aphrodite and a Man Weighing Erotes*. The mixed technique floor from Alexandria with *Three Erotes Hunting a Stag* adapted its composition from earlier hunting scenes with mortals.

The female head shown growing from a calyx among flowers on a pebble floor from Dyrrhachion in Epiros (now Albania) must have a religious or mythological significance, but the interpretation is not certain. This subject is frequent on South Italian vases, but the identity of the figure seems to vary. One is named Aura (personified 'Breeze'), and some (perhaps most) probably represent Aphrodite. The female half-figures depicted growing from florals at the corners of a mosaic floor at Aigai (Vergina) must belong in the same category.

Other scenes, in pebble and tessera alike, are not mythological but generic or historical. The *Lion Hunt* in House 1 at Pella is one of a group of lion hunts of the late 4th century BC, executed in various media, which are thought to have been inspired by a famous bronze statue group by Lysippos and Leochares, dedicated at Delphi by Alexander the Great's friend Krateros after he had saved the King's life in a hunt. However, it is doubtful that the hunters in the mosaic are specifically intended to portray Alexander and Krateros. The sudden popularity of hunting subjects probably owes more to Alexander's calculated espousal of the traditional sport of eastern kings; Gnosis' *Stag Hunt* in the other house at Pella no doubt reflects Macedonian aristocratic pursuits.

Subjects taken from everyday life include what are probably copies of a portrait of a Ptolemaic queen, most likely Berenike II (*reg* 246–221 BC), represented in two tessera emblemata from Thmuis (now Tall Timay) near Alexandria. Both were previously interpreted as personifications of Alexandria. The pebble floor of a bathhouse at Chersonesos in southern Russia is appropriately adorned with a group of two naked women at a wash-basin. In the altar room at Pergamon the only survivor of three emblemata ranged side by side shows a parrot in bright colours on a dark ground, and at Delos there are several still-lifes with prizes, for example a bronze hydria or a Black-figure Panathenaic amphora with a palm and a wreath.

2. History and development. The early history of the craft is fragmentary and obscure, and evidence for dating is woefully inadequate, but since the 1970s important work has been done, and it is now possible to give a rational outline of the development. Areas of great uncertainty remain, however, especially between the fully developed art of the pebble floor in the later 4th century BC and the established tessera style of a hundred years later.

(i) Origins. (ii) Dating. (iii) Stylistic development.

(i) Origins. Remains of a Bronze Age floor from Tiryns (14th century BC) show dark and light pebbles arranged in rows, but no direct connection can be postulated with later Greek mosaic developments. In some Near Eastern countries, there was a continuous tradition of patterned pebble floors, such as those of *c.* 700 BC from palace buildings at Gordion in Phrygia, where one large, nearly square floor (*c.* 10×10 m) is covered with geometric patterns evidently laid as the craftsman went along without reference to a preliminary design. More regular strips of chequerboard pattern occur on a floor there from the first half of the 6th century, and a building in which five rooms

have floors decorated with regular rows of meander squares dates to *c.* 500 BC. However, there is little formal resemblance between the decorative pebble floors from Gordion and those that first appeared in Greece, and it is now generally held that the idea developed independently in Greece.

Yet the sudden popularity of elaborate floor decoration in Greece in the late 5th century BC and the early 4th may have had some particular impulse behind it. While it is still highly conjectural, there is evidence to suggest that the use of fine floor mosaics was a fashion begun and elaborated in Macedonian and imitation-Macedonian palaces and later taken up for private dwellings. The Macedonian capital was moved from Aigai (probably Vergina) to Pella during the reign of Archelaos of Macedon (*reg* 413–399 BC). He built a new palace at Pella and had it decorated by the Greek painter Zeuxis. Nothing is said of mosaic floors, but given the importance of Pella in the later history of the craft, it seems plausible (though undemonstrable) to suppose that it was Archelaos and Zeuxis who, perhaps aware of a tradition of decorated palace floors in the Near East, evolved the notion of more elaborately patterned and figured pebblework. One of the earliest mosaic sites, Olynthos, is situated on the Chalcidian peninsula, which borders Macedonia, and it was due to Perdikkas II of Macedon (*reg c.* 452–*c.* 413 BC) that Olynthos was established in 432 BC as chief city of a Chalcidian League, which led to the building of the 'new city', in which so many mosaics were found. The sack of Olynthos in 348 BC by Philip II of Macedon (*reg* 359–336 BC) was part of the absorption of the whole area into Macedonia.

It has been suggested that the first mosaics owe much to imported eastern textiles, which the Greeks are known to have prized, but this is not borne out by the character of the textiles discovered since the theory was advanced. On the other hand, some of the mid- to late 4th-century BC pebble mosaics from Pella are extremely pictorial and seem to show strong connections with South Italian vase painting. The finest examples of the distinctive Floral style that characterized both vases and mosaics of that period are from Sikyon, Macedonia and Epiros. Epiros was ruled by members of the Macedonian royal house, and there is evidence of cultural and artistic contact in the 4th century BC between Macedonia and the cities of South Italy. There is also a link between Macedonia and Sikyon. During the reigns of Philip II and Alexander the Great (*reg* 336–323 BC), Sikyon was ruled by their ally, the tyrant Aristratos. A famous school of painting flourished there, patronized by Aristratos. The second and most celebrated head of the school, Pamphilos, came not from Sikyon but from Amphipolis, a Thracian city absorbed into Macedonia by Philip II in 357 BC. One of the greatest Sikyonian painters was Pausias, who alone among Greek artists was famed as a flower painter. It has been suggested that Pausias was the inventor of the Floral style, so important in the history of pebble mosaic. While this cannot be proved, Pausias's flower pictures and the Floral style found on the floors and vases surely belong to the same movement. It is significant that he worked in a city that was ruled by a monarch who had close ties with the rulers of Macedonia and in which outstanding mosaics in this style were also produced. The only contemporary reference to 4th-century BC decorated floors comes from Douris of Samos (cited by Athenaeus: *Deipnosophists* XII.542d). Writing in the early 3rd century BC about the ruler of Athens in the Macedonian interest, Demetrios of Phaleron (*reg* 317–307 BC), Douris referred to his outdoing the Macedonians themselves in expenditure on dinners and to many of the floors in his *andrones* being flowery with patterns made by craftsmen.

It is likely that the invention of tessera mosaic also took place in the ambience of Hellenistic courts. In the decades following Alexander the Great's death in 323 BC his generals, all Macedonian aristocrats, fought each other for his empire but finally settled down as kings of their separate provinces. The first tessera mosaics could well have been made at Pella or elsewhere in Macedonia, at the new capital, Kassandreia, or at Thessaloniki, both founded by Kassandros *c.* 315 BC, or at Antioch, founded by Seleukos and his son Antiochos in 300 BC as capital of the huge eastern kingdom known as Syria. None of these palaces has been excavated, but fine floors in royal dwellings of the 2nd century BC have been found in Pergamon, which was ruled from *c.* 200 BC by another Macedonian dynasty, the Attalids.

The theory that tessera was invented in Sicily and introduced from there to Alexandria is based primarily on the supposed early date (before the mid-3rd century BC) of the *Rape of Ganymede* mosaic from Morgantina, but this is doubtful (s, pp. 60–62). According to one story, Hieron II of Syracuse (*reg* 270–215 BC) sent as a present to a Ptolemaic king in Alexandria a luxury galley made under the supervision of Archimedes (*c.* 287–212 BC), which included among its lavish furnishings three dining-rooms with what are thought to have been tessera floor mosaics illustrating the *Iliad.* Even if both the story and the early date are accepted, it is still just as likely that the tessera technique had already been invented in the courts of Greece and the east and was simply being imitated in the west.

As with pebble mosaics, though the fashion for tessellated floors may have been set in palaces, it soon spread to private houses. The merchants' houses on Delos (2nd–1st century BC) are the most conspicuous surviving examples, and here a new influence is discernible. The Romans established a free port there in 166 BC as part of their takeover of the Hellenistic world. Macedonia and Greece were absorbed in the 140s BC, Pergamon and Asia Minor in 133 BC. Many of the merchants on Delos were Italian, and they, like the Romans at home, were beginning to be interested in Greek products. Mosaics in the Greek manner became increasingly popular at Pompeii in the later 2nd century BC and the 1st, and these were surely often the work of Greek craftsmen who adapted their tradition to houses of Roman design and to the artistic tastes of another culture.

(ii) Dating. As has become increasingly clear from the preceding discussion, there are few fixed points for the absolute dating of pebble mosaics. A floor with animals from Motya in western Sicily was long thought to antedate the sack of the city by Dionysios I of Syracuse in 397 BC, but the architecture of the house has been shown to be later. The archaeological context of one fragment from Corinth is not, as had been stated, late 5th century BC but late 4th, though another floor in a bath building from the same site can be securely dated to the end of the 5th century. The large body of pebble mosaics from Olynthos must have been laid between the founding of the 'new city' in 432 BC and its destruction in 348 BC, and floors found in the city of Rhodes cannot be earlier than its foundation in 408/7 BC. Another important series of more sophisticated floors comes from the 'old city' of Sikyon, which was abandoned for a new site in 303 BC. The floors from the two great houses in Pella, which exemplify the art of pebble mosaic at its most masterly, are now shown to have been laid above a fill in which the latest pottery is of the third quarter of the 4th century BC. They cannot be earlier than that, and surely in fact belong to that time. At Eretria, pottery from the end of the 5th century BC was found under one floor, and the house containing it and two others, all with accomplished animal and patternwork, seems to have been built early in the 4th century BC and destroyed about a hundred years later. The city was sacked by the Romans in 198 BC, but habitation and building went on later. Of buildings with simple pattern floors, the Sanctuary of Isis was put up before the sack, the gymnasium and the baths after.

Since technical and stylistic differences are clearly distinguishable in surviving pebble mosaics, these fixed points can be used as the basis for tracing a chronological development. The problem is complicated, however, by wide geographical distribution and by the differing character of the various classes of building with mosaic decoration, as well as by variations in their quality. Yet developments paralleled in other branches of art, for example the Floral style vases produced by Greeks in South Italy from the second quarter of the 4th century BC to the 3rd, the chronology of which is established with some degree of precision, can also help in the dating of mosaics.

(iii) Stylistic development.

(a) Pebble. (b) Mixed and intermediate. (c) Tessera.

(a) Pebble. There is no reason to think that any formally patterned or figural mosaic floor in Greece is earlier than the Corinth bath dating from the end of the 5th century BC. It has a large wheel motif surrounded by narrow concentric pattern circles, with the corners of the square floor occupied by animals orientated to be seen from the centre. Fragmentary remains of an even cruder floor from Megara and a rather better one from Sikyon are similarly designed and probably also early. Another from Megara has a similar design but is unique in having white pebbles used for the outlines of some figures; for this reason it is sometimes dated to the second quarter of the 3rd century BC, though this is inconclusive.

Similar to the Corinth bath is the large body of mosaics from Olynthos, which must belong in the first half of the 4th century BC, with the *andron* mosaic from House B.v.1 near the beginning of the series, and perhaps the casually patterned courtyard mosaic even earlier. Most of the Olynthos mosaics consist of patternwork, some with beasts introduced in a floral border or an animal border with a few human figures substituted for a pattern band, but there are five with mythological scenes. One of these, a fragment from a courtyard, has unusual dark-on-light borders, including a cymation of architectural character. The surviving figure, a warrior, recalls figures in 4th-century BC carved friezes. The style seems later than most of the Olynthian mosaics, but the technique is coarse, with ungraded stones set loosely. Two of the other mythological scenes come from the *andron* and anteroom of a large free-standing house, known as the Villa of Good Fortune, which has a modified plan and was probably not an ordinary private house (it may have been a *pandokeion* or lodging-house). Both are rectangular designs framed in bands of geometrical and floral pattern. The florals in the *andron* are traditional palmettes, but the anteroom has a scroll with flowers, and a similar scroll is found among traditional pattern bands encircling the tondo on another *andron* floor, showing *Bellerophon on Pegasos Attacking the Chimaera*. The Villa of Good Fortune has two more mosaic floors in adjoining rooms, evidently not an *andron* complex, since neither has a plaster surround. These floors are not figured but have simple patterns and dark and light strips with inscriptions in praise of 'Good fortune' and Aphrodite, picked out in pebbles of the opposite hue.

Floors of generally similar character to the Olynthian examples but often more neatly laid are found at Corinth, Sikyon, Athens and Eretria, and these are dated in the second and third quarters of the 4th century BC, overlapping the dates of the Olynthian floors and leading on to the sophisticated ones at Pella, which are dated to the third or last quarter of the 4th century BC.

Of the same character as the scrolls on two of the mosaics at Olynthos, but of far greater accomplishment and used in a new way, is the scrollwork on an *andron* floor from Sikyon. On the threshold is a heraldic griffin, but the whole rectangle of the floor is covered with a floral complex. The effect is still basically two-dimensional: the central flower is flattened, as are the broad stalks that issue from under its petals and, by their scrollings, build up the design. The leaves in which they end, however, are no longer traditional palmettes; they create an effect of growth and show some foreshortening, as do four big bell-flowers that accent the centre of each side. Similarly foreshortened bells appear in the more conventional floral motif of another floor at Sikyon and one from Eretria, as well as in rather summary form in the two Olynthos scrolls. This is the beginning of the distinctive Floral style so important for dating. The two Olynthos scroll mosaics have been dated to 380/70 BC and 370/60 BC, that at Sikyon to 360/50 BC and that at Eretria to 350/40 BC. However, it is unlikely that the mosaicists at Olynthos were pioneers: the primitive technique they used does not necessarily put their floors earlier than the beautiful one from Sikyon. A direct descendant of the latter is the magnificent floor from one of the huge *andrones* in the palace at Aigai (Vergina). Here the complex occupies a circle in the square, with female half-figures rising from floral volutes in the corners. The big central flower has a pictorial chiaroscuro effect, the leaves between the petals being slightly darker in colour, and three-dimensionality is emphasized by corkscrew tendrils that proliferate from the stalks. The floor is dated to the end of the 4th century BC or after (thus later than those from the two big houses at Pella), which may be the same date as the floor of a circular building in Pella. The omission of corkscrew tendrils there makes for a flat effect reminiscent of the Sikyon floor, but the virtuoso execution of the varied, foreshortened flowers supports the later date.

The Floral style is seen at its peak in these and the mosaics of the two main houses at Pella. Only one floor was found with overall floral decoration, and this in a much ruined state (House 5), but the style was developed with extraordinary skill and charm in the broad borders of two others: the badly damaged *Lion Hunt* (House 1) and the perfectly preserved *Stag Hunt* (House 5), signed by Gnosis. There are also remains of a third such border in House 5 (from a destroyed floor). The border of Gnosis' *Stag Hunt* is formed of two 'plants' that spring from calyces of acanthus leaves at the bottom left and top right corners and meet at the other two in fans of leaves. Their twisting lengths are loaded with flowers of many kinds and innumerable tendrils that cover the dark ground with three-dimensional corkscrew curls. The naturalistic detail, however, is subdued to the strong formal decorative effect. Flowers and spiralling tendrils frame a female head rising from a calyx in the centre of the floor at Dyrrhachion, a motif common on the South Italian vases. The large floor (the head is 1 m high) is damaged, but the centre is intact. The room was not an *andron* (it had semicircular niches at either side), and its purpose is not known.

Gnosis' *Stag Hunt* is the most pictorial of all pebble mosaics. The pebbles are carefully graded and used to produce surprising nuances of chiaroscuro and colour. While one hunter is in profile, the other is almost frontal and set back behind the stag, one foot hidden by a rock. They stand on uneven ground, though the upper part of the background is dark in the traditional way. Whether the floral frame of the *Lion Hunt* was as fine as this one is hard to say. The figural element is simpler and less pictorial, and it also seems a little mechanical. From the waist down the two figures are almost identical, apparently taken from one cartoon. Another floor in the same house, however, is even simpler and of stunning quality: within a narrow border of white pebbles young Dionysos, naked, thyrsus in hand, rides across an undifferentiated dark ground on a feline, probably a cheetah. The pictorialism of the *Stag Hunt* and the more relief-like character of the *Lion Hunt* are eschewed. There is some modelling with shadow, but it is very light, and colour is used discretely to pick out detail. This is traditional flat surface decoration, the beautiful effect achieved by the contour of the light figure against the dark ground. But if the design here was more traditional than that of the *Stag Hunt*, the technique, using other materials, was innovative: terracotta strips were added in the hair, beads of the same material (originally coloured) in the ivy wreath and strips of lead for some contours (e.g. the eyebrow and eyelid, and the fingers holding the thyrsus). Such lead and terracotta strips are also found in the *Lion Hunt* and in the much damaged *andron* threshold with two centaurs. The fourth mosaic from House 1, the smaller threshold of the *andron* with *Dionysos Riding a (?)Cheetah* shows a *Griffin Attacking a Stag* and is without lead or terracotta additions.

House 1 at Pella also has two large rooms floored from wall to wall with pebbles in simple geometric patterns, while in House 5 another very large room without a platform for couches has the largest of the figure mosaics: the *Abduction of Helen*. This has no floral border but instead a band of meander inside another of lozenges. The scene shows Theseus carrying off the girl Helen protesting from her distraught duenna Deianeira while Phorbas holds his chariot ready (the names are in white pebbles on the dark ground, like Gnosis' signature on the *Stag Hunt*). This is the only floor in House 5 with lead strips, which are used in the horses' contours and the figures' hands. The figures are arranged on relatively level ground, in a friezelike composition, but there is a striking pictorialism in Deianeira's windblown drapery. Much is now lost, especially in the group of Theseus and Helen, making the effect difficult to judge, but it seems less visually satisfying than either the *Stag Hunt* or *Dionysos Riding a (?)Cheetah*.

Also dated to the last quarter of the 4th century BC are several fragments from Athens: a splendid *andron* with patterns and a threshold with animals, which seem particularly like the Pella circular mosaic though the only preserved florals are palmettes, and the much damaged fragment with traces of the signature of . . . *ōn*. The scroll with corkscrew tendrils is found again on a fine mosaic from Assos, now lost except for fragments but recorded in a drawing. The mosaic is a wide rectangle framed in a broad meander and divided into three fields: a central square with the circular scene of *Aphrodite and a Man Weighing Erotes* surrounded by the scroll and with Erotes filling in the corners; this is flanked by two outer rectangles, orientated on the short ends, at right angles to the central field, each showing two *nikai* (Victories) confronted over a tripod. Both the subject and the design are unparalleled on other pebble floors (this cannot have been an *andron*), and a date of *c.* 300 BC seems appropriate.

The further history of the pebble floor is hard to trace with precision. Several carefully constructed floors have been found in Rhodes. One from an *andron* has a *Triton* within a square frame and a floral motif with spiralling tendrils, which appears also on the threshold. The modelling of the figure is much more linear than at Pella, and the floral motif is simpler and, in spite of the corkscrews, creates a less three-dimensional effect. Comparison with vase painting suggests that these are early 3rd-century BC characteristics. Two other *andron* floors from Rhodes show similar linear modelling: one, with a centaur, has no floral; another, representing *Bellerophon Attacking the Chimaera*, has a further simplified scroll without spiralling tendrils. The composition of the latter is rectangular, but the odd position of the chimaera's hind legs suggests that it was adapted from a circular prototype (not, however, that represented earlier at Olynthos). Similar is the fragment from Chalkis showing *Eros* within a circle framed in dark-on-light ivy, with light-on-dark palmettes in the corners. Also dated to the first half of the 3rd century BC are the bathhouse floor from Chersonesos, with two naked women at a wash-basin, and the patterned floor from Olbia (Ol'viya). Four crude *andron* floors from Eretria with circle in square figural scenes have been convincingly dated to the mid- and later 3rd century BC, while only the very simple patterned floors can be dated after the sack of Eretria in 198 BC. A rather crude floor from Tarsus with floral motifs and animals (partly dark-on-light) is archaeologically dated to the late 3rd century BC or the early 2nd, and many other mosaics from various sites seem to go with it, including one from AI KHANUM, which may date from the mid-2nd century BC. There seem no grounds for dating any pebble floor later than that.

(b) Mixed and intermediate. The introduction of lead and terracotta elements in floors at Pella and elsewhere was already a modification of the pure technique of pebble laying. However, at Pella the basic unit remained the unshaped pebble, and the floors there are thus always classed as pebble mosaics, though they certainly point the way to change. Several other floors are borderline: they employ only pebbles, but some of these are cut to make them suitable for particular purposes. A tradition of laying undecorated floors in chips of stone and terracotta also existed in the 4th century BC, obviously a way of making use of waste material. 'Chip floors', as these are known, may have influenced the development of intermediate mosaic techniques. *Opus sectile*, in which compositions are built up from larger pieces of stone cut to shape, is a Roman development, but such pieces occur in some floors made up of mixed pebbles and tesserae. Such practices may derive partly from chip floors, as may also a type of floor laid in irregular and usually rather large tesserae (*see* §(c) below).

An example of a pebble floor in which cut stones were used for details is in the porch of the 5th-century BC Temple of Zeus at Olympia. This has now largely perished, but a corner showing this peculiarity survives *in situ*. A coin found underneath dates to after the mid-3rd century BC. Other floors elsewhere in Greece, often of poor quality, show the same mixture or a mix of pebbles and tesserae. They probably belong to the 3rd and 2nd centuries BC, but their dates are not fixed. One from Lebena in Crete (*c.* mid-3rd century BC) has an irregularly divided field, a larger rectangle framed in wave-crests with a hippocampus, and a narrower strip with two palmettes. The dark ground and the framing pattern are in pebbles, the palmettes and hippocampus in tesserae of marble and terracotta, some irregular and some regular.

Some scholars believe that there is no direct development from pebble mosaics to floors laid in regular tesserae. They suggest that figural floors in irregular tesserae were developed during the 3rd century BC, influencing some later pebble floors and encouraging the shaping of pebbles and mixing of techniques; the use of regular tesserae then developed only in the later 3rd century BC, virtually driving the other techniques out during the first half of the 2nd. This theory makes good sense and fits much of the evidence. However, there are other factors that point to a different conclusion.

Two well-known floors from ALEXANDRIA combine pebbles and regular tesserae. One, a fragment, is composed principally of pebbles; the other, an almost complete *andron* floor, is composed largely of marble, limestone and terracotta tesserae, both regular and irregular. The fragment is the left-hand edge of a floor, trimmed off on the right and completed by a broad band of tesserae at some later date in antiquity; within a border of animals a man is shown beside a leafless tree, moving violently to the left, his shield out behind him, thrusting back with a spear, perhaps in the act of hunting rather than fighting. The other floor shows *Three Erotes Hunting a Stag*, likewise within a frieze of animals (which has two leafless trees). The pose of the figure on the left wielding an axe resembles that of the spearman on the fragment. The second figure leans forward with a sword swung behind his head. These two figures are very similar in pose and action to the two hunters in the *Lion Hunt* at Pella. The third figure, largely lost, advances from the right with a spear. The picture is separated from the animal frieze by a narrow white band with a black ivy wreath; outside the frieze is a double guilloche and a narrow band of polychrome chequerboard. The last was also carried around the threshold, now largely lost, which had a frame of meander and bead and reel. The couch platform was made not of smooth plaster but of white tesserae. Lead strips were used in both floors for contours and details. In the fragment the background, figure and animals are almost entirely of unshaped pebbles, but the spear shaft and shield are in tesserae, which were also used alongside pebbles in the hair and in parts of the animals and background. The man's eye is a black pebble between two bits of shaped white stone, framed by a strip of lead. In the *andron* floor yellow pebbles were introduced alongside the tesserae for the Erotes' hair and for hair-tufts on some of the animals. The menagerie includes (besides the usual griffins, lions, panthers, boars, bull and deer) a hyena and a mythical monster in the form of a horned lion, like an Achaemenid Persian griffin without wings. The only other known appearance of this unusual monster is carved on a built tomb from Athens (Peiraeus, Archael. Mus.), dated to the later 4th century BC. The various dates suggested for these two mosaic floors range over the whole Hellenistic age, starting from the foundation of Alexandria in 332/1 BC.

(c) Tessera. No example of a floor in regular tessera is proven to be earlier than the late 3rd century BC, and there are few for which it is possible even to argue an earlier date. The date of the much damaged *Rape of Ganymede* from Morgantina, originally published as mid-3rd century BC, may be near the end of the century (*see* §(i) above). The finer of the two emblemata from Thmuis showing a bust of a woman wearing a headdress in the form of a ship's prow, now thought to portray Queen Berenike II, is rectangular and bears the signature *Sophilos epoiei.* It is framed in isometric meander and guilloche and, at the outer edge of the white floor, crenellation, while the other, a circular fragment, is framed in scale pattern. The mosaics were probably copied from a contemporary painted portrait of the Queen. Sophilos has been dated to just before *c.* 200 BC, the other *c.* 150 BC or later. Lead strips were used in the pattern border of the first and in the headdress. They occur regularly in pattern borders of later mosaics, but this seems to have been their last appearance in figural elements in tessera (unless the Alexandrian *Three Erotes Hunting a Stag* really is late). A third emblema from Thmuis (mid- or late 2nd century BC), framed in guilloche and isometric meander with leaden strips, shows an erotic group of a satyr and a maenad, close in composition to a similar group in a later mosaic floor from Pompeii.

Securely dated to the first half of the 2nd century BC are remains of important floors from Pergamon, found in two buildings identified as parts of a royal quarter erected by Eumenes II (*reg* 197–159 BC). In Palace IV only fragments from the floor of one big room, with patterns and garlands, were discovered, but in Palace V the layout and some details of floors in two rooms were preserved. One, with an altar opposite the door, was evidently a shrine. It had a white floor with two panels depicting theatrical masks flanking the altar, but only that on the left, with a tragic mask, is substantially preserved. Between these and the door was a broad rectangle with a lozenge pattern frame enclosing three long panels, the upper and lower with garlands, the central one divided into three emblemata, with a parrot in the largely preserved left-hand one. This disposition is unique, while that of the other room, perhaps an *andron*, is more usual. Along the walls of this large square room (8.5×8.5 m) was a broad band of white tesserae, probably for couches; in the centre of the mosaic is an emblema, now almost totally destroyed, within concentric squares of pattern band on a white ground: these are, from the centre, a double isometric meander, small black-and-white triangles, wave-crests between coloured strips, a leaf-scroll on a dark ground, with insects among the leaves and an occasional Eros, guilloche, a broader band (probably once containing figures) that was carefully and totally removed and, at the outer edge, a double crenellation between coloured strips. All that survives of the emblema is the remains of a myrtle-spray and, in the centre bottom, on a blue-grey ground, the vivid representation of a small cartellino with Hephaistion's signature.

Of the large body of Hellenistic floors on Delos, one is in *opus signinum* (an Italian technique using large, widely spaced fragments of different coloured stone or clay set in coloured plaster). This must have been done by an Italian craftsman or to the specifications of an Italian owner, but the rest of the mosaics adhere to Greek traditions. Tessera floors are subdivided into the ordinary *opus tessellatum* and the more refined *opus vermiculatum*, in which the small and closely set tesserae are used to achieve extremely subtle pictorial and colouristic effects. *Opus vermiculatum* was often employed for special detail in floors mainly of *opus tessellatum* (as two centuries earlier Gnosis had used tiny pebbles). Most of the well-preserved floors at Delos are from ground-floors, in which *opus tessellatum* prevails; but the fragments from lost upper storeys are often in fine *opus vermiculatum*. Some floors have overall geometric patterns; more common are concentric squares or rectangles of pattern bands on a white ground with a framed emblema in the middle. Both the emblema and the threshold may have either geometric or floral patterns or a figural representation. Some unusual designs are found. On one *andron* floor from the House of the Masks a large rectangular pattern frame on a white ground encloses a square emblema with *Dionysos Riding a (?)Cheetah*, flanked by two lozenge-shaped emblemata with centaurs (a layout faintly reminiscent of that of the altar room at Pergamon). The central emblema, in a Hellenistic 'baroque' style, is highly pictorial in treatment. The house was named after another unusual mosaic floor with an overall decoration of *trompe l'oeil* cubes and a garland hung with theatre masks down each side.

One of the finest of the Delian floors is that signed by (Askle)piades. The square floor is in the courtyard, surrounded by the colonnade, and has a single overall design consisting of a large circle reaching almost to the square of black crenellation at the outer edges. The circle within a square design, so popular in pebble mosaics, is not found elsewhere in regular tessera and only once in irregular tessera at Maroneia in Thrace (mid- to second half of the 3rd century BC). Unlike earlier Floral style pebble mosaics, in which the whole circle is filled with an intricate floral motif, (Askle)piades' mosaic has a series of separate pattern circles of great variety and complexity, with the floral motif at the centre. One of the circles has horned griffin heads and horned lion heads rising from calyces of leaves set on an arcade pattern. Animal ornament of this kind is extremely rare in Greek art, but there is a curiously close parallel on an Orientalizing Cretan vase of the 7th century BC (Herakleion, Archaeol. Mus.). Each of the corners of the mosaic has a pair of dolphins, one ridden by an Eros who leads the other on a rein, exquisitely rendered in *opus vermiculatum*—a new and enchanting invention, very much of the Hellenistic age. The outer border of crenellation resembles that of earlier tessellated floors at Alexandria and Pergamon. Thus the floor demonstrates the interplay between tradition and invention in Greek mosaics at this time. The conventional colouring, disposition and treatment of the figures in some works, such as an emblema on a dark ground with a tritoness carrying a rudder and an Eros flying above, suggests deliberate imitation of the pebble mosaic tradition. Elements in other floors at Delos, as well as at Pergamon and Alexandria, seem to anticipate developments at Pompeii and the beginning of the great Roman tradition of mosaic.

J. Overbeck: *Die antiken Schriftquellen zur Geschichte der bildenden Künste bei den Griechen* (Leipzig, 1868/*R* Hildesheim, 1959)

G. Kawerau and T. Wiegand: *Die Paläste vom Hochburg* (1930), V/i of *Altertümer von Pergamon* (Berlin, 1885–)

B. Brown: *Ptolemaic Paintings and Mosaics and the Alexandrian Style* (Cambridge, MA, 1957)

K. M. Phillips jr: 'Subject and Technique in Hellenistic and Roman Mosaics from Sicily', *A. Bull.*, xlii (1960), pp. 244–62

M. Robertson: 'Greek Mosaics', *J. Hell. Stud.*, lxxxv (1965), pp. 72–89

M. Robertson: 'Greek Mosaics: A Postscript', *J. Hell. Stud.*, lxxxvii (1967), pp. 133–6

P. Bruneau: 'Prolongement de la technique des mosaïques de galets en Grèce', *Bull. Corr. Hell.*, xciii (1969), pp. 308–32

P. Bruneau: *Les Mosaïques*, Explor. Archéol. Délos (Paris, 1972)

K. M. Dunbabin: 'Technique and Materials of Hellenistic Mosaics', *Amer. J. Archaeol.*, lxxxiii (1979), pp. 265–77

M. Robertson: 'Early Greek Mosaic', *Macedonia and Greece in Late Classical and Early Hellenistic Times*, ed. B. Barr-Sharrar and E. N. Borza, Stud. Hist. A., x (Washington, DC, 1982), pp. 241–50

D. Salzmann: *Untersuchungen zu den Kieselmosaiken* (Berlin, 1982)

W. A. Daszewski: *Hellenistic and Early Roman Period* (1985), i of *Corpus of Mosaics from Egypt* (Mainz, 1985–)

K. M. D. Dunbabin: *Mosaics of the Greek and Roman World* (Cambridge, 1999)

III. Roman.

Floor mosaic (*opus tessellatum*) and wall and vault mosaic (*opus musivum*) were two distinct arts in ancient Rome and were practised by different, specialist craftsmen. Diocletian's *Edict on Prices* (AD 301) stipulates a higher rate of pay for wall mosaicists (*musearii*) than for floor mosaicists (*tessellarii*), which may reflect the former's more difficult working conditions: an inscription (*Corp. Inscr. Lat.*, ix, 6281) tells of a young mosaicist who fell to his death while working on a mosaic. There are also differences of style and technique between the two crafts. Floor mosaics had to be laid pefectly flat and the tesserae were mainly of durable natural stone, such as marble and limestone, while vault mosaics could be laid unevenly or with the tesserae angled to catch the light, and more delicate materials, such as shells, glass and pumice, could be used. Floor mosaics were often black and white and based on linear patterns, though many were also figural, whereas wall and vault mosaics were more closely related to wall painting in their consistent preference for polychromy, figural scenes and pictorial effects. Floor mosaics became rather neutral in character by the end of the Roman Empire, since with the beginning of the Early Christian period there was a growing feeling that it was wrong to walk on sacred images. Soon the main pictorial religious mosaic cycles were reserved for walls and vaults, and were executed solely by *musearii*. This may explain why the word 'mosaic', derived from *opus musivum*, remained in common use in medieval Latin (instead of a word derived from *tessellatum*) and is now used to denote both wall and floor mosaic, and more commonly the latter.

1. Floor.

(i) Forms, techniques and craftsmen. The use of mosaics for floors was adopted by the Romans from the Hellenistic Greek world (*see* §II above). They first appeared in two distinct forms, the earlier one being ornamental pavements of *opus signinum* and related techniques (3rd century BC; derived from Sicily and South Italy); the pavements are of mortar and aggregate, the latter predominantly ceramic. Fairly large tesserae or other coloured materials set in mortar emphasize the surface, drawing their effects from the colours and contrasts in the materials or from simple two-dimensional patterns. Mosaics of the other form, which appeared in the late 2nd century BC, are polychrome, consisting of small tesserae, and resemble those of Delos, Pergamon and other Hellenistic centres. These latter, if figured, aimed to imitate the effects of painting, using a wide range of shades; they are usually composed as emblemata, small central rectangular panels manufactured separately and inserted to produce 'pictures in the floor'; even the geometric designs are often three-dimensional in effect. Much of the subsequent history of Roman mosaics describes the reconciliation of these two traditions: the abandonment of the concept of the picture in the floor, and the introduction of new methods of treating the floor as a two dimensional surface to be decorated, while retaining the rich repertory of the Hellenistic tradition. This development took place at different rates in different parts of the Empire, depending on the relative strength of the Hellenistic tradition, as well as on economic considerations, such as the nature of

the materials available. The various solutions include Black-and-white style mosaics, characteristic of Rome and Italy; widespread compartmented compositions, where the floor is divided into a series of geometric compartments, each containing separate motifs, ornamental or figural; all-over polychrome figural scenes, developed particularly in North Africa, but found over a wide area in the late Empire; and both floral and figural carpet designs.

Opus sectile, a technique related to mosaic that involves cutting pieces of coloured stone to the shape of specific parts of a pattern and setting them accordingly, appeared at Rome and Pompeii by *c.* 100 BC, and the increasing availability of coloured marbles encouraged its popularity under Augustus; it became the preferred type of pavement for the most luxurious or grandest settings and continued in that function throughout the period of the Empire, although it was comparatively rare outside Italy. A wide range of coloured marble was used, as well as purple and green porphyry, limestone, slate and occasionally glass. In the most common type pieces were cut into simple geometric forms (triangles, rectangles, hexagons, lozenges or circles) and fitted together in a design often based on the repetition of prefabricated elements. Guidobaldi (1981–3) distinguished three different types according to the size of this basic module. More complex designs including floral and vegetal elements, or motifs such as the pelta (semicircular shield), may be combined with these, as in the remains of Nero's Domus Transitoria on the Palatine in Rome, numerous pavements of Hadrian's Villa at Tibur (Tivoli), the Diocletianic floor of the Curia Senatus in Rome or the House of Cupid and Psyche at Ostia.

Ancient sources provide scant information about floor mosaics. Pliny the elder (*Natural History* XXXVI.184–9) mentioned briefly the origins of mosaics and other types of pavements, and their introduction to the Roman world, though his technical terms are difficult to interpret. Vitruvius (*On Architecture* VII.i.3–4) gave directions for laying the foundations of various types of pavement. Other ancient sources mention mosaics only in passing, usually as an example of luxury. Inscriptions, often on the mosaics themselves, provide technical terms in Greek and Latin and give some information about the men who commissioned or laid them, and occasionally about the procedures followed.

Vitruvius' instructions for laying the foundations of pavements (VII. i. 3–4) prescribe successive layers of mortar of different fineness above a rubble foundation. Practice broadly followed these directions, but the number of layers and the composition of the mortar varied. Tesserae were cut from every variety of marble and natural stone, predominantly from those available locally; further colours were sometimes added from glass paste and terracotta; other materials were seldom used. Tesserae vary widely in size, from 1 mm square or less in the finest technique, the so-called '*opus vermiculatum*' (from Lat. *vermiculus*: 'worm'), to over 20 mm in coarse pavements; the average size is halfway between the two. Mosaicists gradually used larger tesserae in looser settings, and tesserae of different sizes were sometimes used within the same pavement to set off different figures or features.

Emblemata were prepared separately in the craftsman's workshop and could be exported overseas. *Opus sectile* pavements were often prefabricated, but most other types must have been laid on the spot. A few examples have been found in excavations of guidelines or simple *sinopie* painted or incised on the mortar beneath the tesserae, or of traces of the preparatory work, such as marble chippings (e.g. those found at Neapolis (now Nabeul, Tunisia)).

No names of mosaicists of the Roman period are recorded in literary sources. A few dozen signatures, in both Greek and Latin, are preserved on the mosaics themselves, not always on those of the highest quality; they do not allow any distinct artistic personalities to be identified. Several signatures use the formula 'From the workshop of . . .', or mention the collaboration of more than one man; there is occasional mention of a separate draughtsman who prepared a cartoon on which the mosaic was based, but there is insufficient evidence to show if this was normal procedure. Characteristics of style and subject-matter have permitted identification of workshops (or at least groups of workshops) in, for example, Britain, the Rhône Valley and Tunisia. But individual figures or groups of figures were often repeated with little variation over long periods of time and huge distances, and are evidently based on stock motifs; it is disputed whether these motifs were derived from circulating copybooks, or simply from the basic training and visual memory of the craftsmen. The extent to which the mosaicists themselves travelled is also disputed.

(ii) Subject-matter and setting. Fine mosaic was at first a luxury item, confined to the wealthiest houses, though the more practical decorated pavements are more widespread. Cheaper methods of production led to mosaic pavements such as those in the Black-and-white style becoming common in domestic contexts in Italy from the Augustan period onwards. They spread throughout the Empire over the next 200 years and were used extensively in public buildings such as baths, where they adapted well to the demands of the architecture, although *opus sectile* was preferred in the grandest buildings. Mosaics are seldom found in temples, but occasionally in the places of worship of other cults, such as Mithraea; in the 4th century AD they came to be used widely in Christian churches and baptisteries and in Jewish synagogues. Tombs, both pagan and Christian, may be completely paved with mosaic, or a panel of mosaic may be placed only over the actual burial, or a mosaic-covered sarcophagus may in rare instances project above the ground; the latter types are characteristic of Christian tombs in North Africa. The function of a building or a room was sometimes

indicated on the mosaic either through the subject-matter or through the layout of the design (e.g. in dining-rooms and bedrooms different designs were sometimes used for different portions of the room). A few mosaics from dining-rooms represent illusionistically the debris of a meal as if lying on the floor, in imitation of the famous *asarotos oikos* or 'unswept room' of the Hellenistic Sosos of Pergamon (Pliny the elder, *Natural History* xxxvi.184), for example that in the ex-Lateran Collection (probably early 2nd century AD; Rome, Vatican, Mus. Gregoriano Profano).

The vast majority of extant Roman floor mosaics are geometric and ornamental rather than figured. The geometric repertory is rich and varied; certain motifs (e.g. meander, guilloche) never went out of use, though most developed unevenly at different periods and in different regions, thus serving as criteria for both dating a mosaic (often more reliable than the style of the figures) and identifying regional workshops. Geometric designs were used as borders, as all-over compositions, or as filling motifs within the compartments of a geometric framework. Floral and vegetal designs were used in the same three ways, for example as border patterns such as scrolls or laurel wreaths, as all-over floral carpets and as individual rosettes.

The figure repertory was also extensive. Greek mythology provided a large number of scenes, some derived from famous Greek paintings, but most later mosaics used stock motifs. Literary and theatrical subjects such as portraits of authors, possibly derived from manuscript illumination, were popular in the Greek-speaking eastern Mediterranean. Subjects from Roman myth and literature are much less common and are confined to the most obvious, such as *Romulus and Remus* from Aldborough, N. Yorks (4th century AD; Leeds, City Mus.), the portrait of *Virgil with Two Muses* from Hadrumetum (Sousse) in Tunisia (probably 3rd century AD; Tunis, Mus. N. Bardo) and *Dido and Aeneas* at Low Ham, England (4th century AD; Taunton, Somerset Co. Mus.); historical subjects are rare. Scenes of contemporary life most often reflect the interests of the class of patrons who commissioned them: hunting, circus and amphitheatre scenes, life on the country estate. Personifications of the seasons are common, while illustrations of seasonal activities and cycles of the months are occasionally found, e.g. those from Saint Romain en Gal (probably first quarter of 3rd century AD; Saint-Germain-en-Laye, Mus. Ant. N.). Complex allegories and personifications occurred most often in the eastern Empire, perhaps reflecting current philosophical preoccupations. A fashion for Nilotic landscapes started with the Egyptomania of the late 2nd century to the 1st century BC (e.g. Praeneste), but continued with little reference to real Egyptian prototypes. Marine subjects, such as nereids, sea-monsters, fish and boats, were always popular, especially in baths; so also were displays of animals and birds. Commonly depicted traditional deities were Dionysus, Neptune and Venus, while some designs were inspired by astrology. Oriental and local provincial religions had little impact, except in Mithraea, which at Ostia were decorated with cult symbols; a few floors were presumably directly connected with the practice of mystery cults, for example the mosaic from the Kornmarkt in Trier (late 4th century AD; Trier, Rhein. Landesmus.). Biblical subjects occurred occasionally in Christian churches (e.g. the story of *Jonah* in Aquileia Cathedral; early 4th century AD), though more neutral or symbolic decoration was normally preferred; synagogues were decorated with symbolic designs, including the zodiac, and a few biblical subjects (e.g. Gaza, *King David*, probably 6th century AD; fragments in Jerusalem, Rockefeller Mus.).

Mosaic floors were also used for apotropaic purposes, to exclude dangerous influences or hostile forces from a building. Thus the Evil Eye is depicted at Rome (2nd century AD) in the Basilica Hilariana and in the vestibule of a house at Jekmejeh near Antioch (early 2nd century AD; Antakya, Hatay Mus.); Phthonos (Envy) torn by wild beasts is depicted on the Greek island of Kephallinia (probably 3rd century AD; *in situ*). Phallic symbols were frequently apotropaic, and motifs such as the gorgoneion probably served the same function; more positive good luck signs included a wide range of plants (palm, ivy, millet). Finally, mosaic was frequently used for inscriptions. These may identify figures or scenes, or contain a message independent of the rest of the decoration; often they record the dedication of the building or the accomplishment of its decoration.

(iii) History and development. The stylistic development of Roman mosaics reflects the general trend in Roman art away from the naturalistic canons of the Classical tradition towards greater abstraction and simplification. As with changes in form and technique, the speed of this development varied in different regions; in general, between the 2nd and the 4th centuries AD there was less interest in the correct depiction of anatomy and in the modelling of figures; more linear effects, heavily dependent on outline and on the contrast of a limited range of colours, were substituted for fine 'painterly' shading; features were treated in an expressive manner, often with exaggeratedly large eyes; decorative schematization replaced realistic treatment of drapery and of floral and vegetal elements; three-dimensional space and perspective were abandoned. In all these ways the mosaic medium was exploited for its own potential rather than as a substitute for painting, thus preparing the way for the great achievements of Early Christian and Byzantine mosaics.

(a) Italy. The earliest decorated pavement found in Rome (late 3rd century BC) is of *opus signinum*; pavements in various forms of this technique were common throughout the late Republic, and continued under the Principate for more utilitarian functions. Tessellated floors with geometric designs, both polychrome and black and white, were in use by the late Republic (e.g. House of the Griffins at Rome,

c. 90 BC), as were *opus sectile* floors of limestone. Emblemata in '*opus vermiculatum*' and other fine figural mosaics in the Hellenistic tradition were certainly established in Campania by *c.* 100 BC (e.g. House of the Faun at Pompeii); the Nilotic and Fish mosaics at Praeneste were probably made around the same date. The emblemata at Pompeii date predominantly from the 1st century BC, when these pictorial mosaics were most fashionable. During the same period polychrome geometric mosaics often showed three-dimensional patterns such as the perspective meander and trellis (e.g. Villa of Volusii at Lucus Feroniae nr Rome), or patterns of coffers (e.g. Lion mosaic, Teramo). Black-and-white two-dimensional geometric designs also appeared in the 1st century BC, probably as a cheaper substitute for polychrome. At first they took the form of small panels at the centre of the room or on thresholds, which were increasingly replaced by all-over designs.

In the Augustan period polychrome mosaics almost disappeared, expelled partly by the growing fashion for *opus sectile* in the richest settings, partly by the increased use of pictorial panels in wall painting. The Black-and-white style became the dominant mosaic type and remained so in Italy until the 3rd century AD. Patterns were comparatively austere in the 1st century AD, but became more complex, with a steady increase in the range of ornamental motifs. Fine floral and curvilinear arabesques are especially characteristic of the Floral style in the time of Hadrian, as, for example, in the guest quarters of Hadrian's Villa at Tibur (Tivoli) and in the House of Bacchus and Ariadne at Ostia. Under the Severans (*reg* AD 193–235) the contrast of black and white had become heavier, and patterns tended to be overloaded with ornament.

A few figures were introduced into the Black-and-white style before the end of the 1st century BC (e.g. House of the Menander at Pompeii); by the mid-1st century AD the Silhouette style had emerged (e.g. Forum Baths at HERCULANEUM; Baths of Via dei Vigili at Ostia). The figures are in black silhouette with white interior detail; the floor is treated as a two-dimensional surface, without suggestion of depth; background and setting are minimal or non-existent. Figures or groups may be isolated in compartments of a geometric pattern or spread freely over the surface. Numerous different viewpoints are frequently offered, with figures facing different sides of the room, adapting themselves to the requirements of the architecture. Such pavements are characteristic of great public buildings such as baths, and are seen at their best at Ostia (e.g. Baths of Neptune). In the 3rd century AD the Black-and-white style became much more schematic, with less concern for anatomical accuracy, and often with densely crowded compositions; it virtually disappeared in the 4th century AD.

The Black-and-white style never completely replaced polychromy, and emblemata continued to be produced. Some or all of those in Hadrian's Villa at Tibur may have been Hellenistic works reused; but the numerous emblemata from the Roman villa at Baccano near Rome (Rome, Mus. N. Romano) probably date to the late 2nd century AD to the early 3rd, and others are found as late as the 4th century. They are normally much coarser in technique and use larger tesserae than Hellenistic emblemata, and some may have been intended for use on walls, not floors. A general revival of polychromy took place under the Antonines (*reg* AD 138–93), with both ornamental and figural all-over designs. These no longer aimed at a three-dimensional effect, or attempted to reproduce a single scene in its setting. Usually the figures are distributed within the compartments of a geometric design; occasionally the free composition of black-and-white mosaics is imitated in colour (e.g. marine pavement from Baccano; Rome, Mus. N. Romano). In the late 3rd century AD to the 4th this trend prevailed, under the influence of fashions in other parts of the western Empire, especially North Africa. Many Italian mosaics of this period show large, all-over figural scenes, often with subjects from the hunting field or amphitheatre (e.g. the hunting pavement from the Esquiline, Rome (formerly in Antiquarium Comunale, Rome); scenes of gladiatorial combat from Torrenuova, near Rome (Rome, Gal. Borghese)).

(b) Western provinces. From the 1st century AD the use of mosaics and decorated pavements spread from Rome and Italy through the western provinces. The direct influence of migrant Italian craftsmen is attested by the adoption of the Black-and-white style (e.g. at Fishbourne in W. Sussex, England), but the regions rapidly developed their individual local styles, with Black-and-white giving way almost everywhere to polychromy. In Gaul pavements of the compartmented type were common; the region of Vienna (Vienne) and the Rhône Valley is noted for pavements of the 'Multiple Décor' style, in which a wide range of ornamental motifs is distributed through the compartments of an all-over grid, sometimes with a central figured panel. Another important workshop was centred in Lugdunum (Lyon), and the villas of Aquitaine continued the use of mosaics into the 5th century AD, with a range of ornamental floral and vegetal motifs peculiar to them. Mosaics in the German and Alpine provinces developed in similar ways to those of Gaul; both Augusta Treverorum (Trier) and Colonia Claudia Ara Agrippinensium (Cologne) were important centres. In Britain several workshops have been distinguished on the basis of their repertory of ornamental patterns and methods of composition; in the 2nd century AD mosaics occurred principally in towns, such as Verulamium (St Albans), and in the 4th century in country villas. Characteristic of the latter are the pavements depicting *Orpheus Charming the Animals with his Music* from the region of Corinium (Cirencester, Corinium Mus.); on these the beasts are arranged around Orpheus in concentric rings, as at Woodchester, Glos (*in situ*).

In the Iberian Peninsula mosaics were at first produced under strong Italian influence; pavements in black and white or four colours (black, white, red, yellow) were common. To these was added influence from Gaul, and in the 4th century AD from North Africa; occasionally also from the East. In Italica near Seville several rich houses had mosaics from the 2nd century AD onwards; distinctive geometric and figural designs have been found at Conimbriga in Portugal. Unique in the western Empire is the cosmological mosaic in the House of the Mithraeum at Augusta Emerita (Mérida), a huge panel with personifications of the sky, sea and other cosmic forces. Numerous villas from the late Empire have mosaics, with both realistic scenes (e.g. hunting, circus) and a wide range of mythological subjects.

In North Africa, Punic Carthage had its own tradition of decorated pavements—mortar mixed with multicoloured stones and potsherds and set with tesserae in simple designs—which must have influenced the *signinum* pavements of Sicily and Italy. After the Roman conquest a few pavements of Italian type appeared, but not until the 2nd century AD did the African mosaic workshops develop fully. In Tripolitania (now in Libya) fine polychrome mosaics have been found near Leptis Magna, at Zliten (Tripoli, Archaeol. Mus.) and at Silin (*in situ*); in the proconsular province of Africa (now in Tunisia) the main centres were Carthage, Hadrumetum (Sousse) and Thysdrus (El Djem); in Mauretania (now in Algeria) it was Caesarea (Cherchel). From there mosaic spread throughout the African provinces; by the late 2nd century AD it was used even in small towns. Large quantities have been found in Tunisia at Thuburbo Maius (now Henchir Kasbat), Bulla Regia and Utica; in Algeria at Thamugadi (now Timgad) and Cuicul (now Djemila); and in Morocco at Volubilis. The North African style is marked by strong polychromy, using the local marbles and limestones; by inventive handling of geometric and floral patterns, for instance in the floral carpet mosaics of Thamugadi; and by a free approach to the composition of figural scenes, breaking away from the single-viewpoint scene and the three-dimensional treatment of space. Figures here are spread over the surface in a way resembling the Black-and-white style mosaics of Italy, but often with a schematic landscape setting. Also characteristic is the expanded repertory of figures. Although mythological scenes were still produced, for example in the House of the Nymphs at Neapolis (Nabeul), scenes from contemporary life became much more popular, especially the hunting field, for example in the House of Isguntus at Hippo Regius (now Annaba in Algeria); the amphitheatre (Zliten (Tripoli, Archaeol. Mus.), Carthage and Thysdrus) and circus (Silin (*in situ*), Carthage (Tunis, Mus. N. Bardo)); and rural activities, such as in a mosaic from Caesarea depicting the labours of the fields. The deities most commonly represented were Dionysus, Venus and the mask of Ocean. In the 4th century AD the style and subject-matter introduced by the North African workshops became widespread throughout the western Mediterranean. A direct North African influence, probably through immigrant craftsmen from Carthage, is to be seen in Sicily, especially in the Piazza Armerina Villa and the Tellaro Villa, and in Sardinia. The influence was less direct in mainland Italy and Spain.

(*c*) *Eastern provinces.* The eastern provinces retained the tradition of polychrome pictorial mosaics much longer than the West, though direct continuity with Hellenistic mosaics is not documented. Little material is datable from before AD 100 except in Palestine, where mosaics from the period of Herod the Great (*reg* 37–4 BC) show a mixture of Hellenistic and Italian characteristics. Some influence from Italy is to be seen in Greece and Asia Minor alongside the more conservative tradition, especially the use of black-and-white mosaics and compartmented compositions. Subject-matter here ranges from traditional mythological scenes to scenes of athletes (e.g. Patras, Archaeol. Mus.) and the amphitheatre (e.g. Kos, *in situ*; probably 3rd century AD). Literary themes include portraits of poets and philosophers (e.g. at Sparta and Seleucia in Pamphylia, Turkey); on the island of Mytilene a portrait of Menander (probably second half of 3rd century AD) was accompanied by a series of scenes from his comedies. A rich series of mosaics on Cyprus includes gladiatorial scenes at Kourion (probably second half of 3rd century AD; *in situ*); the House of Dionysos at New Paphos (probably late 2nd century AD), with some unusual mythological scenes (e.g. Dionysos, Ikarios and 'the first wine-drinkers'); and the so-called Palace of Theseus at New Paphos. Influences from both East and West may be seen here, while much closer to Syrian productions are the mythological scenes of the late 4th century AD from the House of Aion at New Paphos, with a mass of personifications identified by name.

In Syria and the Near East an unbroken sequence runs from *c.* AD 100 to the 6th and 7th centuries; the principal sites are ANTIOCH (i) and APAMEIA. Mosaics here are characterized by pictorial polychrome compositions set in one or more panels resembling over-large emblemata; subject-matter is taken mainly from the traditional mythological repertory, although sometimes favouring stories with a local reference, such as Cassiopeia and the Nereids, from Apameia (*c.* AD 350–*c.* 375; Apameia, Archaeol. Mus.); derivation from famous Greek prototypes is sometimes demonstrable. Geometric designs were more limited in range than in the West, though often of striking polychromy. From the 3rd century AD onwards there was a taste for complex allegorical subjects, the figures often identified by name; most remarkable is the mosaic showing Aion (Time) and the Seasons with other personifications from Philippopolis (Shahba') in Syria, whence comes also a series of traditional scenes from Classical mythology (Marine Venus, Diana and Actaeon). Characteristics of the Late Antique style, such as the loss of interest in depth, perspective and realistic anatomy, appeared in the 4th century AD, but compositions in single panels continued, now often enlarged to occupy most of the room. Mythological scenes remained popular; philosophical interpretations sometimes dictated the choice of subjects, such as the mosaic of Cassiopeia and the Nereids from Apameia. An exceptional work with a subject from contemporary life is the mosaic depicting musicians from Mariamin (late 4th century AD; Hama, Mus. Hama). In the 5th century AD allover compositions were predominant. Geometric décor became richer and more complex, and was used especially to decorate the growing number of Christian churches; the 'Rainbow' style uses strong contrasts of colour and materials. Hunting and animal themes were popular and were often treated as two-dimensional figured carpets, as in a mosaic from Apameia (Brussels, Mus. Royaux A. & Hist). Highly stylized floral and vegetal designs cover entire floors, with semis (scatter designs of small motifs over plain surfaces) and trellises of florets or rosettes, perhaps inspired by textiles.

The use of mosaics spread to the Roman frontiers and even beyond. Those from Palmyra conform to the general pattern of the eastern provinces, but the 3rd-century AD funerary mosaics from Edessa (now Urfa) in Turkey owe nothing but their technique to the Greco-Roman tradition and belong stylistically to the funerary art of Parthia and the East. The palace of the Sasanian King Shapur I (*reg* AD 241–72) at Bishapur was decorated after AD 260 with mosaics, probably the work of captive craftsmen from Antioch. Geometric motifs and ornamental details belong to the Greco-Roman world, but the figural scenes of dancers and harpists are purely Iranian.

M. E. Blake: 'The Pavements of Roman Buildings of the Republic and Early Empire', *Mem. Amer. Acad. Rome*, viii (1930), pp. 7–160

M. E. Blake: 'Roman Mosaics of the Second Century in Italy', *Mem. Amer. Acad. Rome*, xiii (1936), pp. 67–214

E. Pernice: *Pavimente und figürliche Mosaiken* (Berlin, 1938–41), vi of *Die hellenistische Kunst in Pompeji*

M. E. Blake: 'Mosaics of the Late Empire in Rome and Vicinity', *Mem. Amer. Acad. Rome*, xvii (1940), pp. 81–130

D. Levi: *Antioch Mosaic Pavements* (Princeton, 1947/*R* 1971)

Recueil général des mosaïques de la Gaule, suppl. 10 of *Gallia* (Paris, 1957–)

K. Parlasca: *Die römischen Mosaiken in Deutschland* (Berlin, 1959)

V. von Gonzenbach: *Die römischen Mosaiken der Schweiz* (Basle, 1961)

I. Lavin: 'The Hunting Mosaics of Antioch and their Sources', *Dumbarton Oaks Pap.*, xvii (1963), pp. 179–286

La Mosaïque gréco-romaine: Colloques internationaux du Centre National de la Recherche Scientifique: Paris, 1963 (Paris, 1965)

G. Becatti: *Mosaici e pavimenti marmorei* (1967), iv of *Scavi di Ostia* (Rome, 1953–79)

Mosaici antichi in Italia, Istituto Poligrafico dello Stato (Rome, 1967–)

G. Becatti: *Edificio con opus sectile fuori Porta Marina* (1969), vi of *Scavi di Ostia* (Rome, 1953–79)

S. Germain: *Les Mosaïques de Timgad* (Paris, 1969)

D. J. Smith: 'The Mosaic Pavements', *The Roman Villa in Britain*, ed. A. L. F. Rivet (London, 1969), pp. 71–125

Corpus des mosaïques de Tunisie (Tunis, 1973–)

La Mosaïque gréco-romaine II, IIe colloque international pour l'étude de la mosaïque antique: Vienne, 1971 (Paris, 1975)

J. Balty: *Mosaïques antiques de Syrie* (Brussels, 1977)

K. M. D. Dunbabin: *The Mosaics of Roman North Africa* (Oxford, 1978)

Corpus de mosaicos de España (Madrid, 1978–)

J. Clarke: *Roman Black and White Figural Mosaics* (New York, 1979)

III colloquio internazionale sul mosaico antico: Ravenna, 1980

J. Balty: 'La Mosaïque antique au Proche-Orient, i: Des origines à la Tétrarchie', *Aufstieg und Niedergang der römischen Welt*, II/xii/2 (Berlin, 1981), pp. 347–429

P. Bruneau: 'Tendances de la mosaïque en Grèce à l'époque impériale', *Aufstieg und Niedergang der römischen Welt*, II/xii/2 (Berlin, 1981), pp. 320–46

F. Guidobaldi: 'Pavimenti in *opus sectile* di Roma e dell'area romana: Proposte per una classificazione e criteri di datazione', *Marmi antichi*, ed. P. Pensabene, *Stud. Misc.*, xxvi (1981–3), pp. 171–233

A. Carandini, A. Ricci and M. de Vos: *Filosofiana: The Villa of Piazza Armerina* (Palermo, 1982)

La Mosaïque gréco-romaine IV, IVe colloque international pour l'étude de la mosaïque antique: Trèves, 1984

C. Balmelle and others: *Le Décor géométrique de la mosaïque romaine* (Paris, 1985)

Fifth International Colloquium on Ancient Mosaics: Bath, 1987

M. Dondere: *Die Mosaizisten der Antike und ihre wirtschaftliche und soziale Stellung* (Erlangen, 1989)

C. Kondoleon: *Domestic and Divine: Roman Mosaics in the House of Dionysus* (Ithaca, 1994)

VI Colloquio Internacional sobre Mosaico antiguo, Palencia-Mérida 1990 (Guadalajara, 1994)

J. Balty: *Mosaïques antiques du Proche-Orient: Chronologie, iconographie, interprétation* (Besançon, 1995)

M. Blanchard-Lemée and others: *Mosaics of Roman Africa: Floor Mosaics from Tunisia* (New York, 1996)

A. Cohen: *The Alexander Mosaic: Stories of Victory and Defeat* (Cambridge, 1997/*R* 2000)

S. H. Auth: 'Mosaic Glass Mask Plaques and the Ancient Theater', *J. Glass Stud.*, xli (1999), pp. 51–72

K. M. D. Dunbabin: *Mosaics of the Greek and Roman World* (Cambridge, 1999)

C. Cicirelli and M. P. Guidobaldi: *Pavimenti e mosaici nella Villa dei misteri di Pompei* (Naples, 2000)

J. Cull: *Roman Woodchester: Its Villa and Mosaic* (Andover, 2000)

S. Scott: *Art and Society in Fourth-century Britain: Villa Mosaics in Context* (Oxford, 2000)

R. Jacoby: 'The Four Seasons in Zodiac Mosaics: The Tallaras Baths in Astypalaea, Greece', *Is. Explor. J.*, li/2 (2001), pp. 225–30

P. Moreno: *Apelles: The Alexander Mosaic* (Milan, 2001)

A. Zettler: *Offerenteninschriften auf den frühchristlichen Mosaikfussböden Venetiens und Istriens* (Berlin, 2001)

R. Amedick: 'Die Schone, das Seeungeheuer und der Held: Antike Bildbeschreibungen und die Ikonographie mythologischer Bilder', *Ant. Welt,* xxxiii/5 (2002), pp. 527–38

D. S. Neal and S. R. Cosh: *Roman Mosaics of Britain* (London, 2002–)

P. C. Baum-vom Felde: *Die geometrischen Mosaiken der Villa bei Piazza Armerina: Analyse und Werkstattfrage* (Hamburg, 2003)

A. B. A. Ben Khader, E. de Balanda and A. Uribe Echeverría, eds: *Image de Pierre: La Tunisie en mosaïque* (Paris, 2003)

A. Kankeleit: 'Fisch und Fischer: Mosaikbilder in Griechenland', *Ant. Welt*, xxxiv/3 (2003), pp. 273–8
S. Tebby: *Geometric Design in Roman Tessellated Pavements: Comparative Analytical Drawings* (Lutterworth, 2003)
La mosaïque gréco-romaine IX: Actes du IXe Colloque international pour l'étude de la mosaïque antique et médiévale: Rome, 2001
L. Becker and C. Kondoleon: *The Arts of Antioch: Art Historical and Scientific Approaches to Roman Mosaics and a Catalogue of the Worcester Art Museum Antioch Collection* (Worcester, 2005)
E. Bleiberg: *Tree of Paradise: Jewish Mosaics from the Roman Empire* (Brooklyn, 2005)
L. M. De Matteis: *Mosaici di Cos: Dagli scavi delle missioni italiane e tedesche, 1900–1945* (Athens, 2005)
P. Witts: *Mosaics in Roman Britain: Stories in Stone* (Stroud, 2005)
F. Zevi and others: 'Nature and History, Comedy and Tragedy', *F.M.R. Mag.*, x (Dec 2005–Jan 2006), pp. 1–26
A. B. A. Ben Khader: *Stories in Stone: Conserving Mosaics of Roman Africa: Masterpieces from the National Museums of Tunisia* (Los Angeles, 2006)
A. B. A. Ben Khader: *Tunisian Mosaics: Treasures from Roman Africa* (Los Angeles, 2006)
V. Vassal: *Les pavements d'opus signinum: Technique, décor, fonction architecturale* (Oxford, 2006)

2. Wall and vault.

(i) Italy. (ii) Provinces.

(i) Italy.

(a) Antecedents: 1st century BC*–mid-1st century* AD. *Opus musivum* developed from the shell and pumice decoration applied to nymphaea (sometimes called *musaea*), the artificial grottoes that became fashionable in the large villas of the late Roman Republic (1st century BC). The nymphaea were either semicircular in shape or rectangular barrel-vaulted rooms with a recess or semicircular apse at one end. The latter type was often incorporated into the undercrofting of a terraced villa, such as that under the Villa of Cicero at Formia (*c.* 100–*c.* 50 BC); it is covered with a coved vault supported by four columns inlaid with shells, and at one end is a barrel-vaulted recess containing a fountain. The walls are covered with pumice outlined by rows of shells to imitate ashlar masonry. The barrel vault has an elaborate coffered design done entirely in shells, marble chips and pellets of Egyptian blue, a pigment used in wall painting and shell incrustations. Pellets of Egyptian blue were used in the nymphaeum of the Villa of Horace at Tibur (Tivoli; *c.* 50–*c.* 40 BC) to create a simple ribbon pattern against a background of white marble chips.

Another method of adding colour was to paint the plaster ground into which the shells and marble chips were inserted, as in a late Republican nymphaeum at Tibur (later occupied by Hadrian's Villa), where the background plaster is painted red, green and blue. On the same site is a Republican cryptoporticus with an elaborate coffered vault decorated with shells, Egyptian blue and marble chips; the plaster ground is painted red, blue and green, with swags, garlands and birds in Egyptian blue.

The last stage in the transition from shell incrustation to true mosaic is marked by the addition of pieces of coloured glass, probably as a result of Augustus' establishment of glass factories in Italy in 27 BC. Pliny the elder (*Natural History* XXXVI.189) made it clear that glass pieces were not used in the Baths of Agrippa (25–19 BC), but they can be seen in a semicircular nymphaeum of early Augustan date under the Via degli Annibaldi near the Colosseum in Rome. Its walls are encrusted not only with shells and pumice but also large pieces of coloured glass pressed into the painted plaster. The orange, blue, green and brown pieces with white and yellow streaks add to the range of colour and catch the light. By the early 1st century AD twisted glass rods were incorporated into shell encrustations, for example in the mosaic fragments from the Villa dei Centroni on the Via Anagnina and the mosaic fountain in the House of the Grand Duke at Pompeii (*c.* AD 35). The latter is a particularly good example of the transition from shell incrustation to true mosaic. It has a shell mosaic with pumice and pieces of coloured glass on the sides, while the front of the fountain is decorated with Egyptian blue, shells, twisted glass rods and glass tesserae. Below the fountain niche is a Nilotic scene in a panel framed by a row of cockle shells set into red-painted plaster. The mosaic of the Columbarium of Pomponius Hylas at Rome dates to the same period and is the first surviving example of a wall mosaic in a tomb. Presumably the reflective and impermeable qualities of glass made it a suitable decorative medium for a dark, damp environment.

(b) Mid-1st century AD*–2nd century.* By the end of the 1st century AD all other materials except pumice had largely fallen out of use and henceforth wall and vault mosaics were composed almost exclusively of tesserae, mainly of glass, but sometimes of marble or limestone. Glass mosaic remained a favourite decoration for the tall niched fountains that adorned so many houses until the eruption of Vesuvius (AD 79). Some 40 have been found; one of the finest is in the House of the Fountain with Columns at Pompeii and displays exquisitely modelled miniature figures against a ground of Egyptian blue. The fashion may have been established by Tiberius (*reg* AD 14–37) whose grottoes at Sperlonga and Capreae are lavishly decorated with encrusted glass and shell. Both at Sperlonga and in several Pompeian houses mosaic columns or half-columns have been found, and several villas in the Bay of Naples had fountains decorated with mosaic. A fine fountain niche from Baiae (Cambridge, Fitzwilliam) has a garden scene in mosaic reminiscent of that from the Villa of Livia at Prima Porta. In AD 64 Seneca remarked (*Letters* LXXXVI.6) how fashionable wall mosaic had become, which explains why several of the mosaic fountains of Pompeii are sited exactly in line with the front door so that they can be seen from the street.

The earliest surviving vault mosaics date to around the middle of the 1st century AD. Nero (*reg* AD 54–68) had an elaborately decorated nymphaeum in his

Domus Aurea at Rome, with a mosaic frieze outlined in shells running round the upper part of the walls. The vault is covered in red-painted pumice, and in it were inserted five roundels, the central one with a glass mosaic of *Odysseus Offering Wine to the Cyclops*. In the years before AD 79 the fountains of Pompeii became more elaborate. A large nymphaeum near Porta Marina has mosaic half-columns supporting an entablature, and in the fountain niche is a mosaic panel showing Mercury and three cupids on a blue ground. In the open-air triclinium of the House of Neptune and Amphitrite at Herculaneum is a finely executed mosaic fountain showing speckled deer pursued by hounds, and on an adjacent wall a mosaic panel with the figures that give the house its name.

By the middle of the 1st century AD mosaic decoration was also used on walls and vaults not specifically associated with a nymphaeum, such as the mosaic of horses and sea creatures that decorates the pediment of the House of the Stags at Herculaneum. In the decade before AD 79 wall mosaic began to be used to decorate baths at Pompeii, for example in the niches around the *frigidarium* (cold room) of the Stabian Baths, and the plunge bath in the House of Julia Felix. Several baths from the 2nd century have walls and vaults decorated with mosaic, including those at Massaciuccoli and Baiae. In the Baths of the Seven Sages at Ostia the half-dome, lunette and arch soffit of an exedra are covered in a mosaic of acanthus, tendrils and dolphins in yellow, grey, brown and blue tesserae on a mainly white ground. Mosaic became a great favourite for decorating large domed or vaulted structures, especially at the time of Hadrian (*reg* AD 117–38), for example in Hadrian's Villa at TIBUR (Tivoli), where there are vault mosaics in several buildings, including the Piazza d'Oro, the Small Baths and the Serapeum. Vaults and domes of complex profile, which were much in vogue at the time, did not lend themselves to more conventional decoration such as coffering or stucco, while mosaic provided the ideal decorative medium. It was two-dimensional, which meant that it followed every facet of a ribbed dome or irregular vault; it also created a richer and livelier effect than painting, caught the light and sparkled, and was more durable in damp conditions.

Wall and vault mosaic was also frequently used in tombs during the 2nd century AD. At Ostia one tomb has a mosaic inscription and another has a mosaic *arcosolium* (niche for sarcophagus) showing the dead man reclining on his funeral couch. A white mosaic with green scroll patterns covers the dome and niches of a splendid circular hypogeum (underground tomb chamber) of Hadrianic date at Sette Camini near Rome. Vault mosaics were also used to decorate Mithraea, which appeared in Italy from the 2nd century AD. As semi-subterranean buildings representing the cave in which Mithras slew the bull, they lend themselves very well to mosaic decoration. The Mithraeum under the church of S Clemente in Rome has a vault covered in pumice with a plain strip of coloured glass mosaic running around the edges. The light-wells in the vault are also lined with mosaic. Several other Mithraea both in Rome and Ostia have glass mosaic decoration, a notable example being the Mithraeum in the Palazzo Imperiale at Ostia, which has a niche decorated with a figure of the rustic god Silvanus on a green background.

(c) 3rd and 4th centuries AD. Wall and vault mosaics became increasingly common in the late Empire. By the 3rd century AD vault mosaics were used extensively, for example in the *frigidarium* and several adjacent rooms of the Baths of Caracalla in Rome. A mosaic plaque (Rome, Mus. Conserv.), which came from the nymphaeum of an early 3rd-century house on the Quirinal in Rome, shows a lighthouse and a finely modelled ship under sail. In the Baths of Diocletian glass mosaic was used throughout the *frigidarium* and on the vaults flanking the *natatio* (bathing room). Although only scanty traces of turquoise, cobalt, emerald green and maroon tesserae survive and no overall design can be made out, these huge mosaic vaults must have glowed with colour and created a similar impression of jewel-like richness as the 5th- and 6th-century AD churches of Ravenna.

Vault mosaics were used in a Christian context long before the 4th century AD. The mid-3rd-century AD Tomb M under St Peter's, Rome, has a groin vault covered with polychrome figured mosaics that extend to the lunettes below. The vault is covered in a vine scroll in three shades of green on a bright yellow background, and in the centre is a beardless figure of Christ as Helios driving a four-horse chariot. In the 4th century AD, mosaics were commonly used in catacombs, particularly to decorate arcosolia. The so-called Temple of Minerva Medica at Rome (early 4th century AD), with its dome covered in purple, green and gold mosaic (now destr.), must have looked very similar to the great Early Christian baptisteries. Indeed the craftsmen who laid the mosaics on the high vault of the Baths of Diocletian could well have been the masters of the mosaicists working on the Constantinian church building programme. The most celebrated surviving mosaics of the Constantinian period in Rome adorn the annular passage of the church of S Costanza, which was built as a mausoleum for Constantine's daughter. Although they date to the mid-4th century AD, there is no Christian iconography anywhere in the scenes. The mosaics are a series of floor designs adapted to the curve of the vault, a fact that has led some scholars to believe that vault mosaics were derived from floor mosaics. Although the large numbers of wall and vault mosaics that have come to light make this conclusion untenable, the mosaics of S Costanza still pose a problem, because in style and material they are more like floor than vault mosaics. However, the dome of S Constanza was also once decorated with mosaics (destr.), which according to a series of drawings had scenes of putti in boats, water-birds and fish, and a curtain covered in scrolls, all on a deep blue ground. The style of these dome mosaics is much more in keeping with the character of the wall and vault mosaics up to that time. It may thus be no more than a misleading coincidence that only the mosaics of the annular passage survive, mosaics that are atypical and which, for whatever reason, may have been laid by *tessellarii* rather than *musearii*.

(ii) Provinces. Wall and vault mosaics occurred frequently in the Roman provinces, particularly North Africa. In several baths, such as the Antonine Baths at Carthage and the Hadrianic Baths at Leptis Magna, large fragments of polychrome mosaic vault have been found. The Hunting Baths at Leptis Magna have apse mosaics in the *frigidarium* with Nilotic scenes and a crocodile in grey, green, white, black and pink tesserae. A bath at Banasa in Morocco has a vault mosaic showing a male figure, perhaps an attendant or masseur of the baths, and the baths at Salamis in Cyprus have several niches decorated with mosaic, one with a reclining figure of Eurotas with a swan and a winged cupid beside him. A number of North African fountains are decorated in mosaic such as those at Bulla Regia, Utica, Hadrumetum (now Sousse) and Oudna in Tunisia; at Caesarea (now Cherchel) in Algeria; and at Volubilis (now Ksar Pharaoun) in Morocco. Small fragments of glass mosaic frequently turn up in Europe; the best preserved are at Augusta Treverorum (Trier), where a niche in the basilica is decorated with blue scrolls on a gold ground (*c.* AD 325); at Pfäffikon in Switzerland, where a figured mosaic showing one of the Four Seasons adheres to the heating tubes of a Roman bath; and at Centcelles in Spain, where the dome of the great 4th-century AD Roman mausoleum is decorated with zones of figural scenes from the Old and New Testaments. A few fragments of wall mosaic have also been found in Britain, mainly in baths.

T. Ashby: 'The Columbarium of Pomponius Hylas', *Pap. Brit. Sch. Rome*, v (1910), pp. 463–71

G. B. Hallam: 'Notes on the Cult of Hercules Victor in Tibur and its Neighbourhood', *J. Roman Stud.*, xxi (1931), pp. 276–82, fig. 29

M. Santangelo: 'Il Quirinale nell'antichità classica', *Mem. Pont. Accad. Romana Archeol.*, v (1941), p. 147

J. B. Ward-Perkins and J. C. Toynbee: 'The Hunting Baths at Lepcis Magna', *Archaeologia* [Soc. Antiqua. London], 93 (1949), pp. 179–80, 182, 191–2

G. Calza: *Scavi di Ostia* (Rome, 1953–79), iv, p. 136, no. 269 and pp. 291ff

J. Toynbee and J. B. Ward-Perkins: *The Shrine of St Peter and the Vatican Excavations* (London, 1956), pp. 72–4

M. J. Vermaseren: *Corpus inscriptionum et monumentorum religionis Mithriacae* (The Hague, 1956), pp. 156–7, no. 338

V. von Gonzenbach: *Die römischen Mosaiken der Schweiz* (Basel, 1961), pp. 201, no. 100

T. Hauschild and H. Schlunk: 'Vorbericht über die Arbeiten in Centcelles', *Madrid. Mitt.*, ii (1961), pp. 119–82

H. Lavagne: 'Le Nymphée au Polyphème de la Domus Aurea', *Mél. Ecole Fr. Rome: Ant.*, lxxii (1970), pp. 673–722

C. F. Giuliani and M. Guaitoli: 'Il ninfeo minore della villa detta di Cicerone a Formia', *Röm. Mitt.*, lxxii (1972), pp. 191–219

H. Lavagne: 'Villa d'Hadrien: La Mosaïque de voûte du cryptoportique républicain et les débuts de l' *"opus musivum"* en Italie', *Mél. Ecole Fr. Rome: Ant.*, lxxxv (1973), pp. 197–246

F. B. Sear: 'The Earliest Wall Mosaics in Italy', *Pap. Brit. Sch. Rome*, xliii (1975), pp. 83–97

F. B. Sear: 'Wall and Vault Mosaics', *Roman Crafts*, ed. D. Strong and D. Brown (London, 1976), pp. 231–9

F. B. Sear: 'Wall and Vault Mosaics', *Mitt. Dt. Archaol. Inst.: Röm. Abt.*, suppl. xxiii (1977)

M. Mazzei and others: 'Furstengraber, Luxushauser und Delphine: Archaologische Neuentdeckungen im Daunischen Arpi (Nordapulien)', *Ant. Welt*, xxxi/3 (2000), pp. 261–8

J. Harris: 'Grape Harvest Mosaic Discovered in Rome', *Archaeology Odyssey*, viii/4 (July–Aug 2005), p. 12

Mummy portrait. Often highly individualistic portraits painted on wood or canvas that were positioned over the head of a mummy. They came into use in Egypt during the Roman Imperial period and partly replaced the more traditional, idealized masks. Some 900 to 1000 examples are currently known; particularly significant collections are in the British Museum and Petrie Museum in London, the Louvre in Paris, the Staatliche Museen in Berlin and the Egyptian Museum in Cairo. Mummy portraits were found throughout Egypt from the delta to Nubia, but were concentrated in a few cemeteries in the Nile valley, such as Akhmim and Antinoöpolis, and particularly in the FAIYUM (er-Rubayat and Hawara), so that they are sometimes also known as 'Faiyum-portraits'.

The portraits were sometimes painted using very elaborate encaustic techniques, involving layers of coloured, heated wax that produced vivid chromatic tones, but cheaper versions in tempera on white backgrounds and even watercolour also occur. The insufficient state of publication of many portraits has generally not been conducive to studies into workshop connections or the isolation of individual painters; more detailed research on these aspects exists only for examples from Antinoöpolis.

Mummies with painted portraits were found in all types of burial place, from elaborate, freestanding monuments to simple, shallow graves, but nearly always without any further grave goods. Labels on the mummies suggest that they may in some cases have been sent to particularly sacred places rather than have been buried in their home cemeteries. Much information on the socio-cultural context of the portraits was lost in the 19th century, when they were prized out of their tombs and presented as isolated art objects. More recent studies have tried to rectify this dearth of contextual information; they suggest that the deceased belonged to the local élites and more generally privileged sections of society (based on personal names, iconographic elements, the costly detail on the mummies themselves), but more specific information remains sparse. Women in particular regularly appear with a fine array of jewellery (earrings, chains, bracelets, etc, all of recognizable types worn in real life; magic amulets are also frequent). Dress details of some men imply that they may have belonged to the military or administrative class; children, boys in particular, sometimes show hairstyles relating them to the cult of Isis or otherwise comfortable backgrounds. The hairstyles of the portrayed in general are, nearly without exception, fashionable coiffures common in all parts of the empire, often following trends set at the imperial court in Rome, sometimes with certain modifications found throughout the eastern provinces. Comparisons with similar coiffures of sculptured portraits have in recent years helped to provide a much firmer chronology for many of the mummy portraits. The portrayed tend to be clad in the standard Greek-style pallium and palla, not the distinctly Roman toga.

It has been claimed that the portraits were painted during the lifetime of the deceased and put on the mummies only after their deaths, but there is little evidence to support this contention. However, it is possible that the mummies together with their painted portraits were displayed in the house or regularly visited in the tomb over a prolonged period.

A particular appeal of mummy portraits lies in their seemingly striking realism. In the rare cases, however, where portraits by one particular artist or at least from one workshop can be compared, a degree of stylization and the application of recurring formulae are clearly in evidence.

Mummy portraits continued to be in use from the 1st to perhaps the 4th century AD; the end of the practice is disputed and may have already occurred in the 3rd century, due perhaps to changes in the cultural aspirations of the people involved.

K. Parlasca: *Repertorio d'arte dell'Egitto greco-romano: Serie B, I. Ritratti di mummie. I–IV* (Rome, 1969–2003)

B. Borg: *Mumienporträts und verwandte Monumente—Chronologie und kultureller Kontext* (Mainz, 1996)

M. L. Brierbrier, ed.: *Portraits and Masks: Burial Customs in Roman Egypt* (London, 1997)

S. Walker, ed.: *Ancient Faces: Mummy Portraits from Roman Egypt, A Catalogue of Roman Portraits in the British Museum*, iv (London, 1997)

B. Borg: '*Der zierlichste Anblick der Welt*': *Ägyptische Porträtmumien* (Mainz, 1998)

Bilder aus dem Wüstensand. Mumienporträts aus dem Ägyptischen Museum Kairo (exh. cat., ed. W. Seinel; Vienna, Ksthist. Mus., 1998–9)

Murlo. *See* POGGIO CIVITATE.

Mycenae. Site in the north-eastern Peloponnese in southern Greece, 30 km south-west of Corinth. It is renowned for its Late Bronze Age (LBA) palace, tombs and fortifications. In Homeric epic it was the capital city of Agamemnon, leader of the Greek forces at Troy, and it now gives its name to the Mycenaean civilization.

In this article relative dates for the Bronze Age are used; for discussion of chronology *see* HELLADIC, §4.

1. Introduction. 2. The site outside the citadel. 3. The citadel. 4. Artefacts.

1. INTRODUCTION. Mycenae stands on an isolated hill separated by two ravines from Mt Zara and Mt Ayios Ilias and forms a natural strongpoint controlling the route from the Peloponnese to central Greece. Combined with its proximity to the sea, this made Mycenae the key point on the trade routes between the Aegean and the eastern Mediterranean on one side and Greece and central Europe on the other. Originally occupied in the Neolithic period, the area was thickly settled after Early Helladic (EH) III, and the hill became the seat of increasingly powerful rulers. The first fortification wall was built in Late Helladic (LH) IIIA, turning the rock into a citadel (see fig. 1), and a network of roads was established, leading inland and to the ports. Mycenae soon became a powerful state and the cultural centre of LBA Greece, subordinating many mainland strongholds and Aegean islands, including the Cyclades and Crete (*see* HELLADIC, §4(iii)(b), CYCLADIC, §4(iii) and MINOAN, §4(iii)). In LH IIIB, at the height of its prosperity, the city was devastated by an earthquake, though most buildings were reconstructed and more were added. A succession of later fires, however, destroyed various structures, which could not be repaired owing to the decline of Mycenaean palace civilization. The site was gradually abandoned in LH IIIC, and Mycenae later re-emerged as a mere village. A few Geometric (*c.* 900–*c.* 700 BC) huts were set up over the ruined palace, followed by an Archaic temple (6th century BC). Small Mycenaean contingents fought at Thermopylai (480 BC) and Plataia (479 BC), but in 468 BC the village was destroyed by the Argives. It was resettled in the 3rd century BC by farmers, who reconstructed the temple and built a theatre and fountain house outside the walls; it was finally deserted after the 2nd century AD. The site was rediscovered in the 18th century, and in 1841 the Archaeological Society at Athens cleared the Lion Gate (figs 1b and 2). Systematic excavations (1874, 1876) were initiated by HEINRICH SCHLIEMANN and have been continued by the Greek Archaeological Society and the British School at Athens.

2. THE SITE OUTSIDE THE CITADEL. On the southern approach is a truncated sub-Mycenaean viaduct across the Chavos ravine, built of flat blocks in almost level courses. The remains of an earlier Cyclopean bridge lie further north. Beyond the ravine, the Panayia ridge and the ground to its west and north are honeycombed with chamber tombs of the LH IIA–LH IIIC periods. There are nine tholos tombs of LH I–IIIB. Six, on both sides of the ridge, are named after their architectural forms, location or alleged occupants: the Treasury of Atreus (for illustration *see* ARCHITECTURE, fig. 2 and THOLOS TOMB), the Tomb of the Genii, the Epano Phournos and Kato Phournos, the Cyclopean Tomb and the Panayia Tomb. Three further tholoi (the Tomb of Aigisthos, the Tomb of Klytemnestra and the Lion Tomb) are situated on the west slope of the citadel hill. Nearby are the House of Lead, Lisa's House and the

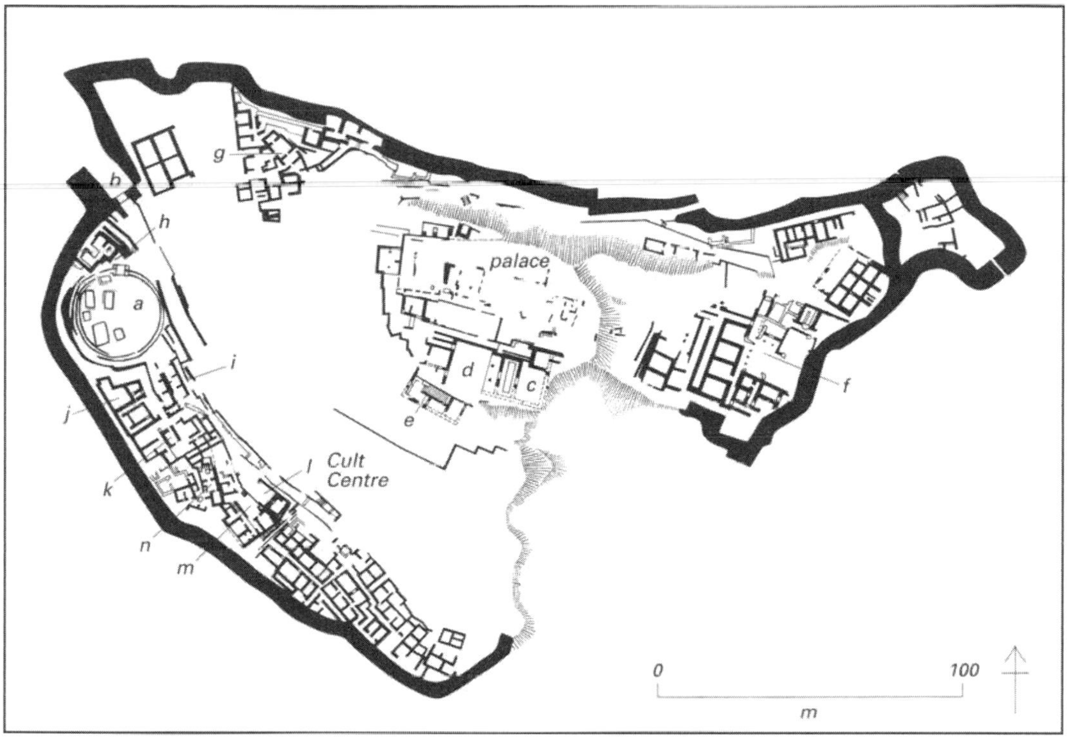

1. Mycenae, plan of the citadel, Late Helladic IIIA:2–IIIC: (a) Grave Circle A; (b) Lion Gate; (c) megaron; (d) Great Court; (e) Grand Staircase; (f) House of Columns; (g) House M; (h) granary; (i) Ramp House; (j) House of the Warrior Vase; (k) South House; (l) temple; (m) Tsountas's House; (n) sanctuaries

Panayia houses. Further north lies the Oil Merchant's quarter, and some distance north-west of the citadel were Petsas' House (probably a potter's workshop) and the House of the Wine Merchant. One more house was excavated at Plakes, on the west slope of Mt Ayios Ilias. Only the Panayia houses, the Oil Merchant's quarter and the Plakes house have been thoroughly investigated. The first two groups were built along the ancient road to the citadel, in an area already settled in Middle Helladic (MH) times and reoccupied in LH IIB–IIIB. The Panayia group consists of three houses (LH IIIB) built close together. Of these, House I is a megaron-type building (*see* MEGARON) fronted by a small court. In LH IIIB it was destroyed by the earthquake, as were House II and House III, which have less clear and more cramped plans. Both the latter were repaired, but House II was burnt down shortly afterwards. House III survived in use for some time.

The Oil Merchant's quarter (LH IIIB) was a complex comprising four buildings, all eventually destroyed by fire: the House of the Oil Merchant, the House of Sphinxes and the House of Shields were built in a row and are named after some oil jars, some ivory plaques representing sphinxes and some others representing shields found in their ruins. Behind them and higher up the slope is the West House, the earliest of the group. Built partly on top of an MH structure, it had a paved court in front of a megaron, which was separated by a corridor from a row of five rooms along its west side. Behind its rear wall there was a large double fireplace, which clearly formed part of a perfume workshop, since clay tablets inscribed in Linear B listing quantities of oil and herbs were found nearby (all artefacts now in Athens, N. Archaeol. Mus., unless stated otherwise). Of the other three houses only the basements survive. The House of Sphinxes contained stone vases, ivory inlays and further tablets mentioning spices; the House of the Oil Merchant, where the fire had been fed by the oil stored in jars in the basement, contained 38 inscribed tablets relating to oil, wool, spices and a list of bakers, all fallen from the living quarters above; and from the House of Shields, built on a massive terrace, came 24 stone vases, cracked and discoloured by the fire. The house at Plakes consisted of a row of four rooms behind a court, with three basement rooms below them. The earthquake precipitated part of it downhill, and its basement rooms were filled with falling debris, which crushed beneath it three adults and a child.

A short distance past the Oil Merchant's quarter the road to the citadel formed a loop around Grave Circle B, which was surrounded by a strong circular wall and contained 14 richly furnished shaft graves, marked with funerary stelai. Between the shafts were 12 individual burials in shallow cists. The enclosure clearly formed part of an MH cemetery that extended eastwards to the foot of the citadel hill. There lay the other royal burial enclosure, Grave Circle A (see fig. 1a), containing six shaft graves and mistakenly identified by Schliemann as belonging to Agamemnon and his entourage. Grave Circle B predates it by a generation or two, but they were used concurrently during the LH I period, when the Tomb of Aigisthos was also built nearby. In LH IIA Shaft Grave Rho in Grave Circle B was dug up and extended to accommodate a built tomb of a type otherwise known only from Cyprus and Ugarit. Then when the Tomb of Klytemnestra was built (LH IIIB), its dome demolished part of the enclosure of the no longer visible Grave Circle B. The last three tholos tombs (i.e. the Treasury of Atreus, the Tomb of the Genii and the Tomb of Klytemnestra), built in the same style as the citadel's Lion Gate (see fig. 2), have walls of square-cut blocks lining their entrance passages, ashlar façades with sculptural decoration and vaults of polished conglomerate ashlars laid in regular horizontal courses. The use of sawn blocks of locally quarried conglomerate is a feature unique to Mycenaean architecture when compared with that of other Helladic sites.

3. THE CITADEL. MH graves and remains of buildings on the west, north and north-east slopes of the citadel hill show that at the time of the grave circles it was already inhabited, and some rock cuttings on the summit suggest that there may have been a palace there. The hill, however, was not fortified until LH IIIA, when the first Cyclopean circuit wall was built along the brow of the rock. The main gate seems to have been above Grave Circle A, with another entrance at the north-east corner. About this time the peak was surrounded with terraces built to support a new palace, approached by a stairway on the north side. The south-west fortification wall was dismantled in LH IIIB, and a new entrance, the Lion Gate (see figs. 1b and 2), was erected, protected by an outwork on the right. The regular courses of rectangular stone blocks around the Lion Gate and the North Gate contrast strikingly with the rough Cyclopean masonry of the earlier fortification wall. From the outwork a new wall was built around the foot of the hill, taking in the west slope and Grave Circle A, which was filled in to the level of the new entrance and embellished with a parapet of stone slabs. Inside the gate, a steep ramp rising southwards replaced the old approach to the palace, while another gate, also flanked by an outwork, was built in the north wall. In LH IIIB the fortifications were extended to the north-east, mainly to protect the underground fountain that provided the citadel with a constant supply of water. Meanwhile, the palace, which had been damaged by fire, was repaired and extended by the addition of a megaron (1c; for illustration of plan *see* MEGARON) and the Great Court (1d) on the south side, accessible through a new approach, the Grand Staircase (1e). It expanded also to the east as far as the circuit wall. In its final form, it comprised four wings, separated by corridors and open spaces. The north wing, of which practically nothing survives, apparently housed the royal quarters, while the middle area formed a terrace in front of them and the south wing contained the state apartments. Workshops, store-rooms, the House of Columns (1f) and two other structures were located in the east wing. All were destroyed by fire in LH IIIB but were immediately repaired and reoccupied. House M (1g), built on the north slope after the reconstruction of the palace and used until its final abandonment, seems to have been another palace dependency. Three further houses within the circuit wall above the Lion Gate were damaged by the great earthquake and are preserved only to basement level.

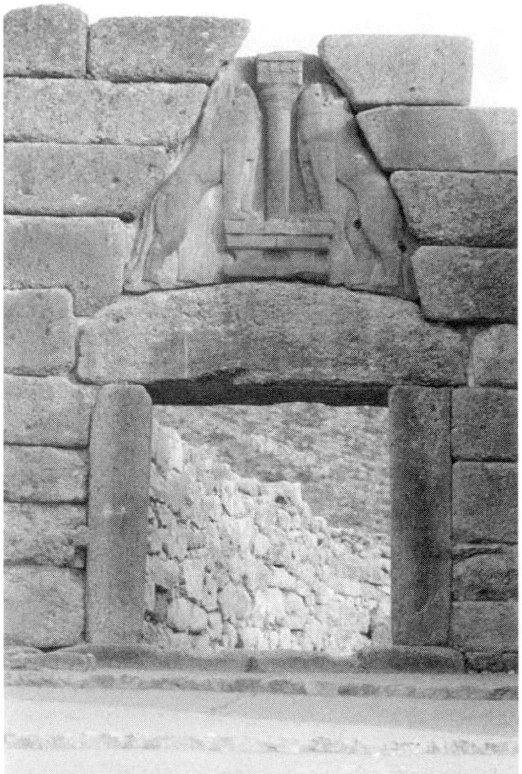

2. Mycenae, Lion Gate, Late Helladic IIIB

Buildings on the west slope include the granary (1h), the Ramp House (1i), the House of the Warrior Vase (1j) and the South House (1k). All date from LH IIIB, were built around Grave Circle A (1a) and continued in use until LH IIIC, after being damaged and rebuilt. The block of buildings next to the South House constituted the cult centre of the citadel, accessible by a processional road leading to a square temple (1l), which had an altar and a flat stone in front of it. At a later date the walls of the temple had to be reinforced from inside, while the altar area was filled in, and a new altar was erected near the precinct's entrance. From the temple, a few steps led down to Tsountas's House (1m; named after its excavator), which was probably occupied by a religious official. Lower still were LH IIIB sanctuaries (1n) containing idols (Navplion, Archaeol. Mus.) and religious frescoes, organized around a small court with a circular altar in the middle. Soon after the sanctuaries' construction, the altar was buried under an accumulation of debris and plastered over with white clay, while the doors to the court were blocked. Some walls, however, were shored up, and new floors were laid, and the shrines continued in use until they were burnt in LH IIIB:2, together with Tsountas's House and part of an adjacent building to the south. The area was then reoccupied until the citadel was finally abandoned. Further south the slope was covered with houses, built in LH IIIB and arranged in superimposed levels. No traces of burning are apparent, and the houses were finally deserted without having been destroyed.

For further discussion of Mycenaean architecture *see* ARCHITECTURE, §III.

4. ARTEFACTS. The best works of Late Helladic (LH) art were found at Mycenae. They come from three main find groups, which succeed and complement each other: the royal shaft graves (LH I); the chamber tombs of the civilian population (LH I–IIIC); and the non-funerary buildings (LH IIIB–IIIC). The first group reflects the impact of Minoan and Cycladic artistic styles on the plain MH local styles at a stage when the copying of Cretan prototypes had given way to the attempt to master foreign techniques and to amalgamate the Minoan elegance of style with Helladic subject-matter, full of action and movement.

By LH II, however, Mycenaean artists had developed their own artistic tradition, distinguished by the tectonic arrangement of shapes and by frugal ornament, evolving from realism to formal stylization. The magnificent hammered, inlaid and cloisonné gold and silver artefacts from the shaft graves (see colour pl. 1:XV, fig. 3) are followed by the silver cup inlaid with bulls' heads in gold and niello (probably LH IIIB) and by the repoussé, granulated and enamelled jewellery from the chamber tombs. The masterpieces of ivory-carving, such as the tusk engraved with a man and a tree flanked by ibexes (probably LH IIIA–B), also found in the chamber tombs, were paralleled by artefacts from the houses and palace, including a group of two women (apparently goddesses) and a child (LH II or IIIA). The only surviving larger-scale sculptures, however, are the primitive stelai, carved in low relief, from the grave circles, the fragmentary decoration from the façade of the Treasury of Atreus (London, BM), the Lion Relief, and the plaster head from the cult area (LH IIIB).

The buildings were decorated with frescoes representing scenes of battle, hunting or ritual processions, of which the fragment known as the '*Mykenaia*' (LH IIIB; *see* PAINTING, fig. 3) is justly famous for the elegance of its pose and its fine workmanship. Nothing of quality seems to have been created after LH IIIB.

H. Schliemann: *Mykenae* (Leipzig, 1878/*R* Darmstadt, 1966)

A. J. B. Wace and others: 'Excavations at Mycenae', *Annu. Brit. Sch. Athens*, xxv (1921–3) [whole vol.]

G. Karo: *Die Schachtgräber von Mykenai* (Munich, 1930–33)

A. J. B. Wace: *Chamber Tombs at Mycenae* (Oxford, 1932)

A. J. B. Wace: *Mycenae: An Archaeological History and Guide* (Princeton, 1949)

G. E. Mylonas: *Ancient Mycenae: The Capital City of Agamemnon* (Princeton, 1957)

A. J. B. Wace: *Mycenae and the Mycenaean Age* (Princeton, 1966)

A. J. B. Wace: *O Taphikos Kyklos B ton Mykenon* [Grave Circle B at Mycenae] (Athens, 1973) [Eng. summary]

W. D. Taylour and others: *Well-built Mycenae: the Helleno-British Excavations within the Citadel at Mycenae 1959–1969* (Warminster, 1981–2001) [published in fascicules]

S. E. Iakovidis: *Late Helladic Citadels on Mainland Greece* (Leiden, 1983), pp. 23–72

G. E. Mylonas: *Mycenae Rich in Gold* (Athens, 1983)

A. Xenaki-Sakellariou: *Oi thalanokoi taphoi ton Mykenon: Anaskaphes Chr. Tsountas, 1887–1898* [The chamber tombs of Mycenae: excavations of C. Tsountas, 1887–1898] (Paris, 1985) [Fr. summary]

I. Mylonas-Shear: *The Panagia Houses at Mycenae* (Philadelphia, 1987)

I. Tournavitou: *The "Ivory Houses" at Mycenae* (London, 1995)

E. B. French: *Mycenae: Agamemnon's Capital: The Site and its Setting* (Stroud, 2002)

E. Andreadi, ed.: *Archaeological Atlas of Mycenae* (Athens, 2003)

E. Spathare: *Mycenae: A Guide to the History and Archaeology* (Athens, 2004)

M. Cultraro: *I Micenei: Archeologia, storia, società dei Greci prima di Omero* (Rome, 2006)

C. Gere: *The Tomb of Agamemnon* (Cambridge, MA, 2006)

Mycenaean [Achaian]. Civilization that flourished in the Late Bronze Age (*c.* 1600–*c.* 1100 BC) on the Greek mainland. The Mycenaean civilization is covered under the last phase of HELLADIC culture.

Myra. Site in LYCIA, Turkey, 1.5 km north of Demre. The inscriptions and rock-cut tombs indicate that it was an important settlement at least as early as the 5th century BC. In the 2nd century BC it became a member of the Lycian League and continued to flourish under Roman rule (1st century BC–3rd century AD). The miracles performed by its bishop, St Nicholas (*b c.* 300), brought Myra widespread fame, and under Theodosios II (*reg* 408–50) it became the provincial capital of Lycia. The rock-cut tombs include a wide variety of types that imitate local wooden and masonry techniques.

Among the more elaborate examples are seven tombs decorated with external reliefs that reflect the process of Hellenization in the 4th century BC. Contrary to earlier scholarly opinion, the façades of these tombs are not based on Lycian houses or Greek temples, but on the banqueting halls within Lycian dwellings. The reliefs frequently contain life-size figures in a mixed setting such as that of a battle scene combined with a funeral repast.

The town's prosperity under the Romans is demonstrated by the marble sarcophagi imported from Athens and Pamphylia (south-west Turkey) and by the theatre (diam. 120 m), much of which is well preserved, including the stage building with its frieze of theatrical masks. Myra's importance in the administration of imperial grain is reflected by Hadrian's granary (60×30 m) in the harbour of Andriake, 2.5 km to the south west.

E. Petersen and F. von Luschan: *Reisen im südwestlichen Kleinasien*, ii (1889), pp. 28ff
J. Borchhardt: *Myra. Eine lykische Metropole in antiker und byzantinischer Zeit* (Berlin, 1975)
A. Bruns-Özgan: *Lykische Grabreliefs des 5. und 4. Jahrhunderts v. Chr.* (Tübingen, 1987)

Myron of Eleutherai (*fl c.* 470–*c.* 440 BC). Greek sculptor. He was a leading Early Classical bronze sculptor of the Attic school. Pliny (*Natural History* XXIV.xix.49) dated his floruit to 420–417 BC, but this is probably inaccurate. The only firm dates for his career are statues of Olympic victors in 456 BC, 448 BC and perhaps 444 BC. Epigraphic evidence suggests that his son Lykios was active in the 440s and 430s BC. These dates suggest that Myron began his career around 470 BC at the latest, and there is no evidence that he worked after *c.* 440 BC.

Later writers counted Myron among the most distinguished Greek sculptors, listing him, together with Pheidias and Polykleitos, as a pupil of Ageladas of Argos and comparing him to Pythagoras of Rhegion, perhaps a slightly older contemporary, as a rival (Pliny: *Natural History* XXXIV.xix.57–9). In their analyses of the development of sculptural forms, Cicero (*Brutus* xviii.70) and Quintilian (*Principles of Oratory* XII.x.7) placed him after Kalamis but before Polykleitos. An obscure passage in Pliny's *Natural History* (XXXIV. xix.58) indicates that the sculptor considerably expanded the compositional repertory and that, in the number of his formal schemes and possibly also in the methods used to determine their proportions, he contrasted with Polykleitos. Indeed, the subject-matter of the works attributed to him suggests a range and versatility unequalled among Early Classical sculptors.

Myron's statues of athletes were greatly admired, especially that of the runner *Ladas* (untraced). Its daring pose and sense of physical exertion were celebrated in epigrams (*Greek Anthology: Planudean Appendix* IV.54; Catullus, *Poems* lviiib.3), suggesting similarities with his *Diskobolos* (Discus-thrower; see fig.). The latter was described in detail by Lucian (*Philopseudeis* xviii) and has been securely identified in Roman copies (e.g. Rome, Mus. N. Romano). The most famous example of Myron's ability to imbue sculpture with an almost deceptive naturalism was his *Heifer* on the Athenian Acropolis. His statues of divinities, however, were criticized for a lack of spiritual depth. His colossal *Apollo* at Ephesos (untraced) and the mid-5th century BC group of the *Introduction of Herakles to Olympos* at Samos, the base of which still survives, indicate his willingness to experiment in scale as well as in pose. Another *Apollo* was a prized possession of the people of Akragas. A group of *Athena and Marsyas* attributed by Pliny to Myron (*Natural History* XXXIV.xix.57) was probably the one seen by Pausanias (*Guide to Greece* I.xxiv.1) on the Athenian Acropolis. The modern restoration of the group from Roman copies of individual figures (*Athena*, Frankfurt am Main, Liebieghaus; *Marsyas*, Rome, Vatican, Mus. Gregoriano Profano) is usually accepted as correct, though doubts still remain. Surviving marble heads (London, BM; Rome, Mus. Conserv.) may be copies of his famous *Perseus after the Killing of Medusa*, which stood on the Athenian Acropolis (Pausanias: *Guide to Greece* I.xxiii.8). The Riccardi *Hero* (Rome, Villa Borghese) may also be based on his work, since it is similar to the head of the *Diskobolos*. Attempts to identify copies of figures from the Samian group, however, have proved unconvincing. It is plausible that Myron's skills were needed for architectural sculptures during the mid-5th-century BC Periclean building programme at Athens; the metopes of the Hephaistion and the south metopes of the Parthenon have subjects in which his talent for momentary poses and for animal sculpture would have been put to good use.

R. Carpenter: 'Observations on Familiar Statuary in Rome', *Mem. Amer. Acad. Rome*, xviii (1941), pp. 3–25
B. S. Ridgway: *The Severe Style in Greek Sculpture* (Princeton, NJ, 1970), pp. 84–6
M. Robertson: *A History of Greek Art* (Cambridge, 1975), pp. 339–44

Myrtos. Village on the river of the same name on the south coast of Crete, 17 km from Ierapetra. It has two important Minoan settlements (Pyrgos and Phournou Koriphi), as well as a large Roman baths (2nd century AD) and residential area, both with

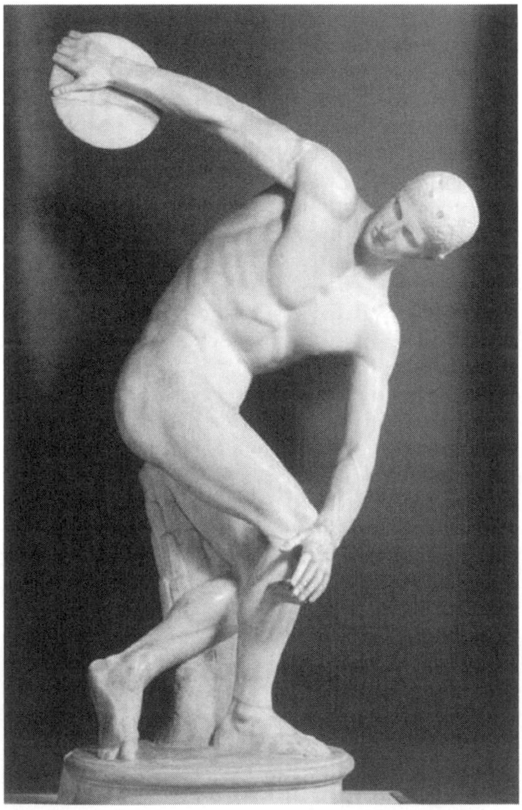

Myron of Eleutherai: *Diskobolos*, bronze original of *c.* 450 BC; Roman copy, marble, h. 1.55 m (Rome, Museo Nazionale Romano)

mosaic pavements. Pyrgos, half a kilometre east of the modern village, on a prominent hill above the mouth of the river, was a long-lived (Early Minoan [EM] II to Late Minoan [LM] I, *c.* 2900/2600–*c.* 1425 BC) and prosperous settlement measuring at least 95×70 m. Excavated by G. Cadogan, largely between 1970 and 1973, the settlement has four principal Minoan phases, of which three (Pyrgos I: EM II, *c.* 2900/2600–*c.* 2200 BC; Pyrgos III: Middle Minoan [MM] II–III, *c.* 1800–*c.* 1600 BC; Pyrgos IV: LM I, *c.* 1600–*c.* 1425 BC) ended in the site's destruction by fire.

The earliest architectural remains are of Pyrgos II (EM III–MM I, *c.* 2200–*c.* 1800 BC), when a house-like communal tomb, similar to those at GOURNIA and MOCHLOS, was built at the south-west corner of the settlement, with a paved yard approached by a stairway and road from the top of the hill. A clay dove rhyton (Knossos, Stratig. Mus.) was part of a probable foundation deposit for this tomb, which continued in use intermittently throughout the Minoan occupation of the settlement. Pyrgos III shared a pottery style, and probably a regional culture, with Mallia, Gournia and other sites in and around the Lasithi Mountains. Finds included a remarkable lobed kantharos (Herakleion, Archaeol. Mus.) containing miniature versions of the same shape. The principal extant monuments of Pyrgos III are two cisterns and a square tower.

In Pyrgos IV a grand country house (which may have had a predecessor in Pyrgos III) built in ashlar masonry was terraced into the hilltop above the settlement, facing south across a courtyard towards the Libyan Sea, its position comparable to that of the contemporary 'palace' at Gournia. Its architecture displays interesting polychrome effects. At the heart of the building is a light well bordered by a gypsum staircase with a stepped parapet, as in the palace at Knossos. A gypsum bench faces the light well. A room on an upper floor probably served as a shrine; its contents included a Linear A tablet (Ayios Nikolaos, Archaeol. Mus.), a red-glazed faience triton shell (Herakleion, Archaeol. Mus.) comparable to one from Grave Circle A at Mycenae (Athens, N. Archaeol. Mus.), two clay sealings (Herakleion, Archaeol. Mus.), a Marine style jug (LM IB, *c.* 1480–*c.* 1425 BC) and four clay tubular stands, with fixed or movable bowls for offerings (Herakleion, Archaeol. Mus.). However, no cult image was found. Another upstairs room, above the house's store-rooms, contained stone vases, a pair of elaborate clay amphorae with decoration copying similar vases in marble and three Cycladic jugs, probably imported from Thera (all in Knossos, Stratig. Mus.). The Pyrgos IV settlement was built with streets following the contours of the hill and with a block system comparable to that at Gournia. Objects discovered there include a Cycladic Black-and-red bird jug and a large globular alabastron with conglomerate decoration (LM IB; Knossos, Stratig. Mus.). A Hellenistic shrine (from Pyrgos V) of Hermes and Aphrodite was built over the ruins of the country house. On top of that stood Pyrgos VI, the Venetian and Turkish watchtower (Gr. *pyrgos*) that gives the site its name.

Phournou Koriphi is about 2 km east of Pyrgos. Uncovered by P. Warren in 1967–8, it is the only completely excavated EM II settlement. Some 90 rooms and associated spaces have been preserved in an area of about 55×35 m, representing two EM II phases of occupation. As at Pyrgos, the second phase ended in destruction by fire, but, unlike Pyrgos, Phournou Koriphi was not reoccupied except by a solitary circular building on the top of the hill (date and function uncertain). Finds from Phournou Koriphi provide important evidence for dating the earliest Minoan stone vases and seals. A vase in the shape of a goddess (Ayios Nikolaos, Archaeol. Mus.) from the settlement's shrine holds a miniature jug of the Myrtos ware type used during EM II at both the Myrtos settlements.

G. Cadogan: 'Clay Tubes in Minoan Religion', *Praktika tou tritou diethnous Kritologikou synedriou: Rethymnon, 1971* [Proceedings of the third international Cretan congress: Rethymnon, 1971], i, pp. 34–8

P. Warren: *Myrtos: An Early Bronze Age Settlement in Crete*, British School at Athens Suppl. Paper, vii (London, 1972)

V. Hankey: 'Stone Vessels at Myrtos Pyrgos', *Praktika tou tetartou diethnous Kritologikou synedriou: Heraklio, 1976* [Proceedings of the fourth international Cretan congress: Herakleion, 1976], i, pp. 210–15

G. Cadogan: 'Pyrgos, Crete, 1970–77', *J. Archaeol. Rep.*, xxiv (1977–8), pp. 70–84

T. M. Whitelaw: *Community Structure and Social Organization at Fournou Korifi, Myrtos* (MA thesis, U. Southampton, 1979)

G. Cadogan: 'A Probable Shrine in the Country House at Pyrgos', *Sanctuaries and Cults in the Aegean Bronze Age: Proceedings of the First International Symposium at the Swedish Institute: Athens, 1980*, pp. 169–71

T. M. Whitelaw: 'The Settlement at Fournou Korifi, Myrtos and Aspects of Early Minoan Social Organization', *Minoan Society: Proceedings of the Cambridge Colloquium: Cambridge, 1981*, pp. 323–45

I. F. Sanders: *Roman Crete* (Warminster, 1982), pp. 18, 138

V. Hankey: 'Pyrgos: The Communal Tomb in Pyrgos IV (Late Minoan I)', *Bull. Inst. Class. Stud. U. London*, xxxiii (1986), pp. 135–7

G. Cadogan: 'Myrtos-Pyrgos', *The Aerial Atlas of Ancient Crete*, ed. J. W. Myers, E. E. Myers and G. Cadogan (Berkeley, 1992), pp. 200–209

P. Warren: 'Myrtos-Phournou Koryphi', *The Aerial Atlas of Ancient Crete*, ed. J. W. Myers, E. E. Myers and G. Cadogan (Berkeley, 1992), pp. 196–9

C. Knappett: 'Assessing a Polity in Protopalatial Crete: The Malia-Lasithi State', *Amer. J. Archaeol.*, ciii/4 (Oct 1999), pp. 615–39

Myson (*fl* first quarter of 5th century BC). Greek vase painter. His name is given by the Greek inscription, 'Myson painted and made [me]', on a small Attic Red-figure column krater (Athens, N. Archaeol. Mus., Acropolis 806). His importance lies in his influence on his milieu and on the craft itself. He is best known for his picture of *Kroisos on his Pyre* on an amphora (Paris, Louvre, G 197; see fig.). This and other early work show ambition and indicate an

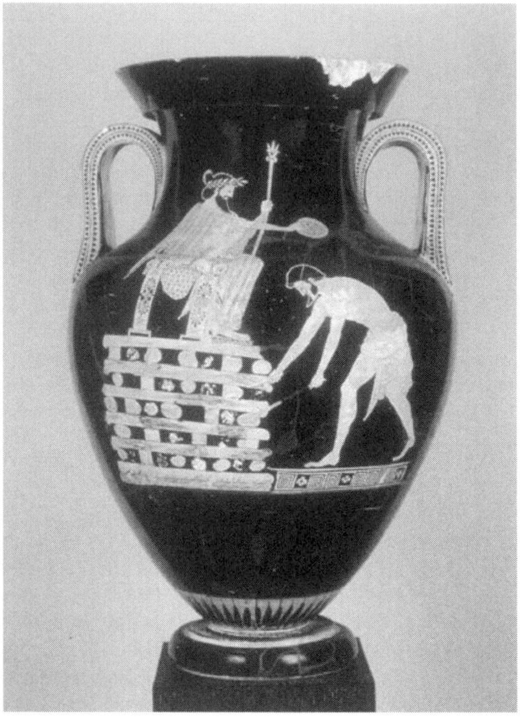

Myson: amphora depicting *Kroisos on his Pyre*, h. 595 mm, Attic Red-figure, from Vulci, *c.* 500–*c.* 490 BC (Paris, Musée du Louvre, G 197)

apprenticeship among the Pioneers. Crossing paths with the Eucharides Painter, the Göttingen Painter and the Chairippos Painter, he then specialized in column kraters, the first in Athens to do so in quantity. Of some 90 vases attributed to him, most are column kraters, usually with a single figure on each side, a style made popular by his contemporary the BERLIN PAINTER. Myson combined a certain grace with a heavy line; his style tightened, then grew flabby. Details in his later work often parallel work of much earlier artists. His preferred subjects were revellers, athletes and Dionysiac scenes; the exceptions are often interesting or unusual. Myson taught the earliest members of the MANNERIST WORKSHOP, which was active for over 50 years.

E. Pottier: 'Deux silènes démolissant un tertre funéraire', *Mnmts Piot*, xxix (1927–8), pp. 149–92

J. D. Beazley: *Red-figure* (1942, 2/1963), i, pp. 237–44; ii, pp. 1592, 1638

A. B Follmann: *Der Pan-Maler* (Bonn, 1968), pp. 70–74 [relationship with Pan Painter]

J. D. Beazley: *Paralipomena* (1971), pp. 349, 510

J. Boardman: *Athenian Red Figure Vases: The Archaic Period* (London, 1975/*R* 1983), p. 112

L. Burn and R. Glynn: *Beazley Addenda: Additional References to* ABV, ARV2 *and* Paralipomena (Oxford, 1982, rev. T. H. Carpenter, 2/1989)

L. Berge: *Myson: A Craftsman of Attic Red-figured Vases* (Chicago, 1994)

N

Nabataea. Kingdom in north-west Arabia (now Jordan and north-west Saudi Arabia) that flourished from the 4th century BC to the 4th century AD and became one of the greatest trading kingdoms of the Ancient Near East. By the late 4th century BC a group of pastoral nomads had settled in the region in the ancient Edomite stronghold of PETRA, and they were known as the Nabatu or Nabataeans. As nomads, the Nabataeans had gained wide experience of the Arabian caravan routes; they monopolized the lucrative frankincense and myrrh trade from the south and then expanded it to include other luxury items prized by the Hellenized West. A royal line developed in the 2nd century BC, and Petra became the capital city of the kingdom, which remained virtually autonomous until Roman annexation by the emperor Trajan (*reg* AD 98–117) in AD 106. Even then Nabataean culture survived at Petra, until the city was destroyed by an earthquake in AD 363. Due perhaps to the previously nomadic lives of the people, as well as to their unusual talent, Nabataean culture developed an eclectic character, most obvious in art and architecture. Public and private monumental architecture abounded, the former including theatres, temples, roads and hydraulic systems, the latter including the tomb façades that have become the Nabataeans' most famous architectural relics.

1. Architecture. 2. Sculpture, ceramics and other arts.

1. ARCHITECTURE. Earlier studies of Nabataean architecture concentrated mainly on the rock-cut funerary monuments at Petra and MADA'IN SALIH. With the excavation of temples and other public buildings at Petra and elsewhere, however, knowledge of Nabataean building methods, decoration, models and influences has increased. The initial work on the numerous tomb façades, by Rudolph E. Brünnow, Alfred von Domaszewski and others, produced only broad typologies, which were neither firm chronologies nor true pictures of actual architectural development. They did recognize, however, that the Nabataeans adapted elements from Mesopotamia, Egypt and the Hellenized West and incorporated them into their own structures; examples of this are the crow-step, the Egyptian cavetto, the Corinthian column and, finally, Roman orders, modified to suit Nabataean taste. The Nabataean capital, for example, is distinctive, composed of projecting 'horns' instead of the volutes of the Corinthian order. Less obvious modifications are reductions in standard heights and in module sizes, and the lack of columnar entasis, apparent only after careful analysis. By contrast, the lavish use of floral decoration, often with applied elements, the typical diagonal dressing of interior walls and the sheer size of the façades and tomb chambers are typically Nabataean contributions.

Nabataean buildings were more varied in their construction techniques and quality than the superbly carved rock tombs. Heavy plastering often covered rather poorly fitted blocks or took the place of elements that might be expected to have been stone-carved, for example in the interior of the Temple of Allat (the Temple of the Winged Lions) at Petra. At the same time innovative approaches to construction can be seen in the use of numbers and letters of the alphabet to designate the location for ashlars and column drums, in the use of ring-bases for columns, in the keying nails and tacks used in plastering walls and in the devices used for affixing *crustae* (plaster wall attachments).

Certain features in Nabataean architecture, at least in the reign of Aretas IV (9 BC–AD 40), were probably based on examples in Vitruvius' *On Architecture*, either directly or indirectly via artisans trained in Rome. Hence the plans of such buildings as theatres and temples tend to conform to those commonly found throughout the Hellenized Roman Empire. The impressive architectural contributions made by Aretas IV were perhaps the result of rivalry with the equally impressive record of HEROD THE GREAT (*reg* 37–4 BC), himself part Nabataean, in the nearby kingdom of Judaea.

Architectural decoration was similarly eclectic. Scattered fragments of reliefs, often copies of Hellenistic works showing Greek deities, sculpture in the round, patterned mosaic floors, mystery-cult fresco panels, scrolls depicting faces and animals, naturalistic or highly conventionalized cult images, vine-covered column drums and other examples intermingle throughout Nabataean territory. Oriental elements are apparent in the pouting lips and protruding eyes of faces and in the use of attributes to symbolize deities. Purely Nabataean are the eye-idols (stylized faces with prominent eyes) and the Dushara blocks (rectangular blocks of rock in niches symbolizing the chief male deity) still *in situ* in Petra.

In hydraulic engineering the Nabataeans surpassed most other cultures in the neighbouring regions, especially in their incorporation of natural features into water-supply systems. Innumerable dams, cisterns and other devices for storing water have been found throughout Nabataea. These are most remarkable at Petra. In drier regions circles of stone may have been an architectural feature designed to curtail run-off and permit the arid soil to soak up the maximum amount of rainfall.

2. Sculpture, ceramics and other arts. Although the names of sometimes successive generations of tomb-façade artisans are known (e.g. at Mada'in Salih), the authorship of the innumerable examples of other types of sculpture found in the region is not. It is difficult, therefore, to determine whether any given sculpture is the work of a local artist or that of an itinerant one. If the work is of local stone, the place of execution is obvious, but the origin of the artist is not. Classical motifs, such as deities, or symmetrical arrangement could have been executed by either local or visiting artists, as could local motifs. The Nabataeans were skilled in many other crafts, suggesting they also possessed technological and artistic ability in the realm of sculpture, but it is not possible to be certain of this. Examples of sculpture found in the region can be seen on Nabataean sites, in the Petra Museum and in the Jordan Archaeological Museum, Amman. The basalt head in the Louvre shows the typical almond-shaped eyes and Nabataean hairstyle but lacks the characteristic 'pouting' lips that are often found.

Nabataean ceramics are distinctive. The fine, thin, red-painted wares were first identified with the culture by Horsfield and Horsfield, who looked to Persia for their origin, although their affinity in form with the West Slope ware of the Athenian Agora suggests a Western source. They display a remarkably high level of expertise in clay preparation, throwing, standardization of size and shape, wall thinness, slip-paint decoration and firing. Decorated plates are common, but a wide variety of small cups, jugs and bowls also occurs). Decoration includes floral, linear and occasional zoomorphic motifs. In the early examples (1st century BC–1st century AD), which represent the highest technological level achieved, the decoration appears in red tones. Later, the decoration on generally less well-executed specimens (late 4th century AD) is done in black, although this may simply represent poor firing. The fine ware class appeared suddenly, probably in the last quarter of the 1st century BC, and represented an advanced stage of ceramic production. The transition to the black decorated class occurred probably around the last quarter of the 1st century AD.

The common wares found on Nabataean sites sometimes followed the forms of the fine ware class (especially the small plates), but proliferated according to the demands of domestic need. Thus cooking pots, strainer jugs, jars, storage jars, 'pilgrim flasks', bowls and other everyday vessels are found. In general, these conform to similar assemblages found throughout the Middle East, as well as in the West, during the Roman period and later. Decoration includes coloured slips, combing and ribbing, along with occasional examples of 'drip' painting on exteriors. Especially notable in the common ware class are the containers thought to be for ointments and known as *unguentaria*. Early examples at Petra (probably 4th century BC) were in the typical Hellenistic form of the spindle bottle, but these were later completely replaced by a series of high-necked types with round to ovoid bodies of varying and apparently standardized forms (1st century BC onwards). The quantity present at Petra in particular suggests local manufacture, linked to the local production of myrrh and other unguents that the Nabataeans traded. The appearance of the same forms in Western sites also suggests that the Nabataeans may have traded in finished products, as well as in raw materials. Some examples of local duplication of imported items have also been found, for example varieties of *terra sigillata* and Roman red wares, indicating that the local potters were aware of techniques not generally used in their own productions.

Allied to the production of household ceramics was the production in large quantities of figurines and lamps. These were commonly made in two moulds and joined before firing. The figurines include naturalistic examples of animals (particularly the horse and camel—the animals of desert caravan transport—but also monkey and ibex), deities, warriors and other motifs. The lamps, typically with slash-and-rosette or similar decoraton, had short nozzles decorated with volutes, round bodies and wide filling holes. They are based on types prevalent during the Roman period.

Nabataean coins are also derivative (examples in London, BM, and Petra Mus.). The earliest coins—those of Harithath II (*reg* 110–95 BC) until Maliku II (*reg c.* 50–28 BC)—portray the head of the king on the obverse but with reverse types borrowed from types issued by their Seleucid neighbours. Later, from the reign of Obidath III (28–9 BC) onwards, the reverses began to show individuality, and they were inscribed with the name of the monarch and, eventually, with that of his queen. The quality of the obverse designs tends to be rather primitive, although successive issues show some variation in features.

Metalwork items, both commonplace and artistic, have been recovered from Nabataean sites. The range includes architectural fixtures for *crustae*, nails for plastering, door keys, chains, diminutive bells and household vessels, as well as cast busts of deities and mythological creatures. The degree of refinement of the metals (especially copper) found in these artefacts is astonishing. It is highly probable that some objects were of local manufacture, but the origin of certain well-made pieces of jewellery and of the finely cast bronze busts is uncertain. None of the art works displays unique stylistic or obviously developmental features; the motifs vary in style from Hellenistic to Oriental.

R. E. Brünnow and A. von Domaszewski: *Die Provincia Arabia*, 3 vols (Strasbourg, 1901–9)

J. Cantineau: *Le Nabatéen* (Paris, 1930)

G. Horsfield and A. Horsfield: *Q. Dept. Art. Palestine*, ix (1941), pp. 105–218 ['Sela-Petra, the Rock of Edom and Nabatene, IV: The Finds'; 'Excavations in Palestine and Trans-Jordan, 1938–9'; 'Bibliography of Excavations in Palestine and Trans-Jordan, 1938–9']

N. Glueck: *Deities and Dolphins: The Story of the Nabataeans* (London, 1966) [good pls]

P. C. Hammond: *The Nabataeans: Their History, Culture and Archaeology* (Göteborg, 1973)

A. Negev: *The Nabataean Potters' Workshop at Oboda* (Bonn, 1974)

G. Bowersock: *Roman Arabia* (Cambridge, MA, 1983)

L. S. El-Khouri: *The Nabataean Terracotta Figurines* (Oxford, 2002)

B. J. Dolinka: *Nabataean Aila (Aqaba, Jordan) from a Ceramic Perspective: Local and Intra-regional Trade in Aqaba Ware during the First and Second Centuries AD: Evidence from the Roman Aqaba Project* (Oxford, 2003)

E. Netzer: *Nabatäische Architektur* (Munich, 2003)

A. Retzleff: 'A Nabataean and Roman Domestic Area at the Red Sea Port of Aila', *Bull. Amer. Sch. Orient. Res.*, cccxxxi (Aug 2003), pp. 45–65

Y. W. Eddinger: 'A Nabatean/Roman Temple at Dhat Ras, Jordan', *Near Eastern Archaeology*, lxvii/1 (March 2004), pp. 14–25

Naos. Term for the architectural core or sanctuary of a building. In ancient Greek architecture it refers to the cella or main sanctuary of a temple. The epinaos is the open rear vestibule of the naos.

Naples. *See* NEAPOLIS (ii).

Narrative Art. Narration, the relating of an event as it unfolds over time, is in principle a difficult task for the visual arts, since a work of art usually lacks an obvious beginning, middle and end, essential features of any story. Nevertheless, many works of ancient Greek and Roman art have as their subjects figures or tales from mythology, legend and history. The artists overcame the inherent limitations of visual narrative by representing stories which the viewer might be expected to know, and which the viewer would retell in his or her mind while taking in the representation. Much of the scholarship on narration in ancient Greek and Roman art consists of attempts to classify the various techniques employed by artists to convey stories visually. The multiplicity and complexity of these techniques is due mainly to two factors: the changing means by which stories were transmitted in antiquity; and the great variety of media and formats in which ancient art occurs. Concurrent with the development of narrative art, Greek culture gradually transformed itself from a culture reliant upon an oral tradition into a literate society; public performance of poetry and song gave way to erudition and to private enjoyment of literature in books (although this was restricted to a small literate minority). These changes in the ways that myths and stories were experienced inevitably led to changes in the techniques of visual narration. As for the diversity of media and of forms, narrative art was represented in sculptural friezes, metopes and pediments, for example the *Gigantomachy* from the north frieze of the Siphnian Treasury at Delphi (*see* SCULPTURE, fig. 12); and on sarcophagi and funerary urns; there were also narrative statuary groups. Narrative scenes were represented in monumental wall paintings (now lost) for public buildings and in wall paintings and mosaics for private houses, for example the pebble mosaic from Olynthos depicting *Thetis Bringing Armour to Achilles*. The largest number of representations of narrative art from ancient Greece consists of the decorative schemes on thousands of painted vases from Athens and other centres, such as that of *Ajax and Achilles Playing a Board Game* by EXEKIAS on an amphora (Rome, Vatican, Mus. Gregoriano Etrus). Different formats encouraged the use of different narrative techniques: tondi and statuary groups permitted the representation of only a few figures and a single episode in a story, whereas sculptural friezes and wall paintings encouraged the proliferation of figures and scenes.

The earliest figural scenes in Greek art, those on Geometric pottery of the 8th century BC, are problematic with respect to narrative. It is unclear whether they are purely descriptive scenes of everyday life, or representations of specific narratives. If they are narrative scenes, it is uncertain whether the events depicted are contemporary or legendary. The difficulty lies in the lack of individualization of the figures and actions. The contemporary viewer would have had to have information external to the images themselves, such as the specific contexts in which they were viewed, to determine whether they were narrative scenes.

By contrast, in the Archaic period (*c.* 700–480 BC) the narrative content of many works of painting and sculpture manifests itself through the use of attributes and inscriptions to identify specific figures, usually gods or heroes, and through the depiction of actions and situations unique to specific stories. A characteristic feature of Archaic narrative art is the depiction of objects, events or figures from several different moments in the tale, rather than the representation of a single moment in a story. This is often described as the simultaneous or synoptic method, and its aim was to render a narrative scene more immediately or more fully intelligible through the inclusion of as much detail as possible from a story. This method has been compared to epic poetry, which is similarly characterized by a great interest in detail.

During the Classical period (*c.* 480–323 BC) the content or action of a narrative scene was often expressed through subtle details of appearance and gesture; the climactic moment in the story was often passed over in favour of a quiet moment before or after the main action, as in the east pediment from the Temple of Zeus at Olympia showing *Preparations for the Chariot Race between Pelops and Oinomaos* (*c.* 470–457 BC; Olympia, Archaeol. Mus.; see fig.). This approach is sometimes called narration by allusion, and its purpose is to draw attention to the nature or state of mind of the characters in a story and thereby not only to relate what happened but also to indicate why it happened. Narrative art of this period also tended to represent one moment in a story, rather than several, and to include in a scene only those figures and objects relevant to that one moment; this method of visual narration, often called the monoscenic method, is closer to written narrative than the simultaneous method is, in so far as it visually maintains the temporal distinctions between successive events in a narrative text. This development, as well as the interest in character and internal states of mind, has been thought to be related to the rise of Athenian drama in the 5th century BC. As means of representing stories, drama and art are similar in that both rely on visual spectacle. Drama, however, also relies for its full effect on the orderly unfolding of events over time (including, for example, dramatic peripeteia or reversal of fortune), and this heightened concern for the temporal aspect of the narrative may have influenced Classical artists. The staging, choreography and costumes of Athenian drama were only occasionally represented in art, but the many reworkings of traditional stories by Athenian dramatic poets served as the point of departure for much narrative art from the 4th century BC on.

Two further developments in narrative art during the Classical period should be noted. First, narrative scenes in painting began to include not only figures but also simple indications of landscape or architectural setting; in a few instances elements of setting seem to have conveyed not merely the location of the action but also a sense of the space in which it occurred. Second, in addition to representations from legend and mythology, there were representations of actual historical events, the mid-5th-century BC painting (untraced) of the *Battle of Marathon* by PANAINOS, originally in the Painted Stoa (Stoa Poikile) at Athens, being perhaps the earliest known example. This new type of subject-matter remained exceptional until the second half of the 4th century BC, when it seems to have greatly increased in importance due to Macedonian patronage, as, for example, in the *Alexander Mosaic* (*c.* 100 BC; Naples, Mus. Archeol. N.; *see* POMPEII, fig. 7) from the House of the Faun at Pompeii, which probably represents the Battle of Issus between Alexander the Great and Darius III and was copied from an earlier painting of the ?4th/3rd century BC.

In the Hellenistic period (323–7 BC) a far-reaching development in narrative art was the practice of illuminating texts. Illuminated texts appear to have served as sources for many works of narrative art in this and in the Roman period, and to

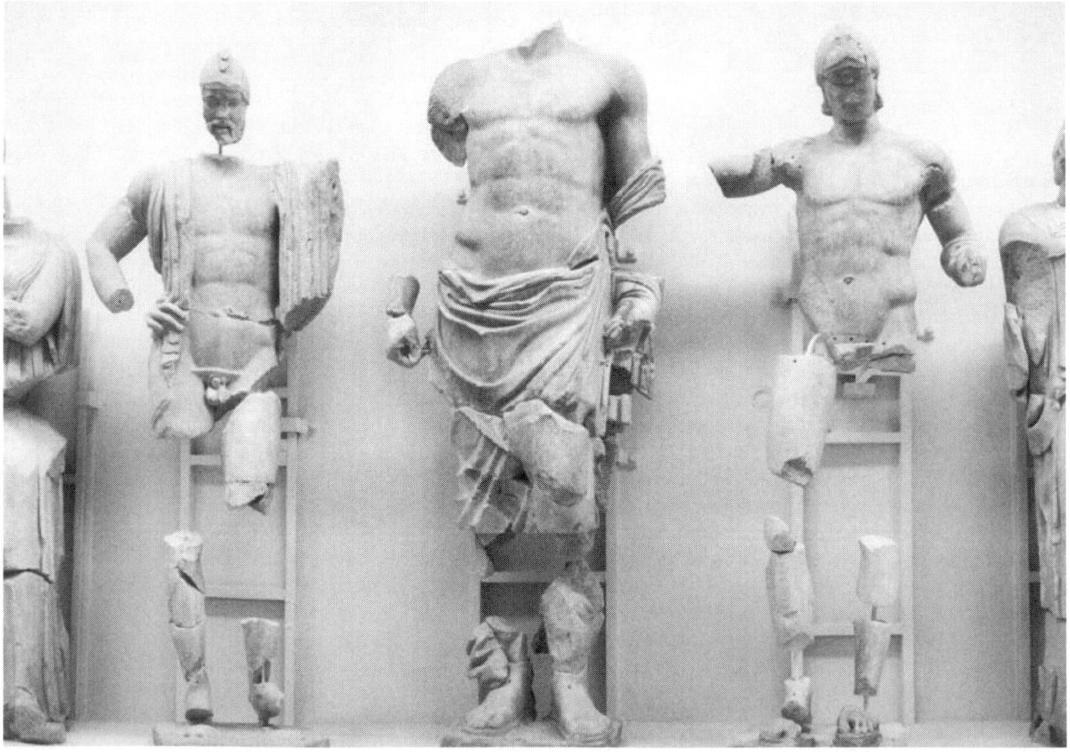

Ancient Greek narrative scene depicting *Preparation for the Chariot Race between Pelops and Oinomaos,* h. 3.3 m, east pediment of the Temple of Zeus at Olympia, *c.* 470–457 BC

have increased the number of situations in Greek myth and legend that were given visual form. This type of visual narrative, sometimes called the cyclic method, presumes that the viewer has a detailed knowledge of the specific textual source of a narrative scene, since the representation was originally embedded in the text itself. As a result, works of art based on these manuscript illuminations, such as Roman sarcophagi decorated with mythological scenes, are very often obscure, learned in character and less immediately comprehensible than earlier works of narrative art.

The technique of continuous narrative, in which a figure appears more than once in the same setting, was also developed during the Hellenistic period. It can be seen in the Telephos frieze showing the *Building of the Boat for Auge* (*c*. 180–*c*. 160 BC; Berlin, Antikensamml.) from the Great Altar at Pergamon. Use of continuous narrative was, however, a characteristic feature of Roman art, and it has been the subject of frequent discussion since Franz Wickhoff (1895) advanced the argument that it was a uniquely Roman, rather than Greek, development. Studies in the 20th century by Kurt Weitzmann (1947) and Peter Heinrich von Blanckenhagen (1957) showed that continuous narrative was a Hellenistic, not Roman, innovation. The principal development of continuous narrative in the Roman period is that of the relation of figure to background. Many Roman paintings of the 1st century BC and the 1st century AD are characterized by expansive landscapes peopled with diminutive figures from Greek mythology, whose actions are subordinate to the setting and the general ambience; the best known example is the painting showing scenes from the *Odyssey* (*c*. 40–*c*. 20 BC; Rome, Vatican, Sala della Nozze Aldobrandine). While the concern for setting and mood is not completely unattested in Greek art, it was of particular interest and importance to Roman patrons. The representation of historical events became the most important function of public narrative art in the Roman Imperial period, the scenes on Trajan's Column (AD 112–13) being well-known examples.

C. Robert: *Bild und Leid: Archäologische Beiträge zur Geschichte der griechischen Heldensage*, Philologische Untersuchungen, v (Berlin, 1881/*R* New York, 1975)

F. Wickhoff: *Die Wiener Genesis* (Vienna, 1895); Eng. trans. by E. Strong as *Roman Art: Some of its Principles and their Application to Early Christian Painting* (London, 1900)

K. Weitzmann: *Illustrations in Roll and Codex: A Study of the Origin and Method of Text Illustration*, Stud. MS. Illum., ii (Princeton, 1947, rev. 1970)

P. H. von Blanckenhagen: 'Narration in Hellenistic and Roman Art', *Amer. J. Archaeol.*, lxi (1957), pp. 78–83

G. M. A. Hanfmann: 'Narration in Greek Art', *Amer. J. Archaeol.*, lxi (1957), pp. 71–8

N. Himmelmann-Wildschütz: 'Erzählung und Figur in der archäischen Kunst', *Abh. Geistes- & Sozwiss. Kl.* (1967), pp. 73–100

A. M. Snodgrass: *Narration and Allusion in Archaic Greek Art* (London, 1982)

R. Brilliant: *Visual Narratives: Storytelling in Etruscan and Roman Art* (Ithaca, and London, 1984)

M. Stansbury-O'Donnell: *Pictorial Narrative in Ancient Greek Art* (Cambridge, 1999)

G. Hedreen: *Capturing Troy: The Narrative Functions of Setting in Archaic and Early Classical Greek Art* (Ann Arbor, 2000)

P. J. Holliday: *The Origins of Roman Historical Commemoration in the Visual Arts* (Cambridge, 2002)

Naukratis [now Kawm al-Gi'eif]. City in ancient Egypt that flourished during the 26th Dynasty (664–525 BC) in the north-western Delta. Discussions about the links between the Aegean and Egypt during the late Orientalizing and Archaic periods of Greece focus erroneously on Naukratis, which was not occupied by the Egyptians before the 7th century BC. Tradition maintains that Psammetichus I (*reg* 664–610 BC) introduced the eastern Greeks into Egypt as a resident class of foreign mercenaries in the service of the pharaoh. Before Amasis (*reg* 570–526 BC), Naukratis was allegedly the only trading post in the whole of Egypt in which an alien merchant might conduct business. It is best regarded as an Egyptian establishment of no earlier than the 26th Dynasty (rather than as a Greek foundation in the literal sense) in which alien merchants from eastern Greece were obliged to reside. During the course of the 4th century BC Naukratis became a true city-state and survived into the 7th century AD.

The northern part of the site is earlier than the rest. Excavations have revealed a Milesian temple to Apollo, a Samian temple to Hera, a temple to the Dioskouroi, a temple to Aphrodite, fronted by a stepped altar, and a factory that produced scarabs, small portable amulets and figurines in faience. Numerous fragments of limestone statuettes, apparently in an Archaic Greek style, found scattered about the site of the Temple of Aphrodite, are most closely paralleled by a group of sculptures excavated on Cyprus. The Greek pottery recovered from Naukratis provides little evidence of the site's supposed connections with the eastern Greeks, since it appears to derive mainly from the Corinth and Attica of the late 7th century BC. Moreover, it is unlikely that the Naukratis sanctuary to the Dioskouroi would have arisen in an eastern Greek context, since these deities were not particularly associated with Asia Minor (the homeland of the eastern Greeks). The archaeological record and the literary tradition are therefore not in accord, and sweeping generalizations about Naukratis' key role in Egyptian influence on emerging Greek art should be avoided. The city's relations with the Carians and the island of Cyprus during this same period are also open to discussion.

F. W. von Bissing: 'Naukratis, Studies in the Age of Greece and Egyptian Settlements at Naukratis', *Bull. Soc. Royale Archéol., Alexandrie*, xxxix (1951), pp. 33–82

W. M. Davis: 'Ancient Naukratis and the Cypriotes in Egypt', *Götting. Misz.*, xxxv (1979), pp. 13–23

G. P. Schaus: 'A Foreign Vase Painter in Sparta', *Amer. J. Archaeol.*, lxxxiii (1979), pp. 102–6

W. D. E. Coulson and A. Leonard jr: *Naukratis: Preliminary Report on the 1977–1978 and 1980 Seasons*, i of *Cities of the Delta* (Malibu, 1981)
W. M. Davis: 'Egypt, Samos and the Archaic Style in Greek Sculpture', *J. Egyp. Archaeol.*, lxvii (1981), pp. 61–81
W. D. E. Coulson: *The Survey at Naukratis and Environs* (Oxford, 1996)
A. Leonard jr: *Ancient Naukratis: Excavations at a Greek Emporium in Egypt,* 2 vols (Oxford, 1997 and 2001)
A. Möller: *Naukratis: Trade in Archaic Greece* (Oxford, 2000)
U. Höckmann and D. Kreikenbom, eds: *Naukratis: Die Beziehungen zu Ostgriechenland, Ägypten und Zypern in archaischer Zeit* (Möhnesee, 2001) [papers in German, French and English]

Naukratis Painter (*fl c.* 575–*c.* 550 BC). Greek vase painter. Together with the BOREADS PAINTER, he represents the 'old generation' in Lakonian Black-figure. His name vase, a cup from NAUKRATIS, Egypt (London, BM, B 4), depicts a standing female figure holding a plant and surrounded by winged daemons. This has been interpreted as the nymph Kyrene but is more likely to be the vegetation deity Artemis Orthia. Such representations of single divine or daemonic figures, outside any narrative context, were favoured by the Naukratis Painter. Two cups attributed to him (Paris, Louvre, E 668; Taranto, Mus. N., IG 4988) show a seated *Zeus* with an eagle flying towards him, and a cup from Cerveteri (Mus. N. Cerite, 90287) depicts *Poseidon Riding a Hippokampos.* The interiors of other cups variously show a daemon (a sphinx, a Gorgon, a Boread, or Pegasos), and there are also some symposion scenes with winged daemons surrounding the diners (e.g. cup, Paris, Louvre, E667). The Naukratis Painter may have invented the characteristic high foot of the Lakonian cup, and he also worked on other shapes including lakainai, kraters and hydriai. He was a good draughtsman and produced fine decorative friezes and rich floral patterns. From Corinthian vase painting he borrowed such designs as the animal frieze, which he used on both small and larger vases.

The Naukratis Painter had a strong influence on all the later important Lakonian vase painters, and his manner was also imitated by lesser followers until the end of the 6th century BC.

See also POTTERY, §IV, 5(iii).

E. A. Lane: 'Lakonian Vase-painting', *Annu. Brit. Sch. Athens*, xxxiv (1933/4), pp. 139–40
B. B. Shefton: 'Three Laconian Vase-painters', *Annu. Brit. Sch. Athens*, xlix (1954), pp. 303–6
C. M. Stibbe: *Lakonische Vasenmaler des sechsten Jahrhunderts v. Chr.*, 2 vols (Amsterdam and London, 1972), pp. 45–85, pls. 1–26

Naukydes (*fl c.* 420–*c.* 390 BC). Greek sculptor. He was born in Argos and during the Classical period produced works in bronze, which are mentioned in ancient sources but no longer survive. Pliny (XXIV. xix.50) dated his floruit to 400–397 BC. His statue of *Cheimon* at Olympia (Pausanias: VI.ix.3) celebrated a victory of 448 BC but may have been made later. A statue of the boxer *Eukles*, also at Olympia (Pausanias: VI.vi.2), belongs to the late 5th century BC or early 4th, and his gold and ivory *Hebe* (Pausanias: II.xvii.5), which stood beside the cult statue, attributed to Polykleitos, in the Temple of Hera at Argos, must date after 423 BC, probably near the end of the century. Pausanias stated that Naukydes was the brother of Polykleitos (II.xxii.7) and that he was the teacher of a different, probably younger Polykleitos (VI.vi.2). The statue base of *Eukles*, however, names Naukydes' father as Patrokles, who was also the father of the sculptor Daidalos of Sikyon.

Naukydes seems to have specialized in statues of athletes, though his *Hermes, Hebe* and a *Hekate* at Argos show an interest in divine figures. Whether a pupil of Polykleitos or not, Naukydes seems to have been a follower and probably continued and experimented with the ideas of the master (*see* POLYKLEITOS, §2). Pliny stated that Naukydes made a *Diskobolos* (*Natural History* XXXIV.xix.80). This statue has long been associated with Roman copies representing an athlete preparing to throw a discus (e.g. Rome, Pal. Conserv., Mus. Nuo.). The stance, with right foot advanced, can be compared to the position of the sockets for feet on the *Eukles* base. Similarly, the Roman *Hermes of Troizen* (Athens, N. Archaeol. Mus.) may copy Naukydes' *Hermes* (Pliny: XXXIV.xix.80). The connection between Naukydes' group of a man sacrificing a ram (Pliny: XXXIV.xix.80) and the statue of *Phrixos* seen by Pausanias on the Athenian Acropolis (I.xxxiv.2) is more problematical.

A. M. U. Linfert: *Von Polyklet zu Lysipp* (Giessen, 1966)
D. Arnold: *Die Polykletnachfolge* (Berlin, 1969)
G. Despinis: 'Zum Hermes von Troizen', *Mitt. Dt. Archäol. Inst.: Athen. Abt.*, xcvi (1981), pp. 237–44

Naxos. Greek island at the centre of the Aegean Cyclades. It is the largest and most fertile of that island group and has been an important centre since prehistoric times. As well as agricultural wealth, the island also possesses extensive marble deposits and is a rare source of the abrasive mineral emery, which was used for working marble objects.

1. Bronze Age. 2. Greek.

1. BRONZE AGE. By the end of the 20th century the most significant prehistoric finds on Naxos had been from Early (EC) and Late Cycladic (LC) contexts (*c.* 3500–*c.* 2000 BC and *c.* 1600–*c.* 1050 BC respectively). The earliest excavations, mainly of EC cemetery sites, were conducted by C. Tsountas in the late 19th century, his work being augmented by that of C. Doumas in the 1960s. The most important Bronze Age settlement, Grotta (the northern and north-western coastal area of modern Naxos town), as well as the neighbouring ec and lc cemetery on the hill of Aplomata, were investigated from 1949 onwards by N. Kondoleon and, after his death, by V. Lambrinoudakis. Grotta poses exceptional problems for the excavator, since much of the deposit is

now below sea-level. Finds from the early work of Tsountas are in the National Archaeological Museum in Athens; the remainder is in the Archaeological Museum in Naxos and in a collection in the village of Apeiranthos.

Early Cycladic cemeteries are widely scattered over the island. At one important cemetery (Ayioi Anargyroi) the graves may have been grouped into those that were richer and those that were poorer, suggesting some kind of social distinction. In general, the richer burials may have marble figurines and vases, and occasionally bronze jewellery, tools or weapons; the poorer may have only pottery, perhaps together with a few beads or other modest offerings. Ayioi Anargyroi also had an interesting structural feature in the form of a stone-built platform, apparently for ceremonial purposes. Other EC architectural remains are the simple houses of the Grotta settlement and the tiny fort at Panormos in the south-west of the island, where the rooms are squeezed into a walled circuit with towers. Unique stone slabs, apparently EC, with scenes showing hunting, fighting and boating, have been found at Korfi t'Aroniou. The figures are depicted with a sort of pointillé technique (Apeiranthos, Archaeol. Col.). Folded-arm figurines from the cemetery of Spedos constitute one of the most important types of EC stone figurine (see fig. 1).

The Middle Cycladic (MC) period (*c.* 2000–*c.* 1600 BC) is not well known, although there are clear signs (at Grotta and Mikre Vigla) of occupation. A group of cist graves at Aila, which span the transition from MC to LC, produced, as well as characteristic pottery, an important group of bronze tools and weapons.

Like other major Cycladic centres, Naxos seems to have succumbed to Minoan influence at the beginning of the LC period. There is some evidence of this in the Aila pottery, as well as at other sites on the island, and an earlier view that Naxos might have escaped this otherwise universal trend must now be discarded. Many of the discoveries from Grotta belong to LC III (*c.* 1390–*c.* 1050 BC) and are predictably Mycenaean in character. The settlement itself was extensive, although the precise limits have not yet been determined. The best-preserved finds of this period come from three chamber tombs on the hill of Aplomata and the nearby site of Kamini, which was probably part of the same cemetery. Most striking are the series of 'stirrup jars' decorated with stylized octopuses and other pictorial schemes (*see* POTTERY, fig. 7c). Some ritual vases have clay snakes attached to them. Also of interest is a cylinder seal of Near Eastern type, some gold-leaf rosettes (*see* METALWORK, §II, 1), pierced probably for attachment to garments, bronze swords and iron dress pins (from Kamini; all Naxos, Archaeol. Mus.). Iron occurred only at the very end of the Bronze Age in the Aegean, and its appearance at Kamini supports the conclusions of excavations at Grotta that the area was occupied continuously during the transition from Bronze to Iron Age.

C. Tsountas: 'Kykladika', *Archaiol. Ephimeris* (1898), cols 137–212; (1899), cols 73–134

K. Scholes: 'The Cyclades in the Later Bronze Age: A Synopsis', *Annu. Brit. Sch. Athens*, li (1956), pp. 9–40

N. Kondoleon: 'Mykenaike Naxos' [Mycenaean Naxos], *Epeteris Etaireias Kykladikon Meleton*, i (1961), pp. 600–08

C. Doumas: *Early Bronze Age Burial Habits in the Cyclades* (Göteborg, 1977)

C. P. Kardara: *Aplomata Naxou: Kineta euremata taphon A kai B* [Aplomata on Naxos: movable finds from Tombs A and B] (Athens, 1977)

V. Fotou: 'Les Sites de l'époque néolithique et de l'âge du bronze à Naxos', *Les Cyclades*, Centre National de la Recherche Scientifique (Paris, 1983), pp. 15–57

M.V. Kosmopoulos: *He Naxos kai to kreto-mykenaiko Aigaio: Stromatographia, keramike, oikonomike organose tou hysteroelladikou I-IIIB oikismou tes Grottas* (Athens, 2004)

2. GREEK. Naxos has relatively few architectural remains from the Classical and Roman periods, although there are two important Archaic buildings. The island was an early centre of monumental sculpture, and the known quarry sites (especially that at Apollona) probably produced stone for building as well as for sculpture.

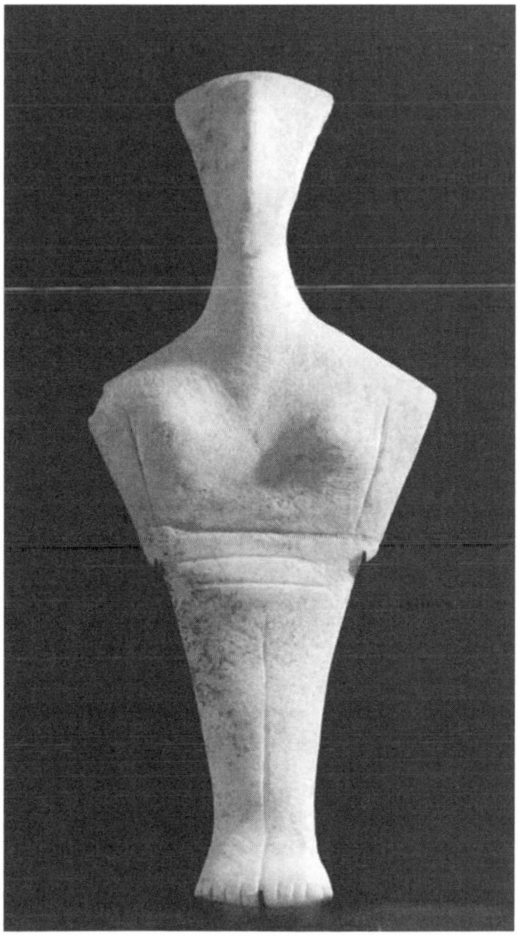

1. Naxos, Early Cycladic folded-arm figurine, marble, h. 275 mm, *c.* 2700–2300 BC (Paris, Musée du Louvre)

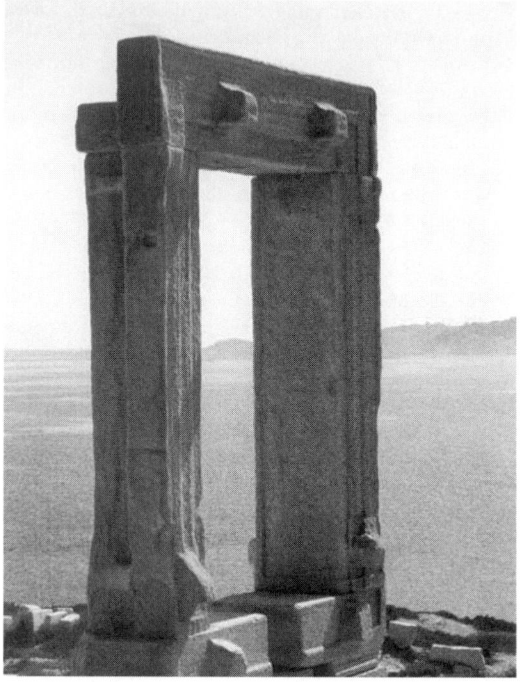

2. Naxos, reconstructed doorway to the Temple of Apollo, *c.* 530 BC

(i) Architecture. A temple, probably dedicated to Apollo and of the time of the tyrant Lygdamis (*c.* 530 BC), stood on the islet of Palati, now a promontory, opposite Naxos town. Apart from the reconstructed doorway to the cella (see fig. 2) nothing survives beyond the foundations, although it is clear that the temple was in the Ionic order and to some extent followed the grandiose tendencies of Archaic Ionic architecture, with double colonnades at its front and rear. Like other buildings on the island it was converted into a church in Early Christian times. At Naxos town the site of the ancient acropolis is presumably marked by the impressive Venetian fortifications. Architectural remains on the lower ground around the citadel are chiefly Hellenistic and Roman and include the colonnades of an agora. Just outside Naxos town, at Hyria, are the remains of a large granite and marble temple probably dedicated to Dionysos (jointly, perhaps, with some lesser goddess, hitherto unidentified). It was first erected in more modest materials in the 8th century BC but was rebuilt in the 7th, now with a four-column prostasis adorning its front; a new, more lavish, temple was built in the 6th century BC and survived into Roman times. As recent excavations have shown, the sanctuary enclosure also included a monumental propylon and a complex of banquet halls (*hestiatoria*), active already in the late 7th century BC and into the Classical period.

At Yiroulas, near the village of Sangri, another Archaic temple (*c.* 530 BC) underlies a three-aisled Early Christian basilica. It was dedicated to Demeter and Kore and had an unusual square plan, like the Archaic telesterion at Eleusis, the chief sanctuary of these divinities. From a porch, with five columns *in antis*, two doors led into the cella, where five further columns of unequal height supported the pitched roof. The whole structure, including the roof tiles, was of marble. The variety of architectural fragments found have allowed a complete reconstruction on paper. The style was Ionic, although the column capitals were Aiolic with leaf decoration. Parts of the masonry are crudely finished, perhaps to suggest a cave, and the interior decoration included painted plaster. In front of the temple, to its south-west, was a repository within a setting of columns. A precinct wall was added (or rebuilt) in the 4th century BC and inscribed boundary stones set up. A secular village seems to have grown up around the sanctuary at the time of its conversion into a basilica (?6th century AD). Some architectural features of the temples at Yiroulas and Palati can be related to those of Naxian buildings in the Sanctuary of Apollo on DELOS.

In an elevated position in the interior of Naxos and commanding impressive views of the south of the island is the remarkable Pirgos Cheimarrou, a Hellenistic tower (probably 3rd or 2nd century BC) preserved to about 20 m in height (the third floor). The masonry is of excellent quality, and the internal cantilevered spiral staircase is partly preserved.

N. M. Kondoleon: 'Anaskaphe en Naxo' [Excavation on Naxos], *Praktika Athen. Archaiol. Etaireias* (1954), pp. 330–38

G. Gruben and W. Koenigs: 'Der "Hekatompedos" von Naxos', *Archäol. Anz.* (1968), pp. 693–717

V. K. Lambrinoudakis, G. Gruben and M. Korres: 'Anaskaphes Naxou' [Excavations of Naxos], *Praktika Athen. Archaiol. Etaireias* (1977), pp. 378–86; (1979), pp. 249–58; (1981), pp. 293–7; (1983), pp. 297–8

A. W. Lawrence: *Greek Aims in Fortification* (Oxford, 1979), pp. 192–3, 470

H. W. Catling: 'Archaeology in Greece', *Archaeol. Rep.: Council Soc. Promotion Hell. Stud. & Managing Cttee Brit. Sch. Archaeol. Athens*, xxxiii (1986–7), p. 47

G. Gruben: *Architektur auf Naxos und Paros* (Berlin, 1991)

V. Lambrinoudakis: 'The Sanctuary of Iria on Naxos and the Birth of Monumental Greek Architecture', *Stud. Hist. A.*, xxxii (1991), pp. 172–88

V. K. Lambrinoudakis and others: 'Six Years of Excavations at Hyria, Naxos', *Archaiol. Ephimeris* (1992), pp. 201–16 [in Greek]

E. Simantoni-Bournia: 'The Early Phases of the Hyria Sanctuary on Naxos: An Overview of the Pottery', *Excavating Classical Culture: Recent Archaeological Discoveries in Greece*, eds M. Stamatopoulou and M. Yeroulanou (Oxford, 2002), pp. 269–80

(ii) Sculpture. Naxos was the first major centre of monumental marble sculpture production in Greece. This was due partly to its marble sources, from which raw material for the majority of early Archaic sculptures came and partly to its proximity to the Sanctuary of Apollo on Delos, for which dedications were commissioned (*see* SCULPTURE, §IV, 2(ii)(b)). Occupying a geographical position between two key areas

of sculpture production, Ionia and Attica, work from the island sometimes displays characteristics of both. Its influence, however, seems to have declined before the end of the Archaic period. Of outstanding interest for the development of both style and technique of Archaic sculpture are the kouroi, broken and/or unfinished, found still lying in quarries near Melanes and Apollona. The original block of stone was drilled round and then detached from its quarry bed by the insertion of damped wedges beneath. The figures were worked, at least in part, before they left the quarry, which explains why sculpture workshops tended to be located nearby. A number of finished kouroi have also been found on the island, for example in the Sanctuary of Demeter at Yiroulas, near Sangri (Naxos, Archaeol. Mus.). However, the best-known early works are mainly from Delos: they include the Naxian *Colossos* (*c.* 600 BC; Delos, Archaeol. Mus. and London, BM) and the Nikandre Kore (*c.* 650 BC; Athens, N. Archaeol. Mus.), as well as a base signed by Euthykartides (*c.* 600 BC; Delos, Archaeol. Mus.). The row of monumental lions (early 6th century bc; *in situ*) along the approach to the Temple of Leto at Delos may also be Naxian, as certainly is the famous sphinx (*c.* 560 BC; Delphi, Archaeol. Mus.; see fig. 3) from Delphi. The latter's similarity to two korai (*c.* 560–*c.* 550 BC; Athens, Acropolis Mus., 619 and 677) from the Athenian Acropolis suggests that they too are Naxian. Some of the kouroi from the Ptoion Sanctuary in Boiotia are of Naxian marble and probably of Naxian workmanship: a late Archaic grave stele (*c.* 490 BC; Athens, N. Archaeol. Mus.) from the same area signed by Alxenor of Naxos further attests to the peripatetic activities of Naxian sculptors at this time.

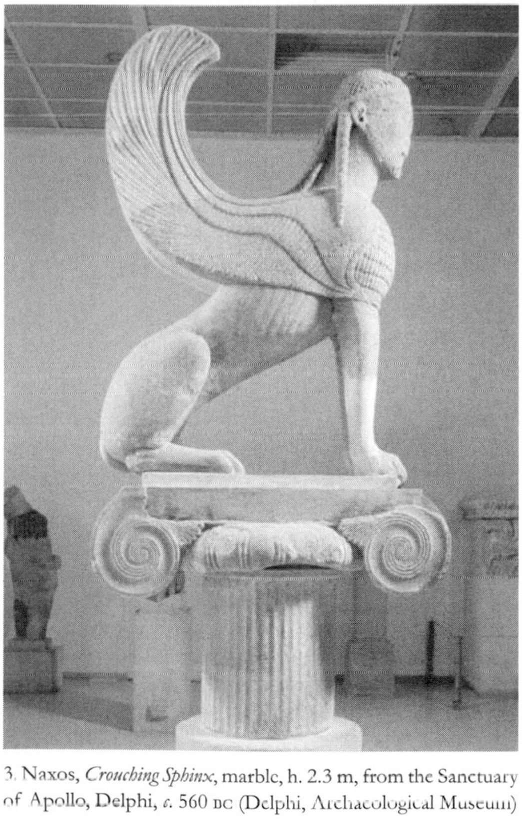

3. Naxos, *Crouching Sphinx*, marble, h. 2.3 m, from the Sanctuary of Apollo, Delphi, *c.* 560 BC (Delphi, Archaeological Museum)

J. G. Pedley: *Greek Sculpture of the Archaic Period: The Island Workshops* (Mainz, 1976)

W. Fuchs and J. Florens: *Die geometrische und archaische Plastik* (1987), i of *Die griechische Plastik* (Munich, 1987–), pp. 150–60

E. Semantone-Bournia: *Anaskaphes Naxou: Hoi anaglyphoi pithoi* (Athens, 1990)

G. Kokkorou-Alewras: 'Die Archaische Naxische Bildhauerei', *Ant. Plast.*, xxiv/1993 (1995), pp. 73–130

Nea Anchialos. *See* PYRASOS.

Nea Nikomedia [Nea Nikomedeia]. Site of Neolithic settlement of the 7th millennium BC, on the Macedonian plain west of the River Vardar-Axios, Greece. The site comprises a low settlement mound that yielded a wide range of craft products (including painted pottery and anthropomorphic figurines) and timber-framed buildings, including a shrine. It was partially excavated from 1961–3 by Robert Rodden, and the material recovered is in the Archaeological Museum, Veria. The low but extensive mound had two main levels from early in the north Greek Neolithic sequence, and a much later Neolithic phase; of these, the early phases, equivalent to the 'Proto-Sesklo' phase of Thessaly to the south, are the most significant.

The hand-formed pottery included simple bowls, ring-footed bowls, globular vessels and *askoi* (spouted pouring vessels); some examples were decorated with red paint on a white slip, or occasionally with white paint on a red ground or slip. The accomplished, mainly geometric, designs employed included zigzags, chevrons, triangles and lozenges. Fired clay anthropomorphic figurines were in the general Balkan tradition of the time. One notable complete female figurine, 175 mm high, has bulbous legs, a narrow waist and broad shoulders, with raised, folded arms and the hands resting on small breasts. The head is a tall, rod-like cylinder with a pinched nose and eyes delineated by incised slits; the legs, torso and head were modelled separately and then pegged together before drying. Other cylindrical forms are pierced at the top and have an encircling incised line; these have been interpreted as phallic representations. Stamps with individual geometric designs were also made from fired clay. Stone was skilfully worked into small axes, studs and plugs, which may have been decorative; a few stylized creatures, probably frogs or toads, were made from serpentine. Simple square and rectangular timber-framed buildings were constructed; clay house models from other northern Greek sites suggest that these would have had pitched roofs (see fig.). In one phase six smaller buildings surrounded a structure measuring *c.* 10 m square, with two internal partitions. Since this building also contained five

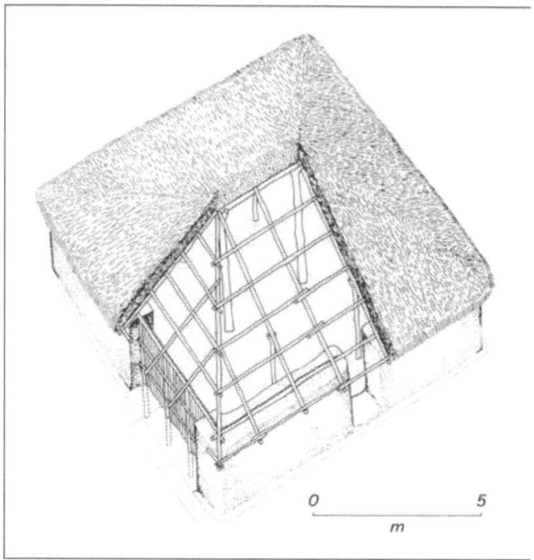

Nea Nikomedia, house, 6th millennium BC; reconstruction drawing

female figurines of the type described above and three serpentine toads, it has been interpreted as a special structure, possibly a shrine.

R. Rodden: 'Excavations at the Early Neolithic site of Nea Nikomedeia, Greek Macedonia', *Proc. Prehist. Soc.*, xxviii (1962), pp. 267–88

R. Rodden: 'An Early Neolithic Village in Greece', *Sci. Amer.*, ccxii (1965), pp. 82–92

J. Nandris: 'The Development and Relationships of the Earlier Greek Neolithic', *Man*, v (1970), pp. 191–213

D. Theocharis: *Neolithic Greece* (Athens, 1973)

M. Gimbutas: *The Goddesses and Gods of Old Europe* (London, 1982)

K. A. Wardle, ed.: *Nea Nikomedeia I: The Excavation of an Early Neolithic Village in Northern Greece, 1961–1964* (London, 1996)

Nea Paphos. *See* PAPHOS, NEW.

Neapolis (i). Site of the capital of the Scythian kingdom in the Crimea on a plateau on the outskirts of modern Symferopol' in Ukraine. Archaeological investigations began in the 19th century, but they were conducted intensively from the 1940s to 1960s. The city was founded in the late 4th century BC, reaching its zenith in the 2nd century BC under the rulers Skiluros and Palakos. Neapolis maintained close contact with the Greeks in the cities on the north coast of the Black Sea whose culture strongly influenced the Scythians; Greeks also formed part of the city's population. In the 3rd century AD Neapolis was destroyed by the Goths. Excavations have uncovered underground dwellings, grain storage pits, large houses with three chambers, public and religious buildings, the city square with a grand porticoed building, and a massive defensive wall with towers and gateways. Other finds are reliefs in stone of King Skiluros and Palakos (a joint portrait) and of the young Palakos on horseback, fragments of sculpture, Greek inscriptions and a variety of household objects of both Greek and local provenance. Outside the town walls lay a necropolis. Noteworthy are the rock-cut burial vaults with wall paintings, one of which (1st–2nd century AD) portrays a Scythian with a lyre, a horseman, a boar hunt and a carpet with a chequered pattern of yellow, black and red squares. There is also a stone mausoleum with 72 richly furnished tombs (2nd century BC–2nd century AD) probably belonging to members of the royal dynasty. Horse skeletons, weapons and a mass of ornaments, including gold rings and earrings, were found in the burial chamber.

Y. P. Zaytsev: *The Scythian Neapolis: 2nd Century BC to 3rd Century AD: Investigations into the Graeco-barbarian City on the Northern Black Sea Coast* (Oxford, 2004)

Neapolis (ii) [now Naples; It. Napoli]. Italian city on the Bay of Naples, overlooking the Tyrrhenian Sea, to the west of Mt Vesuvius. The city began as a Greek settlement. When the Greek colony of CUMAE reached its optimum size in the mid-6th century BC, the residents established a new settlement to the south. Known either as Parthenope in honour of the siren or as Palaiopolis (Gr.: 'the old city'), this settlement on the Bay of Naples was encompassed by a protective tufa wall. When more immigrants arrived in the mid-5th century BC, they established Neapolis ('the new city') to the north-east; Palaiopolis became a mere suburb. The new city had a Hippodamean grid (*see* HIPPODAMOS) with narrow rectangular blocks within an irregularly shaped city wall. Three broad streets (*decumani*) ran east-west, crossed by *c.* 20 narrower north-south streets. With an excellent harbour, Neapolis assumed a leading role among the colonies of South Italy. The Greek town covered approximately 60 ha and had a population of *c.* 30,000. Only a few traces of Greek houses, temples and burials have been discovered under the modern city. In 326 BC the Romans occupied Palaiopolis; Neapolis surrendered without resistance and became a favoured ally of Rome. Hellenic influence remained strong: Greek was commonly spoken, and the city boasted a Greek-style gymnasium erected in the Augustan age (27 BC–AD 14). Most notable of the few Roman urban buildings visible today is the Temple to the Dioscuri, erected under Tiberius (*reg* AD 14–37) and clearly evident within the later church of S Paolo Maggiore. Wealthy citizens from Rome spent winters in the pleasant environment of Neapolis. The surrounding areas boasts hundreds of villas, including that of L. Licinius Lucullus with its famous fishponds in the area of Palaiopolis. In AD 79 the eruption of Vesuvius damaged the town. Soon after, Rome settled a contingent of veterans on the site and awarded Neapolis the title and benefits of a Roman colony. The Imperial city spread over 100 ha with a population of *c.* 35,000. During the late Empire repeated barbarian onslaughts compelled the residents to strengthen the city walls. In AD 552 Neapolis came under Byzantine suzerainty. Ancient art and archaeological material from the area are on display in the grand Museo Archeologico Nazionale.

M. Napoli: *Napoli greco-romana* (Naples, 1959)
A. G. McKay: *Naples and Campania* (Exeter, NH, 1962)
J. D'Arms: *Romans on the Bay of Naples* (Cambridge, MA, 1970)
C. De Seta: *Storia della città di Napoli* (Rome and Bari, 1973)
S. De Caro and A. Greco: *Campania*, Guide archeologiche Laterza (Bari, 1981)
F. Zevi: *Neapolis* (Naples, 1994)
A. Lazzarini: *Marechiaro: Il bello, il sacro, l'antico* (Naples, 1998)

Nearchos (*fl c.* 560–*c.* 550 BC). Greek vase painter and potter. His signature appears on seven Attic Black figure pots and one clay plaque, once as potter and painter, otherwise, as far as preserved, only as potter. His significance as a potter is hard to assess because of the fragmentary state of his vases. His four early lip cups have exceptionally thin walls, while his two signed kantharoi dedicated on the Acropolis were unusually large (estimated h. 500 mm; Athens, N. Archaeol. Mus., Acropolis 611, 612). Five of Nearchos' signed works were painted by him, while the remaining three cups bear so little painting that this cannot be attributed. Finally, fragments of a further kantharos have been ascribed to Nearchos on stylistic grounds.

Nearchos' fame as a true artist is based mainly on the fragments of the only vase he signed as painter: a kantharos showing *Achilles with his Chariot* (Athens, N. Archaeol. Mus., Acropolis 611 and AP 67). This painting does not illustrate any specific scene from the *Iliad*. Instead, Nearchos created his own image of the hero setting out for battle by linking two complementary scenes that otherwise only occur separately: the *Nereids Bringing Achilles' Weapons* and the *Harnessing of Achilles' Chariot*. The names of the horses and of the charioteer are not those traditionally associated with Achilles. Nonetheless, the depiction of the hero gently fitting a bridle on one of his steeds suggests the intimate relationship between Achilles and Xanthos, the divine horse who foretold his death (*Iliad*, XIX.400–24). Achilles' attitude of calm dignity and the scene's general evocation of solemnity point forward to the art of EXEKIAS.

The pictures on Nearchos' kantharoi are painted in the Black-figure technique, but are unusually colourful and give some idea of the lost wall paintings of the period: one of the horses is completely red, another white with black outlines, while the tongue pattern above the pictures is painted on a white ground. Nearchos was the first Attic artist to depict the harnessing of a chariot team, a theme that became highly popular in the second half of the 6th century BC, and he was also the first to represent *Herakles and Atlas* (inside a cup; Berne, priv. col.). In addition, he signed a remarkable aryballos (New York, Met., 26.49) with delicate comic pictures around the mouth and on the handle which show his talent as a miniaturist. Nearchos' two sons TLESON and Ergoteles were also miniaturists, and, since both their signatures included their father's name, Nearchos may have remained in charge of their workshop in his old age. This conjecture is supported by Nearchos' dedication of a marble statue by the well-known sculptor ANTENOR on the Acropolis at a time (*c.* 520 BC) when he can no longer have been active as a painter or potter. At any rate the dedication testifies to the continuing commercial success of the pottery workshop.

G. M. A. Richter: 'An Aryballos by Nearchos', *Amer. J. Archaeol.*, xxxvi (1932), pp. 272–5
J. D. Beazley: *Development of Black-figure* (1951, 3/1986), pp. 37–8
J. D. Beazley: *Black-figure* (1956), pp. 82–3, 347, 682
D. von Bothmer: 'Five Attic Black-figure Lip-cups', *Amer. J. Archaeol.*, lxvi (1962), pp. 255–8
J. D. Beazley: *Paralipomena* (1971), pp. 30–31, 70, 523
H. Jucker: 'Herakles und Atlas auf einer Schale des Nearchos in Bern', *Festschrift für Frank Brommer* (Mainz, 1977), pp. 191–9
I. Scheibler: 'Griechische Künstlervotive der archaischen Zeit', *Münchn. Jb. Bild. Kst*, xxx (1979), pp. 9–10
L. Burn and R. Glynn: *Beazley Addenda: Additional References to* ABV, ARV2 *and* Paralipomena (Oxford, 1982, rev. T. H. Carpenter, 2/1989), p. 23

Neck amphora. Ancient pottery form, used as a storage jar (*see* POTTERY, fig. 15(i)d).

Nemausus [now Nîmes]. French city. Originally a Celtic tribal capital, Nemausus became a Roman colony in 27 BC. Augustus developed and fortified the settlement, and fine monuments of the Augustan period survive, including the PONT DU GARD aqueduct. By the 2nd century AD Nemausus was capital of the province of Gallia Narbonensis and one of the richest cities in Gaul. The city converted to Christianity in the late 3rd century and became a bishopric in the 4th. The prosperity of Nemausus ended with the barbarian invasions: it was sacked by the Vandals in 407, and *c.* 470 it was taken by the Visigoths, who built a fortress within the walls of the Roman amphitheatre.

The pre-Roman town of the Volcae Arecomici was within a fortified enclosure on the hill north-east of a spring sacred to the god Nemausus. The Roman city was laid out on the lower ground to the south, where the Via Domitia, the main Roman route from Italy to Spain, had probably attracted settlement. The town's increased importance earned it the rights of a Latin colony between 51 and 37 BC. After Augustus promoted it to the status of a Roman colony, he paid for the appropriate defences, a gift recorded on the inscription of 16 BC on the east gate, the Porte d'Auguste. The gate's two main carriageway arches remain, with foot passages either side, each with a niche for statues above it; originally there were twin projecting towers and an arcaded gallery above, as on the gates at Aosta and Autun. The south gate, the Porte de France, also survives, with a single arch and pilasters decorating the upper storey. The city walls had circular external towers, and enclosed an irregular area of 223 ha. In a reentrant of the walls above the spring of Nemausus the Tour Magne, an octagonal tower 40 m high, was built round a tower of the pre-Roman defences; it has been interpreted variously as a watch-tower, a mausoleum or a triumphal monument.

The best-known Roman building of Nîmes is the Maison Carrée (see fig.), the Corinthian temple preserved almost intact, owing to its conversion into a church in the early medieval period. Its dedication, *c.* AD 4, has been deduced from the holes on the front entablature for the bronze lettering of an inscription honouring Augustus's grandsons Caius and Lucius Caesar. At that time the Roman Corinthian order was still at an evolutionary stage in Rome itself. The ornament and refinements of the building show that the architect was fully aware of metropolitan developments, although Amy and Gros have detected the work of different groups of provincially trained masons. In the proportions of its ground plan it closely resembles the Temple of Apollo in Circo (*c.* 20 BC) in Rome. The detail of the Corinthian capitals and bases is closely related to the ornament of the Temple of Mars Ultor (dedicated 2 BC) in Rome, and the frieze is one of the earliest examples of continuous acanthus scrolls, inspired by the decoration of the Ara Pacis (dedicated 9 BC). The temple is pseudoperipteral with six columns along the front, a pronaos three bays deep and the remaining eight of the eleven side columns attached to the cella wall. It stood facing north within a rectangular precinct, probably the southern part of the forum. Its dimensions and proportions can be related to two modules, the height of the architrave and the intercolumniation.

The city required a well-organized water supply. North of the temple precinct there remains the *castellum aquae*, the circular settlement tank for water from the aqueduct, of which the Pont du Gard is a part, with apertures for ten distribution pipelines. A monumental complex of buildings was also begun around the spring of Nemausus in the Augustan period. In the mid-18th century the laying out of new basins and terraces for the Jardin de la Fontaine revealed much of the Roman structures and reproduced their form to some extent. The water was collected at the foot of the hill in a large, irregularly shaped pool, the south side of which, with two semi-circular stepped exedrae and the foundation of what was probably a temple, was aligned with the street grid. From there the water was channelled into a rectangular sunken area (18×24 m) surrounded by colonnades with fountains in niches; an altar was later built in the centre. Dedicatory inscriptions indicate that this was a nymphaeum. The sanctuary buildings were enclosed to east, south and west by a large portico. There was a theatre to the north-west and another large pool and what appear to have been baths to the south. Adjoining the west portico is the 'Temple of Diana', a building unlikely to have been a temple, although its unusual character makes its purpose uncertain. The façade, with two large niches on either side of the entrance steps, fronts a central hall, barrel-vaulted in stone, with engaged

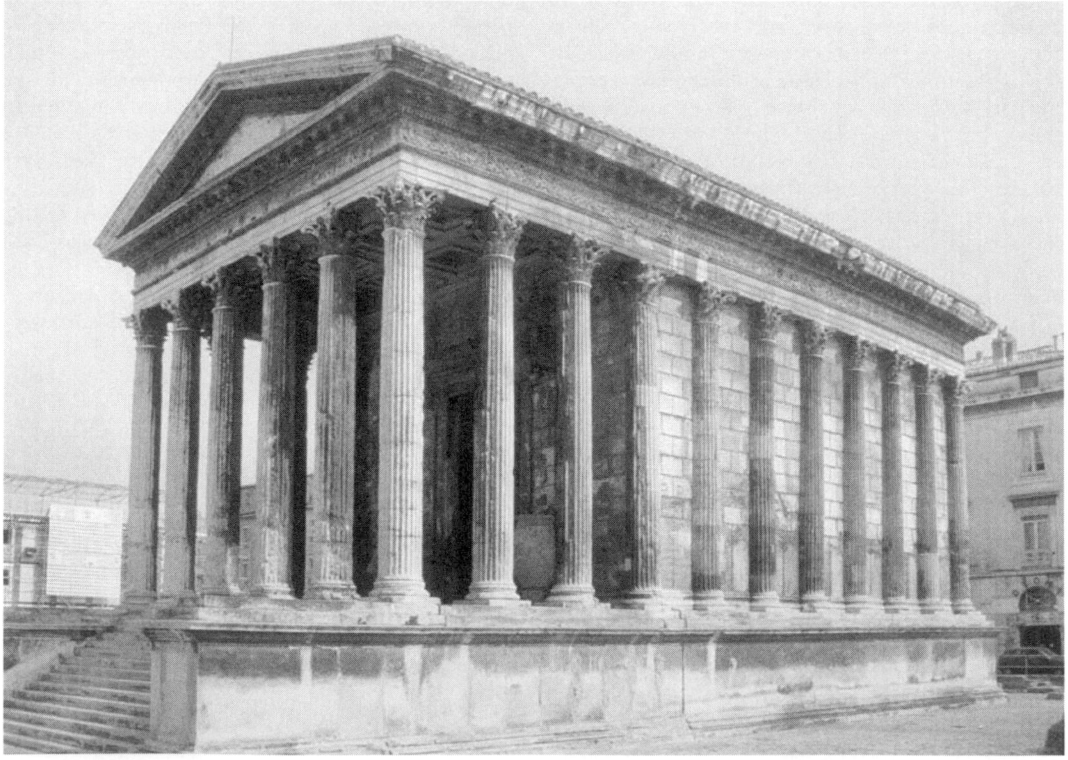

Nemausus (Nîmes), Maison Carrée, *c.* AD 4

pilasters dividing the sides into five bays containing niches set in aediculae with alternating triangular and segmental pediments. At the west end, opposite the entrance, there was a chamber, three metres square, and passages leading to an upper floor. The use of cut stone vaulting and the aediculae are more typical of Roman architecture in the East, whence the builders therefore seem to have come. The ornament indicates a date in the 2nd century AD.

The amphitheatre at Nemausus, with an estimated capacity of 25,000 spectators, is the best preserved in Gaul, and is very similar to that at ARELATE (Arles). The seating is carried on radial vaults, and the dressed-stone exterior, with two tiers, each of 60 arches, mostly survives to its full height. The lower tier is decorated with engaged piers, the upper with engaged columns standing on pedestals, both of the Tuscan Doric order. Although there is a general resemblance to the Colosseum at Rome (begun 80 BC), the projections of the entablatures above the capitals of both levels, and the pedestals of the upper level, combine to give a vertical emphasis and suggest a somewhat later date, probably the late 1st century AD or the early 2nd. Projecting from the parapet at the top are blocks with vertical holes for masts from which the awnings that shaded the seating were raised and lowered.

A. Grenier: *Manuel d'archéologie gallo-romaine*, i (Paris, 1931), pp. 314–23; iv/2 (Paris, 1960), pp. 493–506

R. Naumann: *Der Quellbezirk von Nîmes* (Berlin, 1937)

G. Lugli: 'La datazione degli anfiteatri di Arles e di Nîmes in Provenza', *Riv. Ist. N. Archeol. & Stor. A.*, xiii xiv (1964–5), pp. 145–99

R. Amy and P. Gros: 'La Maison Carrée de Nîmes', *Gallia-Suppl.*, xxxviii (Paris, 1979)

C. Imbert: *Les spectacles à Nîmes et en Gaule Romaine: Ier et IIe siècle après Jésus-Christ* (Nîmes, 1988)

J.-C. Bessac and M.-R. Aucher: *La pierre en Gaule narbonnaise et les carrières du Bois des Lens (Nîmes): Histoire, archéologie, ethnographie, et techniques* (Ann Arbor, 1996)

Nemea. Site of the ancient Greek Nemean Games, 5 km from the modern village of Nemea and 30 km south-west of Corinth, Greece. The remains of the Temple of Zeus (*c.* 340–*c.* 320 BC; see fig.) stand on the east bank of the River Nemea. Its architect is unknown, but Skopas has been suggested because of similarities between the temple and that of Athena Alea at Tegea, known to have been built by Skopas. Local marly limestone was the principal construction material while the sima was of marble, and there is evidence that marble tiles were used for the roof, with acroteria at the corners. This gleaming roof surmounted a peristyle coated with stucco to look like marble. It has six columns on the east and west façades and twelve along each flank; the Doric columns are extremely attenuated, like those of Pergamene architecture a century later. A ramp at the front leads to an altar 41 m long. The cella, on a raised stylobate, had a free-standing Corinthian colonnade along both side walls and across its west end. This was surmounted by Ionic half-columns attached to piers, with quarter-columns at the two ends. A sunken crypt that may have been used for oracular purposes lies in the adyton (inner chamber) behind the cella. There is no opisthodomos. Painted decoration, including a Doric frieze in red and blue, has been discovered. Enough of the pediment floor is preserved to show that it never had statuary. To the south-west are the foundations of other buildings of the 4th century BC: one (l. 85 m) probably served as a *xenon* (guest house) and another as a bathhouse. A Christian basilica was built over the west end of the *xenon* in the 5th century AD, using blocks from the temple.

B. W. Hill, L. T. Lands and C. K. Williams: *The Temple of Zeus at Nemea* (Princeton, 1966)

F. A. Cooper, S. G. Miller and S. G. Miller: *The Temple of Zeus at Nemea: Perspectives and Prospects* (Athens, 1983)

D. E. Birge, L. H. Kraynak and S. G. Miller: *Excavations at Nemea* (Berkeley, 1992–2005)

D. J. Pullen: 'A Lead Seal from Tsoungiza, Ancient Nemea, and Early Bronze Age Aegean Sealing Systems', *Amer. J. Archaeol.*, xcviii (Jan 1994), pp. 35–52

S. G. Miller: *Excavations at Nemea II: The Early Hellenistic Stadium* (Berkeley and London, 2001)

M. K. Dabney and others: 'Mycenaean Feasting on Tsoungiza at Ancient Nemea', *Hesperia*, lxxiii/2 (April June 2004), pp. 197–215

N. Makris and T. Psychogios: *The Reconstruction of the Temple of Zeus at Nemea: Progress Report and Future Perspectives* (Patras, 2004)

S. G. Miller and J. Bravo: *Nemea: A Guide to the Site and Museum* (Athens, 2004)

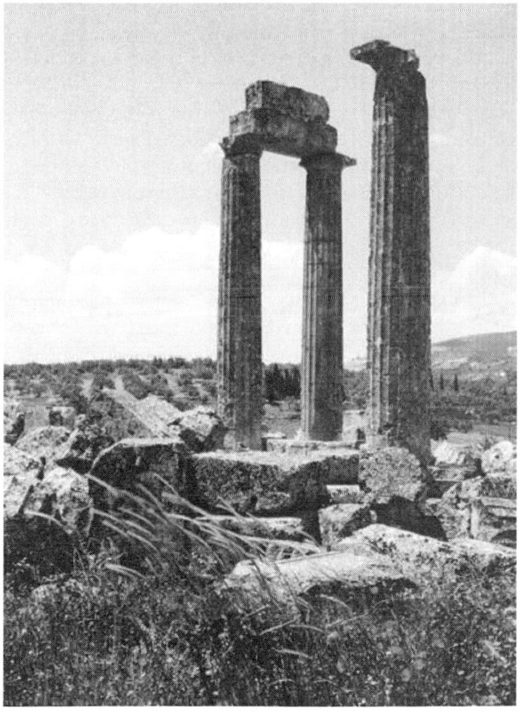

Nemea, Temple of Zeus, *c.* 340–*c.* 320 BC

A. Gutsfeld and others: 'Vom Wettkampfplatz zum Kloster', *Ant. Welt*, xxxvi/2 (2005), pp. 33–41

R. C. Knapp and J. D. Mac Isaac: *Excavations at Nemea III: The Coins* (Berkeley and London, 2005)

Nemi. Site with sanctuary of the goddess Diana beside the lake of the same name that fills a volcanic crater in the Alban hills 25 km south-east of Rome, Italy. Both lake and town take their name from the *nemus* (Lat.: 'sacred wood'). The sanctuary originated before the 6th century BC as the centre for a local cult in the territory of the Latin town of Aricia; it continued to flourish under Roman rule until the 4th century AD. The peculiar slave priesthood of Diana Nemorensis was the inspiration for Sir James Frazer's *The Golden Bough* (London, 1890–1915).

The main remains of the sanctuary now visible to the north-east of the lake are of a large rectangular terraced precinct (*c.* 44,000 sq. m), with retaining walls constructed as a series of arched niches faced in pseudo-reticulate masonry. Archaeological discoveries made there are recorded from the mid-17th century onwards, but the first systematic excavations were by Sir John Savile Lumley (later Lord Savile) in 1885. He identified a large masonry podium in the western half of the precinct as the Temple of Diana itself, but this does not correspond with Vitruvius' description of that temple (*On Architecture*, IV.viii.4), which is probably the still unexcavated building shown on a plan of 1856 as standing further up the hillside. Lumley also explored several rooms on the north side of the precinct and selected areas within it, finding numerous votive and architectural terracottas, coins and some sculpture (see fig.). His own share of the finds, presented to the Castle Museum at Nottingham, England, is now the main archaeological collection from the sanctuary. Much of what was found in further digging after 1885 on behalf of the landowner, Prince Orsini, is now untraceable, but the Ny Carlsberg Glyptotek in Copenhagen acquired most of the best sculpture as well as material from earlier antiquarian collections, while the bronzes and terracottas went elsewhere (e.g. Rome, Villa Giulia).

On the basis of these finds a broad chronology of the site can be defined. Initially the sanctuary consisted merely of a triple image of Diana in bronze (*c.* 500 BC), standing in a clearing in the sacred wood, an image shown on coins issued in 43 BC (e.g. Oxford, Ashmolean). In the late 4th century BC to the early 3rd, however, the site began to receive buildings decorated with architectural terracottas, and it became a focus for votive offerings made for health and fertility. The third phase (*c.* 100 BC) consisted of the large-scale landscaping of the sanctuary, with a terraced precinct and new temples. Finally, in the early Roman Empire, the sanctuary was eclipsed by the summer villas of emperors and aristocrats attracted by Nemi's scenic beauty. A theatre adjoining the sanctuary, excavated by Morpurgo in 1928, was rebuilt early in the 1st century AD by Volusia Cornelia, the proprietor of the luxurious villa nearby. The emperor Caligula (*reg* AD 37–41) had a sumptuous floating palace on a ship moored in the lake, one of two vessels uncovered in spectacular excavations between 1928 and 1931, during which the lake was partially drained. The ships were preserved in a specially built museum near the lake (Nemi, Mus. Navi), but they were largely destroyed during hostilities in 1944.

G. Ucelli: *Le navi di Nemi* (Rome, 1940)

F. Poulsen: 'Nemi Studies', *Acta Archaeol.* [Copenhagen], xii (1941), pp. 1–52

Mysteries of Diana: The Antiquities from Nemi in Nottingham Museums (Nottingham, 1983)

F. Coarelli: *I santuari del Lazio in età repubblicana* (Rome, 1987), pp. 165–85

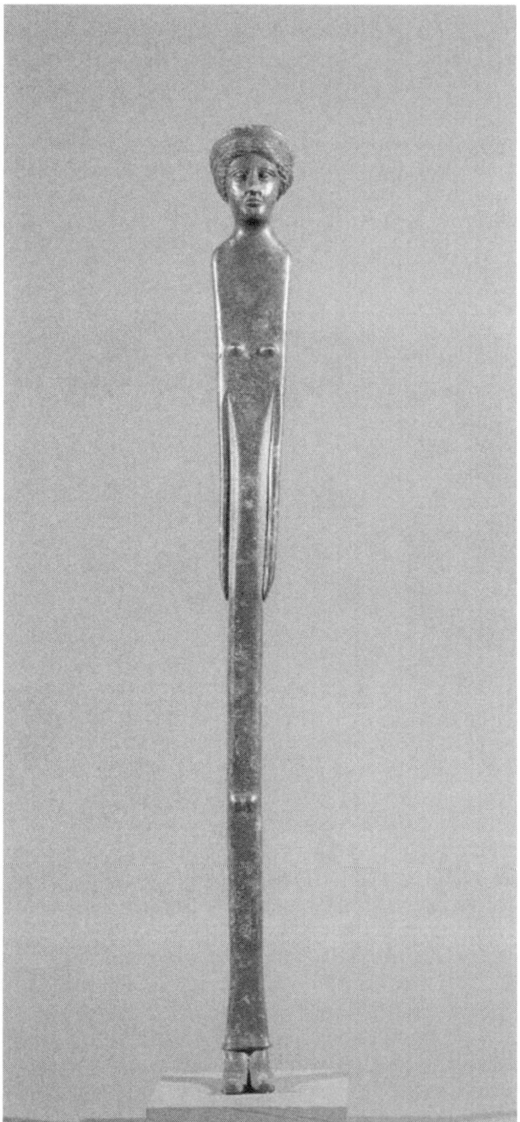

Nemi, bronze female statuette from the Sanctuary of Diana, h. 505 mm, *c.* 350 BC (Paris, Musée du Louvre)

M. Moltesen: *I Dianas hellige lund: Fund fra en helligdom i Nemi/ In the sacred grove of Diana: Finds from a Sanctuary at Nemi* (Copenhagen, 1997)
J. R. Brandt, A.-M. Leander Touati and J. Zahle: *Nemi-status quo: Recent Research at Nemi and the Sanctuary of Diana* (Rome, 2000)
F. Gentili and R. Luciani: *Il Santuario di Diana a Nemi* (Rome, 2001)
M. Moltesen and P. G. Bilde: *A Catalogue of Sculptures from the Sanctuary of Diana Nemorensis in the University of Pennsylvania Museum, Philadelphia* (Rome, 2002)

Neo-Attic. Term coined by Heinrich Brunn in his *Geschichte der griechischen Künstler* (Stuttgart, 1853) to designate sculptors of the 1st century BC to the 2nd century AD who added the epithet *Athenaios* ('the Athenian') after their signatures. The sculptors produced copies and adaptations of earlier statues, such as the bronze herm of *Apollonios*, son of Archias, based on the head of the *Doryphoros* by Polykleitos (?2nd half of the 1st century BC; Naples, Mus. Archeol., 4885), and marble reliefs on kraters, candelabra etc also derived from earlier works. The style arose from the Attic neo-Classical movement of the mid- to late 2nd century BC, and Neo-Attic workshops served rich patrons in Pergamon, Alexandria and above all Rome and Italy, as well as in Greece itself. Important Neo-Attic works include those from the MAHDIA SHIPWRECK near Tunis (*c.* 100 BC; Tunis, Mus. Alaoui), and various reliefs found at Peiraeus, including those based on the shield of the *Athena Parthenos* by Pheidias (2nd century AD; Peiraeus, Archaeol. Mus.). Typical of the Neo-Attic style are a volute krater by Sosibios (mid-1st century BC; Paris, Louvre), which combines disparate figures (maenads, dancers with weapons, nymphs etc), modelled on prototypes of different dates into a unified decorative scheme, and a marble rhyton by Pontios (late 1st century BC; Rome, Mus. Conserv.) with three maenads around its neck, perhaps based on a series by KALLIMACHOS. Although Neo-Attic art with its eclectic formalism and artificiality was the antithesis of the realism of Roman art, the style was extremely important, as it helped to transmit Classical Greek forms to Roman, and thus to western European, art.

F. Hauser: *Die neuattischen Reliefs* (Stuttgart, 1889)
E. Loewy: *Neuattische Kunst* (Leipzig, 1922)
W. Fuchs: *Die Vorbilder der neuattischen Reliefs* (Berlin, 1959)
W. Fuchs: *Der Schiffsfund von Mahdia* (Tübingen, 1963)
W. Fuchs: 'Paralipomena', *Kotinos: Festschrift für Erika Simon*, ed. H. Froning, T. Hölscher and H. Mielsch (Mainz, 1992), pp. 199–203
T. Stephanidou-Tiberiou: *Neoattica* (Athens, 1979)
M. A. Tiberios: 'Saltantes Lacenae', *Archaiol. Ephimeris,* cxx (1981), pp. 25–37, pls 5–6
H.-U. Cain: *Römische Marmorkandelaber* (Mainz, 1985)
H.-U. Cain: 'Neoatticismo', *Enciclopedia dell'Arte Antica Classica e Orientale*, Sec. Suppl. III (Rome, 1995), pp. 893–6
M.-A. Zagdoun: *La sculpture archaïsante dans l'art hellénistique et dans l'art Romain du Haut-Empire* (Paris, 1989)
D. Grassinger: *Römische Marmorkratere* (*Monumenta Artis Romanae XVIII*) (Mainz, 1991)
G. Hellenkemper Salies and others, eds: *Das Wrack* (Cologne, 1994); review by W. Fuchs in *Thetis*, ii (1995), pp. 302–5
L. A. Touchette: *The Dancing Maenad Reliefs: Continuity and Change in Roman Copies* (*BICS Suppl. 16*) (London, 1995)
'Neue Forschungen zum Schiffsfund von Mahdia', *Bonn. Jb.*, cxcvi (1996), pp. 197–370 (various authors)
T. M. Golda: *Puteale und verwandte Monumente: Ein Beitrag zum römischen Ausstattungsluxus* (Mainz, 1997)

Neo-Platonism. Philosophical movement that developed in the 3rd century AD and reinterpreted the ideas of PLATO. It was inaugurated by Plotinus (AD 204/5–70) and continued by Porphyry (232–*c.* 305), Iamblichus (*c.* 250–*c.* 325), Proclus (410 or 412–85) and others, flourishing first in Rome, then at Apamea in Syria and later in both Athens and Alexandria. Pagan Neo-Platonism died out during the 6th century, but Neo-Platonic thought continued to be influential in Byzantium and the medieval West as well as in medieval Islamic and Jewish philosophy. Many Neo-Platonic ideas were taken over by Christian thinkers, in particular by St Augustine (354–430) in the West and Pseudo-Dionysius (*c.* 500) in the East.

The Neo-Platonists' views on art were based on their metaphysics. Plotinus (*Ennead* I.vi) follows Plato's account in the *Symposium* of the ascent to the Form of Beauty, stressing that things perceived by the senses are beautiful only because they imitate the Form. He further argues (*Ennead* V.viii.1) that an artist in creating his work imitates the Form directly. This implicitly contradicts Plato's argument (*Republic* X) that the artist can only imitate sensible particulars; it thus opens the way to a higher evaluation of art than in Plato. Ultimately, however, art cannot reveal the highest reality but must be superseded by philosophical understanding and mystical experience. Plotinus mentions PHEIDIAS' statue of *Zeus* as an example of a sculpture whose model is in the intelligible, not the sensible, world (V.viii.1). This example, already traditional when Plotinus used it, is used again by Proclus. Proclus' point, however, is not quite the same. He declares that Pheidias' model was Zeus as described by Homer; if Pheidias had succeeded in imitating the Zeus of the intelligible world, the result would have been even finer. Proclus was more interested in poetry, especially Homer, than visual art. He offered extensive allegorical interpretations of Homeric myths in an attempt to answer Plato's attack on poetry. His underlying theory, that art can imitate what lies beyond the sensible world, is the same as that of Plotinus, and like Plotinus he holds that art, revealing as it is, cannot penetrate the very highest metaphysical level. For Proclus, Homeric poetry is inspired and so able to present some metaphysical realities in symbolic terms. It can even go beyond the intelligible world to impart truths about the divine henads. Nevertheless, such poetic symbols must ultimately be discarded if full union with the One is to be achieved.

R. T. Wallis: *Neoplatonism* (London, 1972)
S. Rappe: *Reading Neoplatonism: Non-discursive Thinking in the Texts of Plotinus, Proclus, and Damascius* (Cambridge, 2000)
H. D. Saffrey: *Le néoplatonisme après Plotin* (Paris, 2000)
K. Corrigan: *Reading Plotinus: A Practical Introduction to Neoplatonism* (West Lafayette, 2005)

Nereid Monument. *See under* XANTHOS.

Nero [Nero Claudius Drusus Germanicus Caesar] (*b* Antium [now Anzio], 15 Dec AD 37; *reg* AD 54–68; *d* Rome, 9 June AD 68). Roman emperor and patron. His influence on Roman architecture was profound, despite his premature death from suicide. In AD 59 he completed the Circus of Caligula in the valley of the Vatican, in which he introduced Greek games (the Ludi Juvenales) to Rome. The Baths of Nero (AD 62–4), built to the west of Agrippa's Pantheon, stunned his contemporaries by their splendour. As restored by Alexander Severus (AD 227), the baths comprised a symmetrical building with an adjoining gymnasium, but it is impossible to say whether its Neronian form anticipated the great Imperial *thermae* (*see* ARCHITECTURE, §VI, 1(i)(d)). The Emperor was blamed for a fire that broke out during the night of 18 July AD 64 and destroyed many parts of the city, not only because of the many crimes he had committed, but also because of the grandiose works he had undertaken for the renewal of the city. Although Nero's direct responsibility for the fire remains doubtful, the city was in fact rebuilt to his taste. New building standards were adopted to prevent the repetition of such vast fires, including the restriction of the height of buildings to 70 feet (*c.* 21.35 m), and the replacement of the narrow, winding alleys of the old town by regular, broad streets.

To replace the imperial palace on the Palatine—the Domus Transitoria which the fire had destroyed when it was still incomplete—Nero began the Domus Aurea, an enormous complex of buildings that was to extend from the Caelian to the Esquiline (*see* ROME, §IV, 5). It was designed on the lines of a country villa, with thermal baths, porticos, nymphaea, tempietti and other purely scenographic architectural features. The palace incorporated ingenious mechanical arrangements worked out by the architects SEVERUS AND CELER, including ceilings that scattered perfumes and flowers, and a great banqueting hall with a revolving vault or ceiling. The building was not yet finished when Vespasian (*reg* AD 69–79) drained the lake that lay at the centre of the complex and built the Colosseum in its place. Most of the palace was destroyed by fire (AD 104), although the Baths of Trajan (AD 109) incorporated some decorative elements in its foundations.

N. Dacos: *La Découverte de la Domus Aurea et la formation des grotesques à la Renaissance* (London, 1969)
M. T. Griffin: *Nero: The End of a Dynasty* (London, 1984)
M. Henig: *Architecture and architectural sculpture in the Roman Empire* (Oxford, 1990)
L. Crescenzi with S. Gizzi and P. Vigilante: *Anzio, Villa di Nerone: restauri 1989–1992* (Rome, 1992)
S. Gizzi: 'Villa di Nerone ad Anzio: Perderla o restaurarla?', *Boll. A.*, lxxxi/96–7 (April-Sept 1996), pp. 97–126
M. Bradley: 'Fool's Gold: Colour, Culture, Innovation and Madness in Nero's Golden House', *Apollo*, cdlxxxv (July 2002), pp. 35–44
E. Champlin: *Nero* (Cambridge, MA, 2003)
J. Malitz: *Nero* (Malden, MA, 2005)

Nesebr. *See* MESEMBRIA.

Nesiotes. *See* KRITIOS AND NESIOTES.

Nestora. *See* KAKOVATOS.

Nettos Painter (*fl c.* 620–*c.* 600 BC). Greek vase painter. The Nettos Painter is named from the Attic spelling of the Centaur Nessos, who is depicted in the episode of *Herakles Slaying Nessos* on the neck of the splendid Attic Black-figure neck amphora, the artist's masterpiece (Athens, N. Archaeol. Mus.). He is the earliest Attic Black-figure vase painter to have left sufficient vases (about 30) for it to be possible to chart his chronology and to establish his artistic personality. Most of these vases were found in Attica, where they served as grave markers or tomb furnishings. Four vases formerly ascribed to the Chimaera Painter were recognized by Beazley as examples of his early work.

The Nettos Painter preferred to decorate large shapes, chiefly amphorae and skyphos-kraters, though he also painted some lekanides and a plaque. The best examples of his large-scale work are his name piece, three skyphos-kraters from the cemetery at Vari (Athens, N. Archaeol. Mus., 16382, 16383, 16384), a fragmentary amphora (Aegina, Archaeol. Mus., 585) and two well-preserved amphorae (Athens, Agora Mus., P 1247, and Eleusis Mus., Z 21). The lekanides from Vari (Athens, N. Archaeol. Mus., 16363–16369, 16414 and 16416e) offer good examples of his smaller paintings.

Early works by the Nettos Painter generally depict single figures occupying most of the available surface (e.g. the sphinx on Eleusis Mus., Z 21) or, more often, pairs of animals, such as the sphinxes on the stand of Athens 16382 or the two felines attacking a bull depicted on its bowl. (This theme has a long history in both sculpture and painting.) Similarly, a skyphos-krater (Athens, Kerameikos Mus., 154) presents a powerful version of the confrontation between Bellerophon and the Chimaera, and an amphora (Athens, Agora Mus., P 1247) shows a sphinx on each side, probably intended as guardians of a tomb since the vase is weathered and probably stood out of doors for quite a while. A skyphos-krater of his middle phase (Athens 16383) has a vivid scene of a galloping cavalcade, and this is also the time when his sequence of lekanides begins. He decorated these smallish bowls with friezes of animals, a scheme inherited from Corinth. His louterion (Berlin, Antikensamml., 1682; destr. during World War II) may have been of a later date. It was decorated with two panels. One depicted Harpies, the other Perseus, and the figures were labelled, as are those of Herakles and Nessos on the artist's namepiece, where Herakles is shown killing Nessos, who had tried to ravish his wife, Deianeira, while carrying her across the River Evenus. The stumbling centaur raises both hands in supplication, and his long, shaggy beard and coarse features contrast sharply with the trim moustache and refined features of Herakles. This deliberate contrast between man and monster later became a frequent theme in Attic vase painting. On the body of the vase, Medusa's two sisters fly over a 'sea' of wave-like spirals surmounted by a frieze of leaping dolphins. On the viewer's far left Medusa sinks down on one knee, blood spilling from her severed neck. Perseus himself is omitted, but his presence is clearly felt. Equally ambitious is the scene on a skyphos-krater (Athens, N. Archaeol. Mus., 16384) of *Herakles Freeing Prometheus from the Eagle*. Prometheus is shown still fettered, while Herakles, who has already wounded the bird in the neck, is drawing his bow and aiming another arrow. On the stand of the same vase a dignified procession of four women depicts a quieter moment from this artist's repertory. Each woman is holding a palmette, and a Doric column, perhaps representing a temple, flanks the scene at each side. This is the first appearance in Attic Black-figure of an architectural element. Equally dignified is the lyre player on the fragmentary plaque (Athens, Agora Mus., A-P 1085).

The Nettos Painter's flexibility makes him one of the masters of Attic Black-figure. He preferred large vessels that let his figures extend unrestrained over their surfaces, but he was also adept at painting smaller vessels with figural friezes framed above and below by ornamental bands. He also produced some unforgettable mythological scenes, including those on Athens, National Archaeological Museum, 1002 and 16384, and Kerameikos Museum, 154. His drawing style is for the most part expansive and bold, with sure and competent incision, and the black glaze is often enlivened by skilful application of additional white or red. He was the first Attic painter to master the Black-figure technique and to break completely with Proto-Attic style, thus opening the way for later painters.

J. D. Beazley: *Development of Black-figure* (1951, 3/1986), pp. 13–15

J. D. Beazley: *Black-figure* (1956), pp. 4–6, 679

A. Boegehold: 'The Nessos Amphora: A Note on the Inscription', *Amer. J. Archaeol.*, lxvi (1962), pp. 405–6

S. Karouzou: *Angeia tou Anagyrountou* [Pots from Anagyrous] (Athens, 1963)

J. D. Beazley: *Paralipomena* (1971), pp. 1–5

J. D. Beazley: *Addenda* (1989), pp. 1–2

L. Palaiokrassa: 'Ein neues Gefass des Nessos-Malers', *Jb. Dt. Archäol. Inst.*, cix (1994), pp. 1–10

Nike [Gr.: 'victory'] **of Samothrace.** Ancient Greek marble sculpture of winged Victory (h. *c.* 2 m; Paris, Louvre; see fig.). It may have been made by a pupil or follower of Lysippos or Skopas and was perhaps commissioned by Demetrios I of Macedonia between 295 and 287 BC, or it may date to *c.* 200 BC. It was discovered in 1863 on the island of Samothrace during a series of excavations conducted by Charles Champoiseau. The statue was taken to Paris, where it underwent restoration to replace the wings and parts of the drapery, which were found in fragments. It was first exhibited at the Musée du Louvre in the Salle des Caryatides. In 1866 another campaign of excavations was organized on the island, but this proved fruitless. Champoiseau himself returned to Samothrace in 1879 and found the fragments of a rostrate prow, which had served as the pedestal of the statue. The fragments were sent to Paris, and in 1884 the *Nike*, raised on a block above the prow and placed with great scenographic effect at the head of the Escalier Daru, where it can still be admired. Although a later work, it has been compared to the sculptures of the Parthenon. Much of its fame is due to its suggestive placement, which brings out its dramatic qualities; these are perhaps emphasized by the absence of the arms and head. Many hypotheses have been advanced concerning the position of the arms and the objects originally held by the statue. It used to be supposed that the figure held a trumpet or a laurel crown in the right hand. In 1950 new excavations produced fragments of the right hand, and in the same year the thumb and part of the index finger of the same hand were identified among some pieces found at Samothrace in 1873 and 1875 by the

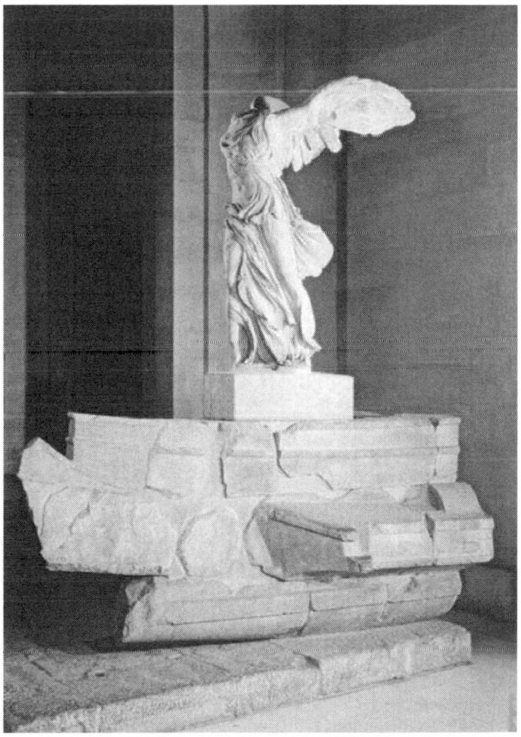

Nike of Samothrace, marble, h. 2.4 m, 3rd century BC (Paris, Musée du Louvre)

Austrians and taken to the Kunsthistorisches Museum in Vienna. These finds suggest that the *Nike* was holding nothing at all in her hand, or at most a fluttering metal fillet between the thumb and index finger.

C. Champoiseau: 'La Victoire de Samothrace', *Rev. Archéol.*, xxxix (1880), pp. 11–17

K. Lehmann: 'Samothrace: Fifth Preliminary Report', *Hesperia*, xxi (1952), pp. 19–43

P. W. Lehmann and K. Lehmann: *Samothracian Reflections: Aspects of the Revival of the Antique* (Princeton, 1973)

F. Haskell and N. Penny: *Taste and the Antique: The Lure of Classical Sculpture, 1500–1900* (New Haven and London, 1981), pp. 333–5

H. Knell: *Die Nike von Samothrake: Typus, Form, Bedeutung und Wirkungsgeschichte eines rhodischen Sieges-Anathems im Kabirenheiligtum von Samothrake* (Darmstadt, 1995)

M. Ellenberger: *La Victoire de Samothrace: Surgie d'un théâtre de statues* (La Rochelle, 2000)

M. Hamiaux: 'La victoire de Samothrace: étude technique de la statue', *Monuments et mémoires de la fondation Eugène Piot, 83* (Patis, 2004)

Nikias (*fl* Athens, second half of the 4th century BC). Greek painter (not to be confused with the NIKIAS PAINTER). He was the son of Nikomedes, the pupil of Antidotos and the master of Omphalion. Pliny (XXXV.xl.133) speculated as to whether the famous Nikias was the painter assigned by some to the 112th Olympiad (332–329 BC), and this dating is possible. Pausanias (I.xxix.15) called him the best of all his contemporaries in painting from life. None of his work survives. He was buried in the Athenian cemetery along the road to the Academy.

The principal technical advance ascribed to Nikias involved his treatment of light and shade. Pliny (XXXV.xl.130–31) reported that he took special care to make his figures stand out from the background, adding that he took great pains in his paintings of women. It may be that Pliny's two assertions should be combined to credit Nikias with the introduction of shading on female skin. He was the first painter to use burnt white lead (*cerussa*), perhaps another indication of his interest in the representation of shading and cast shadows. Nikias painted in the encaustic technique on marble, applying the colours in a wax medium and burning them on to the stone. Pausanias (VII.xxii.6) saw near Triteia a marble tombstone bearing two pictures by Nikias: one of a lady, the other of a youthful hunter. This tombstone would have commemorated the shared grave of a man and wife, and Nikias also produced a painting for the tomb of a priest of Artemis at Ephesos (Pliny XXXV.xl.132). His greatest achievements in the use of encaustic on marble, however, were in the application of colour to the statues of Praxiteles. Indeed, Praxiteles was said to have preferred above all his other statues those coloured by Nikias. It is unclear whether encaustic was Nikias' preferred technique or the only one he used.

Although he was a renowned painter of animals, particularly dogs, Nikias seems to have advised against insignificant subjects, such as flowers or birds. He preferred the complex compositions of naval or cavalry battles, in which men and horses could be depicted in a great variety of poses. His painting of *Hyacinthos*, said to be so beautiful that the viewer could sense Apollo's love for the youth, was taken from Alexandria by Augustus and later placed by Tiberius in the Temple of the Deified Augustus at Rome. Other paintings, too, were brought to Rome: a *Dionysos* hung in the Temple of Concord; and Silanus (Governor of Bithynia 76–75 BC) brought a picture of the nymph *Nemea* from Asia, which Augustus placed in his new senate house. Pliny (XXXV.x.27) described the *Nemea*, which would have been commissioned to commemorate a victory in a chariot race in the Nemean Games. Nikias' signature stated that he had 'burnt it in' (i.e. painted it in encaustic). His most famous picture, however, was the *Questioning of the Dead* (*Nekyomanteia*), based on book XI of the *Odyssey*. Nikias was said to have been so absorbed while painting it that he lost all sense of time and had to ask his household if he had washed or eaten. According to Plutarch (*Moralia* 1093d-e), he refused to sell it to Ptolemy Soter (ruler of Egypt 306–284 BC), even when offered 60 talents, preferring instead to give it to his native Athens. Pliny related the same story (XXXV.xl.132), but anachronistically claimed that it was Attalos I of Pergamon (*reg* 241–197 BC) who made the extravagant offer.

Several paintings by Nikias were large. They included an *Alexander*, perhaps a portrait of Alexander the Great or a depiction of the mythological Paris of Troy (Gr. Alexandros), which was displayed in the Portico of Pompey in Rome; an *Io*; a *Perseus and Andromeda*; a (?standing) *Calypso* and a *Seated Calypso*. The pictures of *Io, Perseus and Andromeda* and *Calypso* seem to have inspired a group of wall paintings at Rome and Pompeii, since several versions of all three subjects exist (e.g. *Perseus and Andromeda* from the House of the Dioscurides, Pompeii; Naples, Mus. Archeol. N). All share a similarity of composition and of contrast between male and female flesh tones, perhaps reflecting Nikias' development of shading on female flesh.

J. Overbeck: *Die antiken Schriftquellen zur Geschichte der bildenden Künste bei den Griechen* (Leipzig, 1868/*R* Hildesheim, 1959), nos 1109, 1294, 1726, 1810–26

H. Lucas: 'Die Kalypso des Nikias', *Österreich. Archäol. Inst. Wien*, xxxii (1940), pp. 54–9

A. Rumpf: *Malerei und Zeichnung* (1953), IV/i of *Handbuch der Archäologie* (Munich, 1939–), pp. 143–6

Nikias Painter (*fl c.* 420–*c.* 400 BC). Greek vase painter (not to be confused with the painter NIKIAS; see above). Active in Athens, he was a contemporary of the MEIDIAS PAINTER and is named after the potter Nikias, who signed one of his bell kraters (London, BM, 1898.7-16.6). There are 37 vases or fragments attributed to him, primarily bell kraters but also some hydriai and oinochoai and one rhyton. He frequently depicted athletes, revellers, symposia and sacrifice scenes; the reverse sides of his bell kraters almost always bear the same three draped youths. Among his more unusual themes are *Leda and the Egg*, armed runners casting lots at a statue of Athena and two scenes with crouching dancers. His hydriai carry typical Meidian subjects: two show the *Judgement of Paris*, while three others depict brides accompanied by divinities and women. The artist's name vase shows the end of a torch-race, with Nike flying up to the winning runner with the sash of victory; a wreathed old man leaning on a staff stands behind the altar. This may be the god or hero, perhaps Prometheus, in whose honour the race was run; the inscription on the wreath of the victor identifies him as the tribal hero Antiochos. The scene seems to represent simultaneously both mythical and contemporary torch races. The Nikias Painter's style is casual rather than precise: the facial features recall works by AISON and the Meidias Painter, but the musculature is sketchy; the drapery, though fussy and elaborate, bears very little correspondence to either the forms or the movements of the limbs beneath it.

J. D. Beazley: *Red-figure* (1942, 2/1963), ii, pp. 1333–5

W. Johannowsky: 'Due vasi del Pittore di Nicia al Museo Nazionale di Napoli', *Boll. A.*, n. s. 3, xlv (1960), pp. 202–12

W. Real: *Studien zur Entwicklung der Vasenmalerei im ausgehenden 5. Jahrhundert v.Chr.* (Münster, 1973), pp. 37–40

J. H. Oakley: 'A Calyx-Krater in Virginia by the Nikias Painter with the Birth of Erichthonios', *Ant. Kst,* xxx/2 (1987), pp. 123–30

J. Boardman: *Athenian Red Figure Vases, the Classical Period* (London, 1989), pp. 167–8

M. B. Moore: '"Nikias made me": An Early Panathenaic Prize Amphora in the Metropolitan Museum of Art', *Met. Mus. J.,* xxxiv (1999), pp. 37–56

Nikomachos of Thebes (*fl* mid-4th century BC). Greek painter. He was the son and pupil of the elder ARISTEIDES and the father and master of the younger Aristeides. None of his work survives. Pliny (*Natural History* XXXV.50) listed him among the four-colour painters, while Cicero (*Brutus* xviii.70) distinguished him from them. It is reasonable to suppose that painters occasionally restricted themselves to four colours (yellow, red, black and white) but at other times used a wider palette. Nikomachos was renowned for the speed with which he painted. When Aristratos, tyrant of Sikyon, commissioned a painting and set a date for its completion, the painter waited until the last moment to begin. Nevertheless, he completed the painting on time. Some said he was the first to give Odysseus his pointed hat, while others gave credit to APOLLODOROS. Although Nikomachos had great talent, unlucky circumstances robbed him of the highest reputation. His paintings included *Apollo and Artemis, Cybele Riding on a Lion* and *Maenads Stalked by Satyrs.* Several were brought to Rome: the *Rape of Persephone* that hung above the shrine to Youth in the Temple of Minerva on the Capitol; *Victory Taking a Four-horse Chariot Heavenward* that the general L. Munatius Plancus (*fl* mid-1st century BC) dedicated on the Capitol; and *Scylla* in the Templum Pacis. Nikomachos' *Rape of Persephone* has been linked to a picture from the same period of the same subject found in Tomb II at AIGAI (ii) (Vergina) in Macedonia. A *Tyndaridai* was unfinished at his death.

J. Overbeck: *Die antiken Schriftquellen zur Geschichte der bildenden Künste bei den Griechen* (Leipzig, 1868/*R* Hildesheim, 1959), nos 1067, 1672–3, 1723, 1754, 1771–6

J. Pollitt: *Art in the Hellenistic Age* (Cambridge, 1986), p. 191, fig. 204

E. Thomas: 'Nikomachos in Vergina?', *Archäol. Anz.,* ii (1989), pp. 219–26

Nikopolis [Gr.: 'city of victory']. Site of an ancient city 6 km north of Preveza in the Epeiros region of Greece. It was founded by Emperor Augustus (*reg* 30 BC–AD 14) to commemorate his victory in the Battle of Actium (31 BC), which took place nearby (*see* ACTIUM MONUMENT). Its exceptional position on a peninsula between the Ionian Sea and the Ambrakian Gulf, with harbours on both waters, and the privileges given to it by many emperors made it a particularly important centre. It was a free Roman city; its initial settlers came from neighbouring cities in Epeiros, Aitolia and Akarnania that had suffered decline during the long years of war. From the time of Emperor Diocletian (*reg* AD 285–305) it was the capital of the region of Epirus Vetus, and it had its own mint. In the Christian era it was the seat of a bishopric and a centre of influence in the ecclesiastical art and liturgical practice of eastern Illyricum. In AD 267 it was pillaged by the Heruli, and it was damaged by an earthquake probably in the last quarter of the 4th century. In 474 the city was captured by the Vandals and in 551 pillaged by the Ostrogoths.

Excavations were begun at Nikopolis in 1913, and they have continued intermittently. The Roman city covered an area of 150 ha, and it was built on a grid plan: its surrounding wall was more symbolic than defensive. Most of the surviving monuments from this period date to the reign of Augustus: they include a large theatre, an odeion (see fig.), baths and a nymphaeum. Two large cemeteries have also been excavated to the west and to the east of the city, while to its north a few traces remain of the 'Temple of Apollo' built by Augustus to commemorate his victory at Actium. The positions of a stadium and gymnasium have also been ascertained nearby, and a villa with mosaic floors has been uncovered. The aqueduct, which carried water over a distance of about 50 km from the River Louros, also served as a defensive rampart on the western edge of the city.

E. Kitzinger: 'Mosaics at Nikopolis', *Dumbarton Oaks Pap.*, vi (1951), pp. 83–102

M. Karamesine-Oikonomidou: *E nomismatokopia tes Nikopoleos* [The Nikopolis mint] (Athens, 1975)

Nikopolis A'. Praktika tou protou diethnous symposiou gia ti Nikopoli: Preveza, 1984 [Nikopolis A. Proceedings of the first international symposium on Nikopolis: Preveza, 1984]

D. K. Samsares: *He Aktia Nikopole kai he "chora" tes (Notia Epeiros-Akarnania): Historikogeographike kai epigraphike symvole* (Thessalonika, 1994)

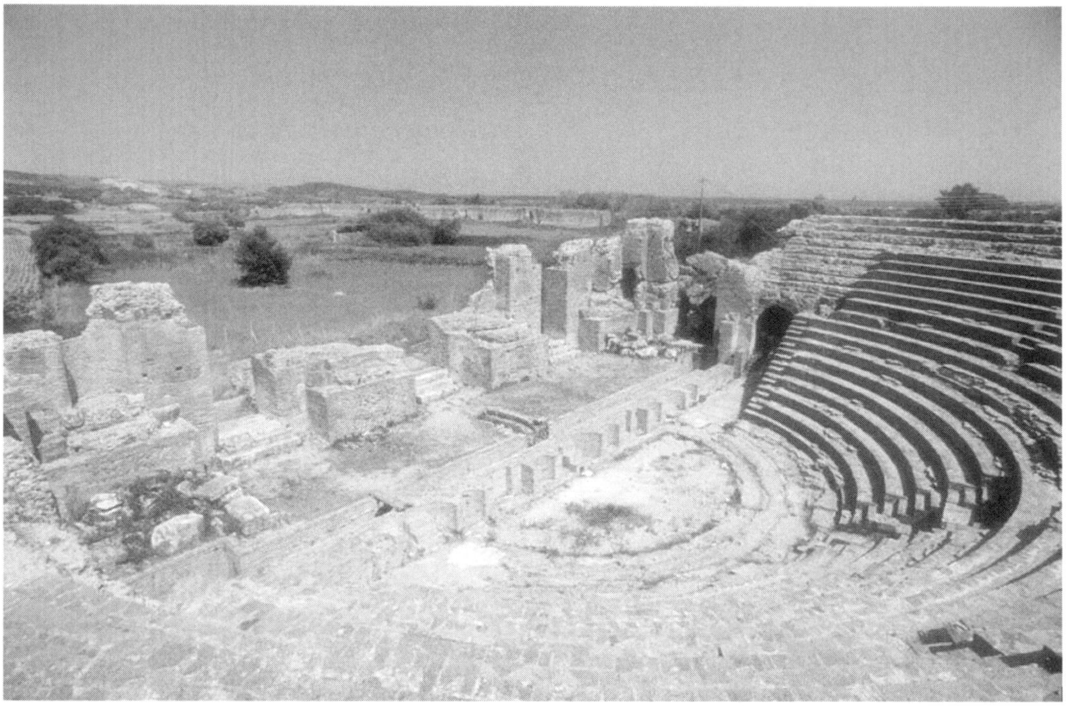

Nikopolis, odeion, 30 BC–AD 14

P. Chrysostomou and P. Kephallonitou: *Nikopolis* (Athens, 2001)
J. Isager, ed.: *Foundation and Destruction, Nikopolis and Northwestern Greece: The Archaeological Evidence for the City Destructions, the Foundation of Nikopolis and the Synoecism* (Athens, 2001)
K. L. Zachos and J. Wiseman: *Landscape Archaeology in Southern Epirus, Greece, vol 1: The Nikopolis Project* (Athens, 2003)

Nikosthenes (*fl c.* 550–*c.* 505 BC). Greek vase workshop owner. He was owner-operator of one of the largest potteries in 6th-century BC Athens, and he signed over 150 vases as their potter or manufacturer (see fig.). He is notable for having opened up new export markets by imitating foreign shapes and for having developed new vase painting techniques to compete with Red-figure work. His earliest signed vase, a band cup (Berlin, Antikensamml., F 1801), is also signed by Anakles, whose name appears on earlier vases. It seems likely that Nikosthenes entered a partnership with him but later had sole control of his workshop. Near the end of the 6th century BC, the workshop's production seems to have been taken over by Pamphaios, Nikosthenes presumably having retired or died around 505 BC. The workshop apparently ceased activity after the Persian invasion of 480 BC.

Nikosthenes was probably originally trained in Chalkis, given his use of the Chalkidian kylix and his frequent use of masks and other decorative motifs that are typical of Chalkidian pottery, such as banding below the figural scenes. However, his arrival in Athens coincided with Athenian domination of the market for fine painted pottery, which he exploited

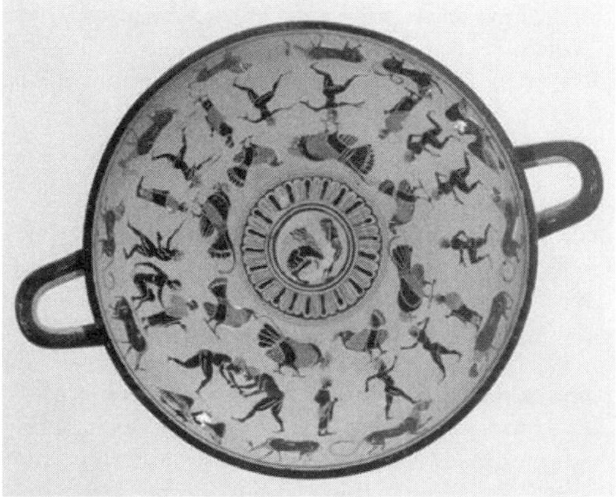

Nikosthenes workshop: kylix depicting sphinx surrounded by athletes and animals, Attic Black-figure, *c.* 550–*c.* 505 BC (Berlin, Antikensammlung, Staatliche Museen zu Berlin, 1805)

by expanding trade links with Etruria. He mainly produced small vases, particularly kylikes and skyphoi. However, a few less usual shapes remain, such as a psykter (Houston, TX, Menil Col.).

Nikosthenes is best known for his 'Nikosthenic amphorae' (h. *c.* 300 mm), which were exported to Caere. These imitated Etruscan Bucchero shapes but were taller and more graceful and were decorated in the Greek style. Several different decorative schemes occur, all attributable to the Group N painters. The commonest scene is a revel with dancing satyrs and maenads (e.g. Cleveland, OH,

Mus. A., 74.10). Similarly, Nikosthenes copied the Etruscan kyathos (h. with handle *c.* 150 mm). Some Black-figure specimens, manufactured, sold and used in pairs, are attributed to Group N, Psiax, the Group of Vatican G 57 and the Leafless Group, and some Red-figure examples to Oltos and the Oinophile Painter: all were exported to central Etruria. The workshop also produced a few quite large acorn-shaped pyxides with an elevated foot. The approximately 135 amphorae, 400 kyathoi and 45 pyxides that survive may represent about a quarter of the workshop's production and were apparently made to order for specific markets: given the small number of vases involved, the exporter must have exploited existing trading systems.

When the workshop of the Andokides painter invented Red-figure around 530 BC, Nikosthenes sent Psiax there to learn the new technique, and subsequently Psiax and others produced a few Red-figure vases for him. However, Red-figure was probably too difficult a technique for many lesser Black-figure artists, and Nikosthenes' workshop developed several ways of 'modernizing' Black-figure (*see* Pottery, §IV, 7). The most successful technique used a white slip to lighten the background and traditional black figures without any added white. Another, known as 'Six's technique', involved painting the vase black and adding white figures with their details incised and emphasized in red. While the result resembled Red-figure, the technique was essentially that of Black-figure. Nikosthenes' workshop also occasionally revived the old system of outline painting: but from about 520 BC all these innovations were virtually abandoned.

Nikosthenes' workshop seldom produced exceptional Black- or Red-figure paintings; among the best are a Black-figure kylix and pyxis (Berlin, Antikensamml., 1805; Florence, Mus. Archeol., 76931) and two Red-figure neck amphorae by Oltos (Paris, Louvre, G 2). Otherwise, apart from a very few incompetent pieces, the general artistic level is typical of Athens *c.* 530–*c.* 500 BC. Typical Black-figure products come from the BMN Painter and Theseus Painter, while the poorest examples are by the Leafless Group and the Haimon Painter and his followers. Though many themes occur, the workshop favoured Dionysiac scenes, gorgoneion masks and athletic contests. Common decorative motifs include large eyes, banding below the scene and ray patterns on kylikes (though these are not exclusively Nikosthenic), while the vases often had unique forms of feet.

Many painters were employed in Nikosthenes' workshop over the years. Some have already been mentioned: other Black figure artists included the painters of Chalkidian cups, all the kyathoi painters and the White Heron Group; the Lysippides painter may have produced his gorgoneion tondo kylikes while briefly employed at the workshop. Other Red-figure artists included the Nikosthenes Painter and the Euphiletos Painter. On the evidence of his workshop's output, Nikosthenes was apparently artistically competent but lacking in flair; technical innovation and marketing were his especial strengths.

J. C. Hoppin: *A Handbook of Greek Black-figure Vases* (Paris, 1924)
J. D. Beazley: *Red-figure*, i (1942, 2/1963), pp. 122–7
J. D. Beazley: *Black-figure* (1956), pp. 216–35, 690
J. D. Beazley: *Paralipomena* (1971), pp. 108–9
J. Boardman: *Athenian Black-figure Vases* (London, 1974)
M. M. Eisman: 'A Further Note on EPOIESEN Signatures', *J. Hell. Stud.*, xciv (1974), p. 172
M. M. Eisman: 'Nikosthenic Amphorai: The J. Paul Getty Museum Amphora', *Getty Mus. J.*, i (1974), pp. 43–54
M. M. Eisman: 'Attic Kyathos Production', *Archaeology*, xxviii (1975), pp. 76–83
T. Rasmussen: 'Etruscan Shapes in Attic Pottery', *Ant. Kst*, xx–viii (1985), pp. 33–9
V. Tosto: *The Black-figure Pottery Signed Nikosthenesepoiesen* (Amsterdam, 1999)
M. Tiverios: 'Zur Geschichte einer Nikosthenischen Pyxis', *Mitt. Dt. Archäol. Inst.: Athen. Abt.*, cxv (2000), pp. 73–81

Nîmes. *See* Nemausus.

Niobe Group. Name given to a group of ancient statues now in the Galleria degli Uffizi, Florence. The group is made up of five marble statues representing Niobe with a daughter; three daughters of Niobe (see fig.); and a son of Niobe. The first and largest is 2.28 m in height. They illustrate the Ovidian myth of Niobe, who was destroyed together with her numerous children by Apollo and Diana. The figures are probably copies of originals by Skopas or Praxiteles, or sculptors contemporary with them, perhaps

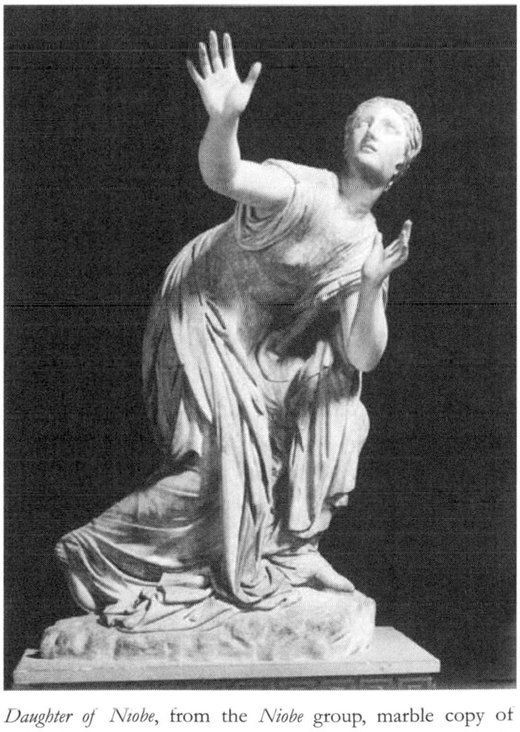

Daughter of Niobe, from the *Niobe* group, marble copy of original of the 4th century BC (Florence, Galleria degli Uffizi)

the sculptures mentioned by Pliny (*Natural History* XXXVI.28) that were sent from Seleucia to Rome to adorn the Temple of Apollo Medicus. They were found in fragments near Porta S Giovanni in Rome in 1583 and bought in the same year by Cardinal Ferdinando I de' Medici (1548–1609). They must have been immediately restored, as plaster casts arrived in Florence in 1588. The group was then exhibited in the gardens of the Villa Medici on the Pincio. In 1769 the statues left Rome, and they were carried by sea to Tuscany. In Florence in 1770 a new restoration was begun by Innocenzo Spinazzi (1726–98): this was finished only in 1776. The figures were later displayed in a hall of the Uffizi especially prepared for them. One of the three daughters and the prostrate son were taken to Palermo in 1800 during the French invasion of Italy, but three years later they were returned to the Uffizi. Some other statues that were discovered with the *Niobe* group are now thought to be unconnected with it. This is the case with a male figure identified as the *Husband of Niobe*, exhibited with the others after its discovery, and the statue of the Muse *Polyhymnia* (both Paris, Louvre). In the same way, the group was exhibited alongside statues of other provenances, such as the rearing horse found in the sea off the coast of Latium, or the *Anchirrhoe* bought by Cardinal Ferdinando I de' Medici from the della Valle collection in 1584 (both Paris, Louvre).

M. Bieber: *The Sculpture of the Hellenistic Age* (New York, 1961), pp. 74–7

R. M. Cook: *Niobe and her Children* (Cambridge, 1964), pp. 30–40

F. Haskell and N. Penny: *Taste and the Antique: The Lure of Classical Sculpture, 1500–1900* (New Haven and London, 1981), pp. 274–9

W. A. Geominy: *Die Florentiner Niobiden* (Bonn, 1984)

Niobid Painter (*fl c.* 470–*c.* 445 BC). Greek vase painter and potter. He is named after a scene on an Attic calyx krater depicting the *Killing of the Niobids* (Paris, Louvre, G 341; see fig.), and some 130 vases and fragments have been attributed to him. He was trained in the workshop of the BERLIN PAINTER, but *c.* 470 BC he set up his own workshop along with the Altamura Painter and the Blenheim Painter. This specialized in producing large vases and was subsequently taken over by his pupil POLYGNOTOS.

The Niobid Painter's work reflects the transition from the Archaic style of Red-figure vase painting to the Classical style. His early compositions, figures and drapery were stiff and simple (e.g. lekanis, Naples, Mus. Archeol. N., 2638). Subsequently, however, his compositions became more complex, his figures began to interact, and his drapery became softer and more substantial with increasingly sharply differentiated details, culminating around 450 BC in works such as his name vase. His draughtsmanship was always careful and assured. His figures are tall and slender and have broad heads with idealized profiles and clearly differentiated features. Their ears are elongated and their eyes wide open and surmounted by a long flat brow, while the eye socket is suggested by a second line on the upper eyelid. The mouths have downturned corners and full bottom lips, while the chins are heavy and prominent. The men's bodies are muscular and their garments substantial.

The Niobid Painter followed the Berlin Painter's tastes in vase shapes and ornament. Thus he favoured kraters, neck amphorae, hydriai and pelikai, generally decorating them with an edging consisting of a meander interrupted by crosses in squares, with a band of lotus palmettes round the mouth and lyre palmettes and palmette trees near the handles. The ornament is distinguished by its varied and meticulously drawn tendrils and leaves.

The Niobid Painter's commonest scenes are of lovers pursuing each other, sacrifices, the *Departure of Triptolemos* and great battles involving Amazons, centaurs, giants or Trojans. The depictions of sacrifices generally consist of three figures, and are skilfully composed to suggest the emotional bonds between them and give a sense of timeless universality. The artist also seems to have been intent on glorifying Athens. Thus he preferred the Athenian hero Theseus to the more generally Greek hero Herakles and drew inspiration from Athens' role in the recent Persian wars, while using Triptolemos, originally an Eleusinian hero, to embody Athens' claim to be the cultural and political centre of Greece.

Many scenes by the Niobid Painter and his followers may reflect lost wall paintings by Polygnotos of Thasos or Mikon. The most famous (on his name vase, on the opposite side to the *Killing of the Niobids*)

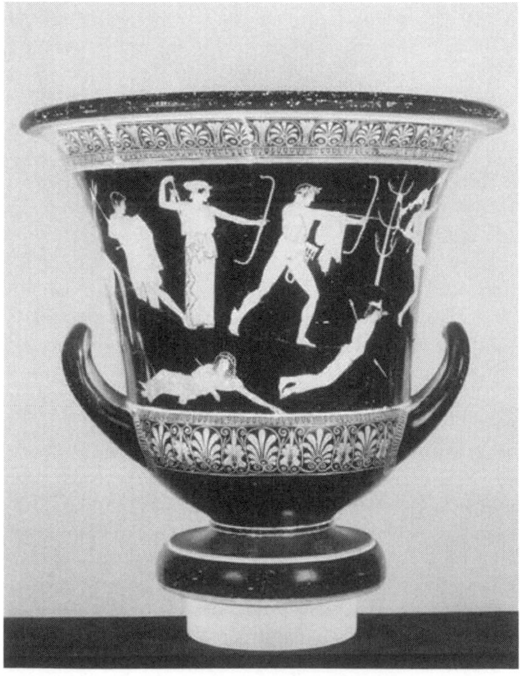

Niobid Painter: calyx krater depicting the *Killing of the Niobids*, h. 540 mm, Attic Red-figure, *c.* 460–*c.* 450 BC (Paris, Musée du Louvre, G 341)

was originally thought to depict the Argonauts but probably represents the gathering of the Athenian heroes before the Battle of Marathon (490 BC). In it the artist abandoned the single ground line usual in vase painting to create an illusion of depth. However, while this device was almost certainly borrowed from murals, the style of painting was adapted to suit the smaller field provided by the vases.

T. B. L. Webster: *Der Niobidenmaler* (Leipzig, 1935)

J. D. Beazley: *Red-figure* (1942, 2/1963), i, pp. 598–608

E. Simon: 'Polygnotan Painting and the Niobid Painter', *Amer. J. Archaeol.*, lxvii (1963), pp. 43–62

P. E. Arias: 'Problemi stilistici, iconologici e cronologici sul Pittore dei Niobidi', *Atti Pont. Accad. Romana Archeol.*, liii–liv (1984), pp. 145–79

S. Bonomi: 'Una nuova pelike del Pittore dei Niobidi', *Archäol. Anz.*, (1985), pp. 29–47

T. J. McNiven: 'Odysseus on the Niobid Krater', *J. Hell. Stud.*, cix (1989), pp. 191–8

M. Prange: *Der Niobidenmaler und seine Werkstatt* (Frankfurt am Main, 1991)

E. D. Reeder: 'The Niobid Painter in Baltimore', *J. Walters A.G.*, lii–liii (1994–5), pp. 113–15

M. Denoyelle: *Le cratère des Niobides* (Paris, 1997)

Nude. Term used to describe the depiction of a naked human figure in works of art. The definition of the nude as a subject for art is an essentially Western tradition, since attitudes towards nudity were fundamentally different in most pre-Renaissance, non-Western cultures, and notably in the Greco Roman world. The modern Western world is accustomed to the notion of 'artistic' nude, male and female, as a result of a long rehabilitation process, whereby Classical antiquity and its art were received, and in effect recreated, by the emerging Renaissance and Neo-classical aesthetics. In visual arts today, including sculpture and painting, film, video and even advertising, as well as the performing arts (chiefly in dance), the nude is considered respectable and sometimes indispensable. Though not acceptable in public life, nudity is used in art as an expression of emotion or disposition, largely based on the way the Classical nude has been received by modern taste. Artistic nudes are often cast as 'heroic', another presumed attribute to their antique models.

Effigies of naked divinities existed in the Near East since prehistory, and in the 1st millennium BC found their way to Greece, triggering some imitation. In the 8th and 7th centuries BC, Greek sculptors adopted Near Eastern types of the female nude in order to represent goddesses such as Astarte or her Greek counterpart Aphrodite. The male nude was acceptable in everyday life in Classical Greece: athletes and soldiers were seen in the state of near or full nakedness, and although women (at least free maidens and matrons) were banned from such spectacles, the idea of male nudity was quite common and natural. Male nudity, with a particular attention to the genitals (especially the erect male organ, the *phallus*) were the object of veneration and worship, treated as symbols of fertility, good fortune and wealth. This behaviour was considered idiosyncratic even in antiquity: foreigners often expressed their distaste for Greek nudity, and the Greeks themselves were aware that this habit was yet another factor emphasizing their collective identity, as opposed to the placid 'barbarians'. It has been argued (notably by Boardman) that in Greek art the nude is neither 'artistic' nor 'heroic', but comes as a matter of fact, based on Greek practice and ideology, chiefly from the view that man (and woman, more often than not) holds a central role in the political and religious life of the society. Greek art imitates nature in order to idealize it, and the nude, based on natural observation, elaboration of pattern and exploration of proportion, seemed an ideal art form for that purpose. Chiefly employed to portray the young and the divine, the nude was a generic category applied to Greek philosophical principles, which seem untranslatable to the non-Greek taste, even that of the Romans, who copied Greek statuary and art in general for their own intents and purposes. The Romans appreciated Greek art for its aspiration to realism and its pursuit of narrative, but were, however, indifferent to the alien ethos it primarily expressed. In Rome Greek culture was accessible only to the educated élite, with particular interests and tastes. Greek statuary was used to emphasize an affinity with the 'Hellenism' of its owners, despite its original identity: as Pliny states (*Natural History* 34.18), statues of naked Greek athletes removed from Greek gymnasia to be set up in Roman houses and baths were christened 'Achilles' as a mythical identity was considered to render nudity more palatable.

The first conventionally realistic male-nude statues, kouroi, appeared in Greek art *c.* the mid-7th century BC. The KOUROS, a life-sized, free-standing naked youth, left foot forward, fists hard against the thighs and smiling enigmatically, is influenced by Egyptian art, although the nature of this influence remains controversial. The early kouroi, which were probably votive or funerary figures, have a formal physique, the musculature of the torso being indicated by shallow incision, and over the next two centuries Greek sculptors strove for ever greater realism. By 490 BC this had been attained, exemplified by the so-called 'Kritios Boy' (*c.* 480 BC; Athens, Acropolis Mus.), still a static, upright figure, but relaxed, with a convincing musculature, and signalling the end of the Archaic period and the emergence of the Classical.

Greek sculptors of the Classical period, having mastered anatomy, turned their attention to idealization. Three cast-bronze statues, over life-size and dating from the first half of the 5th century BC, epitomize the balance attained between perfect form and intense naturalism: the Artemision statue identified as *Zeus* or *Poseidon* (Athens, N. Archaeol. Mus.; for illustration *see* ARTEMISION BRONZES) and the warrior figures known as the RIACE BRONZES. The latter may be the work of Pheidias, who developed ideal proportions based upon fixed numbers (later formalized into a canon by Polykleitos), which avoided the coarseness and disparity of nature and the excesses of imagination, and resulted in symmetry and spiritual beauty.

Polykleitos' *Doryphoros* (*c.* 440 BC; most complete copy Naples, Mus. Archeol. N.; for illustration *see* POLYKLEITOS) introduced the lastingly influential concept of contrapposto, a method of arranging the limbs asymmetrically and creating a sense of vitality through the contrast between a tense, weight-bearing leg and one that is relaxed and free. Technical advances also allowed free-standing statues to be depicted in vigorous movement, as in the *Diskobolos* of Myron of Eleutherai (*c.* 450 BC; untraced; copy Rome, Mus. N. Romano; for illustration *see* MYRON OF ELEUTHERAI).

The female nude is much rarer in Greek art. Originally reserved for exotic divinities, sorceresses and courtesans, it made a firmer appearance in Greek art only in the 4th century BC, chiefly in representations of Aphrodite. Erotic appeal remains the chief connotation of showing a human being (boy or girl) nude in Greek art. In the Black- and Red-figure vases created from the early 6th century BC, examples of erotic art occur among the mythical and everyday subjects (*see* EROTIC ART). Here the figures are stylized and, with heads and legs in profile, suggest Egyptian influence. Male nudes outnumber females, which, on the whole, are treated more sketchily, little attempt being made to produce convincing female anatomy. Generally, the female nude is used to evoke weakness and vulnerability, undoubtedly two characteristics associated with female nature in common thinking. Praxiteles created the first totally naked free-standing female sculpture, the monumental marble *Aphrodite of Knidos* (*c.* 360–340 BC; untraced; copy Rome, Mus. Pio-Clementino; *see* PRAXITELES, fig. 2). This was a startlingly new concept and created a lasting ideal of female beauty. In the subsequent Hellenistic period, in which art became more expressive and warmly naturalistic, the female nude became an increasingly common subject, and many celebrated works, known in copies, were influenced by Praxiteles' work, including the Capitoline *Venus* (Rome, Mus. Capitolino) and the VENUS DE' MEDICI (Florence, Uffizi). The most original and openly sensual Hellenistic nude is perhaps the crouching *Aphrodite at her Bath* (*c.* 250 BC; Roman copy, Paris, Louvre).

In the Late Classical period male nudes were often shown in violent poses, and Pergamese sculptors particularly favoured dramatic subjects, with a strong emotional impact, such as the *Dying Gaul* (*c.* 230–220 BC; Rome, Mus. Capitolino), or the superhuman, exaggeratedly contorted LAOKOON (Rome, Vatican, Mus. Pio-Clementino).

Greek wall painting is known only through later copies excavated at Pompeii and Herculaneum, but such works as *Theseus Slayer of the Minotaur* (Naples, Mus. Archeol. N.) suggest that Greek artists painted from the nude. The sources suggest that painters, like sculptors, were concerned with an ideal beauty, and Zeuxis is said to have created an ideal female nude by uniting the most perfect parts of five models, an anecdote often cited by Renaissance theorists.

In the Roman period Greek sculptors worked well into the 3rd century AD but to a cultural agenda dictated by the Romans. The ideal was eroded by the real, and even the many nude statues of ANTINOUS (*d* AD 130; e.g. Delphi, Archaeol. Mus.), the favourite of the most Hellenistic of emperors, Hadrian, lack the elegance of Classical Greek art. The sole important Roman contribution to the development of the nude was the creation of the infant putti, who were widely used as followers of Bacchus, typified by those on the frieze from the Temple of Venus Genetrix (*c.* AD 113; Rome, Mus. Capitolino) and later converted to Christianity as cherubs.

This peculiar amalgam of Greek ethos and its Roman translation, rediscovered (or rather recreated) in the framework of the *restitutio antiquitatis* attempted by the Renaissance, was systematized for the modern viewer by the emotive and wilful vision of JOHANN JOACHIM WINCKELMANN. Casting a strong, admiring gaze onto Greek art, Winckelmann maintained that it embodied the totality of Greek culture, expressing the eternal ideal of humanity, now lost to mankind, but privy to the Greeks. From a post-Enlightenment, historicist point of view, Winckelmann pursued the study of Greek art as a historical phenomenon, albeit as one with great reference to the present. His intense eroticized longing for the male beauty sought its expression in the idealized forms of Greek statuary—significantly though, as these were modified or even altered by Roman copyists and their clientele. Even though later contacts with Greek originals (such as the Parthenon marbles taken to London in the beginning of the 19th century) suggested that Greek sculptors portrayed the essential and not the ideal state of nature, Winckelmann's homoerotic gaze has deeply influenced the modern, Western view of the nude and its significance for art and life.

K. Clark: *The Nude* (London, 1956)
M. Robertson: *Greek Painting* (London, 1959)
G. M. A. Richter: *Kouroi: Archaic Greek Youths* (London, 1970)
M. Levey: *The Nude* (London, 1972)
M. Cormack: *The Nude* (Oxford, 1976)
E. H. Gombrich: *Art and Illusion: A Study in the Psychology of Pictorial Representation* (London, 1977, 5th edn)
M. Walters: *The Nude Male* (London, 1978)
J. Lewinski: *The Naked and the Nude* (London, 1987)
J. Boardman: *The Diffusion of Classical Art in Antiquity* (London, 1994)
A. Stewart: *Art, Desire, and the Body in Ancient Greece* (Cambridge, 1997)
A. Potts: *Flesh and the Ideal: Winckelmann and the Origins of Art History* (New Haven and London, 2000)
G. Ferrari: *Figures of Speech: Men and Maidens in Ancient Greece* (Chicago, 2002)
G. Greer: *The Boy* (London, 2003)
C. H. Hallett: *The Roman Nude: Heroic Portrait Statuary 200 BC–AD 300* (Oxford, 2005)

Numidia. Term originally used to denote the territory of the nomadic tribes of the Numidae, occupying roughly the modern equivalent of Algeria north of the Sahara. By the late 3rd century BC they comprised two main tribal groupings, the Masaesyli in the west with their capital at Siga (near the coast 90 km west of Oran), and the Massyli further east, centred on Cirta (modern Constantine). The latter tribe rose to prominence under Masinissa (*reg* 203–148 BC), who defeated the Masaesylan king Syphax in 203 BC and then with the help of his cavalry assisted Rome in crushing the Carthaginians at the Battle of Zama in 202 BC. As well as being a successful general, the remarkable Masinissa was also a noted linguist (reputedly the inventor of the Libyan written alphabet), an agronomist, a philosopher and the father of 44 children; he was also a great civilizer, encouraging settled agriculture rather than nomadism, adopting Punic (rather than Libyan) as the language of court, and much influenced too by Greek culture. His vast kingdom was divided at his death but forcibly reunited by his illegitimate grandson Jugurtha, whose sack of Cirta in 112 BC, when Roman businessmen resident there were massacred, prompted the intervention of Rome and the Jugurthine War (112–105 BC). When Jugurtha's grand-nephew Juba I allied himself with Pompey, who lost to Julius Caesar at the Battle of Thapsus (46 BC), the consequence was the extinction of the Numidian kingdom and the organization of the area as a Roman province ('Africa Nova', New Africa); the historian Sallust was its first governor.

Little is known of Numidian settlements, since the principal royal capitals, which included HIPPO REGIUS (Annaba) in north-east Algeria and Bulla Regia in north-western Tunisia (as their 'royal' titles show), were overlain by Roman cities, and by the late 20th century excavation had yet to touch Numidian occupation levels. By contrast the great tombs of the Numidian kings and princes, even if the exact identity of the deceased for whom each was intended is disputed, survive in a striking state of preservation. That at Siga (*c.* 200–*c.* 180 BC), originally 30 m high, is basically triangular in shape and has a complicated series of tomb chambers beneath. The Medracen near Batna (*c.* 200–*c.* 150 BC), a great circular mausoleum 59 m in diameter with a stepped pyramidal roof, has Doric engaged capitals and an overhanging cornice of Punic-Egyptian inspiration. El Khroub, 14 km south of Constantine, a tower-tomb 8.4 m square and perhaps once 30 m high, where the grave chamber yielded late 2nd-century BC Rhodian and Italian wine amphorae and Greek Hellenistic silverware when excavated in 1916, is decorated with Doric capitals as well as false doors in the manner of Hellenistic mausolea. Another tower-tomb at THUGGA (Dougga) in Tunisia of *c.* 150 BC has Ionic and Phoenician-Cypriot Aeolic capitals and much free-standing and relief sculpture. Finally, the later 'tomb of the Christian woman' near Tipaza on the north Algerian coast (*c.* 100–*c.* 50 BC) is another circular mausoleum (61 m in diameter, 32 m high) with a stepped pyramidal roof like the Medracen. All, with the exception of Thugga, stand in stunning locations, commanding views in all directions for miles around. The multi-storey tower-tombs owe something to Greco-Punic mausolea in North Africa (such as the 3rd-century BC one at SABRATHA), as well as to the mausoleum at HALIKARNASSOS (*c.* 353 BC) in Asia Minor and its imitators, but the stone circular mausolea are unique to Numidia at this period and very probably influenced Augustus' choice of a circular monument for his great dynastic mausoleum in Rome (28 BC); this in turn spawned many imitations, both imperial (such as the tomb of Hadrian, now Castel Sant'Angelo) and private.

In 30 BC the province of Africa Nova was transferred to the pro-Roman client king Juba II, but in 25 BC he was moved westwards to the area henceforth known as Mauretania (with his capital at Caesarea (Cherchel)); the eastern part of the former Numidian kingdom then merged with the original province of Africa to become 'Africa Proconsularis'. In BC 198/7, however, provincial reorganization created a new Roman province called Numidia, an approximately triangular area with a short coastline centred on Rusicade (modern Skikda) and broadening out southwards to include a long stretch of the Roman frontier with its forts and watch-towers on the edge of the Sahara. This was controlled from the military nerve centre at LAMBAESIS (Tazoult), where the Third Augustan Legion had been stationed since the early 2nd century; its 21-hectare fortress is the most substantial visible example of its type in the entire Roman Empire. The adjacent civilian settlement grew into a sizeable and impressive city in its own right and became the capital of the new Numidian province. Two Roman cities elsewhere in the province, CUICUL (Djemila) and THAMUGADI (Timgad), which were founded *c.* AD 97 and 100 respectively as colonies with retired soldiers (veterans) as their first citizens, are among the most impressive and extensively excavated Roman cities anywhere in the Empire.

Their prosperity, and that of other cities in Numidia, depended above all on agriculture: Numidia, like other North African provinces, was a major exporter to the Roman world of grain and oil. Its fauna were also famous and in demand for amphitheatre spectacles all over the Empire. Elephants were particularly numerous (one place near Constantine, for example, was called 'Castellum Elephantum', 'Castle of the Elephants'), and Numidia was also an important source in antiquity of lions, leopards, bears and horses. The label 'Numidian' was also applied to the products of a much wider area: the fine yellow marble, for example, that came from the quarries at Chemtou (Simitthu) in western Tunisia was known to the Romans as *marmor Numidicum*, 'Numidian marble'. This handsome material was first used by the Numidian kings in the 2nd century BC (one of their capitals, Bulla Regia, lies nearby), and an impressive rectangular temple of that date on a hilltop at Chemtou, with intricate relief decoration depicting shields and armour, is an early witness of the exploitation of the quarries. From Augustan times onwards this yellow Numidian marble (*giallo antico*) was widely exported, especially to Italy: columns of it can be seen, for example, inside Hadrian's Pantheon in Rome (AD 118–25).

E. Fentress: *Numidia and the Roman Army* (Oxford, 1979)
H. G. Horn and C. Rüger, eds: *Die Numider* (Bonn, 1979)
Y. Le Bohec: *Le Troisième Légion Auguste* (Paris, 1989)
J. Fedak: *Monumental Tombs of the Hellenistic Age* (Toronto, 1990), pp. 133–40

O

Octastyle. Term applied to a building with a portico of eight columns.

Octavian. *See* AUGUSTUS.

Odeion [Lat. *odeum*]. Type of concert hall where musical performances and recitations took place in the Greek and Roman world; the word derives from *ode* (Gr.: 'song'). The oldest known odeion was built for musical contests by Pericles (mid-5th century BC) at the foot of the Acropolis next to the Theatre of Dionysos. It was almost square (*c.* 68×62.4 m) and covered with a pyramidal roof, said to have been based upon the roof of the tent of Xerxes, King of Persia. The forest of columns needed to support the roof must have created visual and acoustic problems. There is no archaeological evidence for any other odeion until the 1st century BC, although there are many examples of a related type of building, the BOULEUTERION or ekklesiasterion. The ekklesiasterion at Priene (*c.* 150 BC), for example, has rectilinear seating on three sides, while the bouleuterion at MILETOS (*c.* 170 BC) has semicircular seating enclosed within rectangular walls. Both are roofed and have windows in the upper part of the walls.

The earliest surviving Roman odeion, the *theatrum tectum* (covered theatre) or small theatre at Pompeii, is related to this type of building. It was built in the early years of the Sullan colony (*c.* 75 BC), as an inscription records (*Corp. Inscr. Lat.*, x, 844). The semicircular seating is inscribed into a rectangle that measures 34.8×28.6 m. Access to the seating is from the *orchestra*, although there are two small staircases that lead from the passageway behind the theatre up to the top seats of the *cavea*. The semicircular *orchestra* is paved in coloured marbles, and two semicircular staircases give access to the steps for the seats of honour and the passageway behind. The entrances to the *orchestra* are vaulted, and the magistrates' seats over them are accessible by staircases that lead from the stage up to the *versurae* (rooms used for props or as foyers). There is a curtain slot behind the wall at the front of the stage and three doorways in the rectilinear *scaenae frons* (stage building), as well as two narrow lateral doorways, now blocked. According to Murolo, the building was probably covered up to the *scaenae frons* with a hipped roof, with its ridge running north-south, an area almost square (30.0×28.6 m), while a separate lower roof covered the backstage area. The *theatrum tectum* forms part of the same complex as the large theatre at Pompeii. The combination of theatre and odeion is also found at Neapolis (Naples), Tauromenion in Sicily, Lugdunum (Lyon) in France, Philadelphia (Amman) in Jordan and Termessos and Sagalassos in Turkey.

Only one odeion is attested in Rome, that built by Domitian (*reg* AD 81–96) in the Campus Martius in AD 86 (Suetonius: *Domitian* v). The Augustan theatre at Aosta is of a similar type to the *theatrum tectum* at Pompeii, with semicircular seating inscribed into rectangular walls. The great height of the walls, the presence of large windows higher up and the rectangular shape of the building all suggest that the building was roofed, although not all scholars are convinced of this. Another building of this type, the Odeion of Agrippa in the Athenian agora (*c.* 15 BC; see fig.), is particularly closely related to such bouleuteria as that at Miletos. It measures 51.38×43.20 m, and its semicircular auditorium could accommodate 1000 spectators; it had a semicircular *orchestra* and long, narrow stage. There were windows in the upper part of the walls, and the building was covered with a wooden roof with the wide span of 25 m. The roof collapsed in the 2nd century AD, and the auditorium had to be rebuilt with a cross-wall, which reduced its capacity to 500. It was perhaps for this reason that the wealthy benefactor Herodes Atticus undertook to build a third odeion at Athens, in memory of his wife, who had died in AD 161 (Philostratos: *Lives of the Sophists*, II.ii). The odeion of Herodes Atticus rests against the south slope of the Acropolis and takes the form of a typical Roman theatre of the eastern type. A large amount of wood-ash was found all over the *cavea* at the time of its excavation. This and the fact that there are windows in the upper part of the *scaenae frons* have been taken as evidence that it was roofed. It is, however, a large building, which could seat 5000 spectators, and its sheer size (w. 76 m) makes this unlikely.

Other odeia, such as those at APHRODISIAS, Argos, Carthage, Nikopolis, Patras and Thessaloniki are semicircular and in many respects resemble small theatres. The main distinguishing features of semicircular odeia, apart from the fact that they were roofed,

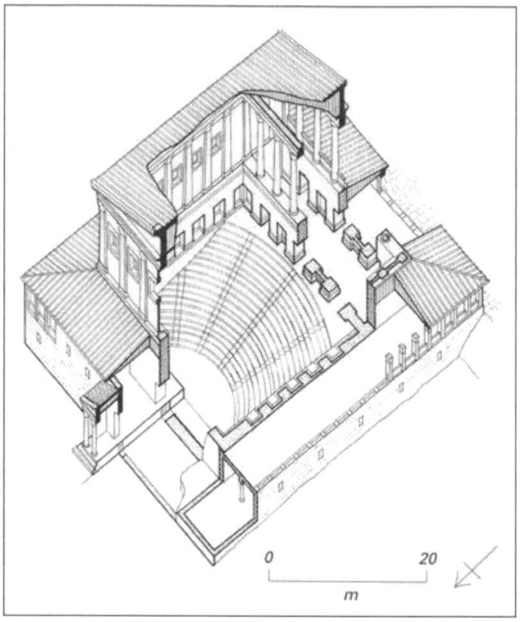

Odeion of Agrippa, Athens, *c.* 15 BC; cut-away axonometric reconstruction

are that they generally have a plain, rectilinear *scaenae frons*, often unadorned with columns, and smaller and simpler annexes behind and at the sides of the stage. This was probably because musical concerts and recitations required less elaborate staging than the plays, mimes and other spectacles that were put on in the great theatres. At the same time musical recitals would have required a hall with better acoustics than the usual large open-air theatre. The roof was probably essential for that reason.

O. Broneer: *The Odeum* (1932), x of *Corinth: Results of Excavations Conducted by the American School of Classical Studies at Athens* (Cambridge, MA, 1929–)

W. A. McDonald: *The Political Meeting Places of the Greeks* (Baltimore, 1943)

O. Broneer: 'The Tent of Xerxes and the Greek Theater', *U. CA Pubns Class. Archaeol.*, i/12 (1944), pp. 305–12

G. Spano: 'Osservazioni intorno al theatrum tectum di Pompei', *An. Ist. Sup. Sci. & Lett. 'S Chiara'*, i (1948–9), pp. 111–39

H. Thompson: 'The Odeion in the Athenian Agora', *Hesperia*, xix (1950), pp. 31–141

P. Wuilleumier: *Fouilles de Fourvière à Lyon* (Paris, 1951), pp. 44–50

M. Murolo: 'Il cosidetto "odeo" di Pompei ed il problema della sua copertura', *Rendi. Accad. Archeol., Lett. & B.A.*, n. s., xxxiv (1959), pp. 89–101

M. Bieber: *The History of the Greek and Roman Theater* (Princeton, 1961), pp. 220–22

J. Travlos: *Pictorial Dictionary of Ancient Athens* (London, 1971), pp. 365–92

A. Hadidi: 'The Excavations of the Roman Forum at Amman (Philadelphia), 1964–1967', *Annu. Dept. Ant. Jordan*, ix (1974), pp. 89–91

R. Meinel: *Das Odeion* (Frankfurt am Main, 1980)

'Troy Update', *Archaeology*, xlvii (Jan–Feb 1994), p. 18 [further excavation and restoration of the Roman Odeion]

T. G. Papathanassopoulos: *Monuments on the South Slope of Acropolis: The Sanctuary and Theatre of Dionysos: The Choregic Monuments, the Stoa of Eumenes, the Odeion of Perikles, the Asklepieion, the Odeion of Herodes Atticus* (Athens, 1995)

K. Aslanidis: 'The Roman Odeion at Epidaurus', *J. Roman Archaeol.*, xvi (2003), pp. 300–11

Oecus [Gk. *oikos*]. Apartment, hall or large room in an ancient Roman house.

Olba [Diocaesarea; anc. Gr. Diokaisareia; now Uğura]. Site of the city of the priestly kings of Cilicia Tracheia (Rough Cilicia), Turkey, in mountainous country 22 km north-east of Seleucia. It is now a village with impressive Hellenistic and Roman remains. The local tribes became Hellenized under the SELEUCIDS and were ruled by a dynasty of potentates, the high priests of the sanctuary of Olban Zeus; according to Strabo, the priests traced their line back to Ajax (son of Teucer, the brother of the Homeric Ajax, who had settled in Rough Cilicia after founding Salamis in Cyprus). The Temple of Zeus is among the most interesting and conspicuous buildings of the Hellenistic period at Olba. It is of the Corinthian order, peripteral and hexastyle with 12 columns (h. 13 m) on its flanks. It was built in the first years of the 3rd century BC with funds donated by Seleukos Nikator (*c.* 358–281 BC) and is the earliest known Corinthian temple. The interesting Corinthian capitals are somewhat experimental in form. All but two of the columns are still standing, although many have lost their upper parts. The lower third of the shafts is not fluted but has facets, the earliest surviving example of this columnar style. The magnificent tower of the priestly kings (2nd century BC) is another notable building; this has walls of fine ashlar masonry, which still stand to a height of over 22.5 m. The structure is rectangular (15.7×12.5 m). About a mile to the west of the sanctuary of Zeus stands a remarkable tower-like, square building (h. 16 m) in a good state of preservation. It has a pyramidal top, the only part of the structure that has suffered dilapidation. This may have been the tomb of one of the priestly dynasts and is probably Hellenistic since its encircling frieze is decorated with triglyphs and metopes of the Doric order.

Until the days of the emperor Vespasian (*reg* AD 69–79) the priestly kings of Olba were able to retain a considerable degree of independence, though under the more or less nominal suzerainty of Achelaos of Cappadocia, Polemon II of Pontus and Antiochos IV of Commagene in succession. Under Vespasian, however, Olba was renamed Diocaesarea and came under more direct Roman control, although it still retained a measure of local autonomy. The sanctuary prospered and grew into a sizeable city issuing its own coins. Ruins surviving from the Roman period include the remains of a colonnaded street, a part of the Tychaion, which was a temple dedicated to the goddess Fortune, the city gate and the 2nd-century AD theatre which still has some remains of the scene building.

J. T. Bent: 'A Journey in Cilicia Tracheia', *J. Hell. Stud.*, xii (1891), pp. 206–24
A. C. Headlam: *Ecclesiastical Sites in Isauria (Cilicia Trachea)* (London, 1893)
R. Heberdey and A. Wilhelm: *Reisen in Kilikien* (Berlin, 1895)
F. X. Schaffer: 'Archäologisches aus kilikien', *Jhft. Österreich. Archäol. Inst. Wien*, v (1902), pp. 106–27
J. G. Frazer: *Adonis, Attis, Osiris* (1914), IV/i of *The Golden Bough* (London, 1890–1915), pp. 143–52
A. H. M. Jones: *The Cities of the Eastern Roman Provinces* (Oxford, 1950)
D. Magie: *Roman Rule in Asia Minor* (Princeton, 1950), p. 269
T. S. MacKay: *Olba in Rough Cilicia* (diss., Bryn Mawr Coll., PA, 1968)
G. M. Staffieri: *La monetazione di Olba nella Cilicia Trachea* (Lugano, 1978)
G. M. Staffieri: *La monetazione di Olba e di Diocaesarea in Cilicia: Addenda e corrigenda* (Lugano, 1987)
C. Taskiran and I. Yilmazer: *Guidebook for Tourists to Uzuncaburç (Olba Diocaesarea) and its Environs* (Silifke, 1987)

Olbia [Olvia; now Ol'viya]. Site of a Greek city on the Bug estuary near Parutino, *c.* 100 km east of Odessa in Ukraine. It was founded by settlers from Miletos and other Ionian cities in the first half of the 6th century BC. Excavations by Boris Farmakovsky (1896, 1901–15 and 1924–6), by L. M. Slavin (from 1936) and others have uncovered a city built on the rectangular grid system of Hippodamos. At its peak (5th–3rd centuries BC) Olbia covered about 50 hectares, encircled by a stone wall with towers. At the centre, in the upper town, stood the agora surrounded by public buildings; the foundation of a gymnasium (5th–3rd centuries BC) with a limestone half-length figure of a kouros (end of 6th–beginning of 5th centuries BC) in a niche, and rows of shops have been excavated. To the north of the agora stood a temenos with the temples of Apollo Delphinios (4th–2nd centuries BC) and Zeus (3rd century BC), with sanctuaries, altars and sacrificial tables. The buildings were constructed of mud-brick on polygonal stone socles. The homes of the richer citizens had peristyles and reception rooms with wall paintings and mosaic floors.

The public areas and the necropolis have yielded large finds of painted pottery. Roughly 2000 3rd-century BC terracotta votive figurines, including *Cybele, Demeter* and *Aphrodite*, came from the cistern near the temple of Apollo. Fragments of marble sculpture have also been discovered, such as a statue of a griffin and a marble altar (both 5th century BC), a statue of *Athena* and a frieze depicting a procession (both 4th century BC) and works showing Alexandrian influence: a head said to be of *Hygeia* and a head of *Asklepios* (both 3rd century BC; both St Petersburg, Hermitage). An example of Olbian coinage is a silver stater (350–320 BC) with Athena's head on the obverse and an eagle and dolphin on the reverse. The city was abandoned in the face of barbarian aggression in the 3rd–4th centuries AD. Artefacts from the Olbia region can be seen in St Petersburg (Hermitage), Moscow (Hist. Mus.) and Odessa (Archaeol. Mus.).

B. V. Farmakovsky: *Ol'viya* (Moscow, 1915)
N. Yachmenev, ed.: *Ol'viya*, 2 vols (Kiev, 1940–58)
V. Gajdukevitch: *Ol'viya: Temenos i agora* [Ol'viya: the temenos and agora] (Moscow, 1964)
L. M. Slavin: *Zdes' byl gorod Ol'viya* [Here stood the town of Ol'viya] (Kiev, 1967)
S. D. Kryzhitsky: *Ol'viya* (Kiev, 1985)
M. Grant: *The Rise of the Greeks* (London, 1987/*R* 2001)
I. U. G. Vinogradov and S. D. Kryzhitskii: *Olbia: Eine altgriechische Stadt im nordwestlichen Schwarzmeerraum* (Leiden, 1995)
L. Dubois: *Inscriptions grecques dialectales d'Olbia du Pont* (Geneva, 1996)
A. Wasowicz and W. Zdrojewska: *Monuments en plomb d'Olbia Pontique au Musée National de Varsovie* (Torun, 1998)
G. I. Sokolov: *Ol'viia i Khersones: Ionicheskoe i doricheskoe iskusstvo* (Moscow, 1999)
M.V. Skrzhinskaia: *Budni i prazdniki Ol'vii v VI–I vv. do n. e.* [on social life and customs] (St Petersburg, 2000)
P. O. Karyshkovskii: *Monetnoe delo i denezhnoe obrashchenie Ol'vii: VI v. do n.e.–IV v.n.e.* (Odessa, 2003) [on coinage]
S. N. Rosliakov: *Ol'viia: zhizn' i smert' tsivilizatsii* (Nikolaev, 2003)
A. I. Ivantchik: 'Dedication to the Goddess Ma from Olbia (IOlb 74)', *Ancient Civilizations from Scythia to Siberia*, x/1–2 (2004), pp. 1–14
A. S. Rusíâeva and M. Rusíâeva: *Ol'viiâ Pontiiskaîâ: Gorod schast'iâ i pechali* (Kiev, 2004)
N. A. Frolova and M. G. Abramzon: *Monety Ol'vii v sobranii Gosudarstvennogo istoricheskogo muzeia* (Moscow, 2005) [catalogue of coins]

Oliaros. *See* ANTIPAROS.

Olkion. *See* VULCI.

Oltos (*fl c.* 525–*c.* 500 BC). Greek vase painter. He was an important early Athenian Red-figure artist. He apparently trained in the workshop of NIKOSTHENES and initially specialized in bilingual eye cups, decorating more extant specimens than any other artist. Indeed, most of his over 150 surviving works are cups, including the two potted by Euxitheos that bear Oltos' painter-signature (Berlin, Staatliche Mus. Antikensamml., 2269; Tarquinia, Pal. Vitelleschi, RC 6848). He was particularly influenced by the earliest Red-figure artists, the ANDOKIDES PAINTER and PSIAX, while his Black-figure output recalls Psiax in motif and the ANTIMENES PAINTER in style. Oltos employed Black-figure exclusively for scenes on eye-cup tondos, such as the *Running Dionysos Carrying a Rhyton and Vine* (Rome, Vatican, Mus. Gregoriano Etrus. 498) or the *Spear-bearing Trumpeters* (Rome, Vatican, Mus. Gregoriano Etrus., 46; Bryn Mawr Coll., PA,

Riegal Mem. Mus.), using fine incision and substantial added red. Between the large eyes on the cups' exteriors he painted Red-figure trumpeters, warriors, athletes, women, beasts, plants or inanimate objects. The genre suited his forthright, repetitive style.

Oltos' characteristic *kalos* inscriptions praising Memnon first appeared on the hastily painted bilingual vases and Red-figure palmette-eye cups of his middle period. The various potters' signatures on his works (e.g. Nikosthenes, Pamphaios, Chelis, Kachrylion and Euxitheos) attest to the late Archaic painter's mobility between workshops. The mature Oltos learnt much from the younger artist EUPHRONIOS, whom he surely met at the potteries of Kachrylion and Euxitheos. Thus, his stately *Assembly of Gods* on the exterior of a Red-figure cup (Tarquinia, Pal. Vitelleschi, RC 6848; see fig.) rivals works of the Pioneer group in its intricately detailed composition and sure draughtsmanship. Oltos, however, always remained more interested in elegant decoration than in naturalism. Contact with the Pioneers may also explain why his masterpieces occur on unusual or innovative shapes. Thus, he painted special Red-figure Nikosthenic amphorae (Paris, Louvre, G 2, G 3) and a special Red-figure stamnos (London, BM, E 437) potted by Pamphaios, placing Red-figure palmettes at the handles of both, as he generally did on his Red-figure cups.

The pictures on his two psykters (wine coolers) typify his style and personality with their deceptively simple figures drawn with a supple relief line over the vessels' sharply curving surfaces. Athletes and their trainers encircle one (New York, Met., 10.20.18): as usual, the figures have downturned lips, hands in affected gestures and long feet, and are drawn in profile but without great anatomical detail. On the other (New York, Met., 1989.281.69) the frieze of singing warriors mounted on dolphins is a clever creation for a vessel designed to float within a krater. Oltos was an energetic and enterprising painter whose long career extended from the early development of Red-figure to the experiments of the Pioneers.

F. P. Johnson: 'Oltos and Euphronios', *A. Bull.*, xix (1937), pp. 537–60

J. D. Beazley: *Red-figure* (1942, 2/1963), i, pp. 53–67, ii, pp. 1622–3, 1700

A. Bruhn: *Oltos and Early Red-figure Vase Painting* (Copenhagen, 1943)

P. E. Arias and M. Hirmer: *Tausend Jahre griechischer Vasenkunst* (Munich, 1960): Eng. trans. and rev. by B. Shefton as *A History of Greek Vase Painting* (London, 1962), pp. 320–22

J. D. Beazley: *Paralipomena* (1971), pp. 326–8

J. Boardman: *Athenian Red Figure Vases: The Archaic Period* (London, 1975), pp. 56–7

B. Cohen: *Attic Bilingual Vases and Their Painters* (New York, 1978), pp. 322–99

L. Burn and R. Glynn: *Beazley Addenda: Additional References to* ABV, ARV2 *and* Paralipomena (Oxford, 1982, rev. T. H. Carpenter, 2/1989), pp. 162–6

G. Ferrari: 'Eye-cup', *Rev. Archéol.*, i (1986), pp. 5–20

J. Harnecker: *Oltos, Untersuchungen zu Themenwahl und Stil eines frührotfigurigen Schalenmalers*, Europäische Hochschulschriften,

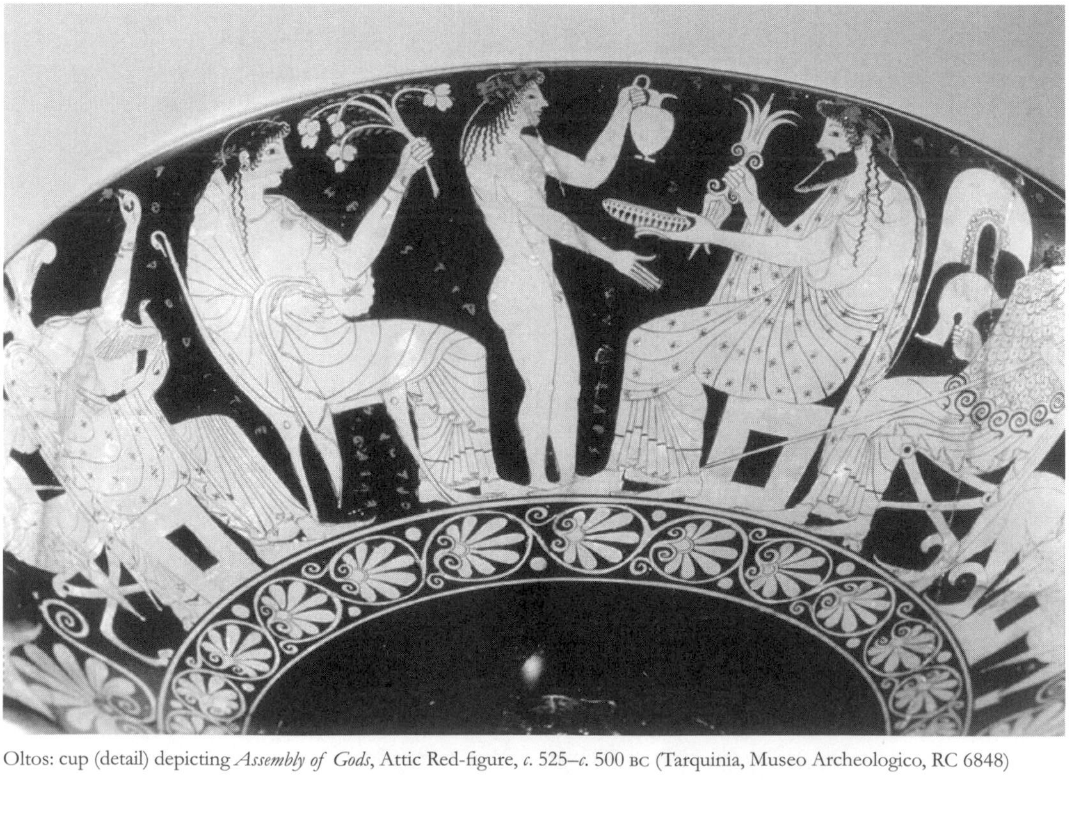

Oltos: cup (detail) depicting *Assembly of Gods*, Attic Red-figure, *c.* 525–*c.* 500 BC (Tarquinia, Museo Archeologico, RC 6848)

Reihe XXXVIII, Archäologie, xviii, (Frankfurt am Main, 1992)

M. Robertson: *The Art of Vase-painting in Classical Athens* (Cambridge, 1992), pp. 16–18, 20–23, 33–34, 38

S. Klinger: 'The Sources of Oltos' Design on the One-piece Amphora London E 2588', *Arch. Anz.* (1993), pp. 183–200

P. J. Connor: 'A Leaper, a Rivet, and Graffiti on a Bilingual Eye cup of the Early Red-figure Period', *Archäol Anz.*, iii (1996), pp. 363–70

M. B. Moore: *Attic Red-figured and White-ground Pottery, The Athenian Agora*, xxx (Princeton, 1997), pp. 84, 87–8, 316

Ol'viya. *See* OLBIA.

Olympia. Site of one of the oldest and most famous ancient Greek sanctuaries. It lies in the western Peloponnese, 18 km inland from the Ionian Sea, at the confluence of the rivers Alpheios and Kladeos and just south of Mt Kronos. Olympia flourished from Late Mycenaean to Roman times; its fame stemmed largely from the quadrennial Olympic Games, the most important pan-Hellenic festival, held there regularly from 776 BC to AD 393. By the 6th century AD most of the site was in ruins, and alluvial silt eventually covered nearly the whole sanctuary to a depth of 7 m. The Kladeos changed its course, sweeping away much of the west side of the site. In 1829 the Temple of Zeus was partly excavated by the French Expédition du Morée, and systematic excavation by the Deutsches Archäologisches Institut began in 1875, continuing since in several phases (for plan see fig. 1).

1. Architecture. 2. Sculpture.

1. ARCHITECTURE.

(i) Early remains. (ii) Archaic to Hellenistic. (iii) Roman.

(i) Early remains. An early settlement on the site was inhabited continuously from the Early Helladic to the Late Helladic periods (*c.* 3600/3000–*c.* 1050 BC), and remains include those of apsidal, rectangular and elliptical buildings. An extensive cemetery containing Late Mycenaean chamber tombs has also been found some 100 m to the north of the main site. The settlement appears to have become a religious centre during the Late Mycenaean period or soon after, when the hero demi-gods Pelops and Hippodameia were worshipped. Of their tumuli only the remains of the circular peribolus of Pelops have been found, beneath the Pelopion of historical times. The cults of Kronos, Rhea, Gaia, Eileithyia, Themis and Idaian Herakles must also have been introduced at an early period. Their shrines were at the southern foot of Mt Kronos, where most of the prehistoric finds were discovered. Following the Dorian invasion (*c.* 1100 BC), the worship of Zeus was introduced. The Olympic Games, which were already held by this time, were initially part of a local religious festival but gradually attracted participants from further afield. In the Geometric and Early Archaic periods (10th century BC–late 7th) the Altis

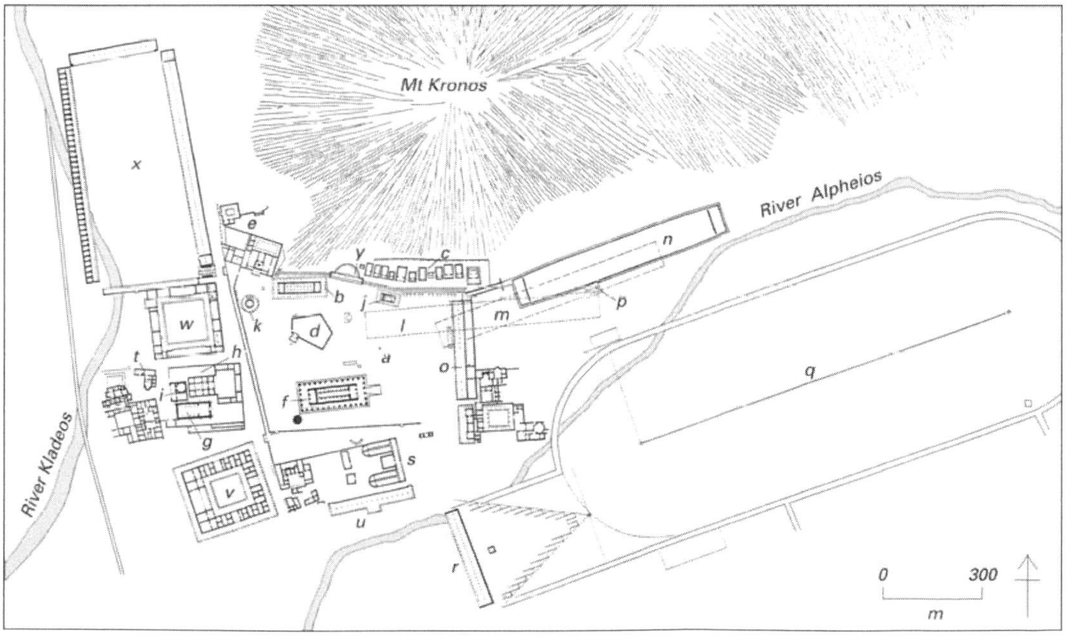

1. Olympia, plan of the sanctuary: (a) Altis; (b) Temple of Hera (Heraion); (c) treasuries; (d) Pelopion; (e) prytaneion; (f) Temple of Zeus; (g) workshop of Pheidias; (h) theokoleon; (i) heroon; (j) metroon; (k) Philippeion; (l) Stadium I; (m) Stadium II; (n) Stadium III; (o) Echo Stoa; (p) exedra for Hellanodikai; (q) hippodrome; (r) Stoa of Agnaptos; (s) bouleuterion; (t) baths; (u) South Stoa; (v) Leonidaion; (w) palaestra; (x) gymnasium; (y) nymphaeum

(sacred grove; fig. 1a) at Olympia contained a few simple structures, including altars and the shrine–tombs of Pelops and Hippodameia. A single column from the palace of Oinomaos apparently survived until the time of Pausanias (2nd century AD). The stadium at this time probably occupied the same site as in the later Archaic period.

(ii) Archaic to Hellenistic. From the Archaic period (7th–6th century BC) onwards the sanctuary became increasingly important and was embellished with its first monumental buildings. These were erected gradually, some of them being sacred structures while others provided for the growing administrative needs of the sanctuary. In the 5th century BC it reached its zenith. The strict observance of the Holy Truce, which operated during the Olympic Games, and the recognition of the controlling city-state of Elis as 'sacred and unassailable', as Polybios affirmed, secured the unhampered development of the whole area of Olympia. At this time the most important building, the gigantic Temple of Zeus, was erected. New building activity continued in the Late Classical period, despite internal problems and external conflicts for Elis. For the first time both the Ionic and Corinthian orders were used on buildings in the sanctuary, which had earlier been dominated by the Doric order. In the newer buildings white marble was frequently employed. By the end of the 4th century BC the sanctuary had broadly acquired its final definitive architectural appearance.

(a) Religious buildings. (b) Recreational and other buildings.

(a) Religious buildings. The first monumental structure was the Temple of Hera (Heraion; fig. 1b), built at the foot of Mt Kronos. This was once considered to have been an enlargement *c.* 600 BC of an earlier small Doric building: research has shown, however, that the whole temple was completed at one time around 600 BC. The Heraion, a narrow building with heavy proportions (18.76×10.00 m; 6×16 columns), is one of the oldest monumental temples in Greece. The lower part and the huge orthostat blocks of the cella are preserved. These are of local shelly limestone, while the upper parts of the walls were of mudbrick, supporting a wooden superstructure roofed with terracotta tiles. At the peak of both gables was a terracotta disc acroterion, one of which has been restored (diam. 2.42 m). The original wooden columns were replaced over a long period by stone Doric ones. Each of the stone columns was in the style of its own period, so that they provide overall a paradigm of the development of the Doric order. The bench on which the stone statues of Hera and Zeus rested is preserved at the back of the cella. In the 6th century BC numerous treasuries (fig. 1c above) were built in a row along a natural terrace on the south slope of Mt Kronos, bordering the north edge of the Altis above the Heraion. Dedicated by the Greek cities, particularly by colonies, these treasuries took the usual form, resembling small temples. The oldest is the Sikyonian treasury, its first phase being roughly contemporary with the Temple of Hera. Later treasuries belong to the first half of the 5th century BC (e.g. the treasuries of Sikyon and of Gela in their second phase, and also of Syracuse and of Byzantium). Pausanias gave the names of ten treasuries, although the remains of twelve are preserved. Only five are securely identified: the treasuries of Sikyon, Selinus, Metapontion, Megara and Gela. There are numerous architectural fragments of the first, fourth and last, although only a few pieces of the pedimental sculptures survive. The stepped supporting wall in front of the treasuries dates from the 4th century BC.

The Pelopion (fig. 1d), a grove containing an altar to Pelops, was renewed in the 6th century BC. It had a pentagonal peribolus and a propylon, which was replaced in the 5th century BC by a more monumental one. An alternative theory dating the Pelopion to the 4th century BC does not seem well founded. The older prytaneion (fig. 1e), which contained the sacred hearth, is at the north corner of the Altis. It dates from the early 5th century BC, although it was enlarged and continually altered in the following centuries. No trace of the Great Altar of Zeus south-east of the Temple of Hera is preserved: a mound slowly built up from the ashes of sacrifices and from the altar of the prytaneion, it was simply washed away after worship at the sanctuary ceased.

The Temple of Zeus (fig. 1f), in the middle of the Altis, was begun *c.* 470 BC and completed in 456 BC. This Doric peripteral temple (27.68×64.12 m; 6×13 columns) was the work of the Elian architect Libon. The largest temple in the Peloponnese, it was considered the finest expression and the 'canon' of the Doric order. It was constructed of local shelly limestone covered with white stucco, with only the roof, sima and lion-head waterspouts of Parian marble. Later, the frequent local earthquakes made replacements of Pentelic marble necessary. The marble pedimental groups are among the finest examples of Early Classical sculpture. The temple housed Pheidias' chryselephantine (gold and ivory) statue of *Zeus*, which was installed at the back of the cella soon after 430 BC.

For the making of this colossal statue a workshop was erected west of the temple (fig. 1g), which survived with various alterations until late Roman times. It measured 14.57×32.18 m, and in and around it were found numerous tools, moulds and other materials from the period of the chryselephantine *Zeus*, obviously used by Pheidias and his assistants. There are two other late 5th-century BC buildings north of the workshop of Pheidias. One is rectangular with a peristyle court, probably the theokoleon (fig. 1h) where the priests of Olympia (*theokoloi*) met. The other, west of the theokoleon, has a plan consisting of a circle inside a square and is named as the heroon (fig. 1i) in a Late Hellenistic inscription found there.

In the Late Classical period the main sanctuary was separated from the surrounding complex by a monumental peribolus with five gates, three on the west side and two at the south. At the beginning of the 4th century BC the metroon (the Temple of

Kybele, mother of the gods; fig. 1j) was built in front of the terrace on which the treasuries stood. Of this Doric peripteral temple (10.62×20.67 m; 6×11 columns) only the stylobate and portions of the stone architrave are preserved. From the time of Augustus the metroon was used for the worship of the Roman emperors, and it contained portrait sculptures of many of them. Around the late 5th century BC–early 4th the South-east Building was erected, which has been thought to be the Sanctuary of Hestia (14.66×36.42 m). It was destroyed in the 1st century AD to provide foundations for a peristyle villa, considered at one time probably to have been built for Nero. However, later excavations showed that Nero's villa was the one to the north of the prytaneion.

The Philippeion (fig. 1k), an elegant circular peripteral building (diam. 15.24 m) south of the prytaneion, was begun by Philip II of Macedonia after the Battle of Chaironeia (338 BC) but finished by his son Alexander the Great. It stood on a marble stylobate, mostly preserved, and was surrounded by an Ionic colonnade. Corinthian half-columns were placed at intervals around the interior of the circular cella, at the back of which were five chryselephantine portrait statues by Leochares representing Alexander the Great between his parents and his grandfathers. This type of tholos (circular building), used earlier for worship of the gods, was here employed for the first time for the hero cult of the Macedonian dynasty.

(b) Recreational and other buildings. The Archaic stadium (Stadium I; fig. 1l), which was simple in form, extended along the slope in front of the treasuries. Stadium II (fig. 1m), constructed around the late 6th century BC–early 5th, was in roughly the same position, possibly further to the east. Towards the mid-5th century BC the stadium was moved 82 m to the east and 7 m to the north (Stadium III; fig. 1n). Excavations have shown that the embankment of the narrow western side was truncated after the mid-4th century BC, when the Echo Stoa was built, which entirely separated the stadium from the sanctuary. The track of this new stadium was 215.54 m long and *c.* 28.5 m wide. The banks that enclosed it on four sides could accommodate 45,000 spectators, most of whom would sit on the sloping ground, the few stone seats being kept for dignitaries. The stone exedra for the Hellanodikai (judges; fig. 1p) was opposite the Altar of Demeter Chamyne. In the late 3rd century BC the north-west corner of the stadium was linked with the sanctuary through a narrow roofed corridor.

The hippodrome (fig. 1q), which was four stades long (*c.* 780 m), had not been excavated by the 1990s and probably had been at least partly washed away by the River Alpheios. It was south of the stadium and parallel to it. To the west the hippodrome ended at the Stoa of Agnaptos (fig. 1r), also unexcavated by the end of the 20th century. The south end of the sanctuary was closed off in the mid-6th century BC by the north building of the bouleuterion (14.0×30.5 m; fig. 1s). This was a rectangular apsidal structure. In the 5th century BC a second apsidal building was added, parallel to the first, and between these a rectangular room housing the altar of Zeus Horkios, where the athletes made their vows (*horkoi*) before the Games. The three buildings constituting the bouleuterion were enlarged in the 4th century BC by an Ionic portico across the east façade. To the west of the sanctuary, beyond the theokoleon and near the River Kladeos, were the baths (5.75×21.56 m) and a swimming pool (16×24 m; fig. 1t).

When the stadium was shifted east, the isolation of the Altis was completed with the construction of the Echo Stoa (fig. 1o), with its base course and steps of marble measuring 12.5×98.0 m along its west side. It was built shortly after 350 BC and had two colonnades, with rooms along the back. The south boundary of the sanctuary in its larger sense was defined by the South Stoa (l. 80.56 m; fig. 1u), which took the form of a T with a colonnaded extension in its centre towards the River Alpheios. Built at the same time as the Echo Stoa, its base course and steps were similarly of marble. In the west part of the sanctuary, south of the workshop of Pheidias, stood the hostel called the Leonidaion (fig. 1v), built in 330 BC and named after its donor and architect Leonidas of Naxos. It is almost square in plan (74.82×81.08 m) and was originally intended for distinguished visitors, although it was later used as a residence for Roman officials.

In the Hellenistic period (3rd–1st century BC) there was no new building in the Altis, although vigorous building activity outside it involved new accommodation for the athletes and spectators at the Games. To the west of the Altis, near the Kladeos, the palaestra (fig. 1w) was built in the mid-3rd century BC as a training ground for wrestling, boxing and jumping. It was nearly square (66.35×66.75 m), with a peristyle court around which were covered areas. To the north of the palaestra and connected with it was the gymnasium (fig. 1x), an enclosed rectangular building (120×220 m) with a wide court in the centre and colonnades on the four sides. There the athletes trained for such contests as throwing the javelin and discus, and running. It was built in the late 2nd century BC, while the monumental entrance between it and the palaestra, in the form of an amphiprostyle Corinthian propylon, was erected soon after.

(iii) Roman. In 146 BC the consul Mummius dedicated 21 gilded shields, fixed to the metopes of the Temple of Zeus, after his victory over the Greeks at the Peloponnesian Isthmus. Later, the dictator Cornelius Sulla decided to move the Olympic Games to Rome and organized the 175th Olympiad there (80 BC). Olympia recovered its prestige under Augustus, and after 31 BC Roman emperors and magistrates endowed the sanctuary in accordance with their political programmes in Greece. Under Nero the Altis was enlarged and surrounded by a new peribolus, and the simple gates of the sanctuary were replaced by monumental propylaia.

At about the same time new baths were erected west of the Greek baths and north of the prytaneion. Later still, other baths were built north-east of Nero's villa and west of the bouleuterion. Another hostel was built west of the workshop of Pheidias, and the older buildings were maintained or altered. Finally, in AD 160 Herodes Atticus built a magnificent fountain, the nymphaeum or exedra (w. 33 m, h. *c.* 13 m; fig. 1y), in the form of a semicircle with a circular naiskos (small shrine) at each end. The walls were of brick with polychrome marble facing. Above the semicircular, probably two-storey wall, and in the apsidal recesses that made up the central façade, were 22 statues of Antoninus Pius (*reg* AD 138–61) and his family as well as the family of Herodes Atticus. The space between the two naiskoi was occupied by two superimposed basins. The water, from an abundant spring 4 km east of Olympia, ran from the nymphaeum via a network of conduits throughout the sanctuary.

With the threat of the Herulian invasion in AD 267, a strong wall was built to protect the richer treasuries and the statue of *Zeus*. This wall, formerly thought to be Byzantine, surrounded the Temple of Zeus and the south part of the sanctuary up to the South Stoa. It was built with material from buildings demolished for the purpose, although the Temple of Hera escaped destruction. Although Olympia continued to decline, there were some restorations in the 3rd century AD, particularly under Diocletian. In AD 393–4 the decree of Theodosios I prohibiting pagan worship ended Olympia's role as a sanctuary, and in AD 426 an edict of Theodosios II caused the destruction of the monuments of the Altis, completed by two earthquakes in 522 and 551. In the 5th and 6th centuries the workshop of Pheidias was transformed into a Christian basilica.

A. Bötticher: *Olympia* (Berlin, 1883, rev. 1886)
E. Curtius and F. Adler: *Olympia: Die Ergebnisse*, 5 vols (Berlin, 1890–97/*R* 1966)
B. Leonardos: *Olympia* (Athens, 1901)
J. K. Smith: 'The Restoration of the Temple of Zeus at Olympia', *Mem. Amer. Acad.*, iv (1924), pp. 153–68
N. E. Gardiner: *Olympia: Its History and Remains* (Oxford, 1925)
E. Curtius: *Olympia* (Berlin, 1935)
W. Dörpfeld: *Alt-Olympia* (Berlin, 1935/*R* 1966)
Berichte über die Ausgrabungen in Olympia, Deutsches Archäologisches Institut (1937–)
Olympische Forschungen, Deutsches Archäologisches Institut (1944–)
I. Kontes: *To ieron tis Olympias kata ton d'aiona p.kh.* [The sanctuary at Olympia in the 4th century BC] (Athens, 1958)
F. Kunze: *Neue deutsche Ausgrabungen im Mittelmeergebiet und im Vorderasien: Olympia* (Berlin, 1959)
H. Berve and others: *Griechische Tempel und Heiligtümer* (Munich, 1961), pp. 10ff, 118ff
H. V. Herrmann: 'Zur ältesten Geschichte von Olympia', *Mitt. Dt. Archäol. Inst.: Athen. Abt.*, lxxvii (1962), pp. 3ff
G. Gruben: *Die Tempel der Griechen* (Munich, 1966, rev. 1976), pp. 43ff
B. Ashmole and N. Yalouris: *The Sculptures of the Temple of Zeus* (London, 1967)
L. Drees: *Olympia* (New York, 1968)
S. Miller: 'The Prytaneion at Olympia', *Mitt. Dt. Archäol. Inst.: Athen. Abt.*, lxxxvi (1971), pp. 7ff
H. V. Herrmann and M. Hirmer: *Olympia: Heiligtum und Wettkampfstätte* (Munich, 1972)
A. Mallwitz: *Olympia und seine Bauten* (Munich, 1972)
N. Yalouris: *Olympia Altis and Museum* (Munich, 1972/*R* 1983)
K. Herrmann: 'Beobachtungen zur Schatzhaus-Architektur Olympias', *Mitt. Dt. Archäol. Inst.: Athen. Abt.* (1976), pp. 321ff
A. Yalouris and N. Yalouris: *Olympia: Guide to the Museum and the Sanctuary* (Athens, 1987)
C. Morgan: *Athletes and Oracles: The Transformation of Olympia and Delphi in the 8th century* BC (Cambridge, 1990)
J. Rambach: 'Dorpfelds Bau VII in der Altis von Olympia: Ein fruheisenzeitliches Apsidenhaus und "Haus des Oinomaos"?', *Archäol. Anz.*, i (2002), pp. 119–34
U. Sinn and others: 'Olympia—eine Spitzenstellung nicht nur im Sport', *Ant. Welt*, xxxiv/6 (2003), pp. 617–23
W. Decker: 'Spiele für die Gotter: Olympia und die anderen grossen Sportfeste des antiken Griechenlands', *Ant. Welt*, xxxv/4 (2004), pp. 8–19
T. Perrottet: 'Walking to Olympia: Who Went, How They Got There, and Where They Stayed', *Archaeology Odyssey*, vii/4 (July–Aug 2004), pp. 22–9, 52–3
I. Triante and P. Valavanes: *Olympia kai olympiakoi agones: Ta mnemeia tora kai tote* (Athens, 2004)

2. Sculpture. Literary sources reveal that in ancient times the sanctuary of Olympia was exceptionally rich in architectural and commemorative sculpture, although only a limited number of works and fragments survive, dating from the Archaic to the Hellenistic periods. Pausanias visited the site in the late 2nd century AD, and his description (*Guide to Greece*, V.x.2–xii.8) provides the main ancient source of information on the sculpture.

Unless otherwise stated, all works discussed below are housed in the Archaeological Museum, Olympia.

(i) From the Temple of Zeus. (ii) Other works.

(i) From the Temple of Zeus. The pedimental figures and metopes from the Temple of Zeus are of particular interest. This temple also once housed Pheidias' colossal chryselephantine statue of *Zeus*, considered one of the Seven Wonders of the Ancient World. The metopes and pedimental sculptures represent the high point of the Early Classical (Severe) style and are among the most important of all Greek architectural sculptures. They are of Parian marble and by the 1990s had not yet been attributed. The east pediment, as described by Pausanias, portrays the *Preparations for the Chariot Race between Pelops and Oinomaos*. The hero Pelops, founder of the Olympic Games, had been worshipped at Olympia since its early history. In the centre of the composition Zeus is flanked by the contestants, female standing figures, chariot teams and attendants, and seated or reclining spectators. The site of the race, Olympia itself, is indicated by the figures of the river gods Alpheios and Kladeos in the angles of the pediment. Zeus

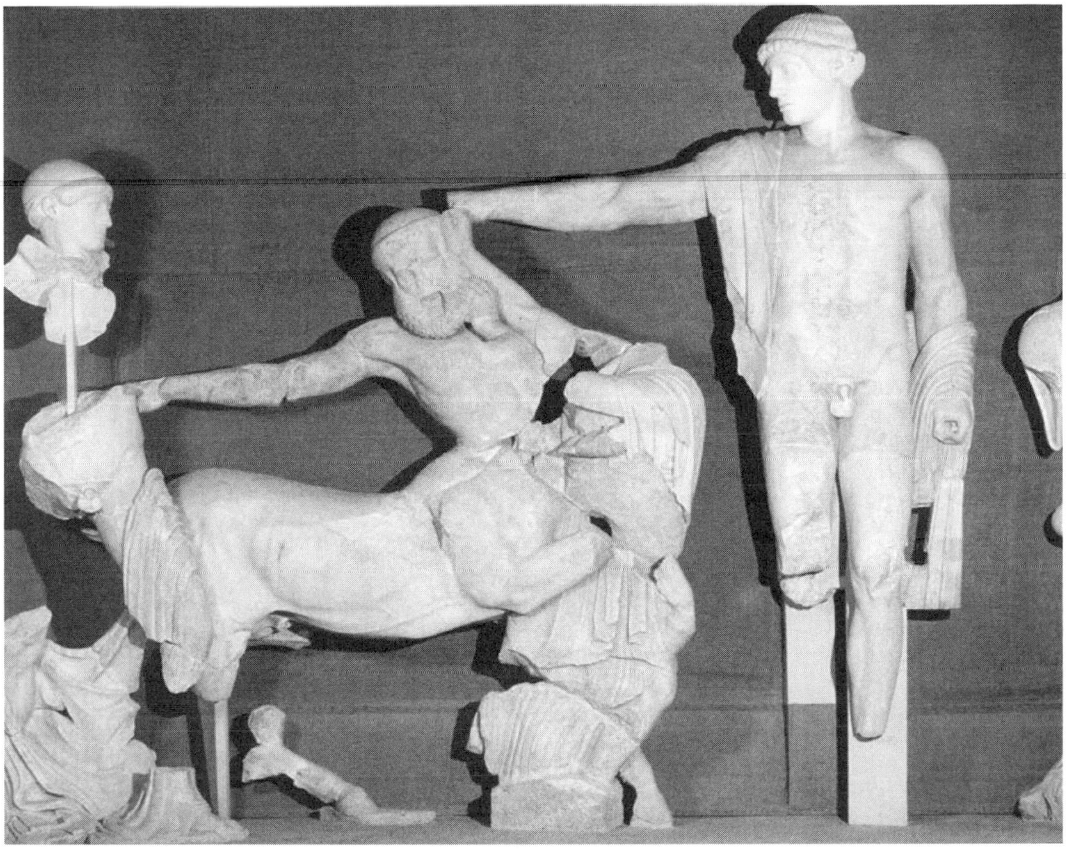

2. Olympia, fragments of sculpture from the west pediment of the Temple of Zeus showing the *Battle of the Lapiths and Centaurs at the Wedding of Perithoos*, marble, h. 3.1 m, *c.* 460 BC (Olympia, Archaeological Museum)

inclines his head toward Pelops, the eventual victor, as a worried seer looks on. Overall, the poses are quiet, since the scene represents the preparation for the race, not its enactment. The west pediment depicts the *Battle of the Lapiths and the Centaurs at the Wedding of Perithoos*. Apollo, the central figure, dominates the scene as he stretches out his right hand to calm the uproar (see fig. 2). On both sides groups of Lapiths and Centaurs are struggling, and Lapith women recline at both corners. The struggling groups and their drapery patterns create a flowing, rhythmic movement that gives unity to the pedimental composition. In general the human figures appear calm in contrast to the agitated, enraged centaurs, and this may be intended to express the superiority of civilized humanity over the bestial, barbarian centaurs, as may the presence of Apollo, patron of the arts. In contrast to the east pediment, the action on either side of the stabilizing figure of Apollo is tumultuous. In keeping with their status as gods, however, the figures of Apollo and Zeus in the pediments play no physical role in the action, although their gestures and expressions suggest their decisive role in the course of human events.

Details of original arrangements of the figures in the pediments are debated, yet it seems clear that they were the product of a unified design. Pausanias attributed the pediments to Alkamenes and Paionios, but problems of chronology and style suggest that he was mistaken, and the unidentified sculptors were probably of a local Peloponnesian school. In any case, the figures were executed in a homogeneous style, probably supervised by a single master. The bodies are anatomically correct, and the poses represent an important stage in the development of Greek sculpture between Archaic and Early Classical (see fig. 3). The figures were undoubtedly painted, probably in a few bold colours, particularly red and blue, with a light tone for women's flesh and brown for men, as was much added detail. The carving is not highly detailed, both because of the use of paint for this purpose and because the figures were placed at least 16 m above the ground.

The external metopes of the Temple of Zeus remained undecorated, but inside the main colonnade, above the columns *in antis* of the pronaos and the opisthodomos, there were 12 high-relief metopes depicting the canonical version of the *Labours of Herakles* (in mythology the great-grandson

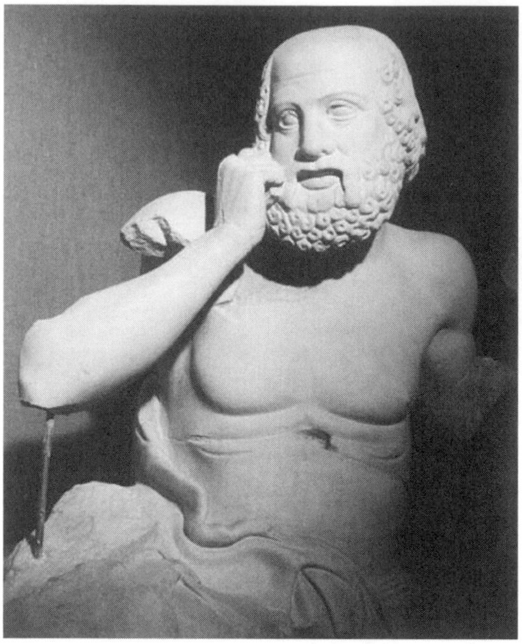

3. Olympia, *Seer*, from the east pediment of the Temple of Zeus, *c.* 470–457 BC (Olympia, Archaeological Museum)

of Pelops). The metopes measure 1.60×1.52 m, and the figures are only slightly under life-size. As in the pediments, the subjects represent both subdued and active scenes; some of the compositions have a vertical emphasis that repeats the design of the framing triglyphs, while the more active scenes often use diagonals to dynamic effect. The depiction of *Herakles with the Cretan Bull*, for example, is based completely on diagonals, while in the scene of *Atlas Presenting Herakles with the Apples of the Hesperides* (see fig. 4) the three vertical figures echo the triglyph composition. Overall, the image of Herakles depicted in the metopes is strong but without the brutishness attributed to him in later art and literature, and his representation alongside Athena in four of the metopes associates him with the Olympian deities. Fragments of some of the metopes are in the Musée du Louvre, Paris.

Originally dominating the interior of the temple was Pheidias' colossal chryselephantine cult statue of *Zeus*, probably completed several years after the temple itself. The framework was probably made of wood on to which plates of gold for the drapery and sheets of ivory for the flesh were attached. Pausanias described the work in detail (V.xi): the god was seated on a gold throne inlaid with jewels, ebony and ivory and decorated with paintings and statuettes, including winged Nikai (Victories) and various

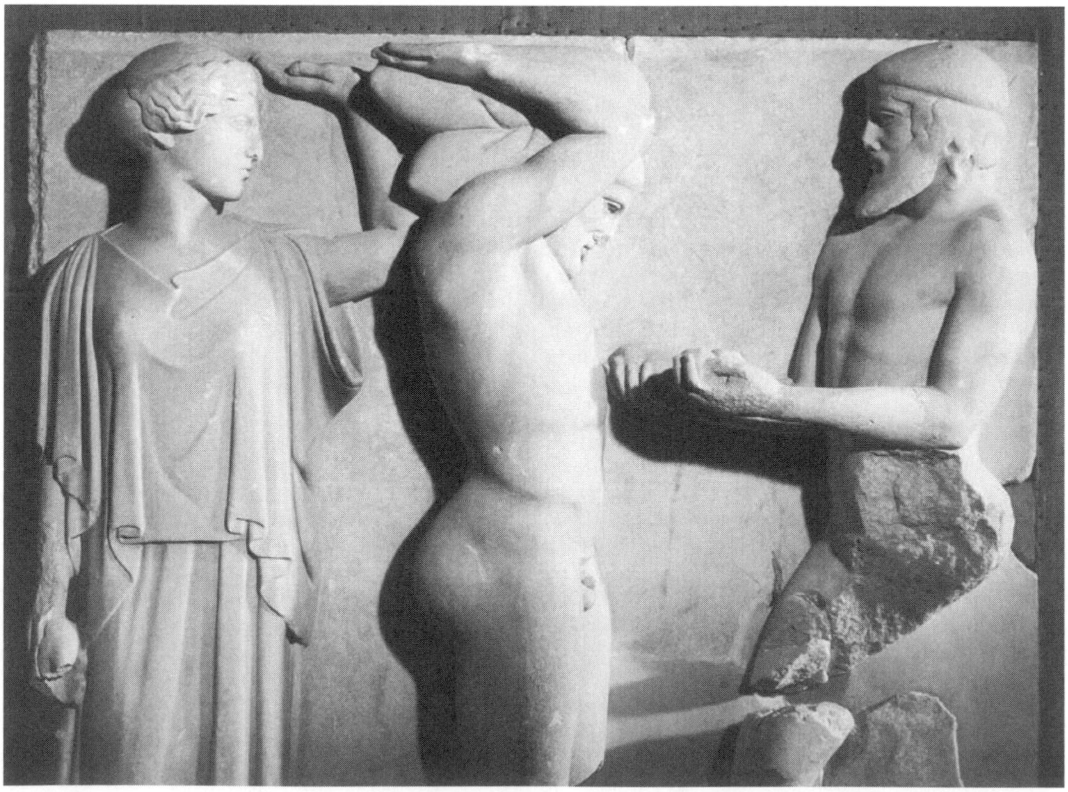

4. Olympia, metope from the Temple of Zeus showing *Atlas Presenting Herakles with the Apples of the Hesperides*, marble, 1.60×1.52 m, *c.* 470–457 BC (Olympia, Archaeological Museum)

mythological scenes. Zeus' head was wreathed in olive; in his right hand he held a Nike and in his left an ornamented sceptre surmounted by an eagle. On the god's feet were gold sandals, and his robe was decorated with flowers and animals. The sculpture is said to have been seven times life-size or about 12 m high. In addition to Pausanias' description, the colossal sculpture is represented on Hadrianic coins from Elis (e.g. in Florence, Mus. Archeol.). It may have been removed to Constantinople (now Istanbul) after the sanctuary fell into disuse in the 4th century AD and destroyed there in a fire of AD 475.

(ii) Other works. The *Nike of Paionios* was dedicated to Zeus and possibly erected at the Peace of Nikias in 421 BC by the Messenians and Naupaktians. It survives as an example of the many statues of gods, heroes and Olympic victors that must have adorned the sanctuary. The dedicatory inscription on the plinth not only identifies the sculptor but also states that PAIONIOS OF MENDE won the competition to design the acroteria for the Temple of Zeus. The central acroteria of the temple were in fact also Nikai. The *Nike* of the dedicatory sculpture, leaning forward with her cloak blown back, is an impressive figure. The sense of movement and windblown effect of the drapery mark it as a highly innovative work, and its original base, a triangular pillar *c.* 9 m high, would have added to its impact.

A marble statue of *Hermes Holding the Child Dionysos*, discovered in the 19th century in the Temple of Hera, was attributed to PRAXITELES on the basis of Pausanias' brief mention of a marble of this subject 'in the manner of Praxiteles' (V.xvii.3). The work is controversial and may be a Roman copy after Praxiteles' original or by a later sculptor of the same name. It has also been suggested that it was carved between 330 and 320 BC, perhaps to commemorate an alliance of 343 BC. If so, it is one of the best-preserved of all Classical sculptures. It was intended to be placed against a wall, as indicated by the lack of detail in the back.

The Philippeion, a tholos constructed after 338 BC, housed a group of five chryselephantine statues by Leochares. These represented Philip of Macedon, his mother and father, his wife Olympias and his son Alexander. Only fragments of the carved base have survived. Other sculptures from Olympia include a smaller than life-size terracotta statue of *Zeus Abducting Ganymede* (*c.* 500–*c.* 470 BC), a transitional work between Archaic and Early Classical, possibly an acroterion. A *Head of Hera* (*c.* 600–*c.* 560 BC) came from a monumental stone group of Zeus and Hera once in the Temple of Hera. A number of small bronze figures of athletes and horses probably represent only a small sample of the innumerable votives that must have been offered to the Olympian deities by athletes and patrons.

G. M. A. Richter: *A Handbook of Greek Art* (Oxford, 1959, 9/1987) [well illust.]
R. Lullies and M. Hirmer: *Greek Sculpture* (New York, 1960)
B. Ashmole and N. Yalouris: *Olympia: The Sculptures of the Temple of Zeus* (London, 1967)
B. S. Ridgway: *The Severe Style in Greek Sculpture* (Princeton, NJ, 1970), pp. 12–28
M. L. Säflund: *The East Pediment at Olympia* (Göteborg, 1970)
M. Robertson: *A History of Greek Art*, 2 vols (Cambridge, 1975), pp. 271–91
J. Boardman: *Greek Sculpture: The Classical Period* (London, 1985/*R* 1991), pp. 33–50
H. V. Herrmann, ed.: *Die Olympia-Skulpturen* (Darmstadt, 1987)
A. Moustaka: *Grossplastik aus Ton in Olympia* (Berlin, 1993)
J. Heiden: *Die Tondächer von Olympia* (Berlin, 1995)
B. Borell and D. Rittig: *Orientalische und griechische Bronzereliefs aus Olympia: Der Fundcomplex aus Brunnen,* xvii (Berlin, 1998)
E. Guralnick: 'A Group of Near Eastern Bronzes from Olympia', *Amer. J. Archaeol.,* cviii/2 (April 2004), pp. 187–222; errata cix/1 (Jan 2005), p. 133
H. Philipp and H. Born: *Archaische Silhouettenbleche und Schildzeichen in Olympia* (Berlin, 2004)
J. M. Barringer: 'The Temple of Zeus at Olympia, Heroes, and Athletes', *Hesperia,* lxxiv/2 (April–June 2005), pp. 211–41
K. Paterakes: *To anatoliko enaetio tou naou tou Dia sten Olympia* (Rethymno, 2005)

Olynthos [Olynthus]. Site of an ancient Greek city on the Chalcidian peninsula in northern Greece. It provides some of the best examples of houses and the most complete plan of a Classical Greek city. Olynthos was the site of a Neolithic village, later inhabited as a small town on the South Hill from the 7th century BC. In 432 BC the surrounding Greek communities joined together to form the Chalcidian League as a defensive measure against Athenian aggression, and Olynthos became its capital, expanding on to a flat-topped hill to the north and down to the plain to the east. Olynthos flourished as such until 348 BC, when it was destroyed by Philip II of Macedonia and the population sold into slavery. A few survivors reoccupied part of the site until 316 BC, but the city was never fully rebuilt or resettled. The ruins were excavated between 1928 and 1938 by an American team led by David M. Robinson.

S. Psoma: *Olynthe et les Chalcidiens de Thrace: études de numismatique et d'histoire* (Stuttgart, 2001)

1. Architecture. 2. Mosaics.

1. ARCHITECTURE. The city was surrounded by a mud-brick wall, outside which, along the main roads into the city, were at least three cemeteries. Excavation has uncovered a number of public buildings. Near the south end of the North Hill or 'new city' is an open agora, flanked by a fountain house, a stoa and a public building with an internal colonnade. Another public building, possibly a council hall, in the older 'civic centre' of the South Hill was apparently torn down and built over during the 4th century BC, while a stoa or arsenal at the north end of the South Hill continued in use until the city's destruction. No sanctuaries have been discovered, and the main

temple was probably outside the city walls. It is, however, the excavation of more than 100 houses that has made the most important contribution to the study of Greek architecture and culture.

The North Hill was laid out in a regular grid plan, with blocks measuring *c.* 86×35 m separated by avenues and streets *c.* 4.8 m wide. One avenue running up the centre of the hill is wider than usual (*c.* 7 m), forming a main thoroughfare. The blocks consist of two rows of five houses each, separated by a narrow alley for rainwater run-off. The basic planning unit seems to have been a parcel consisting of one block plus half a street on all sides. It probably measured 120×270 Greek feet, giving it the proportions of 4:9, the 'golden ratio'. The houses themselves share many common features. The standard plan is square (approx. 17×17 m), generally with a central courtyard. On the north side of the court was a *pastas* (pillared portico), from which this type of house takes its name (*see* ARCHITECTURE, §IV, 1(i)(c) and fig. 7). This provided a sheltered, yet well-lit, space for working and other activities. A row of rooms along the north side of the house opened on to the *pastas*, while other rooms opened directly on to the court (see fig.). Many houses had a complex of two or three rooms for cooking and bathing, with a large workroom or kitchen, a bathroom and a 'flue' open to the sky and used for cooking. The better-built houses had a formal dining-room (*andron*), more finely constructed and decorated than the rest of the house. The *andron* is distinguished by a raised border that supported dining couches ranged around the sides of the room. Some houses had shops and workrooms opening on to the street. In general, there were no architecturally self-contained sections of the house, and most rooms were entered from either the court or the *pastas*. Stair-bases and other features show that some houses had a second storey, and it seems that all the houses on one row had the same number of storeys and shared a common roofline. The roofs were mostly tiled, although a few houses apparently had flat clay roofs over certain rooms, which may have been used for work or sleeping.

The houses were of mud-brick on stone foundations. The foundations of a few outside walls were of cut stone in a rusticated style, but in general the stonework is unworked rubble. Wood was used for doors and doorsills, ceilings and roofs, and pillars, but little has survived. Interiors were sometimes coated with lime plaster, and some rooms, especially the *andron*, and the *pastas* were painted in red and white and occasionally yellow, black and blue. The most elaborate rooms are decorated in a style resembling the Pompeian First Style, with a base painted to resemble ashlar masonry and the walls above in a single colour. More frequently, however, the walls are entirely in a single colour, or only the wall base is decorated. One *andron* was painted with red garlands on a white ground, and another has floral motifs and palmettes, but these are the only designs so far known. The floors of most rooms are simply packed earth, but

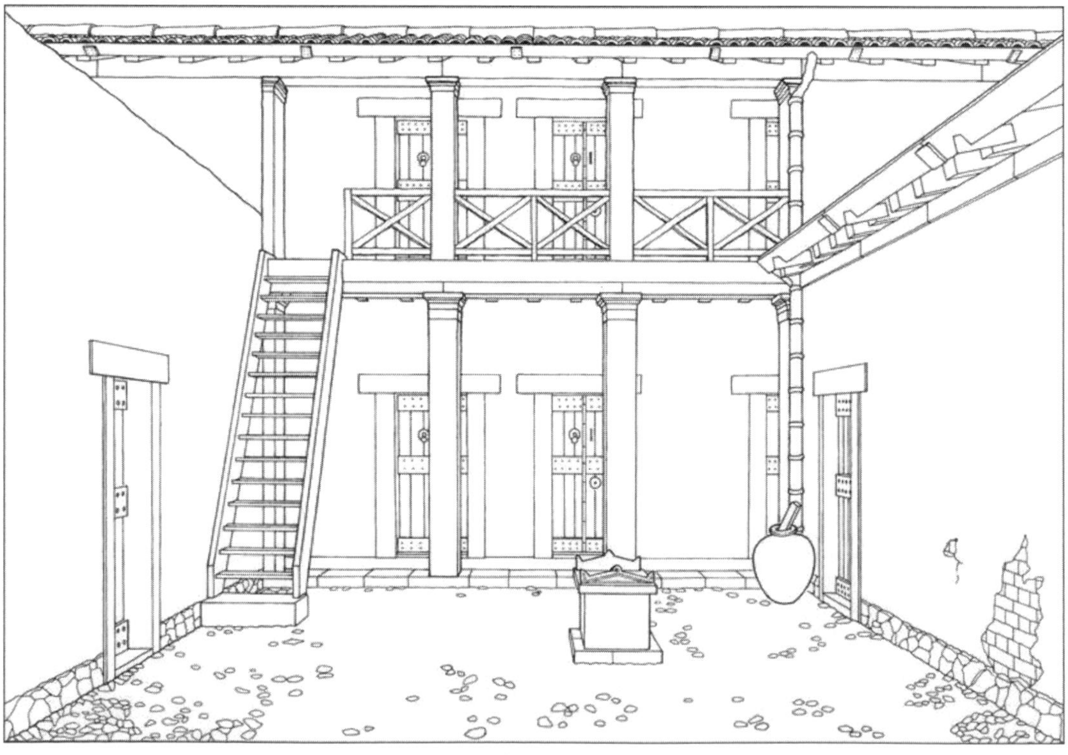

Olynthos, house of the *pastas* type, late 5th century BC to mid-4th; reconstruction of courtyard looking north

*andron*s and some other rooms have cement floors. Courtyards are often cobbled, and the more formal rooms of some of the better-constructed houses have figural pebble mosaics.

Although each household was allotted an equal parcel of land (*kleros*) during the initial planning of the city, and although the houses share features of design and construction, there are significant differences between houses in different parts of the city. Houses in one block may be regularly planned and well-constructed, while houses in the next are less carefully built and more irregular in design. This coherence suggests that the house blocks formed social, as well as physical, units of the city.

G. E. Mylonas: *The Neolithic Settlement* (1929), i of *Excavations at Olynthos* (Baltimore, 1929–52)

D. M. Robinson: *Architecture and Sculpture* (1930), ii of *Excavations at Olynthos* (Baltimore, 1929–52)

D. M. Robinson and J. W. Graham: *The Hellenic House* (1938), viii of *Excavations at Olynthos* (Baltimore, 1929–52)

D. M. Robinson: *Domestic and Public Architecture* (1946), xii of *Excavations at Olynthos* (Baltimore, 1929–52)

J. W. Graham: 'Olynthiaka', *Hesperia*, xxii (1953), pp. 196–207

J. W. Graham: 'Olynthiaka', *Hesperia*, xxiii (1954), pp. 320–46

N. Cahill: *Household and City organization at Olynthus* (New Haven, 2002)

2. Mosaics. Some of the earliest pebble mosaics in Greece were found at Olynthos (*see* Mosaics, §II, 2(iii)(a)). They are all from private houses, except those from the 'Villa of Good Fortune', which may have served as a lodging house (*pandokeion*). The rooms most commonly decorated with mosaics were the *andron*s, but in two houses the courtyard was also paved with mosaic, and in another house the *pastas* was so decorated. Among the finest mosaics, from the *andron* of House A.vi.3, is a scene depicting *Bellerophon on Pegasos Attacking the Chimaera*, with the threshold mosaic showing *Two Griffins Attacking a Stag*. The court of this house was decorated with a *Centauromachy*. Another mosaic, only partly preserved, from the *pastas* of an adjoining house, shows *Three Nereids Riding Dolphins and a Hippocamp*, perhaps a scene relating to the Wedding of Poseidon and Amphitrite. Above the *Nereids* is a second panel depicting animal combat. Four rooms of the Villa of Good Fortune were paved with mosaics. One *andron* has a scene of *Dionysos in a Panther-drawn Chariot with Eros and ?Pan*. The panel is surrounded by a border of dancing maenads. The entrance to the room was set with another panel, depicting two figures of Pan leaning over a krater. The anteroom to this *andron* had a mosaic of *Thetis Bringing Armour to Achilles*. This panel is orientated towards the *andron*, so that the diners could enjoy the scene. Two other rooms in the villa were decorated with mosaics bearing the following inscriptions: 'Good fortune', 'Aphrodite is beautiful' and 'Good fortune is beautiful'. Other mosaics from the site show hunts, animal combats and geometric patterns. The last frequently comprise a circular design, such as a wheel or star, within a square border. Six of the eighteen excavated mosaics, including some of the finest examples, come from one block of houses, which seems to have been occupied by particularly affluent families.

The Olynthian mosaics were composed from unworked, smooth river pebbles (average diam. *c.* 10–20 mm), set in grey cement on a cobble bedding. One fragment of white tessellated mosaic has been found. Tiny pebbles were occasionally used for details, and elongated ones laid end to end were used in linear designs. Figures were shown in white pebbles on a background of black or dark blue, with details picked out in dark or coloured stones (red, green, blue, yellow, pink or purple). The average dimensions of an *andron* mosaic were *c.* 3×3 m. The mosaics date to the main period of occupation of Olynthos (432–348 BC). The exact dates of individual mosaics are disputed. The figural mosaics mentioned above have been dated to *c.* 380–350 BC on the basis of the style of their floral decoration, and other mosaics to the end of the 5th century BC. All are still *in situ*.

D. Salzmann: *Untersuchungen zu den antiken Kieselmosaiken* (Berlin, 1982)

Onatas (*fl* Aigina, first half of the 5th century BC). Greek sculptor. He was one of several important Aiginetan sculptors of the Early Classical period (*c.* 480–*c.* 450 BC). Although Onatas is considered by many scholars to have worked exclusively in bronze, the sculptures from the east pediment of the Temple of Aphaia (Munich, Glyp.; *see* Aigina, §2) have also been attributed to him, as has a head of *Athena* (Paris, Louvre) and a *Sphinx* (Aegina, Archaeol. Mus.). The taut contours of these pieces are illustrative of the regional style of Aiginetan sculpture. His bronze *Herakles* at Olympia (Pausanias, *Guide to Greece* V.xxv.12) survives in various copies: a colossal marble statue (Cherchel, Mus. Archéol.), a variant in Alexandria (Gr.–Roman Mus.) and a head in London (BM 1734). A statue of *Hermes with the Ram of Pheneos* (Paris, Bib. N. 313) corresponds to a description by Pausanias (V.xxvii.8), and a copy of the head also exists (Athens, Acropolis Mus. 2344); the irregular line of the edge of the hair indicates that there was a separately worked *pilos* (felt cap). The Borghese *Hero* (Rome, Mus. Capitolino), the Somzée *Warrior* (La Louvière, Mariemont Mus.), a torso that has been completed as a *Herakles* (Rome, Mus. Torlonia) and a torso in the courtyard of the Palazzo Odescalchi in Rome are thematically and stylistically related to each other and probably derive from Onatas' sculptural group *Achaians Drawing Lots* at Olympia (Pausanias, V.xxv.8), which showed the nine heroes tensely awaiting lots, which Nestor, standing on a separate base, draws from the helmet in his hand.

J. Dörig: *Onatas of Aegina*, i of *Monumenta Graeca et Romana* (Leiden, 1977); review by B. Ridgway in *Amer. J. Archaeol.*, lxxxii (1978), pp. 260–61

A. Stewart: *Greek Sculpture: An Exploration* (New Haven and London, 1990), pp. 147–8, 252–3

M. Denti: 'Typologie et iconographie de la statue masculine de Mozia', *Rev. Archéol.,* i (1997), pp. 107–28

Onesimos (*fl c.* 505–*c.* 480 BC). Greek vase painter. Active in Athens, he specialized in decorating cups, mostly of Type B (*see* POTTERY, §IV, 6(i)(b)), and his work evinces a lively, energetic personality. His name is known from the signature on a cup (Paris, Louvre, G 105) also signed by EUPHRONIOS as potter. At least 10 other cups painted by him bear Euphronios' signature, and others have been attributed on the basis of the potting style.

Onesimos worked in steady collaboration with Euphronios, who also profoundly influenced his drawing style. His preferred *kalos* name was 'Panaitios', which led to his also being called the Panaitios Painter, sometimes identified as a different and earlier artist. J. D. Beazley listed vases attributed to the Panaitios Painter (Beazley, 1942), but these are all now usually considered the work of Onesimos. In addition, some of the vases attributed by Beazley to the Eleusis Painter or Proto-Panaetian Group probably represent Onesimos' earliest work. Besides the *kalos* inscription 'Panaitios', Onesimos frequently praised Athenodotos and, less often, Leagros on his early cups. Later, the names Erothemis, Boukolos, Lykos and Aristarchos occur: the first two are unique to Onesimos, the second two also occur on the vases of his pupil the Antiphon Painter. Onesimos' early work is marked by large tondi with big, boldly drawn figures in complex action poses, often with frontal limbs or heads, for example the satyr in the tondo of a cup (10.179) in the Museum of Fine Arts, Boston, MA. Satyrs and maenads occur especially often in his early work, as do themes drawn from the legends of Troy, Theseus or Medea, for which Onesimos invented new and unusual compositions, often filling his tondi with figures, as on a kylix depicting Theseus visiting Amphitrite accompanied by Athena and a small triton (Paris, Louvre, G 104).

With his associates in Euphronios' workshop, the BRYGOS PAINTER, DOURIS and the Antiphon Painter, Onesimos experimented with less familiar techniques, such as White-ground or coral-red. He sometimes used White-ground for the entire interior of a cup, as on early fragments from Eleusis (Eleusis Mus., 518 and 519), or, unusually, only in the zone around the tondo. He also painted a Red-figure zoned cup with a *Gigantomachy* surrounding the picture of *Selene* in the tondo (Athens, First Ephoria Store). Among the ornamental motifs he employed were a variety of meander types. He came to prefer the stopt meander as a border for tondi, and one or two reserved lines for the ground-line on the exterior. Though he specialized in cups, Onesimos also decorated a few small vases, an alabastron and several kyathoi.

In his mature work Onesimos turned from mythological subjects to those taken from daily life. Scenes involving athletes, lovers or party guests gave scope for his mastery of foreshortening and zest for lively action with twisting back views and various unsavoury poses. He noted realistic details, such as hairy male bodies, receding hairlines or sagging female breasts. He also painted genre scenes, for example a school scene, a fisher boy, a boy reading or a black African groom. Several of these cups carry inscriptions. Some have 'spoken' inscriptions, such as the lovers in the tondo of a cup in the Museum of Fine Arts, Boston, MA (65.873). Onesimos' later work is distinguished by smaller, more graceful figures with quieter, almost introspective attitudes. He was one of the most forceful representatives of the generation of vase painters that followed the Pioneer group, continuing their experiments in the representation of the human body. He had a discernible influence on his contemporaries, and his style was carried on by several pupils, including the Brygos Painter.

J. D. Beazley: *Attic Red-figured Vases in American Museums* (Cambridge, MA, 1918), pp. 14–18

J. D. Beazley: *Red-figure* (1942, 2/1963), i, pp. 313–30; ii, pp. 1645–6, 1701, 1706

J. D. Beazley: 'Some Fragments by the Panaitios Painter', *Amer. J. Archaeol.*, lxvi (1962), pp. 235–6

J. D. Beazley: *Paralipomena* (1971), pp. 358–61, 511

D. Williams: 'The Ilioupersis Cup in Berlin and the Vatican', *Jb. Berlin. Mus.*, xviii (1976), pp. 9–23

M. Ohly-Dumm: 'Medeas Widderzauber auf einer Schale aus der Werkstatt des Euphronios', *Getty Mus. J.*, ix (1981), pp. 5–21

L. Burn and R. Glynn: *Beazley Addenda: Additional References to* ABV, ARV2 *and* Paralipomena (Oxford, 1982, rev. T. H. Carpenter, 2/1989), pp. 166–9

I. Wehgartner: *Attisch weissgrundige Keramik* (Mainz, 1983), pp. 81–4

R. J. Blatter: 'Tod und Schlaf: Zu einem Fragment des Onesimos', *Ant. Welt,* xvi/2 (1985), pp. 55–6

B. A. Sparkes: 'Aspects of Onesimos', *Greek Art: Archaic into Classical*, ed. C. Boulter (Leiden, 1985), pp. 18–39

H. R. Immerwahr: *Attic Script* (Oxford, 1990), pp. 84–5

M. Robertson: *The Art of Vase-Painting in Classical Athens* (Cambridge, 1992), pp. 43–51

M. J. Anderson: 'Onesimos and the Interpretation of Ilioupersis Iconography', *J. Hell. Stud.,* cxv (1995), pp. 130–35

Opisthodomos [Gr.: 'back room'; Lat. *posticum*]. Room at the rear of a Classical TEMPLE, typically used as a treasury.

Oplontis. [now Torre Annunziata]. Roman settlement on the seaward slopes of Mt Vesuvius about five km north-west of Pompeii, in what is now Torre Annunziata. The name Oplontis is attested in the *Tabula Peutingeriana*, a 13th-century copy of an ancient map of the Roman Empire (Vienna, Österreich. Nbib., Cod. 324). Baths were discovered at the locality of Punta Oncino in 1834 while systematic excavations between 1964 and 1984 unearthed two villas and remains of a portico in the nearby area of Mascatelle.

Villa A is a grand residence with origins in the 1st century BC and extended in the Claudian period (mid-1st century AD). It is also known as Villa of Poppaea, after Poppaea Sabina, second wife of the Roman emperor Nero (an amphora inscribed with the name of one of her freedmen was found on the site). The villa was empty and undergoing restoration work at the time of the eruption of Mt Vesuvius in AD 79; its entrance and main façade are still buried. The original central section of the building contained a spacious atrium with fine wall-decoration in the Second Style, flanked in the east by a series of peristyles and internal gardens, and in the west by kitchens and service areas, as well as a series of dining and bedrooms. Furthest west in the excavated area is a large, splendidly decorated *oecus*, probably a dining room, originally overlooking the sea, accompanied further north by a private bathing suite. To the north of the atrium follows a grand hall with frescoes in the fourth style, flanked by porticoes on either side that create a monumental façade giving way to a large garden. A grand passageway leads to the east wing, where a series of rooms overlook a rectangular pool (61×17 m). The rooms have mosaic floors and are decorated throughout with high-quality frescoes, often showing illusionary architecture, further embellished with masks, birds, baskets of flowers and fruit. The villa also contained numerous marble sculptures, mostly Roman versions of Hellenistic works of the 3rd and 2nd centuries BC.

Villa B, discovered some 250 m to the east of Villa A, was much more rustic in appearance and may have been the property of a certain Lucius Crassius Tertius, whose bronze seal was found at the site. Partially excavated between 1974 and 1991, the villa occupied a large insula, extending over two floors grouped around a monumental peristyle with a double row of tufa columns; in the north it bordered a street and series of rooms on this side served as shops. Many rooms were simply whitewashed, some not even plastered, with floors of beaten earth. Storerooms adjacent to the peristyle contained some 400 wine amphorae; others served for manufacturing purposes. Various weights found in the excavations further attest to commercial activities. It is thought that the villa, whose origins date back to the late 2nd century BC, was closely connected with agricultural business, mainly wine production and trade. Living quarters were situated on the first floor. In one of the rooms, the remains of 75 fugitives from the eruption of Mt Vesuvius were discovered, some probably poor workers, others with substantial amounts of jewellery and money.

S. de Caro: 'Sculture dalla Villa di Poppea in Oplontis', *Cron. Pompeiane,* ii (1976), pp. 184–225

C. Melandrino: *Oplontis* (Naples, 1977)

A. de Franciscis: 'Oplonis', *La Regione sotterrata dal vesuvio. Studi e prospettive. Atti del Convegno internazionale: 1979*, pp. 907–25

S. de Caro: 'The Sculptures of the Villa of Poppaea at Oplontis: A Preliminary Report', Ancient Roman Villa Gardens: Dumbarton Oaks Colloquium on the History of Landscape Architecture: Washington, 1984, 10, pp. 77–103

J. R. Clarke: 'The Early Third Style at the Villa of Oplontis', *Mitt. Dt. Archäol. Inst.: Röm. Abt.,* xciv (1987), pp. 267–94

Gli ori di Oplontis: Gioielli romani dal suburbia pompeiano. VI Mostra europea del turismo, artigianato e delle tradizioni culturali: Rome: 1987

J. R. Clarke: 'Landscape Paintings in the Villa of Oplontis', *J. Roman Archaeol.,* ix (1996), pp. 81–107

P. G. Guzzo and L. Fergola: *Oplontis: La villa di Poppea* (Milan, 2000)

L. Fergola, A. Biasiotti, V. Castiglione Morelli: 'Oplontis', *Storia da un'eruzione: Pompei, Ercolano, Oplontis* (Milan, 2003)

L. Fergola: *Oplontis e le sue ville* (Naples, 2004)

Opus Africanum. Type of masonry used in Roman North Africa, in which a framework of dressed stone is infilled with panels of mud brick or rubble.

Opus Caementicium. *See* CONCRETE.

Opus Incertum [opus antiquum]. Small, irregular blocks inserted into thick mortar to create a crude masonry surface to a rubble or concrete wall. It appears in Roman Republican architecture, certainly by the 3rd or 2nd century BC at Ostia, and perhaps earlier (*see* ARCHITECTURE, fig. 21).

Opus Mixtum. *See* OPUS TESTACEUM.

Opus Reticulatum. Roman decorative device using small, square slabs of stone embedded into a regular, tightly knit diamond pattern (see fig.), used by 55 BC in the Theatre of Pompey, Rome (*see* ARCHITECTURE, fig. 21).

Opus Sectile. *See under* MOSAICS, §III, 1(i).

Opus Testaceum. Concrete faced with regular courses of brick, used in the Roman period, as in the Theatre of Marcellus, Rome (13 BC). When panels of *opus reticulatum* are combined with vertical strips of *opus testaceum* the technique is known as *opus mixtum* (*see* ARCHITECTURE, fig. 21).

Orange. *See* ARAUSIO.

Orchestra. Area in a theatre between the stage and the audience's seating area. In the ancient Greek theatre this was a large circular space used by the chorus and dancers; in the ancient Roman theatre it was semicircular and reserved as seating for distinguished spectators (see fig.).

Orchomenos. Site in Boiotia in central Greece, 40 km north-north-west of Thebes, at the foot of

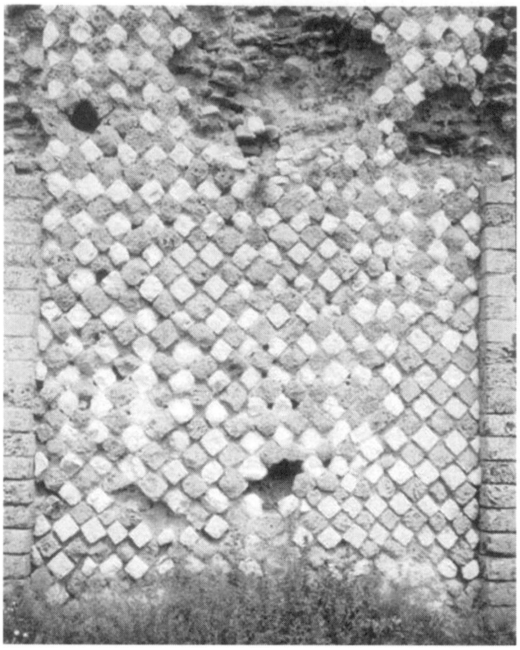

Opus reticulatum at the amphitheatre in Interamna (now Terni), Italy, AD 32

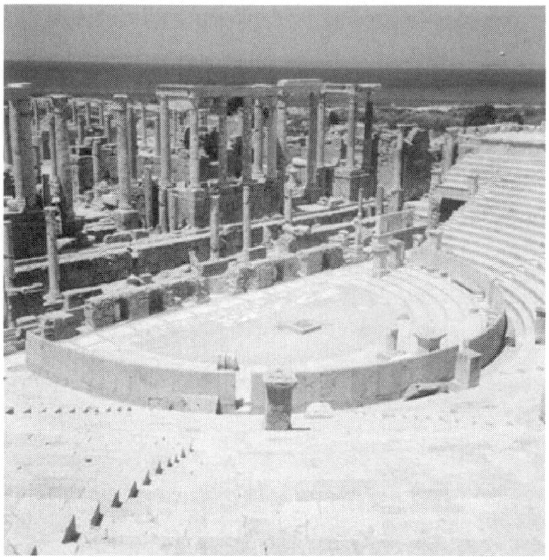

Orchestra and *scaena* of the Roman theatre, Leptis Magna, AD 1–2

a rocky ridge known in antiquity as Akontion. First inhabited in the Late and Final Neolithic periods (*c.* 5500–*c.* 3600/3000 BC) and expanded during the Bronze Age (*c.* 3600–*c.* 1100 BC), it lay on the shores of Lake Kopais, and it is first recorded in Homer's *Iliad* (ii: 511). Among the traces of fine Early Helladic (EH; *c.* 3600/3000–*c.* 2050 BC) architecture uncovered above the remains of the Neolithic city are circular granaries 6 m across with thick mud-brick walls. A city of the Middle Helladic period (MH; *c.* 2050–*c.* 1600 BC) included examples of the apsidal house and rectangular megaron; there Heinrich Schliemann, excavating in 1880–86, found articles of a pottery type that he called Minyan ware (*see* POTTERY, §III and fig. 9).

The 'Minyans', who were traditionally thought to have come to Boiotia from the Thessalian seaboard, are now considered by some to have been settlers from the east Mediterranean area and from Egypt itself around 2,500 BC. Though unlikely to have been original creators of Minyan ware, they settled in Boiotia during the 3rd millennium BC and made Orchomenos their capital. They also drained Lake Kopais during the second half of the 3rd millennium BC, and this task is reasonably connected with their Egyptian provenance. Orchomenos, already the leading economic power of EH–MH central Greece, was to become an important political and cultural centre of the Late Helladic (LH) or Mycenaean period (*c.* 1600–*c.* 1050 BC). This pre-eminence is reflected in the magnificent Treasury of Minyas, a Mycenaean tholos tomb at the eastern end of Akontion excavated by Schliemann and recalling the Treasury of Atreus at Mycenae. The side chamber has a flat roof with a sandstone ceiling exquisitely decorated in low relief with spirals, rosettes and fan-shaped lotus leaves. A large altar in the middle of the tholos suggests that it was used in the Hellenistic period (323–27 BC) as a place of worship.

Furtwängler and Bulle further excavated Orchomenos in 1903–5, to be followed by Kunze, who in the 1930s published works on the pottery of the Neolithic and EH periods. The finds of the German excavations are kept in the National Archaeological Museum, Athens. The resumption of archaeological work in 1970 (finds at Thebes Mus.) by Spyropoulos led to the uncovering of an extensive cemetery of the MH, LH I (*c.* 1600–*c.* 1500 BC) and LH IIIA (*c.* 1390–*c.* 1335 BC) periods, with cists and shaft graves, the latter of monumental size and similar to those at Mycenae. Although some of the graves had been plundered, a spectacular shaft grave at the cemetery's eastern end yielded fine LH IIIA pottery vases. This was undoubtedly a royal grave, which remained in use until *c.* 1300 BC, when the cemetery was abandoned. In another shaft grave was the richest collection of LH IIIA carved sealstones and bronze weapons ever found in Orchomenos. The cemetery was enclosed by an LH IIIA wall (peribolus) of orthogonal shape, and it had a small guard-room erected among the graves.

The abandonment of the cemetery was prompted by an increase in the power of Orchomenos by the end of LH IIIA, which led to the construction of the Treasury of Minyas and of a palatial complex a little further to the east near the 9th-century AD church of Skripou. This site was chosen to take advantage of the refreshing northern winds during the great heat of summer. The palace consists of two main residential buildings. One, on the northern side of the plateau lying to the east of Akontion, is the Little Palace, or Queen's Megaron, which follows the architectural plan of the palace-complex at TIRYNS. The other, on the southern side of the plateau, is the main palace, or Men's Megaron. This measures 8×40 m and is divided as usual into three rooms, with a large ovoid hearth. Most of the building and its contents were destroyed by later intrusions, mainly of the Byzantine era from the 9th century AD onwards, when the whole area was densely covered by constructions and graves. The Little Palace, measuring 4×20 m, was preserved to a height of 1.80 m below the surface, and it has the same tripartite division. It was built at the end of LH IIIA 2 (*c.* 1335 BC) on the layers of older (EH and MH) buildings. Early in the 13th century BC the whole complex was seriously damaged by an earthquake but was not abandoned. It was restored and rebuilt, its frescoes were repaired, and the building remained in use until the end of LH IIIB, *c.* 1180 BC. By the late 1990s the storerooms of the palace and the other installations of the complex had yet to be excavated.

The main finds of the excavation are masses of pottery, especially cups and kylikes of the LH IIIB period (*c.* 1335–*c.* 1180 BC) and well-preserved fragments of wall paintings of fine quality from the Little Palace. There are at least three groups of themes from the Little Palace. One represents boar- and deer-hunts, a theme known from the palace at Tiryns. The scene is depicted according to the well-known Mycenaean artistic convention, paratactic representation of figures giving illusory coherence and movement. Another theme represents a grove, where young attendants bring offerings to priests dressed in long robes. The third theme deals with representations of architectural constructions, houses, perhaps the palace itself, frames and other details; there are also many fragments with decorative motifs, spirals and imitations of wooden frames and marbles. It is very possible that below the Mycenaean palace another palace or palaces of the MH and EH periods are hidden.

A cemetery of chamber tombs, probably of the LH period, is reported from the area south-east of the site, and a tumulus structure containing Mycenean sherds was excavated to the south of Orchomenos between 1903–7. LH IIIC (*c.* 1180–*c.* 1100 BC) pottery is missing, but there are Sub-Mycenaean and Protogeometric (*c.* 1050–*c.* 900 BC) graves. The area covered by the outstanding monuments of the Bronze Age was occupied during the historical period by public monuments, the theatre of the late 4th century BC next to the royal cemetery, and the Archaic Temple of Dionysos (later 6th century BC) above it. A remarkable shrine (late Archaic to late Roman period) to the Graces, who may have been worshipped first at Orchomenos, covers the area of the Mycenaean palace. The city grew southwards in Classical (*c.* 480–323 BC) and Hellenistic times, although shrines, such as the Temple of Asklepios on a terrace that borders the western end of the acropolis, were sited near the acropolis, which lies to the east. The last floruit of Orchomenos coincided with the Macedonian occupation (338 BC–end of the 2nd century BC), when its principal monuments were re-erected and enlarged, only for the city to be destroyed and deserted during the expedition of Sulla (86 BC). The early Roman Imperial period (27 BC–AD 330) marks another temporary revival, during which, to judge from the hoard of inscriptions found at Potza in the area of Coronea, on the southern side of Kopais at the foot of the Helikon mountain, the city's monuments and the hydraulic works in Kopais were well cared for. Orchomenos thereafter followed the common fate of Greek cities and states and fell into poverty and oblivion.

H. Schliemann: 'Exploration of the Boeotian Orchomenos', *J. Hell. Stud.*, ii (1882), pp. 122–63
A. de Ridder: 'Fouilles d'Orchomène', *Bull. Corr. Hell.*, xix (1895), pp. 137–224
H. Bulle and E. Kunze: *Orchomenos*, 3 vols (Munich, 1907–34)
T. G. Spyropoulos: 'A Late Mycenaean Bronze Founder's Hoard from Orchomenos', *Athens An. Archaeol.*, iii (1970), pp. 266–7
T. G. Spyropoulos: 'Orchomenos', *Athens An. Archaeol.*, vi (1973), pp. 392–3, 395 [Eng. summary]
T. G. Spyropoulos: 'To Anaktoron tou Minyou eis ton Boiotikon Orchomenon' [The Palace of Minyas in Boeotian Orchomenos], *Athens An. Archaeol.*, vii (1974), pp. 313–25 [Eng. summary]
T. G. Spyropoulos: *Ampheion* (Sparta, 1982)
P. A. Mountjoy: *Orchomenos V: Mycenaean pottery from Orchomenos, Eutresis and Other Boeotian Sites* (Munich, 1983)
K. Fittschen: 'Archaologische Forschungen im boiotischen Orchomenos', *Archäol. Anz.*, ii (2003), pp. 126–8

Orders, architectural. Identifiable structural units comprising a column and entablature, which may be repeated and combined to make up the elevation of a building and its architectural vocabulary (including the frames around openings). In Classical buildings columns are more than mere cylinders; they are divided into distinct parts: a shaft, which is often fluted (*see* FLUTING) and usually tapers or swells (*see* ENTASIS), with a decorative capital and, usually, a base. Neither is the entablature simply a beam; it too is divided into separate parts: the architrave, FRIEZE and cornice, and it is articulated by mouldings. The giant (or colossal) order of engaged columns or pilasters rises through two or more storeys to the roof of a building.

I. The standard orders. II. Giant order.

I. The standard orders.

From the beginnings of Western architecture in Egypt and the eastern Mediterranean until the present day there have existed, for reasons that remain elusive, relatively few types of column. In ancient Egypt the most common types were the palm, papyrus, lotus, 'tent-pole' and proto-Doric, while a column with a shaft enlarging towards a cushion-shaped capital dominated Minoan architecture. In neither Egyptian nor Minoan buildings, however, does there seem to have been a conscious link between the form of the column and that of the entablature it supports.

It was the Greeks who brought together the column and entablature as a recognizable unit governed by design principles, and in their pure form the orders of columns and entablatures constituted the entire exterior structure of Greek temples (*see* TRABEATED CONSTRUCTION). In ancient Greece there were just three main orders: Doric, Ionic and Corinthian, although the CARYATID and ATLANTID were also used as columns. The Romans developed the use of the orders, adapting them to arcuated structural systems and applying or implying them in a range of different contexts. The Romans also added the Composite and Tuscan orders, and, for the most part, all later Western architecture with classical leanings adopted these five orders almost as if sacrosanct.

1. TYPES.

(i) Doric. This is the earliest and most robust of the Classical orders, invented, according to Vitruvius (*On Architecture* IV.i.3), by Dorus, King of Achaia. The original Greek Doric (see fig. 1a) is characterized by the absence of a base, whereas Roman Doric (1b) nearly always has one, although not prescribed by Vitruvius; both Greek and Roman Doric have a tapering shaft with shallow concave flutes (usually 20 in number) and distinct forms of capital and entablature. The capital is divided into three main parts: neck, echinus and abacus. The lowest part of the capital, the neck, is a continuation of the shaft where the flutes are usually terminated. The middle section, the echinus, is a concentric projecting cushion, usually smooth except for some fine rings towards the bottom. Above the echinus is the abacus, a square capping piece receiving the load of the entablature; it is usually plain, but the addition of a cymatium moulding became fairly common from Hellenistic times (323–27 BC). The entablature also follows a tripartite horizontal division: architrave, frieze and cornice. The essential characteristic of the Doric order is the regular articulation of the frieze by triglyphs, a 'grille' of three chamfered vertical bars. The intervening spaces are known as metopes, which were either left smooth or decorated in low relief. In Archaic and Classical times there were typically two triglyphs and metopes per column bay, with the centre of alternate triglyphs aligned over the centre of the column. The architrave, otherwise plain, has under each triglyph a narrow projecting strip, or taenia, the soffit of which is decorated by six tapering 'pegs', or guttae. The soffit of the cornice is regularly divided up by shallow flat projections, or mutules, which reflect the spacing of the triglyphs below but at twice the rhythm. The leading face of the cornice is either flat or formed as a cyma recta moulding, and, when following the run of a roof, it is usually pierced by decorative rain-water spouts, often in the shape of lion heads.

As Vitruvius was aware (IV.ii), the logic and details of Doric point to its derivation from timber construction, although there is little archaeological evidence of the gradual development from timber to stone that this would imply. If Doric motifs were intended to recall timber construction, they did so in a symbolic rather than a literal manner. They were no doubt also inspired indirectly by Egyptian stone architecture and by vestiges of Bronze-Age buildings still visible in the Peloponnese. The single column in relief over the Lion Gate at Mycenae incorporates all the elements of early Doric capitals (*see* MYCENAE, fig. 2).

See also ARCHITECTURE, §IV, 1(iii)(c) and figs 6 and 12.

(ii) Ionic. Whereas the Doric order belonged primarily to the Greek mainland, the Dorian peoples and their colonies (notably Sicily), the Ionic order was initially associated with the Aegean and western Asia Minor (Samos, Ionia, Lydia, Caria) and the Ionian peoples, by whom it was devised, according to Vitruvius (IV.i.7), as a new style of 'feminine' architectural beauty in contrast to the Doric. The first known archaeological record of Ionic (mid-6th century BC) dates it slightly later than Doric and shows that it was, from the outset, more ornate and elegant. Ionic columns (1c) rise from a decorative base, while the shaft flares gracefully at the top and bottom and has more frequent and deeper flutes (usually 24 or 32 in number), which meet at flat fillets. The voluted capital is the main distinguishing feature, for the base and entablature were appropriated by the later Corinthian and Composite orders. The origin of the Ionic capital and what it represents has been variously interpreted. Vitruvius, pursuing anthropomorphic parallels, likened the volutes to curly ringlets on a woman's head. Alternatively, they appear to resemble a scroll of parchment that is held open by the abacus and curls into two spirals on either side. Between the volutes is a small echinus, often decorated with EGG-AND-DART. The abacus, rectangular in early versions and later square, is delicate and edged with a cyma recta profile. Alone of the orders, the Ionic capital has a linear emphasis, as the sides differ from the front and back. This gave rise to a problem at the corners of colonnades and hence to two principal solutions: one was to abut two fronts and two sides, so that the capital was symmetrical about its diagonal; the other was the invention of the canted capital, in which all four faces were made as fronts.

While no fixed types existed for the base and entablature of the Ionic order, characteristic details are seen time and again. The base usually included a (convex) torus above a (concave) scotia, but otherwise varied greatly, being perhaps enriched by spira, a further torus and a plinth. From the 2nd century BC the Attic base (plinth-torus-scotia-torus) became prevalent. The entablature always comprised an architrave and cornice, but not always a frieze. The architrave was usually composed of two or three

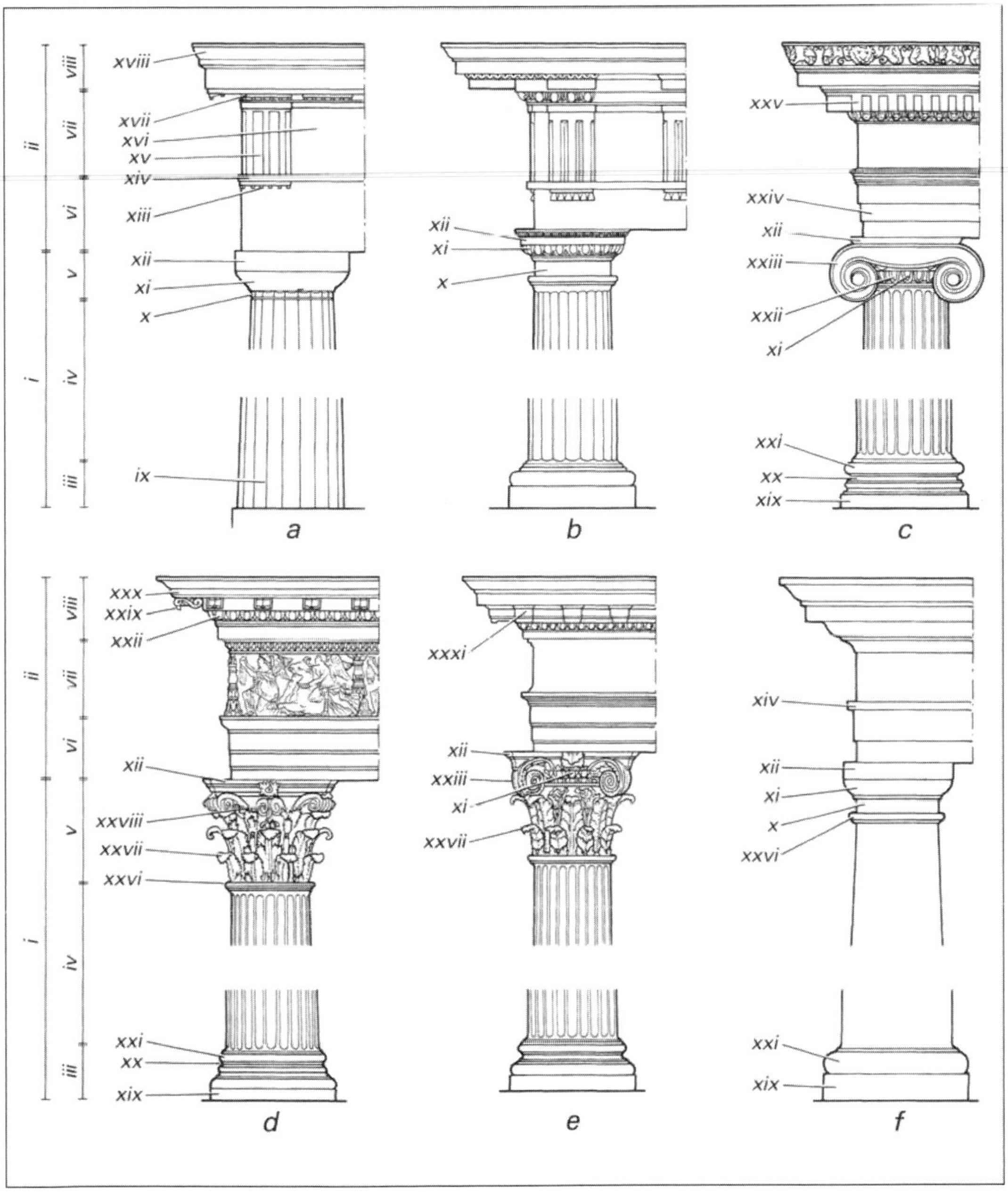

1. Architectural orders. (a) Greek Doric; (b) Roman Doric; (c) Ionic; (d) Corinthian; (e) Composite; (f) Tuscan; parts of the orders: (i) column; (ii) entablature; (iii) base; (iv) shaft; (v) capital; (vi) architrave; (vii) frieze; (viii) cornice; (ix) fluting; (x) neck; (xi) echinus; (xii) abacus; (xiii) guttae; (xiv) taenia; (xv) triglyph; (xvi) metope; (xvii) mutules; (xviii) cyma recta; (xix) plinth; (xx) scotia; (xxi) torus; (xxii) egg and dart; (xxiii) volutes; (xxiv) fascia; (xxv) dentils; (xxvi) astragal; (xxvii) acanthus; (xxviii) caliculi; (xxix) modillion; (xxx) cyma reversa; (xxxi) brackets

fasciae and terminated in a cyma recta moulding. The frieze was either plain or decorated with representational or vegetal motifs. In Roman times it was sometimes given a convex or pulvinated profile. Early cornices resemble Doric (without the mutules); they were later enriched by various sequences of mouldings, including bands of dentils and egg and-dart.

See also Architecture, §IV, 1(iii)(c) and figs 11 and 16.

(iii) Corinthian. The form of the Corinthian capital was allegedly inspired by chance, after a basket containing the few possessions of a young girl from Corinth, who had recently died, was covered with a tile and laid on her tomb. The basket happened to be

over the roots of an acanthus plant, and when spring came, the foliage sprouted up around the basket, the leaves curling outwards under the tile's weight. This poignant effect caught the eye of the Athenian sculptor Kallimachos, according to Vitruvius (IV.i.9–10). The Corinthian column (1d) appropriates the Ionic shaft and base, the latter being usually the relatively simple Attic or Asiatic (double scotia) versions. The early capital comprises two parts, a bell- or basket-shaped body and a four-sided abacus placed on top; the bell is decorated with two tiers of acanthus leaves, from which rise stylized plant stems. Later developments continued inexorably towards the 'normal' Corinthian capital, so called because, after hesitant beginnings in the 3rd century BC, it enjoyed widespread predominance by the time of the Roman Empire. In the normal capital one set of stems terminates in a flower at the centre of each side, usually on the abacus; the others, known as calculi, divide between helices, which turn in towards the flower, and paired volutes, which join under the diagonal corners of the abacus. The abacus usually has a cyma recta profile and characteristically has concave sides, which meet either as a point or, more usually, as a small chamfer. In different periods and geographical areas the morphology and style vary in matters of detail: for example, until it was supplanted by the normal style, a distinct type was prevalent in republican Italy, characterized by squatter proportions, fleshier leaves, larger flowers and separate stems for the volutes and helices.

The entablature initially followed later Ionic forms, with a tendency towards further enrichment. Only in Roman times did the cornice take on its characteristic form, with decorative brackets, or modillions, that support a deeper cornice, an innovation that may be attributed to architects working in Alexandria. It became common for coffers to be inserted in the cornice between the modillions, further enhancing the effectiveness of this order viewed from below, an important factor in Roman buildings with their emphasis on height and perhaps on the superimposition of orders, one above the other.

(iv) Composite. Although the Composite is the only one of the five orders to have been invented by the Romans, it was paradoxically not mentioned by Vitruvius. At the time he wrote *On Architecture* (40–25 BC), a period of ferment and experimentation for architects in Rome, the development of the Composite had only just begun. It subsequently became generally accepted as a distinct variant of Corinthian, justifying the Renaissance view of the Composite as an order in its own right. It is essentially the Corinthian order united with aspects of the Ionic, particularly the volutes of the capital (1e). Otherwise the base, shaft, entablature and the overall proportions remain essentially interchangeable with Corinthian. Renaissance architects liked to link the Composite order with a specific type of entablature, incorporating a pulvinated (curved) frieze and rectangular brackets instead of the usual scrolled modillions in the cornice. This distinction, however, did not apply in Antiquity: rectangular brackets, for example, were in fact used for either order, being particularly popular in the time of Emperor Hadrian (*reg* AD 117–38).

The Composite capital is based on the Corinthian, with the characteristic curving abacus and a bell or basket decorated with a double tier of acanthus leaves. In between are inserted the volutes and echinus of the Ionic canted capital (i.e. with four identical faces). The earliest examples of the Composite capital appear on small-scale sculptural decoration; only gradually was it assimilated into the repertory of monumental architecture. The most complete early set of capitals of medium size are known only out of context, having been reused in the 4th century AD for the construction of S Costanza, Rome. The full acceptance of the Composite is signalled by its use on the Arch of Titus (AD 81), and by the early 2nd century it became widely used throughout the Roman Empire and was particularly popular in Asia Minor. Along with Corinthian, it seems to have had particular associations with Rome, so that together these orders underpinned the bulk of state-sponsored Imperial architecture. Potentially the most ornate of the orders, the Composite was often chosen to convey opulence. It was of particular value as a means of providing emphasis or generally enlivening either Ionic or Corinthian compositions.

(v) Tuscan. The name of the Tuscan order derives from its Etruscan origins. Well before the conquest of Etruria by Rome (from 396 BC), Tuscan columns were in use in temples and tombs there, and presumably also in domestic architecture, as the form of Etruscan tombs reflected that of houses for the living. Tuscan columns can be traced to *c.* 500 BC (e.g. tomb at Vignanello), but the development of the order is somewhat obscure, largely due to the use of timber rather than stone for much of the superstructure. The logic of timber construction is particularly evident in the broad overhanging eaves of such Etruscan temples as those at Veii (late 6th century BC), Tarquinia and Alatri. In Roman practice canonic Tuscan orders do not seem to have conformed with Etruscan precedents or with Vitruvius' rather academic treatment (IV.vii). Instead, the Tuscan order became a sort of 'Romanized' Doric, that is Doric stripped down and adapted in accordance with the perceived tone of architecture in Italy. The overall proportions of the column and its capital are essentially those of later Doric usage, with relatively slender columns and compact capitals (1f). The shaft is unfluted but sits on a simple base comprising only a broad torus and plinth in the manner of Etruscan columns. It was not uncommon to vary the Tuscan order by replacing the segmental mouldings of the base or the capital with a cyma recta moulding. The entablature often resembles Doric without its triglyphs and associated decoration, but it might have an architrave and bed mouldings of a more Ionic character. Indeed, the bottom

two storeys of the Colosseum (AD 80) in Rome, Ionic above Tuscan, have entablatures that are almost identical.

The Tuscan order seems to have been used to convey an impression of naturalness, integrity and vigour, qualities that were commonly held to be indigenous or Latin, in contrast with Greek artifice (as in the Doric). In monumental architecture Tuscan is most commonly found in amphitheatres, temples and such utilitarian buildings as granaries. In Julio-Claudian times the connotations of this order were often amplified by the use of rustication, as may be seen in the amphitheatre (3rd century AD) at Verona and the Temple of Claudius (AD 54) at Rome.

2. History and theory. The earliest allusion to an architectural order dates from 5th-century BC Greece, in a reference by Euripides to Doric triglyphs (*Orestes* 1392). When the Roman architect Vitruvius wrote his treatise *On Architecture* he took the orders (*genera*) for granted, describing in detail each of the five except for the Composite. It was not until the Italian Renaissance, however, that the Classical orders (*gli ordini*) were codified in a systematic way, conforming to a hierarchical progression (robust to slender, plain to ornate) from Tuscan to Composite, each with its own type of pedestal.

(i) The three principal orders. (ii) Selection and variants. (iii) Vitruvius.

(i) The three principal orders. The history of the orders is essentially that of Doric, Ionic and Corinthian, Composite being a derivative of the latter and Tuscan playing a relatively minor role.

(a) Doric. Monumental architecture was absent in the Greek world during the 'Dark Age' between 1100 and 700 BC, but by 500 BC there appeared everywhere carefully built temples recognizable as Doric. The rapid development of Greek building skills in the 7th century BC seems to have been fostered by new links with Egypt, recently liberated from Assyrian rule. Early Doric colonnades certainly resemble their Egyptian counterparts in terms of general effect and proportions, if not in style.

Proto-Doric temples of the 7th century BC survive in the north-east Peloponnese, notably in Isthmia and Corinth. The columns of such buildings were relatively slender, but by the beginning of the 6th century BC the familiar stout features of archaic Doric, complete with wide-spreading capitals supporting a heavy entablature, appeared in Olympia (e.g. Temple of Hera) and Corfu (Temple of Artemis). Doric subsequently evolved gradually, with a trend towards more slender and compact proportions, lighter entablatures and more sophisticated refinements; the late 6th-century BC Temple of Athena at Paestum, for example, also had unusually elaborate decoration. In the second quarter of the 5th century columns tended to be around 4½ lower diameters tall (e.g. Temple of Poseidon at Paestum: 41/3; Temple of Zeus at Olympia: 42/3); in the third quarter of the 5th century BC the slenderness of the columns of the Parthenon (*see* Athens, §II, 1(i) and fig. 6) advanced to about 5½ diameters, and by the Hellenistic period slenderness ratios of around 7 or 8 were standard. Vitruvius (IV.i.8) recommended that Doric columns be 7 diameters tall, but his contempories were already using finer proportions (e.g. Theatre of Marcellus, Rome: 7¾). This development is most graphically seen at sites with a range of buildings of different dates, for example at Paestum, or in individual buildings that took a long time to complete, for example Temple G at Selinus. Doric reached a peak of expression in the latter part of the 5th century BC with such buildings in Athens as the Parthenon and the Temple of Hephaistos; thereafter it changed little and was gradually eclipsed by the Ionic and Corinthian orders.

The use of the Doric order was not without its problems. Doric design involved an exacting attention to details and architectonic logic. This logic demanded general regularity (perceived if not actual) and an adherence to certain conventions, for example the vertical axial alignment of a triglyph over a column and complete triglyphs at the corners. The different aims, however, tended to be mutually contradictory at crucial points, best illustrated by the problem of how to resolve the Doric frieze at the corner. In practice, achieving the separate ideals of a regular frieze at the same time as a complete corner triglyph typically demanded either stretching the elements of the frieze or slightly contracting the spacing of the corner column compared to the norm elsewhere in the building. Partly due to the complexity of the problem and partly due to the relative unfamiliarity of Greek architects with drawing, the junctions of Doric elevations are frequently unresolved. Such imperfections, together with the rigidity of Doric and the lack of scope for ornament, led to the demise of the order in Classical Greece from the 4th century BC. In Vitruvius' words, its 'embarrassments and incongruities' (IV.iii.1) made it unsuitable for monumental civic architecture. Nevertheless, in the hands of Hellenistic and Roman architects, Doric was subsequently treated with greater flexibility than Ionic, which proved to be a problem at corners because of the directional emphasis of the capital. No longer was it considered essential to have only two or three triglyphs per column interval; four or five became admissible, along with decidedly non-canonic corners and junctions.

(b) Ionic. The early development of Ionic took place in the eastern Aegean, taking about half a century longer than Doric to reach an equivalent stage of maturity. The earliest known proto-Ionic capitals are known as Aiolic. These are essentially formed by a pair of spiral volutes, although they spring out of the shaft and are not laid on top of other elements as in Ionic. While it has been suggested that Ionic was a development of Aiolic, it seems more likely that both were inspired by unknown precursors from

further east. The earliest known recognizable Ionic columns are found in the mid-6th century BC monumental temples of Hera at SAMOS and of Artemis at EPHESOS. From the outset other characteristics distinguished it from Doric: the increased number of flutes (32, 44 and even 48), more slender overall proportions, and relatively complex bases involving alternating convex and concave mouldings. In the eastern Aegean the use of dentils—recalling the protruding ceiling rafters of early timber buildings—was common in cornices; as the Ionic order spread to the western Aegean, however, the Ionic FRIEZE was usually employed for carved representational decoration.

The next formative phase of Ionic was in Athens, in such buildings on the Acropolis as the Propylaia (437–432 BC), the Temple of Athena Nike (*c.* 425 BC) and the Erechtheion (421–405 BC; *see* ATHENS, fig. 8). Here, a relative purity and severity of approach permitted its successful integration with the predominantly Doric context. Important later developments occurred in Asia Minor, with the work of the 4th-century BC architect PYTHEOS at the Temple of Athena Polias, PRIENE, and the Mausoleum at Halikarnassos, and of the 2nd-century BC architect HERMOGENES at the Temple of Artemis, MAGNESIA ON THE MAEANDER, and the Temple of Dionysos, Teos. Hermogenes is attributed with the introduction of the subsequently predominant Attic base as well as with an important treatise, on which Vitruvius was heavily dependent. The Romans took their inspiration from Asia Minor and subsequently altered Ionic little in substance. In contrast to Doric, the proportions of Ionic underwent few changes, having already, in the second half of the 5th century BC, attained the proportions (slenderness ratios between 8¾ and 10) that became standard in Roman times.

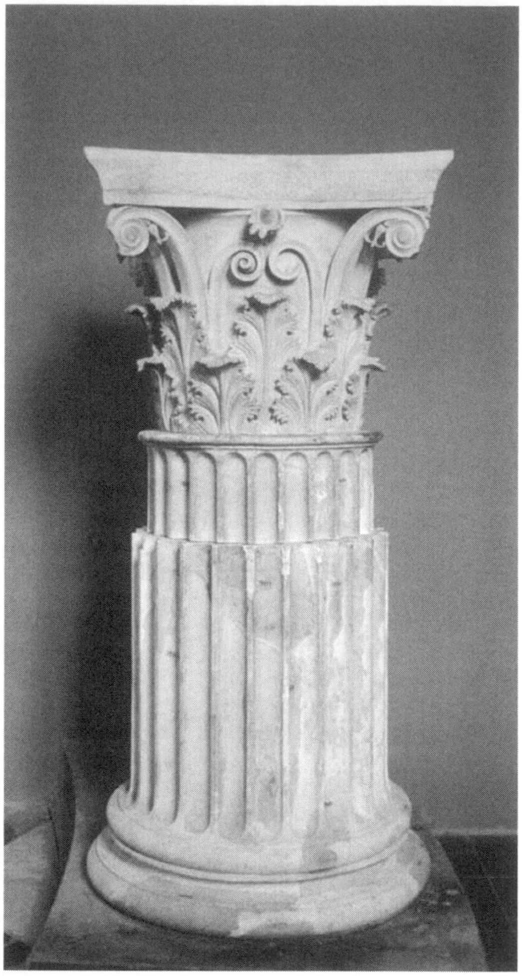

2. Corinthian order, capital, from the thymele (tholos) by Polykleitos the younger, Epidauros, *c.* 350 BC (Epidauros, Archaeological Museum)

(c) Corinthian. The Corinthian order is notably more flexible than either Doric or Ionic. The earliest known example was a free-standing column (untraced) in the interior of the Temple of Apollo (*c.* 430–*c.* 400 BC) at Bassai (*see* ARCHITECTURE, fig. 13). The order may have originated as a response to the awkwardness of the Ionic corner capital as much as for the decorative and iconographic character of the new style. The emphasis on the diagonal and the curving abacus made the Corinthian especially successful for corners and for curvilinear ground plans. The most successful early examples are indeed found in the interior of the circular tholos (thymele; *c.* 360–*c.* 320 BC) at Epidauros (see fig. 2) and the Monument of Lysikrates (335–334 BC), Athens, the latter being the first known example of the exterior use of Corinthian, albeit with a stylistically unique capital.

In Hellenistic times the Corinthian order began to appear as the main exterior order in such prestigious projects as the vast Temple of Olympian Zeus (*c.* 174 BC) in Athens; *see* ATHENS, fig. 15). Roman architects came into contact with Corinthian both through Greek architects working in Italy and through the gradual spread of small-scale Italian variants north from Sicily, which earlier had been a Greek colony. The mature form of Corinthian, including the distinctive cornice, coincided with its popularity in Augustan times (27 BC–AD 14). From then on it superseded Doric and Ionic in terms of quantity, to the extent that it is almost as if Augustus promoted the Corinthian order as a symbol of empire: its diffusion parallels that of statues of the Emperor himself.

Given its dependence on Ionic, Corinthian shared with it similar overall proportions (the height of the shaft being reduced to compensate for the taller capital), with slenderness ratios normally ranging between 8¾ (Temple of Olympian Zeus, Athens) and 10 (Temple of the Dioscuri, Cori) before Imperial times. Thereafter, columns 10 diameters tall remained popular (e.g. Temple of Mars Ultor, ded. 2 BC, Rome), with 9½ or 9 and three fifths diameters preferred where monolithic shafts were used, these being 8 diameters tall. The slenderness of the Imperial Roman Corinthian column, however, was not necessarily its most important proportional characteristic, as the following relationships are often found to be constant in columns of differing slenderness: the height of the shaft is equal to 5/6 the height of the whole column: the height of the capital is equal to the cross-sectional width of its abacus; and the diagonal width of the abacus is equal to the diagonal width of the base, both being double the lower diameter of the shaft and that of the astragal at the top.

It may seem paradoxical that mature Corinthian, which was more varied and luxurious than any other order, conforms to a relatively consistent set of proportions. The explanation lies in the approach of Roman architects to design: the most consistent proportions are precisely those that are not immediately obvious to the eye. At the same time, those that are more obvious were less strictly regulated in the interest of variety and freedom of workmanship and expression. There were also practical pressures: in Imperial times column shafts and capitals were subject to a degree of dimensional standardization. A sizeable percentage of monolithic shafts were produced in multiples of 5 (Roman) feet, a practice that helped to ensure that shafts from various distant quarries matched each other. Corinthian capitals were also often partly completed at quarries and associated workshops before exportation, under which circumstances simple proportional guidelines, such as 1:1 and 1:2, must have been invaluable. If some proportions were relatively fixed, however, flexibility in the way they were related generated a range of permutations. Rules were not rigid: Roman architects enjoyed scope to modify standard proportions, particularly in matters of detail. Together with an undogmatic approach to the selection of mouldings and decorative enrichments, this resulted in spectacular variety in the appearance not only of Corinthian but also of the orders in general in Roman times.

(ii) Selection and variants. Only the initial development of the orders may be linked with distinct geographical areas and their indigenous peoples. With time the orders became less strictly regional and were used more according to their associations. Doric carried with it overtones of the austere outdoor life of the Dorians, their masculinity, economy and frankness. Ionic conveyed associations of the indoor life of civic communities, of learning, culture and feminine values. Corinthian may have been invented in Corinth, but it carried no lasting regional connotations; indeed, this was probably a positive attraction in the politically sensitive contexts of Dorian–Ionian conflict. In mood, Corinthian had more in common with Ionic, with an additional aura of prestige, the afterlife and, more significantly, healing and regeneration. A common hierarchy seems to have existed, from the ordinary (Doric) to the special (Corinthian), with Ionic somewhere in between. The significance of Composite is unclear, but it is interesting to note that its use in temples is quite rare, possibly because its associations with luxury made it unsuitable; it may also have had nationalistic connotations, representing the Romans' emulation of Greek culture in fusing the best of Ionic and Corinthian. Regional overtones again became important in promoting the use of the Tuscan order. Moreover, Tuscan and Doric were the least expensive and vulnerable of the orders, factors that recommended their use in mainly functional and military contexts.

For theorists, columns could have direct anthropomorphic associations. To Vitruvius (IV.i.7–8), Doric embodied the proportions and strength of the male body and Ionic the grace and slenderness of the female, while Corinthian reflected the delicacy of a young girl. Thus, for example, according to his principle of Propriety (*decorum*; *see* §(iii) below), he recommended the plain and 'virile' Doric for the temples of such deities as Hercules, Mars and Minerva; the slender and ornamental Corinthian for temples dedicated to feminine deities and demi-gods, such as Venus, Flora, Proserpina, the nymphs and spring-water deities; and the Ionic order, as an intermediary between those two, he regarded as suitable for such deities as Juno, Diana and Bacchus (I.ii.5).

As the cultural life of the Mediterranean became more sophisticated and mobile, however, general patterns become more elusive. The distinct meanings of the orders became blurred by sheer quantity and arbitrariness, as well as by such factors as habit, fashion and the origin of the architect or patron. In Roman times the search for decorative effects may often have been the guiding principle. Bridges could be decorated with Corinthian; Tuscan and Corinthian could be intermingled on the same structure (e.g. Porta de' Gavi at Verona); and Ionic, Corinthian, Composite and Pergamonese columns share the same entablatures in the Bath–Gymnasium (completed early 2nd century AD) at SARDIS. The Composite order, in particular, was often used as a distinctive feature with the other orders, appearing, for example, with Ionic in the Temple of Zeus (completed *c.* AD 125) at AIZANOI and with Corinthian in the Library of Celsus (completed *c.* AD 120) at Ephesos (*see* EPHESOS, fig. 3).

Structural arguments supporting the adoption of one or other of the orders are also elusive. Because of their differing slenderness and load-bearing capacities it might seem natural to support the superimposition of Corinthian on Ionic on Doric, so that the girth of the shaft increases towards the bottom of a building. This archetypal progression is, however, surprisingly rare. In Athens the Stoa of Attalos (*c.* 150 BC) does have a slighter Ionic order placed over Doric, but in the Stoa (ded. 418 BC) of the Asklepieíon, Athens, the smaller upper order is the same as that below (Doric over Doric, Ionic over Ionic). Where an ascending sequence of orders is found, as at the Colosseum (Tuscan–Ionic–Corinthian–Corinthian), each set of half columns has the same width, their proportions and dimensions being a response primarily to theoretical and aesthetic issues. Classical columns are generally over-sized in terms of structural necessity. Structure and function affected the orders only in limited respects: the tendency for large columns to be closely spaced and small ones loosely spaced probably reflects the spanning limitations of stone architraves at the large scale, and the need for circulation space at the small scale.

While the five orders do represent meaningful categories, history has tended to exaggerate their predominance. The typologies inherited from Vitruvius (*see* §(iii) below) and Renaissance theorists oversimplify the heterogenous character of ancient architectural design. First, there were numerous other distinct forms of capital: Doric with a cyma recta echinus; fluted capitals with one tier of acanthus and a square abacus (also common in Pergamon); and so-called 'sofa' capitals with large volutes like chair armrests and one tier of acanthus (common in Pompeii). There are also numerous non-specific 'Corinthianized' forms involving a variety of vegetal motifs and animal and/or human forms. Second, variety was also manifest within the use of mixed orders, where elements from two or more of the main categories were consciously combined. In such places as Alexandria, Labraunda and Petra, mixed orders were quite common. Other examples include a Doric–Ionic capital at Selinus; shafts with Doric flutes but Ionic fillets in the bouleuterion at Miletos; Doric triglyphs over Corinthian capitals at Philae and Aosta; Pergamonese Corinthian capitals over Doric flutes at Ephesos; and a thoroughly mixed Doric–Corinthian temple at Pompeii. Third, there is a considerable range of mouldings and decorative effects within the ambit of the conventional orders. Shafts may be left smooth (especially if monolithic), have spiral fluting or flutes filled with cabling, or may even be rusticated (e.g. Porta Maggiore, AD 52). Bases take different forms and may or may not include plinths. Entablatures may be entirely plain (e.g. those of the Colosseum), partly enriched (e.g. those of the Pantheon, *c.* AD 120), or have every surface encrusted with ornament.

Finally, apart from a relative conservatism in temple design, Hellenistic and Roman architects displayed considerable exuberance in the way in which the orders were disposed. New effects were constantly sought. The orders might be engaged to walls and arches as piers, half columns, quarter columns and pilasters. Alternatively, columns could be detached from a wall behind them while sharing a projecting section of entablature. Pedestals, columns, entablatures and pediments could be stacked one upon the other in an endless variety of permutations (e.g. Library of Celsus, Ephesos). The enduring success of the five orders and their variations lies in the reconciliation they effect between convention and variety, as well as in the main issues addressed by Classical architects, notably questions of theory, propriety, practicality and visual effect.

For more information on the use of the orders *see* ARCHITECTURE, especially §IV, 1(i)(a), 1(iii), 2(ii)(b) and 3(iv).

Vitruvius: *On Architecture*; Eng. trans. by M. H. Morgan as *The Ten Books on Architecture* (Cambridge, MA, 1914/*R* New York, 1960)

W. B. Dinsmoor: *The Architecture of Greece and Rome* (New York, 1902); rev. as *The Architecture of Ancient Greece* (New York, 1927, rev. 3/1950)

D. S. Robertson: *A Handbook of Greek and Roman Architecture* (Cambridge, 1929, rev. 2/1943); *R* as *Greek and Roman Architecture* (London, 1969)

A. W. Lawrence: *Greek Architecture*, Pelican Hist. A. (Harmondsworth, 1957, rev. 4/1983, with additions by R. A. Tomlinson)

F. Cali: *L'Ordre grec* (Paris, 1958)

J. Summerson: *The Classical Language of Architecture* (London, 1963, rev. 1980)

R. E. M. Wheeler: *Roman Art and Architecture* (London, 1964)

M. Lyttelton: *Baroque Architecture in Classical Antiquity* (London, 1974)

A. Boëthius: *Etruscan and Early Roman Architecture*, Pelican Hist. A. (Harmondsworth, 1978)

J. Onians: *Bearers of Meaning: The Classical Orders in Antiquity, the Middle Ages and the Renaissance* (Princeton, 1988)

R. A. Tomlinson: *Greek Architecture* (Bristol, 1989)

B. A. Barletta: *The Origins of the Greek Architectural Orders* (Cambridge and New York, 2001)

(iii) Vitruvius. The principal source for the theory of the Classical architectural orders was VITRUVIUS' treatise *On Architecture*, the only complete treatise on architecture to survive from antiquity. In it he accounted for the development of the three principal orders, Doric, Ionic and Corinthian (*see* §§1 and 2(i) above). He derived the name of each from the form of its column, giving its origins and features (IV.i.1–10), and he described the proportions of each (IV.iii, III.v and IV.ii.11–12), noting that the essential differences lay in the proportion of the column height to lower column diameter, originally in Doric and Ionic respectively, 6:1 and 8:1 (later 7:1 and 9:1) and the degree of ornamentation of the capital. Vitruvius recognized that the exact forms of each of the orders varied in different places and at different times, although he discounted these geographical and chronological factors in favour of his theory of architecture and of the architectural orders based on fundamental principles (I.ii), including Proportion (*symmetria*) and Propriety (*decorum*). Discussing Symmetry (*symmetria*) and Proportion (I.ii.4 and III.i), he maintained that the proportional harmony between the parts of the body of a well-shaped man should be emulated in the design of a perfect building, particularly a temple, and included the parts of the orders calculated as multiples or fractions of a module.

In the exposition of his own theory, however, Vitruvius subordinated his treatment of the orders to his discussion of Propriety, which he divided into three parts: established religious custom or prescription (*statio*), social usage or habit (*consuetudo*) and natural causes (*naturae*). He ascribed the existence of the different orders to prescription and, moreover, believed that the three sets of characteristic features distinguishing the three principal orders in fact represented all the possible lines of evolution. This threefold emphasis is probably based on contemporary rhetorical theory, as developed by Cicero in his treatise *On Oratory*. Vitruvius' principle of Propriety classified the orders according to their anthropomorphic characteristics and proper dedication: the plain and sturdy Doric for the temples of 'virile' deities, the slender and ornamental Corinthian for temples of feminine deities and demigods, and the graceful Ionic for temples where it was appropriate to mediate between the severity of the Doric and the delicacy of the Corinthian. In relation to each of the orders, Vitruvius had in mind specific temples that epitomized the evolution of the order and could serve as prescriptive models, for example the Doric Temple of Athena (Parthenon) at Athens; the Corinthian Temple of Venus at Corinth; and the Ionic Temple of Hera (Juno) at Samos and Temple of Artemis (Diana) at Ephesos. Hence, from Vitruvius' perspective, architectural history was reconciled with architectural theory in terms of the principle of Propriety. In his specifications Vitruvius followed HERMOGENES in his treatment of Ionic proportions, but he presented Doric proportions according to a modular system that reflected such Italian examples as the Temple of Hercules at Cori.

Because of his desire to present architecture as a theoretical science rather than as a craft with a history of evolved practices, Vitruvius was obliged either to ignore or to assimilate into his established orders such diverse forms as the Etruscan temple, which he incorporated into the section on the Doric order as something of an anomaly (IV.vii). Combinations of the orders (e.g. Ionic dentils in the cornice of a Doric entablature, or Doric triglyphs in an Ionic one), such as might be found in the late Hellenistic architecture of Vitruvius' own time, he condemned as abuses of Propriety in his discussion of usage (I.ii.6). In his attempt to raise the status of architecture, Vitruvius introduced a prescriptive classicism into the theory and practice of the orders, which, as a consequence of the lasting influence of his treatise, has become impossible to separate from the notion of the architectural orders.

Vitruvius: *On Architecture*; Eng. trans. by M. H. Morgan as *The Ten Books on Architecture* (Cambridge, MA, 1914/*R* New York, 1960)

A. Horn-Oncken: *Über das Schickliche*, *Abh. Akad. Wiss. Göttingen*, Philol.-Hist. Kl., iii/70 (1967)

P. Gros: 'Vitruve: L'Architecture et sa théorie, à la lumière des études récentes', *Aufstieg & Niedergang Rom. Welt*, II, 30.1 (1982), pp. 659–95

G. L. Hersey: 'Vitruvius and the Origins of the Orders: Sacrifice and Taboo in Greek Architectural Myth', *Perspecta*, xxiii (1986), pp. 66–77

J. Onians: *Bearers of Meaning: The Classical Orders in Antiquity, the Middle Ages, and the Renaissance* (Princeton, 1988)

M. W. Jones: 'Doric Measure and Architectural Design 2: A Modular Reading of the Classical Temple', *Amer. J. Archaeol.*, cv/4 (Oct 2001), pp. 675–713 [with appendix]

H. J. Kienast: 'Zum dorischen Triglyphenfries', *Mitt. Dt. Archäol. Inst.: Athen. Abt.*, cxvii (2002), pp. 53–68

II. Giant order.

A large order of pilasters or engaged columns, usually Corinthian, it runs from ground or plinth level through two or more storeys to the roof of a building, with the appropriate entablature. The giant order was used in Classical architecture to articulate a wall, with rows of niches or doors between the columns.

Although Vitruvius described a giant order in the basilica (unlocated) that he allegedly built at Fano (*On Architecture*, V.i.6), giant orders are rarely found in the Roman period except in the province of Syria, which contains the present-day Lebanon. More common in the Classical period were rows of superimposed columns, as in the stage building of the theatre at ASPENDOS. Roman giant orders were either engaged columns or pilasters and all surviving examples are Corinthian.

There is a giant Corinthian order down the long sides of the interior of the Temple of Bacchus (2nd century AD) at BAALBEK, where engaged columns articulate the walls, while the bays between the columns are decorated with rows of round-headed niches in the lower part and rectangular niches above, crowned by triangular pediments. There is also a giant order in the semicircular exedrae of the courtyard of the Temple of Jupiter (2nd century AD), where it consists of pilasters articulating the wall and framing two rows of superimposed niches. The pilasters here are unfluted, unlike the engaged columns in the Temple of Bacchus. The round Temple of Venus (3rd century AD) at Baalbek also has a giant order decorating its interior consisting of unfluted pilasters, and the wall between has two rows of superimposed niches. The scheme is similar to that of the Temple of Jupiter, which seems to have often been copied in the interiors of small temples throughout the area. At Gerasa the propylaeum of the Temple of Artemis (late 2nd century AD) has two wings with a giant order of pilasters framing the small doorways with niches faced above them. There is a similar arrangement in the wings of the nymphaeum at Gerasa (late 2nd century AD) where the giant order of unfluted pilasters frames two superimposed niches.

Outside Syria giant orders are found articulating the so-called Arch of Trajan at Thamugadi in Algeria (*c*. AD 200) and in the Severan basilica at LEPTIS MAGNA in Libya (ded. AD 216). On the arch at Thamugadi the giant order consists of four engaged Corinthian columns with unfluted shafts on either side of the main north archway. The columns are grouped in pairs to frame the subsidiary archway, which is surmounted by a niche for statues, and they support segmental pediments. In the other parts of the Empire the articulation of Roman buildings is not sufficiently well preserved to determine whether giant orders were employed.

R. Wood: *The Ruins of Balbek, Otherwise Heliopolis, in Coelosyria* (London, 1757)

T. Weigand and others, eds: *Baalbek*, i–ii (Berlin and Leipzig, 1921–3)

C. H. Kraeling: *Gerasa: City of the Decapolis* (New Haven, 1938)

Ornament and pattern. Decorative devices applied or incorporated as embellishment. Ornament and pattern are not generally essential to the structure of an object, but they can serve a number of other purposes: they can emphasize or disguise structural elements, particularly in architecture, and they can fulfil an iconographic role. In the Classical world, architectural ornament was part of the system of orders (*see* ORDERS, ARCHITECTURAL). Classical ornament applied in non-architectural contexts was selected as much for decorative qualities and convenient shape as for any emblematic significance, though what significance did exist might change through history: pagan imagery often assumed new meaning when absorbed into the Christian or Jewish repertory. The repertory of Classical ornament and the concept of decorum, the theory of appropriate degree and type of ornament, influenced the application of ornament in all European classical revivals from the Renaissance onwards.

1. Architectural. 2. Other.

1. ARCHITECTURAL. The orders are the most important element of Classical architecture. They comprise horizontal entablatures raised on columns, each of which is composed of a shaft, capital and base. The configuration of the earliest order, the Greek Doric, was largely derived from early timber temples, although certain features, such as the triglyphs and guttae, became decorative rather than structural when translated into stone (*see* ORDERS, ARCHITECTURAL, §I, 1 and fig. 1). Columns themselves tended to be load-bearing in Greek buildings but were generally ornamental in Roman architecture. In his treatise *On Architecture* the Roman writer VITRUVIUS attempted to elevate the status of architecture by codifying the orders. He described them in terms of human characteristics dictated by the proportions of the column and the decoration of the friezes and capitals. His discussion was restricted to three orders—the Doric, Ionic and Corinthian—and their application to sacred buildings. Vitruvius believed that temples of Minerva, Mars and Hercules should be executed in the unadorned Doric, suggestive of manliness (*virtus*), while the Corinthian, with its connotations of feminine grace, befitted temples dedicated to Venus, Flora and Proserpina; the intermediate Ionic was suitable for Juno, Diana and Bacchus. Thus he introduced *decorum*, the theory of appropriate degree and type of ornament, in which the enrichments chosen—the mouldings associated with each order, and any mythical, historical or military decoration—were important in establishing mood and purpose.

(i) Greek. (ii) Roman.

(i) Greek. Early temple ornament consisted of repeated geometric patterns similar to those found on vases, mass-produced in moulded terracotta and coloured dull red, buff, brown and purple. From the late 6th century BC designs became bolder and were incised and painted in bright colours. Carved bands of such motifs as BEAD AND REEL, EGG AND DART, egg and tongue, dentils, scrolls, the GUILLOCHE, the PALMETTE, the ANTHEMION, the water-leaf and the rosette, were applied singly or in parallel rows, to enrich mouldings on columns and to frame architectural features, such as doorways and pediments. Free-standing adornments, initially in terracotta, later in stone or marble, varied the silhouettes of temple exteriors. ANTEFIXES, used to conceal tile-ends, were disguised as palmettes; acroteria were applied to the outer angles of pediments (*see* ACROTERION). The heads of lions or occasionally hounds, with mouths agape, constituted the spouts on gutters.

Doric entablatures were composed of metopes carved with figural reliefs or single rosettes against a red ground, alternating with black or dark blue triglyphs. Pediments were embellished with boldly coloured or gilt figurative sculpture. The Parthenon (447–432 BC) in Athens, with its elegant Doric columns and refined sculpture, represented the culmination of this style (*see* ARCHITECTURE, §IV, 2(iii)(a)).

The Ionic, with voluted capital possibly deriving from fronded Aiolic prototypes, originated in Asia Minor. By the 5th century BC a single building might embrace both orders: the Doric applied externally—perhaps an expression of the outdoor character of the Dorian race—and the Ionic used internally, reflecting the more feminine indoor life of the Ionians. The Erechtheion (421–405 BC) in Athens has meticulously carved Ionic capitals on its north porch, enriched with gilt eyes in the volutes, and bands of guilloches filled with coloured glass beads, egg and dart motifs and delicate anthemia (*see* SCULPTURE, §IV, 1(iii)(b)). Black Eleusian limestone acts as a contrasting ground for the marble relief figures on the frieze, and the doorway is profusely carved. The south porch is raised on heavily draped female CARYATIDS in place of columns, with dentils instead of a frieze. Both porches have coffered ceilings, the north one originally hung with bronze rosettes.

Capitals of the Corinthian order were carved in imitation of ACANTHUS fronds, the acanthus being the first truly naturalistic motif in the Greek repertory and the most ornate. This order, which originated in the late 5th century BC, was initially confined to interiors but was subsequently applied externally and exclusively on the small and elaborate choregic monument of Lysikrates in Athens (*c.* 334 BC). The elongate capitals were composed of curling acanthus dotted with a row of flower-heads, above rushlike foliage. The six columns were free-standing, disposed around a hollow drum with a small frieze and row of miniature dentils; a mass of acanthus foliage supporting Lysikrates' bronze tripod rose from the convex roof, which was carved in an overlapping pattern simulating bay-leaf thatching. Despite its Greek origins, however, the Corinthian order was not applied extensively until the Roman era.

See also ARCHITECTURE, §§IV, 1(iii) and MOSAIC, §II, 1(iv)(a).

(ii) Roman. The arches, vaults, domes and niches of Roman public buildings were often executed in concrete, a material that allowed a greater freedom of form but required decorative facings to disguise it (*see* ARCHITECTURE, §VI, 1(ii)(c) and fig. 21). Piers, the principal load-bearing members in these structures, were spaced more widely than columns, creating an increased floor area and greater potential for interior decoration. Walls faced with stonework in a tightly-knit diamond pattern (*opus reticulatum*) and floors of herringbone brickwork (*opus spicatum*) were popular, while arrangements of chevrons, octagons, diamond shapes and swastikas were used on tile or mosaic floors, often bordered by Greek key patterns (*see* MEANDER), guilloches or cross-banding. The painted walls and mosaic flooring favoured during the Republic were succeeded by elaborate schemes of imported coloured marble. The stone was carved into columns and pilasters, arranged in geometric, curvilinear and polygonal paving designs (*opus sectile*; *see* MOSAIC, §III, 1(i)) and composed into increasingly complex patterns of wall panelling. Gilded and painted stucco and polychrome mosaics were also applied to vaults. These materials acted as internal veneers, heightening the disassociation of decoration from the underlying structure. Typically, the decoration of the Pantheon in Rome (begun *c.* AD 118) was concentrated on the interior, where the curved walls were veneered with porphyry and granite and articulated by columnar and pedimented recesses. The vast concrete dome, encased externally with gilded bronze plates, was coffered, thereby reducing its overall weight. The monumental vaulted imperial baths of the city were heavily embellished, incorporating complex patterns of coffering that enclosed vignettes of figures, as well as filigree and candelabra ornament.

Greek motifs continued to be employed widely. The entablature on the Temple of the Deified Vespasian in Rome (*c.* AD 80) includes stiff leaves, anthemia, fluting, acanthus-enriched consoles, egg and dart mouldings, dentils and chevrons. Below them is a frieze carved with bucrania and implements; similar carvings also survive of sacrificial instruments and naval symbols. The Ara Pacis in Rome (dedicated 9 BC; *see* ROME, §IV, 4 and fig. 8) featured richly carved acanthus leaves, the leitmotif of Roman ornament, elaborated from the conventionalized Greek version into densely foliated scrolls. Other typical exterior ornament included scale patterns, pulvinated friezes of bound and overlapping leaves, and such examples of rustication as city gates, originally applied to buildings, intended to denote security.

Since most Roman buildings were arcuated, the orders were usually applied ornamentally, both internally and externally, to give an expressive quality to flat and curved surfaces. In addition to the Greek orders, stocky, unfluted Tuscan columns were employed during the late Republic (*see* ORDERS, ARCHITECTURAL, §I, 1(v)). The Corinthian order was the most popular, its long shafts either fluted or plain, and its capital comprising two rows of acanthus leaves, occasionally incorporating human heads, winged horses or a large flower. The new, highly embellished Composite order was developed, combining Ionic and Corinthian elements. The Colosseum at Rome (inaugurated AD 80; *see* ARCHITECTURE, §VI, 2(i)(d)) consisted of three tiers of arcaded galleries with engaged columns one above the other, Doric, Ionic and Corinthian, plus a crowning storey of Corinthian pilasters—a sequence that became an architectural convention. An upper internal colonnade featured the Corinthian and Composite orders.

TRIUMPHAL ARCHES also featured superimposed orders, but they employed Corinthian and Composite orders only. The tripartite Arch of Constantine in Rome (dedicated AD 315; *see* ROME, §IV, 12) has an entablature breaking forward over its four columns, each marked by a pedestal supporting a figure. The winged Victories and reliefs of contemporary events are characteristic enrichments. Another important Roman monument was Trajan's Column (dedicated AD 113; *see* ROME, §IV, 7 and fig. 12), which depicted a vigorously coloured dramatized historical narrative of Trajan's Dacian wars in a continuous spiral frieze running from base to capital. It stood in a forum celebrating these victories in splendid fashion, with colonnades surmounted by large roundels and caryatid figures of Dacian soldiers, and copious gilded and polychrome statuary, all focused on the monumental equestrian portrait of Trajan. The Markets of Trajan (*c.* AD 100–112; *see* ARCHITECTURE, §VI, 2(i)(e)) exploited the architectural repertory for decorative ends, with round-headed windows framed by pilasters, and a continuous entablature broken out of shallow relief to form a series of aediculae with triangular and segmental pediments and triangular half-pediments. The ostentatious Library of Celsus at Ephesos (*c.* AD 135; *see* EPHESOS, fig. 3) exhibited a more complex configuration, with bicolumnar aediculae supporting alternating curved and triangular pediments.

Private houses—most notably 1st-century AD examples at Pompeii and Herculaneum—were sometimes lavishly decorated internally. The *opus tessellatum* mosaic floors were commonly composed of geometric borders framing a central picture (emblema) executed in the finer *opus vermiculatum*. The frescoed walls depicted representational subjects, such as deities, hunt scenes and fish, illusionistic architecture and grotesques—fantastic concoctions of trellis, grapevines, candelabra raised on tripods and scrolling acanthus, with masks, putti, nymphs, mythical creatures and trailing tendrils. The sumptuous interior of Nero's Domus Aurea in Rome (designed AD 64) was inlaid with mother-of-pearl, gold glass mosaic and jewels. Grotesques embellished the walls, and tent patterns spanned the ceilings. The scheme may have celebrated Nero's reign in celestial terms, since other imperial residences were recorded as having sophisticated cosmological allegories and astrological symbols as part of their decoration.

See also ARCHITECTURE, §VI, 1(iii)(a).

2. OTHER. The wide diversity of motifs used in non-architectural contexts can be broadly classified into geometric, botanical, zoomorphic, mythological and figurative, marine and military categories. Early Greek vase ornament was entirely geometric; Greek key patterns—sometimes incorporating paterae or rosettes—running scrolls, ivies and floral motifs framed more complicated designs later (*see* POTTERY, §IV, 1(ii)(b) and 3). Acanthus, anthemia and palmettes appeared prolifically in borders, mouldings and as general decoration on furniture, ceramics and silver. Oak, laurel and olive leaves bound into wreaths, cornucopias overflowing with fruit, and festoons of flowers and fruit were copied from nature in marble and fresco friezes. Roses and rosettes featured on tombs and stelae.

Some animal motifs derived from sacrificial and ritual practices: altars, sarcophagi and funerary urns depicted aegricanes (heads of rams or goats) and bucrania (bulls' heads), frequently linked by ribbons and swags of fruit. Hunting scenes and gladiatorial contests with wild beasts were favourite subjects for mosaics. Seated sphinxes and griffins were depicted round the bases of altars and candelabra, which might also display the heads of rams, satyrs or lions at their upper corners. Lions also figured on Greek stelae commemorating dead warriors. Furniture, candelabra and bronze tripods sometimes had animal legs terminating in hoof-, paw- or claw-feet. Monopodia, consisting of a griffin surmounting a large foot or leg, functioned as table supports, as did pairs of winged lions; curving serpents made elegant handles. (For further discussion *see* FURNITURE.)

Images of deities enhanced all kinds of domestic artefacts. Finely detailed portraits of mythological and historical characters appeared on engraved gems and on cameos mounted in jewellery and furniture. More complex scenes were shown on vases, either painted or carved, while sarcophagi depicted friezes of figures, sometimes against an architectural backdrop, including hunting and marriage scenes, battling centaurs, dancing maidens, cavorting cupids, and groups of nereids and sea-creatures amid rolling waves. Narrative subjects associated with death and rebirth were also common, for example the rape of Proserpina and the deaths of Adonis, Meleager and Endymion. Bacchic processions and dancing maenads decorated sarcophagi, candelabrum bases and marble vases. Bacchus or his attributes—grapes, vines, ivy, thyrsi, cymbals, satyrs—commonly embellished silver, glass and ceramic drinking vessels. Fountains were decorated with reclining river gods, the water pouring from their urns symbolizing the water's source, and with tritons, dolphins, scallop-shells and giant pine-cones. The heads of lions and gorgons provided waterspouts. The TROPHY was another common motif in the Roman world; comprising armour, plumed helmets, weapons, anchors and insigia, it celebrated Roman martial superiority. Fasces (bundles of rods bound together and often enclosing an axe head) ornamented tombs; legionary standards bore Jupiter's eagle; and panoplies of arms, winged Victories, laurel wreaths and gorgon masks all featured in military contexts.

G. Richter: *Ancient Furniture: A History of Greek, Etruscan and Roman Furniture* (Oxford, 1926)
D. S. Robertson: *A Handbook of Greek and Roman Architecture* (Cambridge, 1929, rev. 2/1943); *R* as *Greek and Roman Architecture* (London, 1969)
A. W. Lawrence: *Greek Architecture*, Pelican Hist. A. (Harmondsworth, 1957, rev. 4/1983)
M. Wheeler: *Roman Art and Architecture* (London, 1973)
J. Boardman: *Athenian Red Figure Vases: The Archaic Period* (London, 1979)
J. Summerson: *The Classical Language of Architecture* (London, 1980)
G. Hersey: *The Lost Meaning of Classical Architecture: Speculations on Ornament from Vitruvius to Venturi* (Cambridge, MA, and London, 1988)
J. Onians: *Bearers of Meaning: The Classical Orders in Antiquity: The Middle Ages and the Renaissance* (Princeton, 1988)
S. McNally: *The Architectural Ornament of Diocletian's Palace at Split* (Oxford, 1996)
J. L. de la Barrera Anton: *La decoración arquitectónica de los foros de Augusta Emerita* (Rome, 2000)
L. S. Meritt and I. E. M. Edlund-Berry: *Etruscan and Republican Roman Mouldings* (Philadelphia, 2000)
T. Mattern: *Gesims und Ornament: Zur stadtrömischen Architektur von der Republik bis Septimius Severus* (Münster, 2001)
T. F. C. Blagg: *Roman Architectural Ornament in Britain* (Oxford, 2002)
H. Heinrich: *Subtilitas novarum scalpturarum: Untersuchungen zur Ornamentik marmorner Bauglieder der späten Republik und frühen Kaiserzeit in Campanien* (Munich, 2002)
S. Hales: *The Roman House and Social Identity* (Cambridge, 2003)
S. Braun and J. Hampé: *Le Jura Roman: Architecture et sculpture* (Besançon, 2004)
F. E. Winter: *Studies in Hellenistic Architecture* (Toronto, 2006)

Orvieto. *See* VOLSINII VETERES.

Ostia [now Ostia Antica]. Port city for ancient Rome that flourished *c.* 325 BC–*c.* AD 400. Situated 25 km south-west of Rome at the mouth (Lat. *ostium*) of the Tiber, Ostia controlled access to the river and the approach to Rome from the sea. It was important originally for defence and later for servicing the massive imports essential to sustain the capital of an empire. It was therefore always of concern to the Roman authorities, who laid out whole areas and built conspicuously within it. This makes it unlike Pompeii, which was influenced as much by the Samnites and the Greeks: Ostia, with a longer history and reaching its peak in the 2nd century AD, is more typically Roman and gives evidence, which is absent for Rome itself, of the impact of Roman planning skills on everyday life. The site, now several kilometres from the coast, was at the beginning of the 20th century a large grass-covered plateau about 6 m above the surrounding plain. Systematic excavation, which started in the late 19th century, was accelerated between 1938 and 1942, rapidly uncovering about two thirds of the ancient town. Since then the prime aims have been consolidation and publication of the finds, with some prudent test excavations within or on the edge of the uncovered area. A site museum (Ostia Antica, Mus. Ostiense) displays a selection of sculptures (see fig. 1) and paintings. Most of the mosaics are still *in situ*.

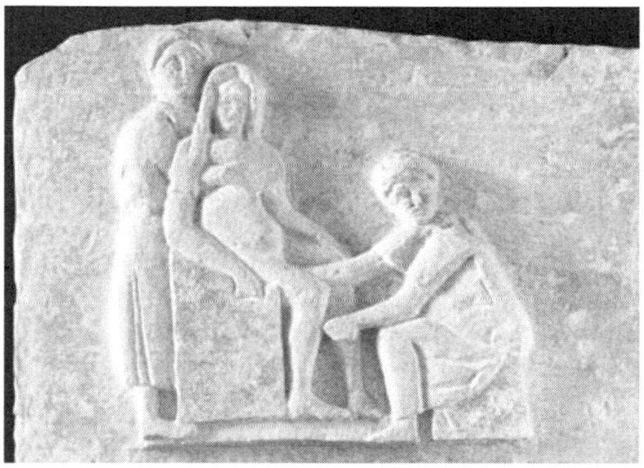

1. Ostia, funerary relief showing midwife delivering a baby, painted terracotta, second half of the 2nd century AD (Ostia Antica, Museo Ostiense)

1. Architecture. 2. Mosaics.

1. ARCHITECTURE.

(i) History and urban development. (ii) Buildings.

(i) History and urban development. At the centre of the site lies the outline of the 4th-century BC castrum (fig. 2a), a fort of some 2 ha built about 200 m south of the Tiber, originally near its mouth. It was large enough for about 300 families and surrounded by strong walls of tufa blocks. No trace of the settlement said to have been made by the king Ancus Marcius in the 6th century BC has yet been discovered. From this fort the later town developed, as is shown by the layout of the roads entering the city. Expansion came with Rome's victory over Hannibal in the late 3rd century BC and the rapid growth of Rome's imports from overseas. In the early 1st century BC this expanded area of some 64 ha was enclosed within new town walls, beyond which the cemeteries developed. These inhibited further lateral expansion when the population grew quickly, to perhaps 50,000 people by the 2nd century AD.

The Tiber was navigable in antiquity as far as Rome by seagoing ships with a capacity of up to 200 tonnes, but merchant ships with their square-rigged sails found it difficult to go upstream on a winding course, and the silting of the river forced them to unload out at sea into lighter vessels. In the mid-1st century AD,

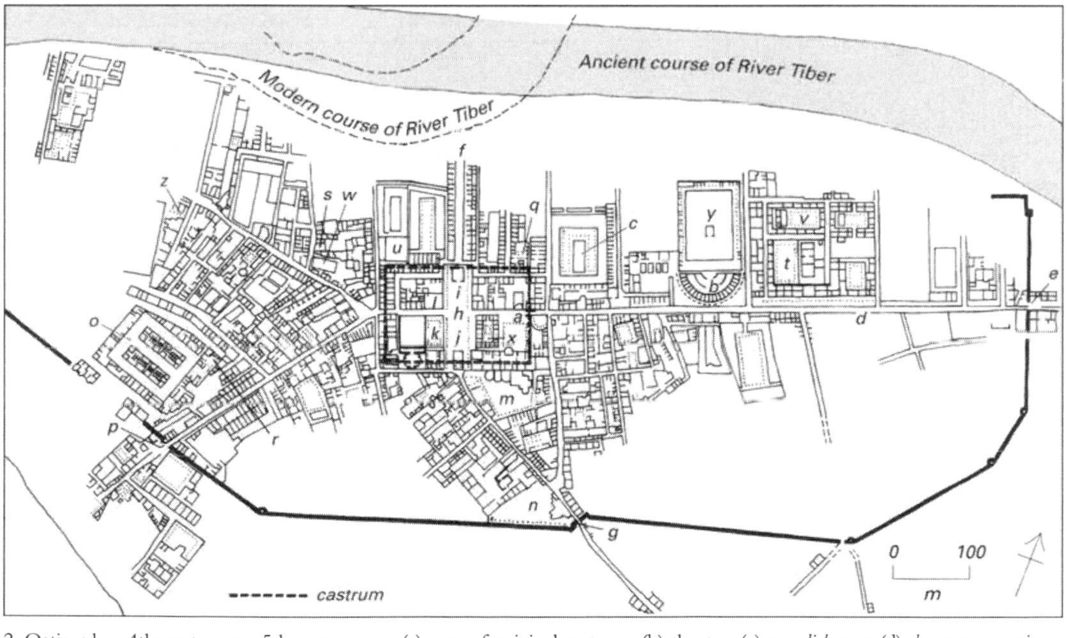

2. Ostia, plan, 4th century BC–5th century AD: (a) gate of original castrum; (b) theatre; (c) *grandi horrea*; (d) *decumanus maximus*; (e) Porta Romana; (f) *cardo maximus*; (g) Porta Laurentina; (h) forum; (i) Capitolium; (j) Temple of Rome and Augustus; (k) basilica; (l) curia; (m) Forum Baths; (n) Sanctuary of the Magna Mater; (o) Garden Houses; (p) Porta Marina; (q) House of Diana; (r) House of the Muses; (s) House of Cupid and Psyche; (t) Baths of Neptune; (u) Horrea Epagathiana et Epaphroditiana; (v) barracks of the Vigiles; (w) Temple of Hercules; (x) headquarters of the builders' guild; (y) Piazzale delle Corporazioni; (z) House of Bacchus and Ariadne

therefore, the emperor Claudius built a large artificial harbour of some 80 ha in a natural bay about 3 km north of the Tiber mouth and linked it to the river by two canals. With a lighthouse at its entrance and 2000 m of quayside, it had room for 250 ships. As this was also liable to silt up and was too big to guarantee calm conditions, a smaller, hexagonal, inner harbour of 32 ha was excavated by Trajan in the early 2nd century AD, and both basins were linked to the river by a new single canal, the Fossa Traiana. There was room for a further 200 ships at the quaysides and guaranteed safety. These arrangements created a new independent centre, Portus, although the immediate effect was beneficial to Ostia.

In Ostia itself, during the reign of Augustus, Agrippa built a theatre capable of seating 3000 spectators (fig. 2b), and in the early 1st century AD an aqueduct for the first time brought water into the city from the high land 6 km to the east to supplement the earlier wells and cisterns. Claudius built the *grandi horrea* (fig. 2c), the greatest of the Ostian grain warehouses. But it was Domitian in the late 1st century AD who started the major redevelopment of Ostia, raising the building level by at least a metre, with an infilling of earth and rubble to avoid flooding and provide deep and stable foundations for the new high blocks of *insulae* (apartments) needed for the expanding population. The present city was substantially rebuilt and completed under Trajan, Hadrian and Antoninus Pius in the first half of the 2nd century AD, the period of Ostia's greatest prosperity. Its architecture reflected the improved standards in building and planning achieved in the reconstruction of Rome by Nero after the great fire of AD 64; wide streets and orderly *insulae* were laid out there, and brick-faced concrete came into use (*see* INSULA and ARCHITECTURE, §VI, 2(i)(c)). The results were handsome substantial buildings of up to five storeys. At Ostia the experience gained in Rome half a century earlier reached fruition in the new town of Hadrian and Antoninus Pius. It provides some of the best evidence for what the new Rome must have been like.

The main street, the *decumanus maximus* (fig. 2d), ran from the Porta Romana (fig. 2e; one of the three main gates in the town walls) from east to west parallel to the former course of the Tiber. It was 9 m wide and about 1500 m long. To the north, in an area important for trade and strictly controlled, lay mostly public buildings, as well as warehouses, baths, the barracks of the fire brigade, the theatre and its colonnaded square, a bakery and some *insulae*. The *decumanus* crossed the other main road, the *cardo maximus* (fig. 2f), which ran south from the Tiber to the Porta Laurentina (fig. 2g), at the forum. The forum (fig. 2h) dates from the early 1st century AD and was a rectangular area of more than 1800 sq. m, dominated by the Capitolium to the north (fig. 2i) and the Temple of Rome and Augustus to the south (fig. 2j). It was flanked by colonnades, behind which on the west lay the basilica (fig. 2k) and the 'curia' (town council chamber; fig. 2l). South-east of the forum lay the gracious Forum Baths (fig. 2m), while near the Porta Laurentina was the Sanctuary of the Magna Mater (fig. 2n). Beyond the forum to the west lay rather more diverse areas with more warehouses, to be expected near the Tiber; while to the south along the continuation of the *decumanus* was a mixture of public and private buildings, including the spacious residential quarter called the Garden Houses (fig. 2o), near the Porta Marina (fig. 2p). This area, constructed under Hadrian, was not all rectangular, but it was rationally laid out and splendidly built.

Ostia had lost its prosperity and power by the 3rd century AD, as Portus became increasingly favoured; its population declined, and the *insulae* and granaries fell into disrepair. Although it declined as a port, it became popular among the wealthy as a seaside resort in the 3rd–4th century AD, finally losing its importance in the 5th century when the towpath from Ostia to Rome along the left bank of the Tiber disappeared (the towpath from Portus to Rome on the right bank remained). In the 9th century the town was evacuated by Pope Gregory IV (*reg* AD 827–44) and its inhabitants removed to the small fortified settlement of Gregoriopolis, east of the ruins, which itself gradually became covered over.

(ii) Buildings. Beneath the 2nd-century AD town, south and west of the forum, are traces of Pompeian-type houses, that is inward-looking houses with atria and peristyles (*see* POMPEII, §II). Only a couple survived into the Empire and in a modified form (the House of Jupiter the Thunderer and the House of the Mosaic Niche). As the population grew and land became valuable, *insulae* began to provide accommodation for all classes and replaced the individual *domus*. The House of Diana (fig. 2q), for example, was a substantial structure of at least three and possibly five storeys, with two sides facing on to the street to the south and the west, while its other two sides adjoined other buildings (see fig. 3). In the centre was a small courtyard for air and light containing a cistern. There was also a small latrine under the stairs. On the ground floor a series of shops opened on to the

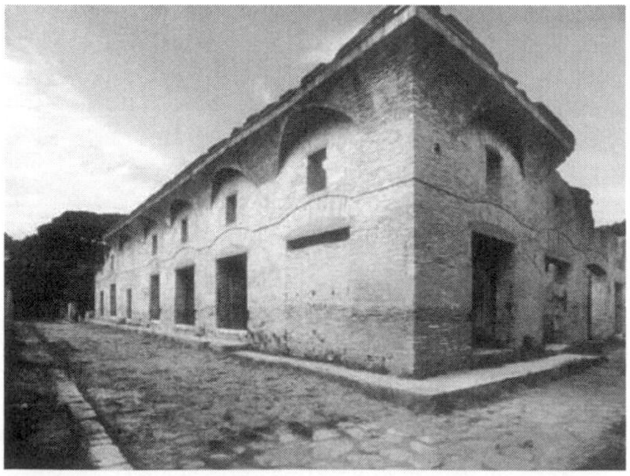

3. Ostia, House of Diana, view from the south-east with shops opening onto the streets, mid-2nd century AD

street, with windows above their doorways to light the mezzanine floor, reached by a small staircase at the back of the shop, where the shopkeeper lived and slept. Between the shops narrow doorways gave access to the ground-floor apartments and to staircases to the upper storeys. The appearance of the whole block, with its narrow vaulted balconies and uncovered brickwork, was handsome and unfussy. The apartments varied in size, but often the rooms opened off a wide corridor that replaced the atrium, with the largest rooms for reception and dining at each end. A simple version of the plan, with only one main room, appears in modest artisans' houses under Trajan (e.g. the Casette Tipo). It could, however, be elaborated in better-class housing, as in the Garden Houses. In neither case was there any need for a central courtyard, although this feature is present in the House of the Muses (fig. 2r above) where the decoration of the ground-floor rooms with paintings and mosaics suggests that the tenants were wealthy.

The ground-floor rooms formed the superior quarters in an *insula*, and they contain the extant painting and mosaic at Ostia. What little wall painting survives is in general disappointing (*see* PAINTING, §VI, 2). The main effects in the Hadrianic period were achieved by contrasting masses of colour, especially yellow and red, in the lower parts of the wall. The central zone might have large panels depicting single figures or groups, mainly mythological in character, for example *Jupiter and Ganymede* and the *Desertion of Ariadne*. Later the whole surface of the wall tended to be treated more as a unit, and white was used more often than yellow. Mosaic was far more of a distinctive feature of the decoration at Ostia (*see* §2 below). (For further discussion and illustration of Ostian *insulae see* INSULA).

Several attractive private houses were built or reconstructed in the 3rd and 4th centuries AD, when Ostia was a popular resort of the wealthy, such as the House of Cupid and Psyche in the west of the town (fig. 2s). Here a living-room was approached by a central corridor, flanked on the left by a series of small rooms, lavishly decorated with marble floors and wall panels. Beyond, on the right, was a little colonnade by a small garden, backed by an elegant nymphaeum.

Baths played an important part in the social life of Ostia, where 17 suites have been discovered. Three of these were large establishments, probably imperial benefactions in the first half of the 2nd century AD. The first, on the coast outside the Porta Marina, was built under Trajan. The Hadrianic Baths of Neptune on the north side of the *decumanus* (fig. 2t) had a rectangular plan, with the main rooms, leading from cold to hot, arranged from south to north on the east side of the building; the west side was occupied by a colonnaded palaestra. The Forum Baths, built under Antoninus Pius, were the grandest; constructed of concrete, they were typical of the new vaulted style of building. While the entrances and cold rooms in the north part were conventionally rectangular, the heated rooms to the south, facing on to a triangular, colonnaded palaestra, were octagonal, elliptical or curved, with windows, later enlarged, to catch the sun. All were decorated with statues and mosaics and distinguished by the variety of marbles and granites used. Most of the baths in Ostia were not on this scale, however. Often they were fitted within an existing building block and run as private businesses. Some were quite humble, such as the Baths of the Drivers, inserted in the 3rd century AD into Republican industrial premises near the Porta Romana. Its mosaics, showing men at work with their mules and carts, are a reminder, like the bakeries with their millstones still intact, of the ordinary life of a busy port town.

It was essential to store the goods for Rome properly until they could be passed up river; Ostia and Portus are our greatest sources of knowledge about the design and structure of horrea (storebuildings) in the Roman world, and they help to give Ostia its peculiar distinction. They were functionally designed and built with the finest materials and methods (usually brick-faced concrete) available in the 1st and 2nd centuries AD. They were normally rectangular in plan with a series of rooms opening on to a courtyard or central corridor. The small and elegant Horrea Epagathiana et Epaphroditiana (*c.* AD 145–50; fig. 2u), owned by two freedmen named in the inscription over the main entrance, was used for storing valuable items. It had 16 rooms on the ground floor, with perhaps two more storeys above, and there were elaborate locking devices throughout the building. Storage of grain, the most important of the commodities needed by Rome, demanded special devices. The grandi horrea west of the theatre were massive structures, with outer walls of tufa blocks and limited access to guarantee security. Porticos supported wide eaves to protect the grain from sun and rain, while gutters prevented accumulation of surface water within the building. Staircases were often partially in the form of ramps to help porters carrying heavy loads. The rooms were built with raised floors to allow a cooling draught of air to pass under the thresholds and circulate below the stored grain. Such wine and oil as was not kept in containers for shipment to Rome was stored in *dolia defossa*, great earthenware jars sunk into the ground to keep them cool. Four of these deposits are known; the largest, north-east of the forum, has more than 100 jars with a total capacity of over 84,000 litres. As the greatest hazard to the docks and the corn supply was fire, Hadrian detached a section of the Vigiles (trained fire-fighters) from Rome to be stationed at Ostia and built a barracks to house them, behind the Baths of Neptune between the *decumanus* and the Tiber (fig. 2v).

As a port town, Ostia reflects a wide range of religious practices. The forum was dominated by two temples; that of Rome and Augustus and the Capitolium. The former, of which little remains, was built under Tiberius. The Capitolium, dedicated to Jupiter, Juno and Minerva, was rebuilt under Hadrian on a podium to a height of *c.* 21 m so as to compete with the *insulae* around it. Only the brick-faced core remains, the marble facing having been robbed. Known by the local people as 'the red house', it protruded for centuries some 15 m out of the Ostia mound. The most important cult at Ostia was that of Vulcan, but its temple remains unidentified. The earliest surviving temple (first half of the 1st century BC) is dedicated to Hercules, in the west part of the town outside the old castrum (fig. 2w). There were many other traditional gods worshipped at Ostia, but one of the most striking features of the 2nd-century AD town is the popularity of oriental cults. Just inside the Porta Laurentina on the south side of the town a large triangular area was dedicated to Cybele, the Phrygian Magna Mater, and the associated cults of Attis and Bellona. A temple of Egyptian Serapis was erected under Hadrian in the west part of the town, and inscriptions refer to a temple of Isis. The most popular cult, however, seems to have been Mithraism: no fewer than 15 mithraea have been found. Built between the mid-2nd century AD and the late 3rd, most of them are small. A large and handsome synagogue has also been found, near the seashore. Evidence for Christianity in Ostia is slight. A hall near the Porta Marina was decorated with *opus sectile* (cut designs in coloured marble); it was destroyed before completion during the late 4th-century pagan reaction.

Most of the free population of Ostia were involved with a guild. They had handsome premises for meetings, dinners and religious ceremonies, such as the headquarters of the builders' guild, on the south side of the *decumanus* just east of the forum (fig. 2x). Its rooms opened on to a porticoed courtyard and included a chapel, five rooms equipped with permanent dining couches, a kitchen and a latrine. The most striking illustration of the guilds in Ostia is the 2nd-century AD Piazzale delle Corporazioni (Square of the Guilds; fig. 2y), a double colonnade behind the theatre, off which opened 61 small rooms fronted by mosaic floor designs, sometimes with inscriptions that appear to illustrate the occupation of the owners or tenants. They were used as offices (*stationes*), where representatives of overseas shippers, from Narbonne, Cagliari or Sabratha, for example, and of Ostian business firms could take orders and give information.

L. Paschetto: *Ostia colonia romana* (Rome, 1912)

Scavi di Ostia, 10 vols (Rome, 1953–79)

R. Calza and E. Nash: *Ostia* (Florence, 1959)

R. Meiggs: *Roman Ostia* (Oxford, 1960, rev. 2/1973)

J. E. Packer: 'The Insulae of Imperial Ostia', *Mem. Amer. Acad. Rome*, xxxi (1971) [whole volume]

G. E. Rickman: *Roman Granaries and Store Buildings* (Cambridge, 1971)

G. Hermansen: *Ostia: Aspects of Roman City Life* (Edmonton, 1981)

C. Pavolini: *Ostia: Vita quotidiana* [Daily life of Ostia] (Ostia Antica, 1983)

J. S. Boersma: *Amoenissima civitas* [The most pleasant city] (Assen, 1985)

R. Chevallier: *Ostie antique: Ville et port* (Paris, 1986)

C. M. Watts and others: 'Geometrical Ordering of the Garden Houses at Ostia', *J. Soc. Architect. Hist.*, xlvi (Sept 1987), pp. 265–76

C. de Ruyt: 'Un exemple de discontinuité des fonctions monumentales dans un quartier de la ville romaine d'Ostie (reg. III, ins. II)', *Rev. Belge Archéol. & Hist. A.*, lxv (1996), pp. 5–16

A. G. Zevi and A. Claridge, eds: *'Roman Ostia' Revisited* (London, 1996)

S. Gallico: *Guide to the Excavations of Ostia Antica: With a Section about the Renaissance Borgo* (Rome, 2000)

G. R. Storey: 'Regionaries-type Insulae 1: Architectural/Residential Units in Ostia', *Amer. J. Archaeol.*, cv/3 (July 2001), pp. 389–401

A. Gering: 'Die Case a Giardino als unerfullter Architektentraum: Planung und gewandelte Nutzung einer Luxuswohnanlage im antiken Ostia', *Mitt. Dt. Archäol. Inst.: Röm. Abt.*, cix (2002), pp.109–40

L. B. Van der Meer: 'Travertine Cornerstones in Ostia Antica: Odd Blocks', *Amer. J. Archaeol.*, cvi/4 (Oct 2002), pp. 575–80

J. DeLaine: 'Designing for a Market: 'Medianum' Apartments at Ostia', *J. Roman Archaeol.*, xvii (2004), pp.146–76

2. Mosaics. A few pavements survive from the Republican period (up to 27 BC), predominantly of *opus signinum* and related techniques. Black-and-white geometric pavements first appeared in the Augustan period (27 BC–AD 14) and continued to be made until the 4th century AD; they were used extensively to decorate the ground floors of *insulae*. Ostia is, however, noted chiefly as the main source of black-and-white figured silhouette mosaics; the earliest are from the Baths of the Via dei Vigili (*c.* AD 40–*c.* 50), and they were common in the 2nd and 3rd centuries AD. Many place the figures within the compartments of a geometric framework. Two other characteristic types of design are all-over marine scenes (especially common in baths) and designs of the floral style. The marine scenes are best represented in the Baths of Neptune (dedicated AD 139). There Neptune is depicted driving his team of four sea-horses amid a cortège of sea creatures, while Amphitrite, his consort, rides towards him in the next room. The figures are in black silhouette, with interior detail of fine white lines, against a plain white background (the sea is hardly indicated), and are distributed around all four sides of the room. On later marine scenes the composition becomes much more rigid; in the Severan Maritime Baths (early 3rd century AD) central heads of Ocean are flanked by symmetrical Tritons at the corners, or regularly arranged sea monsters. The sea is represented by broken black lines, which by the mid-3rd century fill the whole background (e.g. in the Lighthouse Baths). The floral style is found on floors of the Hadrianic (AD 117–38) and Antonine (AD 138–92) periods; elegant examples are in the House of Bacchus and Ariadne (see fig. 2z above). The rotunda of the Baths of the Seven Sages is covered with an all-over scroll, within which are figures of hunters and their prey.

Black-and-white mosaics were used at Ostia for didactic purposes as well as for decoration. In the Piazzale delle Corporazioni mosaics advertise the offices of the trade guilds of shippers and represent ships, dolphins and lighthouses, or allude to the products in which they dealt. In Mithraea (shrines of Mithras), mosaics may portray the symbols of the cult, grades of initiation or the planetary deities, as in the Mithraeum of Felicissimus and the Mithraeum of the Seven Spheres. Polychrome mosaics, much rarer than black-and-white, enjoyed a limited revival in the 4th century AD; in the House of the Dioscuri, a *Triumph of Marine Venus* resembles examples found in North Africa. *Opus sectile* was used from the Augustan period, but it is found principally in the late 3rd century AD–4th; a luxurious example is in the House of Cupid and Psyche. Extensive mural *opus sectile* work was found in the hall near the Porta Marina; it includes lions devouring their prey and a bust apparently of Christ, bearded and with a halo (Ostia Antica, Mus. Ostiense).

Almost all the mosaics are *in situ*, some now in poor preservation.

M. E. Blake: 'Roman Mosaics of the Second Century in Italy', *Mem. Amer. Acad. Rome*, xiii (1936), pp. 69–214

G. Becatti: *I Mitrei* (1954), ii of *Scavi di Ostia* (Rome, 1953–79)

R. Meiggs: *Roman Ostia* (Oxford, 1960, rev. 2/1973), pp. 446–54

G. Becatti: *Mosaici e pavimenti marmorei* (1961), iv of *Scavi di Ostia* (Rome, 1953–79)

G. Becatti: *Edificio con opus sectile fuori Porta Marina* (1969), vi of *Scavi di Ostia* (Rome, 1953–79)

J. Clarke: *Roman Black-and-white Figural Mosaics* (New York, 1979)

M. Floriani Squarciapino: 'Nuovi mosaici Ostiensi', *Rend. Pont. Acc.*, lviii (1985–6), pp. 87–114

I. Bragantini: 'Mosaico policromo con iscrizione di consecratio da una tomba dell'Isola Sacra', *J. Roman Archaeol.*, x (1997), pp. 271–8

W. D. Heilmeyer: 'Schwarz und weiss: Zwei Mosaiken aus Ostia als Dauerleihgabe in Berlin', *Ant. Welt*, xxviii/3 (1997), pp. 269–70

C. P. Jones: 'The Pancratiasts Helix and Alexander on an Ostian Mosaic', *J. Roman Archaeol.*, xi (1998), pp. 293–8

Oxyrhynchus [anc. Egyp. Per-Medjed; Copt. Pemdje; now el-Bahnasa]. Site on the Bahr Yusuf, 50 km north of el-Minya in Egypt. Little is known of the town in the Dynastic period (*c.* 2925–332 BC), when it was the capital of the 19th Upper Egyptian nome and played an important role in the mythology of Osiris. Its main importance is as a source of Roman-period (30 BC–AD 395) papyri, which were preserved by the dry climate, encaustic mummy portraits and Early Christian funerary sculpture.

The rubbish heaps of Oxyrhynchus were first excavated by Bernard Grenfell and Arthur Hunt in 1896, and they have since yielded over 10,000 papyri, the largest number from a single site. They provide unique examples of Roman book illustrations, including circus scenes and stories from mythology, as well as more ephemeral works such as preliminary sketches in wash for wall paintings and coloured designs for textiles (all now Oxford, Ashmolean). Papyrus rolls with fine manuscripts of literary texts attest the art of the calligrapher in Roman Egypt; some luxury books found at the site may have been produced in Alexandria. High-quality manuscripts include works of Sophocles (Cambridge, U. Lib., Add. MSS 5895) and Plato (Toledo, OH, Mus. A., 1400). Non-literary papyri document the organization of artistic life in the city and record the now-vanished public buildings, including gymnasia, temples to Serapis, Isis and Thoeris, an amphitheatre and the baths of Hadrian, which the painter Aurelius Artemidoros undertook to decorate with architectural frescoes in AD 316.

Mummy portraits from Oxyrhynchus are artistically comparable with those from Antinoöpolis (e.g. Malibu, CA, Getty Mus., 78.AP.62). The Early Christian funerary sculpture includes portrait stelae showing heavily draped, partly engaged frontal figures (e.g. Leiden, Rijksmus. Oudhd., F1972/8.1) and decorated stone niches in a variety of shapes. As at Kom Abu Billo, these sculptures were originally brightly painted and set into the mud-brick tomb superstructures.

B. P. Grenfell and others: *The Oxyrhynchus Papyri* (London, 1898–2006) [70 vols to date]

W. M. F. Petrie: *The Tombs of the Courtiers and Oxyrhynchos* (London, 1920)

H. Rink: *Strassen- und Viertelnamen von Oxyrhynchus* (Geissen, 1924)

J. Harris: 'Coptic Architectural Sculpture from Oxyrhynchus', *Fasti Archaeol.*, xvi (1964), pp. 526–59

E. G. Turner: *Greek Manuscripts of the Ancient World* (Oxford, 1970, rev. by P. J. Parsons, London, 2/1987)

J. Krüper: *Oxyrhynchos in der Kaiserzeit* (Frankfurt am Main, 1990)

PQ

Paestum [Lat.; Gr. Poseidonia]. Site on the east coast of Italy near the mouth of the River Sele (anc. Silaris), 96 km south of Naples. The Greek colony of Poseidonia was founded by the city of Sybaris on the Gulf of Taranto, probably in the late 7th century BC. It flourished until *c.* 400 BC, when it was overwhelmed by the indigenous population, the Lucanians. In 273 BC it became the Latin colony of Paestum. Much of the city dates from Roman times, although it clearly follows an underlying Greek scheme. When originally founded it was situated on the coast, but silting created by the River Sele, possibly associated with changes in land levels, caused the coastline to recede, so that it is now in the middle of a plain. It is built on flat ground and has no acropolis. The surviving city walls are nearly 5 km long and were constructed by the Lucanians and the Latin colonists, although they appear to follow the lines of the original Greek fortifications. They have some distinctly Hellenistic characteristics, such as towers decorated with elements of the Greek orders, as at Pompeii. Only part of the trapezoidal area that they enclosed has been excavated, but it is clear that the city had a grid plan of straight streets crossing at right angles, creating long narrow blocks. These were subdivided in the residential area into square or rectangular building plots for houses, and the whole scheme belongs to the period of Latin colonization. The grid system differs from the normal Greek town plan, which created shorter, wider blocks, but it may well have been adapted from the original Greek layout.

At the centre of the town were the public spaces. To the north was a Sanctuary of Athena and to the south a Sanctuary of Hera. Between these stood various individual structures and a forum, in this case a relatively narrow rectangular colonnaded courtyard. The original Greek agora was north of the forum, close to the Sanctuary of Athena, and excavations have revealed several of its buildings. These include a late 6th-century BC underground shrine (hypogeum), possibly a heroön regarded as the tomb of a founder-hero, and a bouleuterion. Though underground and small (3.78 × 3.86 m), the heroön resembles a 'real' building, with walls built of limestone blocks and a pitched roof of full-size tiles.

The most important remains of the Greek city are its temples. The Sanctuary of Hera contains two, popularly misnamed the 'Basilica' and the 'Temple of Poseidon'. The 'Basilica', or first Temple of Hera (*c.* 550–525 BC; see fig. 1), is a pseudo-dipteral Doric building with 9 × 18 columns and measuring 24.51×54.27 m. Its odd number of façade columns seems to be an unusual device to make the plan more regular than is normal in Doric temples built before Hellenistic times (*c.* 323–27 BC) and probably evinces Ionic influence. It enabled the roof span to be divided into four equal parts supported by the flank colonnades, the cella walls and the single row of internal columns. The various crosswise elements in the cella, the porch column and antae, entrance wall and two rear divisions (probably the front and back walls of an adyton rather than the columns and wall of an opisthodomos) were apparently aligned, at least approximately, with flank columns in the peristyle. The columns have distinctive Archaic profiles, with marked tapering curvature (ENTASIS). The undersides of the capitals of those on the west façade have elaborate mouldings (half rounds, lotus and rosette, guilloche, lotus and palmette, and petals) instead of the conventional Doric annulets. The architrave had a continuous Ionic-style moulding instead of the usual taenia.

The second Temple of Hera (see fig. 2) probably dates from *c.* 460 BC, although comparisons with mainland Greek temples are unreliable, and allowance needs to be made for the relatively poor quality limestone used, which resulted in the adoption of heavier proportions than in 5th-century BC Athenian marble temples. It too is Doric, but this time the peristyle (24.26 × 59.57 m) has 6×14 columns, and its entablature is conventional. The cella's side walls are aligned with the second and fifth columns of the façades and there are two rows of internal columns, a mainland Greek feature that became more widespread in Sicily and South Italy at this time. The marked thickness of the outer columns, with heights equivalent to less than 4.25 times their lower diameters, may be compared with the proportion of 4.66 at the roughly contemporary Temple of Zeus at Olympia (a limestone building with abnormally heavy proportions by mainland standards). In this way, the free space between the columns is restricted. The cella includes an internal staircase immediately behind the porch, which probably led to the roof space, since there is no sign that the unusually well-preserved two-storey internal colonnades supported side galleries. These

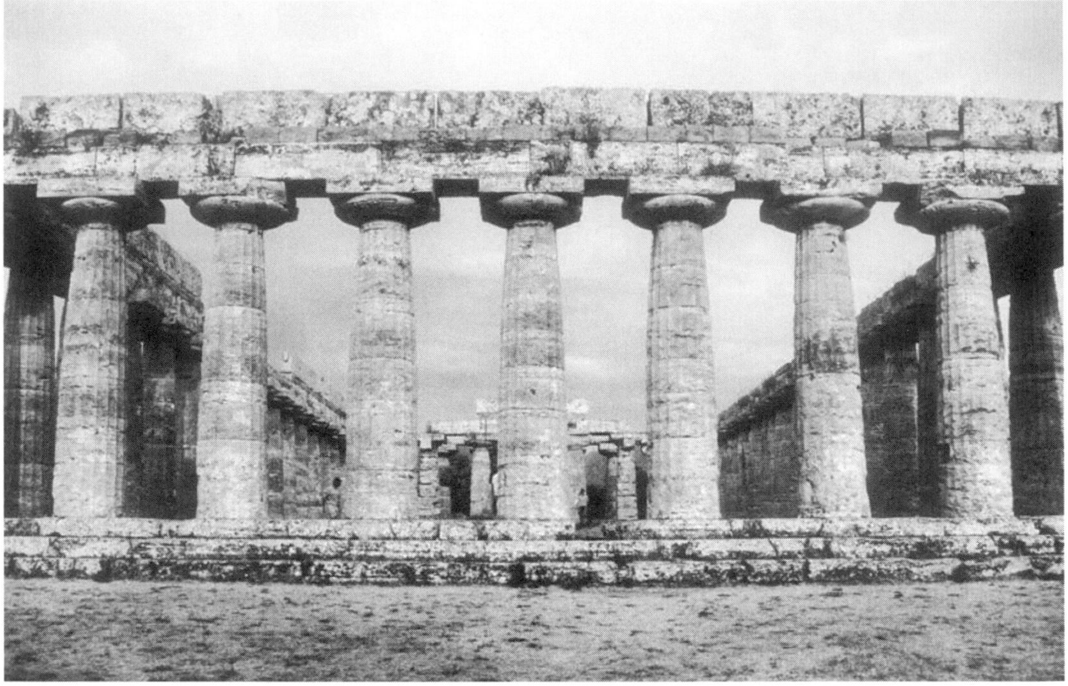

1. Paestum, Sanctuary of Hera, 'Basilica', *c.* 550–525 BC

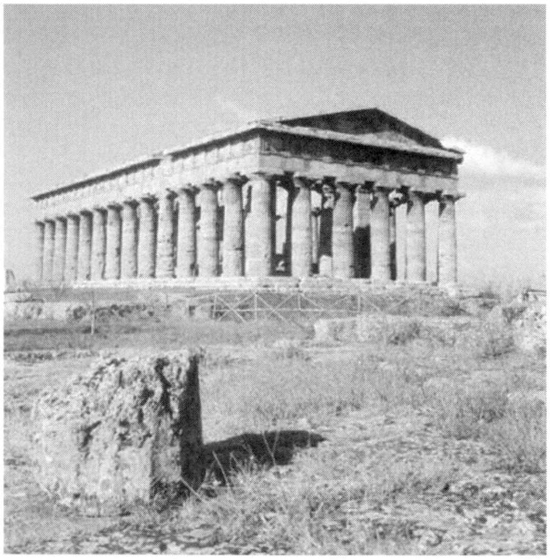

2. Paestum, 'Temple of Poseidon', *c.* 460 BC

internal staircases are typical of western Greek temples, especially those in Sicily, and two occur just inside the door of the third major temple at Paestum, that in the Sanctuary of Athena.

The Temple of Athena (late 6th century BC) is again Doric, but has 6×13 columns and measures 14.54×32.88 m. Like the first Temple of Hera, it was unusually elaborately decorated: the undersides of the column capitals bore bead and reel mouldings instead of conventional annulets, and the architrave was surmounted by an Ionic style moulding. Another moulding ran beneath the cornice, which was not ornamented with Doric mutules and guttae but with square coffers. The cella had no opisthodomos or adyton, and no internal colonnades. It was fronted by an unusually deep Ionic prostyle porch, with four columns across its front, an extra column behind each end and engaged half columns in place of antae. The Ionic influence on Paestan temple architecture is probably a result of Sybaris' close trading connections with East Greek cities, particularly MILETOS.

A much later temple in the Roman Forum stands on an Italian-style podium and has a Doric frieze, but capitals in a variant form of Corinthian, decorated with projecting heads between their corner volutes. Abandoned unfinished, perhaps in the 3rd century BC, this temple was not completed until the 1st century BC, the date of its superstructure. Another sanctuary, originally dedicated to the Greek goddess Damia, then later to her Roman counterpart, the Bona Dea, lies just outside the south gate. It seems to have been in use continuously from the 6th century BC to Roman times.

The cemeteries around Paestum contain several painted tombs. Although many date from the period after the Lucanian occupation, they maintain a Greek tradition of tomb decoration. The most spectacular is the Tomb of the Diver (first half of the 5th century BC; see colour pl. 2:I, fig. 1) in the southern cemetery. It is named after the painting on the underside of its cover slab, which depicts a naked youth diving into a pool from a structure resembling a modern diving-board. Beside the pool are two rather spindly trees, and the whole is framed with palmette decoration. The tomb's side walls both have symposion scenes with men reclining on couches (*see* PAINTING, fig. 4), and one end wall depicts a garlanded youth in front of a table supporting a krater; the other shows two men preceded by a flute player. The paintings are brightly coloured, with blue coverlets on the couches and male bodies painted in a brown wash with details added in thin black lines.

Not far from Paestum, at the mouth of the River Sele, is an important Sanctuary of Hera. This accommodated a 6th-century BC pseudo-dipteral Doric temple measuring 18.7×38.9 m, with 8×12 columns and with internal stairs but no inner colonnade. This again shows Ionic influence, evident in the regularity of its plan and in certain details, such as the mouldings used in its entablature. There is also an important treasury with lavishly carved metopes depicting various mythological scenes. These resemble the decoration on numerous metal vessels found both in tombs and in the underground heroon at Paestum (Paestum, Mus. Archeol. N.).

For Paestan Red-figure vases *see* POTTERY, §IV, 6(ii).

F. Krauss and R. Herbig: *Der korinthisch-dorische Tempel am Forum von Paestum* (Berlin, 1939)

F. Krauss: *Paestum: Die griechischen Tempel*, suppl. D. Mertens (Berlin, 1941, rev. 3/1976)

P. Zancani-Montuoro and U. Zanotti-Bianco: *Heraion alla foce del Sele*, 4 vols (Rome, 1951–4)

F. Krauss: *Die Tempel von Paestum*, I/i (Berlin, 1959)

M. Napoli: *Il Museo di Paestum* (Naples, 1969)

E. Greco and D. Theodorescu: *Poseidonia–Paestum*, i: *La 'Curia'* (Rome, 1980); ii: *L'agora* (Rome, 1983)

J. de Waele: 'Der Entwurf der dorischen Tempel von Paestum', *Archäol. Anz.* (1980), pp. 367–400

M. Bertarelli Sestieri: 'Nuove ricerche sull'Ipogeo di Paestum', *Mél. Archéol. & Hist.: Ecole Fr. Rome*, xcvii/2 (1985), pp. 647–91

A. D. Trendall: *The Red-figured Vases of Paestum* (London, 1987)

Poseidonia–Paestum: Atti del ventisettesimo Convegno di studi sulla Magna Grecia: Taranto–Paestum, 1987

J. G. Pedley: *Paestum, Greeks and Romans in Southern Italy* (New York, 1990)

J. G. Pedley, M. Torelli and T. V. Buttrey: *The Sanctuary of Santa Venera at Paestum* (Rome, 1993–)

M. Cipriani: *The Lucanians in Paestum* (Paestum, 1996)

E. Greco and others: *Archaeological and Historical Guide to the Excavations, the Museum and the Antiquities of Poseidonia Paestum* (Taranto, 1996)

E. Greco and F. Longo: *Paestum: Scavi, studi, ricerche: Bilancio di un decennio: 1988–1998* (Paestum, 2000)

R. A. Ammerman: *The Sanctuary of Santa Venera at Paestum II: The Votive Terracottas* (Ann Arbor, 2002)

E. De Carolis: *Paestum: A Reasoned Archaeological Itinerary* (Torre del Greco, 2002)

M. Skele: *The Poseidonian Chora: Archaic Greeks in the Italic Hinterland* (Oxford, 2002)

Paestum ad Aquileia (exh. cat. by M. Buora and M. Cipriani; Aquileia, Museo civico del Patriarcato, 2003)

H. W. Horsnaes: 'Romanization at Paestum in the 3rd *c.* BC: A Note on the Chronology of the Paistano Coins and the Interpretation of the Wall-paintings from the Spinazzo Cemetery', *J. Roman Archaeol.*, xvii (2004), pp. 305–11

A. Pontrandolfo Greco, A. Rouveret and M. Cipriani: *The Painted Tombs of Paestum* (Salerno, 2004)

Painting. Pigment applied to a relatively flat, smooth surface to create an ornamental effect or to depict a scene (figural, landscape or still-life). This article discusses wall paintings and panel paintings, for information on vase paintings *see* POTTERY.

See also ENCAUSTIC PAINTING, GENRE *and* LANDSCAPE PAINTING.

I. Minoan. II. Cycladic. III. Helladic. IV. Greek. V. Etruscan. VI. Roman.

I. Minoan.

The largest number of extant Minoan wall paintings and reliefs comes from the palace at KNOSSOS, the main administrative and religious centre on Crete. Wall paintings adorned the rich town houses around the palace and important villas on Crete, but surprisingly little has been found in the other Cretan palaces. Poorer houses in Knossos, provincial towns and the country had no pictorial paintings, only striped bands or spiral friezes.

The earliest pictorial wall paintings date from Middle Minoan (MM) IIIA, walls having previously been painted monochrome white or red or with simple bands or patterns. While it is difficult to date Minoan painting precisely—paintings remain on walls long after their execution, so that the destruction or abandonment of a building provides only a *terminus ad quem*, and the contexts themselves are often not secure—the paintings fall roughly into two periods: MM IIIA to Late Minoan (LM) IB throughout the island, and LM II to LM IIIA at Knossos and AYIA TRIADA. Some themes (griffins, bulls) continued in both periods; others disappeared in the later period (nature), while new ones emerged (processions, libation, chariots, soldiers, shields).

When excavated, Minoan paintings are found in small fragments, fallen from the walls and usually thrown with collapsed floors from upper storeys to basements. In time, paints flake, plaster is pulverized, and many of the fragments are irretrievable. In the early years of Minoan archaeology, at the beginning of the 20th century, the fragments were overzealously restored, and much of what is on exhibition in the Herakleion Archaeological Museum on Crete is modern reconstruction into which the original fragments have been fitted. Only the Theran paintings permit full-scale restoration, owing to their excellent state of preservation (*see* §II below *and* THERA, §1). Otherwise, reconstructions are today more likely to occur on paper.

1. Materials and techniques. 2. Subject-matter.

1. Materials and techniques. Dispute surrounds the issue of whether the technique of Minoan wall painting was true *buon fresco* (painting directly onto wet plaster) or *fresco secco* (painting onto dried plaster). The uncertainty may arise because a mixed technique was employed, guidelines and background washes being applied to the wet plaster, details to dry plaster. The term 'fresco' is traditionally used in naming (e.g. miniature frescoes, *Procession* fresco), but the term 'wall painting' is more neutral.

Lime plaster was applied to the walls onto a backing plaster of mud, and the borders and overall design were planned while it was wet. Taut string was pressed into the plaster to mark the border bands; these string lines were also used for alignment of features, such as architecture or complex patterns on garments. Dividers or compasses were used for rosettes. A monochrome wash was applied to the wall, reserving spaces for the figures. At the same time the border bands were coloured. Preliminary sketches were then made in red or yellow. In painting, each colour was applied separately and the details—hair, eyes, outlines, dress patterns—applied last. Finally the surface was polished.

The colours used were red (haematite) and yellow ochre, from natural iron oxides; black, from carbonaceous shale; white, from calcined lime; and blue, from a manufactured frit coloured by copper–calcium silicate imported from Egypt or from the mineral glaucophane (these were expensive, so blue was used sparingly outside Knossos). Green was made by mixing yellow and blue. Opaque or water-diluted paint was applied mainly with the brush, though sponges were occasionally used to dab it on to the wall. White impasto was sometimes applied in dots. In the earlier paintings, backgrounds may be white or red or a combination of both. Later, blue and yellow were favoured at Knossos and Ayia Triada. Sometimes the background was divided into wavy vertical or horizontal zones of colour.

Some MM IIIA–LM IB paintings were executed in relief, either built up in a single layer (low relief) or with added layers of plaster supported by wooden pegs (high relief, used especially for anatomy). Flat and relief techniques can appear together in a single painting (e.g. *Jewel* fresco from Knossos, now destr.). Occasionally the in cavetto technique (reverse of relief) was employed, especially for floors: areas of plaster were cut out and filled with thick paint or another layer of painted plaster.

Paintings usually decorated the upper storeys of buildings, though at Knossos large-scale processional figures were painted along the ground-floor corridors. Paintings either covered the whole wall, were applied to panels or formed a broad frieze with a wide dado or a continuous narrow frieze set at eye-level or above the lintel (see colour pl. 2:I, fig. 2). Border bands defined the upper and lower limits of the painting. Dados often imitate variegated gypsum veneer, others imitate wood. Ceilings painted with spirals and rosette filling motifs were favoured at Knossos. Some floors were painted red, while others were stone-flagged with red-painted stucco in the interstices; a few had in cavetto patterns, and one from a Knossos town house (Royal Road) imitates an animal skin. Floor paintings from Knossos and Ayia Triada feature dolphins and small fish in seascapes.

Some representational conventions are similar to those of Egyptian painting, but Minoan painting is freer, more rhythmic and less hierarchic. Men are painted red, women white. Figures are shown with heads in profile, and their bodies are defined in outline, sometimes with black lines indicating leg muscles (e.g. *Toreador* frescoes; see fig. 1 below). In the Miniature frescoes, the crowds are drawn in a lively shorthand technique, without detail. In landscape scenes, rocks descend as well as rise, like stalactites and stalagmites, and the rockwork is variegated, like the interiors of cut stone. Plants are painted from observation and imagination, sometimes resulting in artistic hybridization.

2. Subject-matter. Minoan wall painting is characterized by a vivid sense of life and an empathy with the natural world. Plants and animals abound, a reflection of the world of the nature goddess, who herself appears life-size in paintings from town and country houses. In the palace of Knossos, a wider variety of subjects was depicted but still within a defined range: processions, cult scenes, bull-sports, festivals, protective griffins. Life expressed through the paintings is without war, old age or daily labour. It is an idealized world filled with joyful observation of the natural environment and youthful celebration through ritual.

(i) The natural world. (ii) Nature cult and the female figure. (iii) Miniatures. (iv) Bull-sports. (v) Griffins. (vi) Processions and palatial cult scenes. (vii) Martial themes. (viii) Programmes.

(i) The natural world. The earliest Minoan paintings (MM IIIA) consist of spirals, bands, foliate bands, lattice, chequers and imitation stone and woodwork. During the same period, the first representational paintings, from town houses by the Royal Road at Knossos, draw their inspiration from the rich plant life of Crete, depicting reeds, myrtle, grass, lilies or vetch.

After MM IIIA until LM IB nature scenes predominate in the houses and country villas. Plants are the most popular subject, with examples (sometimes difficult to identify owing to artistic hybridization) from the Knossos town houses (Royal Road, Hogarth's houses, Savakis's Bothros, Unexplored Mansion), nearby Amnisos, Archanes, a villa at Tylissos and the palaces of Knossos and Phaistos. The most commonly depicted are white (madonna) lilies, a flower shown by the iconography of seals and later Aegean wall paintings to have been a cult plant and an offering to the deity. Paintings of white and red lilies also came from the Cycladic islands of Thera and Melos (*see* §II below) and the Minoan settlement of Ialysos on Rhodes. At Amnisos, two panels of white lilies and one of iris and reeds were found in a room with a painted offering table. Here nature is cultivated: the iris and reeds rise from a built, stepped base, and the lilies stand against an architectonic background. The offering table shows that the room was a shrine.

Animals and birds in a landscape are the subject of paintings in some of the Knossos town houses. From the South-east House, a fragment shows mice among sedges; lilies and rocks were associated. A bird ('swallow'), reeds, pebbles and a water-pool came from the South House. At the Caravanserai, a building assumed to have been used to accommodate visitors, a narrow frieze of partridges ran along the top of a wall of one of the rooms. The partridges stand on a rocky terrain, delineated by wavy lines and interspersed with variegated rocks. Tall, leafy plants stand between the birds, and the background is part white, part blue. On a bush or small tree sits a hoopoe. The landscape is stylized but evocative and the birds stately and still.

A magnificent frieze of birds and monkeys was found in the House of the Frescoes (Herakleion, Archaeol. Mus.). The frieze ran continuously around three walls. The background is part red, part white. Veined rocks in blue, red and yellow rise sinuously into the picture leaving reserved areas for the animal action and the rich plant life of spring or early summer: rock rose, vetch, crocus, honeysuckle, myrtle, mallow, ivy, dwarf iris, lily. Waterfalls gush down past grey rocks, and a stream meanders through the painting, reeds and papyrus following its course. Doves, painted blue with pink dots circling their necks, fly with outstretched wings or perch on rocks. The monkeys, blue with distinctive facial markings, scramble among the rocks and plants, apparently looking for birds' eggs in the summarily depicted nests. One holds an egg to its mouth. Monkeys may have been imported to Crete as exotic park animals from East Africa via Egypt. Fragments of an associated painting show two wild Cretan goats (agrimi), an olive tree, crocuses and undulating bands.

The *Saffron Gatherer* fresco was found north-west of the Central Court at the palace of Knossos (area of the Early Keep). The frieze had at least two blue monkeys in a rocky landscape with crocuses. The head of the best-preserved monkey is missing from the fragments, and when the painting was discovered the convention of a blue figure was misunderstood, so it was reconstructed as a boy (it remains in this form; Herakleion, Archaeol. Mus.). It is now known that blue is the conventional colour for the depiction of monkeys, and the figure has been reconstructed correctly on paper. The background is red. White crocuses appear as large single heads with prominent stamens growing from the tips of rocks that rise from the bottom of the painting and fall from the top, framing the monkey in the central field of the picture. The monkey strides forward, bending at the waist to place crocuses into pots resting on the rocks. Instead of being represented as a creature roaming in a natural landscape, as seen in the House of the Frescoes, the monkey is anthropomorphized in a mythic role associated with the crocus. This role is further developed in the paintings from Thera; for example, in the *Saffron* (or *Crocus*) *Gatherers* fresco the flowers are collected by young girls and offered by a blue monkey to a seated nature goddess.

(ii) Nature cult and the female figure. A goddess of nature among plants is the most prevalent theme of wall paintings in Minoan villas. Most of the figures are fragmentary, their identification circumstantial. In a town house at Palaikastro a woman's arm in relief was found associated with a crocus fragment. Other fragmentary female figures represented with plants occurred in villas at Prasa and Epano Zakros and at the palace of Knossos. A miniature fragment with birds and reeds from a house at Katsamba, the harbour town of Knossos, has been identified as belonging to the girdle or skirt of a goddess. Relief paintings of seated women from the offshore island of PSEIRA presumably belong to the same cycle of goddess figures, while at the villa of Nirou Chani a painting of a sacral knot (a feature of priestly robes, cf. the figure of *La Parisienne* from Knossos; see fig. 2 below) may have been a symbol of the goddess. Garlands, found in a painting in a house at Knossos, may have been sacred emblems of the Minoan gods or goddesses and perhaps symbolize those worn in ritual dances and processions. They were found in association with fragments of female figures (skirts), a built structure and landscape.

The only unequivocal cult scenes from Crete in which female figures are set within a true landscape are the related paintings covering three walls of Room 14 at the villa (or summer palace) of Ayia Triada. On one wall was a nature scene with wild cats stalking birds and with two running deer, set in a rocky landscape with ivy, myrtle, papyrus and other plants (cf. the elements of the landscape miniature frieze from Thera; *see* §II, 1(i) below). On another, a female figure kneels among crocuses and lilies, the two main plants of the Minoan cult. On a narrower wall between these two stood the goddess (or priestess) in a flounced skirt, with a built shrine behind her. Here the two main themes of wall paintings in Minoan houses—the natural world and a female priestess or deity associated with plants—come together, the cult scene providing evidence of their religious function.

In the palace of Knossos, large-scale female figures occur in a number of fragmentary compositions. Women wearing richly decorated textiles have been termed the *Ladies in Blue* and the *Ladies in Red.* Their open bodices expose their breasts, and they are adorned with multiple necklaces. One fragment shows a hand fingering a necklace, recalling the *Jewel* fresco relief, in which a male hand places a necklace on a female, perhaps in a robing ceremony. A fragment of a woman found near the Queen's Megaron was dubbed the *Dancing Lady*, from her flowing locks and outstretched arm; she has since been interpreted as holding out a staff in a reverential gesture.

(iii) Miniatures. In Minoan art, miniature painting is the term applied to narrow painted friezes that ran along the tops of walls and depicted small-scale figures in public festivals. These are action pictures, with a large number of figures accommodated in a small space. They are known from the palace of Knossos and a villa at Tylissos, as well as from the islands of Thera and KEA (*see* §II, 1(ii), 2 and 3 below).

The miniature friezes at Knossos came from a small room off the north-west side of the Central Court and probably ran around three of the walls. (A spiral-relief ceiling came from the same area and would have completed the decoration of the room, which was no doubt a shrine.) Two friezes have been reconstructed from the extant fragments. In the *Shrine* frieze, spectators are crowded into areas around a central tripartite shrine. Next to it are seated women in flounced skirts, engaged in lively conversation, painted against a white background. To the sides, more women stand on stepped platforms with pillars. Crowds of male spectators appear above and below. Only their heads are visible, painted against a red background in shorthand strokes of black, with white dots for eyes and necklaces. The tripartite shrine has columns supporting the roofs, on which are rows of horns of consecration. Both are features of Minoan architecture, the latter being imitation bulls' horns of stone or stucco, used to designate an area as sacred. An actual tripartite shrine existed on the west side of the Central Court and would have been visible from the room with the miniatures. Presumably the spectators are watching an event taking place in the Central Court, conceivably the bull-sports. In the *Sacred Grove and Dance* frieze, crowds of male and female spectators watch a dance in an outdoor area with pathways and olive trees. Some men in loincloths stand in lines; those at the top (i.e. back) wave their arms. A ritual dance is performed by women in flounced skirts moving from left to right, arms held high. The location has been identified as either the West Court or the Theatral Area at Knossos.

Two fragments found in the North-west Fresco Heap show women in architectural frames—one of windows, one a balustrade—that should be related to the main scenes. Other fragments on a slightly larger scale and by a different hand were found in the Thirteenth Magazine. They show a miniature shrine, male spectators and the head of a bull, suggesting a bull-leaping scene.

Several fragments from the palace have miniature designs (bird, griffin, sphinx, bucranium, flutes), as do some from houses near Knossos (plant designs from Knossos town, Prasa, Katsamba), but these probably represent clothing patterns belonging to large-scale figures. A miniature frieze decorated a room of a villa at Tylissos. The extant fragments show a building, a tree, and men and women moving from right to left. The men, in loincloths, carry poles with large pots slung over them. The women may have been dancing, as at Knossos. One fragment shows male spectators facing to the right. The condition is fragmentary, but enough remains to suggest an outdoor festival similar to those shown in the miniatures of Knossos and the islands.

(iv) Bull-sports. The theme of bull-leaping has a long history in the Aegean; it appears on other media (seals, ivory, metal, clay and in miniature painting on a crystal plaque) as well as in Mycenaean painting. In Minoan painting the theme reflects an important event of ritual competition, which took place in the palatial court(s) at Knossos. Depictions of bulls and bull-sports were thus restricted to Knossos, where they were extremely popular. The earliest depictions in relief date from MM IIIB–LM IA. The animals' heavy bodies and the bull-leapers' sinuous musculature were ideal for relief modelling. A scene in relief of a charging bull, fragments of bull-leapers, an olive tree, myrtle and rocks were found in the North Entrance area at Knossos; a bull above a dado was found *in situ* at the West Entrance, and there were also earlier versions. Thus two of the main entrances, from the Royal Road and the West Court, greeted the visitor to the palace with an image of a bull. From the Central Court, the antechamber to the Throne Room was also decorated with a bull, found *in situ* above a stone bench. Other fragments of bulls were found in the House of the Sacrificed Oxen (relief, flung from the south-east angle of the palace), the North-west Treasury (bull and tree) and the Royal Road, while the theme of bull-leaping is reflected in fragments from the Residential Quarters (bull with plant, associated with miniature female bull-leapers) and in the Thirteenth Magazine (miniature, associated with a shrine and spectators). In high reliefs associated with a presumed Great East Hall, fragments of boxers, (?)wrestlers and acrobats were found along with relief fragments of bulls.

The best-known depictions of the sport are the series of *Toreador* frescoes from the Court of the Stone Spout. Fragments of five panels were found, one of which has been restored (see fig. 1). Each had three figures, male and female, wearing the same loincloths but distinguished by colour. One holds the bull's horns, one vaults over the back and one stands at the back either waiting to catch the leaper or having landed after vaulting (three participants or three stages in the sport). The bulls have dappled hide and facial-hair markings. Backgrounds are blue or yellow (indicating a later date, probably LM II), and the friezes are bordered by imitation variegated stone, like rows of cut pebbles, simulating stone dados. Unusually (since Minoan paintings generally show an ideal world) a bull-leaping accident is shown in a fragment from the same area.

(v) Griffins. Griffins—mythical creatures, half lion, half bird, which frequently had a guardian role in Aegean iconography—were a common theme at Knossos. A relief fresco shows griffins tied to a pillar, an abbreviation for a shrine. The Throne Room at Knossos was

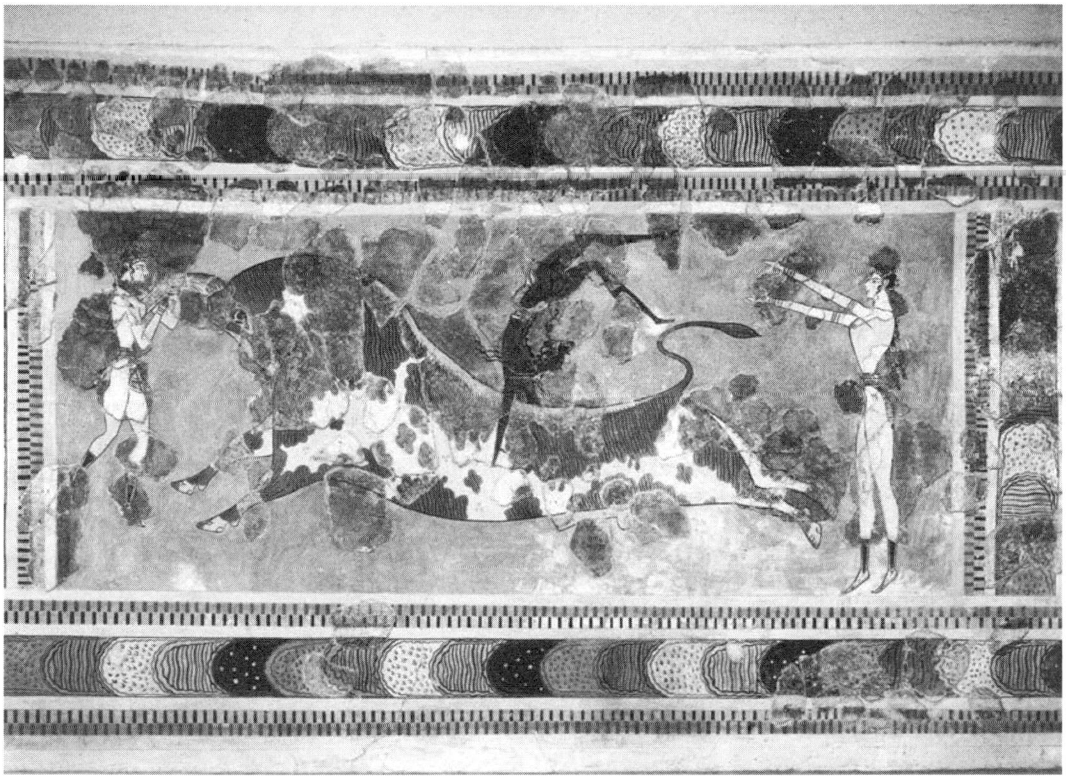

1. Minoan wall painting depicting *Bull-leapers*, from the Toreador frescoes, Court of the Stone Spout, palace of Knossos, late Late Minoan II or early Late Minoan III (Herakleion, Archaeological Museum)

painted with heraldic griffins in a setting of papyrus and palm against a wavy (riverine) background, resting on an imitation marble dado above a row of stone benches. On the north wall, the seated griffins appear to have flanked the throne, as though guarding its occupant, who, based on comparison with scenes of heraldic griffins on seals, may have been a priestess, perhaps enacting an epiphany of the goddess. On the west wall, griffins faced the door to the 'inner shrine'. The theme recurs in the Mycenaean throne-room at PYLOS.

(vi) Processions and palatial cult scenes. Leading along the corridor from the West Entrance into the palace of Knossos was the *Procession* fresco. It was still standing on the walls at the time of the final destruction of the palace and was painted by Cretan artists during the Mycenaean occupation (LM II–IIIA). A row of feet was found *in situ*. The procession of life-size figures, mainly male, walks towards the interior of the palace, bearing offerings. At the front of the reconstructed section is a female figure, the priestess or epiphany of the goddess, in front of whom more men walk backwards in reverence. The procession continued from the long corridor up the main staircase to the upper storey. Only one figure, the *Cupbearer*, is well preserved. Fallen from the west wall of the South Propylaion, he wears a patterned Mycenaean kilt and jewellery and carries a funnel shaped vessel used for libations. Here the figures may have been painted in registers, as in contemporary Egyptian painting. Hundreds of figures must have been painted on the walls of the long corridor and the South Propylon at the end of it. A comparable procession, surviving only in fragments haphazardly thrown out, has been attributed to the Grand Staircase on the east side of the palace.

From the passageway on the south side of the palace came the *Priest-King* or *Lily Prince* relief fresco. The painting survives in three pieces: a torso wearing a lily necklace, a leg and a feathered crown of lilies. The pieces have been variously interpreted as male (from the anatomy) or female (from the colour), as a priest-king leading a griffin, a parading bull-leaper leading a bull prior to the games, a boxer or a god holding a staff. The pieces are reconstructed in the Herakleion Museum as a single figure facing left and wearing a feathered crown; but in a subsequent reconstruction (Niemeier, 1987, p. 95), one figure stands to the right holding a staff (torso), flanked by a male votary (leg), with either a priestess or a sphinx wearing the lily crown.

The only paintings on Crete outside Knossos at this time (*c.* 1400 BC) also depict processions. These come from a shrine within the late (LM IIIA) settlement at Ayia Triada. All are cult scenes. In one, a woman leads deer to an altar. A fragment of a man in a long robe may have belonged to the same composition. Rosettes form a lower frame to the picture. In another, a line of dancing women approaches a sanctuary. These paintings were associated with what is known as the Marine Floor.

Fragments of another painting found just outside the village may have decorated a tomb. On a blue background with rosette border is depicted a procession of male and female figures carrying vessels or playing musical instruments (the man at the front of the procession plays a lyre). Remarkably similar scenes were painted on the sides of a sarcophagus found in a tomb nearby (LM IIIA; Herakleion, Archaeol. Mus.). On one of the long sides, women carrying similar vessels pour libations between two pillars, and behind them a man plays a lyre, while three other men approach a tomb or shrine bearing funerary offerings (two calves and a boat). Receiving the offerings before the tomb is a figure presumably representing the deceased. On the other long side, a procession of women approaches a shrine, a bull has been trussed up for sacrifice and a man plays the double flute. Other scenes pertaining to the funerary cult were painted on the short sides: women ride chariots, one drawn by horses, the other by griffins. The pictures are bordered by rosettes, as in the wall paintings, and the same painter seems to have been at work.

A cult scene from Knossos, known as the *Camp Stool* fresco, fell from an upper-storey hall on the north-west side of the palace. The figures are arranged in two, perhaps four, registers divided by horizontal bands, with a background of blue and yellow vertical divisions. Seated on folding stools are male figures in long robes. They face one another, exchanging a cup (Mycenaean kylix) or chalice. A female figure, known by her curls, retroussé nose and red lips as *La Parisienne* (see fig. 2), wears a sacral knot at her shoulder suggesting that she is a goddess or priestess.

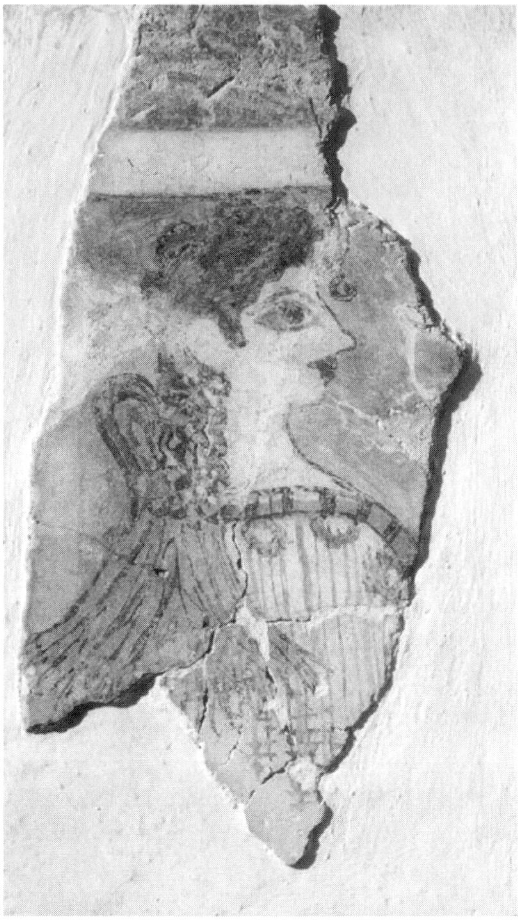

2. Minoan wall painting of *La Parisienne*, fragment of a priestess, from the Camp Stool fresco, palace of Knossos, Late Minoan IIIA:2 (Herakleion, Archaeological Museum)

The so-called *Palanquin* fresco, depicting a male figure seated in a structure (previously thought to be a sedan chair but now interpreted as a shrine), has been associated with pieces of a *Chariot* fresco found nearby (Cameron, *Archäol. Anz.*, 1967). The latter show a man standing in a dual chariot led by horses and followed by a bull, presumably intended for sacrifice. Chariots became a common theme of Mycenaean art.

(vii) Martial themes. Fragments of a painting known as the *Captain of the Blacks* were found near the House of the Frescoes. On an alternating blue and yellow background, a male (red) figure wearing a kilt and a horned cap and carrying two spears leads foreign soldiers, black-skinned and also in kilt and cap. This is the only instance of a martial theme in Cretan painting, but life-size paintings of oxhide figure-of-eight shields, restored in the Hall of the Colonnades adjacent to the Grand Staircase, symbolically reflect the militaristic emphasis of much Mycenaean art and recur in mainland palaces.

(viii) Programmes. According to Cameron (1984, 'The "Palatial" Thematic System…'), a thematic thread, or programme, ran through all the wall paintings of the palace at Knossos. The paintings were thought by him to represent different stages of a major annual religious festival in celebration of the Minoan goddess: procession and offerings escorting a goddess-impersonator into the palace (*Procession* fresco), libations (*Camp Stool*) and adornment (*Jewel* fresco), epiphany of the goddess through a priestess (*Sacred Dance*), gathering of the people for the spectacle (*Triparte Shrine, Ladies in Blue*), ritual games (bull-sports), seating of the goddess-impersonator in the cult room (Throne Room). Although the surviving paintings are of differing dates, the supposition is that a thematic unity was retained on the walls of the palace at any one time. The fragmentary nature of the surviving material has made wall painting programmes difficult to reconstruct, but the spectacular

discoveries on Thera since the late 1960s have provided many new insights into the religious themes of Aegean wall painting.

General Bibliography

N. Heaton: 'Minoan Lime Plaster and Fresco Painting', *RIBA J.*, xviii (1911), pp. 697–710

P. Duell and R. J. Gettens: 'A Review of the Problem of Aegean Wall Painting', *Tech. Stud.* (1942), pp. 179–223

H. A. Groenwegen-Frankfort: *Arrest and Movement* (London, 1951)

W. Schierung: 'Steine und Malerei in der minoischen Kunst', *Jb. Dt. Archäol. Inst.*, lxxv (1960), pp. 17–36

W. Schierung: 'Die Naturanschauung in der altkretischen Kunst', *Ant. Kst*, ix (1965), pp. 3–12

W. S. Smith: *Interconnections in the Ancient Near East* (New Haven and London, 1965)

M. A. S. Cameron: 'New Restorations of Minoan Frescoes from Knossos', *Bull. Inst. Class. Stud. U. London*, xvii (1970), pp. 163–6

M. A. S. Cameron: 'On Theoretical Principles in Aegean Bronze Age Mural Restoration', *Temple University Aegean Symposium*, i (1976), pp. 20–41

B. Kaiser: *Untersuchungen zum minoischen Relief* (Bonn, 1976)

E. S. Hirsch: *Painted Decoration of the Floors of Bronze Age Structures on Crete and the Greek Mainland*, Stud. Medit. Archaeol., lii (Göteborg, 1977)

J. Schafer: 'Zur kunstgeschichtlichen Interpretation altägäischer Wandmalerei', *Jb. Dt. Archäol. Inst.*, xcii (1977), pp. 1–23

M. A. S. Cameron: 'Theoretical Interrelations among Theran, Cretan and Mainland Frescoes', *Thera and the Aegean World*, ed. C. Doumas, i (London, 1978), pp. 579–92

S. Hood: *The Arts in Prehistoric Greece*, Pelican Hist. A. (Harmondsworth, 1978), pp. 48–77

E. S. Hirsch: 'Another Look at Minoan and Mycenaean Interrelationships in Floor Decoration', *Amer. J. Archaeol.*, lxxxiv (1980), pp. 453–62

J. Coulomb: 'Les Boxeurs minoens', *Bull. Corr. Hell.*, cv (1981), pp. 27–40

S. A. Immerwahr: 'The People in the Frescoes', *Minoan Society: Proceedings of the Cambridge Colloquium: Cambridge, 1981*

S. Peterson: *Wall Paintings in the Aegean Bronze Age: The Procession Frescoes* (diss., Minneapolis, U. MN, 1981)

R. Hägg: 'Iconographical Programs in Minoan Palaces and Villas', *L'Iconographie minoenne: Actes de la Table Ronde Athènes*, ed. P. Darque and J. C. Poursat, *Bull. Corr. Hell.*, suppl. xi (1985), pp. 209–17

S. A. Immerwahr: 'A Possible Influence of Egyptian Art in the Creation of Minoan Wall Painting', *L'Iconographie minoenne: Actes de la Table Ronde Athènes*, ed. P. Darque and J. C. Poursat, *Bull. Corr. Hell.*, suppl. xi (1985), pp. 41–50

S. A. Immerwahr: *Aegean Painting in the Bronze Age* (Pennsylvania and London, 1990)

L. Morgan, ed.: *Aegean Wall Painting: A Tribute to Mark Cameron* (London, 2005)

Knossos

T. Fyfe: 'Painted Plaster Decoration at Knossos with Special Reference to the Architectural Schemes', *RIBA J.*, x (1902–3), pp. 107–31

N. Heaton: 'The Mural Paintings of Knossos: An Investigation into the Method of their Production', *J. Royal Soc. A.*, lviii (1910), pp. 206–12

H. Reusch: 'Zum Wandschmuck des Thronsaales in Knossos', *Minoica: Festschrift Johannes Sundwall*, ed. E. Grumach (Berlin, 1958), pp. 334–58

M. A. S. Cameron: 'An Addition to "La Parisienne"', *Kritika Chron.* (1964), pp. 38–53

M. A. S. Cameron: 'Notes on Some New Joins and Additions to Well-known Frescoes from Knossos', *Europa: Studien zur Geschichte und Epigraphik der frühen Aegaeis* (Berlin, 1967), pp. 45–74

M. A. S. Cameron: 'Unpublished Fresco Fragments of a Chariot Composition from Knossos', *Archäol. Anz.*, iii (1967), pp. 330–44

M. A. S. Cameron and S. Hood: *Catalogue of Plates in Sir Arthur Evans' Knossos Fresco Atlas* (London, 1967)

M. A. S. Cameron: 'Unpublished Paintings from the "House of Frescoes" at Knossos', *Annu. Brit. Sch. Athens*, lxiii (1968), pp. 1–31

M. A. S. Cameron: '"The Lady in Red": A Complementary Figure to the "Ladies in Blue"', *Archaeology*, xxiv (1971), pp. 35–43

M. A. S. Cameron: 'Savakis's Bothros: A Minor Sounding at Knossos', *Annu. Brit. Sch. Athens*, lxxi (1976), pp. 1–13

C. W. Hawke-Smith: 'The Knossos Frescoes: A Revised Chronology', *Annu. Brit. Sch. Athens*, lxxi (1976), pp. 65–76

M. A. S. Cameron and R. E. Jones: 'Scientific Analyses of Minoan Fresco Samples from Knossos', *Annu. Brit. Sch. Athens*, lxxii (1977), pp. 121–84

J. Coulomb: 'Le Prince aux lis de Knossos reconsidéré', *Bull. Corr. Hell.*, ciii (1979), pp. 29–50

C. Boulotis: 'Nochmals zum Prozessionsfresko von Knossos: Palast und Darbringung von Prestige-Objekten', *The Function of the Minoan Palaces: Proceedings of the Fourth International Symposium at the Swedish Institute in Athens. Athens, 10–16 June 1984*, pp. 145–56

M. A. S. Cameron: 'The Frescoes', *The Minoan Unexplored Mansion at Knossos*, ed. M. R. Popham (Oxford, 1984), pp. 127–50

M. A. S. Cameron: 'The "Palatial" Thematic System in the Knossos Murals: Last Notes on Knossos Frescoes', *The Function of the Minoan Palaces: Proceedings of the Fourth International Symposium at the Swedish Institute in Athens: Athens, 10–16 June 1984*, pp. 321–8 [résumé by N. Marinatos]

E. Davis: 'The Knossos Miniature Frescoes and the Function of the Central Courts', *The Function of the Minoan Palaces: Proceedings of the Fourth International Symposium at the Swedish Institute in Athens: Athens, 10–16 June 1984*, pp. 157–61

W.-D. Niemeier: 'On the Function of the "Throne Room" in the Palace at Knossos', *The Function of the Minoan Palaces: Proceedings of the Fourth International Symposium at the Swedish Institute in Athens: Athens, 10–16 June 1984*, pp. 163–8

P. M. Warren: 'The Fresco of the Garlands from Knossos', *L'Iconographie minoenne: Actes de la Table Ronde Athènes*, ed. P. Darque and J. C. Poursat, *Bull. Corr. Hell.*, suppl. xi (Paris, 1985), pp. 41–50

R. B. Koehl: 'The Reconstruction of a Marine Style Floor from the Palace at Knossos', *Amer. J. Archaeol.*, xc (1986), pp. 406–17

W.-D. Niemeier: 'The "Priest King" Fresco from Knossos: A New Reconstruction and Interpretation', *Problems in Greek*

Prehistory: Papers Presented at the Centenary Conference of the British School of Archaeology at Athens: Athens, April 1986, pp. 235–44

W.-D. Niemeier: 'Zur Deutung des "Thronraumes" im Palast von Knossos', *Mitt. Dt. Archäol. Inst.: Athen. Abt.*, ci (1986), pp. 63–95

W.-D. Niemeier: 'Das Stuckrelief des "Prinzen mit der Federkrone" aus Knossos und minoische Götterdarstellungen', *Mitt. Dt. Archäol. Inst.: Athen. Abt.*, cii (1987), pp. 65–98

Elsewhere

M. C. Shaw: 'The Miniature Frescoes of Tylissos Reconsidered', *Archäol. Anz.*, lxxxvii (1972), pp. 171–88

C. R. Long: *The Ayia Triadha Sarcophagus: A Study of Late Minoan and Mycenaean Funerary Practices and Beliefs*, Stud. Medit. Archaeol., xli (Göteborg, 1974)

M. A. S. Cameron and R. E. Jones: 'A Note on the Identification of Fresco Material from the British Campaigns at Palaikastro, 1902–1906', *Annu. Brit. Sch. Athens*, lxi (1976), pp. 15–19

M. C. Shaw: 'A Minoan Fresco from Katsamba', *Amer. J. Archaeol.*, lxxxii (1978), pp. 27–34

II. Cycladic.

Cycladic painting had a brief but rich life covering a few decades at the beginning of the Late Bronze Age. Major excavations on the three Cycladic islands of THERA, MELOS and KEA have revealed towns with wall paintings that clearly owe much to Minoan painting on Crete yet have distinctively local characteristics. Features that set Cycladic painting somewhat apart from that of Minoan Crete include complexes of rooms with related sequences of paintings, miniature paintings and the juxtaposition between cult activity and the natural world, especially in themes related to the sea and to presentation and robing ceremonies. Although Cycladic paintings share these features, they were clearly painted by different artists. The painters were apparently local rather than specialized travelling artists. Yet a common tradition (perhaps in some cases a shared apprenticeship) and a free exchange of ideas led to the development of characteristically Cycladic formats and themes.

S. Hood: *The Arts in Prehistoric Greece*, Pelican Hist. A. (Harmondsworth, 1978)

S. A. Immerwahr: *Aegean Painting in the Bronze Age* (Pennsylvania and London, 1990)

1. Thera. 2. Melos. 3. Kea.

1. THERA. The paintings from Akrotiri on Thera (Thera, Archaeol. Mus.; on long-term dep. Athens, N. Archaeol. Mus.) are extraordinarily well preserved, having been covered in volcanic ash following the eruption that destroyed the settlement. Like Minoan murals, they decorated the upper storeys of houses and were found fallen in small fragments, but their excellent state of preservation has enabled them to be extensively reconstructed. Akrotiri was a town rich in wall paintings. Every house or house-complex had a painted room, and those known as the West House and Xeste 3 had programmes of paintings covering two or three adjoining rooms. All the paintings date from the latter part of LC I.

(i) Large-scale works. The theme of nature is expressed in the *Spring* fresco (see colour pl. 2:II, fig. 1), a painting that ran continuously around three walls in a small house shrine (Delta 2). Red lilies in bud, opening and in bloom perch on top of multicoloured rock formations reminiscent of the bright volcanic rocks of the island. Swallows fly singly or in pairs between the flowers, some in the process of courtship feeding. Other paintings, such as the *Boxing Boys* (for illustration *see* THERA) and *Antelopes* (see colour pl. 2:II, fig. 2) found in a small room of a shrine complex (Beta 1), seem to draw a comparison between human and animal nature in scenes of confrontation or contest. There pairs of male antelopes were painted on three walls; their posture, with their heads turned, eyes meeting and tails raised, expresses the competitive aggression typical of the species. On the south wall a pair of young boys engage in ritualized play: each has a boxing glove and is naked except for knotted belts and jewellery. From their blue (shaved) heads stream long black locks, a distinctive style indicating status and youth. A frieze of ivy leaves ran continuously above the figures, linking the images of each wall.

In the House of the Ladies, two life-size female figures were represented alongside large papyrus plants, which, like lilies, were associated with cult in Aegean iconography. A mature woman bends forward with her arms outstretched, a garment in one hand, the other touching the sleeve of the second woman. The rest of this figure has not survived, but she has been reconstructed as seated. The scene has been interpreted as depicting a robing ceremony, in which a garment is presented to a priestess or goddess. The same ceremony was apparently represented elsewhere, for instance in Xeste 3 at Akrotiri, where a man in a procession holds an offering of a cloth, and at Phylakopi on Melos (*see* §2 below).

Another common motif in Aegean painting was the blue monkey. A painting at Thera of *Blue Monkeys*, in which they are shown climbing among stylized rocks above a river, appears to be a scene from nature (Beta 6). Its prototype is the *Birds and Monkeys* frieze from Knossos, but while some Minoan paintings give the impression that the monkey was an imported pet roaming in parks, at Thera it seems to have had a different iconographic role. In another, fragmentary painting from Akrotiri blue monkeys are shown worshipping before an outdoor shrine with a sacred papyrus column and horns of consecration. Fragments with human scenes—a woman, a man before a palm—came from the same area (Alpha 1).

Blue monkeys were also clearly associated with cult scenes in the cycle of paintings from Xeste 3. This building is divided into areas for domestic and ritual activity. The entrance leads directly to the cult area, suggesting that it was a public rather than a private shrine. A life-size mural of a man was painted in the anteroom, facing towards the stairway that led upstairs to the cult area. Plants among a rocky landscape flanked the stairs. The cult area was itself split into two levels, linked by a small staircase. Entry was from the south on the lower level. The walls on both levels were covered with near life-size figures. On the lower-level west wall was a procession of young men carrying offerings (a similar scene was discovered in the partly excavated building Xeste 4 nearby), and on the upper-level west wall was a fowling scene of birds among reeds. On the south wall was a procession of women.

The main action, with young women in a rocky landscape with crocuses, took place on the north and east walls. Their hairstyles—blue shaven head with locks, short curly hair or long hair tied at the neck—differentiate them according to age. On the lower-level east wall were three female figures (*Adorants*), one woman holding a necklace, one bending down to her bleeding foot and a young girl draped in a transparent cloth turning to look behind her towards an altar with horns of consecration dripping with blood. On the upper level were the *Saffron Gatherers*: young girls collecting crocuses into baskets. The crocuses were then offered by a blue monkey to a nature goddess seated on a raised platform, with necklaces of ducks and dragonflies and crocuses on her dress and cheek; behind her is a protective griffin. Saffron was probably exported from the island, and economics and religion are linked in these scenes. The theme of blue monkeys is elaborated in a frieze from near the sanctuary entrance: one monkey holds a lyre, another wields a sword at a snake. Monkeys and crocuses were shown together in wall paintings from Crete (for example the *Saffron Gatherers* from Knossos), but here on Thera the mythic association is explicit. The paintings have been interpreted as initiation scenes for girls approaching womanhood, and it has been suggested that such rituals took place within the sanctuary itself.

Although it is not always possible to relate the activities depicted in the paintings at Akrotiri with rituals that could have taken place indoors, there is evidence to suggest that the paintings reflect Cycladic religious beliefs, which must have revolved around the relationship between humans and the natural world. Even apparently pure nature scenes, such as the *Spring* fresco, relate to a specific time of year of crucial importance in the cyclical life of those dependent on their environment.

(ii) Miniatures. A wealth of information on the culture, environment and cosmopolitan outlook of the Theran people is contained in the miniature friezes that ran above the windows and doorways of one of two painted rooms in the West House. Thera was a central port of call in an international trading network, a maritime role that is reflected in the miniature paintings.

In the *Meeting on the Hill* from the north wall, men in Theran priestly robes and Minoan loincloths are gathered on a rocky summit—the first known representation of rituals at Aegean 'peak sanctuaries'. A pastoral scene on the right shows flocks of sheep led by shepherds and women at a well. Akrotiri had a local wool-producing industry, and sheep were an important commodity. The inhabitants were also sailors, traders and fishermen, and their concern with the sea is expressed in the scene below. Warriors (potential raiders) march up the coast, and in the sea is a shipwreck. This scene has been variously interpreted as an invasion and sea battle (though no fighting is shown) or as a reflection of the typical dangers faced by a coastal people. Depicted on the east wall was a *Landscape* frieze, in which a cat chases birds and a griffin pursues a deer in a river landscape, where the wildness of nature is somewhat domesticated by the inclusion of cultivated palms.

On the south wall was the *Ship Procession* frieze (see colour pl. 2:III, fig. 1). There is a town at each end of the frieze, that on the left set in a hilly landscape with trees and a river, the grander, fortified city on the right around a harbour with fishermen and boats. Horns of consecration mark the sanctity of the city wall and the building closest to the sea. Young men walk beneath the wall, one leading a calf for sacrifice. Men run to look-out buildings on top to see the incoming procession of seven large ships, one rowing boat and one sailing ship, as the townsfolk watch from windows and rooftops. In the harbour multicoloured rocks rise from the sea, and dolphins play around the ships, which have been decorated with dress-ship lines, emblems on mast-tops and prows, painted hulls and stern figureheads of lions and griffins. The large ships are paddled, a traditional method used for ceremonial occasions. Elite passengers sit beneath awnings, some dressed in the ceremonial robes worn by the men in the *Meeting on the Hill*. At the stern of each ship is a cabin, a feature derived from Egyptian ceremonial vessels. This cabin is repeated in large-scale paintings that decorate the walls of the adjoining room. Near them was the painting of a *Priestess*, wearing an oriental-style ceremonial robe; her lips and ear are red, and on her blue head is perhaps a snake, cult symbol of the Minoans. She holds a plant (possibly saffron) over an incense burner, presumably an offering in blessing of the ships.

The occasion represented in this miniature cycle has been variously interpreted. The excavator (Spiridon Marinatos, who began work in 1967) postulated an expedition to Libya, and though that destination was largely rejected, others followed his martial emphasis. Since then, study of the ships' features has led scholars to interpret the scene as a nautical festival, more specifically the resumption of the navigation season in May (Doumas, ed., 1878, pp. 629–44; Morgan, 1983, 1988). This suggestion is based on the seasonal element that runs through the paintings. Lilies in pots were painted on the window-jambs of Room 4. Beneath the miniatures on two walls of Room 5 was a panel of a life-size naked fisherman holding mackerel, which is caught in bulk in early summer. Both the new sailing season and the time for moving flocks to the uplands coincide with the beginning of summer, and both sailors and shepherds participate in the north-wall ritual of the *Meeting on the Hill.* Other scholars have proposed different theories for the festival of ships: a victory celebration (N. Marinators, 1984), sacred marriage (Säflund), jubilee (Polinger Foster); while still others have sought to link the images with the origins of epic Greek poetry (Morris, Hardy and Renfrew, eds, pp. 229–36).

S. Marinatos: *Excavations at Thera*, i–vii (Athens, 1968–76)

S. Marinatos: 'Das Schiffsfresko von Akrotiri, Thera', *Seewesen*, ed. D. Gray, *Archeol. Homerica* (Göttingen, 1974), pp. 140–51

H. G. Buchholz: 'Bemerkung zum Schiffsfresko von Thera', *Hellas ewig unsere Liebe: Freundesgabe für Willy Zschietzschmann zu seinem 75. Geburtstag, 15 Februar 1975*, ed. S. Oppermann (Giessen, 1975)

L. Casson: 'Bronze Age Ships: The Evidence of the Thera Wall Paintings', *Int. J. Naut. Archaeol. & Underwtr Explor.*, iv (1975), pp. 1–10

G. C. Gesell: 'The "Town Fresco" of Thera: A Reflection of Cretan Topography', *Pepragmena tou 4 Diethnous Kretologikou Synedrion: Athina, 1976* [Proceedings of the 4th Annual Cretological Conference: Athens, 1976], pp. 297–304

D. L. Page: 'The Miniature Frescoes from Akrotiri, Thera', *Praktika*, li (1976), pp. 135–52

E. Sapouna-Sakellarakis: 'Oi toíchographiés tés Théras se schesé me tén Minóïké Krété [The wall paintings of Thera in relation to Minoan Crete], *Pepragmena tou 4 Diethnous Kretologikou Synedrion: Athina, 1976* [Proceedings of the 4th Annual Cretological Conference: Athens, 1976], ii, pp. 532–8

M. Benzi: 'Gli affreschi dell'ammiraglio a Thera', *Prospettiva*, x (1977), pp. 3–15

S. A. Immerwahr: 'Mycenaeans at Thera: Some Reflections on the Paintings from the West House', *Greece and the Eastern Mediterranean in Ancient History and Prehistory: Studies Presented to Fritz Schachermeyr on the Occasion of his Eightieth Birthday*, ed. K. H. Kinzl (Berlin and New York, 1977), pp. 173–91

C. Doumas, ed.: *Thera and the Aegean World I* (London, 1978), pp. 571–92, 599–604, 617–56

P. Haider: 'Grundsätzliches und Sächliches zur historischen Auswertung des bronzezeitlichen Miniaturfrieses auf Thera', *Klio*, lxi (1979), pp. 285–307

P. M. Warren: 'The Miniature Fresco from the West House at Akrotiri, Thera, and its Aegean Setting', *J. Hell. Stud.*, xcix (1979), pp. 115–29

G. Säflund: 'Cretan and Theran Questions', *Sanctuaries and Cults in the Aegean Bronze Age. Proceedings of the First International Symposium of the Swedish Institute at Athens: Athens, 1980*, pp. 189–208

A. Sakellariou: 'The West House Miniature Frescoes', *Thera and the Aegean World II*, ed. C. Doumas (London, 1980), pp. 147–53

A. B. Knapp: 'The Thera Frescoes and the Question of Aegean Contact with Libya during the Late Bronze Age', *J. Medit. Anthrop. & Archaeol.*, i (1981), pp. 249–79

N. Marinatos: 'Minoan Threskeiocracy on Thera', *The Minoan Thalassocracy: Myth and Reality. Proceedings of the Third International Symposium at the Swedish School at Athens: Athens, 1982*, pp. 167–76

E. Davis: 'The Iconography of the Ship Fresco from Thera', *Ancient Greek Art and Iconography*, ed. W. G. Moon (Wisconsin, 1983), pp. 1–14

C. Doumas: *Thera: Pompeii of the Ancient Aegean* (London, 1983)

N. Marinatos: 'The West House at Akrotiri as a Cult Centre', *Archäol. Anz.*, xcviii (1983), pp. 1–19

L. Morgan: 'Theme in the West House Paintings at Thera', *Archaiol. Ephimeris* (1983), pp. 85–105

N. Marinatos: *Art and Religion in Thera: Reconstructing a Bronze Age Society* (Athens, 1984)

N. Marinatos: 'An Offering of Saffron to the Minoan Goddess of Nature: The Role of the Monkey and the Importance of Saffron', *Gifts to the Gods: Proceedings of the Uppsala Symposium: Uppsala, 1985*, pp. 123–32

N. Marinatos: 'The Function of the Theran Frescoes', *L'Iconographie minoenne: Actes de la table ronde d'Athènes*, ed. P. Darcque and J.-C. Poursat, *Bull. Corr. Hell.*, suppl. 11 (Paris, 1985), pp. 221–32

E. Davis: 'Youth and Age in the Thera Frescoes', *Amer. J. Archaeol.*, xc (1986), pp. 399–406

L. Morgan: *The Miniature Wall Paintings of Thera: A Study in Aegean Culture and Iconography* (Cambridge, 1988)

K. Polinger Foster: 'Snakes and Lions: A New Reading of the West House Frescoes from Thera', *Expedition*, xxx/2 (1988), pp. 10–20

M. B. Hollinshead: 'The Swallows and Artists of Room Delta 2 at Akrotiri, Thera', *Amer. J. Archaeol.*, xciii (1989), pp. 339–54

S. P. Morris: 'A Tale of Two Cities: The Miniature Frescoes from Thera and the Origins of Greek Poetry', *Amer. J. Archaeol.*, xciii (1989), pp. 511–35

D. A. Hardy and C. Renfrew, eds: *Thera and the Aegean World III* (London, 1990), i, pp. 214–36, 252–82, 309–26; iii, pp. 229–36

A. Doumas: *The Wall-paintings of Thera* (Athens, 1992)

The Wall Paintings of Thera: Proceedings of the First International Symposium: Thera, 1997

2. Melos. At Phylakopi on Melos, the walls of the Pillar Crypt shrine complex were decorated with paintings at the beginning of LC II, but little was found elsewhere in the town (all Athens, N. Archaeol. Mus.). Some pieces of plaster were found outside the city walls, where they must have been dumped at the time of the Mycenaean occupation in LC III. Among them was a fragment of a miniature frieze, showing a man's booted leg and the head of a second figure below. The rest of the frieze is lost, but the fragment suggests that each Cycladic settlement at this time had a cycle of miniatures.

From the original excavations (British School at Athens, 1896–9), fragments of narrow friezes of *Flying Fish in a Seascape* were found in the Pillar Crypt. Dabs of blue paint indicate the sea that surrounds the swooping fish, with marine rocks above and below. Found in the same room was a painting of two half life-size women, one seated facing right and holding a blue cloth. She wears a skirt with designs (now faded) of birds among rocks; the head has not survived. Only the upper torso of the other figure survives. She faces left and extends her arms. The presentation of a garment suggests the figures are part of a robing ceremony, like that depicted in the House of the Ladies at Thera. The seated figure who has received the cloth offering should thus be understood as the goddess or priestess. The birds and rocks on her skirt, together with the associated *Flying Fish* frieze, suggest the cult of nature, embracing the domains of air, land and sea. Fragments of white lilies, which often occur as offerings in Aegean iconography, were painted on a red background in the adjacent room. They have no stems or leaves, characteristic of ceramics rather than wall paintings. In the 1970s a stratigraphical sounding in the room immediately to the east was undertaken in order to date the Pillar Crypt paintings. The sounding revealed that a frieze of *Blue Monkeys* had decorated the room with a festoon spiral frieze above or nearby.

T. D. Atkinson and others: *Excavations at Phylakopi in Melos* (London, 1904)

3. KEA. Compositions of large-scale human figures were apparently not favoured at Ayia Irini on Kea; only a few stray pieces were found (House B). The characteristic format of Kean painting (all Kea, Archaeol. Mus.) was the frieze. *Bluebirds* (doves) and *Dolphins*, shown in various poses against a monochromed background and devoid of context, form the subjects of two friezes (Houses A and J). This abstraction of nature contrasts with the vivid landscapes and seascapes of Minoan paintings of the same subjects (*see* §I above), though it was characteristic of Mycenaean painting some 200 years later (*see* §III below). The *Bluebirds* frieze ran around three walls of a room, on the fourth of which, on a larger scale, was a painting of a griffin seated within a shrine. A nearby room was decorated with a 'splash pattern': paint flicked on to the wall to imitate marble.

A miniature frieze ran around three walls of a large room within the fortification wall (North-east Bastion), which was perhaps intended for public religious gatherings or banquets. Less well preserved than the Theran miniatures, this frieze is harder to interpret. The theme is again a festival set by the sea, with two building complexes and many figures, mainly male. Some, dressed in long robes, take part in a procession, and others dance. A hunter carries a flank of deer, and there are fragments of a chariot and horses. By the seashore men bend over large cauldrons. Fragments of large ships and a small paddled boat show that activity continued at sea. A scene of deer hunted by dogs was painted on one of the walls. The landscape in which the human activity is set is richly diverse, with a river, a marsh, a variety of plants and multicoloured rocks. In the adjoining room were large painted panels of plant compositions. Some of these features—chariot, hunter and dogs—appear for the first time in Aegean painting at Kea, recurring as popular components of Mycenaean painting.

K. Coleman: 'Frescoes from Ayia Irini, Keos: Part I', *Hesperia*, xlii (1973), pp. 284–300

K. Abramovitz: 'Frescoes from Ayia Irini, Keos: Parts II–IV', *Hesperia*, xlix (1980), pp. 57–85

III. Helladic.

Little is known of the earliest paintings on the Greek mainland. All that survives is from the late Helladic (LH), or Mycenaean, period.

1. INTRODUCTION. Mycenaean painting was rooted in the traditions and techniques of wall painting in Minoan Crete (*see* §I above). Unfortunately, architectural remains for the LH II period, the time of greatest Minoan influence on the mainland, are largely missing; yet a few fragments—from Mycenae, Tiryns, Argos and Kokla—show that painting did exist in LH II. The majority of surviving paintings, however, date to LH IIIA and especially LH IIIB. With the collapse of the Mycenaean palaces at the end of the Bronze Age, wall painting as an art came to an end in mainland Greece, not to be revived for centuries.

Wall painting was essentially a palatial art. Most extant works come from the major palaces—at MYCENAE, TIRYNS, PYLOS, THEBES, and ORCHOMENOS—with some fragments from centres such as GLA, ARGOS and ASINE. Some private houses (perhaps of palace officials) at Mycenae and Tiryns were painted, as were sanctuary buildings at Mycenae and a few tombs. As on Crete, most Helladic wall paintings were found in small fragments fallen to the ground. The relationship of scenes to one another is thus frequently lost, leaving vignettes whose place in the architectural space is unclear. Many paintings were recovered from dumps, having been stripped from the walls when the artists redecorated. Those paintings that were still on the walls at the time of the final destruction of the palaces are invariably burnt and difficult to read. The best indications of painting programmes are the remains from the cult centre at Mycenae and the final phase at Pylos.

Mycenaean painting of the LH IIIB period is characterized by a tendency towards schematization and a concentration on the human figure. The rich expression of the natural world found in Minoan art is absent. The few indications of landscape are reduced to stylized trees and conventionalized rocks. Animals do not appear in their natural surroundings but are hieratically and solemnly arranged, for example guard ing a throne or in rows. Close relationships in theme and execution suggest that artists travelled between the palaces. Themes were repeated, and in some cases, the similarities of execution suggest the same hand.

2. SUBJECT-MATTER. Spirals, rosettes, griffins and bull-sports continue the Minoan iconographic tradition, but the procession (*see* §(iii) below), a theme that began at Knossos, was transformed into something quintessentially Mycenaean. Divergence from Minoan ideals is also particularly evident in the secular themes of Mycenaean painting: here the male domain of warfare and the hunt predominate (*see* §(v) below), reflecting a heroic society of aristocratic palace lords such as is described in the later Homeric epics.

(i) Abstraction from the natural world. (ii) Bull-sports. (iii) Processions and religious programmes. (iv) Shields. (v) Hunting and warfare.

(i) Abstraction from the natural world. In Mycenaean painting nature takes second place to the human figure. Vestiges of Minoan themes (e.g. the *Bluebird, Nautilus* and *Women and Deer* friezes at Pylos) repeat their motifs but with little variation and minimal context. Floor decoration, such as the squares of dolphins and octopus from Tiryns, take the tendency to abstraction still further. The *Deer* frieze from Tiryns has more variety of pose, but the hides of the animals are schematized with rows of crosses, and the background is an empty blue. At Pylos, griffins and lions take an emblematic stance, flanking the throne or arranged in a frieze.

(ii) Bull-sports. Of the three known Mycenaean examples of bull-leaping, a theme clearly inspired by Minoan prototypes, two are early. The fragments of toreadors and bulls from Mycenae came from a deposit below the Ramp House (LH II/IIIA). The figures are smaller than those in the Minoan *Toreador* paintings at KNOSSOS (see fig. 2 above), also arranged in panels with both male and female participants. Associated with toreadors and bulls at Mycenae were representations of architectural features, including one fragment with women watching from windows, from which hang festoons attached to double axes. These are on a miniature scale (comparable to the *Shrine* frieze from Knossos) and suggest a relationship between sport and audience. A single fragment of a bull-leaper (LH IIIA) was found at Pylos. At Tiryns, in the only later example from the mainland (LH IIIB), the artist has depicted, with an unsure hand, a dappled bull with a vaulting figure. Like the scenes from nature and the miniature frieze, bull-sports died out as a theme and gave way to the religious and secular subjects of Mycenaean palace art.

(iii) Processions and religious programmes. The procession is the most frequently repeated theme of Mycenaean painting and is known for all the main palaces. Stately figures are shown carrying offerings, and though the recipient is rarely preserved, a goddess or her representative may have been intended; two female recipients appear in the Mycenae Cult Centre processions (see below). Earlier, Cretan processions differ substantially from those of the Mycenaean palaces, not least in that they are composed of male figures, whereas the large-scale Mycenaean processions are, except at Pylos, of female figures. The theme may also have derived inspiration from Egyptian painting, though it is much transformed.

The procession represented in the palace at Thebes may be the earliest on the mainland (LH II–IIIA). From nine to twelve life-size figures wearing Minoan-style flounced skirts with open bodices are set against a background of undulating horizontal colour zones. Most face right. They hold offerings of either flowers, (ivory) boxes or a stone jar. The earliest processional theme at Mycenae, from the Ramp House, is similar to that from Thebes and may be contemporary. Other depictions of the theme at Mycenae, most of them fragmentary, include two from the Pithos area (female, life-size and half life-size); one from the House of the Oil Merchant (man carrying a (?)palanquin, with women and a charging bull); and a single male figure from the area of the megaron. The Tiryns procession had at least eight life-size women moving in both directions. The background is blue, and the figures walk on simulated wood. The stylization and exaggeration of their profile pose suggest a date late in LH IIIB. Fragments of an earlier frieze of smaller women were also found.

Both male and female processional figures occurred at Pylos in several paintings found in the North-west Slope Dump, including a '*Cup-bearer*' and the '*White Goddess*', thought to be a recipient of offerings. The life-size women may be compared with those from the other palaces. These paintings have lost their context, unlike those found within the palace itself. There the figures are shown entering the palace, moving towards the Throne Room. A single fragment suggests a life-size procession in the Outer Propylon. (The wall-fill of the Inner Propylon revealed a miniature male procession.) Part of a processional male figure was preserved *in situ* in Corridor 13 adjacent to the Vestibule, which leads from the Propylaia and Court to the Throne Room. In the Vestibule itself, male processional figures accompany a large sacrificial bull, all moving left towards the door to the Throne Room. Some dressed in kilts carry portable furniture. Others in robes bring offerings in boxes or shallow bowls and walk in pairs (man and boy or priest and acolyte). A single woman dressed in a flounced skirt is perhaps a priestess or member of the ruling family. The background changes colour vertically along wavy lines. The figures must have been in two registers, perhaps either side of the massive bull. On the south-east wall of the Throne Room (i.e. the other side of the Vestibule procession wall) was a male procession moving towards the throne situated on the east wall. A central hearth in the Throne Room, facing the throne, suggests the resting place for the bull. These paintings must be visual echoes of actual religious processions that took place in the palaces.

The large megaron-style Throne Room was the goal of the processional figures. Entering the door from the Vestibule, the figures led to the major composition on the wall behind the throne, which depicted large-scale protective griffins and lions, a theme that echoes that of the Throne Room at Knossos (*see* §I, 2(v) above). (These creatures were repeated in a frieze from Hall 46, the only other room in the palace to have a central hearth.) To the right (south-east) of the throne came the scene known as the '*Bard at the Banquet*'. A small-scale, robed figure sits high up on a multicoloured rock and plays a lyre, as a large crested bird flies in front of him. Below him, to the left, are two small pairs of robed men seated on stools at tables. Further to the left, towards the throne, is a large-scale bull, presumably the sacrificial animal brought through the Vestibule by the men. Next come the griffins and lions, and on the opposite wall is a painting of deer with papyrus, an animal that is iconographically the prey of the protector predators.

At Mycenae, the processional theme is central to the iconographic programme of the Cult Centre. From Area B came numerous fragments of a procession of women wearing Minoan-style flounced skirts. The best preserved, the *Mykenaia*, holds an offering of a necklace (see fig. 3). Two fragments belong to a scene in which a statuette is offered to a seated figure. The *Mykenaia* and the recipient of the statuette appear to be the focal-points of two processions on neighbouring walls. In another (apparently later) painting from nearby a woman holds an offering of a lily. Area A and the adjacent Tsountas's House yielded fragments of a procession of ass-headed daemons holding a rope, a palm tree, a shrine and a female warrior carrying a miniature griffin. The themes suggest a programme concerned with life-giving protection: the daemon nurtures (in glyptic scenes he waters leaves); the warrior goddess and the emblematic griffin protect.

A series of cult images was found along the east wall of the Citadel House, to the north-west of the Cult Centre. On the lower level is a priestess or goddess holding sheaves of (life-giving) grain, and a small animal (?griffin). They face towards an altar platform, on which are painted horns of consecration and 'beam-ends', images that denote a holy area. Above the altar are two (?) goddesses, one with the warrior attribute of a sword, the other with a staff or spear. Between them hover two tiny figures, schematically rendered, one red, one black, their arms outstretched. These may well be unique renderings of souls.

(iv) Shields. Large-scale figure-of-eight shields with oxhide markings appeared on the walls of most palaces. By the time of the palace wall paintings this previously functional shield type had become purely emblematic. A frieze of shields at Knossos (Late Minoan II) is the ancestor of the mainland shield friezes for which there is evidence at Tiryns, Thebes (single fragment) and Mycenae (two friezes). Those from Mycenae came from the Cult Centre in association with the female processions. This religious context for the motif is not unique. A painted plaque found nearby shows two female figures flanking a figure-of-eight shield with a (?)small head above, which has been identified as emblematic of a warrior goddess. The association between a female figure and warfare is repeated in the paintings from the Citadel House—goddess with a sword—and in a miniature fragment from Thebes that shows a female warrior wearing a helmet and carrying a small griffin.

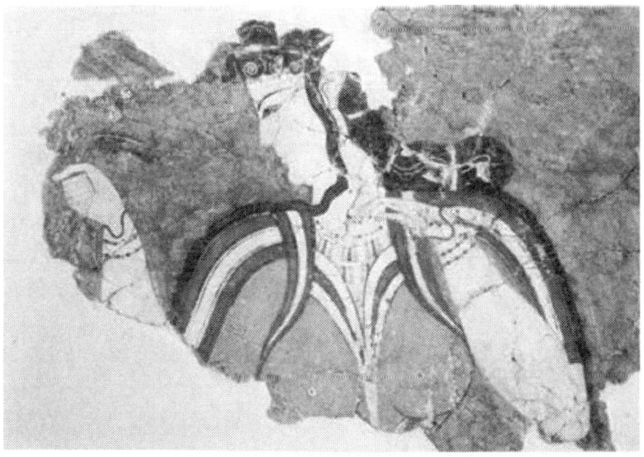

3. Helladic fragment of a processional wall painting depicting *Mykenaia*, from the Cult Centre, Mycenae, Late Helladic IIIB (Athens, Archaeological Museum)

(v) Hunting and warfare. The walls of the megaron at Mycenae were painted with friezes relating to warfare. The figures appeared at different levels, associated with horses, chariots and buildings. The fragments (of LH IIIB date) were badly burnt. On the (?) entrance wall was a scene of preparation for battle: horses led by grooms wearing greaves, an unyoked chariot and horse-drawn chariots. (Chariots in Mycenaean society seem to have been used only to convey men to the battle or the hunt.) A fragmentary battle scene on two levels shows a horse galloping above (reconstructed with a chariot) and a warrior falling below, hurtling past a building with a woman at a window. Other fragments show women standing before a palace façade and more warriors, some in hand-to-hand combat.

The theme was evidently popular at Mycenae. Another, slightly earlier (LH IIIA–IIIB:1) preparation scene came from the entrance to the palace (western portal). Grooms with their horses stand on a single plane, and an indication of setting is provided by descending rockwork in the upper zone. Fragments of architectural constructions, women and horses (unpublished) were also found in the House of the Oil Merchant, and a scene with men and a chariot was found in the vestibule leading into the cult area. Fragments comparable to the Mycenae megaron frieze were also found at Orchomenos, with buildings, a horse and chariot, and men wearing greaves. Two men often interpreted as bull-leapers probably belong instead to this scene.

Warfare was also important at Pylos. Its scenes are unlike those at any other centre and include a *Battle Scene* from Hall 64 depicting Mycenaean warriors in protective kilts, greaves and boar's-tusk helmets fighting sheepskin-clad barbarians. (This 'barbarian' theme also occurred in an earlier painting, found in the North-west Slope Dump, in which there are two men wearing animal skins and one (in a (?) tunic) holding up an animal.) The men in the *Battle Scene* fight in pairs, as in the Homeric duel, with daggers and spears, limbs flailing and bodies tumbling to the ground. Below this painting was a frieze of some 20 life-size, overlapping, seated dogs, a hunting adjunct to the theme of warfare.

The hunt was as popular a theme as the battle. Examples are known from Tiryns, Pylos and Orchomenos. The elements of the scenes are often similar to those of warfare—men, horses and chariots—and the themes are closely linked. Two hunt scenes are known from Tiryns: an earlier (LH IIIA–IIIB) version with horses and charioteers and men carrying spears, and a later, better preserved version (LH IIIB) with aristocratic ladies (?spectators or participants) riding in chariots while men, accompanied by hunting dogs, attack wild boar in a setting with stylized plants and trees. The Mycenaeans hunted boar for its tusks, which were sliced and mounted on a leather cap to make the prized boar's-tusk helmets; clearly a prestige item, the helmet symbolized the strength of man. Pieces with a small stag and a hare may have belonged to the scene. Also found with these pieces (in the West Slope Dump) were fragments of a *Deer* frieze, probably part of the same programme. Fragments of a very similar boar hunt were found at Orchomenos, with hunters carrying spears, some wearing boar's-tusk helmets; dogs attacking a boar; and ladies of the palace watching from their chariots.

The *Hunt Scene* from Pylos is more closely related to the Pylos *Battle Scene* than to the hunts of the other palaces. From a large room above Hall 46, it has the same background as the *Battle Scene* (with undulating colour changes) and shows men in tunics and greaves carrying spears, a stag speared by a man and large hunting dogs. The *Hunt* frieze ran on one side of the room, and on the opposite was the *Return from the Hunt*, with men carrying tripods for a feast. Pieces of an earlier hunt scene were found in wall-fill in Room 27.

H. Bulle: *Orchomenos*, i (Munich, 1907)

G. Rodenwaldt: 'Fragmente mykenischer Wandgemälde', *Mitt. Dt. Archäol. Inst.: Athen. Abt.*, xxxvi (1911), pp. 221–50

G. Rodenwaldt, ed.: *Die Fresken des Palastes* (1912), ii of *Tiryns* (Athens, 1912); see especially N. Heaton: 'Report on the Nature and Method of Specimens of Painted Plaster from the Palace of Tiryns', pp. 211–12

W. Lamb: 'Excavations at Mycenae: Frescoes from the Ramp House', *Annu. Brit. Sch. Athens*, xxiv (1919–21), pp. 189–99

G. Rodenwaldt: *Der Fries des Megarons von Mykenai* (Halle, 1921)

W. Lamb: 'Excavations at Mycenae: Palace Frescoes', *Annu. Brit. Sch. Athens*, xxv (1921–3), pp. 249–55

H. Reusch: 'Ein Schildfresco aus Theban', *Archäol. Anz.*, lxviii (1953), pp. 16–25

H. Reusch: 'Vorschlag zur Ordnung der Fragmente vom Frauenfries aus Mykenai', *Archäol. Anz.*, lxviii (1953), pp. 26–56

H. Reusch: *Die zeichnerische Rekonstruktion des Frauenfrieses im böotischen Theben* (Berlin, 1956)

E. Vermeule: *Greece in the Bronze Age* (Chicago, 1964, rev. 1973), pp. 184–202

W. H. Smith: *Interconnections in the Ancient Near East* (New Haven and London, 1965)

M. L. Lang: *The Frescoes* (1969), ii of *The Palace of Nestor at Pylos in Western Messenia* (Princeton, 1966–73)

W. D. Taylour: 'Mycenae 1968', *Antiquity*, xliii (1969), pp. 91–7

W. D. Taylour: 'New Light on Mycenaean Religion', *Antiquity*, xliv (1970), pp. 270–80

G. E. Mylonas: *Ton kentron thriskeutikou ton Mykinon* [The Cult Centre of Mycenae] (Athens, 1972)

E. S. Hirsch: *Painted Decoration of the Floors of Bronze Age Structures on Crete and the Greek Mainland*, Stud. Medit. Archaeol., liii (Göteborg, 1977)

M. A. S. Cameron: 'Theoretical Interrelations among Theran, Cretan and Mainland Frescoes', i of *Thera and the Aegean World I*, ed. C. Doumas (London, 1978), pp. 579–92

S. Hood: *The Arts in Prehistoric Greece*, Pelican Hist. A. (Harmondsworth, 1978)

C. Boulotis: 'Zur Deutung des Freskofragmentes Nr. 103 aus der Tirynther Frauenprozession', *Archäol. Korrbl.*, ix (1979), pp. 59–67

E. S. Hirsch: 'Another Look at Minoan Mycenaean Interrelationships in Floor Decoration', *Amer. J. Archaeol.*, lxxxiv (1980), pp. 453–62

M. Shaw: 'Painted "Ikria" at Mycenae?', *Amer. J. Archaeol.*, lxxxiv (1980), pp. 167–79

N. Marinatos: 'The Fresco from Room 31 at Mycenae', *The Excavations* (1981), i of *Well-built Mycenae, the Helleno-British Excavations within the Citadel at Mycenae, 1959–69*, ed. W. D. Taylor, E. B. French and K. A. Wardle (Warminster, 1981–92)

S. Peterson: *Wall Paintings in the Aegean Bronze Age: The Procession Frescoes* (diss., Minneapolis, U. MN, 1981)

I. Kritseli-Providi: *Toichographies tou thriskeutikou kentrou ton Mykinon* [The wall painting from the Cult Centre at Mycenae] (Athens, 1982) [Eng. review by L. Morgan: *Amer. J. Archaeol.*, lxxxviii (1984), pp. 77–8]

N. Marinatos: 'The Fresco from Room 31 at Mycenae: Problems of Method and Interpretation', *Problems in Greek Prehistory: Centenary Conference of the British School of Archaeology at Athens: Manchester, 1986*, pp. 245–52

C. Boulotis: 'Mycenaean Wall Painting', *The Mycenaean World: Five Centuries of Early Greek Culture, 1600–1100 BC*, Ministry of Culture, The National Hellenic Committee, ICOM (Athens, 1988), pp. 35–7

S. A. Immerwahr: *Aegean Painting in the Bronze Age* (University Park, PA, and London, 1990)

L. Kontorli-Papadopoulou: *Aegean Frescoes of Religious Character* (n.p., 1996)

T. Angelines: *He anaviose tes Kreto-Mykenaikes toichographias* (Athens, 2000)

L. Morgan, ed.: *Aegean Painting: A Tribute to Mark Cameron* (London, 2005)

IV. Greek.

Painting was practised by Greek-speaking peoples as wall painting and also in the form of panel pictures. Other applications included architectural ornament (*see* ARCHITECTURE, §IV, 1(iii)(c)), painting of statues (*see* SCULPTURE, §IV, 1(iii) and (iv)) and pottery decoration (*see* POTTERY, §IV, 1(ii)(b) and (iii)(c)), notably the work of the VASE PAINTERS. Very few Greek wall and panel paintings survive, and the works of most named painters, among them the most celebrated artists of their day in any media, are known only from literary sources. Nevertheless, the history of Greek painting can be inferred from developments in related arts, from large-scale sculpture to gem-carving, and from the Roman period survive hundreds of copies of Greek works, made as wall paintings or mosaics.

J. L. Benson: *Horse, Bird & Man: The Origins of Greek Painting* (Amherst, 1970/*R* 1990)

S. Woodford: *The Art of Greece and Rome* (Cambridge, 1982)

S. Woodford: *An Introduction to Greek Art* (Ithaca, 1986)

J. J. Pollitt: *The Art of Ancient Greece: Sources and Documents* (Cambridge, 1990)

1. Introduction. 2. Historical survey. 3. Theory and criticism. 4. Collections and collectors.

1. Introduction.

(i) Materials and techniques. (ii) Subject-matter. (iii) Painters and society.

(i) Materials and techniques.

(a) Supports. Ancient literary sources and surviving fragments alike testify to the importance of painting as an art form in ancient Greece. All sorts of materials were painted, either in their natural state or specially prepared: wood, canvas, clay, marble and other stone, even leather, ivory and, in later periods, glass. Wall paintings were executed on specially prepared plaster, and the most important material for Greek easel painting was the wooden panel (*pinax*), either plain, framed or with protective folding doors. Sketchy comments in literary sources suggest that the lost great masterpieces of Greek painting were done on wooden surfaces, but the perishability of organic surfaces makes the reconstruction of the techniques and media used in such painting difficult. Only a few small examples of mediocre quality have been discovered: two panels at Saqqara, Egypt (one now in London, BM) and one whole panel and two fragments of a further three at Pitsa in Achaia (after *c.* 540 BC; Athens, N. Archaeol. Mus.). Wall paintings on stone, plaster and clay, however, may to some extent serve as a substitute. Stone, in particular, was much favoured in most periods, and many murals have been discovered, particularly in tombs. Ceramic painting (as on vases, architectural terracottas etc) constitutes a different category.

(b) Techniques. Apart from a few slight literary references, no ancient handbooks or instructions for painters have survived, and most material evidence comes from painted stone funerary stelai. For murals, the surface of plaster itself was an adequate ground, and it may reasonably be assumed that wooden panels were first given a ground. By contrast, stone was simply polished but does not appear to have been grounded. Surviving paintings on plaster, stone (including polychromy on marbles) and clay all show that the painter first scratched a rough design on the surface itself. Such sketches survive on large painted Archaic-period (*c.* 700–*c.*480 BC) marble funerary stelai (examples in Athens, Kerameikos Mus.) or Archaic clay metopes (e.g. from Thermon; Athens, N. Archaeol. Mus.). Similar preliminary sketches, invisible to the naked eye under the finished picture, have been detected under murals from the early Classical period (*c.* 480–323 BC) onwards (e.g. the Tomb of the Diver, Paestum (see fig. 4); Persephone Tomb, Aigai (Vergina)). Preliminary designs were also done in red brushwork (e.g. the Lyseas Stele; Athens, N. Archaeol. Mus.).

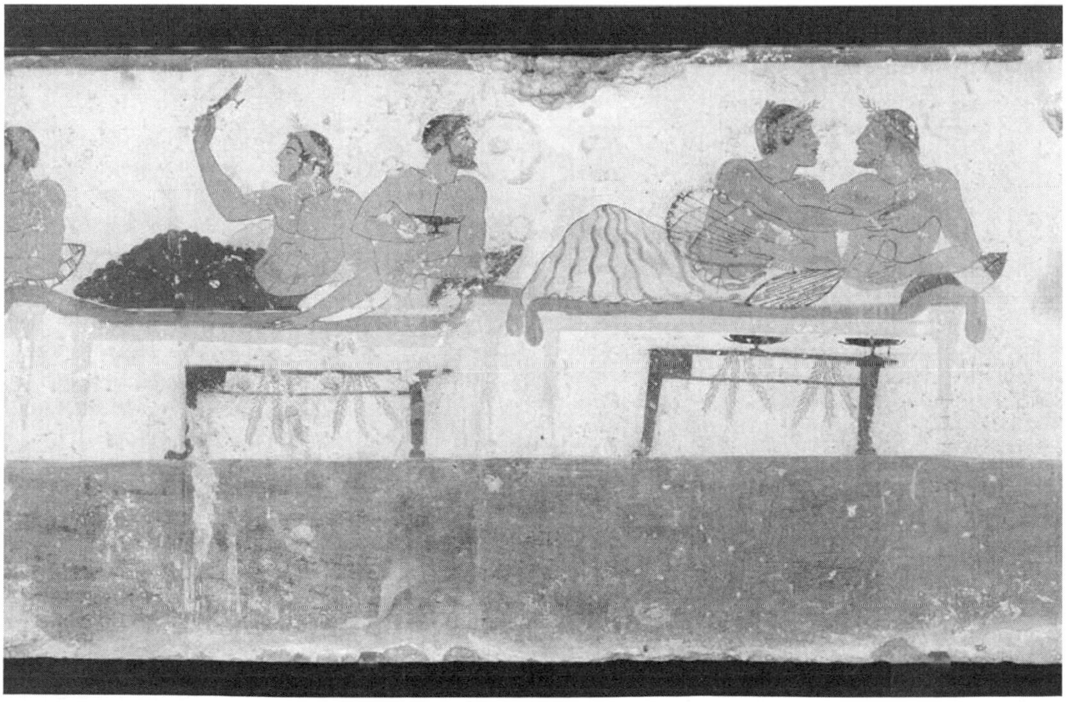

4. Ancient Greek wall painting depicting a funeral banquet, from the Tomb of the Diver, Paestum, early 5th century BC (Paestum, Museo Archeologico Nazionale)

Before the development of chiaroscuro in Greek painting (late 5th century BC), the final picture was composed of precise linear contours and areas of intense natural hues. By the Hellenistic period (323–27 BC) at the latest, technique and execution had become more complex. The rough preliminary design gave way to a detailed monochrome brush drawing, usually in black (as on a stele in Volos, Athanassakeion Archaeol. Mus.). This preliminary drawing is more than a design: it predetermines the tonal effects of the finished picture. The next step was to apply successive washes of different hues and tones until the desired effect had been achieved, with a final layer of shading and lights. For the application of pastose paints, besides the brush, some sort of blunt tool was used for spreading. Once completed, easel paintings were given a coat of varnish: according to Pliny, Apelles invented a varnish that also intensified the colour effects. This careful method of building up a picture was not always used. An alternative, attested from the Late Classical period onwards, was to dispense with the preliminary drawing and paint the picture directly in its final form with quick brushwork, for example Late Classical funerary stelai from Aigai (ii) (now Vergina; e.g. Thessaloniki, Archaeol. Mus.; Vergina, Archaeol. Mus.) and Hellenistic funerary stelai from Alexandria (e.g. Alexandria, Gr.–Roman Mus.; New York, Met.; Paris Louvre). Even unexceptional painters used this method for ordinary funerary stelai, though one may presume that it was originally developed in the more prestigious and advanced field of panel painting. Direct painting was also used for copying works from other sources.

Surviving literary sources on Greek painting deal almost exclusively with the encaustic technique. This involves mixing pigments with wax, either hot or cold, and fixing the mixture to the surface with a hot instrument. For centuries attempts have been made to revive it, with varying success. In the body of surviving Greek painting itself, examples of encaustic painting are extremely rare (e.g. the metopes from Cyrene; Paris, Louvre). However, given the overall evidence for the range of painted materials, it is clear that tempera was the normal medium, and the frequent mention of encaustic painting may simply represent the attention attracted by a special technique.

(c) Composition of paints. Scientific analyses have revealed that the emulsions used on surviving painted stelai consisted of either the egg-yolk or the white or both, as well as oils. Although the polychromy of marble statues has not yet been similarly analysed, it appears that the medium normally used here was tempera too, not wax. Chemical analyses will doubtless disclose many secrets of Greek tempera emulsions; contrary to modern assumptions, those used on both buildings and sculptures in the open were able to withstand the weather for many centuries.

The fullest list of pigments used in ancient painting is given by Pliny (*Natural History* XXXIII and XXXV). Chemical analyses of ancient Greek works have identified various pigments, of which the most common are Egyptian blue, a synthetic pigment made from lime, sand and copper ore; bone black (Pliny's *elephantinum*); lead white or ceruse; calcium carbonate, a white pigment; malachite, a copper carbonate, a green pigment; massicot, a synthetic monoxide, a yellow photosensitive pigment discolouring to reddish-brown; ochre, in yellow, brown and red varieties; red vegetable dye, probably lichen, used for pink; vegetable black (Gr. *tryginon*); lampblack; vermilion, both natural and synthetic mercury sulphide; and green earth, the most common green pigment in murals, though not found in paintings on stone.

E. Berger: *Die Maltechnik des Altertums* (Leipzig, 1904)
S. Augusti: *I colori Pompeiani* (Rome, 1967)
M. Napoli: *La Tomba del Tuffatore* (Naples, 1970), pp. 167–71
R. Büll: *Das grosse Buch vom Wachs: Geschichte, Kultur, Technik*, 2 vols (Munich, 1977)
V. von Graeve and F. Preusser: 'Zur Technik griechischer Malerei auf Marmor', *Jb. Dt. Archäol. Inst.*, xcvi (1981), pp. 120–56
F. Preusser, V. von Graeve and C. Wolters: 'Malerei auf griechischen Grabsteinen: Technische und naturwissenschaftliche Aspekte eines archäologischen Materials', *Maltechnik, Rest.*, lxxxvii/1 (1981), pp. 11–34
M. Andronikos: *Vergina: The Royal Tombs* (Athens, 1984), pp. 86–95
N. J. Koch: *De picturae initiis: Die Anfänge der griechischen Malerei im 7. Jahrhundert v. Chr.* (Munich, 1996)

(ii) Subject-matter. As with other aspects of ancient Greek painting, the content and pictorial treatment of lost originals may often be inferred from literary sources, vase painting and other arts, and Roman wall paintings and mosaics reproducing Greek designs.

(a) Geometric to Archaic (*c.* 900–*c.* 480 BC). (b) Classical (*c.* 480–323 BC). (c) Hellenistic (323–27 BC).

(a) Geometric to Archaic (c. 900–c. 480 BC*).* In the late 8th century BC in Ephesos, BOULARCHOS apparently painted the *Defeat of the Magnetes*; this must be associated with the battle scenes on Geometric pottery. An oinochoe in Munich (Staatl. Antikensamml.) bears a depiction of a shipwreck with a surviving sailor, which is either a primitive *ex voto* or a reference to the *Odyssey*. Mythological themes are clearly present on Orientalizing pottery (*see* POTTERY, §IV, 4). The polychrome decoration on Corinthian wares shows parades of carts and cavalrymen, hunting and scenes of everday life. Dramatic tension informs a scene on a krater (Paris, Louvre) of the banquet held in the palace of Eurytos in Oechalia, with Herakles and Iole; a restless dog under the table is outlined in the Black-figure technique. The contest between Apollo and Herakles for the Delphic tripod, held before Artemis, is the subject of the oldest mythological panel painting still extant, which decorates the Archaic limestone slate of Persepolis (*see* §2(i) below).

(b) Classical (c. 480–323 BC*).*

Early–mid-5th century BC. The cycle commissioned for the Sanctuary of Athena at Plataia, after the

Athenian victory there over the Persians and Boiotians in 479 BC, revisited epic tradition in the light of history, with such subjects as *Odysseus Trapped by the Suitors* by POLYGNOTOS OF THASOS and the *Seven Against Thebes* by Onasias. Polygnotos also painted the *Greeks after the Sack of Troy* in the Stoa Poikile in the Agora at Athens, where MIKON painted the *Amazonomachy*. The portrayal of the *Battle of Marathon*, conceived by these two masters, was probably completed by PANAINOS when Pericles took power in 462–461 BC.

The panels painted by ZEUXIS were sometimes criticized by ancient writers for a concern with visual trickery, but his depictions of everyday life, conversation and games, for example, seem to have been innovative in their use of highlights rather than hatching or outline. *A Young Boy with Grapes* and an *Old Woman* are among titles that have survived; he is also known to have explored mythological and epic subjects such as *Eros, Pan*, a *Centaur Family* and a *Helen* perhaps painted for a Temple of Hera Lakinia at Akragas or at Kroton in southern Italy. Further works are attributed to him through later copies: the *Abduction of Helen* by Theseus represented in a mosaic in PELLA (ii) (*c.* 325–*c.* 275 BC; Pella, Archaeol. Mus.) and the small scene on a marble slate from Herculaneum depicting *Women Playing Astragals* (*c.* 27 BC–AD 14; Naples, Mus. Archeol. N.).

PARRHASIOS produced small paintings with erotic subjects; feelings and pain he tended to express in his more monumental works, such as *Odysseus Feigning Madness, Prometheus in Chains* (tradition holds that a tortured slave was used as a model) and *Philoktetes on Lemnos*. He included such dramatic themes as the *Destruction of Troy* and the *Centauromachy* among the cartoons he was said to have prepared for engravings by the metalworker Mys; these works included acanthus racemes to emphasize the elegance of the line. The images of Silenus and a chariot race decorate the silver pieces inspired by Parrhasios' style found at Douvanli, Bulgaria.

TIMANTHES defeated Parrhasios in contest and painted the famous *Sacrifice of Iphigenia* for a competition against one Kolotes of Teos. He so exhausted all possible expressions of sorrow in his depiction of those attending the sacrifice of Agamemnon's daughter that he veiled the father's head rather than attempt to suggest his grief. Commissions for a portrait of the supreme priest were awarded to Zeuxis and Parrhasios by the Temple of Artemis in Ephesos.

The painting of *Scylla* by Androkydes of Kyzikos (*fl* early 4th century BC) reproduced a theme already widespread in Kyzikos coins, with the addition of space devoted to the representation of creatures (e.g. London, BM). This desire to explore natural subjects together with mythological ones brought to painting the knowledge of nature acquired through experiment and theoretical speculation in the East Greek context, particularly since the Archaic period.

Mid-5th century BC–late 4th. The next step was taken by Pauson (*fl c.* 425–*c.* 388 BC). In Athens, the advances in technique coincided with the breaking of the unity of form and content that had marked painting during the age of Pericles (*c.* 495–429 BC) and made alternatives to traditional themes possible. The description survives of a painting by Pauson of a galloping horse raising a cloud of dust (Aristotle: *Poetics* I, 2, *Politics* VIII, 5, 7; Aristophanes: *Archarnians* 354, *Thesmophoriazusae* 948, *Plutus* 602); if it was inverted, the animal seemed to be rolling on its back in the soil, exactly the image the patron had specified. The novelty lay not only in this exploitation of illusion but also in the autonomy of the animal subject, which existed irrespective of any link with a human being. Aristotle (384–322 BC) advised young people against looking at the works of Pauson, whom he used as a pretext to define the different modes of imitation: 'because those who represent, reproduce human beings in an action, such human beings have to be good or bad that is better or worse than us, as they are represented by painters. In fact Polygnotos represented them better than us, Pauson worse, Dionysios in a way similar to ours.' (*Politics* VIII, 5, 7). This preoccupation with representing the human being experimentally rather than morally constitutes the key to the new painting.

The incorporeal quality of the figures painted by NIKOMACHOS OF THEBES derives from their loss of weight and lack of apparent effort. This quality can be seen in *Cybele Riding on a Lion*, which is similar to *Dionysos Riding a (?)Cheetah* represented in a mosaic in Pella (*c.* 325–*c.* 275 BC; Pella, Archaeol. Mus.) *Maenads Stalked by Satyrs*; *Victory Taking a Four-horse Chariot Heavenward*, a painting brought to Rome and reproduced on *denarii* under Julius Caesar; and the *Rape of Persephone*, the subject of a painting moved to Rome and of a fresco at AIGAI (ii) (Vergina), which can be attributed to Nikomachos on the basis of the light handling of Hermes, who leads Hades' horses (*see* §2(ii)(b) below).

Paintings of the 12 Olympian gods dominated the southern wing of the Stoa of Zeus in the Agora at Athens, painted *c.* 360 BC by EUPHRANOR; on the northern wing the Demos ('people') of Athens was represented as a person, crowned by Demokratia (the constitution) in Theseus' presence; a rendering of the cavalry clash that preceded the Second Battle of Mantinea in 362 BC occupied the central niche. The subject of Demos and Democracy is known from a record relief from the Agora (Athens, Agora Mus.), which conveys solemnity and strength. A man with a beard, seated in meditation next to a container of writing scrolls, appears on a marble slab, dated *c.* 340–338 BC, from the tomb of Hermon in the Kerameikos in Athens, the only original painting attributable to the circle of Euphranor.

NIKIAS projects a solid realism, whether in battle scenes or portraits, and a keen interest in animals; such realism was transmitted to him by his master Antidotos (*fl* late 4th century BC), who was in turn a pupil of Euphranor. Three of his mythological scenes of captivity and liberation are known through Roman and Pompeiian copies in several versions (e.g. *Perseus and Andromeda* from the House of the Dioscuri, Pompeii; Naples, Mus. Archeol. N.); the other two subjects are *Seated Calypso* and *Io and Argus*. Descriptions survive of some of his other works, which have been used to argue for the attribution to him of the hunting scene painted on the tomb of Philip II in Aigai (336 BC). Different episodes of the hunt, involving stags, wild boar, lions and bears, are coerced into a temporal unity by means of a vigorous composition within a vast landscape.

PAMPHILOS compiled a catalogue of *Paintings in Alphabetical Order*, demonstrating his interest in their subject-matter. With the help of his followers, he painted the tyrant Aristratos (*fl* late 4th century BC) next to Nike on a chariot. Aratos (271–213 BC) furiously scratched out the image of Aristratos from the painting, suggesting that Nike's political significance was more important than her role as the symbol of victory. The emphasis was moving from private and municipal patronage of artists, commissioned to produce paintings of the best athletes, to the exploitation of artists as a means of strengthening the central power of the ruler.

A sizeable number of paintings has been attributed to APELLES on the evidence of copies and of elements in others' paintings borrowed from his known works; among his principal works mentioned by written sources, which would have inspired later paintings, are the *Heracules Aversus*, reproduced in a Herculaneum fresco, and *Alexander Holding the Thunderbolt* in the House of the Vettii in Pompeii. Many of those represented by Apelles belonged to the circle of Alexander the Great. Among his works produced after Alexander's death are some allegories, such as the *Charis* ('Grace') at Smyrna, reproduced in a mosaic from Byblos (Beirut, Mus. N.) and the *Calumny*, executed at the court of Ptolemy I (*reg* 305–283 BC), echoes of which can be found in the judicial scenes on a black background from the Villa Farnesina, Rome (40–20 BC; Rome, Mus. N. Romano). Apelles is the first painter for whom there is evidence of a self-portrait.

PROTOGENES' subjects included a portrait of *Aristotle's Mother*, allegories and minor gods set in a landscape. His *Ialysos*, a young hunter sitting with his dog, is reproduced in a cup by the Hesse Painter (London, BM). Protogenes was the author of a catalogue of 'schemes' (Pliny: *Natural History* XXXV.cii), which was of great importance in the dissemination of his iconographic creations. From a contest between Apelles and Protogenes, the Romans acquired the panel on which the two masters competed to draw the thinnest line. Pliny stated that it was burnt during the first fire on the Palatine (Pliny: *Natural History* XXXV.lxxxi–lxxxiii).

(c) Hellenistic (323–27 BC). During the Hellenistic period an interest in surroundings developed out of the mythological and historical genres and so gave rise to the landscape painting, either frankly naturalistic or with an idyllic and bucolic tone inspired by literature. The portrait acquired a more private character, as foreshadowed by Nikias, Apelles and Protogenes. A minor genre, in terms of picture size and character, depicting scenes from ordinary life, erotic groups, animals and still-lifes, became widespread.

In Macedonia, from the mythic and heroic themes of the earliest painted tombs evolved the illusionism of the Lyson and Kallikles tomb in Leukadia. Here the armour and weapons of the two commanders seem to hang within a bright pavilion, demonstrating the decorative solutions of the so-called Second Style of Roman mural painting (*c.* 90–*c.* 15 BC). In Athens the historical manner was perpetuated both by Hyppis, who painted an allegory in celebration of a naval victory (perhaps by the Macedonian Demetrios I Poliorketes, *reg* 294–288 BC) employing the images of Poseidon and Nike, and by Olbiades, who portrayed the strategy of Kalippos, leader of the Athenian army against the Galatians during their incursion in 279 BC. Kratinos, whose work exalted the glories of civilization, decorated the interior of the Pompeion in the Athenian Kerameikos with figures of playwrights; there is an inscription from Menander, possibly reproduced in the House of the Menander wall painting in Pompeii. Eirene, the daughter and pupil of Kratinos, painted a *Kore* in Eleusis, evidence of the growing interest in mystery cults. Realism, pioneered by Pauson, was adapted to the then prevailing taste in the simple *Scenes in a Shop* painted by PEIRAIKOS.

Theon of Samos (*fl* late 4th century BC), who painted a portrait of *Demetrios I Poliorketes*, was celebrated in eastern circles for a cycle on the Trojan War, later brought to Rome in the Portico di Filippo and frequently imitated in Pompeiian decoration. Timomachos of Byzantium (of uncertain date) painted not only the traditional mythological subjects, such as *Ajax, Medea, Orestes and Iphigenia among the Taurians* and the *Gorgon*, but also a portrait of the juggler *Lekythion* and family conversation groups. Frescoes in Delos and later mosaics in Lemnos reproduced scenes from a comedy in the Kalates style.

The adventures of Odysseus gave painters opportunities for grandiose landscapes, much as they were exploited for the large statuary groups of Rhodes and Pergamon, placed by the artists inside grottoes or in the middle of expanses of water. Vitruvius noted the success of these themes in Roman wall painting. Examples of it have been found in a house on the Esquiline, *c.* 50 BC, where *Polyphemos* (untraced), *Laestrygonians, Circe, Odysseus in the Underworld, Sirens* (incomplete) and *Scylla* (untraced) appeared side by side.

In Alexandria, the versatile ANTIPHILOS explored both royal themes—for example, in *Ptolemy I of Egypt Hunting*, which can be reconstructed thanks to the consistency between a wall painting in Stabiae and a mosaic in Sétif—and subjects from everyday life. Hints of a realism that points towards *trompe l'oeil* can be found in the necklaces, shoes and other objects painted in polychrome technique on a light background on the Hadra vases. Caricature, already practised by Apelles, acquired a grotesque dimension, such pictures being known as *grylloi*. Dionysios of Alexandria (*c.* 170–90 BC), known as Thrax, was both a grammarian and a painter; he executed a portrait of the philologist Aristarchos (*c.* 215–143 BC) alongside a personification of Tragedy, an erudite use of allegory. Demetrios (*fl* mid-2nd century BC), known as Topographos, cultivated the art of landscape first at the court of Ptolemy VI Philometor (*reg* 181–145 BC) and later, *c.* 165 BC, in Rome. The *View of the Nile*, reproduced in the Praeneste mosaic (late 2nd century BC; Praeneste, Pal. Barberini), was painted around this time. However, the fairy-tale expanse of water, populated by ducks, cranes, hippopotamuses, crocodiles and snakes among reeds, palm-trees and lotus flowers, is characteristic of the Alexandrian school, which derived the motifs from ancient Egyptian funerary iconography; the mosaic copy in Pompeii's House of the Faun (*c.* 100 BC; Naples, Mus. Archeol. N) is the earliest surviving example in a Roman context.

K. Jex-Blake and E. Sellars: *The Elder Pliny's Chapters on the History of Art* (London, 1896)
C. M. Robertson: *Greek Painting* (Geneva, 1959)
T. Hölscher: *Griechische Historienbilder des 5. und 4. Jahrhunderts v. Chr.* (Würzburg, 1973)
P. H. von Blanckenhagen: 'Painting in the Time of Alexander and Later', *Macedonia and Greece in Late Classical and Early Hellenistic Times*, ed. B. Barr-Sharrar and E. N. Borza (Washington, DC, 1982)
A. Barbet: *Le Peinture murale romaine* (Paris, 1985)
F. Ducatti: *Pittura antica* (Milan, 1987)
S. Woodford: *The Trojan War in Ancient Art* (London, 1993)
S. Woodford: *Images of Myths in Classical Antiquity* (New York, 2003)

(iii) Painters and Society. According to Pliny, monumental polychrome painting originated in Corinth, a centre of trade and a meeting-place *en route* from Syria and Phoenicia to the western Greek colonies. The splendid court of Kypselos (*reg c.* 657–*c.* 625 BC) and Periander (*reg c.* 625–*c.* 585 BC) attracted the first figurative artists as well as poets.

In 479 BC the paintings of Plataia celebrated the unity of the Greeks, and in Athens the activity of POLYGNOTOS OF THASOS and his circle was favoured by the policy of Kimon (*c.* 512–449 BC). In 477 BC, when Lemnos entered the Athens-led Delian League, Polygnotos' brother Aristophon was commissioned to paint a picture representing the *Wounded Philoktetes*. Athens' annexation of Skyros led to Polygnotos' painting of the island's founder Achilles with the daughters of Lykomedes, its legendary sovereign. Kimon (*c.* 512–449 BC) claimed to have found the bones of Theseus, legendary king of Athens, at Skyros; these were taken as a symbol of Athenian power, and Theseus' exploits were represented in a frieze by MIKON that adorned the Sanctuary of Apollo showing battles against the Amazons and the Centaurs and Theseus' descent to the bottom of the sea for the miraculous recovery of a ring. Mikon later returned to the theme in painting the Stoa Poikile in the Athenian Agora during the last years of Kimon's regime. 'Polygnotos was not an artisan', declared Plutarch, and the poet Melanthios was the first among his contemporaries to understand that Polygnotos as a painter had a social role, illustrating the ideal of 'virtuous behaviour' (*ethos*) on the part of the heroes.

The arrival of ZEUXIS in Athens was as important for painting as the 427 BC visit of Gorgias of Leontini (*c.* 485–*c.* 380 BC) was for the birth of rhetoric. Like the Sophists, the new painters were attracted by Athens but remained essentially itinerant. In public they behaved with the pomp of 'masters of knowledge': Zeuxis displayed his name woven in his cloak in letters of gold; PARRHASIOS dressed in purple with gilt accessories. Like the Sophists, Zeuxis was accused of making too much money from his work, but he also gave away paintings declaring that no payment would be truly adequate. Socrates observed that the King of Macedonia had obtained Zeuxis' services at a very high price. APOLLODOROS scorned him for bringing with him the art 'stolen' from others and criticized him for treating his artistic experience as merchandise. Hence a painting that Zeuxis exhibited for a fee was called *Helen Hetaira*.

Plato compared the lesson to be learnt from Zeuxis with that imparted by the Sophists. And it was from the need to cultivate specific skills for each form of production, taught by the Sophists, that a system of education arose that addressed different areas of human activity. The dignity of Zeuxis and Parrhasios came from the new idea of the artist as a 'master'. While Socrates and the Sophists came into conflict in various ways with the city's constitution, painters came to depend less on social and political activity and public commissions. Zeuxis criticized the willingness of AGATHARCHOS to collaborate with the plans of Pericles, declaring that he preferred to work for posterity. Zeuxis had an idea of aristocratic perfection that ill accorded with Athenian democracy but found justification in the circle of the statesman Alcibiades (*c.* 450–404 BC).

The end of the Peloponnesian War in 404 BC marked a turning-point in painting; faith in the old institutions generally was weakened, and painters could no longer aspire to absolute truths in their work. From the beginning of the 4th century BC the Greeks in Asia Minor were particularly sensitive to the centralization of power that was taking place in the coastal satrapies of the Persian Empire. The naturalism introduced by Androkydes of Kyzikos (*fl* early 4th century BC) into mythological painting rested on the preferences of a nascent class that might be termed 'bourgeois': fish-plates with realistic reproductions of marine fauna have been found among the furnishings of a rich house in Olynthos, with numbers incised on the bottoms. Other pieces reached the flourishing mercantile cities on the Black Sea coast.

In Athens the comedies of Aristophanes (*c.* 448–*c.* 388 BC), with their numerous criticisms of Pauson (*fl c.* 425–*c.* 388 BC), denounce the production of pictures that do not celebrate the city: Pauson was considered a 'depraved' caricaturist, and in a climate of economic competition and social division, failure to appeal to wealthy patrons could condemn an artist to destitution. Nor did the social upheaval assure nobly born citizens the free practice of art: even Klisthenes of the Theopropides was a 'scenographer', a poor man. Around 340 BC Demosthenes (*c.* 383–322 BC) expressed a distinction between art and craft. He accused the painter Philochares of being a mere decorator of religious objects, although Pliny later attributed to him an 'immense artistic power'.

Painting of this period reflects the developments in the Athenian *polis*, whether it tends towards mystic and allegorical visions, in the tradition of ARISTEIDES, or accords with the general spirit of the expanding economy, with EUPHRANOR and his followers. The ideology of Isokrates (436–338 BC), master and political inspiration of the *strategos* ('general') Timotheos (*fl* early 4th century BC), can be discerned behind the decorative programme of the Stoa of Zeus in the Athenian Agora. He was responsible for the inscription that accompanied Euphranor's *Theseus*, presenting him as the founder of Athenian democracy. The Demokratia who crowned the Demos of Athens in the presence of armed cavalry represented the moderate democracy of Isokrates, intended to recognize the merits of a privileged minority. The fallen warriors immortalized in the painting had not only redeemed the 'glory of their fathers' at the Battle of Mantinea, as Xenophon recounted, but had also defended the *patria politeia*. From this watershed in historical painting the greatest developments have come to light at sites within the empire of Alexander the Great. NIKOMACHOS OF THEBES, in a dialogue with the Macedonian regent Antipater (395–319 BC), advanced a sense of the dignity of the artist, which was of use in negotiating prices. His work on the Tomb of Persephone at Aigai (Vergina) and the fact that his pupil PHILOXENOS OF ERETRIA worked for Kassander (*reg* 305/4–297 BC), the son of Antipater, confirm the presence of Attic painters at the Macedonian court.

NIKIAS turned to the text of the *Odyssey*; to him, Homer was a part of cultural history, and the artist had no interest in bringing him up to date, as had been done in the time of Polygnotos. This explains Nikias' success in a cosmopolitan society that had no common goals: what had formerly been praised for giving a good example to the contemporary citizen now became important as a record of the past. Nikias was preoccupied with formal refinement, and with this aesthetic rather than moral ideal, he took the social role of the painter as far as it could go in the economic context of the Hellenistic realms. Ptolemy I (*reg* 306–284 BC) was said to have offered 60 talents for a picture of Odysseus descending into the underworld, the *Questioning of the Dead* (*nekromanteia*). But Nikias refused 'because he had abundant wealth' and donated the panel to Athens.

At Sikyon, the tradition of *Chrestographia* ('beautiful painting') expressed an aristocratic ideal. In harmony with Platonic principles, PAMPHILOS did not hide his élitist views of art. In his treatise *On Painting and the Illustrious Painters* he identifies his approach with the greatest achievements of Greek painting. Like the late Sophists, he was in sympathy with the oligarchic party and with Sparta; in 369 BC, with the arrival of the Thebans and the democratic regime of Euphron, he had to leave Sikyon. In exile he painted the *Victory of the Athenians at Phlious*, a reversal for the citizens of the town. After the demise of the Theban rule, Pamphilos returned to Sikyon. With MELANTHIOS, PAUSIAS and APELLES, who shared the aristocratic ideology of their master, he collaborated in celebrating the tyrant Aristratos (*fl* late 4th century BC), who upheld the policies of Philip II (*reg* 359–336 BC). The society that had supported the school of Sikyon was the largest to enter the union of the Greek states under monarchial rule; painting was in the service of political power, and the support Philip II gave to the aristocratic party was reflected in allegorical works of the kind already produced to exalt the local ruler.

In 343 BC Apelles was brought into the Macedonian court through the good offices of Aristratos and the relations Pamphilos maintained with his native city. The sovereign's goodwill towards the artist was matched by the latter's readiness to produce political propaganda, and Philip and Alexander discovered the Sikyonian organizational ability to produce paintings that could project the new image of the sovereign. The meeting between Apelles and PROTOGENES at Rhodes illustrates the opposing approaches prevalent in that period: Apelles, working in the context of monarchic power, requested payment in gold; Protogenes, originally an artisan, lived in the last Aegean city-state to retain a certain independence, and he sold his paintings to the inhabitants of Rhodes at prices so modest as to worry Apelles.

During the Hellenistic period, the difference between the artisan and the successful artist grew more pronounced. The papyri archives of Zenon, an estate manager, established in 256 BC at Philadelphia in the Faiyum in Egypt, have revealed the modest financial position of Theophilos, a painter from Alexandria. He charged only 53 drachmai, of which 23 were spent on coloured paints, to decorate the walls of three rooms and a ceiling. On completing the work, Theophilos wrote to the buyer: 'If you require any further paintings, be so good as to commission me, so that I can earn a living. If you cannot do this, be so good as to send me a viaticum so that I can go back to my brothers in the city.' The Athenian painter and philosopher Metrodoros, by contrast, was invited by the consul Paullus Macedonicus in 168 BC to Rome, where he helped form the aristocratic circle of Attic artists. And DEMETRIOS OF ALEXANDRIA, who had come to Rome from Egypt, achieved such status at this period that he was able to shelter his own exiled king, Ptolemy VI Philometor (*reg* 181–145 BC). During the last century of the Republic, Iaia competed successfully against the noted portrait painters Sopolis and Dionysios for the best clientele between Naples and Rome.

J. J. Pollitt: *The Art of Greece, 1400–31 BC: Sources and Documents* (Englewood Cliffs, NJ, 1965)
C. M. Robertson: *A History of Greek Art* (Cambridge, 1975)
J. J. Pollitt: *Art in the Hellenistic Age* (Cambridge, 1986)

2. Historical survey.

(i) Geometric to Archaic (*c*. 900–*c*. 480 BC). (ii) Classical (*c*. 480–323 BC). (iii) Hellenistic (323–27 BC).

(i) Geometric to Archaic (c. 900–c. 480 BC). After the Mycenaean period (*c*. 1600–*c*. 1050 BC) and the so-called Dorian invasion (*see* Helladic, §4 (iii)(a) and §III above), the first artistic phase of historical Greece was defined by the taste for a wider use of pictorial decoration of pottery: the Protogeometric style (*c*. 1000– *c*. 900 BC) followed by the Geometric (*c*. 900–*c*. 725 BC) and the Orientalizing (*c*. 725–*c*. 600 BC) styles. According to tradition, the origin of figural painting lay in *skiagraphia* ('drawing the shadow'). Saurias of Samos was said by the 2nd-century AD philosopher Athenagoras to have drawn the contours of a horse's shadow; Pliny attributed a similar practice to the anonymous precursors of painting in Sikyon and Corinth. Literary references to this phase of Greek painting correlate the silhouette figures of men and animals on Geometric pottery. The decoration on later Geometric pottery accords with the technique that Pliny attributed to the painters Aridikes of Corinth and Telephanes of Sikyon of giving more substance to the silhouette by adding internal lines within the outline. Pliny (*Natural History*, VII.cxxvi, XXXV.lv) cites as belonging to this period a monumental painting (untraced) by Boularchos. Fragments of mural decoration have been found in the first Poseidon Temple at Isthmia (*c*. 690–*c*. 650 BC).

The use of uniform colours is typical of the 7th century BC, inspired by Neo-Assyrian painted reliefs. Links with Egypt can be discerned in the works of the painter Philokles from Naukratis. In Orientalizing pottery the figures are given more rounded profiles, coordinated movements and more complex narrative contexts. Polychrome painting originated in Corinth, in the works of Ekphantos. The Chigi Vase (*c*. 640–*c*. 630 BC; Rome, Villa Giulia, 22, 697) decorated by the Macmillan painter represents the masterpiece of early polychrome Proto-Corinthian painted pottery (*see* Pottery, §IV, 4(ii)). The palette was that used until the time of Apelles (late 4th–early 3rd century BC): white, black, red and yellow.

In Corinth at the beginning of the Archaic period, the use in pottery decoration of shapes outlined with black paint and with an engraved margin appears side by side with freely rendered outlines in brown lines. Vase painters from Corinth spread the new technique to Athens, where they became the basis of the Black-figure style of vase painting). The François Vase (Florence, Mus. Archeol.; *c*. 570 BC) by Kleitias displays all the characteristics that Pliny attributed to masters of the Archaic style: the clear distinction between females and males, the representation of figures without stiffness and the ability to overlap and foreshorten. In the depiction on this vase of the *Kalydonian Boarhunt*, for example, the heroes pursue the animal from both sides, so that the movement is placed in a tangible space: these are the 'slanting images' (*katagrapha*) introduced into large-scale painting by Kimon of Kleonai. A generation later, Exekias adapted to the needs of Athenian ceramics the resources of monumental painting, in which he was evidently skilled.

Cypress panels from Pitsa (*see* §1(i) above), dating from *c*. 525 BC and after, demonstrate the techniques of painting on wood and are comparable both with contemporary vase painting and with the limestone slate found in the Achaemenid Treasury, Persepolis, which depicts Greek myth. To the same period belong the wall paintings at Gordion and Elmalı, and the vivid Etruscan tomb paintings, which show Ionian influence (*see* §V below).

(ii) Classical (c. 480–323 BC). The Persian destruction of the Acropolis in Athens in 480 BC caused the loss of the legacy of the earlier tradition of Attic painting. It is clear, however, that Archaic painters had already given their figures a fluidity and a sensitivity to narrative context; these qualities are even more marked in the figures of the Classical period, which are part of, and are influenced by, a real environment.

(a) 5th century BC. (b) 4th century BC.

(a) 5th century BC. The flowing graphics of the Red-figure style made it easier for vase painters to borrow themes from the great masters, so that the subject-matter, as described by Pausanias (IX.iv.1–2), of the cycle painted by Onasias (*fl* first half of 5th century BC) and Polygnotos of Thasos for the Sanctuary of Athena in Plataia can be identified in contemporary pottery. The vase painter who most closely follows the style of the masters is the Penthesilea Painter (*fl* 460s–440s BC): the face and the human body are arranged in a series of postures as if in accordance with a poetic code. The impression of monumentality stems from the rhythmic distribution of such schemes within geometric grids.

Stage sets for one of Aeschylus' tragedies (written *c*. 460 BC) were painted on wooden panels by Agatharchos, who gave an impression of depth by his use of undulating ground, rocks and trees, among which figures were interspersed to suggest different planes, thus giving concreteness and credibility to the story. The plastic effect was enhanced by the handling of shadows. Polygnotos began with neutral shading, crosshatching and toning down, and Panainos added flesh-tints to the chromatic scale. Apollodoros varied the colour according to the intensity of the light, mixing different 'earths', from yellow to brown. He also studied the phenomenon of the *ombra portata* (chiaroscuro), which appears for the first time in ceramics just after 450 BC with the Chiusi Cup. This is how Apollodoros made his figures seem so realistic, a revolutionary quality found in his panel paintings even more than in his large wall paintings. He also developed, in his paintings on the cylindrical surfaces of lekythoi, the preference of the Achilles painter for a white ground, so creating easy and harmonious postures.

Zeuxis, who arrived in Athens *c*. 430 BC and died in Macedonia, took the Classical style to its highest point. The lightness of his draperies probably corresponded to the flowery style of the MEIDIAS PAINTER. The decorations engraved on the silver vases of Douvanli recall the Attic lekythoi of Group R with their white grounds, inspired by the perspective of PARRHASIOS' drawings: the line only suggests foreshortening, cancelling the solidity of background. TIMANTHES, a leading figure in the painting competitions that flourished among his generation of artists, on several occasions beat both Parrhasios and the otherwise unknown Kolotes of Teos.

(b) 4th century BC. At the end of the Peloponnesian War (404 BC), three distinct schools existed: one typical of East Greece, centred on Ephesos; an Attic school; and a particularly prestigious school at Sikyon in the Peloponnese. The 'Asian genre', as Pliny called it, was the oldest. Kolophon was the home town of Dionysios, contemporary and imitator of Polygnotos; in Ephesos, Euenor and his son Parrhasios were active; from Samos came Agatharchos. Androkydes was born in Kyzikos, a colony of Miletos; he was named by Pliny as a rival of Zeuxis but outlived him: a painting commissioned from Androkydes by the city of Thebes remained unfinished *c.* 180 BC. Aetion, active during the era of Alexander the Great (*reg* 336–323 BC), is reputed to have come from Miletos. APELLES, born in Kolophon *c.* 375 BC, received his education in Ephesos under Ephoros, but as an artist he was pan-Hellenic. Through his longstanding contact with the most important schools of his time and his presence at the courts of Philip II (*reg* 359–336 BC), Alexander, and Alexander's warring successors, he absorbed the whole experience of Classical style, creating the vocabulary that became universal in Hellenistic art.

In Athens, the school was started by ARISTEIDES, a native of Thebes, who was trained *c.* 400 BC by Euxenidas. Two styles predominated: one, largely represented by his son Ariston and later descendants, featured allegorical subjects; the other, promoted by EUPHRANOR, is more natural, inspired by historical events. The first style can be regarded as of Theban origin, the second Athenian.

NIKOMACHOS OF THEBES, pupil of Ariston and creator of fantastic compositions, is one of the earliest Greek painters to whom a surviving original work can be attributed, the decoration of the Tomb of Persephone at Aigai (Vergina). In *Hades and Persephone* Hades' hair—brown, yellow and purple—floats in the air; his facial features are delineated by hatching, in the same colours as the hair, with yellow used for highlights. The outline of the Hades group, with Persephone being dragged into the carriage, is repeated in the battle scene in the *Alexander* Mosaic at Pompeii (*see* POMPEII, fig. 6): this supports the attribution of the battle scene from which the mosaic was possibly copied to PHILOXENOS OF ERETRIA, who was a pupil of Nikomachos. Another piece by Philoxenos, the *Banquet of the Three Sileni*, known through its reproduction in an engraving on the back of an Etruscan mirror, indicates the painter's influence over neighbouring Thrace, where the Tomb of Kazanluk bears a painting with a very similar perspective illustrating the offer of food to the dead.

Euphranor decorated the Stoa of Zeus in the Athenian Agora in 362 BC. Through his disciple Antidotos (*fl* late 4th century BC), his teaching was transmitted to NIKIAS, a versatile artist who flourished in the second half of the 4th century BC and may have painted the hunting scene on the façade of the Philip II's tomb in Aigai (336 BC). The hunters, with the dogs and the game, are set in a landscape punctuated by rocks and trees, with snow-covered mountains in the background. The palette is rich, from the white of the background and of the King's horse, through the warm tones of yellow–orange, red, brown, pale violet and purple, to the colder green and blue shades and the sombre tones of the rocks.

The founder of the Sikyonian school, Eupompos (*fl* early 4th century BC), argued *c.* 375 BC for the crowd scene as the natural subject, eschewing a moral selection based on the subject's heroic character. For his successors PAMPHILOS and MELANTHIOS, the objective was symmetry, founded on mathematical and geometric schemes; for PAUSIAS, realism was achieved by use of shading and foreshortening. The newly introduced encaustic painting had a parallel in the bright overpainting on West Slope ware and Gnathia vases.

Apelles arrived at Sikyon already possessing the powers of observation characteristic of Ionian art from the beginning. In his painting the Classical organic whole is broken up by the highlighting of peripheral detail. In addition to the plasticity achieved by the perspective, the colour and the light, interpreted in different ways by Melanthios and Pausias, there is what Pliny termed *splendor*: the representation of the source of light within the painting and the study of reflections on figures and objects. Novel but typical of the Sikyon school was a sparing use of shadow, limited to the four colours of the Archaic tradition (black, white, yellow and red). A remarkable technique was used for applying the colours, the 'glazing' sharply observed by Aristotle: 'colours show one through the other, an effect painters sometimes achieve by laying one colour on top of a brighter one'.

Invited by Philip, Apelles moved from Sikyon to Macedonia *c.* 343 BC. Later he returned to Ephesos, where he worked for Alexander; after the King's death, he worked at the court of Ptolemy I (*reg* 305–283 BC) in Egypt. He visited Rhodes, where he met PROTOGENES, then on his way back from Athens. Finally he established his residence in Kos, where he painted his unfinished masterpiece, the *Aphrodite Anadyomene*, between 306 and 301 BC.

(iii) Hellenistic (323–27 BC). During the Hellenistic period, the quest for space, colour and light was enriched by techniques comparable to those used in modern painting from the Baroque period to the Neo-classical and Impressionist. The kingdom of Macedonia continued to attract artists of

different origins, as is shown by the commissioning of Philoxenos by Kassander (*reg* 305/4–297 BC) and of Theon of Samos by Demetrios I Poliorketes (*reg* 294–288 BC).

North of Aigai (Vergina), on the Macedonian plain, a series of remarkable discoveries includes a tomb with a façade on two levels (?3rd century BC), found at LEUKADIA. The whole is designed like the gate of a city, denoting the entrance to the underworld. Two wall paintings depict the deceased as a military leader in armour together with Hermes, the guide of souls, and the infernal judges Aiakos and Rhadamanthys. Of slightly later date is the monument at Naousa, the interior decoration of which, now lost, was reproduced in watercolour at the time of its discovery; it represented a knight in combat against an Oriental. Another tomb, dated 250 BC, was explored there in 1971; this has beautiful floral motifs painted at the entrance and a married couple on the façade. The most recent work is painted on the tomb discovered in Leukadia in 1942 inscribed with the names of the brothers Lyson and Kallikles, officers of the Macedonian army; decorative panels depict armour, shields, helmets and swords in brilliant colours. Perhaps the two occupants had fallen at the Battle of Cynoscephalai (197 BC).

The Leukadia façade shows an artist working according to the internal demands of painting, no longer 'applying to each part the colour that suits it', as Plato recommended. The effect derives from the proximity of colours: employing a type of 'pointillist' technique, bodies and draperies are represented by the overlapping of small, differently coloured touches of the brush that are not mixed with one another but blend only when seen from a distance. This technique was disseminated by a master active at the Macedonian court; he painted the original of the allegorical and dynastic cycle that was reproduced in the Boscoreale Villa (Naples, Mus. Archeol. N.; New York, Met.). Another native of Macedonia was Heraklides, who moved to Athens in 168 BC after the fall of the Macedonian king Perseus (*reg* 179–168 BC).

In Athens, the investigation of light was further advanced by Hyppis, who painted the *Marriage of Pirotoo*, presenting an interior heavy with drapery and gold, lighted by a flaming chandelier.

In Sikyon, Timanthes the younger painted the vigorous *Victory of Aratos over the Aitolians at Pellene*; Leontiskos represented the general next to a trophy. Nealkes, who produced mythological and genre paintings, examined relations between Aratos (271–213 BC) and the Ptolemies, thus recalling the battle between Darius II Ochos (*reg* 423–404 BC) and the Egyptians a century before. His daughter Anaxandra and Erigonos, who in turn was master to Pasias, are mentioned as his disciples.

In Pergamon, the artist Pytheas, educated in Sikyon but a native of Bura in Arcadia, painted an elephant that is echoed in a fresco at the House of Sacello Iliaco in Pompeii, probably depicting the 'Battle of the Elephants', at which Antiochos I (323–261 BC) of Syria defeated the Galatians in 275 BC. Pausanias mentioned a painting in Pergamon, associated with the wars waged by the Pergameni in 238 BC, that celebrated a *Galatomachy*, later reflected in Roman sarcophagi, by artists from Asia Minor such as Milon of Solos. A plasticity derived from Pergamene painting, evident in the wide spaces and shading of atmospheric tones of the *Dionysos Discovering Ariadne*, in the House of Cithara Player in Pompeii, suggests that this work was modelled on a 3rd-century BC original. The neo-Classical taste became popular *c.* 140 BC, as is evidenced by the despatch of the painters Asklepiades (*fl c.* 100 BC), Gaudotos and Kalas to Delphi by Attalos II (*reg* 160–139 BC) to copy famous originals. When Pergamon became part of the Roman Empire in 133 BC, the painter Iaia of Kyzicos, a woman, went to Italy. Around 290 BC Artemon worked at the court of Seleukos of Antioch (*reg* 305–281 BC). His paintings depicting Herakles were moved to the Porticus of Octavia in Rome, where they are said to have inspired the decoration of the House of Octavius Quartone in Pompeii, which is dominated by an intense chiaroscuro, with a rich impasto of colours and specks of light. To the same milieu belongs the exuberant painting representing stories of Dionysos and Herakles in the House of Marcus Lucretius Fronto.

In Rhodes, Protogenes developed the observation of social reality, a course followed by Philiskos (*fl ?c.* 100 BC), who portrayed a shop-boy blowing on a fire in the artist's studio, and by Simos, who painted a dyer's shop. The iridescent effect obtained in the theatrical scenes, as evidenced in mosaic copies signed by Dioskourides of Samos (Naples, Mus. Archeol. N.), derives from developments in technique in Asia Minor and the offshore islands during the 2nd century BC. In this case the technique is used to suggest the transparency of dresses made of Kos silk.

In Alexandria, ANTIPHILOS progressed from chromatic harmony to tonal painting, in the manner of Apelles. The elaboration of *splendor* enabled fire to operate as a source of light in an enclosed space. It seems to have been in Alexandria too, in a reaction against the neo-Attic fashion, that the *a macchia* style was born. There are several examples of this in wall paintings at Rome, including the yellow frieze in the House of Livia on the Palatine representing a scene on the Nile, as well as a nocturne in Pompeii relating to the cult of Isis, authentic *plein-air* paintings.

J. Overbeck: *Die antiken Schriftquellen zur Geschichte der bildenden Künste bei den Griechen* (Leipzig, 1868/*R* Hildesheim, 1959)

K. Jex-Blake and E. Sellars: *The Elder Pliny's Chapters on the History of Art* (London, 1896)

E. Pfuhl: *Malerei und Zeichnung der Griechen* (Munich, 1923)

E. Pfuhl: *Masterpieces of Greek Drawing and Painting* (Munich, 1926)

C. M. Robertson: *Greek Painting* (Geneva, 1959)

V. J. Bruno: *Form and Colour in Greek Painting* (London, 1977)

3. THEORY AND CRITICISM. For the Greeks, painting was perhaps the most highly regarded art form. Travellers, writers and poets from Simonides

(*c*. 556–*c*. 468 BC) until the Byzantine age consistently rated painters higher than other artists.

(i) 5th century BC. (ii) 4th century BC. (iii) 3rd century BC.

(i) 5th century BC. PAUSANIAS' description (X.xxv–xxxi) of the paintings by Polygnotos on the walls of the *lesche* (clubhouse) built by the Knidians *c*. 450 BC at Delphi helps explain why Simonides thought of Polygnotos when he declared, 'Painting, silent poetry; poetry, speaking painting'. The mastery of *techne* ('craft', 'skill') became the artistic equivalent of poetic *sophia* ('wisdom'). But Polygnotos' work was not seen simply as an illustration of a literary text: the artist was credited with the power to elaborate his material independently. Avoiding immediate realism and dramatic excess, painters treated myths and heroes with the detachment of the epic, and human sentiments with the sublimation of the lyric. The *ethos* or depiction of character attributed to Polygnotos by his contemporaries represents the perfect balance between descriptive observation and formal perfection. Ancient critics connected the new expressive possibilities shown by Panainos in the physiognomies of the combatants in his *Battle of Marathon* with the increased use of colours, which they thought had already created a 'perfect' art. Progress coincided with technical experimentation: Panainos had elsewhere used an original milk tempera and a yellow made from crocuses.

In the 5th century BC, among those who developed the perspective theories of Agatharchos, the sculptor Anaxagoras inspired Pheidias, who was originally a painter, and Demokritos was the theorist of painting as illusion, the adviser of Apollodoros. With his treatise on perspective, Anaxagoras, the teacher and friend of Pericles, taught artists a new visual language. He asserted that our weak senses cannot discern the truth but that we can understand it through experience, memory and art, since the world of appearances reflects invisible truths. His rational, scientific approach and faith in the intellect were expressed in the concept of perspective. Demokritos held that our senses perceive not real things but insubstantial images emanating from the atoms that compose matter. According to Pliny, Apollodoros was a painter of 'appearance' (*species*); indeed, Apollodoros had been called *skiagraphos* ('painter of shadows', i.e. phantoms or illusory figures). The term *skiagraphia* was also used to refer to primitive painters, a usage that persisted. Plato confirmed this in the famous myth of the cave in the *Republic*, where the ignorant inhabitants live in a world of 'shadows' thrown by a fire, which they believe to represent reality. For Plato, art was merely the shadow of shadows. In Demokritos space is conceived as a visual field, and Apollodoros was known for the execution of single pictures rather than large wall paintings. This marks the beginning of painting in the modern sense, as a view opening on the world; Pliny said that, among Greek paintings, Apollodoros' were the first from which the observer could not tear his gaze away.

Once they had liberated their art from the directives of civic morality and politics, Greek painters of the late 5th–early 4th century BC engaged in a refined skirmish over formal qualities: theirs was an art of perfection, intended to be understood by other artists. Apollodoros declared that his works were easier to criticize than to imitate. Parrhasios described himself as the 'holder of first place in art among the Hellenes'; Zeuxis retorted that he did not consider himself second; and, in a third epigram, Parrhasios declared that his own heights were 'insuperable'. The figurative artistic vocabularly of this period was so secure in its expressive means that painters were conscious of having reached full self-realization. The preference that Parrhasios gave to line and Zeuxis to chiaroscuro allowed them both to take one technique to its furthest point. Zeuxis' attentive study of proportions was paralleled by that of the sculptor POLYKLEITOS in his Canon. This could be seen as the fulfilment of Pythagorean numerical speculation. Following Apollodoros' lead, Zeuxis also developed a theory of shading, apparently making use of the 'superposition' of transparent colours (i.e. glazing).

Thus Zeuxis continued to feature at the forefront of innovation and controversy. He had lived through the highpoint of the Classical period (*c*. 475–323 BC), but he had also experienced the crisis of the Peloponnesian War (431–404 BC), the elegance of the Athenian nobility, the intolerance of the new intellectuals and the exhausting search for beauty. In the end he escaped into an extroverted kind of painting; his scenes of life, conversation and play were addressed to refined art lovers, and the artist's expertise was exhausted in a process that was increasingly pitched at a specialist level. Art for art's sake was born, and so was the figure of the misunderstood artist.

When the process of formation of strictly Classical iconography, begun by Polygnotos, had come to an end, Parrhasios was credited with the power of a 'lawgiver', because his images of the gods, which were not based solely on natural models, had prevailed for centuries. In Parrhasios, creation arose from imagination rather than observation, and this approach absorbed following generations: Theon became famous, according to Quintilian, 'for his faculty of conceiving visions, which are called *phantasiai*'.

With Timanthes the aesthetic of the *ethos* (portrayal of essential character) became an almost hermetic art. The gifts attributed to Zeuxis and Parrhasios had been technical experience, search for the ideal type, elegance of invention and sympathy for the different aspects of human emotion; the painters were associated with Timanthes, to create an artistic synthesis appropriate for the age of the Sophists. In his painting, for the first time, critics looked beyond formal structures, recognizing that a work's reality lies beyond its appearance and that 'genius goes beyond art'. Hellenism marked the exploration of realism of Greek painting; it remained to Timanthes, in the allusive play he derived from the theatre, to situate the real in extreme situations.

(ii) 4th century BC. After the Peloponnesian War, this tradition was replaced by the schools that flourished particularly in the years of Alexander the Great (*reg* 336–323 BC) and his successors. The Theban–Attic school (*see* §2(ii)(b) above) seems to have been orientated towards mediating between a realistic portrayal or experience and the need to depict events outside human history. The lightness of Nikomachos of Thebes is countered by the realism of Euphranor: the Athenians said that their *Theseus* was fed on meat, while that of Parrhasios was fed on roses. On the Theban side, painting showed a taste for ideal constructions close to Plato's view of the world. In the Athenian tradition, art's profane context allowed the painter a freedom of choice, invention and aesthetic unknown in the earlier Classical world. Its rich possibilities were not to be fully realized until the Renaissance.

A treatise on eloquence saved the artistic vocation of Nikias. He declared that history was a 'grandiose subject...and that this subject was part of pictorial art like the myths of the poets'. This corresponds to Aristotle's opposition of history, which comments on real events, and poetry, which suggests the possible. Similarly, Nikias attributed to history a greatness that placed it between the painting of myths and that of 'little things like birds and flowers'.

The preference accorded in Asia Minor to Androkydes' realism explains why he was subjected to the general condemnation of 'passions' in terms of the residual Athenian aristocratic ethic. Following Plato's critique of the emotions, Androkydes was accused of 'having obeyed his passion [*pathos*] because by nature [*physis*] he was a lover of that food—fish—that he had skilfully introduced into his painting'.

When Eupompos, founder of the Sikyon school, was asked *c.* 375 BC which painters he followed, he pointed to the crowd in the road and answered that one should follow nature, not another artist. This assertion represented the mature development of the culture of the Sophists, who similarly resolved the relation between law (*nomos*) and nature (*physis*), that is to say between convention established by man and what the world offers in its native state: they were in favour of the *physis*, source of all good for mortals. The Sophists, like their antagonist Plato, were engaged in discovering the natural character of techniques (extended later by Pliny): they wanted man to model his own enterprises on the multiform life of plants and animals. Eupompos infused these values into the artistic production of Sikyon.

In his essay on the art of drawing, Pamphilos expressed the approach of one who was 'first among painters to be erudite in every discipline'. He maintained that it was necessary to study mathematics and geometry, to introduce drawing into the education of the young and to teach the encaustic technique. Quintilian praised him for the exactness of his proportional calculation (*ratio*). Plutarch spoke of the Sikyon artists' awareness in cultivating 'perfect painting' (*chrestographia*) and their desire to realize an unchangeable beauty.

According to ancient criticism the process of discovery embarked on by Classical painters culminated in the late 4th century BC–early 3rd with Apelles. It seems that he had not intended to break with the past; he expressed admiration for exponents of different schools and had reworked earlier experiences in a wider synthesis. But on the level of theory he had boldly advanced the innovations of the masters of Sikyon, reaching an awareness of the relativity and subjectivity of representation. From the surviving fragments of his theoretical writings, it seems that he believed 'genius' and 'grace' to be natural gifts of the artist. An epigram from a papyrus speaks of Apelles as a 'demon', whose force fascinates and ensnares the viewer. And he had personified *charis* (grace) in a painting at Smyrna; it was reproduced in a mosaic of the Imperial period (27 BC–AD 330) from Byblos (Beirut, Mus. N.), a composition of a girl exhibiting *kairos* (propitious moment) and *akme* (flowering). In his essay on painting Protogenes confessed his uneasiness about the technical expertise he had achieved: he 'did not like the art that could not be attenuated, and seemed excessive, and moved too far away from the truth'. Pliny attributed to Protogenes the assertion that in painting 'verisimilitude' is not enough: in the soul of the former artisan, still caught up in myth and Classical language, the morality of 'truth' was born.

(iii) 3rd century BC. During the first half of the 3rd century BC, the Athenian sculptor and writer XENOKRATES introduced into art criticism both a parallel between painting and plastic art and the idea that the 'inventions' of the great masters had evolved out of the work of their predecessors. Thus Apollodoros' innovative use of chiaroscuro was developed by Zeuxis in his theory of shading and by Parrhasios' use of symmetry, and following Euphranor's study of colour, Apelles brought it to perfection. Xenokrates' work was continued in Pergamon by Antigonos of Karystos (*fl c.* 250–*c.* 200 BC), who extended art criticism to include terms more appropriate to rhetoric. Polemon in turn introduced the idea of scholarly description of paintings according to their arrangement. Pasiteles developed this a century later in a work of five volumes, one of which was devoted to painting. He took account of the new organization of masterpieces in Rome, paving the way for Varro. The legacy of Greek artists and theorists can be traced in the development of Roman painting, of which many more examples survive.

K. Jex-Blake and E. Sellars: *The Elder Pliny's Chapters on the History of Art* (London, 1896)

4. COLLECTIONS AND COLLECTORS. The idea of the picture gallery itself comes from the Classical Greek world. In the mid-5th century BC, at the time of Pericles, the first building expressly designed to contain

paintings was constructed: Mnesikles planned the north wing of the Propylaia on the Acropolis (*see* ATHENS, §II, 1(i)) to house the collection of precious votive pictures. Good light was assured by south-facing windows, and a cornice of grey marble marked the lower limit of the surface designated for the paintings.

In the Hellenistic period (323–27 BC) collections of paintings of different periods were assembled in the courts of rulers at Pergamon (where specially made copies were also hung), in Antioch and in Alexandria. After their independence was ended in 31 BC by the Romans, the Greeks themselves saw the places of their history more as art museums than as religious and political centres. In Strabo's *Geography*, written in the time of Augustus (*reg* 27 BC–AD 14), a description of the Temple of Hera at Samos gives that site, which had been so lively in the Archaic period (*c.* 700–*c.* 480 BC), the atmosphere of an involuntary museum: 'an ancient sanctuary and a great temple, which today is an art gallery; apart from the quantity of little pictures inside the cella, there are other buildings for the collection of pictures and numerous shrines that are also full of ancient works of art'.

With the conquest of the western Greek cities in the 2nd century BC, the Romans obtained their first substantial collections of pictures, which, after adorning their triumphal processions, were placed in the temples and porticos of the city. Other masterpieces came from Corinth, sacked by Lucius Mummius in 146 BC. It was then that Polybius saw the paintings of the Athenian and Sikyonian masters scattered on the ground, while soldiers played dice on them. Pliny recounted an episode that illustrates the difficulty the Romans had in understanding the commercial value of Greek painting, which was already fuelling the Hellenistic princes' passion for collecting: part of the booty of Corinth was sold at auction, and the Consul was astonished that Attalos II of Pergamon (*reg* 160–139 BC) offered 600,000 *denarii* for the *Dionysos* of Aristeides; concluding that the painting had magic powers, he withdrew it from sale and had it placed in a temple in Rome.

At the end of the Republic, Rome was a precious public art gallery, though many works had ended in private hands. Hortensius, a lover of art and rival of Cicero, had a special shrine built to hold a painting by Cydias depicting the *Argonauts*: the structure adorned his park at Tusculum, near the present Frascati. Agrippa (64/63–12 BC), the son-in-law of Augustus, promoted a cultural policy that even today seems advanced: he held that the works of the greatest Greek artists should not be owned by private individuals but should be offered for the enjoyment of the public, because of their aesthetic and moral value. He was overruled by wealthy collectors, who liked to link their own prestige to the possession of famous works. In the same years Vitruvius recommended that special rooms should be reserved for displaying paintings in houses. He conceived these galleries as little salons with seats and loggias. Following a more advanced ideal than Mnesikles, he advised that sources of light be opened on the north side rather than the south, so that the sun's rays could not reach the paintings, which would have the benefit of constant moderate light.

Petronius (*fl* 1st century AD) reflected on the end of Greek painting, imagining that Eumolpus, the protagonist of his romance *Satyricon*, entered the art gallery of a city in Campania (identified as Neapolis (Naples) or Pozzuoli), where one could admire originals of Zeuxis and drawings by Protogenes. In Neapolis, PHILOSTRATOS Lemnios (*b c.* AD 187–91) visited a large Greek gallery and left a detailed account: the paintings, by different artists, were divided according to great themes. The first hall was dedicated to the personifications of rivers, the second to Dionysos, the next to Aphrodite, the fourth to myths of the origin of the world and the last to Herakles.

The Imperial picture collection had a special position in Rome compared to the civic and private collections. It came from the collections of Hellenistic monarchs and may have maintained a certain continuity through the dynasties. Augustus preferred the paintings of Nikias. Attic vases painted in the Archaic Black-figure technique were collected in an immense museum in the 1st-century AD Grotto of Tiberius at Sperlonga. Philo Judaeus, an Alexandrian Jew who came to Rome in AD 40, described how Caligula (*reg* AD 37–41), reconstructing a villa on the Esquiline, personally studied the proper environment for displaying Greek paintings. A funerary inscription from the time of Antoninus Pius (*reg* 138–61 AD) gives the names of the Director of the Imperial gallery, Flavius Apollonius, and of his Vice-Director, Capito.

Numerous Greek pictures were held in Constantinople, as evidenced by descriptions in medieval epigrams, and these contributed to the continuity of Hellenistic features in Byzantine painting, a continuity now supported by technical evidence.

Turning to modern collections, a fragment of painted panel from the Hellenistic period, from Saqqara, is on display at the British Museum. The small Archaic panels from Pitsa (*see* §1(i) above) are at the Archaeological Museum of Sikyon, near their place of origin. In Italy, the decoration of the Tomb of the Diver at PAESTUM has been transferred to the Museo Archeologico Nazionale there, with the whole stone support represented by the large slabs that closed the sepulchre; these scenes, together with the numerous paintings on the tombs of the Lucan age, form a collection of 5th- and 4th-century BC painting. This is supplemented with examples from other sites in Campania and Apulia in the Museo Archeologico Nazionale at Naples. Painted stelai can be seen in Greece in the museums of Veria, Volos, Thebes and Athens, as well as in Istanbul and Alexandria. Original wall paintings usually remain *in situ*. Many museum collections contain indirect evidence of Greek painting in Greek ceramics (*see* POTTERY, §IV, 10) and Etruscan and Roman painting (*see* §§V and VI, 3 below). Of particular importance for understanding the development of Greek monumental painting are the great collections of figured Attic and South Italian vases in New York (Met.), London (BM), Paris (Louvre), Munich (Staatl. Antikensamml.), Rome (Villa Giulia), the Vatican (Mus. Gregoriano Etrus.), Taranto (Mus. N.) and Athens (N. Archaeol. Mus.).

A. Andronikos, M. Hadjidakis and V. Karagiorgis: *The Greek Museums* (Athens, 1974)

A. Kokkou: *I Merimna ghia tis Ellinikes Archaeotites kai ta prota Mouseia* [The care for Greek antiquities and the first museums] (Athens, 1977)

See also COLLECTION AND DISPLAY OF ART, §I, 1 and II, 4.

V. Etruscan.

The sheer quantity of extant Etruscan painting, from the 7th to the 2nd century BC, on tombs and terracotta slabs, makes it unique in Classical art.

1. INTRODUCTION. Most equivalent Greek painting has perished, although such examples as do survive suggest that its thematic and stylistic features can be related to contemporary Etruscan work. Detailed study of paintings on Greek vases, many of which were deposited in Etruscan tombs, has helped to establish the chronology of Etruscan wall painting.

How far Etruscan painting reflects the innovations of the great Greek painters, such as Polygnotos of Thasos, Zeuxis and Parrhasios, is uncertain. Ironically, while the names of the Greek artists survive, along with detailed descriptions of their works, their paintings have disappeared entirely. Conversely, although no Etruscan painter's name is known and no Etruscan painting is described in contemporary literature, many original works remain. The only possible ancient allusion to Etruscan painting occurs in Pliny (*Natural History* XXXV.xliii.152), who related that three craftsmen accompanied the Corinthian Demaratos when he settled in Etruria. One of these, Eugrammos ('the good draughtsman') sounds like a painter, even though Pliny actually credited the trio with the introduction of sculpture to Etruria. Significantly, Pliny went on to refer to Damophilos and Gorgasos, the artists who decorated the Roman Temple of Ceres in the Circus Maximus, as renowned sculptors and painters, implying early links between terracotta sculpture and painting. Otherwise, Pliny only recorded that he admired some 'extremely old' paintings in buildings at Ardea, Lanuvium and Caere (Cerveteri), without giving details (*Natural History* XXXV.vi.17–18).

Etruscan painting helps towards an understanding of wider developments in Classical art, but its location in religious and burial sites makes it primarily valuable in reconstructing the socio-religious history of Etruria itself, including details of funerary rituals, changes in beliefs in the afterlife and the status of those who commissioned the paintings. Only a small proportion of Etruscan tombs are painted, which implies that they were confined to the wealthy élite. There is evidence that paintings also adorned Etruscan sanctuaries, but almost all that survive occur on the walls of rock-cut family tombs (*see* ARCHITECTURE, §V).

Most of the painted tombs occur in southern Etruria, at Veii, Caere, Tarquinia, Vulci, Volsinii Veteres (Orvieto) and moreover at Clusium (Chiusi), with isolated examples in San Giuliano, Blera, Orte and elsewhere. There are significant regional variations in both quantity and date. The oldest extant fresco occurs in the Tomb of the Ducks (*c.* 680–*c.* 670 BC), at Veii. The painted tombs at Tarquinia are all later, but they are far more numerous than at any other site, so that the history of Etruscan tomb painting is largely a history of Tarquinian tomb painting. The tombs discussed below are all Tarquinian, unless stated otherwise. At Tarquinia itself the painted tombs belong to a single necropolis on the Monterozzi hillside, which has attracted attention at least since the Middle Ages.

Tomb paintings should ideally be viewed in their original setting. The Tarquinian tombs themselves were reached by way of a staircase and dromos (passageway) leading via a vestibule to the main rectangular or squarish chamber. In the Archaic and Classical periods this rarely exceeded 14 sq. m in area, and it contained two or three funeral couches. However, in the 4th and 3rd centuries BC the main chambers became larger and sometimes had pillars, and they were supplemented by further rooms. This reflected the development of the concept of an extended family and the internal layout of the houses of the living. Inscriptions in such tombs often specify family links and provide evidence for dating. Tomb robbing at Tarquinia and elsewhere left few intact tombs, so that the chronology of Etruscan painting is based more on stylistic than on archaeological evidence.

2. TECHNIQUES AND CONSERVATION. Tomb paintings are especially vulnerable when accessible to the public and their effective conservation involves detailed study of how they were executed. In the earliest tombs the paintings were made directly on the smoothed rock walls of the burial chamber. However, most Etruscan paintings are a form of fresco, which was applied in various stages. First, the soft volcanic tufa in which the tombs were cut was roughened and prepared for the application of plaster. This was made of clay and powdered stone, and was often coated with a final layer of lime wash. The plaster varied in thickness, tending to be thinner in Archaic tombs (*c.* 575–*c.* 480 BC). Coated plaster was also used to fill cracks in the rock, but it was not usually applied to ceilings. The origins of the technique are uncertain, but the admixture of peat and plaster, as in the Tomb of the Chariots at Tarquinia (*c.* 490 BC) also occurred in Asia Minor and Mesopotamia. The damp underground conditions and the use of a lime wash, which reacted with groundwater, created a constant level of humidity and paintings could thus be executed without any interruption in the process (unlike later fresco techniques).

The basic decorative scheme on tomb walls consists of three horizontal zones: an upper panel of geometric motifs; a large central zone bearing the principal figural frieze, which occupies about two-thirds of the height of the wall; and a base line. Cords soaked in paint were used to define each area. The figures in the main frieze were first sketched or incised in outline. Cartoons may sometimes have been used as models, as was probably the case for the drawing of the boxers on the Tomb of the Monkey, Clusium (Chiusi, *c.* 480–*c.* 470 BC), where the artist possibly reversed a cartoon to produce identical profiles for both fighters. Some figures were apparently sketched in red outline with inner details, especially clothing, picked out, and many were clearly painted freehand. Once outlined, the figures were filled with broad brushstrokes, while the outline itself was often improved. When this colouring in was completed, both the inner details and the outlines were revised with a black outline, and at this stage a 'master' probably took over, if assistants had been responsible for other aspects of the work. Artists probably worked from 'pattern books' with figures sketched on a small scale. In the Archaic period the craftsmen who painted vases sometimes also decorated tombs, and it is possible to observe that they were accustomed to painting smaller surfaces, such as vases.

The Archaic and Classical painters, in particular, used a restricted palette of white, yellow, black, red, blue and green, with some intermediate tones. Some pigments were easy to obtain (e.g. red from earth containing oxidized iron); others, which were used more sparingly, had to be imported. Thus blue was made from an artificial compound known as Egyptian frit, traces of which have been found at Gravisca, the ancient port of Tarquinia.

Decorating a tomb cannot have taken more than a few days. Paintings may not have been commissioned until after a death by members of the deceased's family, to be completed during the *prothesis* (lying in state).

Etruscan painting techniques underwent certain changes between the 7th and the 2nd century BC. The most important was the shift from Archaic and Classical colour-based painting to a Hellenistic system based on light and shadow. Greek influence resulted in the use of crosshatching (e.g. Orcus Tomb II; *c.* 375–*c.* 350 BC), chiaroscuro highlighting (e.g. Tomb of the Charuns; *c.* 250–*c.* 200 BC), the 'stain' process (e.g. Tomb of the Garlands; *c.* 300–*c.* 250 BC) and the use of swift brushstrokes to paint figures (e.g. later frieze of the Tomb of the Cardinal; *c.* 240 BC). References in Pliny (*Natural History* XXXV.xxxvi.110) and Petronius (*Satyricon* II.ix) to Roman *picturae compendiariae* (shorthand methods of painting) have led some scholars to describe late Etruscan painting as 'impressionistic'.

The conservation of tomb paintings is problematic. Insects, plant roots and micro-organisms can cause extensive damage, but changes in humidity are the most crucial factor. Damp, caused by groundwater infiltration as well as condensation, can make the paintings swell and the plaster come away from the rock, while dryness causes flaking of pigments and plaster and surface growths of crystalline salts. Thus the tombs need to be kept at constant temperatures. Even short visits by small groups of people can have dramatic effects on their microclimates. Thus, restoration involves not only fixing the colours of the paintings but also coating them with a protective film, as at the Tomb of the Augurs (*c.* 530–*c.* 520 BC) and the Tomb of Hunting and Fishing (*c.* 520–*c.* 510 BC), among others. Previously, the only effective remedy was to transfer the paintings to museums, as in the case of the Tomb of the Chariots, the Tomb of the Olympic Games (*c.* 530–*c.* 520 BC), the Tomb of the Triclinium (*c.* 470 BC), the Tomb of the Funeral Couch (*c.* 460 BC), the Tomb of the Black Sow (*c.* 460 BC), the Tomb of the Ship (mid-5th century BC) and the Bruschi Tomb (3rd century BC; all Tarquinia, Pal. Vitelleschi).

3. SUBSIDIARY ORNAMENT. A continuous series of tomb paintings at Tarquinia from the second half of the 6th century BC onwards provides vital evidence for the general characteristics of funerary decoration. Subsidiary ornament served two main functions, emphasizing the architectural structure of the tomb and breaking up the wall space into distinct areas. The latter is achieved by the series of polychrome bands above the main figural frieze, and the further polychrome bands, or dado, that form a base line below it. Sometimes the dado is accompanied by figural decoration, such as dolphins leaping over a wave pattern.

The sloping ceilings of the tombs were sometimes untreated, or simply whitewashed, but often they were painted. The decoration may consist merely of bands of red and white, imitating rafters, or it may take the form of chequers or small floral motifs, petals, dots and circles on a white background, probably based on textile designs. The fake ridge beam (*columen*) was simply painted on in red, but sometimes it was decorated with large discs and bands running lengthways.

The front and back walls of the tombs provided three decorative areas: dado, main frieze and 'pediment'. The latter was divided into two parts by a fake king-post under the end of the *columen*. The king-post's outer corners may be filled with volutes and circles and sometimes animal protomes, while the body of the pediment depicts either heraldic animals (lions, panthers, hippocamps, and deer being savaged by felines) or banqueting scenes. The long triangular space suits the recumbent figures of banqueters, but creates problems of consistency of scale. In some tombs (e.g. the Tomb of the Leopards; *c.* 480–*c.* 470 BC) the painted king-post is omitted, while the lower pitch of Hellenistic roofs meant that the pediment was then no longer decorated.

Some tombs contain more elaborate painted architectural elements. The Tomb of the Lionesses (*c.* 520 BC), for example, has six decorative Tuscan columns at its corners and in the middle of its side walls, rising from floor to ceiling. Some Classical tombs (e.g. Tomb of the Triclinium and Tomb of the Black Sow) have vines painted on their roofs and pediments, and painted props for a bower or pergola at their corners. The Tomb of the Funeral Couch is festooned with painted drapes, while the Tomb of the Hunter (*c.* 500 BC) resembles a tent, so that both probably mimic the awnings and temporary structures that covered the corpse during the *prothesis* and apparently sheltered the guests at the funeral banquet.

4. Subject-matter. From the late 6th century BC to the early 4th, the content of Etruscan tomb paintings remained fairly consistent. Since they were closely associated with funerary ceremonies which were themselves the prerogative of aristocratic families, they probably represented both a form of perpetuated homage and an emblematic assertion of status. Certain themes had particularly strong symbolic values. The banquet was one of the most often repeated, especially during the 5th century BC (see colour pl. 2:III, fig. 2). The theme of the banquet may relate not only to funeral feasts but also to the Etruscan love of 'luxury' in general. Ancient sources are confirmed by the subject-matter of the tomb paintings: Diodorus Siculus might almost have been describing one of these when he wrote:

> They spread their tables for sumptuous meals twice daily, so that the tables groan with the weight of the luxurious fare, while they are shaded by canopies woven with flowers. The services are of solid silver, and the banqueters are waited on by countless slaves, some remarkable for their beauty, others for their lavish costumes. (*Historical Library* V.xl.3)

Typically, banquet scenes show between one and five couches, each bearing two recumbent banqueters. The couches are elaborate, with finely turned legs and embroidered covers. In front of them are small stands for the diners' sandals. The youths in attendance are naked or in loincloths, and hurry to and fro with jugs of wine, filled from large kraters on tables in the corner. Under the couches, domestic animals (e.g. dogs, cats, pigeons, hens and sometimes more exotic felines) wait for scraps of food. The banqueters, wearing garlands and intricately decorated cloaks, lie propped on cushions. They are shown talking, eating, drinking and playing *kottabos*, a messy game which involved flicking wine from a cup into a saucer balanced on a bronze stand. Both sexes participated at these banquets, a fact that aroused the indignation of the Greeks and Romans, who regarded it as a sign of immorality in Etruscan women, who were also reputed to be formidable drinkers. However, it actually reflects the higher legal status enjoyed by Etruscan women, who could inherit property in their own right in the absence of a male heir.

The 'banquet' in tomb paintings usually represents not the feast itself but the symposion that followed it, when guests drank, sang and talked under the supervision of a master of ceremonies. Thus minstrels are depicted beside the couches, usually playing some form of lyre or flute. Again this corroborates ancient literary sources, which not only credit the Etruscans with the invention of certain instruments, but state that they did everything to musical accompaniment, including boxing, kneading bread and even beating their slaves.

Dancing also occurs frequently, either as an element in the funerary ceremonies or simply as part of the general festivities (see fig. 5). Dancers in fine costumes and apparently performing the *tripudium* (three-step jig) sometimes seem from inscriptions to be not 'actors' but members of aristocratic families. Whenever the inner wall of a tomb is taken up by the main symposion scene, the side walls are painted with dancing figures, sometimes alternating with trees and shrubs.

The iconography of Etruscan banquets derives from representations of symposia on Athenian vases, while the banquet in its ideological aspects may be Near Eastern in origin. Another funerary ritual often depicted in Etruscan tombs is the athletic contest held in honour of the dead. This may have originated in prehistoric times and the events involved are similar to those described at the funeral of Patroklos (*Iliad* XXIII). Scenes of boxing predominate, and though the combatants sometimes perform to flute music, these are brutally vivid: one competitor in the Tomb of the Funeral Couch is offered a sponge to mop up a spectacular nose-bleed. Wrestling also occurs, as in the Tomb of the Augurs, and bronze bowls or tripods are shown as prizes. Running, long-jumping and discus-throwing appear in the Tomb of the Olympic Games, so-called both for this reason and because it was discovered shortly before the 1960 Rome Olympics. This tomb also features a race between four chariots: the leading charioteer is shown glancing back over his shoulder to assess the size of his lead or to watch a dangerous crash involving the last chariot. The Tomb of the Chariots depicts preparations for a similar race, with grooms and judges milling about. Some spectators sit attentively on the canopied grandstand, while others make love underneath it. The Etruscan armed dance, midway between ballet and athletics, was related to the Greek Pyrrhic dance and the Roman dance of the Salii. It is depicted in the Tomb of the Funeral Couch, where the dancer has a mantle knotted about his chest and wears a plumed helmet, while similar dancers appear in the Tomb of the Monkey and the Poggio al Moro Tomb (*c.* 480–*c.* 470 BC) at Clusium (Chiusi).

Certain games in Etruscan tomb paintings suggest country fêtes rather than athletic competitions; for example the tug-of-war depicted on the entrance wall of the Tomb of the Augurs, and the quoit-throwing and balancing acts that give its name to the Tomb of the Jugglers (*c.* 520–*c.* 510 BC). Various equestrian sports are also depicted, as might be expected given the social prestige attached to horse ownership. Riders demonstrate their prowess by leaping from one galloping horse to another. Hunting also features as a sport of the Etruscan aristocracy, the pursuit of

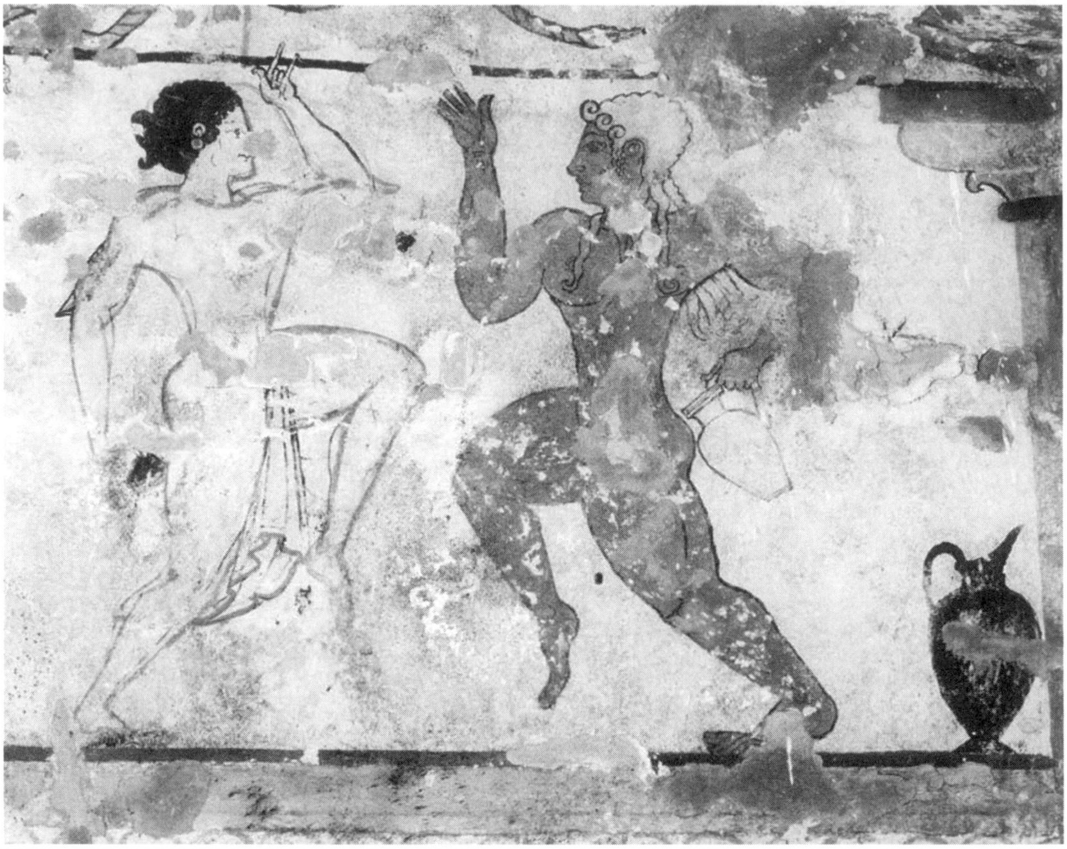

5. Etruscan wall painting with dancing scene, Tomb of the Lionesses, Tarquinia, *c.* 480–470 BC

fierce prey giving ideal opportunities for displaying courage and practising military skills. According to one literary source (Athenaeus: *Deipnosophists* I.xviii.1), Macedonian youths had to hunt wild boar alone and without nets or traps, as a rite of passage before being admitted to the banqueting table, and the same custom may have been followed in Etruria. Boar hunts are vividly depicted in the Tomb of the Black Sow and the Querciola I Tomb (*c.* 450 BC), which show beaters and hounds along with hunters on horseback and on foot. The return from the hunt is shown on the pediment of the first room of the Tomb of Hunting and Fishing. The mounted hunters are followed by pairs of valets carrying the carcasses slung on poles. In one corner a dog worries a hare. In the second room youths are shown aiming slingshots at flocks of multicoloured birds and lowering nets into the sea from a boat.

Representations of the aristocratic way of life predominated during the Archaic and Classical periods, but the subject-matter favoured in tomb paintings changed markedly in the Hellenistic period, with vivid depictions of the underworld. The walls of the Orcus Tomb II are covered with paintings of the gods and heroes of Hades, and in the Golini Tomb I at Volsinii Veteres (Orvieto, *c.* 350 BC) they even participate in the funerary banquet. This is apparently meant to be located in the underworld, and from about this time ceases to feature in painted tombs and is transferred instead to the decoration of cinerary urns and sarcophagi. The banquet was replaced in tomb painting by more explicit emblems of status, such as magisterial insignia, files of toga-clad figures led by lictors, and inscriptions listing public offices held by the deceased. The inscriptions are sometimes so extensive that they cover the walls of an entire room; they include genealogies and may be accompanied by portraits, creating a detailed record of the family's achievements. The change in subject-matter may stem in part from the vicissitudes of Etruscan politics during the 5th and 4th centuries BC, and partly from the spread of Orphic–Pythagorean doctrines concerning the afterlife. The latter clearly influenced the decoration of Orcus Tomb II, which shows small souls scattered among the asphodels.

At this time, some aristocratic families apparently died out, while other, new names came to the fore and the painted tombs became a means of asserting acquired political and social status. Good examples of this are the Pumpu family with the Tomb of the Typhon (first half of the second century BC) and the eponymous Aninas family with its tomb used for a long period (3rd century BC). Etruscan tomb painting eventually ceased altogether when even these families' fortunes waned after the Roman conquest of Etruria (3rd century BC).

5. Historical survey.

(i) *c.* 675–*c.* 500 BC. (ii) *c.* 500–*c.* 150 BC.

(i) c. 675–c. 500 BC. Orientalizing tombs of the 7th century BC mark the beginning of Etruscan painting. The earliest example is the Tomb of the Ducks at Veii, which depicts a file of five ducks painted in a style so close to that of Italo-Geometric vase painting that it may be by a vase painter, especially since close connections existed between Archaic tomb painting and vase painting. However, the late 7th-century BC Campana Tomb, also at Veii, is more significant. The end wall of the first of its two rooms is covered with registers of men, animals and monsters, with an abundant filling of floral and geometric designs. The second room contains six painted shields, which imitate the huge bronze shields frequently hung on tomb walls. The paintings are now faded, but watercolours by Luigi Canina suggest that they recalled Corinthian and Etrusco-Corinthian vase painting in both composition and colour. Several painted tombs of the 7th century BC occur at Caere (Cerveteri), but again they are poorly preserved. Their subjects were typical of the Orientalizing style: animal friezes containing lions, panthers, dogs, deer, dolphins, griffins, centaurs and sphinxes. The sarcophagus (*in situ*) in the Tomb of the Painted Animals (*c.* 650–*c.* 625 BC) had similar decoration to that on the tomb walls. In the Tomb of the Painted Lions (*c.* 650–*c.* 625 BC) the animal friezes included a 'Master of the Beasts' standing between two white-and-red lions, and, finally, the coeval Tomb of the Ship I (not the 5th-century BC tomb of the same name at Tarquinia) had an unusually early representation of a ship. Further Orientalizing tombs occur in various places, including Clusium (Chiusi), San Giuliano, Cosa and Magliano.

Caeretan plaques are a separate but related development in the 6th century BC. These are a series of painted rectangular terracotta plaques from Caere, measuring *c.* 1200 × 600 mm, which were once attached to the walls of sacred buildings or tombs to make a unified frieze. Some may have been transferred from buildings to tombs, since one has been sawn to fit its tomb's sloping roof. The technique used in decorating the plaques resembles vase painting: a stylus was used to incise the bands of decoration and figures on the white ground. The tops of the plaques may be painted with a frieze of tongues, guilloches or meanders and the bases are usually decorated with vertical two-tone stripes. Some of the earliest group (*c.* 560 BC; Rome, Villa Giulia) have two figural friezes, while others depict the Gorgons fleeing after Perseus' killing of Medusa. Of the five funerary Boccanera slabs (*c.* 560–*c.* 550 BC; London, BM), two show squatting sphinxes, while the remaining three each depict three figures. The identity of these is uncertain and interpretation depends largely on the order in which the plaques are juxtaposed. The Judgement of Paris is one possible subject, but at least two slabs may depict a funerary rite. Stylistically, they already show Ionic influence. The final group (*c.* 530–*c.* 520 BC; Paris, Louvre) were clumsily restored, and one may not even be authentic. Their subject is again uncertain, though the presence of an altar with a fire on it suggests a sacrifice scene.

The great period of Etruscan tomb painting began in the mid-6th century BC, although it was anticipated at Tarquinia by the Tomb of the Panthers (*c.* 600 BC), still in the Orientalizing style, and the Tomb of the Hut (*c.* 575–*c.* 550 BC). The former features two large felines on either side of a mask, a motif paralleled on many Etrusco-Corinthian vases; the latter an architectural design in brown wash, including a false door and rafters. Several later 6th-century BC tombs only have pedimental decoration or simple polychrome bands at the tops of their walls. These can be dated on the basis of stylistic comparisons with vase painting. Thus the Tomb of the Lotus Flower (*c.* 520 BC), the Tomb of the Jade Lions (*c.* 530–*c.* 520 BC), the Tomb of the Red Lions (*c.* 530 BC) and the Tomb of the Tritons (*c.* 520 BC) show affinities with the La Tolfa group of vases produced at Caere (*see* Pottery, §V, 7).

The most significant Tarquinian Archaic painted tomb is the Tomb of the Bulls (*c.* 530 BC). Two of its three rooms have pedimental decoration alone, in the form of animal friezes, but the main chamber features the *Ambush of Troilos by Achilles*. This is one of the few depictions of a known Greek myth in an Etruscan tomb and both subject and style connect it to the 'Pontic' vases produced at nearby Vulci. The Ionic influence on Etruscan vase painting in the second half of the 6th century BC also affected tomb art and may reflect the arrival of East Greek artists and craftsmen. Thus Phokaian artists have been credited with the paintings in the Tomb of the Augurs, the Tomb of the Jugglers and the Tomb of the Olympic Games, because of stylistic affinities with both Anatolian painting, exemplified by the frescoes at Gordion in Phrygia, and Caeretan hydriai, which were clearly produced by an East Greek immigrant in Etruria itself.

In addition to funeral games, the Tomb of the Augurs depicts two professional mourners on either side of a mock door symbolizing the passage between the living and the dead, as well as a gory scene involving a figure labelled Phersu. The latter represents a form of punishment inflicted on the condemned and prisoners. (The Roman gladiatorial games probably derived from this form of punishment.) Phersu, masked and dressed like a harlequin, incites a dog on a long lead to attack a naked man with a sack over his head. The man has a club with which to beat off the dog, but he can only do so blindly. The Tomb of the Jugglers depicts acrobats entertaining the deceased, who sits on a folding stool. It also includes an oddly scurrilous scene of a man defecating, identified in an inscription as the slave of Heracanas. This figure may represent the artist himself, adding a humorous touch to his signature.

The Tomb of the Olympic Games again in East Greek style possibly reflects familiarity with East Greek mythology, since the five figures at sides of the mock door resemble protagonists in the Judgement of Paris. Stylistic connections explain resemblances between the Tomb of Hunting and Fishing and works by the Samian Little Master cup painters. Influences of the Ionic style and of the workshop of 'Pontic' vases appear in the Bartoccini Tomb (*c.* 520 BC), with its elegantly tapestried ceiling and walls, and almost miniaturistic banquet scene in white and red on a dark background. The painting in the Tomb of the Lionesses (*c.* 520 BC; see fig. 5 above) seems less accomplished, not only because of inconsistencies in scale, but also because of discrepancies between the preliminary design and what was actually painted, especially in the figure of the dancer with her index and little finger raised in an apotropaic gesture. Finally, despite retouching done in the 19th century, the painting in the Tomb of the Baron (*c.* 510–*c.* 500 BC) still retains an impressive Ionic, perhaps Klazomenian clarity.

(ii) c. 500–c. 150 BC. Athenian Black-figure and Red-figure vase painting influenced Etruscan tombs at the start of the 5th century BC. Old tradition and new stylistic solutions are illustrated by the Tomb of the Hunter, which is painted to resemble a hunter's tent, so that the animal friezes on the upper zones of its wall become herds of game. In the Tomb of the Chariots a frieze of dark figures on a light background is placed directly above another with light figures on a dark background, suggesting the influence of Attic bilingual vases (i.e. with both Red-figure and Black-figure work on a single vase). The draughtsmanship resembles that of early Attic Red-figure vase painters such as EUPHRONIOS, EUTHYMIDES and EPIKTETOS, while some foreshortenings and three-quarter views recall the *katagrapha* ascribed to KIMON OF KLEONAI (Pliny: *Natural History* XXXV. xxxiv.56). Subsequently, the painters of the Tomb of the Triclinium and the Tomb of the Leopards must have been familiar with the developments in Athenian vase painting made by DOURIS and the KLEOPHRADES PAINTER. Thus the arrangements of the couches in the banqueting scenes recall the compositions of Douris, and several tombs (no. 994, of the Varnie family, and nos 4255, 4260 and 4021; all first half of the 5th century BC) share the same delicate workmanship.

The Tomb of the Monkey and the Tomb of the Hill (*c.* 475–*c.* 450 BC) at Clusium (Chiusi) both perpetuate earlier Tarquinian themes and styles. The Tomb of the Monkey contains scenes of chariot racing, wrestling, boxing and armed dancing, while the Tomb of the Hill features both banqueting and athletics. However, the friezes are significantly lower than in Tarquinian tombs.

Two important Tarquinian tombs of the second quarter of the 5th century BC are the Tomb of the Funeral Couch and the Tomb of the Black Sow. In the former the banquet takes place on either side of an imposing catafalque, and the scene, involving ballerinas, armed dancing and athletics, is composed with the same finesse as in the Tomb of the Triclinium. The Tomb of the Black Sow is named after a pedimental scene depicting the hunting of a great sow with prominent pink teats. In the banquet scene the diners are entertained not only by professional musicians, but also by a young female guest playing the zither. Several other tombs belong to the same workshop tradition. The figures in tomb no. 3697, which contained a cup signed by the potter Hieron, have similar profile-view eyes to those in the Tomb of the Black Sow, while tomb no. 5187 and the Tomb of the Stag Hunt both show similar hunting scenes, and tomb no. 5517 features another armed dancer. A hunt also occurs in the Querciola I Tomb, which is related to tomb no. 6071 and the four-roomed tomb no. 1560 (all *c.* 470–*c.* 450 BC).

The mid-5th-century BC Tomb of the Ship contains several banqueting scenes as well as its eponymous picture of a merchant vessel about to set sail. The execution is accomplished and suggests familiarity with the work of POLYGNOTOS OF THASOS. However, Tarquinian tomb painting in the later 5th century BC was undistinguished. Only a few works demonstrate any originality. Thus in the Tomb of the Maiden (*c.* 430–*c.* 420 BC) a painted temple façade, complete with a palmette acroterion and a pediment containing a winged gorgoneion, forms a framework for a burial niche containing the first burial. On the back wall of the niche is a pair of winged genii of the sort that first appear in tomb no. 4813 (first half of the 5th century BC), reappear in the Tomb of the Warrior (*c.* 420–*c.* 400 BC) and become common in the 4th century BC. Here they are shown preparing a shroud for the deceased. The painter of the Tomb of the Cock (*c.* 420–*c.* 400 BC) coordinated his colours well but was a poor draughtsman. The Tomb of the Blue Demons, discovered in 1985, is the oldest representation in Tarquinian funeral painting of the world of the dead (*c.* 420–*c.* 400 BC); it is clearly derived from Greek models, particularly the *Nekyia* painted at Delphi by Polygnotus of Thasos. On the end wall the banquet is depicted; on the left is the journey of the deceased; and on the right is his arrival in the other world among blue demons.

The earliest 4th-century BC tomb at Tarquinia is the Tomb of Orcus. It is in fact two tombs, the earlier designated Orcus I (*c.* 400–*c.* 375 BC) and the later Orcus II (*c.* 375–*c.* 350 BC), linked by an intermediate chamber. It belonged to the Spurinna family, whose most celebrated member was Velthur Spurinna, the *praetor Etruriae* who took the Etruscan fleet to help Athens in the battle against the Syracusans in 413 BC. The paintings are accomplished: Orcus I features a banquet, laid out under a pergola but apparently located in the underworld in the presence of demons; Orcus II contains a form of *nekyia* (summoning of the dead) which includes Hades and Persephone, the three-bodied Geryon and Kerberos on the end wall, and Agamemnon, Ajax, Tiresias, and winged demons on the left. The entrance wall depicts Sisyphos and his boulder, and the right wall shows Theseus and Perithoos, guarded by the winged demon Tuchulcha, with a rapacious look and snakes for hair. Finally, the intermediate room is decorated with the blinding of Polyphemos by Odysseus. Features of technique include a restrained use of crosshatching to give depth to the figures in Orcus I, while Orcus II evinces complete mastery of this device. The Tomb of the Shields (*c.* 340–*c.* 330 BC), named after the shields painted in its end room, belonged to the Velcha family, and its central room contains portraits of its first incumbent, Larth, and his father Velthur. Both are shown with their wives, and are represented twice, on different panels. Larth is also depicted on his journey to the underworld, accompanied by buglers and lictors. The painting is less sophisticated than in the Orcus complex, recalling contemporary Etruscan Red-figure vase painting.

The extent to which 4th-century BC Etruscans had assimilated Greek culture is clearly apparent in the François Tomb, Vulci (*c.* 350 BC; paintings in Rome, Villa Albani). Here the tomb's founder, Vel Saties, is depicted in a richly decorated toga, about to take auspices from the flight of a bird, and several scenes from Etruscan history are interspersed with a host of Greek mythological figures. In one room amid scenes that include the *Duel between Eteokles and Polyneikes*, the *Rape of Kassandra* and *Sisyphos with his Boulder*, the Etruscan Marce Camitlnas is shown killing one of the Roman Tarquins. In the adjacent room Achilles is depicted slaughtering Trojan prisoners to avenge the death of Patroklos and, on the opposite wall, the Etruscan leader Mastarna liberates Caile Vipinas amid combats between Etruscans from various named cities. The Etruscan scenes probably allude to the same events: the struggle that brought Servius Tullius (possibly identified with Mastarna) to the throne of Rome in place of the Tarquins. The scene with Achilles probably represents a piece of contemporary propaganda. Rome was beginning to take control of Etruria, capturing Veii in 396 BC, and the painting is doubtless intended to contrast Etruscan claims to be descended from the (victorious) Greeks with Roman claims of descent from the (defeated) Trojans.

Three painted tombs at Volsinii Veteres (Orvieto) belong to the second half of the 4th century BC. The best preserved, Golini I (*c.* 350 BC), is also the most interesting because, in addition to a fairly conventional banquet scene showing the Leinie family dining with Hades and Persephone, it also depicts the meal being prepared. Thus servants are shown in the kitchens, including one grinding something with a pestle and mortar to the accompaniment of a flute, while the entrance walls depict an ox, a hare, a kid, and various fowl suspended from hooks.

Highlighting was introduced into Etruscan painting under Greek influence. The *splendor* referred to by Pliny (*Natural History* XXXV.xi.29) took the form of brushstrokes of white paint which were first used to represent gleaming metallic objects and later figures. Shadows were created by crosshatching and depth was suggested by 'staining' the luminous areas. The results are illustrated by the paintings in the Giglioli Tomb (*c.* 300 BC) at Tarquinia, although they only depict a frieze of arms, which appear to hang on hooks in the walls. The tomb belonged to the Pinie family, and the shield blazons are especially interesting. They include not only magisterial insignia but also the symbols used on Tarquinian coinage. Powerful chiaroscuro depictions of shields also occur in the Tomb of the Garlands, belonging to the Curunas family, framed by a continuous band of wreaths. The flat ceiling of this tomb has blue panels, decorated with strands of foliage and erotes in the 'stain' technique. Its entrance is guarded by serpent-haired demons.

In the Aninas Tomb two winged demons standing on guard either side of the entrance perform a similar function. One, Vanth, is female and carries a torch; the other, Charun, bears a hammer. The tomb was used for some generations, and decoration, mostly in the form of garlands, was added with each new burial. Consequently, the painting is disorganized and stylistically disparate. The lack of planning in this and similar tombs has also been attributed to the status of their owners: middle-class 'new men' who assumed positions of power, such as the *zilath* (prime magistrate) Larth Aninas. However, the owners of the Tomb of the Cardinal, which was also restructured several times, were the illustrious Vestarcnie family, and its painting also inevitably varies in style. Thus the painting on the pilasters is more accurate than that on the walls. The subject-matter is of considerable interest, since it probably illustrates Etruscan eschatological texts. Further images of the afterlife occur in the Tomb of the Charuns, named after the green-fleshed demons standing either side of the mock doors, which are carved in relief and painted. The doors and the Charuns, which are labelled with names and epithets, decorate a vestibule probably used for cult rituals, while the actual burial chambers are at a lower level.

Only detached painted panels survive from the Bruschi Tomb (3rd century BC) depicting processions of toga-clad figures, including members of the Apuna family, bearing insignia and musical instruments. Some figures are painted in a chiaroscuro technique, exploiting subtle changes of colour and tone, while others are simply drawn in outline. The whale and dolphin frieze on the dado recalls Archaic models. Funerary processions also occur in the Tomb of the Congress (3rd century BC; no longer accessible) and an elderly, white-haired man features particularly prominently. He is represented twice, each time in the centre of a toga-clad throng of people carrying various emblems of office, including whips and double axes. None of the figures overlaps and, while the heads are painted carefully, the bodies are treated more sketchily, with cursive brushstrokes used for the togas. Even the heads show little modelling, though some, in three-quarter view, have an air of pathos. Also among the last significant Tarquinian painted tombs is the Tomb of the Typhon, which belonged to the Pumpu family and is named after the two typhons on the sides of its central pillar. It too portrays a toga-clad procession, but here the figures do overlap, giving some impression of depth. A secondary frieze again depicts waves and dolphins.

M. Pallottino: *Etruscan Painting* (Geneva, 1952)
F. Roncalli: *Le lastre dipinte da Cerveteri* (Florence, 1965)
M. Moretti: *Nuovi monumenti della pittura etrusca* (Milan, 1966; Eng. trans., Philadelphia, 1970)
M. Moretti: *Pittura etrusca in Tarquinia* (Milan, 1974)
E. Poulsgaard Markussen: *Painted Tombs in Etruria: A Bibliography* (Odense, 1979)
S. Steingräber, ed.: *Etruskische Wandmalerei* (Stuttgart, 1985); Eng. trans. as *Etruscan Painting* (New York, 1986)
H. Blanck and C. Weber-Lehmann: *Malerei der Etrusker in Zeichnungen des 19. Jahrhunderts* (Mainz, 1987)
M. A. Rizzo, ed.: *Pittura etrusca al Museo di Villa Giulia* (Rome, 1989)
S. Steingräber: *Etruscan Wall Painting: From the Geometric Period to the Hellenistic Period* (Los Angeles, 2006)

VI. Roman.

The surviving pictorial production of the Roman world consists almost exclusively of wall paintings, some of which are exquisite.

1. Introduction. 2. History and development. 3. Collections and collectors.

1. Introduction.

(i) Subject-matter. (ii) Materials and techniques. (iii) Painters and society.

(i) Subject-matter. Wall paintings were used in a wide variety of contexts, including public, private, religious or funerary buildings. The architectural setting often influenced the choice of subject-matter, though this also varied according to its date. The disposition of the various elements followed well-established practices.

(a) Organization and setting. (b) Literary and mythological subjects. (c) Scenes of daily life.

(a) Organization and setting. Painting adorned both internal and external walls, ceilings, vaults and even ornamental pools, shop-fronts, lararia (small public or private shrines) and, occasionally, floors, where it was used to imitate *opus sectile* (paving made of shaped tiles of coloured marble), as in the dancing floor of the theatre at Caesarea, Israel (*c.* 73–*c.* 4 BC).

The walls of a room were usually divided horizontally, with the lowest section decorated with dark, muted colours and simple patterns, such as various flecks, imitations of marble and other stone blocks, friezes of animals or clusters of plants. The figural scenes, which could be painted in small framed panels or executed on a large scale, according to taste or fashion, occupied the middle section at eye-level. The upper section became particularly elaborate in wall paintings in Italy in the second half of the 1st century AD, but at other times, particularly in the provinces, was restricted to painted or actual cornices. Motifs derived from architecture often served to divide and frame compositions. Imitation columns separating both small and large panels sometimes support false entablatures, at some periods including a stucco cornice. Ceiling and vault decoration often imitated architectural features, such as coffering, rows of beams, a cupola with lunettes or a groin vault. Sometimes, however, it depicted natural motifs, such as birds, a starry sky or a vine trellis against a clear blue sky.

The overall composition was dictated by practical considerations and hardly ever varied. Not only did the painters' scaffolding make it necessary to divide the wall into three horizontal sections, but this division also corresponded to the human field of vision as well as the demands of daily life. Furniture partly hid the lowest section, while the upper section was awkward to view, narrow or even completely absent, making the middle section the obvious field for the figural scenes.

The way in which Roman painting is adapted to its setting and function is among its most distinctive characteristics and makes it a decorative art in the true sense of the term. Some Roman decorative schemes were revived and frequently imitated in later times. Paintings in houses had certain practical and social functions. Some landscapes and perspectives were intended to make a room or a garden appear larger, and house owners liked to display their erudition or piety by evoking well-known literary and religious themes. Passageways and corridors were not decorated in the same way as public reception rooms, which were designed to impress visitors, or private bedrooms, where erotic scenes were not uncommon. Both public and private baths were embellished with subjects connected with the palaestra, sometimes involving athletes or gladiators. Scenes to do with water also occur, for example Venus with her retinue of sea creatures, a subject often associated with nymphaea and fountains, as was the story of Narcissus. Gardens were made to appear larger by illusionistic paintings depicting birds drinking from fountains or flying about among luxuriant foliage (e.g. House of the Marine Venus, Pompeii; *c.* AD 50–79), jets of water, and sometimes idyllic scenes with Orpheus enchanting the animals. The decoration of religious buildings reflected the beliefs of devotees. Roman forms were adapted to the needs of newly introduced Oriental cults. Thus paintings in Mithraic sanctuaries adhered to traditional Eastern iconography when depicting Mithras sacrificing the bull (e.g. Mithraeum of Marino; late 2nd century AD). Similarly, paintings in the synagogue at DURA EUROPOS (*c.* AD 245; Damascus, Mus. N) or in the catacombs in Rome (3rd century AD) combine themes borrowed from the funerary art of earlier times with scenes from the Bible.

Both historical and mythological funerary scenes were common. They include the deaths of such heroes as Hector, and the rape of Persephone by Hades, a symbol of death and resurrection. The daily lives of the deceased are also shown. Paintings in the tomb of the young aedile Vestorius Priscus at Pompeii depict him giving judgement, as well as showing his funerary banquet, and a gladiatorial contest that he presumably funded. At Caivano near Naples an allegorical tomb painting (later 2nd century AD) shows boats leaving the earthly shore for the distant islands inhabited by the souls of the blessed. There are also touching portraits of the deceased, for example medallions representing adolescents from the Via Tarento at Rome (2nd century AD), full-length portraits from Palmyra (*c.* AD 250–*c.* 300) and from Silistra (end of 4th century AD) showing male and female servants carrying clothes and toilet items to their masters. The practice of strewing flowers on graves gave rise to the fashion of painting them profusely on the walls, vaults and ceilings of tombs of all types.

(b) Literary and mythological subjects. These were the most popular. Episodes from the *Iliad* and the *Odyssey* were represented over a long period, either as continuous friezes or in separate panels, each illustrating one particular event. Paintings in a house on the Esquiline in Rome show a row of imitation pilasters against a landscape with scenes from the *Odyssey* labelled in Greek (*c.* 40–*c.* 20 BC; Rome, Vatican, Sala della Nozze Aldobrandine). In the atrium of the House of the Tragic Poet at Pompeii panels in the centre of each wall represent theatrical scenes and episodes from tragedy, such as the *Meeting of Achilles and Briseis* (*c.* AD 62–79; Naples, Mus. Archeol. N.). The most important mythological paintings depict the love affairs of the gods and the punishment of foolish and arrogant mortals. Jupiter appears often, as in the *Rape of Europa* (e.g. from Pompeii, House of the Fated Love; *c.* AD 1–*c.* 33; Naples, Mus. Archeol. N.), the *Rape of Ganymede* or *Leda and the Swan*. There are also several representations of *Apollo and Daphne* (e.g. from Pompeii, House of the Dioscuri; *c.* AD 62–79; Naples, Mus. Archeol. N.). Sometimes the artists chose particularly idyllic scenes, as in *Diana Bathing* (from Pompeii, House of Loreius Tiburtinus; *c.* AD 50–79; Naples, Mus. Archeol. N.), where the goddess's plump, white body contrasts with the rough bronzed features of Actaeon, spying on her from behind a rock. In some cases, a second panel depicts the terrible punishment of Actaeon who, still standing, is savaged by the dogs, with blood beginning to flow from his thigh and stag's horns sprouting from his forehead.

This rather disturbing taste for almost sadistic, nightmarish scenes of men and women as victims of beasts recurs frequently, as in *Dirce Tied to the Bull* (e.g. from Pompeii, House of the Vettii; *c.* AD 50–79; Naples, Mus. Archeol. N.). In other scenes, Achilles' horses drag Hector's corpse, or Phaëthon falls from his chariot as the wild horses of the Sun carry him away towards the rocks and the sea. The mood is similar in a depiction of the *Fall of Icarus* from the House of the Priest Amandus, Pompeii (*c.* AD 1–*c.* 33; Naples, Mus. Archeol. N.), where Icarus crashes to earth in a fantastic landscape while grieving figures look on, thus symbolizing human pride humbled by the gods.

Scenes of explicit violence are, however, rare. Most illustrate the moment just before the brutal event. Scenes of Medea's infanticide, for example, allude grimly to the impending event and depict her standing aloof with wild, staring eyes while her children play happily nearby (e.g. from Pompeii, House of the Dioscuri; *c.* AD 62–79; Naples, Mus. Archeol. N., 8977). The realistic and rather clumsy depiction of *Pyramus and Thisbe* near a fountain in the House of Loreius Tiburtinus at Pompeii (*c.* AD 62–79) is an exception: blood spurts from Thisbe's breast as she kills herself beside Pyramus, who is stretched out, covered in blood.

Some gods proved more popular subjects than others, for example Dionysus. A wall painting from Herculaneum depicts the *Education of Dionysus* (*c.* AD 55–79; Naples, Mus. Archeol. N.), and his love for Ariadne is shown in the *Ariadne Discovered by Dionysus* from the House of the Great Altar, Pompeii (*c.* AD 50–79; Naples, Mus. Archeol. N.), in which the half-naked Ariadne is represented asleep in a languid and sensual pose as the god comes to her. At some periods vine shoots and Dionysiac cult objects became the dominant decorative motifs. Dionysiac ritual was also depicted, as in the celebrated frieze in the Villa of the Mysteries, Pompeii (*c.* 60 BC; see colour pl. 1:VIII, fig. 1), which probably shows Dionysus, Ariadne (or his mother, Semele), Pan and a retinue of maenads and satyrs participating in the initiation of a young woman. The exploits of mythological heroes inspired some scenes, including a long frieze in the House of Loreius Tiburtinus at Pompeii with the *Labours of Hercules* (*c.* AD 62–79), and, from the House of the Vettii at Pompeii, the *Rape of Auge*, depicting a beautiful young woman kneeling and weeping as the unsteady and drunken Hercules unveils her. Other heroes, such as Perseus, were also popular. A wall painting in the House of the Priest Amandus at Pompeii shows *Perseus and Andromeda* (*c.* AD 1–*c.* 33).

It is sometimes possible to trace scenes to specific Greek tragedies, particularly when they include the theatrical setting. One famous painting apparently reproduces a scene in Euripides' play *Iphigeneia in Tauris* in which the priestess Iphigeneia is obliged to sacrifice two strangers, whom she recognizes as her brother, Orestes, and his friend Pylades. The scene is imposing: Iphigeneia descends the steps of the palace of King Theras, who is shown sitting in profile in the foreground with the two strangers in chains in front of him (from Pompeii, House of the Cithara Player; *c.* AD 62–79; Naples, Mus. Archeol. N., 9111). Another Pompeian painting, from the House of the Tragic Poet, depicts the moment in Euripides' *Iphigeneia in Aulis* when the heroine is carried away to be sacrificed, while her father, Agamemnon, covers his face in grief (*c.* AD 62–79; Naples, Mus. Archeol. N., 9112).

Scenes from comedy also occur, with actors wearing grotesque masks. One unusual painting shows an actor dedicating his mask, sitting contemplatively in his dressing-room (mid-1st century AD; Naples, Mus. Archeol. N., 9019). Theatrical motifs, such as props and scenery, formed the basis of one popular style of decoration. Masks were represented as if placed on top of partitions or hung on walls, while actors were depicted in the airy, fantasy buildings which adorned the upper sections of walls in the late 1st century AD. Imaginary buildings, with skilfully handled *trompe l'oeil* effects, occurred often in Roman painting, especially in Italy, although Vitruvius (*On Architecture* VII. v.5) criticized Apatourios of Alabanda for indulging in this kind of scenery painting.

Personified abstractions (e.g. the Seasons) are sometimes represented, and minor mythological beings (e.g. cupids) also occur frequently. Cupids are shown engaged in various activities in the famous frieze in the House of the Vettii at Pompeii (*c.* AD 50–79). Eros is associated with Psyche and Venus, and is shown either being punished or playing with Mars' weapons. The celebrated sentimental scene of the '*Cupid-seller*' from Herculaneum was much copied after its discovery in the 18th century, and the scene also exists in a version from Stabiae (*c.* AD 1–*c.* 33; Naples, Mus. Archeol. N.).

(c) Scenes of daily life. Depictions of ordinary daily activities were usually confined to the decoration of functional buildings. A painting of a large guard dog in the courtyard of the Inn of Sotericus (first third of the 1st century AD) at Pompeii warned thieves to keep away (cf. Petronius: *Satyricon* xxix). Shop signs showed various types of craft and trade. One on the front of the Shop of Verecundus at Pompeii (*c.* AD 50–79) depicts feltmakers using bellows and above them Venus, their guardian deity, on a chariot drawn by elephants. Another Pompeian sign shows in detail the work of fullers and carders, with a statue of a god being carried on a litter (mid-1st century AD); children tread the cloth in basins, while a woman cards wool and a man carries the semicircular wicker basket used for bleaching the cloth. The golden-brown loaves painted above a baker's shop (*c.* AD 62–79; Naples, Mus. Archeol. N., 9071) were clearly intended to entice passers-by.

Inns were decorated inside with different subjects, for example an argument between dice-players seated around a gaming-table (*c.* AD 50–79; Pompeii). The entrances to the small alcoves in a brothel at Pompeii were adorned with pairs of lovers in various positions (*c.* AD 62–79); here, the execution is rudimentary, if explicit, but paintings in the inner rooms of houses of the wealthy represent lovers embracing in a more elegant style (e.g. House of the Red Walls; *c.* AD 62–79). It seems clear that shop signs and finer decorative work in houses were produced by different groups of specialist painters.

Some paintings at Pompeii depict religious scenes, including sacrifices to particular gods, occasionally Isis, whose cult became fashionable during the craze for things Egyptian that occurred in the late 1st century BC to early 1st century AD. The figure of a priest of Isis is sometimes identifiable, holding a sistrum or organizing a ceremony, as in the House of Loreius Tiburtinus at Pompeii (*c.* AD 62–79). Even so, the profusion of Egyptian motifs, frequently in adapted forms, tended to reflect current taste rather than a real attachment to Egyptian religion. Lararia had their own distinctive painted decoration. This could represent the lares, altars, a priest making a libation, a flute-player, a small servant, a pig being taken to sacrifice, snakes or occasionally divine figures, such as Hercules performing a sacrifice or Mercury, the protector of merchants, at the entrance to a shop. In spite of the variety of themes, the treatment is sometimes monotonous.

Even though the basic themes are somewhat stereotyped, scenes of daily life occasionally include realistic details and remain recognizable, despite having been removed from their original contexts. For example schoolboys are shown studying in a portico while one of them is being beaten (*c.* AD 50–79; Naples, Mus. Archeol. N., 9066). In a banqueting scene (*c.* AD 50–79; Pompeii, House of the Triclinium; Naples, Mus. Archaeol.) a slave supports a sick and drunken guest. No picturesque details of this kind occur in representations of funerary banquets, however. Occasionally, contemporary events may be represented, for example the riot in the amphitheatre at Pompeii (AD 59) in which many people from Nuceria and Pompeii were killed (Naples, Mus. Archeol. N., 112222; see fig. 6). The organizers of gladiatorial games sometimes commissioned paintings of contests between famous fighters.

The production of portraits is another sign of the Romans' interest in the present and their desire to commemorate the past (see fig. 7). The tradition of the *imagines maiorum* (images of ancestors usually made of wax) gave rise to some fine painted portraits. The most famous of these is *Terentius Neo and his Wife* (*c.* AD 50–79; Naples, Mus. Archeol. N., 9058; see colour pl. 2:V, fig. 2) from the tablinum ('study room') in the House of Paquius Proculus at Pompeii. Apart from realistic portraits, archetypal or 'abstract' portraits also occur, such as those of philosophers and the Muses.

The backgrounds of the paintings evoke everyday settings: there are landscapes, neat gardens with paths lined by trees or wicker fences, luxurious villas at the water's edge, with landing stages and long porticos decorated with statues, as in Poppaea's villa at Oplontis (mid-1st century BC, enlarged 1st century AD). There the decoration also includes representations of small pictures painted on wooden panels with folding wings and highly ornate candelabra spaced at regular intervals around the walls; they are more fanciful than the real ones on which they were based, showing how the Roman artists' imaginations exaggerated the real world around them. Numerous still-life paintings also occur, clearly derived from offerings to the gods and to hosts.

A. Maiuri: *La Peinture romaine*; Eng. trans. by S. Gilbert (Geneva, 1953)

P. Williams Lehmann: *Roman Wall Paintings from Boscoreale in the Metropolitan Museum of Art* (Cambridge, MA, 1953)

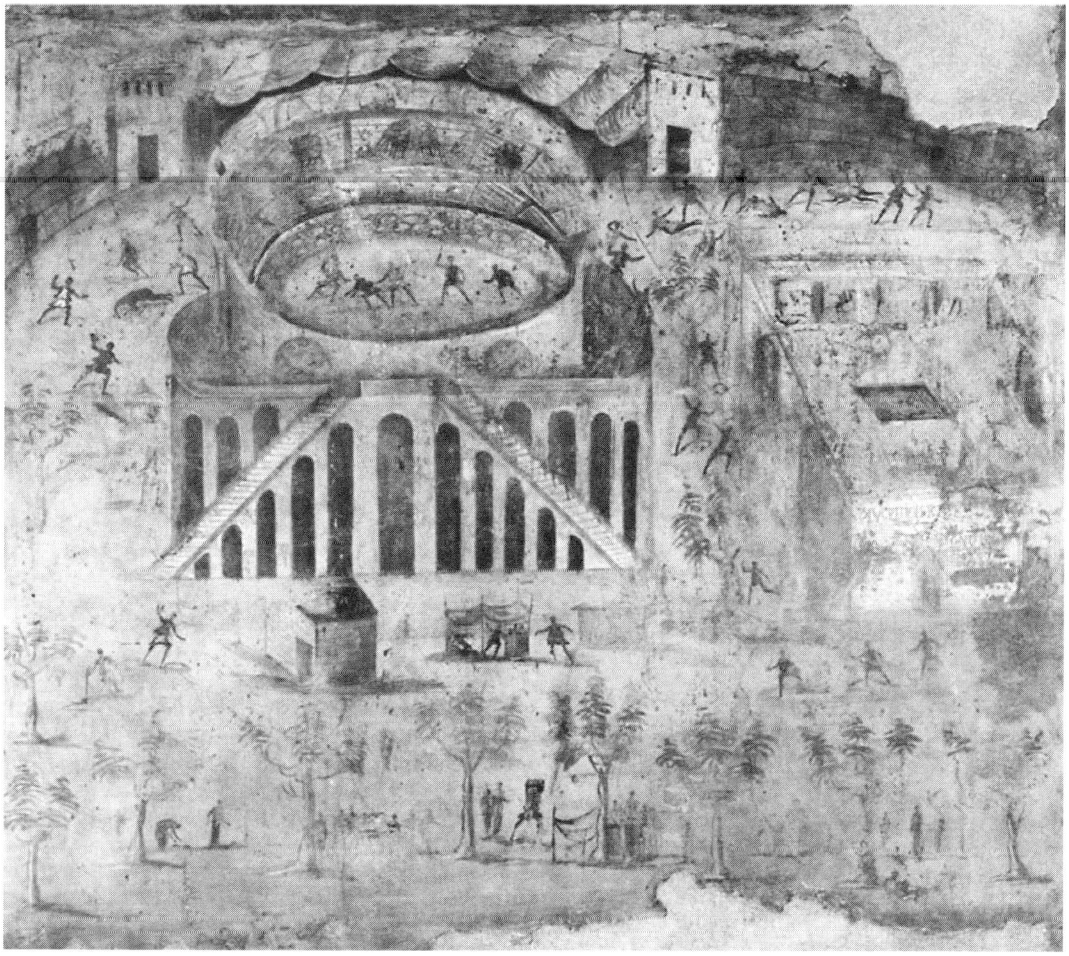

6. Roman wall painting depicting the riot between Pompeians and the Nucerians at the amphitheatre, from House 1 3, 23, Pompeii, *c.* AD 60–79 (Naples, Museo Archeologico Nazionale)

M. Borda: *La pittura romana* (Milan, 1958)

A. De Franciscis: *Die pompejanischen Wandmalereien in der Villa von Oplontis* (Recklinghausen, 1975)

A. Barbet: *La Peinture murale romaine: Les Styles décoratifs pompéiens* (Paris, 1985)

E. W. Leach: *The Rhetoric of Space: Literary and Artistic Representations of Landscape in Republican and Augustan Rome* (Princeton, 1988)

J. Guillaud and others: *La Peinture à fresque au temps de Pompéi* (Paris, 1990)

J. R. Clarke: *The Houses of Roman Italy, 100 BC–AD 250: Ritual, Space, and Decoration* (Berkeley, 1991)

Functional and Spatial Analysis of Wall Painting: Proceedings of the Fifth International Congress on Ancient Wall Painting: Amsterdam, 1992

P. J. Holliday: *Narrative and Event in Ancient Art* (Cambridge and New York, 1993)

I. Baldassarre: *Pittura romana: Dall'ellenismo al tardo antico* (Milan, 2002)

S. Woodford: *Images of Myths in Classical Antiquity* (New York, 2003)

M. Bussagli: *Rome: Art & Architecture* (Colgone, 2004)

J. D. Uzzi: *Children in the Visual Arts of Ancient Rome* (Cambridge, 2005)

(ii) Materials and techniques. Roman paintings were executed on numerous types of support, including wood, stone, marble, pottery, linen, hide and papyrus, though the evidence for their use is fairly sparse. More is known of painting on walls, ceilings, vaults and occasionally floors, and in this context the Romans showed great mastery of their materials and techniques.

(a) Walls, ceilings and vaults. The plaster ground consisted essentially of lime and sand, bonded with water. To ensure its durability it was applied in several layers, which became progressively finer towards the surface, culminating in a smooth *intonaco* or surface coat, sometimes enriched with marble powder. Powdered terracotta was sometimes used to waterproof plaster on exteriors or in damp places, while

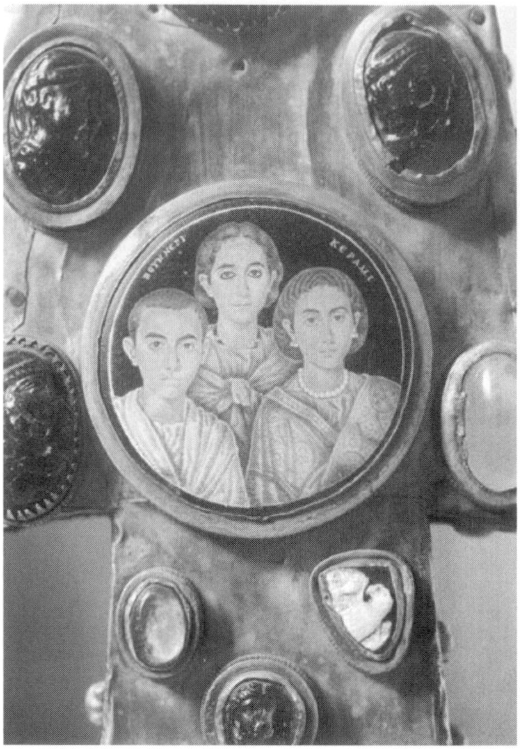

7. Roman painting of the family of Vunnerius Keramus, portrait medallion on a cross, inscribed, engraved gold leaf, glass, *c.* AD 250; cross, 8th century AD (Brescia, Museo Civico dell'Età Romana)

pozzolana or pumice might be employed to lighten plaster on vaults or ceilings. Vitruvius (*On Architecture* VII.iii.5–9) advised the application of seven coats, three containing marble powder, followed by a thorough polishing. Various methods were used to ensure that the plaster adhered to its support. Mud-brick walls were incised with herringbone patterns while plaster on stone walls sometimes contained potsherds. Plaster on ceilings and vaults was applied directly to an armature of reeds, wooden laths or thin interlaced poles. Once the surface was prepared, guidelines for the decoration were traced with a sharp point or with a string which might be dipped in paint; less frequently the design was sketched in with a brush. Circles were usually traced with compasses, but sometimes irregular spirals suggest an improvised system employing a sharp point, brush and string. Grids of regular or oblique geometrical shapes were used for repetitive tracery designs, for example on coffered ceilings, or for complex geometric friezes such as meanders. However, simple notches were also used.

Since most Roman paintings were frescoes, that is applied to fresh plaster, the work that could be completed at any one time was limited to the area covered by scaffolding, which explains the regular appearance of three horizontal sections corresponding to the levels of scaffolding, and of joins between the sections painted at different times. The way in which some paintings have flaked suggests that other techniques were also used, including secco, which involves re-moistening the dried plaster before applying the paint, and lime secco, in which the pigments were mixed with a whitewash for better adherence, resulting in pale colours.

Sometimes particular areas of decoration were reserved, then plastered and painted separately by specialist craftsmen. This technique was applied to some figural scenes, including circular medallions in the Villa S Marco at Stabiae (*c.* AD 20–79) and in the House of the Vettii at Pompeii (*c.* AD 62–79), and even full-length figures such as those in the Villa of the Mysteries at Pompeii (*c.* 60 BC). Some wall paintings at Pompeii left unfinished at the eruption of Vesuvius, for example in the House of the Lararium (before AD 62), reveal the different sections executed in sequence from top to bottom and rough square panels in the centre of the middle sections reserved for the figural scenes.

Roman colours were obtained from a variety of sources. Cinnabar, a bright red pigment extracted from mercury ore, became unstable when overexposed to damp and heat, darkening and eventually turning black (changing to black metacinnabar). A more commonly used and less fragile red was obtained from natural ochres coloured by iron oxides, such as haematite. Yellow was obtained from goethite or limonite. Green was often made from a green clay (argillaceous earth) enriched with a few grains of Egyptian blue. Vitruvius (VII.xi.1) gave a full description of the manufacture of Egyptian blue, an artificial compound made from sand, fine copper grindings and calcium salt, crushed and kneaded into balls with a little water, then fired; actual samples survive. Various mixtures of red and blue provided a range of purples, while black was obtained from carbonized wood or bone. These mineral pigments were supplemented by vegetable pigments, though their importance is only becoming clear through new technical analyses: organic pigments were long thought to be unsuitable for wall paintings because of the caustic action of the lime in the plaster. A blue-grey has been identified as a mixture of flower juices (anthocyanin) and Egyptian blue, while a purple found at Stabiae is a lac, as is a red used at Petra as a ground for gold leaf. In addition, hardstones were mixed with paint on the vault of the Domus Transitoria in Rome (*c.* AD 54–64), as also were shells, pumice stones and glass tesserae, especially on nymphaea and fountains. Finally, gold leaf attached to a yellow ochre or red ground with organic glues is found in stuccowork on vaults (Rome, Aula of Isis; *c.* 20 BC) or at the tops of walls.

(b) Other contexts. The most notable extant examples of Roman painting on wood are the Faiyum portraits (sarcophagus lids from Egypt, 1st–4th century AD) and some shields from Dura Europos (3rd–4th century AD; New Haven, CT, Yale U. A.G.). Nothing is known of the techniques or designs

used in other regions, though many wooden objects were painted, such as the ex-votos dedicated at spring sanctuaries in Gaul (e.g. Chamalières in the Puy-de-Dôme), and the portable pictures protected by folding leaves which are represented in Campanian wall paintings. Stone sculptures and other architectural elements received polychrome decoration on a layer of whitewash, and traces of blue background, yellow ochre flesh, green drapery and foliage, and reddish brown details such as hair, weapons and tools often survive. Paint presumably containing an organic binding agent was applied directly to marble and ivory statuettes to pick out the hair and jewellery, as on the *Venus Bathing* from Pompeii (1st century AD; Naples, Mus. Archeol. N.). Pottery statuettes, tiles and vases were also occasionally painted, though mass-produced mould-made terracotta reliefs were left undecorated. A few surviving military artefacts show that linen and hide were sometimes painted. A hide-covered shield from Dura Europos (3rd century AD; Paris, Bib. N.) depicts a journey, while a standard from Egypt (Moscow, Pushkin Mus. F.A.) shows a Victory standing on a globe and holding a palm. Finally, Pliny the elder (*Natural History* XXXV.xxxiii.51) mentioned an enormous portrait of Nero as a charioteer on a piece of cloth almost 35 m high.

S. Augusti: *I colori pompeiani* (Rome, 1967)

A. Barbet and C. Allag: 'Techniques de préparation des parois dans la peinture murale romaine', *Mél. Ecole Fr. Rome: Ant.*, lxxxiv (1972), pp. 935–1069

A. Barbet: 'L'Emploi des couleurs dans la peinture murale antique, "marquers" chronologiques et révélateurs du "standing" social', *Actes du colloque international du Centre National de la Recherche Scientifique (CNRS). Pigments et colorants de l'antiquité et du moyen-âge: Orléans, 1988*, pp. 255–71

F. Delamare and others: 'Couleur, nature et origine des pigments verts employés en peinture murale gallo-romaine', *Actes du colloque international du CNRS. Pigments et colorants de l'antiquité et du moyen-âge: Orléans, 1988*, pp. 103–116

V. Guichard and B. Guineau: 'Identification de colorants organiques naturels dans des fragments de peinture murale de l'antiquité; exemples de l'emploi d'une laque rose de garance à Stabies et à Vaison-la-Romaine', *Actes du colloque international du CNRS. Pigments et colorants de l'antiquité et du moyen-âge: Orléans, 1988*, pp. 245–54

R. Ling: *Roman Painting* (Cambridge, 1991), pp. 198–220

(iii) Painters and society. Information on Roman painters and their social status is provided by three principal ancient sources: literature, inscriptions and legal documents. Although Roman texts frequently refer to lost Greek works, they scarcely ever mention surviving Roman paintings. This is because almost all the extant specimens are wall paintings, and usually derivative works by anonymous minor artists; the Romans generally considered the mural to lie midway between the fine arts and crafts; they valued true pictures more than murals and painters more than decorators. Nonetheless, some wall paintings and their creators enjoyed a certain renown: for although Pliny the elder claimed that only the painting of pictures brought glory to an artist, he went on to denounce the selfishness of householders who decorated walls that few but they would be able to enjoy (*Natural History* XXXV. xxxvii.118). Similarly, though in theory murals could not legally be taken into account in determining the value of a damaged property, a modest estimate of their worth was actually allowed (Justinian: *Digest* XXXIX.ii.40; AD 533).

Efforts to identify individual artists of wall paintings have centred on five surviving signatures. A certain Alexandros Athenaios signed two marble plaques from Herculaneum, one a monochrome of *Niobe and Latona* (early 1st century AD; Naples, Mus. Archeol. N., 9562), the other found in the House of Neptune and Amphitrite; a graffito in the Farnesina House in Rome (*c.* 25 BC; Rome, Mus. N. Romano) records the name Seleukos; and a certain Lucius signed a painted couch (*c.* AD 70–79) in the House of Loreius Tiburtinus at Pompeii. Similarly, in Spain the vault of the tomb of Postumius at Carmo (*c.* AD 200–*c.* 250) bore the name of C. Silvanus, while the House of the Amphitheatre at Augusta Emerita contained that of Quintosus, though both names have now disappeared. It is difficult to draw any conclusions from such sparse data, though it may be significant that the Greek names appear on artistically superior works, and the Latin on mediocre ones; it is not even certain that the names are artists' signatures.

In Book XXXV, Pliny mentioned several artists whose works are now lost. These include Fabius Pictor and Pacuvius (vii.19), Cornelius Pinus and Attius Priscus (xxxvii.120), all history painters; Turpilius (vii.20), one of the *equites* (wealthy non-senators) who painted small pictures; Titaedius Labeo (vii.20), a senator and rhyparographer (encaustic painter or 'painter of base things'); and Quintus Pedius (vii.21), Arellius (xxxvii.119) and Serapion (xxxvii.113). More is known of the Augustan painter Ludius or Studius, whose scenes of villas and ports are praised (xxxvii.116) as 'the pleasantest of all wall paintings', while the Neronian artist Fabullus or Famulus is said to have worked exclusively in the Domus Aurea which was referred to as 'the prison of his art'; he painted there for a few hours each day and, to distinguish himself from the journeyman decorators, never removed his toga (xxxvii.120).

Diocletian's *Edict on Prices* (AD 301), which laid down rates of pay for all craftsmen, provides important evidence for the relative status of painters and other artists, as well as of the different types of painter. While the average daily wage for craftsmen was 50 denarii, wall painters received 75 and picture painters 150. The edict did not mention the *picturae professores* (painting masters), but in the late 4th century AD they enjoyed important privileges in the province of Africa (*Codex Theodosianus* XIII. iv.4). Similarly, although not listed in the edict, scenery painters, garland painters, chariot painters and the *perfector* ('finisher'), whose duties are unclear, are mentioned in inscriptions which give some indication of their social status. Unlike sculptors, painters were never depicted working on funerary stelae, nor do they seem to have been represented at Pompeii by an electoral guild. Painters' studios seem to have been little more than informal groupings set up or disbanded according to the commissions available, though evidence for their existence is provided by at least one inscription dedicated by members of a studio to dead colleagues. Another refers to the artist P. Cornelius Philomusus as both a scenery painter and a supplier of materials (*Corp. Inscr. Lat.*, Academia Literarum Regiae Borussicae, iii, 4222 and vi, 9794). Finally, in addition to illustrating the close control that wealthy patrons exercised over the decoration of their villas, the letters of Q. Aurelius Symmachus (late 4th century AD) show that the development of painters' careers was determined by contacts with powerful individuals (see *Epistles* IX.l on the painter Lucillus).

J. M. C. Toynbee: 'Some Notes on Artists in the Roman World', *Latomus*, ix (1950), pp. 175–82

I. Calabi-Limentani: *Studi sulla società romana: Il lavoro artistico* (Milan, 1958)

K. Visky: 'Sulla qualifica della pittura è della scultura nelle fonti del diritto romano', *Studi in onore di G. Grosso*, iv (Turin, 1971), pp. 333–57

A. Burford: *Craftsmen in Greek and Roman Society* (London, 1972)

E. W. Leach: 'Patrons, Painters and Patterns: The Anonymity of Romano-Campanian Painting and the Transition from the Second to the Third Style', *Actes du congrès: Literary and Artistic Patronage in Ancient Rome, Austin, 1979*, pp. 135–73

S. Roda: *Commento storico al libro IX dell'epistolario di Q. Aurelio Simmaco* (Pisa, 1981)

F. Lucrezi: 'Pictura alios nobilitans', *Index quaderni camerti di studi romanistici*, 13 (1985), pp. 561–72

2. History and development. Research has revealed no trace of the legacy of earlier Italian painting (e.g. Oscan, Etruscan, Lucanian) on Roman wall painting. It seems instead to have had its origins in the large-scale painting of the Hellenistic period, and it continued to develop over the centuries. At first contemporary Italian styles predominated throughout the Empire, but gradually each province developed its own characteristic forms of decoration.

(i) Italy. (ii) Provinces.

(i) Italy.

(a) Pompeian (2nd century BC–late 1st century AD). (b) Post-Pompeian (late 1st century AD–early 2nd century). (c) Ostian (2nd and 3rd centuries AD). (d) Constantinian (early 4th century AD).

(a) Pompeian (2nd century BC*–late 1st century* AD*).* Early Roman wall paintings are termed 'Pompeian' or 'Campanian', since most extant examples occur in Campanian villas destroyed in the eruption of Vesuvius (AD 79), notably those at Pompeii, Herculaneum and Stabiae. Pompeian painting spanned three centuries and its chronology is divided in terms of four distinct styles, first suggested by the German scholar A. Mau in 1881.

First Style (c. 200–c. 90 BC*).* This was the longest-lived and most homogeneous Pompeian style, derived from the Classical Greek structural style first found in the 5th century BC. In Italian versions, painted stucco relief work was used to simulate masonry of marble and hardstones. It first appeared in Italy in the 2nd century BC and differed from the structural style of Delos, for example. The same characteristic scheme occurs in the Samnite House at Herculaneum and in the House of the Faun and the House of Sallust at Pompeii. The lowest painted wall zone is taller than in contemporary Greek examples, while the stucco cornices are in higher relief, and there is even an example of small, free-standing columns. It was probably these excessive relief effects that precipitated the decline of this style and its subsequent replacement by a simple imitation of the same schemes in paint alone.

Second Style (c. 90–c. 20 BC*).* This first appeared in the House of the Griffins at Rome (early 1st century BC). The walls are decorated as in the First Style, with painted panels and simulated blocks of masonry, often almost indistinguishable from real marble, finely outlined in contrasting colours to give the impression of relief. An illusion of depth is also created by *trompe l'oeil* representations of a podium, panels and columns on different planes, but there are no illusionistic landscapes. The latter first appeared in the villa of P. Fannius Synistor at Boscoreale (*c.* 50–*c.* 40 BC; paintings in New York, Met.) and in the Villa of the Mysteries at Pompeii (*c.* 60 BC), where a painted wall occupies half the height of the real wall, while above it are perspective views of palaces and porticos. The foreground is decorated with doors, entrances to sanctuaries and human figures. An exceptional, life-size depiction (*megalographia*) of 29 figures celebrating the Dionysiac mysteries occurs in one room, hence the villa's name (see colour pl. 2:IV, fig. 1). This grandiose composition may be based on an older work, but its originality stems from the fact that each figure seems almost to be a portrait. A *megalographia* from Boscoreale depicts some imposing figures, which have been interpreted as Hellenistic princes.

Around 40 BC there seems to have been a new desire to go beyond the limits of real space by creating an imaginary space. Spacious landscapes with mythological scenes began to be placed at the centre of each wall, like large openings. Architectural elements were no longer depicted solidly and realistically but in attenuated forms. Thus pilasters often became thin posts decorated with floral motifs and were sometimes replaced by caryatids. Compositions were frequently divided by festoons of flowers, as in the House of the Cryptoporticus or the House of the Silver Wedding at Pompeii. Artists at Rome were the chief innovators. They favoured ornamental friezes with lotus motifs and delicate shades of green, mauve and pink, as in the inventive and elegant decoration in the House of Livia (*c.* 30–*c.* 25 BC) and the House of Augustus (*c.* 36–*c.* 28 BC), both on the Palatine at

Rome. Their townscapes with human figures and the increasingly fantastic architectural settings clearly reflect the influence of the theatre, which was attested to earlier by frequent depictions of theatrical masks. The theatre was to remain a source of inspiration for Roman Imperial art.

Decorative schemes were naturally adapted to their settings (*see also* §1(i)(a) above). Thus painted colonnades often occur on the inner walls of peristyles, while in bedrooms the space is divided into two separate zones: the antechamber is often modestly decorated, while elaborate architectural paintings of arcades, porticos and broken pediments are concentrated in the bedchamber itself. In the bedrooms of the Villa of Poppaea at Oplontis near Naples, semicircular vaults with painted coffers and stucco edgings cover each alcove like bed testers. In dining-rooms too the passageway is less elaborately decorated than the eating area. The transition is indicated by a mosaic threshold and painted pilasters, while the flat ceiling of the passageway is generally replaced by a vault. This differentiation between areas became less pronounced during the Third Style and disappeared with the Fourth Style.

Third Style (c. 15 BC–c. AD 45). Around 20 BC there began to be a reaction against the illusionistic tricks of the Second Style. Buildings are still depicted in the Farnesina House in Rome, commissioned by Agrippa (*c.* 25–*c.* 20 BC), but they are increasingly attenuated and accompanied by new painted motifs: candelabra, a profusion of decorative stripes, and Egyptianizing motifs. Around 15 BC this reaction became still more pronounced. Walls were decorated with candelabras, small, slender columns and flying figures, while architectural elements became linear or were submerged by miniaturist ornament, as at the Imperial Villa at Pompeii and the Villa of Agrippa Postumus at Boscotrecase. Rooms were monochrome; often black but sometimes yellow, white or red. Black walls eliminated all illusion of depth but effectively set off the pastel coloured decorative motifs. The walls of small gardens or rooms with few doors or windows were often adorned with scenes of neatly cultivated orchards with fruit trees and flowers enclosed by trellises. Examples with blue backgrounds occur in Livia's villa at Prima Porta (late 1st century BC; Rome, Mus. N. Romano; for illustration *see* LANDSCAPE PAINTING) and the House of the Orchard, Pompeii, which also contains an example with a black background. The latter includes a vault decorated with a naturalistic trellis with bunches of grapes, panpipes, a drinking-horn, birds and a small cupid among the foliage. Painted lines often divided the lowest wall zone into elaborate compartments with geometric patterns or clusters of foliage. The flat panels of the middle zone bore vignettes with miniature landscapes or flying figures which remained popular in the Fourth Style. Aediculae with fantastic pediments and spindly columns reappeared as frames for mythological scenes, often with dramatic subjects. Several new schemes were also applied to ceilings and vaults. Simulated coffering was replaced by geometric tracery, particularly stars composed of eight lozenges, bearing floral motifs. A more complex type of ceiling was developed too, perhaps inspired by stuccowork, with a vaulted recess in the centre, fasciae and sometimes a small secondary vault at the edge. At the same time, naturalistic compositions with flying figures or vine trellises also occurred. The decorative motifs were the same as on the walls: ornamental friezes, 'moon-like' masks, birds and various other objects.

Fourth Style (c. AD 40–c. 90). From around AD 40 the *trompe l'oeil* architectural decoration, theatrical settings and fake marble wall zones superseded by the Third Style returned to fashion. Under Nero there was a clear emphasis on monumentality, as in the Domus Aurea (*see* ROME, §IV, 5 and see colour pl. 2:IX, fig. 2). Painted podia reappeared, along with columns decorated with golden foliate scrolls and aediculae with side pavilions. Mythological scenes at the centres of walls often depicted love affairs between gods and mortals, or the punishment of the impious. The highest wall zones were covered by fantastic, web-like 'architectural' structures, which often included small human figures, as in the House of the Vettii at Pompeii, creating an atmosphere of mystery (see colour pl. 2:IV, fig. 2). In the Domus Aurea some figures of this kind have human or animal upper bodies but lower bodies in the form of foliate scrolls. (These were rediscovered in the 16th century, when the Domus Aurea was buried beneath ground-level like a vast 'grotto', reached by tunnels. This was the origin of the name 'grottesche' which artists gave to these fantastic creatures.

The favourite colours were red, black and golden yellow, which, although garish, stand out effectively against a white background. Theatrical settings sometimes featured actors in scenes from plays, as in the House of Iphigenia (also called the House of Pinarius Cerealis) at Pompeii. In the later 1st century AD the decorative repertory of the Fourth Style became more systematized, sometimes even formulaic. It was based on the devices used in earlier periods: from the Second Style, the solid architectural frameworks; from the Third Style, the elaborate ornamental devices from which the various openwork borders of the Fourth Style derive (e.g. candelabra, flying figures, clusters of plants, animal friezes and birds in the lowest wall zone). The richness of the repertory varied between workshops: some individual workshops have been identified at Pompeii, while those at Herculaneum and Stabiae also differed in their choice of colours and subjects. The Pompeian style survived the destruction of the Campanian towns in AD 79 but disappeared around AD 90.

(b) Post-Pompeian (late 1st century AD–early 2nd century). The same oscillation between illusionistic and decorative styles persisted from the 2nd century AD onwards. Earlier schemes were re-adopted, but the colours and forms were less rich. At Ostia, traditional Roman family houses were replaced by blocks of *insulae* (rented

apartments) in which the decoration was simplified or even omitted depending on the occupant's status. Even so, the survival of theatrical scenes, designed to display a householder's erudition and culture, is attested by the House of the Muses (*c.* AD 117–*c.* 138). Thus, in Room 5, painted curtains adorn the upper wall zone, above columns on a low podium framing yellow and red panels with the figures of Apollo and the Muses among architectural vistas including porticos with small, schematic columns. In a more modest room, unobtrusive buildings on a white background frame flying figures of satyrs and maenads, clearly copied from works of the previous century.

Though wall decoration was somewhat repetitive, the decoration of ceilings and vaults was novel and luxurious, remaining so even during the later and more austere Ostian phase. Thus, in the House of the Hierodules at Ostia (*c.* AD 130–*c.* 140), one complex composition consists of figural scenes in compartments disposed in a cross, with a plain, concave-sided square crossed by diagonal lines at the centre. Its ornamental motifs—a dancing satyr, shells, crouching animals and heart-shaped foliate scrolls—are rendered in great detail and rich colours. Fragments of a similar ceiling from a house beneath the Baths of Caracalla at Rome (*c.* AD 130–*c.* 140; Rome, Antiqua. Palatino) show that it bore human figures in small panels and theatrical masks in aediculae garlanded with foliage derived from Pompeian painting. On its diagonals were figures perched on foliate scrolls, while at either side of them were cupids driving chariots. The same devices were used in Hadrian's Villa at Tibur (Tivoli), though some of its decoration is known only from 18th-century drawn copies. The elaborate ceiling decoration of Post-Pompeian painting reflects the variety of architectural forms, such as groin vaults, cupolas and arched niches, used at the time. Its compositions emphasize the main structural features of these forms with large concentric circles, lunettes and diagonal bands.

(c) Ostian (2nd and 3rd centuries AD). From the early 2nd century AD the influence of Pompeian painting waned. Particularly in Ostia, where most examples of the period have been found, the compositions are far simpler and depict less varied subjects in fewer colours. The backgrounds are usually white, while wide bands of colour, instead of architectural motifs, separate the three wall zones. Central painted panels bear vignettes, such as hunters and animals rendered in a somewhat stylized and impressionistic fashion, as in the House of the Charioteers (*c.* AD 140).

In the 3rd century AD a new, linear, allusive style became dominant, an early example being the decoration beneath the church of S Sebastiano on the Via Appia. The background was invariably white, while the divisions between panels were reduced to single lines and garlands were represented by mere curves with vertical strokes denoting their loose ends. The old division into principal and secondary panels persisted, with flying figures, objects and animals at their centres. The seemingly three-dimensional architectural schemes inherited from Hellenistic artists and perfected in the mid-1st century AD ceased, while decorative motifs became simplified abstractions, though their original forms remained recognizable. From the end of the 3rd century AD domestic paintings became rare, while the funerary paintings in the catacombs had quite different themes. Nonetheless, the latter retained the same simplified forms, while their circular and radial ceiling and vault compositions depicting *Christ in Majesty* derive from earlier works, particularly of the 2nd century AD.

(d) Constantinian (early 4th Century AD). Constantine used art to identify himself with earlier Roman emperors, and Constantinian painters often returned to the *trompe l'oeil* effects and architectural motifs of the Pompeian Second Style. Imitations of marble veneers are common in Ostian houses, as well as in the hypogeum of the Via di Livenza in Rome, the walls of which bear figural scenes on their middle zones depicting both pagan myths and Christian subjects: *Diana the Huntress* on one side; *St Peter and the Converted Centurion* on the other.

(ii) Provinces. Though Roman styles affected every province of the Empire, the particular style adopted depended on the date of the region's conquest, and its local development was conditioned by indigenous artistic traditions.

(a) Gaul. The Pompeian First and Second Styles occur only in southern Gaul, where wall paintings in both public and private buildings depict columns, masonry blocks with real or imitation bosses and panels simulating oriental alabaster or commoner types of marble. Under Augustus, however, the Third Style spread through the province from south to north, with a concentration of examples around Lugdunum (Lyon). As in Italy, two main periods can be distinguished: a 'severe' style, and a richer, more colourful style involving numerous friezes of waterbirds; candelabra decorated with figures, objects and animals; medallions; small landscape panels; precious vases; and fantastic columns with shafts which may be twisted or in the shape of the trunk of a palm tree. In the mid-1st century AD the candelabra style incorporated certain elements of the Pompeian Fourth Style—though not its distant views of complex and precarious buildings—by combining candelabra, columns and sometimes pediments with animal friezes. The compositions have only two horizontal zones, except at Narbo Martius (Narbonne) in the south, where the use of three zones and the flying figures and openwork borders of the central panels represent a closer adherence to Italian models.

In the 2nd century AD two major stylistic tendencies appeared in both northern and southern Gaul. The first was the adoption of *trompe l'oeil* architectural devices just when Italian artists were resorting to simpler compositions. In the principal wall zone colourful buildings, embellished with clipei (round shields) and sculpted heads or statues of gods, framed large allegorical, mythological or religious figures, while the lower zone was lavishly decorated with imitations of marble. The later style, popular for several decades in the 3rd century AD, was characterized by the execution of old motifs, such as schematized garlands, ribbed pilasters and simplified frames, in a linear technique using a few bright colours on a white background.

(b) Germany. The development of wall painting in neighbouring provinces followed a similar pattern. In Germany the earliest paintings (late 1st century BC) were also derived from Roman models. On the border with Gaul, in Belgium and around Augusta Treverorum (Trier) and Colonia Claudia Ara Agrippinensium (Cologne), panels and candelabra were frequently depicted throughout the 1st century AD, though *trompe l'oeil* buildings were less common. Thereafter, they were replaced by the *Tapetenmuster* (all-over pattern) style, also attested in the adjoining areas, with repetitive designs creating an effect similar to that of modern wallpaper. This style was apparently employed for both walls and ceilings, and it epitomizes the rejection of any illusion of depth.

In the 3rd century AD certain works were apparently influenced by local folk art, for example a landscape with a rural villa and peasants at work, one of whom is wearing the traditional German cowl (Trier, Rhein. Landesmus.), and an incomplete *megalographia* of a hunting scene (Cologne, Röm.–Ger.-Mus.). The masterpiece of painting in Augusta Treverorum, dating from the 4th century AD, is the magnificent coffered ceiling reconstructed from pieces found under the Basilica of Constantine there (Trier, Bisehöf. Dom- & Diözmus.). This seems to represent the marriage of an imperial prince, with portraits in the coffers and cupids bearing attributes. The large figures are vigorously depicted against a rough blue ground and framed by egg-and-dart mouldings painted in *trompe l'oeil.*

(c) Britain. Roman painting styles reached Britain later than other parts of the Empire, soon after its conquest in AD 43. The most luxurious decorative schemes are found mainly in the towns and villas in the south. The pattern of development was the same as in Gaul: after the decline of candelabra, architectural forms returned to favour, but with effects of depth as clumsily achieved as they were elsewhere in the Empire. In the 3rd century AD *megalographiai* reappeared, but, as in Gaul, they were executed on a rough ground, not on a smoothly painted one as in 1st-century AD examples, with the colour applied in flat tints.

(d) Spain. The evidence for painted decoration in the southern provinces of the Empire is sparse. In Spain there are paintings comparable with Pompeian-style works found in Italy, but their candelabra decoration soon became excessively heavy and ornate. Imitations of marble seem to have been more successful. Much later small panels with hunting scenes from Augusta Emerita (4th century AD) anticipate medieval descriptive paintings, while designs in tombs resemble those found in North Africa and the Near East.

(e) North Africa. Few paintings have been found here. However, a fine ceiling at Thina, painted to resemble a cupola, has at its centre a depiction of *Dionysus on a Panther* accompanied by allegorical figures (mid-3rd century AD; Tunis, Mus. N. Bardo) ; it is surrounded by vine shoots and theatrical masks, with further figures reclining on the cornices. This type of composition was popular later. In Libya there is another depiction of *Dionysus on a Panther* (end of the 1st century AD; Villa of Zliten), this time against a plain white background surrounded by figures placed along the axes, with no concern for realism, with landscape panels reminiscent of the Italian examples.

(f) Egypt and the Near East. Civic and domestic paintings rarely occur in Egypt and the Near East, so that Roman styles, which were combined with local artistic traditions, are best attested in tombs. Thus in Egypt traditional pharaonic religious scenes were given a Roman setting, above a lower wall zone painted to resemble marble. In a tomb at Alexandria traditional Hellenistic imitations of alabaster occur alongside two very different scenes: a picture on one wall, combining the mundane and the idyllic, shows oxen working a water-wheel while a cupid plays the pipes; a painting on another wall depicts the biblical subject of *Jonah under the Gourd*, attesting the tomb's long use. Egyptian art influenced works as far away as Palestine. In a 2nd-century BC tomb at Marissa, Egypto-Hellenistic buildings are depicted amid Doric architectural elements.

Though artistic fashions from the centre of the Empire also had a discernible effect on the East, traditional figural scenes, sometimes labelled with names from Greek mythology, persisted with remarkable vitality into the 4th century AD. A tomb at Tyre depicting carefully selected and highly symbolic Greek mythological scenes (the *Rape of Persephone, Hercules Leading Alcestis from the Underworld*, the *Punishment of Tantalus, Hercules Leading Cerberus* and the *Ransom of Hector*) represents the acme of the region's funerary art, while similar work (3rd century) occurs at Hermopolis West (Tuna el-Gebel) and in a tomb (mid-2nd century) at Capitolias (Beit-Ras) in Jordan depicting part of the Trojan Cycle. The complex decorative scheme in the Tomb of the Three Brothers at Palmyra (*c.* AD 142/3–259) was clearly influenced by several artistic traditions. Mythological scenes, such as *Odysseus with King Lycomedes* and the *Rape of Ganymede*, occur along with paintings of Victories holding medallions with portraits of the deceased in rich Oriental costumes. The pilasters of the arched entrance bear figures of women holding children, which resemble later Italian depictions of the Virgin and Child.

The paintings at Ephesos from the 1st century AD onwards were influenced by Fourth Style Pompeian works. Walls bear panels with openwork borders, and central vignettes frequently depict the same figures, such as Socrates and the Muses; their bases are decorated with numerous imitations of marble of varying sophistication. Paintings of the 4th century AD depict skilfully wrought *opus sectile*, including magnificent colonnades. One of the most striking features of Near Eastern painting—the use of flowers to cover walls and ceilings—which occurs in various forms along the coast of Asia Minor, lasted three centuries at Ephesos, until well into the 6th century AD.

The wall paintings at Dura Europos are unique: the plaster is rough and the colours were applied in thin layers, while the figures are frontal with dark outlines. These characteristics pertain as much to the scene of hunting wild asses (AD 194; Paris, Louvre) and the scenes in the Mithraeum with their slightly Sassanid appearance (*c.* AD 240) as to the cult scene from the Temple of Bel (2nd century AD; Damascus, Mus. N.), showing a procession of priests in tall, conical white hats set against a magnificent architectural background. The religious solemnity of the ritual panels is balanced by picturesque details and the richness of the costumes, the latter contrasting with the rigid frontality of the figures. The scene in two registers depicting the tribune Terentius (*fl c.* AD 239) making a sacrifice (New Haven, CT, Yale U. A.G.), with its outline figures on a white background, gives no illusion of depth and heralds a rather contrived narrative style also apparent in the synagogue. Its main characteristics became the hallmark of Early Christian art.

A. Mau: *Geschichte der dekorativen Wandmalerei in Pompeji* (Berlin, 1882)

F. Wirth: *Römische Wandmalerei vom Untergang Pompejis bis ans Ende des dritten Jahrhunderts* (Berlin, 1934)

M. I. Rostovtzeff: *Dura-Europos and its Art* (Oxford, 1938)

H. G. Beyen: *Die pompejanische Wanddekoration vom zweiten bis zum vierten Stil*, i–ii/2 (The Hague, 1938–60)

W. Drack: *Die römische Wandmalerei der Schweiz* (Basle, 1950)

L. Richardson jr: 'The Casa dei Dioscuri and its Painters', *Mem. Amer. Acad. Rome*, xxiii (1955)

M. Borda: *La pittura romana* (Milan, 1958)

A. Barbet: *Recueil général des peintures murales de la Gaule*, 2 vols (Paris, 1974)

V. M. Strocka: *Die Wandmalerei der Haughäuser in Ephesos* (Vienna, 1977)

F. L. Bastet and M. de Vos: *Proposta per una classificazione del terzo stile pompeiano* (The Hague, 1979)

H. Joyce: *The Decoration of Walls, Ceilings and Floors in Italy in the Second and Third Centuries A.D.* (Rome, 1981)

L. Abad Casal: *La pintura romana en España* (Alicante, 1982)

I. Bragantini and M. de Vos: *Le decorazione della villa romana della Farnesina* (Rome, 1982)

N. Davey and R. J. Ling: *Wall-painting in Roman Britain* (London, 1982)

A. Barbet, ed.: *La Peinture murale romaine dans les provinces de l'empire*, Brit. Archaeol. Rep. Intl Ser. (Oxford, 1983)

G. Krahe and G. Zahlhaas: 'Römische Wandmalereien in Schwangau, Lkr. Ostallgäu', *Bayer. Landesamt Dkmpf.*, xliii (1984)

'La Peinture romaine', *Doss. Hist. & Archéol.*, lxxxix (1984) [whole issue]

V. M. Strocka: *Casa del Principe di Napoli (VI, 15, 7–8)* (Tübingen, 1984)

A. Barbet: *La Peinture murale romaine: Les Styles décoratifs pompéiens* (Paris, 1985)

H. Kenner: *Die römischen Wandmalereien des Magdalenburges* (Klagenfurt, 1985)

A. Laidlaw: *The First Style in Pompeii: Painting and Architecture* (Rome, 1985)

D. P. Dimitrov and M. Čičikova: *The Late Roman Tomb near Silistra* (Sofia, 1986)

W. Drack: *Römische Wandmalerei aus der Schweiz* (Feldmeilen, 1986)

A. Barbet and others: *Pictores per provincias* (Lausanne, 1987)

G. W. Meates and others: *The Wall Paintings and Finds*, ii of *The Lullingstone Roman Villa* (Maidstone, 1987)

B. Philp: *The Roman House with Bacchic Murals at Dover*, Kent Monograph Series, Research Report no. 4 (Dover Castle, 1989)

P. H. von Blanckenhagen and others: *The Augustan Villa at Boscotrecase* (Mainz, 1990)

J. R. Clarke: *The Houses of Roman Italy, 100 BC–AD 250: Ritual, Space, and Decoration* (Berkeley, 1991)

D. Mazzoleni, U. Pappalardo and L. Romano: *Domus: Wall Painting in the Roman House* (Los Angeles, 2004)

3. Collections and collectors. The early history of the discovery and collecting of Roman paintings is poorly documented and little studied. Most of the surviving paintings, which derive from the 1st century BC and the 1st century AD, remain in or were once on the walls of houses and villas in Pompeii, Herculaneum, Rome, their environs and in other sites around the Mediterranean. The fact that many paintings survive in their original setting rather than in public or private collections is unusual in the preservation of ancient art; because of the nature and size of Roman mural paintings, they are not easily incorporated into collections. The once accepted practice of excising the finest portions of murals for display in museums, the results of which are seen in the Museo Archeologico Nazionale, Naples (e.g. portrait of a young woman), ended in the 19th century. It is unfortunate that more murals were not left *in situ*, because once the paintings are removed they are deprived of their visual and architectural context, without which much of their meaning is lost.

Pompeii and its environs offer the most extensive *in situ* examples of Roman paintings because of their preservation following the eruption of Mt Vesuvius (*see* Pompeii, §IV). In Pompeii the House of the Vettii and the suburban Villa of the Mysteries contain some of the most complete mural decorations. In the House of the Vettii the entire decorative scheme of architectural friezes, mythological scenes and a frieze of cupids in the *triclinium* can be seen. A large hall in the Villa of the Mysteries is decorated with frescoes of a Dionysiac subject. In Herculaneum (*see* Herculaneum, §IV) such houses as the House of the Great Portal and the House of the Stags retain their original frescoes, although they are fragmentary.

In Oplontis, located between Pompeii and Herculaneum, the Villa of Poppaea retains a large and complete cycle of paintings.

In addition to Roman paintings *in situ*, others are preserved in the collections of major museums. The extensive collection at the Museo Archeologico Nazionale in Naples includes fragments of paintings from Pompeii, Herculaneum and Stabiae. In the mid-18th century the Bourbon kings (Charles III and Ferdinand IV) encouraged excavations in these cities for exhibition in the Palazzo Reale, the Royal Palace of Portici, where the fragments were displayed as framed pictures. Examples of the holdings at the Museo Archeologico Nazionale are *Perseus and Andromeda* from the House of the Dioscuri in Pompeii, *Achilles and Briseis* from the House of the Tragic Poet in Pompeii and *Hercules and Telephus* from the Basilica in Herculaneum. Fragments from Stabiae, such as *Primavera* from the cubiculum of a villa, are also housed there, as are paintings from Boscoreale, located between Vesuvius and Pompeii.

In Rome the Museo Nazionale Romano contains a reconstruction of a room with landscape motifs from the Prima Porta Villa of Livia, the wife of the emperor Augustus. Also displayed are Augustan paintings from the Farnesina House. The Museo Gregoriano Profano in the Vatican houses the *Odyssey* landscapes from the Esquiline.

In London the British Museum collection includes paintings, mostly in fragmentary form, from Pompeii and its environs, Capreae (Tiberius' palace) and Rome (the Domus Aurea of Nero; *see* ROME, §IV, 5) and its environs (the Tomb of Nasonii). The Louvre, Paris, houses paintings from Pompeii and Herculaneum as well as from Rome, its environs, Ostia, Tusculum and Tibur (Tivoli). The first acquisitions were made in 1802; in 1825 the king of the Two Sicilies presented frescoes to King Louis XVIII of France, and in the 1860s several works were acquired from the Campana collection in Rome.

By the end of the 19th century in the USA, when public museums were being established and private fortunes allowed for the amassing of art collections, scientific rather than amateur excavations precluded any large-scale importation of antiquities from Pompeii and Herculaneum. The greatest collection of Roman paintings outside Italy, in the Metropolitan Museum of Art, New York, thus consists primarily of works from the environs of Pompeii, but not from the major Vesuvian excavations, which were more carefully controlled. This collection includes the cubiculum from the Villa of Publius Fannius Synistor at Boscoreale.

Funerary portraits painted on wooden panels, most of which were discovered at Faiyum in Egypt, can be found in many collections, including the Ny Carlsberg Glyptotek in Copenhagen, the Graf collection in Vienna, the Pushkin Museum of Fine Arts in Moscow and the Metropolitan Museum of Art in New York.

See also COLLECTION AND DISPLAY OF ART, §§I, 2 and II, 6.

M. H. Swindler: *Ancient Painting* (New Haven, 1929)
R. P. Hinks: *Catalogue of the Greek, Etruscan and Roman Paintings and Mosaics in the British Museum* (London, 1933)
P. Williams Lehmann: *Roman Wall Paintings from Boscoreale in the Metropolitan Museum of Art* (Cambridge, MA, 1953)
A. Maiuri: *Paintings from Pompeii, Herculaneum and Stabia in the Museo Nazionale at Naples* (Milan, 1959)
T. T. Tran: *Catalogue des peintures romaines (Latium et Campanie) du Musée du Louvre* (Paris, 1974)
Rediscovering Pompeii (exh. cat., New York, IBM Gal. Sci. & A., 1990)
R. Ling: *Roman Painting* (Cambridge, 1991)

Paionios of Mende (*b* Mende, Thrace; *fl c.* 430–*c.* 420 BC). Greek sculptor. His famous over life size marble *Nike* (*c.* 420 BC; Olympia, Archaeol. Mus.; see fig.) is the only extant work that is securely attributed to him. Pausanias (*Guide to Greece* V.x.8) stated erroneously that Paionios worked on the pedimental sculptures of the Temple of Zeus at Olympia. However, the information given by the inscription of the monumental base of the Olympian *Nike* is that Paionios won the competition for the acroteria of the Temple of Zeus (*c.* 430–*c.* 420 BC), a gilded bronze Nike at the middle and tripods at the corners.

The extant *Nike* is made from Parian marble and lacks her face and part of the neck, her wings and most of her mantle and arms. The figure originally stood south-east of the east front of the Temple of the Olympian Zeus, overlooking the procession

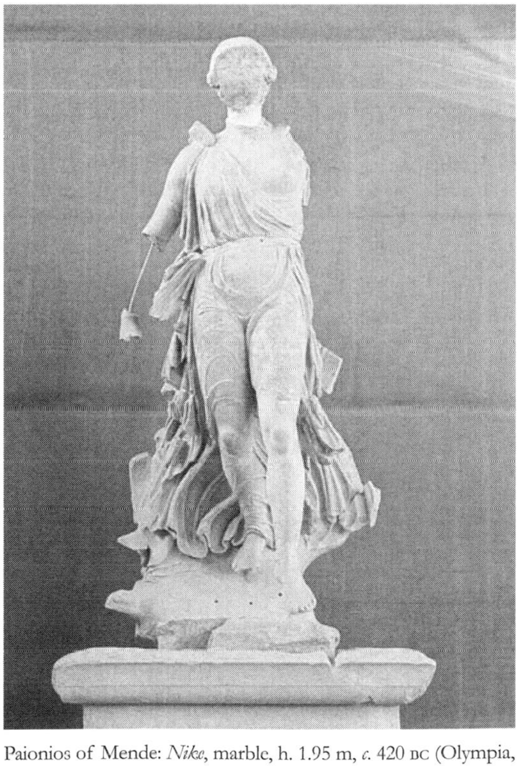

Paionios of Mende: *Nike*, marble, h. 1.95 m, *c.* 420 BC (Olympia, Archaeological Museum)

road, on a tapering pillar-base (h. 9 m) of triangular section. According to the inscription on the front part of its pedestal, *Nike* was a dedication of the Messenians and the Naupaktians of Akarnania in western Greece, made from the spoils of their victory against their enemies. The date of the statue based on stylistic grounds and the information given by Pausanias (V.xxvi.1) suggest that the dedication is related primarily to the battle of Sphakteria in south-west Peloponnese in 425 BC, a victory won together with the Athenians against the Spartans during the Peloponnesian War.

The *Nike*, depicted while alighting, tilting slightly to the left, is considered to be the first successful attempt in Greek sculpture to show a three-dimensional figure in flight. This is facilitated by an absence of Classical weight and by the open wings and the mantle, open at her back, which the figure holds with both her hands. She is clad in a *peplos*, exposing the right breast and leg, her skirts blown back. The impression of movement in the wind is enhanced by the eagle flying under her feet.

The style of the *Nike* is highly decorative; the combination of the drapery clinging to the body and the drapery flourishing free of it is distinctive of the Rich style, the leading Attic style of that period in sculpture (*see* SCULPTURE, §IV, 2(iii)(b)). The head type of the *Nike* is a variation of the head of the Nike held by the *Athena Parthenos* of Pheidias (*c.* 438 BC).

Hofkes-Brukker, relying on the stylistic and compositional features of the Olympian *Nike*, assigned to Paionios the conception and to some extent also the execution of the friezes from the Temple of Apollo at Bassai (late 5th century BC; London, BM), and tried to prove that Paionios' work betrays his north Ionian origins. She also argued for a late period in his career in Athens, where he allegedly took part in the execution of the Erechtheion frieze on the Acropolis (409–406 BC; Athens, Acropolis Mus.). But neither her attributions, nor the earlier effort of Carpenter to identify Paionios as his Master B of the Nike temple parapet on the Athenian Acropolis (*c.* 410 BC; Athens, Acropolis Mus.), have been generally accepted.

R. Carpenter: *The Sculpture of the Nike Temple Parapet* (Cambridge, MA, 1929), pp. 23–35

C. Hofkes-Brukker: 'Die Nike des Paionios und der Bassaefries', *Bull. Ant. Besch.*, xxxvi (1961), pp. 1–40

C. Hofkes-Brukker: 'Vermutete Werke des Paionios', *Bull. Ant. Besch.*, xlii (1967), pp. 10–71

K. Hermann: 'Der Pfeiler der Paionios-Nike in Olympia', *Jb. Dt. Archäol. Inst.*, lxxxvii (1972), pp. 232–57

E. B. Harrison: 'Two Pheidian Heads: Nike and Amazon', *The Eye of Greece: Studies in the Art of Athens: A Collection of Essays in Honor of M. Robertson* (Cambridge, 1982), pp. 33–65

W. Ramonat: 'Der Nike des Paionios in Olympia', *Thiasos ton Mouson: Studien zu Antike und Christentum: Festschrift für Josef Fink* (Cologne, 1984), pp. 77–83

A. Stewart: *Greek Sculpture: An Exploration* (New Haven and London, 1990), pp. 92–8, 271

P. Schultz: 'The Akroteria of the Temple of Athena Nike', *Hesperia*, lxx/1 (Jan–March 2001), pp. 1–47

Palace. The word derives from the Palatine Hill in Rome, where the residence of the Emperor Augustus (*reg* 27 BC–AD 14) was sited. This building was later developed as the Palace of the Caesars, covering the entire hill, and the name began to be applied to all other royal and imperial residences, including those of earlier eras.

1. Greek. 2. Roman.

1. GREEK. The building of palaces in the ancient Mediterranean before the rise of Rome is mainly associated with the Bronze Age civilizations of Crete and mainland Greece, and with the Hellenistic kingdoms that flourished in the Near East between the late 4th century BC and the establishment of Roman hegemony in the region. The civilizations of Archaic and Classical period Greece (and of Etruscan Italy) created monumental architecture, but their types of social and economic organization did not give rise to the construction of palaces. The first palaces on Crete date from the early Middle Minoan I period (after *c.* 2050 BC) and were constructed around a central courtyard, generally on a north-south axis (*see* ARCHITECTURE, §I). Successive phases have been excavated at KYDONIA, KNOSSOS, KATO ZAKROS, MALLIA and PHAISTOS. Most appear not to have been fortified but to have served as royal residences, cult centres, government offices and storehouses. After the collapse of Minoan civilization (*c.* 1400 BC), the centre of power in the Aegean shifted to the Mycenaean civilization of mainland Greece (*see* ARCHITECTURE, §III, 3). Fortified palaces began to be built by local rulers, often with defensive walls encircling all or part of the dependent settlement. Mycenaean palaces and larger houses were characteristically centred on a hall of MEGARON type, decorated with sculpted dados or wall paintings; major examples include MYCENAE, Phylakopi (*see* MELOS), PYLOS and TIRYNS. In the eight centuries after the fall of Mycenae (*c.* 1100 BC), palaces ceased to be built in the Greek world, and most monumental structures were either religious or civic in function.

With the rise of the Argead dynasty in Macedonia, and especially after the death of Alexander the Great in 323 BC and the fragmentation of his empire, the city-states of mainland Greece and their colonies were superseded as focuses of power and patronage by such Hellenistic dynastic centres as Alexandria and Antioch, and royal palaces (the Greek term *basileia* denotes the palace of a city), began again to be constructed on a grand scale. Magnificent peristyles and *andrones* for royal entertainment formed key features, often highlighted by monumental facades and propylaia and a domineering landscape setting; the palace in AIGAI (ii), perhaps Philip II's, provides an excellent early example. Recent research has stressed that palaces such as Aigai and those at PELLA and PERGAMON, despite a scale and magnificence reminiscent of Near Eastern models, essentially drew on precedents set by large and luxurious private mansions of the Late Classical period. In turn, the basileia became the main drivers of architectural innovation during the following period. Large areas of the new royal capitals were reserved for them and gradually built up, often including important sanctuaries and administrative buildings; the need to represent on an ever grander scale seems to have led to intense rivalry between the various courts. Further east, on the fringes of the Greek world, local influences, cultural traditions and building materials led to architectural solutions independent of the main Greek tradition.

J. W. Graham: *The Palaces of Crete* (Princeton, 1962, rev. 2/1987)

G. Cadogan: *Palaces of Minoan Crete* (London, 1976)

Basileia: Die Paläste der hellenistischen Könige: Internationales Symposion: Berlin, 1992

I. Nielsen: *Hellenistic Palaces: Tradition and Renewal* (Aarhus, 1994)

M. B. Hatzopoulos: 'Macedonian Palaces: Where King and City Meet', *The Royal Palace Institution in the First Millennium* BC: *Regional Development and Cultural Interchange Between East and West* (Aarhus, 2001), pp. 189–99

2. ROMAN. The official residence of the Roman emperors on the Palatine Hill in Rome until the Tetrarchy (est. AD 293) was the Palatium, and this term was later used for any building in which the emperor resided. The nucleus of the Palatium was a Republican domus near the south-west corner of the Palatine (*see* ROME, §IV, 3), acquired *c*. 40 BC by Augustus (*reg* 27 BC–AD 14) while he was still a private citizen. The area had strong associations with Romulus and the early history of Rome. Under the Julio-Claudian emperors (Tiberius, Caligula, Claudius and Nero; *reg* AD 14–68), the palace was extended towards the Forum Romanum (Domus Tiberiana) and along the ridge overlooking the Circus Maximus as part of Nero's Domus Aurea. Domitian (*reg* AD 81–96) rebuilt the Domus Tiberiana and created a new palace, the Domus Augustana, designed by RABIRIUS and completed by AD 92; this remained the main residence of the emperor in Rome until the 6th century. Including the later extensions under Hadrian (*reg* AD 117–38) and Severus Alexander (*reg* AD 222–35), the palace covered over 11 ha. The architecture of the palace was based originally on the Republican domus. The emperor, like the senator, required grand public reception areas suited to his status (Vitruvius: *De Architectura*, VI.v) and more private rooms for family and close associates. While the basilica was adapted from public architecture to replace the traditional atrium as the main audience hall, the peristyle, originally a feature of Hellenistic palaces, was retained. The columns and pedimental fronts (*fastigia*) of the audience halls derived from temple architecture. Although the residential wing of the palace was modest (*see* ARCHITECTURE, §VI, 2(i)(b)), Augustus built a splendid temple to Apollo flanked by porticos and libraries within its bounds, enhancing its religious and public associations. The arrangement is strongly reminiscent of the Hellenistic palaces at Pella (ii) and Pergamon.

The official wings of the later palaces employed similar architectural forms but were extraordinary in their scale and richness. Caligula used the temple of Castor in the Forum Romanum as a vestibule to a new domus that included an enormous tetrastyle atrium (26.5×22.3 m). The audience hall (31.4×32.1 m) and the triclinium (29.1×31.6 m) of the Domus Augustana were lofty rectangular rooms with an apsidal end, in which the emperor sat enthroned, and lavish columnar interiors. Contemporary writers compared them, with reason, to the temple of Jupiter Capitolinus (Statius: *Silvae*, IV.ii; Martial: *Epigrammata*, VII.lvi). In contrast, the rooms in the residential wing, organized like the official sector around peristyles, were on a smaller scale, impressing instead by complex shapes and lavish decoration. There was, however, an imposing public façade overlooking the Circus Maximus and a sunken garden in the shape of a circus (Hippodrome).

The influence of the Palatine palace on later imperial architecture remains unclear. The Stadium and adjacent buildings of Hadrian's Villa (AD 118–34) at Tibur (Tivoli) may reflect elements of the Domus Augustana. Several Imperial residences of the late 3rd century and early 4th (e.g. villa of Maxentius on the Via Appia; Diocletian's palace at SPALATUM (Split) and palaces at Nicomedia, Thessaloniki and Trier) featured large apsidal basilical halls and incorporated a circus; while this mainly reflects the growing importance of the circus in Imperial ceremony, their similarity to the Domus Augustana and the Circus Maximus suggests that the latter clearly provided a model.

B. Tamm: *Auditorium and Palatium* (Lund, 1963)

C. F. Giuliani: 'Note sull'architettura delle residenze imperiali dal I al III secolo d.C.', *Aufstieg und Niedergang der römischen Welt*, II/xii (Berlin, 1982), pp. 233–58

Le tranquille dimore degli dei (exh. cat., ed. M. Cima and E. La Rocca; Rome, 1986)

H. Hurst: 'Nuovi scavi nell'area di Santa Maria Antiqua', *Archeol. Laziale*, ix (1988), pp. 13–17 [Caligula's domus]

J. C. Mannell: *The Architectural Ornament of Diocletian's Palace at Split* (diss., Minneapolis,U. MN, 1992)

Palaestra [Gr. palaistra]. Ancient Greek building for exercise and education. Though in early use the term 'palaestra' generally denoted a privately owned wrestling-school, by the mid-4th century BC it referred to the principal peristylar building of the Greek GYMNASIUM. Indeed, in ancient usage the words 'palaestra' and 'gymnasium' were often interchangeable.

The introduction of the rectangular palaestra seems to have arisen from the development of Hippodamian urban planning in the 4th century BC, since none of the pre-Classical and Classical Athenian gymnasia appears to have had an independent palaestra building. According to Vitruvius (*On Architecture* V.xi.1–3), writing in the late 1st century BC, the Greek palaestra contained a club for the young men (*ephebeum*), classrooms (*exedrae*), exercise-rooms, storerooms for sports equipment and an unheated washroom (*loutron*).

The most sophisticated form of palaestra was a peristylar building surrounding all four sides of a courtyard. The first example in a gymnasium occurs at Delphi (*c.* 334 BC); however, the best specimens occur in the 3rd-century BC gymnasia at Olympia and Epidauros. Sometimes one side of the peristyle was emphasized by taller columns, as at Miletos (*c.* 180 BC), or by a double colonnade, as in the Lower Gymnasium (late 2nd century BC) in Priene and the Granite Palaestra (mainly mid-2nd century BC) on Delos.

Although under the Roman Empire traditional palaestras were still built in Asia Minor and Greece, most formed part of bath-gymnasium complexes. In Italy and the West they became simple exercise-courts attached to baths, except in the great Imperial *thermae* where they featured more prominently.

E. N. Gardiner: *Athletics of the Ancient World* (Oxford, 1930)
R. E. Wycherley: *How the Greeks Built Cities* (London, 1949, rev. 2/1962/*R* 1976)
J. Delorme: *Gymnasion* (Paris, 1960)
F. K. Yegul: 'The Palaestra at Herculaneum as a New Architectural Type', *Stud. Hist. A.*, xliii (1993), pp. 368–93
D. M. Bailey: 'A Ghost Palaestra at Antinoopolis', *J. Egyp. Archaeol.*, lxxxv (1999), pp. 235–9
B. Schmaltz: 'Die sogenannte Palastraterrasse in Kaunos: Bericht über die Grabungen 1995–1998', *Archäol. Anz.*, i (2000), pp. 17–55
Z. Newby: 'Sculptural Display in the So-called Palaestra of Hadrian's Villa', *Mitt. Dt. Archäol. Inst.: Röm. Abt.*, cix (2002), pp. 59–82
M. Stamatopoulou and M. Yeroulanou: *Excavating Classical Culture: Recent Archaeological Discoveries in Greece* (Oxford, 2002)
B. Schmaltz: 'Die sogenannte Palastraterrasse in Kaunos: Bericht uber die Grabungen 2000–2002', *Archäol. Anz.*, ii (2003), pp. 1–4, insert 4–insert 5, 5–38

Palea Paphos. *See* PAPHOS, OLD.

Palestrina. *See* PRAENESTE.

Palmette. Motif consisting of a fan of graded spines or lobes supported by spirals. Its origins are obscure, but similar motifs are first recorded in Syria and Mesopotamia and in the islands of the eastern Mediterranean in the course of the 2nd millennium BC.

Palmettes, together with many other Near Eastern decorative motifs, appeared in Greece *c.* 720 BC on pottery of the Geometric (*c.* 900–*c.* 725 BC) and Orientalizing (*c.* 725–*c.* 600 BC) periods. The motif was further developed on Attic pottery in the 6th and 5th centuries BC, replacing the buds in the traditional Egyptian lotus-and-bud border. In another variant, linked palmettes developed, as did single palmettes in association with spiral scrolls. Although these designs were secondary to the main painted scenes in vase painting, the palmette became a major motif in architectural decoration. Typical lotus-and-palmette borders, made more vegetal by the addition of acanthus leaves, occur on the carved friezes of the Erechtheion (late 5th century BC) on the Acropolis at Athens. Much confusion is caused by describing this variant, as well as the entire border motif, as ANTHEMION or honeysuckle. Apart from its use in repeated patterns as a frieze or border, the single palmette was the principal motif for antefixes, acroteria and the finials of funerary stele, as on an example (late 6th century BC; Tekirdağ, Mus.) from Perinthos (now Marmaraereğlisi, Turkey). Split down the centre, half-palmette was used in compositions in which it resembles a stylized leaf; such designs may be known as either half-palmette or ACANTHUS.

The palmette adapted from Greek prototypes became a prominent decorative feature in Etruscan art, typically placed diagonally in undulating scrolls as architectural enrichment or framing the figurative designs on, for example, bronze mirrors. From Italy the design was disseminated north of the Alps, where Celtic scroll motifs were ultimately based on lotus-and-palmette borders and scrolls. Roman architecture also exploited the versatility of the palmette, and it was used increasingly with the acanthus motif, which added vegetal features to the abstract palmette. Varied and sometimes flower-like palmette motifs, such as those carved at the base of some of the columns in the Hellenistic Temple III (*c.* 300 BC to Roman times) at Didyma, became especially influential, eventually adopted throughout the Empire and assimilated into indigenous decoration.

A. Furumark: *The Mycenaean Pottery: Analysis and Classification* (Stockholm, 1941)
W. Stevenson Smith: *Interconnections in the Ancient Near East: A Study of the Relationship between the Arts of Egypt, the Aegean and Western Asia* (New Haven and London, 1965)
P. P. Betancourt: *The Aeolic Style of Architecture: A Survey of its Development in Palestine, the Halikarnassos Peninsula and Greece, 1000–500 BC* (Princeton, 1977)
E. Wilson: *8000 Years of Ornament: An Illustrated Handbook of Motifs* (London, 1984), pp. 113–23
J. Rykwert: 'On the Palmette', *Res*, xxvi (Aug 1994), pp. 10–21
U. W. Gans: 'Antefixe aus Megalopolis', *Mitt. Dt. Archäol. Inst.: Athen. Abt.*, cx (1995), pp. 261–72

Palmyra [Arab. Tadmor]. Site of an oasis city in Syria that flourished *c.* 60 BC–AD 273, for most of this period under Roman rule (see fig. 1). The oasis, bounded on the west by limestone hills and with a spring called Efqa (1a), attracted inhabitants from Stone and Bronze Age times (*c.* 2300–*c.* 2200 BC). The name Tadmor appears soon after 2000 BC. By *c.* 1110 BC (Semitic) Aramaeans were installed, who with more recently arrived (Semitic) Arabs comprised the main population in the Roman period. The Seleucids ruled the small community in the Hellenistic period, but they were ousted in 64/63 BC and Syria became a province of the expanding power of Rome. For decades the Romans apparently controlled only the coast, leaving the oasis dwellers semi-independent and profiting from trans-desert caravan routes between Mesopotamia and the Mediterranean. Perhaps under Augustus (*reg* 27 BC–AD 14), certainly by the time of Tiberius (*reg* AD 14–37), the oasis settlement was fully incorporated into Roman Syria, with tribute-paying status, army presence, city organization into

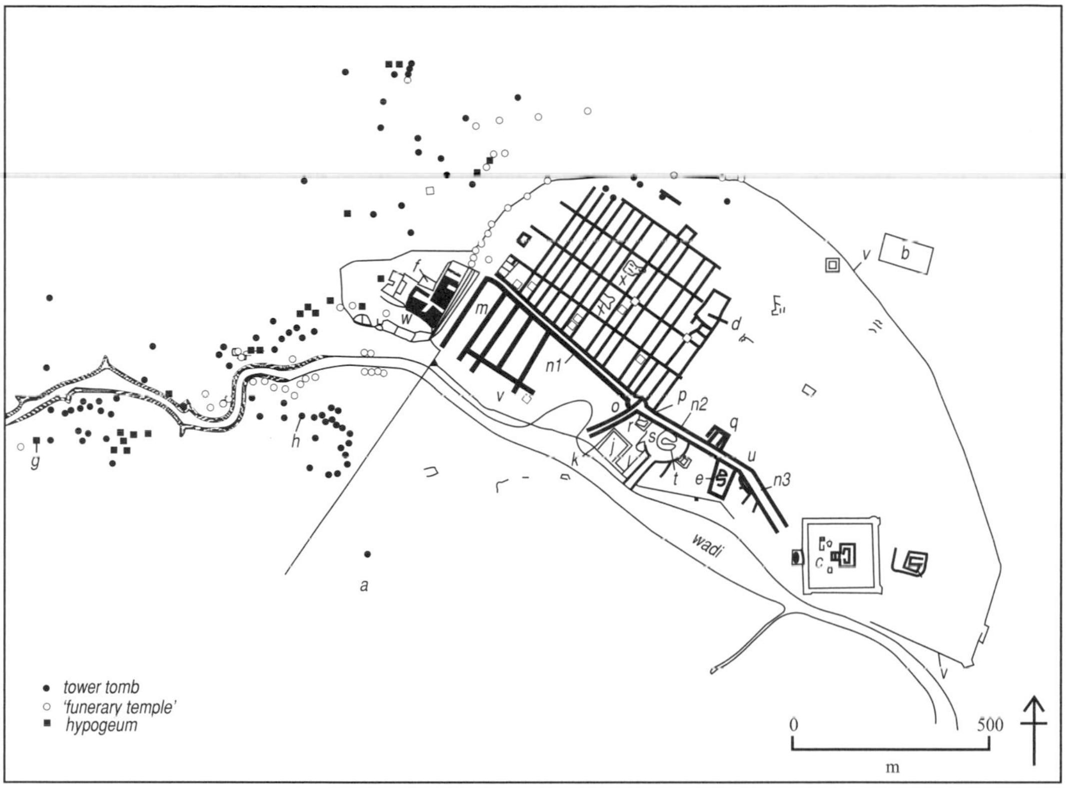

1. Palmyra, plan of the site: (a) Efqa spring; (b) museum; (c) Sanctuary of Bel; (d) Sanctuary of Baalshamin; (e) Sanctuary of Nebu; (f) Sanctuary of Allat; (g) tomb of 'Atenatan; (h) tomb of Iamliku; (i) tomb of Elahbel; (j) agora; (k) banqueting room; (l) court or depot; (m) Transverse Colonnade and Oval Piazza; (n) Great Colonnade (sections 1, 2, 3); (o) tetrapylon; (p) nymphaeum; (q) Baths of Diocletian; (r) Caesareum; (s) senate house; (t) theatre; (u) tripylon; (v) walls of Diocletian; (w) camp; (x) Byzantine churches

four geographical tribal areas, a tariff law, the name Palmyra and soon a 'senate' and 'people'.

Wealth promoted architectural activity. The Emperor Hadrian (*reg* AD 117–38) made 'Hadriana Palmyra' a 'free city' and probably visited (*c.* AD 129). Caracalla (*reg* AD 211–17) gave 'colony' status and citizen rights (AD 212). About AD 227 the Sasanian dynasty supplanted the Parthian dynasty. Disruption and warfare followed. In the chaotic mid-3rd century AD Palmyra gained its independence (*c.* AD 251–73) under the family of 'King' Septimius Odainat, assassinated in AD 267, whose queen Zenobia, ruling through their son Wahballat, conquered Syria and Egypt. In AD 273 the Emperor Aurelianus (*reg* AD 270–75) finally reconquered Palmyra and ended its greatness. Towards AD 300 Diocletian (*reg* AD 284–305) remodelled the declining city as a military stronghold. Justinian I (*reg* AD 527–65) undertook a programme of refurbishment. In AD 634 Palmyra capitulated to the Islamic Arabs and again became Tadmor; later it came under Ottoman rule.

From the 17th century Europeans became reacquainted with the site. The Britons Robert Wood (*c.* 1717–71) and James Dawkins (1722–57) published engravings of its architectural ruins in 1753 and thereby influenced British and European Neoclassicism. Most popular was plate 19, the south thalamus ceiling from the Temple of Bel, which inspired the ceiling of Robert Adam's drawing-room at Osterley Park House, London (1775–6). Scholarly investigation has included the German expeditions of T. Wiegand (1902, 1917) and excavations under French and Syrian authorities by French, Swiss, Polish, German and Syrian expeditions. Many of the finds are displayed in the local museum (1b). Structures dedicated to deities are known either as temples or sanctuaries, and sites are associated with the gods of various cultures.

1. Architecture. 2. Sculpture.

1. Architecture.

(i) Until *c.* AD 14. (ii) *c.* AD 14–273. (iii) After AD 273.

(i) Until c. AD 14. Excavation has shown that oasis habitations were concentrated from at least the Bronze Age on a low mound beside the wadi (a dry river bed), now beneath the Sanctuary of Bel (1c); rebuilding occurred *c.* 300 BC. In the Hellenistic period dwellings seem to have spread around, and westward of, the mound. Tadmor's earliest

surviving structure, a Mesopotamian-style hypogeum 'underground tomb' with arched stone doorway and brick-vaulted corridor containing nine loculi (burial compartments) and graves, used *c.* 150 BC–AD 11, was probably away from housing, but later, as dwellings advanced, it was preserved within the Sanctuary of Baalshamin (1d). The real spur to development seems to have come with semi-independence (*c.* 64 BC–*c.* AD 14), when stone began to supplement and supplant mud-brick. East, west and south-west tracks became commercial routes; and two underground aqueducts (mentioned in a later tariff law) may have been tunnelled. Streets must have developed, and more houses, mainly of mud-brick, must have been built. Sanctuaries were organized according to Semitic religious needs, which included a rectangular open space, an altar, and a *hamana* (a squarish, sometimes solid stone shrine). From the Sanctuary of Bel (equated with Zeus and Jupiter; see fig. 2) came enclosure traces and soft limestone fragments (Palmyra, Mus. Palmyra) in 'Parthian' architectural and sculptural styles (Asiatic with Greek elements) and Tadmor's earliest dated inscription (44 BC), in Aramaic, mentioning 'priests of Bel'. The sanctuary may have had two opposed *hamanas*. The Sanctuary of Babylonian Nebu (equated with Apollo;(1e)) may have possessed a *hamana* and (?Doric) columns. Below the western hills further sanctuaries developed, indicated by traces of *hamanas*: the Arab goddess Allat (later equated with Athena) may have had a sanctuary (1f) by *c.* 50 BC, with an altar dated 6 BC and improvements by *c.* AD 1–60.

Semitic customs demanded burial of the dead and a memorial or dwelling-place for the soul of the deceased, frequently marked by stones, a stone plaque or monument. From *c.* 50 BC striking, rectangular sandstone and limestone tower tombs (1g–i) lined routes away from the village, developing an eastern tradition and creating Tadmor's still unique skyline. Early examples were of rough masonry, solid, with base burial slots (e.g. tomb 52, west necropolis), but they soon began to be made with a hollowed centre and surrounding steps, and by the time of ? Atenatan an internal staircase led to upper chambers with loculi containing successive mummified burials closed with plaster or a plaque (the earliest of these tombs dates from 9 BC). From the late 1st century BC to *c.* AD 150 a cemetery was used to the north-east, with coffin burials beneath limestone markers (Mus. Palmyra). A town wall in mud-brick on limestone may also belong to this period: the village was becoming a city.

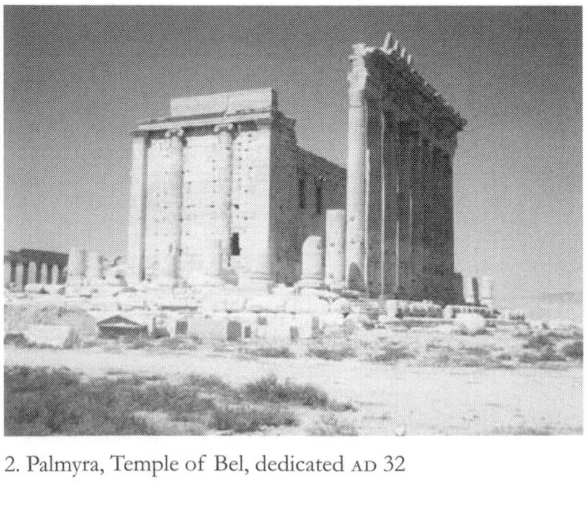

2. Palmyra, Temple of Bel, dedicated AD 32

(ii) c. AD 14–273. With full incorporation into Roman Syria, and peace, the Tadmoreans (now 'Palmyrenes' in Western documents) could devote caravan trade profits collectively and individually to building. Much would have been in traditional mud-brick, which has largely disappeared, but longer-lasting local limestones were also used, with cut-stone techniques adapting the methods and forms of Hellenistic Greek, Roman and occasionally Parthian architecture to local Semitic needs.

The Sanctuary of Allat seems to have been refurbished *c.* AD 1–*c.* 60. The cosmic god Baalshamin (equated, like Bel, with Greek Zeus) had a new, walled three-court sanctuary, recalling that at Seeia in southern Syria, laid out with a northern shrine (*c.* AD 11–*c.* 23), a portico (AD 67) and a ritual banquet room. Most spectacular, however, was the colossal, hard, originally creamy (now golden) limestone Temple of Bel, Iarhibol (sun) and 'Aglibol (moon), dedicated AD 32 and remarkable for mixing a finely carved, outwardly Hellenistic Greek appearance with many oriental features. Much of the Temple survives. Above foundations up to 15 m deep was raised a stepped platform, the stylobate (top step) of which measured 55.60×30.05 m, and a cella measuring 39.45×13.86 m (h. 14.16 m), with exterior Ionic half-columns at each end, lit by eight pedimented windows and entered by means of a ramp and a doorway off-centre in the west wall. A large, separately built thalamus at the northern end of the cella had steps up to a Corinthian pilaster façade with three bays and a wide doorway into a chamber with planetary reliefs on the ceiling and a stairway up to a tower or roof terrace. A spacious pseudoperipteral surrounding colonnade had 8×15 fluted columns (h. 15.81 m) with 'Attic' bases and 'blind fluting' on the lowest metre of the shaft. These were undoubtedly surmounted by bronze Corinthian capitals (destr.) on a stone core. There were roof merlons, ceiling coffers and 20-tonne trapezoidal cella beams with soffit *rinceaux* and, uniquely, religious relief scenes on the side fields. Mouldings recalled Hellenistic Anatolia and Egypt, and proportions the work of the Hellenistic architect HERMOGENES. Graffiti, masons' marks and texts indicate the involvement of Greek-speaking craftsmen as well as Palmyrenes, and possibly of Romans too. Soon after this initial building phase, the present richly ornamented portal was added to the west peristyle to emphasize the entrance, and a complementary interior southern cella thalamus was erected with steps and a Corinthian pilaster façade of five bays, a doorway, a chamber with a deeply carved ceiling acanthus and lotus rosette within a meander and octagonal rosette coffers, and two further staircases. Thus was created a great temple of the ancient world.

Existing sanctuaries were Romanized on the model of an axial podium temple with a columned porch within a rectangular walled court, usually with a Corinthian colonnade. The court of the Temple of Bel was lowered 920 mm and the stepped platform walled to create a podium (*c.* AD 50–*c.* 80). Additions included an altar, basin, banquet chamber, ramp and a walled court (*c.* 205×210 m) with double south, east and north colonnades (before AD 108), and a huge single west colonnade (*c.* AD 100–*c.* 150) with a handsome, three-door central gateway (by AD 175). The Sanctuary of Nebu incorporated a hexastyle, peripteral podium temple with interior staircase, *hamana* and a Doric court (*c.* AD 50–*c.* 99), and the Temple of Baalshamin (well-preserved; see fig. 3) had a porch, pilasters, two pedimented windows and an elegant, apsidal interior thalamus built by Male Agrippa (AD 130/131) with an adjoining 'Rhodian peristyle' court. The Temple of Allat incorporated earlier features, including benches and a marble Athena (*c.* AD 150). The Temple of Arsu and the Efqa spring were integrated into the new development. A disused city wall tower became Belhammon's shrine (AD 89). Romanization spread to rustic shrines north-west of Palmyra, with the rebuilding of the shrine of Abgal (AD 195).

Families continued to surround the city with dramatic tomb architecture, 150 above ground and more below. Some contained over 300 burial spaces, and some were partly leased to outsiders. Dated stone towers run from 9 BC to AD 128. Rising up to five storeys on a stepped socle, from *c.* AD 1–*c.* 50 they had irregular masonry and inward-leaning chamber walls, but thereafter were of ashlar, with narrow staircases and vertical walls, enabling each burial slot to be closed by a squarish plaque, often made of limestone and carrying a named relief bust of, and for, the deceased. Ground-floor interiors were sometimes richly ornamented with Corinthian pilasters, mouldings, coffered ceilings and colouring (e.g. Iamliku family, AD 83; Elahbel family, AD 103). In the 1st century AD hypogea were sometimes added to towers, with steps, limestone doors and interiors variously arranged around corridors lined with burial slots. Later hypogea were created independently, with examples dated AD 81–232, often containing architectural and sometimes painted embellishment. The latest and richest tombs were squarish, white limestone 'house' or 'temple' tombs, dated AD 143–253 (and apparently alternating in popularity with hypogea). Façades echoed Nabataean rock tombs, Parthian palaces or Roman temple fronts; interiors comprised chambers with burial slots or sarcophagi, or a colonnaded court, sometimes two-storey, sometimes open-air. One (tomb 36, Worod family, *c.* AD 200) had measurements in a Persian yard (277.5 mm) and several proportions of 7:4, testifying to Palmyra's opulent cultural mix.

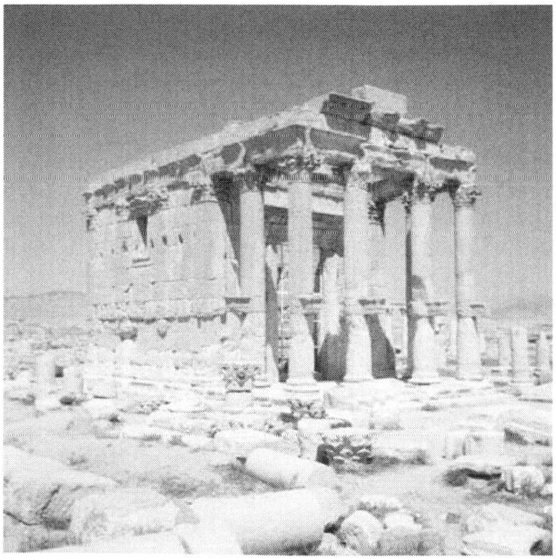

3. Palmyra, Temple of Baalshamin, 2nd century AD

The gradual creation of impressive public and private buildings, primarily in limestone, accompanied Palmyra's greatest prosperity (from the later 1st century AD). These were concentrated north of the wadi. Greco-Roman ideas were imaginatively adapted, and the Corinthian order reigned supreme. Single honorific columns dated AD 64, 74 and 139 supported statuary. The agora (see fig. 1j above) became a vast, walled, pilastered court (71×84 m; *c.* AD 86–*c.* 108), with eleven gates, two little fountains, a tribunal, pedimented windows on the east wall and wall brackets for statuary. Colonnades comprising columns with consoles halfway up for statuary became standard at Palmyra. Out of *c.* 200 surviving texts, 145 (AD 75 [recopied later] to AD 218) indicate the presence of statues of senators (east colonnade), the Severan imperial family (on the east gate, *c.* AD 200), Palmyrene and Roman officials (north colonnade), soldiers (west colonnade) and caravan leaders (south colonnade, flanking the principal gate). Adjoining the agora on the west was a banqueting room (1k) and on the east a similarly huge walled and windowed court, perhaps a depot (1l), where a tariff law of AD 137 was found.

Colonnaded streets were popular in Roman Near Eastern cities; in Palymra, individual columns (usually with consoles) created the north–south Transverse Colonnade street (w. 22 m, *c.* AD 89–*c.* 179), with the Oval Piazza (1m; recalling that at Gerasa) and Damascus gate, and the splendid east–west Great Colonnade (1n), 11 m wide and over 1 km long (partly surviving). A western section (*c.* AD 100–*c.* 150), possibly provided with a fountain, opened on to side streets with wealthy, eastern Roman-style peristyle houses, one perhaps with an iwan (a Parthian-style vaulted room) and a basilica-like structure; later, a 3rd-century AD columned tomb ended its western vista. A slight change in direction was marked by a tetrapylon (1o) on a stepped base (*c.* AD 150), like one at Gerasa and consisting of four groups of four huge red granite Corinthian columns from Aswan, each surrounding a statue. From this a street ran south towards the Temple of Arsu. After *c.* AD 150 the use of fewer column drums and the alternation of large and narrow wall blocks speeded limestone construction. The next, well-preserved portion of the Great Colonnade (*c.* AD 150 to *c.* early 3rd century) ended at the Sanctuary of Nebu. On its north side were a four-column curved and niched nymphaeum (1p) and a bath or royal palace, and a peristyle building with a four-column red granite portico (1q; the later Baths of Diocletian). On the south side, arches and streets led to houses, a fine peristyle building (1r; the Caesareum), banquet rooms, a triangular space with the peristyle apsed senate house (1s) and, in a curved street, a well-preserved Roman-style theatre (1t; see fig. 4) with semicircular *orchestra* 20 m across and a five-door, niched, colonnaded stage front. A richly ornamented, wedge-shaped monumental arch (the tripylon, *c.* AD 200; 1u) concealed the next change of Colonnade direction, leading past shops, banqueting rooms and another fountain to the central gateway of the Sanctuary of Bel. Mid-3rd century AD peristyle houses with painted, mosaic and figured plaster ornamentation were located east of the Sanctuary of Bel and near the Efqa spring. Zenobia's palace remains undiscovered. Urbanization continued until the fall of Palmyra.

(iii) After AD 273. Aurelian's onslaught permanently reduced the city's significance. Inscriptions became rare; the last known Aramaic text was bilingual (AD 279/280), recording roof repairs to the Great Colonnade. In AD 293–303 Diocletian and Maximian's governor Sosianus Hierocles probably repaired, rather than built, the city baths that bear his name in Latin, and made Palmyra a stronghold like Split, Croatia, with square-bastioned walls (see fig. 1v) enclosing a reduced circuit. The refashioned western hillside camp (1w) around the Temple of Allat included a colonnaded street grid, a central columned tetrapylon, forum, staircase and upper chambers, as well as a central apsed Temple of the Standards and boastful Latin text (now an impressive ruin). In AD 328 Constantine's 'curator' Flavius Diogenes restored the roofing of the Great Colonnade. The Temple of Allat received a canopied Athena statue, but it was closed and destroyed when the Christian Theodosius I (*reg* AD 379–95) abolished pagan cults. The Bel and Baalshamin temples became churches. Two basilicas (1x) were built; one preserves six nave columns and an arch. Justinian I almost certainly added round bastions to the city wall.

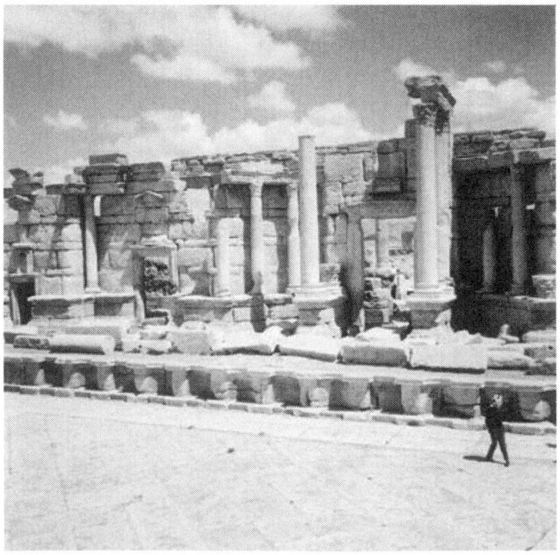

4. Palmyra, theatre, 2nd century AD

J. Dawkins and R. Wood: *The Ruins of Palmyra, Otherwise Tedmor, in the Desert* (London and Paris, 1753)

J. Cantineau: *Inventaire des inscriptions de Palmyre*, 9 vols (Damascus, 1930–36)

T. Wiegand and others: *Palmyra: Ergebnisse der Expeditionen von 1902 und 1917* (Berlin, 1932)

J. Cantineau: *Grammaire du palmyrénien épigraphique* (Cairo, 1935)

D. Schlumberger: *La Palmyrène du nord-ouest* (Paris, 1951)

K. Michalowski, A. Sadurska and M. Gawlikowski: *Palmyre: Fouilles polonaises*, 8 vols (Warsaw, 1960–84)

P. Collart and J. Vicari: *Le Sanctuaire de Baalshamin à Palmyre: Topographie et architecture*, 2 vols (Rome, 1969)

A. Ostrasz: 'Note sur le plan de la partie médiane de la rue principale de Palmyre', *An. Archéol. Arabes, Syr.*, xix (1969), pp. 109–20

R. Fellmann: *Die Grabanlage* (1970), v of *Le Sanctuaire de Baalshamin à Palmyre*, 6 vols (Rome, 1969–75)

M. Gawlikowski: *Monuments funéraires de Palmyre* (Warsaw, 1970)

K. Michalowski: *Palmyra* (London and New York, 1970)

D. Van Berchem: 'Le Premier Rempart de Palmyre', *Acad. Inscr. & B.-Lett.: C. R. Séances* (May 1970), pp. 231–7

M. Gawlikowski: *Le Temple palmyrénien* (Warsaw, 1973)

A. Ostrasz: *Le Développement urbain de Palmyre* (diss., U. Warsaw, 1973)

M. Gawlikowski: 'Les Défenses de Palmyre', *Syria*, li (1974), pp. 231–42

M. Lyttelton: *Baroque Architecture in Classical Antiquity* (London, 1974)

H. Seyrig, R. Amy and E. Will: *Le Temple de Bel à Palmyre*, 2 vols (Paris, 1975)

H. J. W. Drijvers: 'Das Heiligtum der arabischen Göttin Allât im westlichen Stadtteil von Palmyra', *Ant. Welt*, vii/3 (1976), pp. 28–38

H. J. W. Drijvers: *The Religion of Palmyra*, Iconography of Religions (Leiden, 1976)

M. Gawlikowski: 'Le Temple d'Allat à Palmyre', *Rev. Archéol.* (1977), pp. 253–74

H. Stern: *Les Mosaïques des maisons d'Achille et de Cassiopée à Palmyre* (Paris, 1977)

I. Browning: *Palmyra* (London, 1979)

M. Gawlikowski: 'Le Sanctuaire d'Allat à Palmyre: Aperçu préliminaire', *An. Archéol. Arabes, Syr.*, xxxiii (1983), pp. 179–98

J. Starcky and M. Gawlikowski: *Palmyre* (Paris, 1985)

M. Gawlikowski: 'Le Premier Temple d'Allat', *A Joint Tribute to Adnan Bounni*, ed. P. Matthiae, M. Van Loon and H. Weiss (Istanbul, 1990), pp. 101–8

A. Schmidt-Colinet, K. As`ad and C. Müting-Zimmer: *Das Tempelgrab Nr. 36 in Palmyra: Studien zur palmyrenischen Grabarchitektur und ihrer Ausstattung* (Mainz, 1992)

V. Bougault: 'Palmyra, la Venise des sables', *L'Oeil*, dxxix (Sept 2001), p. 103

S. Blin: 'En Syrie, sur le chemin des paradis', *Conn. A.*, dci (Jan 2003), pp. 68–77

A. Schmidt-Colinet: *Palmyra: Kulturbegegnung im Grenzbereich* (Mainz, 2005)

2. Sculpture. Encouraged by the local availability of limestone, artists at Palmyra produced numerous relatively homogeneous and highly original sculptures, most of which date to the first three centuries AD, although some 'archaic' pieces were made in the 1st century BC. Sculpture in the round was rare, but a few funerary statues survive. Many honorific statues of important figures were also erected on the consoles projecting from columns bordering the streets, in the agora and in temples, but most were in bronze, and were plundered or melted down. The largest collections of Palmyrene sculpture are housed in the Musée de Palmyra and in the National Museum of Damascus.

Most of the surviving sculptures from Palmyra are funerary reliefs, which take three forms: stelae erected on individual tombs; plaques intended to seal the loculi in funerary towers, hypogea and 'temple tombs'; and sarcophagi also placed in collective tombs. The earliest are the stelae, which were initially left unadorned but later decorated, either with symbolic motifs such as palmettes and a curtain, or with a figure of the deceased, often with the curtain as a backdrop. The loculi plaques carried a bust of the deceased in high relief, sometimes also against a curtained background. The abundance of these funerary busts and the fact that several were dated by an inscription allowed H. Ingholt to establish a tentative chronology of Palmyrene sculpture, which still forms the basis for modern study. A so-called 'archaic' era (50 BC–AD 50), at the end of the Hellenistic period and at the beginning of the Roman occupation, characterized by rather schematic reliefs and a strictly frontal view, was succeeded by three major periods dating respectively to AD 50–150, AD 150–200 and AD 200–272. These showed a marked development in the treatment of clothing and faces, although figures were still invariably in frontal view, eyes were pre-eminent and features were geometrically regular. The limestone sarcophagi (late 2nd century AD to *c.* AD 250) were carved to resemble couches with turned legs and mattresses covered in decorative motifs. The spaces between the feet were sometimes decorated with busts or, more rarely, whole figures in relief. Above the couch a great slab, carved in high relief, showed the deceased reclining at a banquet in the presence of one or more family members. These luxurious sarcophagi, reserved for only the most monumental tombs, were often arranged in groups of three to suggest a dining-room at the end of the central gallery or the lateral exedrae of a hypogeum.

Large numbers of religious sculptures have also been discovered. One group comprises decorative reliefs with mythological scenes and scenes of worship, the finest of which were found in the Temple of Bel (early 1st century AD). Examples on the ceiling beams of the peristyle include depictions of a god on horseback fighting a snake-footed monster in the presence of a row of divinities, and a procession featuring a camel and a number of veiled women. Certain other decorative reliefs are non-narrative in character and show divinities, sometimes accompanied by animals and various symbols. A third and particularly large group of religious sculptures comprises votive reliefs, of which some were found in Palmyra itself but most were discovered in neighbouring villages and the small temples built along the great caravan routes. Dedicated to the major Palmyrene gods and to the protective divinities of the nomads, these reliefs sometimes show a single deity, sometimes two or more in a line facing the observer, and often include a worshipper offering incense on an altar. When deities were shown mounted on horses or camels, only their mounts were depicted in profile. Such reliefs were produced in every era of Palmyrene art and are particularly representative of the fundamental traits of Palmyrene sculpture. Strict frontality is maintained even in scenes with more than one figure and, where several figures occur, they are merely juxtaposed in a monotonous disconnected line, even when engaged in a common activity.

The influences on Palmyrene sculpture are difficult to determine with any precision. Although various Western elements are apparent, particularly in later works, Palmyrene art, with its emphasis on frontality and hieratic images, also assimilated a combination of Mesopotamian, Greco-Iranian and Parthian elements, which gave it a profoundly Oriental character.

H. Ingholt: *Studier over palmyrensk skulptur* (Copenhagen, 1928)

H. Seyrig: 'Note sur les plus anciennes sculptures palmyréniennes', *Berytus*, 3 (1936), pp. 137–40

M. Morehart: 'Early Sculpture at Palmyra', *Berytus*, 12 (1956–7), pp. 53–83

T. Borkowska: 'Les Bas-reliefs votifs de Palmyre', *Stud. Palmyr.*, 1 (Warsaw, 1966), pp. 96–124 [Polish text with Fr. summary]

A. Sadurska: 'Recherches sur la sculpture funéraire de Palmyre', *Archeol. Class.*, xxvii (1975), pp. 301–16

M. A. R. Colledge: *The Art of Palmyra* (London, 1976)

K. Parlasca: 'Probleme palmyrenischer Grabreliefs', *Palmyre: Bilan et perspectives*, ed. E. Frézouls (Strasbourg, 1976), pp. 33–43

M. Gawlikowski and M. Pietrzykowski: 'Les Sculptures du temple de Baalshamîn à Palmyre', *Syria*, 56 (1980), pp. 421–52

K. Parlasca: 'Probleme der palmyrenischen Sarkophage', *Marburg. Winckelmann-Programm* (1984), pp. 283–96

K. C. Makowski: 'Recherches sur le banquet miniaturisé dans l'art funéraire de Palmyre', *Stud. Palmyr.*, 8 (1985), pp. 119–30

K. C. Makowski: 'La Sculpture funéraire palmyrénienne et sa fonction dans l'architecture sépulcrale', *Stud. Palmyr.*, 8 (1985), pp. 69–117

K. Tanabe, ed.: *Sculptures of Palmyra* (Tokyo, 1986)

A. Sadurska: 'Die palmyrenische Grabskulptur', *Das Altertum*, xxxiv/1 (1988), pp. 14–23

K. Parlasca: 'La Sculpture grecque et la sculpture d'époque romaine impériale en Syrie', *Archéologie et histoire de la Syrie*, ii, ed. J.-M. Dentzer and W. Orthmann (Saarbrücken, 1989), pp. 544–51

Les Antiquités de Palmyre au Musée du Louvre (Paris, 1993), pp. 65–81 by J. Dentzer-Feydy, 133–246 by J. Dentzer-Feydy and J. Teixidor

A. Sadurska and A. Bounni: *Les sculptures funéraires de Palmyre* (Rome, 1994)

H. Nehls: 'Palmyra in der Gelehrtenvilla: Ein wiederentdecktes Grabrelief aus der Sammlung F. Sarre', *Ant. Welt*, xxvi/4 (1995), pp. 271–2

G. Ploug: *Catalogue of the Palmyrene Sculptures, Ny Carlsberg Glyptotek* (Copenhagen 1995)

Pamphilos (*fl* early 4th century BC). Greek painter. He came from Amphipolis in Macedonia but worked in Sikyon; he was the pupil of Eupompos. Pamphilos charged his own pupils extravagant fees. Among them were Melanthios, Apelles and PAUSIAS, the last of whom seems to have come to Pamphilos to learn the encaustic technique of laying on colours in a wax medium and burning them in, a technique for which the Sikyonian school was famous. Pamphilos was praised for his *ratio*, the intellectual quality of his painting. He especially emphasized arithmetic and geometry. Through his influence painting on wooden panels became the first step in a liberal education for freeborn boys, first at Sikyon and later throughout Greece. Among his paintings, none of which survives, were a family group, perhaps a grave monument or a votive offering; the *Victory of the Athenians at Phlios*, perhaps the battle fought in 367 BC; and *Odysseus on his Raft*. The comic playwright Aristophanes (*c.* 450–*c.* 385 BC) ascribed to Pamphilos the *Daughters of Herakles Coming as Suppliants to Athens* (*Wealth* 385). Although most scholiasts confirmed Aristophanes' attribution, one attributed it to Apollodoros. The Sikyonian statesman Aratos (271–213 BC) sent paintings by Pamphilos to Ptolemy II Philadelphus of Egypt.

J. Overbeck: *Die antiken Schriftquellen zur Geschichte der bildenden Künste bei den Griechen* (Leipzig, 1868/*R* Hildesheim, 1959), nos 1642, 1745–53, 1828

Pamukkale. *See* HIERAPOLIS.

Panainos (*fl* second half of the 5th century BC). Greek painter from Athens. He was the son or grandson of Charmides of Athens and the nephew or possibly brother of the sculptor Pheidias, with whom he worked at Olympia; none of his work survives. He painted parts of Pheidias' chryselephantine cult statue of *Zeus*, particularly the drapery. Pausanias (*Guide to Greece* V.xi.1) described lilies and animals on the drapery, and these may have been Panainos' work. He also decorated barriers around the statue: those opposite the door were plain blue, while the others bore nine two-figure scenes. Panainos painted the interior of the shield of the chryselephantine statue of *Athena* in the goddess's temple at Elis, the work of either Pheidias or his pupil Kolotes. He also painted the walls of the temple—Pliny (*Natural History* XXXVI.177) claimed that saffron and milk were mixed with the plaster to prepare the walls. The most famous painting attributed to Panainos was the *Battle of Marathon* in the Painted Stoa (Stoa Poikile) in the Athenian Agora. The earlier artist MIKON was, however, also credited with this work, once in conjunction with Polygnotos of Thasos; perhaps Panainos completed the work that Mikon had begun. Some of the figures in the *Battle of Marathon* seem to have been attempted portraits (e.g. of the Athenian playwright Aeschylus and the Persian general Artaphernes). Ancient sources record that the general Miltiades, depicted urging his men forward, was not named, implying that the names of other figures were inscribed. Pliny (XXXV.57) mentioned the extensive range of colours used in the portraits. Competitions among painters were instituted at the Pythian and Isthmian Games in the time of Panainos, who lost to Timagoras of Chalkis in the Pythian Games.

J. Overbeck: *Die antiken Schriftquellen zur Geschichte der bildenden Künste bei den Griechen* (Leipzig, 1868/*R* Hildesheim, 1959), nos 696, 698, 1094–1108

Panaitios Painter. *See under* ONESIMOS.

Pan Painter (*fl* *c.* 480–*c.* 450 BC). Greek vase painter. Active in Attica, he was associated with the MANNERIST WORKSHOP and named by Beazley after the picture on the obverse of a Red-figure bell krater (Boston, MA, Mus. F.A., 10.185) showing *Pan in Pursuit of a Young Goatherd*. More than 160 vases have been attributed to him, one of the earliest being a psykter in Munich (Staatl. Antikensamml., 2417), usually thought to date from the 480s BC, although dates as late as 460 BC have been suggested. The end of his career is represented by a bell krater (Palermo, Mus. Reg., V778) and some other vases with less generous use of relief lines.

The Pan Painter's drawing style is distinctive. The heads of his figures are round, with rounded and heavy chins and thick necks in which the musculature is sometimes indicated by one or two brown lines. White hair is usually indicated by reserved areas. His rendering of male anatomy relates to that of MYSON, with two divisions of the abdominal muscles rather than the usual three. The arms are strong, with upper muscles sometimes shown by brown-glaze opposed semicircles and lower ones by a brown-glaze line running diagonally from the inside of the elbow to the wrist. Frontal feet are common, occasionally with more than five toes, which are drawn as small arcs. Boots, elegant high leather shoes and sandals strapped to the calves also occur often, as on works by the Mannerists, the Niobid Painter and others. Rocks, sometimes covered with a yellow wash and with stylized cracks, are another distinctive feature. Garments fall in straight folds, frequently grouped in fours, and stacked pleats. The *chiton* often forms a bolster either side of the waist when belted.

Some of the Pan Painter's compositions are outstanding. On a pelike (Athens, N. Archaeol. Mus., 9683) Herakles is shown holding an Egyptian by his feet, with a group of two other Egyptians forming a dynamic triangular composition around a centrally placed altar. The range of vase shapes is exceptionally wide, including cups; hydriai; oinochoai; loutrophoroi; both neck and belly amphorae; bell, calyx and volute kraters; lebetes; stamnoi; alabastra; a kantharos and a psykter. His favoured shapes, however, appear to have been lekythoi, including two White-ground examples, column kraters, pelikai and Nolan amphorae, nearly all with triple handles. With the exception of those on two of his pelikai, his pictures, even on large vases, are unframed. Eight small pelikai seem to come from the same potter's workshop, and most of these have a distinctive pattern of ovolos with blackened centres on the neck. The Pan Painter's patterns are usually simple: keys or broken stopt meanders in pairs or threes, alternating with saltires, sometimes with dots, or crosses in squares.

The Pan Painter's subjects are equally varied, including gods, heroes and scenes of daily life, often with unusual touches (see fig.). The psykter in Munich shows *Apollo Fighting Idas for the Love of Marpessa*, a subject also depicted by the Triptolemos Painter, with whose workshop he seems to have had connections. Two vases depict *Artemis Turning Actaeon's Dogs against their Master*. On the earlier, a volute krater (Athens, N. Archaeol. Mus., Akr. 760) the scene alludes conventionally to Actaeon's metamorphosis into a deer by dressing him in a deerskin, but on the reverse of the later vase (the artist's name-piece; see above) no transformation is suggested. Two paintings depict scenes from the *Iliad*, with *Achilles Slaying Penthesilea* on a calyx krater (Cambridge, Fitzwilliam, GR 3.1971), and the *Ransom of Hector* on a stamnos (Paris, Louvre, C108221). The former also shows *Herakles with Syleus*, and two vases depict *Herakles Killing the Egyptian King Busiris* (Athens, N. Archaeol. Mus., 9683; Leipzig U., Archäol. Inst., T651). On the

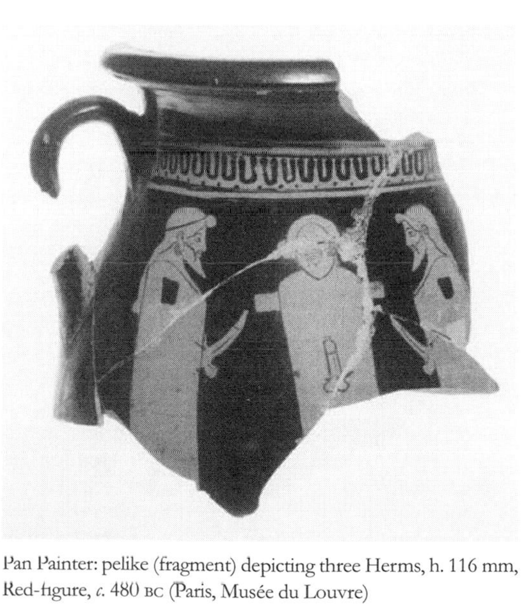

Pan Painter: pelike (fragment) depicting three Herms, h. 116 mm, Red-figure, *c.* 480 BC (Paris, Musée du Louvre)

vase in Athens, a pelike, the detail is remarkable. The Egyptians, who have negroid features, are correctly shown as being circumcised. The altar is adorned with mouldings, palmettes and volutes. A rare depiction of the *Infant Herakles Killing the Snakes in his Cradle* (a cup; Leipzig, Karl-Marx-U., Archäol. Inst., T3365) is also by the Pan Painter. *Theseus Fighting the Minotaur* occurs on a skyphos (New York, Met., X.22.25 (GR85)), and both this and the *Infant Herakles* were subjects popular with the other Mannerists. So too were the *Death of Kaineus* (column krater; London, BM, E473), *Triptolemos Bringing Man the Gift of Corn* (pelike; Ferrara, Mus. N. Archeol., 83(42)) and *Perseus and Medusa* (hydria; London, BM, E181). Scenes of daily life include sacrifices and musical and domestic scenes, and often depict herms.

The Pan Painter was possibly a pupil of Myson (Beazley, 1963), but some scholars consider his teacher to have been a colleague of Peithinos and the Sosias Painter or the Berlin Painter. There are certainly connections between the works of the BERLIN PAINTER and the Pan Painter, since the former decorated an equally wide range of shapes, but also favoured lekythoi and Nolan amphorae. His preference for single, grand figures can be paralleled in the Pan Painter's work, as can his choice of ornament. The Pan Painter's treatment of male anatomy does, however, suggest that Myson taught him and that he was only later influenced by the Berlin Painter. Myson was the founder of a Mannerist workshop that lasted to the end of the 5th century BC, but, while the Pan Painter can be classed as a Mannerist, he differed from the others in quality and character, and his style is in fact 'subarchaic' (Beazley, 1944): both his early and later vases tend to be more elaborately decorated, while the figures are more slender, posing rather than acting, and the drapery shows decorative rather than realistic treatment.

No pupils of the Pan Painter are known, though his influence has been noted in the scenes of revellers by the Cleveland Painter, the Alkimachos Painter and the earlier Mannerists. There is no known example of the Pan Painter's signature. The word *kalos* (Gr.: 'beautiful') occurs on two of his vases, though without the customary named youth, while a vase from his circle praises Hippon.

J. D. Beazley: 'The Master of the Boston Pan-Krater', *J. Hell. Stud.*, xxxii (1912), pp. 354–69

J. D. Beazley: *Red-figure* (1942, 2/1963), i, pp. 550–61

J. D. Beazley: *The Pan Painter* (Oxford, 1944)

A. B. Follmann: *Der Pan-Maler* (diss., U. Bonn, 1968)

C. Sourvinou-Inwood: 'Who Was the Teacher of the Pan Painter?', *J. Hell. Stud.*, xcv (1975), pp. 107–21

M. Robertson: 'Two Pelikai by the Pan Painter', *Greek Vases in the J. Paul Getty Museum*, iii (Malibu, 1986), pp. 71–90

Pantheon [Gr.: 'all gods']. Circular temple dedicated to all the gods. The best-known example is the Pantheon in Rome (*see* ROME, §IV, 8 for a detailed account), built by the Emperor Hadrian in AD 118–25.

Paphos, New [Nea Paphos; now Kato Paphos]. Town on the south-west coast of CYPRUS and capital of the island from the 2nd century BC to the 4th century AD. As Kato Paphos it now occupies the southern part of the modern town of Paphos. New Paphos was founded *c.* 320 BC by Nikokles, king of Old Paphos. Soon afterwards Cyprus came to form part of the Ptolemaic kingdom of Egypt under which it remained throughout the Hellenistic period. New Paphos was vital to the Ptolemys both as a military outpost and as the main port from which Cypriot corn, minerals and above all timber were exported to Egypt. As the capital of the island it played a leading role in the development of culture and the arts on Cyprus.

The little of Hellenistic New Paphos that has been excavated shows that the hellenization of the island, already widespread in the preceding period, was given a new impetus by the Greek-orientated Ptolemaic rule. The city was built on a regular grid with streets forming rectangular blocks, and was surrounded by high walls. Inscriptions mention a gymnasium and many temples, but only the Sanctuary of Apollo Hylates, consisting of two subterranean chambers, has been identified (late 4th century BC). A theatre, apparently the largest on the island, has also been located, and remains of private houses show that these were of the atrium type (i.e. with a central colonnaded court) and richly decorated with frescoes and pebble mosaics like their counterparts in Greece and Asia Minor. Some of the finest rock-cut tombs of the period (e.g. the 'Tombs of the Kings', 3rd century BC) show a similar architecture with stepped entrance passages leading to atria surrounded by Doric porticos with triglyphs and metopes. Some preserve rich painted decoration, which, like the architecture, finds its closest parallels in Alexandria. Tombs and buildings were decorated with imported Attic sculpture, but excavated remains of workshops, furnaces and moulds show that bronze statues were made locally.

New Paphos attained its greatest importance in the 2nd and 3rd centuries AD under the Antonine and Severan emperors, and acquired the title 'Sebaste Claudia Flavia Paphos, the sacred metropolis of the towns of Cyprus'. The city had a large civic centre comprising an odeion, an Asklepieion and an agora. It even had an amphitheatre, but its splendour can best be appreciated in such private dwellings as the houses of Orpheus, Dionysos and Aion, where rich decoration of all kinds has been found. This includes numerous statues, mostly of deities, made of marble and probably imported ready-made. There were also wall paintings, and mosaics of extremely high quality from productive local workshops, which betray links with East Mediterranean workshops. They exhibit a wealth of mythological scenes including some unique in the ancient world. This tradition continued into the 5th century, well after the establishment of Christianity, as witnessed by some of the mosaics of the Villa of Theseus. This vast building was the proconsul's residence, built on a characteristic late Roman plan and decorated with marble veneer, frescoes and many statues. It had several building phases, a major one after the disastrous earthquakes of the 4th century. At this date political reasons dictated that the capital of Cyprus be moved from New Paphos to Salamis, which was renamed Constantia. In spite of this, New Paphos continued to be a major centre, no doubt partly because it was the seat of a bishop. The Arab invasions, however, which started in the mid-7th century, brought an end to the glory of New Paphos; it was abandoned by its population in favour of the upper town, which probably dates from this time.

K. Nicolaou: *Nea Paphos: An Archaeological Guide* (Nicosia, 1966)

K. Nicolaou: 'The Topography of Nea Paphos', *Mélanges offerts à K. Michałowski* (Warsaw, 1966), pp. 561–601

W. A. Daszewski: 'Les Fouilles polonaises à Nea Paphos, 1972–1975: Rapport préliminaire', Rep. Dept Ant., Cyprus (1976), pp. 185–225

W. A. Daszewski: *La Mosaïque de Thésée* (1977), ii of *Nea Paphos* (Warsaw, 1976–7)

G. S. Eliades: *The House of Dionysos* (Paphos, 1984)

F. G. Maier and V. Karageorghis: *Paphos: History and Archaeology* (Athens, 1984)

W. A. Daszewski: 'Researches at Nea Paphos, 1965–1984', *Archaeology in Cyprus, 1960–1985*, ed. V. Karageorghis (Nicosia, 1985), pp. 277–91

S. Hadjisavvas: 'Excavations at the "Tombs of the Kings", Kato Paphos', *Archaeology in Cyprus, 1960–1985*, ed. V. Karageorghis (Nicosia, 1985), pp. 262–8

A. Papageorghiou: 'L'Architecture paléochrétienne de Chypre', *Corsi Cult. A. Ravenn. & Biz.*, xxiii (1985), pp. 299–324

W. A. Daszewski and D. Michaelides: *Guide to the Paphos Mosaics* (Nicosia, 1988)

Paphos: *The coins from the House of Dionysos* (cat. by I. Nicolaou, Nicosia, 1990)

C. Kondoleon: *Domestic and Divine: Roman Mosaics in the House of Dionysos* (Ithaca, 1994)

A. H. Rowe: 'A Current Late Roman Site in Nea Paphos, Cyprus', *Near Eastern Archaeology*, lxi/3 (Sept 1998), p. 179

M. Droste: 'XAIPE KAI CY—Freue Dich, Auch Du: Zur Deutung der Mittelfigur im Jahreszeitenmosaik im "Haus des Dionysos" von Paphos (Zypern)', *Ant. Welt*, xxxii/6 (2001), pp. 563–70

'Archaeology in Cyprus 1997–2002', *J. Hell. Stud.*, 1 (2003–4 suppl. Archaeological Reports), pp. 93–111 [special section]

Paphos, Old [Palea Paphos; formerly Paphos; Med. Covocle]. Site of an ancient city near the modern village of Kouklia on the south-western coast of Cyprus, *c.* 45 km west of Limassol, famous for its Sanctuary of Aphrodite. First inhabited in the Chalcolithic period (*c.* 3800–*c.* 2300 BC), the site was settled by Greek immigrants beginning in the 12th century BC and was capital of the kingdom of Paphos from the 8th century BC to the start of the 3rd, when Cyprus was conquered by the Ptolemies. The foundation in 320 BC of the nearby harbour town of New Paphos led to the adoption of the name Old Paphos.

The city was an important centre of worship throughout antiquity. A local fertility cult was transformed by the Greeks into a cult of Aphrodite, which assimilated elements of the Syrian goddess Astarte. Gradually the sanctuary at Old Paphos, situated close to the place where the 'foam-born goddess' was believed to have risen from the sea, became the most famous sanctuary of Aphrodite in the Greek and Roman world, and its temple formed the chief architectural feature of the city. The first monumental buildings date from *c.* 1200 BC and comprise a type of Near Eastern court sanctuary, combining a large open temenos with a smaller, covered hall. The hall probably housed the conical idol of the goddess, aniconic worship being a legacy of the original autochthonous cult. The workshops of the Late Bronze Age (*c.* 1600–*c.* 1050 BC) city produced refined pottery, jewellery and ivories, which exhibit a characteristic fusion of Cypriot, Aegean and Near Eastern traditions (Nicosia, Cyprus Mus.; Kouklia, Archaeol. Mus.). The potter's craft lived on into the Iron Age, as shown by remarkable vessels in the rather severe Paphian style, which relies mainly on geometric decoration (Kouklia, Archaeol. Mus.).

The Archaic and Classical periods were the most flourishing phase in the history of the city, and their architectural heritage is considerable. In the Sanctuary of Aphrodite the buildings of these periods were destroyed by a thorough Roman remodelling, although the continuity of the cult is amply attested by thousands of votive terracottas (Kouklia, Archaeol. Mus.). An imposing Archaic II period (*c.* 600–*c.* 475 BC) ashlar building, modelled on Achaemenid prototypes, probably served as a royal residence (*see* CYPRUS, §II, 2(iii)). A large Late Classical (*c.* 400–320 BC) peristyle mansion may have been its successor. A unique monument of military architecture is represented by the north-east gate, which forms part of the circuit of walls built in the Archaic I period (*c.* 750–*c.* 600 BC) and maintained to *c.* 300 BC. Elaborate siege and countersiege works excavated on this site enable us to reconstruct in detail the Persian siege of Old Paphos during the Ionian Revolt (498 BC). The debris of a sanctuary outside the walls was used to construct a vast siege ramp. From it comes the largest group of Archaic sculpture found so far in Cyprus, testifying to a considerable local school of sculptors (examples at Nicosia, Cyprus Mus.; Kouklia, Archaeol. Mus.). Combining Egyptian trends with Greek influences, they created some of the finest Cypriot statues known.

At the beginning of the 3rd century BC Old Paphos lost part of its population and importance to New Paphos but retained its fame as a religious centre. The sanctuary was rebuilt around AD 100, possibly after earthquake damage, but not as a temple of Classical Greco-Roman design: the architecture retained the basic character of an open court sanctuary, reminiscent of the Near Eastern antecedents of the cult. The shrine, with the longest cult tradition in Cyprus, did not survive the outlawing of pagan religions by Theodosios I in AD 391.

F. G. Maier, ed.: *Ausgrabungen in Alt-Paphos*, 4 vols (Konstanz, 1977–86)

F. G. Maier and V. Karageorghis: *Paphos: History and Archaeology* (Nicosia, 1984)

F. G. Maier: *Alt-Paphos auf Cypern* (Mainz, 1985)

O. Masson and T. B. Mitford: *Les inscriptions syllabiques de Kouklia-Paphos* (Konstanz, 1989)

A. H. Simmons: 'Early Neolithic Settlement in Western Cyprus: Preliminary Report on the 1992–1993 Test Excavations at Kholetria Ortos', *Bull. Amer. Sch. Orient. Res.*, ccxcv (Aug 1994), pp. 1–14

Papyri, Villa of the. *See under* HERCULANEUM.

Papyrus. Plant of the sedge family (*Cyperus papyrus*). It was widespread in the uncultivated, swampy areas of the ancient Nile Valley and was exploited for many practical purposes including the making of baskets and boats. As a material for the use of scribes and artists, it has a history going back to at least the 3rd millennium BC.

Little direct evidence has survived from the dynastic period regarding methods of manufacture and the organization of the papyrus trade, and caution is necessary when applying to earlier periods the relatively copious evidence from Greco-Roman Egypt. Ancient Egyptian tomb reliefs, illustrating scenes of daily life, show only the gathering of bundles of papyrus stalks. Papyrus was probably manufactured during all periods by numerous small workshops, close to sources of supply. These workshops must always have been most abundant in the Delta and Faiyum, but papyrus may also have been made elsewhere. The cost of papyrus has been much discussed, some writers being more impressed by, for example, the vast amounts of new papyrus used by the bureaucracies of the New Kingdom and later, others by the frequent reuse of papyrus scraps and the employment of ostraca as substitutes. Until the Greco-Roman period there is very little direct evidence of cost, apart from a few prices from the Ramesside period. In pharaonic times, as in the Greco-Roman period, papyrus was no doubt too expensive for the very poorest (who would hardly need it) but involved what would have seemed merely trivial expenditure to the wealthy.

In favourable conditions the triangular stems of the papyrus plant grow to a height of 3–4 m and can be 50 mm or more thick. To manufacture the writing material (the Roman writer Pliny the elder gives a detailed account of the process in his *Natural History*, xiii.74–82), the outer rind was removed and very thin strips prepared from the pith, with a width of anything from 10 to 30 mm. Their lengths were cut to correspond roughly to the dimensions of the sheets to be made; as the sheets measured only a fraction of the full height of the plant, all but the best portions of the stalks could be discarded. Individual sheets of papyrus were made by arranging first one layer of parallel strips, laid down just touching one another or very slightly overlapping, and then a second, similar layer on top, with its strips running at right angles to those of the first layer. In freshly-cut papyrus strips, the three-armed cells that form the bulk of the pith readily interlock, so that no paste needed to be added. Some hammering or pressing seems to have been all that was required for the strips to cohere as they dried out to form a strong, supple sheet. The sheet's thickness varied according to that of the constituent strips, while the colour and flexibility depended on the quality of the papyrus stalks used. In pharaonic Egypt, a very thin and nearly white sheet was considered ideal, although it was already noted in antiquity that papyrus yellowed with age. The surface was well sized by the plant's juices, so the carbon ink of the pharaonic period, which was also the commonest ink of Greco-Roman Egypt, hardly penetrated the surface. The same was true of the various pigments used by artists, although some have subsequently had a destructive effect on the papyrus. Erasures could be made by wiping or washing away the ink, wet or dry, or, once dried, an eraser, such as a piece of sandstone, could be used. The surface of papyrus sheets is also naturally smooth: the 'fibres', which, to modern eyes, are such a conspicuous feature of ancient papyrus (they are actually the fibro-vascular bundles running through the pith of the plant), do not seem to have greatly concerned the Egyptians, and they did not provide any marked obstacle to painting or writing. It is uncertain whether or not the manufacturer needed to smooth the surface mechanically; more likely burnishing was applied only to local irregularities, chiefly by the user. Papyrus was evidently never supplied to scribes and artists in sheet form. The manufacturer made up rolls by pasting together overlapping sheets (Gr. *kollema*); about 20 sheets was the standard size.

Papyrus paper was essentially an Egyptian product. The plant yields only modest stalks in less than ideal conditions, and reports of its production elsewhere in the ancient world are either dubious or of minor significance. Manufactured papyrus rolls formed an Egyptian export of growing importance through the course of the 1st millennium BC. The introduction into Egypt, shortly before the Ptolemaic period, of the stiff Greek style of pen, which was liable to puncture the writing surface, seems to have led to the deliberate adoption of a thicker style of papyrus. Exports to all parts of the Classical world, quite apart from the increase in the Egyptian population, must have meant that production in the Greco-Roman period was on a far greater scale than, for instance, in the Old Kingdom. In the Roman period, papyrus for writing material was apparently specially cultivated, but it is not clear at how early a date this may have begun to be necessary. Pliny and Isidore of Seville (AD 560–636) quote a seven-step grading scheme for papyri, ranging from *augusta* (the best and most expensive) *to emporitica* (the cheapest).

Although several alternative, quite different, writing grounds were used in Egypt—usually for particular purposes—papyrus had no rival as a general writing material until parchment became widely used in the 4th century AD. Papyrus was only finally, but gradually, superseded by this and by true paper (made from linen) after the Arab conquest. The first evidence of the use of the codex form of book in Egypt is from the 2nd century AD. For perhaps two centuries the pages were predominantly of papyrus, even though the codex particularly exposed two of the weaknesses of papyrus: the fact that it is damaged by creasing, and the ease with which it frays at unprotected edges. The inconvenience of cutting codex leaves from the raw material of a pasted-up roll with its frequent joins seems to have led to a final, exceptional development in papyrus manufacture: the making of extremely broad sheets for this particular purpose.

Outside the dry conditions of Egypt, papyrus has rarely survived, despite being the writing material of choice of the Greco-Roman world for many centuries. A rare exception is the scrolls from the Villa of the Papyri in HERCULANEUM that were carbonized during the eruption of Mt Vesuvius in AD 79. An important collection of later material from Egypt itself are the Oxyrhynchus Papyri (named after the ancient town of OXYRHYNCHUS in the Faiyum) that preserve copies of Classical texts as well as important information on the administration and every day life in Greek and Roman Egypt.

L. Borchardt: 'Bemerkungen zu den ägyptischen Handschriften des Berliner Museums', *Z. Ägyp. Spr. & Altertknd.*, xxvii (1889), pp. 118–22

A. Lucas: *Ancient Egyptian Materials and Industries* (London, 1926, rev. 4/1962)

V. Täckholm and M. Drar: *Flora of Egypt*, ii (Cairo, 1950)

J. Černý: *Paper and Books in Ancient Egypt* (London, 1952/*R* Chicago, 1977)

E. G. Turner: *Greek Papyri: An Introduction* (Oxford, 1968, rev. 2/1980)

N. Lewis: *Papyrus in Classical Antiquity* (Oxford, 1974)

M. Weber: *Beiträge zur Kenntnis des Schrift- und Buchwesens der alten Ägypter* (diss., U. Cologne, 1979)

H. Ragab: *Le Papyrus* (Cairo, 1980)

W. E. H. Cockle: 'Restoring and Conserving Papyri', *Bull. Inst. Class. Stud. U. London*, xxx (1983), pp. 147–65

C. H. Roberts and T. C. Skeat: *The Birth of the Codex* (London, 1983)

J. M. Robinson: 'The Kollemata', *The Facsimile Edition of the Nag Hammadi Codices* (Leiden, 1984), pp. 61–70

M. L. Bierbrier, ed.: *Papyrus: Structure and Usage* (London, 1986)

R. Parkinson and S. Quirke: *Papyrus* (London, 1995)

Parodos. Lateral passage in an ancient Greek theatre, dividing the THEATRON from the SKENE.

Paros. Greek island at the centre of the Aegean Cyclades (*see also* ANTIPAROS). It is dominated by Mt Profitis Ilias, on the slopes of which are the marble quarries that prompted the island's sculptural florescence in the Classical period (5th–4th century BC). Paros also has remains, chiefly architectural, dating from the Greek Bronze Age.

1. Architecture. 2. Sculpture.

1. ARCHITECTURE. As well as several cemeteries of the Early Cycladic (EC) period (*c.* 3500/3000–*c.* 2000 BC), with cist tombs of standard EC type, and some house remains, there is on Paros an important Mycenaean fortified settlement (excavated since 1976 by D. U. Schilardhi) on the acropolis of Koukounaries, near Naoussa, which was preceded by some EC occupation. The Mycenaean buildings, constructed of schist slabs, occupy the flat top of the plateau. The surviving remains are mostly those of basements—rectangular rooms off two main corridors that meet at right angles. The floor above may have included a MEGARON of standard Mycenaean palatial type. The top of the only practicable route of ascent (on the southern side of the hill) is barred by a heavy fortification wall of large, roughly worked blocks, which also serves to retain the buildings behind. The indentations in its face recall those of Mycenaean counterparts. A covered drainage channel relieved the settlement of surplus effluent. After destruction by fire in an enemy attack in the early 12th century BC, the site was reoccupied by a sizeable Geometric settlement (9th century BC) of apsidal and rectangular houses, before its final abandonment in the 8th century BC. At this point houses were built on the lower and more accessible southern slopes of the hill. To this last phase belong the remains of a small, plain rectangular Temple of Athena (*c.* 700 BC). Built in the usual local schist-slab style, its roof was supported by wooden interior columns on stone bases. There were traces of a large two-leaved door. The temple was set, with its altar, in a sacred enclosure bounded by a wall. Secular houses were later built nearby.

On a hillock in Parikia, the Classical and modern capital of the island, part of the prehistoric settlement that underlies the later acropolis was excavated (by O. Rubensohn) in the early 20th century. The buildings investigated, some of which were apsidal in plan, belong to EC III (*c.* 2300–*c.* 2000 BC). These remains are no longer visible, but the blue-domed church of Ayios Konstantinos, which is prominent today on the summit, incorporates part of the foundations and lower courses of a large Archaic Temple of Athena (*c.* 550 BC). It was in the Ionic order and had some points of resemblance to the Temple of Apollo at Palati on Naxos. Architectural fragments from the Temple of Athena and from other buildings of the Classical town are built into the Venetian fort (AD 1260) in Parikia, which also contains half of a round Hellenistic building (4th-century BC tholos) reconstructed as the apse of a church.

The other main site of importance on Paros, though the remains are not substantial, is the Delion (sanctuary of the Delian gods) on the opposite side of the bay from Parikia. The boundary wall of marble that surrounds the flat top of the hill dates to the 5th century BC. It contains a small Doric temple (*in antis*) with altar, a stepped platform and some ancillary structures. There are traces of earlier buildings and the original altar may have been an outcrop of rock in the centre of the complex. The base of the cult statue and part of the statue itself have been reassembled (late 1970s).

In Parikia, the Byzantine church of Katapoliani was apparently erected on the site of a Roman building that contained mosaics of the *Labours of Hercules*. Outside the town are the insubstantial remains of two sanctuaries—an Asklepieion and a Pythion. At Tris Ekklesies, an Early Christian basilica incorporated the remains of various ancient buildings, perhaps including the tomb of the Parian poet Archilochos, which, though dating to the Archaic period, was apparently refurbished in Hellenistic times.

O. Rubensohn: 'Die prähistorischen und frühgeschichtlichen Funde auf dem Burghügel von Paros', *Mitt. Dt. Archäol. Insts: Athen. Abt.*, xlii (1917), pp. 1–96

O. Rubensohn: *Das Delion von Paros* (Wiesbaden, 1962)

G. Gruben and W. Koenigs: 'Der Hekatompedos von Naxos und der Burgtempel von Paros', *Archäol. Anz.* (1970), pp. 135–53

D. U. Schilardhi: 'The LH IIIC Period at the Koukounaries Acropolis on Paros', *The Prehistoric Cyclades*, ed. J. A. MacGillivray and R. L. N. Barber (Edinburgh, 1984), pp. 184–206

H. W. Catling: 'Archaeology in Greece', *Archaeol. Rep.: Council Soc. Promot. Hell. Stud. & Managing Cttee Brit. Sch. Archaeol. Athens*, xxxii (1985–6), pp. 76–8

M. Schuller: 'Die Dorische Architektur der Kykladen in spätarchaischer Zeit', *Jb. Dt. Archäol. Inst.*, c (1985), pp. 319–98

G. Gruben: *Architektur auf Naxos und Paros* (Berlin, 1991–)

M. Schuller: *Der Artemistempel im Delion auf Paros* (Berlin, 1991)

D. Berranger: *Recherches sur l'histoire et la prosopographie de Paros a l'époque archaïque* (Clermont-Ferrand, 1992)

M. Stamatopoulou and M. Yeroulanou: *Excavating Classical Culture: Recent Archaeological Discoveries in Greece* (Oxford, 2002)

K. Müller: *Hellenistische Architektur auf Paros* (Berlin, 2003)

A. Ohnesorg: 'Die "neue" Gorgo von Paros—das Akroter eines Bauwerks', *Mitt. Dt. Archaol. Instituts.: Athen. Abt.*, cxviii (2003), pp. 125–38

2. SCULPTURE. Paros was an important source of fine marble for sculpture in antiquity. Quarry sites have been identified (near the monastery of Ayios Minas) and a strong tradition of sculptural craftsmanship was established on the island around the middle of the 6th century BC. This was rather later than on neighbouring Naxos, the importance of which subsequently declined.

Some kouros and kore figures have been found on or can be associated with the island, but later Archaic works signed by Aristion of Paros have been found in Athens and Attica. These include grave stelai and a fine kore (*Phrasikleia*) from Merenda in Attica and perhaps also the kouros found with her (*c.* 550 BC; both Athens, N. Archaeol. Mus.). There are a number of votive and funerary reliefs from the island. Two Early Classical (*c.* 500/480–*c.* 450 BC) grave stelai of girls with doves in a soft and sensitive style are Parian (e.g. New York, Met.), as is probably the well-known Giustiniani stele (Berlin, Antikensamml.). At the Sanctuary of Zeus at Olympia, the sculptures of the temple (and the roof tiles) are in Parian marble, and Parian artists were perhaps involved in their creation. From the island itself is an important Nike (Victory) figure (Paros, Archaeol. Mus.), the first example of a new type, shown descending through the air, rather than in the conventionalized Archaic posture for movement. Much of the base for the cult statue from the Delion sanctuary (and some of the statue itself) has been reassembled (late 1970s) from fragments collected on the site. Major names in Classical (*c.* 500/480–323 BC) sculpture associated with Paros include AGORAKRITOS, whose cult statue of Nemesis at Rhamnous in Attica has been identified in a copy, and some fragments have been recovered (Athens, N. Archaeol. Mus.). SKOPAS, a 4th-century BC artist of unusual power, was responsible for the sculptures of the Temple of Athena Alea at Tegea in the Peloponnese, and his hand has been seen behind some of the work from the Mausoleum at Halikarnassos.

For the Plastiras type of prehistoric stone figurine, named after its place of discovery on Paros, *see* SCULPTURE, §II, 1.

J. G. Pedley: *Greek Sculpture of the Archaic Period: The Island Workshops* (Mainz, 1976), pp. 38–45

J. Boardman: *Greek Sculpture: The Archaic Period* (London, 1978)

A. Despinis: *Problemata tis parianes plastikes tou 5ou aiona B.C.* [Problems of Parian sculpture of the 5th century BC] (Athens, 1979)

J. Boardman: *Greek Sculpture: The Classical Period* (London, 1985)

N. J. Norman: 'Asklepios and Hygieia and the Cult Statue at Tegea', *Amer. J. Archaeol.*, xc (Oct 1986), pp. 425–30

W. Fuchs and J. Florens: *Die geometrische und archäische Plastik* (1987), i of *Die griechische Plastik* (Munich, 1987–), pp. 160–72

S. Lattimore: 'Skopas and the Pothos', *Amer. J. Archaeol.*, xci (July 1987), pp. 411–20

P. Kranz: 'Der sogenannte Herakles Hope [Frühwerk des Skopas oder neuerlicher Fall kaiserzeitlicher Privatdeifikation?]', *Mitt. Dt. Archäol. Inst.: Röm. Abt.*, xcvi (1989), pp. 393–405

L. J. Roccos: 'Apollo Palatinus: The Augustan Apollo on the Sorrento Base', *Amer. J. Archaeol.*, xciii (Oct 1989), pp. 571–88

Paria lithos: Latomeia, marmaro kai ergasteria glyptikes tes Paros: Praktika 1. Diethnous Synedriou Archaiologias Parou kai Kykladon, Paroikia: Paros, 1997

G. Hoffmann, ed.: *Les pierres de l'offrande: Autour de l'oeuvre de Christoph W. Clairmont* (Kilchberg, 2001)

M. Stamatopoulou and M. Yeroulanou: *Excavating Classical Culture: Recent Archaeological Discoveries in Greece* (Oxford, 2002)

Parrhasios (*b* Ephesos; *fl* last quarter of the 5th century BC–first quarter of the 4th). Greek painter. The son of the painter and sculptor Euenor (see Athenaeus: *Deipnosophists* XII.543d; Harpakration: *Lexicon*, 'Parrhasios'; Pliny XXXV.xxxvi.60), he worked chiefly at Athens, becoming one of the most celebrated painters in antiquity. Ancient texts offer conflicting dates for his career, ranging from the mid-5th to the mid-4th century BC. Pausanias (*Description of Greece* I.xxviii.2) stated that Parrhasios did the drawings for the scenes engraved by Mys on the bronze shield of the *Athena Promachos* (*c.* 465–456 BC; lost) by PHEIDIAS. If so, Parrhasios must have made the drawings as a boy. Quintilian (*Institutio oratoria* XII.x.4) placed him at the time of the Peloponnesian wars (431–404 BC), citing a conversation between Parrhasios and Socrates (*d* 403 BC) recorded by Xenophon (*Memorabilia* III.x.1–5). The most plausible date is given by Pliny (XXXV.xxxvi.64–5), who stated that Parrhasios was a contemporary and rival of the painter ZEUXIS, the start of whose artistic career he dated to the 95th Olympiad (400–397 BC). The latest date associated with Parrhasios derives from Seneca's story (*Controversiae* X.v) that he bought an old man taken prisoner during the capture of Olynthos (348 BC) to torture him as a model for a painting of Prometheus; but this tale is probably apocryphal.

The alleged rivalry between Parrhasios and Zeuxis apparently relates to two contrasting stylistic methods in 4th-century BC Greek painting. Pliny (XXXV.xxxvi.67) and others praised Parrhasios for his ability to suggest three-dimensional forms using line drawing alone. This technique (then considered conservative) was a continuation of the linear tradition of APOLLODOROS and contrasted with Zeuxis' method, in which three-dimensionality was suggested by shading, with outline virtually eliminated. Though no works by Parrhasios survive, his style, or at least his technique, may be reflected by the late 5th-century BC Athenian GROUP R funerary lekythoi with their sophisticated line drawings on a white ground.

At least 15 paintings by Parrhasios are listed by ancient writers, almost all cited by Pliny, who also recorded that Parrhasios made drawings on parchment (XXXV. xxxvi.68). Their subjects were diverse, most being mythological (e.g. *Herakles, Theseus, Odysseus, Philoktetes*), but a few depicted daily life (children, a Thracian nurse, a priest). Two of his paintings were taken to Rome: his *Theseus*, commissioned in Athens, was later displayed on the Capitoline, and the emperor Tiberius (*reg* AD 14–37) kept his painting of an *Archigallus* in his bedroom. Pliny also remarked that Parrhasios painted obscene pictures for his own amusement (XXXV.xxxvi.72).

Parrhasios' most famous painting was apparently his *Demos of Athens*, praised for the ingenious manner in which it depicted simultaneously both the noble and ignoble characteristics of the Athenian populace (*demos*). Ancient writings do not specify the way in which this was achieved, but the emphasis on character (*ethos*) represents another conservative aspect of his work. It was for his ability to evoke *ethos* that the Early Classical painter POLYGNOTOS OF THASOS was famous; both Plato (*Phaedo* 69b) and Aristotle (*Metaphysics* 1024b.23) considered this, rather than the creation of visual illusions that preoccupied most 4th-century BC artists, to be the true measure of a painter's talent. Similarly, Parrhasios' painting of *Philoktetes on Lemnos* was noted for its depiction of the abandoned Greek's helpless isolation and misery. Finally, whether factual or not, Xenophon's account of the conversation between Parrhasios and Socrates also reflects the painter's concern with the representation of *ethos*.

What is preserved of Parrhasios' own view of himself seems to confirm Pliny's opinion that he was arrogant. In some verses recorded by Athenaeus (XII.543d–e) Parrhasios adopted the surname *Habrodiaitos* ('He who lives in luxury'), and he also called himself the 'prince of painting', declaring that he had brought the art of painting to perfection and that he was the foremost practitioner of art among the Greeks. While acknowledging his father, Euenor, he also allegedly claimed to be descended from Apollo.

J. Overbeck: *Die antiken Schriftquellen zur Geschichte der bildenden Kunste bei den Griechen* (Leipzig, 1868), nos 1649, 1680, 1692–1730
A. Rumpf: 'Parrhasios', *Amer. J. Archaeol.*, lv (1951), pp. 1–12
J. J. Pollitt: *The Ancient View of Greek Art* (New Haven, 1974)
K. Gschwandtler: *Zeuxis und Parrhasios: Ein Beitrag zur antiken Künstlerbiographie* (diss., Graz, Karl-Franzens-U., 1975)
V. J. Bruno: *Form and Color in Greek Painting* (New York, 1977)

Parthian Monument. *See under* Ephesos.

Paseas [Cerberus Painter] (*fl c.* 520–*c.* 510 BC). Greek vase painter. Formerly called the Cerberus Painter (after a plate, Boston, MA, Mus. F.A., 01.8025, showing *Herakles Leading Kerberos*), he was a minor Athenian Red-figure painter, primarily of plates and small vases (e.g. cups, an alabastron and a standlet); he also decorated several votive plaques of Athena (Athens, N. Archaeol. Mus., Acropolis 2583–5, 2587–9, 2591) in Black-figure on white ground. On some, flesh is emphasized by outline as well as a second white, while one preserves his unique signature: 'one of the paintings of Paseas'.

Paseas' energetic figures, with over-large heads and simple bodies, derive from the Andokides painter, but also recall Oltos and the Pioneers: in several techniques his skill recalls Psiax. He commonly reserved hair borders and used red inscriptions, yet his style remained naively old-fashioned. His subjects include *Theseus* (Paris, Louvre, G 67), *Dionysos* (New Haven, CT, Yale U. A.G., 170) and male athletes (U. Amsterdam, Pierson Sticht., 2474; London, BM, E 138), all on plates; female dancers on a standlet (London, BM, E 809); and charming erotica such as a woman with phallus bird on a chalcicup (Rome, Villa Giulia; Heidelberg, Ruprecht-Karls-U., 20). A plate depicting an *Archer on Horseback* (Oxford, Ashmolean, 310) carries a *kalos* inscription praising Miltiades, while Paseas' masterpieces, the *Kerberos* scene and a touching *Rape of Kassandra* (New Haven, CT, Yale U. A.G., 169), are also on plates.

C. Roebuck: 'White-ground Plaques by the Cerberus Painter', *Amer. J. Archaeol.*, xliii (1939), pp. 467–73
J. D. Beazley: *Red-figure* (1942, 2/1963), i, pp. 163–4, ii, p. 1630
J. Boardman: 'A Name for the Cerberus Painter?', *J. Hell. Stud.*, lxxv (1955), pp. 154–5
J. D. Beazley: *Black-figure* (1956), pp. 352–3, 399–400
J. D. Beazley: *Paralipomena* (1971), pp. 160, 174, 337
J. Boardman: *Athenian Black Figure Vases: A Handbook* (New York, 1974), p. 106
J. Boardman: *Athenian Red Figure Vases: The Archaic Period* (London, 1975), p. 18
A. Greifenhagen: 'Fragmente eines rotfigurigen Pinax', *Essays in Archaeology and the Humanities, Otto J. Brendel in Memoriam*, ed. L. Bonfante and H. von Heintze (Mainz, 1976), pp. 43–8
J. R. Mertens: *Attic White-ground: Its Development on Shapes Other than Lekythoi* (New York and London, 1977), pp. 105–8
L. Burn and R. Glynn: *Beazley Addenda: Additional References to* ABV, ARV2 *and* Paralipomena (Oxford, 1982, rev. T. H. Carpenter, 2/1989), pp. 95, 104, 182

Pasiteles (*fl* Rome, 1st century BC). Greek sculptor and writer from South Italy. He is generally regarded as the head of a school producing eclectic, neo-Classical statuary related to Neo-attic decorative reliefs. Virtually everything known about Pasiteles is derived from a few literary references. No signatures of his are extant, although a marble statue of a youth (*c.* 50 BC; Rome, Villa Albani) is signed by Stephanos as his pupil. Pasiteles received Roman citizenship around 89–88 BC, when enfranchisement was extended as a result of the Social War (Pliny XXXIII.lv.156; XXXVI.iv.40). He is mentioned as an expert in the chasing of metal (*caelatura*), especially elaborately decorated silver vessels (Pliny XXXV.xlv.156; Cicero: *On Divination* I.xxxvi.79). Despite being both a sculptor and metalworker, Pasiteles is never mentioned by Pliny in his section on sculptors in bronze. Rather, he is specifically identified as a modeller and ivory carver (XXXV.xlv.156; XXXVI.iv.40). He must have worked in marble as well, since his name occurs twice in book XXXVI, where marble sculpture is treated, and his student Stephanos certainly sculpted stone. He may also have been the Pasiteles whose pupil Kolotes made a chryselephantine table at Olympia (Pausanias: *Guide to Greece* V.xx.2), given his expertise in working both gold and ivory.

Pliny complained (XXXVI.iv.40) that his source (Pasiteles' contemporary and fellow antiquarian Varro) noted Pasiteles' prolific output without listing specific works. Indeed, an ivory *Jupiter* in Metellus Macedonicus' Temple of Jupiter Stator (146 BC) is the only statue certainly attributed to him. Given the temple's date, this could not have been the original cult statue, which seems anyway to have been the work of Polykles and Dionysios. Pliny (XXXVI.iv.35) also mentioned 'other works' by Pasiteles in the adjacent Temple of Juno Regina (146 BC), but this passage is corrupt, and in any case nothing is known of the appearance of any of these works.

Pasiteles apparently wrote five books on works of art, entitled either *Mirabilia opera* or *Nobilia opera* (i.e. 'masterpieces'; Pliny XXXVI.iv.39). This work may have presented a viewpoint, typical of late Hellenistic times, that elevated the works of Pheidias and Polykleitos as the acme of artistic achievement, in contrast with the Xenokratean view that saw Lysippos as the culmination of artistic development (*see* Xenocrates). This impression of Pasiteles as a neo-classicist is corroborated by the eclectic classicizing work of Stephanos. Pliny (XXXV.xlv.156) also commented that Pasiteles never made a work without making a model beforehand. Although this is to be expected of an artist casting bronze through the lost-wax process, Pasiteles appears to have been better known for his sculpted works, in which models were not necessary. Thus Pliny may have been referring to casts rather than preliminary models, and Pasiteles may have been prominent among those who developed the pointing technique for creating copies in stone—an increasingly important industry during the 1st century BC. Such a conclusion is consistent with our understanding of Pasiteles as a scholarly, eclectic and retrospective craftsman with a good understanding of the Roman art market.

M. Borda: *La scuola di Pasiteles* (Bari, 1953)

G. M. A. Richter: *Ancient Italy* (Ann Arbor, 1955)

J. J. Pollitt: *The Ancient View of Greek Art* (New Haven, 1974), pp. 78–9

J. J. Pollitt: *Art in the Hellenistic Age* (Cambridge, 1986), pp. 163, 174–5

E. Simon: 'Kriterien zur Deutung pasitelischer Gruppen', *Jb. Dt. Archäol. Inst.*, cii (1987), pp. 291–304

M. Fuchs: *In hoc etiam genere Graeciae nihil cedamus: Studien zur Romanisierung der späthellenistischen Kunst im 1.J.H. V. CHR.* (Mainz, 1999)

Patronage.

1. Greek. 2. Roman.

1. Greek.

(i) Architecture. (ii) Sculpture, painting and other arts.

(i) Architecture. Communities, not individuals, commissioned monumental buildings in the Greek world. Examples of personal patronage are virtually unknown before the Hellenistic period (323–27 BC), apart from the Leonidaion (4th century BC), built by a rich Naxian, and the Philippeion (*c.* 338 BC) of Philip II of Macedon, both at OLYMPIA. Powerful individuals such as tyrants sometimes provided impetus for particular building projects: tradition associates the large Temple of Olympian Zeus at Athens (begun mid-6th century BC; completed 2nd century AD; *see* ATHENS, §II, 4) with PEISISTRATOS and the gigantic Temple of Zeus at AKRAGAS (early 5th century BC) with the tyrant Theron. Tyrants, however, did no more than exploit an existing interest in public works: when Herodotus discussed 6th-century BC SAMOS, he attributed the public works of the period—the mile-long rock-cut tunnel, the harbour mole and the great Temple of Hera—not to the tyrant Polykrates but to 'the Samians: they are responsible for three of the greatest buildings and engineering feats in the Greek world' (*Histories* III.xxxix–lx).

Decisions to build were made in much the same way in every community, as shown by a decree from mid-5th-century BC Athens: 'It seemed good to the council and popular assembly....Glaukos proposed: that a priestess of Athena Nike be appointed, and that her sacred place be closed by a door...and that a temple and a stone altar be constructed according to Kallikrates' designs' (*Inscr. Gr./2*, i, 24). The pan-Hellenic sanctuaries were also largely administered by their local communities: the city-state of Elis oversaw the construction of the Temple of Zeus at Olympia (*c.* 470–457 BC); building at Delphi was supervised by a board of Delphic citizens and representatives from elsewhere; at Epidauros the city officials decided what should be built in the Sanctuary of Asklepios. The patriotic need to emulate or outdo a rival city-state was often a major motive for building, as in the Sicilian cities of SELINUS and AKRAGAS, where at least seven large temples were built at both places within four generations. Once a temple had been built, however, it was not replaced by a new structure unless the existing building became unusable. This happened, for example, on Samos, where the earliest stone Temple of Hera (*c.* 650 BC) burnt down and was soon replaced by a new temple (*c.* 560 BC); and the magnificent Periclean building programme on the Athenian Acropolis (*see* PERICLES) might have been far less ambitious had the Persians not sacked the city in 480–479 BC. The communities responsible for the pan-Hellenic sanctuaries seem to have been under obligation to meet the needs of worshippers. Nevertheless, at Olympia, Zeus was accorded no more than an open-air altar and a share of the Temple of Hera until *c.* 470 BC, when the Eleans took charge of the sanctuary. The great Temple of Zeus built then thus marked Elis' new regional influence as much as it honoured the god. At EPIDAUROS, by contrast, the wider following gained by the cult of Asklepios prompted the city to enhance its rural sanctuary; the buildings of the city itself remained modest.

Funds for building might come from war booty, as at Elis; loot from piracy, as in Polykrates' Samos; or reserves from the allies' tribute, as in 5th-century BC Athens. Often, however, the regular city revenues were all that could be used, and when these failed, contributions were called for from citizens. At Delphi, for example, contributions were solicited both from other cities and from private individuals, and personal patronage may often have gained public recognition by the inclusion of the donor's name in a published list of contributors. The total cost of only one temple is definitely known; the Asklepion of Epidauros cost something over 23 talents, or about 280 times the architect's annual salary. The Parthenon, by comparison, may have cost about 450 talents—equivalent to one year's tribute from Athens' allies. Shortage of money may have contributed to slow progress on the later Temple of Apollo at Delphi, or on the Temple of Zeus at Akragas, though delays could also be caused by such factors as war, political unrest or the need to import skills and materials, for example fine limestone or marble, not available in a particular city-state.

The details of an architectural project seem to have been entrusted to a select few with the advice of an expert. The Athenian decree quoted above continues: 'Hestiaios proposed: that three men are to be chosen...and they are to draw up specifications with the architect KALLIKRATES and demonstrate to the council [how the work] will be contracted out.' At most building sites, the project was divided into manageable sections, which were advertised and put out on contract to the best bid. Rich and influential men who wanted to take an active part could guarantee contracts, use their contacts to gain access to foreign quarries or craftsmen or even take up contracts themselves as entrepreneurs, at generously low prices. For example, in the 6th century BC the Alkmaionids, exiled from Athens, gained renown for themselves as well as for the new Temple of Apollo at Delphi (*c.* 525–*c.* 500 BC) by using Parian marble for the pedimental sculptures, instead of the cheaper limestone specified in their contract.

It is not clear who ultimately determined the design of a building. Records of some architects' specifications, as presented to the deliberating body, suggest that the public took some interest in the technical detail of a proposed building. Presumably the building commissioners themselves were selected partly for their understanding of such matters, though they must have depended heavily on the architect's professional expertise. To what extent the public could appreciate such architectural refinements as the upward swell and taper of column shafts (*see* ENTASIS) or the subtle divergences from strict vertical and horizontal lines incorporated into some buildings it is impossible to say. If they were readily apparent, as were the themes and designs of the architectural sculptures, which were probably widely debated, they no doubt attracted admiration, as did simple and satisfying proportional relationships throughout the building. But the introduction of Pythagorean mathematics into the measurements and proportions of a design, as in some 4th-century BC structures, seems unlikely to have been at the behest of an architect's patrons. Though arguments doubtless often arose concerning building schemes, the only evidence for outspoken opposition is the condemnatory reference in Plutarch's *Life of Pericles* (xii.1–2) to the 'thousand-talent temples' at Athens. This was, however, less an aesthetic or moral criticism of the Acropolis buildings themselves than a political judgement on the democratic government and its means of financing them.

(ii) Sculpture, painting and other arts. In many cases the purposes served by monumental sculpture imply the presence of a patron or patrons. Votive statues in sanctuaries, athlete statues commemorating victories in pan-Hellenic games, funerary sculptures and honorific public statues all come into this category. In some instances the names of statues' dedicators or donors survive, but there is little to indicate the exact relationship between sculptors and their patrons. The domain of public patronage included such works as the cult statues inside temples, among the most celebrated examples of which were Pheidias' colossal chryselephantine *Athena* at Athens and *Zeus* at Olympia (both destr. in antiquity). However, sculpture clearly provided more scope for private commissions than did monumental architecture. Occasionally there is a literary tradition linking an artist with an eminent patron, and among sculptors Pheidias has always been closely associated with Pericles.

Literary sources suggest that painters, like sculptors, relied on several forms of patronage, including public commissions and competitions as well as privately commissioned work. Unlike sculpture, however, the record of ancient Greek painting is almost exclusively literary, since hardly any important original works survive. Panel painting was evidently highly regarded, and the names of several famous painters are associated with strong anecdotal traditions. Pliny's celebrated account of Apelles and Alexander the Great suggests an intimacy between artist and patron in which the painter's skill allowed him to transcend normal social barriers. The finest surviving Greek paintings, those from the tombs at AIGAI (ii) (Vergina), also represent Macedonian royal private patronage.

In other arts, the careers and even the names of the most accomplished artists are usually undocumented. The presence of the patron or buyer can be glimpsed, for example, in precious artefacts such as engraved gems (*see* GEM-ENGRAVING), which sometimes bear their owner's name; and the everyday subjects depicted on painted vases include scenes of life in well-to-do households and of artists and craftsmen at work (*see* POTTERY, §IV, 1(iv)).

A. Burford: *The Greek Temple Builders at Epidauros* (Liverpool, 1969)

A. Burford: *Aspects of Greek and Roman Life: Craftsmen in Greek and Roman Society* (London, 1972)

J. J. Coulton: *Greek Architects at Work* (London, 1977); pubd in USA as *Ancient Greek Architects at Work* (Ithaca, 1977)

2. ROMAN. Roman sources preserve much information concerning patronage but little concerning the activity of architects, sculptors and painters. (Roman law expressly forbade the use of an architect's name in the dedicatory inscription of a building, while it demanded, even in private buildings, record of the dedicator or title-holder.) Such an attitude towards architectural patronage is consistent with a culture that valued the thing represented more highly than it valued the representation (*see also* ARCHITECTURE, §VI, 1(iv)).

Under the Republic, the property of the State was entrusted first to the consuls, later to the censor. These officials could also let contracts for new works when, in the course of their duties, they discerned a need. The fact that the censor, the same person responsible for a general accounting of the property of the state, was responsible for state patronage in public works introduced a high degree of fiscal conservatism into Roman building. Counterbalancing constitutional inertia were the needs that arose from the significant growth of the state during the middle and late Republic, and the fact that such contracting and subcontracting could be very profitable. On occasion, temples were vowed or constructed by persons other than reigning magistrates. Special boards might be created for the purposes of building a temple. The aediles, who were the magistrates charged with responsibility for the streets and public places, occasionally undertook projects such as the building of public porticos and shops. Their supervision of the streets also brought them into contact with the owners of private property.

In the late Republic an aesthetic factor, Greek architectural design, was introduced as a technical skill heretofore unavailable to and undesired by Romans. Romans of a traditional nature were incapable of distinguishing between the new Greek import and luxury. Magnificence in public building might therefore be justified to the conservative Romans when it resulted from military victory; the expense was borne by the conquered. Public architecture intended for such spectacles as triumphs or theatrical performances had, on the other hand, to be constructed of wood and pulled down after use. Thanks to philhellenic censors and the justification of conquest, sophisticated Greek architectural materials and design first appeared in Rome about the time of the sack of Corinth (146 BC), with the construction of the Portico of Q. Caecilius Metellus, which included Hermodoros of Salamis' marble Temple of Jupiter Stator.

In apparent reaction to the fashionable Greek building style and the throng of Greek architects, the general C. Marius built a temple to Honour and Virtue in 101 BC using a Roman architect, C. Mucius. Although his work was praised by Vitruvius, Mucius was an anomaly at this time, a patriotic choice.

During the late Republic, the wealth of the patrons and the needs of the populace increased dramatically. Powerful men, such as L. Cornelius Sulla (dictator 82–80 BC), Pompey (106–48 BC) and JULIUS CAESAR, engaged in building on a scale never before seen in Rome. Sulla is the first figure in Roman history with whom a coherent scheme of architectural patronage can be associated (i.e. the Capitoline temple, the Tabularium and extensive building throughout Italy in consequence of settling his veteran soldiers in confiscated cities such as Pompeii, all at public expense). Even more impressive constructions were undertaken by Pompey and Caesar at their own expense. Pompey built the first permanent THEATRE in Rome (55 BC), seeking to avoid moral opprobrium by associating it with a temple to Venus Victrix (*see* ARCHITECTURE, §VI, 2(i)(a)). Caesar poured his immense booty from the Gallic Wars into an extension of the Forum Romanum and the construction of the Forum Julium (begun 51 BC) and its Temple of Venus Genetrix (*see* ROME, §IV, 2). Death prevented him from undertakings of an even more remarkable nature, such as the construction of a harbour at OSTIA and a canal across the isthmus of Corinth.

By far the greatest architectural patron in Roman history was the emperor AUGUSTUS. Although Augustus was able to claim the rights of patronage according to the Republican constitution, having been consul 13 times before the writing of his testament, his patronage in general was more like that of a king than of a Republican magistrate. While some of the money expended went to private property holders, as in the building of the Theatre of Marcellus, most of it was undoubtedly paid back into the imperial coffers.

Under the Empire, the control of public building remained in the hands of the emperor and was usually delegated to freedmen of the imperial household or to *equites* (wealthy non-senators), known as procurators. Care of existing public works was given to specially appointed curators (*curatores operum publicorum*) in addition to the magistracies that had survived from the Republic. Production and supply of building materials came fully under the control of the imperial household. Public works increasingly became an imperial monopoly connected with the personal prestige of the ruler. The reputation of NERO depends much upon the consequences of the fire of AD 64: the building of some greatly improved residential areas but also the appropriation of large sections of the city for the Emperor's palace. The reputation of the Flavian emperors similarly rests much upon their programme of returning much of the land appropriated by Nero to the people in the form of the Baths of Titus (ded. 80) and the Colosseum (or Flavian Amphitheatre; ded. 80). Under the emperors TRAJAN and HADRIAN, the architects RABIRIUS and APOLLODOROS OF DAMASCUS managed to gain notice as much for their involvement with the imperial family as for their considerable professional talents. Their example remains exceptional in Roman architectural history.

Imperial patronage extended beyond the city of Rome to the rest of Italy and to the provinces, where it competed increasingly with local patronage. The history of the later Empire marks the increasing failure of local patronage of public institutions, including public building. The buried cities of HERCULANEUM and POMPEII each preserve a rich fund of epigraphical information on imperial and local patronage up to AD 79, which documents the emergence of a new class of patrons whose parents were slaves. The excavations of the Roman port of Ostia, covering the period from its origins in the middle Republic until the end of the Empire in the West, extends this chronological spectrum and provides a glimpse of a brief period of private aristocratic patronage at the end of Imperial times.

Private patronage in the form of expenditure on domestic architecture and tombs began to increase markedly in the late Republic. Such builders as the politicians L. Licinius Lucullus and M. Aemilius Scaurus scandalized Republican sensibility with their luxurious houses, though they found a defender in VITRUVIUS. During the early Empire, private construction grew dramatically under the security from pirates, brigands and civil war provided by the Pax Augustana.

Roman patronage in the art of sculpture follows an evolution similar to that of architecture. During the short period from the capture of Syracuse (211 BC) to the sack of Corinth, sculptures in their thousands were plundered from the conquered lands and imported to form huge collections at home for the generals and nobles. Special pieces were commissioned to complete ensembles within the collections. C. Asinius Pollio had a famous sculptural collection of old masterpieces; the collections of CICERO were more modest. In the provinces, the Roman governors acted as patrons in the grand Hellenistic tradition.

In Sicily the rapacious C. Verres was accused of having statues to himself and his family erected all over the province at the locals' vast expense (Cicero: *Against Verres*). Cicero himself refused such honours when governor of Cilicia, although an EXEDRA with statues dedicated to himself and his family has been excavated in the Heraion at SAMOS. Under the Empire, the emperor became the supreme patron. Most of the quarries and much of the trade came under State control. Some local rulers also became major patrons, such as HERODES ATTICUS, whose statues commissioned for his nymphaeum at Olympia tactfully represented his own and the imperial family in equal measure. Public spaces and buildings continued to benefit from private patronage, which allowed individuals to show their munificence by statuary dedications.

Roman patronage of the art of painting is best demonstrated by the excavations of private houses in Herculaneum, Pompeii, Ostia and Rome itself. Literary descriptions can, however, provide evidence of patronage intention such as can only be inferred from the archaeological remains. The *Imagines* of PHILOSTRATOS LEMNIOS may be a literal description of a cycle of wall paintings that reflected the ideas of one patron in his villa near Naples. The letters of Q. Aurelius Symmachus (late 4th century AD) illustrate another example of the close control that wealthy patrons exercised over the decoration of their villas.

T. Mommsen: *Römisches Staatsrecht, Handbuch der römischen Alterthümer*, ii/1, 3 vols (Leipzig, 1881–8)

A. Mau: *Pompeji in Leben und Kunst*; Eng. trans. by F. W. Kelsey as *Pompey: Its Life and Art* (New York, 1899/*R* 1908)

L. Friedländer: *Sittengeschichte Roms*; Eng. trans. of 7th edn by J. H. Freese and L. A. Magnus as *Roman Life and Manners under the Early Empire*, 4 vols (London, 1902)

T. Frank: *Roman Buildings of the Republic: An Attempt to Date them rom their Materials*, Papers and Monographs of the American Academy in Rome, 3 (Rome, 1924)

T. Frank: *An Economic Survey of Ancient Rome* (Baltimore, 1933)

K. Lehmann: 'The *Imagines* of the Elder Philostratus', *A. Bull.*, xxiii (1941), pp. 16–44

R. Meiggs: *Roman Ostia* (Oxford, 1960, 2/1973)

M. L. Thompson: 'The Monumental and Literary Evidence for Programmatic Painting in Antiquity', *Marsyas*, ix (1960–61), pp. 36–77

K. Gast: *Die zensorischen Bauberichte bei Livius und die römischen Bauinschriften* (Göttingen, 1965)

P. Gros: *Architecture et société à Rome et en Italie centro-méridionale aux deux derniers siècles de la république*, Collections Latomus, 156 (Brussels, 1978)

E. W. Leach: 'Patrons, Painters, and Patterns: The Anonymity of Romano-Campanian Painting and the Transition from the Second to the Third Style', *Literary and Artistic Patronage in Ancient Rome*, ed. B. K. Gold (Austin, 1979), pp. 135–73

Architecture et société de l'archaïsme grec à la fin de la république romaine: Actes du colloque international organisé par le Centre national de la recherche scientifique et l'Ecole française de Rome: Rome, 1980

S. Roda: *Commento storico al libro IX dell'epistolario di Q. Aurelio Simmaco* (Pisa, 1981)

G. Lahusen: *Untersuchungen zur Ehrenstatue in römische literarische und epigraphische Zeugnisse* (Rome, 1983), chaps 3–4

J. J. Pollitt: *Art in the Hellenistic Age* (Cambridge, 1986), chaps 7–8

P. Zanker: *Augustus und die Macht der Bilder* (Munich, 1987); Eng. trans. by A. Shapiro as *The Power of Images in the Age of Augustus* (Ann Arbor, 1988)

C. Eilers: *Roman Patrons of Greek Cities* (Oxford, 2002)

P. Stewart: *Roman Art* (Oxford, 2004)

Pausanias (*fl c.* second half of 2nd century AD). Greek traveller, writer and geographer. Possibly born in Lydia, he is known for his *Guide to Greece* in ten books, which contains detailed descriptions of monuments and the works of specific artists, as well as substantial information about Greek mythology and history.

Information concerning Pausanias' own life is deduced from references in the *Guide to Greece*, where he repeatedly referred to the area around Magnesia-ad-Sipylum (I.xxiv.8; V.xiii.7; IX.xxii.4 etc.). This is, therefore, where he was probably brought up, while his assertion (VIII.ix.7) that he had not himself seen Hadrian's favourite, Antinous (*d* AD 130–31), though this would evidently have been possible, suggests that Pausanias was born *c.* AD 115. The earliest events that he specifically stated to have occurred during his own lifetime were the construction of a shrine and temple of Asklepios at Smyrna (II.xxvi.9; VII.v.9) and the Odeion of Herodes Atticus in Athens (VII.xx.6), all of which date from the 150s and 160s AD. The latest event recorded is Marcus Aurelius' victory over the Germans and Sarmatians (VIII.xliii.6) of AD 175. Since the Odeion of Herodes Atticus is not mentioned in its proper place, in Book I, but instead in Book VII, it appears that Book I was completed before AD 160. Since Book VIII mentions an event of AD 175, the last two books are presumably later than that. Consequently, the generally agreed dates for the *Guide to Greece* are AD 150–80.

With the exception of Book I, all the books are organized topographically. The account moves from the edge of a region to its capital, describes the city itself and then covers all the major routes extending from it to the border of its territory. Book I describes Attica, including Athens, and Megara; Book II Argolis, including Corinth, Sikyon, Nemea, Mycenae, the Heraion, Argos, Tiryns, Epidauros and Aigina; Book III Lakonia, including Sparta, Amyklai and Kythera; Book IV, which is largely historical, Messenia, including Messene, Asine and Sphakteria; Books V and VI Elis, including Olympia; Book VII Achaia; Book VIII Arcadia, including Mantineia, Megalopolis, Bassai and Tegea; Book IX Boiotia, including Plataia, Thebes, Aulis, Tanagra, Helikon, Orchomenos and Chaironeia; Book X Phokis, including Delphi. Pausanias was deliberately selective in the monuments he recorded (I.xxxix.3; III.xi.1), and his choices reflect his own artistic tastes. He particularly admired works of the 5th and 4th centuries BC and preferred sacred objects and sites to secular ones. Of the approximately 179 sculptors that he described, his favourites were the 5th-century BC sculptors Pheidias and Alkamenes

(VI.iv.5; V.x.8). Of the 16 painters he mentioned, his favourites were Nikias (I.xxix.15) and Polygnotos of Thasos (X.xxxi.12). Similarly, he lavished praise on the architecture of the Propylaia on the Athenian Acropolis (I.xxii.4) and the Temple of Apollo at Bassai (VIII.xxii.8), both of the 5th century BC, and the Temple of Athena Alea at Tegea (VIII.xlv.5) and the theatre at Epidauros (II.xxvii.5), constructed in the 4th century BC. Pausanias' most detailed descriptions are of monuments in religious sanctuaries: the Temple of Zeus at Olympia (V.x.2–xii.8); the chest of Kypselos from the Heraion at Olympia (V.xvii.5–xix.10); the reliefs on the throne of Apollo at Amyklai (III.xviii.9–xix.5); and the paintings by Polygnotos of Thasos at Delphi (X.xxv.1–xxxi.12).

Although some of Pausanias' passages concerning art are lengthy, they are not analytical or critical. When discussing an object, he simply gave a description and a date, and when dealing with an artist he merely indicated his homeland, age and teacher. Here Pausanias' statements about teacher and pupil relationships are not entirely reliable, since they seem sometimes to be based on perceived stylistic similarities, rather than on documentary sources. This limits the usefulness of his account for students of art criticism, though the thoroughness and scope of his descriptions make them an important source for visualizing numerous objects that no longer survive. Archaeologists have, in contrast, found his work indispensable when attempting to identify remains and locate lost sites. Though some early scholars even doubted that Pausanias had actually visited the sites that he described, and suggested instead that he had simply copied his account from sources such as the 2nd-century BC writer Polemon of Ilium, excavation has frequently confirmed his reliability, suggesting that he did indeed write from first-hand knowledge.

F. W. Imhoof-Blumer and P. Gardner: *A Numismatic Commentary on Pausanias* (London, 1887, rev. Chicago, 1964)

H. Hitzig and H. Blümner: *Der Pausanias-Beschreibung von Griechenland*, 3 vols (Leipzig, 1896–1910)

J. G. Frazer: *Pausanias's Description of Greece*, 6 vols (London, 1898)

A. Trendelenburg: *Pausanias in Olympia* (Berlin, 1914)

G. Daux: *Pausanias à Delphes* (Paris, 1936)

G. Roux: *Pausanias en Corinthie* (Paris, 1958)

R. E. Wycherley: 'Pausanias in the Agora of Athens', *Gr., Roman & Byz. Stud.*, ii (1959), pp. 21–44

R. E. Wycherley: 'Pausanias at Athens, ii', *Gr., Roman & Byz. Stud.*, iv (1963), pp. 157–75

F. Imhoof-Blumer, P. Gardner and A. N. Oikonomides: *Ancient Coins Illustrating Lost Masterpieces of Greek Art: A Numismatic Commentary on Pausanias* (Chicago, 1964)

M. H. Rocha-Pereira: *Pausaniae Graeciae descriptio*, 3 vols (Leipzig, 1973–81)

C. Habicht: *Pausanias' Guide to Ancient Greece* (Berkeley, 1985)

K. W. Arafat: *Pausanias' Greece: Ancient Artists and Roman Rulers* (Cambridge, 1996)

Editer, traduire, commenter Pausanias en l'an 2000: Actes du colloque de Neuchâtel et de Fribourg: 1998: Autour des deux éditions en cours de la Périégèse

M. Pretzler: *Pausanias' Arkadia* (diss., U. Oxford, 1999)

W. K. Pritchett: *Pausanias Periegetes* (Amsterdam, 1999)

S. Aneziri: 'Vom Haus des Pulytion zum Temenos des Dionysos Melpomenos: Funktionsänderung und Lokalisierungsversuch eines viel besprochenen Grundstücks in Athen', *Mitt. Dt. Archäol. Inst.: Athen. Abt.*, cxv (2000), pp. 259–79

S. E. Alcock, J. F. Cherry and J. Elsner: *Pausanias: Travel and Memory in Roman Greece* (New York, 2001)

J. Akujärvi: *Researcher, Traveller, Narrator: Studies in Pausanias' Periegesis* (Lund, 2005)

W. Hutton: *Describing Greece: Landscape and Literature in the Periegesis of Pausanias* (Cambridge and New York, 2005)

Pausias (*fl* *c.* 350–*c.* 300 BC). Greek painter from Sikyon. None of his work survives. Pausias' first master was his father Bryetes. He then studied under Pamphilos, probably in order to learn the technique of encaustic, of which he became the first acknowledged master. The technique of laying on and burning in colours in a wax medium, was time-consuming, but he acquired such facility in it that he completed a picture of a boy in just one day, earning it the title *The Day's Work*. His restoration of wall paintings by Polygnotos of Thasos at Thespiai in Boiotia are the only known example of Pausias using brushwork rather than encaustic. This was thought to be inferior to the originals because he was not working in his own style or technique.

He painted small pictures, particularly of boys, which may account for his later reputation as a painter of pornography. He was also famous for his pictures of garlands. A charming story relates that he invented painted garlands in competition with his lover Glykera, a weaver of garlands with real flowers. Some of his depictions of garlands were perhaps still-lifes, but most were probably incorporated into figural scenes or perhaps used to frame them. His picture of Glykera with a garland (the *Garland Weaver* or *Garland Seller*) was one of the most famous pictures in the ancient world. Lucius Lucullus (Roman official in Athens, 88–87 BC) paid the enormous price of two talents for a copy of it. The style of Pausias' garlands may be reflected by contemporary Apulian vase painting and mosaics.

Two of his pictures hung in the Tholos at Epidauros: *Eros with a Lyre*, here depicted with a lyre instead of a bow, and a personification of *Drunkenness (Methe)*, whose face appeared through a transparent goblet as she drank from it, the earliest known example of a motif popular in Hellenistic art and Roman wall painting. Among Pausias' large paintings was the *Sacrifice of Oxen*, which hung in the Portico of Pompey at Rome. It was perhaps one of the paintings taken from Sikyon to Rome by the aedile M. Aemilius Scaurus in 56 BC. Pliny the elder attributed to Pausias unparalleled skill in modelling with dark colours and using extreme foreshortening to suggest the full length of an entirely black ox depicted in front view (Pliny: XXXV.xl.126). This achievement may have inspired the depiction of the black horse in the foreground of the *Alexander* Mosaic, which copies a Hellenistic painting.

Pliny's assertion (XXXV.xl.124) that Pausias painted ceiling coffers and vaults may be correct, though the claim that he was the first to paint the former is certainly erroneous. Vaults are rare in Greek architecture, as is domestic wall painting, and if Pausias decorated either vaults or ceiling coffers they must have been in public buildings such as temples, or perhaps in the palace of Aristratos, tyrant of Sikyon (*fl* later 4th century BC).

J. Overbeck: *Die antiken Schriftquellen zur Geschichte der bildenden Künste bei den Griechen* (Leipzig, 1868/*R* Hildesheim, 1959), nos 1062, 1726, 1760–65

Pediment. Triangular area over the portico of a building formed from a gable by the addition of a horizontal cornice at a level with the eaves. By extension it also designates a triangular or rounded decorative area framed by cornices, which may crown façades without porticos or individual façade elements such as doors, windows or niches. The apex or base of a pediment may be interrupted, or 'broken', in the middle.

Pediments originated in ancient Greek temple architecture around 650 BC, when the invention of heavy roof tiles led to the use of the pitched roof. Earlier gables, as in isolated examples from Phrygia and in 8th-century BC models of Greek temples, which combine steep ridged roofs with horizontal porch roofs, can be seen to anticipate this development. Pediments provided a symmetrical, monumental façade to buildings of simple megaron form, in which the entrance was on the short side. Raking (i.e. sloping) cornices bound them from above, and the underside or soffit of their horizontal cornices slanted downwards slightly in imitation of the eaves. Since the horizontal cornice ran around the whole building, it created a horizontal plane to which the pediment appeared to be a crowning addition. Almost from the outset the Greeks exploited the decorative potential of the recessed inner area (tympanum) of the pediment with pedimental sculptures. The proportion of the height of the tympanum to the length of its base was worked out for each building, but tended to be roughly 1:8. The Etruscans and Romans adopted pediments from the Greeks, and the Romans developed their use for the decorative articulation of walls and niches, later revived in the architecture of the Italian Renaissance. The broken pediment, which was common in European Baroque architecture of the 16th and 17th centuries, has precedents in late Hellenistic and Roman decoration.

1. Architecture. 2. Sculpture and decoration.

1. ARCHITECTURE. In Greek architecture the combination of a ridged roof with a straight front led naturally to the concept of the façade as a rectangle topped by a triangle. Terracotta models such as the house model from the Argive Heraion (*c.* 700 BC) show the porch as a separate unit preceding the main structure. Beginning with such a model, a triangular pediment could have been created by extending the roof over the porch as far as the plane of the façade. The introduction of stone masonry in the 7th century BC led to the construction of the pediment wall by means of horizontal courses (e.g. the unfinished temple at SEGESTA, Sicily, 5th century BC or a combination of a horizontal course with a row of upright stone blocks (orthostats) in front (e.g. the Parthenon, 447–438 BC).

Other factors subject to change were the angle of inclination of the roof and the relation of the plane of the pediment wall with the plane of the colonnaded façade. Further development concerned the integration or separation of the pediment wall with the horizontal and raking mouldings of the projecting cornice (geison). The pediment wall (and accompanying relief) of the Temple of Artemis at Corfu (*c.* 590 BC) had its own ornamental border consisting of a raking chevron pattern and a horizontal meander, all enclosed within the triangle formed by the projecting cornice mouldings. Later temples avoided the duplication of framing ornament. Late Archaic temples (e.g. the Temple of Aphaia at Aigina, *c.* 490–*c.* 480 BC) that employed free-standing sculpture instead of relief for pedimental ornament tended to move the pediment wall back, counter-balancing the weight of the architrave with that of the pedimental sculptures. Temples of the Doric order employed slightly steeper pediments than temples of the Ionic order: the proportions of Doric pediments range from 1:7 (height to width) for the Temple of Artemis at Corfu to 1:8.8 for the Temple of Hephaistos in Athens (*c.* 450–*c.* 445 BC). The pediments of the Parthenon exhibit a moderate proportion of 1:8.2. Vitruvius, reflecting Classical Greek theory, recommended a ratio of 1:9 for temples of the Ionic order (*On Architecture*, III.v.12).

Roman pediments differ from Greek in their general preference for greater base angles and for relief rather than free-standing ornamentation. Despite the extensive Greek influence over temple designs of the late Republic and early Empire, Roman temples such as the Pantheon (*c.* AD 118–25) employ steep pediments (1:5) reminiscent of earlier Italic models, for example the capitolium at Cosa (*c.* 170–*c.* 150 BC). Innovations associated with the Hellenistic and Roman baroque include the segmentally arched pediment, used in conjunction with aedicular window-frames (e.g. on the Porta dei Borsari at Verona, third quarter of the 1st century AD), the 'broken' or interrupted pediment (e.g. the mausoleum of al-Dayr, Petra, 1st–2nd century AD) and the pediment interrupted by the arching of the entablature of the central intercolumniation (the arcuated lintel or 'Syrian' arch, as found in the gateway to the hexagonal forecourt at Baalbek, *c.* AD 250). Especially in these later elaborations but also in the Classical form, the pediment may symbolize the celestial region in programmatic decoration.

The pediment form was subject to imitation and further evolution in other, non-architectural contexts, such as Attic grave stelai (5th century BC), South Italian *naiskoi* (small shrines; 4th century BC), Asiatic sarcophagi (from the 4th century BC), altars of the Hellenistic and Roman periods and, especially, in Roman wall painting.

E. Saglio, E. Pottier and G. Lafaye, eds: *Dictionnaire des antiquités grecques et romaines d'après les textes et les monuments*, v (Paris, 1919), pp. 559–66

K. Friis Johansen: *The Attic Grave-reliefs* (Copenhagen, 1951)

A. Boethius: *Etruscan and Early Roman Architecture*, Pelican Hist. A. (Harmondsworth, 1979)

J. B. Ward-Perkins: *Roman Imperial Architecture*, Pelican Hist. A. (Harmondsworth, 1981)

L. Haselberger: 'Antike Bauzeichnung des Pantheon entdeckt [Planfragment ist Teil der vor 60 Jahren freigelegten Werkrisse vor dem Augustusmausoleum]', *Ant. Welt*, xxv/4 (1994), pp. 323–39

L. Haselberger: 'Ein Giebelriss der Vorhalle des Pantheon: die Werkrisse vor dem Augustusmausoleum', *Mitt. Dt. Archäol. Inst.: Röm. Abt.*, ci (1994), pp. 279–308

F. Dohna: 'Gestaltung öffentlichen Raumes und imperiale Ideologie am Beispiel des Kapitols von Thugga [imperial cult on pediment relief, Tunisia]', *Mitt. Dt. Archäol. Inst.: Röm. Abt.*, civ (1997), pp. 465–76

2. Sculpture and decoration.

(i) Greek. (ii) Roman.

(i) Greek. The triangular gable ends at the front and rear of ancient Greek buildings provided an awkward field for decoration. The earliest solution, found in Corinth and regions under Corinthian influence, such as south Italy and Sicily, involved filling this area with tympanum slabs made from light, easily worked materials such as clay, the flat or relief surfaces of which could be adorned with painted designs. Further experimentation during the 6th and 5th centuries BC gradually led to the development of free-standing sculpted figures and more unified compositions.

By the 6th century BC porous limestone was the usual material for important buildings, but, after a period of co-existence, it was widely replaced by marble. The earliest extant limestone pediment is probably that from the front of the Temple of Artemis on Corfu (*c.* 590 BC), which graphically illustrates the problems of fitting a sculptural group into a triangular frame. The pediment is dominated by a central figure of Medusa, flanked by her offspring, Pegasus and Chrysaor. Beyond them are two reclining panthers and two unrelated scenes from the Trojan War and the *Gigantomachy*; two dead giants occupy the corners (all Corfu, Archaeol. Mus.). The primitive features of this pediment include the prominence given to non-Olympian deities; the absence of thematic unity in the composition; large variations in the scale of the figures, which diminishes markedly towards the corners; a 'painted' impression caused by the exceptionally low relief; and a rigid emphasis on symmetry. These features are typical of many Archaic pediments, but all were eventually eliminated except for symmetrical design. This survived, albeit in a subtler form, because the concept of symmetry was central to ancient Greek aesthetics.

During Archaic times, pedimental compositions increasingly became three-dimensional as the separate figures were carved in higher relief until finally developing into free-standing statues. Since porous stone was relatively easy to carve compared with marble, sculptors were already experimenting with form and mass by the first quarter of the 6th century BC, although subject-matter and composition remained primitive. Thus fragments of a large example from the Athenian Acropolis (*c.* 590–570 BC) depict huge opposed lions devouring their prey, flanked by entirely unconnected mythological figures (Athens, Acropolis Mus.). In contrast, two slightly later stone pediments (*c.* 570 BC and *c.* 560 BC; Athens, Acropolis Mus.) from the Athenian Acropolis depict more developed mythological scenes: *Herakles and the Hydra* and the *Apotheosis of Herakles* respectively. The emphasis, particularly in the latter, had shifted to anthropomorphic mythological figures, rather than primitive daemons, and to unity of theme and composition.

Achieving a uniform scale for both the central and flanking figures in pedimental sculpture was less easy. Even in the marble east pediment of the Temple of Apollo at Delphi, which depicts *Apollo's Epiphany* (520 BC), the side figures were carved standing rigidly erect and thus diminishing in scale towards the corners, which were filled by fighting animals (Delphi, Archaeol. Mus.). Towards the end of the 6th century BC, however, the solution to this problem was achieved in the *Gigantomachy* (510–500 BC; Athens, Acropolis Mus.) from the Athenian Acropolis, the *Amazonomachy* (500–490 BC; Chalkis, Archaeol. Mus.) of the Temple of Apollo at Eretria and the battle scenes on the west and east pediments (510–500 BC and 490–480 BC respectively; Munich, Staatl. Antikensamml.; see fig. 1) of the Temple of Aphaia on Aigina. In these scenes, figures in a wide variety of poses, suiting the narrative emphasis of Archaic Greek art, were employed in a unified composition adapted to the triangular decorative field.

Following Greek victories in the Persian Wars (490–479 BC), pedimental scenes conformed to the mood of other Classical works of art by avoiding excessive violence and suggesting emotion through subtle gestures. The pediments (*c.* 460 BC; Olympia, Archaeol. Mus.) of the Temple of Zeus at Olympia depicting the *Rivalry of Pelops and Oinomaos* and the *Centauromachy at the Wedding of Peirithoos* provide good examples of this trend. It is epitomized, however, by the depiction of the *Birth of Athena* and the *Contest between Athena and Poseidon* on the Parthenon pediments (438/7–433/2 BC; London, BM; see fig. 2), although their exact schemes are still disputed. Other, more fragmentary Classical Athenian pediments include those from the Hephaisteion (*c.* 449–430 BC) and the Temple of Ares in the Athenian Agora (*c.* 450–425 BC; Athens, Agora Mus., Acropolis Mus. and N. Archaeol. Mus.), the Temple of Athena Nike on the Acropolis (*c.* 427–424 BC; Athens, N. Archaeol. Mus.) and the Temple of Poseidon at Sounion (*c.* 440 BC; Athens, N. Archaeol. Mus.). At the same time, the pedimental sculptures of two Peloponnesian temples, the Argive Heraion (*c.* 410 BC; Athens,

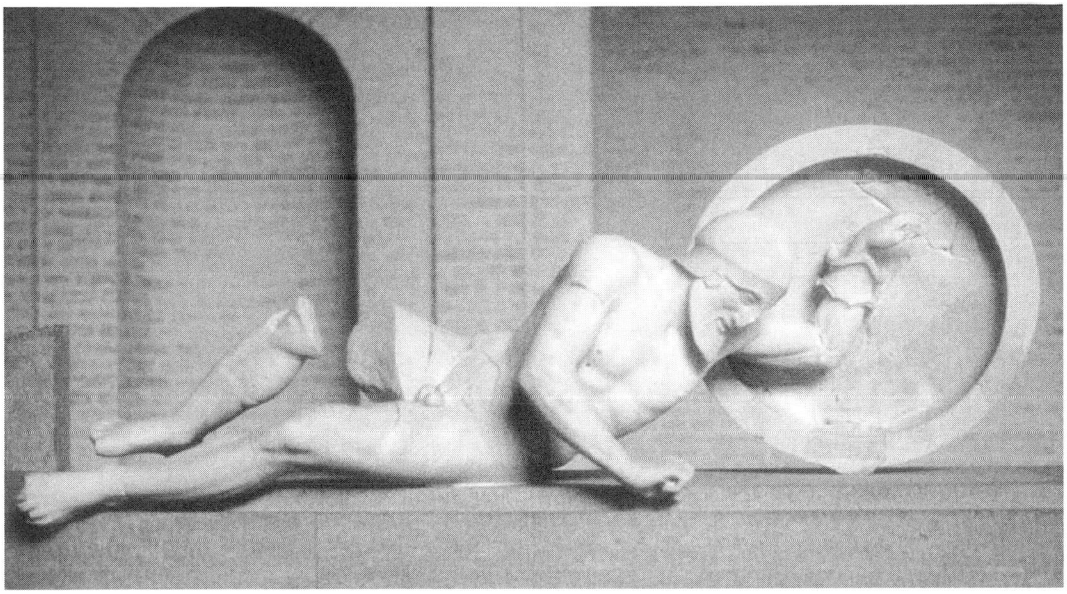

1. Ancient Greek pedimental sculpture, *Dying Warrior*, Parian marble, h. 640 mm, from the east pediment of the Temple of Aphaia at Aigina, Late Archaic period, *c.* 490–*c.* 480 BC (Munich, Glyptothek)

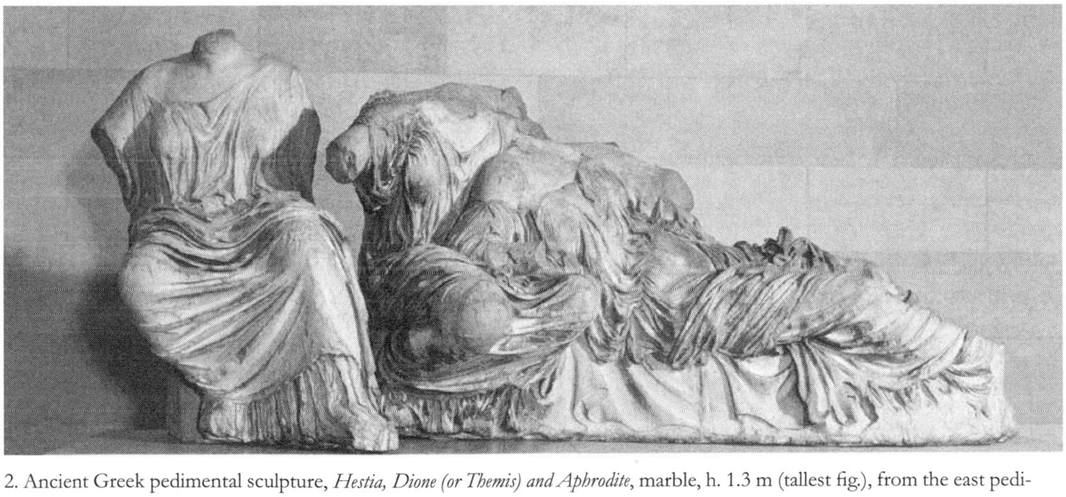

2. Ancient Greek pedimental sculpture, *Hestia, Dione (or Themis) and Aphrodite*, marble, h. 1.3 m (tallest fig.), from the east pediment of the Parthenon, Athens, High Classical period, *c.* 437–*c.* 432 BC (London, British Museum)

N. Archaeol. Mus.) and the Temple of Athena at Mazi in Elis (*c.* 400–390 BC), foreshadow the aesthetic preferences of the 4th century BC.

The few extant 4th-century BC pedimental compositions reflect the new historical reality and are characterized by strong emotional content and impressionistic forms; examples include the *Fall of Troy* and the *Amazonomachy* (390–380 BC; Athens, N. Archaeol. Mus.) from the Temple of Asklepios at Epidauros and, especially, the *Kalydonian Boar Hunt* and the *Fight between Telephos and Achilles* (*c.* 350 BC; Tegea, Archaeol. Mus.; Athens, N. Archaeol. Mus.) from the Temple of Athena Alea at Tegea. Towards the end of the 4th century BC, however, there is evidence of a return to more conventional compositions, notably at the Temple of Apollo at Delphi (*c.* 330 BC; see Pausanias: *Guide to Greece* X.xix.3). This tendency persisted during the first half of the 2nd century BC, judging by the fragments of pedimental sculpture (Samothrace, Archaeol. Mus.) from the Hieron on Samothrace. Even so, analysis of the development of ancient Greek pedimental sculpture is made difficult by the paucity of surviving material and its dispersal to different collections. Some works were in any case looted in antiquity to be re-used in temples at Rome, for example an *Amazonomachy* (*c.* 440 BC; Rome, Mus. Capitolino) used for the Temple of Apollo Sosianus.

E. Lapalus: *Le Fronton sculpté en Grèce des origines à la fin du IVe siècle* (Paris, 1947)
A. Delivorrias: *Attische Giebelskulpturen und Akrotere des 5. Jhs.* (Tübingen, 1974)
E. Touloupa: *Ta enaetía gluptà tou naoú tou Apóllonos Daphnephórou sten Eretría* [The pediment statues of the Temple of Apollo Daphnephoros, Eretria] (Ioánnina, 1983)
E. La Rocca: *Amazzanomachia: Le sculpture frontonali del tempio di Apollo Sosiano* (Rome, 1985)
E. Walter: *Karydi: Die äginetische Bildhauerschule: Werke und schriftliche Quellen* (Mainz, 1987), pp. 129ff
M. Oppermann: *Vom Medusabild zur Athenageburt* (Leipzig, 1990)
O. Palagia: *The Pediments of the Parthenon* (Leiden, New York and Cologne, 1993)
N. Yalouris: 'Die Skulpturen des Asklepiostempels in Epidauros', *Ant. Plast.*, xxi (1993)
W. J. Diebold: 'The Politics of Derestoration: The Aegina Pediments and the German Confrontation with the Past', *A. J.*, liv (Summer 1995), pp. 60–66
H. Kyrieleis: 'Zeus and Pelops in the East Pediment of the Temple of Zeus at Olympia', *Stud. Hist. A.*, xlix (1995), pp. 12–27
O. Palagia: 'First among Equals: Athena in the East Pediment of the Parthenon', *Stud. Hist. A.*, xlix (1995), pp. 28–49
D. Buitron-Oliver: *The Interpretation of Architectural Sculpture in Greece and Rome* (Washington, 1997)
E. Walter-Karydi: '"Die letzten Agineten": Gibelplastik und die Aginetischen Meister', *Rev. Archéol.*, ii (1999), pp. 283–304
M. B. Cosmopoulos: *The Parthenon and its Sculptures* (New York, 2004)
J. M. Barringer: 'The Temple of Zeus at Olympia, Heroes, and Athletes', *Hesperia*, lxxiv/2 (April–June 2005), pp. 211–41

(ii) Roman. Roman architects did not learn the use of figured pediments from contemporary Greek architects. Sculpted pediments enjoyed a sudden popularity throughout Italy from the 2nd century BC, probably the result of a Classical revival in the course of Roman importation of hellenizing architectural styles. Archaeologists have classified pedimental sculpture into two categories: mythological and 'assembly' pediments. Mythological pediments were preferred in Etruria. Among the mythological pediments that survive, discontinuity with the Greek tradition is apparent both in the composition and in the structure. The source of narrative compositions such as *Dionysus Discovering Ariadne* (late 2nd century BC; Bologna, Mus. Civ. Archeol.) from Cività Alba may have been Hellenistic painting. In the Cività Alba pediment the composition consists of densely packed figures executed in high relief on a series of plaques that fit together to form the pediment wall. The result bears only a superficial resemblance to the Classical Greek pediment. Assembly pediments were the type preferred in Rome and her colonies: in this type the pediment was filled less densely with an array of symbols or with a static arrangement of figures expressing an abstract message.

Evidence for the use of pedimental sculpture in major works of Roman architecture comes mostly from depictions on coins and in marble reliefs, such as the Hartwig relief (see below). Other city temples that have been identified from secondary representations include the temples of Mars Ultor in the Forum Augustum (see below), the Magna Mater on the Palatine and Juno Regina in the Portico of Metellus. Such representations indicate that the pediment (as opposed to the dedicatory inscription) could play an important role in signifying the identity of a given temple. Surviving pediments show that Roman architects preferred to place the pediment wall much shallower than did Greek architects of the Classical period. This practice dictated the use of relief rather than free-standing sculpture in all but the largest temples built by Roman architects in the Greek style. Roman temples generally employed steeper gables than did Greek temples, resulting in greater emphasis on the vertical median. In most cases the central axis is occupied by a single commanding figure or symbol.

In Vitruvius' time (late 1st century BC) there were still to be seen in Rome temples in the Etruscan style with mythological groupings in bronze and terracotta (*On Architecture* III.iii.5). Imperial architects, in contrast, preferred the assembly pediment. The array of seven pedimental figures (Palatine, Romulus, Venus, Mars, Fortuna, Roma, Tiber) on the Temple of Mars Ultor completed under Augustus in 2 BC relate to each other only in their common association to Augustus. The pediment represented on the Hadrianic Hartwig relief (Rome, Mus. N. Romano) is more complex. Most would identify the temple as that of Quirinus on the Quirinal, Rome, as restored by Augustus in 16 BC. It has been proposed that the figures be identified as Aeneas, Vesta, Romulus–Quirinus, Mars, Victory, Mercury (with his foot on the gate of heaven), Maia, Hercules, Acca Laurentia and Faustulus. By pairing Aeneas and Vesta with Acca Laurentia and Faustulus the designer compared the origins of the Julian family with the origins of Rome. By pairing Romulus–Quirinus with Hercules he emphasized the common apotheoses of the two heroes, alluding as well to the apotheosis of Julius Caesar. Mars and Victory are balanced by the blessings of peace in the persons of Mercury and Maia, both pairings well known to Augustan propaganda. Finally, above the gate located in the centre of the composition is a flight of vultures, the *auspicium augustum* ('holy sign'), which inspired the choice of Augustus' name (Suetonius: *Augustus* vii). In sum, by means of its typology the pediment presents Romulus–Quirinus as a prefiguration of Augustus.

The Augustan preference for the assembly pediment with its contextual use of symbols is characteristic of the modes of signification employed in Roman art generally. Moreover, with the greater scale, hence greater symbolic importance, implicit in the centre of the composition, assembly pediments anticipated compositional developments in the late Roman style.

P. Hommel: *Studien zu den römischen Figurengiebeln der Kaiserzeit* (Berlin, 1954)
O. J. Brendel: *Etruscan Art*, Pelican Hist. A. (Harmondsworth, 1978)

R. Paris: 'Propaganda e iconografia: Una lettura del frontone del tempio di Quirino sul frammento del "rilievo Hartwig" nel Museo Nazionale Romano', *Boll. A.*, lii (Nov–Dec 1988), pp. 27–38
P. Zanker: *The Power of Images in the Age of Augustus* (Ann Arbor, 1988)
G. Hafner: 'Die beim Apollotempel in Rom gefundenen griechischen Skulpturen', *Jb. Dt. Archäol. Inst.*, cvii (1992), pp. 17–32
'The Interpretation of Architectural Sculpture in Greece and Rome', *Stud. Hist. A.*, xlix (1995), pp. 9–217 [11 article special issue]

Peiraeus [Piraeus]. Greek port on the Saronic Gulf, serving Athens, of which it is now a suburb. Peiraeus is situated on a promontory *c.* 8 km south-west of the city centre and is dominated by the hill of Mounychia. To its west is the great harbour of Kantharos, to the east the smaller harbours of Zea and Mounychia. A fort was established on the hill of Mounychia in the late 6th century BC, but it was not unitl 493/2 BC that the sheltered harbours were exploited and the promontory fortified. Peiraeus flourished until 86 BC, when it was sacked by Lucius Cornelius Sulla. The walls were not rebuilt and Peiraeus declined. The settlement was of little importance until after 1834, when Athens became the capital of Greece. The town's rapid expansion was further encouraged by the opening of the Corinth Canal in 1893.

1. Architecture. 2. Sculpture.

1. ARCHITECTURE. Peiraeus was fortified by Themistokles in 493/492 BC as part of his naval strategy against the Persians. The town was probably redesigned with a grid plan, attributed to HIPPODAMOS, some time after the defeat of Xerxes' invasion in 479 BC. All three of its harbours were enclosed by the city walls and developed for commercial purposes, with an agora adjacent to Kantharos. The harbours were also used as bases for the Athenian fleet during the 5th and 4th centuries BC and were lined with impressive ship sheds. Epigraphical evidence (*Inscr. Gr./2*, ii, 1627–31) demonstrates that there were 94 such sheds at Kantharos, 82 at Mounychia and no less than 196 at the main naval harbour of Zea. Some of those at Zea have been excavated, though they are no longer visible, and have provided valuable evidence for reconstructing the ships that they held. Also near Zea was a 4th-century BC arsenal, designed by Philon of Eleusis, which held ropes and other naval tackle. Parts of this have been found, confirming drawn reconstructions based on the precise specifications laid down in its building inscription (*Inscr. Gr./2*, ii, 1668; *see* ARCHITECTURE, §IV, 3(ii)).

Excavations during building work in the 19th century uncovered traces of the original streets and an area of houses. Though not well preserved, and inadequately studied, the latter clearly had standard plans and dimensions. The chief visible remains of ancient Peiraeus are considerable stretches of fortification walls, especially between Zea and Kantharos. They were built as part of the refortification of Athens and Peiraeus at about the time of the battle of Knidos (394 BC). Traces of earlier walls also survive, particularly on the hill of Mounychia. There are remains, too, of a small 2nd-century BC theatre near Zea, though the large 5th-century BC theatre is now buried.

I. X. Dragatzes: 'Ekthesis peri ton en Peiraiei anaskaphon' [Account of excavations at Peiraeus], *Praktika Athen. Archaiol. Etaireias* (1885), pp. 63–71
R. Martin: *L'Urbanisme dans la Grèce antique* (Paris, 1956; 2/1974)
K. Jeppesen: *Paradeigmata* (Aarhus, 1958), pp. 69–101
E. Lorenzen: *The Arsenal at Piraeus* (Copenhagen, 1964)
W. Hoepfner and E.-L. Schwandner: *Haus und Stadt im klassischen Griechenland* (Munich, 1986; 2/1994), pp. 12–20
R. Garland: *The Piraeus from the Fifth to the First Century* BC (London, 1987)
W. Hoepfner, ed.: *Geschichte des Wohnens: 5000 v. Chr.–500 n. Chr.* vol. I (Stuttgart, 1999)

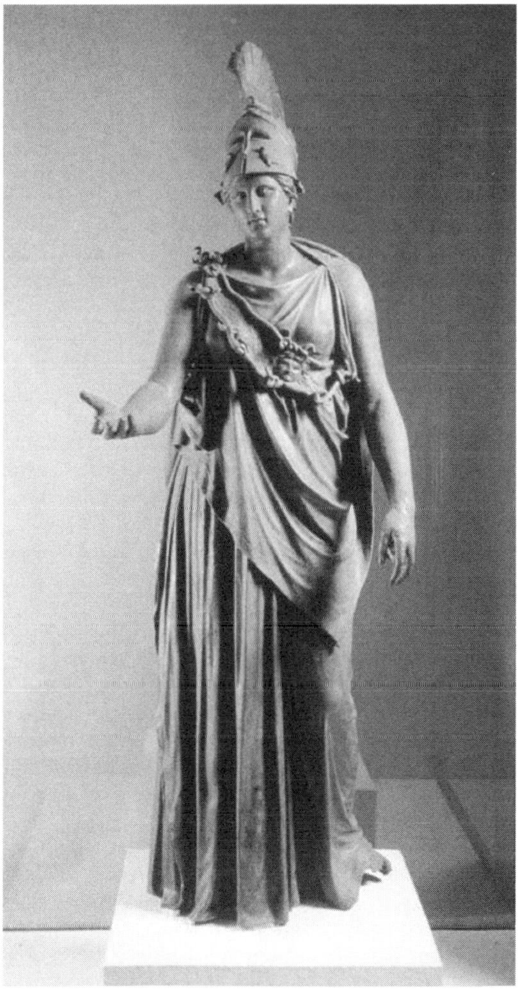

1. Peiraeus, statue of *Athena* attributed to Euphranor, bronze, h. 2.35 m, Late Classical period, *c.* 350 BC (Peiraeus, Archaeological Museum)

2. Sculpture. In 1959 a cache comprising four bronze statues, a bronze tragic mask, a bronze shield, two marble herms and one marble sculpture (all in Peiraeus, Archaeol. Mus.) was discovered. Excavation was carried out immediately by the Greek Archaeological Service. It is generally agreed that these marbles and bronzes were being stored in a warehouse that burnt down, perhaps during Sulla's sack of Athens in 86 BC. Some scholars believe that the statues were removed to Athens from Delos during the Mithridatic wars and that they were at Peiraeus in transit to Rome. Others argue that the bronzes were made in Athens. Stylistically, the bronzes appear to be of different dates, possibly having been made over a period of time for one sanctuary, though it is more likely that they are simply made in styles that we would assign to different dates. The three largest bronzes are similar enough in size, in the alloys used and in their poses and attributes to suggest that they could have belonged to a single commission.

It is the four large bronze statues that have received most attention: they represent *Apollo, Athena* and two figures of *Artemis*. The Peiraeus *Apollo* (h. 1.91 m) is a figure of the kouros type. The heavy, smooth hair, bound with a fillet, falls to the shoulders in thick beaded tresses ending in points. The head is inclined, which is very unusual for an Archaic statue, and the arms are free of the body, extending forwards from the elbow: the flattened right palm probably once held a phiale (cup); the left hand clasped a bow. The right foot is stepping forwards, a reversal of the normal position for kouroi. On stylistic and technical grounds, the *Apollo* is usually dated from as early as *c.* 530–*c.* 520 BC to as late as *c.* 480–*c.* 470 BC, though it could well be Archaistic rather than Archaic. The thick-walled, one-piece casting of the body and legs, however, with only the arms and head separately cast, is characteristic of bronzes from the Archaic and Classical periods, and the eyes of the *Apollo* were cast with the head, in a manner found on some other large Archaic bronzes.

The massive bronze *Athena* (h. 2.35 m; see fig. 1) wears a *peplos* (long heavy woollen tunic) and an aegis adorned with a gorgoneion and serpents. The crested Corinthian helmet is decorated with griffins and owls in relief. The figure's right hand is outstretched and once had something attached to it, again perhaps a phiale, and there may have been a spear in the left hand. The closest parallels for this statue are found among sculptures dated to the first half of the 4th century BC (i.e. the Late Classical period). The *Athena* has been compared with the marble *Apollo Patroos* from the Athenian Agora, a work attributed to Euphranor, and with the marble copies of the group of *Eirene and Ploutos* by Kephisodotos. Both Euphranor and Kephisodotos are reputed to have worked in Athens during the second quarter of the 4th century BC (Pliny, *Natural History* XXXIV.50). Comparisons have also been drawn between the Peiraeus *Athena* and the marble Mattei *Athena* (Paris, Louvre), which has been called an adaptation of the bronze. The large *Artemis* (h. 1.94 m; see fig. 2), which was at first tentatively identified as a Muse, wears a *peplos*, has a quiver strapped across the right shoulder and probably held a phiale in the raised, extended right hand and a bow in the lowered left hand. The weight is borne on the right foot, and the left foot trails. The eyes, lips and teeth are inset. Because the proportions, pose and drapery closely resemble those of the marble *Apollo Patroos*, the large *Artemis* has, like the *Athena*, been dated to the 4th century BC. The small *Artemis* (h. 1.55 m) is more severely corroded than the other bronzes, with the result that the style is more difficult to assess. Certain stylistic features have suggested a date later than that assigned to the *Athena* or to the large *Artemis*, perhaps in the 3rd century BC. The turn of the head is slightly more acute than that of the large *Artemis* and the extension of the arms is more pronounced. The pose reverses that of the large *Artemis*. Like the large *Artemis*, this statue wears a *peplos*, but with a short cloak added. The quiver-strap that runs over the right shoulder is inlaid with a silver meander, and the eyes are inset. It has been argued that the sandals worn by the small *Artemis* and by the *Athena* are of a type that did not appear until the second half of the 2nd century BC.

The tragic mask (h. 0.45 m) is usually dated to the later 4th century BC or to the Hellenistic period. It has heavy cascading locks of hair, raised bulging brows and huge round eyes that were once inlaid, a wide

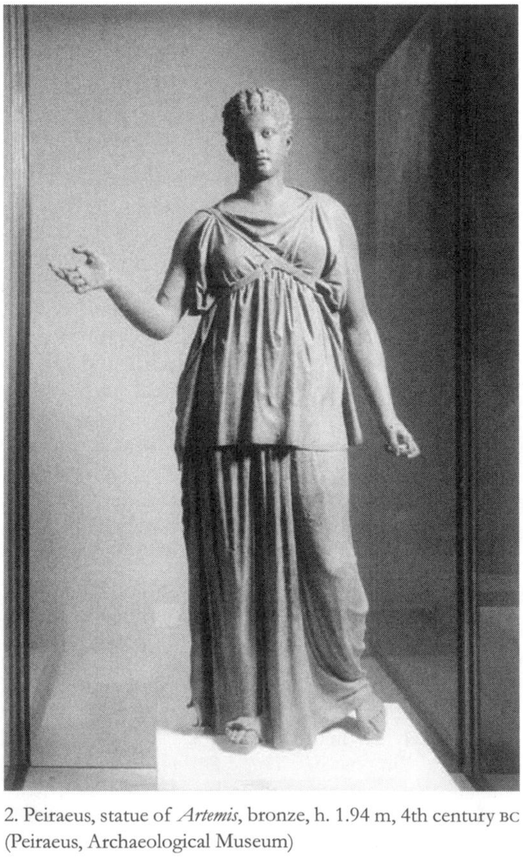

2. Peiraeus, statue of *Artemis*, bronze, h. 1.94 m, 4th century BC (Peiraeus, Archaeological Museum)

open mouth and a tightly curled beard. It has been suggested that the sculptor of the mask was Silanion. The remaining finds from the Peiraeus cache include two marble herms representing the bearded *Hermes* (both h. 1.43 m), a marble statue of a veiled *Artemis Kindyas* and a bronze shield.

M. Paraskevaidis: *Ein wiederentdeckter Kunstraub der Antike?* (Berlin, 1966)
G. Dontas: 'La Grande Artémis du Pirée: Une Oeuvre d'Euphranor', *Ant. Kst*, xxv (1982), pp. 15–33
C. Houser: *Greek Monumental Bronze Sculpture* (New York, 1983), pp. 50–69
K. D. Morrow: *Greek Footwear and the Dating of Sculpture* (Madison, WI, 1985), pp. 71–6
G. Dontas: 'Ho chalkinos Apollon tou Peiraia' [The bronze Apollo of Peiraeus], *Archaische und klassische griechische Kunst* (Mainz, 1986), pp. 181–92
B. S. Ridgway: *Hellenistic Sculpture*, i (Madison, WI, and Bristol, 1990), p. 363
C. C. Mattusch: *Classical Bronzes: The Art and Craft of Greek and Roman Statuary* (Ithaca and London, 1996), pp. 129–40
O. Palagia: 'Reflections on the Piraeus Bronzes', *Greek Offerings*, ed. O. Palagia (Oxford, 1997), pp. 177–95
G. Stainchaouer: *Ta mnemeia kai to Archaiologiko Mouseio tou Peiraia* (Athens, 1998)

Peiraikos. Greek painter. He is known from one passage in Pliny (*Natural History* XXXV.112). A corrupt reference to a painter of 'small art' by Propertius (*Elegies* III.ix.12) may refer to Peiraikos but is generally restored to read Parrhasios. None of Peiraikos' works survives. He was called *rhyparagraphos*, the painter of mean subjects. His pictures were painted with a brush, and his subjects included the shops of barbers and cobblers, food, perhaps in still-life, and humble animals such as asses. Although Pliny claimed that the painter's reputation was limited by the small scale and insignificant subjects of his pictures, nevertheless his popularity was great, and his paintings sold for more than the large pictures of lesser artists.

Peiraion. *See* PERACHORA.

Peisistratos (*d* Athens, 527 BC). Greek tyrant and patron of the arts. His policies and those of his sons, Hippias and Hipparchos, produced an increase in trade that made Attic Black-figure pottery (*see* POTTERY, §IV, 5) the most widely used vessels in the Greek world and Attic coinage one of the foremost currencies. The Peisistratid building programme at Athens included the rebuilding of the Temple of Athena (identified as the Hekatompedon or 'Hundred-footer') on the Acropolis; the Enneakrounos ('nine-headed') fountain-house by the Ilissos river, south of the Acropolis; the foundation of the Temple of Olympian Zeus, finally completed by the Roman emperor Hadrian (*reg* AD 117–38; *see* ATHENS, §II, 4); and a temple to Dionysos at the foot of the Acropolis. He also enlarged the Panathenaic festival to Athena and established the Greater Dionysia, from the choral performances of which developed Classical Greek drama.

A. Andrews: *The Greek Tyrants* (London, 1956)
S. Angiolillo: *Arte e cultura nell'Atene di Pisistrato e dei Pisistratidi: 'O epi kronou bios* (Bari, 1997)
A. S. Blachos: *Peisistratos o filoprotos* (Athens, 1998)
H. Sancisi-Weerdenburg: *Peisistratos and the Tyranny: A Reappraisal of the Evidence* (Amsterdam, 2000)
B. M. Lavelle: *Fame, Money, and Power: The Rise of Peisistratos and 'Democratic' Tyranny at Athens* (Ann Arbor, 2005)

Pelike. Ancient form of vessel, used as a storage jar (*see* POTTERY, fig. 15(i)e).

Pella (i) [anc. Pihil; Pihir; Arab. Khirbet Fahil; now Ṭabaqat Faḥl]. Site of a settlement in Jordan inhabited from the Natufian period, *c.* 10,000 BC, to medieval times. It lies at sea-level in the foothills of the Gilead range, 25 km south of the Sea of Galilee and 3 km east of the River Jordan. Under the early Seleucids from *c.* 300 BC Pella became a major Hellenistic foundation, when it also acquired the Hellenized form of the name. Later it was successively one of the cities of the Roman Decapolis, then the seat of a Byzantine bishopric. It was identified as Pella of the Decapolis in the early 19th century and was briefly investigated in 1957 and 1967. Since 1979 Pella has been excavated and surveyed by a joint expedition from the University of Sydney and Wooster College, OH, under Hennessy and Smith. Most of the finds are in the Jordan Archaeological Museum in Amman and in the Museum of Jordanian Heritage in Irbid.

Apart from the Bronze Age city walls, no monumental architectural remains of the earlier periods have been discovered at Pella. However, there are remains of major public and religious buildings from the late Hellenistic period onwards. Many of these have been restored and are visible at the site. They include a small theatre and temple of the Roman period (part of a much larger civic complex). City coins of Pella show a monumental staircase leading to a hill temple; these can be identified with buildings that are partly visible on Tell Husn.

There is a wealth of glassware from Roman and Byzantine tombs and Umayyad buildings, and charming ivories from late Roman tombs. One fragmentary bronze object of the mid-4th century AD is of considerable interest: on the remains of a small, twin-sided, bronze repoussé reliquary (Amman, Jordan Archaeol. Mus.) is the earliest known depiction of the cross on Calvary. The cross, the hill of stones (reminiscent of the obverse designs of some Byzantine coins) and the cave of the burial are framed by monumental arches, and the scene probably commemorates the building by Empress Helena and Emperor Constantine of the Church of the Holy Sepulchre in Jerusalem, dedicated in AD 335. On the reverse is shown a figure kneeling before a man riding a donkey in procession, perhaps the entry of Jesus into Jerusalem.

G. Schumacher: *Pella of the Decapolis* (London, 1888)
J. Richmond: 'Khirbet Fahil', *Palestine Explor. Fund Q.*, lxvi (1934), pp. 18–31
R. H. Smith: *Pella of the Decapolis*, i (London, 1973)
A. W. McNicoll, R. H. Smith and J. B. Hennessy: *Pella in Jordan*, 2 vols (Canberra, 1982–7)
R. H. Smith: 'Excavations at Pella of the Decapolis', *N. Geog. Res.*, cxiv (1985), pp. 470–89
A. McNicoll: *Pella in Jordan 2: The Second Interim Report of the Joint University of Sydney and the College of Wooster Excavations at Pella, 1982–1985* (Sydney, 1992)
F. V. Richards: *Scarab Seals from a Middle to Late Bronze Age Tomb at Pella in Jordan* (Freiburg, 1992)
T. Weber: *Pella Decapolitana: Studien zur Geschichte, Architektur und Bildenden Kunst einer Hellenisierten Stadt des nördlichen Ostjordanlandes* (Wiesbaden, 1993)
S. J. Bourke: 'Pre-classical Pella in Jordan: A Conspectus of Ten Years' Work (1985–1995)', *Palestine Explor. Q.*, cxxix (July–Dec 1997), pp. 94–115
'Pella Hinterland Tomb Project 1996 Season', *Palestine Explor. Q.*, cxxix (Jan–June 1997), p. 90
K. A. Sheedy and others, eds: *Pella in Jordan, 1979–1990: The Coins* (Sydney, 2001)
P. B. McLaren: *The Military Architecture of Jordan during the Middle Bronze Age: New Evidence from Pella and Rukeis* (Oxford, 2003)

Pella (ii). Capital of the ancient Macedonian kingdom in northern Greece, about 30 km north-west of Thessaloniki and astride the Via Egnatia. In antiquity the area was connected with the Thermaic Gulf of the Aegean Sea, on which Thessaloniki lies. The Macedonian capital was transferred to Pella from Aigai by Archelaos (*reg c.* 413–*c.* 399 BC), who had at his court the painter Zeuxis, the poet Agathon and the dramatist Euripides, who died there in 406 BC. The city prospered particularly under Antigonos II Gonatas (*reg* 285–239 BC) but when Pella fell to Aemilius Paullus after the Battle of Pydna (148 BC), Thessaloniki grew at its expense.

Finds to the south of Pella suggest that there was a prehistoric settlement there. Chance finds in 1957 showed the exact site of the ancient Macedonian city, which is not overlaid by any modern settlement. The site has been extensively excavated by the Greeks, under Prof. Makaronas and Dr Petsas. It is possible, but unlikely, that the royal palace has been uncovered; here were paintings by Zeuxis, and here Philip II (*reg* 359–336 BC) and Alexander the Great were born; no traces of the theatre where Euripides' *Bacchae* was first performed in 408 BC have been found. The most spectacular finds are the mosaics of the ancient houses, made of pebbles of different colours depicting life-size figures.

1. Architecture. 2. Mosaics.

1. Architecture. Although excavations at Pella have uncovered the remains of many buildings, it is difficult to build up a complete and reliable picture of its architecture because publication of the findings has been so limited and fragmentary. Pella was built on the grid system attributed to Hippodamos of Miletos. The extant buildings do not belong to the first phase of construction of the city (late 5th century BC); almost all date to the end of the 4th century BC, the period following the campaigns of Alexander the Great, when there was intense building activity throughout Macedonia. Pella's architectural remains can conveniently be discussed in four categories: the central agora, private houses, the palace and the fortifications.

The agora is situated roughly in the middle of the north–south axis of the city; a central avenue 15 m broad, the widest in the city, bisects the area and allows the movement of people and traffic to and from it. Its buildings are laid out around a huge central courtyard (200.15×181.76 m), which represents ten blocks on the street plan. Despite its impressive dimensions, the quality of construction of the various buildings is mediocre, although only the east wing has been excavated. It is clear from the many small finds that the area included pottery workshops and shops that produced and sold clay vessels and statuettes. Metal workshops were also situated in this part of the city. Archaeological evidence suggests that the agora was destroyed and abandoned suddenly at the beginning of the 1st century BC, along with a large part of the ancient city, almost certainly as a result of a powerful earthquake.

The largest private houses are situated south of the agora. Two of the best preserved are houses I 1 and I 5 (often called the House of Dionysos and the House of Helen after their mosaic floors). The House of Dionysos is 69×47 m, measured according to the theory that all the rooms leading off the two courtyards belong to a single building. One courtyard has Ionic porticos on all four sides leading to sizeable rooms on the west, north and east. To its south is a second courtyard, apparently without colonnades, on the west and north sides of which are situated the main rooms of the house, those containing the famous central floor mosaics of *Dionysos* and the *Lion Hunt*. The walls were of local limestone and although only the lower courses or foundations remain it seems clear that they were painted; good evidence for this is a polychrome wall painting in another house, the architectural framework of which may have influenced the Pompeian First Style (*c.* 200–*c.* 90 BC). The House of Helen, containing the wonderful mosaic of the *Abduction of Helen* in its largest room (situated north of the central peristyle courtyard), measures 50×47 m and is a typical example of a Greek house, organized around an open-air courtyard. It was constructed in the same way as the first house but is less well preserved.

Excavations on a hill to the north of the town uncovered several parts of a large residential complex measuring roughly 60,000 sq. m. The various buildings may belong to the royal palace, although the published drawings make it difficult to construct a clear architectural picture. At the centre of the complex are two huge peristyle courtyards; to the east of these stands the most monumental of the buildings with an area of 7500 sq. m, consisting of a central courtyard surrounded by a Doric portico from which the rooms lead off. Only further excavations will determine if this was the private residence of the king.

2. MOSAICS. The 11 pebble mosaics discovered at Pella on the floors of private houses (Pella, Archaeol. Mus.) can be dated to the last quarter of the 4th century BC and the beginning of the 3rd (*see* MOSAICS, §II, 2(iii)(a)). The two most important groups (four mosaics in each) belong to the two large houses situated south of the large agora. The House of Dionysos had rooms with pebble mosaic floors arranged in geometric patterns; two further rooms had central mosaics with subsidiary mosaics decorating the thresholds. One of the central mosaics depicts *Dionysos Riding a ?Cheetah* (2.72×2.69 m), an example of fine but unoriginal draughtsmanship. The *Lion Hunt* in the same house offered the craftsman greater creative scope. In this long, narrow panel (4.90×3.20 m) two young men, one with a spear and the other with a sword, attack a lion that stands between them. The foreshortened view of the lion and the sense of movement and mass created by the two figures are noteworthy. Terracotta strips are used to emphasize details, as is the case in the first mosaic, but the *Lion Hunt* makes greater use of colour (mainly reds). The two threshold mosaics represent a griffin dismembering a deer and a male and a female centaur; the latter is a most unusual subject in Greek art.

The mosaics in the House of Helen are more painterly and show greater skill in composition. The largest of these, and the most inspired of all the mosaics at Pella, is the *Abduction of Helen*. The unusually long and narrow panel (8.48×2.84 m) and the handling of the subject strongly imply that the mosaicist was faithfully copying a painted prototype, such as the *Rape of Persephone* found in a tomb at AIGAI (ii) (Vergina). The *Stag Hunt* mosaic in the same house is much better preserved (4.31×4.24 m incl. border). It is signed by GNOSIS, who is thus the earliest Greek mosaicist known by name. The third mosaic in this house (an *Amazonomachy*; 2.36×2.12 m) is far less accomplished and less well preserved, while of the fourth only a corner with plant motifs has survived. Two interesting mosaic floors with floral decoration, one circular (diam. 5.80 m) and the other square (5.55×5.60 m), have been discovered in two other buildings in Pella. The plant motif in both develops around a central element and is fashioned with great sensitivity to the shape of the space it fills, like the scheme of the palace mosaic at Aigai. Such plant motifs may have influenced the art of the painter Pausias.

M. Andronikos and others: *The Search for Alexander: An Exhibition* (Boston, 1980)

M. Robertson: 'Early Greek Mosaic', *Macedonia and Greece in Late Classical and Early Hellenistic Times*, ed. B. Barr-Sharrar and E. N. Borza (Washington, DC, 1982), pp. 241–50

M. Stamatopoulou and M. Yeroulanou: *Excavating Classical Culture: Recent Archaeological Discoveries in Greece* (Oxford, 2002)

Pemdje. *See* OXYRHYNCHUS.

Pentastyle. Term applied to a building with a portico of five columns.

Perachora [Gr. Peiraion]. Site near Corinth, at the end of a promontory projecting into the Gulf of Corinth on the west side of the isthmus connecting the Peloponnese with mainland Greece. To the north Mt Geraneia makes land access difficult, but its position commanding the Gulf of Corinth gave Perachora unique strategic importance to the Corinthians, under whose control it flourished from the 8th–4th century BC. Its principal remains are those of the Sanctuary of Hera by a small harbour. Excavations have been conducted there by the British School at Athens, initially during 1930–33 under the direction of Humfrey Payne. All finds are now in the National Archaeological Museum, Athens.

The sanctuary itself is rarely mentioned in ancient literature, although Xenophon (*Hellenica*, IV.v) related its capture by the Spartan king Agesilaos in 390 BC, and Strabo described it as oracular (*Geography*, VIII. vi.22). The earliest remains date from the Dark Age, and from the mid-8th century BC there are the rubble foundations of a small apsidal temple, which originally had mud-brick walls and a thatched roof, as demonstrated by terracotta models deposited in the sanctuary as offerings (e.g. Athens, N. Archaeol. Mus.). This building, however, can only have been short-lived. There may also have been a spring by the harbour, which would explain the siting of the sanctuary and its dedication to Hera, but no trace of it survives.

Away from the harbour to the east, in the shallow 'Heraion Valley', a rectangular building was constructed in the 7th century BC on the uppermost of a series of terraces. This too was largely of mud-brick but had a more carefully worked footing and a tiled roof. By the end of the 6th century BC, a rectangular hearth, lined with reused blocks of stone carrying dedicatory inscriptions, had been placed at its centre. Payne believed that this was a second temple, of the 'hearth-altar' type, dedicated to Hera Limenia ('of the harbour'), and that the sanctuary was therefore a double one. More recent arguments suggest, however, that there was only ever one cult of Hera at Perachora, that of Hera Akraia ('of the promontory'), 'Limenia' being merely a nickname. Thus the terraced area was ancillary to the harbour area, and the building with a hearth (that occurs in other local sanctuaries; e.g. the Sanctuary of Zeus at Megara) probably served for ritual feasting. By this time any original spring had been superseded by an artificial pool below the terraced area, probably supplied by rain-water. In this were found over 200 bronze libation bowls of the 7th and 6th centuries BC, which may have been offerings or simply deposited there by an accident, perhaps an earthquake.

The surviving temple is by the harbour and dates from the end of the 6th century BC. It perhaps replaced an earlier temple of which no trace survives. Because of the restricted area available, it was abnormally long in proportion to its width, with a distyle in antis Doric porch. Parts of its foundations survive, as do scattered blocks of the superstructure. Immediately in front to the east was an altar of similar date with the triglyph decoration characteristic of altars from Corinth and the Argolid. Unusually, it was later embellished with a 'baldacchino' probably supported on eight Ionic columns. Beyond it, a series of steps leads to a sheer cliff and presumably formed a stand for viewing the sacrifices and other rituals. Additional space for worshippers and offerings was made by levelling the 'West Court' south of the temple. This was later enlarged and furnished with a stoa supported on wooden posts. Below the terraces, a large double apsidal cistern of unique form was built (?late 6th–early 5th century BC), perhaps replacing the artificial pool. This had a wooden roof supported on a row of plain square internal pillars, some of which incorporate stone crossbeams to brace the side walls against the pressure of the surrounding soil. Access was provided by a distinctive cantilevered stone staircase, and the cistern was fed by rain-water from the terraces. To its south is a solidly constructed dining building of similar date, comprising an antechamber leading to two rooms (both 6.34 sq. m) with stone couches lining their walls. There was a new phase of construction at the end of the 4th century BC, probably initiated by the ruler of Corinth at that time, Demetrios I Poliorketes, and a two-storey stoa was built to the east of the altars with a Doric ground-floor and an Ionic upper storey. By the 2nd century BC the sanctuary was abandoned.

Other remains connected with the sanctuary occur above and beyond the 'Heraion Valley'. They include at least one further sanctuary and a hexastyle prostyle fountain-house with extensive underground reservoirs fed by an elaborate supply system including giant water-wheels turning bucket-chains.

Artefacts from the sanctuary site include many offerings, particularly from the upper terraces, where they may have been dumped after periodical cleaning of the temple area. These include large quantities of 7th–6th-century BC Proto-Corinthian and Corinthian pottery.

H. G. G. Payne and others: *Perachora: The Sanctuaries of Hera Akraia and Limenia*, i (Oxford, 1940)

T. J. Dunbabin, ed.: *Perachora: The Sanctuaries of Hera Akraia and Limenia*, ii (Oxford, 1962)

J. J. Coulton: 'The Stoa by the Harbour at Perachora', *Annu. Brit. Sch. Athens*, lix (1964), pp. 100–31

H. Plommer and F. Salviat: 'The Altar of Hera Akraia at Perachora', *Annu. Brit. Sch. Athens*, lxi (1966), pp. 207–15

J. J. Coulton: 'The West Court at Perachora', *Annu. Brit. Sch. Athens*, lxii (1967), pp. 353–71

R. A. Tomlinson: 'Perachora: The Remains outside the Two Sanctuaries', *Annu. Brit. Sch. Athens*, lxvi (1969), pp. 155–258

J. Salmon: 'The Heraeum at Perachora and the Early History of Corinth and Megara', *Annu. Brit. Sch. Athens*, lxvii (1972), pp. 159–204

R. A. Tomlinson: 'The Perachora Waterworks: Addenda', *Annu. Brit. Sch. Athens*, lxxi (1976), pp. 147–8

R. A. Tomlinson: 'The Upper Terraces at Perachora', *Annu. Brit. Sch. Athens*, lxii (1977), pp. 197–202

A. Villa: 'Una statuetta arcaica da Perachora', *Annu. Scu. Archeol. Atene & Miss. It. Oriente*, lvii–lviii (1979–1980), pp. 213–16

R. A. Tomlinson and K. Demakopoulou: 'Excavations at the Circular Building, Perachora', *Annu. Brit. Sch. Athens*, lxxx (1985), pp. 261–80

U. Sinn: 'Das Heraion von Perachora, eine sakrale Schutzzone in der korinthischen Peraia', *Mitt. Dt. Archäol. Inst.: Athen. Abt.*, cv (1990), pp. 53–116 [with appendices]

R. A. Tomlinson: 'Perachora', *Le Sanctuaire grec: Entretiens sur l'antiquité classique*, xxxvii (Geneva, 1990)

A. Menardier: 'The Western Chamber of the 6th century Temple of Hera Akraia at Perachora', *Amer. J. Archaeol.*, xcviii (1994), p. 313

B. Menadier: *The Sixth Century BC Temple and the Sanctuary and Cult of Hera Akraia, Perachora* (diss., U. Cincinnati, 1995)

M. Weber: 'Ein Tempelabbild in Perachora für Hera Akraia', *Archäol Anz.*, iii (1998), pp. 365–71

Perati. Late Mycenaean cemetery on the east coast of Attica between Brauron and Portorafti, consisting of 192 chamber tombs (some with lateral niches) and 26 small pit graves. They were mostly family sepulchres, but 61 contained single interments. The dead, of which there were *c.* 600, were inhumed, except 18 persons of all ages and both sexes who had been cremated. The chronological sequence of the grave goods covers the entire Late Helladic (LH) IIIC period (*c.* 1180–*c.* 1050 BC) and reflects an uninterrupted stylistic evolution, best reflected by the pottery. The vase shapes evolve from globular to oval to conical. The decoration is applied more and more closely until it covers the greater part of the surface of the vessel. It consists of solidly painted surfaces, linear motifs or pictorial representations, some stylized to the point of abstraction (flowers, whorl shells) and some highly simplified but still recognizable (birds, fishes, a man, a horse, a landscape). To this category belong some of the best examples of Late Mycenaean stirrup jars, decorated with octopuses and birds or fishes between their symmetrically arranged tentacles (*see* POTTERY, §III, 2(iii) and fig. 12c). There are also a few terracotta figurines, both human and animal.

Other artefacts were made of bronze (swords, a spearhead (Athens, N. Archaeol. Mus.), cleavers, razors, chisels, fishing hooks, tweezers, fibulae); lead (wire, fishing net weights); gold; hardstones; glasspaste; faience (jewellery); ivory (spindles, inlays); bone (handles) and stone. Of special interest are two Ramesses II (*reg c.* 1279–*c.* 1213 BC) cartouches and some scarabs (all Athens, N. Archaeol. Mus.) imported from Egypt, jewellery, an amulet (Athens, N. Archaeol. Mus.) and two cylinder seals (Athens, N. Archaeol. Mus.) from Cyprus and the Levant, vases from Melos, Naxos, Crete, Cos and Rhodes, a double-spiral bronze ring (Athens, N. Archaeol. Mus.) of central European design and two of the first iron knives to be introduced to Greece from the Levant (from where cremation was also introduced).

S. E. Iakovidis: *Perati, to nekrotapheion* [Perati, the cemetery], Library of the Archaeological Society at Athens, no. 67, vols A and B, (Athens, 1969–70) [in modern Gr., with Eng. summary in vol. B, pp. 418–70]
S. E. Iakovidis: *Excavations of the Nekropolis at Perati*, Occasional Paper 8, Institute of Archaeology, UCLA (Los Angeles, 1980)
L. Phialon and others: 'Réflexions sur l'usage des larnakes et cercueils en Grèce mycénienne', *Rev. Archéol.*, ii (2005), pp. 227–54

Pergamon [Turk. Bergama]. Site of an ancient Greek city in Asia Minor (now Turkey), later part of the Roman Empire. Pergamon (Gr.: 'fort' or 'stronghold') occupies a steep-sided hill (h. 355 m) 110 km north of Smyrna and *c.* 15 km from the Aegean. It is flanked by two tributaries of the River Kaikos, the Selinos to the west and the Ketios to the east. Pergamon flourished especially under Attalid rule (282–133 BC).

1. History. 2. Architecture. 3. Sculpture.

1. History. When Pergamon was visited by Xenophon in the early 4th century BC, it was merely the stronghold of a local dynast, and it continued as such during early Hellenistic times. In the partition of Alexander the Great's empire by his 'Successors' (*Diadochi*), Lysimachos, one of Alexander's bodyguard, received Pergamon as part of a province comprising Thrace and north-west Asia Minor. There he established a military stronghold in which he deposited his treasury, his portion of Alexander's wealth. Before the battle of Ipsos (301 BC) Lysimachos appointed Philetairos (*c.* 343–263 BC) as commander of Pergamon; he was the son of Attalos, who may have been a Macedonian. In 281 BC Lysimachos was killed by his former ally Seleukos I (*c.* 358–281 BC), leaving Philetairos in sole command of Pergamon and its treasury. He defected to Seleukos and thus remained ruler of Pergamon under Seleucid suzerainty. He consolidated his dynastic position by adopting his nephews, one of whom succeeded him as Eumenes I. Over the next 150 years a succession of enlightened monarchs—accomplished soldiers and diplomats nonetheless—raised Pergamon almost to the status of such powers as Macedonia, Egypt and Syria, and the city became a major centre of Hellenistic culture, famous for its library and celebrated school of sculpture. These kings were discerning, active and enthusiastic patrons of literature and the arts, who turned their capital into a city of outstanding beauty and splendour. Their victories over the invading Gauls (Galatians) prompted them to assume the role of champions of Hellenism and inspired the most striking achievements of Pergamene art.

Eumenes I (*reg* 263–241 BC), like his uncle, never adopted the title of king. He maintained the independence of Pergamon by throwing off Seleucid suzerainty (262 BC) and then by buying immunity from the Gauls while increasing his military strength. He was succeeded by Attalos I Soter (*reg* 241–197 BC), son of a cousin. Attalos refused to buy immunity from the Gauls, and defeated them in battle (before 230 BC). At this point he adopted the title of king. After 222 BC he turned for help to Rome, which in the long term led to Pergamon becoming a pawn in Roman foreign policy. Eumenes II Soter (*reg* 197–160 BC) succeeded his father; his reign marked Pergamon's greatest period of prosperity and included the construction of several outstanding monuments and a huge expansion of the city. Attalos II (*reg* 160–139 BC) succeeded his brother and continued the same foreign and domestic policies. Attalos III (*reg* 139–133 BC), son of Eumenes II, played little part in public affairs. In his will, however, he bequeathed his kingdom to Rome, thus precipitating an anti-Roman revolt led by Aristonikos, which was not suppressed until 128 BC. The Pergamene kingdom became the Roman province of Asia and continued to flourish under the Roman Empire.

A. H. M. Jones: *The Cities of the Eastern Roman Provinces* (Oxford, 1937, 2/1971)
E. V. Hansen: *The Attalids of Pergamon* (Ithaca, 1947, 2/1971)
R. E. Allen: *The Attalid Kingdom* (Oxford, 1983)
W. Radt: *Pergamon* (Cologne, 1988)
R. A. Tomlinson: *From Mycenae to Constantinople: The Evolution of the Ancient City* (London and New York, 1992)
M. Klinkott: *Die Stadtmauern* (Berlin and New York, 2001–)
M. Kohl: 'Das Nikephorion von Pergamon', *Rev. Archéol.*, ii (2002), pp. 227–53

2. Architecture.

(i) Urban planning and development. (ii) Materials and techniques. (iii) Buildings.

(i) Urban planning and development. Below the acropolis, the city developed mainly on the south-facing slopes of the hill, and on the river plain below. Because of the steepness of the hillside, Pergamene architects developed the earlier Greek tradition of building on terraced platforms, especially for the major public monuments. For this, it was impractical to lay out on the hillside the grid-like plan of streets that was applied to most planned Greek cities. Streets had to follow contours to ease the gradients, and the location of terraces was determined by the lines of the principal roads and the availability of suitable terrain. The plan thus appears as a series of irregularly placed but substantial platforms, each developed independently of the other. The city also grew in size. In the time of Eumenes I it extended only part of the way down the hillside and was enclosed with a fortification wall. This wall was later demolished, and a much larger area was included within the splendid fortifications of Eumenes II: these include gateways, the passages of which, even when turning at right angles, are given most competently constructed vaults. In Roman times the area on the plain was developed with a regular street plan.

The published plans of the upper city show merely the isolated major structures: it is mainly these that have been cleared by the German archaeologists who have been working at Pergamon since the late 19th century. Much of the intervening space, however, was covered, often densely, with lesser structures and private houses. A typical section of these has been cleared, revealing a network of irregular alleyways.

(ii) Materials and techniques. The scale of Pergamene buildings is impressive, but this was achieved by economical methods. The main material of construction is the dull local stone, andesite. There were no local sources of marble, but since Pergamon was not far from the sea, it could easily have been imported. Nevertheless, in Hellenistic times its use was restricted largely to decorative elements applied to the basic andesite structure. Monuments were soundly built, but there were frequent economies in the structure. Whereas Greek architects traditionally built walls of solid masonry, Pergamene architects developed the system of using thinner slab-like blocks as facings, filling the space between with loose rubble; they were kept in place by alternate courses of single blocks lying flat. The result was a distinctive Pergamene pattern of alternate tall and low courses, easily recognizable even when employed in marble structures put up at Pergamene expense elsewhere. The placing of stoas against the terrace walls as well as on the platforms themselves is another distinctive feature (*see* STOA). Terrace walls at Pergamon were often made stronger, economically, by the use of buttresses, never a regular feature in Classical architecture; there is a fine series in the terraces supporting the stoa below the theatre. Pergamene architects also developed a distinctive form of bell-profiled column capital decorated with out-turned hollowed palm leaves (often called 'palm' or 'Pergamene' capitals): these were frequently used for the inner colonnades of stoas and were probably cheaper to carve than the more complex Ionic capitals used in this context elsewhere. The apogee of Pergamene architecture was the 2nd century BC, when it clearly moved away from the Classical tradition—probably along with other Hellenistic cities—by relaxing the rules governing the forms of the orders, the arrangements of their entablatures and the details of mouldings and capitals. Architecturally as well as politically, Pergamon bridged the gap between Classical Greece and Imperial Rome.

(iii) Buildings. The summit of the hill of Pergamon forms the acropolis proper (see fig. 1), with its own massive fortifications. Parts of these undoubtedly date back to early Hellenistic times, though they were later improved; there are no traces of the earlier stronghold visited by Xenophon. The acropolis continued to serve as a place of garrison, and there are remains of barracks and military storerooms (1a and 1b). It was also the site of the Attalids' 'palace' (1c), a surprisingly modest structure comprising nothing more than normal, comfortably built houses. Fragments of mosaic floors survive and are among the earliest extant mosaics made with cut tesserae, rather than natural pebbles, and with polished surfaces (Berlin, Antikensamml.). The fragments are composed of large numbers of small tesserae, including some of glass, in a wide variety of colours, enabling the artist, in effect, to paint in stone. Although the most famous ancient mosaicist, Sosos, worked at Pergamon, none of his work is known, and the fragments in the palace are signed by HEPHAISTION.

The earliest major public building was the Temple of Athena Polias (late or early 3rd century BC), which was placed on the edge of a terrace on the acropolis adjacent to the palace so that it could be seen from below (1d). It is Doric, peripteral (6×11 columns; 12.72×21.77 m) and built of andesite. The Doric order was used at Pergamon through the influence of Macedonia (either Lysimachos or the Attalids who claimed to be Macedonians), but the columns are unfluted, and the entablature was made

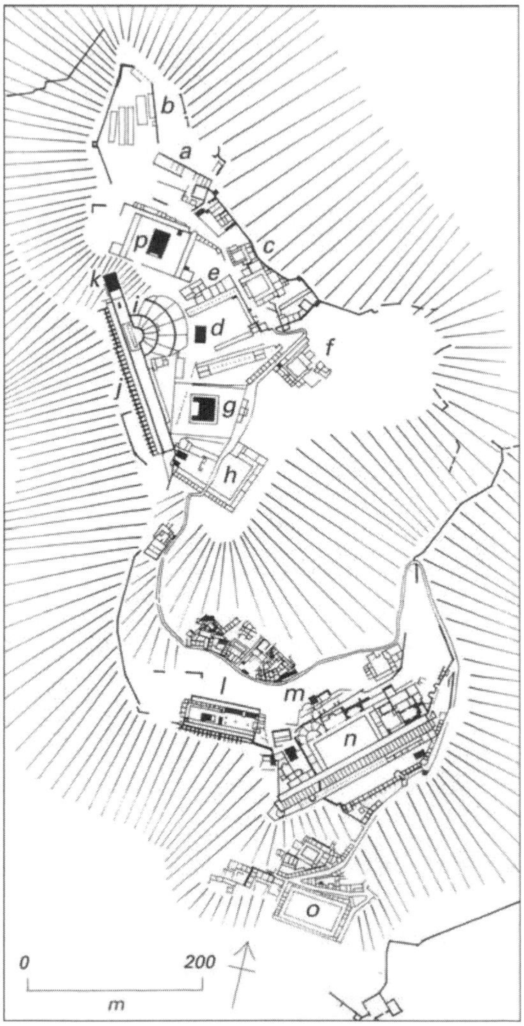

1. Pergamon, plan of upper city, 2nd century BC: (a) barracks; (b) military storerooms; (c) palace; (d) Temple of Athena Polias; (e) library; (f) sanctuary; (g) Great Altar; (h) upper agora; (i) theatre; (j) theatre terrace; (k) Temple of Dionysos; (l) Sanctuary of Demeter; (m) Temple of Hera Basileia; (n) gymnasium; (o) lower agora; (p) Temple of Trajan (2nd century AD)

abnormally low by having three, not two, metopes to each pair of columns, the system used in Asia Minor for stoas. Pergamene use of Doric for temples was later successfully challenged by the Ionian architect Hermogenes, who worked for Eumenes II. The temple was later given a colonnaded precinct with a two-storey propylon, Doric on the lower floor, with four metopes to each spacing, and Ionic above. This precinct led to the famous library of Pergamon (1e), which contained a statue of *Athena*, a marble derivative of Pheidias' gold and ivory *Athena* in the Parthenon, Athens.

Slightly below the acropolis are two more courtyard structures. To the east is a small, poorly preserved sanctuary (1f), probably devoted to the cult of the rulers, which was allowed to decay in Roman times. West of this, surrounded by an open courtyard, is the Great Altar or Altar of Zeus (see fig. 2). This took the form of a podium (36.44×34.20 m) on a five-stepped base, with a wide staircase recessed into the middle of its west face. On the podium was a wall enclosing the altar itself and embellished outside with Ionic columns that returned across the top of the steps, together with an internal colonnade. The whole monument was lavishly decorated with relief sculpture. The date of the altar has been much discussed: it is probably best attributed to the last years of Eumenes II. By the altar is the upper agora (1h), with Doric stoas on three sides. On the hillside below the Sanctuary of Athena is the large, steep-sided theatre, its eighty rows of seats divided into three tiers. Below it, the largest of the Pergamene terraces (1j) supports both the stage building and a double colonnade (l. 246.5 m), which faces the theatre on the north-east and looks out over the hillside to the south-west. At the northern end of the hillside is the small Ionic prostyle Temple of Dionysos (11.80×20.22 m; 2nd century BC; 1k).

Lower down, but still largely within the 3rd-century BC fortifications, is another group of major structures, again on terraced platforms. To the west is the Sanctuary of Demeter (early 2nd century BC), a long shallow platform reached from the east by way of a PROPYLON and with a temple towards its western end, flanked by colonnades and lined on its north side by steps that provided a viewing terrace for worshippers (1l). Behind the west end of the colonnade are three formal dining-rooms, similar to those in mainland Greek sanctuaries. The temple and altar were erected by Philetairos and Eumenes I, though the sanctuary was particularly developed through the interest of Apollonis, wife of Attalos I. To the east is the small Doric Temple of Hera Basileia (*c.* 159–*c.* 138 BC)

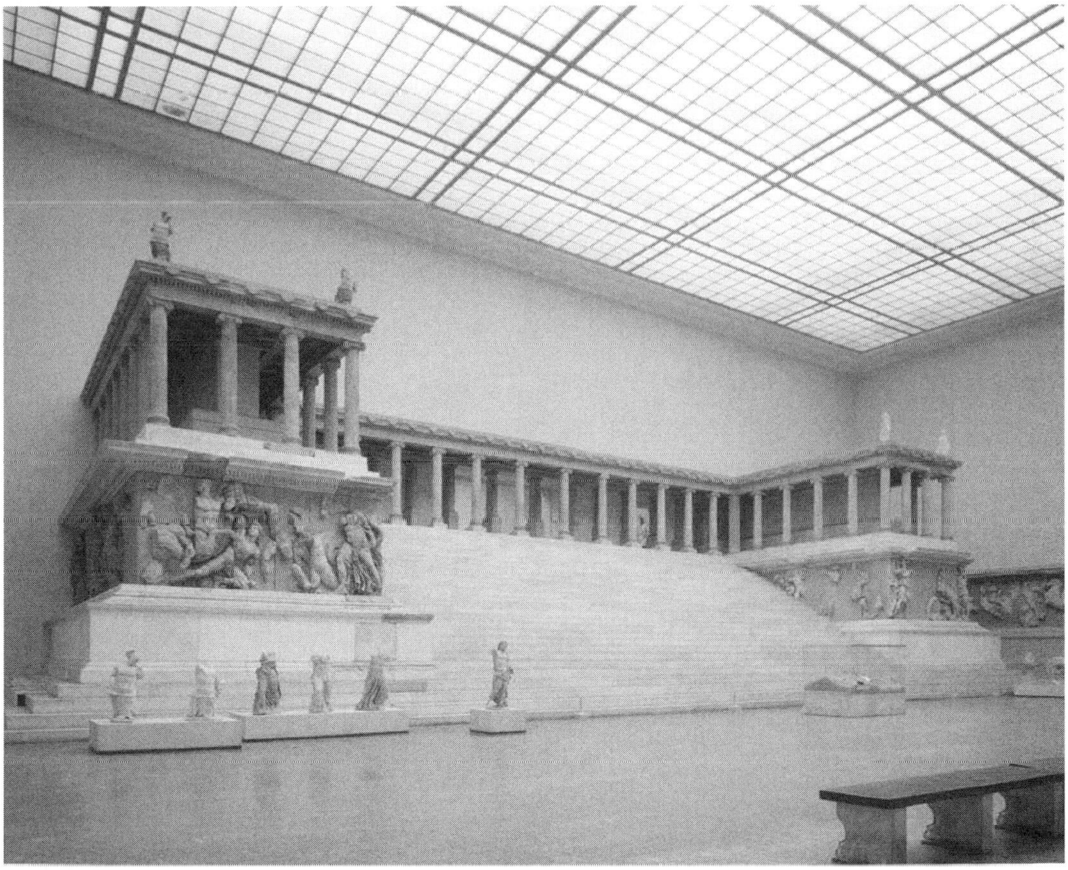

2. Pergamon, Great Altar, *c.* 165 BC; reconstruction (Berlin, Antikensammlung, Staatliche Museen zu Berlin)

and behind this the great gymnasium, on three main levels, all supported by long terrace walls (1m and 1n). At the top is a courtyard (*c.* 200×45 m), flanked by rooms similar to those of gymnasia elsewhere but which were completely altered in Roman times to accommodate a substantial bath building. On the south side a running course extends the full length of the terrace. Below this is the middle section, with a large stoa, again much altered in Roman times. This section straddles the 3rd-century BC fortifications that were by then obsolete. The third and lowest part of the gymnasium was reserved for children. At its eastern end, by the main street that leads up through the town, is the propylon to the middle terrace. Lower down this street, outside the 3rd-century BC walls but within the 2nd-century BC circuit, is the lower agora (1o), a straightforward enclosed court. Unlike the remote and formal upper agora, it was quite easily accessible and served as the market in the 2nd-century BC and later.

The most prominent building below the later fortifications is the so-called Red Basilica, a sanctuary of the Egyptian gods. This consists of a courtyard (*c.* 200×100 m) that crosses the River Selinos, here diverted into two extant vaulted tunnels. At its east end was the temple, a hall with a vast western door. It was built of red brick and mortar and embellished with marble elements. To either side were elliptical rooms, each with its own marble forecourt, and linked to the great hall. The northern room, converted to a mosque, survives with its dome intact. The whole complex is Hadrianic in date (AD 117–38). Slightly earlier, though not completed till Hadrian's reign, is the Temple of Trajan within the acropolis area (1p). This is of Roman form, on a podium with steps only at its front, and with 6×9 Corinthian columns. This is short for Roman temples, but it was necessary to fit the temple into an area defined by colonnades. Its conspicuous position suggests that there may have been a Hellenistic predecessor on this site, but nothing has been found.

There are important buildings outside the city. On the north side of the hill are the remains of an inverted siphon that raised water to the acropolis under pressure. West of the Selinos is a group of Roman structures: a stadium, a second theatre and an amphitheatre. These are badly ruined and have not been investigated in any detail. Past them the sacred way led to the major extramural sanctuary, that of Asklepios. This dates back to the time of Pergamene independence, since it was attacked and plundered by the Gauls; it probably even antedates the development of the Hellenistic city, though virtually nothing is left from its early period due to its total redevelopment in Roman times. The sacred way (l. 820 m) was lined near the Asklepieion itself by colonnades, much of which survives and has been re-erected. It led obliquely to a colonnaded courtyard fronting the sanctuary's formal propylon. The sanctuary itself was enclosed with colonnades on three sides. Within stood the Hellenistic temple, which has left only the slightest traces, and a long underground passage of Roman date. This led from near the centre of the precinct to the southernmost of the principal Roman buildings, which were on the east side of the court. A two-storey circular structure, flanked at its lower level by a series of rooms with curving walls, probably accommodated the ritual of incubation whereby patients were healed while sleeping within the SANCTUARY. To the north is the Roman Temple of Asklepios, the gift of the Roman consul L. Cuspius Pactumeius Rufinus in AD 150; it is clearly modelled, though to a smaller scale (diam. 23.5 m), on the Pantheon at Rome (diam. 43.2 m), an interesting example of direct influence of Imperial Roman architectural form on Asia Minor. To the north of this temple, beyond the propylon, is the square library building. There was yet another theatre at the north-west corner of the precinct, as was the practice in major sanctuaries of Asklepios.

Altertümer von Pergamon (Berlin, 1885–)
H. Kaehler: *Pergamon* (Berlin, 1949)
E. Schmidt: *Der grosse Altar zu Pergamon* (Leipzig, 1961; Eng. trans., London, 1965)
E. Akurgal: *Ancient Civilizations and Ruins of Turkey* (Istanbul, 1969, rev. 2/1983)
O. Deubner: 'Das Heiligtum der alexandrinischen Gottheiten in Pergamon genannt "Kızıl Avlı" ("Rote Halle")', *Istanbul. Mitt.*, xxvii/8 (1977–8), pp. 227–50
P. J. Callaghan: 'On the Date of the Great Altar of Zeus at Pergamon', *Bull. Inst. Class. Stud. U. London*, xxviii (1981), pp. 115–21
H.-J. Schalles: 'Untersuchungen zur Kulturpolitik der pergamenischen Heerschaft', *Jahrhundert vor Christus Istanbuler Forschungen*, xxxvi (1985)
W. Radt: *Pergamon* (Cologne, 1988)
B. Andreae: 'Phyromachos-Probleme', *Mitt. Dt. Archäol. Inst.: Röm Abt.*, iv/31 (1990) [suppl. issue]
K. Grewe and others: 'Antike Welt der Technik VII: Die antiken Flussüberbauungen von Pergamon und Nysa (Turkei)', *Ant. Welt*, xxv/4 (1994), pp. 348–52
U. Wulf: 'Der Stadtplan von Pergamon', *Istanbul. Mitt.*, xliv (1994), p. 135
W. Hoepfner: 'Der vollendete Pergamon Altar', *Archäol. Anz.* (1996), p. 115
W. Radt: 'Reports of Recent Excavations, with Overall Plan', in *Archäol. Anz.* (1996), pp. 443–54
K. Nohlen: 'Ästhetik der Ruine: Zur Prasentation antiker Baukomplexe am Beispiel des Traian-Heiligtums zu Pergamon [restoration of Temple of Trajan]', *Ant. Welt*, xxviii/3 (1997), pp. 185–99
W. Radt: *Pergamon: Geschichte und Bauten einer antiken Metropole* (Darmstadt, 1999)
W. Raeck: 'Ein Gott für den Kaisertempel: Archäologisches vom Trajaneum im Pergamon', *Ant. Welt*, xxx/2 (1999), pp. 105–11
H. Halfmann: *Städtebau und Bauherren im römischen Kleinasien: Ein Vergleich zwischen Pergamon und Ephesos* (Tübingen, 2001)
S. M. C. Bilsel: *Architecture in the Museum: Displacement, Reconstruction and Reproduction of the Monuments of Antiquity in Berlin's Pergamon Museum* (diss., Princeton U., 2003)
B. Kidd: *The Doric Revival under the Attalids of Pergamon* (diss., U. Missouri-Columbia, 2003)

3. SCULPTURE. The sculptures produced at Pergamon during the period of Attalid rule (282–133 BC) are among the most important examples of Hellenistic court art. Although some major sculptures are known only from Roman copies, many original works have been uncovered during more than a century of excavations at Pergamon itself. Several accomplished sculptors of this period are known by name: Antigonos of Karystos (who wrote treatises on art), the Pergamene sculptor Epigonos and Stratonikos of Kyzikos all worked on the great monuments commemorating the Pergamene victory over the Gauls (Pliny: *Natural History* XXXIV.xix.84). The signature of Epigonos occurs on several works. Stratonikos also worked for the Attalids during the 3rd century BC, as did the Attic sculptors Nikeratos and PHYROMACHOS in the 2nd.

(i) Portraits. (ii) Victory monuments. (iii) The Great Altar. (iv) Early copying.

(i) Portraits. A Roman herm (Naples, Mus. Archeol.) may be a copy of an early Hellenistic statue of the founder of the Attalid dynasty, Philetairos, judging by the portrait head on his coins (260s BC). An over life-size portrait head (Berlin, Antikensamml., P. 130) has been identified as Attalos I; other portraits suggested as Pergamene rulers are disputed. A portrait head of *Alexander the Great* (Istanbul, Archaeol. Mus., 538.1138; see fig. 3) probably dates from the second quarter of the 2nd century BC.

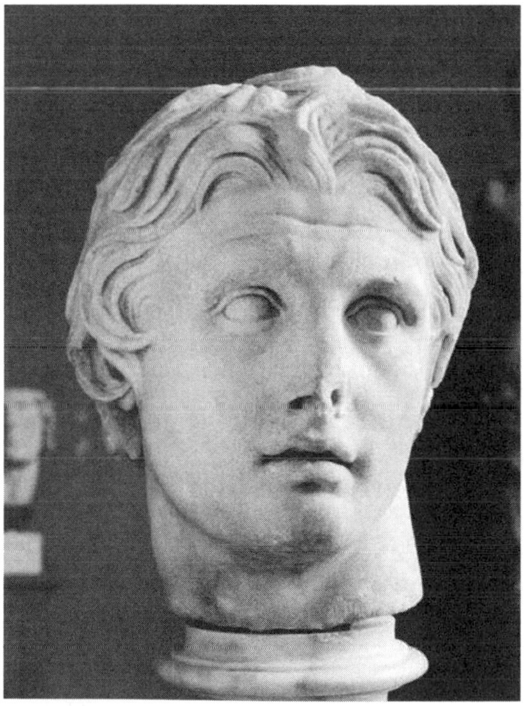

3. Pergamon, *Alexander the Great*, attributed to Lysippos, head from marble copy of lost original of *c.* 4th century BC (Istanbul, Archaeological Museum)

(ii) Victory monuments. It was after a series of battles against the neighbouring Seleucid empire and invading Gauls that Attalos I became King of Pergamon. To commemorate these victories he erected several grand monuments in the Sanctuary of Athena on the acropolis. These included over life-size bronzes, now preserved only in Roman marble copies. These probably stood on a base over 19 m long and *c.* 1.1 m high, rather than the circular podium restored by earlier scholars. This base, erected shortly after 223 BC and signed by Epigonos, was divided into several sections, each with inscriptions relating to a specific victory. Only the vanquished non-Greek foes were represented, their alien appearance captured brilliantly, as in the most important group, the Ludovisi *Gaul* group (Rome, Mus. N. Romano; see fig. 4), which represents a Gaul killing his wife and himself. This was designed to be viewed so that the true nature of the subject was only gradually revealed. Seen from his left, the Gaul appears to be glaring at an imaginary enemy, while taking a long, lunging step over his discarded shield and drawing his wife close to him. His stance, his raised sword-arm and the way he holds the sword are all characteristic of Greek depictions of warriors striking their opponents. The ancient theory of physiognomy supports this impression: the long

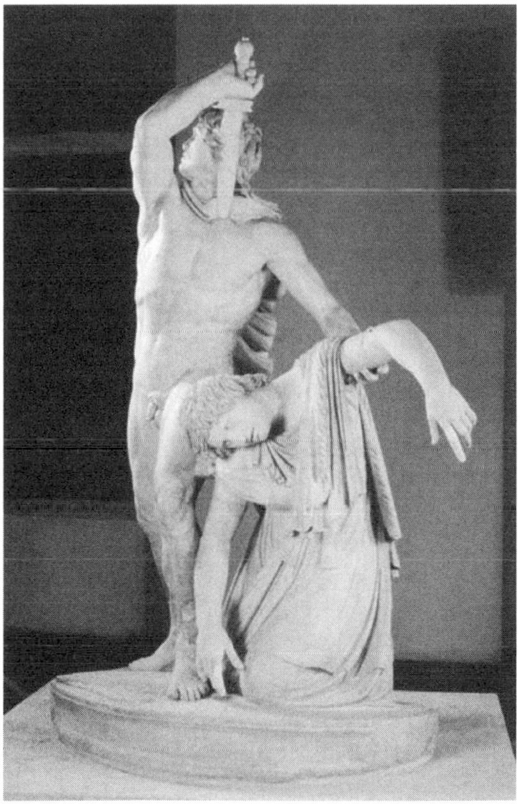

4. Pergamon, Ludovisi *Gaul* group, original bronze, *c.* 230–*c.* 220 BC; marble copy, h. 2.11 m without base (Rome, Museo Nazionale Romano)

stride indicating a daring, purposeful man of action and the erect posture suggesting bravery. A frontal view, however, gives quite a different impression: the composition opens out like a frieze of juxtaposed figures. The Gaul's face is covered, so that the vivid depiction of his wound and the sudden realization that his powerful sword-thrust is suicidal are all the more striking. Finally, from the right, the composition suggests weakness. The centre of gravity is above the female figure, and the Gaul himself seems about to topple over her. These contradictory impressions recall Classical descriptions of the character of the Gauls and their style of warfare: they apparently showed courage, strength and boldness, but also naivety and stupidity, and ultimately lack of stamina. Their lack of the admired Greek quality of moderation (*metriótes*) was regarded as typical of 'barbarians'; the idea that there was an antithesis between the cultured Greek and the uncivilized barbarian, who, as far back as the Persian wars of the 5th century BC, had submitted to Greek genius, had lost nothing of its efficacy. A Persian's head from the same monument (Rome, Mus. N. Romano, 603) reflects similar ideas, and other extant sculptures from it are the *Dying Gaul* (Rome, Mus. Capitolino; *see* SCULPTURE, fig. 14) and a head of a *Gaul* (Rome, Vatican, Mus. Chiaramonti, 1271). By implication the monument commemorates the triumph of the Attalid cultural supremacy through rationalism, intelligent courage and strength, though these are not themselves represented.

The Gaulish theme was taken up again around the mid-2nd century BC when the Attalids placed groups of fighting Gauls on the Acropolis of Athens (Pausanias: *Guide to Greece* I.xxv.2). The claim to be a second Athens is manifested even more clearly in this monument, since the Pergamene victories were linked directly with great historical and mythological models: the fighting Gauls formed part of a greater ensemble depicting battles between Greeks and Persians and Greeks and Amazons, as well as a gigantomachy. A similar monument was probably erected at Pergamon, and ten under life-size Roman marble statues may have been derived from it. They comprise five figures of Gauls (Venice, Mus. Archeol., 55–7; Naples, Mus. Archeol. N., 6015; Paris, Louvre, 324), three Persians (Rome, Vatican, Mus. Chiaramonti, 2794; Aix-en-Provence, Mus. Granet, 246; Naples, Mus. Archeol. N., 6014), a *Dying Amazon* and a *Dying Giant* (both Naples, Mus. Archeol. N., 6012–13).

(iii) The Great Altar. The first fragment of the Great Frieze of the Great Altar at Pergamon was excavated in 1871 by Carl Humann (1836–96), which led to the discovery of the biggest relief cycle known from antiquity. Large parts of this frieze, which has over life-size figures and is almost 120 m long and 2.3 m high, now constitute the principal exhibit of the Pergamonmuseum in Berlin; a few fragments are in England (Worksop Mus. and Fawley Court, Bucks.). The frieze ran all the way round the altar between its undecorated socle and its superstructure, as well as part way up the stairs. Nothing is known of the occasion on which the Great Altar was built, since the only legible words on its dedication read 'for the proven favours'. This may refer to the victories of King Eumenes II (*reg* 197–160 BC) over the Gauls and the neighbouring kingdom of Bithynia in 183 BC and implies a date in the 180s BC. The altar was almost certainly built after the last victorious Gallic War (168–165 BC). It is uncertain whether the structure was dedicated to Zeus alone, to Zeus and Athena, or to all the gods. Another possibility is that it was a HEROÖN of Telephos, the legendary founder of Pergamon.

The Great Frieze depicts a traditional theme in Greek art: the *Gigantomachy*, in which the gods suppressed a revolt by the giants, descendants of the earth mother Ge, and preserved order in the world, though only with the help of a mortal, Herakles. The combatants embodied moral principles, the gods representing stable order and reason, and the giants crude nature and wanton arrogance. The Great Frieze casts the Attalids and the Gauls in the roles of gods and giants respectively, and in this way both underlines Attalid claims to be descended from Herakles and gives their victories heroic status. The positions of the gods in the frieze largely follow genealogical principles. Because of the number of combatants required to fill the frieze, several new figures had to be introduced into the traditional scene. All are labelled with inscriptions, and some are evidently based on Classical models, especially Attic ones of the 5th and 4th centuries BC. This is particularly clear in the east frieze (see fig. 5), the first to confront the viewer, which was devoted to the Olympian gods. On the right Zeus and Athena, accompanied by Herakles and Nike, goddess of victory, are framed on one side by the chariot of Hera and on the other by the charging horses of Ares. The composition is based on the west pediment of the Parthenon (*see* ATHENS, §II, 1(ii)). In the scene, on the eastern half of the frieze, of Apollo and Artemis fighting with their mother Leto against the giants, the figure of Apollo recalls the *Apollo Belvedere* (*c.* 330 BC; Rome, Vatican, Mus. Pio-Clementino) attributed to the Attic sculptor Leochares. The adjoining section of the south frieze begins with gods belonging to the clan of Apollo. In accordance with the comprehensive nature of the *Gigantomachy*, a further family is added to the Olympian deities of the eastern frieze—the gods of day and night. The coherence of this group of gods is emphasized by various compositional devices. The mounted figures of Eos, the goddess of the dawn, and Selene, the moon goddess, flank Helios, the sun god, who stands in his chariot. Here the battle involves the giants' attempts to disrupt the harmony of time. The end of the south frieze and the relief panels adjoining it on the west side of the altar depict eastern gods: Cybele, the mother goddess and ruler of wild nature, riding on a lion, and Dionysos, the god of vegetation and fertility. As divine patron of the Attalids, Dionysos is prominently displayed at the centre of the front wall of the southern projecting

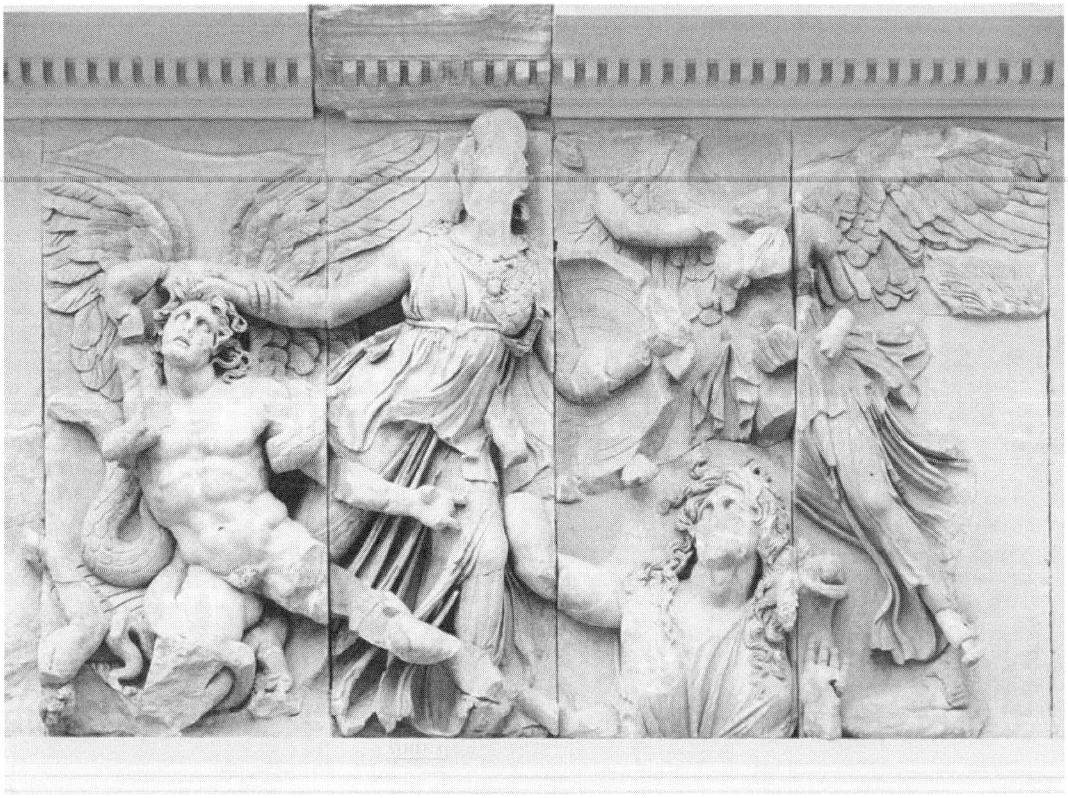

5. Pergamon, Great Altar, detail of the Great Frieze (east) showing the *Gigantomachy*, h. 2.3 m, *c.* 180–*c.* 160 BC (Berlin, Antikensammlung, Staatliche Museen zu Berlin)

bay. The composition on the front of the northern projecting bay is similar, depicting the sea deities Triton, the son of Poseidon, and his mother Amphitrite. On the section of the frieze adjoining it to the north Poseidon himself enters the fray, followed by figures who probably represent the Graiai, daughters of the sea god Phorkys. There are gaps in the adjoining relief panels, so that their interpretation is problematical. It has been suggested that the fighting female figures may be the Moirai and the Erinyes, since it would be appropriate to place them alongside Graiai as they are all goddesses of fate and revenge. Similarly, although at the end of the north frieze Aphrodite, wife of Ares, is labelled, the identities of the other gods in its left half are uncertain. They may belong to Ares' entourage.

The ingenious way in which the Great Frieze blends elements derived from Classical art with allusions to local Pergamene politics and cults to create a battle scene based on family groups among the gods implies that its composition was worked out according to a grand plan. Attempts to trace it back to a single extant literary source (Hesiod's *Theogony*) have been unconvincing. It is possible, however, that the composition was glorified in an epic by a contemporary court poet. The figures are carved in such high relief that they are almost free standing, and their proximity to each other, virtually obscuring the background, emphasizes the intensity of the conflict. The action is so completely integrated into the architectural setting that the giants appear to charge up the stairs of the Great Altar. Attention was also closely focused on the textures of costumes, of laces and ornaments on the footwear, of metalwork, feathers, scales of snakes and fish.

The Little Frieze surrounding the altar platform (h. 1.58 m; Berlin, Antikensamml.), of which fewer than half the figures are preserved, is quite different in style. Its calm sequence of scenes depicts the life of Herakles' son, Telephos. The figures are carved in varying depths and more strongly integrated into the background, while trees, rocks and architectural details define the individual settings. Some individual figures are modelled on Late Classical funerary and votive reliefs (*see* SCULPTURE, §IV, 2(iii)(c)). The stylistic differences between the two friezes are in accord with their different subject-matter: the *Gigantomachy* is a single violent event, while the Telephos frieze is a narrative.

(iv) Early copying. Besides their frequent imitations of Classical reliefs, Pergamene sculptors of the 2nd century BC were also the first to copy and adapt earlier Greek statues, thus establishing a tradition of

copying that was later to dominate Roman art. The library of Pergamon was decorated with an updated version of the *Athena Parthenos* (*see* PHEIDIAS) about a third of the size of its prototype (h. with bases 3.1 m; Berlin, Antikensamml., P. 24), clearly emphasizing the retrospective view of Classical Athens and the cultural pretensions of the Attalids. The *Athena with the Cross-band Aegis* (Berlin, Antikensamml.) is an eclectic combination of features from various statues of *c.* 450–*c.* 400 BC. These adaptations are, like the earliest copies (*Meleager*, Athens, Agora Mus., S 2035; *Athena Giustiniani*-type head, Athens, N. Archaeol. Mus., 3004; both probably from the Stoa of Attalos, *c.* 150 BC, in Athens), clearly the result of a theoretical dispute about Classical art at the Pergamene court.

J. Schrammen: *Der grosse Altar: Der obere Markt* (1906), III/i of *Altertümer von Pergamon* (Berlin, 1885–)

H. Winnefeld: *Die Friese des grossen Altars* (1910), III/ii of *Altertümer von Pergamon* (Berlin, 1885–)

F. Winter: *Die Skulpturen mit Ausnahme der Altarreliefs* (1908), VII/i and ii of *Altertümer von Pergamon* (Berlin, 1885–)

A. von Salis: *Der Altar von Pergamon* (Berlin, 1912)

W.-H. Schuchhardt: *Die Meister des grossen Frieses von Pergamon* (Berlin, 1925)

A. Schober: 'Das Gallierdenkmal Attalos' I. in Pergamon', *Mitt. Dt. Archäol. Inst.: Röm. Abt.*, li (1936), pp. 104–24

E. V. Hansen: *The Attalids of Pergamon* (New York, 1947, rev. 2/1971), pp. 299–389

H. Kähler: *Der grosse Fries von Pergamon* (Berlin, 1948)

A. Schober: *Die Kunst von Pergamon* (Vienna, 1951)

M. Bieber: *The Sculpture of the Hellenistic Age* (New York, 1955, rev. 2/1961), pp. 106–22

U. Westermark: *Das Bildnis des Philetairos von Pergamon* (Stockholm, 1960)

E. Rohde: *Pergamon: Burgberg und Altar* (Berlin, 1961, rev. Munich, 8/1982)

D. E. Haynes: 'The Worksop Relief', *Jb. Berliner Mus.*, v (1963), pp. 1–13

D. E. Haynes: 'The Arundel Marbles', *Archaeology*, xxi (1968), pp. 85–91, 206–11

E. Künzl: *Die Kelten des Epigonos von Pergamon* (Würzburg, 1971)

E. Simon: *Pergamon und Hesiod* (Mainz, 1975)

K. Stähler: 'Überlegungen zur architektonischen Gestalt des Pergamonaltares', *Studien zur Religion und Kultur Kleinasiens: Festschrift für F. K. Dörner* (Leiden, 1978), pp. 838–67

R. Wenning: 'Die Galateranatheme Attalos' I.', *Pergamenische Forschungen*, iv (1978)

B. Palma: 'Il piccolo donario pergameno', *Xenia*, i (1981), pp. 45–84

J. P. Niemeier: *Kopien und Nachahmungen im Hellenismus* (Bonn, 1985)

H.-J. Schalles: 'Untersuchungen zur Kulturpolitik der pergamenischen Herrscher im 3. Jahrhundert v. Chr.', *Istanbul. Forsch.*, xxxvi (1985)

H.-J. Schalles: *Der Pergamonaltar: Zwischen Bewertung und Verwertbarkeit* (Frankfurt am Main, 1986)

B. Andreae: 'Phyromachos-Probleme', *Mitt. Dt. Archäol. Inst.: Röm. Abt.*, iv/31 (1990) [suppl. issue]

M. Kunze: *The Pergamon Altar: Its Rediscovery, History and Reconstruction* (Berlin, 1991)

The Telephos Frieze of the Pergamon Altar (exh. cat., New York, Met., 1996)

N. T. De Grummond and B. S. Ridgway: *From Pergamon to Sperlonga: Sculpture and Context* (Berkeley, 2000)

P. Kranz: *Pergameus Deus: Archäologische und numismatische Studien zu den Darstellungen des Asklepios in Pergamon während Hellenismus und Kaiserzeit; mit einem Exkurs zur Überlieferung statuarischer Bildwerke in der Antike* (Mönnesee, 2004)

Perge. Site in Pamphylia, now southern Turkey. It was celebrated in Greek and Roman times for its worship of Artemis, in whose honour annual festivals were held. The deity was of Anatolian origin, but the city was a Greek foundation, according to legend dating back to the wave of Greek settlers led by Kalchas and Mopsos after the fall of Troy. An inscription found in the older gate of the city bears the names of these two mythical heroes. Perge spread and flourished at the foot of the acropolis on which the first settlement had been established but where only some Byzantine remains survive. No traces of the Temple of Artemis have been found, but the cult of the goddess brought about an accumulation of valuable offerings from the whole region; they were plundered by Verres in 79 BC. Practically nothing is known of the history of Perge until Alexander the Great, to whom it peacefully surrendered (333 BC), and to which period the earliest remains belong. Its Hellenistic remains show that the city was already flourishing in the 3rd and 2nd centuries BC. Most of the impressive extant ruins are of the Roman age, when Perge enjoyed a time of great prosperity. The family of the Plancii (late 1st century AD to early 2nd) played a prominent part as liberal benefactors.

Just outside the city walls the theatre and the stadium have survived in a remarkably good state of preservation. The theatre was originally a Hellenistic structure, with later Roman modifications. Its *cavea* (auditorium), which could accommodate up to 15,000 spectators, is of the Greek type, built against the hillside and exceeding a semicircle, with the *parodoi* (passages) uncovered and separating the *cavea* from the stage-building. The arcaded gallery along the top of the *cavea* is, however, a Roman feature, as is the impressive stage-building. At a later date its exterior side was converted into a nymphaeum. The stadium (2nd century AD; l. 234 m) is almost as large and as well preserved as the stadium of Aphrodisias, with a seating capacity scarcely less than that of the theatre. Barrel-vaulted chambers support the seats and provide access. One end of the stadium is rounded, the other open, in the traditional style.

Most of the city walls are Hellenistic, and large sections are well preserved. They include perhaps the most interesting structure at Perge, the 3rd-century BC gate at the southern end of the city, within the later walls and gate of the 4th century AD. It consists of a horseshoe-shaped court flanked by two attractive round towers, the main parts of which are still standing. The court was transformed and enriched under Hadrian (*reg* AD 117–38) by Plancia Magna, daughter of the Proconsul of Bithynia and a prominent priestess of Artemis. The ruins of the city within the walls are mainly of the 2nd century AD. Two great colonnaded streets cross at right angles with several other colonnaded streets in-between; many of their columns are still standing (see fig.). Buildings include a colonnaded stoa surrounding the 4th-century AD agora with a circular building in the centre, perhaps a temple to Tyche; a palaestra dedicated to Emperor Claudius (*reg* AD 41–54); and a nymphaeum built at the time of Hadrian. There are also considerable ruins of Roman baths and, between the older and later gate on the west side, a monumental propylon and another nymphaeum, dedicated to Artemis Pergaia and Emperor Septimius Severus (*reg* AD 193–211).

K. Lanckoroński, G. Niemann and E. Petersen: *Städte Pamphyliens und Pisidiens*, i (Vienna, 1890), pp. 33–63
A. M. Mansel: *Excavations at Perge* (Ankara, 1949)
D. Magie: *Roman Rule in Asia Minor*, 2 vols (Princeton, 1950)
A. M. Mansel: 'Perge', *Türk Arkeol. Derg.*, xviii (1967), pp. 101–6
G. E. Bean: *Turkey's Southern Shore* (London, 1968, 2/1979), pp. 25–38
E. Akurgal: *Ancient Civilizations and Ruins of Turkey* (Istanbul, 1970)
J. Inan: 'Neue Porträtstatuen aus Perge', *Mansel'e Armağan (Mélanges Mansel)*, ii–iii (Ankara, 1974), pp. 643–61, pls 195–218
A. M. Mansel: 'Die Nympheen von Perge', *Istanbul. Mitt.*, xxv (1975), pp. 367ff
H. J. Colin: *Die Münzen von Perge in Pamphylien aus hellenistischer Zeit* (Cologne, 1996)
M. Heinzelmann: 'Städtekonkurrenz und kommunaler Bürgersinn: Die Säulenstrasse von Perge als Beispiel monumentaler Stadtgestaltung durch kollektiven Euergetismus', *Archäol. Anz.*, i (2003), pp. 197–220
W. Martini: 'Die Akropolis von Perge in Pamphylien', *Archäol. Anz.*, ii (2003), pp. 135–6

Peribolus [peribolos]. Wall enclosing a sacred area, such as a temple or church grounds.

Pericles [Perikles] (*b c.* 495 BC; *d* Athens, 429 BC). Athenian statesman. He was the son of Xanthippos and Agariste, niece of Kimon, and was the leading political figure of his generation. Though an aristocrat by birth, he appears to have courted the people in the Assembly. He is credited with persuading the Athenians to move the Treasury of the Delian League to Athens and convincing the people that this money should be used for lavish rebuilding of the temples on the Acropolis destroyed by the Persians. It was apparently said that he advocated 'tarting up the city with thousand-talent temples'

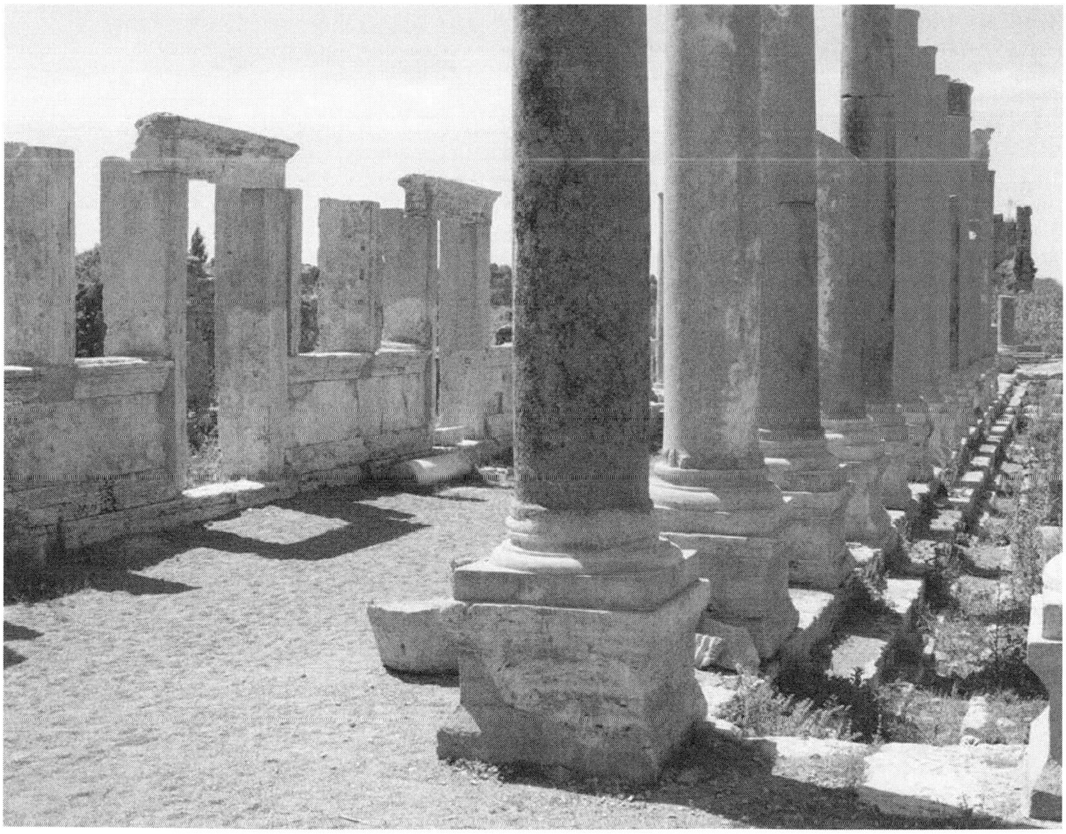

Perge, colonnaded street, 2nd century AD

(Plutarch: *Pericles* xii); his friend PHEIDIAS, who had worked on the cult statue of *Athena* for the most celebrated and ambitious of these, the Parthenon, was subsequently exiled. Pericles' lasting attachment to the courtesan Aspasia also attracted considerable criticism. He was reputed to have had an onion shaped head and was thus usually shown wearing a helmet, as in a Roman bust (London, BM), possibly a copy of a portrait statue by KRESILAS.

M. Revermann: 'Cratinus' Dionysalexandros and the Head of Pericles', *J. Hell. Stud.*, cxvii (1997), pp. 197–200
H. Aird: *Pericles: The Rise and Fall of Athenian Democracy* (New York, 2004)
J. M. Hurwit and A. D. Newton: *The Acropolis in the Age of Pericles* (Cambridge and New York, 2004)
L. J. Samons: *The Cambridge Companion to the Age of Pericles* (Cambridge and New York, 2006)

Peripteral. Term applied to a building surrounded by a single row of columns.

Peristyle [pteron]. Architectural term for a series of columns built either externally (for which 'pteron' is sometimes used) around a temple or internally around a courtyard. Early temples or other sacred buildings on the Greek mainland and islands appear not to have had external peristyles, for example the first Temple of Hera on Samos (*c.* 800 BC) or the Oikos of the Naxians on Delos (*c.* 650 BC). The original presence of a peristyle, however, is often difficult to ascertain before the construction of the earliest monumental stone temples in the 7th century BC.

From the late 7th century BC to the early 6th, some Greek temples seem to have had peristyles; this can be seen in the Temple of Hera at Olympia (*c.* 590 BC) and the second Temple of Hera on Samos (*c.* 650 BC), where a ring of columns was added later to the existing temple. This type of temple plan, termed peripteral, became the norm, and fine examples from the Classical period include the Temple of Apollo at Bassai (*c.* 430–400 BC; *see* BASSAI, fig. 1) and the Parthenon at Athens (447–432 BC; *see* ATHENS, fig. 6). In Asia Minor, Greek temples were often built with two rows of surrounding columns (dipteral), as in the Hellenistic Temple of Apollo at Didyma (3rd century BC onwards). The Temple of Artemis at Ephesos (*c.* 560–460 BC) and the later temples of Hera on Samos were also dipteral.

The secondary use for the term peristyle is in describing courtyards with columns around them. In the Hellenistic period such colonnaded courtyards were much developed in secular architecture. The gymnasium at Olympia (3rd century BC), for example, included a peristyle court, as did many Hellenistic houses on Delos. At the same period it became common to treat agoras, or market-places, as peristyle courts surrounded by colonnaded stoas. At this time the use of individual stoas much declined in favour of courtyards with linked colonnades forming a peristyle around them, as at Miletos. This form of peristyle court, dominated by a temple at its far end, became the normal form of SANCTUARY in the Hellenistic and Roman periods, and many of the Imperial Fora in Rome also followed this pattern. In such sanctuaries there was normally an axial approach to the temple from a monumental entrance in the centre of the opposite side of the courtyard. From the Hellenistic period onwards architects appear to have striven for a hierarchy of related buildings, culminating in the temple itself.

D. S. Robertson: *A Handbook of Greek and Roman Architecture* (Cambridge, 1929, rev. 2/1943); repr. as *Greek and Roman Architecture* (London, 1969)
W. B. Dinsmoor: *The Architecture of Ancient Greece* (London, 1950)
A. W. Lawrence: *Greek Architecture*, Pelican Hist. A. (Harmondsworth, 1962, rev. with additions by R. A. Tomlinson 4/1983)
J. J. Coulton: *The Architectural Development of the Greek Stoa* (Oxford, 1976), pp. 168–83
S. P. Ellis: 'The End of the Roman House', *Amer. J. Archaeol.*, xcii (Oct 1988), pp. 565–76
L. Frey: 'Medietes et approximations chez Vitruve', *Rev. Archéol.*, ii (1990), pp. 285–330
R. Tolle-Kastenbein: 'Zur Genesis und Entwicklung des Dipteros', *Jb. Dt. Archäol. Inst.*, cix (1994), pp. 41–76
J.-A. Dickmann: 'The Peristyle and the Transformation of Domestic Space in Hellenistic Pompeii', *Domestic Space in the Roman World: Pompeii and beyond*, eds R. Laurence and A. Wallace-Hadrill (Portsmouth, RI, 1997), pp. 121–36

Per-Medjed. *See* OXYRHYNCHUS.

Petra [Semit. Reqem; Heb. Sela'; Arab. Ḥiṣn Sal']. Site in the southern desert of Jordan, 262 km south of Amman and 133 km north of the Gulf of Aqaba, near the modern village of Wadi Musa. It is famous for its rock-cut monuments. The site, which may be that of the biblical Rock of Edom, was strategically located adjacent to the 'King's Highway', the major north–south communication line between Aqaba and Amman, and protected on both east and west by parallel massifs of sandstone; it was supplied with perennial springs. As the capital of the ancient kingdom of Nabatea from *c.* 312 BC to AD 106, it was cited by Strabo, Pliny and other Classical writers under its Greek name Petra (Gr.: 'rock'). In AD 106 it was incorporated into the Roman province of Arabia by the emperor Trajan (*reg* AD 98–117). It was destroyed by earthquake in AD 363; during the Byzantine period it was occupied by anchorites. In the 11th–12th centuries the Crusaders knew it as the Valley of Moses, following established Bedouin folklore; with the fall of Jerusalem in 1187, it fell into obscurity. It was discovered by the Swiss explorer Jean-Louis Burckhardt in 1812. The earliest survey and classification of the monuments was carried out in 1897–8 by Rudolph E. Brünnow and Alfred von Domaszewski; they numbered, described and photographed over 800 funerary, hydraulic, cultic and other structures found on and around the site, of which 523 were identified as funerary, including façade-tombs. Actual excavation of the site, by George Horsfield, began in 1929.

Although Petra may have been occupied from Palaeolithic times, documentary and material evidence of substantive occupation exists only from the Iron Age (*c.* 1200 BC). At some time in the 4th century BC the site was occupied by the Nabataeans, nomad Arabs from northern Arabia. Their success as traders in frankincense, myrrh and other luxury items ensured prosperity and an influx of diverse trade items from other cultures. This factor, added to their own remarkable ingenuity and natural talent, contributed to an eclectic and wide-ranging artistic and architectural achievement in which art forms from all over the Hellenized world were combined with native oriental elements. Under the Nabataeans there was a period of intense urban development, during which Petra acquired all the accoutrements of a civilized city of the Greco-Roman period. Tomb façades became monumental, public buildings proliferated, the main street was paved and other facilities were established. Many of the most impressive public buildings can be dated to one of Nabataea's most energetic rulers, Aretas IV (*reg* 9 BC–AD 40), including the main theatre, the Temple of Dushara, now known as the Qasr Bint Fir'awn (Arab.: Palace of the Pharaoh's Daughter), the Temple of Allat (the Temple of the Winged Lions) and possibly the Khaznat al-Fir'awn (the Treasury of the Pharaoh). Rivalry with the adjacent kingdom of the Jews, governed by Herod the Great (*reg* 37–4 BC), may have contributed to this rapid urban embellishment. Roman occupation from AD 106 appears to have had little impact on the architecture of Petra, except in the remodelling of the main theatre.

1. Public architecture. 2. Domestic and funerary architecture.

1. PUBLIC ARCHITECTURE. Once the north and south wall lines had been built to enclose the city, a hydraulic system was constructed to augment the city's springs. This was one of the major architectural achievements of Petra and was the finest of the systems constructed by the Nabataeans. Rock-cut cisterns provided large storage capacity, their plastered walls still retaining water to this day. The installations, however, were inadequate for a growing population and a vast system of ceramic pipe-lines was installed to bring water from springs outside the city. Using gravity feed, the water was carried into the city along the walls of the narrow defile (now called al Siq) that cuts through the eastern cliff and, by overhead arches, into storage cisterns on the top of the eastern peak. A barrage dam at the entrance to the defile diverted the winter torrents from the entrance through a tunnel cut through the mountain, affording both protection for the entrance and a controlled flow of additional water inside the city. Revetted walls were erected along the natural torrent bed to guide the flow, with bridges built across it to connect both sides of the city.

The main theatre (1st century BC), excavated in 1961–2, was cut into the face of a peak just inside the city, a conspicuous site along the main road. A few earlier tombs cut into the same cliff face had to be sacrificed to make room for the *cavea* (auditorium), which seated *c.* 4000 people. The plan followed that generally seen throughout the Greco-Roman world, with the *scaenae frons* (stage building) constructed of ashlar and faced with attachments of white-mottled breccia. Some modifications were made to the height of the entrance passages (after AD 106), and that on the left was never completed. Other features include huge stone-carved chairs for dignitaries, an over life-size marble statue of *Herakles* and a life-size statue of *Aphrodite* (both *c.* 1st century AD; Petra Mus.).

The Temple of Dushara, the chief male deity of the Nabataeans, occupies a prominent location in the city centre but has not yet been fully excavated; among the findings is a stone bust of Zeus-Sarapis. It is surrounded by a temenos and was entered via a broad stairway on the north side. It measures *c.* 27 sq. m and was originally tetrastyle *in antis* at the front. It was constructed in well-cut ashlar, with wooden beams set into the outer walls, perhaps as a cushioning device against earthquakes. It had a Doric frieze of grooved triglyphs and carved metopes. From the pilaster capitals of the rear angles, the order appears to have been Corinthian, with floral spirals taking the place of the usual helices. What appears to be a concealed stairway at the rear indicates some use of an upper balcony or floor, perhaps for cultic demonstrations. The cella was probably divided. Traces of intricate stucco decoration may still be seen on the external face of the rear wall, depicting a tholos or circular shrine framed by columns supporting broken pediments, a scheme found in Pompeian wall paintings of the Second Style (*c.* 90–*c.* 15 BC).

Across the torrent bed, on the northern slope of the city centre, stands the temple dedicated to Allat, the chief female deity of the Nabataeans. On the basis of a fragment of a wall inscription, the completion of the temple has been set to AD 278; remodelling has been attributed to Malichos II (*reg* AD 40–70/71). It measures some 17×17 m, the cella being divided into bays by a row of columns on each side, with the altar platform placed towards the rear and elevated. A wide front entrance apparently necessitated folding doors and may have been approached by a stairway on one side. Huge prostyle columns formed the porch in front of the main doorway. The temple complex also included workrooms and living quarters for the priests. The building was linked across the torrent bed to the main street of the city by a bridge connected to a colonnaded stairway. This building was less carefully constructed than the Temple of Dushara, and the deficiencies were remedied by plastering. Traces of holes on the front side suggest the use of facing attachments, as in the theatre. The cella and altar platform were paved with local marble. The walls were first covered with a thick layer of coarse plaster keyed to the ashlar by large iron nails, and then finished with a coat of fine plaster keyed by small copper tacks. Although the Nabataeans excelled in stone-carving, the mouldings and architectural elements were almost entirely worked in plaster. Columns were constructed from drums, with final dimensions achieved by plastering. A marble torus was then applied to each finished column. In one stage of the temple's construction, the column plaster was fluted, but in the later remodelling a smooth treatment was used, with applied floral decoration.

The wall columns were engaged and cut from the ashlar building blocks. Around the altar platform the same method was used up to the height of the top of the platform, above which true drum-built columns were erected. The capitals on the wall and bay columns were of a Nabataeanized Corinthian order, with lavish use of the vine motif and augmented by the insertion of small painted moulded plaster flowers. The columns of the altar platform had capitals on which the volutes of the Corinthian order were replaced by couchant winged felines. These show great individuality, even on the same capital, suggesting that different artisans may have worked on separate parts of the same capital. Niches were left in the walls between the engaged columns, and some were decorated, initially with mystery-cult scenes, later replaced by plain-coloured panels. Mouldings and other architectural elements were garishly painted in Pompeian red, black, white, yellow, blue, green and other colours, as well as gilded in certain cases.

2. Domestic and funerary architecture. Few private houses have been excavated at Petra. A series of successive residential structures to the east of the Temple of Allat and the residential quarters of the temple complex itself exhibit plans that appear to follow those still seen in the Near East today: a series of small rooms with paved or clay floors, an open court for cooking, and storage facilities (cellar-like pits). Roofs were probably flat, as indicated by a roof roller recovered in the temple complex. Specialized use of rooms is also evident. Interior walls were plastered, cupboards were built in, and doors (with locks) were used throughout. A mosaic floor was found in a house on the southern slope of the city centre, and there is some evidence of mosaic and tessellated floors in the temple residences. Early excavations also revealed the use of natural caves as dwellings, perhaps reflecting the class stratification of the population.

It is the funerary architecture of Petra that is now most apparent at the site. Tomb façades are carved everywhere in the sandstone cliffs, only one of which (the Turkumaniyya tomb) bears any inscription, and that is undated. This phenomenon is quite unlike that found at Mada'in salih, where most tomb façades are inscribed, supplying dates and naming owners, professions and often even the individual artisans.

The façade-tombs were classified by Brünnow and von Domaszewski into ten distinct stylistic types, and a relative chronological development postulated. Although their stylistic ordering is disputed, it remains the most useful for descriptive discussion.

Beginning with the simplest façades, the 'pylon' type, with variations in crow-step organization, they proceeded to partially and fully 'free-standing' 'pylon' façades, then to a 'step' form, with a series of subtype variations in attic and cavetto mouldings. The next development they identified was a further stage of the 'step' form, resulting from Hellenistic influence, the 'proto-Hegr' type, which appeared to have affinities with the examples at Mada'in Salih and showed more elaboration in the architraves. The true 'Hegr' type followed, with much more elaboration of attic, architrave, gable decoration, pilasters and other features. They brought the series to a conclusion with the 'Roman' or 'Roman temple' type, with façades resembling temple entrances. These are perhaps the most impressive of Petra's monuments, outstanding examples being the Khaznat al-Fir'awn, al-Dayr (the Monastery), the Urn Tomb and the Palace Tomb.

The Khaznat (see fig.) was carved into the face of the cliff above al-Siq. Its façade appears to be an example of the linear perspective found in Pompeian wall paintings: its lower order may represent the ground-level of a temple prototype, the stage above representing the side wings of the building, and the circular turret-like structure of the upper order representing a circular shrine between the two wings. The monument was probably a royal tomb, perhaps that of Aretas IV, as indicated both by its location and by its impressive size. The façade is 24.90 m wide, plus an additional 4.70 m in side cutting, and rises to a height of 38.77 m to the top of the urn that crowns its circular tholos or shrine in the centre of the upper order. Six portico columns of the local Nabataeanized Corinthian type (a simplified, blocked out version of the Corinthian capital) stood before the entrance, decorated ornately with floral motifs. The

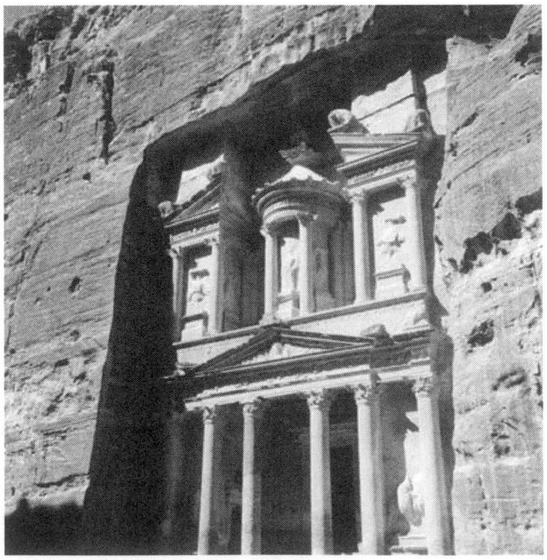

Petra, Khaznat al-Fir'awn (Treasury of the Pharaoh), 1st century AD

pediment also shows floral decoration, above which two broken pediments are placed, along with the circular shrine. Niches in the lower order contain badly eroded half-round sculpted figures. Approached by a wide flight of steps, a portico opens into the main tomb chamber, with two ornate doorways opening into smaller side chambers. The tomb chamber itself is undecorated, except for the characteristic diagonal dressing found throughout Nabataea, and contains two burial loculi to the sides, with a third, slightly elevated, on the wall facing the entry.

Al-Dayr is on the top of a peak *c.* 1.5 km northwest of the city. Its pilastered façade, cut into the cliff face, is the largest to have been executed at Petra (*c.* 43×30.5 m). It has no entrance portico, but otherwise is similar in design to the Khaznat. The lower order is divided into three zones, each set off by engaged columns as if provision was being made either for relief-carvings or for free-standing statues. The upper order similarly has three registers separated by open spaces, the central one forming a tholos and capped by a free-standing urn. The side registers have broken pediments, with small acroteria. This monument, which was never completed, was probably a royal tomb dating from the final period of Petra's independent political life (late 1st century AD–early 2nd). Still later, minor interior changes were made, and the tomb chamber was apparently used as a Christian place of worship.

Along the western face of the mountain ridge that forms Petra's eastern boundary a series of tomb façades was cut, known as the Royal Tomb group, because of their location overlooking the city and huge size. Most impressive is the Urn Tomb, named after the small urn above the pediment series, its façade cut back into the cliff face, leaving a broad front esplanade bordered on each side by a rock-cut colonnaded portico, reached by a series of stairways carried on arches rising from the valley below. Apart from the front portico, the façade of this tomb is unimpressive. It displays frontal engaged columns, three high 'windows', with a triple cornice with squat capped pilasters in the highest, and unadorned frieze and attic. The remains of a red-painted Byzantine inscription on the rear wall of the tomb chamber indicate later use of this tomb by Early Christian inhabitants of Petra.

Also common at Petra are a number of *triclinia*, 'high places' and other funerary or cultic installations carved into the cliffs. The *triclinium* of the Roman Soldier Tomb provides the only example of a carved interior and is decorated on all four walls with fluted engaged pillars separated by rectangular niches.

R. E. Brünnow and A. von Domaszewski: *Die Provincia Arabia*, 3 vols (Strasburg, 1901–9)

J. Cantineau: *Le Nabatéen* (Paris, 1930, 2/1932)

C. M. Bennett: 'The Nabataeans in Petra', *Archaeology*, xv (1962), pp. 233–43

P. C. Hammond: *The Nabataeans: Their History, Culture and Archaeology* (Göteborg, 1973), pp. 43–57

A. Hadidi: 'Nabatäische Architektur in Petra', *Bonn. Jb. Rhein. Landesmus. Bonn & Ver. Altertfreund. Rheinlande*, clxxx (1980), pp. 231–6

J. McKenzie: *The Architecture of Petra* (Oxford and Oakville, CT, 1990/*R* 2005)

T. R. Paradise: *Analysis of Weathering-constrained Erosion of Sandstone in the Roman Theater of Petra, Jordan* (diss. Tempe, AZ State U., 1993)

P. C. Hammond: *The Temple of the Winged Lions, Petra, Jordan, 1973–1990* (Fountain Hills, AZ, 1996)

H. G. Gebel with Z. A.-K. Kafafi and G. O. Rollefson: *The Prehistory of Jordan: Vol 2. Perspectives from 1997* (Berlin, 1997)

D. Tarrier: *Art and History, Petra* (Florence, 2000)

L.-A. Bedal: *The Petra Pool-complex: A Hellenistic Paradeisos in the Nabataean Capital: Results from the Petra 'Lower Market' Survey and Excavations, 1998* (Piscataway, NJ, 2003)

U. Bellwald and I. Ruben: *The Petra Siq: Nabataean Hydrology Uncovered* (Amman, 2003)

E. Netzer: *Nabatäische Architektur* (Munich, 2003)

Petra Rediscovered: The Lost City of the Nabataeans (exh. cat. by G. Markoe; Cincinnati, OH, A. Mus., 2003)

F. Zayadine, F. Larché and J. Dentzer-Feydy: *Le Qasr al-Bint de Pétra: L'Architecture, le décor, la chronologie et les dieux* (Paris, 2003)

L. El-Khouri and others: 'A New Nabataean Inscription from Wadi Mataha, Petra', *Palestine Explor. Q.*, cxxxvii/2 (Oct 2005), pp. 169–74

S. M. Rababeh: *How Petra was Built: An Analysis of the Construction Techniques of the Nabataean Freestanding Buildings and Rock-cut Monuments in Petra, Jordan* (Oxford, 2005)

Phaistos [Festos]. Site on Crete of a Minoan palace that flourished *c.* 1900–2nd century BC. Phaistos is situated on the southern side of central Crete, about 7 km from the coast and at the western end of the large, fertile Mesara Plain. The palace stands on the top of a hill that forms the eastern end of a low ridge and commands wonderful views. The position cannot have been chosen for defensibility as the land rises to the west. The site was first recognized by the English naval officer Captain Spratt on his travels round Crete in 1851–3, and in 1884 was visited by the Italian archaeologist F. Halbherr. Cretan independence in 1898 created a suitable background for excavations, which were begun in a systematic way in 1900 by an Italian mission under the direction of Halbherr and L. Pernier. The later or Second Palace had been substantially revealed by 1909, although supplementary excavations continued. In 1950 a major series of excavations was begun by Doro Levi, which revealed a remarkably well-preserved and interesting section of the First Palace, as well as town buildings of the Minoan, Geometric and Hellenistic periods. Major finds from the excavations are housed in the Archaeological Museum at Herakleion.

1. First Palace. 2. Second Palace.

1. First Palace. Traces of Neolithic occupation occur in many places on the hill, while Early Minoan (*c.* 3500/3000–*c.* 2050 BC) house remains have also come to light around and beneath the palace. The First Palace itself was built about the time of those

at Knossos and Mallia in Middle Minoan (MM) IB (*c.* 1900–*c.* 1800 BC; see fig. 1). Traces of Proto-Palatial (*c.* 1900–*c.* 1625 BC) walls and floors were recognized by the excavators in many parts of the later palace, including the central court, which presumably had a Proto-Palatial predecessor. Phaistos is, though, unique in the preservation of extensive Proto-Palatial remains that were not built over in later periods. This is due to the fact that the west façade of the later palace was not built directly above that of the First Palace, but was moved nearly 8 m to the east. The original west façade of the First Palace can thus clearly be seen (1b), with the remains of a north and south wing behind it.

The south wing, excavated by Levi, was the better preserved of the two. It had an orthostat façade with salients and re-entrants, looking on to a paved west court. Inside, Levi revealed a remarkable series of rooms of mixed rubble, stone and mud-brick construction and superimposed to a great height. He recognized four successive Proto-Palatial building periods—although others have thought that two of these should be conflated—and that the remains preserve the upper and lower storeys of the same period. If so, the ceilings of the lower rooms were very low, and some of the rooms themselves must have been rather dark. In fact the ground-floor rooms of both the north and south wings were probably used for storage: magazines with pithoi (large pottery jars) were found in both, as was pottery apparently stored by type.

While the slightly later north wing, excavated by Pernier, was by no means as well preserved as the south, it too had a fine orthostat façade; the early palace at Phaistos was clearly a building of some refinement. The surviving remains do not include state rooms or obviously important quarters, but it is nonetheless clear that the architecture included the use of porticos, light wells and multistorey construction, and refinements included the use of fine alabaster slabs for floors and dados as well as painted plaster on benches and walls.

While the precise building phases of the First Palace remain somewhat controversial, it seems that in MM II (*c.* 1800–*c.* 1675 BC) it was destroyed at least once by earthquake and later by fire. Attempts to strengthen the constructions in the south wing perhaps reflect a history of difficulties encountered by the builders on this steeply sloping part of the site, leading to the eventual decision to reposition the west façade of the later palace further to the east.

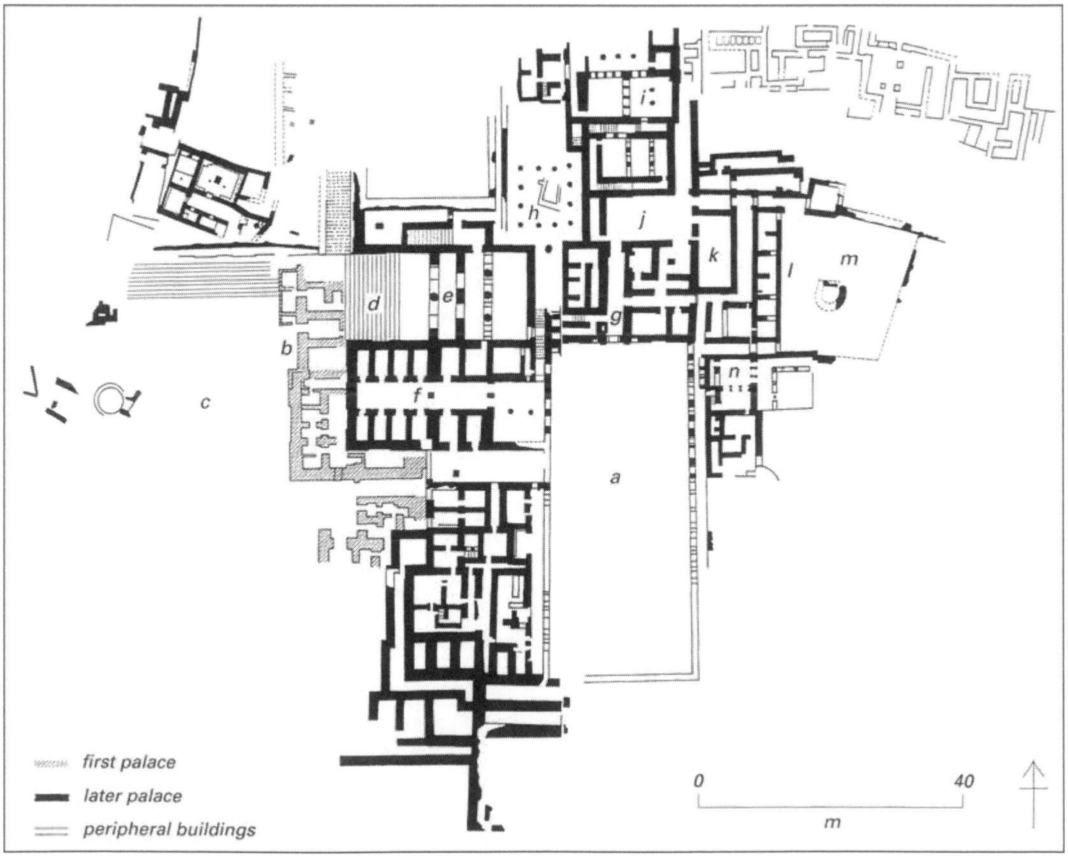

1. Phaistos, plan of the Minoan palace, *c.* 1900–*c.* 1450 BC: (a) central court; (b) west façade (First Palace); (c) west court; (d) staircase; (e) propylon; (f) west wing (Second Palace); (g) corridor; (h) peristyle hall; (i) royal apartments; (j) north court; (k) pen or garden; (l) workshops; (m) east court; (n) east wing suite

2. Second Palace. This is widely held to be one of the most attractive buildings to have survived from the Minoan world. Dating to Late Minoan (LM) IA (*c.* 1600–*c.* 1480 BC), it was built mainly in grey limestone and incorporated spacious and airy rooms, halls, stairways and courtyards. Again the details include such features as the use of thin sheets of alabaster to face the inner walls of the most important rooms, as well as the extensive use of painted plaster. The excavators restricted themselves only to the most basic and restrained restorations, which contrast with the more obtrusive (though perhaps also more necessary) restorations at Knossos to give an air of understated elegance. Above all, the beauties of the position of the palace seem to have been fully appreciated and exploited by the Minoan builders.

The palace is smaller than that of Knossos, covering an area of about 8000 sq. m, but shares the same basic layout as all the known Minoan palaces, with rooms and areas built around a rectangular central court, oriented in a north–south direction. The west court (1c), also a typical feature of Minoan palaces, has steps that could have been used for seating if ceremonies or performances were staged there. From this courtyard an imposing staircase (1d) leads to the grand propylon or entrance (1e), which has a column flanked by pilasters, a wall with two doorways, and a light well beyond. It is typical of Minoan palatial architecture that the grandeur of this entrance way peters out into a winding and irregular approach to the central court and the main rooms of the palace. Such surprises were obviously much to Minoan taste and may also have been intended to make the palaces more secure.

South of the propylon, the west wing of the Second Palace (1f) had extensive magazines housing the pithoi that were used by the Minoans to store large quantities of agricultural produce. A broad east–west corridor provides the most direct access to the central court on this western side, and separates the magazines from a cluster of small rooms. At least some of these seem to have been shrines: a room with piers belongs to the type sometimes described as a pillar crypt, while a sunken room reached by stairs is a typical lustral basin.

The central court at Phaistos was flanked on each long side by a colonnade of alternating columns and piers. The south-east corner of both court and palace are not preserved, having fallen down the hill. At the north end of the central court, though, is the impressive façade of the northern quarter of the palace: an unusually monumental and symmetrical piece of Minoan architecture. The central feature of this façade is the entrance to a large corridor (1g) leading northwards, flanked by half columns and niches, perhaps for sentries. The columns, originally of wood on stone bases, may have had carved decoration, while the niches were plastered and painted with a lozenge pattern.

The northern quarter of the palace contains some of the most impressive areas. A large peristyle hall in the north-west corner (1h) perhaps originally had a central open garden, although remains of a Pre-Palatial house are now visible. North and east of this, extending to the very northern edge of the palace, lie a series of rooms (1i) that may have been apartments belonging to the ruler of Phaistos and his family. These rooms, with their formal layout, careful arrangements of multiple doors and light wells, and extensive use of gypsum and painted plaster, are clearly important and would have provided a suitable setting for the private lives of the royal family, and perhaps also for some of their smaller-scale official and ceremonial activities.

South of the royal apartments lies the small north court (1j), connected with the central court of the palace by the north–south passageway mentioned above. The existence of a drain in the passageway may indicate that it was originally open to the sky. Small rooms on each side perhaps acted as service areas for large state or banqueting rooms above them at first-floor level.

A large enclosed space in the north-east area of the palace has been interpreted as a pen for holding animals for slaughter for the palace kitchens, or it may simply have been a garden (1k). A corridor separates this from a series of small rooms to the east that seem to have been workshops of various kinds (1l). East of these lies the east court of the palace (1m), in which are remains of a semicircular structure, perhaps a furnace used in metalworking.

Directly to the east of the central court lie the remains of a further formal suite of rooms (1n) that have also been interpreted as royal apartments, possibly for a junior member of the ruling family as they are on a smaller scale. The suite has a main hall reached from an anteroom through double doors, a bathroom or lustral basin in which fine pottery was found (LM I, *c.* 1600–*c.* 1425 BC) and a courtyard with rows of columns on two sides that looks out over the Mesara Plain. Bedrooms may have been at first-floor level. The Second Palace was destroyed in LM IB (*c.* 1450 BC).

Parts of the Minoan town around the palace have also been explored, and remains of houses of both the Proto-Palatial and Neo-Palatial periods can be seen on the slopes and at the foot of the hill. A row of buildings lies directly to the north-east of the palace and seems almost to form a continuation of it. These may partly have been occupied by dependants of the palace. In the one nearest to the palace itself was found the famous Phaistos Disc (Herakleion, Archaeological Museum): a clay disc impressed on each side with symbols in a spiral arrangement, the significance of which is unknown (see fig. 2).

The remains of post-Minoan Phaistos are predominantly Hellenistic houses, several of which were removed during the excavation of the Minoan palace. The town was destroyed by neighbouring Gortyn in the 2nd century BC.

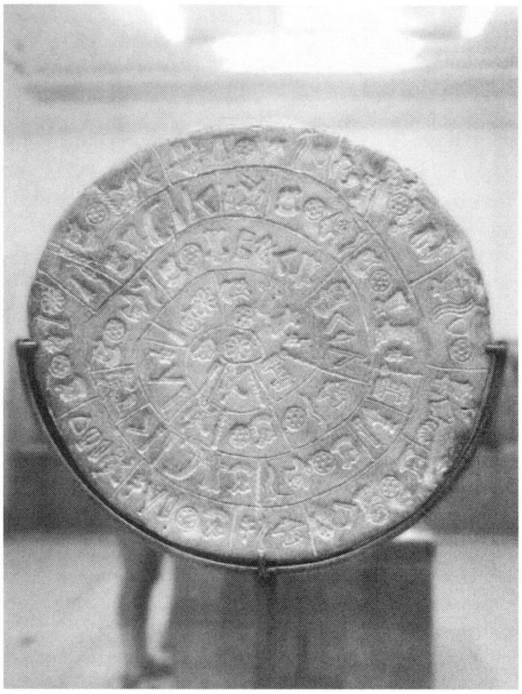

2. Phaistos Disc, clay, diam. 160 mm, *c.* 1650 BC (Herakleion, Archaeological Museum)

L. Pernier and L. Banti: *Il palazzo minoico di Festos*, 2 vols (Rome, 1935–51)

J. W. Graham: *The Palaces of Crete* (Princeton, 1962, rev. 2/1987)

D. Levi: *The Recent Excavations at Phaistos*, Stud. Medit. Archaeol., xi (Lund, 1964)

G. Cadogan: *Palaces on Minoan Crete* (London, 1976)

D. Levi: *Festòs e la civiltà minoica*, 4 vols (Rome, 1976)

D. Hadzi-Vallianou: *Phaistos* (Congleton, 1989/*R* 1993)

P. Warren and V. Hankey: *Aegean Bronze Age Chronology* (Bristol, 1989)

V. La Rosa: 'Phaistos', *The Aerial Atlas of Ancient Crete*, ed. J. W. Myers, E. E. Myers and G. Cadogan (Berkeley and Oxford, 1992), pp. 230–41

V. La Rosa and N. Cucuzza: *L'Insediamento di Seli di Kamilari nel territorio di Festòs* (Padua, 2001)

P. Militello and O. Palio: *Gli affreschi minoici di Festòs* (Padua, 2001)

L. V. Watrous and others: *The Plain of Phaistos: Cycles of Social Complexity in the Mesara Region of Crete*(Los Angeles, 2004)

Pheidias (*c.* 490–430 BC). Greek sculptor. He was the son of Charmides and pupil of Hegias; he became the foremost figure in an Attic school of artists that included Agorakritos, Alkamenes, Kolotes, Theokosmos, Panainos and Mys, and exercised a profound influence on contemporary and later Greek art. He acted as Athenian state artist under Kimon (476–463 BC) and Pericles (462–429 BC), but he also received commissions from allied states such as Plataia, and eventually from the great pan-Hellenic sanctuary of Olympia and nearby Elis. None of his original works survives, but some can be reconstructed from descriptions in ancient literary sources and from later copies. Pheidias has always been regarded as the Classical artist *par excellence.*

1. Early Classical phase, 470–446 BC. 2. High Classical phase, 446–430 BC. 3. Technique and style.

1. EARLY CLASSICAL PHASE, 470–446 BC. In his early career Pheidias seems to have favoured bronze. His earliest datable commission was a group of Athenian heroes with Athena, Apollo and Miltiades, the victor of the Battle of Marathon (490 BC), erected at Delphi as an Athenian thank-offering for victory against the Persians. The inclusion of Miltiades suggests a date during the administration of his son, Kimon. These statues are lost, though some scholars have suggested that the RIACE BRONZES come from the group. Another bronze statue by Pheidias erected from the spoils of Marathon was the colossal *Athena Promachos* on the Athenian Acropolis. Part of its marble base survives between the Propylaia and the Erechtheion, and its shield was decorated by Mys with a *Battle between Lapiths and Centaurs*, based on a drawing by Parrhasios. Roman coins with views of Athens show the statue dominating the Acropolis rock.

Pheidias was also responsible for the bronze *Athena Lemnia*, dedicated on the Acropolis between 451 and 446 BC by Athenian settlers sent out to the island of Lemnos. Ancient authors recorded that the statue was bareheaded and had a fine nose and delicate cheeks. Although the original is untraced, the theory that a Roman marble torso and head (Dresden, Skulpsamml.) represents copies of it seems plausible. A finer version of the head (the Palagi *Head*; Bologna, Mus. Civ. Archeol.) also exists. Furtwängler reconstructed the statue with a helmet in its right hand on the basis of several Roman gems. Athena's short hair is tied with a wide band, and she wears a large aegis diagonally across her chest. This is a new conception of Athena, suggesting the work of a great artist.

2. HIGH CLASSICAL PHASE, 446–430 BC. The reconstruction of the Attic sanctuaries damaged during the Persian invasion (480–479 BC), which Pericles began in 449 BC, gave Pheidias a magnificent opportunity to exercise his skill and influence. His commission to produce the cult statue of *Athena Parthenos* (446–438 BC) for the Parthenon is partly documented by contemporary building accounts, though Pheidias is only named in literary texts. This was the first colossal chryselephantine statue, designed also as a means of storing state gold reserves. Its construction coincided with the early building phase of the Parthenon, and Pheidias' influence is also apparent in the temple's architectural sculptures. (*See also* ATHENS, §II, 1(ii).)

The *Athena Parthenos* was about 13 m high, covered with a tonne of gold. It stood on a marble base and had marble eyes, but its face, arms, hands and feet were of ivory. The original was destroyed by fire in the 3rd or 4th century AD, but its general appearance is clear from the remarks of Pausanias (*Description of Greece* I.xxiv.5–7) and Pliny (*Natural History* XXXVI.iv.18–19) and from numerous later copies of inferior quality and on a reduced scale. The most reliable evidence for the form of the goddess comes from the 2nd-century AD Varvakeion Statuette (Athens, N. Archaeol. Mus.; see fig. 1). This has long hair and wears a *peplos*, a long, heavy woollen tunic, girded at the waist. An aegis carrying a gorgoneion covers the upper part of the chest. The figure is bedecked with jewellery and wears an Attic helmet with three crests springing from a sphinx flanked by winged horses or griffins. Its left hand rests on a shield (original diam. 4.90 m) with Athena's sacred snake coiled inside it, while its outstretched right hand, which is supported by a column, holds a flying Victory (original h. 1.8 m). Coin and gem reproductions depict a spear resting against the original statue's left wrist, and literary sources attest that the Victory held a golden crown, and a gorgoneion of gilt silver was placed in the centre of the shield (see *Inscr. Gr./2*, ii, 1388.53–4). The original statue's subsidiary decoration included a gilded *Amazonomachy* on the exterior of the shield with a *Gigantomachy* painted on the interior, a *Centauromachy* around the soles of its sandals and the *Birth of Pandora* carved on the stone base. No copy of the *Centauromachy* is known, but the *Gigantomachy* is thought to have inspired an unusual scene on an Attic red-figure calyx krater (Naples, Mus. Archeol. N., 2045). In its circular composition the action spreads over several registers with an arched line dividing the giants on earth from the gods in heaven, whom they are trying to reach by piling up rocks. The scene is framed by the Sun driving his chariot above the canopy of heaven and the Moon riding down. The exterior of the statue's shield depicted the *Battle of Theseus and Other Athenian Heroes against the Amazons*. Its composition is preserved by several miniature reproductions in marble (notably in Rome, Vatican, Mus. Chiaramonti, 1738 and Mus. Nuo. 916; London, BM; Patras, Archaeol. Mus.; sarcophagus in Aphrodisias Mus., 75.17, 75.78, 75.104). Individual groups of fighters were copied to scale on marble slabs of the 2nd century AD from Athens, intended for the decoration of Roman villas (Peiraeus, Archaeol. Mus.; Chicago, IL, A. Inst., 1928.257; Berlin, Antikensamml., 1842; Copenhagen, Ny Carlsberg Glyp., 2016). The figures are in groups of two fighting up and down a hill around the central gorgoneion. It may be that the Acropolis citadel formed the original background, though walls are only shown on a few slabs. The bald warrior wielding a rock at the apex of the composition is presumably a mythological figure, though later Greeks took him to be a self-portrait of Pheidias. Some details of the scene of the *Birth of Pandora* on the statue base are preserved by an unfinished miniature statuette (the Lenormant *Athena*; Athens, N. Archaeol. Mus.) and a fragmentary Hellenistic copy from Pergamon (Berlin, Antikensamml.). It consisted of figures standing quietly on either side of Pandora, framed by the Sun and Moon, thus representing the tranquil prelude to the disastrous opening of Pandora's box.

After the completion of the *Athena Parthenos*, Pheidias fell victim to a wave of persecution against Pericles' friends. Accused of appropriating some of the ivory, he had to flee to the Peloponnese (perhaps after a term in jail). It was here that he created his last and greatest masterpiece, the colossal cult statue of *Zeus*, for the god's temple at Olympia. Made of gold, ivory, glass, ebony and hardstones, the work was executed in collaboration with the sculptors KOLOTES and THEOKOSMOS and the painter PANAINOS. Excavations at Pheidias' workshop on the site have uncovered some of his tools and raw materials, including small clay moulds for glass drapery, datable from pottery from the site to the 430s BC.

The form of the complete statue is known only from representations on Roman coins and from Pausanias' account (*Description of Greece* V.xi.1–10). The *Zeus* was seated on a throne more lavishly decorated even than the accessories of the *Athena Parthenos*. Painted panels by Panainos formed barriers between the legs of the throne, while the base was gilded, depicting the *Birth of Aphrodite*, again framed by the Sun and Moon. The Athenian bias of many of the mythological scenes suggests that the subjects were chosen by Pheidias himself. Pausanias' description enables the identification of copies of the subsidiary decoration from the armrests of the throne. These were decorated with two friezes representing the *Slaughter of Niobe's Children by Apollo and Artemis*, and, at the front, by a pair of Theban youths captured by

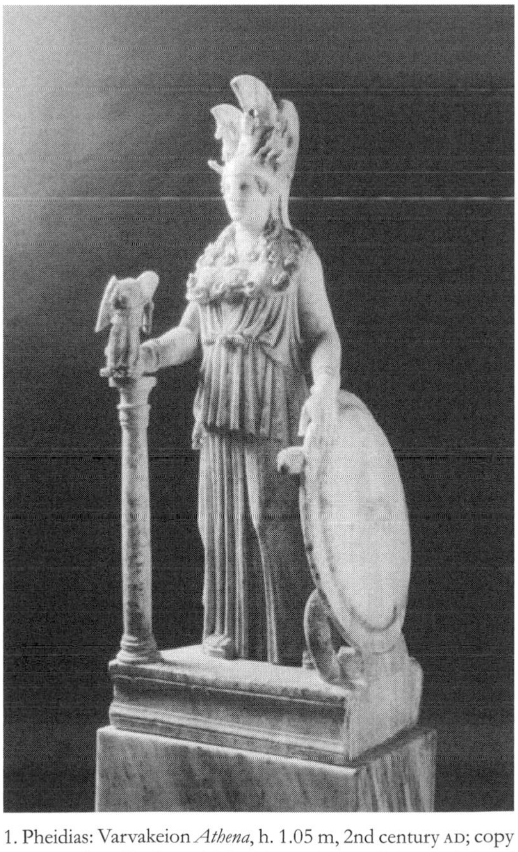

1. Pheidias: Varvakeion *Athena*, h. 1.05 m, 2nd century AD; copy of the *Athena Parthenos*, 446–438 BC (destr.) (Athens, National Archaeological Museum)

sphinxes (Roman copies from Ephesos in Vienna, Ksthist. Mus.; see fig. 2). The exact position of the friezes is revealed by an Attic red-figure krater from Baksy (St Petersburg, Hermitage, Baksy 8), while parts of them are reproduced to scale in Roman reliefs, such as the Campana Relief (St Petersburg, Hermitage) and one in Rome (Villa Albani, 3232), and on a marble disc (London, BM, 2200). The flamboyant treatment of the individual figures, with abundant billowing draperies and a great range of poses representing various stages of collapse, gives some indication of Pheidias' late style.

While at Olympia, Pheidias also produced a chryselephantine cult statue of *Aphrodite Ourania* for her temple at Elis, and a statue of a boy athlete tying his hair with a band (the *Anadoumenos*), dedicated after a victory in the Olympic games. The heads of both works have been tentatively identified in Roman copies (*Aphrodite*, Naples, Mus. Archeol. N.; *Anadoumenos*, Petworth House, W. Sussex, NT and New York, Met.). Both have a large band tied tightly around their luxuriant hair, with a cluster of curls above the ears.

3. Technique and style. Pliny (*Natural History* XXXIV.xix.54) remarked vaguely that it was Pheidias who first revealed the potential of bronze statuary, and there is also evidence that he developed a special technique for creating colossal chryselephantine works. The ivory parts were expanded by means of a technique now lost, so that the statues had to be kept damp, with pools of water and olive oil placed in front of the *Athena Parthenos* and the *Zeus* respectively. The statues were built of clay and plaster on a hollow wooden frame supported by a central pole inserted into the statue base, and covered with gold and ivory plaques held in place with glue. Pheidias' close collaboration with painters is reflected in the pictorial quality of his compositions, many of which were innovative and highly influential. Some of his motifs are unmistakably personal, including the warrior shown from the rear or hiding his face behind his raised arm, the wounded warrior pulling a spear or arrow out of his back, the warrior pulling his adversary's hair and the repeated use of the Sun and Moon to frame compositions; so too are some anatomical details, such as large eyes, full cheeks and curls over the ears.

J. Overbeck: *Die antiken Schriftquellen* (Leipzig, 1868), nos 618–807

A. Furtwängler: *Meisterwerke der griechischen Plastik* (Leipzig, 1893; Eng. trans., London, 1895)

E. Langlotz: *Phidiasprobleme* (Frankfurt, 1947)

G. Becatti: *Problemi fidiaci* (Milan, 1951)

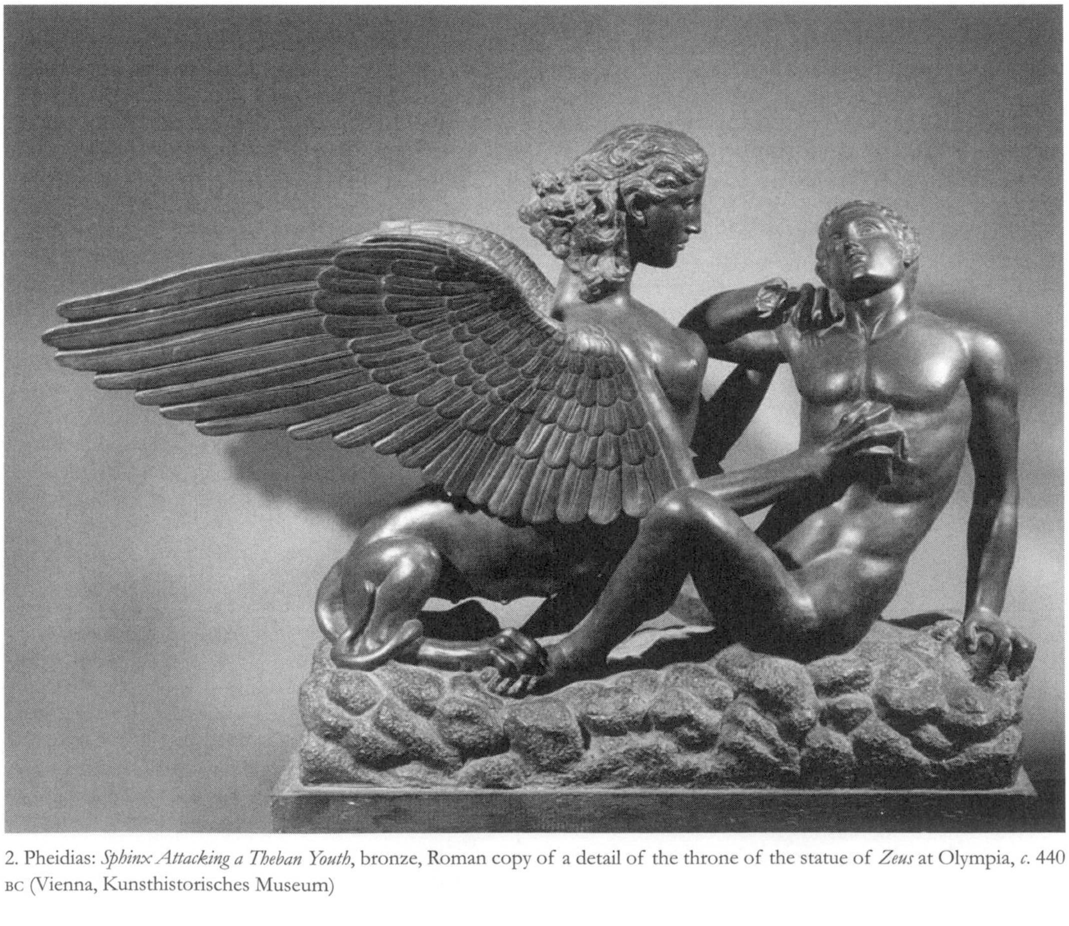

2. Pheidias: *Sphinx Attacking a Theban Youth*, bronze, Roman copy of a detail of the throne of the statue of *Zeus* at Olympia, *c.* 440 BC (Vienna, Kunsthistorisches Museum)

W. Schiering and A. Mallwitz: *Die Werkstatt des Pheidias in Olympia*, i (Berlin, 1964)
N. Leipen: *Athena Parthenos* (Toronto, 1971)
T. Stephanidou-Tiberiou: *Neoattika* (Athens, 1979)
E. B. Harrison: 'Motifs of the City-siege on the Shield of Athena Parthenos', *Amer. J. Archaeol.*, lxxxv (1981), pp. 281–317
E. B. Harrison: 'Two Pheidian Heads', *The Eye of Greece*, ed. D. C. Kurtz and B. Sparkes (Cambridge, 1982), pp. 53–88
A. Linfert: 'Athenen des Pheidias', *Mitt. Dt. Archäol. Inst.: Athen. Abt.*, xcvii (1982), pp. 57–77
E. B. Harrison: 'A Pheidian Head of Aphrodite Ourania', *Hesperia*, liii (1984), pp. 379–88
H. Protzmann: 'Antiquarische Nachlese zu den Statuen der sogenannten Lemnia Fürtwanglers in Dresden', *Jb. Staatl. Kstsamml. Dresden*, xvi (1984), pp. 7–22
K. W. Arafat: 'A Note on the Athena Parthenos', *Annu. Brit. Sch. Athens*, lxxxi (1986), pp. 1–6
T. Stephanidou-Tiberiou: 'E synthese tes Pheidiakes Amazonomachias kai oi Eroes Theseas kai Kekropas' [The composition of the Pheidian Amazonomachy and the heroes Theseus and Kekrops], *Festschrift M. Andronikos*, ii (Thessaloniki, 1986), pp. 839–57
B. Conticello and others: *Alla ricerca di Phidia* (Padua, 1987)
D. Mauruschat: 'Ein neuer Vorschlag zur Rekonstruktion der Schildamazonomachie der Athena Parthenos', *Boreas*, x (1987), pp. 32–58
O. Palagia: 'In Defense of Furtwängler's Athena Lemnia', *Amer. J. Archaeol.*, xci (1987), pp. 81–4
E. B. Harrison: 'Lemnia and Lemnos: Sidelights on a Pheidian Athena', *Festschrift Ernst Berger* (Basle, 1988), pp. 101–7
A. H. Borbein: 'Phidias-Fragen', *Festschrift für N. Himmelmann* (Mainz, 1989), pp. 99–107
W. Schiering, A. Mallwitz and W. Schierung: *Die Werkstatt des Pheidias in Olympia* (Berlin, 1991)
O. Palagia and J. J. Pollitt: *Personal Styles in Greek Sculpture* (Cambridge and New York, 1996)
N. J. Spivey: *Understanding Greek Sculpture: Ancient Meanings, Modern Readings* (New York, 1996)

Phiale Painter (*fl c.* 450–*c.* 425 BC). Greek vase painter. He is named after an Attic Red-figure phiale depicting a *Dancing School* (Boston, MA, Mus. F.A., 97.371), and he is attributed with over 200 extant vases, all but seven of which are also Red-figure. These few White-ground works are his best, and include some genuine masterpieces.

Although he also decorated other shapes, the Phiale Painter preferred Nolan amphorae and lekythoi. His deployment of two rows of pictures on calyx kraters and of shoulder figures on his lekythoi is unusual but characteristic. Though he was a pupil of the ACHILLES PAINTER, his vigorous figures, painted with rapid, sketchy lines, contrast with the static, precisely drawn figures of his teacher. His medium-sized figures are the most successful, the larger ones being somewhat sparsely drawn and the smaller ones poorly proportioned.

The Phiale Painter's range of subjects is remarkable, and some of his mythological scenes seem inspired by Greek tragedy. His hydriai with *Thamyras and the Muses* (Rome, Vatican, Mus. Gregoriano Etrus., 16549: Naples, Mus. Archeol. N., 81531) may reflect Sophocles' *Thamyras*, and the scenes on his White-ground calyx kraters of *Perseus and Andromeda* (Agrigento, Mus. Reg. Archeol.) and *Hermes Bringing the Infant Dionysos to Papposilenos and the Nymphs of Nysa* (Rome, Vatican, Mus. Gregoriano Etrus., 16586; See colour pl. 2:IV, fig. 3) may derive from Sophocles' *Andromeda* and *Dionysiskos* respectively. Rare subjects also occur, such as *Perseus and the Graiai* on a fragment (Delos, Archaeol. Mus.) and *Bendis* on a cup (Verona, Mus. Archeol. Teat. Romano, 52). There are also some unusual scenes from daily life—for example the *Unveiling of the Bride* on a loutrophoros (Boston, MA, Mus. F.A., 10.223) and a chorus of muffled dancers on a double-register calyx krater (Rome, Vatican, Mus. Gregoriano Etrus., Astarita 42)—while recurrent scenes include a youth or god pursuing a woman, a dancing girl and mistress, *Europa and the Bull* and women in domestic settings.

The subject-matter of his White-ground work and its unusual treatment often distinguish it from that of his contemporaries. On a lekythos (Munich, Staatl. Antikensamml., 6248) Hermes, leader of souls on their last journey, beckons gently to a woman standing in front of a tomb and adjusting a wreath on her head before departing for the underworld. On another (Athens, N. Archaeol. Mus., 19355), a woman stands to the left of a tomb, holding a pet hare, while an old maidservant kneels wailing at the other side.

The Red-figure paintings vary more in quality. Some have a certain monumentality, for example the scene on a stamnos (Warsaw, N. Mus., 142465) depicting women preparing for a Dionysiac ritual. Others, especially on Nolan amphorae and lekythoi, are less carefully drawn, though their compositions still give an attractive impression of unrestrained movement which contrasts with the works of many contemporary painters, notably the Achilles Painter, who seem to have been more profoundly influenced by the serenity of the Parthenon sculptures.

J. D. Beazley: *Red-figure* (1942, 2/1963), ii, pp. 1014–26, 1678
G. M. A. Richter: *Attic Red-figured Vases* (New Haven, 1946, 2/1958), pp. 122–3
P. E. Arias and M. Hirmer: *Tausend Jahre griechischer Vasenkunst* (Munich, 1960), trans. and rev. by B. Shefton as *A History of Greek Vase Painting* (London, 1962), pp. 364–5, 367, 374
D. C. Kurtz: *Athenian White Lekythoi* (Oxford, 1975), pp. 48–50
J. H. Oakley: *The Phiale Painter*, Kerameus, viii (Mainz, 1990)
J. H. Oakley: 'Attische rotfigurige Pelike des Phiale Malers und weitere Addenda', *Archäol. Anz.* (1995), pp. 495–501, iii

Philadelphia [Arab. 'Amman; anc. Rabbath Ammon]. Site of a city that flourished between the 2nd millennium BC and the 14th century AD, which is in the modern city of Amman, the capital of the kingdom of Jordan. The site lies in a fertile, well-watered area in the tableland to the east of the River Jordan, on the biblical King's Highway (the ancient Roman Via Nova Traiana), which ran from Bostra in the north to the Red Sea in the south.

The ancient city consisted of the citadel, or acropolis, built in three terraces rising from west to east on a steep-sided, L-shaped hill, and the lower town in the valley of the Wadi ‘Amman to the south. The earliest material found on the citadel dates to the 3rd millennium BC; from *c.* 1100 BC until 582 BC the city was the capital of the kingdom of Ammon. Excavations around the perimeter of the hill have uncovered Ammonite tombs and Hellenistic and early Roman occupation from the 3rd century BC, when the city was renamed Philadelphia in honour of Ptolemy II Philadelphus of Egypt (*reg* 285–246 BC), to the 1st century AD. Older remains were levelled when the citadel was rebuilt after the city's annexation by Rome in AD 106; the Roman fortifications incorporated Ammonite and Hellenistic work.

Of the temples built (or rebuilt) on the citadel during the Roman period, one stood at the northern end on a projecting platform; only the double wall of its enclosure survives. The podium and some of the mouldings remain from another, the Corinthian Temple of Hercules (AD 166–9), which was at the south-east corner, dominating the lower town; fragments of a huge statue, perhaps that of Hercules, have been found. A residential settlement, including a church, occupied the citadel from the 4th century onwards. Below the citadel, along the south bank of the wadi, were the forum, the odeium, the theatre and the nymphaeum, all built under the Roman Empire. The theatre (2nd century) is built into the hill; its auditorium has been restored, and part of the stage building, with Corinthian columns and curved exedra, remains in place.

C. R. Conder: *The Survey of Eastern Palestine* (London, 1889)

H. C. Butler: *Architecture*, 4 vols (1913–19), division II of *Publications of the Princeton University Archaeological Expedition to Syria in 1904–1905, and 1909* (Leiden, 1907–4)

A. Hadidi: 'The Roman Town-plan of Amman', *Archaeology in the Levant*, ed. P. R. S. Moorey and P. J. Parr (Warminster, 1978), pp. 210–22

A. Northedge, ed.: *Studies on Roman and Islamic ‘Amman I: History, Site and Architecture. The Excavations of Mrs C.-M. Bennett and Other Investigations* (Oxford, 1992)

C. Kanellopoulos: *The Great Temple of Amman: the Architecture* (Amman, 1994)

A. Koutsoukou: *The Great Temple of Amman: the Excavations* (Amman, 1997)

Philip II, King of Macedon (*b* 382 BC; *reg* 359–336 BC; *d* Aigai [Vergina], 336 BC). Greek monarch. The son of Amyntas III, King of Macedon (*reg c.* 393 BC), of the Argead family, he learnt the art of war as a hostage at Thebes. Subsequently he brought the whole of Greece under his control in a series of military campaigns culminating in the Battle of Chaironeia (338 BC), thereby laying the foundation on which his son, ALEXANDER THE GREAT (Alexander III; *reg* 336–323 BC) was able to embark on the rapid conquest of Persia. Philip was murdered by a disaffected noble during a festival at Aigai (Vergina). A vaulted tomb there, sumptuously provided with armour and weapons, vessels of gold and silver, jewellery and other items (Thessaloniki, Archaeol. Mus.), discovered by MANOLIS ANDRONICOS in 1977, is now generally accepted to be Philip's tomb (*see* AIGAI (ii)). The partly cremated bones in a solid gold casket include a skull with an injury to the right eye socket, surely the result of the arrow wound Philip sustained at the siege of Methone (355 BC), which blinded him in that eye. The scene painted above the entrance to the tomb is a masterpiece of Greek art representing both Philip and Alexander on horseback in a lion hunt.

J. R. Ellis: *Philip II and Macedonian Imperialism* (London, 1976)

G. Cawkwell: *Philip of Macedon* (London, 1978)

N. G. L. Hammond and G. T. Griffith: *A History of Macedonia*, ii (Oxford, 1979)

M. B. Hatzopoulos and L. D. Loukopoulos, eds: *Philip of Macedon* (Athens, 1980)

A. S. Bradford: *Philip II of Macedon: A Life from the Ancient Sources* (Westport, CT, 1992)

N. G. L. Hammond: *Philip of Macedon* (Baltimore, 1994)

J.-N. Corvisier: *Philippe II de Macédoine* (Paris, 2002)

Philippi. Greek site in eastern Macedonia overlooking the plain to the east of Mt Pangaios. Originally a Thasian settlement known as Krenides, Philippi received its name on its capture by Philip II of Macedon in 357/356 BC. The Hellenistic city is known only from isolated fragments, including several tombs and a temple; almost all of Philippi's visible remains date from the Roman and Early Christian periods. Philippi was the first city in Europe where Christianity was preached by St Paul (Acts xvi:8–40). Excavations at the site have been conducted by the French School since the 1920s.

The urban plan belongs to that of a Roman military colony; in this form Octavian (*reg* as Augustus 30 BC–AD 14) refounded the city in 42 BC to commemorate his victory over Brutus and Cassius on the nearby plain. The key to the city's prosperity was its location on the Via Egnatia, the course of which underlies the modern highway that bisects the site. Along the south side of this central axis lies the forum, replanned apparently between AD 161 and 179. Its paved central court is embraced on three sides by long uniform porticos, with the tribune (speakers' platform) located at the centre of the north side and flanked by a pair of fountains and Corinthian tetrastyle temples. The macellum (market) lies to the south, accessible by a Corinthian hexastyle vestibule, and other shops, offices and a library stand nearby. Also identified by excavations are a bath building with mid-3rd-century AD mosaics (destr.) and a large hillside theatre, rebuilt in the 2nd century AD and transformed in the 3rd century AD into an amphitheatre. On the lower slopes of the acropolis are the remains of a 2nd-century AD sanctuary of the Egyptian deities Isis, Serapis and Harpocrates, and a large number of rock shrines (most dating from the late 2nd and early 3rd centuries AD) embellished with reliefs.

P. Collart: *Philippes, ville de Macédoine, depuis ses origines jusqu'à la fin de l'époque romaine* (Paris, 1937)

D. I. Lazaridis: *Philippoi: Romaike apoikia* [Philippi: Roman colony] (Athens, 1973)

P. Collart and P. Ducrey: *Les Reliefs rupestres* (1975), i of *Philippes* (Paris, 1975)

S. Provost: 'City Walls and Urban Area in Late-antique Macedonia: The Case of Philippi', *Recent Research in Late-antique Urbanism*, eds L. Lavan and W. Bowden (Portsmouth, RI, 2001), pp. 123–35

Philiskos of Rhodes (*fl* ?*c.* 100 BC). Greek sculptor and ?painter. Pliny (*Natural History* XXXVI.iv.34–5) saw several of his marble statues in Rome: an *Apollo* and a group consisting of *Leto, Artemis, the Nine Muses and a Nude Apollo* in the Temple of Apollo near the Portico of Octavia and an *Aphrodite* in the Temple of Juno in the Portico of Octavia. None of his works survives, however. Nothing is known of the style of these statues, and no sure connection can be made between them and later copies of similar subjects based on lost Greek originals. A base from Thasos for a female statue, of which a fragment perhaps survives (Istanbul, Archaeol. Mus.), is signed by Philiskos, son of Polycharmos of Rhodes, in lettering of the late 2nd century BC or early 1st. However, this need not be the same sculptor.

Perhaps to be identified with Philiskos of Rhodes is a painter, none of whose works survives, who according to Pliny (XXXV.xl.143) painted an *Artist's Studio with a Boy Blowing on a Fire*, perhaps the fire necessary to burn in the wax-based colours employed in the encaustic technique. ANTIPHILOS painted a picture with a similar subject (Pliny: XXXV.xl.138).

M. Bieber: *The Sculpture of the Hellenistic Age* (New York, 1955, 2/1961), pp. 129–30

Philostratos. Greek family of writers and philosophers.

(1) Philostratos Lemnios [Philostratus Lemnius] (*b* Lemnos, *c.* AD 187–91). Author of a descriptive work on painting known as the *Imagines* (Gr. *Eikones*). Couched within the literary conceit of the ekphrasis, the *Imagines* is presented as a description of various paintings displayed in a gallery in Naples in the 3rd century AD. The long-debated question of whether the pictures Philostratos described were real or not is irrelevant: Philostratos and the other art writers of the late 2nd century and early 3rd, such as Philostratos the younger (see below) and LUCIAN OF SAMOSATA, are interested in combining the art of ekphrasis with other literary possibilities to create a blend of *logos* and *Kunstwerk*. Philostratos' intention was not only to describe a picture, but also to play with its literary potentialities. This is seen most clearly in his *Imagines*, where, for instance, Philostratos added to his description of a painting of the murder of Kassandra: 'if we examine this scene as a drama, a great tragedy has been enacted on a small stage, but if we look at it as a painting, you will see more in it than a drama' (II.x.1). Although popular in the Renaissance, Philostratos' *Imagines* became even more important after the discovery of frescoes at Pompeii and Herculaneum, and had an important influence on the art critical works of Winckelmann and Goethe.

Philostratos' descriptions, whether or not they were of actual paintings, would have had to be conceivable as such for his literary work to be comprehensible; and in general his descriptions do reflect the themes of the 3rd-century AD paintings that have survived. Almost all of the 64 paintings in his fictitious gallery are variants on stock mythological themes. For example, the scenes of the education of Achilles by the centaur Cheiron (II.ii), of Perseus and Andromeda (I.xxix), of Narcissus entranced by his own reflection (I.xxiii) and of Herakles among the pygmies are all well attested in wall paintings from Pompeii, Ostia and elsewhere in the Roman Empire. Philostratos Lemnios was particularly interested in paintings composed of a single central figure (often Herakles) surrounded by a crowd of smaller figures: thus we have descriptions of Herakles surrounded by vengeful pygmies, by Diomedes' carnivorous mares and by his own captors (II.xx, xxiii.3, and xxv). This composition enabled Philostratos to exploit the rhetorical potential of the contrast between the central figure and the crowd.

Philostratos' aesthetic was a conventional one for his time, dominated by an emphasis on the painter striving for a *trompe l'oeil* realism that can deceive the viewer. The painter of the Narcissus, for example, 'has such regard for realism that he even shows drops of dew dripping from the flowers and a bee settling on them. Whether a real bee has been deceived by the painted flowers or whether we are to be deceived into thinking that a painted bee is real, I do not know.' (I.xxiii.2).

A. Kalkmann: 'Über die Ekphrasis des älteren Philostrat', *Rhein. Mus.*, xxxvii (1882), pp. 397–416, 585–630
E. Bertrand: *Un Critique d'art dans l'antiquité: Philostrate et son école* (Paris, 1887)
A. Lesky: 'Bildwerk und Deutung bei Philostrat und Homer', *Hermes*, lxxv (1940), pp. 38–53
K. Lehmann-Hartleben: 'The *Imagines* of the Elder Philostratos', *A. Bull.*, xxiii (1941), pp. 16–44
Philostratos Lemnios: *Imagines: Text und Kommentar*, ed. K. Kalinka and O. Schönberger (Munich, 1968)
C. Michel: 'Die Weisheit der Maler und Dichter in den Bildern des älteren Philostra', *Hermes*, cii (1974), pp. 457–66
I. Avotins: 'The Year of Birth of the Lemnian Philostratus', *Acta Class.*, xlvii (1978), pp. 538–49
G. Anderson: *Philostratus: Biography and Belles-Lettres in the Third Century AD* (London, 1986)
R. H. Webb: *The Transmission of the 'Eikones' of Philostratos and the Development of 'Ekphrasis' from the Antiquity to the Renaissance* (diss., U. London, Warburg Inst., 1992)
A. Billault: *L'Univers de Philostrate* (Brussels, 2000)

(2) Philostratos the younger (*fl* late 3rd century AD). Grandson of (1) Philostratos Lemnios. Like his grandfather he was the author of a work on painting known as *Imagines* (Gr. *Eikones*). As with the art critical writings of his grandfather, upon which he is heavily dependent, it is difficult to ascertain whether Philostratos the younger's book describes actual works of art or creates imaginary pictures as a vehicle for exemplary exercises in the art of rhetorical depiction. The strong parallels with his grandfather's book and the difficulty of equating Philostratos' descriptions with extant examples of 3rd-century AD art suggest that the latter theory is more likely.

The most interesting section of Philostratos the younger's *Imagines* is the introduction, where his theories on the functions of representational art are outlined. According to the introduction these functions are fourfold: to 'be able to discern the external signs of men's character' and thus represent the inner landscape of the individual; to create a sort of realism whereby one may 'confront objects that do not exist as though they existed, and believe that they do exist'; to follow the well-established canons of symmetry and proportion; and to explore the relationship between poetry and painting, because both arts require an element of imagination to appreciate them. Detailed descriptions of 18 different scenes follow, mostly drawn from mythology: the principal exception is the encomium to Sophocles, apparently a counterpart to Philostratos Lemnios' panegyric on Pindar. Philostratos the younger's descriptions diverge from the realism-based approach of Philostratos Lemnios by emphasizing that the success of a work of art stems from clever expression of the personalities and private feelings of the subjects: particularly vivid examples are his descriptions of the distraught, lovelorn Medea among the Kolchians (vii) and of Marsyas' terror and apprehension as he waits to be flayed alive (ii).

Philostratos the younger: *Imagines*, trans A. Fairbanks (Cambridge, MA, 1960), pp. 283–365 [Eng. and Gr. text]

G. Anderson: *Philostratus: Biography and Belles-lettres in the Third Century AD* (London, 1986), pp. 259–82 and app. I

L. H. Hoffman-Schwab: *Philostratus, Physiognomy and the Boundaries of the Body* (diss., U. Chicago, 1992)

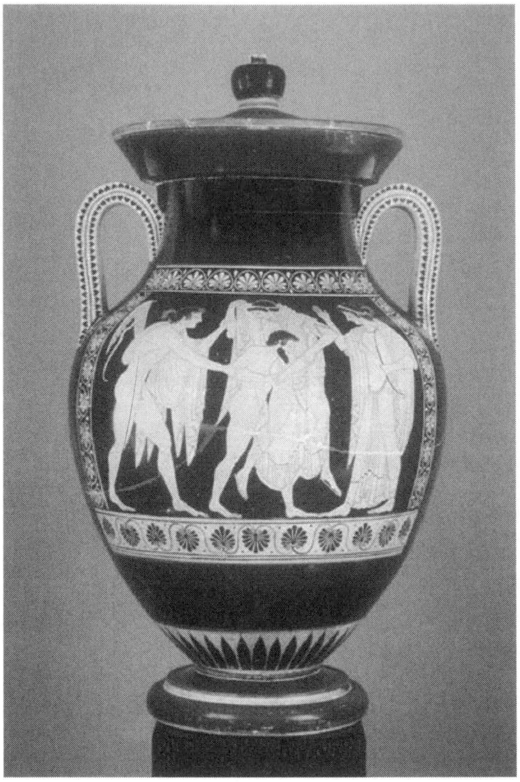

1. Phintias: amphora depicting *Leto Abducted by Tityos*, h. 600 mm, Red-figure, from Vulci, *c.* 515 BC (Paris, Musée du Louvre, G 42)

Philoxenos of Eretria (*fl* late 4th century BC). Greek painter. He was the pupil of NIKOMACHOS OF THEBES and imitated the quickness of his master's technique, inventing other ways of his own in which to increase the speed of painting. The nature of these advances is unknown, and none of his work survives. He painted a picture of *Three Silenoi Revelling*, but his most famous picture was a *Battle between Alexander the Great and Darius III*, painted for King Kassander of Macedon (*reg* 305/4–297 BC), although the painting may have been commissioned before Kassander assumed the throne as he was the most powerful figure in Macedonia from 319 BC. The battle depicted was either that at Issus (333 BC) or that at Gaugamela (331 BC), and the picture was perhaps the model for the *Alexander* Mosaic (House of the Faun, Pompeii; now Naples, Museo Archeologico Nazionale), although the connection cannot be proved.

H. Fuhrmann: *Philoxenos von Eretria; archäologische Untersuchungen über zwei Alexandermosaike* (Göttingen, 1931)

S. Lydakes: *Ancient Greek Painting and its Echoes in Later Art* (Los Angeles, 2004)

Phintias (*fl c.* 520–*c.* 500 BC). Greek vase painter and potter. Phintias signed six vases as painter and three, which he did not paint, as potter. The spelling of his name varies, suggesting that he was not highly literate. Altogether, less than 20 vases ascribed to him survive, but these display considerable variety of shape, including Type A amphorae, a pelike, a volute krater, calyx kraters, both kalpis and shoulder-type hydriai, a psykter and drinking cups.

Phintias was one of the so-called Pioneer group of vase painters (which also included the more gifted EUTHYMIDES and EUPHRONIOS), who explored and developed the new, Red-figure technique. His drawing is bold and simple and avoids over-embellishment of garments and armour. He was, however, attentive to detail, as in his careful drawing on an amphora (Paris, Louvre, G 42; see fig. 1) of the soles of Leto's sandals. Like other Pioneers, he mastered the art of bold anatomical foreshortening, a good example being the figure of Apollo on an amphora (Tarquinia, Pal. Vitelleschi, RC 6843). His compositions seldom contain many figures, usually only three or four, and spread comfortably over the surface of the vase.

Phintias' subjects vary considerably and do not reveal particular preferences for specific myths or scenes of daily life. Among his most impressive paintings is *Herakles and Apollo Struggling for the Delphic Tripod* (on Tarquinia, Pal. Vitelleschi, RC 6843). It shows a youthful-looking Herakles firmly grasping one leg of the tripod and threatening Apollo with his club. The other side of the amphora shows *Satyrs with Maenads in the*

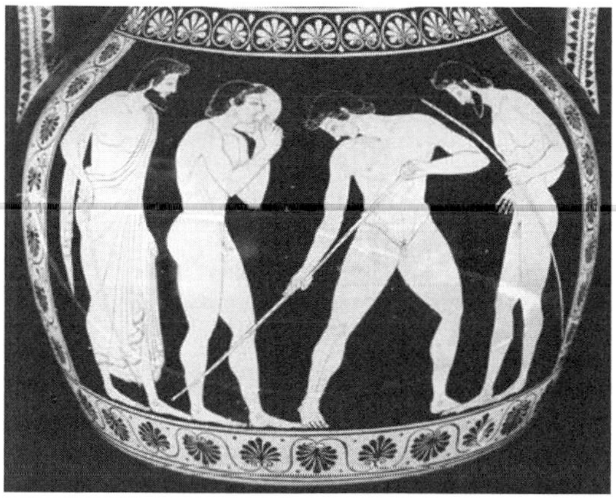

2. Phintias: Amphora depicting *Palaestra Scene*, h. 600 mm, Red-figure, *c.* 515 BC (Paris, Musée du Louvre, G 42)

Presence of Dionysos. A satyr depicted full-face and a close-knit group comprising a satyr and maenad recall similar groups in the work of the Amasis Painter, and the figure of Tityos carrying off Leto probably derives from such groups as the wrestlers on an amphora by the Andokides Painter (Berlin, Antikensamml., 2159). On Phintias' pelike (Paris, Louvre, Cp 10784) a satyr and a maenad make music and dance while Dionysos looks on. The scenes of revelling on the body of a hydria (Munich, Staatl. Antikensamml., 2422) are in a similar vein, and the shoulder of this vase depicts *Satyrs Molesting a Deer.* Other mythological scenes painted by Phintias involve heroes and their exploits. One side of a cup (Munich, Staatl. Antikensamml., 2590 (J401)) shows *Herakles Wrestling with the Giant Alkyoneus*; the other depicts *Herakles and Apollo Struggling for the Delphic Tripod.* A calyx krater (St Petersburg, Hermitage, 1843) shows *Theseus Struggling with a Beast* (probably the bull of Marathon), and a fragment (Limenas Mus.) depicts *Achilles Fighting Memnon.* An amphora (Paris, Louvre, G 42; see fig. 2) and a psykter (Boston, MA, Mus. F.A., 01.8019) both show scenes of youthful athletes with their trainers. Other images of daily life include a *Music Lesson* on another hydria (Munich, Staatl. Antikensamml., 2421) and *Youths at a Fountain* and *A Boy Buying a Vase* on a cup (Baltimore, MD, Mus. A.). Symposia are depicted on the shoulders of two hydriai (London, BM, E 159 and Munich, Staatl. Antikensamml., 2421).

J. D. Beazley: *Red-figure* (1942, 2/1963), i, pp. 23–25

J. D. Beazley: *Paralipomena* (1971), pp. 323, 507, 509

D. L. Cairns: 'Veiling, Aidos, and a Red-figure Amphora by Phintias', *J. Hell. Stud.*, cxvi (1996), pp. 152–8

Phournou Koriphi. *See under* MYRTOS.

Phthiotic Thebes. *See* PYRASOS.

Phyromachos (*fl* late 3rd–2nd century BC). Athenian sculptor. He worked in the service of the Pergamene kings and made the colossal marble cult statue of *Asklepios* at Pergamon (*c.* 180 or *c.* 170 BC), carried off by King Prusias II of Bithynia in 156 or 155 BC (Polybius: *Histories* XXXII.xxv; Diodorus Siculus: *World History* XXXI. xxxv). The bearded head of the god on Pergamene coins may be derived from the statue, while a Roman Imperial copy of it has been seen in the colossal marble head in Syracuse (Mus. Archeol. Reg., inv. 693), and the type of his body in the seated marble *Asklepios* in Cherchel (Mus. Archéol., inv. no. S. 136). The same Phyromachos, presumably, was described as a bronze-worker by Pliny (*Natural History* XXXIV.li), who set his *floruit* in the 121st Olympiad (296–292 BC). This date, however, might have been an attempt by Pliny to set Phyromachos just before the dead period (293–156 BC) in the evolution of Greek art, which only he accepted to have existed. Phyromachos is known from his signatures to have worked with his native Nikeratos on Delos, at Pergamon and at Kyzikos in the late 3rd century BC. According to an inscription from Ostia, Phyromachos also made the portrait of the Cynic philosopher *Antisthenes* (*c.* 200 or *c.* 160 BC; best copy is the herm in Rome, Vatican, Mus. Pio-Clementino). He is also reported to have worked on the Gallic monuments of the Pergamene kings Attalos I Soter (*reg* 241–197 BC) and Eumenes II Soter (*reg* 197–160 BC; Pliny: XXXIV.lxxxiv), although all the other homonym kings of Pergamon have been proposed by scholars. It has been assumed that Phyromachos worked on the Gigantomachy frieze of the Great Pergamene altar (Berlin, Antikensamml.). It is also possible that there was at least one other sculptor with the name Phyromachos, who may have worked in the 3rd century BC. Moreover, according to an inscription a Phyromachos was an Athenian master known to have executed some of the relief figures (408/407 BC) on the frieze of the Erechtheion on the Acropolis of Athens.

A. Stewart: *Attika: Studies in Athenian Sculpture of the Hellenistic Age* (London, 1979), pp. 3–25

B. Andreae: 'Antisthenes Philosophos: Phyromachos epoiei', *Eikones: Studien zum griechischen und römischen Bildnis, Hans Jucker zum sechzigsten Geburtstag gewidmet* (Bern, 1980), pp. 40–48

A. Andreae, ed.: *Phyromachos: Probleme* (Mainz, 1990)

A. Andreae: 'Phyromachos: Schöpfer des Pergamonaltars', *Ant. Welt*, xxiii/1 (1992), p. 65

A. Andreae: 'Vom Pergamonaltar bis Raffael: Vorbilder, Eigenart und Wirkung der römischen Sarkophage', *Ant. Welt*, xxiii/1 (1992), pp. 41–64

F. Queyrel: 'Phyromachos: Problèmes de style et de datation', *Rev. Archéol.* (1992), pp. 367–80

A. Andreae: 'Laurea coronatur, der Lorbeerkranz des Asklepios und die Attaliden von Pergamon', *Mitt. Dt. Archäol. Inst.: Röm. Abt.*,c (1993), pp. 83–106

P. Moreno: *Scultura ellenistica*, i (Rome, 1994), pp. 265–8

I. Leventi: 'E Ygeia tou Nikeratou tou Athenaiou. Symbole ste melete tes proimes glyptikes tes Pergamou (Hygieia by Nikeratos the Athenian. Contribution to the Study of the Early Sculpture of Pergamon)', *Regional Schools in Hellenistic Sculpture*, ed. O. Palagia and W. D. E. Coulson (Oxford, 1998), pp. 101–16

Piazza Armerina. Town in central southern Sicily, known for the Roman villa situated 5 km to the south-west, in the Casale district. The villa (4th century AD) is one of the most opulent country dwellings known anywhere in the Roman Empire. Its secluded site lies 6 km north of the Roman agricultural settlement of Philosophiana, a road station on the main Roman trunk road from Akragas to Catania. First noted in 1761, the villa was partly uncovered in 1881, 1929 and 1935–41, but the principal excavations took place in 1950–54; there was further work in 1970 and in 1983–5. It contains some 45 rooms, nearly all of them still paved with mosaic (or in one case marble) flooring preserved *in situ*. It is estimated that the total area of mosaic paving covers about 3500 sq. m, more than in any other known single building in the Roman Empire. The date has been disputed, but it falls within the first quarter of the 4th century AD, probably *c.* AD 310–25; there was also an earlier villa on the site, of which the bathhouse and some other elements, but no mosaics, are known. The sumptuousness of the later villa's decoration has prompted many theories about ownership. At first it was believed that only an emperor could have afforded such a mansion, and the names of both Maximianus (*reg* AD 286–305) and his son Maxentius (*reg* AD 306–12) were advanced as possible candidates. Now there is general agreement that a private individual owned the villa, clearly a member of the rich land-owning senatorial aristocracy, one probably but not certainly based in Rome rather than in Sicily. Both L. Aradius Valerius Proculus (governor of Sicily *c.* AD 325–8 and later Prefect of Rome) and the family of the Ceionii Rufii (for whom, however, no direct Sicilian connections can be proved) have been suggested.

1. Architecture. 2. Mosaics.

1. Architecture. The large single-storey building, covering about 1.5 ha, consists essentially of four elements (see fig.): a grandiose triple-arched entrance with horseshoe-shaped court behind (1a); the main heart of the residential villa arranged around a peristyled garden (1b), on the far side of which lay a great hall (the 'basilica') for receptions and other functions (1c), flanked on either side by the private apartments of the owner and his family (bedrooms to the north of the hall (1d), and the private suite of living-rooms to its south, itself arranged around an intimate interior court (1e); another set of rooms to the south, probably also for banqueting as its focal point is a spacious three-apsed hall facing an elliptical court (1f); and a large bath complex opening off the north-west corner of the peristyle (1g).

The villa was constructed throughout of mortared rubble faced with irregular pieces of the local brown stone; the walls stand up to 8 m high in places, and they are everywhere preserved to at least 2 m (so in part accounting for the good state of preservation of

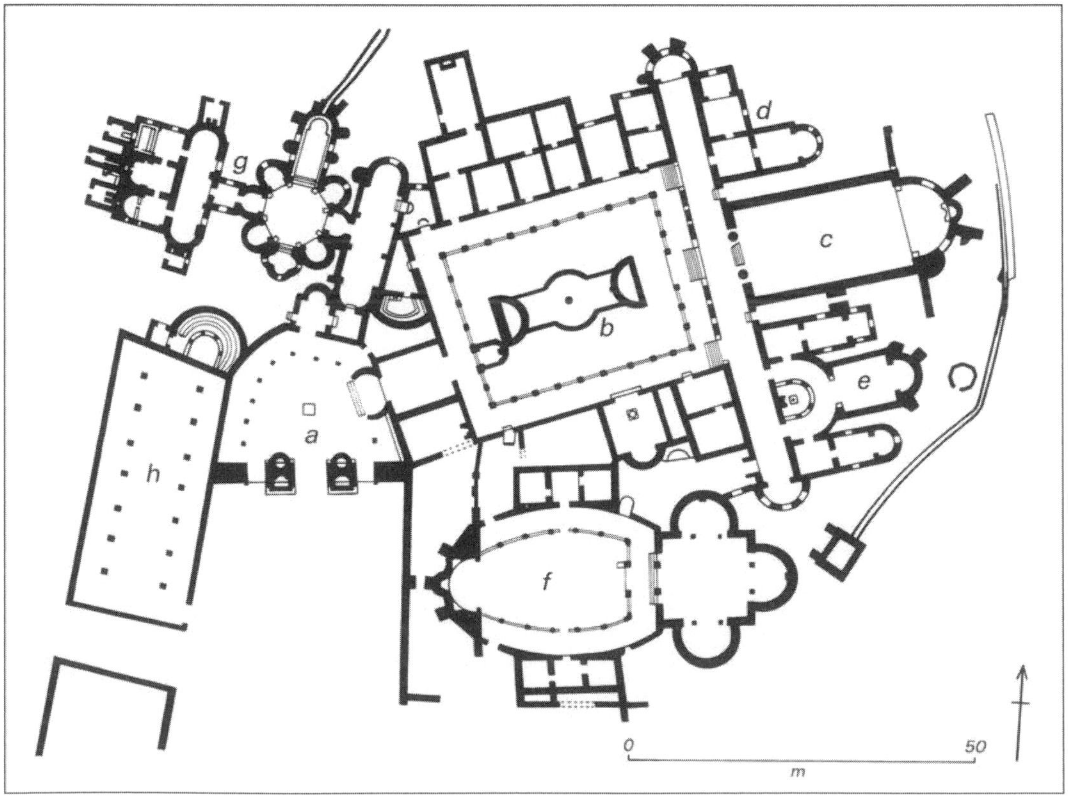

Piazza Armerina, early 4th century AD, plan: (a) entrance court; (b) peristyled garden; (c) reception hall ('basilica'); (d) bedrooms; (e) living-rooms; (f) banqueting rooms; (g) bath complex; (h) granary or stores

the mosaic floors), buried beneath soil that was washed down the slope on which the villa lies. Concrete vaulting was used for roofing in the baths, and terracotta interlocking vaulting tubes of the type popular in North Africa were used to cover the furnaces and the apse of the 'basilica'; elsewhere conventional tile roofs on timber beams are likely. In addition to the floor mosaics, other elements of the villa's decoration are preserved: extensive frescoes on the walls, vibrant with gaudy colours and themselves sometimes featuring figural compositions, as though in competition rather than as a complement to the mosaic floors; marble wall veneer when fresco was not being employed, with an astonishingly wide range of coloured marbles from North Africa, Greece, Egypt and Asia Minor; columns of marble and/or granite in the peristyle, at the entrance to the three-apsed dining hall and elsewhere in the villa; and marble statuary, of which 13 examples have been found. Water was brought to the villa by two aqueducts (whether both came from the same source is unknown), one discharging into a cold-water pool in the baths, the other into a cistern behind the three-apsed hall. There were three latrines, the largest probably intended for estate workers rather than for the villa dwellers as such; water was also used to feed half a dozen playing fountains. Service quarters (kitchens, accommodation for servants etc) have yet to be located; they may lie to the north. It seems likely that the villa lay at the centre of an active farming estate; the 1980s excavations have shown that a large aisled building (perhaps a granary or stores) and other structures are situated to the west of the main entrance to the villa (1h).

Each of the four main elements of the villa is arranged on a different axis. Some scholars have interpreted this as evidence for different building periods, but the study of the structural abutments and the style of the mosaic pavements both suggest that the villa is essentially the product of a single building programme. In choosing a deliberately relaxed overall plan, more reminiscent of the loose grouping of the individual units of Hadrian's Villa at TIBUR (Tivoli) in the 2nd century AD than of known 4th-century AD aristocratic villas, the architect opted for variety and surprise instead of the usual predictable regularity of the standard peristyle house; indeed, the secluded setting of the villa, which does not enjoy an extensive panorama, and the deliberate exclusion of possible vistas (there is a high wall at the far end of the elliptical court in the banqueting area), suggest that a maximum degree of privacy was insisted on by the owner. Few other fully excavated rich villas from the 4th century AD have been explored in Italy or North Africa, and the precise place of Piazza Armerina in late Roman villa architecture is therefore uncertain; but other known contemporary villas, both in Sicily, at Patti Marina on the north coast and at Caddeddi south of Syracuse, as well as elsewhere in the Roman Empire, do not share the relaxed sprawl of Piazza Armerina's layout. Some features of the villa's architecture can be paralleled in North Africa, for example the three-apsed dining hall (also present at Patti Marina), the horseshoe-shaped court with rooms opening off it, and the use of interlocking tubular tiles in vaulting; and in view of the fact that the mosaicists certainly came from North Africa, a case for an African architect at Piazza Armerina can certainly be made. The architecture of Roman North Africa was, however, itself shaped at every turn by developments on the Italian mainland, and the Sicilian villa is essentially an example of the Classical peristyle house that, while ultimately of Greek origin, took on its more developed and elaborate form, in both urban and rural contexts, in late Republican and early Imperial Italy.

2. MOSAICS. The principal figural scenes represented in the villa are as follows: scenes of hunting, both local (hare, boar, deer) and Empire-wide (the rounding up of a wide variety of exotic beasts, such as leopards, tigers, ostriches, an elephant, a hippopotamus and a rhinoceros, for despatch to the amphitheatres of Italy, carpeting a corridor on the east side of the peristyle some 70 m long); circus scenes, both real (a chariot race in the Circus Maximus in Rome) and fantasy (boys driving bird-drawn chariots); other scenes featuring children, shown hunting, acting and practising music (both floors in the owner's private quarters); marine scenes, including three floors of cupids fishing, and a wide variety of fantastical sea creatures, depicted both in the octagonal cold room of the baths and in the Arion mosaic in the owner's private quarters; mythological scenes featuring (in addition to Arion) *Eros and Pan*, *Orpheus Charming the Animals with his Music* (in a small dining- or music-room in the south wing), *Polyphemus with Ulysses* (in the antechamber to a bedroom) and the *Carnage Resulting from the Labours of Hercules* (in the great three-apsed banqueting hall); and heads or foreparts of animals, enclosed individually within laurel wreaths (in the peristyle corridor around the main garden court) or within a running acanthus scroll (in the corridor around the elliptical court). Other floors show cupids harvesting and treading grapes, couples dancing, a couple kissing and, most celebrated of the villa's floors, girls in bikini-style garments engaged in some sort of athletic competition (see colour pl. 1:XVI, fig. 1). The last floor is a little later than the main series as it overlies an earlier geometric mosaic (?*c*. AD 330–40).

Much speculation has been offered about the number of artistic personalities supposed to have been responsible for designing the mosaics (at least three have been suggested), and the time taken by the mosaicists to execute the whole programme (50 years has been proposed, but no owner would have been prepared to be so patient); indeed, the wide variety in the standard of the mosaics suggests not that different mosaic firms were being employed over a long period of time to work on the floors, but that a single mosaic workshop was being stretched to the limits of its available supply of talent to complete the commission within as short a timespan as possible. Internal stylistic links between individual pavements not only suggest close contemporaneity but also strengthen the likelihood that most if not all of the floors were laid by a single workshop; and close parallels in North

Africa for pavement after pavement in the Sicilian villa demonstrate beyond all reasonable doubt that the mosaicists who worked at Piazza Armerina were based in Africa, almost certainly at Carthage.

The arrangement of the rich and varied subject-matter varies a great deal from floor to floor. In some the individual figured panels are contained within a predominantly geometric framework; but most of the pavements with figured decoration are 'all-over' compositions covering the entire area of floor from wall to wall, ranging from schematic arrangements in a series of superimposed registers (as in the 'Small Hunt', or in the mosaic depicting *Children Hunting*) to the more fluid but still effective placing of the figures in the three-apsed banqueting hall or the long corridor with the great hunting scene; the latter is unmatched among ancient hunting mosaics for its organizational skill, endless variety and restless vitality. The approach to figure drawing throughout the villa is largely two-dimensional, with the use of a strong line and bold colours to achieve an immediate impact; naturalism or three-dimensional effects with subtle polychromatic shading are not attempted, except for a few details in the *Labours of Hercules* compositions. The standard of draughtsmanship of the figures is generally competent rather than outstanding, and some of the attempts at foreshortening are bold and striking rather than wholly successful. Indeed, the mosaics at Piazza Armerina impress not so much by their artistic standard as by the sheer quantity of them, the richness of the polychromy, and the varied subject-matter with its wealth of carefully observed detail. They give us an insight into the tastes and interests of the owner who commissioned them such as is obtainable nowhere else on this scale in a late Roman country villa.

G. V. Gentili: *La villa erculia di Piazza Armerina: I mosaici figurati* (Rome, 1959)

G. V. Gentili: *The Imperial Villa of Piazza Armerina* (Rome, 1966)

H. Kähler: *Die Villa des Maxentius bei Piazza Armerina* (Berlin, 1973)

A. Carandini, A. Ricci and M. de Vos: *Filosofiana: The Villa of Piazza Armerina* (Palermo, 1982)

N. Duval: 'Pourquoi une identification? La Place de Piazza Armerina dans l'architecture de l'antiquité tardive après la récente publication', *Opus Int.*, ii (1983), pp. 559–72

A. Giardina: 'Il pane nel circo: Su una scena dell'atrio termale di Filosofiana', *Opus Int.*, ii (1983), pp. 573–80

D. R. Whittaker: 'Filosofiana: The Villa of Piazza Armerina Reconsidered', *Opus Int.*, ii (1983), pp. 553–8

R. J. A. Wilson: 'Luxury Retreat, 4th-century Style: A Millionaire Aristocrat in Late Roman Sicily', *Opus Int.*, ii (1983), pp. 537–8

R. J. A. Wilson: *Piazza Armerina* (London, 1983)

G. Di Giovanni: *Piazza Armerina: Roman Civilization through the Mosaics of the Villa del Casale* (Palermo, 1987); rev. as *Piazza Armerina: The Roman Villa of Casale: An Insight into the Way the Romans Lived* (Agrigento, 2000)

G. Rizza, ed.: *La villa romana del Casale di Piazza Armerina* (1988)

R. J. A. Wilson: *Sicily under the Roman Empire* (Warminster, 1990), chap. 6

F. Ghedini: 'Iconografie urbane e maestranze africane nel mosaico della piccola caccia di Piazza Armerina', *Mitt. Dt. Archäol. Inst.: Röm. Abt.*, xcviii (1991), pp. 323–35

R. Amedick: 'Herakles im Speisesaale', *Mitt. Dt. Archäol. Inst.: Röm. Abt.*, ci (1994), pp. 103–19

L. Villari: *L'Ibla sicana e il sito della Villa imperiale di Piazza Armerina* (Rome, 1995)

G. V. Gentili: 'Piazza Armerina e Faenza: Due mosaici con esaltazioni imperiali', *Boll. A.*, lxxxi/98 (Oct–Dec 1996), pp. 1–16

G. Di Giovanni: *Piazza Armerina: La civiliat romana attraverso i mosaici della villa del casale* (Palermo, 1997)

L. Centonze: *Vizi, costumi e peccati nelle ville romane di Sicilia: Il Casale di Piazza Armerina* (Palermo, 1999)

G. V. Gentili: *La Villa romana di Piazza Armerina Palazzo Erculio* (Osimo, 1999)

F. S. Brancato and R. Mingoia: *Piazza Armerina: Apud thermas apud Hennam: La cosiddetta villa romana del casale* (Comiso, 2002)

P. C. Baum-vom Felde: *Die geometrischen Mosaiken der Villa bei Piazza Armerina: Analyse und Werkstattfrage* (Hamburg, 2003)

Piazza Armerina: The Roman Villa of Casale, Morgantina (Messina, 2003)

N. J. Mactague: 'Die geometrischen Mosaiken der Villa bei Piazza Armerina', *Amer. J. Archaeol.*, cx/2 (April 2006), pp. 338–9

Pihil [Pihir]. *See* PELLA (i).

Piraeus. *See* PEIRAEUS.

Pisidian Antioch. *See* ANTIOCH (ii).

Pithekoussai [Lat. Aenaria; It. Ischia]. Largest island in the Bay of Naples. Strabo (*Geography* V.iv.9) recorded that Pithekoussai was settled by Eretrians and Chalkidians from Euboia, and Livy (*History of Rome* VIII. xxii. 5–6) hinted that the Chalkidian founders of Cumae on the nearby mainland came from Pithekoussai. Excavations conducted since 1952 at Lacco Ameno d'Ischia confirm the establishment by Euboians (by c. 750 BC at the latest) of a major trading centre with an acropolis, a suburban industrial quarter where bronze and iron were worked, and a vast cemetery. Finds from the latter include imports from north Syria, Phoenicia, Egypt (scarabs) and Corinth, as well as from Etruria and other parts of Italy. A Rhodian kotyle (*c.* 720 BC; Naples, Sopr. Ant., 166788) has an incised metrical inscription boasting jokingly that it rivals Nestor's cup (see *Iliad* XI.632–5), and a locally painted wine bowl (*c.* 725–700 BC; Naples, Sopr. Ant., 168813) shows a dramatic shipwreck, possibly the oldest extant example of narrative art from Italy. A shoulder fragment of a krater (*c.* 725–700 BC) bears the earliest known Greek potter's signature formula, while a few locally made vases bear early Semitic inscriptions. During the second half of the 8th century BC the island was the main western base of a far-flung trading network that brought Aegean and Levantine ideas, crafts and craftsmen to Italy, and influenced the orientalizing artistic styles of 7th century BC Campania,

Latium and Etruria. Although a well-stocked votive deposit bears witness to continued sophistication in the 7th century BC, the importance of Pithekoussai clearly declined with the rise of Cumae.

D. Ridgway: *The First Western Greeks* (Cambridge, 1992)
G. Buchner and D. Ridgway: *Pithekoussai I* (Rome, 1993)
A. d'Agostino: 'La "Stipe dei Cavalli" di Pitecusa', *Atti e Memorie della Società Magna Grecia*, iii (1994–5 [1996]), pp. 9–108

Pityoussa. *See* CHIOS.

Planning. The deliberate application of principles relating to the desirable form and nature of urban settlements.

I. Greek. II. Roman.

I. Greek.

1. Sanctuary planning. 2. Town planning.

1. SANCTUARY PLANNING. These were originally simply areas set aside and recognized as the property of a particular deity. From the Archaic period onwards, however, many sanctuaries became the focus for major building projects, and these now form collectively by far the most important ancient Greek sites in terms of their architectural remains.

(i) Location. (ii) Organization. (iii) Landscaping.

(i) Location. Sanctuaries could be situated either within a city boundary or in country districts. There are no obvious rules for the selection of particular localities, and various factors may be postulated. Several important sanctuaries are in places that appear to have been occupied in the Late Bronze Age, and in some instances these were already sacred sites, raising the question of continuity of worship through the Dark Age. This may have been the case in the important but comparatively remote sanctuaries at Delos and Delphi. However, the material evidence for such continuity is never strong, and any connection may be nothing more than the sense of atmosphere that resulted from the remains of earlier occupation. In other instances there may have been a change of function: in Bronze Age communities the focus of society was the ruler, and his palace was the architectural expression of this, often sited on a fortified hilltop. After the disintegration of Late Bronze Age society, the gods and the sites allocated to them emerged as the corresponding focus. Fortified sites might still defend the later community: an obvious example is the Sanctuary of Athena on the Athenian Acropolis. Elsewhere, the choice of site derived from natural features: springs in particular attracted religious usage. Sanctuaries are frequently sited in prominent places, such as the Acropolis at Athens or the long ridge crowned with a succession of temples at AKRAGAS. Some important sanctuaries, however (e.g. those of Hera at Samos and Artemis at Ephesos), are in low-lying, marshy areas, while others are on the slopes of hills rather than the summits (e.g. that of Demeter at Corinth).

The extent of a sanctuary depended on the importance of its cult. Where sanctuaries were recognized as important throughout the Greek world, the area allocated to the gods was substantial (for example at Delphi, Delos and Olympia). The patron deity of a city would receive a major sanctuary, usually within the city itself, as at Athens, but at times outside (e.g. at Samos and Didyma). Lesser deities naturally had less prominent sanctuaries: some were restricted to a few devotees or were even small private places of worship.

(ii) Organization. The arrangements within each sanctuary varied according to usage, the numbers of worshippers and the particular character of the cult. Sanctuaries were arranged primarily to accommodate the festivals of the resident deity. These normally occurred only once a year, though they might last for several days, and some particularly important festivals took place at four-yearly intervals. Thus a major sanctuary had to be able to receive large numbers of worshippers.

The climax of the festival was the offering of sacrifices. These were normally animals, brought to the sanctuary and ritually slaughtered, token parts of the animal being burnt on the altar as the god's portion. Consequently, the altar itself was always the central feature and marked the most sacred area. The worshippers assembled round it to watch the sacrifices, and there was thus generally no need for an enclosed, roofed building for worship. Thus the planning of sanctuaries is in principle external rather than internal, open rather than closed off, except in the case of mystery cults, which required a process of initiation, for example the cult of Demeter and Kore at Eleusis.

It was usual to mark off the sanctuary as the property of the god, but it was not necessary to enclose it within a wall, and simple marker stones were often used. Minor sanctuaries were often informally accessible from the street. Major festivals frequently included a formal procession to the sanctuary, and for this a particular street was designated as a 'sacred way'. The procession at Athens for the festival of Athena gathered at the Sacred Gate and made its way along the Sacred Way through the Agora up to the Acropolis. Similarly, the worship of Eleusinian Demeter required a procession from Athens to Eleusis, and the festival of Asklepios at Epidauros began with a procession to the rural sanctuary some 10 km distant. The entrance to the sanctuary might, therefore, be marked by a gateway or PROPYLON, which was as much symbolic as functional. The propylon to the Athenian Acropolis replaced a military gate and had doors that could be bolted. At Epidauros, on the other hand, the propylon had no doors and served a purely ritual function. The processions included sacrificial animals and thus eventually proceeded to the ALTAR. This could take many forms, ranging from a simple podium or even, as at Olympia, a pile of accumulated ashes to elaborate architectural structures.

The temple was the house of the god and as such provided shelter for the cult image. It was usually a prestigious building, intended to demonstrate both the piety and the wealth of the sanctuary authorities, and temples soon became the dominant, most splendid structures in most Greek sanctuaries. The temple's position within the sanctuary varied. In smaller sanctuaries it tended to be placed at one end, allowing a space in front for the altar and worshippers. The temple was, however, usually free-standing within the sanctuary and could thus be viewed from all directions. Some temples may have been placed to achieve a three-quarter view from the main approach. Most faced east towards the point at which the sun rose on the day of festival and sacrifice, so that the exact orientation of temples varied according to the local skyline and the time of the festival (and its position within the variable system of the Greek calendar). Exceptions to the eastwards alignment include the north-facing Temple of Apollo at Bassai (429–*c.* 400 BC) and the west-facing Temple of Artemis at Ephesos (*c.* 560–*c.* 460 BC). Ideally the door gave a direct view from the cult statue inside to the altar. Again there were exceptions: the altar of Athena on the Athenian Acropolis was in front of the position occupied by her original temple, but remained unchanged even when the final version of that temple was destroyed, and her cult image moved to a new building on the adjacent site; neither this (the Erechtheion) nor the Parthenon faced the altar. Where possible the approach from the sanctuary entrance was to the front of the temple, though the easiest access to the Athenian Acropolis was from the west, and all the temples, therefore, turn their backs on the sacred approach.

Other buildings served ancillary functions. Some provided shelter for worshippers and those dedicatory gifts that were not kept in the temple itself. Extended colonnades (*see* STOA) were normal for this and might be placed on the sanctuary boundary, facing inwards. Other buildings provided accommodation for privileged persons (e.g. priests, magistrates) to consume the sacrificial meat in formal dining-rooms (*hestiatoria*; examples at Perachora, Epidauros and Delos); these are often erroneously described as 'priests' houses'. Such buildings might be located in a secondary area of the sanctuary, away from the principal temple, as at Perachora and on the Athenian Acropolis, where it has been suggested that the north-west wing of the Propylaia was arranged for this purpose. Ordinary worshippers presumably ate their share of the meat alfresco.

Specialized cults required special buildings. There is no discernible regular plan for the sanctuaries of oracular cults, which varied considerably in their practice. Usually the plan of the temple was modified in some way, as at Delphi and probably Didyma, though the officials operating the oracle at Didyma also had a separate office. The healing cult of Asklepios required dormitories for the sick. This type of building (*abaton*) resembles the stoa, though *abata* are always close to the heart of the sanctuary. The initiatory cults needed enclosed buildings for the ritual of admission (e.g. at Eleusis and SAMOTHRACE), though these vary considerably both in form and in placing within the sanctuary.

Most sanctuaries required water supplies, which might receive architectural embellishment in the form of a fountain house, not necessarily within the sanctuary itself. All sanctuaries were adorned with free-standing statues and other monuments, which tended to be grouped around altar, temple and sacred way.

Thus the internal planning of sanctuaries varied considerably. With the development of planned cities in the Hellenistic period, the area set aside for a sanctuary often became more regular, giving rise to rectangular precincts bordered by continuous stoas, with the temple towards one end and the altar axially aligned in front of it (e.g. the Sanctuary of Artemis Leukophryene at Magnesia on the Maeander; 2nd century BC). Such sanctuaries are uncommon, though the loss of such important Hellenistic cities as Antioch and Alexandria doubtless contributes to this. Their influence can be seen, however, in the developed sanctuary arrangements of Roman architecture (*see* §II below).

R. D. Martienssen: *The Idea of Space in Greek Architecture* (Johannesburg, 1956, rev. 2/1964)

H. Berve, G. Gruben and M. Hirmer: *Griechische Tempel und Heiligtümer* (Munich, 1961); Eng. trans. as *Greek Temples, Theaters and Shrines* (New York, 1963)

H. F. Mussche, ed.: *Greek Architecture* (1963), ii/1 of *Monumenta Graeca et Romana* (Leiden, 1963–)

B. Bergquist: *The Archaic Greek Temenos* (Lund, 1967)

E. Melas, ed.: *Temples and Sanctuaries in Ancient Greece* (London, 1973)

R. A. Tomlinson: *Greek Sanctuaries* (London, 1976)

N. Marinatos and R. Hägg: *Greek Sanctuaries: New Approaches* (London and New York, 1995)

N. Bookidis and R. S. Stroud: *The Sanctuary of Demeter and Kore: Topography and Architecture* (Princeton, 1997)

P. J. Perlman: *City and Sanctuary in Ancient Greece: The Theorodokia in the Peloponnese* (Göttingen, 2000)

A.V. Bujskikh and others: 'The System of City Planning in Chersonesos Tauricos', *Archäol. Anz.*, i (2002), pp. 273–303

J. Ito: *Theory and Practice of Site Planning in Classical Sanctuaries*(Kumamoto, 2002)

(iii) Landscaping. Whatever system (if any) was used for the internal planning of a sanctuary, individual constructions or an entire sanctuary complex, urban or rural, often required alteration of the terrain. Foundations in general offset the instability or irregularity of sacred terrain; but construction on uneven surfaces sometimes made it necessary to cut into bedrock (e.g. the Sanctuary of Asklepios, Corinth), build terraces (e.g. the Temple of Apollo, Delphi; Temple of Zeus, Stratos) or platforms (e.g. the later Temple of Artemis, Ephesos; Temple of Athena, Smyrna) and lay deep stone substructures (e.g. the earlier shrine on the site of the Parthenon on the Athenian Acropolis). In gently sloping areas,

sanctuaries could be constructed on one or more large terraces (e.g. the Sanctuary of Asklepios, Kos); but sanctuaries on steep mountainsides required a series of smaller terraces, as at Delphi. Small terraces or outworks could also support single buildings in rocky locations (e.g. the Temple of Athena Nike on the Athenian Acropolis; the Athenian Treasury, Delphi). Larger terraces provided unity as much as stability for groups of buildings (e.g. the treasuries at Olympia). Different levels were linked by stairs or inclined paths, as at Delphi. Exigencies of the terrain may also have produced unusual temple orientation, as perhaps at the Temple of Apollo at Bassai, which is aligned north-south. The location of particular sacred spots apparently sometimes necessitated anomalous buildings, for example the Erechtheion on the Athenian Acropolis.

Temples were not the only large, important structures at sanctuaries. Long narrow stoas required careful siting and extra support in hilly terrain, as on the acropolis at Lindos. Their back walls, however, could provide support for terraces, either above (e.g. the South Stoa, Sanctuary of Hera, Argos) or below (e.g. the Stoa of Apollo Maleatas, Epidauros). The seating in stadia and theatres also required structural support. The siting of a theatre could conform to a convenient hillside, minimally altering the landscape, as at Epidauros. On flat terrain, however, walls were needed, as at Dodona. Stadia could be built with one long side cut into a hillside, as at Delphi, supported by earth in a flat area, as at Olympia, or at right angles to a slope, making use of both the natural hillside and earth fill, as at Nemea.

Simple rural shrines and sanctuaries, which might only contain trees, a rough altar and dedications overseen by a caretaker (Dio Chrysostom: *Orationes* i.52 4), required little alteration of the landscape. They were, nevertheless, influenced by physical features. Mountain ranges forming political boundaries, for instance, dictated the siting of border shrines. Other shrines, for instance those on mountain-tops or at springs, may reflect a particular aspect of the environment controlled by the patron deity. For instance, it was appropriate to worship Zeus the rain-giver on a mountain-top. Sanctuaries where springs were important range from the comparatively simple (e.g. the grove and spring of Apollo near Pharai in Messenia; Pausanias: IV.xxxi.1) to the extremely complex (e.g. the Hellenistic oracle of Apollo at Didyma). The realistic description of a spring and sanctuary of the nymphs of Ithaka (*Odyssey* XVII.205–11) shows how a simple rural shrine might integrate everyday practicality with worship.

The Greeks commonly used trees and bushes at shrines, probably to enhance an atmosphere of age, provide shade and demarcate sacred territory. No doubt they also intensified the sacredness of shrines founded in observation of some quality of nature. Few sites have, however, yielded any archaeological evidence for plantings. The best example is the Temple of Hephaistos at Athens; others include the Temple of Zeus at Nemea and traces of planting for a single tree at Dodona. The abbreviated, sometimes symbolic depiction of landscape in ancient Greek art is usually unhelpful, though written evidence shows that sacred groves were common at urban, suburban and rural shrines.

Every major deity possessed at least one sanctuary where there were trees, and numerous heroes and heroines had trees at their shrines. Particular species were not exclusive to one deity or hero (thus groves of wild olives were sacred to Zeus, Poseidon and Apollo), while groves of a single deity could have different kinds of trees, so that not only laurels but also cypresses (Daphne in Syria) and myrtles (Delphi) are recorded in groves of Apollo. Some sacred groves were said to have been planted in legendary or mythical times; in other instances the deliberate planting of trees at sanctuaries in the recent historic past was recorded. Citizens were honoured for their donation and maintenance of trees, and laws against grazing and woodcutting at shrines were designed to keep groves intact. Many sanctuaries, therefore, must have had pleasant, parklike grounds (e.g. Olympia, see Pindar: *Olympian Odes* iii.17–24; Patrai, see Pausanias: VII.xxi.11). Descriptions of ancient Athens provide a good indication of how trees were used in a city: they grew, for instance, in the Agora (Plutarch: *Kimon* xiii.8; not necessarily sacred) and at various suburban shrines (e.g. Kolonos Hippios, see Pausanias: I.xxx.4; Sophocles: *Oedipus at Colonus*) and gymnasia (e.g. Plato's Academy, see Plutarch: *Kimon* xiii.8, *Sulla* xii.3). An olive tree on the Acropolis, burnt by the Persians, apparently miraculously recovered (Herodotus: *Histories* VIII.lv). Around the Temple of Hephaistos planting pits and terracotta pots for seedlings have been found, evincing an extensive planting programme.

C. A. Doxiadis: *Raumordnung im griechischen Städtebau* (Heidelberg, 1937); Eng. trans. as *Architectural Space in Ancient Greece* (Cambridge, MA, 1972)

D. B. Thompson: 'The Garden of Hephaistos', *Hesperia*, vi (1937), pp. 396–425

A. Philippson: *Die griechischen Landschaften* (Frankfurt am Main, 1950–59)

R. Stillwell: 'The Siting of Classical Greek Temples', *J. Soc. Archit. Hist.*, xiii (1954), pp. 3–8

S. I. Dakaris: 'To hierón tis Dodonis' [The sanctuary at Dodona], *Archaiol. Deltion*, xvi (1960), pp. 4–40

V. J. Scully: *The Earth, the Temple and the Gods* (New Haven, 1962, rev. 3/1979)

M. K. Langdon: 'A Sanctuary of Zeus on Mount Hymettos', *Hesperia*, suppl. xvi (1976)

D. Birge: *Sacred Groves in the Ancient Greek World* (diss., Berkeley, U. CA, 1982)

R. Osborne: *Classical Landscape with Figures: The Ancient Greek City and its Countryside* (London, 1987)

A. J. Ammerman: 'The Eridanos Valley and the Athenian Agora', *Amer. J. Archaeol.*, c (Oct 1996), pp. 699–715 [transformation of the original setting for urban use in the sixth century BC]

A. Bakirtzis: 'The Urban Continuity and Size of Late Byzantine Thessalonike', *Dumbarton Oaks Pap.*, lvii (2003), pp. 35–8, insert 1–insert 16, 39–64

C. Morgan: *Early Greek States beyond the Polis* (London, 2003)
S. D. Kryzhitskii: 'On the Types of Houses on the Island of Berezan', *Ancient Civilizations from Scythia to Siberia*, xi/3–4 (2005), pp. 181–97

2. TOWN PLANNING.

(i) Early urban development. Many of the towns in mainland Greece developed from small settlements of the Geometric period (*c.* 900–*c.* 700 BC). These included widely scattered groups of farmsteads, as at Athens and Argos, as well as densely packed clusters of small houses. The plans of these settlements were not based on right angles but took shape in accordance with the natural terrain, so that they were characterized by crooked alleys, irregular terraces and squares and small houses of varied design.

Of decisive importance in the development of more sophisticated urban planning was the foundation of numerous Greek colonies from the 8th century BC onwards at sites on almost all Mediterranean coasts. These colonies were entirely new foundations, and they thus had to have a more imposing form that would maintain their identities and independence amid alien peoples. For example, Megara Hyblaia in Sicily was laid out in the 8th century BC with parallel streets. The marking out was so inaccurate, however, that the lengths of the blocks (*insulae*) varied considerably. All the early colonial strip cities had similar plans, with long rows of houses ranged along relatively narrow streets and hardly any transverse streets. The town walls were irregular and followed the most appropriate line of defence. Within the walls a fairly large site was reserved for sanctuaries, and an open space in the residential area formed the agora (market place), which was lined by public buildings. The strip layout was still usual in the Archaic period, though it was improved by the increased use of transverse streets.

In mainland Greece also new towns were constantly being founded. These generally developed from a *synoikismos* ('settling together'), when the inhabitants of several small villages jointly founded a town so that they could pursue a more organized way of life. The first generation of settlers must have supported extensive building programmes, but by the 6th century BC ordinary citizens throughout Greece became more prosperous, and the construction of towns expanded still further. Many had populations of more than 10,000, which necessitated major public works, notably the installation of piped water supplies, as at Athens and on Samos. Agoras began to develop into civic centres and were provided with public buildings.

(ii) The science of urban planning. Scientific urban planning developed at the beginning of the 5th century BC and was connected with political changes following the democratic reforms of Kleisthenes in 508/7 BC. Among the greatest building projects after the Persian Wars (490–479 BC) were the rebuilding of Miletos and the laying out of the port of Peiraeus. The new MILETOS may have been the first regularly planned city with a dense grid of streets. The width of these streets varied, with some genuine ceremonial ways 40 m wide. Large open spaces at the centre of the city were reserved for public buildings. House plots were of uniform size and united to form relatively small *insulae* (*see* INSULA).

The layout of PEIRAEUS was probably determined by the famous town planner HIPPODAMOS, who came from Miletos. It too was based on a closely knit, differentiated street system, and house plots and *insulae* were relatively small. The most important innovation, probably attributable to Hippodamos, was the introduction of standard housing units. These terraced houses, which were partly two-storey, were divided into three distinct areas to suit the needs of a large family and reflected the concept of the equality of all citizens in a democratic state. The agora in Peiraeus was called the 'Hippodamic Agora' (Suidas: *Hippodameia*). Its location and form are uncertain. Ancient sources suggest, however, that Hippodamos divided the town into separate districts according to function, as in modern urban planning. Characteristically, the planned Greek city employed an orthogonal grid centred on the agora, as at Dura Europos in Mesopotamia, founded *c.* 300 BC by Hellenistic Greeks (see fig. 1).

The port of RHODES, laid out in 408/7 BC, is the only Classical metropolis that has been systematically studied. It shows that 'building according to the Hippodamic method' (Aristotle: *Politics* IV.1330b24) meant using a consistent, close-knit street grid involving a hierarchy of rectangular blocks, with proportions determined by simple Pythagorean ratios. The basic unit was a standard house plot, of which the size and shape depended on the land available and the house type involved. Areas known vary from 207 sq. m at PRIENE to about 400 sq. m at Rhodes. Most plots were of about 250 sq. m. They were linked together in groups of three (Rhodes), six (Miletos), eight (Peiraeus, Priene, Dura Europos) and, exceptionally, sixteen houses (Abdera), to form *insulae*. Individual *insulae* were surrounded by relatively narrow residential streets, but at Rhodes, for example, wider streets were used to group the blocks into residential districts of equal size. Such a division, involving perhaps more than a thousand people, was of course feasible only in large cities.

Besides Hippodamian foundations there were also new settlements based on a development of the strip city scheme, which did not depend on carefully proportioned rectangular plots. These include OLYNTHOS, founded in 432 BC and destroyed in 348 BC, where *pastas*-type houses stood on almost square plots (360 sq. m) joined together in rows to form *insulae* of various lengths. As in the Archaic strip cities, two rows of houses backed on to each other, giving an interval of 30–40 m between streets. Between the backs of the houses ran a narrow passage (0.8 m

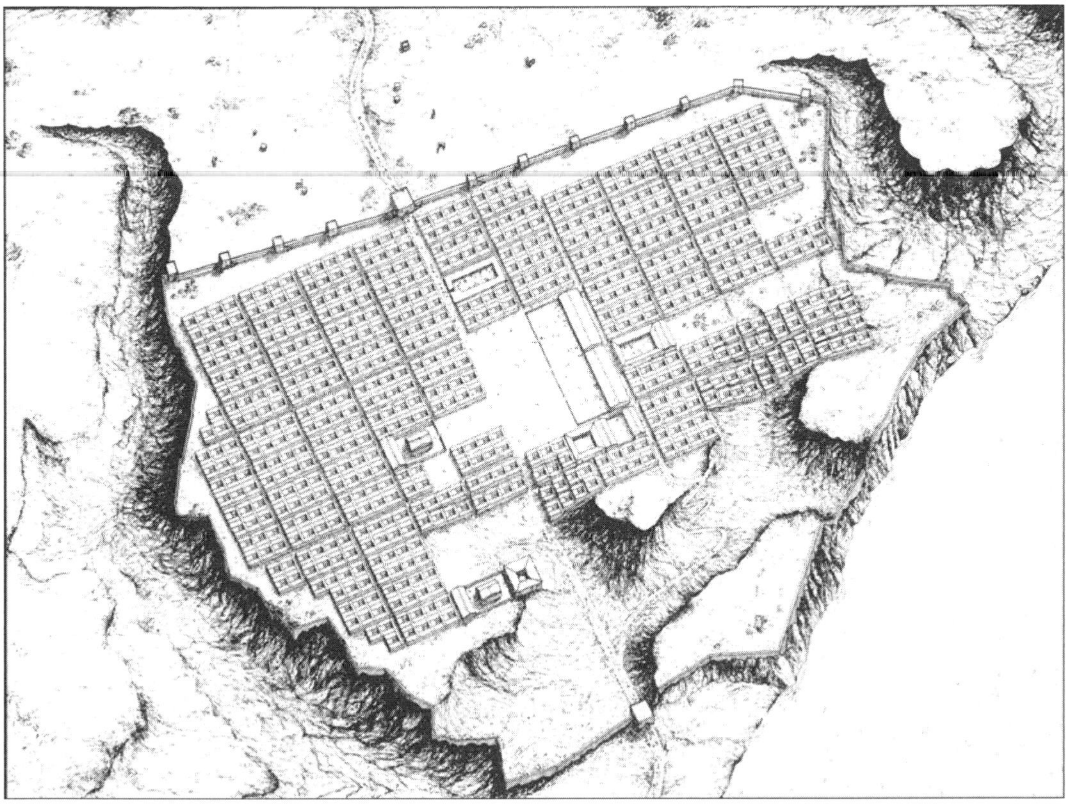

1. Dura Europos, plan of the city *c.* 300 BC; reconstruction drawing

to 1.2 m wide) that served for drainage and light. At another Late Classical strip city, Kassope in Epiros, the houses were again joined together to form long *insulae*. The rigid grid of the residential area did not, however, extend to the agora, situated on the edge of the city, and the public buildings around it. The prytaneion, market building and hall are aligned with the streets, but the bouleuterion (council house) and the great altars are completely off axis, presumably to counteract the geometric order.

From the mid-5th century BC onwards, newly founded cities nearly always had a precise southerly orientation to exploit sunlight, as advocated by Xenophon (*Memorabilia* III.viii.8–10). The high summer sun was excluded from the colonnaded areas of the houses (both *prostas* and *pastas* types), while the oblique winter sun penetrated deep into them, even warming rooms behind. Even so, the main orientation of Dura Europos was instead designed to exploit cooling breezes.

In the newly founded Classical cities the central sanctuary was erected on a dominant site, as shown by the Temple of Athena at Priene, which stood on a high, specially reserved terrace in the middle of the residential city, near the agora. Similar schemes apparently existed at Rhodes and Olynthos. Hippodamos seems to have attached great importance to sanctuaries (Aristotle: *Politics* II.1267b 33–5) and wanted to designate a third of the area of any city as 'sacred land'. Many cities also developed special ceremonial avenues or 'sacred ways', which were used in annual processions to important sanctuaries, though almost all were built over in Hellenistic times and reduced to narrow streets.

The most important act during the foundation of any new colonial city was probably the allocation of equal plots of agricultural land to the settlers. In addition, every family was presumably also allocated a plot for a garden. These were in the lowest and dampest areas of the city. Similarly, plots in the cemeteries flanking the main streets outside the city were probably also distributed among the citizens when the city was founded.

The newly founded Classical cities were based on strict geometric principles. In Hellenistic times, however, a more romantic approach to urban planning developed, employing parks, groups of trees and fountains. Again, whereas earlier domestic architecture had been modest, the elaborate architecture of royal palaces now became a prominent feature of many city centres.

R. E. Wycherley: *How the Greeks Built Cities* (London, 1949, 3/1969)

R. Martin: *L'Urbanisme de la Grèce antique* (Paris, 1956, rev. 2/1974)

E. Greco and M. Torelli: *Storia dell'urbanistica: Il mondo greco* (Rome, 1983)
W. Hoepfner and E. L. Schwander: *Haus und Stadt im klassischen Griechenland* (Munich, 1986, 2/1993)
K. Mitchell: *Town Planning in Ancient Athens: A Theory of Origins* (diss., Seattle, U. WA, 1996)
M. E. H. Walbank: 'The Foundation and Planning of Early Roman Corinth', *J. Roman Archaeol.*, x (1997), pp. 95–130
N. Robertson: 'The City Center of Archaic Athens', *Hesperia*, lxvii/3 (July–Sept 1998), pp. 283–302
N. Cahill: *Household and City Organization at Olynthus* (New Haven, 2002)
M. Korres and C. Bouras: *Athens: From the Classical Period to the Present Day (5th century BC–AD 2000)*(New Castle, DE, 2003)
D. N. Schowalter and S. J. Friesen: *Urban Religion in Roman Corinth: Interdisciplinary Approaches*(Cambridge, MA, 2005)
G. C. R. Schmalz: 'The Athenian Prytaneion Discovered?', *Hesperia*, lxxv/1 (Jan–March 2006), pp. 33–81

II. Roman.

Roman planning began with the conquest of Italy when the expanding power was exposed to existing regularly planned towns and began to colonize for military and strategic reasons. The planning of sanctuaries was strongly influenced by the Hellenistic Greek tradition, whereas Roman military architecture was always an important additional influence on the planning of towns. Improved communications systems and water supplies were also a characteristic Roman feature.

1. Sanctuary planning. 2. Town planning. 3. Road and aqueduct planning.

1. Sanctuary planning. The earliest Roman sanctuaries were simply natural features, for example springs or groves such as that of Diana at Nemi. These were thought to be haunted by deities who required propitiation through sacrifice. In the course of time they acquired other functions, as votaries actively sought out the help of the gods to fortell the future and especially to heal diseases. From early Republican times these sanctuaries acquired an architectural form with temples and other buildings, based directly on models in the Greek East, or on Etruscan adaptations of them. The Roman temple, although similar to the Greek in its simple division into porch and cella and in its use of columns, employs all of these features with distinctive modifications and is set at the back of its enclosure on a high podium. Even the late 6th-century BC Temple of Jupiter Capitolinus was not simply a Greek temple consecrated in Rome but the home of a native, albeit Hellenized, cult. Not all Roman sanctuaries had temples this early—at Nemi, for example, the temple seems to date only to the late 4th century BC, although a cult statue in the Classical Greek style may have been erected before then—with time, however, they became a standard feature. The major development of many Roman sanctuaries took place in later Republican times, when subsidiary buildings for assembly such as theatres were constructed. Strong Greek influence is once more apparent: for example the axial arrangement of the terraces in the great Sanctuary of Fortuna Primigenia at Praeneste (*c.* 80 BC) closely resembles the layout of the Hellenistic Sanctuary of Asklepios on Kos. The actual cult of Asklepios was introduced to Italy in 295 BC and established on the Tiber Island, which was developed as a sanctuary with a perimeter in the shape of a ship. More exotic cults were also imported, such as that of Cybele with its eunuch priests, established on the Palatine in Rome in 204 BC with a temple and a theatre.

When Greece itself became part of the Roman Empire (146 BC) its ancient sanctuaries such as Olympia, Delphi, Epidauros and Eleusis continued to flourish. Pausanias, a doctor from Asia Minor, who travelled around Greece in the 2nd century, wrote an invaluable guidebook describing the sites as they existed at this time. Indeed, conditions of peace and prosperity led to their embellishment with more statues, the reconstruction of principal buildings and the provision of lavish baths. More people were initiated into the Eleusinian mysteries and consulted the Delphic oracle than ever before, while previously less important oracles such as that of Apollo at Klaros in Asia Minor assumed greater significance: some completely new oracular sanctuaries were established, for example that of Glykon at Abonouteichos (2nd century AD), founded by a charlatan called Alexander (see Lucian of Samosata's amusing account: *Alexander*).

In the Levant ancient Eastern deities were venerated in sanctuaries combining a veneer of Hellenism with far older elements, such as that of Jupiter (Zeus) Heliopolitanus at Baalbek (1st–3rd century AD) with its axial arrangement of courts culminating in the temple proper, and the Jewish Temple at Jerusalem, last rebuilt by Herod the Great but almost entirely destroyed during the Jewish revolt of AD 70: despite its emphasis on monotheism, the Jewish religion resembled other cults in centering on sacrifices and visits to a sanctuary. Even more rooted in a local past were the great temple sanctuaries of Egypt; the Roman emperors followed the precedent of the Ptolemies in patronizing the construction of traditional pharaonic religious structures.

In the West, in most of Spain, in Gaul and in Britain, the Romans encountered sanctuaries even less sophisticated than their own rural shrines, though perhaps recalling what the very earliest Italian sanctuaries had been like. Lucan (*Civil War* III.399–425) gave a graphic description of a sacred grove near Marseille used for bloody human sacrifices, and similar shrines were to be found in Britain. The Romans (or, often, Romanized natives) tamed such cults and provided buildings similar to those in Italy and elsewhere in the Empire. At Bath, for example, in a temple probably built by a pro-Roman British client king called Tiberius Claudius Togidubnus [Cogidubnus], the local goddess Sulis was equated with Minerva, probably because both deities were associated with healing, and was venerated in a splendid sanctuary (*c.* AD 70–4th century; see fig. 2). It comprised a temple containing the cult statue, a sculpted altar, a

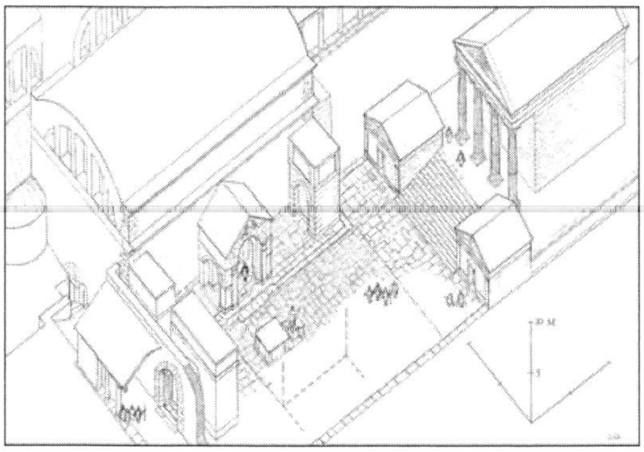

2. Sanctuary of Sulis Minerva, Bath, England, in the 4th century AD; axonometric reconstruction drawing from B. Cunliffe and P. Davenport: *The Temple of Sulis Minerva at Bath* (Oxford, 1985)

sacred spring with an impressive architectural surround, lavish baths, a tholos, almost certainly a theatre and perhaps an *abaton* (Gr.: 'untrodden'), for those not in a state of ritual purity, where the sleeping votary could receive the deity. Similar great healing complexes occur in Gaul, for example that of Sequana at the source of the Seine (mainly 2nd century AD), while other large rural sanctuaries include those at Vieil-Evreux in Eure (1st–3rd century AD) and at Sanxay in Vienne (2nd century AD). A lesser healing sanctuary of Nodens at Lydney, Glos, in England (4th century AD) includes an *abaton*, which suggests affinities with the Sanctuary of Asklepios at EPIDAUROS, as does the discovery there of votive figurines of hounds, perhaps temple hounds that assisted in healing rites; while a votive bowl (2nd century AD) depicting the Sanctuary of Mercury at Berthouville in Eure (1st–3rd centuries AD) shows that it contained a sacred tree and two monumental columns, features that probably recurred frequently elsewhere.

Some sanctuaries were situated in towns, but the larger religious centres in the countryside also acquired urban structures such as houses and inns. At major festivals they must have been enlarged by considerable temporary accommodation and by the stalls of traders, turning the sanctuaries themselves into important meeting-places. Many of the most frequented were concerned with healing, and votive models of parts of the body in various materials occur throughout much of the Empire, while inscribed testimonials such as those at Epidauros and at the Temple of Aesculapius on the Tiber Island record miraculous cures. The gods could punish as well as heal, and lead tablets recovered from various shrines, for example the spring at Bath, ask the deity to punish malefactors. Finally, the Romans seem to have founded some sanctuaries for overtly political motives. The Sanctuary of the Three Gauls at Lugdunum (Lyon) with its altar and accompanying structures was dedicated in 12 BC to Rome and Augustus: the focus of worship, the goddess Roma, was effectively the power of Rome itself. A similar shrine at Camulodonum (Colchester) was destroyed in the revolt of Boudicca (AD 60; later rebuilt) as being the 'citadel of eternal domination', but elsewhere shrines of the imperial cult appear to have been well received, especially in the Greek East, probably because the festivals associated with them offered the same range of spectacle, sacrifice, splendid architecture, art, theatre, choral singing and sport as did those of the older gods.

R. MacMullen: *Paganism in the Roman Empire* (New Haven, 1981)

A. G. MacCormick, ed.: exhibition catalogue *Mysteries of Diana. The antiquities from Nemi in Nottingham Museum* (Nottingham, 1983)

M. Henig: *Religion in Roman Britain* (London, 1984)

S. R. F. Price: *Rituals and Power: The Roman Imperial Cult in Asia Minor* (Cambridge, 1984)

B. Cunliffe and P. Davenport: *The Temple of Sulis Minerva at Bath: 1. The Site* (Oxford, 1985)

T. W. Potter: 'A Republican Healing-sanctuary at Ponte di Nona near Rome and the Classical Tradition of Votive Medicine', *J. Brit. Archaeol. Assoc.*, cxxxviii (1985), pp. 23–47

A. K. Bowman: *Egypt after the Pharaohs, 332* BC–AD *642* (London, 1986)

M. Henig and A. King, eds: *Pagan Gods and Shrines of the Roman Empire* (Oxford University Committee for Archaeology, Monograph no. 8, 1986)

R. Lane Fox: *Pagans and Christians in the Mediterranean World from the Second Century* AD *to the Conversion of Constantine* (Harmondsworth, 1986)

B. Cunliffe, ed.: *The Temple of Sulis Minerva at Bath: 2. The Finds from the Sacred Spring* (Oxford, 1988)

R. Jackson: *Doctors and Diseases in the Roman Empire* (London, 1988), pp. 138–69

G. M. Rogers: *The Sacred Identity of Ephesos: Foundation Myths of a Roman City* (London and New York, 1991)

P.-H. Mitard: *Le Sanctuaire Gallo-Romain de Genainville (Val-d'Oise)* (Guiry-en-Vexin, 1993)

M. Henig: 'From Classical Greece to Roman Britain: Some Hellenic Themes in Provincial Art and Glyptics', *Periplous: To Sir John Boardman from his Pupils and Friends*, eds G. R. Tsetskhladze, A. J. N. W. Prag and A. M. Snodgrass (London, 1999), pp. 124–35

P. Richardson: *City and Sanctuary: Religion and Architecture in the Roman Near East* (London, 2002)

C. M. C. Green: *Roman Religion and the Cult of Diana at Aricia* (Cambridge, 2007)

2. TOWN PLANNING. It has often been noted that Classical civilization was based, as the word suggests (Lat. *civis*: 'citizen'), on the idea of a city. In the Roman world cities provided the social and commercial amenities for themselves and their surrounding territories as well as organizational potential for future development. The Greek writer Pausanias, writing in the mid-2nd century AD, considered that a city was only worthy of the name if it included a temple, theatre, nymphaeum and gymnasium. Added to these buildings of Hellenistic ancestry a Roman city would also contain markets, council chambers, baths and public lavatories with attendant water supplies and drainage

systems. The grandest cities even boasted lighting along their main thoroughfares.

(i) Principles and procedures. (ii) Regional survey.

(i) Principles and procedures. New foundations are the most revealing for the history of Roman town planning, as pre-existing settlements could only be adapted and embellished. (Rome itself was more of an organic growth, developing across the seven hills of its Iron Age predecessor; *see* ROME, §II, 1.) New cities were defined and planned by *mensores* and *grommatici* (surveyors) from all over the Empire. The foundations were accompanied by a certain amount of ritual, probably Etruscan in origin. Once the site had been chosen, the line of the walls was marked by a ploughed furrow, the plough being lifted at the points for gates, and an open area (the *pomerium*) was left between the walls and the fields beyond. There were grades of Roman settlements, each one having civic organizations that were to varying extents based on that of Rome. Foremost were the *coloniae*, originally military in function and representing the highest form of urban life, followed by *municipia* or *civitas* capitals.

Several Roman writers, such as Hyginus Grommaticus or SEXTUS JULIUS FRONTINUS, touched on town planning in their works, but only the architect VITRUVIUS provided specific guidelines in his *On Architecture*. Thus sites chosen for new towns should be within healthy environments with adjacent pasturage, and the effects of nearby coasts and marshlands should be noted. (A fresh water supply was not an indispensable requisite for new sites because Roman engineering skills enabled water to be brought from miles away on aqueducts; *see* §3 below). Vitruvius then discussed the layout and construction of the city walls, arguing against a square plan. A street pattern should provide the internal division, the forum being placed either in the centre of the town or, if a coastal city, nearer the sea side, with the basilica on the warmest side of the forum. Temple location depended on the deity worshipped but theatres should be placed facing south and baths situated in the warmest part of the city.

The rigid planning most readily associated with Roman cities was based on the orthogonal planning developed by the Greeks in the 8th century BC (*see* §I above), although in the Roman case there was little of the accompanying philosophy of social organization. The grid pattern of streets proved to be admirably practical, and the Romans developed infinite variations on the theme. Given the importance of the agricultural hinterland, town planning was ideally, but not universally, linked to the centuriated division of the newly acquired surrounding countryside; stone plans (*c.* 35 BC) of the territory around Arausio (now Orange) survive. The town plans of Forum Cornelii (now Imola) and other cities in northern Italy were linked to the surrounding centuriation, and this relationship gave rise to the urban nomenclature of civic streets as *cardines* and *decumani*, which started out as terms from rural surveying. The most common arrangement was a *cardo* (main street), ideally running north-south, with two transverse *decumani*, all intersected by smaller parallel roads.

New settlements were also planned in relation to the great communication routes of the Roman Empire. The Via Aemilia, for example, also formed the *cardo* of Forum Cornelii and Parma. Earlier settlements on the line of the road such as Piacenza (Placentia, founded 218 BC) only adopted a grid pattern after the building of the road in 187 BC, while Forum Livi (now Forlì) emerged as an organic growth after 187 BC around the place where several roads converged on the line of the Via Aemilia. The anomalies of the town plan of Pompeii, founded as a Roman colony *c.* 80 BC but based on an earlier settlement, are due to the incorporation of pre-existing suburban roads. A similar case exists at Verulamium (now St Albans) where the plan incorporates an oblique stretch of Watling Street, thus making a nonsense of the strict grid. Advances in constructional engineering led to the greater imposition of a standard plan on the natural terrain. At Herdonia (now Ordona, founded in the 2nd century BC) the forum area was artificially built up and levelled above the valley floor. Many a later forum was enhanced by a cryptoporticus developed out of this constructional necessity.

One of the most distinctive elements in Roman town planning was the arrangement of the FORUM and the juxtaposition of public buildings with it. The forum was the focal point of any city and therefore associated with aspects representing the civic and sacred nature of the settlement as a whole. The usual form was with the BASILICA at one end and a temple at the other, often the capitolium dedicated to the dominant three deities of the Roman pantheon. Next to or near the forum was often found the curia (council chamber), and where a second or even third forum was built in an expanded city it was always the one with the curia that remained the most important in civic terms. Forum and basilica together became increasingly planned as a single architectural theme. This integrated development can be seen at Glanum (1st century BC), Veleia (early 1st century AD) and Alba Fucens and Herdonia a little later. The main *decumanus* often bisected the complex between the temple and the forum, for example at Brixia (now Brescia). The ultimate development of this form can best be seen at AUGUSTA RAURICA (now Augst), where by the mid-2nd century AD the entire complex of forum, basilica and capitolium was welded together by rows of uniform shop porticos. In Rome the series of cramped Imperial Fora also culminated in this form under Trajan. Further afield there were infinite variations on the theme. In Londinium (now London), for example, the forum appears to be independent of a temple to the west but was situated to take advantage of its position on a rise overlooking the river.

The extramural expansion of existing towns was usually a salutary lesson for the dogmatic planner. Only in very few instances was there a planned growth, such as Hadrian's new quarter at Athens (early 2nd century AD). At THAMUGADI (now Timgad) suburbs that also contained public buildings almost doubled the size of the original foundation (AD 100) in less than a century. Here and elsewhere there appears to have been no attempt to regulate any expansion, which was increasingly caused by military circumstances. At Eboracum (now York) the expanded city was redesigned in the 3rd century AD to define separate military and civilian spheres either side of the river.

(ii) Regional survey. Towards the end of the 1st century BC and especially after the establishment of the Empire under Augustus, greater prosperity brought a growth in population and an increase in the pressure of space even in the smaller towns. It was therefore at this time that many cities and towns were remodelled and new ones founded on more regular plans. The definitive Roman town emerged largely in the flat lands of northern Italy, where the plans and the architecture influenced much of Rome's urban expansion in the western and northern Empire. In the West the idea of a town was new and the standard grid pattern was admirably practical for new foundations. Roman cities were often sited on the plains at the base of existing hill settlements. The foundation of Lugdunum (now Lyon) in 43 BC, however, is one example of the superimposition of a new city on the site of an earlier one, and subsequent expansion of new cities such as CALLEVA ATREBATUM (now Silchester) in Britain also covered the pre-Roman settlements. Many of the cities of southern France that had been founded in the 1st century BC within irregular walls, such as Arelate (now Arles) and Glanum, were extensively remodelled with internal grids towards the end of the century. The strength of the grid plan allowed the architectural development of a town to retain a uniform pattern over a century or more. It also endured fluctuations of the wall circuit, for example at Calleva Atrebatum.

Increasingly town plans became more regular and cities in northern Italy such as Comum (Como) and Veleia were laid out on rectangular plans. The plan of Augusta Praetoria (23 BC; now Aosta) was divided into 16 equal rectangular blocks, each 180×140 m. Internal division by elongated blocks, a Hellenistic influence, was continued, but there was a movement towards the square block or INSULA, a term that originally referred to an apartment building not always comprising one block. As the wealthier population of cities moved out to villas in the country, their larger town houses were increasingly converted into apartment blocks. The gradual placement of the main street junction and the forum in the centre of the town provided more unitary plans. It was originally the town plan that influenced the military camp, but new garrisons in parts of the Empire now pacified were themselves sometimes influential, for example in the displacement of the transverse axis at Augusta Praetoria. In Britain in the later 1st century AD Camulodunum (now Colchester), Glevum (now Gloucester) and Lindum (now Lincoln) all developed directly from the fortresses that preceded the civilian colonies.

This Western style of planning was also evident in Roman Africa and at its extreme form is found in the rigid plan of Thamugadi. In contrast, CUICUL (now Djemila) was sited on a high crest typical of Punic settlements, thereby precluding a strict orthogonal plan. To the east, LEPTIS MAGNA emerged in Roman form under Augustus, west of the original Punic settlement (see fig. 3a). Its centre was the forum (now known as the Old Forum), the regular layout of which provided the basis for the continued and uniformly axial development of public buildings around it (3b). The market, theatre and Chalcidicum were originally built on the southern outskirts of the city, their appearance linked to the progression of the main street to the rich agricultural hinterlands in the south (3c). This road changed direction with each new phase of construction, resulting in a shift of the city's centre (3d) and providing much opportunity for the skilful masking of awkward angles in the street pattern with arches or larger buildings. Only the Baths of Hadrian in the south-east used up vacant land without much regard to any part of the street grid (3e). In the 3rd century AD the emperor Septimius Severus created a whole new quarter to the east, with a forum-basilica complex to the west of a monumental colonnaded street (3f). The continued

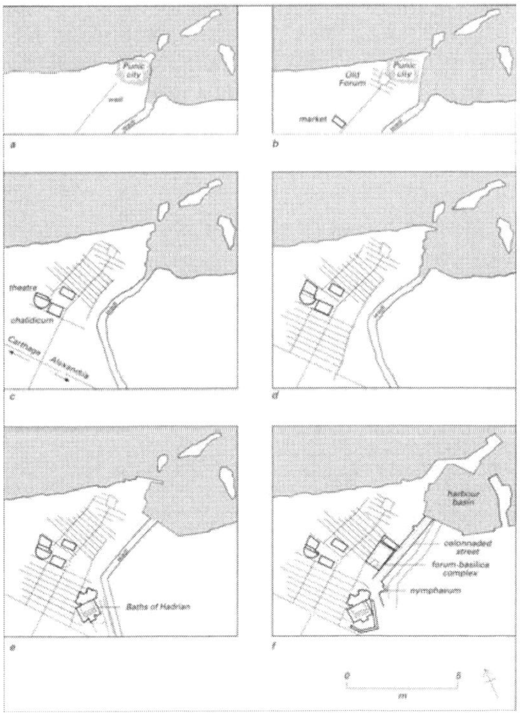

3. Leptis Magna, Libya, plans showing Roman development: (a) pre-Roman nucleus; (b) first Roman city, late 1st century BC (c) 8 BC–AD 12; (d) 1st century AD; (e) 2nd century AD; (f) early 3rd century AD

adaptation and development of existing plans at Leptis Magna is one of the most innovative examples of Roman planning.

Rome's original conquest of the East revealed a rich urban heritage and the Hellenistic plans of cities in Asia Minor and Syria were largely respected. There was little fresh development but an adaptation of existing plans provided an increased interest in axiality and monumentality that has been described as 'baroque'. In some cities, such as EPHESOS, new and magnificent buildings were added piecemeal to the plan. By the 2nd century AD it was common for many of the cities in this area to have had their main streets widened and colonnaded, changing a 'mere means of circulation into an independent monumental feature' (Lyttelton). These new long vistas were often enhanced by a focal point at either end, sometimes a temple but often a gateway, arch or intersecting tetrapylon. Where new plans were established, they could display Hellenistic inspiration. GERASA, begun in the 1st century AD and developed into the 3rd, showed a remarkable exploitation of natural features. Its *cardo* was situated on a long terrace up on the western side of the river valley and contours were used to exhibit monumental effects. One of the last new cities founded here, and never completed, was Philippopolis (Shahba, Syria), founded by Philip the Arab (*reg* AD 244–9). The almost forgotten origin of its plan is reflected in an irregular square with two main streets that intersect off-centre and smaller streets that are not entirely right-angled.

The introspective nature of late Roman architecture had little need for grandiose civic plans. Earlier buildings were often redefined in shape and function and traffic became utilitarian in contracted cities whose only development was organic.

Urbanism and Town Planning, iv of *Acta Congressus Madvigiani: Proceedings of the 2nd International Congress of Classical Studies: Copenhagen, 1954*

E. Nash: *A Pictorial Dictionary of Ancient Rome*, 2 vols (London, 1961–2, 2/1968)

A. Piganiol: *Les Documents cadastraux de la colonie romaine d'Orange* (Paris, 1962)

J. B. Ward-Perkins: 'From Republic to Empire: Reflections on the Early Provincial Architecture of the Roman West', *J. Roman Stud.*, lx (1970), pp. 1–19

O. A. W. Dilke: *The Roman Land Surveyors* (Newton Abbot, 1971)

F. Castagnoli: *Orthogonal Town Planning in Antiquity* (Cambridge, MA, and London, 1972)

M. Lyttelton: *Baroque Architecture in Classical Antiquity* (London, 1974), p. 223

J. B. Ward-Perkins: *Cities of Ancient Greece and Italy: Planning in Classical Antiquity* (New York, 1974)

A. Segal: 'Roman Cities in the Province of Arabia', *J. Soc. Archit. Hist.*, xl/2 (1981), pp. 108–21

J. B. Ward-Perkins: *Roman Imperial Architecture*, Pelican Hist. A. (Harmondsworth, 1981)

F. Grew and B. Hobley, eds: *Roman Urban Topography in Britain and the Western Empire* (London, 1985)

W. L. MacDonald: *An Urban Appraisal* (1986), ii of *The Architecture of the Roman Empire* (New Haven, 1965–86)

A. Segal: *Town Planning and Architecture in Provincia Arabia: The Cities along the Via Traiana Nova in the 1st–3rd Centuries CE* (Oxford, 1988)

D. Alicu and A. Paki: *Town-planning and Population in Ulpia Traiana Sarmizegetusa* (Oxford, 1995)

I. M. Barton: *Roman Public Buildings* (Exeter, 1995)

'Bulletin de la Société française d'Archéologie classique (XXXI, 1998–1999)', *Rev. Archéol.*, i (2000), pp. 119–223 [16 article special section]

M. Bussagli: *Rome: Art & Architecture* (Cologne, 2004)

3. ROAD AND AQUEDUCT PLANNING.

(i) Roads and water supply lines. The earliest Roman roads were local ones, such as the Via Salaria (Salt Road) to the harbour at Asculum and the Via Tiberina following the Tiber valley to the Sanctuary of Lucus Feroniae. However, in the 4th century BC and early 3rd Rome's conquest of Italy was accompanied by the construction of great highways bearing the names of the magistrates who had commissioned them. The earliest, the Via Appia, was begun in 312 BC during the Samnite Wars, though it was extended many times later, becoming the principal route to southern Italy and the port of Brundisium (Brindisi). By the late 3rd century BC, Rome was at the centre of a road network including the Via Flaminia (334 km), the Via Aurelia (280 km) and the Via Cassia (416 km). Initially the roads were unsurfaced, but some sections of the Via Appia were paved as early as 296 BC. Main roads were generally 4–4.5 m wide, and surfaces consisted of well-fitted polygonal trachite blocks on a pounded earth and pebble bed. Kerbs lined both sides, while, from the 3rd century BC on, *cippi* (milestones) were also erected. These were small columns marked with their distance from the Forum Romanum, where Augustus set up the *milliarium aureum* (20 BC), a column of gilded bronze with the names of Italian cities and their distances from Rome.

In Republican times even important towns, such as Pompeii, often depended for their water on wells, rainwater cisterns and springs within the urban area. However, Roman cities in the East sometimes inherited Hellenistic long-distance supply lines, while the earliest supply line to Rome itself, the Aqua Appia, was built in 312 BC. Roman supply systems fell into two main categories: jointed terracotta, or even wooden, pipes and stone or terracotta channels, designed to carry water at or near atmospheric pressure; and heavy duty pipes of lead, stone or thick terracotta (sometimes reinforced at the joints by stone blocks, or encased in cement) designed to withstand a considerable head. Builders of long-distance supply lines generally eliminated high pressures by maintaining gentle downhill gradients and avoiding full pipe flows. Indeed, most such systems were of simple channel type, presumably because these were easier to maintain and produce than a series of pipelines of equivalent capacity. However, many pipelines within towns were of lead as they had to supply water flowing at high pressures, notably over undulating terrain or to upper storeys. On reaching a city, an external supply line discharged into the *castellum urbanum* (best examples at Pompeii and Nemausus (Nîmes), both probably Augustan), a large distribution basin that sometimes also served as a sedimentation and/or storage tank and could be incorporated into a nymphaeum, as at Miletos (late 1st century AD). Subsidiary distribution tanks also occur, notably at Pompeii, where they were raised on brick towers or arches to maintain a sufficient head in the branch lines. These towers are usually accompanied by small basin fountains with sculpted inlets. Distribution was generally on a priority basis, using weirs or outlets at different heights. Adjustable sluices also occur, but calibration using different pipe diameters seems to have been rare, though Frontinus (*On Aqueducts* xxxvi) used *calices* (bronze tubes with standard bores) as crude gauges of flows. From Augustan times, *cippi* were also placed along water supply lines to help locate access points. They resembled milestones but were more closely spaced and marked with distances from the *castellum*.

(ii) Cuttings, tunnels and embankments. Roman roads were remarkably straight: if obliged to deviate, as the Via Aurelia was when crossing the River Mignone, they resumed their original courses as soon as possible, even if this required a large cutting, as in the Montagna Spaccata, with sides faced in concrete and *opus reticulatum* (Augustan). Cuttings for mountain roads were major engineering feats. The 220 m long and 3 m wide Donnaz cutting in the Val d'Aosta (*c.* 25 BC) is hewn through solid rock. Tunnels were rare, but occasionally unavoidable; thus a remarkable specimen was bored through the hills of Posillipo to connect Puteoli and Naples (late 1st century BC, l. 705 m). Sometimes embankments were also needed, as on the valley side of the Via Appia on its long descent towards Fondi.

In contrast, Roman water supply lines meandered along the contours of hillsides and often made large detours to avoid obstacles. Under the Republic external water supply systems were almost entirely underground to prevent sabotage by enemies, and though visible structures subsequently became more common, underground schemes were still preferred, probably mainly for economic reasons, though also to combat accidental damage and contamination and to keep supplies cool. These supply systems took the form of lined and waterproofed trenches with buried covers, incorporating simple channels or, more rarely, containing pipes. The earliest channel systems were often small (e.g. 400×350 mm at Patara, probably 1st century BC), but later specimens were generally made large enough for the passage of workmen and equipped with manholes. Early examples often had slab covers (e.g. the Mont d'Or channel, Lugdunum (Lyon), probably 1st century BC), but later concrete vaults predominated (e.g. in the Eifel channel to Colonia Claudia Ara Agrippinensium (Cologne), perhaps 1st century AD). Tunnels were generally only used to penetrate abrupt barriers and where a detour would have been even more costly. When the tunnel was only a short distance below the ground surface it was generally cut by sinking a series of shafts at regular intervals and linking them together; this speeded construction and provided ready-made aeration and access holes. Deep tunnels were bored from one end, if relatively short, and from both—again to speed construction—if longer (e.g. the Mons Aeflanus tunnel at Saldae in North Africa, *c.* AD 150). Cuttings were often used too, to negotiate lesser obstacles. Some were large rock-cut passages covered with slabs or vaults (e.g. at Side, 2nd century AD), but others are simple beddings for pipelines (e.g. at Oinoanda, later 1st century AD; and Ephesos, perhaps partly early 1st century AD), while pipelines were also placed on walled embankments (as again at Oinoanda and Ephesos) when their position on a steep slope made them vulnerable to landslips.

(iii) Aqueducts and bridges. The most striking remains of Roman water systems are above ground. Raised structures were frequently required to carry water supplies and roads over obstacles such as rivers, but also to maintain a suitable level or gradient on undulating terrain. Those over rivers needed arches to allow the passage of water, whereas those across dry depressions could be solid causeways with only small drainage openings. However, arched construction might be chosen where the savings in materials offset the extra labour costs; hence, probably, the use of vast arched AQUEDUCTS to cross the plains around Rome. Good examples of plain causeways are provided by the aqueduct at Patara (later 1st century AD) and the viaduct at Itri (*c.* 312 BC). Significantly, both were made of polygonal masonry, in which it was difficult to incorporate conventional arches. Changes in aqueduct forms also doubtless reflected increasing expertise in the use of arches. The earliest aqueducts, on the Anio Vetus (272 BC), were short and had few spans. More elaborate arched construction began with the Aqua Marcia (144 BC) and resulted in spectacular individual structures such as the PONT DU GARD (273 m long and up to 48.77 m high, late 1st century BC) and the markedly different aqueduct at Segovia (818 m long and up to 28.5 m high, early to mid-1st century AD). With its wide, relatively low, arches and thick piers, the Pont du Gard looks solid and functional; in contrast, the tall, narrow arches and thin piers of the aqueduct at Segovia make it seem a towering, airy structure, despite its lesser height. The aqueducts at Augusta Emerita (Mérida; probably early 2nd century AD) are closer in form to that at Segovia, but more sophisticated structurally in their use of cruciform pier sections, concrete cores and false lower arches; yet also more severe, despite their decorative bands of brickwork. If possible, the Romans tried to bridge a

fast-flowing river in a single span, since abutments in the stream could be undermined by water scour. Thus the central spans of many bridges are wider than those at the sides and, because the Romans used round-headed arches, the central span starts lower than its neighbours to maintain a level road surface. The highest extant Roman bridge, at Alcántara (47 m, *c.* AD 106), illustrates the mastery of such technical problems. The resilience of Roman bridges is attested to by the number still carrying traffic over the Tiber, notably the Pons Milvius (109 BC), the Pons Fabricius (62 BC) and the Pons Aelius (AD 134). Roman causeways also sometimes had sloping surfaces: the viaduct at Ariccia (2nd or 1st century BC) is a continuous masonry ramp ascending 13.2 m over a length of 231.25 m.

Aqueducts carrying water at atmospheric pressure had to be above the discharge points of their supply systems and could only slope downhill. However, some were also used in inverted siphons, that is pressurized pipelines crossing depressions below both their sources and end points. The *venter* ('belly') of these siphons was a device designed to smooth the transition between the downslope and upslope of the pipeline and so prevent damage at this point, for example at Aspendos (see Vitruvius: *On Architecture* VIII.vi.5–6). In Gaul, inverted siphons with lead pipelines were used at Lyon and elsewhere to cross depressions too deep to be spanned by conventional aqueducts. In Asia Minor, however, stone versions were used to cross much shallower obstacles, although because of the unreliability of their material, some still required substantial substructures to reduce the head of pressure.

Frontinus: *De aquis urbis Romae*; modern edn as *Wasserversorgung im antiken Rom* (Munich, 1982)

E. B. Van Deman: *The Building of the Roman Aqueducts* (Washington, 1934)

T. Ashby: *The Aqueducts of Ancient Rome* (Oxford, 1935)

M. Ballance: 'The Roman Bridges of the Via Flaminia', *Pap. Brit. Sch. Rome*, xix (1951), p. 86

P. Duval: 'La Construction d'une voie romaine après les textes antiques', *Bull. Soc. N. Antiqua. France* (1959), pp. 176–86

P. Gazzola: *Ponti romani*, 2 vols (Florence, 1963)

F. Ulrix: 'Recherches sur la méthode de traçage des routes romaines', *Latomus*, xxii (1963), p. 162

G. Radke: 'Die Erschliessung Italiens durch die römischen Strassen', *Gymnasium*, lxxi (1964), pp. 204–35

P. Fustier: *La Route* (Paris, 1968), pp. 64–148

T. P. Wiseman: 'Roman Republican Road-building', *Pap. Brit. Sch. Rome*, xxxviii (1970), pp. 122–52

R. Chevallier: *Roman Roads* (London, 1976)

G. Radke: *Viae publicae romanae* (Rome, 1981)

A. T. Hodge: 'Siphons in Roman Aqueducts', *Pap. Brit. Sch. Rome*, li (1983), pp. 174–221

E. C. Stenton and J. J. Coulton: 'Oinoanda: The Water Supply and Aqueduct', *Anatol. Stud.*, xxxvi (1986), pp. 15–59

I. M. Barton: *Roman Public Buildings* (Exeter, 1995)

K. Rheidt: 'Romischer Luxus—anatolisches Erbe, Aizanoi in Phrygien: Entdeckung, Ausgrabung und neue Forschungsergebnisse', *Ant. Welt*, xxviii/6 (1997), pp. 479–99

Plato (*b* ?Athens, *c.* 429 BC; *d* 347 BC). Ancient Greek philosopher. He was the son of a distinguished and wealthy Athenian family and grew up in turbulent times; the Peloponnesian War and the bitter struggles between local oligarchic and democratic factions made life unstable and justice difficult. In 399 BC the restored democracy put to death Plato's beloved teacher Socrates (469–399 BC), reinforcing his dislike of democratic institutions. During the following years Plato travelled widely, beginning his friendship with Dion of Syracuse (409–353 BC). Around 385 BC he returned to Athens, where he remained for most of the rest of his life. He began teaching in a school that was later the first to be called an 'Academy', after the grove in which it stood. Plato made two further visits to Syracuse, attempting at Dion's request, but without success, to make a philosopher of the young ruler Dionysius II (*reg* 367–343 BC).

Plato's writings include 25–30 dialogues, the *Apology*, which is meant to represent the thought of Socrates who had not written anything himself, and a group of letters of dubious authenticity. The order of the dialogues is uncertain, but most scholars agree on a tentative division into three periods. During the first period Plato represented the character Socrates as pursuing a search for adequate ethical definitions and accounts that probably is close to the activity of the historical Socrates. The middle period shows increasingly the influence of Plato's mathematical studies. Here he continued his ethical concerns but also pursued more general epistemological and metaphysical questions, developing his Theory of Forms, according to which all genuine knowledge is based on the intellect's apprehension of immaterial paradigms such as the Beautiful itself and the Just itself. Knowledge cannot be gained from the perceptible world alone; insofar as we do attain it, it is through a process of recollection of our prenatal experience of forms (*Phaedo*) and/or through a dialectical and mathematical training (*Republic, Symposium*). The *Republic* argues that if cities are to be well governed, they must be ruled by philosophers who possess such knowledge. The dialogues of the last period raise numerous questions about both the Theory of Forms, and these moral and political ideas. Scholars disagree about how far Plato endorsed these criticisms and how far he altered Socrates' views.

In each of the three periods can be found substantial and influential reflection about beauty and the arts. In the early Socratic works Plato focuses on the inability of alleged experts to give adequate accounts of the concepts they employ. In the *Ion*, Socrates establishes that the well-known rhapsode of that name can perform poetry brilliantly, but cannot explain it. He is inspired rather than rational. In the *Hippias Major* Socrates reveals that the famous sophist, who prides himself on his understanding of beauty, cannot explain it.

The *Republic* develops a more comprehensive criticism of art and artists; it constitutes one of the harshest indictments of mimetic art in Western philosophy. In Books II–III Socrates considers the education of young children of the guardian class in the imagined ideal city. He argues that since the soul is extremely malleable, and since its emotional character, in particular, will depend upon the influences to which it is exposed, great care should be taken to censor the stories and poems the young may hear. His argument here is ethical rather than metaphysical. If people are to be trained to have the appropriate belief that goodness or virtue is sufficient for good life, it is undesirable to give them works that represent gods or heroic figures as experiencing grief, fear or other emotions that imply a deep concern about events and persons outside of personal virtue. Nor should the arousal of such emotions in the young be permitted. They may be permitted to hear poetry praising the goodness of good people, but more or less all traditional literature must go.

Book X reinforces this ethical argument, with special reference to tragedy. However, Socrates now adds to it a more general metaphysical argument that seems to imply, as the ethical argument does not, the rejection of all imitative art. Artists, Socrates claims, not only do not grasp the paradigmatic forms that show the true essence of qualities such as justice and beauty but also have a defective relation to the perceptible things that exemplify (imperfectly) these characteristics. Artists can represent the look or appearance of something, but not its essence or structure; they can, for example, show the manner of a just person but not show what his justice is. Thus when dealing with artists' works, people are further from, for example, a grasp of the essence of justice than when dealing with the perceptible objects, which are themselves imperfect paradigms. The *Symposium* continues this line of argument, urging the philosopher who pursues a true understanding of beauty to turn aside from perceptible appearances and representations, seeking the incorporeal and intangible eternal essence of beauty.

The later dialogues present a complex picture. The *Philebus*, consistently with the *Republic*, condemns art that represents worldly objects, while it praises, for both visual art and music, the creation and contemplation of pure forms and structures. The *Phaedrus*, however, appears far more hospitable to some forms of mimetic activity. The inspired poet is praised for his divine madness, and philosophy itself is held to be an activity inspired by the muses. The soul learns best when it is stirred by an erotic madness inspired by the sight of a beautiful body. The dialogue's deepest insights on love are expressed in the form of a myth that employs self-consciously literary language.

Plato was a writer about art; he was also an artist of the first rank. These two elements are not easy to understand together, since frequently Plato's condemnations of the arts occur in work that is consummately artful. His influence upon thinkers and artists of later centuries (*see also* ARISTOTLE, NEO-PLATONISM and AESTHETICS) has been pervasive and many-sided. It has also been as contradictory, as full of conflicting tendencies, as the writing itself. Thus it is possible to be a Platonist by either espousing asceticism and pursuing the separation of soul from body or following the *Phaedrus*' account of erotic madness; by repudiating artistic imitation in favour of mathematics and dialectic or finding in art access to the inspiration of true beauty.

W. Verdenius: *Mimesis: Plato's Doctrine of Aesthetic Imitation* (Leiden, 1949)

W. D. Ross: 'Plato's Theory of Forms', *An Examination of Plato's Doctrines*, ed. I. Crombie (London, 1962–3)

G. Sörbom: *Mimesis and Art* (Uppsala, 1966)

W. K. C. Guthrie: *A History of Greek Philosophy*, iv and v (Cambridge, 1975 and 1978)

I. Murdoch: *The Fire and the Sun* (Oxford, 1977)

J. Moravcsik and P. Temko, eds: *Plato on Beauty, Wisdom and the Arts* (New Jersey, 1982)

S. Halliwell: *Plato, Republic: Book X* (Bristol, 1988)

D. T. Benediktson: *Literature and the Visual Arts in Ancient Greece and Rome* (Norman, 2000)

S. Stern-Gillet: 'Art as Error: Collingwood's Early Reading of Plato', *Brit. J. Aesth.*, xl/2 (April 2000), pp. 251–63

K. Corrigan: 'Altruism and Artistic Apprehension in the Ancient World: Plato, Aristotle, Plotinus', *The Structurist*, xli–xlii (2001–2), pp. 4–10

Pliny. Roman family of writers.

(1) Pliny the Elder [Gaius Plinius Secundus] (*b* Comum [now Como, Italy], AD 23 or 24; *d* Bay of Naples, 24 Aug 79]. He was the author of the encyclopedic *Natural History* in 37 books, of which Books XXXIII–XXXVII on stones and metals offer the sole surviving history of art from antiquity. The text is eclectic, combining excerpts of earlier treatises from the 5th to the 1st century BC with Pliny's own topical comments about the setting and meaning of art in mid-1st century AD Rome. Preserved through the Middle Ages, the *Natural History* exerted an enormous influence on artists and theoreticians from the Renaissance on. In particular Pliny's historical scheme of an artistic evolution culminating in Greek art of the 5th and 4th centuries BC, with its vivid anecdotes about individual works and artists, fuelled movements of classicism and provided a foundation for the discipline of art history.

1. Life and work. 2. *Natural History*. 3. Sources.

1. LIFE AND WORK. Born in Comum of an equestrian family, Pliny was educated at Rome. At 23 he began a military career and spent 12 years with the armies of the Rhine, where he wrote a monograph on an aspect of cavalry tactics and started both a history of the Roman campaigns against the Germans and a biography of his patron, the scholar and writer Pomponius Secundus (*d c.* AD 60). Pliny's official career came to an abrupt halt after his return to Italy in 57 or 58, perhaps due to differences with Emperor Nero, and he spent the next decade studying rhetoric, grammar and possibly law. It was not until the succession of the Flavians in 69 that Pliny became active again, undertaking a series of procuratorships

in Gaul, Africa and Spain. During this time he wrote a history in 31 books, completed by 77 but published posthumously, and the *Natural History*, begun in the 50s and dedicated to Emperor Titus in 77. In his last years Pliny served as counsellor to the emperors Vespasian and Titus and commanded the fleet at Misenum. In August 79 he sailed to the area of Stabia to observe the eruption of Vesuvius and died from the fumes, an event vividly recorded in a letter by his nephew Pliny the younger to Tacitus (*Letters* VI.16). Pliny the younger also left a rough chronology of his uncle's works (of which only the *'Natural History'* survives) and anecdotes about his working habits that help explain many idiosyncracies of the text. Thus we know that the elder Pliny was constantly active, taking notes and having books read to him, probably by slaves who translated and transcribed earlier texts.

2. 'Natural History'.

(i) Introduction. (ii) Book XXXIII: gold and silver. (iii) Book XXXIV: bronze. (iv) Book XXXV: painting. (v) Book XXXVI: marble. (vi) Book XXXVII: gems.

(i) Introduction. Pliny's history is essentially a work of classification and description that seeks to define the relationship between nature and civilization. The 37 books include: a Preface which states that the text contains 20,000 important facts obtained from 100 principal authors and 2000 books (symbolic numbers meant to stress the magnitude of the work: the total number recorded in the index is in fact much higher); Book I with a summary of the following 36 books and an index of topics and earlier authors consulted; Book II on the universe; III–VI on geography; VII on man; VIII–XI on other animals; XII–XIX on botany; XX–XXVII on botany in medicine; XXVIII–XXXII on zoology in medicine; and XXXIII–XXXVII on metals and stones and their use in medicine, art and architecture.

Pliny presented the *Natural History* as something new in Rome, and it is the only surviving ancient work with a table of contents. The literary genre originated in the Hellenistic period and differed from the modern encyclopedia in its lack of any strict distinction between scientific analysis and rhetoric. Thus Pliny organized his heterogeneous compendium of facts and anecdotes with a few rhetorical devices, such as antithesis (of past and present, nature and culture, Greek and Roman), in order to establish an historical perspective within which he could express his own moralizing views about art and society.

Any reading of the *Natural History* raises the question of originality. Pliny explicitly distanced himself from his sources, which he divides between Romans and 'others' (*externi*), yet it is not always possible to tell what he adopted and what is his own. While 19th-century scholars focused on the Greek sources cited in the indexes, regarding them as intrinsically more valuable and informative, more recent studies have highlighted Pliny's own Roman contribution and recognized his invaluable commentary on the complex, ongoing process of hellenization in Italy that informed both the collecting and copying of objects as well as the Latin literature written about them.

In general Pliny was not interested in the intrinsic qualities of a work of art, for which he provides a title but rarely descriptive adjectives. We can glean most information about individual works of art or artists from the biographical anecdotes he took from earlier sources. Due to the diversity of those sources, Pliny's aesthetic evaluations of earlier art often contradict each other. In contrast Pliny was clear that in the contemporary scene the importance of art lay in its social function or association with a particular person or group. Paradoxically, a pervasive theme in his text is the abuse of art for private pleasure (*luxuria*), yet it is likely that his Roman audience was educated and included collectors and connoisseurs who would have appreciated his frequent citing of prices of works of art.

An important ingredient of Pliny's books on bronze, marble and the minerals employed as colours are the biographies of craftsmen. These begin in the time of Greek legends, and then from the first Olympiad (776 BC) follow artists by generations of about 60 years. According to his historiographical scheme, art progressed from a state of 'rude antiquity' (*rudis antiquitas*) through a series of formal inventions by artisans who carried art (*ars, techne*) towards its zenith (*arche*). This paradigm can be traced back to Aristotle (*Poetics* 1449a9) and posits that the goal of art is the replication of an objective reality, a view that makes eminent sense in a work on nature. Yet Pliny's praise of the *trompe l'oeil* illusionism (*veri similtudo*) attained in the 4th century BC does not correlate with his frequent exaltation of the idealizing art of the 5th century BC nor with his curious exclusion of Hellenistic sculpture, so exemplary for its illusionism.

For Rome as well as Greece, Pliny presented the artistic fashions of different historical periods. A nationalistic tone informs his account of the Italic origins of bronze and painting as occurring independently of the Greek inventions. From the 2nd century BC, however, the emphasis of his account shifts to the conquest and importation of Greek works and materials into Rome, which he recorded as if they were inventions. After this came a gradual decline of values in Roman society, marked by a loss of interest in such venerable materials as wood and clay and in the arts of bronze, silver-chasing and panel painting. In his own day greed and materialism (*luxuria*) had replaced the idealistic value of art, and many artisans who had come as prisoners to Rome now competed for money rather than fame. Although Pliny noted the diminishing opportunities for importing Greek originals, he failed to discuss the lively private market for copies and adaptations, as he did Roman Imperial state art.

Throughout the history Pliny expressed an attitude typical of popular Stoic thought in the mid 1st-century AD, namely the human violation of nature. This he saw especially manifest in the new 'un-Roman' *luxuria*, a view that probably reflects his background in the municipal governing class. Repeatedly he returned to the way art was brought to Rome as plunder, exhibited in triumphs, dedicated in public buildings and finally hoarded in the private sphere. In Pliny's view the display of famous Greek art, which imparted honour to those who imported and erected it, should be reserved for the State and for the emperor.

The *Natural History* remains the principal source for the contents of public collections in early Imperial Rome, which Pliny indicated were eclectic, comprising Greek art from the Archaic to the Hellenistic period as well as Roman copies. Because he listed twice as many (*c.* 100) Greek marble statues as bronze on public display, his source may have been a register of art works in Rome made with the census of AD 73 or catalogues of Augustan collections. Pliny's political alliance is clear in his persistent focus on both the present Flavian and Augustan regimes and especially in his inclusion of these emperors' works in lists of wonders (*mirabilia*). In contrast, Mark Antony and Nero are associated with *luxuria*: Nero kept bronzes under lock and key in his private Domus Aurea, Vespasian offered them to the public in his forum, the Templum Pacis.

Over 200 manuscripts of the *Natural History* exist, the oldest dating to the 5th century AD. All the pre-Carolingian manuscripts are fragmentary. A small group of manuscripts from the 10th–11th century forms the basis for modern editions. The Codex Bambergensis (10th century; Bamberg, Staatsbib., MS. Class. 42 [m.v. 10]) is most commonly used for the last six books of Pliny, followed in authority by the Codex Riccardianus (Florence, Bib. Riccardiana, MS. 488).

(ii) Book XXXIII: gold and silver. According to Pliny it is in the mineral realm that nature has suffered the most abuse. Beginning in Book XXXIII with the most precious metal, gold, then proceeding to silver and later in Book XXXIV to copper and bronze, Pliny gave historical examples of *luxuria* from Greece and Rome along with inventions, prices, medicinal uses and technical methods of extraction. Of the dying art of silver-chasing he singled out a few works for their realism or subject-matter. He mentioned cheap imitations of silver and the late Republican invention of the art of reflection through mirrors. Continuing his diatribe against moral corruption, he pin-pointed as status symbols gold statues and rings and interpreted the transition from bronze to gold coinage as a sign of the decline of Roman society that reached bottom with Nero, a development that, like many others Pliny described, is contradicted by the archaeological evidence.

(iii) Book XXXIV: bronze. In this book Pliny first described artistic activity in Rome and then listed selected Greek artists, thereby correlating Greek and Roman chronologies. In Italy he focused on the making of bronze in local regions, its use in public sculpture and architecture, and the passion for Corinthian bronzes, a label given to the Achaian statues brought to Rome following the capture of Corinth in 146 BC. After attributing the origins of bronze statuary to Italy, Pliny turned to the mass of Greek bronzes in Rome. By his own day bronze had been largely replaced by marble, but was still employed for equestrian statues of the emperor, quadrigas on triumphal arches and *colossi*. In this context Pliny explained the function of the triumphal arch, invented after the honorific column, namely to elevate one individual above other mortals.

He then listed famous Greek and Roman artists, their various works and where they could be seen, many of which we can identify from Roman marble copies. Pliny's development begins with those 5th-century BC artists engaged in the competition of the Amazons for the Temple of Artemis at Ephesos. Sculpture was 'opened up' by PHEIDIAS, the maker of the famous statue of *Zeus* at Olympia, and 'refined' by POLYKLEITOS, creator of the *Doryphoros, contrapposto*, and author of the *Canon* of proportion. MYRON OF ELEUTHERAI used greater variety in his compositions and gave more attention to *symmetria* (the commensurability of parts). PYTHAGORAS OF RHEGION surpassed Myron in rendering certain details such as sinews, veins and hair. Finally, in the 4th century BC LYSIPPOS, self-taught, surpassed all by altering the *Canon* and perfecting anatomical details. With Lysippos' pupils in 296–293 BC 'the art ceased' (*cessavit ars*) followed by a revival in 156–153 BC by 'inferiors, yet still men of repute', a controversial phrase because of Pliny's apparent dismissal of the Hellenistic Baroque and the Pergamene school. (One explanation may be that Pliny was referring specifically to bronze as the art that ceased; another would translate *ars* as Classical theory, which saw a revival in Neo-Attic workshops in the 2nd century BC.) Although Pliny's is the only extant chronological list of bronze sculptors by Olympiads, the archaeological evidence reveals significant errors and omissions; for example Myron, Pheidias and Polykleitos were contemporaries, while Pythagoras, who comes fourth in the series, was earliest. Of his concluding alphabetical catalogue of minor Greek artists and their works, which must have been familiar to Pliny's Roman readers, we have no identifiable remains.

(iv) Book XXXV: painting. Pliny's treatment of the types of earth and mineral used by painters as pigments has always been considered important because of the ephemeral nature of its subject. The evolution of painting parallels that of bronze and sculpture, reaching a high point in 5th- and 4th-century BC Greece but following an independent development in Italy.

Dismissing the theory that the art originated in Egypt, Pliny claimed that painting and clay sculpture were brought to perfection in Italy. Famous Roman painters were Fabius Pictor (*fl c.* 450 BC) and the poet Pacuvius (*fl c.* 220 BC), after which the status of painters fell, with a few notable exceptions such as

Famulus, who painted the walls of Nero's Domus Aurea while wearing a toga, and Iaia of Kyzikos (116–26 BC), a woman who specialized in female portraits and commanded higher prices than male painters. In Pliny's time painting had lost its importance, for marble panelling replaced fresco as a way of decorating a room, and bronze shields with silver faces hung in the Roman atrium instead of the traditional wax masks and painted *imagines* of ancestors.

In Greece painting began either at Sikyon or Corinth and developed from a simple tracing to a tonal harmony of colours. From drawing the outline of a man's shadow, artisans adopted the use of a single colour (monochrome) and then linear drawing inside the outline (bichrome), after which they wrote on the picture to identify the subject. EUMAROS was the first to distinguish between men and women (possibly by skin colour). KIMON OF KLEONAI invented foreshortening through three-quarter views (*katagrapha*). POLYGNOTOS OF THASOS improved such details as transparent drapery and facial expression. APOLLODOROS began the mature era of painting in the late 5th century BC by developing *skiagraphia*, a technique of shading. ZEUXIS refined the rendering of light and shade, while his rival PARRHASIOS introduced *symmetria* into painting and emphasized the clarity of draughtsmanship (his drawings on parchment were still in use in Pliny's day). EUPHRANOR 'made *symmetria* his own' and improved facial expression. Finally, in the last quarter of the 4th century BC, APELLES brought all these achievements to perfection and introduced new techniques, notably highlights to bring shapes forward and a thin dark coating (*atramentum*) over his finished paintings to protect them from dust.

Although scholars have attempted to substantiate Pliny's development, there is no surviving evidence before the Roman period for the Greek genres of caricature, everyday scenes, and still-life, nor for the many famous paintings such as Apelles' *Alexander Holding the Thunderbolt* or TIMOMACHOS' *Medea*. The use of contemporary vases, frescoes in Macedonian tombs or later Roman adaptations such as the Alexander Mosaic (House of the Faun, Pompeii; now Naples, Mus. Archeol. N.), to corroborate Pliny's succession of formal inventions has proved to be speculative and tendentious.

Pliny's overview of the techniques and colours used by the most famous painters had great influence on later artists, even though it is not always clear which pigments correspond to which colours and precisely how encaustic and tempera were composed and applied. Pliny distinguished colours as *austeri* (mat) and *floridi* (the luminous and intense shades of red, blue, purple and yellow). He referred to a technique of colour gradation for modelling as *tonos* (tension) and *harmoge* (the joining together of the transition of colours). And in his earlier section on metals Pliny reviewed the yellow and blue pigments extracted in the mines and their pictorial uses, for example blue as a dividing line separating shadows from light (XXXIII.lvii). Because of Pliny's direct adoption of Greek concepts, many terms such as *skiagraphia* (a kind of shadow-painting), *skenographia* (scene-painting, but also a form of linear perspective) and *pictura compendiaria* (a shorthand technique interpreted as a form of impressionism or the use of ready-made patterns) cannot be precisely defined.

Especially influential in the Renaissance and thereafter were Pliny's anecdotes about the verisimilitude of certain works achieved through an artist's mastery of illusionistic techniques. For example, Pliny related the famous contest in which Zeuxis created such a lifelike rendering of grapes that birds flew down to peck at them; still proud of his achievement, Zeuxis himself was tricked by Parrhasios' painted curtain when he asked that it be drawn back to reveal the picture beneath (XXXV.xxxvi). The elevation of individual skill also underlies Pliny's inclusion of last and unfinished works, which he saw as evidence of an artist's creative process (XXXV.cxlv), a phrase ('Another most curious fact and worthy of record is, that the latest works of artists and the pictures left unfinished at their deaths are valued more than any of their finished paintings') that may have inspired Michelangelo to leave some of his works unfinished. And Pliny's treatment of such specialists as the landscape painter Studius (*fl c.* 10 BC) and the Hellenistic painter of barbers' shops, Pyreikos, whom he called a 'filth painter' (*rhyparographos*), added to the estimation of genre painting in later academic theory, for despite the pejorative title, Pliny claimed that Pyreikos' lively pieces achieved a higher price than works by more famous masters (XXXV.cxii).

Certainly Pliny had seen many of the 32 famous Greek paintings he mentioned firsthand. Most listed on display were of the 4th century BC: four paintings by Apelles in Augustan buildings, two by Zeuxis, one by Parrhasios (two more in Tiberius' private collection), three by ARISTEIDES, four by Nikias and six by the early Hellenistic painter ANTIPHILOS. Julius Caesar had first introduced the habit of displaying famous Greek paintings in public places as a practice that, as with bronze sculpture, should memorialize an individual's contribution to the Roman people.

Finally Pliny turned to *plastice*, the ancient art of modelling in clay (*terracotta*) and the requisite for silver-chasing and sculpture in marble and bronze. He recorded the beginnings of clay portraiture, plaster casts of living people and famous works in clay and plaster. Two 1st-century BC artists, PASITELES and Arkesilaos, had worked first from clay models (*proplasmata*), which were still in high demand. Inevitably Pliny's section on early Italian terracotta art leads to a critique of modern *luxuria*, in which he stated his own preference for clay statues of gods to those in gold and silver. Then, in his characteristically disjointed way, he closed with remarks on the unrelated topic of miniature art.

(v) Book XXXVI: marble. This book on different types of stone begins with the invention of marble sculpture by Dipoinos and Skyllis in 580–577 BC but, unlike the preceding books on bronze and painting, presents no evolutionary history. Pliny treated only

free-standing statues, thereby omitting the significant category of Roman architectural relief, and in the rest of the book covered various subjects, notably architectural *mirabilia*. Again emphasis is placed on Augustus, whose marble architecture and sculpture became a hallmark of Imperial Rome. In contrast Pliny disapproved of the lavish columns and inlay of variegated marbles in baths, theatres and private homes.

Pliny began by singling out works by the great Greek artists on public display and the persons, primarily Augustus and Vespasian, who put them there. These include works by Pheidias, the sculptors of the Mausoleum at Halikarnassos, APOLLONIOS and TAURISKOS (the Hellenistic sculptors of the Farnese *Bull*) and Pasiteles and Arkesilaos. Of PRAXITELES, one of the Greek artists best known among Romans, Pliny related how the sculptor made two statues of the goddess, one draped, the other naked (*Aphrodite of Knidos, c.* 365 BC), and how the latter was sexually assaulted in her shrine, an event that greatly added to her fame. But Pliny complained that many high-quality works on view in prominent places in the city were still not adequately attributed.

In presenting the wonders of the world created out of marble, Pliny reshaped the conventional list compiled in the 3rd century BC by making his own selection and providing Italian counterparts. The wonders progress from ancient Egypt through 800 years to culminate in the Imperial city of Rome. Among Rome's 18 wonders rank the greatest sewer (Cloaca Maxima), theatres, art collections and Augustus' sundial complex in the Campus Martius.

As usual, Pliny provided interesting technical information, such as the methods for cutting marble, the places from which various marble-types derive, the kind of sand used for cutting polished marble and the transport of Egyptian obelisks to Rome, but many 'facts' are false or misleading. Thus, attempts to reconstruct the Mausoleum of HALIKARNASSOS based on his measurements and description of architectural details have foundered both because of the text's intrinsic shortcomings and the many corruptions resulting from its transmission.

Another famous work, the LAOKOON group, was immediately identified upon its discovery on the Esquiline Hill on 14 January 1506, based on comments in Pliny (XXXVI.iv.37), and has since aroused intensive debate. Pliny evidently regarded the work as an original. He claims that it was carved out of one block of marble by HAGESANDROS, POLYDOROS and ATHENODOROS OF RHODES, and that it surpassed all works in painting and bronze. In fact the *Laokoon* is pieced together from seven blocks of stone and is now generally thought to be a marble copy of a bronze original, dated some time between the 2nd century BC and the 1st century AD. Significantly, Pliny stressed its location in Titus' palace, and we know from the finds at the Tiberian complex at Sperlonga that artists from Rhodes and Asia Minor were working for the Imperial house throughout the 1st century AD.

Book XXXVI ends with a discussion of floor pavements, mosaics and glass. Pliny noted the spread of mosaics from floors to walls, one development that can be corroborated with surviving finds. He also recorded the shift in fashion from silver and gold to glass in the making of drinking vessels.

(vi) Book XXXVII: gems. Pliny's presentation of stones, jewellery and gems followed the pattern used in his other books. We are first told their origin, then the time they were first admired, and those most popular, such as pearls, rock-crystal, amber and diamonds. Some famous pieces, such as the magical signet ring of Polykrates of Samos, could be seen in Roman temples. After citing the diverse geographical locations where the most valuable stones were found, Pliny ended with a panegyric to Italy as the greatest source of natural wealth and beauty.

3. SOURCES. Much of modern scholarship on Pliny has been devoted to identifying and reconstructing the content of the Greek and Latin texts listed in his book-by-book bibliographical index. These represent Pollitt's (1974) four categories of ancient art criticism: professional (by and for artists), philosophical, rhetorical and literary, and popular (including epigrams and travel guides). Pliny used these in various ways, transcribing passages directly into his treatise and reorganizing and expanding them with new information. Like the Latin writers before him, he adopted the Greek canonical chronologies, lists of artists' names, critical terms and evaluations, but other technical passages also include borrowings from Celtic and Spanish.

Since the 19th century the sculptor XENOKRATES of Athens has been considered Pliny's most influential Greek source. Xenokrates' volumes on sculpture and painting are cited twice in the indexes, and these may have been based on technical treatises of still other artists. Pliny adopted many of his popular biographical anecdotes from two other Hellenistic sources. ANTIGONOS of Karystos, a sculptor of the Attalid dedications in Pergamon, seems to have expanded Xenokrates' catalogue of artists; even more significant was the compiler Douris of Samos (340–260 BC), whose treatise on sculpture and painting was filled with marvellous tales. In addition Pliny consulted works by the professional painters Apelles, Euphranor and Parrhasios.

Of writers in Rome most important were PASITELES, whose five volumes on *nobilia opera* (masterpieces) described the classicizing sculptures by members of his school in Rome. Pasiteles may have been Pliny's source for the famous phrase *cessavit ars*, in which case *ars* would be understood in the sense of Classical, formal theory. Even more influential was Marcus Terentius Varro (116–27 BC), author of over 55 treatises, who was also a transmitter of the texts of other writers such as Pasiteles. In fact, it is unclear how much Pliny actually took from the earlier works and how much he found in Varro.

Writings

K. Jex-Blake and E. Sellers, eds: *The Elder Pliny's Chapters on the History of Art* (London, 1896, rev. Chicago, 1968, 2/1977)
S. Ferri, ed.: *Storia dell'arti antiche* (Rome, 1946)
H. Rackham, ed. and trans.: *Libri XXXIII–XXXV* (1952), ix of *Natural History*, Loeb Class. Lib. (London and Cambridge, MA, 1938–62)
H. Le Bonniec and H. Gallet de Santerre, eds: *Histoire naturelle, livre XXXIV* (Paris, 1953)
D. E. Einchholz, ed: *Libri XXXVI–XXXVII* (1961), x of *Natural History*, Loeb Class. Lib. (London and Cambridge, MA, 1938–62)
R. König and G. Winkler, eds: *Naturkunde, Buch XXXV: Farben, Malerei, Plastik* (Munich and Zurich, 1978)
J. André, R. Bloch and A. Rouveret, eds: *Histoire naturelle, livre XXXVI*, Collection de l'Association Guillaume Budé (Paris, 1981)
H. Zehnacker, ed.: *Histoire naturelle, livre XXXIII*, Collection de l'Association Guillaume Budé (Paris, 1983)
R. König and G. Winkler, eds: *Naturkunde, Buch XXXIII: Metallurgie* (Munich and Zurich, 1984)
J.-M. Croisille: *Histoire naturelle, livre XXXV*, Collection de l'Association Budé (Paris, 1985)
G. B. Conte, A. Barchiesi and G. Ranucci, eds: *Gaio Plinio Secundo: Storia naturale*, v (Turin, 1988) [Books XXXIII–XXXVII, ed. and trans. by A. Corso, R. Mugellesi and G. Rosati]
R. König and K. Bayer, eds: *Naturkunde, Buch XXXIV: Metallurgie* (Munich and Zurich, 1989)
J. F. Healy, ed.: *Natural History: A Selection* (London, 1991)
R. C. A. Rottländer, ed.: *Plinius Secundus d.Ä., Über Glas und Metalle* (St Katharinen, 2000)
M. Beagon, ed.: *The Elder Pliny on the Human Animal: Natural History, Book 7* (Oxford, 2005)

Bibliography

A. Furtwängler: 'Plinius und seine Quellen über die bildende Kunst', *Jb. Klass. Philol.*, suppl. 9 (1877), pp. 3–78
G. Oehmichen: *Plinianische Studien zur geographischen und kunsthistorischen Literatur* (Erlangen, 1880/*R* Hildesheim, 1972)
A. Kalkmann: *Die Quellen der Kunstgeschichte des Plinius* (Berlin, 1898)
B. Schweitzer: *Xenocrates von Athen: Beiträge zur Geschichte der antiken Kunstforschung und Kunstanschauung* (Halle, 1932)
M. Bieber: 'Pliny and Graeco-Roman Art', *Hommage à J. Bidez et F. Cumont*, Collection Latomus, ii (Brussels, 1949), pp. 39–42
G. Becatti: *Arte e gusto negli scrittori latini* (Florence, 1951)
J. J. Pollitt: *The Art of Ancient Greece: Sources and Documents* (Cambridge and New York, 1965/rev. 1990)
J. J. Pollitt: *The Art of Rome* c. *753 BC–AD 337: Sources and Documents* (New York, 1966/*R* Cambridge, 1983)
G. Becatti: 'Plinio e Vasari', *Studi di storia dell'arte in onore di Valerio Mariani* (Naples, 1972), pp. 173–82
A. Labarre: 'Diffusion de l'Historia naturalis de Pline au temps de la Renaissance', *Festschrift für Claus Nissen*, ed. E. Geck and G. Pressler (Wiesbaden, 1973), pp. 451–70
J. J. Pollitt: *The Ancient View of Greek Art: Criticism, History, and Terminology* (New Haven and London, 1974)
W. D. E. Coulsen: 'The Reliability of Pliny's Chapters on Greek and Roman Sculpture', *Class. World*, lxix (1976), pp. 361–72
P. Gros: 'Vie et mort de l'art hellénique selon Vitruve et Pline', *Rev. Etud. Lat.*, lvi (1978), pp. 289–313
R. Schilling: 'La Place de Pline l'ancien dans la littérature technique', *Rhein. Philol.*, lii (1978), pp. 272–83
A. Daneu Lattanzi: 'A proposito dei libri sulle arti', *Plinio il vecchio sotto il profilo storico e letterario: Atti del convegno: Como, 1979*, pp. 97–107
R. L. Gordon: 'The Real and the Imaginary: Production and Religion in the Graeco-Roman World', *A. Hist.*, ii (1979), pp. 5–34
G. Gualandi: 'Plinio e il collezionismo d'arte', *Plinio il vecchio sotto il profilo storico e letterario: Atti del convegno: Como, 1979*, pp. 259–98
C. G. Nauert jr: 'Caius Plinius Secundus', *Catalogus translationum et commentariorum*, iv (Washington, DC, 1980), pp. 297–422
Plinio: I suoi luoghi, il suo tempo (Como, 1984)
R. French and F. Greenaway, eds: *Science in the Early Roman Empire: Pliny the Elder, his Sources and Influence* (London, 1986)
G. Serbat: 'Pline l'ancien: Etat présent des études sur sa vie, son oeuvre et son influence', *Aufstieg & Niedergang Röm. Welt*, xxxii/4 (Berlin, 1986), pp. 2069–200
I. Pigealdus and I. Orozius: *Pline l'ancien: Témoin de son temps* (Salamanca and Nantes, 1987); also in *Helmantica*, xxxvii (1986), pp. 8–320 and xxxviii (1987), pp. 5–322
A. Wallace-Hadrill: 'Pliny the Elder and Man's Unnatural History', *Greece & Rome*, xxxvii (1990), pp. 80–96
S. Citroni Marchetti: *Plinio il vecchio e la tradizione del moralismo romano* (Pisa, 1991)
J. Isager: *Pliny on Art and Society: The Elder Pliny's Chapters on the History of Art* (London and New York, 1991)
M. Beagon: *Roman Nature: The Thought of Pliny the Elder* (Oxford, 1992)
J. F. Healy: *Pliny the Elder on Science and Technology* (Oxford, 1999)
V. Naas: *Le Projet encyclopédique de Pline l'ancien* (Rome, 2002)
S. Carey: *Pliny's Catalogue of Culture: Art and Empire in the Natural History* (Oxford, 2003/*R* 2006)
L. Cotta Ramosino: *Plinio il Vecchio e la tradizione storica di Roma nella Naturalis historia* (Alessandria, 2004)
T. M. Murphy: *Pliny the Elder's Natural History: The Empire in the Encyclopedia* (Oxford and New York, 2004)

(2) Pliny the Younger [Gaius Plinius Caecilius Secundus] (*b* Comum (now Como, Italy), *c.* AD 61; *d* Bithynia-Pontus, *c.* 112). Nephew and adoptive son of (1) Pliny the elder. Although he never discussed art formally, his nine books of literary letters, published sporadically between 100 and 109, give a unique insight into artistic patronage among the Flavian aristocracy in Rome and the provinces, and the interior design of the wealthy house. His tenth book, of official correspondence conducted with the emperor Trajan while Pliny was governor of Bithynia, is informative about municipal building schemes and spending on public architecture in the cities of Nicaea, Nicomedia, Claudiopolis and Amastris.

As a wealthy landowner, Pliny was able to decorate his various properties in accordance with contemporary taste, apparently presiding over their planning himself. His accounts of the decoration of his villas at Laurentum near Rome (*Letters* II.xvii) and in the Apennine countryside (V.vi) give a vivid picture of Trajanic decorative schemes, for which there is otherwise comparatively little evidence. In these elegant country retreats, wall-paintings, carved marble fountains, columns and topiarized trees were juxtaposed to create an idyllic world of nature luxuriant but tamed within the parameters defined by the social and domestic space of the house (II.xvii; V.vi; IX.vii). The Laurentum villa had elaborately decorated bedrooms, bath-suites and gardens; the dining-room walls of the Apennine house were 'adorned with marble as far as the ceiling and a fresco of birds perched on the branches of trees', recalling the themes used in the earlier *triclinia* at Pompeii and Empress Livia's villa at Prima Porta. He also mentions the *Kleinkunst* of these houses, such as table silver shaped like birds or boats (V.vi), and copies of portraits of well-known writers to be hung in the library. Here Pliny expressed concern that a good artist be found so that these portraits may be as lifelike as possible, because in his opinion artists were liable to take liberties when making copies (IV.xxviii).

Pliny alluded to the Roman élite as artistic patrons, both public and private, elsewhere in his literary letters. Regulus obsessively commissioned portraits of his dead son in various different media (IV.vii); Calpurnius Fabatus commemorated his family by setting up a public colonnade with decorated bronze doors at his own expense (V.xi); Pliny himself endowed a temple at Tifernum to house the collection of Imperial statues he had acquired (III.iv; IV.i; X.viii). He also mentioned patronage of more ephemeral minor arts such as wax-moulding, which was the medium used for busts of deceased persons placed in the domestic ancestor shrine (IV.vii) as well as for miniature objects of vertu (VII.ix).

Most of the artistic references in Pliny's tenth book of letters are connected with the municipal mismanagement of architectural commissions in the cities of Bithynia-Pontus. Building rivalries between neighbouring towns were a feature of civic life in the Roman world. Such rivalry led inevitably to jerry-building and poor architectural standards, and Pliny arrived in Bithynia to find that considerable amounts of public and private money had been wasted on such projects. The city of Nicomedia had squandered over 3,000,000 sesterces on two unusable aqueducts (X.xxxvii). The nearby city of Nicaea was constructing a gymnasium on an enormous scale, but it was badly planned and built, and the theatre there was subsiding badly because of inadequate foundations. At Claudiopolis money was being lavished on a public baths in an unsuitable location (X.xxxix). Pliny recommended pragmatic solutions to all these problems, including abandoning the building programme when it would prove impracticably expensive to continue it.

A. N. Sherwin-White, ed.: *Pliny's Letters: A Social and Historical Commentary* (Oxford, 1966/*R* 2003)

F. Gamberini: *Stylistic Theory and Practice in the Younger Pliny* (Hildesheim and New York, 1983)

P. de la R. Du Prey: *The Villas of Pliny from Antiquity to Posterity* (Chicago, 1994)

I. K. McEwen: 'Housing Fame: In the Tuscan Villa of Pliny the Younger', *Res (Cambridge, MA.)* xxvii (Spring 1995), pp. 11–24

F. Beutel: *Vergangenheit als Politik: Neue Aspekte im Werk des jüngeren Plinius* (Frankfurt am Main, 2000)

J. Henderson, ed.: *Pliny's Statue: The Letters, Self-portraiture & Classical Art* (Exeter, 2002)

L. Castagna and E. Lefèvre: *Plinius der Jüngere und seine Zeit* (Munich, 2003)

K. Bartels: 'Die Villa auf dem Land—eine Statte stiller Musse', *Ant. Welt*, xxxvi/4 (2005), p. 112

P. G. Walsh, ed.: *Complete Letters* (Oxford, 2006)

Plutarch [Lucius Mestrius Plutarchus; Gr. Ploutarkhos] (*b* Khaironeia, *c.* AD 50; *d* Delphi, after 120). Greek priest and author. Plutarch's prolific writings include many metaphors drawn from art and artistic production, but his principal contributions to art history are two antiquarian works on Greek and Roman religious customs, *Quaestiones graecae* (Gr. *Aitia hellenika*) and *Quaestiones romanae* (Gr. *Aitia romaika*). Cast in dialogue question-and-answer form, these works attempt to offer mythological or historical explanations for some of the arcana of Greek and Roman cultic observance, incidentally providing interpretations of religious iconography and much specific information on the layout of shrines and temples which would otherwise be lost. At *Quaestiones romanae* xxii and xli, for instance, Plutarch discussed the reasons for the portrayal of the god Janus as two-headed, and at *Quaestiones graecae* xlv the form of the cult statue of Labrandeian Zeus in Caria, who was represented holding an axe instead of the usual spear or thunderbolt. Elsewhere we learn that at Sparta the shrine of Odysseus was juxtaposed with that of the daughters of Leukippos (*Quaestiones graecae* xlviii). The *Quaestiones* are also an important source for the Greek and Roman usage of sacred space, something that is notoriously difficult to reconstruct from the archaeological record alone. Thus Plutarch is our only source for various areas of the Temple of Saturn at Rome being used as muniment offices, treasuries or reception rooms for ambassadors (*Quaestiones romanae* xlii–xliii), and for the display of ex votos and other temple treasures (xxxvii).

H. J. Rose, ed.: *The Roman Questions of Plutarch: A New Translation with Introductory Essays and Running Commentary* (Oxford, 1924)

W. R. Halliday, ed.: *The Greek Questions of Plutarch* (Oxford, 1928)

R. H. Barrow: *Plutarch and his Times* (London, 1967)

C. J. Gianakaris: *Plutarch* (New York, 1970)

C. P. Jones: *Plutarch and Rome* (Oxford, 1971)

D. T. Benediktson: *Literature and the Visual Arts in Ancient Greece and Rome* (Norman, 2000)

Poggio Civitate [now Murlo]. Site of an Etruscan building complex near Siena. The single large building is on raised ground controlling the valley of the River Ombrone, to which it is connected by a tributary. It is usually considered to have been an aristocratic palace, but it may possibly have been a sanctuary.

One of the most important sites in northern Etruria, it was excavated by a team from Bryn Mawr College, Pennsylvania.

Two main phases of construction can be discerned. The first dates from the early 7th century BC, and, while it has been only partially excavated, it appears to have provided the basic layout for the later phase. The second (*c.* 575 BC) clearly suggests an imposing structure, almost square in plan (*see* ARCHITECTURE, fig. 18e). The foundations show 18 openings arranged around a courtyard, three sides of which had a portico supported by columns resting on stone bases. The fourth, west side had no inner portico, and it may have housed the shrine of an ancestor cult. The walls were of *opus craticium* (wattle and daub on a timber framework), and the roof was adorned with architectural terracottas. In the earlier phase these were humanoid mask antefixes; the later sculptures include free-standing figures as acroteria (as at the Portonaccio Temple, Veii) and moulded figural friezes. Some terracottas retain traces of the fire that destroyed the complex *c.* 530 BC. The site was not resettled but enclosed by an earthen embankment. Its overall development belongs in the context of smaller, rural Etruscan centres, and its demise may be connected with the territorial expansion of such cities as Clusium (Chiusi) and Velathri (Volterra) in the late 6th century BC.

Poggio Civitate (exh. cat., Siena, Pal. Pub., 1970)
K. M. J. Phillips: 'Terrecotte architettoniche con protomi di leopardo da Poggio Civitate', *Boll. A.*, lxviii (March–April 1983), pp. 1–24
S. Stopponi, ed.: *Case e palazzi d'Etruria* (Milan, 1985)
S. Bruni: *Antiquarium di Poggio Civitate* (Florence, 1988)
I. E. M. Edlund-Berry: *The Seated and Standing Statue Akroteria from Poggio Civitate (Murlo)* (Rome, 1992)
K. M. Phillips: *In the Hills of Tuscany: Recent Excavations at the Etruscan Site of Poggio Civitate (Murlo, Siena)* (Philadelphia, 1993)
R. D. De Puma and J. P. Small: *Murlo and the Etruscans: Art and Society in Ancient Etruria* (Madison, WI, 1994)
D. M. Newland: *The Akroterial Sculpture and Architectural Terracottas from the Upper Building at Murlo* (diss., Bryn Mawr Coll., 1994)
'Murlo (Italien): Ein etruskisches Reservat in toskanischer Idylle', *Ant. Welt*, xxvii/4 (1996), p. 343
J. M. Berkin: *The Orientalizing Bucchero from the Lower Building at Poggio Civitate (Murlo)*(Boston, MA, 2003)

Pojan. *See* APOLLONIA.

Pola [now Pula]. City in the Republic of Croatia, at the southern tip of the Istrian Peninsula. The site with its sheltered harbour was first settled by Illyrian tribes in the Bronze and Iron Ages. It was known to early Greek voyagers, and it is mentioned in the Argonaut legend of Jason and Medea. Conquered by the Romans in 178 BC, it was elevated to colonial rank, Colonia Julia Pola Pollentia Herculanea, between 42 and 31 BC.

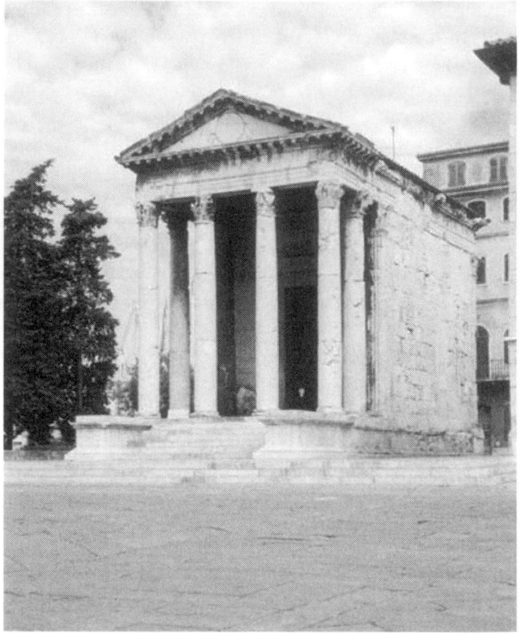

1. Pola, Temple of Roma and Augustus, 2 BC–AD 14

The city contains several notable examples of Roman municipal architecture (1st century BC–2nd century AD) in the fine local limestone. Among the earliest are the gates in the extant stretches of the city walls. The single-passage Hercules Gate (4.0×3.6 m) is named after the bearded figure of the god carved in high relief on the keystone of the arch, with his club on the adjoining voussoir. The inscribed names of magistrates date the structure to the mid-1st century BC. The more ornate Arch of the Sergii was originally a city gate, paid for by Sergia Postuma to honour the municipal and military careers of three members of her family not long after 29–28 BC. Their statues (destr.) stood on inscribed bases incorporated into the attic, below which a frieze depicts cupids, garlands and bucrania on either side of the dedicatory inscription. The single entrance is flanked by pairs of engaged Corinthian columns, and there are winged victories in the spandrels. The Porta Gemina (mid-2nd century AD), which replaced an earlier gate, has two arched entrances flanked by engaged columns on the outer façade, a plain architrave and an ornate frieze. Near the waterfront the Augustan forum was bordered on the north side by a pair of temples (each *c.* 17.6×8.0 m; 2 BC–AD 14). The temple to the west, dedicated to Roma and Augustus (see fig. 1), is one of the most complete Roman temples to survive. Only the rear elevation of the other temple, probably dedicated to Diana, is preserved.

Elsewhere in the city other remains include two theatres: the larger (diam. *c.* 100 m; 1st century AD) was erected on the southern edge of the city, the smaller (diam. *c.* 50 m; 2nd century AD) near the centre. These are eclipsed in scale by the amphitheatre

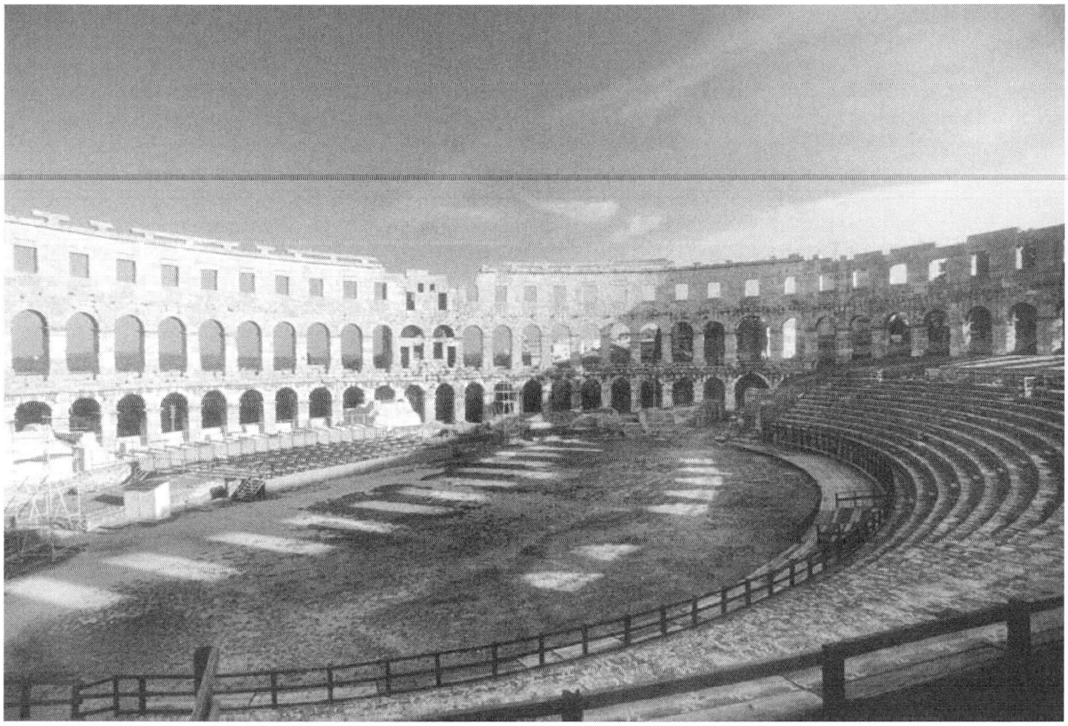

2. Pola, amphitheatre, 1st century AD

(1st century AD), which is the sixth largest surviving Roman arena (see fig. 2). It was built near the sea to the north-east of the city. Seating approximately 23,000 spectators, it is enclosed by a wall (h. 32.5 m) with three storeys on the seaward side and two on the inland side, where the seating rested directly on the sloping ground.

P. Kandler: *Cenni al forestiere che visita Pola* (Trieste, 1845)
T. G. Jackson: 'Pola', *Dalmatia: The Quarnero and Istria*, iii (Oxford, 1887), pp. 280–304
B. Benussi: *Manuale di geografia, storia e statistica della regione Giulia* (Parenzo, 1903/*R* Trieste, 1987)
S. Mlakar: *The Amphitheatre in Pula* (Pula, 1957)
S. Mlakar: *Ancient Pula* (Pula, 1958)
S. Mlakar: *The Amphitheatre at Pula* (Pula, 1997/rev. 7 and supplemented ed.)
G. Pavan: *Il tempio d'Augusto di Pola* (Trieste-Gorizia, 2000)
Voda kao izvor zivota anticke Pule: Izlozba (exh. cat. by V. Girardi-Jurkic and K. Dzin; Pula, 2001)
W. Letzner: *Das römische Pula: Bilder einer Stadt in Istrien* (Mainz, 2005)

Polion (*fl c.* 430–*c.* 410 BC). Greek vase painter. About 21 vases or fragments have been ascribed to him, ranging from kraters to oinochoai and lekythoi. Active in Athens, his name is known from the signature on a large Red-figure volute krater (New York, Met., 27.122.8) depicting *Apollo Preparing to Mount his Chariot*. The scene covers both sides of the vase, showing Apollo taking his lyre from Leto, while Artemis, holding the reins, looks back at him. Hermes stands at the horses' heads, Athena behind them, and Zeus, Hera, Dionysos, Poseidon and Herakles are also present. The figures are statuesque and rather static, and are arranged along a single ground-line. Most are swathed in drapery, with their bodies and legs in three-quarter view and their heads in profile. The painting is careful, the effect dignified, yet both subject and composition seem unenterprising. Polion was apparently aware of new advances in composition though not altogether comfortable with them. This impression is confirmed by scenes on a second large volute krater (Ferrara, Mus. N. Archeol., T. 127) showing *Thamyris Playing his Lyre before the Muses* and the *Return of Hephaistos*. Here, though the figures are not set on a single ground-line, they are not dispersed freely over the field in the more progressive manner of the Meidias Painter and other contemporaries. Instead they are simply arranged on two discrete levels. While Polion's subjects are often conventional, some are more unusual. The scene of Thamyris is remarkable for its representation of the *xoana* (wooden statues) of the Muses and may show the influence of a dithyramb, as may a scene on a bell krater (New York, Met., 25.78.66) depicting comic silenoi dancing and strumming their lyres below an inscription referring to the Athenian festival of the Panathenaia.

J. D. Beazley: *Red-figure* (1942, 2/1963), ii, pp. 1171–3
W. Real: *Studien zur Entwicklung der Vasenmalerei im ausgehenden 5. Jahrhundert v. Chr.* (Münster, 1973), pp. 28–34
J. Boardman: *Athenian Red Figure Vases, the Classical Period* (London, 1989), p. 167

Polychromy. Decoration of architecture, both internally and externally, and of sculpture by using differently coloured materials or by the addition of colour by painting or other means.

1. Architecture. The application of colour, which often provided a protective cover as well as improving a building's aesthetic appearance, and the selection of coloured building materials may be traced back to the earliest civilizations, including Mesopotamia and Egypt. Architectural mouldings and sculpture on Greek buildings were decorated with elaborate, brightly painted designs in tempera, encaustic and fresco. Although the wall surfaces of monumental stone buildings were usually left uncoloured, except when decorated with wall paintings, domestic architecture was commonly painted. Polychrome effects could also be achieved using different coloured limestones and terracotta. This practice was followed by the Romans, who used coloured column shafts to contrast with white marble capitals, bases and entablatures. Their technique of concrete construction faced with brickwork or stone encouraged geometric designs in different coloured materials, including tile. The Early Christian traditions of polychromatic stone cladding and mosaic decoration, which developed from Roman practices, survived in Italy into the Middle Ages.

F. T. Kugler: *Über die Polychromie der griechischen Architektur und Plastik und ihre Grenzen* (Berlin, 1835)
A. Paccard: *Restauration polychrome du Parthénon* (Paris, 1847)
J. I. Hittorff: *Restitution du temple d'Empodocle à Sélinonte ou l'Architecture polychrome chez les Grecs* (Paris, 1851)
C.-E. Beulé: *L'Acropole d'Athènes*, 2 vols (Paris, 1853–4)
C. Garnier: *Le Temple de Jupiter panhellenien à Egine* (Paris, 1881)
W. Hoepfner: 'Farbe in der griechischen Architektur', *Colour in Ancient Greece. The Role of Colour in Ancient Greek Art and Architecture, 700–31 B C: Proceedings of the Conference held in Thessaloniki, 2000*, pp. 37–45

2. Sculpture. It is impossible to be certain when the first polychrome sculpture was produced, due to the fragility of the material, but one may assume that a significant proportion of the earliest forms of three-dimensional representation was coloured at the time of production. The Greeks routinely painted all their sculpture, but the importance of colour seems to have declined in ancient Rome.

Recent research has greatly enhanced our understanding of the original polychromy, especially of Greek marble sculpture. Pigments fade at a different rate, accordingly exposing the initially protected marble surface to differential weathering. As a result of this differential weathering, even if all the pigment has been lost, the sculpture will still show a very fine undulation in its surface relief that can be detected through a range of scientific methods (from strong raking light to infrared and UV lighting techniques). This allows a reconstruction of patterns, motifs, inscriptions etc that were originally painted rather than carved, and as the relative durability of specific pigments is known, in some cases full approximate colour reconstructions are possible. The method has been applied with great success to the pedimental figures of the Temple of Aphaia on Aigina (now Munich, Glyp.), and the friezes of the Siphnian Treasury at Delphi, where the discovery of names written in antiquity next to individual figures to facilitate their identification has led to a new understanding of some scenes. Other examples include archaic sculptures from the Athenian Acropolis and Classical grave stelae. There is a great potential in applying these analytical techniques to sculptures of different periods and cultures.

V. Brinkmann: *Beobachtungen zum formalen Aufbau und zum Sinngehalt der Friese des Siphnierschatzhauses*, i of *Studien zur antiken Malerei und Farbgebung* (Ennepetal, 1994)
V. Brinkmann and U. Koch-Brinkmann: *Der prächtige Prinz* (Munich, 2003)
V. Brinkmann and O. Primavesi: *Die Polychromie der archaischen und frühklassischen Skulptur* (Munich, 2003)
Bunte Götter. Die Farbigkeit antiker Skulptur (exh. cat., eds V. Brinkmann and R. Wünsche; Munich, Glyp., 2003–4)

Polydoros. *See* Hagesandros, polydoros and athenodoros.

Polygnotos (*fl c.* 450–*c.* 425 bc). Greek vase painter. He was a prolific Athenian Red-figure artist of the High Classical period (*c.* 450–*c.* 400 bc), who was trained in the workshop of the Niobid painter, from whom he derived his monumental style. This was apparently based on Early Classical wall paintings, notably by Mikon and Polygnotos of thasos, after whom this vase painter was probably named, and is characterized by the use of an uneven groundline to suggest landscape, as on Polygnotos' early pelike showing *Apollo Attacking Tityos* (Paris, Louvre, G 375).

Like other vase painters in Periclean Athens, Polygnotos modelled some of his figures on the sculptures designed by Pheidias for the Parthenon. Thus the two horsemen on his stamnos (Oxford, Ashmolean, 1916.68) echo the riders on the Parthenon frieze (442–438 bc), while many of his other figures recall the frieze in their stateliness or in more specific details.

Polygnotos decorated large pots, primarily amphorae, stamnoi and kraters, and depicted an unusually wide variety of subjects for his time. He favoured combat scenes, including ones from epic poetry, such as *Greeks Fighting Amazons, Kaineus and the Centaurs, Apollo and Tityos, Perseus and Medusa, Ajax and Kassandra* and the *Death of Laios*. He also portrayed quieter traditional subjects, including *Triptolemos*, scenes of lovemaking, symposia, sacrifices and departing warriors. Five vases signed by Polygnotos survive, among them two stamnoi (Brussels, Musées Royaux A. & Hist., A 134; London, BM 96.7–16.5), and nearly 70 more have been attributed to him, mostly by Beazley, who also regarded him as having supervised a large workshop, including the Peleus Painter and KLEOPHON PAINTER. Painters associated with Polygnotos are now known as the Group of Polygnotos, to which many vases are now assigned, such a fine pelike showing a musician (Paris, Louvre, G 543; see fig.).

J. D. Beazley: *Red-figure* (1942, 2/1963), ii, pp. 1027–33

P. E. Arias and M. Hirmer: *Tausend Jahre griechischer Vasenkunst* (Munich, 1960), Eng. trans. and rev. by B. Shefton as *A History of Greek Vase-painting* (London, 1962)

M. Halm-Tisserant: 'La représentation du retour d'Hephaistos dans l'Olympe: Iconographie traditionnelle et innovations formelles dans l'atelier de Polygnotos, 440–430', *Ant. Kst*, xxix/1 (1986), pp. 8–21

S. B. Matheson: 'Polygnotos: An *Iliupersis* Scene at the Getty Museum', *Greek Vases in the J. Paul Getty Museum*, iii (Malibu, 1986)

L. A. Burkhalter: *An Iconographic Analysis of the High Classical Greek Neck-amphora Attributed to the Group of Polygnotos, High Museum, Atlanta*(diss., Atlanta, GA, Emory U., 1988)

A. Bowtell: *The Group of Polygnotos*, 3 vols (diss., U. Oxford, 1994)

S. B. Matheson: *Polygnotos and Vase Painting in Classical Athens*(Madison, WI, 1995)

Polygnotos of Thasos (*fl c.* 475–450 BC). Greek wall painter and sculptor. He came from a family of painters, which included his father and teacher, Aglaophon (see Harpokration: *Lexicon* 'Polygnotos'; Plato: *Gorgias* 448b), his brother, Aristophon, and, probably, his son or nephew, Aglaophon (Pliny: XXXV.xxxvi.60). Though born on the island of Thasos, Polygnotos worked in Athens and Delphi

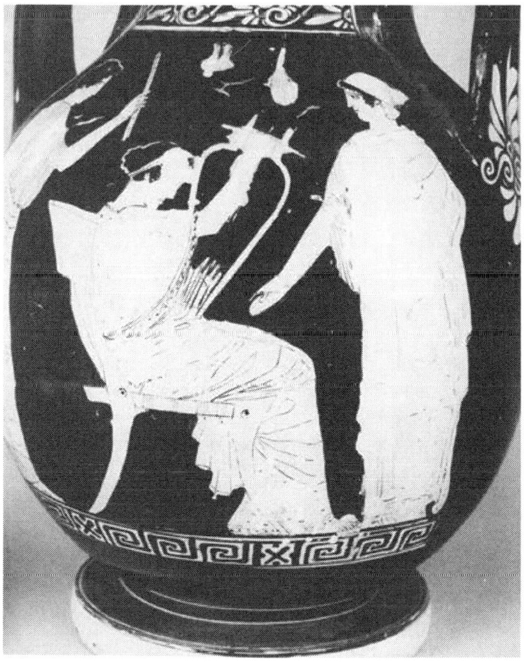

Polygnotos: pelike depicting female musicians, h. 354 mm, Attic Red-figure, *c.* 440 BC (Paris, Musée du Louvre, G 543)

and became an Athenian citizen, allegedly as a result of producing without renumeration a painting for the Stoa Poikile (Painted Stoa; *c.* 460 BC) or another Athenian building (see Harpokration). If so, he was perhaps aided by the Athenian statesman, Kimon (*c.* 512–449 BC), who may have been his patron. Kimon's sister, Elpinike, was said to have been his mistress (Plutarch: *Kimon* iv.5), and it was Kimon's brother-in-law, Peisianax, who founded the Stoa Poikile. According to Pliny (XXXV.xxxv.58) Polygnotos was active before 420 BC, while the style of his works and his association with Kimon place him firmly within the Early Classical period (*c.* 480–*c.* 450 BC). Pliny maintained (XXXIV.xix.85) that he was also a sculptor but mentioned no specific works, so that no statues have been attributed to him.

Ancient sources ascribed numerous artistic innovations to Polygnotos' wall paintings, but two are particularly important. He was said to have been the first painter to depict emotion by such devices as 'opening the mouth, showing the teeth and giving variety to the face' (Pliny: XXXV.xxxv.58), and his ability to portray character (*ethos*, not simply *pathos*) prompted comparisons between his works and those of the great Greek tragedians. Aristotle claimed that Polygnotos painted men as 'better than they are' (*Poetics* 1448a.5–6; 1450a.23–8). He was also accredited with the introduction of important new techniques for creating spatial effects, as in his paintings in the *lesche* ('clubhouse') of the Knidians at Delphi (*c.* 450 BC; see Pausanias: X.xxv–xxxi). For the first time, he abandoned the single ground line characteristic of all earlier Greek painting. Pausanias described certain of his figures as being 'above' or 'higher up than' others, or 'beneath' or 'beyond' them, suggesting that they appeared to recede into the field. Similarly, some figures were partially hidden by the landscape, while others sat on rocks or leant against trees. Nearly contemporary vase paintings, such as that on the NIOBID PAINTER's calyx krater (Paris, Louvre, G431), appear to reflect these innovations.

The paintings from the *lesche*, which may either have been applied directly to its interior walls or painted on separate wooden panels, are lost, so that the precise disposition of their figures is disputed. They depicted the *Sack of Troy* and the *Underworld*, and clearly conveyed a psychological dimension in the relations between the characters, as well as their individual emotions, such as fear, anger and despair. Polygnotos' painting for the Stoa Poikile in the Athenian Agora (see Pliny: XXXV.xxv.59; Pausanias: I.xv.1–4) was accompanied by works by Mikon and Panainos, two other famous Early Classical painters. It depicted the *Greeks after the Sack of Troy*, with Ajax and Cassandra and captive Trojan women. Though the Stoa Poikile itself has recently been identified, no trace of the paintings remains.

Finally, Pausanias referred briefly (I.xviii.1) to a Polygnotan painting of the *Marriage of the Leukippidai* in the Sanctuary of the Dioscuri in Athens (I.xviii.1), to one of *Odysseus Trapped by the Suitors* in a Sanctuary of Athena at Plataia (IX.iv.1–2) and to two or more paintings, almost certainly on wooden panels, in the north wing of the Propylaia on the Athenian Acropolis (I.xxii.6–7). Pliny (XXXV.xxv.42; XXXIII. lvi.160) provided some technical details concerning Polygnotos' paintings in general.

C. Robert: *Die Nekyia des Polygnot* (Halle, 1892)
C. Robert: *Die Iliupersis des Polygnot* (Halle, 1893)
E. Simon: 'Polygnotan Painting and the Niobid Painter', *Amer. J. Archaeol.*, lxvii (1963), pp. 43–62
M. D. Stansbury-O'Donnell: 'Polygnotos's *Iliupersis*: A New Reconstruction', *Amer. J. Archaeol.*, xciii (1989), pp. 203–15
J. J. Pollitt: *The Art of Ancient Greece: Sources and Documents* (Cambridge, 1990)
M. D. Stansburg-O'Donnell: 'Polygnotos's *Nekyia*: A Reconstruction and Analysis', *Amer. J. Archaeol.*, xciv (1990), pp. 213–35

Polykleitos (*b* Argos or Sikyon, *fl c.* 450–*c.* 415 BC). Greek sculptor. Along with Pheidias, with whom he is often compared in the sources, Polykleitos was the most important sculptor in bronze of the 5th century BC. He wrote a manual (the Canon) and headed the first recorded major 'school' of sculptors, which lasted three generations, and he influenced not only the sculpture of his own time but also Hellenistic and Roman sculpture.

1. Life and work. 2. Followers.

1. LIFE AND WORK. The birthplace of Polykleitos is disputed, Plato (*Protagoras* 311C) citing Argos, Pliny the elder (XXXIV.xix.55) Sikyon. The period of his activity is dated by Roman copies of his works, and Pliny's notice (XXXIV.xix.49) implies that he did his greatest work at the end of his career (420–417 BC). His teacher was Ageladas of Argos, whose oeuvre is not identifiable and who also taught Pheidias and Myron. Several other artists were also called Polykleitos, and literary sources do not always clearly distinguish between their works.

(i) Theory of art. Few original quotations from Polykleitos' manual, the Canon, survive. The exact meaning of the most important (Plutarch: *Quomodo quis suos in virtute sentiat profectus* 85.F and *Quaestiones convivales* 636.C) is disputed, but it clearly gives minutely detailed instructions concerning the final touches to clay models. A quotation derived from Xenokrates via Varro (Pliny the elder: XXXIV.xix.56) is more significant, stating that Polykleitos 'had conceived the idea that statues should stand firmly on one leg only; yet despite that, they are made squarely (*quadrata*) and almost as an example' or 'according to a pattern'. Both these translations suggest rules for a grammar of forms that could well underlie the emergence of a 'school'. The first clause may allude to an intensification of the contrapposto stance common from *c.* 480 BC, or may simply mean that Polykleitos' statues always stood on the same leg. Either interpretation suits those works definitely attributed to him, in which the figures stand on the right leg, with the left stretched back and to the side creating uncertainty over whether they are standing or walking; seen from the front, they appear to be standing on one leg. The upper parts of the figures are chiastically structured: the arm above the weight-bearing leg is relaxed, while that over the flexed leg is tensed and active, and the head turns towards the supporting leg. This chiastic rhythm persists in the anatomical details of the trunk, but in a non-naturalistic way. From the raised hip above the weight-bearing leg the horizontal lines (*inscriptiones*) articulating the trunk stretch obliquely to the shoulders, where the shoulder of the tensed arm is higher than that of the relaxed arm. This goes against any idea of naturalism but perhaps explains Quintilian's statement (*Principles of Rhetoric* XII.x.7) that Polykleitos' works 'lack weight' (*deesse pondus*) and have a 'charm beyond truth' (*decorem … supra verum*). The pose does indeed create an impression of lightness, as the lifting of the shoulder above the tensed arm suggests the slightness of its burden. It is manifestly contrived, and Polykleitos was probably not seeking to capture a fleeting pose, so much as to express essential forms. Pliny's reference to 'squareness' is readily intelligible. The shoulders are square, while the areas of abdominal musculature are more or less rectangular in form, the lines defining the pectorals being equally angular and enlarging upwards into regular pentagons. At the same time, Pliny may also mean that the figures appear to be enclosed by a rectangular field.

The heads too are artificial. The individual planes of the faces are distinct and generally built up at right angles to each other. The artificiality of the hair is more evident, with layers of hooked or S-shaped curls overlapping like scales and radiating from a spider-like whorl on the crown of the head. Precisely over the centre of the forehead is a parting like a pair of pincers: two curls are swept to the side, but their tips curve back towards the centre. Roman copies suggest that Polykleitos virtually always adhered to this fundamental scheme, as shown most clearly in the *Doryphoros*.

(ii) Works and development. The few works certainly attributed to Polykleitos survive only in Roman copies, which have been affected in varying degrees by Roman taste. Polykleitos' originals appear to have been consistently *c.* 2 m high, thus slightly over life-size. His earliest established work (*c.* 450–*c.* 440 BC) is the so-called *Diskophoros* ('discus bearer'; copies in Rome, Mus. Torlonia, 76, and Vatican, Galleria delle Statue, 251; Wellesley Coll., MA, Mus., 1904.1, and elsewhere), which is probably in fact a *Doryphoros* ('spear bearer'). Significantly, it is only life-size and is not yet a canonical *Doryphoros*. Its free leg is placed sideways and slightly forward in the old, Early Classical manner. Otherwise, the figure essentially follows the Polykleitan scheme. It may be 'the leader putting on his armour' (Pliny the elder: XXXIV.xix.56), perhaps Theseus.

The *Doryphoros* (*c.* 440–*c.* 435 BC; best copies: statue, Minneapolis, MN, Inst. A.; herm and statue, Naples, Mus. Archeol. N.; see fig.; torso, Berlin, Antikensamml; torso, Florence, Uffizi) was apparently Polykleitos' masterpiece and almost certainly the work 'which artists called the Canon, and from which they derived the patterns of art as if from a law' (Pliny the elder: XXXIV.xix.55). It was perhaps an Achilles, since Pliny refers to the use of the term *Achilleae* for statues of spear bearers in gymnasia (XXXIV.x.18). Slightly later Attic works, such as the Borghese *Ares* (*c.* 430 BC; Paris, Louvre, 866), perhaps by ALKAMENES, show the influence of the *Doryphoros*.

Polykleitos' *Hermes* was made *c.* 430 BC and taken, probably in the early 3rd century BC, to Lysimacheia (Pliny the elder: XXXIV.xix.55). In Pliny's time it apparently stood in Rome. A bronze statuette (Paris, Petit Pal. Dut. 1) gives a fairly reliable idea of its overall appearance. Copies of the head also survive (e.g. Boston, MA, Mus. F.A., 98.641) and already suggest

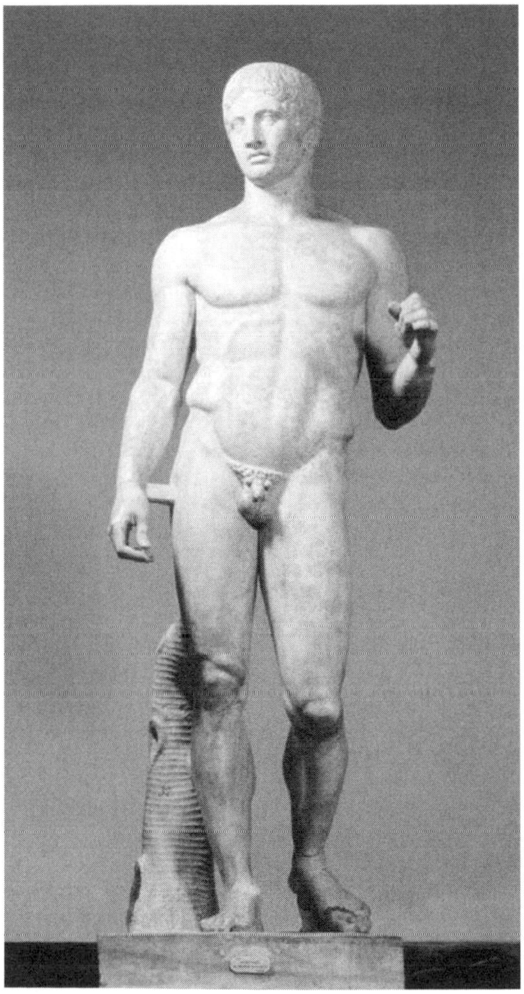

Polykleitos: *Doryphoros*, original bronze, *c.* 440–*c.* 435 BC; Roman copy, marble, h. 2 m (Naples, Museo Archeologico Nazionale)

some relaxation of the Canon: the face is less angular and the pincer-like parting looser.

The *Herakles* 'in Rome' (Pliny the elder: XXXIV.xix.56) was created in the 420s BC and also shows that Polykleitos allowed himself some freedom within the Canon. The 'active' left arm is active in repose; it is supported. The body is considerably more muscular than that of the *Doryphoros*, but has a similar scheme of articulation, while the head, with its pincer-like hairstyle, shows an even closer resemblance. However, the most important copies (statuette, Rome, Mus. Barracco, 109; torso with head, Rome, Mus. N. Romano, 11616 + 54226; head, Rome, Pal. Conserv., Braccio Nuo., 1887) exhibit little stylistic uniformity.

Pliny the elder (XXXIV.xix.55) considered the *Diadoumenos* (a young victor tying a ribbon around his head; *c.* 423–*c.* 419 BC; best copies: statues, Athens, N. Archaeol. Mus., 1826, and London, BM, 500; torsos, Basle, Antikenmus and New York, Met; several heads, Oxford, Ashmolean Mus., 1918.67) to be Polykleitos' most famous work, marking the peak of his career. Pliny recorded that 100 talents were once offered for it. On the basis of a Hellinistic epigram, he contrasted the *Diadoumenos* as a 'tender youth' with the *Doryphoros* as a 'manly boy'. This is readily apparent in collections with copies of both works (e.g. Rome, Pal. Mattei; Tripoli, Archaeol. Mus.; Side Mus.). The *Diadoumenos*, possibly a representation of Apollo, is certainly canonical, but, in what is probably Polykleitos' last work, the Canon was losing its stringency. The pose of tying the victor's ribbon did not allow such a marked contrast between the actions of the two arms, while the *Diadoumenos'* musculature is also less pronounced, and its hair parting is hidden by the ribbon.

The *Amazon of Ephesos* (*c.* 430 BC; Lansdowne-Sciarra type: best copies in Berlin, Antikensamml.; Copenhagen, Ny Carlsberg Glyp., 54; New York, Met.) is the only statue of a female figure definitely attributed to Polykleitos by ancient sources. However, it is uncertain which of the types of Amazon he originated. As between the Sosikles/Capitol type and the Landsdowne-Sciarra type, the latter seems more likely, since it follows Polykleitos' canonical scheme, with the active left arm and hand holding a weapon (not, as in some copies, leaning on a pillar) and the right hand placed on the head in the Classical gesture of repose. The drapery of the short *chiton* is also strictly schematized, with shallow curved folds between heavily-bunched vertical pleats.

Other works have been attributed to Polykleitos, either wrongly or without sufficient evidence. Some sculptures, such as the Westmacott *Ephebe* and the so-called *Narkissos/Hyakinthos*, are probably works of his school. Other pieces, such as the IDOLINO (Florence, Mus. Archeol.) and perhaps the Petworth *Oil-pourer* (Petworth House, W. Sussex, NT), are possibly Roman imitations. Some works named in the sources still remain unidentified.

2. FOLLOWERS. The school of Polykleitos is the earliest school of sculpture known to have exercised

a wide influence. About 20 pupils' names survive, including two mentioned in a list of outstanding sculptors of 400–396 BC (Pliny the elder: XXXIV. xix.50) who are also known to have worked on the statues dedicated by Lysander at Delphi between 405 and 396 BC (Pausanias: X.ix.10). Nevertheless, there is disagreement over the school's 'family tree'. About half the names preserved are of first-generation artists; but known works can be ascribed with confidence only to Naukydes, who may in fact belong to the second generation. Works by two second-generation artists—another Polykleitos of Argos (Polykleitos II) and Daidalos of Sikyon—can probably be identified. The earliest work by a pupil may be a statue of a victorious athlete by Naukydes mentioned by Pausanias (VI.ix.3). The athlete gained his victory in 448 BC; however, the statue may actually date to the end of the 5th century BC. The latest work (of the third generation) may be a portrait of *Hephaisteion*, the friend of Alexander the Great (Pliny the elder: XXXIV.xix.64), but this too is uncertain and no copy has been identified.

Some statues of male figures occasionally attributed to the first Polykleitos (Polykleitos I) may in fact have been produced by first-generation members of his school. The decisive factor is the extent to which the Canon of Polykleitos was carefully and hesitantly developed. The process is well illustrated by an original bronze statuette from Sikyon (*c.* 430 BC; Athens, N. Archaeol. Mus., 7474), which corresponds closely in stance, proportions and articulation to the *Doryphoros*. Even the head, including the hair, is reminiscent of Polykleitos' work but, contrary to the Canon, it is turned towards the free leg; the figure thus becomes labile, even lively. Much the same applies to the Dresden *Boy* (best copy at Dresden, Skulpsamml.), though it is more youthful and delicate. Some scholars have seen this as a late work by Polykleitos I, linking it with the Westmacott *Ephebe* (copy, London, BM, 1754), which presents something of a reverse image; others have seen in it an early work, the so-called *Kyniskos*, or an *Apoxyomenos* (man using a strigil). The *Narkissos/Hyakinthos* (*c.* 400 BC; Roman copies e.g. Paris, Louvre, 456, 457) also shares these childlike features; but its pose is so unstable that it requires a support, later a favourite motif of Praxiteles, while the treatment of the hair lacks the precision of Polykleitan works.

Though the chryselephantine (gold and ivory) cult statue for the Temple of Hera at Argos is usually attributed to Polykleitos I, it can only have been installed in the late 5th century BC, after the roofing of the cella of the new temple that replaced the temple burnt down in 423 BC, and so may well have been by Polykleitos II. A seated torso (1st century AD; Boston, MA, Mus. F.A., 03.749), a head (London, BM, 1792) and an unpublished relief of Roman date (Argos, Archaeol. Mus.) may give an idea of its appearance: the way in which the drapery moulds the body is particularly distinctive. The same is true of the standing Borghese *Hera* (Roman, 1st century AD; Copenhagen, Ny Carlsberg Glyp., 247) and the standing *Aphrodite* from Epidauros (Claudian copy of an original of *c.* 400–*c.* 390 BC; Athens, N. Archaeol. Mus., 262). Their stances lack the stiffness characteristic of works by Polykleitos I.

NAUKYDES of Argos is known mainly for male figures, although he also made female statues (e.g. *Hebe*, which stood beside the *Hera of Argos*). He must have been active in *c.* 410–*c.* 380 BC.

Daidalos of Sikyon (*fl c.* 390–*c.* 360 BC) apparently produced the prototype of the bronze *Apoxyomenos* from Ephesos (Flavian copy at Vienna, Ksthist. Mus., 3168) and the *Oil-pourer* (several variants; Trajanic copy at Florence, Pitti), which should perhaps also be restored with a strigil. The stances and musculature are recognizably Polykleitan, though the latter is rather less angular, and the free legs are placed simply to the side. Notably, while the curls of their hair are again of Polykleitan pattern, though somewhat livelier, the characteristic pincer-like fringe is replaced by horizontal strands spreading out high above the forehead. Among the female figures attributed to Daidalos is the prototype of the Colonna *Artemis* (e.g. Roman copy at Berlin, Antikensamml., K 243), which again is characteristically modelled by its drapery (a long, undergirdled *peplos*), albeit somewhat differently than in works by Polykleitos II; it probably stood in Monogissa in Caria.

Attributions to third-generation artists are less reliable, even when the works concerned are clearly in the Polykleitan tradition. The chief characteristics of works by the Polykleitan school are the precise articulation of the anatomy, even of draped figures, and an adherence to the Canon of Polykleitos, which was only gradually and partially abandoned. Polykleitos and the first generation of his pupils also influenced Attic artists such as KEPHISODOTOS and the early works of his son Praxiteles, and to a lesser extent Skopas and Lysippos. The latter's imitation was clearly conscious, since he apparently called the *Doryphoros* his teacher (Cicero; *Brutus* lxxxvi.296). Yet Lysippos was the first Peloponnesian sculptor to reject the Polykleitan tradition, to which even the Corinthian artists EUPHRANOR and KALLIMACHOS conformed. Polykleitos was also studied in Hellenistic times and especially in the early Roman Empire. His strong influence on Roman works is exemplified by the *Augustus* of Prima Porta (Rome, Vatican, Braccio Nuo., 14).

General Bibliography

J. Overbeck: *Die antiken Schriftquellen zur Geschichte der bildenden Künste bei den Griechen* (Leipzig, 1868/*R* Hildesheim, 1959), pp. 166–75, nos 103, 978–1014, 1492

C. Anti: 'Monumenti Polycletei', *Mnmnt. Ant.: Lincei*, xxvi (1920), pp. 501–792

R. Bianchi Bandinelli: *Policleto* (Florence, 1938)

G. Lippold: 'Griechische Plastik', *Handbuch der Archäologie*, iii/1 (Munich, 1950), pp. 162–9, figs 59–60

P. Amandry: 'A propos de Polyclète: Statues d'olympioniques et carrière de sculpteurs', *Charites* (Bonn, 1957), pp. 63–87

P. E. Arias: *Policleto* (Milan, 1964)

H. Lauter: *Zur Chronologie römischer Kopien nach Originalen des V. Jh. v. Chr.* (diss., Bonn, 1966)

A. Linfert: *Von Polyklet zu Lysipp* (Giessen, 1966, rev. Cologne, 1969)

D. Arnold: *Die Polykletnachfolge* (Berlin, 1969)

C. Vermeule: *Polykleitos* (Boston, MA, 1969)

T. Lorenz: *Polyklet* (Wiesbaden, 1972)

P. Zanker: *Klassizistische Statuen* (Mainz, 1974), pp. 4–48

E. Berger: 'Zum von Plinius (Nat. Hist. 34.55) überlieferten "nudus talo incessens" des Polyklet', *Ant. Kst*, xxi (1978), pp. 55–62

E. La Rocca: 'Policleto e la sua scuola', *La Grecia nell'età di Pericle: Le arti figurative*, ii/4 of *Storia e civiltà dei Greci* (Milan, 1979)

A. H. Borbein, *Göttingische gelehrte Anzeigen*, ccxxxiv (1982), pp. 184–241

G. V. Leftwich: *Ancient Conceptions of the Body and the Canon of Polykleitos* (diss., Princeton U., 1987)

D. Kreikenbom: *Bildwerke nach Polyklet* (Berlin, 1990)

Polyklet: Der Bildhauer der griechischen Klassik (exh. cat., ed. H. Beck, P. C. Bol and M. Bückling; Frankfurt am Main, Liebieghaus, 1990), pp. 240–94

W. G. Moon: *Polykleitos, the Doryphoros, and Tradition* (Madison, WI, 1995)

O. Palagia and J. J. Pollitt: *Personal Styles in Greek Sculpture* (Cambridge and New York, 1996)

Specialist Studies

E. Pfuhl: 'Bemerkungen zur Kunst des vierten Jahrhunderts', *Jb. Dt. Archäol. Inst.*, xliii (1928), pp. 10–11

P. Zahcani Montuoro: 'Repliche romane di una statua fidiaca'. *Bull. Comm. Archeol. Mun. Com. Roma*, lxi (1933), pp. 25–58

P. Wolters: 'Polyklets Doryphoros in der Ehrenhalle der Münchner Universität', *Münchn. Jb. Kstgesch.* (1934), p. 139

P. M. Robinson: 'The Cyniscus of Polyclitus', *A. Bull.* (1936), pp. 133–49

G. Hafner: *Zum Epheben Westmacott* (Heidelberg, 1955)

T. Lorenz: *Polyklet: Doryphoros* (Stuttgart, 1966)

H. Marwitz: 'Antiken der Sammlung Hermann Bünemann, München', *Ant. Plast.*, vi (1967), pp. 31–8

H. von Steuben: 'Kopf des polykletischen Herakles', *Ant. Plast.*, vii (1967), pp. 95–105

H. von Steuben: *Der Kanon des Polyklet* (Tübingen, 1973)

B. Sismondo Ridgway: 'A Story of Five Amazons', *Amer. J. Archaeol.*, lxxviii (1974), pp. 1–17

M. B. Comstock and C. C. Vermeule: *Sculpture in Stone* (Boston, 1976), p. 95, no. 148

M. Weber: 'Die Amazonen von Ephesos', *Jb. Dt. Archäol. Inst.*, xci (1976), pp. 28–96; xcix (1984), pp. 75–126

R. Fleischer: 'Zur Deutung des "Diskophoros" Polyklets', *Österreichische Jahreshefte*, lii (1978–80), pp. 1–9

T. Dohrn: 'Altes und Neues über die ephesischen Amazonen', *Jb. Dt. Archäol. Inst.*, xciv (1979), pp. 112–26

B. Vierneisel-Schlörb: *Klassiche Skulpturen*, ii of *Katalog der Skulpturen*, Munich, Glyp. cat. (Munich, 1979), pp. 208–15, no. 19

G. Despinis: 'Zum Hermes von Troizen', *Mitt. Dt. Archäol. Inst.: Athen. Abt.*, xcvi (1981), pp. 237–44

E. Berger: 'Der sogenannte Diskophoros: Eine Theseusstatue (?) des Polyklet', *Numi. & Ant. Class.*, xi (1982), pp. 59–105

Polykles [Polycles] (*fl* ?mid-2nd century BC). Greek sculptor(s). Although Pliny (*Natural History* XXXIV.xix.52) listed Polykles among those sculptors who flourished in the 156th Olympiad (156–153 BC), the numerous testimonia show that at least two sculptors of that name were active during the 2nd century BC. Members of a successful dynasty that also attained considerable social prominence, they may be considered the main exponents of the Classical revival in 2nd-century BC Athens (*see also* DIONYSIOS, TIMARCHIDES and TIMOKLES). Their family tree is controversial, and it is often unclear which sculptor made what. Polykles seems to have been responsible for a *Hermaphrodite* in bronze, often identified with one preserved in several replicas (the most famous in Paris, Louvre); a *Boy Victor* in Olympia; a statue at Elateia in Aitolia; and several works in Rome: a *Hercules* in the Temple of Ops; a marble *Jupiter* and *Juno* in their temples within the Portico of Octavian (*c.* 146 BC and 179 BC respectively), joint works with Dionysios; a set of bronze *Muses*; and a statue of a Macedonian, *Koinos*. In addition, nine works are recorded for other family members in Olympia, Aitolia and Rome. Since the Aitolian League honoured a Polykles in 210 BC, and several of his works have an Aitolian context, the family may have made its reputation working for the League. Some of their statues probably went to Rome when the Romans conquered and looted Aitolia in 189 BC, and commissions for others swiftly followed. At the end of the 2nd century BC a Polykles and Dionysios, the last two known members of the family, were recorded as working for the Romans on Delos. Preserved works are few. Among the attributions, most plausible is a colossal head of *Hercules* (Rome, Mus. Capitolino), which imitates Praxiteles, following his Aberdeen head (London, BM). In Italy the style thrived well into the next century: as late as the 50s BC a colossus from Pompey's theatre complex at Rome imitates it closely.

J. Overbeck: *Die antiken Schriftquellen zur Geschichte der bildenden Künste bei den Griechen* (Leipzig, 1868/*R* Hildesheim, 1959), nos 1146, 2206–13

F. Coarelli: 'Polycles', *Stud. Misc.*, xv (1969–70), pp. 75–89

A. F. Stewart: *Attika: Studies in Athenian Sculpture of the Hellenistic Age* (London, 1979)

A. Stewart: *Greek Sculpture: An Exploration* (New Haven and London, 1990), chaps 18.3, 24.5

Polyphemos Painter. (*fl c.* 670–*c.* 650 BC). Greek vase painter. He was active either in Athens or on the island of Aigina in the Saronic Gulf. An imaginative innovator in mythical representation on a grand scale, he was named after the Middle Proto-Attic amphora from Eleusis (Eleusis Mus.) showing the intoxicated Polyphemos blinded by Odysseus. His early work owes something to the Early Proto-Attic (*c.* 700–*c.* 670 BC) Mesogeia Painter (*see* POTTERY, §IV, 4(iii)), who was perhaps his teacher. On the Eleusis amphora his style is mature, exploiting black and white paint equally. His human figures are in silhouette, except for outlined faces; heads are rounded above, with receding forehead and chin, and bull neck. Minimal use is made of incision, and figures do not overlap. On the neck the giant Polyphemos, blinded while asleep, holds a wine cup to explain his misfortune. On the body Perseus, having beheaded Medusa, escapes from her two enraged Gorgon sisters, protected by Athena; uniquely, the Gorgons' faces are portrayed as Near Eastern metal cauldrons with serpents appended. The confronting lion and boar on the shoulder of the vase bare their teeth, typically aggressive specimens of this painter's animal repertory.

A krater stand (ex-Pergamonmus., Berlin; see Corp. Vasorum Ant., Berlin i, pp. 24–5, pls 31–3), a later work of this painter, shows, among an assembly of chieftains, a figure named, in Aiginetan script, Menelas (Menelaos). The stand, like several other works by this hand, is from Aigina but made of Attic clay; Aiginetan clay is unsuitable for the production of fine painted pottery. It follows either that the Polyphemos Painter was an Aiginetan resident in Athens, or that he worked on Aigina in the Proto-Attic tradition.

Corp. Vasorum Ant., Berlin, i

G. E. Mylonas: *Ho Protoattikos amphoreus tis Eleusinos* [The Protoattic amphora, from Eleusis] (Athens, 1957)

E. T. H. Brann: *Late Geometric and Protoattic Pottery, Mid 8th to Late 7th Century* BC (1962), viii of *The Athenian Agora* (Princeton, 1953–), pp. 11, 23–4

S. P. Morris: *The Black and White Style: Athens and Aigina in the Orientalizing Period* (New Haven, 1984), pp. 37–51

R.G. Osborne: 'Death Revisited, Death Revised: The Death of the Artist in Archaic and Classical Greece', A. Hist., xi (March 1988), pp. 1–16

Pompeii. Roman site in southern Italy, located 24 km south-east of Naples. Destroyed by an eruption of Mt Vesuvius in AD 79, it was preserved under layers of ash and lava until rediscovered in the 18th century.

I. Introduction.

Situated in the Sarno River valley, on a gentle slope facing the sea to the south of Vesuvius, Pompeii was already famous in the ancient world, according to Seneca (*Naturales Quaestiones* VI.i.1) and Tacitus (*Annals* XV.22). The original town must have existed at least as early as the 6th century BC. Little is known of its beginnings, and even its name, believed to be Oscan, is something of an enigma; some mythologists link it, without any evidence, to the Latin word *pompa* or 'procession' in celebration of the myth of Hercules. Archaeological evidence indicates that the Oscan city came first under Etruscan political influence (525–474 BC) and then under that of the Greeks (474–425 BC). It was occupied by the Samnites at the end of the 5th century BC and was apparently politically dependent on the nearby town of Nuceria (Livy: *History of Rome* IX.xxxviii.2–3) during the Second Samnite War; during this period it served mainly as a harbour town for its more important neighbours Nuceria and Nola and for smaller towns in the Sarno Valley.

During the Social War of 90–89 BC, Pompeii took an active part in the insurrection against Rome. The town was besieged by Sulla in 89 BC and held out for a year, thanks to its fortifications. In 80 BC, Publius Sulla (the nephew of the famous dictator) set up the first veterans' colony there, and Pompeii became the Colonia Cornelia Veneria Pompeianorum. A second wave of veterans was settled there under Augustus (*reg* 30 BC–AD 14).

As with any Roman municipality, Pompeii was administered by a college of four elected magistrates, two *duoviri* and two *aediles*, under the supervision of a non-elected town council (*ordo decurionum*). Each quarter (*vicum*) elected its own *magistri vici*, and the suburbs (*pagi*) elected their *magistri pagi*. An earthquake on 5 February AD 62 caused significant damage (Seneca: *Naturales Quaestiones* VI.i.1–2). Vesuvius began to erupt in the late morning of the 24 August AD 79, and by the end of the day some 2 m of ash had fallen on the town. The first 3 m also contain lava pebbles (*lapilli*), followed by layers of pumice, the solidified volcanic magma. Pompeii ultimately lay buried under some 4 m of debris.

The city was undisturbed for some 1700 years until excavations in the mid-18th century following the discovery of HERCULANEUM, about 15 km further up the coast.

G. Fiorelli: *Descrizione di Pompeii* (Naples, 1875)

J. Overbeck and A. Mau: *Pompeji in seinen Gebäuden, Alterthümern und Kunstwerken* (Leipzig, 1884)

A. Mau: *Pompeji in Leben und Kunst* (Leipzig, 1900, 2/1908); Eng. trans. by F. W. Kelsey as *Pompeii: Its Life and Art* (New York, 1902/*R* 1982)

T. Kraus and L. von Matt: *Pompeii and Herculaneum: The Living Cities of the Dead* (New York, 1975)

J. Ward-Perkins and A. Claridge: *Pompeii AD 79* (Boston, 1978)

II. Architecture.

Pompeii's architectural development can be divided into three phases that also reflect the political evolution of the city: the Pre-Samnite period (525–425 BC), the Samnite period (425–80 BC) and the Roman phase (80 BC–AD 79); the last may be further subdivided by the establishment of the Roman Empire under Augustus in 30 BC and by the earthquake of AD 62. Doric capitals and column bases still visible in the Triangular Forum, as well as various artefacts uncovered during excavations, particularly in the Temple of Apollo, are evidence of Greek and Etruscan influence during the pre-Samnite period. During the succeeding Samnite period Pompeii enjoyed great economic prosperity, especially from *c.* 250 BC onwards, thanks to its agricultural activities and maritime trade. The town fortifications were strengthened, and a number of public monuments were built, including the forum, the Temple of Zeus Meilichios, the Temple of Apollo, the basilica and the Stabian Baths. Construction continued after 80 BC but at a different rhythm and with a more grandiose vision: the amphitheatre, the odeion, the Temple of Capitoline Jupiter, the Temple of Venus and the Forum Baths were built, and starting under Augustus the town was further embellished with new public buildings, including the Temple of Fortuna Augusta, the Eumachia, the macellum, the great palaestra and the Central Baths. After the earthquake of AD 62, which destroyed a large part of the town, the Pompeians rebuilt and restored both public and private monuments, until the eruption of Vesuvius in AD 79 put an end to all this dynamic activity.

1. Town planning. 2. Religious. 3. Civic and recreational. 4. Domestic. 5. Funerary.

1. Town planning. The oldest nucleus of Pompeii appears to have been in the southern part of the later town: the remains of a Doric temple (to ?Hercules) on the terrace of the Triangular Forum, the remains of the forum itself and the irregular layout of the streets in areas VII and VIII (see fig. 1) all suggest that this was the site of earliest, pre-Samnite, construction. It is possible that the blocks in area VI, marked off with orthogonal streets, date from as early as the 5th–3rd century BC. The present layout, with orthogonal streets in areas I, II, III, IV, V and IX, suggests that Samnite urban developments continued into the Roman period. The north-east-to-south-west layout of the main avenues (*decumani*) and the perpendicular lines followed by the transverse streets (*cardines*) gave Pompeii's urban fabric its claim to nobility and distinguished it from provincial Roman towns with less sophisticated urban plans. Very little is known about the distribution of the quarters of the town (*vici*), the existence of which is indicated by Samnite and Latin inscriptions, or about the location of the suburbs (*pagi*), which are only known from Latin epigraphical sources.

Archaeological excavation indicates that by the 6th century BC the town was already protected by walls made out of blocks of soft black lava (*papamonte*). In the 5th and 4th centuries BC these fortifications were replaced by Italic-style limestone constructions. In the 3rd and 2nd centuries BC an internal curtain wall was built out of blocks of tufa and the external wall out of limestone. Some 12 quadrangular towers were added at the end of the 2nd century BC, reinforcing the walls to such an extent that the Pompeians were able to hold out for a year against besiegement by Sulla in 89 BC. The walls had seven, possibly eight, openings, some dating to the Samnite period; these are conventionally known as the Vesuvius Gate to the north-west, the Nola Gate to the north and the Stabian Gate and Nucerian Gate to the south-east, the Sarno Gate to the east. Dating to the Roman

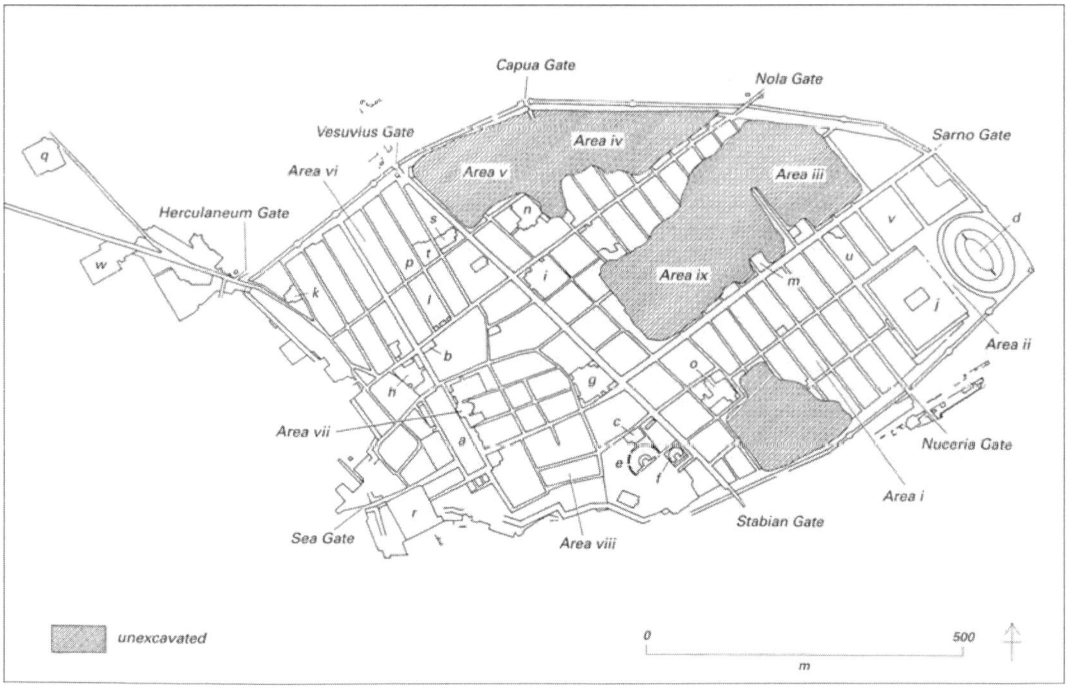

1. Pompeii, plan of the site: (a) forum; (b) Temple of Fortuna Augusta; (c) Temple of Isis; (d) amphitheatre; (e) theatre; (f) odeion; (g) Stabian Baths; (h) Forum Baths; (i) Central Baths; (j) great palaestra; (k) House of Sallust; (l) House of the Faun; (m) House of Julius Polybius; (n) House of the Silver Wedding; (o) House of the Menander; (p) House of the Labyrinth; (q) Villa of the Mysteries; (r) Temple of Venus; (s) House of the Gilded Cupids; (t) House of the Vettii; (u) House of Loreius Tiburtinus; (v) House of Julia Felix; (w) Villa of Diomedes

period are the Herculaneum Gate to the west, the Sea Gate to the south and probably the Capua Gate to the north.

These gateways were linked to the centre of the town by straight roads 7–12 m wide. Several of these, paved with great blocks of volcanic stone, still show the deep grooves left by the passage of cartwheels. They are flanked by high pavements, and squared-off blocks of stone were placed at the intersections to allow pedestrians to cross the road without getting their feet wet and to force carts and chariots to reduce their speed. These features are indicative of a highly developed sense of urban planning, as well as evidence of heavy traffic.

Another admirable aspect of Pompeian town planning is the arrangements made for the supply and distribution of water, beginning under Augustus. Drinking water arrived via the Serino aqueduct and filled a great water-tower near the Vesuvius Gate, from which it flowed through a fairly complex but rational system of channels towards smaller water-tanks erected on distribution towers built near crossroads. Water was piped from these to the public buildings, especially the baths and palaestrae, to the public fountains installed every 100–200 m in the streets and finally to a number of industrial installations and private houses. In no other town in the ancient world, except Rome itself, has such a sophisticated hydraulic system been found.

The FORUM remained in the oldest part of town over the centuries. The existing rectangular area, 157×35 m (see figs 1a and 2), was surrounded in the 4th–3rd century BC by taverns and shops. In the 2nd century BC it was embellished with two-storey porticos, the columns built of tufa. During the Samnite and Roman periods the forum was a religious centre, with the Temple of Capitoline Jupiter (2a) to the north, the Temple of Apollo (2b) to the west and

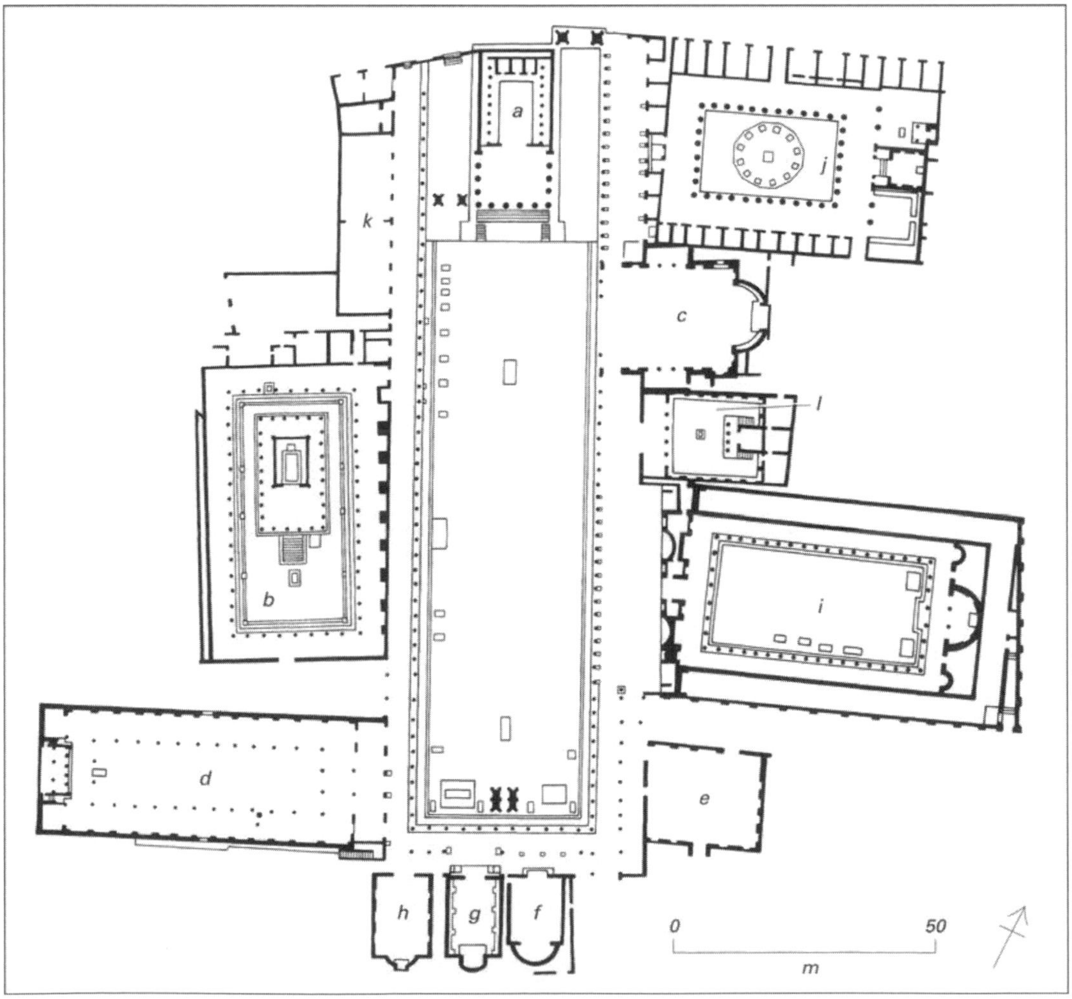

2. Pompeii, plan of the forum: (a) Temple of Capitoline Jupiter; (b) Temple of Apollo; (c) sanctuary of the Lares; (d) basilica; (e) voting hall (*comitium*); (f) chief magistrates' (*duoviri*) office; (g) council chamber; (h) junior magistrates' (*aediles*) office; (i) Eumachia; (j) macellum; (k) Forum Olitorium; (l) Temple of Vespasian

on the eastern side a number of shrines dedicated to the Genius of Augustus and to the public Lares (2c); it was a civic centre, with the basilica (2d) to the west, the administrative buildings to the south (2e–h) and the bases of statues of honour in the centre; and it was a commercial centre: the building (Eumachia; 2i) that served as head office to the corporation of fullers and the macellum (2j), a covered market comprising a quadrilateral portico and a central tholos for the fishmongers, both lay to the east and the Forum Olitorium (cereals market; 2k) to the west.

2. Religious. All the temples in Pompeii suffered significant damage in the earthquake of AD 62, and almost all were in the process of being restored in 79. The Temple of Apollo, in which Oscan and Latin inscriptions dating from the establishment of the colony in 80 BC have been found, was a Corinthian hexastyle building set on a high podium, reached by means of a flight of 14 steps. The *pronaos* (porch) was quite wide, the *naos* (sanctuary) beginning only from the 5th column; the temple was surrounded by a peristyle comprising 9 by 17 fluted tufa columns. The building as a whole revealed a subtle marriage of Hellenistic, Italic and Roman traditions. The Temple of Capitoline Jupiter showed a similar artistic amalgam. Erected under the dictatorship of Sulla, it was also hexastyle prostyle, built in the Corinthian order on a high podium, and in its last phase the *naos* was preceded by a deep *pronaos*. As in any Capitoline temple, the *naos* was divided into three naves to house the images of the Capitoline Triad.

The Temple of Fortuna Augusta was built during the reign of Augustus at the intersection of the Via del Foro and the Via di Nola. This was a more modest building in the Roman style, as were the Temple of Vespasian (AD 81; 3l) and the shrine to the public Lares on the east side of the forum, which were probably erected after AD 62. Very little remains of the Temple of Venus Physica, which stood on the southern promontory near the Sea Gate. The reconstruction of the Temple of Isis (1c above) began after AD 62 and was completed well before the eruption of Vesuvius. It occupied a trapezoidal space hemmed in by the Temple of Zeus Meilichios and the theatre, encroaching on the so-called Samnite palaestra. Built on a podium, its cella was surrounded by a peristyle of seven by eight columns, with four columns supporting the pediment of the *pronaos*. Within the shallow *naos*, over the hollow podium, were foundations for two statue bases. The temple was decorated with paintings in a Greco-Roman style with a number of Egyptianizing elements, representing the iconography, rituals and ceremonies in honour of Isis; a shrine to the child-god Harpocrates stands to the east. The followers of Isis in Pompeii formed one of the largest communities of her worshippers in the first century AD.

3. Civic and recreational. The basilica of Pompeii is both one of the oldest such buildings to have survived in the Italic world and one of the most handsome public structures built in the Hellenistic tradition. It was at once a court, the site of political rallies and a general meeting-place, built at the end of the 2nd century BC in accordance with standards that were to be set down and codified at a later date by the architect Vitruvius. It consisted of a wide, rectangular space (55×24 m) divided by colonnades into a nave and two aisles, ending in a raised podium that served as a platform for the judges. Its First Style decorations and Oscan graffiti are evidence of the building's great age. When roofed over, as it can be assumed that it was, this basilica must have been a remarkable example of technical ingenuity in its day.

Although it was only a small provincial town, Pompeii prided itself on the fact that the first amphitheatre (1d above; see fig. 3) in the whole of the Empire was built there shortly after 80 BC (well before Rome) for gladiatorial games and wild animal fights. Erected at the far eastern end of the town in the form of an oval (140×105 m), it could accommodate 20,000 spectators and was equipped with a mechanism for stretching an awning from the top tiers to shade the public from the heat of the sun.

The theatre (1e above) and the odeion (covered theatre; 1f above) are situated near the Triangular Forum. The layout of the former with its horseshoe-shaped *orchestra* was Greek, possibly from the 2nd century BC, though the existing remains date from its restoration under Augustus. The stage is less than a metre high and is decorated in the Roman style, with the front adorned by seven arched rectangular niches, each containing a fountain. The walls of the stage building (*scaenae frons*) were in the process of being restored in AD 79. The mechanisms for raising a curtain in front of the stage, the wells built below the stage—probably for stage machinery—and basins found underneath the *orchestra* all offer precious information on the nature of the spectacles played out there in ancient times. The Odeion was built shortly after 80 BC. Of typical Roman design, it occupied a rectangle measuring 34.8×28.6 m, with a semicircular orchestra, *tribunalia* (platforms) at the sides and broad tiers of marble seating in the *ima cavea*. The ends of the walkway separating the lower seats from the upper ones were adorned with two kneeling telamones.

Also well before Rome, Pompeii indulged in the luxury of a well-built bathhouse—the Stabian Baths (1g above; *see* Bath, fig. 1), the construction of which began during the Samnite period in the 4th century BC (*see* Architecture, §VI, 1(i)(d)). They underwent various improvements and restorations during the 80s BC and after AD 62. The baths had male and female areas, and in each of these bathers had the use of a changing room (*apodyterium*), a hot bath room (*caldarium*), a steam room (*tepidarium*) and a cold bath room (*frigidarium*). Ultimately the establishment also had its own palaestra, an open-air swimming pool and a library. There are magnificent stucco reliefs in the *apodyterium* and in front of the library, the beauty of which is surpassed only by the reliefs in

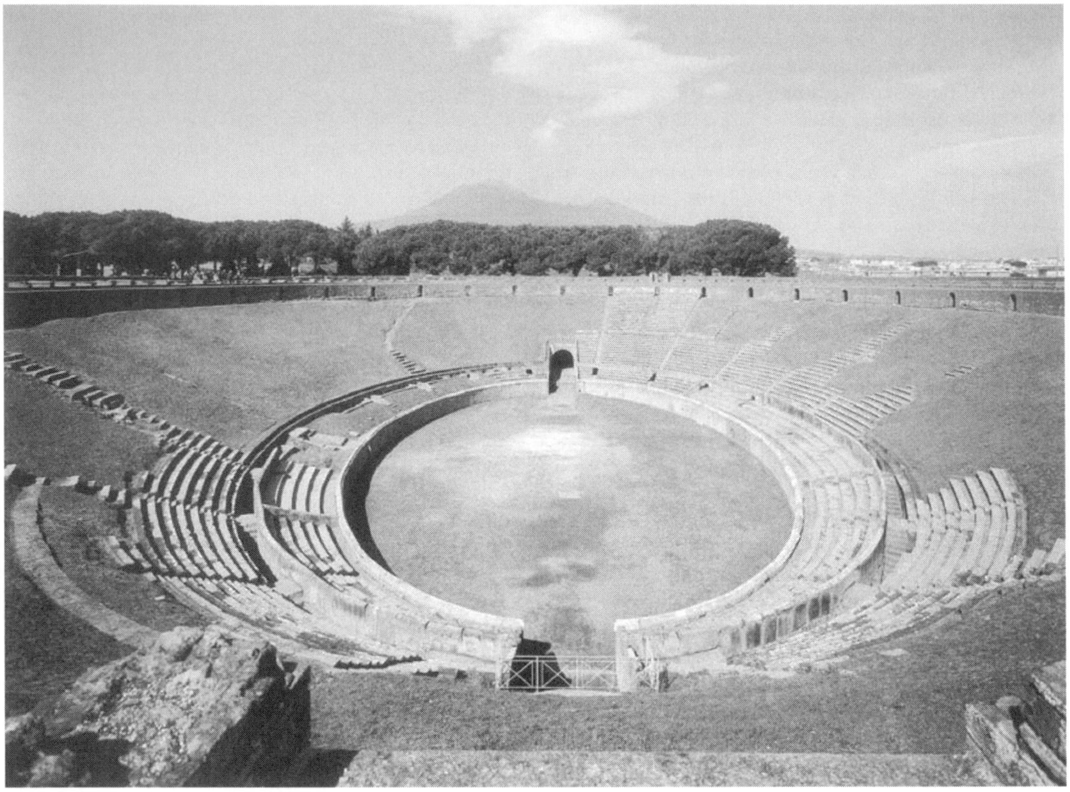

3. Pompeii, amphitheatre, *c.* 80 BC

the Forum Baths (1h above). These baths, built after Sulla's dictatorship, were smaller but had a more sophisticated heating system for the *caldarium* that distributed hot air under the floor and within the walls. It is notable that rotundas were used for the *frigidaria* and vaulted rooms for the *caldaria*. Of the town's two other bathhouses, the baths just outside the town near the Sea Gate appear to have been built outside the ancient town walls at the water's edge, as were the baths just outside HERCULANEUM; the Central Baths (1i above; mid-1st century AD; *see* ARCHITECTURE, §VI, 2(i)(c)) had not yet been restored. In addition to the small palaestrae of the bathhouses, the youth of Pompeii could enjoy other, more spacious exercise grounds, including the Samnite palaestra near the theatre and the great palaestra (1j above) neighbouring the amphitheatre. This last (142×170 m) was built under Augustus and had a handsome swimming pool in a shady setting.

4. DOMESTIC. The houses of Pompeii comprise one of the richest and most complete of any known sources of information on the domestic architecture of ancient Italy up to the end of the 1st century AD, reflecting both the Italic tradition and Hellenic influences. The main Italic element was the atrium, the centre of domestic activity, covered in a few rare cases (*atrium testidunatum*) but more usually lit by an opening in the roof (*compluvium*) formed by the ends of four sloping sections of roofing. Below the *compluvium* lay a rectangular pool for collecting rainwater (*impluvium*; *see also* WELL-HEAD). The atrium was *tuscanicum* (of Tuscan type) when the *impluvium* was supported solely by beams, *tetrastylum* when it was supported by four columns and *corinthium* when the number of these columns was greater than four. The water collected by the *compluvium* was channelled into an underground tank either directly below the ornamental tiling or, occasionally, outside. Before running water was supplied via the aqueduct, these architectural features were essential for everyday life. The most important room opening onto the atrium was the tablinum, the living room of the head of the family. The other main rooms included the *alae*—two rooms situated symmetrically on either side of the atrium that often housed images of the family's ancestors—and the triclinium, or dining room, which was furnished, as its name indicates, with three stone couches on which guests would recline. The earliest Pompeian houses had no upper storeys, but during the Imperial period the rising population led to the frequent addition of a first floor either above the lateral rooms off the atrium or overlooking its back or front sides. The Hellenic element of these houses was the peristyle built around the garden (see fig. 4). This peristyle, often surrounded by rooms, including an *exedra* that usually served as a summer triclinium, was present in all Pompeian middle-class homes.

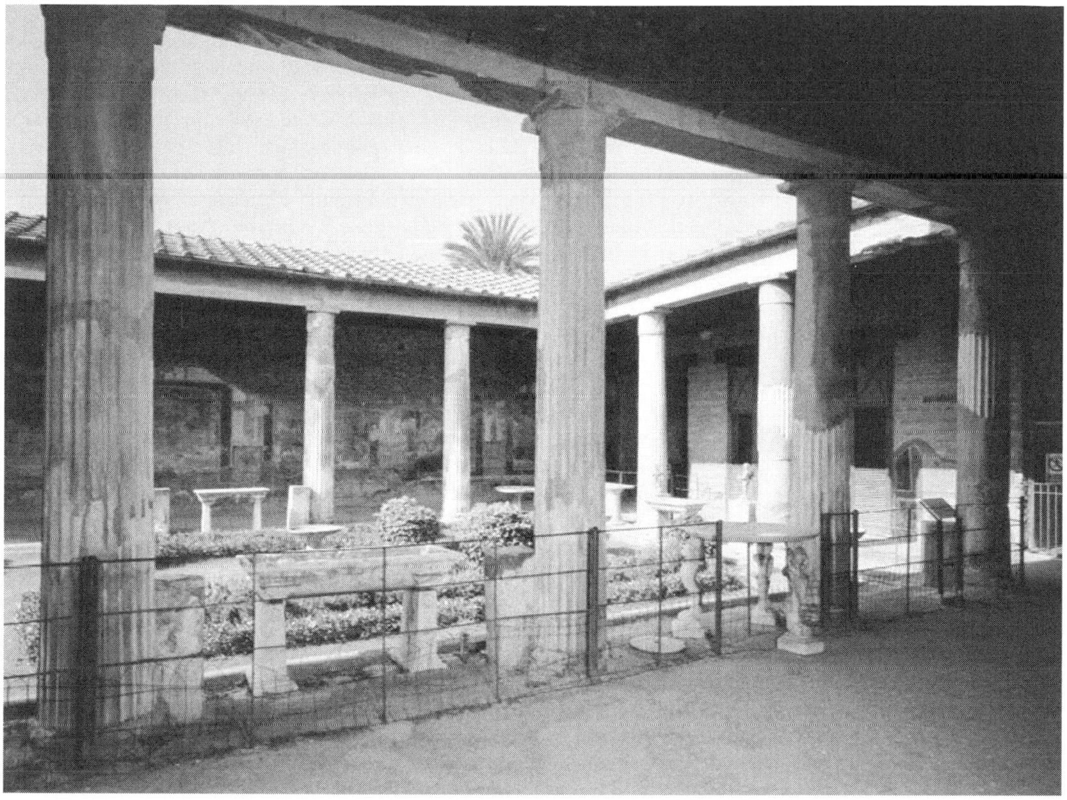

4. Pompeii, House of the Vettii, view of the peristyle garden, mid-1st century AD

Peristyle gardens were often decorated with *oscilla* (small panels suspended in the intercolumniations of peristyles), nymphaea, statues and hermes, and busts of Mercury.

The evolution of domestic architecture went hand in hand with the development of construction technology and painting. During the Samnite period (until 80 BC) construction was dominated by the use of ashlar blocks of tufa for grandiose gateways and façades, and the use of *opus incertum*—lava and tufa rubble embedded in mortar—(*see* ARCHITECTURE, §VI, 1(ii)(a)) to build walls; the walls themselves were decorated with First Style paintings characterized by stuccowork imitating coloured or veined plaques of marble. Pompeii's economic prosperity allowed landowners to build great houses, several of which still retain typical early features despite later alterations; there are perhaps a dozen representative houses of this period. The House of Sallust (1k above), which opens on to the Via Consolare, is a famous example of the *atrium tuscanicum* type of early Pompeian house. The building is wide and tall, has no peristyle and is decorated in the First Style. The House of the Faun (1l above) is the most grandiose residence of the period, however; it is here that the famous mosaic depicting Alexander's defeat of Darius III was found in the tablinum (see fig. 6 below). Its monumental gateway opens on to the Via della Fortuna, and the house occupies an entire city block. It has two atria: an *atrium tuscanicum*, where excavations unearthed the beautiful statue of a faun, after which the house is named, and a smaller *atrium tetrastylum*, as well as two broad gardens surrounded by colonnades. Smaller but no less splendid, the House of Epidius Rufus is distinguished from the others by its magnificent *atrium corinthium* with 16 Doric columns made of tufa; *alae* were built in the middle of each side of the *compluvium*, their doorways decorated by two Ionic tufa columns. The House of Julius Polybius (1m above) is similar to the House of the Faun in that it has a double atrium, but in this case the atrium is covered (*testidunatum*). As was the House of the Faun, this house was built towards the end of the 2nd century BC, and it retains a splendid false door in the First Style.

The buildings erected after 80 BC typically had walls of *opus incertum* made of travertine and lava rubble. The houses were decorated with *trompe-l'oeil* paintings referred to as Second Style. In the House of the Silver Wedding (1n above) there was a great atrium bathed in light; curtains (the hooks still survive) were used to dim the full force of the sunlight coming through the *compluvium* (see colour pl. 2:V, fig. 3). Later improvements in the house included domestic baths, the most sophisticated found anywhere in Pompeii, which contained all the rooms to be found in the public baths and even a small swimming pool. The House of Menander (1o above; named after a painting of the poet on the wall at the south side of the peristyle) also had a large *atrium tuscanicum* and sophisticated baths decorated with Second Style paintings and splendid mosaics. The House of the Labyrinth (1p above), named after a mosaic that depicts a labyrinth with Theseus fighting the Minotaur in the middle, is a large house decorated in the Second Style situated behind the House of the Faun. As in the House of the Silver Wedding, the House of the Labyrinth includes a room richly adorned with columns that reinforce the illusions created by the *trompe-l'oeil* wall paintings.

With the exception of the great villas in Boscoreale and Oplontis near Pompeii, which date to the same period (the villa at Oplontis is thought to be that of Poppaea, wife of Nero (*reg* AD 54–68)), the Villa of the Mysteries (1q above; named after its magnificent painting apparently depicting the mysteries of Dionysus) is one of the most remarkable constructions of the Republican period. A typical suburban villa in plan, it has two separate parts: the stately apartments and grounds designed for the pleasure of its owner, and the slaves' quarters and agricultural land. This villa shows a harmonious combination of two different design concepts: the typical Pompeian house with a large atrium and peristyle on the one hand, and on the other a country villa characterized by halls commanding a panoramic view and surrounded by porticos, each supported on a solid cryptoporticus, making it possible for someone standing in the portico above to see the sea, which was then closer to the town than now.

Apart from *opus incertum*, which continued to be employed, the main technique used between the beginning of the Imperial period and the first earthquake in AD 62 was that of *pseudo-reticulatum*. This consisted of squared but somewhat irregular stones arranged obliquely, in imitation of the meshes of a net. The decorations that accompanied this technique were Third Style—decorative and not *trompe-l'oeil*. The remains of houses from this period leave considerable gaps in the information they offer. The houses tend to be fairly small, such as the House of Sacerdos Amandus, which is famous particularly for the paintings in the tablinum; or the House of the Fruit, which is bright with Egyptian-style paintings and Third Style landscapes. Others include the House of Marcus Lucretius Fronto, with its square atrium and asymmetric garden decorated with marble statues and a nymphaeum, and the House of Jason and the House of Spurius Mesor, both known for their paintings. The decoration of the Villa of Agrippa at Boscotrecase was more elaborate, but its architecture was of no special interest.

There was a significant new element in Pompeii's urban development before AD 62: the beginning of construction work that ultimately swallowed up the city's ramparts. In the so-called Imperial Villa (*c.* AD 50), situated to the south of the Sea Gate and below the Temple of Venus (1r above), one of the porticos ran along the town wall itself. This villa had a number of rooms handsomely decorated in the Third Style (presumably meeting rooms or banqueting rooms), which were completely unrelated to any atrium.

The last phase of Pompeii's construction, from AD 62 to 79, was rich and complex. After the earthquake of 62, landowners restored and renovated their properties according to their means, and some aristocratic houses were converted into shops. The eruption of Vesuvius 17 years later took the population by surprise in the middle of their rebuilding work. The construction techniques used during this period included small rectangular stones (*opus vittatum*), squared stones arranged obliquely (*opus reticulatum*), bricks (*opus latericium*) and a combined system in which several of these bonds appeared together (*opus mixtum*). For want of more suitable materials, workers on several building sites added filler material to the mortar of the *opus incertum*—fragments of marble, brick and tile—in other words, any debris that came to hand from buildings destroyed in the earthquake. The wall paintings of this period are referred to as Fourth Style.

Although the main elements of Italic and Hellenistic architecture were generally retained, this period saw the beginning of an important change: a taste for the Baroque now began to play a part in the arrangement and decoration of some of the large houses, which can be classified in several groups. In the houses of the first group, the atrium and tablinum were still present, but the design emphasized the peristyle, through which one could stroll while contemplating the fountains and *objets d'art* in the garden, and the triclinium overlooking the flower beds, where fine meals could be enjoyed. Among these houses, the House of the Gilded Cupids (1s above) invites the admiration of visitors with its great peristyle of five by seven columns and a garden adorned with a central pool and brightened by pillars, statuettes and busts of Mercury; the guests reclining in the triclinium on the western side must have enjoyed the beauty of these works of art scattered among the greenery. The plan of the garden in the House of the Vettii (1t above) is more impressive still, for despite the beauty of its high *atrium tuscanicum*, the visitor's eye is irresistibly drawn to the rectangular peristyle comprising wide porticos of seven and four columns. The garden was enlivened with multiple fountains, fountains in the form of bronze statues, marble objects and sculptures arranged artistically amid flowers and plants. The vast triclinium, richly decorated with friezes of cupids, adjoins the north side of the garden. The House of Meleager also had a vast garden surrounded by wide porticos and equipped with a rectangular marble fishpond in its centre.

In the second group of houses, the centre of attraction was not the peristyle but the garden. The most typical example is the House of Loreius Tibertinus (1u); its charm lay in its large rectangular garden overlooked by a wide portico of six columns bordered by a chapel to Isis on the east and a triclinium with a nymphaeum on the west. The water from the nymphaeum flowed towards an upper canal that ran alongside the colonnade and then flowed into a lower canal, perpendicular to the first (the two together forming a long T); there was a marble waterfall in the centre of this second canal. In the garden of the House of Julia Felix (1v above), a canal was placed facing a chapel dedicated to the trinity of the cult of Isis. Elsewhere, gardens occupied a level below that of the house, as in the case of the House of the Black Anchor or the Villa of Diomedes (1w above). Water also played an important role in the design of some 20 other houses; among these were the Casa of the Great Fountain, the House of the Small Fountain, the House of the Bear, the House of the Grand Duke and the House of the Scientists, in each of which water streamed from sparkling nymphaea covered in glass mosaics.

A new concept of the use of space in domestic architecture was established at this time, as seen in the new constructions of the third group of houses. The most striking examples are the House of Fabius Rufus and several houses built between the Herculaneum Gate and the Sea Gate. Built astride the old town walls, which had by then become obsolete, these houses had upper storeys and a considerable number of *diaetae* (summer rooms), balconies and wide openings to allow their inhabitants to enjoy the beauties of the landscape—a privilege hitherto reserved for those who lived in villas outside the town, such as the Villa of the Papyrus in Herculaneum or the Villa of Tiberius on Capri. Another series of houses with more than one upper storey was built above the south-west section of the fortifications, also apparently catering for a taste for views. These were more modest in construction, often built to a new plan in which the atrium was absent; they seem to be more like groups of apartments or rooms for rent than houses. The new taste for landscape views may also be seen in the rooms built with large windows and balconies overlooking the Via dell'Abbondanza in area IX, dating from after AD 62. The increasing population and the rise of a new, well-to-do merchant class changed the face of Pompeian streets. Patrician families rented or sold rooms or parts of their houses to craftsmen, shopkeepers, tavern managers and other workers, converting them into apartments, workshops or shops opening on to the streets. This resulted in the break-up and distortion of traditional atrium-based houses and changed the appearance of their façades; the *decumani* and the main *cardines* filled up with fullers' workshops, shops and taverns, whose owners did business on the ground floor and lived on the floor above. These changes can be seen, for example, in the fulling establishments of Marcus Vesonius Primus or Lucius Veranius Ipseus, in the industrial installations that invaded the peristyles of patrician-type houses, and in the Via dell'Abbondanza, where an unbroken line of shops and taverns bears witness to the prosperity of this rising merchant class.

5. FUNERARY. The main necropolises of Pompeii lay outside the Herculaneum Gate, the Vesuvius Gate and the Nocera Gate. Pompeian funerary architecture was rich and varied in both form and decoration and included many different types of tomb: tombs in the form of chapels, such as that of the priestess Eumachia; hemicyclic exedrae, such as the tomb of the priestess Mamia; circular tombs, such as that of the Istacidi; *colombaria* (tombs with niches for cinerary urns) often crowned by an altar decorated with reliefs; tombs in the form of altars; cylindrical mausolea; and tombs decorated with statues or portraits of the dead. Life was a close neighbour to death for the Pompeians. It was on the Via dei Sepolcri, next to the tombs, that the wealthy owners of the Villa of the Mosaic Columns, the Villa of Cicero and the Villa of Diomedes chose to build their homes. The architects of Pompeii used the same techniques and revealed the same artistic tastes, whether they were building for the dead or for the living.

M. Della Corte: *Case ed abitanti di Pompei* (Naples, 1914, 3/1965)

A. Maiuri: *L'ultima fase edilizia di Pompei* (Rome, 1942)

A. Maiuri: *Pompei* (Novara, 1957)

H. Eschebach: *Die städtebauliche Entwicklung des antiken Pompeji* (Heidelberg, 1970)

A. Maiuri: *Alla ricerca di Pompei preromana* (Naples, 1973)

E. La Rocca and others: *Guida archeologica di Pompei* (Rome, 1976)

J. P. Adam: *La Construction romaine: Matériaux et techniques* (Paris, 1984)

P. Zanker: *Pompeji: Stadtbilder als Spiegel von Gesellschaft und Herrschaftsform*, Trierer Winckelmannsprogramme (Mainz, 1987)

L. Richardson jr: *Pompeii: An Architectural History* (Baltimore, 1988; Baltimore and London, 2/1989, 1997)

A. Wallace-Hadrill: *Houses and Society in Pompeii and Herculaneum* (Princeton, 1994)

A. De Franciscis and I. Bragantini: *Pompeii: Monuments Past and Present* (Rome, 1995)

S. E. Bon and R. Jones: *Sequence and Space in Pompeii* (Oxford, 1997)

R. Laurence and A. Wallace-Hadrill: *Domestic Space in the Roman World: Pompeii and beyond* (Portsmouth, RI, 1997)

R. Ling and others: *The Insula of the Menander at Pompeii*, 4 vols (Oxford, 1997–2006)

M. Grahame: *Reading Space: Social Interaction and Identity in the Houses of Roman Pompeii, a Syntactical Approach to the Analysis and Interpretation of Built Space* (Oxford, 2000)

M. Staub Gierow: *Casa della Parete nera (VII 4, 58–60) und Casa delle Forme di creta (VII 4, 61–63)* (2000), x of *Häuser in Pompeji* (Munich, 1984–)

P. M. Allison and F. Sear: *Casa della Caccia antica: (VII 4, 48)* (2002), xi of *Häuser in Pompeji* (Munich, 1984–)

P. M. Allison: *Pompeian Households: An Analysis of Material Culture* (Los Angeles, 2004)

W. Ehrhardt, P. Grunwald and J. Kramer: *Casa delle Nozze d'Argento: (V 2, i)* (2004), xii of *Häuser in Pompeji* (Munich, 1984–)

III. Sculpture.

Excavations at Pompeii reveal that sculpture was common and exceedingly varied in its materials and forms. Probably more important, certainly more expensive than painted mural decoration, sculpture is found in virtually every context and in every scale, from miniature to colossal. Two obstacles prevent the full appreciation of Pompeii's sculpture: first, the fact that the city was salvaged extensively in antiquity despite official prohibition, and second, the removal of nearly all sculpture from its context, transferred to the Museo Archeologico Nazionale in Naples, or to magazines at Pompeii. Unless otherwise noted, all the pieces discussed below are in the Museo Archeologico.

That salvaging after the destruction of the city affected the survival rate of sculpture is apparent from the fact that three of the smallest temples held full complements of sculpture, whereas Pompeii's larger temples were comparatively bare. In the small Temple of Zeus Meilichios, focus of a pre-Roman Greek cult, were found two cult images, life-size terracotta statues of *Jupiter* and *Juno* (1st century AD). The Temple of Isis held an acrolithic cult statue of *Isis* (untraced), another Egyptianizing statue of the goddess, a statue of *Dionysus with a Panther*, and numerous other works. The Temple of Fortuna Augusta contained life-size images of private citizens: an unidentified man, the so-called '*Cicero*', and a woman, '*Livia*'. These statues may represent patrons, moved into spaces left vacant when images of the family of Augustus were transferred to the macellum (market building) adjoining the forum. Statues depicting two members of the family of Augustus, '*Marcellus*' and '*Livia*' (both 27 BC–AD 14), were discovered in the macellum. The reigning Flavians were apparently honoured in the Temple of Vespasian; the absence of their portraits there is presumably the result of salvaging. A fine relief of a public sacrifice remains *in situ* on an altar there. Fragments of a colossal *Jupiter* (1st century BC–AD 79), among them a fine head, were found in the cella of the Temple of Capitoline Jupiter at the north end of the forum. The city's other large temples, to Apollo and Venus, yielded a few interesting pieces, including a bronze *Apollo with Bow*.

It has been estimated that the forum once contained some 18 equestrian statues honouring local dignitaries and six more colossal monuments to members of the imperial family, though none remains. However, two honorary statues placed well away from the forum did survive. Near the intersection of two of Pompeii's main streets was found a cuirassed statue (?*c*. 1 BC) identified by inscription as that of *M. Holconius Rufus*, one of the city's most distinguished citizens, who was responsible for the rebuilding of the theatre. Hidden in a chapel behind the building she had given to the city was the statue of *Eumachia* (27 BC–AD 14), paid for by the fullers' guild. A portrait herm of *Norbanus Sorex*, a famous mime of Augustus' time, stood in Eumachia's building (amid a gallery of distinguished citizens); it does not survive, although another from the Temple of Isis—like the first, paid for by the town council—is preserved in Naples.

Private statuary survives in greater numbers than public works, due to its location away from the centres of the town. The range of quality and materials is considerably greater than that of public monuments. A few workshops, such as that in the House of the Bronzes, have been identified from their concentration of artefacts, and parts of several likely original pairs have been found in separate households, probably through sale or inheritance. Half life-size, archaizing statues of Diana and Apollo were found in different locations, as were quarter-scale terracotta statuettes of *Pittakos* (1st century AD; Pompeii, Antiqua.) and *Antisthenes* (1st century AD).

Funerary monuments from the roads leading out of the principal city gates, most commonly portrait busts, togate statues and biographical narrative relief, provide rich commentary upon civic life. In a study of the monuments outside the Herculaneum Gate, Kockel concluded that the decoration was directed almost exclusively to the tomb exterior (i.e. to a living audience), and that the subject-matter was concerned, almost exclusively, with the life of the deceased rather than with the afterlife. A single, late instance of *apotheosis in deum*, the depiction of M. Cerrenius Restitutus as *Mercury*, has been interpreted as an example of a fashion that became common elsewhere in the Roman world at a later date.

Lararia (household shrines), found in many houses, held terracotta, bronze or silver statuettes representing the genius and the tutelary divinities of the household. Among the latter, Jupiter, Juno, Venus, Apollo, Minerva, Mercury, Fortuna and Hercules are common. Symmetrical, dancing figures, traditionally called lares (household gods) but more correctly of Dionysiac nature, are also common. The contents of many *lararium* groupings have been reconstructed from excavation reports.

Life-size bronze heads may be identified as ancestral portraits, judging from their prominent display in several atrium houses. Apparently identical heads, representing either L. Caecilius Iucundus or an ancestor (27 BC–AD 14 or mid-1st century AD) and set into marble herms, flanked the tablinum of the House of Caecilius Iucundus. Similar placement, at one *anta* of the tablinum, has been noted for portraits in the House of Cornelius Rufus, the House of Vesonius Primus and the House of the Citharist. The bronze head of a woman (AD 14–68) from the latter house may also represent an ancestor, having been found in a wing of the atrium adjoining the tablinum, where a male portrait was found. Two celebrated portraits (27 BC–AD 14) found in another part of the House of the Citharist are more likely to represent famous persons than ancestors.

Portraits of famous men (philosophers, orators, poets) include, besides the statuettes of *Pittakos* and *Antisthenes* mentioned above, a number of marble portrait herms (e.g. '*Pseudo-Seneca*', *Epicurus, Demosthenes, Menander*); these were placed separately or used as decorative ensembles in some gardens. Large marble statuettes of gods or demi-gods are common in garden ensembles, where the theme of nature is appropriate; often a dais or shrine provided a focus for the sculptural programme, usually occupied by Venus, Dionysus, Cupid or Silenus. Secondary subjects included satyrs and satyr-children engaged in dramatic poses, such as the famous *Dancing Faun* from the House of the Faun (*c.* 300–100 BC; see fig. 5), and animals, including hunting groups. Less common are such statues as the fine bronze *Apollo with Lyre* (1st century AD) and the marble archaizing *Diana*. Bronze youths bearing lamps (1st century BC–AD 79) were probably used to illuminate nocturnal banquets.

Marble relief panels—circular, lunate or rectangular—were employed either as *oscilla*, suspended in the intercolumniations of peristyles, or as *pinakes*, reliefs set atop pilasters about a metre in height within the area of the garden, as in the House of the Gilded Cupids). The subject-matter of *oscilla* and *pinakes* often has direct association with the theatre—tragic, comic and satyr masks being among the most common subjects. There is much evidence that Pompeii's decorative marble sculpture, both free-standing and relief, was painted in several colours, and some marble statuettes were gilded. Some decorative marbles were sculpted locally, but most pieces were imported, as were other classes of sculpture.

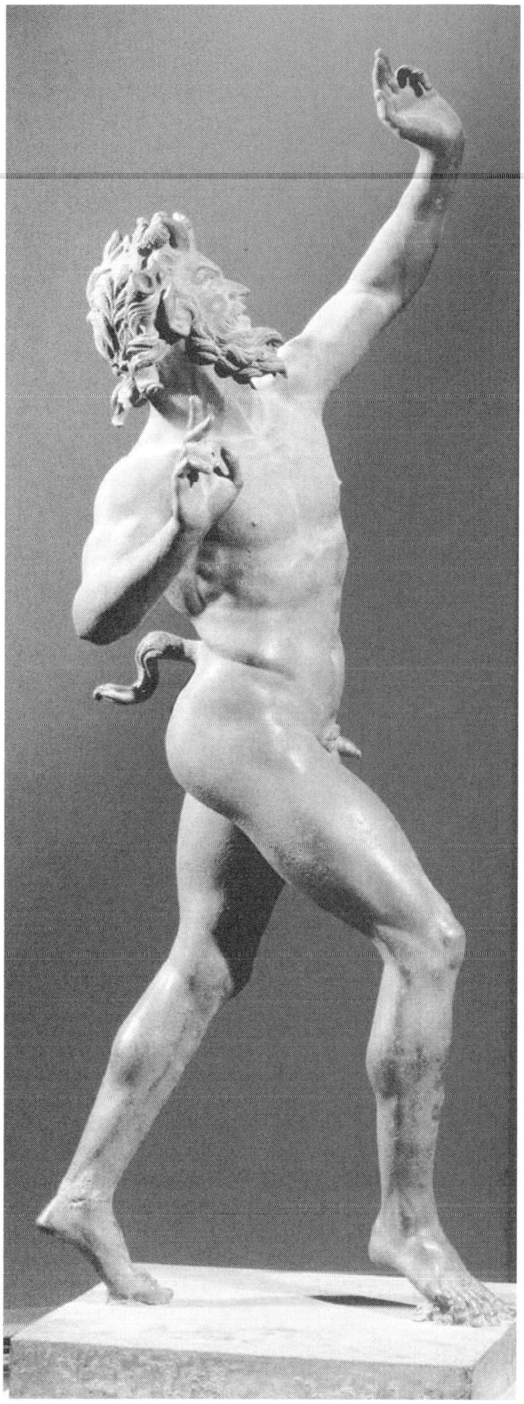

5. Pompeii, *Dancing Faun*, bronze, h. 700 mm, from the House of the Faun, *c.* 312 BC (Naples, Museo Archeologico Nazionale)

J. Overbeck and A. Mau: *Pompeji in seinen Gebäuden, Alterthümern und Kunstwerken* (Leipzig, 1856, 4/1884/*R* 1968)
H. von Rohden: *Die Terrakotten von Pompeji*, (1880), i of *Die antike Terrakotten* (Stuttgart, 1880–1911)
A. Ruesch: *Guida illustrata del Museo nazionale di Napoli* (Naples, 1908)
E. Pernice: *Gefässe und Geräte aus Bronze* (1925), iv of *Die hellenistische Kunst in Pompeji* (Berlin and Leipzig, ?1925–38)
A. Levi: *Le terracotte figurate del Museo nazionale di Napoli* (Florence, 1926)
V. Spinazzola: *Le arti decorative in Pompei e nel Museo nazionale di Napoli* (Milan, 1928)
E. Pernice: *Hellenistische Tische, Zisternmündungen, Beckenuntersätze, Altäre und Truhen* (1932), v of *Die hellenistische Kunst in Pompeji* (Berlin and Leipzig, ?1925–38)
A. Maiuri: *La Casa del Menandro e il suo tesoro di argenteria* (Rome, 1933)
G. K. Boyce: 'Corpus of the Lararia of Pompeii', *Mem. Amer. Acad. Rome*, xiv (1937) [whole vol.]
A. de Franciscis: *Il ritratto romano a Pompei* (Naples, 1951)
V. Spinazzola: *Pompei alla luce degli scavi nuovi di Via dell' Abbondanza, 1910–1923* (Rome, 1953)
E. J. Dwyer: *Pompeian Domestic Sculpture: A Study of Five Pompeian Houses and their Contents* (Rome, 1982)
V. Kockel: *Die Grabbauten vor dem Herkulaner Tor in Pompeji* (Mainz, 1983)
W. Wohlmayr: *Studien zur Idealplastik der Vesuvstädte* (Buchloe, 1991)
Domus, viridaria, horti picti (exh. cat., Pompeii Casina dell'Aquila; Naples, Bib. N.; 1992)
R. Bonifacio: *Ritratti romani da Pompei* (Rome, 1997)
H. Weinstock: 'Zur Statuenbasis in der samnitischen Palastra von Pompeji [plinth of Doryphoros sculpture]', *Mitt. Dt. Archäol. Inst.:Röm. Abt.*, civ (1997),pp. 519–26
W. M. F. Jashemski and F. G. Meyer: *The Natural History of Pompeii* (Cambridge and New York, 2002)
F. W. von Hase: 'Pompeji: Die Stunden des Untergangs [Exhibit: Reiss-Engelhorn-Museen, Mannheim]', *Ant. Welt*, xxxv/6 (2004),p. 67

IV. Painting.

Of all the art genres represented in Pompeii, the wall paintings are the best preserved and the most numerous. Since the 18th century they have rightly been so famous that Pompeian painting has become synonymous with late Republican–early Imperial Roman painting (1st century BC–1st century AD), and the chronological scheme of the four Pompeian styles is also applied outside Pompeii. (All examples cited are *in situ* unless otherwise stated.)

In most of the private houses and in some of the public buildings and baths, several painted rooms, and in some cases many such rooms, have been found, although in varying states of preservation. Some of the painted walls have been found still standing to their full height of 3 to 6 m. Not until the 20th century, however, has care been taken to preserve and reassemble fragments of fallen ceilings. Until the late 19th century, well-preserved figural paintings or decorative motifs were cut from the walls and transferred to the museum of Portici and later to the Museo Nazionale in Naples, and the rest either destroyed for fear of theft (18th century) or so inadequately protected from the weather (19th century) that most of the older finds are now only known in fragments or from old engravings and watercolours. Giuseppe Fiorelli was the first to take pains, from 1863, to preserve the paintings complete and *in situ*, but much has still been lost since—through inadequate roofing, lack of conservation and the effects of tourism. As late as the 19th century it was mistakenly assumed that encaustic or tempera paints with binding agents were used in Pompeii. It has been proved, however, that *buon fresco*, i.e. painting on damp plaster, was generally used. Only occasionally did painters supplement this with tempera painting on a dry ground (*a secco*), for example for vignettes (*see* PAINTING, §VI, 1(ii)).

For a long time only the content of the figure paintings or the decorative character of the compositions at Pompeii were of interest, not their historical development. From 1873, however, the German archaeologist August Mau demonstrated a temporal sequence of four different decorative styles. Although occasionally disputed, and much refined since, his chronological system has survived into the early 21st century. Paintings of the First Style (*c.* 300–*c.* 100 BC), such as in the House of Sallust, imitate architectural elements (hewn stones, pilasters, cornices etc) in painted stucco relief. Figural painting is generally limited to low friezes or the surfaces of individual stones. In the Second Style (*c.* 100–*c.* 20 BC) the system of the First Style is at first translated into illusionistic painting by the use of perspective and shading, such as in the Villa of the Mysteries (see colour pl. 2:IV, fig. 1). In especially lavish decorations the illusionistic opening up of space sometimes includes views through openings on to integrated structures. The vista through an opening develops within the Second Style into a central space for mythological landscape paintings, at first framed by architectural features—as in the bath-suite of the House of the Cryptoporticus. After a mannerist transitional phase, with fantastically animated and elongated architecture, the classicizing Third Style (*c.* 20 BC–*c.* AD 40/50), ostensibly simple and severe, emphasizes surface effects once more. Disembodied architectural elements articulate the wall into broad, still areas of colour, from which framed figural compositions stand out. Colours become pale and cool. This style represents the Augustan-Tiberian era. In the Fourth Style (*c.* AD 40/50–79, outside of the Vesuvian towns to *c.* AD 100), under the reign of Emperor Claudius, there was a shift to painterly, representational forms, warm, strong colours, violent movement and contrast, and rich, luxuriant vegetal ornamentation. Elements of the late Second Style were mingled with the innovations of the Third Style. For example, perspectivist vistas through fantastic architectural forms alternate with the fields of the main zone. In a clear rejection of calm, empty surfaces, strips of filigree ornamentation, or gleaming metal or vegetal candelabra and garlands, have been inserted wherever there is room, as in Triclinium K from the House of the Prince of Naples. Pictorial compositions are now full of figures and movement, organized three-dimensionally and dramatized by shadow and highlights.

Despite the changes between the styles, from the Second to the Fourth Style and for long afterwards the wall articulation remained basically the same. Ceremonial rooms were, of course, more lavishly equipped than secondary rooms or corridors. There was no fundamental difference, however, between the decoration of public and private rooms. Utility rooms were decorated very simply or not at all. But there was no type of articulation that was limited to a particular room function. Usually the walls were divided horizontally into the socle, the main zone and the upper zone, and vertically into what were usually three or five axes, while the short sides had two or three axes.

In the main rooms the articulation of the walls, some more elaborate than others, was usually done by architectural elements. The middle part of the wall could (in the Second Style) open in a vista or (in the Third and Fourth Styles) have an aedicule above a mythological image. From the Third Style the upper zone contained bizarre structures. Field painting created simpler types of wall, in which vertical, rectangular, paratactic fields above the narrow socle zone were varied by colour changes and diverse frames and vignettes. For greater elaboration, narrow strips were inserted between the different fields of the main zone and filled with the most diverse ornamentation, usually candelabra or vine foliage, while in the Fourth Style there were often also vistas of bizarre architectural structures. Because of its uniform rhythm, field-painting was especially suited to long walls like those of porticos or corridors.

Patterns formed of repeated elements covered the walls of small rooms above the socle, although they are fairly rare and limited to the Fourth Style. Sometimes the walls consist only of horizontal, frieze-like ornamental bands. The hewn stones of the First and Second Styles live on in the Third and Fourth as simple, brightly coloured surface patterns, but only on the main and/or upper zones of atria, entrances, staircases or courtyard walls. Ceilings imitate either coffers (in the Second and Third Styles) or are embellished with ornamental strips and fields arranged concentrically or endlessly repeated (in the Third and Fourth Styles).

As early as the Second Style interior rooms display vistas of gardens or landscapes animated by mythological figures, each framed by architectural features. Central paintings with landscapes containing mythological scenes in miniature format are a speciality of the Third Style. A number of the preceding elements are brought together in a style transitional between the Third and Fourth Styles. In the Fourth Style small pictorial panels with landscape sketches are widespread. Large garden scenes, covering the main and upper zones, with or without architectural articulation, are found in the Third and Fourth Styles, both in small rooms and on extensive courtyard and garden walls. On the latter, in the Fourth Style, large-format paintings of hunts and indigenous or exotic wild animals, or Nile landscapes are found, sometimes with burlesque pygmy scenes.

The great majority of figural scenes are taken from Greek and occasionally Roman mythology. They are found in frieze form and as small panels, but usually as centre panels. Historical subjects are extremely rare (e.g. the *Death of Sophonisba*; from Pompeii I 10, 7 (8) and Pompeii VIII 2, 38–39, now Naples, Mus. Archeol. N., inv. no. 8968; or a scene of fighting in the amphitheatre of Pompeii in AD 59; from Pompeii I 3, 23, now Naples, Mus. Archeol. N., inv. no. 112222). Genre scenes also occur (cult ceremonies, scenes at the forum, tavern pictures, depictions of craftsmen, pornography), and still-lifes may be found both as centre panels or as unframed vignettes or small panels (for an example from the House of Lucretius Fronto). Portraits of people, mostly idealized types, appear alone or in pairs (see colour pl. 2:V, fig. 2), often inside tondi in side panels but rarely as main images. *Lararia*, images of domestic and other deities in small niches or on façades, form a special group. The image types are taken from high art, although the quality of depiction, depending on the pretensions of the worshipper, can be 'popular' or even quite primitive.

Attempts to distinguish workshops and the hands of individual painters have long been made, but with little success. The range of quality is very wide. There are no two identical walls in Pompeii: the painters were always trying to vary the treatment, even in the case of mythological paintings that clearly followed the same model. With few exceptions it has proved futile to try to identify Greek paintings, only known to us from literature, as models. But it is certain that pattern books were used, in which both entire compositions and individual figures and ornament types were recorded.

The originality of Pompeian wall painting lies in the infinite variation of a rich tradition going back to Late Classical and Hellenistic art, both in the compositions and in the figures. The quality of the pictorial programme—the close relationship of several mythological images within one room—was a particular achievement. The myths are often related by contrast: heroes and miscreants, divine rewards and punishments, but also clear injunctions to pleasure or virtuous conduct.

W. Zahn: *Die schönsten Ornamente und merkwürdigsten Gemälde aus Pompeji, Herculaneum und Stabiae* (Berlin, 1828–59)

W. Helbig: *Die Wandgemälde der vom Vesuv verschütteten Städte Campaniens* (Leipzig, 1868)

A. Mau: *Geschichte der decorativen Wandmalerei in Pompeji* (Berlin, 1882)

P. Herrmann and F. Bruckmann: *Denkmäler der Malerei des Altertums* (Munich, 1906–50)

G. Rizzo: *La pittura ellenistico-romana* (Milan, 1929)

H. Beyen: *Die pompejanische Wanddekoration vom zweiten bis zum vierten Stil*, 2 vols (The Hague, 1938–60)

K. Schefold: *Pompejanische Malerei: Sinn und Ideengeschichte* (Berne, 1952)

K. Schefold: *Die Wände Pompejis: Topographisches Verzeichnis der Bildmotive* (Berlin, 1957)

K. Schefold: *Vergessenes Pompeji* (Berne and Munich, 1962)

W. Peters: *Landscape in Romano-Campanian Mural Paintings* (Groningen, 1963)

S. Augusti: *I colori pompeiani* (Naples, 1967)

A. Barbet and C. Allag: 'Techniques de préparation des parois dans la peinture murale romaine', *Mél. Ecole Fr. Rome: Ant.*, lxxxiv (1972), pp. 935–1069

F. Bastet and M. de Vos: *Proposta per una classificazione del terzo stile pompeiano*, Archeologische Studien van het Nederlands Instituut te Rome, 4 (The Hague, 1979)

V. M. Strocka, ed.: *Häuser in Pompeji*, 8 vols (Tübingen and Munich, 1984–94)

F. G. Andersen: 'Pompeian Painting: Some Practical Aspects of Creation', *Anlct. Romana Inst. Dan.*, xiv (1985), pp. 113–28

A. Laidlaw: *The First Style in Pompeii: Painting and Architecture* (Rome, 1985)

W. Ehrhardt: *Stilgeschichtliche Untersuchungen an römischen Wandmalereien von der späten Republik bis zur Zeit Neros* (Mainz, 1987)

G. Cerulli Irelli and others, eds: *Pompejanische Wandmalerei* (Stuttgart, 1990)

G. Pugliese Caratelli, ed.: *Pompei: Pitture e mosaici* (Rome, 1990)

T. Fröhlich: *Lararien- und Fassadenbilder in den Vesuvstädten* (Mainz, 1991)

R. Ling: *Roman Painting* (Cambridge, 1991)

R. Thomas: *Die Dekorationssysteme der römischen Wandmalerei von augusteischer bis in trajanische Zeit* (Mainz, 1995)

I temi figurativi nella pittura parietale antica: IV sec. a. C. – IV sec. d. C.: Atti dei VI Convegno internazionale sulla pittura parietale antica: Bologna, 1995

Still Lifes from Pompeii (exh. cat. by S. De Caro: Paris, Maison de l'Unesco, 1999)

P. G. Guzzo and V. Scarano Ussani: *Veneris figurae: Immagini di prostituzione e sfruttamento a Pompei* (Naples, 2000)

L. Richardson: *A Catalog of Identifiable Figure Painters of Ancient Pompeii, Herculaneum, and Stabiae* (Baltimore, 2000)

E. De Carolis: *Gods and Heroes in Pompeii* (Los Angeles, 2001)

The Villa of Mysteries in Pompeii (Pompeii, 2001)

E. Heinrich: *Der Zweite Stil in pompejanischen Wohnhäusern* (Munich, 2002)

F. Pesando, M. Bussagli and G. Mori: *Pompei: La pittura* (Florence, 2003)

D. Mazzoleni, U. Pappalardo and L. Romano: *Domus: Wall Painting in the Roman House* (Los Angeles, 2004)

L. Fierz-David and N. Hall: *Dreaming in Red: The Women's Dionysian Initiation Chamber in Pompeii* (Putnam, CT, 2005)

V. Mosaics.

The earliest surviving pavements date from the period when First Style painting was popular (*c.* 300–*c.* 100 BC) and belong to the South Italian and Sicilian traditions. *Opus signinum* (plaster made with lime and potsherds) was decorated with white limestone tesserae set in rows or in a limited range of geometric patterns (meanders, trellis, imbrications), with a few vegetal elements (scrolls, palmettes). Later in the same period appeared pavements made of irregular fragments (*crustae*) of coloured limestone loosely set into a plain background of cement, and terrazzo floors of irregular chips of white limestone; floors of plain white tesserae are also found, sometimes with a single black border. All these types continued into the period of Second Style wall painting (*c.* 100–*c.* 20 BC), and floors of *opus signinum* and *crustae* were made throughout the history of Pompeii, the former with a steady enrichment of the decorative repertory, the latter with increasing use of multicoloured marbles and a background of black or white tesserae. Different techniques were frequently combined within a single floor.

A different tradition, undoubtedly of Greek derivation, appears in a small number of rich houses dating to *c.* 100 BC: that of the fine, figured 'picture-mosaic', usually in the form of emblemata (separately made panels). These are mostly small, rectangular panels in the fine technique known as *opus vermiculatum*, with minuscule tesserae and a very wide range of colours. Subject-matter includes animals, fish and birds, among them variants of the *Drinking Doves* of Sosos of Pergamon (the best is in house VIII.2.34); Nilotic motifs, notably the frieze from the House of the Faun; Dionysiac motifs such as the *Tiger-rider* from the same house; and a few mythological scenes, for example *Theseus and the Minotaur*, once at the centre of a two-dimensional black-and-white labyrinth in the House of the Labyrinth. The theatre is also represented, notably by the two emblemata signed in Greek by Dioskourides of Samos from the so-called Villa of Cicero, with scenes from two of the comedies of Menander (Naples, Mus. Archeol. N.). Without parallel are the portrait of a woman and the allegorical mosaic with a skull, from a triclinium table (both Naples, Mus. Archeol. N.). The tradition of such pictorial mosaics was declining towards the end of the Republic, and it is not certain if any are to be dated after this.

The greatest number of fine mosaics in any one house came from the House of the Faun, dating to *c.* 100 BC. Outstanding here is the *Alexander* Mosaic (see fig. 6), probably representing the Battle of Issus in Cilicia between Alexander the Great (*reg* 336–323 BC) and Darius III (*reg* 335–331 BC). The panel contained an estimated four million tesserae, all of natural stone, in a four-colour technique recalling that of Greek Late Classical painting; it was undoubtedly copied from an original painting, usually ascribed to PHILOXENOS OF ERETRIA, done shortly after the battle itself.

Polychrome geometric mosaics appeared at the end of the First Style of painting and were common in the late Republic; they frequently had three-dimensional perspective designs. Alongside these appeared two-dimensional black-and-white geometric pavements, which came to predominate at the end of the 1st century BC. Small panels at the centre of the room or on thresholds were succeeded by all-over designs; the decorative repertory grew steadily, as did the complexity of the geometric framework, and floral elements were frequent. Figured motifs were introduced into the Black-and-white Style, at first tentatively; the Full Silhouette Style appeared by the last decades of the city's life. In the baths (*c.* 20 BC) of the House of the Menander swimmers and bath attendants are shown in black silhouette, with a limited use of colour for some details. Vestibules with black-and-white figured mosaics, especially of animals, were popular in the final years of the town and included the *cave canem* (Lat.: 'beware of dog') designs of watchdogs in the House of the Tragic Poet and the House of Paquius Proculus. *Opus sectile* limestone pavements appeared *c.* 100 BC, often in combination with other techniques; from the Augustan period (30 BC–AD 14) there was increasing use of marble and, occasionally, coloured glass. Three examples show figured intarsia of marble used on walls: one (from a Fourth Style (*c.* AD 40 or 50–79) setting) shows Venus lacing her sandal (house I.2.10).

In addition to floors, Pompeii contains numerous examples of mosaic used to decorate fountains and nymphaea, and a few examples (from the last period) of the application of mosaic to other wall surfaces. Seashells, pumice, Egyptian blue frit and glass fragments were used, as well as stone and glass tesserae. Figures appear in the later examples, which include a marine Venus in her shell in the House of the Fountain with Columns and the House of the Bear. Figured panels might also be inserted in the walls, as was the *Achilles and the Daughters of Lycomedes* in the House of Apollo.

See also MOSAICS, §III.

M. E. Blake: 'The Pavements of Roman Buildings of the Republic and Early Empire', *Mem. Amer. Acad. Rome*, viii (1930), pp. 7–159

E. Pernice: *Pavimente und figürliche Mosaiken* (1938), vi of *Die hellenistische Kunst in Pompeji* (Berlin and Leipzig, ?1925–38)

B. Andreae: *Das Alexandermosaik aus Pompeji* (Recklinghausen, 1977)

P. Meyboom: 'I mosaici pompeiani con figure de pesci', *Meded. Ned. Inst. Rome*, xxxix (1977), pp. 49–93

F. Sear: *Roman Wall and Vault Mosaics* (Heidelberg, 1977)

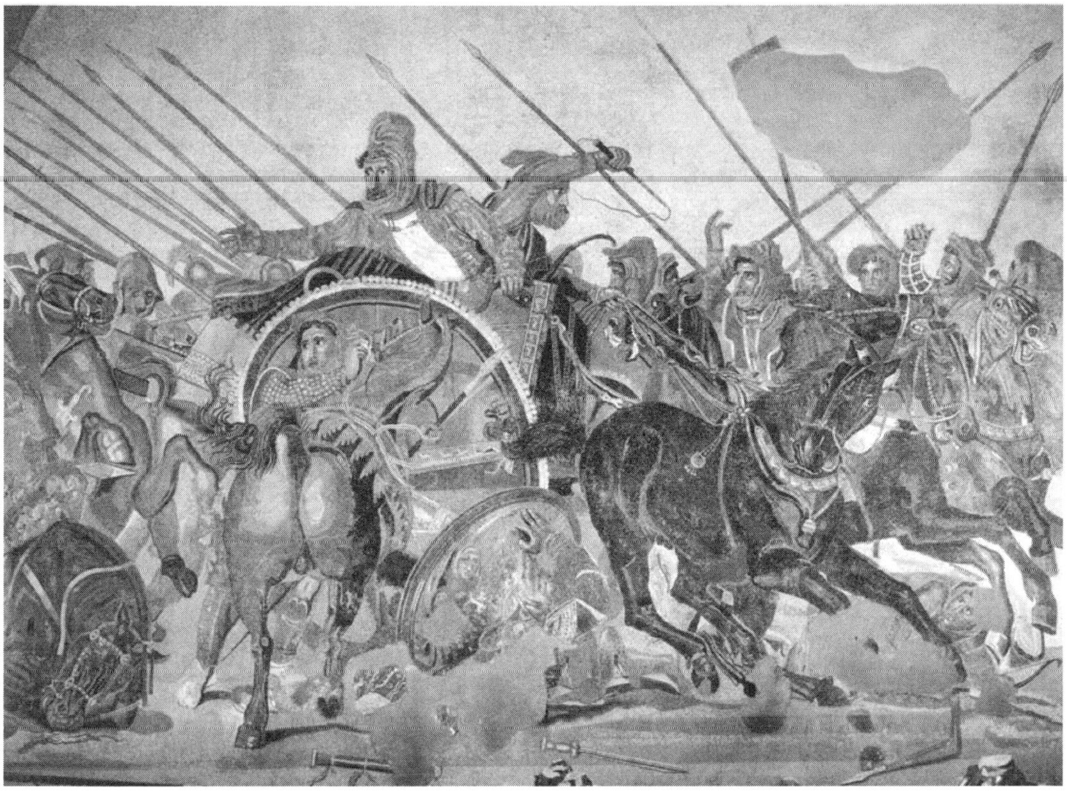

6. Pompeii, mosaic of *Darius*, detail from the *Alexander* Mosaic, from the House of the Faun, *c.* 100 BC (Naples, Museo Archeologico Nazionale)

M. de Vos: 'Pavimenti e mosaici', *Pompei 79*, ed. F. Zevi (Naples, 1984), pp. 161–76

I. Baldassarre and others, eds.: *Pompei: Pitture e mosaici* I–VIII (Rome, 1990–98)

F. Zevi: 'Die Casa del Fauno in Pompeji und das Alexandermosaik', *Mitt. Dt. Archäol. Inst.: Röm. Abt.*, cv (1998), pp. 21–65, pls. 10–17

K. P. Stähler: *Das Alexandermosaik: Über Machterringung und Machtverlust* (Frankfurt am Main, 1999)

Still Lifes from Pompeii (exh. cat. by S. De Caro; Paris, Maison de l'Unesco, 1999)

C. Cicirelli and M. P. Guidobaldi: *Pavimenti e mosaici nella Villa dei misteri di Pompei* (Naples, 2000)

P. Moreno: *Apelle: La battaglia d'Alessandro* (Milan, 2000)

S. De Caro: *I mosaici la casa del Fauno: Guida alla collezione* (Naples, 2001)

P. Moreno: *Apelles: The Alexander Mosaic* (Milan, 2001)

W. M. F. Jashemski and F. G. Meyer: *The Natural History of Pompeii* (Cambridge and New York, 2002)

F. Zevi and others: 'Nature and History, Comedy and Tragedy', *F.M.R. Mag.*, x (Dec 2005–Jan 2006), pp. 1–26

VI. Rediscovery and influence.

Allusions in Classical sources to the buried cities of Campania aroused the interest of Italian Renaissance scholars. Martial (*Epigrams* IV.44) and Dio Cassius (*Roman History* LXVI.xxiii.3) indicated their general location and fate, and Pliny the younger wrote a vivid contemporary account of the disaster (*Epistles* VI.xvi and xx). Yet when workers constructing an aqueduct from the Sarno River struck the ruins of Pompeii in 1594, no apparent connection was made with the ancient city. In 1738 Charles of Bourbon, King of Naples and Sicily (*reg* 1734–59), initiated systematic excavation at HERCULANEUM; while searching for more readily accessible sites ten years later, engineers again excavated at the site known simply as Civita until inscriptions found in 1763 identified it as Pompeii.

As Royal Proprietor, Charles continued the tradition of removing objects and sending them to his palace at Portici. In 1755 he established the Accademia Ercolanese, whose 15 scholars published the discoveries from Campania in *Le antichità di Ercolano esposti* (1757–96). This vast study consisted of five volumes on wall paintings, one on lamps and candelabra and two on bronzes; a projected volume on marble sculpture did not appear. Each folio was illustrated with handsome engravings and excellent descriptions of the objects by members of the academy; later reprinted in several languages, these volumes were instrumental in popularizing Pompeian motifs throughout Europe and became invaluable guides for designers and decorators intent on selling the 'Pompeian style' to a public sated with the Rococo.

The newly unearthed wall paintings inspired Giovanni Battista Piranesi (1720–78), Joseph-Marie Vien (1716–1809), Anton Raphael Mengs (1728–79), Jean-Auguste-Dominique Ingres (1780–1867), and especially Jacques-Louis David (1748–1825), to whose influence Eugène Delacroix attributed the replacement of the Pompadour style by the Pompeian. However, although Neo-classical artists incorporated Pompeian-inspired decoration and furniture into their works, the style became less specific and somewhat arbitrary; only occasionally did artists produce paintings of the site and history of Pompeii itself. Architects such as Robert Adam (1728–92), and a fashionable group of decorative painters including Pietro Borgnis (1739–after 1810), Giovanni Battista Cipriani (1727–85), William Hamilton (1751–1801), Angelica Kauffman (1741–1807), John Francis Rigaud (1742–1810) and Antonio Zucchi (1726–95) used Pompeian motifs for Neo-classical interiors. Excavated objects provided the archetypes for furniture designers and makers to complete an appropriately antique setting (e.g. Charles Percier (1764–1838) and F.-H. Jacob-Desmalter (1770–1841) in France, and George Smith (*fl c.* 1786–1828), Thomas Hope (1769–1831) and C. H. Tathum (1772–1842) in England). Ceramicists at Sèvres and Vienna, as well as Josiah Wedgwood (1730–95) in England, and designers of textiles at Gobelins, Jouy and Lyon, also found inspiration in the *Antichità*. As a consequence, Johann Wolfgang von Goethe observed that no catastrophe in history had yielded as much pleasure as the burial of Pompeii and Herculaneum.

Although the Neo-classical movement originated with the desire for a rational, perfect world based upon the Classical ideal, the complex image of Vesuvius also evokes a dramatic blend of the terrible and sublime and thus continued to influence 19th-century Romantics. Percy Bysshe Shelley (1792–1822) and Giacomo Leopardi (1798–1837) recorded melancholy reflections after visiting the site, while plays and opera culminating in the eruption were numerous, for example Edward Bulwer-Lytton's *The Last Days of Pompeii* (1834) and Théophile Gautier's *Arria Marcella* (1852). A similar morbid fascination has continued up to the present, inspiring several films on the subject. More serious students of antiquity produced scholarly works on Roman architecture, decoration and furniture based on the continuing excavations, the most notable being Sir William Gells's *Pompeiana: The Topography, Edifices and Ornaments of Pompeii* (with Joseph Gandy, London, 1817–19) and *Pompeiana: The Topography, Edifices and Ornaments of Pompeii: The Result of Excavations since 1819* (2 vols, London, 1832), François Mazois's *Les Ruines de Pompéi* (4 vols, Paris, 1824–38), Wilhelm Zahn's *Die schönsten Ornamente und merkwürdigsten Gemälde aus Pompeji, Herkulaneum und Stabiae* (3 vols, Berlin, 1829–59) and Owen Jones's *The Grammar of Ornament* (London, 1856).

Undisciplined and random digging on the site came to an end in 1861 with the appointment of Giuseppe Fiorelli (1823–96) as Director of Excavations. He replaced the disastrous practice of tunnelling vertically into buildings with careful, layer-by-layer excavation. He made diagrams and measurements, removed rubble from the site for the first time, tightened security and established a more systematic plan of excavation. He also stopped the constant stream of artefacts to the Museo Archeologico Nazionale at Naples by instituting a policy of leaving objects *in situ*. In the 20th century, in which time nearly three-quarters of the city was uncovered, the techniques developed at Pompeii were continually refined, and influenced modern archaeological practice.

Le antichità di Ercolano esposti, Accademia Ercolanese, 8 vols (Naples, 1757–92)

A. Maiuri, ed.: *Pompeiana: Raccolta di studi per il secondo centenario degli scavi di Pompeii* (Naples, 1950)

H. Honour: *Neo-classicism* (Harmondsworth, 1968)

F. Haskell and N. Penny: *Taste and the Antique: The Lure of Classical Sculpture, 1500–1900* (London and New Haven, 1981)

E. Pozzi, ed.: *Le collezione del Museo Nazionale di Napoli* (Rome, 1989)

F. Bologna: 'The Rediscovery of Herculaneum and Pompeii in the Artistic Culture of Europe in the 18th Century', *Rediscovering Pompeii*, ed. B. Conticello (Rome, 1990), pp. 78–91

J. Harris: *Pompeii Awakened: A Story of Rediscovery* (London, 2006)

Pont du Gard. This Roman bridge of arches built across the River Gardon, 3 km north-west of Remoulins, France, carries the late 1st-century BC aqueduct that supplied water from the Fontaines d'Eure, near Uzès, to Nemausus (Nîmes), a distance of 50 km. It remains virtually intact, with three tiers of arches, rising to a height of 48.7 metres above the river, and measuring 273 metres long at the top (see fig.). Mérimée (1803–70), as inspector-general of historic monuments, was influential in arranging restoration work in 1843–50. The road bridge next to it was added in 1743–7.

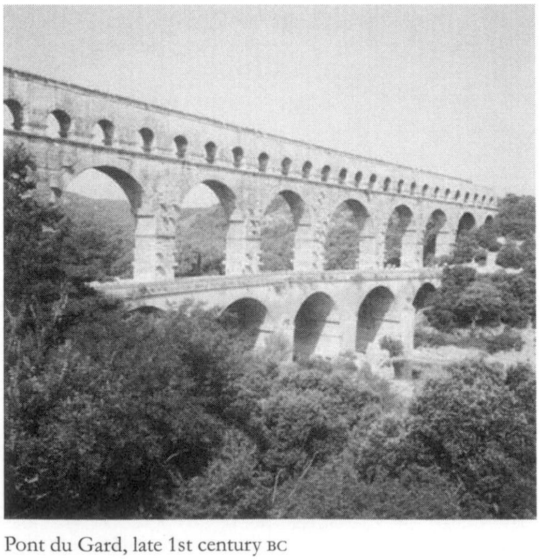

Pont du Gard, late 1st century BC

The aqueduct, built of dressed limestone quarried from the north side of the valley, was planned with a slight convex curvature upstream, its piers founded on bedrock. In the lower tier, the widest arch (24.52 m) across the deep river channel is closer to the left (north) bank and has one arch to the left and four to the right, diminishing in width from 19.2 to 15.5 m. The middle tier is of nearly equal height and has eleven arches, corresponding in width with those below. The visual harmony of the structure is effected by the regularity of the upper arcade of small arches beneath the water channel, with 35 openings of equal width (4.8 m), 4 over the largest arch below and 3 over each of the others. The diminution of the latter was resolved by decreasing the width of the piers between the small arches. Blocks that supported the scaffolding were left projecting from the face and from the intrados of the arch, and others retain incised letters and numbers indicating where they were to be placed.

E. Espérandieu: *Le Pont du Gard* (Paris, 1926, 2/1932)

A. Grenier: *Manuel d'archéologie gallo-romaine*, iv/2 (Paris, 1960), pp. 88–101

G. F. W. Hauck: *The Aqueduct of Nemausus* (Jefferson, NC, 1988)

G. Fabre: *The Pont du Gard: Water and the Roman Town* (Paris, 1992)

G. Fabre, J.-L. Fiches and J.-L. Paillet: *L'Aqueduc de Nîmes et le Pont du Gard: Archéologie, géosystème, histoire* (Paris, 2000)

G. Fabre: *Le Pont du Gard: L'Aqueduc antique de Nîmes* (Barbetane, 2001)

Populonia [Etrus. Pupluna]. Italian village situated on a promontory *c.* 15 km north of the port of Piombino. In ancient times Populonia was an Etruscan city and the only major Etruscan centre sited directly on the coast (all other 'coastal' cities were in fact several km inland). There was already an important settlement there at the end of the Bronze Age, and in Etruscan times there were two main centres of habitation: on the summit of the acropolis hill at Poggio del Molino and at its foot on the Bay of Baratti. The acropolis had its own ashlar wall; the lower town was also defended by an outer wall, which effectively cut off the whole of the peninsula. Few remains of the buildings in either area have been uncovered, although excavations at Poggio del Molino, begun in 1980 by A. Romualdi, have revealed the platform of a large temple of Hellenistic date, along with fragments of its exterior terracotta decorations.

The Orientalizing and Archaic period cemeteries are extensive. A fully developed type of corbelled chamber tomb appeared here as early as the 9th century BC, and there are many monumental tumuli dating from the 7th century BC. The latter had plinths of ashlar masonry with earth piled above; inside, a dromos leads to the chambers. A few tombs of the 6th and 5th centuries BC were built in stone throughout in imitation of houses with ridged roofs (see fig.). Many of the burials were lavish, and the tomb contents included many items of gold jewellery and

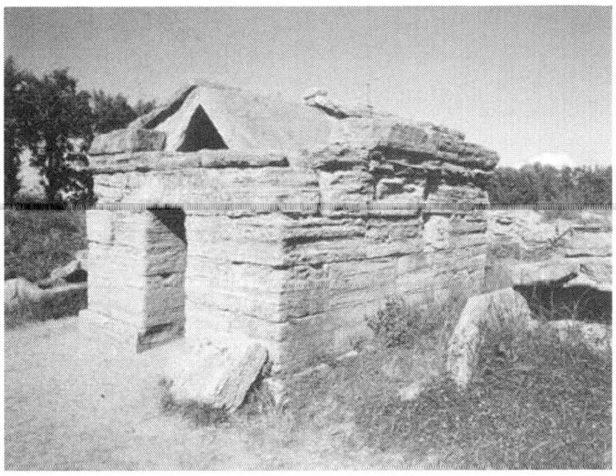

Populonia, necropolis, Etruscan tomb with aedicule

bronzework (examples in Florence, Mus. Archeol.). Two Hellenistic tombs have chambers painted with wave patterns and dolphins.

Beyond the walls of the lower town an industrial quarter, in use from the 6th to the 3rd century BC, was excavated in 1977–80 by M. Cristofani and M. Martelli at Poggio della Porcareccia. Buildings for accommodation were laid out there to a regular plan, with areas set aside for foundries and furnaces. This quarter must have been typical of much of ancient Populonia, for it was the most important metal-processing centre in the Mediterranean, primarily for iron but also for bronze. The iron ore was obtained from the nearby island of Elba and from the Campigliese region immediately inland, where much copper and some tin were also mined. This natural wealth, and the prosperity it generated through trade, explains the richness of the tombs as well as the fact that more imported Attic pottery has been found at Populonia than at any other site in northern Etruria. Populonia's mint was the most prolific in Etruria (*see* COINS, §2). Some of the coins show the Greek god Hephaistos, an appropriate emblem for a metalworking centre, together with his hammer and tongs.

The processing of metal ores over many centuries has covered much of the area with vast quantities of slag, even burying some of the earlier cemeteries. The industry continued well into Roman times, although Strabo (*Geography*, V.ii.6), writing in the time of Augustus, described the upper town as almost wholly deserted.

A. Minto: *Populonia* (Florence, 1943)

M. Martelli: *Gli Etruschi in Maremma*, ed. M. Cristofani (Milan, 1981), pp. 153–74

F. Fedeli: *Populonia: Storia e territorio* (Florence, 1983)

The First Iron in the Mediterranean: Proceedings of the Populonia/Piombino 1983 Symposium

G. Camporeale, ed.: *L'Etruria mineraria* (Milan, 1985), pp. 84–95

F. H. Massa-Pairault: 'Etrurie minière [Porto Ferraio, Massa Marittima, Populonia]', *Rev. Archéol.*, ii (1986), pp. 354–5

D. W. J. Gill: 'METRU.MENECE: An Etruscan Painted Inscription on a Mid-5th-century BC Red-figure Cup from Populonia', *Antiquity*, lxi (March 1987), pp. 82–7

S. Bruni: 'Attorno alla tomba del bronzetto d'offerente di Populonia', *Mitt. Dt. Archäol. Inst.: Röm. Abt.,* xcvi (1989), pp. 267–84
A. Romualdi: *Populonia in età ellenistica: I materiali dalle necropoli* (Florence, 1992)
F. Fedeli, A. Galiberti and A. Romualdi: *Populonia e il suo territorio: Profilo storico-archeologico* (Florence, 1993)
S. MacDonald: *Monumental Inhumation Burial at Populonia*, 2 vols (diss., U. Coll. Dublin, 1994)
L'Architettura funeraria a Populonia tra 9. e 6. secolo A.C.: Atti del convegno, Castello di Populonia, 1997
S. Rossi: 'La citta etrusche', *L'Architettura*, xlv/528 (Oct 1999), p. 607
F. Cambi and others: *Materiali per Populonia*, 4 vols (Florence, 2002–5)

Porphyrousa. *See* KYTHERA.

Portico. Term used in Western architecture for a covered area before the entrance to a building, of grander proportions than a simple porch and usually forming the central element in the façade. In Classical Greek and Roman contexts the term portico can also describe a free-standing roofed colonnade, of the kind used for shelter in public spaces such as market places and sanctuaries. In Greek temples the porch or vestibule at the entrance is termed the pronaos. At some point in later architectural writings in Latin this came to be translated as *porticus* (a word used by Vitruvius to render the Greek term *stoa*). Viewed externally, a Greek temple's configuration of columns in the pronaos surmounted by a pediment simultaneously both constituted the portico's solid form and comprehended a covered open space. This configuration received stronger emphasis in Etruscan and, later, Roman temples, which were typically not peripteral (i.e. surrounded by columns) in the Greek manner, but frontally orientated, often with columns in the porch alone, as in the Maison Carrée at NEMAUSUS (Nîmes).

Porticos can be divided into several types, with the number of columns at the front as one determinant. A portico of four columns is termed tetrastyle; if there are six or more columns, it becomes hexastyle, octastyle and so on. A further classification is made according to whether a portico is integral to a building, with its row of columns flush or aligned with the façade, when it is known as *in antis*, or projects from the façade, when it is known as prostyle. Sometimes a portico can be either, if it is half in and half out, or if the row of columns stands between projecting side walls, or *antae*, depending on the degree of projection. A final classification depends on the number of columns by which the portico projects or advances from a façade, which is determined by the space between the columns expressed as a multiple of their diameter: pycnostyle (one and a half diameters), systile (two), eustyle (two and a quarter), diastyle (three) and araeostyle (four). Porticos are thus structures in which the ARCHITECTURAL ORDERS may be used to great effect, each building type having the order appropriate to its destination, character and function.

Essential functions of the portico are that it should enclose some significant space and provide shelter. It constitutes an intermediary or transitional space—covered, but open at the sides—between the exterior and the fully enclosed interior of a building, and between public and private spaces (engaged columns or pilasters surmounted by an applied pediment providing no shelter are more properly considered as articulating a building's façade rather than as a portico). Compositionally the portico is used to emphasize centrality on a façade—acting as either the climax to a composition or as a fulcrum—and to indicate the prospect of an entry. It must welcome and impress simultaneously; and the means of access thus vary widely, ranging from an approach level with the ground to steps of one or more flights the full width of the portico, and from either lateral curved perrons or internal spiral staircases to more complex stairs with one or more quarter landings. Cicero recorded that the Senate granted a special dispensation permitting Julius Caesar to erect, as one of several trophies and honours, a pediment on his house, probably over the principal entrance, or *porta*, columned or otherwise, at the centre of the main façade (*Philippicae* II. xliii, 110). Talking of propriety and the Capitol, Cicero also considered any significant building, earthly or celestial, to be entirely without dignity unless pedimented. The pediment itself and the pedimented portico were thus meant to be read as architectural, metaphorical and aesthetic features in their own right, signifying power and distinction.

J. J. Coulton: *The Architectural Development of the Greek Stoa* (Oxford, 1976)
W. L. MacDonald: *The Pantheon* (Cambridge, MA, 1976)
J. A. Null and A. Stelian: *The Portico di Ottavia and the Teatro di Marcello: Evolution & Transformation* (Rome, 1984)
K. L. Gleason: 'The Garden Portico of Pompey the Great: An Ancient Public Park Preserved in the Layers of Rome, Expedition, xxxii/2 (1990), pp. 4–13
J. F. Bommelaer: 'Les Portiques de Delphes', *Rev Archéol.,* i (1993), pp. 33–52
L. Haselberger: 'Ein Giebelriss der Vorhalle des Pantheon: Die Werkrisse vor dem Augustusmausoleum', *Mitt. Dt. Archäol. Inst.: Röm. Abt.,* ci (1994), pp. 279–308
M. Pausch: 'Mockenlohe (Deutschland): Eine wiederaufgebaute villa rustica', *Ant. Welt*, xxxii/1 (2001), pp. 96–7
J. F. D. Frakes: Framing Public Life: The Portico in Roman Gaul (diss., New York, Columbia U., 2002)
'Engendering Space: Octavia's Portico in Rome', *Aurora (Woodcliff Lake, NJ)*, iv (2003), pp. 13–33
R. Taylor: 'Roman Oscilla: An Assessment', *Res (Cambridge, MA.)*, xlviii (Autumn 2005), pp. 83–105
C. K. Quenemoen: The Portico of the Danaids: A New Reconstruction', *Amer. J. Archaeol.,* cx/2 (April 2006), pp. 229–50

Poseidonia. *See* PAESTUM.

Post and lintel construction. *See* TRABEATED CONSTRUCTION.

Pottery. Items of clay fashioned using a variety of techniques and hardened by heat. This article discusses the manufacture and decoration of clay vessels, for other uses *see* LAMPS *and* TERRACOTTA.

I. Minoan. II. Cycladic. III. Helladic. IV. Greek. V. Etruscan. VI. Roman.

I. Minoan.

Minoan pottery styles, particularly in the Early Minoan (EM) period, developed slowly, but occasionally the transformations were sufficiently dynamic and deep-seated to allow the study of individual workshops and craftsmen. Indeed, many Minoan vases were unique creations that arguably may be described as high art.

For chronological overview *see* MINOAN, §4.

1. Materials and techniques. 2. Final Neolithic. 3. Early Minoan. 4. Middle Minoan. 5. Late Minoan.

1. MATERIALS AND TECHNIQUES. By the Neolithic period European and Asian craftsmen understood that clays moistened with water became plastic enough to form objects or containers, which hardened if heated. By the time the craft reached Crete during the Early Neolithic period, the basic techniques were well developed. Tempering, the addition of crushed stone or some other aplastic material, which prevented breakage by reducing shrinkage during drying and firing, was routine. Rubbing the surface before firing, a process called burnishing, was used to create a smoother surface that was more resistant to liquids and soiling. Decoration included the addition of knobs or strips of clay, scratched or pecked motifs, and designs painted on in a contrasting colour of clay (slip). Even the burnishing could create a design of sorts. Most Cretan slips were coloured by iron oxides, red if fired in the presence of oxygen and grey or black if fired in unventilated kilns. Most Neolithic vases were relatively simple utilitarian containers. Open-mouthed bowls and jars predominated, with cursory geometric ornament limited mainly to incised lines and dots. At the end of the Neolithic period, however, several stylistic changes occurred, and though their causes and sequences are disputed, they heralded the emergence of the Minoan civilization, a time of outstanding artistic achievement in many media; among these artistic products ceramic vases occupied an important position.

2. FINAL NEOLITHIC. The transitional Final Neolithic period was a time of profound change in the development of Minoan pottery, during which several new styles were introduced. How much these styles overlapped with the earlier and later phases is not really known. Crete was evidently inhabited by small groups of agriculturalists, some of whom were very conservative in their pottery styles, so that it is not always clear how soon a new feature was adopted throughout the island.

Final Neolithic pottery was dark-surfaced, with most pieces fired brown to black. Shapes included open jars and bowls, cups, bottles or jars with closed mouths, small rounded pyxides (boxes) with cylindrical lids, and several other vases. Horns and lugs were common, placed either on rims or on shoulders. Usually the surface was burnished by rubbing it with a tool such as a smooth pebble or a wooden burnisher; on the pottery known as Pyrgos ware, burnishing was used to produce linear decoration. Other decorative systems included pricking or incising geometric designs before firing, scoring the surface with the sharp ends of a bundle of reeds or with a comblike instrument (Scored ware) and painting simple lines in red ochre directly on to the clay. Some of these characteristics are also found in the pottery of north-western Asia Minor (Anatolia), but its relationship to Final Neolithic Cretan pottery is unclear. Since Anatolian tomb types and other cultural features did not occur in Crete, it is possible the ceramic products represent technological diffusion rather than a movement of population.

3. EARLY MINOAN. EM pottery was more diverse than that of either earlier or later periods. It could be red, buff or grey, coarse or fine, with decorative methods that included incising, stamping, painting in several styles, and modelling to create three-dimensional images. Perhaps because of experimentation, some pieces were fanciful, while others were so unusual in shape that their function is unknown.

(i) Early Minoan I. Several new pottery styles were introduced in EM I, of which the most important was Ayios Onouphrios I ware, named after a site near Phaistos. Small pyxides and askoi (closed vases with a small opening at one upper corner) became characteristic Minoan pottery shapes, and askoi were already being made in the shape of animals. At the same time improvements in kiln design and construction enabled potters to control their results more consistently. Evenly coloured, grey or buff pottery could be achieved at will.

In addition to new styles, Pyrgos ware and Scored ware persisted in EM I. The parallel scratches on Scored ware were much the same as in Final Neolithic times, though they were applied to new shapes such as spouted jugs. EM I Pyrgos ware, however, was considerably more advanced than its predecessor. It was most common in north-central Crete, where it was used for bowls, cups and a few closed shapes. Its most striking product was the footed chalice, a cup on a high base (see fig. 1a). The decoration often consisted of simple horizontal or vertical burnished lines, but some better specimens combined several different burnished patterns, of which the most common were solid areas, zigzags, crosshatching and parallel lines.

Painting began in earnest in EM I. Ayios Onouphrios I ware had parallel or crosshatched red lines long enough to sweep around the curvature of the

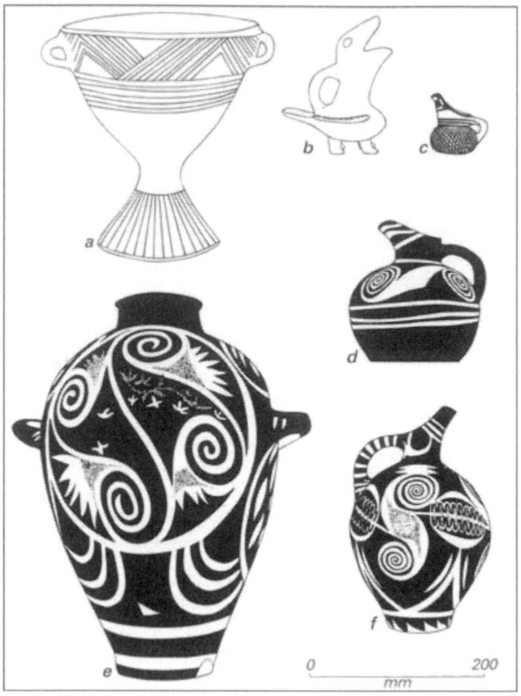

1. Early and Middle Minoan pottery: (a) chalice, Pyrgos ware with burnished horizontal, vertical and diagonal lines, h. 280 mm, from Pyrgos Cave, EM I; (b) bird-shaped jug, h. 172 mm, from Koumasa, EM II; (c) jug, Koumasa ware, h. 73 mm, from the type site, EM II; (d) jug, h. 165 mm, from Mochlos, EM III; (e) narrow-necked jar decorated with quadruple spiral motif, h. 460 mm, from Phaistos, MM II; (f) jug, Kamares ware, h. 267 mm, from Phaistos, MM II (all Herakleion, Archaeological Museum)

buff clay vessel. The style, particularly common in central Crete, was used on a range of new shapes, especially spouted jugs with rounded bottoms designed to be suspended rather than set on a flat surface. Well finished and skilfully painted, the pottery was probably regarded as the best ware of its time. Its only counterpart was Lebena ware. Most common in southern Crete, it employed the same geometric linear patterns as Ayios Onouphrios I ware, applied in white paint on a solid red slip.

(ii) Early Minoan II. Many new towns were founded in Crete during EM II, and the island probably supported a much larger population. Pottery styles changed appreciably. Existing shapes improved, with jugs that sat on small feet (see fig. 1b) or rested on flat bases, an advance on the rounded bottoms of EM I. New shapes, such as teapots and small goblets, reflected changes in tastes or customs.

Two varieties of linear-painted pottery spread throughout Crete in EM IIA: Koumasa ware, decorated with dark paint, and Ayios Onouphrios II ware, ornamented with red paint. In both cases the decoration consisted of well-painted crosshatched triangles and other simple geometric designs (see fig. 1c), usually on the upper shoulder of closed shapes such as jugs and jars and on the interiors or exteriors of bowls and cups. The style differed from Ayios Onouphrios I ware in its tighter control, with patterns that seem more stilted, more restricted and less related to the rounded form of the vessel. The contemporary Fine Grey ware was finer textured than earlier grey pottery, fired to a uniform tint all the way through the wall. A geometric decoration was usually incised before firing; especially popular were herringbones and other simple linear designs.

During the second half of EM II, painted and incised vases became less popular. Most vases were plain, but an elaborate ware named after a site in eastern Crete spread to a few sites in the central and western districts: Vasiliki ware was entirely covered with a coat of slip mottled during firing to achieve a brilliant variegated effect. It was the first Minoan pottery to be decorated in more than one colour: the mottling varied from browns to yellowish browns to reds to black. The unusual slip effects were used on a long series of shapes, some of them bizarre, with exaggerated forms such as teapots with long spouts, jugs with tall beaked spouts or tiny goblets sometimes with unnecessary handles or spouts. The technique used to achieve the mottling is not completely understood, but it clearly involved exposing selected parts of a vessel to oxidation and reduction at the end of the firing cycle, perhaps after it had been removed from the kiln.

(iii) Early Minoan III. Painted pottery regained its popularity in EM III, and Vasiliki ware ceased to be made. Painted ornament had first re-emerged in the form of a few white lines on the red to dark surface of EM IIB Vasiliki ware, but it soon commanded almost the entire fine ware production. Called White-on-dark ware, the new pottery had crisp geometric motifs in off-white paint applied to an even, dark coat of slip. New designs included spirals, quirks, elaborate circles and fancy diagonal bands (see fig. 1d). Such was the popularity of this ware in EM III–MM IA that on some sites it accounts for more than 90% of the fine pottery of this date. Although White-on-dark ware was used throughout Crete, its most dynamic production centres were north-eastern sites. The ware has been found at MALLIA, GOURNIA, PSEIRA, VASILIKI, Palaikastro and MOCHLOS. Its repertory of spirals, complex circle motifs and other curvilinear designs suggests that White-on-dark ware was probably the main forerunner of Kamares ware, the finest ceramic achievement of the Middle Minoan period.

4. MIDDLE MINOAN. During the Middle Minoan (MM) period Cretan pottery followed the fortunes of a series of palatial centres. In MM IB, new palaces were built at Knossos and Phaistos, probably expanding on pre-existing structures levelled to make way for the new establishments. The pottery of these two centres was dynamic and innovative, influencing production throughout the island, while that from

the palace at Mallia was also of a high quality. Most other pottery centres produced humbler ware, imitating the shapes and a few of the less complex designs used in the palatial workshops.

(i) Middle Minoan I. MM IA pottery was still made entirely by hand; it is chiefly distinguished by the use of red paint alongside the off-white of earlier times. As in EM III, the white and red designs were applied to a contrasting solid dark slip. Almost all were abstract and linear, exhibiting great variety and far more elaboration than in EM III: spirals, circle designs, quirk bands, dot bands, straight or diagonal lines and a few cursory foliate designs were regularly used. These gradually increased in complexity, and often several were used on the same vessel. Shapes included jars and jugs of several types, as well as bowls and cups. Often the jugs had only a small upturned spout, much shorter than in the Early Bronze Age. The small stemmed goblet (or egg-cup) was particularly common in central Crete; in the region of PHAISTOS it almost died out at the end of the period, but in the north-central area it persisted much longer. Handmade carinated cups, tall conical cups without handles (tumblers) and cylindrical cups with one vertical handle were all typical of the period.

Plain wares also acquired forms that distinguished them from their EM ancestors. The conical cup, a small handleless bowl or cup, was the most common unpainted shape, while pithoi for large-scale storage, tripod pots for cooking, small lamps and the first bathtubs were among the other characteristic products.

Although a few tentative wheelmade saucers are known from MM IA, the introduction of the potter's wheel marks the transition to MM IB, an innovation that led to developments that continued over several centuries. The clay discs from several Minoan potters' wheels survive: they are always thick and heavy to enhance the wheel's centrifugal force, with the upper surface smoothed from use and the underside having a socket at the centre for attachment to a vertical axle. The wheels were probably mounted close to the ground and were turned by assistants, as shown in contemporary Egyptian wall paintings.

The potter's wheel was evidently not introduced to all workshops at once. Many MM IB pots were still handmade, even including fine cups, and numerous pieces can barely be distinguished from their MM IA predecessors. New shapes included a thin, well-made carinated cup with a cylindrical upper half, a conical lower part and a thin, metallic-looking handle, bowls and cups with crinkled or undulating rims and wheelmade bridge-spouted jars with two horizontal handles for lifting. Handmade vessels, both plain and painted, continued the styles of MM IA: tumblers, jars, jugs, tripod cooking pots, bowls of many types, amphorae, pithoi and bathtubs. Eggcups were common in the north. Thousands of conical cups were produced, either plain or with just a band or with a trace of decoration, and for the next 600 years they would be a ubiquitous feature of Minoan houses.

As early as the Neolithic period, Cretan potters had experimented with roughening the surface of a vase, a texture that became popular at the beginning of the Middle Bronze Age, giving rise to Barbotine ware. It was mostly produced in the MESARA near Phaistos, but examples were also made around KNOSSOS and Mallia, and pieces occur sporadically throughout the island. Several types existed, the clay worked up to form irregular ridges, or with knobs, bumps or rough bands applied to the surface. This relief decoration often formed spirals, triangles or other typical Minoan motifs and was usually combined with painted designs. After reaching its high point in MM IB, the ware remained popular into MM IIA but then declined, only a few examples being produced in the later stages of the MM period.

(ii) Middle Minoan II. Following the dramatic rise of the palace workshops in MM II, the contrast between village and palace productions increased. Especially at the palaces of Knossos, Phaistos and Mallia, potters began turning out a sequence of sophisticated ceramic designs superior in both shape and ornament to anything produced in the provinces. The technology of the potter's wheel permitted the production of extremely delicate walls, sometimes literally as thin as eggshells. Handles, spouts and other details were often copied from metalware. New ornaments were invented, especially by stylizing the curvilinear tendrils and leaves of plants (see fig. 1e). With an increased use of orange and crimson paints to supplement the white and red of MM I, Cretan pottery reached new artistic heights.

Plain and less expansively decorated vases were also made at the palaces as well as in village workshops. The conical cup remained the most common open shape. Other cups had carinated, straight-sided or S-shaped profiles, as in MM I. Jugs with small raised spouts, jars of various kinds, especially with bridged spouts, amphorae with two opposed handles extending from rim to shoulder, and most other MM I shapes continued. As before, it was not unusual for a potter, even in a remote village, to invent unique details of shape or decoration. Among the new shapes was the rhyton, a closed vessel with two openings, one at the top for filling and one at the base so that liquid could stream out. Its use, whether in ritual or in daily life, is often debated. Some rhyta took the form of animal heads, especially bulls', while askoi were occasionally shaped like complete animals, as they had been in earlier times.

The main palatial pottery of MM II was Kamares ware, often regarded as a highpoint in Minoan art. Its clay was first covered with the same dark slip used in MM I, and a rich assortment of ornaments in several colours was added (see colour pl. 1:XIII, fig. 1). Small vases were almost always wheelmade, though the hand methods of earlier times were retained, principally for larger vessels. Floral motifs, especially curvilinear, were prolific, though geometric designs and a few carefully selected figural devices were also used. Since the decoration usually comprised several well-proportioned designs and two or three different colours, the effect was richly ornamental. Kamares ware adopted sophisticated decorative principles: each motif, whether figural, floral or geometric, was reduced to a simple two-dimensional form. Overlapping of colours was employed to enrich the ornamentation, as when red dots were placed on a white line, but not to create an illusion of depth. Most motifs incorporated curves, so were well suited to rounded forms. They were arranged on the vessels in various compositional schemes, often with two or more opposed diagonals twisting around the vase (see fig. 2). This device, known as torsion, was a major Minoan artistic innovation, designed to produce a sense of suspended movement from the balancing of opposed compositional forces. First attested on seals and pottery, it became a feature of the finest Minoan art in other media for several centuries. A bridge-spouted jar from Knossos (Herakleion, Archaeol. Mus.) illustrates the exuberant qualities of the ware. Petals and tendrils flow and whirl around small circles of linked diamonds, creating a brilliant 'skin' of painted decoration on the vase's surface, and handles and spout are an integral part of the overall ornament.

(iii) Middle Minoan III. In many ways, MM III was a transitional period: its earliest pottery essentially represented a continuation of MM II types. During a later phase, best called MM IIIB, the pottery advanced along several fronts, until it had left its Middle Bronze Age style well behind and was anticipating LM I.

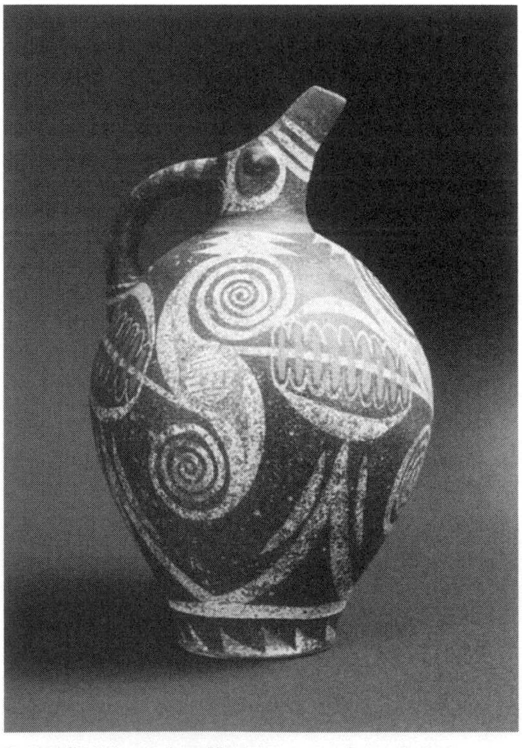

2. Middle Minoan jug, Kamares ware, from Phaistos, MMII (Herakleion, Archaeological Museum)

The potting and the pyrotechnology changed substantially. By MM IIIB, most ceramic products were thicker-walled than their MM II counterparts, and their clay was grittier. The paint often flaked badly. Clay fabrics in central Crete tended to be less dense than in MM II, indicating a lower firing temperature or a shorter time in the kiln or possibly comprising a different mixture of raw materials. The shapes developed as well: cups were larger, closed vessels were taller and more slender, and rounded vases such as bridge-spouted jars and piriform jars were often given a constricted lower body. A few shapes, such as the carinated cups, were no longer made.

The decoration of MM III vases is so different from that of MM II that it is sometimes termed Post-Kamares. Orange and red paint were used more sparingly, and compositions were greatly simplified, as were the decorative motifs themselves, leading to the gradual elimination of most types of rosettes, petals and other elaborate floral designs. In contrast, spirals, especially large retorted ones, became more common. At the same time, an important class of vase began to be decorated in a more naturalistic style, perhaps related to the beginning of wall painting in the palaces. Its most characteristic motifs are lilies, crocus blossoms and palms, combined with elaborate spirals set in series with areas of solid white.

A new ceramic technology also appeared. Its products were harder and glossier and soon supplanted the earlier MM dark-surfaced vases. The earliest specimens belonged to a class of vases decorated with ripple designs and wavy bands. The most common pottery of the new group, known as Tortoise-shell Ripple ware, occurs throughout Crete. Closely spaced vertical lines were burnished before firing to create a rippled effect in the ornament as the burnishing compressed and polished the surface. When spirals and floral decorations were added in the new technique, the Middle Bronze Age was over.

5. LATE MINOAN. The construction of the new palaces at the beginning of the Late Bronze Age stimulated dramatic developments in many artistic media, but especially in pottery, given its widespread use at all levels of Minoan society. The role of the new palaces as patrons of the arts cannot be overemphasized.

(i) Late Minoan I. The earliest Late Minoan (LM) vases were only slightly more advanced in style than those of MM IIIB, but there was an essential difference: spirals and floral designs were painted in dark-firing slip on the pale ground of the vase, not in white on the dark slip. Using the dense, burnished fabric of Ripple ware, which was painted with a wide range of motifs, the LM I potters gave their ceramics a wholly new appearance. By LM IA the new styles were being diffused throughout Crete, and by LM IB Minoan ceramic products were so uniform that sometimes only clay analysis can distinguish the products of widely separated areas. Except for the Special Palatial tradition, a

small but highly influential palatial production, many of the LM IB styles were so widely spread that they constituted a common ceramic tradition.

Pottery shapes developed considerably during LM I. The handleless conical cup continued to be the most common plain shape among the finer pieces, while straight-sided, semi-globular and bell-shaped cups, all with handles, were the most numerous of the painted cups. The latter were usually well made, with even walls and well-shaped ribbon handles. Among the closed shapes, the jug was still predominant. Many varieties occur: globular, squat or pear-shaped bodies, flat or rising spouts or no spout at all, mouths that range from constricted to wide. By the end of the period the most common closed form, used for small decorated jars and amphorae as well as for jugs, had a pear-shaped body with a small neck. Its widest diameter was at the shoulder, where the main decoration was placed. Rarer shapes included the rhyton, the most notable specimens being of conical (see fig. 3a), ostrich-egg or bull's-head form. Sometimes made in moulds, bull-shaped askoi and bull's-head rhyta were now much more naturalistic.

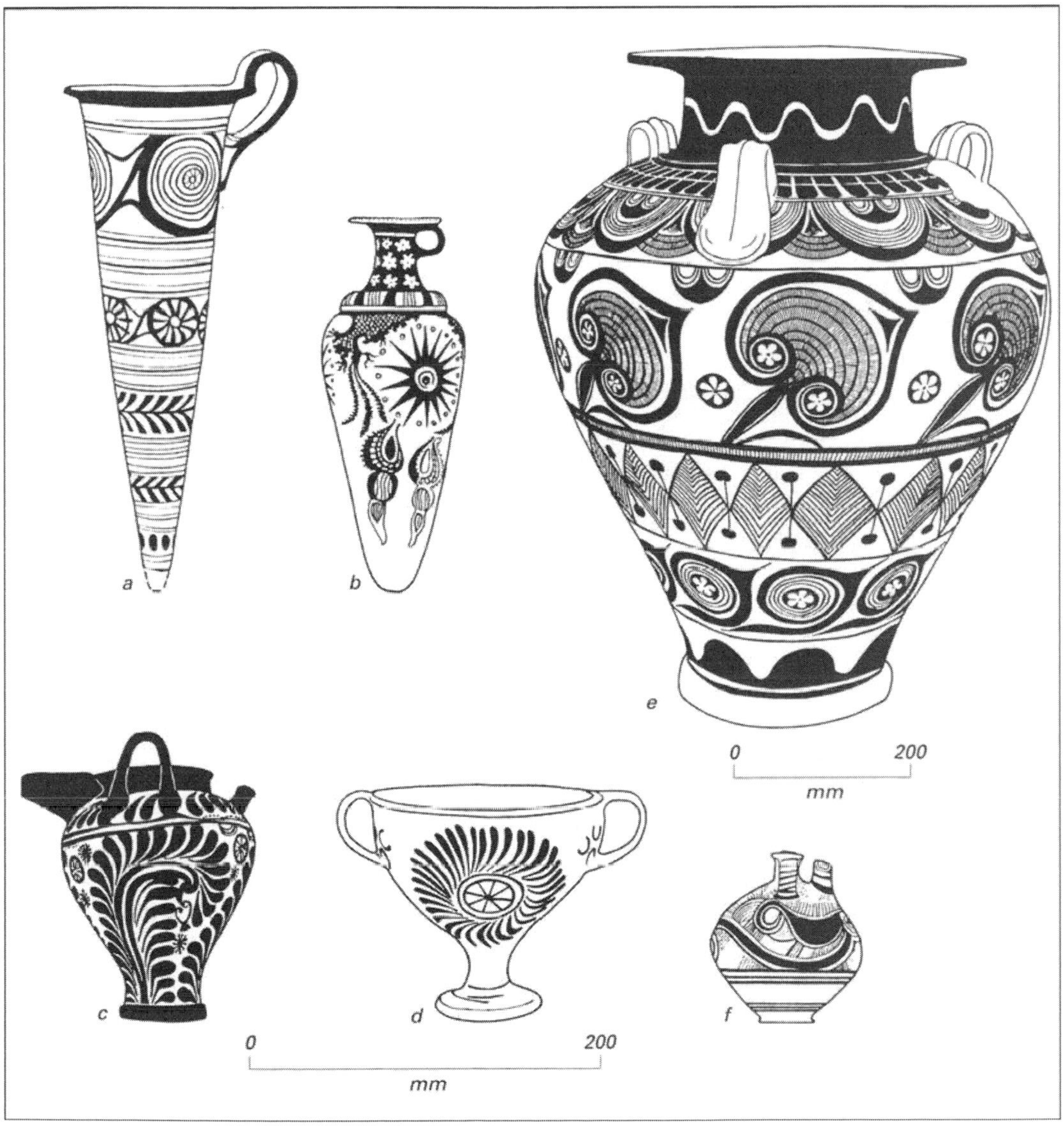

3. Late Minoan pottery: (a) conical rhyton, h. 325 mm, from Gournia, Room C58, LM IB; (b) ovoid rhyton, Marine style, h. *c.* 240 mm, from Palaikastro, LM IB; (c) bridge-spouted jar, Special Palatial tradition, Floral style, h. 165 mm, from Knossos, LM IB; (d) 'Ephyraean' goblet, h. 150 mm, from the Temple Tomb, Knossos, LM II; (e) jar, Palace style, h. 850 mm, from Knossos, LM II–IIIA:1 (all Herakleion, Archaeological Museum); (f) stirrup jar, Close style, h. 105 mm, from a tomb at Tourloti, LM IIIC (Philadelphia, PA, University of Pennsylvania, University Museum of Archaeology and Anthropology)

Decorative schemes continued the principles of the Middle Bronze Age, with two-dimensional floral motifs, especially ivy leaves, flowers, rosettes, grasses and branches, accompanying spirals and other geometric designs. The development of a few individual motifs can be traced in detail. The LM IA spiral, for example, often had a large dot as its centre surrounded by tiny white dots, but by the end of LM IB this type had been abandoned and was usually replaced by a quickly made whorl, drawn from the inside out. Similarly, the foliate band developed from a fairly naturalistic representation of a branch with leaves on both sides to an abstract design composed of two rows of dots or crescents with a line between them. In general, LM IA vases were more carefully painted than those of LM IB.

A large jar from Pseira (Herakleion, Archaeol. Mus.) illustrates the LM IA decoration at its most elaborate. The motifs in its largest frieze are unusual for the period: bulls' heads in front view alternate with double axes, with leafy branches placed vertically between them. Bulls were important sacrificial animals in Minoan religion, and the axe, probably used to slaughter them, had become a religious symbol. Axes also adorn the jar's rim, while elaborate ivy leaves and typical LM IA spirals decorate the lower body.

The LM IB vases of the Special Palatial tradition excelled even the finest LM IA works in the inventiveness of their shapes and the vividness of their marine and floral decoration. The Marine style, the most attractive aspect of the tradition, used argonauts, octopuses, starfish, coral, shells and other such details in a lively evocation of underwater life (see fig. 3b). The best-known example is a flask by the so-called Marine Style Master (Herakleion, Archaeol. Mus.; see colour pl. 2:VI, fig. 1), which was found at Palaikastro in eastern Crete, though its style and fabric suggest that it was almost certainly exported from Knossos. Each side bears an octopus in front view, with fierce eyes and writhing tentacles. Small sea creatures and plants act as filling motifs. A feeling of suspended motion, especially appropriate for a subject floating beneath the Aegean, is projected by the diagonal curved lines and the sinuous tentacles and seaweed.

A Floral style and an Abstract and Geometric style also formed part of the Special Palatial tradition. In the first, flowers, especially imaginary hybrids based on papyrus plants, palms or lilies, were painted exuberantly (see fig. 3c). In the second, new kinds of spirals and foliate bands were invented; and in addition to geometric devices, abstract motifs from the natural world (e.g. double axes) were used. Since many of the shapes were also new to pottery, the tradition seems very innovative, but in fact it depended on a wide range of immediate sources, especially metalware and monumental painting. A late variation of the tradition, known as the Alternating style, used individual motifs in strict alternation around the vase in an empty field.

Also during LM I, the pithos, a large storage jar that had gradually developed during the Early to Middle Bronze Ages, reached a peak of size and splendour. In EM times pithoi had been plain jars, perhaps a metre high, but during LM I they became much more elaborate and increased in height to almost 2 m. The most common of several shapes of giant pithoi had a heavy rim and rather wide mouth, a slightly swelling shoulder and straight walls that contracted a little towards the base. Decoration usually consisted of raised bands indented with finger impressions and known as ropework, though some workshops added circular medallions or other simple plastic designs. Each pithos had several handles, designed to receive a hoisting rope. However, the giant pithoi are chiefly remarkable for their manufacture and firing. They were built by hand, by the addition of successive slabs of clay to build up the walls, probably while the vessels were rotated on a turntable. Firing a pithos of great size demanded a kiln of sophisticated design because breakage would occur if the temperature were not uniform. Taken together, the giant pithoi and the eggshell-thin Kamares ware productions indicate the astonishing versatility of Minoan potters in forming techniques, kiln design and general pyrotechnology.

(ii) Late Minoan II. This stage of the Late Bronze Age, which was probably of short duration, followed a time of widespread destructions in Crete, and many of the burnt towns were either not rebuilt or experienced a loss of population. Several new influences entered the local ceramic traditions. Most of the new shapes, which included the squat alabastron and the krater (a deep bowl with two opposed horizontal handles), had already occurred on the Greek mainland, so the influences were probably Mycenaean (*see* § III, 2(III)). Among other Mycenaean shapes adopted by the Minoans, the 'Ephyraean' goblet (also called the 'Ephyraean' kylix) is noteworthy (see fig. 4d above): the vessel consisted of a conical bowl on top of a stemmed base, but it possessed a smooth, unbroken curve from rim to base and had opposed vertical handles extending from rim to body.

Mycenaean Greece and Minoan Crete had been in contact for many centuries, but before LM II most of the ideas in pottery-making had gone from the island to the mainland. The change in direction of influence was sudden and fundamental: besides the Mycenaean shapes, the Minoans adopted several mainland ornamental motifs and something of the Mycenaean pyrotechnology. Many scholars see the destructions in Crete at the end of LM IB as inflicted by invading Mycenaeans.

Yet despite the fact that LM II pottery absorbed new influences, especially Mycenaean, it was still firmly in the Minoan tradition. For instance, not all LM II vase shapes came from Mycenaean Greece. Many, such as the conical cup, semi-globular cup, jug, bridge-spouted jug and jar, piriform jar, alabastron, rhyton and most of the storage vessels, were simple developments of LM I shapes. Unpainted pottery, especially conical cups, remained in vogue.

The ornament on painted LM II vases was more abstract than that on LM IB specimens. 'Ephyraean' goblets often had only a single element on each side of the body, set cleanly on the pale Minoan clay. Other vases, especially cups and conical bowls, usually bore a single frieze, with only a few painted bands on their lower bodies. The Marine style persisted but without much of its former energy. Octopuses were more attenuated and often more symmetrical. Florals were stylized, as if the artists were copying designs rather than nature. Open space became more of a force in compositional design.

The most exciting development of LM II was the Palace style. Although it originated exclusively from Knossos, it profoundly influenced ceramics throughout Crete. The style basically represented a movement towards the grandiose. Vases, particularly large ones, were decorated with expansive and often elaborate and symmetrical compositions, featuring floral and geometric motifs and occasionally unusual elements such as marine ornaments or even a warrior's helmet. Many of the style's ornamental elements were borrowed from the Special Palatial tradition, especially the Alternating style, of LM IB. A major difference is that motifs used previously as small filling ornaments were now enlarged and employed as the main focus of a vessel. In addition, they were occasionally abstracted and used in a more formal, symmetrical way. The style continued into LM IIIA, with many of the best examples dating from late in the tradition (see fig. 4e).

(iii) Late Minoan III. This period has been divided into three phases, the first having two parts. Although these phases closely follow the chronology of Mycenaean Greece, Minoan sequences are not as easily unravelled, because each contains more variations than those of Late Helladic III.

LM IIIA vase painting continued the stylization and abstraction of LM II, which led to a series of motifs whose natural origins were not readily visible. But technology was greatly improved. Except at a few centres, such as Knossos, LM II fabrics were softer than those of LM IB, though the potting was always expertly done. By LM IIIA the firing could achieve a dense, firm fabric, and it continued to improve during LM IIIB. LM IIIA ornament was more abstract than that of LM II, and bands of repeated designs became the standard for semi-globular cups and bowls and for many closed shapes. The direction faced by individual motifs often alternated between bands, creating a zigzag, flowing movement. A few of the finest LM IIIA vases depict stylized landscapes in which birds and floral motifs, including some very elaborate plant designs, were used to create lush scenes probably related to the more naturalistic Nilotic scenes of LM I, known from monumental paintings, inlaid metal daggers and a few other art objects.

The shapes of LM IIIA vases developed naturally from those of LM II. The plain conical cup was still used, but its popularity was already declining. It may have been replaced by the unpainted kylix and by an increasingly large output of painted cups. The kylix was taller than it had been in LM II, with a more conical bowl. The one-handled cup was quite different from the earlier varieties; all the LM I–II types had coalesced into a hemispherical shape with a tiny ledge rim, which died out at the end of LM IIIA:1 in favour of a nearly straight rim. A new type of stemmed goblet with one handle (usually called a champagne cup) appeared at the beginning of LM IIIA:2. Kraters, bowls, jugs, amphorae and jars continued to be produced, and storage pithoi had become smaller and plainer. Stirrup jars, now an important transport vessel, were made in many sizes, both painted and plain.

During LM IIIB the repertory of shapes was more standardized. Conical cups had almost vanished. Kylikes, cups and bowls, both painted and plain, were used for drinking. The occurrence of large numbers of amphorae and kraters, and dippers with long handles, suggests that the Classical Greek practice of mixing water with wine was already well established. All of the LM IIIA:2 shapes continued to be used.

Motifs became still more abstract, and those in decorative friezes were usually more widely spaced; alternating the direction in which they faced became rare. LM IIIB designs thus lacked the flowing character of the earlier bands and seemed more monotonous. Most of the designs were also greatly simplified, continuing the tendency that had begun much earlier and in some cases descending to absurdity, such as replacing the octopus and its many sinuous tentacles with a single wavy line. Usually several variants of a motif coexisted, so that, for example, more complete octopuses were painted at the same time as vestigial ones.

Human or animal figures had occasionally appeared on Minoan pottery since the Early Bronze Age, but only at the end of LM IIIA did they become common. A new fashion in figural work appeared on kraters and a few other large shapes. Probably inspired by a contemporary Mycenaean tradition, the usually symmetrical compositions are less lively.

During LM IIIC, Minoan vase painting effectively ended; the Sub-Minoan period that followed was as much a transition to the next phase as a continuation of existing practices. Simplification of the existing motifs continued, while the disappearance of many of the designs left an impoverished and overly repeated repertory. At the same time, potting and firing declined in quality at many centres, so that vases were softer and more likely to flake. An Open style of decoration (also called Plain style), which left most of the vessel unpainted except for a simple design such as irregular concentric triangles or semicircles or a wavy line and bands, coexisted with a Close style characterized by elaborate ornament and fine hatching over the whole surface. Close-style vases, especially small stirrup jars with symmetrical octopuses whose tentacles were more ornament than animal (see fig. 4f above), exhibit the last really vigorous Bronze Age painting in Crete, and with a revival of expert potting and firing they became popular for some time, a number being exported to several regions, including Rhodes. Thereafter, Cretan pottery went into decline until it was revived by the influence of Attic Protogeometric.

A. J. Evans: *The Palace of Minos at Knossos*, 4 vols and index (London, 1921–36, 2/1964)
A. Furness: 'The Neolithic Pottery of Knossos', *Annu. Brit. Sch. Athens*, 48 (1953), pp. 94–134
C. Zervos: *L'Art de la Crète néolithique et minoenne* (Paris, 1956)
M. R. Popham: *The Last Days of the Palace at Knossos: Complete Vases of the Late Minoan IIIB Period* (Lund, 1964)
M. R. Popham: *The Destruction of the Palace at Knossos: Pottery of the Late Minoan IIIA Period* (Göteborg, 1970)
D. Levi: *Festòs e la civiltà minoica*, i (Rome, 1976)
G. Walberg: *Kamares* (Uppsala, 1976)
L. Vagnetti and P. Belli: 'Characters and Problems of the Final Neolithic in Crete', *Stud. Micenei & Egeo-Anatol.*, xix (1978), pp. 125–63
G. Walberg: *The Kamares Style: Overall Effects* (Uppsala, 1978)
P. Betancourt and others: *Vasilike Ware: An Early Bronze Age Pottery Style in Crete* (Göteborg, 1979)
A. Kanta: *The Late Minoan III Period in Crete* (Göteborg, 1980)
B. J. Kemp and R. S. Merillees: *Minoan Pottery in Second Millennium Egypt* (Mainz, 1980)
G. Walberg: *Provincial Middle Minoan Pottery* (Mainz, 1983)
P. Betancourt, ed.: *East Cretan White-on-dark Ware* (Philadelphia, 1984)
P. Betancourt: *The History of Minoan Pottery* (Princeton, 1985)
W. D. Niemeier: *Die Palaststilkeramik von Knossos* (Berlin, 1985)
A. Walberg: *Kamares: A Study of the Character of Palatial Middle Minoan Pottery* (Göteborg, 1987)
A. Walberg: *Middle Minoan III: A Time of Transition* (Jonsered, 1992)
Late Minoan III Pottery: Chronology and Terminology: Acts of a Meeting Held at the Danish Institute: Athens, 1994
J. A. MacGillivray: *Knossos: Pottery Groups of the Old Palace Period* (London, 1998)
J. W. Shaw: *A LM IA Ceramic Kiln in South-central Crete: Function and Pottery Production* (Princeton, 2001)
A. Simandiraki: *Middle Minoan III Pottery from Building B of the Peak Sanctuary of Mount Juktas, Crete, and a General Re-assessment of the Middle Minoan III Period* (diss., U. Bristol, 2002)
K. A. Barnard, T. M. Brogan and P. M. Day: *Mochlos IB: Period III, Neopalatial Settlement on the Coast, the Artisans' Quarter, and the Farmhouse at Chalinomouri, the Neopalatial Pottery* (Philadelphia, 2003)
E. Borgna: *Il complesso di ceramica tardominoico III dell'Acropoli mediana di Festòs* (Padua, 2003)
Pottery and Society: The Impact of Recent Studies in Minoan Pottery: Gold Medal Colloquium in Honor of Philip P. Betancourt: 104th Annual Meeting of the Archaeological Institute of America: New Orleans, 2003
K. S. Christakis: *Cretan Bronze Age Pithoi: Traditions and Trends in the Production and Consumption of Storage Containers in Bronze Age Crete* (Philadelphia, 2005)

II. Cycladic.

The Early and Middle Cycladic periods were times of innovation and individuality in island pottery. Subsequently, although local features can be discerned, they are insignificant compared with the stylistic influences of Minoan Crete and, later, Mycenaean Greece. Although wheelmade pots from the end of the Early Bronze Age have been found, they were not common until the Late Cycladic period.

For chronological overview *see* Cycladic, §4.

C. Zervos: *L'Art des Cyclades du début à la fin de l'âge du bronze: 2500–1100 avant notre ère* (Paris, 1957) [excellent pls]
R. L. N. Barber: *The Cyclades in the Bronze Age* (London, 1987)
A. G. Papagiannopoulou: *The Influence of Middle Minoan Pottery on the Cyclades* (diss., U. London, 1987)

1. Early Cycladic. 2. Middle Cycladic. 3. Late Cycladic.

1. Early Cycladic. The earliest Cycladic pottery is relatively crude. The fabric is thick and coarse, though the surfaces are often burnished to a high and attractive lustre, most commonly in black, brown or reddish-brown. All the vessels are handmade, and decoration, when it occurs, always consists of incised rectilinear patterns. There are no curvilinear or figurative motifs. The incisions are filled with a white substance, making the patterns stand out sharply from the dark background, though the original effect is now usually diminished by the loss of the white filling or the deterioration of the burnish over time. The uses of the various vases are not always easy to determine, though pottery containers certainly fulfilled a wide range of functions. Two forms, the purposes of which are unknown, may be taken as examples: a globular flask (of which copies or exported specimens occur in northern Crete) and a circular pyxis

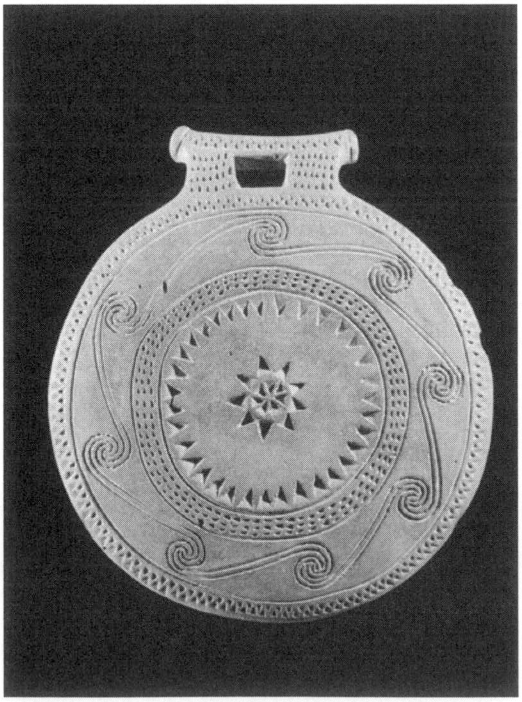

4. Early Cycladic pottery, 'frying pan' with incised and stamped decoration, diam. 203 mm, EC I (Paris, Musée du Louvre)

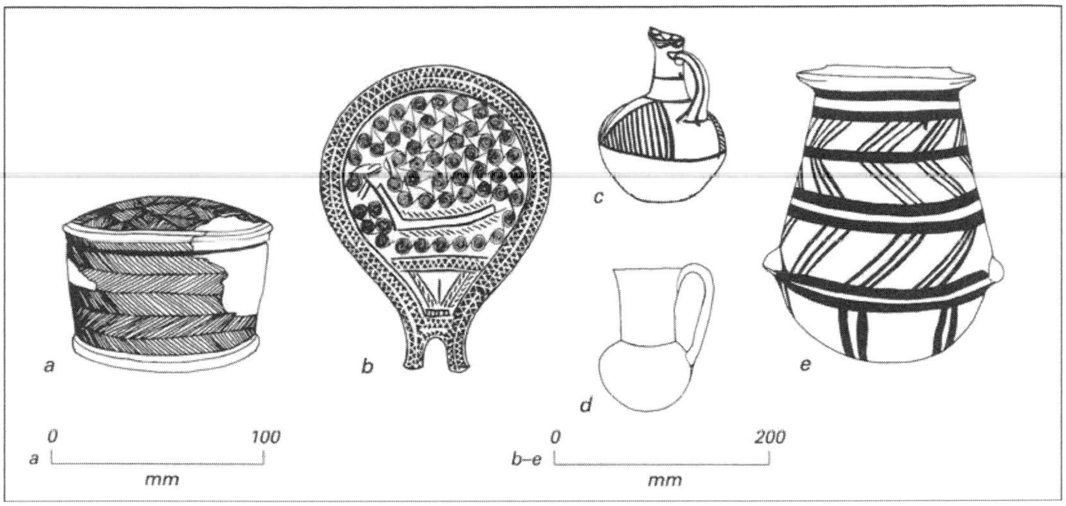

5. Early Cycladic pottery: (a) circular pyxis with incised decoration, h. 83 mm, EC I; (b) 'frying-pan' with incised and stamped decoration, h. 280 mm, EC II; (c) jug with painted decoration, h. 160 mm, EC II; (d) tankard with burnished surface, h. 132 mm, EC IIIA; (e) barrel jar with painted Geometric designs, h. 274 mm, EC IIIB

(see fig. 5a). Some shapes found more commonly in cemeteries than in settlements may have had some specifically funerary purpose. One example is the 'hat-vase', which resembles an upturned hat and apparently contained offerings.

Towards the end of EC I the range of shapes increased, and some curvilinear motifs, such as running spirals, were introduced. A notable new form was the 'frying-pan', a shallow bowl with flat bottom, straight sides and a projecting handle that varies in form (see fig. 4). The circular, flat area of the base was extensively and sometimes elaborately decorated with incised patterns. This vessel type is thought by some to have been filled with water and used as a mirror, though the fact that the handles are sometimes decorated to resemble the female vulva may suggest a more complex function. Later 'frying-pans' sometimes bear representations of boats (5a), providing some of the earliest evidence for shipping in the Aegean. Others are decorated with a frieze of running spirals encompassing a large star pattern.

During EC II the variety of shapes and motifs again increased, and two new decorative techniques were used: painting and stamping. The painted designs, which are neat and rectilinear, occur on a new fine fabric with a pale surface. Stamps were carved, probably from wood, and their designs were then pressed into the damp clay. In this sense stamping was simply a variation on the traditional practice of incision. A common stamped pattern, the *kerbschnitt*, is composed of a series of solid triangles set alternately in opposite directions. On some EC II 'frying-pans' the exuberance of the earlier incised spiral patterns was replaced by a dull, mechanical repetition of isolated spirals made by stamping. Important new shapes in EC II were the jug (5c) and 'sauceboat'. The latter is an odd and distinctive shape, again of uncertain function, which is often regarded as a typically mainland form (EH II; see fig. 9 below) but is possibly of Cycladic origin. Another typical shape in EC II was the pedestalled jar with a trumpet-shaped or conical foot. Its decoration was relatively simple, comprising one or two friezes of incised herringbone patterns or running spirals around the neck and shoulder. This shape is also found in stone. Indeed, as in the preceding period, stone and clay vessels shared many forms.

Pottery fabrics, forms and motifs established in EC I and II did not entirely disappear with the radical changes that occurred in EC IIIA (though their range was certainly reduced). But the innovations of this late phase of EC are striking and appear to be due to Anatolian influence. The potter's wheel began to be used, especially for plates, though handmade vases remained predominant. The most interesting new fabric had a highly burnished finish, usually black or red, and some distinctive shapes, including the tankard (5d), the two-handled tankard (*depas amphikypellon*) and the high-beaked jug, immediately betray their Anatolian origin. There was little decorated pottery, but incised and painted designs persisted, the latter usually in the form of cross-hatching on stemmed cups. Some innovations in this period were purely local, such as the duck vase, a squat, humped vessel with a projecting spout, which became more common later. Spout-ends have an attractive leaf shape, which also continued in fashion.

The last phase of the Early Cycladic period (EC IIIB), which overlaps with the early Middle Bronze Age in neighbouring Aegean areas, is notable for local developments and for the influence it exerted on the Matt-painted pottery of the Greek mainland (*see* §III, 2(ii) below). The tradition of incised decoration continued on roughly burnished 'Dark-faced' vases (e.g. the duck vases, which sometimes bear modest figural scenes), but there was a great expansion of painted designs in the so-called Geometric style, which apparently originated on MELOS. Most of the designs are in dark matt paint on a light surface, provided by covering the vase with a thin pale wash. (This decorative technique was then widely used in Syria and Cilicia in southern Anatolia.) Initially the painted motifs were probably almost entirely rectilinear, but they increasingly incorporated curvilinear elements. They were applied to some distinctive shapes: the barrel jar (5e), also found on the mainland, and the beaked jug, a developed version of the earlier type. At the end of the EC period, however, after the use of white-filled incision had ceased, patterns were sometimes painted in white on a dark ground, perhaps in an attempt to reproduce the effect of incising.

J. E. Coleman: 'Early Cycladic Clay Vessels', *Art and Culture of the Cyclades*, ed. P. Getz-Preziosi (Karlsruhe, 1977), pp. 109–17 [Eng. trans. of *Kunst und Kultur der Kykladeninseln im 3. Jahrtausend v. Chr.* (exh. cat., ed. J. Thimme; Karlsruhe, Bad. Landesmus., 1976]

R. L. N. Barber and J. A. MacGillivray: 'The Early Cycladic Period: Matters of Definition and Terminology', *Amer. J. Archaeol.*, lxxxiv (1980), pp. 141–57 [incl. summaries of the pottery of each phase and further refs]

2. MIDDLE CYCLADIC. Although some aspects of the pottery of the Middle Cycladic (MC) period are directly derived from that of the preceding phase (e.g. the barrel jar and the beaked jug), some of the similarities are only general (e.g. the widespread use of a dark burnished fabric); and some elements are completely new, such as the Cycladic White fabric and the motifs that decorate it. There is a good deal of variation between the pottery of different islands, mostly in details of fabric and finish.

The two major classes of MC pottery are Cycladic White and Dark Burnished (see fig. 6). Of these, the most conservative is the Dark Burnished. Its fabric is fairly crude, but the surfaces, which were sometimes slipped first, are finely finished and can have a very high lustre. This pottery was most common in the earlier part of the period, when it was occasionally exported to sites in mainland Greece, including Lerna, Athens and Magnesia. Shapes were limited, consisting primarily of bowls, jars, stemmed goblets (6b) and angular vases imitating those found in Helladic Grey Minyan pottery, which, although imported into the Cyclades, is primarily associated with the mainland (*see* §III, 2(ii) below). Designs, occasionally quite elaborate, were sometimes painted in white and, less frequently, in black on the dark burnished surfaces. This kind of pottery occurs on all Middle Cycladic sites, but at the end of MC and in the Late Cycladic period it was replaced by a less prominent Red-washed variety with a thick, matt, cherry-coloured surface coat.

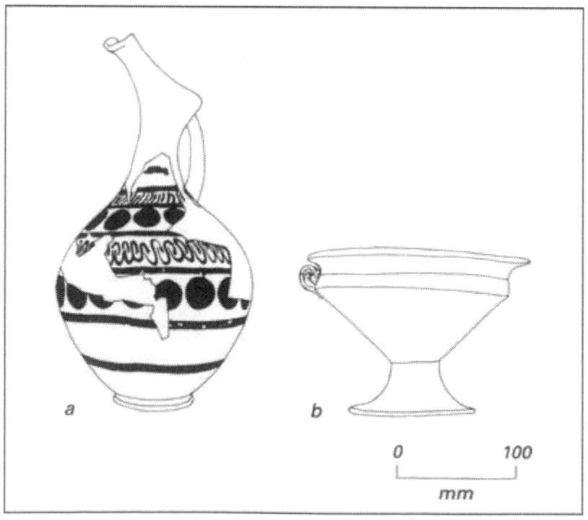

6. Middle Cycladic pottery: (a) Cycladic White beaked jug, h. 330 mm; (b) Dark Burnished stemmed goblet, h. 70 mm

The finest examples of the second main type, Cycladic White, have a thin, smooth and well-levigated fabric and a consistent creamy colour, though there are many coarser pieces. Cycladic White pots are normally decorated with designs in a rather dusty matt black paint; however, there is an attractive subgroup particularly associated with Melos, the Black-and-red style, which combines burnished red elements, mainly large circles, with other motifs in the standard matt black against a white ground. The shapes of Cycladic White consist partly of adaptations of traditional forms such as the beaked jug (6a), with a taller neck and a longer spout, flanged at the tip (see colour pl. 2:VI, fig. 3); partly of local innovations (e.g. the 'panelled' cup, so called because the decoration is set in a panel on the visible side); and partly of forms borrowed from other areas, such as the bridge-spouted jar from Crete.

The decorative motifs of Cycladic White are sometimes divided into a 'curvilinear' and a 'naturalistic' style. The earlier, curvilinear style consists mainly of non-figural designs, usually large spirals or irregular running loops arranged in zones, some clearly of Cretan derivation. One striking motif is the 'imp', a figure composed of essentially abstract elements, which appears on some Cycladic White beaked jugs. The later, naturalistic style comprises vegetable, floral and bird motifs, some again with parallels in Crete. Particularly common are the round-bodied birds, with wings, head and legs added in outline, that appear on Black-and-red jugs. Before the end of the MC period, the attractive Cycladic White fabric began to have a more sandy tinge, and some of its painted decoration was almost lustrous, changes that anticipated the most common local decorated pottery of the Late Cycladic period.

R. L. N. Barber: 'The Cyclades in the Middle Bronze Age', *Thera and the Aegean World I*, ed. C. Doumas (London, 1978), pp. 367–79

J. C. Overbeck: 'Stratigraphy and Ceramic Sequence in Middle Cycladic Ayia Irini', *The Prehistoric Cyclades*, ed. J. A. MacGillivray and R. L. N. Barber (Edinburgh, 1984), pp. 108–13

J. L. Davis: *Ayia Irini: Period V* (1985), v of *Keos* (Mainz, 1977–) [incl. pottery of the later MC period only]

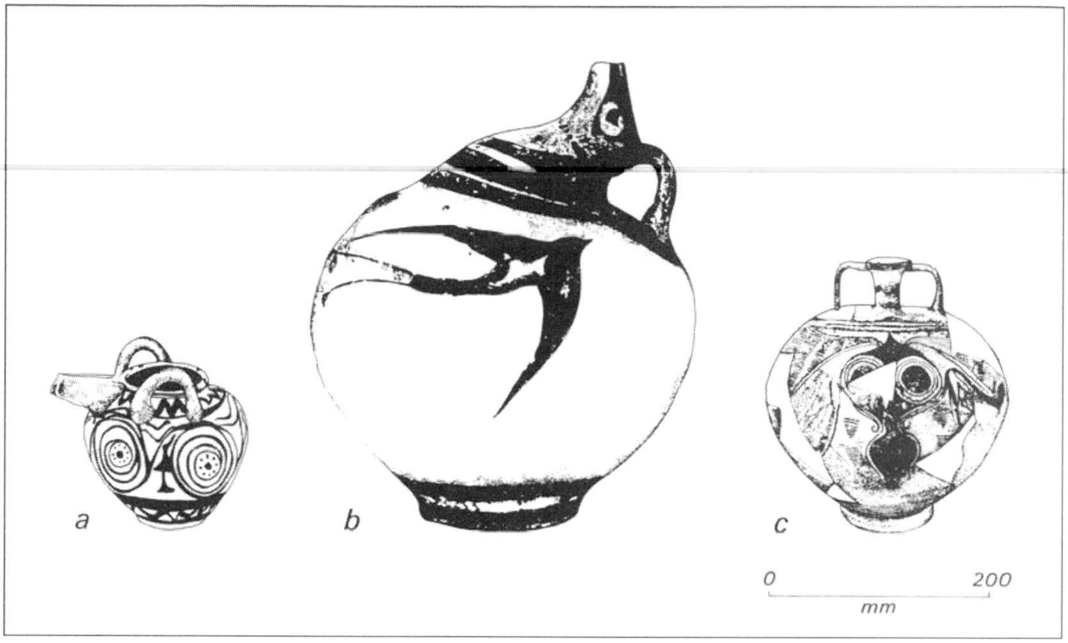

7. Late Cycladic pottery: (a) Minoanizing bridge-spouted jar with Black-and-red style decoration, h. 130 mm, LC I; (b) breasted ewer with painted bird motif, h. 435 mm, from Akrotiri, Thera, LC I; (c) Stirrup jar with stylized octopus decoration, h. 250 mm, LC IIIC

3. LATE CYCLADIC. During the two early phases of the Late Cycladic (LC) period Minoan vases were imported from Crete and imitated to a remarkable extent. Minoan teacups, Vapheio cups and bridge-spouted jars (*see* FIG. 7a) were typical shapes, and, as in Crete, many of the decorative motifs were floral or vegetable. Spirals were also common.

Two decorative schemes characterize the copious finds of the early LC period from Akrotiri on THERA. One is arranged in zones and is close to Minoan designs; the other disposes motifs in a free field and seems characteristically Cycladic. The motifs are both abstract and figural, including dolphins, fish, quadrupeds and birds (7b). Colours used are either the traditional matt black or a mixture of red and black, sometimes with added white detail. Pottery of the LC I and II periods is also well represented at Phylakopi on Melos and Ayia Irini on Keos, and local variations of the Minoanizing trends are identifiable.

About the beginning of LC III, the Minoan stylistic influence on Cycladic pottery was replaced by Mycenaean. Typical Mycenaean forms—the kylix and, later, the deep bowl—became common. Though a period of change, it was not one of renewed local artistic initiative, and there were no longer any truly local shapes. It remains unclear how much of the pottery of the earlier part of LC III was locally produced and how much was imported. The fabric of most of the decorated vases suggests that they were produced abroad, but it seems improbable that all the fine wares were imported. Mycenaean imports certainly declined drastically during the later 13th century BC (LC IIIB), and subsequent production was locally based, even though remaining strongly Mycenaean in character. Cycladic pottery of the final stage of the Bronze Age (LC IIIC) essentially mirrors that of contemporary Mycenaean pottery on the mainland, though there are some local trends, the stirrup jars with stylized octopus decoration (7c), particularly well known on Naxos, being attractive examples.

C. Kardara: *Aplomata Naxou: Kineta euremata taphon A kai B* [Aplomata on Naxos: Portable finds from Tombs A and B] (Athens, 1977) [numerous illus. of octopus vases]

C. Doumas: *Thera: Pompeii of the Ancient Aegean* (London, 1983), pp. 108–13

P. A. Mountjoy: 'The Pottery', *The Archaeology of Cult: The Sanctuary at Phylakopi*, ed. C. Renfrew (London, 1985), pp. 151–208

J. C. Overbeck: *Ayia Irini: Period IV: 1. The Stratigraphy and the Find Deposits* (1989), vii of *Keos* (Mainz, 1977–)

III. Helladic.

Pottery is found in great quantities on Helladic sites in all Bronze Age phases, but kilns have been identified only rarely and deposits of wasters, which would indicate the range of a kiln's production, only once or twice. Conclusions about the organization and processes of manufacture must therefore be deduced almost entirely from the pottery itself; little analysis bearing on these questions has yet been undertaken, however. Traditionally, the main wares have been identified in visual terms, with a concentration on the finer material; only the shapes and motifs of the Mycenaean style have received intensive study, resulting in a sophisticated classification. Scientific studies have been concerned mainly with methods of decoration, and fabric study has concentrated on establishing provenance. A promising development in this field, which suggests that fabrics and the traditional 'wares' do not necessarily coincide, is still in its early stages.

Within the Helladic region the provinces of the Argolid, Corinthia, Attica and Boiotia frequently played a leading role in pottery production as in other fields, and they will be referred to collectively below as the 'central Helladic region'.

For a chronological overview *see* HELLADIC, §4.

1. MATERIALS AND TECHNIQUES. Pottery had been made for several millennia in mainland Greece before the Bronze Age, and the Helladic potters inherited considerable technical knowledge from their Neolithic predecessors. They knew how to choose clays, tempering them, if necessary, with fragments of stone or other materials (inclusions), and they knew how to fire them to achieve a special appearance or quality. However, their technical equipment and level of organization do not appear to have been complex. Although some pottery may have been produced within the household, particularly in the earlier stages of the Bronze Age, most was doubtless produced by specialists, though these are likely to have been part-timers who also farmed land, unless they were directly supported by a palace or similar establishment. The evidence suggests a wide spread of potters established in separate workshops. These may have specialized in particular fabrics, as the study of fabrics is beginning to suggest, and in some cases their products may have been widely distributed from a single centre, but mostly they seem to have served small neighbourhoods.

For most of the Early Helladic (EH) period all pottery was handmade, and some of the finer ware, at least, must have been kiln-fired. It is widely believed that late in the period a form of potter's wheel, probably a simple turntable on a pivot, was introduced, but there is continuing disagreement over what proportion of the pottery was wheel-thrown before the Late Helladic (LH) period, though much was evidently kiln-fired. In the LH period, use of the wheel has often been assumed to have been almost universal, and even cooking pots are reported to be wheel-thrown at Mycenae and other central sites. LH decorated pottery is so homogeneous for most of the period and so well adapted to mass production that it seems likely that Mycenae gave the stylistic lead, and it is quite possible that the pottery was produced to a standard by provincial centres serving wide regions. There is, however, evidence for local variation to a limited extent at several major southern Peloponnesian sites, and certain household wares, perhaps even a large proportion of total production in remote regions such as Thessaly, may have continued to be handmade, as did a class of miniature decorated pots even in the Argolid. But in all probability most if not all pottery was kiln-fired by this time, if in rather small and, to judge from their rarity, often impermanent structures.

In all Helladic phases several qualities of pottery were produced; in LH times this reflects the choice of different clays, and the same is likely earlier. The finest wares, often only a few millimetres thick, were generally fired a light colour, although dark wares fired under reducing conditions were sometimes favoured. The most popular shades were light buff, yellow or near-white, and where local clays did not produce these naturally a slip of such a colour might be applied. Polishing or burnishing was normally used to give fine wares a lustrous surface and to improve the glossiness of paint. Other wares of good quality can have even surfaces but feel rough to the touch even when decorated, and when thick may contain large inclusions. These are different, however, from true coarse ware, which is generally of a distinctive red or brown fabric (containing much tempering matter) and which tends to have an uneven surface that is variegated in colour, whether from the original firing or from constant use on the hearth, for this is the ware of cooking pots. (Late Helladic cooking ware, however, though of similar fabric, is of much higher quality.) Finally, large storage jars (pithoi) were produced throughout the period; their fabric, normally several centimetres thick, contains many stone inclusions and other tempering matter but is generally light-surfaced and often smooth. They may even be slipped and painted, although decoration with applied bands of clay is more common.

2. HISTORICAL SURVEY.

(i) Early Helladic. The earliest EH wares had likely antecedents in the latest Neolithic phases. These include not only the red-slipped and burnished ware characteristic of Attica and central Greece that has traditionally been termed EH I, which has a range of simple rounded shapes, principally bowls, jars and jugs, but also a newly defined group, 'Talioti ware', which is particularly well represented in the Argolid. The finer pieces in this group have a slightly glossy red or brown-red coating and are decorated with incision, while the coarser storage vessels often have finger-impressed bands; there is a wider range of shapes than in central Greek EH I wares, including fruit-stands. How these relate to each other and how the far more sophisticated style of EH II developed from them are questions that need investigation.

'Classic' EH II wares were of a remarkable quality and homogeneity throughout the Helladic region. The finest are light in colour, hard-fired and often extremely thin, almost certainly the product of specialized workshops (one of which may be represented by pottery deposits, identified as wasters, at Vouliagmeni, near Corinth). They might be coated partly or wholly with dark paint that is often lustrous, probably as a result of burnishing ('Urfirnis'), or have a burnished slip, which could be deliberately mottled; the evidence from Lerna suggests a trend from painted to plain surfaces during the period. The most characteristic shapes are the ring-based small bowl or saucer and the 'sauceboat', the hallmark of EH II (see fig. 8a–b); the popularity and relative quantities of both might suggest their use in ceremonial drinking parties as drinking and pouring vessels respectively. The 'sauceboat' developed over the period from a shallow to a deep open-spouted vessel, the purpose of which is unclear; the taut curves of its profile can be matched in other shapes such as the askos (8c), and there is no compelling reason to relate its shape to metalwork (the extant gold examples are of the mature form, so can hardly represent the original inspiration). These two shapes constituted the great bulk of pottery exports, which were popular in the Cyclades and reached as far as Crete, Macedonia and Troy.

Another class of pottery of particular interest consists of the large pithoi of the Argolid, also clearly produced by a specialist workshop. These were decorated with running patterns in relief on raised bands, produced by some form of roller; one of the most elaborate patterns, two rows of running spirals with doglike creatures neatly fitted between, is found on examples from Lerna, TIRYNS and ZYGOURIES, which must therefore have been distributed from a single centre or made by an itinerant group (as pithoi have been in modern times).

The relative chronology of the late EH period, when the preceding homogeneity broke up, is controversial. On the view preferred here, a new pottery tradition, often known as 'Lefkandi I' from the Euboian site where it was first identified, appeared before the end of EH II in Euboia, central Greece, Aigina and some north Cycladic islands, most often mixed with EH II or Early Cycladic II types (*see* §II, 1 above). It has good parallels in the Troad and neighbouring regions, and there are other grounds for suspecting some movement of population from that area into the Aegean at the time, but the nature of this movement is still unclear. The most characteristic shapes are plates (8d) and bowls, two-handled drinking vessels and beaked jugs, all in black-, brown- or red-burnished wares; traces of a potter's wheel have been recognized on this material.

The characteristic fine shapes of EH III probably represent a fusion of Lefkandi I and EH II forms, first developed in central Greece and spread, perhaps by local migration, to the northern Peloponnese. This provides the best evidence for a link between the two phases, although it does not explain all the new features of the pottery attributed to EH III, a phase of notable heterogeneity in which at least two distinct traditions can be detected in the central Helladic region alone. These have in common most shapes and many motifs but differ in a preference for white decoration on a dark coat (Ayia Marina ware) in central Greece, and dark decoration on a light ground (Lerna IV Patterned ware) in the northern Peloponnese. The patterns are mainly variations on large upright triangle groups on the shoulders of the bigger shapes and arrangements of horizontal line groups on the smaller ones, such as the characteristic tankard (11e); the style may draw on rare earlier classes of decorated pottery in the Helladic and Cycladic regions and on basketry patterns. Wholly or partly coated and plain burnished wares are also common, the two-handled bowl being an especially popular shape (11f). A rare grey ware seems particularly associated with use of the potter's wheel and is clearly the direct ancestor of Middle Helladic Grey Minyan ware.

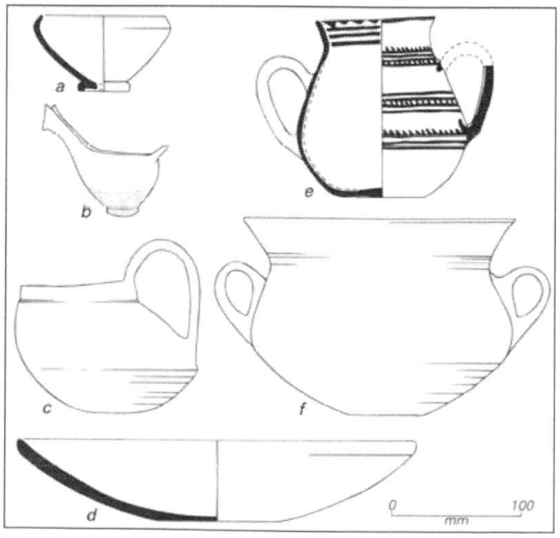

8. Early Helladic pottery: (a) saucer, EH II; (b) 'sauceboat', EH II; (c) askos, EH II; (d) plate, Lefkandi I; (e) tankard, Lerna IV Patterned ware, EH III; (f) two-handled bowl, EH III

A. J. B. Wace and C. W. Blegen: 'The Pre-Mycenaean Pottery of the Mainland', *Annu. Brit. Sch. Athens*, xxii (1916–18), pp. 175–89

J. L. Caskey: 'The Early Helladic Period in the Argolid', *Hesperia*, xxix (1960), pp. 285–303

J. B. Rutter: *Ceramic Change in the Aegean Early Bronze Age. The Kastri Group, Lefkandi I, and Lerna IV: A Theory Concerning the Origins of Early Helladic III Ceramics*, Occasional Paper 5, Institute of Archaeology, UCLA (Los Angeles, 1979)

J. B. Rutter: 'Fine Gray-burnished Pottery of the Early Helladic III Period: The Ancestry of Gray Minyan', *Hesperia*, li (1983), pp. 327–53

R. E. Jones: *Greek and Cypriot Pottery: A Review of Scientific Studies* (Athens, 1986)

H.-J. Weisshaar: 'Die Keramik von Talioti', *Tiryns Forschungen und Berichte*, xi (1990), pp. 1–34

J. B. Rutter: 'Early Helladic Pottery: Inferences about Exchange and Production from Style and Clay Composition', *Proceedings of the International Conference 'Wace and Blegen: Pottery as Evidence for Trade in the Aegean Bronze Age, 1939–1989': Amsterdam, 1993*, pp. 19–37

O. T. P. K. Dickinson: 'Pottery', *The Aegean Bronze Age*, Cambridge World Archaeology (Cambridge, 1994)

(ii) Middle Helladic. The obscurity surrounding the final EH stages extends to the process whereby the MH pottery tradition spread, since a relatively full sequence has been discovered at only a few sites. It has become clear, however, that the traditional description of MH pottery, which laid much stress on Grey Minyan and Matt-painted wares, gives the wrong impression. The only truly universal MH ware was the domestic coarse ware; Grey Minyan and Matt-painted were characteristic only of the central Helladic region, and the classic Matt-painted ware is now believed, on the basis of its fabric, to be Aiginetan in origin. However, the basic pattern of complementary fine wares, plain burnished or polished and dark-painted, was widespread, and it is possible to detect a family resemblance between the local fine pottery traditions of all the mainland regions south of Thessaly. Both groups had clear EH III antecedents in shapes and techniques, but the use of manganese-based matt paints, rather than potentially lustrous iron-oxide-based paints, was a new phenomenon, with Cycladic affinities. These are particularly clear in the Aigina-derived ware, whose shapes, like the popular barrel jar (see fig. 9c), often have Cycladic parallels.

The burnished group consists almost entirely of open vessels, especially two-handled bowls and kantharoi. Its best-known manifestation is Grey Minyan, the finest ware produced for most of the MH period. This was of well-levigated clay, polished (rather than burnished) on all surfaces, evenly fired in a reducing kiln; somewhat inferior grey and dark burnished varieties with a very similar range of shapes were produced in slightly different fabrics, and comparable plain wares occur throughout the mainland. At first the shapes were round-bodied like their EH III ancestors, but by the mature stage the well-known angular shapes were standard (9a–b). These often have elaborately modelled rims, sharply carinated bodies and horizontal faceting or rilling on the shoulder, all features that, like the ringed stem on the most elaborate shape, the goblet (9a), seem to require use of a wheel; any traces of the wheel's use have generally been removed by polishing or burnishing. The frequent suggestion that these features reflect metallic originals is implausible, both because the MH culture was scarcely rich enough to support the production of metal vessels and because far from being naturally suitable for metal, such features will place a strain on plate. However, these shapes, particularly the goblet, were undoubtedly very popular, being imported and imitated in the Cyclades and Macedonia, and at Troy.

The painted wares are largely closed vessels, jars and jugs, with simple ovoid or near-globular shapes, though bowls and kantharoi are also found; in general, they seem to be handmade. The decoration is simple, consisting generally of hatched or nested triangles set on bands or a coated area on the upper body (9d); slightly more adventurous patterns can be found on the Aiginetan Matt-painted shapes, especially the barrel jars. A ware well known in the eastern Peloponnese, particularly the Argolid, is decorated with semi-lustrous dark paint but has very similar shapes and motifs; nevertheless, it seems from its fabric and technique of manufacture to be a product of the 'Minoanizing' workshop that is likely to have been based at either Lerna or Ayios Stephanos in Lakonia, since most of the products have been identified at these two sites. This 'Minoanizing' pottery is the only Helladic class to show marked foreign influence for most of the period; it has particularly close links with the local Minoan style of KYTHERA, presumably the source of the workshop's founders. It includes both fine and coarse wares, in which cups, bowls, jugs and larger closed vessels were produced; they were decorated in white and other colours, principally red, on a dark coat in a manner similar to the simpler Middle Minoan styles of Crete (*see* §I, 4 above).

In the latest stages of the MH period light-coloured fine wares were increasingly favoured. In some parts of the central Helladic region Grey Minyan was largely supplanted by Yellow Minyan, a similar ware fired in oxidizing conditions, in which low-stemmed goblets were produced; closed vessels with burnished exteriors are of similar fabric. But unburnished plain wares were also common, and the graves of the period, which supply much of the available evidence, contain a wide range of plain and painted small vessels as Cycladic origins, as do motifs used on them, such as spiral-based forms, plants and birds. Yet these wares do not imitate any Aegean ware closely and seem

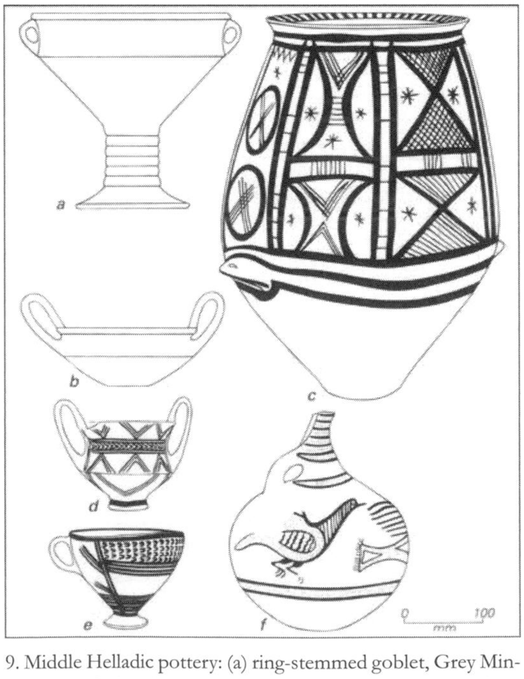

9. Middle Helladic pottery: (a) ring-stemmed goblet, Grey Minyan ware; (b) kantharos, Grey Minyan ware; (c) barrel jar, Aiginetan Matt-painted ware; (d) kantharos, Matt-painted ware; (e) Matt-painted cup, with 'panelled' style of decoration; (f) jug, Mainland Polychrome style

rather to be local developments, particularly in parts of the central Helladic region. Especially notable are the Matt-painted burnished ware and its characteristic 'panelled' style of decoration, which seems to have been a product of the northern Peloponnese (9e), and the Mainland Polychrome style, which may have been based in central Greece (9f). These and other wares overlap substantially with the earliest Mycenaean pottery. Their relative chronology has not yet been fully worked out, but their earliest forms probably preceded the development of LH I pottery, and their diversity reflects the atmosphere of experiment in which the first Mycenaean pottery was produced.

A. J. B. Wace and C. W. Blegen: 'The Pre-Mycenaean Pottery of the Mainland', *Annu. Brit. Sch. Athens*, xxii (1916–18), pp. 175–89

R. J. Buck: 'Middle Helladic Matt-painted Pottery', *Hesperia*, xxiii (1964), pp. 231–313

J. B. Rutter and S. H. Rutter: *The Transition to Mycenaean*, Monumenta Archaeologica, iv (Los Angeles, 1976)

J. L. Davis: 'The Mainland Panelled Cup and Panelled Style', *Amer. J. Archaeol.*, lxxxii (1978), pp. 216–22

R. E. Jones: *Greek and Cypriot Pottery: A Review of Scientific Studies* (Athens, 1986)

H. B. Siedentopf: *Matthemalte Keramik der mittleren Bronzezeit*, Alt-Agina, iv/2 (Mainz, 1991)

C. W. Zerner: 'New Perspectives on Trade in the Middle and Early Late Helladic Periods on the Mainland', *Proceedings of the International Conference 'Wace and Blegen: Pottery as Evidence for Trade in the Aegean Bronze Age, 1939–1989': Amsterdam, 1993*, pp. 39–56

O. T. P. K. Dickinson: 'Pottery', *The Aegean Bronze Age*, Cambridge World Archaeology (Cambridge, 1994)

(iii) Late Helladic. The terms 'Late Helladic' and 'Mycenaean' have become almost interchangeable, but the adoption of a new pottery style was in fact one of the latest developments in the evolution of the Mycenaean culture; nevertheless, it was to become the most widespread and characteristic of all Mycenaean features. Analysis of Lerna fabrics strongly suggests that the new style was created in the well-established 'Minoanizing' workshop, and there is good reason to suppose that at first it was produced in only a few Peloponnesian centres.

The first stage of the style, LH I, is characterized by a fine decorated ware with a restricted range of shapes and motifs, both of which had most often a Minoan origin. But there is a non-Minoan, presumably local, element that includes one of the most popular shapes, the squat jug (see fig. 10b), and while the style is close to that of Late Minoan IA (*see* §I, 5 above), particularly

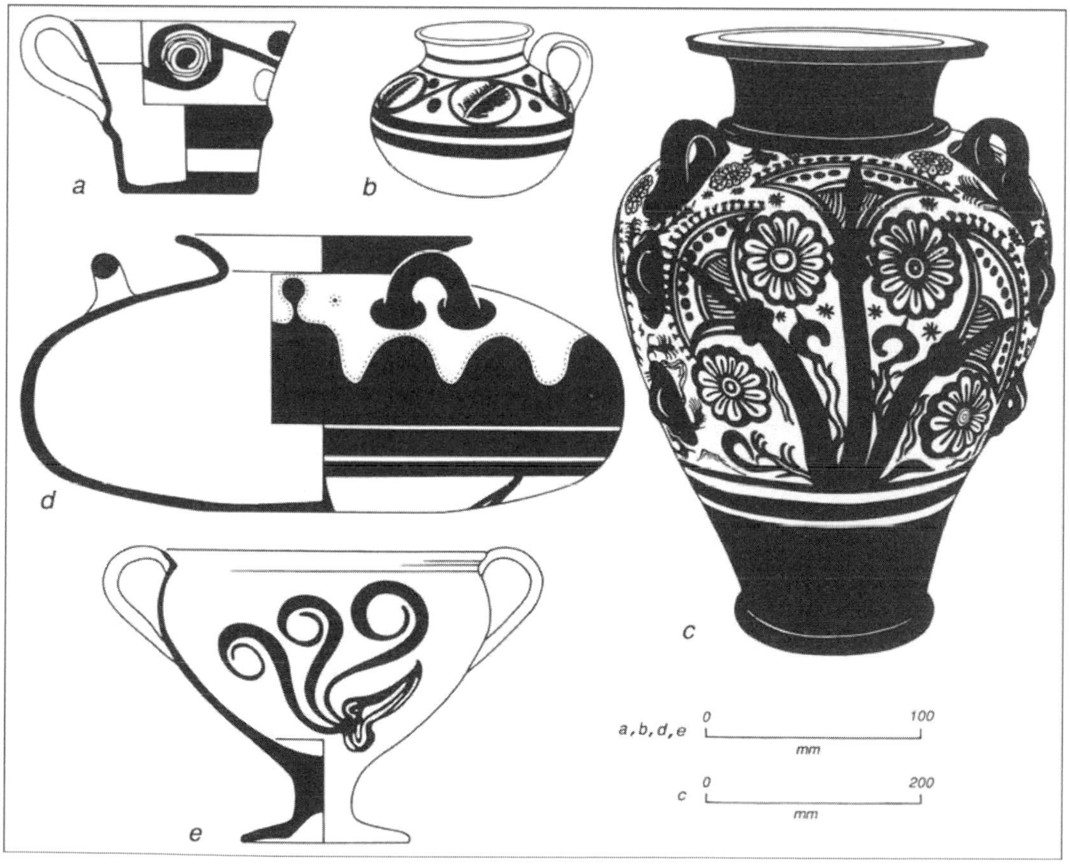

10. Late Helladic pottery, LHI–II: (a) Vapheio cup, LH I; (b) squat jug, LH I; (c) pithoid jar, Palatial style, LH IIA; (d) alabastron, LH IIB; (e) 'Ephyraean' goblet, LH IIB

the variant produced in Kythera, it has a distinctive character. Ideally, the ware is thin and hard-fired, having a light polished surface decorated with lustrous paint that normally fired red or near-black; dots and lines in dull white paint were frequently superimposed on painted areas, particularly exterior rim-bands. Decoration is normally confined to a single zone on the upper body, bounded by bands or coated areas and subdivided by the handles if there are more than one; usually the same motif occurs in each subdivision. All accessory parts of the body were normally coated (cup-handles might be obliquely barred), and a band runs round the inside of the rim. The motifs are a mixture of geometric and stylized natural forms; variants of running spiral and linked circle motifs and plant forms, particularly foliate bands, dominate (10a–b). The shapes are mostly small cups, jugs and jars with rounded profiles, the major exception being the Vapheio cup (10a), which is essentially a flaring cylinder, most often divided by a midrib (a common feature on metal examples of the shape); a liking for piriform profiles, sometimes extremely compressed, is apparent in the closed shapes.

There are indications of primitive technique in the shaping and finishing of many vases, though there are clear signs of the use of the wheel, and interiors of open shapes were commonly left unslipped and unpolished; encircling bands were often unevenly painted, and some motifs could be inexpertly handled (e.g. spirals can have a 'squashed' look). In such features LH I pottery compares poorly with the best examples of the late wares in the MH style, which still commonly appeared in northern Peloponnesian contexts and continued to dominate in central Greece. (After the LH I period the Mycenaean style became wholly dominant, and only a few simple forms of Matt-painted decoration survived on large vessels.) However, the plain and domestic wares found with LH I pottery essentially continued MH traditions, though improving in quality. The commonest shapes are low-stemmed goblets and other open vessels that are clearly in the Minyan tradition, although more often rounded than angular in profile; in some regions these could still be produced in grey and dark wares, but light wares were to become the norm. The only Minoan introductions so far identified in this class are the tripod cooking pot, conical cup and lamp, none of which was common by Cretan standards.

The preferences in shape and the decorative principles established in LH I remain characteristic of the Mycenaean style for the rest of its history, although the range of motifs and shapes was greatly extended. The deployment of the motifs was standardized, seeming to obey quite strict rules, so that identical vases are commonly found; this mass-producible quality may have been a factor in the style's success. At first Minoan influences continued to be strongly felt, particularly in the 'Palatial' class of LH IIA, which consists of elaborately shaped and decorated closed vases that have many parallels in contemporary Late Minoan IB pottery. But even here there are distinctive Mycenaean features, such as the fondness for pithoid jars decorated with plant patterns (10c), which may be attributed to local stylistic development.

The ability to reproduce elaborate Minoan shapes and motifs argues for considerable increases in the skills of mainland potters, some of whom may have been immigrants from Crete or the 'Minoanized' Cycladic islands; there is also a detectable improvement in the quality of the ordinary decorated ware. This remained essentially separate from the 'Palatial' class, although it adopted some of the motifs in a simplified form, and the typical LH I shapes continued to be popular, joined by the characteristically Helladic alabastron (10d), a low three-handled shape that was made increasingly so squat that it must have been quite difficult to throw on the wheel, and the goblet (10e), which became more popular as a drinking vessel at the expense of the cup shapes. These two shapes appear in the Late Minoan II pottery style, providing plausible evidence for Helladic influence on Minoan pottery at a subsequent stage.

By LH IIIA:1 the Mycenaean style was fully formed, and the plain ware had become as standardized as the decorated, at least in the central Helladic region. The best is of comparable quality to the decorated, with a finely polished surface, but the majority is only smoothed. The decorated and plain wares continued to have largely distinct ranges of shapes, coinciding particularly in the open shapes, not least the kylikes, which now largely replaced the goblets and which, with their tall stems and shallow, gracefully curved bowls, are among the most attractive Mycenaean shapes (see fig. 11a). Other common decorated types are the two-handled deep bowl (11a and 12a), which is one of the hallmarks of LH IIIB; a variety of containers, including the alabastron, pyxis, piriform jar and stirrup jar (11c–e); and a range of jugs. The cooking wares are dominated by tripod pots and broad-mouthed jug/jar types; specialized forms of the kind found in earlier Minoan pottery are rare, but this class remains poorly researched. Ceremonial or ritual forms are rare in any ware.

The same range of motifs was now used on large and small bases; the 'Palatial' class had effectively disappeared at the end of LH II, and the only distinctive class is the Pictorial, which consists largely of kraters. These deep, broad-mouthed vessels are rare and probably prestigious, perhaps used as mixing bowls for drink, like their Classical successors; their decoration, perhaps inspired by frescoes, most often centres on bulls or chariot processions (11f; see colour pl. 2:VI, fig. 2). Clay analysis supports the view that, although popular in Cyprus, the majority of the standard examples were made in the Argolid, perhaps principally at Berbati, where wasters from a potters' establishment include Pictorial pieces; at a late stage, local versions (the so-called Pastoral, or Rude, style) began to be produced in Cyprus (*see* CYPRUS, §IV, 3). They may well have been produced largely as an 'export' ware, and the same workshop(s) may be the source of Cypriot and Levantine shapes decorated in Mycenaean style.

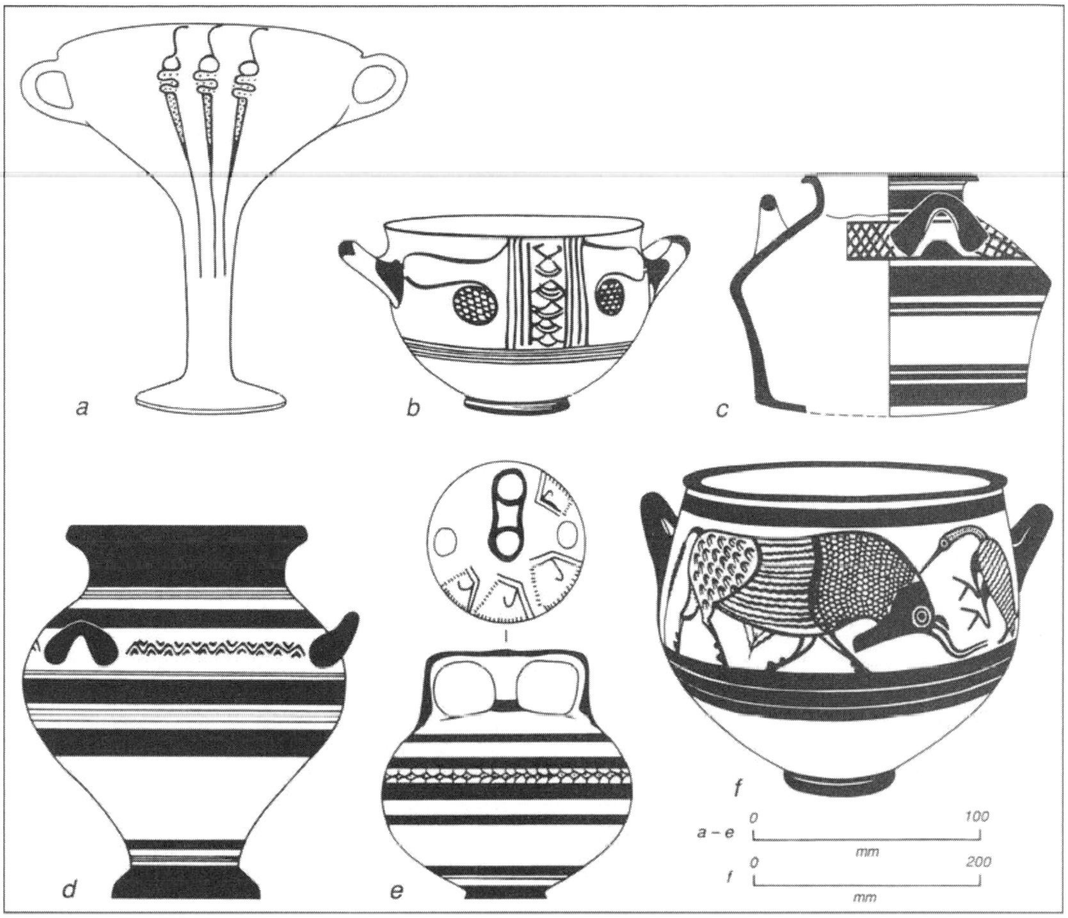

11. Late Helladic pottery, LH III–IIIB:1: (a) kylix, LH IIIB:1; (b) deep bowl, LH IIIB; (c) pyxis, LH IIIA:2; (d) piriform jar, LH IIIB:1; (e) stirrup jar, LH IIIB:1; (f) krater, Pictorial style, LH IIIB:1

Such sophistication in production was not to be found everywhere, but the LH IIIA:1, IIIA:2 and IIIB:1 phases represent a peak of quality and homogeneity in Mycenaean pottery, in which the standard set by the Argolid was followed without significant variation elsewhere. The ideal was a neatly balanced arrangement of one or at most two decorative zones and groups of bands, painted with great dexterity, which covered most of the vase on small closed shapes but was confined mainly to the upper body on others. On some classes of vessel, chiefly open shapes, the mannerism of isolating a motif in the centre of the vase with little or no accessory decoration was used to great effect (11a), but such classes always remained isolated developments.

Motifs could run through a zone, be spaced along it or be arranged in it to flank a more elaborate central motif; they include such geometric forms as the ever-popular spiral and groupings of bars, such zone-fillers as scale and net patterns, and increasingly stylized versions of flowers, octopuses, argonauts and shells. There are many parallels with contemporary Late Minoan III styles, but Mycenaean and Minoan are readily distinguishable; any influences went from the former to the latter.

The Mycenaean pottery of these phases was widely exported in the east and central Mediterranean, and imitation wares were produced in many areas, a striking testimony to its popularity. Small containers such as the stirrup jar were particularly popular, no doubt primarily for their contents (probably perfumed oil), and were imitated in faience and stone in Egypt and Palestine. Open vessels and ceremonial types were also exported in smaller quantities. After LH IIIB:1 there was a marked falling off in identifiable exports, which may have prompted increasing production of a local Mycenaean style on Cyprus.

In fact, there are signs of general decline in pottery of the LH IIIB:2 phase. The 'filled' or 'Metope' style (see fig. 12a) was influential over a much more restricted area, outside which there was little independent development but rather stagnation. Some shapes ceased to be produced, or like the kylix are found only in their plain form, and there was a narrowing of the range of motifs and more

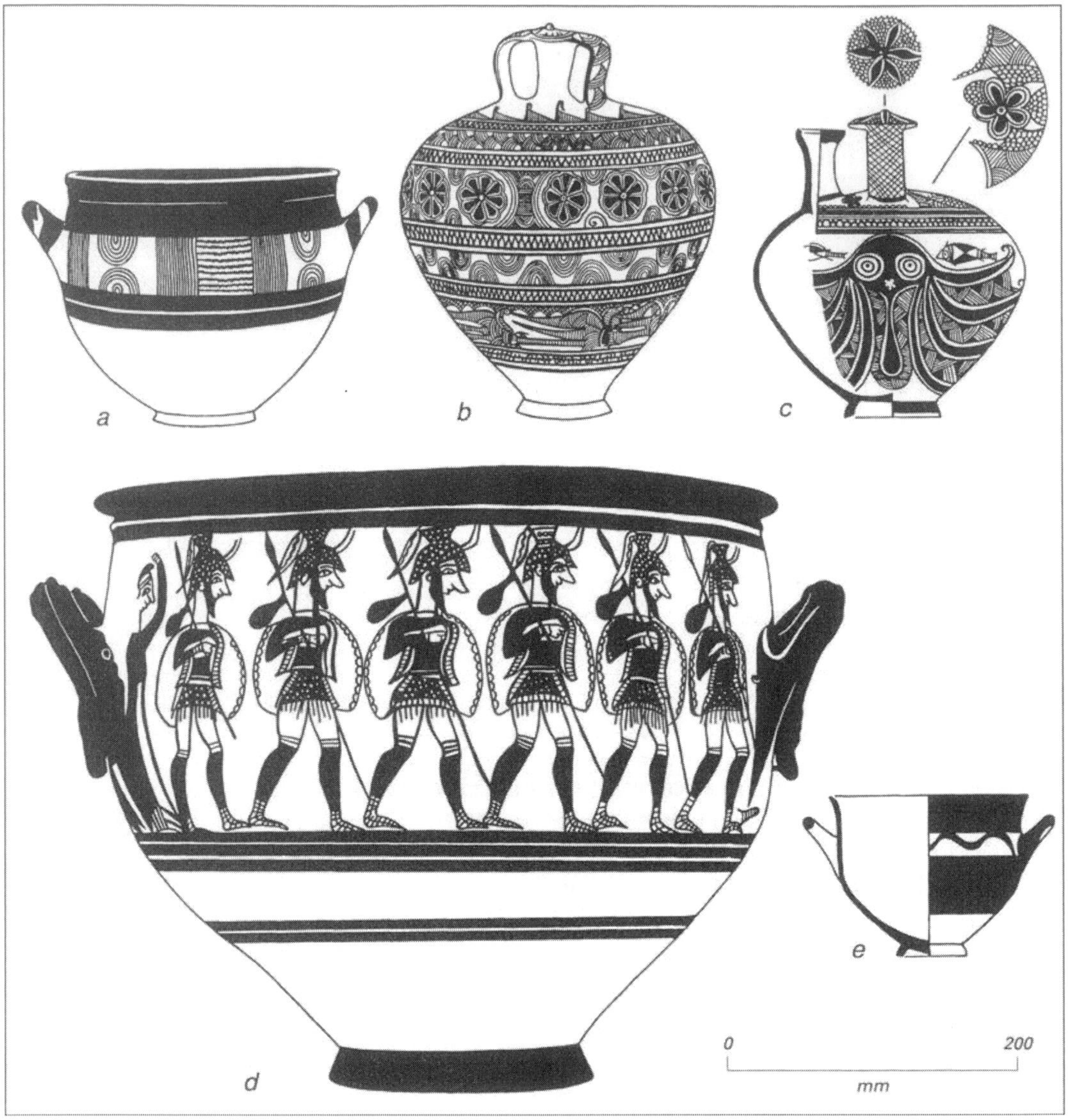

12. Late Helladic pottery, LH IIIB:2–IIIC: (a) deep bowl, 'filled' or Metope style, LH IIIB:2; (b) stirrup jar, Argive Close style, LH IIIC; (c) stirrup jar, Octopus style, LH IIIC; (d) krater, Pictorial style, LH IIIC; (e) deep bowl, LH IIIC

common use of simple banding and coating. These features represent the prelude to the collapse of homogeneity in the final, LH IIIC phase, when increasingly the different parts of the Mycenaean world developed divergently. The bulk of the pottery produced in LH IIIC continued to be of fair quality, but the range of shapes was progressively limited, until by the end only about ten were common and such standards as the kylix and stirrup jar had disappeared from many areas. Decoration was increasingly simplified; the wavy line was one of the commonest motifs (12e), and much use was made of banding and coating (the plain ware was ultimately absorbed into this minimally decorated class).

Side by side with this limited and monotonous material small classes of extremely elaborate vases were produced in a number of related but distinctive local styles. The impetus for this development seems to have come from the Dodekanese and Cyprus, which were linked with each other and Crete in a pattern of cross-influences from the beginning of the phase, but important centres of the mainland and Cyclades also produced well-known styles (*see* §II, 3 above). Common to all is the use of narrow zones filled with linear motifs, which might be arranged between band-groups to cover the bulk of the vase, as in the Argive Close style (12b), or might be used as bordering or dividing motifs for broader zones of pictorial decoration, in which octopuses (12c) and other

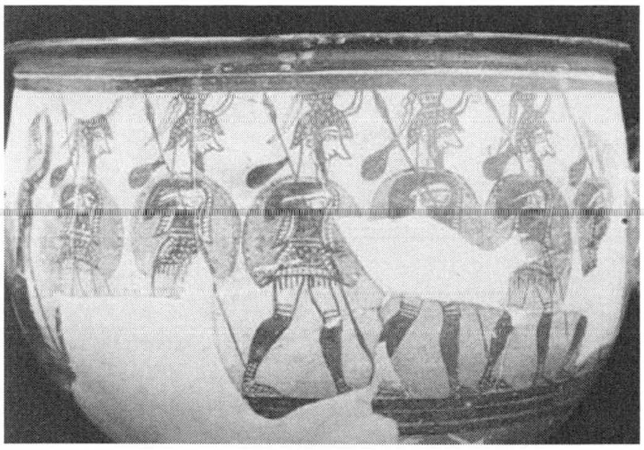

13. Late Helladic krater, h. 410 mm, from Mycenae, Pictorial style, LH IIIC (Athens, National Archaeological Museum)

animals, especially birds, marching warriors (12d; *see also* fig. 13) or more complex scenes are displayed. Only a few shapes, principally the stirrup jar and krater, were decorated in these styles. They may have been a response to the disappearance of higher forms of art, but they did not last long. In the final stages of LH IIIC, production was reduced to a narrow range of functional shapes, still wheel-thrown and technically good but showing little trace of creativity in the decoration. Yet this reduced remnant was the direct ancestor of Protogeometric (*c.* 1000–*c.* 900 BC), the first true Greek style of vase painting (*see* §IV, 2 below).

A. J. B. Wace and C. W. Blegen: 'The Pre-Mycenaean Pottery of the Mainland', *Annu. Brit. Sch. Athens*, xxii (1916–18), pp. 175–89

A. Furumark: *Mycenaean Pottery: Analysis and Classification*, Skrifta utgivna av Svenska Institutet i Athen, xx (Stockholm, 1941/*R* 1972)

E. S. Sherratt: 'Patterns of Contact: Manufacture and Distribution of Mycenaean Pottery, 1400–1100 B.C.', *Interaction and Acculturation in the Mediterranean*, eds J. G. P. Best and N. M. W. de Vries (Amsterdam, 1980)

E. S. Sherratt: 'Regional Variation in the Pottery of Late Helladic IIIB', *Annu. Brit. Sch. Athens*, lxxv (1980), pp. 175–202

E. Vermeule and V. Karageorgis: *Mycenaean Pictorial Vase-painting* (Cambridge, MA, 1982)

R. E. Jones: *Greek and Cypriot Pottery: A Review of Scientific Studies* (Athens, 1986)

P. A. Mountjoy: *Mycenaean Decorated Pottery*, Stud. Medit. Archaeol., lxxiii (Göteborg, 1986) [contains citations of almost all significant stud. of Mycenaean pott. since Furumark]

Å. Åkerström: *Berbati, II: The Pictorial Pottery*, Skrifta utgivna av Svenska Institutet i Athen, xxxvi/2 (Stockholm, 1987)

O. T. P. K. Dickinson: 'Pottery', *The Aegean Bronze Age*, Cambridge World Archaeology (Cambridge, 1994)

K. S. Shelton: *The Late Helladic Pottery from Prosymna* (Jonsered, 1996)

M. Lindblom: *Marks and Makers: Appearance, Distribution, and Function of Middle and Late Helladic Manufacturers' Marks on Aeginetan Pottery* (Jonsered, 2001)

E. Andrikou and others: *Thèbes, fouilles de la Cadmée* [Vol 2. Les tablettes en linéaire B de la odos pelopidou. Le contexte archéologique. 2. La céramique de la odos pelopidou et la chronologie du linéaire B] (Pisa, 2006)

IV. Greek.

Ancient Greek pottery was produced in most areas around the Mediterranean and is among the most distinctive in the history of the craft. The pots were intended for a wide variety of uses—domestic, funerary, commercial and ceremonial—and range from plain kitchenware to elaborately decorated cups and bowls. Thousands of specimens, many in excellent condition, have been recovered and are now eagerly sought by museums and private collectors as well as providing study material for both the archaeologist and the art historian. The archaeologist finds pottery remains helpful in reconstructing the histories of particular sites; such information does not depend on the quality of the pottery, though decorated ware is usually more closely datable than other types. Pottery can also provide information about social behaviour, customs, economic trends and trade connections and in some cases be connected with historical events. Art historians, by contrast, are concerned primarily with the development of manufacturing techniques, the aesthetics and uses of different shapes of the fine decorated wares and especially the stylistic development and subject-matter of their painted decoration. They have also sought to identify individual painters and workshops using Morellian techniques, first applied by J. D. Beazley to the study of Attic vase painting.

1. INTRODUCTION. A continuously developing tradition of Greek pottery-making can be traced from *c.* 1000 BC to the end of the 1st century BC, by which time Rome had taken over the Greek areas of the eastern Mediterranean and was already imposing her ceramic styles and techniques on the provinces of her empire. Excluding the Sub-Mycenaean phase, during which pottery styles were essentially debased versions of their Mycenaean precursors (*see* §III, 2(iii) above), Greek pottery spanned five historical periods: Protogeometric (*c.* 1000–*c.* 900 BC), Geometric (*c.* 900–*c.* 700 BC), Archaic (*c.* 700–*c.* 480 BC), Classical (*c.* 480–323 BC) and Hellenistic (323–27 BC). The extent to which the development of the pottery styles described below follows these conventional historical divisions is, however, debatable. While Protogeometric and Geometric pottery have provided the key datings and identity for the cultural periods they have been used to define, the same cannot be said of the later periods. The development of the Orientalizing style at the beginning of the Archaic period can be associated with the establishment of trade links with the Near East, but the emergence of the important Black-figure technique in the same period seems unrelated to known historical events, as does the introduction of Red-figure and White-ground pottery at the end of the Archaic period. The Classical period was dominated by the Red-figure style, though there were also important examples of White-ground and Black-glaze

(unpainted) pottery. The Hellenistic period is characterized by the continuation of unpainted pottery and the development of several new techniques. Although the evolution of pottery styles and techniques after the Geometric period was only marginally influenced by developments in Greek cultural and political history, production in certain regions does seem to have been affected by such events as the fall of cities, foreign invasions and the creation of new settlements, which in their turn provide some evidence for dating. The chronology of Greek pottery is thus firmer for some periods than for others, and it would be unwise to consider it finally established.

By the beginning of the 1st millennium BC the Greeks had colonized not only mainland Greece but also the Aegean islands and the west coast of Asia Minor: over the following five centuries they established settlements in South Italy, Sicily, southern France, Spain, coastal north Africa and the shores of the Black Sea. All these areas either produced their own distinctive range of pots or imported from other Greek areas what they themselves lacked. Local pottery shapes and decoration were often severely practical, tending towards heavy-duty, plain and coarse wares: but in some areas both the potting and decoration were of the highest quality. The decoration might simply be linear patterns, as on Geometric wares; though figured narrative scenes gradually became dominant, and it is these which are in a sense the hallmark of Greek ceramic decoration, allowing art historians to follow the development of figure drawing from early schematized renderings to the three-dimensional effects of 5th-century BC and later vase painters. This development cannot be traced in other media, since the panel and wall paintings that undoubtedly pioneered such effects as chiaroscuro and perspective are almost entirely lost.

P. E. Arias and M. Hirmer: *Tausend Jahre griechischer Vasenkunst* (Munich, 1960); enlarged Eng. trans. by B. B. Shefton as *A History of Greek Vase Painting* (London, 1962)

R. M. Cook: *Greek Painted Pottery* (London, 1960/*R* 1972)

H. A. Shapiro: *Myth into Art: Poet and Painter in Classical Greece* (London and New York, 1994)

M. J. Vickers and D. W. J. Gill: *Artful Crafts: Ancient Greek Silverware and Pottery* (Oxford, 1994)

B. A. Sparkes: *The Red and the Black: Studies in Greek Pottery* (London and New York, 1996)

R. M. Cook: *Greek Painted Pottery* (London and New York, 1997)

R. M. Cook and P. Dupont: *East Greek Pottery* (London and New York, 1998)

T. Schreiber: *Athenian Vase Construction: A Potter's Analysis* (Malibu, 1999)

M. Vickers: *Ancient Greek Pottery* (Oxford, 1999)

C. M. Stibbe: *Laconian Oil Flasks and Other Closed Shapes* (Amsterdam, 2000)

J. Boardman: *The History of Greek Vases: Potters, Painters, and Pictures* (New York, 2001)

J. N. Coldstream, L. J. Eiring and G. Forster: *Knossos Pottery Handbook: Greek and Roman* (London, 2001)

M. Lindblom: *Marks and Makers: Appearance, Distribution, and Function of Middle and Late Helladic Manufacturers' Marks on Aeginetan Pottery* (Jonsered, 2001)

M. K. Risser: *Corinthian Conventionalizing Pottery* (Princeton, 2001)

A. J. Clark, M. Elston and M. L. Hart: *Understanding Greek Vases: A Guide to Terms, Styles, and Techniques* (Los Angeles, 2002)

S. Lewis: *The Athenian Woman: An Iconographic Handbook* (London and New York, 2002)

V. V. Stissi: *Pottery to the People: The Production, Distribution and Consumption of Decorated Pottery in the Greek World in the Archaic Period (650–480 BC)* (n.p., 2002)

S. I. Rotroff and others: *The Hellenistic Pottery from Sardis: The Finds through 1994* (Cambridge, MA, 2003)

J. Whitley: *Style and Society in Dark Age Greece: The Changing Face of a Pre-literate Society 1100–700 BC* (Cambridge, 2003)

C. Isler-Kerényi: *Civilizing Violence: Satyrs on 6th-century Greek Vases* (Fribourg, 2004)

M. B. Moore: *Greek Geometric and Protoattic Pottery* (New York, 2004)

B. Cohen and K. D. S. Lapatin: *The Colors of Clay: Special Techniques in Athenian Vases* (Los Angeles, 2006)

(i) Subject-matter. The exceptional interest in the human figure on ancient Greek, and especially Athenian, fine pottery grew gradually. The Protogeometric and earlier Geometric styles are concerned almost wholly with abstract ornamentation; animals made their first appearance in the early 8th century BC, at first singly and then in files of single species. In the 7th century BC the Orientalizing animal style dominated, where both real fauna such as the lion and fabulous beasts such as the griffin and siren are clearly borrowed from Near Eastern art, along with many floral ornaments. Corinth was the most creative, even playful, centre in depicting animals, inventing new hybrids such as the lion-siren and phallus-bird as well as new complex varieties of lotus and palmette (*see* §4(ii) below). Corinth is also important for the early development of scenes with human figures, but from *c.* 550 BC produced only pots with floral decoration or simple patterns. Similar unpretentious styles are found throughout the Greek world. Even more popular, from the later 6th century BC onwards, were the plain black wares (*see* §8 below). The finely drawn and complex figural compositions found on some Greek vases are the exception rather than the rule.

Human figural scenes first appeared at Athens around the mid-8th century BC. Many Geometric pots were intended for the grave or as grave-markers; consequently the depictions on them are frequently funerary in nature: figures in mourning around the bier, the transport of the dead to the cemetery, chariot processions at the funeral. There are also scenes of warfare by land and at sea, and at Argos, another great centre of Geometric pottery, men 'taming' horses are a popular motif. The pure silhouette style of Geometric, however, made it difficult to tell visual stories of any complexity.

Although the appearance of mythological narrative after *c.* 700 BC has often been connected with the contemporary rise of literary epic, it is more likely that artists drew for inspiration on stories told informally. There are many scenes specifically connected with the *Iliad*, far fewer of the *Odyssey*, with the exception of Odysseus' escape from Polyphemos' cave, and some of the most frequently shown Trojan scenes, such as the Ambush of Troilos, are from non-Homeric parts of the epic cycle. Of Greek heroes Herakles is by far the most popular in all periods, and his fight with the Nemean lion is the most favoured scene of all. This is the first of his labours, but some of the most numerous episodes with Herakles are not the canonical labours but other incidents in his career such as his struggle with Apollo over the Delphic tripod or his confrontation with the centaur Nessos. Among the gods all the Olympians get depicted to some degree, sometimes grouped together without narrative thrust as on Oltos' famous cup (late 6th century BC; Tarquinia, Pal. Vitelleschi, RC 6848), sometimes shown singly (Aphrodite on her goose, Dionysos standing quietly with his son Oinopion, Artemis as Mistress of Beasts), more often interacting with other gods and mortals in narrative contexts (Athena helping various heroes in their tasks, Zeus' many and varied love affairs, Apollo and Artemis shooting down the children of Niobe.

Archaic vase painters preferred vigorous, even violent, scenes that emphasize the monstrous or bizarre, such as the Birth of Athena from the head of Zeus. In the Classical period the focus of attention was more on the psychology of the situation before the climax of the action or during its aftermath. True, there are many action stories, such as the Gigantomachy, that never went out of vogue, but some narratives undergo considerable modification of treatment. On Black-figure vases the Judgement of Paris is a scene of movement as the goddesses are brought in procession to the shepherd prince, who stands or makes to run away. In the 5th century BC the atmosphere is quieter: Paris is calmly seated, the goddesses stand by. The more subtle, fluid drawing of Red-figure, and in particular the development of the profile eye in the human face, made it possible to convey dramatic interaction between even quietly posed figures, as in *Polyneikes Bribing Eriphyle with the Necklace of Harmonia* (Chicago Painter; Lecce, Mus. Prov. Sigismondo Castromediano) or *Odysseus with Elpenor's Shade* (Lykaon Painter; Boston, MA, Mus. F.A.). In Black-figure only a superlative artist such as Exekias could inject psychological power into his scenes by effectively transcending the Archaic conventions of his time.

Where a vase displays more than one scene they may be connected, especially obverses and reverses; but often they are not, in particular scenes set one above the other, although presumably at the subconscious level the juxtaposing of scenes was rarely arbitrary.

Vase painters employed various devices to make their story-telling clear to the viewer, of which the most important is the inclusion of attributes. Athena sported her spear and aegis, Zeus his sceptre and thunderbolt, Herakles his club, often in contexts in which they are not needed or where their presence is illogical, simply as a means of identification. Thus the necklace with which she has been secretly bribed may be carried as an attribute by Eriphyle in public. Another helpful device is the addition of painted inscriptions, though their use is by no means universal (*see* §(vi) below). It is presumably for clarity's sake too that artists made free play with time sequences. Whereas most scenes show only one moment of time, others imply different moments of the same story: so Polyphemos may carry the cup with which he has drunk himself into a stupor while the stake is being driven into his eye. But rarely is the same character shown more than once to create a 'continuous' narrative, the exception being a series of Red-figure cups depicting on the exterior the adventures of Theseus. It is not always an easy matter to distinguish mythological from theatrical scenes, which figure most prominently on South Italian vases (*see* §6(ii) below), for often the same narratives are common to both. The problem is greatest with representations of tragedy, where props such as masks are rarely shown, and yet in scenes of comedy and farce not only are masks and the comic padded costume with phallus usually included but even details of the stage setting. The satyrs of satyr plays are shown sometimes as actors and sometimes as real satyrs; the most revealing illustration of the former is provided by the Attic Red-figure Pronomos vase (late 5th century BC; Naples, Mus. Archeol. N.), which shows a full satyr chorus warming up, complete with elaborate costumes, masks, musical accompaniment and dance movements. This whole aspect of vase painting is important for the illustration of plays for which only the title has otherwise survived.

Scenes of everyday life are more common in the 5th century BC than the 6th, but the data offered is uneven in its scope. There are plentiful scenes of banqueting and drinking, of sexual encounters with *hetairai*, music (especially on flute and lyre), dance and other entertainments, as in *Pandora and Chorus*. The vases are also a mine of information about homosexual courtship and copulation. Sporting activities are very common, and it may be that the opportunity to study nude male athletes in the palaestra inspired vase painters to experiment with and modify their renderings of poses and anatomy so rapidly in the Late Archaic period. There are, however, few representations of hoplites in battle formation (most battles are split into individual duels in the heroic/epic manner) and of trade and industry, although pottery production—appropriately enough—is shown in some detail.

Most painters, however, showed little in the way of setting. A mirror or pot suspended in the background is enough to indicate an interior, a single stylized tree an exterior. Occasionally there is something more, as in the Priam Painter's scene of women swimming in a stretch of water fronted by large trees (*c.* 520

BC; Rome, Villa Giulia), but most of the numerous hunting sequences show no setting at all. Fuller treatment of landscape would involve more complex recession and spatial relationships that are unsuited to curving vase surfaces; the multiple hilly ground-lines favoured by some artists from the mid-5th century BC onwards are derived almost certainly from contemporary monumental painting.

In choosing a subject the vase painter took into account not only the shape of the field offered by the vase but also the function of the vessel. Many of the most popular vase shapes are connected with the drinking, serving or storage of wine; consequently Dionysos as wine-god features conspicuously, along with his entourage of satyrs and maenads. So too, on the human level, are featured symposia, drinking parties organized by the wealthy young urban males (see fig. 14), and the vases show all the stages of such an evening: the cavorting through the streets, the symposiasts drinking as they recline on their couches, the singing and dancing and party games, the effects of over-drinking and the sexual pleasures of the later evening. The only women shown participating are *hetairai* and prostitutes; other depictions of women occur on hydriai, pots specifically handled by women for carrying water. On these, scenes of fetching water from the fountain-house are often shown, as well as other female domestic activities: spinning, weaving, dealing with maidservants and children. The latter subject is also found on white lekythoi—tall flasks for oil that at Athens came to have an exclusively funerary use—where we are probably to imagine the deceased among the figures shown. But the funerary context of the painting on these is often made explicit: the tomb itself is depicted with mourners around it, or the dead person is taken by Hermes and Charon to the underworld. Where the close correspondence between shape and decoration is concerned, the Panathenaic amphora is a special case. On these prize vases it was traditional to place an armed Athena on one side and on the other a scene of the victor's sporting event.

The study of iconography is far less advanced than connoisseurship, and most studies are inevitably Athenocentric or based on South Italian Red-figure. Yet other regional schools are of considerable interest and may offer surprises. One of the most detailed versions of the Ambush of Troilos is on a Chiot chalice, while Lakonian Black-figure abounds with winged youths ('Boreads'), whose significance is obscure, and a late Black-figure workshop in Boiotia specialized in lively mythological and low-life

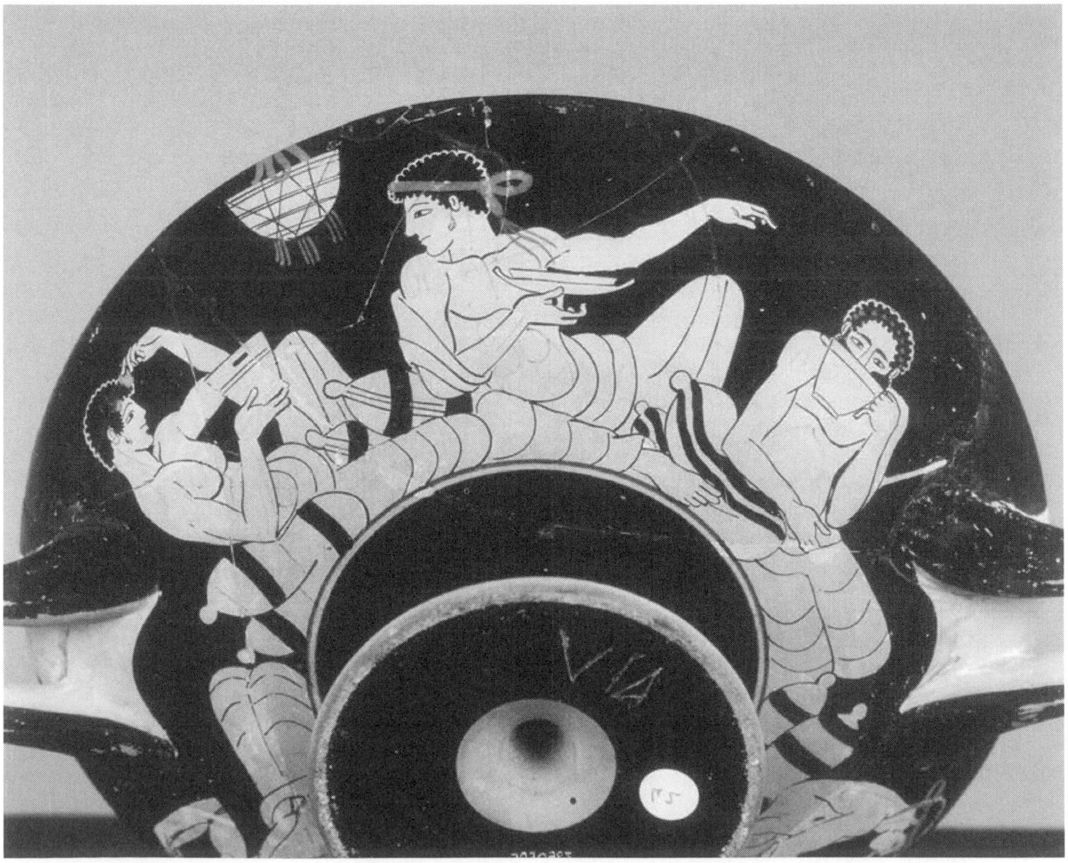

14. Ancient Greek cup depicting *Youths at a Banquet,* diam. 240 mm, Red-figure, *c.* 480 BC (Paris, Musée du Louvre)

burlesque. But wherever Greek pottery is produced it is astonishing how few scenes repeat each other precisely; there is endless variation of story and detail. The overwhelming impression is of artists working freehand, without any degree of mechanization or recourse to pattern books, and that they did so is proved by preliminary sketches on the pots themselves, together with details that have been erased. It is even true of stock scenes such as the draped youths that occur on the reverses of innumerable Red-figure kraters.

Recent studies have attempted to elucidate choice of decoration in terms of historical events, religious attitudes, political ideology and cultural values. Possible links between the images and the final destinations of the vases (tombs, sanctuaries, particular export localities) have begun to be explored. Scenes of actual historical figures and events are rare; more often—as in architectural sculpture—historical events may be alluded to in mythological terms. A case has been made out for the popularity at Athens of Herakles and later of Theseus being fostered by different political regimes, and it is likely that the introduction of new cults may explain the sudden cultivation by vase painters of particular gods. These kinds of approaches are on the increase and have much to offer, although their conclusions are hardly susceptible to proof.

K. Schefold: *Myth and Legend in Early Greek Art* (London, 1966)

T. B. L. Webster: *Potter and Patron in Classical Athens* (London, 1972)

Lexikon iconographicum mythologiae classicae (Zurich, 1981–)

W. G. Moon, ed.: *Ancient Greek Art and Iconography* (Wisconsin, 1983)

C. Bérard and others: *A City of Images* (Princeton, 1989)

T. H. Carpenter: *Art and Myth in Ancient Greece* (London, 1991)

T. Rasmussen and N. Spivey, eds: *Looking at Greek Vases* (Cambridge, 1991)

B. A. Sparkes: *Greek Pottery: An Introduction* (Manchester, 1991), chap. 5

K. Schefold: *Gods and Heroes in Late Archaic Greek Art* (Cambridge, 1992)

(ii) Shapes, uses and decoration. Almost all Greek pots were intended for specific practical uses, which in turn determined their form and decoration. The appearance of finer wares, however, was also influenced by current aesthetics or fashion. The names currently used to designate pottery shapes have developed largely through convention and are not always used consistently or with precision. Though some of the more firmly established terms have ancient Greek origins, few are used in their original sense. Some other names are those of modern forms of pots and vary from language to language; yet others are hybrid terms (e.g. neck amphora), and a few are pure inventions (e.g. bolsal, formed from *Bol*ogna and *Sal*onica, where two examples of this type of low cup occur).

Knowledge of the uses to which particular shapes were put derives from several sources. The shapes themselves often declare their function: a spout and a single handle, for example, suggest that a vase was used for pouring liquids. Figural scenes on decorated pottery often show vases in use, and some vases are labelled with their original names, though the significance of these terms is not always clear. Literary sources are surprisingly unhelpful since they are rarely specific, and it is often uncertain whether a term in modern usage had the same connotations in ancient times. They do, however, show that the Greeks often used anatomical terms such as 'body', 'foot' and 'ears' (i.e. handles) to designate parts of vases, much as is done today. Moreover, since few potters signed their vases (*see* §§(iv) and (vi) below), shapes can be useful in identifying the work of individual craftsmen; but this area remains to be researched more fully.

(a) Shapes and uses. (b) Decoration.

(a) Shapes and uses. Though they were a utilitarian product, not all pots were intended for uses that are currently familiar: for example, large Geometric amphorae served as grave markers, while Apulian kraters were produced specifically as tomb offerings. Other shapes were dedicated in sanctuaries and generally differed in size and elaboration from their more utilitarian counterparts, while others again were made in direct imitation of foreign pottery shapes (e.g. the kyathos and rhyton) or to reproduce the appearance of the non-ceramic item (metal container, basket, drinking-horn etc) they were designed to replace.

Nonetheless, the underlying emphasis on practicality of design probably helped to limit the number of shapes produced: a vase's function defined the essential features of its various components, while hygiene and durability were additional considerations. The skill of the Greek potters lay in their ability to produce vases that were clearly articulated and well-proportioned, with tight, lively contours; the relative emphasis given to practical sturdiness or elegance varied at different times and in different centres of production. Though a discussion of the shapes of Greek vases can be organized in various ways, the utilitarian emphasis noted above makes it most suitable to consider them in the context of their functions (see fig. 15). Since most research has centred on Attic pottery and, to a lesser extent, on Corinthian and South Italian, the shapes of these wares inevitably form the main basis for study.

Storage and transport vessels. One of the main functions of pottery was the bulk storage of liquids or solids. The heavy-duty pithos was the principal shape used for this purpose. Goods in transit, particularly wine, were usually carried in the transport amphora, which had a long body, small toe, narrow, offset neck and two vertical handles from shoulder to mouth. The mouth could be sealed, and the shape facilitated stacking during transit. The vase could also be handled easily by using the toe as an extra grip and could even be fixed in the ground. Smaller sizes of amphorae, with plumper bodies, wider mouths and

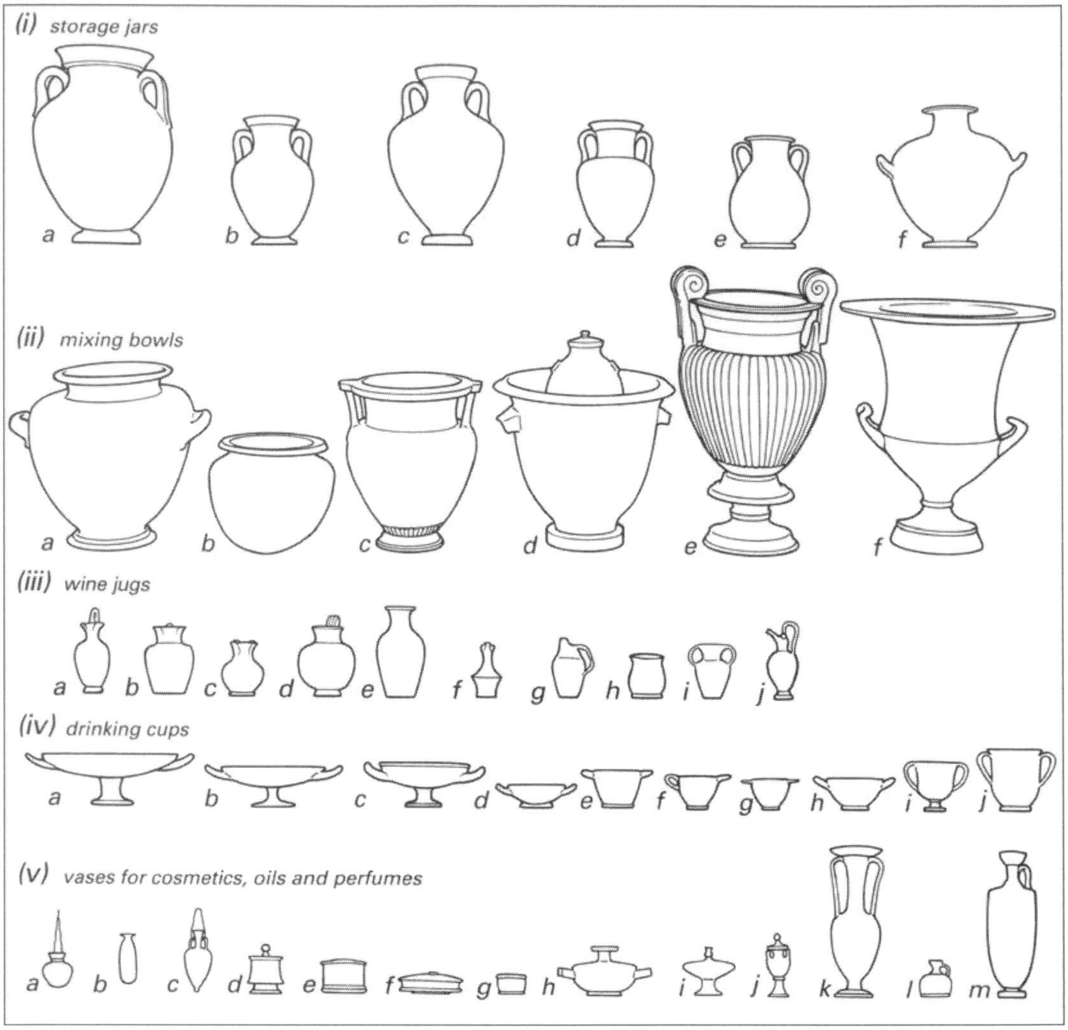

15. Ancient Greek vase shapes from Attica, 6th–4th centuries BC: (i) a–c one-piece or belly amphora, d neck amphora, e pelike, f hydria; (ii) a stamnos, b lebes, c column krater, d bell krater, e volute krater, f kalyx krater; (iii) variously shaped wine jugs (oinochoai), some with named shapes: c chous, e olpe, j lagynos; (iv) a–d kylix, e Attic skyphos, f skyphos, g Corinthian skyphos, h cup skyphos, i–j kantharos; (v) a aryballos, b alabastron, c amphoriskos, d–g pyxis, h lidded lekanis, i kothon, exaleiptron, plemochoe or smegmatotheke, j lebes gamikos, k loutrophoros, l squat lethythos, m lekythos

more stable feet, were produced in various finishes for temporary storage (19(i)a–d).

For fetching and carrying water either a hydria (15(i)f) or a kados was used. The hydria was produced in metal and in both coarse and fine clays but invariably had a capacious body, sturdy foot, wide mouth and three handles, one rising vertically from shoulder to neck for dipping, pouring and carrying when empty and two horizontal handles at the sides of the body for lifting when full. Illustrations of hydriai are common in fountain scenes on Attic Black-figure vases and in depictions of *Achilles' Ambush of Troilos*. The kados was a form of bucket used exclusively for drawing water from courtyard wells, and pottery versions were invariably of coarse clay. It had a broad body, wide mouth and plain foot, with two small vertical handles on its shoulder for attaching a rope when letting it down the well.

Among the finest examples of Greek pottery are the vessels used at aristocratic drinking parties. Since wine was mixed with water and drunk in large quantities, great mixing bowls (*see* below) were provided. The wine itself was stored in amphorae, which could double as mixing bowls and were varied in shape. The neck amphora, with a neck meeting the body at an abrupt angle (15(i)d), was popular in most areas from Protogeometric times onwards, with certain regional and chronological variations such as the Nolan amphora, named from its principal findspot in South Italy, which is small with a high neck. The one-piece or belly amphora, with a neck and body profile forming a continuous double curve (15(i)a–c), was mainly an Athenian shape of the 6th and 5th centuries BC.

It is on examples of one-piece amphorae that some of the most outstanding Attic Black- and Red-figure painting occurs. An Attic and South Italian alternative to the wine amphora was the pelike (15(i)e), which closely resembles the one-piece amphora but has its broadest diameter near the base of the body. It was particularly popular in the 4th century BC and seems also to have served as a container for perfumed oil.

Mixing Vessels. The ancient Greek word for mixing bowl (*krater*) is now used to designate a group of large pots with mouths wide enough to admit jugs and ladles (see fig. 15(ii)). The earliest are Protogeometric plain open bowls, but the four best-known forms were produced by Archaic and Classical Athenian potters. The first of these was the column krater (15(ii)c), apparently invented in Corinth and probably known in antiquity as the Corinthian krater. Its stepped foot is topped by a round body, steep neck and wide mouth, while two columnar handles stretch from the shoulder to the handle plates, which are extensions of the overhanging lip. In Attica this form attracted few first-rate artists. The volute krater, known also from bronze examples such as the 6th-century BC Vix Krater (Châtillon-sur-Seine, Mus. Archéol.) and the 4th-century BC Derveni Krater (Thessaloniki, Archaeol. Mus.), is the most elaborate of the four and was sometimes furnished with a separate stand (15(ii)e above). Its neck was usually given figure decoration, as was the body, though the latter is sometimes covered with vertical ribs. Its most distinctive feature is its pair of handles, which were formed with increasingly tightly curled volutes overhanging the lip. The most elaborate decoration occurs on Red-figure funerary examples from Apulia, which sometimes have relief clay figures and mascaroon handles. The calyx krater (15(ii)f), which first appeared in the mid-6th century BC, had quite a different profile and an even wider mouth. On top of the foot a short stem opens out to form the lower body; above this is the splaying flower-like 'calyx', the transition being marked by two horizontal handles. Like other forms of krater, this type tended to become taller and narrower, and in the 4th century BC the best pieces were plain black with relief decoration added in gilt clay. The bell krater (15(ii)d) is the latest of the four types and consists simply of a sturdy foot and a body shaped like an inverted bell. Two horizontal handles or, more rarely, lugs are set near the top of the bell, and the shape may have been based on that of a wooden tub. It was popular in Athens during the later 5th century BC and the 4th, and it tended over the years to acquire a more strongly outcurved mouth and incurved lower body. Other shapes that served the same purpose as the kraters include the stamnos (15(ii)a), with a bulbous body, high shoulder and flaring mouth. Two horizontal handles were placed just below the shoulder, occasionally with small projections at either side as though they had been woven into the vase's wall. Another mixing bowl, the lebes (15(ii)b), consisted simply of an almost spherical body with short neck and wide mouth and was often produced in metal. It had no handle or foot and was placed on a separate round stand. In the late 6th century BC a wine cooler, the psykter, began to be used at Athens. It was a mushroom-shaped pot containing cold water that floated inside a krater (shown in the bell krater, 15(ii)d). One version had a lid and pierced tubes at the sides, which vase paintings show were used for attaching cord handles.

Jugs and Cups. After mixing, wine was poured out using an oinochoe. Many shapes and sizes of oinochoai were produced, as demonstrated by the range of Attic examples (see fig. 15(iii)a–j above). The basic form is a jug with one vertical (high or low) handle and a narrow neck (15(iii)a). Its mouth is often modelled into a trefoil shape to aid pouring; but round and beak-shaped examples also occur, and some of the more elaborate versions have animal heads as necks and mouths. Body shapes also vary: some are conical, others concave, but most are convex, either with a single curve from mouth to base or with the neck offset from the body. Some variants have their own specific names: the olpe (15(iii)e) was a slender form with an uninterrupted curve, and the mug (15(iii)h) may also have been used for drinking. The chous, with a plump body and trefoil mouth (15(iii)c), figured prominently in the Anthesteria festival at Athens, when miniature versions decorated with pictures of children's games were given to the young. Similar miniatures were also placed in the graves of children too young to have received them in the normal way. A popular shape in Hellenistic times was the lagynos, with a bulbous body, low foot, tall narrow neck and tall vertical handle.

The most elegant of the many types of Greek cup (15(iv)) was the kylix (15(iv)a–d). Protogeometric examples tended to be deep with a high foot; in Geometric times they became squatter. The most exquisite forms, however, occurred in Athens in the 6th and 5th centuries BC and are designated by various names, such as komast cups, Siana cups, lip cups, band cups and eye cups, of which there are three further variants, Types A, B and C (15(iv)a–c). They consisted essentially of a wide low body with a high stem and thin footplate, and two spreading horizontal handles attached near the rim or lip. A less elegant stemless form had a ring foot attached directly to the body (15(iv)d). The skyphos, sometimes called the kotyle, is a smaller and deeper cup, with two handles attached just below the rim. Usually both of the latter are horizontal, but in one variant one of the handles is vertical (15(iv)f). The two main varieties of skyphos, called Corinthian (15(iv)g) and Attic (15(iv)e) after their places of origin, differ in the curvature of the wall and the shape of the foot, and the Corinthian type also has a thinner wall, finer rim and foot and daintier handles. There are also hybrid forms of the kylix and skyphos, such as the cup-skyphos (15(iv)h). A special form of cup, the kantharos, was closely associated with Dionysos; it consisted essentially of a deep bowl with two vertical handles. Some extravagant versions have a tall stem and high handles curving in a wide arc from the base of the body to the rim, but others have low handles and stem (15(iv)i), and yet others low handles and no stem (15(iv)j). The shape was popular at Athens and in Boiotia. The kotyle krater was a deep, two-handled cup on a high, flaring pedestal, while a kotyle pyxis was a deep, two-handled cup with a lid.

Less important varieties of drinking cup are the phiale, which was generally used in libation ceremonies; the different forms of rhyta, shaped as horns or animal heads; the sturdy one-handler; the delicate bolsal; and the breast-shaped mastos. In addition there are also various mugs moulded into the shape of human and animal heads. In Hellenistic times mould-made hemispherical bowls with relief patterns and figures, once called 'Megarian' bowls, replaced all other shapes in popularity.

Vases for cosmetics, oils and perfumes. Oil and perfume were stored in containers of various sizes (see fig. 15(v) above), the smallest of which had very narrow openings so that they could be sealed with a tiny stopper and used to pour out droplets or thin streams. The alabastron (15(v)b) was based on Oriental alabaster prototypes and developed in Corinth in the 7th century BC for use by women; it remained popular until the 4th century BC in South Italy and Sicily. It was a long, slender flask, usually with a round bottom and sometimes with two small lugs high up on the body. Though its top was flat and wide, its opening was only large enough for a dip-stick used to perfume the hair and body. A less widespread shape was the amphoriskos (15(v)c), a miniature version of the pointed amphora with a small toe, an egg-shaped body and two vertical handles running from shoulder to neck. Few examples have figural decoration, most being black with impressed or incised patterns. A larger container for perfume, or perhaps for perfumed water, is variously referred to as a kothon, exaleiptron, plemochoe or smegmatotheke (15(v)i). This is a stemmed and lidded bowl with a deep, downcurved mouth designed to prevent its contents from spilling. The small lydion may have been used as a container for the Lydian perfume *bakkaris*. The heavy, bulbous body, small foot and thick rim of the Lydian original were, however, frequently refined by Greek craftsmen. In the absence of soap, men used olive oil to cleanse themselves after exercise, carrying it with them in a small flask, the aryballos (15(v) a). It was usually ovoid or round and fitted easily into the palm of the hand. A cord attached to one or two small vertical handles was fastened around the wrist. Again, though its top is flat, the actual opening is narrow. The lekythos was a more important type of oil container. It usually had a small vertical handle from shoulder to neck, a narrow neck and wide mouth above a broader body. Early examples are ovoid, but later ones were increasingly elongated, culminating in the large cylindrical White-ground lekythoi used for funerary purposes in 5th-century BC Athens (15(v)m). A variant represented by both Black- and Red-figure specimens is the squat lekythos (15(v)l). Some aryballoi and lekythoi, mainly from Corinth, Athens and Greek Asia Minor, take the form of human or animal figures, human heads or other anatomical features such as feet, while others simply have mouths in the shape of human or animal heads. Small lekythoi, particularly from Attica, can also take the shape of such objects as acorns and cockleshells; larger examples sometimes bear relief figures or scenes or are treated as statuettes, for example of sphinxes or Erotes.

Vase paintings show that the large pelike, in addition to being used for wine, was employed for pouring oil into lekythoi and alabastra, while the Black-figure Attic amphorae presented to victors in the Panathenaic Games each contained a prize of almost 40 litres of oil. Since these had to be transported they had the same general shape as transport amphorae, with narrow, easily sealed mouths and small feet, rather than adhering to the conventional forms for other painted examples. Miniature Red-figure versions substituting for lekythoi were also produced as souvenirs.

Vases associated with women. The marriage gifts received by Greek women may traditionally have included a pyxis (see fig. 15(v)d–g), a round, lidded box without handles used to store cosmetics, trinkets and powder. Depending on date and place of manufacture, the precise form of pyxides varied. Attic Red-figure examples are small and often bear dainty scenes of weddings and home-life. A similar but larger shape is the lidded lekanis (15(v)h) with handles, usually ribbon-shaped. Such vases were also given as wedding presents, and Red-figure specimens bear similar scenes to those on pyxides and probably also contained trinkets or heirlooms. Both shapes occur among vases found as grave goods, and large Geometric pyxides may have been produced specifically for funerary use.

Two other shapes particularly associated with Athenian women were the loutrophoros and the lebes gamikos. The loutrophoros (15(v)k) is basically a thin neck amphora with an exaggeratedly elongated neck; some examples have two side handles and one long vertical handle in the manner of hydriai. Loutrophoroi were used to carry water for the bridal bath but were also buried with those who died unmarried, and the scenes painted on them reflect these two functions. Indeed, a few show battle scenes and presumably constituted funeral offerings for men who had died fighting. Those made specially for the grave often had no floor, perhaps to enable libations to enter the ground. In Apulian Red-figure examples the elaboration of the shape became extreme, with ribbed upper and lower bodies, concave sides, tendril-shaped handles and separate stands. The lebes gamikos (15(v)j) has a bulbous body, short neck, pointed lid and horizontal hooplike handles on its shoulders. It occurs in two forms, one with an attached stand, the other with a low foot. These vases carry wedding and domestic scenes and probably held the heated water for the bride's bath; they were also deposited in graves.

(b) Decoration. The production of high-quality Greek pottery involved maintaining a fine balance between shape and decoration. Floral and geometric designs, which continued to be used throughout

the history of Greek pottery, were relatively easily accommodated to the various parts of the vases they adorned. By contrast, figural scenes, which began to be used to decorate pots towards the end of the Geometric period, posed greater challenges to the potter. Nonetheless, from their introduction in the 8th century BC until the later 5th century BC their disposition was also largely determined by a vase's form. However, when the influence of wall paintings led to a striving for three-dimensional effects and the abandonment of a single ground-line, figural scenes no longer reflected the physical shapes of their vases so precisely.

There were essentially three decorative fields available to the vase painter. One was the long horizontal band on the outside of cups and kraters, which suited figural friezes or repetitive floral patterns. Another was the large, squarish 'metope' shape provided, for example, by the body of an amphora and best suited to depictions of large single figures or small groups of large figures. The third was the circular tondo inside a cup or on the surface of a plate, which was treated differently in different regions. Lakonian Black-figure painters ignored the circular surround and treated the area as a 'porthole' for viewing a conventional, square-framed scene. By contrast, Attic cup painters fitted their compositions carefully into the circular field, producing designs of great subtlety. The most accomplished painters, however, invariably used their pictures to enhance the shapes that they were decorating, leaving their contours unbroken and adapting their compositions to the space available (e.g. a cup-skyphos by Epiktetos; late 6th century BC). Indeed, when a vase was both made and painted by the same artist its shape and decoration may have been conceived as a unity from the outset.

It is often unclear why particular subjects from the wide repertory were associated with certain vase shapes. Some are clearly related to a shape's function. This is perhaps especially evident on funerary wares. Paintings on Geometric funerary vases usually depict the deceased lying in state or being taken away for burial, or allude to the circumstances of death with battle scenes. Similarly, 5th-century BC Attic White-ground lekythoi bear graveside scenes and depictions of such mythological characters associated with the dead as Hermes, Charon, Hypnos and Thanatos, as well as pictures of soldiers departing and quiet domestic activities designed to evoke a sense of pathos. The relevance of scenes on certain other classes of pots is also readily apparent. Examples include the representations of weddings and home-life, both real and mythological, on pyxides and lebetes gamikoi; scenes of drinking, singing and lovemaking on cups and wine containers; the depictions of women at the fountain so frequent on hydriai; and the children's games shown on choes. More specific still are the scenes on the reverse sides of Panathenaic amphorae depicting the particular athletic event for which the vase was to serve as prize, though these are a special case. Finally, some fish plates have depictions of seafood arranged around a central dip for sauce.

Painted designs or figural scenes were not the only form of pottery decoration: incised decoration is found from Geometric times (*see* §3(iv) below), while plain Black-glaze ware (*see* §8(i) below) probably constituted the most popular pottery type in Classical and Hellenistic times, partly because the glaze could make the pot look like patinated silver. These pots were decorated with vertical or horizontal ribbing, by incised or stamped patterns and by the addition of moulded reliefs representing persons, animals or plants or imitating the rivets seen on silverware. Moulded reliefs of heads or figurines were also a frequent aspect of Hellenistic pottery (*see* §9 below), either appliqued to wheelmade wares or moulded integrally with the vessel, while on painted vases three-dimensional pictures or designs were created by the application of a thick clay, which was subsequently gilded or painted, to the glazed surface.

G. M. A. Richter and M. J. Milne: *Shapes and Names of Athenian Vases* (New York, 1935)
W. Schiering: *Griechische Tongefässe: Gestalt, Bestimmung und Formenwandel* (Berlin, 1967, rev. 2/1983)
M. G. Kanowski: *Containers of Classical Greece: A Handbook of Shapes* (St Lucia, Queensland, 1984)
B. A. Sparkes: *Greek Pottery: An Introduction* (Manchester, 1991)
M. Vickers and D. W. J. Gill: *Artful Crafts* (Oxford, 1994)
T. Schreiber: *Athenian Vase Construction* (Malibu, 1999)
J. Boardman: *The History of Greek Vases: Potters, Painters, and Pictures* (New York, 2001)
G. Bishop: *Classification of Greek Pottery Shapes and Schools Using Image Retrieval Techniques* (diss., New York, Pace U., 2006)

(iii) Materials and techniques. The labours involved in the production of ancient Greek pottery included digging and purifying the clay, wedging it, throwing the vase on the potter's wheel, joining separately made sections, turning and finishing, decorating and firing. Fine wares were made from well-settled clays and generally turned on a fast wheel to ensure crispness of profile. Coarse wares used for cooking and other domestic purposes were made from fire-resistant clay and shaped on an anvil with a beater, possibly a stone, while heavy-duty storage vases such as pithoi were usually built up by hand: some other heavy-duty shapes such as mortars were made in moulds. In the smallest potteries a single potter and his wheel-turning apprentice probably performed all these tasks, but an average Athenian pottery employed four to six workers and the largest perhaps a dozen, permitting much greater specialization. In particular, though a potter sometimes decorated his own vases, the vase painter was usually a separate artist.

(a) Clay. (b) Forming the vase. (c) Decorative techniques. (d) Firing

(a) Clay. Fine pottery requires a large amount of fine clay, and Greece and its neighbouring Mediterranean regions had abundant deposits of good-quality secondary clay, which fired to an attractive reddish-orange

colour due to its contamination by iron oxide. The clay that occurred around Corinth was purer and fired to a light creamy colour, but pure primary white clay was rare and was used sparingly as an accessory colour or on White-ground vases as a coating applied in a thin, uniform layer as the vase rotated on the potter's wheel.

Before use the clay was purified through a process of sedimentation. This was particularly important, because the presence of such impurities as quartz or limestone might cause spalling or cracking during firing. This rarely happened in Attic pottery; in South Italian pottery, however, many spalls were caused by limestone pebbles. After sedimentation the purified clay was matured to improve its cohesion and finally wedged to make it suitable for working.

(b) Forming the vase. The earliest forming technique for pottery, practised in prehistoric times, was by pinching and shaping a lump of clay. This process eventually led to the development of the coil method, in which strands of clay were rolled out and coiled around a flat base disc of clay. They were pinched and smoothed to form a good joint, and additional strands were added to achieve the desired height and shape. This process could produce remarkably fine pottery with walls of uniform thickness, and even after the introduction of the potter's wheel the coil method continued to be used for the construction of extremely large plain ware such as storage jars and unglazed utilitarian pottery.

Wheelmade pottery dating to *c.* 2500 BC has been found at Troy, and the use of the potter's wheel subsequently spread throughout the Greek world. Most Classical Greek pottery was formed on the wheel, although some pieces were mould-made and a few decorative elements were hand-formed and then added to wheelmade vases. The Greek potter's wheel was a sturdy disc of wood, terracotta or stone about 600 mm in diameter, with a socket underneath that fitted over a low fixed pivot. The wheel was carefully balanced to run true without wobble or vibration. An apprentice boy turned it by hand and adjusted the speed at the command of the potter. Once in motion its size and weight provided ample momentum to keep it running freely, and the potter was able to use both hands to form the vase and to give it his undivided attention. The vase shapes were based on the cylindrical or spherical forms most naturally produced on the wheel and were formed freehand using only a pair of dividers and a ruler as guides. There is no evidence that a template was used either to form the vases or even to check their measurements.

By these simple means the Greek potter achieved an elegant balance between utilitarianism and beauty. The emphasis was on perfecting existing designs and forms rather than exploring the development of radically new shapes. This repetition of form could have encouraged mass production without artistic development; it was, however, the striving for perfection within a limited framework of shapes that caused Greek pottery to develop in such a splendid manner. The proportions of the vases are harmonious: the size of the mouth relates to the size of the neck, the neck to the body and the entire vase to its foot. Handles, which were modelled separately and added before firing, do not appear as mere appendages but as organic parts of the whole composition; for structural reasons they widen at the point where they join the vase, and this requirement for strength causes them to emerge gracefully. In some vases the contour is a single, unbroken curve; most, however, have their sections clearly articulated, and their beauty is based on the harmonious relationship between the various areas of the vase. This articulation enabled the potter to contrast a straight line with a strongly curved one and a swelling form with an incurving plane.

The production of wheelmade pottery required a high degree of manual dexterity and a continual application of artistic judgement. The shape of the vase had to evolve gradually; too slowly, however, and the damp clay slumped and the vase collapsed. A simple bowl or plate could therefore be formed in a single operation, but vases taller than about 300 mm were composed of several sections thrown separately on the wheel, left to dry a little, then joined together with wet clay slip. The joints were carefully smoothed and usually located at points where they could be concealed, such as the points of articulation between foot and body, body and neck, neck and mouth. In the case of some exceptionally large vases the bodies themselves had to be thrown in several sections, their joints being located on a continuous curved area where they were not hidden by articulation. They were turned and smoothed so skilfully that the joints are still invisible on the outside of the vase, though on the inside they can often be detected in the occasional crack or variation in thickness. Vases as tall as 1.5 m required four or five sections to be joined in this way.

Two techniques, though widely used in other parts of the world, were only occasionally employed by the Greeks: one was the freehand modelling of ornamental elements such as the snakes on certain ritual or funerary vases; the other was the cutting or carving of a vase before firing to create patterns, for example the Black-glaze Attic ware (*see* §5(II) below) carved with flutes or ribs in imitation of metal vessels. A small quantity of Greek pottery, for instance the so-called 'plastic' vases, usually in the form of animals' heads, and a series of Hellenistic bowls (*see* §9 below), was produced using moulds. The first stage in this process involved the creation by a sculptor of a clay master model of the vase, which was then fired and used to form a two-part clay mould designed to separate on a line where there was no undercutting. After being dried and retouched the mould itself was fired. To form the pot a layer of soft clay was pressed into each section of the mould, its edges scored and coated with a clay slip, and the mould sections were bound together: within a few hours the new clay had dried and shrunk sufficiently for the mould to be removed. Most mould-made vases had separate mouths, and sometimes feet, that were made on the wheel and added prior to decoration and firing, using wet clay slip as an adhesive. The fingerprints of the potter can often be seen on the inside of such mould-made vases.

(c) Decorative techniques. A major feature of Greek pottery is the use of a black 'glaze' with a pronounced metallic lustre, quite different from conventional ceramic glazes in use today. Indeed, the substance was not a mixture of silica and mineral pigments but a fine solution of the same reddish clay that was used for the main body of the vase, with no additional colouring agents. The contrast between the black glazed and red unglazed areas was only achieved by means of a complex and ingenious method of firing, based on the fact that iron oxide present in the clay is red in colour if fired in an oxidizing atmosphere and black if fired in a reducing atmosphere (*see* §(D) below). The process was probably discovered by accident in the Bronze Age, when an observant potter noticed that a coating of purified clay over a coarse-bodied vase was susceptible to partial fusing or sintering and locking in streaks of black on a red background.

Only clays that possessed very small particles and platelets were suitable to produce the black glaze matter. The separation of these particles from the coarser materials in the clay was accomplished by sedimentation. A solution of clay and water mixed with potash to prevent flocculation was allowed to stand for 48 hours until it separated into three areas. The sediment of sand and coarse particles at the bottom was discarded; the middle zone of clay slip was used for the body of the vase; at the top the colloidal suspension of very fine particles was carefully removed and thickened by evaporation to form a brownish liquid slightly darker than the clay itself. When this was applied to the vase and allowed to dry before firing, it already had a slight metallic sheen caused by the horizontal alignment of the platelets; this could be enhanced by burnishing the surface with a smooth pebble or piece of bone and polishing it with a cloth. However, it was only after firing that the glaze became black. The greater sheen of Attic black glaze helps to distinguish Attic vases from those of South Italy and perhaps reflects minor differences in the quality of the clay.

Black-glaze achieved particular prominence after the introduction of the Black-figure technique, when it was used to produce silhouette figures: when the glaze had dried, anatomical and other details were incised using a sharp point, revealing the red clay underneath. In the later and more realistic Red-figure technique, figures were drawn in outline and then left red, while the entire background was covered over with black glaze. Minor details and occasionally shading were painted in with a dilute black glaze solution that remained brown even after firing. However, outlines and more significant details were executed in relief lines of extremely concentrated black glaze, which projected appreciably from the vase's surface. These cannot have been painted with brushes in the usual way and must have been applied with a syringe, probably a tapered nozzle of bone or bronze pierced with a fine hole and attached to a piece of animal intestine filled with the glaze: this is most apparent where blobs were used to denote grapes or curly hair. The two paint pots shown in certain depictions of vase painters (e.g. Milan, Torno Col.) probably contained glazes of different consistencies. The blacking in of the background was usually done by apprentices, who sometimes carelessly painted over parts of figures and decorative borders. On some pots with entirely black grounds, pale lines formed by unglazed areas of the underlying clay were used to emphasize or clarify certain elements such as a black-glazed head of hair or to articulate the concentric panelwork on Geometric vases. This technique is called reservation.

During Classical and Hellenistic times many vases were coated entirely in a plain black glaze similar to that used on figured pots, and decorated with incised, stamped, moulded or impressed patterns, figures or scenes (*see* §8 below). Stamped or impressed designs were made with terracotta punches while the clay was still quite soft. As the vase rotated on the potter's wheel a vibrating tool was held against it, producing a series of uniform dots. Occasionally mould-made appliqué ornaments were also added: these were applied to the unfired vase while they were still moist, using clay slip as a binder, and when dry were covered with black glaze along with the rest of the vessel. From the 3rd to the 1st century BC floral patterns and other ornament such as decorative series of dots were produced in relief using a white or red clay slip, as on Attic West Slope ware (*see* §9 below).

The reddish clay of Black- and Red-figure vases was usually covered with a burnished coat of thin yellow ochre wash before the black glaze was applied, thereby accentuating the contrast, while both Red- and Black-figure artists also made sparing use of accessory colours. Added white was made from a pure white primary clay and used for details of clothing, architectural elements and statues; added red was made from red ochre and used for details of clothing or to depict blood. Both pigments were rather friable and have often flaked off, though their original presence on areas of black glaze is indicated by dull matt patches. For another important class of pottery known as White-ground (*see* §7 below) the part of the pot's surface to be painted on was given a preliminary coating of liquid clay containing kaolinite: Black- or Red-figure or in later times polychromatic scenes or decoration were then painted on to this prepared surface.

The method of decoration known as Six's Technique, used by some Black-figure artists on small vases, involved painting figures in added white or red on top of a black-glaze ground and incising details so that the black glaze showed through. The effect is similar to Red-figure, though less refined.

Small objects on later Red-figure vases were sometimes executed in relief lines made from a plain clay slip and covered with thin gold leaf. The gold was glued with egg white, pressed into shape with a brush and burnished with a small pointed instrument: it could be applied before the vase was fired because the melting-point of gold was well above the firing temperature. The restrained colour scheme on Greek vases was not by choice; these were the only colours available that would withstand firing. A wider palette of colours, such as pink, blue and green, made from vegetable and mineral pigments, was occasionally employed. However, these were too fragile to withstand high temperatures or daily use and so were painted on after firing and confined to funerary vases, notably Attic White-ground lekythoi and the elaborate Hellenistic pottery from Canosa in South Italy.

Before they began work on a vase, painters may well have made trial sketches, at least of their most complex compositions, though none has survived. Some were possibly based on sculptural groups or wall paintings. However, the vases' curved surfaces limited the usefulness of conventional drawings, and sketching must have been done directly on to the vases themselves with a stick of lead or charcoal. The resultant lines generally burnt away during the firing process, but when a vase was not as dry as it should have been, the stick left slight indentations, which have been preserved. Figures were usually first sketched nude to render their movement correctly, and the clothing added later. If a Red-figure artist made a mistake while executing the actual vase painting, he could easily erase it with a moist sponge. Such corrections have sometimes left telltale brown smudges, while slightly roughened patches show where dry glaze was removed by scraping. Although some scenes on different vases show a close similarity, they were always drawn freehand and never duplicated by tracing.

(d) Firing. Ancient Greek pottery was fired only once, partly to economize on fuel but principally because the black glaze so frequently used adhered better to an unfired surface. For decorated vases this single firing was accomplished in three phases. The first was an oxidizing phase during which the temperature reached about 900°C and air was allowed to enter the kiln freely, so that both the clay of the pot itself and the black glaze turned red. The second was a reducing phase during which the potter covered the air vent at the top of the kiln, threw in large quantities of green wood, leaves or dung and closed the stoking door. Because the kiln was deprived of oxygen from the outside, combustion was incomplete and a reducing process began, releasing carbon monoxide, which united with the oxygen in the clay and the glaze, turning both into black ferrous oxide. During this phase the temperature reached about 950°C, but before the start of the third phase it was allowed to decline to about 875°C. This final phase was a reoxidizing one, during which the potter opened both the air vent at the top of the kiln and the kiln door to allow oxygen free access. The oxygen readily entered the porous clay and turned its black ferrous oxide back into its red ferric form. However, because the glaze had sintered, its black ferrous oxide was sealed off from contact with the oxygen, and at this temperature it remained black. The kiln was allowed to cool down slowly, and the following day, when the vases were removed, they displayed their characteristic red and black colour combination. The dramatic transformation is illustrated by modern plaques painted in Black- and Red-figure techniques and shown before and after firing.

In Athens in the 6th and 5th centuries BC a special red glaze was sometimes produced to be used in conjunction with the standard black glaze. It was achieved by creating a black-glaze mixture with such a high sintering-point that at the customary firing temperature it reoxidized and turned red during the final phase, while preserving the shiny surface quality of the glaze. At the same time, adjoining areas in the conventional black glaze with a lower sintering-point turned black. However, the process was very hard to control and was soon abandoned.

Funerary vases that were to be decorated only with delicate pigments were fired in a single oxidizing phase before painting but after receiving their white slip. This provided the artist with an excellent white background for painting.

The entire firing cycle probably lasted six to eight hours, though it must have taken at least a further twelve hours for the kiln to cool down to the point at which the fired pottery could be removed safely. The potter judged the temperature of the various phases by looking through a spy-hole and monitoring changes in the colour of the fire or by withdrawing small test-pieces. These were unfired plaques or fragments of vases coated with black glaze and equipped with holes so that they could be hooked out through the spy-hole using a wire or stick. They would indicate when the pottery had been correctly fired and had achieved a satisfactory black glaze.

Much ancient pottery was fired in the open by piling fuel under and around the vases to be fired. Greek pottery, however, had to be fired in a kiln in order to control the atmosphere for oxidation and reduction. Most of the essential features of an operating kiln are shown on a fragment of a Corinthian Black-figure pinax (Berlin, Antikensamml.), which has been restored on the basis of similar ancient depictions. As a rule, the kiln was a domed structure about 1.8–2.4 m in diameter, fronted by a short stoking tunnel with a removable door. The lowest level was occupied by the firing chamber, separated from the main kiln chamber above by a perforated clay floor. The chamber was filled with pottery through a loading door incorporating the spy-hole (not illustrated) and surmounted by the small chimney or vent that was closed during the reducing phase of firing. In the painting two perforated test-pieces are shown near the chimney, and the boat-shaped vessel beneath the kiln chamber perhaps contained water to provide extra moisture during the reducing phase. The unfired vases themselves had to be thoroughly dry, as otherwise the steam released from their clay would have burst them. In the painting they are spaced out to display their shapes, but in practice they would have been tightly stacked to economize on fuel. Small bowls could even be nested inside larger ones, since the black glaze would not fuse to the glaze of other vases. Lidded pots were almost certainly dried and fired at the same time as their lids to ensure that they shrank by the same amount, while a temper of sand, crushed stone or terracotta was added to the clay of large storage jars to stiffen them during forming, so that they did not slump under their own weight, and to minimize shrinkage during drying and firing. The firing of elaborate monumental funerary vases required a large kiln doorway, which was presumably bricked up and sealed with wet clay. If the vase had a large mouth, it was fired upside down for greater stability or else propped up with fired terracotta struts. Perhaps also the kiln was not so tightly packed, allowing the heat to circulate freely around the huge vessel; and the libation openings in the feet of many funerary vases must also have helped ensure even firing. Because their size made them more prone to damage while being manoeuvred into and out of the kiln, some large South Italian pots had separately fired feet and decorative attachments, such as masks and figurines, which were glued on with a casein adhesive made from milk or with pine pitch or asphalt. The adhesives and the unfired colours made such vases impractical for daily use, but these gaudy assemblages were highly prized as offerings for the dead (*see* §(c) above).

Many mishaps could occur during firing. A stack of vases could topple and be broken. One part of the kiln might be at a higher or lower temperature than it should have been due to a draught, and this would result in red streaks and blemishes in the black glaze. Various Black-glaze batches had slightly different correct firing temperatures, and this could produce a dull black glaze rather than the metallic gloss of the best Greek pottery. Despite these pitfalls, the ancient potters normally achieved excellent results by controlling the firing temperatures.

Vases placed on funeral pyres as offerings were usually broken by the unequal expansion caused by rapid and uneven heating. Such fragments can be identified because they tend to have irregular wavy edges rather than the straight edges caused by normal impact breakage. They would be badly discoloured by carbon smudging from the smoke, and the iron in the clay body would have been reduced by the lack of oxygen, which also caused a change in colour, often to grey. Unless there has been permanent warpage or destruction of the glaze, it is possible to eliminate the disfiguring appearance of these fragments by reversing the chemical process through refiring. It is important for uniformity that all surviving fragments of the vase be refired at the same time, including those that do not show any discolouration. It is also possible to correct blemishes suffered at the time of production by using the three-stage firing process exactly as if the pieces had never been fired previously. Both under- and overfired vases can be restored to the original appearance of the black glaze as intended by the ancient vase painter.

G. M. A. Richter: *The Craft of Athenian Pottery* (New Haven, 1923)
C. F. Binns and A. D. Fraser: 'The Genesis of the Greek Black Glaze', *Amer. J. Archaeol.*, xxxiii (1929), pp. 1–9
T. Schumann: 'Oberflächenverzierung in der antiken Töpferkunst: Terra sigillata und griechische Schwarzrotmalerei', *Ber. Dt. Ker. Ges.*, xxiii (1942), pp. 408–26
J. D. Beazley: 'Potter and Painter in Ancient Athens', *Proc. Brit. Acad.*, xxx (1946), pp. 87–125
M. Farnsworth: 'Draw Pieces as Aids to Correct Firing', *Amer. J. Archaeol.*, lxiv (1960), pp. 72–5
J. V. Noble: *The Techniques of Painted Attic Pottery* (New York, 1965, rev. London, 1988)
H. A. G. Brijder, ed.: *Ancient Greek and Related Pottery: Proceedings of the International Vase Symposium: Amsterdam, 1984*
J. Boardman: *Early Greek Vase Painting* (London, 1998)
T. Schreiber: *Athenian Vase Construction, a Potter's Analysis* (Malibu, 1999)
A. J. Clark, M. Elston and M. L. Hart: *Understanding Greek Vases: A Guide to Terms, Styles, and Techniques* (Los Angeles, 2002)
B. Cohen and K. D. S. Lapatin: *The Colors of Clay: Special Techniques in Athenian Vases* (Los Angeles, 2006)

(iv) Potters, painters and society. The social position of pottery workers in any Greek city was complex and is now largely unclear, since the effects of various factors are hard to assess, and the available evidence is often meagre. While a little is known about some aspects of pottery production in Classical Athens (*c.* 500–300 BC), and there are occasional insights into conditions at other places and during other periods, conclusions are frequently hypothetical. Most artisans seem likely to have been free men, working to order or developing their own styles and iconography; but the statutory distinction between slave and free man had only developed in the years between *c.* 600 and *c.* 450 BC, as had the use of official coinage for everyday transactions. Contemporary or later literary documentation, even of Classical Athenian pottery production, is scant; the contrast with numerous references to work in other media during the same period probably indicates the low status of painted pottery.

Evidence for the social status of pottery workers is ambiguous and largely confined to Athens. Outside Attica, a few potters and painters signed their vases between *c.* 700 and 580 BC, after which the practice began at Athens and ceased elsewhere, except for Boiotia. However, the signatures rarely give any indication of social status. Many appear to be slave names (e.g. Lydos 'the Lydian', or Thrax 'the Thracian'), and there is clear evidence in other areas of production of slaves working for citizen or resident alien shop-owners. One signature of *Lydos* has the added phrase *being a slave*, but the piece is too late to have been made by the famous Lydos, and the words could be jocular. The potter and painter Syriskos, the 'little Syrian', perhaps acquired the sobriquet Pistoxenos, 'trusty stranger', after displaying his loyalty to Athens during the Persian Wars (490 and 480–479 BC). Scenes of potters' shops on vases certainly appear to depict both slaves and free men, while two vases, one Boiotian and one Attic, show a woman at work, though female participation is not otherwise documented. That pottery production could be a family tradition is clear from a few signed Athenian vases on which the potter or painter mentions a father known from earlier signatures: TLESON, for example, succeeded his father NEARCHOS.

Evidence for the economics of the pottery industry is again confined largely to Athens. Overhead costs are uncertain. Smaller neighbouring potteries probably shared kilns that would have been used to fire all kinds of terracotta objects, including figurines and tiles as well as the plain or Black-glaze pots that must have been the staple of production even in 5th-century BC Athens. No information has come to light concerning the cost of clay and other materials, notably fuel. Inscriptions under the feet of 5th-century BC Attic vases record some 50 prices, probably wholesale. They range from 1/20 obol for a small Black-glaze handleless bowl to 3 drachmas (18 obols) for a large Red-figure hydria with two rows of figures. The pricing is not entirely consistent, but there are no wild fluctuations during the century, throughout which a drachma represented a good day's wage. Two pairs of nearly identical vases indicate the relative price for Black-glaze and Red-figure wares, with a mark-up of 33% in one case and 100% in the second. This, however, is insufficient to build up a true picture of relative profits or of the additional labour required to produce a figured piece. Such prices as we know are those likely to have been paid by the 'shipper' at Athens. There is extremely little evidence for prices asked at the end of the many routes that Attic vases travelled, and so for merchants' profits.

Scale of production must be judged by a measure that converts the amount of preserved material into a percentage of the original total. The most plausible figure may come from counting preserved, if often fragmentary, prize Panathenaic amphorae and comparing them with the known production run. In the first half of the 4th century BC at least 1450 were awarded every four years at the greater Panathenaia. This would yield a preservation rate of about 0.25%, but the result depends on two major assumptions: that all the amphorae were decorated and that the same number was awarded in earlier centuries. The first assumption is plausible, but the second is debatable. Another method of estimating production figures is to consider the debris from three potters' shops unearthed in Athens. The painters involved are in two cases known only from a few other works. If a 1% survival rate were hypothesized, the formula would mean that the debris from perhaps one firing would constitute up to a quarter of the painter's life-time output—an unlikely result. Here too 0.25% seems more reasonable.

Potters are rarely mentioned in contemporary documents. Inscriptions show that two 4th-century BC Athenian potters, Kittos and Bakchios, emigrated to Ephesos and received honours there, while earlier references occur on inscribed stone bases in the debris from the Persian sack of the Athenian Acropolis (480 BC). Thus a base for a large sculpted kore (Athens, Acropolis Mus., 681) apparently refers to its dedicator Nearchos as *kerameus* (Gr.: 'potter'), though the word is largely restored. The word certainly does accompany the names of Euphronios, Peikon, Mnesiades and Andokides, who dedicated smaller marble or bronze offerings, implying that potters enjoyed a modicum of wealth.

Indeed, the larger Athenian potteries were probably run by men of substance, whose names may be preserved in the most frequently occurring signatures. However, wealth need not imply high social status. True, a figure in a (frequently aristocratic) symposium scene on a stamnos by Smikros (*c.* 515–*c.* 510 BC; Brussels, Musées Royaux A. & Hist., A 717) is labelled with the artist's own name; but this may have been wishful thinking, and those making and painting pots would normally have been classed as artisans or tradesmen.

In addition to Kittos and Bakchios, other pottery workers are known to have travelled abroad. While many were surely small-scale operators, some may have run more substantial establishments. An East Greek painter was active in Etruria *c.* 600 BC, while *c.* 525 BC the Athenian Teisias signed Boiotian pots, and *c.* 400 BC the Athenian Suessula Painter decorated some Corinthian Red-Figure before returning to Athens. Potters accompanied Greek colonists in the 8th and 7th centuries BC, while South Italian Red-figure production was started *c.* 430 BC, probably at Herakleia, by artists from the Attic workshop of POLYGNOTOS.

It is difficult to untangle the relationships between pottery producers and their clients and to distinguish between commissioned and uncommissioned works, despite the frequent implicit assumption that producers enjoyed 'artistic freedom'. Whether the greatest vase paintings were specially commissioned is disputed. Webster argued that vases with *kalos* inscriptions must have been made specifically for an admirer of that person to use in a symposium, and that many other pieces were commissioned. However, *kalos* names appear on several vases set aside for traders, and while such names do appear on some 'masterpieces', these may not be unique works, since some have duplicates or near duplicates; for example, there are fragments of a piece close to the Chigi Vase (Rome, Villa Giulia), of a krater similar to the François Vase (Florence, Mus. Archeol.) and of doublets by the painter EXEKIAS.

In addition, although special types of pottery were used in a variety of cultic rites throughout Greece, not all scenes of cult on vases appear to have been commissioned. Thus Attic White-ground funerary lekythoi often depict generic scenes, although the particular details on a few suggest individual orders, and there are a few vases with painted inscriptions, mostly dedications to a deity by a named individual, which were clearly specifically commissioned. The most numerous are plain Chiot chalices from sanctuaries at Naukratis and on Aigina. However, even commissioned works sometimes ended up far from the homes of those who had ordered them. A dinos (a large wine-bowl with no handles) with Exekias' signature on the rim, accompanied by a dedication in the distinctive Sikyonian script, ended up in Etruria. A similar route was taken by those prize Panathenaic amphorae found in Etruria, since they could be won only by Greeks. They were a particularly distinct class of commissioned work, and, significantly, none bears a 'trademark'.

Sets of vases used in funerary rites can sometimes be identified, though whether or not they were commissioned is hard to say. One example is provided by 7th-century BC White-ground vases from the Kerameikos at Athens, another by the sets of Red-figure vases painted by a single artist, which often accompanied 4th-century BC Athenian burials; such sets are rare elsewhere. Some paired vases also exist, each decorated with half a scene or even half a figure, and the Siren Painter, in the early 5th century BC appears to have decorated a whole set of stamnoi with *Adventures of Odysseus*; but 'services' of vases for symposia comprising kraters, oinochoai and cups are difficult to isolate. From the mid-5th century BC some merchants scratched identificatory marks and prices for batches of pots under the foot of one 'master' vase, but again these groups cohere into no recognizable set.

Finally, 4th-century BC Apulian vase painters specialized in producing a group of huge volute kraters without bottoms, depicting scenes from Greek tragedies and clearly intended exclusively for funerary use. One tomb of *c.* 400 BC at Herakleia, near Taras (Taranto), contained so many vases with theatrical scenes that they may well have been commissioned for the funeral of a playwright or actor. Although most intact Greek vases come from burials, this is a rare example where it is possible with any confidence to suggest that the scenes on them reflected the interests and achievements of the occupant.

J. D. Beazley: 'Potter and Painter in Ancient Athens', *Proc. Brit. Acad.*, xxx (1944), pp. 87–125

A. E. Raubitschek: *Dedications from the Athenian Akropolis* (Cambridge, MA, 1949)

C. M. Robertson: '"Epoiesen" on Greek Vases: Other Considerations', *J. Hell. Stud.*, xcii (1972), pp. 180–83

T. B. L. Webster: *Potter and Patron in Classical Athens* (London, 1972)

M. M. Eismann: 'A Further Note on "Epoiesen" Signatures', *J. Hell. Stud.*, xciv (1974), p. 172

J. Ziomecki: *Les Représentations d'artisans sur les vases attiques* (Warsaw, 1975)

A. W. Johnston: *Trademarks on Greek Vases* (Warminster, 1979)

Ancient Greek and Related Pottery. Proceedings of the International Vase Symposium: Amsterdam, 1984

R. M. Cook: 'Pots and Pisistratan Propaganda', *J. Hell. Stud.*, cvii (1987), pp. 167–9

J. H. Oakley: 'An Athenian Red-figure Workshop from the Time of the Peloponnesian War', *Les Ateliers de potiers dans le monde grec aux époques géométrique, archaique et classique*, ed. F. Blondé and J. Perreault, *Bull. Corr. Hell.*, suppl. xxiii (Paris and Athens, 1992), pp. 195–203

Athenian Potters and Painters (exh. cat. by W. D. E. Coulson, J. H. Oakley and E. M. Langridge-Noti; Athens, Amer. Sch. Class. Stud., 1994)

The Complex Past of Pottery: Production, Circulation and Comsuption of Mycenaean and Greek Pottery (Sixteenth to Early Fifth Centuries BC): Proceedings of the ARCHON International Conference: Amsterdam, 1996

J. H. Oakley, W. D. E. Coulson and O. Palagia, eds: *Athenian Potters and Painters: The Conference Proceedings* (Oxford, 1997)

T. Schreiber: *Athenian Vase Construction: A Potter's Analysis* (Los Angeles, 1999/*R* 2000)

J. Boardman: *The History of Greek Vases: Potters, Painters, and Pictures* (New York, 2001)

(v) Trade. Down to Hellenistic times all Greek cities used Greek pottery, as did many other peoples of the West and of Anatolia. From the 7th to the 4th century BC most of these places relied on imports for their fine wares and sometimes for their coarse wares as well. Corinth and Athens then dominated the fine export trade from Late Geometric times (*c.* 760–*c.* 700 BC) until the end of the 5th century BC: thereafter the market fragmented, and in the following century there was a general decline in decorated pottery manufacture. Little evidence is available for the mechanics of the pottery trade, whether internal or international, though the scope and, to a limited extent, the volume of the latter is indicated by the distribution of pottery find-spots.

There is no evidence to suggest that potters themselves organized the export and sale of their wares in other markets, and the entrepreneurs who performed this function are shadowy figures indeed. A significant proportion of the Athenian and Corinthian exports may have been carried by foreigners, for the flow of vases suffered little interruption when manufacturing states were at war, suggesting that traders may have been neutrals. As well as shiploads heading directly to a targeted market, it is clear from excavated wrecks that a large share of the trade was in the hands of general carriers plying a coastline with a mixed cargo that was partly sold off and replenished at each port of call. Merchants must have expected a retail profit that compared well with that derived from more easily shipped commodities such as corn or oil.

The principal evidence for the extent of the vase export trade is gained by plotting find maps for each style of pottery. Such evidence must be used with caution, especially when it is based only on a handful of items, since allowance must be made for the dissemination of heirlooms, gifts etc. The large numbers of Panathenaic amphorae (*see* §5(ii) below) in Etruscan tombs and, some have argued, the wide distribution of vases bearing *kalos* names also indicate the existence of a second-hand market. A city-state's colonies would often be a major market for its potteries, but export patterns were much broader, and decorated pottery formed only one part of any cargo. Traders were often residents of other states, supplying goods that were readily saleable throughout the Mediterranean. A large amount of decorated ceramics exported is of high aesthetic quality, one would judge, but there is the corollary that the originating workshops would also have produced much second- and third-rate material to satisfy the markets that they had created.

The percentage of pots that any given centre exported varied widely, from minimal to vast. During the 7th century BC Attic figured vases and Cycladic and Cretan relief pithoi, some with mythological scenes, travelled little, but these are rare exceptions; comparatively productive centres do export much of their output. The Corinthian Thapsos cups, for example, are commonly found in the West from *c.* 730 BC onwards, and it has been suggested that they were produced specifically for the use of emigrating Greeks. Even earlier, the functionally similar Euboian skyphoi, decorated with sets of pendant semicircles, were used in many parts of the Mediterranean, not least the eastern seaboard. Later, Corinthian figured ware was extremely popular in Etruria (notably Caere), as, of course, was Attic ware. There is a little evidence for migrant potters working in foreign cities, and it would be natural for the most talented artists to gravitate towards the state whose mercantile expertise was currently generating the greatest wealth.

It is impossible to build up any coherent picture of the vase export trade in Protogeometric and Geometric times, but it is clear from the distribution of finds that with the recovery from the political chaos of the post-Mycenaean Dark Ages, vases were an element in cargoes on the newly opened trading routes around the Mediterranean. Thus in the 9th century BC the trading primacy enjoyed by the Euboian cities Chalkis and Eretria gained markets all round the Aegean and even in Cyprus and the Levant for an Euboian sub-Protogeometric ware that was by Athenian standards stuck in something of a rut. Middle Geometric ware (*c.* 850–*c.* 760 BC) from Athens achieved a high artistic standard and had an unusually wide distribution for the period, but in the Late Geometric period (*c.* 760–*c.* 700 BC) Attic ware was exported little. Instead, Corinthian workshops, producing a range of very different shapes, provided an increasing percentage of Greek exported wares, and over the next two centuries Corinth's export trade continued to grow; she became the principal supplier of fine Black-figure vases to the whole Greek world.

By the beginning of the 6th century BC Attica was establishing a market for her Black-figure wares, which appear at the Greek trading post of Naukratis on the Nile delta, around the Black Sea coast and a little later in great numbers in the graves of Etruria. It is harder to explain Athens' displacement of Corinth in the pottery export trade by the mid-6th century BC. Corinth had suffered no political or economic setback, and the early 6th-century Athenian product shows no manifest artistic superiority, though its orange clay (which the Corinthians came to imitate) may have made the wares visually more attractive, and there is some evidence that superior firing may have made Attic pottery more durable. Attic dominance of the market continued through the Red-figure period until her political decline at the end of the century. Competing Red-figure workshops had also been established in South Italy, a major export area for Attic products, between 440 BC and 400 BC. In the 4th century Athenian exports of figured pottery were concentrated more in the Black Sea and eastern Mediterranean areas; South Italian production expanded, with limited amounts of exports. The final period of Red-figure production at Athens persisted into the last quarter of the century.

Other centres gained significant secondary shares in the pottery export trade. Finds of Orientalizing Fikellura ware (*see* §4(IV) below) are plentiful at Naukratis, south Ionia and the Black Sea coast, while in the 6th century BC Lakonian ware led the smaller Black-figure producers, with especially strong trade to Sicily, South Italy and Etruria in the west and Samos, North Africa and Egypt in the east. Klazomenian ware was plentiful in north Ionia and Egypt.

Although some Corinthian and Athenian vases bear trading marks that indicate their inclusion in specific bulk consignments, there is only limited evidence that potters produced special shapes, scenes or decorative schemes to satisfy foreign demand. In the 6th century BC Athenian potters in the circle of NIKOSTHENES copied Etruscan shapes, and there are a few Athenian Red-figure copies of native South Italian shapes; but basically the same vases were sold abroad as at home. Some individual vases were made to order for foreign clients: two Athenian examples have pre-fired painted inscriptions in Etruscan, one of them indicating that the vase was a gift.

R. M. Cook: 'Die Bedeutung der bemalten Keramik für den griechischen Handel', *Jb. Dt. Archäol. Inst.*, lxxiv (1959), pp. 114–23

J. Boardman: 'The Athenian Pottery Trade: The Classical Period', *Expedition*, xxi/4 (1979), pp. 33–4

I. Scheibler: *Griechische Töpferkunst: Herstellung, Handel und Gebrauch der antiken Tongefässe* (Munich, 1983)

J. Boardman: *Athenian Red Figure Vases: The Classical Period* (London, 1989)

A. W. Johnston: 'Greek Vases in the Marketplace', *Looking into Greek Vases*, ed. T. Rasmussen and N. Spivey (Cambridge, 1991), pp. 203–31

M. Vickers and D. Gill: *Artful Crafts: Ancient Greek Silverware and Pottery* (Oxford, 1994)

The Complex Past of Pottery: Production, Circulation and Consumption of Mycenaean and Greek Pottery (Sixteenth to Early Fifth Centuries BC): Proceedings of the ARCHON International Conference: Amsterdam, 1996

J. Luke: *Ports of Trade, Al Mina, and Geometric Greek Pottery in the Levant* (Oxford, 2003)

(vi) Inscriptions. Incised (graffito) inscriptions occurred on Greek pottery from the time of the invention of the Greek alphabet in the 8th century BC, while painted (*dipinto*) inscriptions are found only from the 7th century BC; both types continued to be used on figured vases until the end of the Classical period in the late 4th century BC. In the Hellenistic period they were much rarer. The majority occurred on Attic pots, of which about one in ten was inscribed, giving a total of some 8000–10,000 extant examples. Their principal uses were to identify the characters

or objects depicted or to record the names of persons involved in the commissioning or manufacture; some record remarks passed between the characters portrayed or the comments of the painter himself.

(a) Introduction. (b) Mythological names. (c) Names of contemporary persons. (d) Artists' signatures. (e) Other texts. (f) Scripts.

(a) Introduction. Like the adoption of the alphabet, the custom of incorporating inscriptions in works of art was a feature of the Orientalizing movement (*see* §4 below). In the art of the Near Eastern cultures, the inscribing of monuments (especially sculpted reliefs) was a long-standing tradition, but their syllabic writing systems are not directly comparable with the Greek. However, the Aramaic inscriptions on a relief from Zincirli (*c.* 730–*c.* 700 BC; Berlin, Antikensamml.) identifying King Barrakab and the god Baal of Harran provide a closer parallel: Aramaic script is sufficiently closely related to the Greek to have inspired Greeks to use a similar technique for naming figures. Whatever the inspiration, two elements indigenous to Greek culture greatly encouraged the use of such inscriptions: the development of mythology as transmitted in the early epic poems of Homer and Hesiod, and the rise of individualism as evidenced by the earliest lyric poetry. Inscriptions were used not only in vase painting: in early sculpture too, identifying labels or dedications were sometimes placed on the figures themselves or near them on the background.

The earliest surviving inscriptions (of *c.* 750 BC from Lefkandi on Euboia and the Euboian colony of Pithekoussai) are casual graffiti on the vase's shoulder; their content is unrelated to the pot's decoration. The message of those that can be interpreted is often of the 'I belong to X' type, leading scholars to suggest that those that consist merely of a couple of letters or of some non-alphabetic device may also be indications of ownership applied by the purchaser to safeguard his property; similar marks appear on the shoulders of a long series of Attic amphorae dating from *c.* 730 BC to *c.* 570 BC.

A second important class of non-artistic vase inscription is the trading mark that is sometimes found on the foot of a vase. Its exact purpose remains unclear: perhaps to identify the merchant to whose bulk order the vase was assigned or perhaps simply to serve as the potter's 'trademark' in the modern sense. The earliest examples are red *dipinti* on Corinthian vases of *c.* 625–*c.* 575 BC: they coincide with the foundation of the Greek trading post at Naukratis in Egypt (*c.* 620–*c.* 610 BC). While the use of painting or incision of trading marks was probably partly determined by which would show up better against the background of the pot, graffiti eventually became dominant, and *dipinti* are rare on Attic Red-figure vases. The most frequent incidence of trading marks is on Attic pottery of *c.* 550–*c.* 450 BC, and relatively few are found on Corinthian or East Greek vases or indeed on the earliest Attic Black-figure. Even on Attic Red-figure their incidence gradually declined after 450 BC, and by the end of the 5th century BC they were rare.

In the Archaic period inscriptions were used in several regional schools, such as Naxian, Rhodian, Lakonian, Boiotian and Chalkidian. Indeed, some of the earliest painted inscriptions are on pottery from Ithaka and include some hexameter lines of *c.* 700 BC and a potter's signature (*c.* 675–*c.* 650 BC). Ithaka had close connections with Corinth, and it was in Corinth that the main types of inscriptions were developed in the 7th century BC, to be taken over by Attic artists in the following century when their pottery dominated the market.

The painted inscriptions on Attic Black-figure vases were usually executed in the same paint as the figures, although added red also occurs. In the later Red-figure style inscriptions were initially sometimes incised or even reserved, but later they were usually in added red (and even later, pink or white) painted on the black background, making them more evanescent and often hard to read. Red-figure artists used a soft brush, which allowed a more casual style, so that their letter forms are much more variable than those on stone inscriptions. Vase inscriptions were normally written by the painters in their own handwriting, although some may have been based on models of some kind or even be in the potter's hand; copybooks were probably not used at this early date. Several inscriptions refer to the projected use of the vases as dedications or gifts; more frequently they allude to the drinking parties for which the pots were intended, in the form of exhortations to drink and praise for handsome youths. The idea that most of the finest vases were made for specific clients, however, has been overstated.

(b) Mythological names. These are perhaps the most common inscriptions in figural scenes. They first appeared *c.* 675 BC on Proto-Corinthian vases, and slightly later specimens include the famous Chigi Vase (*c.* 640–*c.* 630 BC; Rome, Villa Giulia, 22,697), which has a subsidiary scene of the *Judgement of Paris* under its handle. Here the figures are named *Al*[exand]*ros* (Paris's other name), *Athanaia* and *Aphrod*[ite] in large letters (not in the Corinthian alphabet) aligned at their tops in the Early Archaic manner. Contemporary is a row of warriors on a stand from Aigina (*c.* 640 BC; destr.) in a style related to Proto Attic. One of the warriors is named *Menelas* in a non-Attic dialect and an alphabet that may not be Attic. Without the inscription there would be no way of identifying this figure, which is not the case in the *Judgement of Paris* scene or indeed in most mythological scenes: labels often appear in scenes where they are not needed and are frequently absent from scenes where they are. Their function is therefore not necessarily one of identification. One of the principal motives for adding inscriptions to such scenes may have been to connect the pictures with the world of the *logos*, the literary or oral stories told about gods and heroes. This is demonstrated by a famous lost monument, the gold and ivory chest dedicated by the Corinthian

tyrant Kypselos (*c*. 657–*c*. 625 BC) at Olympia (Pausanias: *Description of Greece* V.xvii.5–xix.10). Here, in addition to the labels, were some explanatory inscriptions in verse, which gave the scene a certain 'literary' quality: it certainly did not need this explanation. Similar inscriptions inspired by epic poetry also occur on vases. There may also have been an ornamental function to this writing, for Archaic artists did not favour large empty spaces, and inscriptions therefore doubled as filling ornaments.

(c) Names of contemporary persons. During the 6th century BC genre scenes became increasingly popular on Attic vases, especially those depicting symposia and athletics. A common practice was to add the word *kalos* ('handsome'), even where no such figure appeared in the scene, with or without reference to a specific person; in the former case the formula became 'So-and-so is handsome' or 'So-and-so appears handsome to So-and-so'. These *kalos* names (or lovenames) mostly belong to aristocratic males, although female names, no doubt referring to courtesans, also occur; those that can be associated with known historical figures have played an important role in establishing the chronology of Attic vase painting, for they were presumably written when the named person was young, although some have questioned this. There are also large numbers of contemporary aristocratic names attached to figures in symposium and athletic scenes, and most of these must also be names of real people, since the same names sometimes appear elsewhere with *kalos*. Both categories include well-known figures: among the *kalos* names are the Athenian general Miltiades (*c*. 550–489 BC; Oxford, Ashmolean, 310) and Euaion, a son of the dramatist Aeschylus (525/4–456 BC) and himself a poet or actor, while labelled figures include the poet Anakreon (*c*. 570–after 514 BC; Copenhagen, Nmus., 13365) and Phayllos, a South Italian athlete who fought at Salamis (480 BC).

(d) Artists' signatures. The signatures of both potters and painters can be found in Beazley's *Black-figure, Red-figure* and *Paralipomena*. Additional signatures appear in T. H. Carpenter's *Beazley Addenda*, appendix 2. They are among the earliest painted inscriptions on vases, appearing soon after the beginning of the 7th century BC. Signatures are of three kinds: some are accompanied by *egraphsen* ('painted it'), indicating that the named person furnished the painted decoration; some are followed by *epoiesen* ('made it'), which may refer either to the potter or the owner of the workshop (it is probable, however, that the former is meant, even where the latter is also true: since they occur at random and are not easily interpreted as advertising a factory, they may indicate pride in individual achievement); third, some artists (e.g. EXEKIAS) sometimes signed as both potter and painter.

The tondo of a Red-figure cup by DOURIS depicting *Eos Carrying the Dead Memnon* (*c*. 490–*c*. 480 BC; Paris, Louvre, G 115; see fig. 16) illustrates most of the types of inscriptions mentioned above. The names of Eos and Memnon are written beside their heads; near the former is the painter's signature (*Doris egraphsen*); below the latter, that of the potter (*Kalliades epoiesen*); in the left part of the field is the praise of a youth (*Hermogenes kalos*); and along the left margin is an unintelligible inscription, perhaps some miswritten comment by the painter.

(e) Other texts. There are well over a hundred Attic vases bearing more unusual texts that show a close involvement of the painters or their clients with their work and the subjects represented, as well as a considerable interest in the spoken and even the written word. Most examples date to the late 6th century BC and early 5th, but some are earlier. Already on the François Vase (*c*. 570 BC; Florence, Mus. Archaeol., 4209), objects are labelled 'altar', 'fountain', 'hydria' and 'seat'. On a Black-figure hydria (late 6th century BC; Münster, Westfäl. Wilhelms-U., 565) the winged figure of the dead Patroklos hovering over his tomb is named as his spirit, *psyche*. Several pots bear laudatory references to themselves, such as 'I am a fine drinking cup' (Rhodes, Archaeol. Mus., 10527) or 'Greetings and buy me' (Paris, Louvre, EL. 98). Vases by the Pioneer group often bear comments on the quality of their figures. The painter Euthymides placed along the margin of one of his amphorae (Munich, Staatl. Antikensamml., 2307) the bold 'Euphronios never did this', which is probably a taunt addressed to his famous rival.

Many of these inscriptions provide the remarks of the characters portrayed. On two vases courtesans playing the game of *kottabos*, in which wine dregs were hurled from the drinker's cup against a metal stand or basin, are made to say: 'I throw this for you'; one (a hydria by Phintias; Munich, Staatl. Antikensamml., 2421) bears the *kalos* name of Euthymides, the other (a psykter by Euphronios; St Petersburg, Hermitage, 644) that of Leagros; if the throws are successful, these are their predicted lovers. 'Dysniketos' horse has won', says a herald on a Black-figure Panathenaic amphora (London, BM, B 144). 'Zeus, make me rich' and 'It is full, full already, it has spilt', exclaims the oil-seller in two scenes on a Black-figure pelike (*c*. 530 BC; Rome, Vatican, Mus. Gregoriano Etrus., 413). On a Red-figure vase depicting *Oedipus and the Sphinx* (*c*. 470 BC; Rome, Vatican, Mus. Gregoriano Etrus., 16541) the latter says 'and three' as part of her riddle. Snatches of song occur on early Red-figure vases, as on a fragmentary calyx krater by the Kleophrades Painter (Copenhagen, Nmus., 13365) depicting a banqueter singing what was probably a drinking song of Theognis. Poetry appears on representations of book rolls, such as on the famous School cup by Douris (Berlin, Antikensamml., 2285), which has lines resembling the openings of Homeric hymns.

Sometimes characters engage in conversations. In two Black-figure scenes depicting *Achilles and Ajax Playing a Board Game* (lekythos, Boston, MA, Mus. F.A., 95.15; amphora, Rome, Vatican, Mus. Gregoriano Etrus., 344), each hero calls out his score, while a Red-figure pelike (St Petersburg, Hermitage, 615)

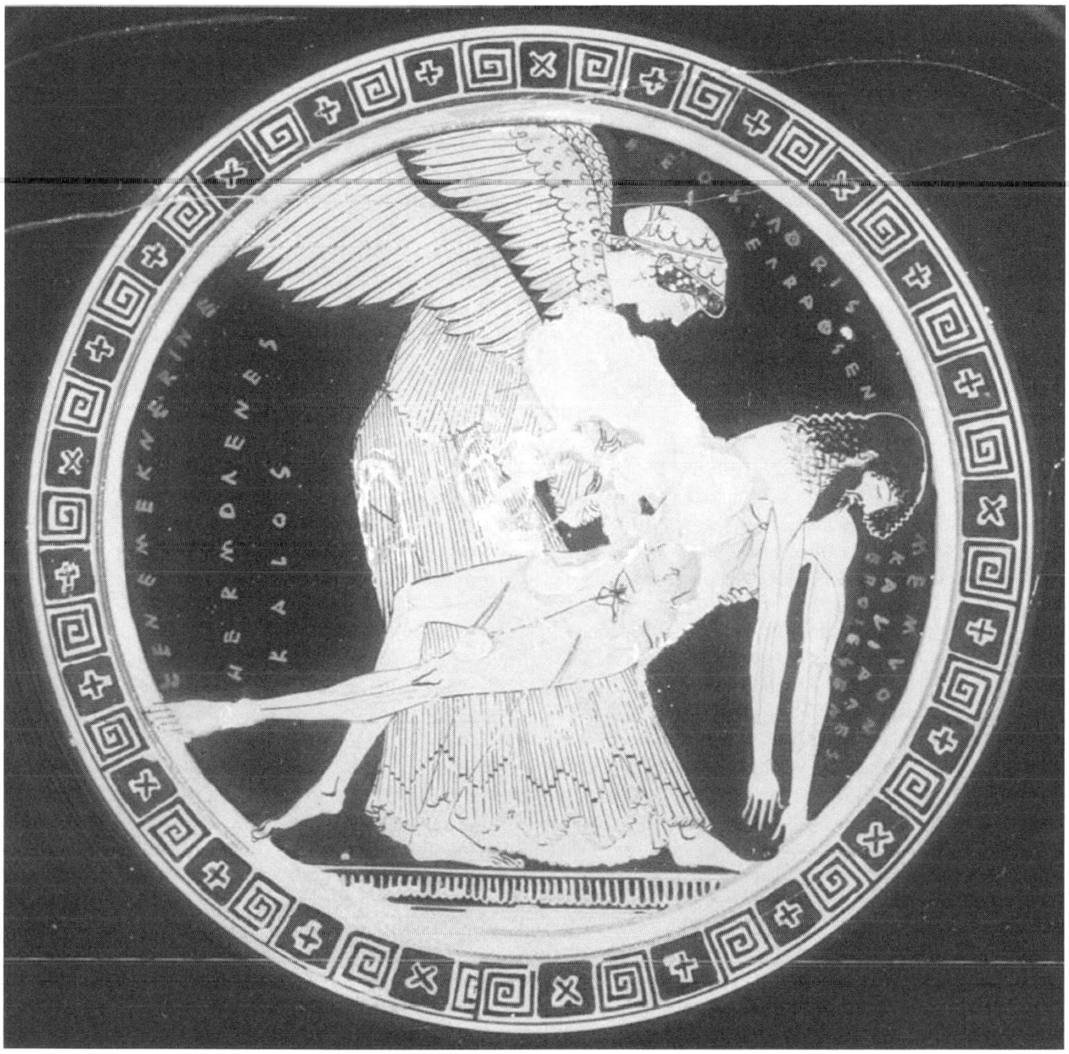

16. Ancient Greek inscription on the tondo on an Attic Red-figure cup by Douris: *Eos Carrying the Dead Memnon,* diam. 260 mm, *c.* 490–*c.* 480 BC (Paris, Musée du Louvre, G 115)

related to works by the Pioneer group depicts the *Three Ages of Man*: a youth says 'Look, a swallow!', a man replies 'Yes, by Herakles!', and a boy says 'Spring has come'. On a slightly earlier oinochoe (Munich, Staatl. Antikensamml., 2447), which has no figural decoration, there is a rather inane conversation: 'Nikolas is handsome. Dorotheos is handsome. Yes, I think so too. That other boy, Memnon, is also handsome. He is a good friend of mine, too'.

Some everyday scenes are also identified by inscriptions. One Black-figure hydria (*c.* 550–*c.* 500 BC; London, BM, B 331) identifies a fountain as the famous Athenian fountain Kallirhoe, while on a late 5th-century BC Red-figure bell krater (New York, Met., 25.18.66), lyre-playing satyrs are identified as actors by the inscription 'Singers at the Panathenaic Festival'. Finally, an early Red-figure psykter by Oltos (Kings Point, NY, N. Schimmel priv. col.) has six warriors riding on dolphins (an early example of a comic chorus), each figure accompanied by the words 'on a dolphin', perhaps part of a song or a kind of title to the picture.

(f) Scripts. Attic vase inscriptions include specimens of individual handwriting closer to everyday script than are the more formal inscriptions on stone; they are therefore important evidence for the development of script as well as for attitudes towards ornamentation. In the 7th century BC inscriptions were usually integrated with the filling ornament, which may explain their large scale; it was not until *c.* 570 BC that the Attic script finally developed regular, more geometric letter forms and writing was organized into more consistent lines. Around 575–550 BC the alphabet was revised, perhaps in conjunction with the production of Homeric texts for recitation at

Athens, and beautiful writing occurs on large vases by such painters as Kleitias and Nearchos. Such was the enthusiasm for writing in the Archaic period that meaningless inscriptions frequently occur, often written by vase painters who were otherwise perfectly literate but also by those who were wholly or partially illiterate.

On the 6th-century BC Little Master cups inscriptions are very much a part of the standard decoration. There are more signatures on these small vases than on any other class of pottery, as well as drinking inscriptions and meaningless strings of letters. Vase painters were prominent in developing the new script, and the most elegant lettering of the period, and perhaps of any period, is that of Exekias, who established a fine counterpoint between the varied poses of his figures and the margins of his scenes by carefully calibrated lines of inscriptions.

Towards the end of the 6th century BC, and perhaps reflecting the establishment of democracy at Athens, inscriptions came to be used more freely and the writing formed more casually, contrasting strongly with the elegance of the figures executed in the new Red-figure technique. This is particularly evident in the works of the Pioneer group, but such exuberance had already diminished by the early 5th century BC, as shown by the works of Douris, for example. Soon after the Persian Wars (490 and 480–479 BC) vase painters began to be influenced by the 'chancellary script' developed by the Athenian State for official use, but for the rest of the century there was a gradual decline in the number of inscriptions, and towards the end they were executed in small lettering running horizontally above the heads of the figures, sometimes more as a symbol of erudition than for their decorative value. This style of inscription also occurs on some 4th-century BC Attic vases as well as on pottery from South Italy, especially Apulia and Paestum, where scenes were frequently influenced by the theatre.

Vase painters had turned to the Ionic alphabet several decades before it was adopted officially at Athens in 403 BC, replacing local Attic; but they participated little in the concurrent development of monumental, plain official and cursive scripts. However, some Panathenaic prize amphorae of the period bear inscriptions in a calligraphic script paralleled in the earliest papyri. Particularly noteworthy are the elegantly curved strokes and the thickening of the end points on a fragmentary specimen of 316 BC (Athens, Kerameikos Mus., PA 29). Important 4th-century BC inscriptions also occur on South Italian vases and on Boiotian vases connected with the cult of the Kabeiroi. A class of Black-glaze drinking vessels also bears one-line inscriptions in a calligraphic style referring to divinities presiding over the symposium: 'Of Zeus the Saviour', 'Of Dionysos' etc; these were known as 'lettered drinking cups' by contemporary writers and were still produced in the Hellenistic period. A more informal style occurs in inscriptions on the numerous 3rd-century BC funerary vases from the cemetery of Hadra at Alexandria, while certain faience vases from Egypt bear inscriptions connected with the cult of Hellenistic queens. Finally, the so-called Megarian bowls, which were widely produced in the Hellenistic period and decorated in relief, sometimes carried scenes from the Homeric poems with copious inscriptions added in a bookish manner for didactic purposes. Generally, however, vase inscriptions were not of great importance in the Hellenistic period: most writing, both formal and informal, was now done on papyrus; inscriptions on stone were more common; and most pottery production had sunk to a lowly craft no longer at the centre of artistic creation.

J. D. Beazley: *Red-figure* (1942, 2/1963)
J. D. Beazley: *Black-figure* (1956)
A. G.Woodhead: *The Study of Greek Inscriptions* (Cambridge, 1959, rev. 1981)
L. H. Jeffery: *The Local Scripts of Archaic Greece* (Oxford, 1961, rev. 1990)
H. R. Immerwahr: 'Inscriptions on the Anacreon Krater in Copenhagen', *Amer. J. Archaeol.*, lxix (1965), p. 153 and no. 10
J. D. Beazley: *Paralipomena* (1971)
J. Boardman: *Athenian Black-figure Vases* (London, 1974)
M. Guarducci: *Epigrafia greca*, iii (Rome, 1974), pp. 456–95
M. A. Lang: *Graffiti and Dipinti* (1976), xxi of *The Athenian Agora* (Princeton, 1953–)
F. Lorber: 'Vaseninschriften', *Das Studium der griechischen Epigraphik*, ed. G. Pfohl (Darmstadt, 1977), pp. 97–115
A. W. Johnston: *Trademarks on Greek Vases* (Warminster, 1979)
F. Lorber: *Inschriften auf korinthischen Vasen* (Berlin, 1979)
L. Burn and R. Glynn: *Beazley Addenda* (Oxford, 1982); rev. by T. A. Carpenter and others (Oxford, 1989), appendix 2
H. R. Immerwahr: *Attic Script: A Survey* (Oxford, 1990)
A. Cohen: 'The Literate Potter: A Tradition of Incised Signatures on Attic Vases', *Met. Mus. J.*, xxvi (1991), pp. 49–95
N. K. Rutter and B. A. Sparkes: *Word and Image in Ancient Greece* (Edinburgh, 2000)

2. PROTOGEOMETRIC. The term derives from the abstract decorative designs on Greek pottery of the Early Iron Age (*c.* 1050–*c.* 900 BC), which precede the more fully developed and varied ornament of the Geometric style.

(i) Introduction. (ii) Attic. (iii) Other regional styles.

(i) Introduction. After the collapse of Mycenaean civilization in the 12th century BC, fine painted pottery was the only art form that maintained a continuous tradition throughout the ensuing Dark Age. The latest Mycenaean pottery had been decorated chiefly with highly stylized floral and marine motifs; in the intervening Sub-Mycenaean phase (*c.* 1125–*c.* 1050 BC) these motifs were further simplified to create abstract patterns of wavy lines, languettes and concentric arcs or semicircles. Without more sophisticated art forms for inspiration, Protogeometric (PG) vase painters still relied on these simple abstract motifs, carefully subordinated to the shapes of their vases. On this limited repertory, however, they imposed a geometrical precision by using a multiple brush attached to a compass, with which sets of concentric semicircles or circles could be executed

with a deft flick of the wrist. At the same time standards of potting improved: a fast wheel fashioned the vessels in crisper contours and more harmonious proportions, and a higher firing temperature gave the paint—a fine solution of the clay—a more brilliant lustre.

After the severe disruption following the Mycenaean demise, the appearance of PG pottery indicates a return to more settled conditions of life and a recovery of ceramic finesse. One result of the Mycenaean collapse had been a decline in communications within the Aegean world. Thus a common Mycenaean idiom in pottery style (*koinē*) gave way to wide local variations. The Attic PG style, first to emerge, gradually influenced the output of most other Aegean areas through exported pottery, thereby restoring a limited *koine*; but each regional style nevertheless retained its own character. Such styles evolved throughout the Greek world, including the seaboard of Asia Minor recently settled by Ionian Greeks; to the north, however, potters on Lesbos and in the Aiolian Greek coastal settlements produced instead grey Bucchero ware in a traditional Anatolian technique.

(ii) Attic. The finest PG pottery was produced for funerary use, and in Attica, where cremation had become the usual burial rite, exceptional care went into the making and decoration of ash urns. A continuous sequence of whole vessels offered in single cremations illustrates the development of the Attic PG style over *c.* 150 years. The shapes prefigure those of Archaic and Classical Athenian vases and are remarkable for their excellent proportions, which became progressively more refined. The larger closed forms have a taut ovoid body and a tall concave neck; open vessels are roughly hemispherical, often resting on a high and skilfully turned conical foot.

The chief closed shape is the amphora, designed as a cremation urn. Those for the ashes of men have vertical strap handles springing from the shoulder to the middle of the neck (neck-handled amphorae), as in an example from the Athenian Kerameikos (*c.* 980–*c.* 960 BC; Athens, Kerameikos Mus., 572), while those for women have more globular bodies, initially with round horizontal handles attached to their bellies and later with vertical strap handles on their shoulders (shoulder-handled amphorae). Other common closed shapes are the oinochoe, trefoil-lipped to facilitate pouring; the narrow-necked lekythos, which replaced the Mycenaean stirrup jar as the standard oil flask; and the globular pyxis with a short, everted lip and a fitted lid. The largest open shape is the krater, while the most common drinking vessels are the skyphos and a deep cup with one vertical handle; both rest on high conical feet, but the cup also occurs in a shallow flat-based variety. Less frequent is the kantharos; rarer shapes of special interest include clay miniatures of bronze tripod cauldrons and a lentoid pilgrim flask of Cypro-Levantine character. The conical foot was probably also of Cypriot origin; otherwise, apart from the pyxis and the kantharos, all the standard shapes were developments of the less sophisticated Attic Sub-Mycenaean forms.

The decoration gradually changed from light to dark ground during Attic PG. Except on the largest belly-handled amphorae, the ornament was usually confined to a single zone: the shoulder of a closed vessel or the area between the handles of an open one. A major role was played by compass-drawn sets of concentric circles and semicircles, the latter emphasizing the vigorous curve of a shoulder, the former employed on flatter areas such as the handle zone of a deep skyphos. The repertory adopted large wavy lines from the Sub-Mycenaean style and admitted some rectilinear patterns: latticed triangles provided an alternative to the semicircles, and rectangular panels of chequerboard or diagonal latticing were sometimes inserted between two sets of circles. Typical of the latest Attic PG were narrow horizontal strips of rectilinear ornament (e.g. dogtooth, single zigzag, oblique bars) reserved between large areas of shiny dark paint: other late vessels, near the change to Geometric, carried heavy accumulations of chequerboard and latticing to the exclusion of circular motifs. The few instances of figural designs among an otherwise wholly abstract repertory are sketchily rendered in silhouette: they are confined to four amphorae from the Kerameikos cemetery in Athens, on which horses make an unobtrusive appearance (e.g. Athens, Kerameikos Mus., 560T18 and 1260), and an Attic skyphos exported to Lefkandi with birds tucked under its handles (Eretria, Archaeol. Mus.).

(iii) Other regional styles. These arose at different times and display varying combinations of local and Attic elements. Closest to Attic are the PG wares of Boiotia, Corinth, the Cyclades (notably Naxos) and the newly established Ionian settlements in the east Aegean. The Argolid, once the heartland of Mycenaean civilization, developed a more individual PG style, sharing some features with Attic but also deriving much from the latest Mycenaean pottery, perhaps without any intervening Sub-Mycenaean phase: Argive decoration consists largely of rectilinear motifs, especially latticed triangles; the same is true of vases from the Dodekanese, which also have some links with contemporary pottery on Cyprus.

Furthest from the Attic style are the PG wares of Lakonia, the western Peloponnese, Achaia and Ithaka, which nevertheless share the common decorative principle of heavily latticed triangles and lozenges placed in square or rectangular panels. A distinctive Lakonian shape is a grooved and baggy skyphos, the ancestor of the Archaic lakaina; the most usual drinking vessel in Achaia and Ithaka was the tall kantharos. In Thessaly, Attic and Euboian features were grafted on to a local style derived from handmade pottery in the Macedonian tradition.

The Euboian PG style is well documented from numerous grave offerings at Lefkandi. It developed from a local Sub-Mycenaean tradition, displaying throughout some affinity with Attic, especially in its late phase. Almost all the Attic shapes are present, often furnished with high conical feet. Cremation, as in Attica, was the normal rite at Lefkandi, but not urn cremation; hence the rarity of large and elaborately decorated amphorae, and their relatively unpretentious ornament, characterized by the wavy line. Nevertheless, there were some adventurous experiments: a small hydria (early 10th century BC) bears the earliest post-Mycenaean figural Greek vase painting, comprising two archers crudely rendered in silhouette; under the handle of a vast krater, probably a marker for a royal grave, is depicted an oriental Tree of Life; and a ritual vessel takes the form of a centaur, with modelled limbs added to a wheelmade body (*c.* 900 BC; all Eretria, Archaeol. Mus.). The PG tradition enjoyed a long life in Euboia, persisting far into the period of Attic Geometric. During the 9th century BC and into the early 8th the Euboians took the initiative in maritime trade and established a common Sub-Protogeometric pottery style shared by parts of Thessaly, Boiotia and the northern Cyclades. Its most characteristic shape, the low-footed skyphos decorated with pendent concentric semicircles, was widely exported around the Aegean and even to Cyprus and the Levant.

Crete suffered less than the Greek mainland in the upheaval at the end of the Bronze Age; hence its pottery reveals an exceptionally smooth transition from the Minoan past. A Sub-Minoan phase throughout the island preserved many Minoan shapes decorated with spare curvilinear ornament on a light ground. Afterwards there was much local variation, but the subsequent PG style was most fully developed around Knossos, the area most open to outside influences. Knossian PG, well represented in collective chamber tombs, evolved in the early 10th century BC as a hybrid style, combining Sub-Minoan elements with Attic late PG: Attic types of amphora were common alongside the stirrup jar of Minoan origin; the local deep bell krater was decorated with Attic concentric circles; and globular pithoi, also decorated with circles, were designed as ash urns, cremation having by then become the rule. This style developed on its own lines until *c.* 850 BC when, before the arrival of true Geometric, there followed an interlude of florid and ebullient decoration known as Protogeometric B, unique in the Greek world: to the usual PG repertory was added a profusion of freehand curvilinear motifs—cables, spirals and massed arcs—probably derived from metalwork made by immigrant Levantine craftsmen. The chief shape of PG B is a straight-sided pithos used as an ash urn.

Knossian PG includes several experiments in figure drawing. Wild goats appear several times, once as prey in a hunting scene on a bell krater (*c.* 900 BC; Herakleion, Archaeol. Mus.); another bell krater (*c.* 850 BC) depicts a warrior struggling with two lions on one side and heraldic sphinxes on the other. The most outstanding example of PG B is a straight-sided pithos on which is boldly portrayed a nature goddess with trees, birds and fish (late 9th century BC; Knossos, Stratig. Mus., T.107.114).

W. Kraiker and K. Kübler: *Die Nekropolen des 12. bis 10. Jahrhunderts* (1939), i of *Kerameikos: Ergebnisse der Ausgrabungen* (Berlin, 1939–)

K. Kübler: *Neufunde aus der Nekropole des 11. und 10. Jahrhunderts* (1943), iv of *Kerameikos: Ergebnisse der Ausgrabungen* (Berlin, 1939–)

V. R. d'A. Desborough: *Protogeometric Pottery* (Oxford, 1952)

J. K. Brock: *Fortetsa: Early Greek Tombs near Knossos* (Cambridge, 1957)

E. L. Smithson: 'The Protogeometric Cemetery at Nea Ionia, 1949', *Hesperia*, xxx (1961), pp. 147–78

V. R. d'A. Desborough: 'The Dark Age Pottery from Settlement and Cemeteries', *Lefkandi*, i, ed. M. R. Popham, L. H. Sackett and P. G. Themelis, *Brit. Sch. Athens*, Suppl. vol. xi (London, 1980), pp. 281–350

B. Wells: *The Protogeometric Period* (1983), iv/2–3 of *Results of the Excavations East of the Acropolis 1970–1974*, ii of *Asine* (Stockholm, 1938–)

J. N. Coldstream: 'A Protogeometric Nature Goddess from Knossos', *Bull. Inst. Class. Stud. U. London*, xxxi (1984), pp. 93–104

W. D. E. Coulson: 'The Dark Age Pottery of Sparta', *Annu. Brit. Sch. Athens*, lxxx (1985), pp. 29–84

R. W. V. Catling and I. S. Lemos: *The Protogeometric Building at Toumba: The Pottery*, ii.1 of *Lefkandi, Brit. Sch. Athens,* Suppl. Vol. xxii, ed. M. R. Popham, P. G. Calligas and L. H. Sackett (London, 1990)

J. N. Coldstream: 'The Protogeometric and Geometric Pottery', *Knossos, North Cemetery: Early Greek Tombs, Brit Sch. Athens, Suppl. Vol.* xxviii, ed. J. N. Coldstream and H. W. Catling (London, 1996), pp. 311–420

3. GEOMETRIC. Geometric pottery (*c.* 900–*c.* 700 BC), a style characterized by abstract rectilinear designs, evolved in Attica from a Protogeometric (PG) phase in which the motifs were predominantly circular. It was always subject to wide regional variations, initially as a result of poor communications during the Dark Age, later reflecting the emergence and growth of the independent city-state (*polis*) and its pride in local tradition. Of the many regional styles, Attic Geometric was the most fully developed and the most influential.

(i) Introduction. (ii) Attic. (iii) Other mainland styles. (iv) Island styles.

(i) Introduction. Painted Geometric pottery, almost always made on the wheel, is found in Greek settlements, sanctuaries and cemeteries. Its export outside the Aegean, eastwards to Cyprus and the Levant, westwards to the newly founded Greek colonies in Italy and Sicily, attests the expanding horizons of the Greek world, especially in the 8th century BC. The best-preserved specimens come from graves, and special care was often taken in the manufacture of vessels designed for funerary purposes. Groups of whole vessels offered in individual graves illustrate the development of local styles; but their absolute chronology is determined, however indirectly, by exported specimens found in datable contexts overseas.

Geometric pottery is divided into Early (EG; *c.* 900–*c.* 850 BC), Middle (MG; *c.* 850–*c.* 760 BC) and Late (LG;

c. 760–*c.* 700 BC) phases; in the Attic and related styles, each phase is subdivisible into two further stages, thus EG I (*c.* 900–*c.* 875 BC) and EG II (*c.* 875–*c.* 850 BC), MG I (*c.* 850–*c.* 800 BC) and MG II (*c.* 800–*c.* 760 BC), LG I (*c.* 760–*c.* 735 BC) and LG II (*c.* 735–*c.* 700 BC). During EG and most of MG, ornament was almost always abstract, with a few cautious experiments in representational drawing. Then, from MG II onwards, Attic vase painters introduced extended scenes that constituted the first consistent figural style in Greek art. Funerals and battles were portrayed, notably on enormous vessels (LG I) designed as monuments to mark aristocratic graves. During LG figural scenes became quite common on Argive, Euboian and Boiotian pottery; but the preoccupation with elaborate funerary and warlike themes was peculiar to Attica. The battle scenes may reveal interest in a heroic past, though attempts to identify specific events in Homeric and other epic poetry remain inconclusive. In LG II, however, the introduction of centaurs and other supernatural creatures implies an awakening interest in the portrayal of myth. The rendering of human figures and animals, almost always drawn in full silhouette, was conceptual rather than representational; the artist drew not what he saw from any one viewpoint, but the sum of what he knew to be there. Despite their simplicity, minor variations in figure drawing have led to the identification of individual painters and workshops.

(ii) Attic. The EG and MG stages of the Attic styles are best represented in the Kerameikos cemeteries of Athens, where the vase forms evolved naturally from their Protogeometric precursors. The amphora cremation urn remained the leading closed shape, its proportions more attenuated than before, but the placing of its handles still varied according to the sex of the deceased. The oinochoe developed a plumper body and a ring base. Pyxides were globular or pointed in EG, but a new broad and flat form appeared in MG I; the lips were inset to receive lids. The chief drinking vessels, the skyphos and the kantharos, were shallower than in PG, and a ring base replaced the PG conical foot; the kantharos with high-swung handles was introduced in MG II. The krater occurs only in the graves for male cremations and gradually developed a tall pedestal with a ribbed stem.

As in mature PG, decoration in EG and MG was still predominantly executed on a dark ground, but the motifs were new. Concentric circles were replaced by rectilinear designs applied in reserved panels and zones to emphasize the focal points of the vase. The principal motif was the key meander with diagonal hatching. Multiple zigzags and battlements were also frequent. Ornament in EG was usually simple and austere, small units of decoration being dominated by large expanses of dark paint. In MG I the decorated areas became larger, producing a fine balance between light and dark and emphasizing the form and articulation of the vase, in which there is complete harmony between shape and decoration, with the reserved panels coinciding with the handle attachments. In MG II the decoration spread still further, covering the upper part of large vases and organized round a central meander panel.

Whereas representations of living creatures had previously been exceptional and confined to isolated figures inconspicuously placed, from late MG II to late LG I there was a sudden abundance of funerary and battle scenes painted on gigantic vessels up to 1.7 m high. They stood as markers over aristocratic graves in the Dipylon cemetery of Athens, enabling libations to be poured to the dead through holes pierced in their bases. For female graves these monuments took the form of especially large belly-handled amphorae with figured panels surrounded by geometric ornament, which depicted the deceased lying in state on a bier among mourners (*prothesis*). On the vast pedestalled kraters provided for men, the *prothesis* also included retinues of warriors and chariot teams; scenes of war on land or sea might be added on other parts of the vase. The figural decoration occasionally included depictions of deer and goats, often in continuous decorative friezes. The Dipylon cemetery gives its name to the leading vase painter of the LG I phase, the DIPYLON MASTER. Most of the monumental grave vases (e.g. Athens, N. Archaeol. Mus., 804) are attributed to him, his younger contemporary the HIRSCHFELD PAINTER or their close associates. The human figures are stiff and static, hardly less abstract than the surrounding ornament, but these painters achieved clarity by avoiding overlapping bodies and representing every limb. To soften the contrast between the silhouettes and the hatched geometric motifs, light filling ornaments were inserted into the figured panels.

In LG I decoration covered virtually the entire surface of the vase. On the vessels without figures important zones were emphasized by large and complex meanders or by rows of square panels ('metopes'); usually containing quatrefoils, swastikas, lozenges, chequerboards or water-birds with hatched bodies. During the final phase, LG II, figure drawing became more fluid and more varied in theme, while the geometric ornament lost its discipline, both in execution and in its arrangement on the vase. The monumental Dipylon cemetery vases passed out of fashion, but much figured pottery was still made for funerary purposes. The chief shape was a neck handled amphora of moderate size, its lip encrusted with freely modelled serpents, the guardians of the dead. The neck panel often contained a condensed *prothesis* scene, with female mourners distinguished by long hair and latticed skirts. Processions of chariots and foot soldiers filled the main body zones, conveying a greater sense of movement than their precursors on the Dipylon vases; narrower zones contained friezes of grazing deer, or hounds pursuing a hare. Towards the end of LG II the *prothesis* was sometimes replaced by a chain of female dancers, while lions, bulls, centaurs and winged goats joined the repertory of animals in subsidiary friezes. Other important shapes included the large round-mouthed pitcher and the shallow skyphos decorated inside with concentric figural bands in the manner of embossed metal bowls imported from the Levant.

The figure drawing on Attic LG II varies greatly in style and quality. Many different artists and workshops have been distinguished, but the most significant vase painters followed the tradition of the Dipylon Master. Humans and animals were still depicted conceptually and in silhouette but gradually became less rigid. This process began with the Sub-Dipylon group, which includes a krater (London, BM, 1899.2–19.1) showing an unusual scene of a man and a woman departing by ship, perhaps alluding to the legend of Theseus and Ariadne, an early experiment in mythological representation. The style was developed further by the Philadelphia Painter and led to the prolific output of the workshop that produced an amphora in Athens, NM 894 (N. Archaeol. Mus., St. 222).

Attic Geometric vases were copiously exported during the two MG phases, influencing the pottery of almost every region, but the export and influence of Attic pottery declined sharply in LG, when the regional styles diverged most widely.

(iii) Other mainland styles. The best-known and most important Geometric styles in the Peloponnese were the Argive and Corinthian, which evolved from the local PG a little later than their Attic equivalent. Both displayed a close affinity with Attic shapes and decoration during their EG and MG I phases, but subsequently they developed on more original lines.

Argive LG is distinguished by both its linear ornament and its figural motifs. The best and most characteristic work occurs on large kraters and amphorae found in graves. Their purely geometric compositions, covering most of the vessel, are elaborate but less carefully structured than those of Attic: the result is often a patchwork of zones, long panels and metopes without the central emphasis of the Attic designs. The meander appears in a stepped form, giving the composition a diagonal thrust. Smaller motifs were mass-produced with a multiple brush; most typical are rows of leaf-shaped lozenges and small birds in silhouette. Figural scenes were not funerary but drawn from everyday life, the favourite subject being a man reining in one or two horses (e.g. Argos, Archaeol. Mus., C 201 and C 1). The field sometimes also contained small filling ornaments such as fish, large birds or T-shaped objects, perhaps representing mangers or tripods. Rows of female dancers entered the repertory in LG II, linking hands and carrying branches. The chief manufacturing centre was Argos, where many different artists and workshops have been distinguished. Asine, on the gulf of Argos, produced a slightly different style, still influenced to some degree by Attic. Unlike its Attic and Corinthian counterparts, Argive LG was not succeeded by any consistent Orientalizing style; deep kraters with Sub-Geometric decoration were made throughout the 7th century BC and even imitated at Syracuse (Syracuse, Mus. Archeol. Reg.).

Quite different was the character of Corinthian LG, which excelled in small shapes with simple and restrained decoration. Thin zones of vertical chevrons or sigmas were preferred to heavy motifs such as the meander, and much of the surface was covered with fine horizontal lines. Corinthian LG potters eschewed figure drawing almost entirely; the only living creature to appear regularly in the repertory is the marsh bird, at first drawn singly or in confronted pairs, and later mass-produced in miniature silhouette files using the multiple brush. An important innovation in shape was the kotyle, which at once became the favourite Corinthian drinking vessel.

Corinthian pottery of this phase was already remarkable for its well-levigated yellow clay, its precise potting and its thin walls; it was thus becoming the most widely and abundantly exported fine ware in the Greek world and often inspired local imitations elsewhere. Most exports went west to Delphi, Ithaka and to the new colonies of Magna Graecia, whose foundation dates—given by Thucydides and others—help to establish absolute dates for the Corinthian pottery found there and thence for all other LG schools.

During the last two decades of the 8th century BC Corinthian artists were the first to develop an Orientalizing style. Even so, the bulk of their output was still of Geometric character. The most important shapes of these years, both of outstandingly fine fabric, were the globular aryballos and a deeper version of the kotyle. In a grave group at the Euboian colony of Pithekoussai (Ischia), several globular aryballoi are accompanied by an Egyptian scarab of the pharaoh Bocchoris (*reg* 717–712 BC), thereby providing another dating point for Geometric pottery.

In Lakonia, finds of Geometric pottery are limited to fragments from sanctuaries at Sparta and Amyklai. Little is known of the Geometric sequence there before the rise of the distinctive LG style. It is characterized by tall and baggy shapes inherited from the local PG tradition, including the lakaina, the normal Lakonian drinking vessel. The decoration, usually applied over a creamy slip, was at first influenced by Argive LG, especially on large vases; subsequently delicate ornament of Corinthian character appeared on the smaller vessels. Figures were rare and confined to scenes of dancing and horse-taming. A Sub-Geometric or 'Transitional' phase persisted through the early 7th century BC until the appearance of the local Orientalizing style.

Like Lakonia, other parts of the Peloponnese show little sign of any settled EG or MG phase. Arcadian LG was strongly influenced by the pottery of the Argolid. The other regions—Achaia, Elis and Messenia—shared a West Greek LG style that lasted well into the 7th century BC and spread to Aitolia, Acarnania and Ithaka. There are local differences between the LG pottery of these regions, but all shared a preference for a tall kantharos and a common debt to Corinth in the decoration, consisting of small, widely spaced motifs in narrow zones encased between large numbers of fine horizontal lines.

The Boiotian style was closely related to that of its Attic neighbour until the outset of LG, when individual characteristics emerged. The most distinctive vessels were large oinochoai, their decoration becoming increasingly rich, with funerary serpents modelled on their handles; they were produced at Thebes, along with kraters, kantharoi and pyxides in a similar style. The linear ornament is compounded of Corinthian, Attic and Euboian elements; the wide range of figural themes includes warriors with horses, dancers, hunters, boxers and a nature goddess flanked by beasts and birds. From outside Thebes comes a very different Boiotian group of mainly Sub-Geometric pottery: high-footed burial amphorae with wide necks, coated with a thick white slip and decorated with a different repertory of motifs derived from Euboia.

Thessaly was the most northerly region to manufacture wheelmade Geometric pottery. Its local style was influenced from the south by Attica and Euboia and from the north by the handmade painted ware of Macedonia. The chief northern shapes adopted were the jug with cut-away neck, the high-handled kantharos and the trigger-handled cup. The profusion of densely packed rectilinear ornaments on 9th century BC vases was derived from the north, but from MG II onwards the new influences were from Attica and Euboia.

(iv) Island styles. In Euboia and the Cyclades the transition from PG to Geometric was very slow: throughout the 9th century BC and even in the early 8th both areas continued essentially in the local PG tradition, which Thessaly also shared to some extent. The chief drinking vessel in this Sub-Protogeometric style was the Euboian skyphos with pendent concentric semicircles; its wide Mediterranean distribution, from al Mina in northern Syria to Veii in Etruria, attests the trading enterprise of the Euboians even before their foundation of the first western colonies.

Much Euboian Sub-Protogeometric pottery has been found in the graves and settlement at Lefkandi, where the usual shapes were amphorae, oinochoai, lekythoi, globular pyxides, kraters, skyphoi, kalathoi and cups. Apart from the rendering of ships on two 9th-century BC vessels (Eretria, Archaeol. Mus.), decoration was unadventurous. On a dark ground, concentric circular motifs still play a leading part, supplemented by groups of diagonal bars, silhouetted double-axes and hour-glasses, and latticed triangles. Occasional imitations of Attic Geometric appear from MG I onwards, while at Eretria (founded *c.* 800 BC) the earliest pottery echoes the Attic MG II phase, with little sign of Sub-Protogeometric features.

The change to Euboian LG is associated with the Cesnola Painter, who decorated a vast ovoid krater (New York, Met., 74.51.965) found at Kourion in Cyprus, which is now generally thought to be Euboian rather than Naxian. Though much influenced in style by the Attic Dipylon Master, the Cesnola Painter evolved a typically Euboian repertory of figural themes, all of which appear on the Kourion Krater; the horse at the manger with a double-axe in the field, the frieze of grazing horses and the oriental Tree of Life flanked by deer or goats. Pottery by this painter or his workshop was widely exported and profoundly influenced a colonial Euboian school on Pithekoussai. The decoration of Euboian LG skyphoi and other small shapes was at first adapted from the Attic metopal friezes, with local variations; later miniature bird files were introduced from Corinth, and some motifs were painted in added white. Towards the end of LG large high-footed amphorae were produced, with thick vertical wavy lines on their broad necks.

In the 9th century BC a Sub-Protogeometric style like that of Euboia flourished in the Cyclades, especially on the northern islands of Andros and Tenos, but influence from Attic MG gradually permeated the entire archipelago. The Attic connection persisted into the beginning of Cycladic LG with its metopal decoration on the smaller shapes; subsequently distinct schools on Naxos, Paros, Melos and Thera moved away from Attic. Naxos and Paros produced most of the pottery offered at the sanctuary on Delos: Naxian figural and linear decoration was close to that of Euboia, and the most individual shape was a very slim neck-handled amphora with bands on its body and birds on its neck (e.g. Mykonos, Archaeol. Mus.); Parian linear decoration was light and airy, often confined to sigmas, vertical dashes and dots floating in a wide field. A Melian workshop, specializing in kraters, amphorae and unusual fenestrated stands, rendered apparently tail-less birds, and animals in the manner of the Attic Hirschfeld Painter. On Thera a retarded LG style lasted through much of the 7th century BC. Its amphorae and neckless pithoi, made to contain cremations, were conservatively decorated with meanders, wheel motifs and other linear Geometric designs. Meanwhile artists on Tenos specialized in large amphorae made of coarse clay and decorated in relief with a wide variety of figural motifs.

The main Geometric style of Crete originated at Knossos, where copious offerings in family chamber tombs have been found. It again came to its fullest expression in the decoration of cremation urns, usually in the form of neckless ovoid pithoi with lids and two or four handles. A true Geometric style was not established until the end of the 9th century BC; instead of evolving directly from orthodox PG, it was preceded by an interlude of florid curvilinear decoration known as Protogeometric B. During a fleeting EG phase, the PG B repertory was combined with meanders and other motifs borrowed from Attic Geometric, but the Attic element predominated in MG, and the decoration became more disciplined and rectilinear. In the LG period Attic influence waned, and though a dark ground was still used, it was often enlivened by ornament in white paint. Figural motifs were scarce, but there was a refreshing variety in the depiction of birds, including some with multiple heads (e.g. Herakleion, Archaeol. Mus., Fortetsa 1501). The influence of Cypriot imports can be seen in the globular lekythos with a ridge on the neck, which was often decorated with circles in the Cypriot manner.

The Knossian Geometric style spread over most of Crete but failed to reach either extremity. In the east an Eteocretan style, with wild curvilinear decoration, flourished throughout the 8th century BC, while the little-known Kydonian school in the far west seems to have been even further removed from the central Cretan style.

A fairly homogeneous East Greek Geometric style was shared by the Dodekanese, Samos, Chios and the Greek coastal settlements of Asia Minor. It even spread to the non-Greek inhabitants of Caria; further north, however, the Greeks of Lesbos and Asiatic Aiolis preferred to produce Greek vase shapes using the native Anatolian technique of a grey Bucchero fabric with incised decoration.

For EG and MG in East Greece the cemeteries of Kos and Rhodes provide the fullest sequence. On closed shapes, as in PG, the main decoration was confined to the shoulder with dark paint below. Concentric semicircles surviving from PG were supplemented by latticed or hatched rectilinear ornament: hour-glasses, lozenges and triangles in EG, followed in MG by battlements and nets of lozenges inside triangles. Attic influence was very slight, except on some MG wares from Samos and Miletos, and a few MG II vessels from Rhodes. From MG onwards, lekythoi acquired a ridge on the neck in imitation of Cypriot imports, but their decoration was still often in the local dark-ground Geometric manner.

The use of a dark ground persisted into East Greek LG, when the decoration was often broken up into metopal squares. Samos was unusual in maintaining links with Attic LG I: elsewhere a purely local stock of metopal motifs developed, including outlined and latticed lozenges, meander hooks, birds and the so-called 'Rhodian tree', composed of a latticed triangle with two square hooks attached to its apex. This repertory appeared on high-footed kraters, round-mouthed jugs and especially on the most popular drinking vessel, a local adaptation of the Corinthian hemispherical kotyle. Also typical of Dodekanesian LG are Geometric versions of the cable and the palm tree, adapted from Levantine ivories. Imitations of Cypriot unguent vessels continued, and Rhodian aryballoi of Oriental character, decorated with a spaghetti-like combination of concentric circles and wavy lines, were widely exported. Figure drawing is extremely rare, though a *prothesis* scene appears on a fragmentary Samian kantharos (Kolonna, Heraion Mus., K 76), and several vase fragments from Chios (Chios, Archaeol. Mus.) show scenes involving ships and human figures, including a warrior confronting a lion.

In the East Greek world a Sub-Geometric manner persisted well into the 7th century BC. Especially conservative was the shallow 'bird bowl', a descendant of the LG kotyle, which preserved the purely Geometric format of a latticed bird between lozenges until around 600 BC.

C. Dugas and C. Rhomaios: *Les Vases préhelléniques et géométriques* (1934), xv of *Exploration archéologique de Délos* (Paris, 1909–)

S. S. Weinberg: *The Geometric and Orientalizing Pottery* (1943), vii/1 of *Corinth: Results of the Excavations Conducted by the American School of Classical Studies at Athens* (Princeton, 1932–)

K. Kübler: *Die Nekropole des 10. bis 8. Jahrhunderts* (1954), v/1 of *Kerameikos: Ergebnisse der Ausgrabungen* (Berlin, 1939–)

J. K. Brock: *Fortetsa: Early Greek Tombs near Knossos*, Brit. Sch. Athens, Suppl. Paper no. 2 (Cambridge, 1956)

K. F. Johansen: 'Exochi: Ein frührhodisches Gräberfeld', *Acta Archaeol.* [Copenhagen], xxviii (1958) [whole issue]

R. M. Cook: *Greek Painted Pottery* (London, 1960, rev. 1972), chap. 3

J. M. Davison: 'Attic Geometric Workshops', *Yale Class. Stud.*, xvi (1961) [whole issue]

E. T. H. Brann: *Late Geometric and Protoattic Pottery, Mid 8th to Late 7th Century BC* (1962), viii of *The Athenian Agora* (Princeton, 1953–)

P. Courbin: *La Céramique géométrique de l'Argolide* (Paris, 1966)

J. N. Coldstream: *Greek Geometric Pottery* (London, 1968)

B. Schweitzer: *Die geometrische Kunst Griechenlands* (Cologne, 1969); Eng. trans. by P. Usborne and C. Usborne as *Greek Geometric Art* (London, 1971), chaps 1–4

G. Ahlberg: *Prothesis and Ekphora in Greek Geometric Art* (Göteborg, 1971)

J. N. Coldstream: 'The Cesnola Painter: A Change of Address', *Bull. Inst. Class. Stud. U. London*, xviii (1971), pp. 1–15

A. Ruckert: 'Frühe Keramik Böotiens', *Ant. Kst*, x (1976) [suppl. issue]

J. N. Coldstream: *Geometric Greece* (London, 1977)

L. Morricone: 'Sepolture della prima età del ferro a Coo', *Annu. Scu. Archeol. Atene & Miss. It. Oriente*, lvi (1978), pp. 9–427

V. R. d'A. Desborough: 'The Dark Age Pottery from Settlement and Cemeteries', *Lefkandi*, i, ed. M. R. Popham, L. H. Sackett and P. G. Themelis, *Brit. Sch. Athens,* Suppl. vol. xi (London, 1980), pp. 281– 350

J. Boardman with M. J. Price: 'The Late Geometric Pottery', ibid., pp. 57–79

M.-G. Bock: *The Development of Narrative on Geometric Vases* (diss., Albion College, 1996)

J. N. Coldstream: 'The Protogeometric and Geometric Pottery', *Knosses, North Cemetary: Early Greek Tombs, Brit. Sch. Athens,* Suppl. Vol. xxviii, ed. J. N. Coldstream and H. W. Catling (London, 1996), pp. 311–420

J. Boardman: Early Greek Vase Painting (London, 1998), chap. 3

J. Luke: *Ports of Trade, Al Mina, and Geometric Greek Pottery in the Levant* (Oxford, 2003)

A. M. Leatherman: *The Italian Geometric Pottery: Workshops and Interactions* (diss., Providence, RI, Brown U., 2004)

M. B. Moore: *Greek Geometric and Protoattic Pottery* (New York, 2004)

4. ORIENTALIZING. By the time Greece emerged from its Dark Age, significant trade links had been re-established between Greece and the eastern Mediterranean, and after the disintegration of the Geometric style in the late 8th century BC, Greek vase painters began to look to the Near East for fresh ideas, creating an Orientalizing movement. There was still little direct contact with the major artistic centres of Egypt and Assyria; the immediate sources

of the new designs were chiefly the small-scale arts of the Neo-Hittite principalities of north Syria and the Phoenician trading cities, especially their ivories and metal bowls. Metalwork from the Anatolian kingdoms of Urartu and Phrygia also exercised some influence.

Curvilinear plant motifs, notably the lotus, palmette and rosette, formed striking contrasts with the predominantly abstract and rectilinear designs of the previous Geometric style. Animal friezes became more varied and naturalistic under eastern influences; the usual stock of Orientalizing animals, often varied within the same frieze, comprised lions, panthers, bulls, boars, birds, deer and goats, as well as fantastic creatures such as sphinxes, griffins and sirens. Human figures were affected too: facial features, hardly rendered at all in the simple Geometric silhouette technique, assumed exaggerated proportions, especially in the outline drawings on early Orientalizing vases.

(i) Introduction. (ii) Proto-Corinthian. (iii) Proto-Attic. (iv) Other areas.

(i) Introduction. As in the Geometric period, regional schools differed widely. Corinth and Athens produced the most ambitious Orientalizing styles, making much use of the human figure and thereby enabling the identification of individual painters and workshops. Since they anticipate the riper Archaic vase painting of the two cities (*see* §5(i) and (ii) below), these styles are called Proto-Corinthian and Proto-Attic. Other Orientalizing styles arose in Lakonia, on Crete, in the Cyclades, in various parts of the East Greek world and sporadically in the western colonies. In Boiotia and the Argolid, apart from a few Orientalizing experiments, a Sub-Geometric style prevailed; indeed, even at Corinth much Sub-Geometric pottery was contemporary with the masterpieces of Proto-Corinthian. There and elsewhere the Orientalizing style was initiated by a few innovative artists who tempered the local Geometric style with an eclectic repertory of oriental features always adapted to Greek taste.

In the rendering of figures, Orientalizing vase painters progressed from the plain silhouette of Geometric times towards outline drawing, silhouette with incised details, and the use of additional colours. Outline was suitable for large surfaces but not for the miniature unguent vessels in which the leading Proto-Corinthian artists specialized; here incision on silhouette achieved finer detail, and such was the origin of the incised Black-figure technique. The most frequently added colour was a purplish red, although Proto-Attic artists at first preferred white. During the mid-7th century BC polychrome vase painting was briefly attempted in Corinth, Athens and the Cyclades, perhaps prompted by the revival of large-scale wall painting in the first monumental temples. These technical innovations were skilfully exploited in the rendering of extended figural scenes; the incised silhouette technique in particular allowed the figures to overlap in tightly knit compositions without loss of clarity.

As Homeric and other epic poetry circulated around the Greek world, scenes of myth were more frequently attempted and are more recognizable than the tentative experiments of Attic LG vase painters. Many Orientalizing scenes portray violent conflicts between heroes and monsters: Herakles fighting Nessos or other centaurs, Perseus beheading Medusa, Bellerophon slaying the Chimaera, Odysseus and his companions blinding Polyphemos, or episodes from the Sack of Troy, as in the relief decoration on a coarse storage amphora found on Mykonos (Mykonos, Archaeol. Mus.). Sometimes personal attributes were added to identify individual deities or heroes, for example Apollo's lyre or Herakles' bow. In rare instances the artist painted names beside the figures, as on a Proto-Attic stand (*c.* mid-7th century BC; Berlin, Antikensamml., A 42; destr.), on which the single word *Menela*[o]*s* identified a gathering of the Greek commanders at Troy. Another purpose of inscriptions was to identify the artist or potter.

The wide distribution of Orientalizing pottery outside the Aegean reflects the expansion of Greek trade and the establishment of more distant colonies, such as the shores of the north Aegean, the Sea of Marmara, the Black Sea and Libya. Corinth was the most prolific exporter to the western colonies, while from the late 7th century BC East Greek pottery predominated in the Black Sea, Cyprus, the Levantine coast and the Greek trading post of Naukratis in the Nile Delta. The absolute chronology of Orientalizing pottery is deduced from specimens found in datable contexts outside the Aegean. The foundations of Sicilian colonies from Gela (689 BC) to Selinus (*c.* 625 BC) supply clues for the dating of Proto-Corinthian, while for the East Greek styles a useful dating point is provided by finds from Meshad Hashavyahu in Palestine, occupied by Greek mercenaries only between 621 and 609 BC.

R. M. Cook: *Greek Painted Pottery* (London, 1960, rev. 1972), pp. 41–160

K. Fittschen: *Untersuchungen zum Beginn der Sagendarstellungen bei den Griechen* (Berlin, 1969)

(ii) Proto-Corinthian. Corinth was the first centre to develop an Orientalizing style. Though its earliest products were the Cumae group of oinochoai (*c.* 720 BC), combining Late Geometric (LG) decoration on their necks with lotus and other bold floral designs on their bodies, the evolution of the style is best illustrated by the series of miniature aryballoi (h. seldom over 80 mm). The changes in their shape reflect the chronological subdivision of Proto-Corinthian into Early (EPC; *c.* 720–*c.* 690 BC), Middle (MPC; *c.* 690–*c.* 650 BC) and Late (LPC; *c.* 650–*c.* 640 BC): the aryballoi were globular in EPC; they became ovoid and increasingly attenuated in MPC; and they eventually assumed a slim piriform shape during LPC and the Transitional phase (*c.* 640–*c.* 625 BC) before Early Corinthian.

Figure drawing was very rare in Corinthian LG, but it often appeared on EPC globular aryballoi. Strutting cocks, grazing animals, fish and floral motifs were painted in an uneasy combination of silhouette, outline and reserve techniques, with occasional touches of incision. The limitations of this combination are apparent in the scene depicting a warrior and a mounted hunter on the only EPC aryballos to portray human figures (*c.* 700 BC; London, BM, 1969.12–15.1). In a scene only 35 mm high, even the finest painted line would be too heavy for anatomical details, especially of the human face.

Consequently the main figural zones on the bodies of the ovoid MPC aryballoi were rendered almost completely in the new Black-figure technique. Much finer detail could be obtained through incision on a full black silhouette, enlivened by touches of added red. Floral motifs, however, remained in outline and were relegated to the shoulder. Animal friezes often occupied the main zones, but the more ambitious hands began to experiment with mythical scenes. The most adventurous artist of the First Black-figure style (*c.* 690–*c.* 660 BC) was the Ajax Painter, named after an aryballos showing the hero falling on his sword (Berlin, Antikensamml., 3319). On another aryballos (Boston, MA, Mus. F.A., 95.12) he depicted probably Herakles (or perhaps Zeus) using a firebrand to attack a centaur, while a puzzling scene on a third (Paris, Louvre, CA 617) is often explained as the rescue of the young Helen from Theseus and Peirithoos by her twin brothers Castor and Pollux. Although this painter's drawing is vigorous, his human figures are ill-proportioned, with arms and faces too large for the body; his compositions are episodic rather than unified, and the representation of movement is unconvincing.

The possibilities of Black-figure were also explored on larger MPC shapes, especially the oinochoe, the flat pyxis and the large kotyle. Three kotylai demonstrate growing mastery over the new technique. On the earliest, depicting a procession of horsemen (Aegina, Archaeol. Mus., 191), incision is virtually confined to the excessively large horses, but much more assured painting and incision distinguishes the 'Hound Kotyle' (London, BM, 1860.4–4.18) in the Second Black-figure style (*c.* 660–*c.* 650 BC): the animals are full of springy curves and latent energy, with touches of red on their necks. The third vessel is the finest example of the Second Black-figure style, the fragmentary 'Bellerophon Kotyle' (Aegina, Archaeol. Mus. 253), which depicts the Corinthian hero mounted on his winged horse Pegasus, confronting the fire-breathing Chimaera in a spacious and airy composition flanked by attendant sphinxes, all drawn with a graceful finesse of line never equalled in subsequent Corinthian vase painting.

The finest and most elaborately decorated aryballoi also belong to this decade, and despite their miniature scale some even incorporate subsidiary figural zones. The main Black-figure scenes show a new mastery of movement and even give an impression of depth through the use of overlapping figures clearly separated by incision. The compositions are now much more unified, as though first sketched out on a flat surface; this, together with occasional experiments in polychromy, may imply that they were to some extent inspired by temple murals. Two masters of the Second Black-figure style were the Boston Painter and the MACMILLAN PAINTER. The Boston Painter's name-piece (Boston, MA, Mus. F.A., 95.11) shows a hero confronting an oriental lion-man, while a more mature work (Paris, Louvre, CA 931) has a grim hoplite duel as the main scene, and a mouth modelled as a human face in the Daidalic style of contemporary sculpture. This painter achieves a monumental dignity on a miniature scale; his style is austere and restrained, with a minimum of incision and, unusually, no filling ornament. Very different was the approach of the Macmillan Painter, an exuberant virtuoso. His name vase, for example, the Macmillan Aryballos (London, BM, 1899.4–18.1), has a Neo-Hittite lion-head mouth and three miniscule figural zones on its body, of which the main one depicts eighteen embattled hoplites bearing various blazons on their shields. The two tiny friezes below, a horse race and a fox hunt, are studies in rapid movement. On a larger scale, the LPC Chigi Jug (Rome, Villa Giulia, 22679; see colour pl. 1:XIV, fig. 2) is a later work by the same hand, showing a scene of hoplites marching into battle, a second broad frieze combining a cavalcade, a lion hunt and a (fragmentary) representation of the Judgement of Paris, and another lively fox hunt below. The vase also displays the painter's experimental polychrome scheme: in addition to the usual black and red, two shades of brown were used for human flesh and body armour.

The LPC phase was on the whole a time of consolidation rather than invention. New shapes included the baggy round-mouthed olpe and the drop-shaped alabastron; added white on black was used for some narrow animal zones, and a red-and-black scheme was used for incised tongue and scale patterns. Figural decoration rarely ventured beyond the animal frieze, which became increasingly stereotyped and perfunctory with the transition to Ripe Corinthian Black-figure style.

H. G. G. Payne: *Protokorinthische Vasenmalerei* (1933), viii of *Bilder griechischer Vasen*, ed. J. D. Beazley and P. Jacobsthal (Berlin, 1930–)

T. J. Dunbabin and M. Robertson: 'Some Protocorinthian Vase-painters', *Annu. Brit. Sch. Athens*, xlviii (1953), pp. 172–81

T. J. Dunbabin: *Protocorinthian Pottery* (1962), ii of *Perachora*, ed. T. J. Dunbabin (Oxford, 1940–), pp. 4–132

J. L. Benson: 'Middle Protocorinthian Periodization', *Corinthiaca: Studies in Honour of D. A. Amyx* (Columbia, MO, 1986), pp. 97–106

D. A. Amyx: *Corinthian Vase-painting of the Archaic Period*, 3 vols (Berkeley, 1988)

(iii) Proto-Attic. Unlike Corinth, Athens had a firmly established Late Geometric (LG) figural style but little first-hand acquaintance with Near Eastern art. Consequently, the Proto-Attic style appeared later

than the Proto-Corinthian and involved a gradual modification of the Geometric tradition, perhaps only under indirect oriental influence. It is divided into Early (EPA; *c.* 700–*c.* 670 BC), Middle (MPA; *c.* 670–*c.* 630 BC) and Late (LPA; *c.* 630–*c.* 600 BC) phases. The finest painting occurs on large vessels that seem to have been produced mainly for aristocratic burials. Outline drawing was introduced in EPA, chiefly for facial features; white was added to the usual colour scheme in MPA; little use was made of incision until LPA when, under Corinthian influence, a true Black-figure technique was developed.

The pioneer of Proto-Attic vase painting was the ANALATOS PAINTER, whose style was inspired by the latest products of the LG Athens 894 workshop. The Analatos Painter's name vase is a hydria (*c.* 700 BC; Athens, N. Archaeol. Mus., 313) from Analatos, near Athens, which is decorated with Orientalizing plant motifs and heraldic lions; the dancing men and women on the neck are still in silhouette, but their features are accentuated in an un-Geometric manner. Throughout the next two decades the Analatos Painter experimented with outline faces and more fluent renderings of the human body than was achieved in Geometric vase painting. Typical of his mature style are squarish faces with over-emphasized features. Most EPA artists, however, clung more tenaciously to Geometric conventions. The Mesogeia Painter developed a lively if rough figural style derived from that of the Analatos Painter, but he crammed his backgrounds with Sub-Geometric filling ornament. Two other artists retained the angular contours of Geometric figure drawing: the N Painter, who introduced the cock into the repertory, is named after his preferred filling ornament, while the Passas Painter's best-known amphora (New York, Met., 21.88.18) shows a commanding figure with robe, sceptre and eagle, perhaps an early representation of Zeus. Around 680 BC the Passas Painter and the Analatos Painter collaborated in decorating two elaborate cauldrons with high stands for an aristocratic funeral (Mainz, Johannes Gutenberg-U., 153 and 156) which explored the possibilities of adding white and red to the colour scheme. White was preferred by these early artists and often used for subsidiary details on the latest EPA works of the 670s BC.

By MPA the Geometric heritage had been forgotten. The old themes of funerals, rows of dancers and chariot processions gave place to scenes of dynamic action, especially hoplite battles and mythical combats. White paint was used as much as black, and the combination—the Black-and-white style—could produce effective contrasts, as on a stand (Berlin, Antikensamml., A 40) with silhouetted warriors wearing white armour. Without incision, however, there could be confusion when bodies overlapped, as in two scenes showing Herakles rescuing Deianeira from the centaur Nessos, one on a stand (Athens, N. Archaeol. Mus.), the other on an amphora (New York, Met., 11.210.1). Both works are typical of a Wild style early in MPA, also remarkable for curious disparities in the scale of both figures and subsidiary motifs. Nevertheless, mastery of this new Black-and-white style was soon achieved by the POLYPHEMOS PAINTER *and the* RAM JUG PAINTER, though they were chary of overlapping figures and restrained in their choice of filling ornaments; the features of their outlined human faces assumed more naturalistic proportions. Rounded crowns, receding foreheads and bull necks are characteristic of the Polyphemos Painter, as in the eponymous scene on his amphora (Eleusis Mus.) showing the giant being blinded, whereas squarer faces, more in the tradition of the Analatos Painter, with long curved eyebrows and aquiline noses, were preferred by the Ram Jug Painter.

Soon after 650 BC a short-lived polychrome style using up to six colours was applied to some funerary vessels; but the main development in MPA was the gradual replacement of the Black-and-white style by an incised Black-figure technique derived from Proto-Corinthian pottery and accompanied by the use of red instead of white paint for subsidiary details. The fragmentary Kynosarges Amphora (*c.* 640 BC; Athens, N. Archaeol. Mus., 14497) combines Black-figure animal friezes, human scenes still in outline and luxuriant filling ornament everywhere; in the 630s BC the amphorae of the Pair Painter likewise combine opposed pairs of animal *protomes* in Black-figure with elaborate spirals of Cycladic origin.

Full Black-figure was achieved during LPA, and though the technique had first been perfected for miniature Corinthian work, it was now employed on grandiose Attic funerary vessels. Majestic lions and sirens were favourite subjects; filling ornament, sparser than before, was dominated by the Corinthian rosette, dotted or incised. Two important new shapes appeared: the kotyle krater, an enlargement of the lipless kotyle, and the one-piece amphora, often decorated with *protomes* of women or horses inside reserved panels. A Chimaera scene on a fragmentary kotyle krater (Athens, Kerameikos Mus., 154) may be an early work by the NETTOS PAINTER, the outstanding artist of this phase, who by the end of his career (*c.* 600 BC) had helped to lay the foundations of the Attic Black-figure style.

Apart from some sparsely decorated wine amphorae, Proto-Attic pottery was rarely exported beyond immediate neighbours. The abundance of MPA finds on Aigina, together with the Aiginetan letter forms of the inscription *Menela*[o]*s* on a Proto-Attic stand, have prompted the suggestion that Aigina, not Athens, was the chief centre for the MPA Black-and-white style.

J. M. Cook: 'Protoattic Pottery', *Annu. Brit. Sch. Athens*, xxxv (1934–5), pp. 165–219

K. Kübler: *Altattische Malerei* (Tübingen, 1950)

J. D. Beazley: *The Development of Attic Black Figure* (Berkeley, 1951), pp. 1–16

K. Kübler: *Die Nekropole des späten 8. bis frühen 6. Jahrhunderts* (1959), vi/1 of *Kerameikos: Ergebnisse der Ausgrabungen* (Berlin, 1939–)

E. T. H. Brann: *Late Geometric and Protoattic Pottery* (1962), viii of *The Athenian Agora* (Princeton, 1953–)

S. Papaspyridi-Karouzou: *Angeia tes Anagyrountos* [Pottery from Anagyrous] (Athens, 1963)

S. P. Morris: *The Black and White Style: Athens and Aigina in the Orientalizing Period* (New Haven, 1984)

(iv) Other areas. At Corinth the Orientalizing style had established itself by the end of the 8th century BC, and within a generation or two most other local schools were beginning to adopt it, though not regularly copying Corinthian models. Of these schools the Cretan was the earliest, indeed about as early as Corinthian; but though it lasted around a century it was more wayward than progressive, and invention was mainly restricted to forms of vegetable and abstract ornament. Birds occur fairly frequently, often in forms of pretty fantasy, notably with multiple heads. Animal and human figures are rare but may be adventurous. A spectacular early group of vases, perhaps peculiar to Knossos, is that of the so-called Polychrome pithoi, which have a white slip and bright red and indigo painted decoration; since both slip and paint wore badly, they were probably only for mortuary use.

In the Peloponnese, Argos had a robust Geometric school and admitted Orientalizing novelties reluctantly, but an impressive Orientalizing scene of the blinding of Polyphemos occurs on an exceptional polychrome krater (660s BC; Argos, Archaeol. Mus.). Presumably proximity to Corinth was fatal. There may, though, be Argive influence on the early 7th-century BC Fusco kraters of Syracuse, with their loose Orientalizing ornament and, in one instance, creditable animals; and a little later a more ambitious workshop, known from vases found at Megara Hyblaia, also in Sicily, attempted bolder figural scenes in a polychrome technique. However, in the Greek West as well, no independent new style took root.

In Lakonia, Orientalizing ornament became common early in the 7th century BC (Lakonian I): most was abstract, but some unpretentious little Lakonian I Fine ware pots (*c.* 650–*c.* 625 BC) bore rows of engagingly misshapen animals, and by the end of the century a Black-figure style had developed. Lakonian usually has a cream slip over a body fired pinkish to brown. Other finds suggest that some potters in the western Peloponnese experimented with the Orientalizing style but did not persevere.

Boiotian pottery was usually a debased version of that produced by its neighbours Athens, Corinth and Euboia. The first large group of Orientalizing vases, mainly big amphorae with tall conical feet, flaunt bands of thick zigzags, and their principal decoration, vegetable or animal, is often clumsily composed. This group may have continued throughout the 7th century BC or even longer. More remarkable is the 'Bird cup' group (*c.* 575–*c.* 500 BC), clumsy dishes, sometimes with a tall foot, and slightly less clumsy kantharoi; the decoration consists largely of flying birds and palmettes, generously coloured with red and later also yellow paint on a creamy (or later white) slip and drawn in a folksy style that is surprising for the period. In Euboia an Orientalizing group of big amphorae parallels those from Boiotia but are of better quality; and at Eretria a few artists towards the end of the 7th century BC misguidedly attempted human figures, though even these compare well with the ostensibly Black-figure work of the early 6th.

In the Cyclades the Orientalizing style was more welcomed, though only one school survived long. Lack of contextual information and close stylistic comparison makes dating and attribution to particular islands hazardous. The Ad group (?*c.* 700–*c.* 675 BC), now usually assigned to Paros, is a curious but enjoyable parody of Geometric. It is best represented by its broad amphorae, though other shapes occur. The neck usually depicts an elongated horse, which may be winged, the shoulder a tableau of animals, and the rest of the body carries bands of coarse ornament; often a creamy slip is used. Probably contemporary, but more innovative, is the Heraldic group, perhaps from Naxos. Its narrow amphorae have fronts bearing sinuous animals on the neck and below the shoulder, framed by ornament that is sometimes Orientalizing, while their backs are covered with rough scrawling, and the lower part of the body is banded; again a creamy slip is usual. Much more numerous is the Linear Island group (early to ?mid-7th century BC; see fig. 17); these mostly largish amphorae are staider in style and less provincial than their counterparts in Euboia and Boiotia. Decoration is concentrated on the upper part and consists of a few bold ornaments and some occasionally imaginative Orientalizing birds and beasts in panels on the shoulder. Except for the Linear Island vases, these and other early Orientalizing groups seem to be the products of independent workshops rather than regional schools, too individual to consolidate into a tradition, unless 'Melian' vases were descendants of the Ad group. The 'Melian' group was the longest-lived and the most successful of the Cycladic ventures. The vases, usually assigned to Paros or Melos (or both) between the mid-7th century BC and the early 6th, usually took the form of amphorae, hydriai and plates. The staple decoration consists of female heads, animals and big volutes, with gaudily coarse ornaments covering the rest of the pot. There are also some big amphorae with high feet, which have ineptly ambitious figural scenes in a polychrome technique. 'Melian' works are generally dull and unoriginal, borrowing from the East Greek Wild Goat style (see below) and increasingly from Corinthian.

East Greek Orientalizing had a long and mainly undistinguished existence, and despite the extent of the region, comprising all the west coast of Turkey and the islands offshore, the style was remarkably uniform. Unluckily, though there has been much excavation, finds have been patchy and often inadequately published: little is known of important cities such as Miletos, Smyrna and Phokaia, and there is disagreement over local schools and dating. Producers on Lesbos and to some extent mainland Aiolis adhered to the traditional, usually undecorated, grey Bucchero ware, but elsewhere most larger pots were made of a coarsish clay with a whitish slip, while

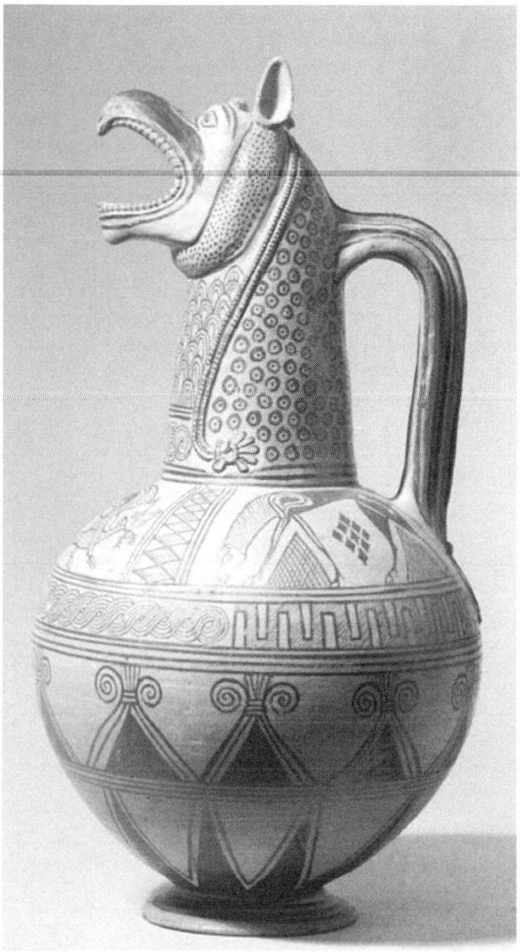

17. Ancient Greek Orientalizing jug with a griffin-head spout, Linear Island group, h. 415 mm, from ?Paros, *c.* 675–650 BC (London, British Museum, 1873.8-20.385)

cups were of finer clay and, except on Chios, were unslipped, following normal Geometric practice. During the 7th century BC the favourite type of cup was the 'Bird bowl', a shallow, two-handled vessel with a low foot, decorated with a neat Geometric-style bird in a panel flanked by lozenges. About the end of the century this formula was replaced by a loose scatter of Orientalizing ornaments, most often dotted rosettes, and the execution became coarser. Clay analysis has revealed them to be mainly north Ionian, particularly from Klazomenai. A rarer form was the rather taller Vroulian cup, which was produced from *c.* 600 BC to after 550 BC, probably on Rhodes, and was among the most elegant of all Greek vases. Specimens were covered inside and out with blackish paint and decorated with incised motifs, notably palmettes and lotuses, picked out in red paint. There are also innumerable cups decorated with simple bands of paint, which are used by the less wary as evidence of Ionian influence in Etruria.

The staple East Greek Orientalizing style has had various names, but now is most often known as the Wild Goat style. Graves on Rhodes have provided accurate dates for specimens from the last quarter of the 7th century BC, and judging by the extent of stylistic development and the paucity of earlier pieces that have been found, the style seems not to have arisen until *c.* 650 BC, being preceded by some Sub-Geometric and experimental Orientalizing, of which tantalizing scraps remain. After a little diversification the Wild Goat style settled into a routine—decorative but monotonous and increasingly arid. Largish oinochoai are the most frequent shape in the Rhodian burials, but dinoi, dishes and plates were also common, as, in the north, were amphorae. The principal decoration usually consists of animals, either filing round the body or grouped on the shoulder: goats occur most frequently, but the repertory includes spotted deer, geese, sphinxes, griffins and, less often, dogs and felines, all surrounded by well-spaced filling ornaments. On subordinate fields large versions of lotus flower and bud are characteristic. Heads and anatomical details are generally reserved; and purple was soon used to enliven the dark paint over the whitish slip. Typical of this Middle Wild Goat period is an oinochoe in London (*c.* 625–*c.* 600 BC; BM, 67.5–8.928). Clay analyses suggest that early production was dominated by south Ionia and primarily by Miletos. But around 600 BC north Ionian workshops adopted from Corinth the Black-figure technique, with its animal forms and often its filling ornament, while retaining the old reserving technique, frequently using both—in different fields—on the same pot. Coarse though they were, vases in this Late Wild Goat style were exported in greater numbers than their south Ionian precursors, perhaps simply because there was a wider market. The Late style is usually said to have ended in the 570s BC, but that may be too early, since in its reserving version it survived with minor modifications on Klazomenian sarcophagi well into the 5th century BC.

Contemporary developments in south Ionia are obscure, but it seems unlikely that vase painters adopted the Black-figure technique, since around the 560s BC a new reserving style appeared there, again, according to clay analysis, at Miletos. This, usually called the Fikellura style (named after the site in Rhodes), is closer to the Middle Wild Goat style than to the Late, though its practitioners abandoned the outlining of heads and showed greater originality. The commonest shape is a squat amphora (e.g. London, BM, 61.4–25.47); the decorative scheme ranges from close bands of ornament to a single figure in an empty field. Animals occur frequently, as do human figures, often revellers. Typical ornaments include crescents, simplified lotus flowers and buds and thick volutes, which may spread all round the body. The quality of workmanship is very uneven, even on the same pot, but Fikellura continued to be the liveliest of East Greek Orientalizing styles until the end of the 6th century BC, when it flagged and died out.

The pottery of Chios, recognizable by its very white slip, developed differently. Its best-known shape, the 'chalice', is a conical cup, later supported on a conical or near-conical foot. In the 7th century BC a fairly orthodox if rather clumsy variant of the Wild Goat style was current. In the 6th century BC this reserving style continued, notably on chalices bearing a single sphinx or animal or occasionally a human figure, and no longer encumbered by filling ornaments. More elaborate scenes of human action, sometimes in a polychrome technique, are featured in the Grand style of *c.* 575–*c.* 550 BC; at about the same time and a little earlier a form of Black-figure became popular, with rows of lions, sphinxes or revellers, generally depicted in a perfunctory Corinthianizing style. There may have been Chian workshops at Naukratis (particularly since Grand style vases have been found there but not yet in Chios), though the clay seems to be uniform. Imitation, sometimes inventive, is more certain on Thasos.

Pottery in the East Greek style was also produced in the adjoining non-Greek areas of Caria and Lydia. Carian specimens exhibit only debasement of its models, but Lydia had its own ceramic traditions, and its style was more fanciful. Elsewhere East Greek pottery influenced only 'Melian' vases.

E. Pfuhl: 'Der archaische Friedhof am Stadtberge von Thera', *Mitt. Dt. Archäol. Inst.: Athen. Abt.*, xxviii (1903), pp. 1–288, esp. pp. 183–93

H. G. G. Payne: 'Early Greek Vases from Knossos', *Annu. Brit. Sch. Athens*, xxix (1927–8), pp. 224–98, esp. pp. 277–98

R. M. Cook: 'Fikellura Pottery', *Annu. Brit. Sch. Athens*, xxxiv (1933–4), pp. 1–98

E. A. Lane: 'Lakonian Vase Painting', *Annu. Brit. Sch. Athens*, xxxiv (1933–4), pp. 99–189, esp. pp. 107–21

C. Dugas and C. Rhomaios: *Les Vases préhelléniques et géométriques* (1934), xv of *Exploration archéologique de Délos* (Paris, 1909–), pls 20–25

C. Dugas: *Les Vases orientalisants de style non mélien* (1935), xvii of *Exploration archéologique de Délos* (Paris, 1909–)

J. Boardman: 'Pottery from Eretria', *Annu. Brit. Sch. Athens*, xlvii (1952), pp. 1–48

J. K. Brock: *Fortetsa: Early Greek Tombs near Knossos*, Brit. Sch. Athens, Suppl. Paper no. 2 (Cambridge, 1956)

R. M. Cook: *Greek Painted Pottery* (London, 1960, rev. 1997)

C. Kardara: *Rhodiake angeiographia* [Rhodian vase painting] (Athens, 1963)

J. Boardman: *Excavations in Chios, 1952–1955: Greek Emporio* (London, 1967)

H. Walter: *Frühe samische Gefässe* (1968), v of *Samos* (Bonn, 1961–)

E. Walther-Karydi: *Samische Gefässe des 6. Jahrhunderts v. Chr.* (1973), vi/1 of *Samos* (Bonn, 1961–)

A. Ruckert: 'Frühe Keramik Boötiens, *Ant. Kst*, x (1976) [suppl. issue]

B. Schmalz: 'Zur Chronologie der böotischen Vogelschalen', *Marburger Winckelmann-Programm, 1977–8*, pp. 21–60

P. Dupont: 'Classification et détermination de provenance des céramiques grecques orientales archaïques d'Istros: Rapport préliminaire', *Dacia*, n. s., xxvii (1983), pp. 19–43

P. Zapheiropoulou: *Problemata tes Meliakes angeographias* [Problems relating to Melian vase painting] (Athens, 1985)

G. P. Schaus: 'Two Fikellura Vase Painters', *Annu. Brit. Sch. Athens*, lxxxi (1986), pp. 251–95

E. Moignard in J. N. Coldstream and H. W. Catling: *Knossos, North Cemetery: Early Greek Tombs, Brit. Sch. Athens, Suppl. Vol.* xxviii (London, 1996)

R. M. Cook and P. Dupont: *East Greek Pottery* (London, 1998)

5. Black-figure. Ancient Greek Black-figure vase painting is a silhouette technique in which black glaze is applied to the surface of the vase and enlivened by incision as well as accessory red and white. Vase painters at Corinth during the early 7th century BC were probably the first to incise lines through black glaze, a decorative approach very likely inspired by metalwork. From *c.* 620 to *c.* 480 BC, during the middle and late Archaic period, artists working there and in several other regions of the Greek world decorated vases in the Black-figure technique. Each of these fabrics takes its name from the region or city that produced it, with the exception of Chalcidian, which is named after inscriptions in the Chalcidian alphabet on many of the vases. The length of time these different fabrics were produced varied considerably, with Attic having the longest lifespan and the greatest quantity of surviving pieces.

(i) Corinthian. (ii) Attic. (iii) Lakonian. (iv) Boiotian. (v) East Greek and islands. (vi) Chalcidian. (vii) Caeretan. (viii) Euboian.

(i) Corinthian. During the 7th century Corinth was an especially active commercial centre, and from *c.* 625 to *c.* 580 BC it was the most productive ceramic centre in Greece. Corinthian vases are mostly small vessels, especially alabastra and aryballoi, and they are found in all areas of the Greek world. The figural decoration usually consists of animal friezes, horsemen or warriors. The rise of the rival Attic ceramic industry by *c.* 580 BC led Corinthian artists to produce larger shapes, especially column kraters and amphorae, which were often decorated with specific mythological themes. They also disguised the yellow Corinthian clay with a covering of red slip so that the finished products appeared to be direct imitations of Attic wares. Nevertheless, Attic vases soon dominated the market, and by *c.* 550 BC Corinthian Black-figure had declined steadily, although production of small vases, decorated just with ornament, continued.

(a) Introduction. Corinthian Black-figure vase painting is still usually classified in terms of the three stylistic periods defined by H. G. G. Payne: Early (EC; *c.* 625–*c.* 600 BC), Middle (MC; *c.* 600–*c.* 575 BC) and Late (LC; *c.* 575–*c.* 425 BC). Late Corinthian is subdivided by some scholars into two phases and by others into three: the stylistic characteristics of LC I (*c.* 575–*c.* 550 BC) are fairly well agreed on, but those distinguishing LC II AND III (*c.* 550–*c.* 425 BC) are not. Since Payne's work scholars have concentrated primarily on identifying the hands of individual painters and workshops by tracing the influence of one painter on another. More than 190 painters have been distinguished, comprising around 60 EC, 95 MC

and 60 LC artists; about 20% of these were active in more than one period. Only two painters, Chares of Lindos and Timonidas, signed their vases; the names of a few others are known from literary sources.

Transitions from one period to another were so gradual that many vases cannot be classified with certainty. Changes in style were accompanied by changes in vase shapes, and workshops usually specialized in manufacturing either small scent bottles or a selection of the larger vessels. Some painters seem to have decorated only one or two types of vase. The decoration is largely the same as that on Proto-Corinthian vases.

(b) Early. Animal friezes developed from those of the Proto-Corinthian Transitional phase. The new style is signalled by the widespread use of cross-incised rosette filling motifs, and its development is most easily followed by noting the evolution in the character and placement of these elements. Early forms are simply and neatly drawn and evenly but sparsely distributed in the field, as on several alabastra (St Petersburg, Hermitage; Brussels, Mus. Royaux A. & Hist., A51 and A52).

Soon the more innovative painters sought new effects and a new balance of proportions. They created new filling motifs, producing stronger contrasts between dark and light areas: some EC vases are quite baroque in this respect (e.g. an alabastron at U. Würzburg, Wagner-Mus., 254). Animals were made larger in relation to their friezes and friezes taller in relation to their vases. These changes probably reflect not only artistic but also economic factors, since vase paintings with larger animals and friezes could be made more quickly. But many painters resisted the pressure to sacrifice work of high quality and the pursuit of new interests to increased production. The variety of animals and filling ornaments was in fact greater than ever: the Dodwell Painter, for example, used at least 50 different filling ornaments. Panthers and goats became more numerous, lions and bulls rarer, and symmetrical compositions with pairs of animals flanking floral centrepieces occurred more frequently, as on the kotyle pyxis by the Royal Library Painter (*c.* 620–*c.* 600 BC; Brussels, Bib. Royale Albert 1er). A hallmark of this painter is the form of the rosette just above the rear inner leg of the panther. The figures were also drawn in greater detail than before and embellished more often with touches of red and white. The decoration of different parts of vases became systematized, for example with petals on the mouthplates of aryballoi and rays at the bases of kotylai, though there were characteristic variations from workshop to workshop.

The Figure style of EC displays more naturalism than its Proto-Corinthian forerunner. Eyes and noses are smaller, rounder and more correctly related to each other and to the face; waves of hair are looser and less artificially arranged; figures are more slender. At the beginning of the period, although narrative scenes occur, human figures are usually merely elements in a frieze alongside the animals (e.g. aryballos; Rhodes, Archaeol. Mus., 13008). Increasingly, however, groups of human figures formed scenes in the centres of friezes, while the animals either appeared to be spectators or entirely disappeared. Towards the end of the period large narrative scenes appeared on column kraters, a new shape of vase (e.g. Paris, Louvre, E 635). The use of each side of a large vase for a single important figural composition was a momentous development in Greek vase painting. Most scholars look to Athens for the origins of monumental Black-figure painting, although the column krater is generally agreed to be a Corinthian invention. A significant consequence of this innovation was the relegation of the animal frieze to a subordinate position on these kraters.

(c) Middle. The period is one of transition for the Animal style. At first painters followed the trends of EC by continuing to invent new animal poses and combinations of animals and floral centrepieces, but there was less experimentation with the filling ornaments, which are usually either large and incised or small and unincised; the crowded fields and varied forms typical of some phases of EC are rarer. There was a growing tendency to use dots to echo the contours of animals; single rows of unincised dots along the backs of goats and deer are almost a trademark of the period. Painters yielded increasingly to the pressures of mass production and enlarged their animals to fill friezes more quickly; some succeeded with only two.

Later in the period painters showed interest in new effects that, fully developed, became characteristic of the LC I period. They favoured highly symmetrical compositions, choosing proportions and arrangements with a view to greater decorative effect. Their routine work shows that they had lost interest in the filling motifs and subsidiary ornamentation: the petals on the mouthplates of aryballoi, for example, were replaced by more quickly drawn groups of bands.

The greatest works of the period were those with human figures, skilfully creating exquisitely cadenced patterns of movement and serene figures of noble bearing and elegant proportions. Some painters sought greater naturalism in anatomical details and proportions, while others pursued elegance through attenuation of form and refinement of line, seen at its extreme in the long-legged horses on a krater by the Detroit Painter (New York, Met. 27.116). The repertory of narrative scenes was extended and improved by the use of inscriptions and props such as furniture, architecture and landscape elements. A red slip was usually applied to the background, and figures were often painted largely in white, creating a very colourful effect (e.g. krater; Paris, Louvre, E 29).

(d) Late. In LC I the Animal style friezes display, in fully realized form, the tendencies begun in MC. In their routine work, which was rather lifeless, painters neglected incision, often content to sketch or suggest

details, and skimped or abandoned filling ornament. On their better work, however, which included some exquisite pieces, the more innovative artists cultivated a taste for large elaborate ornaments arranged in formal patterns, concentrating on the decorative, the symmetrical and the colourful at the expense of variety and animation. They drew animals with the attenuated proportions and elegant calligraphic lines developed for the human-figure scenes (e.g. Copenhagen, Nmus., 1630, 1631) and adopted from the Figure style the colourful scheme of red ground with large areas of white. Despite a general decline in ceramic production at Corinth after the mid-6th century BC, the Figure style continued to flourish. Painters developed greater facility in representing action, a good example being the figured frieze on a column krater showing the *Departure of a Warrior* (Berlin, Antiken-samml., 1959.1). They exploited the colourful combinations of the red ground, white figures and black silhouettes, with details picked out in red.

During LC II and III the production of Black-figure vases at Corinth declined. Those made are of two types. A number of vases from *c.* 525 to *c.* 475 BC were decorated in close imitation of Attic Black-figure ware, some of excellent quality. But some painters continued to decorate vases in a graceless Animal style with rough silhouettes and slapdash incision. The filling ornament, though meagre, is sometimes distinctive, and a few vases have an engaging charm, though most are routine works. Fragments from a well (*c.* 450–*c.* 410 BC) provide the latest evidence for Black-figure production at Corinth.

H. G. G. Payne: *Necrocorinthia: A Study of Corinthian Art in the Archaic Period* (Oxford, 1931)

M. T. Campbell: 'A Well of the Black-figured Period at Corinth', *Hesperia*, vii (1938), pp. 557–611

D. A. Amyx: 'A Corinthian Kotyle in Mainz', *Jb. Ger. Zentmus. Mainz*, vi (1959), pp. 101–9

P. Lawrence: 'The Corinthian Chimaera Painter', *Amer. J. Archaeol.*, lxiii (1959), pp. 349–63

D. A. Amyx: 'The Medallion Painter', *Amer. J. Archaeol.*, lxv (1961), pp. 1–15

D. A. Amyx: 'The Honolulu Painter and the "Delicate Style"', *Ant. Kst*, v (1962), pp. 3–8

T. J. Dunbabin, ed.: *Perachora: The Sanctuaries of Hera Akraia and Limenia*, ii (Oxford, 1962)

P. Lawrence: 'Notes on the Chimaera Group', *Amer. J. Archaeol.*, lxvi (1962), pp. 185–7

J. L. Benson: 'The Laurion Painter', *Oudhdknd. Meded. Rijksmus. Ouden Leiden*, xlvi (1965), pp. 76–86

D. A. Amyx: 'Observations on the Warrior Group', *CA Stud. Class. Ant.*, ii (1969), pp. 1–25

J. L. Benson: 'The Three Maidens Group', *Amer. J. Archaeol.*, lxxiii (1969), pp. 109–22

E. G. Pemberton: 'The Vrysoula Classical Deposit from Ancient Corinth', *Hesperia*, xxxix (1970), pp. 265–307

J. L. Benson: 'A Floral Master of the Chimaera Group: The Otterlo Painter', *Ant. Kst*, xiv (1971), pp. 13–24

D. A. Amyx and P. Lawrence: *Archaic Corinthian Pottery and the Anaploga Well* (1975), vii/2 of *Corinth: Results of the Excavations Conducted by the American School of Classical Studies at Athens* (Princeton, 1932–)

C. W. Neeft: 'The Dolphin Painter and his Workshop', *Bull. Ant. Besch.*, lii–liii (1977–8), pp. 133–58

M. Blomberg: *Observations on the Dodwell Painter* (Stockholm, 1983)

A. N. Stillwell, J. L. Benson and others: *The Potters Quarter: The Pottery* (1984), xv/3 of *Corinth: Results of the Excavations Conducted by the American School of Classical Studies at Athens* (Princeton, 1932–)

D. A. Amyx: *Corinthian Vase-painting of the Archaic Period*, 3 vols (Berkeley, 1991)

C. W. Neeft: *Addenda et corrigenda to D. A. Amyx, 'Corinthian Vase-painting in the Archaic Period'*, Allard Pierson series (Scripta Minora), iii (Amsterdam, 1991)

A. A. Amyx and P. Lawrence: *Studies in Archaic Corinthian Vase Painting*, Hesperia Supplement, xxviii (Princeton, 1996)

J. S. Schaeffer, N. H. Ramage and C. H. Greenewalt: *The Corinthian, Attic, and Lakonian Pottery from Sardis* (Cambridge, MA, 1997)

V. Tosto: *The Black-figure Pottery Signed Nikosthenesepoiesen* (Amsterdam, 1999)

M. J. Bennett and others: *Magna Graecia: Greek Art from South Italy and Sicily* (Cleveland, 2002)

N. R. Bahl: *An Investigation of Black-figure Greek Pottery Depicting Women at the Fountain House* (Ann Arbor, 2003)

(ii) Attic. During the late 7th century BC Attic artists began to decorate vases in the incised Black-figure technique they had learnt from their Corinthian colleagues, and by the second quarter of the 6th century BC Attic Black-figure was the leading fabric in Greek ceramics. By *c.* 480 BC production of this technique had ceased, except for Panathenaic amphorae awarded as prizes in the Panathenaic games, which lasted until late in the Roman era. Many Attic vases are signed by potters and painters, and these provide the starting-points around which unsigned vases may be grouped. In turn, analysis of the drawing provides a chronological framework into which new finds may be fitted. Attic Black Figure is found in all areas of the Greek world, but the largest quantity comes from Etruscan tombs. Of all the Black-figure fabrics, Attic has the greatest variety of shapes and sizes, ranging from impressive monumental vases that marked tombs to miniature vessels that may have been toys for young children. Attic Black-figure exhibits for the most part a restrained effect, sometimes with drawing that is understated and sober, and in the case of true masterpieces the result is one of brilliant elegance. Almost from the beginning, the Attic Black-figure artist, more than any other, was interested in depicting mythological scenes from the various poems that comprised his literary heritage. The result is a rich and imaginative repertory of subjects.

(a) c. 625–c. 600 BC. Of the first generation of Attic Black-figure vase painters, the NETTOS PAINTER is the only one whose work has survived in sufficient quantity to reconstruct his artistic personality. He takes his name from the scene on a neck amphora

(Athens, N. Archaeol. Mus., 1002) showing *Herakles Slaying Nessos*. His contemporaries, such as the Painter of Berlin A 34 (formerly called the Woman Painter), the Piraeus Painter, the Bellerophon Painter and the Lion Painter, have left far fewer vases, but, taken together, their works give a good idea of the activity in the Athenian Kerameikos (potters' quarter) during the last quarter of the 7th century BC. All of them preferred to decorate large funerary vessels (amphorae or kraters), allowing their figures to spread out over the surface as much as possible, containing them only with ornamental frames that articulated the various parts of the vase (neck, shoulder etc). The scenes themselves often depict monsters such as sirens and sphinxes, savage beasts such as lions, or occasionally mythological events, especially Bellerophon confronting the Chimaera and Perseus chased by the Gorgons, besides Herakles slaying Nessos.

(b) c. 600–c. 560 BC. At the start of the 6th century BC there was a change in direction away from the large and monumental towards small shapes, especially oinochoai and lekythoi. Large vessels continued to be made, but their surfaces were divided into ornamental and figured friezes, a good example being the namepiece (dinos with stand; Paris, Louvre, E 874) of the GORGON PAINTER. He is the first known artist to take up the challenge of decorating smaller vessels, and he may have helped to initiate the splendid series of 'Horse-head amphorae' (*c.* 600–*c.* 550 BC). These are one-piece amphorae with a horse's head set in a panel on each side; they may have been intended for funerary use.

Contemporary with the later works of the Gorgon Painter are those of the Komast group, the KX Painter and the KY Painter (for Komast X and Komast Y respectively) as well as those painting in their manner. These were the first Attic painters to be influenced directly and primarily by Corinthian vase painting, which was still at its zenith. From Corinth they borrowed the column krater and the komast cup as well as the komast dancer, a cheerful, bulky reveller that gives the group its name. Animal friezes, borrowed earlier from Corinth by the Nettos Painter for his lekanides, were also popular with painters of the Komast group. Occasionally a human figure or a mythological theme was inserted into the frieze, such as *Achilles Receiving his Armour*, which may be depicted on a lekanis (Rhodes, Archaeol. Mus., 5008).

SOPHILOS is the first Attic vase painter whose name is known from signatures; two vases may bear his potting signature as well. His colourful, exuberant style is demonstrated nowhere better than in the mythological scenes comprising his mature work (*c.* 580 BC). Sophilos continued the tradition of setting his human figures in friezes, and he painted many animal friezes, but his main contribution to Attic Black-figure was his imaginative treatment of mythological subjects, for he was the first Attic vase painter to be genuinely interested in narrative. He was also the first to identify many of his figures by inscription; at this early date visual attributes had not yet been invented. A fragment of a dinos or lebes (Athens, N. Archaeol. Mus., 15499) illustrates both innovations: it depicts the *Funeral Games of Patroklos* (the scene is labelled on the vase) with its excited crowd cheering from the grandstand. Other good examples include the dignified procession of guests at the *Marriage of Peleus and Thetis* on a dinos (Athens, Acropolis Mus., 587; with stand, London, BM, 1971.11–1.1) and the fierce fight between Herakles and the Centaurs on fragments of a krater or kettle (Athens, N. Archaeol. Mus., 15918, 15492). These are big, ambitious scenes that pave the way for the grand narratives of the second and third quarters of the 6th century BC.

Less able contemporaries of the Gorgon Painter, the Komast group and Sophilos include the Panther Painter, the Kerameikos Painter, painters from the Group of the Dresden Lekanis, and the Polos Painter, whose career may have extended beyond 550 BC. In the early years of the 6th century BC Attic pottery was exported for the first time, chiefly to Greek colonies such as Naukratis and later to Etruria. This is well demonstrated by the poorly turned and abysmally painted pots of the Polos Painter, which seem to turn up everywhere.

Sophilos' style was continued by KLEITIAS, who may have been his pupil. Kleitias, one of the undisputed masters of Attic Black-figure, always signed as painter in collaboration with the potter Ergotimos. He preferred to decorate small shapes and divided large ones into friezes. His famous volute krater, the François Vase (Florence, Mus. Archeol., 4209; see colour pl. 2: VI, fig. 4), is a prime example. Kleitias had a precise, refined and delicate style that maintained a careful balance between the decorative and the plain. He was interested in mythological narrative and introduced many new themes into the Attic repertory. Nearly all his vases have inscriptions identifying the figures and enhancing the composition. His slightly younger contemporary NEARCHOS signed as both potter and painter. Like Kleitias, Nearchos preferred to decorate small vessels in a refined and precise drawing style, and he too was interested in narrative.

Around 560 BC the painters of Siana cups present the first evidence of Attic artists specializing in a particular shape. This sturdy, practical vessel with deep bowl, offset lip and echinus foot takes its name from the pair found at Siana in Rhodes (London, BM, B 379 and B 380). The best-known painters of these cups are the C PAINTER, who exhibits Corinthianizing elements in his work, and his more able contemporary the HEIDELBERG PAINTER. Lesser artists specializing in these cups include the Griffin Bird Painter.

Contemporary with these artists were the painters of the Tyrrhenian group who continued to be active until *c.* 550 BC. They decorated ovoid neck amphorae almost exclusively, and their products, judging from the known provenances, were intended for the Etruscan market. Among the painters belonging to this group were the Castellani Painter, the Kyllenios Painter and the Goltyr Painter. Human figures appear on the shoulder of their neck amphorae; below are animal friezes or ornament; on the neck there may be figures or patterns. The work of these painters is vivid and decorative, with abundant use of incision and accessory colour; their themes are most often mythological, frequently in unconventional compositions.

(c) c. 560–c. 520 BC. Whereas the earliest Attic painters decorated mostly small vessels or divided the format of large ones into friezes, by *c.* 560 BC a more monumental style began to develop. One of the first to display this trend was the PAINTER OF ACROPOLIS 606, whose name-piece (Athens, Acropolis Mus., 606) is a large dinos depicting a battle scene in its main zone. Equally powerful, though more restrained, are the horsemen on each side of his two one-piece amphorae (Berlin, Antikensamml., 4823, and Tübingen, Eberhard-Karls-U., Antikensamml., S./10 1298).

The work of LYDOS ('the Lydian') also belongs to this period: he was active in the Athenian Kerameikos *c.* 570–*c.* 540 BC or even a little later. He signed as painter on an early amphora (Paris, Louvre, F 29) and on a dinos from his mature phase (Athens, Acropolis Mus., 607). He decorated a wide variety of shapes, from large ones such as dinoi, column kraters and amphorae to small ones such as lekythoi and cups, skilfully adapting figural compositions to varied formats. His earliest work, which overlaps with Kleitias and the Siana cup painters, is rather severe and restrained, exemplified by two hydriai (Munich, Staatl. Antikensamml., 1681, and Paris, Louvre, E 804), both demonstrating an economical use of incision. More mature works show a more decorative use of incision tempered by areas of plain black glaze. His best vases date from after 550 BC: these are ambitious compositions with densely overlapping figures, the groups rendered clear and legible through the juxtaposition of black glaze with areas of incision and accessory red and white. The effect resembles richly woven tapestry; a good example is a column krater depicting the *Return of Hephaistos* (New York, Met., 31.11.11). Lydos had two companions of decidedly less talent, the Painter of Louvre F 6 and the Painter of Vatican 309, who produced a series of neck amphorae and column kraters, often decorated with pairs of opposed sphinxes or procession scenes.

The mature work of Lydos coincides with the output of the painters of GROUP E and the very early work of EXEKIAS, the greatest master of Attic Black-figure, from whom Group E takes its name (the 'E' stands for Exekianizing). Shapes preferred by the Group E painters are the Type B amphora with cylindrical handles, round foot and straight lip, the neck amphora and a precursor of the Type A amphora (which has a stepped foot and flaring lip) perfected by Exekias. They painted a variety of mythological subjects, especially the labours of Herakles, Theseus killing the Minotaur and scenes from the Trojan cycle. Their drawing style is generally sober and restrained, making economical use of incision and accessory colour. More colourful work was produced by the Towry Whyte Painter and the Painter of the Vatican Mourner on the periphery of Group E.

Like Sophilos and Kleitias, Exekias signed as both potter and painter. His perfection of the Black-figure technique and his sensitive approach to the subject-matter were unsurpassed and perhaps equalled only by his great contemporary, the AMASIS PAINTER (see below). Exekias preferred themes that depicted a broad range of human emotions, which he treated quietly and subtly. Good examples are the two scenes on a belly amphora (Rome, Vatican, Mus. Gregoriano Etrus., 344), one the intense concentration of *Achilles and Ajax Playing a Board Game*, and the other the *Homecoming of the Dioskouroi* with its exchange of glances between parents and sons. Occasionally he reworked well-known themes to give them new emphasis, as on two neck amphorae (Berlin, Antikensamml., 1718; Munich, Staatl. Antikensamml., 1470) showing *Ajax Carrying the Body of Achilles*. Some of his subjects are rare, for example the archer grazing his horse (amphora; Philadelphia, U. PA, Mus., MS. 4873), and others unique, such as Dionysos sailing in his boat (cup; Munich, Staatl. Antikensamml., 2044). Exekias' tendency to depict the moment in a theme before its greatest action links him more with the narrative approach of artists of the high Classical period than it does with those of his own time.

Other good painters contemporary with those of the Group E workshop and Exekias include the Painter of Berlin 1686, whose name-piece (amphora; Berlin, Antikensamml.) shows a procession in honour of Athena and who specialized in decorating amphorae. The Princeton Painter also preferred amphorae, and his most interesting piece is a Panathenaic amphora in New York (Met., 53. 11. 1) showing Athena in front of her altar and a flute-player behind it. More prolific than these two was the SWING PAINTER, whose work extended well into the 520s BC. His drawing is seldom first rate; his contribution to Attic Black-figure lies in his varied choice of subject-matter.

These painters represent a monumental aspect of Attic Black-figure, for they mostly decorated large vessels with amply proportioned figures. This tradition continued in the work of their successors, but a different approach is revealed by the Amasis Painter and other artists working during the mid-6th century BC. The Amasis Painter, who is named after several vases signed by the potter Amasis, is a true master of Black-figure, matched only by Exekias. His career spanned nearly five decades (*c.* 560–*c.* 515 BC), his earliest work being contemporary with that of Kleitias, Nearchos, the C Painter and the early Lydos and his latest overlapping with the early Red-figure vases decorated by the ANDOKIDES PAINTER, OLTOS, EPIKTETOS and the Pioneer group. The Amasis Painter decorated a wide variety of shapes, though usually preferring smaller vases. Like Kleitias, from whom he may have learnt some of his craft, he excelled at integrating ornamental patterns with friezes and inscriptions so that his vases exhibit perfect harmony between shape and decoration. This is particularly apparent on some larger vases, such as the neck amphora depicting *Dionysos and Maenads* (Paris, Bib. N., 222), but also on exquisite smaller pieces, such as the Montclair Lekythos (Montclair, NJ, priv. col). Between them, Exekias and the Amasis Painter exploited the decorative and narrative possibilities of Attic Black-figure technique almost to the full. Although good Black-figure continued to be produced until well into the 5th century BC, the Red-figure technique, invented *c.* 530 BC, increasingly attracted the more ambitious and talented artists.

A vase painter active during this same period but whose style is highly distinctive was the AFFECTER, so called because his drawing style is affected, mannered and often old-fashioned. His career extended from *c.* 550 to *c.* 520 BC, but because his style remained relatively unchanged throughout it is difficult to place his vases chronologically. His favourite shape was the ovoid neck amphora, the type generally preferred in the second quarter of the 6th century but which went out of fashion by *c.* 550 BC. The Affecter's drawing style is precise, with liberal use of accessory colour, especially red. His figures have a delicate, fresh appearance; his ornamental patterns are tightly controlled and carefully related to the parts of the vase which they articulate. Associated with the Affecter is Elbows Out, named after the peculiar manner of depicting most of his figures with their arms akimbo. A colourful group of small vases, especially unusually shaped neck amphorae, come from the workshop of the potter Nikosthenes, whose signature is the most frequent in the history of Black-figure. He seems to have had a long career, for his latest vases date from *c.* 515 BC.

Just as in earlier times, there were workshops and painters in the third quarter of the 6th century BC who almost exclusively produced cups, in this case the 'Little Master' cup. These elegant cups are lightly made with crisply articulated profiles. Two systems of decoration prevail. The first, the lip cup, has figural decoration on the lip (one or two figures, not a frieze) and further figures in the tondo; since much of the exterior surface is unglazed, the visual effect is light and bright. The second, the band cup, has its figural decoration in the handle zone with the tondo left plain; since much of the outside is glazed, the appearance is dark. When signatures appear on these cups they are nearly always those of potters—the painter Sakonides being the exception—who thus lend their names to the painters. The former include Eucheiros (son of the Ergotimos who collaborated with Kleitias), Glaukytes, Hermogenes, Taleides, TLESON (the son of Nearchos) and Xenokles.

Besides cup specialists there were also painters during these years just before the invention of Red-figure who preferred to decorate lekythoi. These founded a long tradition of lekythos painting that reached its zenith during the Persian Wars (490–479 BC). The lekythoi are generally rather modest little vessels that stand in sharp contrast to the work of the masters. Their chief painters were from the Cock group and the Dolphin group.

(d) c. 520–c. 480 BC. The Attic Black-figure produced during these decades overlaps with the more progressive and eventually more popular Red-figure, and a few painters tried their hands at both techniques, producing 'bilingual' vases (i.e. with Black- and Red-figure on a single vessel). The tradition of monumental compositions and heroic mythological subjects preferred by Exekias was continued by the LYSIPPIDES PAINTER, who may have been his pupil. Many vases attributed to the Lysippides Painter overlap with the mature and late work of Exekias, but the former continued to be active until *c.* 515–*c.* 510 BC. Like Exekias, he preferred one-piece amphorae (both types A and B), neck amphorae and hydriai. He has, however, also left the largest known Black-figure cup (London, BM, B 426). The drawing of the Lysippides Painter is looser and less precise than that of Exekias, but never is it slipshod.

Contemporary with the Lysippides Painter is the ANTIMENES PAINTER, who is called after a *kalos* name on a hydria in Leiden (Rijksmus. Oudhd., PC 63) that shows *Youths in a Palaestra*. His early work seems to recall that of Lydos, who may have been his teacher. The Antimenes Painter decorated many standard neck amphorae, but one of his favourite shapes was the hydria, which offered him a variety of formats for his figural compositions (a frieze on the shoulder, a panel on the body and a narrow predella below). He often depicted rather well-known subjects, for example the exploits of Herakles or the departure of a warrior on a chariot, while his scenes of the harnessing of a war chariot, together with those by Psiax (see below), provided the model for those to come. But the Antimenes Painter is most memorable for some of his unusual themes, such as the full palaestra scene on the name-piece hydria in Leiden or the olive pickers on two neck amphorae (London, BM, B 226; Berlin, Antikensamml., 1855). His drawing is crisp and sure, and his sparing use of accessory colour gives his vases a sober look.

Closely related to the Antimenes Painter, enough to be designated his 'brother' by Beazley, is PSIAX, an elegant, refined artist who also painted in Red-figure (as on his signed pieces, two alabastra: Karlsruhe, Bad. Landesmus., 242 (B120), and Odessa, A. Mus.); he also experimented with White-ground, Coral Red and Six's technique. Occasionally he decorated large vessels, such as the hydria formerly in Berlin (destr) showing the harnessing of a war chariot. But his best work appears on small vases such as the exquisite alabastron in St Petersburg (Hermitage, 381) or elegant kyathos in Würzburg (U. Würzburg, Wagner-Mus., 436). Two painters active in the last decade of the 6th century BC who may have been pupils of Psiax are the PRIAM PAINTER and the RYCROFT PAINTER. They preferred large vessels, chiefly amphorae and hydriai. Their incision is often quite fine with little accessory white or red added to the figures: the effect is one of sleek elegance.

The largest single group of good Black-figure pots that may be dated to the late 6th century BC comes from the workshop of the LEAGROS GROUP.

These painters were contemporaries of the Red-figure artists known as the Pioneer group because of their innovative exploration of the new technique, and vases by painters of the Leagros group often reflect the boldness and spirit of their colleagues. Beazley (1956, pp. 354–9) identified several painters within the group, notably Painter A, Painter S and the painters of the Antiope group. The Leagros group preferred to decorate large vessels, in particular hydriai, amphorae (including neck amphorae and Panathenaics) and column kraters, but they also produced some splendid large lekythoi. Most of their subjects are drawn from myth, with episodes from the Trojan cycle and the exploits of Herakles being clear favourites. Often these are scenes of chilling violence, as on three hydriai depicting respectively *Achilles Hurling the Severed Head of Troilos at his Would-be Rescuers* (London, BM, B 326), *Herakles Stoning Kyknos to Death* (Munich, Staatl. Antikensamml., 1709) and *Neoptolemos Killing Priam* (U. Würzburg, Wagner-Mus., 311). A good artist on the periphery of this group is the ACHELOOS PAINTER; two other contemporaries are the Nikoxenos Painter and his more able pupil, the Eucharides Painter. Both of the latter also worked in Red-figure, and their latest vases belong to the early years of the 5th century BC.

Other vase painters of this period specialized in small shapes; foremost among these artists is the Edinburgh Painter, whose style derives from the Leagros group. He perfected the White-ground cylindrical lekythos, and he also left a number of small neck amphorae; his drawing is simple and precise. Between *c.* 510 and *c.* 480 BC other painters also specialized in lekythoi, especially the Theseus Painter, the ATHENA PAINTER, the Sappho Painter and the Diosphos Painter. Most productive of all were the painters of the Haimon group, who decorated small mass-produced and rather hastily painted lekythoi, which were often used as humble furnishings for Athenian graves during the time of the Persian Wars.

A special class of Attic Black-figure vases are Panathenaic amphorae: large, handsome vessels filled with oil that were awarded as prizes in the games in honour of Athena that took place in Athens every four years. The earliest extant specimen dates from *c.* 560 BC, shortly after the games are said to have been reorganized by Peisistratos, but the series continued into the late Roman era. The vases have a set format: on one side Athena strides to the left between columns surmounted by cocks, her spear poised and her shield at the ready, and in front of her, written alongside the shaft of the column, is the prize inscription *ton athenethen athlon* ('a prize from the games at Athens'); on the other side is a representation of the contest for which the prize was awarded. The earliest Panathenaics are stylistically related to Lydos; the one surviving example by Exekias (*c.* 540 BC; Karlsruhe, Bad. Landesmus., 65.45) is slightly later. In *c.* 520 BC the Euphiletos Painter was commissioned to produce the amphorae; in the early 5th century BC the KLEOPHRADES PAINTER received the commission, which passed to the BERLIN PAINTER and some years later to his pupil the ACHILLES PAINTER. During the first half of the 4th century BC the figure of Athena was reversed so that she is seen striding to the right, the name of the archon in power in the year that the oil was produced was inscribed next to the right-hand column, and often the columns themselves were surmounted by small figures, which were probably the insignia of the archon in office in the year that the vase was made.

J. D. Beazley: *Development of Black-figure* (1951, 3/1986)
J. D. Beazley: *Black-figure* (1956/*R* 1978)
J. D. Beazley: *Paralipomena* (1971)
J. Boardman: *Athenian Black Figure Vases* (Oxford, 1974)
M. B. Moore and M. Z. P. Philippides: *Attic Black-figured Pottery* (1986), xxiii of *The Athenian Agora* (Princeton, 1953–)
J. D. Beazley: *Addenda* (1989)
A. J. Clark: *Attic Black-figured Olpai and Oinochoai* (diss., New York U., 1992)
M. C. Miller: *Adoption and Adaptation of Achaemenid Metalware Forms in Attic Black-gloss Ware of the Fifth Century* (Berlin, 1993)
C. Morgan and G. R. Tsetskhladze: *Attic Fine Pottery of the Archaic to Hellenistic Periods in Phanagoria* (Leiden and Boston, 2004)

(iii) Lakonian. The Black-figure technique was introduced to Lakonia around 620 BC, when it succeeded a short-lived Orientalizing style (Lakonian I). Its experimental stage (Lakonian II; *c.* 620–*c.* 580 BC) is characterized by the production of small vases (lakainai, chalices, mugs, plates and bowls) with a few human figures, animals often in outline and primarily abstract subsidiary decoration. It is in this period that export began, particularly of cups. When a fully developed Black-figure style made its appearance (Lakonian III and IV; *c.* 580–*c.* 500 BC) the vases were widely exported: indeed, most extant specimens come from Samos, Olympia, Naukratis on the Nile delta, Cyrene, Etruria and South Italy (especially Taras and Sicily). The location of the Lakonian pottery workshops is problematic: some appear to have been located in Sparta itself, but most were in the surrounding towns, such as the port of Gytheion, since it was presumably their inhabitants (*perioikoi*) who had the major role in the practice of arts and running of commerce in Lakonia.

Decorated with a simple and lively figure style and rich floral ornament, Lakonian vases owed much to Corinthian Black-figure and were also influenced by East Greek and by Attic pottery (after *c.* 560 BC). However, they never lost their native character and strong originality. The clay is pink to light brown, the black glaze usually good, and much use was made of added purple. Until the middle of the 6th century BC a pale cream slip covered the surface as a background for the decoration, but its use declined thereafter. These vases used to be ascribed to the Theran colony of Cyrene in North Africa, mainly because of the subject-matter on some of them, for example *King Arkesilaos of Cyrene Supervising the Weighing and Packing of (?)Silphion* on a cup (Paris, Bib. N., Cab. Médailles,

189) and the *Nymph Cyrene Struggling with a Lion* on another cup (Taranto, Mus. N., IG 4991). However, British excavations in Sparta at the beginning of the 20th century brought to light a large quantity of pottery that demonstrated a continuous ceramic production from Geometric times onwards, though with the degeneration of Lakonian Black-figure at the end of the 6th century BC Lakonian figured pottery as a whole fell into decline.

Absolute dates for Lakonian Black-figure have been provided mainly by grave finds from Taras, where Lakonian vases have been discovered side by side with Corinthian examples adequately dated by other criteria, while development in the shape of the cup, its most characteristic vessel, has helped to establish a relative chronology: Lakonian cups of the late 7th century BC and the early 6th were small and footless or medium-sized with a short foot, but after *c.* 580 BC they acquired an elegant form with a higher stem, shallow bowl and high lip. A new type, the Lakonian 'Droop cup', appeared *c.* 550 BC, with thick walls, a concave lip, deep bowl and medium-high stem with horizontal grooves.

Unlike their Attic and Corinthian colleagues, Lakonian vase painters made the interior of the cup the main surface for their figural decoration, an odd choice since the circular tondo was not appropriate for the development of narrative. Under the main scene there is normally a narrow exergue filled with animal figures or floral patterns, recalling East Greek Orientalizing practice. The exterior of the cup carries characteristic decorative friezes—pomegranates, lotus buds, myrtle wreaths, tongues, rays or crescents—or sometimes animal friezes in the Corinthian manner. Horizontal palmettes normally flank the handles. Lakonian cups seem to have been made mainly for export, since few have been found in Sparta, where the usual drinking vessel was probably the lakaina. Other shapes of Lakonian Black-figure are the hydria, dinos, volute krater, amphora and oinochoe, apart from the smaller shapes mentioned above.

The scenes decorating Lakonian vases were taken both from myth and everyday life and generally from the stock Archaic repertory. Of the heroic scenes the most frequent are those featuring Herakles; other popular stories include Achilles' ambush of Troilos, the Boreads chasing the Harpies, Bellerophon and the Chimaera and perhaps the Kalydonian boar hunt. Gods are often shown alone (e.g. Zeus, Poseidon on a hippocampus, a nature goddess), but a characteristic scene is that of a seated deity (or deities) with worshippers approaching. Daemonic creatures such as Gorgons and Boreads are similar to those on Corinthian vases, but peculiar to Lakonia and difficult to interpret are the small winged daemons surrounding symposiasts, riders and a nature goddess. Everyday scenes include symposia, komasts, lyre-players, warriors fighting and the return from battle.

Apart from some minor artists with just a few vases attributed to each, five major Lakonian vase painters have been identified. Earliest are the NAUKRATIS PAINTER and the BOREADS PAINTER, who worked *c.* 575–*c.* 550 BC mainly under Corinthian influence and established the canonical Lakonian Black-figure style. The ARKESILAOS PAINTER was a younger contemporary influenced by them but with a strong originality. The HUNT PAINTER was a prolific artist who flourished *c.* 565–*c.* 530 BC and whose work exhibits Attic influence, while finally, the lesser RIDER PAINTER worked *c.* 570–*c.* 535 BC and imitated most of his predecessors. There are also works in the manner of these painters, particularly of the Naukratis Painter, who was imitated until the end of the 6th century BC. No signature of potter or painter has survived, but most of the major painters seem to have been literate, since there are inscriptions on some of their vases.

J. P. Droop: 'The Laconian Pottery', *The Sanctuary of Artemis Orthia at Sparta*, ed. R. M. Dawkins (London, 1929), pp. 52–116

E. A. Lane: 'Lakonian Vase-painting', *Annu. Brit. Sch. Athens*, xxxiv (1933–4), pp. 99–189

B. B. Shefton: 'Three Laconian Vase-painters', *Annu. Brit. Sch. Athens*, xlix (1954), pp. 299–310

P. Pelagatti: 'La ceramica laconica del Museo di Taranto', *Annu. Scu. Archeol. Atene & Miss. It. Oriente*, xxxiii–xxxiv (1955–6), pp. 7–44

P. Pelagatti: 'Laconici, vasi', *Enciclopedia dell'arte antica*, iv (Rome, 1961)

C. M. Stibbe: *Lakonische Vasenmaler des sechsten Jahrhunderts v.chr.*, 2 vols (Amsterdam and London, 1972)

Studi sulla ceramica laconica. Atti del seminario: Perugia, 1981

M. Pipili: *Laconian Iconography of the Sixth Century BC* (Oxford, 1987)

J. S. Schaeffer, N. H. Ramage and C. H. Greenewalt: *The Corinthian, Attic, and Lakonian Pottery from Sardis* (Cambridge, MA, 1997)

(iv) Boiotian. Boiotian Black-figure was produced at numerous local centres, and its study is therefore less a matter of tracing continuous lines of development than of identifying significant groups of pots, some of which can be attributed to specific painters and workshops. Little Boiotian pottery was exported, and there has been relatively little excavation in Boiotia itself, so that there is only a small amount of material involved.

Although Boiotian pottery is distinctive in both shape and decoration, proximity to Athens led to the continuous borrowing of Attic ideas, techniques and even subject-matter; some of the painters appear to have been Athenian immigrants. The influence of Corinthian pottery was strongest in the 7th century BC but continued in the 6th, transmitted both directly through trade and indirectly through Athenian borrowings. The commonest Corinthian exports found on Boiotian sites are aryballoi and piriform alabastra, which Boiotian artists were quick to copy; one of the earliest groups of Boiotian Black-figure vases, the Horse Bird group of alabastra (*c.* 600 BC), set the pattern for much that followed. Though very close to its Corinthian models, the group was produced by an immigrant Athenian painter whose work at

Athens had also been Corinthianizing. The vases feature groups of animals, birds, hybrid monsters and the occasional human figure set amid rosettes and painted in rather thin black glaze; details are incised on the figures, less often on the florals.

The four distinguishable painters of the Boiotian Dancers group (*c.* 575–*c.* 550 BC), named after the frolicking komasts who appear in most of their scenes, were influenced strongly by the Athenian KY Painter, a decorator of cups and small vases in a miniaturizing style. The workshop of this group may have been near Tanagra, and their shapes, including tripod kothons (boxes with flared feet) with lion-paw feet and a kyathos (a small, single-handled type of kantharos) shaped like a ship and with a boar's-head spout (e.g. Paris, Louvre, CA 577), suggest links with the local terracotta industry. The komasts—dancing, drinking and playing games—are sometimes accompanied by other scenes of drinking and sacrifice or by mythological subjects such as Perseus and the Gorgon (e.g. Berlin, Staatl. Mus., F 1727), and by some Corinthianizing animals. Incision enhances what would otherwise be lively but undistinguished drawing. A number of these komast scenes appear on kantharoi, which remained a particularly popular shape in Boiotia, especially a type with a tall, deep lip and two high-swung handles with struts and thumb rests. The shape allowed for the occasional attempt at more complex mythological scenes such as the Kalydonian boar hunt (e.g. Athens, N. Archaeol. Mus., 432) or the ambush of Troilos (e.g. Berlin, Staatl. Mus., 3778), both popular in Athens and better executed there. In general, however, parades of humans and animals are more common; they are frequently used as friezes on lekanai, of which several groups survive from the mid- and late 6th century BC, such as those by the Protome Painter and the Triton Painter. These were produced near Tanagra, with incision and filling ornament influenced by East Greek fabrics, especially Fikellura. Some contemporary groups of pots feature unincised Black-figure designs; these were quickly executed and more popular in Boiotia and Euboia than at Athens.

Added red and white on a group of skyphoi testifies to the Boiotian love of colour. Vases of this shape were imported in quantity from Athens *c.* 500 BC and were imitated locally. The Athenian originals use red, white and even yellow; the Boiotian copies exhibit similar colourful effects, although their handling of mythology is inept but enthusiastic and their figure drawing sketchy. After Boiotian painters began to produce Red-figure pottery around 480 BC, they readily used both techniques on the same pot, so that Red-figure vases often have Black-figure lids. Black-figure was clearly the more popular, and towards 400 BC local production of Black-figure cups revived; they were often decorated in an unincised style and featured large palmettes with figures or groups between them.

The Kabeirion style, so called because most specimens were found at the Kabeirion sanctuary near Thebes, is notably different from normal Boiotian Black-figure. It was produced from the later 5th century BC until well into the 4th, and although it is a true Black-figure style, using incision and added white paint, it derives—and distorts—many features from contemporary Attic Red-figure. Its subjects are burlesque treatments of myths and scenes of everyday life; its figures have ill-proportioned bodies, circular heads and stick-like limbs. The most notable subjects include Kabeiros at the feast (e.g. Athens, N. Archaeol. Mus., 10426)—heroes feasting are a popular Boiotian subject—and illustrations of the *Odyssey* (e.g. Oxford, Ashmolean, G 429), especially those episodes that lend themselves to grotesque treatment; some of the scenes may have had connections with theatrical farce. Even in this style, however, vases with florals are more common than those with figures. The most usual shape is a deep kantharos with thumb and finger rests on its ring-handles. Some individual painters, including the Mystae Painter, can be distinguished.

A. D. Ure and P. N. Ure: *Sixth and Fifth Century Pottery from Excavations at Rhitsona* (London, 1927)

A. D. Ure: 'Boeotian Geometricising Vases', *J. Hell. Stud.*, xlix (1929), pp. 160–71

A. D. Ure and P. N. Ure: 'Boeotian Vases in the Akademisches Kunstmuseum, Bonn', *Archäol. Anz.* (1933), pp. 1–42

A. D. Ure: 'More Boeotian Geometricising Vases', *J. Hell. Stud.*, lv (1935), pp. 227–8

P. Wolters: *Das Kabirenheiligtum bei Theben*, i (Berlin, 1940)

G. M. A. Richter: *A Handbook of Greek Art* (Cambridge, MA, 1953/*R* London, 1977)

K. Schauenburg: *Heidelberg I: Germany X*, Corp. Vasorum Ant. (Munich, 1954), p. 11, nos 24–30

A. D. Ure: 'Krokotos and White Heron', *J. Hell. Stud.*, lxxv (1955), pp. 90–103

B. A. Sparkes: 'The Taste of a Boeotian Pig', *J. Hell. Stud.*, lxxxvii (1967), pp. 116–30

K. Kilinski II: 'Boiotian Black Figure Lekanai by the Protome and Triton Painters', *Amer. J. Archaeol.*, lxxxi (1977), pp. 55–65

K. Kilinski II: 'The Boiotian Dancers Group', *Amer. J. Archaeol.*, lxxxii (1978), pp. 173–91

K. Kilinski II: *Boiotian Black Figure Vase Painting of the Archaic Period* (1990)

J. Boardman: *Early Greek Vase Painting* (London, 1998), pp. 213–15, figs. 437–457

(v) East Greek and islands. In north Ionia the Late Wild Goat style had made much use of the Black-figure technique, and various experiments led to several genuine Black-figure styles *c.* 575–*c.* 550 BC. By this time a standard had been set by the Attic artists, whom the newcomers followed in rejecting slip, though not consistently in anything else. Because they were exported, and by the chances of discovery and publication are more available for study, the best-known vases are those of the so-called Klazomenian groups (*c.* 550–*c.* 525 BC), at least some of which seem from clay analysis to have been made at Klazomenai itself. Amphorae—one type abnormally narrow—and hydriai are frequent; also known are kraters and at the beginning an over-sized form of

pyxis. The main decorative fields generally carried human figures, particularly files of women, as on an amphora at Tübingen (*c.* 550–*c.* 540 BC; Eberhard-Karls-U., Antikensamml., S 12.2656), while sirens, sphinxes, animals and birds (notably feeding cranes) were relegated to subsidiary positions. Vegetable ornament lost the importance it had on Orientalizing vases; instead there was a preference for scales with white centres and initially for white or alternate white and red crescents. A row of white dots between incised lines was a favourite embellishment, and white was sometimes used for male as well as female flesh; inner details on white were more often painted than incised. The workmanship is inconsistent, even on the same pot, and does not display much concern for anatomical accuracy.

Two groups of vases tenuously related to Klazomenian were also exported. The Knipovitch class is notable for the forepart of a winged horse, which fills the decorative panels on many of its sloppy amphorae. The Enmann class is a looser group, consisting mostly of amphorae with one or two large figures in their panels, carelessly drawn and without merit. Its chief interest is its connection with the Campana group of dinoi and hydriai: from the distribution of finds the Campana painters should have been working in Etruria and the Enmann painters in Asia Minor, and if (as some maintain) pots from both groups were painted by the same hand, it implies that the artist emigrated from East Greece to Italy. Though much superior in technique and draughtsmanship, the Northampton group also has connections with the Campana group and was probably made in Etruria by an Ionian immigrant. These groups all date to *c.* 540–*c.* 520 BC: later evidence for the emigration of East Greek artists is hard to find, though one of the painters of Caeretan hydriai (the Busiris Painter) used Ionic script.

Other north-Ionian Black-figure vases occur in a range of styles; although a few are of high quality, only some column kraters from Old Smyrna have yet been classified into a fairly coherent group. Their effect is drab, though one more ambitious piece depicts a camel led by a man in Scythian dress, suggesting a date after 546 BC, when Cyrus brought his camels from Persia to Sardis. There are also some poor late 6th-century BC imitations of Attic pottery, though there may be some earlier and better specimens. The general impression of all the north-Ionian groups is of a multiplicity of local workshops operating without discipline or much reference to each other.

Some Klazomenian clay sarcophagi were also decorated in a Black-figure style, though not the full technique, since the inner details were painted and not incised. The earliest examples (?530s BC) show some affinities with Klazomenian pottery, but the latest (early 5th century BC) conform to Attic principles in their depiction of anatomy, though some details are East Greek and their compositions tend to feature symmetrical and often meaningless arrangements of stock figures.

In the south a small number of cups of Attic shapes, which are given the mistranslated name of Ionian Little Masters, rivals Attic products in technical excellence and sureness of draughtsmanship. The inner details of their figures may be incised, sometimes with microscopically fine lines, or meticulously reserved in imitation of incision. Again, no coherent school developed. The date suggested by stylistic comparisons is *c.* 560–*c.* 525 BC, and they were perhaps produced on Samos. Some of these cups have close affinities with Fikellura vases, where reserved detail is also sometimes as fine as incision.

Clay analysis assigns a final Black-figure group, the East Greek situlae (deep cylindrical vases), still further south to Rhodes. These tall, neckless jars were divided into three deep decorative zones: the lower two were separated by reserved lines and adorned with large pendent lotus flowers and palmettes, incised and picked out in purple on a black ground after the manner of Vroulian cups, while the uppermost usually carried a Black-figure group or single figure in a panel on each side between the ring handles; the quality of the drawing ranges from good to bad. Discovery contexts and stylistic comparisons date the group to between 550 and 500 BC, though a few rather earlier situlae, sturdier and technically superior, are still Orientalizing in spirit.

E. Kunze: 'Ionische Kleinmeister', *Mitt. Dt. Archäol. Inst.: Athen. Abt.*, lix (1934), pp. 81–122

R. M. Cook: 'A List of Clazomenian Pottery', *Annu. Brit. Sch. Athens*, xlvii (1952), pp. 123–52

CVA British Museum, viii (London, 1954)

J. M. Cook: *Greek Painted Pottery* (London, 1960, rev. 1972), pp. 134–41, 158

J. M. Cook: 'Old Smyrna: Ionic Black-figure and Other Sixth-century Figured Ware', *Annu. Brit. Sch. Athens*, lx (1965), pp. 114–42

R. M. Cook: *Clazomenian Sarcophagi* (1981)

R. M. Cook and P. Dupont: *East Greek Pottery* (London, 1998/*R* 2003)

J. Luke: *Ports of Trade, Al Mina, and Geometric Greek Pottery in the Levant* (Oxford, 2003)

(vi) Chalcidian. This name is given to the approximately 300 surviving vases produced *c.* 580–*c.* 510 BC by a Black-figure school, the exact site of which is disputed, and comes from the inscriptions in the Chalcidian alphabet on many of the vases. The vases have no visible predecessors, and this may indicate the work of a small group of painters. Chalcidian vases show a close awareness of developments in Attic Black-figure, although obvious borrowings are not constant, and dating depends on this close contact. Animal friezes, which appear on many vases and continue to do so later than in Athens, suggest the influence of Corinth, perhaps filtered through Athens. East Greek details also appear on some of the later vases.

The most usual shapes are short-necked amphorae, flat-shouldered hydriai very like the Attic shape, column kraters with distinctive kinked handles, and cups. The potting evidently imitated contemporary

Attic models, and its quality is extremely high. The fine-textured clay varies in colour from pale pinkish-orange to reddish-brown. As in Attic practice, artists used added reddish-purple and white as well as dark brown paint, but the overall effect is perhaps more reminiscent of East Greek prototypes. A notable practice was dipping the necks of the vases in paint instead of painting them by hand.

The appearance of the vases resembles that of any other mature Black-figure works, with large figures in the main field framed by subsidiary decoration including animal friezes, fat interlaced buds, stepped, slanted zigzags, and square designs framed by interlaced lotuses and palmettes. The crisp, bright effect of the figures and patterns is often more striking than the scenes themselves. The Inscription Painter, conventionally regarded as the originator of the school, frequently adapted stock scenes to show specific mythological figures by using inscriptions. His figures are well separated from one another and delineated with flat areas of colour: there is little internal detail or clarity of outline (e.g. a krater, *c.* 540 BC; U. Würzburg, Wagner-Mus.). The spacing of the figures and the balance of dark and light areas are characteristic and may owe something to Corinthian influence. The figures of the Phineus Painter, who followed the Inscription Painter (later 6th century BC), are also solid and heavy, though he used much more linear detail, especially on cups. In general, even the figures on late Chalcidian vases tend to resemble those on earlier Attic examples of *c.* 565 BC. Some mythological scenes do appear, including Herakles, the Trojan War, Dionysos and even the occasional rarity such as Phineus and the Harpies, but the lack of internal detail prevents serious exploration of the subject-matter, and together with the use of colour, the style suggests a greater interest in decoration than in narrative art.

A. Rumpf: *Chalkidische Vasen*, 3 vols (Berlin, 1927)

H. R. W. Smith: *The Origin of Chalcidian Ware* (Berkeley, 1932)

L. Banti: 'Calcidesi vasi', *Enciclopedia dell'arte antica*, ii (Rome, 1959), pp. 260–65

E. Simon, M. Hirmer and A. Hirmer: *Die griechischen Vasen* (Munich, 1976, rev. 1981), pp. 62–4

J. Boardman: *Early Greek Vase Painting* (London, 1998), pp. 217–19, figs. 468–82

(vii) Caeretan. The term is applied almost exclusively to a group of 40 odd hydriai of markedly individual style (*c.* 530–*c.* 500 BC), all found in Etruria and very probably made at Caere (Cerveteri). The same workshop produced other forms of vases, but these are hardly decorated and have nothing in common with the remarkably colourful style of painting of the hydriai. The form and decoration of the hydriai differ from contemporary examples produced elsewhere in the Greek world. The ornamentation comprises elaborate wreaths, generally of ivy, and polychrome lotus and palmette friezes. The figural scenes are mostly mythological and include no less than eleven depictions of Herakles and four of Dionysiac subjects; many are consciously humorous. The drawing is often exceptionally fine: the Eagle Painter used decoratively sweeping incised lines, and his younger colleague, the Busiris Painter, worked with swift sketchy strokes, as on his name piece depicting *Herakles Killing the Egyptian King Busiris* (*c.* 510 BC; Vienna, Ksthist. Mus., 3576). In contrast, the pots themselves—most of which were apparently also potted by these artists—are often carelessly produced and ineptly fired.

Though working in Etruria, these two vase painters were clearly of East Greek origin, probably fugitives from the Persian conquest of Ionia (546 BC), since their paintings have definite East Greek features: male flesh may be white or even red, and reservation was often used instead of incision to separate the various elements of ornamental motifs. However, while the paintings have close stylistic affinities with East Greek sculpture, they bear surprisingly little detailed resemblance to any particular East Greek style of vase painting, prompting speculation that these vase painters came from a family of producers of architectural terracottas. During the 16 or so years between the fall of Ionia and the establishment of the Caeretan workshop they appear to have travelled widely, and paintings on a piece of wood from Saqqara in Egypt closely resemble the style of the Eagle Painter. Once in Etruria the two artists remained largely uninfluenced by Etruscan art throughout their careers, in contrast to other immigrant artisans. However, the poor quality of some ornamental motifs suggests that they were executed by Etruscan assistants, who used templates. Some assistants may have become vase painters in their own right, and these perhaps included the Painter of Munich 833; the Caeretan hydriai also influenced Etruscan La Tolfa pottery and works by the Etruscan Tityos Painter. Those studying these vases should be aware of the production of fakes, some of which are quite skilful.

J. M. Hemelrijk: *Caeretan Hydriae* (1984), v of *Kerameus* (Mainz, 1975–)

H. A. Cahn: in *Enthousiasmos, Essays on Greek and Related Pottery* (Amsterdam, 1986), pp. 35–8 ff.

J. Boardman: *Early Greek Vase Painting* (London, 1998), pp. 221–2, figs. 494–9

J. M. Hemelrijk: 'Three Caeretan Hydriae in Malibu and New York', *Greek Vases in the J. Paul Getty Museum* 6. Occasional Papers on Antiquities, vol. 9 (Malibu, 2000)

(viii) Euboian. Knowledge of Euboian Black-figure is based on a small number of vases mainly, when their provenance can be traced, from Eretria. Earlier Euboian vases show links with the Cyclades, Attica and Corinth; the most characteristic shape is a large, krater-like amphora with a tall, conical foot and a wide neck, which had begun in the late 7th century BC to be decorated with figures and animals. Incision, the distinctive feature of the Black-figure technique, also began to appear on vases that continued to show outline drawing.

True Euboian Black-figure first appeared *c.* 540 BC on a group of amphorae whose shape owed something to the earlier krater-like Euboian vases and to the Attic lebes gamikos. The amphorae were found at Eretria and were decorated in a style so close to Attic that their painters must have trained in an Attic workshop. Two specimens (Athens, N. Archaeol. Mus., 1004 and 12076) carry wedding scenes, which are usual on the lebes gamikos, while a third (Athens, N. Archaeol. Mus., 12075) depicts *Herakles Fighting the Hydra.* Added red and white paint were used more freely than on Attic vases, especially for the subsidiary florals, and all of the vases have animal friezes, which continued to be fashionable in Euboia and Boiotia later than at Athens. The animals on the Herakles vase are unincised, as on the 7th-century BC vases and contemporary Euboian lekythoi and on the lekane, the most popular small shape. Lekanai of various forms continued to be produced in the Black-figure technique until the 4th century BC. The earlier ones carry depictions of animals and the occasional human figure, painted in much the same style as those on incised Black-figure pots; the later ones, and other small vases, have almost exclusively floral decoration, with large palmettes, honeysuckle and related designs.

L. A. Amyx: 'The Gorgon Hydria from Eretria', *Amer. J. Archaeol.*, lxv (1941), pp. 64–9

J. Boardman: 'Pottery from Eretria', *Annu. Brit. Sch. Athens*, xlvii (1952), pp. 1–48

J. Boardman: 'Early Euboean Pottery and History', *Annu. Brit. Sch. Athens*, lii (1957), pp. 1–29

A. D. Ure: 'Unincised Black Figure', *Bull. Inst. Class. Stud. U. London*, vi (1959), pp. 1–5

A. D. Ure: 'Euboean Floral Black Figured Vases', *Annu. Brit. Sch. Athens*, lv (1960), pp. 211–17

A. D. Ure: 'Euboean Lekanai', *J. Hell. Stud.*, lxxx (1960), pp. 160–67

A. D. Ure: 'Four Lekythoi in Chalcis', *J. Hell. Stud.*, lxxxii (1962), pp. 138–40

A. D. Ure: 'Small Vases from Euboean Workshops', *Annu. Brit. Sch. Athens*, lviii (1963), pp. 14–19

A. D. Ure: 'Euboean Floral Black Figured Vases: Additions and Corrections', *Annu. Brit. Sch. Athens*, lxv (1970), pp. 265–70

A. Andreiomenou: 'Archaïke kerameike ex Eretrias' [Archaic pottery from Eretria], *Archaiol. Chron.* (1976), pp. 1–7

6. RED-FIGURE. In this painting technique, the visual antithesis of Black-figure, the figures were drawn in outline and the surrounding surface was blacked in. The less significant details of the figures were then painted with dilute glaze, and their more important features emphasized with relief lines, which also sometimes gave well-defined outer contours. Initially reddish-purple and white were used for some details, and later other colours were also employed. The technique was invented in Athens *c.* 530 BC, probably by the ANDOKIDES PAINTER. Many of its earliest exponents also worked in Black-figure, often using both techniques on the same ('bilingual') vase. After 500 BC, however, Red-figure became increasingly dominant, and, except for Panathenaic prize amphorae, little Black-figure was produced after *c.* 450 BC. During the 5th century BC Attic Red-figure was the most important fine ware in the Mediterranean region, where it was widely distributed (*see* §1(v) above). Production in Athens stopped *c.* 330–320 BC, possibly due to Macedonian control of the city. In South Italy there was significant production, with five recognized schools: Lucanian, Campanian, Apulian, Sicilian and Paestan. Etruria too became an active centre (*see* §V below), especially its Faliscan school. Various other centres in Greece in the 5th and 4th centuries BC, including Boiotia, Corinth, Lakonia, the Chalcidici and Elis, made Red-figure pottery largely in imitation of Attic ware. Red-figure production ceased entirely at the beginning of the 3rd century BC.

(i) Attic. (ii) South Italian. (iii) Other areas.

(i) Attic. Attic Red-figure is regarded by many scholars as the highest achievement of Greek vase painting. Its earliest artists (late 6th century BC) used the revolutionary technique to break new ground in the depiction of anatomical detail and complex poses. Within 50 years of its inception Attic Red-figure had driven most other figured pottery from the market, and its artistic quality remained high throughout its history.

(a) The first generation (*c.* 530–*c.* 500 BC). (b) Late Archaic (*c.* 500–*c.* 480 BC). (c) Early and High Classical (*c.* 480–*c.* 425 BC). (d) Late 5th century BC. (e) 4th century BC.

(a) The first generation (c. 530–c. 500 BC). The Red-figure technique was probably invented by the ANDOKIDES PAINTER, who is named from the potter with whom he worked. He decorated mainly amphorae and a few cups; most of his later amphorae are bilingual, with the Black-figure side being decorated by the LYSIPPIDES PAINTER, who may have been the same person. The Andokides Painter's drawing style shows uncertainty with the new technique and clear vestiges of Black-figure. Thus he incised some details, especially the outer contour of the hair, and added purplish-red to colour parts of his figures. His subjects were also generally taken from Black-figure, as on his amphora depicting *Ajax and Achilles Playing a Board Game* (Boston, MA, Mus. F.A., 01.8037). His richly dressed figures rarely overlap and have a statuesque dignity; most retain the standard Black-figure pose of chest frontal or in profile and legs and head in profile. Their anatomical details are stiffly rendered and recall those on relief sculpture, especially the frieze of the Siphnian Treasury in Delphi, with harsh relief lines used for details depicted by later artists in dilute glaze.

Similar features characterize the work of other early artists such as PSIAX, although he attempted more inventive poses and was a better draughtsman. A versatile artist who also worked in Black-figure, White-ground, Coral Red and Six's technique (*see* §1(iii)(c)), he preferred to decorate a variety of such smaller shapes as alabastra and mastoi.

The Pioneer Group. These were the first artists fully to explore the potential of the new technique. Their camaraderie suggests that they knew they were breaking new ground; theirs is the first identifiable movement in Western art. No longer do their figures stand isolated and stiff in profile; they overlap and entangle in a multiplicity of new poses: back views, frontal faces and twisted torsos. Earlier artists had experimented with foreshortening for drawing objects; now it was used for human figures, not always successfully but with increasing assurance. Even so, some Black-figure traits remained, including the selective use of incision, Black-figure subsidiary ornament and reserved lettering in early inscriptions. However, Red-figure floral bands became increasingly common, while later inscriptions began to be painted in added red or white, and the artists fully developed the use of dilute glaze to render details of anatomy.

The Pioneers preferred large vases such as kraters, stamnoi and amphorae, which provided large surfaces on which to experiment; they also decorated a few cups. They introduced new shapes, such as the psykter and pelike, and new versions of older shapes, such as neck amphorae with twisted handles. They were observant, depicting symposia, athletes, music lessons, jumping dancers and a youth pointing to a flying bird. The compositions are lively, and the poses allow the figures to interact more naturally: the dry repetitiveness of much Black-figure work is gone. The compositions are not arranged haphazardly, for there is a sense of balance and often symmetry. New mythological subjects appeared, and new compositions for older themes. The painters no longer looked to Black-figure models; rather, the Black-figure painters were influenced by them. Many of the vases have inscriptions, attesting to the painters' literacy. They labelled figures with their colleagues' names and challenged one another in friendly rivalry (*see* §1(vi)(e) above).

The greatest Pioneer was EUPHRONIOS, who signed as both painter and potter and continued to pot for other painters after abandoning painting. He preferred kraters but may also have invented the large neck amphora with twisted handles. More than any other Pioneer, he took delight in depicting anatomical detail: sometimes his figures almost seem flayed. His interest in mythology is evident in such masterpieces as a calyx krater depicting *Sleep and Death Lifting the Corpse of Sarpedon* (*c.* 515 BC; New York, Met., 1972.11.10). The balance and harmony of the scene is typical of Euphronios, with the majestic, fallen figure of Sarpedon raised on either side by Sleep and Death. Especially striking are the contrasts between the limp body and the taut limbs of its bearers, and between the moving figure of Hermes in the centre and the static warriors at either side.

EUTHYMIDES, Euphronios' younger rival and colleague, also signed as potter and painter. His father was Pollias, probably the sculptor of the same name who dedicated bases on the Acropolis in Athens, which indicates that he had some social standing. Euthymides preferred amphorae; his figures are more substantial than Euphronios' and his scenes more simply constructed.

PHINTIAS, probably the eldest member of the Pioneer group, also both potted and painted. His work retained more Black-figure features than that of his colleagues, and his figures are stiffer. Lesser members of the group include Smikros, the Dikaios Painter and the Sosias Painter.

Cup painters. Nearly three-quarters of extant early Red-figure vases are cups, and many painters specialized in decorating them. The earliest specimens are normally bilingual. Type A cups have Red-figure exteriors consisting of a single figure on each side between palmettes and eyes, and a Black-figure tondo. Types B and C cups were introduced later; the most common scheme for the former is a Red-figure frieze between the handles on either side and a Red-figure tondo, for the latter simply a Red-figure tondo.

OLTOS, possibly a student of the Andokides Painter, worked with at least seven different potters. His best work is on the few large vases he decorated, including a psykter with *Dolphin-riders* (New York, Met., 1989.281.69) and a Type B cup with *The Assembled Gods* (Tarquinia, Pal. Vitelleschi, RC 6848). His figures are squat and drawn with an economy of line, but they are powerful and lively embodiments of the vitality offered by the new technique. He had an interest in scenes from epic and mythological subjects, including the exploits of Herakles and Theseus.

Oltos' younger contemporary EPIKTETOS also worked for several potters and painted a few large vases; in addition he decorated plates, including such masterpieces as the *Boy Riding a Cockerel* (New York, Met., 1981.11.10). Many of his cups are bilingual. He was the master of the circular format: his light and graceful figures elegantly fill the tondos of his cups and plates in new and varied poses. Everyday life inspired him, and he shared his contemporaries' interest in the rendering of action.

Several lesser artists specialized in cups, notably the Euergides Painter, the Nikosthenes Painter and Skythes, whose work is generally superior to most contemporary Black-figure. The names of many other potters survive too; Kachrylion, Nikosthenes and Pamphaios are among the most important.

(b) Late Archaic (c. 500–c. 480 BC). The next generation of painters took the Red-figure technique to its highest artistic level. By *c.* 480 BC most of the problems of foreshortening had been successfully overcome: figures could now bend, twist, stoop or stretch successfully, and standing figures with one leg in profile and the other viewed frontally became the norm. There was less attention to detail and more selective use of relief lines, which are often replaced by lines in black glaze. Likewise, the amount of ornament decreased, and most was executed in Red-figure. Drapery is characterized by stacked folds arranged in a symmetrical, linear fashion, while depictions of muscles are also normally linear. The frontal eye on a profile head gradually changed to one truly viewed in profile; the process was completed by *c.* 460 BC in the Early Classical period, into which the careers of many Late Archaic painters extended.

A wider range of shapes was decorated, but only the askos, a wide flask with a small spout and a handle across its top, was new, the rest being new versions of old, such as Nolan amphorae, and shapes previously decorated only by Black-figure artists, such as the dinos and phiale. More artists specialized as painters either of pots or cups, and more worked exclusively with one potter. Production doubled, and many new genre and mythological subjects appeared, while the frequent depiction of Theseus may be connected with the founding of democracy.

Pot painters. The two greatest pot painters were the BERLIN PAINTER and the KLEOPHRADES PAINTER. The Berlin Painter is named after a Type A amphora (Berlin, Antikensamml., F 2160). His long career (*c.* 500–*c.* 460 BC) began at the time of the Pioneers, and his style heavily influenced both contemporaries and students. He decorated a wide range of shapes; in 1976 a new shape was attributed to him, a pair of phialai (Malibu, CA, Getty Mus., 76.AE.16.1–2). His best work is on large vases from his early period; his late drawing is stiffer and mechanical and mainly confined to Nolan amphorae and lekythoi, the former shape possibly invented in his workshop. His charming, slender and graceful figures often stand isolated against a lustrous black background, frequently extending their arms to make them look broader and assert their forms. Subsidiary ornament is minimal or sometimes completely absent, so that his figures seem to float in space; the effect is powerful and immediate. One masterpiece, a Type A amphora (*c.* 490 BC; Basle, Antikenmus., BS 456), shows Athena standing in profile, solemnly holding out an oinochoe to fill the kantharos of Herakles on the other side of the vase. Elsewhere too the figures on different sides of his vases work together to tell the story. Hair is sometimes rendered in clay relief, an early Red-figure technique; he also decorated Black-figure Panathenaic amphorae and a few White-ground vases.

The KLEOPHRADES PAINTER is named from the potter's signature on a large cup (Paris, Bib. N., 535, 699 and other fragments). However, he was primarily a pot painter, decorating the shapes favoured by the Pioneers. His style is closer to the Pioneers' than to the Berlin Painter's: indeed, he was a pupil of Euthymides, and some of his early work resembles that of his master. He was one of the last Red-figure artists to use incision for outlines of hair, and he used subsidiary Black-figure friezes on some Red-figure vases. He also produced Black-figure Panathenaic amphorae and neck amphorae. Though his compositions are generally more static than those of the Berlin Painter, the scale of the figures gives them considerable power. The outer figures often face outwards, drawing the focus away from the centre. Foreshortening is of less interest, and he was normally better at drawing figures in relaxed poses. The pathos common to many of his scenes is well illustrated by the Vivenzio Hydria (Naples, Mus. Archeol. N., 2422) with its moving depiction of the *Sack of Troy*. The artist apparently had a special interest in scenes from the Trojan War, but otherwise he painted many stock themes: Dionysiac revels, athletics, the exploits of Herakles and Theseus and scenes from everyday life. His late work declined sharply in quality.

There were many other competent pot painters, some of whom produced flashes of brilliance. MYSON, who specialized in column kraters, also painted a splendid amphora (Paris, Louvre, G 197) with the unusual subject of *King Kroisos on his Funeral Pyre*, while the Copenhagen Painter, Syriskos Painter and the Geras Painter produced some interesting mythological scenes. Artists specializing in particular shapes include the Tsyzkiewicz Painter (stamnoi and pelikai) and the Flying Angel Painter (pelikai).

Cup painters. These include some of the greatest Greek vase painters: Onesimos, Douris, the Brygos Painter and Makron. Most of their cups are Types B and C, which had virtually supplanted Type A. They regularly outlined the tondos with ornamental bands of meanders and patterned squares, which were also sometimes placed beneath the figures on the exterior. Some cups have White-ground interiors.

The early style of ONESIMOS was dependent on the Pioneers, especially Euphronios, who potted some of Onesimos' vases when he stopped painting. Onesimos' compositions are imaginative and harmonious, especially those in tondos with more than one figure. He was a master of the curved line, as exhibited in the expressive hands of his vigorous, thin-limbed figures. His early works show more interest in myth, such as his cup with *Theseus' Visit to Amphitrite* (Paris, Louvre, G 104), but he later favoured scenes of athletics, komos, symposia and youths with horses.

DOURIS signed over forty vases—more than any other painter—including two as potter. He began as a colleague of Onesimos and worked initially with the potters Kleophrades and Euphronios, and with Python throughout his career. Four phases in his work have been identified on the basis of drawing style, ornament and *kalos* names. Especially distinctive is the 'Dourian meander' of his third phase, with meander squares alternating with blackened cross squares. His figures were drawn with a fine line and are often charming, but there is an increasing dullness and repetitiveness in his late works. He painted several interesting Trojan War scenes but mostly favoured conventional scenes of everyday life. He decorated mainly cups but also a few other shapes, including some fine White-ground works such as a lekythos with *Atalanta and Erotes* (Cleveland, OH, Mus. A., 66.114).

The BRYGOS PAINTER is named after the potter of some of his cups. His style derives from the early work of Onesimos, and in addition to cups he decorated a variety of other, mostly small, shapes, including rhyta, skyphoi and lekythoi. Some cups have White-ground interiors. He was a masterly painter of action, and his revel scenes are unrivalled for excitement and movement. The artist could depict scenes of tenderness as well, however. One particular cup (*c*. 480 BC; U. Würzburg, Wagner-Mus., 479) illustrates both aspects. The outside depicts wild revelry, while the inside shows a *Sick Reveller and Hetaira*, the young courtesan gently supporting the head of the vomiting youth. He excelled at rendering realistic gestures and poses and different human ages. His subjects include a good range of myth and genre; much of this vitality, however, is absent from his late work.

MAKRON was more prolific than any other Red-figure artist, with well over 400 vases attributed to him. However, he painted a more limited range of shapes than the other major Late Archaic vase painters: all are small, and almost all are cups. Mythological subjects occur, especially the Trojan War, but erotic scenes predominate. His figures are heavy; those of women are particularly well drawn. Though there is much repetition, the quality of his work remained consistently high.

These four major cup painters developed followings, and several major artists can be associated with each. Thus the style of the Antiphon Painter derives from the early style of Onesimos, while the Colmar Painter was also influenced by Onesimos and probably belonged to the same workshop. At least six painters worked in the 'Brygan Circle'. Some, such as the Foundry Painter, could equal the quality and mood of the master's work. Others, such as the Briseis Painter and Dokimasia Painter, were less intense. Similarly, the Triptolemos Painter (*fl c*. 480s–*c*. 470 BC) was linked to Douris by both potting and painting style: indeed, one of his cups (Berlin, Antikensamml., F 2286) is even signed as if it were by Douris. He began as a cup painter but later decorated various large shapes, including stamnoi and kraters, with notable mythological scenes.

(c) Early and High Classical (c. 480–c. 425 BC). The careers of many painters spanned the Early Classical (*c*. 480–*c*. 450 BC) and High Classical (*c*. 450–*c*. 425 BC) periods, and the major stylistic schools continued through both. In the Early Classical period figures became stockier and faces heavier, especially at the chin. The depiction of movement became less important than conveying a sense of seriousness and sometimes pathos; drapery became less linear and more plastic (see fig. 18); tragedy began to have an important influence on the choice of scenes and their iconography.

In the High Classical period figures became slimmer, and pathos gave way to a godlike serenity. The draughtsmanship appeared more assured, and compositions became simpler and more symmetrical, giving a sense of balance and harmony. Drapery was more realistically drawn, hanging correctly on the body; its folds became increasingly varied and suggested greater depth. Although the artists did not gratuitously devise difficult poses, they could successfully render back views, frontal faces and so on as required. The influence of the Parthenon sculptures (*see* ATHENS, §II, 1(ii)) was the major impetus for these developments. Pots rather than cups were favoured, while White-ground vases, particularly

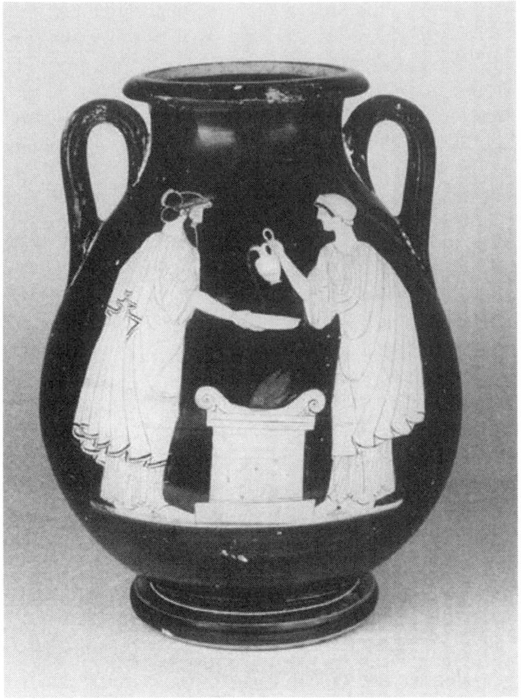

18. Ancient Greek Attic Red-figure pelike by the Argos Painter: *Couple Pouring a Libation above an Altar*, h. 299 mm, *c*. 480–*c*. 470 BC (Paris, Musée du Louvre, G 236)

lekythoi, grew increasingly popular; many artists worked in both techniques. Inscriptions occurred less frequently.

Mannerists. Not all Early Classical painters followed these trends; the MANNERIST WORKSHOP in particular retained many Archaic features in their work, including stacked, linear drapery folds and stiff poses. However, they combined these with various degrees of Early Classical innovation to produce a very distinctive style characterized by slim, small-headed figures with exaggerated gestures. The Mannerists originated from the workshop of Myson and apparently all worked together, mainly on column kraters, pelikai and hydriai, which they often adorned with old-fashioned Black-figure patterns. The first Mannerist was the Pig Painter, whose early works are particularly close to those of Myson. The Leningrad Painter and his younger contemporary the Agrigento Painter were also capable artists, but the consummate Mannerist was the PAN PAINTER, named after an unusual scene, *Pan Pursuing a Goatherd*, on a bell krater (Boston, MA, Mus. F.A., 10.185). Both the range of shapes he decorated and the variety of scenes are remarkable; he even worked in White-ground. Many of his subjects are original and some humorously lustful. They include such outdoor scenes as hunting and fishing as well as interesting scenes of sacrifice and sanctuary, all in well-ordered compositions. Many of his figures adopt somewhat affected but original poses, displaying a dramatic vitality. His followers never equalled this last successful use of the Archaic style in vase painting. Of the later Mannerists, the most important were the members of the Nausikaa and Hephaistos Painters' (or NH) group, who decorated the same shapes as their forebears. The Nausikaa Painter was the earliest: mythological scenes predominate in his work, many of them interesting and original, though his figures are awkward and affected. The latest Mannerists perpetuated the style until the end of the 5th century BC in a decadent form exemplified by the excessively linear work of their main artist, the Academy Painter.

The tradition of the Berlin Painter. The Providence Painter, Hermonax and the Achilles Painter were three important pupils of the Berlin Painter who used similar stylistic devices to those of their teacher and often similar iconography. The earliest was the Providence Painter (*fl c.* 480–*c.* 460s BC), who was a competent artist specializing in Nolan amphorae and lekythoi, shapes favoured by the Berlin Painter late in his career. The Providence Painter was fond of depicting moving figures and gods, as on his name piece showing *Apollo* (Providence, RI Sch. Des., Mus. A., 15.005).

Hermonax (*fl c.* 470s–*c.* 450s BC) signed ten vases. He painted Nolan amphorae and lekythoi, as well as several larger vases, especially stamnoi and pelikai. Some of his cups, mainly early works, recall Makron. Like other artists in the Berlin Painter's tradition he favoured pursuit scenes, while his rare mythological scenes can have unusual and interesting subject-matter, as on a hydria (Athens, Kyrou Col.) with *Hermes Bringing the Infant Dionysos to Athamas and Ino.*

The youngest pupil of the Berlin Painter was the ACHILLES PAINTER. Although his career began in the Early Classical period he became the Classical vase painter *par excellence*, reflecting the spirit of the Parthenon sculptures more than any other painter. Approximately half his extant vases are White-ground, and he was the undisputed master of White-ground lekythoi, whose development he greatly influenced. He also apparently took over from the Berlin Painter the commission for producing Black-figure Panathenaic amphorae. His Red-figure, mainly on medium-sized vases, varies in quality, but his best is excellent. His name piece (*c.* 450–*c.* 440 BC; Rome, Vatican, Mus. Gregoriano Etrus., 16751) depicts *Achilles* standing serenely in three-quarter view. The relaxed but commanding pose of the hero is reminiscent of the *Doryphoros* of POLYKLEITOS, the canon of Classical Greek sculpture, while the solitary figure against a black background recalls the Berlin Painter.

The PHIALE PAINTER was the pupil of the Achilles Painter and the last major artist working in the Berlin Painter's tradition. Although he is credited with several excellent White-ground vases, he worked primarily in Red-figure, decorating a wide range of shapes, but like his teacher favouring Nolan amphorae and lekythoi. He painted a wide variety of everyday and mythological scenes; many are rare and interesting, but his most memorable pictures feature young dancing girls and their mistresses (e.g. phiale; Boston, MA, Mus. F.A., 97.371).

The tradition of the Niobid Painter. The NIOBID PAINTER, his older colleague the Altamura painter (*fl c.* 470–*c.* 450s BC) and several followers, including the Painter of the Woolly Satyrs and the Painter of the Berlin Hydria, formed a school of artists whose scenes were sometimes clearly influenced by contemporary wall painting. Thus the figures on the Niobid Painter's name piece, a calyx krater (*c.* 460–*c.* 450 BC; Paris, Louvre, G 341) showing *Apollo and Artemis Slaying the Niobids*, are dispersed on different levels in a rocky landscape, not on the normal single groundline. Other vases by the group portray grandiose, multi-figured scenes such as Amazonomachies, Gigantomachies, Centauromachies and the Sack of Troy. They exhibit bold attempts at foreshortening and monumental figures. Similar characteristics are ascribed by literary sources to such contemporary wall painters as POLYGNOTOS OF THASOS and MIKON of Athens, although none of their work survives.

Both the Niobid Painter and the Altamura Painter favoured scenes involving myths and gods and preferred large vases, particularly kraters, though the latter specialized also in oinochoai. An innovation introduced by their workshop was the use of two registers of figures on kraters and hydriai. The Niobid Painter has often been underrated: although his figures are often stiff, their crisp lines and monumentality give them more solid substance than those of his contemporaries, and his work maintained a consistently high quality.

One of his younger pupils was POLYGNOTOS, who led the workshop during the next generation. His drawing is mellower and less stiff than the Niobid Painter's and betrays the influence of the Parthenon sculptures, but it still recalls the master's early work. He too preferred large shapes with combat scenes and other monumental subjects, such as the *Centauromachy* on a stamnos (Brussels, Musées Royaux A. & Hist., A 134). His large following included the Hector Painter, the Peleus Painter, the Lykaon Painter and the Christie Painter.

The KLEOPHON PAINTER was one of Polygnotos' younger followers. His work shows an even stronger influence of the Parthenon. His harmonious figures are full and fleshy, their heads often exquisite, as for example on a stamnos illustrating *A Warrior's Departure* (Munich, Staatl. Antikensamml., 2415). He continued the workshop's tradition of decorating large vases but favoured scenes from daily life, particularly those of sacrifice, procession and a warrior's departure. His pupil was the Dinos Painter (*fl c.* 420s–*c.* 410 BC), who maintained a monumental quality in his figures while adopting the elaborate and decorative style of his contemporaries; this he infused with greater excitement and movement, both trends being especially noticeable in the Dionysiac scenes he preferred. Kraters were his favourite shape; he did not continue his predecessors' interest in stamnoi.

Cup painters. After the Late Archaic period cups lost their popularity. However, some of the great Late Archaic cup painters created followings that persisted into the Classical period. Of the later followers of Douris, the Euaion Painter (*fl* mid-5th century BC) is the most important. His numerous but monotonous works exhibit well the Classical spirit. The Clinic Painter and the Telephos Painter, the principal followers of Makron, painted in a softer version of their master's style.

The most productive workshop was that of the Penthesilea Painter (*fl c.* 460s–*c.* 440s BC) and his followers, in which, most unusually, more than one artist often worked on the same vase. The Penthesilea Painter's work varies considerably in quality; his style is normally playful and sketchy, the bulbous heads of his figures contributing to this effect. His name piece depicting *Achilles and Penthesilea* (Munich, Staatl. Antikensamml., 2688) and a few other vases are more serious and monumental. He painted some mythological scenes, particularly pursuits involving Eos, but mostly he depicted youths, horses, athletes, women and satyrs with maenads. Some scholars have regarded the output of the Pistoxenos Painter (*fl c.* 475–*c.* 460 BC) as early works by the Penthesilea Painter, but the former's drawing is softer and more elegant; both produced notable White-ground vases. The Penthesilea Painter had numerous followers, including the Splanchnopt Painter and the Veii Painter: his workshop ceased production in the 420s BC.

Some later cup painters such as the Eretria Painter (*see* §(D) below), his colleague the Calliope Painter and the Codrus Painter are also notable: their output continued into the last quarter of the 5th century BC. The Codrus Painter was a particularly fine artist who painted several interesting scenes from Attic myth.

Other painters. Some other schools can be traced for more than one generation but had little influence. The VILLA GIULIA PAINTER was a repetitive artist, but his works are harmonious and tranquil. He decorated both large and small vases and sometimes worked in White-ground; his stamnoi with scenes of women before a rustic idol of Dionysos are his trademark. His main pupil, the CHICAGO PAINTER, continued his style in a less rigid manner. The Boreas Painter and the Florence Painter, the principal members of the Boreas–Florence group, produced mainly second-rate column kraters *c.* 475–*c.* 450 BC in a style continued by the Naples Painter. The Lewis Painter, an Early Classical specialist in skyphoi, was succeeded in the High Classical period by the Penelope Painter. The Sabouroff Painter specialized in cups, lekythoi and Nolan amphorae, an unusual combination. His better work is in White-ground; his cups recall the Brygos Painter, while some of his other works associate him with the Achilles Painter.

Other productive artists who specialized in particular shapes include the Painter of the Louvre Centauromachy (column kraters); the Bowdoin, Carlsruhe and Aischines painters (lekythoi); and the Shuvalov Painter (oinochoai), a transitional artist whose work continued into the last quarter of the 5th century BC. The workshop of the potter Sotades specialized in plastic (i.e. modelled) vases, many of which are strikingly beautiful.

(d) Late 5th century BC. Attic vase painting of this period reflected the developments of the Rich style in Attic sculpture exemplified by the Nike Balustrade (*see* ATHENS, §II, 1(ii) below). There is a move toward the effeminate, with female figures modelled by elaborate, diaphanous drapery. Jewellery and other objects were commonly emphasized in relief and often gilded, while the use of added white and yellow became more frequent. Individual strands of hair were delineated, male bodies lost their muscular definition, and poses became more affected. Subject-matter was taken mainly from domestic life; Dionysos and Aphrodite were the preferred deities. These changes may be an attempt to escape from the horrors of the Peloponnesian War (431–404 BC) into a charming fantasy world.

Although no wall paintings survive from this period, literary sources attest major advances in shading and perspective, and both are evident on vases. Many have figures set on different levels and sometimes in different scales, giving a sense of spatial depth. Linear perspective was often applied to small objects (e.g. altars and stools), and some shading is evident, particularly on White-ground lekythoi.

Most of the best work of this period appears on smaller vases. Some of the smaller shapes used in the boudoir, such as the squat lekythos and the pyxis, became popular, as did lekanides, bell kraters, oinochoai and hydriai.

The Meidias Painter. The leading instigator of the new style was the MEIDIAS PAINTER, named after the potter of his magnificent hydria (*c.* 410 BC; London, BM, E 224). His work recalls that of AISON and the ERETRIA PAINTER; each has been proposed as his teacher. The Eretria Painter mainly painted cups with repetitive scenes of satyrs, maenads and athletes, but the elegant, miniature female figures on his many other small vases, such as an amphoriskos with a *Seated Woman* (Oxford, Ashmolean, 537), clearly foreshadow the Meidias Painter.

The Meidias Painter preferred smaller shapes—squat lekythoi, choes, pyxides and lekanides—but he also decorated hydriai, often with two registers of figures. His graceful figures are frequently set on several levels in landscape and are often arranged with a good sense of symmetry. Many scenes depict Aphrodite and her world, and the artist led the way in depicting personified abstractions, many of them named on the vases. Scenes of violence and physical exertion are rare and invariably softened when they could not be avoided. On his name piece depicting *Herakles in the Garden of the Hesperides* the hero obtains the apples with no apparent effort, while in the upper register the *Rape of the Leucippidae* seems a mere flirtatious encounter. The tilted heads and outstretched hands holding folds of drapery are typical of the artist's figures, as are the rich clothes and elaborate hairstyles.

Although fewer than 40 vases are ascribed to the Meidias Painter, he influenced numerous other artists, notably the Painter of the Carlsruhe *Paris* and Aristophanes. Many vases are assigned to his 'manner', some so close that they may indeed be his, others clearly poor imitations.

Other painters. The other major tradition in this period was that of the Dinos Painter, the last successor of the Niobid Painter. Other pot painters, such as POLION and the Painter of Munich 2335 (*fl c.* 430s–*c.* 410s BC), also favoured this more traditional style, although their works someimes recall the Meidian school: many minor painters showed similar conservatism. The Painter of Munich 2335 was one of the last artists to work in both Red-figure and White-ground, and he had connections with several workshops, including those of the Achilles Painter and the Shuvalov Painter.

Painters who shared characteristics of both movements include the KADMOS PAINTER and the Pothos Painter: their large, statuesque, Polygnotan figures were often set in Meidian landscapes, while the NIKIAS PAINTER was conservative early in his career and Meidian later. Finally, the TALOS PAINTER and the PRONOMOS PAINTER produced several large, ornate vases at the end of the 5th century BC.

(e) 4th century BC. Vase painting of the 4th century has not been as well studied as that of earlier periods. At the start of the century two stylistic trends predominated, the Ornate style and the Plain style. The former derived from the Talos Painter, the Pronomos Painter and the Meidias Painter: its best exponents were the Meleager Painter (*fl c.* 400s–*c.* 380 BC) and the Painter of the New York *Centauromachy*. It is characterized by crowded, multi-level scenes, richly decorated drapery and coloured accessories, and more figures are shown in white than in earlier work. The Plain style developed from the Dinos Painter's tradition, its best exponents being the Jena Painter (*fl c.* 390s–*c.* 380s BC), who decorated some exquisite cups, and the Erbach Painter. Their uncrowded compositions lack depth, more heads are shown in profile, and fewer lines are used for drapery and anatomical details. Many other painters shared the characteristics of both schools.

The KERCH STYLE, named after the region where many of the vases were found, appeared *c.* 370 BC and reached its acme by *c.* 350 BC. In many ways it is an amalgamation of both earlier styles, but it owes more to the Ornate. Its compositions are still crowded, but there is more balance and harmony; the figures are statuesque, perhaps even influenced by the contemporary sculpture of Praxiteles and others, and complement the shapes of the pots so that each accentuates the other. The figures are drawn with many short, sketchy lines, with the occasional addition of wash to suggest volume and shadow. Accessory blue and green were also used, and some figures were rendered completely in relief with applied clay; towards the end of the 4th century BC some vases were produced with all their figures in relief.

The MARSYAS PAINTER was the best of the Kerch Painters. His pelike depicting *Peleus Abducting Thetis* (*c.* 350 BC; London, BM, E 424) epitomizes the style. The bodies of Thetis and Eros are white and placed centrally, as often with coloured figures; other areas are gilded or painted in blue and green. The elongated figure of the fleeing Nereid in three-quarter back view to the upper right blends with the lines of the vase, as do Aphrodite and her assistant on the left.

Far fewer shapes were decorated in this period, and cups of all types disappeared by *c.* 375 BC. Pelikai were the favourite, although hydriai, calyx kraters, bell kraters, skyphoi, squat lekythoi and oinochoai were also common, and the lekanis was popular in the first half of the 4th century BC. Women remained the most common subject-matter, although there were several interesting cult scenes; Dionysos and Aphrodite were the most popular deities, Herakles the favourite hero. Oriental costumes and animals are often found, but inscriptions are rare.

It is unclear why Attic Red-figure production ceased *c.* 330–*c.* 320 BC. Perhaps the development of the technique had run its course, or the end may simply reflect a change in taste. Very likely it is connected in some way with the Macedonian domination of Greece.

J. D. Beazley: *Red-figure* (1942, 2/1963)

G. M. A. Richter: *Attic Red-figured Vases* (New Haven, 1946, rev. 1958)

M. Robertson: *Greek Painting* (Geneva, 1959)

P. E. Arias and M. Hirmer: *Tausend Jahre griechischer Vasenkunst* (Munich, 1960); enlarged Eng. trans. by B. B. Shefton as *A History of Greek Vase Painting* (London, 1962)

J. D. Beazley: *Paralipomena* (1971)

J. Boardman: *Athenian Red Figure Vases: The Archaic Period* (London, 1975)

E. Simon, M. Hirmer and A. Hirmer: *Die griechischen Vasen* (Munich, 1976)

R. F. Sutton: *The Interaction between Men and Women Portrayed on Attic Red-figure Pottery* (diss., Chapel Hill, U. NC, 1981)

J. Boardman: *Athenian Red Figure Vases: The Classical Period* (London, 1989)

L. Burn and R. Glynn: *Beazley Addenda* (Oxford, 1982); rev. by T. A. Carpenter and others (Oxford, 1989), appendix 2

M. Robertson: *The Art of Vase-painting in Classical Athens* (Cambridge, 1992)

M. B. Moore: *Attic Red-figured and White-ground Pottery* (Princeton, 1997)

(ii) South Italian. The Greek settlers who colonized South Italy and Sicily in the 8th century BC produced vases imitating the style prevalent in their mother-city, although they imported the finer vases from Greece, especially those made in Athens and Corinth. The situation changed in the second quarter of the 5th century BC, when Athenian potters and vase painters established workshops on the Gulf of Taranto, as first suggested by Adolf Furtwangler in 1893. His hypothesis associated the beginning of South Italian

Red-figure vases with the foundation of Thurii by Athens in 443 BC. Eighty years after Furtwängler's hypothesis, two potter's kilns were discovered at Metapontion (now Metaponto), 80 km north-east of Thurii and 40 km west of Taras (now Taranto). Fragmentary vases have permitted the identification of one of them with the workshop of the Creusa Painter and Dolon Painter, two important Lucanian artists active in the first third of the 4th century BC. The second was used by the Amykos Painter, one of the first Lucanian vase painters, towards the end of his career late in the 5th century BC. The finds in Metapontion are of the utmost importance, since these are the earliest workshops involved in the production of Red-figure vases in South Italy to be discovered and scientifically studied. It is perhaps not surprising that the Red-figure technique appeared early at Metapontion, for the city was one of Athens' allies in the region. The new technique spread rapidly, and by the middle of the 4th century BC each Hellenized region produced its own Red-figure vases. Hence we speak today of Lucanian, Apulian, Sicilian, Campanian and Paestan vases.

The great interest in such a production lies in the wide range of myths, sometimes inspired by the Athenian tragedies, that they depict. They also shed some light on the life of the native population and Greek colonists: warriors and banqueters are frequently depicted, and the private life of women and funerary subjects are favoured by many painters. Especially in late Apulian, the funerary scenes are omnipresent, perhaps reflecting the growing insecurity of the time as the natives contested the domination of Taras. The following description of the five fabrics owes much to the work of Dale Trendall (1909–1995), whose carefully annotated lists of vase painters provide the indispensable framework that has long been needed in this field.

(a) Lucanian. The first Lucanian vase painters were active in the last third of the 5th century BC. These artists, namely the Pisticci Painter and the Amykos Painter, are very close to such contemporary Attic vase painters as the followers of the Achilles Painter and the members of the Polygnotan group. It is therefore possible that they were trained in Athens, although none of their vases has yet been found in Greece. The Pisticci Painter seldom departed from genre scenes, but some vases show that mythological subjects also appealed to him. The reverses of his vases are rather monotonous, and their draped youths are somewhat stiff when compared with Attic models. The Amykos Painter was keener on mythological subjects, and around the end of the 5th century BC he decorated monumental vases probably under the influence of the Tarentine school. Among the various shapes he used, there is one of Messapian (local) origin called a nestoris.

A second workshop may have been located at Herakleia (now Policoro), a Tarentine colony near Metapontion. Three important artists worked there: the Palermo Painter, Karneia Painter and Policoro Painter, known as the PKP group. They produced vases of high quality with a predilection for mythological subjects on large vases. A pelike attributed to the Policoro Painter (Policoro, Mus. N. Siritide, 35297) and showing the *Punishment of Dirce* gives some idea of the painter's neat drawing, balanced composition and successful three-quarter views.

The second generation of Lucanian artists was led by the Creusa Painter and Dolon Painter working in Metapontion. The Creusa Painter was perhaps a pupil of the Amykos Painter, although he preferred genre scenes. The Dolon Painter was more original, treating mythology in an almost caricatural manner that perhaps reflects the work of the great painter Zeuxis, who worked in nearby Herakleia. His style was also influenced by the Tarporley Painter, an Apulian artist with whom he might have worked for a while. In a separate workshop, the Brooklyn-Budapest Painter was an artist of considerable importance. At the beginning of his career he remained close to the Amykos Painter, but he may have moved to Taras, since he shows considerable influence of the Iliupersis Painter in his work. Nevertheless, he used Lucanian patterns and decorated some nestorides, which distinguishes him from contemporary Apulian artists. He returned to Lucania *c.* 380 BC and started a workshop in northern Lucania, perhaps at Anzi.

Most Lucanian vase painters followed him, a migration that proved to be fatal since the artists lost contact with the major artistic developments of the time. Their repertory of subjects became more limited, and their stock figures were repeated without much variation. The most significant vase painter of this period is the Primato Painter, who directed a large workshop possibly located at Armento. He was probably trained in Taras by the Lycurgus Painter, since he liked to decorate large vases in the Apulian manner. His floral and ornamental patterns are finely drawn and show much originality for an isolated workshop; his choice of subjects is likewise remarkably large. One of his finest works is a large volute krater with *Herakles* (Paris, Louvre, K 518). His profile heads are rather squarish, while his three-quarter figures are well rendered. The Lucanian fabric died out early (*c.* 320 BC) because of the remote location of the workshops.

(b) Apulian. The Apulian fabric is by far the most important in South Italy, its production reflecting the level of wealth attained by the Tarentines during the 4th century BC, especially under the guidance of the philosopher Archytas (*fl* 367–361 BC). Red-figure vases began to be made in Taras in the last quarter of the 5th century BC, but no trace of the potters' quarter has yet been discovered. Since the cemetery of Taras lies under the modern city and has been only sporadically excavated, most Apulian vases have been discovered at other sites such as Ruvo and Canosa, where excavations have taken place since the

early 19th century. Vases of the second half of the 4th century BC, especially those with funerary scenes, depict perhaps some of the products (weapons, bronze vessels, horses etc) that the Greek colonists were willing to trade with the native populations in exchange for wheat, wool and salt.

Two major trends are consistently discernible throughout the Apulian fabric, the Plain and Ornate styles. The Plain style includes most of the smaller vases, which present simple compositions involving a restricted number of figures and a limited choice of decorative patterns. The emblematic vase of this style is the bell krater. The subjects are limited to Dionysiac and genre scenes; many of the later vases are decorated solely with female heads. While myths are rarely depicted in the Plain style, they are very popular in the Ornate, together with funerary subjects. Vases are decorated with intricate floral and geometric patterns, which find an interesting parallel in the subsidiary decoration of temples and funerary monuments. The ornaments are enlivened by the use of added colours. The shapes favoured are the larger ones, such as volute kraters, amphorae and, from *c.* 350 BC, loutrophoroi.

The early vases are well-proportioned in the Attic tradition, but from *c.* 370–*c.* 360 BC much larger vases were produced, some of them over a metre in height. This phenomenon can perhaps be linked to changes observed in funeral practices, as wealthy families now occupied spacious chamber tombs. The increased size of vases allowed the painters to indulge in more complex multi-figural compositions. Although the Apulian artists were able to deal satisfactorily with problems of perspective and foreshortening, their ambitious compositions lack spatial unity: scenes are often divided into separate groups of figures that appear to float on the black background.

The Painter of the Berlin Dancing Girl and the Sisyphus Painter are the most important artists of the original Tarentine workshop. They worked in both Plain and Ornate styles and must be considered the pioneers of the Apulian fabric. They were fond of mythological subjects but decorated a sizeable number of their vases with Dionysiac or genre scenes. The influence of the Sisyphus Painter on later vase painters was substantial. On his name vase, a volute krater depicting a rare version of the myth of Sisyphus, Ornate style characteristics such as the multi-figural composition, rich decorative patterns and monumental look of the vase are already evident.

For the next 50 years painters specialized: a large group, led by the Tarporley Painter, decorated vases in the Plain style, while a somewhat smaller group continued the tradition of the Ornate style. The Tarporley Painter preferred to decorate bell kraters with Dionysiac scenes or scenes from phlyax plays (farces); the reverses of his vases show two or three draped youths. Despite his association with the Plain style he occasionally depicted mythological scenes. The followers of the Tarporley Painter have been grouped around his three principal pupils: the Schiller Painter, the Hoppin Painter and the Painter of Karlsruhe B 9. These artists continued the tradition established by their master, bringing few novelties in subject-matter.

Evolving in parallel with the Tarporley school, the artists working in the Ornate style followed the Painter of the Birth of Dionysos. His favoured shape was the volute krater. Its increasing size allowed him to depict various mythological scenes in which the many figures are placed at different levels, sometimes giving the impression that the artist is afflicted by *horror vacui*. The greater surface available and the particular morphology of the volute krater called for an increased use of decorative patterns. In this Apulian artists followed Attic volute kraters, which were still exported to Apulia towards the end of the 5th century BC, although their fondness for decorative patterns led them to combine the Attic models in new ways and later to create their own. With added colours, these patterns gave a cheerful look to late Apulian vases.

Few immediate followers of the Painter of the Birth of Dionysos are well known. Their work has survived mainly in fragments from the occasional excavations of the cemetery under modern Taranto. These vases do, however, present perhaps some of the best drawn figures in Apulian ware, such as Priam on a large fragment of a calyx krater attributed to the Black Fury group (New York, Met., 20.195). The richness of the patterns depicted on the clothes suggests some kind of stage performance. The whole vase must have been a masterpiece.

Around 360 BC a new decorative scheme was introduced by the Iliupersis Painter for the larger vases. The obverse is generally reserved for a mythological, bridal or funerary scene arranged on different levels. The reverse depicts a Dionysiac scene, but later this is replaced by a scene around a stele or naiskos (small shrine). The naiskos is a novelty, reflecting actual stone monuments, fragments of which have been retrieved from the Tarentine cemetery. A volute krater attributed to the Iliupersis Painter has one of the earliest depictions of one of these monuments. Youthful visitors bringing various offerings are grouped around the naiskos in which the figure of the deceased stands. Both the naiskos and the deceased are in added white, perhaps to reflect the marble or stony look of the building. Usually two or four visitors, of both sexes, are grouped around the monument. These figures were repeated from vase to vase as stock figures with little variation. The Iliupersis Painter also modified the subsidiary decoration on the neck of volute kraters and amphorae by replacing the small figural or animal scenes by a head, usually female, in a floral setting. Likewise, the introduction of moulded frontal female heads on the volutes of kraters must be attributed to him or at least to his workshop. Finally, he made more extensive use of added colours in conjunction with elaborate new patterns. His followers include the Lycurgus Painter, who showed improvements in foreshortenings and overlappings and who succeeded in rendering emotions on faces in three-quarter view.

Around the middle of the 4th century BC, the Varrese Painter and his followers were clearly at ease in both Plain and Ornate styles. They are, however, best known for their monumental vases in the Ornate style, which reveal an ever-increasing use of added colours and decorative patterns. Two new shapes were introduced: the loutrophoros and the situla. Curiously, they were made in two similar variants, the body being either concave or slightly convex. New myths were also introduced, such as the mourning Niobe or rare personifications. An excellent example is on a loutrophoros (type I: Malibu, CA, Getty Mus., 86.AE.680) attributed to the Painter of Louvre MNB 1148, a pupil of the Varrese Painter. The obverse shows the legend of Leda and the Swan with Hypnos ('Sleep'). Over them, Zeus and Aphrodite are depicted inside a palace. Astrape ('Lightning'), Eniautos ('Year') and the personification of Eleusis—the only certain representations of these figures in Greek art—stand slightly apart. All have their names inscribed. The Painter of Louvre MNB 1148 and his colleague, the Metope Painter, exhibit great care and refinement in their work, sometimes even surpassing their master.

These artists were succeeded by two groups of painters who began to specialize in particular subject-matter, some of them preferring funerary scenes, others myths. The first group is best represented by the Painter of Copenhagen 4223. He gave the funeral scene its canonical form by using a naiskos for the obverse and a stele for the reverse. Both are surrounded by visitors, and the deceased are almost exclusively youths, often with a horse or a dog. The second group is more complex, involving a growing number of artists of outstanding quality illustrated by a very limited number of surviving vases. They offer unusual myths or new renditions of popular ones. The reverses often show a funeral scene. Among these talented artists is the De Schulthess Painter, who was unknown until 1986. One of his volute kraters (New York, Shelby White and Leon Levy Col., 381) shows a vivid *Gigantomachy*. The bending legs of the two giants are improperly rendered, indicating the limits attained in foreshortening. Of interest also are the dancing women on the vase's neck: their pose and the contrasting colours of their dresses recall the decoration on the walls of the 'Dancers' tomb' in Ruvo (Naples, Mus. Archeol. N., inv. 9355). These artists are very close in style to the Darius Painter and were either his immediate forerunners or colleagues at an early stage in his career.

The DARIUS PAINTER was the finest representative of the Ornate style. He preferred to decorate large vases that provided the appropriate space for his complex renditions of myths. His repertory seems to reflect in part a remarkable knowledge of the Classical Athenian tragedies, especially those of Euripides. One of his monumental volute kraters, which shows the *Funeral of Patroklos*, exemplifies the mature phase of the Ornate style. The subsidiary decoration begins to invade such new areas as the 'blinkers' of the volutes as well as the foot. The principal scene lies in the centre of the composition, around which the secondary scenes are clustered, providing clues to the myth depicted. Frequently, though, the Darius Painter felt it was necessary to clarify his subject by means of inscriptions identifying key figures or by giving a title, as on the Patroklos vase. His chief follower in the Ornate style was the UNDERWORLD PAINTER, a competent artist who followed his master closely. His inspiration was more limited, but he was still able to depict rare myths in a vivid manner, such as the unique representation of the story of Melanippe on a volute krater (Atlanta, GA, Emory University, Michael C. Carlos Mus., 1994.1).

Until the time of the Darius Painter, the major workshops were presumably located at Taras. In the later years of the fabric, however, a new centre, possibly located at Canosa (northern Apulia), supplied the rich local market. The artist responsible was perhaps the Patera Painter (*fl c.* 340–*c.* 320 BC), who may have been trained in Taras by the Painter of Copenhagen 4223 and who later moved to Canosa. His style and subjects were much influenced by those of the Painter of Copenhagen 4223. Like his master, he preferred funerary scenes to myths. On some of his vases the reverse is decorated solely with a large female head, which may be the work of an associate. The same is true for the GANYMEDE PAINTER, who is best known for the intricate and colourful floral patterns on the neck of his volute kraters and amphorae.

These artists were followed by a second workshop, in which the principal artist was the BALTIMORE PAINTER. His early works reflect the influence of the Patera Painter, whose pupil he must have been. Later on he was much closer to the Underworld Painter, his contemporary in Taras. He decorated large vases with mythological scenes, although his repertory lacks originality. His naiskoi tend to accommodate more figures, often three, with patterned clothes enlivened by added colours. When the deceased is a man, there is frequently a cuirass beside him or suspended from the ceiling. Such a practice is characteristic of the Canosan artists. The presence in the scene of M-handled hydriai is a characteristic of both the Baltimore Painter and his follower, the White Saccos Painter. They occur, for example, on a loutrophoros (type III) attributed to the White Saccos Painter, a type of loutrophoros only decorated by Canosan artists. The upper register shows a toilet scene, while the lower depicts two women at a stele. The women of the upper register wear white *sakkoi*, hence the painter's name. It is a feature confined almost entirely to this painter.

Towards the end of the 4th century BC the Red-figure technique declined rapidly. Some artists tried to retain originality in their compositions or subject-matter, such as the Arpi Painter and the Virginia Exhibition Painter, but many confined themselves to funeral scenes and female heads until the whole fabric died out *c.* 300 BC.

(c) Sicilian. Despite the Athenian expedition against Syracuse in 415 BC, Sicilian production of Red-figure vases began towards the end of the 5th century BC with the help of Athenian artists. The first Sicilian Red-figure vase painter, the Chequer Painter (*fl c.* 410–*c.* 380 BC), remained very close to contemporary Athenian vase painters, especially to the Jena Painter. His name refers to his fondness for using chequer patterns. His subjects show a marked preference for Eros and genre scenes. The Dirce Painter, his immediate follower, introduced a number of typical Sicilian features, such as the wreath of ivy around the rim of kraters. He also depicted phlyax scenes and some rare myths in a colourful manner.

The death of Dionysios I, tyrant of Syracuse, in 367 BC opened a period of political turmoil in Sicily that might explain the significant diminution in production as well as a possible migration to Campania, where Sicilian vases have been found. This may have led to the foundation of local fabrics in Campania and at Paestum, hence explaining the many similarities between Sicilian, Campanian and Paestan vases. One of these migrants was the Locri Painter, who was previously thought to be Lucanian and working in Lokroi Epizephyrioi (now Locri). Recent discoveries of some of his vases in Sicily, however, suggest that he worked there before moving to Lokroi Epizephyrioi after Dionysios II's expulsion from Syracuse in 356 BC.

The arrival of Timoleon at Syracuse in 342 BC marked a return to stable government in Sicily and enabled an important revival of Red-figure vase painting. The workshops were apparently still concentrated in eastern Sicily, with the exception of one probably located on Lipari Island. Three main groups have been identified: the Lentini-Manfria group, the Etna group and the Lipari group. The Lentini-Manfria group (*c.* 340–*c.* 320 BC) produced some monumental vases that are among the best Sicilian vases. They show an unusual interest for mythological subjects treated in the grand manner with added colours, perhaps reflecting free painting. One of the masterpieces is a skyphoid pyxis attributed to the Gibil Gabib group and showing a bridal scene. The figures are drawn with unusual care and delicacy, echoing the finest Attic vases of the KERCH STYLE. Further development of the Lentini-Manfria group may be seen in the Borelli group (*c.* 320–*c.* 300 BC), which exhibits some decline in the drawing of figures and decorative patterns but offers such examples of polychromy as the Falcone pyxis (Palermo, Mus. Reg., GE 4730), on which Greek letters specifying the required colours are inscribed in order to help the painter. The vases of the Etna group are much smaller. The most popular shape is the lekanis, which accommodated only a limited choice of subjects, namely women, Nike, Eros and confronted female heads. The principal artist of the group was the Cefalù Painter. His delicate style and sense of composition permitted him some successful attempts at mythological subjects. His lekanis (Lipari, Mus. Archeol. Eoliano, 749 A), for example, shows Apollo and Artemis at Delphi.

The Lipari Painter (*fl c.* 320–*c.* 300 BC) stood at the head of a group whose vases are easily recognizable by the extensive use of added colours; not only the usual white, yellow and red, but also blue, pink and green. A skyphoid pyxis attributed to the Lipari Painter (Lipari, Mus. Archeol. Eoliano, 276 L) shows two naked women. The lid displays the usual decoration of laurel wreaths to which ovoid objects decorated with blue ribbons, recalling Easter eggs, are attached. The Lipari Painter had a fondness for three-quarter views and feminine subjects; the reverses of his vases often depict a large female head. His latest vases coincide with the end of the Sicilian Red-figure vases *c.* 300 BC.

(d) Campanian. The production of Red-figure vases in Campania started late in the second quarter of the 4th century BC. Three fabrics have been identified, two at Capua and one at Cumae. Campanian potters preferred smaller vases, and among the various shapes employed the most original is the bail amphora, which is restricted to Campanian. The body is close to a neck amphora, but the handles are replaced by a single one arched over the mouth. Mythological scenes were rare, while funerary scenes around a stele were quite popular. Women's flesh is often added in white. Native elements play an important part in the repertory, such as the cuirass with three metal discs and feathered helmets worn by Samnite warriors. Female heads were often used as subsidiary decoration on the necks of amphorae and below the handles of hydriai.

The first fabric in Capua was established by the followers of the Dirce Painter, who emigrated there from Sicily *c.* 370 BC. The Cassandra Painter owed much to their style but very soon departed from them and affirmed his originality. The ground on his vases is often enlivened by black and white spots perhaps representing the volcanic Campanian soil (e.g. Berlin, Antikensamml., 3238). His followers took separate paths. The Parrish Painter owed much to his master, although his drawing is less careful and his style much cruder. By contrast, the Laghetto Painter (*fl c.* 350–*c.* 320 BC) departed rapidly from the Cassandra Painter to develop a polychromatic style. His most important follower was the Caivano Painter, whose influence on contemporary Paestan vase painters is so clear that he perhaps worked at Paestum for a while; he was once thought to be Paestan himself. One of the distinctive features of his works is the depiction of what appears to be solidified lava. It is composed of parallel, slightly undulant black lines, as on a bell krater depicting the *Ambush of Dolon* (Naples, priv. col.). His choice of subjects is fairly extensive, with a good selection of myths, though some are difficult to recognize. He may well have been the first to include Samnite warriors in his repertory. This is perhaps a reflection of his clientele, which was part Greek colonists, part native.

The fabric is well represented in late Campanian by the Ixion Painter (*fl c.* 330–*c.* 300 BC), who favoured monumental vases with scenes treated in the grand manner, often with multi-level compositions comparable to contemporary Apulian. His mastery of the complex composition is exemplified by a bell krater showing *Boreas Ravishing Oreithyia* (Oxford, Ashmolean, 1894.5). The Ixion Painter offered an unusually wide choice of subjects for a Campanian artist. His warriors do not wear the typical Samnite armour and helmet. After him, vases declined drastically in quality.

The second Capuan fabric presents some interesting contrasts with the first; funerary scenes and native peoples are more frequently depicted, for example, which suggests that the vases might have been produced specifically for the Samnite market. There are also a greater number of phlyax vases. The first artist was the Capua Painter (*fl c.* 360–*c.* 330 BC), who decorated a large number of vases but whose subjects were restricted mainly to funerary and Dionysiac themes. He was followed by three groups of artists known collectively as the AV group. The Whiteface/Frignano Painter led the first group. He recalls the Capua Painter in his limited choice of subjects but is best known for the Praxitelean-like pose of his youths. In the second group, headed by the Libation Painter, a popular scene is the departure or arrival of a warrior to whom a woman makes a libation. A good example is represented on a bell krater attributed to the Libation Painter. The warriors wear the characteristic feathered helmet of the Samnites, while the woman is represented in a native costume with a distinctive headdress. The painter seems equally at home with funerary and mythological subjects. The Danaid group (AV III) began its production a little later than the others (*c.* 340 BC). The choice of subjects shifted away from libation and stele scenes to Dionysiac, mythological and genre scenes. The influence of Paestan is important in composition, patternwork and the presence of a multiple lid on lebetes gamikoi, such as one attributed to the Danaid Painter and showing a naked mistress and her maid (London, BM, F 207). The female flesh is now rarely added in white. The AV group was succeeded by the Fillet group and an unusually swift barbarization of production.

In Cumae, the vases are classified in three succeeding groups known as Cumae A, B and C. The unity of style, patterns and subject-matter suggests a single large workshop (*c.* 350–*c.* 300 BC); the choice of subjects is even more restricted than on Capuan ware. The pioneer was the CA (= Cumae A) Painter (*fl c.* 350–*c.* 325 BC), who seemed to devote himself almost exclusively to funerary scenes showing women at a stele; these are occasionally accompanied by a Samnite warrior, as on a bell krater (Budapest, Mus. F.A., 51.41). Later in his career, during the Apulianizing phase, he depicted naiskoi and 'xylophones'. The 'xylophone' first appeared on Apulian vases. It is a musical instrument in the form of a small ladder which might be identified as the rattle of the philosopher Archytas.

The Apulianizing phase marked a turning-point in Cumaean ware. It has been suggested that the Tarentine embassy to Naples *c.* 330 BC might have brought Apulian artists, at least two of whom came to Cumae: the Ivy-leaf Painter and the APZ Painter. Vases by the Ivy-leaf Painter have been found at Canosa in Apulia, where he may have worked at the beginning of his career. The APZ Painter (*fl c.* 330–*c.* 320 BC) is the great figure of the Apulianizing phase, adding such Apulian features as the naiskos and 'xylophone' to the Campanian repertory. Nevertheless, he immersed himself quite rapidly in the local artistic environment, since he decorated neck and bail amphorae and used added white for women's flesh.

Cumae B ware (*c.* 330–*c.* 315 BC), the work of the second generation of vase painters, reflects a better understanding of the new Apulian elements present in Campanian. There was, however, a steady decline in its style, associated with a restricted use of added colours and a narrowing range of subject-matter, with monotonous repetition of figures from one vase to another. Some originality in style and subject-matter, however, is exhibited in the work of such artists as the Branicki Painter and the Painter of B.M. F 229 in the Rhomboid group. These vases are easily recognizable by the presence of rhomboids (lozenges) in the field. The female heads decorating the small vases of the Branicki Painter wear a unique headdress known as a 'tennis-racket' saccos, for example on a plate (Birmingham, Mus. & A.G., 1297.85). The fabric came to an end with the artists of Cumae C (*c.* 315–*c.* 295 BC). The influence of Sicilian is manifested by the introduction of a vase in the shape of a bottle, by subjects centred on women's daily life and by the return of polychromy. By this time, however, the drawing had declined irreversibly.

(e) Paestan. Most Paestan vases have been found in and around Paestum (anc. Poseidonia), hence indicating their probable production at that site. They present a remarkable unity of style, subject-matter and pattern-work. In fact, the canon established by the painters Asteas and Python was maintained throughout the life of the fabric, with the exception of the Apulianizing phase from *c.* 330 BC. The use of 'framing palmettes' is one of the characteristic features of the Paestan style: the palmette, to which a sinuous leaf is attached to each side, is placed below the handle and serves as a frame for the figural scenes on the vase. The so-called 'Asteas flower', restricted to the workshop of Asteas and Python, is also easily recognizable. The preferred shape was the bell krater, while the lebes gamikos, with its multiple lid, was the most original contribution of Paestan potters. Such lids are bold and complex creations composed of up to four elements, mainly miniature lekanides and lebetes gamikoi.

Scenes of women's daily life and Dionysiac subjects were favourite Paestan themes; mythology played a minor role, and funerary scenes and those involving native warriors are extremely rare. On larger vases a row of onlookers is often placed above the scene. These are represented as busts or heads looking down from a window. The reverses often show a pair of draped youths who may hold various objects. The drapery is patterned with a distinctive dot-stripe border going back to the Dirce Painter in Sicily, where Paestan ware must have originated.

The principal vase painter was Asteas (*fl c.* 360–*c.* 330 BC) who, along with his colleague Python, was the only South Italian vase painter to sign his products. Eleven of his surviving vases bear his name. His repertory is mostly confined to Dionysiac and phlyax scenes, but his larger vases present a good selection of myths. His most ambitious work may be a signed calyx krater showing the *Rape of Europa*. Although he took great care in the rendering of such complex mythological scenes, his best work is his simpler but vivid depiction of phlyax scenes. Like him, Python represented mythological scenes on his larger vases, and it is sometimes difficult to distinguish his works from those of Asteas. His signature appears on two vases.

There were a number of other vase painters in the same workshop. They show strong stylistic affinities with the two masters, while their subjects are restricted to Dionysiac and genre scenes. The Aphrodite Painter (*fl c.* 340–*c.* 320 BC), an outstanding figure among these artists, probably trained in Apulia before moving to Paestum, a situation recalling that of the APZ Painter in Cumae. The Aphrodite Painter brought elaborate floral ornaments and pattern-work with him, as well as hollow rocks and 'xylophones'. He assimilated rapidly by decorating such non-Apulian shapes as the neck amphora and by using such Paestan features as the 'Asteas flower' and the dot-stripe border for his draped figures.

The Paestan style of the last quarter of the 4th century BC is best represented by the Painters of Naples 1778 and 2585. The production of their workshop reflects the swift decline of the Red-figure technique. Around 330 BC a group of Apulian vase painters came to Paestum, probably after its liberation from Lucanian domination by Alexander the Molossian. They used some local shapes and pattern-work but mostly remained apart, probably in a distinct workshop.

P. Wuilleumier: *Tarente: Des origines à la conquête romaine* (Paris, 1939)

A. D. Trendall: 'Phlyax Vases', *Bull. Inst. Class. Stud. U. London*, suppl. 19 (London, 1959, rev. 2/1967)

A. G. Woodhead: *The Greeks in the West* (London, 1962)

A. D. Trendall: *The Red-figured Vases of Lucania, Campania and Sicily*, 2 vols (Oxford, 1967; 1st suppl., London, 1970; 2nd suppl., London, 1973; 3rd suppl., London, 1983)

A. Oliver jr: 'The Reconstruction of Two Apulian Tomb-groups', *Ant. Kst*, suppl. 5 (Berne, 1968)

H. R. W. Smith: *Funerary Symbolism in Apulian Vase-painting* (Berkeley, 1976)

A. Kossatz-Diessmann: *Dramen des Aischylos auf westgriechischen Vasen* (Mainz, 1978)

A. D. Trendall and A. Cambitoglou: *The Red-figured Vases of Apulia*, 3 vols (Oxford, 1978–82; 1st suppl., London, 1983; 2nd suppl., London, 1991–2)

H. Lohmann: *Grabmäler auf unteritalischen Vasen* (Berlin, 1979)

D. Adamesteanu, ed.: *Metaponto I* (Rome, 1980), pp. 355–452

G. Schneider-Herrmann: *Lucanian and Apulian Nestorides* (Amsterdam, 1980)

B. R. Macdonald: 'The Emigration of Potters from Athens in the Late Fifth Century BC', *Amer. J. Archaeol.*, lxxxv (1981), pp. 159–68

H. Lohmann: 'Zu technischen Besonderheiten apulischer Vasen', *Jb. Dt. Archäol. Inst.*, xcvii (1982), pp. 191–249

The Art of South Italy: Vases from Magna Graecia (exh. cat., ed. M. E. Mayo and K. Hamma; Richmond, VA Mus. F.A., 1982)

D. von Bothmer: 'Observations on the Subject Matter of South Italian Vases', *A. VA*, xxiii/3 (1983), pp. 28–41

M. W. Frederiksen: *Campania* (London, 1984)

R. Hurschmann: *Symposienszenen auf unteritalischen Vasen* (Würzburg, 1985)

Napoli antica (exh. cat., ed. G. Macchiaroli; Naples, Mus. Archeol. N., 1985)

A. D. Trendall: 'On the Divergence of South Italian from Attic Red-figured Vase-painting', *Greek Colonists and Native Populations. Proceedings of the First Australian Congress on Classical Archaeology: Sydney, 1985*, pp. 217–30

Le Peintre de Darius et son milieu (exh. cat. by A. Cambitoglou, C. Aellen and J. Chamay, Geneva, Mus. A. & Hist., 1986)

I. McPhee and A. D. Trendall: 'Greek Red-figured Fish-plates', *Ant. Kst*, suppl. 14 (Basle, 1987)

A. D. Trendall: *The Red-figured Vases of Paestum* (London, 1987)

F. Villard: 'L'Art: Céramique et peinture', *Un secolo di ricerche in Magna Grecia. Atti del ventottesimo convegno di studi Magna Grecia: Taranto, 1988*, pp. 177–97

A. D. Trendall: *Red Figure Vases of South Italy and Sicily*, World A. (London, 1989)

M. R. Jentoft-Nilsen and A. D. Trendall: *The J. Paul Getty Museum, Malibu*, iii–v, Corp. Vasorum Ant. USA, 26–7, 30 (Malibu, CA, 1990–91, 1994)

I. McPhee and A. D. Trendall: 'Addenda to *Greek Red-figured Fish-plates*', *Ant. Kst*, xxxiii (1990), pp. 31–51

A. D. Trendall: 'Farce and Tragedy in South Italian Vase-painting', *Looking at Greek Vases*, ed. T. Rasmussen and N. Spivey (Cambridge, 1991), pp. 151–82

A. D. Trendall and A. Cambitoglou: *Second Supplement to the Red-figure Vases of Apulia* (London, 1991)

E. Greco: *Archeologia della Magna Grecia* (Bari, 1992), pp. 321–40

Principi Imperator Vescovi: Duemila anni di storia a Canosa (exh. cat., ed. R. Cassano Marsilio; Bari, Monastery of Santa Scolastica, 1992)

J. M. Padgett and others: *Vase-Painting in Italy: Red-Figure and Related Works in the Museum of Fine Arts, Boston* (Boston, 1993)

A. D. Trendall: 'An Introduction to the South Italian Vases', *Greek Vases in the San Antonio Museum of Art*, ed. H. A. Shapiro, C. A. Picon and G. D. Scott, III (San Antonio, 1995), pp. 199–203

M. Schmidt: 'La ceramica italiota e siceliota', *I Greci in Occidente* (exh. cat., ed. G. Pugliese Carratelli; Venice, Palazzo Grassi, 1996), pp. 443–56

A. Cambitoglou and J. Chamay: *Céramique de Grande Grèce: La collection de fragments H. A. Cahn* (Geneva, 1997)

(iii) Other areas. In the second half of the 5th century BC, particularly during the Peloponnesian War (431–404 BC), local Red-figure fabrics began to be produced in various areas of Greece, especially Boiotia, Corinth, Lakonia, Elis and the Chalcidice, in imitation

of, and sometimes in competition with, Attic Red-figure vases. The earliest and most inventive workshop was located in Boiotia. Its output apparently included an Early Classical pelike (*c.* 470–*c.* 460 BC; Munich, Staatl. Antikensamml., 2347) indebted to Athenian work by such artists as the Syleus Painter and the Geras Painter, but large-scale production only begins *c.* 430–*c.* 420 BC with the lekythoi and bell kraters from a mass burial at Thespiai. These vases still closely resembled their Athenian models—in the case of the lekythoi, works by the ACHILLES PAINTER—but contemporary or only slightly later calyx kraters and skyphoi by the Painter of the Judgement of Paris exhibit pronounced non-Attic elements in shape, decoration and style. This local Red-figure style flowered *c.* 425–*c.* 375 BC, probably at Thebes. Though the vases were largely for local use, some were exported as far as Spina at the mouth of the Po. A wide variety of shapes occur, many derived from Attic, but some, such as the Kabeiric skyphos and the kantharos, are derived from popular local forms. The principal artists were the Argos Painter, the Painter of the Large Athens Kantharos, whose works include a calyx krater depicting *Athena in a Quadriga* (*c.* 400 BC; London, BM), and the Thetis Painter, who produced vases in both red- and black-figure. Subject-matter is varied, combining standard genre or mythological scenes with ones derived from local cults, such as those on the Kabeiric skyphoi; a large number of small bell kraters bear a head, usually female, on one side and a palmette on the other. Though many isolated Boiotian vases of the first half of the 4th century BC have been discovered, the later phase of the fabric is poorly understood and needs more research. Considerable production of local Red-figure is likely *c.* 375–*c.* 350 BC during the age of Boiotian military domination. Since the light brown colour of Boiotian clay is often indistinguishable from that of Attic, some vases now thought to be Attic may actually be Boiotian.

Corinth also produced considerable Red-figure pottery *c.* 440–*c.* 350 BC, mainly for local use, though some pieces reached Boiotia, Phokis, Olympia and perhaps even South Italy. The fabric is easily distinguished from Attic by the pale (cream to light brown) colour of the fired clay, the orange slip sometimes used and the flaking of the glaze. The most common shapes are the bell krater and calyx krater, but the range is large, including pelikai, hydriai, oinochoai of various types, squat lekythoi, cups, stemless cups, skyphoi, lekanides and even plates. All these are derived from the Attic repertory of the late 5th century BC and early 4th; but one remarkable Corinthian form is the stemless bell krater, a shape adopted in Apulia and decorated in the Gnathia technique. The subject-matter of Corinthian Red-figure is similar to that found on contemporary Attic, though scenes involving torch racers are surprisingly common, and the influence of the theatre is evident in certain paintings depicting comic actors who resemble the *phlyakes* of South Italian vases. Stylistic resemblances between Corinthian and Attic are very close: indeed, the Athenian Suessula Painter decorated at least one vase made of Corinthian clay and strongly influenced early Corinthian Red-figure works. Few individual artists have been identified due to the fragmentary nature of the evidence, apart from the Pelikai Painter (late 5th century BC) and the Dombrena Painter (early 4th century BC).

Lakonia also apparently produced Red-figure pottery *c.* 430–*c.* 375 BC, including large one-handled mugs, which must have served a cult function. Many fragments were unearthed at Sparta, and whole vases were found at Analipsis in Kynouria, including a colossal mug showing a traditional Spartan story, the *Birth of Helen* (*c.* 410–*c.* 390 BC; Athens, N. Archaeol. Mus., 19447). The fabric is coarser than Attic and fired light red to reddish brown, often with a grey core; its surface was sometimes coated with a light brown slip.

Production of Red-figure pottery in the vicinity of Elis from *c.* 430 BC was probably initiated by Athenian artisans working at Olympia during the construction of the cult statue for the Temple of Zeus. Many fragments have been found at Olympia and ancient Elis, and a few at Elean Pylos and Mazi. The bell krater is the most common shape, and the fired clay is light brown to orange and easily mistaken for Attic: indeed, Elean pottery showed close stylistic links with Attic until *c.* 400 BC, when it began to look to Apulian Red-figure for inspiration. Whether the pottery was made in Olympia or Ancient Elis or both is not clear, but production apparently ceased by *c.* 350 BC.

The so-called 'Agrinion group' of small squat lekythoi decorated with figures reserved and painted white occurs along the north-western coast of Greece, at sites in Albania and the former Yugoslavia, and even in Italy (Spina, Policoro, Vaste). To judge from the fabric, these vases may be imports from Elis rather than local productions, but some pottery in the museums at Agrinion, Arta and Ioannina may be local, and there is no doubt that many Red-figure vases were made in the Greek colonies at Dyrrhachion and/or Apollonia on the Adriatic coast of Albania, their style and iconography deriving from the pottery of South Italy.

In northern Greece, local Red-figure vases characterized by their micaceous, yellowish-brown clay were produced *c.* 425–*c.* 350 BC at Olynthos or another Greek settlement in the Chalcidice. Two main painters have been identified, the Painter of Olynthos 5.141 and the Painter of Olynthos 5.156, both of whom decorated various shapes but specialized in skyphoi and lebetes gamikoi. Finally, less significant Red-figure workshops seem to have existed also at Eretria (*c.* 430–*c.* 420 BC) and on Crete (*c.* 400 BC) as well as, perhaps, at Tegea and at Sikyon or Argos.

C. Dugas: 'Vases et bronzes de Tégée', *Bull. Corr. Hell.*, li (1927), pp. 329–44

R. Lullies: 'Zur boiotisch rotfigurigen Vasenmalerei', *Mitt. Dt. Archäol. Inst.: Athen. Abt.*, lxv (1940), pp. 1–27

A. D. Ure: 'Boeotian Vases with Women's Heads', *Amer. J. Archaeol.*, lvii (1953), pp. 245–9

A. D. Ure: 'The Argos Painter and the Painter of the Dancing Pan', *Amer. J. Archaeol.*, lxii (1958), pp. 389–95

P. Pelagatti: 'Vasi di fabbriche della Beozia', *Arch Cl* 11 (1959), pp. 70–76
P. Pelagatti: 'Nuovi vasi di fabbriche della Beozia', *Archeol. Class.*, xiv (1962), pp. 29–41
W. Schiering: *Die Werkstatt des Pheidias in Olympia. Rotfigurig bemalte Keramik* (Olympische Forschungen V, Berlin, 1964), pp. 248–66
B. A. Sparkes: 'The Taste of A Boeotian Pig', *J. Hell. Stud.*, lxxxvii (1967), pp. 116–30
J. J. Maffre: 'Collection Paul Canellopoulos (VIII): Vases béotiens V: Vases à figures rouges', *Bull. Corr. Hell.*, xlix (1975), pp. 511–20
S. Herbert: *The Red-Figure Pottery* (1977), vii/4 of *Corinth: Results of Excavations Conducted by the American School of Classical Studies at Athens* (Princeton, 1932–)
I. McPhee: 'The Agrinion Group', *Annu. Brit. Sch. Athens*, lxxiv (1979), pp. 159–62
K. Braun: *Bemalte Keramik und Glas aus dem Kabirenheiligtum bei Theben* (Berlin, 1981)
I. McPhee: 'Some Red-figure Vase-painters of the Chalcidice', *Annu. Brit. Sch. Athens*, lxxvi (1981), pp. 297–308
I. McPhee: 'Local Red Figure from Corinth, 1973–1980', *Hesperia*, lii (1983), pp. 137–53
S. Karouzou: 'I Eleni tis Spartis' [Helen of Sparta], *Archaiol. Ephimeris.* (1985), pp. 33–44
K. Gex-Morgenthaler: 'Der Berner Maler', *Ant. Kst.*, xxix (1986), pp. 115–25
I. McPhee: 'Laconian Red-figure from the British Excavations in Sparta', *Annu. Brit. Sch. Athens*, lxxxi (1986), pp. 153–65
I. McPhee and A. D. Trendall: 'Six Corinthian Red-figure Vases', *Corinthiaca, Studies in Honor of Darrell A. Amyx* (Columbia, 1986)
I. McPhee: 'The Painter of the Large Egg-Patterns: A Elean Red-figure Vase-painter', *Numismatica e antichità classiche* xv (1986), pp. 169–77
A. Eggebrecht: *Albanien, Schatze aus dem Land der Skipetaren* (Mainz, 1988)
B. Cook: 'Cretan Red-figured Lekythoi', *Annu. Brit. Sch. Athens*, lxxxv (1990), pp. 69–70
I. McPhee: 'Local Red-figured Pottery from Ancient Elis: The Austrian Excavations of 1910–1914', *Jhft. Österreich. Archäol. Inst. Wien*, lx (1990)
I. McPhee: 'A Corinthian Red-figured Calyx-krater and the Dombrena Painter', *Oxford J. Archaeol.*, x (1991), pp. 325–34
K. Gex: *Eretria IX: Rotfigurige und weissgrundige Keramik* (Lausanne, 1993)
K. Gex and I. McPhee: 'The Painter of the Eretria Cup: A Euboean Red-figure Vase-painter', *Ant. Kst*, xxxviii/1 (1995), pp. 3–10
P. Pelagatti: 'Vasi beotici a figure rosse: Il pittore di Argos', *Boll. A.*, xcii (1995), pp. 33–48
M.-X. Garezou: 'Whitebait or Pottery? A Case of an Attic Import in Fourth-Century Boeotia', *Athenian Potters and Painters: The Conference Proceedings* (Oxford, 1997), pp. 371–81
V. Sabetai: 'Marriage Boiotian Style', *Hesperia*, lxvii (1998), pp. 323–34

7. White-ground. Greek painted pottery with a light background produced by applying liquid clay containing kaolinite was made at various dates and in different regions. Only in Athens, however, did White-ground become a recognized class of pottery, equivalent to Black- and Red-figure, and associated with particular shapes of vessel, certain workshops, painters and techniques of painting. The White-ground technique relates, therefore, essentially to Attic pottery.

White-ground painting was not as durable in use as Red-figure or Black-figure work and was thus confined to funerary vessels and votive or possibly other special gifts, such as wedding presents. The vases' functions influenced the choice of subjects and motifs used. Only that part of the vase surface used for pictures or ornamentation had a white ground, and White-ground painting was often combined with Black- or Red-figure work. Athenian White-ground production started *c.* 530–*c.* 520 BC and continued uninterrupted until *c.* 400 BC. A series of different painting techniques developed in different workshops, though these overlapped to an extent, some being used only for specific shapes of vessel.

The use of Black-figure painting on a white ground was the earliest form of White-ground painting and was introduced to Athens by the potter Nikosthenes, presumably under the influence of Ionian models. It was adopted by other workshops and used mainly on small- and middle-sized vases, differing from normal Black-figure only in the changed background colour and the associated practice of not using white for women's skin. The ground was rarely pure white, tending to be yellowish or brownish. The oldest examples are two oinochoai (Paris, Louvre, F 116 and F 117) signed by Nikosthenes.

The technique of outline drawing was adapted from Red-figure painting for use on White-ground pottery towards the end of the 6th century BC and was applied particularly to cups and smallish ointment containers (alabastra and small lekythoi). The outer contours of a figure were first executed with relief lines similar to those used in Red-figure, an example being the *Dancing Maenad* on a cup by the Brygos Painter in Munich (Staatl. Antikensamml., 2645). From the start of the 5th century BC, however, outlines were increasingly drawn in the same diluted glaze as the subsidiary detail. Individual parts of the drawing were given a yellowish or brownish tone, also with diluted glaze, and red was occasionally used for minor details (e.g. hair ribbons). The so-called 'semi-outline technique' combined the outline technique with the Black-figure silhouette technique and was used only in the first half of the 5th century BC, almost exclusively on lekythoi and alabastra.

Four-colour painting using black and diluted glaze and earth colours was a technical development of *c.* 500–*c.* 475 BC, probably originating from the workshop of Euphronios, which specialized in cups. It combined pure outline drawing with areas of solid colour. Parts of the body and garments of thin material were drawn in outline, generally with diluted glaze, whereas garments of thick material were coloured in entirely. Details within the coloured areas such as patterns or folds were executed either in diluted glaze or in red or white paint as appropriate.

Such objects as jewellery, fruit, parts of weapons and vessels or containers were often modelled in relief and gilded. Though the palette of colours was effectively reduced to shades of red by the exclusive use of earth colours, the painters could produce shades of black and yellow by varying the strength of the glaze. White was still largely reserved for the ground, though also employed for patterns on garments. Painting was completed before firing. Four-colour painting was used mainly on cups and pyxides. Even in the 5th century BC alabastra were generally decorated purely in outline, while special painting techniques were developed in the Classical period for lekythoi. White-ground was virtually confined to these four shapes, though it was used occasionally on others.

The most beautiful four-colour cups were made *c.* 475–*c.* 460 BC and are attributed to the Pistoxenos Painter. They include a cup in Athens (N. Archaeol. Mus., Acropolis 439) depicting the *Death of Orpheus*, and one in London (BM, D2) depicting *Aphrodite.* Most four-colour pyxides seem to have come from the workshop of the Penthesilea Painter, whose pyxis depicting the *Judgement of Paris* (New York, Met., 07.286.36) is a good example of the graphic potential of four-colour painting.

Early Classical lekythos painting using black and diluted glaze, earth colours and non-ceramic matt colours belongs to the second quarter of the 5th century BC. This technique was employed for painting large lekythoi used exclusively in burial rites, and it was the first to exploit non-earth colours such as cinnabar and 'Egyptian' blue, though glaze and earth colours still predominated. Compared with four-colour cup and pyxis painting, it made possible more marked colour contrasts and an altogether richer palette: purely linear elements became subordinate to coloured surfaces. Flesh tints on female figures were painted over with a second white, and even thin garments were now rendered in colour. Other typical features include black robes with red folds and hemlines, and painters also strove for greater realism in reproducing the colours of objects: stones were painted white, wooden objects black or brown. Most of these Early Classical lekythoi paintings depict scenes in women's apartments, the best-known being by the ACHILLES PAINTER.

About the middle of the 5th century BC a new polychrome technique of lekythos painting using matt colours was introduced. The use of second white was abandoned as was that of large areas painted with glaze, while the use of non-ceramic colours increased. The ground was now usually chalky white, and large parts of the picture, including flesh and funerary stelai, were again drawn in pure outline. At the same time red or blackish-grey matt paint began to replace diluted glaze for outlines. The Sabouroff Painter was apparently the initiator of this new painting technique, though several painters, such as the Achilles Painter, still employed diluted glaze for contours, a practice that persisted until about 430 BC. Outlines in matt colours were still drawn before firing, but the rest of the painting was completed after firing, making it even less durable. The original colours on these lekythoi have now largely disappeared, and the scenes depicted can be recognized—if at all—only from their outlines, while a few painters (e.g. the Sabouroff Painter) no longer bothered to outline those parts of the picture that were to be coloured. Thus it is no longer easy to recapture the original colourful effect of these Classical lekythoi, which must in their day have been striking. The pigments used included cinnabar and haematite for red and malachite and copper hydroxide chloride for green, together with yellow ochre and 'Egyptian' blue. Other pigments, such as those used for pink and matt black, have not yet been identified. The most important painters of lekythoi during the Classical period were: the Achilles Painter, the Sabouroff Painter, the Thanatos Painter, the Triglyph Painter, the Bird Painter, the Quadrate Painter, the Woman Painter, the REED PAINTER, the PHIALE PAINTER and the painter of GROUP R. Towards the end of the 5th century BC the influence of contemporary panel painting on lekythos painting increased noticeably, with the first attempts at shading on human bodies (*see* GROUP OF THE HUGE LEKYTHOI).

In the second half of the 5th century BC White-ground was used exclusively in sepulchral contexts and was largely confined to lekythoi, generally with paintings of grave scenes. When the production of funerary lekythoi ceased *c.* 400 BC, Attic White-ground painting also came to an end.

D. C. Kurtz: *Athenian White Lekythoi: Patterns and Painters* (Oxford, 1975)

J. R. Mertens: *Attic White-Ground: Its Development on Shapes other than Lekythoi* (New York, 1977)

I. Wehgartner: *Attische weissgrundige Keramik: Maltechniken, Werkstätten, Formen, Verwendung* (Mainz, 1983)

I. Wehgartner: 'Neue Untersuchungen zur weissgrundigen Lekythenbemalung', *Ancient Greek and Related Pottery. Proceedings of the International Vase Symposium: Copenhagen, 1987*, pp. 640–51

M. B. Moore: *Attic Red-figured and White-ground Pottery* (Princeton, 1997)

8. UNPAINTED. This section deals with pottery having no painted design or picture. Such pottery was, however, often painted or dipped in a single overall colour or decorated with bands of plain paint and might bear stamped, incised or moulded decoration.

(i) Black-glaze. (ii) Domestic wares.

(i) Black-glaze. Black-glazed (or, perhaps more accurately, black-glossed) pottery was one of the most popular forms of fine ceramics in the Classical and Hellenistic periods and was produced at various sites throughout the Mediterranean. In the eastern Mediterranean, workshops have been located at Athens, Corinth, Olynthos and Izmir, and in Boiotia and Lakonia; production centres in the west are being traced by scientific analysis. The vase shapes are often similar, possibly the result of the influence of a particular centre such as Athens or of another medium such

as metalwork. That Athenians made Black-glaze pottery outside Attica is attested by an Ephesian decree bestowing temporary citizenship on two potters and by the appearance at Corinth of a series of Attic and Corinthian Black-glaze pots that share a common stamped design.

The popularity of Black-glaze pottery is demonstrable in several ways: for example, it accounts for some 99% of the imported Attic pottery at the north African port of Sabratha, and it is also the most frequently found ware at rural sites, such as the Classical and Hellenistic houses excavated at Dema and Vari in Attica. Indeed, many Classical and Hellenistic rural sites discovered by field surveys in Greece are characterized by the presence of Black-glaze wares. As for its market value, although Black-glaze Nolan amphorae may have cost half an obol less than Red-figure ones, a plain bell krater at nine obols cost twice as much as its Red-figure counterpart.

The shapes of Black-glaze vessels correspond closely to figure-painted ones. However, some of the larger shapes, such as amphorae, early hydriai, psykters and kraters, occur rarely, and often the examples are confined to Athens. Smaller shapes such as oinochoai, mugs, skyphoi and lekanides seem to have been made in roughly equal numbers of Black-glaze and figure-painted. In addition, Black-glaze vessels include many shapes that were rarely, if ever, figure-painted: bowls, one-handlers (a low cup with a single handle), stemmed plates, feeders, amphoriskoi, bolsals and Rheneia cups.

The glaze used on Attic Black-glaze pottery is generally similar to that used on figure-painted ware, although some shapes, such as the 'bare-bottom' lekanides, were simply dipped and were not of such high quality; these shapes seem to have been confined mostly to Attica. The use of reserving and added purple and white resembles that on figure-painted pottery. One of the most striking means of decoration was the use of large areas of 'coral red'. This technique is particularly common on stemless cups and phialai dating from after the Persian Wars (490–479 BC), on which the red body contrasts strikingly with the black lip and handles. These shapes may have been produced at Athens under the influence of Persian metalwork, and it is possible that the colour was intended to evoke gold. In a similar way, the 'metallic' finish of the black glaze itself may reflect a taste for patinated silver in different areas and periods. The use of 'glazes' to evoke metalwork is corroborated by one of the few ancient literary references to the decoration of pots, in which the potters of Naukratis are described as 'baptizing' their wares to make them appear like silver (Athenaeus: *Deipnosophists* XI.cdlxxx.e). Other decorative devices included garlands in added clay, which were frequently gilded.

The bodies of many Black-glaze shapes were also enhanced by ribbing. In the first half of the 5th century BC this was often horizontal, formed either by concave depressions or moulded rings. This technique is most commonly found on phialai and mugs. Later in the 5th century BC vertical ribbing became more popular, particularly on mugs, though it is also found on cups, stemless cups, squat lekythoi and amphoriskoi. This change may have been due to the appearance of a new type of vessel, the thericleian, which is attested in various literary and epigraphic sources, including a series of inscriptions on Black-glaze pottery from Kafizin on Cyprus. Thericleians were also made in silver, terebinth wood and later in gold. One characteristic seems to have been their dark colour.

One of the main forms of decoration on unpainted pottery was the use of incised and stamped patterns. These techniques were used to decorate the insides of various shapes, such as stemless cups, bowls and plates, and the outsides of other vessels, including mugs, oinochoai, hydriai and amphoriskoi. The stamps were created from moulds and given convex faces, which allowed them to be applied with a rotary action to curved surfaces as well as flat. The patterns were impressed prior to glazing, while the clay was still moist.

Stamping and incision were not confined to unpainted wares but were also used in the decoration of Red-figure stemless cups and cup-skyphoi. Although it has been suggested that incised decoration preceded stamping in these workshops, the evidence from unpainted Attic wares from Stryme in Thrace shows that they were in fact introduced simultaneously. In the earliest designs, rays and arcs were used in conjunction with palmette stamps and sometimes in elaborate patterns, such as the ivy leaves on a stemless cup from Kameiros on Rhodes (*c.* 450–*c.* 440 BC; London, BM, 64.10–7.1591). By far the commonest stamp was the palmette, although such other shapes as the meander, ovule and boxed triangle were also used. The complex stamped and incised patterns of the mid-5th century BC soon evolved into monotonous designs of enclosed ovules surrounded by, or enclosing, linked palmettes. By the end of the 5th century BC even these patterns had degenerated into simple palmette crosses. During the 4th century BC the technique known as 'rouletting' or 'chattering' was introduced, whereby a bent strip of metal left a series of indentations as the pot was turned on the wheel: this pattern was often combined with a zone of palmettes linked by short arcs.

Although much stamped decoration is repetitive, some designs are extremely attractive. The most unusual are found on two kantharoi (Boston, MA, Mus. F.A., 01.8023; Brussels, Musées Royaux A. & Hist., A741) and a mug (*c.* 435–*c.* 430 BC; London, BM, G90), which depict the *Slaying of Medusa.* On one side Hermes is shown leading Perseus, who clutches a sickle in his left hand and a bag containing the head in his right, to Athena; the other shows two gorgons in pursuit, Medusa sinking to the ground with Pegasus flying about her and the baby Chrysaor to her right. The scene is framed by Ionic columns surmounted by sphinxes. Related to these are two kantharoi (Newcastle upon Tyne, U. Newcastle upon Tyne, Gr. Mus., 58, and Naples, Mus. Archaeol. N., 166455; the latter found at Pithekoussai) decorated with horses and boxed triangles, and a fragment of another from Perachora (Athens, N. Archaeol. Mus.) stamped with lions.

A further type of decoration found on Black-glaze pottery consists of reliefs moulded to the upper surfaces of askoi and depicting various subjects, ranging from heads of Herakles, Helios, maenads or others, to actual scenes, such as a mounted Amazon. Several of these rare pieces have been found at Marion on Cyprus. This decorative tradition continued into the Hellenistic period, when reliefs were applied to mould-made bowls.

The lack of painted decoration on Black-glaze pottery has led scholars to examine the relationships between different shapes in their potting technique and stamped decoration. Thus the carefully moulded feet of certain oinochoai (e.g. Leiden, Rijksmus. Oudhd., NL7) also occur on hydriai (e.g. Leiden, Rijksmus. Oudhd., GNV 57), and the heavy lips and reserved feet of Castulo cups are also found on cup-skyphoi, one-handlers, small bowls and askoi. These associations are sometimes strengthened by the use of common stamps on different shapes. Thus a swastika meander can link kantharoi, mugs and askoi, while a large, spindly palmette (which may represent a silphium plant, as on coins from Cyrene) is found on amphoriskoi, 'baby-feeders', bolsals and miniature kantharoi.

Black-glaze pottery was also produced in the same workshops as figure-painted wares. The Red-figure palmettes at the handles of otherwise plain bell kraters (e.g. Leiden, Rijksmus. Oudhd., NL1) associate them with kraters by the PHIALE PAINTER and the Cassel Painter. Some of the earliest plain-walled mugs were produced in the workshop of the Painter of Berlin F2268. Similarly, some fragments of Black-glaze mugs are attributable to the same workshop as Red-figure mugs decorated by a follower of Douris or by the Painter of Philadelphia 2449, a follower of Makron. The Black-glaze Castulo cup appears to have originated from the workshop of the Amphitrite Painter and the Carlsruhe Painter. Black-glaze stemless cups, many from Stryme, have a prominent moulded cone on the underside, which is also a feature of cups decorated by the Amphitrite Painter, while the concave moulded and reserved rings on the undersides of stemmed bowls are also found on products by the Dish Painter.

There can be little doubt that Black-glaze pottery was influenced by metalwork, especially given the availability of silver at Athens. A Black-glaze mug from Douvanli in Thrace was found in the same tomb as a silver one of the same shape; the tomb also contained a figure-decorated silver Rheneia cup, a shape frequently decorated in Black-glaze though not in Red-figure. Likewise, silver cups from Chemyrev parallel Black-glaze and Red-figure vessels, and a silver perfume pot from Selenskaya is identical to a series of Black-glaze vases.

(ii) Domestic wares. The domestic wares of antiquity were essentially utilitarian vessels used for cooking, the processing of foods, storage and transport. They occur in the archaeological record of most ancient dwellings. Among the mostly highly decorated pieces were louteria (wash-basins on stands), a shape also represented in marble at sanctuaries. Their broad rims were often decorated with impressed mouldings, including tongues, ovules and wreaths; those made from the same material as Corinthian tiles could also be decorated with bands of red paint and black glaze. The pedestals of louteria were invariably fluted. Pithoi also carried some impressed decoration, though their motifs were generally quite different, including linked spirals, guilloches, concentric circles and lotus bands. Glazed lines were sometimes used to decorate table and storage amphorae, hydriai, jugs and lekanai; this simple decoration is also found on transport containers.

B. A. Sparkes and L. Talcott: *Pots and Pans of Classical Athens* (1953), i of *The Athenian Agora* (Princeton, 1953–)

P. E. Corbett: 'Palmette Stamps from an Attic Black-glaze Workshop', *Hesperia*, xxiv (1955), pp. 172–86

B. A. Sparkes: 'Black Perseus', *Ant. Kst*, xi (1968), pp. 3–16

B. B. Shefton: 'Persian Gold and Attic Black Glaze: Achaemenid Influences on Attic Pottery of the 5th and 4th Centuries BC', *Proceedings of the IXth International Congress of Classical Archaeology: Damascus, 11–20 Oct 1969*, pp. 109–11

B. A. Sparkes and L. Talcott: *Black and Plain Pottery of the 6th, 5th and 4th Centuries BC* (1970), xii of *The Athenian Agora* (Princeton, 1953–)

S. I. Rotroff: *Hellenistic Pottery: Athenian and Imported Moldmade Bowls* (1982), xxii of *The Athenian Agora* (Princeton, 1953–)

D. W. J. Gill: 'The Workshops of the Attic Bolsal', *Ancient Greek and Related Pottery. Proceedings of the International Vase Symposium: Amsterdam, 1984*, pp. 102–6

A. J. N. W. Prag: 'Neutron Activation Analysis of Black-glazed Pottery: A Report on Work in Hand', ibid., pp. 54–8

S. I. Rotroff: 'Ceramic Workshops in Hellenistic Athens', ibid., pp. 173–7

D. W. J. Gill: 'Classical Greek Fictile Imitations of Precious Metal Vases', *Pots and Pans. A Colloquium on Precious Metals and Ceramics in the Muslim, Chinese and Graeco-Roman Worlds: Oxford, 1985*, pp. 9–30

D. W. J. Gill: 'Attic Black-glazed Pottery', *Excavations at Sabratha, 1948–1951*, ed. P. M. Kenrick (London, 1986), pp. 275–96

K. L. Nicholas: *Interpreting Religious Ritual in Magna Graecia: An Analysis of the Archaic and Classical Black Glaze Ceramics from the Rural Sanctuary at Pentanello (Metaponto)* (diss., Los Angeles, UCLA, 1999)

9. HELLENISTIC. Although early Hellenistic potters often imitated Athenian models, they soon developed their own diverse regional variations of shapes and decoration; in newly Hellenized areas the local ceramic tradition often continued alongside the hellenizing one. Nonetheless, certain general characteristics are apparent: the pots developed from low, stable forms to tall, elegant ones, often imitated metal prototypes and shared ornamental motifs with works in other media such as glassware and wall painting.

Hellenistic pottery is difficult to date. Most is undecorated, much was carelessly made, and style is of little use in determining the date of mechanically reproduced mould-made products. There are a few archaeological contexts for which historical events can provide latest possible dates; for Attic pottery the most useful are the destruction of Olynthos (348 BC), the occupation of the Ptolemaic camp at Koroni in Attica (260s BC), the destruction of Corinth (146 BC) and the sack of Athens by Sulla (86 BC). Since Attic pottery was widely exported and imitated, at least in the early Hellenistic period, its dating has more than local importance: study of the material from Koroni caused a general downdating of some 35 years for early Hellenistic ceramics found throughout the eastern Mediterranean.

The most common Hellenistic tableware was Black-glazed, with a gradual shift to Red-glazed beginning in the 2nd century BC, heralding the red wares of Roman times. The earliest well-defined Hellenistic red ware, Eastern Sigillata A (formerly called 'Pergamene'), probably originated in Syria or Palestine *c.* 150 BC. Grey wares, with black or dark grey glaze and grey fabric, were made in several centres, notably in Sicily (e.g. Campana C ware) and in Asia Minor.

Though Red-figure vase painting died out at the end of the 4th century BC, Black-figure continued to be used for Panathenaic amphorae, their depictions of Athena providing early evidence for the emergence of archaism in Greek art. The commonest type of painted pottery, however, was West Slope ware, named after finds from the west slope of the Athenian Acropolis. Its designs were executed in tan-coloured dilute clay and white paint on a Black-glaze background, sometimes with incised details. In Athens it evolved from 4th-century BC gold-decorated ware, with decoration painted on to the glazed surface in thick clay and gilded after firing. Increasingly gilding was omitted and designs enlivened with white paint. Local versions of West Slope ware were produced throughout the Hellenistic world from the early 3rd century BC to the 1st. Motifs are usually simple, consisting of wreaths, rosettes, leaping dolphins and charm bracelets, while figural scenes are rare. Occasionally there are painted inscriptions naming a divinity (e.g. Zeus Soter, Dionysos, Aphrodite) or a quality (e.g. friendship). Cretan West Slope ware is exceptionally fine, with a larger proportion of figural scenes and occasional use of pink and blue paint. Links between Crete, South Italy and Alexandria were strong enough for Cretan vase painters to have been influenced by the South Italian Gnathia ware produced at several centres in Apulia from the 360s to *c.* 250 BC; its designs are painted on a dark ground in red, white and 'gold'—a dilute clay wash on white—with more delicate, elaborate and carefully composed decoration than on most West Slope ware from the eastern Mediterranean.

Decoration in dark paint on a light background is restricted to only a few ceramic centres, several still unidentified. Hadra vases, hydriai used as cremation urns in 3rd- and 2nd-century BC ALEXANDRIA, are of two types. Those of coarse clay, with the surface whitewashed after firing to receive polychrome decoration, were probably made locally. Clay-ground Hadras, with glazed designs applied directly to the clay surface in silhouette or Black-figure technique, seem to have been produced on Crete, to judge from clay analyses and similarities with Cretan West Slope ware. Both floral and figural designs occur, the former probably being the earlier. The chronology is in part based on painted inscriptions giving the name of the deceased and a regnal year but omitting the name of the reigning monarch.

Another variety of dark-on-light ware was probably produced *c.* 200–*c.* 50 BC on the west coast of Asia Minor, to judge from its distribution. Its most common shape was the lagynos, though large pyxides and thymiateria (small incense altars) also occur. Glaze ranging from black to orange was applied either directly to the clay or over a white slip. Wreaths, garlands and musical instruments were the favourite motifs. The variety of fabrics and decorative schemes suggests the existence of several regional workshops.

Polychrome decoration was particularly common on South Italian pottery, such as the series of large vases, mostly lidded kraters and lekanides, from Centuripe in Sicily, many with moulded decoration (e.g. New York, Met., 53.11.5). Against a pink (or, earlier, black) background appear scenes of marriages or Dionysiac ceremonies painted in tempera after firing in a figural style reminiscent of 1st-century BC wall painting. Their size, the placement of decoration on one side only and certain technical features (e.g. lids sometimes fired in one piece with bodies, fugitive paint) imply that they were grave goods. Stylistic and iconographic similarities suggest that Centuripe ware derived from late 4th-century BC Red-figure with polychrome details produced at Lipari off the coast of Sicily and that it dates to the 3rd century BC. A series of funerary vases produced at Canosa in northern Apulia from the late 4th century BC to the mid-2nd has painted decoration (floral designs, horses, chariots) on a pink background, sometimes combined with mould-made appliqués (often gorgoneia) and attached mould-made figurines (principally *nikai*, erotes, women and horse *protomes*).

Large-scale use of moulds for pottery production began *c.* 225 BC with the emergence of the hemispherical relief bowl (formerly called the 'Megarian' bowl), a footless and handleless cup, developed in imitation of silverware and possibly invented at Athens, which became a standard drinking vessel. Floral and figural designs were the norm until *c.* 150 BC, the former derived from silverware, the latter mostly a ceramic development belonging to a repertory that spanned many centuries and media. The composition of the *Rape of Persephone* on an Attic example (Athens, Agora Mus., P 28545) is paralleled in late 4th-century BC tomb painting (Vergina, Macedonia, Tomb I) and later on Roman sarcophagi and wall painting. Other specimens known as 'Homeric bowls' represent subjects from epic and tragedy, often with quotations or identifying labels; they were probably manufactured in Macedonia in the 2nd century BC and perhaps slightly earlier, their compositions possibly deriving from manuscript illumination. By 150 BC various linear schemes had become popular. 'Shield bowls' decorated with concentric semicircles imitated the traditional Macedonian shield also pictured on Macedonian coins; 'Long-petal' bowls, covered with tall, contiguous, rounded petals, derived ultimately from Achaemenid silver prototypes.

Mould-made appliqués were frequently added to wheelmade wares. Heads or busts in high relief, usually of mythological figures but sometimes portraits, were placed on the floors of hemispherical bowls, below the handle attachments of pitchers, on the covers of pyxides and in other appropriate places. Particularly fine is the Black-glaze 'Calenian' ware produced in Apulia, Campania and Etruria from the mid-4th century BC to the 3rd. Its most common shapes are *gutti* (oil jugs) with appliqué medallions on top and phialai with elaborate relief scenes on their interiors; exact parallels in metal have been found. Low-relief appliqués appear on fine, often red-fired ware from Pergamon (Pergamene appliqué ware; mid-2nd century BC to the 1st). The most common shape is a low skyphos; decoration includes ivy garlands, mythological figures and erotic scenes. Similar in technique are the Black-glaze *Plakettenvasen*, mostly bigger, closed shapes with large-scale reliefs of mythological figures on their reeded walls; they were probably made at several sites (Corinth, Taras, Crete) from the mid-4th century BC to the mid-3rd.

Relief-ware cups with a distinctive green, lead-based glaze were produced *c.* 50 BC–*c.* AD 50 in one- or two-piece moulds or on the wheel with added appliqué designs; floral decoration is more common than figural. This short-lived experiment with vitreous glaze probably began in the East, since several workshops have been identified in Asia Minor, but was imitated in the West; there are close parallels in silver.

Hellenistic kitchen ware has been little studied. While plain jugs and bowls were often locally made, there was considerable trade in vessels considered superior in material, method of manufacture or appearance: for example, elaborate braziers with figural appliqué decoration and mould-made lugs in the shape of bearded satyr heads were produced at several sites and widely exported.

G. Leroux: *Lagynos* (Paris, 1913)

F. Courby: *Les Vases grecs à reliefs* (Paris, 1922)

G. Libertini: *Centuripe* (Catania, 1926)

H. A. Thompson: 'Two Centuries of Hellenistic Pottery', *Hesperia*, iii (1934), pp. 311–480

F. O. Waagé: 'Hellenistic and Roman Tableware of North Syria', *Ceramics and Islamic Coins* (1948), iv/1 of *Antioch-on-the-Orontes*, ed. G. W. Elderkin, J. Lassus and R. Stillwell (Princeton, 1934–)

F. F. Jones: 'The Pottery', *The Hellenistic and Roman Periods* (1950), i of *Excavations at Gözlü Kule, Tarsus*, ed. H. Goldman (Princeton, 1950–63), pp. 149–296

G. R. Edwards: 'Panathenaics of Hellenistic and Roman Times', *Hesperia*, xxvi (1957), pp. 320–49

U. Hausmann: *Hellenistische Reliefbecher aus attischen und böotischen Werkstätten* (Stuttgart, 1959)

P. W. Lapp: *Palestinian Ceramic Chronology, 200 BC–AD 70* (New Haven, 1961)

E. Vanderpool, J. R. McCredie and A. Steinberg: 'Koroni: The Date of the Camp and the Pottery', *Hesperia*, xxxiii (1964), pp. 69–75

L. Forti: *La ceramica di Gnathia* (Naples, [1965])

J. Schäfer: *Hellenistische Keramik aus Pergamon* (1968), ii of *Pergamenische Forschungen*, ed. E. Bochringer (Berlin, 1965–)

D. M. Bailey: *Greek, Hellenistic, and Early Roman Pottery Lamps* (London, 1975)

G. R. Edwards: *Corinthian Hellenistic Pottery* (1975), vii/3 of *Corinth: Results of Excavations Conducted by the American School of Classical Studies at Athens* (Princeton, 1932–)

U. Wintermeyer: 'Die polychrome Reliefkeramik aus Centuripe', *Jb. Dt. Archäol. Inst.*, xc (1975), pp. 136–241

V. R. Anderson-Stojanovic: *Pottery of the Late Hellenistic and Early Roman Periods at Stobi* (diss., Austin,U. TX, 1977)

A. Hochuli-Gysel: *Kleinasiatische glasierte Reliefkeramik (50 v. Chr. bis 50 n. Chr.) und ihre oberitalischen Nachahmungen* (Berne, 1977)

A. Laumonier: *La Céramique hellénistique à reliefs: Ateliers 'ioniens'* (1977), xxxi of *Exploration archéologique de Délos* (Paris, 1909–)

G. Siebert: *Recherches sur les ateliers de bols à reliefs du Péloponnèse à l'époque hellénistique* (Paris, 1978)

U. Sinn: *Die homerischen Becher: Hellenistische Reliefkeramik aus Makedonien* (Berlin, 1979)

J. P. Morel: *Céramique campanienne: Les Formes*, Bibliothèque des écoles françaises d'Athènes et de Rome (Rome, 1981)

S. I. Rotroff: *Hellenistic Pottery: Athenian and Imported Moldmade Bowls* (1982), xxii of *The Athenian Agora* (Princeton, 1953–)

L. Rossi and F. van der Wielen-van Ommeren: *Canosa*, ii (Bari, 1983)

P. J. Callaghan: 'Knossian Artists and Ptolemaic Alexandria', *Studi in onore di Achille Adriani*, iii (Rome, 1984), pp. 789–94

F. A. Winter: *Late Classical and Hellenistic Pottery from Gordion: The Imported Black Glazed Wares* (diss., Philadelphia, U. PA, 1984)

T. Dohrn: 'Schwarzgefirniste Plakettenvasen', *Mitt. Dt. Archäol. Inst.: Röm. Abt.*, xcii (1985), pp. 77–106

A. H. Enklaar: 'Chronologie et peintres des hydries de Hadra', *Bull. Ant. Besch.*, lx (1985), pp. 106–51

A. H. Enklaar: 'Les Hydries de Hadra, ii: Formes et ateliers', *Bull. Ant. Besch.*, lxi (1986), pp. 41–65

D. B. Thompson, H. A. Thompson and S. I. Rotroff: *Hellenistic Pottery and Terracottas*, 4 vols (Princeton, 1987)

G. Hübner: *Die Applikenkeramik von Pergamon* (1993), vii of *Pergamenische Forschungen*, ed. W. Radt (Berlin, 1965–)

S. I. Rotroff and others: *The Hellenistic Pottery from Sardis: The Finds through 1994* (Cambridge, MA, 2003)

C. Morgan and G. R. Tsetskhladze: *Attic Fine Pottery of the Archaic to Hellenistic Periods in Phanagoria* (Leiden and Boston, 2004)

10. Collecting and collections. The ancient Greeks acquired painted pottery only for utilitarian purposes, and though the vast numbers of Greek vases imported into Etruria during the 6th and 5th centuries BC were prized items apparently displayed at parties, as shown in the paintings in the Tomb of the Ship at Tarquinia (end of 5th century BC), they too were put to practical use and were not mere collectors' items. Indeed, prior to the 17th century AD there is only sporadic evidence of interest in Greek vases.

A Tuscan altarpiece by Bonaventura Berlinghieri (*fl* 1228–74) (13th century; Pescia, S Francesco) depicts buildings adorned with palmette scrolls remarkably similar to those on 4th-century BC Apulian vases, while later, another Tuscan artist, Antonio Pollaiuolo (*c.* 1432–98), may have imitated lost works by the Niobid Painter or one of his followers in his frescoes of nude dancers at the Villa la Gallina, Arcetri, near Florence (1460s; *in situ*), or in his engraving of the *Battle of the Ten Nudes* (*c.* 1470–75). That Greek pottery was collected and studied at that time is confirmed by a letter of 1491 from Angelo Poliziano offering Lorenzo de' Medici (1449–92) a large vase and two smaller pots and implying that Lorenzo already had similar pieces: unfortunately, no further details are known. In his life of Battista Franco (*Vite* (1550, rev. 2/1568); ed. G. Milanesi (1878–85), vi, p. 571), Vasari referred to vases with Red- and Black-figure painting, though he mistook them for Roman works and commented that they were inferior to maiolica from Urbino. Around the same time Ulisse Aldrovandi recorded a few vases in the varied collection of Cardinal Rodolfo Pio da Carpi (1500–84) at Rome (*Delle statue antiche che per tutta Roma in diversi luoghi . . . si veggono*; Venice, 1556). Both Black- and Red-figure vases were excavated at Orbetello in 1565. The collection of Gerolamo Garimberto at Rome, inventoried in 1576, contained some 80 fictive vases.

In the 17th century Cassiano dal Pozzo (1588–1657) included drawings of vases (five clearly Attic and five South Italian) in his vast *Museum chartaceum* (Lat.: 'Paper Museum'; now at Windsor Castle, Royal Lib., and London, BM), which was intended to be a comprehensive record of ancient sculpture and smaller antiquities known in his day. A few Attic, South Italian and Italo-Corinthian vases owned by the antiquarian Giovanni Pietro Bellori (1613–96) and sold to Frederick III of Brandenburg (later Frederick I, King of Prussia; *reg* 1701–13) were published along with other items from his collection by L. Beger (*Thesaurus regius et electoralis brandenburgensis*, iii (Berlin, 1701)). Soon afterwards Greek vases came to be of considerable interest to both collectors and scholars: Filippo Buonarroti's edition of Thomas Dempster's *De Etruria regali* (Florence, 1723–4) includes drawings of over 30 vases and a discussion of their origins, while his notes refer to several contemporary collections. A number of the vases mentioned were in the Medici collection, but the holding most frequently cited was that of the Orvietan cardinal F. A. Gualterio, containing 183 items from the Neapolitan collection of Giuseppe Valletta (*d* 1714) and from excavations at Chiusi (Clusium) and elsewhere; it passed to the Vatican after Gualterio's death in 1728, becoming the most substantial collection of Greek vases in the city of Rome. In Naples, the Marchese F. M. Mastrilli amassed a collection of nearly 400 vases between *c.* 1740 and 1755. Buonarroti's work had profound consequences. He argued that the vases could not be Roman, since they had never been discovered in Rome itself, and that they did not fit stylistically with either Greek or Roman art: he concluded that they must be Etruscan. This view was widely held for nearly a century, and Greek vases shared in the popularity of genuine Etruscan artefacts during the later 18th-century craze for all things Etruscan. Thus Johann Wolfgang von Goethe recorded (*Italian Journey*, Naples, 9 March 1787) that every visitor to Italy wanted to acquire an Etruscan vase, for which extravagant prices were being paid. As a consequence, Giovanni Battista Passeri's *Picturae etruscorum in vasculis* (Rome, 1767–75) includes 300 plates illustrating specimens in some 40 collections in Italy and elsewhere.

The most famous collector of the period, Sir William Hamilton (1730–1803), amassed and disposed of two great collections and profoundly influenced contemporary attitudes. As British Plenipotentiary to the King of the Two Sicilies (1764–1800), Hamilton obtained his vases by excavation in southern Italy as well as by purchase; 65 specimens, for example, were selected from the Mastrilli collection. Unlike previous students of Greek vase painting, who had been interested primarily in the subjects depicted, he drew attention to the style of the paintings by publishing clear, attractive drawings to serve as models for contemporary designers. The publication of his first collection (P. F. Hugues [P. V. d'Hancarville]: *The Collection of Etruscan, Greek and Roman Antiquities from the Cabinet of the Honble Wm Hamilton*, 4 vols (1766–7)) was so successful that the British Parliament decided to purchase his pottery for £8400: thus in 1772 the British Museum, London, became the first public museum to display Greek vases. Hamilton's second collection had a much more eventful history. It, too, was published, in four lavish volumes edited by Wilhelm Tischbein (*Collection of Engravings from Ancient Vases . . .* (Naples, 1791–5)), but during shipment to England 8 of the 24 crates in which it was packed were lost when the *HMS Colossus* sank off the Scilly Isles. The remaining 16 crates were sold in London to the Amsterdam merchant Thomas Hope (1769–1831); their contents were dispersed throughout the world at the sale of the Hope collection in 1917. The wreck of the *Colossus* was rediscovered in 1975, and some 30,000 vase fragments were retrieved and deposited in the British Museum.

During the neo-Classical era motifs based on Greek vase paintings were incorporated in the designs of the brothers Robert (1728–92) and James Adam (1732–94) and others for the décor of many 18th-century English country houses. In Johan Zoffany's painting of *Charles Towneley's Library in Park Street* (1781–3; Burnley, Towneley Hall A.G. & Mus.), a genuine Red-figure amphora may be seen, as well as copies of famous sculptures, while George Hammond Lucy placed a fine Black-figure hydria (*in situ*) on the cornice of the bookshelves in his antiquarian library at Charlecote House in Warwickshire (1820s), and Spencer Joshua Alwyne Compton, 2nd Marquess of Northampton (1790–1851), displayed his splendid collection of vases acquired in Rome (1820–30) along with other antiquities at Castle Ashby, Northants; vases were also acquired by collectors of more modest means, who could afford the price of what were then regarded as minor Classical items.

Although some 18th-century scholars had suspected that the so-called 'Etruscan' vases were really Greek, this was only widely accepted after the publication of Luigi Lanzi's *De' vasi antichi dipinti volgarmente chiamati etruschi* (Florence, 1806), which stresses that the vases' inscriptions, mythological subjects and representations of architecture are all Greek. By this time there was such great enthusiasm for these objects, as well as for all things Greek, that collectors continued to prize them. Soon afterwards, the excavations of Lucien Bonaparte, Prince of Canino (1775–1840), unearthed over 3000 specimens of decorated wares at the Etruscan cemeteries on his estates at Vulci (1828–9), while plain pottery was simply trampled underfoot on site; little record was kept of the vases' original contexts. Purchasers included Ludwig I of Bavaria (*reg* 1825–48) and William I of the Netherlands (*reg* 1813–40); other specimens went to the Louvre, the British Museum and the Berlin Museum. O. Jahn's catalogue of Ludwig's vases (*Beschreibung der Vasensammlung König Ludwigs in der Pinakothek zu München* (Munich, 1854)) includes a detailed survey of other important European private and public collections of the period.

Among the most prominent 19th-century collectors was the archaeologist Giampietro Campana, Marchese di Cavelli (1808–80), who amassed at Rome through excavation and purchase one of the most important private collections of vases and other antiquities. Unfortunately, his collecting activities were financed through embezzlement, and after his imprisonment his whole collection was sold. The catalogue prepared in 1857 includes 3791 vases, the largest number of which was purchased by Napoleon III (*reg* 1852–70) and exhibited first in the Musée Napoleon III and then in the Louvre, where they now form the basis of one of the most important collections of Greek vases in the world.

Some ten years before its sale and dispersion the Campana collection was visited and described by George Dennis (*The Cities and Cemeteries of Etruria*, ii (London, 1848), pp. 528–31), whose account gives an impression of how a mid-19th-century private collection of Greek vases was displayed. Most of the selected specimens, which were predominantly Red-figure, were set up on shelves around a large room, while a few choice pieces stood on central pedestals that allowed a view from all sides. In the same volume (pp. 497–512) Dennis also gave an excellent description of the Museo Gregoriano Etrusco at the Vatican, despite an official ban on taking notes. Many of its specimens had been excavated by the Campanari family of Toscanella on papal estates at Vulci, Cerveteri (Caere), Tarquinia and elsewhere in Etruria, and four rooms were devoted exclusively to vases. The specimens were again mainly displayed on shelves, with a few special pieces on pedestals (e.g. the Black-figure amphora 344 depicting *Ajax and Achilles Playing a Board Game* by Exekias and the White-ground krater with *Hermes Bringing the Infant Dionysos to Papposilenos and the Nymphs of Nysa* by the Phiale Painter, both from Vulci). The organization of the display was based at least partly on vase shape: one room contained only kylikes, while another featured amphorae.

Numerous sales catalogues attest the heavy trade in Greek pottery during the 19th century, and Italian adventurers continued to excavate vases for sale to private collectors, especially in Paris. The most important Italian collectors after Campana were the members of the Castellani family, especially the brothers Alessandro (1823–83) and Augusto (1829–1914). The latter sold 250 vases to Vienna (now in the Kunsthistorisches Museum), while other parts of his collection ended up in the Museo dei Conservatori and the Museo Nazionale di Villa Giulia in Rome. Alessandro was active in Paris and London, but most of his collection was sold in lots in Rome after his death in 1883. After the unification of Italy in 1870 private excavation in Etruria was made illegal, limiting considerably the number of newly discovered vases entering the market; but pieces from existing collections continued to be traded, and items from clandestine digs still found their way on to the market.

Greek pottery from Greece itself was never traded in such vast quantities as that from Italy. Indeed, it excited little interest before excavators in the 1830s began to record it, and in any case, the export of Greek antiquities was forbidden by law from 1827. As a result many finds were put into the National Museum that was set up at Aegina in 1829 and subsequently moved to Athens. However, some vases, particularly those from outside the Greek mainland, did find their way into other European collections. For example, Red-figure vases from Kerch in south Russia were sent to the Hermitage in St Petersburg, pottery from Rhodes and Naukratis went to the British Museum, vases from Crete collected by Sir Arthur Evans went to the Ashmolean Museum in Oxford, and pieces from Cyprus went to the Kunsthistorisches Museum in Vienna and the Metropolitan Museum of Art in New York.

More sophisticated study of Greek vases in the late 19th century and the 20th inevitably influenced the market for antiquities. Following Jahn's emphasis in his Munich catalogue on the importance of provenance and his attempt to distinguish particular styles and schools, J. D. BEAZLEY began to identify individual hands and workshops. The publication in 1923 of the first fascicle of the *Corpus vasorum antiquorum* marked the start of an attempt to catalogue Greek vases in collections throughout the world. Well over 200 fascicles have been published, constituting a basic reference work for scholars, museums and indeed private collectors, who are not only more numerous than ever but also far more knowledgeable. Vases signed by important Attic artists now command extraordinary prices: in 1972 a krater by Euphronios purchased by the Metropolitan Museum of Art in New York became the first Greek pot to cost a million dollars. To discourage further price

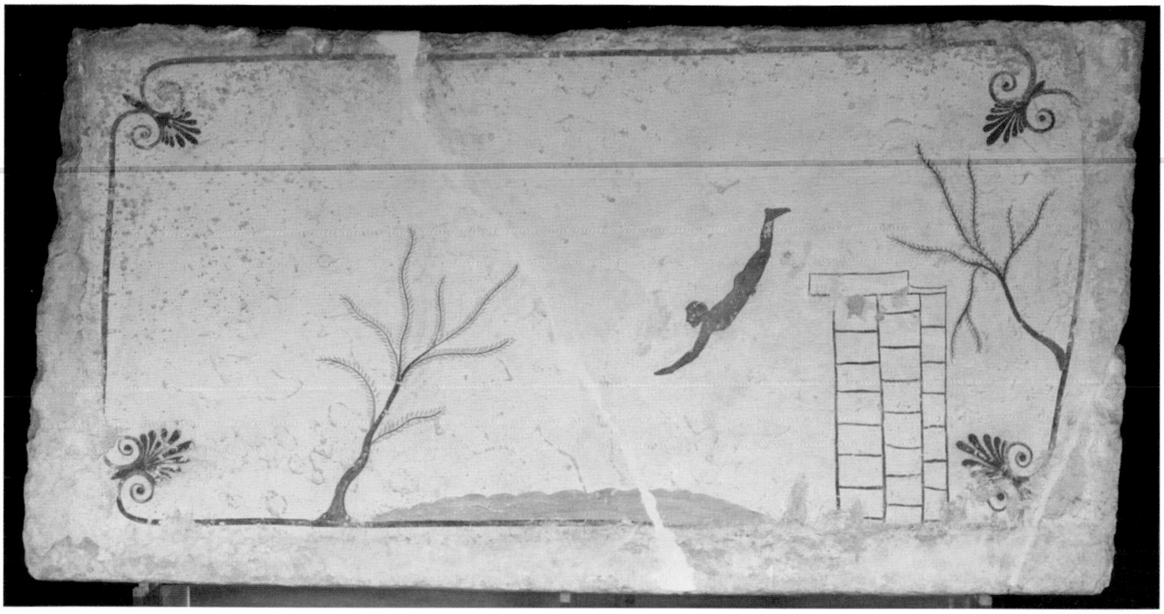

1. Paestum, ceiling painting depicting a youth diving, from the Tomb of the Diver, first half of the 5th century BC (Paestum, Museo Archeologico Nazionale); *see* Paestum

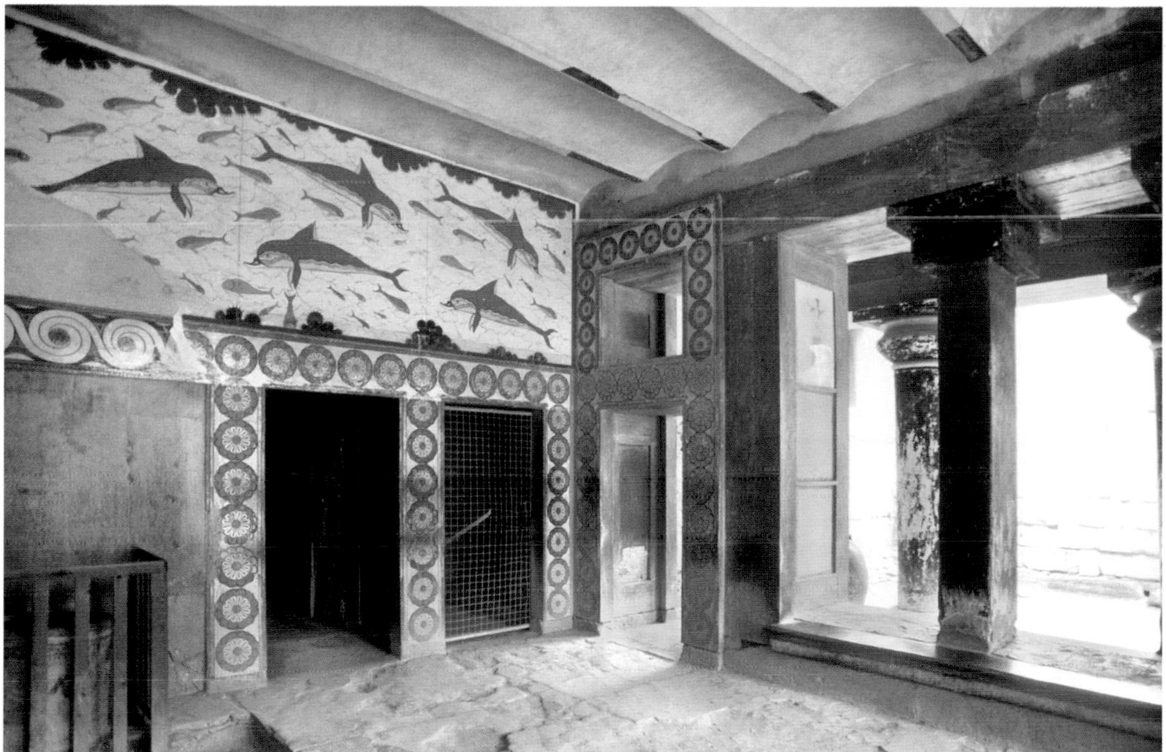

2. Minoan wall painting depicting dolphins and small fish, Queen's Megaron, palace of Knossos, Middle Minoan II–Late Minoan IIIB; *see* Painting (Minoan)

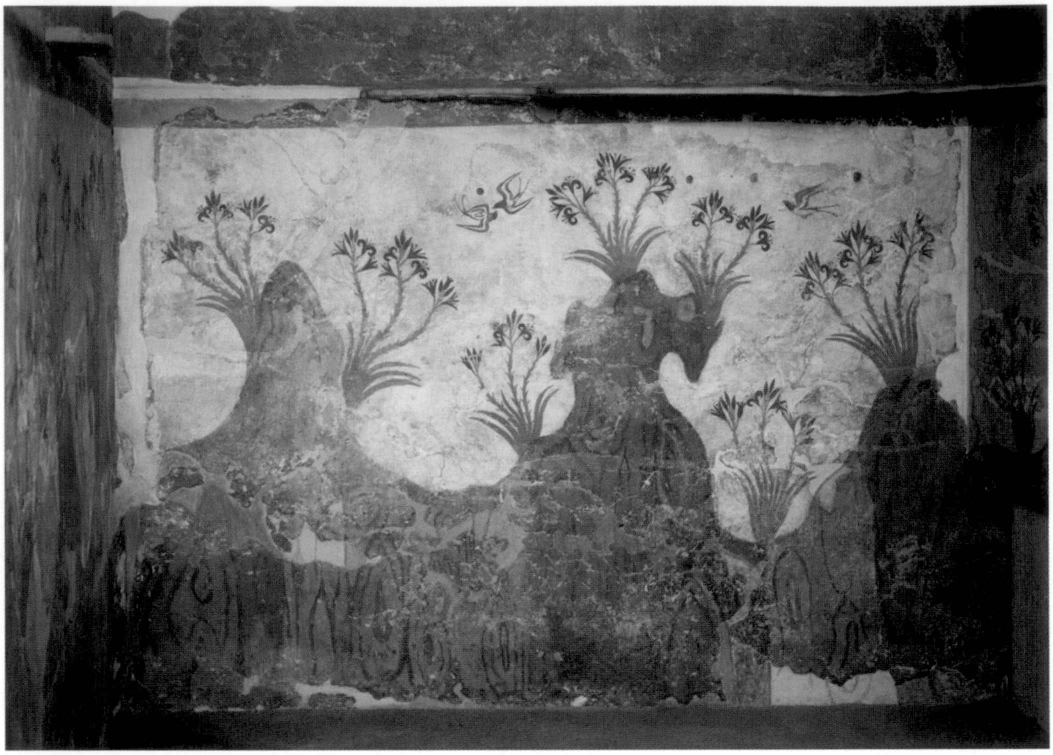

1. Cycladic wall painting depicting *Spring*, from Room Delta 2, Akrotiri, Thera, Late Cycladic I (Thera, Archeological Museum: on deposit at Athens, National Archaeological Museum); *see* Painting (Cycladic)

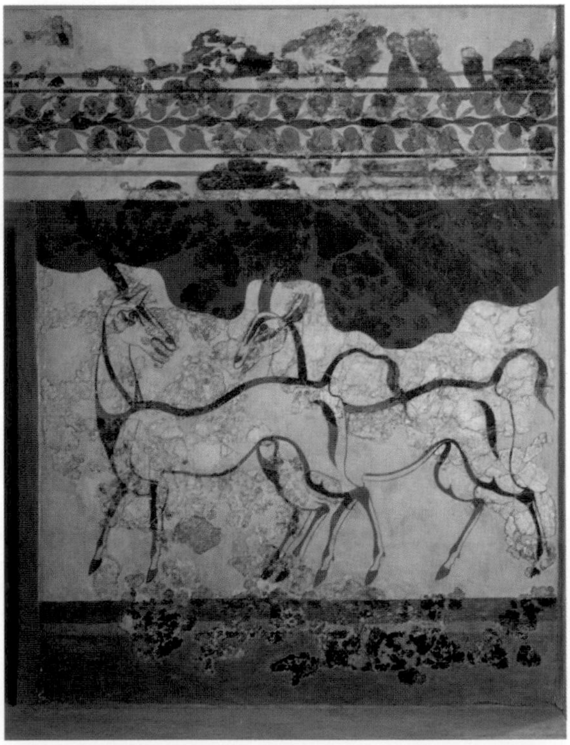

2. Cycladic wall painting depicting *Antelopes*, from Room Beta 1 of a shrine complex, Akrotiri, Thera, Late Cycladic I (Thera, Archaeological Museum: on deposit at Athens, National Archaeological Museum); *see* Painting (Cycladic)

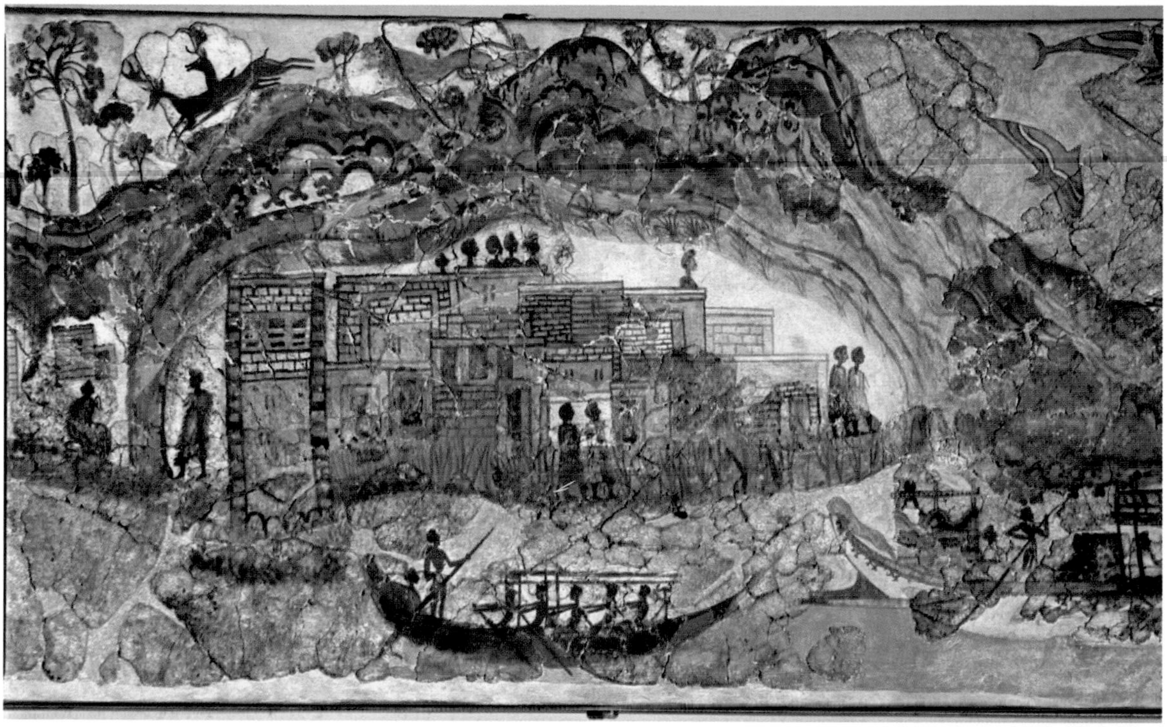

1. Cycladic wall painting of *Ship Procession* frieze (detail), from the south wall of the West House, Akrotiri, Thera, Late Cycladic I (Thera, Archeological Museum: on deposit at Athens, National Archaeological Museum); *see* Painting (Cycladic)

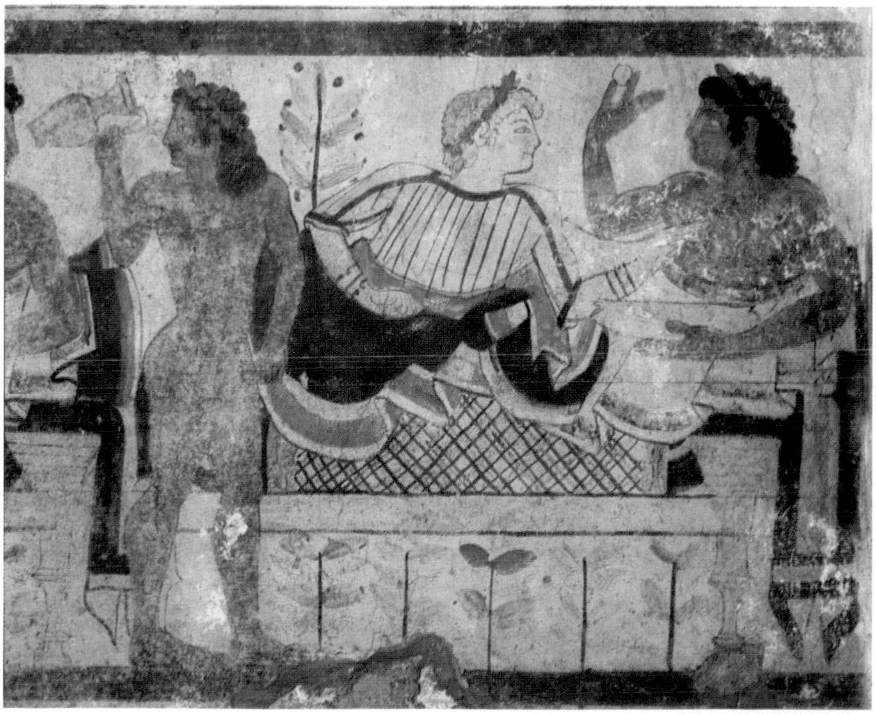

2. Etruscan wall painting with banquet scene (detail), Tomb of the Leopards, Tarquinia, *c.* 480–*c.* 470 BC; *see* Painting (Etruscan)

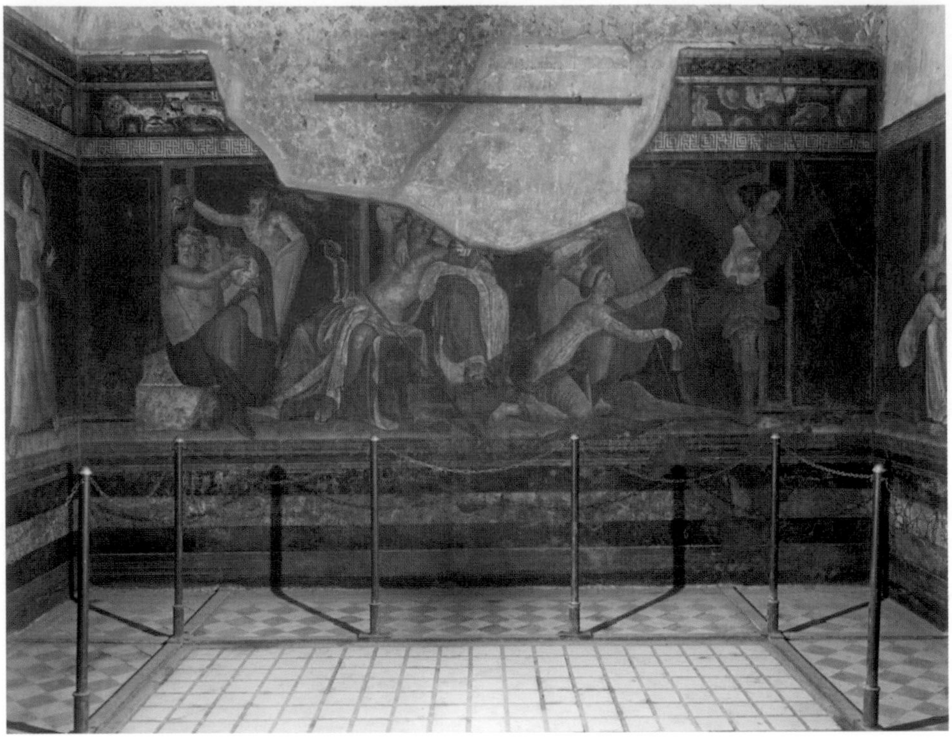

1. Pompeian Second Style painting, *megalographia* of Room 5, Villa of the Mysteries, Pompeii, *c.* 60 BC; *see* Painting (Roman)

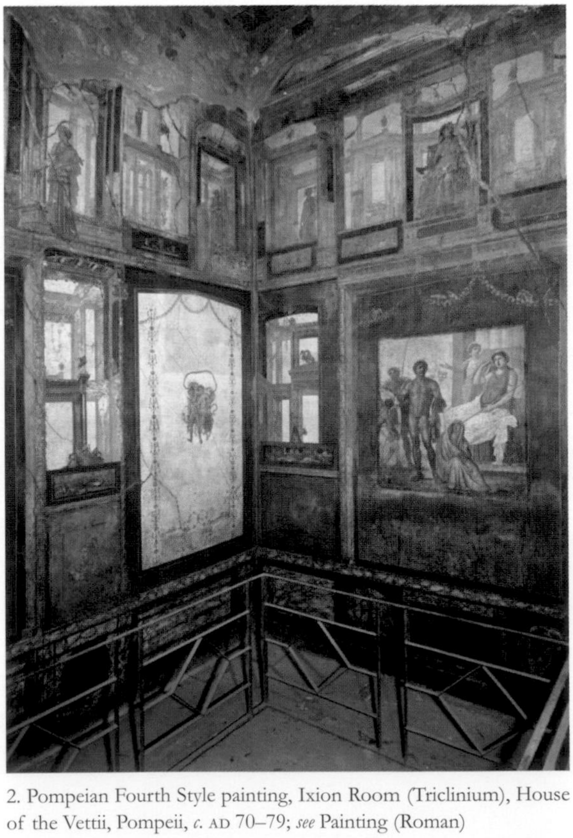

2. Pompeian Fourth Style painting, Ixion Room (Triclinium), House of the Vettii, Pompeii, *c.* AD 70–79; *see* Painting (Roman)

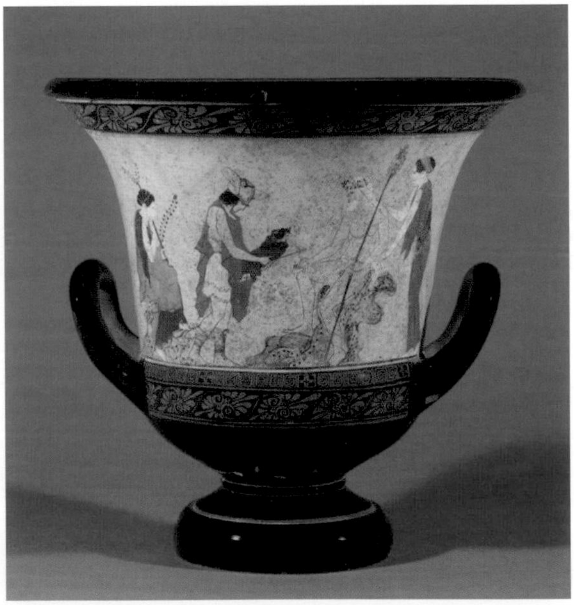

3. Phiale Painter: calyx krater depicting *Hermes Bringing the Infant Dionysos to Papposilenos and the Nymphs of Nysa*, h. 356 mm, Attic White-ground, *c.* 440–435 BC (Rome, Vatican, Museo Gregoriano Etrusco, 16586); *see* Phiale Painter

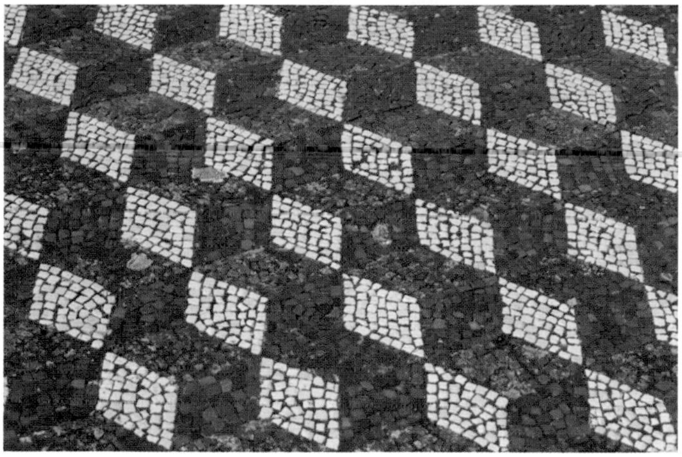

1. Greek floor mosaic with geometric design, from Delos, late 2nd–early 1st century BC; *see* Mosaic (Greek)

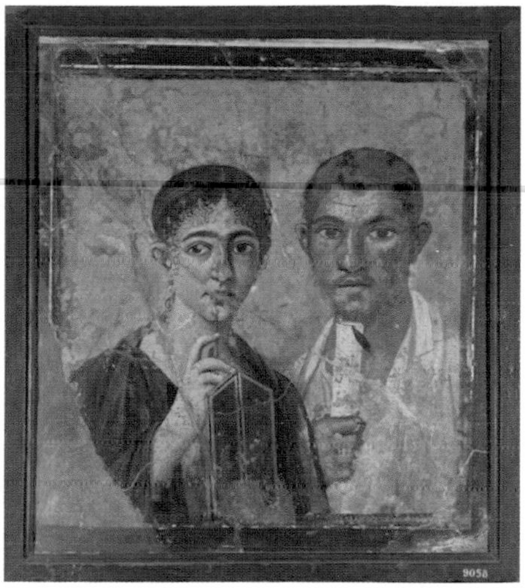

2. Pompeii, portrait of *Terentius Neo and his Wife*, wall painting from the House of Paquius Proculus, *c.* AD 50–79 (Naples, Museo Archeologico Nazionale); *see* Pompeii

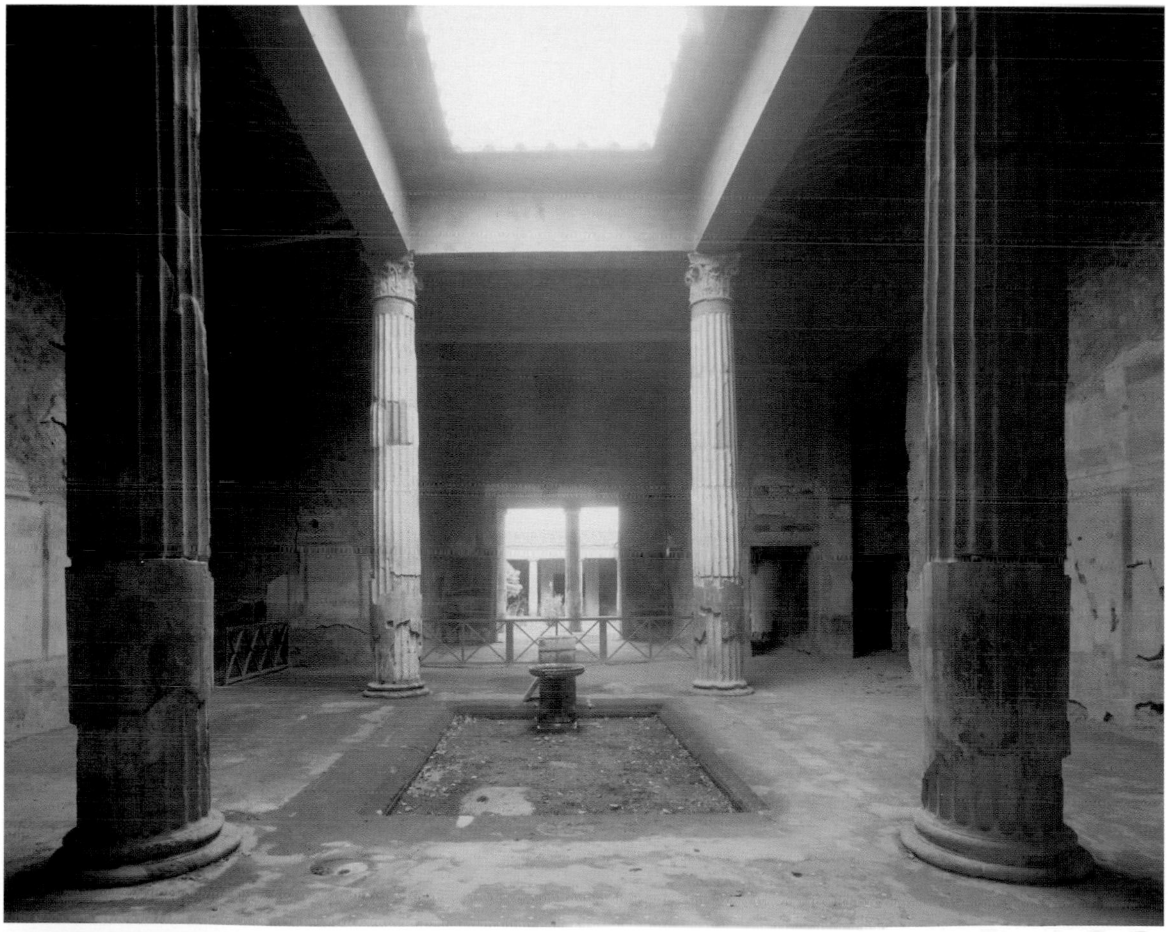

3. Pompeii, House of the Silver Wedding, interior view of the atrium; *see* Pompeii

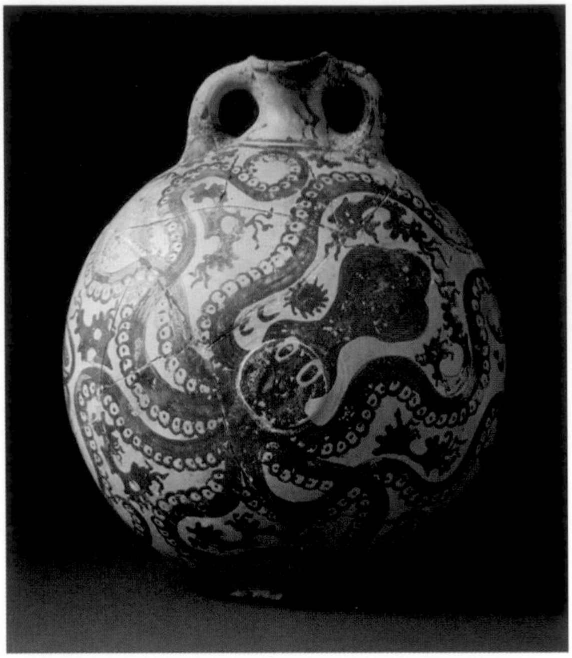

1. Late Minoan lentoid flask, Special Palatial tradition, Marine style, h. 270 mm, from Palaikastro, LM IB (Herakleion, Archaeological Museum); *see* Pottery (Minoan)

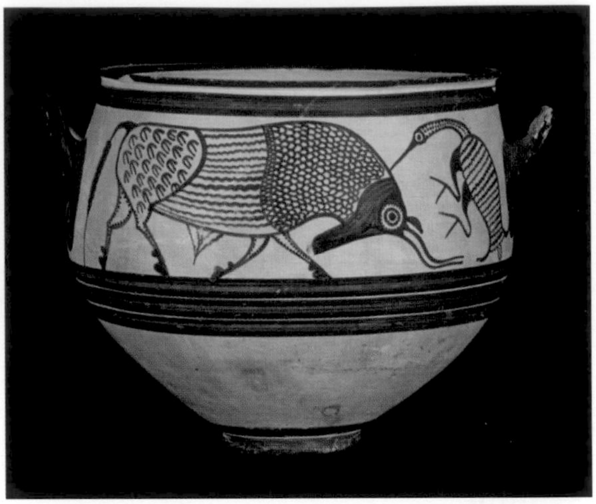

2. Late Helladic vase decorated with bulls and birds, Pictorial style, h. 272 mm, from Tomb 83, Enkomi, LH IIIB:1 (London, British Museum, 1897.4-1.1150); *see* Pottery (Helladic)

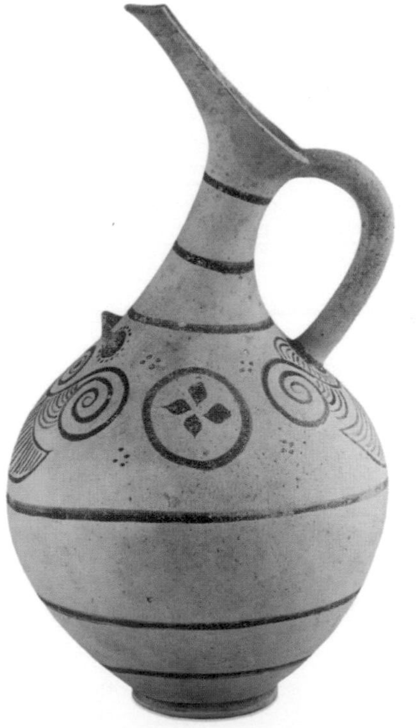

3. Middle Cycladic White beaked jug, h. 390 mm, from Melos, MC (London, British Museum); *see* Pottery (Cycladic)

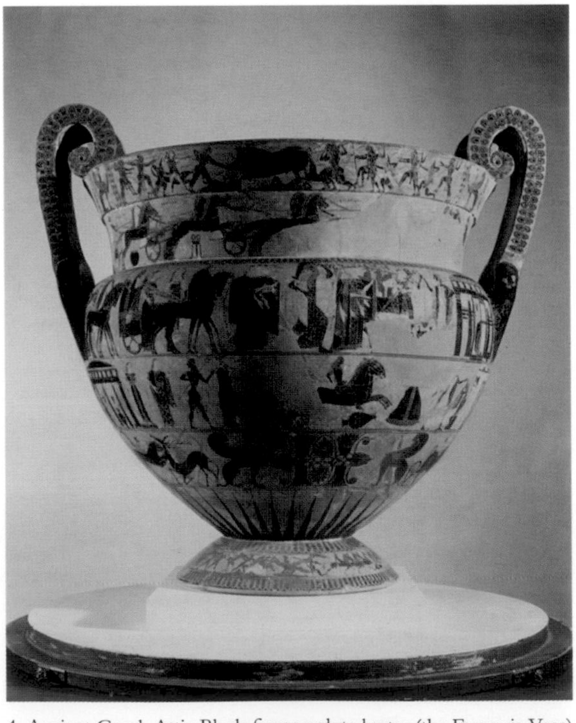

4. Ancient Greek Attic Black-figure volute krater (the François Vase) by Kleitas and Ergotimos, h. 660 mm, *c.* 600–*c.* 560 BC (Florence, Museo Archeologico di Firenze, 4209); *see* Pottery (Greek)

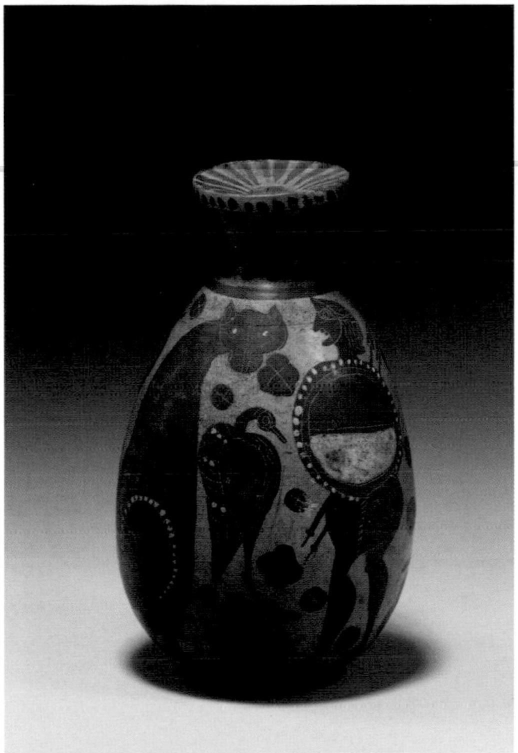

1. Etrusco-Corinthian alabastron by the Pescia Romana Painter, depicting a warrior, h. 157 mm, *c.* 590–580 BC (London, British Museum, 1928.6-14.1); *see* Pottery (Etruscan)

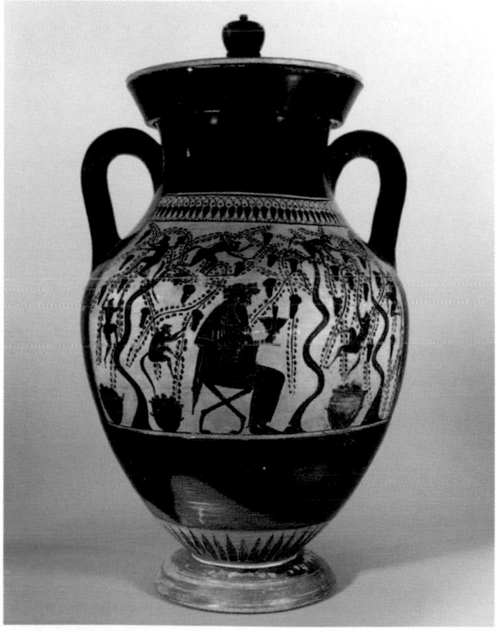

2. Priam Painter: amphora depicting *Dionysos Sitting under Grape Vines*, Attic Black-figure, *c.* 515–*c.* 500 BC (Rome, Museo Nazionale di Villa Giulia e Soprintendenza alle Antichita per l'Etruria Meriodionale); *see* Priam Painter

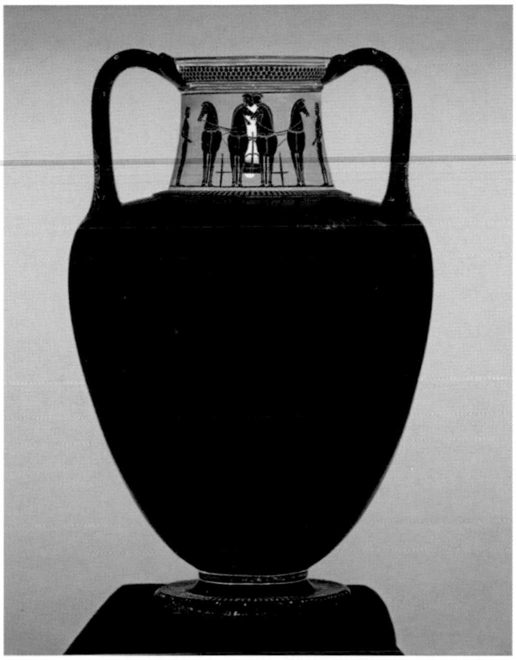

3. Psiax: neck amphora depicting a chariot, h. 395 mm, Attic Black-figure, *c.* 530–520 BC (London, British Museum, 1980. 10-29.1); *see* Psiax

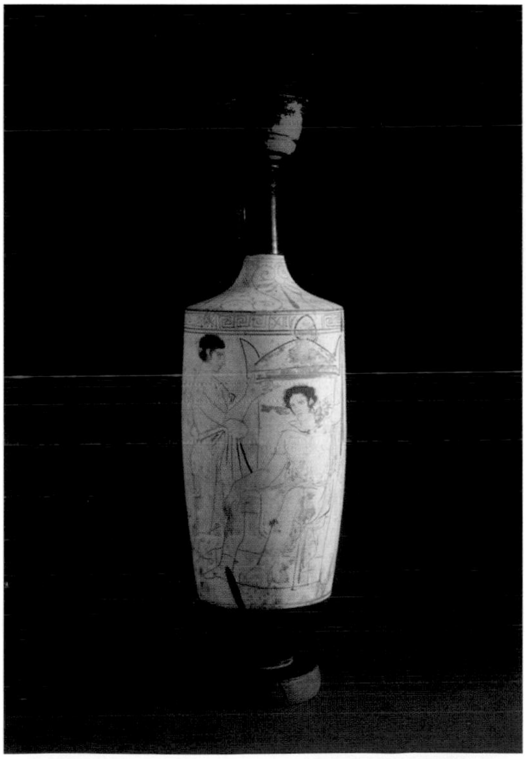

4. Reed Painter: lekythos depicting a soldier in his tomb, Attic White-ground, *c.* 420–*c.* 410 BC (Athens, National Archaeological Museum); *see* Reed Painter

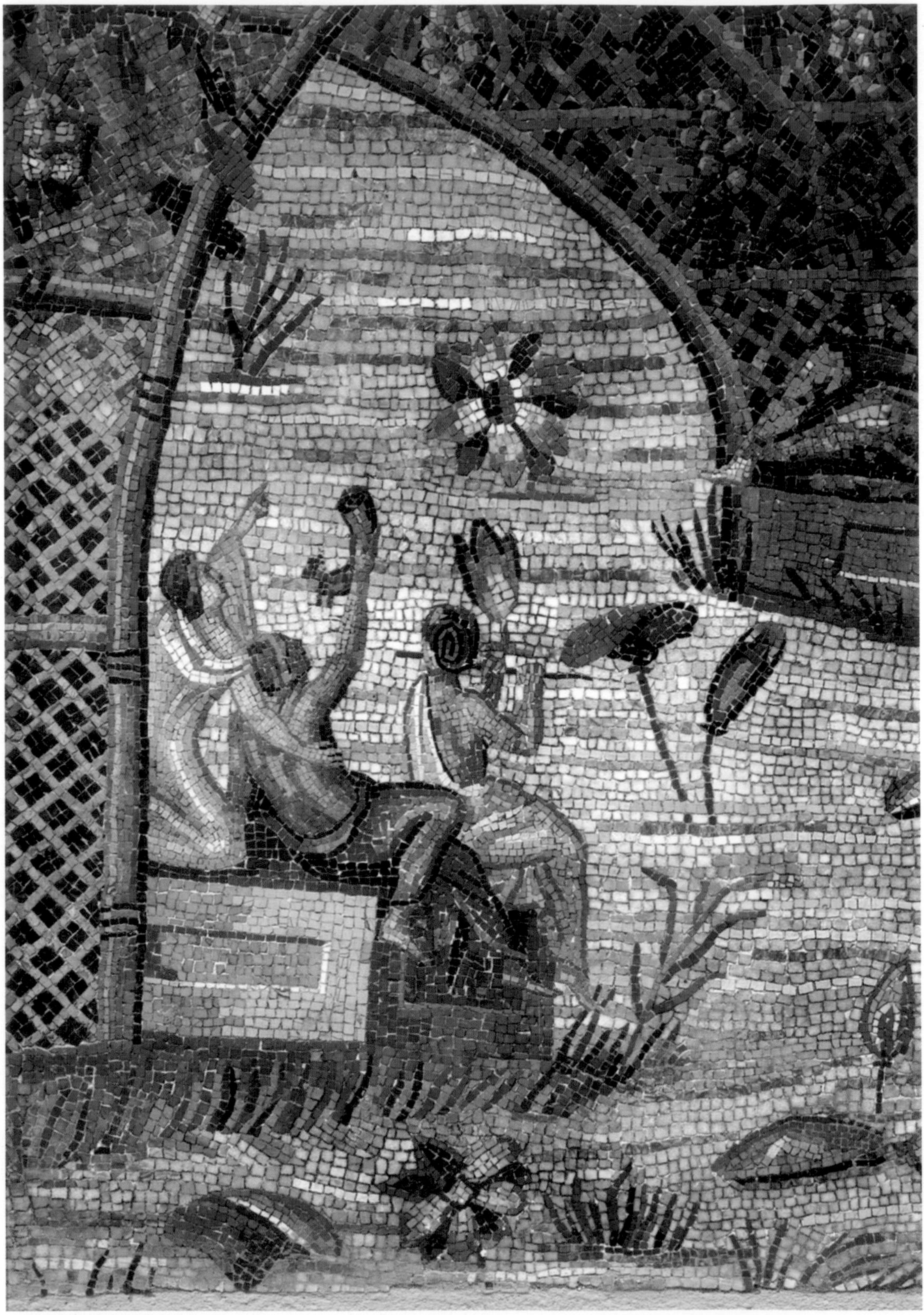

Praeneste, mosaic of *Bathers*, detail of the *Nile* mosaic from Sanctuary of Fortuna Primigenia, late 2nd century BC (Palestrina, Museo Archeologico Nazionale, Palazzo Barberini); *see* Praeneste

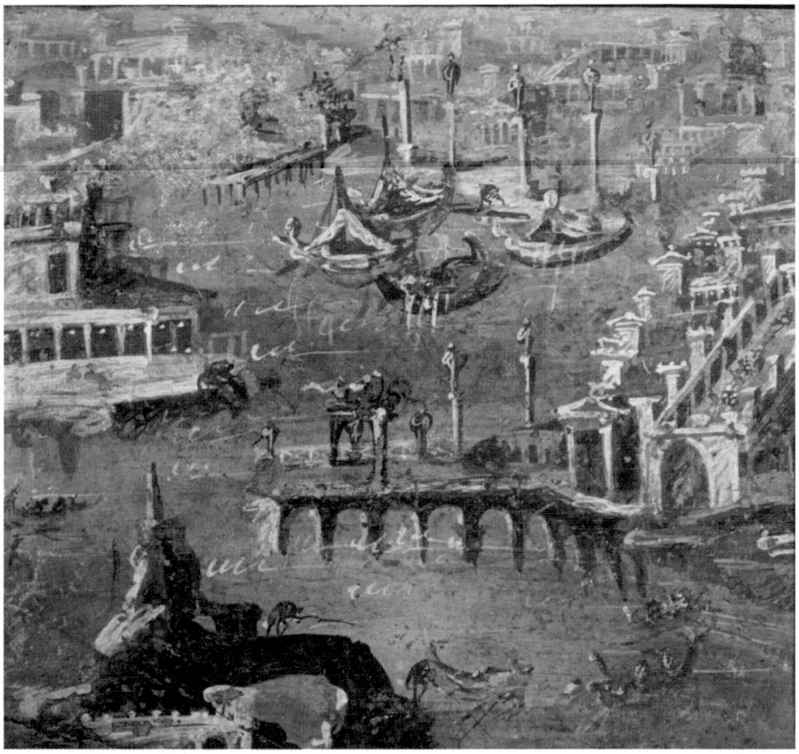

1. *View of a Harbour (? Puteoli)*, Roman fresco from Stabiae, *c.* AD 55 (Naples, Museo Archeologico Nazionale); *see* Puteoli

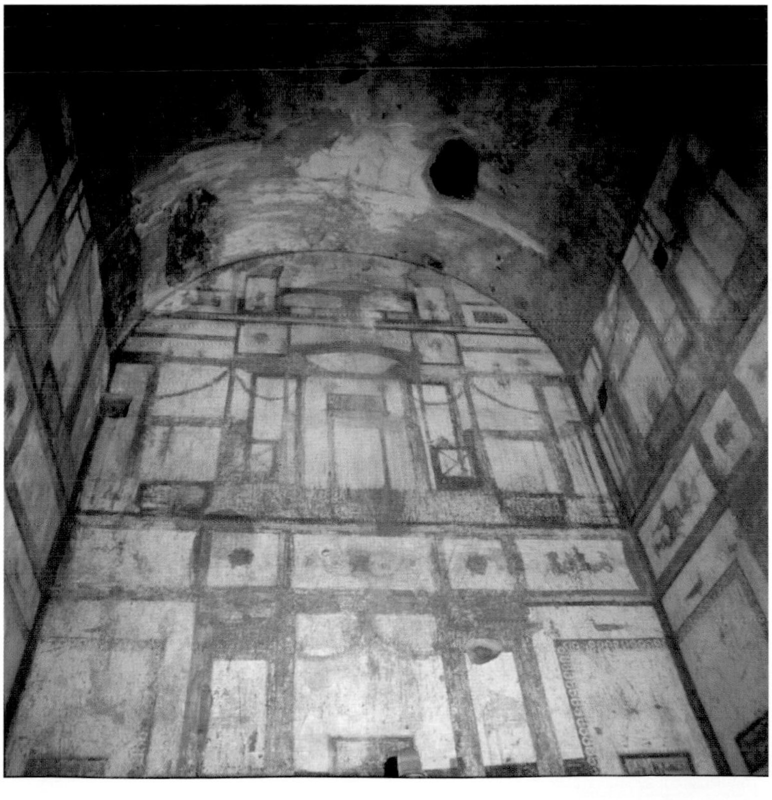

2. Rome, Domus Aurea, Fourth Style wall paintings, after *c.* AD 64; *see* Rome

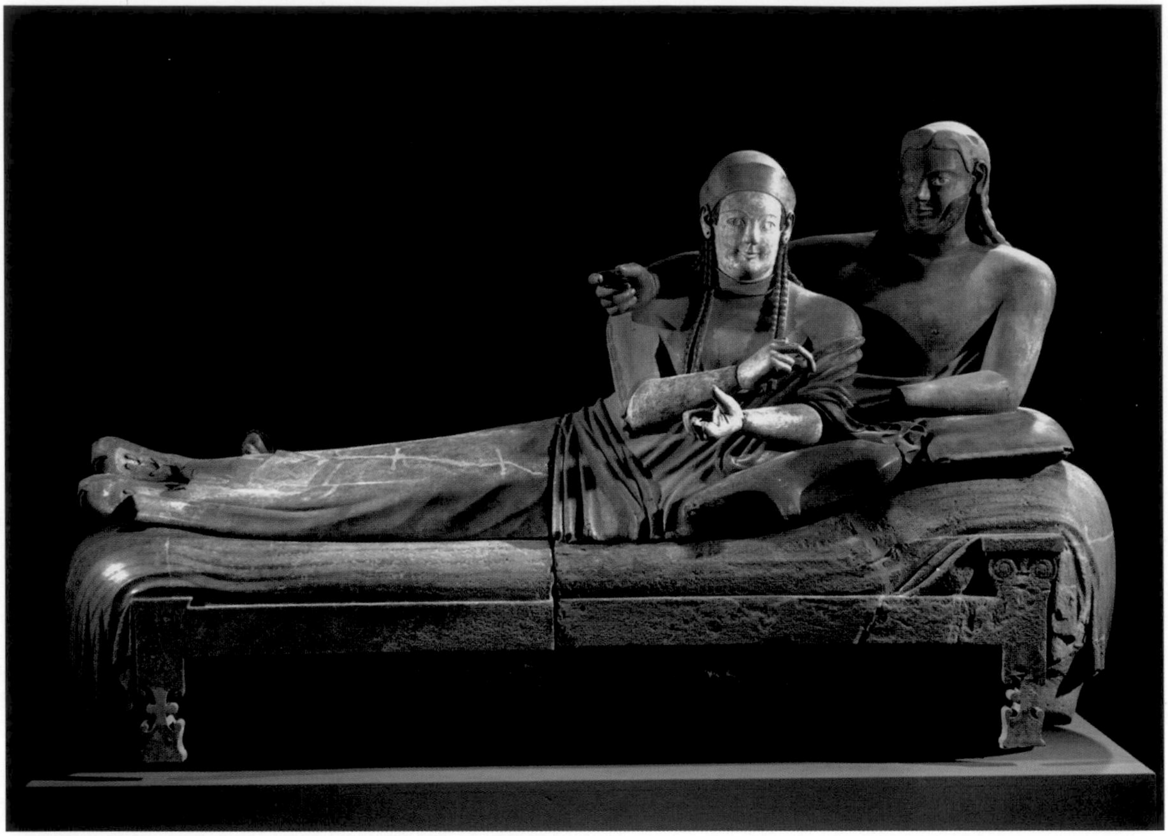

1. Etruscan terracotta sarcophagus with reclining figures of a man and woman, h. 1.11 m, from Caere (Cervetari), *c.* 520–510 BC (Paris, Musée du Louvre); *see* Sculpture (Etruscan)

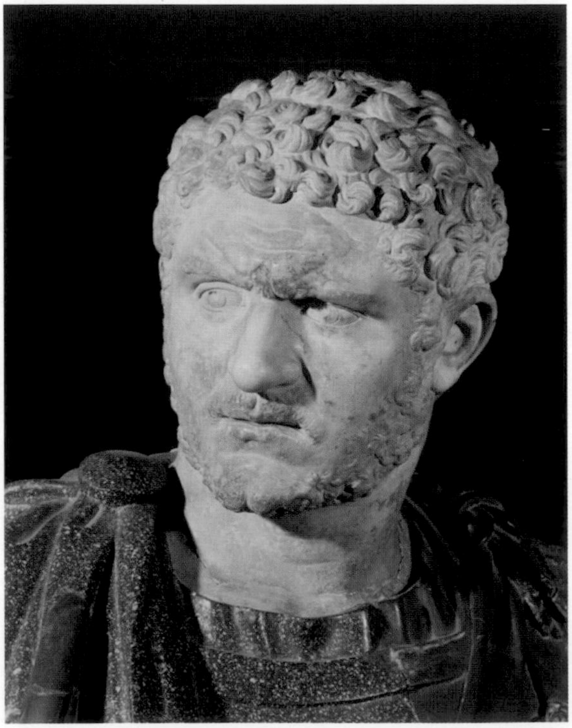

2. *Caracalla*, marble, *c.* 3rd century AD (Rome, Musei Capitolini); *see* Sculpture (Roman)

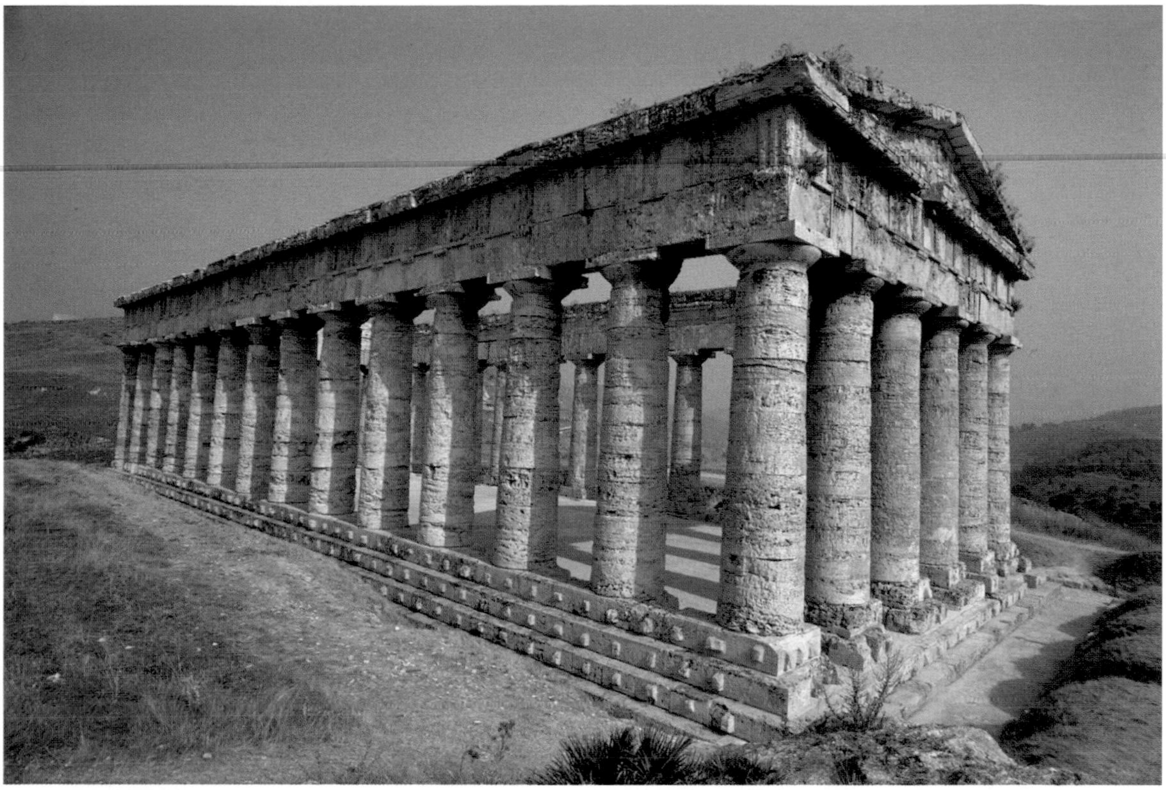

1. Segesta, Doric temple, late 5th century BC, unfinished; *see* Segesta

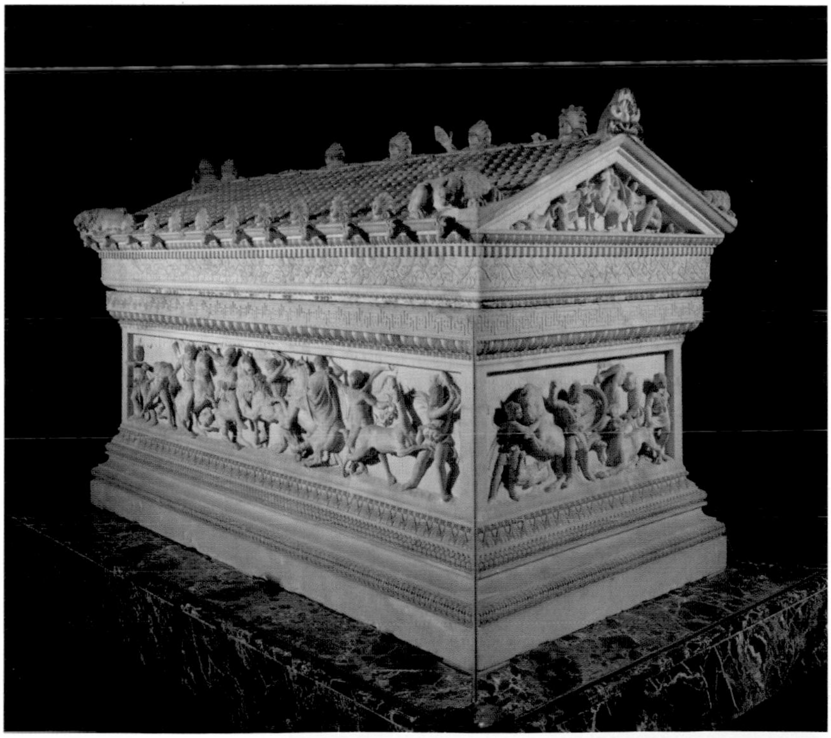

2. Sidon, 'Alexander Sarcophagus', marble, 1.95×3.18×167 m, late 4th century BC (Istanbul, Archaeological Museum); *see* Sidon

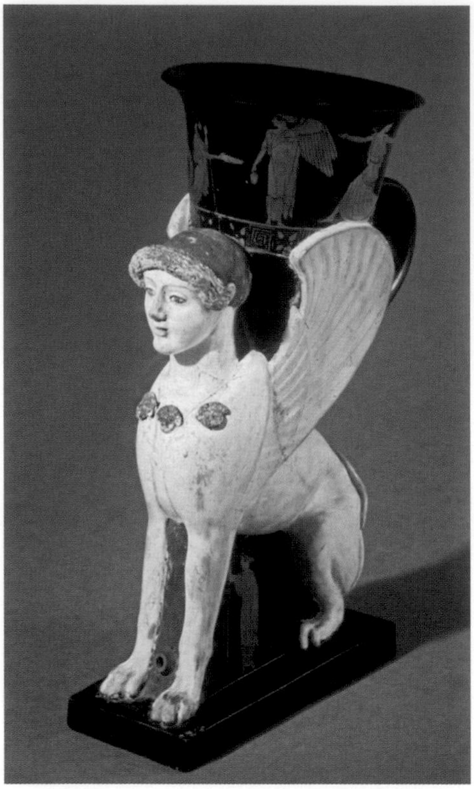

1. Sotades Painter: sphinx rhyton depicting King Kekrops, h. 290 mm, Attic Red-figure, from the Brygos tomb at Capua, *c.* 470–*c.* 460 BC (London, British Museum, E 788); *see* Sotades Painter

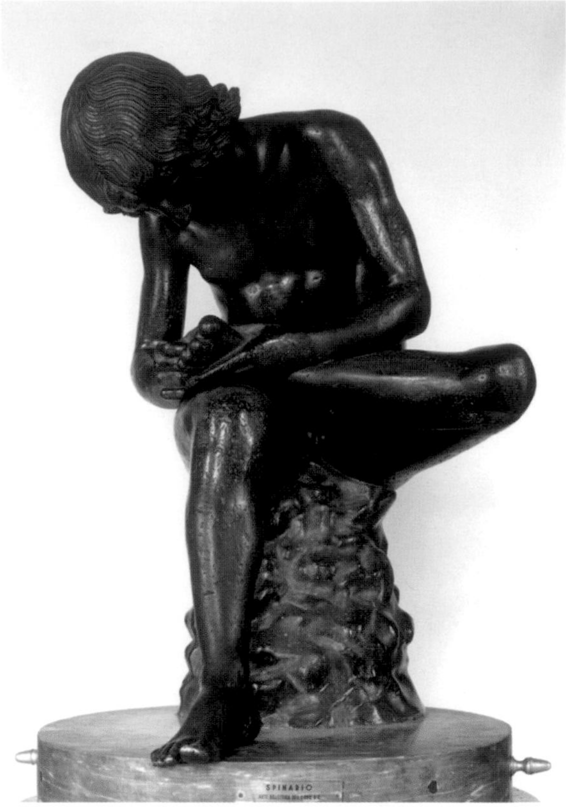

2. *Spinario*, bronze, h. 730 mm, ?1st century BC (Rome, Museo dei Conservatori); *see* Spinario

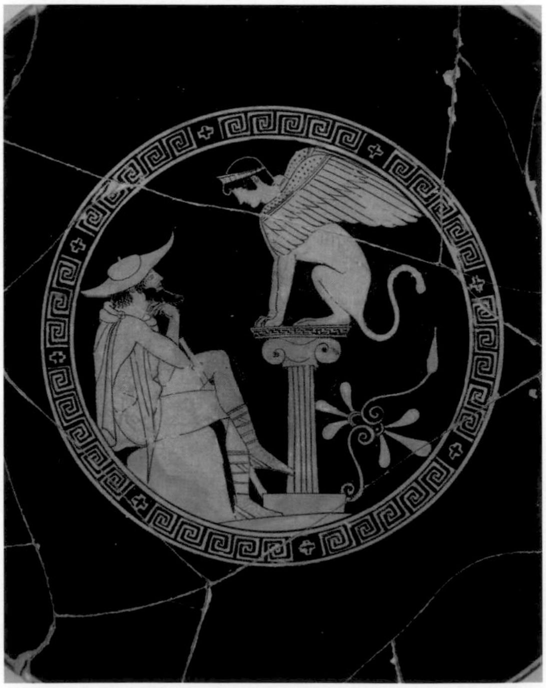

3. *Oedipus and the Sphinx* depicted on an Attic Red-figure cup by the Oedipus Painter, diam. 264 mm, *c.* 480–*c.* 470 BC (Rome, Vatican, Museo Gregoriano Etrusco); *see* Sphinx

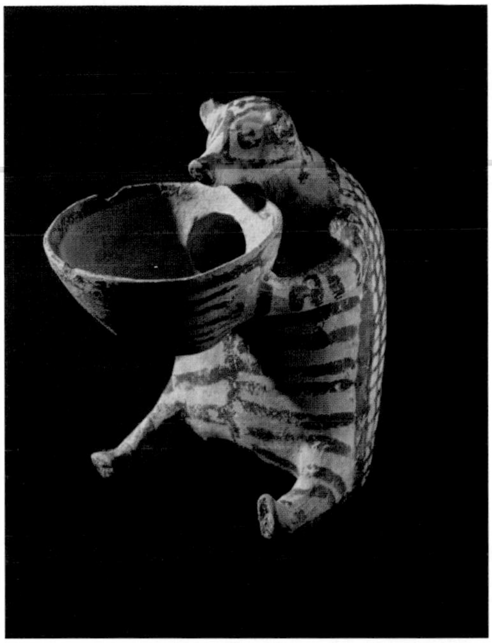

2. Syros, Cycladic hedgehog-shaped pink micaceous clay vase with partly effaced black-brown and dull red paint on white veneer, h. 110 mm, from Kastri, 3rd millennium BC (Athens, National Archaeological Museum); *see* Syros

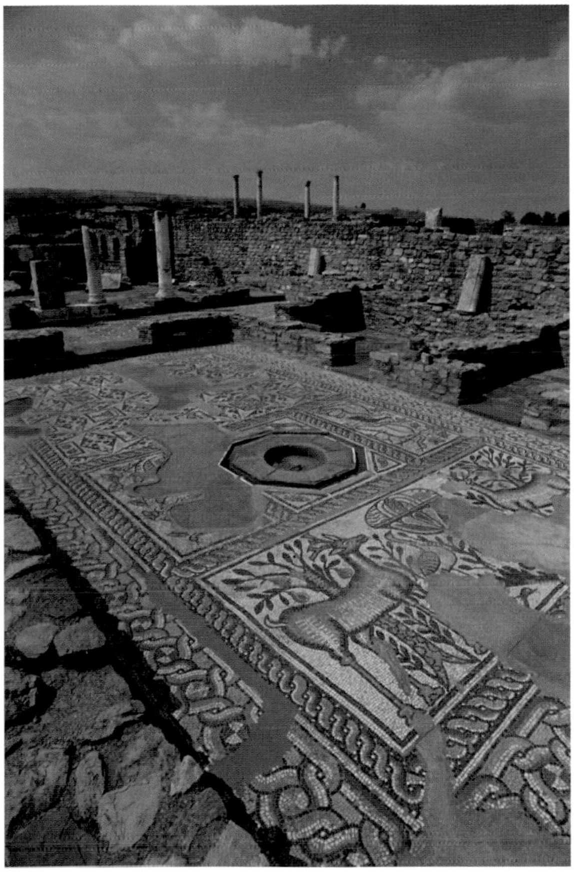

1. Stobi, House of the Psalms, 4th century AD; *see* Stobi

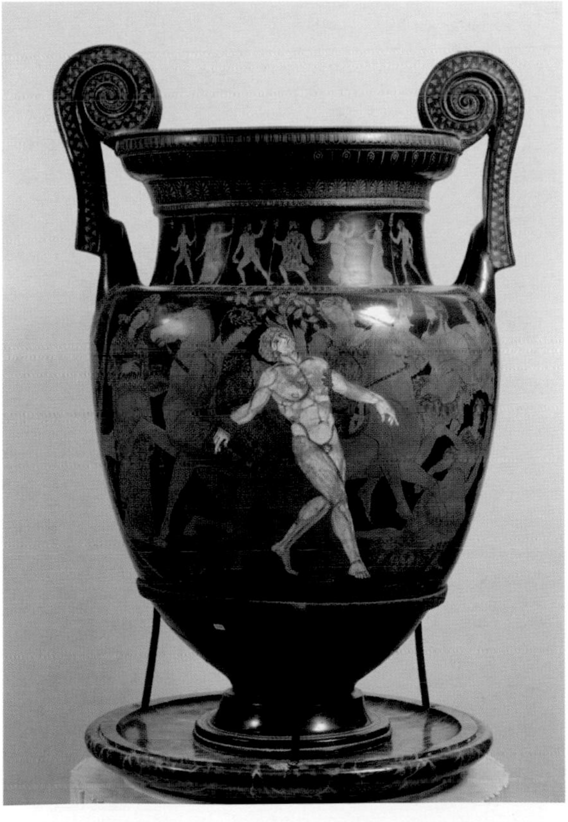

3. Talos Painter: volute krater depicting the *Death of the Bronze Giant Talos*, Attic Red-figure, *c.* 410–*c.* 390 BC (Ruvo di Puglia, Museo Jatta, 1501); *see* Talos Painter

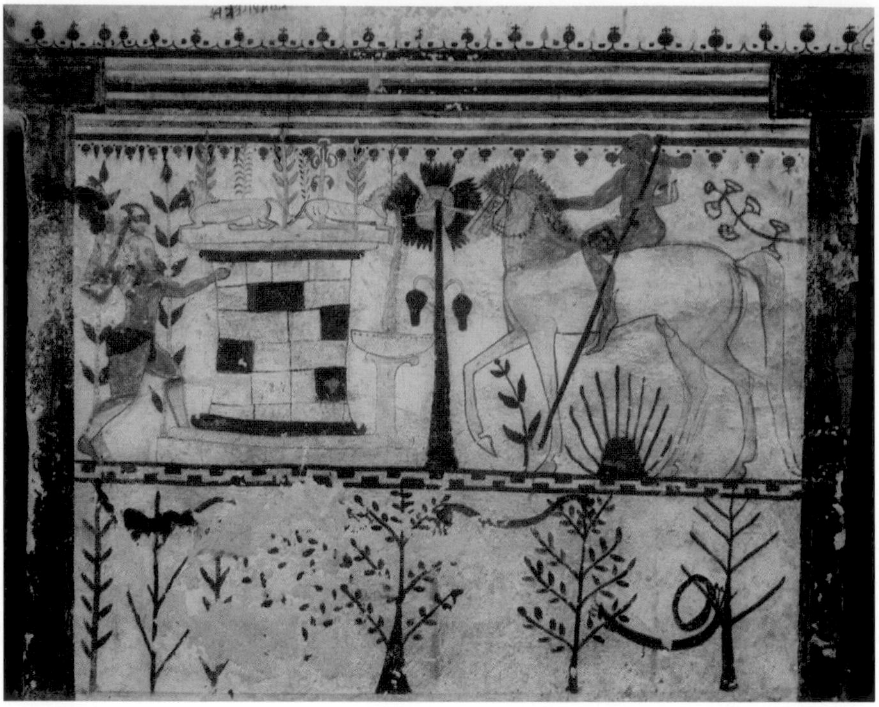

1. Tarquinia, wall painting with the *Ambush of Troilos by Achilles*, Tomb of the Bulls, *c.* 530 BC; *see* Tarquinia

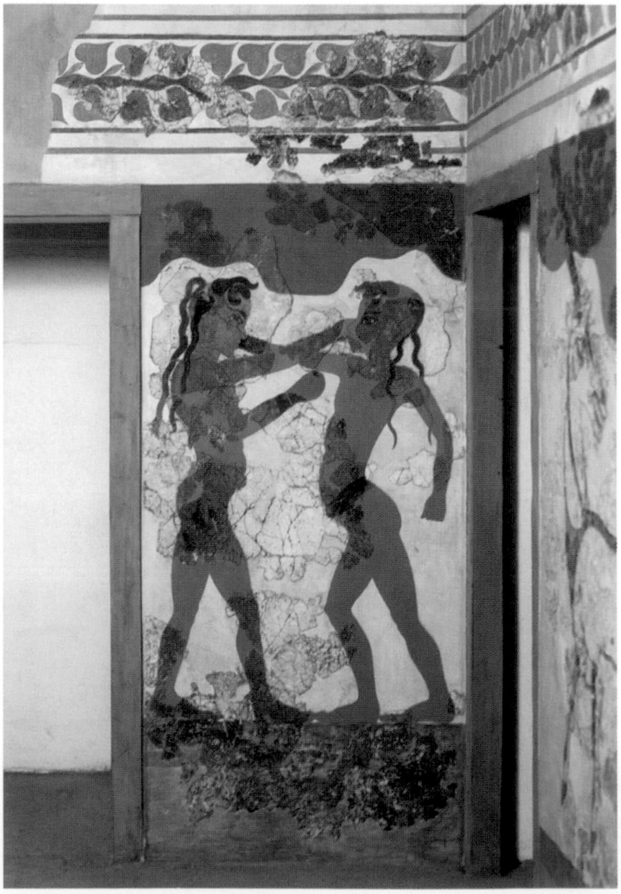

2. Thera wall painting depicting *Boxing Boys*, from Room Beta 1 of a shrine complex, Akrotiri, Late Cycladic I (Thera, Archaeological Museum: on deposit at Athens, National Archaeological Museum); *see* Thera

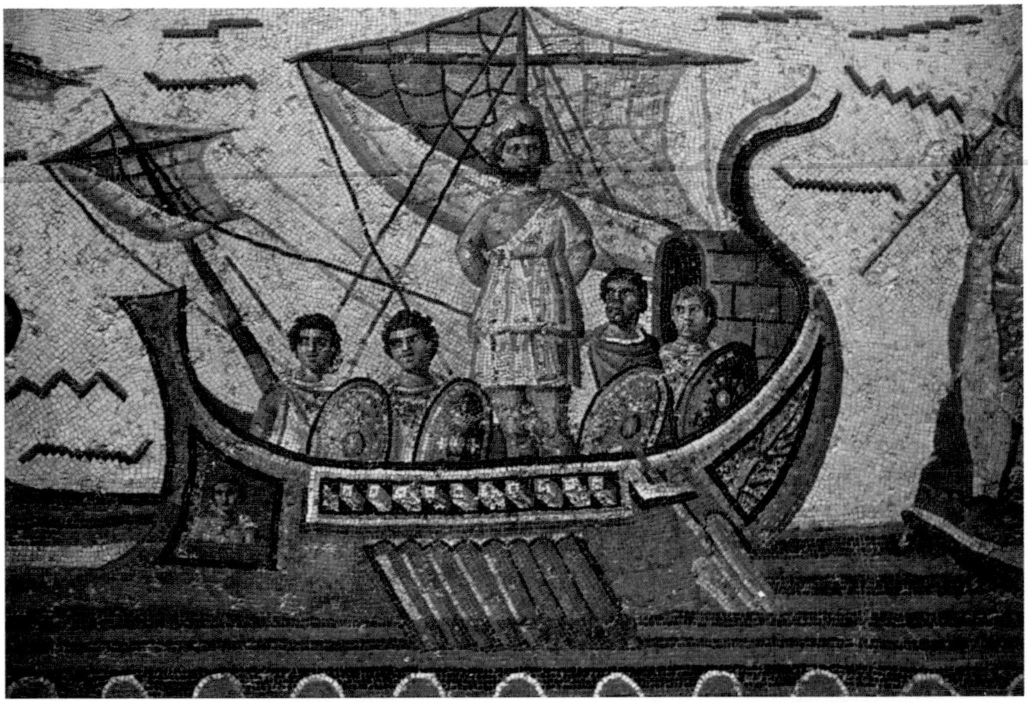

1. Thugga, mosaic of *Odysseus and the Sirens*, 3rd century AD (Tunis, Musée National du Bardo); *see* Thugga

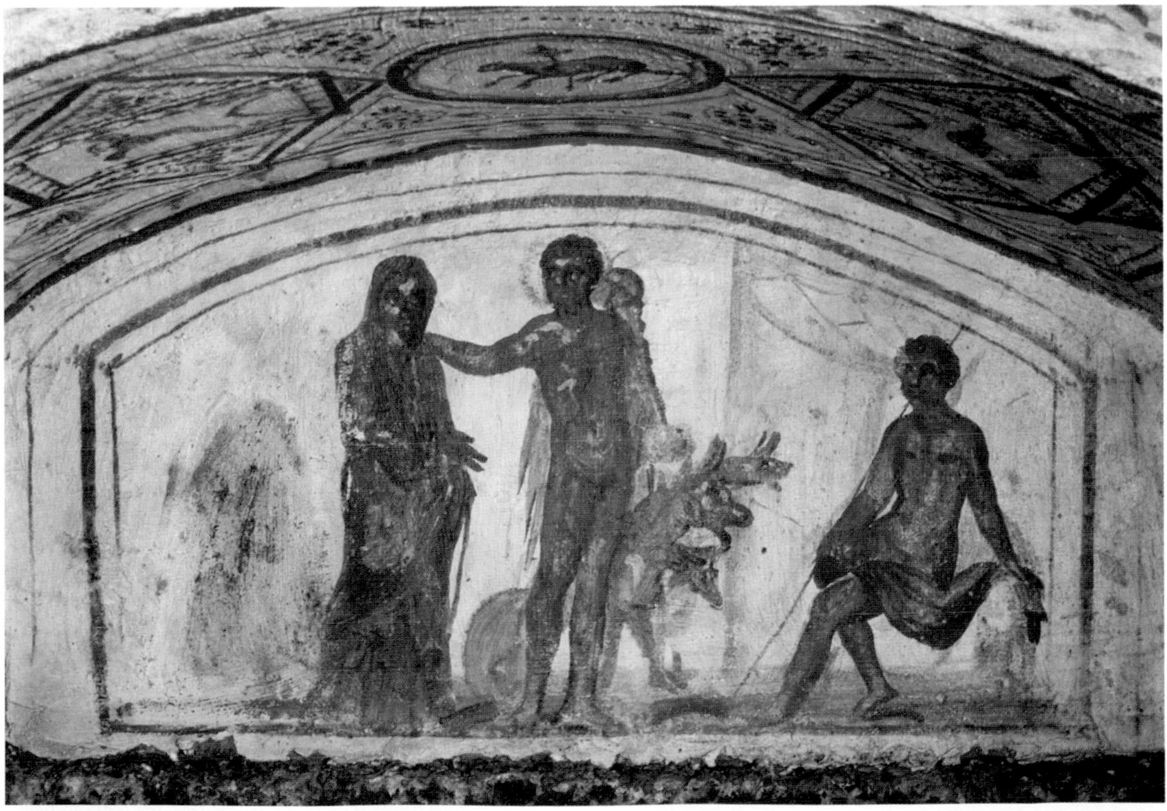

2. Cubiculum N in the Via Latina catacomb, Rome, decorated with scene depicting *Hercules Leading Alcestis from the Underworld*, *c.* AD 320–50; *see* Tomb

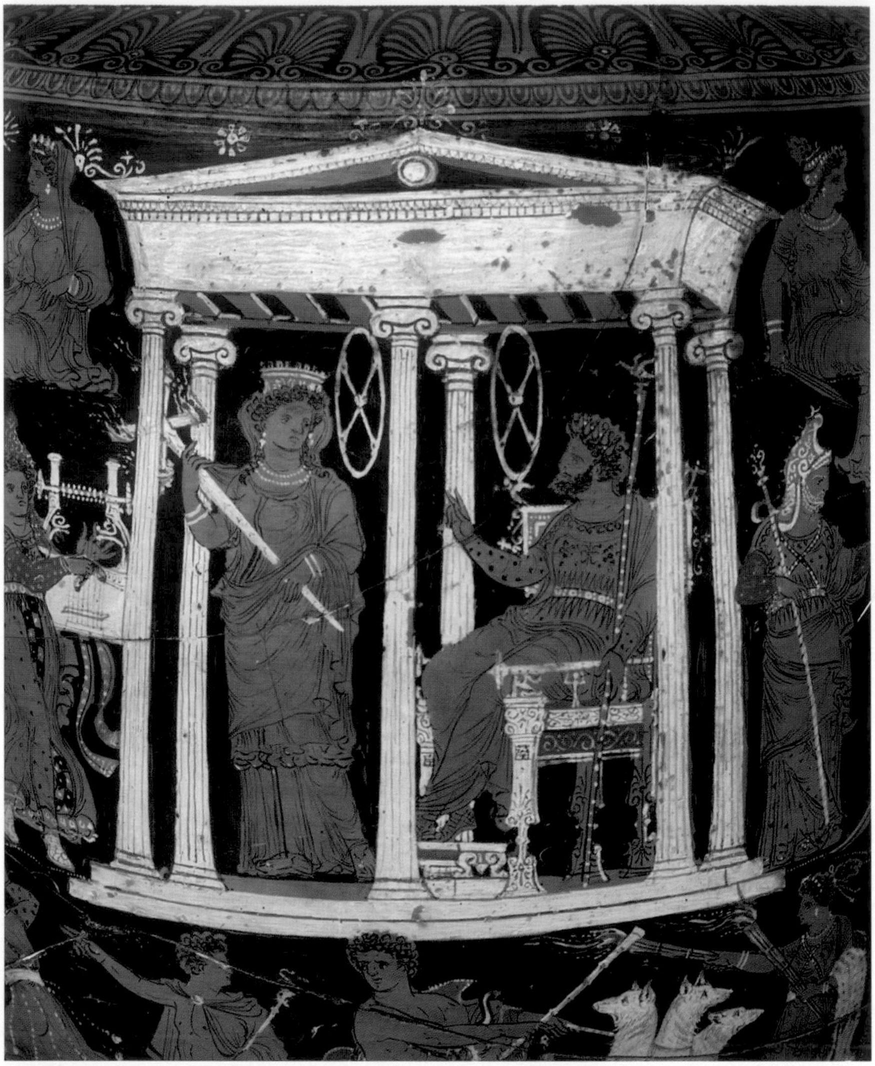

1. Underworld Painter: volute krater depicting *Pluto and Persephone in their Palace* (detail), Apulian Red-figure, from Canosa, *c.* 330–*c.* 310 BC (Munich, Staatliche Antikensammlung, 3297); *see* Underworld Painter

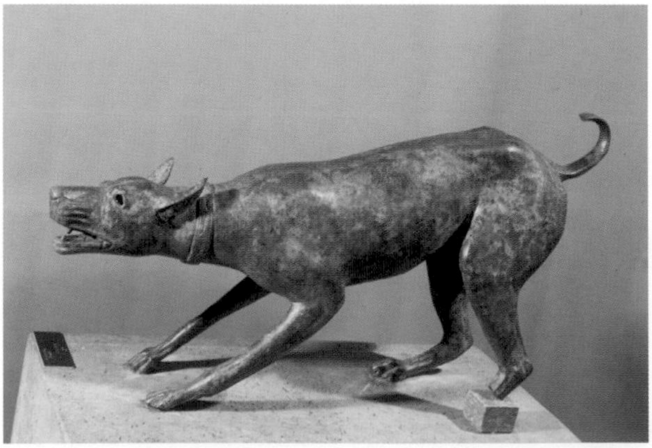

2. Volubilis, bronze sculpture of a barking dog, h. 355 mm (Rabat, Musée des Antiquités); *see* Volubilis

inflation, with its incentives to the illicit excavator, museums have tended since the 1970s to avoid making further purchases to complete their collections, collaborating instead to mount travelling loan exhibitions, which assemble items from a number of public and private collections to give a comprehensive view of the output of a particular period or area: an exhibition mounted at the Metropolitan Museum of Art in New York in 1985, for example, was able to concentrate exclusively on the works of a single ancient artist, the Amasis Painter. In modern displays the shelf-lined walls of 19th-century collections are usually replaced by free-standing glass cases that protect the pottery and allow it to be viewed from all sides. Labels supply information with varying degrees of precision, while the vases are carefully grouped by periods or schools, provenance, forms, subject-matter or manufacturing technique.

E. M. W. Tillyard: *The Hope Vases: A Catalogue and a Discussion* (Cambridge, 1923)

P. Mingazzini: *Vasi della collezione Castellani*, 2 vols (Rome, 1930)

R. M. Cook: *Greek Painted Pottery* (London, 1960, rev. 1972)

Select Exhibition of Sir John and Lady Beazley's Gifts to the Ashmolean Museum, 1912–1966 (exh. cat., ed. R. W. Hamilton; Oxford, Ashmolean, 1967)

P. Mingazzini: *Catalogo dei vasi della collezione Augusto Castellani*, 2 vols (Rome, 1971)

M. Vickers: 'A Greek Source for Antonio Pollaiuolo's *Battle of the Nudes* and *Hercules and the Twelve Giants*', *A. Bull.*, lix (1977), pp. 182–7

D. von Bothmer: 'Notes on Collectors of Vases', *Wealth of the Ancient World* (exh. cat., ed. J. F. Tompkins; Fort Worth, Kimbell A. Mus., 1983), pp. 37–44

R. Morris: 'Ancient Pottery from the Scillonian Seabed', *Int. J. Naut. Archaeol. & Underwtr Explor.*, xiii (1984), pp. 156–63

M. Vickers: 'Value and Simplicity: Eighteenth-century Taste and the Study of Greek Vases', *Past & Present*, 116 (Aug 1987), pp. 98–137

N. H. Ramage: 'Sir William Hamilton as Collector, Exporter and Dealer: The Acquistion and Dispersal of his Collections', *Amer. J. Archaeol.*, xciv (1990), pp. 469–80

A. L. Lyons: 'The Museo Mastrilli and the Culture of Collecting in Naples, 1700–1755,' *J. Hist. Col.*, i/4 (1992), pp. 1–26

V. Etruscan.

For Etruria, as for the Classical world generally, pottery represents the largest and best defined body of available archaeological material. Scholarly attention has been mostly taken up by figured and decorated vases, even if they constitute only a fraction of all pottery production. The excavation of domestic settlements has demonstrated that the utilitarian pottery in everyday use was mostly coarse or undecorated. Pottery production as a specialized craft sector began in the 8th century BC through the acquisition of techniques from the Greek world and the settlement of immigrant craftsmen. Workshops were set up in many Etruscan centres to meet the demand for pottery, a demand fuelled by the influx of Greek vases, which were imported continuously into Etruria from the first half of the 8th century BC to the mid-4th. As Etruscan trade developed, Etruscan pottery was itself widely exported; its distribution reveals patterns of trade and communication that are invaluable for reconstructing economic history. (A number of shapes are of purely local origin, but for the identification of the Greek-influenced shapes of Etruscan vases *see* §IV, 1(ii) and fig. 15 above.)

1. Impasto ware. 2. Etrusco-Geometric. 3. Orientalizing. 4. Bucchero. 5. Red ware. 6. Etrusco-Corinthian. 7. Black-figure. 8. Red-figure. 9. Black-glaze.

1. Impasto ware. During the Iron Age (9th–8th century BC) impasto was the fabric used for vases. It consisted of unpurified clay containing calcareous, siliceous and other matter, which was fired at low temperatures. It was either hand-modelled or slow-turned, and air-dried before being smoothed and sometimes decorated, then fired in an open kiln at about 800°C. This method produced robust vessels of irregular shape, in a range of earth colours from black to red.

During the 8th century BC finer wares began to be made, but impasto remained in use for domestic vessels. Many impasto vases were decorated with pointing tools and combs, or impressed *a cordicella* (given moulded cordons and pseudo-cordons). Punched impressions, notches, grooves and fingerprints also occur. Such decoration, mostly on the body and neck, emphasized the vases' structural features, and the formulaic geometric patterns include concentric circles, meanders, zigzags and other motifs. Less frequently, amber overlays (Verucchio), bronze chains and rings, bronze bosses and tin sheets were also used, the latter especially at Vulci, continuing into the Orientalizing period. Painted impasto ware, again with geometric decoration, was found at Veii, Tarquinia, Vulci, Poggio Montano and Civitavecchia. Stamped impasto occurs more commonly at northern Etruscan sites, such as Vetulonia and Populonia, and especially Felsina (Bologna) and Verucchio. Modelled decoration included human and animal figures, singly or in various configurations.

Impasto was used for both domestic and ritual, often funerary, vessels, and such shapes as the biconical urn clearly belonged in both contexts. Hut urns were obviously funerary, as were urns with peaked or crested helmet-shaped lids, miniature ships and miniature three-footed tables. Shapes mainly for domestic use included multiple vases, cups, saucers, pitchers, beakers, jugs, amphorae, plates and zoomorphic askoi, such as an example from Felsina (Benacci necropolis) in the form of a bull-bird surmounted by an armed warrior on horseback (Bologna, Mus. Civ. Archeol.). The warrior wears the characteristic triangular-crested Villanovan helmet and has a round shield at his back. The stoves and dolium-jars, the latter used for containing foodstuffs, were also made of impasto, as were models of wagons and miniature horses, thrones, spindle whorls and loom weights. The shape range is conservative, but regional specialities occur: 'candelabra' from Tarquinia; from Felsina situlae, cists and so-called *presentatoi*; from Latium small ollas (jars) with modelled lattice decoration; and from Sardinia askoid jugs. With the introduction of the fast potter's wheel more regular shapes were produced, including spiral amphorae, jugs with oblique spouts and chalices with hemispherical or carinated bowls. Some impasto vases, ribbed phialai and stands (*holmoi*) have been influenced by metallic Oriental shapes: the three-footed plates produced at Caere (Cerveteri) derived from Levantine tripod-bowls, while skyphoi and kotylai are essentially Greek shapes.

In the 7th century BC a distinctive type of carved decoration with the design filled in with white or red ochre occurs alongside more traditional techniques, impasto wares show the influence of Etrusco-Geometric and Bucchero pottery shows new figural, floral and geometric motifs. From the first half of the 7th century BC several impasto vases had their Etruscan names inscribed (e.g. chalices (*thafna*) and plates (*spanti*)). A dedicatory inscription on an olla with horseshoe cordons certainly made at Vulci (*c*. 675–650 BC; Rome, Villa Giulia, 63189) has letters formed from clay lines applied before firing, and surely relates to a special commission. A particularly fine local variety of 7th-century BC impasto with a red sheeny slip was produced at Caere. It was used for pithoi, ollas, amphorae, oinochoai, chalices, plates, large pyxides and cinerary urns with sloping roofs, and it was decorated with motifs in added white (so-called 'white-on-red'). It is distinct from the Caeretan Red ware, generally used for pithoi and braziers.

2. Etrusco-Geometric. Vases in this style were produced from *c*. 775 to *c*. 630 BC. They were wheel-made from purified clay, and their painted decoration, in black, brown or orange-red, directly derives from Greek Geometric pottery. Until *c*. 675 BC Euboein-Cycladic pottery of the Middle–Late Geometric style was a main model. From *c*. 675 to *c*. 630 BC more exotic, Orientalizing motifs occurred, along with Proto-Corinthian, Proto-Attic and Western Greek influence.

The first imports of Greek Geometric pottery to Etruria, the Faliscan region and Latium occurred at the beginning of the 8th century BC, before the founding of the Greek colonies in South Italy. With the establishment between *c*. 770 and *c*. 760 BC of the Euboian settlements at Pithekoussai and Cumae, imports greatly increased, with drinking vessels predominating. The few larger vases may be evidence of gift-exchanges between Greeks and Etruscan leaders. From about 730 BC Etruscan imitations of Greek wares proliferated, with the increasing refinement both of the clay used and of the painted decoration. In fact it is sometimes difficult to distinguish imported Greek originals from south Etruscan imitations, many of which were in any case probably made by immigrant Greek craftsmen, who set up workshops and introduced new shapes, such as the skyphoi and round-mouthed jugs that occur at Veii, Caere (Cerveteri), Tarquinia, Poggio Montano, Vulci, Bisenzio and around Rome and Felsina (Bologna). New decorative formulae such as groups of chevrons or vertical strokes, rows of concentric circles, and dotted rosettes also appeared. From about 730 BC workshops at Vulci assumed a leading role in producing Etrusco-Geometric pottery to judge by the quantity of pots recovered from the city and its territory. Other regional centres were Bisenzio, Veii (probably the earliest centre), Caere and Tarquinia. The range of vases, apparently mainly for ceremonial or ritual functions, includes Greek shapes (e.g. kraters with stirrup handles, amphorae, high-stemmed dinoi, hydriai, oinochoai, a type of ring kernos) and Etruscan ones (e.g. ollas, holmoi, plastic or bottle-shaped askoi and biconical urns).

Decorations became richer from the third quarter of the 8th century BC, with elements from the Euboein-Boiotian-Cycladic common style of the Late Geometric period. Metopes frames enclosing hatched birds, swastikas, asterisks, chequers, zigzags, star-rosettes, running or isolated meanders, sequences of dots, crosshatched triangles and lozenges appeared, as did grazing horses, recumbent goats and rampant beasts. These were followed by the first narrative scenes: deer hunts, on foot (bird-shaped askos; Norbert Schimmel priv. col.) and horseback (holmos); horsemen on parade (dinos; Los Angeles, CA, Co. Mus. A.); and an armed dance led by a phorminx player (krater; Basle, Antikenmus., BS 403.1963), all of which originate from Vulci workshops, as may the first possibly mythological scene, the *Crane-dance of Theseus and Ariadne*, on the neck of an oinochoe (London, BM, 49.5–18.18). A boat, with helmsman and two oarsmen perhaps hunting a deer (olla; Rome, Villa Giulia, 57069A), and a chorus scene, presumably threnodic (olla; Florence, Mus. Archeol., 85629), both come from Bisenzio. The so-called 'Metopengattung' shows the development of some Euboian motifs, such as squares enclosing chequered lozenges, and horizontal wavy lines, used routinely in the decoration of domestic vessels produced around Vulci and Tarquinia from the last quarter of the 8th to the mid-7th century BC. Again, the vase shapes are both Greek influenced (stamnoid ollas, oinochoai) and indigenous (e.g. biconical urns, ollas without handles, cups on high feet). Contact with Corinth is attested by a few Late Geometric Corinthian vases occurring at Veii, Tarquinia and Narce, and an increased number of early Proto-Corinthian vases, including kotylai, conical lekythoi, oinochoai, low pyxides and squat aryballoi, found at Narce, Veii, Tarquinia, Vulci and most notably at Caere. At Tarquinia a workshop was set up specializing in oinochoai and kotylai of Proto-Corinthian-Cumaean type. The Bocchoris Painter and Palms Painter were both active here from *c*. 700 to 690 BC, and added a number of Orientalizing elements, such as hybrid bird-felines and palm leaves, to the stock Proto-Corinthian-Cumaean motifs. The latter also depicted maritime experiences (e.g. on oinochoai; St Louis, MO, A. Mus., 71.114; Haifa, N. Mar. Mus.).

3. Orientalizing. The Orientalizing style succeeded Etrusco-Geometric gradually, the latter continuing in evidence into the 7th century BC. Early Orientalizing pottery includes much stereotyped work with Corinthian-derived linear decoration organized in registers or concentric zones, often alternating with files of fish and marsh birds. Parallels with contemporary metal and Bucchero vessels appear in vase shapes (e.g. kylikes imitating Proto-Corinthian types, bridge-handled situlae and vertical-handled cups). Although produced in southern Etruria, these vases were distributed widely within central Italy. Caere (Cerveteri) was a major centre, producing the distinctive 'Heron class' vases, which show elongated aquatic birds with filiform beaks and silhouette bodies and tails, and a series of large vases, predominantly amphorae, dated *c.* 700–*c.* 625 BC. An important krater (Rome, Mus. Capitolino) depicting a *Sea-battle* and the *Blinding of Polyphemos* was signed by its craftsman, Aristonothos, a Greek immigrant, and it exemplifies a new Caeretan decorative approach, which introduced figural scenes executed in outline drawing filled in with dots entailing the break-up of traditional zoomorphic motifs. Effectively, the routine sub-Geometric schemata were relegated to filling motifs, and the principal decorative field was occupied by real or fantastic animals and narrative scenes, either from real life or from Greek myth and epic. One amphora (*c.* 650–*c.* 630 BC; Amsterdam, Allard Pierson Mus., 10188) shows a female figure confronting a three-headed serpent: this scene must be *Medea and the Dragon of Kolchis*. Two individual painters identified in this school are the Heptachord Painter and the Cranes Painter (both active *c.* 680–*c.* 670 BC). These developments are to some extent paralleled by work in fine impasto (so-called 'white-on-red'). Scenes painted in cream-white on a reddish slip include the *Birth of Athena* and the *Hunt of the Kalydonian Boar* (pyxis; *c.* 630 BC; Paris, Louvre, D151) and naval fights (pyxis; Paris, Louvre, D150). Stylistic affinities between impasto and fine ware production are also shown by two fine-ware amphorae from Caeretan tombs, made by the same potter as a pair of impasto pithoi (all four vases in Rome, Villa Giulia).

4. Bucchero. Produced continuously between *c.* 675 BC and the beginning of the 5th century BC, this distinctively Etruscan ware was made from a clay similar to that of impasto but purer, which fired to a black tone with a lustrous, almost metallic brilliance (see fig. 19). Bucchero was in fact produced as a deliberate substitute for metal vases, and its shapes and decoration were based, especially at first, on metallic prototypes. Bucchero was extremely versatile and was used for a wide range of shapes. Etruscan Bucchero is usually divided into three types: fine (*c.* 675–*c.* 625 BC), transitional (*c.* 625–*c.* 575 BC) and heavy (*c.* 575–*c.* 500 BC), according to the thickness of the pottery walls. Northern Etruscan Bucchero followed a different development: the oldest was a type of buccheroid impasto, which gave way in the Archaic period to a heavy Bucchero. 'Grey' Bucchero

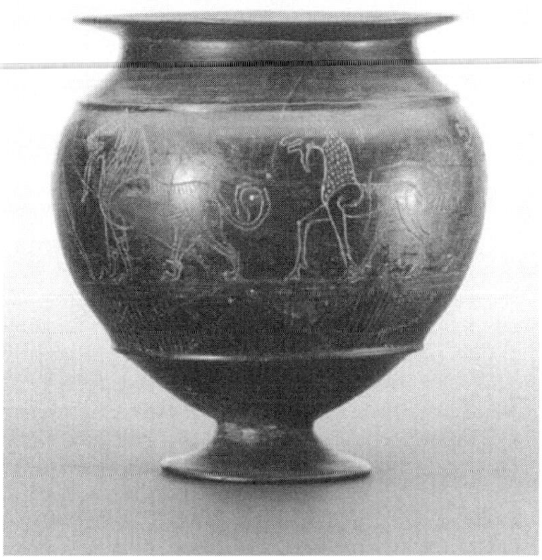

19. Etruscan incised bucchero bowl with animal frieze decoration, h. 140 mm, from ?Caere (Cerveteri), *c.* 630–600 BC (London, British Museum, 1927.1-10.1)

appeared only in the second half of the 6th century BC and was used for less than a century for a limited range of shapes.

Fine Bucchero production in southern Etruria began in Caere (Cerveteri), followed by Veii and Tarquinia. The vase shapes partly conformed to types established in the impasto repertory: double spiral amphorae, 'Phoenician-Cypriot' oinochoai, hemispherical or carinated chalices, kotylai, skyphoi and kylikes based on Proto-Corinthian types, olpai, plates, kantharoi and kyathoi with crested handles. Decoration also followed impasto techniques, being impressed, incised, stamped, relief and occasionally carved. Specific to Bucchero, however, are motifs of open and closed fans, and the 'diamond-point' notching that underlines carinations and relief cordons, both derived from metalwork. Towards the mid-7th century BC a workshop at Caere produced relief decoration with human and animal figures, in clear imitation of metal embossed vases, with iconographic formulae taken from Syro-Phoenician models. The shapes on which such decoration appears include pyxides, situlae, kotylai, plates, kantharoi and kyathoi, and some of these have been found at Clusium (Chiusi) and even Vetulonia. Mid- to late-Orientalizing relief-decorated Bucchero was produced at Vulci, and possibly also in northern Etruria at Rusellae (Roselle) and Populonia. At Caere some one-off commissions were produced, including the 'ink pot' inscribed with a syllabary (*c.* 650–*c.* 640 BC; Rome, Vatican, Mus. Gregoriano Etrus.) and the phiale from the Tomb of the Painted Lions (Rome, Villa Giulia) that, with its human heads, reproduces a prestigious Levantine metal type. Bucchero gradually acquired its own range of shapes, but new ones derived from ivory and metal vessels, or indeed from Proto-Corinthian, Transitional and Corinthian pottery (e.g. oinochoai, olpai, kylikes and aryballoi) and East Greek shapes (e.g. bird bowls), were constantly added.

The frieze-like incised decoration that was first produced at Caere in the early 7th century BC derived from metal originals and featured an Orientalizing bestiary supplemented by horsemen, hunters, boxers, chariots and combat scenes, where influences from the Near East and, later, from Corinth are to be seen. Such decoration was also produced after *c.* 630 BC at Veii, Tarquinia and Vulci. Some of these vases, particularly kantharoi, were exported at least as far afield as Naxos and Megara Hyblaia in Sicily, and Bucchero ware in general has been found throughout the Mediterranean region. Furthermore, it sometimes exerted its own morphological influence on Attic Black-figure vases, which were mainly exported in Etruria (*see* §IV, 5(ii)): amphorae produced in the workshops of NIKOSTHENES and Pamphaios around 530–510 BC clearly reflect a Caeretan shape of *c.* 575–*c.* 550 BC, with a stemmed foot, two relief cordons around the top half of the body, and a pair of band-shaped handles, vertically decorated with openwork or stamped animals. These were exported back to Caere, and Nikosthenes' workshop also adapted both the high- and low-footed kyathos from Bucchero prototypes typical of Vulci, carefully imitating both the modelled projections at the top of the handle and the peculiar relief ornament inside it.

Transitional Bucchero was produced in Campania and probably Latium too. Towards the end of the 7th century BC a new technique of decoration was developed, and used primarily on chalices: carved wooden cylinders were run over the pot before firing. They impressed the negative areas of the desired design, resulting in small, shallow relief friezes, crudely executed, with simple motifs or a motley of schematic human and animal figures, the former seated, running, riding chariots, fighting, hunting or dancing. The technique persisted at Tarquinia up to the early 6th century BC and into the second half of the 6th century BC at Volsinii Veteres (Orvieto) and Clusium.

The increased availability of imported Greek painted pottery during the Archaic period meant the relegation of Bucchero to ordinary domestic use, except in certain sanctuaries, where Bucchero vessels served cult purposes (e.g. a 'chest' dedicated to Menerva at the Portonaccio Sanctuary, Veii; Rome, Villa Giulia). The main shapes were oinochoai, including the beaked type, chalices, kantharoi (usually low-footed) and kyathoi. The influence of metal forms persisted, reasserting itself around the second quarter of the 6th century BC, first at Vulci and then at Tarquinia, Volsinii Veteres and especially Clusium, with the manufacture of complete table services in heavy Bucchero with plastic decoration in the forms of human heads, 'acorns', animal protomes or relief motifs, clearly imitating contemporary bronzework. From the mid-6th century BC Bucchero undecorated plates, bowls and cups were widely made. Specialized vessels included 'filter' vases and libation cups. Occasionally, extra ornament was in the form of silver or gold foil, and polychrome decoration was painted after firing.

Northern Etruscan Bucchero had a more limited range of shapes and only local distribution. Decoration was dominated by geometric or linear motifs continuing the Iron Age tradition and small stamps with swastikas, rosettes, human and animal figures etc. Inland centres such as Clusium and those in the Florence-Fiesole district produced from the late 7th century BC onwards chalices, kantharoi and kyathoi, and also perfume vases, alabastra, ring-askoi and kotyle-pyxides, with inscriptions attesting gift-exchange, and special objects such as the 'incense burner' or, more likely, lamp from Artimino (Artimino, Antiqua.), made up of a number of interlocking components and with an inscription denoting either its owner or maker. Although some imitations of southern Etruscan fine Bucchero with stamped figures were produced at Clusium, most of the consistent output was heavy Bucchero, which, from the mid-6th to the beginning of the 5th century BC, had abundant modelled decoration, such as human masks, heads and figures of cocks and 'doves', and stamped relief ornament. The shapes made were predominantly local ones and only occasionally related to South Etruscan or Greek types: kraters, amphorae, hydriai, oinochoai, handled trays, foculi, simpula, infundibula, cylindrical stands, cups etc. The stamped relief ornaments, whether floral or figural, show Greek and some specifically Ionic influence.

5. RED WARE. A slightly purified impasto, granular in texture, with a blackish core and a shiny red surface, Red ware was used for stamped pithoi and braziers produced at Caere (Cerveteri) and in the Caeretan hinterland from the late 7th century BC throughout the Archaic period to *c.* 500 BC. The pithoi are *c.* 700–900 mm high, with flat bases, flared mouths and ovoid bodies with vertical ribbing, bounded by relief cordons in such forms as zigzags, connected bows or double circles on the shoulders. Around the shoulder, and sometimes beneath the ribbing as well, there is often subsidiary decoration, whether stamped or cylinder-impressed. The braziers, in two typical sizes from 300 to 600 mm in diameter, have only cylinder-impressed ornament around the border. While pithoi were food containers, braziers might be used for the presentation of cooked food. The stamped or cylinder-impressed decoration relates technically to that of both transitional and heavy Bucchero, and the variety of subjects is rich, including a wide range of both animal and human scenes. Horsemen, archers, hoplites, gorgoneia, centaurs and Acheloos all feature, showing clear late Orientalizing and Corinthian influence. In the more complex subjects (e.g. hunting, chariot-racing, banquets, sacrifices, Apollo and Tityos, Achilles and Troilos), Ionic influence is evident. At a lesser

workshop at San Giovenale, in Caeretan territory at this time, the owner added his name, Larice Crepu, to the stamped decoration. At Caere, a good deal of pithoi and braziers was found in both the settlement site and the necropolis; they have also been found at Pyrgi (Santa Severa), Tuscania and various settlements in the Mignone Valley, the Tolfa Hills and the area around Lake Bracciano, and, less frequently, at Veii, Tarquinia, Gravisca and Vulci.

6. ETRUSCO-CORINTHIAN. Southern Etruscan pottery was copiously produced in imitation of Proto-Corinthian and Corinthian vases imported into Etruria from the 8th century BC to the first half of the 6th. It was in its own turn exported, both within central Italy and to other Mediterranean sites. Its initial phase (*c*. 630–*c*. 600 BC) shows shapes and decoration influenced by late Proto-Corinthian and Transitional, with the familiar filling motif of dot-rosettes. One of the Dot-rosette group artists, the Bearded Sphinx Painter, may have trained at Corinth, and was active at Vulci, being attributed with the decoration of more than 100 vases. He is notable not only for his predilection for the masculine sphinx, but also for his animal friezes; his dot-rosettes gradually degenerated into mere blobs and discs. His rare narrative scenes include the *Sack of Troy* on an oinochoe (Paris, Bib. N., 179), and warriors and chariots on an olpe (Ischia di Castro, Antiquarium Com. Pietro Lotti). He decorated mostly olpai and oinochoai, with a few alabastra, amphorae and large amphorae of the 'scale' type (*anforoni squamati*). His contemporary, the Swallow Painter, also active at Vulci, was from East Greece and has been ascribed ten vases including oinochoai, olpai, amphorae, an alabastron and a large kylix similar to the Type A Ionic cup. He painted files of steinbock and geese and subsidiary decoration, essentially East Greek designs drawn from the Wild Goat style, to which he added some elements from the local repertory. At Caere (Cerveteri) many large amphorae with scale decoration were produced between *c*. 620 and *c*. 590 BC. These have animal decoration of Late Proto-Corinthian-Transitional type yielding to that of early Corinthian, with its files and heraldic schemata. Below these animal friezes, expansive areas of scales were incised on a dark background, although this repetitive format was occasionally altered by the Pilgrim Flask Painter, who sometimes included human subjects, for example in a hunting scene.

In the last quarter of the 7th century BC the Etrusco-Corinthian Black-figure technique coexisted with the more widely practised polychrome technique involving incised figures, almost invariably animals, on a brownish surface glaze, heightened by white and purple overpaint. This technique is related to the incised decoration employed at the same time in Bucchero and impasto, and possibly also metalwork. It is exemplified by the Polychrome group of vases, made at Veii, Caere and Vulci. At Veii the Castellani Painter painted small vases, preferring the piriform aryballos; at Caere the style was applied to amphorae with large but incoherent figures by the Monte Abatone cycle; slightly later, at Vulci, the main centre of Black-figure production, artists such as the Pescia Romana Painter, the manneristic Painter of the Polychrome Bows and the Garovaglio Painter used some polychrome decoration. During the early 6th century BC simple linear or floral polychrome decoration was used for a relatively wide range of vases.

The middle phase of Etrusco-Corinthian (*c*. 600–*c*. 560 BC) was marked by the predominance of Vulci and the development of an industry to meet growing demand. The range of shapes was extended, with olpai remaining the most popular, while ring-askoi and kraters are very few. Modelled balsamarics in many forms (e.g. monkey, fawn, dead hare, swan, head of Acheloos, eagle's head, human leg, porcupine, piglet) came into vogue, inspired by East Greek and Corinthian models. Among the many groups of pottery identified from this period are the Olpai and Rosoni cycles. All employed repetitive animal friezes and filling motifs, but some exceptional pieces exist, including a krater by the Painter of the Rosoni Kraters depicting *Herakles and Alkyoneus* (Paris, Louvre, E631) and a krater (Cerveteri, Mus. N. Cerite) with *Herakles Stealing the Cattle of Geryon* and, possibly, the *Sacrifice of Polyxena*. The Feoli Painter depicted some of the few human subjects of Etrusco-Corinthian, notably a male and female couple (olpe; Turin priv. col). The bilingual Pescia Romana Painter was distinguished by vigorous and fluid drawing (see colour pl. 2:VII, fig. 1), and the Boehlau Painter produced exuberant and undisciplined work. The Carnage Painter and the Wolf Heads Painter apparently initiated production at Tarquinia, where the Vitelleschi group, the Grasmere group and the 'Senza Graffito' Painter and his workshop specialized in plates, phialai and bowls from *c*. 590 to *c*. 560 BC.

During the third and final phase of Etrusco-Corinthian (*c*. 560–*c*. 540 BC) fewer small-scale vases such as cups, alabastra, globular aryballoi and plastic balsamaries were decorated and the formulae derived from the Vulci workshops in the preceding phase were rigidly applied. The Bobuda Painter, one of the 'Little Masters', was an uninspired imitator of the Pescia Romana Painter, and the Human Mask group simply transferred to Caere and brought to an end the Rosoni group. Also possibly from Caere were the artisans of one of the latest groups, the Heraldic Cocks cycle, which, with the Bird cycle, produced the banal stereotypes that marked the end of the Etrusco-Corinthian.

7. BLACK-FIGURE. Etruscan Black-figure ware was produced from *c*. 550 to *c*. 480 BC, and coincided with the highest percentage of importation of Athenian Black-figure and Red-figure (*see* §IV, 5(II) and 6(I) respectively). It was probably introduced by East Greek immigrants, who came to Vulci from the early 6th century BC, though in much greater numbers after the Persian invasions in the East. Their presence explains the exclusively Etruscan provenance

of Caeretan hydriai and dinoi of the Campana group, and the Ionic quality of some Etruscan tomb paintings from 540–500 BC. The first phase (*c.* 550–*c.* 520 BC) is notable for the Pontic style developed by the Paris Painter and his followers. Over 200 vases are attributed to the Pontic painters, who were apparently based at Vulci and included the Paris Painter, the Amphiaraos Painter, the Tityos Painter, the Silen Painter and the Painter of Bibliothèque Nationale 178. They specialized in neck-amphorae, influenced by the 'Tyrrhenian' amphorae produced in Attica from *c.* 575 to *c.* 550 BC, mainly for the Etruscan market. They adopted the Tyrrhenian partitioning of the vase-space: a shoulder scene often depicting Greek myths (e.g. Herakles episodes connected with Troy and Thebes cycles), while the body of the vase was filled with animal files and friezes of subsidiary ornament, such as partridges, meanders, stars, ivy leaves and lotus buds. The effect is fluid and eclectic and shows strong North Ionic influence, such as the Caeretan painted plaques and Archaic architectural terracottas. The genre scenes include departure and arming, the hunt, horsemen, fights, symposia and centaurs. The shape range may have been influenced by local Bucchero, and includes chalices, kantharoi, kyathoi, oinochoai, lydia, plates, and also types that were uncommon, such as hydriai, nikosthenic amphorae, phialai and dinoi.

The Ivy Leaf group and the La Tolfa group, at Vulci and Caere (Cerveteri) respectively, are slightly later. The Ivy Leaf group, named after a decorative motif frequently used, includes more than 50 vases, mostly Type B amphorae. Greek themes appear on both sides of these amphorae (often involving Dionysos, but also Herakles, Bellerophon and Odysseus), and apotropaic eyes, dancers and animals also occur. The predominant influence is that of Attic Black-figure, in particular the work of the AFFECTER and the AMASIS PAINTER. The La Tolfa workshop, to which some 30 vases have been attributed, produced neck-amphorae influenced by the North Ionic or 'klazomenian' winged, running figures, animals and hippocamps, as well as rare mythological scenes (e.g. Achilles and Troilos). The style is monumental and may owe something to the Caeretan hydriai.

In the second phase of production (*c.* 530–*c.* 500 BC) the Micali Painter ran a workshop, again at Vulci. His work shows signs of early contact with the Pontic painters, but clearly soon developed its own idiom of fantastic themes dominated by sphinxes and sirens. He painted athletes, chariot-racing and, occasionally, mythological subjects including Herakles, Achilles and Troilos, and the *Suicide of Ajax*. His mature style reveals a more conscious study of contemporary Attic style, with more added white and subsidiary vase-space filled with palmette florals. Among his followers the Painter of Vatican 238 is notable for his hydria depicting the *Transformation of the Tyrrhenian Pirates into Dolphins* (Toledo, OH, Mus. A., 82.134).

A third phase (*c.* 500–*c.* 480 BC) is characterized by shoddier work, only dependent on Attic models of the late 6th and beginning of the 5th century and manufactured at Vulci, Volsinii Veteres (Orvieto) and Clusium (Chiusi). Some of the painters who trained at Vulci may have set up the inland workshops as well as others in Campania. The uniform conventionality of these products makes attribution difficult. There are rarely more than three figures and ornament is restricted to palmette chains and lotus buds, all executed mostly in silhouette, with touches of white. The subject-matter is unambitious. More than 100 vases can be assigned variously to the Painter of Munich 892, the group of Munich 883 and the group of Vatican 265, with many more still unattributed. The Volsinii Veteres group is distinguished by the coarse vigour of its style. It can be divided into patterned vases (geometricizing and floral decoration on chalices, plates, oinochoai and stamnoi) and vases with figural decoration, rarely mythological, ultimately inspired by Attic models. Minor groups include the local Clusium pyxides, two non-figural groups of vases from Vulci, the 'Dot-wreath plates', and the bowls and plates of the Spurinas group, the latter with pre-fired onomastic inscriptions. Finally, the more individualistic work of the Painter of the Dancing Satyrs, probably active at Caere, includes depictions of satyrs and actors impersonating satyrs, the *Killing of the Minotaur* with Herakles, not Theseus, as the hero, and the instruction of the armed dance.

8. RED-FIGURE. The earliest examples are not strictly Red-figure but applied red painting and belong to the Praxias group, named from a signature on one amphora (Paris, Bib. N., 913). Arnth Praxias was probably a Greek artisan naturalized in Etruria, active at Vulci from *c.* 480 to *c.* 460 BC. Some 80 vases are ascribed to the Praxias group, distributed well into the Etruscan inland (Volsinii Veteres (Orvieto), Clusium (Chiusi)). These may not all have come from a single workshop, but they share a common dependence on Late Archaic Attic style, and the inscriptions that occur for mythological subjects are in Greek.

Red-figure proper did not fully develop in Etruria until the end of the 5th century BC or the beginning of the 4th, a generation after the rise of the South Italian Red-figure workshops. In the first of its phases (*c.* 400–*c.* 350 BC) production centred at Falerii (Civita Castellana), Vulci and in northern Etruria; from Falerii about 300 vases survive. Late Attic influence, especially that of the Meleager Painter and Jena Painter, is evident in the kylikes. Kraters and stamnoi show Attic floridness and intricacy, with a basic repertory of Dionysiac and erotic subjects. As the Faliscan style evolved, it absorbed elements of South Italian, notably Apulian vase painting, as in the work of the Aurora Painter and the Nazzano Painter. Vases believed to be from Vulci are less easy to classify. The large-scale vases of the Painter of London F 484, the Vatican Biga Painter and the Perugia Painter seem influenced by the work of the MEIDIAS PAINTER, but curious archaizing also occurs (Rodin kylix, Vich amphora). Overall, however, the dominant influence is South Italian, whether in the accessory decoration or in the subjects of the main scenes. A South Italian theatricality is evident in the work of the Poggio Sommavilla Painter (e.g. Oedipus, satyr dramas), the Paestan-style stamnoi of the Settecamini Painter and the Campanizing group vases. Workshops in northern inland Etruria produced smaller vases, in particular kylikes, decorated with stock figures derived from late 5th-century BC Attic vases. One such painter, Pheziu Paveś, signed before firing a cup found at Grotti, near Siena (Siena, Mus. Archeol.).

In the second phase (*c.* 350–*c.* 300 BC) a marked increase in quantity occurred, as some workshops began to specialize in funerary vases. Quality, however, declined, with one or two exceptions. Workshops proliferated at Falerii, Caere (Cerveteri), Tarquinia, Vulci, Volsinii Veteres, Clusium and Velathri (Volterra). At Falerii and Caere, a repetitive series of vases was produced featuring Dionysiac or erotic subjects or simply female heads. The Caeretan vases were distributed to Liguria, Gaul, Corsica, Sardinia, Carthage, Malta, Cyrene and elsewhere. At Vulci funerary themes predominated, for example the kraters of the Funnel group. From *c.* 330 to *c.* 300 BC the decorative style became less rigid. The Clusium group is perhaps the most representative of later Etruscan Red-figure: it includes at least five painters, who concentrated at first on kylikes decorated with Dionysiac subjects but then extended their repertory to large funerary vases (calyx kraters) as well as askoi and skyphoi. In the later phase compositions were more complex. At Velathri the Hesione Painter specialized in kelebai and stamnoi for cinerary purposes, and was followed by lesser Red-figure painters active into the early 3rd century BC (e.g. Asciano Painter and Pygmy Trumpeter Painter).

9. Black-Glaze. Black-glaze ware was widely produced in Etruria from the mid-4th century BC, after import of Attic pottery had halted. As in Apulia, the vases were only occasionally decorated with added paint, and so classification depends on clay and glaze features and shape. The shapes produced range from vases for large domestic services to miniaturistic votive vessels, made in both southern and northern Etruria. At Velathri (Volterra) the fine Malacena class vases were produced in a beige-pink clay coated with an ink-blue glaze obviously intended to imitate metal vases. These were distributed throughout northern Etruria and Corsica. Overpainted decoration was less common than relief decoration, but the Sienese workshop produced many kylikes with painted ornament, and the Ferrara T 585 group specialized in skyphoi with a swan between floral motifs or with palmettes. There is evidence that Red-figure painters worked on Black-glaze overpainted vases: a Black-glaze kelebe is attributable to the Asciano Painter, one of the later masters of Red figure painting from Velathri. Production of Black-glaze continued up to *c.* 200 BC, with lesser centres established at Arretium (Arezzo), Rusellae (Roselle), Vulci-Sovana and Volsinii Novi (Bolsena).

Overpainted Black-glaze fabrics from the south include the Sokra group at Falerii (Civita Castellana), named from a Greek signature on a kylix, workshops at Tarquinia, and the Phantom group at Caere (Cerveteri, *c.* 300–*c.* 280 BC), specializing in oinochoai with a single figure. But by the early 3rd century BC Rome was becoming the dominant presence: the Roman cups of the 'Atelier des petites estampilles' were widely distributed throughout Etruria, and *pocola deorum* ('cups of the gods') with polychrome overpainted decoration, were also distributed in Etruria. The Hesse group of vases, produced perhaps at Vulci in the early 3rd century BC, marks the end of local figured pottery production.

Å. Åkerstrom: *Der geometrische Stil in Italien* (Lund-Leipzig, 1943)

J. D. Beazley: *Etruscan Vase-painting* (Oxford, 1947)

G. Camporeale: *Buccheri a cilindretto di fabbrica orvietana* (Florence, 1972)

M. Bonamici: *I buccheri con figurazioni graffite* (Florence, 1974)

F. Canciani: *Corpus Vasorum Antiquorum Italia*, LV/iii (Rome, 1974)

L. Hannestad: *The Paris Painter* (Copenhagen, 1974)

J. G. Szilágyi: *Etruszko-korinthosi vázafestészet* (Budapest, 1975)

L. Hannestad: *The Followers of the Paris Painter* (Copenhagen, 1976)

T. B. Rasmussen: *Bucchero Pottery from Southern Etruria* (Cambridge, 1979)

J.-P. Morel: *Céramique campanienne, les formes* (Rome, 1981)

J. M. Hemelrijk: *Caeretan Hydriae* (Mainz, 1984)

M. Cristofani, ed.: *Contributi alla ceramica etrusca tardo-classica* (Rome, 1985)

B. Adembri: *La più antica ceramografia falisca a figure rosse* (Rome, 1987)

S. S. Leach: *Sub-geometric Pottery from Southern Etruria* (Göteborg, 1987)

M. Martelli, ed.: *La ceramica degli Etruschi: La pittura vascolare* (Novara, 1987)

N. J. Spivey: *The Micali Painter and his Followers* (Oxford, 1987)

Un artista etrusco e il suo mondo: Il Pittore di Micali (Rome, 1988)

L. Cerchiai: *Le officine etrusco-corinzie di Pontecagnano* (Naples, 1990)

J. G. Szilágyi: *Ceramica etrusco-corinzia figurata, Parte I: 630–580 a.C.* (Florence, 1992)

M. Micozzi: *'White-on-Red': Una produzione vascolare dell'orientalizzante etrusco* (Rome, 1994)

I. Werner: *Dionysos in Etruria: The Ivy Leaf Group* (Stockholm, 2005)

VI. Roman.

Several parallel stylistic traditions flourished within the Roman Empire, some with local pre-Roman roots. 'Roman' pottery usually denotes the products of the Roman Imperial period; late versions—'Byzantine' (in Palestinian contexts) or, more normally, 'Late Roman'—persist in some Mediteranean regions until *c.* AD 700. The technology already current in Greek lands—the fast wheel, moulds, sintered (heat-treated) slips—was scarcely improved on, but penetrated to many more regions, where a commercial pottery industry replaced local domestic production. Vigorous hybrid traditions ensued in several outlying areas, while a certain artistic sterility marks the wares of the Mediterranean after *c.* AD 200.

1. TYPES AND TECHNIQUES. The most characteristic Roman ware is a smooth red ware bearing a glossy sintered slip. This has been called *terra sigillata* since the 19th century (see fig. 20); its alternative name, Samian ware (*vasa samia*), attested in antiquity, signified a varnishing technique, not that it was a product of Samos. The finest versions (*c.* 30 BC–*c.* AD 200) come from several centres in Italy and Gaul. Such red wares inherited the traditions of fine Greek pottery, while substituting a single-phase firing in an open kiln. The glossy surface, as in Greek wares, depended on the use of calcitic clays rich in such iron compounds as illite. Kilns were equipped with piping to direct any smoke away from the pots; some kilns were enormous, holding up to 40,000 vessels.

Glossy red wares, some decorated, appeared at Pergamon in Asia Minor by 100 BC; another series (Eastern Sigillata A), from an unlocated Levantine source, was widely marketed in the eastern Mediterranean after 150 BC. Both influenced Sicilian wares. The rise of the classic Arretine ware factories in Italy at Arretium (now Arezzo) and around Neapolis (now Naples) *c.* 40–*c.* 25 BC suggests the imposition of Pergamene and Sicilian practices, presumably via slave craftsmen, on the already strong local Black-gloss ware tradition. Lead-glazed wares also occur, though rarely; the glaze was apparently applied in powdered form. Such vessels were normally inverted for firing in stacks within closed containers (saggars), as is shown by knobs of glaze at their rims; some cups bear the scars of small tripod stilts. Parthian-style, alkali-lead glazes occur in some eastern frontier regions; these parallel the Egyptian 'faience' (glazed glass-frit) series, which survived into Roman times.

Millions of large two-handled clay jars (amphorae) of plain heavy-duty ware and generally elongated form, in hundreds of varieties, served as shipping containers for foodstuffs, as they had done in the Greek world. Such vessels were formed of several wheel-thrown sections luted together before firing and were remarkably standardized within each series. Early Roman examples (2nd century BC) defined a unit of capacity (*amphora*=25.8 litres), but the average size was reduced thereafter. Around AD 1–200 many centres from Syria to Britain produced variants of the Hellenistic 'Koan' shape (from Kos) with its double-roll handles; also typical are the globular Baetican (southern Spanish) oil amphorae, the main constituent of the Monte Testaccio, an immense rubbish dump in Rome.

Other shapes were normally wheelmade: red- and grey-bodied cooking pots, buff-ware jugs and serving vessels, frequently with horizontal ribbing. Heavy buff-ware basins with grit-studded interiors (*mortaria*) were used in preparing food.

Potters' stamps, naming both proprietors and workmen (mostly freedmen and slaves), are standard on Italian *terra sigillata*. One- or two-line stamps were superseded by foot-shaped ones *c.* AD 15–*c.* 30; the latter persisted until production ceased in Italy *c.* AD 150. In Gaul and Spain the rectangular form of stamp persisted, generally with OF (*officina*: 'workshop') or FEC (*fecit*: 'made') accompanying the name. Name-stamps are rarer on 1st-century AD Eastern wares, occurring mostly on the Italian-style products of Pergamon and Tralles (Eastern Sigillata B).

2. REGIONAL TRADITIONS.

(i) The Mediterranean. Prestige silverware provided models for Mediterranean Roman fine pottery. Hence *terra sigillata* flat plates and trays (diam. up to 700 mm) and smaller bowls display complex rim- and foot-profiling. A parallel range of drinking vessels (shallow two-handled cups, small bowls, beakers) current *c.* 100 BC–*c.* AD 100 mimic the extreme thinness of metalware. Their varied decoration includes moulded relief, freehand applied motifs, rouletting (regular mechanical notching) and added sand or clay particles creating a 'rough-cast' surface; others bear a bronze-coloured mica-rich wash. Most such types originated in Italy, but Spain and Gaul were also major producers.

A smaller class of high-footed bowls and cups in *terra sigillata* bear relief patterns cast from moulds that were rotated on the potter's wheel, the rims and moulded feet being thrown freehand. Patterns were either punched individually into the moulds or, less often, cast directly off metalware. Arretine ware typifies the class; many bowl-shaped moulds are known from several named workshops at Arretium (Arezzo), notably those from the workshop of M. Perennius (mostly Augustan; many modern fakes exist). The Perennius workshop repertory, closely following that of silverware, abounds in figural compositions, largely mythological or erotic, skilfully crafted in the delicately refined Neo-Attic style favoured in Augustus' court circles. Yet such products are rarer among other finds: most Arretine and related bowls made until AD 60–70 tend towards lush foliage or plain symmetry, with multiple mouldings on wheelmade

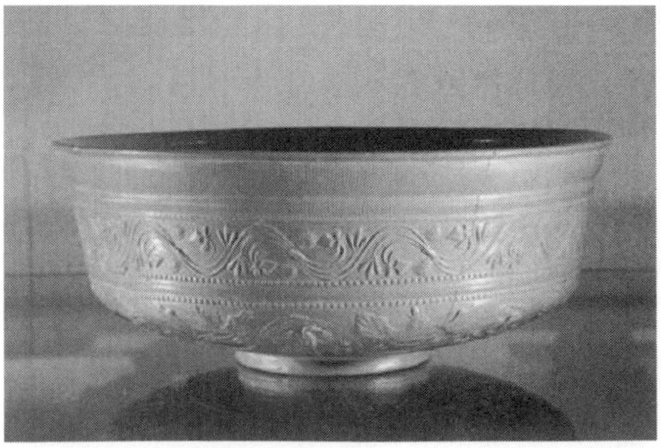

20. Roman *terra sigillata* bowl with moulded relief pattern (Bonn, Rheinisches Landesmuseum)

parts. The many branches of the Ateius workshops established at Arretium, Pisa and Lugdunum (Lyon) adopted this treatment. (It was copied on some early provincial *terra sigillata* from Gaul, where it soon evolved into mere patternwork.)

Arretine-style motifs, similarly produced, ornament the less numerous two-handled drinking-cups and pedestalled bowls with a green or yellow lead glaze. These rather dearer wares patently mimic silverware. Several classes are known from Asia Minor, where they were produced at Tarsus and (probably) Pergamon; others stemmed from Italy. White clay additions may appear under the glaze to create a colour contrast. Some lead-glazed cylindrical tankards (*modioli*) and related red-gloss jugs from north-west Turkey copy metalware with high reliefs; motifs such as skeletons are here rendered in barbotine technique (liquid clay squeezed on to the surface).

Less often, vessels were entirely mould-made, like most Roman lamps and figurines. Knidos in Asia Minor produced the main series (*c.* AD 70–*c.* 230); some copies are known from Africa. 'Novelty' products predominate, mostly wine jugs and sexually explicit forms (possibly to combat magic). Corinth and later Pergamon produced other series.

After AD 150 silver plate with Dionysiac or animal-hunt relief friezes on the rim was repeatedly copied in Roman pottery. Rare lead-glazed, mould-made versions occur in Italy; commoner are red-gloss ones. On African Red Slip ware (mostly from Tunisia), by then the dominant Mediterranean fine ware, the style recurred for almost three centuries; discrete applied figures are set on rims, inside rounded bowls and on small jugs (some bearing labels). Amphitheatre and hunt scenes were favoured, reappearing on some related signed flagons and jugs (by Navigius and others, *c.* AD 300). The mythological, Mithraic and biblical motifs on later bowls recall cut glassware. Rectangular platters dating to *c.* AD 400 combine mould-made 'pictures' with the usual rim ornaments; the Achilles legend, hunt scenes and Christian saints mingle, reflecting cultural diversity. From *c.* AD 320 stamped ornament characterized the ever-popular African red wares; again, both vessel shapes and repertory are 'metallic'. Dishes and shallow bowls exhibit simple radial or concentric patterns based on repeated palm-branch or circle stamps, framed by grooving or rouletting. Small animals—mere crude outlines—and various Christian symbols abound after AD 430. The influence of later (Byzantine) metal platters is clear on footed plates and dishes featuring large Christian motifs: 'saints', 'jewelled' crosses, lambs, fishes. Linear in concept, and lacking relief depth, these stamps form rudimentary patterns within grooved surrounds. The African stamped style was copied in South Gaul and Spain, in Egypt, perhaps in Cyprus, and particularly in the Phokaian ware that was widely marketed in the eastern Mediterranean and featured broad rouletted bands impressed with a multiple-notched tool, and crude figures. The treatments tended to diverge: a series of medallions in sunk relief marked the end of one South Gaulish series, while in the East (Egypt, Jordan) painted scenes largely prevailed. A small orange-ware class from western Turkey, which favoured hunting scenes and crosses, mimicked pictorial plates by engraving and removal of the slip from background areas (a sort of 'Black-figure' style). All such treatments faded out between *c.* AD 550 and *c.* AD 700, signalling the demise of the Roman decorative tradition.

(ii) Gaul and elsewhere. Best known among the non-Mediterranean wares are those from the Rhineland, Gaul and Britain, where many hundreds of kiln sites have been excavated. Some Italian-style *terra sigillata* was made in southern France in the time of Augustus; further north this was copied in the plain burnished 'Gallo-Belgic' wares. Classic Gaulish *terra sigillata* is divided by region into South Gaulish (mostly *c.* AD 20–*c.* 120), with main centres at La Graufesenque (Aveyron), Montans (Tarn) and Banassac; Central Gaulish (*c.* AD 100–*c.* 250), at Lezoux (Puy-de-Dôme) and Les Martres-de-Veyre; and East Gaulish (*c.* AD 40–*c.* 300, mostly 2nd century AD), with various centres in and around Lorraine and Alsace, and later at Rheinzabern and Augusta Treverorum (Trier). The large and long-lived Spanish *terra sigillata* series, produced chiefly in Navarra and Rioja, and in the south at Andújar (Jaén), derived mainly from southern Gaul, while the other series spawned crude copies in the Danubian provinces. Lezoux, the largest 2nd-century AD producer, exerted considerable influence. East Gaulish offshoots include Westerndorf in south-east Bavaria and short-lived workshops at Camulodunum (Colchester) in Britain. The classic Gaulish vessel shapes, like earlier Italian forms, widely influenced coarse-ware products in all northern provinces.

The huge commercial success of the mid-1st century AD wares of La Graufesenque induced a progressive migration of specialist potters to the north and east; indeed, potters' stamps and decorative motifs attest much movement among the various Gaulish centres, and some moulds for decorated wares (notably those of Cinnamus of Lezoux) were also traded around.

Gaulish vessel forms are normally cited by the type numbers assigned to them in the 1890s by Dragendorff. Three types regularly bear moulded decoration. The earliest, an angular 'carinated' bowl (Dragendorff 29), bears two friezes, normally with floral motifs. Around AD 60–90 a round-bodied version with upright rim (Dragendorff 37) took over, continuing until the ware's demise; its single decorated band, narrowing over time, has a repeating egg-pattern (ovolo) at the top. It was the most copied type; in Spain it survived until the 5th century AD. A deep cylindrical bowl (Dragendorff 30), less common, is similarly treated. More numerous were undecorated dishes and bowls, made in standard sizes, bearing makers' stamps in Latin script. These vessels, which soon discarded Italian 'metallic' profiles, were mostly robust, with an impermeable surface gloss.

The classic South Gaulish style featured delicate floral scrolls in low relief, in part traced freehand on the mould. Panel decoration, with some small animal motifs, became popular in the late 1st century AD (mainly on Dragendorff 37). In the 2nd century AD the frieze was often divided vertically and horizontally into variegated panels (cf. mosaics and plasterwork), each bearing a few figural or floral motifs punched deeply into the mould; other vessels display a continuous figural frieze. While hundreds of motifs were borrowed from the Classical mythological repertory, their handling was mostly crude and haphazard, lacking sculptural feeling. By the 3rd century AD repeated copying and remoulding rendered many almost unrecognizable. (The so-called 'Late Italian' series from Pisa, of *c.* AD 80–*c.* 140, parallels the Gaulish treatment, though its figure-types derive mostly from Arretine ware.) Around AD 200 the Gaulish moulded wares were largely replaced by other vessel types: *sigillata* beakers and high-flanged basins with barbotine patterns, vertical-sided basins with applied spouts in the form of a lion's head, and a series with excised patterns copying cut glassware. Lezoux, Rheinzabern and, finally, Trier were major sources. Derivative wares with a poor red gloss, some with crude roller-stamping replacing the reliefs, were still made in the Argonne region (northern France) and the Rhône Valley in the 4th century AD. The late Roman red-slipped Oxfordshire wares mirror these.

Drinking mugs and beakers in fine wares, mostly pale-bodied with a darker surface slip, were also popular in the northern provinces throughout Roman times; most lack handles. They derive in part from local pre-Roman types, some angular and cordoned (decorated with horizontal ribs), some elegantly curved. Italian surface treatments (rough-cast, barbotine) mark some early series, as in central Gaul. Later the barbotine technique was used for whole flowing compositions of animals and foliage, notably on the 'hunt cups' made at Colonia Claudia Ara Agrippinensium (Cologne), Camulodunum, Castor and elsewhere from *c.* AD 130. Most refined in technique are the black-gloss products of Lezoux and the Trier region ('Rhenish ware'). Their decoration includes barbotine scrollwork (some in added white or orange), white slip inscriptions, applied 'fish-scales', indentations and impressed rouletting. Less ambitious barbotine wares occur in the Danubian areas (especially Bulgaria) and in Egypt.

Simpler painted wares, mostly dark-on-light and featuring linear patterns or simple scrollwork, were produced in many regions of the Roman Empire, but form no continuous tradition; plain slip coatings are more widespread. In Athens, white painted scrollwork adorns some 'metallic' forms; comparable motifs can be found on 4th-century AD examples from Britain. Some more fancy treatments appear in the Rhineland, including jugs with striped 'marbling' and a small polychrome series from the Frankfurt region (Wetterau ware). Other dark-on-light series, generally floral, occur in Egypt; later ones there (5th–6th century) are more ambitious, with some sketchy figural scenes. The eggshell-thin bowls from NABATAEA (southern Palestine, mostly 1st century AD) show a refined but un-Classical use of floral elements. Linear burnished patterns, with pre-Roman Celtic origins, are the sole decoration of most coarse cooking wares in the northern provinces.

H. Dragendorff: 'Terra sigillata', *Bonn. Jb. Rhein. Landesmus. Bonn & Ver. Altertfreund. Rheinlande*, xcvi (1895), pp. 18–155

E. Gose: *Gefässtypen der römischen Keramik im Rheinland* (Kevelaer, 1950/*R* Cologne, 1975)

R. J. Charleston: *Roman Pottery* (London, 1955)

H. Comfort and others: *Terra sigillata: La ceramica a rilievo ellenistica e romana* (Rome, [1967])

A. Oxé and H. Comfort: *Corpus vasorum Arretinorum* (Bonn, 1968)

C. Johns: *Arretine and Samian Pottery* (London, 1971, rev. 2/1977)

J. W. Hayes: *Late Roman Pottery* (London, 1972, suppl. 1980)

M. Vegas: *Ceràmica común romana del Mediterráneo occidental* (Barcelona, 1973)

N. Chantel, ed.: *Céramique en Gaule romaine* (Paris, 1975)

V. G. Swan: *Pottery in Roman Britain* (Princes Risborough, 1975)

A. Carandini, ed.: *L'instrumentum domesticum di Ercolano e Pompei* (Rome, 1977)

M. Bulmer: *An Introduction to Roman Samian Ware* (Chester, 1980)

A. King: 'A Graffito from La Graufesenque and "samia vasa"', *Britannia*, xi (1980), pp. 139–43

P. Levêque and J. P. Morel, eds: *Céramiques hellénistiques et romaines* (Besançon, 1980)

H. Cockle: 'Pottery Manufacture in Roman Egypt: A New Papyrus', *J. Roman Stud.*, lxxi (1981), pp. 87–97

D. P. S. Peacock: *Pottery in the Roman World* (London, 1982)

F. Mayet: *Les Céramiques sigillées hispaniques* (Paris, 1984)

V. G. Swan: *The Pottery Kilns of Roman Britain* (London, 1984)

C. Bémont and J.-P. Jacob, eds: *La Terre sigillée gallo-romaine* (Paris, 1986)

T. Dyson, ed.: *The Roman Quay at St. Magnus House, London: Excavations at New Fresh Wharf, Lower Thames Street, London, 1974–78* (London, 1986)

D. P. S. Peacock and D. F. Williams: *Amphorae and the Roman Economy* (London, 1986)

N. I. Khairy: 'The Painted Nabataean Pottery from the 1981 Petra Excavations', *Levant*, xix (1987), pp. 167–81

V. Rupp: *Wetterauer Ware: Eine römische Keramik im Rhein-Main-Gebiet* (Frankfurt and Bonn, 1988)

F. P. Porten Palange: 'Fälschungen in der arretinischen Reliefkeramik', *Archäol. Korrbl.*, xix (1989), pp. 91–9

A. Ettlinger and others: *Conspectus formarum terrae sigillatae italico modo confectae* (Bonn, 1990)

V. R. Anderson-Stojanovic: *Stobi: The Hellenistic and Roman Pottery* (Princeton, 1992)

K. Greene: *Roman Pottery* (Berkeley, 1992)

D. Adan-Bayewitz: *Common Pottery in Roman Galilee: A Study of Local Trade* (Ramat-Gan, 1993)

P. Tyers: *Roman Pottery in Britain* (London, 1996)

A. M. Gibson and A. Woods: *Prehistoric Pottery for the Archaeologist* (London, 1997)

J. W. Hayes: *Handbook of Mediterranean Roman Pottery* (Norman, 1997)
Early Italian Sigillata: The Chronological Framework and Trade Patterns: Proceedings of the First International ROCT-Congress: Leuven, 1999
A. G. Poulter, R. K. Falkner and J. D. Shepherd: *Nicopolis ad Istrum: A Roman to Early Byzantine City: The Pottery and the Glass* (London, 1999)
J. N. Coldstream, L. J. Eiring and G. Forster: *Knossos Pottery Handbook: Greek and Roman* (London, 2001)
M. Augros and M. Feugère: *La nécropole gallo-romaine de la citadelle à Chalon-sur-Saône, Saône-et-Loire* (Montagnac, 2002–)
B. Hoffmann, M. Genin and A. Vernhet: *Céramiques de la Graufesenque et autres productions d'époque romaine: Nouvelles recherches: Hommages à Bettina Hoffmann* (Montagnac, 2002)
C. M. A. De Micheli Schulthess: *Aspects of Roman Pottery in Canton Ticino (Switzerland)* (Oxford, 2003)
J. Tobin: *Black Cilicia: A Study of the Plain of Issus during the Roman and Late Roman Periods* (Oxford, 2004)
J. Faiers and S. Clackson: *Late Roman Pottery at Amarna and Related Studies* (London, 2005)
J. M. Gurt Esparraguera, J. Buxeda i Garrigós and M. A. Cau Ontiveros: *LRCW I: Late Roman Coarse Wares, Cooking Wares and Amphorae in the Mediterranean: Archaeology and Archaeometry* (Oxford, 2005)
J. W. Hayes: *Roman Pottery: Fine Ware Imports—Typology* (Athens, 2005)
V. Malamidou and J. W. Hedges: *Roman Pottery in Context: Fine and Coarse Wares from Five Sites in North-eastern Greece* (Oxford, 2005)
F. Seeley and J. Drummond-Murray: *Roman Pottery Production in the Walbrook Valley: Excavations at 20–28 Moorgate, City of London, 1998–2000* (London, 2005)
M. T. Marabini Moevs: *Cosa: The Italian Sigillata* (Ann Arbor, 2006)

Pozzuoli. *See* PUTEOLI.

Praeneste [now Palestrina]. Latin settlement on the southern slopes of Mt Ginestro, 36 km east of Rome, which is chiefly famous for its oracular sanctuary of Fortuna Primigenia, probably totally rebuilt in the late 2nd century BC, though perhaps after the city's destruction by Sulla in 82 BC. The sanctuary's influence continued until the 4th century AD.

1. INTRODUCTION. Praeneste stood on the main route between Etruria and Poseidonia, and finds from the late 7th-century BC Bernardini Tomb in the necropolis of La Columbella to the south of the city, including jewellery, weapons and metal bowls and cauldrons (Rome, Villa Giulia), show that it was strongly influenced by Etruscan culture. Nonetheless, a famous inscribed fibula from the contemporary Barberini Tomb in the same cemetery (Rome, Villa Giulia) indicates that a form of Latin was already spoken in the region. Fine terracotta revetments of the 6th and early 5th centuries BC imply the existence of temples at Praeneste at this date, but no remains have been identified with certainty. The next substantial finds come from tombs of the 4th to 2nd centuries BC, when the city apparently enjoyed a resurgence of wealth, and include the renowned Ficoroni Cist (*c.* 325–*c.* 300 BC; Rome, Villa Giulia; see colour pl. 1:XV, fig. 4). Praeneste was a founding member of the Latin League, and, although it defected to Rome in 499 BC, it subsequently revolted and only came under Roman domination after the League's defeat in 338 BC. In the late 2nd century BC its close commercial contacts with the East resulted in a period of great prosperity, and Praeneste continued to flourish until the Roman civil war of the 80s BC, when its backing for the Marian cause led to its sack by Sulla, who rebuilt the city and colonized it with veterans from his army.

O. Marucchi: *Guida archeologica dell'antica Preneste* (Rome, 1885); rev. 3 as *Guida archeologica della città di Palestrina* (Rome, 1932)
M. P. Muzzioli: *Praeneste*, ii, Forma Italiae, Regio 1/viii (Rome, 1970)

2. ARCHITECTURE. The earliest architectural remains at Praeneste are probably those of the 4.5 m long wall in polygonal masonry, which surrounds both town and acropolis on top of Mt Ginestro and may date back to the 7th–6th centuries BC, although its southern part was rebuilt in *opus quadratum* (large square stones laid in horizontal courses) in the 2nd century BC. The temple in the forum (partly built into the present cathedral) may have been that of Jupiter Imperator, whose image was taken to Rome in 338 BC, but otherwise the city's principal extant buildings probably date to Praeneste's period of greatest prosperity at the end of the 2nd century BC. Among them is a group of structures on rising ground on the north side of the forum. They stand on a terrace concealed for part of its length by a colonnade of limestone Doric columns, directly above which are the Corinthian columns of the lower storey of the basilica. These latter columns supported either the roof of the south aisle or a third tier of columns, which in turn supported the main roof of the basilica. The basilica had four aisles and was lit by a row of rectangular clerestory windows. Adjacent and at right angles to it was a great rectangular hall terminating in an apse, which was paved with the famous *Nile* mosaic. The interior walls of the hall are lined with statue niches flanked by Ionic half columns and pilasters on a projecting podium capped by a triglyph frieze. The lower part of the external façade was at the same level as the Doric colonnade fronting the terrace below the basilica, and above is the main door flanked by Corinthian columns on the same level as those of the basilica. Features including the Nile mosaic suggest that the hall was perhaps a temple of Isis, while the grotto on the other side of the basilica, the 'Antro delle Sorti', which was also paved in fine mosaic, may have been an Egyptian sanctuary, perhaps a temple of Serapis.

On the slope to the north was the Sanctuary of Fortuna Primigenia (totally rebuilt ?late 2nd century BC), one of the most important in Latium. The problem was to unite the two centres of the cult later described by Cicero (*On Divination*, II.xli.85–7).

These were the Temple of Fortuna, where an olive tree exuded honey, and the statue of the *Infants Jupiter and Juno Being Suckled by Fortuna*, which stood next to the place where a boy drew the lots used when the oracle was consulted. The solution was an elaborate complex (see fig.) built on a series of linked terraces, culminating in a round temple. The terraces rose immediately behind the basilica, with a double ramp leading up to the first main level of the sanctuary. Here the statue of Jupiter and Juno and the place where the lots were drawn was marked by a hemicycle of columns, but as the spot was several metres to the east of the sanctuary's main axis a similar hemicycle was built further west for the sake of symmetry. The actual place where the lots were drawn takes the form of a monopteros of seven Corinthian columns that stand on a podium capped by a triglyph frieze. The upper part of the sanctuary consists of a vast terrace closed on three sides by two rows of Corinthian columns that support a double barrel vault, and of a hemicycle of steps that form the auditorium of a theatre (diam. 59 m). Around the top of the auditorium runs a double row of Corinthian columns, behind which is the temple itself. The inspiration for the complex was probably found in the great Hellenistic terraced sanctuaries, such as those at Lindos and Kos, although at Praeneste only the columns and parts of the façades are of stone, while most of the substructures are of concrete faced in *opus incertum* (irregularly shaped small blocks).

T. Ashby: 'Classical Topography of the Roman Campagna, i: Via Praenestina', *Pap. Brit. Sch. Rome*, i (1902), pp. 125–281 (149–215)

F. Fasolo and G. Gullini: *Il santuario della Fortuna Primigenia a Palestrina*, 2 vols (Rome, 1953)

G. Gullini: 'La datazione e l'inquadramento stilistico del santuario della Fortuna Primigenia a Palestrina', *Aufstieg und Niedergang der römischen Welt*, I/iv (Berlin, 1973), pp. 746–99

L. Quilici: *La Via Praenestina* (Rome, 1977)

H. Lauter: 'Bemerkungen zur späthellenistischen Bakunst in Mittelitaliën', *Jb. Dt. Archäol. Inst.*, xciv (1979), pp. 390–459

F. Zevi: 'Il santuario della Fortuna Primigenia a Palestrina', *Prospettiva*, xvi (Jan 1979), pp. 2–22

L. Quilici: 'L'impianto urbanistico della città bassa di Palestrina', *Mitt. Dt. Archäol. Inst.: Röm. Abt.*, lxxxvii (1980), pp. 171–214

B. Coari: *Urbanistica ed architettura dell'antica praeneste: Atti del Convegno di studi archeologici, Palestrina, 16/17 aprile 1988* (Palestrina, 1989)

J. M. Merz: *Das Heiligtum der Fortuna in Palestrina und die Architektur der Neuzeit* (Munich, 2001)

S. Pittaccio: *Il foro intramuraneo a Preneste: Origini e trasformazioni* (Rome, 2001)

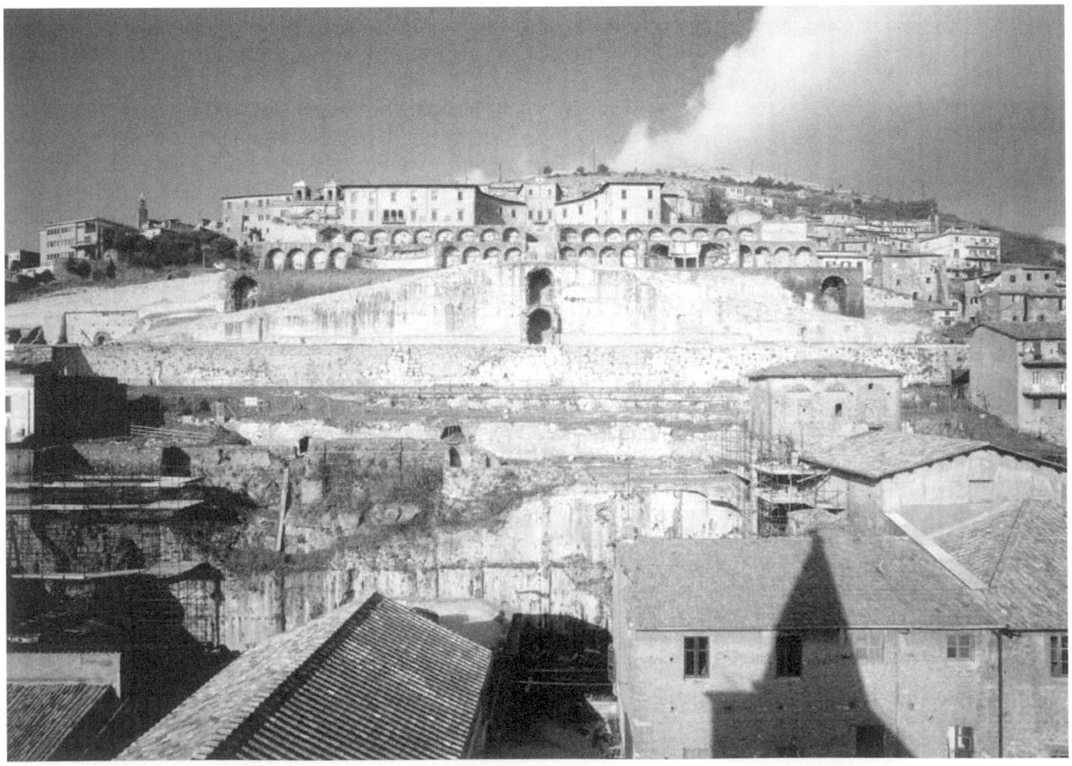

Praeneste, Sanctuary of Fortuna Primigenia, late 2nd century BC

3. Mosaics. A spectacular mosaic was found in the late 16th–early 17th century in the forum at the foot of the Sanctuary of Fortuna Primigenia, the famous *Nile* (or Barberini) mosaic (4.31×5.85 m; Palestrina, Pal. Barberini; see colour pl. 2:VIII). It was executed in the refined *opus vermiculatum* technique and decorated a grotto-nymphaeum in a complex of what were probably public buildings. The mosaic was damaged and heavily but arbitrarily restored in the 17th century, as can be seen from watercolour copies (Windsor Castle, Berks, Royal Col.) made before it was restored; some scenes were lost.

Widely varying interpretations of the mosaic have been offered. On the one hand, it has been suggested that it represents a historical event such as the arrival in Egypt of a Roman emperor, possibly Augustus or Hadrian. On the other hand, it is believed that it depicts only genre scenes. The upper arched area apparently represents Ethiopia, where the Nile rises; the wild animals are labelled with their names in Greek. In the lower part Egypt is shown at the time of the inundation, with the Nilometer (a device for measuring the rise of the Nile) at Aswan. The Temple of Osiris at Canopus near Alexandria may be identified specifically, as can the procession with the sarcophagus of Osiris at the time of the mystery of the rebirth of Osiris in the month Khoiak (symbolizing the revival of the vegetation by the flooding of the Nile), the tomb of Osiris in a grove, and a banquet of high officials that probably originally also included the Ptolemaic sovereigns.

Various dates have been suggested for the *Nile* mosaic, ranging from *c.* 80 BC to the 3rd century AD. However, the similarity of the iconography and style and of a badly damaged mosaic depicting a fishing scene found nearby with a group of mosaics from Pompeii, especially those from the House of the Faun (now Naples, Mus. Archaeol. N.), suggests that they were probably executed by the same workshop towards the end of the 2nd century BC.

The *Nile* mosaic is the earliest and the most elaborate example of an Egyptian scene in Roman Italy. It shows a wealth of accurate detail, illustrating the interest in natural history current during the Ptolemaic period (323–30 BC) and betraying a direct connection with Alexandria, the Hellenistic and Roman capital of Egypt. It is the earliest extant example of a large landscape picture convincingly rendered in perspective from a bird's-eye view. It is therefore a rare example of Hellenistic landscape painting that may be connected to the genre of Alexandrian topographical painting. The choice of the *Nile* mosaic for a public building at Praeneste, where the presiding deity was the Roman goddess Fortuna Primigenia ('first-born, Fortune'), probably reflects the wish to link Fortuna with the Greek goddess of good fortune, Tyche, who was also known as Protogeneia ('first-born') and who was closely identified, especially in Ptolemaic Alexandria, with the Egyptian goddess Isis, wife of Osiris. Isis was associated with Egypt and Osiris with the Nile, and their union regenerated nature (Plutarch, *De Iside et Osiride*, 38). The mosaic may also have been intended to emphasize the commercial relations that existed between southern Italy and Alexandria.

G. Gullini: *I mosaici di Palestrina* (Rome, 1956)

S. Aurigemma: 'Il restauro del mosaico Barberini condotto nel 1952', *Rendi. Adunanze Solenni: Accad. N. Lincei*, xxx–xxxi (1957–9), pp. 41–98

H. Whitehouse: *The Dal Pozzo Copies of the Palestrina Mosaic*, Brit. Archaeol. Rep., Suppl. Ser. xii (Oxford, 1976)

P. G. P. Meyboom: 'I mosaici pompeiani con figure di pesci', *Meded. Ned. Inst. Rome*, xxxix (1977), pp. 49–93

A. Steinmayer-Schareika: *Das Nilmosaik von Palestrina und eine ptolemäische Expedition nach Äthiopien* (Bonn, 1978)

L. Musso: 'Rilievo con pompa trionfale di Traiano al Museo di Palestrina', *Boll. A.*, lxxii (Nov–Dec 1987), pp. 1–46 [with appendix]

F. Rakob and others: 'Die Rotunde in Palestrina [mit einer Bauaufnahme und Rekonstruktion von Martin Kleibrink]', *Mitt. Dt. Archäol. Inst.: Röm. Abt.*, xcvii (1990), pp. 61–92

J. M. Merz: 'Das Fortuna-Heiligtum in Palestrina als Barberini-Villa', *Z. Kstgesch.*, lvi/3 (1993), pp. 409–50 [with appendix]

P. G. P. Meyboom: *The Nile Mosaic of Palestrina. Early Evidence of Egyptian Religion in Italy. Religions in the Graeco-Roman World*, cxxi (Leiden, New York and Cologne, 1995)

J. F. Moffitt: 'The Palestrina Mosaic with a Nile Scene: Philostratus and Ekphrasis, Ptolemy and Chorographia', *Z. Kstgesch.*, lx/2 (1997), pp. 227–47

C. Napoleone: 'A River of Stone', *F.M.R. Mag.*, lxxxviii (Oct–Nov 1997), pp. 59-90 [the Nilotic mosaic at Palestrina, with a text by Claudius Aelianus on Egyptian fauna]

C. La Malfa: 'Reassessing the Renaissance of the Palestrina Nile Mosaic', *J. Warb. & Court. Inst.*, lxvi (2003), pp. 267–71

Praetorium. General's tent pitched at the centre of the marching camps of the Roman army during the Republic. It was used as headquarters, and around it the remainder of the camp was organized. As Roman military installations became more permanent, the name was transferred to the accommodation provided for the senior officer, who in the case of a legion would have been of praetorian rank; the headquarters of fortresses and forts were separate buildings forming a self contained administrative block, the *principia* (*see* Architecture, §VI, 1(i)(c)). In legionary fortresses of the 1st and 2nd centuries AD throughout the Empire, the *praetorium* stood close to the *principia* and was an expansive courtyard-style house modelled on those in Mediterranean Roman towns, with suites of apartments arranged around a series of peristyle courts. The two *praetoria* inside the double legionary fortress of Vetera (*c.* AD 10–70) in Germany were of palatial size (110×78 m and 98×78 m) and, like the rest of the fortress, were built of stone, although neither survives. An entrance hall midway along one of the long sides led to a large atrium surrounded by rooms, which gave access to further subsidiary courtyards, while each building incorporated a long narrow track with rounded ends and a central spine for exercising horses.

These arrangements in legionary fortresses were mirrored in the far more numerous auxiliary forts, although, since their commanding officers were not of praetorian rank, their accommodation was correspondingly smaller. Most took up around 20 or 30 per cent of the available space at the centre of the fort, their scale being comparable with that of a medium-sized provincial town house. The plan of such a *praetorium* comprised several ranges of rooms around a small courtyard. The functions of individual rooms are often obscure, but several have hypocaust heating, and there are clear examples of latrines, small bath suites and kitchens. Stables may also have been provided.

The word *praetorium* also occurred in the Roman world as a place name, and an inscription from Cologne (*Corp. Inscr. Lat.*, xiii, 8170), referring to the massive palace on the banks of the Rhine, indicates that it could also signify the residence of a provincial governor of praetorian rank.

H. von Petrikovits: *Die Innenbauten römischer Legionslager während der Principätszeit* (Opladen, 1975)
A. Johnson: *Roman Forts of the 1st and 2nd Centuries AD in Britain and the German Provinces* (London, 1983)
R. Birley and others: *The 1998 Excavations at Vindolanda: The Praetorium Site: Interim Report* (Carlisle, 1999)
K. G. Holum, A. Raban, and J. Patrich: *Caesarea Papers 2: Herod's Temple, the Provincial Governor's Praetorium and Granaries, the Later Harbor, a Gold Coin Hoard, and Other Studies*, Journal of Roman Archaeology Supplementary Series 35, (Portsmouth, RI, 1999)

Praxiteles (*b* Athens, ?*c*. 400 BC; *d* Athens, *c*. 330 BC). Greek sculptor.

1. Life and work. 2. Sons of Praxiteles.

1. LIFE AND WORK. His career spanned the 370s to the 340s BC. He was the foremost Attic sculptor of the Late Classical period (*see* SCULPTURE, §IV, 2(iii)(c)), son (or possibly son-in-law or brother) and pupil of the sculptor KEPHISODOTOS and father of the sculptors Kephisodotos the younger and Timarchos. Praxiteles' affluence is attested by his practice of fashioning models for statues without having to depend on commissions and by his expensive gifts to his favourite model, the courtesan Phryne. An exceptional amount of information is imparted by the ancient sources on his private life. His elevated social position may well be representative of the status of great artists in Classical Athens. He seems to have had some freedom in choosing his own subjects, of which the Eleusinian deities, Dionysos and his companions, Aphrodite, and Apollo with Artemis and Leto predominate. He produced cult and votive statues as well as private portraits for sanctuaries in Attica, Boiotia, the Peloponnese, Ephesos, Knidos and Kos. The lack of Macedonian commissions suggests that his career had ended before Philip II's conquest of southern Greece in 338 BC. His statues were particularly admired by the Romans and many were removed to Rome. Praxiteles' career is comparatively well documented in the literary sources. Although none of his original works survives, apart from the disputed *Hermes* (Olympia, Archaeol. Mus.), several can be reconstructed from Roman copies; some attributions go as far back as the 18th century. His lost works include the cult statues of *Dionysos* at Elis, *Demeter, Kore and Iakchos* in the Temple of Demeter in Athens, the cult statues of *Apollo, Leto* and *Artemis* in Mantinea and Megara, and of *Trophonios* in Lebadeia, the sculptures on the altar of Artemis in Ephesos and a group of *Dionysos, Drunkenness and a Satyr* in Athens.

(i) Statue bases. (ii) Early works. (iii) Mature works. (iv) Late works. (v) Technique and style.

(i) Statue bases. Praxiteles' portraits are documented by three signed bases. One, found at Leuktra, carried the portrait of Thrasymachos, son of Charmides (Thebes Mus.), and two found in the Athenian Agora held portraits of women: Archippe and Kleiokrateia (Athens, Agora Mus., I 4568 and 4165). A base for two unknown statues signed by Praxiteles was found in the House of the Herm on Delos (Delos, Archaeol. Mus.), another base, once in Olbia, is now lost. Statues by Praxiteles carried to Pergamon and Rome in later periods were given new bases and labelled as his works, as attested by two bases from the Sanctuary of Athena at Pergamon (Bergama, Pergamon Mus., II 16 and II 114) and a base in the Museo Capitolino, Rome.

(ii) Early works. PAUSANIAS (*Guide to Greece* I.xx.1–2) and Athenaios (*Deipnosophists* XIII.591B) related how Praxiteles had promised a gift of his best work to Phryne but refused to name it. She therefore paid one of his slaves to give him a false report that his studio was on fire, which forced him to reveal that the pieces worth saving were the *Satyr* and the *Eros*. Phryne chose the marble *Eros*, which she dedicated in the god's sanctuary in her native town of Thespiai, while the *Satyr*, represented as a slave boy pouring Dionysos a drink, became part of a choregic dedication (perhaps set up by Praxiteles himself) in the Street of the Tripods in Athens. Both statues have been tentatively identified in two closely related types transmitted through Roman copies and dated to the 370s BC. The *Pouring Satyr* (e.g. Rome, Mus. N. Romano, 8597, restored by Alessandro Algardi (1598–1654)) represents a naked boy, with pointed ears and luxuriant hair decorated with ivy berries and tied with a band over the forehead, pouring wine from an oinochoe held over his head. His right leg is drawn back, his head bent in the direction of the weight-bearing left leg. The *Eros Farnese* (e.g. Paris, Louvre, 2266) is of the same basic type but is distinguished as Eros on account of the wings and corresponds to Kallistratos' description (*Descriptions* iii) of a bronze Praxitelean *Eros* holding a bow in the left hand, right hand over his head, weight on

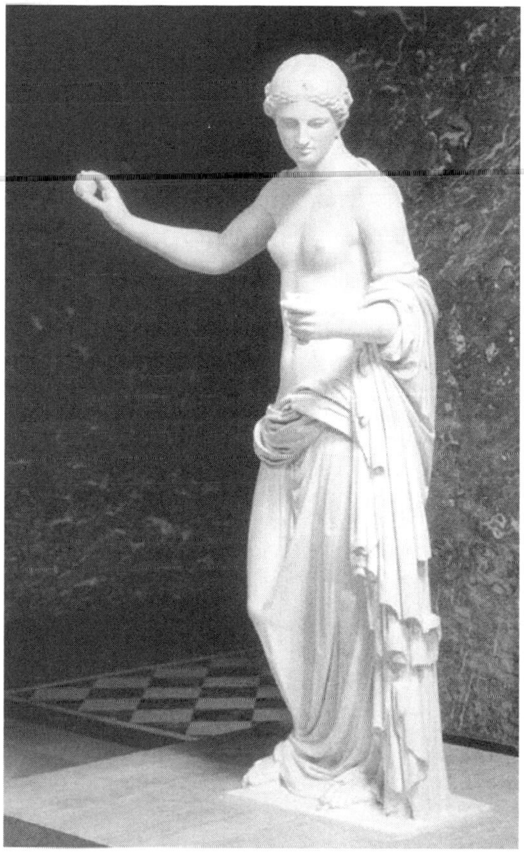

1. Praxiteles: *Aphrodite of Arles*, original 360 BC, Roman copy, marble, h. 1.94 m, late 1st century BC (Paris, Musée du Louvre)

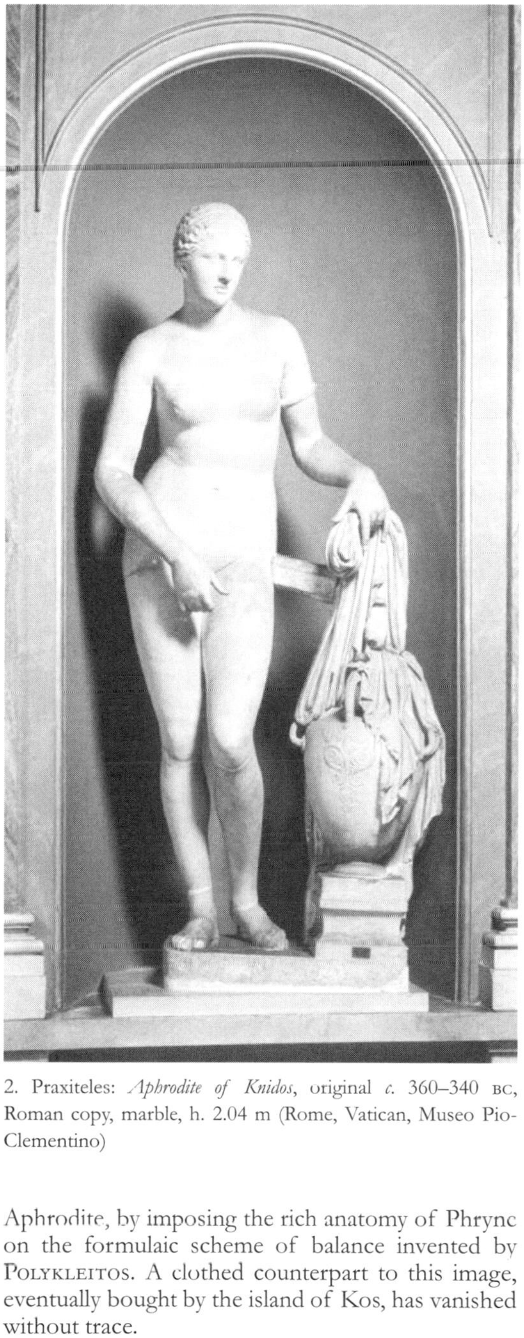

2. Praxiteles: *Aphrodite of Knidos*, original *c.* 360–340 BC, Roman copy, marble, h. 2.04 m (Rome, Vatican, Museo Pio-Clementino)

the left leg. The original *Eros* of Thespiai had its wings gilded in Roman times and was finally taken to Rome by Nero, where it perished in a fire.

Another youthful work is the *Aphrodite of Arles* (Roman copy, e.g. Paris, Louvre, 439; see fig. 1), restored by François Girardon (1628–1715), usually identified with a marble statue modelled on Phryne and also dedicated in the Sanctuary of Eros at Thespiai (Pausanias: *Guide to Greece* IX.xxvii.5). The stance is closely related to that of the *Pouring Satyr*, while the goddess is shown naked to the hips, with a cloak draped round her lower body.

(iii) Mature works. PLINY (*Natural History* XXXIV.xix.50) placed the peak of Praxiteles' career between 369 and 364 BC, the date generally assigned to his masterpiece, the marble *Aphrodite of Knidos* (copy, Rome, Vatican, Mus. Pio-Clementino; see fig. 2). The first female nude in Greek monumental sculpture, she was represented as placing her clothes on a hydria in anticipation of a bath, her right hand modestly concealing her genitals. The bracelet on her left arm betrays the courtesan Phryne as the artist's model. Praxiteles' creation excited the imagination of antiquity and inspired countless later images of Aphrodite, by imposing the rich anatomy of Phryne on the formulaic scheme of balance invented by POLYKLEITOS. A clothed counterpart to this image, eventually bought by the island of Kos, has vanished without trace.

Copies of two portraits of Phryne, one of marble at Thespiai, another of gilded bronze at Delphi, have been recognized in two Roman marble heads in Arles (Mus. Lapidaire A. Chrét.) and Athens (N. Archaeol. Mus., 1762). Their features recall the Aphrodites of Arles and Knidos.

The bronze *Apollo Sauroktonos* (Apollo the Lizard-slayer) has been identified on the basis of ancient descriptions in a boy with long hair tied with fillets, leaning against a tree and preparing to stab a lizard, which runs up its trunk (Paris, Louvre). This statue epitomizes Praxiteles' style, though its unfamiliar iconography cannot be related to any specific cult of Apollo. A mirror-image of this pose occurs in the *Leaning Satyr* (copy; Rome, Mus. Capitolino, 739). Although impossible to relate to any known work by Praxiteles, the attribution seems safe on grounds of style. The attitude of relaxation is belied by the subject's alert features, which betray an element of bestiality (also apparent in the *Apollo Sauroktonos*), while his smooth flesh contrasts sharply with the rough panther skin running diagonally across his chest. The final effect of the work relies on pictorial but subtle gradations of light.

(iv) Late works. Praxiteles' cult statue of *Artemis Brauronia* on the Athenian Acropolis has been tentatively recognized in a Roman copy from Gabii (Paris, Louvre, 529) representing a delicate girl dressed in a long *chiton* (light tunic) drawn up over her knees with two girdles and fastening her cloak at the right shoulder. The cloak is of a ceremonial type rarely shown in 4th-century BC sculpture, while the emphasis on Artemis' dress can be best explained by the importance of votive garments in her cult. Another exceptional feature of the figure is that it is designed to be viewed from several angles.

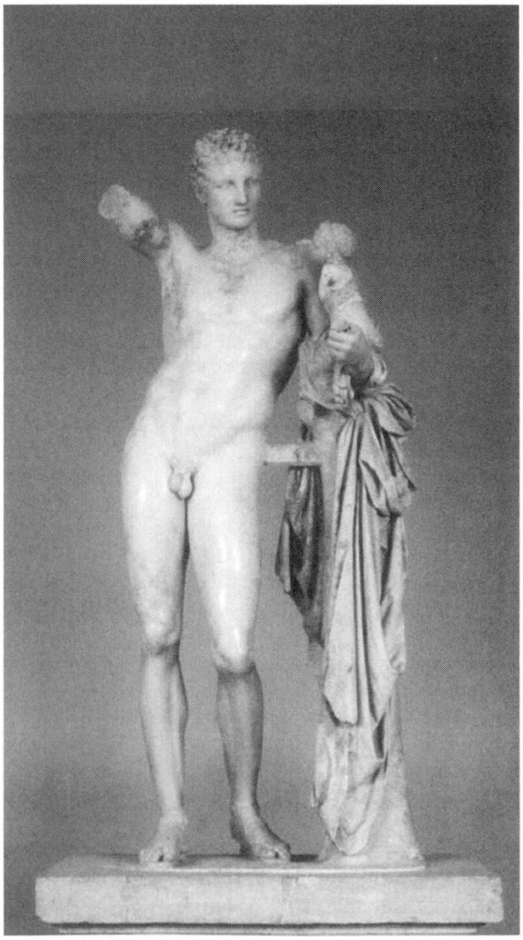

3. Praxiteles: *Hermes Holding the Infant Dionysos*, original *c.* 350 BC, Hellenistic copy, marble, h. 2.16 m (Olympia, Archaeological Museum)

Although the marble *Hermes Holding the Infant Dionysos* (Olympia, Archaeol. Mus.; see fig. 3) is easily acknowledged to be Praxitelean, its date is highly controversial. Pausanias (V.xvii.4) described it as an original by Praxiteles standing in the Temple of Hera at Olympia. It is nevertheless thought to be a late Hellenistic copy because of technical and formal details. The youthful god is shown leaning against a tree trunk covered with his cloak, playing with the baby Dionysos on his left arm, his right hand raised over his head. The expressive qualities and the sentimental overtones of the piece are striking. The dreamy features of Hermes can look either pensive or cheerful depending on the angle of vision. Although traces of red paint on the hair and sandals indicate that they were originally gilded, the nude parts are highly polished to reflect the light like bronze, and the cursory depiction of the sandal thongs as well as the rectangular strut connecting the god's thigh to the tree trunk can be more readily explained if the statue is a copy of a bronze.

(v) Technique and style. Praxiteles produced both bronze and marble sculptures, but his fame rested primarily on his expertise in marble. His heads were particularly admired (Cicero: *De Divinatione* II.xxi.48). His colossal reputation was due in part to the novelty of ideas embodied in an essentially conservative art. For example, he introduced total nudity as a means of enhancing the sensual appeal of mature goddesses; by contrast, he also showed a predilection for the playful activities of adolescent gods. He failed, however, to explore the three-dimensionality of statuary; instead, by shifting the weight of his figures on to an external support he aimed to expand his compositions laterally. His system of balance was based essentially on Polykleitan contrapposto—resulting in a rather limited repertory of pose—tempered by the blurred muscular gradations created by reflected light. The sinuous outlines and luminous surfaces of many 4th-century BC sculptures can be attributed to his influence. He relied for his effects on the contrast of textures, the playful combination of light and shade, and of human and bestial elements, and by exploiting the colouring of marble. This love of contrasts can be exemplified by his double portrait of Phryne as laughing courtesan and crying matron. But his chief contribution to Western art lies in his aesthetic exploration of female sexuality.

J. Overbeck: *Die antiken Schriftquellen zur Geschichte der bildenden Künste bei den Griechen* (Leipzig, 1868), nos. 1190–300

A. Furtwängler: *Masterpieces of Greek Sculpture* (London, 1895), pp. 307–47
E. A. Gardner: *Six Greek sculptors* (Honolulu, 1910, 2004)
G. E. Rizzo: *Prassitele* (Milan, 1932)
C. Picard: *Manuel d'archéologie grecque*, III/ii (Paris, 1948), pp. 406–632
C. Picard: *Manuel d'archéologie grecque*, IV/i (Paris, 1954), pp. 237–410
J. Marcadé: *Recueil des signatures de sculpteurs grecs*, ii (Paris, 1957), pp. 114–22
S. Adam: *The Technique of Greek Sculpture* (London, 1966), pp. 124–8
P. Gercke: *Satyrn des Praxiteles* (Hamburg, 1968)
H. Lauter: 'Zur wirtschaftlichen Position der Praxiteles-Familie im spätklassischen Athen', *Archäol. Anz.* (1980), pp. 525–31
M. Pfrommer: 'Ein Eros des Praxiteles', *Archäol. Anz.* (1980), pp. 532–44
G. Hafner: 'Die Rhea des Praxiteles', *Archäol. Anz.* (1988), pp. 63–8
H. Lauter: 'Der praxitelsche Kopf Athen, Nationalmuseum 1762', *Ant. Plast.*, xix (1988), pp. 19–21
A. Corso: *Prassitele*, i (Rome, 1988), ii (Rome, 1990), iii (Rome, 1991)
C. M. Havelock: *The Aphrodite of Knidos and her Successors: A Historical Review of the Female Nude in Greek Art* (Ann Arbor, 1995)
B. Hinz: Aphrodite: *Geschichte einer abendländischen Passion* (Munich, 1998)
S. R. Martin: *The Apollo Sauroktonos of Praxiteles* (diss., Berkeley, U. CA, 2000)
B. Geoffroy-Schneiter: 'Le Satyre Dansant: Sauve des Eaux', *Beaux-A.*, ccxxx (July 2003), pp. 48–9
A. Corso: *The Art of Praxiteles: The Development of Praxiteles' Workshop and its Cultural Tradition until the Sculptor's Acme (364–1 BC)* (Rome, 2004)

2. SONS OF PRAXITELES (*fl c.* early 3rd century BC). Greek sculptors. They are named as Kephisodotos the younger and Timarchos (Pseudo-Plutarch; 843 e–f) and apparently often collaborated. Kephisodotos was probably the elder, since in double signatures his name is given first, and Pliny (XXXIV. xix.51) named him before Timarchos when giving their floruit as the 121st Olympiad (295–292 BC). Their collaborative works include an altar near the House of Kadmos in Thebes (Pausanias: IX.xii.4) and a marble group in the Asklepieion in Kos, which was praised for its lifelike quality (Herondas: *Mimes* IV.21–34). Fragments associated with the latter include the lower half of a semi-draped female torso and part of a girl's head (Istanbul, Archaeol. Mus.); the delicate carving and *sfumato* treatment of the surfaces indicate that the sons carried on the sculptural tradition of their father. Ancient references and signed bases record a range of portrait statues: wooden representations of *Lycurgus and his Sons* in the Erechtheion (Pseudo-Plutarch: 843 e–f); *Enyo* in the Temple of Ares in Athens (Pausanias: I.viii.4); a *Priestess of Athena Polias* (*Inscr. Gr.*/2, ii–iii, 3455); *Dion and Diokleia* from Megara (*Inscr. Gr.*/1, vii, 54); and *Menander* in the Theatre of Dionysos in Athens (Pausanias. I.xxi.1). The latter's base (*Inscr. Gr.*/2, ii–iii, 3777) indicates that it was bronze, lifesize and probably seated: it was probably erected shortly after the playwright's death (291 BC) and perhaps influenced subsequent portraits of him.

Unlike Timarchos, Kephisodotos signed some works alone, indicating that he worked independently and, perhaps, earlier than his brother. He was apparently renowned for portraits and images of divinities, primarily in marble. Pliny (XXXVI.iv.24) listed several of his works: a *Leto* in the Temple of Palatine Apollo at Rome; an *Aphrodite* owned by Asinius Pollio; an *Asklepios* and *Artemis* in the Temple of Juno in the Portico of Octavia at Rome; and a group called *Symplegma* ('The grapplers') in Pergamon, highly esteemed because the statues' fingers appeared to be pressing into real flesh. Tatian (*Ad Graecos*) mentioned portraits of *Myro of Byzantium* and *Anyte of Tegea*, while statue bases record portraits of *Philylla*, priestess of the Eleusinian goddesses, at Athens (*Inscr. Gr.*/2, ii–iii, 4025); a *Priest of Apollo* at Troizen (*Inscr. Gr.*/1, iv, 766); several statues dedicated to Demeter and Kore at Eleusis (*Inscr. Gr.*/2, ii–iii, 4608, 4304); a statue from the Sanctuary of Athena Pronaia at Delphi; and a bronze from the Athenian Acropolis (*Inscr. Gr.*/2, ii–iii, 4915). Other works attributed to Kephisodotos, such as an *Artemis* and a *Seated Zeus* from Megalopolis (Pausanias, VIII. xxx.10), a group of *The Muses* on Helicon (Pausanias, IX.xxx.1) and a *Priest of Asklepios* (*Inscr. Gr.*/2, ii–iii, 4390), may well be by the elder KEPHISODOTOS, the father or brother of Praxiteles. Little is known of the younger Kephisodotos' style apart from what can be gleaned from the fragments from Kos, the comments on the Pergamon statue group, and Pliny's remark (XXXVI.iv.24) that he inherited the skill of his father.

G. Dittenberger, ed.: *Sylloge Inscriptionum Graecarum* (Leipzig, 1883, 3/1915)
M. Bieber: 'Die Söhne des Praxiteles', *Jb. Dt. Archäol. Inst.*, xxxviii–xxxix (1923–4), pp. 242–75
G. M. A. Richter: *The Sculpture and Sculptors of the Greeks* (New Haven, 1929, rev. 4/1970), pp. 206–7
J. Marcadé: *Recueil des signatures de sculpteurs grecs*, i (Paris, 1953), nos 53–9

Prepesinthos. *See* DESPOTIKON.

Priam Painter (*fl c.* 515–*c.* 500 BC). Greek vase painter. He is named after a Black-figure hydria (Madrid, Mus. Arqueol. N., 10920) depicting *Priam Setting out to Ransom the Body of Hector*. The nearly 60 vases attributed to him cover an unusually wide variety of subjects, which are sometimes accompanied by narrative inscriptions. There is compositional balance between decorated and undecorated areas, costumes and accessories are often elaborate and exotic, and horses are small and fine-boned, with little or no indication of musculature. This refinement recalls works by the ANTIMENES PAINTER and by PSIAX, who may have been his teacher: the

RYCROFT PAINTER was apparently a workshop colleague. Women are frequently depicted in scenes greatly animated by their gestures and poses: in an orchard, bathing in a grotto or fetching water at a fountain. Chariot scenes and depictions of Herakles and other heroes departing are also common, while his *Herakles Fighting Alkyoneus* and *Aeneas Carrying his Father* are among the earliest examples of these scenes. These works are related iconographically to the ANDOKIDES PAINTER and his circle, and both iconographically and compositionally to paintings by the LEAGROS GROUP. Sometimes the frame of the decorative panel interrupts the narrative elements; conversely figures sometimes overlap the frame, a device apparently designed to create elementary spatial relationships and to compete with the innovations of Red-figure painting (see colour pl. 2:VII, fig. 2).

W. G. Moon: 'The Priam Painter: Some Iconographic and Stylistic Associations', *Ancient Greek Art and Iconography* (Madison, 1983), pp. 97–118

Priene. Site in Ionia, now south-west Turkey, which flourished from the mid-4th century BC to late 2nd. It is situated on the southern slopes of Mt Mycale (now Samsun Dağı), close to the River Maeander and *c.* 16 km north of its important neighbour Miletos, which overshadowed Priene economically. An earlier (Archaic) settlement probably occupied lower ground that has since been silted over by the Maeander, but around 352 BC Priene was refounded, and its remains constitute one of the best examples of a planned ancient Greek city. Originally an independent Ionian Greek *polis*, Priene was later ruled by the Attalids of Pergamon, followed by the Romans. In the late 2nd century BC the city was destroyed by fire, although an insignificant settlement remained on the site into Byzantine times. It was rediscovered in the mid-18th century, when architects and scholars, directed by references in Vitruvius, began studying the Temple of Athena. Excavations by the German archaeologists Carl Humann and Theodor Wiegand during the 1890s uncovered about a third of the city, and in the early 21st century work on the Sanctuary of Athena is still in progress.

1. Architecture. 2. Sculpture.

1. ARCHITECTURE.

(i) City plan. Priene was laid out on the type of grid plan advocated by Hippodamos of Miletos, but the architect most closely associated with the city was PYTHEOS, who had earlier worked on the Carian National Shrine at Labraunda and the Mausoleum of Halikarnassos. According to Vitruvius (IV.iii. 1–2; VII. Preface. 12), Pytheos erected the Temple of Athena at Priene (*c.* 350–*c.* 340 BC) and wrote a book about its design, expressing his preference for the Ionic order over the Doric. His alleged assertion (Vitruvius I.i.12) that architects should have greater knowledge in all subjects than the experts in the individual disciplines reflects the great importance attached to architecture in communal life, and it may well entail a view of the ideal planned city as a 'total' work of art. Certainly, the striking regularity of Priene's ground plan and the care with which individual buildings were located suggest that it was conceived as a model city and testify to the high self-esteem that even medium-sized city-states enjoyed in the Classical period.

The new city of Priene was laid out on a south-facing slope 600 m high, which allowed the houses to receive a good deal of sunshine. The steep gradient prevented the passage of carts and made it necessary to introduce terraces and stepped streets, and large amounts of the white marble bedrock were then available as building material. In accordance with the principles of High Classical town planning, Priene was composed strictly of individual rectangular blocks based on multiples of the standard house plot. A block was equivalent to two rows of four house plots, each 30×80 ft (1 Attic or Ionian foot = 295 mm). These larger units measured 120×160 ft, giving a ratio of 3:4. The existence of 500 plots for residential houses indicates a population of about 5000.

Priene is typical of newly founded or transferred Greek cities of the period in that the plots of land were the same size and the houses were built in the same manner, so that the same architect was probably responsible for the designs of both the city plan and the standard house type. The latter represents the smallest (207 sq. m) and most modest in use at any Greek site, but this is surely connected with the limited area available on the rocky plateau.

The street grid of Priene is centred on a relatively narrow main street (w. 24 ft or 7.07 m) linking the city's east and west gates. The residential streets ran north-south and were separated by the width of one block. Their width increased progressively towards the middle of the city, reflecting the greater weight of traffic there. On either side of the central agora, which covered a large square equivalent to two blocks (200×200 ft), ran two broad thoroughfares (w. 20 ft). Next to the agora was the market, which covered an area of one block. The north side of the main street was lined with shops. In accordance with the division of land into standard areas, some blocks were set aside as sites for public buildings, including the Sanctuary of Zeus east of the agora, and, north of the agora, the bouleuterion (identification disputed; possibly an ekklesiasterion), the prytaneion, the upper gymnasium and the theatre. Although some of these building projects could not have been started at the time of Priene's foundation, there seems to have been at the outset a precise plan for each building, as part of the overall concept of the city. Evidence for this procedure exists in the case of the Temple of Zeus, which was not built until the 3rd century

BC but appears to follow plans that could only have been made in conjunction with the city's principal earlier temple, the Temple of Athena.

The original city plan for Priene seems to have determined the pattern of building there for more than 100 years, but in the 2nd century BC it was discontinued. The agora was modernized by the addition of stoas on three sides, and in several places the streets were built over. The new bouleuterion (or ekklesiasterion) erected at this time extended 2 m into the street in order to provide more seats. Similarly, when the theatre was moved and rebuilt in stone, the new building did not keep to the boundaries between blocks. The greatest changes in the city related to its domestic architecture. Because of changing social conditions large houses were created by combining adjacent dwellings, as in the well-known example of House 33, and many small houses were also built, some comprising only one or two rooms.

(ii) Buildings. The standard house plan at Priene was of the *prostas* type. This had three parts, comprising two-storey living quarters north of a central courtyard, with a one-storey shop or workshop on the south side. The main living area was a small *oikos* with a hearth, extended to the side by a subsidiary room and linked by a staircase to the sleeping quarters. The *andron* (dining-room), which was an indispensable feature of houses of the Classical period, was unusually small at Priene and inconveniently situated next to the anteroom. Directly above it was presumably the *gynaikonitis* (women's quarters). The area of the residential part is about 120 sq. m, but the courtyard (58 sq. m) and the flat roof above the subsidiary rooms could also be used for work and leisure. The shop or workshop area (*c.* 40 sq. m) may sometimes have been divided into two or three rooms. Altogether, this type of standard house plan represents a skilful use of the ground area, and the alternation of ridge roofs and flat roofs avoided the usual problems with the run-off of rain water.

The theatre (later 4th century BC in its earliest form) was constructed in the Greek style (i.e. the *cavea* or auditorium is greater than a semicircle) and seated 5000. The *cavea* was separated from the *orchestra* by a *prohedria*, a semicircular bench that incorporated an altar to Dionysos and five marble chairs for dignitaries (see fig. 1). The *skene* (see fig. 2) and *proskenion* are well preserved; from the mid-2nd century BC the roof of the *proskenion* was used for performances. The bouleuterion (20×21 m) dates from the mid-2nd century BC, and it seated *c.* 640 people. Together with the prytaneion next door it formed the administrative centre of the city. The lower

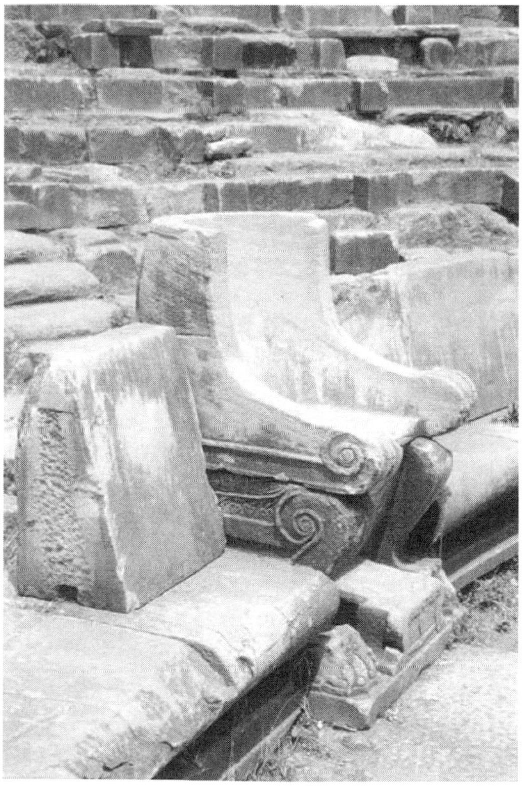

1. Priene, theatre, *prohedria*

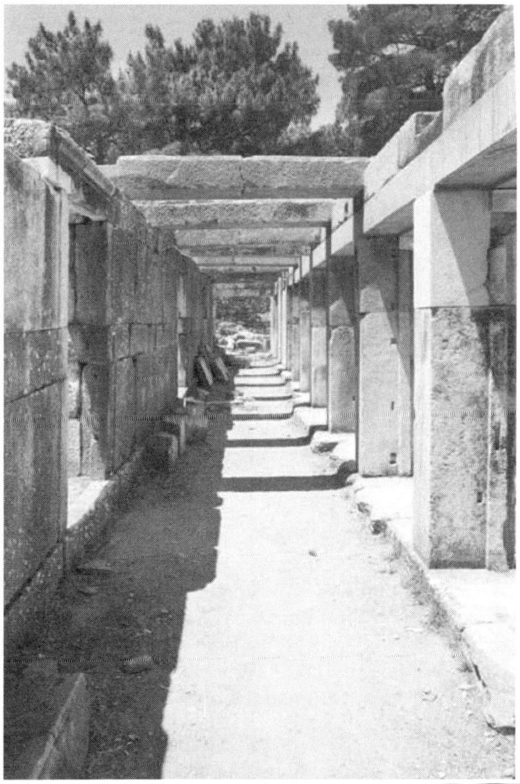

2. Priene, theatre, *skene*

gymnasium south of the agora (*c.* 130 BC) comprised a palaestra surrounded by four Doric stoas. In the north stoa an *ephebeion*, where the young men studied and practised, has walls covered with contemporary graffiti.

The Temple of Athena, designed by Pytheos, stood on a high terrace near the agora. It was a peripteral Ionic building of local white marble with a peristyle of 6×11 columns. The columns on three sides were aligned with the edges of the adjacent housing blocks, and the width of the block (120 ft) was also reflected in the distance between the columns of 12 ft. The cella was 100 ft long, making the temple a *hekatompedos* ('hundred footer'). The ratio of the lower diameters of the columns to the intercolumniations was 1:1¾, which is considerably more close set than in the much smaller Temple of Zeus with its ratio of 1:2, and became canonical for the style system advocated by Vitruvius (III.iii.2). The height of the columns was equivalent to ten lower diameters. The Temple of Athena shows, moreover, that even in the Late Classical period a plan based on a grid was used for temples as well as cities. The bases of the peristyle columns rest on plinths 6 ft square, set at intervals of 6 ft. Pytheos paid particular attention to the column bases and capitals as important architectural elements of the Ionic order. The bases have an Asiatic Ionic form and closely resemble those of the mausoleum at Halikarnassos and the Temple of Zeus at Labraunda, also possibly by Pytheos. The beautiful capitals of the Temple of Athena have a basic ratio of 3 units width, 2 units depth and 1 unit height. These proportions also occur on the Temple of Zeus at Labraunda and again in the mausoleum. The ratio 1:2:3 continued to be usual for Ionic capitals, and it applies to many Hellenistic capitals. It was adopted by Vitruvius, and it became standard throughout the Roman Imperial period.

The fact that the marble Temple of Athena was a peripteral *hekatompedos* shows that the citizens of Priene wished it to be a prestigious architectural monument. The smaller Temple of Zeus was doubtless also designed in connection with the larger temple, and its architect seems to have been particularly concerned to create a unified composition involving both buildings. This problem was again posed more than a century later at Magnesia on the Maeander, where Hermogenes' response clearly related to Pytheos' theories. The solution at Priene was not to repeat the same columnar order in a reduced form for the Temple of Zeus, since in Pytheos' view architectural elements could not simply be scaled up or down. Thus the minor elements in the Temple of Zeus, such as bases and capitals, are relatively larger than those in the Temple of Athena, and this may represent a theoretical principle according to which small buildings should have more prominent details than in large-scale architecture, which should be as unified as possible.

The Temple of Athena was the first building in Priene to be investigated when the site was rediscovered. Attention had been drawn to it by the frequent references in Vitruvius, and after it was published by the Society of Dilettanti (*Ionian Antiquities*, i, 1769, London) the temple became an influential point of reference in the development of the neo-Classical movement in Europe.

T. Wiegand and H. Schrader: *Priene: Ergebnisse der Ausgrabungen und Untersuchungen in den Jahren 1895–1898* (Berlin, 1904)
A. von Gerkan: *Das Theater von Priene* (Munich, 1921)
M. Schede: *Die Ruinen von Priene* (Berlin, 1934, 2/1964)
W. Koenigs: 'Der Athenatempel von Priene', *Istanbul. Mitt.*, xxxiii (1983), pp. 134–75
W. Hoepfner and E. L. Schwandner: *Haus und Stadt im klassischen Griechenland* (Munich, 2/1994), pp. 141–86
F. Rumscheid and W. Koenigs: *Priene: A Guide to the 'Pompeii of Asia Minor'* (Istanbul, 1999)
S. Patronos: *Public Architecture and Civic Identity in Classical and Hellenistic Ionia: The Cases of Miletus and Priene* (diss., U. Oxford, 2002)
C. Schneider: 'Poseidon und sein Volk: Die Ionier feierten ihre Gemeinschaft im Heiligtum des Poseidon Helikonios bei Priene (Turkei)', *Ant. Welt*, xxxv/3 (2004), pp. 17–24
K. Ferla, F. Graf and A. Sideris: *Priene* (Athens, 2005)

2. SCULPTURE. The extant sculpture from Priene comes almost entirely from the Sanctuary of Athena. The excavations of the Society of Dilettanti carried out by Richard Popplewell Pullan in 1868–9 produced rich finds, immediately sent to the British Museum, London. Additional pieces made their way to Berlin (Pergamonmus.) and Istanbul (Archaeol. Mus.) after Wiegand and Schrader's excavations in the 1890s. A few more (now Miletos, Archaeol. Mus.) have been uncovered since 1965. When this scattered material was finally studied as a whole (Carter), it led to a radical reappraisal of the sculpture of Priene.

The reliefs from the Temple of Athena comprise 65 fragments and have been recognized as belonging to lids for the 26 deep coffers of a ceiling above the peristyle. (They had earlier been variously assigned to a hypothetical external frieze, a balustrade inside the temple, or even the altar.) They represent a *Gigantomachy*, with several additional figures of Amazons. Close stylistic comparison with the friezes of the mausoleum strongly suggests that the Priene reliefs were executed by some of the same sculptors, although previously they had been thought to recall the *Gigantomachy* on the Great Altar of Zeus at Pergamon (*c.* 170 BC). They belong, however, to the first phase of the Temple of Athena, executed under Pytheos' supervision between *c.* 350 and *c.* 340 BC. The coffer reliefs rank with the best work of the Late Classical period, and they surpass all in the boldness of their three-dimensional compositions.

Numerous marble fragments of an acrolithic cult statue of Athena were found in the ashy fill of the temple's cella (London, BM), together with two gilded wings of a *nike* figure resembling that held by Pheidias' *Athena Parthenos*. The measurements suggest that the Priene *Athena* was approximately two-thirds the size of the *Parthenos*, and an image of this statue type appears on coins of the Roman period from Priene. Previously assigned to the mid-2nd century BC, as were the coffer reliefs, the Priene *Athena* is in fact more likely to date from the second half of the 4th century BC, when its base appears to have been carved. If so, it would be the earliest extant replica of Pheidias' masterpiece, as well as by far the largest.

The sculptural decoration of the altar to the east of the temple can be reconstructed on the basis of two relief panels (3rd century BC); one represents a standing draped female figure (Berlin, Antikensamml.), the other shows the seated Muse, *Urania* (Istanbul, Archaeol. Mus.), one of the largest and earliest versions of a much-copied presumed original. A third relief representing *Apollo Playing the Lyre* is now lost but is known from Pullan's photographic record (see Carter). The altar itself was a low structure, originally adorned with a cycle of ten such relief panels, together representing *Apollo and the Muses*. Many portraits were erected in the Sanctuary of Athena, as surviving inscriptions attest. There are over 100 fragments in the British Museum, London, including an over life-size female head in the same style and marble as a Hekatomnid portrait from the Mausoleum at Halikarnassos (London, BM). Found in the cella together with the remains of the cult statue, it has been identified as *Ada*, the Hekatomnid princess, a likely benefactress of Priene and the adoptive mother of the first dedicator of the Temple of Athena, Alexander the Great (second half of the 4th century BC). The temple was rededicated to the Emperor Augustus and Athena, probably in the late 1st century BC, and at the same time became an imperial cult place. This would explain the presence in the cella of portraits of the *Emperor Claudius* (London, BM) and other Romans, possibly even including an early provincial portrait of *Julius Caesar* (London, BM).

Antiquities of Ionia IV (London, 1881)
J. C. Carter: *The Sculpture of the Sanctuary of Athena Polias at Priene* (London, 1983) [with bibliog.]
I. Jenkins: *Greek Architecture and its Sculpture* (New York, 2006)

Pronaos. Inner room before the naos in a temple.

Pronomos Painter (*fl c.* 410–*c.* 390 BC). Greek vase painter. He was an exponent of the florid style of Athenian vase painting of the late 5th century BC and early 4th, and he is named after the flute player Pronomos (*fl c.* 400–*c.* 380 BC) depicted on a large volute krater (Naples, Mus. Archeol. N., 3240; see fig.). The Pronomos Painter may have been a pupil of both the Dinos Painter and the Kadmos Painter, and his style is particularly close to that of the Painter of Louvre G 433, with whom he collaborated on one vase (Berlin, Staatl. Mus., 2642). The Painter of Vienna 1089 must have been his pupil. The Pronomos Painter decorated at least one volute krater, two bell kraters and a squat lekythos, and his later works probably included a pelike (Athens, N. Archaeol. Mus., 1333), a calyx krater (Genoa, Mus. Osp. Civ., 1911.163) and a hydria (San Simeon, CA, Hearst State Hist. Mnmt). His subject-matter can be mythological, Dionysiac or even theatrical, for his name-vase shows the actors, chorus and poet of a satyr-play. The florid style in which he worked is exemplified by the depiction of garments richly ornamented with enscrolled palmettes, rosettes or asterisks and by the considerable use of white and golden dilute glaze. His treatment of the male torso in three-quarter view and of the head in profile is also characteristic.

A. Furtwängler and K. Reichhold, eds: *Griechische Vasenmalerei*, iii (Munich, 1932), pp. 132–50 [contribution by E. Buschor]
J. D. Beazley: *Red-figure* (1942, 2/1963), ii, pp. 1336–7
F. Brommer: 'Zur Deutung der Pronomosvase', *Archäol. Anz.* (1964), pp. 109–14
E. Simon: 'Die "Omphale" des Demetrios', *Archäol. Anz.* (1971), pp. 199–206

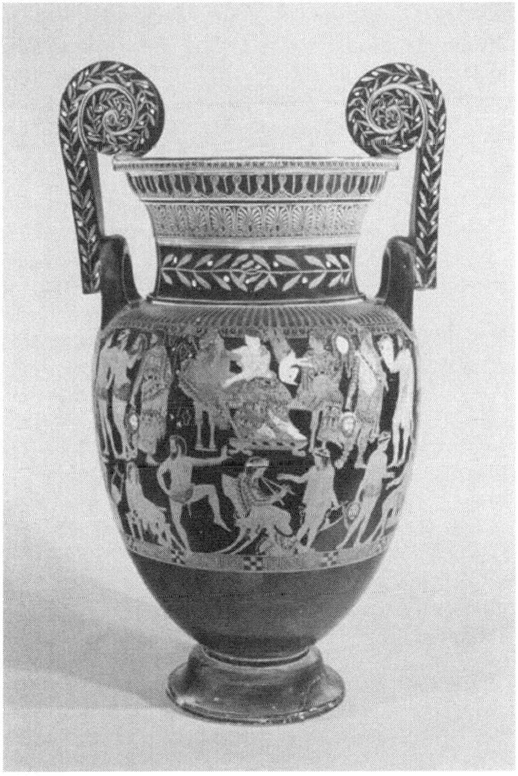

Pronomos Painter: volute krater depicting preparations for a satiric drama, Attic Red-figure, *c.* 410–*c.* 390 BC (Naples, Museo Archeologico Nazionale, 81673)

W. Real: *Studien zur Entwicklung der Vasenmalerei im ausgehenden 5. Jahrhundert v. Chr.* (Münster, 1973)

I. McPhee: 'Turin 4122 and the Pronomos Painter', *Amer. J. Archaeol.*, lxxxii (1978), pp. 551–3

B. Shefton: 'The Krater from Baksy', *The Eye of Greece*, eds D. Kurtz and B. Sparkes (Cambridge, 1982), pp. 149–81

M. Robertson: *The Art of Vase-Painting in Classical Athens* (Cambridge, 1992), pp. 255–9

S. Drougou: 'Krieg und Frieden im Athen des Spaten 5. Jahrhunderts v. Chr.: Die Rotfigurige Hydria aus Pella', *Mitt. Dt. Archäol. Inst.: Athen. Abt.*, cxv (2000), pp. 147–216

Propylon [Gr.: 'gateway'; pl. *propylaia*; Lat. *propylaeum*, pl. *propylaea*]. Ancient Greek monumental gateway, originally to a religious sanctuary; the term was later also applied to civic buildings. The simpler type of propylon consisted of an outer and an inner porch separated by a wall; in the most elementary examples the porches were linked by a single opening. More elaborate gateways, also known as propylaia, had three or more doorways.

Early examples of the propylon occurred in Bronze Age Minoan and Mycenaean palaces. After a long hiatus, and without any evidence of continuity, they reappeared in Archaic times. One propylon (*c.* 625 BC; *c.* 10×5 m), at the Sanctuary of Hera on Samos, consisted of a passage flanked by two rooms on either side with no trace of a door. The early 6th-century BC entrance to the Sanctuary of Aphaia on Aigina probably had two wooden columns *in antis*. It was, however, replaced in the 490s BC by a building of similar plan (7.32×6.25 m) with octagonal stone columns, so slender that they must have carried a wooden architrave. The slighty later 'Old Propylon' on the Athenian Acropolis (*c.* 480 BC) was built on two levels and probably had four Doric columns *in antis* and five gateways, though it was never finished. Another Doric propylon at the Sanctuary of Poseidon at Sounion (440s BC; 13.5×9 m; see fig.), again in Attica, was also on two levels, linked by a single step (a). It was, however, distyle *in antis* and had three doorways, including a central opening approached by a ramp for sacrificial animals. A ramp was also incorporated in the Propylaia on the Athenian Acropolis (437–432 BC), the first building in Classical Greece to accommodate several different units with their respective functions (*see* ATHENS, *§II, 1(i),* and MNESIKLES). Its central element, the gatehouse proper (23.84×21.12 m), again linked two levels, with five steps and five doorways. Its porches each had six prostyle Doric columns, though the deep outer porch also incorporated an inner colonnade of 3×2 Ionic columns. The building was to have been flanked by extensive wings, giving it a total width of 68.16 m, but these were never completed.

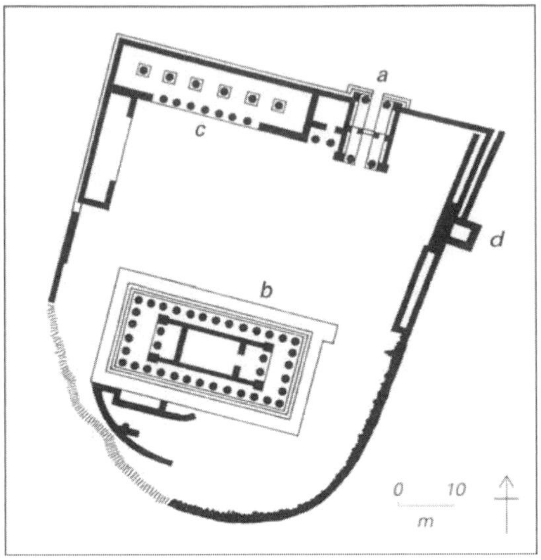

Sanctuary of Poseidon, Sounion, 440s BC, plan: (a) propylon; (b) temple; (c) stoas; (d) bastion

The Hellenistic propylon (*c.* 285–281 BC) dedicated by Ptolemy II (*reg* 285–246 BC) at the Sanctuary of the Great Gods on Samothrace originally doubled as a bridge over a river. Its hexastyle porches were of different architectural orders, the eastern one being Ionic, the western providing what may be the earliest example of the external use of Corinthian columns. At Pergamon the two columns of the outer porch of the propylon to the Sanctuary of Demeter (early 2nd century BC) had Pergamene leaf capitals. Its inner porch, however, had no columns but simply steps leading to a lower level. A novel plan was employed in the so-called Lesser Propylaia at Eleusis (*c.* 54 BC). This had a paved forecourt (10.35×9.80 m) flanked by walls with engaged Ionic columns. The outer porch had two prostyle Corinthian columns, while the inner had two caryatids; the entablatures of both porches combined Doric and Ionic features. The entrance was flanked by niches, those on the outside perhaps for statues, the inner ones containing fountains.

By the late 3rd or 4th century AD, propylaia had generally been superseded by fortified gates.

J. R. Carpenter: *The Propylon in Greek and Hellenistic Architecture* (Ann Arbor, 1979)

V. Lambrinoudakis: *The Propylon of the 'Gymnasium' and the Tholos in the Asklepieion at Epidauros* (Athens, 1988)

G. Gruben: 'Naxos und Delos: Studien zur archaischen Architektur der Kykladen', *Jb. Dt. Archäol. Inst.*, cxii (1997), pp. 261–416

M. M. Miles: 'The Propylon to the Sanctuary of Demeter Malophoros at Selinous', *Amer. J. Archaeol.*, cii (Jan 1998), pp. 35–57

C. Piok Zanon: *The Propylon to the Sanctuary of Demeter at Pergamon* (diss., U. Pittsburgh, 2000)

Prostyle. Term applied to a building with a row of columns or portico at the front end only.

Protogenes (*fl* Rhodes, late 4th century BC). Greek painter and bronze sculptor. He came from Kaunos in Caria, a city dominated by Rhodes in his day, or perhaps from Xanthos in Lycia. He had no known master, and none of his works survives. He painted ships, perhaps their ensigns, before he became a panel painter at the age of 50. APELLES appreciated his talent and promoted his pictures. He held Protogenes to be his equal in all aspects of art except one: he did not know when to stop working on a picture, and consequently his paintings lacked grace. His extreme diligence is the point of many anecdotes about him. His most famous painting was a depiction of *Ialysos*, the eponymous founder of that city on Rhodes. Ialysos was accompanied by a dog and so was perhaps represented as a hunter. The story is told that the foam on the dog's mouth caused the artist so much trouble that, enraged, he threw his sponge at the picture. The sponge struck the dog's mouth and achieved exactly the natural appearance the artist wanted. The *Ialysos* took seven or, in one account, eleven years to complete. Pliny (*Natural History* XXXV.102) added the curious detail that Protogenes applied four layers of colour, so that as one wore away or was damaged, another would take its place. Apelles stood speechless before the painting, and its reputation saved Rhodes. The Macedonian ruler Demetrios Poliorketes (*reg* 294–288 BC) besieged the city in 305 BC and would have destroyed it but was won over by the Rhodians' appeal to spare not so much their city as the *Ialysos*. Cicero (*Orator* II.5) and Strabo reported seeing the painting in Rhodes; Pliny (*Natural History* XXXV.102) saw it in the temple of Peace in Rome, where it was subsequently destroyed in a fire. Protogenes also painted a *Satyr Playing Pipes and Leaning against a Stele*, which included a partridge perched on the stele. However, as the bird won greater fame for its naturalism than the satyr, he painted it out of the picture. He also painted various portraits of heroes and celebrated contemporaries and was commissioned to decorate public buildings at Athens: a picture of *Law Makers* in the bouleuterion and a picture of *Paralos and Hammonias*, personifications of state triremes, in which small warships appeared in the background, in the Pinakotheke of the Propylaia.

J. Overbeck: *Die antiken Schriftquellen zur Geschichte der bildenden Künste bei den Griechen* (Leipzig, 1868/*R* Hildesheim, 1959), nos 803, 806–7, 1067, 1093, 1687, 1840–41, 1897, 1904, 1907–36

Prudentius (, Aurelius Clemens) (*b* ?Saragossa, AD 348; *d c.* AD 410). Spanish writer. Born into a good family, he gave up a successful career in the civil administration to devote himself to the dissemination of Christian doctrine through his Latin Christian poetry and hymns. Loyalty to the Church, however, failed to quench his admiration for Ancient Rome or an awareness of beauty in pagan art forms. His *Peristephanon*, a series of lyrics inspired by veneration for the martyrs of Spain and Rome, offers valuable descriptions of Roman catacombs and churches (e.g. St Peter's, S Paolo fuori le Mura, the basilica near the grave of Hippolytus and the Lateran baptistery) together with their marbles, painting and mosaics.

Prytaneion [Gr.: 'town hall']. Type of civic structure built in most ancient Greek towns around the 7th to the 4th century BC, although the first prytaneion in Athens was probably built in the 9th–8th century BC. It served as a place where official guests dined at the expense of the state, as a law court, a social welfare institution, an archive office and a place of asylum. Its religious significance stemmed from the presence in it of the perpetual fire of the goddess Hestia, which symbolized the existence of the city.

Prytaneia are referred to in inscriptions in more than 100 Greek city-states. There are, however, only three excavated examples of a securely identified prytaneion: on the island of Delos (?early 5th century BC), at Lato on Crete (late 4th century BC) and at Olympia (early 5th century BC). These examples make it clear that this building type had more diversity of plan than, for example, a peripteral temple. Its general features are not unlike those of a house, albeit on a grander scale. Central to the building was a room for the hearth of Hestia with its flame, where sacrifices were offered on behalf of the city-state. The dining-room, perhaps of equal significance in the plan and certainly more easily detectable, was lined with mattress-covered couches upon which reclined the official guests. Ancient sources also indicate that the plan of the prytaneion included a courtyard, rooms for state archives and storage space. Movable objects included statues of distinguished citizens, such as those of Miltiades and Themistokles in the prytaneion at Athens (Pausanias: *Guide to Greece*, I.xviii.3).

The prytaneion was normally located on or near the agora, where it was most accessible. In some cases, however, circumstances required that the immutable hearth of the prytaneion (and hence the building itself) remain in its original location when the agora was moved away. In Athens, for example, the expanded agora north of the Areopagos was some distance from its original location, and a special building, the tholos (officially called the prytanikon or magistrates' hall), was constructed to fulfil some of the functions normally confined to the prytaneion.

S. G. Miller: *The Prytaneion: Its Function and Architectural Form* (Berkeley, Los Angeles and London, 1978)

M. H. Hansen and T. Fischer-Hansen, 'Monumental Political Architecture in Archaic and Classical Greek *Poleis*: Evidence and Historical Significance', *Hist. Einzelschr.*, 87 (1994), pp. 30–37

G. C. R. Schmalz: 'The Athenian Prytaneion Discovered?', *Hesperia*, lxxv/1 (Jan–March 2006), pp. 33–81

Pseira. Minoan town on an island of the same name off the north-east coast of Crete, in the Gulf of Mirabello; it was first excavated by Richard Seager in 1906–7. A Minoan settlement was already established there by the Early Minoan (EM) period; it expanded during the Middle Minoan (MM) period, reaching its largest size in Late Minoan (LM) I, at the end of which period it was destroyed by fire. (For discussion of the absolute dates associated with Minoan chronological periods *see* MINOAN, §4).

The buildings on Pseira were of local stone. Paved lanes and tall staircases divided the town into blocks of houses that followed the topography. Some houses were large and massively built, occupying several terraces on the slope of the hill, while others were more compact; most were two storeys high. One of the finest, the Building of the Pillar Partitions, had an inner court and an L-shaped wall of alternating pillars and doorways, so that the entire wall could be closed off or opened to admit a maximum of light and air to an area with a sunken bathtub. In Pseira's shrine was a fine relief fresco (LM I; Herakleion, Archaeol. Mus.) depicting seated female figures in elaborate costumes. Several ceramic and stone vases have also been recovered from the site. Among the stone objects are a fine rhyton in an attractive red breccia, perhaps made on the island itself (LM IB; Herakleion, Archaeol. Mus.). Several of the pottery vases from the LM IB period are among the best known examples of their class: two standing bulls in a naturalistic style (Herakleion, Archaeol. Mus.), a set of twin pear-shaped rhyta decorated with leaping dolphins (Philadelphia, U. PA, Mus.; Herakleion, Archaeol. Mus.) and several Marine style vases (*see* POTTERY, §I, 5(i)) decorated with argonauts and other designs inspired by the sea (Herakleion, Archaeol. Mus. and Siteia Mus.).

R. B. Seager: *Excavations on the Island of Pseira, Crete* (Philadelphia, 1910)

J. Leatham and S. Hood: 'Sub-marine Exploration in Crete, 1955', *Annu. Brit. Sch. Athens*, liii–iv (1958–9), pp. 263–80

P. P. Betancourt: *Minoan Objects Excavated from Vasilike, Pseira and Other Sites*, i of *The Cretan Collection in the University Museum, University of Pennsylvania* (Philadelphia, 1983–91)

A. Davaras, P. P. Betancourt and W. R. Farrand: 'Pseira', *The Aerial Atlas of Ancient Crete*, ed. J. W. Myers, E. E. Myers and G. Cadogan (Berkeley, 1992), pp. 260–65

P. P. Betancourt and others: *Pseira,* 8 vols (Philadelphia, 1995–2004)

Pseudo-Dipteral. Term applied to a building that appears to have an arrangement of surrounding columns like a dipteral temple, but with only a single outer row of columns, the inner row being omitted and thus leaving a wide space around the inner cella.

Pseudo-Peripteral. Term applied to a building that appears to be surrounded by a row of free-standing columns, although these are actually engaged or attached to the wall.

Psiax [Menon Painter] (*fl c.* 525–*c.* 510 BC). Greek vase painter. He played an important role in the transition from Attic Black-figure to Red-figure. Formerly called the Menon Painter, after the potter's signature on a Red-figure amphora (Philadelphia, U. PA, Mus., 5349), he signed two Red-figure alabastra as painter, both of which bear the signature of the potter Hilinos (Karlsruhe, Bad. Landesmus., 242 (B 120) and Odessa, A. Mus.).

Psiax was an experimenter who mastered several vase-painting techniques, including Black-figure, and variants with White-ground or coral-red glaze, Six's technique and Red-figure. Fewer than 60 works are attributed to him, and these include large vases (e.g. amphorae, hydriai and calyx kraters) and small vases (cups, an aryballos, alabastra, a lekythos, kyathoi, a mastos and plates).

His attractive miniatures recall Black-figure work by the AMASIS PAINTER, who may have been his teacher. Signatures of the potter Andokides on two of his amphorae (London, BM; see colour pl. 2:VII, fig. 3; Madrid, Mus. Arqueol. N.) attest to his connection with the workshop that produced the earliest Red-figure and bilingual vases, and where Psiax worked beside the ANDOKIDES PAINTER. He clearly painted both the Red-figure and Black-figure monumental compositions on his stiffly formal bilingual amphora (Munich, Staatl. Antikensamml., 2302 (J. 373)). The Red-figure scene shows *Dionysos Reclining Between a Dancing Maenad and Satyr*; the Black-figure one, *Iolaos Steadying Herakles' Chariot.* The latter has a *kalos* inscription praising Hippokrates, and elsewhere Psiax praised Aischis, Karystios and Smikrion. Unusually in Red-figure, Psiax's inscriptions are always incised.

He favoured Dionysiac subjects, as on his Black-figure kyathos (Milan, Mus. Poldi Pezzoli, 482), and the exploits of Herakles, for example *Herakles and the Nemean Lion* (Black-figure amphora, Brescia, Mus. Civ. Età Romana), *Herakles with Amazons* (Red-figure aryballos, ex-Bologna, Mus. Civ. Archeol., PU 322), or *Herakles with a Horse of Diomedes* (coral-red cup, St Petersburg, Hermitage). Horses appear in Psiax's best large compositions. Two amphorae, in Brescia and Philadelphia (U. PA, Mus., 5399), show *Horses Led by Youths in Thracian Dress.* The stately chariot-harnessing scene on a hydria (destr.) was Psiax's monumental Black-figure masterpiece. A similar, but livelier, hydria scene (Hartford, CT, Wadsworth Atheneum) recalls the ANTIMENES PAINTER, whom J. D. Beazley termed 'Psiax's brother'.

Psiax's paintings on both Red-figure and Black-figure small vases share the same imagery and delicate, sinuous, vivid draughtsmanship. He combined fine design with sensitivity to colour, as on the perfectly composed tondo of his Red-figure cup showing *A Young Archer in Scythian Dress Grasping the Reins of a Red-maned Horse* (New York, Met., 14.146.1). The warriors' spears on the outside are white with black incised heads. Elsewhere Psiax even added objects in clay relief, and he was among the first Red-figure painters to reserve hair contours. The anatomy of the warriors on his New York cup is detailed, with limbs twisting, shields shown in profile and three-quarter view, and one warrior falling in back view. This interest in anatomy and space anticipates the Pioneer group, and indeed, PHINTIAS and EUPHRONIOS may have been his pupils. Archer, trumpets and warrior recur on Black-figure plates (London, BM) where Psiax retreated to a charmingly old-fashioned decorative realm.

H. R. W. Smith: *New Aspects of the Menon Painter* (Berkeley, 1929)
G. M. A. Richter: 'The Menon painter = Psiax', *Amer. J. Archaeol.*, xxxviii (1934), pp. 547–54
J. D. Beazley: *Red-figure* (1942, 2/1963), i, pp. 6–8; ii, pp. 1617–18
J. D. Beazley: *Black-figure* (1956), pp. 292–5, 692
P. E. Arias and M. Hirmer: *Tausend Jahre griechischer Vasenkunst* (Munich, 1960); Eng. trans. and rev. by B. Shefton as *A History of Greek Vase Painting* (London, 1962), pp. 304–5
J. D. Beazley: *Paralipomena* (1971), pp. 127–8, 321
J. Boardman: *Athenian Black Figure Vases: A Handbook* (London, 1974), p. 106
J. Boardman: *Athenian Red Figure Vases: The Archaic Period* (London, 1975), pp. 17–18
B. Cohen: *Attic Bilingual Vases and Their Painters* (New York, 1978), pp. 194–239, 276–87
J. R. Mertens: 'Some New Vases by Psiax', *Ant. Kst*, xxii (1979), pp. 22–37
L. Burn and R. Glynn: *Beazley Addenda: Additional References to* ABV, ARV2 *and* Paralipomena (Oxford, 1982, rev. T. H. Carpenter, 2/1989), pp. 76–7, 150–51
B. Jeske and C. Stein: 'Eine frührotfigurige Hydria des Psiax', *Hefte des Archäologischen Seminars der Universität Bern* 8 (1982), pp. 5–20
M. Robertson: *The Art of Vase-painting in Classical Athens* (Cambridge, 1992), pp. 9, 12–17, 34, 42, 51
M. B. Moore: *Attic Red-figured and White-ground Pottery, The Athenian Agora*, xxx (Princeton, 1997), pp. 83–5, 343
P. Pelletier-Hornby: 'Deux aspects de Psiax dans la collection Dutuit du Petit Palais (Musée des Beaux-Arts de la Ville de Paris)', *Rev. Louvre,* 1/4 (Oct 2000), pp. 27–37, 117

Pteron. *See* PERISTYLE.

Ptolemais [Arab. Tolmeita; Tolmeta; Tulmaythah]. Hellenistic and Roman city in Cyrenaica, Libya, the only natural harbour between Eusperides-Berenice (now Benghazi) and Apollonia (now Susa). It was probably founded in the reign of Ptolemy III Euergetes (246–221 BC), although the site had been used as the port of nearby Barca since the 6th century BC. Ptolemais came under Roman control in 96 BC and under Diocletian (*reg* AD 284–305) became the capital of Libya Pentapolis. Its buildings extend the whole width of a fertile, 2 km-wide coastal plain, bounded to the south by the foothills of the Jabal al-Akhdar (the Green Mountain).

There are traces of the Hellenistic grid plan with at least five transverse streets (*decumani*) intersected by two main longitudinal ones (*cardines*), enclosing blocks measuring 180×36 m. Most of the major streets are 8.8 m wide, but the principal thoroughfare, the Street of the Monuments, is 14.8 m wide including the colonnades either side. The city walls, as is so often the case, are unrelated to the street-plan. They are punctuated by square towers and extend from the sea to the Jabal, where they enclose a commanding triangle of high ground. There were probably seven gates in the circuit, of which the best preserved is the Taucheira gate, flanked by two massive square towers with finely drafted masonry.

The water supply was assured in early Roman times by a complex of vaulted cisterns enclosed within a platform measuring 65.85×70.60 m, framed by Doric colonnades on three sides. Traces of a Hadrianic aqueduct have been found to the east of the city (*c.* AD 117–38). The best-known monument to survive is the 'Palace of the Columns', a magnificent peristyle house with a columnar Egyptian-style central room paved in fine mosaic; it may date to the 1st century BC, although it was enlarged in the early Imperial period. The upper part of the north side of the peristyle has broken and hollow pediments, features of the so-called Hellenistic Baroque. The house is often regarded as reflecting the grand domestic architecture of Alexandria. To the west is the Roman Villa, another fine peristyle house (1st century AD).

Ptolemais was prosperous in Roman times to judge by the hippodrome and the amphitheatre (?2nd century AD). This prosperity continued into the Late Empire, perhaps after the city became the provincial capital. The Street of the Monuments was colonnaded and framed by a triple arch at the west end and the Byzantine tetrapylon at the east. A former odeion or bouleuterion was transformed into an aquatic theatre, probably in the course of the 4th century AD, and at the same time the public baths were rebuilt. A three-apsed audience hall (the triconchos) was added to an old peristyle house, perhaps when it became the residence of the governor of Libya Pentapolis. In the same period a pair of 1st-century AD buildings were joined to form the house and adjacent offices of Paul, a man of consular rank.

In the early 5th century AD the incursions of desert tribesmen, recorded by Synesius, bishop of Ptolemais, caused great problems. The upper theatre was looted, and a Byzantine theatre was built in a less vulnerable position on the plain. At the same time much of the perimeter wall was demolished to build the forts and defensible buildings. A particularly noteworthy late building is the fortified basilica with an inscribed apse (5th century AD).

G. Pesce: *Il Palazzo delle Colonne in Tolmaide di Cirenaica* (Rome, 1950)
C. H. Kraeling: *Ptolemais: City of the Libyan Pentapolis* (Chicago, 1962)
C. Arthur and A. Bazama: 'The Aqueduct at Ptolemais', *Libya Ant.*, xi–xii (1975), pp. 243–9

G. W. W. Barker, J. Lloyd and J. Reynolds: *Cyrenaica in Antiquity*, BAR International Series (Oxford, 1985)

J. B. Ward-Perkins and others: 'Town Houses at Ptolemais', *Libyan Stud.*, xvii (1986), pp. 109–53

Cyrène, Apollonia, Ptolemais: Sites prestigieux de la Libye antique (Dijon, 1992)

R. Polidori and others: *La Libye antique: Cités perdues de l'Empire romain* (Paris, 1998)

Public monument. *See* MONUMENT, PUBLIC.

Pula. *See* POLA.

Punic art. Term applied to the civilization of the city of CARTHAGE on the north coast of Africa and its colonies in the western Mediterranean and on the Atlantic coasts of North Africa and Spain during the 1st millennium BC. Carthage was founded by the Phoenician people, traditionally in 814/813 BC by the exiled princess Elissa (also known as Dido) from Tyre (now in the Lebanon); this date is widely accepted, although excavations have not revealed any material earlier than the 8th century BC. Carthage became the catalyst for Phoenician power in the western Mediterranean and developed rapidly. The city successfully countered Greek colonization in the west and established a first colony at Ibiza in 654/653 BC; this was soon followed by others in Sardinia and western Sicily. In the 6th century BC the political and economic expansion of Carthage led to a cultural boom in which its colonies participated, particularly Tharros in Sardinia and Motya (now Mozia) in Sicily. Later there were successive wars directed against the Greek settlers in Sicily, and in 264 BC the first of three Punic Wars between Carthage and Rome began, eventually leading to the destruction of Carthage in 146 BC. Nevertheless, Punic art survived in its Neo-Punic form.

1. Architecture. 2. Sculpture and terracottas. 3. Pottery. 4. Metalwork. 5. Seals. 6. Luxury goods.

1. ARCHITECTURE. Following the tradition of the maritime Phoenician city-states, Carthage was founded on a promontory between two sheltered lagoons; other Punic cities were similarly sited. Considerable parts of the harbour (Phoen. *cothon*), with its communicating docks, and the nearby cemetery (Phoen. *tophet*) have been uncovered, but only small parts of the residential areas have been excavated. Surviving evidence confirms Classical descriptions of the city as having square insulae with two- to six-storey houses within the confines of triple battlemented curtain walls. Domestic architecture is best represented by houses of the 6th–3rd centuries BC uncovered at Kerkouane, a fortified town on the east coast of the Cap Bon peninsula (Tunisia), and at Motya in Sicily. The rooms were rectangular, and some were furnished with a bath and drains; they were arranged around a courtyard that held a basin and was decorated with a simple mosaic (*pavimenta punica*) consisting of tesserae set in pink cement, occasionally with a white-outlined symbol such as the Tanit sign (a stylized figure with circular head and arms at the apex of a triangle). A wooden staircase gave access to upper floors or a flat roof. Remains of monumental religious architecture with Egyptianizing architraves have been excavated in Sicily (Motya) and Sardinia (Nora, Antas and Tharros). The most impressive fortifications are three strongholds on Cap Bon that were later reused. The city walls of Motya, which date to the 6th century BC, and those of Eryx, Monte Andranone and Lilybaeum, bear witness to the Greek threat to the Punic enclaves in Sicily. In Sardinia, the most impressive defence system was excavated at Tharros. Fortifications at Monte Sirai in Sardinia and in Spain betray the persistence of Near Eastern casemate building techniques in Punic architecture.

2. SCULPTURE AND TERRACOTTAS. A few stele-like statues of the 3rd century BC, representing the deceased, have been found in the cemetery at Ste Monique and elsewhere in Carthage (Tunis, Mus. N. Bardo); stylistically they recall the clay figurines that were mass-produced in the area of Tyre on the Phoenician coast (5th–4th centuries BC; e.g. Beirut, Mus. N.). Sculpture in the round is represented by a much-damaged statue of a goddess seated on a throne flanked by winged sphinxes (Tunis, Mus. N. Bardo), for which there are also Near Eastern prototypes (5th century BC). The same subject, in alabaster, was found at Galera, near Granada in Spain (Madrid, Mus. Arqueol. N.). The carved lids of stone coffins and ossuaries (4th–3rd centuries BC) are of higher quality and better preserved: they depict priests (and, in one case, a priestess) in a predominantly Greek style that, despite some Egyptianizing features, is in marked contrast to that of the anthropoid sarcophagi of Sidon. One, carved in high relief (Carthage, Mus. N.), shows a robed and bearded priest, holding a box in one hand and raising the other.

A further indication of Punic independence can be seen in the many stelae found at Carthage and Hadrumetum (now Sousse) in Tunisia, and at Cirta (now Constantine, Algeria). The chronological evolution of these grave-markers can best be studied at Carthage, where many were found stratified in the *tophet*. The earliest (7th–6th centuries BC) are shaped like the Egyptian *djed* pillar of Osiris, while others have their upper parts carved like plain thrones, often supporting a *djed* pillar (Tunis, Mus. N. Bardo). During the next two centuries the stelae were shaped to resemble small shrines or doorways, sometimes framing the crudely carved figure of a worshipper (see fig.); or one or more (up to five) column-like cult-stones; or a symbol, generally bottle-shaped (Tunis, Mus. N. Bardo). From the 5th century BC onwards, increasing numbers of triangular-topped stelae were engraved with such symbols as the Tanit sign and motifs from an iconographic repertory that gradually replaced Egyptian motifs with Greek; the number

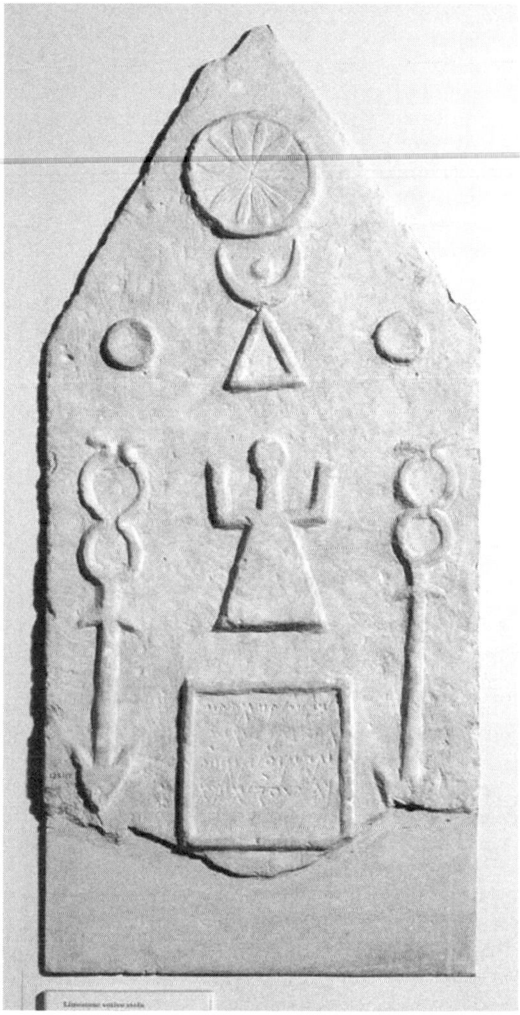

Punic stele from Carthage with a dedication to Baal, limestone, 750×380 mm, 2nd–1st century BC (London, British Museum)

and length of inscriptions increased until the fall of Carthage in 146 BC.

From the 7th century BC to the 6th, Carthaginian terracottas were largely dependent on models imported from Phoenicia, Cyprus and Rhodes, and depict scenes from daily life, such as bread-making (Carthage, Antiqua.), pregnant goddesses and tambourine players (Tunis, Mus. N. Bardo). Bell-shaped and ovoid votive figurines from the *tophet* were copied on Ibiza (Isla Plana; Ibiza, Mus. Arqueol.), Sicily (Motya; Mozia, Mus. Whitaker) and Sardinia (Bithia; Cagliari, Mus. Archeol. N.). Another 7th-century BC tradition, also firmly rooted in the east, was the production of male masks: those from Carthage (Carthage, Mus. N.; Paris, Louvre) often have grotesque features and may betray influences from the African continent. Stereotyped Egyptianizing female protomes were popular during the second half of the 6th century BC (Paris, Louvre) but were soon replaced by those cast from Sicilian moulds, including Silenus masks (Cagliari, Mus. Archeol. N.) and, later still, Greek theatrical masks (Carthage, Mus. N.). The moulds for three-dimensional terracotta figurines found in potters' kilns at Dermech (Carthage) also betray Greek influence. Cross-shaped figurines (5th–2nd centuries BC), clad in the Greek *chiton*, with arms outstretched (Cagliari, Mus. Archeol. N.) have 5th-century BC prototypes in Sidon on the Phoenician coast (Paris, Louvre); this type was to develop in its most 'baroque' form on Ibiza (Ibiza, Mus. Arqueol.). The same pattern of development can be seen in a group of figurines representing seated male and female deities flanked by sphinxes (e.g. the Baal of Thinissut, 1st century AD; Tunis, Mus. N. Bardo). Several figures, some of them adapted as incense burners, emphasize the impact of the Greek cult of Demeter and Kore on Carthage and its colonies (e.g. from Korba on Cap Bon, 1st century BC; Tunis, Mus. N. Bardo). There are many examples of the symbiosis of Greek and Egyptian features in Sardinia and Sicily, but one of the most remarkable is provided by a nearly life-size (h. 1.3 m), terracotta statue of a lion-headed goddess, wearing a garment imitating bird-wings, from Thinissut on Cap Bon (1st century AD; Tunis, Mus. N. Bardo).

Terracottas also took the form of moulds, possibly for sacrificial cakes (6th–3rd centuries BC). These are unknown in the east but have been found in Spain, Ibiza, Sardinia, Sicily and Carthage; they feature human figures, a deity riding a horse, the Egyptian dwarf-god Bes, animals and round or rectangular geometric patterns (Carthage, Mus. N.).

3. POTTERY. Between the 8th and 6th centuries BC the ceramic repertory of the Punic world gradually distanced itself from Near Eastern prototypes. Each centre developed its own distinctive clays, shapes and finishes. Pottery was essentially utilitarian, and decoration was generally restricted to horizontal bands of red or brown paint. Exceptions are a seven-fold vase, incense burners and animal-shaped vessels (Tunis, Mus. N. Bardo). Lamps were derived from Canaanite prototypes; they developed into a two-beaked saucer type, which was eventually closed and, in a final stage, had two tubular extensions to hold the wicks. Luxury wares were all imports from Phoenicia (red-slipped), Greece (Proto-Corinthian and Attic) or Italy (Etruscan, or South Italian polished wares).

4. METALWORK. Figurines and vessels were exported from Phoenicia, but by the 7th century BC Spanish workshops (possibly at Cádiz) were producing a variety of items, including bronze handle-attachments in the shape of a pair of human hands and tripod braziers with one to three rows of lily petals decorating the shaft (Madrid, Mus. Arqueol.

N.). Sardinian bronze figures illustrate the interaction of Near Eastern and local influences (Cagliari, Mus. Archeol. N.). The many copper razors (7th–2nd centuries BC) from Sardinia (Cagliari, Mus. Archeol. N.), Ibiza (Ibiza, Mus. Arqueol.) and Carthage (Tunis, Mus. N. Bardo), though typologically related to Egyptian examples, are most typical of Punic metalwork: the engraved designs on them blend, in various proportions, Egyptian, Greek and Near Eastern art. No native bronzeworking tradition seems to have existed in Carthage. Despite local variations, Punic coins are not distinctive.

5. SEALS. These have been found throughout the Punic world but especially at Carthage, Puig des Molins (Ibiza) and Tharros. The standard type was shaped like a scarab-beetle. From the 7th century BC to the 3rd the designs combined Egyptian and Near Eastern motifs, but from the 5th century BC Greek motifs became increasingly prevalent. It is not always easy to distinguish Cypro-Phoenician imports from locally produced seals, but a Punic style can probably best be defined with reference to Tharros, where more than 3000 seals have been found (e.g. London, BM; Cagliari, Mus. Archeol. N.). Many of these are of greenstone (generally referred to as green jasper), but the source of the stone has not been identified. Common subjects include deities on sphinx-thrones, figures flanking a distinctive palmette, sphinxes, the Egyptian dwarf-god Bes, winged sun-discs with drooping wings, a variety of Egyptianizing motifs, lions and Greek warriors. Some scarabs, found with Phoenicio-Punic examples of the 6th to 4th centuries BC, are faithful copies of imports from Egypt, but examples have also been found in Phoenicia, and it is not certain where they were made.

6. LUXURY GOODS. These include faience and glass objects, carved ivories, various items of jewellery and painted ostrich eggs.

(i) Faience and glass. Faience and glass objects were extremely popular and are widely distributed, but for most categories the extent of the local share in their production has not been established. Sand-core glass unguent vessels, both moulded and hand-worked, occur from the later 7th century BC (Paris, Louvre), and variegated glass beads are found throughout the Punic world. Faience amulets, mostly reproducing Egyptian motifs, both imported and, probably, locally made, were also popular (Tunis, Mus. N. Bardo), as were unguent vessels of faience representing Egyptian figures (Brussels, Mus. Royaux A. & Hist.). Faience amulet cases were probably imported from Egypt. Distinctive amulets in the form of masks in white, blue, black, green and yellow glass were made in Phoenicia, Carthage and perhaps elsewhere in the Punic world (Carthage, Mus. N.).

(ii) Ivories. The art of ivory-carving was doubtless transmitted to the west by expatriate Phoenician craftsmen, a few examples of whose work have been found at Carthage and Málaga (late 8th–7th centuries BC; Carthage, Mus. N.; Málaga, Mus. Arqueol. Prov.). A number of ivories, mostly toiletry objects imitating Near Eastern prototypes, were made in the Iberian peninsula in the 7th–6th centuries BC, for instance combs decorated with incised lions attacking hares, from the Carmona area (New York, Hisp. Soc. America). The tradition of ivory-carving was kept alive in Sardinia, as shown by the numerous amulets and plaques from graves at Tharros (6th century BC; Cagliari, Mus. Archeol. N.) and at Carthage, for example combs with incised decoration and mirror handles (Tunis, Mus. N. Bardo). The tusks of African elephants were shipped from Carthage.

(iii) Jewellery. Near Eastern techniques, such as granulation, filigree and repoussé, characterize gold jewellery found in Punic sites, but it is difficult to identify specifically Punic items. The greatest range is found in the tombs of Tharros (Cagliari, Mus. Archeol. N.; London, BM). The most elaborate types of earrings are leech-shaped, with hawks and teardrop pendants or baskets suspended from them by means of single or double rings. Simpler forms show a cruciform pendant attached to the leech, resembling the Egyptian *ankh*. Others were ring-shaped with gold wire twisted around them. Several earrings with a calf or ox head at the end of the loop illustrate the impact of Achaemenid Persian art from the 5th century BC. Swivel-rings have plaque-shaped bezels decorated with eyes of Horus, palmettes or scarabs; other rings, often with twisted loops, hold oval mounts in which are set scarab seals in hardstones, often greenstone. Four-winged scarabs decorate two gold bracelets from Tharros and rings and diadems of gold and silver from Sardinia and Carthage (Cagliari, Mus. Archeol. N.; Tunis, Mus. N. Bardo). Necklaces were strung with glass and faience beads and amulets (see above), and occasionally with gilded silver and gold pendants in the form of plant motifs, astral or cultic symbols and small shrines containing a bottle- or mountain-shaped symbol flanked by uraeus snakes, sometimes inlaid with coloured paste and hardstones. Repoussé pendants depicting fertility goddesses holding their breasts are depicted round the necks of terracotta bejewelled goddesses from Ibiza (Puig des Molins, 5th–4th century BC; Ibiza, Mus. Arqueol.), and gold examples have also been found (e.g. at Tharros). Cylindrical amulet cases, often with falcon or lioness heads, contained strips of papyrus or gold with magical inscriptions (Tunis, Mus. N. Bardo); these constitute a group of Punic jewellery for which the Phoenician homeland has not yet yielded any prototypes.

(iv) Ostrich eggs. These were painted with geometric and stylized designs and used as dishes and cups (6th–3rd centuries BC). They have been found at Carthage, in Sardinia, Sicily and, especially, in Spain and Ibiza (e.g. Ibiza, Mus. Arqueol.). These ostrich eggs are generally considered to be typically Punic, but the absence of Near Eastern counterparts may be fortuitous.

S. Gsell: *Histoire ancienne de l'Afrique du Nord*, 8 vols (Paris, 1913–29)

J. Vercoutter: *Les Objets égyptiens et égyptisants du mobilier funéraire carthaginois* (Paris, 1945)

P. Cintas: *Amulettes puniques* (Tunis, 1946)

P. Cintas: *Céramique punique* (Tunis, 1950)

G. Pesce: 'Il tempio punico monumentale di Tharros', *Atti & Mem. N. Lincei, Atti Cl. Sci. Morali*, xlv (1961), cols 333–439

A. Lezine: *Architecture punique: Recueil de documents* (Paris, 1962)

G. C. Picard: 'Sacra Punica: Etude sur les masques et rasoirs de Carthage', *Karthago*, xii (1965–6), pp. 1–115

A. M. Bisi: *Le stele puniche* (Rome, 1967)

A. M. Bisi: 'I pettini d'avorio di Cartagine', *Africa*, ii (1967–8), pp. 11–52

G. C. Picard and C. Picard: *The Life and Death of Carthage* (London, 1968)

P. Cintas: *Manuel d'archéologie punique*, 2 vols (Paris, 1970–76)

E. Acquaro: *I rasoi punici* (Rome, 1971)

S. Moscati: *I Fenici e Cartagine* (Turin, 1972)

B. S. J. Isserlin and J. du Plat-Taylor: *Motya: A Phoenician and Carthaginian City in Sicily* (Leiden, 1974)

G. Quattrocchi Pisano: *I gioielli fenici di Tharros nel Museo Nazionale di Cagliari* (Rome, 1974)

P. Bartolini: *Le stele arcaiche del tofet di Cartagine* (Rome, 1976)

B. Quillard: *Bijoux carthaginois* (Leuven, 1979–)

H. Benichou-Safar: *Les Tombes puniques de Carthage* (Paris, 1982)

M. Seefried: *Les Pendentifs en verre sur noyau des pays de la Méditerranée antique* (Rome, 1982)

S. Lancel: 'Ivoires phénico-puniques de la nécropole archaïque de Byrsa, à Carthage', *Atti I Congresso internazionale di studi fenici e punici: Rome, 1983*, pp. 687–92

G. Tore: 'I bronzi figurati fenicio-punici in Sardegna', *Atti I Congresso internazionale di studi fenici e punici: Rome, 1983*, pp. 449–61

M. Fantar: *Kerkouane: Cité punique du Cap Bon*, 3 vols (Tunis, 1984–6)

S. Moscati and M. L. Uberti: *Scavi al tofet di Tharros: I monumenti lapidei* (Rome, 1985)

M. J. Almagro Gorbea: *Orfebreria fenicio-punica* (Madrid, 1986)

P. Bartolini: *Le stele di Sulcis: Catalogo* (Rome, 1986)

W. Culican: *Opera selecta* (Göteborg, 1986), pp. 353–61, 445–65, 549–79

Les Phéniciens et le monde méditerranéen (exh. cat., ed. E. Gubel; Brussels, Gén. de Banque, 1986)

E. Acquaro: 'Gli scarabei in pietra dura del Museo Nazionale "G. A. Sanna" di Sassari', *Rendi. Adunanze Solenni: Accad. N. Lincei*, xli (1987), pp. 227–52

R. D. Barnett and C. Mendleson, eds: *Tharros: A Catalogue of Material in the British Museum from Phoenician and other Tombs at Tharros, Sardinia* (London, 1987)

F. Bertrandy and M. Sznycer: *Les Stèles puniques de Constantine* (Paris, 1987)

M. P. San Nicolás Pedraz: *Las terracotas de la Ibiza punica* (Rome, 1987)

The Phoenicians (exh. cat., ed. S. Moscati; Venice, Pal. Grassi, 1988)

E. Lipiński and others: *Dictionnaire de la civilisation phénicienne et punique* (Turnhout and Paris, 1992)

S. Lancel: *Carthage: A History* (Oxford, 1995)

F. Prados Martínez: *Introducción al estudio de la arquitectura púnica: Aspectos formativos, técnicas constructivas* (Madrid, 2003)

Pupluna. *See* POPULONIA.

Puteal. *See* WELL-HEAD.

Puteoli [now Pozzuoli]. Site of ancient Roman city on the Bay of Naples, Italy, 12 km west of Naples. It was founded in a volatile volcanic region *c.* 520 BC as the Greek settlement of Dikearchia, a dependency of Cumae. Puteoli was conquered by Samnites in 421 BC and fell within the orbit of Rome in the following century, becoming a maritime colony in 194 BC and having full Roman colonial status under Augustus (*reg* 27 BC–AD 14). Its position on the Roman trunk road, the Via Appia, made it a more important city in antiquity than Naples; its territory was enlarged under the Flavians (later 1st century AD) as a reward for being on Vespasian's side during the civil war of AD 68–9.

The fame and prosperity of Puteoli were based on the importance of its port for Rome, especially from the mid-2nd century BC when trade routes with the eastern Mediterranean developed. The city was the principal port of entry in Italy for Egyptian grain and was also the largest importer of eastern slaves. Its population rapidly became cosmopolitan, and not surprisingly it adopted early on the new oriental cults, such as the cult of Serapis introduced in 105 BC. Even after improvements to the harbour facilities at Ostia at the mouth of the Tiber in the mid-1st century AD, Puteoli retained its importance: Nero (*reg* AD 54–68) thought of linking it with Rome by canal, and the huge Alexandrian grain ships continued to arrive there. Puteoli was also a major exporter of Campanian agricultural produce, especially wine and oil, as well as black gloss pottery (of which the area was a major producer) in the late Republic, and later glass and Roman red gloss ware (*terra sigillata*). The latter supplanted the black wares in popularity from the last quarter of the 1st century BC until it too went into decline around the middle of the 2nd century AD (*see* POTTERY, §VI).

Under the Empire the city covered about 80 ha. The lower town has suffered from the phenomenon known as bradyseism (the ground level has sunk *c.* 8 m since Roman times and has then risen again), seen clearly in the now flooded market building, where the central columns show the marks of marine borers. The spacious building (58×75 m), once called the Temple of Serapis from a statue of this god found there in 1750, has a circular pavilion in the centre of a marble-paved court, which is surrounded by shops behind colonnades, except for a large apsed room (probably a shrine) in the centre of the north side; there are latrines in the north-east and north-west corners. The visible market, with its African and Euboian marble columns as well as granite ones, is the result of an early 3rd-century AD rebuilding, replacing an earlier structure (probably late 1st century AD) below.

Other preserved monuments include a temple, two amphitheatres and several tombs. The temple of Augustus (early 1st century AD), in the Corinthian order, incorporates remains of both a 5th-century BC and a later Samnite predecessor. Unusually for a surviving ancient building we know the name of its architect, L. Cocceius Auctus, builder also of the great road tunnel near Cumae. In the upper town is an amphitheatre (130×95 m) of the mid-1st century BC, replaced (or supplemented) by a larger one (149×116 m) nearby, which was constructed by the Puteolans at their own expense during the reign of Vespasian (AD 69–79) but not finished until the early 2nd century AD. With a seating capacity of *c.* 50,000, this was the third largest amphitheatre in Italy, after those of Capua and Rome. The building is mainly of interest for its well-preserved subterranean passages and 80 animal cages, which were winched up to the arena through rectangular trapdoors. The complexity and size of the arrangements give a vivid idea of the sheer quantity of beasts that could be displayed (and despatched) at a single show.

The upper town also contained the Baths of Trajan (the 'Temple of Neptune', from the early 2nd century AD), a solarium portico, a circus, several cisterns and an aqueduct. Several buildings are shown schematically in a series of engraved glass flasks produced in the city (4th century AD). Nothing is now visible of a famous quayside (*c.* 15×372 m) built by Augustus, repaired under Hadrian (*reg* AD 117–38) after storm damage and again, in AD 139, under Antoninus Pius (*reg* AD 138–61): it bore a triumphal arch, a lighthouse and ships' prows. It may have been during the construction of one of the quay's Republican predecessors that the waterproof qualities of the local volcanic brick-earth (pozzolana or 'pit-sand'), one of the vital ingredients of Roman CONCRETE, were first discovered (*see* ARCHITECTURE, §VI, 1(ii)(c)).

Several impressive mausolea survive in the environs of the city, some decorated with stucco and mosaics. One, beside the Via Celle on the west side of the city, which displays a niche relieving the centre of the façade on the lower storey, and a circular pavilion above, shows Baroque tendencies, which is unusual for an Italian building of this early date (1st century BC). Most of the tombs are provided with funerary niches for cremation burial urns. Another tomb (1st century AD) is also unusual in being in the form of a pyramid, like the contemporary but more famous pyramid of Cestius at Rome.

C. de Ruyt: 'L'Importance de Pouzzoles pour l'étude de macellum romain', *Puteoli*, i (1977), pp. 128–39
P. Sommella: *Forma e urbanistica di Pozzuoli romana* (Naples, 1978)
S. E. Ostrow: 'The Topography of Puteoli and Baiae on the Eight Glass Flasks', *Puteoli*, iii (1979), pp. 77–140
'Studi e ricerche su Puteoli romana', *Puteoli*, iv–v (1980–81)
S. De Caro and A. Greco: *Campania: Guide archeologiche Laterza* (Rome and Bari, 1981), pp. 37–53
M. Frederiksen: *Campania* (London, 1984), chap. 14 and pp. 319–58
F. Zevi and M. Jodice: *Puteoli* (Naples, 1993)
H. I. Flower: 'A Tale of Two Monuments: Domitian, Trajan, and Some Praetorians at Puteoli (AE 1973, 137)', *Amer. J. Archaeol.*, cv/4 (Oct 2001), pp. 625–48
C. Gialanella: 'Vicende urbanistiche del Rione Terra', *Boll. A.*, lxxxvi (Oct–Dec 2001), pp. IV, 1–4
C. Valeri: 'Il complesso scultoreo del Rione Terra: Note preliminari', *Boll. A.*, lxxxvi (Oct–Dec 2001), pp. 5–46
Da Puteoli a Pozzuoli: Scavi e ricerche sulla rocca del Rione Terra: Atti della giornata di studio, Istituto Germanico: Rome, 2001
G. Thomas: 'The Cult of Isis: Its Introduction at Roman Puteoli and Pompeii', *Hagion Temenos: Essays on Temples and Sacred Space in the Classical World,* eds R. T. Macfarlane and S. D. Ricks (Provo, 2004)
D. F. Jones: *The Bankers of Puteoli: Financing Trade & Industry in the Roman World* (Stroud, 2006)

Pylos [now Epano Englianos]. Mycenaean palace, built *c.* 1300 BC, on a flat-topped hillock (l. 170 m, w. 90 m, h. 4–7 m) 17 km north of modern Pylos in southern Greece. Preliminary exploration in 1938–9 revealed traces of walls, frescoes, stuccoed floors and Linear B tablets; systematic excavation by C. W. Blegen and the Cincinnati Expedition began in 1952, and the remains of a Mycenaean palace, popularly known as the 'Palace of Nestor', were uncovered. Large-scale investigations resumed in 1990 under F. A. Cooper of the University of Minnesota. The earliest traces of human habitation of the hilltop date to the Middle Helladic (MH) period (*c.* 2050–*c.* 1600 BC), while in its north-easterly corner there are remains of a paved road, gateway, circuit wall and some buildings of Late Helladic (LH) I date (*c.* 1600–*c.* 1500 BC). However, these settlements were largely destroyed when the summit was levelled for the erection of the LH IIIB palace. This occupied just over half the hilltop (85×70 m) but apparently had no fortifications, presumably relying instead on its naturally defensible site. Its buildings were largely of stone, with what were once thought to be horizontal and vertical half-timber reinforcements. Research carried out in the early 1990s showed instead that the walls were built in a series of 750×1050 mm rubble-and-mortar piers, separated by 300 mm slots, on top of a stone socle. The walls were faced outside with limestone ashlar blocks and inside with plaster-coated rubble, sometimes decorated with frescoes. Remains of staircases show that parts of the building had two storeys, the upper walls apparently being of mud-brick. The columns, door surrounds, ceilings and roofs were wooden.

The palace was orientated south-west-north-east and comprised three main units, the most important of which was the central one (50×32 m). It was approached from the south-east via a propylon of H-shaped plan with wooden fluted columns, the stuccoed bases of which remain *in situ*. To the left of this entrance were two rooms that probably constituted the palace archives, containing over 1000 Linear B tablets. Facing across an inner courtyard lay the megaron. Its distyle *in antis* porch and the vestibule had painted stucco floors and frescoed walls. The main chamber (*domos*: 12.9×11.2 m) had a central hearth of stucco-coated clay decorated with flame and spiral patterns, surrounded by four wooden columns on stone bases supporting a balcony, and facing the throne in the middle of the right-hand wall. The walls bore lavish frescoes, with griffins backed by lions arranged heraldically behind the throne and a man sitting on a rock playing the lyre in the eastern corner. The floor was decorated with squares filled with abstract patterns, with a large octopus directly in front of the throne. The megaron was the focal point of a large complex including what appears to be a bathroom, complete with a terracotta bathtub (see fig.) decorated on the inside with spirals, and another large hall with frescoes of griffins and lions or leopards and a central painted stucco hearth. Long corridors on either side of the megaron led to a substantial storage area. Two rooms immediately behind the megaron containing 33 pithoi and some Linear B tablets referring to olive oil and scents for perfuming it were probably oil stores, while five rooms to its west contained over 6000 pots. A separate building to the north-east of the complex clearly served as the wine store, as it held over 35 wine jars and 60 clay sealings, some with the Linear B ideogram for wine.

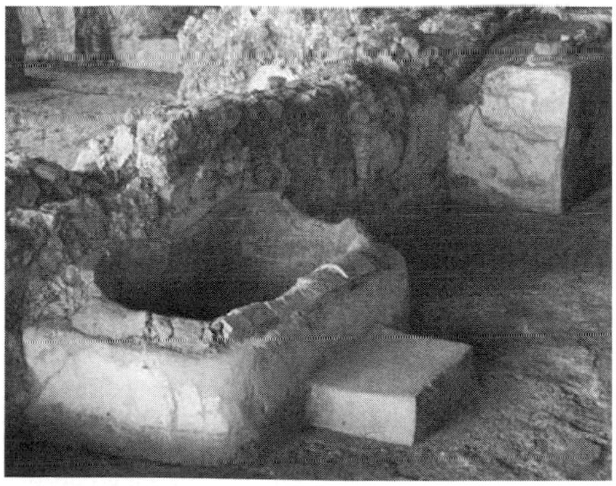

Pylos, megaron, terracotta bathtub, *c.* 1300 BC

A ramp from the central complex led to the palace's separate south-west wing, parts of which have been badly damaged by erosion and modern quarrying. Beyond a courtyard was a large entrance hall with a two-columned façade, stuccoed floor and frescoes including a frieze of pink griffins; a doorway led to a hall that once had four, or possibly six, internal columns. Some parts of the south-west unit were destroyed and rebuilt twice; it probably represents the original palace, which had the large hall as its megaron.

To the south-east of the central complex lay a unit of six rooms linked by a corridor. One small room, an open-fronted chamber with large antae, faced a plastered and decorated rectangular stone base and contained a Linear B tablet referring to the goddess Potnia Hippeia: it may have been a shrine and its altar. The remaining rooms contained pieces of pottery, fragments of bronze and ivory and Linear B tablets referring to chariots and the repair of metal and leather objects, so that they were probably the palace workshops. The original excavator believed that the palace was destroyed *c.* 1200 BC and never reinhabited. Investigations carried out in the early 1990s, however, appear to show that rehabitation took place not long after the destruction of the Mycenaean palace and continued sporadically, possibly as late as the Middle Ages.

C. W. Blegen and M. Rawson: *A Guide to the Palace of Nestor* (Cincinnati, 1962)

C. W. Blegen and others: *The Palace of Nestor at Pylos in Western Messenia*, 3 vols (Princeton, 1966–73)

A. Griebel and M. Nelson: 'The Geometric Occupation at Pylos', *Amer. J. Archaeol.*, xcvii (1993), p. 331

M. L. Galaty: *Nestor's Wine Cups: Investigating Ceramic Manufacture and Exchange in a Late Bronze Age 'Mycenaean' State* (Oxford, 1999)

M. L. Galaty and W. A. Parkinson: *Rethinking Mycenaean Palaces: New Interpretations of an Old Idea* (Los Angeles, 1999)

S. U. Hofstra: *Small Things Considered: The Finds from LH IIIB Pylos in Context* (diss., Austin, U. TX, 2000)

C. W. Blegen and others: *A Guide to the Palace of Nestor: Mycenaean Sites in its Environs and the Chora Museum* (Princeton, 2001)

D. Nakassis: *The Individual and the Mycenaean State: Agency and Prosopography in the Linear B Texts from Pylos* (diss., Austin, U. TX, 2006)

Pyrasos [formerly Phthiotic Thebes; now Nea Anchialos]. Greek town on the Pagasitic Gulf, 17 km south of Volos in the nome of Magnesia. Nea Anchialos was built in 1907/8 to accommodate Greek refugees from Anchialos (now Pomorie) in Bulgaria. Excavations by the Greek Archaeological Service have confirmed the existence of a settlement at this site from as early as the 2nd millennium BC. It was destroyed in 1200 BC and rebuilt after 900 BC. From the 5th century BC it developed as a trading centre and became the port of the inland city of Thebes, gradually absorbing the population of the latter. In 196 BC it was conquered by the Romans, and it became part of the Thessalian League. From the 2nd century AD Pyrasos was known as Phthiotic Thebes, and the city enjoyed a period of particular prosperity from the 4th century to the early 7th. In the second half of the 7th century its fortunes declined, but it continued to be mentioned in inscriptions until the 9th century.

The town preserves a wall from the Roman period, which was repaired under Justinian I (*reg* 527–65). It was fortified with towers, and it stretched from the ancient acropolis of Pyrasos down to the sea. A group of buildings, probably an agora or hospital, with eight phases of construction from the Roman and Early Christian periods, lies in the southern foothills of the acropolis hill. The remains of other secular buildings include those of a paved avenue with arcades and shops, and from the 5th century AD a hypocaust and a private villa. The Roman cemetery was situated on the east side of Pyrasos at a place known as Ta Dodeka ('the twelve'); many tombs from various periods and of all types have been found inside and outside the walls.

J. Koder and Fr. Hild: *Hellas und Thessalia* (1976), i of *Tabula imperii byzantini* (Vienna, 1976–), pp. 271–2
P. E. Lazarides: 'Phthiotides Thebai' [Phthiotic Thebes], *Archaiol. Ephimeris* (1987), pp. 313–35

Pyrgi [now Santa Severa]. Etruscan town on the Tyrrhenian coast *c.* 53 km north-east of Rome. It was one of the ports of CAERE (Cerveteri) and thus an important centre for Etruscan trade and naval power in the Mediterranean. Pyrgi was inhabited from the Bronze Age, but its development as a port dates from the 7th–6th century BC. The Sanctuary of Leukothea (or Eileithyia) at Pyrgi has been excavated by the Institute of Etruscology at the University of Rome (1957–64). It was approached by a wide road (*c.* 10 m) from Caere through a monumental entrance. The sanctuary was enclosed by a wall and bounded to the south by inlets from the sea.

Two temples, apparently dedicated to Uni (the Etruscan Juno), stood either side of a sacred area. Temple B, the older and smaller structure (*c.* 500 BC; *c.* 28×19 m) was peripteral with a pronaos and single cella, following Greek models. Finds from its site include numerous fine architectural terracottas, notably a terracotta relief plaque depicting the *Seven against Thebes*. Temple A, slightly later (*c.* 460–*c.* 450 BC) and considerably larger (*c.* 34×24 m), appears to have been a characteristically Etruscan tetrastyle temple with a deep pronaos and probably three cellae. The architectural terracottas from Temple A include a series of plaques depicting the *Labours of Hercules* and antefixes representing divine figures. Between the two temples the remains of a third building, a chapel, contained three gold plaques, two inscribed in Etruscan and one in Punic, dedicated by Thefarie Velianas, lucumon (king) of Caere (*c.* 500 BC; Rome, Villa Giulia). The sanctuary was sacked in 384 BC by Dionysios of Syracuse.

'Pyrgi (Santa Severa)', *Not. Scavi Ant.* (1970), suppl. II/i–ii
L. S. Olschki, ed.: *Die Göttin von Pyrgi* (Florence, 1981)
A. Colonna, ed.: *Santuari d'Etruria* (Milan, 1985)
A. Morandi: 'Die Goldbleche von Pyrgi [Indizien für eine neue Lesung]', *Ant. Welt*, xxii/2 (1991), pp. 119–26
L. Pieraccini: *The Sanctuary at Pyrgi* (diss., San Francisco State U., 1992)
L'Altorilievo di Pyrgi: Dei ed eroi greci in Etruria (exh. cat. by G. Colonna; Rome, La Sapienza, 1996)
M. Pittau: *Tabula cortonensis: Lamine di Pirgi e altri testi etruschi* (Sassari, 2000)
S. Battaglini: *Le lamine di Pyrgi: La bilingue etrusco-fenicia e il problema delle origini etrusche* (Rome, 2001)

Pyrgos. *See under* MYRTOS.

Pyrgoteles (*fl* 4th–3rd century BC). Greek gem-engraver associated with the glyptic portraits of Alexander the Great (*reg* 336–323 BC). According to Pliny (*Natural History* 7.125), Pyrgoteles was one of the three court artists authorized to depict Alexander's likeness in art (the others being Apelles for painting and Lysippos for sculpture). The same author (*Natural History* 37.8) adds that Alexander had issued an edict forbidding anyone to engrave his image on emeralds, other than Pyrgoteles, 'who was without a doubt the most illustrious master of his art'. According to Plutarch (*Life of Alexander*, 4.1), it was Alexander himself who designed his public image, and saw that it was widely publicized through art, as a means to cultivate his own legend. Plutarch also relates that Alexander demanded from his court artists, in order to convey his royal qualities through his idealized portrait, that 'the poise of the neck turned slightly to the left and the melting of the eyes', in order to broadcast 'his manly and leonine quality' (Plutarch, *On the Fortune or the Virtue of Alexander* 2.2). These elements of physical likeness, as well as of attitude, were widely and systematically imitated by Alexander's successors. The imagery created by the three court artists had a wide impact in Hellenistic art, as well as folklore: its echoes may be detected as far the The Alexander Romance, a mythical tale ostensibly narrating the life of Alexander, most likely compiled by a Greek living in Alexandria between AD 140 and 130, versions of which exist today in 24 languages.

Despite the impact Pyrgoteles' contribution to Alexander's imagery had in the ancient world, we are today unable to identify his actual output, as no signed pieces of his survive. The phrasing of various texts suggests that, next to gem-engraving, Pyrgoteles was responsible for coin dies as well. Coinage was the standard medium for diffusing royal imagery in the Hellenistic period. Alexander never had his actual portrait cut on his coins during his lifetime, though it is possible that Pyrgoteles was responsible for designing Alexander's first coin dies, which depict Herakles, Alexander's patron god. Following Alexander's premature death, Pyrgoteles would have continued his career in the courts of his successors, as we know Lysippos and Apelles did.

In the royal imagery of Alexander's successors, the portrait of Alexander became a central point of reference. His head appeared on the coinage of his successors soon after his death, anticipating the series of coin-portraits of the kings themselves. Pyrgoteles is often associated with the so-called Lysimachi, a long series of silver tetradrachms and gold octodrachms issued by King Lysimachos of Thrace starting in 297/6 BC. Lysimachos was at the time emerging victorious from the wars against his fellow-claimants of Alexander's political and territorial legacy, and he chose to illustrate his coins with a posthumous portrait of their common predecessor. The obverse of the coins shows the head of the deified Alexander, wearing the royal diadem and the ram's horn, a direct allusion to his being the son of the Egyptian deity of Zeus Ammon. This paying respect to Alexander carries the implicit connotation of Lysimachos' own regal and military qualities, admirably demonstrated through his victory at the crucial battle of Ipsos in 301 BC. As it appears on the coins, Alexander's head comes close enough to Plutarch's descriptions and the extant marble heads in the Lysippan tradition, for it to be quite possible that Pyrgoteles was responsible for the design of the Lysimachi, presumably working for the Thracian court after the dissolution of Alexander's empire.

An exceptionally large ringstone, now in the Ashmolean Museum in Oxford, has also been associated with Pyrgoteles, on the grounds of its subject-matter, a portrait of Alexander the Great wearing the ram's horn. Since Alexander is shown deified, it seems more likely that the stone dates from the period after Alexander's death, and presumably derives its iconographical stimulus from the Lysimachi. The stone bears a minute inscription, unreadable to date, in a script that has been tentatively recognized by various authorities as South Indian (Kharoshti or Brahmi) or even South Arabian.

Although Pyrgoteles' oeuvre remains elusive, and his career is much more obscure than that of his two fellow court-artists, sources suggest that his work had been instrumental in the creation, propagation and diffusion of Alexander's (and other rulers') royal imagery in the early Hellenistic period. Archaeological evidence, moreover, might provide, albeit anonymously, direct or indirect evidence of the portrait types he created, motivated by the ideas of his royal patron and the expectations of his followers.

J. Boardman: *Greek Gems and Finger Rings: Early Bronze Age to Late Classical* (London, 1970)

J. Boardman and M.-L. Vollenweider: *Catalogue of the Engraved Gems and Finger Rings in the Ashmolean Museum: I. Greek and Etruscan* (Oxford, 1978)

J. J. Pollitt: *Art in the Hellenistic Age* (Cambridge, 1984)

O. Mørkholm: *Early Hellenistic Coinage from the Accession of Alexander to the Peace of Apamea (336–188 BC)* (Cambridge, 1991)

D. Plantzos: *Hellenistic Engraved Gems* (Oxford, 1999)

Pythagoras of Rhegion (*fl c.* 475–*c.* 450 BC). Greek sculptor. According to ancient writers, there were two sculptors named Pythagoras, one from Rhegion, the other from Samos (Pliny: *Natural History*, XXXIV.xix.59–60; Diogenes Laertius: VIII.xlvii). They were said to have been contemporaries and identical in appearance. Modern scholars, however, generally equate the two, supposing that Pythagoras was among the Samians who migrated to Zankle-Messana in 494 BC and became subject to Anaxilas of Rhegion (Herodotus: *Histories*, VI.xxii–xxiii). Pythagoras was the student of Klearchos of Rhegion (Pausanias: *Guide to Greece*, VI.iv.3) and the teacher of Sostratos (Pliny: XXXIV.xix.60). Ancient authors credited him with victory monuments for Olympic and Pythian athletes, a statue of the citharode Kleon of Thebes, and various mythological works, including *Europa and the Bull, Eteokles and Polyneikes, Apollo Killing Python* and a *Winged Perseus.* No copies of his works, all bronzes, have been identified with certainty, although a statue base for the victor Euthymos at Olympia preserves the name Pythagoras of Samos. An interest in evoking pathos is evinced by his statue of a lame man at Syracuse that was said to arouse sympathetic pain in the viewer. Pliny claimed that he was the first to represent sinews and veins, and to pay attention to the treatment of the hair (XXXIV.xix.59). An interest in artistic theory is attested by Diogenes Laertius' assertion that he may have been the first to strive for rhythm and balance (VIII.xlvii).

J. Overbeck: *Die antiken Schriftquellen zur Geschichte der bildenden Künste bei den Griechen* (Leipzig, 1868/*R* Hildesheim, 1959), nos 489–507

A. S. Ridgway: *The Severe Style in Greek Sculpture* (Princeton, 1970), pp. 83–4, 91

A. de Franciscis: *Pitagora di Reggio* (Reggio Calabria, 1996)

Pytheos (*fl c.* 370–*c.* 330 BC). Greek architect who worked in Asia Minor. Vitruvius (*On Architecture* I.i.12–15, VII. Preface. 12) cited the *Commentaries* by Pytheos on his most famous works, the Mausoleum at HALIKARNASSOS and the Temple of Athena Polias at PRIENE; Pytheos has also been credited with the original design for the altar of Athena at Priene. He may have produced new town plans for Halikarnassos and Priene, including, at Priene, provision for the sanctuary of Zeus east of the agora, and he may be Pliny the elder's 'Pythis', the designer of the quadriga on top of the Mausoleum (*Natural History* XXVI.iv.31). He apparently incorporated a traditionally Doric opisthodomos and acanthus-scroll sima in the Temple of Athena at Priene, setting a precedent for later Ionic temples such as the new Temple of Artemis at Ephesos. The Priene temple evidently inspired some features of the new Temple of Zeus (*c.* 355–*c.* 350 BC) at Labraunda, but the attribution of the Labraunda plan to Pytheos is unconvincing. Though Pytheos may have been responsible even for the detail of the Temple of Athena, he can have produced only the overall design of the Mausoleum. Vitruvius' references suggest that Pytheos was the first major Greek architectural theorist. This reputation seems well deserved, for no earlier Greek temple design exhibited the clarity and carefully conceived interrelationships found at Priene. Pytheos' theories clearly affected the design of the early Hellenistic Temple of Hemithea at Kastabos, and were still influential when HERMOGENES built the Temple of Dionysos at Teos (late 3rd century BC). Like Pytheos, Hermogenes favoured the Ionic order (Vitruvius: *On Architecture* IV.iii.1), but the latter's concepts of modular design went well beyond those of Pytheos himself.

H. Drerup: 'Pytheos und Satyros', *Jb. Dt. Archäol. Inst.*, lxix (1954), pp. 1–31

J. C. Carter: *The Sculpture of the Sanctuary of Athena Polias at Priene* (London, 1983), pp. 24–43, 181–201

W. Koenigs: 'Der Athenatempel von Priene', *Istanbul. Mitt.*, 33 (1983), pp. 134–75

W. Koenigs: 'Pytheos: Eine mythische Figur in der antiken Baugeschichte', *Bauplanung und Bautheorie* (Berlin, 1984), pp. 89–94

B. Wesenberg: 'Zu den Schriften der griechischen Architekten', *Bauplanung und Bautheorie* (Berlin, 1984), pp. 39–48

J. C. Carter: 'Pytheos', *Akten des XIII. internationalen Kongresses für klassische Archäologie: Mainz, 1990*, pp. 129–30

E. Friedrich: 'Eudoxos—Pytheos, elementare Mabordnungen in der frühen spharischen Astronomie und in der Architektur der Spätklassik', *Architectura*, xxiii/1 (1993), pp. 1–13

Pyxis [pl. pyxides]. Ancient vessel form, used to contain cosmetics, oils and perfumes (*see* POTTERY, fig. 15).

Qalʿat al-Mudīq. *See* APAMEIA.

Qalʿat as Sālihīyah. *See* DURA EUROPOS.

al-Quds. *See* JERUSALEM.

Quintilian [Marcus Fabius Quintilianus] (*b* Calagurris [now Calahorra], Spain, *c.* AD 40; *d c.* AD 100). Roman rhetorician, writer and teacher. He was educated in Rome, where he studied rhetoric with the orator Domitius Afer; he later returned to the capital in AD 68, becoming himself a highly successful teacher before being appointed by the Emperor Vespasian (*reg* AD 69–79) as the first professor of rhetoric paid by the State. During his retirement he served as tutor to members of the family of Domitian (*reg* AD 81–96), and around AD 95 he completed the *Institutio oratoria* ('Principles of Oratory'), a comprehensive treatise on the training of the orator, which became the foundation of education in the Late Empire. Quintilian's importance derives from his close association with the policy of the Flavian dynasty and the subsequent influence of his writing. He shared with Vespasian a concern to define a distinctively Roman culture after the excesses of the Grecophile Nero, and his description of Roman rhetorical style as 'forceful', 'weighty' and 'copious' (XII.x.36) may have helped to form contemporary taste not only in oratory but also in the visual arts. Equally his observations on the systems of 'signs' and 'places' used by orators to aid the memorization of speeches (XI.ii) may help us to understand the propagandistic use of sculptural compositions in coordinated architectural layouts by the Flavians and their successors. Quintilian himself encouraged his readers to correlate the styles of rhetoric and the visual arts by using a discussion of the concept of style in painting and sculpture to explicate style in rhetoric (XII.x). His comments on the history of art in this connection are among the most important by any ancient writer. His parallel schemes of development in terms of stages, from the rude simplicity of Polygnotos of Thasos to the brilliance and charm of Apelles for painting, and from the hardness and rigidity of Kallon to the truthfulness of Lysippos and Praxiteles for sculpture, are more complete than similar schemes in *Cicero* and are enhanced by revealing comments of two types. One gives importance to *phantasia*, the faculty that allows the artist to go beyond naturalism by exploiting an inner vision, and that enabled Pheidias to make his statue of *Zeus* at Olympia so beautiful that it 'added something to established religion' (XII.x.9). Another matches the emphasis on the personal nature of Pheidias' style with similar comments on the distinctive achievements of other artists. All these observations contributed to shaping the language of art theory in the Renaissance and later periods.

J. Onians: 'Quintilian and the Idea of Roman Art', *Architecture and Architectural Sculpture in the Roman Empire*, ed. M. Henig (Oxford, 1990), pp. 1–8

Qusantiniya. *See* CONSTANTINOPLE.

Quseir [Quṣayr al-Qadīm; al-Quṣayr al-Qadīm; Quseir al-Qadim; el-Kusair el-Kadim; Qusayr; Kuseir]. Port on the Egyptian coast of the Red Sea east of Luxor. Located at the mouth of the Wadi Hammamat, the shortest overland route between the Nile Valley and the Red Sea, the port was known in the 1st and 2nd centuries AD as Leukos Limen. Excavations begun in 1978 have revealed the remains of a Roman port, an industrial area, a Roman villa, glass, ceramics and a wealth of organic remains.

D. S. Whitcomb and J. H. Johnson: *Quseir al-Qadim 1980, Preliminary Report* (Malibu, CA, 1982)
C. Meyer: *Glass from Quseir al-Qadim and the Indian Ocean Trade* (Chicago, 1992)
D. Glazier: *'We Make the Diamond Shine': Archaeological Communities in Quseir, Egypt* (diss., U. Southampton, 2003)
D. P. S. Peacock and L. K. Blue: *Myos Hormos—Quseir al-Quadim: Roman and Islamic Ports on the Red Sea* (Oxford, 2006)

R

Rabbath Ammon. *See* PHILADELPHIA.

Rabirius (*fl c.* AD 80–95). Roman architect. Martial (*Epigrams*, vii.56) identified Rabirius as the architect of the emperor Domitian's palace on the Palatine (completed *c.* AD 92). It is usually assumed that he designed all of the building, although his work may have been restricted to the Domus Flavia, the official wing of the palace. There is no ancient evidence that Rabirius designed any of the other buildings in Rome with which he has sometimes been credited. In the formal reception rooms of the Domus Flavia, Rabirius created a worthy setting for the Emperor as world ruler. The main rooms impress by their sheer size and rich columnar decoration; the focal point of each room was an apse where the Emperor sat enthroned. On the smaller scale of the residential section (the Domus Augustana) Rabirius exploited the potential of concrete construction to create a series of novel interiors, which, although borrowing many elements from Nero's Domus Aurea, show a far more sophisticated manipulation of curvilinear forms within a tightly organized space. There is an emphasis on variety and surprise, achieved through contrasting room shapes, unusual effects of light and water, asymmetrical approaches and unexpected views, often of spaces which were not directly accessible.

W. L. MacDonald: *The Architecture of the Roman Empire*, i (New Haven, 1965)

G. Wataghin Cantino: *La Domus Augustana* (Turin, 1966)

Ram Jug Painter (*fl c.* 665–*c.* 640 BC). Greek vase painter. He is named after the scene on the Middle Proto-Attic Black-and-white-style jug (Aegina, Archaeol. Mus., 566), in which Odysseus' comrades escape from Polyphemos under rams' bellies. The Aiginetan provenance of many vessels attributed to this painter has prompted a view that he worked on Aigina rather than in Athens. He was schooled in the tradition of the Early Proto-Attic (*c.* 700–*c.* 670 BC) style of the ANALATOS PAINTER, and his earliest work may be seen in the Kerameikos Mug group, showing chariot teams, hoplite warriors and mourning women. The ovoid krater in Berlin (ex-Pergamonmus., A32) has also been attributed to his early stage, portraying Apollo, Artemis and a scene identified by some as Orestes slaying Aigisthos.

His mature figure style appears on the Ram Jug and on the fragmentary amphora showing Peleus handing over his infant son Achilles to the care of the centaur Cheiron, who returns from the chase (Berlin, Antikensamml., A9). The squarish human faces are in outlined profile, with a gentle curve on the upper contour; characteristic are the sloping almond eye under a long brow, the large aquiline nose, the short mouth and the curved line of the chin carried up to the ear. The painter's animals have similar eyes; their bodies are in silhouette, sometimes with touches of incision or white paint. An olpe (wine jug) with a large lion head in outline (Athens, Agora Mus., P 22550) is a fine specimen of the painter's late style of animal drawing, which reveals a delight in resilient curves.

J. M. Cook: 'Protoattic Pottery', *Annu. Brit. Sch. Athens*, xxxv (1934–5), pp. 193–4

S. Papaspyridi-Karouzou: 'Archaika mnemeia tou Ethnikou Mouseiou' [Archaic objects from the National Museum], *Archaiol. Ephimeris* (1952), pp. 149–66

E. T. H. Brann: *Late Geometric and Protoattic Pottery, Mid 8th to Late 7th Century BC* (1962), viii of *The Athenian Agora* (Princeton, 1962), pp. 11, 23–4

S. P. Morris: *The Black and White Style: Athens and Aigina in the Orientalizing Period* (New Haven, 1984), pp. 51–9

Reed Painter (*fl c.* 420–*c.* 410 BC). Greek vase painter. He mainly decorated small or medium-sized Attic White-ground lekythoi, exclusively in matt paint, and is named after the reeds that he often depicted (see colour pl. 2:VII, fig. 4) His output was large, but monotonous both in its subject-matter and in its individual motifs. He usually depicted only two figures: generally a youth and a woman, less often two women, on either side of a broad funerary stele; or Charon waiting in his boat among the reeds to ferry the deceased, normally a woman, across the Styx. His more unusual pictures, which include several depicting three figures, battles or horse-riding, and one depicting a prothesis, mostly occur on a few larger lekythoi. The patternwork invariably consists of meanders with saltire squares above the picture and palmettes and scrolls on the shoulder. A few palmette leaves are red, otherwise all the elements are dark grey. The figures have striking red outlines. The figure drawing is competently executed with a sweeping line, but perfunctory and lacking in expression. Bodies are often in three-quarter view, creating some impression of depth, but heads are always in profile. The pictures give an impression of sketchiness, owing to the disappearance of the short-lived matt paint that originally coloured the cloaks and shawls revealing incomplete outlines. Similarities in patternwork, colour scheme and painting technique suggest that the Reed Painter shared a workshop with GROUP R.

J. D. Beazley: *Red-figure* (1942, 2/1963), ii, pp. 1376–82, 1692, 1704

J. D. Beazley: *Paralipomena* (1971), pp. 485–6

D. C. Kurtz: *Athenian White Lekythoi* (Oxford, 1975)

L. Burn and R. Glynn: *Beazley Addenda: Additional References to* ABV, ARV2 *and* Paralipomena (Oxford, 1982, rev. T. H. Carpenter, 2/1989)

Reggio di Calabria. *See* RHEGION.

Regula (i). Narrow band between the taenia and guttae on a Doric entablature.

Regula (ii). Any long, straight piece of wood or metal used in the construction of ancient Roman buildings.

Reqem. *See* PETRA.

Resina. *See* HERCULANEUM.

Rhamnous. Site of Ancient Greek culture on the north-east coast of Attica. It was one of the rural demes (communities) of the city-state of Athens and flourished from about the 6th century BC to the 3rd century AD. Rhamnous was renowned in antiquity for its cult statue and Sanctuary of Nemesis, and its location also gave it strategic importance. Well-preserved fortification walls of the late 5th century BC–4th century BC enclose public buildings and a theatre. The Sacred Way, lined with monumental tombs, led 500 m uphill from the coastal fortress to the Sanctuary of Nemesis and continued beyond it inland towards Marathon. The seat of the cult of Nemesis, goddess of divine retribution, and the associated goddess of justice, Themis, the sanctuary encloses a small Temple of Themis of *c.* 500 BC, the Temple of Nemesis of *c.* 430–*c.* 420 BC, an altar, stoa and fountain. The peripteral, Doric Temple of Nemesis was built of white local marble, with 6×12 columns on a stylobate measuring 9.96×21.43 m. It had a pronaos, opisthodomos and plain cella with no internal columns. The platform and six lower drums of the columns are *in situ*, and many blocks from the superstructure are reconstructed in a storeroom near the site. The over life-size cult statue of *Nemesis* was carved of Parian marble in around 420 BC by AGORAKRITOS and has been reconstructed by G. Despinis from many shattered fragments (most now at Rhamnous; part of the head in London, BM). The statue stood on a base, reconstructed by B. Petrakos, with a sculpted relief depicting *Leda Presenting Helen to Nemesis*, as described by Pausanias (*Guide to Greece* I.xxxiii). Numerous Roman copies of the statue are extant (e.g. Copenhagen, Ny Carlsberg Glyp., 304a).

J. Pouilloux: *La Forteresse de Rhamnonte* (Paris, 1954)

G. Despinis: *Symbole ste melete tou ergou tou Agorakritou* [Contribution to the study of the work of Agorakritos] (Athens, 1971)

Praktika Athen. Archaiol. Etaireias (1975–) [excav. reps by B. Petrakos]

B. Petrakos: 'La Base de la Némésis d'Agoracrite', *Bull. Corr. Hell.*, cv (1981), pp. 227–53

B. Petrakos: 'To Nemesion tou Rhamnountos' [The Sanctuary of Nemesis at Rhamnous], *Philia epe eis Georgion E. Mylonan* [Studies in honour of George E. Mylonas], ii (Athens, 1986–9), pp. 295–326

J. Travlos: *Bildlexicon zur Topographie des antiken Attika* (Tübingen, 1988), pp. 388–403 [excellent pls]

M. M. Miles: 'A Reconstruction of the Temple of Nemesis at Rhamnous', *Hesperia*, lviii (1989), pp. 131–249

B. Vasileios Ch. Petrakos: *Rhamnous* (Congleton, 1991/*R* 1994)

K. D. S. Lapatin: 'A Family Gathering at Rhamnous? Who's Who on the Nemesis Base', *Hesperia*, lxi (Jan–March 1992), pp. 107–19

B. Knittlmayer: 'Kultbild und Heiligtum der Nemesis von Rhamnous am Beginn des Peloponnesischen Krieges', *Jb. Dt. Archäolog. Inst.*, cxiv (1999), pp. 1–18

B. Vasileios Ch. Petrakos: *Ho demos tou Ramnountos: Synopse ton anaskaphon kai ton ereunon (1813–1998)* (Athens, 1999)

Rhegion [Lat. Rhegium; Reggio di Calabria]. City at the southernmost tip of Italy. It was founded *c.* 720 BC by Greek colonists from Chalkis in Euboia and, with the slightly earlier Cumaean and Chalkidian foundation of Zancle (Mod. Messina) in north-east Sicily, ensured Euboian control of the southern approaches to the Tyrrhenian Sea through the Straits of Messina, which were later fortified against the Etruscans by Anaxilas, tyrant of Rhegion (494–476 BC). It was destroyed in 386 BC by Dionysius I, tyrant of Syracuse, but soon rebuilt. Though subject to earthquakes, Rhegion emerged as a thriving centre of Greek culture under the Roman Empire. Little has survived of its Greek buildings, apart from an important series of polychrome architectural terracottas of the late 6th and early 5th centuries BC. However, the major Griso-Laboccetta sanctuary, in use from the Archaic period to Roman times, has yielded so many Chalcidian black-figure vases (later 6th century BC) that they were probably made locally, though widely exported to other Greek colonies in South Italy and to Etruria. The Ionian sculptor Pythagoras (*see* PYTHAGORAS OF RHEGION) lived at Rhegion from 494 BC, and the National Museum in Reggio di Calabria houses the outstanding Greek bronzes found in the sea off Porticello (1969) and Riace Marina (*see* RIACE BRONZES).

G. Vallet: *Rhégion et Zancle* (Paris, 1958)
E. Lattanzi, ed.: *Il Museo Nazionale di Reggio Calabria* (Reggio Calabria, 1987)
E. Lattanzi: 'Il cosiddetto kouros di Reggio Calabria', *Boll. A.*, lxxxvi (Jan–March 2001), pp. 1–22
G. Cordiano and S. Accardo: *Ricerche storico-topografiche sulle aree confinarie dell'antica chora di Rhegion* (Pisa, 2004)

Rhodes [Gr. Rhodos]. Greek island, 11 km from the south-west coast of Asia Minor (now Turkey). It is the largest island in the Dodekanese (1400 sq. km; l. 77 km from north to south; see fig. 1), traversed by a range of hills running north–south along its west centre. It is very fertile and well placed to benefit from the trade between the eastern Mediterranean and the Aegean.

1. Introduction. 2. Bronze Age, *c.* 3500/3000–*c.* 1050 BC. 3. Greek and Roman, *c.* 9th century BC–3rd century AD.

1. Introduction. During the 2nd millennium BC there were settlements on Rhodes first of Minoans and then of Mycenaeans; rich finds have been uncovered from the tombs of this period. From *c.* 1100/1050 BC the island was colonized by Dorians from mainland Greece, and three city-states—Kameiros, Ialysos and Lindos—enjoyed great prosperity. In 408 BC these three cities combined to form a federal capital, Rhodes, on the northern tip of the island. This site has remained capital of the island ever since. The city of Lindos retained some importance as the site of a sanctuary of Athena, which was rebuilt in Hellenistic times. Rhodes grew rich in the Hellenistic period, especially after the victory over Demetrios I Poliorketes of Macedon (304 BC) when the Rhodians used money from the sale of Demetrios' equipment to erect the Colossus of Rhodes, which was considered one of the Seven Wonders of the World. Conquered by the Romans in 42 BC and incorporated into the Roman Empire under Vespasian (*reg* AD 69–79), Rhodes retained its reputation as a beautiful city and centre of learning. It had a bishop at an early date. Its strategic and economic importance increased from AD 330 after the establishment of Constantinople (now Istanbul), the eastern capital of the empire. In AD 395 Rhodes became part of the eastern empire.

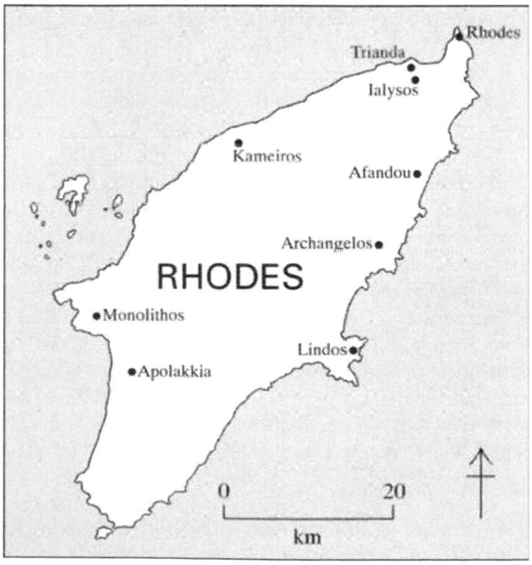

1. Map of Rhodes

A. Gabriel: *La Cité de Rhodes*, 2 vols (Paris, 1921–3)
C. Papachristodoulou: *Istoria tis Rodou apo tous proistorikous chronous eos tin ensomatosi tis Dodekanisou (1948)* [History of Rhodes from prehistoric times to the unification of the Dodekanese with Greece (1948)] (Athens, 1972)
C. Karouzos: *Rhodes* (Athens, 1973)

2. Bronze Age, *c.* 3500/3000–*c.* 1050 BC. Because of a lack of excavation, knowledge of the earlier prehistory of Rhodes is limited; it appears, however, that in the Neolithic period the Dodekanese and Samos comprised a cultural unit, and this may also have been the case in the Early Bronze Age (*c.* 3500/3000–*c.* 2050 BC). A deposit of Middle Minoan I–II (*c.* 2050–*c.* 1675 BC) domestic pottery from the acropolis of Ialysos implies that Cretans were active on Rhodes early in the 2nd millennium BC, but it is not until Late Minoan (LM) IA (*c.* 1600–*c.* 1480 BC) that we have definite evidence of Minoan settlement, at Trianda on the north-west coast. The houses are Minoan in plan and construction and preserve traces of fresco decoration. Minoan pottery was locally produced, and Minoan stone lamps were imported from Crete. The Trianda settlement was apparently abandoned during LM IIIA: 1 (*c.* 1390–*c.* 1360 BC).

By Late Helladic (LH) IIIA: 2 (*c.* 1360–*c.* 1335 BC) there were Mycenaean settlements of mainland Greeks throughout Rhodes. Of their cemeteries Ialysos, which lies just south of Trianda, has proved the richest, no doubt because the site was perfectly positioned to benefit from the trade between the Aegean and the eastern Mediterranean. The first tombs were excavated by Alfred Biliotti in 1868–71, and work was continued by Amadeo Maiuri and G. Jacopi between 1914 and 1928, although many tombs have been excavated illicitly. The LH IIIA tombs were not large but contained fine offerings: bronze swords, knives and spears, and gold, glass and faience jewellery (Rhodes, Archaeol. Mus., and London, BM). The pottery is of excellent quality, and the presence of certain distinctive shapes led some scholars to identify a local Rhodo-Mycenaean style, inspired by but independent of the products of the Argolid. Clay analysis has, however, demonstrated that most of this pottery was in fact imported from the Argolid, where it must have been produced specifically for an eastern Aegean market.

In LH IIIB (*c.* 1335–*c.* 1180 BC) there was a decline in the quantity and quality of grave offerings from Rhodian cemeteries. It is possible that some sites were destroyed or abandoned. The lack of LH IIIB: 2 pottery imports from the Argolid certainly suggests that trade was disrupted. Then in LH IIIC (*c.* 1180–*c.* 1050 BC) there was a revival at Ialysos in particular, which may suggest an influx of settlers from mainland Greece.

A common pottery style of this period, exemplified by the octopus stirrup jar (Rhodes, Archaeol. Mus.; London, BM; see fig. 2), has affinities with the products of Kos, Naxos and Attica. Exotic trinkets imply at least limited contacts between the Aegean and the eastern Mediterranean. The revival was, however, brief. The last Mycenaeans were buried at Ialysos early in the 11th century BC, and there followed a period of complete obscurity from which Rhodes did not emerge until late in the 10th century BC.

C. Mee: *Rhodes in the Bronze Age* (Warminster, 1982)

S. Dietz: *Excavations and Surveys in Southern Rhodes: The Mycenaean Period* (1984), IV/i of *Lindos* (Berlin and Odense, 1931–)

A. Sampson: 'The Neolithic of the Dodecanese and the Aegean Neolithic', *Annu. Brit. Sch. Athens*, lxxix (1984), pp. 239–49

A. B. Knapp: 'Bronze Age Mediterranean Island Cultures and the Ancient Near East', *Bibl. Archaeologist*, lv (June 1992), pp. 52–72

3. Greek and Roman, c. 9th century BC–3rd century AD. Rhodes city was famous in Greek and Roman times first for its Hippodamian urban planning and later for the Hellenistic redevelopment. On both occasions famous sculptors were called upon to embellish the city. Strabo (*Geography*, XIV.ii.5) praised its unparalleled beauty.

(i) Architecture. (ii) Sculpture.

(i) Architecture. Until the late 5th century BC the island of Rhodes was divided between three city-states: Lindos, Kameiros and Ialysos. Lindos and Kameiros each consisted of an urban centre serving as the seat of government, at the foot of an acropolis hill surmounted by a sanctuary of Athena, as well as of various surrounding villages. Ialysos was unusual, however, in consisting entirely of small villages and having its sanctuary of Athena on an isolated hill *c.* 250 m high. When the Rhodians decided in 408 BC to unite the island into one city-state, they entrusted the planning of its new capital, Rhodes, to an urban planner from the school of the great Hippodamos. The site chosen, at the northern tip of the island, was ideal for overseas trade and permitted the construction of five fine harbours, while its sloping terrain ensured good drainage. In accordance with the Hippodamian system, the city's plan was based on a grid of straight, precisely orientated, regularly spaced streets (5–16 m wide) covering the length and breadth of the site. The area within the city walls was divided into various zones: the acropolis; a trade zone comprising the five harbours, with their dockyards, port installations and warehouses; the agora, closely connected to the great harbour; and a residential zone, which occupied the greatest area.

The damage caused by the siege by Demetrios I Poliorketes in 305–304 BC and by an earthquake in 227/226 BC led to the Hellenistic redevelopment of the city. The walls, towers and gates were restored, while outworks and a ditch were added to the exterior of the defences, and the port installations were completed. Terraces were laid out on the east slope of the acropolis, and sanctuaries were redesigned and temples rebuilt in the contemporary Hellenistic Baroque style, tempered by traditional Rhodian classicism, including those of Pythian Apollo, Zeus and Athena on the acropolis, and the Temple of Aphrodite near the great harbour. The city streets, which had previously been dirt tracks, were surfaced, large drainage channels were created and earthenware pipelines laid. Architecture and planning reached their apogee in the great cave-like shrines hewn deep into the rock of the acropolis, with their associated buildings at ground-level and magnificent sculptural groups set in landscaped parks. In addition, large, luxurious private houses and imposing monumental tombs have been uncovered.

At Kameiros the earlier town was completely covered by a Hellenistic settlement of Hippodamian type with large public spaces and sanctuaries, while a huge and splendid stoa was built on the acropolis. At Lindos, where the Temple of Athena had been rebuilt and monumental propylaia erected after a fire in the 4th century BC, a great stoa also completed the architectural complex (late 3rd century BC).

When the Romans conquered Rhodes in 42 BC, they found it already well provided with public buildings, public spaces and private houses and so engaged in little architectural activity. In addition to the construction of a few palatial houses, there was one major renovation project. In the 3rd century AD a central avenue leading southwards from the dockyards of the small harbour was paved and lined with great stoas with colonnades made of imported granite, and its intersection with another road at the heart of the harbour was marked by a monumental marble tetrapylon. However, the Romans also seized

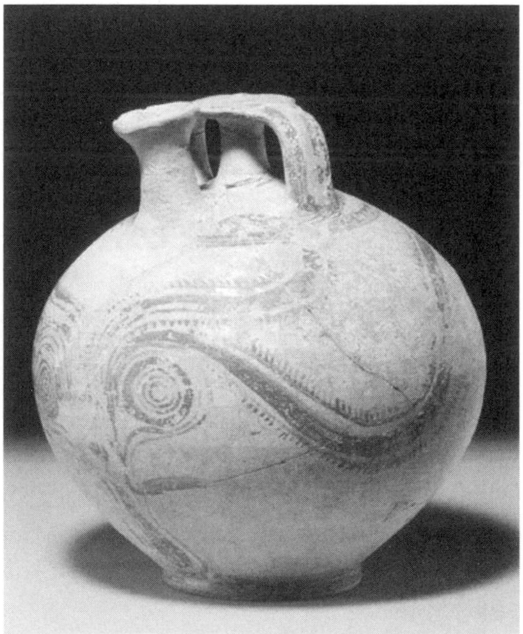

2. Bronze Age octopus stirrup jar from Tomb 10, Ialysos, Rhodes, *c.* 1200 BC, h. 230 mm (London, British Museum, A 932)

enormous amounts of the island's treasures and works of art after the conquest, and destroyed the walls of the city, ever fearful of its power.

J. D. Kondis: 'Zum antiken Stadtbauplan von Rhodos', *Mitt. Dt. Archäol. Inst.: Athen. Abt.*, lxxiii (1958), pp. 146–58

E. Dyggve and V. Poulsen: *Le Sanctuaire d'Athana Lindia et l'architecture lindienne*, 2 vols (1960), iii of *Lindos: Fouilles et recherches, 1902–1914 et 1952* (Berlin, 1931–60)

G. Konstantinopoulos: 'Rhodes: New Finds and Old Problems', *Archaeology*, 21 (1968), pp. 115–23

K. Lauter: 'Kunst und Landschaft: Ein Beitrag zum rhodischen Hellenismus', *Ant. Kst*, xv (1972), pp. 49–59

G. Konstantinopoulos: *Fileremo, Ialysos, Kamiros* (Athens, 1973)

G. Konstantinopoulos: *Lindos* (Athens, 1973)

W. Hoepfner and E. L. Schwandner: *Haus und Stadt im klassischen Griechenland* (Munich, 1986), pp. 21–6

G. Konstantinopoulos: *Archaia Rhodos* [Ancient Rhodes] (Athens, 1986)

G. Pugliese Carratelli: 'Epigrafi dal Tetrapilo di Rodi', *Annu. Scu. Archeol. Atene & Miss. It. Oriente*, lxiv–lxv (1986–7), pp. 267–93 [catalogue]

M. Cante: 'Rodi: L'arco quadrifronte sul decumano massimo', *Annu. Scu. Archeol. Atene & Miss. It. Oriente*, xlviii–xlix (1991), pp. 175–266

(ii) Sculpture. Examples of Archaic Rhodian sculpture include several items from Kameiros, the most important being a fragmentary stone libation vessel originally supported by three figures representing the 'mistress of the beasts' (late 7th century BC; Rhodes, Archaeol. Mus.), two fragmentary kouroi of Cycladic type and three heads of kouroi showing Samian and oriental influence (all third quarter of the 6th century BC; Rhodes, Archaeol. Mus.). From Lindos there is a fragment of a kore (late 6th century BC; Rhodes, Archaeol. Mus.), the head of a small statue of *Athena* (6th century BC; Copenhagen, Nmus.) and a damaged but important relief depicting a seated male figure (*c.* 550–*c.* 525 BC; Copenhagen, Ny Carlsberg Glyp.). Early Classical sculptural remains are confined to two fragmentary reliefs depicting the legs of naked youths such as those commonly found on grave stelai, and a small marble female head (all *c.* 480–*c.* 450 BC; Rhodes, Archaeol. Mus.).

The earliest large funerary relief on a grave stele is that of *Krito and Timarista* from Kameiros, an important work dated to the end of the 5th century BC (Rhodes, Archaeol. Mus.). The theme of two figures embracing seems to have been popular for many years, as it recurs on finds from Rhodes and the surrounding islands. The figures of both the mother (Timarista) and the daughter (Krito) were clearly inspired by the Parthenon frieze, while the emotional intensity of the scene, the expressive treatment of the girl's youthful flesh and the curved top of the stele are strong indications of Ionian influence. Other specimens of Rhodian sculpture of this period are confined to five further funerary reliefs (four in Rhodes, Archaeol. Mus.; one in Istanbul, Archaeol Mus.).

Among the famous artists called upon to embellish the city of Rhodes immediately after its foundation (408 BC) were the sculptors BRYAXIS, who created five colossal statues of gods, and LYSIPPOS, who made a huge, bronze group of *Helios in a Chariot*, as well as a gilded group depicting the same subject that was dedicated by the Rhodians at Delphi. Notable examples of the few surviving 4th-century BC Rhodian works are a complete marble grave stele of Attic type depicting a seated mistress, *Kalliarista*, attended by her standing servant-girl, and the head of a statue of *Herakles* (both Rhodes, Archaeol. Mus.), as well as the head of a woman (Boston, MA, Mus. F.A.) and an exceptionally fine head of a youth from Ialysos (New York, Met.).

In early Hellenistic times the Rhodian victory over Demetrios I Poliorketes (304 BC) led to the erection of the famous Colossus, a bronze image of the god Helios (h. 30–32 m), which cost 300 talents (raised from the sale of spoils left by Demetrios) and numbered among the Seven Wonders of the World. It was made by CHARES OF LINDOS, a pupil of Lysippos, and probably stood in the still unlocated Temple of Helios; it certainly did not bestride the small harbour, as shown in later engravings. It was felled by the earthquake in 227/226 BC.

Inscribed bases show that during the Hellenistic period over 100 workshops operated on Rhodes, producing both stone sculptures and bronzes. In the 3rd century BC there were more than 40 workshops, and in the 2nd century BC another 40 began production. In the first half of the 1st century BC about 16 new workshops were active, while in the second half of the century only another four were added. Statue bases at Olympia, on Delos, at Alexandria, probably on Samothrace, and at Anzio and Sperlonga in Italy, all bear witness to the activity and widespread export of the Rhodian workshops.

Several extremely important Rhodian sculptures either produced in Hellenistic times or based on Hellenistic models are recorded by Greek and Roman authors. One is the original bronze portraying the *Punishment of Dirke* (?*c.* 150 BC), attributed by Pliny (*Natural History*, XXXVI.iv.34) to the Rhodian artists APOLLONIOS AND TAURISKOS and reproduced by the so-called FARNESE BULL discovered in 1545 in the Baths of Caracalla at Rome (mid-3rd century AD; Naples, Mus. Archeol. N.). Others include the sculptures discovered in 1957 at SPERLONGA, signed by the Rhodians HAGESANDROS, POLYDOROS AND ATHENODOROS, as well as the LAOKOON group, assuming that it is the one attributed to the same artists by Pliny (XXXVI.iv.37). Although both works are of early Imperial date (1st century AD), they appear to be at least copies of Rhodian Hellenistic bronzes. The NIKE OF SAMOTHRACE (?early 2nd century BC; Paris, Louvre), a fine Hellenistic marble sculpture, was perhaps also produced on Rhodes, along with other similar representations of Victories, although its attribution to the Rhodian sculptor Pythokritos is now questioned. The most beautiful and best preserved original piece of Rhodian 2nd-century BC Hellenistic sculpture is the famous bronze *Sleeping Eros* (*c.* 150–*c.* 100 BC; New York, Met.; see fig. 3), found on the north slope of the acropolis. It represents a plump, round-cheeked boy with curly hair, stretched out on his cloak on a rock, his legs slightly apart, his left arm under his head

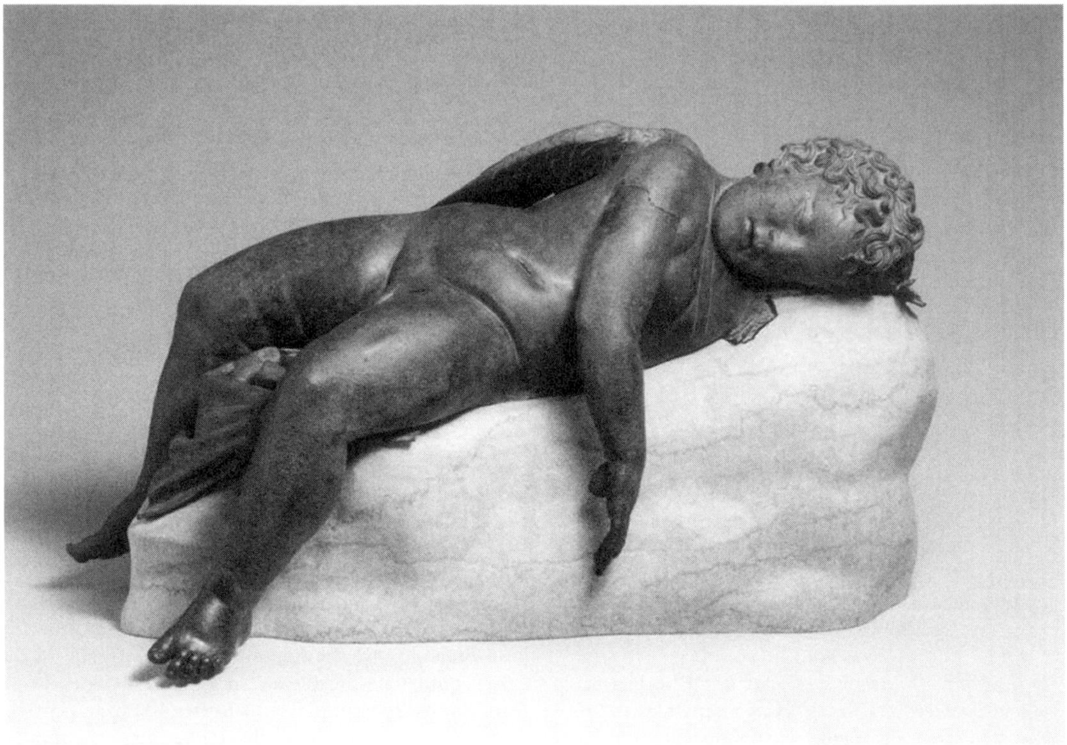

3. *Sleeping Eros,* Hellenistic bronze from Rhodes, *c.* 150–*c.* 100 BC (New York, Metropolitan Museum of Art)

and his right arm hanging down across his chest. The facial features, hair and anatomical details are expertly rendered, and the impression of complete relaxation is absolutely convincing. The piece is also of particular interest because it is the only Rhodian bronze to have survived intact, despite the fact that almost all Rhodian sculpture was executed in this medium because of the lack of local marble quarries.

The latest Hellenistic sculpture from Rhodes is confined almost entirely to small pieces, presumably because when the Romans captured the island they carried off all the most important works to Rome. The principal Rhodian sculptures of Roman date found on the island are in the Archaeological Museum, Rhodes, and comprise several portrait heads, an almost complete marble relief of a hunting scene (3rd century AD) and some fragments of similar reliefs that decorated the piers of the tetrapylon (3rd century AD).

M. Bieber: *The Sculpture of the Hellenistic Age* (New York, 1961), pp. 123–35

G. S. Merker: *The Hellenistic Sculpture of Rhodes* (Göteborg, 1973)

G. Gualandi: 'Sculpture di Rodi', *Annu. Scu. Archeol. Atene & Miss. It. Oriente*, xxxviii (1976), pp. 7–259

P. M. Fraser: *Rhodian Funerary Monuments* (Oxford, 1977)

G. Konstantinopoulos: *Museums of Rhodes. 1 Archaeological Museum* (Athens, 1977–)

E. Pfuhl and H. Möbius: *Die ostgriechischen Grabreliefs*, 4 vols (Mainz, 1977–9)

V. C. Goodlett: 'Rhodian Sculpture Workshops', *Amer. J. Archaeol.*, xcv (Oct 1991), pp. 669–81

G. Zimmer and N. Hachländer: Der Betende Knabe: Original und Experiment (Frankfurt am Main, 1997)

W. Hoepfner: 'Der Koloss von Rhodos', *Archäol. Anz.*, i (2000), pp. 129–53

V. Christopoulou-Alephantou: *Plastike paragoge ton meson Hellenistikon chronon ste demokratia tes Rodou* (Rethymno, 2002)

W. Hoepfner: *Der Koloss von Rhodos und die Bauten des Helios: Neue Forschungen zu einem der Sieben Weltwunder* (Mainz, 2003)

V. Machaira: 'Sculptures Hellénistiques de Rhodes en Contexte Public ou Privé', *Rev. Archéol.*, i (2003), pp. 205–10

Rhoikos and Theodoros (*fl* Samos, mid-6th century BC). Greek architects and ?artists. They are occasionally referred to as father and son, though Herodotus (the only near-contemporary authority) gave their fathers' names as Philes and Telekles respectively (*Histories* III.lx.4, III.xli.1). He described Rhoikos as the 'first architect' of the 'Great Temple of Hera' at the Sanctuary of Hera (Heraion) on Samos (III.lx.4). This probably indicates the third Temple of Hera or 'First Dipteros', now excavated (*see* SAMOS). It was probably built *c.* 560 BC and destroyed by fire *c.* 545 BC, though these dates may be too early. Pausanias (*Guide to Greece* X.xxxviii.6) mentioned a bronze statue attributed to Rhoikos alone, but elsewhere he is only mentioned alongside Theodoros. The latter need not be younger than Rhoikos; Herodotus (I.li.2–3) believed that he had made a silver bowl for Croesus, King of Lydia (*reg c.* 560–546 BC). Like Rhoikos, he too worked on a temple in the Heraion (Pliny: *Natural History* XXVI.

xix.90, XXXIV.xix.83; Vitruvius: *On Architecture* VII. Preface. 12) but this was perhaps the fourth Temple of Hera or 'Second Dipteros', usually dated to the tyranny of Polykrates (*reg c.* 540–*c.* 522 BC). He probably also designed a building at Sparta (Pausanias: III. xii.10). However, there is no firm evidence to support Herodotus' tale (III.xli–xliii) of the emerald ring made by Theodoros that Polykrates threw into the sea in a vain attempt to appease the gods. This is clearly a moral fable, and even Pliny doubted that the emerald exhibited in Augustan Rome could have been the same one (XXXVII.ii.4). Plato (*Ion* 533a–b) mentioned Theodoros as a great sculptor, but no extant statue can be linked to him. In fact, most remaining evidence is untrustworthy. A golden krater by Theodoros may have stood in the King of Persia's bedroom, but he probably did not make the famous golden plane tree and vine that stood nearby (Athenaeus: *Deipnosophists* XII.514f). It has also been asserted that Rhoikos and Theodoros discovered bronze-casting, though this cannot be true (Pausanias: VIII.xiv.8, IX.xli.1, X.xxxviii.6), and that Theodoros and Telekles used Egyptian techniques to make the two halves of a statue separately (Diodorus: *World History* I.xcviii.5–9). Theodoros reputedly put crushed charcoal under the Temple of Artemis at Ephesos to stabilize it (Diogenes Laertius: *Lives of the Famous Philosophers* II.103), made a self-portrait statue (Pliny: XXXIV.xix.83) and invented the set square, water-level, lathe and lever (Pliny: VII.lvi.198). These stories conflate many separate developments, demonstrating the ancient Greek tendency to credit one genius with many independent inventions. So little is known about these artists that ancient, no less than modern, authors have been tempted to fill the gaps in the evidence with speculation.

G. Shipley: *A History of Samos, 800–188* BC (Oxford, 1987), pp. 84, 88

H. J. Kienast: 'Der Niedergang des Tempels des Theodoros', *Mitt. Dt. Archäol. Inst.: Athen. Abt.*, cxiii (1998), pp. 111–31

Rhyton. Ancient drinking vessel shaped like a horn or animal's head, usually with a small hole in the bottom to allow liquid to be consumed directly from it (see colour pl. 1:XV, fig. 2).

Riace bronzes. Two ancient Greek over life-size bronze statues of naked warriors (Reggio Calabria, Mus. N.). They were discovered underwater 300 m off the Calabrian coast near Riace Marina (southern Italy) in 1972. Along with the famous statue of a god (either Zeus or Poseidon) discovered near Cape Artemision (Athens, N. Archaeol. Mus., Br 15161; *see* ARTEMISION BRONZES) and the DELPHI CHARIOTEER, they represent the most important virtually intact large Greek bronzes of the Early Classical period (*c.* 480–*c.* 450 BC). Both the Riace bronzes were produced in similar alloys using the lost-wax technique (*see* SCULPTURE, §IV, 1(iii)), and numerous technical and stylistic resemblances, as well as near identical key measurements and piece molding suggest that they may have come from the same workshop, or at least have been based on the same master model.

The two bronzes are known as Statue A and Statue B. Statue A (h. 1.98 m, *c.* 455 BC; see fig. 1) has a powerful upright posture, with the musculature of its weight-bearing right leg and relaxed left leg clearly distinguished. Its left foot is advanced and turned slightly to one side, but, unlike some later works, is placed flat on the ground. The upper body is not contracted above the supporting leg; indeed the right shoulder is actually somewhat higher than the left. The bent left arm once held a shield, though only the handle remains around the forearm. The right hand is held low, and the positioning of its fingers suggests that it held a spear with the tip pointing downwards. In the modelling of its muscular body and the intricate detail of its head, Statue A surpasses even the Artemision god.

Though Statue B (h. 1.97 m, *c.* 450 BC; see fig 2.) has a posture similar to that of Statue A, the treatment of the body here is different and has suggested to some a slightly later date. For example the right side of the torso, above the supporting leg, is

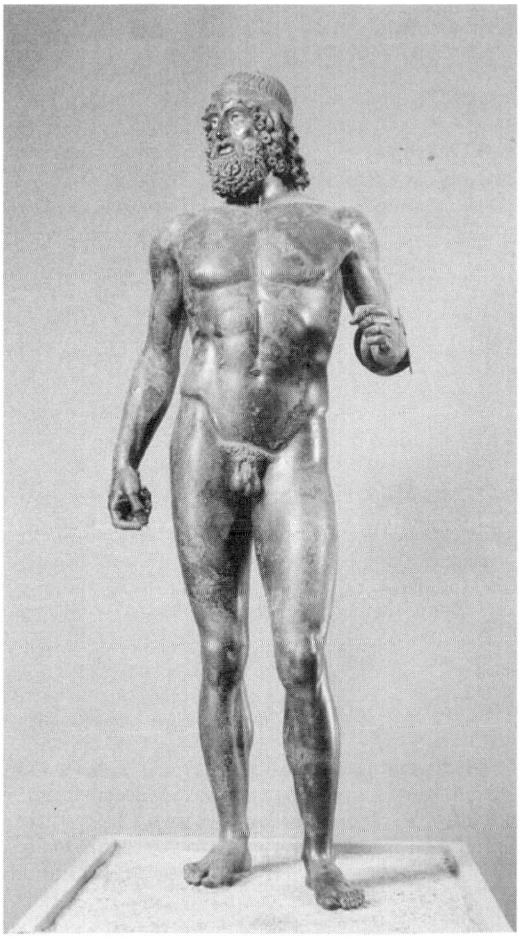

1. *Warrior* (Statue A), bronze, h. 1.98 m, from Riace, *c.* 450 BC (Reggio Calabria, Museo Nazionale)

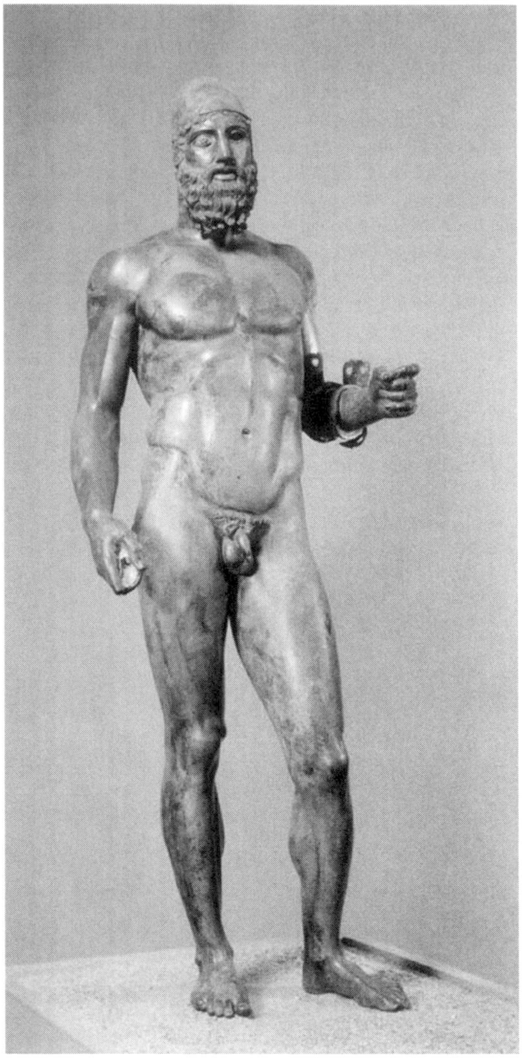

2. *Warrior* (Statue B), bronze, h. 1.97 m, from Riace, *c.* 450 BC (Reggio Calabria, Museo Nazionale)

noticeably contracted, with the right shoulder much lower than the left. This suggests an early form of the Polykleitan contrapposto stance (*see* POLYKLEITOS). The modelling of the upper body, the displacement of the edge of the thorax towards the pelvis and the slightly curved median line of the abdomen also suggest the influence of works by Polykleitos. In contrast to the confident, upright head of Statue A, Statue B has a slightly bowed head. Over a felt or leather skullcap Statue B once had an Attic helmet, of which the plume mounting survives. The right arm, left forearm and left hand and the shield handle were restored in antiquity.

The head of Statue A is turned quite sharply to the right, and since its mouth, with teeth inlaid in silver, is clearly open to speak, it evidently formed part of a group. This must have been a votive offering comprising several figures, dating from the transition between the Severe Style (*c.* 480–450 BC) and the High Classical phase (*c.* 450–*c.* 375 BC) and dedicated at a major Greek sanctuary.

Various features have led to attempts at identification. Statue A closely resembles certain works, now attested only by Roman copies, in particular the Tiber *Apollo* (Rome, Mus. N. Romano), the *Anakreon* (Copenhagen, Ny Carlsberg Glyp.), the *Hermes Ludovisi* (Rome, Mus. N. Romano) and the Kassel *Apollo* (Kassel, Schloss Wilhelmshöhe), all attributed to PHEIDIAS or his circle. An Attic origin for both statues could perhaps be suggested by comparison with contemporary vase paintings, such as those on the name vase of the NIOBID PAINTER (*c.* 460–455 BC; Paris, Louvre, G 341). Given this, and the fact that both statues undoubtedly represent warriors, they may have belonged to a sculpted group of Attic heroes by Pheidias that the Athenians erected at Delphi, probably between 457 and 450 BC, in thanksgiving for their victory at Marathon (490 BC; see Pausanias: *Description of Greece* X.x.1–2)—although such a definite attribution to Pheidias is still debated. This suggestion is perhaps supported by the striking profusion of Statue A's hair and beard, a distinctive feature of Attic heroes, as in the east frieze of the Parthenon. Indeed, Statue A's head also bears a striking resemblance to the head of *Kodros*, the early Attic king, depicted in an impression in glass from a gem by the lapidary Heios (1st century BC; Heidelberg, 61/7), which may be based on the statue of *Kodros* in the Athenian votive group.

Statue B is characterized by his bent head as hesitant and thoughtful, and may represent the great general Miltiades awaiting the outcome of the Battle of Marathon. Though there are significant differences between Statue A and Statue B, these can be explained in terms of the transition *c.* 450 BC from Early Classical to High Classical style (*see* SCULPTURE, §IV, 2(iii)(a) and (b)). They may be separated by more than five to ten years, a reasonable period to assume for the execution of a monument consisting of several figures. Alternative explanations might involve the collaboration of different artists in the commission, or simply an attempt to differentiate the subjects represented: A more aggressive and alert, B more relaxed.

Ultimately, the fact that the statues were removed from their bases (resulting in the loss of the accompanying inscriptions) makes a definitive identification impossible. Multi-figure monuments by artists such as ALKAMENES, AGELADAS, ONATAS and Pheidias were dedicated by a number of Greek cities and are attested in various cities and sanctuaries (Delphi, Olympia, Argos etc). All that seems certain is that the statues were removed from Greece (recent analysis of their core material has confirmed a Greek origin) and that the ship on which they were carried perished on the way to Rome.

A. Busignani: *Gli eroi di Riace: Daimon e techne* (Florence, 1981)

W. Fuchs: 'Zu den Grossbronzen von Riace', *Boreas*, iv (1981), pp. 25–8

A. Giuliano: 'I grandi bronzi di Riace', *Xenia*, ii (1981), pp. 55–62
W. Fuchs: 'Zu den Grossbronzen von Riace', *Praestant Interna: Festschrift für U. Hausmann* (Tübingen, 1982), pp. 34–40
A. Giuliano: 'I grandi bronzi di Riace ii', *Xenia*, iii (1982), pp. 41–6
C. O. Pavese: 'Interpretazione dei bronzi di Riace', *Stud. Class. & Orient.*, xxxii (1982), pp. 13–58
A. Giuliano: 'I grandi bronzi di Riace iii', *Xenia*, v (1983), pp. 5–6
Due Bronzi da Riace: Rinvenimento, restauro, analisi ed ipotesi di interpretazione, 2 vols, *Boll. A.*, special ser., iii (1984)
J. Boardman: *Greek Sculpture. The Classical Period* (London, 1985), pp. 53–4, figs. 38–9
W. Fuchs: 'Zu den Grossbronzen von Riace in Reggio Calabria', *Gymnasium*, xcii (1985), pp. 465–9
J. Marcadé: 'Rapports techniques et publications archéologiques: A propos des bronzes de Riace', *Rev. Archéol.* (1986), pp. 89–100
W. Fuchs: *Zu Neufunden klassisch-griechischer Skulptur* (Gerda Henkel Vorlesung, Opladen, 1987)
O. Deubner: 'Die Statuen von Riace', *Jb. Dt. Archäol. Inst.*, ciii (1988), pp. 127–53
W. Fuchs: *Die Skulptur der Griechen* (Munich, 1993), pp. 78, 587; figs 71a–b
E. La Rocca: 'Bronzi di Riace', *Enciclopedia dell'Arte Antica Classica e Orientale*, Sec. Suppl. IV (Rome, 1996), pp.730–34
C. Mattusch: *Classical Bronzes. The Technique of Greek and Roman Statuary* (Ithaca, 1996), pp. 64–7, figs. 2.18 a-d
P. Moreno: *I bronzi di Riace: Il Maestro di Olimpia e i Sette a Tebe* (Milan, 1998)
J. Pollini: 'The Riace Bronzes: Some New Observations', *Köln. Jb. Vor. & Frühgesch*, xxxiii (2000), pp. 37–55
A. Melllucco Vaccaro and G. de Palma, eds: *I bronzi di Riace: Restauro come conoscenza* (Rome, 2003)

Rider Painter (*fl c.* 570–*c.* 535 BC). Greek vase painter. He was the least important of the five major Lakonian Black-figure vase painters of the 6th century BC, and his work was never innovative. The Rider Painter was a pupil of the BOREADS PAINTER and later imitated in turn the work of the NAUKRATIS PAINTER, the ARKESILAOS PAINTER and the HUNT PAINTER. He is named from the scenes of a rider accompanied by small winged daemons on three cups (St Petersburg, Hermitage, 183; London, BM, B1; Paris, Louvre, E 665), which may be imitations of a lost work by the Naukratis Painter. The least talented of his colleagues, he had a dry, careless style, particularly on his latest vases, and the only interesting aspect of his work is his predilection for lively narrative scenes, often given unusual and humorous renderings. His various mythological subjects include the heroes Herakles, Bellerophon, Achilles and Odysseus, and he also painted such everyday scenes as revels and symposia. Many scenes, however, suffer from clumsy and vague execution, which makes them difficult to interpret. Thus, a scene on a cup depicting a seated figure with an eagle (Tocra, Archaeol. Mus., 932) presumably imitates the Naukratis Painter's scenes of Zeus (e.g. on a cup; Paris, Louvre, E 668), but it in fact looks more like Prometheus bound. A cup that appears to show an unidentified warrior attacking a snake at a fountain (Paris, Louvre, E 669) resembles depictions of Achilles' ambush of Troilos, though it is certainly a different event, possibly Apollo and Python, or Kadmos and the Dragon.

C. Rolley: 'Le Peintre des cavaliers', *Bull. Corr. Hell.*, lxxxiii (1959), pp. 275–84, pl. 12
C. M. Stibbe: *Lakonische Vasenmaler des sechsten Jahrhunderts v. Chr.*, 2 vols (Amsterdam and London, 1972), pp. 151–75, pls 93–112

Rogozen Treasure. Hoard comprising 165 silver and silver-gilt drinking vessels, dating to the late 5th century BC–4th, dug up in a garden in the Vratsa district, north-west Bulgaria, in 1986. The hoard contains vessels of Persian, Greek, Thracian and 'Thraco-Getic' manufacture and appears to represent a collection of known value, buried at a time of unrest and never recovered. The historical context is perhaps the incursion south of the Danube by the Celts at the time of their meeting with Alexander the Great in 335 BC.

There are 33 undecorated and 71 decorated silver *phiale* both of the shallow (Greek) and deep (Thracian) type, some apparently unfinished. One remarkable heavy silver-gilt vessel of Achaemenid inspiration is a technical masterpiece, and is decorated on either side with four interlocking pairs of horned and winged lions with tails curved into palmette motifs. Elements of the design are picked out with amalgam gilding. Another imported vessel is a biconical beaker of AGIGHIOL type, with applied bands of gold leaf. The remainder of the hoard consists primarily of handled jugs, many with elaborate figural repoussé decoration. The meaning of the scenes is not clear despite some recognizable Greek derivations. One jug appears to show female archers mounted on lions, another depicts a griffin with a disembodied human head above. A third jug has a frieze with a hunting scene of aurochs and hounds, above which are human-headed griffins and a winged figure clasping an animal in each hand, that is reminiscent of representations of the Babylonian *Epic of Gilgamesh*.

A. Fol, B. Nikolov and R. F. Hoddinott: *The New Thracian Treasure from Rogozen, Bulgaria* (London, 1986)
T. Taylor: 'The Persian Empire', *The Cambridge Ancient History*, ed. J. Boardman (Cambridge, 1988), pp. 78–94
B. P. Cook, ed.: *The Rogozen Treasure: Papers of the Anglo-Bulgarian Conference, 12 March 1987* (London, 1989)
A. Fol: *The Rogozen Treasure* (Sofia, 1989)

Roman Republic and Empire. Civilization that flourished first in Rome itself (from the 7th century BC) and eventually in the far-flung regions of the Empire. This article surveys the culture of Rome and its empire, ending with the official recognition of Christianity by Constantine the Great in the Edict of Milan (AD 313); an introductory account of the city of Rome can be found in the entry on ROME.

For further information on Roman art *see* ALTAR, §3; ARCHITECTURE, §VI; ARMS AND ARMOUR, §2; CHARIOT, §2(iv); COINS, §3; COLLECTION AND DISPLAY OF ART, §§I, 2 AND II, 6; DRESS, §4; FURNITURE, §3; GARDEN, §2; GEM-ENGRAVING, §3; GLASS, §II; HARNESS AND TRAPPINGS, §3; IVORY AND BONE, §6; JEWELLERY, §5; LAMPS, §2; LEATHER; METALWORK, §VI; MILITARY ARCHITECTURE AND FORTIFICATION, §2; MOSAICS, §III; PAINTING, §VI; PALACE, §2; PATRONAGE, §2; PLANNING, §II; POTTERY, §VI; SARCOPHAGUS, §3; SCULPTURE, §VI; STUCCO, §III; TEMPLE, §2; TERRACOTTA, §II; TEXTILES, §3; TOMB, §2.

1. History and geography. 2. Trade. 3. Religion. 4. Subject-matter.

1. HISTORY AND GEOGRAPHY. 'You Romans, keep your mind on ruling other peoples. These will be your arts,' wrote Virgil in the 1st century BC (*Aeneid* VI.851–2). Indeed, the Romans became masters in the art of conquest, extending their power through the entire Mediterranean and beyond (see fig. 1). The locus of Roman power began modestly. A cluster of independent Neolithic villages first occupied the future site of Rome, inland east of the River Tiber in central Italy. At this advantageous location, hills gave protection from attacks and floods; intervening valleys and the river provided easy communication; and an island facilitated river crossing. According to tradition, Romulus, descendant of Mars and the Trojan Aeneas, founded Rome in 753 BC.

In the 7th century BC the Etruscans pushed southward into Latium, the area of west central Italy around Rome; according to literary sources, an Etruscan king ruled Rome by 616 BC. The Etruscans introduced a more cultivated, urban way of life, instituted a more formalized religion and produced sophisticated figural art, inspired by imported Greek works. Under Etruscan rule, Roman buildings became more substantial: houses replaced huts, permanent structures replaced open-air meeting-places, large funeral monuments replaced pit burials and temples replaced sacred groves. The Etruscans also drained Latium's waterlogged clay subsoil. By the late 6th century BC, the *ager Romanus* (the 'Roman domain', i.e. the part of the territory in which the people were granted citizenship) covered some 910 sq. km of productive farmland.

In 509 BC the Romans expelled the Etruscan kings and instituted an aristocratic Republic. Cultural ties with Etruria remained strong. The new government completed Etruscan building projects and employed Etruscan artisans and soothsayers. The Republic was controlled by the Senate, a council of 300–900 elders representing the leading clans. Two members of the privileged patrician class jointly held the foremost civil and military office, the consulship. The general citizenry of plebeians served in the army and assemblies of the people, and elected their own officers. Resenting exclusion from major magistracies and the harsh laws on debt, the plebeians threatened to secede in 494 BC. Though they gained some slight redress, conflict between the social orders endured for centuries. Despite this inner struggle, Rome's military power increased during the 5th and 4th centuries BC. Through alliances, conquest and colonization, the Romans dominated the peninsula by 270 BC. They connected their disparate territories with a network of well-constructed roads and united them culturally through a common language and artistic vocabulary, as well as through shared religious beliefs and state ceremonies. During this period, Rome's focus was wholly on Italy. In part, the lack of good ports and the buffer of Greek cities to the south and Etruscan cities to the north prompted Rome's geographical introspection. Furthermore, Italy offered a favourable climate, ample arable land and mineral resources.

During the 3rd and 2nd centuries BC, however, Rome became embroiled in Mediterranean politics, as the urbanization of Italy stimulated trade and created a market for imports. Beginning in 264 BC, the Romans fought the three Punic Wars against Carthage for control of the western Mediterranean. Subsequent victories gave Rome access to the rich production and trade centres of Greece, Egypt and Asia Minor. The Romans established provinces or protectorates throughout the East, as well as in Africa, Sicily, Sardinia, Spain and Gaul. By the end of the Third Punic War in 146 BC, the Romans could legitimately call the Mediterranean *mare nostrum* ('our sea'). According to Horace, 'Greece, the captive, made her savage victor captive, and brought the arts into rustic Latium' (*Epistles* II.i.156–7). With each conquest, Roman generals returned home with works of art in huge quantities. A single triumphal procession in 187 BC included 285 bronze and 230 marble statues. The quantity and quality of plundered Greek art changed Roman taste forever. Wealthy Romans and the State displayed imported art as status symbols and as valuable tools for self-promotion.

In the 2nd and 1st centuries BC the rise of acute class consciousness and unrestrained individualism caused a series of social disruptions. The dislocation of small farmers from their land led to uprisings followed by agrarian reforms. The revolt of Rome's Italian allies in the Social War (91–87 BC) culminated with the enfranchisement of the entire peninsula. During these agitations, individuals grappled for personal power: governors exploited provinces; generals acted as warlords with private armies. In 60 BC three powerful and ambitious men—Pompey, Crassus and JULIUS CAESAR—entered an uneasy, unofficial alliance known as the First Triumvirate. Eventually, Caesar dominated. In 49 BC he ignored the Senate's orders and entered Italy at the head of his army trained in Gaul; in 44 BC he became dictator for life. Caesar did little more than explore the principle of personal autocracy, as on the Ides of March 44 BC he was murdered by a group of staunch republicans. The death of Caesar again plunged Rome into civil war. Caesar's heir and grand-nephew Octavian allied with Mark Antony to avenge the dictator, but they soon came into conflict themselves: Octavian defeated Antony and his ally Cleopatra in 31 BC. Awarded the honorific title 'Augustus' in 27 BC, he ruled for the next 40 years. Overtly, AUGUSTUS claimed to have restored the Republic; covertly, he gathered all power into his own hands, to become in effect Rome's

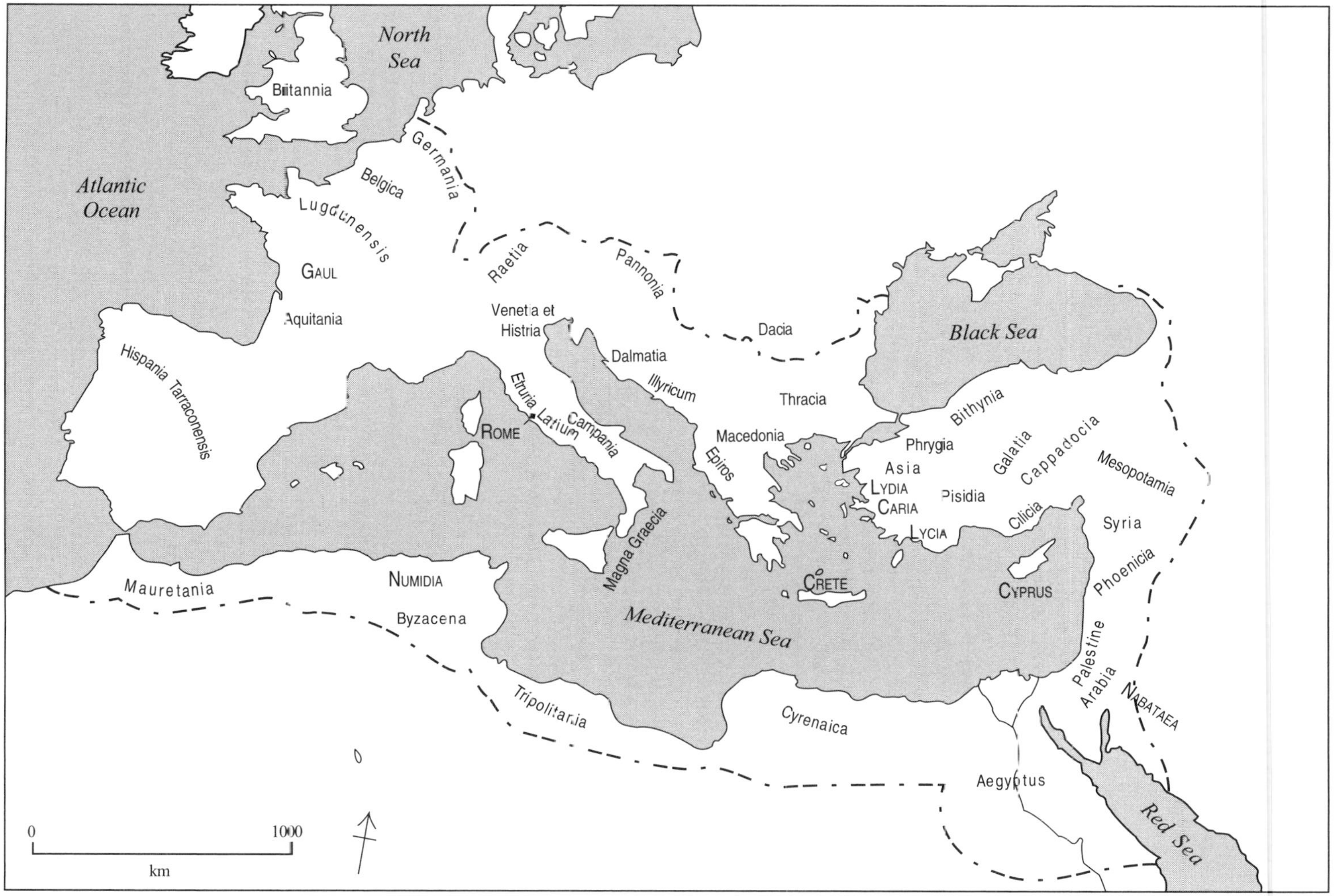

1. Map of the Roman Empire; those areas with separate entries in the encyclopedia are distinguished by CROSS-REFERENCE TYPE

first emperor. He simultaneously held several important administrative and religious positions and reorganized the social orders. To consolidate control over the Empire, Augustus streamlined provincial administration, expanded the road system and stimulated the growth of towns. In addition, he united the Empire through personal allegiance to himself, even allowing worship of his *genius* (protecting deity). Augustus used the arts to promote himself and to champion the themes of his administration: devotion to duty, respect for tradition, fecundity and peace. He also lavished new buildings on the capital to create a city worthy of the great Empire and rightly boasted that he had transformed Rome from a city of mud-brick to one of marble. In effect, Augustus established an Imperial vocabulary, making art the deliberate manifestation of Roman rule. At his death in AD 14 he was proclaimed a god, like Caesar before him.

Succeeding Julio-Claudian emperors dropped all Republican pretence and assumed the trappings of Empire. Increasingly, they relied on a large bureaucracy of freedmen to administer the State. The Julio-Claudians expanded the Empire in the East and consolidated holdings in the West and North. Following NERO, the last of the line, four emperors assumed power in rapid sequence in AD 69, each backed by an army. In the end, VESPASIAN reigned. Of humble lineage, this general eschewed luxury and applied himself to governing. He restored confidence in the State, stabilized the provinces and returned prosperity to the Empire. Vespasian's two sons, TITUS and DOMITIAN, followed in uncontested succession, creating the Flavian dynasty. The exuberance of the art of this period reflects contemporary optimism. The Flavians courted popular support with large buildings for entertainment in Rome, including the Colosseum (the Flavian Amphitheatre) and the Baths of Titus, while Domitian constructed a great imperial residence on the Palatine, an appropriate palace for an emperor who accepted semi-divine honours and was ruthlessly autocratic.

The Empire flourished in the next four decades. Through adoptive succession, five able emperors followed in sequence, establishing an age of civil harmony, prosperity and territorial expansion. TRAJAN pushed the Empire to its greatest limits, including Dacia, Parthia, Romania and the Persian Gulf. HADRIAN was an administrator of Rome's provinces and consolidated the frontiers; he also reworked the Roman legal system, established generous grain doles and erected dozens of buildings. His villa at TIBUR (Tivoli) was filled with art and buildings emulating Greek and Egyptian examples. The 2nd century AD was a golden age for Roman urbanism. Roman legions built cities everywhere, frequently using the grid layout of military camps as at THAMUGADI (Timgad) in North Africa. The prosperous middle class enriched their cities with impressive urban amenities. Libraries, baths and theatres adorned even lesser provincial centres. Some structures imitated famous buildings in the capital, while others reflected local traditions within a Roman context. With a ready market in Rome for foodstuffs and luxury goods, the provinces began to out-perform Italy. The capital received new port facilities and great market halls, such as those of Trajan, to handle imports from as far afield as Scandinavia, India and China.

The euphoria of the period could not mask dark undercurrents. External threats menaced the frontiers; revolts broke out in Britain and Germany; plagues were rife. After the death of his co-regent Lucius Verus (*reg* AD 161–9), MARCUS AURELIUS named his own son Commodus (*reg* 180–93) as heir, thereby ending the successful process of selection by adoption. SEPTIMIUS SEVERUS established a new dynasty based on military power. Italy changed from being the centre of Empire into one of many provinces; Rome became more the container of tradition and less an active capital. Severus expended great sums to aggrandize his African home town, LEPTIS MAGNA, constructing a splendid colonnaded street leading to a new harbour and grand civic buildings. His heir Caracalla (*reg* 211–17) abolished the distinction between Italians and provincials by granting full Roman citizenship to all in 212. In the 3rd century, Roman supremacy was challenged on every side. Fearing foreign incursions, Aurelian (*reg* 270–75) erected a defensive brick wall around Rome. Alternative temporary capitals were established near the frontiers. As belief in the eternity of Empire declined, DIOCLETIAN adopted eastern ideas of the ruler as vicegerent of Jupiter. He stabilized the currency, made taxes more equitable and checked inflation. To prevent wars of succession and facilitate administration of the crumbling Empire he instituted joint rule, whereby he shared power with a co-augustus, each being served by a junior caesar. This Tetrarchy thus divided the Empire into Eastern and Western halves. In 305 Diocletian retired to his fortified palace at SPALATUM (Split), his hopes of peaceful succession destroyed by rival pretenders backed by large personal armies.

CONSTANTINE THE GREAT once again united the Empire under a single ruler. Even more enduring, he officially recognized Christianity (AD 313). Constantine began to transform Rome into a Christian city, erecting large churches on the capital's edges. In 324 he established a Christian capital in the East, CONSTANTINOPLE, inaugurated as the 'new Rome'. From here Roman emperors concentrated on governing the rich Eastern Empire; increasingly, they ignored the impoverished West. The cities of Asia Minor and the rich agricultural areas of North Africa survived the disruptions of the 3rd century. Wealthy cities undertook ambitious renewal projects, including long colonnaded avenues. Elsewhere in the Empire, cities suffered with the collapse of Imperial security and stability. Few residents could afford to hold costly public offices, and power thus gravitated to the large fortified country estates of the aristocracy.

At the death of Constantine in AD 337, his three sons divided the Imperial territories. Thereafter, a few emperors attempted to re-establish the Roman Empire as the sole power in the Mediterranean, but none succeeded. Attempts to revive paganism also failed. Large-scale commissions were made to a Christian, not Imperial, mandate, and thousands of pagan statues were destroyed or were carried off by invading Vandals. In 410 the Visigoths captured Rome. With the deposition of the emperor Romulus Augustulus in 476, the Western Empire ended, and with it Rome's 1000-year-old cultural and political ascendancy in the Mediterranean.

S. A. Cook and others, eds: *The Cambridge Ancient History*, vii–xii (Cambridge, 1922–36, rev. 2/1970–88)

A. E. R. Boak: *A History of Rome to A.D. 565* (New York, 1929, rev. 5/1965)

T. H. Frank, ed.: *An Economic Survey of Ancient Rome*, 5 vols (Baltimore, 1933–40)

M. Cary and H. H. Scullard: *A History of Rome Down to the Reign of Constantine* (London, 1935, 3/1975)

H. H. Scullard: *A History of the Roman World, 753 to 146 BC* (London, 1935, rev. 4/1981)

A. Garzetti: *L'impero da Tiberio agli Antonini* (Bologna, 1960); Eng. trans. by J. R. Foster (London, 1974, 2/1976)

R. Bianchi-Bandinelli: *Rome, the Centre of Power: Roman Art, 500 B.C. to A.D. 200* (London and New York, 1970)

R. Bianchi-Bandinelli: *Rome, the Late Empire: Roman Art, A.D. 200–400* (London and New York, 1971)

G. M. A. Hanfmann: *Roman Art* (New York, 1975)

O. Brendel: *Prolegomena to the Study of Roman Art* (New Haven, 1979)

J. Stambaugh: *The Ancient Roman City* (Baltimore, 1988)

J. Boardman, J. Griffin and O. Murray, eds: *The Oxford History of the Roman World* (New York, 1991)

E. Gruen: *Culture and National Identity in Republican Rome* (Ithaca, 1992)

2. TRADE. The growth of large cities such as Rome led to an increased level of supply to meet the needs of large populations. Much of this trade was linked to the supply of staples, primarily grain, slaves and metals. Yet with the creation of specialized harbours, such as OSTIA at the mouth of the River Tiber, it became easier to transport and tranship bulky items. Aelius Aristides, writing in the mid-2nd century AD, noted how the countries round the Mediterranean sent 'an endless flow of goods' to Rome. These included cargoes of 'agriculture, metallurgy, all the skills that exist and have existed, anything that is begotten and grows' (*Eis Romin* ('To Rome') xi–xiii).

The cost of transport, especially for bulky materials such as marble or metals, would have been much cheaper by sea than by road. The size of ships also increased; some vessels may have been over 40 m in length and may have carried some 500 tons. The expense of travel may be one reason why PLINY the younger (*Letters* X.xli.2), writing to the emperor TRAJAN from Bithynia, proposed constructing a canal from Lake Solophon to the Sea of Marmara. He noted that items such as marble, which had to be taken to the sea for the final part of their journey, were transported there by cart at great expense.

The incorporation of Greece into the Roman Empire (146 BC) led to an increased taste for Greek art. Many of the great sanctuaries of the Greek world were stripped to meet this need, and monumental Greek bronze sculpture recovered from the sea off Italy often appears to have been part of this looting process. The taste for Greek art also led to the demand for marble replicas of famous works of art. Workshops in such places as Athens produced replicas that were shipped to Italy and elsewhere. A batch of 2nd-century AD Roman reliefs from a shipwreck in the Peiraeus were clearly part of such a consignment. Some of them 'quote' elements from the *Amazonomachy* decoration of the shield of the *Athena Parthenos* on the Athenian Acropolis.

Apart from grain, one of the main bulk cargoes in the Roman world was marble, which was used in the construction of buildings as well as for sculpture. As the urban élites in the provinces wished to express their wealth, they gave buildings to their cities as part of major benefactions. Often this involved elaborate structures that needed to use imported marble. Marble sculpture and architectural elements at LEPTIS MAGNA in Tripolitania, home to the emperor SEPTIMIUS SEVERUS, replaced limestone and stucco or sandstone. Isotopic analysis of the new material has suggested that it had been brought from the quarries of Dokimeion, LUNA (now Carrara), Prokonnesos and possibly Thasos.

Marble was also widely used for sarcophagi (*see* SARCOPHAGUS). A will from Andemantuum in Gaul specified that the image inside should be made of 'the finest marble from overseas or else the finest bronze'. Luna marble was used to close the tomb. Thus a member of the urban élite in Gaul could expect his family to erect a monument that would incorporate marble brought from the quarries at Luna in Tuscany.

In the eastern Mediterranean the main quarries that exported both roughed-out and finished sarcophagi were located in Attica (Mt Pentelikon), Prokonnesos in the Sea of Marmara and DOKIMEION. Apart from Greece, Crete and Cyrenaica, Pentelic sarcophagi are also found in Syria. Interestingly they appear to be absent from Tripolitania. This may reflect the regional networks of trade operating within the eastern provinces of the Roman Empire. Prokonnesian marble was widely exported, in part due to the proximity of the quarries to the sea. Sarcophagi seem to have been roughed out *in situ*, to be completed at their point of destination. They were particularly popular at Rome in the 3rd century AD. A wreck, possibly from the 3rd century, was found off San Pietro near Taranto in southern Italy containing a number of these sarcophagi. Prokonnesian sarcophagi are also found around the coast of the Black Sea and the Adriatic. It seems that the marble from these quarries was sent to Nicomedia, the local administrative centre. Moreover Nicomedian or Bithynian sculptors may have gone to cities of the Empire to work on the marble. For example at NIKOPOLIS in modern Bulgaria an inscription on an altar refers to the guild of Nicomedian craftsmen; this coincides with the use of Prokonnesian marble on the site. The same type of organization may have been true for the sculptors from the city of APHRODISIAS in Caria, who also seem to have worked in different cities of the Empire on finishing sculpture and architectural items that had been sent out in half-finished form.

The quarries at Dokimeion seem to have been imperial property. The purple and white marble they produced was particularly valued at Rome. Strabo (*Geography* XII.viii.14) mentioned the difficulty of transporting large blocks of this marble, which were to be used for columns and veneers, to Rome. Some of the exported sarcophagi seem to have travelled by road down through western Anatolia via the Maeander Valley, from where they could be shipped to Greece, Syria and Rome.

Perhaps one of the most impressive examples of the transport of stone for use in sculpture and architecture was the exploitation of porphyry from Mons Porphyrites in Egypt (*see under* SCULPTURE, §VI, 1(iii)(a)). Often this purple-coloured stone was used for colossal statues, and its transport from the quarries overland across the desert to the Nile was a major achievement in itself.

The luxury trade carried out in the Mediterranean in the late 1st century AD was huge and varied: 'And the merchants of the earth shall weep and mourn over her; for no man buyeth their merchandise any more: the merchandise of gold, and silver, and precious stones and of pearls, and fine linen, and purple, and silk, and scarlet, and all thyine wood, and all manner vessels of ivory, and all manner vessels of most precious wood, and of brass, and iron, and marble' (Revelation 18:11–13). Examples of such trade include carpets, cloaks and woollens that were widely exported in the Augustan period from Patavium (now Padua; see Strabo V.i.7, 12). GLASS had a widespread distribution throughout the Empire. It seems to have been produced in major centres such as SIDON, ALEXANDRIA and COLONIA CLAUDIA ARA AGRIPPINENSIUM (Cologne). Glass workshops were also established in the Po Valley of Italy during the 1st century AD, probably by craftsmen moving from the eastern Mediterranean. Significant though these items may be in the archaeological record, especially as pointers to the activity of commerce in the Roman Empire, it is important to remember that such manufactured items played a very small part in the Roman economy.

The resources of the Empire were such that luxury items could be brought in across the frontiers. Pliny the elder (*Natural History* VI.101; XII.84) observed that the trade with India took 50 million sesterces out of the Roman world every year, and that with China and Arabia the total was some 100 million sesterces. An anonymous travel document of the 1st century AD (*Periplus Maris Erythraei* ('Voyage around the Red Sea', xlix and lvi) records the type of trade being undertaken with India. Some of it comprised raw materials: wine, copper, tin, lead, coral, textiles, raw glass and so on. Imports were such exotic items as ivory, pearls and Chinese silk, as well as a range of gems including diamonds and sapphires.

J. B. Ward-Perkins: 'Tripolitania and the Marble Trade', *J. Roman Stud.*, xli (1951), pp. 89–104

J. B. Ward-Perkins: 'The Marble Trade and its Organisation: Evidence from Nicomedia', *Mem. Amer. Acad. Rome*, xxxvi (1980), pp. 325–38

J. B. Ward-Perkins: 'Nicomedia and the Marble Trade', *Pap. Brit. Sch. Rome*, n. s., xxxv (1980), pp. 23–69

H. Dodge: 'Notes on Luxury Building Stones in Asia Minor', *Yayla*, iv (1981), pp. 8–11

R. Duncan-Jones: *The Economy of the Roman Empire: Quantitative Studies* (Cambridge, 1982)

H. Walda and S. Walker: 'The Art and Architecture of Lepcis Magna: Marble Origins by Isotopic Analysis', *Libyan Stud.*, xv (1984), pp. 81–92

M. I. Finley: *The Ancient Economy* (London, 1985)

S. Walker: *Memorials to the Roman Dead* (London, 1985)

K. Greene: *The Archaeology of the Roman Economy* (London, 1986)

D. B. Harden: *Glass of the Caesars* (London, 1987)

B. A. Sparkes: 'Greek Bronzes', *Greece & Rome*, xxxiv (1987), pp. 152–68

H. Walda and S. Walker: 'Isotopic Analysis of Marble from Lepcis Magna: Revised Interpretations', *Libyan Stud.*, xix (1988), pp. 55–9

M. L. Anderson and L. Nitsa, eds: *Radiance in Stone: Sculptures in Coloured Marble from the Museo Nazionale Romano* (Rome, 1989)

M. G. Fulford: 'To East and West: The Mediterranean Trade of Cyrenaica and Tripolitania in Antiquity', *Libyan Stud.*, xx (1989), pp. 169–91

A. J. Parker: 'Classical Antiquity: The Maritime Dimension', *Antiquity*, lxiv (1990), pp. 335–46

W. Scheidel and S. von Reden, eds: *The Ancient Economy* (Edinburgh, 2002)

3. RELIGION. From the earliest times, the Romans believed that success, both in the State and in their private affairs, depended not on their strength but on a harmonious relationship with the gods. A great deal of Roman art explores the theme of *pax deorum* (peace of the gods) in the frequent repetition of sacrificial scenes and other sacral acts by which the favour of the gods was repaid. For example on the Ara Pacis (*see* ROME, §IV, 4) Aeneas, the legendary founder of the Trojan settlements in Italy, is shown clad in a toga, his head covered, about to offer a libation of fruit and wine and then to sacrifice a sow to his ancestral gods (*penates*) who are depicted in a little shrine. A frequent subject is the *suovetaurilia* (see fig. 2), the sacrifice of a boar, a ram and a bull to the chief deities of the State, and especially Jupiter, by an important magistrate or the emperor on behalf of the Roman people. Aeneas' sacrifice was matched in every Roman house by the devotion lavished on the household gods (*lares*) who, together with the *penates* and the *genius* (protecting deity) of the master, were venerated in the household shrines (*lararia*); a splendid example of a LARARIUM, embellished with paintings of two *lares* and a *genius*, stands in the hall of the House of the Vettii at Pompeii (1st century AD). Even the *suovetaurilia* might be offered by the head of an ordinary household on a special occasion, and in

the 2nd century BC Cato the Censor recommended one as a sacrifice to Mars as expiation when thinning the god's sacred grove (*De agri cultura* 139–41). Most religious observances were seasonal, with various feasts and ceremonies being prescribed for specific days throughout the year, a calendar given poetic form by Ovid in his *Fasti* (calendar of feast days).

At first the Roman gods were strictly functional, but under Greek influence the most important ones were equated with those of the Greeks and to some degree acquired their mythological attributes. Jupiter (Zeus), Juno (Hera) and Minerva (Athena) were of especial importance and were venerated together as the Capitoline triad. Mars was more significant than the Greek Ares and was primarily a power of agriculture and a protector, not a war god. Apollo, on the other hand, was an import from the Greek world who became thoroughly acclimatized in the West during the Imperial period. The Romans were ever conscious of the multiplicity of gods, and apart from Greek deities they accepted Cybele (Kybele) the Great Mother from Asia Minor in the late 3rd century BC, the Egyptian Isis in Hellenized form in the 1st century AD and Sol Invictus (the Unconquered Sun) in the 3rd century. Moreover, everywhere local deities were interpreted as though they were Roman ones, so that, for example, Sulis was equated with Minerva at Aquae Sulis (Bath), Caelestis (the North African moon goddess) with Juno and Lenus was invoked at Augusta Treverorum (Trier) as Lenus Mars.

The pantheon was further enriched and expanded by extending the lists of functional powers to include not only important personifications such as Fortune, Health, Hope, Victory, Peace and Fecundity but also Roma and the various provinces such as Britannia. It is not surprising that altars were set up to them. The power of the Roman emperor found expression in the veneration accorded to his *numen* or divine spirit as well as in the worship of dead rulers, subsequently deified, such as Augustus, Claudius and Vespasian. Some of the grandest temples, including the Maison Carrée at NEMAUSUS (Nîmes) and the so-called Temple of Augustus and Livia (late 1st century BC) at Vienna (Vienne), were associated with this imperial cult, as was the Temple of the Deified Claudius (mid-1st century AD) at Camulodunum (Colchester), which was at least as impressive, though nothing of it now remains save its massive substructure.

Central to Roman religion was the legal contract. Men, either as individuals or in communities, made a contract offering gifts in return for a favour. This pronouncement (*nuncupatio*) inevitably led to the payment of the vow (*solutio*) if the request was answered. Apart from sacrifices, the system was a major generator of art; gifts presented as thank-offerings included sculpture, silver plate, figurines and even temples.

The forms of TEMPLES varied from region to region. The classic type of Roman temple was rectangular, standing on a high podium and furnished with a PSEUDO-PERIPTERAL colonnade. In Gaul and Britain this type gave way to a square or hexagonal structure sometimes with a tower-like CELLA and a surrounding ambulatory, whilst in the East the temple was the innermost element of a series of courts or sacred spaces, as for example at BAALBEK. What all these disparate architectural forms have in common is the idea of a house for a god or goddess, generally represented by a CULT STATUE. Temples were not, in fact, essential elements in sanctuaries—the central device on a silver dish from a temple at Berthouville (Paris, Bibl. N., Cab. Médailles) shows Mercury at home in his sanctuary, which is represented simply by means of two columns and a sacred tree. Many works of art, including wall paintings from Pompeii, confirm the omnipresence of the divine, for instance in sacred trees and springs, wayside shrines and in gardens.

Because the gods were everywhere and affected all living things, it followed that it was possible to learn the divine will from unusual events in nature (prodigies) of which Roman history—especially legendary history—is full, and from a close study of natural phenomena, notably the flight of birds. Augury

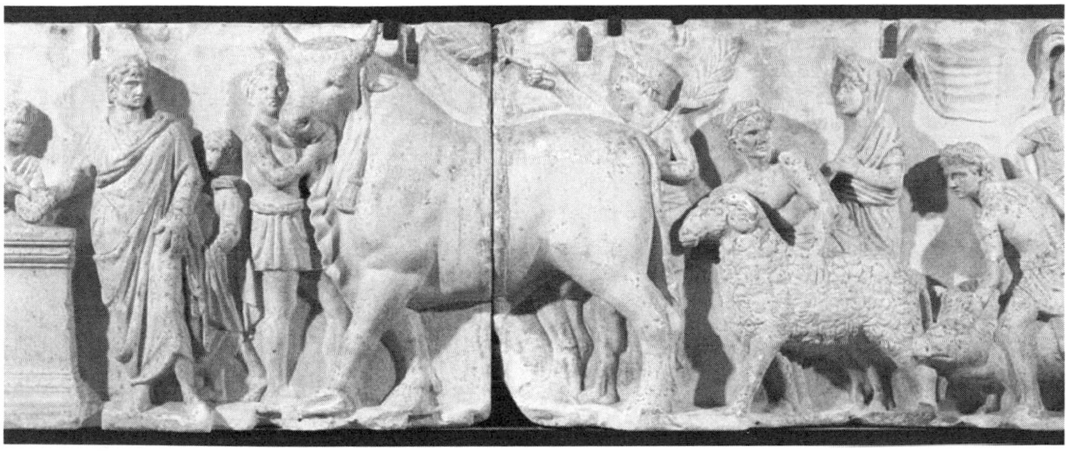

2. *Suovetaurilia* (sacrifice of a boar, a ram and a bull), marble relief, h. 813 mm, possibily from the Temple of Neptune, Rome, *c*. 70 BC (Paris, Musée du Louvre)

played an important part in decision-making; so too did the examination of the livers of sacrificed animals, for they were 'read' as maps of the sky by experts, *haruspices* (the word *haruspex* is Etruscan and means 'gut-gazer'). The use of professionals, as here, was exceptional. For the most part, priesthoods were not onerous and were undertaken as honours just like lay magistracies. There was thus a very wide public participation in religious affairs, not surprising when it is recalled that every *paterfamilias* was a priest in his own household's cult.

There is little doubt that the Roman gods, especially those of the countryside, generated warm affection from their votaries; the poetry of Virgil, Horace and Ovid confirms this. The more esoteric and ecstatic aspects of Roman religion belonged to private, perhaps secret, societies such as one that must have met at the Villa of the Mysteries just outside Pompeii in the 1st century BC to venerate Bacchus, as the initiation ceremony painted on the walls suggests. A cult building in Rome of about a century later, the underground basilica on the Via Praenestina outside the Porta Maggiore, is embellished with fine stuccowork showing mythological scenes (including divine rapes, of Ganymede by Jupiter and of a daughter of Leucippus by one of the Dioscuri) and others concerned with education; this was presumably also dedicated to a mystery cult offering salvation through secret knowledge. A mosaic floor from the Kornmarkt in AUGUSTA TREVERORUM (Trier), dating from the 4th century AD (Trier, Rhein. Landesmus.), depicts a ritual from another cult concerned with the offering of food. Votaries appear carrying dishes or dancing, as doubtless they did in life. Another detail on the mosaic shows that the rituals of this otherwise unknown cult centred on the union of Jupiter with Leda. An important find of jewellery and silver spoons at Thetford, Norfolk, belonged to another religious group venerating Faunus, who was worshipped in Rome and Latium.

The search for religious fulfilment through special rites and sacred meals was always an important aspect of the Roman religious scene. Best known of these mystery cults was that of Mithras, a deity of Indo-Iranian origin, although the cult as practised in the Mediterranean world was entirely Roman, having developed through the officer class of the army and the merchants of the great ports. Every Mithraeum (e.g. that beneath S Clemente in Rome) represented a cave in which the god Mithras slew the primeval bull and thus brought creation, with its life and light, into existence. Mithraists reclined on benches in the aisles of these artificial caves to partake of meals (which the early Christians not unnaturally saw as parodies of the Eucharist). There were various grades of initiation achieved through various trials. Much of what is known about this cult comes from the numerous works of art recovered from these Mithraea, all of them votive gifts just like art works from the public temples.

The adoption of Christianity as the state religion in the Roman Empire in the 4th century AD precipitated major changes. The traditional gods disappeared from public veneration, to the alarm of traditionalists such as Q. Aurelius Symmachus, urban prefect in 384 (*Relatio* iii). The emperor's spiritual power no longer rested on his *numen* or divine ancestors but rather on his status as God's deputy on earth. Christian churches, however large, followed the model of the *collegium* (college) or *schola* (school) rather than the temple; central was a new form of mystery, the Eucharist. The building of churches on the burial sites of martyr tombs was a striking innovation, for no Roman precedents existed and graves were only the places for rites connected with the ancestors on certain limited occasions during the year. Large and striking Constantinian churches such as St Peter's in Rome and the Holy Sepulchre in Jerusalem, built on the sites of tombs of the 'special dead', effectively reversed the boundaries of the sacred and the profane as they had been understood throughout Classical antiquity. However, it is clear from Christian sources, notably the *Liber pontificalis* (the original version of which dates to the 6th century), that the building of churches and the dedication of mosaics and plate simply continued the tradition of votive offering that was central to Roman ideas of piety.

Liber pontificalis (6th century AD); Eng. trans. and intro. by R. Davis as *The Book of Pontiffs* (Liverpool, 1989)

J. Toynbee and J. Ward Perkins: *The Shrine of St Peter and the Vatican Excavations* (London, 1956)

M. J. Vermaseren: *Mithras: The Secret God* (London, 1963)

R. Ogilvie: *The Romans and their Gods* (London, 1969)

J. Ferguson: *The Religion of the Roman Empire* (London, 1970)

R. E. Witt: *Isis in the Graeco-Roman World* (London, 1971)

M. J. Vermaseren: *Cybele and Attis: The Myth and the Cult* (London, 1977)

P. Brown: *The Cult of the Saints* (Chicago, 1981)

R. MacMullen: *Paganism in the Roman Empire* (New Haven, 1981)

H. H. Scullard: *Festivals and Ceremonies of the Roman Republic* (London, 1981)

C. Thomas: *Christianity in Roman Britain in AD 500* (London, 1981)

M. Henig and A. King: *Pagan Gods and Shrines of the Roman Empire* (Oxford, 1983)

M. Henig: *Religion in Roman Britain* (London, 1984)

R. Merkelbach: *Mithras* (Hain, 1984)

S. R. F. Price: *Rituals and Power: The Roman Imperial Cult in Asia Minor* (Cambridge, 1984)

R. Lane Fox: *Pagans and Christians* (Harmondsworth, 1986)

D. Fishwick: *The Imperial Cult in the Latin West: Studies in the Ruler Cult of the Western Provinces of the Roman Empire*, 2 vols (Leiden, 1987–92)

R. Turcan: *Les Cultes Orientaux dans le monde Romain* (Paris, 1989); Eng. trans. A. Nevill: *The Cults of the Roman Empire* (Oxford, 1996)

E. Simon: *Die Götter der Römer* (Darmstadt, 1990)

T. F. Mathews: *The Clash of Gods. A Reinterpretation of Early Christian Art* (Princeton, 1993)

C. M. Ternes and P. F. Burke: *Roman Religion in Gallia, Belgica and the Germaniae* (Luxembourg, 1994)

S. Fine, ed.: *Sacred Realm: The Emergence of the Synagogue in the Ancient World* (New York, 1996)

M. Beard, J. North and S. Price: *Religions of Rome, Vol. 1: A History; Vol. 2: A Sourcebook* (Cambridge, 1998)

T. Derks: *Gods, Temples and Ritual Practices: The Transformation of Religious Ideas and Values in Roman Gaul* (Amsterdam, 1998)
J. B. Rives: *Religion in the Roman Empire* (Oxford, 2007)

4. Subject-matter. The subject-matter of Roman art ranges from humans at work and leisure to animals (sometimes being hunted or butchered in the amphitheatre but often in their natural habitats) to the countryside and the sea, and includes gods, heroes and monsters, myth and history, solemn ritual and caricature.

For more extensive discussions of subject-matter *see* Sculpture §VI, *Painting*, §VI, *Mosaics*, §III and *Textiles*, §III. Portraiture is also discussed under sculpture.

(i) Introduction. (ii) Commemorative and religious art. (iii) Portraiture. (iv) Narrative art. (v) Still-life and the natural world. (vi) Late Roman developments.

(i) Introduction. Roman art is an elusive concept for it changed its meaning through time. At first it was simply the art produced in the city of Rome, basically Etruscan in character (*see* Etruscan, §5) though influenced by Greek and Hellenized settlements to the south. From about the 3rd century BC, however, despite the continuation of strong regional trends, most of Italy was effectively Roman. Later, and especially from the establishment of the Principate by Augustus in 27 BC, major works of art throughout the Mediterranean carried the political aims and cultural values of Imperial Rome, employing the sophisticated visual language and intellectual content of Hellenistic civilization. In its turn this art went through profound changes, and in many ways the hieratic images of Late Antique emperors, the abstract forms of late Roman/Early Christian sculpture and the dazzling colour and esoteric symbolism of Early Christian church mosaics mark the beginning of medieval art.

In Rome of the kings and of the early Republic, with its simple images of household gods and stylized representations of ancestors, art functioned simply to serve the needs of religion. Influenced by Etruscan artists such as Vulca (*fl c.* 500 BC), the Romans embellished their temples with terracotta images of deities (see Pliny the elder: *Natural History* XXXV.xlv.157). Painting too was largely religious and mythological, and even historical narrative scenes, such as those in the 3rd- or 2nd-century BC tombs on the Esquiline, should not be taken at face value as secular works, for the Romans saw the whole of their history from the days of Aeneas and Romulus as an expression of destiny, arising from their intense *pietas*.

The first manifestations of a wider artistic repertory came as a result of contacts with Greek culture. Fine bronzes in a distinctive Greco-Etruscan style were made at Praeneste (Palestrina) in Latium and also in Rome itself, to judge from the evidence of the Ficoroni Cist (see colour pl. 1:XV, fig. 4), made in Rome by Novios Plautios. The theme of the frieze engraved on this cist concerns the Dioscuri, twin saviour-deities who were widely represented on early Roman coinage. Had Rome developed as a typical city-state a native artistic tradition might have flourished. However, conquest in South Italy, Sicily, Macedonia, Greece and the East swamped the city in booty, much of it destined for temples and public places, although a great deal of sculpture, gems, jewellery, inlaid furniture and silver plate ended up in private hands. Later writers such as Livy and Pliny the younger affected to lament this process, especially for its part in destroying the ancient peasant simplicity of the Roman character. Some Greek artists settled in Italy, while Rome and other Italian cities received Hellenistic-style buildings ornamented with sculpture, and Greek taste also influenced art on the domestic scale: in the marble garden furniture, wall paintings (in the First and Second styles) and bronzes. With the consolidation of political power in the hands of Octavian [Augustus] after he had defeated Mark Antony at the Battle of Actium in 31 BC, state art became more focused. It was only then that a confident Roman style emerged, though its execution was largely in the hands of Greeks.

(ii) Commemorative and religious art. Augustan poets such as Virgil and Horace and the sculptors of the Ara Pacis (*see* Rome, §IV, 4) alike celebrated the Roman mission to bring peace and prosperity to the world. On each side of the two entrances to the Ara Pacis is a scene carefully chosen from the repertory of Roman myth, including Aeneas' sacrifice at Lavinium and Romulus and Remus suckled by the She-wolf. The personification of Italy as a mother nurturing two babies between other personifications of the air and the sea is highly reminiscent of such Hellenistic works as the Tazza Farnese cameo cup (mid-1st century BC; Naples, Mus. N. Archeol.), but on the Ara Pacis great care is taken to avoid any suggestion of a ruler-cult. Rome's prosperity is attributed to the piety of its magistrates, priests and people portrayed along the long sides of the screen wall (for illustration *see* Dress).

Commemoration of an event not so much for its own sake as to emphasize harmony between the Romans and their gods is a feature of other State monuments, whether they were arches, altars or columns. They differ from the triumphal monuments of the Near East in their stress on the sacramental nature of Rome's victories as performed in fulfilment of a mission. The Arch of Titus (AD 79–81) at Rome, for example, carries in high relief on the two internal passage walls two extracts from the triumphal procession over the Jews, one of them the display of booty from the war (including the great Menorah from the Temple in Jerusalem) and the other the emperor Titus in his chariot. The purpose of these scenes was not simply to brag. Titus, who had died when the arch was finally completed, is portrayed as divine on the vault above the passageway, being carried up to the heavens by an eagle and the sculptures of the arch remind the Roman people of an emperor who had deserved well of them and now, after death, was amongst the gods as a *Divus*. The reliefs on Trajan's Column take such commemoration to much greater length. They purport to tell the story of the Dacian Wars, and thus military historians have used them as a major source of factual information. They should probably be read, however, in a more symbolic and poetic manner. The *optimus princeps* ('great leader') is figured again and again in close harmony with the Roman people in arms, a fighting army but also an army that regularly sacrifices to the gods that Jupiter himself succours in its time of need. Once again, this monument's skilful execution is the work of Greek artists. Although the column itself was inaugurated by TRAJAN in 113, it has been convincingly argued that the sculpture was added on the orders of Hadrian some ten or fifteen years later, after the column had become Trajan's tomb.

(iii) Portraiture. Greek artists also provided the Romans with other commemorative art, including perhaps the most distinctive of Roman artistic achievements, portraiture. This was once considered simply a native Italian (Etruscan and Roman Republican) achievement, but portraits in the early Republic are far less convincing than those produced later under Greek influence. Portraits of Augustus, for example, were based on those of Alexander the Great and his successors to a remarkable degree. The Prima Porta *Augustus* (Rome, Vatican, Braccio Nuo.; for illustration *see* AUGUSTUS) displays affinities with the late Etruscan *Arringatore* (Florence, Mus. Archeol.; *see* ETRUSCAN, fig. 2), but its pose is based on the Classical Greek type of the Polykleitan Canon, while its physiognomy is Hellenistic. Imperial portraits were set up in temples and public places throughout the Empire, reminding its inhabitants of the power of living rulers and of the divine status of dead emperors whose deeds were still officially remembered. The imperial family was honoured as a whole and so portraits of wives, sons and daughters are also common.

The quality and style of private portraiture was also affected by the desire to commemorate. Some houses contained large numbers of busts of ancestors, political heroes, philosophers and writers. Busts were also placed in or, preferably, on tombs, while tomb monuments themselves often combined the accurate depiction of individuals with scenes of their daily activities, or even set them in mythological contexts (*see* SARCOPHAGUS, §3). In Petronius' *Satyricon* (lxxi) there is a splendid description of Trimalchio's tomb, built in his lifetime so that he could enjoy the prospect of it and 'carry on living after death'. Trimalchio was to be shown seated on a high platform pouring out money at a banquet for the people; trading vessels, the source of his prosperity, were also depicted. Most important of all were the statues of Trimalchio and his wife Fortunata. Examples of such monuments and of reliefs from them abound, not only in Italy but throughout the provinces, such as the elaborate tomb of the Secundinii (*c.* AD 250) at Igel near Trier with its depictions of the production and distribution of cloth coupled with scenes of myth such as the *Apotheosis of Hercules*.

Both public and private monuments were accompanied by inscriptions recording their functions. Roman monumental lettering is far more harmonious than Greek and has remained the standard of excellence down to our own time; each character is beautifully proportioned and designed for maximum legibility (*see also* ARCHITECTURE, §VI, 1(iii)(c)).

See also SCULPTURE, §VI, 1(ii).

(iv) Narrative art. Private works of art display considerable diversity. The large degree of personal and economic freedom enjoyed by the upper classes in Italy and the provinces throughout the early centuries of the Empire meant that private citizens were able to amass vast collections. Workshops of sculptors, painters, mosaicists, glassworkers, potters, jewellers and silversmiths catered for this demand. Local workshops often had distinctive styles or themes, and various regions specialized in particular materials: Greece and Asia Minor, for example, were known for high-quality marble, the Levant for glass and Aquileia for amber.

Taste in subject-matter varied from the gladiatorial and circus scenes common on mosaics from North Africa and elsewhere, as well as on everyday objects such as glass beakers, pots and lamps (Petronius' Trimalchio had these subjects portrayed in wall paintings, on silver plate and even on his tomb), to deliberate displays of erudition, such as the representations of writers in paintings in the House of the Menander at Pompeii (*c.* AD 69–79). The close connection between art and literature is clear from the popularity of mythological scenes, such as the depiction of *Polyphemus and Galatea* on the wall of a room in the villa at Boscotrecase (late 1st century BC; New York, Met.), which recalls Theocritus' 11th Idyll. Sometimes they contain a moral message, as in the paintings of the Theban Room in the House of the Vettii, Pompeii (*c.* AD 54–*c.* 65), which show the *Punishment of Pentheus* and the *Punishment of Dirce*, both guilty of impiety, scenes contrasting with the *Infant Hercules Wrestling with Snakes*. Just as a library contains a good selection of books, the selection of paintings for a house would have been deliberate, designed to stimulate thought and conversation.

The same use of juxtaposition is to be found on mosaic floors, for example in those at Lullingstone in Kent (4th century AD), where *Bellerophon on Pegasus* is contrasted with *Europa on the Bull*, the second scene accompanied by a couplet to the effect that if jealous Juno had seen the bull (Jupiter in disguise) swimming she would have stirred up the winds. The literary allusion is to Virgil (*Aeneid* II, in which Juno drives the Trojan fleet on to the shores of Carthage), but the metre of the poem and source of the myth come from Ovid (*Metamorphoses* II). Sculpture was employed in a similar manner. The pointing process whereby exact copies of statues could be reproduced by measuring distances between fixed points on the original with callipers made it possible to create effects with multiple replicas as well as to juxtapose statues as mirror images. Augustus was able to suggest that Rome was a new and better Athens by placing copies of the caryatids of the Erechtheion in his Forum Augustum; Hadrian used copies of the same figures in his villa at Tibur (Tivoli), reflected in the waters of an ornamental canal, to produce a very different effect, that of Romantic Hellenism.

In a wealth of precious objects, notably gems and silver plate, Romans were able to indulge their tastes for both storytelling and mood-painting. For example, the repoussé decoration on a silver beaker found on the Rhine (Bonn, Rhein. Landesmus.) shows Jason with his wife Creusa and two children next to Medea. What passes for a quiet domestic scene is in fact infused with tragedy: Medea has sent the children with poisoned gifts for Creusa; soon she will slay them too. A scene of Classical tranquillity decorates one side of the masterpiece of cameo glass known as the Portland Vase (*c.* 27–17 BC; London, BM): it probably shows Apollo in the form of a serpent with Atia, the mother of Augustus, welcoming her son into the world; in contrast, the other side portrays Hecuba with a firebrand and her son Paris, whose abduction of Helen brought about the destruction of Troy. The decoration may have political and religious overtones, and the vase probably belonged to a member of Augustus' family.

(v) Still-life and the natural world. Still-life also had an important place in the Roman repertory; this too had Greek roots. The Unswept Room mosaic from a house on the Aventine Hill in Rome (2nd century AD; Rome, Vatican, Mus. Gregoriano Profano) is probably a copy of an original by Sosos of Pergamon (2nd century BC; see Pliny the elder: *Natural History* XXXVI.lx.184). Compositions consisting of the careful arrangement and juxtaposition of objects comprise a large category of Pompeian wall paintings. Allied to such work are themes taken from nature. Detailed studies of plants are sometimes carefully arranged, as with the crossed plane branches on the front of an Augustan altar, or fancifully incorporated into acanthus ornament, as on the screen wall of the Ara Pacis; on occasions they mirror the empathy with the natural world so evident in Virgil's *Georgics* and the *Odes* of Horace.

Gardening was a highly characteristic Roman art, by its very nature bringing order and harmony out of chaos. The remains of GARDENS recovered by excavation at Pompeii and elsewhere give an idea of the planning and even (through the study of plant remains and soils) of what was grown, but it is through such masterpieces as Livia's Garden Room at Prima Porta (late 1st century BC; Rome, Mus. N. Romano) that we can experience the Roman ideal of myriad plants with foliage of distinct tones and flowers of different colours. Birds of several varieties inhabit this grove, at once artificial and natural. In the House of the Marine Venus (mid-1st century AD) at Pompeii, painted statues in the foreground are a reminder of the actual formality of the walks in a Roman garden. In the cubiculum of the villa of P. Fannius Synister at Boscoreale, one section shows a garden containing a pergola, cave and fountain, inhabited by brightly coloured birds.

Although the Romans could appreciate nature in its minute details, a wider awareness of and feeling for landscape is evident in paintings of country scenes, often full of human and animal activity, and depicting buildings such as shrines and bridges as well as natural features such as streams, rocks and trees. This is not the wild Romanticism of the late 18th century but a reflection of the gods of the countryside and man in harmony. One famous landscape painter was a Roman (at least he has a Latin name) called Studius who lived in the reign of Augustus, when the greatest Roman nature poetry was also written.

(vi) Late Roman developments. If the character of early Roman Imperial art can be seen as a brilliant climax to the art of the Hellenistic world rather than a pale shadow of the Greek experience, the art of Late Antiquity is harder to understand. In part it continued the tradition, as can be seen especially in the collections of the late pagan aristocracy. There were tendencies in other directions, however, and novel themes were adopted, especially in commissions from the imperial court after the official espousal of Christianity (AD 313). Portraiture ceased to aim for verisimilitude and established instead a repertory of conventional types. The mask-like face, enormous staring eyes and impassive mouth of the colossal image of Constantine (*c.* 313; Rome, Mus. Conserv.) is the type of the all-seeing ruler, God's deputy on earth (*dominus*). Lesser men aped his style. The great men who appear on ivory consular diptychs and on mosaics (e.g. the 'Great Hunt' at PIAZZA ARMERINA, Sicily) dressed in splendid clothes are ideals of power and authority rather than individuals. Even the self-consciously pagan emperor Julian (*reg* 360–63) and his intellectual circle could not turn back to the artistic forms of the Antonine age, though they substituted the type of the bearded teacher for that of the *dominus*.

In fact Christian art employed both types of image, depicting Christ both as teacher and as world ruler (Pantocrator). His apostles and saints appear in similar ways, both as men of immense power and as pedagogues. Such virtue was believed to be inherent in them that painted icons were held to be sacred mediators between the visible and unseen worlds. Christian artists adopted many of the devices of earlier art—figural scenes, still-life, the world of nature but to very different purpose. Christian art is didactic: the stories chosen are biblical, expounding the scheme of salvation; nature is Eden before the Fall or Paradise; and the elements of still-life are symbols of immediate relevance to the Christian beholder.

The pagan reaction to these developments is best seen on precious objects such as the dish from the Kaiseraugst treasure with its scenes from the *Life of Achilles* (mid-4th century AD; Augst, Römermus.) and the Symmachus–Nichomachus ivory diptych depicting two elegantly clad priestesses engaged in traditional rites in a tranquil countryside (late 4th century; Paris, Mus. Cluny, and London, V&A). Numerous mosaics from Britain to Syria also show the vitality of Greek and Roman myths. Rare survivals of illustrated manuscripts, such as the *Iliad* in the Biblioteca Ambrosiana, Milan, and the *Virgilius romanus*, reveal that the late pagans were strongly conscious of their literary traditions, and this informs their art with a rare harmony.

G. M. A. Richter: *Ancient Italy: A Study of the Interrelations of its Peoples as Shown in their Arts* (Ann Arbor, 1955)
W. J. T. Peters: *Landscape in Romano-Campanian Mural Painting* (Assen, 1963)
J. M. Croisille: *Les Natures mortes campaniennes: Répertoire descriptif des peintures de nature morte du Musée national de Naples, de Pompéi, Herculanum et Stabies* (Brussels, 1965)
J. J. Pollitt: *The Art of Rome, c. 753 BC–AD 337* (Englewood Cliffs, 1966/*R* Cambridge, 1983)
D. E. Strong: *Greek and Roman Gold and Silver Plate* (London, 1966)
D. E. Strong: *Roman Art*, Pelican Hist. A. (Harmondsworth, 1976, rev. 2/1988 by R. Ling)
M. Bieber: *Ancient Copies: Contributions to the History of Greek and Roman Art* (New York, 1977)
C. C. Vermeule: *Greek Sculpture and Roman Taste: The Purpose and Setting of Graeco-Roman Art in Italy and the Greek Imperial East* (Ann Arbor, 1977)
J. M. C. Toynbee: *Roman Historical Portraits* (London, 1978)
K. Weitzmann, ed.: *Age of Spirituality: Late Antique and Early Christian Art, Third to Seventh Century* (New York, 1979)
W. F. Jashemski: *The Gardens of Pompeii, Herculaneum and the Villas Destroyed by Vesuvius*, 2 vols (New Rochelle, 1979–93)
J. Onians: 'Abstraction and Imagination in Late Antiquity', *A. Hist.*, iii (1980), pp. 1–24
K. Weitzman, ed.: *Age of Spirituality: A Symposium* (New York, 1980)
M. Henig, ed.: *A Handbook of Roman Art: A Survey of the Visual Arts of the Roman World* (Oxford, 1983)
R. Brilliant: *Visual Narratives: Storytelling in Etruscan and Roman Art* (Ithaca, 1984)
N. Hannestad: *Roman Art and Imperial Policy* (Århus, 1986)
P. Zanker: *Augustus und die Macht der Bilder* (Munich, 1987); Eng. trans. by A. Shapiro as *The Power of Images in the Age of Augustus* (Ann Arbor, 1988)
R. Ling: *Roman Painting* (Cambridge, 1991)
S. Walker: *Roman Art* (London, 1991)
D. E. E. Kleiner: *Roman Sculpture* (New Haven and London, 1992)
A. Claridge: 'Hadrian's Column of Trajan', *J. Roman Archaeol.*, vi (1993), pp. 5–22
D. Whitehouse and K. Painter: 'The Portland Vase: An Aspect of Roman Cameo Cutting', *Cameos in Context: The Benjamin Zucker Lectures, 1990*, ed. M. Henig and M. Vickers (Oxford and Houlton, 1993), pp. 2–24
J. Elsner: *Art and the Roman Viewer: The Transformation of Art from the Pagan World to Christianity* (Cambridge, 1995)
M. Henig: *The Art of Roman Britain* (London, 1995)
K. Galinsky: *Augustan Culture: An Interpretive Introduction* (Princeton, 1996)
J. Elsner: *Imperial Rome and Christian Triumph*, Oxford History of Art (Oxford, 1998)
L. Farrar: *Ancient Roman Gardens* (Stroud, 1998)
R. Ling: *Ancient Mosaics* (London, 1998)
K. Dunbabin: *Mosaics in the Greek and Roman World* (Cambridge, 1999)
J. Onions: *Classical Art and the Cultures of Greece and Rome* (New Haven and London, 1999)
T. Holscher: *The Language of Images in Roman Art* (Cambridge, 2004)

Rome [It. Roma]. Capital city of the Roman Empire, half-way down the Italian peninsula and *c.* 35 km from the mouth of the River Tiber. The early city spread over the seven traditional hills (Palatine, Capitoline, Aventine, Celian, Esquiline, Viminal and Quirinal).

I. History. II. Urban development. III. Art life and organization. IV. Buildings and monuments.

I. History.

Roman historians established 21 April 753 BC as the date of Rome's foundation, when, according to the myth, Romulus founded a city on the Palatine Hill. Virgil, in the *Aeneid*, also followed tradition by linking Romulus and Aeneas, the famous hero who survived the Trojan War and settled in Latium after an eventful journey. In fact a settlement on the Palatine and small villages on the other hills probably started to appear around the 9th century BC; when they united and elected their own king, Rome was founded. The traditional list of Roman kings (753–509 BC) comprises one group of Latin kings (Romulus, Numa Pompilius, Tullus Hostilius and Ancus Marcius); they were followed by three Etruscans, Tarquinius Priscus, Servius Tullius and Tarquinius Superbus (*see also* ETRUSCAN, §1). In this second phase Rome seems to have peacefully submitted to Etruscan control, which resulted in the development of crafts and trades and some prosperity. The crisis of monarchy and the attainment of public offices by the plebs led to the birth of the Republic (509–27 BC). The city gradually became supreme as head of a confederacy of all Italians, and after successful wars against Carthage (3rd–2nd centuries BC) became a world power. The city itself continued its irregular growth and, at the end of the Republican era, the population reached one million. Roman culture was rapidly hellenized after the conquest of Greece in 146 BC. Simple Roman values were confronted by the refined Greek world, and wealthy Romans competed for the most skilled Hellenistic artists to increase their power and status. The Republican era ended in civil war between JULIUS CAESAR and Gnaeus Pompey, Octavian and Mark Antony, and in social and moral collapse.

Once Octavian had attained absolute power in 27 BC and proclaimed himself AUGUSTUS, he developed a wide-ranging cultural programme to underpin his government; he renewed morals and religion and reorganized and embellished the city. In the following centuries Rome was the capital of an empire, and it reached the peak of its extent and power. Every emperor linked his name to splendid buildings. From the 3rd century AD Rome became more and more isolated, owing to radical changes in army organization; the emperors transferred both their wealth and their interest abroad and left the city to the senatorial class. Social changes were hastened by a religious crisis due to the spread of Christianity. Under CONSTANTINE THE GREAT the city lost its role as political capital of the Empire, but it became the heart of the Christian world: after the Edict of Milan (AD 313),

Constantine established the first organized structure for the Roman Church. The early churches became new poles of attraction in the old Imperial urban system. In AD 395 Rome lost its role as capital of the Western Empire.

E. Gibbon: *History of the Decline and Fall of the Roman Empire* (London, 1776–82)

Storia di Roma, Istituto di Studi Romani, 31 vols (Bologna, 1954–87)

M. T. Boatwright, D. J. Gargola and R. J. A. Talbert: *The Romans, from Village to Empire* (New York, 2004)

J. H. McGregor: *Rome from the Ground Up* (Cambridge, MA, 2005)

II. Urban development.

Only a fraction of the ancient city of Rome has been excavated: the layered evidence of the city's long period of growth lies well below the modern pavements. Thus the evidence of ancient writers, inscriptions, coins showing buildings, and Renaissance and later views of structures now lost are all of primary importance. Most informative of all are pieces of the large, detailed Severan marble plan (*c.* AD 205–8; see fig. 1). Arranging these varied materials in meaningful ways, and solving relationships between them and the existing buildings and ruins, are major scholarly enterprises, especially since Rome has been frequently extended and rebuilt after great fires and floods. It is sometimes only through excavation that it is possible to supplement these data to reveal the form of the ancient city and to correct long-established misinterpretations.

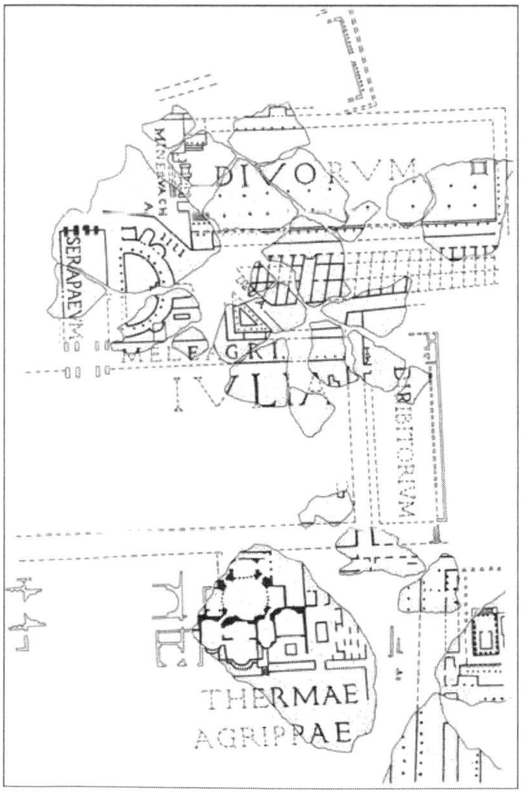

1. Severan marble plan of Rome, detail showing the Porticus Divorum, part of the Saepta Julia and the Baths of Agrippa, *c.* AD 205–8; reconstruction drawing showing elements of the map outside the surviving fragments (Rome, Antiquarium Comunale: on deposit at Rome, Palazzo Braschi)

1. Early and Republican. 2. Imperial. 3. Decline.

1. EARLY AND REPUBLICAN. About 35 km before it reaches the sea the Tiber, flowing south, is divided by an island, the only good crossing place in its lower course (see fig. *2*). The island lies between two large bends in the river. The one upstream loops to the west, enclosing a flood plain later called the Campus Martius; that downstream curves to the east, bordering what is now Trastevere. Three of Rome's seven hills lie just east and south-east of the river (the Capitoline, Palatine and Aventine); the other hills are in effect riverward projections of higher ground further to the east. Between the hills the low ground was swampy, though drained in part by streams emptying into the Tiber. The island crossing and the defensible nearer hills formed a natural setting for trans-Italian trade and a town, though inadequate for the role the future city would play. In spite of marshes and floods, people settled in the valleys and on the hills in the 2nd millennium BC. The Palatine was their common citadel, and by the 7th century BC a common meeting place had been established on the site of the later Forum Romanum (2e; *see* §IV, 1 below). At the end of the 7th century until 510 BC Etruscan kings ruled the city, constructing sanctuaries and assembly places and a monumental Temple of Jupiter on top of the Capitoline (ded. 509 BC; *see* ARCHITECTURE, §VI, 2(i)(a)). The Etruscans imposed urban offices, however primitive, bridged the river and regulated

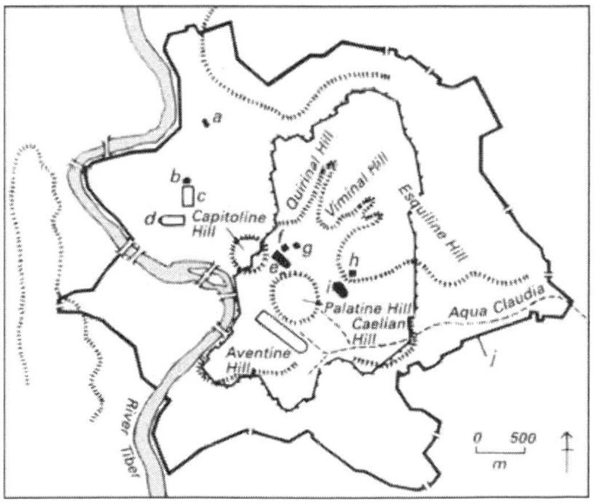

2. Rome before AD 313, plan: (a) Ara Pacis; (b) Pantheon; (c) Baths of Agrippa; (d) Theatre of Pompey; (e) Forum Romanum; (f) Forum Julium; (g) Forum Augustum; (h) Baths of Titus; (i) Colosseum; (j) Aurelian Wall

trade. By also introducing taxes, defence and political organization, they largely laid in place the armature of a proper city.

Internal strife, external conquests in central Italy and increased trade all testify to a growing community. Temple wardens (aediles) in time became city officials. The Gauls sacked the city in 390 BC, after which the five-mile-long Servian Wall was built. The Forum Romanum was partly flanked by shops, and nobles built sizeable houses nearby. In 312 BC the 5 km-long Claudian aqueduct was built, followed in 272 BC by the 64 km Anio Vetus. Urban planning in the modern sense was probably as yet unknown, but the ancient trade-paths, leading to the city gates and thence across country, were at least partly paved. It was Rome's extended conquests outside Italy, begun in 264 BC and continued intermittently thereafter, that transformed Rome. Contacts with the great eastern Hellenistic capitals, the acquisition by many Romans of at least a veneer of Greek culture, and the arrival of foreign artisans and intellectuals helped to make Rome the capital of the West. For a long time no real municipal administration existed. Though aediles, censors and other officials took care of the city as best they could, there was no regularly appointed chief municipal officer, no police force and no detailed civic code. Victorious generals endowed memorials; booty financed civic buildings. By 184 BC the Forum Romanum had a large municipal hall or basilica, and in 179 BC the first stone bridge was built across the Tiber; in 144 BC another aqueduct, the Marcia, was built. The main roads were paved and spanned by triumphal arches, and ancient buildings were renovated. Rome became overcrowded, and tenements, often shoddily built, were hastily erected by speculators.

A series of civil wars, from the late 2nd century BC until 31 BC, slowed or halted planning and construction. The dictator Sulla began restoration of the Capitoline Temple of Jupiter in 83 BC and in 78 BC built a records hall or tabularium overlooking the northern end of the Forum Romanum. Pompey built the first Roman stone theatre (55 BC; 2d), in the Campus Martius but the area remained largely empty, despite the elaborate plans of JULIUS CAESAR for it. Before his assassination in 44 BC Caesar did begin building a new forum (2f), containing a Temple of Venus Genetrix (ded. 46 BC), adjoining the old Forum Romanum on the north; this was the first of several Imperial for a (*see* §IV, 2 below).

2. IMPERIAL. Octavian, later AUGUSTUS, inherited Caesar's plans and in 40 years of rule put many of them in hand, adding ample contributions of his own. In the Campus Martius he built himself a huge round mausoleum of Etruscan design (28 BC); beside the main north–south thoroughfare (now the Via del Corso) he built the beautiful Ara Pacis (2a; *see* §IV, 4 below; now re-erected to the west); nearby he created an immense sundial, its pointer a giant Egyptian obelisk, its vast dial marked in gilded bronze numbers that have in part survived, affixed to their paving.

Though he lived in a fairly modest house on the Palatine, Augustus and his chief lieutenant, AGRIPPA, built other vast works in the capital, as well as in the provinces. The Pantheon (25 BC), commemorated by the inscription extant on Hadrian's successor building (2b; *see also* §IV, below 8), was Agrippa's work. The Emperor himself bought the land for his new forum (ded. 2 BC; 2g), placed between that of Caesar and the Esquiline Hill. It is a striking example of the imperial nature of such designs: rich marble statues mixing Greek and Roman imagery and forms, with themes chosen to glorify Roman origins and in particular the Emperor's preservation and enhancement of Roman traditions. Enclosed by a high wall, its vast central court was extended by curved exedrae, where numerous niches held portrait statues. At one end stood the marble Temple of Mars Ultor (ded. 2 BC); inside were statues of *Mars*, who avenged Julius Caesar's murder, *Venus*, ancestress of the Imperial house, and the deified *Caesar*.

A street plan was begun in the Campus Martius, and new bridges were constructed. The municipal government was organized on a sound footing, with chief administrators reporting to the emperor. Some charitable foundations appeared, and a regiment of guards and a detachment of firemen evolved into a series of barracks and offices in different precincts. The city was divided into 14 regions, and the water supply was put in the charge of a senior official; building regulations multiplied. Rome possessed a copious supply of fresh water, many public fountains and lavatories, but the literature of the 1st and 2nd centuries AD makes it clear that it remained a noisy, noisome and often dangerous city. It was notorious for its poor, its hangers-on and the flood of foreigners that had been arriving since the 2nd century BC. Food supply and employment were constant concerns of the government. Thus as early as the 190s BC immense warehouses had been built along the Tiber; they were followed by many more. Different sections of the Tiber shores below the island were devoted to different products, and soon, near the Aventine Hill, there was an immense dump of used and broken terracotta jars (Monte Testaccio), still to be seen. Labour gangs and certain trades were loosely organized into identifiable groups, a process that developed into more supervised guilds. As public works were an integral part of every imperial administration, some at least of the threatening ranks of the unemployed could be given work. By the 2nd century AD the city may have contained a million or more people; certainly it had at least 600,000 inhabitants.

The Great Fire of AD 64, which destroyed or rendered uninhabitable at least a third of the city, spurred the use of fire-resistant materials in domestic construction—brick, concrete and stone (*see* ARCHITECTURE, §VI, 2(i)(c)). Huge brickyards flourished, and their products were often stamped with indications of the yard owner, the master potter in charge, and even the names of the consuls in office, thus facilitating the dating of the buildings. Another fire occurred in AD 80, again necessitating much restoration. It is clear from ancient texts, however, that the government was not wanting in these emergencies. Demolition slowed or prevented the flames' spread; refugee centres and housing were provided; and the debris cleared by work gangs was taken down-river in food supply boats that normally would have returned empty to Rome's seaport.

That seaport was OSTIA, properly a suburb of the capital with similar commercial and residential quarters. One half excavated, it is one of the most informative sites of all Classical antiquity, where it is possible to study the shops, markets and warehouses, and the brick-faced concrete apartment houses, with which Rome itself was once half-covered. (Many shops can still be seen at Rome, in the Markets of Trajan and along the Via dei Cerchi beside the Circus Maximus, but only a few apartment houses on the Capitoline.) The streets of Ostia are punctuated by fountains; there are a dozen bath buildings, a theatre and a commercial plaza decorated with mosaic house flags of shipping companies. The town clearly reflects aspects of Rome's appearance in the late 1st century AD onwards: it grew as the capital grew, its administration directly under Rome's thumb.

Textual and archaeological evidence shows that the fires encouraged more systematic urban planning. The historian Tacitus described (*Annals* XV.xliii) how broad avenues and lesser streets were neatly laid out after the devastation of AD 64, forming a grid over part of the city, although he added that some thought the old shady alleys were better. Excavations by the Via del Corso have revealed almost exactly what is found at Ostia: a surfaced thoroughfare with pavements, drainage, covered porticos and lines of small shops fronting apartment houses, all of brick-faced concrete (mid-2nd century AD).

The construction of public monuments and facilities also continued unabated. BATH buildings were among the most notable, reaching immense size in the 3rd and 4th centuries AD. Agrippa built one near his Pantheon in the Campus Martius (2c), but it has disappeared, as has one constructed by Nero. The first major municipal bath that is fairly well preserved is that of Titus, opposite the Colosseum and dedicated in AD 80 (2h). A large enclosure with a block of bathing rooms, symmetrically disposed along one end, it featured a huge vaulted central hall and contained lavatories and exercise grounds. In time, hardly a city quarter anywhere in the Empire would be without a larger or smaller version of the type.

Several theatres were built after Pompey's, as well as two amphitheatres (including the Colosseum; 2i; *see* §IV, 6 below), three circuses and a stadium (AD 86) on the Greek model, the outline of which is preserved in the modern Piazza Navona. There were concert halls, auditoria and libraries as well as such government buildings as senate houses, mints, jails and water administration headquarters. Fountains proliferated, both grand scenic ones and mere tubs, while some houses had their own water supplies. Waste water flowed through the city to the Tiber from baths, fountains and commercial establishments. In AD 97 the new *curator aquarum* (director of water supplies), SEXTUS JULIUS FRONTINUS, wrote down the technical and legal record of his office. The work is preserved and gives a rare glimpse of the duties of an imperial administrator of rank and the problems he faced. For all its public services and facilities, however, health, safety and comfort were still the prerogatives of the rich and powerful.

Apart from emperors, businessmen, visiting potentates and high officials also participated in embellishing the city. Some willed their spacious gardens to the public or to the emperor; the latter sometimes opened them to the people. Grand tombs were often public places. The city was fringed with parks large and small, where ornamental waterworks, statuary, benches and exedrae abounded. The fora were crowded with statuary, as were honorific arches. The sculptured tombs of both the affluent and the merely comfortable lined the consular highways leaving the city. Marble was imported from throughout the Empire; rare, coloured varieties were much sought after. Mosaicists decorated not only floors but walls and ceilings, often with glass cubes as well as marble ones. Painted stucco on both outside and inside walls was common; plain outside walls often bore election slogans. Fashions were largely determined by the imperial court, partly because many of the best architects and artists worked there. The ruins on the Palatine Hill preserve much evidence of all this activity. Augustus' immediate successors built there, but it was Domitian who built the large, complex imperial palace there that for so long epitomized the idea of a true palace (begun AD 81; *see* §IV, 3 below); it remained in use until the Dark Ages, and its influence on the numerous, extravagant country villas of the rich, and on architecture in general, was immense.

Meanwhile, official religious architecture remained almost in stasis, the basic temple form including a porch approached by a tall flight of stairs from a large, usually rectangular, sacred area. Hadrian's Pantheon (*c*. AD 128), however, was a revolutionary structure, and his Temple of Venus and Rome (AD 135) opposite the Colosseum had a novel dedication. The Temple of Antoninus and Faustina built a little later beside the Sacred Way in the Forum Romanum was almost the last example of the 600-year-old type built in Rome. Other cult buildings included underground basilicas, such as the one by the Porta Maggiore (1st century AD), circular domed structures, simple alterations of household rooms, such as those used by the first Christians, and Mithraic temples in the form of small underground halls lined with benches, such as that preserved under S Clemente. Ancient shrines were also venerated. Visitors were shown where Virginia died, where the horses of the Dioscuri drank, and other legendary locations. The Forum Romanum was a museum of sculpture and architecture; additions to it ceased only in the 7th century AD. Rome's lengthy colonnades, many enclosed but public porticos, towering columns and a dozen or more huge triumphal arches gave it a distinctive grandeur that many rulers and architects have later emulated.

3. Decline. In the 270s AD, after half a century of civil war, economic difficulties and serious challenges to Rome's authority from beyond the Empire's boundaries, the great Aurelian Wall was quickly thrown up around the city (2j), much of which still stands. It was built without respect to apartment houses and other structures in its way, but was provided with major gates, some of them splendid examples of military architecture, wherever a consular highway entered the city. The walling of the city after so many centuries must have had a profound psychological impact on its population, but worse followed when, in the 320s AD, Constantine moved the Imperial court to Byzantium (now Istanbul). Thereafter, Rome became effectively a provincial city, though its decline was arrested somewhat by the ascendancy of a new administrative power, the bishopric.

Imperial edicts repeatedly emphasized the need to prevent destruction of property, and the decline in population was perhaps accompanied by a decline in public services. Pilgrims came, however, and tourists still visited the city, among them emperors who had never seen it before. Moreover, a 4th-century AD inventory of surviving structures includes 46,600 apartment houses, 1352 fountains, 856 bath buildings, 36 marble triumphal arches and 432 shrines.

Frontinus: *On the Water Supply of Rome*

R. Lanciani: *The Ruins and Excavations of Ancient Rome* (London, 1897)

R. Lanciani: *The Destruction of Ancient Rome* (New York, 1899)

S. B. Platner and T. Ashby: *A Topographical Dictionary of Ancient Rome* (London, 1929)

I. A. Richmond: *The City Wall of Imperial Rome* (Oxford, 1930)

J. LeGall: *Le Tibre: Fleuve de Rome dans l'antiquité* (Paris, 1953)

G. Carettoni and others: *La pianta marmorea di Roma antica: Forma urbis Romae*, 2 vols (Rome, 1960)

E. Nash: *Pictorial Dictionary of Ancient Rome*, 2 vols (London, 1961–2, 2/1968)

A. P. Frutaz: *Le piante di Roma*, 3 vols (Rome, 1962)

W. L. MacDonald: *The Architecture of the Roman Empire*, 2 vols (New Haven, 1965–86; i, rev. 2/1982)

D. R. Dudley: *Urbs Roma: A Source Book* (London, 1967)

F. Castagnoli: *Topografia e urbanistica di Roma antica* (Bologna, 1969)

G. Lugli: *Itinerario di Roma antica* (Milan, 1970)

F. Coarelli: *Guida archeologica di Roma* (Milan, 1971, Verona, 2/1975)

E. Gjerstad: *Early Rome* (1973), vi of *Historical Survey* (Lund, 1953–)

A. Boëthius: *Etruscan and Early Roman Architecture*, Pelican Hist. A. (Harmondsworth, 1978)

E. Rodriguez-Almeida: *Forma urbis marmorea: Aggiornamento generale*, 2 vols (Rome, 1980)

J. B. Ward-Perkins: *Roman Imperial Architecture*, Pelican Hist. A. (Harmondsworth, 1981)

E. B. MacDougall: *Ancient Roman Villa Gardens* (Washington, DC, 1987)

P. Connolly and H. Dodge: *The Ancient City: Life in Classical Athens & Rome* (Oxford, 1998)

A. Gabucci, S. Peccatori and S. Zuffi: *Ancient Rome: Art, Architecture and History* (Los Angeles, 2002)

B. Ward-Perkins: *The Fall of Rome: And the End of Civilization* (Oxford, 2005)

III. Art life and organization.

Little is known about the personalities and organization of artists in the Roman world, let alone in ancient Rome itself, for artists were regarded as no more than craftsmen and, like craftsmen, usually remained anonymous. Early Roman art is difficult to distinguish from the art of central Italy as a whole; then from the 2nd century BC, when foreign artists dominated artistic production and moulded artistic taste in the city, it is difficult to distinguish Roman art from that of the wider Empire.

The major artistic influence on the newly founded city was Etruscan; under the Republic (established 509 BC), Greek contacts became more direct. Two artists of Greek origin, Damophilos and Gorgasos, were commissioned at this time to decorate the Temple of Ceres (Pliny: *Natural History* XXXV.154–5). The first recorded Roman painter was Fabius Pictor, who decorated the Temple of Salus in 303 BC (Pliny: *Natural History* XXXV.19); few Romans who practised the art became famous, however. The city's public monuments were transformed in the 2nd century BC, when generals from the Punic Wars and elsewhere brought back vast amounts of Greek art as booty to embellish the capital. Buildings were designed specifically to accommodate sculpture and painting, and visual art flourished as a result. Not only were public buildings decorated inside and out with sculpture, paintings and mosaics: private houses of the rich and the not-so-rich also displayed fine painting, furniture, silver and gold, ceramics and glass.

Artists flooded to the city to take up commissions. Most were foreign and appear to have come from Greece: sculptors and painters in the late Republic and early Empire were almost exclusively Greek, including some from South Italy. Several families of sculptors travelled to Rome, including some from the Aphrodisian school (*see* APHRODISIAS). Some Aphrodisian work found in Rome was executed in Italian marble, and five signed statues (Copenhagen, Ny Carlsberg Glyp.) and three signed statue bases have been found on the Esquiline Hill, which suggests that a group of artists in Rome worked together on a special monument. In many cases, however, it is difficult to know if art works were produced in Rome itself or were executed in the provinces and shipped to their destination in Italy; certainly both practices occurred. Some foreign artists were so famous that they were summoned to Rome to work. When the general Aemilius Paulus wanted paintings done to celebrate his victory in Macedonia, he invited the Athenian Metrodoros to Rome. Similarly, Nero requested Zenodoros to make his bronze colossus (Pliny: *Natural History* XXXIV.xlvi.47).

At the end of the Republic powerful dictators began to stamp their mark on the city's art and architecture. Sulla carried out a grand scheme of unprecedented public building; Pompey and Caesar followed. Augustus used art as a major propaganda tool, and in rebuilding and adorning Rome he set a trend followed by most of his successors. Statues of the reigning emperor were set up throughout the city (and the Empire) to make his presence ubiquitous; important citizens also honoured themselves, on a smaller scale. The Forum of Trajan in Rome was one of the most popular settings for such statues. From the 3rd century AD, as Rome declined in political importance in relation to the eastern provinces, so the city loosened its grip on the art of the Roman world.

M. F. Squarciapino: *La scuola di Afrodisia* (Rome, 1943)

J. M. C. Toynbee: *Some Notes on Artists in the Roman World*, Collection Latomus, vi (Brussels, 1951)

P. Zanker: *Augustus und die Macht der Bilder* (Munich, 1987); Eng. trans. by A. Shapiro as *Augustus and the Power of Images* (Ann Arbor, 1988)

A. Gabucci, S. Peccatori and S. Zuffi: *Ancient Rome: Art, Architecture and History* (Los Angeles, 2002)

P. Stewart: *Statues in Roman Society: Representation and Response* (Oxford, 2003)

E. W. Leach: *The Social Life of Painting in Ancient Rome and on the Bay of Naples* (Cambridge and New York, 2004)

T. Allan: *Life, Myth, and Art in Ancient Rome* (Los Angeles, 2005)

IV. Buildings and monuments.

1. Forum Romanum. 2. Imperial Fora. 3. Palatine. 4. Ara Pacis. 5. Domus Aurea. 6. Colosseum. 7. Trajan's Column. 8. Pantheon. 9. Castel Sant'Angelo. 10. Baths of Caracalla. 11. Basilica of Maxentius. 12. Arch of Constantine. 13. Temple of Mithras. 14. Villa of Maxentius.

1. Forum Romanum. Administrative, juridical and commercial centre of Republican Rome, which continued to receive increasingly elaborate public buildings throughout most of the Imperial era (after 27 BC). The Forum Romanum came to symbolize Roman power, and its basic form was copied throughout the Roman world. Its buildings have inspired artists for over two millennia. Rome's earliest settlers occupied the hills and plateaux to the east of the River Tiber. Gradually, however, they moved down into the lowlands, and by the mid-7th century BC the central depression between the hills, formerly used for burials, had become a communal assembly and trading place or FORUM. It eventually became known as the Forum Romanum to distinguish it from other gathering points such as the Forum Boarium and Forum Holitorium (the cattle and vegetable markets respectively). The general layout of the site was established under the Etruscan kings in the 6th century BC, when the open area was drained and paved, and buildings oriented to the cardinal points were erected along its periphery. Development accelerated under the Republic. During this period the forum lay at the foot of the city's religious centre, the Capitoline Hill to the north-west. To the south stood the Palatine Hill, favoured residential quarter of the rich; to the north-east were the crowded plebeian residences of the Subura Valley; while to the south-west the Velabrum valley connected it to the Tiber port. This large area, defined by its surrounding hills, comprised two main sections. On the north-west, a large paved area (*c*. 90×60 m) formed the core of the Forum Romanum proper, while the area extending south-east towards the Velia was known as the Forum Adjectum. The focus of Republican government, the senate house or curia (later the Curia Julia), stood on the forum's north-east edge (see fig. 3a). In front of it lay the open-air comitium where various assemblies met, with a speakers' platform on one side, called the Rostra (3b) after the captured ships' prows displayed on its sides.

The Forum Romanum was the locus for numerous activities. Readily accessible, it was a flourishing market in the early Republic, yet the sale of produce was felt to detract from more serious activities, so it was banned in the 4th century BC. Speeches, rituals and tribunals were held in the central open space; triumphal processions marched through the forum along the Via Sacra. During inclement weather, activities moved indoors. In the 2nd century BC the old wooden shops were replaced by large BASILICAS: the Porcia (184 BC), the Aemilia (179 BC; 3c), the Sempronia (170 BC) and the Opimia (121 BC). Here lawyers, money-changers, foreign visitors and senators mingled. From the exterior balconies and roof terraces spectators watched gladiatorial games and other events in the central square.

Other important buildings included numerous shrines. Among the earliest was the circular Temple of Vesta (3d), in which the Vestal Virgins tended the city's sacred fire. It was rebuilt many times, and the Corinthian tholos visible today essentially represents a restoration of AD 191. At the opposite end of the forum was the Temple of Saturn (early 5th century BC; 3e), which replaced an early altar to Hercules. It acted as a visual foil for the curia opposite and doubled as the state treasury, with public documents displayed on its sides. Eight of its tall, Ionic granite columns still stand. The chief priest, the Pontifex Maximus, lived near the Temple of Vesta in the Domus Publica and, by the late Republic, used the adjacent Regia (3f), identified as the palace of Rome's legendary kings, as his headquarters. After a fire in the 30s BC the Regia was lavishly restored in marble. The small but politically important shrine of Janus (3g) stood at the end of the Argiletum street, which entered the forum from the north-east. Covered in bronze, it was perhaps designed to recall a double gate of one of Rome's primitive villages, and at the announcement of peace in the Roman world its doors were closed with a great fanfare. The nearby shrine of Venus Cloacina (3h) was associated with Rome's great drain, the Cloaca Maxima.

Other structures marked the locations of significant events. The Temple of Castor (3i) commemorated the miraculous appearance of the Dioscuri

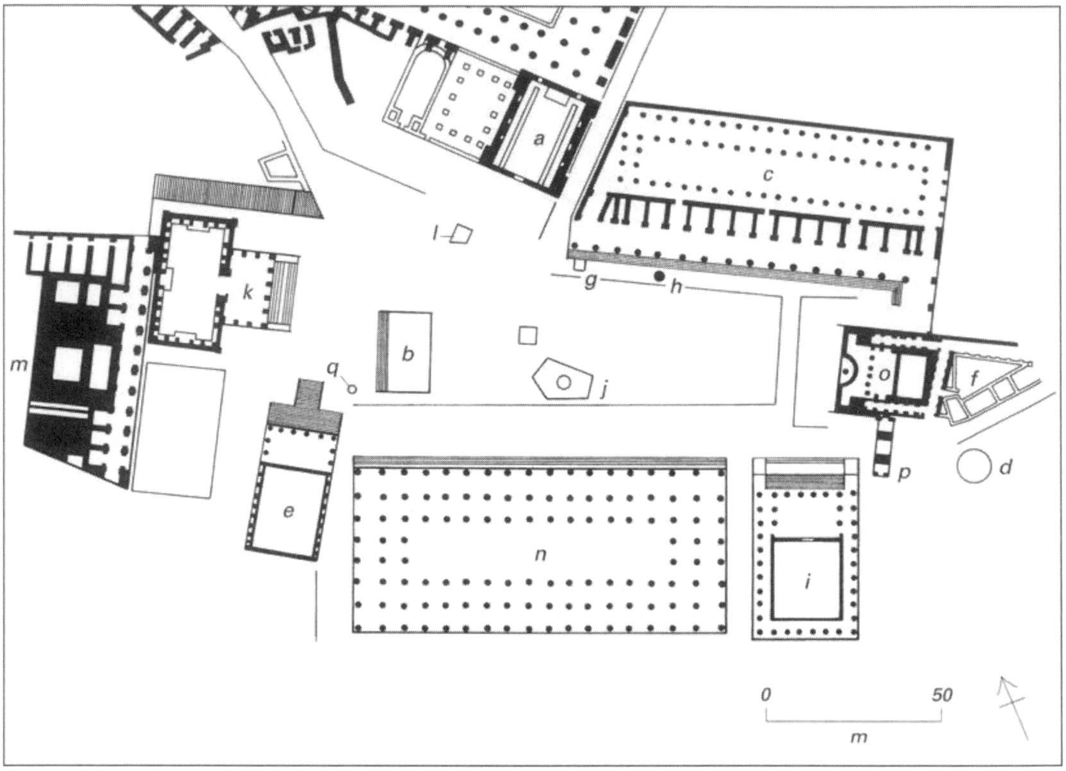

3. Rome, Forum Romanum, layout in the early 1st century AD: (a) Curia Julia; (b) Rostra; (c) Basilica Aemilia; (d) Temple of Vesta; (e) Temple of Saturn; (f) Regia; (g) shrine of Janus; (h) shrine of Venus Cloacina; (i) Temple of Castor; (j) Lacus Curtius; (k) Temple of Concord; (l) Lapis Niger; (m) tabularium; (n) Basilica Julia; (o) Temple of Divus Julius; (p) Arch of Augustus; (q) Milliarium Aureum

during the 5th century BC, while the fenced marshy spot known as the Lacus Curtius (3j) was associated with a myth about the self-sacrifice of a Sabine leader. Similarly, the Temple of Concord (3k) below the Capitoline commemorated the resolution of a major conflict between the patricians and plebs in 336 BC, while the Lapis Niger (3l), a black marble paving by the comitium, covered a stone pillar with an early Latin inscription (*c.* 500 BC; Rome, Antiqua. Forense) believed by some Romans to mark the tomb of Romulus.

The military leaders who dominated Roman politics in the 1st century BC exploited the Forum Romanum as a political arena in which to propagate their policies. In the 80s BC Sulla planned the tabularium (3m), a large structure to house the state archives, on the slopes of the Capitoline, with impressive tufa arcades forming a dramatic backdrop to the buildings on the forum's western edge. In the mid-1st century BC Julius Caesar began to reorder the entire area by moving the curia back and realigning it with the Forum Julium. He also relocated the Rostra on the forum's primary axis and built his own grand Basilica Julia (begun 54 BC; 3n) opposite the Basilica Aemilia. Tunnels underneath the central space accommodated the apparatus for his extravagant gladiatorial combats. Augustus completed many of Caesar's elaborate projects and constructed a Temple of Divus Julius (29 BC; 3o) on the site of the dictator's funeral pyre. With the two arches of Augustus on one side (29 and 19 BC; 3p) and a portico to his heirs on the other, the south-eastern edge of the central forum was closed off with an impressive series of dynastic monuments. At the opposite end Augustus symbolized the forum's status as the centre of the Roman world by erecting the Milliarium Aureum (20 BC; 3q), a column covered with gilt bronze marking the start of the great Roman highways.

During the Empire, the Forum Romanum became less important as the locus of active government and more valued as a historic memorial, stage and museum. The 2nd-century AD reliefs known as the Anaglypha Trajani or Plutei Trajani (now in the Curia Julia) depict the forum as an impressive setting for imperial ceremonies. Sacred trees grew in the central area, plants surrounded the Temple of Divus Julius, and colourful garlands hung on the other temples. Paintings embellished both exteriors and interiors, and statues adorned the central square and its buildings. Tiberius rebuilt the Temple of Concord (ded. AD 10) with a porch on the long axis flanked by large windows to allow a full view of the works of art displayed inside, while

Pliny (*Natural History* XXXVI.xxiv.102) listed the opulent Imperial version of the Basilica Aemilia (rebuilt after AD 22) among the most beautiful buildings in the world.

Commemorative arches also embellished the forum, announcing military achievements, serving as gateways and masking changes in street direction or ground-level. The simple Fornix Fabianus (121 BC) marked the approach from the east. The elaborate arches of Augustus, Tiberius (AD 16) and Septimius Severus (AD 203) marked the entrances to the central paved area, while that of Titus (AD 81) stood at the high point of the Via Sacra. Virtually every emperor left his mark on the Forum Romanum. Nero added a large portico to the south-east (AD 60s) as an entrance to the Domus Aurea, and on part of the same site Hadrian constructed the large Temple of Venus and Rome (ded. AD 135). Vespasian and Titus, and Antoninus Pius and his wife Faustina were honoured posthumously with temples in the forum (late 1st century AD and AD 141 respectively). Around AD 307 Maxentius began constructing a gigantic concrete and brick basilica, completed by Constantine at about the same time he transferred the imperial government from Rome to the East (AD 330). Thereafter, the forum's importance declined. The last ancient monument on the site was a column composed of spolia (AD 608) erected to the Byzantine emperor Phokas.

With neglect came destruction. The ground-level rose, covering the open area, while the Romans plundered the ancient structures for the materials or burnt the marble for lime. Some notable monuments, however, were reused as Christian buildings, including the curia, the Temple of Antoninus and Faustina, the Temple of Venus and Rome and the Arch of Septimius Severus. The so-called Temple of Romulus became the vestibule to the church of SS Cosma e Damiano (*c.* AD 530), containing one of the finest Early Christian mosaics in Rome.

In the 15th and 16th centuries Renaissance scholars refocused attention on the site, though it had become so derelict that the architect Pirro Ligorio (*c.* 1513–83) argued that the centre of Roman power must have been located elsewhere. Hundreds of paintings and drawings of the forum were produced, but by this time the ground-level had reached the tops of the side openings of the Severan arch. In 1536 the forum was partially cleared to allow the Habsburg emperor Charles V to follow the ancient triumphal route, and the site began to flourish again as a market, a ceremonial park and a haunt for artists. Unfortunately regeneration led to the further destruction of ancient buildings, since the very men who so diligently documented antiquities were among the most active in quarrying the site. Scientific excavations began in the late 1700s, and by *c.* 1900 almost the entire extent of the ancient Forum Romanum was uncovered. The rich finds are housed in the Antiquarium Forense on site and the Antiquarium Comunale on the Capitoline. Excavations continue.

P. Ligorio: *Delle antichità di Roma* (Venice, 1553)

C. Huelsen: *Das Forum romanum* (Rome, 1893); Eng. trans. by J. B. Carter (Rome, 1909/*R* London, 1928)

S. B. Platner and T. Ashby: *A Topographical Dictionary of Ancient Rome* (London, 1929), pp. 230–36

G. Lugli: *Roma antica: Il centro monumentale* (Rome, 1946)

M. Grant: *The Roman Forum* (London, 1970)

P. Zanker: *Forum romanum: Die Neugestaltung durch Augustus* (Tübingen, 1972)

F. Coarelli: *Il foro romano*, 2 vols (Rome, 1983–5)

M. Wegner: 'Bauschmuck der Basilica Aemilia am Forum Romanum', *Mitt. Dt. Archäol. Inst.: Röm. Abt.*, xciv (1987), pp. 325–9

M. Wegner: 'Gebalk von den Rostra am Forum Romanum', *Mitt. Dt. Archäol. Inst.: Röm. Abt.*, xciv (1987), pp. 331–2

A. J. Ammerman: 'On the Origins of the Forum Romanum', *Amer. J. Archaeol.*, xciv (Oct 1990), pp. 627–45

K. Welch: 'The Roman Arena in Late-Republican Italy: A New Interpretation', *J. Roman Archaeol.*, vii (1994), pp. 59–80

R. Grussinger: 'Zur Funktion und Bedeutung der kolossalen Marmorgorgoneia vom Tempel der Venus und Roma', *Mitt. Dt. Archäol. Inst.: Röm. Abt.*, cx (2003), pp. 329–43

T. K. Kissel: *Das Forum Romanum: Leben im Herzen Roms* (Düsseldorf, 2004)

2. Imperial Fora. Built in Rome adjacent to and north of the Forum Romanum, the Imperial Fora were five complexes of public buildings constructed over one and a half centuries (see fig. 4). The earliest was that of Julius Caesar and the latest was Trajan's, after which no further architectural additions were made to the area, although it appears that they were in constant use into at least the 5th century AD. After this their marble was routinely plundered for use elsewhere, so that much of their decoration is untraced.

(i) Forum Julium. This was planned in 54 BC by Julius Caesar and begun three years later (4a). The unfinished court (*c.* 160×75 m) and Temple of Venus Genetrix (4b), mythical ancestress of the Julian family, were dedicated in 46 BC but completed by Augustus. The octastyle pseudo-peripteral marble temple with high podium was placed at the end of a forecourt, abutting the enclosure wall, which eliminated the rear colonnade. The cella probably housed a cult statue by Arkesilaos, sculptures of Caesar and Cleopatra, and collections of gems and paintings (all untraced). Most of the forum's remains date to a Trajanic rebuilding; an inscription reveals a rededication in AD 113. The forum was damaged by fire (*c.* AD 283) but restored soon after by Diocletian. Until 1932 the area was beneath a slum district; remains now include a few arches incorporated into the walls of houses, the temple's foundations and three columns.

(ii) Forum Augustum. The forum (l. *c.* 125 m; w. 85 m, and 118 m including the hemicycles) and incomplete

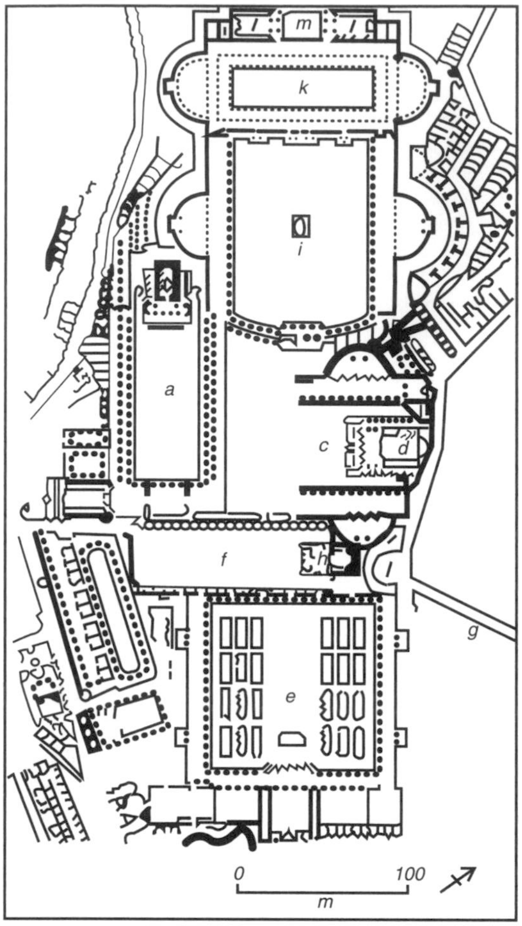

4. Rome, Imperial Fora, early 2nd century AD, plan: (a) Forum Julium; (b) Temple of Venus Genetrix; (c) Forum Augustum; (d) Temple of Mars Ultor; (e) Templum Pacis; (f) Forum of Nerva (Forum Transitorium); (g) Argiletum; (h) Temple of Minerva; (i) Porticus Absidata; (j) Forum of Trajan; (k) Basilica Ulpia; (l) libraries; (m) Trajan's Column

Temple of Mars Ultor were dedicated in 2 BC. It followed the basic plan of the Forum Julium, but was more elaborate and compact (4c and see fig. 5). The octastyle temple (4d) was placed at the far end of the forecourt, abutting the enclosure wall. It was flanked by porticos (h. 35 m) that masked two roofed semicircular exedrae, each containing 15 niches filled with statues. The central niches were twice as large as the others and aligned with the temple's façade. The attic storey of the porticos, in typical Augustan classicizing style, sported caryatids copied from the Erechtheion in Athens, which carried a coffered entablature. Between each caryatid was a relief roundel of a divinity's head. An exterior altar was centrally located on the temple's 17 front steps leading to the stylobate, while the apsidal end of the cella held statues of Venus and Mars and possibly one of Julius Caesar (all untraced). In AD 19 Tiberius built a triumphal arch on either side of the temple, while in AD 128, as indicated by a rededication inscription, Hadrian made repairs to the

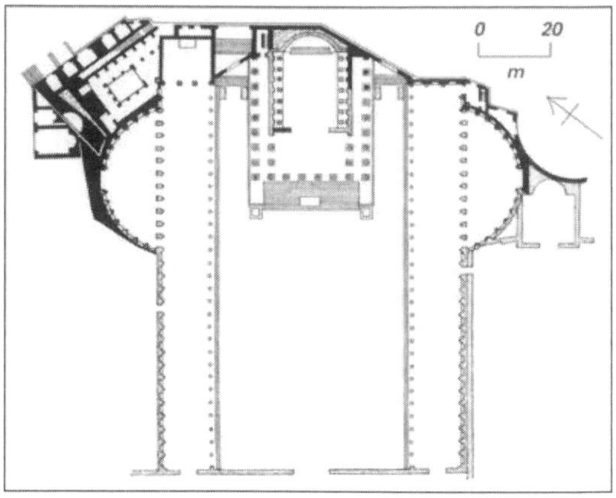

5. Forum Augustum, Rome, dedicated 2 BC, plan

complex. Today the south-west half of the forum is still buried, but remains at its north-east end include the temple platform and three Corinthian columns, and the hemicycles. Much of the dedicatory inscription has also survived (Corp. Inscr. Lat., vi, 8709).

Excavations begun in 2005 have focused on a small semicircular wall that has been identified as part of an apsidal basilica placed across the axis of the Forum opposite the Temple of Mars Ultor. That such a structure would have interrupted the Forum and blocked the view to the Temple of Mars Ultor is peculiar, and much about this (including the date of the proposed basilica) is uncertain and hypothetical at this date.

(iii) Templum Pacis. At the end of the Jewish War (AD 71) Vespasian vowed to construct a temple. Completed four years later, it housed the spoils from Jerusalem and an art collection and was designed to identify the imperial family with peace (4e). Officially named Templum Pacis, it was not called a forum until after the 4th century AD and differed from the other Imperial Fora because the precinct was squarish (*c.* 135×110 m) and contained a large formal garden, while the temple lacked a high podium and did not project into the forecourt. A colonnaded portico of red Egyptian granite ran along three sides of the enclosure wall. The fourth side, opposite the temple, was simply lined by large columns of African marble. The lateral porticos contained four square exedrae, although excavations have confirmed the existence of only one. The temple façade was emphasized by six columns that were taller and more widely spaced than the others and probably carried an entablature. The temple itself was flanked by large halls serving as libraries. The complex was destroyed by fire in AD 191 and probably restored by Septimius Severus, since the Severan marble plan of Rome (*c.* AD 205–8; Rome, Antiqua. Com., on dep. Rome, Pal. Braschi) hung on a wall of the south library, which was incorporated into the church of SS Cosma e Damiano (6th century AD). Apart from this wall, all that remains

of the complex are one large fallen column and one exedra, so that its reconstruction depends largely on the marble plan itself.

(iv) Forum of Nerva. The addition of this forum (45×150 m; 4f) began the process of uniting the Imperial Fora, since it was constructed between the Forum Augustum and the Templum Pacis, enclosing the Argiletum thoroughfare (4g), hence its alternative name, Forum Transitorium. It was planned by Vespasian, built by Domitian and dedicated by Nerva (AD 97). The architect may have been RABIRIUS, who designed Domitian's Flavian Palace. The plan had few parallel lines, since even the precinct walls converged slightly in the north-east. The long forecourt was too narrow to accommodate a peristyle, but near the side walls stood a marble colonnade backed by pilasters. The columns (h. 10 m) were free-standing yet the capitals were attached to the entablature which projected and recessed to form a series of bays. This entablature style was Hellenistic in origin and had long been common to interior decoration, but its exterior use may have been a Flavian innovation. Fragments of relief sculpture from the attic storey and frieze remain *in situ*, depicting the arts and crafts of which Minerva was the patron goddess. The Temple of Minerva itself (4h) was Corinthian hexastyle prostyle and stood on a high podium at the end of the court. Walls on either side of the cella extended to the colonnade, one masking the projecting hemicycle of the Forum Augustum. Behind the temple the semicircular Porticus Absidata (4i) created a grand entrance to the forum.

Renaissance drawings and the Severan marble plan provide evidence for the appearance of this complex, much of which is now beneath the Via dei Fori Imperiali. Remains include the concrete core of the temple's podium, the foundations of the Porticus Absidata, a single bay of the south lateral wall ('Le Colonnacce') and the foundations of the curved enclosure wall.

(v) Forum of Trajan. The largest and most magnificent of the Imperial Fora was built with the spoils of the Dacian Wars and dedicated by Trajan in AD 113 (4j). Its architect was APOLLODOROS OF DAMASCUS. The main entrance was marked by a triumphal arch erected in AD 117 soon after Trajan's death; coins verify that it had six columns in front and was crowned by a sculpture of a six-horse chariot carrying Trajan. A high colonnaded retaining wall enclosed the forum proper (89×118 m exclusive of exedrae) and masked two large hemicycles (diam. 41 m). Statues of Dacian prisoners decorated the attic storey of the colonnades. The centre of the court was dominated by an equestrian statue of Trajan. At the west end was the Basilica Ulpia (4k), so-called after Trajan's family name, Ulpius. The appearance of its façade can be restored from coins. A flight of stairs ran the length of the building, which had a triple entrance. Each door was flanked by columns that carried a high attic storey. Above the central door, which was aligned on the triumphal arch, was a sculpture of a chariot led by Victories, while groups of soldiers appeared above the side openings. The interior comprised a central nave (w. 25 m), two side aisles and an apse at either end. Its pavement was decorated with coloured marble in geometric patterns, of which fragments remain *in situ*. Its concrete walls were faced with marble, and its timber ceiling had gilded bronze tiles. The 96 nave columns were taller and thicker than those of the side aisles, which implies a clerestory.

Behind the basilica stood two libraries (4l), perhaps begun by Trajan, although the large number of Hadrianic bricks suggests that Hadrian completed the buildings. Between them rose Trajan's Column, with the unprecedented continuous spiral reliefs that still decorate its surface. The Temple of the Deified Trajan, identified by fragments of its dedicatory inscription (Rome, Vatican, Gal. Lapidaria), was long thought to have been behind Trajan's Column, but excavations begun in Rome's Jubilee year, 2000, have failed to find it there. The Italian excavator has suggested that the Temple stood in the southern side of the porticoed square (but it lacked a podium or platform, which would have been very unusual for such a temple) or that there was a forecourt there. Other scholars have speculated that the Temple may have been further back under the current Palazzo Valentini, where substructures have been found (this has not yet been excavated).

Another problem raised by recent excavations is the location of the Forum's monumental entrance gate, which traditionally was placed on the southern side of the Forum. No corresponding remains have been uncovered here, and the Italian excavator suggests a location on the north side behind the Column. The results of the excavations of 2000 remain highly controversial.

R. Lanciani: *The Ruins and Excavations of Ancient Rome* (London, 1897, 2/1967)
S. B. Platner and T. Ashby: *A Topographical Dictionary of Ancient Rome* (London, 1929)
D. M. Robathan: *The Monuments of Ancient Rome* (Rome, 1950)
P. H. von Blanckenhagen: 'The Imperial Fora', *J. Soc. Archit. Historians*, xiii/4 (1954), pp. 21–6
E. Nash: *Pictorial Dictionary of Ancient Rome*, i (New York, 1981)
J. B. Ward-Perkins: *Roman Imperial Architecture*, Pelican Hist. A. (Harmondsworth, 1981)
J. C. Anderson: *The Historical Topography of the Imperial Fora* (Brussels, 1984)
C. F. Giuliani and P. Verduchi: *L'Area centrale del Foro Romano* (Florence, 1987)
R. Meneghini: *Il Foro e i Mercati di Traiano* (Rome, 1994)
S. Panciera: *Iscrizioni greche e latine del Foro romano e del Palatino: Inventario generale, inediti, revisioni* (Rome, 1996)
E. La Rocca and others: 'Fori Imperiali', *Mitt. Dt. Archäol. Inst.: Röm. Abt.*, cviii (2001), pp.171–285
M. Milella: 'Il Foro di Traiano', *Il Museo dei Fori Imperiali, dallo studio alla pubblicazioni* (Rome, 2001)
J. E. Packer: *The Forum of Trajan in Rome: A Study of the Monuments in Brief* (Berkeley, 2001)
J. W. Stamper: *The Architecture of Roman Temples: The Republic to the Middle Empire* (Cambridge, 2005)

3. Palatine. One of Rome's hills and site of the official imperial residence until the 4th century AD. The hill itself is roughly rectangular with steeply sloping sides and is situated at the centre of the city overlooking the valley of the Forum Romanum to the north-east, with its slightly lower north-western extension, sometimes called the Germalus, rising sharply from near the Tiber. In Roman times the Palatine (Lat. Palatium) was thought to have been the site of the citadel of the legendary king Evander and of the original walled city founded by Romulus; it was certainly inhabited in remote antiquity: the remains of three huts discovered at the western corner date back to the 8th century BC. From around the beginning of the 2nd century BC it became one of the city's most fashionable districts and was the setting of a number of well-appointed houses belonging to wealthy patricians. Residents during the 1st century BC included Cicero, Mark Antony and the future emperor Augustus (*reg* 27 BC–AD 14). Almost all these houses, however, were swept aside by the end of the following century to make way for the fast encroaching domain of Augustus' imperial successors and the spectacular Flavian Palace (the Palatium) subsequently built there by Domitian, which covers the highest ground and which gave its name to all such future buildings (*see* Palace). Following the ruination of the palace and all the other buildings at the end of antiquity, the Palatine was abandoned. During the Renaissance, the 'caverns and abysses' of the deserted palace mentioned by Onofrio Panvinio were certainly visible, but the area was never thoroughly explored, and in the 1540s much of the Germalus was made inaccessible to archaeologists when it was converted into formal gardens for Cardinal Alessandro Farnese. After the early investigations of Monsignor Francesco Bianchini in 1720–24, whose plan reconstructions of the palace were published posthumously, and those later on of Antonio Nibby and others, systematic exploration eventually began when Pietro Rosa commenced excavations in 1860 on behalf of Emperor Napoleon III.

There are remains of several buildings of distinction dating from the Republican and early Imperial periods. One of the earliest, at the hill's western corner, is the Temple of Magna Mater (or Cybele; ded. 191 BC; see fig. 6a), which was restored under Augustus (AD 3) with an imposing hexastyle Corinthian

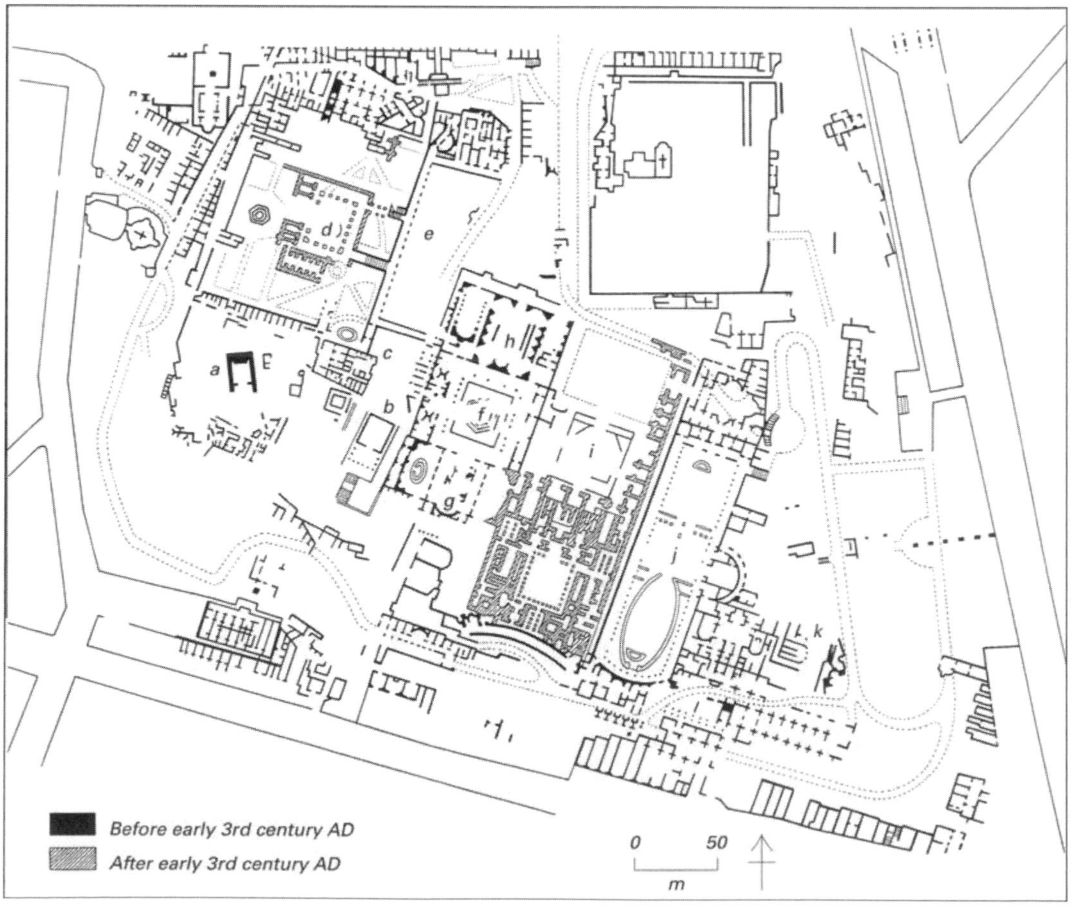

6. Rome, Palatine, early 2nd century BC–early 3rd century AD, plan: (a) Temple of Magna Mater; (b) Temple of Apollo; (c) House of Livia; (d) Domus Tiberiana; (e) cryptoporticus; (f) Domus Flavia; (g) banqueting chamber; (h) Aula Regia; (i) Domus Augustana; (j) stadium or garden; (k) Palace of Septimius Severus

façade (recorded in a mid-1st-century AD relief in the Villa Medici). Not far to the east is the site of the once splendid Temple of Apollo vowed by Augustus in 36 BC (completed 28 BC; 6b), which had walls built entirely of Luna marble, a roof embellished with two gilded chariots, and a Corinthian façade facing on to a forecourt bordered by porticos and a Latin and a Greek library. Remains of two Republican houses with impressive Second Style wall paintings, the House of the Griffins and the Aula of Isis, survive beneath the halls of Domitian's palace. The late Republican complex immediately to the west and north of the Temple of Apollo, which was preserved during the Imperial period, is the one lived in by Augustus himself, who had prudently bought up several houses in the vicinity; the complex includes the finely decorated House of Livia (6c) dating back to the early 1st century BC and designed on a conventional atrium plan. The area behind, overlooking the Forum Romanum, which appeared as a series of buildings abutting one another along the crest of the hill, was developed by Tiberius as the Domus Tiberiana (6d), and then by Caligula (*reg* AD 37–41), who converted the Temple of Castor below into an entrance vestibule fronting an enormous atrium on the site of the later S Maria Antiqua. The Domus Tiberiana and surrounding area was subsequently redeveloped by Nero as a palace complex organized around a central peristyle and built on an enormous podium (still surviving), fronted on one side by a lengthy cryptoporticus (6e). As part of his Domus Transitoria and Domus Aurea, Nero also built other structures on the higher open ground to the east, including the elaborate and ostentatiously ornamented dining complex buried beneath Domitian's palace.

Domitian's palace, conceived on an enormous scale by the architect RABIRIUS and begun soon after AD 81, consists of a public and a private sector, now usually referred to as the Domus Flavia and Domus Augustana respectively. The Domus Flavia (6f), situated next to the Temple of Apollo and the Domus Tiberiana, incorporates on one side a group of three assembly halls facing on to a large peristyle, and on the other a banqueting chamber (6g) of unprecedented size positioned between two fountain courts. Internally, the massive brick and concrete structure was once reveted with exotic marbles and richly articulated with columns and niches. It seems probable that the largest hall, the awesome Aula Regia (6h), and the banqueting chamber were once covered with vaulted ceilings made of wood and perhaps adorned, as other rooms were, with celestial decorations. Externally, to judge from a sestertius of AD 95/96, the building appeared as a series of superimposed terraces, with the Aula Regia surmounted by a temple-like arrangement of columns and pediments. The Domus Augustana to the east (6i) is organized axially about three courtyards on two levels; the most intimate rooms were arranged in two storeys around the lowermost courtyard, which is shelved into the hillside and fronted by a sweeping concave façade overlooking the Circus Maximus. The remarkable intricacy and geometric complexity of the planning developed tendencies already apparent in Nero's Domus Aurea but now to an extreme and obsessive degree. Immediately beyond the Domus Augustana is a long open space the shape of a stadium, which presumably served as an enclosed garden (6j). Of the structures added subsequently to the south, the most notable were the Palace of Septimius Severus (*reg* AD193–211), a development of the Flavian Palace on enormous substructures (6k), and the Septizodium (completed AD 203, partly surviving until 1588), a monumental three-storey columnar screen-façade with apsidal recesses and a statue of the Emperor at the centre. The enormous raised terrace at the hill's eastern corner, on which S Sebastiano now stands, was perhaps constructed under Domitian but may have later served as the platform for the Temple of Sol Invictus Elagabalus built by the infamous Heliogabalus (*reg* AD 218–22).

Since 2005 Dr Andrea Carandini has excavated a spacious aristocratic house or palace on the Palatine Hill. Extending to 3700 square feet, the residence included 1130 square feet of roofed space, while the remaining spaces were courtyards or porticos. The structure was supported by at least two big wooden beams, and had a banquet hall. Pottery was also found at the site. Carandini suggests that the grandeur of the dwelling indicates it was fit for a king, perhaps the first king of Rome, Romulus. Thus the house and surrounding structures (the Sanctuary of Vesta) supports the claims of Rome's legendary history of early kings and state formation, and refutes more conventional attitudes about a backward and primitive Rome in the 8th century BC. Carandini's finds are not yet published, and his interpretation has raised scepticism.

F. Bianchini: *Del palazzo de' Cesari* (Verona, 1738)
B. Tamm: *Auditorium and Palatium* (Lund, 1963)
W. L. MacDonald: *The Architecture of the Roman Empire*, i (New Haven, 1965, rev. 2/1982)
C. F. Giuliani: 'Domus Flavia: Una nuova lettura', *Mitt. Dt. Archäol. Inst.: Röm. Abt.*, lxxxiv (1977), pp. 91–106
C. Krause: 'Rapporti di lavoro', *Domus Tiberiana: Nuove ricerche, studi di ristauro*, ed. R. Locher (Zurich, 1985), pp. 73–154
M. Royo: *Domus imperatoriae. Topographie, formation, e imaginaire des palais imperiaux du Palatin* (Rome, 1990)
C. Giavarini and M Biritognolo. *Il Palatino: Area sacra sud-ovest e Domus Tiberiana* (Rome, 1998)
C. Cecamore: *Palatium: Topografia storica del Palatino tra III sec. a.C. e I sec. d.C.* (Rome, 2002)
P. Zanker: 'Domitian's Palace on the Palatine and the Imperial Image', *Representations of Empire, Rome and the Mediterranean World*, ed. A. Bowman (London, 2002), pp. 105–130
J. P. Ikäheimo: *Late Roman African Cookware of the Palatine East Excavations, Rome: A Holistic Approach* (Oxford, 2003)
A. St Clair: *Carving as Craft: Palatine East and the Greco-Roman Bone and Ivory Carving Tradition* (Baltimore, 2003)
A. Carandini: *Palatino, Velia e Sacra Via: Paesaggi urbani attraverso il temp*, Workshop di archeologia classica, Quaderni, i (Rome, 2004)
A. Hoffmann and U. Wulf: *Die Kaiserpaläste auf dem Palatin in Rom: das Zentrum der römischen Welt und seine Bauten* (Mainz, 2004)

4. Ara Pacis. Monumental 'Altar of Peace' in the Campus Martius, consecrated after the victorious return of Augustus from Spain and Gaul in 13 BC and dedicated four years later. It was reconstructed on a nearby site in 1938 from fragments, most of which were excavated from beneath the Palazzo Fiano in 1903 and 1937–8 (see fig. 7). The altar was originally erected at the east edge of the Campus Martius, between the obelisk of Augustus, which served as a needle for his gigantic sundial, and the Via Flaminia, parallel with both and related to the lines of the equinox and the winter solstice. The altar, made of Carrara marble, is horseshoe-shaped and surrounded by a virtually square enclosing wall (11.63×10.66 m) with—unconventionally—two entrances from the east and the west, the measurements of which were determined by the equinoctial line running through them. In this way the altar was directly connected with the dates of the conception and birth of Augustus (on 23 September, Augustus' birthday, the obelisk's shadow fell directly on the centre of the Ara Pacis), just as the Mausoleum of Augustus lying further to the north was also integrated into the sundial system.

The enclosure wall is decorated both inside and out with reliefs, in two horizontal zones. Inside is a simple relief above a half-height close-set paling, depicting large garlands composed of a variety of agricultural produce, that hang from bucrania (bulls' skulls); it serves as a reminder of the annual sacrifice made at the altar. The exterior is much richer. A flowery filigree latticework of acanthus shoots growing up from powerful central leaf bases, the scrolls ending in a variety of calyxes and inhabited by innumerable small animals and a row of swans along the top, is cleverly arranged to run parallel with and overlap the lower zone. Above the frieze on the entrance sides there are four panels with scenes relating to Roman mythology: to the west, Aeneas after his arrival in Latium at the sacrifice in Lavinium and the discovery of Romulus and Remus being suckled by a she-wolf; corresponding to these at the east end are on one side Roma and on the other a mother figure, probably Tellus (the earth; see fig. 8), whose fruitfulness was linked with peace. The long friezes on the north and south sides arranged on three superimposed levels depict the train of the inaugural sacrificial procession, with individual portraits of Augustus and his retinue. The ramp-like staircase from the sundial to the west entrance carries on inside the wall across the stepped pedestal, rising towards the platform of the altar. A small frieze depicting another sacrificial procession runs around and inside the top of the altar proper, which is covered by more of the typical metallic scrolls; most of the later reliefs have been destroyed.

The whole relief programme represents the Pax Augusta, crediting Augustus with the blessings and prosperity that result from peace and accustoming the viewer to the idea of dynastic rule (while declining official triumphs for his successes in Spain and Gaul, Augustus had granted permission to build the altar). The Ara Pacis is also an outstanding example of Augustan classicism (*see* SCULPTURE, §VI, 2(ii)): it continues the development of techniques used in late Hellenistic relief sculpture, while reflecting the art of Classical Athens, for example on the Parthenon frieze. Its scenes and motifs were hugely influential for Imperial art.

G. Moretti: *Ara Pacis Augustae* (Rome, 1948)
S. Weinstock: 'Pax and the "Ara Pacis"', *J. Roman Stud.*, l (1960), pp. 44–58
E. Simon: *Ara Pacis Augustae*, Monumenta Artis Antiquae (Tübingen, 1967)
A. Borbein: 'Die Ara Pacis Augustae: Geschichte, Wirklichkeit und Programme', *Jb. Dt. Archäol. Inst.*, xc (1975), pp. 242–66
E. Buchner: 'Solarium Augusti und Ara Pacis', *Mitt. Dt. Archäol. Inst.: Röm. Abt.*, lxxxiii (1976), pp. 319–65
E. La Rocca and others: *Ara Pacis Augustae: In occasione del restauro della fronte orientale* (Rome, 1983)
G. M. Koeppel: 'Die historischen Reliefs der Kaiserzeit, v: Ara Pacis Augustae', *Bonn. Jb. Rhein. Landesmus. Bonn & Ver. Altertfreund. Rheinlande*, clxxxvii (1987), pp. 101–57; clxxxviii (1988), pp. 97–106
G. Sauron: 'Le Message esthétique des rinceaux de l'Ara Pacis Augustae', *Rev. Archéol.* (1988), pp. 3–40
S. Settis: 'Die Ara Pacis', *Kaiser Augustus und die verlorene Republik* (exh. cat., Berlin, Berlin. Gal., 1988), pp. 400–427
J. Elsner: 'Cult and Sculpture: Sacrifice in the Ara Pacis Augustae', *J. Roman Stud.*, lxxxi (1991), pp. 50–61
R. Billows: 'The Religious Procession of the Ara Pacis Augustae: Augustus' Supplicatio in 13 BC', *J. Roman Archaeol.*, vi (1993), pp. 80–92
D. Castriota: *The Ara Pacis Augustae and the Imagery of Abundance in Later Greek and Early Roman Imperial Art* (Princeton, 1995)
D. A. Conlin: *The Artists of the Ara Pacis: The Process of Hellenization of Roman Relief Sculpture* (Chapel Hill, NC and London, 1997)
N. Hannestad: 'Late-antique Reworking of the Ara Pacis?', *J. Roman Archaeol.*, xiii (2000), pp. 311–18

5. Domus Aurea. Great imperial palace built by NERO. The Domus Aurea (Lat.: 'Golden House'), spreading between the Palatine, Caelian and Oppian hills, is among the most evocative Classical buildings, and its painted decorations inspired many artists from the Renaissance onwards. It was designed soon after the Great Fire of Rome (AD 64) by the architect-engineers SEVERUS AND CELER (see Tacitus: *Annals* XV.xlii) to replace Nero's earlier Domus Transitoria, but was apparently never completed. It was largely destroyed in a fire of AD 104, and shortly afterwards the substantial remains of a domestic wing on the Oppian hillside were incorporated into the substructures of the Baths of Trajan. This ensured the preservation of their painted decoration and, together with literary sources, these remains provide a reasonably detailed impression of the original appearance of the Domus Aurea.

The main palace buildings were erected on a series of terraces above a vast artificial lake, later drained for the construction of the Colosseum in AD 80 (see fig. 9). The surviving range, which faces due south, was apparently fronted by colonnades and consisted of two wings separated by a large polygonal recess with a further wing to the right. The central section, at least, had an upper storey, which extended backwards to form part of the terrace above, where there were

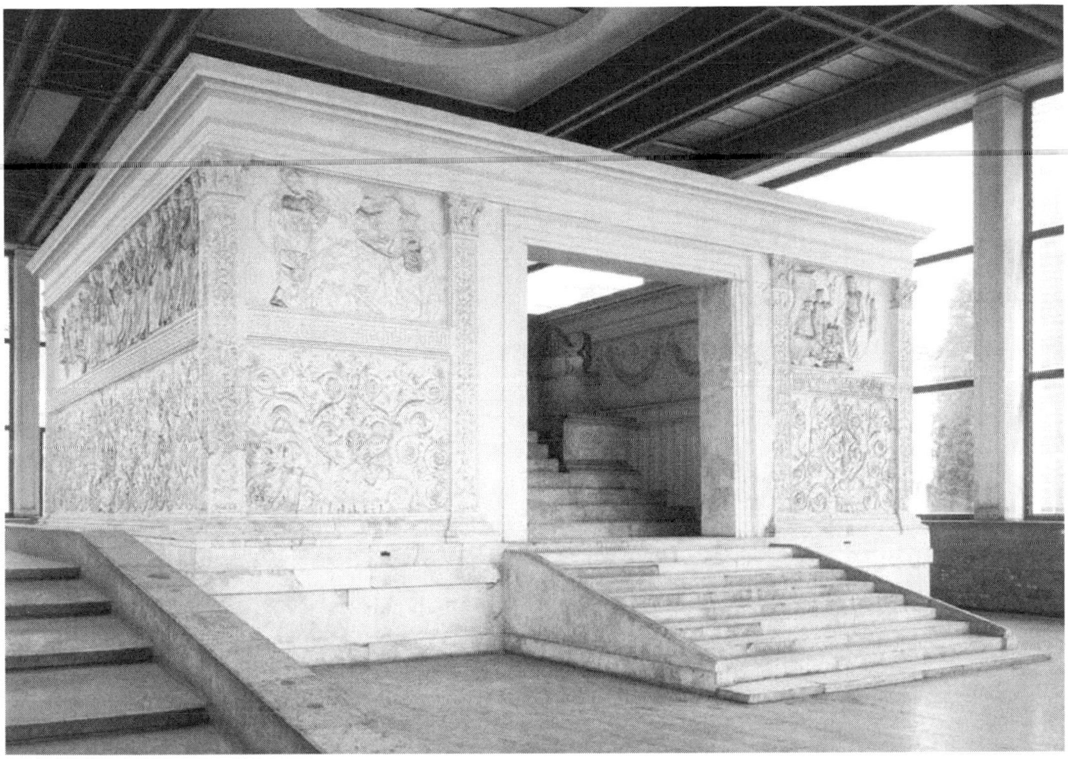

7. Rome, Ara Pacis, dedicated 9 BC

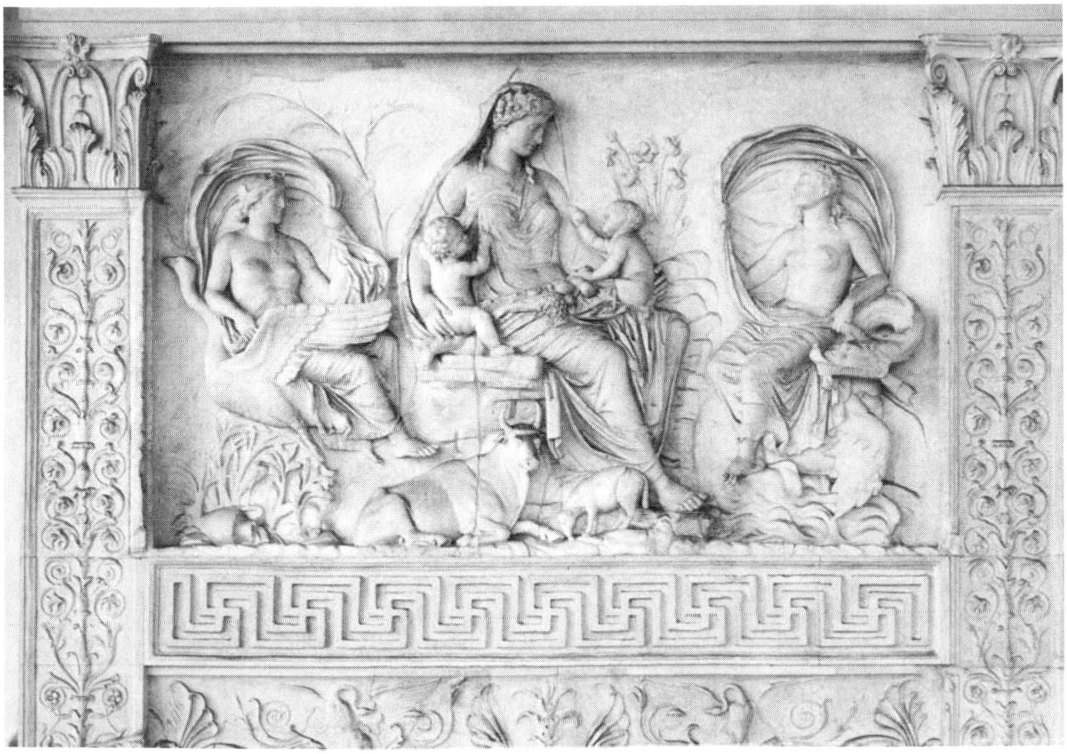

8. Rome, Ara Pacis, relief on the east side showing ?*Tellus*, marble, dedicated 9 BC

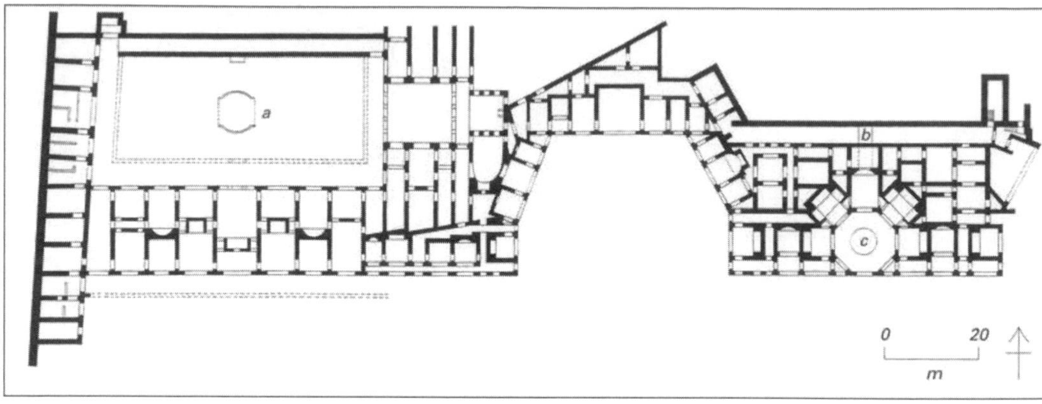

9. Domus Aurea, Rome, begun AD 64, plan of the domestic wing: (a) columned court with fountain; (b) cryptoporticus; (c) octagonal hall

courtyards and ornamental gardens. The complex may well have occupied the entire hilltop. The building's dimensions, with a frontage nearly as long (*c.* 360 m) as the garden façade of Versailles, surpassed those of any earlier palace. Other palace buildings included a nymphaeum on the platform intended for the Temple of Claudius on the Caelian Hill, and perhaps also the building on the Palatine later known as the Domus Tiberiana, and the baths next to the Oppian wing named after Titus (*reg* AD79–81). The site, covering at least 200 acres, was dotted with numerous other buildings, some public. Other areas were made to resemble natural countryside and were reserved for wild animals. In the entrance court, facing the Forum Romanum, was a gigantic bronze statue of *Nero* (*c.* 30 m: high i.e. about as tall as the Colossus of Rhodes), which probably represented the emperor as the Sun god.

Both gold and jewels were extensively employed in the decorations, and the palace was filled with choice statuary, much of it pillaged from Greece. The architectural marvels apparently included a banqueting hall with a rotating dome. The architecture of the surviving wing is also remarkable, especially that of an ingeniously planned group of rooms in the central section. This consists of a large domed octagonal hall (not discovered until the 20th century) surrounded by five vaulted chambers, one housing a cascade. Only the building's concrete skeleton survives, stripped almost entirely of its original surfacing, but this clearly demonstrates the architects' daring exploitation of concrete's plasticity and strength.

The Domus Aurea conforms in several ways to well-established traditions in Roman domestic architecture. The plan of the Oppian wing, for example, closely resembles that of the late Republican villa (*c.* mid-1st century BC) at Oplontis (mod. Torre Annunziata), near Naples, while its façade was evidently similar to those of the villas depicted in Pompeian wall paintings. Terracing was a common feature of hillside villas (e.g. at Baiae or Tibur (Tivoli)), as were artificial landscapes and even wild animal reserves. It is possible that the gardens and pleasure buildings of the late Republican and early Imperial estates at Rome itself influenced the scheme. Nevertheless, both Nero and his architects also presumably intended to emulate the great royal palaces of the Hellenistic world, above all that of the Ptolemies at Alexandria, which consisted of a series of sumptuous buildings surrounded by gardens and overlooking the waterfront. Similarly, though the octagonal hall, which was almost certainly articulated with columns, closely resembles such Roman structures as the vaulted Ninfeo Minore in the so-called Villa of Cicero at Formiae, the complex design and tent-like appearance of its faceted dome may have been inspired by Athenaeus' description (*Deipnosophists* v.196a–197c) of the famous banqueting pavilion of Ptolemy II Philadelphus (*reg* 285–246 BC) in Alexandria or by similar structures.

The direct architectural influence of the Domus Aurea was limited, although it probably inspired Domitian's palace on the Palatine (begun AD 81). The painted decoration, which is partly attributed to the celebrated painter Famulus, was, however, much more influential (see colour pl. 2:IX, fig. 2). It is among the earliest examples of Fourth Style painting, a development in Roman painting that may have been promoted by Nero himself, and was presumably instrumental in establishing the new fashion. When the Oppian wing began to be explored in the late 15th century and the early 16th, its murals and painted stucco vaults profoundly affected architectural and interior decoration and gave rise to a style known as the 'Grotesque' after the 'caverns' (*grotte*) that they appeared to adorn. Much of the Domus Aurea's ornament is known only from drawings and from splendid engravings made in the late 18th century, when the Oppian wing was still supposed to be part of the overlying Baths of Trajan (misidentified as the Baths of Titus). Recognized early in the 19th century as part of the Domus Aurea, the Oppian wing continues to be studied, although its paintings are rapidly fading.

A mosaic depicting naked harversters has been found under the Baths of Trajan on the Oppian Hill (reported in the international. press on 1 Feb 2005).

The polychrome mosaic (1.83×3.05 m) is thought to date from *c.* AD 64–100. Of the five male figures represented in the mosaic, one is shown placing bunches of grapes in a wicker container while a second, seen from behind, is playing a double-flute. Three other figures are crowned with leaves and dance on harvested grapes in a large rectangular vat. The mosaic may have decorated a house built in this zone between Nero's extensive redevelopment and Trajan's reclamation of the hill.

C. C. Van Essen: 'La Topographie de la Domus Aurea Neronis', *Meded. Kon. Ned. Acad. Wét.*, xvii (1954), pp. 371–89

A. Boethius: *The Golden House of Nero* (Ann Arbor, 1960)

M. P. O. Morford: 'The Distortion of the *Domus Aurea* Tradition', *Eranos*, lxvi (1968), pp. 158–79

N. Dacos: *La Découverte de la Domus Aurea et la formation des grotesques à la renaissance* (London, 1969)

H. P. L'Orange: 'Domus Aurea: Der Sonnenpalast', *Likeness and Icon: Selected Studies in Classical and Early Medieval Art* (Odense, 1973), pp. 292–312

L. Fabbrini: 'Domus Aurea: Il piano superiore del quartiere orientale', *Atti Pont. Accad. Roman Archeol.*, xiv (1982), pp. 5–24

W. J. T. Peters and P. G. P. Meyboom: 'The Roots of Provincial Roman Painting: Results of Current Research in Nero's Domus Aurea', *Roman Provincial Wall Painting of the Western Empire*, ed. J. E. A. Liversidge (Oxford, 1982), pp. 33–74

L. Fabbrini: 'Domus Aurea: Una nuova lettura planimetrica del palazzo sul colle Oppio', *Anlct. Romana Inst. Dan.*, suppl. x (1983), pp. 167–85

D. Hemsoll: 'The Architecture of Nero's Golden House', *Architecture and Architectural Sculpture in the Roman Empire*, ed. M. Henig (Oxford, 1990), pp. 10–38

M. N. Pinot de Villechenon: *Domus Aurea: La decorazione pittorica del palazzo neroniano nell'album delle "Terme di Tito" conservato al Louvre* (Milan, 1998)

M. N. Pinot de Villechenon and G. Guadalupi: *Domus Aurea: Les fresques du palais de Néron à travers les "Bains de Titus" conservés au Louvre* (Milan, 1999)

Nerone: la vita, le follie, le meraviglie della Domus Aurea (Milan, 1999)

L. F. Ball: *The Domus Aurea and the Roman Architectural Revolution* (Cambridge and New York, 2003)

E. Segala and I. Sciortino: *Domus Aurea* (Milan, 2003)

P. Bennet: 'Rome's Basement', *N. Geog.*, ccx (July 2006), pp. 88–103 [with illustration of mosaic on p. 89]

6. COLOSSEUM. Officially called the *Amphitheatrum Flavium*, but soon nicknamed after a nearby colossal statue of the sun god, the *Colosseum* became the principal amphitheatre in the Roman Empire. Its construction finally gave Rome a venue for its gladiatorial games and wild beast hunts (*venationes*) worthy of the imperial capital. Work was begun by Vespasian (*reg* AD 69–79) early in his reign on the site of the artificial lake of Nero's Domus Aurea and continued by his son Titus, who inaugurated the amphitheatre in AD 80. Late sources attributed the top storey to Domitian, but this is disputed, though it is generally believed that he was responsible for the subterranean service corridors.

The building is the largest of all Roman amphitheatres, with a regular elliptical plan measuring 188×156 m externally on its major axes (see fig. 10). The foundations are a ring of concrete 13.5 m high and 54 m wide, set 9 m deep into the clay bed of the former lake. The superstructure is composed of a network of radial and annular barrel-vaulted passages on three levels, linked by staircases, with the seating supported on raking barrel vaults, a pattern established already in the Theatre of Pompey (55 BC). The façade and the main piers up to the vaults of the second level are in travertine ashlar, while the radial walls up to the start of the second level are of large tufa blocks. The rest of the structure is in brick-faced concrete. Cozzo (1928) suggested that the travertine skeleton and second-storey vaults were built first, to allow subsequent work to proceed at two levels, so increasing the speed of construction. He also attributed the four quadrants of the ellipse to four different gangs of workmen. His analysis is not, however, universally accepted.

The floor of the arena itself (79×47 m along its major axes) is missing but originally consisted of wooden boards covered with sand. These rested on the walls of a complex series of subterranean passages. The animals were driven along annular corridors into 32 cells on the arena's periphery, from where they were hoisted to an upper level and released up ramps into the arena, appearing simultaneously from all sides if required. A system of winches and counterweights also allowed scenery to appear suddenly in the arena from the central longitudinal passages. A heavy net, supported by stout wooden posts and topped by rolling bars made from elephant tusks, surrounded the arena to prevent the animals escaping. A subterranean passageway linked the Colosseum to the nearby *ludus magnus*, Rome's main gladiatorial barracks.

The *cavea* (auditorium) is estimated to have held 50,000–75,000 people (see fig. 11). Most of the seating does not survive, although one section has been restored. Around the edge of the arena ran a podium supporting marble seats for important guests. This was interrupted at the ends of the long axis by the processional entrance and the exit of the arena, and on the short axis by loggias on either side. The northern loggia was the *pulvinar*, the imperial box, while the southern one was reserved for the president of the games, the Vestal Virgins and the consuls. Behind the podium were 3 ranges of seating: the *ima cavea*, comprising 7 rows of marble seats for the senators, with 12 rows behind for the equites (wealthy non-senators); the *media cavea*, with 19 rows divided into wedges for different classes of citizens; and a further 7 rows comprising the *summa cavea*. A broad passage and a high wall with 36 doors opening on to the passage separated the *media cavea* and *summa cavea*. A portico in the Composite order crowned the *cavea*, behind which were a further 11 rows of wooden seats for women and slaves. The passages and staircases were so arranged that, with the help of wooden barriers, a spectator entering the amphitheatre at any of the 76 numbered openings would be led automatically to the appropriate section of seating.

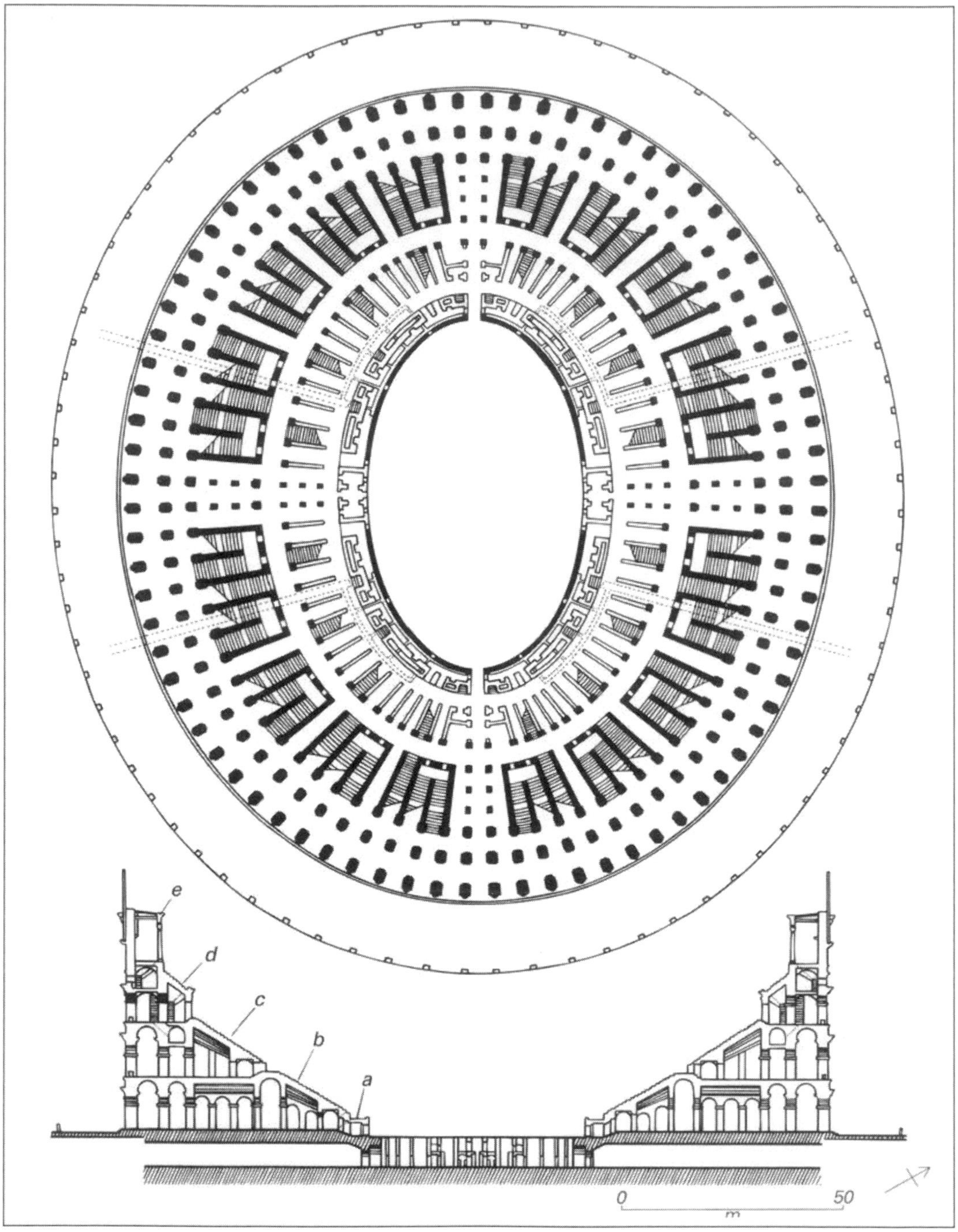

10. Rome, Colosseum, AD 69–80, ground plan and section: (a) podium; (b) *ima cavea;* (c) *media cavea;* (d) *summa cavea;* (e) portico

Together with the Circus Maximus, the Colosseum quickly became the main venue for the emperor's interaction with the Roman public. Through the games, the emperor and his senior magistrates re-enacted fundamental principles of Roman culture and society, whose power balance and hierarchical structure the architecture visibly reinforced.

In the outer façade (48 m high) the ends of the radial passages appear as three superimposed tiers of 80 regular arched openings, above which is a tall attic separated from the arcades by a high basement. In ascending order the arches of the three tiers are framed by engaged Tuscan, Ionic and Corinthian columns. All bear Ionic entablatures with plain

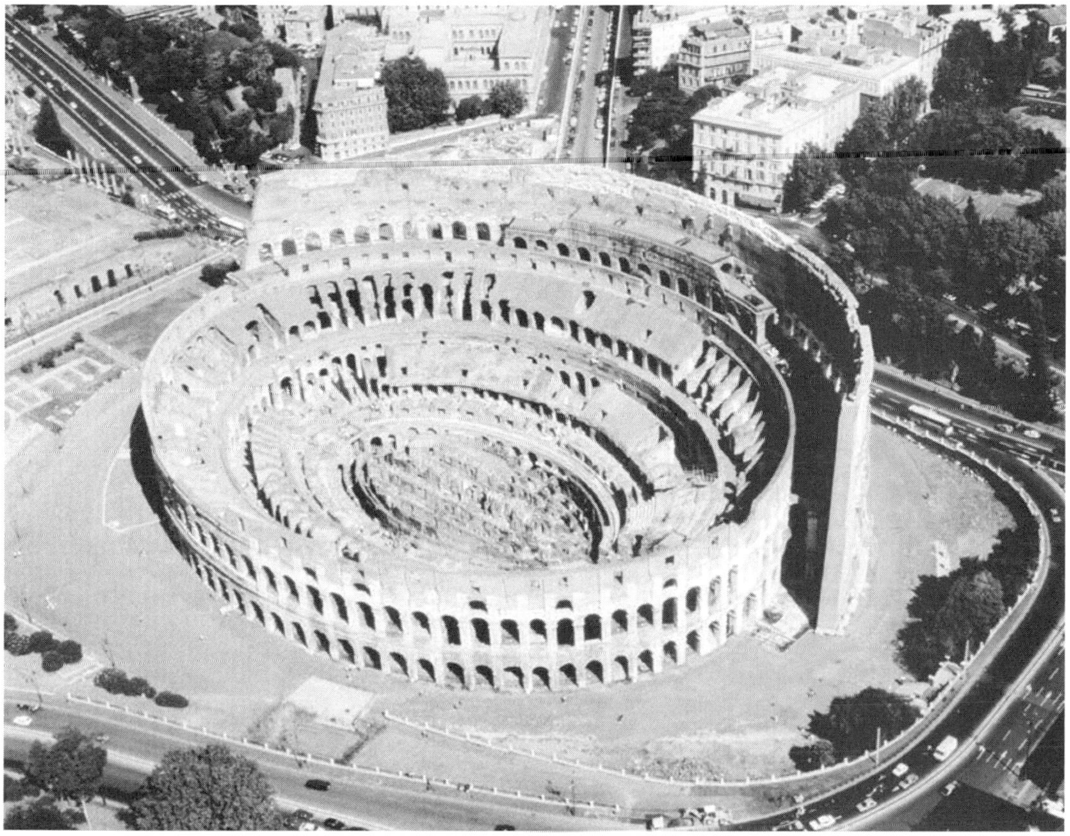

11. Rome, Colosseum, aerial view, AD 69–80

friezes, while the Corinthian cornice alone has a row of dentils. The Ionic and Corinthian columns rest on pedestals. The entrance to the *pulvinar* was lavishly decorated in the manner of a triumphal arch, and it is possible that the other three entrances on the main axes were also given special treatment. Although coins of Titus and Gordian III (*reg* AD 238–244) show statues in the upper arcades, no trace of these survives. The attic was divided into bays, decorated alternately with rectangular windows and gilded bronze shields, by tall Corinthian pilasters on pedestals corresponding to the engaged orders below. In each bay stood three masts for a great awning sheltering the *cavea*. These passed through holes between the modillions in the heavy crowning cornice and were supported by large consoles above the line of the windows. Corresponding to the masts at ground level was a row of travertine bollards, set 17.6 m from the façade, on top of which were fixed capstans for manipulating the ropes of the awning. A special detachment of 1000 sailors from the fleet at Misenum was stationed at Rome to operate the system.

The Colosseum was restored several times following fires (in AD 217, 250 and 320) and earthquakes (AD 429 and 443); signs of rebuilding can still be clearly seen in the attic zone. The last recorded *venationes* were held in the 7th century AD, after which the building was plundered for marble and for the iron clamps used to bond its ashlar blocks, but it seems to have remained structurally intact until the earthquake of 1349. The mound of travertine created by its fallen masonry was quarried throughout the Renaissance and used for, among other things, the Cancelleria and the steps of St Peter's. The remaining arches were often studied by architects and inspired a number of façades with superimposed orders flanking arcades (e.g. the cortile of the Palazzo Farnese in Rome). It has been restored several times since the 18th century, not least by Raffaele Stern (1774–1820) after the earthquake of 1806.

P. Colagrossi: *L'Anfiteatro flavio nei suoi venti secoli di storia* (Florence, 1913)
G. Cozzo: *Ingegneria romana* (Rome, 1928), pp. 195–253
M. di Macco: *Il Colosseo: Funzione simbolica, storica, urbana* (Rome, 1971)
J. Pearson: *Arena: The Story of the Colosseum* (New York, 1973)
C. Mocchegiani Carpano and R. Luciani: 'I restauri dell'Anfiteatro flavio', *Riv. Ist. N. Archeol. & Stor. A.*, ser. 3, iv (1981), pp. 9–69
J.-C. Golvin: *L'Amphithéâtre romain: Essai sur la théorisation de sa forme et de ses fonctions* (Paris, 1988), pp. 173–83
A. Gabucci, ed.: *The Colosseum* (Los Angeles, 2001)

K. Hopkins and M. Beard: *The Colosseum* (Cambridge, MA, 2005)

L. C. Lancaster: 'The Process of Building the Colosseum: The Site, Materials and Construction Technique', *J. Roman Archaeol.*, xviii (2005), pp. 57–82

7. Trajan's Column. Monument in the Forum of Trajan, covered in relief carving, which was dedicated 18 May AD 113. The inscription over its door (Corp. Inscr. Lat., vi, 960) indicates that it commemorated Trajan's accomplishment in excavating the Quirinal Hill and building his forum and markets, which are visible (through 43 windows) from the inner stair and crowning platform. Eight blocks form the base (26.83 sq. m, h. 5.37 m), entered by a door in the south-east face; its chamber received Trajan's ash-urn at his death in AD 117 (Dio: *Roman History* XLVIII.xvi.3); if Titus' ashes (*d* AD 81) were in the attic of the Arch of Titus, intramural burial had precedent. The Tuscan Doric column held a colossal bronze *Trajan c.* 5.5 m tall, of which the head (now lost) was 694 mm; coins of AD 113 show a heroic nude, a spear in the right hand. The 29.78 m Luna marble shaft (17 drums, each 1.44 m high with diameters tapering from 3.83 m to 3.66 m) made with the capital a *columna centenaria* of 100 Roman feet. Column portraits were traditional in Rome from the 5th century BC; new were the shaft's spiral narrative relief and internal stair of 185 steps. The carved shaft of this first *columna historiata* (a modern term) was imitated in antiquity by the columns of Marcus Aurelius (AD 176–93; *see* SCULPTURE, §VI, 2(vii)) and *Arkadios* (AD 400–402). In 1540 Pope Paul II cleared the base; a 9th-century church of St Nicholas built against it had damaged the inscription. In 1588 Sixtus V installed on the egg-and-dart echinus a new platform and statue of St Peter; his artists imitated the column. The fascination of artists (such as Piranesi) and rulers alike culminated in the project of Napoleon III (*reg* 1852–70) to cast the column reliefs. These 114 panels (Paris, Louvre; London, V&A; ex-Lateran Pal., Rome; Rome, Mus. Civiltà) document details now eroded by pollution, although restoration in the 1980s has allowed detailed re-examination. Modern 'scene' numbers (1–155) follow Cichorius, 1896–1900.

The column was set in Trajan's Forum between the Greek and Roman halls of the library behind the north entrance court to the Basilica Ulpia. Its statue may have been visible from the forum court on the other side of the basilica; the column was certainly prominent to those travelling south into the city centre along the Via Flaminia. Amid structures for learning and law, the column, like the decorations of his forum, honoured Trajan for his *virtus* as *imperator*. The shaft rises from a torus carved as a triumphal laurel garland; on the base, carved as a trophy pile of Dacian arms, flying Victories uphold the inscription *tabula*; at its corners Jupiter's eagles with spread wings suspend oak garlands from their beaks. (Oak, Jupiter's tree, supplied the *corona civica* awarded for saving Roman lives.) The shaft reliefs (which Claridge suggested are Hadrianic) describe Trajan's two Dacian campaigns (AD 101–2, 105–6) in a spiral frieze of 23 turns edged by a rocky ground-line, peopled by *c.* 2500 figures (*c.* 1×200 m; relief depth 34 mm; see fig. 12). Between depictions of the two wars Victory inscribes a shield between two trophies; in the last spirals after the dramatic death of the Dacian leader Decebalus his people are rounded up and trail off with their animals. These reliefs glorified Trajan and his army, the only Romans depicted. The two or three officers who always back Trajan sometimes have portrait features (e.g. Licinius Sura and possibly Hadrian). Apollodoros of Damascus, architect of the forum, perhaps supervised the column. Teams worked together from a master plan, each carving a given width of frieze moving up the shaft; these workshops are believed to be responsible also for the Great Trajanic Frieze and Trajan's Arch at Beneventum (Benevento; for both *see* SCULPTURE, §VI, 2(v)). Metal attachments once supplied armament details; the extent of added colour in the form of paint and gilding is debated.

This is a rich lexicon of Roman historical relief iconography and stylistic conventions, which long served European artists and illustrators as a sourcebook. It documents Roman architecture and engineering; for military historians it usefully chronicles military engines, specialized weaponry (such as chainmail) and legionary insignia. The reliefs represent, not reproduce, the historical conquest of Dacia; the legible exposition is a careful selection of episodes

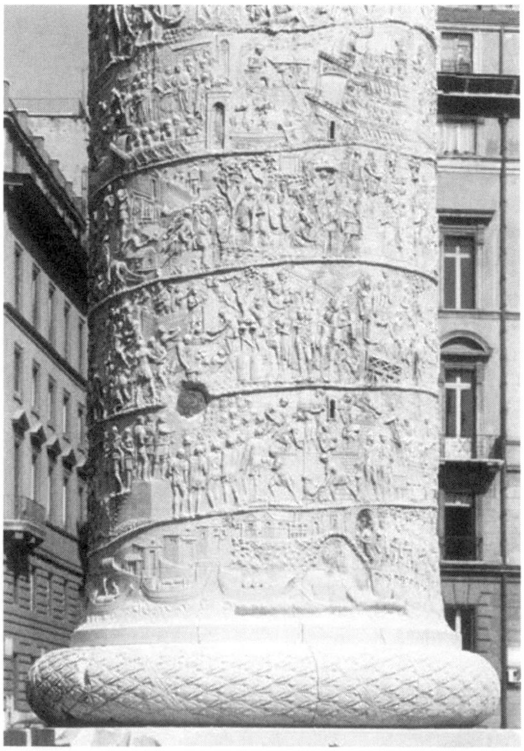

12. Rome, Trajan's Column, detail of lower part showing the spiral frieze, dedicated AD 113

that have not just narrative but thematic, typological significance (*virtus*, clemency, piety etc): the ubiquitous Trajan never actually fights, for his mere presence ensures victory. The frieze is an important exemplar of episodic narration, a continuous landscape in which protagonists recur. Although such details as weaponry and topography are in fact often confused, the reliefs intended an impression of authentic reportage, analogous to Julius Caesar's or Trajan's own war commentaries; this seeming candour underpins their panegyric to the army's skills and Trajan's genius. The action unfolds in a detailed natural and man-made Dacian setting that locates and demarcates events, depicted in bird's-eye, or panoramic, perspective. Figures, details and small groupings seem realistic, but consistent illusionism in perspective and relative proportion is irrelevant to this vivid expository style. Late Antique devices such as multiple ground-lines and hierarchic scale already appear. The full episodic sequence spirals, but a story could be read from fixed points set by the sides and corners of the base; these vertical sequences make sense from several vantage points. To help spectators the designer repeated figures and motifs on these axes, such as the Emperor, major constructions (e.g. bridges thrown across the Danube, contemporary marvels) and set-piece compositions (e.g. sacrifices, barbarian submissions). The sources of this mode of decoration, thus its value to other reconstructions, are debated. The old theory that the frieze reproduced a book-scroll is discredited. Columns had had spiral decoration, or carved figures, but not both; however, historical narration in stacked frieze bands was a Roman genre, as on painted Republican tombs (e.g. Rome, Esquiline Tomb) or the 3rd-century AD Arch of Galerius in Thessaloniki. The pictorial mode may have imitated types of expository painting carried at Roman triumphs, as did panels of the Arch of Septimius Severus in the Forum Romanum; the selection of motifs conforms with texts describing such paintings.

G. B. Piranesi: *Trofeo o sia magnifica colonna coclide di marmo* (Rome, 1775–6)

C. Cichorius: *Die Reliefs der Traianssaüle*, 3 vols (Berlin, 1896–1900)

K. Lehmann-Hartleben: *Die Trajanssaüle: Ein romisches Kunstwerk zu Beginn der Spätantike* (Berlin, 1926)

G. Becatti: *La colonna coclide istoriata* (Rome, 1960)

E. Nash: *A Pictorial Dictionary of Ancient Rome*, i (New York, 1961, 2/1968), pp. 283–6

J. J. Pollitt: *The Art of Rome, c. 753 B.C.–A.D. 337: Sources and Documents* (Englewood Cliffs, 1966/*R* Cambridge, 1983), pp. 51–2, 65–6, 169

F. Coarelli: *Guida archeologica di Roma* (Rome, 1974), pp. 54, 117–24 [drawings of entire frieze]

D. Strong: *Roman Art* (Harmondsworth, 1976, rev. and ed. R. Ling, 2/1988), pp. 141–51, 351

W. Gauer: *Darstellungsprogramm und künstlerischer Entwurf* (1977), i of *Untersuchungen zur Trajanssaüle* (Berlin, 1977)

G. Becatti: 'La Colonna traiana: Espressione somma del rilievo storico romano', *Aufstieg und Niedergang der römischen Welt*, II/xii/1 (Berlin, 1982), pp. 536–78

R. Brilliant: *Visual Narratives: Storytelling in Etruscan and Roman Art* (Ithaca, 1984), pp. 90–114

F. Lepper and S. Frere: *Trajan's Column: A New Edition of the Cichorius Plates: Introduction, Commentary and Notes* (Gloucester, 1988)

S. Settis, ed.: *La Colonna Traiana* (Torino, 1988)

La Collona Traiana e gli artisti francesi da Luigi XIV a Napoleone I (exh. cat., ed. G. Agosti, V. Farinella and G. Simoncini; Rome, Villa Medici, 1988)

A. Claridge: 'Hadrian's Column of Trajan', *J. Roman Archaeol.*, vi (1993), pp. 5–22

M. Wilson-Jones: 'One Hundred Feet and a Spiral Stair: The Problem of Designing Trajan's Column', *J. Roman Archaeol.*, vi (1993), pp. 23–38

F. Coarelli and others: *The Column of Trajan* (Rome, 2000)

G. Martines: *Colonna Traiana: Corpus dei disegni, 1981–2001* (Rome, 2001)

R. Bianchi Bandinelli: *Il maestro delle imprese di Traiano* (Milan, 2003)

G. Calcani and M. Abdulkarim: *Apollodorus of Damascus and Trajan's Column: From Tradition to Project* (Rome, 2003)

M. Rich: *Women at War: The Depiction of Women on the Column of Trajan* (diss., Norman, U. OK, 2003)

D. Richter: *Das römische Heer auf der Trajanssäule: Propaganda und Realität: Waffen und Ausrüstung: Marsch, Arbeit und Kampf* (Mannheim, 2004)

8. PANTHEON. Circular domed temple erected on the Campus Martius between *c.* AD 118 and 125 (see fig. 13). Preserved almost intact, it is a unique achievement in Roman architecture and one of the most celebrated buildings in all architectural history. It was converted into the church of S Maria ad Martyres in AD 609. Study of brick stamps and limited excavations in 1891–2 show that the whole structure was built by Hadrian. The inscription on the porch entablature stating that it was built by M. Agrippa refers to an earlier Pantheon under the present one, a dynastic monument to honour Augustus and the Julio-Claudian family. Despite the importance of the building, the only ancient reference to it is by Dio Cassius (early 3rd century AD), who mistook it for the earlier building of Agrippa and referred to the building as a temple dedicated to many gods (*History of Rome*, LIII.xxvii.2).

The Pantheon was surrounded by the Baths of Agrippa to the south, the immense porticos of the Saepta Julia to the east and the Baths of Nero to the west. A rectangular forecourt to the north provided the traditional approach, its long colonnades making the brick rotunda, so conspicuous today, appear less dominating; a tall, octastyle pedimented porch on a high podium with marble steps also created the impression of a traditional Roman temple. Inside the huge bronze doors, however, the worshipper was enveloped by the vast interior space and the hemispherical dome soaring to a height of 43.3 m, exactly equal to the diameter of the drum, and illuminated dramatically by a slanting shaft of light coming from the great oculus (diam. 8.15 m).

The Pantheon is composed essentially of two architectural entities: a porch and a cylindrical drum covered by a dome. Between these is a transitional

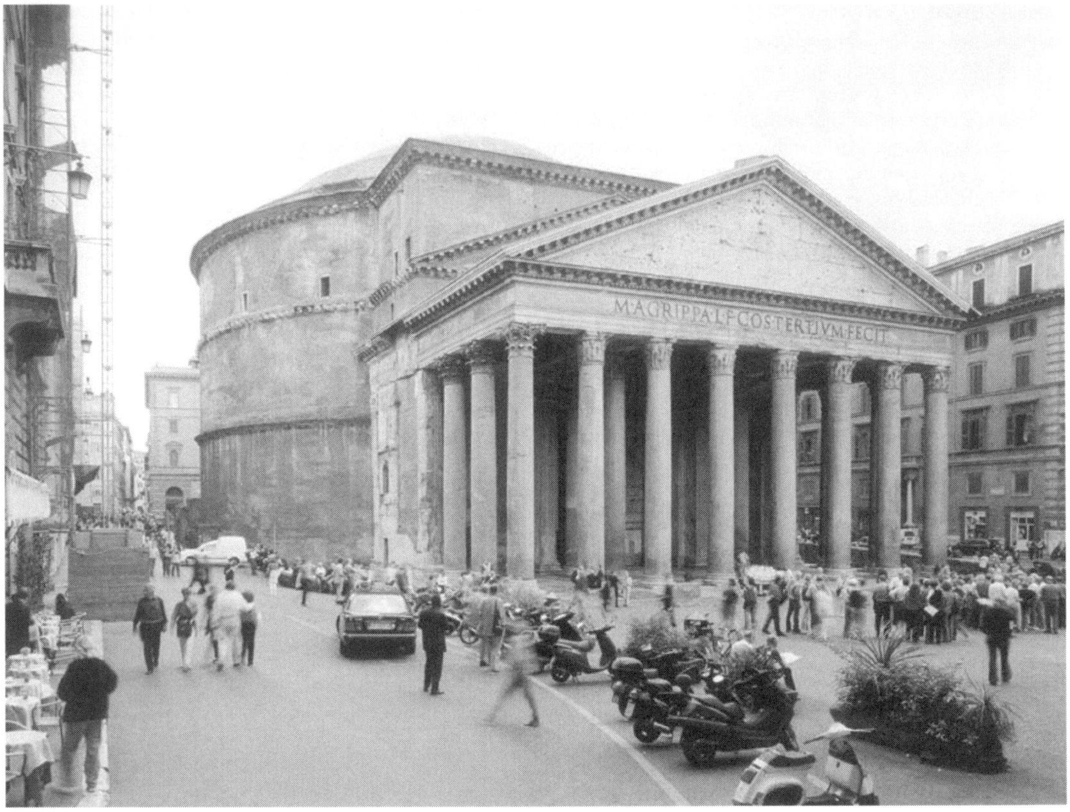

13. Pantheon, Rome, *c.* AD 118–125

rectangular structure, which contains a pair of large niches flanking the bronze doors. These niches probably housed the statues of *Augustus* and *Agrippa* and provided a pious and political association with the original Pantheon. The inside wall of the circular chamber is articulated by eight deep recesses, alternately rectangular and semicircular, including the striking barrel-vaulted entrance alcove and the 'apse' at the south end of the building's axis. The six simple recesses are screened off from the chamber by pairs of marble columns, while aediculae (small pedimented shrines) raised on tall podia project in front of the curving wall between the recesses. A tall entablature and a strongly projecting cornice surround the lower zone above the recesses. The original decoration of the upper zone was a row of closely spaced, thin porphyry pilasters on a continuous white marble plinth. A small portion of this scheme has been restored; the rest belongs to an 18th-century restoration. Another continuous cornice runs around the base of the dome. The great expanse of the floor, largely original, is paved in a checkerboard pattern of alternating squares and circles in squares, the attractive polychromatic marbles, granites and porphyry creating an appropriate visual reflection of the 140 square coffers of the dome. The latter are arranged in five superimposed rows, their centres originally decorated by gilt-bronze rosettes. Each coffer recedes in a series of steps with faces of varying slope; a swirling sense of movement is created by the shadows.

The Pantheon is entirely of concrete except for the porch and some marble and travertine decoration. The brickwork of the drum is only a veneer. Although brick-faced concrete was widely used in large-scale Imperial architecture, and concrete domes and vaults had covered some exceptionally daring spans, the Pantheon represents the apogee of Roman building technology. Its logical and sophisticated structure is a tribute to the efficiency of Roman building methods, whereby large numbers of unskilled labourers worked under a few highly skilled specialists. The entire building was cast in horizontal layers of concrete, with the dome poured over a vast and complex wooden formwork. Even the aggregate in the concrete was carefully graded for structural reasons, with the heaviest in the foundations and becoming lighter as the building height increased. Reinforcement was provided by double-tiered, radiating brick vaults penetrating the entire thickness of the walls and spanning the great niches, which distributed the load on to the eight great 'piers'.

The design and symbolism of the Pantheon may reflect the complex, even contradictory character of Hadrian himself. The centralized, domed design is unprecedented in a Roman temple, yet the porch is traditional. Again, although its structure is the culmination of a long period of experimentation with concrete, the Pantheon was not a progressive building. Instead, its quiet, trabeated interior, with numerous columnar screens and strong continuous cornices, can be seen as conforming to a conservative line of classicism. The Pantheon's unusual design may be explained by Dio's claims that it was dedicated to many gods (in addition to the imperial family) and that Hadrian even used it as a law court (LXIX.vii.1). Whether it was consequently intended to evoke the dome of heaven (LXIX.xxvii.2) or the universality and permanence of the Empire remains conjectural.

The Pantheon was much admired during the Renaissance. Later work on the building included two turrets added in front by Gianlorenzo Bernini (1598–1680; popularly known as the 'ass ears of Bernini' and removed in 1883), restoration of the portico by Giuseppe Paglia (*fl* 1665–82) and of the interior of the atrium by Paolo Posi (1708–76).

L. Beltrami: *Il Pantheon* (Milan, 1898)

A. M. Colini and I. Gismondi: 'Contributi allo studio del Pantheon', *Bull. Comm. Archeol. Mun. Com. Roma*, liv (1926), pp. 67–92

L. Beltrami: *Il Pantheon rivendicato ad Adriano* (Milan, 1929)

A. Terenzio: 'La Restauration du Panthéon de Rome', *Mouseion*, xx (1952), pp. 52–7

C. L. V. Meeks: 'Pantheon Paradigm', *J. Soc. Archit. Historians*, xix (1960), pp. 135–44

H. Kähler: 'The Pantheon as Sacral Art', *Bucknell Rev.*, xv/2 (1967), pp. 41–8

K. de Fine Licht: *The Rotunda in Rome: A Study of Hadrian's Pantheon* (Copenhagen, 1968)

W. L. MacDonald: *The Pantheon: Design, Meaning and Progeny* (London and Cambridge, MA, 1976)

H. Geertman: 'Aedificium celeberrimum: Studio sulla geometria del Pantheon', *Bull. Ant. Besch.*, lv/2 (1980), pp. 203–17

W. C. Loerke: 'Georges Chédanne and the Pantheon: A Beaux-Arts Contribution to the History of Roman Architecture', *Modulus* (1983), pp. 41–55

D. Moore: *The Roman Pantheon: The Triumph of Concrete* (Mangilao, 1995)

E. Thomas: *The Architectural History of the Pantheon in Rome from Agrippa to Septimius Severus via Hadrian* (Lüneburg, 1997)

W. L. MacDonald: *The Pantheon: Design, Meaning, and Progeny* (Cambridge, MA, 2002)

9. CASTEL SANT'ANGELO. Mausoleum of Hadrian erected on the right bank of the Tiber opposite the Campus Martius (see fig. 14). It was begun by Hadrian in AD 130 and completed in AD 139, the year after his death, by his successor, Antoninus Pius, who dedicated it to the deified Emperor. It served as a sepulchre for Hadrian and Sabina, their adopted son L. Aelius Caesar, the Antonines until Commodus, and Caracalla, who in AD 217 became the final emperor entombed here. The original appearance of the tumulus-shaped building can be reconstructed from ancient descriptions and Renaissance drawings (which indicate that the sculptural decorations were influenced by those of the Temple of Venus and Rome, AD 135) as well as modern archaeology. Constructed of concrete and travertine and faced with

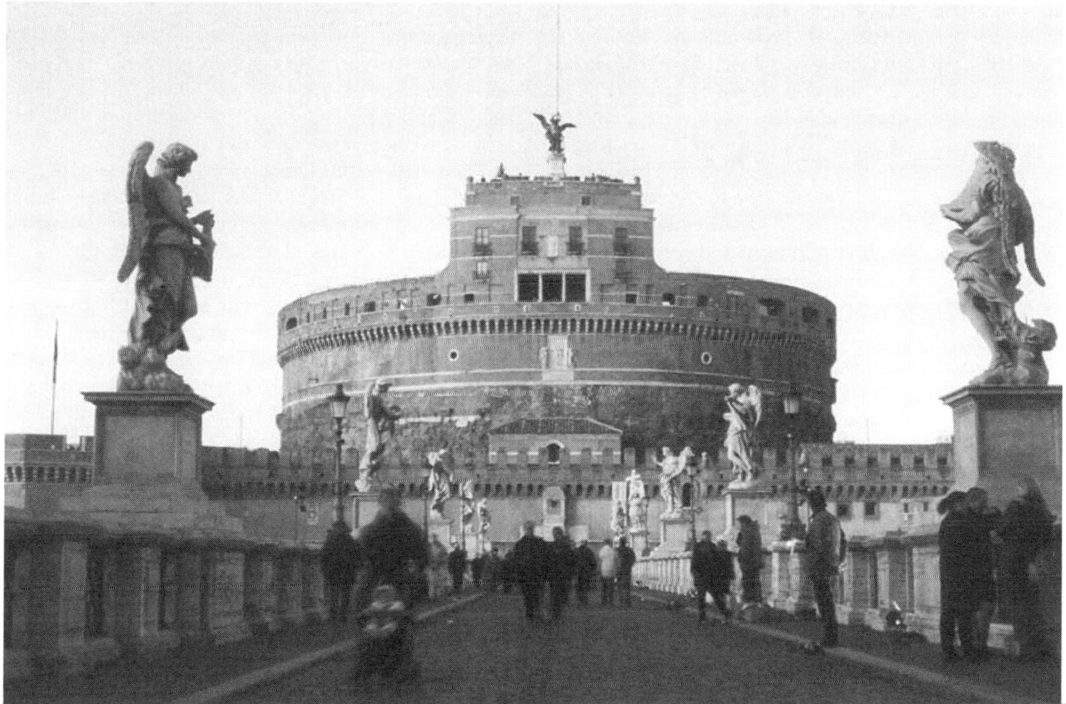

14. Rome, Castel Sant'Angelo, AD 130–39, with later additions and alterations

marble, it consisted of a square podium-like base that supported the main drum, the top of which was planted with cypress trees. Above the drum's centre rose a smaller base and drum crowned with statuary, probably Hadrian in a four-horse chariot. The building was surrounded by a pedestrian pavement and enclosed by a low wall with a gilt railing, which was supported by marble pillars topped with gilt peacocks. A bridge, the Pons Aelius (ded. AD 134; now the Ponte Sant'Angelo), was built to facilitate construction and access.

The podium (84 sq. m, h. 10 m), much of which has been covered by later masonry, was decorated with Corinthian pilasters, of which one capital is preserved (Rome, Mus. N. Romano), and an entablature. Relief garlands and ox skulls decorated the frieze. The centrally placed entrance door, above which hung a dedicatory plaque inscribed with Hadrian's name, faced the river. Inside the base were several concrete vaulted chambers. The extant spiral ramp, still containing some traces of wall decoration and mosaic pavement, led to the tomb chamber. A series of engaged columns supporting an entablature encircled the main drum (diam. 64 m, h. 21 m); above stood marble sculpture, one corresponding to each column. In AD 537 these statues were hurled down on top of attacking Ostrogoths. The barrel-vaulted tomb chamber is located in the centre of the drum; it is almost square and contains a niche on each wall, presumably for sarcophagi. The original gilt fittings and statuary are untraced. The Antonine emperors were buried in a square room above the central chamber, which has the same dimensions as the main room below but lacks the two side niches and has a lower ceiling. Above this storey was a chamber divided into two rooms, also apparently for burials.

Early in the 5th century AD Castel Sant'Angelo became a fortress. During the plague of AD 590, Pope Gregory the Great had a vision of the archangel Michael, which resulted in a statue of Michael being placed on top of the building, hence its modern name. In the late 14th century the Castel Sant'Angelo became the private residence of the popes, many of whom made substantial additions and alterations. The castle now houses a military and artistic museum.

R. Lanciani: *The Ruins and Excavations of Ancient Rome* (London, 1897, rev. 1967)

S. R. Pierce: 'The Mausoleum of Hadrian and the Pons Aelius', *J. Roman Stud.*, xv (1925), pp. 75–103

D. M. Robathan: *The Monuments of Ancient Rome* (Rome, 1950)

E. Nash: *Pictorial Dictionary of Ancient Rome*, ii (New York, 1981)

C. Cundari and others: *Rilievo degli appartamenti papali in Castel Sant'Angelo* (Rome, 1994)

10. Baths of Caracalla. Vast baths south of the Porta Capena. Known in Latin as the Thermae Antoninianae, they are the best preserved of the Imperial *thermae* (*see* ARCHITECTURE, §VI, 1(i)(d)) and the only ones in which the combination of monumental architecture and garden setting can still be appreciated. Begun *c.* AD 211, the baths were dedicated by Caracalla (*reg* AD 211–17) in AD 216, although the outer precinct was not completed until the reign of Severus Alexander (*reg* AD 222–35). There were several later restorations, and an apse was added to the *caldarium* in the 4th century AD. Fifth-century AD sources record the baths as one of the wonders of Rome, while brick-stamps of the Ostrogothic king Theodoric (*reg* AD 493–526) suggest that they continued in use into the 6th century AD.

The site chosen for the baths was terraced to create a platform (328×323 m) from which rose the bathing block proper, surrounded by gardens. Incorporated in the platform were extensive subterranean service areas, including a water-mill and a large Mithraeum. Two tiers of barrel-vaulted chambers formed an impressive façade overlooking the Via Nova, while a monumental staircase led down from the Aventine Hill at the rear. The hillside was buttressed by a series of cisterns fed from an aqueduct built especially to serve the baths. Tiered rows of seats masked the cisterns and provided an area for performances; flanking this were libraries. Either side of the garden between the bathing block and the theatre area were broad exedrae housing other halls for cultural and social activities.

The bathing block (218×111 m excluding the *caldarium*) follows the normal pattern for the imperial *thermae*, with a groin-vaulted *frigidarium* at the centre of an axially symmetrical scheme. One end of the short axis is marked by the open-air *natatio*, the other by the huge circular domed *caldarium* (diam. 35 m), which has been identified as the *cella solearis* ('room with hot pools') referred to in the *Augustan History* (*Life of Caracalla* ix.4–5). Secondary areas—entrances, lounges, dressing rooms and *caldaria*—are duplicated about this axis, while a pair of porticoed palaestrae close the ends of the transverse axis. The complex but functional planning extends to the elevations, where varying room heights are exploited to admit maximum light and provide terraces for public use or maintenance.

The baths were once lavishly decorated with mosaic and marble floors, marble wall veneer, gilded stucco and glass mosaic vaults, and numerous statues and marble columns. The north wall of the *natatio* was particularly rich, with an elaborate display of columns framing niches in the manner of the *scaenae frons* of a theatre. The stripping of this decoration began in the medieval period. In the 12th century some capitals were used in the building of S Maria in Trastevere, Rome. Many sculptures were unearthed in the 16th century (Naples, Mus. Archeol. N.), including the Farnese *Hercules*; excavations in 1824 uncovered the athlete mosaics (Rome, Vatican, Mus. Gregoriano Profano).

G. A. Blouet: *Restauration des thermes d'Antonin Caracalla à Rome* (Paris, 1828)

S. A. Iwanoff and C. Hülsen: *Architektonische Studien*, iii: *Aus den Caracallathermen* (Berlin, 1898)

E. Brödner: *Untersuchungen an den Caracallathermen* (Berlin, 1951)

M. Marvin: 'Freestanding Sculptures from the Baths of Caracalla', *Amer. J. Archaeol.*, lxxvii (1983), pp. 347–84

D. Kinney: 'Spolia from the Baths of Caracalla in Sta Maria in Trastevere', *A. Bull.*, lxviii (1986), pp. 379–97
J. DeLaine: 'The "cella solearis" of the Baths of Caracalla: A Reappraisal', *Pap. Brit. Sch. Rome*, lv (1987), pp. 147–56
L. Lombardi and A. Corazza: *Le Terme di Caracalla* (Rome, 1995)
J. DeLaine: *The Baths of Caracalla: A Study in the Design, Construction, and Economics of Large-scale Building Projects in Imperial Rome* (Portsmouth, RI, 1997)
M. Piranomonte: *The Baths of Caracalla* (Milan, 1998)

11. Basilica of Maxentius. Basilica erected on the site of the earlier Horrea Piperataria (Spice Market), in a prominent position overlooking the eastern end of the Forum Romanum (see fig. 15). It was begun by the Emperor Maxentius (*reg* AD 306–12), possibly following the fire of AD 307, which severely damaged the nearby Temple of Venus and Rome, but was only completed, in slightly altered form, after his death in the Battle of the Milvian Bridge (AD 312). The Senate subsequently dedicated it to his victorious rival Constantine. The collapse of the nave and south aisle in the medieval period created the imposing ruin visible today. It was a popular subject for Renaissance artists, who identified it mistakenly as the Templum Pacis, and it may have inspired Bramante's design for St Peter's in Rome.

Unlike most earlier basilicas, which had internal colonnades and trabeated timber roofs, the Basilica of Maxentius was built with brick-faced concrete walls and concrete vaults, to a design based on the *frigidaria* of the Imperial *thermae*. The nave (82.6×25.3×*c.* 39.0 m) was roofed with a triple groin vault decorated with oval and octagonal coffers and lit by arched clerestory windows. It was the largest vaulted space ever created by Roman architects. Three parallel barrel-vaulted chambers, 15.8 m deep and averaging 23.6 m wide, connected by broad arched openings, formed each aisle and acted as buttresses for the piers supporting the central vault. In front of these piers stood giant Corinthian columns with fluted monolithic shafts, 15.8 m high, in Prokonnesian marble, which appeared to support the vault but were almost entirely decorative. The last remaining column was removed by Pope Paul V in 1613 to its present location in front of S Maria Maggiore in Rome.

As originally planned the basilica was oriented east–west, with the entrance from a narrow street to the east, which also served the Temple of Venus and Rome. Immediately inside the entrance was a long narrow narthex at right angles to the building's main axis, which gave access to the nave and aisles through five arched doorways. At its west end the nave terminated in a broad apse, perhaps originally intended for the tribunal. Constantinian alterations to the nearly completed building changed its axis by creating a new entrance from the Via Sacra to the south and a new apse in the north aisle opposite it. This entrance consisted of a portico of four porphyry columns added to the terrace in front of the central bay of the south aisle, with a monumental staircase leading to the street below. The new apse was decorated with two superimposed rows of eight niches flanking a central pedestal and partitioned off by a columnar screen; a marble bench below the niches probably served as seating for the tribunal. The original west apse was adapted to house an acrolithic statue of Constantine, surviving fragments of which include the colossal marble head (Rome, Mus. Conserv.; see fig. 16).

A. Nibby: *Del Tempio della Pace e della Basilica di Costantino* (Rome, 1819)
A. Minoprio: 'A Restoration of the Basilica of Constantine, Rome', *Pap. Brit. Sch. Rome*, xii (1932), pp. 1–25
H. W. Henry: *The Basilica of Maxentius* (diss., Providence, RI, Brown U., 1975)
U. Kultermann: *Die Maxentius-Basilika: Ein Schlüsselwerk spätantiker Architektur* (Weimar, 1996)
C. Giavarini and C. M. Amici: *The Basilica of Maxentius: The Monument, its Materials, Construction, and Stability* (Rome, 2005)

12. Arch of Constantine. A three-vaulted structure, dedicated in AD 315, which stands between the Caelian and Palatine hills, on the triumphal way from the Circus Maximus to the Arch of Titus. Inscriptions on both north and south faces of the arch (on the part of the attic storey above the central span and on the entablatures over the side openings) record that it was erected by the Roman people after the victory

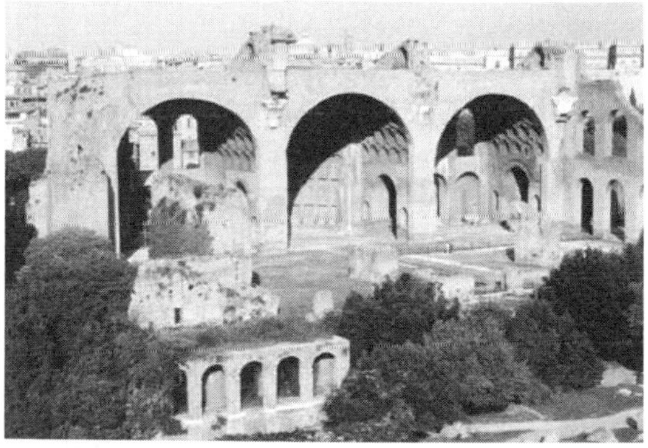

15. Rome, Basilica of Maxentius, AD 306–13

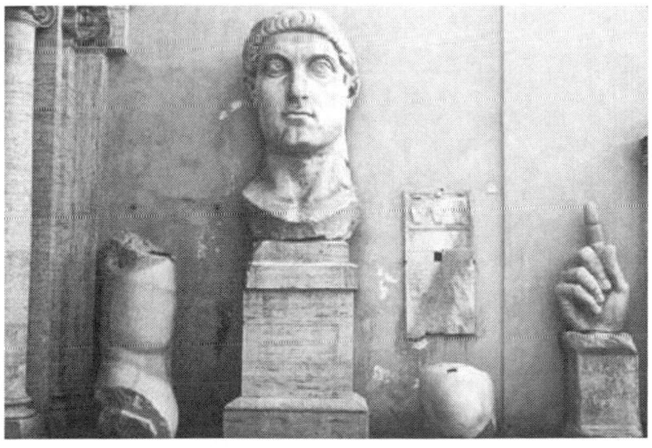

16. Rome, fragments of the colossal statue of Constantine from the Basilica of Maxentius, marble, *c.* AD 315–30 (Rome, Palazzo dei Conservatori)

of Constantine over Maxentius at the Milvian Bridge (28 Oct AD 312) in gratitude for his first decade as emperor and as a votive offering for his second. Contemporary literary sources, however, make no mention of the arch, and the first extant reference to it is in the anonymous Carolingian Itinerary of Einsiedeln (*c.* 800; Einsiedeln Abbey).

The Arch of Constantine faces north and south, and both of these longer sides are articulated by four Corinthian columns in yellow Numidian marble, with four pilasters and statues fronting the flat-topped attic storey. It is the largest triumphal arch to survive intact (h. 20 m, w. 25 m), with a central opening measuring 11.45×6.50 m and openings either side of 7.40×3.35 m. Its elevation is entirely of marble, except for the brick fill of the attic storey. Part of the material for its construction was, however, obtained from Flavian buildings. Even the sculptures vary in date. Among those of Constantine's own period are the reliefs on the eight tall plinths for the columns. Those of the south façade depict Victories with trophies and barbarian prisoners, as do the two outer plinths of the north façade. The inner plinths flanking the central opening (north) depict Victories writing on shields, and further Victories bearing trophies appear with Genii of the Seasons in the spandrels of the central arch, while river gods occupy those of the side openings. The historical frieze running round most of the arch just above the side openings is also of Constantinian date. On the west side, six panels illustrate the *Departure of Constantine's Army from Milan*, and the narrative continues on the south façade with the *Siege of Verona* on the left and the *Battle of the Milvian Bridge* on the right. This is followed on the east side by *Constantine's Entry into Rome*, and the frieze finishes on the north façade with *Constantine's Oratio in the Forum Romanum* (left) and the *Congiarium* or distribution of money to the populace (right). On the east and west sides of the arch are two Constantinian tondi. That on the west depicts the two-horse chariot (*biga*) of the Moon, that on the east the four-horse *quadriga* of the Sun.

The sculpture above the historical frieze on the north and south faces consists entirely of bas-reliefs from earlier monuments. Immediately above the frieze panels are eight tondi of Hadrianic date (AD 117–138), all in Luna marble surrounded by panels of red porphyry. The four on the south face depict, from left to right: the *Emperor's Departure for the Hunt*; a *Sacrifice to Sylvanus*; a *Bear Hunt*; and a *Sacrifice to Diana*. Those on the north face depict: a *Boar Hunt*; a *Sacrifice to Apollo*; a *Lion Hunt*; and a *Sacrifice to Hercules*. In the hunting scenes Hadrian's head has been rechiselled to represent Constantine, in the sacrifice scenes to represent Constantine's co-emperor Licinius. The eight *pavonazzetto* (purple veined marble) statues at attic level above the projecting entablature of the façade columns depict Dacian prisoners and were sculpted for the Forum of Trajan (AD 113). Each of the sections of the attic storey above the side openings is decorated with two panels from a monument to Marcus Aurelius, illustrating his campaigns against the Quadi and the Marcomanni. The four panels on the south face depict, from left to right: the *Presentation of a Barbarian Chief to Marcus Aurelius*; *Prisoners Being Led to the Emperor*; *Speechmaking*; and *Sacrifices on the Battlefield*. Those on the north show: the *Emperor's Arrival in Rome*; the *Emperor Setting off for War*; the *Congiarium*; and the *Surrender of a Barbarian Chief*. Finally, the east and west sides of the attic storey and the inner surfaces of the central vault bear splendid friezes in Pentelic marble, probably from the Basilica Ulpia in the Forum of Trajan. A cast of all four sections in sequence (Rome, Mus. Civiltà) forms a frieze 18 m in length and 3 m high. This so-called Great Trajanic Frieze shows a battle scene with decapitated barbarians (west side); Trajan on horseback overwhelming the Dacians, with a Constantinian inscription above (west side of central vault); a battle scene with barbarians trampled by horses (east side); and Trajan's entry into Rome, crowned by Victory, again with a Constantinian inscription above (east side of central vault).

The Arch of Constantine has remained relatively undamaged, despite the decapitation of the eight Dacians, probably around 1534. The first attempts at restoration were as early as 1498–9, followed by genuine conservation work in 1570 and, in 1732 under Clement XII, reconstruction of the heads of the Emperor in the reliefs of Marcus Aurelius and the heads and hands of the Dacians. Restoration carried out from 1955 to 1959 involved reinforcing the structure and replacing missing parts of the sculpture. Work begun in 1981 (and still continuing in the early 21st century) involves projects including petrological study of the polychrome marbles and analysis of surface pigments, cleaning the arch without removing its patina, which is probably antique, and re-roofing the attic storey and improving its drainage.

G. B. De Rossi: 'L'iscrizione dell'arco trionfale di Costantino', *Boll. Archeol. Crist.*, i (1863), pp. 57–60; rev. in *Nuovo Boll. Archeol. Crist.*, xix (1913), pp. 21–8

A. L. Frothingham: 'Who Built the Arch of Constantine?', *Amer. J. Archaeol.*, xvi (1912), pp. 368–86; xvii (1913), pp. 487–503; xix (1915), pp. 1–12

C. Gradara: 'Restauri settecenteschi fatti all'arco di Costantino', *Bull. Comm. Archeol. Com. Roma*, xlvi (1918), pp. 161–4

H. P. L'Orange and A. von Gerkan: *Der spätantike Bildschmuck des Konstantinsbogens* (Berlin, 1939)

A. Giuliano: *Arco di Costantino* (Milan, 1955)

P. P. Bober and R. Rubinstein: *Renaissance Artists and Antique Sculpture* (London, 1986), pp. 214–16, pl. 182

S. De Maria: *Gli archi onorari di Roma e dell'Italia romana* (Rome, 1988), pp. 203–11, 316–19

G. Tedeschi Grisanti: 'Arco di Costantino: Manutenzioni e restauri nei documenti degli archivi di Roma', *Boll. Un. Stor. & A.*, n.s., xxxi (1988), pp. 71–4

A. Cassatella and M. L. Conforto: *Arco di Costantino: Il restauro della sommità* (Rimini, 1989)

D. Cirone: 'I risultati delle indagini stratigrafiche all'arco di Costantino', *Rendi. Pont. Accad. Romana Archeol.*, lxvi (1993–4), pp. 61–76

A. Melucco Vaccaro and A. M. Ferroni: 'Chi costruì l'arco di Costantino? Un interrogativo ancora attuale', *Rendi. Pont. Accad. Romana Archeol.*, lxvi (1993–4), pp. 1–60

P. Pensabene and C. Panella: Reimpiego e progettazione architettonica nei monumenti tardo-antichi di Roma, *Rendi. Pont. Accad. Romana Archeol.*, lxvi (1993–4), pp. 174–283

P. Pensabene and C. Panella, eds: *Arco di Costantino tra archeologia e archeometria* (Rome, 1999)

M. L. Conforto: *Adriano e Costantino: Le due fasi dell'arco nella valle del Colosseo* (Milan, 2001)

L. Pirzio Biroli Stefanelli and R. Valeriani: *Venti bozzetti in cera rossa: Raffiguranti rilievi dell'Arco di Costantino in Roma* (Milan, 2003)

F. Zeri and N. Criscenti: *L'Arco di Costantino: Divagazioni sull'antico* (Milan, 2004)

13. Temple of Mithras (S Clemente). Beneath the apse of the Early Christian basilica of S Clemente (which is in turn below the 12th-century basilica) are the remains of a Mithraeum (2nd–3rd century AD) that had been inserted into the earlier Imperial building. Mithraism was an Eastern cult that became popular in Rome in the 1st century AD, especially among soldiers; it rivalled Christianity for a time, like Christianity promising eternal life to its initiates. The position of this Mithraeum immediately below and with precisely the same orientation as the later Christian church suggests an interesting continuity of cult in the transition from pagan to Christian Rome.

The temple, which is reached from a staircase from the southern aisle of the lower church, consists of a pronaos with an ornamental stuccoed ceiling; a well-preserved *triclinium*, the main room of the temple, its vaulted ceiling carved to resemble a cave; and a room that may be the Mithraic school, where catechumens were instructed in the rituals of the cult, its vaulted roof also stuccoed and with a mosaic floor. In the *triclinium* stone benches for initiates line the flanking walls; the marble altar, with carved reliefs relating to the struggle of Mithras with the bull, stands in the centre of the room. In the niche behind is a statue of Mithras.

14. Villa of Maxentius. A palace complex (AD 309–12) on the Via Appia Antica on the outskirts of Rome built by the self-appointed emperor Maxentius (*reg* 306–12). Occupying more than a square mile of property between the second and third Roman milestones of the Via Appia Antica, the extramural imperial estate of Maxentius comprised a palatial residence, a 520-metre long circus for chariot racing and a massive, rotunda-like mausoleum. Once attributed erroneously to the Severan emperor, Caracalla, fragmentary inscriptions discovered during the 19th-century excavations of the circus by Antonio Nibby identified the extant remains as projects of the early 4th-century usurper, Marcus Valerius Maxentius. The large complex may have been built in conjunction with the funerary celebrations in honour of the young son and heir of Maxentius, Romulus, who drowned in the Tiber River in 309. More likely, Maxentius constructed the suburban palace to rival similar structures built by legitimate tetrarchs elsewhere in the empire. The ultimate model for many of these self-contained Tetrarchic palaces may have been the arrangement of the early imperial residences on the Palatine Hill above the Circus Maximus in the heart of Rome. Maxentius was defeated at the hands of Constantine at Saxa Rubra and died at the Battle of Milvian Bridge in 312. The remains of the Villa of Maxentius were a significant feature of the modern archaeological park on the Via Appia Antica that also included pagan tombs, Christian and Jewish catacombs, early Christian churches and vast suburban ancient Roman estates.

The legitimate son of the tetrarch Maximian (*reg* 286–305), Maxentius ruled Italy and North Africa for a brief and turbulent period from 306 to 312. With overt disregard for the tetrarchic succession system established by Diocletian, political factions in Rome elevated Maxentius to the office of augustus in October 306. In an effort to justify his illegal position, and in imitation of the benefactions of his father in Rome, Maxentius constructed and refurbished numerous structures in the capital city. A self-declared 'saviour of the city' (*conservator urbis*), Maxentius rebuilt the heavily damaged Hadrianic Temple of Venus and Rome and constructed anew the enormous, vaulted Basilica Nova (see above) on the Velian located east of the Forum Romanum. Thus, the suburban palace on the Via Appia was only one element in Maxentius' extensive building campaign designed to underscore his claims for political legitimacy and imperial power.

(i) Circus of Maxentius. (ii) Mausoleum of Romulus. (iii) Residential quarter.

(i) Circus of Maxentius. The relatively well-preserved Circus of Maxentius (see fig. on p. 1:272) displayed all the major architectural features characteristic of Roman circuses, long elliptical buildings for funerary games, cult worship, chariot races and other spectacles. Circus games were closely associated with Roman conceptions of cyclical time, dynasty, life and death, and the cult of the sun-god Helios/Sol. Nestled in a shallow valley between two low hills, the Circus of Maxentius was one of the best-preserved ancient Roman circuses in Italy. Almost 50,000 square metres in area with seating for approximately 10,000 spectators, the circus was oriented east–west with a large arched ceremonial entrance (*porta triumphalis*) at the curved east end. Substantial remains of 12 starting gates (*carceres*) for the chariots survived at the west end of the circus. Decorated with earlier sculptures reused during the Maxentian construction, the chariot stalls stood between two curved towers, each preserved to the third storey. Remains of the long low barrier (*spina*) that divided the elliptical arena into two parallel courses were excavated and restored in the 1960s. Originally the spina (296 metres in length) was covered with marble veneer and surmounted by sculptures, fountains and other elaborate monuments, fragments of which have been recovered. To adorn the centre of the *spina*,

Maxentius relocated a granite obelisk dedicated to the Flavian emperor Domitian (*reg* 81–96) that stood in the Campus Martius; under the orders of Pope Innocent X (*reg* 1644–55), the obelisk was removed from the circus in the 17th century, restored and then re-erected at the center of Gianlorenzo Bernini's Four Rivers Fountain in the Piazza Navona. Also characteristic of Roman circus design are two conical turning posts or *metae*, which marked each end of the *spina* at the Circus of Maxentius.

In addition to the partially preserved substructures for the six rows of spectators' seats (*cavea*), the circus contained the remains of two major viewing platforms: the imperial box (*pulvinar*) and the judges' box (*tribunal iudicum*). Positioned high above the northern side of the *cavea* and connected to the adjacent residential quarter by a long, walkway (*ambulacrum*), the *pulvinar* would have permitted the emperor and his attendants to observe the races and, simultaneously, be observed by the spectators with dramatic spectacle. The ornate *tribunal iudicum* on the southern side afforded an unobstructed panorama of the arena for the judges who presided over Roman circus races. Excavation of the sandy floor of the arena has suggested that very few, if any, chariot races occurred at this circus.

(ii) Mausoleum of Romulus. Although long identified as the tomb of 'Divus Romulus', the young son of Maxentius who drowned in 309, the circular burial chamber was most likely built to serve as a dynastic mausoleum for Maxentius, his family and future descendents. The tomb and its surrounding enclosure walls were positioned close to and parallel with the paved course of the Via Appia. Of the original circular mausoleum, only the lower brick and mortar core has survived, and careful examination of the building has suggested that the tomb was not completed before Maxentius' death in 312. Situated partially below modern ground level, the core contained a 7-metre wide, barrel-vaulted circular corridor surrounding a central, octagonal pillar almost 9.5 metres in diameter. Like the walls of the corridor, the surface of the pillar was pierced by eight large rectangular and semi-circular niches. No funerary sarcophagi, floor surfaces or decoration have been found inside the structure, lending further support to the hypothesis that the mausoleum was never finished. In the 19th century, the aristocratic Torlonia family attached a farmhouse to the south side of the concrete core and used the vaulted subterranean interior of the tomb as both a stable and a storage room. After the property was acquired by the Comune di Roma in 1943, the front exterior porch of the Maxentian tomb was excavated. However, although architectural historians have made several hypothetical reconstruction drawings of the tomb over the centuries, the original exterior superstructure of the tomb remained uncertain.

Surrounding the circular tomb, a large, four-sided enclosing wall (*quadriporticus*) constructed in *opus vittatum* (small rectangular stones) defined the perimeter of the sacred space and isolated the mausoleum from the rest of the suburban estate. Only the west, north and east walls have survived up to the level of the springing arches for the cross-vaults. Excavations inside the perimeter of the walls revealed that the area was filled and levelled for construction in the early 4th century and, in the process, an earlier small bath building was incorporated into walls. The cross-vaulted passageway that ran along the interior perimeter of the quadriporticus might have been intended for funerary processions.

In addition to the Mausoleum of 'Romulus, the concrete core of an early imperial tomb of the Augustan period was preserved on the estate grounds. Abutting the exterior side of the west wall of the *quadriporticus*, the circular Tomb of the Servilii has been stripped of its exterior decoration. In the interior, a narrow annular corridor encircled the central tomb chamber (cruciform plan, pyramidal roof). The design of the interior represented a simplified version of the interior layout of the roughly contemporary Mausoleum of Augustus. As in Augustus' mausoleum, the corridor in the Tomb of the Servilii may have been used for circumambulation rituals connected with the funerary rites of Roman aristocrats and military officers.

(iii) Residential quarter. The residential sector was located on a series of artificial terraces and cut bedrock on the hill that overlooked the circus and the mausoleum. Exploratory excavations conducted by G. Pisani Sartorio in the 1960s uncovered architectural remains that permitted the identification of four major construction phases for the residential buildings. Two phases of walls constructed in *opus reticulatum* indicate a late Republican residence that was refurbished during the early imperial period (early 1st century AD). These structures, which included a double-corridor underground passageway (cryptoporticus), were built on property that probably belonged to the prominent Annii family of late Republican Rome. Since the structures were heavily damaged or redesigned by later imperial building projects, little has been discovered about these early periods of occupation.

The third phase of construction coincided with the acquisition of the property in the mid-2nd century by the wealthy Athenian philanthropist and imperial tutor, HERODES ATTICUS. Atticus had acquired the property following his marriage to the Roman aristocrat Annia Regilla, a member of the Annii family. Following Annia Regilla's death in 160, Atticus transformed the villa buildings and properties into a vast memorial park (*Pagus Triopion*) for the worship of his deceased wife, the gods of the underworld, Diva Faustina and Ceres. Columns from a possible temple to Ceres and Diva Faustina were incorporated into the nearby church of S Urbano at Caffarella. Perhaps in conjunction with Atticus' rededication of the property, the earlier cryptoporticus was remodelled to include two semi-circular buildings at each end and interior rooms decorated with polychrome frescos. Marble sculptures discovered over the centuries in the area of the residential buildings and the circus represented a fraction of the lavish decorative program of Atticus' Triopion. Many of these 2nd-century sculptures were reused by Maxentius for the decoration of the circus.

In the early 4th century Maxentius began construction of his suburban palace on top of the pre-existing early imperial and 2nd-century structures. In the course of construction for the terraced platform of the palace, some earlier buildings were demolished while others were integrated into the new Maxentian structures. The walls of the earlier cryptoporticus were reinforced and extended approximately 70 metres east to create a two-storey grand walkway (*ambulacrum*) that connected the residential quarter to the *pulvinar* of the circus. Just to the north of the cryptoporticus, Maxentius' palace was dominated by the large apsidal hall (*aula palatina*), a type of grand room that was common in late Roman aristocratic homes. Measuring approximately 30 metres by 20 metres, the walls and coffered apse of the basilica hall were constructed in *opus vittatum*, a technique of alternating courses of brick and tufa stones that was common in the 4th century. In addition to the impressive rectangular vestibule located at the southern end of the structure, two side entrances to the hall have been identified. Equipped with ceramic heating pipes and furnace arches along the lateral walls, the function of the apsidal hall as a major architectural feature in the residential quarter remained unclear. The requisite furnace (*praefurnia*) to supply warm air for the heating system has not been discovered. Comparisons with other late Roman apsidal halls suggested that the space was intended to serve as a formal reception room. Like the mausoleum, the residential quarter may not have been completed before Maxentius' death. The uncertain fate of the palace complex following the victory of Constantine at the Battle of the Milvian Bridge in 312 has been the focus of excavations of the residential quarter conducted since 2005 by the University of Colorado at Boulder and Kalamazoo College under the auspices of the Sovraintendenza ai Beni Culturali di Comune di Roma.

A. Frazer: 'The Iconography of the Emperor Maxentius' Buildings on the Via Appia', *A. Bull.*, xlviii (1966), pp. 385–92

G. Pisani Sartorio and G. Calza: *La Villa di Massenzio sulla Via Appia* (Rome, 1976)

J. Rasch: *Das Maxentius-Mausoleum an der Via Appia in Rom* (Mainz, 1984)

R. de Angelis Betolotti, G. Iopolo and G. Pisani Sartorio: *La Residenza imperiale di Massenzio: Villa, mausoleo e circo* (Rome, 1988)

M. Cullhead: *Conservator urbis suae: Studies in the Politics and Propaganda of the Emperor Maxentius* (Stockholm, 1994), pp. 45–67

J. Curran: '*Conservator Urbis*: Maxentius in Rome', *Pagan City to Christian Capital* (Oxford 2000), pp. 43–69

Roof. In Bronze Age Greece both flat and pitched roofs were known. The flat roof was standard for the architecture of Minoan Crete (including Thera), and it was used extensively on mainland Greece by the Mycenaeans. The pitched form may have been used for the MEGARON at the heart of the Mycenaean palace. With the Dorian invasion of Greece (*c.* 1000 BC) pitched roofs became the norm for Greek buildings, and by *c.* 600 BC they were virtually universal. This primacy resulted from two factors: their superior rain-shedding qualities, doubtless appreciated by the Dorians, who reputedly came from wetter regions to the north of Greece; and the invention of TERRACOTTA roof tiles, which rapidly replaced the previous roofing materials of thatch, rushes or (for flat roofs) packed mud. Tiles made a simple, cheap and watertight roof, but they required a slope and thus the support of a timber frame.

In the Classical Greek temple the roof timbers were always hidden. Both the cella and the peristyle were invariably covered with flat ceilings, leaving above them a triangular attic space (roughly corresponding in level and proportions to the pediment). The tie-beam truss was still unknown, so the timbers were arranged in the trabeated pattern that formed the basis of Greek architecture (see fig). The ridge-beam (a) was supported on a series of vertical props (b), each situated at the mid-point of a heavy cross-beam (c), which itself rested on the side walls of the cella, or on the internal colonnade in large temples. This arrangement imposed a heavy load on the mid-point of the crossbeam, which therefore had to be of massive proportions; the availability of large trees became a significant factor in determining a temple's size. Even with the biggest beams the clear span that could be bridged was relatively narrow. The widest was that over the centre of the cella in the Parthenon, which measured only 11.05 m, a striking contrast to the spans achieved in Roman buildings. Parallel to the ridge-beam ran the purlins (d), which were also very large (*c.* 1 sq. m cross-section in the Parthenon). Usually there was a single pair, aligned on and supported by the side walls of the cella, but large temples (e.g. PAESTUM, second Temple of Hera) sometimes had a second pair aligned on the internal colonnade, and the Parthenon, exceptionally, had a third. Like the ridge-beam, the purlins were supported by vertical props: these could be of any length, so that the crossbeams supporting them could be set at whatever level was desired. This meant that the ceiling carried by the crossbeams was independent of the roof and could also be set at any suitable level to accommodate the attic space—a scheme impossible with a truss roof, where the ends of the crossbeam are attached to the ends of the rafters.

The Greek temple's rafters (e), which were laid on top of the ridge-beam and the purlins, were not under tension, and since they were directly supported from below at ridge, mid-point (purlin) and eaves, they exerted no outward thrust on the side cornice, enabling the roof to have an extremely shallow pitch. On the rafters were laid cross battens and, on top of them, laths parallel to the rafters. On this might be laid a layer of rushes, and then one of clay in which the

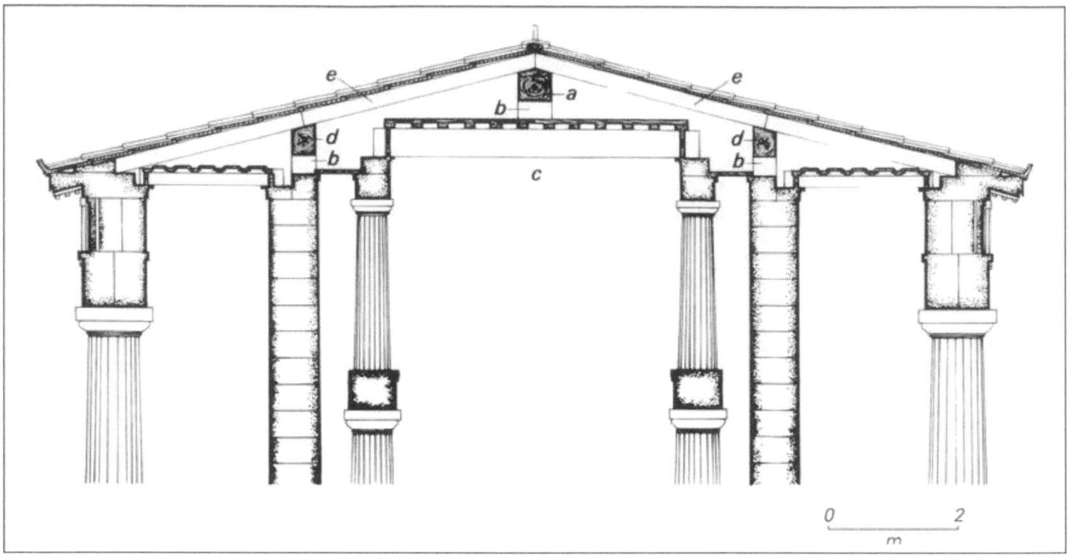

Ancient Greek timber-frame roof structure of the Hephaisteion, Athens, *c.* 449 BC: (a) ridge-beam; (b) vertical props; (c) cross-beam; (d) purlins; (e) rafters

roof tiles were embedded. Some elements could be omitted, depending partly on the type of tiles used: marble tiles, which were only employed in the most opulent structures, did not need clay and rushes, and perhaps could even be set directly on the rafters. The tiles were never nailed down but simply laid in place; this dictated the pitch of the roof, the configuration of the timberwork and hence the profile of the whole temple. Too shallow a pitch and the roof would leak; too steep and the tiles would slide off. The usual slope was *c.* 1 in 4. Remarkably the Greeks seem never to have realized that the strength of a beam is determined by its depth. Rafters were often planks, while the major timbers were generally square in cross-section. The preferred material was silver fir, the best of which came from Macedonia. No timber fragments survive, and reconstructions of roofs are based on beam sockets in stonework and specifications preserved in inscriptions, notably the Arsenal of Philon at Peiraeus (*Inscr. Gr.*/2, ii–iii, no. 1668) and the gallery on the walls of Athens (*Inscr. Gr.*/2, ii, no. 463). Certain elements of the Doric entablature almost certainly represent stone versions of wooden prototypes, but attempts to reconstruct the original carpentry remain inconclusive.

The trabeated roofing systems of 5th- and 4th-century BC Greece were eventually succeeded by designs using the triangulated roof truss, in which principal rafters were joined to the tie-beam to provide a rigid frame equivalent to a stone gable. Purlins could then be laid on the principals. Hellenistic architects may have invented the truss, since they designed buildings with clear spans of 14 m or more, which could hardly have been roofed using earlier Greek methods. Still less could the large basilicas of the Augustan period at Rome. Much less is known of Roman timber roofs, partly because the Romans normally built their walls in concrete, rather than cut stone, which in collapse exhibit their beam sockets; collapsing concrete erodes and fragments, destroying the evidence. Although Vitruvius' descriptions of roof designs are obscure, it seems that they included trussed structures. Roman ruins seldom provide firm evidence of roof design, which is nevertheless revealed for the late pagan period by votive offerings in the form of aediculae or tempietti as excavated at Carnuntum. The forms include a simple triangle with tie-beams and principals; a conventional strutted king-post truss; a more elaborate truss with multiple struts rising from the king-post and corner struts from tie-beam to principals; and raised *stridsuler* between tie-beam and principals. Semicircular trusses with more complex bracing are also shown.

Drawings made before the destruction of the roofs of the 2nd-century AD Pantheon porch and the 4th-century basilicas of St Peter and S Paolo fuori le Mura at Rome provide more detailed evidence. The Pantheon porch was treated like an aisled basilica. The nave had a braced collar truss with an upper king-post, and the aisles miniature king-post trusses. Although the roofs of both basilicas included medieval repairs, the similarity of the 9th-century replacement trusses at S Paolo to those recorded in the 16th century at St Peter's suggests that the restorers retained the original design. The aisles of both churches had struts to principal rafters. The nave trusses, however, embedded in the walls and projecting outside them, each included a king-post and a collar, which at St Peter's was apparently halved to the principals. The rafters, tie-beams and collars were paired, with the king-posts keyed between them. The surviving 6th-century roof of St Catherine's Monastery at Sinai, Egypt, like St Peter's, an imperial foundation, has classic king-post trusses with butt-cogged and face-pegged struts. On the principal rafters of all four buildings were laid many purlins of small scantling, which supported boards at the Pantheon, common rafters in the churches. Traces of late Roman roofs with closely spaced trusses and very light purlins, which probably allowed common rafters to be eliminated altogether, have been recorded in Syria.

See also ARCHITECTURE.

A. T. Hodge: *The Woodwork of Greek Roofs* (Cambridge, 1960)

P. Varène: 'La Charpente de comble chez les Grecs et les Romains', *Doss. Archéol.*, xxv (1977), pp. 92–9

R. F. Liebhart: *Timber Roofing Spans in Greek and Near Eastern Monumental Architecture during the Early Iron Age* (diss., Chapel Hill, U. NC, 1988)

N. K. Cooper: *The Development of Roof Revetment in the Peloponnese* (Jonsered, 1989)

G. Izenour: 'The Ancient Roman Roofed Theater', *Perspecta*, xxvi ([1990]), pp. 69–82

N. A. Winter: *Greek Architectural Terracottas: From the Prehistoric through to the Archaic Period* (Oxford, 1993)

N. L. Klein: 'Evidence for West Greek Influence on Mainland Greek Roof Construction and the Creation of the Truss in the Archaic Period', *Hesperia*, lxvii/4 (Oct–Dec 1998), pp. 335–74

Roselle. *See* RUSELLAE.

Rotunda. Name applied generally to a circular building, predominantly domed or vaulted (sometimes entitled 'Pantheon'). The rotunda form derives from the THOLOS, a circular building used for commemorative purposes, such as that (*c.* 470 BC; destr. AD 267; rebuilt 4th century) within the Agora, Athens, the Tholos of Athena Pronaia (*c.* 390–380 BC) at Delphi and the Philippeion (after 338 BC) built for the Macedonian royal family at Olympia. The circular form was not used by the Greeks other than for structures within a temple sanctuary. The temple dedicated to Vesta (rebuilt AD 191) in the Forum Romanum, however, has a circular central space (or cella), while other notable Roman circular temples include the 'Temple of Vesta' (late 2nd century BC) at Tibur (Tivoli), the 'Temple of Venus' (3rd century AD) at Baalbek and the 'Temple of Minerva Medica' (early 4th century AD; collapsed 1828) in the Licinian Gardens, Rome. In discussing the planning of antique temples, Vitruvius implied the ideal status of the circular form through its embodiment of the perfect proportions of an outstretched man (III.i.3). The rotunda form was also frequently adopted for Imperial mausolea in Rome, most notably by Hadrian (AD 130–39; now the Castel Sant'Angelo; *see* ROME, §IV, 9), following that of Augustus (28–23 BC; ruined). The most intact and grandest example of a Late Antique rotunda is the Pantheon (*see* ROME, §IV, 8), erected by Hadrian between AD 118 and 125. The drum and semicircular dome are equal in height—thus enclosing a sphere, with the attached portico set out around a square—and as such the Pantheon became the prototype of the perfect rotunda. Its diameter (43.3 m or 150 *pedes*) was transposed in the Island Villa (*c.* AD 125) at TIBUR (Tivoli), while the so-called Tor de' Schiavi (early 4th century AD) on the Via Praenestina and the tomb of Romulus (or Mausoleum of Maxentius; *c.* AD 307) on the Via Appia are small rotundas on the Pantheon model.

In addition to a rectangular basilica, the normal form for Early Christian church architecture, one of the most important sites in Christendom was marked by the rotunda of the church of the Holy Sepulchre in Jerusalem. Embracing the Rock of Calvary, this was erected as a martyrium to Christ by Constantine between 326 and 337 (destr. 614; rebuilt *c.* 1148). It subsequently became a natural model for churches and baptisteries of rotunda form, complemented by the circular S Costanza (*c.* 320), Rome, which was built as the mausoleum of Constantine's daughter Constantina (*d* 354) and later converted into a church.

P. Godfrey and D. Hemsoll: 'The Pantheon: Temple or Rotunda?', *Pagan Gods and Shrines of the Roman Empire*, ed. M. Henig and A. King (Oxford, 1986), pp. 195–209

P. Davies and others: 'The Pantheon: Triumph of Rome or Triumph of Compromise?', *A. Hist.*, x/ii (June 1987), pp. 133–53

M. Wilson Jones: 'Principles of Design in Roman Architecture: The Setting Out of Centralised Buildings', *Pap. Brit. Sch. Rome*, lvii (1989), pp. 106–51

W. C Loerke: 'A Rereading of the Interior Elevation of Hadrian's Rotunda', *J. Soc. Archit. Hist.*, xlix (March 1990), pp. 22–43

J. R. McCredie, G. Roux and S. M. Shaw: *The Rotunda of Arsinoe* (Princeton, 1992)

Rusellae [It. Roselle]. Site of an Etruscan city *c.* 10 km from Grosseto, Italy. It is situated on two elevated points, once an island in the shallow gulf that became, in Roman times, the salt-water Lake Prilius and later degenerated into malarial swamps, drained and cultivated in modern times. The settlement dates back to the 9th century BC, although there are few remains of the city before the 6th century BC, by which time a city wall of crude brickwork on stone foundations had apparently been constructed (*see* ARCHITECTURE, §V, 4). In the second half of the 6th century BC a new, more substantial wall of irregular but firmly jointed blocks was erected, and there is evidence that the town had become a specialized manufacturing centre. Rusellae's development seems to have been at the expense of nearby Vetulonia. Rusellae continued to prosper in the Classical and Hellenistic periods, although it appears to have expanded less than other major Etruscan cities. During the 4th century BC the city wall was rebuilt in places with blocks in almost regular courses. At least one area of the city was rebuilt in the Hellenistic period. Rusellae was taken by Rome in 294 BC, and the last main phase of building activity was during early imperial times, when the Emperor Augustus and the local nobility provided the city with a forum, an amphitheatre and other public buildings. Decline was rapid after the 2nd century BC.

Roselle: Gli scavi e la mostra (exh. cat., Grosseto, Mus. Archeol., 1975)

Rycroft Painter (*fl* *c*.510 BC). Greek vase painter. He painted in the Black-figure style at a time when most of his contemporaries were turning to Red-figure, and intimations of the new outline technique may be seen in his figures. Beazley associated him with PSIAX and the PRIAM PAINTER, and Boardman compared his work with the Pioneer group of Attic Red-figure painters. His name vase (Oxford, Ashmolean, 1965.118), a belly amphora of Type A, bears a scene of *Leto Mounting a Chariot* with Apollo, Artemis and Hermes in attendance; indeed, chariot scenes occur more often than any other theme in his work. Several amphorae and hydriae show wedding scenes with chariots, and they also occur in some of his Dionysiac scenes, another favourite theme (see fig.). In addition to vases, a plaque from the Acropolis at Athens is attributed to him, painted with a scene of *Athena Watching the Vintage*.

J. D. Beazley: *Black-figure* (1956), pp. 335–8
J. D. Beazley: *Paralipomena* (1971), pp. 148–9
J. Boardman: *Athenian Black Figure Vases: A Handbook* (London, 1974), p. 113
W. G. Moon: 'Some New and Little-known Vases by the Rycroft and Priam Painters', *Greek Vases in the J. Paul Getty Museum* (Los Angeles, 1983/*R* 1990), pp. 41–70
E. J. Holmberg: *On the Rycroft Painter and Other Athenian Black-figure Vase-painters with a Feeling for Nature* (Jonsered, 1992)

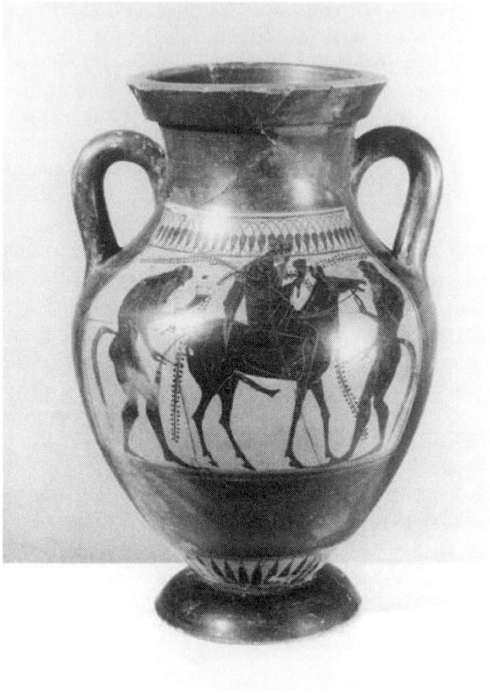

Rycroft Painter: amphora depicting *Dionysos on a Mule between Two Satyrs*, Attic Black-figure, *c*. 510 BC (Laon, Musée Archéologique Municipal, 37977)

S

Sabratha. Roman town on the coast of Libya, 64 km west of Tripoli, originally established as a Phoenician trading post. The most conspicuous surviving monument from this period is a 2nd-century BC tower tomb. In the Augustan period (27 BC–AD 14) a rectangular forum was laid out, which in the course of a century acquired a curia, basilica and several frontally planned temples. To the prosperous Antonine period (AD 138–93) belong the paving of the forum, the porticos of Corinthian columns with granite shafts and the extensive marbling of most of the temples, except that of Liber Pater, which dominates the east side. At the same time a new quarter of the town was laid out further to the east, dominated by the late 2nd-century AD Severan theatre (w. 92.6 m; see fig.). As well as being the best-preserved Roman theatre in North Africa, it is the most sophisticated in plan. It is chiefly remarkable for its three-tier *scaenae frons*, which was completely rebuilt by the Italian Archaeological Service in 1937. Its circulation system is much more sophisticated than that of LEPTIS MAGNA, which in many respects it resembles, although it lacks the temple at the top of the *cavea*. Part of its outer wall, which has arched openings flanked by Corinthian pilasters, has also been rebuilt. Sabratha is important for the large number of domestic and commercial buildings that have been excavated there. The houses had lower storeys of squared stone masonry and upper ones of mud-brick. The roofs were flat, and large underground cisterns were used to store water. From the end of the 4th century AD the town was extensively rebuilt; it was severely affected by the Arab conquest in the 7th century AD.

G. Caputo: *Il teatro di Sabratha* (Rome, 1959)

D. E. L. Haynes: *An Archaeological and Historical Guide to the Pre-Islamic Antiquities of Tripolitania* (Tripoli, 1962), pp. 107–34

P. M. Kenrick: 'Excavations at Sabratha, 1948–51', *Libyan Stud.*, xiii (1982), pp. 51–60

G. Caputo and F. Ghedini: *Il Tempio d'Ercole di Sabratha* (Rome, 1984)

E. Joly, F. Tomasello and S. Garraffo: *Il Tempio a divinità ignota di Sabratha* (Rome, 1984)

P. M. Kenrick and others: *Excavations at Sabratha, 1948–1951*, 2 vols in 3 parts (London, 1986–1994)

R. Polidori and others: *La Libye antique: Cités perdues de l'Empire romain* (Paris, 1988)

G. Barone and E. Epifanio Vanni: *Gessi del Museo di Sabratha* (Rome, 1994)

E. M. Ruprechtsberger: *Sabratha—eine antike Stadt in Tripolitanien* (Mainz, 2001)

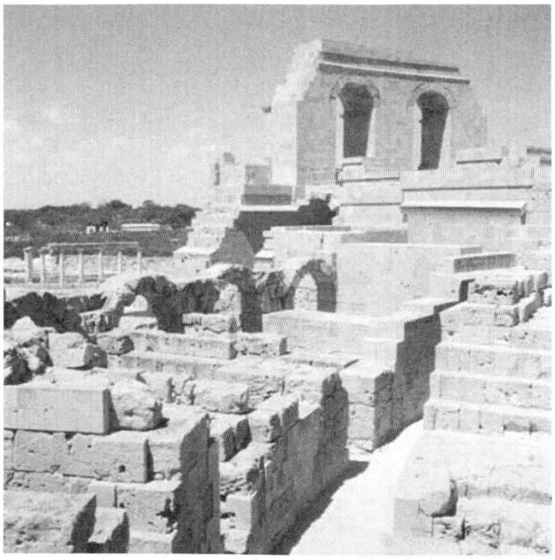

Sabratha, theatre, late 2nd century AD

Sagalassos [Ağlasun]. Site in Pisidia, south-west Turkey, which flourished *c.* the 4th century BC–*c.* the 4th century AD; it occupies a naturally defensible position some 1650 m above sea-level. It was the leading city of Pisidia at the time of Alexander the Great, who attempted to capture it, and throughout the Imperial period, when it was an ally of Rome and part of the province of Galatia, with territory extending some 45 km west. Its civic titles and abundant coinage proclaim its prosperity during the Imperial period.

The city axis is directed south–north, being almost level in the south yet rising steeply to the upper agora in the north. During the Hellenistic period the civic centre was situated on the upper ridge, where a Doric temple and bouleuterion (council chamber) are located (both 2nd century BC). A well-preserved frieze of dancing maidens came from a heroön (before 150 BC). The upper agora was laid out with porticos in the 2nd century BC but was much rebuilt in the Imperial period. Also pre-Roman is the *cavea* of the impressive theatre, although its elaborate two-storey stage-building dates to the late 2nd century AD. Buildings from the Roman period include the Ionic Temple of Apollo Klarios (early 1st century AD); the Corinthian peripteral Temple of Antoninus Pius (2nd century AD; 26.83×13.87 m) enclosed within a porticoed temenos; a macellum of the period of Commodus (*reg* AD 180–93) near the upper agora; a nymphaeum at the north of the Claudian lower agora; and a paved street, once colonnaded, connecting the Antonine temple to the lower agora. The necropolis of the city, in the valley below, contains Roman sarcophagi, while the cliffs behind the site contain numerous rock-cut arcosolium tombs from the Imperial period.

K. Lanckoroński, G. Niemann and E. Petersen: *Städte Pamphyliens und Pisidiens*, ii (Vienna, 1892), pp. 127–60
R. Fleischer: 'Der hellenistische Fries von Sagalassos in Pisidien', *Ant. Welt*, xii/1 (1981), pp. 3–16
M. Waelkens, S. Mitchell and E. Owens: 'Sagalassos 1989', *Anatol. Stud.*, xl (1990), pp. 185–98
M. Waelkens and others, eds.: *Sagalassos,* 5 vols (Leuven, 1993–2000)
L. Vandeput: *The Architectural Decoration in Roman Asia Minor: Sagalassos: A Case Study* (Leuven, 1997)
XIII. Arkeometri Sonuçları Toplantısı (Ankara, 1998)
J. Poblome: *Sagalassos Red Slip Ware: Typology and Chronology* (Turnhout, 1999)
R. Degeest: *The Common Wares of Sagalassos: Typology and Chronology* (Turnhout, 2000)
B. De Cupere: *Animals at Ancient Sagalassos: Evidence of the Faunal Remains* (Turnhout, 2001)
M. Waelkens: *Ontdekking van het verloren Sagalassos* (Leuven, 2002)
H. Vanhaverbeke and M. Waelkens: *The Chora of Sagalassos: The Evolution of the Settlement Pattern from Prehistoric until Recent Times* (Turnhout, 2003)
M. Vermoere: *Holocene Vegetation History in the Territory of Sagalassos (Southwest Turkey): A Palynological Approach* (Turnhout, 2004)
V. Köse: *Nekropolen und Grabdenkmäler von Sagalassos in Pisidien in hellenistischer und römischer Zeit* (Turnhout, 2005)

Saida. *See* SIDON.

St Albans. *See* VERULAMIUM.

Saintes. *See* MEDIOLANUM SANTONUM.

Salamis [Constantia]. Site of an ancient city on the east coast of Cyprus *c.* 10 km north of Famagusta and 3 km north-east of Enkomi, that flourished from *c.* the 11th century BC to *c.* the 8th century AD. The ancient city extended over more than 2 km along the sea front to the north of the mouth of the River Pedieios, on the edge of the fertile Mesaoria Plain. The hinterland supplied it with agricultural produce (cereals and olives), wood for construction and copper for making bronze, while the position of its port made it a staging post on the sea routes from the Greek world to the Syrio-Palestinian coast and Egypt. The principal excavations on the site have been carried out by the British under J. A. R. Munro and H. A. Tubbs (1880), the Cypriots under P. Dikaios and later V. Karageorghis (1957–72) and the French under J. Pouilloux and later M. Yon (1964–74).

According to literary tradition, Salamis was founded by the hero Teucer on his return from the Trojan War. Teucer came from the island of Salamis off Attica and was of mixed Greek and barbarian extraction; this twin ancestry perhaps reflects the history of the kingdom and highlights the diversity of the cultural links that it had with Greece, Phoenicia, the Semitic world and the Orient. The site appears to have been first settled in the 11th century BC, probably by refugees from Enkomi (itself perhaps known as Salamis), which was destroyed *c.* 1050 BC. The city's Greek foundation legend finds support in the Mycenaean style of the 11th-century BC rock-cut tombs and accompanying pottery finds, which are probably the work of Aegean settlers dislodged from their homelands in the turmoil that accompanied the final collapse of the Mycenaean palace civilization in the last years of the Bronze Age. From the 10th to the 6th century BC the extension of the city and its monumental necropolis bore witness to the wealth of the princes who ruled Salamis. Large tombs (8th–7th century BC) were built in blocks of dressed stone with an entrance passage up to 13 m wide and 25 m long leading by way of a paved propylon to the funeral chamber. They were covered by a high barrow of brick and earth (e.g. Tomb 3; h. over 10 m, diam. 60 m). Their contents recall the funeral rites of Homeric Greece (e.g. that of Patroklos in *Iliad* XXIII) and include chariots decorated with bronze fittings and buried along with their horses, furniture decorated with finely carved ivories, ceremonial weapons, bronze cauldrons decorated with the heads of realistic animals such as lions and birds or of fantastic creatures such as griffins and hundreds of pottery vessels for offerings. Most of the objects are in a style common to the whole of the Levant and display the influence of Egypt, the Orient and the Urartian bronzesmiths. The pottery finds, on the other hand, reflect current local decorative styles, including floral designs typical of eastern Cyprus, as do the votive terracotta figurines that filled the shrines.

During the Classical period (*c.* 475–323 BC) Salamis seems to have gained a predominance over the other kingdoms on the island, while in cultural matters the influence of the Greeks became predominant. Euagoras I, King of Salamis (*reg* 411–374/3 BC), championed the cause of Hellenism in the eastern Mediterranean against the Great King of the Persians as well as playing the part of protector of learning. He rebuilt and extended the city, but no large monuments of the period have so far been recovered. Sculpture at the site reflects the contemporary innovations and criteria of Greek sculpture; finds range from small korai (late 6th century BC; Nicosia, Cyprus Mus.) recalling those of the Acropolis at Athens to a Grecian head of *Aphrodite/Hygieia* in white marble.

Greek influence can also be traced in more popular works, such as the terracotta figurines and ceramics.

At the end of the 4th century BC Salamis lost its status as an independent kingdom. The last king, Nikokreon, was conquered by Ptolemy (later Ptolemy I Soter, *reg* 305–283 BC) in 311 BC; his tomb was an exceptional monument, perhaps reflecting the spectacular ceremonies that accompanied the funeral. A great pyre-cenotaph was built in brick, comprising a stepped platform (17.0×11.5 m; h. 1 m) with a ramp in front of it. The numerous valuable offerings and clay statues within included both realistic and idealized near life-size portraits, executed in the style of Classical Greece. During the Hellenistic period Salamis was politically integrated into the Lagid empire and lost its position as capital of the island to NEW PAPHOS. The construction of the great Temple of Zeus Olympios to the south of the town was begun as part of a major urban development at the end of the 2nd century BC. The temple was a peripteral building (8×6 columns), with capitals related to the Corinthian style and entablatures that included both Corinthian and Doric elements (triglyphs and metopes); it was built on a podium (27.5×22.2 m; h. over 2 m) with a stepped base. Salamis regained its pre-eminent position under Roman rule. The Temple of Zeus was completed, and an access ramp was added to it (late 1st century BC–early 1st century AD); it also became a temple of emperor worship, and bronze portraits of the emperors were placed there, including a life-size head, probably of the Emperor Claudius (mid-1st century AD; Nicosia, Cyprus Mus.). Another major public building programme included a theatre (early 1st century AD; remodelled 3rd century AD; see fig.), gymnasium (early 1st century AD) and palaestra (early 2nd century AD): the remains of this work are still clearly visible to the north of the city.

The arrival and spread of Christianity in Cyprus gave Salamis a new position of importance in the empire from the 4th century AD onwards. It was rebuilt after an earthquake, renamed Constantia and became the metropolis of Cyprus. The town grew, with the addition of luxurious houses, numerous churches and monumental basilicas. Salamis–Constantia later fell into decline, hastened by the raids of the Arab conquerors in the 7th century AD, and the site was finally abandoned to the sand and vegetation.

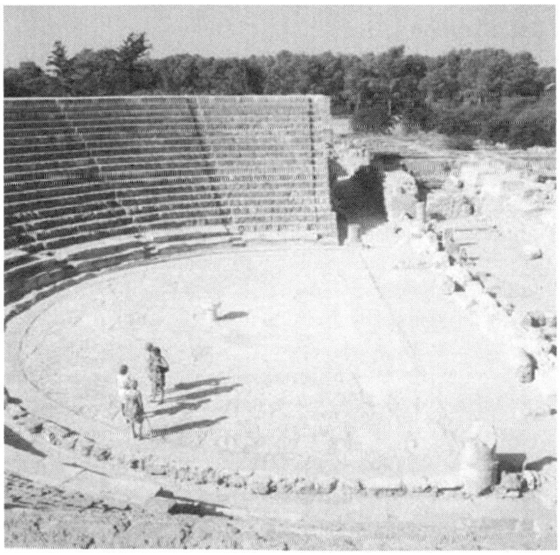

Salamis, theatre, 1st century AD; remodelled 3rd century AD

A. Palma di Cesnola: *Salaminia (Cyprus): The History, Treasures and Antiquities of Salamis in the Island of Cyprus* (London, 1882)

J. A. R. Munro and H. A. Tubbs: 'Excavations in Cyprus, 1890: Third Season's Work: Salamis', *J. Hell. Stud.*, xii (1891), pp. 59–198

V. Karageorghis and others: *Salamis*, 7 vols (Nicosia, 1964–78)

V. Karageorghis: *Salamis in Cyprus: Homeric, Hellenistic and Roman* (London, 1969)

J. Pouilloux and G. Roux, eds: *Salamine de Chypre*, 14 vols (Paris, 1969–94)

M. C. Taylor: *Salamis and the Salaminioi: The History of an Unofficial Athenian Demos* (Amsterdam, 1997)

V. Karageorghis: *Excavating at Salamis in Cyprus, 1952–1974* (Athens, 1999)

M. W. Jones: 'Doric Measure and Architectural Design 1: The Evidence of the Relief from Salamis', *Amer. J. Archaeol.*, civ/1 (Jan 2000), pp. 73–93

N. Erkan: *Salamis 2000 kazilarinda ele geçen kandiller* (Ankara, 2001)

M. Polojiorghi: 'Die Grabstele des Eleusiniers Pythogenes', *Mitt. Dt. Archäol. Inst.: Athen. Abt.*, cxvi (2001), pp. 125–33

Salamis in Cyprus: A Violation of Scholarly Ethics (Nicosia, 2001)

T. A. Pantele: *Salamina: Poreia sto chrono* (Athens, 2003)

M. Polojiorghi: 'Ein lernbegieriger Ephebe auf einer Grabstele aus Salamis', *Mitt. Dt. Archäol. Inst.: Athen. Abt.*, cxviii (2003), pp. 337–47

Salona [anc. Colonia Martia Iulia Salona; Salonae; now Solin]. Site in Dalmatia, Croatia, at the mouth of the River Jadro, 5 km north-east of Split. Since the site of the Roman town was not built over, it has been possible to conduct extensive excavations, notably those undertaken in the late 19th century by Frane Bulić (1846–1934).

Salona was established as a trading settlement as early as the Hellenistic period and became important as the point where the Via Egnatia branched off from the coast road towards the interior. Salona sided with Julius Caesar against Pompey in 48 BC and was given the status of a colony before 27 BC. It became the provincial capital of Dalmatia after AD 9 and by the 2nd century AD had developed into a thriving town with a population of *c.* 60,000. Salona reached its peak under the patronage of Diocletian (*reg* 284–305), who was born nearby and built his palace at SPALATUM (now Split). A Christian community was established by then and several martyrs are recorded during his reign. The growth of the community after the persecutions had ceased is indicated by the presence of numerous Early Christian basilicas, of which ten have been excavated.

The town probably developed in three phases (see fig.). The central area (Urbs Vetus) was first extended to the west (Urbs Occidentalis) and then to the east

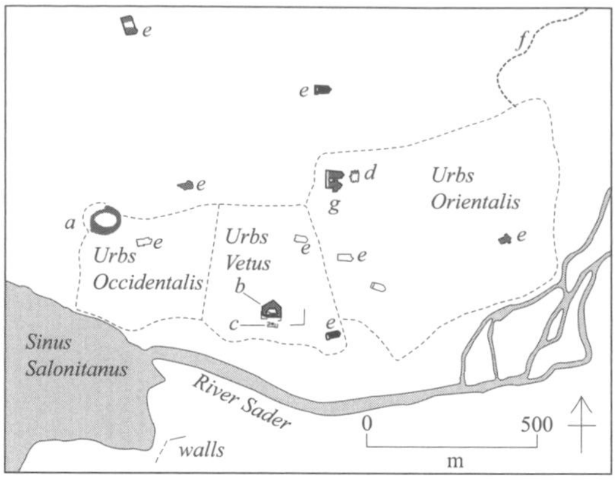

Salona, plan: (a) amphitheatre; (b) theatre; (c) temple; (d) baths; (e) basilicas; (f) aqueduct; (g) episcopal complex

(Urbs Orientalis). An amphitheatre (a; 2nd century AD), a theatre (b), temple (c), baths (d) and an aqueduct (f; late 3rd century–early 4th) indicate a high standard of living. New defensive walls were built in AD 170 and numerous towers were added along the northern, landward section in the 6th century.

W. Gerber, E. Dyggve and R. Egger: *Forschungen in Salona*, 3 vols (Vienna, 1917–39)

E. Dyggve: *Recherches à Salone*, 2 vols (Copenhagen, 1928–33)

E. Dyggve: *History of Salonitan Christianity* (Oslo, 1951)

E. Ceci: *I monumenti pagani di Salona* (Milan, 1962)

E. Ceci: *I monumenti cristiani di Salona* (Milan, 1963)

T. Hauschild: 'Das "Martyrium" von La Alberca (Prov. Murcia)', *Madrid. Mitt.*, xii (1971), pp. 170–94

C. W. Clairmont: *Excavations at Salona, Jugoslavia, 1969–72* (Park Ridge, 1975)

Vjesnik Arheol. & Hist. Dalmat., lxxvii (1984) [issue devoted to Salona]

D. Rendić-Miočević: 'Anastasio "aquileiese", martire a Salona, e il cimitero che da lui prende nome', *Ant. Altoadriat.*, xxvi/2 (1985), pp. 315–29

E. Marin and I. Britvić: *Don Frane Bulić: Po ruševinama stare Salone* [Don Frane Bulić: at the ruins of old Salona] (Split, 1986)

E. Marin: 'Nouvelles recherches sur Marusinac à Salona', *Akten des 12. Internationalen Kongresses für Christliche Archäologie: Münster 1995*, pp. 1016–23

S. McNally: *The Architectural Ornament of Diocletian's Palace at Split* (Oxford, 1996)

E. Marin: *Salona, Narona: Razgovori* (Sarajevo, 1998)

E. Marin: *Narona: Vid kod Metkovica* (Metkovic, 1999)

N. Duval, ed.: *Salona. Recherches aechéologiques franco-croates à Salone/III, Manastirine: Etablissement préromain, nécropole et basilique paléochrétienne à Salone* (Rome, 2000)

N. Duval, E. Marin and M. Bonacic Mandinic: *Manastirine: Etablissement préromain, nécropole et basilique paléochrétienne à Salone* (Rome, 2000)

E. Marin : *Longae Salonae* (Split, 2002–)

Salonica. *See* THESSALONIKI.

Samaria [Bibl. Shomeron; Gk. Sebaste; Arab. Sebastiyah]. Ancient capital of the northern kingdom of Israel from the time of Omri (*reg* 882–871 BC) until the final conquest of the kingdom by the Assyrian king Sargon II in 721 BC. It has been identified with the modern Arab village of Sebastiyah, which lies *c.* 10 km north-west of Nablus and 40 km west of the River Jordan. The site is situated on a hilltop about 90 m above a large and extremely fertile agricultural plain; more importantly, it stands at the crossroads of two ancient major routes, one passing west to east from the coastal plain, through Shechem to the Jordan Valley, and the other leading north from Judah to Megiddo and the Jezreel Valley. According to biblical tradition (1 Kings 16:24), the hill on which the capital was to be established was purchased by Omri from Shemer (hence the name Shomeron) for two talents of silver. During the reign of Herod the Great (37–4 BC) the name of the city was changed to Sebaste in honour of the Emperor Augustus, and this name has been preserved in that of the modern village of Sebastiyah.

Two major archaeological expeditions have excavated at Samaria. The first, from 1908 to 1910, by Harvard University of Cambridge, MA, was initially directed by G. Schumacher but subsequently by G. A. Reisner and C. S. Fisher. The second expedition, directed by J. W. Crowfoot, worked at the site from 1931 to 1935 and was sponsored by four further institutions. Between 1965 and 1967 limited excavations were undertaken by the Department of Antiquities of Jordan, directed by F. Zayadine, mainly concentrated on the Temple of Augustus, but an Iron Age tomb was also uncovered, dating to the 9th century BC and containing more than 200 pottery vessels. Finds are in a number of museums, including the Rockefeller Museum, the Hebrew Museum and the Institute of Archaeology of the Hebrew University in Jerusalem and the British Museum in London.

The site consists of two elements: an upper city, or acropolis, which contained the Israelite royal quarter, and a lower city, extending over the slopes and around the foot of the hill, which contained extensive remains of the Hellenistic and Roman periods. Although both expeditions examined these areas, researches into the pre-Hellenistic periods were concentrated on the acropolis, and very little information was retrieved concerning the contemporary settlement in the lower city, although it is likely that during the period of the Israelite kingdom, at least, the whole of the area enclosed by the later Roman defences was fully occupied. Pottery found in the pre-constructional levelling fills on the acropolis included Early Bronze Age and Iron Age sherds, suggesting that there had been small settlements of the 3rd millennium BC and of the 10th century BC before the establishment of the royal capital.

At the beginning of the Hellenistic period the Israelite walls were repaired and strengthened with a number of round towers, one of which, measuring 13 m in diameter, is preserved to a height of over 8.5 m. Traces of the city wall of the 4th century BC were found near the later Roman gate; there, it may be assumed, the Hellenistic gate also stood. In the latter part of the Hellenistic period (2nd century BC), the defences of the acropolis were strengthened by the addition of a massive wall, 4.2 m thick at its base, which followed generally the line of the Israelite wall and was reinforced with substantial square towers. It was destroyed, along with the rest of the city, in 108 BC by John Hyrcanus (*reg* 134–104 BC). A Hellenistic temple, dedicated to the goddess Kore, was excavated in the area to the north of the later Roman Temple of Augustus. It measured 36×15.5 m and stood in a large temenos that may have been surrounded by columns. This temple was also destroyed in 108 BC, but was subsequently rebuilt in the Roman period.

During the Roman period, Samaria, now called Sebaste, reached the peak of its Classical splendour. The city walls, which included the acropolis, enclosed an area of about 69 ha. The main city gate was on the western side and was flanked by two massive round towers, 14 m in diameter. Under Septimius Severus a colonnaded street with 600 columns was constructed, running 800 m from the west to the east gates. It was about 12.5 m wide and had a roofed portico with shops on either side.

The residential quarter, in the western part of the acropolis, was probably built during the time of Gabinius (*d* 47 BC). Rising above it, on the highest part of the hill, and partly overlying the Israelite royal quarter, was a huge temple built by Herod and dedicated to Augustus. The temple itself measured *c*. 35×24 m and was approached through a spacious forecourt on the south side. This was constructed over an artificial platform supported by vaulted corridors. A wide flight of steps led up from the court to the temple, which stood on a podium, 4.5 m high. The temple was destroyed, but was rebuilt by Septimius Severus, who added an altar in the forecourt and a new flight of steps to extend the earlier ones.

In the north-eastern part of the lower city was the stadium, which has been only partially excavated. It was enclosed by four porticos with Doric columns and walls coated with coloured plaster. It was originally built during the reign of Herod and was remodelled in the 2nd century AD in the Corinthian style. In a cistern near the stadium was found a statue of the goddess Kore.

On the north-eastern slope of the acropolis was a relatively well-preserved theatre of the 3rd century AD. It had an external diameter of about 65 m, and the façade of the stage was decorated with niches, alternately rounded and rectangular. The forum was erected on a platform (128×72.5 m) east of the acropolis and was enclosed on all sides by roofed porticos (see fig.). A door in the middle of the western wall led to a basilica of the 2nd century AD, which measured 68×32.6 m and was divided internally into nave and aisles by three rows of columns. Close to the forum and basilica were found parts of the aqueduct that brought water to the city from the hills to the east.

A mausoleum of the Roman period (late 2nd–early 3rd century AD) was found in the village of Sebaste. The stone-built, domed structure (5.5×5.5 m) has walls decorated with pilasters and a façade that had a portico of two rows of four columns each. The

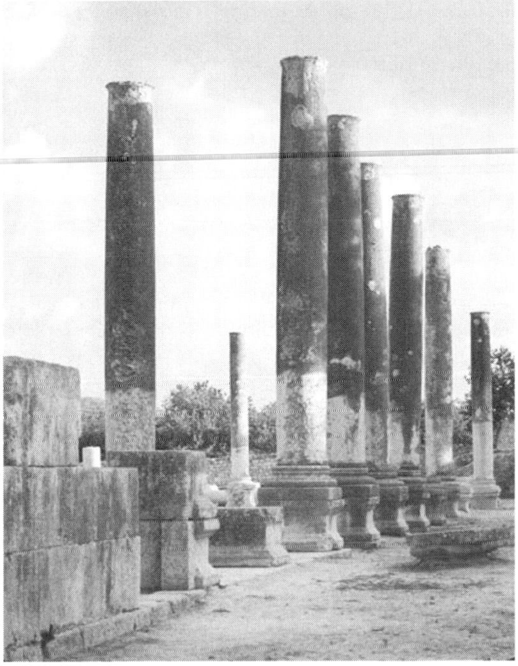

Samaria, colonnaded street, AD 193–211

tomb consists of a single chamber (3.3×3.3 m) with arched niches on three walls for stone sarcophagi. One sarcophagus, found outside the tomb, was richly decorated with columns, garlands, masks and human figures. Several rock-cut tombs in the area east of the city have produced a variety of finds, including sarcophagi, glass vessels, lamps and jewellery.

G. A. Reisner, C. S. Fisher and D. G. Lyon: *Harvard Excavations at Samaria (1908–1910)*, 2 vols (Cambridge, MA, 1924)

J. W. Crowfoot and others: *Samaria-Sebaste*, 3 vols (London, 1938–57)

R. W. Hamilton: *Guide to Samaria-Sebaste* (Jerusalem, 1944)

A. Parrot: *Samaria: The Capital of the Kingdom of Israel* (London, 1958)

F. Zayadine: 'Une Tombe du Fer II à Samarie-Sébasté', *Rev. Bib.*, lxxv (1968), pp. 562–85

I. Roll and others: 'Roman Roads in Western Samaria', *Palestine Explor. Q.*, cxviii (July–Dec 1986), pp. 113–34

J. H. Humphrey: *The Roman and Byzantine Near East: Late-antique Petra, Nile Festival Building at Sepphoris, Deir Qal'a Monastery, Khirbet Qana Village and Pilgrim Site, 'Ain-'Arrub Hiding Complex and Other Studies* (Portsmouth, RI, 2002)

Samos. Greek island in the eastern Aegean near the coast of Asia Minor (now Turkey). It was inhabited in the 3rd millennium BC or earlier, and from the Archaic period onwards it was a major centre for the ancient Greek cult of Hera. Samos flourished during the 6th century BC under the tyrant Polykrates (*reg c*. 540–*c*. 522 BC), who initiated a series of ambitious building projects, including the Tunnel of Eupalinos and the fourth Temple of Hera. As part of the Roman Empire the island's fortunes were varied, but during Byzantine times it suffered steep decline. Though there are later buildings of interest, most of the important remains on Samos are of ancient Greek or Roman date.

1. Architecture. 2. Sculpture.

1. Architecture.

(i) Greek. The information provided by ancient writers regarding Samian architecture is meagre. Thus Herodotus' assertion (*Histories* III.lx.1) that the people of Samos carried out the largest building projects of the Late Archaic period supplements the archaeological remains with a unique indication of the importance of the ancient city of Samos (now Pithagório). The harbour was protected by a huge mole with boathouses (Herodotus: III.xlv.4, lx.3), and the city had at least one agora and several sanctuaries, though only a Sanctuary of Artemis and Aphrodite has been uncovered (Temple of Artemis, mid-6th century BC; Temple of Aphrodite, only remains of Hellenistic date). The long city wall (6 km) is noteworthy. Built of mud-brick on a stone foundation, it was one of the first city walls to have its course determined by the site's strategic needs and not merely by the extent of the inhabited area. A water supply system 2.5 km long included a spectacular tunnel (l. 1036 m), which was bored simultaneously from both ends through the acropolis hill under the direction of the Megarian engineer Eupalinos (*c.* mid-6th century BC). There is no information concerning the palace of the tyrant Polykrates or the layout of the city and its houses. Quite a large villa, however, stood on the Kastro Hill (3rd century BC), and one with remarkable mosaics was constructed on the slopes of the acropolis (2nd century BC). An extensive Hellenistic gymnasium has been excavated in the south-west part of the city (*c.* 270 BC, with later additions).

The most impressive remains on Samos are, however, those in the Sanctuary of Hera (Heraion) on the south-east coast of the island about 6 km west of the ancient city. It is one of the most important sites in terms of the evolution of the Ionic order (*see* Orders, architectural, §I, 1(ii) and 2(i)). It was excavated by the German Archaeological Institute under T. Wiegand (1910–14) and E. Buschor (1925–39 and 1952–61). The origins of the cult go back to Mycenaean times, but the first extant altar was erected about 1000 BC, and the first substantial Temple of Hera was built about 800 BC. The latter was a non-peripteral 'hundred-footer' (*hekatompedos*) with a characteristically elongated Archaic plan (*c.* 33.0 × 6.5 m). Its remains are confined to parts of the wall foundations, and flat stone bases for a central row of pillars in the cella, which partially obscured the cult statue on a pedestal near its inner end. The building resembled contemporary houses in having mud-brick walls and a steep ridge roof. The suggestion that a peristyle was added to the main building is dubious. The building was, however, probably replaced in about 650 BC by a second *hekatompedos*, probably a peripteral temple with a cella of the same size and orientation. It was constructed from ashlar masonry and decorated with a frieze, of which a section bearing the incised outlines of warriors has been preserved (Samos, Archaeol. Mus.). Another early building, the South Stoa (*c.* 630 BC), on the west boundary of the sanctuary, was the first monumental Greek hall (69.0×5.9 m). It was divided into three adjacent compartments, had an inner and outer colonnade, and must have been covered with a pentroof.

The sanctuary was expanded considerably around 600 BC and transformed by a series of building projects: the construction of the 'First Dipteros', the substantial enlargement of the altar, the erection of several treasuries and the addition of a sacred way, which was lined by lavish votive offerings and connected the sanctuary with the city. This comprehensive replanning is linked with the names of Rhoikos and Theodoros. The third Temple of Hera, also known as the 'Temple of Rhoikos' or 'First Dipteros' (*c.* 560 BC), was on a scale and of a type unparalleled in Greece at that time and must have been inspired by Egyptian models. The temple platform, composed of two steps, measured *c.* 52.5×105.0 m, and the cella measured *c.* 25.0×52.5 m. The peristyle had 2 rows of 21 columns on the flanks and 2 rows of 8 and 10 columns at the front and rear respectively, while a further 30 columns stood in the pronaos and cella (see fig. 1). The only surviving traces of the temple, however, are the remains of foundations, the paving of the peristyle, the steps and numerous column bases. The latter were the first examples of canonical Ionic form, comprising a spira and torus. They were renowned for the precision with which they had been turned (Pliny: *Natural History* XXXVI.xix.90). The columns themselves were of tufa, and each had 40 flutes separated by sharp arrises of Doric type. None of the entablature survives, but numerous fragments of roof tiles and antefixes indicate that the building was completed and confirm its date. Unlike earlier altars, the new 'Altar of Rhoikos' stood precisely on the main axis of the temple, at a distance from its façade carefully calculated to suit its proportions. It was, however, of traditional form, with a U-shaped wall enclosing a great stepped structure that supported the sacrificial altar proper. The enclosing wall was adorned with an animal frieze, rich Ionic mouldings and huge antae capitals. Besides these two central buildings there was a series of subsidiary

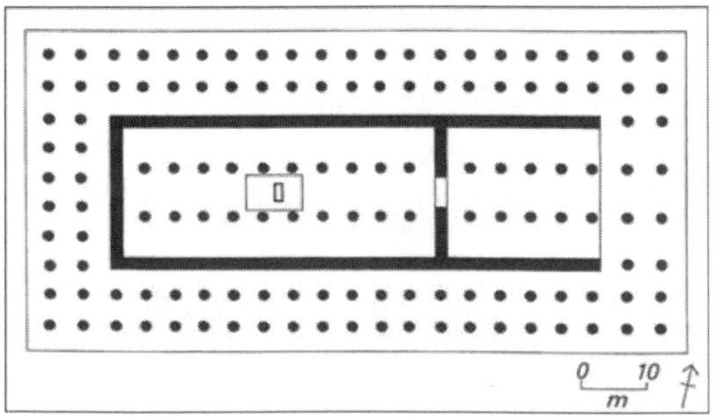

1. Samos, plan of third Temple of Hera, *c.* 560 BC

ones: the North-west Stoa, two treasuries erroneously known as 'Temple A' and 'Temple B', and two massive peripteral structures of unexplained significance.

Only a few decades after the reorganization of the sanctuary, the third Temple of Hera was destroyed, owing to bad foundations, and replaced by a new building, the fourth Temple of Hera or 'Second Dipteros'. Doubtless because of the poor state of the site, this was built 40 m to the west of its predecessor and with a slightly different orientation. It was probably started towards the end of the 6th century BC, and it can be reconstructed on the basis of the surviving foundations and one remaining column. The peristyle of 24 × 8 columns (9 along the back of the building) was dipteral at the sides and tripteral along the ends, while the pronaos contained 2×5 columns and the cella 2 × 11 columns. The walls and internal columns were of tufa, while the peristyle was of marble. The outer columns were unfluted but had richly decorated necks and capitals with volutes; the inner columns had egg-and-dart capitals with strong convex profiles. The gigantic building was never completed, since the Persian Wars, followed by Samos' subjection to Athenian hegemony, led to a decline in the island's fortunes.

(ii) Roman. In 129 BC Samos was incorporated into the province of Asia. It became a favourite resort of several Roman emperors, and during the reign of Augustus it was even granted its 'freedom'. Building activity at the city itself included the renovation of the villa on the Kastro Hill, the conversion of the gymnasium into Roman baths, the construction of a theatre on the slopes of the acropolis and the improvement of the water supply by the addition of a second aqueduct. The benevolence of the imperial family is particularly noticeable at the Sanctuary of Hera, which, after a long interruption, regained some of its earlier prestige. A grand staircase was added to the front of the half-finished fourth Temple of Hera, and a fine Corinthian temple (late 2nd century AD) and a small shrine or naiskos (1st–2nd century AD) were erected between it and the altar. The cult statue of Hera was probably placed in a peripteral marble temple built almost directly in front of the altar. This had an unusual ground-plan and columns with archaizing Ionic bases and Doric capitals. The details of its superstructure are unclear. The most important building work undertaken in Roman times was the complete reconstruction of the altar, using marble and adhering strictly to its Archaic forms, with Ionic leaf profiles, an animal frieze and huge antae capitals. The last sacred building was a small Roman-style temple north of the Sacred Way, constructed in the 3rd century AD, by which time the sanctuary was increasingly being encroached on by private houses.

E. Buschor: 'Heraion von Samos: Frühe Bauten', *Mitt. Dt. Archäol. Inst.: Athen. Abt.*, lv (1930), pp. 1–99

H. Schleif: 'Heraion von Samos: Das Vorgelände des Tempels', *Mitt. Dt. Archäol. Inst.: Athen. Abt.*, lviii (1933), pp. 211–47

G. Gruben: 'Die Südhalle', *Mitt. Dt. Archäol. Inst.: Athen. Abt.*, lxxii (1957), pp. 52–64

O. Reuther: *Der Heratempel von Samos* (Berlin, 1957)

O. Ziegenaus: 'Die Tempelgruppe im Norden des Altarplatzes', *Mitt. Dt. Archäol. Inst.: Athen. Abt.*, lxxii (1957), pp. 87–151

R. Tölle: *Das Kastro Tigani* (1974), xiv of *Samos* (Bonn, 1961–)

H. Walter: *Das Heraion von Samos* (Munich, 1976)

H. Kienast: *Die Stadtmauer von Samos* (1978), xv of *Samos* (Bonn, 1961–)

H. Kyrieleis: *Führer durch das Heraion von Samos* (Athens, 1981)

W. Martini: *Das Gymnasium von Samos* (1984), xvi of *Samos* (Bonn, 1961–)

H. Kienast: 'Der sogenannte Tempel D im Heraion von Samos I', *Mitt. Dt. Archäol. Inst.: Athen. Abt.*, c (1985), pp. 105–27

G. Shipley: *A History of Samos, 800–188 BC* (Oxford, 1987)

A. E. Furtwängler and H. J. Kienast: *Der Nordbau* (Bonn, 1989)

M. Tiede: 'Hellenistische Pfeilermonumente im Heraion von Samos und in Magnesia am Maeander', *Mitt. Dt. Archäol. Inst.: Athen. Abt.*, cv (1990), pp. 213–58

K. Muller: 'Hellenistische Architekturglieder im Heraion von Samos [architectural fragments from Doric entablatures]', *Jb. Dt. Archäol. Inst.*, cix (1994), pp. 199–225 [with catalogue]

S. Westphalen: 'Die frühchristliche Basilika im Heraion von Samos und ihre Ausstattung', *Jb. Dt. Archäol. Inst.*, cix (1994), pp. 301–35 [with appendix]

H. Kienast: 'Der Niedergang des Tempels des Theodoros', *Mitt. Dt. Archäol. Inst.: Athen. Abt.*, cxiii (1998), pp. 111–31

B. Kreuzer: *Die attisch schwarzfigurige Keramik aus dem Heraion von Samos* (Bonn, 1998)

H. Kienast and T. Schulz: *Die römischen Tempel im Heraion von Samos* (2002), xxiv of *Samos* (Bonn, 1961–)

2. SCULPTURE. During the 6th century BC Samos was one of the most important centres of production of Greek sculpture. This was partly because of its flourishing economy and partly because of the availability of high-quality marble on Samos and the Fourni islands to the west. Though mainly fragmentary, there are rich finds of sculpture from the Heraion and around the ancient capital, Samos, as well as from the necropolis near Myli and from Misokampos.

The earliest marble sculpture is a fragmentary mid-7th-century BC kore (female figure) from the Heraion. It is of Naxian marble and was probably the work of a Cycladic artist. The first evidence of local workshops is provided by fragments of small korai from the late 7th century BC onwards (Samos, Archaeol. Mus.). These already prefigure the masterpieces of the earlier 6th century BC, which include two over life-size korai from the Heraion (*c.* 570 BC; Paris, Louvre; see fig. 2). Each of these bears the inscribed name of the dedicator, Cheramyes, and both korai together with a kore of similar type made for the same dedicator, the *Kore Holding a Hare* (Berlin, Antikensamml.) and the statue of a kouros of which only the feet and a fragment of the leg with the inscription of Cheramyes are preserved, probably belonged to a group monument of the dedicator's family. The Cheramyes korai are characterized by a successful combination of almost abstract columnar form with subtle modelling and drapery rendered in ornamental linear folds. An important work dating from *c.* 560 BC is the family group signed by the sculptor Geneleos, which stood

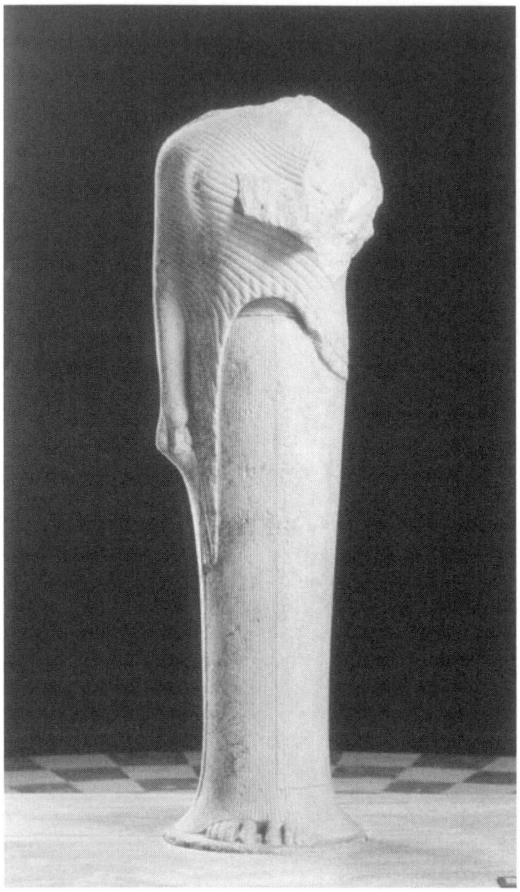

2. Samos, Cheramyes kore, marble, h. 1.92 m, *c.* 570 BC (Paris, Musée du Louvre)

on a rectangular base beside the Sacred Way of the Heraion. Of the original row of statues, the recumbent figure of the donor, the seated figure of his wife, two figures of girls and smaller fragments of two other statues (all without heads) survive and are identified by inscriptions (Berlin, Antikensamml.; Samos, Archaeol. Mus.). The Geneleos group is the only extant large-scale Archaic sculptural group and the only Archaic Samian work signed by its sculptor. Stylistically, these figures mark the transition from the strictly controlled forms of the Cheramyes korai to the more lively korai of the later 6th century BC with elaborately variegated drapery folds, as typified by the *Kore Holding a Bird* (*c.* 540–530 BC; Berlin, Antikensamml.). A statue of an enthroned man in a long robe (*c.* 540 BC), of a type well known from Didyma, is identified by an inscription as Aiakes, possibly the father of the tyrant Polykrates.

The many Samian examples of kouroi (male figures) include some of the most important versions of this type of statue. The series apparently began with colossal statues, including a three-times life-size kouros inscribed on the left thigh with the name of its donor, Isches (*c.* 580 BC; Samos, Archaeol. Mus.). It is the largest extant Greek kouros in this state of preservation, though fragments of a second colossal kouros have been found in the south part of the Heraion. The Isches kouros is also remarkable for its sensuous facial features and powerful modelling. The head of a rather later over life-size kouros is also well preserved (Istanbul, Archaeol. Mus.). Otherwise, only torsos survive, the least damaged being that of a kouros dedicated by Leukios to Apollo (*c.* 560 BC; Samos, Archaeol. Mus.), though several small bronzes give an idea of the appearance of the missing heads. Other notable sculptures include the fragment of a colossal bearded figure found west of the town of Samos (*c.* 540 BC; Samos, Archaeol. Mus.) and the upper part of the figure of a warrior in armour from the Heraion (*c.* 520 BC; Berlin, Antikensamml.). Only a few poros fragments of the friezes from the Late Archaic fourth Temple of Hera survive, but these testify to the excellent quality of Samian architectural sculpture, now largely lost.

The finest Archaic sculpture on Samos was produced *c.* 580–*c.* 530 BC and was stylistically intermediate between works from the Cyclades and from Asia Minor. Its characteristic features are strong three-dimensional forms with gently modelled surfaces and decorative linear treatment of drapery folds and hair. These traits persisted into the Early Classical period (*c.* 480–*c.* 450 BC), though few works remain apart from the torso of an athlete (Samos, Archaeol. Mus.), fragments of some sensitively carved funerary reliefs (Samos, Archaeol. Mus.; Pithagório Mus.) and some fine relief palmettes from grave stelai (Pithagório Mus.). The only extant High Classical sculptures are a beautiful head of an athlete (*c.* 440 BC; Samos, Archaeol. Mus.) and a fragment of an important funerary relief with the figure of a youth (*c.* 420 BC, Samos, Archaeol. Mus.). Part of the base for the bronze group by Myron of Eleutherai representing the *Introduction of Herakles to Olympos* (Strabo: *Geography* XIV.i.14) was found in the Heraion. The rarity of Classical sculpture is probably connected with the political decline of Samos, and no noteworthy sculptures survive from the period of Attic hegemony in the 4th century BC. When Samos regained some economic prosperity in the Hellenistic period, however, its sculptors again produced significant works. These include fragments of draped female figures from statue groups in the Heraion (Samos, Archaeol. Mus., and Berlin, Antikensamml.) and funerary banquet reliefs from the necropolis (Pithagório Mus.; Samos, Archaeol. Mus.; St Petersburg, Hermitage), as well as a few portrait heads. A distinctive Samian style is, however, no longer discernible in these sculptures. Relatively few sculptures from the Roman Imperial period are preserved, but they include some portraits of high quality. Among these are heads of *Augustus* and *Claudius* and a statue of *Trajan* (all in Pithagório Mus.). After the mid-2nd century AD sculpture production on Samos seems to have ceased.

T. Wiegand: 'Antike Skulpturen in Samos', *Mitt. Dt. Archäol. Inst.: Athen. Abt.*, xxv (1900), pp. 145–214

E. Buschor: *Altsamische Standbilder*, i–v (Berlin, 1934–61)

W. H. Schuchhardt: 'Zum grossen Weihrelief in Samos', *Essays in Memory of Karl Lehmann*, ed. L. Freemann Sandler (New York, 1964), pp. 293–9

G. Hiesel: *Samische Steingeräte* (diss., U. Hamburg, 1967)
G. Schmidt: *Kyprische Bildwerke aus dem Heraion von Samos* (1968), vii of *Samos* (Bonn, 1961–)
R. Horn: *Hellenistische Bildwerke auf Samos* (1972), xii of *Samos* (Bonn, 1961–)
B. Freyer-Schauenburg: *Bildwerke der archaischen Zeit und des strengen Stils* (1974), xi of *Samos* (Bonn, 1961–)
H. Kyrieleis: 'Ein samischer Athlet', *Mitt. Dt. Archäol. Inst.: Athen. Abt.*, xciii (1978), pp. 171–9
U. Kron: 'Eine archaische Kore aus dem Heraion von Samos', *Archaische und klassische griechische Plastik: Akten des internationalen Kolloquiums: Athen, 1985*, i, pp. 47–65
H. Kyrieleis: 'Neue archaische Skulpturen aus dem Heraion von Samos', *Archaische und klassische griechische Plastik: Akten des internationalen Kolloquiums: Athen, 1985*, i, pp. 35–45
H. Kienast: 'Die Basis der Geneleos-Gruppe', *Mitt. Dt. Archäol. Inst.: Athen. Abt.*, cvii (1992), pp. 29–42
H. Kyrieleis: *Eine neue Kore des Cheramyes, Ant. Plast.*, xxiv (1995), pp. 7–36
H. Kyrieleis, H. J. Kienast and G. Neumann: *Der grosse Kuros von Samos* (1996), x of *Samos* (Bonn, 1961–)
V. H. Bohm: 'Herkunft geklärt? Die Bronzen von Cartoceto und die Exedra der Ciceronen auf Samos', *Ant. Welt,* xxxi/1 (2000), pp. 9–22
B. Freyer-Schauenburg and others: 'Die Statue des Trajan auf Samos: Mit einem Beitrag von Klaus von Woyski', *Mitt. Dt. Archäol. Inst.: Athen. Abt.,* cxvii (2002), pp. 257–98
U. Gehring: *Die Greifenprotomen aus dem Heraion von Samos* (2004), ix of *Samos* (Bonn, 1961–)

Samothrace. Mountainous Greek island in the north-east Aegean. It was famous in antiquity for its Sanctuary of the Great Gods (see fig.). These included a pre-Greek Great Mother goddess (Axieros, in the native tongue; Gr. Demeter), her spouse (Kadmilos; Gr. Hermes), Axiokersos and Axiokersa (Gr. Hades and Persephone) and attendant daemons (Gr. Kabeiroi or Dioskouroi). The Great Gods were special protectors of those at sea, and through their mysteries the initiate gained protection, moral improvement and probably the hope of immortality. The nocturnal rites were available to men and women, freemen and slaves, a feature unique to Samothrace. Although the initiation buildings were accessible only to initiates, the sanctuary was otherwise open to all visitors. Samothrace was inhabited in Neolithic times and was settled *c.* 700 BC by Greek-speaking colonists from north-west Anatolia or Lesbos. They mingled with the local population, whose original Thracian tongue is documented as the ritual language of the cult until the late 1st century BC. Under the patronage of the Macedonian royal house and Alexander the Great's 'successors', the Sanctuary was embellished with buildings that remained in use until the cult ceased in the late 4th century AD. In the 6th century AD the Sanctuary was destroyed by an earthquake. In the second half of the 19th century the site was excavated by French and Austrian expeditions, then by a Czech–French team in 1923–5. Since 1938 systematic excavations have been conducted by the Institute of Fine Arts, New York University.

1. Architecture. 2. Sculpture.

1. Architecture.

(i) Buildings for initiation ceremonies. The latest remains of the succession of buildings for the initiation into the first degree of the mysteries (*myesis*) are those of the early 1st-century AD Anaktoron (a). This was a rectangular building of polygonal limestone construction, entered through three doors on its western side. White stucco originally covered the walls and piers that supported beams for the roof. The building was divided into two sections: a hall lined at north and east by a wooden grandstand, from which previous initiates witnessed the ceremonies, and a smaller inner chamber accessible only after initiation. In the rear inner corner was a *bothros* (pit) for pouring libations. Nearby was a circular wooden platform on which the initiate sat while dances were performed around him. The inner chamber was closed by a wooden partition, a marble stele outside forbidding any but the initiated to enter. Within it the initiate must have performed some ritual action and been shown sacred symbols. Next to the Anaktoron was the Sacristy (b), a room equipped with benches and with marble stelae in the walls commemorating previous initiates. Here the initiate was prepared for the *myesis* and provided with a lamp for the nocturnal rites.

Only after he had become a *pious mystes* could the initiate acquire the higher degree of *epopteia*. This took place in a second building, the Hieron (c). Its Doric columnar porch, completed in the mid-2nd century BC, gave access to a hall dating from the late 4th century BC. A preliminary outdoor ceremony was conducted near the entrance, where two marble stepping-stones, for the *mystes* and the priest, were separated by a stone for a torch. Here the initiate had to confess his most serious sins and be purified to be eligible for *epopteia*. This requirement was one peculiar to Samothrace. Two lateral doors in the hall allowed access to previous *epoptai*, who sat on marble benches lining the side walls. After performing a lustration rite, the *mystes* sacrificed at a hearth in the central aisle before proceeding to a curtained apse at the rear of the building, where a further ceremony included pouring libations to the underworld gods. The Hieron was built of Thasian marble with walls of drafted-margin masonry, two high courses alternating with a low binding course (a scheme that occurs here for the first time in ancient Greek architecture). The entire building, including the later porch, was crowned by a Doric entablature topped by a *rinceau* gutter with lion's-head waterspouts and palmette antefixes. Inside, the building terminated in an apse, invisible from the rectangular temple-like exterior. The interior walls were stuccoed to reflect the drafted-margin masonry of the exterior, and painted scarlet with a black dado and white upper section. Wooden coffers and beams concealed the trussed roof, and the floor was of marble. The Hieron was repaired after an earthquake in the early 1st century AD. Later,

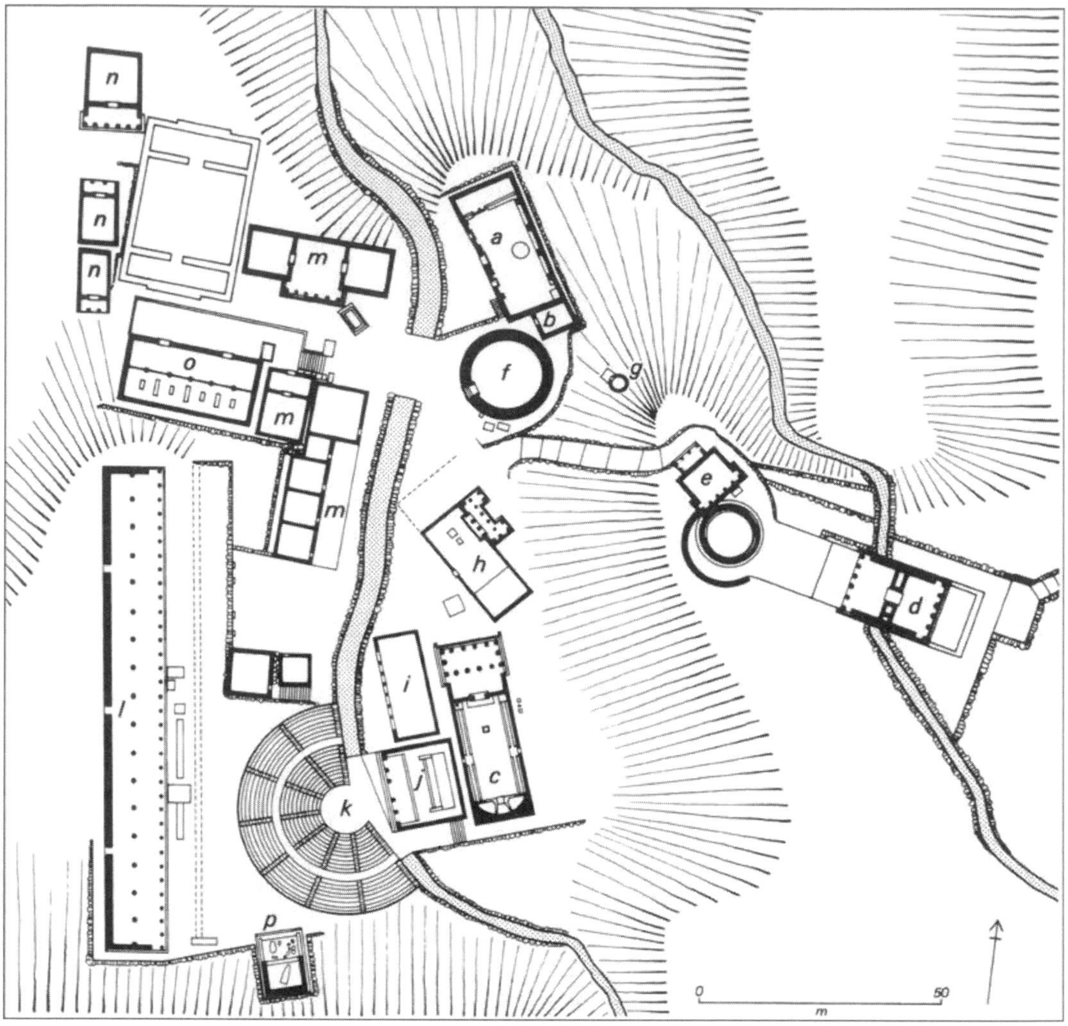

Samothrace, Plan of the Sanctuary of the Great Gods, 1st century AD: (a) Anaktoron; (b) Sacristy; (c) Hieron; (d) Propylon of Ptolemy II; (e) Doric building dedicated by Philip III and Alexander IV; (f) Rotunda of Arsinoe; (g) Doric rotunda; (h) Temenos; (i) Hall of Votive Gifts; (j) Altar Court; (k) Theatre; (l) Stoa; (m) dining-rooms; (n) treasury-like buildings; (o) Warship building; (p) *Nike* fountain

c. AD 200, a crypt was installed in the apse for the introduction of new rites, the *kriobolia* and *taurobolia* (ram- and bull-slaying) of the Magna Mater, a divinity equivalent to the Samothracian Axieros. Within the apse, traces were found of two predecessors of the 4th-century building, one 5th century BC, the other Archaic.

(ii) Other buildings. After 275 BC the Sanctuary was entered from the east through the Propylon of Ptolemy II (d), a marble gateway dedicated to the Great Gods by its donor. Its exterior Ionic porch faced the ancient city of Palaiopolis; its interior Corinthian porch faced the Sanctuary. This was the first use in Greek architecture of the Corinthian order as a structural member. The porches were separated by a wall with a double door and a chamber to the left and right of the single portal. Over the banded architrave, the frieze was carved with alternating bucrania (bull's-head decorations) and rosettes topped by dentils, a cornice and a gutter with lion's-head waterspouts. Its limestone substructure contains an oblique barrel-vaulted tunnel spanning the torrent that formed the eastern boundary of the sanctuary. Originally the Propylon of Ptolemy was linked to the Eastern Hill by a causeway; later, after the 1st-century AD earthquake, by a wooden bridge.

Between the Propylon of Ptolemy and the Eastern Hill was a Doric building (e) dedicated between 323 and 317 BC by Philip III Arrhidaios, Alexander the Great's half-brother and eventual successor, and his son, Alexander IV. This had an Ionic porch added at the rear, perhaps for the display of statues. From here the processional road led to the sanctuary proper, forking towards the Rotunda of Arsinoe on the right, and the Propylon to the Temenos on the left. The Rotunda (f), dedicated to the Great Gods *c.* 275 BC by Queen Arsinoe II of Egypt, lies just south of the Anaktoron. It is the largest closed circular building or tholos in ancient Greek architecture (for illustration *see* THOLOS). The circular marble drum was topped by a course of carved anthemia (plant ornaments) and palmettes, echoing its base moulding. On the exterior, below the Doric entablature, a gallery of pilasters separated by parapets was decorated with rosettes between bucrania. On the interior, Corinthian half-columns were separated by parapets carved with bucrania and paterae (round vessels). The drum, dressed smooth on the exterior, had on the interior drafted-margin masonry above the dado. The floor was of earth. The conical roof was originally covered with scale-shaped tiles. After the earthquake its timbers were altered and the roof was converted into an octagonal pyramid crowned by a marble finial. Directly to the east of the Rotunda of Arsinoe stood a tiny late 4th-century BC Doric Rotunda (g), which appears to have been a cenotaph.

The Temenos (h) was an open-air precinct, again with a hearth and *bothros*. To its north-east side was attached an Ionic Propylon, built *c.* 340 BC as a donation by Philip II of Macedon. Its colonnaded façade consisted of a central section flanked by projecting wings, from which three doors led into the Temenos. The columns were crowned with richly carved drums, and the entablature (a banded architrave, frieze, dentils, cornice-gutter) is the earliest known example of a scheme destined to become standard in later Ionic and Corinthian architecture. The frieze was decorated with dancing maidens and musicians in an archaizing style, and the coffers of the ceiling were also sculpted. The designing architect–sculptor of the propylon may have been SKOPAS.

To the west of the Hieron stood the Archaic Hall of Votive Gifts (i) and the Altar Court (j). The hall, a rectangular limestone building, stuccoed on both exterior and interior, had a Doric colonnade on one long side. The Altar Court, an open enclosure containing an altar, had as its façade a marble Doric colonnade attached to walls of stuccoed limestone. Metal grilles and doors linked the columns. The inscribed architrave names Philip III Arrhidaios as dedicator. The Altar Court faced the Theatre (k), built *c.* 200 BC. The Western Hill is dominated by the Stoa (l), the largest building in the Sanctuary, erected in the first half of the 3rd century BC to shelter pilgrims. Built of limestone covered with white stucco, its façade of Doric columns and entablature contrasted with its inner Ionic order, and its walls were stuccoed and painted red, white and blue-grey. Inscriptions listing initiates were incised on the walls. Here, the *rinceau* gutter, waterspouts and antefixes were of terracotta rather than the marble employed on the other buildings. To the north and north-east of the Stoa lay a series of dining-rooms (m) erected in the 4th and 3rd centuries BC, and to the north, near a group of treasury-like buildings (n), stood a rectangular Hellenistic structure housing a warship (o). This was divided by a colonnade and grille, and lighted by large windows. The ship was contained in the inner section and viewed by spectators through the grille. Only one comparable structure is known, the Neorion ('Monument of the Bulls') on Delos. The dedicator of both the ship and building was apparently Antigonos Gonatas, king of Macedon from 276 to 239 BC.

2. SCULPTURE. The most famous work from the island is the NIKE OF SAMOTHRACE found in 1863 (3rd century BC). Of Parian marble, the *Nike* is shown with wings spread wide, as if having alighted on the prow of a grey marble warship. It originally formed part of a fountain, with the ship set in water in an open horseshoe-shaped enclosure. Part of the right hand of the *Nike*, which had been held aloft in a gesture of greeting, was discovered in 1950 (Paris, Louvre). The archaizing frieze of dancing maidens and musicians from the Propylon to the Temenos (*c.* 340 BC; Samothrace, Archaeol. Mus.) is the earliest example of this style in Greek sculpture. In the coffers of the ceiling divinities, legendary figures and 'heroic' initiates honoured in the sanctuary were represented. Sculptures from the northern pediment of the Hieron represent the *Nurturing of Aetion* (the legendary infant destined to establish the Samothracian mysteries; mostly in Vienna, Ksthist. Mus.). The southern pediment contained busts of the Great Gods worshipped in the Sanctuary, and sculptures in the coffers of the porch chiefly represent centaurs. Acroteria embellished both pediments, openwork sculptures of acanthus leaves, stalks, flowers and palmettes at the apex (the best-preserved floral acroteria in ancient Greek sculpture), and at the sides draped, winged figures pouring libations in honour of the life-giving power symbolized by the floral acroteria.

K. Lehmann: *Samothrace: A Guide to the Excavations and the Museum* (Locust Valley, NY, 1955, rev. 6/1998)

P. W. Lehmann and others: *Samothrace,* 11 vols (Princeton, 1958–96)

P. W. Lehmann and K. Lehmann: *Samothracian Reflections* (Princeton, 1973)

S. G. Cole: *Theoi Megaloi: The Cult of the Great Gods at Samothrace* (Leiden, 1984)

J. Bouzek and others: *Samothrace: 1923, 1927, 1978* (Prague, 1985)

N. M. Dimitrova: *Theoroi and Initiates in Samothrace* (diss., Ithaca, NY, Cornell U., 2002)

A. J. Graham: 'The Colonization of Samothrace', *Hesperia,* lxxi/3 (July–Sept 2002), pp. 231–60

N. Dimitrova and others: 'An Archaic Inscription from Samothrace', *Hesperia,* lxxii/2 (April–June 2003), pp. 235–9

San Giovenale. Site of an Etruscan town on a tufa plateau *c.* 15 km south-west of Viterbo, Italy. Some scholars have identified it as ancient Contenebra.

Both the town and its necropolises have been excavated by the Swedish Institute at Rome. The earliest evidence of habitation dates from the Middle Bronze Age, and by the Late Bronze Age there was a village of large oval huts. This was succeeded during the Early Iron Age by a village of similar oval-plan huts. The main building phase of the Etruscan town began around 700 BC and was characterized by houses with rectangular plans, tufa block foundations, walls of *opus craticium* (wattle and daub on a timber framework) and drainage channels. The plan of one house shows clear similarities with that of the Tomb of the Thatched Roof, Caere (Cerveteri; early 7th century BC), and pottery finds, both from the town and the necropolises (the most important of which is the Porzarago), reveal strong Caeretan influences: like the nearby Tolfa mountains, San Giovenale probably came under the political and economic sway of Caere. In the 5th century BC the acropolis hill was enclosed by a defensive wall, but the town already appears to have been in decline. It was eventually abandoned after the Roman conquest of Etruria during the 3rd century BC. As at many Etruscan sites, fortifications were later built at San Giovenale in medieval times, and the remains of a 13th-century castle surmount those of 4th-century BC walls.

Etruscan Culture, Land and People: Archaeological Research and Studies Conducted in San Giovenale and its Environs by Members of the Swedish Institute in Rome (New York, 1962)

San Giovenale: Materiali e problemi (Stockholm, 1984)

Architettura etrusca nel viterbese: Ricerche svedesi a San Giovenale e Acquarossa, 1956–1986: Viterbo, 1986

Sanctuary. Term derived from the Latin *sanctuarium* (holy place); it is used in Classical contexts to denote a sacred precinct (anc. Gr. *temenos*) and the buildings belonging to it. Greek and Roman sanctuaries were areas where worshippers performed religious rituals, particularly offerings of animals or other food. This generally required an altar on which the parts offered to the god were burnt or, in the case of certain chthonic deities, a pit. The sanctuary needed sufficient space for worshippers to watch the ritual, and the whole area had to be clearly demarcated, though not necessarily walled or fenced. Within this area special religious laws and taboos prevailed: human death, whether violent or natural, was sacrilege and the terminally ill might be removed; but fugitives could seek asylum there, notably at the altar (a custom that later prevailed in Christian churches). The deity was usually represented by an image, generally a statue of a conventionalized form, which was normally housed in a richly decorated temple, according to the resources of the cult. Even at the height of Roman prosperity, however, statues in many sanctuaries were set in simple shrines or in the open air, and deities were sometimes represented in other ways. The existence of early phases in a sanctuary is often indicated by the discovery of offerings, rather than structures, and it is clear that in many cases the establishment of a sanctuary considerably pre-dates its architectural development.

1. FUNCTION AND DEVELOPMENT. Offerings to the gods ranged from sculpture, paintings and valuable objects, such as gold and silver cups, to various curios (e.g. the tusks of the Kalydonian Boar at Tegea; see Pausanias: *Guide to Greece* VIII.xlvi.2), humble pottery vessels and figurines representing human worshippers. All offerings required space, and those valuable or perishable (for example the ropes used by Xerxes to build his bridge of boats across the Hellespont for his invasion of Greece in 480 BC) needed shelter. Many valuable objects were kept in the temples, which became veritable storehouses and may even have served as city treasuries: Athens' financial reserves were stored in the Parthenon, and the Temple of Saturn at Rome was called the 'Treasury of Saturn' (aerarium Saturni). Other objects could be kept in specially constructed buildings: several Greek sanctuaries contain such TREASURY buildings. These were themselves offerings, in addition to the offerings they contained, and were generally made to deities in sanctuaries of universal importance (e.g. Delphi and Olympia) as tokens of gratitude from individual cities. Other buildings included extended porticos (*see* STOA), which provided shelter both for offerings and worshippers.

Other aspects of cult sometimes required special architectural arrangements. For example, the oracular sanctuaries, which were particularly important in the Archaic period (*c.* 600–480 BC), but often continued to flourish under the Roman Empire, needed to accommodate both the oracle itself, which was often housed within the temple, and those wishing to consult it. Ritual usually included a procession to the sanctuary, and this might require assembly buildings at some distance from it. Gateways (*see* PROPYLON) emphasized the transition from secular to sacred, and Roman sanctuaries often had a single closable entrance. Sanctuaries of healing deities such as Asklepios might require dormitories to enable the sick to sleep close to the temple (as at EPIDAUROS), so that the god could easily visit them. Healing cults were popular and widespread in the Roman Empire, and, for these and other similar cults, water was an essential element. Their sanctuaries were often situated at abundant sources, thermal sources being particularly lavishly developed by the Romans. Their sanctuaries often contained structures for storage and access to water supplies.

Contests were another prominent element of Greek and Roman cult. Athletic competitions were important from early times, the first Olympic games traditionally being held in 776 BC. They were not restricted to the most prestigious sanctuaries, such as Olympia, but were widespread. At first they were simply held on open ground, adjacent to the sanctuary or nearby, rather than actually within the sacred area; but gradually formal structures were developed to accommodate them, ranging from stoas surrounding the competition area to genuine stadia (*see* STADIUM) with stone seating and even larger hippodromes for chariot racing. The contests varied considerably. They normally included all-in wrestling, throwing the discus and racing in full armour. Particularly in Italy and Rome, however, they also involved gladiatorial combats between individuals or groups; these acquired a distinctive architectural setting, the AMPHITHEATRE. Such combats probably originated in some form of sacrificial ritual, despite their later secular nature under the Roman Empire, though the miasma of human death meant that the place of combat always lay outside the sanctuary proper (*see also* CIRCUS). Contests of music and dance were also held. Again, space was the first requirement: a floor for the contestants and room for the spectators, and specialized theatres and music halls (*see* ODEION) were constructed from at least the 5th century BC. These were usually attached to the sanctuaries, as with the theatre of Dionysos (original structure rebuilt in stone 342–326 BC) and odeion of Pericles (?shortly before 446 BC) on the south slopes of the Acropolis at Athens, although, like the other ancillary areas, they often lay outside the main sacred precinct. Geographical constraints, however, such as the need for a hillside to support the auditorium, occasionally necessitated greater separation.

2. LAYOUT. The architectural arrangement of sanctuaries varied considerably. When present, temples generally faced east, often towards the specific point on the skyline at which the sun rose during their annual festivals. Their orientation, therefore, imposed some order on the plans of sanctuaries.

The altar was generally directly in front of the temple, to allow the cult image in the temple to view the sacrifice. Etruscan temples, which inspired those at Rome, often stood on a podium fronted by steps, rather than standing on a platform with steps on all four sides, as did Greek temples. This strong frontal emphasis explains the axial arrangement typical of Roman sanctuary plans. Conversely, the axiality of Greek sanctuaries is normally confined to the temple–altar alignment, and even this is not universal. The altar of Zeus at Olympia substantially pre-dates both the early 6th-century BC Temple of Hera and the 5th-century BC Temple of Zeus and is aligned with neither. Instead, it constitutes in itself the focal point for the sanctuary. Where the altar is in fact aligned with the temple, it is often close to the temple façade, as at the Temple of Aphaia, Aigina (early 5th century BC). In Roman sanctuaries the intervening space is frequently small; indeed, several extant altars are incorporated in the steps of the podium.

The disposition of other structures appears to have been more in accordance with their religious significance than with aesthetic principles. Processional routes extended inside larger sanctuaries, and probably served to link specific areas where ritual acts, such as the singing of hymns in the procession at Epidauros, traditionally took place, although the religious importance of such areas is not always archaeologically attested. Monuments were also often placed so as to be viewed from the processional route, as is apparent at Olympia and, most clearly, on the zigzagging Sacred Way in the Sanctuary of Apollo at Delphi. The route of the Sacred Way might also determine the placing of viewing stands: tiers of steps apparently accommodated those watching the procession at the Argive Heraion (Sanctuary of Hera), and there were tiered steps or benches in the forecourt to the original gateway of the Athenian Acropolis.

In Greek sanctuaries the temples generally stood near the centre, so that they could be viewed from all sides, particularly if they were major buildings with peristyle colonnades. The locations of sanctuary entrances vary, therefore, and often seem determined by external factors, such as the approach route. One example is the entrance to the Acropolis at Athens, which was sited to exploit the easier gradients of the west slope, with the result that approaching worshippers saw the back of the Parthenon rather than its front. Consequently, the west end of the Parthenon was as magnificently decorated as the east, and the back of the Temple of Athena Nike, which also faced the entrance to the sanctuary, was given an Ionic façade, despite its cramped situation. Elsewhere, entrances sometimes afforded a three-quarter view of the temple, and, though this may have been unintentional, it argues against a predilection for an axial approach.

From the Hellenistic period (323–27 BC), contacts with the East and the increased role of urban planning prompted the development of more formal sanctuary layouts. Egyptian and Near Eastern religious and architectural traditions possibly influenced the elaborate terracing and imposing central stairways of the Sanctuary of Asklepios on Kos (enlarged 2nd century BC). In the Sanctuary of the Syrian gods on Delos (2nd century BC), Near Eastern influence is unmistakable: the architectural focus is not a traditional Greek temple but a theatre-like structure from which worshippers presumably observed religious enactments (though Greek theatres themselves had religious associations). The most elaborate example of Oriental influence is found in the Sanctuary of Fortuna Primigenia at PRAENESTE (late 2nd or early 1st century BC), which has no conventional temple but instead a combination of staircases, ramps and a small viewing stand, undoubtedly inspired by Hellenistic Syrian architecture.

More importantly, Hellenistic urban planners made increasing use of the enclosed courtyard surrounded on all four sides by stoas, particularly in such cities as Miletos and Priene that had been newly laid out on Hippodamian grid patterns; these enclosed spaces also became a feature of sanctuary planning, as at the Sanctuary of Artemis Leukophyrene at Magnesia on the Maeander, in Ionia. Here a Hellenistic grid-plan city developed around a much older temple. Though the temple was rebuilt in the 2nd century BC, it did not conform with the layout of the streets. Nonetheless, it was, or was to be, completely surrounded by a regular courtyard with stoas at right angles to each other on three sides, and a building belonging to the agora on the fourth, running slightly askew to conform to the street plan. The temple stood at the east end of the courtyard with a large open area in front containing the altar and an axially aligned entrance leading from the agora at the west end.

Such formal arrangements suited Roman sanctuaries, which had a traditional axial emphasis (see above). Some temples—for example those scattered around the Forum Romanum—were placed in the open in the Greek manner, but the combination of temple and colonnaded courtyard soon predominated. The Temple of Venus Genetrix dedicated by Julius Caesar and completed by Augustus had such a courtyard, known as the Forum Julium. Augustus later built a similar forum, at right angles to it, with a temple to Mars the Avenger. In both, the temple stood at the rear of the courtyard, which became in effect a forecourt, an arrangement that suited the frontal emphasis of Roman temples. Not all Roman temples were positioned in this way, and the Hellenistic Greek tradition continued particularly in eastern areas, for example at Baalbek and Gerasa.

See also ARCHITECTURE, §§IV, 1(i)(a) and 2, VI, 1(i)(a); *and* PLANNING, §§I, 1 and II, 1.

A. Furtwängler, E. R. Fiechter and H. Thiersch: *Aegina: Das Heiligtum der Aphaia* (Munich, 1906)

T. Wiegand, ed.: *Baalbek*, 3 vols (Berlin and Leipzig, 1921–5)

R. M. Dawkins, ed.: *The Sanctuary of Artemis Orthia at Sparta* (London, 1929)

D. M. Krencker and W. Zschietzschmann: *Römische Tempel in Syrien* (Berlin and Leipzig, 1938)

H. Payne and others: *Perachora: The Sanctuaries of Hera Akraia and Limenia*, i (Oxford, 1940)

F. Fasolo and G. Gullini: *Il santuario della Fortuna Primigenia a Palestrina* (Rome, 1953)

A. W. Lawrence: *Greek Architecture*, Pelican Hist. A. (Harmondsworth, 1957, 4/1983)

P. Bruneau and J. Ducat: *Guide de Délos* (Paris, 1965)

B. Bergquist: *The Archaic Greek Temenos* (Lund, 1967)

R. J. Hopper: *The Acropolis* (London, 1971)

A. Mallwitz: *Olympia und seine Bauten* (Munich, 1971)

P. Zanker: *Forum Romanum* (Tübingen, 1972)

R. A. Tomlinson: *Greek Sanctuaries* (London, 1976)

J. B. Ward Perkins: *Roman Imperial Architecture*, Pelican Hist. A. (Harmondsworth, 1981)

R. A. Tomlinson: *Epidauros* (London, 1983)

J. G. Pedley, M. Torelli and T.V. Buttrey: *The Sanctuary of Santa Venera at Paestum* (Rome, 1993–)

N. Bookidis and R. S. Stroud: *The Sanctuary of Demeter and Kore [at Corinth]: Topography and Architecture* (Princeton, 1997)

W. E. Mierse: *Temples and Towns in Roman Iberia: The Social and Architectural Dynamics of Sanctuary Designs from the Third Century BC to the Third Century AD* (Berkeley, 1999)

E. Bispham and C. J. Smith: *Religion in Archaic and Republican Rome and Italy: Evidence and Experience* (Edinburgh, 2000)

M. Yeroulanou: *The Architecture of Greek Treasures and Other Foreign Dedications: Stylistic Developments and the Role of Dedicating States and Workshops* (diss., U. Oxford, 2001)

P. Richardson: *City and Sanctuary: Religion and Architecture in the Roman Near East* (London, 2002)

M. Stamatopoulou and M. Yeroulanou: *Excavating Classical Culture: Recent Archaeological Discoveries in Greece* (Oxford, 2002)

Santa Maria Capua Vetere. *See* CAPUA.

Santa Severa. *See* PYRGI.

Santiponce. *See* ITALICA.

Santorini. *See* THERA.

Sarcophagus. Chest for inhumation. The term (from anc. Gr. *sarkophagous*: 'flesh eating', from a type of limestone thought to consume the bodies laid in it) is generally applied to substantial or decorated types of coffin, of which there are examples from many different contexts worldwide.

1. Greek. 2. Etruscan. 3. Roman Empire.

1. GREEK. The earliest sarcophagi in the Greek world are the Bronze Age larnakes of Late Minoan Crete. From the 14th century BC, these coffins were shaped as rectangular chests with low feet and pitched lids. Mostly of terracotta, they are thought to derive from wooden storage chests, and many were painted with figural scenes comparable to contemporary vase decoration. On mainland Greece an outstanding group of Mycenaean terracotta larnakes of the 13th–12th century BC was found at Tanagra (Thebes Mus.). Many are decorated with scenes of funeral rites, vividly painted in black and red on a white slip.

From the 9th century BC, inhumation was practised in Greece alongside the more common rite of cremation. Sarcophagi were a relatively rare and expensive alternative to cists. Greek sarcophagi were of marble, limestone or terracotta, and many were stuccoed or plastered and painted. Too heavy for carrying the body of the deceased to the tomb, they were not intended to be seen by visitors to the grave. The most distinctive of regional types are the terracotta sarcophagi from Klazomenai (now in Western Turkey). These were made of rough clay of the sort used for tiles and painted with figural decoration, almost all in the Black-figure technique, on the upper rim of the chest. The workshops remained active *c.* 550–*c.* 450 BC.

A much more cosmopolitan mixture of styles is found in sarcophagi from the royal cemeteries of Phoenicia. The tombs of the kings of Sidon (Lebanon) contained anthropoid sarcophagi of 5th-century BC date made of imported Egyptian basalt and shaped like Egyptian mummy-cases. Other cemeteries in the area have yielded anthropoid sarcophagi in marble, probably imported from Paros (Beirut, Mus. N.), and an impressive array of other royal sarcophagi of imported Greek marble was also excavated at Sidon (Istanbul, Archaeol. Mus.). These include a chest decorated with scenes portraying a Persian satrap, a figured sarcophagus of the Lycian type with an ogival roof (*c.* 400 BC), and more Hellenized chests of later 4th-century BC date, including the Sarcophagus of the Mourning Women and the Alexander Sarcophagus. As on earlier larnakes, scenes of hunting and funerary rites were popular subjects for decoration, in these cases carved in relief and painted.

Regional types include Lycian sarcophagi, which reproduce in local stone the characteristic local forms of timber construction. From Cyprus there are examples of anthropoid and other sarcophagi in local stone decorated with local motifs, and wooden sarcophagi are known from Egypt and the Crimea. The Phoenicians' taste for anthropoid sarcophagi extended to their dependencies in the western Mediterranean, where the chests were made of imported marble (probably Parian) or terracotta. Sarcophagus lids of Parian marble, decorated with figures of Phoenician priests or votaries, are known from Carthaginian and Etruscan tombs. The 4th-century BC trade in chests and lids of Parian marble ranged from the Black Sea to Spain, anticipating the much better known Roman Imperial trade in half-finished sarcophagi from north Aegean island quarries.

F. Matz and B. Andreae, eds: *Die antiken Sarkophagreliefs* (Berlin, 1890-)

D. C. Kurtz and J. Boardman: *Greek Burial Customs* (London and Ithaca, 1971), pp. 267–72

V. von Graeve: 'Der Alexandersarkophag und seine Werkstatt', *Istanbul Forsch.*, xxviii (1978) [whole issue]

R. Fleischer: 'Der Klagefrauensarkophag aus Sidon', *Istanbul. Forsch.*, xxxiv (1983), pp. 48–62

A. Schmidt-Dounas: 'Der lykische Sarkophag aus Sidon', *Istanbul. Mitt.*, suppl. 30 (1985) [whole issue]

A. Pasinli: *The Book of Alexander Sarcophagus* (Istanbul, 1997)

M.-T. Langer-Karrenbrock: *Der lykische Sarkophag aus der Königsnekropole von Sidon* (Münster, 2000)

E. E. Perry: 'Iconography and the Dynamics of Patronage: A Sarcophagus from the Family of Herodes Atticus', *Hesperia*, lxx/4 (Oct–Dec 2001), pp. 461–92

L. Atkins: *The Amazon Sarcophagus* (diss.,Tallahassee, FL State U., 2002)

B. Burke: 'Materialization of Mycenaean Ideology and the Ayia Triada Sarcophagus', *Amer. J. Archaeol.*, cix/3 (July 2005), pp. 403–22

2. Etruscan. There was a long tradition of decorated sarcophagi in the southern cities of Etruria, where inhumation had been the custom since the 7th century BC. In some cities in northern Etruria, such as Volterra, where cremation was practised, no sarcophagi were produced, while at Clusium the two rites coexisted. Etruscan sarcophagi were of painted terracotta or local stone (nenfro). The deceased was often portrayed supine or reclining on the lid, sometimes with a spouse. Some chests formed a supporting bed, while others were decorated with mythological or dramatic scenes including Homeric subjects such as the monster Scylla, a popular figure in Hellenistic funerary art. Some chests were simply rough-finished. Although the production of sarcophagi in Etruria was very localized, the influence of Hellenistic Greek art is clearly evident on later chests and cinerary urns. Sarcophagi ceased to be produced in Etruria when the area came under Roman administration.

See also Sculpture, §V, 3.

3. Roman Empire. Apart from a few noble families, such as the Scipii, most Romans practised cremation. A few plain sarcophagi of early Imperial date are known from Rome. These were of Carrara marble in the form of long low boxes with incised decoration on the lid. In the 2nd century AD the dominant rite changed to inhumation and sarcophagi became more fashionable, with many of the features of Etruscan sarcophagi and cinerary urns revived at Rome. Like their Etruscan predecessors, Roman sarcophagi were displayed in alcoves and were therefore carved only on the front and sides. The long, low box remained popular, with the lid flat or lightly ridged and a decorative panel along the front.

Since the Romans did not have a strong religious belief in life after death, the decoration on their sarcophagi was often concerned with cultural interests rather than intimations of death or life beyond the grave. They shared the Etruscan taste for scenes from Greek mythology and drama; Bacchic scenes were popular, while other subjects, such as Medea slaying her children, appear inappropriate for funerary use. Sarcophagi made at Rome often depict the lives of their occupants, which may be represented by conventionalized biographies, genre scenes of childhood, or scenes of civic and imperial ceremonies. In the 3rd century AD portraits of individuals in reclining poses appeared on the lids of some *lenoi* (vat-shaped chests) and on the chests of a much wider group of sarcophagi. Most portraits were set in medallions or frames, but some individuals were portrayed in mythological scenes: the sleeping shepherd Endymion was a popular subject.

Sarcophagi were revived at the same time in the Greek-speaking eastern provinces of the Empire. As in Bronze Age and later Greek art, forms were localized, but production was now based at a number of marble quarries. The main centres were Athens (Pentelic marble), Thasos, Prokonnesos and Dokimeion (Phrygia), and several local workshops are also known, especially in western Asia Minor. By the end of the 2nd century AD, chests and lids were exported to Mediterranean destinations: thus the north Aegean island quarries of Thasos and Prokonnesos became the principal suppliers of roughed-out chests to Rome, apparently supplanting the Carrara quarries in this respect. In the Greek-speaking provinces of the eastern Roman Empire, Athens supplied Greece, Crete, Cyrenaica and Lycia; Prokonnesos supplied Thrace and the Black Sea coast, southern Asia Minor, the Levant coast and Alexandria. There was apparently little overlap between the markets for finished and unfinished sarcophagi.

The eastern centres mostly produced large sarcophagi designed to be seen from all sides. In the 2nd century AD gabled lids were fashionable, and many chests were decorated with garlands resembling those hung on altars, expressing the sacred status accorded in Roman law to containers of human remains. Vignettes or portrait busts were often carved above the garlands, but scenes from myth and epic gradually became more popular. Reclining figures appeared on the lids of Attic and Asiatic sarcophagi by the end of the 2nd century AD (see fig. 1). The chests of Attic sarcophagi took the form of beds, often with carved legs or caryatids at the corners to support the lids. The characteristic form from Dokimeion was an articulated columnar façade, with figures set on low pedestals between the columns in narrative sequence, imitating the decoration of public buildings. These were the most sumptuous of contemporary sarcophagi; some were exported as far as Italy, and many imitations were made in more easily available marble. Visual references to the tomb are frequent in sarcophagi of all types: doors and altars appear in scenes on chests, and griffins, the traditional tomb guardians, occur with torches or candelabra as subsidiary decoration.

Fine sarcophagi were made at Rome throughout the troubled years of the 3rd century AD (see fig. 2), though the Attic workshops seem to have ceased production following the Herulian raids on Athens in 267. From the later 3rd century, sarcophagi were made for Christian burials, and the Carrara workshops at Rome revived, producing small-scale chests decorated with Christian scenes. Pagan motifs were ingeniously adapted for Christian use, and many pagan sarcophagi were reused, especially those decorated with strigil-shaped channels and lion's head protomes, which were apparently inoffensive to Christians.

See also SCULPTURE, §VI, 1(iv)(b).

F. Matz and B. Andreae, eds: *Die antiken Sarkophagreliefs* (Berlin, 1890-)

G. Koch and H. Sichtermann: *Römische Sarkophage* (Munich, 1982)

M. Waelkens: *Dokimeion: Die Werkstatt der repräsentativen kleinasiatischen Sarkophagen*, Deutsches Archäologisches Institut: Archäologische Forschungen, xi (Berlin, 1982)

E. S. Malbon: *The Iconography of the Sarcophagus of Junius Bassus* (Princeton, 1990)

A. T. Christ: *The Sarcophagus of Junius Bassus: Patron, Workshop, and Program* (diss., U. Chicago, 1992)

M. L. Woodhull: *The Deer Hunters Sarcophagus at the San Antonio Museum of Art: An Exploration of Carving Techniques and Style* (diss., Austin, U. TX, 1993)

F. G. J. M. Müller: *The So-called Peleus and Thetis Sarcophagus in the Villa Albani* (Amsterdam, 1994)

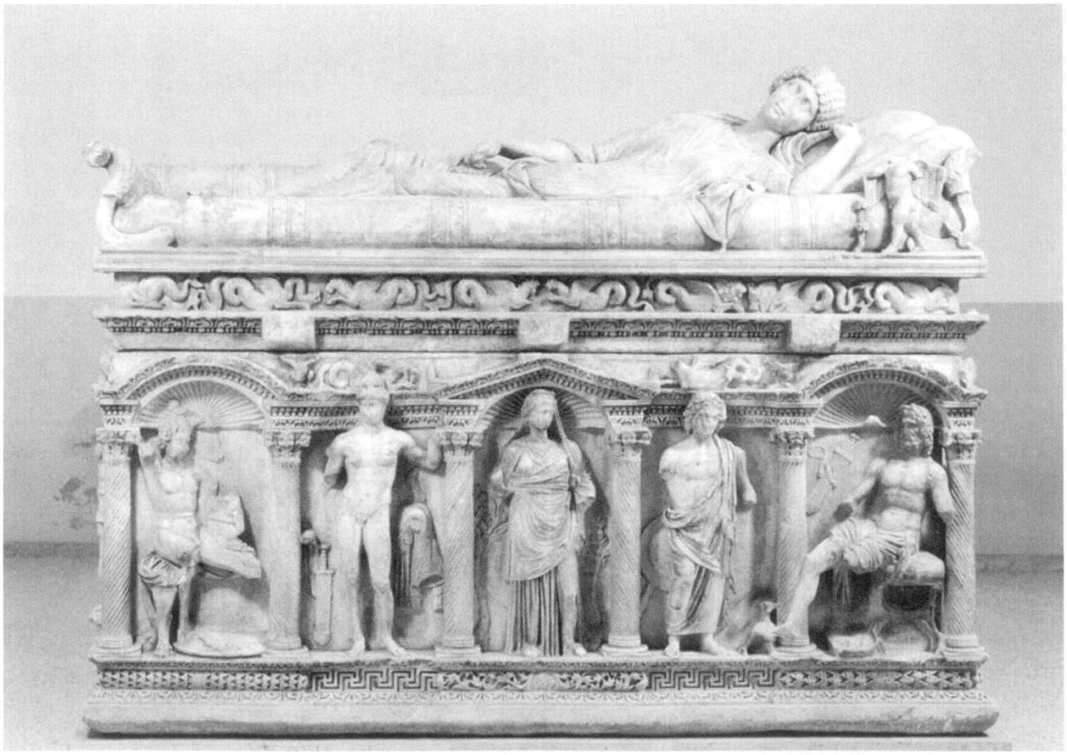

1. Roman sarcophagus of a woman, from Rapolla, Italy, marble, h. 1.7 m, *c.* AD 165–170 (Melfi, Museo Nazionale Archeologico del Melfese)

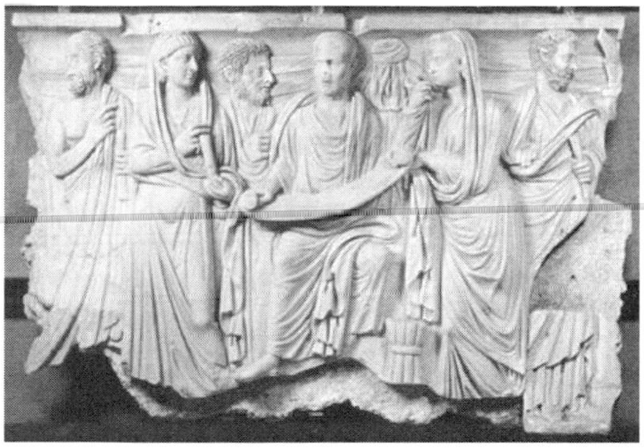

2. Roman sarcophagus of ?*Plotinus,* marble, h. 1.5 m, *c.* AD 270–80 (Rome, Vatican, Museo Gregoriano Profano)

M. Koortbojian: *Myth, Meaning, and Memory on Roman Sarcophagi* (Berkeley, 1995)

F. Giraud: 'Le Serment d'Adonis sur un Sarcophage Romain Conservé au Musée du Louvre', *Ant. Kst,* xlv (2002), pp. 80–85

R. Bielfeldt: 'Orest im Medusengrab: Ein Versuch zum Betrachter', *Mitt. Dt. Archäol. Inst.: Röm. Abt.,* cx (2003), pp. 117–50

S. Bohm: 'Ein früher Girlandensarkophag in Arles: Kleinasiatisches Formengut in der Gallia Narbonensis', *Mitt. Dt. Archäol. Inst.: Röm. Abt.,* cx (2003), pp. 287–301

M. Immerzeel: 'A Day at the Sarcophagus Workshop', *Visual Resources,* xix/1 (March 2003), pp. 43–55

F. G. J. M. Müller: 'New Arms for Achilles: The So-Called Peleus and Thetis Sarcophagus in the Villa Albani Reconsidered', *Mitt. Dt. Archäol. Inst.: Röm. Abt.*, cx (2003), pp. 85–115

E. Angelicoussis: 'Sarcophagi from Ince Blundell Hall', *Mitt. Dt. Archäol. Inst.: Röm. Abt.,* cxi (2004), pp. 239–78

P. Zanker and B. C. Ewald: *Mit Mythen leben: Die Bilderwelt der römischen Sarkophage* (Munich, 2004)

Sardis [now Sart]. City at the foot of Mt Tmolus (now Boz Dağ) in western Turkey; it was the capital of the Lydian kingdom (7th and 6th centuries BC) and subsequently flourished in Greek and Roman times.

1. ARCHITECTURE. The Lydian city under King Croesus (*reg c.* 560–546 BC) fell to Cyrus of Persia in 547 BC. Its most notable architectural remains are the royal tombs of Bin Tepe, enormous earthen mounds covering chambers of finely tooled and precisely fitted limestone or marble blocks (Hipponax: frag. 42; Herodotus: *Histories* I.xciii), while remains of terraces on the north and north-east slopes of the acropolis display masonry of comparable quality (*see* LYDIA). The city itself, however, which extended into the valley of the gold-bearing Paktolos River, was an agglomeration of mud-brick houses (Herodotus: V.ci.1; Pliny: *Natural History* V.xxx.110). A 6th-century BC monumental mud-brick structure on a 20-m-thick stone socle may belong to its defences, since it resembles the contemporary walls of Babylon.

The Temple of Artemis in the Paktolos Valley shows that the city had become fully Hellenized by the early 3rd century BC. This pseudo-dipteral building with columns 17.8 m high was the fourth largest Greek Ionic temple (*c.* 99.2×45.7 m) and displays superb workmanship in marble, although it was never finished. Its cella was divided into two, apparently in the reign of Antoninus Pius (*reg* AD 138–61), to accommodate the Roman Imperial cult. In AD 17 a devastating earthquake levelled Sardis, and the Emperor Tiberius (*reg* AD 14–37) initiated a redevelopment programme (Tacitus: *Annals* II.xlvii). Following the alignment of its Hellenistic predecessor, a marble-paved east–west colonnaded avenue was crossed at right angles by a secondary, north–south street. The city centre at the juncture of the thoroughfares provided the site for one of the largest of the Imperial-type bath–gymnasium complexes in Asia Minor (completed early 2nd century AD), with massive vaulted halls arranged symmetrically about its east–west axis. Opening on to the palaestra, which occupies the eastern half of the complex, is the rectangular marble court (now restored), which displays richly decorated columnar aediculae (shrine-like structures) in two storeys. A dedicatory inscription to Caracalla, Geta and Julia Domna dates the court to AD 211 and suggests that it was actually a hall for the Imperial cult. Along the south side of the baths runs a long row of shops (*c.* AD 400–*c.* 600). At the end of the 3rd century AD the south wing of the palaestra was transformed into a synagogue of basilica type (for illustration *see* LYDIA). The colossal size, prominent position and lavish decoration of this synagogue attest to the peaceful co-existence of the Christian and Jewish populations at this time. A small church with two apses, one behind the other, at the south-east corner of the Temple of Artemis and a Constantinian basilica in the Paktolos Valley (overlaid by a well-preserved Middle Byzantine church with a cross-in-a-square plan) are the principal Christian remains from this period.

Like many other Anatolian citadel and valley towns, Sardis clearly developed organically. While the flat land north of the marble avenue was the public quarter with important civic areas and structures, the rising ground to the south was largely residential. There, clusters of one- or two-storey peristyle houses hugged the slopes of the acropolis, interrupted by irregular winding streets and occasionally by such large public buildings as a theatre and stadium (both early Hellenistic) and an early Imperial Corinthian temple. Buildings known only from inscriptions include the odeion, the Gymnasium of the Elders, the Precinct of Zeus and Men, and the Council Building of the Elders, the Gerousia; according to Vitruvius (*On Architecture* II.viii.10), this was once the palace of Croesus. The royal past of Sardis was recalled as late as the Severan period (early 3rd century AD), when the town was described with nostalgia as the 'metropolis of Greece, of Asia, of all Lydia'.

H. C. Butler: *The Excavations: 1910–1914,* Publications of the American Society for the Excavation of Sardis, I/i (Leiden, 1922)

G. M. A. Hanfmann and J. C. Waldbaum: *A Survey of Sardis and the Major Monuments outside the City Walls*, Archaeological Exploration of Sardis, Monograph 1 (Cambridge, MA, 1975)
C. Foss: *Byzantine and Turkish Sardis*, Archaeological Exploration of Sardis, Monograph 4 (Cambridge, MA, 1976)
G. M. A. Hanfmann: *Sardis from Prehistoric to Roman Times* (Cambridge, MA, 1983)
C. Ratté and others: 'An Early Imperial Pseudodipteral Temple at Sardis', *Amer. J. Archaeol.*, xc (Jan 1986), pp. 45–68
F. K. Yegül: *The Bath-Gymnasium Complex at Sardis* (Cambridge, MA, 1986)
F. K. Yegül: 'Roman Architecture in Sardis', *Sardis: Twenty-seven Years of Discovery*, ed. E. Guralnick (Chicago, 1987), pp. 46–61
C. Ratté: *Lydian Masonry and Monumental Architecture at Sardis* (diss., Berkeley, U. California, 1989)
C. Ratté : Archaic Architectural Terracottas from Sector Byz-Fort at Sardis', *Hesperia*, lxiii (July–Sept 1994), pp. 361–90
L. M. Gadbery: 'Archaeological Exploration of Sardis', *Harvard University Art Museums Bulletin*, vi/1 (1996–7) pp. 51–4
E. R. M. Dusinberre: *Satrapal Sardis: Aspects of Empire in an Achaemenid Capital* (diss., Ann Arbor, U. MI, 1997).

2. Sculpture. Although sculpture from Sardis ranges in date from the Bronze Age to late Roman times, no evidence of a local stone-carving workshop is known. The greyish marble used most frequently, however, is a local stone, found in the quarries in the foothills of Mt Tmolos. In works from the Lydian period (*c.* 680–547 BC), recumbent lions are the most frequent subject (see fig.). Three (*c.* 570 BC; two, Manisa Mus.; frag. *in situ*) were found embedded in the corners of the later Altar to Cybele. Among the several representations of Cybele herself, of various dates, are the Cybele Shrine (h. 620 mm, *c.* 540–530 BC; Manisa Mus.), where the goddess stands in relief, framed by an Ionic temple, and a relief showing two people worshipping Artemis and Cybele together (h. 990 mm, *c.* 400 BC; Manisa Mus.). Under the Persians (546–334 BC), the Lydians continued to carve lions. Two pairs of addorsed lions (h. with base 790 mm, *c.* 450–350 BC; Manisa Mus.) were reused as supports for a table in the later synagogue. Eastern themes such as that of the funerary feast were also represented in this period. The Hellenistic cult statues in the Temple of Artemis were replaced in Roman times by colossal statues of the Emperor *Antoninus Pius* (*c.* AD 140) and *Faustina the Elder* (h. 1.45 m, *c.* AD 140; London, BM) as well as the newly identified (by R. R. R. Smith) *Marcus Aurelius* (formerly identified as Zeus) and a recently discovered fragment of *Commodus*. Portraits of distinguished citizens abound, such as that of *Claudia Antonia Sabina* on her sarcophagus (h. 2.11 m, late 2nd century AD–early 3rd; Istanbul, Archaeol. Mus.) and the late Roman *Head of a Sage* (h. 300 mm, late 3rd century AD; Manisa Mus.). The most notable examples of architectural sculpture are the capitals with sculpted heads (AD 211–12; most *in situ*), which decorated the Roman gymnasium complex.

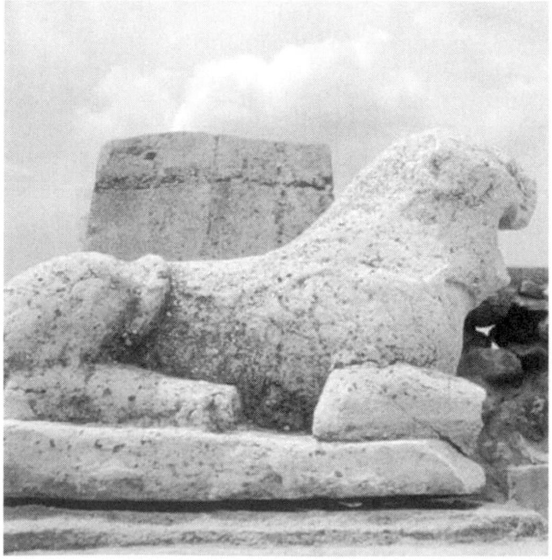

Sardis, Altar to Cybele, lion

G. M. A. Hanfmann: 'On Late Roman and Early Byzantine Portraits from Sardis', *Hommages à Marcel Renard*, ed. J. Bibauw, ii (Brussels, 1969), pp. 288–95
G. M. A. Hanfmann and J. C. Waldbaum: 'Kybele and Artemis: Two Anatolian Goddesses at Sardis', *Archaeology*, xxii (1969), pp. 264–9
G. M. A. Hanfmann and N. H. Ramage: *Sculpture from Sardis: The Finds through 1975* (Cambridge, MA, 1978)
G. M. A. Hanfmann and P. Erhart: 'Pedimental Reliefs from a Mausoleum of the Persian Era at Sardis: A Funerary Meal', *Studies in Ancient Egypt, the Aegean and the Sudan: Essays in Honor of Dows Dunham*, ed. W. K. Simpson and W. M. Davies (Boston, 1981), pp. 82–90
M. Hamiaux: 'Deux lions archaïques grecs méconnus au musée de Louvre', *Rev. Archéol.*, i (1994), pp. 19–32

Satra. *See* Eleutherna.

Sbeïtla. *See* Sufetula.

Scaena [*scena*; Gr. *skene*]. Covered structure for the players, chorus and dancers behind the acting stage of a Classical Theatre. The term *scaena frons* is applied to the decorated front of the *scaena*, which serves as the backdrop for the performance (*see* Aspendos).

Schliemann, (Johann Ludwig) Heinrich (Julius) (*b* Neubukow, Mecklenburg, 6 Jan 1822; *d* Naples, 26 Dec 1890). American archaeologist and businessman of German birth. The death of his mother in 1831 and accusations of embezzlement against his father (a pastor) in 1833 disrupted his schooling. A consequent sense of under-achievement propelled him to Amsterdam, where he studied bookkeeping and foreign languages. In 1844 he secured a position with the merchant bankers B. H. Schröder & Co., and in 1846 he was posted as the firm's agent to St Petersburg, where he established himself as a commodity dealer and spent the next 20 years. There followed a short period in America as a banker of doubtful integrity during the California gold-rush (1850–51), a marriage (1852) and three children, travels (1858–9) and a world tour resulting in an undistinguished travel diary, *La Chine et le Japon* (Paris, 1867).

By 1866 Schliemann was 44 and restless; leaving his wife and family he moved to Paris, ostensibly to study at the Sorbonne. In 1868 he toured the sites of Ithaka, the Peloponnese and the Troad where Frank Calvert, British Consul at the Dardanelles, drew his attention to Hisarlık and its claims to be the site of Homer's Troy. In *Ithaka, der Peloponnes und Troja* (1869) Schliemann recounted his journey and claimed to have had an interest in Troy since his childhood. In 1869 he obtained American citizenship (by perjury), was divorced, gained a doctorate from the University of Rostock, and in Athens married Sophia Kastromenos, 30 years his junior, whom he subsequently tried to involve in his excavations.

From 1870 to 1873 he excavated at TROY in the hope of uncovering Priam's city. He missed the relevant 2nd-millennium remains and so erroneously found the legendary city among the Early Bronze Age strata of the 3rd millennium. His most spectacular find was a hoard of Early Bronze Age metalwork ('Priam's Treasure'; *see* TROAD, §(ii)), which he smuggled to Athens. He published the excavation results in *Troy and its Remains* (1875) and the *Atlas trojanischer Alterthümer* (1874), though not in a form to endear him to scholars.

After friction with the Greek government he gained permission to dig at MYCENAE in 1876. There he did find the 2nd-millennium deposits and revealed the gold masks, weapons, vessels and jewellery of the shaft graves (Athens, N. Archaeol. Mus.), publishing his results in *Mycenae* (1878). The wealth and solidity of Mycenae contrasted strangely with the poverty of Troy, to which he therefore returned in 1878–9. His new excavations clarified the stratigraphy and were published in *Ilios* (1881), a book that also renewed his autobiographical claim of an obsession with archaeology since childhood. He dug briefly at ORCHOMENOS in 1880 (*Orchomenos*, 1881), and in 1881 he donated his Trojan collection to the German nation in return for public honours; the valuables were taken to Moscow in 1945.

In 1882 he formed a redeeming partnership with the young German architect Wilhelm Dörpfeld. Schliemann's keen but erratic interest in objects and stratigraphy was matched and disciplined by Dörpfeld's interest in the precise recording of architecture. Fruitful excavations followed at Troy in 1882 (*Troja*, 1884), at TIRYNS in 1884–5 (*Tiryns*, 1885) and, under pressure of ill-informed public attacks, at Troy again in 1890. This final season produced Mycenaean pottery from 2nd-millennium strata previously missed and so corrected the earlier conclusions.

Native intelligence, good observation, phenomenal drive and a flair for publicity, aided by prompt publication, assisted Schliemann; dishonesty, lack of technique and prickly arrogance did not. His work improved greatly in collaboration with Dörpfeld. His outstanding achievement was to open Aegean prehistory to the public. Others would probably have dug the same sites (all previously known) later and no doubt better, but with less effect on public interest.

H. Schliemann: unpublished diaries and correspondence (Athens, Amer. Sch. Class. Stud., Gennadius Lib.)
H. Schliemann: *Ithaka, der Peloponnes und Troja* (Leipzig, 1869)
H. Schliemann: *Atlas trojanischer Alterthümer* (Leipzig, 1874)
H. Schliemann: *Troy and its Remains* (London, 1875)
H. Schliemann: *Mycenae* (London, 1878)
H. Schliemann: *Ilios* (London, 1881)
H. Schliemann: *Orchomenos* (Leipzig, 1881)
H. Schliemann: *Troja* (London, 1884)
H. Schliemann: *Tiryns* (London, 1885)
E. Ludwig: *Schliemann: The Story of a Goldseeker* (London, 1931)
E. Meyer: *Heinrich Schliemann: Kaufmann und Forscher* (Göttingen, 1969)
D. F. Easton: 'The Schliemann Papers', *Annu. Brit. Sch. Athens*, lxxvii (1982), pp. 93–110
W. M. Calder III and J. Cobet, eds: *Heinrich Schliemann nach hundert Jahren* (Frankfurt am Main, 1990)
J. Herrmann, ed.: *Heinrich Schliemann: Grundlagen und Ergebnisse moderner Archäologie 100 Jahre nach Schliemanns Tod* (Berlin, 1992)
D. A. Traill: *Excavating Schliemann* (Atlanta, 1993)
C. Moorehead: *Lost and Found: The 9,000 Treasures of Troy: Heinrich Schliemann and the Gold that Got Away* (New York, 1996)
S. H. Allen: *Finding the Walls of Troy: Frank Calvert and Heinrich Schliemann at Hisarlik* (Berkeley, 1999)
D. Coulmas: *Schliemann und Sophia: Eine Liebesgeschichte* (Munich, 2001)
R. Vollmann and H. Schliemann: *Trojanische Träume in Mecklenburg* (Stuttgart, 2001)
D. F. Easton: *Schliemann's Excavations at Troia, 1870–1873* (Mainz, 2002)
C. N. Runnels and H. Schliemann: *The Archaeology of Heinrich Schliemann: An Annotated Bibliographic Handlist* (Boston, 2002)
Führer durch die ständige Ausstellung (exh. cat. by W. Bölke and R. Witte; Mecklenburg, Heinrich-Schliemann-Museum, 2003)
H. Bompou-Protopapa and S. K. Schliemann: *Sophia Enkastromenou-Sleman: Grammata ston Erriko* (Athens, 2005)
S. E. Gutker de Geus: *Een masker van goud* (Utrecht, 2005)
M. La Ferla: *L'Ultimo tesoro* (Viterbo, 2006)

Sculpture. Carved, cast or modelled artworks that can be either free-standing pieces (usually figural) or relief decoration on monuments or buildings (either figural or abstract).

I. Minoan. II. Cycladic. III. Helladic. IV. Greek. V. Etruscan. VI. Roman.

I. Minoan.

Figures of humans and animals were made throughout the Minoan period in a variety of materials, including stone, clay, terracotta and metal (discussed in this section), as well as ivory and faience (treated in separate sections; *see* Ivory and bone, §1(ii) *and* Faience, §1(ii)). Most sculptures were relatively small, and many served as votive offerings, the human figurines representing worshippers, the animals perhaps sacrificial victims. Some female figurines have been identified as goddesses, and these may have had larger counterparts in wood (the bronze locks of hair found by Sir Arthur Evans at Knossos may have belonged to such works). Large-scale relief frescoes, in which the figures are built up in plaster, were certainly made by the Minoans (*see* Painting, §I), but unlike the contemporary Egyptians, they apparently did not produce large stone sculptures or reliefs. This difference may partly be explained by Crete's shortage of suitable stone, or it may simply be that the Minoans preferred small-scale works. Given their skill at stone-carving, as is demonstrated by stone rhyta (ritual vessels) in the shape of animals' heads and by relief scenes on stone vases, it seems certain that they would have been capable of working on a larger scale. What Minoan figurines lack in monumentality, however, is more than compensated for by their inventiveness, carefully observed detail and imaginative design.

1. Neolithic and Early Minoan. The earliest Cretan figurines date from the Neolithic period, when both male and female figures were made in stone or clay. They include obese female figurines, usually seated, belonging to a type found throughout the Aegean area at this time and sometimes identified as fertility goddesses. Early Minoan (em) figurines are much more common and come from both settlements and cemeteries. They are profoundly influenced by the distinctive white-marble folded-arm figurines produced in large numbers in the Cyclades (*see* §II, 1 below) in the Early Cycladic ii period. Cycladic figurines were imported into Crete, and Cycladic types were extensively imitated in local marble, as well as in such other materials as ivory, bone and steatite. In Crete, as in the Cyclades, they comprise both schematic and naturalistic types. Typical Cretan schematic forms include peg-shaped examples with a rounded head, separated by a grooved neck from a long, roughly cylindrical body, and others with squat, rounded bodies. Limbs and facial features are only occasionally indicated, though the latter are carefully depicted on the otherwise completely schematic figures of the Ayios Onouphrios group (Herakleion Archaeol. Mus.).

Naturalistic folded-arm figurines are also found on Crete, and a typically Cretan variant, known as the Koumasa type, evolved. These thin and angular figures with broad shoulders and short legs may have been carved by Cycladic craftsmen resident on Crete. Unusual forms also occur, including a pair of steatite figurines sharing a single base, from Teke near Knossos (Herakleion, Archaeol. Mus.). The bone figurines from the Lasithi Plain represent another Cretan variety. Their legs are separated and their arms folded with the left below the right (contrary to normal Cycladic practice), while their faces have a sharp ridge down the middle and carved features. In late em and early mm times more naturalistic stone figurines were produced, which increasingly broke away from Cycladic conventions.

2. Middle Minoan i and ii. During mm i and ii, peak sanctuaries flourished on Crete. Among the main cult practices associated with them was the dedication of human and animal figurines, which seem usually to have been thrown into sacred fires. The ashes containing the offerings were swept up and preserved in fissures in the rocks. Most of these figurines were of clay, though some were of bronze. Terracotta figures representing worshippers are rarely over 200 mm high. The women characteristically have bell-shaped skirts, short-sleeved tops that either leave the breasts bare or have very low necklines, and various elaborate hairstyles, tall headdresses or hats. While some are rather roughly made with pinched, birdlike faces, others have finely modelled facial features and detailing of clothing and coiffure. The male figures often wear a loincloth and dagger and have the arms raised in gestures of worship: sometimes both hands rest on the chest, sometimes one hand is raised to the forehead. Both male and female terracotta figures were painted. Earlier examples often have red or brown decoration on a light ground, in a manner no doubt influenced by em pottery, while some mm figures are covered with a dark, lustrous wash and decorated in red and white, again like contemporary vases. The terracotta animals were also mostly small. Domestic animals predominate, especially bulls, oxen, sheep and goats. Wild animals are rare but include weasels and wild goats. These figurines may have been substitutes for real sacrifices, perhaps dedicated with prayers for the protection of livestock. Similarly, while the human figurines were probably left by worshippers as a substitute for continual presence at the shrine, the pieces representing parts of bodies and single limbs that also occur were no doubt left with prayers for the healing of specific afflictions.

3. Middle Minoan iii and Late Minoan. From mm iii more elaborate groups and models were included among terracottas. One, from a tholos tomb at Kamilari, near Phaistos, apparently depicts worshippers bringing offerings to two pairs of seated deities, while another shows four figures dancing, and a third depicts a woman kneading dough (all Herakleion, Archaeol. Mus.). While these scenes may all have religious significance, a fine model of a two-storey house from Archanes seems purely secular (Herakleion, Archaeol. Mus.).

Most of the finest bronze figurines date from lm i. Elsewhere in the Aegean, bronze figures were rare before the Iron Age, so their production was a specifically Minoan accomplishment. Again, most are small, usually under 250 mm high, and most seem to have been made as votive offerings, since several come from peak sanctuaries and even more from sacred caves. Both male and female human figures have been found, the males usually given the same typical Minoan costumes as their terracotta counterparts and the females attired in long, flounced skirts and open-fronted jackets. They are generally shown in attitudes of prayer. Many animal figures, including horses, deer, goats, bulls and oxen, were also dedicated. One particularly fine LM I bronze group (London, BM; see fig. 1) shows an acrobat leaping over the back of a bull. He is attached to the bull's head by his long, trailing hair and so caught in arrested motion. His forearms and his lower legs may have been lost during casting.

Minoan bronzes were cast solid using the lost-wax method, in which a wax model is enclosed in a clay mould and then heated. The melted wax runs out of the mould, to be replaced by molten metal. The surfaces of Minoan figurines are rough and bubbly, and almost no finishing work seems to have been carried out once the bronze was removed from the mould. Poor casting technique and the nature of the metal may partly account for this surface, but leaving it in that state was clearly deliberate. Lead figurines also survive, and there may have been others in precious metals. Certainly gold was sometimes combined with ivory in the most precious of all extant Minoan sculptures.

An impressive series of terracotta figurines has been found on the Cycladic island of KEA (Kea, Archaeol. Col.; *see* CYCLADIC, §4(iii)). Their size and elaboration have led to their interpretation as goddesses and perhaps as cult statues, though it is possible that they are simply representations of worshippers. The figures are Cretan in style and dress but far larger than anything yet known from Crete, many of them originally standing 1.5 m high or more. They may therefore shed some light on the possible nature of large-scale Minoan statues in wood.

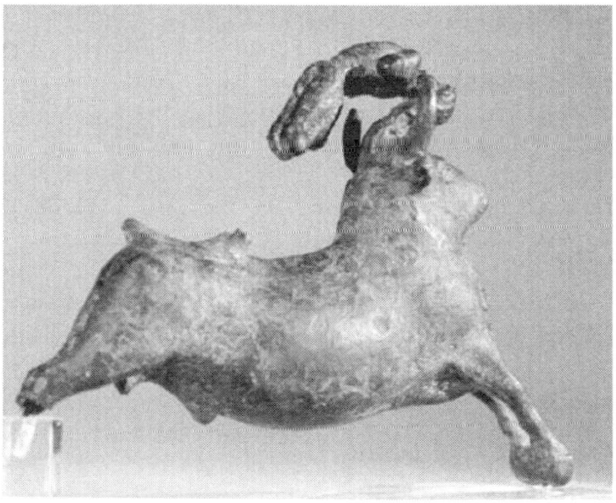

1. Minoan sculptural group of an acrobat leaping over the back of a bull, bronze, h. 114 mm, from ?Rethymnon, Late Minoan I (London, British Museum)

Fairly large (*c.* 500–800 mm high) terracotta figurines with wheelmade skirts were produced in Crete during the LM period, and these too have been identified as goddesses. Angular and somewhat ungainly, with upraised arms, they often wear diadems bearing a variety of motifs, such as birds and poppyheads. The earliest may date from as early as the first half of the 15th century BC, but they continued to be made into Sub Minoan times. The potter's wheel was also used to make the bodies of certain animal figurines produced in Crete towards the end of the Bronze Age (probably from *c.* 1200 BC). The heads and legs were handmade, and the animals had painted decoration similar to that on contemporary vases. This style was widely imitated elsewhere in Greece, persisting beyond Minoan times.

A. J. Evans: 'On a Minoan Bronze Group of a Galloping Bull and Acrobatic Figure from Crete', *J. Hell. Stud.*, lxi (1921), pp. 247–59

C. Zervos: *L'Art de la Crète néolithique et minoenne* (Paris, 1956)

S. Alexiou: 'E Minoike thea meth'upsomenon cheiron' [The Minoan Goddess with Raised Arms], *Kritika Chron.*, xii (1958), pp. 179–299

R. A. Higgins: *Greek Terracottas* (London, 1967)

R. A. Higgins: *Minoan and Mycenaean Art* (London, 1967)

P. J. Ucko: *Anthropomorphic Figurines* (Richmond, VA, 1968)

K. Branigan: 'Cycladic Figurines and their Derivatives in Crete', *Annu. Brit. Sch. Athens*, lxvi (1971), pp. 57–78

M. S. F. Hood: *The Arts in Prehistoric Greece*, Pelican Hist. A. (Harmondsworth, 1978)

C. Verlinden: *Les Statuettes anthropomorphes crétoises en bronze et en plomb, du IIIe millénaire au VIIe siècle av. J-C* (Providence, RI, 1984)

B. Rutkowski: *The Cult Places of the Aegean* (New Haven, 1986)

B. Rutkowski: *Petsophas: A Cretan Peak Sanctuary* (n.p., 1991)

S. Krause: *Die Typologie der frühminoischen Idole: Versuch einer evolutionären Typologie* (Hamburg, 1992)

A. Pilale-Papasteriou: *Minoika pelina anthropomorpha eidolia tes sylloges Metaxa: Symvole ste melete tes Mesominoikes peloplastikes* (Thessalonika, 1992)

G. Cipollone: *Simmetria, asimmetria ed altre caratteristiche della ceramica minoica di Festòs* (Rome, 1996)

A. L. D'Agata: *Haghia Triada: Vol 2. Statuine minoiche e post-minoiche dai vecchi scavi di Haghia Triada (Creta)* (Padua, 1999)

J. A. MacGillivray, J. Driessen and L. H. Sackett: *The Palaikastro Kouros: A Minoan Chryselephantine Statuette and its Aegean Bronze Age Context* (London, 2000)

G. Rethemiotakes: *Minoan Clay Figures and Figurines: From the Neopalatial to the Subminoan Period* (Athens, 2001)

II. Cycladic.

The abundance of white marble on most of the Cycladic islands, especially NAXOS and PAROS, resulted in a strong tradition of stone-carving in the Early Cycladic (EC) period. Stone figurines of the EC period—sometimes referred to as idols—are arguably the best-known and most highly appreciated productions of Cycladic art. Their appeal to modern taste has led to an increased demand for them on the international antiquities market, and extraordinary prices have been paid for individual items at auction (for example, £2.09 million for the Merrin Head, sold New York, Sotheby's, 1 Dec 1988, lot 83). One consequence has been the intensification since the 1960s of illicit digging of EC tombs. But even this proved unable to satisfy the demand, and the manufacture of forgeries has reached the status of a 'growth industry'. Disputes have also arisen over the ownership of authentic pieces: in July 1990, in a precedent-setting case, Greece failed to obtain a court order halting the sale of a private collection of Cycladic sculptures at auction, despite the Greek government's insistence that the works had been removed from Greek soil illegally.

The fact that most Cycladic stone figurines come from illicit excavations has added to the confusion surrounding their function and significance. Several interpretations of their purpose have been proposed, none of which is universally accepted. They may have been magical representations of venerated ancestors, companions for the dead, images of divinities, status symbols or even toys. Those of known provenance are mainly from burials, but not all graves contained them. Moreover, some were evidently repaired in antiquity, suggesting that they were items of personal property for everyday use. Finally, some are too large to have been buried in the small and narrow graves: these may perhaps be cult images of an unknown deity.

1. EARLY CYCLADIC. Figurines of the EC I phase, whose origins can be traced to the Neolithic period, rarely exceed 200 mm in height. Initially they seem to have been fashioned from white flattened beach pebbles, the earliest types being natural pebbles worn by the waves into schematic human forms. Other early types were more substantially worked with tools, probably of obsidian, stone, emery or wood; abrasives such as emery powder and pumice stone were also used. The flat, violin-shaped figurines, which occasionally have anatomical details such as breasts, genitalia and arms, are more sophisticated than the pebble figurines. Their predecessors were the Neolithic squatting female figures such as the Fat Lady of Saliagos (Paros, Archaeol. Mus.). Later in date, though still in EC I, and far more naturalistic is the Plastiras type of figurine, named after its place of discovery on Paros. This figurine seems to have evolved from the standing variety of the Neolithic Aegean figurines. Both male and female figures of the Plastiras type have an almond-shaped head with facial details in low relief (nose, eyes, mouth, ears), arms bent at the elbows with hands meeting on the stomach, legs set apart and feet with flat horizontal soles suggesting a simple upright pose (see fig. 2). The introduction of metal tools in EC II enabled sculptors to attempt larger, more three-dimensional figures. But schematic forms, such as the Louros type, which is an abstract version of the earlier Plastiras type, continued.

The most characteristic EC II type is the folded-arm figurine, ranging in size from *c.* 100 mm to almost life-size (*c.* 1500 mm). Its body is three-dimensional but never fully rounded. The main features are a triangular, spade- or almond-shaped head turned upwards,

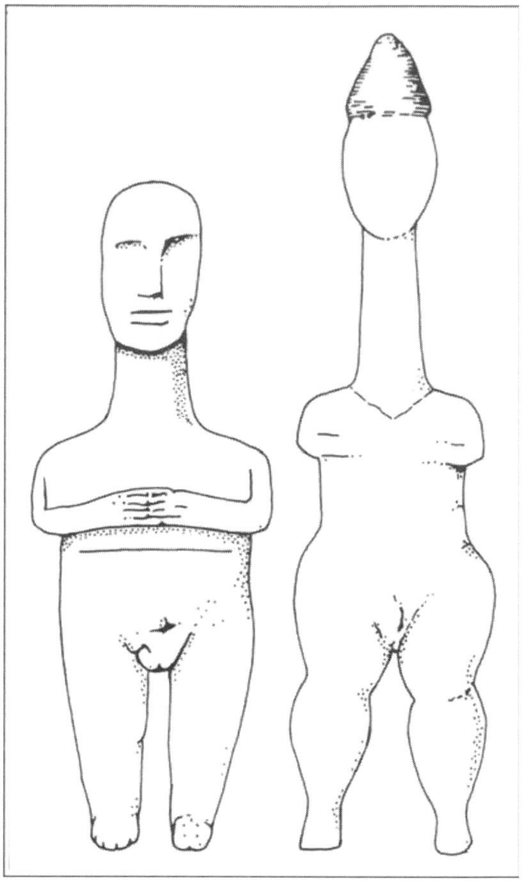

2. Early Cycladic male figurines of Plastiras type, marble, EC I

an elongated and stylized nose (no eyes or mouth), arms folded left-over-right across the stomach and legs usually slightly bent at the knees and separated by means of a groove both at the front and back. The feet have slanting soles, suggesting a tip-toe position for the figurine. Few other anatomical details were carved, but some, mainly the facial features and hair, were painted. Variants of this popular type, named after the sites where they were first discovered, are ascribed to different phases of EC II. The Kapsala variety, characterized by narrow shoulders, heavy, convex head and clearly indicated breasts, as well as by generally rounded forms, was common in the central Cyclades, while the Dokathismata group (*see* AMORGOS), consisting of thin, long, angular and very elegant figurines, was more widely distributed among the islands. Spedos-type figurines, which are the most numerous and were produced over the longest period, are well built and have spade-shaped heads (see fig. 3). The Koumasa variety comprises short, broad and rather flat figurines found exclusively on Crete, and the Chalandriani variety consists of figures with rather square, flat torsos and the right arm folded over the left (which gives rise to the group's alternative title of 'post-canonical', to distinguish them from the standard folded-arm type). A small group of

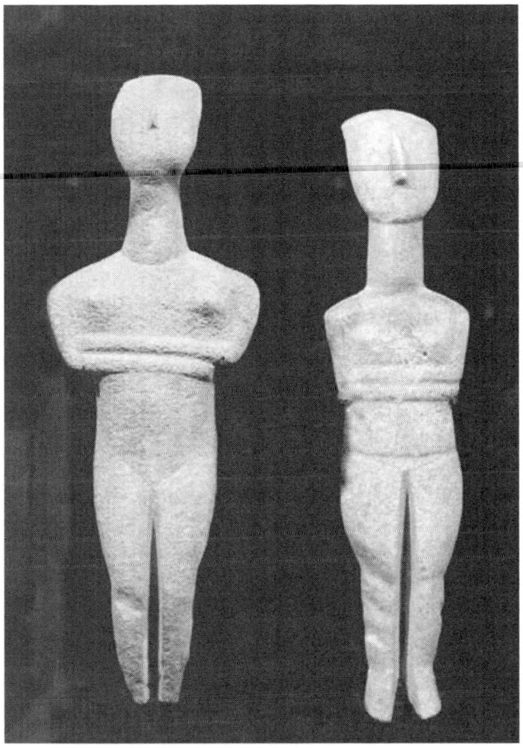

3. Early Cycladic female folded-arm figurines, marble from Paros, h. of tallest figure 393 mm, Spedos-type, EC II (Paris, Musée du Louvre)

typical folded-arm figurines depict pregnant women; another special category, the 'occupational' figurines, depict mainly male figures engaged in a specific activity: common figures include the 'hunter' or 'warrior', the lyre-player (*see* CYCLADIC, fig. 2), the flautist and the seated figure proposing a toast.

Systematic study of the EC figurines has led to the recognition of individual artists to whom certain pieces can be attributed on stylistic grounds. Among these artists are the Goulandris Master, the Naxos Museum Master, the Ashmolean Master, the Steiner Master and the Copenhagen Master. They all produced figurines of the Spedos variety. It has become clear through study and experimentation that the Cycladic figurines were not sculpted at random but that specific canons were applied in the planning of the various types, in order that standard proportions should be met in their execution.

A quite significant, though often neglected, aspect of Early Cycladic sculpture is the application of starkly coloured pigments. Quite often figurines of all types carry traces of black, blue, red, or green colouring: black and blue is used to denote or accentuate anatomical details and facial features such as eyes and eyebrows, ornate hairdos or the pubic triangle, and reds are employed to emphasize incised details and ornaments on face and body, often interpreted as tattoo marks. The substances used are azurite (copper carbonate) for blue, various iron oxides, cinnabar (mercuric sulfide) or red ochre for red, and malachite or azurite hydroxide for green. Cinnabar in particular is a remarkable choice, as it is not native to the islands, but had to be imported from elsewhere (most likely the coast of Asia Minor). The presence of pigments has left visible traces ('paint ghosts') on the surface of the figurines, as it preserved the stone from further corrosion, compared to those parts of the surface left plain.

The widespread use of pigments in Early Cycladic sculpture seems to have carried a much deeper significance than the mere indication or accentuation of anatomical detail or the enhancement of line and contour. Even though the use of colour seems to increase the naturalist aspect of the statuettes, closer examination suggests that the overall impression of a fully-fledged Cycladic figurine would be even more abstract, certainly less naturalistic than what they now look like, having lost their original pigments. In short, Cycladic figurines would have originally stood as works of painting as well as sculpture (Birtacha). The colouring of the figurines seems related to the widespread presence of pigments on burial sites, be that in the form of actual chunks of raw materials such as azurite or cinnabar inside the graves themselves, or inside clay or stone pigment containers (*see* STONE VASES, §1). Miniature clay pots (aryballoi) or fine receptacles made of bone are often found inside graves containing colours of the types described above, as well as great numbers of stone vases (phialai, palettes etc) seemingly used for the preparation of pigments. A practice of ritual application of colour onto the bodies of the dead or the living, carrying perhaps symbolisms of fertility, healing, afterlife and so on, has usually been suspected to explain these finds. Tattooing, as a means of social distinction or ritual marking of the living, transferred onto the figurines, has also been suggested. In more recent years, socio-anthropological theory has been employed in the further understanding of the figurines and the cultural aspects associated with them (Hendrix; Hoffman).

D. G. Hogarth: 'Aegean Sepulchral Figurines', *Essays in Aegean Archaeology Presented to Sir Arthur Evans* (Oxford, 1927), pp. 55–62

M. L. Erlenmeyer and H. Erlenmeyer: 'Von der frühen Bild kunst der Kykladen', *Ant. Kst*, viii (1965), pp. 59–71

J. Thimme: 'Die religiöse Bedeutung der Kykladenidole', *Ant. Kst*, viii (1965), pp. 72–86

C. Doumas: *The N. P. Goulandris Collection of Early Cycladic Art* (Athens, 1968)

O. Höckmann: 'Zu Formenschatz und Ursprung der schematischen Kykladenidole', *Berlin. Jb. Vor- & Frühgesch.*, viii (1968), pp. 45–75

C. Renfrew: 'The Development and Chronology of the Early Cycladic Figurines', *Amer. J. Archaeol.*, lxxiii (1969), pp. 1–32

P. G. Preziosi and S. S. Weinberg: 'Evidence for Painted Details in Early Cycladic Sculpture', *Ant. Kst*, xiii (1970), pp. 4–12

F. Zafiropoulou: 'Early Cycladic Finds from Ano Koufonisi', *Athens An. Archaeol.*, iii (1970), pp. 48–51

K. Branigan: 'Cycladic Figurines and their Derivatives in Crete', *Annu. Brit. Sch. Athens*, lxvi (1971), pp. 57–78
J. L. Caskey: 'Marble Figurines from Ayia Irini in Keos', *Hesperia*, xl (1971), pp. 113–26
J. L. Fitton, ed.: *Cycladica: Studies in Memory of N. P. Goulandris* (London, 1984)
P. Getz-Preziosi: *Early Cycladic Sculpture: An Introduction* (Malibu, 1985, R/1994)
P. Getz-Preziosi: *Early Cycladic Art in North American Collections* (Richmond, VA, 1987)
P. Getz-Preziosi: *Sculptors of the Cyclades: Individual and Tradition in the Third Millennium BC* (Ann Arbor, 1987)
C. Renfrew: *The Cycladic Spirit* (New York, 1991)
E. Hendrix: 'Painted Ladies of the Early Bronze Age', *Met. Mus. A. Bull.* (Winter 1997–8), pp. 4–15
C. G. Doumas: *Early Cycladic Culture: The N. P. Goulandris Collection* (Athens, 2000)
E. Hendrix: *The Paint Motifs on Early Cycladic Figures* (diss., New York U., 2000)
P. Getz-Gentle and J. de Vries: *Personal Styles in Early Cycladic Sculpture* (Madison, WI, 2001)
C. G. Doumas: *Silent Witnesses: Early Cycladic Art of the Third Millennium BC* (New York, 2002)
K. Birtacha: 'Pigments and Colouring during the Early Bronze Age in the Cyclades', *Argonaut: Festschrift for Professor Christos G. Doumas by his Students at the University of Athens (1980–2000),* ed. A. Vlachopoulos and K. Birtacha (Athens, 2003), pp. 263–76 [in Greek]
G. L. Hoffman: 'Painted Ladies: Early Cycladic II Mourning Figures?', *Amer. J. Archaeol.*, cvi (2005), pp. 525–50
P. Sotirakopoulou: *The 'Keros Hoard'; Myth or Reality? Searching for the Lost Pieces of a Puzzle* (Athens, 2005)

2. Rediscovery. The Cycladic culture and its material remains fell into obscurity after *c.* 2000 BC, with minor exceptions of survival or accidental discovery and partial reuse in later periods. Towards the end of the 18th century, however, Cycladic figurines began once more to see the light of day, in the hands of travellers and archaeophiles, whose neo-Classical tastes could hardly accommodate the striking simplicity and abstraction of the prehistoric statuettes. Accidental finds of Cycladic figurines on the Aegean Islands were dubbed 'idoli' and 'idoletti' by Pasch van Krienen in his 1773 work *Breve descrizione dell' Arcipelago.* In the course of the 19th century many antiquarians came across Cycladic figurines in their travels and identified them as 'creations of a barbaric hand', judging them as 'primitive', 'naïve', 'rudimentary', 'incomplete' and even 'repulsively ugly'. By the end of the 19th century, systematic excavation of Cycladic sites and publication of their finds made clear that the figurines were the product of a prehistoric Aegean culture, flourishing on the islands in the pre-Hellenic 3rd millennium BC.

Travellers on the Grand Tour were, therefore, indifferent to Cycladic figurines, which were appreciated by better informed figures, such as the British antiquarian James Theodore Bent, who excavated many examples during his trips to the Cyclades in 1883–4 (subsequently acquired by the British Museum). Oxford and Cambridge acquired their pieces at about the same time, as did other European museums, such as the Staatliche Kunstsammlungen in Dresden and the Badisches Landesmuseum in Karlsruhe.

Familiarity with Cycladic culture and its creations did little to lessen European dislike towards them, however, until some of the greatest modernist artists of the 20th century had the chance to view some of the figurines, appreciate their aesthetic values and be inspired by them. As artists were turning to non-Western, pre-Renaissance art for their inspiration, the 'primitive' idols from the Cyclades were seen in a different light, on a par with tribal art from other parts of the non-Classical world, such as Africa or Oceania. Simplicity of form, abstraction and clarity became the essential qualities of 'beauty' in modernist eyes: Constantin Brancusi (1876–1957), Amedeo Modigliani (1884–1920) and Alberto Giacometti (1901–66) produced work that evokes, directly or indirectly, Cycladic prototypes. Henry Moore (1898–1986), Pablo Picasso (1881–1973) and Barbara Hepworth (1903–75) often expressed their interest in Cycladic art. (Moore is known to have owned three Cycladic figurines, and Picasso, who also owned one, is quoted by André Malraux as having expressed a preference for the ancient originals over Brancusi's own works.) As these artists gradually became established, and their views on art and beauty were accepted as the new orthodoxy, Cycladic figurines (along with other such 'primitive' or 'tribal' arts) were allowed into the mainstream. This encouraged further studies, as well as collecting, state or private, with the deplorable result of mass looting on the islands, in order to produce more finds to satisfy the needs of an ever growing market.

Initially, modernists viewed Cycladic art as primarily non-Classical, as the negation of the conventional, over-abused, and trivialized models of Renaissance art (itself based on the Greco-Roman tradition). According to Henry Moore, in the 1930s Greece and the Renaissance were 'the enemy', due to their ties to academia. This break with tradition expressed the modernists' rejection of the way contemporary culture formed and communicated an established truth. Gradually, however, through the efforts of thinkers such as Christian Zervos, the Greek émigré who established himself in France and became one of the leading art critics of his time, Cycladic art came to be viewed (by many at least) as a mystic anticipation of what was in the 1st millennium BC to emerge as the 'Hellenic spirit'. As Cycladic culture was increasingly accepted into the realm of Hellenism (by exponents of modernism such as Le Corbusier (1887–1965) and Maurice Raynal (1884–1954)), the boundaries between pre-Classical and Classical art became blurred. Thus, since the 1930s, Cycladic art has become in many ways emblematic of Hellenic culture and its roots, even though it pre-dates Hellenism as such. In this way, many contemporary approaches to Cycladic art, and the figurines in particular, are deeply influenced by the same post-Renaissance sensitivities that initiated Classical archaeology as an independent academic discipline.

See also COLLECTION AND DISPLAY OF ART, §II, 2 *and* III, 2.

C. Zervos: *L'Art en Grèce du troisième millénaire au IVe siècle avant notre ère* (Paris, 1934)
C. Zervos: *L'Art des Cyclades du début à la fin de l'âge du bronze: 2500–1100 avant notre ère* (Paris, 1957)
A. Malraux: *Picasso's Mask* (New York, 1976)
C. Renfrew: *The Cycladic Spirit* (New York, 1991)
D. W. J. Gill & C. Chippindale: 'Material and Intellectual Consequences of Esteem for Cycladic Figures', *Amer. J. Archaeol.*, xcvii (1993), pp. 601–59
C. G. Doumas: *Silent Witnesses: Early Cycladic Art of the Third Millennium BC* (New York, 2002)
V. Chryssovitsanou: 'Les figurines cycladiques: De la répulsion à la fascination', *Le Métamorphose des ruines: L'Influence des découvertes archéologiques sur les arts et les lettres (1870–1914)*, ed. S. Basch (Athens, 2004), pp. 33–8
R. Labrusse: 'Dieux cachés, mirages des origins', *Cahiers d'art: Musée Zervos à Vézelay*, ed. C. Derouet (Paris, 2006), pp. 39–59

III. Helladic.

1. EARLY AND MIDDLE HELLADIC. The only known Early Helladic (EH) sculptural works are an ithyphallic terracotta figurine from Zerelia in Thessaly (Volos, Athanassakeion Archaeol. Mus.); another highly stylized human figurine from Zygouries (EH II; Corinth, Archaeol. Mus.); some abstract zoomorphic vessels and figurines from Eutresis (Thebes Mus.), Zygouries, Palaiopyrgi, Tiryns (Navplion, Archaeol. Mus.) and Corinth (Corinth, Archaeol. Mus.); and a series of carefully modelled, almost naturalistic bovine figurines from Lithares in Boiotia (EH III; Thebes Mus.). Middle Helladic (MH) works are even rarer, being confined to two terracotta bull rhyta from Eleusis (Eleusis Mus.). They too are stylized, but their muscular bodies, hunched shoulders and lifelike heads are clearly and forcefully portrayed.

2. LATE HELLADIC. Examples of Late Helladic (LH), or Mycenaean, sculpture are better known; they were produced in stone, clay and plaster, in the round and in relief. The tools available to Mycenaean artists for stonework were stone hammers, chisels, drills, saws and abrasives such as emery, pumice or sand. Drills were reeds or bronze tubes turned back and forth by a rope or bow, which thus bored rings, rather than complete holes; to create holes the stone core within the drilled ring was broken out. Saws were straight or curved toothless bronze blades, or pieces of wire. Both were used as grinding implements in conjunction with sand or emery powder, probably applied wet. When carving reliefs, the sculptor outlined the composition by drilling a series of closely packed rings and then hammering out their cores and the thin walls between them. Then he cut the surface back to the level of the background with stone hammers or emery chisels and effaced tool marks and sharp edges using an abrasive. A compass was sometimes employed for cutting circles, and borers and small stone or bronze chisels were used for detailed work.

(i) Sculpture in the round. About two dozen examples have survived, all belonging to LH IIIB–C and thus representing the final phase of LH sculpture. They comprise the plaster head of a goddess or sphinx and the small head of a statuette, both from MYCENAE (Athens, N. Archaeol. Mus.), a small fragmentary clay head from Athens (Athens, Acropolis Mus.) and another from Asine (Navplion, Archaeol. Mus.), all probably originally attached to wooden bodies. The large head from Mycenae is two-thirds life-size and is made of white plaster, with the features (eyes, mouth, ears, facial tattoos, headband and cap) indicated or enhanced by paint. It is more expertly fashioned than the small head from the same site, which is closer to the examples from Athens and Asine; these are also painted white and embellished with added colour. The modelling of the Mycenae and the Athens heads is stylized but fairly regular, and their proportions are roughly correct: the Asine head, known as the Lord (or Lady) of Asine, is much cruder, with protruding eyes, a triangular nose, beardlike chin and flat ears. However, all four share one basic trait: unlike the smoothly rounded contemporary Cretan and Cycladic statues they are modelled in four distinct planes (face, sides and back) that meet rather than merge.

There are also 19 wheelmade female terracotta idols from the Cult Centre at Mycenae (LH IIIB; Navplion, Archaeol. Mus.). These are even more rudimentary and conventional than the heads. Their tubelike bodies with small, pointed breasts support spherical heads with long noses and incised mouths, while their short, stunted arms are raised up on either side, stretched forwards or folded across the chest. Their eyes, mouths and hair are either moulded or painted, while perishable accessories such as plaits or jewellery were inserted into small holes made before firing.

In addition to the large-scale sculptures, there are a few anthropomorphic or zoomorphic vessels and thousands of small, stylized terracotta figurines (see fig. 4) of women (or goddesses), animals and birds,

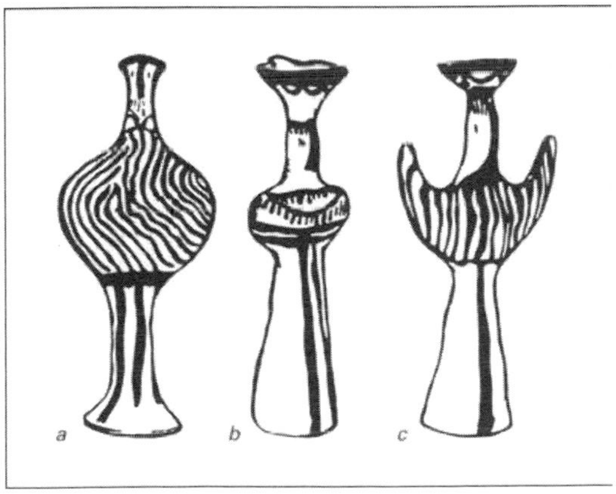

4. Late Helladic terracotta figurines, LH III: (a) Phi type, h. 80 mm, probably from Melos; (b) Tau type, h. 95 mm, from Athens; (c) Psi type, h. 115 mm, probably from Athens (London, British Museum)

discovered on practically all LH sites. The terracotta figurines, cylindrical from the waist down and with flattened torsos and arms, are so abstracted that the general shape of the human body is barely recognizable. Their only moulded details are a flat-topped hat, a pinched-out nose, pellets for breasts and occasionally a tress at the back. All other features (eyes, clothes, jewellery) are simply painted on. Most are female figures with upraised or crossed arms, but some represent women kneading dough (Athens, priv. col.), holding a child or seated on either a throne (Navplion, Archaeol. Mus.) or a pack animal (Athens, N. Archaeol. Mus.). Other figurines depict chariots, with or without charioteers (Navplion, Archaeol. Mus.), and horsemen (Navplion, Archaeol Mus.). The animal figurines (mostly bovines) are even more schematic, so that when they have no obvious distinguishing features such as horns or manes it is often impossible to identify them. The features on the plastic vessels, mainly rhyta, are equally sketchy and stereotyped but are painted rather than modelled. Some represent humans, but there are also birds (Patras, Archaeol. Mus.), a pack animal with wine skins (Rhodes, Archaeol. Mus.), an oxhead (Rhodes, Archaeol. Mus.), a fish (Navplion, Archaeol. Mus.) and two high boots with upturned toes (Athens, N. Archaeol. Mus.).

(ii) Reliefs. Again, about two dozen have been preserved, of which the 14 or so soft limestone tomb markers from the royal graves at Mycenae are the earliest (LH I; Athens, N. Archaeol. Mus.). They were decorated with spiral, meander or rosette patterns or with crudely designed and inexpertly incised or carved scenes involving chariots, such as hunting, racing or warfare scenes. The flat, single-plane designs were outlined to a uniformly shallow depth using a wood-carving technique: only on one slab is there a rudimentary attempt at modelling.

The next extant works are a few scraps of well-modelled architectural reliefs from Mycenae, Thebes and Tiryns, produced three centuries later. These were carved in coloured stone or alabaster and ornamented respectively with spirals, a net pattern and bisected rosettes. Similar but more sophisticated are the spiral and floral designs sculpted on the ceiling of the side chamber of the Treasury of Minyas (LH IIIB), a tholos tomb at Orchomenos, and the bead-framed zigzag bands of spirals on the half columns of the Treasury of Atreus at Mycenae (LH IIIB; parts now at London, BM; Munich, Staatl. Antikensamml.; Athens, N. Archaeol. Mus.; Navplion, Archaeol. Mus.); from this tomb also a few frieze fragments depicting the feet and head of a bull standing next to a tree survive.

The most significant LH relief is that on a limestone slab concealing the relieving triangle over the lintel of the Lion Gate at Mycenae (LH IIIB; *in situ; see* MYCENAE, fig. 2). It represents two confronted rampant lions who rest their front paws on a double altar surmounted by a column supporting a length of entablature. The lions' heads, now missing, were probably of softer stone, perhaps steatite. Their musculature is modelled in fairly low relief with a few bold planes. There is little anatomical detail, and the proportions are stylized, but overall the work creates a naturalistic impression of raw power.

Another relief occurs on the menhir-like stone slab from Soufli Magoula in Thessaly (late LH IIIB; Larissa, Archaeol. Mus.), though its style is unusual and its date uncertain. It represents a barely recognizable life-size human figure wearing a pointed helmet, five necklaces, a dagger and a belt, flanked by wriggling snakes. Its right hand hangs down by its hip, while its left is held across its chest. The design and execution are so crude that only its find spot and the shapes of the helmet and dagger link the piece to other Mycenaean works.

W. A. Heurtley: 'Mycenae: The Grave Stelai', *Annu. Brit. Sch. Athens*, xxv (1921–3), pp. 126–46

G. E. Mylonas: 'The Figured Mycenaean Stelae', *Amer. J. Archaeol.*, lv (1951), pp. 134–47

H.-G. Buchholz and V. Karageorghis: *Altägäis und Altkypros* (Tübingen, 1971); Eng. trans. by F. Garvie as *Prehistoric Greece and Cyprus* (London, 1973)

E. French: 'The Development of Mycenaean Terracotta Figurines', *Annu. Brit. Sch. Athens*, lxvi (1971), pp. 101–87

S. Hood: *The Arts in Prehistoric Greece*, Pelican Hist. A. (Harmondsworth, 1978), pp. 94, 96–112

IV. Greek.

The Greeks produced sculpture in many different materials for display or use in various contexts. This article focuses mainly on the development of large-scale sculpture, while smaller-scale or mass-produced works, such as bronze statuettes or terracotta figurines, are discussed in separate articles (*see* METALWORK, §IV, 2(i) *and* TERRACOTTA, §I, 2).

1. Overview. 2. Historical survey. 3. Theory and criticism. 4. Collections, museums and exhibitions.

1. OVERVIEW. Together with painting, monumental sculpture, particularly free-standing statues and prestigious architectural ensembles, was associated with the most accomplished Greek artists and was the medium in which new techniques and aesthetic trends first became manifest. While hardly any original ancient Greek paintings survive, however, numerous datable and (if not always securely) attributable sculptures are known, and the evidence they provide can be compared with descriptions by ancient writers. Particularly important early sources, constantly referred to in the survey that follows, are the works of the Roman writer PLINY THE ELDER and the Greek traveller and geographer PAUSANIAS. Most large-scale Greek sculptures come from public and religious contexts—sanctuaries, agoras, cemeteries. Important categories include the gravestones of the Archaic period (*c.* 700–*c.* 500/480 BC) and the contemporary KORE and KOUROS statue types; the architectural sculptures associated with the great marble temples of the Archaic and Classical

(*c.* 525/480–323 BC) periods; and the statues dedicated in sanctuaries.

In the 2nd and 1st centuries BC, as the Romans conquered the ancient Greek world, they looted the finest works of art, which often found their way to the private collections of wealthy individuals in Italy. The most famous statues of the Classical period, many of which were cast in bronze, were reproduced by Roman copyists in marble. Except for the chance survival of a few important works, such as the RIACE BRONZES or ARTEMISION BRONZES, the original bronzes—more easily destroyed than marble—are lost. It was Roman marble copies in papal and other collections, rather than authentic Greek sculptures, that inspired interest in ancient Greek art in Renaissance Europe and at the time of the neo-Classical movement of the later 18th century. Even today, these white marble copies continue to underlie the popular notion of the ancient Greeks' artistic achievements and ideal of beauty. To the Romans and later European collectors, such pieces represented desirable possessions and were acquired and displayed as works of art rather than as sacred objects. The attitude of the Greeks themselves to sculpture is harder to recapture; for example, deities were both represented by and embodied in their cult statues, and it would have been unimaginable to separate such works from the context of worship.

Because of its extraordinarily wide-reaching influence on the formation of Western aesthetics, Greek sculpture—hard as it is now to view it objectively—has been among the most intensively debated and researched subjects in art history, and the associated scholarly literature is immense. The consensus is still frequently revised on such matters as the date, attribution and meaning of specific works.

G. M. A. Richter: *The Sculpture and Sculptors of the Greeks* (New Haven and London, 1929, 4/1970)
G. Lippold: *Griechische Plastik* (Munich, 1950)
R. Lullies and M. Hirmer: *Greek Sculpture* (New York, 1957/R London, 1960)
R. Carpenter: *Greek Sculpture: A Critical Review* (Chicago, 1960)
B. Rowlands: *The Classical Tradition of Western Art* (Cambridge, MA, 1963)
S. Adam: *The Technique of Greek Sculpture in the Archaic and Classical Periods* (London, 1966)
C. Blümel: *Greek Sculptors at Work* (London, 1969)
M. Robertson: *History of Greek Art*, 2 vols (Cambridge, 1975)
J. Barron: *Greek Sculpture* (London, 1982)
A. F. Stewart: *Greek Sculpture: An Exploration*, 2 vols (New Haven and London, 1990)
N. Yalouris: *Ancient Sculpture* (1994), iii of *Greek Art* (Athens, 1994–6)
D. Buitron-Oliver: *The Interpretation of Architectural Sculpture in Greece and Rome* (New England, 1997)
B. S. Ridgway: *Prayers in Stone: Greek Architectural Sculpture ca. 600–100 BCE* (Berkeley, 1999)
D. Steiner: *Images in Mind: Statues in Archaic and Classical Greek Literature and Thought* (Princeton, 2001)
S. Woodford: *The Art of Greece and Rome* (Cambridge and New York, 2004)

(i) Forms and functions. (ii) Subject-matter. (iii) Materials. (iv) Techniques. (v) Craftsmen and society.

(i) Forms and functions.

(a) Free-standing. (b) Architectural. (c) Non-architectural reliefs.

(a) Free-standing. In the absence of any surviving works by the great ancient Greek panel painters, free-standing sculpture is the most sensitive indicator of the stylistic development of Greek art. It was the field in which the most important sculptors worked and from which innovations and new tendencies spread to other branches of sculpture. Again with the exception of panel painting, it was the art form that commanded the highest respect among contemporaries: architectural and relief sculpture, by contrast, are seldom mentioned in ancient literary sources, though they now account for most of the surviving original large-scale Greek works. Most Greek sculpture is concerned with the human figure, though other subjects occur throughout its history. In free-standing sculpture, single figures are generally much commoner than group compositions (see below).

Formal development. By the mid-7th century BC at the latest, life-size and over life-size sculptures in stone were being produced. These works were not determined by the direct observation of nature, and there was no straightforward development towards an increasing naturalism. However, from the austere stylization of the figurines of the preceding Geometric period, the proportions of the human body were brought into a fixed, recognizable and measurable relation to each other. Firm rules were established, clearly influenced by the Egyptian canon of proportion, though, unlike it, they included the whole head, did not imply a back support and could be developed freely and continuously by individual artists. Even so, the mode of representation remained in principle two-dimensional, being applied to only two sides of the block, with mediation at the edges. Later in the Archaic period there appeared a playful tendency to stylize certain motifs ornamentally, for example hair or parts of the body. Despite the unity that can be seen in the overall development of Archaic Greek sculpture, as in the KOUROS type (a striding nude male figure), regional styles occurred, particularly in the Late Archaic period, and these sometimes perpetuated technical and stylistic peculiarities. Though conforming to certain basic patterns, Late Archaic statues show a greater openness to every kind of variation and to increasingly rich adornment, as is seen most clearly in the KORE statues (draped female figures). At the same time, sharp transitions and stylization within the modelling of the body were reduced. For example, the musculature of the abdomen was treated more subtly, making it possible to show turning movements of the body. About the end of the 6th century BC a new stage was imperceptibly reached, even though the kouros pattern, as in the Aristodikos Kouros, was still applied. Though at first sight this work is similar to the *Kritios Boy* from the Acropolis at Athens, the latter marks the decisive transition from Late Archaic sculpture to the Severe style of the Early Classical period. In the *Kritios Boy* (see fig. 13 below) the realization of the shifting of weight from one leg to another, distributed through all parts of the body, signals the end of the simple conventions of the Archaic portrayal of the human being. Body structure and movements had to be elaborated plausibly as a whole. Such careful analysis of the interrelatedness of all the details of the body presupposes a close observation of nature by the leading sculptors, who must have been responsible for the new direction. In keeping with this development there is, from the beginning of the Severe style, an increasing diversity of subjects and poses, elaborated especially with figures in motion: only slight gestures or changes of position were needed to convey a new interpretation of the human figure in the manner of a code.

These new possibilities were rapidly elaborated in the mid-5th century BC, with the dynamic potential of the human figure treated in such works as the Artemision *Zeus* and Myron's *Diskobolos*. This formal development was also connected with advances in bronzeworking techniques. Bronze succeeded stone as the preferred medium for free-standing sculpture (though many of the most important works are known only from Roman copies in marble). The next decisive step was the perfection of the balanced asymmetrical type of pose known as Classical contrapposto, realized by POLYKLEITOS in his 'Canon' (both a written treatise, now lost, and a statue, probably the *Doryphoros*). This work set new standards for Greek sculpture, since Polykleitos' theoretical system, which he derived in a revolutionary way from the old canon of proportions, involved the precise harmonizing of proportions and symmetries. By comparison, other types of the balanced stance, such as the standing pose with the unweighted foot forward, found in Attica up to the late 5th century BC, were soon only marginal.

Of almost equal importance to Polykleitan contrapposto were the variations in the treatment of textiles in relation to the body in High Classical sculpture, so that a sense of movement in draped figures was clearly conveyed and even accentuated. At the same time, drapery folds were composed into complex figures that emphasized the underlying forms of the figure. Thus the High Classical form of the traditional *peplos*-wearing female figure was joined in the last quarter of the 5th century BC by other female statue types, for example those showing the garment adhering to the body as if wet, as in Paionios' *Nike* at Olympia and the Fréjus *Aphrodite*.

The end of the 5th century BC and the early 4th thus brought a working-out of the possibilities discovered by High Classical sculpture and a continuation of its tradition, first in a mannered calligraphic form, then with greater reserve and severity. This transitional period is exemplified by such works as Kephisodotos' *Eirene and Ploutos*. New tendencies gradually emerged within this framework in the mid-4th century BC, notably in the work of Praxiteles. He varied the standing figure by crossing the legs and using a leaning pose, already found in a late 5th-century BC *Aphrodite* from the circle of Pheidias (Naples, Mus. Archeol. N.), and he thus entirely reinterpreted contrapposto. The new nudity of the female figure in Praxiteles' statues of *Aphrodite* was accompanied by a continuation of the technique of contrasting drapery folds, as seen also in figures from Herculaneum. There was also a tendency to frame individual statues, such as cult statues or famous masterpieces, in small shrines (*naïskoi*) on a high pedestal. Some sought-after effects included equally the violent, sometimes opposed, turning poses exemplified by Skopas' *Maenad* (Dresden, Skulpsamml.); the overemphatic representation of rest and weight, as in the figures of *Herakles* by Lysippos; the suggestion of actions extending out into space in a single figure; and the alteration of the canonical proportions to yield still slenderer forms with smaller heads—a tendency originated by Lysippos that remained influential in the Hellenistic period. However, around the mid-4th century BC there were also retrospective tendencies, especially in the field of sacred subjects, in which an Archaic structure might be combined with Late Classical drapery folds, in a way that may have been influenced by a restoration of old cult statues. Such tendencies could also take the form of an archaizing treatment of hair and folds, as practised occasionally by Alkamenes in the High Classical period. Though such experiments still adhered firmly to Classical assumptions, they also prepared for new developments in the late 4th century BC that diverged more sharply from the Late Classical style.

At this time the beginnings of Early Hellenistic sculpture emerged, discarding some of the Classical conventions and even in some respects running counter to Late Classicism. At first, a trend can be discerned towards terse, stiff figures that do not reach beyond themselves. The sculpture of the following High Hellenistic period of the later 2nd century BC is almost the converse of this, with the figures characterized by violent movements and twists. Entirely new subjects, poses and group arrangements were tried out in large sculptures, especially at Pergamon, in works commemorating victories over the Gauls (e.g. the *Dying Gaul;* see fig. 14 below, and the Ludovisi *Gaul* group; *see* PERGAMON, fig. 4). These played an important role in combining the Classical tradition with the latest tendencies.

In the mid-2nd century BC there was a gradual return to the forms and models of Classical sculpture, which might be used as a stimulus and developed in their own terms, taken further in the style of the time, or merely copied. Sculptors continued, especially on Rhodes, to develop the High Classical style, while works were produced elsewhere that were purely Hellenistic in conception. Characteristic of such Late Hellenistic works is the restriction to a single viewing side, determined by the original siting of the sculpture. This is particularly noticeable in group compositions, though some groups are exceptions. From the early 1st century BC an increasingly clear neo-Classicism emerged, with new works produced in an earlier style and a flourishing production of straightforward copies of famous Classical works. At this time the market for sculpture was increasingly dominated by rich Romans, whose preference for earlier masterpieces over contemporary art stimulated the making of copies. This phase of Greek sculpture thus passed seamlessly into the early Roman Empire, where there was no room for the unfettered formal developments of the Hellenistic period. The influence of Roman taste can also be seen in the verist emphasis in portraiture that spread from Hellenistic central Italy.

Group compositions occurred from the Archaic period onwards. To begin with, they were usually formed simply by lining up figures on an extended common base, and only in the Early Classical period was the row of figures given a clear group connection. Later in the Classical period the multi-figure offerings by Greek states at the large pan-Hellenic sanctuaries provided opportunities for many different solutions to this problem, and from the Late Classical to the Hellenistic period increasingly large and complex groups were constructed. A reaction to this is represented by some Late Hellenistic groups, which adopt symmetrical arrangements with only one possible viewing side.

Functions. The forms and subjects of free-standing sculpture were closely related to their functions, almost all of which must be understood, at least to begin with, in a religious context. They include the representation of deities as cult statues in sanctuaries and the decoration of religious sites, which included the votive offerings made there. An honorific statue was also primarily a votive offering, even if this is not immediately evident in a secular context. Such statues were usually only legitimate after the death of the person honoured, though this was less in deference to the deity than to protect the state from excessive self-display by an individual citizen using sacred means. Though tomb statues also served the purpose of commemorating the dead and their families, they arose from an Archaic practice of marking graves with a sculpted stele. Sanctioned by this tradition, they soon took over modes of representation from sacred sculpture, a pattern that was often to be repeated.

Not until the Hellenistic period were statues, rather than mere utensils, used to decorate the living areas of palaces and houses, a practice that constituted an extension of the domestic shrine. In the Late Hellenistic period the acquisition of works of art by private collectors sometimes led to separate displays of statues, for example in the palaces of kings such as the Attalids of Pergamon. This practice was widely imitated in the villas of wealthy Romans, though even then an attempt was usually made to retain the sacred context, for example by displaying the works in a gallery dedicated to a 'presiding deity' in imitation of the votive collection at a shrine, or in a section of a library laid out as a shrine.

By the Hellenistic period, sculptures with similar subjects served widely differing functions, and a clear division into distinct genres occurred, though outstanding individual works continued to transcend these categories.

G. Krahmer: 'Stilphasen der hellenistischen Plastik', *Mitt. Dt. Archäol. Inst.: Röm. Abt.*, xxxviii–xxxix (1923–4), pp. 138–89
G. Krahmer: 'Die einansichtige Gruppe und die späthellenistische Kunst', *Nachrbl. Ges. Wiss. Göttingen, Philos.-Hist. Kl.* (1927), pp. 53–91
R. Horn: 'Stehende weibliche Gewandstatuen in der hellenistischen Plastik', *Mitt. Dt. Archäol. Inst.: Röm. Abt.*, suppl. 2 (1931)
G. Krahmer: *Figur und Raum in der ägyptischen und griechisch-archaischen Kunst* (Halle, 1931)
C. Karusos: *Aristodikos: Zur Geschichte der spätarchaisch-attischen Plastik der Grabstatue* (Stuttgart, 1961)
R. Kabus-Jahn: *Studien zu Frauenfiguren des vierten Jahrhunderts vor Christus* (Darmstadt, 1962)
U. Knigge: *Bewegte Figuren der Grossplastik im Strengen Stil* (diss., Munich, Ludwig-Maximilians U., 1965)
G. M. A. Richter: *The Portraits of the Greeks*, 3 vols (London, 1965; abridged and rev. by R. R. R. Smith (Oxford, 1984)
B. Fehr: *Bewegungsweisen und Verhaltensideale* (Bad Bramstedt, 1970)
B. S. Ridgway: *The Severe Style in Greek Sculpture* (Princeton, 1970)
P. Kranz: 'Frühe griechische Sitzfiguren: Zum Problem der Typenbildung und des orientalischen Einflusses in der frühen griechischen Rundplastik', *Mitt. Dt. Archäol. Inst.: Athen. Abt.*, lxxxvii (1972), pp. 1–55
A. H. Borbein: 'Die griechische Statue des 4. Jahrh. v. Chr.: Formalanalytische Untersuchungen zur Kunst der Nachklassik', *Jb. Dt. Archäol. Inst.*, lxxxviii (1973), pp. 43–212
H. von Steuben: *Der Kanon des Polyklet: Doryphoros und Amazone* (Tübingen, 1973)
R. R. Holloway: *Influences and Styles in the Late Archaic and Early Classical Greek Sculpture of Sicily and Magna Graecia* (Leuven, 1975)
H. L. Schanz: *Greek Sculptural Groups: Archaic and Classical* (New York and London, 1980)
R. Tölle-Kastenbein: *Frühklassische Peplosfiguren: Originale* (Mainz, 1980)
B. S. Ridgway: *Fifth-century Styles in Greek Sculpture* (Princeton, 1981)
H. Jung: *Thronende und sitzende Götter: Zum griechischen Götterbild und Menschenideal in geometrischer und früharchaischer Zeit* (Bonn, 1982)
C. Vorster: *Griechische Kinderstatuen* (Cologne, 1983)
P. Karakatsanis: *Studien zu archaischen Kolossalwerken* (Frankfurt, 1986)
H.-H. von Prittwitz und Gaffron: *Der Wandel der Aphrodite: Archäologische Studien zu weiblichen halbbekleideten Statuetten des späten Hellenismus* (Bonn, 1988)
B. S. Ridgway: *The Styles of c. 331–200 BC* (1990), i of *Hellenistic Sculpture* (Bristol, 1990–)
A. F. Stewart: *Greek Sculpture: An Exploration*, 2 vols (New Haven and London, 1990)
L. Todisco: *Scultura greca del IV secolo: Maestri e scuole di statuaria tra classicità ed ellenismo* (Milan, 1993)
S. Woodford: *The Art of Greece and Rome* (Cambridge and New York, 2004)

(b) Architectural. Greek architectural sculpture developed as decoration for stone temples in the Doric and Ionic orders, but it occurs on other imposing formal buildings and on smaller structures, often in temple form. Only certain parts of any building were adorned, typically the pediment, the frieze section of the entablature and, less often, columns, cella walls and other parts. Mythological battle scenes appear to have been subject-matter particularly well suited to architectural sculpture. Individual themes recur, particularly when there was concern to find a motif with local reference. In general, weight-bearing elements were decorated only with reluctance and particularly not in high relief. The most important decorated areas could be viewed as having a masking function: metope friezes and pediment fields cover the ends of ridge beams, for example.

Pediments. Pedimental sculpture occurs mainly in the Doric order and only exceptionally in the Ionic. The triangular field formed by the PEDIMENT created particular compositional problems that were not satisfactorily solved until the end of the Archaic period (see below). The earliest temple pediments may simply have had a central terracotta revetment (a tradition that continued in Etruscan architecture until the Late Hellenistic period); the use of stone reliefs began in the late 7th century BC soon after the first stone temples were built.

The earliest large-scale ensemble, from the Temple of Artemis at Corfu (*c.* 600 BC), has three distinct figural groups on different scales. The running Gorgon at the centre (for illustration *see* CORFU) is both fearsomely apotropaic and, with the smaller-scale figures on either side, part of a mythological narrative (Perseus and Medusa), while the recumbent lions flanking this group further suggest the motif of the Mistress of the Animals. The corners contain small three-figure scenes from a *Gigantomachy* and the *Trojan War*, both subjects that were later of great importance in architectural sculpture. Contemporary with the Kerkyra pediment are the symmetrical facing lions tearing apart a steer, which appear on a pediment on the Acropolis at Athens (Acropolis Mus.). Here fish were used to effect closure in the narrowing corners. In two later examples there the discontinuities between unrelated pictorial motifs were removed by the placing of figures of diminishing size within the pediment to form a unified thematic framework. By the mid-6th century BC sculpture in high relief or, for large pediments, in the round increasingly became the norm, as at the earlier Temple of Apollo at Aigina, where figures were not finished in detail on their backs. The tendency was towards thorough finishing, however, and in addition limestone was superseded by marble. In the older Temple of Apollo (*c.* 520–*c.* 510 BC) at Delphi, for example, the west pediment was limestone, but the east was marble. The latter had rows of kouroi and korai either side of Apollo's chariot, a far more static composition than the *Gigantomachy* on the west pediment, with its battle scenes unfolding either side of a central figure. In the slightly later Temple of Apollo (*c.* 510–*c.* 500 BC) at Eretria, chariot groups were used to make the transition from the central figures and the lateral groups, a device that often recurs in later pediments. The pediments of the Temple of Aphaia on Aigina demonstrate the transition from Archaic to Early Classical. Both have the same subject (Athena flanked by fighting warriors), but the east pediment, replaced in the early 5th century BC, shows a new, bravura approach to the overall composition in the foreshortening of the figures and other details.

The two great pedimental ensembles of the 5th century BC come from the Temple of Zeus (*c.* 470–*c.* 457 BC) at Olympia and the Parthenon (447–432 BC) at Athens. In both sets, mythological subjects of local significance were used, and as at the Temple of Apollo, Delphi, there are clear differences between the relatively static compositions on the east sides (at Olympia, the *Preparations for the Chariot Race between Pelops and Oinomaus*; at Athens, the *Birth of Athena*) and the stronger sense of movement in the west pediments (at Olympia, a *Centauromachy, see* OLYMPIA, fig. 2; at Athens, the *Struggle between Athena and Poseidon for Possession of Attica*). In terms of composition, the central fighting pair, as originally in the Parthenon's west pediment, was to become a more important element than the quietly standing central figure. One of the last great sculptural pediments with subjects of local significance was created by Skopas, as architect-sculptor, on the Temple of Athena Alea at Tegea. Here the *Kalydonian Boar Hunt* and the *Legend of Telephos* were rendered with a strong, unquiet sense of movement quite different from High Classical sculpture.

Pedimental sculpture is rare in the Hellenistic period, the more so since the Doric order was steadily eclipsed by Ionic and Corinthian. An important exception is the pediment (first half 2nd century BC) of the Hieron of the Kabeiroi at Samothrace.

Metopes. This form belongs to temples in the Doric order. Sculpted metopes could be placed on the exterior entablature or inside, over the pronaos and opisthodomos, where they provided a series of rectangular fields separated by triglyphs, suitable for at most three figures. During the Archaic period a single scene was sometimes divided between two or three metopes, and this device developed into metopal cycles consisting of a series of related individual scenes.

Painted terracotta metopes were used on the late 7th-century BC Temple of Apollo at Thermon, and from the first half of the 6th century BC relief metopes in stone occur, for example on the Sikyonian Treasury at Delphi. The first extensive series comes from the Treasury (*c.* 530 BC) in the Sanctuary of Hera at Foce del Sele in South Italy. These are still relatively simple, in low relief and often with only one figure, but they are notable for their representation of the *Labours of Herakles*, which was to become one of the main subjects in the metopal repertory. The tendency towards thematic structuring is already evident in the Athenian Treasury (*c.* 510–*c.* 490 BC) at

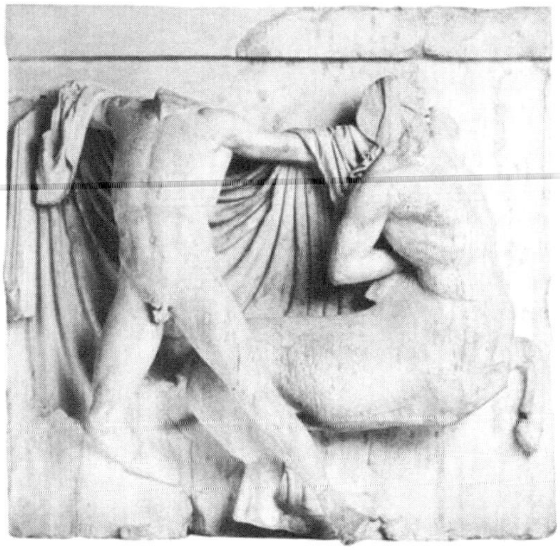

5. Metope showing a *Centauromachy*, marble, h. 1.72 m, from the south side of the Parthenon, Athens, High Classical, *c.* 440 BC (London, British Museum)

Delphi, with its parallel cycles of the *Labours of Herakles* and the *Exploits of Theseus*. Mostly two-figure groups, these metopes show an extensive mastery of physical perspective.

In the Temple of Zeus (*c.* 470–*c.* 457 BC) at Olympia the canonical cycle of the *Twelve Labours of Herakles* was divided between the pronaos and the opisthodomos (*see* OLYMPIA, fig. 4). These two- or three-figure reliefs relate not only to each other, forming an integrated cycle, but also to their positions on the building itself. However, the high point of metopal sculpture is undoubtedly the Parthenon (447–432 BC). Each of the temple's four sides had a different battle subject: a *Gigantomachy*, an *Amazonomachy*, a *Centauromachy* (see fig. 5) and *Trojan War* scenes. In the metopes of Skopas' Temple of Athena Alea at Tegea the form reached its technical limits, with figures carved almost fully in the round (as a result, only fragments now remain).

With the decline of the Doric order, the metope ceased to be an important form, though the concept of the metopal series was continued in figurative coffer reliefs (e.g. the Early Hellenistic *Centauromachy* from the heroön at Belevi).

Friezes. Unlike metopes, the frieze formed an uninterrupted horizontal field. The external frieze is an Ionic feature originating in the marble architecture of the Cyclades, but in the High Classical period friezes were even used to adorn Doric buildings, both on the inside of the peristyle and on the cella walls. Early Archaic frieze-like sculptures are known from Crete, but the first important Ionic frieze is that of the Late Archaic Siphnian Treasury (*c.* 525 BC) at Delphi. This may well represent the work of two sculptors, one more progressive than the other, and its subjects are the *Judgement of Paris*, the *?Abduction of Helen*, *Trojan War* scenes and a masterful *Gigantomachy*, densely composed, with bold overlappings.

The high point of frieze sculpture is again the Doric Parthenon, with its external cella frieze showing the *Panathenaic Festival* (see fig. 6). This further provides the most comprehensive expression of the formal language of High Classical Attic sculpture, since it was produced by several sculptors collaborating under Pheidias' direction. Ionic friezes from the Acropolis include those of the Temple of Athena Nike (*c.* 425 BC), with battle scenes that probably depict a historical rather than mythological conflict and figures of the *Consulting Gods* over the entrance, and the Erechtheion (421–405 BC), where the relief figures were attached to slabs of black Eleusinian marble. Athenian sculptors were responsible for the internal cella frieze (*c.* 410 BC) of the High Classical Temple of Apollo at Bassai, which shows an *Amazonomachy* and a *Centauromachy*.

Between the end of the 5th century BC and the 2nd century BC (e.g. the Temple of Artemis at Magnesia on the Maeander), friezes generally ceased to be a feature of large temples, though the tradition was continued on other types of monument. These included altars, cult statue pedestals and tombs, most notably the Mausoleum (completed *c.* 349 BC) at Halikarnassos, the Nereid Monument at Xanthos (*c.* 425–400 BC) and the Tomb of Pericles (mid-4th century BC) at Limyra. The Monument of Lysikrates (336/5 BC) at Athens has a circular frieze of *Dionysos Transforming the Pirates into Dolphins*, which neatly fits the architecture, though with its single plane of figures that do not overlap, it belongs rather to the genre of subsidiary ornamental friezes than to the temple frieze tradition. Among the most important Hellenistic friezes are those from the colossal altars at Ephesos, Magnesia on the Maeander and Pergamon. The Altar of Zeus at Pergamon had an extremely vivid *Gigantomachy* (the 'Great Frieze') on the exterior of the socle and a series of scenes from the *Legend of Telephos* on the interior of the altar enclosure. The latter shows a development of illustrative technique that was important for Roman Imperial relief sculpture.

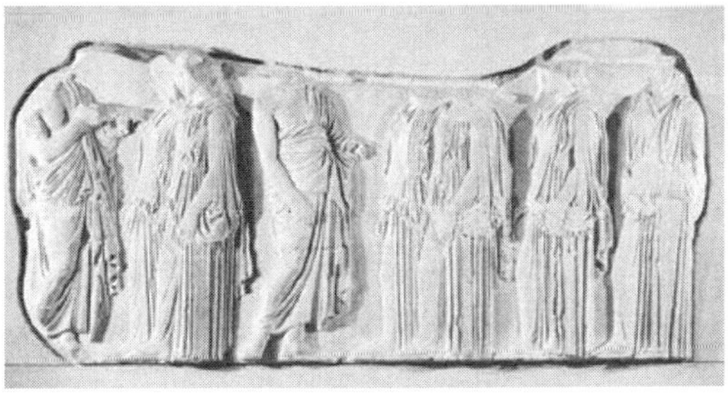

6. Ancient Greek relief known as the 'plaque of the Ergastines', from the east frieze of the Parthenon, showing young women (ergastines) and two marshals (one holding a basket which would have contained the sacrificial knife) in the Panathenaic procession, marble, h. 960 mm, *c.* 445–*c.* 438 BC (Paris, Musée du Louvre)

Acroteria and other forms. Acroteria (*see also* ACROTERION) ornamented the slanting cornices of pediments (one at the apex, one on each side). Favoured types of subject were figures that could leap or fly or move easily through water (e.g. winged *nikai*, riders, dolphins), or vegetal palmette-scroll forms. Groups were also sometimes used, as in *Boreas Abducting Oreithyia* from the Athenian Temple of Apollo on Delos.

The other special forms of architectural sculpture were mostly developed in the Archaic period by the more experimental East Greeks. Metopes might be combined with a frieze (e.g. the Doric Temple of Athena, Assos; *c.* 540 BC), columns were carved as figures (e.g. the Siphnian Treasury, Delphi, and the Erechtheion; *see also* ATLANTID *and* CARYATID) or given relief decoration on part of the shaft (e.g. the Temple of Apollo, Didyma, and the Temple of Artemis, Ephesos, 6th and 4th centuries BC). Wall reliefs, of which there are many 7th-century BC examples from the Sanctuary of Hera on Samos, perhaps developed out of the plastic enhancement of murals. They were later abandoned, but since the interiors of houses were a favourite location for wall paintings, the same interiors later offered a place for mural reliefs.

P. Demangel: *La Frise ionique* (Paris, 1932)

W.-H. Schuchhardt: *Archaische Giebelkompositionen* (Freiburg, 1940)

E. Lapalus: *Le Fronton sculpté en Grèce des origines à la fin du quatrième siècle* (Paris, 1947)

B. S. Ridgway: 'Notes on the Development of the Greek Frieze', *Hesperia*, xxxv (1966), pp. 188–204

B. Ashmole: *Architect and Sculptor in Classical Greece* (London and New York, 1972)

A. Delivorrias: *Attische Giebelskulpturen und Akrotere des fünften Jahrhunderts* (Tübingen, 1974)

A. Schmidt-Colinet: *Antike Stützfiguren* (diss., U. Cologne, 1977)

N. Bookidis: *A Study of the Use and Geographical Distribution of Architectural Sculpture in the Archaic Period (Greece, East Greece and Magna Graeca)* (Ann Arbor, 1979)

E. Schmidt: *Geschichte der Karyatide* (Würzburg, 1982)

F. Felten: *Griechische tektonische Friese archaischer und klassischer Zeit* (Waldsassen, 1984)

P. Knell: *Mythos und Polis: Bildprogramme griechischer Bauskulptur* (Darmstadt, 1990)

P. A. Webb: *Hellenistic Architectural Sculpture: Figural Motifs in Western Anatolia and the Aegean Islands* (Madison, WI, 1996)

D. Buitron-Oliver: *The Interpretation of Architectural Sculpture in Greece and Rome* (New England, 1997)

B. S. Ridgway: *Prayers in Stone: Greek Architectural Sculpture ca. 600–100 BCE* (Berkeley, 1999)

A. E. Herring: *Reconnecting Architectural Sculpture to its Building: A Study of Ionic Friezes on Fifth Century BC Doric Buildings* (diss., Los Angeles, UCLA, 2005)

I. Jenkins: *Greek Architecture and its Sculpture* (New York, 2006)

(c) Non-architectural reliefs. There are four main types of Greek non-architectural reliefs, distinguished by their forms and functions: grave reliefs, votive reliefs, record reliefs and base reliefs.

Graves. Funerary reliefs (stelai) form the largest and most widespread group. Their development can be traced from the late 7th century BC to the 2nd century AD. The earliest examples come from Athens and its surrounding countryside, where they appeared among other types of grave markers erected by wealthy families. Occasionally made of limestone but generally of marble, these reliefs bear a marked resemblance to grave statues of the period. The narrow slabs, often of monumental size, represent a single standing figure in profile. Initially only male figures occurred (*see also* KOUROS). Attributes such as swords, spears and flowers indicate upper-class status.

From the mid-6th century BC onwards, the images became more varied, highlighting aristocratic preoccupations by showing naked athletes, armed warriors or men wearing patterned cloaks and accompanied by dogs. The stelai frequently also included a small area at the bottom depicting animals or scenes from everyday life and a top section representing an animal, a palmette, or a mythical creature, such as a sphinx, gorgon or siren. The few reliefs made for women differ in shape and structure, showing the deceased enthroned. Rare in the Archaic period (*c.* 700–*c.* 500/480 BC), they were prevalent during the Classical period (*c.* 500/480–323 BC).

During the first half of the 5th century BC, sumptuary laws restricted the size and appearance of graves, but sepulchral reliefs were produced again in Attica from *c.* 440 BC. These monuments were commonly erected for married women but also for unmarried young people and sometimes for adult men. The Stele of Hegeso exemplifies a widespread type of relief, depicting a deceased matron in the company of her servant. The servant is handing Hegeso a box from which the latter lifts an object that was once painted. Such gravestones were erected alongside other monuments to display the family group as an important unit in the community. Unity was also expressed by the motif of the handshake, which became increasingly popular in the 4th century BC. At the same time, the number of family members and servants represented increased, while the deceased were occasionally marked by their names. The representative character of such reliefs was accompanied by a stylistic development, with figures in the foreground positioned frontally, in high relief.

The production of grave reliefs ended in Attica after 317 BC with the introduction of laws restricting burial practices. Other Mediterranean regions, however, developed their own traditions, profiting from a favourable political and economic environment. The sepulchral reliefs of Samos and Smyrna (now Izmir) are examples of the many such idiosyncratic styles. On Samos, grave stelai (Pithagorio Mus.) borrowed the iconography of votive reliefs, depicting the deceased banqueting with relatives. Tombstones from Smyrna (e.g. Izmir, Kültürpark, 31, 164, 3277, 519; Oxford, Ashmolean, Michaelis 204), on the other hand, show single or paired figures, attended by their servants and among objects reflecting the values of a prosperous Hellenized world. The architecturally shaped frames often carry inscriptions and a wreath symbolizing honours received by the citizens from their community (*demos*).

Votives. Early Greek votive reliefs of marble or limestone show the epiphany of the god or represent a shrine's donor. The first reliefs carved with what was to become the typical arrangement of divine or semi-divine beings and worshippers in a single scene were made shortly after 600 BC (e.g. *c.* 580–*c.* 570 BC, Athens, Acropolis Mus., 586–7, 622; *c.* 570–*c.* 560 BC, Munich, Glyp., 241). These are of various sizes, generally square or rectangular, and were set up in urban and rural sanctuaries. Reliefs dedicated to Hermes, Pan and the nymphs often take the shape of a cave. Lakonian hero reliefs are a special case; these were erected in sanctuaries as well as on grave tumuli. One of the best-known votive reliefs is the so-called Mourning Athena.

Large numbers of votive reliefs were produced in Athens between the late 5th century BC and the 4th. Most show processions of men, women and children, some carrying offerings, others driving animals to be sacrificed. They approach a god or, more commonly, groups of deities represented on a considerably larger scale than the worshippers. Some reliefs represent the god or hero banqueting or show Dionysian and bucolic scenes. Changes in religious beliefs found expression in the range of deities addressed by humans in the Late Classical (*c.* 375–*c.* 323 BC) and Hellenistic (323–27 BC) periods. Healing deities, semi-divine beings connected with fertility and vegetation, Oriental gods, heroes such as Herakles, and mythical founders of cities had replaced the Olympian gods as the focus of worship. From their predominantly humble size and quality and from occasional inscriptions it can be concluded that votive reliefs were mainly dedicated by the middle classes.

Records. Record reliefs were erected by decree to publish documents of private or public institutions. They were simple marble plates displaying the text of the decree. In some instances modestly sized, rectangular reliefs, paid for privately, were included above the inscription. Most of the numerous published documents were made in Athens (and set up mainly on the Acropolis) from *c.* 430 BC to the early 3rd century BC. They record, for example, treaties, accounts by treasurers and honours given to individuals in recognition of services to the city. Simple, often repeated representations reflect the content of the inscribed texts. For example, on some reliefs from the 5th century BC and early 4th, Athena, the patron goddess of Athens, is shown shaking hands (*dexiosis*) with another deity, thus expressing alliance between Athens and a foreign Greek state. On others, Athena or Demos (the personification of the Attic people) honours individuals with a wreath. Motifs similar to those on votive reliefs were also used, especially in decrees concerning religious matters. As a result of changed political and economic circumstances (including the rise of Macedonia), production of record reliefs almost completely ceased in the early 3rd century BC.

Bases. Attic sculptors of the Archaic period were the first to decorate the marble bases of stelai and statues. Depending on the character of the monument, the bases were adorned with reliefs showing animals, sports activities, mythical contests and heroic deeds. Several Archaic square bases of excellent quality display scenes reflecting the aristocratic lifestyle. A round base of the same period in Istanbul (Archaeol. Mus., 5370) shows young people dancing. Bases of commemorative votive monuments for athletic victories, mainly from the 4th century BC, often represent sports scenes on three sides with an explanatory inscription on the fourth. Another form of base relief comprises the plaques of *c.* 330/20 BC that once decorated the base of the cult group in the temple in Mantinea (Athens, N. Archaeol. Mus., 215–16), depicting the *Musical Contest between Apollo and Marsyas.*

G. M. A. Richter: *The Archaic Gravestones of Attica* (London, 1961/*R* Bristol, 1988)
E. Mitropoulou: *Attic Votive Reliefs of the 6th and 5th Centuries BC* (1977), i of *Corpus* (Athens, 1977–)
E. Pfuhl and M. Möbius: *Die ostgriechischen Grabreliefs*, i–iii (Mainz, 1977–9)
G. Neumann: *Probleme des griechischen Weihreliefs* (Tübingen, 1979)
B. Schmaltz: *Griechische Grabreliefs* (Darmstadt, 1983)
M. Meyer: 'Die griechischen Urkundenreliefs', *Mitt. Dt. Archäol. Inst.: Athen. Abt.*, suppl. 13 (1989) [whole vol.]
C. W. Clairmont: *Classic Attic Tombstones* (Kilchberg, 1993)
A. Muller: *Les terres cuites votives du Thesmophorion: De l'atelier au sanctuaire* (Athens, 1996)

(ii) Subject-matter. By far the most popular subject in monumental Greek sculpture was the human figure. It was used to represent a divinity, a mythological personage, an abstract concept, a particular individual or a typical mortal. Inscription, attribute or context was usually sufficient to make the intended meaning clear. Animals were also represented, occasionally in their own right but more usually in conjunction with the human figure. Monsters were sometimes depicted; plant life is rare and generally stylized; other subjects are exceptional.

(a) Free-standing sculpture. (b) Free-standing reliefs. (c) Architectural sculpture.

(a) Free-standing sculpture.

Divinities. The major divinities differed broadly in character—Apollo was always depicted as young, Zeus and Poseidon as mature—but their identities were usually specified by means of attributes. Thus Athena is recognized by her aegis (and often her helmet as well), Apollo by his bow or kithara, Hermes by his traveller's hat and winged shoes and Eros by his wings. Traces of Poseidon's trident or Zeus' thunderbolt would establish beyond dispute the identity of the bronze god (Athens, N. Archaeol. Mus.,

Br. 15161; for illustration *see* ARTEMISION BRONZES) found in the sea off Cape Artemision. The characterization of some gods changed in the course of time; thus Dionysos and Hermes, generally bearded in the Archaic period, were usually represented as youths in the Hellenistic period, and Eros gradually changed from a youth to a baby. An image of a god could serve as a CULT STATUE or a dedication and could also appear in narrative contexts as a part of a mythological representation. Aniconic or roughly shaped images, despite their professed holiness, will not be treated here, but something of an intermediate form is represented by the herm, a pillar topped by a head of Hermes and graced with male genitals, which was popular from Archaic times and stood at entrances of houses and along roadsides, providing protection to residents and wayfarers. Eventually heads other than those of Hermes were placed on herms, sometimes even double heads (Janus-like) or portraits.

Other mythological figures. These are usually identified in one of four ways: first, by inscription, usually on the base; second, by attribute (e.g. Herakles' lionskin and club); third, by the use of a unique and characteristic type, for instance the seated figure of the mourning Penelope; and fourth, by means of particular features specific to the type (e.g. tails and horse-ears on satyrs, horse-bodies on centaurs, fish-tails on Tritons or monstrous visages on gorgons).

Monsters appeared in sculpture from the Archaic period onwards. Sphinxes frequently surmounted Archaic grave stelai or sometimes served as dedications in their own right (e.g. the *Crouching Sphinx* on the Naxian Column at Delphi). Sirens are shown in funerary contexts in the 4th century BC, and centaurs, satyrs and figures of Pan, with his goat-legs and horns, became increasingly popular in the Hellenistic period, often interacting piquantly with human or divine figures. Other monsters, for example Skylla (e.g. London, BM), also occur occasionally in narrative contexts or in isolation.

Personified abstractions. It is not always easy to draw the line between genuine divinities and personified abstractions. Vividly anthropomorphic personifications exist in Homer and Hesiod; Nike (Victory) appears in sculpture already in the Archaic period (e.g. the *Nike of Archermos*) and is probably a *bona fide* goddess; Eirene (Peace) was accorded a cult and a statue, made by Kephisodotos, in Athens at the same time (*c.* 375 BC); but Kairos (Opportunity), an ingenious invention by Lysippos in the late 4th century BC (see Posidippos: *Greek Anthology* XVI.275), seems to be a fully-fledged personification of an abstract concept. Personified abstractions became increasingly popular in the Hellenistic period (e.g. the *Tyche* of Antioch by Eutychides) and could be incorporated into complicated allegories.

Generic figures. Archaic standing nude male figures (kouroi; *see* KOUROS), which were neither placed on graves as memorials nor equipped with special attributes (e.g. a bow for Apollo), may simply have represented non-specific votaries of a god, particularly when they were found in a sanctuary, for instance the kouroi (Athens, N. Archaeol. Mus., and Thebes Mus.) found in the Ptoion sanctuary to Apollo in Boiotia. The same may apply to draped female figures (korai; *see* KORE), for example those found on the Athenian acropolis. Most athlete statues, now known chiefly through Roman copies and literary references, were probably votive offerings placed in sanctuaries to commemorate victories. According to Pliny the elder (XXXIV.viii.16), it was customary for those who won a victory in a sacred contest, particularly at Olympia, to dedicate a statue of themselves, but only those who won three times were allowed to dedicate a statue that bore a physical resemblance to the dedicator. Some figures that appear generic may originally have been representations of mythological characters: for instance, the *Doryphoros* (for illustration *see* POLYKLEITOS) may have been a representation of Achilles and the *Diskobolos* one of Hyacinthus.

During the Hellenistic period there was an immense expansion of the sculptor's repertory. Generic figures, which we might call 'ideal' or perhaps better 'non-specific', became rarer, and a wide variety of specific characterizations far more popular. Not only did portraiture of both real and imaginary sitters increase, but sympathetic and highly individualized representations were made of barbarians (Gauls, Africans, Scythians etc) and deformed people (grotesques), and even the extremes of age (chubby babies and desiccated elderly people) came in for artistic scrutiny. Along with representations of a wide range of humanity came representations of a wide range of activities: people were shown at work or at play, making war or making love; genre subjects became acceptable for major works of sculpture.

Representations of individuals. Individuals could be identified by inscriptions or by means of specific characterizations. Kouroi or korai placed as memorials on graves were identified as representations of the deceased by means of inscriptions (e.g. 'Kroisos', 'Aristodikos', 'Phrasikleia'; all Athens, N. Archaeol. Mus.). Portraits, which attempted to capture the physical appearance of an individual, may have begun as early as the 5th century BC; but characterization always remained more important, as is obvious from the imaginary portraits the Greeks felt free to create (e.g. of *Homer*) and the portraits of real people that they felt free to re-create (e.g. of *Socrates* or *Alexander the Great*). Greek portraits were full-length; a truncated or abbreviated image was not felt to be an adequate representation, except when portraits were made as herms. Portraits were normally either commemorative or honorary, with the result that most (though not all) were of the famous and powerful: poets, statesmen, orators, rulers or philosophers.

Groups. Free-standing statues could be grouped either as loose assemblages (e.g. the *Geneleos Group*; Berlin, Antikensamml. and Samos, Archaeol. Mus.) or tightly knit entities (e.g. the *Gaul Killing Himself and his Wife* (Ludovisi *Gaul* group; Rome, Mus. N. Romano; *see* PERGAMON, fig. 4) or something in between, for example the *Tyrannicides* (Naples, Mus. Archaeol. N.; *see* TYRANT SLAYERS). Groups could commemorate individuals (as seems to have been the case with the *Geneleos Group*, which consisted of several figures—standing, seated and reclining—lined up along a single base), a group (as in the case of the Messenian statues at Olympia in honour of 35 boys lost at sea along with their trainer and flautist; Pausanias, V.xxv.2–4), heroic action (e.g. the *Tyrannicides*; Pliny the elder, XXXIV.ix.17) or a victory (e.g. the *Gaul Killing Himself and his Wife*, a copy of part of an Attalid monument at Pergamon, of which this was the centrepiece). Not only were real people assembled in groups (as in the above examples) but mythological figures also—or even a mixture of the two, as in the Athenian dedication at Delphi, which included Athena, Apollo, a group of heroes and the general Miltiades (Pausanias, X.x.1) or the nearby Lacedaemonian dedication comprising the Dioskouroi, Zeus, Apollo, Artemis and Poseidon with Lysander accompanied by his soothsayer and helmsman (Pausanias, X.ix.7). From the 4th century BC groups were occasionally composed of a naturalistic figure combined with an archaistic image, for instance *Artemis* leaning on a statue of herself (Vienna, Ksthist. Mus.).

Myths could be represented by means of figures loosely assembled, as in Myron of Eleutherai's representation of *Athena and Marsyas* (Pliny the elder, XXXIV.xix.57; copy of *Athena*, Frankfurt am Main, Liebieghaus; copy of *Marsyas*, Rome, Vatican, Mus. Pio-Clementino), or in tighter groups where a hero is shown in conflict with his adversary, the adversary often serving to identify the hero (e.g. *Theseus and the Minotaur*). Lysippos is said to have sculpted a series of representations of the *Labours of Herakles* (Strabo: *Geography* X.459), which would have consisted of tightly-knit groups showing Herakles in combat with the lion or the deer or carrying the boar (compositions that seem to be reflected on many Roman sarcophagi). More complex groups were favoured in the Hellenistic period (e.g. *Menelaos with the Body of Patroklos* (Florence, Loggia Lanzi); *Artemis Rescuing Iphigeneia* (Copenhagen, Ny Carlsberg Glyp.); the *Laokoon* (Rome, Vatican, Mus. Pio-Clementino); the Farnese *Bull* (Naples, Mus. Archaeol. N.)).

Representations of men and horses were frequently grouped together to form equestrian statues, one of the earliest being the Rampin *Horseman* (Athens, Acropolis Mus., 590, and Paris, Louvre, 3104; see fig. 11 below), or chariot groups (e.g. the one now lost to which the bronze DELPHI CHARIOTEER (Delphi, Archaeol. Mus.) originally belonged). Men were shown carrying animals (e.g. the *Calf-bearer*, Athens, Acropolis Mus., 624; see fig. 10 below) or carried by them (e.g. *Odysseus under the Ram*; Rome, Gal. Doria-Pamphili) or sacrificing them (Pliny the elder, XXXIV.xix.79 and 80). Children were shown with pets—the representation of infants with various sorts of geese was particularly popular in the Hellenistic period—and those beloved of the gods with amorous divinities in animal disguise (e.g. *Leda and the Swan* (Boston, MA, Mus. F.A., 04.14) or the *Ganymede and the Eagle* (Pliny the elder, XXXIV.xix.79)).

Animals. As well as appearing in groups animals were occasionally shown on their own. Lions from early times were represented as guardians of the grave, for example the *Lion of Menekrates* (Corfu, Archaeol. Mus.), and probably continued to serve the same function, though in an attenuated form, on the Mausoleum at Halikarnassos. Sometimes the meaning imputed to a lion used as a commemorative image could be deeper, as with the lioness set up to commemorate Leaina, the mistress of Aristogeiton (Pausanias, I.xxiii.2 and Pliny the elder, XXXIV.xix.72) or the Lion of Chaironeia, which, according to Pausanias (IX.xl.10), alluded to the spirit of the men who died fighting Philip of Macedon. Under Oriental influence, a whole sequence of lions was erected to line the Sacred Way at Delos. Of domestic animals, the noble horse was always admired and occasionally represented without rider or chariot. Bulls were represented (Pausanias, X.ix.3), and a bronze *Heifer* by Myron was much admired (Pliny the elder, XXXIV.xix.57). Dogs became a subject of interest in their own right (Pliny the elder, XXXIV.xix.90), especially in the Hellenistic period. Even reptiles and insects were occasionally represented, for instance the lizard slain by Apollo in the *Apollo Sauroktonos* by Praxiteles (copy, Paris, Louvre) or the tree-cricket and locust sculpted by Myron (Pliny the elder, XXXIV.xix.57).

Plant life. Flowers and trees are rare in Greek sculpture, though stylized plant forms were often used for architectural decoration, and 'palm trees' in sculptural form were set up at Delphi and on Delos and even within the Erechtheion in Athens (Pausanias, I.xxiv.7).

(b) Free-standing reliefs. Free-standing reliefs fall into three main categories: grave monuments, document reliefs and votive offerings. Grave stelai in their most elaborate form were topped by free-standing sphinxes, but in time a palmette finial was considered sufficient. Archaic grave stelai were usually carved with a single standing figure representing the deceased, who might be characterized as a boxer by a broken nose and a boxing glove on his upraised hand (Athens, Kerameikos Mus.), as a warrior in armour (Athens, N. Archaeol. Mus.) or as an athlete carrying an oil flask (New York, Met.), but neither at this time nor later is there any hint of real portraiture in grave reliefs. Occasionally two figures were shown: a brother and sister (New York, Met., 11.185) or a mother and child (Athens, N. Archaeol. Mus., 3845). In the second half of the 5th century BC, with the introduction of more varied formats, seated figures gradually came to be preferred, often accompanied by standing ones, as on the Hegeso Stele (Athens, N. Archaeol. Mus.). In the 4th century BC the number of figures increased; a seated figure often grasps the hand of a standing one in the presence of others

(Athens, N. Archaeol. Mus.). Standing figures, alone or with others (e.g. the Ilissos Relief; Athens, N. Archaeol. Mus.), and commemorative scenes of battle (e.g. the Dexileos Stele; Athens, Kerameikos Mus.) were also occasionally carved, until the production of Attic grave stelai came to an end *c.* 310 BC. Occasionally some hint was given as to the deceased's way of life but only in the most general way (e.g. huntsman, athlete etc).

Documents such as treaties that were carved on stone were frequently headed by a figured relief. The figures often represented the signing parties—for example a relief from the Acropolis shows *Athena Clasping the Hand of Hera* (Athens, Acropolis Mus., 1333), the two goddesses representing Athens and Samos respectively—or glossed the contents of the document with abstractions, as with *Democracy Crowning the Seated Demos* (Athens, Agora Mus., I.6524).

Votive reliefs usually show worshippers bringing homage to deities. The deities were carved on a large scale, which contrasts with their minute votaries (e.g. *Worshipper with (?)Triptolemos, Persephone, Demeter and a God*; Copenhagen, Ny Carlsberg Glyp., 197). Such reliefs sometimes hint at a landscape setting, such as a cave or a tree or a shrine. Other miscellaneous reliefs can be religious (e.g. the Eleusis Relief; Athens, N. Archaeol. Mus.) or mythological. The Hellenistic period favoured elaborate allegories, such as the *Apotheosis of Homer* (London, BM) or simple slices of nature.

(c) Architectural sculpture. Temples, treasuries and other buildings were frequently decorated with sculptures, almost without exception illustrating myths. These can usually be identified by means of the attributes carried by the principal figures or by their characteristic opponents (Gorgon, Hydra, Minotaur etc). Sometimes, however, only a literary source can explain the subject as in the case of the east pediment of the Temple of Zeus at Olympia, which Pausanias' description (V.x.6–7) reveals as the *Preparation for the Chariot Race between Pelops and Oinomaos* (see fig. 7).

Pediments. The awkward triangular shape of the pediment made it difficult for artists to fill with a unified and coherent subject. In the first half of the 6th century BC and sometimes later, animals were used to cope with some of the problems presented by pediments, snakes filling the corners, lions devouring cattle in the centre (Athens, Acropolis Mus.) and reclining panthers (Corfu, Archaeol. Mus.) mediating the slope between the centre and the corners. Later this last role was taken over by horses, which could be integrated into the story being told, as on the east pediment of the Temple of Zeus at Olympia (Olympia, Archaeol. Mus.) and probably on the west pediment of the Parthenon. The pediment in the early Temple of Artemis at Corfu (Kerkyra; Corfu, Archaeol. Mus.) has the story of the Gorgon Medusa and her progeny told in the centre, but a *Gigantomachy* is squeezed into one (or both) of the corners. Later artists were usually able to fill the whole pediment with a single story. Scenes of action were most adaptable, and mythological battles were therefore popular, for instance the two Trojan wars depicted in the pediments of the Temple of Aphaia at Aigina (Munich, Glyp.) and the *Battle between the Lapiths and the Centaurs* in the west pediment of the Temple of Zeus at Olympia (Olympia, Archaeol. Mus.). But Classical sculptors could also effectively deploy subjects without overt conflict, for example the *Preparation for the Chariot Race between Pelops and Oinomaos* in the east pediment of the Temple of Zeus at Olympia or the *Birth of Athena* (central figures now lost) in the east pediment of the Parthenon (Pausanias, I.xxiv.5).

Metopes. Being nearly square in shape, metopes required stories to be condensed and usually illustrated by no more than two or three figures. The themes chosen for illustration could be loosely or tightly organized. A series of metopes could present either a miscellany of heroic deeds (e.g. *Perseus and Medusa* and *Herakles and the Kerkopes* among others on Temple C at Selinus (Palermo, Mus. Reg); the *Argonauts*, the *Kalydonian Boar Hunt* and *Europa and the Bull* on the Sikyonian Treasury at Delphi (Delphi, Archaeol. Mus.); *Herakles and the Amazon* and *Zeus and Hera* among others on Temple E at Selinus (Palermo, Mus. Reg.)), a sequence of related incidents pertaining to a

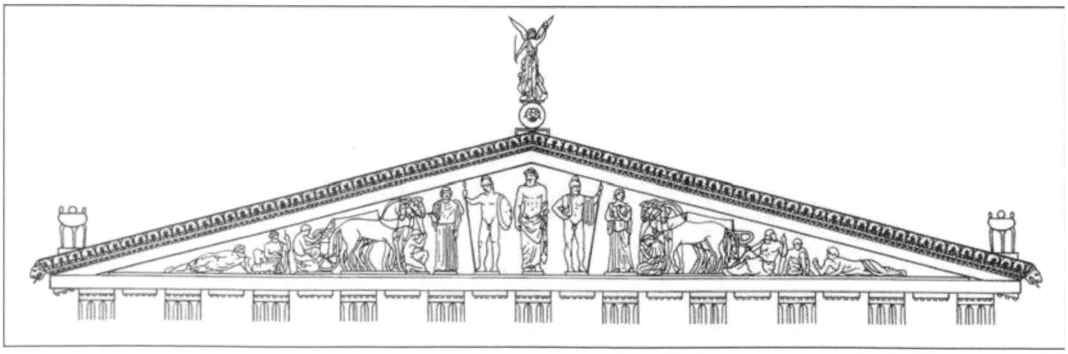

7. *Preparation for the Chariot Race between Pelops and Oinomaos,* h. 3.3 m, l. 26.4 m, east pediment of the Temple of Zeus at Olympia, Early Classical, *c.* 470–457 BC; reconstruction

single myth (e.g. the *Gigantomachy* on the east front of the Parthenon (Athens, *in situ*); various deeds of Herakles on the east front of the Temple of Hephaistos at Athens (*in situ*)) or a single theme embracing the whole metopal decoration (e.g. the *Labours of Herakles* on the east and west metopes over the porches of the Temple of Zeus at Olympia (Olympia, Archaeol. Mus.; *see* OLYMPIA, fig. 4)).

Friezes. In contrast to metopes, friezes (or friezelike decoration) required subjects that could easily be extended by the addition of as many figures as were necessary to fill up the space available. For this reason battles were particularly popular; hunts, processions, revels and assemblies could also be used. Gigantomachies were used on one of the friezes on the Siphnian Treasury at Delphi (Delphi, Archaeol. Mus.) and on the 'Great Altar' at Pergamon (Berlin, Antikensamml.; *see* PERGAMON, fig. 5), and amazonomachies and centauromachies at Bassai (*see* BASSAI, fig. 2) and on the mausoleum at Halikarnassos (both London, BM; *see* HALIKARNASSOS, fig. 2). A new style, continuous narration, was used to present the biographical cycle illustrating the *Legend of Telephos* on the small frieze from the 'Great Altar' at Pergamon (Berlin, Antikensamml.). The Doric architrave of the temple at Assos (Paris, Louvre; Boston, MA, Mus. F.A.) was used to carry friezelike decoration illustrating *Herakles' Fight with the Centaurs.* Action, generally combat, was preferred for friezes, but occasionally peaceful assemblies were illustrated, as on the east frieze of the Temple of Athena Nike at Athens (*in situ*), or processions, as on the Parthenon (Athens, Acropolis Mus.; London, BM, and elsewhere).

Friezes may sometimes have been decorated with historical rather than mythological scenes; it has been suggested that the battle friezes on the Temple of Athena Nike in Athens (*in situ* and London, BM) reflect the Battle of Marathon and events in the Peloponnesian War, that the frieze on Aemilius Paulus' Monument (Delphi, Archaeol. Mus.) at Delphi reflects part of the Macedonian War, and that the Parthenon frieze is an idealized portrayal of the Panathenaic procession, perhaps the last before the Battle of Marathon in 490 BC.

Acroteria. These were usually graced with stylized floral decoration, but they could also carry winged figures, such as *nikai* or sphinxes. More elaborate ones could even portray abductions or other mythological scenes, for example *Theseus Throwing Skiron into the Sea* and *Hemera Carrying off Kephalos*, once on the Stoa Basileos (Royal Stoa) in Athens (Pausanias, I.iii.1).

G. Rodenwaldt: *Das Relief bei den Griechen* (Berlin, 1923)
H. Kähler: *Das griechische Metopenbild* (Munich, 1949)
K. F. Johansen: *The Attic Grave Reliefs of the Classical Period* (Copenhagen, 1951)
U. Hausmann: *Griechische Weihreliefs* (Berlin, 1960)
G. M. A. Richter: *The Archaic Gravestones of Attica* (London, 1961/*R* Bristol, 1988)
G. M. A. Richter: *The Portraits of the Greeks* (London, 1965); abridged and rev. by R. R. R. Smith (Oxford, 1984)
Å. Åkerström: *Die architektonischen Terracotten Kleinasiens* (1966)
M. Bieber: *The Sculpture of the Hellenistic Age* (New York, 1967)
G. M. A. Richter: *The Sculpture and Sculptors of the Greeks* (New Haven, 1970)
B. S. Ridgway: *The Severe Style in Greek Sculpture* (Princeton, 1970)
B. S. Ridgway: *The Archaic Style in Greek Sculpture* (Princeton, 1977, rev. Chicago, 1993)
J. Boardman: *Greek Sculpture: The Archaic Period* (London, 1978/*R* 1988)
G. Neumann: *Probleme des griechischen Weihreliefs* (Tübingen, 1979)
H. C. Ackermann and J. R. Gisler, eds: *Lexicon iconographicum mythologiae classicae* (Zurich, 1981–)
B. S. Ridgway: *Fifth Century Styles in Greek Sculpture* (Princeton, 1981)
B. Schmaltz: *Griechische Grabreliefs* (Darmstadt, 1983)
F. Felten: *Griechische tektonische Friese archaischer und klassischer Zeit* (Stiftland, 1984)
J. Boardman: *Greek Sculpture: The Classical Period* (London, 1985)
J. J. Pollitt: *Art in the Hellenistic Age* (Cambridge, 1986)
H. Wrede: *Die antike Herme* (Mainz, 1986)
M. Meyer: *Die griechischen Urkundenreliefs* (Berlin, 1989)
J. J. Pollitt: *The Art of Ancient Greece: Sources and Documents* (Cambridge, 1990)
B. S. Ridgway: *Hellenistic Sculpture I* (Bristol, 1990)
A. F. Stewart: *Greek Sculpture: An Exploration*, 2 vols (New Haven and London, 1990)
R. R. R. Smith: *Hellenistic Sculpture* (London, 1991)
C. W. Clairmont: *Classical Attic Tombstones* (Kilchberg, 1993)
J. Boardman: *Greek Sculpture: The Late Classical Period* (London, 1995)
B. S. Ridgway: *Fourth-Century Styles in Greek Sculpture* (London, 1997)
S. Dillon: *Ancient Greek Portrait Sculpture: Contexts, Subjects, and Styles* (Cambridge, 2006)
I. Jenkins: *Greek Architecture and its Sculpture* (New York, 2006)

(iii) Materials. In their choice of materials, Greek sculptors did not apparently feel bound by the Apolline law of moderation. Clay, wood, stone, bronze, iron, silver, gold and ivory were all employed, sometimes in combination, and, where appropriate, were painted or further embellished with precious stones, enamel, glass, copper and tin.

(a) Introduction. (b) Terracotta. (c) Wood. (d) Limestone. (e) Marble. (f) Bronze. (g) Chryselephantine.

(a) Introduction. The choice of materials for a given sculpture was conditioned by factors as diverse as skill, cost, availability, appropriateness to context or subject, and simple delight in experiment and variety. The nature of the materials themselves was also important. Clay, wood and limestone generally ceased to be used for major sculpture after *c.* 500 BC, for these materials are not only less durable but are also duller than the others, which are extolled in Homeric and later poetry as both long-lasting and visually exciting. All have 'radiance' or 'gleam' (Gr. *aigla*) and can 'flash' or 'sparkle' (*marmairein*; hence *marmaros*, marble). Not only do these

materials fulfil the requirement of a monument to be lasting, but they also engage and delight the spectator.

From the sculptor's point of view, other considerations besides appropriateness to context or the material's effect may be more relevant, for example hardness or tensile strength. In addition, some sculptors worked in several media, while others specialized. Particularly after *c.* 500 BC, when bronze came to dominate large-scale, free-standing sculpture, a clear distinction emerged between sculptors in marble, who were often Athenians or islanders, and sculptors in bronze, often Peloponnesians. In part a matter of availability of materials in different regions, this distinction also corresponds to a practical difference between glyptic work, which involves direct carving of hard materials whose properties must be absolutely familiar to the sculptor, and fictile work, which involves the modelling of soft clay to produce hollow-cast bronzes. Yet it was only in the Hellenistic period that the forms attainable in freely modelled clay began to influence bronzes; earlier Greek sculpture in all media had remained glyptic throughout.

A Greek sculptor's relationship to his materials was complex and differed in several respects from that of medieval, Renaissance or modern sculptors. In particular, unlike Renaissance sculptors, the Greeks never regarded themselves as locked in hopeless combat with their materials. Nor, unlike modern sculptors, did they have the concept of 'truth to materials'. Rather, they viewed their materials as resources, to be exploited as fully and daringly as possible. Aristotle wrote of the way in which skill (*techne*) could allow the artist to transcend the limitations of nature (*Physics* ii.8, 199a15–20). More pragmatically, a 6th-century BC sculptor's dedication explains that 'skilled craftsmen do well to show their cunning in their *techne*, for whoso possesses *techne* has a better life' (*Inscr. Gr./2*, ii, 678): thus improved technical control brought both material and psychological rewards in the battle for commissions.

(b) Terracotta. Clay was the earliest sculptural material and was apparently the only one to continue in use throughout the Greek Dark Age. Its popularity, at least for small-scale work, continued into Roman times. Hundreds of thousands of TERRACOTTA figurines survive, ranging from cheap votive offerings to the high-quality 3rd-century BC figurines from Tanagra (examples in London, BM, and elsewhere) and the extraordinary grotesques of Hellenistic Alexandria. Most such figurines were painted in rather garish colours and were sometimes even gilded. In large-scale terracotta sculpture, Corinth and the Greek cities of Sicily and South Italy dominated production during the Archaic and Early Classical periods, principally because marble was not easily available in these areas. The making of hollow-cast bronzes, which utilized many of the same skills, supplanted this industry during the 5th century BC.

(c) Wood. Though hardly any wooden sculpture survives, ancient sources record that the earliest Greek cult images were wooden *xoana* ('scraped things'), some mere logs, others hewn roughly into human form. The existence of *xoana* has been challenged, but the literary references, chiefly in Pausanias' *Guide to Greece*, cannot be explained away. Some woods, such as Lebanese cedar, were chosen for their sculptural qualities and durability; others were selected for religious or patriotic reasons. Thus, the statue of *Athena Polias* (destr. in antiquity) on the Athenian Acropolis was made of olive wood, since she was said to have given the olive tree to Attica. Wood was also used for statuettes, at least in the Archaic period, though since most of the finds are due to the unique conditions for preservation at the Sanctuary of Hera on Samos, it is uncertain how widespread or long-lived this practice was. Like clay, wooden sculpture could be painted or gilded, and cult statues were often further adorned with real jewellery and clothing. After the Archaic period wood all but disappeared in mainland Greece as a sculptural medium, though in such areas as Sicily or Egypt, where marble was scarce or had to be imported, acrolithic statues, consisting of wooden bodies with stone limbs and heads, were not uncommon. Wood-carving also survived as the basis for chryselephantine sculpture, which succeeded the Archaic *sphyrelaton* technique, in which bronze plates were applied to a wooden core.

(d) Limestone. The earliest limestone sculpture occurred on Crete around 700 BC, apparently stimulated by contact with the Neo-Hittite kingdoms of north Syria. Free-standing statues and architectural sculpture were both carved in this medium, knowledge of which soon spread to the rest of the Aegean, then to the Greek colonies of South Italy and Sicily. Yet by the time the Cretan tradition died out in the early 6th century BC, marble had supplanted limestone in mainland Greece for all but architectural sculpture. Attic limestones were the finest of the mainland varieties and were used for architectural sculpture until the late 6th century BC, when a general preference for marble emerged. In the western Greek world, limestone architectural sculpture is to be found until the mid-5th century BC, though the latest examples, from Temple E at Selinus (*c.* 470–*c.* 460 BC), often have limbs and heads of imported marble. This mixed technique, a variant of acrolithic sculpture, was also used for a colossal statue of a goddess of *c.* 400 BC (Malibu, CA, Getty Mus., 88.AA.76). In the Late Classical and Hellenistic periods (mid-4th century BC-late 1st), limestone sculpture was popular both at Taranto (anc. Taras) and in Egypt. Tarentine grave shrines (*naïskoi*) were embellished with small reliefs in the local soft limestone (*pietra tenera*) from *c.* 330 BC to *c.* 250 BC, and in Egypt the local Pharaonic tradition of limestone-carving never died out but was simply applied to Greek genres and iconography.

(e) Marble. Marble was first used as a material for sculpture in Greece in the mid-7th century BC, and even though the earliest example is a statue of a woman, the Nikandre Kore dedicated on Delos, its

introduction was closely related to the development of the KOUROS statue-type, a striding nude male figure. This fact, coupled with the apparent use of a grid to lay out the proportions of the kouroi (*see also* §(iv)(a) below), suggests that the inspiration for using such a hard stone came not from the Near East but from Egypt, where grid-based statues in hard stones of striding, kilted males had been produced for centuries. The date of the Nikandre Kore (*c.* 660–*c.* 650 BC) coincides with the successful use of East Greek mercenaries by Psammetichus I (*reg* 664–610 BC) to establish himself on the throne of Egypt and with the subsequent founding of an East Greek trading colony at Naukratis in the Nile Delta. Sculptors on Naxos and Samos pioneered the technique of marble-carving, which soon spread throughout the Aegean. By the later 6th century BC Samian marble was no longer used, while Naxian had been largely supplanted by the sugary Parian marble and by the fine-grained stone from the Pentelic quarries just north of Athens. Local marbles, such as Thasian, Prokonnesian, Ephesian and Doliana (from the Peloponnese), were also occasionally used, but only Parian and Pentelic were consistently and widely exported before Roman times. Piecing was common, at least for draped statues, as sculptors progressively attempted to transcend the limitations of the block, including making outstretched arms or heads separately. As with limestone, terracotta and wood, marble sculpture was usually at least partly painted: traces of paint have been found on hair, eyes and lips, and patterns and borders were painted on to clothes and armour. Earrings, bracelets and sandals were painted as appropriate. The background of relief sculpture was also coloured. Figures were further embellished with attributes, jewellery or other attachments in bronze and other metals. By the end of the 6th century BC marble dominated all forms of sculpture in the Aegean, yet within a few decades hollow-cast bronze, with its greater tensile strength, had virtually supplanted it for free-standing work. Though some Attic cult statues were still made of marble, it was otherwise restricted to architectural and funerary sculpture until Praxiteles initiated a revival around 350 BC with his marble *Aphrodite of Knidos* (copy, Rome, Vatican, Mus. Pio-Clementino; *see* PRAXITELES, fig. 2). The few large-scale, free-standing Classical works in marble, such as the *Nike of Paionios*, show sculptors striving to overcome the limitations of their material and to rival bronze. Meanwhile, acrolithic statues continued to be produced in such areas as Sicily and South Italy, where marble was difficult to obtain.

The *Aphrodite of Knidos*, with its unrivalled surface finish, including a more subtle coloration invented by the painter Nikias, reawakened interest in free-standing marble sculpture. Though bronze was still regularly used for portraits and groups, Hellenistic marble sculptures of all sizes abound at such sites as Delos, Pergamon and Alexandria. Inscriptions reveal a distinction emerging between cult statues (*agalmata*), which were often of marble, and statues of mortals (*andrianta*), normally of bronze; the reasons for this distinction remain unclear.

(*f*) *Bronze*. Bronze is usually defined as an alloy of about nine or ten parts of copper to one part of tin. In antiquity, however, these proportions varied widely, and large admixtures of other elements, such as lead, were sometimes introduced. The Greek term *khalkos* covered all variations from pure copper to heavily leaded tin-bronze, and the range is demonstrated by the published analyses of surviving bronzes. Some 'bronze' statuettes, for example, contain almost no tin, while the arms of one of the RIACE BRONZES included up to 14.5% lead. The small number of surviving large-scale Greek bronzes (total *c.* 30) further complicates the issue. Though many seem to conform to the standard alloy, others do not. Two factors that undoubtedly influenced the sculptors' choice of alloy were ductability and ease of working when cold: alloys with large amounts of lead flow well into the mould but are hard to work cold, whereas alloys with much tin and little lead tend to be less ductile but take chiselled detail much better. The Greeks apparently preferred the latter formula for large-scale bronzes, which are characterized by a compelling attention to detail, while the Etruscans and Romans, less concerned with detail, adopted the former.

Bronze statuettes, solid-cast using the lost-wax method, occur from the 8th century BC, and large-scale bronzes from around 700 BC. The latter initially fall into two classes, both employing Near Eastern technology. The first are statues made using the *sphyrelaton* technique, which involved hammered and riveted bronze plates; the second are griffin protomes of Near Eastern type attached to bronze cauldrons (examples in Olympia, Archaeol. Mus.). The earliest of these protomes were hammered, but hollow-casting soon became the norm. The technique of indirect casting via piece-moulds taken from a prototype in wood or clay may be Egyptian, since Samian bronze-casters are reputed to have visited Egypt, and many Egyptian bronzes were found in the Sanctuary of Hera on Samos, where the bronze industry flourished as almost nowhere else during the Archaic period. Indirect casting allowed the sculptor to produce several versions of a prototype without destroying the original, as the direct method necessitated, but the detailing, done cold after casting, was always individualized.

The advantages of indirect casting were soon applied to sculptures of the human figure. Already by 600 BC Samian merchants had dedicated a giant bronze griffin-cauldron supported by three bronze women, each over 3 m tall (lost in antiquity), at the Sanctuary of Hera, which has also yielded bronze statuettes with identical torsos and heads but with limbs in various poses (examples in Vathy, Archaeol. Mus.). By the mid-6th century BC the *sphyrelaton* technique, with its sharp transitions and doll-like articulation, was obsolete. At about this time the earliest life-size, indirect-cast bronzes also began to appear, and once established, the new technique soon became widely popular. Remains of statue bases from the Athenian Acropolis show that free-standing bronzes equalled marble works by *c.* 500 BC and far exceeded them by *c.* 480 BC. Novelty apart, the burgeoning demand for statues of victors in the Panhellenic games and other contests may have stimulated this change, for not only could polished and burnished bronze evoke a sense of the tanned, oiled body of the athlete, but its excellent tensile strength also made it the perfect medium for the action poses increasingly favoured for both statues of athletes and narrative groups. Eyes were usually inset in ivory and glass, teeth silvered, hair gilded and nipples coppered. Drapery and other attributes were inlaid with patterns in various metals, gilded or even painted. Sometimes whole statues were gilded, either using wafer-thin gold leaf applied over size or glue or, more expensively, using sheet-gold hammered into grooves cut into the bronze. Fire-gilding by a solution of gold in mercury is not attested before Roman Imperial times.

(g) Chryselephantine. Statues of cast silver or gold were always rare in antiquity. The preferred chryselephantine technique, which used much less metal, derived from the Near East, where it had been in use for centuries. The earliest remains of chryselephantine sculptures come from Delphi (6th century BC; Delphi, Archaeol. Mus.). They are about half life-size, technically all but identical to the colossal statues of *Athena Parthenos* at Athens and *Zeus* at Olympia by Pheidias, erected a century later (both destr. in antiquity). As in the *sphyrelaton* technique, gold sheets for the drapery were hammered over a wooden core, but exposed flesh surfaces were of ivory; solid in the examples from Delphi, applied in thin strips over wood on the Pheidian statues. Both gold and ivory often occur in ancient Greek poetry in metaphors for divine perfection, yet in the case of the *Athena Parthenos* a more prosaic motive for the choice of chryselephantine also applied: the one and a half tons of gold involved formed part of the State treasury and could be removed in an emergency and later replaced. In 295 BC, however, the tyrant Lachares permanently despoiled the statue, which Athens subsequently had only sufficient resources to cover with gold leaf. Further effects applied to chryselephantine works included rouging cheeks and lips, setting eyes in aquamarine and embellishing drapery with silver, copper and enamel inlay. The moulds found at Pheidias' workshop at Olympia, once thought to be for the golden drapery of his *Zeus*, were in fact for glass pieces set into the clothing of an over life-size goddess, perhaps his *Athena* or *Aphrodite* at Elis. Several versions of many of these moulds survive, in increasingly detailed series, showing that the glass was heated and then 'slumped' into them in stages to prevent cracking.

Normally used exclusively for statues of deities, and even then only rarely, chryselephantine was selected by Philip II of Macedonia (*reg* 359–336 BC) for the images of himself and his family in his Philippeion at Olympia, erected after his defeat of Athens and Thebes at Chaironeia in 338 BC. The intended message was clearly that his deeds approached divine status, and though few later monarchs followed his example directly, gilded cult statues of Hellenistic kings and eventually even of important benefactors were later commonly erected in sanctuaries and temples.

C. Blümel: *Griechische Bildhauer an der Arbeit* (Berlin, 1927, 3/1934); Eng. trans. by L. Holland (London, 1955, 2/1969)

S. Adam: *The Technique of Greek Sculpture in the Archaic and Classical Periods* (London, 1966)

R. A. Higgins: *Greek Terracottas* (London, 1967)

J. J. Pollitt: *The Ancient View of Greek Art* (New Haven and London, 1974)

R. Meiggs: *Trees and Timber in the Ancient Mediterranean World* (Oxford, 1982)

L. Mannoni and T. Mannoni: *Il marmo: Materia e cultura* (Genoa, 1985); Eng. trans. by P. J. Hammond-Smith as *Marble: The History of a Culture* (New York, 1985)

C. Rolley: *Greek Bronzes* (London and New York, 1986)

A. Donohue: *Xoana and the Origins of Greek Sculpture* (Atlanta, 1988)

C. C. Mattusch: *Greek Bronze Statuary: From the Beginnings through the Fifth Century BC* (Ithaca, 1988) [analyses of bronzes on pp. 14–15]

A. F. Stewart: *Greek Sculpture: An Exploration* (New Haven and London, 1990), i, pp. 36–40

I. Haynes: *The Technique of Greek Bronze Statuary* (Mainz, 1992)

J. A. MacGillivray, J. Driessen and L. H. Sackett: *The Palaikastro Kouros: A Minoan Chryselephantine Statuette and its Aegean Bronze Age Context* (London, 2000)

K. D. S. Lapatin: *Chryselephantine Statuary in the Ancient Mediterranean World* (Oxford, 2001)

I. Jenkins: *Greek Architecture and its Sculpture* (New York, 2006)

O. Palagia: *Greek Sculpture: Function, Materials, and Techniques in the Archaic and Classical Periods* (Cambridge, 2006)

(iv) Techniques.

(a) Stoneworking. (b) Clay-modelling and moulding. (c) Bronze-casting. (d) Models and reproduction.

(a) Stoneworking. Evidence for ancient Greek stoneworking methods and tools is abundant. Greek sculptors in marble are known, for example, to have used a range of tools similar to those of a modern sculptor, comprising chisels, drills and abrasives. Even on such highly finished work as the Parthenon sculptures (mainly in London, BM) there are recesses where the marks of tools were not smoothed away, and the numerous carved grave stelai of the Archaic and Classical periods have many areas where the use of drills and chisels shows clearly. Similar methods appear to have been widely employed throughout the Aegean islands and mainland Greece, and the changes that occurred during the Archaic and Classical periods were also general rather than local.

Marble from the islands of Paros and Naxos was especially prized, and on Naxos there is good evidence of marble quarrying from early times. Instead of being cut from deep vertical faces, large blocks could be removed across the surface of the hills. Drills were used to cut vertically into the rock around a block, forming a row of perforations that could then be knocked into continuous channels to separate the block from the surrounding marble. Wedges were driven in underneath the block until they detached it from its bed.

As well as the quarry sites, a number of unfinished Archaic statues have been found on Naxos. These are of the kouros type, which probably derived from Egyptian models. It seems clear that the Greeks also adopted Egyptian methods when they began to produce sculpture in stone. The Egyptians marked the block to be carved with a grid of equal squares, producing a canon of proportion. Thus the medial line was fixed, and the sculptor would be able to visualize the finished statue in terms of the grid, which could be continually renewed as the work progressed. The Archaic Greek kouroi from Naxos show, rather surprisingly, that a statue might be shaped almost down to its final surface while still at the quarry, possibly in order to reduce the weight for transportation. While the Egyptians produced over life-size statues to a similar design for centuries, the Greeks broke away from their original format in just over a hundred years to develop a wide formal repertory of smaller-scale sculpture, though there was little change to the sequence of tools employed.

First, a pointed chisel was used to shape the general outlines of the figure. Though a pointed chisel can remove large flakes of stone, evidence from Greek statues suggests that sculptors preferred to use short strokes, holding the chisel almost at a right angle to the block and removing only small flakes. The sculptor could finely control the contours he was shaping, because his attention at any one time was closely focused on a small area, which he worked slowly. The drill was also important from an early stage of the work. Drills were simply chisels that were whirled round while being pressed into the stone. The sculptor might have assistants to turn the drill by means of a thong round its shaft, or he might work single-handed with a bow drill. Drill holes can be seen between the arms and body of certain kouroi, in the ringlets of the hair of female statues, in drapery channels on statues of all periods and around heads in profile in relief sculptures. In the drapery channels of figures on the Parthenon frieze (*c*. 442–*c*. 438 BC) rows of holes made by repeated use of a small drill are visible in places. The use of a running drill, which could be moved along the surface to carve simplified lines and planes, does not appear until the 4th century BC. The flat chisel was used for more detailed shaping, to give crisp edges to eyelids, locks of hair and drapery channels and to prepare the surfaces for their final smoothing. There is a striking contrast between the short, careful strokes of the flat chisel in early work and the long, unsubtle strokes on some later pieces, where all the varied contours of an arm may be reduced to a few facets. Metal rasps were sometimes used next. The final smooth, burnished but not shining finish to the marble was given by emery blocks or powder.

C. Blümel: *Griechische Bildhauer an der Arbeit* (Berlin, 1927, 3/1934); Eng. trans. by L. Holland (London, 1955, 2/1969)

S. Casson: *The Technique of Early Greek Sculpture* (Oxford, 1933)

S. Adam: *The Technique of Greek Sculpture in the Archaic and Classical Periods* (London, 1966)

B. Ashmole: *Architect and Sculptor in Classical Greece* (London and New York, 1972)

O. Palagia: 'Les Techniques de la sculpture grecque sur marbre', *Marbres helléniques* (Brussels, 1987)

P. Rockwell: *The Art of Stoneworking: A Reference Guide* (Cambridge, 1995)

B. S. Ridgway: *Prayers in Stone: Greek Architectural Sculpture ca. 600–100 BCE* (Berkeley, 1999)

A. E. Phlorakes: *Hagion Oros lithanaglypha* (Athens, 2000)

I. Jenkins: *Greek Architecture and its Sculpture* (New York, 2006)

O. Palagia: *Greek Sculpture: Function, Materials, and Techniques in the Archaic and Classical Periods* (Cambridge, 2006)

(b) Clay-modelling and moulding. Free-standing terracotta sculpture could be either mould-made or handmade. It includes both statuettes, of which great numbers survive, and a few larger statues that range in height from under half life-size to approximately three-quarters life-size. In handmade statues the body was built up from coils of clay and modelled to give the figure its basic shape. Earlier statues sometimes had an internal clay support in the form of a solid wall dividing the statue from front to back, but in the Classical period only small clay supports might be used, or none at all. Once the body of the statue had dried, the separately modelled head, neck, arms, feet and plinth were added. Scoring marks made during attachment can often be seen. The face was sometimes made in piece-moulds. During the Archaic period, tempered clay was used to reduce the risks of cracking and shrinkage, but by the Classical period it was no longer needed for free-standing statues, though it was still used sparingly for architectural sculpture. The entire figure was covered with a layer of fine clay, in which details, such as of face, hair and drapery, were cut or modelled. During the Archaic period, the figure was painted after drying, then fired at a low temperature. By the 5th century BC, however, a white slip was fired with the clay, and the more delicate colours were added after firing. Finally, vent holes left for the escape of gases were plugged, and the statue was burnished to produce the finished surface.

(c) Bronze-casting. Greek sculptors used the lost-wax technique for casting both large and small bronzes. Large-scale works were widely produced in this way from the 6th century BC onwards in a diversified industry, adapted to the idiosyncrasies of individual artists and the requirements of specific commissions. Despite the reproductive nature of lost-wax casting, bronze statues were generally individualized by details given to the wax working model. Workshops were temporary establishments, closed down after casting was completed. Small statuettes (*see* METALWORK, §IV, 2(i)) might be cast solid, but larger figures were always cast hollow and in pieces that were then fitted or soldered together.

Lost-wax casting in ancient Greece essentially differed little from the process used in modern foundries. It involved the construction of a preliminary full-size model of the sculpture, probably usually of clay, though wax, wood or stone could also have been used. A clay master mould was taken from the model in separate but joining pieces, then dried. The pieces of the master mould were then reassembled in manageable groups: a nude figure might have as few as four major parts (e.g. head, arms, trunk and legs), but a draped statue might have many pieces, since it was easy to conceal joins within folds. Next, each of the master mould assemblages was lined with a beeswax layer, either poured in, brushed on or applied in slabs. A liquid clay core was then poured into the hollow wax model and sometimes reinforced with simple iron rods or armatures. After this, the master moulds were removed, and the wax working model was worked over in what could be an extensive process, involving the addition of more wax for such features as locks of hair and beard and the tooling of surface details, such as ears and eyebrows. The wax working model was now ready for casting, and a wax 'gate' system was attached to it, comprising a pouring funnel and gates for admitting the molten bronze. In one-piece casting, vents were also needed for the escape of gases from within the core, though in piece-casting the core was partly exposed. To hold the core in position when the wax layer was melted out, pins or chaplets made of iron or bronze were driven through the wax into the core at several points, with their outer ends left exposed. A final investment mould was applied in two or more layers, covering the entire model and gate system but leaving the lip of the wax funnel and the tops of the vents exposed. Its innermost layer was fine enough to ensure that the wax was completely coated, while its outer layers were of coarser clay with rough sandy inclusions or 'temper' to prevent cracking and reduce shrinkage during drying and baking.

Next the mould was placed on a base inside a hole or casting pit, and a fire was built around it to melt out the wax and evaporate any moisture. The elimination of the wax left a moulded cavity for the bronze, and the wax gates, vents and funnel became channels for admitting the molten bronze and evacuating any gases. After cooling, the moulds were packed firmly in sand in the casting pit. Bronze was heated to 1000–1100°C, either in an adjacent shaft furnace or in a crucible furnace, and poured into the funnels. Once the bronze had cooled, the sand packing was removed and the investment moulds were broken away. The clay core was either left in place or removed as far as it could be reached inside the bronze statue. Inlays of other materials, such as copper, stone and silver, were set in the bronze to emphasize the eyes, eyelashes, eyebrows, teeth, nipples and sometimes even finger- and toenails. Finally, the pieces of the statue were fitted together (see fig. 8) and sometimes soldered. Joins and imperfections were smoothed and patched, and the bronze was polished to a high gleam.

To produce a statue with many projecting parts would have required special procedures: for example, loose locks of hair would surely have been best produced by being individually modelled in wax, cast solid, then attached to the statue. Similarly, the model for a statue's head might be so rough as to provide only an indication of scale and general contours, with most of the detailing left until the wax working model with its clay core had been prepared. Thus irregularities in the thickness of the walls of some Greek bronzes testify to additions made to the wax working model. Where the inner surface of a bronze is visible, the drips, brushmarks or seams resulting from the application of the wax to the master moulds are sometimes evident.

P. C. Bol: *Antike Bronzetechnik* (Munich, 1985)

C. C. Mattusch: *Greek Bronze Statuary: From the Beginnings through the Fifth Century* BC (Ithaca, 1988) [analyses of bronzes on pp. 14–15]

G. Zimmer: *Griechische Bronzegusswerkstätten* (Mainz, 1990)

D. Haynes: *The Technique of Greek Bronze Statuary* (Mainz, 1992)

C. C. Mattusch: *Classical Bronzes: The Art and Craft of Greek and Roman Statuary* (Ithaca, 1996)

I. Formigli, ed.: *I Grandi bronzi antichi: Le fonderie e le techniche di lavorazione dell'età arcaica al Rinascimento* (Siena, 1999)

W. Hoepfner: *Der Koloss von Rhodos und die Bauten des Helios: Neue Forschungen zu einem der Sieben Weltwunder* (Mainz, 2003)

U. Gehring: *Die Greifenprotomen aus dem Heraion von Samos* (Bonn, 2004)

S. A. Hemingway: *The Horse and Jockey from Artemision: A Bronze Equestrian Monument of the Hellenistic Period* (Berkeley, 2004)

(d) Models and reproduction. The introduction of the use of full-scale models in clay or other materials was part of the technical and stylistic revolution that was responsible for the development of the Classical style of sculpture in the 5th century BC. Models are first attested for bronze statuary in the early 5th century BC, with the development of the indirect lost-wax technique, which involved the construction of a clay model on an iron armature from which clay piece-moulds were then taken. The stage of fashioning this type of clay model for a bronze statue is illustrated on an Attic Red-figure oinochoe of *c.* 460 BC (Berlin, Antikensamml., F 2415), showing *Athena Modelling a Horse in Clay*. A similar process employing piece-moulds may have been used to produce plaster models for marble sculptures from the 5th century BC onwards. The existence of full-scale models for marble statues of the Classical period is suggested by references to models in wax, wood and plaster for architectural members, such as lion-head spouts, ornaments for ceiling coffers and mouldings, in the building accounts of the Erechtheion at Athens (408–406 BC) and of the Temple of Asklepios and the Tholos at Epidauros (4th century BC; *Inscr. Gr./2*, i, 374; iv, 102a and 102b; iv, 103 respectively). The use of plaster in monumental sculpture was already known in the 5th century BC. Pausanias (*Guide to Greece* I.xl.4) described an unfinished chryselephantine statue of *Zeus* by

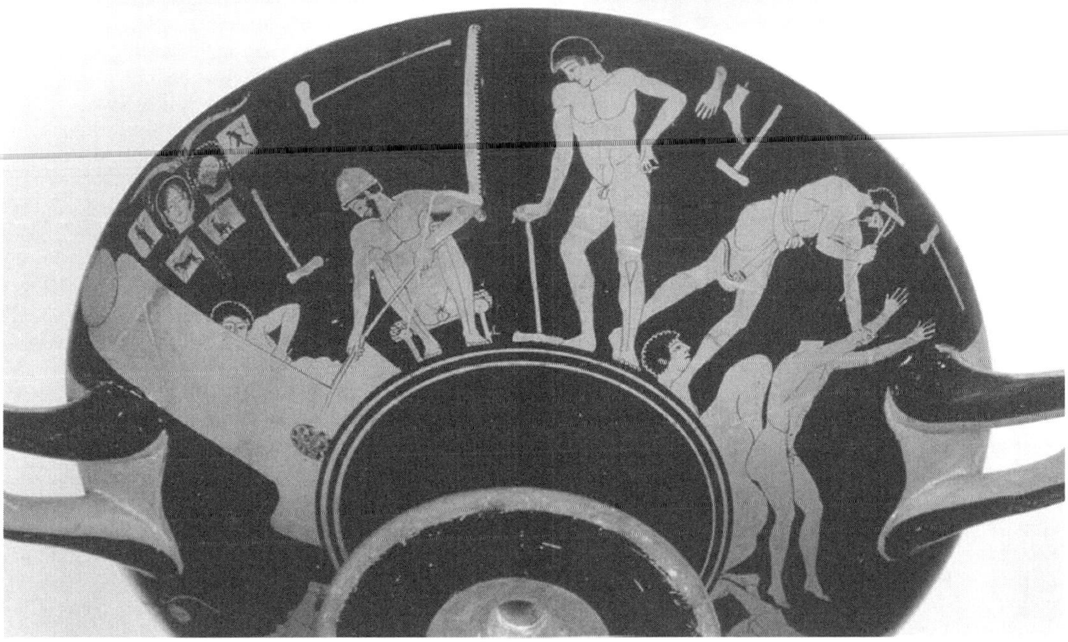

8. Two workmen heating a metallurgical furnace, while a third pieces together a life-size bronze statue of an athlete, detail from the Berlin Foundry Cup, Attic Red-figure, diam. 305 mm, from Vulci, Late Archaic, *c.* 490–*c.* 480 BC (Berlin, Antikensammlung, Staatliche Museen zu Berlin)

Theokosmos of Megara, modelled in clay and plaster, over a wooden core, and in the 4th century BC Lysistratos, the brother of Lysippos, is credited with the invention of life masks in plaster, of which he took wax impressions. Further evidence for the use of models in marble sculpture is provided by traces of measuring points on unfinished pieces.

The earliest examples of the use of a copying device are the bosses and the grooves left by the removal of bosses on the foreheads of a few figures from the metopes and pediments of the Temple of Zeus at Olympia (*c.* 470–*c.* 457 BC; Olympia, Archaeol. Mus.). These bosses may have served as fixed points for the attachment of plumb-lines for taking measurements both horizontally and vertically, so that the sculptor could determine the angles of his planes and the depth to which he had to cut. Another copying method perhaps employed in antiquity involves the use of three calipers. It is extremely precise and can also be employed for enlargement or reduction.

Copying methods made possible the production of more than one 'original' work at a time. Duplicate original sculptures of the 5th century BC include not only votive reliefs, which may have been duplicated freehand, but also free-standing marble statues. One example is the marble *Mourning Penelope* from the ruins of Persepolis (*c.* 460 BC; Tehran, Archaeol. Mus.). Persepolis was destroyed by Alexander the Great in 331 BC, but Roman copies of an identical work (Rome, Vatican, Mus. Pio-Clementino, 754; Copenhagen, Ny Carlsberg Glyp., 1944) imply the existence of a second original. Similar circumstances are also postulated for the bronze Peiraeus *Athena* (*c.* 350 BC; Peiraeus, Archaeol. Mus.). The extant statue was buried in the 1st century BC, but copies of this type were still being made, presumably after a second original, in the 2nd century AD (e.g. the *Athena Mattei*; Paris, Louvre, MA 530).

The mechanical reproduction of marble statuary was facilitated by the introduction of an early form of pointing machine in the 1st century BC. This served to transfer measurements taken in three dimensions from the model to the marble block. It consisted of a movable needle calibrated on a fixed axis, which could bore a network of holes on the surface of the marble. The machine was hung from a hook mounted on a perforated boss on top of the figure and was also supported by a pair of symmetrical protrusions at its base. As the statue was carved, measuring points in the form of bosses punctuated its surface and were only removed on completion of the work. Unfinished pieces from Delos, sacked in 69 BC, have bosses that show they were carved with the aid of a primitive pointing machine. This device was, however, not strictly accurate and therefore required some freehand adjustment by the sculptor. On the other hand, it allowed a piecemeal approach, with parts of a statue being thoroughly finished while others were still roughly formed. However, it was never the only method in use for the reproduction of copies of Classical or contemporary works in the Hellenistic or Roman periods.

C. Blümel: *Griechische Bildhauer an der Arbeit* (Berlin, 1927, 3/1934); Eng. trans. by L. Holland (London, 1955, 2/1969)

C. Blümel: 'Griechische Bildhauerarbeit', *Jb. Dt. Archäol. Inst.* (1927), suppl. 11 [whole issue]

F. Brommer: 'Vorhellenistische Kopien und Wiederholungen von Statuen', *Studies in Honor of D. M. Robinson*, i (St Louis, 1951), pp. 674–82

J. J. Pollitt: *The Ancient View of Greek Art* (New Haven and London, 1974), pp. 204–15

V. M. Strocka: 'Variante, Wiederholung und Serie in der griechischen Bildhauerei', *Jb. Dt. Archäol. Inst.*, xciv (1979), pp. 143–73

M. Pfanner: 'Über das Herstellen von Porträts', *Jb. Dt. Archäol. Inst.*, civ (1989), pp. 157–257

B. S. Ridgway: 'Defining the Issue: The Greek Period', *Retaining the Original*, Stud. Hist. A., xx (Hannover and London, 1989), pp. 13–26

(v) Craftsmen and society. Monumental stone sculpture first appeared in Greece in the first half of the 7th century BC, though it is not until some time thereafter that sculptors can be named with any assurance and related to extant statues, or that one can gain any real sense of their place in society. The sculptor's profession clearly had important links with earlier image-makers, who made not only figurines in ivory, terracotta and metal but also larger representations of deities in wood, and sculptors would have been credited, like their legendary forerunner DAIDALOS, with mysterious skills. The legend of Daidalos in fact reflects many aspects of the sculptors' real situation and may have owed much of its persistence to the sculptors themselves. Later literary sources preserve extensive information on attributions, individual sculptors' techniques and the judgements of connoisseurs, but they have little to say about other aspects of sculptors' lives, except when these are mentioned in anecdotes about famous patrons. Pheidias is thus less obscure than other sculptors because of his connection with Pericles, and Lysippos because he was Alexander the Great's favourite sculptor.

Despite sculpture's importance from its inception, little more can be said of the initiators of the craft than that they learnt it through contact with Egyptian sculpture. Naxian stoneworkers were among the first to exploit the new medium, and one of the first sculptors known by name from his 'signature' is the Naxian Euthykartides, who dedicated a statue he had made to Delian Apollo (feet and base in Delos, Archaeol. Mus.). The Naxians' role in the early development of sculpture, however, is scarcely remembered in literary sources. Instead sculptors from elsewhere—the Cretan Dipoinos and Skyllis, Smilis of Aigina, Klearchos of Rhegion or Rhoikos and Theodoros of Samos—are counted among the first great practitioners.

(a) Professional skills and organization. (b) Working environment and conditions. (c) Status.

(a) Professional skills and organization. The versatility characteristic of the leading sculptors in every age is demonstrated by Rhoikos and Theodoros (*fl* early and mid-6th century BC). Their skills may have included bronze-casting, monumental temple architecture and jewellery. A similar versatility was shared by the Classical sculptors Pheidias of Athens and Polykleitos of Argos. Pheidias designed and worked on the Parthenon sculptures, and he made two colossal chryselephantine statues, of *Athena* at Athens and of *Zeus* at Olympia (destr. in antiquity). Polykleitos, most famous for his work on harmony in the sculpted figure, also probably made a chryselephantine statue of *Hera* and, like Pheidias, cast statues in bronze. Many other sculptors worked in bronze and may customarily have overseen the alloying of the metal itself, as the scene on the Berlin Foundry Cup indicates (see fig. 7 above), together with the accounts for Pheidias' *Athena Promachos*, which include payments for tin, copper, fuel and a furnace.

Sculpture was both an art dependent on the inspiration of its leading exponents for its development and a craft held together by strength of tradition. There were many lesser sculptors whose competence was limited to one or two processes only, including assistants and apprentices in an established sculptor's workshop or sculptors who worked only on such small projects as grave reliefs or monuments for private dedication. Nevertheless, many such sculptures, especially of the 6th and 5th centuries BC, demonstrate an expertise that could only have existed within a tight-knit craft in which there was close communication between the various branches. For example, the sculptors brought together at Athens to work on the Parthenon, like those employed on the Erechtheion a generation later, no doubt included some who came from the more workaday section of the profession. Their workshop training and the cohesiveness of the craft as a whole enabled them to reach the same high standard of work, under proper direction.

The sculptural tradition was fostered in workshops, where masters and fathers taught apprentices and sons. Many sculptors were born to their craft, as the literary records together with many sculptors' signatures indicate: for example, when some Parian sculptors signed their work as 'the sons of Charopinos', they surely intended to acknowledge not their family descent but their professional indebtedness. In some instances the sculptor's craft was handed down through several generations: the late 6th-century BC Athenian Antenor was the son and nephew of sculptors, and Kritios and Nesiotes, who made the replacement for his *Tyrannicides* group, were probably younger relatives. Praxiteles, too, was the son and nephew of sculptors, whose descendants in the craft can be traced to *c.* 200 BC.

(b) Working environment and conditions. The most notable sculptors and the best examples of family descent are found in connection with places that could offer inducements to skilled workers to congregate and settle down. Prosperity of the kind that encouraged artistic activity was one factor and the availability of raw materials another. Athens in the 6th and 5th

centuries BC was such a centre, and vase painters especially offered sculptors a challenge in dealing with perspective and the human body. This cross-professional competitiveness may be seen in the fine relief (Athens, N. Archaeol. Mus.) by the Naxian Alxenor, on which he experimented with foreshortening in much the same way as contemporary Athenian vase painters, and to which he appended the comment, 'You have only to look and see!' Athens could also offer good marble, as did Naxos and Paros. Sikyon in the 4th century BC was a centre for painters as well as sculptors, the most famous of whom was Alexander the Great's portraitist Lysippos (his brother was a painter, as was the brother of Pheidias).

But how had a sculptor like Paionios of Mende in Thrace entered the profession? There can usually have been little more than competent stone masonry called for in such a place. Yet he acquired the skill to win the competition for sculpting the acroteria on the Temple of Zeus at Olympia and to make the fine *Nike* for the Messenian and Naupaktian dedication there. The fact that he included his home town in his signature to this piece, together with the information about the competition, suggests that he wished his rise from provincial obscurity to be advertised. He perhaps owed his opportunity to a chance encounter with an established sculptor temporarily working in Thrace, and at some point he came under Athenian influence, possibly that of Pheidias himself (both sculptors worked at Olympia).

Although there were times and places in which sculptors could find more or less continuous employment, for example Periclean Athens, 6th-century BC Samos and Olympia in the mid-5th century BC, they often had to travel to find work. No city remained permanently prosperous: for example, the defeat of Athens in 404 BC meant that a large nucleus of skilled labour was broken up. Moreover, few communities were ever prosperous enough to be regular bases for accomplished craftsmen. When the Epidaurians developed their Sanctuary of Asklepios during the 4th century BC, they had to call on imported skilled labour: architects and masons came in from Corinth and Argos, and among the sculptors were Timotheos of Athens and Thrasymedes of Paros.

Mobility was characteristic of good sculptors at all periods; for example, Myron of Eleutherai may have worked not only at Athens but also at Olympia, on Aigina and Samos, at Ephesos, Orchomenos and Akragas (now Agrigento). This mobility facilitated both the exchange of ideas and the influence of styles that had evolved in one centre on sculptors brought up in different traditions. The need to search out work would have enhanced competitiveness to the benefit of the craft, though it may often have kept prices, and thus earnings, down. Though some sculptors could doubtless command high prices, the scanty evidence (mainly from public works) suggests that a sculptor's earnings generally provided little more than a bare living. Sculptors were conceived of first and foremost as craftsmen; valuable for their skill and often hard to find when needed, but nonetheless not deserving of vast payments.

The sculptors of figures for the Erechtheion frieze were paid a standard rate of 60 drachmas per figure, which may have worked out at around 1 drachma a day, in other words, not much more than was earned by the masons who fluted the columns. At Epidauros the Athenian Timotheos provided reliefs for pronaos of the Temple of Asklepios at 150 drachmas apiece, but the cost of the marble and its transportation were included. Thrasymedes of Paros, on the other hand, received a large sum simply for decorating the temple ceiling, the materials being provided. Chryselephantine statue-making was probably well rewarded, but otherwise the only unequivocal indication that sculptors could do well is Pliny's reference (*Natural History* XXIV.xxxvii) to Lysippos' savings from his many sales. Nevertheless, competition among patrons for the services of famous sculptors may have allowed them to charge more than the usual rate for public projects.

(c) Status. Sculptors appear to have had much the same status as other manual workers, regardless of sculpture's cultural importance as Greek connoisseurs themselves saw it. Yet even though there was some intellectual sympathy between sculptors, who were concerned with the principles of harmony, and philosophers, who considered number and proportion in the abstract, it was not close enough to break down the prejudice against banausic occupations. The admirers of works of art did not value their makers equally, and sculptors were no less banausic than smiths, cobblers or potters, as the Berlin Foundry Cup suggests, with its portrayal of workers hunched over the furnace or swinging hammers at the bronze statue under construction.

There is little evidence that sculptors were ever rewarded for good work on a public monument, for example with political privileges (apart from those of the resident alien, a status enjoyed by numerous craftsmen in Greek cities), and no sculptor is known to have held political office. A few sculptors' dedications are known, showing entirely conventional religious observance, and many sculptors displayed a public personality by signing their works. A sculptor who, like Thrasymedes, could sign the chryselephantine statue of *Asklepios* and so have his name preserved in the god's temple, had no other need of public reward. A few signatures are accompanied by personal statements of pride in the work.

J. Overbeck: *Die antiken Schriftquellen zur Geschichte der bildenden Künste bei den Griechen* (Leipzig, 1868)

G. M. A. Richter: *The Sculpture and Sculptors of the Greeks* (New Haven and London, 1929, 4/1970)

J. J. Pollitt: *The Art of Greece, 1400–31 BC: Sources and Documents* (Englewood Cliffs, 1965)

B. Ashmole: *Architect and Sculptor in Classical Greece* (London and New York, 1972)

A. Burford: *Craftsmen in Greek and Roman Society* (Ithaca, 1972)

C. C. Mattusch: *Greek Bronze Statuary: From the Beginnings through the Fifth Century BC* (Ithaca, 1988)

H.-P. Müller: *Die gesellschaftliche Stellung des griechischen bildenden Künstlers im 4. Jahrhundert v.u.Z.*, Ethnographisch-Archäologische Zeitschrift, xxix (1988), pp. 139–45

A. F. Stewart: *Greek Sculpture: An Exploration* (New Haven and London, 1990), i, pp. 19–99

2. Historical Survey. The following discussion traces the development of large-scale Greek sculpture from the 7th century BC, when during the Early Archaic period Greek sculptors began carving life-size and over life-size marble statues of nude male youths (*see* Kouros) and draped female figures (*see* Kore), until the end of the Hellenistic period (27 BC). It begins, however, with a discussion of the small-scale precursors to these monumental sculptural forms. For further discussion of small-scale Greek sculpture of all periods *see* Metalwork, §IV *and* Terracotta, §I.

(i) Antecedents. (ii) Archaic (*c.* 700–*c.* 500/480 BC). (iii) Classical (*c.* 500/480–323 BC). (iv) Hellenistic (323–27 BC).

(i) Antecedents.

(a) Dark Age and Geometric (*c.* 1050–*c.* 700 BC). (b) Proto-Daidalic (*c.* 700–*c.* 675 BC). (c) Early Archaic Daidalic (*c.* 675–*c.* 600 BC).

(a) Dark Age and Geometric (c. 1050–c. 700 BC). When the palatial civilization of the Bronze Age Aegean collapsed around 1200–1100 BC, the Minoan-Mycenaean traditions of creating figures and reliefs in stone, ivory and metals also collapsed (the Minoans of Crete are noted for their cast bronze figurines, but the Mycenaeans, though they used bronze for many other purposes, do not seem to have favoured it as a material for sculpture). Some Mycenaean cult statues may have retained their function after the end of the Bronze Age, and indeed the break with Minoan-Mycenaean traditions was otherwise not clean or absolute. From the ensuing 'Dark Age' (*c.* 1050–*c.* 725 BC) there are, for example, some relatively large terracotta idols found at Karphi on Crete (*c.* 1000 BC; Herakleion, Archaeol. Mus.) that are clearly indebted to Late Bronze Age religious imagery. The use of the potter's wheel to shape their cylindrical skirts was also a Bronze Age technological inheritance. Judging from the evidence, however, Greek sculptors worked at first only in baked clay and did not begin to cast bronze figurines, using the lost-wax technique, until at least the second half of the 9th century BC and possibly only in the early 8th.

Sculpture from the Geometric period (*c.* 900–*c.* 700 BC), named from the style of contemporary pottery decoration (*see* Pottery, §IV, 3), is limited to small-scale figures in bronze, terracotta and, exceptionally; ivory. The terracotta figures are mostly handmade animals, and a few combine a cylindrical wheelmade body with hand-formed head and limbs. A good example is the early terracotta centaur from Lefkandi on Euboia (*c.* 900 BC; Eretria, Archaeol. Mus.). This remarkable work, both animal and human, is painted in the Geometric style and bears a gash intentionally made on the left knee, a wound that probably identifies it as the centaur Cheiron, struck by Herakles' arrow. Whatever the case, the Lefkandi centaur is a creature of the imagination and thus the earliest hint that Greek artists would in time become obsessed with the representation of myth.

Most Geometric sculpture is of bronze rather than terracotta. Bronze statuettes occur almost exclusively as votive gifts, and the pan-Hellenic sanctuaries at Olympia, Delphi and Delos received bronze votives from many regions. The identification of regional styles is based on finds at such local shrines as the Athenian Acropolis, the Sanctuary of Hera at Argos, the Sanctuary of Artemis at Sparta and the Sanctuary of Hera at Perachora. The most important votive dedications were three-legged bronze cauldrons, sometimes 2 m high, with small figures of horses, men or birds placed on or beside the vertical ring-handles (e.g. bronze man, *c.* 750 BC; Olympia, Archaeol. Mus., B4600). Free-standing bronze votives include animals, chariots with drivers, hunters and their prey, goddesses standing nude or riding sidesaddle, circle-dancers, musicians and craftsmen (e.g. helmet-maker, early 7th century BC; New York, Met., 42.11.42). Mythological subjects are rare, though a group of a *Man Fighting a Centaur* (*c.* 750–*c.* 700 BC; New York, Met., 17.190.2072), perhaps from Lakonia, may represent Herakles and Nessos. Bronze figures were solid-cast using the direct lost-wax technique, which was introduced into Greece from Syria-Palestine, along with such Near Eastern figure types as spear-brandishing warriors and nude females, derived respectively from Levantine weather gods and fertility goddesses. A group of apelike seated figures, probably Lakonian, was based on Phoenician ape figurines.

Early human figurines in bronze (*c.* 800–750 BC) have triangular or lozenge-shaped torsos, elongated legs and fluidly curving arms. Their faces are flattened ovals with rudimentary features, attached to the head at a 45° angle as if tilted strongly upwards. In the second half of the 8th century BC, however, the torso gained depth and the waist thickened; shoulders and elbows were articulated as joints; and faces became convex and vertical, with more cleanly defined eyes, nose, lips and ears. The elongated proportions reached their extreme soon after 700 BC, especially in Athens.

There were clear regional variations in style and technique. Athenian bronzesmiths specialized in hammered tripod-cauldrons, and their attached figures of horses and humans have long limbs and slender bodies. By contrast, Argive bronzesmiths cast their tripod-cauldrons, and their men and horses have fuller, rounder forms. Lakonian figures tend to have short torsos and large heads, while Corinthian horses, which combine sharp angles with gracefully curved outlines and rounded volumes with sheet-thin extremities, are the most elegant of Geometric statuettes.

Other late 8th-century BC cult statues, such as the one that stood in the early Temple of Hera on Samos, were primarily wooden *xoana* ('scraped things'). Once routinely considered the 'source' of Archaic statuary (an assumption now challenged), these early wooden icons have in any case all disintegrated. However, the cedars and ebonies out of which many early cult statues were carved came, according to literary sources, from the East, as did many of the ideas that began to infiltrate Greek culture at this time.

Early and Middle Geometric sculpture is not abundant, but the number of terracottas and bronzes rapidly increases towards the mid-8th century BC and in the following Late Geometric period (*c.* 760–*c.* 700 BC), and this is one of several symptoms of the general recovery of 8th-century BC Greece, associated also with the consolidation of the city-state (*polis*) as a political entity and the construction of the first important temples, which were intended to house cult statues. Figurines in Near Eastern ivory also occur at this time. Though Geometric ivories are generally rare, a grave near the Dipylon Gate in Athens produced five nude female figurines, datable from pottery finds to *c.* 735–*c.* 720 BC (Athens, N. Archaeol. Mus., 776–9, 2602), the tallest being 240 mm high. The largest and among the latest of Geometric sculptures are three bronze figures from Dreros, Crete. These were made in the *sphyrelaton* technique using hammered bronze plates over a wooden core, and they probably represented Artemis, Apollo and Leto (h. 400 mm, 800 mm and 450 mm respectively, early 7th century BC; Herakleion, Archaeol. Mus., 2445–7).

(b) Proto-Daidalic (c. 700–c. 675 BC). The formative Geometric period of Greek sculpture may be said to have concluded with a bronze statuette, reportedly from Thebes, known as the *Mantiklos Apollo* (Boston, MA, Mus. F.A., 03.997). Combined with its Geometric-style body are features usually associated with the ensuing Daidalic style, including prominent eyes, triangular face, low forehead and thick vertical locks of hair framing the face. But the face is shorter, with sharply slanted sides and a more pointed chin, than in Early Daidalic examples, and for this reason the piece has been assigned to the transitional Proto-Daidalic phase (*c.* 700–*c.* 675 BC). The identity of the figure is not certain: he represents either the god Apollo (if what his left hand held was a bow) or (if a spear) his mortal votary Mantiklos, whom two lines inscribed across the statuette's thighs name as dedicant, asking 'The Far Darter of the Silver Bow' for a favour in return. It is the earliest Greek sculpture to record the circumstances of its own creation and use, and in its expressiveness and pose, which is upright and rigidly frontal with the left leg slightly advanced, it seems to anticipate the birth, slightly later in the 7th century BC, of Greek monumental statuary.

(c) Early Archaic Daidalic (c. 675–c. 600 BC). The term 'Daidalic' derives from the legendary sculptor DAIDALOS ('cunning worker'). Although the name itself is only a convenience (it eventually came to personify the concept of craftsmanship), it was in fact via Crete, Daidalos' legendary home, that the style—the earliest homogeneous style of Greek Archaic sculpture—seems to have been introduced to the Aegean, probably by *c.* 675 BC. It was an Orientalizing style that fused both Syro-Phoenician and native Geometric elements. The impact of Near Eastern imagery and techniques had often been felt in Greece before, but it was in the 7th century BC that Near Eastern influences were strongest. Bronze protomes of griffins, lions and sirens, all based on foreign types, occur frequently on the rims of tripod-cauldrons, and the idea of supporting stone water basins (*perirrhanteria*) with statuettes of maidens standing beside or on the backs of lions was also suggested by Eastern practice.

While not every 7th-century BC Greek sculpture belongs to the Daidalic style (the maidens of *perirrhanteria* do not), it was rapidly diffused throughout Greece, Ionia, South Italy and Sicily. The chief centres, however, were Dorian: Crete, Rhodes, Sparta and Corinth. The most common Daidalic products are mould-made and mass-produced clay reliefs, but the essentially two-dimensional and decorative character of the style is preserved wherever it occurs, not only in terracotta works but also in ivory, wood, gold jewellery, bronze and limestone. Numerous examples of the terracotta plaques were found at Cretan sites; with their representations of nude female figures, they show a close connection to terracotta plaques from Syria depicting the goddess Astarte (e.g. plaque in Oxford, Ashmolean, AE 403). The Oriental technique of mould-made terracottas reached Greece around 700 BC, and the resulting proliferation helped to spread the Daidalic style.

Daidalic figures are characteristically frontal, with heads flattened on top and low foreheads defined by the straight horizontal line of the hair or headdress (e.g. terracotta bust from Gortyn). The hair falls in front of the shoulders, framing the face, and may take the form either of solid triangular panels with horizontal divisions (the Egyptianizing stepped wig) or thick vertical locks. Both male and female figures often wear a wide belt, and Cretan female figures often have a short cape. Compared with Proto-Daidalic works, Early Daidalic faces (*c.* 670–*c.* 655 BC) were more elongated with U shaped chins, as in the ivory group of two standing females (New York, Met., 17.190.70). In Middle Daidalic works (*c.* 655–*c.* 630 BC), the faces became shorter and wider. The earliest large-scale stone statues of the Archaic Greek world are soft limestone Middle Daidalic works from Crete. It was on Crete, too, that stone statues and reliefs may first have been incorporated into the architecture of temples, for example at Gortyn, where reliefs depicting *Apollo Striding between Two Goddesses* decorated a temple dado or orthostat course of *c.* 630 BC (Herakleion, Archaeol. Mus.); or at Prinias, where a combination of reliefs of felines, deer and riders with statues of seated goddesses decorated lintels or dados and a relieving space above the doorway of Temple A, variously dated between 650 and 620 BC (Herakleion, Archaeol. Mus.). To this phase also belong the marble Nikandre Kore from Delos (Athens, N. Archaeol. Mus., 1) and the famous 'Auxerre Goddess' (Paris, Louvre, 3098; see fig. 9). The limestone 'metope' from Mycenae (Athens, N. Archaeol. Mus., 2869), depicting a cloaked woman with the angular jaw and squared chin of later Middle Daidalic, illustrates the emergence of high-relief sculpture, and the famous bronze statuette from Delphi (Delphi, Archaeol. Mus., 2527) shows the pose of the kouros type fully developed by *c.* 630 BC. Hollow-casting was introduced before the mid-7th century BC and used for larger works, such as the head in Karlsruhe (Bad. Landesmus., F1890), probably once riveted to a hammered bronze body about 500 mm tall. Late Daidalic faces (*c.* 630–*c.* 615 BC) continued to become shorter until the length of the face equalled its width and the line of the chin became level, as in the life-size torso from Eleutherna, Crete (Herakleion, Archaeol. Mus., 47). In general, figures gained volume and plasticity during the 7th century BC. Heads gradually became deeper and foreheads higher, while ears, eyes and lips became smaller and better proportioned to the whole figure. Ears, which were regularly omitted in early phases, later appeared carved in relief against the hair at the sides.

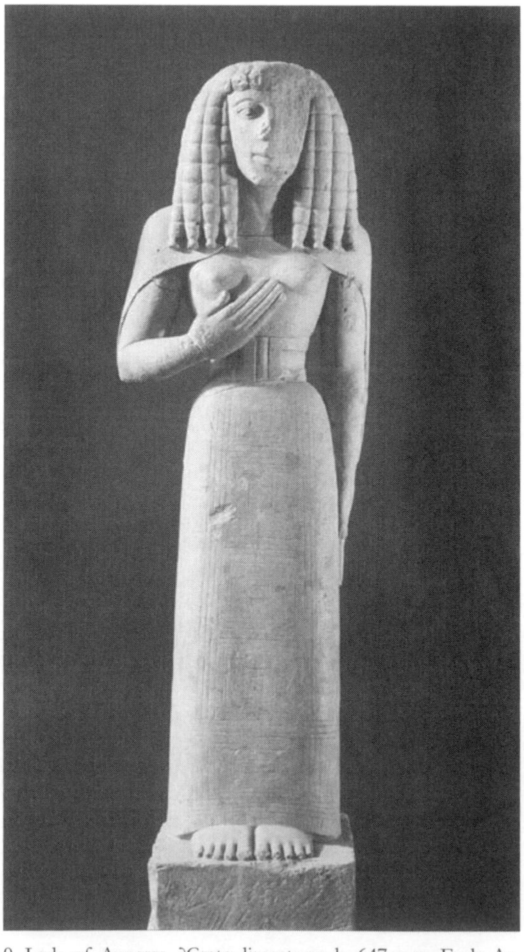

9. Lady of Auxerre, ?Crete, limestone, h. 647 mm, Early Archaic perod, *c.* 650–*c.* 625 BC (Paris, Musée du Louvre)

In the late 7th century BC the Greek fascination with Orientalizing styles and motifs began to fade, and the Daidalic style also declined, essentially reaching the end of its development around 600 BC, though works displaying Daidalic features continued well into the 6th century BC. Before that, however, the Daidalic style was applied to two kinds of statues that Greek sculptors began to carve in emulation of works they saw or heard about in Egypt, the kouros type of striding nude male and the kore type of clothed female statue, as in the Nikandre Kore.

R. J. H. Jenkins: *Daedalica* (Cambridge, 1936)
N. Himmelmann-Wildschütz: *Bemerkungen zur geometrischen Plastik* (Berlin, 1964)
R. M. Cook: 'Origins of Greek Sculpture', *J. Hell. Stud.*, lxxxvii (1967), pp. 24–32
B. Schweitzer: *Die geometrische Kunst auf Griechenland* (Cologne, 1969; Eng. trans. by P. Usborne and C. Usborne, London, 1971)
Dädalische Kunst auf Kreta im 7. Jahrhundert v. Chr. (exh. cat., Hamburg, Helms-Mus., 1970)
C. Davaras: 'Die Statue aus Astritsi: Ein Beitrag zur dädalische Kunst auf Kreta und in den Anfängen der griechischen Plastik', *Ant. Kst*, suppl. 8 (1972)
H. V. Hermann: 'Zum Problem der Entstehung der griechischen Grossplastik', *Wandlungen: Studien zur antiken und neueren Kunst Ernst Homann-Wedeking gewidmet* (Waldsassen, 1975), pp. 35–48
J. N. Coldstream: *Geometric Greece* (New York, 1977)
L. Adams: *Orientalizing Sculpture in Soft Limestone*, Brit. Archaeol. Rep., Suppl. Ser., 42 (Oxford, 1978)
A. C. Brookes: *The Chronology and Development of Dedalic Sculpture* (diss., Philadelphia, U. PA, 1978)
J. M. Hurwit: *The Art and Culture of Early Greece, 1100–480 BC* (Ithaca, 1985)
J. Floren: *Die geometrische und archaische Plastik* (1987), i of *Die griechische Plastik*, ed. W. Fuchs and J. Floren (Munich, 1987-)
A. A. Donohue: *Xoana and the Origins of Greek Sculpture* (Atlanta, 1988)
S. Langdon: 'From Monkey to Man: The Evolution of a Geometric Sculptural Type', *Amer. J. Archaeol.*, xciv (1990), pp. 407–24
A. F. Stewart: *Greek Sculpture: An Exploration*, 2 vols (New Haven and London, 1990)

(ii) Archaic (c. 700–c. 500/480 BC). Whatever the subject, material, genre or scale, the sculpture of Archaic Greece was primarily religious in function. The typical work was made to be dedicated as a 'delight' or 'pleasing gift' (the basic meaning of *agalma*, one of several ancient Greek words for 'statue') in the sanctuary of a deity, to decorate a temple or other structure in the sanctuary or to be placed in or on a grave. Though decorative figurines were often attached as handles or supports to such objects as vessels or mirrors, the idea of 'private' sculpture as the prized possession of individuals was essentially foreign to early Greece.

There are basically three categories of Archaic sculpture: free-standing works; architectural sculpture, including pediments, metopes and friezes; and non-architectural reliefs, such as gravestones. The subject-matter is diverse, encompassing images of deities, heroes and mortals, and even, according to literary sources, portraiture. Animals and monsters, myths and everyday activities are also represented. The range of material is wide, including terracotta, bronze (hammered or cast), various woods, gold, ivory, chryselephantine, silver and stone (primarily limestone and marble). Archaic sculptors were generally regarded as craftsmen rather than as 'artists', and they worked within accepted traditions of image-making, as skilled technicians, whose task was not to innovate but to produce well-made examples of established genres. The names of only a few dozen Archaic sculptors are known from inscribed signatures and ancient literary sources. Of these, a few, such as DAIDALOS, were less historical persons than personifications of early styles, and only a handful of sculptors' names (e.g. Aristion of Paros or Geneleos of Samos) can be plausibly associated with extant works. In some cases groups of unsigned works can be attributed to a single sculptor, who is then given an invented name (e.g. the Rampin Master).

The limits of the Archaic style in sculpture are difficult to define, and the generally accepted chronology has been fiercely, if inconclusively, disputed. The beginning of Archaic sculpture is conventionally placed in the middle of the 7th century BC, when the first large-scale marble statues appear, and there is general agreement that the style did not continue past the Persian destruction of the Athenian Acropolis in 480 BC.

(a) Early (*c.* 700–*c.* 600 BC). (b) Middle (*c.* 600–*c.* 550 BC). (c) Late (*c.* 550–*c.* 500/480 BC).

(a) Early (c. 700–c. 600 BC). The origins of the large statues of draped, standing maidens (korai) and nude youths in an upright pose with left leg advanced and arms held down (kouroi) are complex and controversial. The debate centres on whether they were the product of sudden foreign stimuli or rather of slow, internal development within the Aegean region itself. Most scholars would probably concede at least some degree of Egyptian technological influence, since this was the period of the 'opening up' of Egypt to Greeks during the reign of Psammetichus I (*reg* 664–610 BC). Nevertheless, a Greek kore or kouros can hardly be mistaken for an Egyptian work. Greek sculptors either did not adopt or consciously rejected the relative naturalism of contemporary Egyptian works, and kouroi were not given the clothing and artificial screens and supports of the standard Egyptian prototype. The Greek image of the ideal male figure was balanced on his own two feet and free in space.

The earliest marble korai and kouroi are still Daidalic in style. Probably the earliest is the much-eroded but still impressive kore dedicated in the Sanctuary of Artemis on Delos by Nikandre of Naxos, *c.* 650 BC. While the earliest kouroi are not even as well preserved as this, a belted figurine in bronze from Delphi, dated to *c.* 630 BC, must surely reflect contemporary large-scale examples in marble. Though Crete had been the home of the Daidalic style, the kore and kouros types seem first to have appeared in the orbit of Naxos (the earliest figures are of Naxian marble) and then Samos, spreading from these islands to other, though by no means to all, parts of Greece. These statues were clearly prestige works, affordable primarily by members of Archaic élites, and were in some way emblematic of a 'youth-and-beauty' culture fundamental to Archaic society.

Korai and kouroi could be funerary as well as votive in function, and in some areas of Greece one use predominated over the other. The precise meaning of the types is, however, open to question. It is not clear, for example, whether the Nikandre Kore represents the goddess Artemis, the dedicant Nikandre or just a beautiful woman—a generic 'delight' for Artemis' sanctuary. The identity of the earliest kouroi is similarly uncertain. The scholarly consensus is that from the beginning the kouros was a generic representation of eternal 'handsome youth' that could be given a more specific identity only by inscriptions or attributes. However, some kouroi certainly represent Apollo (e.g. the four-times life-size kouros dedicated on Delos by the Naxians; *c.* 600 BC; fragments, Delos, Archaeol. Mus., and London, BM), and some scholars maintain that the kouros began as an image of Apollo, only later acquiring a generic character that fitted it for a range of purposes that included grave-marking and dedication in the sanctuaries of other gods (and even goddesses).

(b) Middle (c. 600–c. 550 BC). By the beginning of the 6th century BC different regions of Greece were clearly developing local interpretations of the kouros and kore: Naxian kouroi are lean and relatively flat, with oval faces and grooves and ridges indicating anatomical details; Samian kouroi, which could be colossal, are rounded, with spherical heads and soft transitions between anatomical parts; Attic kouroi are angular yet muscular, revealing the sculptor's special interest in anatomical pattern and structure; Argive kouroi, represented by the statues identified as the legendary twins *Kleobis* and *Biton* by [?Poly]medes (*c.* 580 BC; Delphi, Archaeol. Mus.) are thick-set and massive, with short torsos and a suggestion of the Daidalic style about them. Though they differ widely, kouroi seem to illustrate a tendency towards ever-increasing representational accuracy in Greek sculpture in the course of the 6th century BC. The later a statue, the more anatomically 'correct' it appears. Yet it should not be assumed that Archaic sculptors were somehow striving for a lifelike ideal (much less trying to become Classical sculptors) or that each kouros was primarily an experiment in rendering anatomy. Archaic sculptors eschewed the naturalism of Egyptian prototypes and do not seem to have valued naturalism especially highly. Rather, it was the distillation of nature and the imposition of order and pattern (patterns of anatomy, patterns of cloth) that governed Archaic sculpture.

Though kouroi and korai dominate any discussion of Archaic sculpture, many other forms of large-scale sculpture in stone were developed in the first half of the 6th century BC. For example, a seated female and a reclining male figure appeared with a row of korai and a draped youth on a single base in the Geneleos group from Samos (*c.* 560–*c.* 550 BC; Berlin, Antikensamml., and Vathy, Archaeol. Mus.). The kouros type itself could be adjusted for use in high-relief sculpture, as on the Egyptian-influenced limestone pillar-relief of *Dermys and Kittylos* from Tanagra in Boiotia (*c.* 580 BC; Athens, N. Archaeol. Mus.), or could be transformed into an offering-bearer by the addition of an animal in the arms or over the shoulders. On Thasos a colossal *Ram-bearer* was left unfinished around 580 BC, and the history of marble sculpture on the Athenian Acropolis essentially begins in the years before 560 BC with the dedication, by a certain [Rh]onbos, of the *Calf-bearer* (*Moschophoros*; Athens, Acropolis Mus.; see fig. 10). Major cult statues were also created at this time: the Temple of Hera at Olympia, built *c.* 590 BC, contained images of a standing *Zeus* and a seated *Hera*; a huge limestone head (Olympia, Archaeol. Mus.), often said to be from the statue of the goddess, is more likely to have come from a sphinx dedicated on a column outside the temple, like the gigantic *Crouching Sphinx* dedicated by the Naxians at Delphi *c.* 560 BC (Delphi, Archaeol. Mus.). By the mid-6th century BC other important categories of Archaic free-standing and relief sculpture had become established: the earliest stone *Nike*, the *Nike of Archermos*, was set up on Delos *c.* 550 BC (Athens, N. Archaeol. Mus.), while a little earlier a row of 16 lions was placed beside the precinct of Leto, in the Egyptian manner. A life-size *Bull*, made of silver plates in the *sphyrelaton* technique, was dedicated at Delphi in the mid-6th century BC (Delphi, Archaeol. Mus.), and equestrian statues began to occur in large numbers. This type was mainly Attic, and examples include the Rampin *Horseman* (Athens, Acropolis Mus., and Paris, Louvre; see fig. 11). Grave stelai carved in low relief with images of the dead, for example a warrior carrying sword and spear (*c.* 560 BC; Athens, Kerameikos Mus.), began to fill Archaic cemeteries, especially those at Athens.

Equally significant were the emergence in the Middle Archaic period (*c.* 600–*c.* 550 BC) of large-scale stone architectural sculpture and its use for the representation of mythological narrative, in contrast to the earlier non-narrative Daidalic architectural reliefs from Crete. Large-scale stone architectural sculpture required massive stone architecture to carry it: thus the first stone pedimental sculptures, and possibly the first stone metopes, occur on the first all-stone Greek temple, the Temple of Artemis at Corfu (Kerkyra; *c.* 580 BC). Compositionally, the major problem presented by a pediment is how to fill its low triangular space with figures that must vary greatly in either scale or posture. In terms of subject-matter, the problem is one of thematic unity. In the

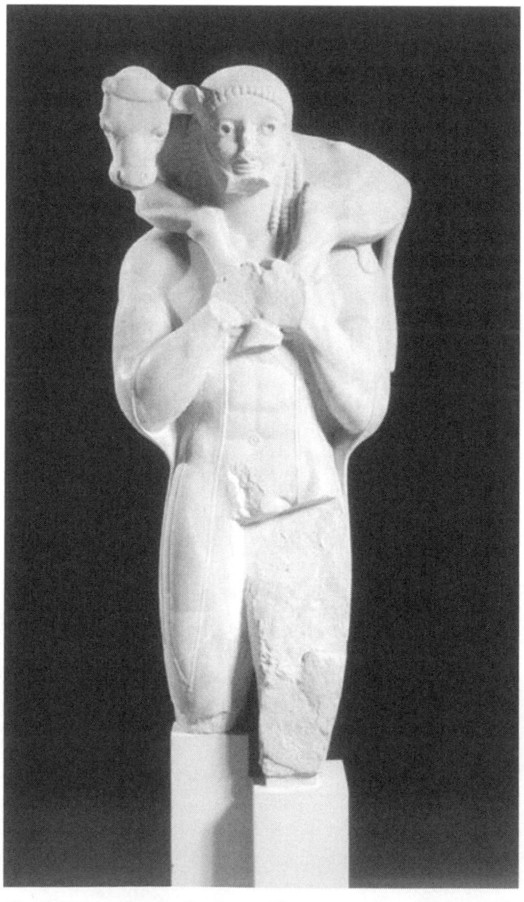

10. *Calf-bearer* (*Moschophoros*), marble, restored, h. 1.65 m, Middle Archaic period, *c.* 560 BC (Athens, Acropolis Museum)

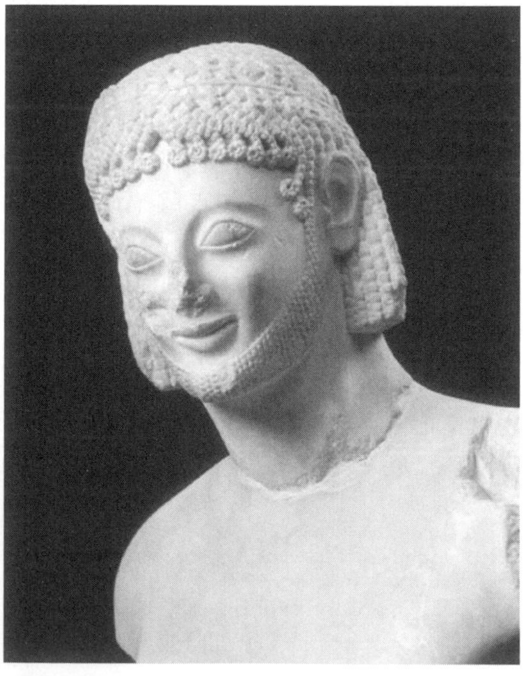

11. Rampin *Horseman*, marble, h. 293 mm, *c.* 560 BC (Paris, Musée du Louvre)

Temple of Artemis the solutions to both problems seem disjointed. At the centre of the west pediment stood a gigantic relief of the Gorgon Medusa (for illustration *see* CORFU), flanked by her children Pegasos and Chrysaor (since they were born only after Medusa's beheading by Perseus, a chronologically plausible narrative is immediately subverted). Two huge leopards flank this central image, offering a sinuous transition to the angles, where there are disconcertingly puny groups of Zeus hurling a thunderbolt at a giant or Titan and, on the other side, a spearman threatening a seated male figure (Priam or Kronos). Crammed into the corners and again on a different scale are two larger Titans or giants, lying dead on their backs. The precise relationship of these parts is unclear. The common theme is violence, which might relate to the ferocity of nature, Artemis' province; but the central group is easier to explain. The Gorgon often appeared in early Greek art as a version of the Near Eastern 'Mistress of the Animals', and she, in turn, was commonly identified with Artemis. Thus, the Gorgon and leopards must not only have been apotropaic temple guardians, transfixing the visitor with their masklike, demonic faces, but must also have been considered as expressions of Artemis and her wild power.

Though sculptural narrative first appeared on Corfu, there are numerous mid-6th century BC examples from the Athenian Acropolis, where brilliantly painted limestone pedimental reliefs and groups adorned a series of temples and small treasury-like buildings. The buildings have not been securely identified and located, and the relationship of the pedimental groups to each other is also controversial. One small building bore a pediment with an incised olive tree and high relief building and figures (Athens, Acropolis Mus.), perhaps representing an early legend relating to the Acropolis itself. Another pediment, in low relief, depicted *Herakles Fighting the Hydra* (Athens, Acropolis Mus.). The pediments of a large temple of Athena built on the Acropolis *c.* 570–*c.* 550 BC were possibly filled with a Gorgon flanked by lions as at Kerkyra, lions savaging a bull, snakes, a narrative group of Herakles wrestling with a sea-god (Triton or Nereus) in one angle and, occupying the opposite angle, a problematic triple-bodied, snaky-tailed monster with bearded human heads (Athens, Acropolis Mus.). No single reconstruction or interpretation of these large mythological groups has yet been agreed upon; one controversial theory is that the narratives dealing with Herakles were political allegories, with the hero standing for the Athenian tyrant Peisistratos, who seized power for the first time *c.* 560 BC. However, at least one, even more fundamental meaning is evident: the actions of such heroes as Herakles were considered appropriate expressions and reinforcements of the divine order, and Athena, goddess of the Acropolis and patron of Athens, would protect those who so honoured the gods with their might and courage.

The history of pedimental sculpture from the mid-6th century BC onwards reflects attempts to replace the narrative and proportional disjunction of the earliest compositions with a unity of theme and scale in which one myth rather than several forms the subject and in which all the figures are as close in scale as possible. The individually carved metopes that alternated with triglyphs in the entablatures of Doric buildings were more suitable fields for the display of mythological diversity, though the separate myths represented in a series of metopes often share thematic associations. Heroic combats filled at least some of the metopes of the Temple of Artemis at Kerkyra (a duel between Achilles and Memnon may have been divided by a triglyph), and a building at Delphi (probably an early treasury built by the city of Sikyon), dating from before the fire of 548 BC, was adorned with metopes representing the *Kalydonian Boar Hunt*, the *Dioskouroi Stealing Cattle*, the *Argo and the Argonauts* and other subjects (Delphi, Archaeol. Mus.). Though individually treated, these myths were not haphazardly chosen: for example, the presence of the Dioskouroi (who were worshipped at Sikyon) at least twice on the treasury was one unifying factor in the series.

The carved metope was, however, not a common feature of mainland Greek temples in the 6th century BC, and there are no certain examples from the Athenian Acropolis, so rich in other forms of architectural sculpture. Metopes seem instead to have been a major feature of Sicilian and South Italian Greek temples: a series of vigorously conceived high-relief panels decorated Temple C at Selinus (*c.* 550 BC; Palermo, Mus. Reg.; *see* SELINUS, fig. 2), and nearly 40 extant metopes, variously depicting the legend and labours of Herakles and the punishment of such impious figures as Sisyphos, filled the entablature of a treasury or temple of Hera at Foce del Sele (*c.* 530 BC). As a medium for narrative, the third main genre of architectural sculpture, the continuous 'Ionic' frieze characteristic of East Greek architecture, did not assume importance until the second half of the 6th century BC (ironically on the mainland, at Delphi).

(c) Late (c. 550–c. 500/480 BC). In 546 BC Ionia became part of the expanding empire of Persia, and *c.* 540 BC workshops on Naxos, the probable birthplace of Greek marble statuary, essentially ceased production of kouroi. In the 530s BC the production of free-standing sculpture on Samos declined: Polykrates was tyrant, and kouroi and korai, the emblems of the rival aristocracy, went rapidly out of favour. Other cities and regions emerged as the sculptural centres of Greece: Paros, with its excellent local marble quarries, became a major centre, with accomplished artists and extensive influence. The most important centre of Archaic sculpture in the second half of the 6th century BC was Athens, which experienced a phenomenal burst of prosperity and cultural activity from 547/6–510 BC under the tyrant Peisistratos and his sons. By *c.* 550 BC even a Parian sculptor, Aristion, had journeyed to Attica to undertake, in a style at least as 'Attic' as 'Parian', such commissions as the brilliant Phrasikleia Kore (Athens, N.

Archaeol. Mus.). Dressed in an elaborately incised and painted *peplos* and bedecked with jewellery and crown, this statue marked the grave of an unmarried girl. Athens, then, was the centre where, in the third quarter of the 6th century BC, many regional styles combined. Presumably introduced by artists attracted by the city's wealth, they seem to have fused into what has been termed an 'International style'.

With a few exceptions, however, korai were not common in Attic cemeteries, where relief stelai and kouroi predominated. The Anavysos Kouros (Athens, N. Archaeol. Mus.; *see* KOUROS, fig. 1), bulgingly muscular and slightly smiling, which was placed over the grave of a certain Kroisos, killed in battle *c*. 530 BC, is an excellent example. Most 'Ripe Archaic' sculpture (*c*. 550–*c*. 510 BC), however, comes from the Athenian Acropolis, where korai were especially plentiful. They were among the earliest marble dedications on the site, but they proliferated after *c*. 550 BC, and 30 or more examples survive. Almost all wear the elaborate Ionian costume of *chiton* and *himation*, and many seem to vie with each other in brilliance of texture, colour and patterning of the dress. This competitive element possibly reflects social rivalry among either the dedicants (often male) or their families. Thus huge statues such as 'Antenor's Kore' (h. 2.15 m; Athens, Acropolis Mus.) claim higher status in terms of their great cost. Artistically, however, the contest between ornamentality and the surface led to a certain decorative unreality by the end of the 6th century BC. Such works as the small but fantastically variegated kore possibly imported from Chios (*c*. 510 BC; Athens, Acropolis Mus.) seem remote from any concern with naturalism.

The Acropolis korai were far from the only free-standing marble statues on the site in the Late Archaic period. Statues of animals (including dogs), horsemen, warriors, draped youths, kouroi, *nikai*, seated figures of Athena, and officials also existed on the Acropolis, as did marble and terracotta reliefs and bronze statues and statuettes. Bronze, in fact, became a favoured medium there and elsewhere towards the end of the Archaic period. Knowledge of large-scale Archaic bronze statuary is derived from such fragments as the head of an under life-size *Zeus* from Olympia (Athens, N. Archaeol. Mus.), from smaller works and statuettes that presumably reflect larger works (for example the striding god (?Zeus) from Ugento in Italy (h. 718 mm, *c*. 525–*c*. 500 BC; Taranto, Mus. N.)) and from rare monumental bronzes, such as the life-size Peiraeus *Apollo* (h. 1.91 m, *c*. 530–*c*. 520 BC; Peiraeus, Archaeol. Mus.).

Independent narrative groups were also dedicated on the Acropolis, for example *Theseus Wrestling with Procrustes* (marble, *c*. 510–*c*. 500 BC; Athens, Acropolis Mus.). However, the mythological compositions that dominated the Late Archaic Acropolis occurred in the pediments of the Old Temple of Athena Polias (possibly as late as *c*. 510–*c*. 500 BC; Athens, Acropolis Mus.), which may have been among the earliest products of the period of Athenian democracy. One pediment was apparently filled with a scene of *Lions Attacking a Bull*, a rather conservative, if suitably apotropaic, way of filling the triangular field. The other pediment contained a single narrative scene, the *Battle between Gods and Giants*. Athena played a major role, with fighting and falling figures occupying the varying heights and angles of the field without violating the unity of scale. The main problems of pedimental sculpture have been solved here, and this temple may also have included a continuous interior frieze representing a divine procession. If so, the presence of an Ionic frieze on an otherwise Doric building anticipates the combination of architectural orders later seen on the Parthenon.

Mythological narrative also flourished at Delphi, where several richly adorned Ionic treasuries and a new Temple of Apollo were built in the last decades of the 6th century BC. The Siphnian Treasury can be dated on historical grounds to *c*. 525 BC, and this remains the first of the very few 'fixed points' in the chronology of Archaic sculpture. The treasury's abundant sculpture (Delphi, Archaeol. Mus.) included acroteria in the form of *nikai*; a pediment representing *Herakles and Apollo Struggling over the Delphic Tripod*; a frieze on all four sides of the building, representing a *Homeric Combat and Council of Gods*, the *Judgement of Paris*, an *Abduction Scene* and a *Gigantomachy* (see fig. 12); and two caryatids in the porch. It seems to have been produced by two distinct workshops, and there even exists the signature of the artist responsible for the north and east sides, carved into the shield of a giant, though the actual name of this master of narrative structure and foreshortening is lost. The Siphnian Treasury, standing as it did in a pan-Hellenic sanctuary, constituted both a sculptural lesson and a challenge to the rest of Greece, answered near the end of the Archaic period by those most contentious of Greeks, the Athenians. Their treasury at Delphi was a Doric structure located along the Sacred Way above the Siphnian Treasury. It was adorned with metopes representing the *Exploits of Herakles and Theseus* and, across the entire east side, a *Battle between the Greeks and the Amazons*. The date of the Athenian Treasury is notoriously controversial, but scholars increasingly accept Pausanias' statement that it was built to commemorate the Athenian victory over the Persians at Marathon (490 BC). If so, the *Battle between the Greeks and the Amazons* would allude to the recent historical struggle between West and East.

The *Battle between the Gods and Giants* on the Siphnian Treasury, with its implicit moral theme of the defeat of *hubris* by wisdom and order, was repeated in the limestone west pediment of the Archaic Temple of Apollo (*c*. 510 BC) at Delphi, though these sculptures are poorly preserved. The marble east pediment, commissioned by an important Athenian family *c*. 513 BC, depicted *Apollo in a Chariot* flanked by kouroi and korai (often stylistically linked to the Antenor Kore from the Acropolis) and, in the angles, by groups of lions attacking animals, apparently an old-fashioned compositional solution though perhaps also an intentional symbol of the suppression of the savage violence of nature to the corners of a

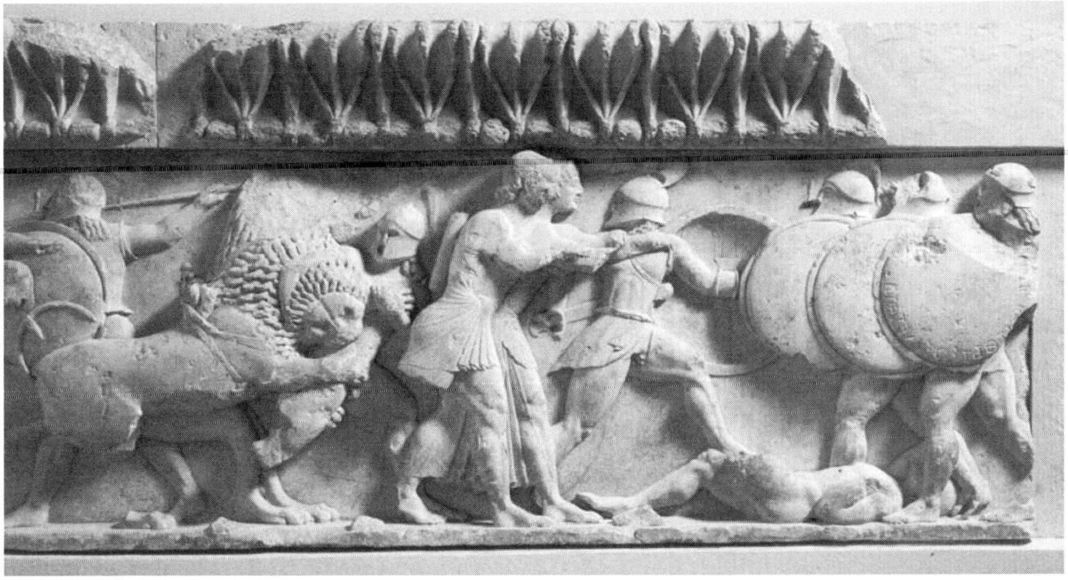

12. *Gigantomachy*, from the north frieze of the Siphnian Treasury at Delphi, marble, h. 640 mm, Late Archaic period, *c.* 525 BC (Delphi, Archaeological Museum)

pedimental cosmos dominated by the calm, civilizing power of Apollo.

Later still are the pedimental sculptures of the Temple of Apollo Daphnephoros at Eretria (*c.* 500 BC or later; Chalkis, Archaeol. Mus., and Rome, Mus. Conserv.), which depicted *Theseus Abducting Antiope under the Protection of Athena*. This alluded to the close political ties between Eretria and Athens, which together raided Persian Sardis in 498 BC. On Aigina, Athens' bitter foe, the Temple of Aphaia had its first set of pediments (*c.* 500–490 BC) replaced by a second set (*c.* 490–480 BC or later; Munich, Glyp.), depicting two legendary sacks of Troy (by Herakles and by Agamemnon). Even though these later pediments do not seem to differ appreciably in date (the east seems slightly later than the west), their radical differences of style and mood embody the transition from the Archaic to the Classical style. The west pediment is stylistically conservative: its *Dying Warrior* is essentially an awkwardly reclining, vacantly smiling kouros. The east pediment, however, is stylistically advanced: its *Dying Warrior* has drama and pathos, vainly struggling to support himself with his shield. These qualities mark it as already essentially Early Classical in spirit.

The end of the Archaic style came quickly. Even by 500 BC such quintessentially Archaic types as the kouros must have seemed old-fashioned, especially when contrasted with vigorous and sophisticated relief scenes on their bases, in which twisting and foreshortened poses were used to create a sense of space (e.g. the *Ball-player* base, *c.* 510 BC; Athens, N. Archaeol. Mus.) or to manipulate perspective (on two sides of a base the same procession of warriors and chariot is depicted as if seen from different angles; *c.* 500 BC; Athens, N. Archaeol. Mus., 3477). Such juxtapositions of old schemata with bold experiments must have seemed increasingly incongruous. Even the elaborate ornamentality of Late Archaic korai no longer appealed: one of the latest Acropolis korai, dedicated by Euthydikos *c.* 490 BC, eschews the elaborate surfaces of earlier examples in favour of a simplicity that emphasizes the form of the body beneath the cloth; and it no longer has the Archaic smile. Perhaps by the same sculptor is the moody *Blond Boy* (Athens, Acropolis Mus., 689), which, like the *Kritios Boy* (see fig. 13), was dedicated on the Acropolis *c.* 480 BC, the year of the Persian sack of Athens. Though little remains of the *Blond Boy*, both figures originally stood with all their weight shifted on to one leg and with the other leg relaxed, thus assuming a pose suggestive of a spontaneous moment, rather than the traditional quadratic pose of the 'eternal' kouros. Both turn their heads to the right, breaking with the accustomed Archaic frontality, and both appear not to look out at the world like a kouros but inwards, in self-conscious contemplation. Whenever they were dedicated on the Acropolis, either just before 480 BC or just after, the Archaic style in sculpture ended with them.

H. Schrader and others: *Die archaischen Marmorbildwerke der Akropolis* (Frankfurt am Main, 1939)

G. M. A. Richter: *Kouroi: Archaic Greek Youths* (London, 1942, 3/1970)

G. M. A. Richter: *The Archaic Gravestones of Attica* (London, 1961)

G. M. A. Richter: *Korai: Archaic Greek Maidens* (London, 1968)

J. Boardman: 'Herakles, Peisistratos, and Sons', *Rev. Archéol.* (1972), pp. 52–72

B. Freyer-Schauenburg: *Bildwerke der archaischen Zeit und des strengen Stils* (1974), xi of *Samos* (Bonn, 1961–)

L. Schneider: *Zur sozialen Bedeutung der archaischen Korenstatuen* (Hamburg, 1975)

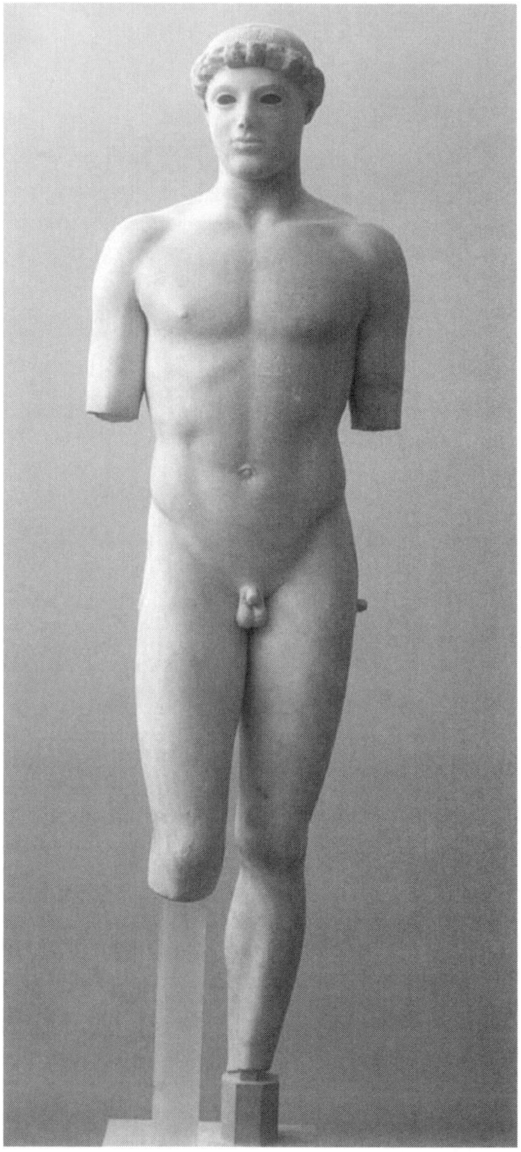

13. *Kritios Boy*, marble, h. 1.17 m, from the Acropolis, Athens, Late Archaic period, *c.* 480 BC (Athens, Acropolis Museum)

J. G. Pedley: *Greek Sculpture of the Archaic Period: The Island Workshops* (Mainz, 1976)
B. S. Ridgway: *The Archaic Style in Greek Sculpture* (Princeton, 1977, rev. Chicago, 1993)
J. Boardman: *Greek Sculpture: The Archaic Period* (London, 1978/*R* 1988)
Archaische und klassische griechische Plastik: Akten des internationalen Kolloquiums: Athen, 1985
J. M. Hurwit: *The Art and Culture of Early Greece, 1100–480 BC* (Ithaca, 1985)
J. Floren: *Die geometrische und archaische Plastik* (1987), i of *Die griechische Plastik*, ed. W. Fuchs and J. Floren (Munich, 1987–)
C. C. Mattusch: *Greek Bronze Statuary: From the Beginnings through the Fifth Century BC* (Ithaca, 1988)
J. M. Hurwit: 'The Kritios Boy: Discovery, Reconstruction and Date', *Amer. J. Archaeol.*, xciii (1989), pp. 41–80
A. F. Stewart: *Greek Sculpture: An Exploration*, 2 vols (New Haven and London, 1990)
J. Boardman: *Greek Sculpture: The Archaic Period: A Handbook* (New York, 1991)
B. S. Ridgway: *The Archaic Style in Greek Sculpture* (Chicago, 1993)
M. A. Eaverly: *Archaic Greek Equestrian Sculpture* (Ann Arbor, 1995)
D. Steiner: *Images in Mind: Statues in Archaic and Classical Greek Literature and Thought* (Princeton, 2001/*R* 2003)
A. Kosmopoulou: *The Iconography of Sculptured Statue Bases in the Archaic and Classical Periods* (Madison, WI, 2002)
K. Karakasi: *Archaic Korai* (Los Angeles, 2003)
C. Marconi: *Temple Decoration and Cultural Identity in the Archaic Greek World: The Metopes of Selinus* (New York, 2006)

(iii) Classical (c. 500/480–323 BC).

(a) Early (*c.* 500/480–*c.* 450 BC). (b) High (*c.* 450–*c.* 375 BC). (c) Late (*c.* 375–323 BC).

(a) Early (c. 500/480–c. 450 BC).

Introduction. Sculpture of this period is termed 'Severe style', being distinguished both from fully developed High Classical sculpture and from the mannerism of the Late Archaic period. It is characterized by new and effective means of representing the human form. Even before the early 5th century BC, there had been experiments in foreshortening, in three-dimensional representation of the human body and in balanced distribution of masses. Although in the few remains of Early Classical free-standing sculpture these attempts can no longer be clearly discerned, they are evident in reliefs and in contemporary vase paintings. Unfortunately, ANTENOR's first group of *Tyrannicides* does not survive, but the group of *Theseus Abducting Antiope*, from the pediment of the Temple of Apollo at Eretria, can be adduced.

Antenor was probably among the important sculptors who brought about the shift from Late Archaic sculpture to the Severe style. About the end of the 5th century BC Antenor worked in Athens, where KRITIOS AND NESIOTES were later of special importance. They were commissioned to produce a new work to replace Antenor's *Tyrannicides* on the Agora, which had been removed by the Persian king Xerxes in 480/79 BC. Other famous sculptors of the early Severe style whose names are known but whose works do not survive include KANACHOS (ii) of Sikyon and PYTHAGORAS OF RHEGION. ONATAS' and KALAMIS' work is much disputed. MYRON OF ELEUTHERAI's *Diskobolos* and *Athena with Marsyas* have been identified, although these statues already demonstrate the transition to High Classical art, also marked by the works of younger sculptors such as POLYKLEITOS, PHEIDIAS or ALKAMENES.

In contrast to the situation with High and Late Classical sculpture, the Romans left few copies of Severe style works. A few original bronzes have been preserved: works from the second quarter of the 5th century BC include the Delphi *Charioteer*, the

ARTEMISION BRONZES, a *Youth* from Selinus (Palermo, Mus. Reg.) and a similar head from the Athenian Acropolis (Athens, N. Archaeol. Mus.), the head of the Chatsworth *Apollo* (London, BM; *see* CYPRUS, fig. 5), a bearded head with portrait-like features from Messina and, at the point of transition from Early to High Classical, the RIACE BRONZES. The stylistic development of marble sculpture can be traced from architectural sculptures, grave and votive reliefs, bronze statuettes (e.g. of sportsmen or *peplos*-clad female figures), especially from the second quarter of the 5th century BC, and through figural bronzes ornamenting such objects as mirror handles. Few large votive statues of victors in pan-Hellenic games are recorded before the end of the Early Classical period.

Sculpture in terracotta remained important. Large pieces frequently took the form of acroteria, still popular in South Italy and also represented at Olympia, including a group of *Zeus Abducting Ganymede* and an *Athena* (Olympia, Archaeol. Mus.). Smaller votive terracottas also provide important evidence, although the reuse of moulds creates problems of dating. Clay reliefs from Melos and Lokroi Epizephyrioi deserve special mention, even though many examples from earlier moulds were probably not cast until after the mid-5th century BC.

Centres of production. Despite the restrictions imposed by sumptuary laws and the effects of the Persian Wars, Athens was an important centre for sculpture in this period, and the destruction of the city by the Persians in 480/79 BC provides an invaluable chronological reference point. Also central to the development of marble sculpture in the first half of the 5th century BC was Paros, where there was an important statue of *Nike*. Ionian relief sculpture also includes a delicate depiction of a funerary banquet from Thasos (Istanbul, Archaeol. Mus.) and grave reliefs, proscribed in Attica at this time. Of these, the best-known type depicts a girl holding a bird. Ionian workshops produced large numbers of broad-format tomb stelai especially suited to family scenes, for example the grave relief from Ikaria. Sculptures from Paros were widely exported; Parian marble was of outstanding quality and, when exported for a temple pediment, might be accompanied by an entire workshop (one reason for the itinerant nature of sculptors and for the 'internationalization' of ancient Greek art). Parian grave reliefs also inspired local imitation, such as the copious if partly provincial production of stelai in Thessaly.

Types and subject-matter. Kouroi (*see* KOUROS) and korai (*see* KORE) continued to be produced as votive offerings, even in Athens, but their character quickly changed, with details, gestures and shaping becoming freer and more individual and new basic types being added. The same applies to cult statues. An important turning point, marking the end of Late Archaic art, is seen in a comparison of the *Aristodikos Kouros* or the *Antenor Kore* (Athens, Acropolis Mus.) with the *Kritios Boy* (see fig. 13 above), whose pose demonstrates a truly balanced distribution of masses, the *Blond Boy* or the closely-related *Euthydikos Kore*. A dating reference shortly after this is provided by the *Tyrannicides* group by Kritios and Nesiotes (477/6 BC). The end of the Severe style is marked by a number of statues of Apollo that, despite a clearer distribution of body masses, have not yet mastered the contrapposto pattern perfected by Polykleitos at around the same time, still having both feet fully on the ground.

Female Severe style statues are usually masked by their garments, quite unlike Late Archaic korai, whose garments clearly reveal the forms of the female body. Examples include the *Angelitos Athena* by Euenor (Athens, Acropolis Mus.), the *Ludovisi Candia*, the so-called *Hestia Giustiniani* (Rome, Villa Albani) and, completely wrapped in her cloak, the *Aspasia* in Berlin (Pergamonmus.). The impression given by these works is governed by the play of folds: the contrast between the simple, ideally formed heads, with their partly veiled but delicate and animated hair styles, and the flat, almost unstructured surfaces of the garments. The same is true of the bronze Delphi *Charioteer* dating from the same time. About the mid-5th century BC this stage, strict and yet rich in contrasts, is taken to its conclusion and transcended by the youthful *Athena* (copy; Frankfurt am Main, Liebieghaus) from Myron's *Athena with Marsyas* group.

Children are infrequent subjects in free-standing sculpture, although they appear as secondary figures in the pediments at Olympia and are sometimes accurately portrayed in Severe style reliefs. At the end of the Early Classical period, however, children begin to be shown in terms of their age (e.g. in the family scenes on the stele in Ikaria).

The character of narrative reliefs and pedimental sculpture slowly changes; the emphasis shifts from pure action to the underlying situation as in the *Preparations for the Chariot Race between Pelops and Oinomaos* on the east pediment at Olympia (see fig. 6 above).

In terms of detail, the folds at the vertical edge of a garment, initially forming a schematic zigzag pattern, become larger and more individual; Archaic embossed locks of hair, still seen in Harmodios in the *Tyrannicides* group, give way to a plastic rendering of crescent locks. Formally, however, a conservative element persisted, evident in the old-fashioned folds with projecting zigzag edges in the *Nike* dedicated by Kallimachos, who died at Marathon in 490 BC (Athens, Acropolis Mus.). Such stylized, sub-Archaic features should not be confused, however, with the archaizing and archaistic tendencies that began somewhat later, around and after the turn of the century.

Although votive reliefs became less common in Athens, pieces of high quality were produced in other regions, for example Thasos and Paros. Two works in a category of their own are the Ludovisi Throne, originating in South Italy, and the Boston Throne (Boston, MA, Mus. F.A.; *see also* LOKROI EPIZEPHYRIOI), perhaps sculptural elements of altars depicting central mythological scenes (the birth of Aphrodite, probably, and the weighing of souls by Hermes respectively) on the front side, accompanied by supplementary sitting figures on the small sides.

The votive offerings at large shrines include various free-standing groups that mostly seem to have been conceived as accumulations of single figures. The two bronze warriors from Riace probably formed part of such a group produced shortly before the mid-5th century BC.

Two-figure groups begin to express an inner relation and a concrete event taking place between the figures; this is particularly true of combat groups—including those on temple pediments—and of figures facing each other, as in reliefs of this time and later. Two-figure grave reliefs also became more common. With regard to the group formation, the *Tyrannicides* of Kritios and Nesiotes are a special case: despite the simple axial symmetry of the concept, a wider context and a complex political statement are evoked. The Severe style also first made possible the depiction not only of figures in motion but of fighters in action on pediments and in groups, for example a torso from the Temple of Zeus at Akragas or the *Leonidas* from the acropolis at Sparta (Sparta, Archaeol. Mus.), with its unusual rotating movements.

Of special importance in the Severe style is the first development in Greece of genuine portrait sculpture, which strove for individual characterization, even emphasizing features that diverged from the ideal of beauty. The portrait of *Themistokles* (Ostia Antica, Mus. Ostiense) still shows a close proximity to the *Tyrannicides*, but the portrait of *Pindar* (Oslo, Nmus.; long mistakenly attributed to Pausanias of Sparta and dated too early) is part of the transition to High Classicism.

The overall contribution made by architectural, especially pedimental, sculpture to the dissemination and unification of Early Classical innovations must be emphasized. The sculpture of the Temple of Aphaia on AIGINA is of major importance: the sculptures in the earlier west pediment are still in the Archaic style, whereas the later east pediment shows new features clearly belonging to the Severe style, as in the difference between the dying warriors in the corners. Still more important are the large sculptural groups from the two pediments of the Temple of Zeus at OLYMPIA. While the traditional difference between the more static east pediment and the more animated west pediment is preserved, both show convincing new solutions in representing movement and depth, thus foreshadowing the sculptures of the Parthenon. They offer the best examples of the attempt to resolve the spatial problems posed by fighting groups. In the treatment of the canonical Twelve Labours of Herakles, the metopes of Temple E at Selinus are close to those of the Temple of Zeus at Olympia. In both series a change in the choice of moment can be noted: instead of the dramatic climax of a struggle, a moment of rest after it is often shown.

E. Langlotz: *Frühgriechische Bildhauerschulen* (Nuremberg, 1927)

P. Jacobsthal: *Die melischen Reliefs* (Berlin, 1931)

V. Poulsen: 'Der strenge Stil: Studien zur Geschichte der griechischen Plastik 480–450', *Acta Archaeol.* [Copenhagen], viii (1937), pp. 1–142

S. Brunnsaaker: *The Tyrant-slayers: A Critical Study of the Sources and Restorations* (Lund, 1955, rev. Stockholm, 1971)

W.-H. Schuchardt: *Die Epochen der griechischen Plastik* (Princeton, 1959)

H. Biesantz: *Die thessalischen Grabreliefs: Studien zur nordgriechischen Kunst* (Mainz, 1965)

U. Knigge: *Bewegte Figuren der Grossplastik im strengen Stil* (diss., U. Munich, 1965)

H. Prückner: *Die lokrischen Tonreliefs: Beitrag zur Kulturgeschichte von Lokroi Epizephyrioi* (Mainz, 1968)

E. Berger: *Das Basler Altzrelief: Studien zur griechischen Grab- und Votivrelief um 500 v. Chr. und zur vorhippokrateischen Medizin* (Basle, 1970)

B. S. Ridgway: *The Severe Style in Greek Sculpture* (Princeton, 1970)

D. Metzler: *Porträt und Gesellschaft: Über die Entstehung des griechischen Porträts in der Klassik* (Munster, 1971)

H. Hiller: *Ionische Grabreliefs der ersten Hälfte des 5. Jahrhunderts v. Chr., Istanbul. Mitt.,* suppl. 12 (1975) [whole vol.]

D. Willers: *Zu den Anfängen der archaistischen Plastik in Griechenland, Mitt. Dt. Archäol. Inst.: Athen. Abt.* suppl. 4 (1975) [whole vol.]

J. Dörig: *Onatas of Aegina,* Monumenta Graeca et Romana, i (Leiden, 1977)

R. Tölle-Kastenbein: *Frühklassische Peplosfiguren: Originale* (Mainz, 1980)

D. Haynes: *Greek Art and the Idea of Freedom* (London, 1981)

R. Tölle-Kastenbein: 'Frühklassische Peplosfiguren: Typen und Repliken', *Ant. Plast.,* xx (1981) [whole vol.]

B. Fehr: *Die Tyrannentöter oder: Kann man der Demokratie ein Denkmal setzen?* (Frankfurt am Main, 1984)

G. B. Triches: *Die bronzi da Riace: Rinvenimento, restauro, analisi ed ipotesi di interpretazione*, 2 vols (Rome, 1984)

J. Boardman: *Greek Sculpture: The Classical Period* (London, 1985/*R* 1991)

W. Fuchs: 'Die Eroberung der Freiheit in der griechischen Kunst', *Spiegelungen*, ed. W. Knopp (1986), pp. 1–20

I. Jenkins: *Greek Architecture and its Sculpture* (New York, 2006)

(b) High (c. 450–c. 375 BC). Towards the mid-5th century BC a new phase of Classical Greek sculpture, different in character from the Severe style, was inaugurated with the discovery of new and even more striking possibilities for representing the human figure in three dimensions. This High Classical period can be subdivided into three phases, each corresponding roughly to a quarter of a century. High Classicism proper reached its peak in the third quarter of the 5th century BC, when the most important and innovative works were produced. Then came a phase in the last quarter of the century, known as the Rich style, during which the successful formulae were perfected, often being lavishly applied, occasionally to the point of mannered exaggeration, with strong graphic tendencies. The Rich style was followed by a late phase in the first quarter of the 4th century BC, when the repetition of these formulae became hackneyed and sometimes meaningless. Almost immediately a reaction set in, characterized by greater plasticity, simplification and hardening of forms, preparing

the way for the Late Classical Plain style in the second quarter of the 4th century BC.

Free-standing works. Although most of the free-standing works by the celebrated masters of the High Classical period, which was regarded already by the Romans as the greatest age of Greek art, are now lost, some of them are known from descriptions in ancient sources, many of them Roman, and from Roman copies. The task of interpreting this evidence, which has occupied scholars since the Renaissance, has produced some convincing results, especially in the 19th and early 20th centuries, and, in some cases, more recently. It is thus possible to gain a vague impression of these lost masterpieces, though the quality of the evidence varies considerably from sculptor to sculptor, and the uncertain methodological basis for interpreting it has sometimes led to quite contradictory conclusions. Moreover, evaluation of copies and written sources can give only an imprecise outline of the lives or development of individual sculptors. Nevertheless, some idea can be formed of lost works by the sculptors Myron, Pheidias, Polykleitos, Alkamenes, Kresilas and Agorakritos and, less certainly, of those by Kalamis and Kallimachos. There is also some record of the early 4th-century BC sculptors Naukydes and Timotheos but almost none of others such as Kolotes and Strongylion.

The most important and versatile sculptor of the 5th century BC, and the most famous even in antiquity, was the Athenian PHEIDIAS, whose career extended from the late Severe style to the Peloponnesian War. However, the attribution of many of the works traditionally assigned to him is disputed, including the two RIACE BRONZES (*c.* 455–*c.* 450 BC; Reggio Calabria, Mus. N.). These demonstrate the striving towards a clearer and more spatially convincing representation of the body in action, a quality shared by copies of other mid-5th century BC works attributed to Pheidias with greater certainty. Among these are the Kassel *Apollo* (*c.* 450 BC; copy, Kassel, Hess. Landesmus.), the *Anakreon* (*c.* 450–440 BC; best copy, Copenhagen, Ny Carlsberg Glyp.), in collaboration with Kolotes, Theokosmos and the painter Panainos, and the *Hermes Ludovisi* (*c.* 450–440 BC; named after copy, Rome, Mus. N. Romano), with its Attic contrapposto (a balanced standing posture with the flexed leg set firmly in front). Pheidias' masterpieces were considered to be two colossal chryselephantine cult statues, which received the longest descriptions of any sculptures in ancient literature. One of these, the *Zeus* (*c.* 430 BC; remains of piece-moulds from Pheidias' workshop, Olympia, Archaeol. Mus.) at Olympia, is reproduced only on Roman Imperial coins. The other, the *Athena Parthenos* (*c.* 440 BC), survives in small-scale copies, the most important of which are the Varvakeion Statuette (h. 1.05 m) and the Lenormant Statuette (h. 420 mm; both Athens, N. Archaeol. Mus.).

On the other hand, the works of POLYKLEITOS of Argos, who is assumed to have been active from the middle to the end of the 5th century BC, present a unified picture. His representations of youths, with their rather uniformly schematized curly hair, reveal a clear pattern of development, especially in his late work. His treatise explaining in theoretical terms the ideal proportions displayed in a sample statue known as the Canon (both now lost) exemplified the Greek belief that the ideal proportions of the human figure were based on fixed mathematical relationships and that it was the artist's task to represent this. The Canon is probably represented by the *Doryphoros* (*c.* 440 BC; most complete copy with best copy of the head, Naples, Mus. Archeol. N.). Developed here for the first time is the definitive Classical contrapposto, a standing posture with equilibrium based on reciprocal antithesis: the unengaged leg bears no weight and is set back, and the overall composition reveals the working of individual parts of the body by means of the clearly recognizable distribution of weight.

Pheidias' fellow sculptors and rivals in Athens, such as ALKAMENES, an exact contemporary who worked until the end of the 5th century BC, AGORAKRITOS and KRESILAS, were strongly influenced by him. Consequently, in several cases the attribution of works is disputed among them, for example two statue-types of Aphrodite from *c.* 420 BC: the Daphne type (copy, Naples Mus. Archeol. N.) and the Seated Olympias type (copy, Rome, Mus. Torlonia). The latter has been thought to represent Alkamenes' famous *Aphrodite in the Gardens* on the slopes of the Acropolis. However, Polykleitos' influence is also apparent in the contrapposto and the formation of hair in other sculptors' work, particularly that of Kresilas (e.g. his *Diomedes*, *c.* 430 BC; full-length copy, Naples, Mus. Archeol. N.), and even in the work of Pheidias himself. Occasionally, sculptors deliberately reverted to the Attic contrapposto, which had been usual in the mid-5th century BC, as in Alkamenes' Borghese *Ares* (*c.* 420 BC; named after copy, Paris, Louvre). This sculptor retained, on purpose, some archaic elements in such works as the *Hecate* and *Hermes Propylaios* on the Acropolis at Athens (*c.* 430 BC; copies, Athens, Brit. Sch. Archaeol. and Panathenaic Stadium, respectively). The famous group of Amazons from Ephesos must all have been made shortly before the Peloponnesian War, though their chronology has been disputed. If the *Amazon* generally associated with Kresilas (Copenhagen-Sciarra type; named after copy, Copenhagen, Ny Carlsberg Glyp.) is compared with those attributed to Pheidias (Mattei type; named after copy, Rome, Vatican, Mus. Pio-Clementino) and Polykleitos (copy signed by Sosikles, Rome, Mus. Capitolino), it can be seen to have borrowed elements from both while also showing an exaggerated tendency in the drapery towards symmetrical and finely delineated folds. Agorakritos seems to have had more of Pheidias' genius, as indeed was his reputation in antiquity. His cult statue of *Nemesis* has been reconstructed from the original fragments found at Rhamnous (*c.* 430 BC; complete Roman copy, Copenhagen, Ny Carlsberg Glyp.).

The introduction of a clearer emphasis on the forms of the female body by means of apparently 'wet' transparent drapery seems to have been initiated by PAIONIOS OF MENDE, whose *Nike* (*c.* 420 BC; Olympia, Archaeol. Mus.) at Olympia has survived, and KALLIMACHOS, to whom is attributed the Fréjus *Aphrodite* (or Venus Genetrix type, *c.* 420–*c.* 410 BC; named after copy, Paris, Louvre). The preference for the lavish treatment of folds that became increasingly apparent in the 430s BC led in the last two decades of the 5th century BC to other mannered works. Many of these, typifying the early Rich style, cannot be securely attributed, for example the *Hera Borghese* (*c.* 410 BC; copy, Copenhagen, Ny Carlsberg Glyp.) and the *Athena Velletri* (*c.* 420–410 BC; copy, Paris, Louvre). By the beginning of the 4th century BC, however, a reaction is apparent in the works of Polykleitos' pupil NAUKYDES (e.g. his *Diskobolos* (*c.* 400 BC; copy, Rome, Pal. Conserv., Mus. Nuovo) and the *Hermes of Troizen* (*c.* 390 BC; copy, Athens, N. Hist. Mus.)), though the Polykleitian tradition is still discernible in them, as in the works of TIMOTHEOS, to whom the *Hygieia* (*c.* 380 BC; copy, Athens, N. Archaeol. Mus.) at Epidauros can probably be attributed. New motifs were explored, with striding figures in vigorous action. The calligraphic treatment of both drapery folds and hair was disrupted though not rejected immediately.

To the Greeks the most important large free-standing sculptures were the cult statues in temples, representing single or paired gods either calmly standing or enthroned (e.g. Pheidias' *Athena* in Athens and *Zeus* at Olympia). Iconographically these were often indistinguishable from votive statues, but other types of sculptures set up in temples and sanctuaries included statues of animals, such as the famous *Heifer* by MYRON OF ELEUTHERAI on the Acropolis at Athens (Pliny: *Natural History* XXXIV. xix.57), and mythological figures and groups, such as the *Trojan Horse* by STRONGYLION, also on the Acropolis (now lost), as well as an increasing number of honorary portrait statues. The latter, which were generally posthumous, are of special historical value, since some can be dated by the names inscribed on copies. The first signs of a concern with the realistic depiction of age and with a subject's individuality are found at the beginning of the High Classical period, for example in a portrait of the poet *Pindar* (*c.* 440 BC; copy, Oslo, Nmus.), who died soon after 446 BC. This contrasts with idealized portraits, such as that of *Pericles* (*c.* 425 BC; copy, London, BM) by Kresilas.

Architectural and relief sculpture. A detailed picture of the stylistic developments of the Classical period is, however, derived less from surviving copies of important free-standing sculptures than from works of relief sculpture. Although often smaller and anonymous (but original), these are more numerous and provide more evidence for making comparisons and historical connections. They include architectural sculptures such as metopes and friezes, funerary and dedicatory reliefs and related works; particularly important among these are the so-called record reliefs.

During the mid-5th century BC important marble statues and reliefs were produced on the Aegean islands, especially Paros, with its supply of high-quality marble, and these were distributed throughout the Aegean. Typical Parian products of the early High Classical period are some children's grave stelai depicting birds, the best known being the Dove Stele (*c.* 440 BC; New York, Met., 27.45). Some of these pieces were found as far away as northern Greece, and they apparently influenced the production of reliefs in Thessaly. These were plentiful until the beginning of the 4th century BC, but they often appear stiff and coarse in their proportions and execution, as do reliefs from other regions. In some regions independent styles also developed. Thus in Boiotia around 430–420 BC, besides Ionian-influenced grave reliefs imported either directly or via Athens, a number of accomplished, finely incised local stelai occur. These were apparently intended to be painted and were clearly influenced by wall painting. In Lakonia, whose rich Archaic artistic tradition had long expired, a small workshop produced extremely provincial flat reliefs. However, most Rich style reliefs come from Athens, which at that time was the most important city-state in Greece, both politically and artistically. During the Periclean building programme, Athens attracted many Ionian artists, above all the celebrated Agorakritos of Paros. Though individual, independent or regional groups existed, most of the works found outside Attica from the late 5th century BC already show the influence of developments in Athens. This influence even appears to have been stimulated by the collapse of Athens at the end of the Peloponnesian War (404 BC), since many artists were apparently forced to seek work and patrons in other Greek states from the Black Sea to Italy. They took with them not only models but also whole workshops with their accumulated expertise and in effect created a common school of Greek sculpture in the 4th century BC, which continued to be dominated by artistic practice in Athens.

For the High Classical period it is precisely the great Periclean religious buildings in Attica itself that provide the most exact sculptural record. The chronological sequence can sometimes be established from the surviving inscriptions of the annual building accounts, which were then customary only in the Attic democracy, though in the 4th century BC they also existed in other city-states. Here the Parthenon on the Acropolis at Athens, the construction of which was in some way overseen by Pheidias, is of the greatest importance. The iconographic programme of its architectural sculpture was certainly conceived by Pheidias himself and became an influential model for all similar later projects. Its full extent was recorded in drawings made by Jacques Carrey (1649–1726) shortly before the Parthenon was blown up in 1687. Enough is preserved (mostly London, BM; also Athens, Acropolis Mus., and elsewhere) to give an idea of the sequence of construction and the corresponding subtle stylistic changes in the 440s and 430s BC. The massive metopes, probably commissioned at the beginning of construction around 447 BC, show traditional mythological battle scenes, though some are imaginatively treated (see fig. 4 above). The earliest metopes only just begin to depart from the Severe style. By contrast, the great Panathenaic frieze, with the inexhaustible variety of its new subject-matter, is more softly modelled. It dates from *c.* 442–*c.* 438 BC, and parts of it were finished *in situ*. Finally, the free-standing sculpture in the two pediments belongs to *c.* 437–*c.* 432 BC. Here Pheidias, who has always been thought to have designed the works, gave a new form to a traditional theme (a divine birth among the Olympians; east pediment) and put a new theme (the quarrel of the gods over the land of Attica; west pediment) into visual form. Despite the loss of the central figures and much other damage, the better preserved east pediment remains a magnificent sculptural ensemble. The completion of Pheidias' chryselephantine statue of *Athena Parthenos* can be dated to 438 BC, when the cella was already roofed. Its sculpted and painted ornament, including the animals on the upper part of the helmet, the reliefs on the outside and the images on the inside of the shield, and the reliefs on the sandals and on the base, evidently reflected the iconographic programme of the temple itself. Small-scale reproductions of the statue and fairly accurate neo-Attic relief copies of the figures on the outside of the shield contribute to a clear overall idea of the High Classical style in sculpture. Despite the collaboration of many sculptors, the Parthenon is characterized by a varied but coherent style, presumably attributable to Pheidias' involvement.

Fragments of pedimental sculpture, acroteria, friezes and metopes survive from several slightly later Periclean temples. The best preserved are the friezes and metopes of the Temple of Hephaistos (Hephaisteion; *c.* 450–*c.* 430 BC; Athens, Agora Mus., and *in situ*). The east frieze, at least, should be dated to the end of the 430s BC, and the increasingly high relief of the friezes led to a denser calligraphic treatment of individual figures, a style subsequently perfected in the frieze of the small Temple of Athena Nike on the Acropolis (slabs *in situ*, Athens, Acropolis Mus., and London, BM). The latter must date from after a change in plan of the Propylaia during the Peloponnesian War, probably *c.* 425 BC. Though all its formulae are High Classical, the effect is sterile and crowded, so that it already represents the long 'mannered' final phase of High Classicism, the Rich style.

Two new developments in Attic sculpture ensure that the evolution of the Rich style is well-documented. One was the rescinding of the Kleisthenic prohibition of luxurious grave monuments, which had been in force from *c.* 500 BC. This meant a rapid increase in the number of Attic sculpture workshops returning to the tradition of funerary sculpture that had been continued since the Archaic period on the Aegean islands and in northern Greece. Instead of free-standing kouroi or korai, however, these now produced various types of funerary reliefs. Besides the traditional tall, narrow single-figure stelai there appeared increasing numbers of the broader stelai, usually with a pedimental top and several figures. This type of relief immediately became widespread, predominating until the end of the Classical period. It was characterized by increasingly high relief accompanied by a tendency to architecturalize the stelai to the point at which they suggest *naïskoi* (grave shrines). Ever more varied requirements led to the development of large grave temples, eventually constructed from several pieces, and small flat stelai with a simple painted frame, both types probably being produced in specialist workshops. The old custom of placing special funerary vases on graves led to the development of marble funerary lekythoi and loutrophoroi adorned with reliefs. Some stood on pedestals, which could have relief decoration, as could the 'funerary tables' on other graves. The production of votive reliefs also increased, but, though some display the architecturalizing tendency evident in grave reliefs, most are still in the form of framed oblong panels (*pinakes*), often placed on high pillars in sanctuaries. The reliefs depicting *Orpheus* and *Peliads* (*c.* 420 BC; copies, Naples, Mus. Archeol. N., 6729, and Berlin, Antikensamml., 925) brilliantly encapsulate a whole myth in a single crucial scene, recalling the plays of Euripides. By contrast, a round base with *Dancing Maenads* (*c.* 410–400 BC; copy, Rome, Mus. Conserv., 1094) illustrates the Rich style sculptors' obsession with the abstract linear play of fluttering drapery.

The second important new development in sculpture was the use of reliefs to decorate public inscriptions in Athens. These record reliefs began to appear early in the Peloponnesian War (431–404 BC), and the series ends in the early 3rd century BC. As a source for the absolute dating of Greek sculpture, record reliefs carry risks, since they cannot be directly compared with large-scale architectural or free-standing sculpture. They usually depict only two figures, representing the partners concerned in the document, and though Late Classical record reliefs of the second half of the 4th century BC occasionally strive for more complex compositions, spatial depth and clearer perspective, reliefs in the Rich style use perspective only for the bodies of stationary figures. Moreover, the workmanship of some record reliefs makes a misleading basis for the stylistic analysis of drapery, which is usually particularly helpful for dating. They are thus best compared with technically similar works, particularly small funerary and votive reliefs or tectonic friezes, though even here slight differences of genre occur.

Early Rich style record reliefs from the 420s BC onwards show a preference for highly calligraphic drapery, sometimes swathing the whole figure with rippling tubular folds. Despite their relatively high quality, this remains an inadequate means of giving expression to the three-dimensional physicality of the figures, as demonstrated by the breasts of figures on the Eleusinian Bridge-building Relief (421/20 BC; Eleusis Mus.) representing *Athena with the Eleusinian Triad*. The rippling folds of drapery on the upper bodies of the three female figures form almost symmetrical triangles. Smaller folds are gathered near the girdle in the female figures, with steep folds in front of the weight-bearing leg and taut, smooth folds over the relaxed leg. The frontally facing pose used for the figures of Demeter and Persephone became usual only at this time. Other record reliefs of before *c.* 410 BC display even more finely differentiated movement of the drapery, sometimes with larger smooth areas of cloth between the folds, which are otherwise still conceived as calligraphically as possible. In stark contrast to the figures on two documentary reliefs of 410/9 BC (Paris, Louvre, 83; Athens, Epig. Mus., 6598), which are particularly vital and delicate, are the figures on reliefs from the end of the Peloponnesian War, which are stiff and hard, with larger smooth areas of drapery. Nevertheless, the Rich style survived a long time. Both the unusual battle frieze from a State grave (Athens, N. Archaeol. Mus., 2744) and the funerary Dexileos Stele (Athens, Kerameikos Mus.), dated by inscriptions to 394/3 BC, cling almost desperately to the calligraphic tendencies of the Rich style. Conversely, the figures of the city goddesses of Athens and Syracuse on the severely damaged record relief from the same year honouring Dionysios I of Syracuse (Athens, Epig. Mus., 6899) already show signs of stylistic changes. They have higher waists and almost conical bodies, and are generally stiff and lifeless. As part of a further reaction, the figures on the record relief for the treaty between Athens and Kerkyra (Corfu) of 376/5 BC (Athens, N. Archaeol. Mus., 1467) are no longer stiff but combine an elegance and ease of posture derived from the Rich style, with individual motifs and a new simplicity that announce the Late Classical Plain style.

The Attic building documents are also useful for dating architectural sculptures, though often not with absolute certainty. Thus, though the frieze of the Temple of Athena Nike (see above) cannot be dated securely, the frieze on the Nike Balustrade (*c.* 415 BC; Athens, Acropolis Mus.), perhaps the purest embodiment of the Rich style, must be later than the long series of statues of Athena with trophies and *nikai* from the years shortly before Athens' catastrophic Sicilian campaign (415–413 BC). The Erechtheion is even more informative. Its relief frieze figures, attached by an unusual appliqué technique to a background of dark Eleusinian marble (Athens, Acropolis Mus.), are apparently mentioned in documents of *c.* 409 BC, which even make it possible to estimate the cost of the sculptors.

By contrast, the breaking down and hardening of Attic forms can be seen in the architecture and the frieze (*c.* 410 BC; London, BM, 540–42) of the Temple of Apollo at Bassai. Though built in the middle of the Peloponnesian War, judged by Attic standards it can appear to be of a later date. And whereas the architectural sculpture of the rebuilt Temple of Hera (*c.* 400 BC; Athens, N. Archaeol. Mus., 1561) at Argos is only fragmentary, the more complete architectural sculpture from the Temple of Asklepios (*c.* 380 BC; Athens, N. Archaeol. Mus., and Epidauros, Archaeol. Mus.) at Epidauros provides examples of the final phase of the Rich style. Within this great ensemble, experiments in the construction of figures and depiction of action were clearly being attempted. This is especially apparent in the *Amazon on Horseback* (Athens, N. Archaeol. Mus.) from the west front or the figure of a *Fallen Man* (Athens, N. Hist. Mus.), which has a contorted pose that is far more vivid than that of any comparable earlier figure. The formation of the drapery folds also shows an acceptance and development of the conventions of the Rich style, while endowing them with a new animation. This contrasts with the simplifying and hardening tendencies of the Plain style and shows how the formal achievements of the High Classical period could be carried over into Late Classical sculpture.

Attic influence and also, to some extent, the presence of Attic craftsmen are behind much of the Rich style architectural and relief sculpture in East Greece. This includes funerary monuments in Lycia, for example the mythological friezes from the Heroön of Trysa (*c.* 410 BC; Vienna, Ksthist. Mus.), the battle reliefs and dancing girls of the Nereid Monument (*c.* 400 BC; London, BM) from Xanthos, the friezes and caryatids from the Heroön of Limyra (*c.* 390 BC) and the friezes on the higher-quality relief sarcophagi from the royal necropolis of Sidon (the Satraps Sarcophagus, *c.* 410 BC, and Lycian Sarcophagus, *c.* 390 BC; both Istanbul, Archaeol. Mus., 9(367) and 63(369)). In both areas Attic iconography combined with subject-matter commissioned by the local ruler to create something radically new in Greek sculpture, as shown by the inclusion of perspective and staggered architecture in continuous frieze narratives, an innovation based on Oriental precedents and methods developed in wall painting.

R. Carpenter: *The Sculpture of the Nike Temple Parapet* (Cambridge, MA, 1929)

G. M. A. Richter: *The Sculpture and Sculptors of the Greeks* (New Haven and London, 1929, 4/1970)

F. Brommer: *Die Skulpturen der Parthenon-Giebel* (Mainz, 1963)

B. Schlörb: *Untersuchungen zur Bildhauergeneration nach Phidias* (Waldsassen, 1964)

G. M. A. Richter: *The Portraits of the Greeks*, 3 vols (London, 1965); abridged and rev. by R. R. R. Smith (Oxford, 1984)

F. Brommer: *Die Metopen des Parthenon* (Mainz, 1967)

D. Arnold: 'Die Polykletnachfolge', *Jb. Dt. Archäol. Inst.*, suppl. 25 (1969)

P. N. Boulter: 'The Frieze of the Erechtheion', *Ant. Plast.*, x (1970), pp. 7–28

T. Bowie and D. Thimme: *The Carrey Drawings of the Parthenon Sculptures* (Bloomington, 1971)

G. Despinis: *Symboli sti meleti tou ergou to Agorakritou* [A contribution to the study of the work of Agorakritos] (Athens, 1971)

A. Delivorrias: *Attische Giebelskulpturen und Akrotere des 5. Jahrh. v. Chr.* (Tübingen, 1974)

D. Willers: 'Zu den Anfängen der archaistischen Plastik in Griechenland', *Mitt. Dt. Archäol. Inst.: Athen. Abt.*, suppl. 4 (1975)

F. Brommer: *Der Parthenonfries* (Mainz, 1977)

E. Mitropoulou: *Corpus of the Attic Votive Reliefs of the 6th and 5th Centuries BC*, i (Athens, 1977)

G. Despinis: 'Zum Hermes von Troizen', *Mitt. Dt. Archäol. Inst.: Athen. Abt.*, xcvi (1981), pp. 237–44
B. S. Ridgway: *Fifth-century Styles in Greek Sculpture* (Princeton, 1981)
L. Alscher: *Klassik* (1982), ii/2 of *Griechische Plastik* (Berlin, 1954-)
C. Houser: *Greek Monumental Bronze Sculpture* (New York and London, 1983)
B. Schmalz: *Griechische Grabreliefs* (Darmstadt, 1983)
J. Boardman: *Greek Sculpture: The Classical Period* (London, 1985/*R* 1991)
J. Boardman: *The Parthenon and its Sculpture* (London, 1985)
Archaische und klassische griechische Plastik: Akten des internationalen Kolloquiums: Athen, 1985
M. Meyer: 'Die griechischen Urkundenreliefs', *Mitt. Dt. Archäol. Inst.: Athen. Abt.*, suppl. 13 (1988)
C. Höcker and L. Schneider: *Phidias* (Reinbek, 1993)
I. Jenkins: *Greek Architecture and its Sculpture* (New York, 2006)

(c) Late (c. 375–323 BC*).* Greek sculpture of the 4th century BC encompasses several styles, beginning with a straightforward continuation of the Rich style during the first quarter century. By *c.* 375 BC new trends were established, constituting what has come to be known as Late Classical sculpture. Though the inception of the Hellenistic period is conventionally set at the death of Alexander the Great in 323 BC, a Hellenistic idiom is in evidence by the 330s BC. A classicizing trend, the Plain style, apparent *c.* 330 BC, continued into the first decades of the 3rd century BC. Throughout the 4th century BC the character of Greek sculpture, previously produced exclusively for the city-states of Greece, was transformed by its dissemination through the kingdoms of Asia Minor, where Greek forms were combined with Asiatic iconography.

Introduction. After its defeat in the Peloponnesian War in 404 BC, Athens was no longer the principal centre of sculptural production. Greek sculptors thus sought employment in the sanctuaries of the Peloponnese, Boiotia and Phokis and in the Hellenized satrapal courts of the disintegrating Persian empire. The main representatives of the Attic school were KEPHISODOTOS, his son PRAXITELES, LEOCHARES, SILANION and EUPHRANOR. Its formal preoccupations include a more sentimental rendering of High Classical prototypes as well as a more intimate treatment of divine images: Kephisodotos was responsible for the first free-standing group of a divine mother and child, his *Eirene and Ploutos* (*c.* 360 BC; copy, Munich, Glyp.), and Praxiteles sculpted the first full-scale female nude in Western art, the *Aphrodite of Knidos* (*c.* 360–*c.* 340 BC; copy, 'Venus Colonna', Rome, Vatican, Mus. Pio-Clementino). At the same time LYSIPPOS in Sikyon and the followers of POLYKLEITOS in Argos developed important workshops specializing in bronze statues, mainly of male athletes, with a market not only in the pan-Hellenic sanctuaries of Greece but also in South Italy and Sicily. Itinerant artists of high calibre, such as SKOPAS and BRYAXIS, produced works throughout the Greek world. Other workshops making architectural sculptures in marble were active in local sanctuaries. Regional schools, however, are not readily distinguished, since new ideas travelled fast and styles could be mixed.

Late Classical sculptors considered themselves the direct successors of 5th-century BC masters, whose works they consciously adapted and emulated. A break with the High Classical period, however, was marked not only by differences in the treatment of draperies, which were given a thicker texture and an individuality of their own, and changes in hairstyles but also by a tendency towards mass production, more rapid working methods, the enhancement of the pictorial qualities of marble and a higher degree of subjectivity. A new awareness of viewing angles began to affect the proportions of figures: by the mid-4th century BC long legs, shorter torsos and smaller heads were common features, while Plato (*Sophist* 236a) complained of sculptors' predilection for 'apparent' as opposed to 'real' proportions. Adaptations by 4th-century BC sculptors of High Classical models can sometimes be distinguished only on grounds of proportions. Any experiments with new forms of expression were ultimately tempered by a streak of classicism, which appears to run through all schools of Late Classical sculpture. Portraiture also flourished, even though many surviving portraits are clearly imaginary, showing prominent men of earlier generations. The highest achievement of the period, however, was the popularization of High Classical art, and it was this new, more accessible version of the Classical that inspired later Greco-Roman art.

Free-standing works. Though many original Late Classical sculptures survive, most are anonymous, often second-rate works. The mutilated cult statue of *Apollo Patroos* by Euphranor (*c.* 330 BC; Athens, Agora Mus., S 2154) is a rare example of a relatively secure attribution. The most outstanding of the anonymous original marble statues are the portraits traditionally identified as *Mausolos* from the Mausoleum at Halikarnassos (*c.* 360–*c.* 350 BC; London, BM, 1000), those of the ancestors and family of Daochos II at Delphi (*c.* 335 BC; Delphi, Archaeol. Mus.), the head of *Zeus Labrandeus* from Mylasa in Caria (*c.* 350 BC; Boston, MA, Mus. F.A., 04.12) and the Bartlett Head from Athens (*c.* 325 BC; Boston, MA, Mus. F.A., 03.743) The colossal *Mausolos* is a masterpiece of characterization of a Hellenized Asiatic prince (*see* HALIKARNASSOS, fig. 3), while among the figures on Daochos' monument the statue of the Olympic victor *Agias* is a prime example of the 'pendulum' stance of a restive athlete. The head of *Zeus Labrandeus* from Hellenized Caria recalls images of Pheidias' majestic cult statue of *Zeus* at Olympia, though on a much smaller scale. The Bartlett Head, from a statue of Aphrodite, has blurred, luminous features contrasting with the roughly modelled hair, high triangular forehead, narrow eyes and dreamy expression associated with works by Praxiteles and his followers.

Two of the most striking bronzes of the 4th century BC seem to be portrait heads: one, the *Boxer* from

Olympia (*c.* 330 BC; Athens, N. Archaeol. Mus., 6439), is a superb characterization that may have come from the statue of *Satyros* by Silanion; the other, from the Porticello shipwreck, represents an elderly man with a long beard (*c.* 380 BC; Reggio Calabria, Mus. N.). The more conventional bronze *Youth* from the shipwreck at Antikythera (*c.* 340 BC; Athens, N. Archaeol. Mus., 13396) is based on Polykleitan models and probably represented Perseus triumphant, holding up the head of Medusa. Both the *Youth* and the Peiraeus *Athena* (*c.* 350 BC; Peiraeus, Archaeol. Mus.; *see* PEIRAEUS, fig. 1), attributed to Euphranor, appear to have distorted proportions, corrected when the statues are viewed from a particular angle. The two statues of *Artemis* from the Peiraeus cache (both Peiraeus, Archaeol. Mus.; *see* PEIRAEUS, fig. 2) differ considerably in proportions and general appearance. The larger (*c.* 340 BC) is of uneven quality, with a squat body, large limbs and dull drapery but an exquisite head. The smaller (*c.* 325 BC) is elegant and well-proportioned, exuding Attic grace and charm. The *Boy* from the Bay of Marathon (?*c.* 340–*c.* 300 BC; Athens, N. Archaeol. Mus., 15118) is an enigmatic work. Sometimes associated with Praxiteles because of its lithe limbs and sinuous outline, it has an athlete's headband but apparently functioned as a lampholder and may in fact be of Roman date.

Architectural sculpture. The fully-blown Late Classical style was anticipated by several important High Classical examples, including metopes from the Tholos at Delphi depicting an *Amazonomachy*, a *Centauromachy*, the *Labours of Herakles* and the *Exploits of Theseus*, and acroteria in the form of *nikai* (*c.* 390 BC; Delphi, Archaeol. Mus.). These represent a new approach to architectural sculpture, which was beginning to shed its formal character in favour of spontaneity. The Tholos workshops also produced sculpted pediments and acroteria for the Temple of Asklepios at Epidauros. The temple pediments depict an *Amazonomachy* and the *Fall of Troy* (or a *Centauromachy*), the latter represent the *Rape of Koronis, Nikai* and *Nereids* or *Aurai* ('breezes'; *c.* 380 BC; Athens, N. Archaeol. Mus.). This project is uniquely documented by detailed accounts, and the work of the four master sculptors involved—TIMOTHEOS, Hektoridas, Theo(?dotos) and one other—seems to blend into a harmonious whole. Although they are, strictly speaking, late High Classical, the Epidauros sculptures are distinguished by their technical virtuosity: their rotating poses, high-waisted figures and new density in the texture of draperies reveal a new approach to the depiction of both form and movement. The fragmentary remains of the Late Classical architectural sculptures showing battle and hunting scenes (*c.* 340 BC; Tegea, Archaeol. Mus., and Athens, N. Archaeol. Mus.) from the Temple of Athena Alea at Tegea are considered a landmark, with their particularly powerful heads in contorted poses. Their affinity with the earlier architectural sculptures of the Temple of Hera at Argos (early 4th century BC; Athens, N. Archaeol. Mus.) and the Temple of Athena at Mazi (early 4th century BC; Olympia, Archaeol. Mus.; Patras, Archaeol. Mus.; Athens, N. Archaeol. Mus.) testifies to the continuity in Peloponnesian workshops of the earlier High Classical tradition.

The large quantities of free-standing and architectural relief sculpture from the Mausoleum at HALIKARNASSOS are notable for their uniformity of inspiration. The ensemble is attributed to the workshops of Skopas, Timotheos, Bryaxis, Leochares, PYTHEOS and Satyros. The colossal portrait statues of Carian magnates, with their mixture of Carian and Greek dress and hairstyles, are particularly striking. Praxiteles is associated by literary sources with the Altar of Artemis at Ephesos, and the single extant *Horse's Head* (*c.* 330 BC; Selçuk, Ephesos Archaeol. Mus.) demonstrates a successful attempt to go beyond the Parthenon type of horse by exploiting a subtle interplay of light and shade. The colossal sculpted column drums from the Temple of Artemis (after 336 BC; London, BM) reproduce the iconography of their Archaic predecessors but in a style indebted to Attic grave reliefs.

Reliefs. The many grave, votive and record reliefs found in Attica are a testimony both to the taste of a flourishing society and to the techniques and practices of lesser 4th-century BC marble workshops. Grave reliefs were ready-made in a wide range of sizes, designed to stand on the edge of a grave plot. Within an architectural frame they depict single figures, family or battle scenes, none of which is individualized. The scenes are restrained in gesture, showing little emotion, and their quality is uneven. The general tendency is for both figural groups and the monuments themselves to become larger, developing into full-scale *naïskoi* (grave shrines) containing free-standing figures. A sumptuary decree ended the practice in Attica between 317 and 310 BC.

Votive reliefs also usually have an architectural frame in the form of a flat roof adorned with antefixes and supported by pilasters. The deities honoured tend to be in groups of three, approached by their votaries. Towards the end of the 4th century BC the gods were depicted frontally in order to establish a more intimate link with the spectator. Both votive reliefs and the more modest record reliefs provide invaluable evidence because, among other things, they reproduce statue types of the 5th and 4th centuries BC. Relief bases are less common and more original in conception. The best relief sculpture is directly indebted to painting in its atmospheric quality, its ingenious exploitation of space and use of perspective diminution of background figures. Pictorial qualities are especially apparent in the relief slabs depicting the *Contest of Apollo and Marsyas* from Mantinea (*c.* 325 BC; Athens, N. Archaeol. Mus., 215–17), where the outlines of the figures merge with the background, and in the relief dedicated by Neoptolemos to Apollo and the nymphs (*c.* 325 BC; Athens, Agora Mus., I 7154), in which the action is broken into small groups spread over different planes. Relief and architectural decoration also featured on certain Oriental sarcophagi: thus the Sarcophagus of the Mourning Women from Sidon (late

4th century BC; Istanbul, Archaeol. Mus.) was treated as a miniature Ionic temple, with relief figures on the eaves and pediment and in the intercolumniations.

A revival of 4th-century BC styles and ideals towards the end of the 2nd century BC was to produce such outstanding works of the Hellenistic period as the *Venus de Milo*, paving the way for the assimilation of Late Classical art by the artists of the Roman Empire.

B. R. Brown: *Anticlassicism in Greek Sculpture of the Fourth Century BC* (New York, 1973)

G. Neumann: *Probleme des griechischen Weihreliefs* (Tübingen, 1979), pp. 42–75

B. Vierneisel-Schlörb: *Glyptothek München: Katalog der Skulpturen*, ii (Munich, 1979), pp. 216–514

O. Palagia: 'An Attic Head in Oxford', *Boreas*, iii (1980), pp. 5–11

O. Palagia: 'A Colossal Statue of a Personification from the Agora of Athens', *Hesperia*, li (1982), pp. 99–113

R. Fleischer: *Der Klagefrauensarkophag aus Sidon* (Tübingen, 1983)

C. Houser: *Greek Monumental Bronze Sculpture* (London, 1983)

B. S. Ridgway: 'Painterly and Pictorial in Greek Relief Sculpture', *Ancient Greek Art and Iconography*, ed. W. G. Moon (Madison, 1983), pp. 193–208

B. Schmalz: *Griechische Grabreliefs* (Darmstadt, 1983)

E. Paribeni: 'Le statue bronzee di Porticello', *Boll. A.*, xxiv (1984), pp. 1–14

J. P. Niemeier: *Kopien und Nachahmungen im Hellenismus* (Bonn, 1985)

C. J. Eiseman and B. S. Ridgway: *The Porticello Shipwreck: A Mediterranean Merchant Vessel of 415–385 BC* (College Station, TX, 1987)

M. Meyer: 'Die griechischen Urkundenreliefs', *Mitt. Dt. Archäol. Inst.: Athen. Abt.*, suppl. 13 (1988)

J. J. Pollitt: *The Art of Ancient Greece: Sources and Documents* (Cambridge and New York, 1990)

J. Boardman: *Greek Sculpture: The Late Classical Period and Sculpture in Colonies and Overseas* (New York, 1995)

J. Boardman and C.-M. Diebold: *La Sculpture grecque du second classicisme* (Paris, 1998)

S. L. Karakas: *Subject and Symbolism in Historical Battle Reliefs of the Late Classical and Hellenistic Periods* (diss., Chapel Hill, U. NC, 2002)

O. Palagia: *Greek Sculpture: Function, Materials, and Techniques in the Archaic and Classical Periods* (New York, 2006)

(iv) Hellenistic (323–27 BC). Given the cultural, political and artistic diversity of the Greek world during the three centuries following the death of Alexander the Great in 323 BC, Hellenistic sculpture is particularly difficult to classify. This article follows a chronological scheme comprising Early, High and Late Hellenistic periods, though these relate far less clearly to corresponding stylistic developments than in the case of Greek sculpture of the Classical period, and apparently contradictory styles sometimes flourished simultaneously.

(a) Introduction. (b) Early (323–*c.* 220 BC). (c) High (*c.* 220–*c.* 150 BC). (d) Late (*c.* 150–27 BC).

(a) Introduction. After Alexander the Great died, his generals soon abandoned any pretence of unity, and the ensuing power struggle took some 40 years to resolve. It left three dominant empires: Ptolemaic Egypt, Seleucid Syria and Antigonid Macedonia. While these contended for hegemony, however, lesser states attempted to assert their independence. The most successful of these were Bactria (now Afghanistan), Pergamon, the Aitolian League and Achaian League in mainland Greece, and later the non-Greek states of Pontus and Hasmonean Israel. In the west, Syracuse and Taras (now Taranto), which had never come under Macedonian control, maintained their power until conquered by Rome in 211 BC and 209 BC respectively.

In a world unprecedented in Greek experience—rich, far-flung, and astonishingly diverse—it is hardly surprising that art, and in particular sculpture, should be characterized by contradiction and confusion. Late Classical Greek sculptors such as Lysippos and Praxiteles had achieved a daunting mastery of styles and techniques, and in the Hellenistic context, where earlier social or stylistic constraints had all but ceased to function, dogged conservatism, unbridled virtuosity, bombastic magniloquence, light-hearted playfulness and sheer bad taste all began to compete. The range of subjects as well as styles expanded. Allegories began to appear on temple pediments and friezes; portraits of the bourgeoisie exceeded those of great men; and contemporary foes took their place alongside, and sometimes replaced, the time-honoured enemies of myth. New subjects were also invented, of which the most radical were the numerous studies of satyrs molesting a variety of erotic partners, and a motley array of low-life characters such as fishermen and peasants. Drawing on pre existing traditions in the minor arts, both genres seem to have begun *c.* 200 BC. This plurality of styles and types was encouraged by the demands of patrons as different as half-Hellenized Levantines, Roman aesthetes, members of the Alexandrian bourgeoisie and Hellenistic monarchs.

Artistic presentation became more a matter of choice than of convention and was determined by a complex interrelationship of genre, patron, school and locale. Styles developed simultaneously, not successively. The task of providing a historical framework is complicated by the loss of all but a few of the thousands of Hellenistic monumental bronzes and an almost complete lack of context for those that survive and is further impeded by the abrupt ending of Pliny's list of famous sculptors. For him 'art' ceased in 292 BC, though he grudgingly recorded half a dozen names under a neo-Classical 'revival' in the year 156 BC. Roman collectors preferred Classical Greek works, and when they did want contemporary sculpture, they usually favoured busts of intellectuals for their libraries and villas and erotic and low-life subjects for their gardens. Original works were seldom copied exactly but were reproduced freehand in an endless series of variations, and novelty was valued more than fidelity to a type or style. This makes it almost impossible to determine what, if anything, is 'original' in much Hellenistic sculpture.

(b) Early (323–c. 220 BC). At Alexander's death, Athens and Sikyon dominated Greek sculpture. The Attic sculptors were the more diverse, cultivating styles that ranged from the somewhat conservative classicism of the carvers of grave monuments (whose staple product was banned by sumptuary legislation in 317 BC) to the extremely delicate manner of the sons of PRAXITELES. The stilted *Themis* from Rhamnous by Chairestratos (*c.* 300–*c.* 250 BC; Athens, N. Archaeol. Mus.) exemplifies the former approach, while the famous *Hermes Carrying the Infant Dionysos* from Olympia (Olympia, Archaeol. Mus.) probably represents the latter, since its technique, drapery and footwear have no 4th-century BC parallels, though they are found in more developed form in 2nd-century BC monuments, such as the 'Great Altar' at Pergamon. Almost all of the most prominent sculptors made portraits, and by 300 BC this had become a leading genre. Surviving copies include representations of *Menander* (?early 3rd century BC; copy, Boston, MA, Mus. F.A.), *Demosthenes* (*c.* 280 BC; copy, Copenhagen, Ny Carlsberg Glyp) and the philosophers *Epicurus* and *Hermarchos* (first half of 3rd century BC; copy, New York, Met.; and early 3rd century BC; copy, Florence, Mus. Archeol. respectively). These testify to the rapid supersession of the Classical 'role portrait' by true character studies. Attic sculptors were in demand throughout the Aegean world and were increasingly encouraged to emigrate by Athens' accelerating economic and political decline. They established workshops in cities as far apart as Syracuse, Rhodes, Pergamon and Alexandria, exercising a profound influence on local tastes.

The Sikyonian school was founded by Alexander's court sculptor, LYSIPPOS. His three sons and numerous followers inherited his Peloponnesian and Macedonian clientele and were frequently commissioned to produce royal portraits and battle and hunt groups (genres pioneered by Lysippos himself) as well as private portraits and statues of athletes, all executed in bronze. The Getty Bronze (?late 4th century BC; Malibu, CA, Getty Mus.), found in the Adriatic Sea, gives a good idea of their approach, which sought to capture the sitter's actual appearance while also subtly idealizing it. With its commanding manner, slim, mobile body, portrait-like features and relatively small head (giving an impression of greater height), the Getty Bronze conforms in every way to Pliny's description of Lysippos' style (*Natural History* XXXIV.xix.65), probably quoted from a handbook by Lysippos' own follower XENOKRATES. The Lysippic school also occasionally made statues of the gods. In antiquity, the most famous of these was the colossal statue of *Helios* (the so-called Colossus of Rhodes; h. 32 m, *c.* 305 BC) by CHARES OF LINDOS. Poised much like the Getty Bronze, this work was a technical feat of the highest order, celebrating the deliverance of Rhodes from the siege of 305 BC. It did not stand astride the harbour, as medieval tradition alleged, but on a hill overlooking the town. It was felled by an earthquake in 224 BC. More innovative in terms of composition was the *Tyche* of Antioch by EUTYCHIDES, made just after the city's foundation in 301 BC (copy in Rome, Vatican, Gal. Candelabri). This representation of Tyche (Fortune), the most characteristic of Hellenistic divinities, was seated in a pose of studied nonchalance on a rock symbolizing the nearby Mt Silpion, with the personified River Orontes swimming below, and it inaugurated a long tradition of similar images produced for eastern cities.

Though literary sources present a vivid picture of the wealth and beauty of ancient Antioch, almost nothing remains of the city. The great statue of *Apollo* made by BRYAXIS for its sanctuary at Daphne is lost, except for a series of miniature reproductions on later Seleucid coins, and the bronze portraits of the Seleucid kings have fared no better. Alexandrian sculpture is only slightly more accessible, chiefly through copies of Bryaxis' *Sarapis* (*c.* 280 BC; copies, Athens, N. Archaeol. Mus.; Rome, Villa Albani) and the numerous portraits of the Ptolemaic kings. The *Sarapis* was enthroned like Zeus and designed to appeal to both Greeks and Egyptians, for it combined the chthonic attributes of Hades with the Egyptian Osiris-Apis cult of death and rebirth. The styles of the portraits range from pure Greek to pure Egyptian, according to their intended context. Indeed, during the 3rd century BC even the Greek-style works began to take on much of the masklike character of Egyptian-style portraits, as the Ptolemaic monarchy sought to create a distinctive court style. Egyptian influence is also recognizable in the growing repertory of miniature grotesque and genre pieces in bronze and terracotta, presumably made for the Alexandrian bourgeoisie (bronzes, e.g. *Dancing Dwarf*, London, BM; *Street Boy*, Paris, Bib. N.; terracottas, e.g. *Hunchback*, New York, Met.). Their mixture of pathos and satire was echoed in contemporary Alexandrian poetry and by *c.* 200 BC also began to appear in monumental sculpture.

Though the Ptolemies and the Seleucids were at war for much of the 3rd century BC, the only evidence for early Hellenistic victory monuments comes from Roman copies of Pergamene dedications commemorating victories over invading Gauls. The most decisive of these occurred around 237 BC and prompted Attalos I (*reg* 241–197 BC) to assume the title of king and declare Pergamon's independence from Syria. Further successes over the Seleucid and Macedonian armies extended Pergamene influence over much of western Asia Minor and the Aegean and occasioned massive construction projects on the acropolis at PERGAMON, as the new monarchy sought to outdo its rivals in grandeur and present itself as the Athens of the East. The sculptural groups of Gauls, made *c.* 230–*c.* 220 BC by the local sculptor Epigonos (*see* ISIGONOS, EPIGONOS, STRATONIKOS AND ANTIGONOS), are extremely problematic, not least because copies of only a few figures survive, and none of these portray the victors. Though represented with an objectivity and sympathy unique in Greek art, the barbarians are nevertheless characterized as mortal threats to civilization. One figure, representing a trumpeter, accepts his fate with dignity (the *Dying Gaul*; copy, Rome, Mus. Capitolino; see fig. 14), while a group of two figures shows a *Gaul Killing Himself and his Wife* (Ludovisi *Gaul* group; copy, Rome, Mus. N. Romano; *see* PERGAMON, fig. 4). The heightened pathos of the latter paralleled contemporary literary developments in 'tragic' history and rhetoric and anticipated the 'baroque' style of the Altar of Zeus at Pergamon. The first sculptor to imbue his works with such intense feeling was apparently the Athenian PHYROMACHOS, whose portrait of the philosopher *Antisthenes* (*c.* 200–*c.* 150 BC) is known from a copy (Rome, Vatican, Mus. Pio-Clementino). The trend may derive from late 4th-century BC paintings, such as the fresco of *Hades and Persephone* (*c.* 340–*c.* 330 BC) from Tomb I at Vergina in Macedonia. At Pergamon, Phyromachos' colossal *Asklepios* (Polybios: *Histories* XXXII.xv.4) may have pioneered the style.

(c) High (c. 220–c. 150 BC). The acknowledged zenith of Hellenistic sculpture coincided with the outbreak of warfare on an unprecedented scale, as Macedonia and Syria each tried one last time for hegemony, and smaller states sought help from Pergamon and from Rome, now the dominant power in the western Mediterranean. Sucked into the conflict, the Romans defeated Macedonia (197 BC) and Syria (189 BC), and many plundered works were taken to Rome. From this point onwards, power and prosperity passed increasingly from the eastern Hellenistic kingdoms westwards to Rome. A final attempt by Macedonia to reassert its authority on a purely local level led to its defeat and dismemberment in 168 BC and its annexation as a Roman province in 146 BC. The immediate beneficiaries of these events, however, were Pergamon, Rhodes and the southern Greek cities that had sided with Rome. To advertise their success, all soon embarked on major sculptural and architectural programmes. The most spectacular of these was the Altar of Zeus at Pergamon (reconstr. in Berlin, Pergamonmus.; *see* PERGAMON, fig. 2), which, as research now suggests, may have been a hero-shrine for the city's legendary founder, Telephos. It dates from *c.* 170 BC, and its extensive podium was embellished with a large-scale frieze (h. 2.3 m) of a *Gigantomachy*, while inside the colonnaded court above ran another, somewhat smaller frieze representing the *Life of Telephos*. Sculptors were hired from throughout the Aegean world, and their signatures advertise the international character of the enterprise. Nevertheless, the style is remarkably uniform, testifying, like the complex iconography, to a meticulously conceived plan. The *Gigantomachy* is generally viewed as the apotheosis of the 'baroque' style in Greek sculpture, and it exploits every device available to drive home its vision of cosmic turmoil and irresistible power, with surfaces ripped open by the drill, muscles that appear to heave and pulsate and drapery that swirls and flares. Classical compositional patterns were rephrased here into a new emotive rhetoric of persuasion, while Stoic notions of a conflict between cosmic order and irrational impulse can be perceived in the carefully designed composition and the contrast between the cool, self-possessed figures of the gods and the wild, often grotesquely deformed giants. In contrast, the frieze

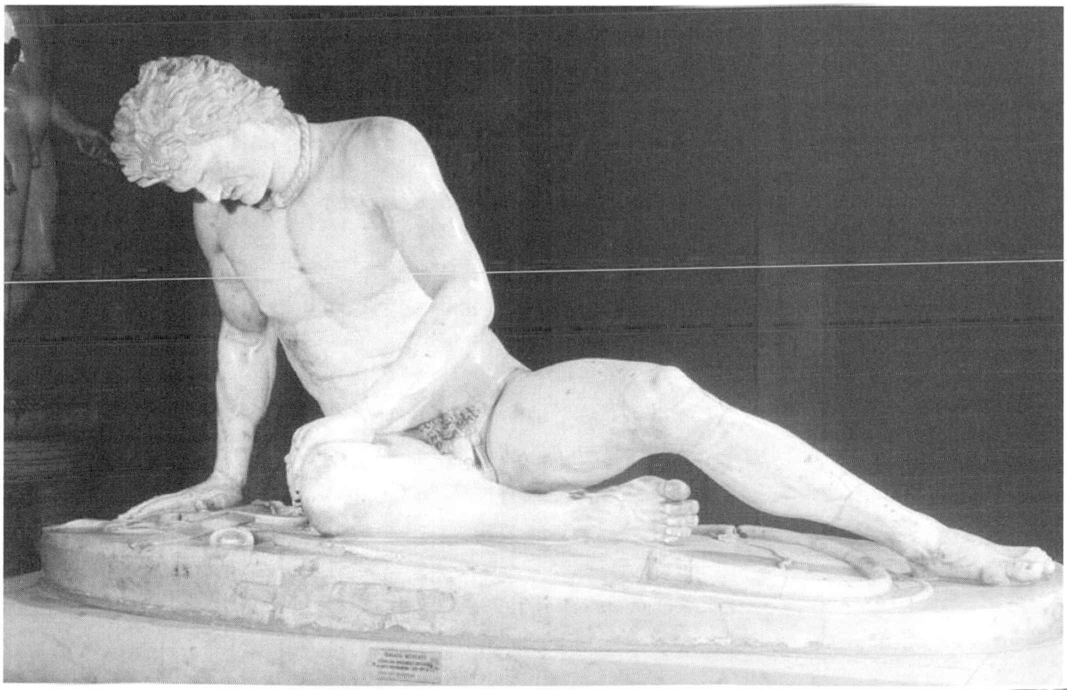

14. Epigonos of Pergamon: *Dying Gaul*, marble copy, h. 930 mm, Hellenistic period, *c.* 230–*c.* 220 BC; (Rome, Museo Capitolino)

depicting the *Life of Telephos* is more subdued and selfconsciously classicizing, though it also shows evidence of experiments with such pictorial devices as perspectival diminution. It charts the hero's life in a series of interconnected episodes that unfold from left to right, making it the earliest monumental example of continuous narration, a method that was to have considerable importance in Roman and medieval art.

From Pergamon, the 'baroque' style spread throughout Asia Minor, overriding both national boundaries and the conventions of genre. The NIKE OF SAMOTHRACE (Paris, Louvre), possibly dedicated by the Rhodians to celebrate their part in the Syrian War of 192–188 BC, is an extraordinary *tour de force* of baroque rhetoric. The figure of the *Nike* stands on the prow of a warship, and her criss-crossing drapery evokes the turmoil of the wind and sea as she guides the victorious vessel safely into port with a hand outstretched in greeting. Other baroque compositions of the period include the originals of the LAOKOON (Rome, Vatican, Mus. Pio-Clementino) by HAGESANDROS, POLYDOROS AND ATHENODOROS of Rhodes, and of their Odysseus groups from SPERLONGA. One of the latter, showing *Odysseus Dragging Achilles' Body out of Battle*, adapts a composition known from numerous other replicas, the Pasquino Group type (2nd century BC; copy, Florence, Loggia Lanzi). The original probably represented the rescue of the corpse of Patroklos by either Menelaos or Ajax. Despite its strongly articulated pathos, the Pasquino Group's pyramidal structure and strict emphasis on the frontal plane betray the growing influence of neo-Classicism.

Neo-Classical touches also appear in several contemporary studies in a lighter vein, showing satyrs grappling with nymphs, hermaphrodites and others, a 'rococo' genre that was evidently popular in Asia. Yet not all such erotica were so violent: one group composition particularly favoured by the Roman copyists featured a young satyr playing castanets and foot-clappers, jauntily inviting a half-naked nymph to dance. The originals apparently stood in Kyzikos (*c.* 200–*c.* 150 BC; copies, Florence, Uffizi). Meanwhile, a replica of Pheidias' *Athena Parthenos* erected in the library at Pergamon *c.* 190 BC inaugurated the neo-Classical movement proper. Soon other centres began to look to Athens' golden age for inspiration and support in the disintegrating Hellenistic world.

The Athenian sculptors themselves, nostalgic for their days of greatness and never particularly comfortable with the 'baroque', responded enthusiastically. Indeed, since the late 3rd century BC, the leading Attic exponents of the neo-Classical style, the POLYKLES family, had produced numerous cult statues for the powerful Aitolian confederacy. One of these, the *Athena* (excavated in the 19th century; untraced) at Elateia, even had a shield bearing a replica of the *Amazonomachy* on the shield of the *Athena Parthenos*, a subject that was later to become a staple product of Athenian neo-Classical decorative sculpture. When the Aitolians were defeated in the Syrian War, Attic sculptors began to work for the victors, the Achaian confederacy and the Romans. In Achaia, however, the leading exponent of the neo-Classical style was the local sculptor DAMOPHON of Messene, best known for his colossal cult group for the Temple of Despoina at Lykosoura in Arcadia (fragments of heads; *c.* 200–*c.* 150 BC, Athens, N. Archaeol. Mus.). At Rome from this period onwards, temples were increasingly embellished with specially commissioned cult statues in the neo-Classical style, designed to stand alongside the artworks looted from defeated Hellenistic kingdoms.

Neo-Classicism also became popular in the eastern Hellenistic world, particularly in Syria under the eccentric Antiochos IV (*reg* 175–164 BC). He sought to revive and unify his battered, truncated realm by adopting a policy of Roman efficiency combined with Attic culture, choosing a replica of Pheidias' *Zeus* at Olympia as his special symbol. Antiochos' attempt to impose the cult on the Jews led, however, to the Maccabean revolt, and his intended invasion of Egypt was repulsed by the threats of a single Roman envoy. Soon after his death, Babylonia fell to the Parthians, cutting off the Greek colonists in Bactria and India entirely. Such sculpture as survives from these areas is decidedly provincial, though a few pieces exhibit a novel blend of surface calligraphy and sensitivity to volume, anticipating the Gandhara style that is usually considered Greek art's greatest legacy to the East.

In Egypt, though High Hellenistic royal portraits were often rather more dramatic than before, it was on genre sculpture that the 'baroque' style made the greatest impact. The rhetoric of the low-life studies in bronze and terracotta intensified, perhaps as a response to increased racial tension as the kingdom declined further and the native population reasserted itself. Numerous marble replicas in the same vein show that by the early 2nd century BC monumental sculpture had responded to the challenge—though no single type can be confidently traced to Egypt. This unlovely array of characters includes virtuoso studies, such as the so-called *Seneca*, actually representing a rheumatic old man (black marble copy, Paris, Louvre), a *Drunken Old Woman* nursing her wine bottle (copy, Munich, Glyp.); and the *Old Market Woman* (New York, Met.), whose ivy-leaf crown indicates that she is a participant in a rustic festival of Dionysos. All three may date to the 2nd century BC, though the *Old Market Woman* betrays a hint of neo-Classicism that suggests a slightly later date. These genre pieces may have embellished the gardens of the Alexandrian élite, even the royal parks of the Ptolemies, but the archaeological record is blank.

Ptolemaic court art proper is best exemplified by the *Apotheosis of Homer* relief by Archelaos of Priene, found in Italy but probably taken there from Alexandria as loot (London, BM). It celebrates the establishment of the cult of Homer by Ptolemy IV (*reg* 221–205 BC), and its inscribed lowest register shows Ptolemy and his wife crowning Homer while an array of figures representing the literary genres inspired by him perform sacrifices. Its three upper registers depict the Muses, Apollo and Zeus gathered on Mt

Parnassos, accompanied by an unidentified poet. The composition emphasizes Homer's status as the central figure in Greek literature and thus, by association, Alexandria's status as the main Hellenistic literary centre. It also symbolically replicates the relationship between the institutions at the heart of Alexandrian intellectual life, with the upper levels representing the Mouseion (the world's first university) and the lowest one its incomparable resource, the great Library. A greater contrast to the thematic and stylistic concerns of Pergamene sculpture, exemplified by the huge *Gigantomachy*, could hardly be imagined.

(d) Late (c. 150–27 BC). Rome's victories over Carthage, Macedonia and Achaia in the mid-2nd century BC greatly accelerated the decline of the Hellenistic world, while Egypt and Syria increasingly succumbed to civil war and the petty kingdoms of Asia Minor remained locked in local conflicts. Pergamon was bequeathed to Rome by its last king, Attalos III, in 133 BC, thus losing its role both as a stabilizing force in the region and as a flourishing sculptural centre. Thereafter the disintegration of the Hellenistic sculptural tradition was inevitable. Neo-Classicism could not substitute for the Hellenistic 'baroque' in every context, and the requirements of an increasingly splintered clientele led to a rapid proliferation of sculptural styles (see fig. 15).

These developments are best illustrated by portraiture, always a barometer of political reality. The characteristics of individual works range from pseudo-Classical repose to 'baroque'-style histrionics and even hard-boiled realism, according to the image that each individual wished to project, see fig. 15. On Delos, members of a colony of Italian slave-traders hired sculptors from Asia Minor and Athens to render their features in the grimly realistic 'verist' manner then in favour at Rome, where it suggested the traditional Roman virtues of self-discipline (*gravitas*) and resolution (*constantia*). These portraits were given idealized heroic bodies, and the combination must have looked almost as offensive to traditionally minded Greeks as the 'Slipper-slapper' group of *Aphrodite Defending Herself with her Sandal against the Amorous Advances of Pan* (Athens, N. Archaeol. Mus., 3335; see fig. 16), dedicated by another foreign trader on Delos, Dionysios of Berytos (Beirut). The Delian workshops also met the needs of this heterogeneous,

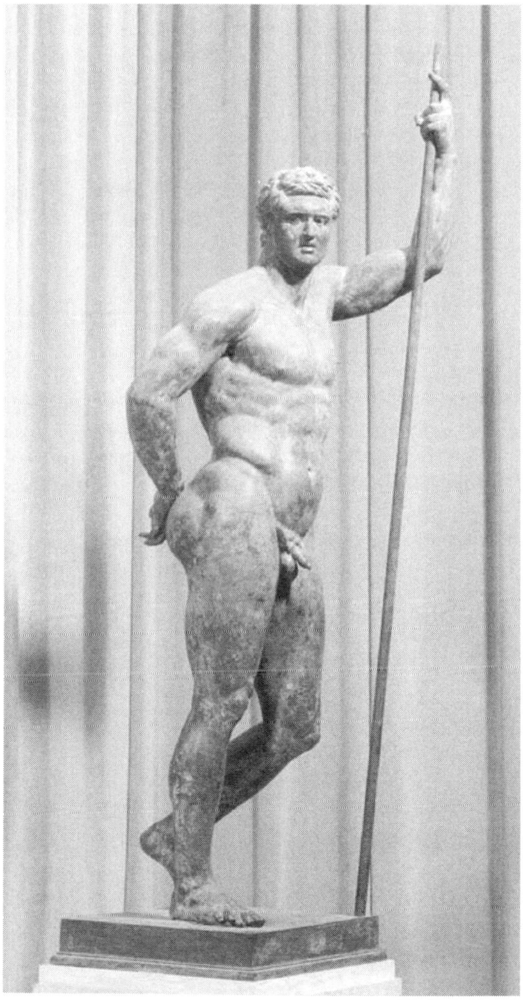

15. Hellenistic ruler, bronze, h. 2.37 m, *c.* 150–140 BC (Rome, Museo Nazionale Romano)

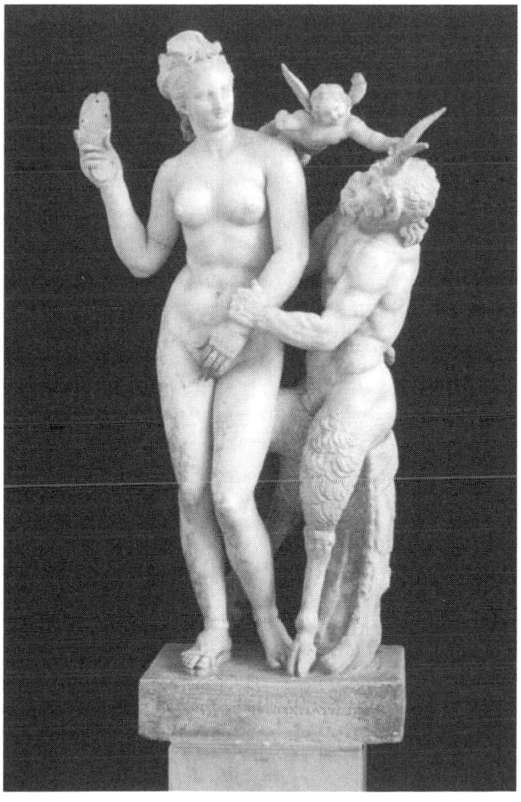

16. *Aphrodite Defending Herself with her Sandal against the Amorous Advances of Pan*, marble, h. 1.32 m, *c.* 100 BC (Athens, National Archaeological Museum)

nouveau-riche clientele by producing vast quantities of decorative sculpture for houses and gardens. At Athens, too, this type of sculpture was turning into a major industry, chiefly devoted to copies of Classical masterpieces, either free-standing or in relief, which were shipped west to embellish Roman temples, public squares and buildings and private villas.

Neo-Classicism also significantly affected other sculptural genres. Thus two of the most famous masterpieces of Greek sculpture of any period, the VENUS DE MILO and the BORGHESE GLADIATOR (both Paris, Louvre), signed by sculptors from Asia Minor (Alexandros of Antioch on the Maeander and Agasias of Ephesos respectively), are strongly classicizing. The *Venus* (or *Aphrodite of Melos*) combines a Pheidian-style head with a Praxitelean body, Pergamene drapery and a highly contemporary Hellenistic 'sprung' rhythm (cf. the *Nike of Samothrace*). The *Borghese Gladiator* blends exaggerated Lysippic proportions and musculature with a dramatic 4th-century BC lunging pose. Other works in a similar vein include a *Sleeping Hermaphrodite* (2nd century BC; copy, Rome, Mus. N. Romano), often attributed to Polykles, and a bronze *Boxer* from Rome (2nd or early 1st century BC; copy, Rome, Mus. N. Romano). Numerous Greek sculptors had by now settled permanently in Rome, though few were as successful as the versatile PASITELES, whose works captivated the Roman upper classes and who wrote an influential five-volume guide to the 'classics' of Greek sculpture. Yet while sculpture at Rome flourished, its decline in the eastern Hellenistic world was hastened by the increasing impoverishment both of cities and of their ruling élites, as well as by the progressive annexation by Rome of almost all the surviving kingdoms, including Syria (64 BC). After the devastation of the Mithridatic Wars (88–66 BC), the Roman civil wars (49–30 BC) and a Parthian invasion of much of Asia Minor (41–39 BC), the combination of huge indemnities levied by the Romans on rebel states, pirate raids and the rapacity of tax-collectors reduced many cities to the last extremity. In portraiture, the prevailing manner became more introverted and morose. Against the assertive individuality of Roman taste, the portraits from Greek Asia Minor oppose a quasi-philosophical sense of introverted reflection, an awareness of the instability and illusoriness of human existence.

In the three main surviving kingdoms, however, conditions were somewhat different. Herodian Israel has yielded no sculpture, but both Commagene (now part of eastern Turkey) and Egypt experienced something of a revival in the mid-1st century BC. In Commagene, the eccentric Greco-Iranian monarch Antiochus I was obsessed with ideas of religious and racial unity between East and West, and his vast tomb on the summit of Nemrut Dağ was approached via terraces with massive reliefs of his ancestors and colossal statues of Antiochos and his gods, constructed in coursed masonry in a dignified, highly formalized Greco-Iranian style (*in situ*). In Egypt, Cleopatra (*reg* 51–30 BC) had taken advantage of the chaos of the Roman civil wars to secure the throne and used first Julius Caesar then Mark Antony to realize her dream of reviving the Ptolemaic empire. A superb portrait (*c.* 50–*c.* 30 BC; Berlin, Antikensamml.) gives expression to these ambitions; it shows her with a fresh, delicate complexion and a look of regal determination: a rival to the great Ptolemaic queens of the 3rd century BC and a virtual double of their common alter ego, Aphrodite. In 31 BC, however, the combined forces of Cleopatra and Mark Antony were defeated by Octavian at Actium. By 27 BC, when Octavian assumed the title Augustus, the power of Rome was supreme and the Hellenistic world effectively at an end. Yet in sculpture, the Hellenistic legacy was tenacious, informing almost every Roman Imperial style from the neo-Classicism of the Augustan 'Golden Age' to the 'baroque' revival exemplified by the *Laokoon* and the works produced by the school of Aphrodisias. It was in these forms that it was later rediscovered by the sculptors of the Renaissance, when Hellenistic art again influenced the mainstream Western sculptural tradition.

W. Klein: *Vom antiken Rokoko* (Vienna, 1921)
E. Buschor: *Das hellenistische Bildnis* (Munich, 1949, 2/1971)
G. Lippold: *Die griechische Plastik* (1950), III/i of *Handbuch der Archäologie* (Munich, 1939-), pp. 293–387
A. Schober: *Die Kunst von Pergamon* (Vienna, 1951)
M. Bieber: *The Sculpture of the Hellenistic Age* (New York, 1955, rev. 1961)
P. H. von Blanckenhagen: 'Narration in Hellenistic and Roman Art', *Amer. J. Archaeol.*, lxi (1957), pp. 78–83
R. Carpenter: *Greek Sculpture: A Critical Review* (Chicago, 1960), pp. 180–254
T. Dohrn: *Die Tyche von Antiocheia* (Berlin, 1960)
A. Adriani: *Repertorio d'arte dell'Egitto greco-romano*, ser. a, i–ii (Palermo, 1961)
J. J. Pollitt: *The Art of Greece, 1400–31 BC: Sources and Documents* (Englewood Cliffs, 1965)
G. M. A. Richter: *The Portraits of the Greeks*, 3 vols (London, 1965); abridged and rev. by R. R. R. Smith (Oxford, 1984)
T. B. L. Webster: *The Art of Greece: The Hellenistic World* (New York, 1966)
E. Buschor: *Das hellenistische Bildnis* (Munich, 1971)
E. Künzl: *Die Kelten des Epigonos von Pergamon* (Würzburg, 1971)
C. M. Havelock: *Hellenistic Art* (London, 1972, rev. New York, 2/1981)
J. Charbonneaux, R. Martin and F. Villard: *Hellenistic Art* (New York, 1973)
G. S. Merker: *The Hellenistic Sculpture of Rhodes*, Stud. Medit. Archaeol., xl (Göteborg, 1973)
B. Andreae: 'Die römischen Repliken der Skulpturengruppen von Sperlonga', *Ant. Plast.*, xiv (1974), pp. 61–108
B. Conticello: 'I gruppi scultorei di soggetto mitologico a Sperlonga', *Ant. Plast.*, xiv (1974), pp. 7–58
H. Kyrieleis: *Die Bildnisse der Ptolemäer* (Berlin, 1975)
E. Simon: *Pergamon und Hesiod* (Mainz, 1975)
A. M. U. Linfert: *Kunstzentren hellenistischer Zeit: Studien an weiblichen Gewandfiguren* (Wiesbaden, 1976)
A. F. Stewart: 'To Entertain an Emperor: Laokoon, Sperlonga, and Tiberius at the Dinner Table', *J. Roman Stud.*, lxvii (1977), pp. 76–90

J. Frel: *The Getty Bronze* (Malibu, 1978)
J. Onians: *Art and Thought in the Hellenistic Age* (London, 1978)
R. Wenning: *Die Galateranatheme Attalos I* (Berlin, 1978)
A. F. Stewart: *Attika: Studies in Athenian Sculpture of the Hellenistic Age* (London, 1979)
B. Frischer: *The Sculpted Word* (Berkeley, 1982)
H. P. Laubscher: *Fischer und Landleute* (Mainz, 1982)
K. D. Morrow: *Greek Footwear and the Dating of Sculpture* (Madison, 1985)
A. Pasquier: *La Vénus de Milo et les Aphrodites du Louvre* (Paris, 1985)
J. J. Pollitt: *Art in the Hellenistic Age* (Cambridge, 1986)
M. Mattei: *Il Galata Capitolino* (Rome, 1987)
E. D. Reeder: *Hellenistic Art in the Walters Art Gallery* (Baltimore, 1988)
R. R. R. Smith: *Hellenistic Royal Portraits* (Oxford, 1988)
B. S. Ridgway: *The Styles of 331–200 BC* (1990), i of *Hellenistic Sculpture* (Madison, 1990-)
A. F. Stewart: *Greek Sculpture: An Exploration*, 2 vols (New Haven and London, 1990)
R. R. R. Smith: *Hellenistic Sculpture* (London, 1991)
A. F. Stewart: *Faces of Power: Alexander's Image and Hellenistic Politics*, ii of *Hellenistic Culture and Society* (Berkeley, CA and Oxford, 1993)
B. R. Brown: *Royal Portraits in Sculpture and Coins: Pyrrhos and the Successors of Alexander the Great* (New York, 1995)
D. Castriota. *The Ara Pacis Augustae and the Imagery of Abundance in Later Greek and Early Roman Imperial Art* (Princeton, 1995)
K. E. Evans: *The Daochos Monument* (diss., Princeton U., 1996)
Regional Schools in Hellenistic Sculpture: Proceedings of an International Conference Held at the American School of Classical Studies: Athens, 1996
B. S. Ridgway: *Fourth-century Styles in Greek Sculpture* (Madison, WI, 1997)
T. M. Brogan: *Hellenistic Nike: Monuments Commemorating Military Victories of the Attalid and Antigonid Kingdoms, the Aitolian League and the Rhodian Polis ca. 307 to 133 BC* (diss., Bryn Mawr Coll., 1999)
B. S. Ridgway: *Prayers in Stone: Greek Architectural Sculpture ca. 600–100 BCE* (Berkeley, 1999)
A. C. Cooper: *Hellenistic Bronze Poseidon* (London, 2000–04)
S.-A. Ashton: *Ptolemaic Royal Sculpture from Egypt: The Interaction between Greek and Egyptian Traditions* (Oxford, 2001)
S. L. Karakas: *Subject and Symbolism in Historical Battle Reliefs of the Late Classical and Hellenistic Periods* (diss., Chapel Hill, U. NC, 2002)
P. E. Stanwick: *Portraits of the Ptolemies: Greek Kings as Egyptian Pharaohs* (Austin, TX, 2002)
B. S. Ridgway: *Second Chance: Greek Sculptural Studies Revisited* (London, 2004)

3. Theory and criticism.

(i) Ancient. The ancient Greeks did not distinguish between fine art and craftsmanship. Both were designated by the word *techne*. By the mid-5th century BC this had come to mean the rational and technical procedure for realizing a desired end result. Thus it could apply equally to carpentry or sculpture. During the 5th and 4th centuries BC, however, the term *sophia* (the 'skill' of the craftsman or artist) gradually acquired connotations of theoretical knowledge (Aristotle: *Metaphysics* 981a.24–982a.2). This distinction was retained by Roman writers on art, who translated *techne* with the Latin word *ars* ('art') but distinguished between *ratiocinatio* (the intellectual and theoretical foundation for art) and *opus* (the practical and technical side of production; see Vitruvius: *On Architecture* I.i.15). Treatises on ancient Greek sculptural theory were produced by several different categories of writers. Particularly during the Classical and Early Hellenistic periods (*c.* 450–*c.* 300 BC) artists themselves wrote books addressing the formal problems of their craft, such as proportion. No ancient sculptural treatises survive, though Pliny apparently summarized portions of a lost critical work by the Hellenistic sculptor Xenokrates, while fragments and paraphrases of a treatise by Polykleitos also survive in ancient authors.

The two crucial artistic concepts, *rhythmos* and *symmetria*, were first formulated in the Early Classical period by Pythagoras of Rhegion (see Diogenes Laertius: VII.x/vii). *Rhythmos* (Lat. *numerus*), or 'form', referred to the way a statue's 'frozen' pose could convey a specific impression of action. Thus the *rhythmos* of Myron's *Diskobolos* captures the poised instant between the discus thrower's backswing and the forward-swinging release of the discus. *Eurhythmia* meant the successful achievement of *rhythmos*, while *symmetria* indicated the 'commensurability of parts' in a work of art, or proportion. Polykleitos wrote a sculptural treatise, the *Canon*, which he probably illustrated with his statue the *Doryphoros*. He apparently described the theoretical ideal of 'the good' (*to eu*) or 'the beautiful' (*to kalon*). This was based on a carefully conceived system of *symmetria*, while the works themselves had to be executed with 'precision' (*akribeia*; Lat. *diligentia*). The sculptor aimed at 'the mean' (*to meson*) between excess and deficiency and thus came to a theoretical understanding of the true nature of his subject (*aletheia*; Lat. *veritas*), and his statues revealed the workings of nature to others. Varro called the works of Polykleitos *quadrata* (Gr. *tetragona*), referring either to their four-square composition or to the chiastic arrangement of their limbs (Pliny: *Natural History* XXXIV.xix.56).

In the Late Classical and Early Hellenistic periods (*c.* 375–*c.* 323 BC), such sculptors as Lysippos are said to have retained an interest in *symmetria* while experimenting with new systems of proportion and torsional compositions. Indeed, Lysippos appears to have addressed the optical problems that derive from the subjective way in which works of art are perceived. Pliny described his works as more 'slender' (*gracilis*) and 'drier' (*siccus*)—that is, leaner—than those of his predecessors (*Natural History* XXXIV.xix.65).

From the mid-5th century BC onwards Greek philosophers such as Plato and Aristotle wrote on artistic issues, though they were primarily concerned with art's moral, political and epistemological value. Art was an 'imitation' (*mimesis*) of the perceived world and had the power to affect man's 'character' (*ethos*). *Mimesis* involved not only the imitation of physical objects but also 'imitation by psychological association' (Pollitt). The latter was the way in which artists could evoke states of mind. Artists could thus communicate both good and bad character, as well as 'suffering' (*pathos*), through the features, poses and forms of their figures (Xenophon: *Memorabilia* III. x.1–8; Aristotle: *Politics* 1340a.30–38). Plato believed in a realm of immutable 'forms' (*eidos*; pl. *eide*) that underlay everything in the visible world and could be comprehended by the mind alone. These *eide* constituted the only 'true reality', and nature merely imitated them. Since art imitated nature, Plato regarded it as 'an imitation of an imitation' and condemned artists for being concerned with the merely illusory 'appearance' of objects, rather than their true essence (*Sophist* 235d-236c; *Republic* X.597a-e).

In the 2nd century BC Greek rhetoricians began to formulate analogies between rhetoric and art on the basis of style. Their works do not survive, but they are reproduced in passages by such Roman authors as Cicero and Quintilian that suggest a view of the history of Greek sculpture as an evolution from a 'stiff and undeveloped' (*durus* or *rigidus*) kind of work to that which was 'supple' (*mollis*). Excellence in sculpture involved 'fidelity to nature' (Gr. *aletheia*; Lat. *veritas*), 'beauty' (Gr. *to kallos*; Lat. *pulchritudo*), 'precision' (Gr. *akribeia*; Lat. *diligentia*) and 'appropriateness' (Gr. *to prepon*; Lat. *decor*). The culmination of this evolutionary scheme was seen in the works of Pheidias, who had suffused his creations with spiritual insight. For the Latin writers, the greatest works of Greek sculpture were characterized by their 'majesty' (*maiestas*), 'presence' (*auctoritas*) and 'grandeur' (*pondus*). The concept of 'intuitive insight' (*phantasia*) replaced the Classical idea of mere *mimesis* as a criterion for excellence, and with the advent of this theory, artists were no longer regarded as mere craftsmen but were thought to possess an inspired, spiritual awareness.

For a discussion of Roman copies of Greek sculpture *see* §VI, 1(ii)(d) below.

J. A. Overbeck: *Die antiken Schriftquellen zur Geschichte der bildenden Künste bei den Griechen* (Leipzig, 1868)

E. Sellers and K. Jex-Blake: *The Elder Pliny's Chapters on the History of Art* (London, 1896/*R* Chicago, 1966)

B. Schweitzer: 'Xenokrates von Athen', *Schr. Königsberg. Gelehrten Ges.: Geistwiss. Klasse*, ix (1932), pp. 1–15

S. Ferri: 'Nuovi contributi esegetici al "canone" della scultura greca', *Riv. Reale Ist. Archeol. & Stor. A.*, vii (1940), pp. 117–52

J. J. Pollitt: *The Ancient View of Greek Art* (New Haven and London, 1974)

C. Cavarnos: *Plato's Theory of Fine Art* (Belmont, MA, 1998)

(ii) Modern. It was between the late 17th century and the mid-18th that ancient Greek sculpture was first recognized as a discrete category of antique statuary, in the writings of André Félibien, (1619–95), the Comte de Caylus (1692–1765) and JOHANN JOACHIM WINCKELMANN. Although all of these authors characterized Greek sculpture as superior to Roman, Winckelmann went beyond his predecessors in offering aesthetic and historical grounds for distinguishing Greek from Roman in his monumental *Geschichte der Kunst des Alterthums* (1764), a chronological survey of ancient sculpture. Invoking the analogy of biological growth, Winckelmann charted the stylistic development of Greek art from its birth in the Archaic period to maturity in the High Classical period and subsequent decline in the Hellenistic and Roman periods, and his essential stylistic and chronological divisions are still accepted. Whereas his predecessors had championed ancient Greek sculpture as a whole, Winckelmann singled out works of the Classical period, especially idealized male nudes, for his highest praise. His theories were widely admired, by Goethe and Hegel among others, and the statues that he extolled became renowned works of art.

Winckelmann had never visited Greece, and he unwittingly based his history not on original statues by Classical Greek masters but on Roman copies that he saw in Italy. His friend Anton Raphael Mengs (1728–79) was among the first critics to recognize that many of the works celebrated by Winckelmann were not in fact Greek. Mengs initiated a critical evaluation that was ultimately to remove such sculptures as the APOLLO BELVEDERE from their exalted position as paradigms of Greek aesthetics. The arrival in England of the architectural sculptures from the Parthenon, brought to London by the 7th Earl of Elgin in the early 19th century, further eroded the reputation of the statues most admired by Winckelmann. Purchased by the British Museum in 1816, the Elgin Marbles (*c.* 442–*c.* 438 BC) set new standards for the evaluation of Greek art. Their weathered, ruined condition helped bring about a shift in popular taste away from the highly polished and restored statues of Winckelmann's day. At the same time, the Elgin Marbles confirmed Winckelmann's judgement that the second half of the 5th century BC was the high point of the Greek achievement in sculpture. Finds from excavations at other ancient Greek sites, however, soon caused that long-standing opinion to be challenged. The discovery of Severe style pedimental figures at AIGINA (Munich, Staatl. Antikensamml.) in 1811, of Archaic statuary on the Athenian Acropolis in the 1860s and 1870s and of the Hellenistic reliefs that once decorated the Altar of Zeus at PERGAMON (Berlin, Antikensamml.) in the 1870s combined to alert the European public to the range and quality of ancient Greek sculpture from outside the High Classical period.

The survival of many ancient literary references to Greek sculptors and their works has inspired scholars and antiquaries since the Renaissance to attempt to link extant statues with the names of artists known from texts and inscriptions. An early example is the 16th-century attribution of the LAOKOON to the Rhodian sculptors HAGESANDROS, POLYDOROS AND ATHENODOROS on the basis of Pliny's account (*Natural History* XXXVI.iv.37). This approach formed the basis of a highly influential work by ADOLF FURTWÄNGLER, *Meisterwerke der griechischen Plastik* (1893). Taking Roman copies to be accurate reflections of lost Greek masterpieces, Furtwängler attempted to reconstruct statues mentioned by the sources as works of the 5th or 4th century BC. On the basis of his reconstructions, he outlined the careers of individual sculptors as well as constructing a detailed stylistic history of Classical sculpture. His methodology has, however, been much criticized for its assumptions both of the stylistic closeness of the copies to lost originals and of the correlation between extant works and ancient descriptions.

No single critic or methodology dominated 20th-century investigations of Greek sculpture. In recent decades scholars have pursued two approaches initially suggested by Winckelmann: the formalist and the contextual. The formalist approach emphasizes style as the primary means for dating and interpreting a statue. Examining such details as drapery, musculature and pose, formalist scholars have devised developmental schemes that assume the ever-increasing attainment of naturalism. Their analyses often ignore the roles both of individual artists and of historical factors. The contextual approach was intended to remedy this deficiency by considering sculpture in a wider context embracing cultural history, the conditions of production or social function. In particular, articles in the German periodical *Hephaistos* (1979) exemplify the more theoretical dimension of this approach.

A. Félibien: *Des Principes de l'architecture, de la sculpture, de la peinture* (Paris, 1697)

Comte de Caylus: *Recueil d'antiquités égyptiennes, étrusques, grecques et romaines*, 7 vols (Paris, 1752–67)

J. J. Winckelmann: *Geschichte der Kunst des Alterthums* (Dresden, 1764); Eng. trans. by G. H. Lodge as *The History of Ancient Art* (Boston, 1856)

A. Furtwängler: *Meisterwerke der griechischen Plastik* (Leipzig, 1893; Eng. trans. and rev., London, 1895)

G. M. A. Richter: *Kouroi: Archaic Greek Youths* (New York, 1942, rev. London, 3/1970)

R. Carpenter: *Greek Sculpture: A Critical Review* (Chicago, 1960)

G. M. A. Richter: *Korai: Archaic Greek Maidens* (London, 1968)

J. J. Pollitt: *Art and Experience in Classical Greece* (Cambridge, 1972)

P. Zanker: *Klassizistische Statuen* (Mainz, 1974)

L. A. Schneider: *Zur sozialen Bedeutung der archaischen Korenstatuen* (Hamburg, 1975)

J. Rothenberg: *'Descensus ad terram': The Acquisition and Reception of the Elgin Marbles* (New York, 1977)

A. D. Potts: 'Greek Sculpture and Roman Copies, I: Anton Raphael Mengs and the Eighteenth Century', *J. Warb. & Court. Inst.*, xliii (1980), pp. 150–73

F. Haskell and N. Penny: *Taste and the Antique* (New Haven and London, 1981)

A. D. Potts: 'Winckelmann's Construction of History', *A. Hist.*, v (1982), pp. 377–407

B. S. Ridgway: *Roman Copies of Greek Sculpture: The Problem of Originals* (Ann Arbor, 1984)

A. F. Stewart: *Greek Sculpture: An Exploration*, 2 vols (New Haven and London, 1990)

E. Perry: *The Aesthetics of Emulation in the Visual Arts of Ancient Rome* (Cambridge 2005)

4. Collections, museums and exhibitions. Ancient Greek architectural and funerary reliefs and free-standing sculptures can be seen in many museums and collections. Many of the extant sculptures are in a badly damaged or fragmentary state, and few are visible *in situ*. Though a high proportion of Greek sculpture has been destroyed, some of the sculptures most famous in antiquity are known today through Roman copies. Examples of Greek sculpture are held in major museums throughout the world, but the greatest concentration is in Greece itself. There are few important private collections of Greek sculpture, and temporary or travelling exhibitions are rare. This article necessarily covers only the most important works; fuller information can be obtained from the selection of museum catalogues listed in the bibliography below.

(i) History of collecting. The ancient Greeks themselves collected sculpture, but interest in the collecting of art did not really flourish until the Hellenistic period. The ruler of Pergamon, Attalos I (*reg* 241–197 BC), for instance, collected sculpture to adorn the city's acropolis, and his successor, Eumenes II (*reg* 197–160 BC), commissioned copies of works when he could not acquire originals. Roman interest in collecting developed following the importation of works of art as war trophies; Sulla, Lucullus and others displayed looted Greek antiquities both publicly and privately. When the desired Greek originals were unobtainable, Roman copies were made. In the late Roman Republic, the concept of the art collection as an investment gained popularity; thus Marcus Agrippa urged that works should be kept in the city and available for the public, instead of being removed to their owners' country villas. Christianity in the West later became a deterrent to the collection and preservation of 'pagan' Greek sculpture, but the humanism of the Renaissance brought about renewed interest in Greek antiquities. Before the 18th century, most collections were private and inaccessible to the public, though the Musei Capitolini, presented to the people of Rome in 1471, were a notable exception.

During the 18th century, popular interest in art became more widespread, and public museums were developed and expanded. The influence of Neo-classicism and the rediscovery of Pompeii and Herculaneum led to a renewed interest in Greek and Roman antiquity generally, and new discoveries and collecting both increased. Archaeology became fashionable, and wealthy Europeans excavated Greek and Roman sites, placing their finds in personal or public collections. Increasingly often, private collections were consolidated and opened to the public. American collectors began to be active in the 19th century, and after 1900 collection was increasingly dominated worldwide by the magnates of American industry. The public display of works of art was disrupted in Europe by World War II, with museums closed and sculptures placed in storage. The Glyptothek in Munich, for example, closed in 1939 and did not reopen until 1972 after its restoration. New directions in research and in the restoration and display of ancient Greek sculpture were stimulated by the discovery off the Italian coast of the Riace bronzes, first exhibited in Florence in 1981.

(ii) Major collections and exhibitions. Unfortunately, no Greek temple complex survives with its architectural sculpture intact. The pediments, friezes and metopes of the Athenian Parthenon, the most extensive programme in all Greek architectural sculpture, survive in a fragmentary state, mostly in the British Museum in London, where they were placed after their removal from Athens by the 7th Earl of Elgin in the early 19th century. Other fragments are in the Acropolis Museum in Athens, the Louvre in Paris and the Kunsthistorisches Museum in Vienna. Fragments of pediments from other buildings on the Acropolis are also displayed in the Acropolis Museum. The magnificent pedimental figures and metopes from the Temple of Zeus at Olympia are in the museum on the site, and the pedimental figures from Aigina, which were severely damaged during restoration, are now in the Glyptothek in Munich. Other important architectural remains include the pediment of the earlier Temple of Athena on the Acropolis (Athens, Acropolis Mus.); figures and friezes from the temple at Bassai (London, BM); the pediment from the Temple of Artemis on Corfu (Corfu, Archaeol. Mus.); the pediment, caryatids and frieze of the Siphnian Treasury at Delphi (Delphi, Archaeol. Mus.); a column base from the Temple of Artemis at Ephesos (London, BM); figures and frieze fragments from the Mausoleum of Halikarnassos (London, BM); the metopes from the Temple of Hera at the mouth of the River Sele (Paestum, Mus. Archeol. N.); and the metopes from the Temple of Hera at Selinus (Palermo, Mus. Reg.). More sculptures were once visible *in situ*, but many architectural or dedicatory sculptures, such as the caryatids of the Erechtheion in Athens and some grave stele in the Kerameikos Cemetery there, are gradually being removed to protect them from the effects of modern pollution.

Many of the most important examples of Greek sculpture of all types are in Athenian museums. The collections of the Acropolis Museum were begun during the cleaning of debris from the Turkish settlement on the Acropolis in 1834, when antique finds were amassed. The Acropolis Museum contains kouros and kore figures from the Acropolis, including the *Kritios Boy*, the Nike Balustrade reliefs from the Temple of Athena Nike and caryatids from the Erechtheion. The National Archaeological Museum in Athens, established in Aigina in 1829 and moved to Athens in 1834, contains the colossal kouros from the Temple of Poseidon at Sounion, several later kouroi, the bronze *Boy* from Marathon, grave reliefs from the Kerameikos Cemetery, the *Dipylon Head* and the bronze *Zeus* (?or *Poseidon*), the most famous of the ARTEMISION BRONZES. Museums at other ancient Greek sites also contain important finds. The Archaeological Museum at Olympia houses a colossal Archaic *Head of Hera*, the terracotta *Zeus Abducting Ganymede*, the *Nike of Paionios* and *Hermes Holding the Infant Dionysos*, perhaps by Praxiteles. The Archaeological Museum at Delphi has the bronze *Charioteer*, fragments of his quadriga and architectural sculpture from the treasuries of the Athenians and Siphnians. Other important site museums include those at Alexandria, Corfu, Corinth, Cyrene, Delos, Eleusis, Ephesos, Epidauros, Paestum, Pergamon, Priene, Rhodes and Thessaloniki.

In Italy, Rome and Naples contain major collections of Greek sculpture and Roman copies of Greek sculpture: the first because of ancient Roman interest in and copying of Greek antiquities, the second because of the discoveries nearby at Pompeii and Herculaneum. These collections include many Hellenistic works and some of the finest Roman copies. Among the works in the Musei Vaticani are the APOLLO BELVEDERE, the LAOKOON and the BELVEDERE TORSO. The Museo Nazionale Romano includes the Ludovisi Throne (from the Ludovisi Collection), the *Venus of Cyrene*, the bronze *Boxer* by Apollonios, the best-preserved copy of Myron of Eleutherai's *Diskobolos* and the bronze *Hellenistic Prince*. The collections of the Musei Capitolini include Roman copies of figures of Gauls from Pergamon (the *Dying Gaul* and the Ludovisi *Gaul* group). The Museo Archeologico Nazionale in Naples houses the impressive ancient works from the Farnese collection. The Museo Civico Archeologico in Bologna has a copy of the head of Pheidias' *Athena Lemnia*, and the Museo Regionale di Palermo, established in 1866, when several local collections were consolidated, also houses important Greek sculptures.

Elsewhere in Europe, other museums with important collections include the Pergamonmuseum in Berlin, which contains the reconstructed frieze from the Altar of Zeus at Pergamon. Acquisitions for the ancient collection at the Glyptothek in Munich, founded by Ludwig I of Bavaria (*reg* 1825–48) from his private collection, began as early as 1804. In addition to the sculptures from Aigina, which Ludwig purchased soon after they were excavated in 1812, the Greek collections include the Tenea Kouros, the Hellenistic *Drunken Old Woman* and the *Sleeping Satyr* (also called the Barberini *Faun*). The Department of Greek and Roman Antiquities at the Louvre in Paris was established in 1800, and its collection includes the *Auxerre Goddess*, the Cheramyes Kore, the Rampin Head, the *Apollo of Piombino*, a bronze head from Benevento, the VENUS DE MILO and the NIKE OF SAMOTHRACE. The Archaeological Museum at Istanbul has a group of sarcophagi found at Sidon in 1887. Other European collections include those of the National Museum in Belgrade, the Museum of Greek and Roman Antiquities in Berlin (Staatl. Museen), the Museum of Fine Arts in Budapest, the Prado in Madrid, the Ny Carlsberg Glyptotek in Copenhagen, the Staatliche Kunstsammlungen in Dresden (Albertinum), the Hermitage in St Petersburg, the British Museum in London and the Kunsthistorisches Museum in Vienna.

In the USA there are important collections at the Metropolitan Museum of Art in New York, the Museum of Fine Arts in Boston and the J. Paul Getty Museum in Malibu, CA. The Metropolitan Museum contains a 7th-century BC kouros, Classical grave stelai and the Hellenistic *Old Market Woman*. The Museum of Fine Arts collection began with the purchase of part of the collection of the excavator

Luigi Palma di Cesnola (1832–1904) in 1872 and was increased from 1895 to 1905, primarily through the work of Edward Warren (1860–1928) and Samuel Warren (1851–1910). It includes the Boston Throne, a counterpart to the Ludovisi Throne, and many Greco-Roman portrait busts. The Getty Museum houses a collection of ancient works begun by J. Paul Getty (1892–1976) in 1939. It includes a 4th-century BC bronze *Victorious Athlete*, acquired in 1977, which has been attributed to a sculptor influenced by Lysippos. Among other American collections with important works are the Walters Art Gallery in Baltimore, the Brooklyn Museum in New York, the Cleveland Museum of Art, the Fogg Art Museum of Harvard University in Cambridge, MA, the Art Institute of Chicago, the Detroit Institute of Arts, the Wadsworth Atheneum in Hartford, the Nelson-Atkins Museum of Art in Kansas City, MO, the Los Angeles County Museum of Art, the Minneapolis Institute of Arts, the Museum of Art of the Rhode Island School of Design in Providence, the Santa Barbara Museum of Art and the Worcester Art Museum. In Canada there is an important collection at the Royal Ontario Museum in Toronto.

There have been few important temporary or travelling exhibitions of ancient Greek sculpture, partly because of the difficulties in moving major works. Representative of such exhibitions have been *Ancient Greek Art* at the Burlington Fine Arts Club in London in 1904, an exhibition of Greek art at the Royal Academy, London, in 1946, *Meisterwerke griechischer Kunst* at Basle in 1960 and *Ancient Art from New York Private Collections* at the Metropolitan Museum of Art in New York in 1959–60.

W. Amelung and G. Lippold: *Die Skulpturen des Vaticanischen Museums*, i, ii (Berlin, 1903–8)

G. Mendel: *Istanbul, Musées impériaux ottomans: Catalogue des sculptures grecques, romaines et byzantines*, 3 vols (Athens, 1908)

H. Stuart Jones, ed.: *The Sculptures of the Museo Capitolino* (Oxford, 1912)

L. D. Caskey: *Catalogue of Greek and Roman Sculpture: Fogg Art Museum* (Cambridge, MA, 1925)

H. Stuart Jones, ed.: *The Sculptures of the Palazzo dei Conservatori*, 2 vols (Oxford, 1926)

C. Blümel: *Katalog der griechischen Skulpturen des fünften und vierten Jahrhunderts vor Christus* (1928), iii of *Berlin: Katalog der Sammlung antiker Skulpturen* (Berlin, 1928–38)

R. N. Pryce: *British Museum: Catalogue of Sculpture*, I/i (London, 1928)

A. Hekler: *Die Sammlung antiker Skulpturen in Budapest* (Budapest, 1929)

J. Charbonneaux: *La Sculpture grecque et romaine au Musée du Louvre* (Paris, 1936)

G. Lippold: *Die Skulpturen des Vaticanischen Museums*, iii/1–2 (Berlin, 1936–56)

Greek Art (exh. cat., ed. J. Chittenden and C. Seltman; London, RA, 1946)

D. B. Harden, ed.: *Summary Guide to the Department of Antiquities, Ashmolean Museum* (Oxford, 1951)

F. Poulen: *Catalogue of Ancient Sculpture in the Ny Carlsberg Glyptotek* (Copenhagen, 1951)

G. M. A. Richter: *Catalogue of Greek Sculptures in the Metropolitan Museum of Art* (Cambridge, MA, 1954)

Meisterwerke griechischer Kunst (exh. cat., ed. C. Schefold; Basle, Ksthalle, 1960)

Ancient Art in New York Private Collections (exh. cat., New York, Met., 1961)

M. A. del Chiaro: *The Collection of Greek and Roman Antiquities at the Santa Barbara Museum of Art* (Santa Barbara, 1962)

W. Helbig: *Führer durch die öffentlichen Sammlungen klassischer Altertümer in Rom*, 4 vols (Tübingen, 1963–72)

S. Karouzou: *National Archaeological Museum, Athens: Collection of Sculpture* (Athens, 1968)

E. Rohde: *Griechische und römische Kunst in den Staatlichen Museen zu Berlin* (Berlin, 1968)

M. B. Comstock and C. C. Vermeule: *Greek, Etruscan and Roman Bronzes in the Museum of Fine Arts, Boston* (Boston, 1971)

C. C. Vermeule and N. Neuerburg: *Catalogue of the Ancient Art in the J. Paul Getty Museum* (Malibu, 1973)

Greek and Roman Portraits in the J. Paul Getty Museum (exh. cat., Northridge, CA State U., 1975)

M. B. Comstock and C. C. Vermeule: *Sculpture in Stone: The Greek, Roman and Etruscan Collections of the Museum of Fine Arts* (Boston, 1977)

C. C. Vermeule and A. Brauer: *Stone Sculptures: The Greek, Roman, and Etruscan Collections of the Harvard University Art Museums* (Cambridge, MA, 1990)

J. B. Grossman: *Greek Funerary Sculpture: Catalogue of the Collections at the Getty Villa* (Malibu, 2001)

V. Etruscan.

Etruscan sculpture includes votive figures, funerary monuments and architectural embellishments. Terracotta and bronze were used in all these contexts, but stone was used only for funerary sculpture. Stone included volcanic tufa in southern Etruria, sandstone and travertine around Clusium (Chiusi), sandstone at Fiesole and, occasionally, marble around Velathri (Volterra) in the north-west.

1. Terracotta. 2. Bronze. 3. Stone. 4. Portraiture.

1. TERRACOTTA. The earliest sculptures from the Iron Age in Italy were small figurines in terracotta and bronze, meant as ornaments or offerings for the dead. A free-standing terracotta figurine of a woman from San Lorenzo Vecchio in the Alban Hills (mid-9th century BC; Rome, Mus. N. Preist. & Etnog) was found in a cremation burial. She holds a bowl on the palm of her right hand, while her left is held open in a gesture of offering or prayer repeated by many later figures. Her body is heavy and shapeless, and the small head on a long tapering neck is featureless apart from a jutting nose and ears, the latter pierced for earrings. Also stylistically rudimentary, a somewhat later terracotta figure forms the handle of a three-legged cup from Bisenzio (Rome, Mus. N. Preist. & Etnog., 51762).

Etruscan Orientalizing sculpture shows a marked increase in scale. Figures were given full, rounded contours suggestive of mass and weight, as in the carefully modelled terracotta ash urns from CLUSIUM (Chiusi). While some Early Iron Age ash urns had lids in the form of helmets, to indicate that the ashes were a warrior's, the Orientalizing Canopic urns from Clusium carried this personification further: the lid became a head, the urn itself a body. Another example from Clusium (h. 445 mm; *c.* 650–*c.* 600 BC; Florence, Mus. Archeol.) combines the ample curves of the new style with such Early Iron Age features as deeply cut eyes, slit mouth and prominent ears with spiral earrings. A rare form of ash urn has a lid carrying a large terracotta statuette surrounded by a ring of griffin protomes and figures of mourning women. The main figure on this urn, raised on a circular base, has a round head too large for her body, with a conical projection on top. The hair makes a striated pattern on the skull and hangs in a long braid at the back. Two little tresses in front of the ears fall to the shoulders. The back braid is an Early Iron Age fashion, while the tresses are Eastern features. The face is round, with a long narrow nose and small slit mouth; the eyes are blank oval bosses. The dress is of chequered material, belted and falling short of the ankles, and a small rectangular cloak fastened at the shoulders hangs down the back. The elbows of her bare arms are bent, the right hand closed as if holding something, the left raised to the chin. This figure may be an effigy of the dead, a mourning woman or an underworld deity.

During the second half of the 7th century BC, terracotta tomb monuments were produced for burials at Caere (Cerveteri). The Tomb of the Five Chairs (*c.* 600 BC) contained fragments of five small, seated figures: one male, almost complete (h. 470 mm; Rome, Mus. Conserv.); the trunks of two others; and two female heads now attached to the headless male bodies (London, BM). All three bodies wear a long tunic of chequered material and a cloak fastened on the right shoulder and covering the left arm. The heads are masterpieces of the Orientalizing style, with rounded skulls, ovoid faces, arched eyebrows and heavy eyelids framing oval eyes, and large noses, soft mouths and high cheekbones. The inspiration for these features may have been the bronze heads on cauldrons imported from the East.

In the second half of the 6th century BC the Ionian style of the Greek cities of Asia Minor captivated the Mediterranean world, and Caere produced some of the finest examples of the new style. Caeretan ash urns now took the form of couches, sometimes the funeral couch, more often the banquet couch, on which figures of the dead reclined, smiling. The two finest (*c.* 525–*c.* 500 BC; Rome, Villa Giulia; Paris, Louvre; see colour pl. 2:X, fig. 1) have life-size figures of a man and woman reclining together, the man's right arm around the woman's shoulders, both smiling and gesticulating animatedly. They have egg-shaped heads, long, oval faces with arched eyebrows and slanting eyes, short noses with rounded nostrils, and the 'Archaic smile'. Fine temple terracottas, female mask antefixes, and revetment plaques showing horse and chariot races were also produced at Caere. The finest Archaic temple terracottas, however, are those from the Portonaccio Temple at Veii (*c.* 515–*c.* 490 BC; Rome, Villa Giulia). These include splendid antefixes, including a gorgon's head in a shell of curving tongues (h. 485 mm) and free-standing over life-size statues of Apollo, Hermes, Herakles and a female figure holding a baby in her arms, which originally stood on the ridge of the temple roof. The heads are still Ionian, but the line of cheek and jaw has filled out and the smiles are less serene.

Fewer temples were given elaborate terracotta decorations in the Classical period than in the Archaic, and none rivalled the magnificent Late Archaic figures at Veii. On Temple B at Pyrgi (Santa Severa), however, the projecting end of the ridge-pole carried a relief showing a combination of two episodes from the story of the *Seven against Thebes* (*c.* 510–*c.* 485 BC; Rome, Villa Giulia). In the background Zeus hurls his thunderbolt at Kapaneus; Tydeus and Melanippos sprawl mortally wounded across the foreground, Tydeus biting into Melanippos' skull while Athena draws back in horror. The figures, which overlap and intertwine, are modelled in high relief on a flat background, and their heads are in the round. Every face, except that of Zeus, shows intense feeling, and both the composition and its emotional charge suggest comparison with the west pediment of the Temple of Zeus at Olympia (*c.* 470–*c.* 457 BC).

Fine terracottas were also produced at Volsinii Veteres (Orvieto) in the Classical period. The figures from the Belvedere Temple (late 5th century BC–early 4th; Orvieto, Mus. Etrus. Faina) are not grouped in scenes, but isolated, standing or seated. Their effect resembles that of the east pediment of the Temple of Zeus at Olympia, but their style is later, based on High Classical Greek statues such as the Borghese *Anakreon* and the Farnese *Diadoumenos*. A bearded man, nude except for a cloak fastened at the throat by a round brooch, stands with the weight on the left leg, the left hand resting on the hip, the right arm hanging easily at the side. His head, with staring eyes and a rather unpleasant open mouth, is lifted towards the left, as though he were watching something. There are several young men in armour: one, who wears a moulded cuirass over a full tunic, stands in the same pose but with the back of the right hand on his hip; his head was apparently turned to the right. Another, in a cuirass of small rectangular plates, stands with the weight on the right leg, the left arm lowered, the hand stretched forward to hold a spear, now missing. Like the figures from Pyrgi, the bodies are in high relief against a flat surface, the heads worked in the round. They are about half life-size (800–870 mm) and thus inadequate for the pediment of the Belvedere Temple (w. 16.3 m), though they may have been revetments for beam ends either side of the ridge-pole, perhaps two figural groups looking towards the ridge-pole where something dramatic was displayed.

Greater numbers of temple terracottas survive from the 3rd and 2nd centuries BC. Some of the finest come from the temple at Lo Scasato, Falerii (Civita Castellana). These include figures modelled in the round at three-quarters life-size, large figures in relief, and fragments of small figures, presumably parts of antefixes.

The most spectacular of these is the 'Apollo', the head and torso of a nude youth (h. 560 mm; late 5th century BC; Rome, Villa Giulia). The head is turned to the right and lifted. The broad face with its deep-set eyes, high cheekbones, strong jaw and half-open mouth, is crowned by a mass of curly hair brushed up in the centre above the forehead and falling loosely to the shoulders. The effect recalls portraits of Alexander the Great. The broad, muscular torso bends forward to the left and the left arm is stretched forward. Other important fragments of temple statuary come from Arretium (Arezzo), though again the pieces are too few to tell their location on the temple or the story they illustrate. The two finest heads are an *Athena* and a young man wearing a Phrygian cap (*c.* 175–*c.* 150 BC; Florence, Mus. Archeol.). The cap suggests that the whole scene may have been the Judgement of Paris. The gentle face of the helmeted goddess has deep-set eyes shadowed by heavy bulges under the outer corners of the thin eyebrows; her nose is short, her lips full and soft. Thick locks of hair straggle from under the visor of the helmet. The head of the young man (?Paris) must have been modelled by the same hand. His face is longer and thinner, but otherwise the heads are alike. The contrast between the man's smooth face and the rough, lively texture of his hair is more noticeable because more of the hair is visible, modelled in high relief and striated, wavy rather than curling, in the manner adopted for portraits of Hellenistic heroes and princes.

2. Bronze. Early Iron Age bronzes are more elegant than their terracotta equivalents; their spindly Geometric style depends as much on space as on form for its effect. A bronze cup from Bisenzio has a vertical handle ending in an openwork disc. This makes a double circle enclosing a nude female with a rod-like torso, arms and legs, and a big round head with loop earrings. The face is slightly flattened, with a long narrow nose, drilled holes for eyes and no mouth. It exemplifies the Wiry Geometric Early Iron Age figural style of the 8th century BC and early 7th. The figure, clearly a 'Mistress of Animals', is accompanied by two Geometric ducks and two four-footed beasts, and two large birds' heads adorn the rim of the disc. The 'Mistress of Animals' was derived ultimately, via Greece, from Minoan iconography, and the pose of this figure, with raised arms and straddled legs, suggests Geometric Greek representations of deities appearing to worshippers. Some Early Iron Age ash urns were also of bronze; one from Tarquinia has a real bronze helmet for a lid (Florence, Mus. Archeol.).

During the 7th and 6th centuries BC bronzes tended to be small votive figures or ornaments for utensils. Large funerary bronzes also survive, apparently made as images of the dead. The oldest is a hammered bronze bust from Marsiliana d'Albegna (Florence, Mus. Archeol.). The head is a globe decorated with repoussé lines and bosses in Early Iron Age style, set on a cylindrical neck attached to the broad shoulders of the torso. Early bronze busts were also produced at Vulci and were perhaps intended to represent figures rising from the underworld. During the second half of the 7th century BC, bronze human figurines dedicated at sanctuaries developed two distinct types: a male figure with long hair, armed with a sword or lance, often shown stepping forward, dressed in short trunks; and a female figure in a full-length dress or cape, with hair in a single long tress at the back, making a gesture of offering. Some of these figurines have the flat bodies and crudely articulated limbs reminiscent of Geometric forms; others, presumably the products of a more cosmopolitan urban culture, show Orientalizing influences.

Bronze reliefs of the 6th century BC are numerous and splendid. They almost always illustrate Greek myths, or mythological creatures, and are used in the decoration of tripods, furniture and chariots (e.g. the Monteleone Chariot; *c.* 550 BC). Archaic votive figurines continued to be produced in quantity, with new types appearing: the Greek-influenced figures of the kouros, kore, hoplite, athlete, and mythological deities and heroes; and the more specifically Etruscan figures of the augur, haruspex, toga-clad male, and various animals and anatomical bronzes. Hollow-cast bronzes of the 5th century BC also show the influence of the Archaic Greek types of the Attic kore and nude kouros (e.g. statuette of a spear thrower, *c.* 470 BC; Paris, Louvre). Large collections of bronze statuary were assembled in Etruscan cities, although few of these pieces now survive. Two statuettes from Monteguragazza (*c.* 470 BC; Bologna, Mus. Civ. Archeol.) represent votaries. The man carries a libation bowl and wears a short cloak around his waist; the fully-clothed woman carries a flower and a fruit and wears Etruscan shoes.

The Etruscan Classical style is exemplified by the Todi *Mars*, which is so close in style to the terracottas from the Belvedere Temple, Volsinii Veteres (Orvieto), that it has been assigned to the same workshop. It was hollow cast in seven pieces: head, arms and legs in piece moulds; the torso in two sections, cast directly from a wax model. It represents a warrior in a cuirass of overlapping plates, its lower part made of two rows of lappets, and worn over a full tunic like that of the Belvedere warrior in the moulded cuirass. The *Mars* stands with the weight on the right leg, hip thrown out, the left leg rather too far to the side, knee bent; both feet are firmly on the ground. The broad, blank face has thin eyebrows, a long nose, full mouth and heavy chin, recalling a terracotta head from Volsinii Veteres. The left eye is a small travertine cone with a pupil of black resin; the right is modern. A libation bowl rests on the palm of his right hand; his left once grasped an iron spear, fragments of which are preserved, on which he leaned. His head is turned to the right, as though looking upwards. Attic Red-figure vases depict similar figures of warriors pouring libations before battle, but these are not part of the usual repertory of Greek sculpture. They do appear, however, among Etruscan and Italic votive bronzes of the Late Classical and Hellenistic periods. The *Mars* too is a votive bronze, and a dedicatory inscription in Umbrian is incised on the centre lappet of the cuirass.

A life-size head of a young man, found on an island in Lake Bolsena, also exemplifies Etruscan adaptation of a Greek style (h. 250 mm; London, BM). The long face has a sober expression; forehead and nose make a single line; iris and pupil are incised. The heavy cap of hair has flamboyantly swirling locks, parted on the forehead and shortened in the centre, framing the forehead like the hair of the *Doryphoros* of POLYKLEITOS. A young beard is lightly chased, not a Polykleitan detail. The bronze is hollow cast, broken probably from a votive statue. Another important Classical votive bronze is the Arezzo *Chimaera* (h. 650 mm; *c.* 375–*c.* 350 BC; Florence, Mus. Archaeol.). The wounded beast appears dangerous, snarling and crouching to spring, the mane and the hair along the back bristling in sharp spikes with slightly curved points and deeply striated surfaces, a stylish archaism. Except for these the body is smooth; ribs and muscles are clearly articulated under its shining surface. On the right foreleg is a votive inscription, 'offering'. The serpent-headed tail is an 18th-century addition.

In the late 4th century BC Etruscan bronzeworkers took inspiration from LYSIPPOS: figures became taller and slimmer, with small heads and long legs, sometimes in gracefully sinuous attitudes, the heel of the free foot lifted, for example a bronze representing a young man offering a libation (h. 288 mm; Florence, Mus. Archeol.). Later bronzes are even more elongated (e.g. a togate figure from Volsinii Veteres; h. 270 mm; Rome, Villa Giulia). One series of elongated bronze figures has nothing to do with Lysippos. They are excessively tall, straight and flattened; very much like yardsticks equipped with heads, hands and feet. They represent men, women, priests or perhaps divinities. The oldest of these is a female figure from the Sanctuary of Diana at Nemi (h. 500 mm; *c.* 350–*c.* 300 BC; Paris, Louvre). In a related series the elongated bodies are three-dimensional, and the women's dresses are more detailed and modelled in relief. The best known of these figures is a nude boy from Velathri (Volterra), the 'Evening Shadow' (h. 570 mm, 2nd century BC; Volterra, Mus. Etrus. Guarnacci). The body has an attractive young boy's head with wavy hair straying over his cheeks and the nape of his neck. He has a snub nose, a smiling mouth and a rounded, childlike forehead. These figures seem strangely out of place in the generally philhellenic history of Etruscan sculpture. They may be descendants of an early Italic votive type, wooden and terracotta examples of which have been found in Campania.

3. STONE. Stone sculpture began to be produced in the 7th century BC, a clear indication that Etruria was becoming a major centre in the Mediterranean world. This new craft was probably learnt from Near Eastern and Greek immigrant craftsmen. Early stone figures are large, imposing and immobile, and were connected exclusively with the cult of the dead. The oldest surviving statues are two almost life-size seated male figures in the vestibule of a mid-7th century BC rock-cut tomb at Ceri in the territory of Caere (Cerveteri). They are carved in high relief in the tufa of the tomb and sit enthroned, facing one another, just within its entrance. Their heads are mutilated, but were obviously once bearded. They wear long tunics and their sandalled feet rest on footstools; one wears a slanting mantle over the tunic and his right hand holds a sceptre topped by a stylized lotus flower. Their forms are stocky, with the vertical and horizontal surfaces emphasized. They may have been carved by an Anatolian or north Syrian craftsman. Throne, footstool and sceptre were signs of rank in the Near East, but Etruscan seated figures were usually images not of living potentates but of the dead. These dignitaries of Ceri are not effigies of the couple whose bodies lay in the tomb chamber beyond, but are perhaps ancestors, doing honour to their descendants.

The Pietrera Tomb at Vetulonia (*c.* 650–*c.* 630 BC) contained parts of at least 18 standing figures, some in high relief, some apparently free-standing. The best preserved head, a woman's (h. 280 mm; Florence, Mus. Archeol.), suggests a Greek model, despite its non-Greek features, as it has similarities with early kouroi from Attica and Boiotia. It has a long, solemn face widening into the jaw, a shallow skull with flattened back and long ears set high and far back. The thin, sharp ridge of the eyebrow is separated from the upper lid by a shallow channel; the eye is a swelling oval framed by a fine line of shadow. The torso that probably belongs with this head has no Greek counterpart; but one of the male figures had the stance of a Greek kouros, with arms at the sides, hands half closed, left leg advanced. Unlike Greek kouroi, however, this figure wears a loincloth, as do other Etruscan male figures of the 7th and 6th centuries BC.

By the second quarter of the 6th century BC at Vulci handsome stone figures were being produced in close imitation of the post-Daidalic style of early 6th-century BC Greece. A gypsum figure from the Isis Tomb may be the earliest of these. It represents a woman standing erect in a frontal pose with feet apart but parallel, upper arms pressed to the body, forearms held out. The head is cubic; the body, except for the forearms, a single mass. Details, however, are softly and delicately worked. The low-crowned head has a deep profile, the face is trapezoidal, with a low forehead, and the horizontal eyes, mouth and chin characteristic of Daidalic figures (*see* §IV, 2(i)(c)). The hair is arranged in a row of snailshell curls across the forehead, two curls fall on each shoulder and nine braids bound together hang down the back. A band circles the head and the hair at the back bulges slightly over this. Under a shawl she wears a long, belted dress; these are smooth, without folds, although the dress bulges a little over the belt. The dress, like the curls and the sandalled feet, is Greek. The shawl has three lappets; one at the back, two falling over the shoulders. This is an Etruscan garment, worn by small votive bronzes of the early 6th century BC. The elaboration of the back braid is also Etruscan, and the pose of the hands recalls some votive bronzes: the right hand open as if to hold a flat bowl, the left closed as if around the handle of a jug or cup. The gesture is that of a libation pourer, and the statue may represent the deceased, a mourner or a deity. It stands on a low, profiled base. Stone tomb guardians were also produced at Vulci. A centaur in local tufa is among the best (h. 770 mm; *c.* 590 BC; Rome, Villa Giulia). Seen from the front he resembles a bearded kouros with a sub-Daidalic head, enormous eyes, stunted arms, the open hands pressed to the thighs; the hindquarters of a horse are attached to the buttocks.

At Clusium, stone tomb guardians and busts of mourning women for tomb doorways were produced in imitation of Vulci's post-Daidalic style. The finest early carving from Clusium is a warrior with a pot helmet and a round shield with a gorgoneion in high relief (h. 490 mm, first half of the 6th century BC; Munich, Staatl. Antikensamml.), presumably a tomb guardian. In the Late Archaic period at Clusium a long series of finely carved grave monuments of a new type appeared, comprising gravestones, ash urns, and some sarcophagi, decorated with low-relief panels, with numerous figures on quite a small scale but in elaborate detail (see fig. 17). The scenes are of Etruscan funerary rites, mourners, funeral games and banquets, a repertory like those of the painted tombs of Tarquinia and Clusium. The reliefs also recall early Attic Red-figure pottery styles. Also of a new type were the stone ash urns made at Clusium from the mid 6th century BC, monumental seated figures with removable heads and cavities in the upper torso for the ashes (see fig. 18). The earliest represent solemn, bearded men with heavy bodies, distantly related to the seated figures that lined the sacred way at Didyma. In the second half of the 5th century BC, the time at which true Classical art began in Etruria, the seated figures were female. Some sit on thrones with arms shaped like sphinxes; some hold a pomegranate in the left hand; one carries a baby (h. 900 mm; Florence, Mus. Archeol.). They look more like underworld deities than mortal women. Classical ash urns from Clusium in the shape of banquet couches may have imitated the Late Archaic terracotta urns from Caere. One shows a couple, the woman sitting, in the Greek manner, at the foot of her husband's couch (late 5th century BC; Florence, Mus. Archeol.). On others the foot of the couch is occupied by a messenger from the other world, who summons the banqueter away (e.g. limestone urn; *c.* 400 BC; Florence, Mus. Archeol.; see fig. 19).

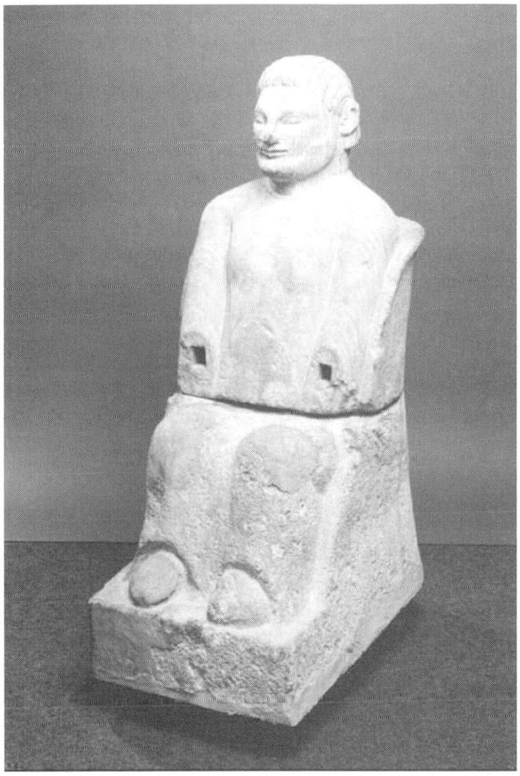

18. Etruscan, stone cinerary urn in the form of seated man, limestone, h. 1.38 m, from Clusium (Chiusi), *c.* 540–520 BC (London, British Museum)

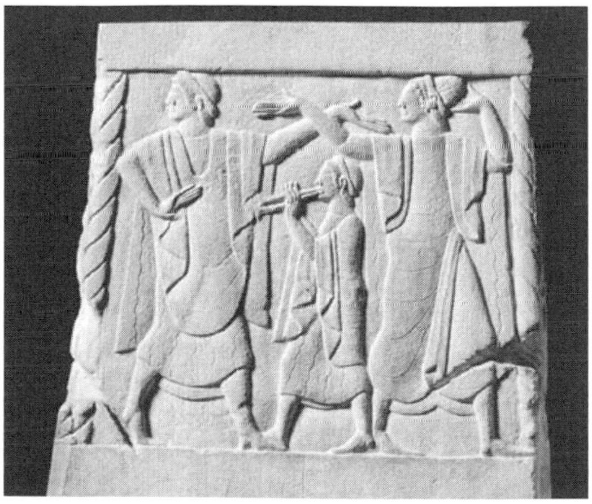

17. Etruscan stone cippus decorated with relief showing musicians, limestone, h. 342 mm, from Clusium (Chiusi), 490–470 BC (London, British Museum)

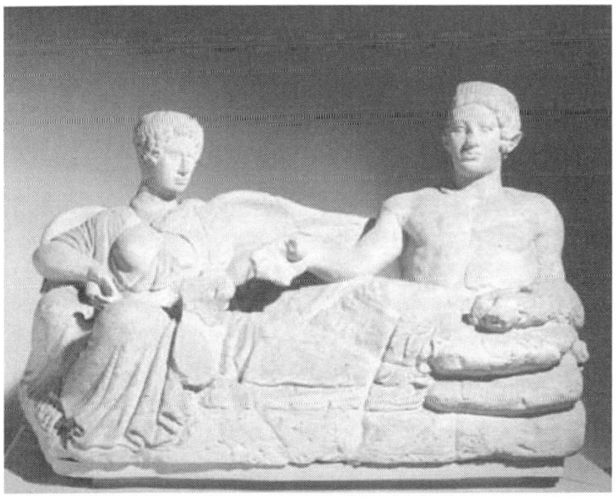

19. Etruscan lid of stone cinerary urn depicting a banqueter and a messenger, limestone, l. 1.19 m, *c.* 400 BC (Florence, Museo Archeologico di Firenze)

By the end of the 5th century BC, burial rather than cremation was almost universal in the cities of southern Etruria, particularly Caere, Tarquinia and Vulci. The oldest stone sarcophagus comes from Caere. The lid is shaped like a couch, the head and foot like temple pediments with sphinxes for acroteria. A bearded man crowned with an elaborate wreath lies on the couch; around his neck is a garland, which he grasps with the left hand, and a necklace with five *bullae*; three more hang from a bracelet on the left upper arm. His upper torso is bare; a cloak covers him from waist to ankles; his right hand grasps a libation bowl. Head and feet are turned slightly to his left, towards the front of the sarcophagus. Although his couch seems to be a funeral couch, the man is not dead, nor even sleeping; his eyes are open. Figural scenes in low relief adorn the front and right end of the sarcophagus itself. On the front, a procession moves to the right, headed by three men in long cloaks. The first carries a large circular trumpet framing his head and walks briskly with both heels off the ground, turning back towards the man who follows, evidently at a slower pace. His heels are firmly on the ground and his right hand holds a staff with a curved end, the Etruscan *lituus*, an emblem of priests and magistrates including those who supervised funeral games, which may be this man's function. Next comes a man with his arms muffled in his cloak except for the left hand, which holds a rod with a twisted top, rather like a cadeuceus; he is hurrying, and looks back at the two men who follow. These have the long, sleeved tunics of musicians; one plays a lyre, the other a double pipe; they walk slowly. Behind them hurry two figures: a bearded man in a long cloak carrying a staff or sceptre in his right hand, preceded by a woman turning her head towards him and laying her hand on his shoulder. Her jewels indicate high rank, and her dress and cloak are diaphanous. Both figures are wreathed; the man may represent the bearded man on the lid, the woman either his wife or her ghost, who has come, like the winged messengers on the urns from Clusium, to escort him. Behind them stands a boy in a long cloak, carrying a stool and blocking the advance of the two-horse chariot driven by the final figure, a young man in tunic and cloak. Except for the boy and the horses, the heads of all the figures touch the upper frame of the chest and, except for the charioteer's, all their feet are on its lower frame. Attendants and musicians have large square heads and broad flat bodies; the figures of the old man, his wife, the boy and the charioteer are more shapely and detailed. The scene is a curiously disorganized procession, and a further scene, on the end of the sarcophagus, reveals its destination. It shows a man with a *lituus* on the left, a lyre player on the right and between them two nude boys preparing for an athletic contest. Thus the procession is on its way to the funeral games and includes the bearded man for whom they are given.

Figures of attendants, musicians, servants and chariots all appear on friezes on later sarcophagi from Tarquinia and on Hellenistic ash urns from Velathri (Volterra), but these represent the cortèges of magistrates, who often drive the chariots themselves, accompanied by lictors. These processions move forward steadily; sometimes an underworld spirit and mourning women take part, but the magistrates are not accompanied by their wives or their ghosts. The destinations are not funeral games but the underworld itself. On early sarcophagi the figures lay supine on the funeral couch, as if dead or sleeping. Later, head and shoulders were half raised on cushions, the left hand supporting the head. Early in the Hellenistic period the figures were shown lifting themselves as if on banqueting couches, looking out at the world. The figures on Hellenistic ash urns assume all of these poses, but the one preferred was that of the banqueter. Sarcophagi and ash urns with such figures continued to be produced well into the 1st century BC. The latest dated sarcophagus (Viterbo, Mus. Civ.), a lamentable work, was made for a burial in 23 BC.

4. PORTRAITURE. In Archaic and Classical Greece, statues honouring the living were uncommon. Portraiture only became important with Alexander the Great and his successors, especially on coins; it became important in Etruria at much the same time, and probably under Greek influence. But it was not used for the same purpose: it honoured the dead. Etruria had a long history of what may be called symbolic portraiture, beginning with the Early Iron Age urns with helmets as lids. The Canopic jars from Clusium (Chiusi) carried on this tradition, and then the figures on Archaic ash urns and sarcophagi from Caere. The earliest stone sarcophagus still presents a symbolic portrait, that of a bearded old man. Perhaps the first sarcophagus to carry a genuine portrait is the fine example from Vulci that shows an elderly man and his wife lying on their marriage couch (mid-4th century BC; Boston, MA, Mus. F.A.). Thereafter, such portraits and near-portraits became common, although, of course, there is no way of verifying that they were actually portraits.

The Greeks, and later the Romans, set up their funeral monuments as public memorials; Etruscan portraits of the dead were hidden in tombs. Public portraits were, however, set in Etruscan sanctuaries. In the Late Classical and Hellenistic periods terracotta heads were popular offerings throughout Italy: most of these are stereotypes, but a few look like individuals. Several splendid Hellenistic bronze portrait heads have been found in central Italy; the Capitoline *Lucius Junius Brutus* (h. 320 mm; Rome, Mus. Conserv), the 'Young General' from San Giovanni Lipioni near Chieti (h. 280 mm; Paris, Bib. N.), a young boy (h. 230 mm; Florence, Mus. Archeol.) and a plump young man from Fiesole (h. 300 mm; Paris, Louvre). These heads have much in common: a cubical solidity, broad face, flat profile, hair in a thick cap of longish locks brushed forward from the crown of the head to fall in strands on the forehead. The greatest difference from the heads on sarcophagi and ash urns is their animated expression. They are not like the terracotta votive heads, either, but are more like parts of free-standing statues such as the Todi *Mars*. They too may have been votive, or honorary, as were the bronzes in the

Forum Romanum described by Pliny (*Natural History* XXXIV.xx–xxx). These are true portraits, idealized but strongly individual; *Brutus* and the 'Young General' have the vigour and intensity of the best of the Greek princely portraits; they may well come from honorary statues. The portrait of the young boy in Florence is less individual and may have been part of a votive statue. The head from Fiesole is the least idealized and most realistic of the four. He looks straight ahead, two vertical frown lines between his heavy eyebrows. His small eyes once had inset irises and pupils; plump cheeks frame his short, broad nose, there is a roll of fat under his chin and his full lips are tightly closed. It is an impressive face, for all its quietness, recalling the head of the 'Magistrate' (Tarquinia, Pal. Vitelleschi) and anticipating Roman heads. It may also be from a votive statue, representing a private citizen who knows his own importance, but does not flaunt it, and thus more Roman than Greek in both feeling and form.

R. Herbig: *Die jungeretruskischen Steinsarkophage* (Berlin, 1952)
A. Hus: *Recherches sur la statuaire en pierre étrusque archaïque* (Paris, 1961)
S. Haynes: 'Zwei archaisch-etruskische Bildwerke aus dem "Isis Grab" von Vulci', *Ant. Plast.*, iv (1965), pp. 13–25, pls 6–11
R. Bianchi Bandinelli and A. Giuliano: *Etruschi e Italici prima del dominio di Roma* (Milan, 1973, rev. 2/1979)
R. D. Gempeler: *Die etruskischen Kanopen: Herstellung, Typologie, Entwicklungsgeschichte* (Küsnacht, 1973)
F. Roncalli: 'Il "Marte" di Todi', *Atti Pont. Accad. Romana Archeol.*, 3rd ser., xi (1973) [whole issue]
M. Cristofani, ed.: *Il Museo Guarnacci, parte prima: Corpus delle urne etrusche di età ellenistica* (1977), ii of *Urne volterrane* (Florence, 1975-)
M. Cristofani: *Statue-cinerario chiusine di età classica* (Rome, 1975)
M. Sprenger and G. Bartolini: *Die Etrusker: Kunst und Geschichte* (Munich, 1977); Eng. trans. by R. Wolf as *The Etruscans: Their History, Art and Architecture* (New York, 1983)
G. Proietti, ed.: *Il Museo Nazionale Etrusco di Villa Giulia* (Rome, 1980)
G. Colonna and F.-W. von Hase: 'Alle origini della santuaria etrusca: La tomba delle statue presso Ceri', *Stud. Etrus.*, lii (1984), pp. 13–59
M. Cristofani: *I bronzi degli Etruschi* (Novara, 1985)
E. Hostetter: *Bronzes from Spina*, i (Mainz, 1986)
F. Jurgeit: *Le Ciste prenestine*, II/i (Italy, 1986)
J. Swaddling, ed.: *Italian Iron Age Artefacts in the British Museum* (London, 1986)
F. Buranelli: *La Tomba François di Vulci* (exh. cat., Rome, 1987)
M. C. Galestin: *Etruscan and Italic Bronze Statuettes* (diss., Rijksuniversiteit Groningen, 1987)
B. van der Meer: *The Bronze Liver of Piacenza*, Dutch Monographs on Ancient History and Archaeology, ii (Netherlands, 1987)
The Gods Delight (exh. cat., Cleveland, OH, Mus. A., 1988)
G. Bordenache Battaglia and A. Emiliozzi: *Le Ciste prenestine*, I/ii (Italy, 1990)
M. Bentz: *Etruskische Votivbronzen des Hellenismus* (Florence, 1992)
M. Söderland: *Late Etruscan Votive Heads from Tessennano: Production, Distribution, Sociohistorical Context* (Rome, 2002)

VI. Roman.

1. Introduction. 2. Historical survey. 3. Collections, museums and exhibitions.

1. Introduction. Works of Roman sculpture survive in great numbers, filling museums and collections worldwide with a bewildering abundance of images, formats and styles; they span centuries of artistic production and originate from the Mediterranean heartland as well as from the far-flung provinces of the Empire. In contrast to the loss of so much Roman painting (although its figural repertory is preserved in sculpture), it is Roman sculpture that survived into the Middle Ages and the Renaissance, providing the most tangible evidence of Classical art. It also inspired many later artists, particularly after 1506 when the Laokoon—a work made by Greek sculptors for a Roman patron in the 1st century AD—was discovered in Rome. Until the rediscovery of Greece in the 18th century by Winckelmann and subsequently by generations of travellers and archaeologists, Classical sculpture was, to all intents and purposes, Roman sculpture.

Roman sculpture was the outcome of an unprecedented scale of artistic production, not equalled until modern times. Large workshops, specializing in architectural commissions, portraits, sarcophagi, devotional images and the replication of masterworks, served a mixed clientele with very different interests and resources. Sculptors' workshops were often associated with quarries in Asia Minor and North Africa, and they could be found at sites of intense activity near large cities; they also engaged in large-scale trade, involving disparate areas of the Empire. Scholarship has begun to define the range of activities and typical specialities of these workshops, but most of the production of Roman sculpture remains anonymous, in part because as handworkers sculptors had low class status although their works might be esteemed, and in part because Roman patrons, especially among the élite, had been educated to prefer the renowned works of the Greek masters. Yet there is ample evidence that great patrons sought out great artists, however nameless they remain, most notably perhaps in the major public commissions and in portraiture, where the artistic personality of individual masters has been extricated from a number of surviving works (*See* §(v) below; *see also* Roman Republic and Empire, §4).

Because of the vast scale of the sculptural enterprise and the anonymity of the sculptors, the study of Roman sculpture has been directed largely to the analysis of general topics, such as that of period style, metropolitan or 'provincial' style, the development of types and programmes of representation, and the interaction between public and private repertories of imagery. Thus, to a large degree, connoisseurship has not been a central issue in the study of Roman sculpture, except where questions of authenticity, the dating and locating of objects and the discovery of 'master portraitists' are concerned. Instead, the social and political history of Roman sculpture has engaged art historians, especially when the matters of differential patronage and highly stratified audiences have become major issues of scholarship. However, connoisseurship is not absent even from these discussions because of the wish to associate art works with particular sources of patronage and the importance of determining contemporary Roman standards of quality, given the varieties of the clientele and the absence of an aesthetic literature devoted to the evaluation of contemporary Roman works. There was a mass market for Roman sculpture, consisting of élite, plebeian and provincial patrons and consumers whose tastes and desires were very different. Therefore the judgement of quality is not simply a matter of aesthetics but, rather, involves the complex and highly variable conditions of the workshop, the art market, the exercise of public and private patronage, and the nature and purposes of display. All these conditions, in turn, were deeply affected by two interrelated phenomena, the operation of period styles—especially strong in the late Republic, under Augustus and Trajan, from the Antonines to the Severans, and in the late 3rd century AD and early 4th—and the force of recurrent revivals that so permeated Roman art throughout its history. Some might consider the latter even more important than the former in shaping the appearance of subject-matter in Roman sculpture, in determining the relative strength of native Italian or borrowed Greek traditions, or in moving Roman art towards greater abstraction in the course of the centuries. The engagement between indigenous traditions and Greek art, often hostile but sometimes accommodating, confuses the history of Roman sculpture as a discrete and continuous art form, introduces into its imagery and programmes pre-Classical, Classical and anti-Classical currents, and challenges the applications of Greek, Greco-Roman or Roman standards of quality to the entire sculptural repertory, if not to individual works of art.

(i) General. (ii) Subject-matter. (iii) Materials and techniques. (iv) Forms. (v) Craftsmen and society.

(i) General. Roman sculpture began under the Etruscan kings with terracotta (*See* §V, 1 above), perhaps because of the lack of good quality stone in Latium. Hand- and mould-made sculptures were applied as architectural decoration to the larger temples in Rome from the 6th to the 2nd century BC. Brightly painted terracotta was the preferred sculptural medium for temple pediments, antefixes and acroterial statues at Rome, Ardea, Signia, Satricum and Cosa; small statuettes and reliefs fulfilled the demand for votive offerings, devotional images and dedications, although occasionally large-scale sculptures were created for important shrines, such as that of Hercules near S Omobono in Rome or the sacred area around Lavinium, south of Rome. The practice of cremation, common among the Etruscans and early Romans, led to the creation of terracotta cinerary urns of varied sculptural complexity; many of these urns displayed stereotyped motifs and were produced in large numbers by local workshops (e.g. at Velathri (Volterra)); sometimes the figural repertory was more ambitious and included narrative scenes from Greek mythology, with the figure of the deceased on the lid. These figures too were stereotyped, but in the course of Roman expansion over the Italian peninsula they became more detailed, displaying by the 3rd and 2nd centuries BC a graphic realism that took on the character of portraiture, if not producing individualized portraits. In the last two centuries of the Republic, terracotta portrait heads appeared in Etruria and Latium that seem quite specific in their characterization, especially in physiognomic detail. Perhaps they reflect the collection of wax images of great ancestors, the so-called *imagines maiorum*, treasured by Roman patrician families and displayed publicly at special occasions of family pride.

The coarse volcanic rock, tufa, was also used in the Republican period for architectural decoration, including historiated capitals (e.g. at Pompeii), but it was quickly replaced by local limestones. Because of its hardiness and the prestige of greater cost, limestone also began to replace terracotta as a preferred sculptural medium by the 2nd century BC; available from a variety of sites in Italy, limestone was used for altars decorated with reliefs, for architectural decorations requiring a more intricate form of carving, for the adornment of city gates with busts, statues or reliefs (e.g. at Perugia) and for funerary monuments. Portraits of the deceased and his family, sometimes with additional reliefs (e.g. the Baker's Tomb at Porta Maggiore, *c.* 30 BC; Rome, Mus. Nuo.), were carved in limestone and attached to large tombs in prominent positions; this practice continued in Italy and in the western and northern provinces well into the Empire. Along the Roman military frontier, local limestones (sometimes sandstone) were used for funerary monuments and sacred images until the 4th century AD. Perhaps the most distinguished of these limestone sculptures are the late Republican/early Imperial commemorative statues of men and women, clad respectively in toga or stola, that adorned public places, fora and tombs. These statues were produced in large numbers by workshops possibly containing a portrait artist who would be called in to finish the work on commission. Thus many were made with large cavities between the shoulders, waiting for the insertion of a separately made portrait head, to give an identity to an otherwise anonymous but well-defined exemplar of a social class.

With the opening of the Luna quarries under Augustus and the growing influence of Greek marble statuary, marble replaced other stone sculpture wherever possible (*see* ARCHITECTURE, §IV, 1(ii)(a)). Greek marble sculptures from the Greek mainland, Asia Minor and Magna Graecia poured into Roman Italy, first as a result of conquest, beginning in the late 3rd century BC, and later as an esteemed commodity, the sign of an educated Roman of high station. Original works of Greek art went on private and public display; when they could not be acquired, more or less faithful copies would be made, following Hellenistic practice, beginning in the late Republic and at periods of intense activity thereafter (especially under Augustus, the early Julio-Claudians, Hadrian and the Antonines, but not unknown even in the 4th century AD; *see* §(ii)(d) below). Other art works in the manner of 5th- or 4th-century BC Greek masters were invented to serve this same clientele, a form of creative revival that was not only retrospective in its attitude but also continued the Greco-Roman artistic tradition in the production of new art. Roman villas, libraries, museums and public places were filled with Greek or Greek-imitation statues, many of them surviving until modern times as the only replicas of lost Greek masterworks. As such they are often housed in the Greek section of museums rather than in the Roman, as if their invisible precedent were more important than their visible presence. Stimulated by the Greek model, Roman sculptors of whatever ethnic origin turned to marble for portrait statues and busts, public sculptures of every kind, elaborate altars and divine images, dynastic ensembles glorifying the imperial house, and large-scale architectural sculpture. Greek originals also served to adorn Roman temples (e.g. the Temple of Apollo Sosianus, Rome, late 1st century BC) but from Augustus on, vast Roman projects such as the Forum Augustum and the Forum of Trajan required new works of sculpture in large numbers, and they in turn served as models for new productions in Rome and elsewhere, especially in the fora and public spaces of Roman towns, where broken fragments and empty podia give mute testimony to the forest of statues that once existed.

Hard stones such as granite, diorite, basalt and porphyry were used in Imperial architecture, especially for their colour and texture. Red porphyry was favoured for Imperial images, especially in the late Empire, perhaps as a sign of permanence, consistent both with the programmatic intention of their commission and with the Egyptian tradition of the sculptors who probably made them, since most of the porphyries came from Egypt. Other hard stones, especially gemstones and glass, were carved and engraved for seals, cameos and small, precious images, even portraits, often superbly crafted and loaded with symbolic messages. Wood sculpture is rare, probably because so much of it has perished, although hundreds of Gallic cult figures have been preserved in sacred deposits in the Seine.

Roman sculptors also employed bronze, silver, gold and lead. The first three metals were used for centuries as coins, while lead was restricted to tokens (for the games, baths and brothels), although it entered the debased coinage of the late Empire. Thousands of small bronze sculptures survive, some of them made as independent works, others attached to furniture; works in gold and silver have largely disappeared, melted down for their monetary value. Lead weights often took the form of small sculptures, especially truncated busts, while sheet lead, decorated with symbolic images in relief, occasionally served as coffin sheathing, especially in the eastern Mediterranean. Roman sculptors achieved great public commissions in bronze, sometimes replicating Greek originals but more frequently departing from those models to create impressive new works. Notable early examples include the *She-wolf* (see fig. 20) and *Lucius Junius Brutus*, neither of them technically Roman although indubitably Italian. From the Republic to the late Empire, bronze statues were erected as a mark of the highest honour or as a sign of the greatest importance of the subject, as on the attic of a triumphal arch or gate. When possible the statues of equestrian commanders would be gilded so as to enhance their visibility and their splendour in the sun; the restored statue of *Marcus Aurelius*, formerly on the Capitoline, gives a good indication of that effect, as does Statius' description (*Silvae* I.1) of Domitian's equestrian statue in the Forum Romanum. Although most of the major bronze statues have perished, their high quality and powerful iconographic charge are revealed in the statue of *Augustus* from Prima Porta (Rome, Vatican, Braccio Nuo.; for illustration *see* AUGUSTUS), believed to be a close marble copy of a bronze original, made shortly after 27 BC.

E. Strong: *Roman Sculpture from Augustus to Constantine* (London, 1907)

O. Vessberg: *Studien zur Kunstgeschichte der römischen Republik* (Lund, 1941)

D. E. Strong: *Roman Imperial Sculpture* (London, 1961)

R. Bianchi Bandinelli: *Rome: The Centre of Power: Roman Art to AD 200* (London and New York, 1970)

R. Bianchi Bandinelli: *Rome: The Late Empire* (London and New York, 1971)

H. P. L'Orange: *Art Forms and Civic Life in the Late Roman Empire* (Princeton, 1971)

R. Brilliant: *Roman Art from the Republic to Constantine* (London, 1974)

C. C. Vermeule: *Greek Sculpture and Roman Taste* (Ann Arbor, 1977)

B. S. Ridgway: *Roman Copies of Greek Sculpture: The Problem of the Originals* (Ann Arbor, 1984)

D. E. E. Kleiner: *Roman Sculpture* (New Haven, 1992)

M. Koortbojian: *Myth, Meaning, and Memory on Roman Sarcophagi* (Berkeley, 1995)

C. C. Mattusch: *Classical Bronzes: The Art and Craft of Greek and Roman Statuary* (Ithaca, 1996)

M. Bertoletti, M. Cima and E. Talamo: *Sculptures of Ancient Rome: Collections from the Capitoline Museums at the Montemartini Power Station* (Milan, 1997)

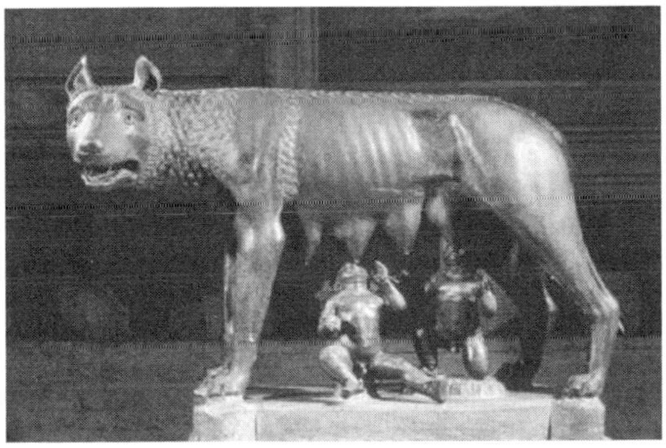

20. *She-wolf*, bronze, h. 750 mm, l. 1.14 m, 5th century BC; figures of Romulus and Remus (*c.* 1484–96) by Antonio Pollaiuolo (Rome, Museo dei Conservatori)

D. A. Conlin: *The Artists of the Ara Pacis: The Process of Hellenization in Roman Relief Sculpture* (Chapel Hill, 1997)

L. Farrar: *Ancient Roman Gardens* (Stroud, 1998)

K. D. S. Lapatin: *Chryselephantine Statuary in the Ancient Mediterranean World* (Oxford and New York, 2001)

Rethinking the Romans: New Views of Ancient Sculpture (exh. cat., Providence, RI Sch. Des., Mus. A., 2001)

J. B. Grossman: *Looking at Greek and Roman Sculpture in Stone: A Guide to Terms, Styles, and Techniques* (Los Angeles, 2003)

N. Kaltsas: *Ancient Greek and Roman Sculpture in the National Archaeological Museum, Athens* (Los Angeles, 2003)

P. Stewart: *Statues in Roman Society: Representation and Response* (Oxford and New York, 2003)

C. H. Hallett: *The Roman Nude: Heroic Portrait Statuary 200 BC–AD 300* (Oxford and New York, 2005)

E. Perry: *The Aesthetics of Emulation in the Visual Arts of Ancient Rome* (Cambridge and New York, 2005)

(ii) Subject-matter. Although Roman sculpture in all its different media and iconographic variety presents a vast repertory of images, four principal themes can be identified. The first is portraiture, a subject long identified as a focus of artistic creativity (*see also* §§(*a*)-(*c*) below); even though the Romans did not invent the portrait as an art form, their exploitation of it was unprecedented in range and variety. Honorific and commemorative, public and private, flattering although often highly realistic, fashionable and revealing, Roman portraits span both the history of Roman art and the history of the Romans' attitude towards themselves and their place in the world. These vivid images of men, women and children appear singly or in groups, are carved in the round or in relief, are fully rendered or reduced to bust form and may bear the distinct mark of a particular artist or the blurred sign of a much reproduced copy. The images move between the individual and the type with great ingenuity. Portraits were grounded on established typologies, reflecting the importance of one's position in Roman society: as the citizen, the priest, the commander, the statesman, the consul, the intellectual (on the Greek model), the *eques* (wealthy non-senator), the successful plebeian, the soldier, the husband and wife—all endowed with a specific reality and presence. That attempt at fixing a type in the person was usually accomplished by emphasizing the portrait head, making possible the ready transfer of specific identities by replacement, when convenient or necessary. (*See* §(iv)(a) below; *see also* ROMAN REPUBLIC AND EMPIRE, §5(iii).)

The visualization of politicized historical and mythological subjects in great works of public art constitutes the second major theme of Roman sculpture. Historical, mythological or allegorical programmes of relief sculpture inform triumphal arches and other monuments across the Empire, for example the series of Hadrianic tondi on the Arch of Constantine in Rome that represent hunting in an allegorical mode, substituting the hunt for battle. In this way Roman sculptors converted politics and political programmes into a public, affective art that aggrandized the nature of Roman life and stimulated the ordinary Roman's consciousness of the greatness of their leaders and their times. (*See* §(iv)(b) below; *see also* ROMAN REPUBLIC AND EMPIRE, §4(iii).)

Carved marble sarcophagi with their rich repertories of imagery offered a creative opportunity to generations of Roman sculptors. Although portraits survive in the thousands, sarcophagi survive in the hundreds, giving evidence of the aspirations of wealthy Romans for themselves and their progeny that they might survive the oblivion of death. From the 1st century AD Roman sarcophagi exhibit a great variety of subjects and treatments on the sides and the lid: scenes from Greek mythology, more or less Romanized; scenes from everyday life, both public and private, domestic and foreign; references to the gods, especially to the divine Dionysus, who saves; the release offered by the philosophical life; the cultivation of the Muses that elevates the spiritual worth of men and women; the cycle of the seasons that promises continuity. Many of the reliefs on the body of the sarcophagus incorporate the portrait of the deceased, thereby conflating the deceased and the heroic character or divine being in the representation. The products of many specialized workshops throughout the Empire, these sarcophagi might be roughed out near the quarry, then shipped to their final destination to be finished by different sculptors working in some metropolitan centre. They provide a good deal of evidence about the marble and art trade and the development of workshop practices in design and carving techniques. In addition, mythological sarcophagi offer another instance of the adoption and adaptation of Greek forms and subjects into the Roman repertory; they also offered Renaissance artists and iconographers a superb entry into the Classical tradition (*see also* SARCOPHAGUS, §3).

The fourth major theme in Roman sculpture is, therefore, the Roman contribution to the formation of the Classical tradition itself through the response to Greek art. The *opus nobile*, or Greek masterwork, provided an extraordinary repertory of images, forms and artistic solutions, as well as value-laden objects. Often an encumbrance on the artist's imagination, but just as often a stimulus to his invention, Greek art served as a foundation for the Roman sculptor (and his patron) and as a repertory that he could use or reject, often self-consciously. By replication, transformation and creative interpretation, Roman artists took the Greek tradition and naturalized it for their own needs (*see* §(d) below). The *Laokoon* and the assemblage of 'Classical' sculptures in the Tiberian villa at SPERLONGA or in Hadrian's Villa at TIBUR (Tivoli) reveal the complexity of the Romans' response to Greek art, their admiration, and yet their departure from its norms when their own needs were paramount. The formation of the Classical tradition was a collaborative enterprise that involved Roman artists' contributions to a received tradition, which, reshaped, became the foundation of European art. But this participation in the formation and redirection of the Classical tradition was only part of a larger, peculiarly Roman phenomenon of artistic creation. In the waxing and waning of the tradition in the face of indigenous patterns of artistic behaviour and strong anti-Classical currents, Roman sculpture also anticipated the state of stylistic pluralism typical of modern mass culture.

H. G. Niemeyer: *Studien zur statuarischen Darstellung der römischen Kaiser* (Berlin, 1968)

G. Koch and H. Sichtermann: *Römische Sarkophage* (Munich, 1982)

K. Fittschen and P. Zanker: *Katalog der römischen Porträts in den capitolischen Museen*, i and iii (Mainz, 1983 and 1985)

G. Lahusen: *Untersuchungen zur römischen Ehrenstatue in Rom* (Rome, 1983)

P. Zanker: *Augustus und die Macht der Bilder* (Munich, 1987); Eng. trans. by A. Shapiro as *The Power of Images in the Age of Augustus* (Ann Arbor, 1988)

N. Taback: *Untangling the Muses: A Comprehensive Study of Sculptures of Muses in the Greek and Roman World* (diss., Cambridge, MA, Harvard U., 2002)

S. Dillon and K. E. Welch: *Representations of War in Ancient Rome* (Cambridge and New York, 2006)

(a) Imperial portraiture. (b) Private portraiture. (c) Portraits of women. (d) Roman copies of Greek statuary.

(a) Imperial portraiture. The most important form of public sculpture in the Roman world was the portrayal of emperors. Early imperial portraits were markedly indebted to Greek precedents. Portraits of AUGUSTUS, for example, were based on those of Alexander the Great and his successors to a remarkable degree; the pose of the image on the Prima Porta Augustus (Rome, Vatican, Braccio Nuo.; for illustration *see* AUGUSTUS) is based on the Classical Greek type of the Polykleitan Canon (*see* POLYKLEITOS), while its physiognomy is Hellenistic. Imperial portraits were set up in temples and public places throughout the Empire, reminding its inhabitants of the power of living rulers and of the divine status of dead emperors whose deeds were still officially remembered. The imperial family was honoured as a whole and so portraits of wives, sons and daughters are also common.

The imperial portraits that were most influential in terms of their effect on subsequent portraiture were those of HADRIAN, partly because his decision to wear a beard influenced both public and private portraiture, but also because the curls of his beard and hair created a fluidity of form that became embedded in the conventions of portraiture. The individuality of imperial portraiture was diminished with DIOCLETIAN's creation of the Tetrarchy in AD 293; thereafter the political need to emphasize the integrated nature of Tetrarchic rule rendered imperial portraiture impersonal, and so the figures of the four rulers were identical. This impersonality was to characterize imperial portraiture throughout the next century.

J. Pollini: *The Portraiture of Gaius and Lucius Caesar* (New York, 1987)

J. Bazant: *Roman Portraiture: A History of its History* (Prague 1995)

C. B. Rose: *Dynastic Commemoration and Imperial Portraiture in the Julio-Claudian Period* (Cambridge 1997)

E. R. Varner: *Mutilation and Transformation: Damnatio Memoriae and Roman Imperial Portraiture* (Leiden and Boston, 2004)

(b) Private portraiture. The sculpted public portrait, still considered to be one of the major contributions of the Romans, has traditionally taken pride of place in the scholarly and popular literature of the field. Much work has been done on portraits depicting emperors, less on their wives and daughters, and even less on the private portrait—an inadequate term used to designate mostly anonymous subjects, usually although not exclusively citizens of the lower social orders. The term indicates that the subjects of the portraits were not the ruling élite, the emperor, his family or members of his court; however, private portraits were erected in public spaces of cities to honour prominent citizens in the towns and provinces of the empire. Now, without inscribed plaques to identify them, the busts or statues offer character studies of distinct personalities whose names and lives are otherwise lost to us. Studies of private portraits have been stymied by the overwhelming interest in identifying images of the great men whose deeds comprise the historical record. With identification and classification of imperial portraits being the focus of the scholarly industry, the private portrait has been deemed less worthy as an object of inquiry.

Freedmen's reliefs. Research on portraits in funerary art, whether portraits on relief panels on tomb façades, on altars erected within tombs or on sculpture representing the deceased in the guise of the gods—and most recently, the painted mummy portraits of Roman Egypt—has looked to social history to analyse the motives of patrons lacking the political careers and high honours of the élite. In this context the private portrait has been considered as evidence of the artistic patronage and self-representation of one low-status group that achieved a high profile, that is, freedmen: ex-slaves manumitted to become citizens. Freedman typically worked in trades or business in the cities and were eager to display their new status and prosperity in the Augustan period, yet their role as patrons of the arts may be overstated in later periods (their notoriety in literary sources may be behind this). Late Republican and Augustan reliefs with group portraits offer poignant glimpses of social mobility: often the freed parents (only recently released from slavery) are represented as stern and upright citizens in togas and with veiled heads (for matrons) with their freeborn children, on whom their ambitions rested. In the early Augustan relief of *L. Vibius Felix* (Rome, Vatican, Mus. Chiaramonti; see fig. 21), the son is proudly displayed as a portrait bust placed between his parents. It is not clear if this indicates that the son had predeceased his parents (and therefore is shown to be properly commemorated) or that the prestige of commissioning a costly form of art determined its representation in the relief. The inscription at the bottom of the panel that once adorned a tomb façade outside of Rome states that L. Vibius Felix was freeborn, that his wife was a freedwoman, but the status of the son is not made explicit. Thus, the group portrait depicts a family in transition.

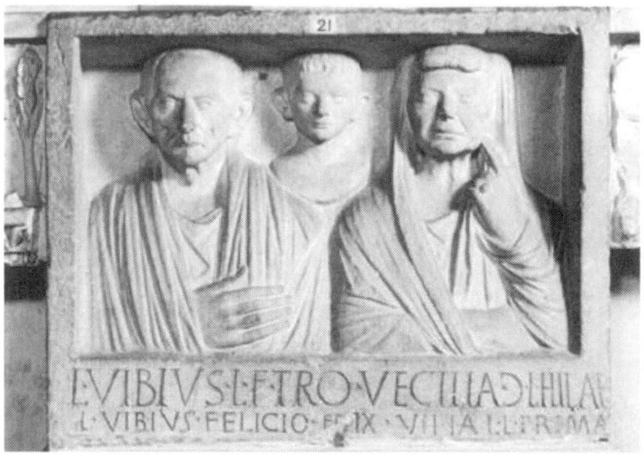

21. Roman funerary relief of *L. Vibius Felix and his Family,* late 1st century BC (Rome, Vatican, Museo Chiaramonti)

Private portraits and the imperial model. The austere, unflattering style of the portraits in the funerary relief of L. Vibius Felix reflects the late Republican veristic style. It is thought that in any given period during the Empire, private portraits followed the style of the dominant imperial portraits. This phenomenon of emulation of features and artistic style can be seen in the Augustan, Flavian, and Trajanic-Hadrianic periods. Vespasian's and Titus's fleshy faces and heavy jowls appear on private portraits in the round or on reliefs, as do the hairstyle and resolute expression of Trajan. Beards came into vogue soon after Hadrian began to be portrayed wearing a beard. Private portraits are usually dated by their resemblance to the imperial models. Rarely is there any external evidence for dating them, and this should make one pause. That the imperial portrait wielded an overwhelming influence may, however, be overstated: there are mid-2nd century AD private portraits with full beards and wavy hair in flamboyant coiffures that go beyond the conservative self-fashioning of the emperor (for example, the mid-2nd century AD portrait bust in the National Museum, Athens, originally from the Theatre of Dionysos).

Mythological portraits. Social status seems to have made a difference in the choice of portrait format or monument type, as we have seen in the group or family portraits of the late Republic and Augustan periods. In the early-mid Imperial period, some imperial freedmen (the emperor's ex-slaves freed to take positions on his staff), privileged to some degree by their proximity to the court and high society, were depicted in the form of the mythological portrait: the bodies copying celebrated statues of the gods and the heads carved as likenesses of the deceased. Men were depicted as the warrior god Mars (occasionally with their wives in the role of Venus), and boys as Apollo or the infant Hercules, among other choices. A statue in the Bardo Museum in Tunis seems to depict a middle-aged man in the guise of Hercules with the attribute of the lion skin tied around his neck. The receding hairline, furrowed brow and sagging skin under the eyes, however, indicate that we are not in the presence of the superhero of antiquity but, rather, of a grim and hardbitten individual in the mid-3rd century AD. The mythological guise honours the subject of the portrait with the comparison to Hercules, the hero made immortal (and his combats are appropriate to commemorate a veteran, as some have suggested the subject was). Women were graced with the resplendent bodies of Venus, girls granted the prowess of the huntress Diana and matrons the authority of goddesses such as Cybele (e.g. a statue of a matron as enthroned Cybele, AD 90–120; Malibu, CA, Getty Mus.). The bodies of these statues conform to well-known statue types, familiar from sanctuaries, theatres and gardens, that endowed the subjects not only with the prestige of a Hellenic work of art, but also with the powers of the particular god or goddess. Within the ranks of freedmen and freedwomen, differences of motivation, taste and cultural background need to be acknowledged.

Private portraits in public. Not all private portraits commemorated the dead; some were erected in public—in religious sanctuaries as well as in fora or marketplaces—and not all of them depicted subjects of the lower social orders (including the freeborn along with freedmen). Portrait heads, broken off from busts or statues and long removed from archaeological contexts that could have provided names of the subjects in inscriptions, depicted members of the senatorial and equestrian orders, as well as members of the provincial élite, even though we are unable to recognize these individuals now. Heads with strikingly similar facial features, now dispersed in different collections, may have depicted the same subject whose stature or wealth required several images to be displayed in the same or diverse locales (e.g. an equestrian honoured with the grant of a statue both in Rome and in his home town as a reward for public service in an administrative post and as a local benefactor or a wealthy individual being represented by an ensemble of portraits in his tomb). Private portraits, therefore, played key roles in many aspects of Roman life: as a means to perpetuate memory of the dead, as emblems of pride and status symbols for both those well established and newly arrived in society, and as one of the perquisites of a life lived prominently and replete with honours.

(c) Portraits of women. Given that portraits of men can serve as an index of their political careers, the female portrait has figured as an intermediary of such relationships in studies of imperial women as wives, sisters or mothers of emperors. The imagery of imperial women is most often treated as an extension of the political programme of their male relatives (this is apparent in the images on the reverses of coins, so useful for identification of imperial subjects and dating). A few more recent studies have taken on Roman attitudes toward gender (i.e. the coiffures as fashionable adornment and as signs of status) or the representation of virtue (clothing conveying the moral standards of the wearer).

Private female portraits, like their male counterparts, have been assumed to have been under the influence of the conventions of the current imperial portrait. In some periods this is more or less true, and can be traced through hairstyles copied from imperial models. The representation of women in imperial Rome, however, cannot entirely be explained by the trickle-down theory of artistic styles and personal adornment. In the 2nd century AD the coiffures of Plotina and Sabina (wives of Trajan and Hadrian) are rarely represented in private portraits and, on the contrary, many private portraits wear more highly-styled and elegant coiffures, for example, the bust of Claudia Olympias (*c.* AD 100; London, BM) with a coiffure featuring meticulously tiered crests and a turban of braids. It is particularly interesting that in the 2nd century AD, the height of production of the marble portrait bust and statue, portraits of imperial women are less easy to distinguish from those of their social inferiors. The beauty depicted displays a sophistication emerging from the cosmopolitan societies of cities across the Mediterranean in the 2nd century.

As Roman men are depicted in their roles as politicians and military commanders, so women are also represented in their domestic roles that correspond to their stage of life: girl, maiden, matron and dowager. Each of these roles entailed different portrait types that may or may not have coincided with those of the current imperial women. Many, but not all, of these portraits are funerary commemorations of beloved mothers, wives and daughters. Given the high rates of mortality and the suddenness of death in the ancient world, it has been suggested that bereaved families and the sculptors they commissioned relied on stock types, that is, conventional portraits of idealized young beauties, stern matrons and haughty dowagers that could be individualized to varying degrees. The mythological portraits of matrons in the guise of Venus, for example, tend to show middle-aged features with dour or wary expressions, while their voluptuous figures invite the viewers' gaze (e.g. statue of the Flavian period, Copenhagen, Ny Carlsberg Glyp.). We may wonder about the contradiction, but for Romans the sexuality of Venus was harnessed to the needs of the state, and recast in productive terms as fertility and the bearing of children. Venus, therefore, was an appropriate model for wives and mothers, and the lined or sagging skin of the portraits was seen as marks of feminine virtue: modesty, reserve and self-control. As there were ideal types of youthful beauty, so there were ideal types for the mature woman, the respectable matron and mother. The striking faces projecting dignity and probity also graced portrait busts and statues of various types, including those of fully draped figures.

Portraits of girls and maidens raise different questions for a society that did not worship youth nor celebrate lives without achievements in the public sphere. Furthermore, portraits frequently commemorate maidens who died before their time, that is, before they married, the culminating rite of passage into adulthood. Grieving parents were often motivated to represent their daughters in terms of their promise, the life taken away from them. Funerary portraits and reliefs occasionally depict deceased girls who look older than their ages at death as indicated in the accompanying epitaphs. It is as if the unfortunate girls were represented as the matrons they would have become if death had not intervened. The funerary altar of *Julia Victorina* (AD 60–70; Paris, Louvre; see fig. 22) commemorates the girl, dead at the tender age of ten, with a portrait carved in relief. Julia Victorina, described as a *filia dulcissima* ('the sweetest girl'), shows a pre-adolescent with wide-open eyes, a short nose and thick shapely lips. If we accept this as a formula for girlish beauty, then we find an appeal in looks defined as lovely and charming by the appearance of inchoate vitality and intelligence, as well as fragility and dependence. The cropped coiffure appears boyish but is offset by her drop earrings. The altar is especially interesting because of the second portrait on the back of the altar, which depicts a woman with an elongated face and sharper, more chiselled features than those of the childish portrait on the front. It is likely that the second portrait depicts an older version of Julia Victorina, as if to bestow on her the second act denied in life.

G. Daltrop: *Die stadtrömischen männlichen Privatbildnisse trajanischer und hadrianischer Zeit* (Münster, 1958)

A. Carandini: *Vibia Sabina* (Florence, 1969)

D. Kleiner: *Roman Imperial Funerary Altars with Portraits* (Rome 1987)

K. Fittschen: 'Ritratti maschili privati di epoca adrianea: Problemi della loro varietà', *Scienze dell'antichità: Storia, archaeologia, antropologia,* vi–vii (1992–3), pp. 445–85

P. Cain: *Männerbildnisse neronisch-flavischer Zeit* (Munich, 1993)

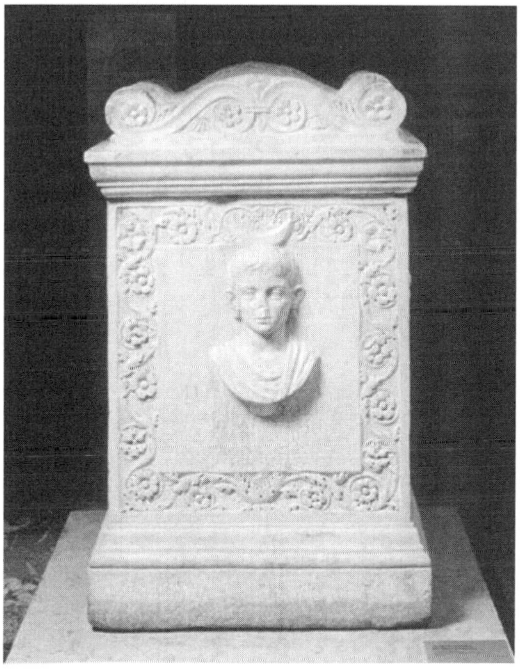

22. Roman funerary altar of *Julia Victorina,* marble, h. 1.14 m, *c.* AD 70–80 (Paris, Musée du Louvre)

E. D'Ambra: 'The Calculus of Venus: Nude Portraits of Roman Matrons,' *Sexuality in Ancient Art*, ed. N. B. Kampen (Cambridge 1996), pp. 219–32
D. Kleiner and S. B. Matheson, eds: *I, Claudia: Women in Ancient Rome* (New Haven 1996)
S. Walker and M. Bierbrier: *Ancient Faces: Mummy Portraits from Roman Egypt* (London 1997)
R. R. R. Smith: 'Cultural Choice and Political Identity in Honorific Portrait Statues and the Greek East in the Second Century AD', *J. Roman Stud.*, lxxxvii (1998), pp. 56–93
D. Kleiner and S. B. Matheson, eds: *I, Claudia II: Women in Roman Art and Society* (Austin, TX, 2000)
K. Olson: '*Matrona* and Whore: The Clothing of Women in Roman Antiquity,' *Fashion Theory*, vi (2002), pp. 387–420
E. D'Ambra: *Roman Women* (Cambridge 2006)

(d) Roman copies of Greek statuary. Roman copies of Greek statuary are prominent due to the sheer quantity of their production. The statues, known as *Idealplastik* (that is works of Greek mythological figures and athletes), adorned temples, theatres, gardens and houses, among other sites. Despite the ubiquity of this work in the archaeological record, it has not received serious scholarly consideration for its own merits until recently. Previous generations of scholars sought to recover the lost Greek masterworks that they thought the Roman statues reflected. They developed the method of *Kopienkritik*, which entailed comparative study of statues of the same subject (gods, heroes etc) in order to retrieve the original. Deviations from what they deduced was the norm of the Greek model were considered to be errors on the part of Roman sculptors. Supported only by a few literary sources on the Greek canon, these studies disdained the Roman evidence at hand by its very terminology, i.e. copy, reproduction, imitation and valourized, that is the notion of the superiority of Greek artistic practice (identified with the original, the masterwork and the authority of famous artists, such as Polykleitos, Pheidias and Praxiteles etc). A prodigious scholarly enterprise was thus devoted to the description and analysis of statues that no longer exist. That the so-called copies were made by Roman artists for Roman patrons and contexts was of little interest until recently.

The Roman market for Greek copies. The older scholarship acknowledged the Roman appetite for Greek art, which first arrived as war booty during the Roman expansion into the eastern Mediterranean in the 3rd-1st centuries BC. It was thought that the Roman élite were of two minds about such imports: one group embraced them and displayed the splendid objects to advance their prestige, while others feared the corrupting influence of foreign and decadent products (*see* COLLECTION AND DISPLAY OF ART, §I, 2). The debate was probably more complex than the polarized and moralizing rhetorical stances found in the literary sources. The intellectual arguments, however, did not stop Romans from acquiring Hellenic works of art, either originals or in the form of reproductions. It is clear that statues from the Greek repertory formed part of the décor of Roman civic and domestic space after the introduction of Greek art during the wars of imperial conquest. Romans sought out marble muses and discus-throwers by commissioning sculptors to produce them. The market in copies was initially spurred by the importation of war spoils but far surpassed it in volume and creative energy.

This vast enterprise required technical expertise. Sculpture is copied through the pointing process (*see* §(iii)(d) below). Taking measurements from at least three fixed points on a plaster cast of the original and from the same three points on the marble block, the sculptor proceeds to make the copy. The points were assumed to have been transferred to the block by a pointing device; in the late 18th century a pointing machine was developed, but the Roman version was probably far simpler. The copy would be more faithful to the original if more points were marked. In 1954 a cache of fragmented ancient plaster casts found in Baiae, a resort in southern Italy near Naples, seemed to provide evidence for the mechanical process of pointing. Although this has been questioned, the casts' subject-matter of famous Greek statues appears to support the goals of *Kopienkritik* with its quest for the lost masterwork.

Roman contributions to the Greek canon. A closer study of the field of Roman copies, however, reveals discrepancies among the corpus of ideal statuary and the claims of the traditional scholarship of the *Kopienkritik*. First of all, the often-cited literary passages on taste and patronage predate most of the sculpture in question and, thus, have little to say about their specific historical contexts. Secondly, most of the ideal statues are not exact replicas of well-known Greek prototypes, but rather, are loose interpretations of their subjects that refer only generally to the Hellenic past and allow for the creative engagement of the Roman artist. Furthermore, there is no evidence for a pointing device in antiquity to provide for the methodical and exacting precision of making an exact replica. In fact patrons in the late Republic, such as Cicero, were not interested in specific masterworks but rather in sculpture that they thought was appropriate for certain settings (e.g. the gymnasium). Thirdly, replication of statue types was a valuable device for Roman patrons to convey messages or to create distinct environments, because a series of works could reiterate a moralizing exemplum in state reliefs or present playful variations on a theme in a villa or garden. Repetition in this manner did not connote a lack of imagination or resources nor did it indicate that the prototype was a Greek work (in many cases, the source of the series was Roman rather than Greek). The APOLLO BELVEDERE (Rome, Vatican, Mus. Pio-Clementino) is no longer considered to be a Greek copy after the artist Leochares, but a Roman creation of the 2nd century AD. In all, the current state of research looks to the Roman context and meanings of ideal statues that functioned quite independently of Greek precedents (some of which were more explicitly evoked than others). The cultural heritage of the Greeks was construed rather differently for ancient Romans of the high Empire than it was for 20th-century archaeologists and art historians in Europe and North America.

A case in point is a sculpture, the so-called *Youth* (or *Athlete*) by STEPHANOS, a student of Pasiteles, the south Italian Greek artist and art historian (*c.* 50 BC; Rome, Villa Albani, 906). It bears certain characteristics of the Greek Severe style of the early 5th century BC, although it is mannered in comparison. Reproduced in nine statues, three statuary groups and five heads, the Stephanos *Youth* evidently wielded influence, yet the work did not have a pedigree in one particular work of Greek sculpture, but was produced from a freehand interpretation of several models. Stephanos appears to have been well-versed in the canon of Greek sculpture and was confident enough to make selections based on his own criteria of values and his own, perhaps highly personalized or idiosyncratic, understanding of Greek practice. Recently, scholars have pointed out that such artists aimed to emulate or even rival their predecessors. They were not passively following age-old tradition, but taking possession of it by creatively altering or adapting it to new forms and uses. The alleged failures of the Roman copyist are recast in terms of the critical reassessment of the Greek achievement by Roman artists. Given the post-modern fascination with appropriation and disenchantment with artists/authors and original works, the field of Roman ideal sculpture provides rich insight into the aesthetics and culture of the Empire.

A. Furtwängler: *Meisterwerke der griechischen Plastik: Kunstgeschichtliche Untersuchungern* (Leipzig 1893)

G. Lippold: *Kopien und Umbildungen griechischer Statuen* (Munich 1923)

P. Zanker: *Klassisistiche Statuen: Studien zur Veränderung des Kunstgeschmacks in der römischen Kaiserzeit* (Mainz, 1974)

R. Haskell and N. Penny: *Taste and the Antique: The Lure of Classical Sculpture, 1550–1900* (New Haven, 1981)

M. Marvin: 'Copying in Roman Sculpture: The Replica Series', *Retaining the Original,* ed. K. Preciado (Washington, DC, 1989), pp. 29–45

B. S. Ridgway: *Roman Copies of Greek Sculpture: The Problem of the Originals* (Ann Arbor, 1994)

E. Gazda: 'Roman Sculpture and the Ethos of Emulation: Reconsidering Repetition', *Harvard Studies of Classical Philology,* xlvii (1995), pp. 121–56

M. Marvin: 'Roman Sculptural Reproductions or Polykleitos. The Sequel', *Sculpture and its Reproductions,* eds. A. Hughes and M. Marvin (London, 1997), pp. 7–28

E. Gazda, ed.: *The Ancient Art of Emulation* (Ann Arbor, 2002), pp. 1–24

E. Perry: *The Aesthetics of Emulation in the Visual Arts of Ancient Rome* (Cambridge, 2005)

(iii) Materials and Techniques.

(a) Materials. (b) Tools and painting. (c) Moulding and casting. (d) Models and copying.

(a) Materials. The materials of Roman sculpture embodied the immense mineral and material wealth of the Roman world. For private commissions almost anything and everything was used, singly or in combination, from wax to gold inset with gems. Public dedications respected a hierarchy largely based on Greek precedent and intrinsic cost, modified by some particularly Roman sensibilities. For IVORY AND BONE and TERRACOTTA see separate entries.

Wood. Major statuary in wood, a traditional material at Rome before the Empire, was an early victim of increasing wealth. Although old wooden cult figures might be venerated for as long as they lasted, the latest recorded new dedications at Rome are two cult statues in cypress for the Temple of Juno on the Capitoline Hill in 207 BC and another two for the Temple of Veiovis in 193 BC. Wooden sculpture (in oak, box, limewood, yew, cypress, cedar or ebony) certainly continued to be produced but mainly in the smaller towns of the Empire and in the countryside. Two roughly shaped portrait busts have been found at Herculaneum (mid-1st century AD; Naples, Mus. Archeol. N.). Other rare survivals include 300 oak ex-votos from Montbouy, the sanctuary at the source of the River Craon (Orléans, Mus. Hist. & Archéol. Orléanais); an over-life-size oak statue of the god *Silvanus* (Geneva, Mus. A. & Hist.), which once marked the entrance to the Roman harbour of Geneva; and a seated cult statue of *Jupiter* with traces of its original paint, from the Faiyum in Egypt (2nd–3rd century AD; Alexandria, Gr.-Roman Mus., 23352).

Bronze. The Romans were well acquainted with small bronze sculptures from early times, through their Etruscan neighbours. In the 3rd and 2nd centuries BC supplies of metal increased vastly, together with Greek craftsmen specialized in the art of casting large-scale statuary. In the 1st century BC bronze was probably more widely used than any other material, for public and private commissions alike (cult statues, honorary, commemorative and votive portrait statues, and much of the statuary that decorated houses, gardens, fountains and palaestrae). Although its importance for cult purposes was regularly challenged by materials of yet higher intrinsic value, namely silver, ivory and gold (and marble came to equal if not actually surpass it in popularity for more general use), bronze remained a significant medium until the end of the Roman Empire. It was especially favoured for colossal statues, for figures on horseback (e.g. the gilded bronze *Marcus Aurelius*), and other particularly large and complicated works, such as victorious emperors in chariots drawn by four or six horses or elephants, often gilded, which surmounted triumphal arches.

White marble. This developed slowly as a Roman sculptural medium but eventually became the most widespread and typical medium of all. The homelands of marble carving were Greece, the Aegean islands and the western coast of Turkey, and in the last two centuries BC those were also the only regions producing the raw material (*see also* ARCHITECTURE, §VI, 1(ii)(a)). Roman officials and merchants in the East became enthusiastic patrons, but supplies of marble for commissions elsewhere were limited. It was not until the establishment of the Principate under Augustus (27 BC) that marble started to become available in quantity in the West. The emperors of the 1st century AD took many quarries under their direct control and invested huge amounts of manpower and other resources in quarrying and providing for long-distance transport. By the beginning of the 2nd century AD white and greyish marble, from varying sources, was a common commodity in cities all around the Mediterranean basin, a potent symbol of empire and the benevolence of imperial rule.

Parian marble, from the island of Paros in the Cyclades, had been the most renowned marble among the Greeks. Of supreme sculptural quality, it retained its special prestige in the Roman period. There were two grades: one, with fine crystals, highly translucent and mostly only available in small blocks, was called lychnites; the other was hardly less translucent but had much larger crystals and could be quarried in enormous blocks.

Pentelic marble takes its name from the principal earlier Greek quarries on Mt Pentelikon, although the Romans opened various new quarries in the mountains of Attica near Athens. A finely crystalled stone, translucent white and rather prone to micaceous faults, together with Parian it was a mainstay of the statuary marble trade until the late 1st century AD. It is not quite so commonly found outside Greece thereafter, perhaps because the quarrying ran into difficulties or because there were so many other good alternatives.

LUNA marble, from the Apuan Alps in Italy (near modern Carrara), was quarried on a grand scale from the mid-1st century BC, probably initiated by Julius Caesar, and supplied a high proportion of the marble used in the western Mediterranean provinces during the first three centuries AD. The usual Roman statuary grades were finely crystalled, rather dull whites, often distinctly greyish in tone but of excellent workability.

Dokimeion marble, from Baçakale in west central Turkey, is a finely crystalled warm white stone quarried alongside the more famous purple-and-white variegated Phrygian marble (see below). Dokimeion white was widely used for statuary and sarcophagi in its own and neighbouring regions and is also found in considerable quantities at Rome.

Thasian marble, from the island of Thasos in the northern Aegean, is a brilliant white with large scintillating crystals. It was much used in Greece and Italy from the mid 1st-century AD to the late 2nd.

Another large and presumably imperially operated source in the East was the island of Prokonnesos in the Sea of Marmara, north-west Turkey. Its medium-coarse crystalled greyish white and banded grey-white marbles were widely employed locally and (at least from the early 2nd century AD to the 4th) also at Rome and in the West, though mainly for architecture and sarcophagi rather than statuary. Other prolific sources of white marble in Turkey, such as Belevi near Ephesos and in the Maeander Valley, notably Aphrodisias, were exploited for predominantly local uses, though some of the stone reached wider markets both at home and abroad. Smaller privately or imperially operated regional quarries were also opened at Hippo Regius and Filfila, both on the Algerian coast; at Saint Béat in the Pyrenees (Haute Garonne); in various parts of Spain, such as Almadén de la Plata, Macael (Almería) and Antequera (Seville); and at Alto Alentejo (Estremoz) in Portugal.

There were few sculptural purposes for which marble was not generally sought after (equestrian and chariot groups, for example, were usually in bronze; see above) and extant works can be counted in their thousands. Initial difficulties of supply (and occasional later shortcomings) are witnessed by the number of works composed of several blocks. The pieces may be of the same kind or two or more different kinds of white marble, carefully joined to achieve statuary of the desired size and type. White limestone was an acceptable substitute among those who could not obtain marble. Grave reliefs commissioned by freedmen at Rome in the 1st centuries BC and AD were often made of the local limestone (travertine, from near Tibur (Tivoli)). Some regions (e.g. northern Greece, northern Italy) developed long traditions of funerary sculpture in their local white stones. White plaster (gypsum) was another cheaper alternative, especially in the dry climates of Egypt and North Africa. Plaster was also quite often used for portable indoor sculpture.

Coloured marbles and other stones. The exotic self-coloured stones sawn into thin slabs to veneer floors and walls, or quarried as monolithic column shafts, were occasionally carved into figural sculpture. The obvious precedents for the practice are in ancient Egypt, the traditions of which the Romans clearly recognized and respected, but Roman sculptural uses of coloured stones were by no means confined to Egyptian themes. The works concerned tend to be of extremely high quality and constitute one of the more original aspects of Roman art. A high proportion appear to have been imperial commissions for major public monuments at Rome, for the great imperial palaces and villas in and around the city, or for imperial benefactions elsewhere. The emperors, who owned and operated most of the quarries and thus presumably had first call on available supplies, may have exercised their rights still further in order to restrict access to others, turning all large-scale statuary in coloured stones into a particular symbol of imperial prestige.

Red porphyry from the mountains of the Eastern Desert of Egypt (Mons Porphyrites) had not been quarried by the Egyptians themselves. Its imperial purple colour made it particularly appropriate for the draped statues of the goddess Roma and emperors wearing the toga, whose heads and exposed arms were inserted in white marble. The emperors of the late Empire sometimes had themselves portrayed completely in red porphyry (see fig. 40 below) and some were buried in red porphyry sarcophagi.

Red marble from Cape Tainaron (Matapan, Greece) and Iasos (south-west Turkey) is wine-red in colour and, perhaps simply by an association of ideas, was used for statues of Bacchus, the god of wine, and the Fauns, his youthful drinking companions. Small pieces are found used for decorative Bacchic herms.

Purple-and-white variegated Phrygian marble was quarried far inland in central Turkey alongside white Dokimeion (see above). Some statues of Marsyas, hanging flayed and bleeding from a tree, exploited the stone to realistic colour effect. By virtue of its provenance, however, it also signified deities and mythological figures of specifically Phrygian or more generally Oriental origin, such as Attis, Ganymede, Mithras, Orpheus and Paris. When carved into captive prisoners wearing barbarian dress it could represent Roman military triumphs in the eastern Empire. After his Parthian victory in 14 BC the Emperor Augustus dedicated in the precinct of the Temple of Apollo on the Palatine in Rome a great tripod supported by three kneeling captives in Phrygian marble (Naples, Mus. Archeol. N., and Copenhagen, Ny Carlsberg Glyp.). According to Pausanias (*Guide to Greece* I.xviii.8) another tripod of the same sort was dedicated in the Temple of Olympian Zeus at Athens. Later, the decoration of Trajan's Forum at Rome (AD 106–12), built with the proceeds of the spoils from campaigns in Dacia (now Romania), included colossal figures of Dacian prisoners carved in Phrygian marble (as well as red-and-green porphyry and black marble).

Black marbles and limestones quarried in Egypt, Turkey, Tunisia and Greece also had many different uses. One of the earliest known examples is a monument set up in 91 BC by King Bocchus I of Mauretania on the Capitoline Hill in Rome to celebrate the surrender of his rival King Jugurtha of Numidia to the Roman general Sulla, in which Bocchus himself took a hand. The protagonists were triumphantly represented in gold, and the significance enhanced by mounting the group on a base composed of blocks of black limestone from Numidia (now Tunisia), carved with figures of Victory and trophies in relief (Rome, Mus. Nuo.). The black marble used for some of the colossal Dacian prisoners from Trajan's Forum in Rome probably came from Greece. There are also some realistic black stone portrait heads of negroes and native Libyans, the original contexts of which are unknown, set in busts or bodies of white marble or other coloured stones. From temples and sanctuaries of the egyptianizing goddess Isis and Isis-Fortuna come statues in black and dark-grey stone (which may or may not be Egyptian in origin), with the exposed parts of the head, arms and feet inserted in white marble, representing not only the deity herself but also the priests and priestesses who administered the cult.

Yellow Numidian limestone from Simitthus (now Chemtou, Tunisia) was realistically employed for animal sculpture, notably lions and leopards, the latter with their spots inset in black marble. There are also some small herms with Bacchic heads carved in Numidian yellow. Alternatively, on a grand scale in triumphal monuments it could, like Phrygian purple marble for the East, be carved into figures of captive 'barbarians' signifying Roman military achievements in the West.

'Bekhen' stone, called 'basanite' by the Romans, quarried from the Wadi Hammamat in the Eastern Desert of Egypt, is a rather special case. Either brownish black or very dark green in colour, it was likened to iron by Pliny the elder (*Natural History* XXXVI.58). The ancient Egyptians had long used it for images of their gods and pharaohs, and the Romans often chose the stone for statues of the same (or Romanized versions of) Egyptian gods, Roman emperors as pharaohs and personifications of the River Nile. (Roman sculptural use of the rose pink granite from Aswan appears to have been almost entirely dictated by its Egyptian precedents.) However, other finds suggest that bekhen stone ranked high as a material in its own right. Two colossal statues of *Hercules* and *Bacchus* (Parma, Mus. N. Ant.) were once part of a set of 12 that adorned the throne room of the imperial palace on the Palatine Hill in Rome. Some villas around Rome could boast large bekhen-stone vases decorated with Bacchic motifs. In addition, there are some exceptionally fine examples of statues of idealized naked youths and a headless draped female statue, perhaps portraying the Empress Livia as imperial priestess (Rome, Mus. Capitolino, 1882).

Green porphyry, often but erroneously termed 'serpentine', was quarried in quantity in the mountains south of Sparta in Greece and highly prized for veneer. Fragments of colossal Dacian prisoners from Rome (Rome, F. Zeri priv. col.) are as yet unique examples of its use for large-scale sculpture. It is possible that the quarries could rarely supply sufficiently large blocks. An impressive statue of a hound from the Gardens of Maecenas on the Esquiline Hill in Rome (Rome, Mus. Conserv., 1110) is carved in real serpentine, from Wadi Atollah, near Wadi Hammamat, in Egypt.

Variegated white-green marble from Karystos (Euboia, Greece), ubiquitous in paving and veneer, was probably very difficult to carve into free-standing sculpture, being prone to split along the micaceous veins that give it its colour. A rare instance is an admirably life-size and lifelike crocodile from Hadrian's Villa at Tibur (Tivoli, Mus. N. Archeol., Villa Adriana, 2326).

Coloured alabasters were also used by the Romans. The individual sources of the many different red, yellow, brown and variegated alabasters are uncertain, but they most probably came from Turkey, Egypt, Tunisia and Algeria. Some 3rd-century AD white marble portrait heads of wealthy aristocratic or imperial ladies have brown alabaster 'wigs' (e.g. Copenhagen, Ny Carlsberg Glyp., 773a). A colossal seated figure of *Minerva* (Rome, Mus. N. Romano, 124 495), whose draped body was made of golden yellow alabaster, the hair in black marble, the face, hands and exposed foot in white Luna marble, possibly evoked a Classical Greek prototype in gold and ivory.

Silver. Practically every province of the Empire produced some silver, but by far the most important mines, from the 2nd century BC until the 2nd century AD, were in southern Spain. The amounts of silver pouring into Rome in the last two centuries BC and the early 1st century AD were such that it may have been as common as, and so almost rated on a par with, bronze. Sculpture in the round ranged from miniatures of intricate detail to huge works: the silver images melted down by Augustus (see below) included equestrian statues and a chariot drawn by four horses. By the 2nd century AD, however, supplies of Spanish silver were declining and values rose accordingly. Substantial silver sculptures mentioned by ancient writers or recorded in inscriptions (stating the weight of silver) are all either gods or members of the imperial family. A life-size silver bust of the Emperor Lucius Verus (*reg* AD 161–9) was found with the Marengo Hoard (Turin, Mus. Ant.). In the early 3rd century AD supplies apparently began to increase again, from unknown sources, and silver returned to more widespread private use. A fine silver portrait bust of a man, dating from the mid-3rd century AD, was discovered in a Roman town house in southern France (Vaison-la-Romaine, Mus. Archéol.). Silver was particularly characteristic of wealthy aristocratic private tastes in the 4th and 5th centuries AD.

Gold. In addition to occasional inputs of enormous amounts of gold booty, Roman gold was obtained from Asia (Armenia, Colchis, the Hermos, Pattolos and Oxus rivers), Africa (Ethiopia), northern Greece and northern Italy, the Iberian peninsula, France, Switzerland, Britain and Dacia. Most Mediterranean peoples, including the Romans, associated the indestructible properties of gold with the gods. Throughout the Roman period most of the gold statues mentioned by ancient writers or recorded in dedicatory inscriptions are major cult statues in temples. In the kingdoms of the Hellenistic East, however, it had also come to be associated with mortals who claimed regal or divine powers. In Republican Rome any such connection was politically sensitive, though exceptions were readily made in the case of military triumphs and, in time, gold portraiture was pragmatically condoned in private: at the end of the 1st century AD Regulus, a wealthy Roman senator who commissioned portraits of his dead son in gold (as well as silver, ivory, bronze, marble and wax), was considered by his peers to be lamentably ostentatious, not dangerous. By then, portrait statues in gold set up in public were the recognized preserve of the emperors, depending on whether they cultivated or rejected divine honours during their lifetimes. Augustus was proud of having ordered 80 public statues of himself in silver to be melted down, the proceeds going to gold offerings not to himself but to Apollo in the temple on the Palatine. Caligula (*reg* AD 37–41), Nero and Domitian, on the other hand, expressly ordered public images of themselves in gold and silver, Domitian dictating that on the Capitoline Hill in Rome they should be of nothing else. His successor Nerva (*reg* AD 96–8), however, refused to be portrayed anywhere in any precious metal. The politically stable emperors of the 2nd century AD were probably less concerned one way or the other. The one sizeable surviving example of Roman sculpture in sheet gold is a bust of *Marcus Aurelius*, a provincial work found and probably made at Avenches, Switzerland (*c.* AD 161–80).

Many statues were not composed of solid or sheet gold but were made of other materials and gilded or covered in gold leaf of varying thickness, with the same basic connotations as the real thing. Pliny the elder noted (*Natural History* XXXIII.61) that especially thick gold leaf was called 'praenestine', after the cult figure of Fortuna Primigenia at Praeneste in Italy. Small cult images of Sol and Mithras in gilded terracotta and gilded plaster (gypsum) have survived from Rome, and southern Russia has produced examples in wood. Bronze statues of deities, especially Hercules, Bacchus, Apollo and Athena, and deified dead or divine living emperors, might be completely or selectively gilded, enhancing the eyes in particular. Gold leaf was also glued to the hair, eyes and details of the dress of cult figures in marble, the combination perhaps imitating works in ivory and gold.

Other. Numerous other materials, and combinations of materials, are known. Small sculptures in amber and rock crystal, to be held in the hand, have been found at Pompeii (Naples, Mus. Archeol. N.). Realistic metal attachments such as diadems, earrings, finger-rings, bracelets, armlets, weapons and helmets, variously in gold, silver or bronze, were made to works in marble and stone. The eyes of statues in all materials could be inlaid in ivory or fine white limestone and hardstones or coloured glass paste, sometimes with eyelashes of silver or bronze. One remarkable Roman work found at Amman and representing *Daedalus and Icarus* (*c.* AD 200; Amman, Jordan Archaeol. Mus.) stretched marble beyond its otherwise possible structural limits by providing the stone limbs with internal metal rods, presumably of bronze or iron.

Pliny the elder: *Natural History* XXXIV.1–99 (bronze); XXXVI.14–43 (white marble); IV.67, V.22, XXXVI.44–63 (coloured marble); XXX.95–8, 151–8 (silver); XXXIII.12–81 (gold)
R. Delbrueck: *Antike Porphyrwerke* (Berlin, 1936)
G. Bendinelli: *Il tesoro di argenteria di Marengo* (Turin, 1937)
A. Grenier: *Manuel d'archéologie gallo-romaine*, II/ii (Paris, 1938), p. 568, pl. 184; IV/ii (Paris, 1960), pp. 730–32
M. Wegner: 'Die Herrscherbildnisse in antonischer Zeit', *Das römische Herrscherbild*, II/iv (Berlin, 1939), p. 278
P. Schatzmann: 'Buste en or représentant l'empereur Marc-Aurèle trouvé à Avenches', *Z. Schweiz. Archäol. & Kstgesch.*, ii/2 (1940), pp. 69–93
J. Iliffe: 'A Heroic Statue from Philadelphia-Amman', *Studies Presented to D. M. Robinson*, i (St Louis, 1951), pp. 705–12
J. Sautel: 'Le Buste en argent de Vaison', *Mnmts Piot*, xlvii (1953), pp. 149–52
P. Reutersward: *Studien zur Polychromie der Plastik: Griechenland und Rom* (Stockholm, 1960), pp. 143–59
R. Gnoli: *Marmora romana* (Rome, 1971, rev. 2/1988)
H. W. Müller: *Il culto di Iside nell'antica Benevento* (Benevento, 1971)
T. Hölscher: 'Römische Siegesdenkmäler der später Republik', *Taina: Roland Hampe zum 70. Geburtstag* (Mainz, 1980), pp. 351–71
R. Meiggs: *Trees and Timber in the Ancient Mediterranean World* (Oxford, 1982), pp. 300–24

J. Maier: *Genavae Augustae: Les Inscriptions romaines de Génève* (Geneva, 1983), p. 9, pl. 1

R. M. Schneider: *Bunte Barbaren: Orientalenstatuen aus farbigem Marmor in der römischen Repräsentationskunst* (Worms, 1986)

M. Cisneros: *Marmoles hispanos: Su empleo en la España romana* (Saragossa, [1988])

J. C. Fant, ed.: *Ancient Marble Quarrying and Trade*, Brit. Archaeol. Rep. (Oxford, 1988)

N. Herz and M. Waelkens, eds: *Classical Marble: Geochemistry, Technology, Trade* (Dordrecht, 1988)

L. Lazzarini: 'Rosso Antico and Other Red Marbles Used in Antiquity: A Characterization Study', *Marble: Art Historical and Scientific Perspectives on Ancient Sculpture* (Malibu, 1990), pp. 237–51

R. M. Schneider: 'Kolossale Dakerstatuen aus grünem Porphyr', *Mitt. Dt. Archäol. Inst.: Röm. Abt.*, xcvii (1990), pp. 235–60

C. C. Mattusch: *Classical Bronzes: The Art and Craft of Greek and Roman Statuary* (Ithaca, 1996)

M. Fischer: *Marble Studies: Roman Palestine and the Marble Trade* (Konstanz, 1998)

(b) Tools and painting. Marble sculptors in the Roman world used the same limited but versatile range of tools as their Greek predecessors: iron-headed picks, pick-hammers, hand-forged iron chisels (pointed, claw or toothed, bull-nosed and flat) of varying lengths and weights struck with iron-headed hammers also of varying weights, and drills, rasps and abrasives. The iron was mainly a low-carbon steel and the marks left on unfinished sculptures attest to skilful tempering. The great increase in the numbers of craftsmen at work in the Empire led to the development of many regional variations in carving method (i.e. the amount of stone that sculptors attempted to remove with a particular type of tool as the work progressed from roughing-out to the final finishing) and technique (the way in which each tool was handled to achieve the desired result). Approaches to free-standing figures, probably in the interest of speed, display a tendency to work primarily from the front and side views, leaving the back as a reserve of solid stone, which was then often left only broadly shaped in the finished work. Roman marble sculptors also became very adept at making a statue out of several pieces of stone, joined with the aid of iron dowels and powerful adhesives.

All Roman carving methods started with pointed tools (pick-hammers or pointed chisels) of different sizes depending on the quantity of stone to be removed in relation to the size of the overall work, and progressed to lighter, finer points as the shaping advanced. Individual techniques ranged from densely grouped single vertical blows (especially when working over convex shapes) to long low strokes at carefully judged parallel intervals (when dressing off flat surfaces). The bulk was done with the point of the tool hitting the stone at about 40°. Some sculptors continued to use pointed chisels to an advanced stage of definition, changing only briefly to claw chisels (with four or five rounded teeth), to prepare their point-worked surfaces for the more delicate edged chisels (flat or slightly curved) with which they would pursue the final detail. There is no sign of the two- or three-toothed chisels that characterize Renaissance and later practice. In fact, many ancient Roman sculptors did not use claw chisels at all, but changed over from pointed chisels directly to bull-nosed chisels, or to strong cross-cut flat chisels. These were handled in long parallel strokes, clarifying the forms as an intermediary between roughing-out and definitive carving, before switching to normal edged chisels for the details.

Strap-drills were used in the course of the major carving, to pierce large gaps or produce deep channels (first as a series of single holes placed close together, later worked into a continuous line with chisels) and to achieve special effects in the finished work. The drills had solid blade-shaped bits (w. 2–15 mm) or larger tubular bits, and were operated with a bow by the sculptor himself, or with a longer thong drawn back and forth by an assistant. Roman drillwork of the 2nd century AD, exemplified by the techniques employed in rendering hair and beards in portraiture, could be highly imaginative. Many sculptors were capable of obtaining a variety of sophisticated effects by bracing the point of the drill at an angle against the stone to produce short curving channels rather than single holes.

The quality of the finish subsequently sought with fine flat chisels, rasps and abrasives depended on the nature and extent of the paint that was to be applied. Few works still preserve traces of their original polychromy, but the treatment appears to have varied according to subject-matter and level of patronage. Clothing, hair, details of the eyes, eyelashes, mouth, nostrils and other attributes would be picked out in colour, sometimes just in red, more often in bright combinations of red, pink, black, brown, blue, yellow or gold. The pigments were probably the same as those used in wall painting, with a coating of wax to protect them. Human flesh was generally left unpainted in the natural colour of the marble: in the 1st century AD flesh surfaces were carefully smoothed, using emery or pumice; by the 2nd century they were often given a high polish (method unknown). In the 2nd and 3rd centuries it also became customary to incise irises and pupils, probably not instead of paint but to enhance the intended gaze and preserve it in the event of repainting.

P. Reuterswärd: *Studien zur Polychromie der Plastik: Griechenland und Rom* (Stockholm, 1960), pp. 181–247

A. Claridge: 'Sulla lavorazione dei marmi bianchi nella scultura dell'età romana', *Marmi antichi: Problemi d'impiego, di restauro e d'identificazione*, ed. P. Pensabene (Rome, 1985, 2/1993), pp. 113–25

P. Rockwell: *Lavorare la pietra* (Rome, 1989), pp. 117–125; Eng. trans. as *The Art of Stoneworking: A Reference Guide* (Cambridge, 1993), pp. 109–16

A. Claridge: 'Ancient Techniques of Making Joins in Marble Statuary', *Marble: Art Historical and Scientific Perspectives on Ancient Sculpture* (Malibu, 1990), pp. 135–54

P. Rockwell: 'Finish and Unfinish in the Carving of the Sebastcion', *Aphrodisias Papers: Recent Work on Architecture and Sculpture*, ed. C. Roueché and K. Erim (Ann Arbor, 1990), pp. 111–18

(c) Moulding and casting. Roman metal sculptors used several moulding and casting techniques derived from their Greek and Etruscan precursors. The principal steps in the making of a bronze statue were preparing a mould, melting and casting the metal and finishing the cast. Various types of mould were employed. Open moulds were made by carving the form of the object to be cast in a slab of stone or refractory clay, and pouring molten metal into the depression: such moulds were suitable only for simple one-sided objects or relief plaques. Bivalve moulds consisted of a pair of carved slabs fastened together, with a canal or opening at one end for pouring in the metal. Moulds of this type were reusable and employed in manufacturing utensils and simple sculptural ornaments.

Free-standing bronze sculptures, however, were normally produced by the lost-wax process from clay moulds. The simplest moulds were made by fashioning a solid wax model and packing the clay around it while leaving an opening at one end. After the clay had hardened the wax was removed by heating, leaving a cavity into which the molten metal was poured. This solid casting technique was used only for figurines or the separately cast parts of larger statues (e.g. locks of hair or extended fingers). More elaborate statues were hollow cast from clay moulds equipped with clay cores. A rough form of the model was made by applying clay on to an iron support. A layer of wax was added and modelled to give the final form of the sculpture. On top of this went the clay mould proper, secured by iron or bronze pins (chaplets) inserted into the core. A system of branched wax rods projecting through the mould created canals into which the molten bronze was poured and through which air and vapours could escape. After casting, the clay mould was chiselled away. Fragments of a mould of this type have been found together with other traces of bronze foundering near Gestingthorpe, England. In this direct lost-wax technique, since both the model and the mould were destroyed in casting, a casting mishap required that the whole process had to be repeated. This danger was avoided, by the Romans as by the Greeks, by the indirect lost-wax technique (*see* §IV, 1(iv)(c) above), in which clay models were employed to prepare reusable plaster auxiliary moulds or master moulds, although the direct technique seems to have been retained for casting smaller parts such as locks of hair and attributes.

The processes of casting and finishing, in furnaces such as that excavated near Kaiseraugst in Switzerland, also differed little from those used by the Greeks, although the Romans intensified the practice of adding lead to lower the melting-point of the alloy and improve the workability of the cast. Separately cast parts of statues were sometimes fitted together using mortice-and-tenon joints and simply hammered together; the joints were frequently strengthened by soft-soldering using an alloy with a low melting-point. The most durable method of joining was welding, whereby molten bronze was poured into the joints. Fine details and sharp edges (e.g. locks of hair and beard) were engraved, while all other surfaces were smoothed with files and scrapers, and the whole statue was given a final polish. In the Republican and early Imperial periods the eyes of bronzes were inlaid with ivory, glass, alabaster or precious stones, but later they were simply engraved. Lips were sometimes plated with copper foil hammered into a recessed surface, while garments were sometimes decorated with silver inlay. Sometimes the entire statue was gilded with gold foil or gold-mercury amalgam.

A specialized use of plaster casts of bronze or marble statues was in the production of full-scale marble copies of famous originals. Such plaster casts could be transported to remote workshops and thus made possible the manufacture of marble copies throughout the Roman world. Although Pliny the elder (*Natural History* XXXV.153) ascribed the invention of this technique to the Greek sculptor LYSISTRATOS, it probably developed from the use of auxiliary moulds in bronze casting (*see also* §IV, 1(iv)(d) *above*). A large number of fragments of plaster casts of Greek bronzes from Baiae, Italy, show that the process involved making a mould and then pouring liquid plaster into it to obtain a cast. Lucian (*Zeus Rants* xxxiii) alluded to the use of a pitch-like material for making moulds, but extant piece-moulds (e.g. one found near Sabratha) were made by applying a piece of wet plaster to part of a statue. The edges of this piece were smoothed with the spatula, fresh plaster was applied next to it and the process was repeated over the entire statue. A second layer of plaster was applied to the outer surface of groups of piece-moulds to form removable caps. Thus the mould of a large statue was divided up into mould sections consisting of groups of piece-moulds (e.g. for the head, arms, legs and rump), each held together in a cap. After the piece-moulds were removed from the statue and reassembled in their caps, plaster was poured in and reinforced with pieces of bone, antler, reed or lead wire. Wooden or iron dowels were inserted into casts of arms and legs to facilitate mounting. Once the separately cast parts had dried they were assembled to form a full-scale plaster replica, from which a copy could be produced by transferring measurements to a marble block using the pointing technique.

K. Kluge and K. Lehmann-Hartleben: *Die antiken Grossbronzen*, 3 vols (Berlin, 1927)

G. Barone: 'I gessi di Sabratha: Anticipazioni e problemi', *Quad. Archeol. Libia*, xi (1980), pp. 35–74

Toreutik und figürliche Bronzen römischer Zeit: Akten der 6. Tagung über antike Bronzen: Berlin, 1980

E. Formigli: 'Indagine tecnica sulla testa di Giove del Kunsthistorisches Museum (Antikensammlung) di Vienna', *Alba Regia*, xxi (1984), pp. 125–8

W.-D. Heilmeyer: 'Neue Untersuchungen am Jüngling von Salamis im Antikenmuseum Berlin', *Archäologische Bronzen, antike Kunst, moderne Technik*, ed. H. Born (Berlin, 1985), pp. 132–8

C. Landwehr: *Die antiken Gipsabgüsse aus Baiae* (Berlin, 1985)

G. Zimmer: 'Schriftquellen zum antiken Bronzeguss', *Archäologische Bronzen, antike Kunst, moderne Technik*, ed. H. Born (Berlin, 1985), pp. 38–49

G. Lahusen and E. Formigli: 'Kunst und Technik: Analysen römischer Bronzebildnisse', *Forsch. Frankfurt*, ii/3 (1987), pp. 34–9

G. C. Marini: 'Le tecniche di fabbricazione', *Bronzi dorati da Cartoceto: Un restauro* (Florence, 1987), pp. 126–9

(d) Models and copying. Model-making was a matter of professional pride among the versatile Greek sculptors who worked for wealthy patrons in Rome in the 1st century BC (Pliny the elder: *Natural History* XXXV.155–6). Their sculptural intentions were ambitious (extreme realism, complex figural compositions, displays of technical virtuosity) and they left nothing to chance. Fine metalwork in relief, bronze statuary and marble sculpture were all preceded by preliminary models in clay (*proplasmata*), sometimes conscientiously modelled from life (Pliny the elder: XXXVI.39–40). For a work to be cast in bronze or silver, the clay model was subsequently carefully converted into a full-scale, fully detailed plaster form (*exemplum e gypso*) from which the necessary moulds would be taken. Equal care was probably taken in the case of a work to be executed in marble, by producing an accurate model from which measurements could be transferred during the processes of carving. By the 2nd century AD, however, technical virtuosity in marble sculpture could mean working without a model at all, composing directly in stone and carving freehand; the most impressive demonstrations of this are the reliefs on the shaft of Trajan's Column (*see* ROME, fig. 12). Sculptural expertise was channelled into producing and reproducing works as quickly and efficiently as possible, along predictable (but not necessarily unimaginative) lines.

Models. In bronze sculpture, the most effective shortcut to production was to use an existing set of moulds, or make new moulds, from an existing work. Bronzeworkers in Athens in about AD 160 apparently repeatedly took moulds from an antique Greek bronze statue which stood in the main public square (Lucian: *Zeus Rants* xxxiii), although it is not clear whether they wished to make a replica of the whole figure or only of the torso, which they wanted to use for purposes of their own. The Roman practice of casting bronze statuary in sections made it relatively easy to combine elements moulded from different sources.

In marble, the main obstacles to using an existing work directly as the model for another were physical. Sculptors could only copy their own works, or anything that could be readily transported (e.g. two female portrait heads from Apollonia, Libya). Otherwise they had to obtain their models second-hand through the medium of plaster casts, an option that was also widely available to metalworkers. Such plaster casts (and also plaster sculpture) are well attested in the 2nd and 3rd centuries AD. The shop of one maker/supplier has been excavated at Thysdrus (now El Djem) in Tunisia, and another at Sabratha in Libya. A significant find of plaster casts from Baiae (on the Bay of Naples) includes elements of eight familiar figure-types which were frequently reproduced in marble.

New models were constantly being made, whenever a bronze had to be executed at a different scale, or something reproduced that was not accessible for plaster casts to be made, or reproduced in marble when the original model (perhaps a bronze) was not directly suitable. The greatest need was in portrait sculpture. Bust forms and bodies tended to be as conventionalized and repetitive as other forms of sculpture, but heads were expected to be individual and often highly realistic. In the best 1st-century BC Greek tradition, a portrait head was sometimes modelled first in clay from life, then cast in plaster. Alternatively, the model took shape directly in plaster or wax over a clay core, incorporating life-casts from the subject's own face (taken in two vertical halves), retouching the eyes and modelling the hair, ears and back of the head freehand. To save time and effort the hair was also sometimes a cast from another portrait of the same person or (since hairstyles were conventional rather than individual) from someone else's portrait. In funerary portraiture, a death-mask sometimes provided a cast of the whole head to behind the ears, although the cast might have had to undergo substantial modifications to make the image sufficiently lifelike for Roman tastes. The genesis of the models used for official imperial portraits (emperors and their families), reproduced all over the Roman world, was similarly varied. It is interesting that imperial portrait types in bronze are not the same as those generally found in marble: each medium had its appropriate models.

Copying. A close relationship between the model and a finished work in bronze was assured, when need be, by the casting process. In marble the operation had to be done by hand. If the model was fairly straightforward in design and the carvers had carved it many times before, they often copied it simply by eye. They may even have been able to carry some models in their heads, having learnt the basic elements of the pose or composition as part of their workshop training.

Where the model was a new one—or new to them—or where it was important to reproduce it precisely to scale, or it presented twisting, interlocking or overlapping elements which were difficult to memorize or pursue in three dimensions by simple rules of thumb, then the carvers provided themselves with some fixed measuring points. This had been done ever since the 5th century BC (*see* § IV. 1(iv)(d) above). Points (small knobs or bosses of stone left isolated on the surface as the carving advanced) can be found on many unfinished and finished Roman works of all types and periods. Sometimes only one or two points on each side of a free-standing sculpture were enough: the back of the statue of *Augustus* from Prima Porta (Rome, Vatican, Braccio Nuo., 14; for illustration *see* AUGUSTUS) has only one, in the centre. In most cases, however, the points form groups of three (e.g. on a head, two over the brow and one on the chin); some are set in closely spaced pairs, at wide intervals. An unfinished over-life-size figure of a Dacian prisoner (Rome, Vatican, Mus.

Gregoriano Profano, 10543) preserves 21 points variously placed on the front and sides. The points rarely mark significant elements of the design: they are points from which those significant elements were plotted, presumably using a ruler or triangulating dimensions within a given area of the work with the aid of callipers. How the main points were set in the first place is not known. They presumably reproduced points fixed in the same positions on the model but even that is not absolutely certain. Modern scholars have been tempted to draw parallels between the ancient evidence and that left by some of the modern (post-1760s) systems of 'pointing-off' but the resemblances are only superficial. The accuracy of the ancient system depended on the skill of the individual sculptor.

Pliny the younger: *Letters* IV.vii

C. Bluemel: *Griechische Bildhauerarbeit* (Berlin, 1927), pp. 30–32

V. Cianfarani: 'Proplasma dell'antiquario Teatino', *Boll. A.*, xxxvii/1 (1952), pp. 1–4

L. Polacco: 'Due ritratti romani da Apollonia di Cirene', *Sculture greche e romane di Cirene*, ed. C. Anti (Padua, 1959), pp. 301–29

G. M. A. Richter: 'How Were the Roman Copies of Greek Portraits Made?' *Mitt. Dt. Archäol. Inst.: Röm. Abt.*, lix (1962), pp. 52–8

G. M. A. Richter: *The Portraits of the Greeks*, 3 vols (London, 1965), i, pp. 24–8

H. Slim: 'Masques mortuaires d'El-Jem (Thysdrus)', *Ant. Afr.*, x (1976), pp. 79–92

C. Mattusch: 'The Bronze Torso in Florence: An Exact Copy of a Fifth-century BC Original', *Amer. J. Archaeol.*, lxxxii (1978), pp. 101–4

G. Barone: 'Gessi di Sabratha: Anticipazioni e problemi', *Quad. Archeol. Libia*, xi (1980), pp. 35–74

C. Landwehr: *Die antiken Gipsabgüsse aus Baiae: Griechische Bronzestatuen in Abgüssen römischer Zeit*, Archäologische Forschungen (Berlin, 1985)

L. D'Alessandro and F. Persegati: *Scultura e calchi in gesso: Storia, technica e conservazione* (Rome, 1987), pp. 18–24, 47–60

M. Pfanner: 'Über das Herstellen von Porträts: Ein Beitrag zu Rationalisierungsmassnahmen und Produktionsmechanismen von Massenware im späten Hellenismus und in der römischen Kaiserzeit', *Jb. Dt. Archäol. Inst.*, civ (1989), pp. 157–257

P. Rockwell: *Lavorare la pietra* (Rome, 1989), pp. 126–52; Eng. trans. as *The Art of Stoneworking: A Reference Guide* (Cambridge, 1993), pp. 116–26

B. S. Ridgway and J. M. Berkin: *Greek Sculpture in the Art Museum, Princeton University: Greek Originals, Roman Copies and Variants* (Princeton, 1994)

L.-A. Touchette: *The Dancing Maenad Reliefs: Continuity and Change in Roman Copies* (London, 1995)

E. Perry: *The Aesthetics of Emulation in the Visual Arts of Ancient Rome* (Cambridge and New York, 2005)

(iv) Forms.

(a) Free-standing. (b) Architectural and relief.

(a) Free-standing. Free-standing statues once decorated virtually every building in every Roman city or sanctuary of importance. Only a small fraction of these images now survives, but the evidence of their statue bases and secondary sources such as coins, paintings and literary references provide a vivid picture of the important role of free-standing sculpture in Rome. As many as 3000 statues are said to have crammed the stage of a theatre in Republican Rome (Pliny the elder: XXXIV.36) and the Forum Romanum was so popular a site for statuary dedications that it had to be periodically cleared of its bronze and marble sculptural accumulation.

Roman free-standing sculpture falls into two broad typological categories: portraits of actual persons and idealized figures. The latter category includes divinities, personifications, mythological characters and animals. Both categories served various purposes for their owners and dedicators; the Romans commissioned free-standing images as CULT STATUES, votives, honorific and funerary monuments and decorative *objets d'art.* Neither category appeared exclusively in a particular context of display and use. Public areas such as fora or theatres and private spaces such as houses or luxury villas drew upon a common repertory of statuary images for their decoration. The collections themselves often mixed sculptural genres, for example the statues found at the Villa of the Papyri in HERCULANEUM which constitute an ensemble typical in its selection if extravagant in its numbers. Free-standing sculpture often followed established principles of display. Most statues were combined with an architectural feature such as an aedicula, arch or column to create a controlled viewing environment. Secondary sources such as coins (e.g. a sestertius of Titus showing statue-filled niches in the façade of the Colosseum; London, BM) or reliefs (e.g. the *oratio* scene from the Arch of Constantine in Rome illustrating statues raised high on columns; see fig. 39 below) depict typical forms of display. The multiple figures used to fill the wall niches of theatres, nymphaea and baths were often selected and displayed in accordance with a particular thematic or formal programme.

Portraits. Like the Greeks, Romans honoured esteemed athletes, statesmen, philosophers and poets, as well as less celebrated individuals such as family members, with portraits set up in public. These portraits took the form of full-length statues, usually life-size or larger, busts and, more rarely, HERMS. In contrast to the generally idealized portraiture of the Greeks, Roman sculptors rendered their subjects with a degree of physiognomic accuracy that sometimes verges on brute realism. (This is thought to be the case even in portraits of persons who lived so long before they were sculpted that their features must be based on literary description rather than direct observation.) Facial appearance, gesture, costume and attribute conveyed the sitter's personality and his social or political rank. The bronze *Arringatore* inscribed as Aulus Metellus (early 1st century BC; Florence, Mus. Archeol.; *see* ETRUSCAN, fig. 2) publicizes his role as a municipal official by means of his toga, high-laced shoes, finger-ring and the rhetorical gesture of his outstretched arm. Like several other bronzes from the Republican period, this life-size figure was probably made by an Etruscan workshop. If the patron was Roman (or, as in this case, probably a Romanized Italian), it is correct to view the work as an expression of Roman artistic taste. Similarly, statues carved by Greek sculptors employed by Roman patrons should be regarded as Roman rather than Greek.

Another famous bronze head, identified without foundation as *Lucius Junius Brutus* (4th–2nd centuries BC; Rome, Mus. Conserv.) is thought to exemplify the traditional character of the Republican patrician: austere, grave, morally upstanding. Countless other Republican portraits extol the virtues of old age. Images such as a head of an old woman (late 1st century BC; Rome, Mus. N. Romano, 124493) or a veiled head of a man (early 1st century BC; Rome, Vatican, 1751) unflinchingly record their subjects' bald pates, blemishes and wrinkles. Because of their unflattering realism these portraits have often (but without substantiation) been interpreted as death masks. The majority probably represent portraits commissioned by Roman aristocrats to commemorate their esteemed ancestors. Such portraits are known to have been kept in the atrium of the house and displayed in public on certain occasions. The Barberini *Togatus* (see fig. 23), depicting an elderly, toga-clad man holding two male portrait busts, provides vivid testimony of their use.

During the Republic modesty of dress prevailed in portraits of both men and women. Men donned the civilian toga or military cuirass and women wore full-length tunics in layers. Under Greek influence in the 2nd century BC male portrait sitters shed their clothes. A life-size marble portrait statue from Delos (1st century BC; Athens, N. Archaeol. Mus., 1828) combines a head with realistic facial features (typically Roman) and a nearly nude, heroically posed body (typically Greek). As Roman exposure to Greek art increased during the late Republic, such Grecisms permanently altered the appearance of Roman portrait sculpture. The *Augustus* from Prima Porta (*c.* 19 BC; Rome, Vatican, Braccio Nuo.) represents a masterful union of Greek and Roman artistic traditions with its adaptation of a recognizable portrait of Augustus in formal military dress to Polykleitos' 5th-century BC *Doryphoros* (*see also* AUGUSTUS). Even at such times as the 3rd century AD when strongly anti-Classical styles prevailed, Greek classicism lingers in the heroic pose, nudity or sculptural type adopted for the portrait. So a brutally ugly face of the emperor Trebonianus Gallus (*reg* 251–3; New York, Met.) sits on top of a well-muscled nude body whose relaxed pose stems ultimately from 5th-century BC models. Similarly, 5th-century AD portraits from Aphrodisias render philosophers or statesmen according to traditional Greek formulae of costume, pose and attitude but without recourse to the idealizing impulse of earlier epochs.

Portrait subjects, particularly those belonging to the imperial circle, were ennobled through divine allusion and colossal scale. Claudius commands as

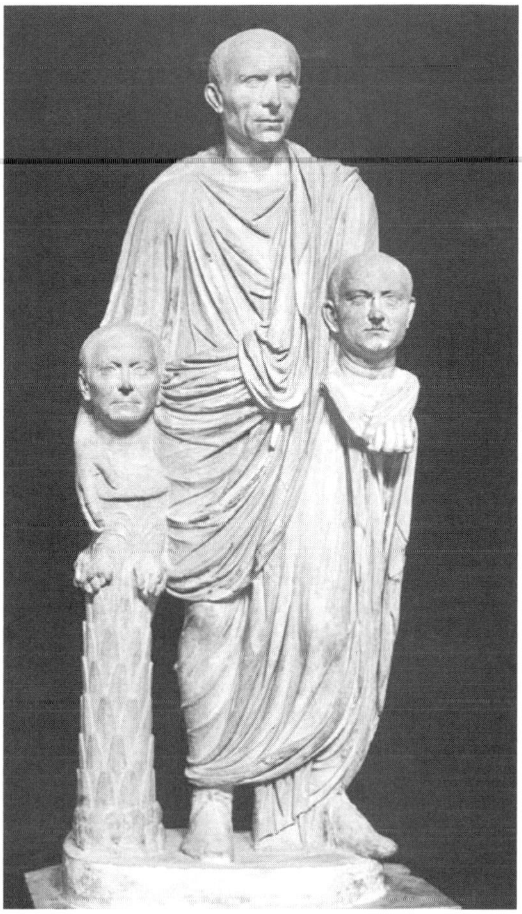

23. Barberini *Togatus*, marble, h. 1.65 m, early 1st century AD (Rome, Palazzo dei Conservatori, Braccio Nuovo)

Jupiter in a portrait from Lanuvium (AD 42; Rome, Vatican) and Commodus is assimilated to Hercules in a magnificent marble bust (*c.* AD 180–*c.* 192; Rome, Mus. Conserv.). Nero achieved superhuman status in a 120-foot gilded bronze portrait that towered in the Domus Aurea (Pliny the elder: XXXIV.45–7). Equestrian statues such as the bronze *Marcus Aurelius* physically elevated their subjects in a more restrained manner. Statues such as the Flavian lady represented as the Venus of Knidos (late 1st century AD; Copenhagen, Ny Carlsberg Glyp.) or a child portrayed as the infant Hercules strangling the snakes (late 2nd century AD, Rome, Mus. Capitolino) demonstrate how divine allusion was not the exclusive prerogative of imperial portraits. Dating primarily to the late 1st century AD and the 2nd, these funerary portraits of private individuals used divine reference to express hope for the afterlife.

Standardized 'official' portrait images for important members of the imperial circle were created in Italy and then disseminated throughout the provinces to be replicated. By erecting portrait statues of the emperor and his family a city and its institutions could express thanks (or hope) for imperial largesse. Long-reigning and respected persons such as Augustus and his wife Livia (see fig. 24) were known in hundreds of portrait images, while emperors enjoying less longevity or popularity were usually represented by a scant number. There is literary evidence that imperial statues were regarded as physical extensions of the emperor himself: defiling an imperial portrait, tantamount to an attack on the emperor's person, could be punished. Beyond their political value, imperial portraits were also important transmitters of court styles. It is not unusual to find local nobles in their funerary or honorific images adopting the coiffures and facial expressions of the reigning imperial family. Not all imperial portraits had a metropolitan style, however. Those executed in the provinces often rendered the official portrait type in accordance with prevailing artistic taste. An over-life-size granite head of *Caracalla* found at Koptos (AD 211–17; Philadelphia, U. PA, Mus.) interprets the emperor's curly locks and scowling visage in the simplified, cubic mode commonly employed in Egyptian portraits in hard stone. A gold bust of *Marcus Aurelius* (*c.* AD 161–80; Avenches, Mus. Romain) has been so schematized in accordance with local styles that its subject is recognizable only by its typologically distinctive hairstyle and beard.

Idealized statuary. In addition to making statues themselves, the Romans also commissioned images of their gods, mythic heroes and certain contemporaries such as servants or barbarians whose generic rather than specific conception did not warrant true

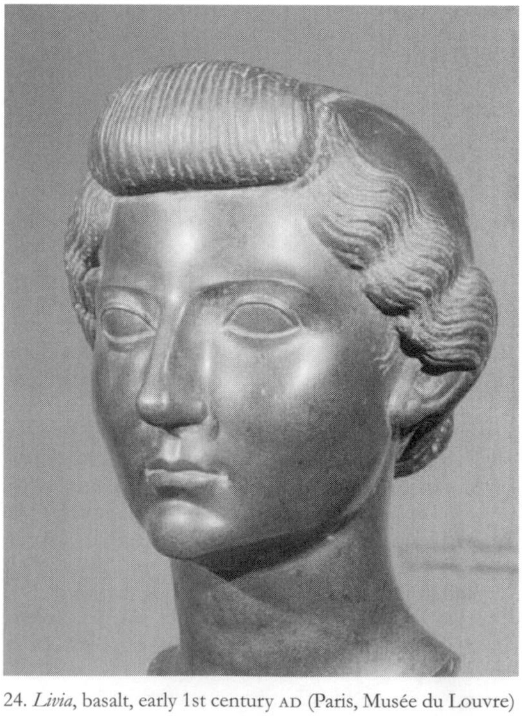

24. *Livia*, basalt, early 1st century AD (Paris, Musée du Louvre)

portrait representation. Because of their certainly Roman theme, statues of contemporaries provide unqualified evidence of the Roman conception and execution of free-standing idealized sculpture. Important examples include a bronze *camillus* (a male attendant at sacrifices, AD 40–50; Rome, Mus. Conserv.) and any of the colossal Dacians carved during the Trajanic period (e.g. AD 110; Paris, Louvre, or Naples, Mus. Archeol. N.). These works are important for expanding our view of Roman sculpture beyond portraits and historical reliefs, two genres in which the Roman sculptor is credited with an original achievement.

The first free-standing idealized images made by the Romans functioned as cult statues or votives in temples and sanctuaries. Literary sources inform us that the oldest image of a god in Rome was that of Jupiter Optimus Maximus, dedicated by Tarquinius Priscus (*reg* 616–579 BC), on the Capitoline (Pliny the elder: XXXV.157). By the 3rd century BC some 60 temples in Rome had cult statues. These images rendered the gods, who were conceived in anthropomorphic terms, as seated or standing figures. The terracotta *Hercules and Minerva* from S Omobono, Rome (6th century BC; Rome, Antiqua. Com.), although perhaps architectural sculptures rather than cult statues, illustrate the stiff frontality and archaism of the first cult images produced at Rome. A number of later cult statues in Rome were actually Greek statues plundered as booty during the 2nd century BC and early 1st. Greek in style if not actually in origin are a colossal gilded bronze *Hercules* from the Ara Maxima in the Forum Boarium (2nd century BC; Rome, Mus. Conserv.) and a female head in marble from the Largo Argentina in Rome (2nd century BC; Rome, Mus. Conserv.). The goddess Roma is represented by a colossal draped female, her left leg resting on a globe, from the Temple of Rome and Augustus at Ostia (early 1st century AD; *in situ*). Numerous cult statues of Mithras, Isis and other exotic gods are also known.

Free-standing votive statues that represent either a divinity or an offerent survive in greater numbers. Fragmentary Dioscuri with their horses from the Lacus Juturnae of the Forum Romanum probably represent a costly marble dedication of the 2nd century BC (Rome, Antiqua. Forense). Numerous other free-standing statues of gods that survive had religious functions other than strictly cultic. Lacking the over-life-size dimensions and static pose that usually define a cult statue, these images probably stood in bathhouses or villas rather than temples. Spectacular examples are the colossal statues of *Hercules* and *Bacchus* from the Domus Flavia in Rome, carved in rare green schist (late 1st century AD; Parma, Mus. N. Ant.).

An *Apollo Citharoedus* from Castelgandolfo, complete with laurel wreath, girded *peplos* and cithara, illustrates the Roman use for attributes as iconographic identifiers and narrative props. Specific costumes, hairstyles and props permitted countless iconographic permutations in an otherwise standardized repertory of ideal forms. With attributes simple idealized figures of draped women could be transformed into personifications of places (e.g. *Africa*; Lambesc, Mus. Mun.) or virtues (e.g. *Abundantia*; Madrid, Prado); mature bearded men could be distinguished as Jupiter, Poseidon, Aesculapius or Hades; and statues of beautiful young men could assume specific identities as Apollo, Hermes, Adonis or Paris. The large number of surviving images of the latter subject illustrate the Roman taste during the 1st and 2nd centuries AD for statues of slightly effeminate youths posed nude and lost in dreamy reverie, such as the Hadrianic sculptures of Antinous. A bronze boy outfitted as a lampholder (from Pompeii; Naples, Mus. Archeol. N.) and a marble *Bacchus* (Rome, Mus. N. Romano) found at Hadrian's Villa in Tibur (Tivoli) are further examples of this sculptural genre. With their hip-shot poses and sinuous contours, these statues recall works made by the 4th-century BC Greek sculptor Praxiteles. A large group of stylistically related statues found inspiration in the oeuvre of the 5th-century BC Greek sculptor Polykleitos. Statues such as the IDOLINO (Florence, Mus. Archeol.) replaced the Polykleitan ideal of hardened muscularity with pre-adolescent softness but retained distinctive Polykleitan features such as the flat and symmetrically combed hairstyle.

The *Idolino* and other Polykleitan-derived statues represent the classicizing mode of Roman idealized sculpture. In their retrospection they are conceptually linked to other sculptural types favoured by the Romans: copies of specific Greek masterpieces as well as more independent creations such as eclectic pastiches attributed to PASITELES and his Neo-Attic school, for example *Orestes and Electra* (1st century BC; Naples, Mus. Archeol. N.), or archaistic statues. Scholars dispute whether certain of the classicizing images are true Roman creations or replicas of pre-existing Greek statues.

Pliny the elder: *Natural History*

B. Andreae: *Römische Kunst* (Freiburg, 1973; Eng. trans., New York, 1977)

P. Zanker: *Klassizistische Statuen* (Mainz, 1974)

D. Strong: *Roman Art*, Pelican Hist. A. (Harmondsworth, 1976, rev. 2/1988)

H. Wrede: *'Consecratio in formam deorum': Vergöttlichte Privatpersonen in der römischen Kaiserzeit* (Mainz, 1981)

H. Martin: *Römische Tempelkultbilder*, Stud. & Mat. Mus. Civil. Romana (Rome, 1987)

M. Fullerton: *The Archaistic Style in Roman Statuary* (Leiden, 1990)

S. Woodford: *The Art of Greece and Rome* (Cambridge and New York, 2004)

(b) Architectural and relief. The modern assessment of ancient Roman art is based in large part on the study of the relief sculpture that decorated both public and private monuments in the capital. Studies begun at the turn of the 20th century sought to determine the unique characteristics of Roman art (*romanitas*) and sparked discussion that continues to this day. Scholars have been struck by the recurring nature of Roman 'classicism', and by the confusing and enriching tendency of Roman art to revive its own past. Sieveking recognized the anti-Classical spatial nature (*Räumlichkeit*) of some reliefs and determined that this quality was a typically Italic phenomenon; Wickhoff also analysed the evolution of 'illusionistic' tendencies of Roman relief. Koepp, however, rejected any deterministic construct of an historical *Zeitstil* (like Riegl's *Kunstwollen*, 'the involuntary yet supreme law of a whole epoch which dominates artistic thought and manifestation') for one in which contemporaneous works could be different in character for a number of reasons. Rodenwaldt distinguished between a classicizing court style dominated by State patronage and a popular style exemplified by an individual preference for non-classicizing reliefs; von Blanckenhagen suggested that the court style predominated when the State wished to represent itself as a lasting force, and that the popular style was influential when the State was weak. Brendel argued for a model in which the multiplicity of autonomous styles were each dependent on the specific genus of representation. Building on these ground-breaking studies, contemporary scholars continue to explore the mechanisms of artistic patronage in ancient Rome and the politically resonant iconography of its relief sculpture.

Relief sculpture on public monuments. The conflicting currents of a classicizing style based on Greek idealism and a popular style drawn from Roman realism are strikingly juxtaposed on the marble 'Altar of Domitius Ahenobarbus', in actuality a monumental rectangular statue base from the late Republican period. On the principal face (Paris, Louvre) sculptors struggled to render the novel Roman subject-matter: combined scenes of census-taking, a lustral sacrifice and the mustered armies of Roman citizens. Close attention is given to the narrative detail of these civic rites. In sharp contrast are the three other faces depicting a mythological marine procession led by Neptune and Amphitrite (Munich, Glyp.); probably of Hellenistic origin, these reliefs were recut for use on this monument to celebrate the triumph of a successful naval campaign. The combined reliefs celebrate a private citizen in the roles of *triumphator*, magistrate and priest. The utilization of public art to further political ambitions is typical of the late Republican period and provided a model for later Imperial patrons.

During the principate of Augustus the Roman practice of artistic self-glorification for personal advancement was harnessed for the State in the person of the emperor. Emblematic of this process is the Augustan Ara Pacis (*see* ROME, §IV, 4), carved between 13 and 9 BC by Greek artists (or artists trained in the NEO-ATTIC style). Marble reliefs decorate the surfaces of the enclosure walls and the altar itself. As was common in Republican monuments, there is a juxtaposition between allegorical scenes drawn from the realm of myth (Mars watching over Romulus and Remus, Aeneas at sacrifice, the goddesses Tellus Italia and Roma on the short end walls) and descriptive narratives based on historical reality (the processions of the senate and imperial family on the long side walls; for illustration *see* Dress). The reliefs emphasize the role played by Augustus in the life of the State and its historical significance. The figures in the processions range from the peculiarities of portraiture to the near ideal; they advance with the stately calm characteristic of Classical Greek friezes, yet the forms, carved in varying depths of relief, overlap and appear to recede into the background. Sieveking argued that Augustan relief first realized a truly 'Roman' form by perfecting the Italic tendency in the representation of space. The Ara Pacis translates the ideological programmes of Augustus into an aesthetically convincing concrete form, not only creating the iconographic type for imperial processions but also defining the classicizing Augustan style which became the foundation for Roman Imperial art. The imitation of Augustan monuments served the political and artistic needs of the Julio-Claudian house: allusions to Augustus, father of both the imperial system and the imperial family, supported their claim to rule.

Spatial relief became even more predominant during the 1st century AD. During the reigns of Nero and the succeeding Flavian dynasty sculptors refined their use of illusionistic devices and were increasingly sophisticated in the use of light and shade to enliven details. The great panel reliefs decorating the interior passage of the Arch of Titus in Rome (AD 81) depict the triumph following the conclusion of the Jewish War of AD 66–70 (see fig. 25). On one panel attendants carry booty from the campaign, including the great Menorah, the Table of the Shew Bread and the silver trumpets sounded at Rosh Hashanah. Twenty massed figures stand for the thousands who were actually present; abbreviated topographical references on the panel localized the scene and amplified its meaning for the people of Rome. The carving and careful placement of reliefs on architectural monuments so that they would engage the spectator was extremely important to Roman designers. The procession appears to approach from out of the background, pass beside the viewer and disappear under an arch shown in the composition. If the spectator proceeds through the Arch of Titus towards the Capitolium in the same direction as on the depicted procession, his illusionistic identification with the reliefs is intensified. On the opposite panel Titus rides in a triumphal chariot, crowned by a winged Victory and greeted by the geniuses of the Roman people and the senate. Portraying such allegorical figures produces more a symbolic than documentary effect. The whole work conveys an illusion of uninterrupted motion, and the subtle use of chiaroscuro endows it with a realistic pictorial quality which owed much to the rich Roman tradition of historical painting, now known to us only through literary sources.

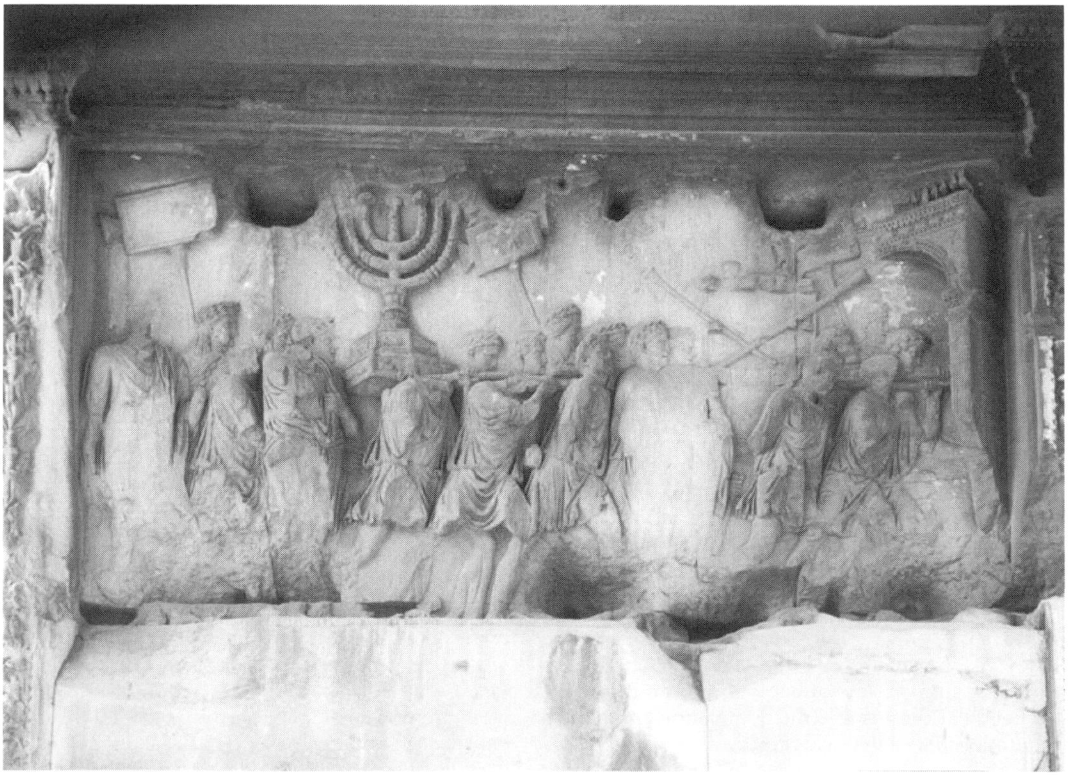

25. Relief from the Arch of Titus, Rome, showing the *Spoils of Jerusalem*, marble, h. 2.03 m, AD 81

In 1937 two marble relief panels from the late Flavian period were discovered beneath the Palazzo Cancelleria in Rome (Rome, Vatican, Mus. Gregoriano Profano). In the first relief Vespasian places his hand upon the shoulder of the young Domitian, a symbolic act indicating the transfer of the father's *imperium* to his son. The geniuses of the Roman people and the senate, the Vestal Virgins and the goddess Roma witness this act of faith, perhaps alluding to Domitian's temporary rule until Vespasian returned from the East (AD 70). In the second relief additional allegorical figures, including Victory, Mars and Minerva, entreat the figure of Domitian (later recut to resemble the Emperor Nerva) to follow them. Both reliefs were propaganda pieces carved to justify the actions of the unpopular Domitian; their effectiveness is evident in a successor's attempt to re-employ them. The pictorial space and the rich treatment of the hair, drapery and other details derive from the earlier Flavian 'Baroque' tradition of the Arch of Titus; the stately figures and coldly polished surface, however, harken back to Augustan classicism.

The forceful, dramatic battle reliefs forming the Great Trajanic Frieze, now on the Arch of Constantine (*see* ROME, §IV, 12), overawe with their scale. The figures are larger than life (2.3 m on average), and the density of the composition, with Romans and Dacians arranged one behind the other, sometimes as many as five deep, heightens their powerful impression. The artists created the impression that the figures are fighting in actual space. Action takes place not only in the plane of the relief but into and out of the background. This type of spatial composition is essentially a pictorial one. Hamberg typified the Great Frieze as representative of the 'grand' or 'monumental' tradition of Roman relief. The dominance of the human figure in the scene and the restrained rendering of topographical features suggested to Hamberg great historical panel paintings, such as the lost 4th-century BC work copied by the Alexander Mosaic from Pompeii (Naples, Mus. Archeol. N.).

In contrast the reliefs spiralling up the 30 m shaft of Trajan's Column (AD 113; *see* ROME, §IV, 7) unwind like a picture-book scroll, an equivalent in stone of the *Commentaries* Trajan wrote of his campaigns in the Balkans. Hamberg described this as the 'epic' or 'documentary' tradition. The frieze length of over 200 m contains 2500 figures populating contiguous scenes which form a kind of continuous narrative. Trajan embodies the ideal general supervising the conduct of warfare through the repetition of typical events, including addressing his troops, battles, departures, embassies and sacrifices. Each scene is clearly composed in shallow relief, the details of forts, bridges and landscapes all carefully delineated. Although partial overlapping exists, a basic characteristic of the composition of the column, in contrast to the Great Frieze, is the preference for a relief depth of only one figure spread out over the surface of the column shaft. Instead of trying to create the impression of recession into depth for the battles, the artists employed a formula known as the 'bird's eye view' in which the ground plane is tilted up so that figures and objects placed on it create the impression of standing on a higher level the further away they are in the background. This abstract rendition of space also has pictorial precedents, such as the 3rd-century BC tomb painting discovered on the Esquiline Hill (Rome, Pal. Conserv., Braccio Nuo.), and the staggering of figures on Etruscan ash urns, which ultimately go back to the Greek Polygnotan school as reflected on the 5th-century BC Niobid Krater (Paris, Louvre; *see* POTTERY, §IV, 6(i)(c)). In Rome the tradition was kept alive in historical paintings, specifically in triumphal paintings used by Roman generals to document the details of their victories for the populace. Since the Renaissance, artists have used the reliefs on Trajan's Column as a storehouse of archaeological detail and ancient figural compositions.

The differences between Hamberg's 'monumental' and 'documentary' types of representation are those of tradition and intention. Although both embody official propaganda, the Great Frieze conveys a more conceptual statement, in which typical incidents were chosen to give the underlying political message a dramatic quality. Personifications and allegorical figures heightened the significance of the scenes for the Roman viewer. The reliefs on Trajan's Column, however, represent a more factual commentary of Roman military action, emphasizing the descriptive presentation of events; nevertheless, their reportorial manner was no less effective in stirring its audience. Polychromy on Roman reliefs may have heightened their effect for the ancient viewer, and also indicates the dependence of both the 'monumental' and 'documentary' relief types on painting traditions.

Under Hadrian simple sacrificial and religious scenes replaced the extensive narrative compositions of the 'documentary' tradition. The circular medallions now on the Arch of Constantine in Rome represent typical scenes of hunting and sacrifice to the gods of the chase. Simpler historical scenes include the *Remission of Taxes* (Chatsworth, Derbys) and two companion reliefs, the *Apotheosis of the Empress Sabina* and *Hadrian Making a Proclamation* (Rome, Mus. Conserv.). Hadrianic reliefs are characterized by neutral backgrounds unencumbered by landscape or architectural details and by a return to the Attic manner of composition, probably due to the influence of sculptors from Aphrodisias in Asia Minor. The smooth technique, the frieze-like arrangement of figures and the accentuation of linear contours by frequent use of the running drill to produce effects of light and shadow are all hallmarks of Hadrianic classicism.

Based on the Column of Trajan, the Column of Marcus Aurelius at Rome (AD 180–93) documents the campaigns against the Marcomanni and the Sarmatians. The later artists vivified their narrative by emphasizing episodes and individual personages to evoke a profound sympathy with human suffering; the Roman discipline extolled by Trajan is here transformed into a series of scenes wrought with expressive emotion. Wegner, of a generation that had experienced the horrors of World War I and saw its own artistic traditions breaking down, articulated this dramatic change. The style is disjointed, dramatic; original traits include more compact groupings and a tendency towards centralized compositions. The drill is used more aggressively to create illusionistic effects. Whether or not its artists arose from the 'popular' tradition, as is frequently argued, the Column of Marcus Aurelius represents a totally different aspect of Roman art from the heavy stateliness and realistic details of the marble panel reliefs carved a few years earlier for a lost triumphal arch celebrating the conclusion of the same campaigns (three in Rome, Mus. Conserv.; eight reused in the Arch of Constantine). The surviving panels reflect the 'monumental' tradition of paintings and sculpted reliefs. Although the contrast of the empty air above and the massed figures below is marked, the sculptors failed to create the illusion of space achieved in the Arch of Titus or Great Trajanic Frieze.

In AD 203 a great triple arch was dedicated in Rome to celebrate the Mesopotamian campaign of Septimius Severus. Among its sculpted decorations are four great panel reliefs with scenes similar to those on the historiated columns. The artists manipulated the large panel format to include the portrayal of mass actions and successive events in a single composition. Although the division of the scenes by ground lines and the explanatory 'bird's eye' views of cities have been elaborated beyond the earlier column compositions, their technique too was probably influenced by triumphal paintings. Despite their vivid treatment of form and line, their figures are even squatter and sketchier than those on the Column of Marcus Aurelius.

The Arch of Constantine (AD 312–15) was the last great triumphal arch in Rome. The architects used spolia from monuments honouring earlier emperors: the Great Trajanic Frieze on the ends of the attic and on the sides of the central bay, eight medallions from Hadrian's reign on the façades and eight panel reliefs of Marcus Aurelius on the attic faces. The actual battles, triumph and benefactions of Constantine are portrayed in a small inconspicuous frieze squeezed between the large river gods in the spandrels and the Hadrianic tondi (see fig. 39 below). The scenes exhibit the prosaic immediacy of popular art. The puppet-like figures, packed in overlapping rows, are carved in a primitive 'woodcut' style in which the use of the drill has almost completely replaced the chisel. The emperor is portrayed frontally as a superhuman ruler in the Oriental tradition. The reliefs have been both decried as the lowest ebb of Roman art and praised as the revolutionary creation of Late Antique expressionism. The Classical traditions evoked by the spolia have all but vanished.

Relief sculpture on private monuments. Reliefs decorating private funerary monuments are as varied as those found in State commissions. The extensive frieze on the tomb of the baker Marcus Vergilius Eurysaces (1st century BC; Rome, *in situ* outside the Porta Maggiore) illustrating the various processes of breadmaking is typical of the scenes of daily life popular on the tombs of freedmen and the lower classes. The frieze composition has traits in common with both the earlier Esquiline tomb paintings and motifs that reappear two centuries later in Trajan's Column where men carrying baskets of earth to build the ramparts resemble the slaves carrying baskets of wheat on the baker's tomb. More modest relief panels, of stone or terracotta, decorated the tombs of wealthy freedmen well into the Imperial period; examples include a funerary relief of a vegetable vendor (see fig. 26) and a funerary relief with a midwife (both Ostia Antica, Museo Ostiense). These show typical scenes of commerce, often featuring a portrait of the deceased at work. The style was in the popular tradition, which emphasized descriptive detail over artistic subtlety.

For reasons still not wholly understood, during the 2nd century AD the Romans abandoned cremation for inhumation. The most common themes used to decorate the marble sarcophagi of wealthy patrons include mythological compositions, hunt and battle scenes and the life of the philosopher (*see* SARCOPHAGUS, §3).

Mythological compositions expressed allegorical schemes in which the myths were interpreted as moralizing poetic metaphors: as the emperors had demonstrated their virtue in the actions commemorated in public monuments, so the dead claimed the virtues possessed by immortal heroes decorating their sarcophagi. Like the wall paintings and mosaics found in Roman houses, the scenes created a kind of

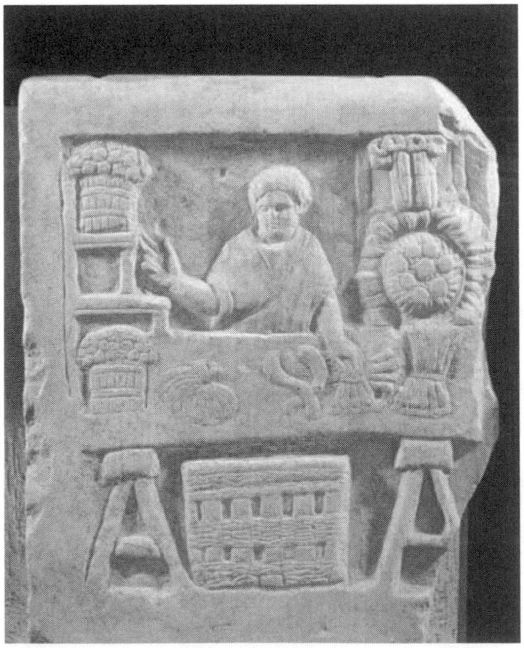

26. Roman funerary relief of a vegetable vendor, terracotta, h. 432 mm, second half of 2nd century AD (Ostia Antica, Museo Ostiense)

visual rhetoric, which in a formalistic manner glorified the traditional aesthetic and educational values. Themes related to mystery religions, such as those associated with Dionysus (the Roman 'Liber Pater' who brings liberation and bliss), often conflated with imagery of the seasons and carved in a classicizing style, created a sophisticated art of escape from the turmoils of 3rd-century AD life.

Scenes of hunting reflected the imagery and spirit of the Hellenistic hunts of Alexander and his successors. Closely packed compositional formats and vivid treatment in the carving compare with the more innovative public monuments of the Antonine period, such as the swirling cavalry parades on the Column of Antoninus Pius (see fig. 27). The funerary reliefs adapted from the great Hellenistic battle scenes, however, demonstrate a more original use of Greek models: heroically nude Greek warriors became realistic Roman soldiers. The mood of the battle scenes reflects the desperate campaigns fought throughout the 3rd century AD.

By the end of the 3rd century AD the *Mousikos aner* ('man of the Muses') began to dominate the imagery of Roman sarcophagi. Contemplative themes appealed to educated pagans who comforted themselves with the promise of an afterlife where they might be united with the great philosophers and cultivate the truths of the mind; other patrons may simply have wanted to be remembered as savants and patrons of culture.

Whether carving public or private commissions, Roman artists tended to soften the strongly modelled forms of the Greek tradition, relied on strong contrasts of light and shadow, carved in flatter relief and reduced the three-dimensionality of their compositions. Abstraction had always been latent in the inherited Classical vocabulary, and although Roman artists worked within that tradition, the effect was that the very essence of sculptural conception was undermined. This was not a steady, unbroken evolution, however; nor was it an oscillating development of relief styles, merging into and out of each other. Rather, Roman relief is best understood as representing the synchronous development of various artistic themes, formats and styles to serve distinct and recognizable purposes. The resulting contrasts and discrepancies did not cause any discomfort for the ancient spectator. On the contrary, as Brendel suggested, Roman relief sculpture reflects an attitude of aesthetic selection according to taste and purpose, a situation in which the patron exercised a choice as free as ours.

Pedimental sculpture. PEDIMENTS and acroteria (*see* ACROTERION) joined reliefs to provide Roman temples with explicit political messages through elaborate sculptural programmes. Although the Greeks and Etruscans had long filled the triangular gable of temple pediments with sculpture, Roman architects did not introduce the practice until the late Republic.

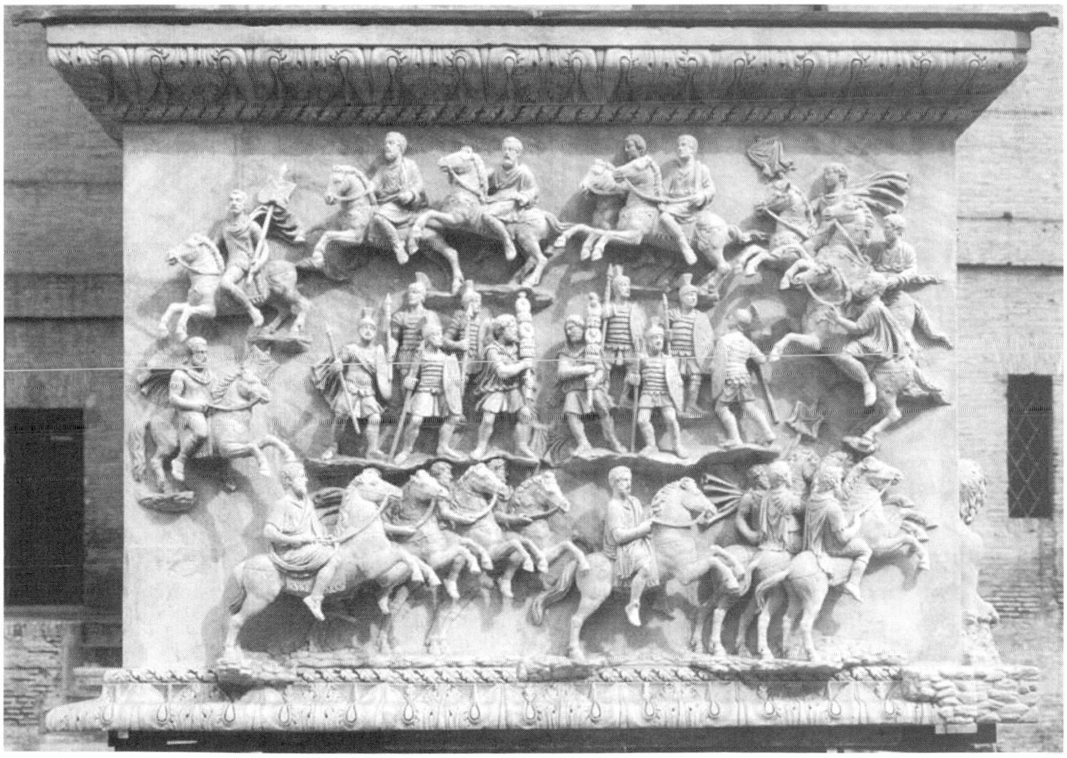

27. Roman relief of a cavalry parade, marble, h. 2.47 m, from the column of Antoninus Pius, Rome, after AD 161 (Rome, Vatican, Cortile della Pigna)

The earliest surviving example, discovered in 1878 at the Via S Gregorio on the Caelian Hill (Rome, Mus. Conserv.), exhibits the eclectic threads that were woven into characteristically Roman traditions. The figures are of terracotta, the favoured material of Etruscans, and include deities (Mars, Venus and Victory) drawn from Greek prototypes combined with mortals conducting an animal sacrifice, the *suovetaurilia*, a thoroughly Roman ritual. The neo-Classical style of the figures suggests a date in the second half of the 2nd century BC; their original location remains controversial.

Classical Greek marble statues decorated the pediment of the early Augustan Temple of Apollo Sosianus (Rome, Mus. Conserv.), in which Athena, Theseus and Hercules lead Greeks against Amazons. The amazonomachy functioned both as war booty and as an allegorical allusion to an historical battle, following the Greek practice.

Few pedimental groups from the Imperial period remain intact. Nevertheless, evidence for their appearance can be obtained from literary descriptions and coin types; in addition, Roman artists depicted buildings as political symbols on historical reliefs, paying careful attention to the delineation of sculptural programmes on temple pediments. For example, the reliefs traditionally associated with the Ara Pietatis Augustae, dedicated in AD 43 (since the 16th century embedded in the walls of the Villa Medici), depict sacrifices performed before important temple façades. A central figure of Mars the Avenger flanked by Venus and Fortuna identifies the Corinthian temple on one relief as the Augustan Temple of Mars Ultor. The Temple of Magna Mater or Cybele on the Palatine on another relief is identified by the goddess's turreted crown displayed on a throne in the centre of the gable, flanked at left and right by *galli* (priests of Cybele); the acroteria consist of dancing figures clad in Phrygian costume. On some Imperial reliefs, however, sculptors demonstrate greater concern for design than for documentary accuracy.

F. Wickhoff: *Die Wiener Genesis* (Vienna, 1895)

A. Riegl: *Die spätrömische Kunstindustrie* (Vienna, 1901)

J. Sieveking: 'Das römische Relief', *Festschrift Paul Arndt* (Munich, 1925), pp. 14–35

F. Koepp: 'Kritische Bermerkungen zum römischen Relief', *Nachrbl. Ges. Wiss. Göttingen, Philos.-Hist. Kl.*, iii (1926)

M. Wegner: 'Die kunstgeschichtliche Stellung der Marcussäule', *Jb. Dt. Archäol. Inst.*, xlvi (1931), pp. 61–174

G. Rodenwaldt: 'Römische Reliefs: Vorstufen zur Spätantike', *Jb. Dt. Archäol. Inst.*, lv (1940), pp. 12–43

P. H. von Blanckenhagen: 'Elemente der römischen Kunst am Beispiel des flavischen Stils', *Das neue Bild der Antike*, ii (Leipzig, 1942), pp. 310–41

P. G. Hamberg: *Studies in Roman Imperial Art* (Copenhagen, 1945)

O. Brendel: 'Prolegomena to a Book on Roman Art', *Mem. Amer. Acad. Rome*, xxi (1953) [whole issue]; as book, ed. J. J. Pollitt (New Haven, 1979)

I. S. Ryberg: 'Rites of the State Religion in Roman Art', *Mem. Amer. Acad. Rome*, xxii (1955)

B. Andreae: *The Art of Rome* (New York, 1977)

B. M. Felletti Maj.: *La tradizione italica nell'arte romana* (Rome, 1977)

G. Koeppel: 'The Grand Pictorial Tradition of Roman Historical Representation during the Early Empire', *Aufstieg und Niedergang der römischen Welt*, II/xii/1 (Berlin, 1982), pp. 507–35

M. Torelli: *Typology and Structure of Roman Historical Reliefs* (Ann Arbor, 1982)

G. Koeppel: 'Two Reliefs from the Arch of Claudius in Rome', *Mitt. Dt. Archäol. Inst.: Röm. Abt.*, xc (1983), pp. 103–9

E. La Rocca: *Amazzonomachia: Le sculture frontonali del tempio di Apollo Sosiano* (Rome, 1985)

P. Zanker: *Augustus und die Macht der Bilder* (Munich, 1987); Eng. trans. by A. Shapiro as *The Power of Images in the Age of Augustus* (Ann Arbor, 1988)

D. E. E. Kleiner: *Roman Sculpture* (New Haven, 1992)

C. C. Hemingway: *Female Archaistic Statue Supports: Motives for Archaizing in Greek and Roman Statuary* (diss., Cambridge, MA, Harvard U., 1999)

J. M. Højte: *Roman Imperial Statue Bases: From Augustus to Commodus* (Aarhus, 2005)

(v) Craftsmen and society. Lucian's *Dream* (ix) has often been quoted as evidence for the low status of sculptors in Roman society, referring even to Pheidias and Polykleitos as mere craftsmen. Although there was a general prejudice in ancient society against manual work, this essay is patently polemic, since it extols the career of a scholar as of higher social standing. In any case, there was a major distinction made between the humble stonecutter carving grave reliefs for a local market and a master sculptor, sometimes also owner, of the great workshops of the metropolis.

When Roman generals began to collect sculpture in the 2nd century BC, they turned to the great workshops of the East, mainly Athens, but increasingly artists moved to Rome (*see* COLLECTION AND DISPLAY OF ART, §I, 2 *and* PATRONAGE, §2). Dynasties of Athenian sculptors covering several generations can be traced. The sculptor POLYKLES had several successors, including DIONYSIOS and TIMARCHIDES, who signed a portrait statue of the Italian businessman C. Ofellius Ferus, found in Delos (late 2nd century BC; Delos, Archaeol. Mus.), both giving their fathers' names and their Athenian origin. In 1st-century BC Rome, PASITELES, a Greek born in South Italy, became a prominent sculptor and engraver. He was also a scholar whose treatises greatly influenced Varro and Pliny the elder. None of his many works can be identified for certain, but the base of a standing nude youth (Rome, Villa Albani, 906) bears the signature 'Stephanos, the pupil of Pasiteles', and a group perhaps representing *Orestes and Electra* (Rome, Mus. N. Romano, 8604) is signed 'Menelaos, the pupil of Stephanos'. The famous sculptural collection of C. Asinius Pollio (76 BC–AD 4) contained Stephanos' *Nymphs of the Appian Water* (untraced).

The State art of Imperial Rome developed new modes of representation, but little is known of the master sculptors themselves, for example those responsible for the portraits of Augustus, more than

250 of which survive, for the design of the Ara Pacis or Trajan's Column. More is known, however, about ordinary craftsmen, mainly through epigraphy and particularly in the early and high Empire. Sculptures were signed more than any other works of art, and inscriptions on plinths and elsewhere often give the artist's full name, patronymic and geographical origins, but many are only short autographs. Even State art was occasionally signed; thus the name M. Ulpius Orestes appears on the foot of a sacrificial bull in a relief from Trajan's Forum (*c.* AD 113; Paris, Louvre, 978). Longer inscriptions, mostly epitaphs, are conventional, but sometimes informative. Almost all are in Greek, Latin being nearly always confined to the western Empire.

Although Rome became the dominant sculptural centre, during the high Empire, and particularly in the East, local centres often connected to quarries became increasingly important, both as local suppliers to the emergent provincial aristocracy and for the long-distance trade. Itinerant craftsmen and even whole workshops were common. The epitaph of Novius Blesamus boasts that 'he embellished the city and the world with his sculptures' (*Corp. Inscr. Lat.*, VI/i, 23083). The most famous of all itinerant artists was ZENODOROS, who worked for ten years on a statue of *Mercury* for the Arverni in Gaul and was paid the vast sum of 40 million sesterces. Such was his reputation that Nero commissioned him to make the bronze colossus for his Domus Aurea (Pliny the elder: *Natural History* XXXIV.xviii.4b). Among the most important and best attested groups of sculptors was the 'School of APHRODISIAS', which was active throughout the Empire but often used the characteristic marble of its native Caria. A poem inscribed on a herm, which is all that survives of the early 2nd-century AD family mausoleum of the sculptor Zenon at Rome, stresses his Aphrodisian origin but also boasts that he visited many cities.

For reasons of access, workshops were usually outside cities, and so are difficult to trace. A few were, however, uncovered in Pompeii. After the earthquake of AD 62 a sculptor moved into an old house close to the large theatre, the House of the Sculptor, using its ground floor to produce minor works in marble, such as statuettes, herms and tables. Finds included a saw still stuck in a marble slab, and unfinished mortar. Many workshops were established around Baiae to supply the villas of wealthy Romans. A collection of plaster casts of old masterpieces to be copied by the pointing technique was found there (Báia, Parco Archeol., 174.479–174.784) along with several sculptures *in situ*. A copy of the *Hera Borghese* in Italian marble from a submerged villa is signed by 'Aphrodisios Libyos from Athens' (Naples, Mus. N. Archeol.). Particularly in the later Roman period finished marble sculptures were also exported, sometimes even in pieces for reassembly.

Many sculptors were freedmen working directly for patrons. Thus C. Avianus Evander, who supplied Cicero in 51 BC, ran a workshop in Athens on behalf of his patron. Later he went to Egypt to work for Mark Antony, but after 30 BC he was taken to Rome as a prisoner of war. There he soon resumed work, and among other things restored old masterpieces for Augustus. The freedmen members of the Cossutii family (*see* COSSUTIUS) traded in sculpture on a large scale, becoming extremely wealthy by the early 1st century BC and continuing business at least until the 2nd century AD. One, Habinnas, appears in Petronius' *Satyricon* as the supervisor of construction of the family mausoleum, and he seems quite content with his social standing.

Portraits were often produced by specialists, and those on sarcophagi were the last part to be executed. Sculptors sometimes worked in other media: Zenodoros, for example, made copies of two precious cups for the governor of Gaul. Some sculptors recorded that they had carved both a statue and its inscription, which could be paid for separately. Conversely, craftsmen were occasionally highly specialized: an epitaph mentions a *faber ocularìarius* (maker of eyes for bronze statues; *Corp. Inscr. Lat.*, VI/i, 9402). The standard of workmanship could attain great precision: identical imperial portraits occur in marble and bronze, while the four horses of S Marco in Venice (?2nd century AD; Mus. S Marco) all have exactly the same weight (897 kg) and dimensions.

When sarcophagi became fashionable in Hadrianic times, they began to be mass-produced, the manufacture being organized with greater efficiency. Athenian workshops monopolized some provinces, Asiatic ones others. Most Attic sarcophagi (*c.* 1000) can be attributed to a single or closely related group of workshops. The coffins were roughly carved in the quarries and could be finished in different workshops, depending on the location of the customer. There was a high level of organization for State art too. An imperial workshop apparently operated at Dokimeion as part of the Phrygian quarry system administered from Synnada, which furnished the colossal Dacians in *pavonazzetto* marble for Trajan's Forum (ded. AD 113), as an unfinished piece in one of its quarries demonstrates.

There is no evidence for contracts for sculptures, nor for the *collegia* that are attested for other craftsmen. Little is known either of sculptors' training. LUCIAN OF SAMOSATA, born into a family of sculptors, was apprenticed to an uncle as a stonecutter, but ran away. According to his epitaph, L. Arrius Secundus was at the age of 17 already considered a sculptor (*Corp. Inscr. Lat.*, X, 7039). Eutychides, only 16, spoke of himself as not inferior to Praxiteles. Pupils were presumably responsible for much of the rough initial carving of statues, and actual training pieces have been found at Aphrodisias, including a double foot joined at the soles. Moreover, when, during AD 193–211, craftsmen were brought in from Asia Minor, apparently from Aphrodisias, to work on the Severan building programme in Leptis Magna, some local Latin-speaking pupils were also employed to boost numbers.

Most evidence for statue prices comes from Italy, but it is generally scanty and inconsistent. Some figures are extraordinary: 1567.17 Roman pounds of silver were spent on a statue of *Hadrian in a Chariot* at Beneventum. Municipal statues, however, commanded fairly standard prices. In Africa most ranged between 4000 and 7000 sesterces, with an average of 5000 sesterces, approximately four times the annual wage of a soldier or municipal clerk. Manufacture probably represented 50%–90% of the total cost of a statue, depending on whether it was of bronze or marble. Even so, the high transport costs of marble could easily offset its lower material and production costs. According to Diocletian's *Edict on Prices* of AD 301, a simple stonemason was paid 50 denarii a day, the price of a pair of sandals. This was equivalent to a carpenter's wage and double that of a farm worker.

In later Imperial times there was a shortage both of skilled craftsmen and of State funds for major projects. The sudden decline in the quality of official reliefs in Severan times indicates the use of forced labour, as in other areas of society, but from the same period marvellous sarcophagi were produced for the upper class in Rome. Edicts of Constantine encouraged the training of skilled craftsmen, and so presumably improved their social standing. In Late Antiquity high-quality sculpture was still produced, even in the Classical tradition, but it had become substantially more expensive. Some early 4th-century AD copies of Classical works from a stately home on the Esquiline in Rome (Copenhagen, Ny Carlsberg Glyp.) are signed by Aphrodisian sculptors, also named in inscriptions at Aphrodisias itself, who clearly belonged to the highest level of society.

M. Squarciapino: *La scuola di Afrodisia* (Rome, 1943)
D. Mustilli: 'Botteghe di scultori, marmorarii, bronzieri e caelatores in Pompei', *Pompeiana* (1950), pp. 206–29
J. M. C. Toynbee: *Some Notes on Artists in the Roman World* (Brussels, 1951)
A. Burford: *Craftsmen in Greek and Roman Society* (London, 1972)
E. Rawson: 'Architecture and Sculpture: The Activities of the Cossutii', *Pap. Brit. Sch. Rome*, xlii (1975), pp. 36–47
K. Erim and C. M. Roueché: 'Sculptors from Aphrodisias: Some New Inscriptions', *Pap. Brit. Sch. Rome*, l (1982), pp. 102–15
G. Zimmer: *Römische Berufsdarstellungen* (Berlin, 1982)
F. C. Albertson: 'A Bust of Lucius Verus in the Ashmolean Museum and its Artist', *Amer. J. Archaeol.*, lxxxvii (1983), pp. 153–63
G. Lahusen: *Untersuchungen zur Ehrenstatue in römische literarische und epigraphische Zeugnisse* (Rome, 1983)
M. Waelkens: 'From a Phrygian Quarry: The Statues of the Dacian Prisoners in Trajan's Forum', *Amer. J. Archaeol.*, lxxxix (1985), pp. 641–53
K. Erim: *Aphrodisias: City of Venus Aphrodite* (London, 1986), esp. chap. 5
J. J. Pollitt: *Art in the Hellenistic Age* (Cambridge, MA, 1986), chaps 7–8

2. Historical survey.

(i) Republic. (ii) Augustus. (iii) Julio-Claudians. (iv) Flavians. (v) Trajan. (vi) Hadrian. (vii) Antonines. (viii) 3rd century AD. (ix) Tetrarchs. (x) Constantine.

(i) Republic. Sculpture in Rome at the advent of the Republic (*c.* 510 BC) belonged to the mainstream bronze and terracotta votive and architectural tradition of south Etruria (*see* §V above), her Latin neighbours and Oscan Campania (e.g. a bronze *Chimaera* from a mythological group). By 300 BC Rome had extended her hegemony over central Italy; 3rd- and 2nd-century BC Roman nobles and their Italian associates had a shared high culture as they moved on the Greek cities of South Italy and Sicily, then the eastern Mediterranean. Conquest resulted in the transfer of sculpture, rededicated publicly and later also retained privately, for example the 2000 statues moved from Orvieto (Pliny the elder: XXXIV.34) and the booty from Syracuse (211 BC) and Corinth (146 BC). From the earliest period, artists from Etruria to Sicily visited Rome to work, with the result that the ethnicity of Republican artists and their stylistic origins are problems, exacerbated by the tendency of Italian artists not to sign their work and the incomplete literary and archaeological record. In the 2nd and 1st centuries BC many Greek sculptors arrived, for example Timotheos, Polykles, Skopas, Pasiteles and Arkesilaos; they often engendered local workshops and schools. Sculptors responded to patronage with art forms not known or exploited in the East, such as theatre and portico groups, small bronzes, statuary for the garden, grotto and nymphaeum, herm statuary and caryatid series. Work in bronze, wood, terracotta and local stones was indigenous; the imported marbles of the 3rd–1st century BC were usually worked by artists linked to their quarry sources in the East, but Italian quarries such as that at Luna opened in the early 1st century BC.

Sculpture thus followed a 'medio-Italic' Hellenistic aesthetic, under the canons of PRAXITELES and LYSIPPOS mediated especially through Greek Taras and Syracuse, and characterized by vivid figure types and multi-figural compositions, sensual poses and drapery styles, and clear texture and contour. Bravura exposition accentuated frontality and expressionistic depiction of the body, emphasizing heads, gestures and physical attributes. From the 2nd century BC new styles appeared, such as neo-classicism, archaism, NEO-ATTIC and Pergamene Baroque (*see* PERGAMON). Colossal statues were popular for deities, miniatures for private display. From the later 2nd century BC the proliferation of luxurious houses and villas and a boom in public construction both necessitated sculptural adornment. This also fuelled the import of older Greek masterpieces, generating an auction and collecting culture; Cicero's diatribes on Verres, the governor of Sicily, for example, document the obsessed patron (*Against Verres*).

Typical of Republican statuary were cult figures, gilt bronze such as the Lysippic *Hercules* in the Forum Boarium (2nd century BC; Rome, Mus. Conserv.) or colossal acroliths with marble limbs and heads and bronze bodies (e.g. a 2nd-century BC head of an archaistic *Dioscurus* from the Lacus Juturnae in the Forum Romanum; Rome, Antiqua. Forense). Architectural sculpture depicts vivid mythological episodes or static *sacra conversazione* groups; the many extant fragments show full mastery of Hellenistic styles, both in Rome and throughout Latium and Etruria. Depictions from Rome's legendary past could reach iconic status, for example the bronze *She-wolf* (5th century BC; Rome, Mus. Conserv., see fig. 20 above) and the 'archaic' portraits of the late Republic such as the bronze bust of *Lucius Junius Brutus*. Honorific bronze and stone statues, the former especially on arches, depicted Victory, chariot and equestrian figures and symbolic combat or submission groups, for example the 2nd-century BC acrolith of a windblown striding *Victory* in Rhodian blue stone from Praeneste and the peperino heads from a Gallic victory monument on the Via Tiburtina, Rome (*c.* 220–*c.* 150 BC). A famous example of a relief-carved statue base is the 'Altar of Domitius Ahenobarbus' (*c.* 100–70 BC; Paris, Louvre and Munich, Glyp). Mythological and genre groups from the 1st century BC include the colossal neo-Classical Muses from the Theatre of Pompey in Rome and Arkesilaos' *Winged Cupids Playing with a Lioness* (both destr.). Coins document styles and sometimes monuments, and such texts as Cicero's *Letters* can reconstruct assemblages and multiple commissions by Pompey, Lucullus, Julius Caesar and others; the bronze caches from the Mahdia (*see* MAHDIA SHIPWRECK) and Antikythera shipwrecks and from the Villa of the Papyri at HERCULANEUM probably represent such collections.

Imitation of past styles and monuments characterized 1st-century BC production; this culture of allusion is illuminated by contemporary literary techniques, especially the rhetorical canons of *imitatio* and *allusio*. In this respect the family workshop and writings of the Italian Greek PASITELES were highly influential: he told contemporaries to paraphrase the Greek masterpieces; thus M. Cossutius Menelaos' signed *Orestes and Electra* (Rome, Mus. N. Romano) draws on a *mélange* of 5th- and 4th-century BC figural styles. Sculptors appreciated not only the High Classical masters but also Late Archaic and Early Classical works, as testified by casts and copies of the Athenian *Tyrannicides* (*see* KRITIOS AND NESIOTES) or the Esquiline charioteer group respectively. Certain subjects had particular resonance, such as the styles and monuments of the Athenian democracy, Alexander the Great and the dynasties of Macedon and Attalid Pergamon (e.g. the *Dying Gaul*, marble copy of 3rd-century BC original; Rome, Mus. Capitolino; see fig. 14 above). The dependence of equestrian statuary on Alexander can be seen in the bronze Granikos monument by Lysippos, which was transferred to Rome from Macedon by its conqueror Metellus in the 2nd century BC and was replicated in bronze and stone on the Capitol (for Scipio; destr.), at Lanuvium (for Licinius Murena; fragments in London, BM) and for Julius Caesar's portrait in the Forum Julium; destr.). Miniature bronzes of individual figures survive from Herculaneum. Hellenistic styles remained popular for decorative sculpture on erotic and Dionysiac themes (centaurs, nude Aphrodites, cupids, satyrs etc), cruel genre studies of the urban and rustic poor and vivid Baroque treatments of mythological themes, for example Pompey's commissioned series of monstrous births (Pliny: VII.34) and Homeric groups such as the LAOKOON (which may be of early Imperial date) and the *Blinding of Polyphemos* groups executed for SPERLONGA and at Ephesos, the latter probably by Mark Antony for a pediment. Iconographic considerations strongly influenced patrons, inspired by the theory of *decor* (appropriateness) and their wish to express personal cultural and political attainment; by the 1st century BC the habit of programmatic display was well established for house decoration (e.g. Villa of the Papyri, Herculaneum) and public complexes.

O. Vessberg: *Studien zur Kunstgeschichte der römischen Republik* (Lund and Leipzig, 1941)

G. Kaschnitz von Wienberg: *Zwischen Republik und Kaiserzeit* (1961), ii of *Römische Kunst* (Reinbeck, 1961–2)

F. Coarelli: 'L'"Ara di Domizio Enobarbo" e la cultura artistica in Roma nel II sec. a. C.', *Dial. Archeol.*, ii (1968), pp. 302–68

P. C. Bol: *Die Skulpturen des Schiffsfundes von Antikythera* (Berlin, 1972)

Roma medio repubblicana: Aspetti culturali di Roma e del Lazio nei secoli IV e III a. C. (exh. cat., Rome, Antiqua. Com., 1973)

E. Dwyer: *Pompeian Sculpture in its Domestic Context* (San Francisco, 1974)

M. Bieber: *Ancient Copies* (New York, 1977)

L'Art décoratif à Rome à la fin de la République et au début du Principat, Collection de l'Ecole Française de Rome (Rome, 1981)

F. Coarelli: *Il Foro Romano: Periodo repubblicano ed augusteo* (Rome, 1985)

E. La Rocca: *L'Auriga dell'Esquilino* (Rome, 1987)

N. Horsfall: 'Patronage of Art in the Roman World', *Prudentia*, xx (1988), pp. 9–29

N. Himmelmann: *Herrscher und Athlet: Die Bronzen vom Quirinal* (Milan, 1989)

E. La Rocca: 'Linguaggio artistico e ideologia politica a Roma in età repubblicana', *Roma e l'Italia: Radices imperii* (Milan, 1990), pp. 289–495

M. Sehlmeyer: *Stadtrömische Ehrenstatuen der republikanischen Zeit: Historizität und Kontext von Symbolen nobilitären Standesbewusstseins* (Stuttgart, 1999)

(ii) Augustus. Artistic excellence and the exemplary status of the first emperor made Augustan styles and monuments paradigmatic to the Julio-Claudian dynasty and the Empire in general (compare the Hadrianic and Constantinian 'renaissances'; see below). Typical late Republican patrons, Augustus and his rivals and associates had unprecedented power and wealth, spurring the unparalleled exploitation of Italian and imported marbles and coloured stones, silver and precious stones, and the employment of Eastern as well as indigenous workshops, especially of Athenian origin. As in Republican times, written texts usually preserve Greek artists' names, especially new ones (e.g. Pliny the elder reported that Diogenes of Athens made caryatids and pediment statues for the Pantheon (XXXVI.38–9)), but only a hidden signature documents the Roman Vibius Rufus at the Forum Augustum. Decorative

and dynastic sculpture was needed in the new elaboration of built theatre *scaenae frons* (stage buildings) and precincts. Libraries, such as those of Asinius Pollio and Augustus in Rome, required statues of eminent authors as well as decorative pieces. Reused 5th-century BC Greek temple pediments are distinctive, although Republican nobles had already used such sculpture privately, for example the 4th-century BC nereid acroterion at Vedius Pollio's villa near Naples (Naples, Mus. Archeol. N.). Both new and reused figures stood in porticos, in temple colonnades and niched interiors and flanking their monumental stairs, for example in the Temple of Concord in the Forum Romanum, as coins show. The Temple of Apollo Sosianus in Rome (ded. 19 BC) incorporated a 5th-century BC pediment, dying Niobids in the porch, and a cult group and statue gallery within, both reused and contemporary. These Niobids and the 50 Danaids in the porticos of the Palatine Apollo temple exemplify a tendency to decorate State monuments with (Greek) mythological themes and figural series in imitation of Republican villa and portico decoration; Augustan complexes, however, attain special magnificence through quantity, such as large series of identical characters and/or figure types. Fashion and propaganda trends converged in the promulgation of caryatid series, a Republican motif, at the Basilica Aemilia (rebuilt after 14 BC), Agrippa's Pantheon (27–25 BC, by Diogenes the Athenian) and, most famously, the Forum Augustum (ded. 2 BC), the attic of which was lined with replicas of the Erechtheion CARYATIDS.

Augustan sculpture was distinguished by high standards of execution, with detailed attention to line pattern, contour and texture, and with flesh surfaces often rasped; pose, drapery and surface elaboration were characteristically classicizing; in sum it exhibited refinement, delicacy and wit. Augustan classicism, Neo-Atticism (*see* NEO-ATTIC) and archaism can be seen as political tools to evoke an idealized Periclean Athens; High Classical body types, drapery effects and contrapposto systems were now preferred, often synthesized with other retrospective and contemporary modes to produce synthetic styles. The finest examples of Augustan neo-Classical sculpture are the Ara Pacis reliefs (for illustration *see* DRESS; *see also* ROME, §IV, 4). Archaizing sculpture often included mannered zones of windblown drapery, as in an *Artemis* (Munich, Staatl. Antikensamml.).

Primary and secondary evidence show that the major private and public displays expanded on Republican taste for stylistic collage between units of large figure groups. There were important assemblages at the Forum Augustum; Agrippa's Pantheon; the Palatine Apollo temple and its porticos (36–28 BC); the curia gallery in the Portico of Octavian (Pliny the elder: XXXVI.28–9); the Temple of Apollo Sosianus; and the Temple of Concord as rebuilt by Tiberius (ded. AD 10). Important collections of the Augustan nobility include those of Asinius Pollio (Pliny the elder: XXXVI.33–4) and of the Villa of the Papyri at HERCULANEUM. Poets such as Virgil, Horace, Ovid and Propertius produced set-piece descriptions and reflections of contemporary assemblages, for example Virgil's fantastic Augustus precinct (*Georgics* III.1–39). Pliny the elder's chapters on art also reflect the continuing prestige of Augustan dedications. The dramatically posed, hyper-realist 'Hellenistic Baroque' styles of the Republic remained popular for Homeric and bucolic genres, and seem to have been used sometimes for figures of State mythology, for example (to judge by paintings and relief versions) for the key groups set in the Forum Augustum exedrae of *Aeneas with his Son and Father*, and *Romulus with the Tropaeum*.

The marked unity of artistic production, and the State-encouraged tendency of client courts and provincial towns, especially in the West, to replicate or evoke monuments in the capital, gave new authority to other arts (silver, ceramics, architectural terracottas) and to relief and provincial sculpture; thus they are a source for the style and iconography of major sculpture at Rome. Examples are the trophy groups, arches and funerary monuments of Gaul, as at Lugdunum Convenarum (Saint-Bertrand-de-Comminges, 25 BC); imitations of the Forum Augustum as at AUGUSTA EMERITA (Mérida); and remains from Juba II's Mauretanian kingdom, especially at his capital CAESAREA (Cherchel). Important provincial reliefs include the sculpture from Pompeii that evokes the *Romulus and Aeneas* from the Forum Augustum; the Caere throne (Etruscan cities; see below); the Algiers relief depicting a Venus-Mars-Amor cult group (Algiers, Mus. N. Ant.) and the Gens Augusta altar depicting an Aeneas group, Roma, sacrifice scene and Apollo, from Carthage; and the Aphrodisias (*see* APHRODISIAS, §3) Sebasteion reliefs. These often flesh out textual accounts, for example the representation on a base (Sorrento, Mus. Correale Terranova) of the contemporary cult statue group in the Palatine Apollo temple showing Leto, Apollo, Artemis and a Sibyl, which illustrates the originals by Timotheos, Skopas and Kephisodotos (Pliny the elder: XXXVI.24–32) and permits identification of existing secondary copies. Among the other arts coinage remains an important documentary source, contemporary Arretine ware often illustrates or paraphrases Republican and Augustan sculpture, and some decorative silver echoes or parodies programmatic literary portraits.

Augustus' massive programme of dedicating or rededicating new or restored temples established an authoritative series of new cult statues. Augustan propaganda reinforced a late Republican practice of giving the features of current rulers to decorative and votive statues of divinities, for example the Octavian/Veiovis herm, or the attribution of Augustus' features to the Villa of the Papyri bronze *Seated Mercury*; a cupid with the features of a dead great-grandson was a decorative piece in Augustus' bedroom and a votive by Livia in a Venus temple (Suetonius: *Caligula* vii). Due to the religious propaganda of Julius Caesar and Augustus, neo-Classical Venus types proliferated, with examples in the temples of Divus Julius,

Mars Ultor, the Pantheon and Venus Victrix on the Palatine; Augustus' new Mars Ultor was an elaborately cuirassed, bearded mature god. The standing Amazon representing Roma, for example that on the Temple of Rome and Augustus, Ostia, was a mandatory presence in the ruler cult shrines that burgeoned under imperial direction around the Empire; Augustan emphasis on Apollo (Augustus' guardian deity at the Battle of Actium in 31 BC) promoted specific neo-Classical types of Apollo Citharoedus, draped or nude.

These iconographies are reflected in decorative sculpture, such as the archaizing *Apollo and Diana* (Naples, Mus. Archeol. N.). The dancing, windblown figures of the new Lares Augusti (guardians of the crossroads), which are generally small bronzes, are also typical; other examples are the dancers in Asian royal dress (New York, Met., and Baltimore, MD, Walters A.G.) or the whirling Amazon statues in the tholos of the Khaznat at Petra. The rushing *Victory* from Taras (Taranto), installed on a globe in the curia at Rome after the Battle of Actium, generated a dominant Imperial iconography, for example the Temple of Mars Ultor acroteria as depicted on a relief from the Ara Pietatis Augustae. A synthesis of Venus and Victory types occurred, for example the bronze *Victory* (Brixia, now Brescia) adapted from the *Venus de Milo* type. God(dess) and infant groups became popular, such as the copies of *Peace and Wealth*, or the goddess on her acanthus rock found at Cumae (updated pendant to a 2nd-century BC original); Augustan Venuses are usually accompanied by an infant cupid hovering at the shoulder, a Hellenistic decorative motif.

Paratactic figural groups were popular in temples (e.g. the Venus, Caesar and Mars cited for the Pantheon) and pediments, for example the temples of Mars Ultor and Quirinus illustrated on later historical reliefs; these tableaux, which influenced relief sculpture, shared similar forms and gestures, a visual complement to the complex allegorical buildings that had become popular. Likewise the bronze dynastic and allegorical groups on arches, as documented by coins and inscriptions, for example the Arch of Gaius and Lucius at Pisa (AD 2; *Corp. Inscr. Lat.*, xi, 1421) and the 50 Danaids in the Palatine Apollo porticos imitated by the Villa of the Papyri's 'Herculaneum Dancers'. Republican honorific genres continued, as did references to Alexander the Great (e.g. the colossal seated *Alexander* in the rear exedra of the Forum Augustum). Newly popular honorific types were elephant groups, both singly (e.g. the obsidian elephants dedicated in the Temple of Concord) or as chariot teams; personified city and province groups, often arranged about honorific portraits, for example the Porticus ad Nationes (Servius on *Aeneid* VIII.721) and the Etruscan cities replicated for the Vatican 'Throne of Claudius' from Caere (Cerveteri); and series of captive Persians, such as those offering trophies on the Arch of Augustus (from coins), the kneeling trio holding a votive tripod on the Palatine and the caryatids of the Basilica Aemilia. In these last two acrolithic series, the exploitation of contrasting coloured marbles may (as in contemporary architecture) have had an iconographic dimension, symbolizing the multinational make-up of the Empire.

P. Hommel: *Studien zu den römischen Figurengiebel der Kaiserzeit* (Berlin, 1954)

V. Poulsen: *République et dynastie julienne* (1962), i of *Les Portraits romains* (Copenhagen, 1962–74)

P. Zanker: *Forum Augustum: Das Bildprogramm* (Tübingen, 1973)

H. P. Laubscher: 'Motive der augusteischen Bildpropaganda', *Jb. Dt. Archäol. Inst.*, lxxxix (1974), pp. 242–59

M. F. Squarciapino: 'Ipotesi sul lavoro sul gruppo scultore da Pan Caliente', *Augusta Emerita: Actas del simposio internacional conmemorativo del bimilenario de Mérida: Mérida, 1975*

K. Fittschen: 'Zur Panzerstatue in Cherchel', *Jb. Dt. Archäol. Inst.*, xci (1976), pp. 175–210

L'Art décoratif à Rome à la fin de la République et au début du Principat, Collection de l'Ecole Française de Rome (Rome, 1981)

B. A. Kellum: 'Sculpture Programs and Propaganda in Augustan Rome: The Temple of Apollo on the Palatine', *The Age of Augustus: Interdisciplinary Conference Held at Brown University, Providence, RI, 1982*, pp. 169–76

G. Koeppel: 'Die historischen Reliefs der römischen Kaiserzeit, i: Stadtrömische Denkmäler unbekannter Bauzugehörigkeit aus augusteischer und julisch-claudischer Zeit', *Bonn. Jb. Rhein. Landesmus. Bonn & Ver. Altertfreund. Rheinlande*, clxxxiii (1983), pp. 61–144

W. Eck: 'Senatorial Self-representation: Developments in the Augustan Period', *Caesar Augustus: Seven Aspects*, ed. F. Millar and E. Segal (Oxford, 1984), pp. 129–67

E. La Rocca: *Amazzonomachia: Le sculture frontonali del tempio di Apollo Sosiano* (Rome, 1985)

E. Simon: *Augustus: Kunst und Leben in Rom um die Zeitenwende* (Munich, 1986)

P. Gros: 'Un Programme augustéen: Le Centre monumental de la colonie d'Arles', *Jb. Dt. Archäol. Inst.*, cii (1987), pp. 339–63

R. R. R. Smith: 'The Imperial Reliefs from the Sebasteion at Aphrodisias', *J. Roman Stud.*, lxxvii (1987), pp. 88–138

P. Zanker: *Augustus und die Macht der Bilder* (Munich, 1987); Eng. trans. by A. Shapiro as *The Power of Images in the Age of Augustus* (Ann Arbor, 1988)

Kaiser Augustus und die verlorene Republik (exh. cat., ed. M. Hofter; Berlin, Gropiusbau, 1988)

M. Fullerton: *The Archaistic Style in Roman Statuary* (Leiden, 1990)

B. A. Kellum: 'The City Adorned: Programmatic Display at the Aedes Concordiae Augustae', *Between Republic and Empire: Interpretations of Augustus and his Principate*, ed. M. Toher and K. Raaflaub (Berkeley, 1990), pp. 283–96

P. J. E. Davies: *Death and the Emperor: Roman Imperial Funerary Monuments from Augustus to Marcus Aurelius* (Austin, TX, 2004)

(iii) Julio-Claudians. After the reign of Augustus the production of official sculpture decreased; Tiberius, Caligula (*reg* AD 37–41), Claudius and Nero were generally more frugal in their building and decorative programmes. Sculpture from the Julio-Claudian period was still overwhelmingly influenced by the ideals and styles of Greek art, known through descriptions, copies and works imported into Italy. Of named

sculptors working in Rome during this period, many were of Greek heritage (such as Zenodoros who, according to Pliny the elder, created a colossus of *Nero*). In function, too, Julio-Claudian works followed Augustan sculpture in establishing credibility for the regime.

The influence of Augustan sculpture upon Julio-Claudian works is also evident: friezes, for example, demonstrate the impact of the Augustan Ara Pacis. A *Suovetaurilia* (animal sacrifice; *c.* AD 48; Paris, Louvre; *see* ROMAN REPUBLIC AND EMPIRE, fig. 2) and the Ara Pietatis (commissioned in AD 22 by Tiberius to commemorate Livia's recovery from illness and completed under Claudius; Rome, Villa Medici and Mus. Nuo) are among the rare examples of surviving monumental reliefs. The *Suovetaurilia* differs from the Ara Pacis in its richer modelling, and the Ara Pietatis is notable for the deliberate rendering of recognizable architecture, smaller units of figural groups and deeper relief. The Claudian *Vicomagistri* relief (Rome, Vatican, Mus. Gregoriano Profano), which depicts a procession of magistrates and priests, reveals a new interest in representing greater spatial depth: the low-relief heads of the figures in the second row are elevated above those of the high-relief, frontal figures in the foreground, while the feet of the figures in both rows remain on the same level.

Sculpture in the round, influenced by Greek and neo-Classical works, decorated homes, fora, baths and gardens. Public and private portraits were common; those of Tiberius, Caligula, Claudius and Nero were executed in much the same style as the portraits of Augustus, although there was a general trend away from strict idealism. Hairstyles vary little, and a similar physiognomy, also found in a number of portraits of youthful Julio-Claudian princes, enforces the idea of family identity; unfortunately, such similarities make specific identification of these portraits difficult. Beginning with representations of Claudius and continuing with those of Nero, there was a greater sensitivity in modelling as well as a new interest in animation and in the psychological aspects of the individual, a development that was to reach its height with the portraits of the Flavian emperors. Vivid chromatic effects, common in the later portraits of Nero, are combined in other sculpted work, such as cippi and cinerary urns, with extravagant ornamentation.

The personal taste and ideology of each emperor also influenced the development of Roman sculpture. This can be seen, for instance, in Tiberius' villa at SPERLONGA, where a grotto housed colossal sculptural groups depicting scenes from the *Odyssey*; in the decorative scheme at Nero's Domus Aurea (Golden House), which illustrates the increasingly important role of sculpture in luxurious interior décor (*see* ROME, §IV, 5); and in the fact that propagandistic art was less common under Tiberius than under Augustus, as indicated by the paucity of monuments with historical reliefs constructed during the Tiberian period. Caligula commissioned a statue of himself as Zeus to be placed in Jerusalem and, because of his insistence upon being treated as divine, ordered that the heads of well-known statues of Greek deities be replaced with his portrait. Nero, unlike Augustus, modelled his portraits on the Hellenistic ruler cult type, as indicated by the style of hair.

The growth of the Empire with the development of provinces in Italy and elsewhere led to an increasing demand for decorative and historical sculpture, as exemplified by the rich reliefs on the Tiberian arch at ARAUSIO. The preponderance of Julio-Claudian portraits among the imperial portraits found in the provinces indicates the importance of portraiture in establishing imperial rule in new territories.

D. E. Strong: *Roman Imperial Sculpture* (London, 1961)

M. Torelli: *Typology and Structure of Roman Historical Reliefs* (Ann Arbor, 1982)

F. S. Johansen: 'The Sculpted Portraits of Caligula', *Ancient Portraits in the J. Paul Getty Museum*, i (Malibu, 1987), pp. 87–106

S. Wood: '*Memoriae Agrippinae*: Agrippina the Elder in Julio-Claudian Art and Propaganda', *Amer. J. Archaeol.*, xcii/3 (1988), pp. 409–26

G. Sauron: 'De Buthrote à Sperlonga: A propos d'une étude récente sur le thème de la grotte dans les décors romains', *Rev. Archéol.* (1991), no. 1, pp. 3–42

D. Kleiner: *Roman Sculpture* (New Haven, 1992)

G. Sena Chiesa: *Augusto in Cisalpina: Ritratti augustei e giulio-claudi in Italia settentrionale* (Milan, 1995)

(iv) Flavians. An exclusively Flavian style of sculpture did not exist. The style of the period (AD 69–96) was already starting to develop under Caligula and Claudius, reached its high point under Vespasian and Titus, and continued to influence works under Domitian and even into the first third of the 2nd century AD. Its softly modelled and richly detailed 'baroque' forms, designed to exploit illusionistic lighting effects, were gradually replaced in the last decade of the 1st century AD by a precise, somewhat austere linear style with which it had initially co-existed. This stressed balance and articulation rather than variety, with friezes of figures standing side by side in rather stiff, self-conscious poses.

The main characteristics of Flavian portraiture are already apparent in a portrait of *Claudius* of the 40s AD (Rome, Pal. Conserv., Braccio Nuo. III.10.2443). Heads are broad and faces puffy or flabby, with loose folds of skin blending into each other and concealing the bone structure. The eyelids are thin, making the gaze undirected; and though the hair is short, its individual locks are treated three-dimensionally to create a tousled, naturalistic effect. Like later portraits of Nero, those of Otho and Domitian have the stepped hairstyles typical of the period. The foppishness of the era is also apparent in the upswept toupee hairstyles of both women and men (see fig. 28), and the emphasis on voluptuousness and well-nourished, plump bodies. The more austere late Flavian style is particularly evident in 'Type 3' portraits of Domitian.

From the time of Caligula and Claudius onwards statues of Roman emperors displayed more overt identification with gods, especially Jupiter, reflecting a more autocratic attitude. A similar approach is also evident in imperial cameos of the 40s AD, executed

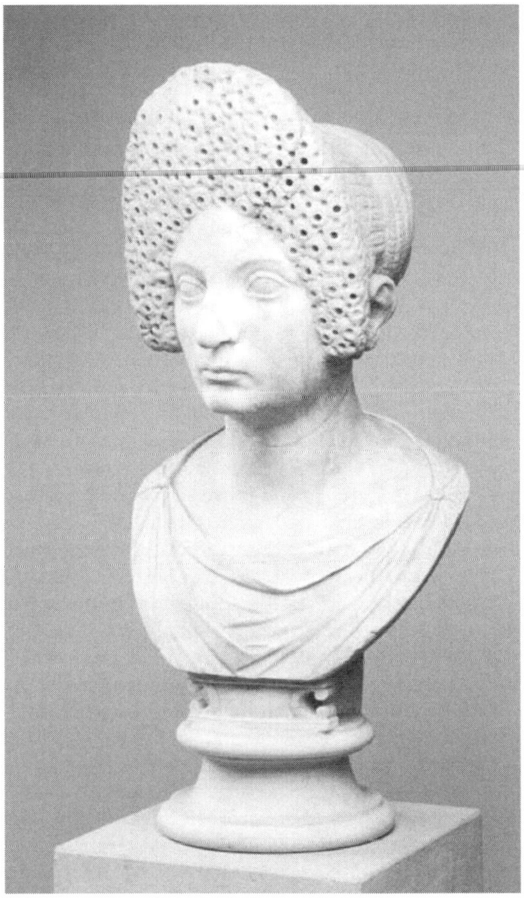

28. Roman bust of a woman, h. 450 mm, late 1st century AD (Berlin, Antikensammlung, Staatliche Museen zu Berlin)

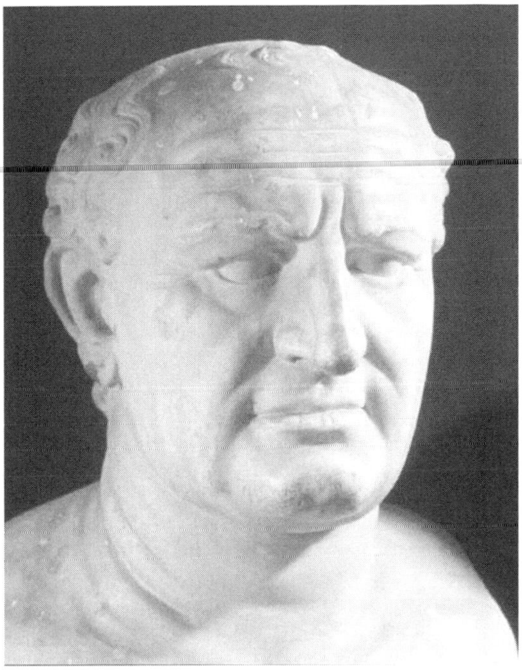

29. *Vespasian*, marble, second half of the 1st century AD (Naples, Museo Archeologico Nazionale)

in a lively, picturesque baroque style. However, by the reigns of Titus and Vespasian such works had ceased, as did overt comparisons between the emperor and Jupiter, though this reflects a change in attitude rather than style. The restrained forms and themes of their sculptures emphasized their close links with ordinary citizens (see fig. 29), in sharp contrast to representations of Domitian, the *dominus et deus* (ruler and god). Even towards the end of Domitian's reign, his official reliefs, such as those on the passage walls of the Arch of Titus (*c.* AD 81) and that from the Temple of the Flavian family on the Quirinal, used complex groups of figures on several planes to create chiaroscuro and an illusion of depth. Both the triumphal procession on the arch and funerary procession on the temple are traditional themes. What is novel is the allegorical depiction of the *pietas* (piety) of the State on a temple for the Flavian family on the site of Vespasian's residence, and the emphasis given to the historical elements of Titus' triumphal procession. The treatment of an actual event in an illusionistic style results in a pleasingly 'naturalistic' work.

Funerary urns adorned with relief sculpture were produced in greater quantities and with more diverse decoration than ever before, though they were still based on Claudian prototypes. Their ornament consists primarily of swags of rampant vegetation carved in high relief to create a chiaroscuro effect, but overlapping and blending together. Funerary altars were also rich in deep-cut symbolic ornament and figural motifs. During Flavian times all classes used collections of statues as symbols of wealth and prestige. The statue galleries of senatorial villas were more lavish than at any other period and encouraged the inclusion of lines of statue niches in increasing numbers of Roman buildings; similar, smaller and less sophisticated statue collections decorated the peristyle gardens of middle-class municipal houses. This also accounts for the unparalleled production of statuettes, marble *oscilla* (little masks of Dionysus), masks and other decorative relief work in the second half of the 1st century AD. The sculptors of funerary monuments also developed a wide repertory of craft and trade scenes to replace earlier depictions of tools, which reveals a greater self-awareness among craftsmen.

P. H. von Blanckenhagen: *Flavische Architektur und ihre Dekoration* (Berlin, 1940)

F. Magi: *I rilievi flavi del Palazzo della Cancelleria* (Rome, 1945)

G. Daltrop, U. Hausmann and M. Wegner: *Die Flavier* (1966), III/i of *Das römische Herrscherbild* (Berlin, 1939-)

H. G. Niemeyer: *Studien zur statuarischen Darstellung der römischen Kaiser* (Berlin, 1968)

M. Bergmann and P. Zanker: '"Damnatio memoriae": Umgearbeitete Nero- und Domitiansporträts', *Jb. Dt. Archäol. Inst.*, xcvi (1981), pp. 317–412

H. Wrede: *Consecratio in formam deorum* (Mainz, 1981)
I. Corswandt: *Oscilla* (Berlin, 1982)
H.-W. Ritter: 'Ein neuer Deutungsvorschlag zum Fries B der Cancelleriareliefs', *Marburg. Winckelmann-Programm* (1982), pp. 25–36
M. Pfanner: *Der Titusbogen* (Mainz, 1983)
H. Herdejürgen: 'Sarkophage mit Darstellungen von Kultgeräten', *Marburg. Winckelmann-Programm* (1984), pp. 7–25
R. R. Holloway: 'Some Remarks on the Arch of Titus', *Ant. Class.*, lvi (1987), pp. 183–91
F. Sinn: *Stadtrömische Marmorurnen* (Mainz, 1987)
H.-U. Cain: 'Chronologie, Ikonographie und Bedeutung der römischen Maskenreliefs', *Bonn. Jb. Rhein. Landesmus. Bonn & Ver. Altertfreunden Rheinlande*, clxxxviii (1988), pp. 107–221
P. Cain: *Männerbildnisse neronisch-flavischer Zeit* (Munich, 1993)

(v) Trajan. Portraits of Trajan have the same harmonious and imposing Classical appearance as 'Type 3' portraits of Domitian during the Flavian period. However, even the earliest are more massive and solid, with the hair simply combed forward on to the forehead following the contour of the skull and only the most important features emphasized (see fig. 30). The elegance of the late Flavian portraits with their fashionable hairstyles was deliberately replaced by an appearance of austere simplicity, suiting the first adopted emperor, whose authority rested on his willingness to serve the State, although in late portraits the modelling of the hair and features is less severe, toning down the emphasis on stern devotion to duty and introducing a hint of charisma. Nonetheless, Trajan's earlier portraits influenced contemporary taste more than those of any previous emperor: his hairstyle and attitude recur frequently in private portraits, especially those of middle-class men. In female portraits the typical Flavian hairstyle with small locks gathered into a vertical toupee at the front persisted in a more solid ornamental form. The most ornate of all Roman imperial hairstyles, stiffened with some form of diadem, was also developed; but apart from this concession to female beauty, the new emphasis on austerity profoundly influenced all forms of Trajanic sculpture, leading to a generally perfunctory and simplified imitation of Classical prototypes. In a new variety of toga-clad figure the toga became shorter, and its folds were treated more simply. Similarly, instead of being adorned with unrealistic ornaments the armour of cuirassed statues was often accurately copied from the actual dress of Roman generals. On clothed female statues the ornate fold-patterns of Flavian times were replaced by heavier and simpler systems, which like other Trajanic drapery often seem crude and monotonous. More profoundly, the iconography of imperial statues no longer emphasized the emperor's divine status: Trajan was rarely represented by a complete nude; more usually by a bust with swordband and aegis. His portraits established the canonical form for the bust, with a large sculptured element on a small moulded section carried by a small circular base. In the first two decades of the 2nd century AD portraits in general began to be more carefully modelled to create a realistic three-dimensional effect.

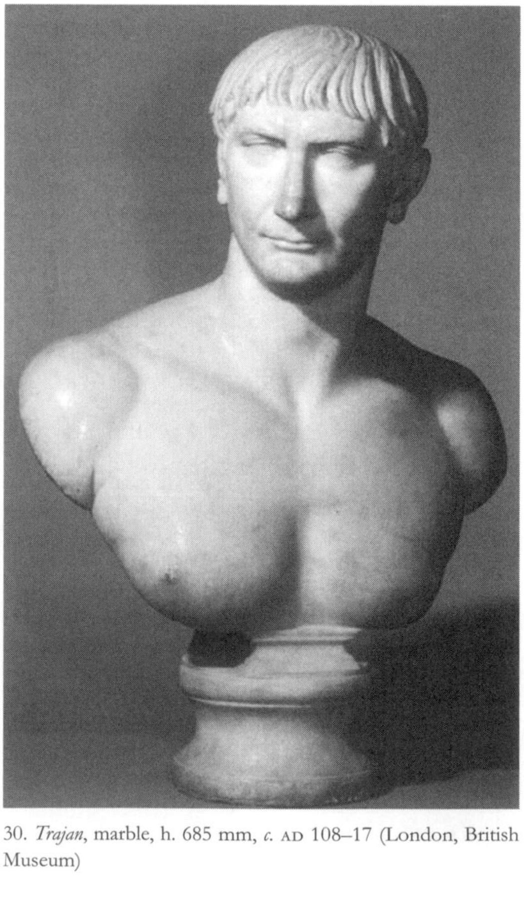

30. *Trajan*, marble, h. 685 mm, *c.* AD 108–17 (London, British Museum)

Many Trajanic historical reliefs survive, and their comparatively realistic depiction of historical events influenced post-Classical art. Their most striking and original feature is the juxtaposition of multiple scenes to suggest the emperor's omnipresence and omnipotence. The packed relief panels on the inner faces of Trajan's Arch at Beneventum (Benevento; *c.* AD 117) probably represent his duties in Rome, and those on the outer faces his activities abroad. His figure appears in such scenes as the conscription of recruits or the care of veterans, never before depicted on official reliefs: they represent day-to-day imperial duties rather than major historical events. Following contemporary Stoic and Cynic ideals of authority, Trajan portrayed himself as the *optimus princeps* (most worthy leader) appointed by the best of his own contemporaries and by Jupiter himself. Similarly, the spiral relief band round Trajan's Column (*see* ROME, §IV, 7) depicts the emperor as the ideal general in the context of his Dacian campaigns (AD 101, 105–6). Though its realistic scenes relate to historical events, it is not a mere chronicle but an instrument of propaganda. The emperor and his retinue are shown in a rather stereotyped and repetitive series of activities, such as sacrificing, addressing the army, setting out, supervising earthworks and directing battles, which are interrelated both horizontally and vertically. That the detailed and realistic treatment of the relief reflects the monument's function rather than contemporary artistic style is clear from comparison with the Great Trajanic Frieze (?*c*. AD 117; other sections now in Paris, Louvre and Rome, Villa Medici) reused in the Arch of Constantine (*see* ROME, §IV, 12). With its densely packed scenes carved in several planes and its more elevated and passionate tone it recalls Hellenistic prototypes, though it also reflects the contemporary image of barbarians such as the Dacians. Like Trajan's Forum (*see* ROME, §IV, 2(v)), with its central equestrian statue of the emperor (destr.) as the culmination of a statuary gallery representing earlier emperors, the State reliefs used their imposing scale and carefully selected scenes to bolster Trajan's image as the *optimus princeps*. The Trajanic sacrificial frieze (late 1st century AD; Paris, Louvre, MA 978, MA 979) may also have been designed to legitimize the emperor's position. Despite allusions to Trajan's civil benefactions (e.g. in the anaglyphs in the Forum Romanum, Curia Julia and in a relief in the opening of the arch at Benevento), a theme that recurred under Hadrian, the main emphasis was on military achievements: this accords with Trajan's expansionist policy.

The densely packed, pictorial scenes and floral decoration of Flavian funerary reliefs persisted under Trajan (see fig. 31), as in the late Trajanic Tomb of the Haterii (Rome, Vatican, Mus. Gregoriano Profano). Similarly, Flavian decoration persisted on funerary urns with an abundance of apparently continuous patterns, though the style became harsher and the compositions more systematized. Flavian schemes also continued to influence funerary altars, but new forms were developed: garlanded altars gave way to column and pilaster altars that emphasized the central decorative device. Greater numbers of sarcophagi were produced, and the forms and iconography of garland sarcophagi, sarcophagi with sacrificial equipment and griffins, and couch sarcophagi began to be established.

W. H. Gross: *Bildnisse Trajans* (1940), II/ii of *Das römische Herrscherbild* (Berlin, 1939–)

G. Daltrop: *Die stadtrömischen männlichen Privatbildnisse trajanischer und hadrianischer Zeit* (Münster, 1958)

F. J. Hassel: *Der Trajansbogen in Benevent* (Mainz, 1966)

P. Zanker: 'Sitzung am 13 Mai 1969', *Archäol. Anz.* (1970), pp. 499–544

T. Lorenz: *Leben und Regierung Trajans auf den Bogen von Benevent* (Amsterdam, 1973)

H.-J. Kruse: *Römische weibliche Gewandstatuen des 2. Jahrhunderts n. Chr.* (Göttingen, 1975)

W. M. Jensen: *The Sculptures of the Tomb of the Haterii* (1978)

P. Zanker: 'Ein hoher Offizier Trajans', *Eikones: Studien zum griechischen und römischen Bildnis* (Basle, 1980), pp. 196–202

J. Pinkerneil: *Studien zu den trajanischen Dakerdarstellungen* (diss., U. Freiburg, 1983)

T. Schäfer: 'Ein neues Denkmal zu Alimentarstiftung Trajans', *Archäol. Anz.* (1983), pp. 247–52

G. Koeppel: 'Die historischen Reliefs der römischen Kaiserzeit, III', *Bonn. Jb. Rhein. Landesmus. Bonn & Ver. Altertfreund. Rheinlande*, clxxxv (1985), pp. 143–213

G. Koeppel: 'Die historischen Reliefs der römischen Kaiserzeit, IV', *Bonn. Jb. Rhein. Landesmus. Bonn & Ver. Altertfreund. Rheinlande*, clxxxvi (1986), pp. 1–90

A.-M. Leander Touati: *The Great Trajanic Frieze* (Stockholm, 1987)

L. Musso: 'Rilievo con pompa trionfale di Traiano al Museo di Palestrina', *Boll. A.*, n. s. 4, xlvi (1987), pp. 1–40

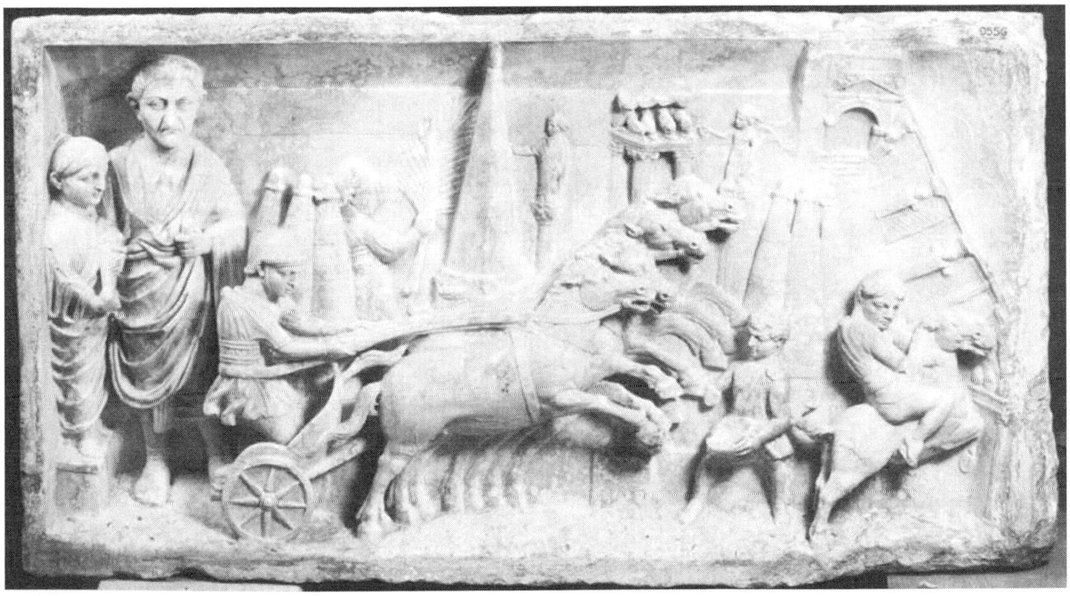

31. Roman funerary relief showing a circus official in the Circus Maximus, from Ostia, marble, h. 508 mm, *c.* AD 110–30 (Rome, Vatican, Museo Gregoriano Profano)

S. Settis and others: *La Colonna Traiana* (Turin, 1988)
D. Buitron-Oliver: *The Interpretation of Architectural Sculpture in Greece and Rome* (Washington, DC, 1997)
J. E. Packer and K. L. Sarring: *The Forum of Trajan in Rome: A Study of the Monuments* (Berkeley, 1997)

(vi) Hadrian. Sculpture from the reign of Hadrian varies in style, and its themes, forms and function display both continuity and innovation. Hadrianic art is generally characterized by a strong classicizing tendency. The emperor's ruling passion was a philhellenism that also served his political aims, providing a unifying and legitimizing paradigm for the Empire. In addition, he linked himself explicitly with his adoptive father, Trajan, and with Augustus.

Portraits of Roman emperors often set the tone for other forms of sculpture. Hadrian's appearance is described in Spartianus' biography (*Vita Hadriani* xxvi.1), and six portrait types are attested, varying in hairstyle, beard and expression (see fig. 32). Nearly all depict him with a contracted brow and vertical lines at the bridge of the nose. The ears curl outward. The richly worked head of hair contrasts strongly with the orderly hairstyles of the 1st century AD. His hair waves forward from short locks at the back and long strands on the top and sides, to end in a fringe of curls framing the forehead like a bonnet. The short beard is most striking of all, a major departure from his predecessors (except when in mourning). Unlike the hair, it is close-cropped and rough, contrasting strongly with the smoothness of the flesh. Besides portrait busts, there are also important cuirassed statues (e.g. Istanbul, Archaeol. Mus., no. 50; Athens, Agora Mus., S 166; Olympia, Archaeol. Mus., 148), one cast in bronze (Jerusalem, Israel Mus.). An interesting portrait from Ostia (Mus. Ostiense, no. 11(32)) resembles Early Classical Greek works: the fringe is regularized into snailcurls and the face is vaguely Periclean.

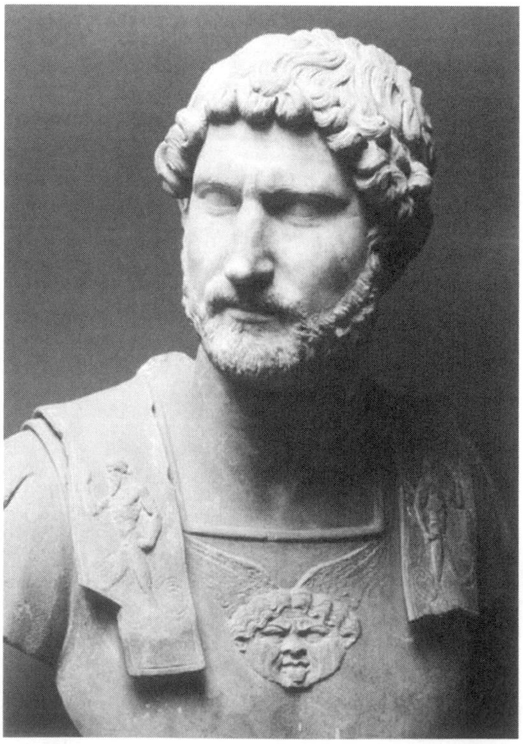

32. *Hadrian*, marble, h. 900 mm, *c.* AD 117–38 (Rome, Museo Capitolino)

Female imperial portraits include those of Hadrian's sponsor, Trajan's wife, Plotina; his aunt, Marciana; his mother-in-law, Matidia; and especially his wife, Sabina. The hairstyle in many portraits of Sabina has a Classical sobriety and clarity that accords with her fine features. Though early specimens depict her with elaborate Flavian coiffures like her mother's, later ones have the hair parted in the centre and its long soft locks pulled back into a loose bun, making her look like a Greek goddess. Her expression is gentle, less forbidding or dramatic than the other women of the imperial household and many Flavian ladies.

Perhaps the most frequent and evocative Hadrianic sculptures are those of the emperor's young Bithynian companion Antinous. Little is known about this youth, who became the emperor's constant companion and who drowned in the Nile in AD 130. After his death, he was assimilated to several deities, including Osiris (see fig. 33), Silvanus, Apollo and Dionysus. The apotheosized youth's adolescent body, stocky proportions and sensual features offer a contrast to more conventional types. A strain of romanticism or mysticism has been discerned in his representations because of the implied erotic relationship between emperor and favourite and the mysterious circumstances of Antinous' death. Yet his form was often posed in Classical stance and dress. Versions were disseminated throughout the Empire, but two portrayals are notable: the colossal Mondragone Head (Paris, Louvre); and a relief from Lanuvium (signed by Antonianos of Aphrodisias; Rome, Banco di Roma) showing Antinous as the god Silvanus.

Many reliefs appear to come from Hadrianic monuments in Rome. Though varied in size and apparently in function, all are in a classicizing style. The original context of two large panels (*c.* 2.5 × 2.0 m; Rome, Mus. Conserv.), which formed part of the Arch of Marcus Aurelius (destr. 1662–4), is lost. Though they perhaps came from an altar, restoration to the figures' heads and limbs and the recutting of certain details somewhat obscures their original appearance. One carries an *adlocutio* (address), the other Sabina's apotheosis. In the former the emperor addresses men, boys and a young man personifying the Roman people from the Rostra (speakers' platform) in the forum; in the latter Sabina is carried to heaven on the back of a winged figure, watched by the emperor, a companion and a personified abstract in the form of a reclining youth. Though the funeral pyre in low relief was added after antiquity and Hadrian's head has been reworked, the subject is clear. The base of

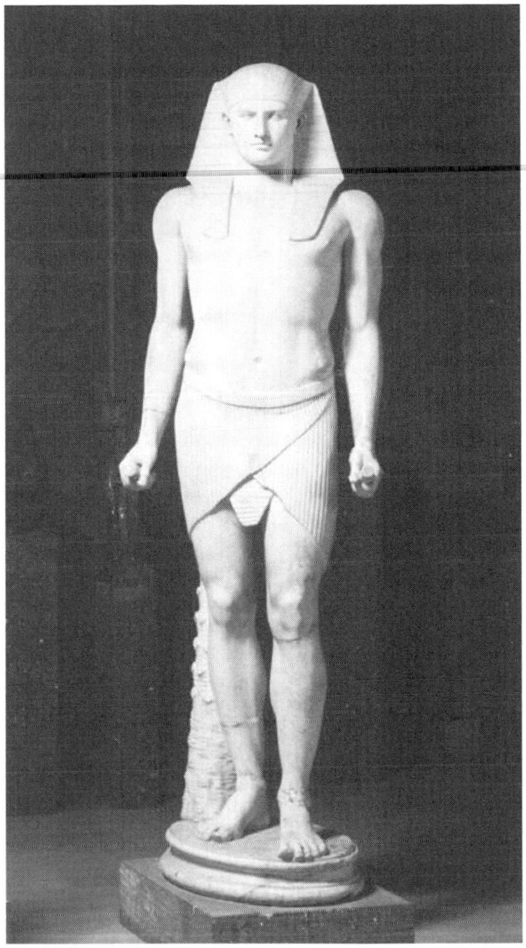

33. *Antinous*, from Hadrian's Villa, Tibur (Tivoli), *c.* AD 130–38 (Rome, Vatican, Museo Gregoriano Egizio)

the Column of Antoninus Pius (*c.* AD 161; Rome, Vatican, Cortile Pigna), showing the apotheosis of Antoninus and his wife, Faustina, affords a comparison. The pendant *adlocutio* represents Hadrian's funerary oration for Sabina (AD 136). These two reliefs exemplify several Hadrianic features: use of rectangular panels in State reliefs, which was followed in succeeding periods; relatively high relief; richly textured hair; short but full beards; and idealized facial features. The drapery is fully modelled, sometimes with the use of deep incision to define folds and the running drill to suggest texture, but without the cut-out effects of Antonine and Severan drillwork. The irises of the eyes often have incised outlines, while the pupils are carved or painted, a treatment applied to statues at least from Trajan's reign, though not widespread until Antonine times.

There is disagreement over the original function and even the Hadrianic date of the two long rectangular friezes known as the Anaglypha Hadriani (or Trajani; Rome, Curia), which were reused in the medieval Torre del Campanaro or della Grascia (destr. 1872). The friezes (*c.* 2×5 m) are made up from several smaller pieces of Pentelic marble. Their rear faces depict a *suovetaurilia* (animal sacrifice), while their front faces portray an *adlocutio* and the burning of tax records, apparently in the Forum Romanum. The two reliefs are meant to be read together: a fig tree and statue of Marsyas, both known features of the Forum, appear at the right edge of the *adlocutio* and the left edge of the burning scene. Hadrian certainly remitted taxes (AD 118), but the Chatsworth Relief (Chatsworth, Derbys), which shows soldiers carrying ledgers and is almost certainly Hadrianic, includes architectural indications of a different locale. Precise dating of the Forum relief is impeded by the fact that most of the heads are missing. Nonetheless, the two surviving heads have the straight noses and richly carved beards and hair typical of Hadrianic works, while the figures show the high relief and deeply carved drapery already noted and are of roughly similar height, in relative proportion to setting and each other.

The Arch of Constantine preserves a unique series of eight roundels in the attic (diam. *c.* 2.5 m) showing Hadrian and his companions hunting lion and wild boar and making sacrifice (see fig. 39 below). Their original setting is unknown and difficult to envision. There may once have been more roundels, since a head (Rome, Antiqua. Forense, 3671) seems to belong to a missing specimen. In style, the reliefs resemble those already discussed, though the round field affects both the depth and complexity of their composition. The love of hunting, which all sources agree characterizes the reign of Hadrian, became in the next century an imperial theme connoting power and victory.

The surviving panels of the Great Antonine Altar from Ephesos (*c.* 2×45 m, *c.* AD 138; Vienna, Ksthist. Mus.) are impressive in sheer size, but the workmanship is uneven and usually characterized as provincial: the figures are rigidly frontal and carved in very high relief with linear drapery, while the composition is awkward in comparison with that of the reliefs in Rome. The best-known scene shows Hadrian presenting his adopted heir Antoninus, together with the young Marcus Aurelius and Lucius Verus.

The ten Spada Reliefs (each *c.* 1.00×1.75 m; Rome, Gal. Spada and Mus. Capitolino), eight of which were found in 1620 during restoration work on S Agnese fuori le Mura, provide examples of non-historical, unofficial relief sculpture, though they are heavily restored and some may actually be early Antonine. They originally formed a cycle (or part of one, since other related examples are known) and probably decorated the peristyle of a villa. All depict individual or paired mythological figures. Their compositions to some extent resemble those of the historical reliefs but are also inspired by wall painting and metalwork. The panels themselves can be paired on the basis of the characters portrayed (e.g. *Bellerophon and Pegasus* with *Perseus and Andromeda*). The figures are in high relief against a very detailed, low-relief background of landscape or architecture; their sculptors mixed allusions to Archaic, Classical and Hellenistic Greek mythology and iconography for the enjoyment of sophisticated viewers.

An important group of Hadrianic copies or adaptations of actual Greek statues occurs at Hadrian's Villa at TIBUR (Tivoli). Among the best known are: the *Caryatids*, based on those of the Erechtheion at Athens (the copies of the 5th-century BC *Amazons of Ephesos* by Pheidias, Polykleitos and Kresilas); and the copy of the *Aphrodite of Knidos* by Praxiteles. There are also personifications of the Nile and Tiber, and a famous portrait of Antinous in pharaonic costume (Rome, Vatican, Mus. Gregoriano Egizio; see fig. 33).

Figured sarcophagi superseded the garlanded type that became popular under Trajan. Scenes were taken from myth; the lids often imitate architecture, with pitched roofs and acroteria at the corners, or a couch with the deceased reclining. The Attic and Asiatic types are so named from the sites of their workshops. Attic versions were more classicizing in both iconography and workmanship than the Asiatic, the sculptors of which used deep drillwork to produce strong contrasts of light and dark.

J. M. C. Toynbee: *The Hadrianic School* (Cambridge, 1934)
L. Maull: 'Hadrians Jagddenkmal', *Jhft. Österreich. Archäol. Inst. Wien*, xlii (1955), pp. 53–67
M. Wegner: *Hadrian: Plotina, Marciana, Matidia, Sabina* (1956), II/iii of *Das römische Herrscherbild* (Berlin, 1939-)
C. W. Clairmont: *Die Bildnisse des Antinous: Ein Beitrag zur Porträtplastik unter Kaiser Hadrian* (Neuchâtel, 1966)
A. Carandini: *Vibia Sabina: Funzione politica, iconografica e il problema del classicismo adriano* (Florence, 1969)
F. Eichler: 'Zum Partherdenkmal von Ephesos', *Jhft. Österreich. Archäol. Inst. Wien*, xlix, suppl. 11 (1971), pp. 102–35
U. Rüdiger: 'Die Anaglypha Hadriani', *Ant. Plast.*, xii (1973), pp. 161–74
M. Torelli: *Typology and Structure of Roman Historical Reliefs* (Ann Arbor, 1982)
J. Raedere: *Die statuarische Ausstattung der Villa Hadriana bei Tivoli* (Frankfurt am Main, 1983) [excluding reliefs]
N. Hannestad: *Roman Art and Imperial Policy* (Århus, 1986)
M. Boatwright: *Hadrian and the City of Rome* (Princeton, 1987)
R. Gergel: 'The Tel Shalem Hadrian Reconsidered', *Amer. J. Archaeol.*, xcv (1991), pp. 231–51
D. Buitron-Oliver: *The Interpretation of Architectural Sculpture in Greece and Rome* (Washington, DC, 1997)
Adriano e il suo mausoleo: Studi, indagini e interpretazioni (exh. cat. by M. Mercalli; Rome, Castel Sant'Angelo, 1998)

(vii) Antonines. Under the Antonines (*reg* AD 138–92) Roman civilization blossomed. Buildings, relief sculpture, portraits, marble sarcophagi and copies of Greek statues are extant in large numbers. A new style became dominant, characterized by effects of light and shade and deep drillwork (see fig. 34). The 'Antonine stylistic shift' also gave rise to exaggeratedly expressive figures.

Most monumental reliefs are in the Classical style, following the tradition of the Ara Pacis and the Benevento arch, with large, impassive figures standing in rows. This is the case, for example, both with the individual personifications of provinces on

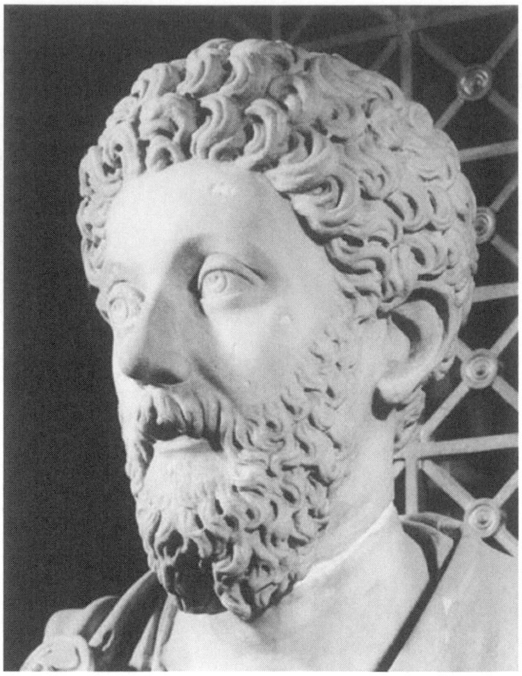

34. *Marcus Aurelius,* marble, second half of 2nd century AD (Vienna, Kunsthistorisches Museum)

the Hadrianeum (ded. AD 145) and with the scenic reliefs on one or two arches of Marcus Aurelius (after AD 176; destr.), of which eight panels were reused for the Arch of Constantine (*see* ROME, §IV, 12) and three are preserved in the Museo dei Conservatori in Rome. The scenes from Marcus Aurelius' Danube campaigns are intended, as on other triumphal arches, to exemplify general ideals of war, military leadership and imperial rule rather than specific historical events; the series of scenes is canonical and appeared frequently on coins. On the 'Parthian Monument' at Ephesos, which was probably erected after AD 166 in honour of Lucius Verus' victories over the Parthians, next to the solemnly arrayed emperors and personifications is a battle scene of the histrionic Hellenistic type, with complex figural and abstract patterns.

Even in scenes on the base of a vanished column in honour of Antoninus Pius (after AD 161; Rome, Vatican, Cortile Pigna; see fig. 35) stock images are used to depict the emperor and Faustina being borne to the sky by a winged Genius, watched by Roma and a personification of the Campus Martius. On the sides of the base a cavalcade of horsemen is depicted riding in a circle on lines denoting terrain, a scene from the imperial funerary ceremony. It derives directly from the tradition of the reliefs on Trajan's Column (*see* ROME, §IV, 7) and indirectly from that of so-called history painting, that is, panoramas of crowded scenes set in detailed landscapes seen from a bird's-eye view, a genre once considered typically Roman, but which should perhaps be regarded as Hellenistic.

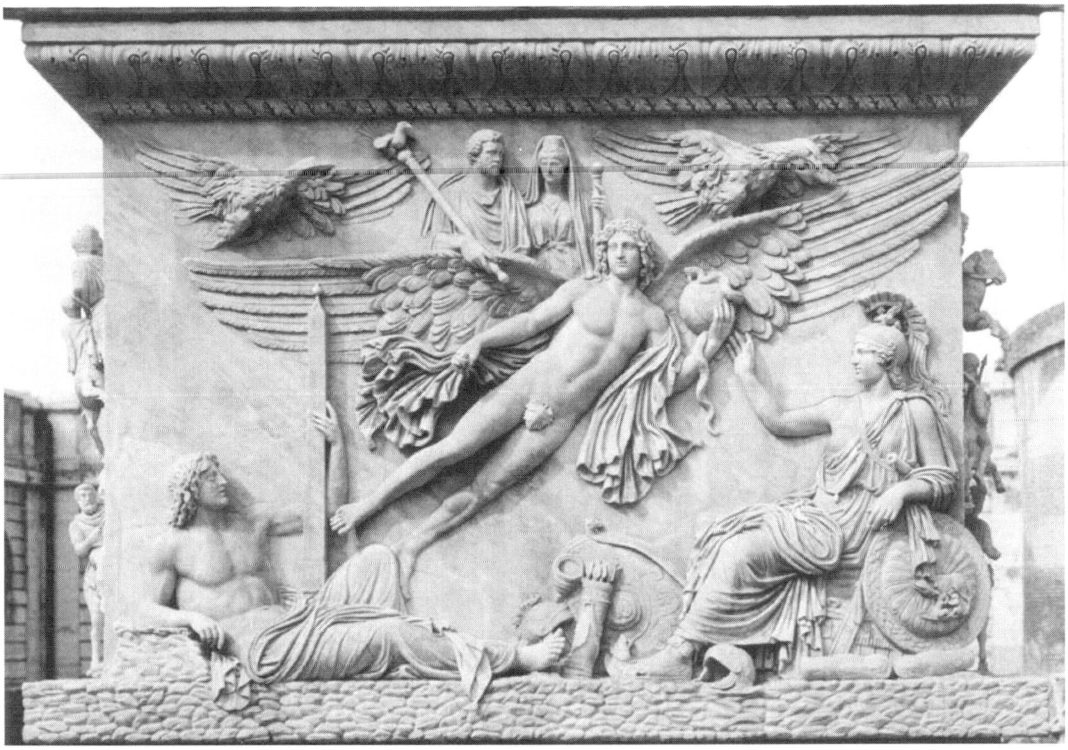

35. *Apotheosis of Antoninus Pius and Faustina,* marble, h. 2.47 m, from the pedestal of the Column of Antoninus Pius, Rome, after AD 161 (Rome, Vatican, Cortile della Pigna)

There is a clear stylistic development in civic monuments of the period, with chiaroscuro contrasts from the harsh modelling of positive and negative, gradually supplanting more plastic forms, and deep drillwork becoming the preferred technique.

This stylistic change is especially evident in portrait sculpture. The Antonine emperors continued the fashion, customary since Hadrian, for groomed curly hair and beards, first short, then long. Their faces are calm and without excessive expression, with no pronounced signs of aging. This stylization reflects the period of 2nd-century AD peace, a greater acceptance of Greek culture and refined ways of life that had previously been rejected and the enlightened and undramatic ideals of the Antonine regime, founded on gentleness and moderation. However, stylization in art moved so far from reality that it proved capable of reversing its original intentions. Coiffures grew more and more artificial and exaggerated, and sculpture depicted an increasingly sharp contrast between the highly polished surface of the face and the exquisitely arranged mass of hair, culminating in such extravaganzas as the bust of *Commodus as Hercules* (*c.* AD 180–*c.* 192; Rome, Mus. Conserv.; for illustration *see* BUST). Portraits of ordinary citizens closely imitated imperial models. In the crisis at the end of the Antonine period, subjects were frequently represented as older and with lively facial expressions; this became the norm in the 3rd century AD. The only equestrian statue of this period to survive is the famous gilded bronze statue of *Marcus Aurelius* (h. 3.52 m; AD 161–80), which stood at the centre of the Piazza del Campidoglio on the Capitol, Rome (now in Rome, Mus. Conserv.).

Frieze sarcophagi became widespread during the Antonine period, when they assumed their ultimate form. Predominant was the type on which mythological scenes were depicted as episodes in continuous sequence. Both scenes and individual figures were modelled on identifiable Greek sources and were sometimes taken from small artefacts. References to the deceased became more direct, as mythical heroes were given their features; scenes from Roman life were also introduced, representing the standard virtues, for example the sacrifice scene denoting *pietas* (piety). The unchanging subject-matter provides the ideal conditions to observe the gradual decline of plastic forms and the increasing use of chiaroscuro effects. (See also below.)

In the bird's-eye-view landscapes with historical scenes, the form of the subject-matter was less rigidly laid down than in other sculptural genres. Innovations in design were permitted, so that content, composition and execution could be given new meaning. This is the case with the Column of Marcus Aurelius, erected in Rome between AD 176 and 193 on the model of Trajan's Column. Its relief band depicts Marcus Aurelius' first Danube campaigns, but whereas the Trajan's Column sculptures celebrate the victories over the Dacians as achieved by imperial strategy and the discipline of the troops, here the message is narrowed to victory alone. Nearly half of the relief band contains scenes in which the Romans massacre the barbarians, who are shown as inferior opponents in cowardly flight or writhing on the ground. This compositional and stylistic change reflects a narrower view of reality and intensifies the statement; in addition, three-dimensionality is reduced in favour of clarity, and the landscape background is restricted to sketch-lines. The scenes are placed on two levels one above the other, sometimes to be understood as above and sometimes as behind each other. For the first time the emperor stands out in frontal view above the centralized composition. Expressiveness is heightened by elongation of the figures, emphasis on the movement of individuals and staccato repetition of these dynamic motifs from one group to another. Individual figures are articulated by notched lines. Elongated figures in lively motion also occur on frieze sarcophagi of the same period, but while the column reliefs are characterized by an expressive rawness aimed at distant viewing, the sarcophagi are refined luxury articles. They are much larger than earlier sarcophagi, their sculptured areas often containing a mass of figures piled on further figures, thus contrasting with the exposed figure outlines on Trajan's Column, but in their own way heightening the dramatic effect. And despite many chiaroscuro effects, they are rich in plastic forms and delicate detail.

As Rodenwaldt discovered, the expressive style of the Column of Marcus Aurelius corresponds with a more general shift in taste that, as he demonstrated in the case of a series of military commanders' sarcophagi, occurred suddenly in the decade AD 170–80. The un-Classical features of frontality, centralized composition and linearity are such marked features of the column that Rodenwaldt took the break with tradition to be one of fundamental principle and designated it the 'Antonine stylistic shift', which conveys at once the rapidity of the phenomenon and the durability of its effect. Expressive agitation, the leading characteristic of Roman sculpture of the 3rd century AD, is the enduring legacy of the Antonine stylistic shift. But this shift is also an interesting phase in itself. Shortly after AD 200 a number of its features, such as the elongation of figures, disappeared from sarcophagi and public monuments. So the stylistic shift proved to be a limited phase of a new taste in art, seeking a new and intense language and permanently destroying the Classical tone that had hitherto been predominant in Roman art. This search for more powerful means of expression is clearly indicative of the general crisis of the late Antonine period. It was a search that found fulfilment in the trappings of refined luxury, and its specific form was promoted by the exaggerated personality of Commodus (*reg* AD 180–92).

As in other genres, in Antonine copies of Greek statues there was a more intense response to their models than before. The garments of female figures exhibit diminished linearity, but they are enlivened by the addition of dynamic detail. Nude male figures are made more interesting by the admixture of detail from various periods, and they are charged with different moods by identification with mythological figures.

C. Robert and others, eds: *Die antiken Sarkophagreliefs* (Berlin, 1890)

E. Petersen, A. von Domaszewski and C. Calderini: *Die Marcussäule auf der Piazza Colonna in Rom*, 3 vols (Munich, 1896)

M. Wegner: 'Die kunstgeschichtliche Stellung der Marcussäule', *Jb. Dt. Archäol. Inst.*, xlvi (1931), pp. 61ff

J. M. C. Toynbee: *The Hadrianic School* (Cambridge, 1934), pp. 152ff, pls 34–5 [reliefs from the Temple of Hadrian]

G. Rodenwaldt: *Über den Stilwandel in der antoninischer Kunst* (Berlin, 1935)

M. Wegner: *Die Herrscherbildnisse in antoninischer Zeit* (1939), II/iv of *Das römische Herrscherbild* (Berlin, 1939-)

P. G. Hamberg: *Studies in Roman Imperial Art* (Uppsala, 1945)

I. S. Ryberg: *Panel Reliefs of Marcus Aurelius* (New York, 1967)

L. Vogel: *The Column of Antoninus Pius* (Cambridge, MA, 1973)

P. Zanker: *Klassizistische Statuen* (Mainz, 1974)

H.-J. Kruse: *Römische weibliche Gewandstatuen des 2. Jahrhunderts n. Chr.* (Göttingen, 1975)

M. Bergmann: *Marc Aurel* (Frankfurt am Main, 1978)

W. Oberleitner et al.: *Funde aus Ephesos und Samothrake* (Vienna, 1978) ['Parthian Monument' at Ephesos]

K. Fittschen: 'Ein Bildnis in Privatbesitz: Zum Realismus römischer Porträts der mittleren und späteren Prinzipatszeit', *Eikones: Studien zum griechischen und römischen Bildnis* (Basle, 1980), pp. 108–14

G. Koch and H. Sichtermann: *Römische Sarkophage*, Handbuch der Archäologie (Munich, 1982)

K. Fittschen and P. Zanker: *Katalog der römischen Porträts in den capitolinischen Museen und den anderen kommunalen Sammlungen der Stadt Rom*, i and iii (Mainz, 1983 and 1985)

H. Jung: 'Zur Vorgeschichte des antoninischen Stilwandels', *Marburg. Winckelmann-Programm* (1984), pp. 59ff

T. Hölscher: *Römische Bildsprache als semantisches System* (diss., Heidelberg, Akad. Wiss., 1987)

(viii) 3rd century AD. During the Severan period (AD 193–235) sculpture of all types was still produced in quantity. The great forum built by Septimius Severus (*reg* AD 193–211) in LEPTIS MAGNA claims comparison with the Imperial Fora in Rome. In the subsequent periods of crisis, however, sculptural output diminished and existing works were reused. No monumental reliefs are extant until the Tetrarchy. Portraits became fewer; only representational marble sarcophagi became more frequent. Monumental reliefs of the early 3rd century AD increasingly show frontal designs common to religious contexts. A typically 3rd-century AD style develops, characterized by expressively distorted lines and movements of figures and garments, and a tendency towards heavy, massive figural forms with sharp chiaroscuro contrasts. The use of flattened light and dark forms rather than more plastic ones is a constant feature of development. This is, however, overlaid by three

stylistic phases in all genres, in part ideologically determined: first, a movement away from the Antonine stylistic shift towards calmer and more solid forms at the beginning of the century; second, a powerful, expressive style with exaggerated figure movement and broken-up surfaces (*c.* AD 230–*c.* 253); third, a classicism that became the vehicle for ossification in Late Antiquity.

Most of the ornamentation on the triumphal arch (completed AD 203) built in the Forum Romanum by Septimius Severus after the Parthian Wars follows conventional designs. The great reliefs over the arches, however, depicting scenes of battle and siege on a landscape background, contain the same image types as those on the columns of Trajan and Marcus Aurelius, and like these they are more open to innovation. Although larger than those on the Column of Marcus Aurelius, the figures are stocky, and their lines covered by thick coats. The panel format combines a unified composition with an attempt to describe a continuous narrative, as on the columns. Other Severan monuments show an increasing preference for the frontal representation of major figures, which leads the viewer's attention away from the context of the action and towards a reverential attitude to the figure, for example the imperial groups depicted on the Arch of the Argentarii built in AD 204 by the silversmiths of the Forum Boarium in Rome. Similar tendencies are apparent in the provinces; they reach an early high point on the Arch of Septimius Severus at LEPTIS MAGNA (*c.* AD 203). Here not only is the imperial group in the triumphal chariot depicted in frontal view; in whole friezes of static and dynamic scenes a paratactic frontal arrangement of figures prevails, tending towards a central axis.

The history of the portrait in the 3rd century AD is the history of the programmatic self-stylization of rulers; the private portrait is influenced in turn. In these times of rapid, mostly violent change (25 rulers in 90 years), with corresponding problems of legitimacy, iconographical references to forebears were as frequent as abrupt breaks with the past and the following of fashion. There is a general tendency to more abstract forms and a rapid falling off of interest in individual personality; in contrast, achievement and charisma are emphasized (see colour pl. 2:X, fig. 2).

After the end of Commodus' reign (AD 192) new modes of appearance and depiction emerged, although some rulers, including Septimius Severus and Macrinus (*reg* AD 217–18), reverted to an Antonine style in order to project themselves as the legitimate heirs. From Caracalla (*reg* AD 211–17), however, the prevalent type of adult man had close-shaven hair, stubble beard, more mature features and a tense expression, indicative of a century moulded by military needs. The hair and beard style—not a military obligation—were practical features that corresponded to a new ideal of rigour. The mature features and tense expression indicated experience, effort and achievement. In the second quarter of the century, through eloquent distortion, this rough-hewn type attained full expression. The likenesses of the mid-3rd-century soldier-emperors Maximinus, Philip the Arab (see fig. 36) and Decius show mounting tension in the facial features and an increasing hardening and splintering of the form.

The emperors Valerian (*reg* AD 253–60) and Gallienus (*reg* AD 253–68) suddenly reverted to a more relaxed appearance, with longer hair, after Severan or even older models (a development called Gallienic classicism). The likenesses of the autocrat Gallienus, however, were charismatic: radical formal experiments in the spirit of Late Antiquity. The long curly hair perhaps alluded to Augustus and Alexander. The almost inert facial expression was heightened by an unrealistic crystalline form with straight contours and inner lines. The likenesses of the later 3rd-century AD Illyrian soldier-emperors Claudius Gothicus, Aurelian and Probus, though they again take up elements of the achievement-oriented portrait, are couched in the same abstract formulae.

In the 3rd century AD sarcophagi decorated with mythological themes and scenes from the Roman canon of virtues, for example those with depictions of military commanders and weddings, continued to be produced. But symbolic representations also assumed great importance, such as that of the deceased as a lion-hunter who conquers death through virtue (e.g. Reims, Mus. St-Remi), or a philosopher who attains eternal life by intellectual achievement.

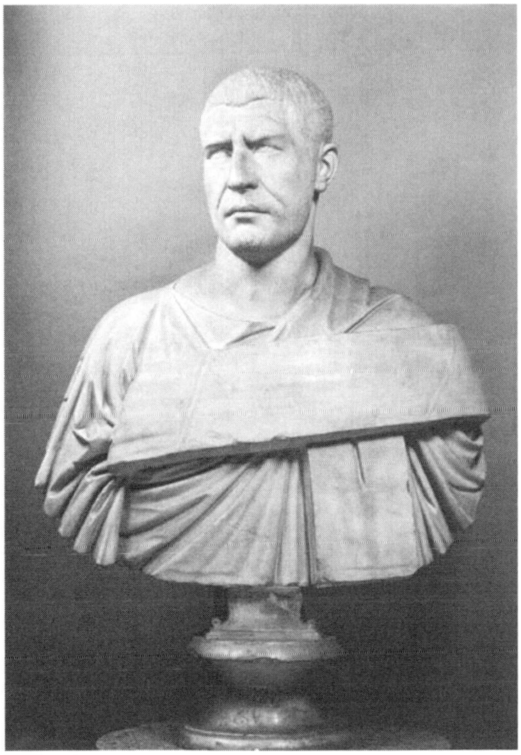

36. *Philip the Arab*, marble, h. 711 mm, *c.* AD 244–9 (Rome, Vatican, Braccio Nuovo)

In the 3rd century AD, as in the 2nd, there was a development towards more abstract forms, in which frontal surfaces of reliefs seem almost to have been squeezed on to a pane of glass, and upper surfaces are divided into light and dark areas. At the beginning of the century the excesses of the Antonine stylistic shift—the elongation of figures, giant scale and overcrowding—were abandoned for more conventional proportions and somewhat less mobile forms. This was rapidly followed, up to the middle of the century, by a heightening of expressive mobility in figures and detail (flame-style hair, for example). As in portrait sculpture, a Classical trend was dominant between AD 250 and 280. From a small circle of workshops came a prolific output of large and ambitious sarcophagi, the ornamentation of which was freed from the intricate detail of their predecessors to give a more serene and monumental effect (e.g. the lion-hunter sarcophagi and the Ludovisi battle sarcophagus, the latter in Rome, Mus. N. Romano; see fig. 37).

The lack of surviving monuments makes it virtually impossible to know the background to the stylistic shifts that took place in the 3rd century AD. It is intriguing that such sumptuous sarcophagi could be produced at the high point of the economic and political crisis after the middle of the century, but perhaps behind Gallienic classicism lay an appeal to the old values of the upper social strata from which Gallienus himself came. Evidence to support this includes the depiction of the celebration of the consular office on sarcophagi, Gallienus' preference for Greek culture, his acquaintance with Plotinus and his appeal to the great rulers of the past.

A. Alföldi: 'Die Vorherrschaft der Pannonier im Römerreiche und die Reaktion des Hellenentums unter Gallienus', *Fünfundzwanzig Jahre römisch-germanische Kommission* (Berlin and Leipzig, 1930), pp. 11–51

D. E. L. Haynes and P. E. Hirst: *Porta Argentariorum* (London, 1939)

R. Brilliant: *The Arch of Septimius Severus in the Roman Forum* (Rome, 1967)

A. M. McCann: *The Portraits of Septimius Severus (A.D. 193–211)* (Rome, 1968)

H. B. Wiggers and M. Wegner: *Caracalla, Geta, Plautilla: Macrinus bis Balbinus* (1971), III/i of *Das römische Herrscherbild* (Berlin, 1939)

D. Soechting: *Die Porträts des Septimius Severus* (Bonn, 1972)

M. F. Squarciapino: *Sculture del Foro Severiano di Leptis Magna* (Rome, 1974)

K. Fittschen: *Der Meleager Sarkophag* (Frankfurt am Main, 1975)

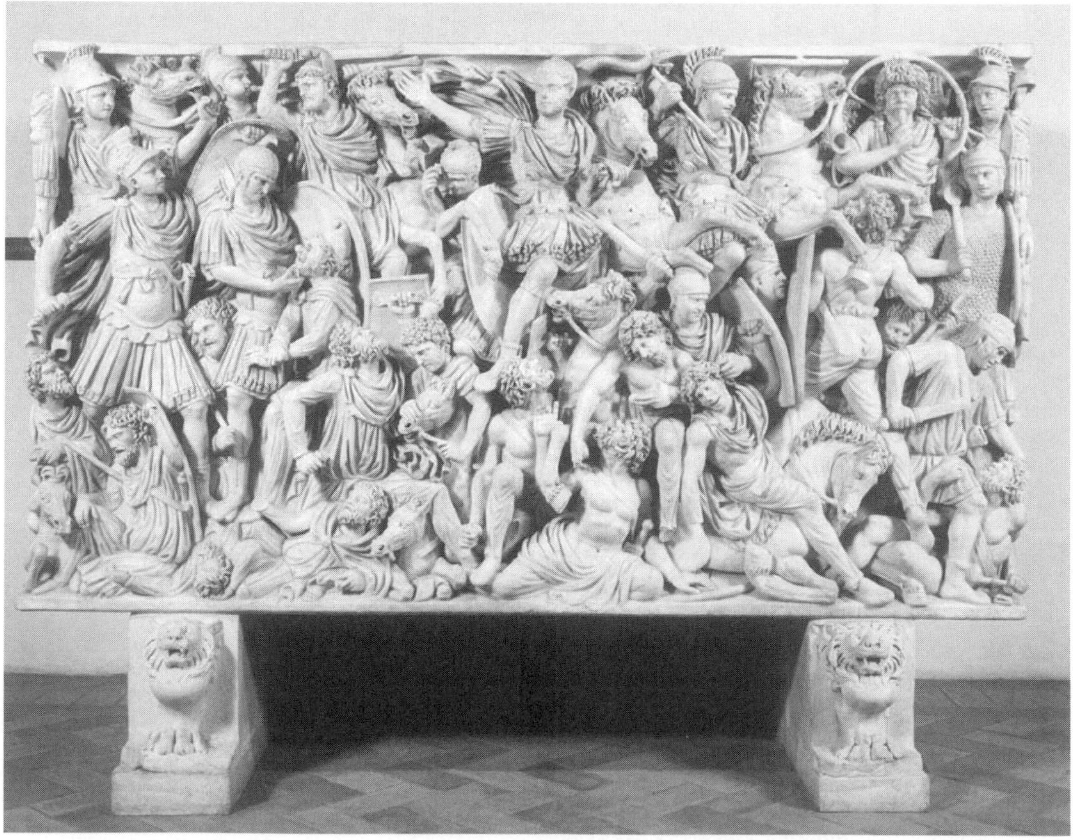

37. Ludovisi battle sarcophagus, depicting a battle between the Romans and the barbarians (detail), found near Rome, *c.* AD 250 (Rome, Museo Nazionale Romano)

M. Bergmann: *Studien zum römischen Porträt des 3. Jhs. n. Chr.* (Bonn, 1977)
B. Andreae: *Die römischen Jagdsarkophage* (Berlin, 1980)
G. Koch and H. Sichtermann: *Römische Sarkophage*, Handbuch der Archäologie (Munich, 1982)
S. Wood: *Roman Portrait Sculpture, 217–260* A.D. (Leiden, 1986)

(ix) Tetrarchs. Under the Tetrarchy, established by Diocletian (*reg* AD 284–305), major state monuments were again erected. The first ten years of the Tetrarchy were celebrated in Rome in AD 303 with the *decennalia* monument in the Forum Romanum. As depicted on the *oratio* relief of the Arch of Constantine (*c.* AD 315), five columns surmounted by porphyry statues were set up just behind the Rostra (speakers' platform): Jupiter in the centre flanked by the four emperors. One of the bases has survived (*c.* 1.00×1.82 m), carved with reliefs of rather dull quality. On the front two Victories hold an inscribed shield above bound barbarians. The other three sides depict the state animal sacrifice, the *suovetaurilia*, seen here for the last time in Roman art. Also in AD 303 Diocletian celebrated his twentieth anniversary by raising an arch, the Arcus Novus, over the Via Lata (the modern Corso) in Rome. Like the later Arch of Constantine, it was partly decorated with reused material, some fragments of which have been preserved. A pair of sculpted column plinths (Florence, Pitti, Boboli Gdns), similar to those of the Arch of Constantine, may also come from this arch.

Major building activity took place in the four new capitals. The main monument of the period was the four-way triumphal arch in THESSALONIKI, the residence of Galerius (*reg* AD 305–11), commemorating the Persian victory (AD 297). On the two pillars (*in situ*) decorated with narrow relief bands, some of the scenes depict specific events such as the capture of the royal Persian harem, but most depict stock themes: Galerius in battle, addressing his soldiers or sacrificing, and, as an expression of the ideology of unity, all four emperors posing frontally, the two senior emperors enthroned and flanked by the two standing juniors. The imperial college is surrounded by gods and personifications, but compared to the High Empire the allegorical compositions have become set-pieces characterized by the formalized imagery of Late Antiquity.

The new abstraction of forms found its best expression in the porphyry groups. The use of the hard, purple-coloured stone from Egypt became an imperial prerogative like the use of purple cloth. The Tetrarchs stand as guardians of the restored order in two pairs of reliefs (h. 1.3 m, *c.* AD 300; see fig. 38) set into the south-west corner of the façade of S Marco, Venice. Each grips his sword with one hand and embraces his partner with the other, thereby symbolizing *virtus* (valour) and *concordia* (friendship). The bearded man on the left of each group is an Augustus, while the clean-shaven one at his side is, by definition, the younger Caesar. The mutual *similitudo* (likeness) is underlined by the Illyrian bearskin cap, used only in this period. In general the sculptural quality of these 'cubic' works is not very high,

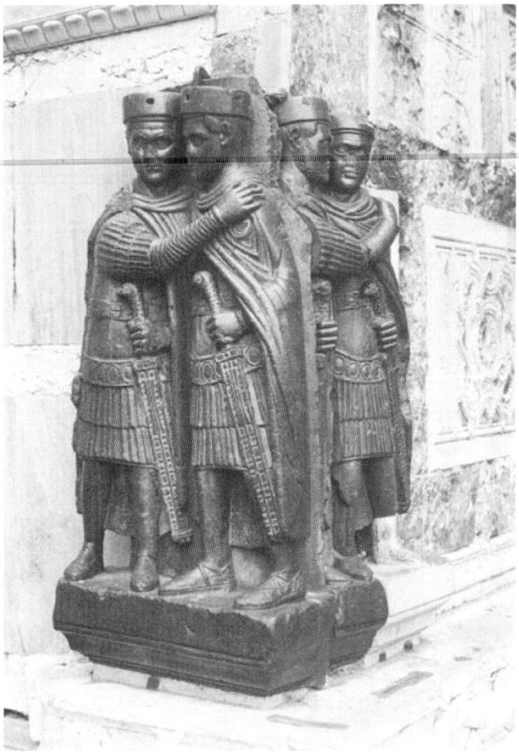

38. Relief sculpture of the Tetrarchs *Diocletian, Maximianus, Galerius and Constantius Chlorus*, on the façade of S Marco, Venice, porphyry, h. 1.3 m, *c.* AD 300

a life-size bust (*c.* AD 300; Cairo, Egyp. Mus. 7257) being an exception. Several tendencies compete in Tetrarchic portrait sculpture, but the often argued Eastern influence in, for example, the 'cubic' style can hardly be maintained. Some pieces still follow the more realistic tradition of the soldier-emperors, but few imperial portraits can be identified, the long series of replicas invented by the Augustan system having now ceased.

H. Kähler: *Zwei Sockel eines Triumphbogens im Boboligarten zu Florenz* (Berlin, 1936)
H. Kähler: *Das Fünfsäulendenkmal für die Tetrarchen auf dem Forum Romanum* (Cologne, 1964)
H. P. L'Orange: *Art Forms and Civic Life in the Late Roman Empire* (Princeton, 1965, 2/1972)
H. P. Laubscher: *Der Reliefschmuck des Galeriusbogens in Thessaloniki* (Berlin, 1975)
H. P. Laubscher: 'Arcus Novus und Arcus Claudii: Zwei Triumphbögen an der Via Lata in Rom', *Nachr. Akad. Wiss. Göttingen*, iii (1976), pp. 65–108
H. P. L'Orange and R. Unger: *Das spätantike Herrscherbild von Diokletian bis zu den Konstantin-Söhnen 284–361 n. Chr.* (1984), III/iv of *Das römische Herrscherbild* (Berlin, 1939-)

(x) Constantine. With the victory at the Milvian Bridge in AD 312, Constantine (*reg* AD 312–37) gained control over the western part of the Empire. As expressed by the conventional formulae of the inscription, the

senate and the people of Rome dedicated to his honour a triumphal arch, the last to be erected in Rome (*see* ROME, §IV, 12). The main part of its sculpture was obtained by stripping monuments of the High Empire—quite a common practice at that time. These recycled elements were not, however, used as pure decoration, but combined with those of a later date to form a single entity. The conventional sculpture, such as the *Victories* in the spandrels of the central arch, is carved in a traditional manner, but appears stiff and clumsy compared to the reused parts, while the historical frieze running round the entire arch continues the harsh Tetrarchic tradition. The main episodes of the campaign are reproduced in a naive and popular way. Allegorical representation is avoided, and the scheme of composition is simplified to appear basically two-dimensional. The resemblance to later Romanesque art is obvious. Best known of the scenes is Constantine's *oratio* (see fig. 39), a long narrow frieze showing the emperor in battle-dress standing frontally on the Rostra (speakers' platform) among his companions and addressing the Roman people. The Rostra is flanked by the surrounding buildings of the forum, in front of which the listening people are strung out. Of quite a different sculptural standard are the reworked portraits: those of the Hadrianic tondi on the façades rendering alternately Constantine and his then co-emperor of the East, Licinius. The latter is depicted in Tetrarchic fashion, with cubic head and short-cut hair and beard, while Constantine (best preserved in the wild boar hunt) becomes the model for the future imperial portrait. Both are masklike images, the political message of Constantine's being that the period of the soldier-emperors has finally come to an end. The new type, which can be traced back to the likeness of Alexander the Great but is also heavily influenced by the portrait of Trajan—the last emperor of an expanding empire—shows a man with a round, softly modelled face, hair in locks and no beard. This portrait type reached its mature expression in the colossal head of a statue of the emperor enthroned from the Basilica of Maxentius (h. 2.6 m, *c.* AD 313; Rome, Pal. Conserv.; for illustration *see* CONSTANTINE THE GREAT *and* ROME, fig. 16). In the grandeur of this portrait the masklike image has found its final form, and afterwards no imperial portrait can be identified on the basis of individual likeness.

The porphyry tradition of the Tetrarchic period was continued in two huge sarcophagi (both Rome, Vatican, Mus. Pio-Clementino), one traditionally ascribed

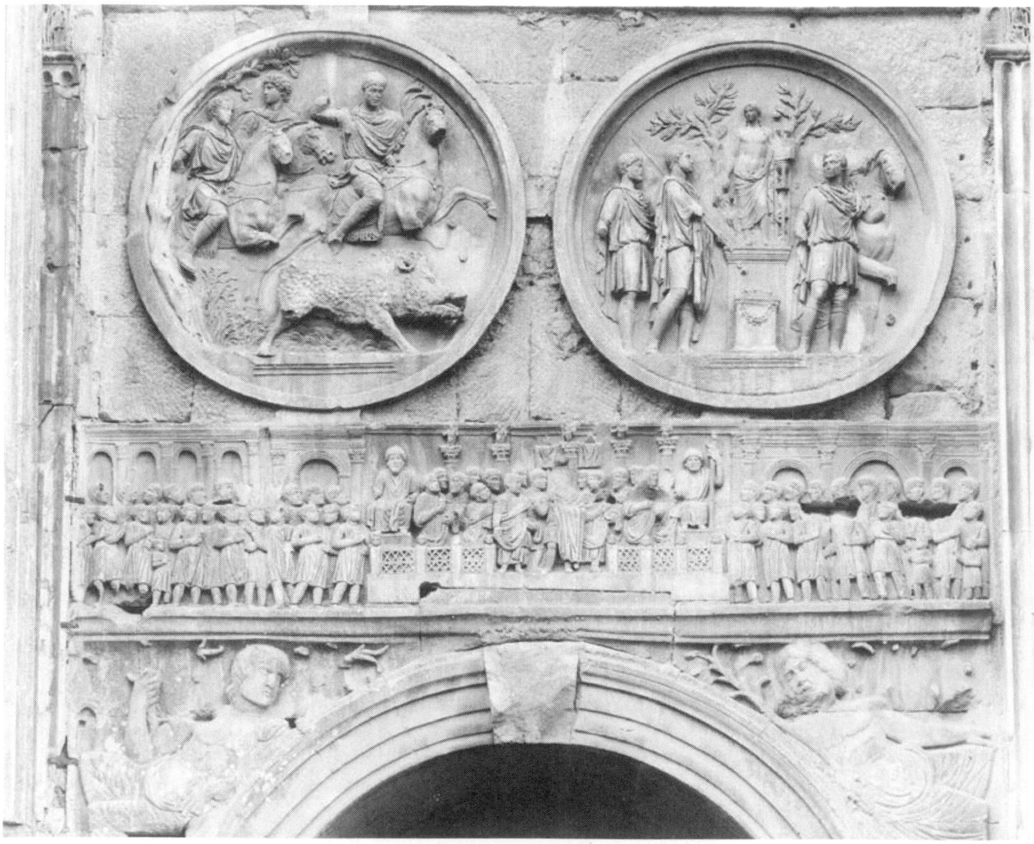

39. Relief sculpture from the north side of the Arch of Constantine, Rome, showing: (above) a boar hunt (left) and a sacrifice to Apollo (right), reused from a Hadrianic monument; (centre) the emperor delivering an oration; (below) a pair of reclining river gods, *c.* AD 315

to St Helen, the mother of Constantine (2.68×2.42 m), the other to Constantina, his daughter (2.33×2.25 m). The first, which may have been made for the emperor himself, shows Roman cavalry subduing barbarians in a strange balletic fashion, while the second depicts putti working in a vineyard of acanthus scrolls. Following the Edict of Milan in AD 313, sarcophagi with purely Christian motifs, often of high quality, began to be made in large numbers. A front in the Vatican (2.23×0.78 m; Rome, Vatican, Mus. Pio-Cristiano) is a typical example, known in several variants. In the middle are placed busts of the deceased couple in a cockleshell tondo, on both sides of which scenes from the Old and New Testaments are rendered in two superimposed registers. Style and mode of representation are related to the historical frieze of the Arch of Constantine, but the figures are slender and more refined. At about the same time the pagan upper class began to show less interest in this type of monument.

Of the new capital, Constantinople (ded. AD 330), little is known. Many works of sculpture were transferred from other parts of the Empire, but Constantine also issued edicts encouraging young men to learn the arts and crafts. Presumably from the Constantinian period is a highly mannered relief from the Hunter's Gate (h. 2.68 m; Istanbul, Archaeol. Mus.) depicting a huge Victory running in a formal way, her drapery folds closely set and rather stiff. With central power re-established, the court style came to play a more significant role, but, as in the previous period, many trends were in vogue, causing severe problems with respect to chronology. Reworking of older sculpture had become common, and several more or less independent centres of sculpture flourished. There is, however, a marked tendency towards classicism, not only of style and type but also in sculptural technique. Portraits in marble, for example, were often rendered with smooth eyeballs, as was the fashion until the late Hadrianic period. Along the same lines also is the continued copying of Greek-style sculpture, mainly ordered by the wealthy pagan aristocracy for their mansions. In this trade, the school of APHRODISIAS seems to have played a major role.

H. P. L'Orange and A. von Gerkan: *Der spätantike Bildschmuck des Konstantinsbogens*, 2 vols (Berlin, 1939)

B. Berenson: *The Arch of Constantine or the Decline of Form* (London, 1954)

J. Ruysschaert: 'Essai d'interprétation synthétique de l'Arc de Constantin', *Rendi. Pont. Accad. Romana Archeol.*, xxxv (1962–3), pp. 79–100

F. W. Deichmann: *Frühchristliche Sarkophage in Bild und Wort* (Olten, 1966)

F. W. Deichmann, ed.: *Rom und Ostia* (1969), i of *Repertorium der christlich-antiken Sarkophage* (Wiesbaden, 1969–)

W. von Sydow: *Zur Kunstgeschichte des spätantiken Porträts im 4. Jahrhundert n. Chr.* (Bonn, 1969), chaps 3–5

Spätantike und frühes Christentum (exh. cat., ed. H. Beck and P. C. Bol; Frankfurt am Main, Liebieghaus, 1983), chap. 4.10

H. P. L'Orange and R. Unger: *Das spätantike Herrscherbild von Diokletian bis zu den Konstantin-Söhnen 284–361 n. Chr.* (1984), III/iv of *Das römische Herrscherbild* (Berlin, 1939–)

N. Hannestad: *Roman Art and Imperial Policy* (Århus, 1986, 2/1988), pp. 301–18

N. Hannestad: *Tradition in Late Antique Sculpture* (Århus, 1994)

3. COLLECTIONS, MUSEUMS AND EXHIBITIONS. Roman portraits, sarcophagi, decorative reliefs, copies of Greek sculptures and other works survive in great numbers, although this should not obscure the fact that most have been destroyed. Examples survive in Rome, at sites throughout the Empire and in museums throughout the world, but there are few private collections of Roman sculpture.

The earliest collections were formed by the Romans themselves, who displayed Greek and Roman sculpture in gardens, homes and public spaces; two well-known ancient sculptural collections are those of Hadrian's Villa at TIBUR (Tivoli) and the Gardens of Sallust in Rome. The collecting and exhibiting of ancient sculpture was revived in the Renaissance, especially in the circle of the Florentine humanists; Cyriac of Ancona reported that the sculptors Donatello (1386/7–1466) and Lorenzo Ghiberti (1378–1455) had collections of ancient works. Popes Julius II (*reg* 1503–13), and Clement XII (*reg* 1730–40) developed collections of Roman art that were enriched by later papal collectors. Before the 18th century most collections were private and inaccessible to the public; the Capitoline Museums, presented by Pope Sixtus IV (*reg* 1471–84) to the people of Rome in 1471, are a notable exception. Public museums were developed and expanded during the 18th century, which experienced a widespread popular interest in art, while Neo-classicism and the rediscovery and excavations of POMPEII and HERCULANEUM led to a renewed interest in Classical antiquity and increased discoveries and collecting. Archaeology became a fad; wealthy Europeans and Americans excavated Greek and Roman sites and placed their finds in private or public collections. Private collections were increasingly consolidated and opened to the public. The USA entered the field of art collecting in the 19th century and, particularly after 1900, collection was dominated by the magnates of American industry. Public display of works of art was disrupted in Europe by World War II when museums were closed and the sculptures placed in storage. The Glyptothek in Munich, for instance, closed in 1939 and did not reopen until 1972 after its restoration. The discovery and attribution of the Riace Bronzes, which were first exhibited in Florence in 1981, have spurred new directions in research and in the reassembly, restoration and display of ancient sculpture.

A number of important examples of Roman sculpture can still be viewed *in situ*, within the context of their architectural and urban settings, although increasingly they are being removed for protection against the disintegration caused by pollution. *In situ* sculpture in Rome includes the reliefs on the restored Ara Pacis, those on the triumphal columns of Trajan and Marcus Aurelius, and those on the triumphal arches of Titus and Constantine; some of the reliefs on the Arch of Constantine were taken from earlier Trajanic and Hadrianic monuments. There are sculpted friezes *in situ* in the Forum of Nerva and on the Temple of Antoninus and Faustina. Examples of *in situ* sculpture outside Rome include the reliefs of the triumphal arches of Trajan at Beneventum (Benevento), of Septimius Severus in Leptis Magna, of Galerius in Thessaloniki, and those on the arches at Arausio (Orange) and Tripoli, as well as the reliefs on the base of the Obelisk of Theodosios at Constantinople (Istanbul) and the friezes on the Temple of Bel at Palmyra. Some of the rock-cut temples at Petra have sculptures carved into the façades. Surviving pedimental sculpture is rare, but the fragments of the pedimental sculpture of the Temple of Augustus at Ephesos have been reconstructed at the museum near the site. Since many antiquities have been discovered during the process of building and enlarging Rome, museums and collections throughout the city contain rich holdings of ancient sculpture. Of particular interest are the Capitoline Museums, the oldest public art collection in Europe. It now encompasses four institutions, two of which are particularly important for the display of antique sculpture: the Museo Capitolino, opened to the public in 1734, which was established by Clement XII from the private collection of Cardinal Alessandro Albani (1692–1779); and the Museo dei Conservatori, which includes sculpture found in the Gardens of Maecenas on the Esquiline. Included in the museums' collections are the Capitoline *Venus*, a fine collection of imperial portraits, busts of Flavian women, a Roman copy of the Hellenistic *Dying Gaul* that was discovered in the Gardens of Sallust, *Commodus as Hercules* and fragments of the colossal statue of the *Emperor Constantine* from the Basilica of Maxentius. In the Capitoline square stands the equestrian statue of *Marcus Aurelius*.

The Vatican Museums, which began with Julius II's private collections, were established at the time of his ascent to the papacy in 1503. The holdings of the Museo Gregoriano Profano and the sculpture gallery of the Museo Pio-Clementino, founded by Clement XIV (*reg* 1769–75) and enlarged by Pius VI (*reg* 1775–80) in the late 18th century, reflect continuing papal interest in Rome's Classical heritage. Included in the collections are the *Apollo Belvedere*, the *Augustus* from Prima Porta, the *Laokoon, Venus Felix, Hercules and Telephus*, a Roman copy of Praxiteles' *Venus of Knidos*, the altar of the Vicomagistri, many portrait busts, and Roman copies of Greek sculptures, including the marble *Marsyas*, a copy of a bronze by Myron.

The Museo Nazionale Romano, also in Rome, was founded in 1889 to display works discovered in Rome since 1870; it includes sculptures from the Kircherian and Ludovisi collections. Included are Roman copies of Greek original works, including the *Diskobolos* of Castel Porziano, which is a copy of a bronze by Myron, portraits such as *Augustus as Pontifex Maximus*, and stucco decorations from the Farnesina House.

There are many other collections in Rome. The Villa Albani (now Villa Torlonia) includes the collections of Cardinal Alessandro Albani as they were arranged by Winckelmann in 1765. The Galleria Borghese has the collection of Cardinal Scipione Borghese (?1576–1633) and additions by later family members. The Museo Barracco, established by Senator Giovanni Barracco (1829–1914), was presented to the city in 1902. Although a small museum at Hadrian's Villa, Tivoli (anc. Tibur), houses some sculptures, many works discovered at the site are now displayed elsewhere in Rome and Europe.

In Naples, the Museo Archeologico Nazionale houses a representative selection of ancient sculpture that includes many important works excavated from the Vesuvian sites, especially Pompeii and Herculaneum. There are sculptures from the Borgia collections, the collections of the Bourbon kings of Naples, and the extensive Farnese collections, which were inherited by King Charles III of Spain (*reg* 1759–88) from his mother, Elisabeth Farnese. Important works include *Aristides*, the *Elder Balbus* and *Younger Balbus* and the Farnese *Bull* and *Hercules*, as well as bronze figures from the Villa of the Papyri (Herculaneum) and Roman portraits including a colossal head of *Julius Caesar* and busts of *Vespasian* and *Antoninus Pius*. Among the Roman copies of Greek works are those of Polykleitos' *Doryphoros* and the *Aphrodite Kallipyges*.

In Florence, the Museo Archeologico di Firenze houses the *Arringatore* and other works, and the Galleria degli Uffizi has a large group of ancient statuary collected by the Medici that includes the *Arrotino* (from a Hellenistic Marsyas group), the *Wild Boar*, the *Idolino*, the Niobe group and the *Wrestlers*. In Mantua there is a collection of Roman sculpture at the Palazzo Ducale, while in Venice the Museo Archeologico exhibits Roman works and the church of S Marco displays the horses of St Mark's, a bronze quadriga now generally thought to be Roman in origin. In Palermo the Museo Regionale di Palermo has a large collection of Roman sculpture, and in Sperlonga portions of the sculptural groups from the grotto of Tiberius are displayed in the Museo Archeologico Nazionale.

The extent of the territory held by the Romans is reflected in the works displayed at such cities and sites as Antioch, Arles (anc. Arelate), Belgrade, Cádiz (anc. Gades), Cologne (anc. Colonia Claudia Ara Agrippinensium), Corinth, Cyrene, Delphi, Ephesos, Leptis Magna, Olympia, Ostia, Palmyra, Pergamon, Thessaloniki, Trier (anc. Augusta Treverorum) and Tunis. The remains from Roman sites in Turkey are displayed in museums at Ankara, Bursa, Izmir and Istanbul.

The British Museum in London incorporates the Townley collection, begun in 1767, which contains portraits, sarcophagi and copies of Greek works. The Department of Greek and Roman Antiquities at the Musée du Louvre in Paris was established in 1800, but it includes ancient works collected by Francis I, king of France (*reg* 1515–47), in the 16th century; works in the collection include Roman portrait busts, the *Lion* from Miletos and important copies after Greek works. Other collections with significant works are the National Archaeological Museum and the Agora Museum in Athens, the Antikensammlung and the Antikenmuseum in Berlin, the Fitzwilliam Museum in Cambridge, the Ashmolean Museum in

Oxford, the Ny Carlsberg Glyptotek in Copenhagen, the Museo del Prado in Madrid, the Glyptothek and Staatliche Antikensammlungen in Munich, the Kunsthistorisches Museum in Vienna, the Hermitage in St Petersburg, the Museum of Fine Arts in Budapest, the Staatliche Kunstsammlungen in Dresden and the Staatliche Kunstsammlungen in Kassel. In Canada there is an important collection at the Royal Ontario Museum in Toronto.

In the USA the most important collections are at the Metropolitan Museum of Art in New York, the Museum of Fine Arts in Boston, MA, and the J. Paul Getty Museum in Malibu. The Metropolitan Museum of Art contains reliefs and portrait sculptures, including a colossal head of *Constantine* formerly in the Giustiniani collection in Rome. The Boston Museum of Fine Arts collection began with the purchase of the Cesnola collection in 1872; it now includes fragments, reliefs and Greco-Roman figures, as well as portraits, most notably from the Julio-Claudian period. The J. Paul Getty Museum houses an ancient collection, begun in 1939, that includes a number of grave reliefs and sarcophagi.

Other American collections with important pieces include the Walters Art Gallery in Baltimore, the Isabella Stewart Gardner Museum in Boston, MA, the Bowdoin College Museum of Art in Brunswick, ME, the Cleveland Museum of Art, the Fogg Art Museum in Cambridge, MA, the Art Institute of Chicago, the Cincinnati Art Museum, the Detroit Institute of Arts, the Wadsworth Atheneum in Hartford, the Nelson-Atkins Museum of Art in Kansas City, the University Museum of the University of Pennsylvania in Philadelphia, the Museum of Art in Santa Barbara, the Museum of Art in Toledo, OH, and the Worcester, MA, Art Museum. William Randolph Hearst, his family and his organizations are largely responsible for the Roman collections at the County Museum of Art in Los Angeles, the Hearst Foundation at San Simeon, CA, and the Robert H. Lowie Museum of Anthropology at the University of California in Berkeley.

Because of the large scale of much Roman sculpture and the fact that the commonly used materials, marble and bronze, present difficulties in moving major works, significant temporary or travelling exhibitions have never been common. Representative exhibitions are *Ancient Art from New York Private Collections* at the Metropolitan Museum of Art, New York (1959–60); *Pompeii AD 79*, at the Museum of Fine Arts in Boston, MA, the Art Institute of Chicago, the Dallas Museum of Fine Arts and the American Museum of Natural History in New York (1978–9); and *The Vatican Collections* at the Metropolitan Museum of Art, New York (1982), which included the *Apollo Belvedere*, the *Augustus* from Prima Porta and Roman portraits.

O. Benndorf and R. Schöne: *Die antiken Bildwerke des Lateranensischen Museums* (Leipzig, 1867)

W. Amelung and G. Lippold: *Die Skulpturen des vatikanischen Museums*, 3 vols (Berlin, 1903–8)

G. Mendel: *Istanbul: Musées impériaux ottomans: Catalogue des sculptures grecques, romaines et byzantines*, 3 vols (Istanbul, 1912)

L. D. Caskey: *Catalogue of Greek and Roman Sculpture, Fogg Art Museum* (Cambridge, MA, 1925)

R. N. Pryce: *British Museum: Catalogue of Sculpture*, I/ii (London, 1931)

C. Blümel: *Römische Kopien griechischer Skulpturen des vierten Jahrhunderts vor Christus: Staatliche Museen zu Berlin* (Berlin, 1938)

A. García y Bellido: *Esculturas romanas de España y Portugal*, 2 vols (Madrid, 1949)

S. Bocconi: *Collezioni capitoline* (Rome, 1950)

F. Poulsen: *Catalogue of Ancient Sculpture in the Ny Carlsberg Glyptotek* (Copenhagen, 1951)

B. M. Felletti sr: *Museo Nazionale Romano: I ritratti* (Rome, 1953)

A. Giuliano: *Catalogo dei ritratti romani del Museo Profano Lateranense* (Vatican City, 1957)

G. A. Mansuelli: *Galleria degli Uffizi: Le sculture*, 2 vols (Rome, 1958–61)

E. Paribeni: *Catalogo delle sculture di Cirene* (Rome, 1959)

Ancient Art from New York Private Collections (exh. cat. by D. von Bothmer, New York, Met., 1961)

J. Charbonneaux: *La Sculpture grecque et romaine au Musée du Louvre* (Paris, 1963)

L. Budde and R. Nicholls: *A Catalogue of the Greek and Roman Sculpture in the Fitzwilliam Museum, Cambridge* (Cambridge, 1964)

E. Rohde: *Griechische und romische Kunst in den Staatlichen Museen zu Berlin* (Berlin, 1968)

M. B. Comstock and C. C. Vermeule: *Greek, Etruscan and Roman Bronzes in the Museum of Fine Arts, Boston* (Boston, 1971)

D. E. Strong: 'Roman Museums', *Archaeological Theory and Practice*, ed. D. E. Strong (London and New York, 1973), pp. 247–64

M. B. Comstock and C. C. Vermeule: *Sculpture in Stone: The Greek, Roman and Etruscan Collections of the Museum of Fine Arts* (Boston, 1977)

Treasures from the National Archaeological Museum, Naples, and the Pompeii Antiquarium (exh. cat., Boston, MA, Mus. F.A., 1978)

C. C. Vermeule: *Greek and Roman Sculpture in America* (Malibu, 1981)

The Vatican Collections: The Papacy and Art (exh. cat., text by C. Pietrangeli and others, New York, Met.; Chicago, A. Inst.; San Francisco, F.A. Museums; 1983–4)

E. Bartman: 'Sculptural Collecting and Display in the Private Realm', *Roman Art in the Private Sphere*, ed. E. Gazela (Ann Arbor, 1991), pp. 71–88

G. Daltrop and H. Oehler: *Katalog der Skulpturen: Museo Gregoriano Profano ex Lateranense* (Mainz, 1996)

M. Bertoletti, M. Cima and E. Talamo: *Sculture di Roma antica: Collezioni dei Musei Capitolini alla Centrale Montemartini* (Milan, 1997)

R. Brilliant: *Mythological Figures and Portraits: The Miller Collection of Roman Sculpture* (Minneapolis, 2004)

Scythian Art. Term used principally to describe the figural toreutic (chased and embossed) metalwork of the Eurasian steppes in the 1st millennium BC. Scythian art is closely connected to Thracian, Iranian, Hellenistic and Central Asian art, and also to the so-called 'Northern' culture of China. The later phase of the art is is closely connected to Dacian art (*see* THRACIAN AND DACIAN ART).

Early Scythian art only rarely depicts human figures. The animal motifs are essentially self-contained and either emblematic or decorative. From the late 6th century onwards, imported Greek objects were included with Scythian pieces in the kurgans; for example a late 5th-century BC Panathenaic amphora was found in the Elizavetinskaya kurgan, near Kerch. These imports introduced ideas of greater iconographic complexity and of providing indigenous themes with a narrative structure. Marking a development in complexity over the shield-boss stags of the preceding period is a fragment of quiver (gorytus) overlay from the Ilychovo barrow (5th century BC; see Piotrowsky, Galanina and Grach). A recumbent stag is attacked by a wolf, eagle and snake. The heads of birds are used to indicate the antler tines, hooves and possibly the entrails of the stag, which are being pecked by the eagle perched on its rump.

Many indigenous metalsmiths of this period were probably itinerant and therefore were exposed to a vast range of regional styles. In this period the steppe emerged as an economic buffer zone connecting the Greek city-states and their colonies to sources of labour, grain and minerals in the forest-steppe and mountain regions. Control of the northern trade routes between China and the Near East gave the nomad élites access to Greek luxury goods, including wine and metalwork; for example the kurgan burials of the so-called Seven Brothers contained Greek imports and Greco-Scythian costume appliqués of sheet-gold in the form of sphinxes, owls and heads of Silenus. Scythian pieces included bronze bridle frontlets and plaques in the form of stag or elk heads (Piotrowsky, Galanina and Grach). Depictions of such animals are more usual in the art of Siberia and reflect the eastern origins of many of the nomad groups.

In the 4th century BC there is a significant change in the nature of the Greek material found in Scythian burials. Much of the metalwork was classically inspired and made in the Greek BLACK SEA COLONIES but depicted scenes from everyday Scythian life. An important aspect of Greco-Scythian art is that it provides a visual record of the Scythians. Human depiction and narrative iconography became an established part of steppe art in the following centuries.

Complex iconography is used to depict particular stories. Sometimes these are clearly Greek, such as the scenes from the life of Achilles on quiver covers from the Chertomlyk and Melitopol kurgans. The influence of Greek conventions on steppe art was not always positive, as demonstrated by the stag on a shield emblem from the Kul' Oba kurgan. Similar in conception to the Kostromskaya stag of 150 years earlier, with inset amber eye, S-curled antlers and folded legs, it is neither as technically accomplished nor as vigorous and is decorated with smaller repoussé animal forms that make no attempt to serve as metamorphosed body parts. A griffin is rendered on the rump, a lion and hare on the belly and a greyhound under the neck. The smaller animals clearly follow Greek prototypes, while the encompassing stag is poorly stylized in the steppe manner.

B. Piotrowsky, L. Galanina, and N. Grach: *Scythian Art* (Oxford, 1987)

T. Taylor: 'Thracians, Scythians and Dacians: 800 BC–AD 300', *Oxford Illustrated Prehistory of Europe*, ed. B. W. Cunliffe (Oxford, 1994), pp. 373–410

M. Vickers: *Scythian and Thracian Antiquities in Oxford* (Oxford, 2002)

Seals. Dies or signets, often in the form of a cylinder or ring, having a raised (cut) or incised (engraved) emblem, such as a heraldic device or monogram. A seal is used to stamp an impression on clay, wax or lead as a means of authentication or to seal closed a document or container.

See also GEM-ENGRAVING.

1. Minoan. 2. Helladic.

1. MINOAN. Crete's long and continuous tradition of glyptic art is assumed to have had its beginnings in Early Minoan (EM) I under the stimulus of contemporary Anatolian and Egyptian cultures. The few seals datable to this period are close in style to the more rudimentary forms of EM II. Designs on EM II stamp seals are simple: random linear scratches, hatching, angle-filled crosses and S-scrolls. Carved from bone, ivory and soft stone, early shapes range from simple conical to more complex forms, such as pear-shaped seals with double animal-head handles, or they are ring-shaped with bezels. In the period of development that followed, while a few parallels can be found with the richer repertory of Early Helladic (EH) II seals, some basic compositional differences are noticeable. Minoan glyptic art evolved its own characteristics independently. As well as symmetrical and static designs, some compositions show a sense of rotation within the confines of the seal face, while others ignore the perimeter and allow all-over patterns notionally to overflow into the surrounding space.

By the end of EM III and the beginning of Middle Minoan (MM) I, there were several centres of seal-carving. A distinctive group of bone or ivory seals, mainly conoids or cylinders engraved at both ends, is associated with the Mesara area of southern Crete, though examples are known from other parts of the island. On the principal face stylized lions with hatched manes pad in an endless procession round the edge, while the secondary face often carries an abstract pattern such as linked scrolls. Another related group is characterized by complex theriomorphic forms (crouching lion, seated monkey, dove sheltering young) with simple crosshatching or meander patterns on the bases. A further group, which made use of soft stone as well as ivory, comprises seals of simple form (disc, cylinder, dome and animal shape) with designs such as leaves, rosettes and animals disposed within a border line. The occasional occurrence of hieroglyphs may be due to influence from a school of seal-carving in north-central Crete that was totally different in character. This school produced crudely cut, three-sided stone prisms, with motifs including men, goats and other quadrupeds, animal heads, birds, fish, scorpions, insects, vases, ships, ornamental designs, and on later examples recognizable hieroglyphs. Broken and unfinished seals of this group were excavated together with lapidaries' tools from a workshop at Mallia.

Early seals, whether of ivory or soft stone such as steatite and serpentine, were carved by means of a hand graver with copper blade or obsidian point, or by a slow hand-held drill. A revolution in technique came in MM II with the introduction of fast-turning rotary tools: the fixed bow-powered lathe with solid and tubular drills and cutting wheels. This allowed harder stones such as quartz, jasper, chalcedony, agate and cornelian to be cut and new styles of engraving and seal shapes to emerge. Typical of this period are prisms with three or more elliptical or rectangular faces, various animal types, the disc seal with convex faces, the 'flattened cylinder' (rectangular, with curved faces) and the stemmed signet, which apparently derived from a metal prototype; contemporary sealings suggest that metal seals were in use at this period. Many of the prism seals are exquisitely engraved with hieroglyphic signs often combined with ornamental devices reminiscent of the patterns painted on Kamares-style pottery. On other seals, single motifs resembling hieroglyphs appear rather as decorative elements, though perhaps with a talismanic function.

From the First Palace at Phaistos (MM IB-II) comes an important deposit of clay sealings bearing impressions of seals in use at the end of MM II, including heirlooms such as an ivory seal of the lion procession group, as well as more recent types. The majority appear to have been soft stone or wooden seals with round faces engraved predominantly with ornamental motifs but also with animal figures. The latest sealings include impressions of metal rings with oval bezels and more naturalistic representations and impressions of hardstone seals—discs, perhaps of rock crystal, with architectonic devices and stemmed signets with motifs in the hieroglyphic style. The impression of a seated owl on one of the sealings may have come from a seal engraved by the same craftsman as produced a signet in the Ashmolean Museum. Apart from a single nodule with impressions of two simple characters from one face of a three-sided prism, the Phaistos sealings include no examples with hieroglyphic inscriptions.

In contrast, further north at Knossos, sealings from the Hieroglyphic Deposit (Herakleion, Archaeol. Mus.), dating from roughly the same period, are dominated by impressions from hardstone prisms engraved with hieroglyphic signs. However, as at Phaistos, stemmed signets with hieroglyphic-style motifs are also represented, as well as more naturalistic scenes such as a rocky seascape with a clearly identifiable dolphin fish (*Coryphaena hippurus*) attacking a cephalopod (Herakleion, Archaeol. Mus.). Three designs of human heads in profile, stylized but with such individual features as to suggest somewhat unsuccessful attempts at portraiture, are also remarkable (Athens, N. Archaeol. Mus. and Herakleion, Archaeol. Mus.). Sealings from the MM IIIB–LM IA Temple Repositories at Knossos also include types represented earlier at Phaistos. In some compositions simple figurative motifs, instead of occurring singly, are grouped formally to produce a pattern perfectly suited to the circular face of the seal—four cockle shells around a central point, for example, or two whorl shells arranged head-to-tail. Other designs display a greater naturalism both in the delicacy of the modelling and in the composition: of these the most delightful fragment depicts a suckling fawn. Human figures are also portrayed in violent action: an acrobat somersaults over the back of a bull, a pugilist strides menacingly with muscles tensed, and divine personages pace beside attendant lions.

By the end of the Middle Minoan period, while engraved motifs showed increasing diversity in subject and technique, seal shapes became more limited, dictated perhaps by the use of the bow lathe. The majority of stone seals were lentoids (a form evolved from the old discoid), amygdaloids (a new form) and the occasional 'flattened cylinder', all biconvex forms on which the rotating drill and cutting wheel could be used to most effect. These, along with the oval-bezelled gold signet ring, continued to be the main shapes of Late Minoan (LM) seals. Some engravers had used the basic cuts of their tools unsoftened to produce the patterns characteristic of the Phaistos sealings, the architectonic designs and stylized animal motifs; others had experimented further with secondary engraving to produce subtler modelling for the more naturalistic representations. Both techniques found their exponents at the beginning of the Late Bronze Age. The so-called 'Talismanic' group, which originated in MM III but seems in certain respects descendent from the early three-sided prisms, is characterized by the economic but effective technique of applying only the basic cuts of drills and wheel with little or no further working. Its repertory is dominated by a limited range of stylized motifs, including some that do not appear in other contemporary groups: vases of various shapes combined with vegetation, marine creatures (fish, cephalopods, crabs), animals, birds, bucrania, papyrus plants, ships, double axes, enigmatic heart shapes and 'bundles', rosettes and panelled ornamentation. Another group related in style is characterized by schematic animal motifs rendered with strong linear cuts.

Working in the east of the island and inspired by the same local traditions as produced the 'Talismanic' group was the Zakros Master, whose bold, deeply modelled compositions transform old subjects into new fantasies. Among his favourite themes are bird-women, minotaurs and other monsters, and animal masks. At other centres, engravers, influenced by the ideas of fresco painters, were producing cult scenes and animal and bird studies in a fluid, naturalistic style, exploring the modelling not only of anatomical details but of subjects in motion and contortion. Contemporary with the fine art of the palace craftsmen working in hardstone or on gold rings there was also a 'Popular' group with moderately naturalistic animals and human figures on lentoids of humble serpentine.

While Minoan glyptic art strongly influenced that of the mainland at the beginning of the Late Bronze Age, the trend was reversed from LM II, with Mycenaean political domination of the island. Fine seals were still produced for a while, including typical Minoan subjects such as studies of waterfowl, but gradually naturalism gave way to more conventional styles, and iconography became more restricted. The finest Minoan and Mycenaean glyptic art was associated with palace bureaucracy, and although when worn on the wrist or as pendants seals might double as jewellery or amulets, their prime function was for official identification and security. With the destruction in LM IIIA of the palace at Knossos and the collapse of the central bureaucracy on Crete, the manufacture of seals rapidly declined.

N. Platon: *Die Siegel der Vorpalastzeit* (1969), i of *Iraklion Archäologisches Museum*, Corpus der minoischen und mykenischen Siegel, ii (Berlin, 1964-)

J. Boardman: *Greek Gems and Finger Rings* (London, 1970)

I. Pini: *Die Siegelabdrücke von Phästos* (1970), v of *Iraklion Archäologisches Museum*, Corpus der minoischen und mykenischen Siegel, ii (Berlin, 1964-)

N. Platon, I. Pini and G. Salies: *Die Siegel der Altpalastzeit* (1977), ii of *Iraklion Archäologisches Museum*, Corpus der minoischen und mykenischen Siegel, ii (Berlin, 1964-)

S. Hood: *The Arts in Prehistoric Greece*, Pelican Hist. A. (Harmondsworth, 1978), pp. 209–32

P. Yule: *Early Cretan Seals: A Study of Chronology*, Marburger Studien zur Vor- und Frügeschichte, iv (Mainz, 1980)

N. Platon and I. Pini: *Die Siegel der Nachpalastzeit* (1984), iii of *Iraklion Archäologisches Museum*, Corpus der minoischen und mykenischen Siegel, ii (Berlin, 1964-)

N. Platon and I. Pini: *Die Siegel der Nachpalastzeit* (1985), iv of *Iraklion Archäologisches Museum*, Corpus der minoischen und mykenischen Siegel, ii (Berlin, 1964-)

The Erlenmeyer Collection of Cretan Seals, text J. Betts (sale cat., London, Christie's, 5 June 1989)

J. G. Younger: *A Bibliography for Aegean Glyptic in the Bronze Age*, Corpus der minoischen und mykenischen Siegel, suppl. iv (Berlin, 1991)

H. Graeme: *The Architectural Iconography on Minoan and Mycenean Seal Rings, Seal Stones, and Sealings* (diss., Boulder, U. CO, 1995)

E. Hallager: *The Minoan Roundel and Other Sealed Documents in the Neopalatial Linear A Administration* (Liège and Austin, TX, 1996)

J. B. Wohlfeil: *Die Bildersprache minoischer und mykenischer Siegel* (Oxford, 1997)

E. Loughlin: *Representations of the Cow and Calf in Minoan Art* (diss., U. Edinburgh, 2000)

C. D. Cain: 'Dancing in the Dark: Deconstructing a Narrative of Epiphany on the Isopata Ring', *Amer. J. Archaeol.*, cv/1 (Jan 2001), pp. 27–49

J. S. Smith: *Script and Seal Use on Cyprus in the Bronze and Iron Ages* (Boston, MA, 2002)

A. Lebessi and others: 'The Runner's Ring, a Minoan Athlete's Dedication at the Syme Sanctuary, Crete', *Mitt. Dt. Archäol Inst.: Athen Abt.*, cxix (2004), pp. 1–31

E. Kyriakidis: 'Unidentified Floating Objects on Minoan Seals', *Amer. J. Archaeol.*, cix/2 (April 2005), pp. 137–54

2. Helladic. On the Greek mainland seal use and production was spasmodic. Though their prime function seems to have been for printing patterns on cloth or hide, large Neolithic clay stamps with deeply incised geometric designs may also have been used as seals. The hatched quadrant common on seals throughout the eastern Mediterranean was already in evidence at this time and continued to be used in the Early Helladic (EH) period on clay and softstone stamp seals. A fine school of seal-carving flourished in the Argolid at Lerna in the Early Helladic (EH) II period. The actual seals (probably of wood) have not survived, but impressions of their circular faces on clay nodules used to seal storage jars and wooden chests (Argos, Archaeol. Mus.) bear witness to a sophisticated sense of design. Their compositions tend to be orientated around a central point, filling the entire field while respecting its circular confines. They exhibit a keen awareness of symmetry, even to the extent of introducing the occasional subtly balanced asymmetrical element. Designs are geometric, based on meanders, interlocking loops, trefoils, swastikas and spirals, the latter betraying Cycladic influence; rare representational motifs, such as a spider or beaked jug, appear only as minor elements in a composition. At Lerna and elsewhere seal impressions also occur on pottery: cylinders probably of wood were used by itinerant potters to decorate earthenware pithoi and hearths, producing continuous bands of geometric patterns based on zigzags, herringbones, wavy lines, spirals and concentric circles. Sometimes the field was divided vertically into panels, or disparate elements were juxtaposed but balanced so that repeat rolling created a unity of design.

The Lerna school had no direct successor: Middle Helladic (MH) communities seem to have had little use for glyptic art. Such seals as are securely dated to this period are few and poor, mostly clay or softstone stamps with simple linear patterns. However, the beginning of the Late Helladic (LH) period saw a new blossoming of glyptic art on the mainland under the influence of Crete. Minoan seals were imported, and hardstone seals and gold signet rings, which were inspired by Cretan models but suited to the mainland taste for more formal and monumental compositions, were made by both Minoan and Mycenaean craftsmen. So interrelated are the styles of the finest work that they are often grouped together as 'Minoan/Mycenaean', though Mycenaean seals tend to be more rigid and heraldic in concept, preferring stylized detail to naturalism and with increasing emphasis on the raw tool marks undisguised by secondary modelling. Subjects include cult scenes and symbols, scenes of combat and hunt, animals (particularly lions) and mythical beasts such as griffins.

Of mainland origin also are a series of mould-made glass lentoids with animal motifs and a cheap 'Popular' group. The latter evolved in LH IIIA following the decline in hardstone engraving and is characterized by lentoids of black steatite crudely gouged in a linear style with a limited repertory of ornamental motifs and quadrupeds—bulls, goats and deer—often so schematized as to be unidentifiable. Although existing seals continued to be used officially until the destruction of the palace at Pylos and were worn as jewellery or amulets and dedicated as votive offerings at shrines, seal manufacture in Greece ceased in the final phases of the Late Bronze Age and was not resumed until the Geometric period.

A. Sakellariou: *Die minoischen und mykenischen Siegel des Nationalmuseums in Athen*, Corpus der minoischen und mykenischen Siegel, i (Berlin, 1964)
J. Boardman: *Greek Gems and Finger Rings* (London, 1970)
I. Pini and others: *Kleinere griechische Sammlungen*, Corpus der minoischen und mykenischen Siegel, v (Berlin, 1975)
S. Hood: *The Arts in Prehistoric Greece*, Pelican Hist. A. (Harmondsworth, 1978), pp. 209–32
J. G. Younger: *A Bibliography for Aegean Glyptic in the Bronze Age*, Corpus der minoischen und mykenischen Siegel, suppl. iv (Berlin, 1991)
H. Graeme: *The Architectural Iconography on Minoan and Mycenean Seal Rings, Seal Stones, and Sealings* (diss., Boulder, U. CO, 1995)

Sebaste [Sebastiyah]. *See* SAMARIA.

Sebaste Claudia Flavia Paphos. *See* PAPHOS, NEW.

Segesta [Gr. Egesta]. Town in western Sicily, *c.* 17 km from Castellammare, that flourished 600–400 BC. It was inhabited by the Elymi, a native people strongly influenced by Greek culture; Segesta came under Carthaginian rule in 409 BC and then from *c.* 260 BC under Roman rule. It was destroyed by Vandals in the 5th century AD. Remains of two successive city walls on the hilltop of Monte Barbaro surround the settlement, which has not been excavated. The site is noted for its unfinished Doric temple (stylobate 23.17×58.07 m), which stands on a hill outside the city (see colour pl. 2:XI, fig. 1). The perfectly preserved exterior was almost completed, except for the fluting of the columns and the removal of the lifting-bosses; a cella and a roof were evidently planned. The four steps of the base (with strong curvature and remains of marks for its construction) and the colonnade with 6 by 14 columns and double angle contraction reflect the Early Classical Sicilian Doric style. The decorative details, however, and the proportional system of the elevations betray a knowledge of buildings constructed in Athens in 440–432 BC under Pericles. The temple was the last of the Classical Doric temples in Sicily and was probably begun around 420 BC and left unfinished at the outbreak of the Greco-Carthaginian war in 409 BC. Investigations have also uncovered remains at the same site of an earlier, primitive temple with an open front and without columns. Capitals and architrave fragments of an Early Classical Doric peripteral temple, not yet excavated, have been discovered at Mango, another suburban site. The theatre, on the hilltop within the walls, was probably constructed for local Phlyax farces *c.* 100 BC. The auditorium is in the shape of a horseshoe, as in Greek theatres, but the *scaenae frons* (stage building), with engaged Doric and Ionic columns in two storeys, and perhaps also a pediment, anticipates Roman forms.

A. von Gerkan: 'Zu den Theatern von Segesta und Tyndaris', *Festschrift A. Rumpf* (Krefeld, 1952), pp. 82–92
V. Tusa: 'Il santuario arcaico di Segesta', *Atti del VII congresso internazionale di archeologia classica: Napoli, 1958*, ii, pp. 31–40
A. Burford: 'Temple Building at Segesta', *Class. Q.*, xi (1961), pp. 87–93
H. Schläger: 'Beobachtung am Tempel von Segesta', *Mitt. Dt. Archäol. Inst.: Röm. Abt.*, lxxv (1968), pp. 168–9
D. Mertens: 'Die Herstellung der Kurvatur am Tempel von Segesta', *Mitt. Dt. Archäol. Inst.: Röm. Abt.*, lxxxi (1974), pp. 107–14
J. A. De Waele: 'La progettazione dei templi dorici di Himera, Segesta e Siracusa', *Secondo quaderno imerese*, ed. N. Allegro and others (Rome, 1982), pp. 1–45
D. Mertens: *Der Tempel von Segesta* (Mainz, 1984), pp. 1–53, 87–92
T. E. Kalpaxis: *Hemiteles: Akzidentelle Unfertigkeit und 'Bossen-Stil' in der griechischen Baukunst* (Mainz, 1986), pp. 138–42
V. Tusa: *Segesta* (Palermo, 1991)
G. Blandi: *I templi di Agrigento, Segesta e Selinunte: Storia, architettura, tecnica* (Palermo, 2000)

Sela'. *See* PETRA.

Seleucids. Name given to the Macedonian kings of Syria and their territories between 311 and 64 BC, whose empire dominated the Ancient Near East from the end of the 4th century BC until the 2nd. Seleukos I Nikator (*reg* 305–281 BC), one of Alexander the Great's generals, founded the empire in Babylon in 311 BC; in 300 BC he moved its capital to ANTIOCH (i), and by his death he controlled most of the region now occupied by Afghanistan, Iran, Iraq, Syria and Turkey (about two-thirds of Alexander's conquests). Continuous warfare on all fronts considerably eroded this vast territory during the 3rd century BC. Antiochos III (*reg* 223–187 BC) succeeded in reversing the situation by the 190s BC and even added Israel to the empire, but his unsuccessful invasion of Greece in 191 BC and subsequent defeat by Pergamon and Rome in 188 BC deprived him of most of Asia Minor and saddled the empire with a huge indemnity. A single Roman envoy prevented the ablest of his successors, the eccentric Antiochos IV Epiphanes (*reg* 175–163 BC), from conquering Egypt, and the latter's sudden death on his way to fight the newly arrived Parthians accelerated the empire's decline. By 100 BC, external enemies and internecine feuding had reduced Seleucid territory to Syria alone. Between 83 and 69 BC Tigranes II of Armenia (*reg* 95–56 BC) even occupied Antioch, and in 64 BC the Roman proconsul Pompey (106–48 BC) abolished the dynasty and turned Syria into a Roman province.

The empire's ethnic and regional diversity was reflected in its art. While the western provinces and the Syrian heartland were extensively Hellenized, Greek settlement in Israel and Mesopotamia was largely confined to such administrative and trading centres as Ake-Ptolemais (now 'Akko), and Seleucia on the Tigris. On the Iranian plateau it was almost non-existent, though Bactria (now Afghanistan) was more densely settled; this territory, however, broke away during the 3rd century BC to form an independent kingdom, which from the mid-2nd century BC was entirely cut off from the west by the Parthians. Broadly speaking, the art of the western provinces was closest to mainstream Hellenism, that of Mesopotamia was most traditional, and that of Bactria was a complex mixture of the two.

Of the splendours of the Seleucid capital, Antioch, almost no trace remains. Seleukos I is reported to have built an agora and a temple of Zeus there, and a splendid temple of Apollo (whom he claimed as his father) and Artemis at nearby Daphne. The city's two most celebrated cult statues were the bronze *Tyche* (Fortune) of Antioch by Eutychides and the colossal *Apollo of Daphne* by Bryaxis. A diademed bronze bust of *Seleukos I Nikator* from the Villa dei Papyri at Herculaneum (Naples, Mus. Archeol. N) is similar to his portraits on coins; its craggy physiognomy and intense gaze emphasize his physical power and personal magnetism. Portraits on coins of the Seleucids (the longest continuous series in the Hellenistic world) show that in its heyday the dynasty modelled its royal style on its mythical ancestor, Apollo; faces are strong, glances determined and hair full and curly. The Seleucids' main surviving monument in the west is the enormous Temple of Apollo at DIDYMA in Asia Minor. Built entirely of marble, it was begun in the late 4th century BC; construction dragged on through the Hellenistic period and was eventually abandoned in Roman times. The temple's embellishment emphasizes the griffin, Apollo's beast and the Seleucids' royal symbol, whose prominence on the contemporary mausoleum at BELEVI also points to the Seleucids.

The eastern cities, though less well preserved, present a quite different picture. Alexander the Great had expressed his intention of restoring the temple and ziggurat of Marduk at Babylon, and the Seleucids swiftly showed their own commitment to the local culture by rebuilding the Anu-Antum temple, its associated ziggurat and other shrines at Uruk in traditional Mesopotamian style, using the local baked brick. The architecture of such colonies as Seleucia on the Tigris, DURA EUROPOS and AI KHANUM is more mixed. Traditional Iranian temple and palace designs, again usually executed in brick, were often given a Greek veneer through such additions as Doric, Ionic or Corinthian porticos or pebble mosaics. Hardly any large-scale Seleucid sculpture has survived, though a big sandalled marble foot, embellished with a thunderbolt, survives from the 'temple à redans' at Ai Khanum; this fragment, presumably from a statue of Zeus, indicates that the cult statues of such Iranian-style temples could take a standard Greek form. Yet the opposite could also be true: coin designs from the western cities show that Oriental goddesses, such as Ishtar/Astarte/Inanna, were worshipped in many guises and could be identified with both Artemis and Athena. The other arts of the eastern Seleucid provinces present a fascinating kaleidoscope, ranging from nude or semi-nude statuettes of Aphrodite-Anahita in 'pure' Greek (namely, Praxitelean) style to sophisticated versions of Iranian and Scythian work in ivory and metal. Town plans, where preserved, are invariably Hippodamian.

The last major Seleucid builder was Antiochos IV Epiphanes, whose lavish gifts of temples and public buildings to Antioch, the cities of Greece and Asia Minor, and the communities of Mesopotamia are profusely documented. He aimed to restore Seleucid power without antagonizing Rome, and he held a great festival at Daphne to celebrate his 'victory' over Egypt in 168 BC. Polybius' description (*Histories* XXX, 25–7) of its main event, a sumptuous procession that included golden images of the Sun, Moon and the Olympians with other luxuries, gives some idea of what has been lost. Antioch and Alexandria dominated the production of Hellenistic luxury arts: indeed, both cities have equal claim to the invention of glass-blowing, which occurred either at the end of the Seleucid period or at the beginning of the Roman. Antiochos was a devotee of Zeus and chose a Pheidian-style statue of the god as the emblem of his new plan of reconstruction. He built a new temple of Zeus at Antioch and put his own neo-Classical image (signalling a revival of Greece's golden age and his own pretensions to cultural leadership) on his coins. The temple seems to have stood in the spacious new suburb, Epiphania, that he donated to the town. His attempts to proselytize, however, met with a mixed reception. Whereas at Athens his offer to reconstruct the great temple of Olympian Zeus was met with enthusiasm (part of it, completed under Hadrian, still stands), his rededication to Olympian Zeus of the temple in Jerusalem helped to touch off the Jewish revolt. The main distinguishing architectural feature of Antiochos' temples and public buildings was their novel use of an external Corinthian order. Equally novel was his employment of a Roman, Cossutius, as architect of the Athenian temple and public works at Antioch, perhaps because of his superior engineering skill, given the scale of the projects involved.

Few important works of art or architecture are known from the period of Seleucid decline. Bronzes (Tehran, Archaeol. Mus.) from a temple complex at Shami in southern Iran dramatically illustrate the decline. A shattered, diademed bronze portrait, perhaps of Antiochos VII Sidetes (*reg* 139–129 BC), who was killed in battle by the Parthians, was supplanted by a huge statue of a moustachioed Parthian, trousered and with feet slightly astride in the traditional Iranian manner. Two other portraits (Antakya, Hatay Mus.), from Iskenderun near Antioch, show Seleukos I and Antiochos IX Kyzikenos (*reg* 115–95 BC): the stereometric forms and soft surface modelling recall

Ptolemaic Egyptian work, and it may be no coincidence that Antiochos was installed on his throne by the Ptolemies. The coins, too, vividly document the empire's disintegration: after the death of Antiochos IX the two warring branches of the family adopted antithetical physiognomies—those descended from Antiochos VIII Gryphos ('Hook-nose'; *reg* 125–96 BC) retained his huge beak of a nose, while the other side of the family, following Kyzikenos, were shown with straight or slightly retroussé noses. Their wild, tousled hair indicates an almost hysterical desire to imitate the royal image of Alexander, and some late Seleucids even had themselves represented as Helios or the new Dionysos, posturing as lords of the East and bringers of eternal prosperity even as their empire dwindled and its wealth drained into the coffers of Rome.

E. T. Newell: *The Coinage of the Eastern Seleucid Mints* (New York, 1938/*R* 1978)
E. T. Newell: *The Coinage of the Western Seleucid Mints* (New York, 1941/*R* 1977)
A. W. Lawrence: *Greek Architecture* (Harmondsworth, 1957, rev. by R. A. Tomlinson, 1983)
G. Downey: *A History of Antioch in Syria from Seleucus to the Arab Conquest* (Princeton, 1961)
A. A. Houghton: *Coins of the Seleucid Empire from the Collection of Arthur Houghton* (New York, 1983)
J. J. Pollitt: *Art in the Hellenistic Age* (Cambridge, 1986)
A. Kuhrt and S. Sherwin-White: *Hellenism in the East* (Berkeley, 1987)
S. B. Downey: *Mesopotamian Religious Architecture: Alexander through the Parthians* (Princeton, 1988)
R. R. R. Smith: *Hellenistic Royal Portraits* (Oxford, 1988)
A. F. Stewart: *Greek Sculpture: An Exploration*, 2 vols (New Haven and London, 1990)
S. Sherwin-White and A. Kuhrt: *From Samarkhand to Sardis* (Berkeley, 1993)
J. D. Grainger: *A Seleukid Prosopography and Gazetteer* (Leiden and New York, 1997)
J. Wolski: *The Seleucids: The Decline and Fall of their Empire* (Kraków, 1999)
A. Houghton, C. C. Lorber and B. Kritt: *Seleucid Coins: A Comprehensive Catalogue* (New York, 2002)

Selinus [Selinunte]. Greek colony on the south-west coast of Sicily, some 13 km south of Castelvetrano. It was founded *c.* 650 BC from Megara Hyblaia, on the east coast of Sicily, and flourished as an independent state until it was taken by the Carthaginians in their conquest of 409 BC; it remained under their rule until abandoned by them in 250 BC in the face of a Roman attack. It occupied two connected hills between the rivers Hypsas and Selinus; the smaller hill near the sea served as an acropolis with two sanctuaries and was surrounded by fortifications (well preserved); the larger hill inland was the site of the settlement, abandoned after 409 BC. Important suburban sanctuaries were located east and west of the rivers. The site is notable for the remains of numerous Doric temples built of local stone, all now ruined (one partly reconstructed), and was first excavated in 1823 by S. Angell and W. Harris.

1. ARCHITECTURE. Several plain temples without Doric features were built in the Archaic period (*c.* 600–*c.* 480 BC; see fig. 1), some of monumental scale, such as the Temple of Demeter Malophoros (9.52×20.40 m). An early temple (?*c.* 600 BC) was discovered under the later Temple E to the east of the town. It had no external columns but did have Doric inner columns, an experimental Doric wall frieze and a tiled roof with polychrome decoration at the eaves. Of a large, early temple on the acropolis, perhaps replaced by the later Temple C, there remain only huge ornamental terracottas. The first peripteral Doric temple at Selinus, Temple Y (*c.* 550 BC), is known only from architectural blocks and metope reliefs reused in the later fortifications; its plan and location are unknown.

The large Temple C on the acropolis (stylobate 23.94×63.72 m; probably *c.* 550–*c.* 525 BC) displays characteristics of the Sicilian Archaic style, being built to a long, narrow plan of 6 by 17 columns, with a double column front emphasized by a wide stair, a colonnade with thick, heavy columns closely set without corner contraction, and a tall entablature decorated at the eaves and under the pediments with ornamental terracottas. The design was modelled on the early temples of SYRACUSE. The long, narrow cella was divided into three rooms, with doors in the porch, a cella without inner columns and an adyton (shrine) for the cult image. Both pediments were decorated with large terracotta gorgon masks, as frequently occurred in Archaic Sicilian temples; the eastern front had relief metopes, partly preserved. A huge, artificial terrace in front of the temple, framed by a stoa in the eastern end, was built as part of the same programme.

Later Archaic temples, D on the acropolis and F in the eastern sanctuary (?*c.* 500 BC and ?*c.* 500–*c.* 480 BC respectively; stylobates 23.63×55.68 m and 24.37×61.88 m), combined the long, narrow

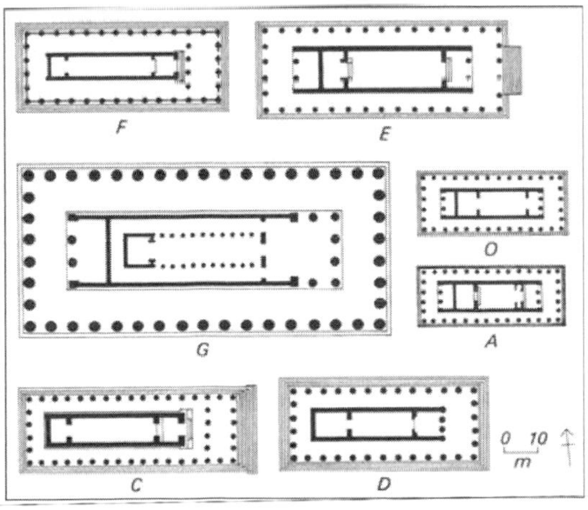

1. Selinus, plans of Doric temples, *c.* 550–*c.* 450 BC

cellae, still divided into three rooms, with shorter colonnades (6 by 13 and 6 by 14 columns respectively). The columns were more widely spaced and the entablatures less heavy, having no ornamental terracottas. Temple D had columns in the pronaos and engaged columns on the antae. Temple F follows more closely the model of Temple C, with a double column front, doors in the cella porch and relief metopes in the front. The colonnade was later closed by a stone screen. Similar to and contemporary with Temple F are the oldest parts of Temple G nearby (also known as Temple GT or Temple of Apollo), one of the largest built in antiquity (stylobate 50.07×110.12 m), which was probably dedicated to Zeus. The use of three different types of column and capital demonstrates changes of plan during a long period of construction. The colonnade (8 by 17 columns) surrounds a cella with an opisthodomos and a prostyle pronaos (probably unroofed, as the cella certainly was); two lines of inner columns lead up to a small sanctum sheltering the cult image. The temple, never completed, was obviously inspired by gigantic temples in Ionia with unroofed cellae, such as the Archaic Artemision at EPHESOS (*c.* 560–*c.* 460 BC).

The Classical (*c.* 525/480–323 BC) Doric style appeared suddenly at Selinus with Temple E in the eastern sanctuary, dedicated to Hera (*c.* 470–*c.* 450 BC; stylobate 25.32×67.74 m). The colonnade of massive and closely spaced columns (6 by 15), with single angle contraction at the corners, probably reflects the so-called Temple of Herakles at AKRAGAS (Agrigento) of *c.* 500 BC; the arrangement of the cella, with an adyton as well as standard pronaos and opisthodomos, is a local feature; the strong curvature in the foundations is unique to Selinus, however. The roof tiles were of bronze. The almost identical temples A (stylobate 16.13×40.30 m) and O (destr.), both *c.* 460–*c.* 450 BC, were smaller and later than Temple E, and were situated in a separate sanctuary on the acropolis. Both had the normal Sicilian colonnades, and Temple A had double angle contraction, still retaining the adyton behind the cella.

2. SCULPTURE. Relief metopes decorated temples Y, C, F and E, mostly following the Sicilian tradition by representing separate subjects without evident narrative connections. But there is no clear stylistic development between the groups from the various temples. The metopes from Temple Y (*c.* 550 BC) were executed in low relief with a figure style clearly influenced by the Aegean (e.g. sculpture from the Sanctuary of Hera on SAMOS; *c.* 570 BC) but foreign to Sicily. The six preserved metopes show divine groups, for example ?Poseidon as horse-god with a consort on a chariot depicted frontally and Apollo with Artemis and Leto.

The metopes from the eastern front of Temple C included a centre-piece of two metopes (one untraced) with divine epiphanies (perhaps of Apollo and Artemis) on chariots depicted frontally (see fig. 2); two other metopes show Perseus killing Medusa assisted

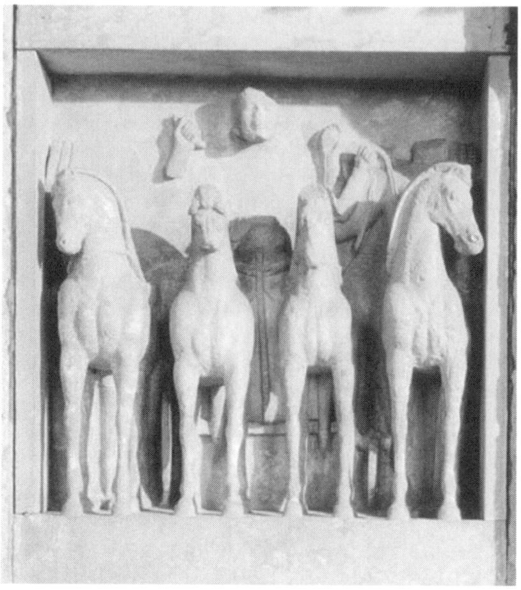

2. Selinus, *Chariot of Apollo (Quadriga of Helios)*, metope from Temple C on the acropolis, *c.* 530–*c.* 520 BC (Palermo, Museo Regionale)

by Athena and Herakles carrying the Kerkopes, both myths of local importance. The high relief and heavy figure style, fundamentally different from the Temple Y metopes, reflect a tradition from eastern Sicily (Syracuse and Gela); the date is disputed, but the drapery and the gorgoneion suggest they were carved *c.* 530–*c.* 520 BC. The metopes from Temple F are still basically Archaic, but they introduce Classical elements hardly possible before *c.* 475 BC. Only two half-metopes remain of a battle between the gods and giants depicted on the ten front metopes; the same subject, also portrayed in the pediments of the Temple of Zeus at Akragas (Agrigento, Mus. Reg. Archeol.) may have decorated the pediment of the inner sanctum of Temple G (one figure preserved).

The metopes from Temple E (*c.* 460–*c.* 450 BC) returned to independent subjects, all with one male and one female figure and chosen and grouped to illustrate Pythagorean and/or Empedoclean philosophical ideas of contrasting elements and different combinations of positive and negative forces. The style reflects earlier works from Akragas. There are numerous fragments of metopes, among them several female heads of marble. The same artists carved a metope from an unknown temple on the acropolis showing Eos pursuing Kephalos.

An Early Classical (*c.* 480–*c.* 450 BC) bronze statue of an ephebe (youth), found in the necropolis, was originally close in style to the Temple E metopes but was disfigured by repairs carried out in later antiquity. Extremely rich finds of minor sculpture, terracotta figurines and reliefs, particularly from the sanctuary of Demeter Malophoros, illustrate the local artistic developments. All finds from Selinus are now in the Museo Regionale, Palermo.

O. Benndorf: *Die Metopen von Selinunt* (Berlin, 1873)
R. Koldewey and O. Puchstein: *Die griechischen Tempel in Unteritalien und Sicilien* (Berlin, 1899), pp. 77–131
G. Fougères and J. Hulot: *Sélinonte* (Paris, 1910)
E. Gabrici: 'Il santuario della Malophoros a Selinunte', *Mnmt. Ant.: Lincei*, xxxii (1927) [whole issue]
P. Marconi: *L'efebo di Selinunte* (Rome, 1929)
E. Gabrici: 'Per la storia dell' architettura dorica in Sicilia', *Mnmt. Ant.: Lincei*, xxxv (1933–5), pp. 137–262
E. Gabrici: 'Daedalica Selinuntia', *Mem. Reale Accad. Archeol., Lett. & B.A., Soc. Reale Napoli*, v (1936), pp. 3–18
W. Fuchs: 'Zu den Metopen des Heraions von Selinunt', *Mitt. Dt. Archäol. Inst.: Röm. Abt.*, lxiii (1956), pp. 102–21
E. Gabrici: 'Studi archeologici selinuntini', *Mnmt. Ant.: Lincei*, xliii (1956), pp. 205–408
G. Gruben: *Die Tempel der Griechen* (Munich, 1966, rev. 4/1986), pp. 274–96
V. Tusa: 'Due nuove metope arcaiche selinuntine', *Archeol. Class.*, xxi (1969), pp. 153–71
V. Tusa: 'Selinunte punica', *Riv. Ist. N. Archeol. & Stor. A.*, n. s., xviii (1971), pp. 47–68
L. Giuliani: *Die archaischen Metopen von Selinunt* (Mainz, 1979)
E. Østby: 'An Early Sicilian Relief-Metope in Copenhagen', *Acta Archaeol. & A. Historiam Pertinentia*, n. s., ii (1982), pp. 1–53
A. Di Vita: 'Selinunte fra il 650 e il 409: un modello urbanistico coloniale', *Annu. Scu. Archeol. Atene & Miss. It. Oriente*, lxii (1984), pp. 7–53
V. Tusa: *La scultura in pietra di Selinunte* (Palermo, 1984)
G. Pugliese Carratelli, ed.: *Sikanie* (Milan, 1985), pp. 187–94, 230–33, 390–97, 417–86
M. Grant: *The Rise of the Greeks* (London, 1987/*R* 2005)
E. Østby: 'Riflessioni sulle metope di Selinunte', *Parola Passato*, facs. ccxxxiii (1987), pp. 123–53
A. Di Vita: 'Selinunte fra il 650 e il 409: un modello di città coloniale', *Annu. Scu. Archeol. Atene & Miss. It. Oriente,* lxii (1984, issued 1988), pp. 7–62
D. Mertens: 'Die Mauern von Selinunt', *Mitt. Dt. Archäol. Inst.: Röm. Abt.*, xcvi (1989), pp. 87–154
C. Marconi: *Selinunte. Le metope dell'Heraion* (Modena, 1994)
C. Marconi: 'Due studi sulle metope figurate dei templi "C" e "F" di Selinunte', *Riv. Ist. N. Archeol. & Stor. A.*, S.III, xviii (1995), pp. 5–68
D. Mertens: 'Die Entstehung des Steintempels in Sizilien', *Diskussionen zur antiken Bauforschung* vi (1995), pp. 25–38
E. Østby: 'Chronological Problems of Archaic Selinus', *Acta Hyperborea* vi (1995), pp. 83–101
D. Mertens: 'Griechen und Punier. Selinunt nach 409 v. Chr.', *Mitt. Dt. Archäol. Inst.: Röm. Abt.*, civ (1997), pp. 301–20
L. Pompeo: *Il complesso architettonico del Tempio M di Selinunte: Analisi tecnica e storia del monumento* (Florence, 1999)
A. Rallo: 'Considerations sur les fouilles récente de Selinonte', *Rev. Archéol.,* i (2002), pp. 194–8
F. De Angelis: *Megara Hyblaia and Selinous: The Development of Two Greek City-states in Archaic Sicily* (Oxford, 2003)
K. Junker: 'Die Reliefmetopen des Heratempels in Selinunt: Mythoskritik und der Wandel des Sagenbildes im fünften vorchristlichen Jahrhundert', *Mitt. Dt. Archäol. Inst.: Röm. Abt.,* cx (2003), pp. 227–61
D. Mertens: 'Die Agora von Selinunt: Neue Grabungsergebnisse zur Fruhzeit der griechischen Kolonialstadt', *Mitt. Dt. Archäol. Inst.: Röm. Abt.,* cx (2003), pp. 389–446
C. P. Presicce: 'Selinunte dalla scelta del sito alle prime fasi di vita', *Mitt. Dt. Archäol. Inst.: Röm. Abt.,* cx (2003), pp. 263–84
'Abteilung Rom', *Archäol. Anz.,* ii (2004), pp. 256–63
R. R. Holloway: 'Megara Hyblaia and Selinous', *Amer. J. Archaeol.,* cx/2 (April 2006), pp. 326–7

Sesklo. Site in Magnesia in central Greece, 18.5 km west of Volos. It was already a flourishing settlement extending over an area of several hectares in the Early Neolithic period. The farmers who lived there cultivated the light soils in this part of coastal Thessaly, growing wheat and barley as well as legumes such as vetch. Their principal source of meat was the domestic sheep, but cattle and pigs were also important. Hunting played only a minor part in food supply. By the Middle Neolithic period, *c.* 4500 BC, it was a substantial community spreading from an acropolis hill with circuit walls.

The site was first excavated in 1901 by Christos Tsountas. The houses, which had several rooms and sometimes more than one storey, had walls of sun-dried brick with stone footings. The largest house on the acropolis, 13 m long with four rooms, belongs to the Late Neolithic period and is an early example of the megaron type. The rich variety of handmade Neolithic pottery to which Sesklo has given its name is decorated with geometric patterns in red or orange on a fine cream fabric. Typical compositions used zigzags or flame motifs on simple but elegant bowls and jars. Occasional examples of stylized human figures also occur. Other artefacts include polished stone axes for tree-felling and carpentry, chipped stone blades for sickles and other tools as well as anthropomorphic figurines and amulets. Objects from Sesklo are held in Athens (N. Archaeol. Mus.) and Volos (Athanassakeion Archaeol. Mus.). Similar wares are found from central Greece to southern Macedonia and indicate the extent of the flourishing culture best represented at Sesklo. As with the majority of Greek Neolithic sites, no cemetery has yet been found and hence there is no information about the physical type of the settlers.

C. Tsountas: *Oi proistorikoi akropoleis Dhiminiou kai Sesklo* [The prehistoric acropoleis of Dimini and Sesklo] (Athens, 1908)
D. R. Theokharis: *Neolithic Greece* (Athens, 1973), pp. 65–6

Settefinestre. Site of a large Roman villa near Cosa in Tuscany, Italy, which flourished 1st century BC–3rd century AD. Its importance lies in the complete plan ascertained from excavations in 1975–81, and in the interior decoration of the *villa urbana*. The excavations provide good evidence for wine production, perhaps linked to the export of Sestius amphorae from Cosa to Gaul. This was associated with the building of the villa in the mid-1st century BC and its *floruit* in the Augustan period (27 BC–AD 14). By the 2nd century AD changes had taken place in the region's agricultural economy, with the result that intensive pig rearing for export replaced wine production to a certain extent. The villa was not so well appointed at this time, and it was abandoned by the mid-3rd century AD.

The villa was built on terraces over a low hill, and is divided along the lines of a *villa urbana/villa rustica* type (*see* VILLA). It can be clearly linked with the description of an ideal villa in Varro (*On Country Matters* i.13). The *villa urbana* is the nucleus, built on vaulting with a cryptoporticus underneath and surrounded by gardens, orchards, workshops, wine and oil presses, slave quarters and animal sheds. It has an axial layout, leading from the entrance courtyard through to the atrium, thence to the tablinum and the peristyle. The main axis continues through an exedra to a porticoed verandah that overlooked the lower terraces and the surrounding countryside. The verandah also served to provide access to a number of other rooms, notably a rare *oecus corintheus*. Some parallels to the whole arrangement can be drawn with the Villa of the Mysteries at Pompeii.

Interior decorative schemes in many of the rooms can be restored with confidence, thanks to the good preservation and restoration of fallen wall plaster. The wall paintings are of fine quality in Pompeian Second Style, featuring, for instance, 'theatre sets' and illusionistic architecture with false doors. There are parallels for the style in the house of Augustus on the Palatine, Rome (30–28 BC). Other wall paintings are in Pompeian Fourth Style and can be dated to the early 2nd century AD. Floor decoration consists mainly of mosaic work in the *villa urbana*, usually in geometric schemes, such as in the atrium (a regular scatter of coloured limestones and marbles on a black ground) or the peristyle and verandah (similar to the atrium but on a white ground). Parallels for these can be seen in the House of the Menander and the House of the Griffins at Pompeii. Elsewhere, simple black-and-white figural decoration is used in threshold mosaics. The *oecus corintheus* is decorated with *opus sectile* (cut marble patterns) in geometric lozenges, as seen in the cella of the Temple of Apollo at Pompeii. Also noteworthy is the use of terracotta lion and gorgon antefixes on the peristyle roof. Material from the excavations is currently in the Museo Archeologico e d'Arte della Maremma, Grosseto. The site itself is partly on public display.

A. Carandini and S. Settis: *Schiavi e padroni nell'Etruria romana: La villa di Settefinestre dallo scavo alla mostra* (Bari, 1979)

A. Carandini and T. Tatton-Brown: 'Excavations at the Roman Villa of "Sette Finestre" in Etruria, 1975–9: First Interim Report', *Roman Villas in Italy: Recent Excavations and Research*, ed. K. Painter (London, 1980), pp. 9–43

A. Carandini and A. Ricci, eds: *Settefinestre: Una villa schiavistica nell'Etruria romana*, 3 vols (Modena, 1985) [main site report]

A. Carandini and others: *Paesaggi d'Etruria: Valle dell'Albegna, Valle d'Oro, Valle del Chiarone, Valle del Tafone: Progetto di ricerca italo-britannico seguito allo scavo di Settefinestre* (Rome, 2002)

Severus, (Lucius) Septimius, Emperor (*b* Leptis Magna, 11 April AD 146; *reg* AD 193–211; *d* York, 11 Feb AD 211). Roman ruler and patron. He established a new dynasty after the murder of Commodus (*reg* AD 180–93). In AD 191, during the reign of Commodus, a fire had destroyed the Templum Pacis, the nearby Horrea Piperataria, the Temple of Vesta and the Palatine. Severus therefore undertook vast works of reconstruction, attested by both literary sources and monumental ruins. (He also created a detailed map of Rome, the so-called Severan marble plan, which he hung on a wall of the south library of the Templum Pacis, AD 205–8; Rome, Antiqua. Com., on dep. Rome, Pal. Braschi). He enlarged the imperial palace on the Palatine, and on a corner of the hill constructed the decorative façade of the Septizodium (ded. AD 203). In AD 202 he began a large bath building on the Aventine and the Via Nova in front of it; he may also have begun the great Baths of Caracalla (ded. AD 216). In AD 203 the senate dedicated to him the triumphal arch in the Forum Romanum commemorating his two campaigns against the Parthians. Above the arch, as can be seen on a coin of the period, there was a bronze four-horse chariot with figures of Severus accompanied by his sons Geta and Caracalla. In the Velabrum, Rome, is the small arch (actually an ornamental gate) dedicated to Severus and his family by the *argentarii* (bankers) and cattle merchants (AD 204). Severus was also responsible for the building of the Domus Lateranorum, the Castra Nova Equitum Singularium (the camp of the imperial bodyguard) and the Excubitorium. Outside Italy, Severus adorned his native city of LEPTIS MAGNA with splendid buildings.

M. Pallottino: *L'arco degli Argentari* (Rome, 1951)

R. Brilliant: 'The Arch of Septimius Severus in the Roman Forum', *Mem. Amer. Acad. Rome*, xxix (1967) [whole issue]

G. A. Mansuelli: *Roma e il mondo romano*, ii (Turin, 1981), pp. 43–57

K. Schilling: *Der neue Hannibal: Lucius Septimius Severus in der Sicht der deutschsprachigen Altertumswissenschaft* (diss., Marburg, Philipps-U., 1991)

A. R. Birley: *Septimius Severus: The African Emperor* (London and New York, 1999)

H. Gitler and M. Ponting: *The Silver Coinage of Septimius Severus and his Family, 193–211 AD: A Study of the Chemical Composition of the Roman and Eastern Issues* (Milan, 2003)

Severus and Celer (*fl* mid-1st century AD). Roman architects and engineers who built Nero's Domus Aurea (*see* ROME, §IV, 5) and landscaped its grounds (after AD 64; see Tacitus: *Annals* XV.xlii). They were previously associated with Nero's ambitious project to engineer a ship canal 160 Roman miles long (*c.* 250 km) joining Lake Avernus near Naples with the mouth of the Tiber, so that grainships from the port of Baiae could reach Rome, avoiding the open sea. The project was soon abandoned. Severus and Celer's engineering skills were more effectively applied to the Domus Aurea; a residential area destroyed in the great fire of AD 64 was cleared, and a country park was created round an artificial lake in the hollow where the Colosseum was later built. According to Suetonius (*Nero* xxxi), the house contained such extravagances as a revolving circular dining room, baths supplied with sea water, and rooms with ivory ceiling panels that opened to shower petals and perfume on the guests below. The remains of the palace that survive, incorporated within the substructure of the Baths of Trajan, are among the first rooms that show architects developing the design potential of brick-faced Roman concrete, exploiting the interplay of straight and curved surfaces and the volumes contained beneath domed and vaulted roofs.

A. Boethius: *The Golden House of Nero* (Ann Arbor, 1960)

Shahhāt. *See* CYRENE.

Sham, al-. *See* DAMASCUS.

Sheikh Ibada, el-. *See* ANTINOÖPOLIS.

Shomeron. *See* SAMARIA.

Sicily [anc. Sikanie; Trinacria]. Italian island, the largest in the Mediterranean (24,089 sq. km), separated from the south-west tip of Italy by the 3–16 km-wide Strait of Messina. It owed its ancient name of Trinacria to its triangular shape; the name Sicily is derived from its first recorded inhabitants, the Sicels and Sicani. It appears as Sikanie in Homer's *Odyssey* (XXXIV.307). The island has three mountain ranges across the north: the Peloritani, Nebrodi and Madonie, and another across the east, which is dominated by Mt Etna (h. *c.* 3200 m), the largest active volcano in Europe. The central plateaux are rich grain-growing areas, while the fertile coastal plains are devoted to wine, olive and fruit production.

Small settlements and the rock-cut necropolis of Pantalica South best document the culture of Sicily *c.* 850–*c.* 750 BC, when the Sicels lived on the east side of the island, the Sicani in the centre and the Elymi at Eryx (now Erice) and Segesta in the west. None of these groups presented strong opposition to Greek colonization, which began in the mid-8th century BC on the eastern coast with the foundation of Megara Hyblaia by the Megarians, Naxos by the Chalkidians and SYRACUSE by the Corinthians, and then moved south and westward over the course of the next century. At the same time, Phoenicians founded Motya (now Mozia), Panormos (now Palermo) and Soloeis (now Solunto) at the western end of the island. Their struggles with the Greeks and later the Romans for control of Sicily made up much of the island's early political history and greatly affected artistic production. So too did tyranny, later called kingship, which persisted longer in Sicily than elsewhere in the Greek world. With the sack of Syracuse in 211 BC by the Roman general Marcus Claudius Marcellus and the defeat of Carthage in the Second Punic War (218–201 BC), the whole island became a Roman province. His export of Greek art treasures from Sicily to Rome, which Gaius Verres continued while proconsul of Sicily (73–71 BC), denuded the island but effectively transmitted Classical culture from Greece to Rome.

The opportunities afforded by colonization and the resources of the island shaped Sicilian Greek art and architecture. New foundations allowed for systematic urban planning. Nearly all of the Greek cities bear traces of a particular type of plan with a few broad avenues crossed by narrower and more closely spaced side streets. In many cities, series of Doric temples were constructed in locally available sand- or limestone and were set side by side in a single precinct (*see* ARCHITECTURE, §IV, 2(ii)(b)). Common features of Archaic Sicilian Doric temples include a deep front porch created by a second row of columns, a long narrow sekos, the frequent use of an adyton rather than an opisthodomos, heavy proportions, emphatic architectural details and richly embellished terracotta roof ornament. Elements of the Ionic order are often deftly interwoven to create a handsome synthesis of bold form and richly active ornament. Classical temples are more akin to mainland Greek examples (*see* ARCHITECTURE, §IV, 2(iii)(b)) but frequently incorporate staircases, retain a slightly longer plan and use double column contraction at the corners. The telamon (male figural support) appears more often in Sicily than elsewhere in the Greek world, as do altars decorated with a Doric frieze. Domestic architecture is best seen in Hellenistic Morgantina, Akragas, Soloeis, and Monte Iato, civic architecture (3rd century BC) in the agora of Morgantina, and urban development on a grand scale in Neapolis (275–215 BC) at Syracuse. Sophisticated defences responding to siege warfare survive at Syracuse and Selinus.

More readily available than imported marble, limestone and terracotta became the chosen media for monumental free-standing and architectural sculpture. Broad surfaces, linear detail and emphatic though sometimes mannered gesture govern western Greek taste. Female representations outnumber male, perhaps owing to the popularity of the cults of Demeter and Proserpina, Artemis and Aphrodite. Distinctively Sicilian works include the Laganello head, a mother-figure suckling twins (possibly *Night Suckling Sleep and Death*) from Megara Hyblaia and several enthroned korai (all early 6th century BC–early 5th, Syracuse, Mus. Archeol. Reg.). The few male kouroi serving as grave markers are carved in imported marble (Syracuse, Mus. Archeol. Reg.), as is the extraordinarily bold work known as the *Motya Charioteer* (early 5th century BC; Mozia, Whitaker Mus.). At Selinus, local limestone sufficed for the sculptured metopes of temples Y, C and F, but on Temple E, the exposed female faces, hands and feet are inset in marble. Western Greek sculptural forms found on Sicily include terracotta horsemen decorating the ridges of roofs, apotropaic satyr and gorgoneion antefixes, life-size terracotta female busts (early 5th century-3rd BC; Syracuse, Mus. Archeol. Reg.; Aidone, Mus. Reg. Archeol.; and Agrigento, Mus. Reg. Archeol.), small terracotta altars decorated with mythological figures (mainly 6th century BC) dispersed throughout Sicily's museums, and marble lamps decorated with female protomes (7th century BC; Palermo, Mus. Reg., and Syracuse, Mus. Archeol. Reg.). Sicilians also commissioned works for the pan-Hellenic sanctuaries, the *Charioteer* of Delphi being the most famous example (*c.* 478–474 BC; Delphi, Archaeol. Mus.; for illustration *see* DELPHI CHARIOTEER.

Around the mid-6th century BC Sicilian cities began to mint coins using imported silver. The issues of the 5th century BC are among the finest in the Greek world both for imagery and style; master engravers signed the dies. Significant motifs include the head of Arethusa surrounded by dolphins and the moving quadriga on Syracusan coins, the head of Dionysos and the foreshortened pose of the drinking satyr on Naxian coins, and the eagles devouring a hare on the coinage of Akragas.

From the late 8th century BC to the second half of the 5th, Sicilians imported quantities of painted pottery from Corinth, Athens and East Greece. They also produced a lively subgeometric and Orientalizing polychrome ware in the late 8th century and 7th (e.g. material from Syracuse and Megara Hyblaia; Syracuse, Mus. Archeol. Reg.). At the end of the 5th century BC, immigrant Athenian Red-figure vase painters started workshops in Sicily (*see* POTTERY, §IV, 6(ii)); early artists include the Chequer Painter (*fl* *c.* 410–380 BC) and an immediate follower, the Dirce Painter. Workshops identified as the Lentini-Manfria Group, the Etna Group and the Lipari Group were active chiefly at the end of the 4th century BC. Representations of females predominate, with other favourite subjects being Dionysiac, theatrical, underworld and Phlyax scenes. A special class of Hellenistic vases found at Centuripe approximates free painting in polychrome.

Sicily's eclipse during the Roman Imperial period is reflected in her public architecture, the amphitheatre (*c.* 1st century AD) at Syracuse and 'basilica' at Tyndaris (now Tindari) being noteworthy exceptions. Villas and houses, however, continued to be built and richly appointed through the late Roman period. In the 4th century AD, following the administrative reforms of Emperor Diocletian, Sicily underwent a political and economic reorganization. A long period of peace, lasting until the first incursions of the Vandals in 440, favoured the repopulation of the countryside and the formation of a class of Roman landowners, who built the great residences of the Late Antique period. One of the most characteristic examples of this culture is the mosaic decoration, attributed to craftsmen of African origin, with scenes of hunting, fishing and daily life in the villa of PIAZZA ARMERINA (*c.* 320). Other settlements include the Roman villa of Helorus (mid-4th century) near the mouth of the Tellaro River, with its splendid mosaic floors, wide peristyle and animal bas-reliefs, and the villa at Patti (76.5 km west of Messina), where excavations began on the 20,000 sq. m site in 1976.

Periodicals devoted to the study of ancient Sicily include *Kokalos* and *Sicilia Archaeol.*

R. Koldewey and O. Puchstein: *Die griechischen Tempel in Unteritalien und Sicilien* (Berlin, 1899)
B. Pace: *Arte e civiltà della Sicilia antica*, 4 vols (Milan, 1935–49)
M. Hirmer and E. Langlotz: *The Art of Magna Grecia* (New York, 1965)
M. Finley: *A History of Sicily* (London, 1968/*R* 1976)
D. Mac Smith: *Storia della Sicilia medievale e moderna* (Rome and Bari, 1970)
R. R. Holloway: *Influences and Styles in the Late Archaic and Early Classical Greek Sculpture of Sicily and Magna Graecia* (Leuven, 1975)
R. Romano, ed.: *Storia della Sicilia*, 10 vols (Naples, 1977–81)
B. Barletta: *Ionic Influence in Archaic Sicily: The Monumental Art* (Göteborg, 1983)
D. Mertens: *Der Tempel von Segesta und die dorische Tempelbaukunst des griechischen Westens in klassischer Zeit* (Mainz, 1984)
G. Pugliese Carratelli: *Sikanie: Storia e civiltà della Sicilia greca* (Rome, 1985)
R. J. A. Wilson: *Sicily under the Roman Empire: The Archaeology of a Roman Province, 36 BC–AD 535* (Warminster, 1990)
R. R. Holloway: *The Archaeology of Ancient Sicily* (London, 1991)
T. Fischer-Hansen: *Ancient Sicily* (Copenhagen, 1995)
G. Vallet: *Le monde grec colonial d'Italie du sud et de Sicile* (Rome, 1996)
C. J. Smith and J. Serrati: *Sicily from Aeneas to Augustus: New Approaches in Archaeology and History* (Edinburgh, 2000)
F. Sezgin and others: *Coins and Coinage of Sicily* (Frankfurt am Main, 2003)
L. Cerchiai, L. Jannelli and F. Longo: *The Greek Cities of Magna Graecia and Sicily* (Los Angeles, 2004)
L. Jannelli and others: *The Greeks in Sicily* (Venice, 2004)
G. Messineo and E. Borgia: *Ancient Sicily: Monuments Past & Present* (Rome, 2005)
Urbanistica e architettura nella Sicilia greca (exh. cat. by P. Minà; Agrigento, Mus. Reg. Archeol., 2005)

Side. Site on the Pamphylian coast of southern Turkey. The city was Greek and Roman; when Captain Francis Beaufort discovered it in 1811 the ruins were overgrown with vegetation, but remarkable remains have come to light as the result of clearing and excavation. Side was founded in the 7th century BC, according to Strabo (*Geography* XIV.iii.2) and Arrian (*Campaigns of Alexander* I.xxvi), by colonists from the Aiolian city of Kyme who forgot their own Greek language, presumably as a result of being absorbed by the local Anatolian people. After Alexander the Great's conquest (*c.* 333 BC) the inhabitants of Side became entirely Hellenized. Early in the 1st century BC they grew rich as the result of the slave trade, the city being the main harbour used by the Cilician pirates. When their power was crushed by Pompey in 67 BC, the prosperity of Side declined. The city flourished again, however, under the Roman peace, particularly in the 2nd century AD; thereafter it experienced periods of decline and partial recovery. In the 10th century AD it was destroyed by fire and permanently deserted.

The somewhat ostentatious ruins are practically all of the Roman age. The Hellenistic buildings, with the exception of a couple of houses and some sections of the city walls, were obliterated by the building activities of the 2nd century AD. The most impressive building extant is the 2nd-century AD theatre, a huge structure of which the *cavea* (auditorium) is in an excellent state of preservation. It rests on a great barrel-vaulted gallery in the Roman style. At the foot of the theatre is the agora, a spacious square courtyard surrounded on four sides by a stoa. In the centre stood a round temple (2nd century AD), perhaps dedicated to Tyche, of which only the base survives. To the east are the remains of a large building known as the state agora. One side, decorated with statues in niches, is still standing virtually complete. To the west of the agora are the 5th-century AD baths, now restored and converted into a museum. Outside the main city gate stand the remains of a monumental nymphaeum (2nd century AD), while at the opposite end of the city, close to the sea, are the ruins of the peripteral temples of Athena and Apollo; a few columns of the former have been re-erected. A large Christian basilica (5th–6th centuries) was built to the east of the two temples.

F. Beaufort: *Karamania* (London, 1817)

K. Lanckoroński, G. Niemann and E. Petersen: *Städte Pamphyliens und Pisidiens*, i (Vienna, 1890), pp. 125–52

D. Magie: *Roman Rule in Asia Minor*, 2 vols (Princeton, 1950), i, pp. 261–2; ii, pp. 1133–4

A. M. Mansel: *Die Ruinen von Side* (Berlin, 1963)

G. E. Bean: *Turkey's Southern Shore* (London, 1968, 2/1979)

A Complete Guide to the Three Major Cities of the Ancient Antalya-Pamphylia: Perge, Aspendos, Side (Antalya, 1997)

P. Verzone: 'Il ninfeo di Side in Pamfilia', *Palladio*, xvi/31 (Jan–June 2003), pp. 5–22

Sidon [Arab. Saida]. City on the coast of Lebanon, 40 km south of Beirut. Sidon has been a rich source of stone anthropoid sarcophagi and elaborately sculptured marble sarcophagi manufactured between the 6th and 4th centuries BC. The anthropoid sarcophagi were inspired by the Egyptian mummy case but the features and hair of the deceased were sculpted in the Greek style; they appear to be a Phoenician invention. Homer and Strabo praise the skill of Sidon's artisans and it occurs frequently in the Old and New Testaments. The city came under Assyrian and Babylonian domination (900–550 BC) and was incorporated in the Fifth Persian satrapy between *c.* 550 BC and 330 BC. Sidon welcomed Alexander the Great and was rapidly Hellenized. At his death the city became a possession of the Ptolemies and the Seleucid kings; it came under Roman rule in 64 BC.

Four sculpted marble sarcophagi from the royal necropolis at Ayaa are outstanding. These are probably the work of Greek artists and show the adaptation of Greek architectural and sculptural motifs to an Oriental ideal. The sculpted reliefs on the sides of the 'Satrap Sarcophagus' (last quarter of the 5th century BC; Istanbul, Archaeol. Mus.) portray scenes from the life of an Oriental potentate. On one side a Persian satrap is seated on a throne flanked by attendants as he gives an order to a youth about to mount a chariot drawn by four horses. The other side represents a hunting scene in which the satrap is seen, after mortally wounding a doe, attacking a panther with a spear. One end has four youths holding lances; the other shows the dignitary reclining on a couch flanked by attendants. The 'Lycian Sarcophagus' (early 4th century BC; Istanbul, Archaeol. Mus.), the shape and decoration of which recall the funerary monuments of Lycia, was made of Paros marble. One side depicts a wild boar attacking a group of horsemen and the other represents a lion hunt with two chariots drawn by four horses each. The ends depict contests with centaurs. On the high curved lid are reliefs of two winged sphinxes and two griffons. The 'Sarcophagus of the Mourning Women' (mid-4th century BC; Istanbul, Archaeol. Mus.) is in the form of a Greek temple surrounded by a portico with Doric columns at the corners. Between pairs of Ionic columns stand 18 statues of women, elegantly draped, about 1 m high, expressing different attitudes of grief. The sarcophagus lid represents the roof of the temple.

The best-known is the 'Alexander Sarcophagus' (late 4th century BC; Istanbul, Archaeol. Mus.; see colour pl. 2:XI, fig. 2). This large pedimented work measures almost 3.18 m in length and weighs over 15 tons; it was carved in Pentelic marble and is unique in being decorated with historical reliefs rather than mythological scenes. There are traces of colouring on the figures. The Greeks, mostly on horseback, had blue eyes, scarlet cloaks, blue tunics, crested helmets and long straight swords and are engaged in battle against their opponents, probably Persians, who have peaked hats and a cloth wrapped about the head. Alexander the Great appears twice on the reliefs. In the main battle scene, probably showing Alexander at Issus, he is mounted on a rearing horse and wears a lion skin over his head like the god Herakles (see fig.). His horse has been wounded by an arrow and, startled, leaps over the prostrate figure of a dying Persian. Alexander pursues an enemy cavalryman and holds a spear poised over his head ready to strike. The Persian, whose horse has stumbled, tries to disengage himself from the fallen steed and points his sword at Alexander. The other side represents both Greeks and Persians hunting a lion and deer. Alexander, this time wearing the Macedonian diadem, gallops towards the lion. The hunting scene is a more open composition and may have taken place in the Persian royal park in Sidon. One end displays another battle scene while the other represents a panther hunt. The two pedimental compositions represent contest and battle scenes. The reliefs are a vivid example of the naturalistic skill of the sculptor. The lid is in the form of a temple roof with tiles, antefixes, acroteria and cornice.

O. Hamdy and T. Reinach: *Une Nécropole royale à Sidon*, 2 vols (Paris, 1892)

G. Mendel: *Catalogue des sculptures grecques, romaines et byzantines* (1912), i of *Musées impériaux ottomans* (Constantinople, 1912–14)

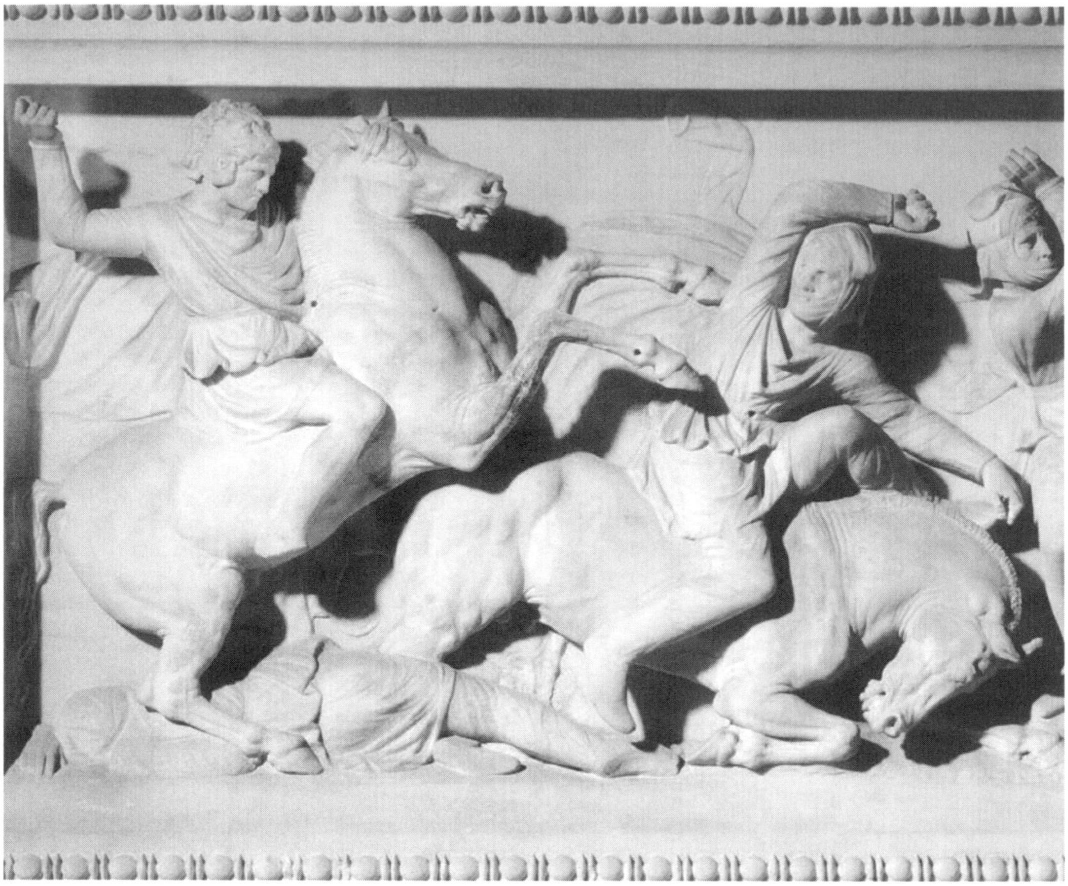

Sidon, *Battle of Issos*, detail from the 'Alexander Sarcophagus', marble, late 4th century BC (Istanbul, Archaeological Museum)

F. Winter: *Der Alexander-Sarkophag aus Sidon* (Strasbourg, 1912)

C. Torrey: 'A Phoenician Necropolis at Sidon', *An. Amer. Sch. Orient. Res. Jerusalem*, i (1919–20), pp. 1, 4, 6, 14, 18–21

G. Richter: *The Sculpture and Sculptors of the Greeks* (New Haven, 1930)

E. Kukahn: *Anthropoïde Sarkophage in Beyrouth* (Berlin, 1955)

I. Kleeman: *Der Satrapen-Sarkophag aus Sidon* (Berlin, 1958)

M. L. Buhl: *The Late Egyptian Anthropoid Stone Sarcophagi* (Copenhagen, 1959)

M. Dunand: 'Rapport préliminaire sur les fouilles de Sidon en 1964–1965', *Bull. Mus. Beyrouth*, xx (1967), pp. 27–44

K. Schefold: *Der Alexander-Sarkophag* (Berlin and Frankfurt am Main, 1968)

M. Dunand: 'La Statuaire de la favissa du temple d'Echmoun à Sidon', *Archäologie und altes Testament* (Tübingen, 1970), pp. 61–7

N. Jidejian: *Sidon through the Ages* (Beirut, 1971); rev. French edn., *Sidon à travers les âges* (Beirut, 1995)

R. A. Stucky: 'Die Skulpturen aus dem Eschmun-Heiligtum bei Sidon: Griechische, römische, kyprische und phönizische Statuen und Reliefs vom 6. Jahrhundert vor Chr. bis zum 3. Jahrhundert nach Chr.', *Ant. Kst*, xvii (1993)

I. Kawabani: 'Le Pseudo-Tribune d'Ichmoun d'après un témoignage oculaire', *Archeology and History in Lebanon* xviii (Autumn, 2003), pp. 120–28

R. Saidah: *Sidon et la Phénicie Méridionale au Bronze Récent: A propos des tombes de Dakerman* (Beirut, 2004)

R. A. Stucky and others: *Das Eschmun-Heiligtum von Sidon: Architektur und Inschriften* (Basle, 2005)

Sikanie. *See* SICILY.

Sikyon. Site in the northern Peloponnese, *c.* 26 km west of Corinth, now partly occupied by the village of Vasiliko. The ancient town, reputed to be one of the oldest in Greece, was originally by the sea, near the modern port of Kiato. During the Classical period it was an important artistic centre: Kanachos, Lysippos and Polykleitos are associated with its school of bronze sculpture, and Pamphilos and Pausias trained at its academy of painting. In 303 BC it was razed by Demetrios I Poliorketes (*reg* 306–285 BC), who built a new town (then called Demetrias) 3 km inland on the site of the old acropolis. Apart from the scattered fragments of an early Doric temple at Kiato, the visible remains of the ancient city are found at the later site. In 301 BC Sikyon became part of the small kingdom based on Corinth that Demetrios succeeded in retaining after the catastrophic defeat of his father,

Antigonos I Monophthalmos (*reg* 306–301 BC), at Ipsos. Most of the surviving buildings date either from this period, and are comparable with Demetrios' architectural projects at Perachora, although on a more lavish scale, or to the subsequent time after 251 BC, when Sikyon was united with the Achaian League by its most famous Hellenistic statesman, Aratos. The theatre on the slopes of the acropolis hill was excavated by the American School at Athens in 1889–91. It is badly damaged but interesting because of the two substantial vaulted passages, one at each side, that lead under the upper rows of seating to the middle levels. Their competent use of keystone vaulting recalls Macedonian-built tombs and the slightly earlier passage into the stadium at Nemea (*c.* 320 BC), which suggests that the theatre was built by Demetrios. Nearby are the remains of a large formal gymnasium with two terraced courtyards, both bordered on three sides by colonnades, the lower Ionic and the upper Doric. Set into the terrace separating the two courts are two small but elaborate Doric fountain-houses. Below the gymnasium is the agora, with the remains of a long stoa and a square bouleuterion. The construction of both the gymnasium and the bouleuterion may reflect the rise to power of the wealthy families who controlled the member-cities of the Achaian League in the 3rd and 2nd centuries BC. The best-preserved structure on the site is a Roman vaulted bath building, which retains its roof and now functions as the local museum. Sikyon has produced good examples of floors decorated with pebble mosaics, coming from the formal dining rooms (andrones) of private houses. A particularly fine one, from a house below the Hellenistic acropolis, has a series of spiralling tendrils and flowers, similar in concept to a floor in the palace at Aigai (ii) (Vergina), but simpler in design, and without the three-dimensional effect. It may well reflect the flower painting which was said to be a specialty of the most famous Sikyonian painter, PAUSIAS.

E. R. Fiechter: *Das Theater in Sikyon* (Stuttgart, 1931)
A. C. Orlandos: 'La Fontaine de Sicyone', *Amer. J. Archaeol.*, xxxviii (1934), pp. 153–7
J. Delorme: *Gymnasion* (Paris, 1960), pp. 99–102
C. M. Robertson: 'Greek Mosaics: A Postscript', *J. Hell. Stud.*, lxxxvii
A. Griffin: *Sikyon* (Oxford, 1982)
D. Bérend, S. Hurter and C. Arnold-Biucchi: *Pour Denyse: Divertissements numismatiques* (Berne, 2000)

Silanion (*fl* late 4th century BC). Greek sculptor. He was active at Athens, where he was born, and at Olympia. Pliny (*Natural History* XXXIV.xiv.51) listed him as a contemporary of the more famous 4th-century BC sculptor Lysippos, who was active in the 113th Olympiad (328–325 BC). Silanion was thought remarkable in antiquity for being self-taught in his craft. Literary sources cite 11 bronze portraits by him; in addition, three statue bases signed by the sculptor have been found in Asia Minor, at Pergamon, Ephesos and Miletos.

Of the 11 portraits, three may be connected with surviving sculptures. A portrait of *Plato*, identified by an inscribed herm (Berlin, Antikensamml.) and known in over 20 marble copies, probably originated with one by Silanion discussed by Diogenes Laertius (*Lives of the Famous Philosophers* III.xxv), which was dedicated in the Academy of Plato by a Persian, Mithridates. The features are individualized by small, close-set eyes under a prominent brow, an aquiline nose and a protruding lower lip under a drooping moustache that flows into a full pointed beard. The second portrait is of a boxer, *Satyros*, which some have identified with a bronze head found at Olympia (Athens, N. Archaeol. Mus., 6439); it shows an older man with rough tousled hair and beard, and the flattened nose and cauliflower ears of a boxer. Third, a marble statuette inscribed with the name Korinna (Compiègne, Mus. Mun. Vivenel, 515) has been rather tenuously associated with the bronze portrait of *Korinna* by Silanion referred to by Tatian (*Speech to the Greeks* liv). The Boiotian lyric poetess was a contemporary of the 5th-century BC poet Pindar, so a portrait by Silanion in the 4th century BC was an invention. The style of drapery and hair on the statuette is, however, consistent with the 4th century BC.

From the descriptions in the sources of the remaining portraits executed by Silanion, it appears that he had a naturalistic and expressive style. A portrait of his contemporary, the sculptor *Apollodoros*, was praised by Pliny (XXXIV.xix.81–2) for having captured the subject's angry intensity. A portrait of *Jokasta*, the mother and wife of Oedipus, showed her dying so realistically that a dubious technical explanation was reported by Plutarch (*Moralia* 674A), namely that the artist mixed silver in the bronze which produced the colour of dying flesh on the surface. Other portraits include those of *Sappho, Achilles, Theseus*, two youthful boxers and an athletic trainer. According to Vitruvius (*On Architecture* VII. Preface. 12, 14), Silanion also wrote on *symmetria*, the commensurability of parts in a work of art, but no further details are given.

K. Bluemel: *Staatliche Museen zu Berlin: Katalog der Sammlung antiker Skulpturen*, ii-v (Berlin, 1938)
J. J. Pollitt: *The Art of Ancient Greece: Sources and Documents* (Englewood Cliffs, 1965, rev. Cambridge, 2/1990), pp. 92–3, 261
G. M. A. Richter: *Portraits of the Greeks*, i (London, 1965)
P. C. Bol: *Grossplastik aus Bronze in Olympia*, Olympische Forschungen, ix (Berlin, 1978)
A. Stewart: *Greek Sculpture: An Exploration* (New Haven and London, 1990), pp. 288–9

Silchester. *See* CALLEVA ATREBATUM.

Sileen [Silene], **Villa.** Roman villa in Libya. The élite of the great city of LEPTIS MAGNA built villas along the Tripolitanian coast, and the Villa Sileen, near the village of Khums (Qums) is an excellent example of this type of domestic architecture in North Africa. Discovered in 1974, the villa was inhabited in the

2nd century AD. It consists of 20 rooms, including domed baths. Wall paintings and mosaics grace the villa, now on the edge of the coast, which are so well preserved because the villa had been covered by sand dunes over the centuries. The subject-matter of the interior decoration includes scenes of hunting and chariot racing, with mosaics depicting scenes of the Nile with pygmies fighting crocodiles, as well as sea nymphs and tritons.

J. Azema: *Footprint: Libya Handbook* (Bath, 2000)
V. Walt: 'Swords and Sandals', *Smithsonian* xxxvi (2005), pp. 24–6 [on a related site]

Silver. *See* METALWORK.

Siracusa. *See* SYRACUSE.

Sirmio [now Sirmione]. Roman site on the Sirmione Peninsula situated at the southern end of Lake Garda, in northern Italy; Sirmione is also the name of the main town at the tip of the promontory. The Romans established an important *mansio* or station here, between Brixia (Brescia) and Verona, along the imperial route that linked the eastern part of the Empire with the west. From about the 1st century BC Sirmio became popular as a holiday resort for wealthy Romans from Brixia and Verona. At the tip of the peninsula stand the ruins of a Roman villa known as the Grotte di Catullo and mistakenly associated with the poet Catullus (*c.* 84–*c.* 54 BC), though he is known to have stayed in Sirmio and praised it in his writing. One of the largest extant Roman villas in northern Italy, it was most likely constructed in the 1st century BC and enlarged in the following century. Fragments of stucco, frescoes and inscriptions found in the vicinity are conserved in the Antiquarium. The extensive villa complex includes residential quarters, baths, dry storerooms, courtyards and granaries. In the late Roman and Byzantine periods Sirmio was an important military stronghold and was fortified, almost certainly in the 4th century (when the Christian Church became organized in the area); remains of these fortifications run the length of the peninsula and include the ruins of several towers.

M. Mirabella Roberti: 'Fortificazioni tardoantiche nella penisola di Sirmione', *Il sistema fortificato dei laghi lombardi in funzione delle loro vie di communicazione* (Como, 1977), pp. 47–56
E. Roffia and E. A. Arslan: *Le 'grotte di Catullo' a Sirmione: Guida alla visita della villa romana e del museo* (Milan, 2005)

Sirmium [now Sremska Mitrovica, Serbia]. Roman town founded in the late 1st century BC on the site of an earlier settlement on what is now the River Sava, *c.* 76 km west of Belgrade. Between AD 79 and 96 it was elevated to the status of a colony, and then became capital of the province of Pannonia. It was one of the most important bases for the Danubian frontier of the Empire, and was often used as a residence by emperors on campaign. In 293, when the Empire was split into four parts (the Tetrarchy), Sirmium became one of the four capitals, and was the seat of the Emperor Galerius. Constantine the Great (*reg* AD 306–37) founded a mint in the city, and several church councils met there during the 4th century. Sirmium fell to the Goths in 409.

Excavations undertaken in the 1960s and 1970s by joint Yugoslav, American and French teams have revealed several ancient monuments beneath the modern city. They include scattered sites of 3rd- to 4th-century Roman housing, granaries and public baths, as well as parts of a circus (l. *c.* 350–400 m; *c.* AD 315) and neighbouring buildings that may have been part of the imperial palace. The latter contain red porphyry columns and a large court with a square decorative structure at its centre. If these buildings can be shown to be directly connected with the circus, the complex would be comparable with contemporary palaces at Constantinople (Istanbul) and Thessaloniki. Of the stretches of city wall that have been recovered the north side is said to date to the 2nd century AD and the south to the late 3rd century AD or the early 4th: not enough has been found to reconstruct the whole circuit.

Sirmium (Belgrade, 1971-) [excav. reps, i-iii (1971–3), ed. V. Popović and L. Ochsenschlager; vii–viii (1977–8), ed. V. Popović and N. Duval]
P. Milošević: *Arheologija i istorija Sirmijuma* (Novi Sad, 2001)

Siros. *See* SYROS.

Situla art. Decorative metalwork style of the 7th–4th centuries BC, characteristic of the bronze situlae (buckets) and other objects discovered in tombs in Slovenia and in the Adige and Bologna regions of Italy.

1. FORM AND CONTEXT. As the name implies, the most important decorated examples of this style are situlae, which are adorned with one or more figurative friezes and ornamental bands. There are also complementary designs on other vessels, metal belts and mirrors. Signs of use on the belts reveal that these objects were not merely part of a cult of the dead but were also used in life. The earliest discoveries of such works date back to before the mid-19th century, but their significance was not realized until the 1870s–1890s, when a whole series of well-preserved examples was discovered, including situlae from Vače in Slovenia (Ljubljana, N. Mus.) and Kuffarn in Austria (Vienna, Nathist. Mus.), as well as the famous Certosa Situla from Bologna, Mus. Bologna (there is another example perhaps from the same place in Providence, RI Sch. Des., Mus. A.). It was clear that these works originated from Upper Italy or Slovenia, and discussions began to determine to what extent the situlae were directly dependent on Greek or Etruscan models and how much they were a reflection of the indigenous ancient cultures of Upper Italy and the south-east Alpine region. Considerable progress in

their evaluation was made in 1961–2 when an exhibition shown in Padua, Ljubljana and Vienna gathered together the most important examples. At the same time there was increased research into the Hallstatt culture that flourished in the east *c.* 750–*c.* 400 BC: the figuratively decorated situlae are a product of its late period. Great emphasis was placed on situlae as a source for historical interpretation.

The situlae usually measure 200–300 mm in height and nearly all are riveted together from a single sheet. The base is joined with a lock seam, and the edge is often rolled around a lead ring. The attachments for the movable handles are riveted on to the indented shoulder or, if present, the narrow neck of the vessel. The decoration usually comprises one, three or four figural friezes bordered by a trim. The figures were beaten from inside before the metal was joined; some parts of human figures, such as the joints, cheeks and lips, were merely raised by using bosses of different sizes. On the outside, the designs were outlined by a small chisel or pointed punch; hasty work, perhaps with too large a chisel, is to be found among works of higher quality. There are only a few examples of completely engraved pieces.

The pictures are relatively primitive. Men or women are seen in profile, and the point of attachment of the arm, which is difficult to depict, is often covered with clothing. However, hands are usually shown with all the fingers or holding clearly detailed utensils, though they are still often too large. Animals are usually distinguished only by such features as horns, tails, hooves or paws. Some pictures are repeated so exactly that the artists must have had fixed patterns.

The earliest examples of Situla art date from the late 7th century BC and belong in the context of the local traditions of Upper Italy. The end of Situla art, taking into account a certain transition period, can be dated to the 4th century BC, after the Celts had advanced into Upper Italy and the south-east Alpine region. These events are related to the end of eastern Hallstatt culture and to a new direction in art.

2. Subject-matter. Situlae with several friezes are usually decorated with two or three registers of human scenes with an animal scene below, following Greek or Etruscan models. The direction of the scenes usually changes between the individual registers. Banquet scenes are particularly common: distinguished men sit on thrones, their rank shown by a broad-brimmed hat or other conspicuous headgear, while servants are depicted either with small caps or bareheaded. The noblemen often hold sceptres, fans or such musical instruments as lyres or panpipes. Women or servants serve them drinks in a bowl or direct from the ladle. The men also stand by the mixing pot, scooping out samples or pouring in spices. Vessels shown on the floor or hanging up form part of the drinking scene, while men with axes lead animals to the slaughter, showing that the preparation of meat was a part of the banquet. Erotic pleasures are also shown. Athletic competitions, usually in the form of a boxing match, form the final part of the feast; horse and chariot races are depicted. Processions are another recurrent subject, sometimes with marching men, who play the flute, or sometimes with led animals, including wild animals. Women figure in some processions, carrying vessels or other loads on their heads. Charioteers and riders appear, and there are many examples of military processions. Less frequent battle scenes include a metal belt from Vače (Vienna, Nathist. Mus.) showing two riders accompanied by foot soldiers, and a situla fragment from Nesactium in Istria depicts a sea battle. Hunting scenes are more common, for example hare-hunting with nets and the deer-hunt on horseback. Finally there are some examples of ploughmen.

In none of the above scenes is there any clear indication that they represent particular myths. Rather they depict the life of the élite and therefore an idealized view of a male world, in which women are only attendants. There is no doubt that these pictures reflect the daily life of the ancient peoples of Upper Italy and the eastern Alpine region. This is evident in the animal friezes, in which fabulous beasts occur only infrequently. Lions often have a bushy tail, thereby becoming local wolves, and in addition to deer, roe deer and ibex, there is even a clear representation of a typical Alpine chamois. The friezes with human scenes have antiquarian details that show that they are not merely copies of Classical models. The soldiers, for example, have characteristic weapons known from finds in burials in the south-east Alpine region. The boxers have dumb-bell-shaped hand protectors not found in contemporary Greek and Etruscan images. The musical instruments and costumes depicted also have unique qualities. On the other hand, influences from the ancient world, particularly from Etruscan art, are clearly visible. These include for instance beasts of prey with a half-devoured animal in their jaws, as well as certain details on the costumes and the fans held by distinguished men. Elements of composition are also taken from Classical models, as can be seen from the zonal arrangement of the decoration and the use of animal friezes. Specific examples are the arrangement of boxers around the victor's prize and the posture of charioteers.

Three works with figural scenes date to *c.* 600 BC and can be regarded as starting-points for the development of Situla art: a pendant (*tintinnabulum*) from Felsina (Bologna) (Bologna, Mus. Civ. Archeol.), the Benvenuti Situla from Este (*see also* Este art) and a helmet fragment from Slovenia (Ljubljana, N. Mus.). The latter depicts only a military procession, but the Benvenuti Situla is more impressive, depicting distinguished revellers, boxers with typical hand protection and soldiers with prisoners. The scenes on the *tintinnabulum* from Felsina, surely a local project, are thematically quite different, as they show noblewomen spinning and weaving, thereby offering a unique insight into the contemporary woman's world. These three works clearly show the influence of middle Italian Etruscan models from the orientalizing period of the 7th century BC. The animal and plant images on the Benvenuti Situla and the plant motif on the helmet fragment clearly belong to the early Este art style, in which animal pictures are dominant, and the origins of Situla art can therefore be placed in the local traditions of Upper Italy. The development of art in Este later took a different path, although it frequently came into contact and mixed with Situla art.

P. Ducati: 'La situla della Certosa', *Mem. Reale Accad. Sci. Ist. Bologna, Cl. Sci. Mor.*, 2nd ser., v–vii (1923), pp. 23–95

Mostra dell'arte delle situle dal Po al Danubio (VI–IV secolo a.c.) (exh. cat., Padua and Florence, 1961)

W. Lucke and O.-H. Frey: *Die Situla in Providence (Rhode Island): Ein Beitrag zur Situlenkunst des Osthallstattkreises* (Berlin, 1962)

J. Kastelic: *Situla Art: Ceremonial Bronzes of Ancient Europe* (London, 1965)

O.-H. Frey: *Die Entstehung der Situlenkunst: Studien zur figürlich verzierten Toreutik von Este* (Berlin, 1969)

J. Boardman: 'A Southern View of Situla Art', *The European Community in Later Prehistory: Studies in Honour of C. F. C. Hawkes*, ed. J. Boardman, M. A. Brown and T. G. E. Powell (London, 1971), pp. 121–40

O.-H. Frey: 'Bemerkungen zur hallstättischen Bewaffnung im Südostalpenraum', *Arheol. Vestnik*, xxiv (1973), pp. 621–36

O.-H. Frey: 'Bemerkungen zu figürlichen Darstellungen des Osthallstattkreises', *Festschrift für Richard Pittioni I* (Vienna, 1976), pp. 578–87

A. Eibner: 'Darstellungsinhalte in der Kunst der Hallstattkultur: Gedanken zum "überhöhten" Leben im Situlenbereich und Osthallstattkreis', *Die Hallstattkultur: Bericht über das Symposium in Steyr, 1980* (Linz, 1981) pp. 261–96

A. Eibner: 'Musikleben in der Hallstattzeit: Betrachtungen zur "Mousiké" anhand der bildlichen Darstellungen', *Musik in Antike und Neuzeit: Quellen und Studien zur Musikgeschichte von der Antike bis in die Gegenwart*, i (Frankfurt, 1986) pp. 271–318

O.-H. Frey: 'Beziehungen der Situlenkunst zum Kunstschaffen Etruriens, Etrusker nördlich von Etrurien', *Akten d. Symposions Wien* (Vienna, 1992) pp. 93–101

Skene. Stage in an ancient Greek theatre.

Skopas (*fl* mid-4th century BC). Greek sculptor and architect. He was probably the son of the Parian Aristandros, who worked on the Spartan dedication for their victory at Aigospotamoi in 405 BC. He was employed as an architect and sculptor at Tegea after 395 BC and as a sculptor on the Mausoleum at HALIKARNASSOS from *c.* 367 BC to *c.* 351 BC, at Ephesos after 356 BC and in Thebes before 336 BC.

Pliny, Pausanias and others recorded 25 works by Skopas in the Peloponnese, Attica, northern Greece, Ionia and Caria. Several were later taken to Rome as loot. All but one were of marble and included 16 studies of the younger gods (e.g. *Aphrodite, Apollo, Ares, Artemis, Asklepios, Athena, Dionysos, Hekate, Hermes* and *Hestia*). The rest comprised the *Furies*; *Eros, Himeros* and *'Pothos'*; *Herakles*; two basket-bearers; a *Maenad*; a carved column-drum for the Temple of Artemis at Ephesos; and two large ensembles, *Achilles, Thetis and Poseidon's Marine Cortège* and the sculptures of the east side of the Mausoleum. Later connoisseurs also attributed the *Niobe* group (Florence, Uffizi), a *'Janus'* and another *Artemis*, all by then in Rome, to Skopas or Praxiteles. Ancient writers listed Skopas alongside Praxiteles and Lysippos as one of the greatest Late Classical sculptors and, with Praxiteles and Pheidias, one of the foremost makers of divine images. Their constant comparisons with Praxiteles are, however, problematic.

Attributions to Skopas have traditionally been based on sculpture fragments from the pediments of the Temple of Athena Alea at TEGEA. Though Pausanias says only that Skopas was the temple's architect and sculpted free-standing statues of *Asklepios* and *Hygieia* for it, these pediments are so innovative and un-Praxitelean that they must be by a major sculptor. Their craggy features, deep eye sockets and upturned gazes suggest intense, if generalized, emotion (pathos), and this conforms with Kallistratos' description of Skopas' *Maenad Tearing a Goat*. A copy of this work (Dresden, Albertinum, 133) was independently identified in 1902 and supports the Tegea attributions. Other works ascribed to Skopas on this basis include several slabs from the Amazon Frieze from the Mausoleum at Halikarnassos (London, BM, 1007-8-10, 1011–12); the Grimani *Triton*, possibly from the *Poseidon* group (Berlin, Antikensamml., 286); two types of Herakles (copies: the Hope-type, Los Angeles, CA, Co. Mus. A., 50.33.22; the Lansdowne-type, Malibu, CA, Getty Mus., B-B 691–92); a *Meleager* (copy: e.g. Copenhagen, Ny Carlsberg Glyp., 387 and Berlin, Antikensamml., Staatliche Museen; see fig.); and a *Winged Youth*, probably *'Pothos'* (Gr: 'yearning'; Rome, Mus. Conserv., 2417). A helmeted head (the De Bry *Head*; Malibu, CA, Getty Mus.) has been conjectured to have belonged to the figure of Achilles in the western pediment at Tegea itself.

This approach to attribution has, however, increasingly been questioned. The attribution of the Tegea pediments themselves has been challenged, and several important pieces have been rejected as alien to them. The De Bry *Head* has been labelled a fake and the two Herakles types have been called Roman pastiches. The *'Pothos'* has been accepted as by Skopas but associated with a quite different group of sculptures, notably the Florentine *Niobe* group. Such challenges remain, even so, inconclusive. Rejections of works ascribed to the Temple of Athena Alea at Tegea because they are too poor or the 'wrong size' take no account of variation in quality within a single workshop and overlook the fact that the two pedimental groups were of different scales, evidently for compositional reasons. The matter of the De Bry *Head*, however, has been decisively resolved by the discovery that its dimensions are identical to one of the Tegea heads, and its material is Parian, as against local Doliana, marble, condemning it as a forgery. With regard to the copies, the Hope-type *Herakles* is indeed awkward and second-rate but conforms so closely with an effigy on a Sikyonian coin that it may well reproduce Skopas' Sikyonian *Herakles*. The pose of the more accomplished Lansdowne-type *Herakles* has good 4th-century BC parallels but none of the Hadrianic period. Similarly, the attempt to attribute the *Niobe* group to Skopas ignores the fact that the one secure Greek original in this style is Attic (Athens, N. Archaeol. Mus., 142).

Though the traditional attributions have, therefore, not been conclusively revised, problems still remain. The originals are workshop pieces and thus can only reflect to a limited extent the style of any individual sculptor. Moreover, the copies of works attributed to Skopas include almost none of the statues of the gods for which he was most renowned in antiquity, and the *'Pothos'*, which is the most securely identified copy, is extremely Praxitelean. This may be a coincidence of subject and original location, since Skopas' *Eros, Himeros* and *'Pothos'* at Megara were grouped with Praxiteles' *Persuasion* and *Consolation*, but the contrast with the sculptures from Tegea is striking.

Skopas' stature as an architect is easier to assess. The Temple of Athena Alea at Tegea was boldly innovative in approach, combining proportions and details derived from buildings such as the Temple of Asklepios at Epidauros with its pi-shaped internal colonnade, recalling the Parthenon and Hephaisteion. Skopas' concern with the articulation of space is apparent in the open proportions of the colonnade, the careful positioning of mouldings, the deep porches and, above all, in the novel layout of the interior. Here, the pi-shaped colonnade was pushed back till engaged in the cella walls to create a single open room, while the Doric columns of its precursors were replaced by a Corinthian lower order and an Ionic upper one. These innovations were frequently copied by Hellenistic architects and appreciated much later by Pausanias, who commented that Skopas' temple was 'far superior to any other in the Peloponnese in both size and style' (*Guide to Greece*, VIII.xlv.5).

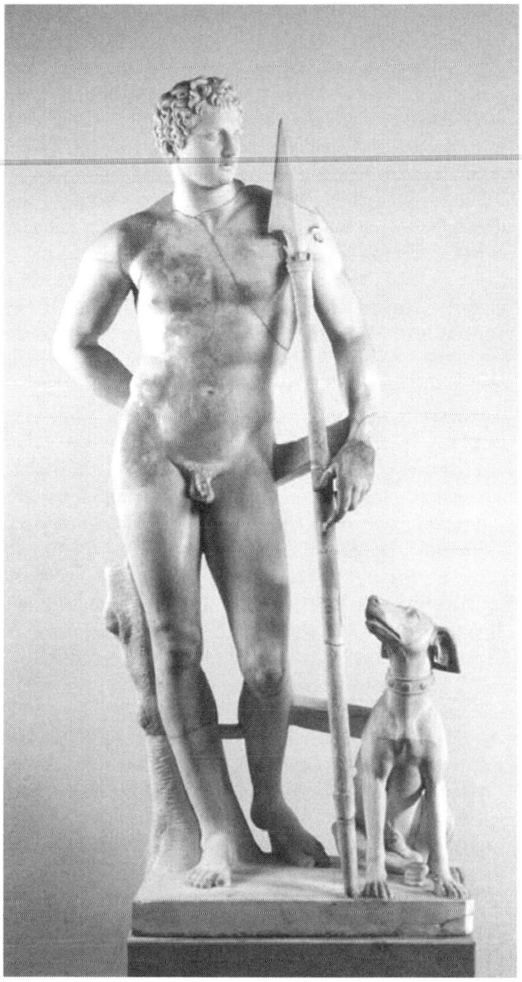

Skopas: *Meleager* (copy), marble, h. 2.09 m, *c.* 340 BC (Berlin, Antikensammlung, Staatliche Museen zu Berlin)

C. Dugas, J. Berchmans and M. Clemmensen: *Le Sanctuaire d'Alea Athena à Tégée* (Paris, 1924)

P. E. Arias: *Skopas* (Rome, 1952)

G. M. A. Hanfmann and J. G. Pedley: 'The Statue of Meleager', *Ant. Plast.*, iii (1964), pp. 61–6

A. Delivorrias: 'Skopadika I', *Bull. Corr. Hell.*, xcvii (1973), pp. 111–35

S. Lattimore: 'Meleager: New Replicas, Old Problems', *Opscula Romana*, ix (1973), pp. 157–66

S. Lattimore: 'Two Statues of Herakles', *Getty Mus. J.*, ii (1975), pp. 17–26

S. Lattimore: *The Marine Thiasos in Greek Sculpture* (Los Angeles, 1976)

A. F. Stewart: *Skopas of Paros* (Park Ridge, NJ, 1977)

G. B. Waywell: *The Free-standing Sculptures of the Mausoleum at Halicarnassus in the British Museum* (London, 1978)

A. F. Stewart: *Skopas in Malibu* (Malibu, 1982)

A. Delivorrias and A. Linfert: 'Skopadika II', *Bull. Corr. Hell.*, cvii (1983), pp. 277–88

W. A. Geominy: *Die Florentiner Niobiden* (Bonn, 1984)

N. J. Norman: 'The Temple of Alea Athena at Tegea', *Amer. J. Archaeol.*, lxxxviii (1984), pp. 169–94

O. Palagia: 'The Hope Herakles Reconsidered', *Oxford J. Archaeol.*, iii (1984), pp. 107–26

G. Hafner: 'Ungemein schön und seelenvoll', *Ant. Welt*, xv (1986), pp. 27–32

J. Marcadé: 'Tegeatika', *Bull. Corr. Hell.*, cx (1986), pp. 317–29

N. J. Norman: 'Asklepios and Hygieia and the Cult Statue at Tegea', *Amer. J. Archaeol.*, xc (1986), pp. 425–30

A. F. Stewart: *Greek Sculpture: An Exploration* (New Haven, 1990), pp. 64, 84–5, 182–5, 284–6

Skyphos. Ancient vessel form, used as a drinking cup (*see* POTTERY, fig. 15(iv)e-h).

Smyrna [now Izmir]. Greek and Roman site at the head of the Gulf of Smyrna in Ionia, now western Turkey. The earlier site, *c.* 4 km to the north, has significant Archaic architectural remains; when it became too small it was refounded, reputedly in 334 BC by Alexander the Great.

1. GREEK. Old Smyrna (now Bayraklı Tepe) occupied what originally seems to have been a peninsula.

It was inhabited in prehistoric times, but Greek settlers may not have arrived before 1000 BC. Foundations of houses have been excavated (1948–51 by E. Akurgal (Ankara U.) and J. M. Cook (Brit. Sch., Athens); 1966– by E. Akurgal), the earliest dating from *c.* 900 BC, followed by levels of densely packed small houses, mainly with curved walls, of the 8th century BC. In the earlier 7th century BC the city began to take on a regular plan with streets on a north-south axis, and, since this seems to have coincided with a spread of population on to the mainland, some form of deliberate urban planning may be assumed. The larger, well-built houses, some at least two-storey, had mud-brick walls on stone socles of up to 1 m high and flat roofs. By the later 7th century BC the city wall, apparently twice enlarged, had become massive (see fig. 1), though it still did not save Smyrna from being sacked *c.* 600 BC by the Lydian king Alyattes. Also of 7th-century BC date is a sanctuary terrace fitted into the axial plan at the north end of the site. The first temple seems to have been small and simple; but the great temple dedicated to Athena, which was being built to supersede it at the time of the Lydian attack, had stone columns with unusual voluted capitals. This is the earliest-known monumental East Greek temple. The sanctuary's partly closed entrance and the adjoining terraces had walls in fine polygonal masonry of contrasting colours. Habitation on the site was resumed not long after the Lydian sack. In the 6th century BC sturdy houses were built, those in the northern part of the site having the same orientation as their predecessors. They seem to have been abandoned at the beginning of the 5th century BC, when the Persians put down the Ionian Revolt, but from the late 5th century BC to the 4th there is again evidence of dense habitation, lasting until the refounding of the city.

Excavation of the sanctuary has yielded costly votive offerings, such as ivories, bronze objects, terracotta and faience statuettes, and engraved tridacna shells (Izmir, Archaeol. Mus. And Paris, Louvre; see fig. 2). Some were imported from Cyprus and the Near East, indicating Smyrna's position on international trade routes. In addition, much fine pottery was found, both there and in the houses. The Geometric pottery, though initially inspired by Athenian wares, was of a general Ionian or East Greek character, as were the 'bird bowls' and related vases. The East Greek orientalizing wares, found in some abundance, seem to be of both north and south Ionian manufacture, and some were clearly produced on Chios. Without scientific tests, however, it is still uncertain whether any of these wares were made locally. Corinthian pottery and 6th-century BC Attic Black-figure vases have also been found in quantity. Much of the East Greek Black-figure seems to have come from neighbouring Klazomenai, and several 'Klazomenian' painted terracotta sarcophagi have been found in the cemetery (Izmir, Archaeol. Mus.). The latter were not definitely produced at Klazomenai itself, but there is no evidence to suggest that either they or any of the Black-figure pottery were in fact produced at Smyrna.

After Smyrna was refounded it quickly became one of the most important Greek cities and, according to Strabo (*Geography* XIV.i.37), the most beautiful of all, famed for its straight and well-paved streets. Though many of its handsome buildings were rebuilt after an earthquake of AD 178, little of Hellenistic and Roman Smyrna survives.

J. M. Cook and others: 'Old Smyrna', *Annu. Brit. Sch. Athens*, liii–liv (1958–9), pp. 1–182

E. Akurgal: *Alt-Smyrna I: Wohnschichten und Athentempel* (Ankara, 1983)

G. Petzl: *Die Inschriften von Smyrna,* 2 vols (Bonn, 1987–90)

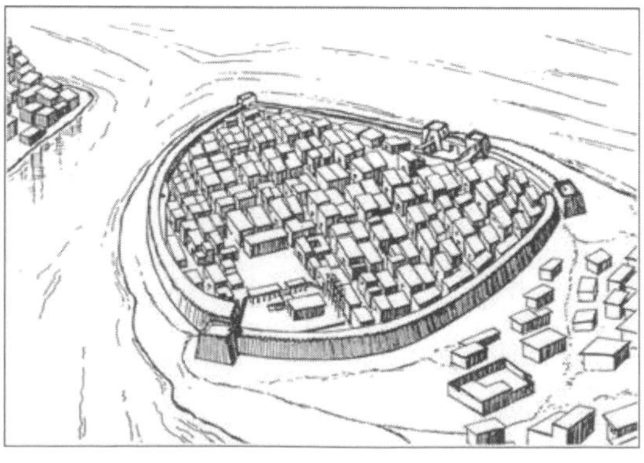

1. Smyrna, reconstruction view from the north-east, showing Old Smyrna in the late 7th century BC

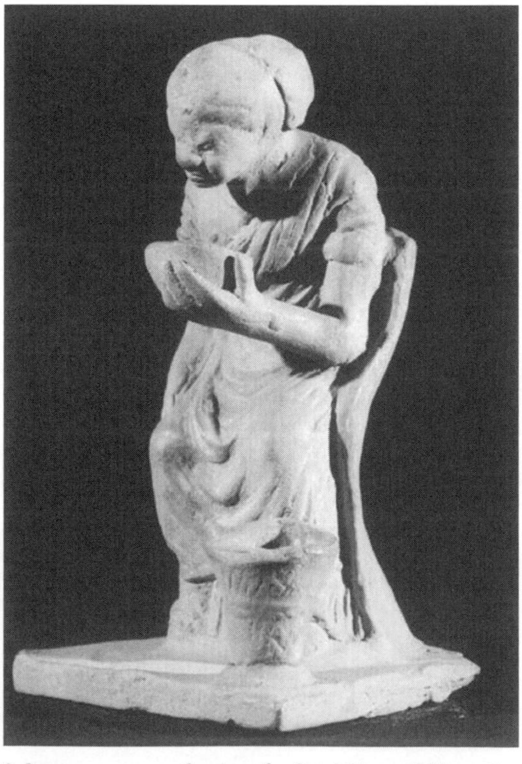

2. Smyrna, terracotta figurine of a *Seated Woman Holding a Cup*, h. 150 mm, 1st century AD (Paris, Musée du Louvre)

P. Zanker: 'The Hellenistic Grave Stelai from Smyrna: Identity and Self-image in the Polis', *Images and Ideologies: Self-definition in the Hellenistic World,* ed. A. W. Bulloch (Berkeley, 1993)

2. ROMAN. By the late 1st century BC New Smyrna had spread down the slope of Mt Pagos and on to the flatland adjoining the harbour, where the commercial agora was probably located. Hadrian (*reg* AD 117–38) built a silo near the docks. The city was severely damaged in the earthquake of AD 178, but the Emperor Marcus Aurelius provided assistance for its rebuilding. Among the monuments restored was the state agora, partly excavated in 1932–40, where a portrait bust of Faustina, Marcus Aurelius' wife, decorates an arch in the west colonnade. The agora had a vaulted substructure, which supported two-storey stoas with three aisles on the east and west sides, and a two-storey basilica with a nave and two aisles (w. 28 m) on the north side. The northern aisle of the vaulted basement beneath the basilica probably contained shops, since it communicated directly with the street outside the agora. The design of the basement itself resembles the cryptoporticus constructions of the western provinces and may have been influenced by them. An altar to Zeus stood in the state agora, to which the life-size high-relief statues of *Demeter* and *Poseidon* found in the excavations probably belonged (*c.* AD 180; Izmir, Archaeol. Mus.).

R. Naumann and S. Kantar: 'Die Agora von Smyrna', *Kleinasien und Bysanz,* Istanbul. Forsch. (Berlin, 1950), pp. 69–114
R. A. Straccioli: 'Gli edifici sotterranei dell'agora di Smirne e, ancora, sui *Criptoportici forensi*', *Latomus,* xvi (1957), pp. 275–92
E. Akurgal: *Ancient Civilizations and Ruins of Turkey* (Istanbul, 1969, rev. 8/1985), pp. 119–24
M. Yenim: *The Izmir Museums and Archaeology of some Ancient Cities* (Izmir, 1969)

Solin. *See* SALONA.

Sophilos (i) (*fl c.* 600–*c.* 570 BC). Greek vase painter. He is the first Attic vase painter whose ancient name is known. It appears on three vases which he signed as painter; a fourth signature is probably to be reconstructed as a potter's signature. Around fifty, mostly large, vessels or fragments of such are attributed to the painter. As it was the fashion of his time, he adapted to the Corinthian animal style, decorating his vases mainly or entirely with mixed processions of wild, tame and mythical creatures, which he executed in a lively and careless style. His importance is due to his rarer many-figured friezes depicting mythological subjects. These appear in his advanced oeuvre and are more ambitious and more detailed than any earlier pictures of myths. Also new are most of the subjects he chose and the very liberal use of inscriptions.

Sophilos' best-preserved mythological frieze occurs on the shoulder of the 'Erskine Dinos' (London, BM, 1971.11–1.1; see fig.). It occupies a rather higher band than the conventional animal friezes beneath it and depicts the *Procession of Gods at the Marriage of Peleus and Thetis.* Peleus is shown standing in front of his

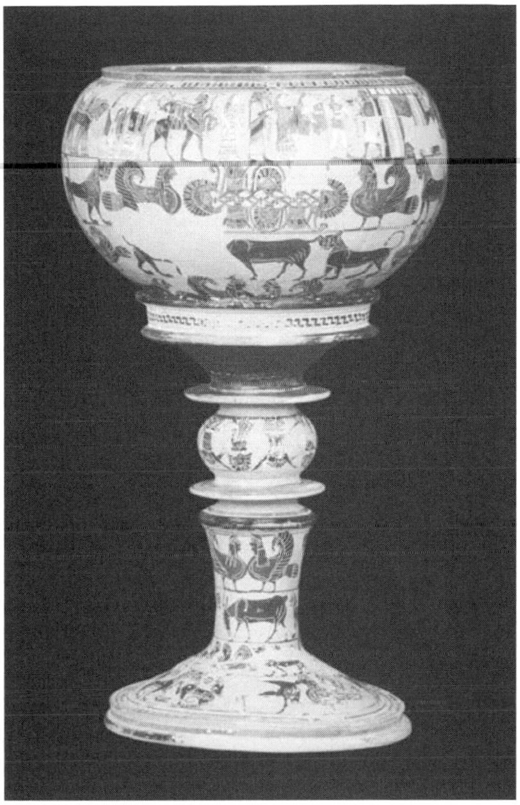

Sophilos (i): dinos depicting the *Marriage of Peleus and Thetis* (Erskine Dinos), h. 710 mm, Black-figure, *c.* 580 BC (London, British Museum, 1971.11-1.1)

house, holding a kantharos for a libation, and greeting a procession of 41 deities in brightly coloured robes arriving on foot or in carriages, led by their messenger Iris. All the figures are labelled with inscriptions in red paint, and some are also identified by special attributes. Sophilos has used his uninhibited drawing style imaginatively to create an animated festive scene with Apollo singing and playing the lyre and a muse playing panpipes. This figural frieze is made to stand out from the animal friezes beneath it by various means: the figures are overlapping freely; female figures and some horses are drawn in outline instead of silhouette; and female clothing is depicted in white paint applied directly on to the clay and outlined in red and decorated with red animal friezes and ornaments. A similar dinos was dedicated by Sophilos on the Athenian Acropolis (Athens, N. Archaeol. Mus., Acropolis 587). Somewhat later, KLEITIAS tackled the *Wedding of Peleus and Thetis* in a strikingly similar way on his famous calyx krater (Florence, Mus. Archeol., 4209) though in a more sophisticated miniaturistic style. Whether he modelled his work directly on that of Sophilos, or whether both artists shared a common source, is uncertain.

Fragments of a third dinos signed by Sophilos (Athens, N. Archaeol. Mus., 15499) depict the *Funeral Games of Patroklos.* The scene has two unique features: an inscription recording its subject, and a representation of a grandstand packed with wildly gesticulating spectators urging on a four-horse chariot. Achilles was also depicted, but only his name and the fingertips of one hand survive. Sophilos also decorated the first extant *lebes gamikos* (Izmir, Archaeol. Mus. 3332), a cult vessel for the bridal bath. His choice of scene was also new: the *Wedding of Helen and Menelaos*, with the bride and groom in one carriage and a second carriage carrying Helen's brothers, the Dioscuri (Castor and Pollux). Only a few other fragments of mythological friezes by Sophilos remain. However, he also produced clay funerary plaques with mourning women (Athens, Vlasto Col.), which were destined to decorate tombs.

J. de La Genière: 'Quand le peintre Sophilos signait ses oeuvres', *Mnmts Piot*, LXXIV (1955), pp. 35–43
J. D. Beazley: *Black-figure* (1956), pp. 37–43, 681, 714
J. D. Beazley: *Paralipomena* (1971), pp. 18–19
G. Bakir: *Sophilos: Ein Beitrag zu seinem Stil* (Mainz, 1981)
L. Burn and R. Glynn: *Beazley Addenda: Additional References to* ABV, ARV2 *and* Paralipomena (Oxford, 1982, rev. T. H. Carpenter, 2/1989), pp. 10–12
D. Williams: 'Sophilos in the British Museum', *Greek Vases in the J. Paul Getty Museum*, i (Malibu, 1983), pp. 9–34
A. B. Brownlee: 'Sophilos and Early Attic Black-figured Dinoi', *Ancient Greek and Related Pottery*, ed. J. Christiansen and T. Melander (Copenhagen, 1988), pp. 80–87
A. B. Brownlee: 'Story Lines: Observations on Sophilan Narrative', in *The Ages of Homer: A Tribute to Emily Townsend Vermeule* (Austin, 1995), pp. 363–72
C. Isler-Kerenyi: 'Dionysos im Götterzug bei Sophilos und bei Kleitias', *Ant. Kst*, xl/2 (1997) pp. 67–81

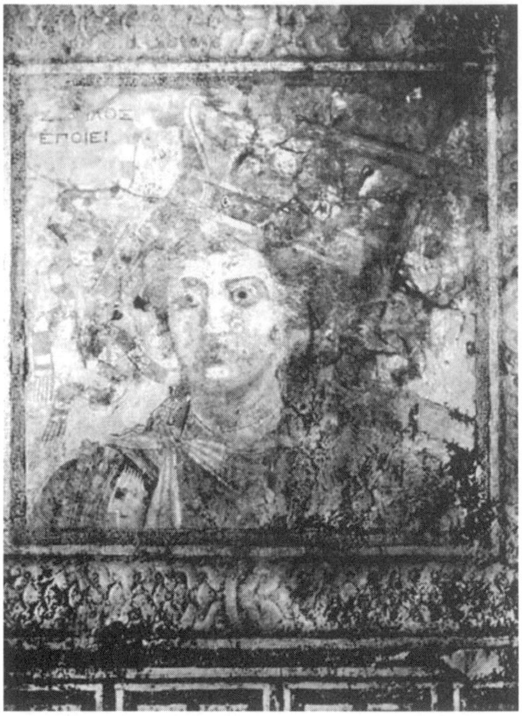

Sophilos (ii): mosaic of a Ptolemaic queen, probably Queen Berenike II, 1.44 sq. m, from Thmuis, *c.* 200 BC (Alexandria, Graeco–Roman Museum)

Sophilos (ii) (*fl c.* 200 BC). Ancient Greek mosaicist active in Egypt. His work is known from a signed floor at Tall Timay (anc. Thmuis) in the Nile Delta (now Alexandria, Gr.-Roman Mus.), in which SOPHILOS EPOIEI (Gr: 'Sophilos made') is set in two lines in black tesserae on a white floor. It appears to date to *c.* 200 BC or possibly a little before. At the edge of the rectangular floor is a frame of black crenellations; in the centre is an emblema in *opus vermiculatum* framed in isometric meander, with the inscription and a bust of a woman wearing a headdress in the form of a ship's prow (see fig.). This representation also appears in a circular emblema of coarser execution and apparently later date from the same site (now Alexandria, Gr.-Roman Mus.). The figure has traditionally been interpreted as a personification of Alexandria, but it seems more likely that these are portraits of a Ptolemaic queen, probably Berenike II (*reg* 246–221 BC), and that the mosaics derived from a contemporary painting. Strips of lead are used to contour forms in the headdress in Sophilos' panel as well as in the pattern border. These were a regular feature of figurework in pebble mosaic from the later 4th century BC onwards, but this is their latest appearance on a tessera figure, although they continued to be used in borders.

W. A. Daszewski: *Hellenistic and Early Roman Period*, i of *Corpus of the Mosaics from Egypt* (Mainz, 1985), pp. 142–58, nos 38–9
A. M. Guimier-Sorbets: 'Les mosaïques d'Alexandrie: Nouvelles découvertes', *Rev. Archéol.*, i (1998), pp. 188–93

Sosos (*fl* Pergamon [now in Turkey], some time between *c.* 250–*c.* 150 BC). Ancient Greek mosaicist. Pliny (*Natural History* XXXVI. lx. 184) named Sosos as the most celebrated Greek mosaicist. He said that Sosos laid a floor at Pergamon that became known as the Unswept Room, because he showed all the scraps from the feast that are usually swept away. Some Roman mosaic floors illustrate the same idea, but none can be claimed as a copy of Sosos' work. According to Pliny, Sosos made another floor, also at Pergamon, depicting a dove drinking and casting the shadow of its head on the water while other doves preen themselves in the sun on the lip of a vessel. Again, there are Roman mosaics of this subject. The earliest example from a dated context is a fine fragmentary emblema of *c.* 100 BC, from House B in the Quarter of the Inopos (now Delos, Archaeol. Mus.). A famous example from Hadrian's Villa at Tibur (now Tivoli; Rome, Mus. Capitolino) has been claimed by Donderer as the original, with particular reference to the character of the frame.

The Delos piece has the same border of small black and white triangles as the emblema from Pergamon signed by HEPHAISTION, but that is not uncommon. The character of Hephaistion's work seems close to what we hear of that of Sosos. Hephaistion worked in a palace built by Eumenes II of Pergamon (*reg* 197–159 BC). Sosos is not given a date, but was working during the time of great Pergamene patronage of the arts in the second half of the 3rd and first half of the 2nd century BC. Sosos is the only mosaicist named by an ancient writer. Modern writers sometimes speak of 'Sosos of Pergamon', but Pliny only says that he worked there, as did many artists from all over the Greek world.

J. Overbeck: *Die antiken Schriftquellen zur Geschichte der bildenden Künste bei den Griechen* (Leipzig, 1868), p. 415, no. 2158

K. Jex-Blake and E. Sellers: *The Elder Pliny's Chapters on the History of Art* (London, 1896), pp. 222–5, app. IX

E. Pfuhl: *Malerei und Zeichnung der Griechen* (Munich, 1923)

M. Donderer: 'The Capitoline Dove Mosaic: A Sosos Original?', *Proc. 5th International Colloquium on Ancient Mosaics: Bath, 1987*

Sotades Painter (*fl c.* 470–*c.* 450 BC). Greek vase painter. Active in Athens, he was among the finest Early Classical vase painters. Like the best of his late Archaic predecessors, he suited his style to his medium, yet he was apparently also influenced by developments in large-scale painting. He is named after the potter's signature on some of his vases, though the decoration often complements the crafting of these so well that potter and painter may have been the same man.

The Sotades Painter was a master of both the Red-figure and White-ground techniques. He was essentially a miniaturist, painting either small vases or vases with only a small field for decoration. His White-ground work appears in the tondi of three small, delicate cups in London (BM, D 5–7), while his Red-figure work includes cups, a skyphos, a kantharos and several rhyta of various forms ranging from conventional animal heads to black boys being eaten by crocodiles (e.g. London, BM, E 789) and a camel flanked by two figures, one Persian and one black (Paris, Louvre, CA 3825), which display the virtuosity of the potter Sotades. Another vase, so far unparalleled, is shaped like a knucklebone (London, BM, E 804). It is decorated on all four sides with a Red-figure scene of a bald-headed man apparently instructing several girl dancers. While three dancers have their feet on the ground, the rest appear to float, and the scene may show Aiolos directing the dance of the clouds. The skilful adaptation of the scene to the shape of the vase typifies works by Sotades and the Sotades Painter. The man stands by the vase's opening, its curved edge suggesting a cave, while the fluid movements of the dancers are accentuated by the vessel's alternately swelling and contracting contours.

The Sotades Painter's figures are neat and precise, and their drapery appears transparent, revealing the forms of the bodies beneath. Their features are small and sometimes quite idiosyncratic, and, despite the miniature scale of the work, the detail is such that, when transparencies of the painter's White-ground scenes are projected on a screen, they resemble genuine murals, suggesting that he had an interest in larger-scale contemporary painting. In his White-ground works particularly, he tries to convey texture by liberally applying extra layers of painted, or perhaps gilded, clay, and experimenting with shading to suggest the feel of a snake's scales or animal fur.

The Sotades Painter's range of subject-matter is wide and interesting. Satyrs occur frequently, as actors or with maenads or animals. There are also several rarer mythological subjects, including King Kekrops on a sphinx rhyton (London, BM, E 788). The camel rhyton (see above) depicts, in Red-figure, a *Combat Between a Greek and a Persian*: most unusually, the Persian is shown winning. Especially intriguing are the subjects of three White-ground cups (London, BM, D 5–7), found together in an Athenian tomb. The scene on D 7, with a rustic, an enormous snake and a recumbent woman, may represent Orion, about to be punished by a serpent for assaulting the goddess Artemis, Kadmos and the Theban serpent, or the beekeeper Aristaios, with Eurydice and the snake that killed her as she fled from his advances. The two girls picking apples on D 6 may represent the Hesperides, and D 5 depicts Glaukos and Polyeidos, perfectly illustrating the Sotades Painter's ability to evoke an entire story in a single scene.

E. Buschor: *Das Krokodil des Sotades* (Munich, 1919)

L. Curtius: 'Der Astragal des Sotades', *Sber. Heidelberg. Akad. Wiss.*, iv (1923)

J. D. Beazley: *Red-figure* (1942, 2/1963), i, pp. 763–73

L. Kahil: 'Un Nouveau Vase plastique du potier Sotadès au Musée du Louvre', *Rev. Archéol.* (1972), pp. 271–84

M. Robertson: *A History of Greek Art* (Cambridge, 1975), pp. 263–6

L. Burn: 'Honey Pots: Three White-ground Cups by the Sotades Painter', *Ant. Kst*, xxviii (1985), pp. 93–105

A. Griffiths: '"What Leaf-fringed Legend?": A Cup by the Sotades Painter in London', *J. Hell. Stud.*, cvi (1986), pp. 58–70

A. Collinge: 'Aristaios, or his Father-in-law?', *Ant. Kst*, xxxi (1988), p. 9

J. Boardman: *Athenian Red Figure Vases, the Classical Period* (London, 1989), pp. 39–40

H. Hoffmann: 'Aletheia: The Iconography of Death/Rebirth in Three Cups by the Sotades Painter', *Res*, 17–18 (1989), pp. 68–88

H. Hoffmann: *Sotades* (Oxford, 1997)

Sounion. Site at the furthest south-east point of Attica, *c.* 70 km east of Athens, Greece. The ancient town occupied the headland of Cape Sounion, with its acropolis on a steep promontory, and its most important remains are those of the Sanctuary of Poseidon. The Temple of Poseidon was investigated by Nicholas Revett in 1765 and again by the Society of Dilettanti in 1812. In 1884 the German archaeologist Wilhelm Dörpfeld excavated the site, followed by the Greek Archaeological Society during 1899–1915. The surviving temple dates from around 440 BC and is one of a series of four temples built to related designs and possibly the work of a single architect. Together with the Temple of Hephaistos at Athens, the Temple of Ares, formerly at Acharnai but later moved to Athens, and the Temple of Nemesis at Rhamnous, it can be interpreted as a thank-offering for the defeat of the Persians in 480–479 BC. The temple at Sounion (see fig.) is Doric and peripteral (6×13 columns) and was built from marble quarried locally at Agrileza. The columns have only 16 instead of the usual 20 flutings, and the shafts are straight-edged, without the usual slight outward curve (entasis), features that may simply reflect reasons of economy. As in the Temple of Hephaistos, the porch façade is aligned with the third columns of the flanks, and a continuous Ionic frieze, replacing the normal triglyphs and metopes, extends across the porch and to the back of the outer entablature. In contrast to the Temple of Ares, the west end (rear) of the building was treated similarly. The temple precinct was walled, and the foundations of a simple propylon and at least two stoas survive (for a plan of the sanctuary *see* PROPYLON). By Roman times the Temple of Poseidon was abandoned; Pausanias mistakenly attributed it to Athena. Parts of its decorated gutter were removed for reuse on the Temple of Ares. The actual Sanctuary of Athena at Sounion was situated to the north of the Sanctuary of Poseidon and contained an Ionic Temple of unusual form: a rectangular cella facing east, its roof supported by two pairs of internal columns, with unfluted external colonnades, linked to it by single columns at the SW and NE corners, only on the south (12 columns) and east (10 columns). These seem to have been constructed at the same times as the cella. It was badly damaged, probably by Philip V of Macedon. Parts of this building were removed to Athens in Augustan times and reused in the Agora. The whole promontory was fortified as a vital naval base during the Peloponnesian War (431–404 BC), and considerable traces of these and later walls survive.

An earlier temple of Poseidon underlies the existing building. It was probably damaged during the Persian Wars. Also damaged at the same time, and afterward deliberately concealed, was a number of early over-lifesize kouroi, including the well-preserved Sounion Kouros now in the National Museum at Athens. These were found in the pits by the Temple of Poseidon in the Athena precinct. They are the only kouroi from Attica known to have been dedicated as votive offerings, not as grave markers.

A relief in Parian marble was found in the precinct of Athena, dedicated to commemorate an athletic victory and not as a funerary monument. It probably dates from around 480, rather than later, as some authorities suggest.

B. Stais in *Archaiologikon Deltion* 2 (1916), parartema 77

B. Stais: 'Sounion anaskaphai' [Excavations at Sounion], *Archaiol. Ephimeris* (1917), pp. 168–213

W. H. Plommer: 'Three Attic Temples', *Annu. Brit. Sch. Athens*, xlv (1950), pp. 78–94

W. H. Plommer: 'The Temple of Poseidon on Cape Sounion: Some Further Questions', *Annu. Brit. Sch. Athens*, lv (1960), pp. 218–33

W. B. Dinsmoor Jr: *Guide to Sounion* (Athens, 1970)

G. M. A. Richter and I. A. Richter: *Kouroi: Archaic Greek Youths: A Study of the Development of the Kouros Type in Greek Sculpture* (New York, 1970/*R* 1988)

H. Knell: *Perikleische Baukunst* (Darmstadt, 1979), pp. 64–7

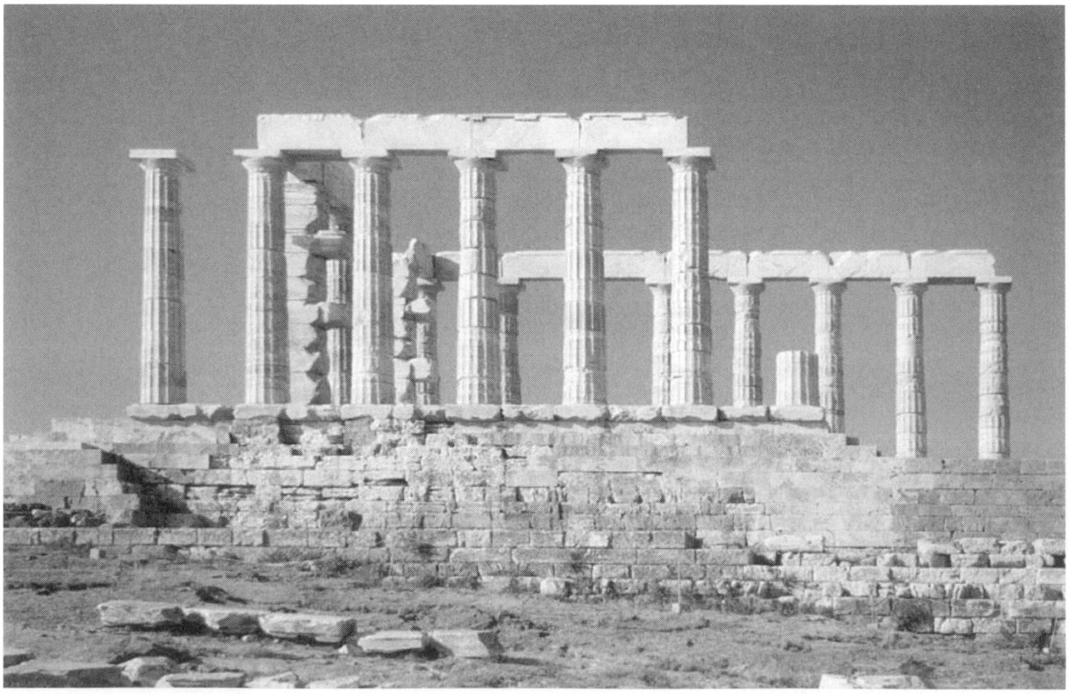

Sounion, Temple of Poseidon, *c.* 440 BC

S. D. Wright: *The Regional Styles of Kouroi from the Sounion Group and their Geographic Relationships to the Greek Trade Route to Egypt* (diss., Atlanta, U. GA, 1988)
A. B. Tataki and D. Hardy: *Sounion: The Temple of Poseidon* (Athens, 1992)
M. Salliora-Oikonomakou: *Sounion* (Athens, 2003)
M. Salliora-Oikonomakou: *Ho archaios demos tou Sounion. Istorike kai topographike episkopese* (Koropi, 2004)
G. Terlakis: *Sounio, Laurio & Thorikos* (Athens, 2004)

Spain, Roman. Roman Spain consisted of the entire Iberian peninsula, both modern Spain and Portugal. As it is twice as large as Italy, Hispania was viewed as a remote subcontinent with the Pyrenees guarding passage to Europe and the Straits of Gibraltar beckoning to Africa (see fig.). Its geography, therefore, played a significant role in its historical development, especially in its early contact with Rome during the Punic wars. The landscape exhibits variety in features, such as a high central plateau bounded on three sides by mountain ranges, a narrow coastal plain bordering the Mediterranean, and the Atlantic seaboard. With a climate ranging from Mediterranean to subdesert conditions, agriculture provided a livelihood for its inhabitants (wheat, olives and grapes being the most important products). Its wealth of resources also included metals (gold, silver, iron, copper, lead) that were mined, and the harvest of the sea (especially for the making of garum, a fish sauce considered a delicacy by the Romans).

1. History. The high mountain passes and rugged terrain proved difficult for the Romans to invade and hold, whose conquest of Spain took about 200 years, from 218–16 BC. Roman Spain was a war zone during the Republican period as the battles between Carthage and Rome were fought there. Carthage had established bases in south-east Spain to advance both their military and economic power, and in 219 BC their general Hannibal destroyed a city, Saguntum,

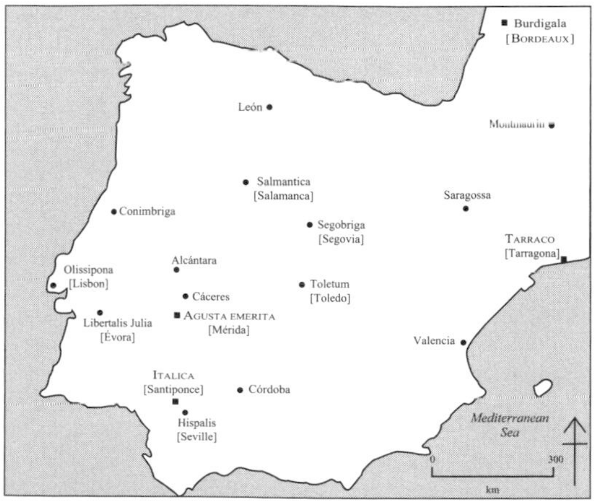

Map of Roman Spain; those sites with separate entries in the encyclopedia are distinguished by Cross-reference type

allied with Rome, and continued onwards to Tarraco (modern Tarragona). Roman forces responded, which culminated in the commander P. Cornelius Scipio's sack of the most important Carthaginian settlement, Carthago Nova (modern Cartagena), in 209 BC (Scipio, later called Scipio Africanus, continued to fight against Hannibal in Africa and pounded the Punic troops in Zama in 202 BC). Once Carthage was defeated, a series of rebellions by the Iberian inhabitants kept the Roman commanders occupied for many years. The peninsula was conquered only very gradually, region by region (and then reconquered after successive insurrections among the Cantabri and Celtiberi in the north, and the Lusitani in the south) because of the fierce resistance of the inhabitants.

Throughout the arduous campaigns of the 2nd and 1st centuries BC, the top talent of the Roman military cut its teeth there: Marcus Porcius Cato (Cato the elder), Tiberius Sempronius Gracchus, Lucius Aemilius Paullus, Decimus Junius Brutus, Fulvius Nobilior, Scipio Aemilianus, Julius Caesar and Augustus among them. Infighting among local tribes, the co-option (and then desertion) of their leaders by Roman governors, and incessant guerrilla warfare that drained well-trained Roman troops, dragged the conflict forward, while a lack of strategic planning and objectives by the conquerors, rivalry among Roman commanders, and the not infrequent brutal retributions inflicted on the local populace, threatened its success. In this grim and haphazard way Spain came under Roman rule.

To govern a pacified and stable Hispania was a challenging task, since the peninsula never had been united by a central authority and remained, in effect, a patchwork of separate communities and ethnic groups living in disparate environments. Early on in the wars of conquest, Rome had divided the territory into two provinces: Hispania Citerior on the Mediterranean coast up to the modern town of Linares, and Hispania Ulterior, which roughly corresponded to modern Andulusia. Between 16 BC and 13 BC Augustus subdivided Hispania Ulterior into two provinces: the southern one was Hispania Baetica, while Hispania Lusitania covered the area to the north and west, with Augusta emerita (now Mérida) as its capital. As part of this reorganization, Hispania Citerior received more land rich in mines, and was renamed Tarraconensis. Its capital was Tarraco (modern Tarragona).

Communication was essential to the governing of such a vast territory. The Romans had constructed a system of roads that followed the course of rivers. Although many had first served the military, the roads provided access for the state postal system and for the conveyance of supplies and trade. Studding the network of highways were towns, which were the focal points of the administrative organization. Milestones marked the roads, inscribed with the distances between towns. Roman rule depended on the growth of urbanization.

The Romans founded towns for their citizens who ran the provinces, they established new settlements for Iberians, and allowed for semi-autonomous outposts in the hinterlands. Towns received different privileges for their residents: *coloniae* were centres of government, run by Roman citizens who were often retired military personnel granted land to farm in the area, while those living in *municipia* were granted Latin rights; some of them received Roman citizenship after serving terms of administrative offices. The oldest Roman town is ITALICA near modern Seville. Founded by Scipio Africanus as a settlement for wounded soldiers in 206 BC, Italica thrived, especially under TRAJAN and HADRIAN, its native sons (it later became a *municipium*). The changing fortunes of Hispania are evident in Emporion, which was a Greek port. In about 100 BC the new Roman town, EMPORIAE, was built behind the Greek settlement on the waterfront. AUGUSTA EMERITA (modern Mérida), established in 25 BC by a decree from Augustus, was founded by veterans of the legions as a military settlement. Prospering as a market town, it eventually became a provincial capital of Lusitania in western Spain. TARRACO (modern Tarragona), a port city situated on a bay close to the mouth of the Ebro River, was the capital of the largest Roman province in Europe, and it took about five days to sail to Rome, depending on the weather.

2. ART AND ARCHITECTURE. Domestic architecture took on the Roman forms of the *atrium* and *peristyle* houses, with central courtyards and colonnaded gardens open to the sky. In the new town of Italica, the Casa de la Exedra extended to about 3000 square metres with shops fronting the street and a large atrium; beyond this was a colonnaded garden with flanking dining rooms and further back were the service quarters of kitchen and baths, which were situated off of a terrace with a water pool. The rooms in this affluent house and others (such as the House of the Amphitheatre in Augusta Emerita) were paved with brightly coloured mosaics depicting themes of some relevance to the hospitality of the owner: Bacchus, the god of wine, often appears, as well as Muses and philosophers, who allude to the ideals of refinement and cultivated taste, among other motifs. Further developments in domestic architecture are found in the great houses of Conimbriga in the late 2nd century AD. Built outside the town walls, the grandest houses had porticoed gardens and large formal dining rooms, as seen in the earlier houses in Italica, for example. Other features, however, were added, such as L-shaped fishponds, extended gardens with apse-shaped beds and more elaborate bath suites. Mosaics adorned the floors with themes from mythology, such as Perseus carrying the head of Medusa and Bellerophon attacking the winged Chimaera. Dining rooms, bedrooms and bathrooms seemed to be the rooms most frequently furnished with mosaics, even in less palatial residences elsewhere.

The funerary art of Roman Spain offers portraits of its people, accompanied epitaphs frequently giving their names, ages and the names of those who were honouring the deceased with memorials. One example, the stele of Lutatia Lupata (Mérida, Mus. N. A. Romano) conforms to a standard format, with the relief portrait set in a niche within an architectural frame and an inscriptional plaque below. It dates to the mid- or late 2nd century AD and served to commemorate her death at the grave or tomb. The epitaph reads, 'Dedication to the gods and departed spirits. Lutatia Lupata aged 16. Lutatia Severa (set this up) in memory of her foster-daughter. Here she lies. May the earth rest lightly upon you' (AE 1959.0029). The letters are irregularly formed and the lines slant—indications of a restricted budget and lower status. The portait represents a girl with smooth features, a broad nose and full chin, wearing her hair parted in the middle and pulled back. She is shown holding a stringed instrument similar to a guitar or lute. With fingers plucking the strings, the figure of Lutatia Lupata is commemorated in the act of making music. The inscription on the stele identifies Lutatia Lupata as the foster-daughter of Lutatia Severa, who dedicated the stele. The lute may represent an occupation by evoking the musical talents of women who entertained for a living. Lutatia Lupata could have been both an apprentice and foster-child to Lutatia Severa, who mourned the loss of her protégé and colleague-in-training. The terse epitaph typically does not offer emotional declarations nor biography, but Lupata may have been a slave who was freed by Severa and then lived in her care in a relationship of quasi-adoption (and had a far better life than the gangs of slaves who worked the gold and silver mines). The Roman museums of Mérida, Tarragona and Seville offer many fine examples of portraits of the citizens and inhabitants of Roman Spain, as well as portraits of the emperors erected in public (e.g. the head of a girl known as 'La Gitana' in Mérida or that of Marcus Aurelius in the Roman Museum of Tarragona).

In the Late Empire, the 3rd and 4th centuries AD, the bureaucracy was strained and the financial responsibilities of local élites burdensome. Invasions of Moors and army deserters (and later, barbarians) disrupted life, and the wealthy retreated from the civic affairs of the cities to their private estates in the countryside. The Roman government was increasingly centralized to the detriment of the provincial capitals. Towns were walled, military fortresses rebuilt, and even villas appear fortified with towers and gates. With a shrinking economy, the luxuries dwindled—far fewer mosaics adorned dwellings. There is at least one example, however, that demonstrates the lasting significance of Rome's urban culture: a mosaic depicting the chariot races in the Circus Maximus in Rome in a 4th-century house in Barcino (modern Barcelona).

E. Badian: *Foreign Clientelae (264–70 BC)* (Oxford, 1958)

A. Garcia Y Bellido: 'Colonia Aelia Augusta Italica', *Bibliotheca Archaeologica* ii (Madrid, 1960)

J. Alvarez: 'El templo de Diana', *Augusta Emerita: Actas del bimilenario de Mérida* (1977), pp. 43–53

A. Blanco: *Mosaicos romanos de Mérida, Corpus de Mosaicos Romanos de España,* i (Madrid, 1978)
J.-G. Gorges: *Les villas hispano-romaines* (Paris, 1979)
S. J. Keay: *Roman Spain* (Los Angeles and San Francisco, 1988)
W. Trillmich and P. Zanker: *Stadtbild und Ideologie: Die Monumentalisierung hispanischer Städte zwischen Republik und Kaiserzeit* (Munich, 1990)
L. A. Curchin: *Roman Spain* (London and New York, 1991)
W. Mierse: *Temples and Towns in Roman Iberia* (Berkeley and Los Angeles, 1999)
G. M. Leather: *Roman Aqueducts in Iberia* (Garstang, Lancs, 2002)
L. A. Curchin: *The Romanization of Central Spain: Complexity, Diversity and Change in a Provincial Hinterland* (London, 2003)
L. A. Curchin: *The Romanization of Central Spain* (London and New York, 2004)
M. Pilar Reis: *Las termas y balnea romanos de Lusitania* (Madrid, 2004)

Spalatum [It. Spalato; now Split]. Roman site in Croatia, mid-way along the coast of the Adriatic. It is an important port, built on a peninsula and backed by a formidable range of mountains. Under the Roman Empire it was the capital of the province of Dalmatia, and it is famous for having the palace of Diocletian at its centre. This was built for the retirement of the Emperor Diocletian following his abdication in AD 305; he lived there until his death in 311.

The site for what since medieval times has been known as the palace of Diocletian was an inlet on the coast *c.* 6.5 km south of Salona, the principal city of Roman Dalmatia, facing south towards the island of Brač. Its ancient name was Aspalathos (Lat. Spalatum), after a thorny shrub that grew in the area. A notion that Spalatum and the subsequent forms of the name derive from 'palatium' or 'palace' is of medieval origin and erroneous: all contemporary accounts refer to the villa of Diocletian. The residence was built of fine local limestone, local tufa and brick. Many columns, in a variety of white and coloured marbles and Egyptian granites, were brought second-hand, probably from Egypt, whence came also several sphinxes of the New Kingdom (16th–11th centuries BC). These were set to guard Diocletian's mausoleum, where one still remains near its original position between the columns of the peristyle.

In plan the palace appears a near rectangle, facing the sea with its longer axis roughly north-east to south-west. The east and west sides are 215.5 m, the north side 175 m and the south side 181 m; the total area is over 3.8 ha. The perimeter wall, which ranges in height from 17 m in the north to 24 m in the south, to compensate for the seaward slope of the ground, incorporates a patrol walk at the upper level flanked by arched openings. The external face of the landward walls is plain; the south façade is more ornate: a long gallery at the upper level has 42 arched openings framed by engaged columns with simplified Corinthian capitals. Three loggias, at the centre and sides, break the monotony, and two openings midway between these are enlarged to signify the central axis and entrance of the principal chambers opening off the gallery. Three of the four corner towers (each 12×12 m) survive; along with the octagonal towers flanking the three landward gates and the six interval towers, they projected *c.* 4 m above the perimeter wall. A gate was placed centrally in each side. The principal gate was on the north, in the direction of Salona. Between the flanking octagonal towers a pair of niches, aligned vertically, was set either side of the entrance. The upper niches were framed by free-standing columns resting on projecting consoles, above which ran a blind arcade surmounted by the cornice. Above this, the four statue bases still visible may have borne statues of Diocletian and his colleagues of the Tetrarchy. The outer façades of the other two landward gates were less ornate, with single niches either side of the entrance at the lower level. Each of the three landward gates had an inner and outer entrance separated by an open court 9–10 m square.

The interior was divided by two colonnaded streets, one leading from the north gate to the centre, where it joined with an east-west cross-street. Building complexes in the two parts of the northern half may have accommodated Diocletian's personal staff and bodyguard. The principal buildings lay south of the cross-street. Opposite the junction of the streets at the centre, the open peristyle (27.0×13.5 m) continued the line of the street from the north gate. It was flanked by arched colonnades that fronted the precincts of the mausoleum and Classical temple and terminated in the monumental vestibule (a massive pediment resting on four columns of crimson granite) of the entrance to the private apartments behind the south façade (see fig.).

East of the peristyle the octagonal mausoleum enclosing a rotunda rests on a massive podium that contains a hemispherical crypt. Restored in the 19th century, the circular chamber (diam. 13.35 m) rises 21.5 m to the centre of its dome. The interior walls are embellished with two storeys of free-standing columns supporting projecting orders and were once decorated with glass mosaic and marble inlay. Around the chamber, just below the upper order, a crudely carved frieze of hunting scenes with cupids, garlands and masks includes a male and female portrait, traditionally identified as Diocletian and his wife Prisca. At the centre of the chamber the body of the emperor was laid in a porphyry sarcophagus. In a similar precinct across the peristyle lay the temple (11×9 m), which is among the finest surviving examples of the small Roman temple. Its outer wall surfaces are plain, save for pilasters at the corners. The frame of the doorway is richly carved, but even this takes second place to the 65 coffers of the barrel-vaulted ceiling, which is like that of the Temple of Venus in Rome (1st century AD). The temple may have been dedicated to Jupiter, the personal deity of Diocletian.

Almost nothing remains of the private apartments. The walls of the great circular vestibule were once covered with mosaic of coloured glass, and the

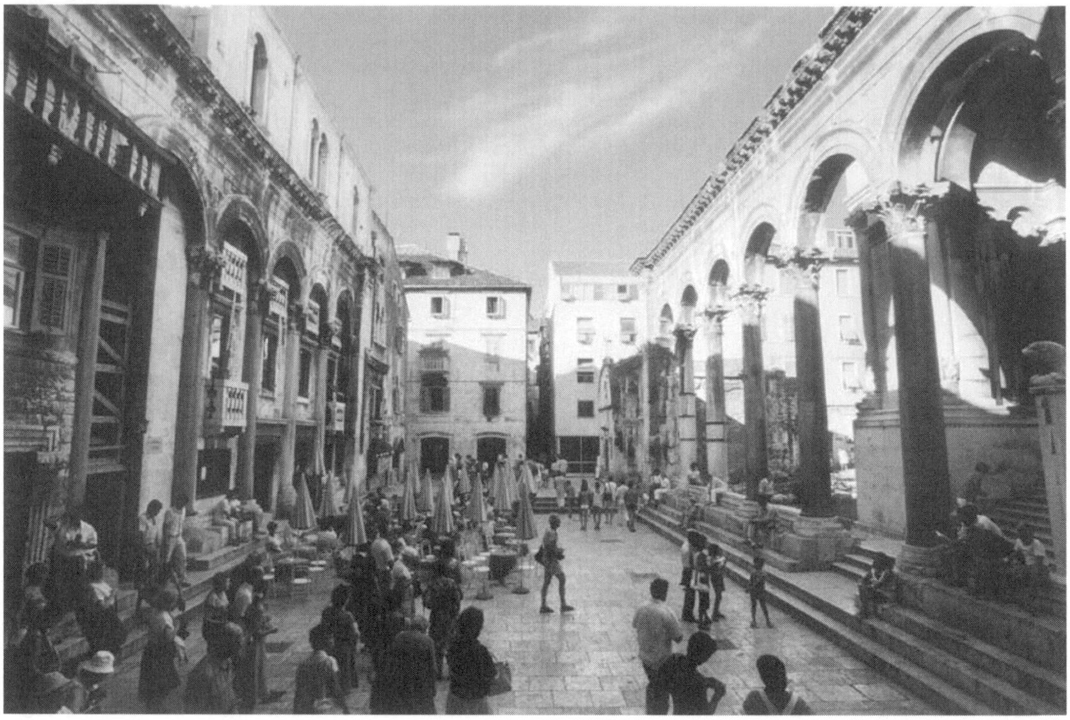

Spalatum (Split), palace of Diocletian, peristyle court, *c.* AD 300

whole residential block was raised on vaulted basements, which have survived intact. The arrangement of the rooms at basement level permits a reconstruction of the apartments at the upper level. At the centre of the block an aisled hall was flanked with rows of small chambers, perhaps service rooms, and on the east there was a monumental dining-room within a complex of smaller chambers. On the west the main feature was a large aisled hall with an apse at the north end, presumably the principal reception chamber. To the west of this lay a block of 14 small interconnected chambers that probably served as the private accommodation of Diocletian. Many small service passages within the thickness of the walls testify to the care taken to ensure an efficient and unobtrusive provision for the privacy and comfort of the retired emperor.

Although the palace was essentially a private residence, it combined the security of a fortress, the grandeur of a city and the elegance and luxury of a villa. The rectangular *castrum* with solid walls, projecting towers and narrow entrances recalls the fortifications constructed by Diocletian and his colleagues on almost every frontier of the Empire. The arrangement of the principal streets recalls that of the *via praetoria* and *via principalis* from fortresses of the early Empire. Within this scheme the residence of Diocletian stands in the place of the *principia* (headquarters) and *praetorium* (commander's residence). The private apartments furnish an example of the Roman villa at a time when it was undergoing profound change. The earlier peristyle arrangement was opened out along a single axis and combined with elements of the corridor villa to produce the portico villa with flanking corner towers. This type, common in the Late Empire, is exemplified by the great villa at Nennig in the Mosel Valley and above all by the villas portrayed on North African mosaics of the 4th century AD. The arrangement of villa and camp at Spalatum was imitated by Diocletian's successor Galerius (*reg* AD 305–11) in his residence at Romuliana (now Gamzigrad in eastern Serbia).

R. Adam: *Ruins of the Palace of the Emperor Diocletian at Spalato* (London, 1764)

G. Niemann: *Der Palast Diokletians in Spalato* (Vienna, 1910)

E. Hébrard and J. Zeiller: *Spalato: Le Palais de Dioclétien* (Paris, 1912)

F. Bulić and L. Karaman: *Kaiser Diokletians Palast in Split* (Zagreb, 1929)

N. Duval: 'La Place de Split dans l'architecture antique du bas-empire', *Urbs*, iv (1961–2), pp. 17–95

S. McNally: 'Ausgrabungen im Diokletianspalast zu Split', *Ant. Welt*, x/2 (1979), pp. 35–46

T. Marasović: *Diocletian's Palace* (Belgrade, 1982)

J. J. Wilkes: *Diocletian's Palace, Split* (Sheffield, 1986, 1993)

S. McNally: *The Architectural Ornament of Diocletian's Palace at Split* (Oxford, 1996)

R. Adam and M. Navarra: *Ruins of the Palace of the Emperor Diocletian at Spalato in Dalmatia* (Cannitello, 2001)

M. Bonacic Mandinic: *Greek Coins Displayed in the Archaeological Museum Split* (Split, 2004)

G. Niemann and A. Conze: *Der Palast Diokletians in Spalato* (Split, 2005)

Sparta [Lakedaimon; now Spárti]. Site in Lakonia in southern Greece on the bank of the River Eurotas; a dominant power on the Greek mainland throughout most of the Archaic and Classical periods.

1. Bronze age. Sporadic activity in the Neolithic, Early (*c.* 3600/3000–*c.* 2050 BC) and Middle (*c.* 2050–*c.* 1600 BC) Bronze ages gave way to the emergence of the central Spartan plain as the leading centre of Lakonia in the Late Helladic (LH) II period (*c.* 1500–*c.* 1390 BC), as attested in the spectacular tholos tomb at Vapheio. The tomb is a large construction (diam. 10.35 m) built, in accordance with local technique, on the hilltop rather than within it. Known since 1805, the collapsed tomb was unsurprisingly looted by the time Tsountas excavated it in 1888. Excavation, however, revealed an intact pit beneath the floor, which the looters had missed. As one of only four tholoi in Greece found with their contents wholly or partially intact, the luxurious abundance of its contents suggests what has been lost in other such tombs. In the stone-lined pit lay the body of a man clad in a profusion of jewellery and surrounded by precious objects and an arsenal of weapons (Athens, N. Archaeol. Mus.). Best known are the pair of gold cups placed beside the hands, which reveal either Minoan origin or strong Minoan stylistic influence; both depict bull-hunting scenes (see fig.; one peaceful, one turbulent). The foreign origin of many gifts in the tomb suggests the prosperity and active commercial relations of the region, and possibly of the tomb's noble owner.

Tradition and legend offer a tantalizing picture of Bronze Age Sparta as the kingdom of Menelaos. The *Odyssey* (IV.37–75) described the richness of the royal megaron. The abduction of Helen, which sparked the Trojan War, attests the prominence of Menelaos' position in the affairs of mainland Greece, as do the 60 ships he commanded (*Iliad* II.581–7). Physical remains at Sparta, however, are only beginning to correlate legend with fact. Surprisingly lacking so far has been a palatial centre to match the Vapheio tomb, although that honour has been tentatively given to the unexcavated site of Palaiopyrgi near Vapheio. To date, the most important signs of life in the Mycenaean period (LH IIIA 2–B 2) cluster around the site of Sparta and particularly the Menelaion, the Archaic shrine of Menelaos and Helen, just east of Sparta on a bluff overlooking the River Eurotas. Mycenaean material discovered here in 1909 was confirmed in the excavations of the British School at Athens conducted by H. Catling from 1973 to 1976 (objects in Sparta, Archaeol. Mus.). The excavated remains represent two successive Mycenaean building complexes, the second following shortly after the first in the late 15th century BC (LH III–A1), with a major change of axis. The mansion was refurbished after a 150-year gap and reoccupied until its destruction *c.* 1200 BC. The main phase constituted a megaron of multiple rooms with interconnecting corridors and an open court. Evidence of Cretan influence in the masonry techniques, as in some of the associated pottery, reinforces the glimpse offered by the Vapheio tomb of active foreign relations and possible Minoan presence in this region. Parts of another important building further west, now badly eroded, suggest a shrine. The site was destroyed by fire of unknown origin *c.* 1200 BC. While the Menelaion site was clearly the principal Mycenaean settlement of the Lakonian plain from the 15th century BC to the 13th, its identification as the home of Menelaos cannot be confirmed. Perhaps a lingering reverence attached to the spot led to the institution of the cult here in the 8th century BC.

Amyklai, about 5 km south of the Menelaion, was the home during historical times of the cult of Hyakinthos, whose pre-Greek name implies Bronze Age origins. Numerous terracotta figurines identified as goddesses and animals were found there together with fragments of nearly life-size clay human figures (Sparta, Archaeol. Mus.). The relation of this cult site to the Mycenaean Menelaion settlement is not yet completely understood, but finds here may indicate activity continuing into the 12th century BC and possibly spanning the Dark Age (11th–9th centuries BC).

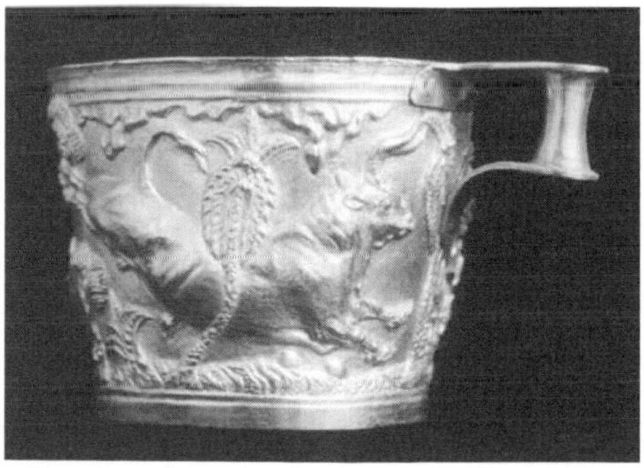

Sparta, gold cup with turbulent scene of bull-hunting, h. 90 mm, from Vapheio, Middle Minoan IIIB–Late Minoan IB (Athens, National Archaeological Museum)

C. Tsountas: 'Erevnai en te Lakonike kai o Taphos tou Vapheiou' [Finds from Lakonia and the tomb at Vapheio], *Archaiol. Ephimeris* (1889), pp. 129–72, pls 7–10

S. Hood: 'Tholos Tombs of the Aegean', *Antiquity*, xxxiv (1960), pp. 166–76

E. T. Vermeule: *Greece in the Bronze Age* (Chicago, 1972), pp. 127–30

J. G. Younger: 'The Vapheio Gems: A Reconsideration of the Find-spots', *Amer. J. Archaeol.*, lxxvii (1973), pp. 338–40

E. N. Davis: 'The Vapheio Cups: One Minoan and One Mycenaean?', *A. Bull.*, lvi (1974), pp. 472–87

H. W. Catling: 'New Excavations at the Menelaion, Sparta', *Neue Forschungen in griechischen Heiligtümern*, ed. U. Jantzen (Tübingen, 1976), pp. 77–90

H. W. Catling: 'Excavations at the Menelaion, Sparta, 1973–76', *Archaeol. Rep.: Council Soc. Promotion Hell. Stud. & Managing Cttee Brit. Sch. Archaeol. Athens* (1977), pp. 24–42

P. A. Cartledge: *Sparta and Lakonia* (London, 1979)

K. Demakopoulou: *To Mykinaiko iero sto Amyklaio kai i IEIII periodos sti Lakonia* [The Mycenaean sanctuary at Amyklai and the LH III period in Lakonia] (Athens, 1982)

K. Killian: 'L'Architecture des résidences mycéniennes', *Le Système palatial en Orient, en Grèce, et à Rome* (Leiden, 1987), pp. 203–17

K. Werner: *The Megaron during the Aegean and Anatolian Bronze Age* (Jonsered, 1993) [esp. pp. 103–105]

2. Greek and Roman.

(i) Architecture. Writing in the later 5th century BC, Thucydides (*History of the Peloponnesian War* I.x.2) predicted that, should Sparta be destroyed, one would not be able to estimate its importance from its unimpressive architecture (the opposite, of course, would be true of Athens). Time has indeed vindicated that prediction, as the remains of the ancient Greek city are very scanty. Only a few foundation blocks survive from the Temple of Athena Chalkioikos ('bronze house') (mid- to late 6th century BC), and the remains of the Temple of Artemis Orthia, though more impressive, are still only foundations (*c.* 700 BC; rebuilt *c.* 575 BC). The typical Spartan temple was a small shrine building, simple in plan, and the only embellished sacred structures known are outside the city itself. The Archaic shrine at the Menelaion, across the River Eurotas, had a surrounding platform surmounted by a triglyph and metope frieze (fallen fragments of which survive at the site), added probably in the late 6th century BC. The Sanctuary of Apollo at Amyklai (late 6th century BC), attributed to the East Greek architect and sculptor Bathykles of Magnesia, was an anomalous structure with a 'throne' consisting of walls and colonnades in a mixture of the Doric and Ionic orders that surrounded a tall, free-standing cult statue. The city itself was architecturally undeveloped, an amalgamation of its four constituent villages. There was an agora and an important portico, the Persian Stoa, constructed apparently with carved figures of Persian prisoners instead of conventional columns (Vitruvius: *On Architecture* I.i.6); a Roman stoa has been identified as its successor. Additions to the Menelaion employ the substantial blocks (normally over 2 m long) typical of the Hellenistic architecture of Sparta. These were also used in Sparta itself in the 'Tomb of Leonidas', probably in fact a small temple. In Roman times Sparta became architecturally more conventional, and there are more substantial remains. They include a well-built theatre (late 1st century BC) and other structures on the acropolis hill, as well as large, though conventional, houses in the area of the modern town, now mostly built over, though some of the mosaic floors (Sparta, Archaeol. Mus.) have been preserved. The Sanctuary of Artemis Orthia was also rebuilt at this time, to provide a theatre-like building (2nd century AD) for viewing the ritual beating of young boys, which seems to have become something of an attraction for visitors.

A. J. B. Wace, M. S. Thompson and J. P. Droop: 'Laconia: I Excavations at Sparta, 1909', *Annu. Brit. Sch. Athens*, xv (1908–9), pp. 108–57

A. M. Woodward: 'Excavations at Sparta', *Annu. Brit. Sch. Athens*, xxvi (1923–5), pp. 116–239; xxvii (1925–6), pp. 173–254; xxviii (1926–7), pp. 1–48; xxix (1927–8), pp. 1–56

R. M. Dawkins, ed.: *The Sanctuary of Artemis Orthia at Sparta* (London, 1929)

R. Martin: 'Bathyclès de Magnésie et le "Trône" d'Apollon à Amyklae', *Rev. Archéol.* (1976), pp. 205–18

P. Cartledge and A. Spawforth: *Hellenistic and Roman Sparta: A Tale of Two Cities* (London, 1989/*R* 2001)

R. A. Tomlinson: 'The Menelaion and Spartan Architecture', *Philolakon: Studies in Honour of Hector Catling*, ed. J. M. Sanders (Oxford, 1992)

N. A. Winter: *Greek Architectural Terracottas* (Oxford, 1993)

G. B. Waywell and J. J. Wilkes: 'Excavations at Sparta: The Roman Stoa, 1988–91: Part 2', *Annu. Brit. Sch. Athens,* lxxxix (1994), pp. 377–432

G. B. Waywell and J. J. Wilkes: 'Excavations at the Ancient Theatre of Sparta, 1992–94: Preliminary Report', *Annu. Brit. Sch. Athens,* xc (1995), pp. 435–60

C. M. Knibbe: *Das andere Sparta* (Mainz, 1996)

W. Cavanagh and S. E. C. Walker, eds: *Sparta in Laconia* (1998)

G. B. Waywell and J. J. Wilkes: 'Excavations at the Ancient Theatre of Sparta, 1995–1998: Preliminary Report', *Annu. Brit. Sch. Athens,* xciv (1999), pp. 427–45

M. Stamatopoulou and M. Yeroulanou: *Excavating Classical Culture: Recent Archaeological Discoveries in Greece* (Oxford, 2002)

(ii) Sculpture. Spartan sculpture is known mainly from small ivories and bronzes. Sculptures in the local Taygetos marble are marked not only by the lack of monumentality characterizing the output of other local workshops but also by a lack of continuity, making it difficult to trace the conditions of their production, the supposed influences of a Cretan tradition and their later development. Indeed, the accepted view that Lakonian sculpture gradually declined after the Peloponnesian Wars (459–446 BC and 431–404 BC) may be due to the scarcity of excavated material from Lakonia, rather than to the reorientation of Spartan politics and the closed nature of the Spartan state. The names of certain Archaic Spartan sculptors who worked at Olympia are known, though none of their work has been identified. One of the earliest surviving sculptures is a nude, kneeling female figure flanked by two smaller male figures (from Magoula; 7th century BC; Sparta, Archaeol. Mus.). A pyramidal base of the early 6th century BC (Sparta, Archaeol. Mus.) has two relief scenes relating to the myth of Menelaos and Helen. Apart from certain notable small-scale works, the main Lakonian sculptures of the 6th century BC are the shallow 'hero reliefs'. These undoubtedly had chthonian significance but may not have been funerary. They continued to be produced up to the Hellenistic period. The reliefs of the Dioskouroi were undoubtedly votive, and examples date from the Archaic period to Roman times. The construction of the 6th-century BC 'throne' of Apollo at Amyklai must have influenced local sculpture production in the following century, to judge from such works as the marble 'Leonidas' (*c.* 480 BC; Sparta, Archaeol. Mus.). Some Lakonian sculptures of similar date from Olympia display the same style,

indicating the spread of Lakonian art elsewhere in Greece. From then on sculpture production apparently decreased, though there are many extant examples in a careless, popular provincial style. During Roman times Sparta flourished once again, though the numerous extant works may have been imported rather than locally produced.

M. N. Tod and A. J. B. Wace: *A Catalogue of the Spartan Museum* (Oxford, 1906)

G. Lippold: *Die griechische Plastik* (1950), III/i of *Handbuch der Archäologie* (Munich, 1939-), pp. 30–33, 89–90

H. Häfner: *Das Kunstschaffen Lakoniens in archaischer Zeit* (diss., Westfäl. Wilhelms-U., Münster, 1965)

G. Steinhauer: *Museum of Sparta* (Athens, 1975)

C. Rolley: 'Le Problème de l'art laconien', *Ktema*, ii (1977), pp. 125–40

L. F. Fitzhardinge: *The Spartans* (London, 1980)

C. M. Stibbe: 'Dionysos in Sparta', *Bull. A. Besch.*, lxvi (1991), pp. 1–44

A. Delivorrias: 'The Importance of Sculptures in the Sparta Museum and the Need for Publication of a New Catalogue', *Acts of the 4th International Congress on Peloponnesian Studies: Athens, 1992*, pp. 225–44

O. Palagia and W. Coulson, eds: *Sculpture in Arcadia and Laconia* (Oxford, 1993)

A. Faustoferri: *Il trono di Amyklai e Sparta: Bathykles al servizio del potere* (Naples, 1996)

Sperlonga. Roman villa on a promontory on the coast of Latium, 121 km south of Rome, made famous by the discovery in September 1957 of a large number of fragmentary sculptures and other antiquities in a nearby cave. Although excavation initially concentrated on the grotto and its sculpture, research later focused on the villa itself.

1. Architecture. The remains of the villa display several distinct building phases. It probably belonged to M. Aufidius Lurcone, grandfather of Livia, the wife of Augustus (*reg* 27 BC–AD 14) and mother of Tiberius (*reg* AD 14–37). The oldest sections are late Republican, given their use of *opus incertum* (concrete faced with irregular stones), while a second Republican phase has pavements in *opus signinum* (concrete with crushed tiles) and marble decoration. A total renovation and remodelling of the villa was undertaken during the late Augustan period, while fragments of several Fourth Style paintings (*see* Painting, §VI, 2(i)(a)) date to a partial redecoration of the villa during the Flavian period (AD 69–98). In late antiquity the villa was used as a convent, and the adaptation of the grotto to a chapel resulted in the systematic destruction of its sculptures. During the Saracen raids of the 9th century AD the community was transferred to the city of Sperlonga, whose name (from Lat. *spelunca*: 'grotto') preserved the memory of the ancient villa. The grotto is a natural cave incorporated into the villa as a *triclinium* (summer banqueting room) during the late Augustan renovations. Its façade was revetted with tufa tesserae and its interior lined with stucco seascapes. At its mouth lay a large rectangular pool containing a small island. A further pool in the front part of the cave was rounded off into a near circle, slightly more than 20 m in diameter, and paved with polychrome marble slabs. Within the depths of the grotto two smaller caves to the left and right were equipped with fountains. The site has long been associated with Tiberius, hence its popular name l'Antro di Tiberio (Grotto of Tiberius). It was probably here that Sejanus, the commander of the Praetorian Guard, protected the emperor from falling rocks when a roof collapsed during a banquet (Tacitus: *Annals* IV.lix.1–2; Suetonius: *Tiberius* xxxix).

2. Sculpture. Important statues from Sperlonga include a *Ganymede*, a *Kneeling Satyr* and a portrait of *Faustina* (all finds in Sperlonga, Mus. Archeol. N.). The most significant of the more than 7000 marble fragments discovered there, however, belong to large sculptural groups from the grotto depicting various exploits of Odysseus, which also reveal the different aspects of the hero's character. Four major subjects have been identified: at the mouth of the cave *Odysseus Rescuing Achilles' Corpse*; to the right *Odysseus with Diomedes and the Palladion*; in the centre of the circular pool *Odysseus' Ship Encountering Scylla*, in which the helmsman of the wreck still clings desperately to the stern, enmeshed in Scylla's tentacles (see fig.); and in the subsidiary grotto on the south side of the pool the *Blinding of Polyphemos*. Careful choice of settings made the sculptures seem more lifelike and dramatic. In the case of the *Scylla* group the pool evoked the sea, while for the *Polyphemos* group the small dark grotto served as the Cyclops' cave.

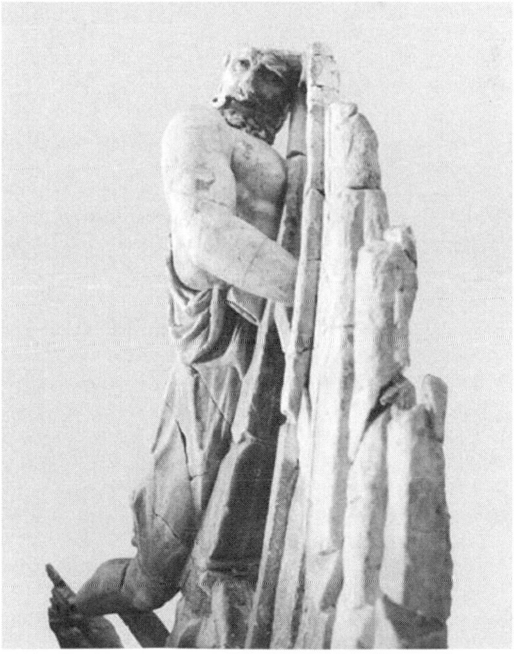

Sperlonga, grotto, *Odysseus' Ship Encountering Scylla* (detail), marble, h. 2.15 m, ?1st century AD (Sperlonga, Museo Archeologico Nazionale)

An inscription on the ship in the *Scylla* group, in lettering assigned to the 1st century AD, identifies the artists as the Rhodian sculptors HAGESANDROS, POLYDOROS AND ATHENODOROS, who also sculpted the LAOKOON. Like the Laokoon, the Sperlonga sculptures have pronounced late Hellenistic 'Baroque' characteristics. Their turbulent surfaces, exaggerated musculature, dramatic expressions and intense theatricality recall the reliefs on the Great Altar at PERGAMON, which originally led scholars to interpret them as Hellenistic works probably made on Rhodes in the 2nd or 1st century BC or as Roman copies of Hellenistic originals. The group of *Odysseus Rescuing Achilles' Corpse* is apparently related to the Pasquino Group, which is generally interpreted as *Menelaos Rescuing Patroklos' Corpse* (restored version of a Roman copy of a late 3rd-century BC original; Florence, Loggia Lanzi), and so may well be closely based on a Greek original, as may the *Odysseus with Diomedes and the Palladion*. However, no extant Greek works rival the *Scylla* and *Polyphemos* groups in size and complexity, and though grottoes containing sculptures certainly existed on Rhodes in Late Classical and Hellenistic times, the sculptures harmonize so well with their setting that they are surely original Roman works made specifically for Sperlonga, though doubtless based on various Hellenistic models. Finally, the setting, arrangement, style and subject-matter of the Sperlonga groups correspond to the taste for grandiose mythological compositions prevalent during the Julio-Claudian period. The sophisticated depiction of the contrasting extremes of Odysseus' character suggests the complex temperament of Tiberius, who not only expressed an interest in the hero (Suetonius: *Tiberius* lxx), but also had been exiled to Rhodes.

P. H. von Blanckenhagen: 'Laokoon, Sperlonga, und Vergil', *Archäol. Anz.*, lxxxiv/3 (1969), pp. 256–75

B. Conticello, B. Andreae and P. C. Bol: 'Die Skulpturen von Sperlonga', *Ant. Plast.*, xiv (1974)

A. F. Stewart: 'To Entertain an Emperor: Sperlonga, Laokoon and Tiberius at the Dinner-table', *J. Roman Stud.*, lxvii (1977), pp. 76–90

F. Coarelli: *Lazio*, Guida archeologiche Laterza (Rome, 1982), pp. 340–54

B. Conticello: 'Sul Gruppo di Scilla e della nave nel Museo di Sperlonga', *Alessandria e il mondo ellenistico-romano: Studi in onore di Achille Adriani* (Rome, 1984), pp. 611–24

B. Andreae and B. Conticello: *Skylla und Charybdis: Zur Skylla-Gruppe von Sperlonga* (Stuttgart, 1987)

M. B. Schultz: *A Study of the Sperlonga Sculptures* (diss., Chapel Hill, U. NC, 1989)

B. Andreae: *Praetorium speluncae: Tiberius und Ovid in Sperlonga* (Mainz, 1994)

N. Himmelmann: *Sperlonga: Die homerischen Gruppen und ihre Bildquellen* (Opladen, 1995)

N. Cassieri: *La grotta di Tiberio e il Museo archeologico nazionale, Sperlonga* (Rome, 2000)

N. T. De Grummond and B. S. Ridgway: *From Pergamon to Sperlonga: Sculpture and Context* (Berkeley, 2000)

H. Broise and X. Lafon: *La villa Prato de Sperlonga* (Rome, 2001)

M. Squire: 'Giant Questions: Dining with Polyphemus at Sperlonga and Baiae', *Apollo*, clviii (July 2003), pp. 29–37

Sphinx. Type of statue and art form, first found in the early 3rd millennium BC in Egypt and the Ancient Near East, in the form of a mythical animal usually with a human head. The sphinx (Gr.: 'strangler') could be male or female, and the female version was often shown with breasts. Lion sphinxes were the most numerous, but there were also many examples in the form of bulls or horses. Occasionally they were depicted with various other attributes such as wings, bulls' horns or snakes' tails. Throughout Egypt and the Near East the sphinx was seen as a guardian; its role diversified in the ancient Greek world, where it often took on a more sinister aspect.

The earliest example of the sphinx in the Greek world is a small terracotta representation (Herakleion, Archaeol. Mus.) discovered in 1972 at the palace of Mallia in Crete. This is dated to *c.* 1750 BC, and was made as an attachment for a princely vase or cup. Its reclining posture, without wings, and its bearded, male face with long curling hair suggested to the excavator that this was a 'portrait' sphinx of a Minoan ruler, inspired directly by Egyptian ideas. By *c.* 1550 BC the female sphinx—now with wings, inspired by Syrian prototypes—was shown with the griffin as decoration for richly embroidered robes, for a deity or priestess, on a fresco in the palace of Knossos (Knossos, Pal. Mus.). From this time the winged, female sphinx, rather than the male sphinx, predominated in the Greek world. The Mycenaeans of the mainland seem to have derived their first sphinx from Syria. A series of gold plaques from the latest shaft grave at Mycenae (*c.* 1550–*c.* 1500 BC; Athens, N. Archaeol. Mus.) bear representations of sphinxes wearing plumed bonnets, and in the seated position of sphinxes on Syrian cylinder seals. In spite of direct influences from both Egypt and Syria, however, the Minoans and Mycenaeans swiftly adapted the sphinx to their own ideas and artefacts. It was given the distinctive, plumed crown of their most important female figures, probably deities, a spiral necklace and, on the upper layer of its wing, a row of spirals. Representations of sphinxes adorned objects of value and significance, notably gold signet rings; gold plaques, which were probably for crowns; ivory combs, which may have been offered to the goddess; ivory pyxides, which were carried in processions; and ornamental plaques for furniture, probably thrones. A fresco fragment from Pylos shows a sphinx above a door, in an architectural setting, with her face and neck painted white, the colour used for female skin.

Mycenaean vase painters, especially those from the Argolid and from Lefkandi in Euboia, portrayed the sphinx with an equine rather than a leonine body; this was because they were used to painting horses, rather than because they intended to alter the composition of the sphinx. It has, however, led to some confusion between sphinxes and the horse-bodied centaurs, which were unknown in the Greek Bronze Age. There is also evidence that, in Crete, the idea of the wingless sphinx survived in terracotta sculptures and in a small example in bronze (London, BM).

Except in representations in ivory, which were always more open to Oriental influences, the sphinx never seems to have been as popular in the Greek world as the other winged, mythical monster, the griffin. It has been suggested that the Greeks were less happy with the mixture of a human and an animal. The griffin, rather than the sphinx, was shown as an accompaniment to important male and female figures. The sphinx's most frequent association was with the stylized tree or column. It was often shown antithetically, with an identical sphinx on each side of the column. On wheeled bronze stands for sacred vessels made in Cyprus, *c.* 1200 BC, sphinxes are shown on either side of a stylized tree. There may have been larger representations in bronze, stone or wood.

It has been suggested that in the Bronze Age the sphinx was associated primarily with death. But its association was with the supernatural rather than merely the underworld. It attended the Tree of Life, and the objects it decorated were offered to the deity and worn by people in life as well as in death. It is assumed that, with the possible exception of the earliest sphinx from Mallia, these sphinxes were not portraits of rulers, but abstract, idealized expressions of supernatural power.

The sphinx disappeared from most of the Greek world at the end of the Bronze Age, except in Crete, where it was shown in Orientalizing metalwork, on bronze shields from the Idaean cave, on bronze stands (of which fragments survive) and on metalwork in relief. On the Greek mainland and especially in Attica the form of the sphinx was re-learnt, during the second half of the 8th century BC, from Oriental imports such as matrices for stamping gold diadems and bronze Syro-Phoenician bowls found at Olympia and Delphi. There is an interesting example of the Greeks' misunderstanding of the sphinx—the first in Attic vase painting—on a Late Geometric skyphos made in imitation of a metal bowl, which shows two winged, antithetical monsters, surely intended as sphinxes because of their curly lion's tails, but each with the body of a horse and raised human arms that Attic vase painters usually gave to centaurs.

Proto-Attic vase painting (7th century BC) depicts both male and female sphinxes, some with beards, some with a floral crown, some with an extra wing oddly shown behind the foreleg. During the first half of the 7th century BC, the sphinx was a very popular motif among Attic and Corinthian vase painters as well as in the Cyclades and Crete. Increasingly naturalistic, and usually female, these sphinxes were shown with helmets, diadems, floral crowns or a spiral lock that has been seen as a symbol of vegetation. At this time they were shown in active, probably mythological, contexts: as an accompanying motif to heroic combat; in a scene of two sphinxes on either side of a warrior, whom they seem to threaten; or, on vases from Samos and Perachora, as companion to the goddess Athena. On vases from Rhodes an inimical female sphinx is shown, with a human hand used to strangle a water-bird—perhaps the origin of her description as the 'strangler'.

The sphinx was sometimes, by the 6th century BC, associated with the forces of death and destruction, especially on Attic grave stelai, which were crowned with capitals bearing seated sphinxes. But the association with the stylized tree or column remained: most conspicuously at Delphi, where, *c.* 560 BC, the Naxians erected a statue of a seated sphinx on top of a column nearly 10 m high. This is one of the earliest Ionic columns to survive and one of the first monumental sculptures to be dedicated at a sanctuary. Monumental votive sphinxes were set on top of Ionic columns at the sanctuaries of Delos and Aigina too. Female, seated, with upraised wings, a diadem or *polos* and long hair, they shared the enigmatic features of Archaic korai. They were also widely used as architectural sculpture, or acroteria, for Archaic temples. They were among the first marble monuments on the Athenian Acropolis, in the second half of the 6th century BC.

The disappearance of the sphinx at the end of the Bronze Age and the fact that the imagery was re-learnt from the East may explain its reputation as a mysterious monster, the setter of riddles and the destroyer of men. The first identification of the art form of the sphinx with the monster of Theban legend, whose riddle Oedipus answered correctly, was probably not earlier than the 6th century BC. The sphinx may have had a sinister significance even before its association with the Oedipus story; it has often been described as a death demon. The destructive sphinx, inspired by Oriental representations of sphinxes trampling prostrate figures, was reproduced on Archaic gems by the end of the 6th century BC and was shown destroying youths on the throne of the statue of *Zeus* at Olympia.

The votive sphinxes of the sanctuaries also served as a model for Classical vase painters in depicting the Oedipus story. On the inside of an Attic Red-figure cup by the Oedipus Painter at the beginning of the 5th century BC, Oedipus sits beside the sphinx, who is crowned and seated on top of a column, looking down at him (see colour pl. 2:XII, fig. 3). The sphinx on an Attic relief vase of *c.* 430 BC is seated on top of a tall column, with Athena standing at its foot, and watches the flight of Perseus from one of the Gorgons. There are few representations of the sphinx in a mythological context that do not show a column.

By Hellenistic and Roman times the image of the sphinx seems to have lost much of its power and to have become mainly a decorative device for furniture and sarcophagi.

N. Verdelis: 'L'Apparition du sphinx dans l'art grec', *Bull. Corr. Hell.*, lxxv (1951), pp. 1–37
A. Dessenne: *Le Sphinx: Etude iconographique* (Paris, 1957)
H. Demisch: *Die Sphinx* (Stuttgart, 1977)

P. Müller: *Löwen und Mischwesen in der archaischen griechischen Kunst* (Zurich, 1978)
P. Bosana-Kourou: *The Sphinx in Early Archaic Greek Art* (diss. U. Oxford, 1979)
K. Schauenberg: 'Zur thebanischen Sphinx', *Festschrift für U. Hausmann* (Tübingen, 1982), pp. 230–36
I. Kraskopf: *Perseus und die Sphinx* (Berlin, 1986)

Spinario ['Thorn-puller']. Bronze statue (h. 730 mm; Rome, Mus. Conserv.; see colour pl. 2:XII, fig. 2), usually considered an eclectic work of the early Imperial period in Rome (late 1st century BC- early 1st cent AD). It reproduces a Hellenistic model (thought to be more closely reflected by the marble Castellani *Spinario* in the British Museum, London; cf. also a Hellenistic terracotta statuette of a peasant boy from Priene (now in Berlin, Staatl. Museen, Antikensamml., TC8626), combined with a head type of the early 5th century BC that is also known in conjunction with a different body type. The *Spinario* represents a young boy sitting on a rock and removing a thorn from his left foot, which he holds on his right knee. The statue was listed by the English antiquary Magister Gregorius between 1165 and 1167 among the ancient bronzes standing outside the Lateran in Rome; reliefs in a number of medieval churches show versions of the figure, attesting its early fame. It was one of the antiquities donated by Pope Sixtus IV (*reg* 1471–84) after 1471 to the Museo dei Conservatori, where it remained until 1797, when it was taken to Paris following the Treaty of Tolentino. On its return to Rome in 1816, it was replaced in the Museo dei Conservatori. The *Spinario*, along with the *Marcus Aurelius* that accompanied it in the Lateran Square, was one of the first antique statues to be admired and frequently copied by artists especially from the early Renaissance onwards. Although it was thought in the Middle Ages to be a pagan idol (identified as Priapus and later as the personification of the month of March) and thus representing Vice, for the artists who studied and reproduced it in their drawings and other works it was, above all, an image of grace and simplicity, and most commonly seen as a young shepherd. A popular story in the 17th and 18th centuries identified him as Gnaeus Martius, the shepherd boy who delivered a message to the senate before removing the thorn from his foot; this idea is still mentioned in tourist guidebooks and on the backs of postcards. Another suggestion is that he was a victorious young athlete in the Greek games. There are well-known replicas in bronze on a smaller scale (late 15th century or early 16th) by the sculptors Severo da Ravenna (*fl c.* 1496–*c.* 1543) and Antico (*c.* 1460–1528). The engravings of Marco Dente (*d* 1527) and Marcantonio Raimondi (*c.* 1470/82–1527/34) as well as the drawings of Parmigianino (1503–40), Maarten van Heemskerck (1498–1574) and Francisco de Holanda (1517–84) are also worthy of mention.

While it used to be thought that the Capitoline *Spinario* not only used an alien head type but, in line with Augustan classicism, also altered the proportions of the statue's body, recent research suggests that this was not the case. Combined with the observation that the alloy used for the head of the Capitoline statue is different from the rest of the body, this leaves open the possibility that the sculpture as we know it is unique and may have been put together from parts of two different statues, rather than represent a new type created during the Roman period and then independently copied.

P. Zanker, *Klassizistische Statuen: Studien zur Veränderung des Kunstgeschmacks in der römischen Kaiserzeit* (Mainz 1974), pp. 71–94
F. Haskell and N. Penny: *Taste and the Antique: The Lure of Classical Sculpture, 1500–1900* (New Haven and London, 1981), pp. 308–10.
C. Parisi Presicce: *The Spinario: London, The British Museum 15 March–14 April 2005* (Rome 2005)

Split. *See* SPALATUM.

Sremska Mitrovica. *See* SIRMIUM.

Stadium. Sports ground, usually uncovered, enclosed by seating or terraces for spectators. The Greek term *stadion* was probably introduced in the 6th century BC, and by the early 5th century BC it had three meanings: a structure for athletic competitions, a distance of 600 feet and a foot-race equal to this in length; its original meaning was probably 'standing place'. The Greek and Roman stadium consisted of two parts, the dromos or racecourse, usually rectangular and always 600 feet in length, and the embankments where spectators stood or sat. It was the setting for various foot-races, the pentathlon (including the discus and javelin throws, the long jump and wrestling), boxing and the pancratium. The stadium was clearly distinct from the GYMNASIUM and PALAESTRA where athletes practised.

Stadia often formed part of Greek rural and urban sanctuaries, and most of those excavated are in mainland Greece and Asia Minor. The earliest remains of Greek stadia, found in the sanctuaries at ISTHMIA and Olympia, date from the 6th century BC, while 5th-century BC stadium remains occur at Isthmia, Olympia and Halieis. These early stadia took the form of simple, level, rectangular dromos *c.* 183 × 30 m, bordered on one or more sides by artificial earth embankments to accommodate the spectators. The gentle slopes of these earth banks (4–9°) suggest that the spectators would probably have stood. It is very unusual to find remains of early seating, but single stone seat blocks are known from Olympia (e.g. the mid-6th-century BC seat of the Spartan representative Gorgos) and may have been provided at Isthmia. The ends of the dromos were defined by rows of stone slabs carved with either single starting grooves or parallel double starting grooves and post holes. From the 5th century BC mechanical starting devices were incorporated into some stadia and probably continued in use throughout antiquity. An early 5th-century BC dromos in Corinth, which is not strictly a stadium since it had no formal facilities for spectators, had a unique starting line consisting of a curved stone platform with starting positions cut into its blocks. The running tracks of most Greek stadia had a cambered surface of hard-packed clay. By the 4th century BC, many had water channels and basins along the sides of the dromos, which were probably used to damp the running track to prevent it becoming hard and uncomfortable for barefoot athletes in the summer.

In Archaic and Classical times the dromos was often situated in the heart of the sanctuary, near the altar and temple of the deity in whose honour the games were held (as at Olympia, Isthmia and Halieis). In some cases the temple steps themselves served as a grandstand: at the Sanctuary of Apollo at Didyma the dromos (*c.* 300 BC) ran parallel to the temple's south side. By the 4th century BC many stadia were enlarged and renovated. Some were actually moved to neighbouring sites, where more spectators could be accommodated. In a number of cases, the enlarged stadia took advantage of valleys or hollows, which provided natural earth banks for spectators, as at Isthmia (late 4th century BC), Olympia (mid-5th century BC) and Nemea (late 4th century BC). In Hellenistic times several stadia were given vaulted entrances (e.g. at Epidauros, Olympia, Nemea and Delphi), which connected them with an adjoining sanctuary. At Nemea the late 4th-century BC vault is over 36 m long. In Hellenistic and Roman times, stadia were sometimes constructed in conjunction with theatres, as perhaps on the Pnyx in Athens as early as 330 BC, and at Aizanoi (AD 76–138), Sardis, Tralles, Rhodes and Pergamon (197–159 BC). Stadia for Greek-style athletics contests continued to be built during the Roman Imperial period. For example the Stadium of Domitian in Rome was erected in AD 92–6 and restored in AD 228 by the Emperor Severus Alexander. The famous Panathenaic stadium at Athens was constructed between AD 140 and 144 by Herodes Atticus, who also renovated the stadium at Delphi. The Panathenaic stadium was especially lavish, being built of Pentelic marble and seating *c.* 50,000 spectators.

In AD 391 the Christian Emperor Theodosios I decreed the closure of all pagan temples and the abolition of cult festivals. After this date stadia were no longer used for athletics contests, although in late Roman times the Panathenaic stadium in Athens continued in use for wild beast shows and gladiatorial combats.

P. M. Mylonas: *Peri stadion* [On stadia] (Athens, 1952)
W. Zschietzschmann: *Das Stadion* (1960), i of *Wettkampf und Übungsstätten in Griechenland* (Stuttgart, 1960–61)
P. Aupert: *Le Stade* (1979), ii of *Fouilles de Delphes* (Paris, 1902–)
D. G. Romano: *The Stadia of the Peloponnesos* (diss., Philadelphia, U. PA, 1981)
D. G. Romano: 'The Stadium of Eumenes II at Pergamon', *Amer. J. Archaeol.*, lxxxvi (1982), pp. 586–9
D. G. Romano: 'The Panathenaic Stadium and Theater of Lykourgos: A Re-examination of the Facilities on the Pnyx Hill', *Amer. J. Archaeol.*, lxxxix (1985), pp. 441–54
E. R. Gebhard and F. P. Hemans: 'University of Chicago Examinations at Isthmia, 1989:I', *Hesperia*, lxi (1992), pp. 1–77
Proceedings of an International Symposium on the Olympic Games: Athens 1992, pp. 33–7, 73–9, 81–6
D. G. Romano: *Athletics and Mathematics in Archaic Corinth: The Origins of the Greek Stadium* (Philadelphia, 1993)
K. Welch: 'Greek Stadia and Roman Spectacles: Asia, Athens, and the Tomb of Herodes Atticus', *J. Roman Archaeol.,* xi (1998), pp. 117–45
K. Welch: 'The Stadium at Aphrodisias', *Amer. J. Archaeol.,* cii (1998), pp. 547–69
S. G. Miller, ed.: *Nemea II, The Hellenistic Stadium* (Berkeley, 2001)
A. Papanicolaou-Christensen: *The Panathenaic Stadium: Its History over the Centuries* (Athens, 2003)

Staircase. Major buildings in the ancient world, from palaces to temples, were symbolically raised well above ground-level, with an external staircase (either flight of steps or ramps) serving as a ceremonial entrance. The addition of columns enhanced the prestige of the principal staircase in the Cretan Palace of Minos (late 14th century BC) at KNOSSOS. Greek temples, which were only slightly raised above ground-level, were surrounded by continuous steps with no particular side being emphasized (e.g. Parthenon, Athens, begun 447 BC). In contrast, Roman buildings, civic and religious alike, were placed on a high podium and given an axial approach. One broad flight led up to the entrance portico, its top platform serving as a rostrum for public proclamations (e.g. Maison Carrée, NEMAUSUS (Nîmes), ded. *c.* AD 4). At the sanctuary of Fortuna Primigenia (?late 2nd century BC), built on a terraced hill at PRAENESTE (Palestrina) near Rome, a series of stairs and ramps, including a huge two branch staircase, provided a scenic approach reminiscent of the ziggurats of Mesopotamia.

Internal staircases had a utilitarian role, but in buildings for public entertainment they had to be large in order to accommodate huge crowds of spectators, and the variety of their types was influential on later centuries. The staircase used in western European AMPHITHEATRES consisted of a long, straight flight that turned back on itself, its steps covered by barrel vaults, and, in variations of this type at VERONA, Limonum Pictonum (Poitiers) and Nemausus, two parallel flights were separated by a central return. Other types included an impressive two-branch, tunnel-vaulted staircase resembling a T-plan, recently excavated in the cryptoporticus under the Temple of Domitian (AD 81–96) at EPHESOS, and a larger version of an Egyptian type, the turning staircase in a square cage, built in the Roman theatre at ASPENDOS (late 2nd century AD). Small-scale spiral staircases were built in the thickness of the walls (e.g. Basilica of Maxentius, Baths of Caracalla and Trajan's Column, all in ROME).

Stamnos. Ancient Greek vessel form, used as a mixing bowl (*see* POTTERY, fig. 15(ii)a).

Statuette [Fr.: 'little statue']. Type of SCULPTURE, smaller than life-size, usually figural and free-standing; often a reduced version of a larger work. The statuette was a significant element of sculptural production during most of Classical antiquity. Made in various materials, of which marble, bronze and terracotta were the most common, it served both sacred and secular functions. Inexpensive terracottas dedicated as votives in sanctuaries (*see* CULT STATUE) outnumber other types of figurines, but statuettes in precious materials, apparently commissioned as decorative objects, are also known. Statuette copies provide the primary evidence for several lost statues: two examples are the 2nd-century AD Varvakeion *Athena* (Athens, N. Archaeol. Mus.), which is a Roman copy of the *Athena Parthenos* by PHEIDIAS, and a seated, draped female recognized as a copy of the *Tyche* of Antioch by Eutychides. Perhaps the best-known ancient statuette was the Palladion, a much venerated image of Athena from Troy. Known from Greek legend, this statuette may actually have existed.

Lacking the technical skills to work on a larger scale, early Greek sculptors created statuettes from necessity. A painted terracotta centaur found in a tomb at Lefkandi (*c.* 900 BC; Eretria, Archaeol. Mus.) represents one of their first surviving efforts. A cast-bronze statuette of a nude male, the 'Mantiklos Apollo' (*c.* 700–*c.* 675 BC; Boston, MA, Mus. F.A), and a group of deities found at Dreros on Crete, made of thinly hammered bronze surmounting a wooden core (*c.* 700 BC; Herakleion, Archaeol. Mus.), illustrate the early achievements in bronze. Several lively bronze figures of athletes made in the early 5th century BC document the continued role of the statuette as a trend-setter into the Early Classical period (*c.* 480–*c.* 450 BC).

Overshadowed during the 5th century BC by statuary of human scale, the statuette rose again to prominence in the Hellenistic era, when the popularity of the private house as a locus for sculptural display spurred the making of small-scale statues. Extensive finds of statuettes at Delos and RHODES document this trend. During this time the sculptor LYSIPPOS is said to have made a statuette of *Herakles* as a table ornament for Alexander the Great (Martial: *Epigrams* ix.43).

The statuette was also important in the Roman world. Household gods (*lares*) were a favourite subject. Hundreds of bronze statuettes rendering figures according to traditional typologies have been discovered in such provincial areas as Gaul and Germany. Although often artistically mediocre, these statuettes disseminated the formal language of Classicism throughout the Empire. Other statuettes of higher quality inspired the small Renaissance bronzes made by Antico and other sculptors.

S. Boucher: *Recherches sur les bronzes figurés de Gaule préromaine et romaine* (Paris, 1976)

J. Boardman: *Greek Sculpture: The Archaic Period* (London, 1978)

J. Boardman: *Greek Sculpture: The Classical Period* (London, 1985)

M. True: *Pre-Sotadean Attic Red-figure Statuette Vases and Related Vases with Relief Decoration* (diss., Cambridge, MA, Harvard U., 1986)

E. Künzl: *Aphrodite Untying her Sandals: A Hellenistic Terracotta and a Roman Alabaster Statuette* (Haifa, 1994)

J. A. MacGillivray, J. Driessen and L. H. Sackett: *The Palaikastro Kouros: A Minoan Chryselephantine Statuette and its Aegean Bronze Age Context* (London, 2000)

J. Pollini: *Gallo-Roman Bronzes and the Process of Romanization: The Cobannus Hoard* (Leiden and Boston, 2002)

M. Albertocchi: *Athana Lindia: Le statuette siceliote con pettorali di età arcaica e classica* (Rome, 2004)

Stele [Gr.; pl. stelai; Lat. stela, pl. stelae]. Stone or pillar set upright in commemoration of some event or as a marker for a grave. In ancient Greece and Rome the term stele is usually applied to grave markers, although slabs carrying decrees are also called stelai. Most grave monuments have inscriptions only, while it is a minority that have carved figures, although these have attracted more attention than the others. Stelai were rare in Greece until Archaic times (*c.* 600 BC), when a series of carved relief stelai occur in Attica. These are usually thin and show only a single figure, often a warrior or an athlete; they are topped by a sphinx or a palmette finial, the latter type originating from the islands of East Greece. About 500 BC the series of Attic grave stelai ended, probably as a result of legislation preventing excessive expenditure on grave stelai and funerals, though this interpretation depends upon an obscure passage in Cicero. (The East Greek type persisted in the islands, however.) Around 438 BC, when the Parthenon at Athens was completed and the sculptors who had been employed to decorate it required work, the series of Attic grave stelai was revived. These Classical stelai are broader and often show far more figures. They do not have scenes of great grief or lamentation: the dead who are represented appear rather distant and aloof. There is never any sign of portraiture, either in the figure of the dead person or in the people surrounding him or her; and it has thus been suggested that the stelai were purchased ready made. Classical stelai often have quasi-architectural decoration consisting of a pediment and pilasters at both sides.

A typical example shows a youth holding a bird (London, BM, 1907.10–25.2), an Athenian work of the early 4th century BC inscribed with the name Stratios. Another example is the grave stele of Xanthippos, which has a pediment and shows Xanthippos sitting in a chair, gazing at a model of a foot, with his two daughters at his knees. The girls are shown as small-scale adults. Around 300 BC Demetrios of Phaleron, the governor of Athens under Macedonian rule, passed further sumptuary laws limiting expenditure on funerary monuments, so the series of carved stelai comes to an end.

F. Johansen: *The Attic Grave Reliefs* (Copenhagen, 1951)

G. M. A. Richter: *The Archaic Gravestones of Attica* (London, 1961/*R* Bristol, 1988)

M. Robertson: *A History of Greek Art*, i (Cambridge, 1975), pp. 363–82
A. Sadurska and Z. Kiss: *Les monuments funéraires: Autels, urnes, stèles, divers dans les collections polonaises* (Warsaw, 1990–)
U. Tocchetti Pollini: *Stele funerarie romane con ritratti dai municipia di Mediolanum e Comum* (Milan, 1990)
I. A. Papapostolou: *Achaean Grave Stelai* (Athens, 1993)
A. Scholl: *Die attischen Bildfeldstelen des 4. Jhs. v. Chr.: Untersuchungen zu den kleiformatigen Grabreliefs im spätklassischen Athen* (Berlin, 1996)
L. Mercando, G. Paci and G. Colonna: *Stele romane in Piemonte* (Rome, 1998)
K. Kissas: *Die attischen Statuen- und Stelenbasen archaischer Zeit* (Bonn, 2000)
J. Moore: *Cultural Identity in Roman Africa: The 'La Ghorfa' Stelae* (diss., Hamilton, McMaster U., 2000)

Stephanos (*fl c.* 1st century BC). Greek sculptor. He worked in Rome during the late Hellenistic and early Imperial eras, and signed a statue of a *Youth* (*c.* 50 BC; Rome, Villa Albani, 906) as a pupil of PASITELES. However, he is mentioned only once in literary sources (Pliny the elder: *Natural History* XXXVI.iv.33), as the maker of a group of *Appiades* (apparently water nymphs associated with the Aqua Appia) in the collection of Asinius Pollio (76 BC–AD 5). The Albani *Youth* is representative of the eclectic and stylistically retrospective sculptures created for the Roman market in later Hellenistic times. While it is largely modelled on Early Classical Apollo types (e.g. the Choiseul-Gouffier *Apollo*; London, BM), it has the elongated proportions, small head and agitated stance typical of Late Classical works. At least replicas of the type are known, including nine statues, three statuary groups and five heads. In the *Orestes and Electra* (1st century AD, but based on originals of 1st century BC; Naples, Mus. Archeol. N.) the youth is paired with a female figure whose body derives from the *Venus Genetrix* type (itself an eclectic Roman version of the High Classical Fréjus *Aphrodite* type) but whose head, with male hairstyle, is Early Classical in style. In the *Orestes and Pylades* group (late 1st century BC; Paris, Louvre) the youth is placed with a statue of another youth executed in the Early Classical style, but in a Praxitelean pose. These examples show that artists in the workshop of Pasiteles not only produced classicizing statues but also combined versions of them in different groupings.

J. Overbeck: *Die antiken Schriftquellen zur Geschichte der bildenden Künste bei den Griechen* (Leipzig, 1868), nos 2265–6
M. Borda: *La scuola di Pasiteles* (Bari, 1953)
G. M. A. Richter: *Ancient Italy* (Ann Arbor, 1955), pp. 112–16
P. Zanker: *Klassizistische Statuen* (Mainz, 1974), pp. 49–68
J. J. Pollitt: *Art in the Hellenistic Age* (Cambridge, 1986), pp. 163, 175

Stereobate. Top part of a foundation, just above ground-level, on which a building is constructed. In ancient Greek and Roman architecture the term refers to the substructure of a temple.

Sthennis (*fl c.* 325–*c.* 280 BC). Greek sculptor. He was the son of Herodotos of Olynthos and the father of Herodoros, both of whom were also sculptors. He was born in Olynthos before 348 BC when the city was destroyed by Philip of Macedon. His later signatures on statue bases record his citizenship as Athenian or from the Attic deme Diomeia. He was a contemporary of Lysippos as well as Leochares, and continued to work during the reign of Lysimachos (287–281 BC). Many of his works were brought to Rome, including statues of *Demeter, Zeus* and *Athena* which were displayed in the Temple of Concord; matrons weeping, praying or sacrificing (Pliny: *Natural History* XXXIV.xc); a portrait of the philosopher *Dion of Ephesos* (*Inscr. Gr./1*, XIV, 1149); and a portrait of *Autolykos*, the founder of Sinope (Plutarch: *Lucullus* xxiii). Other works include a portrait of *Hadeia*, the wife of Autolykos, in the amphiareion at Oropos (*Inscr. Gr./1*, VII, 279); a group of statues representing the family of Pandaites on the Acropolis of Athens, sculpted with Leochares (*Inscr. Gr./2*, II, 3829); two equestrian statues of noblemen of Elis set up in Olympia (Pausanias: *Guide to Greece* VI.xvi.8); and a statue dedicated by Sthennis, the base of which was discovered in the Theatre of Dionysos in Athens (*Inscr. Gr./2*, II, 4902).

J. Overbeck: *Die antiken Schriftquellen zur Geschichte der bildenden Künste bei den Griechen* (Leipzig, 1868/*R* Hildesheim, 1959), nos 1314, 1343–9
E. Loewy: *Inschriften griechischen Bildhauer* (Leipzig, 1885), pp. 63, 81–2, 307
J. Kirchner: *Prosopographia attica*, ii (Berlin, 1903), no. 12641

Still-life. The depiction of an arrangement of diverse inanimate objects, including items of food (especially fruit and game), plants and artefacts. In the Classical world, still-life evolved as a distinct category, probably reaching its height in the 3rd and 2nd centuries BC in the wall paintings, mosaics and panels of Hellenistic Greece. Not a single panel of these has survived, but Greek pottery may be used for comparative analysis, supplemented with Roman decorative paintings and mosaics. Classical writers such as Pliny, Philostratus, Plato and Vitruvius also provide a useful source. Pliny, for example, in his *Natural History*, described the celebrated competition between the Greek painters Parrhasios and Zeuxis that took place as early as 400 BC. Zeuxis had painted grapes so lifelike that birds came to pick at them, but Parrhasios painted a curtain over the panel, which Zeuxis tried to lift, thereby admitting defeat. Pliny also devised a hierarchy of genres, with paintings of deities and mythological subjects as the most noble category. At the lower end of the scale were such unpretentious genres as flower still-lifes and everyday objects (Lat. *humilia*), animal painting (*aselli*), representations of food (*obsonia*) and the representation of food that the Greeks offered to their guests (Gr. *xenion, xenia*). The painters of such everyday items, such as the Greek still-life painter Peiraikos, were called *rhyparographoi*, or painters of vile objects. The *xenia* in the decorative schemes of Classical antiquity are close in content to later still-life paintings and appear in two forms: a niche divided into two zones by a shelf, so that objects are shown in two superimposed levels, or a display of objects on two stone slabs. The *xenia* described by Philostratus and Pliny were probably free-standing easel paintings, which had first appeared in the second half of the 4th century BC and were executed by such painters as Antiphilos, the rival of Apelles. The later works excavated at Pompeii, Herculaneum and elsewhere, however, were either decorative frescoes or mosaics.

The Roman still-life tradition was largely derived from that of Greece. As a rule, Roman still-lifes were realistic, bordering on *trompe l'oeil*, and were part of decorative schemes in dwellings. Sterling has proposed a distinction between four typical, successive styles. The earliest type of Pompeian still-lifes, the so-called First Style, is to be found exclusively in mosaics, such as the *Fish Mosaic* (2nd-century BC) in the House of the Faun, Pompeii. The Second Style, often believed to be the direct heritage of Hellenistic tradition and including the finest still-lifes from antiquity, contains many mural decorations in a sensitive version of realism, some of these in *trompe l'oeil*. The Third Style is a reductionist reaction against the compelling realism of the previous style and resulted in minimalist, small and minutely executed pictures. The *trompe l'oeil* reached its zenith during the Fourth Style, which also included a revival of the *xenion* still-life as part of a decorative, illusionistic scheme or as an addition to a central theme, such as a mythological scene or a landscape. The great majority of the still-lifes in Herculaneum and Pompeii belong to the last category.

The high level of skill in representing the tactile qualities of flowers, fruit, fowl and inanimate objects led to the painting of grotesques, which appeared in the time of Emperor Nero (AD 54–68). Together with simulated architectural elements, grotesques were among the most original mural decorations and were described by Vitruvius. From the 5th century onwards, however, during the Early Christian and Byzantine period, still-lifes were relegated to a strictly symbolic and decorative role.

C. Sterling: *Still Life Painting from Antiquity to the Twentieth Century* (New York, 1959, rev. 2/1982)

Still Lifes from Pompeii (exh. cat. by S. De Caro; Paris, Maison de l'Unesco, 1999)

Stirrup jar. Ancient pottery form (*see* POTTERY, figs 3f, 7c, 11e and 12b–c).

Stoa. Ancient Greek term applied principally to a type of long, narrow, free-standing building with a façade of columns. The stoa was developed as an architectural form in its own right and was popular in ancient Greece between the 7th and 1st centuries BC. *See also* PORTICO.

1. DEFINITION AND FUNCTION. The Greek word *stoa* encompassed the porticos of complex buildings and sometimes even other related buildings for which there was no more suitable name. The term is now generally restricted to the free-standing porticos characteristic of Greek sanctuaries and market squares. The simplest stoas had only three walls and a colonnaded front, but a second, inner colonnade often supported the ridge of the roof. Sometimes a row of small rooms lay behind the portico, while multi-storey stoas, with a substructure below the portico or a second portico above it, also occur. Some stoas had projecting pedimented wings at either end, others formed L- or pi-shaped plans, individually or in combination, to frame open spaces.

Unlike temples or baths, stoas had no dominant function. Some were built for a single purpose, such as the abaton, a dormitory for ritual dream cures (4th century BC) in the sanctuary of Asklepios at Epidauros, but their roles varied, and many stoas were general-purpose buildings. Those in sanctuaries sheltered the visitors attending the main festivals and often stood along processional routes or faced the altar. However, they could also house dedications and provide backdrops for votive sculpture, and they became increasingly important to the aesthetic planning of ancient Greek sanctuaries.

In secular contexts stoas served as magistrates' offices and meeting-places for civic bodies or law courts. However, their function was at least as often commercial: any rooms behind the stoa could be rented out as shops. They also sheltered crowds and provided space for strolling and conversation (whence the development of Stoic philosophy founded by Zeno of Kition *c.* 300 BC). As in sanctuaries, they also served for display, for example of laws, decrees or commemorative art, and to define public areas.

2. HISTORY. Porticos had occurred as parts of some complex buildings in earlier foreign and Aegean civilizations, but the development of the free-standing portico as an important building type was peculiar to Greek architecture. Being inherently simple structures, stoas probably evolved from primitive open shelters with wooden posts. The earliest substantial remains of stoas date from the late 7th century BC, more than a century after the first substantial remains of Greek temples, and stoas were not common until about the mid-5th century BC. Early stoas occurred in all parts of the Greek world, but more commonly in sanctuaries than in secular contexts. Even in the early 6th century BC some had stone columns, ashlar walls and tiled roofs. However, several had only wooden posts, rubble or mud-brick walls, and thatched or flat, clay roofs, while later stoas were often less sophisticated in materials and construction than temples.

The second half of the 5th century BC was an important period in stoa development, particularly in Athens, where the complexities of democratic government required new civic buildings. Thus the small Stoa Basileios (Royal Stoa; date uncertain but restored after 480 BC; see fig.) in the Athenian Agora was joined

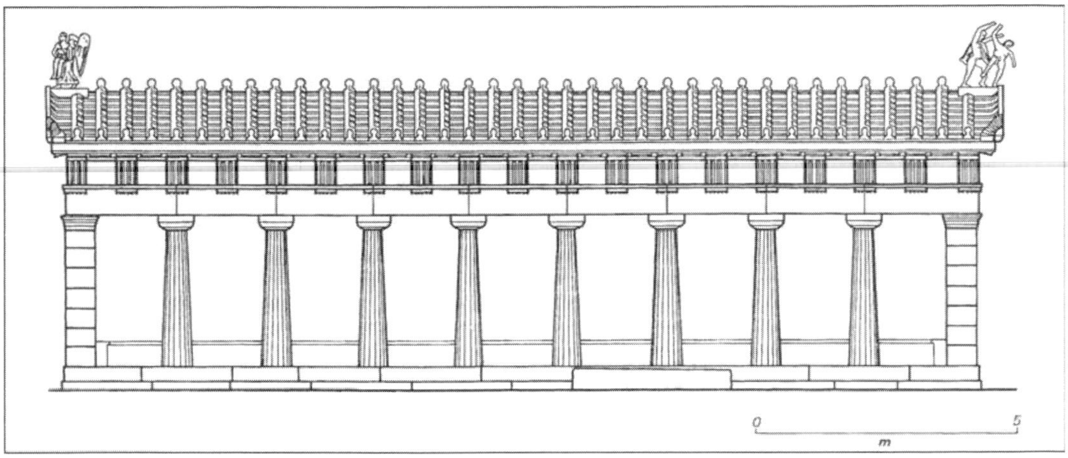

Stoa Basileios (Royal Stoa), Agora, Athens, late 6th century BC; restored elevation

by the Stoa Poikile (Painted Stoa; *c.* 465–460 BC), the Stoa of Zeus (*c.* 425–410 BC), the Stoa of the Herms (*c.* 475–470 BC) and South Stoa I (*c.* 425–400 BC). These, together with the stoa at Brauron in eastern Attica (*c.* 425–415 BC), include the first stoa with projecting wings (Stoa of Zeus), the first stoas with rooms (Brauron and South Stoas), and the first pi-shaped stoa (Brauron). In addition, in the Stoa of Zeus, and probably the Stoa Poikile, Ionic columns supported the roof ridge behind the squatter Doric external colonnade, so that the choice of architectural orders was no longer essentially a question of regional style but became a matter of convenience, context and perhaps of symbolism. Also, to provide more space between the columns of small colonnades, three metopes were placed above each intercolumniation at Brauron, rather than the two that were conventional in temples. Both these features recurred in most later stoas and show how stoa designers were among the first to adapt the architectural orders, created for temples, to buildings with different requirements. The use of stoas to frame open spaces also goes back to the 5th century BC, as at Brauron.

The only major innovation of the 4th century BC was the introduction, towards the end of the century, of two-storey stoas. Stoas also became more widespread, and some, such as the Stoa of Philip at Megalopolis (*c.* 155×20 m; *c.* 340–330 BC), were very large. The use of stoas to frame specific areas also developed at this time. Thus, at Olympia the large Echo Stoa (*c.* 970×11.5 m), begun *c.* 350 BC but completed much later, defined the eastern edge of the Sanctuary of Zeus, with its axis almost perpendicular to those of the two main temples. This function is especially evident in Ionia, for example in the agoras at Priene and Miletos, which were begun in the 4th century BC but not completed until Hellenistic times.

The Hellenistic period (*c.* 323–27 BC) was the great age of stoas, which became vital amenities for any city. In Ionia, where building restarted in the second half of the 4th century BC after *c.* 150 years of inactivity, a characteristic form of agora was developed with L- or pi-shaped stoas partly framing a rectangular space and a road normally running along its fourth side in front of a straight stoa. Here the space, not the building mass, was basic to the design, so that the porticos and other surrounding buildings often merged into each other.

Similarly, stoas often defined regular spaces for sanctuaries, as at the Sanctuary of Artemis at Magnesia on the Maeander (2nd century BC), by creating a symmetrical frame around the temple and incorporating an axial approach. The steep site of Pergamon (developed mainly in the 2nd century BC) meant that its main building complexes had different orientations: stoas were used in several to create approximately regular spaces. Stoas on the downhill sides of terraces often stood on two-storey substructures, retaining the terrace fill as well as raising their porticos to the required level, while two-storey stoas often masked the cut slopes above their terraces. Though known earlier, and also used in Hellenistic Delos, two-storey porticos seem to have been a Pergamene speciality. The stoas donated to the Athenians by Eumenes II (197–?160 BC) and Attalos II (?160–138 BC) of Pergamon were both of this type; the latter, now rebuilt, has the ingenious upper cornice and the hour-glass section of the upper colonnade specially developed for multi-storey façades.

Under the Roman Empire, public porticos were still highly valued, particularly in the eastern provinces, but more specialized building types, such as market courts and basilicas, were also developed for specific purposes. Because of this, and because of changing architectural conceptions, Roman porticos generally form part of larger complexes, such as baths and colonnaded streets or courts. Their builders still called them stoas, but they had lost the independence that so clearly distinguished Greek stoas from the porticos of other cultures.

R. Martin: *Recherches sur l'agora grecque* (Paris, 1951)
O. Broneer: *The South Stoa and its Roman Successors* (1954), I/iv of *Corinth* (Princeton, 1929–)

R. Martin: *L'Urbanisme dans la Grèce antique* (Paris, 1956, rev. 2/1974)
R. Martin: *L'Agora*, i (1959), vi of *Etudes thasiennes* (Paris 1944–)
C. Bouras: *E anastylosis tes stoas tes Brauronos kai ta architecktonika tes problemata* [The restoration of the stoa at Brauron and its architectural problems] (Athens, 1967)
J. J. Coulton: *The Architectural Development of the Greek Stoa* (Oxford, 1976)
W. Koenigs: *Die Echohalle* (1984), xii of *Olympische Forschungen*, ed. A. Mallwitz (Berlin, 1944–)
G. Kuhn: 'Untersuchungen zur Funktion der Säulenhalle in archaische und klassische Zeit', *Jb. Dt. Archäol. Inst.*, c. (1985), pp. 169–317
G. Roux and O. Callot: *La terrasse d'Attale I*, ii of *Fouilles de Delphes* (Paris, 1987)
He Stoa tou avatou sto Asklepieio tes Epidaurou: protase syntereses kai merikes apokatastases (Athens, 1987)

Stobi. Site in the former Yugoslav Republic of Macedonia on a promontory at the confluence of the rivers Crna and Vardar, *c.* 23 km south-east of Titov Veles. It existed as a city by the early 2nd century BC; under the Romans, its commercial and military importance was enhanced with the construction of roads along the Crna and Vardar valleys. In AD 325, the city is recorded as having its own bishop and by the 5th century it had become the capital of the province of Macedonia Secunda. It was severely damaged by the attack of 479 by the Goths and was probably also affected by the earthquake of 518.

Excavations, begun in the 1920s and carried on intermittently since then, have uncovered about a third of the site, which occupies three low terraces that descend towards the Crna. One of the city's earliest features is the Hellenistic grid pattern of streets, which is still evident in the two main streets that run roughly parallel in a north-west to south-east direction, and in the division of the terraces into *insula* blocks. Surviving sections of the Roman wall delineate the extent of the city, which originally stretched along the west bank of the Crna and covered an area *c.* 520×450 m. By the late 4th century AD, Stobi's inhabitants had abandoned the urban quarter nearest the river and retreated behind the rampart built *c.* 75–100 m further up the slope.

Except for the Roman theatre (2nd century AD), virtually every other excavated monument dates from the 4th or 5th century AD, although Hellenistic and Roman levels have been found under a number of buildings. Several secular structures have been uncovered including the House of the Fuller, the House of Parthenius, the House of Peristerias, the Theodosian Palace, the House of the Psalms (see colour pl. 2:XIII, fig. 1), the Casino, and the Little and Large Baths. Most of these buildings preserve remnants of their rich mosaic floors (4th–5th centuries), decorated with a variety of designs: geometric and stylized floral patterns; scenes of land and sea creatures; and, in one instance, a large-scale composition of paired animals. Statues of mythological figures and spirally fluted and variegated columns (*in situ*) were also found in the Theodosian Palace. Stobi had several intramural churches, including the Central Basilica (5th century), which was erected on the site of a synagogue (2nd or 3rd century AD; rebuilt second half 4th century), the North Basilica (late 4th century) and a basilican church (*c.* 360–70), which was replaced by the Episcopal Basilica (*c.* mid-5th century; rebuilt after 518). These churches were lavishly decorated, and the most impressive sequence of wall paintings, floor mosaics and sculptural decorations came from the early basilica and its successor, the Episcopal Basilica. In the former, two phases of predominantly geometric mosaics have been uncovered; the second phase also contains a donor inscription referring to a Bishop Eustathios.

E. Kitzinger: 'A Survey of the Early Christian Town of Stobi', *Dumbarton Oaks Pap.*, iii (1946), pp. 81–162
J. Wiseman and B. Aleksova, eds: *Studies in the Antiquities of Stobi*, i–ii (Belgrade, 1973–5); iii (Titov Veles, 1981)
B. Aleksova: 'The Early Christian Basilicas at Stobi', *Corsi Cult. A. Ravenn. & Biz.* (1986), pp. 13–81
E. Kolarik: 'Mosaics of the Early Church at Stobi', *Dumbarton Oaks Pap.*, xliv (1987), pp. 295–306
K. Hattersley-Smith: *Byzantine Public Architecture between the Fourth and Early Eleventh Centuries AD with Special Reference to the Towns of Macedonia* (diss., U. Oxford, 1988), pp. 72–124
V. R. Anderson-Stojanovic: *Stobi: The Hellenistic and Roman Pottery*, i of *Stobi: Results of the Joint American–Yugoslav Archaeological Investigations, 1970–1981* (Princeton, 1992–)
V. Lilcik: *Anticka gradezna keramika vo Republika Makedonija: Skuti, Stobi, Herakleja, Stibera* (Skopje, 1996)
P. Josifovski: *Rimskata monetarnica vo Stobi* [Roman mint of Stobi] (Skopje, 2001)
I. Mikulcik: *Stobi: An Ancient City* (Skopje, 2003)

Stone vases. Vessels carved and drilled out of a variety of hardstones, such as chlorite, serpentine, marble and obsidian, for funerary use.

1. Minoan. 2. Cycladic.

1. MINOAN. The manufacture of stone vessels in Crete began during Early Minoan (EM) II, at a time when other crafts such as seal-carving and metalwork underwent their first substantial development. These beginnings, joining the long-established pottery industry, mark the onset of specialization of labour, which contributed to the increasingly complex economic and social organization of Cretan villages. The growth of the craft industries was given further impetus in Middle Minoan (MM) IB by the building of the first palaces. Stone vase-making pursued an increasingly brilliant course until the major destruction of the Minoan civilization in Late Minoan (LM) IB.

(i) Early Minoan. The first vessels, similar to those being produced in the Cyclades, were bowls and pyxides in chlorite or steatite, hollowed out with small chisels and usually featuring on the outside incised decoration or relief spirals related to the applied-wire decoration on metal jewellery. These softish green stones were perhaps first chosen because of their similarity in colour to copper-bearing rocks. During EM II a wider range of Cretan rocks was being

selected, including banded marbles and limestones, polychrome breccias, calcites, wavy-veined tufa and mottled serpentines. In addition, two new manufacturing techniques were being used: the extraction of the interior of the vase with drills made from hollow reeds, and the undercutting of the shoulder inside with small transverse bits of different sizes, mounted on a cylindrical piece of wood or bone or perhaps on the reed. Extracted cylindrical cores are found as waste material on many Minoan settlement sites. The range of shapes expanded, and external decoration came to include small inlays of red or white material.

Most EM stone vessels come from tombs (e.g. on Mochlos and in the Mesara), indicating that, as in ancient Egypt, their function was largely funerary. The tombs were in use for families or clans over hundreds of years, so many stone vessels cannot be closely placed within the period EM II–MM II. But there is enough evidence to show that most of the rocks and the most complex shapes, such as the 'teapot', were already in use during EM II.

(ii) Middle Minoan I and II. Alongside the use of many small shapes for tomb offerings a new development occurred at the beginning of the MM period, prompted by increased urbanization and, soon afterwards, by the establishment of the first palaces. This was the manufacture for household use of larger vases, chiefly various forms of bowl, in blue-black mottled serpentine, a Cretan rock employed for about half of all known Minoan stone vases. The increased size of vessels required more advanced techniques of hollowing out the interior. Quite regular horizontal striations around interior walls of vessels show that large, transversely mounted bits, probably of obsidian or quartz, were employed in MM II. By this time, too, hard and beautiful stones had begun to be imported: *rosso antico*, the deep pink, fine-grained marble from southern Mani in the Peloponnese, and white-spotted black obsidian from Gyali in the Dodekanese.

(iii) Middle Minoan III and Late Minoan. The highest attainments of the vase lapidaries came during MM III and LM I, evidenced by the variety and sizes of the shapes produced, the technical skills mastered and the range of attractive and hard rocks used. As well as bowls and bucket-shaped jars, shapes included amphorae, chalices, large ewers and other jugs, jars with bridge-spouts, lamps, offering tables, rhytons (for pouring ritual libations) in conical, inverted-pear, bull's- and lion's-head forms (see fig. 1), and shell imitations. The height of the largest vessels is over 500 mm. A major technical advance was provided by the lathe, its use proved by two unfinished jars from the palace at Mallia (Herakleion, Archaeol. Mus.) and from Akrotiri on the Cycladic island of Thera. A hollow cylinder, probably of copper or bronze, would have been fitted to project from another cylinder, solid, heavy and probably wooden. The cutting would have been achieved by the combination of the lathe's weight, abrasive powder (emery from Naxos in the Cyclades or sand) and water as the lathe was rotated down on to the vessel. The diameter of the circular cutting on the Akrotiri jar is *c.* 300 mm.

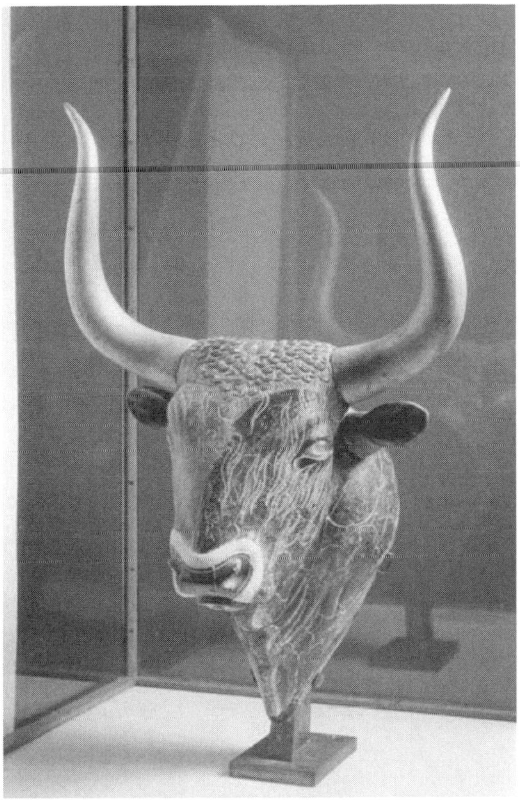

1. Minoan stone rhyton in the shape of a bull's head, steatite, shell, rock crystal and red jasper with gilt-wood horns restored, h. 305 mm, Late Minoan IA (Herakleion, Archaeological Museum)

Much technical skill was also shown in surface decoration, which included precisely parallel horizontal flutings and grooves, ribbing and mouldings, as well as the carving of startlingly naturalistic scenes in relief, with human figures, bulls, birds, flowers, marine creatures and sanctuaries. The most outstanding relief vases are the Boxer Rhyton, the Chieftain Cup, the Harvester Vase from AYIA TRIADA (see fig. 2) and the Peak Sanctuary Rhyton from Kato Zakros (MM III–LM I; Herakleion, Archaeol. Mus.). Gold leaf was sometimes applied over these scenes, in imitation of gold vessels such as the famous cups from Vapheio. Vases were often made in separate parts, cleverly joined by bronze wires through holes. These technical skills were also used to adapt imported Egyptian vessels to Minoan taste, by the addition of new parts or gold sheeting. Some shapes were common to pottery, metal, faience and stone.

As well as rather soft Cretan serpentine, a brilliant range of local and imported hardstones (up to 7 on Mohs' scale) was used, comprising Cretan gabbro and diorite; *lapis Lacedaemonius* and *rosso antico* from the Peloponnese; Gyali obsidian and a jet-black obsidian, very possibly Anatolian; Egyptian alabaster (calcite);

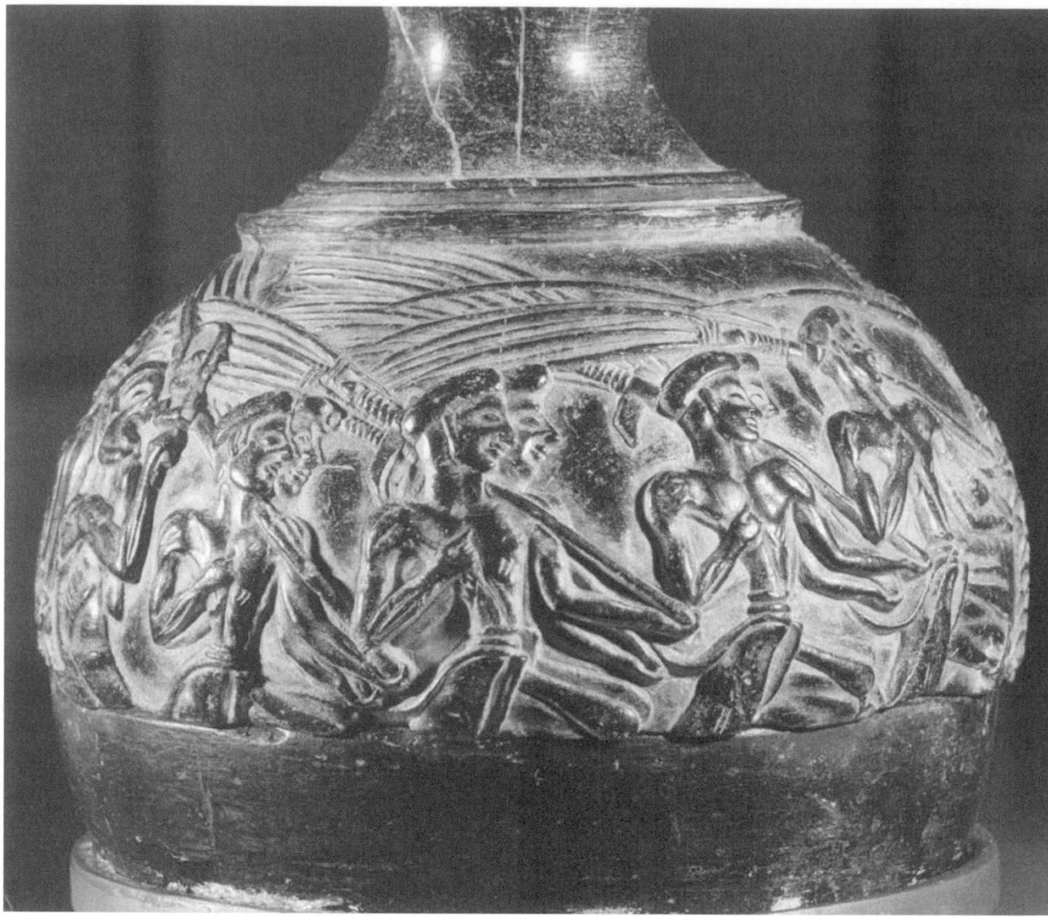

2. Harvester vase (detail), from Ayia Triada, lower part of vase is reconstructed, steatite, diam. 113 mm, Late Minoan IA (Herakleion, Archaeological Museum)

large rock crystals, probably from Egypt; Cycladic or local white marble; and fine polychrome and creamy-white limestones, both similar to marble.

The functions of stone vases also became more diverse during MM III–LM I and included use in religious rituals, many of the finest vessels coming from shrine treasuries; domestic usage in houses and palaces, chiefly vessels of Cretan serpentine; and use as burial gifts, though these were now on a much reduced scale. In addition, vases were exported to Minoan settlements abroad and to other sites in the Aegean. Many of the finer pieces may have been presents or gift exchanges with local rulers, designed to encourage trade.

After the Cretan destructions in LM IB, large vessels (alabastrons and amphorae) were produced at Knossos in a new, soft stone: gypsum. The rulers at this time may have been Mycenaean Greeks, and a new lapidary technique, involving the use of a cutting compass to engrave elaborate spiral decoration, is paralleled in architectural stonework on the Greek mainland.

R. B. Seager: *Explorations in the Island of Mochlos* (Boston and New York, 1912) [fine colour illus. of EM pieces]

S. Xanthoudides: *The Vaulted Tombs of Mesará* (Liverpool, 1924)

C. Zervos: *L'Art de la Crète néolithique et minoenne* (Paris, 1956)

S. Marinatos and M. Hirmer: *Crete and Mycenae* (London, 1960) [excellent pls of vessels with scenes in relief]

P. M. Warren: 'Minoan Stone Vases as Evidence of Minoan Foreign Connexions in the Aegean Late Bronze Age', *Proc. Prehist. Soc.*, xxxiii (1967), pp. 37–56

P. M. Warren: *Minoan Stone Vases* (Cambridge, 1969)

N. Platon: *Zakros: The Discovery of a Lost Palace of Ancient Crete* (New York, 1971) [excellent pls]

P. M. Warren: 'The Unfinished Red Marble Jar at Akrotiri, Thera', *Thera and the Aegean World*, ed. C. Doumas, i (London, 1978), pp. 555–68 [manufacture of stone vases]

C. Baurain and P. Darcque: 'Un Triton en pierre à Malia', *Bull. Corr. Hell.*, cvii (1983), pp. 3–73

P. Darcque: 'Crète. L'Art des sculptures de coquillages: Un Triton en pierre trouvé à Malia', *Archaeologia*, 211 (1986), pp. 30–38

G. Walberg: 'Relationships between Kamares and Minoan Stone Vases', *Ant. Kst,* xxxi/1 (1988), pp. 3–4

P. M. Warren: 'Stone Vessels in Minoan Crete', *Minoan and Greek Civilization from the Mitsotakis Collection* (exh. cat., ed.

L. Marangou; Athens, Mus. Cyclad. & Anc. Gr. A., 1992), pp. 151–5

R. D. G. Evely: 'Minoan Crafts: Tools and Techniques. An Introduction', *Stud. Medit. Archaeol.*, xcii/1 (1993), pp. 172–94 [manuf. of stone vases]

2. Cycladic. The same high quality of Cycladic white marble that inspired the sculptors of stone figurines also led to the creation of an impressive series of stone vessels with similarly clean lines and simple, elegant forms. Like the figurines, these vases were produced chiefly in EC I and II, although there were a few Late Neolithic prototypes, such as a pointed marble beaker from an early 4th-millennium grave on Kea (Kea, Archaeol. Col.). The most common EC I forms are the rounded jar with a tall collar and pedestal foot (the *kandili*), plain open bowls, flat-based beakers and rectangular trough palettes. One or two beakers have seemingly anthropomorphic relief decoration, recalling marble figurines of the EC I Plastiras type as well as Early Minoan (EM) cult statuettes from Crete. The earliest Cycladic stone vessels seem to have functioned mainly as grave offerings. Some are decorated with red ochre, and some contain traces of red or blue pigment used in burial rites. Occasionally the interior of a bowl is coloured red all over; this looks like decoration rather than the result of mixing colouring matter.

During EC II a wider range of forms developed, chiefly elegant open bowls, flaring in profile and sometimes with an open spout or a pedestal foot. Rectangular palettes up to 300 mm long also occur, as do rounded bowls or jars with lug handles (pyxides). The bowls and pyxides are closely paralleled in contemporary pottery shapes. A rarer form is a cylindrical pyxis with horizontal grooves and a close-fitting lid. A special class of lidded box was made of green chlorite or chlorite-schist rather than marble. Such boxes are decorated with incised herringbone patterns, alternating hatched triangles or finely carved low-relief spirals. One example from Melos (Munich, Staatl. Antikensamml.) appears to be a model of a granary, raised on pillars: it portrays a building with an elaborate entrance porch, seven tall cylindrical storage bins and a central courtyard. Others could be models of huts. Vases of the same stone and similar decoration, but of different shapes, occur at the same time in Crete, where they constitute the earliest stone vessels. This suggests direct links between Cycladic and Minoan workshops. As in Crete, the EC II stone vessels were apparently burial gifts, though this cannot be confirmed, as few EC I and II settlements have been excavated.

There were sudden changes at the beginning of EC III, which resulted in the almost complete abandonment of stone vase production, though there were occasionally stone imitations made of the collared and pedestalled pottery jars. This lapse in production lasted several centuries, making the discovery at Akrotiri on Thera of a complete pithos of local grey-black lava (h. 1.18 m; Akrotiri, Thera Excav. Storerooms) all the more astonishing. The vase came from a settlement immediately below the LC I town. Though a unique survival, the jar presupposes the complete mastery of the craft of carving in a Theran volcanic stone. It heralds the resumption of the vase industries during the LC I period, when two distinct classes of vases were produced. One comprises vessels fashioned from local stones: banded marble on Kea and volcanic rocks (dacite, lava and tuff) on Thera. The best Theran works are three-footed mortars, some exported to Crete. The other class comprises a wide range of vessels in foreign materials, chiefly Cretan serpentine but sometimes more exotic stones, such as *rosso antico*. Either the vessels themselves or the stone to make the vessels were imported to the islands from Minoan Crete. A magnificent unfinished jar in *rosso antico* marble found at Thera (Akrotiri, Thera Excav. Storerooms) was in the course of manufacture by either a Theran or Minoan stone-carver when Akrotiri was destroyed in the volcanic eruption late in LC I.

The excavated towns on Kea and Thera have provided the most evidence of imported Minoan pieces, but a few are known from other islands. A small group of gypsum vessels from Thera appears to have come from the Syro-Palestinian region. After the destruction of Thera and the subsequent Minoan destructions, stone vases ceased to be made on the islands, and the few imported items found in later contexts were simply heirlooms.

C. Zervos: *L'Art des Cyclades du début à la fin de l'âge du bronze: 2500–1100 avant notre ère* (Paris, 1957) [excellent pls]

P. Getz-Preziosi: 'Early Cycladic Stone Vases', *Kunst und Kultur der Kykladeninseln im 3. Jahrtausend v. Chr.* (exh. cat., ed. J. Thimme; Karlsruhe, Bad. Landesmus., 1976); Eng. trans. as *Art and Culture of the Cyclades*, ed. P. Getz-Preziosi (Karlsruhe, 1977)

P. M. Warren: 'The Stone Vessels from the Bronze Age Settlement at Akrotiri, Thera', *Archaiol. Ephimeris* (1979), pp. 82–113

Cycladic Art: Ancient Pottery and Sculpture from the N. P. Goulandris Collection (exh. cat., ed. C. Doumas; London, BM, 1983)

T. Devetzi: 'Stone Carving-sculpture: Vessels', *Cycladic Culture: Naxos in the 3rd Millennium BC* (exh. cat., ed. L. Marangou; Athens, Mus. Cyclad. & Anc. Gr. A., 1990), pp. 117–35, nos 113–41

P. Getz-Gentle: *Stone Vessels of the Cyclades in the Early Bronze Age* (University Park, PA, 1996)

C. G. Doumas: *Early Cycladic Culture: The N. P. Goulandris Collection* (Athens, 2000)

C. G. Doumas: *Silent Witnesses: Early Cycladic Art of the Third Millennium BC* (New York, 2002)

Stratonikos. *See* Isigonos, epigonos, stratonikos and antigonos.

Stratos. Site in Akarnania, north-west Greece, on the west bank of the River Acheloos. The largest city and ancient capital of the region, it flourished from the 5th to the 2nd century BC. Preserved at the site are a theatre, traces of an agora with a stoa, a fortification wall, extramural tombs and a temple to Zeus. The site was investigated by the French School at Athens in

1892, 1910–11 and 1924. The Temple of Zeus was built of limestone and orientated east-west. It stood on a platform, partly projecting from the west city wall, with two statue bases, a treasury-like building and a structure that may have been either an altar or a stoa. The orthostat course of the cella wall still stands, and architectural fragments are scattered around, but the workmanship is not good, and the temple was probably unfinished. The stylobate (*c.* 32.5×16.5 m) carried a peristyle of 6×11 Doric columns attached to it with dowels. The profile and proportions of the capitals compare well with those from the South Stoa at Corinth (later 4th century BC). The cella was originally thought to have been unroofed, but a high threshold (h. 450 mm) and the lack of drainage argue against this reconstruction. No fragment of an internal colonnade has been found, although tooling on the orthostata suggests internal Corinthian or Ionic columns. This internal colonnade was probably three-sided, as at the Temple of Artemis at nearby Kalydon. The Temple of Zeus has been dated to the late 4th century BC on the basis of assumed contemporaneity of temple, temple platform and city wall. The city wall dates from *c.* 314 BC, when Stratos became the capital of a city-state comprising various local communities. At the point where the platform breaks through, however, the city wall shows evidence of reworking, suggesting that the temple may have been constructed later. Except for a central acroterion, no architectural sculpture has been found.

A. Joubin: 'Inscriptions de Stratos', *Bull. Corr. Hell.*, xvii (1893), pp. 445–52

A. K. Orlandos: 'O en Strato tis Akarnanias naos tou Dios' [The Temple of Zeus in Akarnanian Stratos], *Deltion Archaiol.*, viii (1923), pp. 1–51

C. Picard and F. Courby: *Recherches archéologiques à Stratos d'Acarnanie* (Paris, 1924)

R. L. Scranton: *Greek Walls* (Cambridge, MA, 1941)

Strongylion (*fl* Athens, late 5th century–*c.* 365 BC). Greek sculptor. Little is known of him although he apparently received some State commissions in Athens. He collaborated with Kephisodotos on a bronze group of *Muses on Mount Helikon* (Pausanias: *Guide to Greece* IX.xxx.1), and his *Artemis Soteira* at Megara (Pausanias: I.xl.2–3) may have been the model for that by Kephisodotos in Megalopolis (Pausanias: VIII.xxx.10; after 368/367 BC). He achieved fame as a sculptor of animals. His *Trojan Horse* (Pausanias: I.xxiii.8; 414 BC) had political connotations, as perhaps did a bronze bull (Pausanias: I.xxiv.2). Two other works seem to have particularly appealed to Hellenistic and Roman taste: an *Amazon* 'with beautiful thighs', which was carried around by Nero's entourage, and a boy, which Brutus, Julius Caesar's murderer, liked so much that it came to be known as 'Brutus' Boy' (Pliny: *Natural History* XXXIV.82). These were perhaps admired for their erotic beauty, but also doubtless for their lifelike appearance.

J. Overbeck: *Die antiken Schriftquellen zur Geschichte der bildenden Künste bei den Griechen* (Leipzig, 1868/*R* Hildesheim, 1959), nos 877–92

G. Lippold: *Die griechische Plastik*, Handbuch der Archäologie (Munich, 1950), pp. 189–90

Stucco. Decorative art that, at its simplest, is a render of mortar designed to decorate a smooth wall or ceiling and, in its more sophisticated form, is a combination of high-relief, sculptural and surface decoration. The words stucco and plaster are used virtually interchangeably and, most flexibly, can be applied to mixtures of mud or clay; more precisely, however, stucco usually means a hard, slow-setting substance based on lime as opposed to quick-setting plaster based on gypsum.

I. Introduction. II. Greek. III. Roman.

I. Introduction.

The origins of stucco probably lie in ancient Egypt, where stucco was employed either to supplement stone, as on the bust of *Nefertiti* (Berlin, Ägyp. Mus.), or to cast plaster busts from a death-mask before mummification. In addition, gypsum was widely used in Ancient Egypt as an architectural element. In Early Dynastic times walls were first coated with mud and plastered with gypsum before being painted. Gypsum was also frequently used to repair defects in the stone before the entire surface was carved; in this way the artist created plaster reliefs.

The Egyptian relief tradition was adopted in Crete during the Second Palatial period (1700–1400 BC), when low-relief stucco panels were used to decorate walls. Several examples of these panels, such as a charging bull (Herakleion, Archaeol. Mus.), decorated the palace at Knossos. In the 6th century BC in Greece, gypsum was used to smooth sculptures carved from porous stone, and actual sculptures made from gypsum are referred to by Pausanias (VIII.xxii.7).

II. Greek.

In seeking to establish the origins of architectural stucco and plasterwork in Hellenistic times, it is important to note that clay, and not gypsum, was widely used for wall-plastering in the Greek world, and it remained a major medium for architectural decoration. This preference for clay does not seem to have been related to the availability of gypsum and may be attributed to architectural tradition and fashion. Indeed, in the most important centres of Hellenism—such as Alexandria in Egypt and Begram in Afghanistan—stucco was used for models for silverwork and not for architectural decoration or sculpture. In other areas under Greek control or influence during the Hellenistic period, such as Etruria, Rome, Mesopotamia and Iran, architectural stucco decoration did develop, and, in spite of the above-mentioned tradition of clay architectural decoration, it has been argued that the Greeks were responsible for introducing it on a substantial scale.

Stucco was employed in both the art and the architecture of ancient Greece, and information about its application and composition is provided by archaeological remains and the accounts of the Roman authors Vitruvius (*On Architecture* VIII.i–iv) and Pliny (*Natural History* XXXVI.liii.174 lv.77). Its primary uses were to camouflage coarse stone or rubble masonry and to protect more perishable materials (e.g. wood), for relief decoration, and to form a base for wall painting. The earliest evidence for the use of stucco in the Aegean comes from Vasiliki on Crete, in buildings from the Early Minoan period (*c.* 3500/3000–*c.* 2050 BC). On mainland Greece the first lime stuccos are attested during the Middle Helladic period (*c.* 2050–*c.* 1600 BC) at palatial centres and other sites.

In the Archaic period (*c.* 700–*c.* 480 BC) evidence for the use of stucco comes mainly from temples and public buildings. It was applied to the surface of imperfect or poor-quality stone (especially the local limestones of Attica and the Peloponnese) to produce a white, marble-like appearance. On the Athenian Acropolis, for example, the '"H" Architecture' of porous limestone was coated with a fine layer of stucco to which marble dust had been added, so that when polished it would present an even surface. The existence of decorative stuccowork on Athenian grave monuments in the 6th century BC is implied by the legislation of Solon specifically prohibiting its use (Cicero: *De legibus* II.xxvi. 64–5), but no examples have survived. Also from the 6th century BC there is evidence for the use of volcanic pumice from the island of Thera to make waterproof stucco for a basin and drain channel in the Sanctuary of Asklepios at Corinth. A similar mixture of volcanic powder with stucco is seen on monuments from the Classical period, when marble architectural members were coated with stucco as a basis for painting. The interior walls in the Temple of Hephaistos at Athens, for example, were covered with a stucco containing a mixture of volcanic powder and straw as a basis for elaborate wall paintings, which are now known only from ancient descriptions.

In the Hellenistic period stuccowork was found in private establishments as well as sanctuaries. The houses from Delos and Olynthos are among the finest preserved examples of private domestic architecture (*see* ARCHITECTURE, §VI, 1(i)(c)) and illustrate the range and technique of decoration. In addition to coating wall surfaces for protection or for painting, stucco was used to imitate such architectural features as panels, stone dado courses, ashlar masonry with drafted edges, and three-dimensional decorative mouldings. One of the more important examples of relief stucco decoration comes from a private Macedonian tomb at Leukadia, dated *c.* 300 BC. Its façade is made completely from stucco applied to stone and moulded to imitate Doric and Ionic elements.

Further artistic uses of stucco are now known only from ancient authors. Pliny (*Natural History* XXXV. xliv.153) recorded that the Sikyonian artist Lysistratos (*fl c.* 350–*c.* 300 BC) was the first to model a likeness in plaster from a living face. This has been understood by some scholars to indicate the beginnings of realistic portraiture in ancient Greece. Pausanias (*Guide to Greece* VIII.xxii.7) saw a temple in the Sanctuary of Artemis at Stymphalos with images of the Stymphalian birds on the roof (probably acroteria), which seemed to be made of either wood or plaster.

R. Martin: *Matériaux et techniques* (1965), i of *Manuel d'architecture grecque* (Paris, 1965–)

A. Orlandos: *Les matériaux de construction et la technique architecturale des anciens grecs* (Paris, 1966)

P. Petsas: *Ho taphos ton Leukadion* [The grave at Leukadia] (Athens, 1966)

S. Hood: *The Arts in Prehistoric Greece*, Pelican Hist. A. (Harmondsworth, 1978)

III. Roman.

1. Introduction. 2. Technique. 3. Regional survey.

1. INTRODUCTION. Etruscan works in stucco from the Hellenistic period have survived in tombs, some of which, unfortunately, can only be roughly dated between the 4th and 1st centuries BC. Outstanding examples are to be seen on the walls and pilasters of the Tomb of the Painted Reliefs (Cerveteri; 3rd century BC), which are decorated with mythological motifs and representations of weapons and household utensils.

In support of the contested theory of the Greek origins for Roman architectural stucco (*see* §3(i)(a) below) is the fact that it was introduced after the absorption of Campania into the Hellenistic world *c.* 343 BC. The stucco decoration of the House of the Griffins in Rome (first half of the 2nd century BC) may demonstrate the influence of Alexandrian metalwork, both in design and execution. Later Roman stucco decoration reveals the existence of two successive schools. The late 1st-century BC stuccos (Rome, Mus. N. Romano) from a house near the Villa Farnesina in Rome, with their freedom of expression and an emphasis on landscapes, were succeeded by an increased use of ornamental elements, which became dominant in the early 1st century AD. During the reign of Hadrian, the Imperial style—a Neo-Attic vision of Greek art—was introduced and can be seen in the emperor's villa at Tibur (now Tivoli; *in situ*). Examples of Roman stucco from the 2nd and 3rd centuries AD have been discovered in tombs and Mithraea (e.g. the Mithraeum of Porta Maggiore, Rome), but the paucity of stucco remains during this late period may be a sign of the art's decreasing importance in Rome. Colour played an important part in stucco decoration: sometimes the whole scene was painted, but in other cases only the background was coloured, leaving the reliefs white.

2. TECHNIQUE. Roman stucco is a mixture with a base essentially of chalk, or occasionally plaster, to which powdered marble or less costly limestone or even sand is added, although the latter naturally produces a coarser and less durable mixture. Craftsmen probably tried to improve the plasticity, colour and

drying time of the paste, as they did in Renaissance times, by adding various ingredients, perhaps of organic origin, which would explain why they fail to be detected by analysis. While the base coat was still fresh a preliminary outline was traced with a point, indicating the general plan of the decoration and the positions of the motifs. Wet paste applied inside these outlines was then modelled with a spatula for the figures and scenes, while cornices and repeated motifs were formed by means of moulds and templates pressed into the stucco. The adhesion of elements in very high relief could be reinforced by attachment systems using nails and pegs of wood or bone. In principle there is no difference between a coating that is painted on and one applied as relief, and the same Latin terms—*opus tectorium* or *albarium*—refer to them both.

3. Regional Survey.

(i) Italy. (ii) Provinces

(i) Italy.

(a) Before *c.* 20 BC. (b) *c.* 20 BC–*c.* AD 50. (c) *c.* AD 50–79. (d) Late 1st century AD–2nd century.

(a) Before c. 20 BC. It was long thought that the art of stuccowork had been first discovered in Hellenistic Alexandria and was introduced to Rome after Sulla's conquest of Campania (89 BC). In fact as early as the beginning of the 2nd century BC this material probably entered the Roman repertory by way of the Pompeian First Style of wall painting (*see* Painting, §VI, 2(i)(a)), in which wall decoration imitates real architectural elements, primarily through the use of painting but also of relief, especially in the upper zones, with cornices and friezes that sometimes carry figural decoration. Indeed the earliest examples, both at Cosa and at Pompeii (*c.* 200 BC), are very similar to decorative schemes of the Hellenistic period at Delos, Priene and Pergamon, the origins of which are possibly Macedonian, as the tombs at Leukadia (*c.* 300 BC) and Aigai (Vergina; *c.* 350 BC) show.

In Rome stuccowork quickly developed into an independent art form, as it began to be used to cover the entire surface of ceilings, for which it was to remain the favourite method of decoration. At first, the stucco decoration followed architectural models, as in the earliest examples, such as the plain coffering on the vault in the House of the Griffins on the Palatine, Rome (variously dated between 100 and 60 BC). That artists were beginning to realize the potential of stucco, however, is shown in the lunette there, with its stiffly modelled high relief of two opposed griffins on either side of an acanthus shoot. Indeed, the exceptional malleability and versatility of the medium soon enabled artists to break free from the constraints imposed by architectural prototypes.

The House of the Cryptoporticus at Pompeii (*c.* 40 BC) provides the earliest example of this development in its full form: on the vault of the cryptoporticus (partially underground vaulted corridor) the traditional coffers have been replaced by a more complex scheme of rectangular panels enclosing lozenges, hexagons and squares decorated with various motifs. But it is, above all, in the small *tepidarium* of the baths that a definite advance is made: there the lunette is decorated with the earliest known figural scene in stucco, depicting cupids carrying the attributes of Hercules against a pastoral background with a tree and an altar.

(b) c. 20 BC–c. AD 50. The stucco decoration of the vaults of the house found under the present Villa Farnesina (*c.* 20 BC; Rome, Mus. N. Romano), carried out during the reign of Augustus, perhaps constitute the masterpiece of the stucco technique. In at least four rooms the rich use of colour in the magnificent wall paintings was balanced by the white barrel vaults divided into panels of various shapes by a complex stucco tracery. These panels are framed by egg-and-dart or wave mouldings and within them unfold stucco friezes of griffins fighting Arimasps, and cupids and Victories rising from vegetal scrolls and carrying weapons or facing each other on either side of candelabra. This building owes its fame above all to its figured panels and especially to the rare Dionysiac scenes, which have been interpreted as depicting the vital moments in an initiation ceremony: the reading of the sacred texts, offerings on the altar and—the climax of the initiate's reception—the unveiling of the *liknon* (winnowing basket) containing the sacred objects of the Mystery. Punctuating these scenes are landscapes of the 'sacral-idyllic' type, a term that conveys their twofold pastoral and religious character. The virtuosity of their expressive treatment was rarely equalled in later periods. They are modelled with an almost miniaturist precision; the relief is hardly more than 10 mm deep, yet it depicts views in perspective with bridges, rivers and small buildings in the shade of trees. Among these rustic buildings are porticos, tombs or sanctuaries with various types of roof, often in the shape of towers or supported by minuscule columns with ornate capitals. They are enlivened by human figures engaged in various occupations: fishermen, neighbours conversing or patting a dog, beggars, women and children engaged in pious acts; grazing cattle add to the bucolic atmosphere. The different planes are suggested by subtle gradations in the relief, the contours of which gradually blend in with the surface, itself applied with a spatula in an almost painterly manner, which the fine and malleable quality of the plaster allows. Several hands were at work, but in spite of their talent they remain anonymous, as do all the Roman stuccoists.

During this period stucco was popular for funerary monuments and baths where, in contrast to ordinary plaster, it proves particularly resistant to the damp conditions. Examples are the Baths of Venus at Baiae (first phase *c.* AD 14) and a tomb (No. 18) on the Via Laurentina at Ostia. The underground basilica near the Porta Maggiore at Rome, long thought to belong to the reign of Claudius but now dated to that of Tiberius, was probably a funerary hypogeum, even though its dimensions are unusually large (the cella with its three naves is 12 m long). In the vestibule stuccowork and painting are combined, but the whole of the cella, both walls and vaults, is covered with a layer of brilliant white stucco bearing narrative scenes (*in situ*). The walls are divided into panels, each one with a small landscape at its centre, of the type already seen in the Villa Farnesina, although much simplified. Most depict a simple enclosure surrounding a column or statue in the shade of a sacred tree, with an occasional figure praying or decorating what must be rural shrines rather than tombs, similar to those depicted in contemporary paintings. The scenes depicted on the vaults are varied and sometimes highly unusual. Serious genre scenes (e.g. pupils at school and in the palaestra) and grotesque scenes (e.g. pygmies dancing and other Egyptianizing themes) alternate with religious scenes and especially mythological subjects such as *Hercules and Hesione, Rape of the Daughters of Leucippus* and the *Rape of Ganymede*, while others are more unusual, for example the *Punishment of the Danaids* and *Apollo and Marsyas*, or apparently even unique, such as the large scene decorating the apse which has been interpreted as Sappho leaping from the cliff on Leukas. The scene, which takes place in Apollo's presence, shows a woman pushed by a cupid into the waves where sea creatures await her. The unconventional subject-matter has presented difficulties of interpretation. Carcopino (1927) believed that the basilica was a meeting-place for the Pythagorean sect and that these images represented the path followed by the wise Pythagorean whom the master's doctrines had rescued from the errors of mortals. Most of the scenes can, however, be explained perfectly well with reference to funerary symbolism, especially the rape scenes which frequently appear in tombs or on sarcophagi in the following century. The treatment of the vault owes much to sculpture, both in the quality of the modelling, which is in fairly high relief, and in the iconographic schemes. Some striking parallels to the terracotta Campana reliefs are evidence of the vitality of this art form, which never lost touch with other decorative techniques. It was able to build up a broad and original repertory of images and arrange them over the whole surface of large monuments.

(c) c. AD *50–79.* From the mid-1st century AD onwards, stucco was important in architectural decoration, as is seen in the Domus Aurea (*c.* AD 65), the house of Nero at Rome. Unfortunately, the present poor state of its wall surfaces means that it is impossible to tell whether it played as influential a role in the history of stuccowork as it played in the history of painting. In the famous *volta dorata*, stuccoed panels, in which some of the relief work was gilded, alternate with painted panels, a combination characteristic of the time of Nero, even though the scheme was known earlier and continued to be used long afterwards.

The most complete and detailed picture of the role of stuccowork in Roman art is provided by the evidence of the towns buried in the eruption of Vesuvius in AD 79. The earthquake of AD 62 had destroyed or damaged many buildings which were then redecorated, and work was still in progress on some when the eruption occurred 17 years later. Most of the stuccos can thus be dated to the reign of Vespasian, although in style there is little to distinguish them from what remains from the Neronian period. The largest and most beautiful stucco schemes occur in the public buildings, especially the baths: the Forum Baths, the Stabian Baths and the Suburban Baths at Pompeii, and the Suburban Baths at Herculaneum. The barrel vaults of the various rooms are covered with stucco reliefs; occasionally a simple fluted motif is enhanced by a cornice with polychrome mouldings, but in most cases the vault is adorned with an intricate if over-ornamental decorative scheme. In the men's *apodyterium* (changing room) of the Stabian Baths stucco tracery made up of octagons, with weapons and flying figures filling their centres, delineates squares arranged like diamonds and decorated with meanders. By contrast, the decoration in the vestibule is characterized by curved lines as rows of medallions alternate with concave-sided octagons decorated with sea-monsters, swans, cupids and other figures picked out against a polychrome background. The same wealth of ornamentation is found in the *tepidarium* of the Forum Baths, where foliated scrolls are juxtaposed with octagons, candelabra and rectangular panels bearing mythological scenes such as the *Rape of Ganymede* or figures such as a handsome Eros leaning on his bow. Often architectural motifs—niches, porticos or caryatids—occupy the lunettes and the wall space; these are inspired by the contemporary Pompeian Fourth Style paintings (*see* PAINTING, §VI, 2(i)(a)), but are sometimes rendered in monochrome as in the Suburban Baths at Pompeii and Herculaneum.

Stucco was also sometimes used to imitate stone, especially to hide rough hewn exteriors like a marble revetment on the entablatures of porticos or on the façades of buildings. In this role it sometimes adopted the same models as architectonic sculpture, for example in the coffered vault of the four-fronted arch in Herculaneum, but more often the material's plasticity encouraged freer and richer ornamentation, as in the divine and heroic couples decorating the walls of the *purgatorium* (building used for purification rites, supplied by water from the Nile) of the Temple of Isis at Pompeii, or the gladiatorial scenes (destr.) on the enclosing wall of the so-called tomb of Umbricius Scaurus. Even inside, sculpture was imitated by very high relief stucco, for example the warriors that stand out from the middle of the walls of a *vestibulum* (entrance-room) in the Suburban Baths at Herculaneum as if they were statues on bases.

Painting was used as the main decoration in private houses, but it was often combined with stucco on ceilings or less frequently on walls, for example in the *Iliad* frieze of the House of the Lararium at Pompeii depicting the *Death of Achilles*. Nevertheless, the joint between wall and ceiling was regularly emphasized by a moulded cornice in stucco, more or less richly decorated with lotus flowers, trefoils, leaf-and-dart mouldings and palmettes in various combinations.

Villas provide examples of some more prestigious works, for example the large niches with standing figures in the nymphaeum of the Villa S Marco at Stabiae and in the baths of the Petraro Villa nearby, the latter including a beautiful Narcissus. Finally, stucco was the favourite medium for funerary decoration, which is well illustrated by the tombs at Pozzuoli, where it covers the whole surface, the vault, the walls and the niches, with a repertory of symbolic figures, mainly Dionysian, as well as purely decorative designs.

(d) Late 1st century AD–2nd century. Extant stuccos from succeeding periods, though less numerous, are of sufficient quality to show that the art form continued to play an important part in architectural decoration alongside painting and mosaic. It was popular in emperors' residences, for example in the Palatine complex at Rome, in Domitian's villa at Castelgandolfo (*c.* AD 80) and in Hadrian's Villa at Tibur (Tivoli; *c.* AD 130–*c.* 140), as well as on some prestigious monuments, such as the coffered vaults in the entrances of the Colosseum (*c.* AD 80). The best preserved examples, however, come from tombs, especially in the cemeteries on the Isola Sacra near Ostia, where many of the decorative schemes date from the reign of Hadrian; the vault and the niches from the tomb of P. Aelius (Ostia Antica, Mus. Ostiense) are unusual in having the names of the protagonists inscribed below the scenes depicted, one being Protesilaus and Laodameia. Two tombs on the Via Latina in Rome are masterpieces, the contrasting styles of which testify to the creativity of the workshops of this period. The tomb of the Pancratii (*c.* AD 165–*c.* 170) has a decorative scheme adapted to fit the surface of the new groined vault, its richness reinforced with the use of polychromy, mainly of blues and reds. Colour is used not only in the still-lifes and painted landscapes which alternate with mythological scenes in relief—the *Judgement of Paris, Priam and Achilles*—but also on the plain background surfaces where it brings out the decorations in relief. On the other hand, the barrel vault in the slightly later tomb of the Valerii, decorated with a regular stucco tracery of medallions and small panels emphasized by volutes, is striking for its whiteness and for the airy grace of the ornaments: sea-monsters, their bodies describing arabesques, carrying on their backs Tritons and Nereids with floating draperies. The contemporary tomb of Valerius Herma in the Vatican cemetery underneath St Peter's in Rome shows another aspect of the stuccowork of this period. Its large niches are decorated with figures in high relief, suggesting statues, which portray gods—Mercury, Diana, Minerva, Somnus—and philosophers as well as members of the family of the tomb's founder.

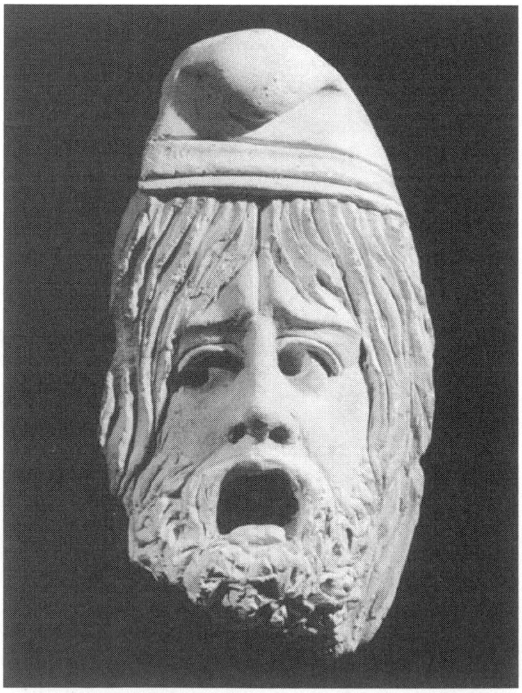

Stucco cornice decoration, modelled on a Hellenistic theatrical mask, from Apameia, Syria (Palmyra, Musée de Palmyra)

(ii) Provinces. Stucco decoration spread throughout the Empire in the 2nd century AD: the most important decorative schemes in the provinces date to this period and to the following centuries. Good examples are the theatrical masks decorating cornices found at Apameia in Syria (Palmyra, Mus. Palmyra; see fig.), the funerary reliefs depicting a reading scene and the dead woman at her toilette found near Carthage (Carthage, Mus. N.), the heads in high relief from Cuicul (now Djemila) in Algeria (Djemila, Mus. Archéol.) or the coffered vaults of Ephesos (Turkey) or Aquincum (Hungary). More modest remains, mainly moulded cornices, have been found in many houses in Gaul. Finally, several buildings at Ravenna attest the continuing popularity of stuccowork in Early Christian art.

K. Ronczewski: *Gewölbeschmuck im römischen Altertum* (Berlin, 1903)

E. Wadsworth: 'Stucco Reliefs of the First and Second Century Still Extant in Rome', *Mem. Amer. Acad. Rome*, iv (1924), pp. 9–102

J. Carcopino: *La Basilique pythagoricienne de la Porte Majeure* (Paris, 1927)

F. L. Bastet: 'Claudius oder Tiberius? Das grosse Hypogaeum bei der Porta Maggiore zu Rom', *Bull. Ver. Bevord. Kennis Ant. Besch.*, xxxv (1960), pp. 1–24

N. Dacos: *La Découverte de la Domus Aurea et la formation des grotesques* (London, 1969)

R. J. Ling: 'Stucco Decoration in pre-Augustan Italy', *Pap. Brit. Sch. Rome*, xl (1972), pp. 11–57

H. Mielsch: *Römische Stuckreliefs* (Rome, 1975) [complete repertory and exhaustive bibliog.]

R. J. Ling: 'Stuccowork', *Roman Crafts*, ed. D. Strong and D. Brown (London, 1976), pp. 209–21

M. Frizot: *Stucs de Gaule et des provinces romaines* (Dijon, 1977)

N. Blanc: 'Le Courant paysagiste dans la décoration en stuc', *Rev. Archéol.*, i/1 (1983), pp. 51–78
N. Blanc: 'Les Stucateurs romains: Témoignages littéraires, épigraphiques et juridiques', *Mél. Ecole Fr. Rome: Ant.*, xcv (1983), pp. 859–907
U. Riemenschneider: *Pompejanische Stuckgesimse des dritten und vierten Stils* (Frankfurt, 1986)
R. Ling: *Stuccowork and Painting in Roman Italy* (Aldershot and Brookfield, VT, 1999)
L. Sonzogni: *Lo stucco lucido: Dall'antichita ai giorni nostri* (Bergamo, 2004)

Stylobate. Term for the upper part of the STEREOBATE in a Classical temple. This platform, which supports the colonnade, usually comprises three steps; strictly, however, only the top step should be referred to as the stylobate, the three together forming the crepidoma.

Sufetula [now Sbeïtla]. Tunisian site on the Roman road from Carthage to Thevestis, on a plateau on the west bank of a deep wadi. The original nucleus of 9 ha was divided into centuriations at the time of the Flavians (*reg* AD 69–96), the name of the new foundation being a diminutive form of Sufes, a castellum situated a journey stage to the north-east. With abundant springs, easily accessible quarries and farmland, it flourished in the 3rd and 4th centuries AD, covering an area of *c.* 50 ha and possessing a population of *c.* 10,000; its principal source of revenue was olive oil (many presses survive). There was a bishop as early as AD 256.

Among the buildings visible today are the forum complex, with a monumental triple archway (AD 139; see fig.) dedicated to Antoninus Pius, an enclosed square with colonnades on three sides and three temples on the fourth side dedicated to the Capitoline triad. The pseudo-dipteral prostyle temples stand on podia and are linked by small arches at the rear; the central temple is in the Composite order, while the flanking temples are Corinthian. Other notable monuments are the Arch of Diocletian (*c.* AD 284–*c.* 305), baths (3rd century AD), fountains (second half of the 4th century), a theatre (late 3rd century to early 4th) and an amphitheatre (*c.* 4th century). Other artefacts discovered during excavation include pottery, sculpture, inscriptions, stelae and coins (some in Tunis, Mus. N. Bardo).

A. Merlin: *Forum et églises de Sufétula* (Tunis, 1912)
F. Cabrol and H. Leclercq: *Dictionnaire d'archéologie chrétienne*, xv (Paris, 1950), cols 949–80
N. Duval: *Les ruines de Sufetula Sbeitla* (Tunis, 1973)
N. Duval: *L'Urbanisme de Sufétula=Sbeïtla, Tunisie* (Berlin, 1982), II/x/2 of *Aufstieg und Niedergang der römischen Welt*, ed. H. Temporini (Berlin and New York, 1972-), pp. 596–632
R. B. Hitchner: *Studies in the History and Archaeology of Sufetula and its Territorium down to the Vandal Conquest* (diss., Ann Arbor, U. MI, 1982)
F. Bejaoui: *Sbeïtla: L'Antique Sufetula* (Tunis, 1994)
W. Kuhoff: 'Tempel, Thermen und Theater', *Ant. Welt*, xxxvi/5 (2005), pp. 55–61

Surveying. In antiquity surveying was necessary both for civil engineering projects and for building construction. The surveyor in the Greek world, whether measuring the land or buildings, used the plumb-line and water-level in association with a geometrical figure implied in both devices, the right-angled triangle. The Hellenistic Temple III at DIDYMA preserves in its fabric the carefully constructed 'drawings' from which it was built. One of the most celebrated of all ancient surveying exercises, the alignment of a water-supply tunnel at Samos, is credited to Eupalinos of Megara (*fl c.* 520 BC), who located the ends of the tunnel on opposite sides of a mountain and guided the engineers with sufficient accuracy to achieve a closing error of *c.* 5 m over a distance of 1.04 km. (On the units and instruments of measurement, *see* ARCHITECTURE, §IV, 3(iii).)

The skills of the surveyors made possible the unprecedented mastery of civil engineering shown in Roman irrigation and dams, roads and bridges, amphitheatres and theatres. Both written sources and surviving artefacts provide evidence of methods and equipment for the Roman period. There were three main instruments: the *groma*, a plumb-line device for setting right angles; the *chorobates*, a large water-level described by Vitruvius with particular reference to aqueduct levelling (*On Architecture*, VIII.v); and the *dioptra*, a more complex and versatile instrument recommended by Heron of Alexandria (*fl c.* AD 60) for surveying land, setting out buildings, tunnels and harbours, and for astronomical observation (*Dioptra*, III–V). Land surveying was fundamental to Roman life, for it was required to settle disputes over boundaries and to allocate land, especially by centuriation,

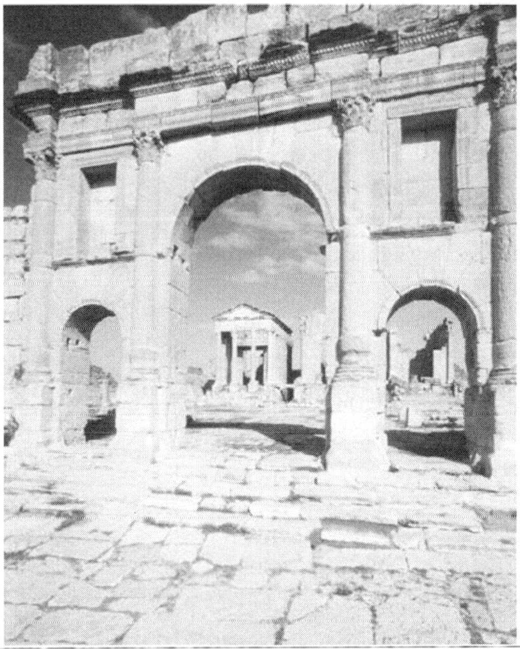

Sufetula, archway dedicated to Antoninus Pius, AD 139

in which the *agrimensores* divided the land into plots of 2400 sq. ft.

J. Goodfield and S. Toulmin: 'How Was the Tunnel of Eupalinus Aligned?', *Isis*, lvi/1 (1965), pp. 46–55
O. A. W. Dilke: *The Roman Land Surveyors* (Newton Abbot, 1971)
M. J. T. Lewis. *Surveying Instruments of Greece and Rome* (Cambridge, 2001)

Swing Painter (*fl c.* 540–*c.* 520 BC). Greek vase painter. He is named after an Athenian Black-figure amphora (Boston, MA, Mus. F.A., 98.918) depicting a demure lady on a swing observed by two men on either side; a similar amphora is in the Louvre. Abandoning the solemn themes and meticulousness of his mentors, he preferred loose compositions of charming half-pious, half-sheepish yokels with large flat feet, slouching posture and drooping heads who 'all look like geese' (Beazley, 1931/2). These scenes are often unusual or humorous (e.g. men walking on stilts or naked and beset by bees); others, however, are more conventional (e.g. warriors preparing for battle or fighting, or Herakles or Athena with their adversaries), though even here the warriors' sweet demeanour makes their warfare unconvincing. The artist's earlier paintings were much closer to the mainstream tradition of such mid-6th-century BC masters as EXEKIAS. They contain dense and intricate compositions, heavy with horses and muscular warriors, in which sombre men and women gather round departing chariots. Though they are often excellent technically, their appeal is evanescent; the artist's fame derives from his later modest, colloquial style and quirky subjects. Though only a lesser painter, the Swing Painter was prolific, decorating over 150 extant pieces (e.g. in Paris, Louvre; Rome, Villa Giulia; St Petersburg, Hermitage; London, BM; Munich, Staatl. Antikensamml.).

J. D. Beazley: 'Groups of Mid-sixth-century Black-figure', *Annu. Brit. Sch. Athens*, xxxii (1931–2), pp. 1–22
J. D. Beazley: *Black-figure* (1956), pp. 304–10
J. D. Beazley: *Paralipomena* (1971), pp. 132–5
E. Böhr: *Der Schaukelmaler* (Mainz, 1982)
E. Böhr: 'Weitere Werke des Schaukelmalers', *Praestant Interna: Festschrift für Ulrich Hausmann* (Tübingen, 1982), pp. 213–20

Symposion [Gr.: 'drinking together']. Highly ritualized drinking party that developed in Archaic and Classical Greece. Initially restricted to aristocratic circles, participants were exclusively male; women, if they attended at all, attended in subordinate roles as servants, dancers, musicians, prostitutes or more refined courtesans (Gr. *hetairai*). A symposion took place in specially constructed room, the *andron* (men's room), fitted to accommodate a series of *klinai* (dining couches) along the walls and usually recognizable in the archaeological footprint of a house through its off-centre doorway. Food was a secondary element; it was offered first and served on small, low tables standing in front of the couches. After the meal and a sacrifice, the drinking began. Revellers elected one of their number as *symposiarch*, or master of proceedings, whose task it was to decide the pace of drinking and ratio of wine to water to be imbibed (Greeks always diluted their wine; drinking it undiluted was considered barbaric); he would also determine a topic for conversation. Symposia could range from highly philosophical discourse (as immortalized in Plato's famous dialogue, *Symposion*; and also in the works of Xenophon) to more straightforward drinking sessions accompanied by rowdy songs and specific games, such as *kottabos*, where the dregs at the bottom of a cup had to be aimed at a specific target. Symposia could include a strong erotic element, sometimes leading to homo- or heterosexual love-making, in the latter case, however, only with prostitutes. The iconography of the Greek symposion is well known through representations on vessels of the type used during the event: mixing bowls, coolers, wine jugs, various types of drinking cups etc. The symposion was a male bonding ritual that encouraged class cohesion. As a private event that encouraged free speech, it could potentially be politically subversive. In 5th-century Athens, wider circles of society appear to have taken up the custom; it is noteworthy that the new standard-type houses in Peiraeus all seem to have featured *andrones*.

In educated circles of the hellenized Roman élite, Greek-style symposia with a focus on Classical entertainment and learned discourse were sometimes staged.

F. Lissarrague: *Un flot d'images: Un esthétique du banquet grec* (Paris, 1987)
O. Murray, ed.: *Sympotica: A Symposion on the Symposion* (Oxford, 1990)
K. Vierneisel, ed.: *Kunst der Schale: Kultur des Trinkens* (Munich, 1990)
P. Schmitt-Pantel: *La cité au banquet: Histoire des repas publics dans les cités greques* (Rome, 1992)

Syracuse [Siracusa]. Site of a city in south-east Sicily. From the early 5th century BC until its destruction by the Saracens in AD 878 it was the leading city of Sicily and, for a time, of the Greek world.

Greek colonists from the Corinthia founded Syracuse in the second half of the 8th century BC (734 BC according to Thucydides) on the island of Ortygia, where the famous Fountain of Arethusa is located (see fig. 1a). Soon after the foundation, a city plan was set out, which continued on to the mainland and connected the early settlement with the contemporary cemetery at Fusco. It became the basis for the regular urban development of the city over the next centuries. Systematic archaeological work has revealed much of the ancient city; finds, including all those mentioned below, are well displayed in the Museo Archeologico Regionale 'Paolo Orsi'.

Syracuse displayed her wealth in boldly innovative architectural monuments built of local limestone. The temples of Apollo (*c.* 565 BC; see fig. 1b)

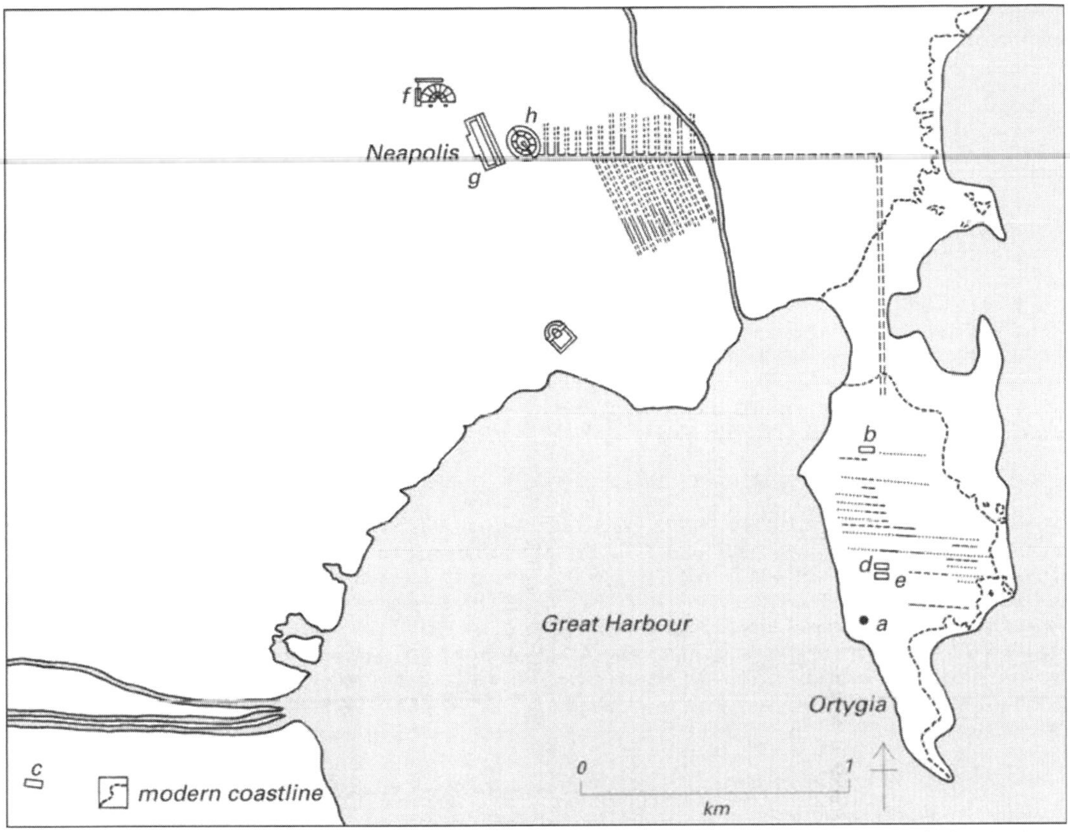

1. Syracuse, plan, 6th century BC–1st century AD: (a) Fountain of Arethusa; (b) Temple of Apollo; (c) Temple of Olympian Zeus; (d) Ionic temple; (e) Temple of Athena; (f) theatre; (g) altar of Hieron II; (h) amphitheatre

and Olympian Zeus (*c.* 550 BC; see fig. 1c) are among the earliest peripteral Doric temples designed entirely of stone. Both are impressively heavy in proportion, with 6×17 closely spaced monolithic columns, a deep porch created by a second row of columns, an adyton and an elaborately patterned terracotta roofing system with trumpet-shaped waterspouts. In the late 6th century BC Syracuse began construction on the only peripteral Ionic temple known in Sicily (1d). To celebrate his victory over the Carthaginians in 480 BC, the tyrant Gelon commissioned a new temple to Athena (1e), parallel to and of the same scale as the Ionic temple, but Doric in order. Early Classical in style, it had 6×14 columns and was crowned by an imported marble sima with lion-head waterspouts.

Neapolis was developed with a theatre (1f), monumental altar 198 m long (1g), stoas, nymphaeum and sacred precincts during the city's Hellenistic resurgence under the rule of Hieron II (*reg* 275–215 BC). The theatre is one of the largest in the Greek world (diam. 138 m) and influenced both Sicilian and Roman design. The nearby amphitheatre (1h; see fig. 2), one of the few in Sicily, probably dates to the refounding of the city as a Roman colony under Augustus. The city's sophisticated defences survive particularly well in the fort and gates at Euryalus.

Finds from the cemeteries of the late 8th century BC to the early 5th include imports from Corinth, East Greece and later Athens. Vibrantly decorated Subgeometric kraters (early 7th century BC) attest to the early development of local workshops. Much of the finest sculpture was crafted in terracotta, for example the Gorgon plaque (early 6th century BC), a large votive relief with *Demeter and Persephone* (late 6th century BC) and richly painted, life-size female busts associated with the cult of Demeter and Persephone (5th–3rd century BC). Early sculpture in stone includes the limestone Laganello head (early 6th century BC) and a marble draped kouros (late 6th century BC). Later works of high quality include a marble statuette of the young *Herakles* in Lysippan style (*c.* 300 BC), two life-size bronze rams (early 3rd century BC; one now in Palermo, Mus. Reg.) and the *Venus Landolina* (2nd-century AD copy after a Greek original of the 2nd century BC).

The city was probably a centre for the production of Sicilian Red-figure vases by such artists as the Chequer Painter and the Dirce Painter in the first half of the 4th century BC and the Lentini-Manfria Group in the second half; favourite subjects include female figures or theatrical and Dionysiac scenes. Syracusan coinage is unparalleled, with the master engravers Eumenes, Eukleidas, Euainetos and Kimon signing

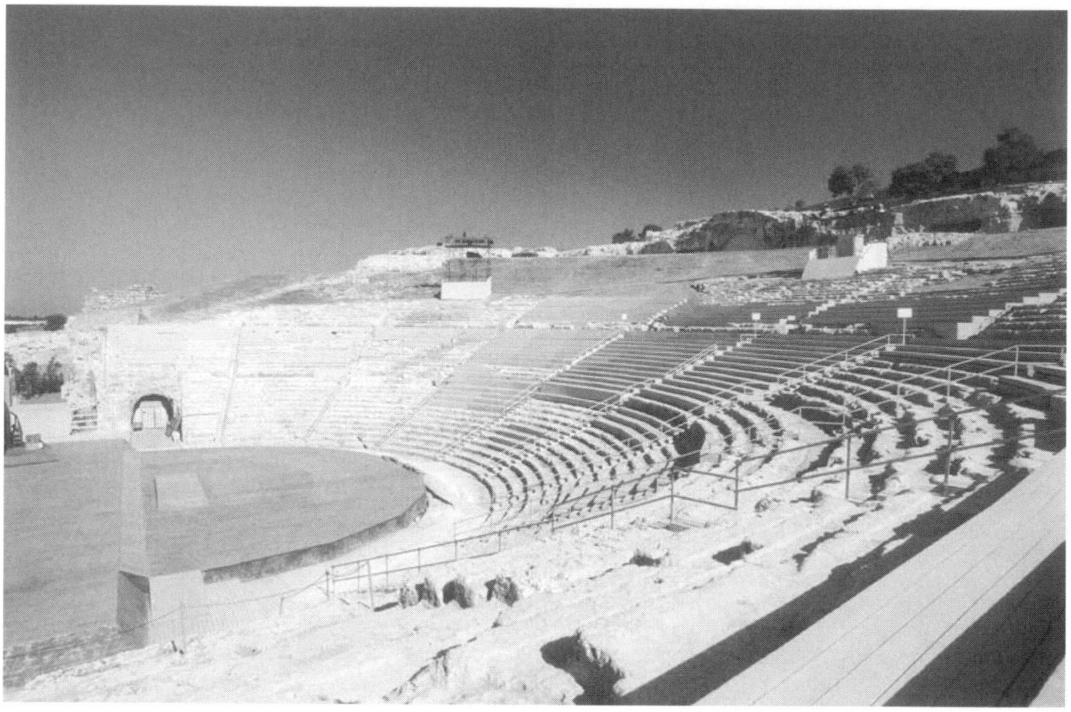

2. Syracuse, amphitheatre, early 1st century AD

their dies. In a series of representations of the female head (of Arethusa, Athena, Persephone, Kyane and Philistis) and the moving *quadriga*, the formal development of Greek art can be traced.

P. E. Arias: *Siracusa*, i, Corp. Vasorum Ant. (Rome, 1941–9)

P. Pelagatti and G. Voza, eds: *Archeologia nella Sicilia sudorientale* (Naples, 1973)

P. Pelagatti: 'L'attività della soprintendenza alle antichità della Sicilia orientale', *Kokalos* (1976–7), pp. 519–50 (548–50); *Kokalos* (1980–81), pp. 694–730 (707–11)

G. Vallet and E. Gabba, eds: *La Sicilia antica*, 2 vols (Naples, 1980)

L. Polacco and C. Anti: *Il teatro antico di Siracusa* (Rimini, 1981/2, 1990)

P. Pelagatti: *Annu. Scu. Archeol. Atene & Miss. It. Oriente*, lx (1982), pp. 117–62

G. P. Pugliese Carratelli, ed.: *Sikanie: Storia e civiltà della Sicilia greca* (Rome, 1985)

Syracuse, the Fairest Greek City: Ancient Art from the Museo Archeologico Regionale 'Paolo Orsi' (exh. cat., ed. B. D. Wescoat; Atlanta, GA, 1989–90)

P. Reichert-Südbeck: *Kulte von Korinth und Syrakus: Vergleich zwischen einer Metropolis und ihrer Apoikia* (Dettelbach, 2000)

Syros [Siros, Syra]. Greek island at the centre of the Cyclades group in the Aegean Sea. It has produced important Early Cycladic (EC) finds, mostly from the enormous EC II–IIIA (*c.* 2800–2150 BC) cemetery at Chalandriani in the north of the island, where about 500 graves were excavated by Tsountas. Much of the decorated pottery is painted in the style characteristic of EC II but some is EC IIIA (see colour pl. 2:XIII, fig. 2). Although the graves are essentially of the standard Cycladic cist type, they have features peculiar to Syros: corbelled upper walls and a false entrance (access being through the roof). The only Bronze Age excavated settlement is the remote EC IIIA fortress of Kastri (near Chalandriani, though the main settlement to which the cemetery belonged was some distance away). This consists of small houses crammed inside a walled circuit equipped with towers. In addition to pottery, some important metal objects were found: tools, weapons, pins, toilet articles and even a remarkable silver diadem (*c.* 2500–2200 BC; Athens, N. Archaeol. Mus.). Moulds and crucibles (Athens, N. Archaeol. Mus.) were also uncovered, together with the remains of a smelting hearth. Another cemetery, Ayios Loukas, produced some Middle Cycladic pottery, but otherwise the prehistoric finds from Syros are exclusively Early Cycladic.

C. Tsountas: 'Kykladika', *Archaiol. Ephimeris* (1899), pp. 73–134

J. L. Caskey: 'Chalandriani in Syros', *Essays in Memory of Karl Lehmann* (New York, 1964), pp. 63–9

E.-M. Bossert: 'Kastri auf Syros', *Archaiol. Deltion*, xxii/A (1967), pp. 53–76

B. Knittlmayer: 'Wiedervereinigte Funde von der Kykladeninsel Syros', *Jb. Berlin. Mus.*, xliii (2001), pp. 37–52

J. J. Hekman: *The Early Bronze Age Cemetery at Chalandriani on Syros (Cyclades, Greece)* (n.p. 2003)

TU

Ṭabaqat Faḥil. *See* PELLA (i).

Tablinum. Main reception room of an ancient Roman house, located at the far side of the atrium. The term probably originally referred to the master bedroom. The tablinum was also used as a study for keeping records and personal documents.

Tadmor. *See* PALMYRA.

Talos Painter (*fl c.* 410–*c.* 390 BC). Greek vase painter. He is named after a large Attic Red-figure volute krater (Ruvo di Puglia, Mus. Jatta, 1501; see colour pl. 2:XIII, fig. 3) depicting a rarely illustrated episode from the voyage of the Argonauts, the *Death of the Bronze Giant Talos.* The artist seems to have preferred such large vases, which he decorated with big figures in a florid style, employing much added white paint. The figures' garments have elaborate patterns, favourite motifs including linked black palmettes, long black rays and waves; some vases have figural borders depicting battle scenes, Nikai, four-horse chariots and sphinxes. Musculature is carefully delineated and often shaded with dilute glaze to produce a strong sense of volume, while some heads are shown in three-quarter view. Garments are sometimes finely pleated in a mannered fashion. Beazley attributed only seven vases to the painter, but he apparently decorated at least four other extant specimens (U. Würzburg, Wagner-Mus., H 5708 a–c; Naples, Mus. Archeol. N., 2883; Rome, Villa Giulia, 2382; Potenza, Mus. Archeol. Prov., 54622). Apart from the story of Talos, the painter's subject-matter includes *Dionysos and Hephaistos Reclining under a Pergola*, the *Apotheosis of Herakles, Theseus and Peirithoos Sacrificing in the Presence of Helen*, a remarkable *Gigantomachy* and warriors fighting on foot and on horseback: some scenes seem to be inspired by contemporary megalographic wall paintings. The artist's own background is unclear, though his style may owe something to the Dinos Painter and the KADMOS PAINTER.

J. D. Beazley: *Red-figure* (1942, 2/1963), ii, pp. 1338–9

J. D. Beazley: *Paralipomena* (1971), p. 481

E. Simon: 'Dionysos und Hephaistos auf einem Kelchkrater des Talosmalers', *Pantheon*, xxxvi (1978), pp. 199–206

G. Greco: 'Un cratere del pittore di Talos da Serra di Vaglio', *Riv. Ist. N. Archeol. & Stor. A.*, n. s. 2, viii–ix (1985–6), pp. 5–35

M. Robertson: *The Art of Vase Painting in Classical Athens* (Cambridge, 1992), pp. 256–8

Tanagra. Site in Boiotia in central Greece, 25 km east of Thebes and 5 km south of Skimatarion.

1. Bronze Age. 2. Later Greek and Roman.

1. BRONZE AGE. The prehistoric settlements of the area have been no more than tested by excavation, especially Late Helladic (LH) or Mycenaean (*c.* 1600–*c.* 1050 BC) habitation sites near the two Mycenaean cemeteries that have been uncovered by T. G. Spyropoulos during excavations (1968–85). During the LH period Tanagra became a place of some importance, to judge from the two cemeteries. The first covers a slope at Gephyra, some 500 m south-east of the modern village of Tanagra, and the second was found 1200 m to the east of the same village, just above the plain and the Hellenic Air Force base. A total of 300 chamber tombs have been unearthed, each with a spacious chamber, irregularly cut in the soft rock, and long dromos (entrance passage). Other types of grave have been found in both cemeteries, the so-called fossa graves, and cist and pit graves. The two cemeteries date from the LH II to the LH IIIB 2 periods (*c.* 1500–*c.* 1180 BC), and their systematic excavation has revealed interesting Mycenaean funeral practices. The skeletal remains, though not very well preserved, prove that the dead were placed on the bottom of the chamber in niches cut in the dromoi of the tombs or, in some cases, buried in clay coffins called larnakes. They were regularly buried with pottery vases (stirrup jars, cups, kylikes, jugs, alabastra, kraters and amphorae), bronze weapons such as swords and knives, personal objects (pins and violin-type fibulae) and tools such as chisels and whetstones. Figurines and sealstones were also found in several tombs. The decorative patterns on the pottery clearly reflect the Mycenaean style as it evolved between LH II and LH IIIB 2.

Of principal interest are the painted Mycenaean clay sarcophagi found in the chamber tombs. These are orthogonal chests with low feet and flat lids (though some are gabled), *c.* 300 mm wide with a maximum length of 1.05 m. They were furnished with funeral gifts, mostly placed on their coverings. Such larnakes are customary in Crete, where they appear in the Prepalatial period, but they are very rare on the mainland.

That those at Tanagra are the richest and most homogeneous collection so far discovered cannot easily be accommodated within the usual assumption of a Minoan influence on mainland funeral practices. Indeed, the decorative as well as the figural representations on the Tanagra sarcophagi testify to a genuine Mycenaean tradition and above all to purely mainland funeral rites that are not encountered in Minoan Crete. Besides the motifs and religious symbols common to both cultural traditions (such as spiral patterns, palm-trees, birds, papyrus, cuttlefish, the double axe, horns of consecration), the whole cycle of funeral rites is represented on the Tanagra sarcophagi, with scenes of lamentation, prothesis and ekphora, funeral games and the cult of the dead. These verify the Mycenaean antiquity of the Homeric funeral rites and practices, an archaeological discovery of great importance to students of the heroic Greek tradition.

All the Mycenaean finds from Tanagra are housed in the Archaeological Museum, Thebes.

P. Ålin: *Das Ende der mykenischen Fundstätten auf dem griechischen Festland* (Lund, 1962), pp. 118–28

E. T. Vermeule: 'Painted Mycenaean Larnakes', *J. Hell. Stud.*, lxxxv (1965), pp. 123–48

Praktika Athen. Archaiol. Etaireias (1969–83) [excav. rep. by T. G. Spyropoulos]

S. P. Marinatos: 'From the Silent Earth', *Athens An. Archaeol.*, iii (1970), pp. 61–8

T. G. Spyropoulos: 'Anaskaphi eis to mykinaikon nekrotapheion tis Tanagras' [Excavations of the Mycenaean cemetery of Tanagra], ibid., pp. 184–97

T. G. Spyropoulos: 'Funèbre mais sensationnelle découverte à Tanagra', *Conn. A.*, ccxxx (1971), pp. 72–7

T. G. Spyropoulos: 'Mycenaean Tanagra: Terracotta Sarcophagi', *Archaeology*, xxv (1972), pp. 206–9

L. Phialon and S. Farrugio: 'Réflexions sur l'usage des larnakes et cercueils en Grèce mycénienne'. *Rev. Archéol.*, ii (2005), pp. 227–54

2. Later Greek and Roman. Apart from a reference to the region on a number of stamped tiles found *c.* 4 km from the site of modern Tanagra and dating from *c.* 700 BC, the earliest historical mention of Tanagra does not occur until 585 BC, when jointly with Megara it established the colony of Heraklei on the shores of the Black Sea and was also involved in the founding of Cumae in Italy. From as early as the 6th century BC Tanagra minted silver coins, which suggests that by that time it must have been prosperous. In 550 BC Tanagra, together with the two other principal Boiotian cities of Thebes and Haliartos, formed the Boiotian League; this alliance lasted until the end of the Persian Wars in 480 BC. Like Corinth in the Peloponnese, Tanagra seems to have been a centre for the manufacture of terracotta roof tiles in the region. Some of these are signed by the makers Dabychos and Priknon. This production must have been of some importance, as exports have been found as far afield as Aigina and other parts of Greece.

Three famous battles were fought near the city: Tanagra and Oinophyta in 457 BC and, in 424 BC, Delion, where many of the city's youth fell—their names are inscribed on a stele now in the museum there. Between 386 and 374/372 BC it was occupied by a Spartan garrison, and in 338 BC it lost its freedom when Philip of Macedon subjugated the rest of Greece. Three years later Thebes revolted against Philip's son and successor, Alexander the Great, and was completely destroyed. Tanagra now became the leading Boiotian city and flourished commercially, if not politically. During the later 4th century BC and much of the 3rd century BC Tanagra was probably the richest of the Boiotian cities. Although part of the Kingdom of Macedonia from 338 to 288 BC, it was precariously independent from 288 to 244 BC, when it reverted to external rule. The affluence of Tanagra in this period is reflected in innumerable sculpted gravestones and the famous terracotta 'Tanagra figurines' (see figs. 1 and 2), which often depict domestic scenes. The return of Macedonian government brought a century of social and political unrest and mob rule, which ended only in 146 BC, when Tanagra fell to the Romans. By 145 BC Rome had granted the city the status of *civitas libera et immunis*. According to Strabo, by the 1st century AD Tanagra and Thespiai were the only wealthy cities in Boiotia.

The site has yet to be excavated systematically. Herakleides, who visited the city in the 3rd century BC, left a vivid account:

> The city stands in a high and rugged situation, and has a white argillaceous appearance. The houses are handsomely adorned with porticos and encaustic paintings. The country does not abound in corn but its wine is the best in Boiotia. The people are blest with substance, but simple in their way of life; they are all farmers, not manufacturers. They are strict to observe justice, honour and hospitality. They give freely of their goods to their needy fellow-townsmen and to tramps, for they are utter strangers to meanness and to cheese-paring. It is the safest city in all Boiotia for a stranger to dwell in.

Writing in the 2nd century AD, Pausanias gave a good description of the city's monuments in his *Guide to Greece*. Unfortunately, no trace can be seen of the temples, public buildings or statues that once adorned the city. Pausanias (*Guide to Greece* IX.xxii.3) also mentioned as a native of Tanagra the poetess Korinna, whose grave he saw during his visit there.

Of all the deities worshipped in Tanagra, the two most important appear to have been Dionysos and Hermes, whose cult statue was the work of the Athenian sculptor Kalamis; a temple at nearby Soros dedicated to the mother of the gods was excavated in 2002. The only ancient building in Tanagra readily identifiable today is the theatre, the bare outline of which can be discerned in the south-west sector of the city. To the north, the ruins of the gymnasium have been identified, famous in Pausanias' time for housing a painting depicting Korinna tying her hair with a ribbon for the victory she won over Pindar at Thebes. The city walls are often considered among the most impressive monuments in Greece, exemplifying Aristotle's dictum (*Politics* VII.x.8) that a wall ought to be an ornament as well as a protection.

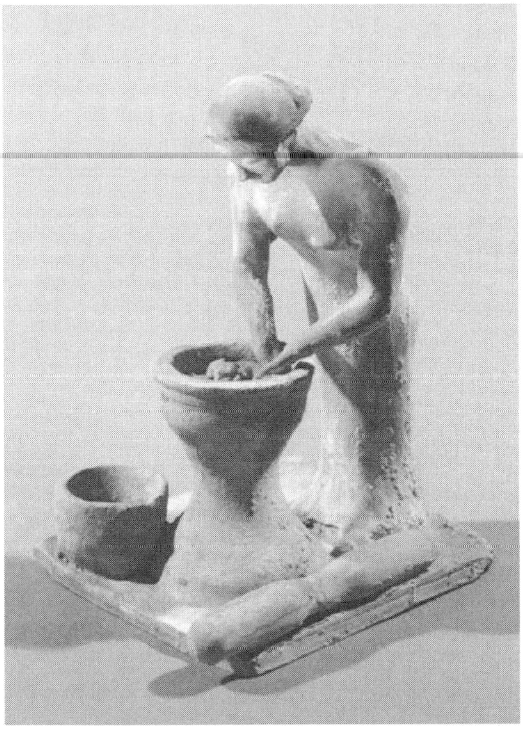

1. Tanagra, terracotta figurine of *Woman Kneading Dough,* h. 110 mm, *c.* 525–*c.* 475 BC (Paris, Musée du Louvre)

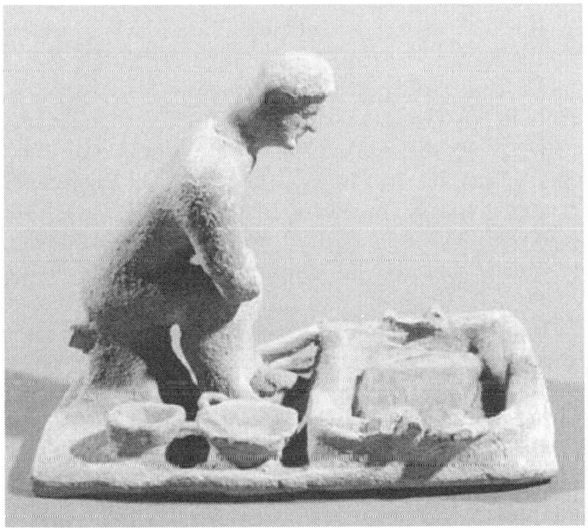

2. Tanagra, terracotta figurine of *Woman Cooking, c.* 575 BC (Paris, Musée du Louvre)

R. E. Wycherley: *How the Greeks Built Cities* (London, 1949, rev. 1962)

F. Pfister: *Die Reisebilder des Herakleides* (Vienna, 1951)

M. Xagorari-Gleissner: 'Das vergessene Heiligtum: Das Heiligtum der Göttermutter in Soros bei Tanagra', *Ant. Welt,* xxxiv/5 (2003), pp. 491–7

Tanagra: Mythe et archéologie (exh. cat., Paris, Louvre; Montreal, Mus. F.A., 2004) [Eng. version: *Tanagra: A Small World in Clay*]

Taras [Lat. Tarentum; now Taranto, Italy]. Site of the easternmost Greek colony in South Italy, founded by Lakonian settlers in the late 8th century BC. Although surrounded by a hostile native population, it had the finest port on the southern coast of Italy and flourished as a trading power, particularly from the late 5th century BC to the 4th, under the philosopher–statesman Archytas. Taras submitted to the advancing power of Rome in 272 BC, after Pyrrhos I, king of Epiros (*reg* 307–302, 297–272 BC), was driven back to Greece. As an important artistic centre, only Syracuse among the western Greek colonies rivalled Taras, and its influence on Roman culture was considerable. (Unless otherwise stated, artefacts discussed below are in the Museo Nazionale di Taranto.)

Some of the many public buildings mentioned by ancient authors (e.g. Strabo: *Geography* VI.iii.1) survived until the 1880s but were destroyed in the process of urban expansion. All that remains of the earliest Greek monumental stone temple in South Italy are the stout columns and substructure, freed from the walls of a former monastery. Its carinated Doric capitals and proportions date it to the first quarter of the 6th century BC and reflect the architectural influence of the Peloponnese and Corfu. This and the substructure of a temple under the medieval church of S Domenico are the only remains of Greek monumental temples, located at opposite ends of the acropolis, at the western end of the narrow peninsula, now an island, where the earliest settlement was made.

Taras expanded eastwards along the peninsula in the 5th century BC, and the eastern city walls, large stretches of which have been uncovered, enclosed both houses and tombs, an anomalous situation that was considered by contemporary visitors to be Taras' single most remarkable feature. The tombs lined the projected grid plan of the city's streets, and, together with the small funerary shrines (*naïskoi*) erected over them, they provide the fullest evidence of Tarentine architecture and sculpture, especially a long series of terracotta antefixes (6th–3rd century BC), which decorated the *naïskoi*. The *naïskoi* of the late 4th century BC–early 3rd display rich decoration. Hybrid figured capitals, ultimately of Near Eastern origin, represent, as do the figured column bases, an intermediate stage between influences from Greece and Asia Minor and later Etruscan and Roman architecture. Early Hellenistic underground tomb chambers reflect the influence of Macedonian funerary architecture as well as native traditions. Tomb walls of the 3rd–2nd century BC were painted with Alexandrian motifs, which later appear on the walls of houses at Pompeii. The many metopes, friezes and acroteria, with scenes from mythology and small figures, like the architectural decorative elements in a fine, white limestone (*pietra terera*), provide the fullest evidence of Tarentine art in the period *c.* 350–*c.* 275 BC. Six exceptionally large reliefs from an impressive tomb, possibly that of an officer in Pyrrhos' army, represent a *Battle between Greeks and Barbarians* and evince a fully developed 'Baroque' style in the first quarter of the 3rd century BC, a century earlier than the Great Altar at Pergamon.

In terms of sculpture, major Tarentine works of the Archaic period are rare, though the bronze *Zeus* from Ugento (*c.* 525–*c.* 500 BC) may have been made at Taras. It is one of the earliest hollow-cast Greek bronzes and was originally mounted on a Doric capital. A marble *Seated Goddess* (*c.* 500–*c.* 450 BC; Berlin, Antikensamml.), possibly by a local sculptor, shows the strong influence of works from Aigina. Metalwork includes a fine silver medallion depicting Aphrodite seated on a rock (*c.* 300–200 BC; London, BM; see fig.); it may originally have decorated a bowl.

Many surviving terracotta figurines, plaques, busts and masks testify to the varied cults of the city. Archaic and Classical terracottas often represent a bearded Dionysos-Hades reclining with Persephone, often accompanied by an infant, and the Dioskouroi are also frequent subjects. Graceful dancers and acrobats reflect the importance of the performing arts in Hellenistic Taras. Local workshops may have produced the numerous examples of filigree gold jewellery with exuberant vegetal motifs, found in Apulian and Tarentine tombs. From *c.* 425 to *c.* 300 BC Red-figure pottery was produced in greater quantity at Taras than at any other ancient centre, and these vases were widely traded. Mythological, theatrical and funerary scenes are the usual subjects.

P. Wuilleumier: *Tarente: Des Origines à la conquête romaine* (Paris, 1939)

Taranto nella civilità della Magna Grecia: Atti del decimo convegno di studi sulla Magna Grecia: Taranto, 1970

J. C. Carter: *The Sculpture of Taras* (Philadelphia, 1975)

A. D. Trendall: *The Red-figured Vases of Apulia*, 3 vols (Oxford, 1978–82)

E. M. De Juliis and others: *Gli ori di Taranto in età ellenistica* (Milan, 1986)

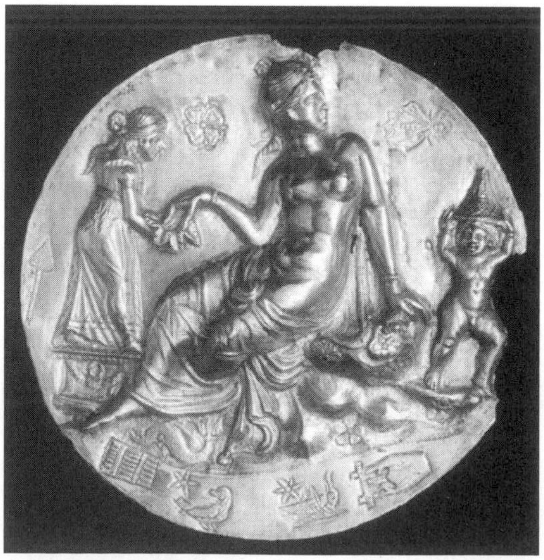

Taras, silver medallion depicting *Aphrodite*, diam. 93 mm, *c.* 300–200 BC (London, British Museum)

P. G. Guzzo and others: *Il museo di Taranto: Cento anni di archeologia* (Martina Franca, 1988)

E. Lippolis and others: *Catalogo del Museo Nazionale Archeologico di Taranto,* 4 vols (Taranto, 1992–2001)

Tarchon. *See* TARRACO.

Tarquinia [Etrus. Tarchuna, Tarxna; Gr. Tarkunia; Lat. Tarquinii]. Site of one of the most important Etruscan cities, on a hill *c.* 5 km from the Tyrrhenian coast and *c.* 92 km north-west of Rome. The modern town of Tarquinia, known as Corneto until 1922, is on a hill slightly to the west of the ancient site. The legendary founder of Tarquinia was Tarchon (Strabo: *Geography* V.cclxxix). During the Early Iron Age several small, dispersed settlements occupied the site, and the cemeteries associated with these, containing many cremation burials, have provided the most copious finds of any Etruscan centre of this period. During the 8th century BC the settlements combined and Tarquinia began to develop into a powerful Etruscan city-state. The occurrence of more elaborate burials at this time (e.g. the Tomb of the Warrior) further suggests the emergence of a ruling élite. In the Orientalizing period large chamber tombs, for inhumation rather than cremation burial, began to be constructed, and a particularly important tomb-group of Orientalizing artefacts was found in the Bocchoris Tomb (*c.* 670 BC). Between the late 7th century BC and the mid-6th the Tarquinian port Gravisca developed into an emporium, facilitating the trade with Greece, and in Tarquinia itself several Etrusco-Corinthian Black-figure pottery workshops were established.

The earliest of the painted tombs in the Monterozzi necropolis, for which Tarquinia is famous, date from around 570–560 BC; these soon show Ionic Greek influence, later succeeded by Attic. Particularly fine 6th-century BC tombs include the Tomb of the Bulls (*c.* 530 BC; see colour pl. 2:XIV, fig. 1); the Tomb of Hunting and Fishing (*c.* 510 BC) and the Tomb of the Hunter (*c.* 510–*c.* 500 BC). Altogether, of the 5735 tombs discovered, 62 have painted interiors. Among the last of these is the Tomb of the Typhon (*c.* 200–*c.* 150 BC). The first phase of the 'Ara della Regina' temple on the acropolis dates to the 6th century BC. It was a monumental structure (77.50×35.55 m) with a tripartite inner arrangement, and was completely restructured during the 4th century BC. Among finds from the site is a terracotta pedimental relief of winged horses in Hellenistic style (see fig.).

During the 5th century BC Tarquinia continued to expand, assuming the leadership of the Etruscan 12-city league and joining Athens in the campaign against Syracuse of 413–412 BC. The affluence of the ruling élite is demonstrated by their sculptured sarcophagi and elaborately painted tombs, for example the Tomb of the Banquet (*c.* 470–*c.* 460 BC) with its scenes of dancers, or the Tomb of the Ship (*c.* 460–*c.* 450 BC) with its depictions of such symbols of wealth as imported Greek vases. Tarquinia was engaged in almost continuous warfare with Rome from the mid-4th century BC until 281 BC, when the city finally lost its territory and

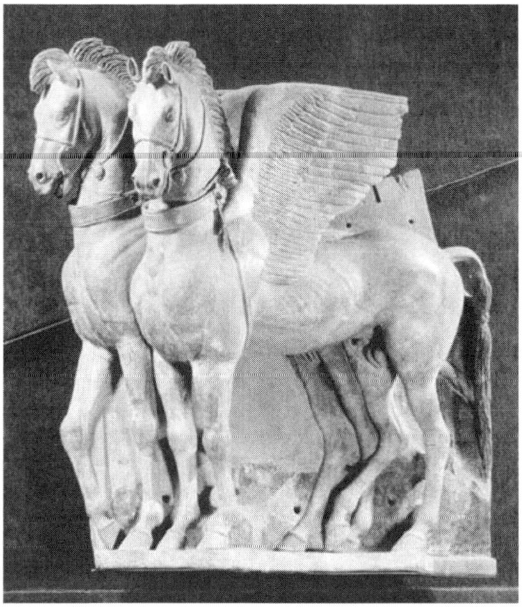

Tarquinia, terracotta pedimental relief of winged horses, from the temple, *c.* 500 BC (Tarquinia, Museo Archeologico)

independence. In tomb paintings the earlier scenes of celebratory gaiety gave way increasingly to scenes redolent of menace and violence, and the tombs also provide evidence that, during this period of political decline, power was passing from the aristocracy to a rising class of magistrates and administrators. From the 1st century BC onwards decline was unremitting, and by the 3rd century AD Tarquinia was virtually extinct. The ancient site was finally abandoned in the 8th or 9th century AD, when Corneto was founded nearby. The first recorded archaeological excavations of modern times took place at Tarquinia in 1489.

H. Hencken: *Tarquinia, Villanovans and Early Etruscans* (Cambridge, MA, 1968)

S. Steingräber: *Catalogo ragionato della pittura etrusca* (Milan, 1984)

M. Bonghi Jovino, ed.: *Gli Etruschi di Tarquinia* (Modena, 1986)

R. Leighton: *Tarquinia: An Etruscan city* (London, 2004)

F. Chiesa: *Tarquinia: Archeologia e prosopografia tra ellenismo e romanizzazione* (Rome, 2005)

M. B. Jovino: *Città sepolte d'Etruria: Storie e memorie dello scavo di Tarquinia* (Milan, 2005)

Tarraco [Phoen. Tarchon; Cat. and Sp. Tarragona]. Roman city in Catalonia, on the north-east coast of Spain. The Iberians established a stronghold on the site, and later the Carthaginian fortress of Tarchon was built. Sections of Cyclopean walls and some of the original gateways (erected during the 3rd century BC) are preserved, with their Roman superstructures. Gnaius Cornelius Scipio Calvus captured the fortress in 218 BC and established one of the earliest Roman strongholds in Spain. The site was fortified against Carthaginian invasion and the harbour was improved. Under the Romans Tarraco became one of the most important cities of the Iberian Peninsula and, with its flax trade and other industries, one of the richest seaports of the empire. Augustus made Tarraco the capital of the province of Hispania Citerior or Tarraconensis, the largest Roman province in Europe.

Laid out in a rectangular grid, the city had an upper and lower town with the circus in between. In the late 1st century AD the upper town was built on two terraces that held the porticoed provincial forum, a broad rectangular space (300×120 metres). In the large forum, assemblies of the provincial council met. Entrance was through stairs set in towers of the Republican walls that enclosed the area. A basilica in which the provincial representatives met has not been uncovered, but statue bases inscribed with the names of the priests of the cult suggest that it is on the south side. On the highest level of the terrace, a temple of the imperial cult, the Temple of Rome and Augustus, was erected in an enclosed precinct (140×120 metres). Marble relief sculpture depicting medallions with heads of Jupiter Ammon decorated the temple and its enclosure, an allusion to the Forum of Augustus in Rome, which was also evoked in the forum of Augusta Emerita. Each of the provincial capitals, it would seem, displayed motifs from the capital that allowed the town's magistrates to lay claim to the majesty of the state. This evocation of Rome was also reiterated in the systematic urban development of these towns with their fora, temples and basilicas.

The upper terrace possessed buildings for various functions: religious worship, administration and sports. The circus for chariot racing (340×116 metres) was built on the lowest level, maintaining the symmetry of the complex through the axis on its long sides. The sports complex and official buildings on the upper terrace, culminating in the Temple of Rome and Augustus at the top, must have created an impressive vista to travellers arriving from the sea.

In the lower town, what once was thought to have been a forum is now interpreted as a basilica with a shrine of Augustus on one side. An amphitheatre, of the late 1st–early 2nd centuries AD, that could seat 11,000 people, was built near the sea. There was also a theatre on the west slope that could accommodate 5000 people. An inscription also mentions baths in the city, and the impressive Els Ferreres aqueduct outside of the city that carried water from the Gaià river ten kilometres away. The aqueduct merits notice due to its *opus quadratum* construction with concrete only used in the water channel. Tarraco was lavishly endowed with the amenities of Roman life.

According to tradition, St Paul, with the help of St Thecla, founded the Christian Church in Spain at Tarraco in AD 60. An Early Christian necropolis of the 3rd–6th centuries AD, with the remains of a basilica and two crypts, is preserved. The 4th-century Christian mausoleum at Centcelles lies 5 km outside the modern city; it has a very fine mosaic cycle.

Tauriskos. *See* APOLLONIOS AND TAURISKOS.

Tazoult Lambèse. *See* LAMBAESIS.

Tebessa. *See* THEVESTIS.

Tegea. Site in south-west Arcadia, Greece, near modern Tripolis. The ancient city was one of the oldest and largest in the region, and it flourished from the Bronze Age to the end of the 4th century AD, when it was destroyed by the Goths under Alaric. Refounded in Byzantine times as Nikli, it became one of the main medieval cities of the Peloponnese. The ancient site was excavated by the French School at Athens during 1889–1910 and by the Greek Archaeological Service in 1965. Its principal remains are those of the Temple of Athena Alea, but the site also includes a stadium and a market, the Sanctuary of Demeter and Kore, and an Early Christian basilica. The Sanctuary of Athena was a famous place of asylum even in the Geometric period. The Archaic Temple of Athena burnt down around 395 BC, leaving only two internal rows of stylobate blocks *in situ*; these suggest that it was monumental, with a wide cella divided into three aisles by a double colonnade. It was replaced by a temple designed by SKOPAS, of which a substantial part is preserved, both *in situ* and in museums at Tegea (Archaeol. Mus.) and Athens (N. Archaeol. Mus., 178–80). Its stylobate (47.52×19.16 m) carried a peristyle of 6×14 Doric columns. Above the columns of the pronaos and opisthodomos were metopes with separately attached sculptures, as in the Erechtheion frieze at Athens. The east metopes showed *Herakles Fighting Kepheus and his Sons*; the east pediment depicted the *Kalydonian Boar Hunt*. The west metopes and pediment showed the *Telephos* myth. It is not certain which surviving sculptures, if any, were carved by Skopas himself. The cella was surrounded on three sides by an engaged two-storey colonnade with Corinthian half-columns below and Ionic half-columns above. The Corinthian capitals resemble those in the Temple of Zeus at Nemea. A cult statue of *Athena*, flanked by statues of *Asklepios* and *Hygieia* by Skopas (all now untraced), stood in the cella in Roman times (Pausanias: *Guide to Greece* VIII. xlvi.1 and xlvii.1). Little remains of the altar, but Pausanias' description (VIII.xlvii.3) suggests that it was modelled on the sculpted altars of such Ionian sanctuaries as that at Ephesos. Thus both altar and temple probably date from after Skopas' work in Ionia, around 345–335 BC.

C. Dugas, J. Berchmans and M. Clemmensen: *Le Sanctuaire d'Aléa Athéna à Tégée au IVe siècle* (Paris, 1924)

G. Gruben: *Die Tempel der Griechen* (Munich, 1976), pp. 129–33

N. J. Norman: 'The Temple of Athena Alea at Tegea', *Amer. J. Archaeol.*, lxxxviii (1984), pp. 169–94

N. J. Norman: 'Asklepios and Hygieia and the Cult Statue at Tegea', *Amer. J. Archaeol.*, xc (1986), pp. 425–30

M. E. Voyatzis: *The Early Sanctuary of Athena Alea at Tegea and Other Archaic Sanctuaries in Arcadia* (Göteborg, 1990)

L. Hammond: *The Miniature Votive Vessels from the Sanctuary of Athena Alea at Tegea* (diss., Columbia, U. MO, 1998)

J. Pakkanen: *The Temple of Athena Alea at Tegea: A Reconstruction of the Peristyle Column* (Helsinki, 1998)

Tekin. *See* MAGNESIA ON THE MAEANDER.

Temenos. Sacred enclosed area around a temple or other holy site.

Temple. Building or site conceived as the dwelling of a deity, whose presence is represented by a holy symbol. The word derives from the Greek word *temenos*, meaning 'an enclosure'. In Latin the word *templum* originally denoted a place marked out for augury by the augur with his staff but later came to mean an area sacred to a particular deity and was also used for a large and elaborate structure dedicated to one or more deities.

1. Greek. 2. Roman.

1. GREEK. Not all Greek temples were freely accessible to the general public. Some were open only to priests or initiates, or to men or women only, and others opened only on festival days, sometimes no more than once a year. In ancient Greece, the temple or *naos* ('home of the god or of his statue') took two forms: the sanctuary-temple, the function of which was primarily religious (e.g. the 5th-century BC Erechtheion, Athens), and the treasury-temple, the function of which was primarily practical (e.g. the slightly earlier Parthenon). Sanctuary-temples were built to shelter sacred places and objects, such as trees that had been worshipped in prehistoric nature cults and tombs of mythical heroes, or ancient cult statues endowed with miraculous powers and made the focus of ceremonies for which these buildings provided an architectural setting. Thus the Erechtheion (*see* ATHENS, §II, 1(i)) housed the olive-wood statue of *Athena Polias*, said to have fallen from heaven in former times, the outline on the rock of Poseidon's trident, the underground crevasse where the sacred serpent, the city's guardian spirit, was alleged to live, the 'sea of Erechtheus', a spring associated with Athens' founder king, the tombs of Erechtheus and Pandrosos, and the altars of Poseidon-Erechtheus, Hephaistos, the hero Boutes and Zeus Hypatos. Finally, in the adjoining courtyard was Athena's sacred olive tree, symbolizing the very existence of the city. Similarly, the cella of the Temple of Apollo (7th century BC) at DELPHI contained the altar of Hestia (*thymele*) and the altar of Poseidon, while its sunken oracular crypt (adyton) contained the crack in the earth from which the Pythia received her prophetic inspiration, the Pythia's tripod, the sacred laurel tree, the omphalos (an ancient stone representing the navel of the world), the tomb of Dionysos, an ancient wooden cult statue of Apollo presented by the Cretans, and, initially, the oracular fountain of Cassotis.

These sanctuary-temples, by their nature, imposed numerous constraints on architects. First, they had to be constructed on the sacred site, irrespective of its suitability. Building the Temple of Demeter (Telesterion) at Eleusis involved cutting deep into the bedrock, and at Delphi massive foundations were needed to raise the Temple of Apollo above its adyton. The five successive temples of Demeter and the six temples of Apollo had, moreover, to be rebuilt on top of each other in exactly the same place. Secondly, since a single building often had to accommodate several sacred places and objects, or be designed for unusual cult practices, the architect was obliged to resort to abnormal plans. The Erechtheion had two cellae, back-to-back, and a portico at the end of each flank, and the Telesterion at Eleusis was a hypostyle hall with rows of seats for initiates. The temple at Delphi had an elongated cella to accommodate its adyton. Moreover, the sacred ground had to remain visible and accessible, resulting in a difference of several metres between the ground levels of the east and west cellae of the Erechtheion. This also explains the sunken adyta at Delphi and in the Temple of Apollo at Didyma, the oracular crypt under the Temple of Apollo at Klaros, and the underground labyrinth beneath the Tholos at Epidauros, leading worshippers to the tomb of Asklepios via its ritual triple circuit.

Sanctuary-temples often contained one or more altars, which either had a fire continually burning (e.g. the *thymele* of Apollo at Delphi) or were employed for particular ceremonies, such as the ground-level hearth (*eschara*) in the Hieron at Samothrace, where sacrifices were made during the initiation ceremonies of the Great Gods. The buildings were ventilated, and the smoke escaped through large openings with grilles, as in the Erechtheion and the Pythion at Delos, through pierced tiles (e.g. the Temple of Apollo at Bassai), or through specially constructed lanterns in the roof (e.g. the Telesterion at Eleusis). Altars in temples were regarded as hearths of the god, so that the temple itself was seen as his home. Thus a sanctuary-temple was sometimes called a megaron or *anactoron* (a term for a palace dating from heroic times) and could be entered only after stringent purificatory rituals.

Although treasury-temples were endowed with a sacred character since they were built in honour of gods, they had no ritual function but were intended to protect precious and perishable offerings, such as chryselephantine statues. Thus the Parthenon was built by the Athenian government simply to house the chryselephantine statue of *Athena Parthenos* by Pheidias in its east chamber and the monetary wealth of the city of Athens and various cults in the west (the opisthodomos). The interior of a treasury-temple did not constitute holy ground, and the Athenians even accommodated Demetrios I Poliorketes of Macedonia (*reg* 306–285 BC) and his concubines in the opisthodomos of the Parthenon, something inconceivable in the Erechtheion. Architecturally, treasury-temples were clearly simpler to design and build than sanctuary-temples. The architect could choose the most suitable site and follow a standard plan. Construction was usually occasioned by the offering of chryselephantine statues, as at the Parthenon, the Temple of Zeus at Olympia, the Philippeion at Olympia (five statues), and the Tholos at Delphi (nine statues). Thus an individual deity could have several neighbouring temples at the same time, in the same sanctuary: Hera had two at Paestum, and Apollo had four at Delos. Treasury-temples were ancillary to sanctuary-temples, and as many were built as were needed to house the offerings made to their deities. In practice, sanctuary-temples also doubled as treasury-temples, but the converse never appears to have been the case.

See also ARCHITECTURE, §IV, 1(i)(a).

G. Gruben: *Die Tempel der Griechen* (Munich, 1966)

G. Roux: 'Le Vrai temple d'Apollon à Delos', *Bull. Corr. Hell.*, (1979), pp. 109–35

W. Burkert: 'The Meaning and Function of the Temple in Classical Greece', *Temple in Society*, ed. M. V. Fox (1988), pp. 27–47

D. Pohl: *Kaiserzeitliche Tempel in Kleinasien unter besonderer Berücksichtigung der hellenistischen Vorläufer* (Bonn, 2002)

J. Pedley: *Sanctuaries and the Sacred in the Ancient Greek World* (Cambridge, 2005)

2. ROMAN. The Roman temple was essentially a simple cella, in which the statue of the deity was housed. It was not designed to accommodate a congregation, and the altar was normally outside, opposite the entrance to the temple, which wherever possible faced east. There was, therefore, a tendency for architects to concentrate on the exterior at the expense of the interior. The façades of Roman temples were treated particularly elaborately because of the Roman practice, inherited from the Etruscans, of aligning temples along the major axis of the sacred precinct with the main door facing the entrance to the enclosure. Several other characteristic features of Roman temples are also of Etruscan origin, such as the high podium, which projected well forward of the porch pronaos to enclose an imposing staircase. Although the Etruscans built several varieties of temple, the Romans seem to have been most influenced by the type with a columnar porch, a cella extending the full width of the podium and a blank rear wall. Some Roman examples are pseudo-peripteral, for instance the 'Maison Carrée' (*c.* 19 BC) at Nemausus (Nîmes).

During Rome's military campaigns in Asia Minor and Greece in the 2nd century BC, Greek architects were brought to Rome and built the first Hellenistic marble temples. However, even when the architectural details of Roman temples had been completely Hellenized, their plans continued to reflect Etruscan models, as in the Temple of Portunus (late 2nd century BC) in the Forum Boarium. During the later 1st century BC the Roman temple began to assume many of its distinguishing features. The Forum Julium (46 BC; *see* ROME, §IV, 1), with its rectangular enclosure surrounded on three sides by a double portico of columns and dominated on the fourth by the Temple of Venus Genetrix, began a long sequence of similar complexes (*see* ROME, §IV, 2), including the Forum Augustum (2 BC) and the Forum of Nerva (AD 97), the Temple of the Deified Claudius (after AD 70) and the Templum Pacis (AD 71–5). At the same time marble became a common building material, and by the end of the Augustan period its frequent use, especially in temples, had transformed the face of Rome. It was also during the Augustan period that the Roman Corinthian order (*see* ORDERS, ARCHITECTURAL, §I, 1(iii)), with its deeply carved capitals and elaborate friezes, reached its full development. It is this order that gives Roman temples their richly detailed and opulent appearance. The temples of Mars Ultor in the Forum Augustum and of the Deified Vespasian in the Forum Romanum are good examples of the orthodox Roman temple, which underwent little modification until the building of the Pantheon (AD 118–25) under Hadrian.

The Pantheon is unusual because, in contrast to earlier temples, its interior, an enormous domed rotunda (diam. 43.2 m), is designed to be at least as impressive as its exterior (*see* ROME, fig. 13). Despite this, however, the Pantheon remained an anomaly and had little influence on temple design. Only after the Roman acceptance of Christianity (4th century AD) did centralized domed buildings again assume importance in religious architecture. Hadrian's Temple of Venus and Rome (AD 135) is also unorthodox, since the emperor insisted on a stylobate in the Greek manner instead of the high podium that the temple required. The architectural details suggest that Asian craftsmen were brought in to finish the project, and several temples built over the next few years, including the Temple of Antoninus and Faustina (AD 141) in the Forum Romanum and the Hadrianeum (AD 145) in the Campus Martius, show similar influence. In terms of sheer size, the culmination of Roman temple architecture is represented by Caracalla's Temple of Serapis (AD 211–18) on the Quirinal, which had 12 columns on its façade, each over 18 m high, and was approached by a staircase 21 m high.

Although official temples such as the 'Maison Carrée' at Nemausus, the Capitolium (2nd century AD) at THAMUGADI (Timgad) and the temple of the Severan family (AD 216) at LEPTIS MAGNA, followed the Roman pattern of high podium, frontal staircase and prostyle porch, temples with traditional local features continued to be built in all provinces. In Gaul they had a square or circular tower-like cella, often surrounded by a portico, seen in the 'Temple of Janus' (2nd century AD) at AUGUSTODUNUM (Autun). In Greece and Asia Minor, temples of Hellenistic type predominated, while in Syria strong Semitic influences persisted, as in the Temple of Bel (AD 32) at PALMYRA, which has crowstep merlons, an entrance doorway inserted into the colonnade of one of the long sides and shrines at each side of the cella. Temple A (2nd century AD) at Niha in Lebanon has a staircase at the end of the cella leading up to a canopied sanctuary at the end, similar to that of a Christian church. Even the massive Temple of Jupiter (1st century AD) at BAALBEK, which is typically Roman in many respects, with its high podium, frontal staircase and colonnaded rectangular enclosure, has 'high places' and other features found in earlier Lebanese sanctuaries. In North Africa too, where Roman influence was particularly strong, some temples of local gods were built on traditional lines, such as the Temple of Mercury (AD 211) at Thuburbo Maius and the Temple of Aesculapius (AD 162) at LAMBAESIS.

By the 1st century AD, several congregational religions had established themselves in Roman Italy. These had unconventional building requirements. Thus the underground basilica (1st century AD) near Porta Maggiore in Rome, built for a neo-Pythagorean sect, has a nave flanked by two aisles and terminates in an apse. Mithraea (temples of Mithras) had to accommodate worshippers and contained a long nave, flanked by banqueting couches, which terminated in a recess containing a painting or sculpture of the deity. The growing popularity of Eastern cults also influenced mainstream religion, giving rise to such temples as that of Jupiter Dolichenus (AD 138) at Rome, which has an aisled prayer hall screened off by high walls. When Constantine's Edict of Milan (AD 313) eventually granted toleration to Christianity and allowed the building of churches, the pagan temple with its comparatively small, dimly lit cella was considered unsuitable for congregational worship, and the model of the more spacious, well-lit basilica was adopted instead.

See also ARCHITECTURE, §VI, 1(i)(a).

A. M. Colini: 'La scoperta del santuario della divinità Dolichene sull'Aventino', *Boll. Comm. Archeol. Com. Roma*, iii (1935), pp. 145–59

J. A. Hanson: *Roman Theater Temples* (Princeton, 1959)

D. E. Strong and J. B. Ward Perkins: 'The Round Temple in the Forum Boarium', *Pap. Brit. Sch. Rome*, xxviii (1960), pp. 7–32

D. E. Strong and J. B. Ward Perkins: 'The Temple of Castor in the Forum Romanum', *Pap. Brit. Sch. Rome*, xxx (1962), pp. 1–39

A. Boethius and J. B. Ward-Perkins: *Etruscan and Roman Architecture*, Pelican Hist. A. (Harmondsworth, 1970)

H. Kähler: *Der römische Tempel* (Berlin, 1970)

F. Rakob and W. D. Heilmeyer: *Der Rundtempel am Tiber in Rom* (Mainz, 1973)

J. B. Ward Perkins: *Roman Imperial Architecture*, Pelican Hist. A. (Harmondsworth, 1981)

F. B. Sear: *Roman Architecture* (London, 1982, 2/1989)

N. R. Armstrong: *Round Temples in Roman Architecture of the Republic through the Late Antique Period* (diss., U. Oxford, 2001)

J. W. Stamper: *The Architecture of Roman Temples: The Republic to the Middle Empire* (Cambridge, 2005)

Teos. Site on the west coast of Turkey, on the isthmus of a small peninsula *c.* 48 km south-west of Smyrna (now Izmir). It was founded by Athenians and Ionians led by Nauklos, a son of King Kodros, though its legendary origin went back to Minyan settlers from Boiotia. The city flourished in the 7th and 6th centuries BC, before falling to Persian invaders (546 BC). Many of its citizens departed and founded the city of Abdera in Thrace, though several later returned after the Persians had been evicted. In the 5th century BC Teos regained its prosperity and, through seaborne trade, became one of the richest Ionian Greek cities. It continued to prosper throughout the Hellenistic period in spite of the conflicts that broke out under Alexander's successors and with the coming of the Romans in the 2nd century BC. Under the Romans Teos gradually declined. The remains of the city lie scattered among olive trees, and the most conspicuous ruins are those of the Temple of Dionysos, the principal deity of Teos, built early in the 2nd century BC by the architect HERMOGENES. This large peripteral temple had 6 by

11 Ionian columns, though little more than the foundations survives. Two columns have been partially re-erected. The theatre, of Hellenistic date with a Roman proscenium, is poorly preserved. The odeion is in a better condition, and there are also remains of another large building, probably the gymnasium.

D. Magie: *Roman Rule in Asia Minor* (Princeton, 1950), pp. 79, 898
E. Akurgal: *Ancient Civilizations and Ruins of Turkey* (Istanbul, 1983)
G. E. Bean: *Aegean Turkey* (London, 1984), pp. 106–15
Klazomenai, Teos and Abdera: Metropoleis and Colony: Proceedings of the International Symposium Held at the Archaeological Museum of Abdera: Abdera, 2001

Tepidarium. *See under* BATH.

Termessos. Site of a Pisidian city that flourished *c.* 150 BC–AD 300, now in the Termessos National Park, near Antalya, Turkey. According to tradition, it was founded by a Central Anatolian tribe, the Solymoi, who were noted warriors. Early record of them is shrouded in legend (e.g. Homer: *Iliad* VI. 184), though Herodotus (I.clxxiii.2) mentioned their conflicts with settling Greeks. Termessos, like all Pisidia, was overrun by the Persians (mid-6th century BC), but due to the city's remote, mountainous location, its citizens were able to retain much of their independence. It submitted to Alexander the Great in 333 BC, though it was not actually captured by him (Arrian: *Anabasis of Alexander* I.xxvii.5–xxviii.2). After Alexander's death in 323 BC, Termessos became involved in the conflicts between his 'Successors'. Siding first with Alketas and then with Antigonos, it surrendered to the Seleukids (301 BC), who eventually ceded it to Rome by the Peace of Apameia in 188 BC. Most of the extant ruins appear to date from the Roman period.

The site of Termessos is dramatic in the extreme. Situated high on a shoulder of Güllük Dağ (Mt Solymos), it is covered with forest and has spectacular views. The area is little excavated, however. The ruins were found by Fellows in 1842 and correctly identified by him. Of particular interest are the dizzily situated Hellenistic theatre, the 'odeion' (probably the bouleuterion; 1st century BC), and the gymnasium with its strange, high, curving gables. The oldest monument is probably a rock-cut tomb thought by many scholars to be that of Alketas (*fl* 323–319 BC). Though much damaged, it retains a life-size, early Hellenistic low relief of a mounted soldier. The pose recalls heroic representations of Alexander the Great, and if this is Alketas' tomb, the carving is an elegant compliment to that maligned 'Successor'. The site has two principal burial grounds. The one to the north is not extensive, but the upper necropolis covers a large area and is a place of considerable archaeological and artistic interest, strewn with huge stone sarcophagi, their lids cast aside in apocalyptic confusion.

K. Lanckoroński, G. Niemann and E. Petersen: *Städte Pamphyliens und Pisidiens*, 2 vols (Vienna, 1890–92)
G. E. Bean: *Turkey's Southern Shore* (London, 1968, 2/1979)
A. Pekridou: *Das Alketas-Grab in Termessos* (Tübingen, 1986)
B. Iplikçioglu: *Epigraphische Forschungen in Termessos und seinem Territorium,* 3 vols (Vienna, 1991–4)
A. Dierichs: 'Termessos', *Ant. Welt,* xxx/1 (1999), pp. 81–2

Terracotta [It.: 'cooked earth']. The commonly used term for a type of natural plastic clay that hardens when dried.

This article discusses the use of clay to make items other than vessels, for the latter *see* POTTERY.

I. Greek. II. Roman.

I. Greek.

1. Introduction. 2. Figurines and statuettes. 3. Reliefs and plaques. 4. Masks, protomes and busts. 5. Architecture.

1. INTRODUCTION. In ancient Greece the maker of small sculpture or figurines in clay was known as a coroplast ('modeller of girls'), a term that probably evolved because of the predominance of the female image in clay (*see also* KORE). The word terracotta refers to the finished product, which was baked in a kiln. Good sources of clay were found throughout the Greek world, a fact that contributed to the development of a thriving terracotta industry at many centres over some 700 years, from the early 7th century BC to the end of the 1st century BC or later. The manufacture of terracotta figurines was complicated but resulted in an inexpensive product. Clay was mined and then purified in settling basins. The purified, liquid clay was solidified to a workable consistency in order to be hand-modelled or pressed into a mould. To make a mould, a hand-modelled prototype was created and fired. Moist clay was pressed around the prototype and, when carefully removed, contained the impression or imprint of the original image. The use of plaster moulds, a technique introduced from Egypt, can be documented from the 3rd century BC onwards but never replaced the standard technique of production from clay moulds.

The earliest mould-made figurines were solid-cast, using a front mould only. By the end of the 7th century BC hollow figurines produced from a double mould were made, although single-mould figurines with simple, handmade backs were more common. Toward the end of the 4th century BC, Greek coroplasts began to use multiple moulds for figures in complicated poses. Separate moulds for heads, torsos, arms, legs, wings and attributes produced individual parts of figurines that could be combined, varied or interchanged by the coroplast. After the figurine was cast, and assembled if necessary, hair and drapery were frequently retouched by hand to produce fine detail. Sometimes hand-modelled components, such as wreaths, flowers and leaves, or jewellery were applied, and in some cases the surface was burnished while in the leather-hard state. A vent hole was cut, usually in the back, and the figurine was fired. After firing, many figurines were decorated with bright colours, such as red, light blue, pink or magenta, as well as black, often over a chalky white coating; occasionally gilding was applied in order to imitate bronze.

2. Figurines and statuettes.

(i) Before *c.* 700 BC. (ii) Archaic (*c.* 700–*c.* 480 BC). (iii) Classical (*c.* 480–323 BC). (iv) Hellenistic (323–27 BC).

(i) Before c. 700 BC. From the 10th to the 8th century BC in Greece, figurines were chiefly made by potters who also hand-modelled small images of animals or humans that were pinched or rolled into shape. Around 700 BC, mould-made faces began to appear on otherwise hand-modelled figurines. The use of the mould was a technique practised in Mesopotamia and Egypt from the 3rd millennium BC onwards. By the mid-7th century BC, particularly at Greek centres with strong trading contacts with the East, such as those on Rhodes, Samos or Crete, the use of a full mould for the figurine became standard. Thus from the mid-7th century BC onwards, nearly all terracottas were produced from moulds, even though the technique of hand-modelling the figure never died out. The earliest mass-produced, mould-made terracottas were small, solid-cast figurines and plaques, made in frontal moulds, in the Daidalic style. Most come from Crete and Lakonia, but sites on the Greek mainland, in the Aegean, East Greece and South Italy also have yielded Daidalic figurines.

(ii) Archaic (c. 700–c. 480 BC). In the last quarter of the 7th century BC, coroplasts at Corinth, on Rhodes and at Miletos began to manufacture small vessels in human or animal form, fitted with an alabastron-type neck and mouth, to act as attractive containers for perfume. Because they were conceived as vessels, a double mould was used, and the resulting casts were thin-walled and pleasant to hold.

Such figural vases and related figurines made in a fine, dusty rose, micaceous clay dominated the market from the last quarter of the 6th century BC to the 2nd. Once widely believed to have originated on Rhodes, they now are scientifically confirmed as coming from Miletos. The types, which collectively make up the 'Aphrodite group', comprise figural vases in the form of a standing kore wearing *chiton* (light, baggy-sleeved linen tunic) and *himation* (pleated and buttoned mantle) and, less commonly, a draped Kouros, a hieratic seated, veiled woman wearing a tall *polos* (cylindrical crown) or low *stephane* (diadem), seated couples, sirens and various animals, as well as small figurines of banqueters, crouching dwarfs and female protomes. The best of these Milesian figural vases and figurines show extraordinarily refined detail and comprise some of the finest examples of Archaic miniature sculpture.

Together with the perfume they contained, the terracottas of the Aphrodite group were traded throughout the Mediterranean and Black Sea areas, where, in the later 6th century BC, they became the basis for local production at many centres, from Cyrene in North Africa to Olbia (Ol'viya) on the Black Sea, as well as at many sites in South Italy and Sicily. On the Greek mainland, however, Milesian terracottas had little impact. Corinth, Athens, Argos and several sites in Boiotia were the most important Archaic terracotta-producing centres on the mainland, although local production also is evident at many other sites. At Corinth, a vigorous coroplastic industry developed towards the end of the 8th century BC and flourished until the destruction of the city in 146 BC. Corinthian coroplasts worked a fine-grained clay that fired to a cream, orange-buff or pale greenish colour with a smooth, almost soapy surface. Apart from a series of Daidalic plaques of the 7th century BC, in the later 7th and 6th centuries BC the figurines were simple and hand-modelled, although moulds often were used for the faces. Principal types included animals, horses and riders, and standing or seated females whose boardlike bodies, bent to approximate a seated position, were supported at the back with vertical struts; applied decoration in the form of pellets and bands imitated earrings, necklaces and pectorals. Corinthian terracottas were distributed throughout the mainland and furnished the prototypes for local production at Aigina, Delphi, Kirrha, Elateia, Kalydon, Corfu, Ithaka and elsewhere.

Terracotta production at Argos may have received its stimulus from Corinth, although Argive figurines in general appear more primitive in technique and in a taste for heavy applied decoration. Primitive, hand-modelled female types with flat bodies and, in the 6th century BC, mould-made heads, are either standing or seated, in the Corinthian manner described above. The upper bodies are ornamented with rows of alternating strips, pellets and braids, seemingly held at the shoulders by large applied rosettes, while elaborate, high hairstyles are held in place by twisted strips of clay.

At Athens, finds from the Agora, Kerameikos and Acropolis suggest that extensive local production began in the early 7th century BC, although terracotta figurines were made earlier. Most of the Attic types of the 7th and 6th centuries BC are hand-modelled, even though, as at Corinth and Argos, moulds were occasionally used for faces. The standing or seated female board-figurine predominates, but protomes, horses and riders, chariots and warriors also are known, as well as a fine series of Late Archaic reliefs. In the last quarter of the 6th century BC a new typology based on the use of a complete, frontal mould appeared. The most influential type was that of a woman with an unarticulated body seated on a wing-back throne; more elaborate versions have detailed garments, a *chiton* and transverse *himation*, while abbreviated varieties were made as protomes. These and other related types, cast solid in a fine, brown clay, were traded along with Attic pottery throughout the Greek world and provided the impetus for local imitations at many sites.

Terracottas from Thebes, Tanagra, Halai, Rhitsona and elsewhere in Boiotia attest to a lively coroplastic industry that flourished from the end of the 7th century BC until the early 2nd. In the Archaic period, Corinthian influence was strong in the development of standing or seated board-figures, but these are more sober in form and in decoration than their Corinthian counterparts. The lustrous glaze and painted decorative motifs of these figures are identical to those on contemporary Boiotian pottery.

Many other cities of the Greek world in the Archaic period had local workshops producing terracotta figurines. In the west, at Taras (Taranto), Metapontion (Metaponto), Lokroi Epizephyrioi (Locri), Medma and Poseidonia (Paestum) in South Italy, as well as at Naxos, Megara Hyblaia, Katane (Catania), Syracuse, Gela, Akragas (Agrigento) and Selinus in Sicily, coroplasts were adapting and reinterpreting imported East Greek, Corinthian or Attic types. Most distinctive among the original western Greek types of the Late Archaic period (*c.* 550–*c.* 480 BC) is a hieratic form of seated or standing goddess, perhaps distantly related to the Corinthian board-figure in its slablike body, although it is entirely mould-made. Best known from hundreds of examples at Selinus and Agrigento, where it probably originated in the last quarter of the 6th century BC, this type is distinguished by a rich series of pectorals that cross the upper body from neck to waist.

(iii) Classical (c. 480–323 BC). In East Greece new types appeared at the end of the 6th century BC but were more common in the early 5th. Believed to originate on Rhodes because of the large numbers found there, these East Greek figurines filled the void throughout the Mediterranean left by the decline of the Milesian workshops at the end of the 6th century BC. The types collectively belong to the 'post-Aphrodite group' and comprise hieratic seated and standing females wearing a *chiton* and *himation*; they are generally carefully executed using a double mould and a refined light brown clay. Local reproductions and imitations were made at Olynthos, Thasos, Halikarnassos, Larissa, Kos, Erythrai, Cyrene and other sites.

During the 5th century BC, Athens was the most important terracotta-producing centre, and its figurines were widely exported. New types of standing and seated women wearing a *peplos* instead of the *chiton* and *himation* were created in response to the sculptural developments of the Early Classical Severe style (*see* SCULPTURE, §IV, 2(iii)(a)), although the older, hieratic type of seated goddess continued to be made in slightly updated variants. The most popular of the new types presents a tall, thin figure with square shoulders, a long neck and an oval face marked by a sombre expression; the type also is known in a version truncated below the waist. In the 2nd half of the 5th century BC, more majestic female types wearing a *peplos* over a *chiton* and carrying a torch and piglet occur at Athens and Eleusis, as do types of *hydrophoroi* ('water-jar carriers') and dolls with articulated limbs.

Local imitations of 5th-century BC Attic figurines were made at most terracotta-producing centres. In Boiotia, the Attic *peplophoros* ('*peplos*-wearer') was modified to wear a tall *polos*. In later 5th-century BC Boiotian versions, the *polos* was substituted for an over-sized, elaborate, braided coiffure and low *kalathos* (basket-shaped hat), elements believed to derive from a local cult statue. Protomes and several standing types of nude youths were introduced from Athens, perhaps to serve the cult of the Kaberioi at Thebes, where most examples have been found; some of these also have elaborate coiffures. In addition to these sculptural types of standing *peplophoroi* and nude youths, Boiotian coroplasts hand-modelled complex scenes reflecting activities from everyday life, such as a woman baking bread, a man sawing wood or a man writing.

At the end of the 6th century BC new types appeared at Corinth, although the old hand-modelled figurines continued to be made. These new figurines, solid and made in a complete, frontal mould, reflected stylistic trends in Late Archaic sculpture. The principal type was flat, almost like a cut-out, and represented a standing kore in *chiton* and *himation*; her hand was occasionally pierced to carry an offering, or it held a flower. Slightly later, other types were introduced: more fully three-dimensional standing and seated females, dolls with articulated limbs, protomes and cut-out reliefs. These continued to be produced with little variation well into the 4th century BC.

The western Greek cities are noted for original contributions to the terracotta repertory of the 5th century BC. A local style and a unique local typology distinguishes the early 5th-century BC seated and standing women from Lokroi Epizephyrioi and Medma, with their squat, blocklike proportions, precise linear detail, exaggerated Severe style characteristics and lingering archaisms; the reliefs are similar, if more decorative. The coroplasts at Taras, aside from other terracottas, produced a type of reclining Dionysos throughout the 5th century BC and into the 4th. Perhaps originally inspired by 6th-century BC East Greek banqueter figurines, the type quickly acquired the locally specific features of the head of Dionysos with an elaborate *stephane* with a central lotus or rosette. In Sicily in the 5th century BC, the Attic *peplophoros* was transformed into a pig-bearer at Syracuse and elsewhere, although local types of pig-bearers were already current in the late 6th century BC at Gela. A type of torch-bearing female figure accompanied the pig-bearer types; both are generally associated with the worship of Persephone, yet both pig- and torch-bearers have been found at sanctuaries in Sicily belonging to other goddesses. Syracuse was the most important terracotta-producing centre in the 5th century BC, but many other sites in Sicily, such as Gela, Akragas, Naxos, Francavilla, Morgantina and Catania, had a flourishing coroplastic industry.

At the end of the 5th century BC and in the first half of the 4th, coroplasts tempered the hieratic character of the standard seated and standing females with rich movement in drapery and elaborately detailed surfaces reminiscent of Attic sculpture of the Rich style. New types were created, first at Athens and then at many other centres from the Ionian coast to Sicily and from North Africa to the Black Sea. Figurines of veiled dancers provided the coroplasts with the opportunity to create twisting movement and swirling drapery, in contrast to the earlier static and hieratic images of goddesses. Small figurines of comic actors, modelled in the miniature style of bronzes and reflecting bronze technique in the use of a double mould, reflect the increased popularity of the theatre at Athens.

In East Greece in the 4th century BC few sites show evidence of terracotta production. Halikarnassos has yielded hundreds of mediocre figurines dating from the end of the Archaic period to the last third of the 4th century BC; types include *hydrophoroi* based on Attic models, protomes, and a long series of standing male figures. In Sicily and South Italy, earlier 5th-century BC types of seated females and standing pig-bearers were brought up to date in the 4th century BC by more fussy drapery. Dancers, loosely based on Attic models, were among the new types to appear. Syracuse and Taras continued to be the main centres for terracotta production, but other centres, such as Morgantina, also were active.

(iv) Hellenistic (323–27 BC). At the beginning of the Hellenistic period terracotta production all over the Greek world was profoundly influenced by developments in Athens. Early in the third quarter of the 4th century BC Athenian coroplasts began to imitate in miniature the style of the Athenian sculptor PRAXITELES in figures of standing, draped women. A variety of graceful standing and sometimes seated poses, complemented by intricate drapery patterns, characterized a new type of female image that reflected a sophisticated secular ideal. The use of the double mould and crisp, metallic detail derived from the slightly earlier theatrical figures. This new repertory was immensely popular and by the beginning of the 3rd century BC was imitated throughout the Greek world, with the exception of Corinth, where coroplasts preferred to revise their religious types with new arrangements of drapery in a more monumental style (see fig.).

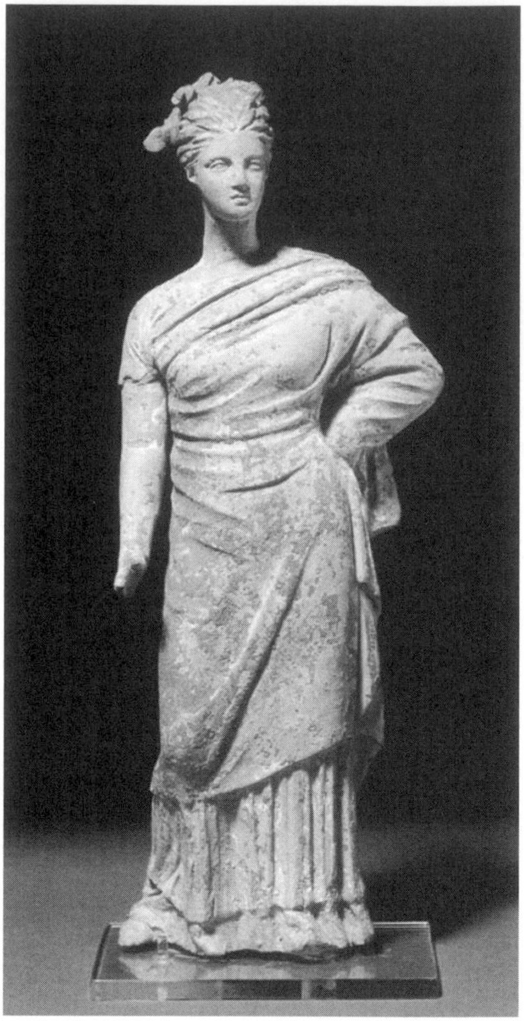
Ancient Greek terracotta figure of a woman, h. 260 mm, from Corinth, 3rd–2nd century BC (London, British Museum)

Boiotian coroplasts were among the first to take up this new style immediately after it appeared in Athens. So many of these figurines were recovered from graves during illicit excavations in the late 19th century at TANAGRA that early scholars believed the types to have originated there and referred to all such figurines as 'Tanagras', a name that is still used. While the standing draped woman typified late 4th-century production in Athens and Boiotia, other 'Tanagra' types (e.g. young men, old nursemaids, standing and seated children, and erotes) were also made. These continued to be produced, with a gradual decline in quality at Athens and its environs and in Boiotia, throughout the 3rd century BC and, for some types, as late as the 1st century BC. In the 3rd century BC and into the 2nd, the Tanagra style exerted a strong influence on workshops in northern Greece, such as those in Thessaly, Macedonia and Thrace, as well as on centres in Hellenistic Asia Minor, such as Troy, Amisos, Myrina, Smyrna, Pergamon, Knidos and Priene and in Alexandria. Some products from these centres rival the best Tanagras from mainland Greece and may have been made by Attic coroplasts.

In the 2nd century BC new influences began to be manifest. From Pergamon came a taste for the grandiose, best represented by a number of female figurines from nearby Myrina. Larger terracotta statuettes replicating well-known monumental sculptures may have been a speciality of Smyrna but can also be documented at Pergamon, Myrina and elsewhere. From Alexandria, probably via the Pergamene court, came a new feminine ideal, characterized by plump faces and small, squinting eyes. At Smyrna and Alexandria, coroplasts seemed particularly interested in chillingly realistic representations of pathology and disease.

Myrina, Smyrna, Amisos, Priene and Alexandria are the best sources for terracotta production in the eastern Mediterranean in the 2nd and 1st centuries BC. At Myrina, alongside the standing draped female figure of Tanagran inspiration, occur many winged *Nike* and Eros ephebe (Eros as a young man) figures in flight, whose backs were provided with suspension holes. Other popular types included Aphrodites and various mythological personages, sirens, youths, children and genre groups, actors, grotesques and caricatures. Over 40 different coroplasts' signatures and

20 monograms marked many of the figurines from Myrina, in contrast to the mostly unsigned figurines from other Hellenistic sites.

In South Italy the influence of the Tanagra style was strong at Taras (Taranto), Poseidonia (Paestum), Neapolis (Naples) and other Greek cities, as well as in Samnite Pompeii, Latin Rome and other centres in central Italy. Tarantine coroplasts personalized the motif of the standing draped woman with characterful expressions and dynamic drapery; scores of handsome figurines have been found in Tarantine tombs. In addition, completely new types, such as acrobats or long-legged male dancers, entered the repertory, which collectively was the richest and most influential in outlying workshops, such as those at Canosa, Herakleia, Egnatia and Ruvo. In Sicily, the products of the Hellenistic workshops of Syracuse provided the dominant influence over the lesser centres at Morgantina, Centuripe, Lentini and Akragas (Agrigento), until Syracuse itself was destroyed in 212 BC. Thereafter, the workshops at Centuripe provided the local markets with stiff and provincial figures in a diluted Tanagra style, as well as dancers, Aphrodites and erotes.

Terracotta production had generally ceased in the West by the end of the 2nd century BC, although workshops at Taras continued to manufacture credible figurines well into the 1st century AD. On the Greek mainland and the islands, output at most centres had dwindled by the 1st century BC, if not earlier, except at Corinth, where the making of terracottas was revived in the 1st century AD after a hiatus of a century and a half. In East Greece, the industry continued unabated into the 2nd century AD or even later at some major centres, until natural disasters or political circumstances intervened.

F. Winter: *Die Typen der figürlichen Terrakotten* (1903), iii of *Die antike Terrakotten* (Berlin, 1880–1911)

G. Kleiner: *Tanagrafiguren: Untersuchungen zur hellenistischen Kunst und Geschichte* (Berlin, 1942, rev. 1984)

A. Laumonier: *Les Figurines de terre cuite* (1956), xxiii of *Exploration archéologique de Délos* (Paris, 1909–86)

E. Paul: 'Die böotischen Brettidole', *Wiss. Z. Karl-Marx-U. Leipzig*, viii (1958–9), pp. 165–206

D. B. Thompson: *The Terracotta Figurines of the Hellenistic Period, Troy*, suppl. monograph 3 (Princeton, 1963)

W. D. Heilmeyer: *Frühe olympische Tonfiguren*, Olympische Forschungen, vii (Berlin, 1972)

G. Olbrich: *Archaische Statuetten eines Metapontiner Heiligtums* (Rome, 1979)

S. Mollard-Besques and others: 'Cinquante ans de découvertes et de travaux sur les figurines de terre cuite grecques et romaines', *Rev. Archéol.* (1985), pp. 77–114

R. A. Higgins: *Tanagra and the Figurines* (Princeton, 1986)

G. S. Merker: 'Corinthian Figurines of the Hellenistic Period', *The Coroplast's Art: Greek Terracottas of the Hellenistic World*, ed. J. P. Uhlenbrock (New Rochelle, 1990), pp. 54–62

M. DeWailly: *Les Statuettes aux parures du sanctuaire de la Malophoros à Sélinonte: Contexte, typologie et interprétation d'une catégorie d'offrandes* (Naples, 1992)

G. S. Merker: *The Sanctuary of Demeter and Kore: Terracotta Figurines of the Classical, Hellenistic, and Roman Periods* (Princeton, 2000)

L. Burn and R. Higgins: *Catalogue of Greek Terracottas in the British Museum* (London, 2001)

R. M. Ammerman: *The Sanctuary of Santa Venera at Paestum II: The Votive Terracottas* (Ann Arbor, 2002)

3. RELIEFS AND PLAQUES. Greek terracotta reliefs can take the form of small, figurine-like objects, large decorative plaques, grave stelai, architectural decoration or revetment (*see* ANTEFIX), *oscilla* (objects to be hung in the breeze) or applied decoration on furniture, pottery, lamps or other portable objects. In the Archaic period at many sites in Sicily and South Italy, terracotta altars (*arulae*) had hand-modelled or mould-made relief decoration. In the 4th century BC, terracotta appliqués, sometimes gilded, ornamented coffins at Taras (Taranto) and large, funerary urns at Canosa. Tiny terracotta reliefs, also gilded, and strung to imitate expensive jewellery, were recovered from tombs at Cyrene, Myrina, Taras and elsewhere.

The earliest terracotta votive reliefs belong to the second half of the 7th century BC and were particularly numerous on Crete, although they also were made at sites on the Greek mainland, in the islands and in East Greece. Independent terracotta reliefs, however, were not particularly popular, and it was not until the 4th century BC that this genre began to be widely explored. At certain periods and at certain centres, however, particular types of reliefs were produced over a short period, evidently for specific purposes. Such was the case at Athens and Brauron from the late 6th century BC to the early 5th, at Corinth, Lokri and Melos in the early 5th century BC, and at Taranto in the 4th (here votive reliefs in the form of shrine façades carried images of the Dioskouroi in various exploits).

The Melian reliefs, dating to *c.* 475–*c.* 450 BC, are thin slabs decorated with mythological scenes; the backgrounds were cut away, and small, discreetly placed holes suggest that they were attached to furniture. The scenes are rendered in a lively if somewhat provincial style, with elongated figures and much surface detail. Very different are the contemporary Lokrian reliefs, which are always in a rectangular format with attachment holes at the corners. They depict scenes relating to Persephone, in whose sanctuary at Lokri most were found. Their compositions conform to a strong gridlike pattern, within which quiet figures are rendered with quasi-metallic detail and delicate, linear ornamentation.

4. MASKS, PROTOMES AND BUSTS. Terracotta masks are most often votive objects but also occur as grave offerings; they were made continuously from the 6th century BC onwards. The most interesting Archaic examples are types of grotesque masks with the eyes and mouth cut out, found in the Sanctuary of Artemis Orthia at Sparta, among other places, and modelled on Phoenician grotesque masks. Terracotta versions of theatrical masks also are known from the 6th century BC to the Hellenistic period, both in miniature and life-size. Most were probably votive offerings to Dionysos, patron deity of the theatre, although some may have been purchased as souvenirs.

A fine series of theatrical masks of the 4th century BC reflecting characters from Middle and New Comedy were found in tombs on Lipari.

Protomes (i.e. half-length or truncated figures) were primarily votive, although they also occur in graves and houses. In the early 6th century BC at Athens female protomes, representing the front of a head wearing a rayed crown or decorated with pendant ornaments over the forehead, were attached to a flat plaque perforated at the corners for suspension. In East Greece female protomes originating in Miletos *c.* 545 BC were modelled in the form of a semi-cylindrical sheath, rounded at the top and cut off horizontally below the neck. At Corinth and in Boiotia protomes comprised a female head, neck and upper, disclike chest. East Greek protomes showed a veiled female whose particular style of headdress probably reflected Cypriot or Egyptian prototypes. Belonging to the Aphrodite group of terracottas, these were by far the most popular and, exported throughout the Mediterranean and Black Sea regions, were widely imitated during the second half of the 6th century BC.

At the beginning of the 5th century BC protomes in East Greece and on the Greek mainland were enlarged to include the upper part of the chest of the image, and by *c.* 450 BC arms were incorporated, so that attributes could be held. Most represent a female image, but several fine 5th-century BC examples from Boiotia portray Dionysos. Without attributes, it is likely that the protome served as a generic image suitable for any divinity, since protomes have been found in sanctuaries belonging to every goddess, as well as to the nymphs and Pan.

In Sicily, the protome was modified; by the end of the 6th century BC the fully modelled female bust was developed, the earliest examples of which came from Agrigento. These represent a female head and neck on unarticulated shoulders, modelled in the round, as if the arms were lowered (Kilmer). Versions from the late 5th and 4th century BC show dress, floral *poloi* and elaborate jewellery. On the Greek mainland and in East Greece, female busts were also made from the late 5th century BC to the Hellenistic period. They have been found in sanctuaries and graves at many sites and in houses at Priene.

P. Jacobsthal: *Die melischen Reliefs* (Berlin, 1931)

R. Lullies: *Vergoldete Terrakotta-Appliken aus Tarent* (Heidelberg, 1962)

H. Prückner: *Die lokrischen Tonreliefs* (Mainz, 1968)

M. Kilmer: *The Shoulder Bust in Sicily and South and Central Italy: A Catalogue and Materials for Dating* (Göteborg, 1977)

F. Croissant: *Les Protomés féminines archaïques* (Paris, 1983)

J. P. Uhlenbrock: *The Protomai from Gela: A Discussion of Local Style in Archaic Sicily* (Rome, 1988)

L. Burn and R. Higgins: *Catalogue of Greek Terracottas in the British Museum* (London, 2001)

5. ARCHITECTURE. Besides being used for statuettes, vases and lamps, terracotta was widely employed for tiling and adorning pitched roofs and for weatherproofing exposed woodwork and cornices of mud-brick or soft stone. The introduction of moulds in the early 7th century BC may have stimulated the manufacture of architectural terracottas, but these remained costly, and during Archaic times they were restricted to temples and other important buildings in sanctuaries. In Italy and Asia Minor, however, they were used from the start on civic buildings, private houses and funerary monuments as well, and by Hellenistic times they occurred on secular structures, such as stoas, in Greece itself.

Although fired clay tiles have been found at some prehistoric sites in Greece, tiled roofs seem to have been rare at this time. The earliest post-Dark Age tiled roofs apparently occurred on temples in the vicinity of Corinth during the first half of the 7th century BC and were undecorated. Each of their combination tiles comprised a slightly concave pan to carry off rainwater and a convex covering element to seal the joint between tiles.

The Corinthian roof, derived directly from this proto-Corinthian scheme, retained combination tiles for some time, although their pans had become flat and their joint covers four-sided with a double slope. In addition, moulded and painted floral antefixes were attached to eaves tiles, which had a painted guilloche pattern, and a raking sima (gutter), initially with a cavetto profile and painted tongues above a single or double guilloche, outlined the pediments. After the mid-6th century BC a new raking sima was introduced, as at the Megarian Treasury at Olympia. This consisted of an ovolo moulding above a vertical fascia, with a double anthemion pattern painted in the dark-on-light style. Handmade acroteria in the form of sphinxes and *nikai* regularly adorned the corners of the pediment, their bases equipped with lion-head water spouts. The ridge bore floral plaques echoing the lotus and palmette antefixes along the eaves.

Several other regional roofing systems evolved in Greece between *c.* 650 and *c.* 625 BC, notably the Lakonian, which developed at Sparta. This used separately made, concave pan tiles and convex cover tiles, regularly glazed black or red. Lakonian temple roofs were embellished with large disc acroteria with mouldings and painted geometric decoration, capping the semicircular ridge tiles at the apex of the pediment, and by antefixes with incised and painted designs, such as crescents, along the eaves. In contrast, figural decoration, including antefixes with heads of men, women and silens or satyrs, was usual in north-western Greece.

Distinctive regional forms of terracotta roof decoration also developed in Italy in Archaic times, though a single 'hybrid' tiling system was universal. This consisted of separately made, flat pan tiles and convex cover tiles. Semicircular antefixes with figural relief decoration, including heads of women, Gorgons, silens or satyrs, and floral patterns, lined the eaves, while raking simas embellished with continuous figural friezes, such as chariot races, horse races or processions, spanned the pediments. In Etruria, flat revetment plaques with figural scenes were nailed to exposed architectural elements, and large-scale statues occasionally lined the roof ridge. In South Italy and Sicily the larger buildings often had sizeable raking and horizontal simas, as at the Treasury of Gela at Olympia, frequently with openwork floral patterns, while smaller buildings had eaves tiles and antefixes. Sicilian pediments sometimes contained terracotta plaques depicting Gorgons. In Asia Minor too, hybrid tiling was usual. Raking simas, horizontal simas and revetment plaques bore floral friezes in metopes or continuous chains, as well as figural friezes, especially chariot races, while antefixes generally bore Gorgoneia, feline heads or floral patterns.

In Classical times (480–323 BC) official buildings in Greece were increasingly roofed with marble tiles. When terracotta was used, however, a highly standardized version of the Archaic Corinthian system was adhered to. This comprised flat pan tiles with four-sided cover tiles; a raking sima, frequently consisting of a weak cyma reversa painted with a light-on-dark anthemion pattern above a low recessed band with a painted maeander; palmette antefixes over eaves tiles with a painted maeander; and occasionally figural acroteria. Private houses, by contrast, were regularly roofed with plain Lakonian tiles. Limited production in Etruria of architectural terracottas is attested by fragments of pedimental sculpture, figural acroteria and antefixes.

By Hellenistic times (323–27 BC), however, terracotta was again widely used for the roofs of public buildings. The Corinthian system still prevailed in Greece but was now characterized by simas with floral reliefs, often surmounted by floral antefixes, as on the Leonidaion at Olympia. Many such simas ran along the eaves of stoas to protect those entering from rainwater shed from the roofs, and these had rows of lion-head spouts. In Etruria, some of the elaborate open-work simas, such as those from temples at Falerii, hand-made pedimental sculpture and friezes, belong to this period, including ones depicting entire mythological scenes.

In Roman times, the use of architectural terracottas became even more widespread, and several different workshops can be identified by tile stamps. Mass-production led, however, to a deterioration in quality. The Corinthian system was still usual for official buildings, but its floral antefixes were schematic versions of Classical and Hellenistic prototypes.

See also ARCHITECTURE, § IV, 1(ii)(d) *and* SCULPTURE, §IV, 1(iii)(b).

F. Alder, E. Curtius, W. Dörpfeld and others: *Die Baudenkmäler*, ii of *Olympia: Die Ergebnisse der von dem Deutschen Reich veranstalteten Ausgrabung*, ed. F. Alder and E. Curtius (Berlin, 1890–97)

H. Koch: *Dachterrakotten aus Campanien* (Berlin, 1912)

D. Brooke: 'Terracottas', *Catalogue of the Acropolis Museum*, ed. S. Casson, ii (Cambridge, 1921), pp. 345–425

E. D. Van Buren: *Figurative Terracotta Revetments in Etruria and Latium in the VI and V Centuries BC* (London, 1921)

E. D. Van Buren: *Archaic Fictile Revetments in Sicily and Magna Graecia* (New York, 1923)

E. D. Van Buren: *Greek Fictile Revetments in the Archaic Period* (London, 1926)

E. Buschor: *Die Tondächer der Akropolis*, 2 vols (Berlin, 1929–33)

I. Thallon-Hill and L. Shaw King: *Decorated Architectural Terracottas*, IV/i of *Corinth* (Cambridge, MA, and Princeton, 1929–)

C. Blinkenberg: *Les Petits objets* (1931), i of *Lindos: Fouilles et recherches, 1902–1914: Fouilles de l'acropole, 1902* (Berlin, 1931–60)

E. Breccia: *Terracotte figurate greche e greco-egizie del Museo di Alessandria* (Bergamo, 1934)

A. Andrén: *Architectural Terracotttas from Etrusco-Italic Temples* (Lund, 1939–40)

R. V. Nicholls: 'Type, Group and Series: A Consideration of Some Coroplastic Fundamentals', *Annu. Rep. Brit. Sch. Archaeol. Athens*, xlvii (1952), pp. 217–26

A. N. Stillwell: *The Potters' Quarter: The Terracottas* (1952), xv/2 of *Corinth: Results of the Excavations Conducted by the American School of Classical Studies at Athens* (Princeton, 1932–)

R. A. Higgins: *Greek: 730–330 BC* (1954), i of *Catalogue of the Terracottas in the Department of Greek and Roman Antiquities, British Museum* (London, 1954–9)

S. Mollard-Besques: *Musée National du Louvre: Catalogue raisonné des figurines et reliefs en terre cuite grecs, étrusques, et romains*, 4 vols (Paris, 1954–92)

S. Mollard-Besques: *Les Terres cuites grecques* (Paris, 1963)

Å. Åkerström: *Die architektonischen Terrakotten Kleinasiens* (Lund, 1966)

R. A. Higgins: *Greek Terracottas* (London, 1967)

C. Le Roy and J. Ducat: *Les Terres cuites architecturales: La Sculpture decorative en terre cuite*, ii of *Fouilles de Delphes* (Paris, 1967)

G. Rizza and V. Santa Maria Scrinari: *Il santuario sull'acropoli di Gortina*, i (Rome, 1968)

E. Töpperwein-Hoffmann: 'Terrakotten von Priene', *Istanbul. Mitt.*, xxi (1971), pp. 125–60

B. Schmalz: *Terrakotten aus dem Kabirenheiligtum bei Theben* (Berlin, 1974)

E. Töpperwein: *Terrakotten von Pergamon*, Pergamenische Forschungen, iii (Berlin, 1976)

M. Bell: *The Terracottas*, Morgantina Studies, i (Princeton, 1981)

L. Bernabò Brea: *Menandro e il teatro greco nelle terracotte liparese* (Genoa, 1982)

R. Miller: *The Terracotta Votives from Medma: Cult and Coroplastic Craft in Magna Graecia* (diss., Ann Arbor, U. MI, 1983)

M. Sguaitamatti: *L'Offrant de porcelet dans la coroplathie géléenne: Etude typologique* (Mainz, 1984)

J. Heiden: *Korinthische Dachziegel: Zur Entwicklung der korinthischen Dächer* (Frankfurt am Main, 1987)

D. B. Thompson, H. A. Thompson and S. I. Rotroff: *Hellenistic Pottery and Terracottas*, 4 vols (Princeton, 1987)

M. Bell: 'Hellenistic Terracottas of Southern Italy and Sicily', *The Coroplast's Art: Greek Terracottas of the Hellenistic World*, ed. J. P. Uhlenbrock (New Rochelle, 1990), pp. 64–70

N. A. Winter: *Greek Architectural Terracottas from the Prehistoric to the End of the Archaic Period* (Oxford, 1993)

II. Roman.

1. Introduction. 2. Regional survey.

1. INTRODUCTION. In the Roman world, the process used in the manufacture of objects in terracotta was similar to that practised in Greece. The raw material, clay, was either hand-modelled, cast in a mould, thrown on the wheel or rolled into slabs or strips, to

suit a variety of purposes, from the production of sewer pipes, building bricks and roof tiles, to pottery, lamps, toys, furniture, sarcophagi, cinerary urns and grave stelae, fountains, monumental sculpture and small, mass-produced, mould-made figurines. Most of these objects were polychromed, and some of the larger figures were gilded to imitate more costly bronze statuettes. Terracotta revetments decorated architecture, and terracotta tubes were incorporated into the masonry of vaulted structures in order to lighten the load. Brightly painted terracotta antefixes and waterspouts, modelled into a variety of figural and floral motifs, were used to enliven the eaves of buildings.

Although terracotta was common to all aspects of industrial and artistic production in the Roman world, its most informative manifestation for the history of style, religious expression and social interaction was the mass-produced, mould-made, terracotta votive. During the middle Republican period, at least, terracotta votive figurines comprised one third of all artistic production documented thus far for central Italy. Indeed, the discovery throughout the Roman world of hundreds of votive deposits containing figured terracottas indicates that the primary purpose behind the manufacture of mass-produced, terracotta images was votive. Yet the frequent appearance of terracotta figurines in graves implies that the motifs represented may have had a protective function as well. In addition, the occasional discovery of terracotta figurines in houses suggests domestic cults or possibly merely an interest in stylish décor.

2. Regional survey.

(i) Rome and Italy. (ii) Western provinces. (iii) Eastern provinces.

(i) Rome and Italy. In Rome itself there is no evidence for the manufacture of mass-produced terracottas before the end of the 4th century BC. At this time political and social factors may have offered a fertile environment for the gradual assimilation of Etruscan votive practices involving the offering of figured terracottas. By the beginning of the 3rd century BC these practices necessitated the large-scale manufacture of terracotta votives within the city, as well as throughout Rome-dominated central Italy. Based on earlier Etruscan models, these Roman, or Etrusco-Roman, terracottas reflected an indigenous, rustic, folk tradition rooted in the fertility and healing cults of the countryside. Popular types, loosely based on current trends in Greek sculpture, included the isolated head or half-head, presenting either a left or right profile; the standing offerant; the *kourotrophos*, or child-carrier; and the swaddled baby. Other more indigenous types included the anatomicals, such as hands, feet, genitalia, hearts, intestines and uteri, models of buildings and altars, animals and fruit. But the most important and widely used type was the votive head or half-head. An example of the latter of the late 4th century BC from a Tiber sanctuary in Rome (Rome, Mus. N. Romano) has the long, straight nose with full nostrils, deeply set eyes, slightly parted lips and richly modelled hair made popular by the school of the Greek sculptor Lysippos.

At the same time that the Etrusco-Roman terracottas were being produced, artisans in Rome began to imitate the motif of the urbane and elegantly draped woman of the refined and cosmopolitan Tanagra style developed in Athens towards the end of the third quarter of the 4th century BC. Thus by the 3rd century BC, within the votive repertory in central Italy, two terracotta traditions representing two distinct classes of society were current, the one rustic and the other sophisticated. It is noteworthy that Tanagras are virtually absent from the votive deposits and graves of the countryside but are well documented in large urban centres such as Rome and Pompeii.

By the early 2nd century BC the Etrusco-Roman votive types had become stereotyped and were widely diffused throughout the sphere of Roman influence in Etruria, Latium and Campania, where they had completely replaced earlier Greek votive types (Comella). However, a gradual shift in the Roman social structure towards the mid-2nd century BC caused the small, rural landowner to drift away from the countryside towards the city. Moreover, near the end of that century a deliberate process of State control began to emphasize the worship of the Capitoline triad of Jupiter, Juno and Minerva, and the old indigenous cults of the countryside lost their importance. Evidence suggests that by the beginning of the 1st century BC Etrusco-Roman terracottas were made no longer. Although terracotta figurines continued to be manufactured, they were produced in considerably reduced numbers, for entirely different purposes and with a completely different emphasis.

In the 1st century BC and particularly during the 1st century AD, elegant, Hellenistic terracotta types, which could suit a decorative as well as religious setting, became more fashionable. Secular Tanagra types continued to be produced but were now accompanied by representations of deities, such as Venus and Bacchus, or members of Bacchus' entourage. Themes referring to the theatre, the circus, the arena and caricature were particularly popular. Yet typically Roman motifs borrowed from early Imperial monumental sculpture were also developed. Such new types, which included the *togatus*, or draped, aristocratic male, the young, well-bred boy wearing the *bulla* and the portrait bust, presented a new form of *pietas* and emphasis on family values, important aspects of Augustus' political programme; the *togatus* and portrait bust types, in particular, often reflected fashions made popular by the imperial family.

Pompeii is a good source of information for late Republican and early Imperial terracotta production, but even here terracottas were found only occasionally. Their discovery *in situ* provides us with some indication of their function in everyday life. Even though a few have been found in *lararia* (domestic shrines), and several others came from sacred contexts, the more interesting discoveries are those from the living quarters of the houses. A small ensemble of terracottas was found in a cupboard among other objects in the atrium of a house (Insula I, 13, 2). One of these, a bust of a woman, one of two from the same mould, illustrates the cool neo-Classicism and generally high quality associated with the arts of the Augustan age. Other terracottas in the cupboard include two from the same mould in the form of a Silenus supporting a lamp (Naples, Mus. Archeol. N.). The terracottas in this cupboard were probably used to decorate the reception area of the house (the *tablinum*), as was the case with the figurines discovered in the *tablinum* of another house at Pompeii (Insula I, 14, 3). A large and handsome statuette of a philosopher (Naples, Mus. Archeol. N.) was uncovered in the garden of the House of Julia Felix and another of an elegant, standing draped woman (Naples, Mus. Archeol. N.), over 1 m high, in the garden of the Albergo del Gladiatore. Terracotta theatrical masks and relief discs were suspended from the architraves of garden porticos to swing in the wind, and gardens could be adorned with terracotta fountains.

(ii) Western provinces. Roman artisans followed the path of Roman colonization northwards into Switzerland and Gaul, where the terracotta industry thrived at a number of important centres. The earliest documented examples of mould-made figurines in the western Empire come from the Allier region of central France, where production based on imports from Italy started around Clermont-Ferrand and Saint-Rémy-en-Rollat by about AD 50. Here, as elsewhere in central Gaul, the manufacture of mould-made terracotta lamps was already well-established. This no doubt facilitated the production of mould-made terracotta figurines, some of which carry the signatures of lamp-makers. By the end of the 1st century AD, production was also flourishing at workshops in Colonia Claudia Ara Agrippinensium (Cologne), while in the 2nd century the Mosel and central Rhineland regions had important centres at Augusta Treverorum (Trier), Nida (Frankfurt am Main) and Mogontiacum (Mainz). At Augusta Treverorum production continued well into the 4th century, although the types, which by the early 4th century had degenerated into featureless forms, were replaced by terracotta toys representing animals and carts.

Even though several different clays have been documented for the major centres of production, the most characteristic for Gallo-Roman terracottas is a white baking clay. Many kiln sites in France, Holland, Belgium and Germany document the production of terracottas, but the prototypes for these figurines originated either in the Allier region of France or in the Cologne or central Rhineland and Mosel areas of Germany.

Scholars have been able to organize the figurines from Gaul into stylistic groups corresponding to centres of manufacture and even to individual artisans, since over 140 artisans' signatures and monograms are known, yet there is a striking uniformity of types and stylistic characteristics. Among the most popular types are a seated nursing mother known as *matrona*; an armed Minerva; Epona, the indigenous female horse goddess; Bacchus; the *togatus*; busts of men, women and children, including the *risus* type of chubby, smiling boy; the hooded boy or *cucullus*; warriors and gladiators; theatrical types and grotesques; dogs, cocks and other animals. But most popular throughout the western Empire were images of Venus. Whether nude or semi-draped, she is invariably shown standing, either as Venus pudica, anadyomene or knidia. A *Venus and Cupid* figurine from a workshop at Colonia Claudia Ara Agrippinensium of the 2nd century AD but found in Holland presents the stereotypical elongated, tear-drop shaped body with a high waist, narrow shoulders and tubular, almost rubbery arms and legs. The extreme distance from the original Roman model is evident in the structureless body, the softened contours and the need for linear touch-up that distinguishes the drapery and hair, while the many small, round protuberances and clay adhesions betray the use of a plaster mould.

Venus figurines such as these and other Gallo-Roman types were widely exported, especially to Britain. Most of the figurines found there were imported from the Allier region of central Gaul and ultimately from workshops at Colonia Claudia Ara Agrippinensium. Londinium (London) was the centre of distribution in Britain for these imported figurines, which were then carried throughout Britain by Roman soldiers.

Gallo-Roman terracottas also found their way to Spain. In general the Hispanic artisans borrowed heavily from either central Gaul or Italy, reworking the types in a highly stylized, rigid and linear idiom. Little is original among the terracottas of Roman Spain, but there is a noteworthy series of female figurines of the 3rd century AD with extraordinarily large and complicated coiffures, believed to have been inspired by fashions from North Africa. Although terracottas were produced locally in Spain from the late 1st century BC to the 4th AD, the paucity of Spanish finds in graves and votive deposits suggests that it was not a flourishing industry.

(iii) Eastern provinces. In the eastern Roman Empire the centuries-old sculptural traditions of the Hellenistic East continued to dominate artistic production well into the 3rd century AD. A true Roman terracotta production with a characteristic Roman typology such as we see in the Roman West never became established east of Italy. On mainland Greece the available evidence indicates that during the 1st century AD and early 2nd there was no figural terracotta production of any consequence, except at Corinth, where the industry experienced a revival in the 1st century after a lapse of 150 years. At Athens, for example, terracotta production picked up only during the 3rd century when figurines were produced in pottery and lamp workshops, using a minimum of means and a

typology that was developed locally, with little influence from the Roman West. An Athenian figurine of a nursing mother signed by the Greek artisan Leonteos (late 3rd century AD; London, BM), may be a distant descendant of the *kourotrophos* figurines of Classical Greece.

In the Hellenistic East during the 1st century AD the terracotta repertory was also relatively unaffected by Roman types, although the Roman coroplasts Gaius and Antistius were working both at Myrina and Pergamon as early as the late 1st century BC. Even though late Hellenistic types continued to be produced well into the early Imperial era at Pergamon, Smyrna, Troy, Myrina, Amisos and Tarsus, among other centres, there nevertheless was a gradual loss of quality, as terracottas were often produced in moulds that were long past their prime. An artless reproduction of types caused proportions to be elongated, while the increasing reliance on moulds in plaster, which broke down easily under moisture, resulted in figurines with imperfect surfaces, softened contours and indistinct details that often required much retouching for legibility. A figurine of an ephebe, signed by Diphilos (Paris, Louvre), epitomizes the gradual stylistic changes that took place over the course of the 1st century BC.

In Roman Egypt, these features contributed to a distinctive and unique style in terracottas. Called Faiyum, after a district west of the Nile in Lower Egypt, this style is also associated with a particular dark brown and coarse terracotta fabric known as 'Nile mud', although Faiyum-style figurines are known in other fabrics. Faiyum terracottas, as characterized by a lantern in the form of a half-length figure of Isis, are rigidly frontal to the point of being relief-like. The obese image has swollen and almost doughy-looking forms, which are the setting for elaborately textured surfaces rich in movement, detail and strong, linear contrasts. The Faiyum typology comprises representations of deities, such as the Egyptian Isis, Harpokrates, Bes and Serapis, or the Greek Demeter, Aphrodite, Dionysos, Eros and Athena, along with dancers and musicians, grotesques and caricatures, erotic subjects and various models of altars and lanterns, among other subjects. This style and typology developed in response to mixed influences from older pharaonic traditions from Greek Alexandria and from the large Roman population of Egypt. In contrast to the votive contexts in which most Roman terracottas have been discovered, in Egypt the contexts are primarily funereal or domestic; to date no votive deposits of Faiyum terracottas have been found.

H. Goldman: *The Hellenistic and Roman Periods* (1950), i of *Excavations at Gözlü Kule, Tarsus* (Princeton, 1950–63)

C. Grandjouan: *Terracottas and Plastic Lamps of the Roman Period* (1961), vii of *The Athenian Agora* (Princeton, 1953–82)

S. Mollard-Besques: *Myrina* (1963), ii of *Musée National du Louvre: Catalogue raisonné des figurines et reliefs en terre cuite grecs et romains* (Paris, 1954–72)

F. Jenkins: 'Some Interesting Types of Clay Statuettes of the Roman Period Found in London', *Collectanea Londiniensa: Studies in London Archaeology and History Presented to Ralph Merrifield*, ed. J. Bird, H. Chapman and J. Clark (London, 1978), pp. 149–62

P. Pensabene: *Terrecotte votive dal Tevere* (Rome, 1980)

A. M. Comella: 'Tipologia e diffusione dei complessi votivi in Italia in epoca medio- e tardo-repubblicana', *Mél. Ecole Fr. Rome: Ant.*, xciii/2 (1981–2), pp. 717–803

A. Ruiz Fernández and F. Molina Fajardo: 'El conjunto de teracotas de una tumba romana in Almuñécar (Granada)', *Madrid. Mitt.*, xxiii (1982), pp. 318–46

V. von Gonzenbach: *Die römische Terracotten in der Schweiz: Untersuchungen zu Zeitstellung, Typologie, und Ursprung der mittelgallischen Tonstattuetten*, vol. B (Berne, 1986)

J. MacIntosh Turfa: 'The Anatomical Votive Terracottas in Etruscan and Italic Sanctuaries', *Italian Iron Age Artifacts in the British Museum*, ed. J. Swaddling (London, 1986)

G. M. E. C. Boekel: *Roman Terracotta Figurines and Masks from the Netherlands* (Groeningen, 1989)

A. d'Ambrosio and M. Borriello: *Le terrecotte figurate di Pompei* (Rome, 1990)

F. Dunand: *Musée du Louvre: Catalogue des terres cuites gréco-romaines d'Egypte* (Paris, 1990)

H. Lange: *Römische Terrakotten aus Salzburg*, Schriftenreihe des Salzburger Museums Carolino Augusteum, 9 (Salzburg, 1990)

Deliciae Fictiles: Proceedings of the First International Conference on Central Italic Architectural Terracottas at the Swedish Institute in Rome, 1990

J. De Bienhouwer: 'Roman Terracotta Statuettes from a Closed Find at Tongeren and their Relation to the Köln, Trier and Central Rhein Production Centers', *Acta Archaeol. Louvan.*, xxx (1991), pp. 61–93

L. Rangel Berrocal: 'Avance al estudio del depósito votivo altoimperial del Castrejón de Campote (Higuera la Real, Badajoz)', *Extremadura Arqueol.*, ii (1991), pp. 331–44

C. Bémont, M. Jeanlon and C. Lahanier: *Les Figurines en terre cuite gallo-romaines* (Paris, 1993)

S. Ciaghi: *Le terrecotte figurate da Cales del Museo Nazionale di Napoli* (Rome, 1993)

S. B. Downey: *Architectural Terracottas from the Regia* (Ann Arbor, 1995)

Deliciae Fictiles II: Proceedings of the Second International Conference on Archaic Architectural Terracottas from Italy Held at the Netherlands Institute in Rome, 1996

Tetrastyle. Term applied to a building with a portico of four columns.

Textiles. Fabrics composed of any form of pliable fibre held together by such techniques as weaving, felting, plaiting, looping etc.

See also DRESS.

1. Greek. 2. Etruscan. 3. Roman.

1. GREEK. Few textiles have survived from ancient Greece. References in literature and evidence from vase painting and sculpture are, however, abundant. Wool was the most commonly used material, because of the plentiful supply of sheep. Linen was also popular but more expensive, because it had to be imported. Greece was not fertile enough for

the growing of flax. Silk was also much prized but obtainable only from the East by those who could afford it. Cotton is mentioned by Herodotus in the 5th century BC as an exotic substance growing in India. The standard textile product was a rectangular piece of wool for use as a cloak or blanket, curtain or whatever was required. The weave and thickness of the material varied.

Wool-making was women's work. The wool was first washed and beaten in the courtyard of the Greek home. Then it was taken indoors and straightened into hanks. To do this, women sat on a chair and spread the wool across their knees, which they would protect with a special kind of leg-shield (*epinetron*). A number of these beautifully decorated objects made of terracotta have survived. They were probably often given to young women as wedding presents. For dyeing the wool, many colours were available, obtained from a variety of mineral and vegetable substances. The favourite, a purple dye, was extracted from the murex shellfish found along the shores of the eastern Mediterranean. After dyeing, the wool was spun with a distaff and spindle. The spindle, made of polished wood and *c.* 304 mm long, was weighted with whorls made of clay (these are often found in the excavation of ancient Greek homes).

After spinning, the wool became a fine yarn, suitable for weaving. The Greek loom was upright and made of wood; the warp hung from the crossbar of the loom with the lower end anchored with loom weights. Miniature looms also existed. These produced delicate patterns on small pieces of cloth, for use as borders and veils. The sprang process, involving the manipulation of a set of stretched threads, was widely used for patterned textiles.

M. G. Houston: *Ancient Greek, Roman and Byzantine Costume and Decoration* (1931/*R* 1966), ii of *A Technical History of Costume* (London, 1920–39)
R. J. Forbes: *Studies in Ancient Technology*, iv (Leiden, 1956)
M. Hoffman: *The Warp-weighted Loom* (Oslo and Bergen, 1964)
G. M. A. Richter: 'The Furnishings of Ancient Greek Houses', *Archaeology*, xviii (1965), pp. 26–32
H. W. Parke: *Festivals of the Athenians* (London, 1977), pp. 38–9
I. Tzachile: *Hyphantike kai hyphantres sto proïstoriko Aigaio: 2000–1000 p.Ch* (Herakleion, 1997)
M. Vickers *Images on Textiles: The Weave of Fifth-century Athenian Art and Society* (Konstanz, 1999)

2. Etruscan. Etruscan textiles were in demand not only for garments, but also for blankets, sheets, cushions, rugs, armour padding, sails and other objects of everyday use. One Etruscan speciality was linen books containing prayers and religious texts, which were used by priests and depicted on their sarcophagi as attributes of office. One of these, the *Liber linteus* (?1st century BC; Zagreb, Archaeol. Mus.), was subsequently taken to Egypt, cut into strips and used to wrap a mummy. The restoration and scientific analysis of this and other textiles provide evidence of, for example, the origin of the flax and the methods of manufacture of both wool and linen, the two fabrics used most by the Etruscans. It is also possible to analyse 'pseudomorphs', the thread marks caused by the chemical reaction of bronze objects with cloth, for example when bronze mirrors were protected by cloth mirror-cases, the latter no longer surviving. Further information on Etruscan textile manufacture comes from finds of all periods, both tombs (women were buried with distaffs and spindles, sometimes made of precious materials) and dwelling sites (thousands of loom weights have been found, some still in place where they were used, tied to the threads of the cloth on the loom).

J. Stage: *Etruscan Textiles* (MA thesis, Tallahassee, FL State U., 1981)
E. Barber: *Prehistoric Textiles* (Princeton, 1992)

3. Roman.

(i) Introduction. (ii) Materials and techniques. (iii) Style and subject-matter.

(i) Introduction. Evidence for Roman textiles has come from fine art, particularly portrait sculpture, from Latin texts and from recovered equipment such as spindles and loom weights. There is now also a growing body of excavated textiles, many well-preserved. The most important groups are from Palmyra and Dura Europos in Syria; Masada and the Cave of Letters in Israel; Mons Claudianus in Egypt; Pompeii and Herculaneum in Italy; Mainz in Germany; and Vindolanda on Hadrian's Wall in England. Isolated finds include several from Rome itself. There are examples of the Roman period among Egyptian Coptic textiles. Late Roman textiles have occasionally survived as Christian relics.

Clothing, usually of wool, consisted principally of a tunic and a draped mantle or cloak (*see also* Dress). Loincloths, socks and women's hair-nets were among a range of smaller garments. Household textiles, of wool or linen, included decorated couch and cushion covers, wall hangings, curtains and carpets as well as plainer towels etc. Outdoors, sacks, sails and awnings were all made from woven cloth. In a society with relatively few personal possessions, textiles were prominent and always costly, whether reckoned in terms of money, if bought, or expenditure of time, if made by women of the household. Some garments differed in outline from region to region; in particular the Roman and Italic man's mantle, the toga, was semicircular, while the mantle worn in the Greek-influenced East was rectangular. But in general textile types were similar throughout the Mediterranean area. Social class was expressed through the choice of raw material: fine white wool was valued far higher than pigmented coarse wool and real purple dye expressed status in direct proportion to its cost. Quantity of material also denoted status: in general the greater the social position the more voluminous the clothes. 'Drapery' in Classical art reflects a style of clothing that was emphatically three-dimensional.

(ii) Materials and techniques. Cloths of wool or linen, the commonest fibres, were supplemented at the bottom of the market by goat-hair and some cotton and at the top by silk (originally imported from the Far East, by the 2nd or 3rd century AD probably being produced within the Roman Empire). Linen was almost invariably left undyed. Wool occurred naturally in a range of colours from cream to dark brown but was also often dyed, as was silk. Dye analysis has shown that primary colours were produced from vegetable dyes: madder for reds, woad or Indian indigo for blues and various plants including weld for yellows; greens, oranges and second-grade purples were created by combining these. The most expensive colours were the real purples, derived from an extract of several Mediterranean sea whelks; very dark tones were particularly admired. Also expensive were dark pinks obtained from certain insects, in particular kermes. Favourite colour combinations usually involved real or imitation purple: a white ground with contrasting areas of purple for men's clothes; a darker colour, often pink, with contrasting purple for women's clothes; green with purple for many furnishings. For exceptional uses real gold thread was combined with wool dyed with real purple.

Despite the fine quality and sophistication of many Roman textiles, the equipment used was mostly simple and unchanged for centuries. Spinning was carried out with a spindle and short distaff, although methods varied. Wool was combed before spinning and the careful preparation of roves made possible extremely fine yarns. Linen yarns were often also very fine. The two major looms were the warp-weighted loom and the two-beam upright loom. But more complex weaves, occurring from the 1st century AD, indicate the presence of a third loom, probably horizontal and with a number of shafts or heddle rods. In the Mediterranean area the predominant wool weave was a weft-faced tabby or plain weave, although more open and crêpe-like tabbies also occur. A thicker 1:2 twill was employed especially for cloaks. Such cloths were usually given a brushed nap. Textiles with a weft pile were also common, as both furnishings and clothing. For clothing, the pile was plain and usually had asymmetrical knots (the original loops are often now missing because of wear). Tapestry, which exploited the natural weft-faced tendency of the wool cloth, was much the most common decorative weave. Compound tabby, the earliest complex weave to appear, was also weft-faced; it was characterized by repeating patterns in two contrasting colours. In the northern provinces the most widely used wool weave was 2:2 twill, often in the form of diamond twill. Northern wool cloths also differed in being 'balanced', with roughly equal numbers of warp and weft threads. Throughout the Empire all-linen cloth was quite plain, decorated only by bands of grouped weft threads.

Minor techniques included sprang, knotless netting, felting and narrow band weaving. Embroidery was known but was not common; there are some late examples in thick wool on a linen ground, evidently furnishings. More important was a technique where a resist medium, probably mainly wax, was painted on to a plain cloth and the cloth afterwards dyed with indigotin. Roman textiles differed much from modern textiles, in particular in that they were never produced as anonymous lengths. Warps were short, sometimes shorter than they were wide, and were always prepared with a particular item in mind. Longitudinal selvages as well as the special transverse starting and closing borders were retained on the finished item (the little tassels at the ends of these borders are often shown on sculpture). The use of cutting and sewing was minimal, and some shaping was even carried out during weaving.

(iii) Style and subject-matter. Textiles made for clothing were generally plain, decorated only with simple weft-faced bands or motifs, most obviously the two vertical *clavi* (bands) on tunics (tunics were made up with the warp of the cloth running horizontally). But some figural decoration might occur within the area of the contrasting colour, for example the narrow tapestry garland on fragments of silk from the Vatican cemetery was probably part of a *clavus* on a woman's tunic. And certain garments were highly elaborate. The *toga picta* (patterned toga), worn with a matching tunic by victorious generals in triumphs, was entirely in gold and purple tapestry; a bronze fragment of a depicted triumphal garment from the Arch of Caracalla at Volubilis (early 3rd century AD) is decorated with captives and trophies of arms.

A favourite style for furnishing textiles had abstract shaded bands: an example is the cloth from the Cave of Letters where, on a green ground, multiple bands shading from purple to red appear to be three-dimensional and overlapping. But furnishings could have large-scale multicoloured figural designs, for example the scenes of Ariadne and Dionysus on a fragmentary set of tapestries (h. 1 m; Hildesheim, Pelizaeus-Mus.). Tapestry decoration was close in style to other Roman decorative art; the fishes on a fragment of a wall hanging from Antinoöpolis, for instance, compare closely with fishes in a wall painting in the House of the Vettii at Pompeii. Designs in coloured loops were by their nature less subtle, but in turn had strong affinities with mosaics. Examples of the blue-and-white resist technique, for instance the cloth with the *Life of Dionysus* in the Louvre, have flowing curvilinear designs which, despite the difference in scale, can be compared to engraved designs on metalwork.

In the late Roman period (3rd and 4th centuries AD) an increased taste for decoration in all areas of life influenced clothing in particular. Schemes of decoration became more complex with roundels or squares and sleeve bands appearing on tunics in addition to *clavi*. These contrasting ornaments were provided with tapestry plant borders and by *c.* AD 400 had begun to be filled with figural scenes in the manner continued in Coptic textiles. At the same time the spread of more complex weaves led to the first appearance of all-over repeating designs on clothing.

R. Pfister: *Textiles de Palmyre*, 3 vols (Paris, 1934–40)
R. Pfister and L. Bellinger: *The Textiles* (1945), IV/ii of *The Excavations at Dura-Europos: Final Reports*, ed. M. I. Rostovtzeff and others (New Haven, 1943–67)
Y. Yadin: *The Finds from the Bar-Kokhba Period in the Cave of Letters* (Jerusalem, 1963)
J. P. Wild: *Textile Manufacture in the Northern Roman Provinces* (Cambridge, 1970)
H. Granger-Taylor: 'Weaving Clothes to Shape in the Ancient World: The Tunic and Toga of the Arringatore', *Textile Hist.*, xiii/1 (1982), pp. 3–25
H. Granger-Taylor: 'Two Silk Textiles from Rome and Some Thoughts on the Roman Silk weaving Industry', *Bull. Liaison Cent. Int. Etud. Textiles Anc.*, lxi (1987), pp. 13–31
M. Flury-Lemberg: *Textile Conservation and Research* (Berne, 1988)
M.-H. Rutschowscaya: *Coptic Fabrics* (Paris, 1990)
A. Sheffer and H. Granger-Taylor: 'The Textiles: A Preliminary Selection', *Masada: The Yigael Yadin Excavations 1963–65: Final Reports*, iv (Jerusalem, 1991)
P. W. Rogers, L. B. Jørgensen and A. Rast-Eicher, eds: *The Roman Textile Industry and its Influence: A Birthday Tribute to John Peter Wild* (Oxford, 2001)
J. C. Batcheller: *Late Roman Textiles from Karanis, Egypt: An Investigation into the Characterization of Archaeological Textiles*, 2 vols (diss., U. Manchester, 2002)
L. L. Lovén: *The Imagery of Textile Making: Gender and Status in the Funerary Iconography of Textile Manufacture in Roman Italy and Gaul* (Göteborg, 2002)

Thamugadi [Timgad]. Site of one of the most completely excavated Roman towns in North Africa (see fig.). It lies on the edge of a plain in Algeria, below the northern flanks of the Aures mountains, some 160 km from the Mediterranean coast. It stood at a nodal point in the road system: to the west lay the legionary fortress at Lambaesis, while to the east was the main route to Thevestis and Carthage. It was founded by Trajan in AD 100 as a colony for army veterans, the Colonia Marciana Traiana Thamugadi, and built by soldiers stationed at Lambaesis. Although its plan is overwhelmingly military, there is little doubt that Thamugadi was intended to be a town, not a military base. Its square shape comprises a grid of 111 blocks, each 20 sq. m; most were subdivided into properties for the individual settlers, while a good number were given over to public buildings.

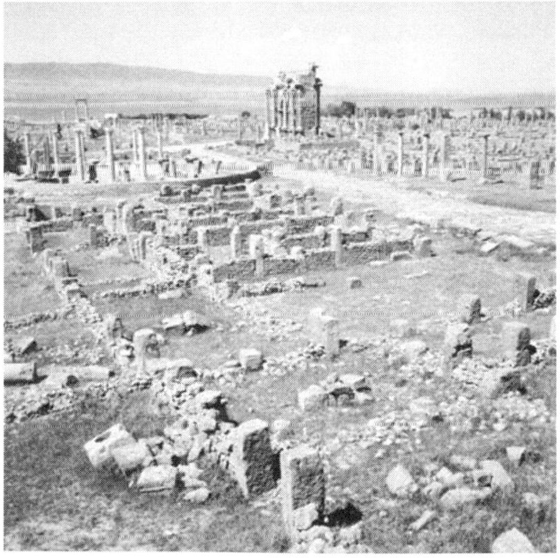

Thamugadi, view of Roman town, begun AD 100

The forum was placed more or less centrally, where the main north–south street met the main east–west street. The square (50×43 m) was surrounded by shops, a public lavatory, the judicial basilica, a temple dedicated to Trajan and his military victories and, in the north-east corner, the so-called Maison des Jardinières. This elegant building was probably the official residence of the legate of the Third Legion, who acted as governor of the province of Numidia. Within the forum were statues of local dignitaries, while many graffiti record games and diversions played in the shade of the porticos; one reads: 'to hunt, to bathe, to play, to laugh, that's living'. Nearby there was a market and a theatre (begun AD 160), while elsewhere in the town no fewer than 14 bath complexes were built; together with the magnificent library (?4th century AD) they illustrate how civilized frontier towns could become. The houses vary greatly in size, style and grandeur, indicating a wide variation in individual wealth; some had mosaic floors from the first, while others acquired them much later, or not at all.

Before long, the town began to expand beyond its walls. The capitolium, a magnificent temple to Jupiter, Juno and Minerva (begun *c.* AD 160), was built on a high podium to the south-west of the town, and private housing soon followed. The orientation of the street grid was largely ignored, a departure from rigid planning that is consistent with spontaneous growth. Eventually large parts of the old town walls were pulled down, while to the west the gate was replaced by a splendid triumphal arch built *c.* AD 200 under Severus, though incorrectly known as the Arch of Trajan. Just outside is a great market (early 3rd century AD), paid for by a rich citizen, M. Plotius Faustus Sertius; his sumptuous house lay at the south-west corner of the town. Great public baths were put up to the north, west and south of the old town, but particular interest attaches to the extra-mural Christian complexes. One, to the south-west, comprises a vast basilica, a baptistery, baths and other buildings, including a house with a 4th-century AD inscription bearing the name of Optatus, a bishop of the Donatist sect. The other main Christian complex, to the north-west of the town, also had a huge cathedral and baptistery, which may have belonged to the Catholic church.

The town was finally deserted in the mid-7th century AD.

J. Lassus: *Visite à Timgad* (Paris, 1969) [good pls]
J. Lassus: *Fouille à Timgad, 1938–56*, i of *La Forteresse byzantine de Thamugadi*, Etudes d'antiquités africaines (Paris, 1981)

Thasos. Greek island in the northern Aegean, close to the Thracian coast. It was colonized by Ionian Greeks from Paros probably *c.* 680 BC. The primary attraction was precious metal, mined on the island itself as well as the mainland opposite, part of which eventually came under Thasian control. This provided a sound basis for prosperity, along with the export of wine: storage amphorae with stamped handles indicating Thasian origin have been found in enormous quantities in the Aegean area and further afield, particularly from the Hellenistic period. The town of Thasos is on the northern side of the island, facing Thrace, with luxuriantly wooded hills rising up behind it to an acropolis. Sites on the island have been excavated since 1910 by the French School in Athens.

Despite the wealth resulting from trade, and the availability of white marble quarried in the southern part of Thasos, the architecture of the island is solid rather than spectacular. There are no large temples, but the buildings of the ancient town, both public and private, are soundly constructed and have therefore left substantial remains. By the end of the 6th century BC a substantial area was included within the stone-built fortifications that run up to and along the ridge leading to the acropolis. The walls are of trapezoidal masonry, and have impressive gateways, flanked by large, upright slabs of stone decorated with figures in relief. Within the fortified area, the town seems to have been the result of haphazard development, and there is no sign of an imposed grid plan. Evidence survives for houses dating back at least to the 6th century BC, though there was constant renewal, and many houses are later. There is no simple, universal house plan. Sizes vary, and layout depends on the often irregular building plots, though most seem to conform to the courtyard arrangement typical of ancient Greek houses.

The principal sanctuary that has been excavated is that of Herakles, again dating back at least to the 6th century BC. The temple was not part of the original arrangement but was added in the mid-5th century BC. It is in the Ionic order, peripteral, but having only eight columns along the sides. Eventually the precinct was closed off, with entrance via a small propylon. Herakles was worshipped here both as a god and as a hero, reflecting the Greek myth of Herakles' birth and translation to deified status. Attempts to identify the dual Thasian cult with that of the Phoenician 'Herakles' (presupposing a Phoenician interest in the trade in precious metals) remain inconclusive, and there is no need to postulate non-Greek influence in the architectural arrangement. An ancillary structure, originally a single rectangular room but later extended to form a set of adjacent rooms, is best interpreted as a building for ritual feasts.

Other public buildings include a conventional theatre on the slopes of the acropolis hill. More interesting are the buildings of the agora, an irregularly shaped area a short distance from the harbour (the submerged remains of substantial artificial harbour walls can still be seen). Surprisingly the buildings of the agora are much later than other parts of the town, being Hellenistic in date. They may represent a resurgence, either under Macedonian royal control or, more probably, in a period of renewed independence after the collapse of the Macedonian Kingdom (167 BC). However, despite its Hellenistic date, the agora does not conform to the regular enclosed courtyard type that evolved in the planned cities of Asia Minor, such as Priene and Miletos, and that was imposed (as far as possible) at this time in the Agora at Athens. The perimeter is marked out by a series of stoas, which were treated as separate architectural entities rather than a mere surround of colonnades. This is particularly emphasized by the stoa on the east side, which is of the *paraskenia* (stage building) plan, with a central section terminated at each end by projecting, pedimented wings, modelled on the Stoa of Zeus at Athens.

There are ancient buildings in other parts of the island. One notable feature is the frequent presence of isolated towers. The only other important site (though not particularly large) is a sanctuary at Aliki on the south side of the island, near the marble quarries, which has not been fully investigated. A building there with two adjacent rectangular rooms of unequal dimensions has been identified as the temple, but would be most unusual in plan if it had been intended to fulfil the normal functions of a temple. It is much more likely to have contained a pair of feasting rooms. No remains of a conventional Greek temple have been found at Aliki.

B. Bergquist: *Herakles on Thasos* (Uppsala, 1973)

J. Servais: 'Les Deux Sanctuaires', *Aliki I* (1980), ix of *Etudes thasiennes* (Paris, 1971–)

R. Osborne: 'Island Towers: The Case of Thasos', *Annu. Brit. Sch. Athens*, lxxxi (1986), pp. 167–78

Thasos: Protes hyles kai technologia apo tous proïstorikous chronous hos semera: Praktika diethnous synedriou, Limenaria Thasou, 1995/ Thasos: Matières premières et technologie de la préhistoire à nos jours: Actes du colloque international

Y. Garlan: *Les Timbres amphoriques de Thasos* (Athens, 1996)

A. Muller: *Les Terres cuites votives du Thesmophorion: De l'atelier au sanctuaire* (Athens, 1996)

A. Coulié: *La Céramique thasienne à figures noires* (Athens, 2002)

Theatre. Place or structure for drama and performance.

1. Greek. 2. Roman.

1. Greek. In its fully developed form the Greek theatre consisted of three components: the *orchestra* (circular performing area), *theatron* (auditorium) and *skene* (the stage building); these may be considered the products respectively of the Archaic, Classical and Hellenistic periods. The *orchestra* (Gr. *orcheisthai*: 'to dance') probably derived its shape from the threshing-floor where in early times religious dances took place on the same spot as was used for laying out grapes to dry. These dances, made in honour of Dionysos (the god of wine), were performed by a chorus. As theatre developed, the orchestra—the

place for music and dancing—remained its nuclear centre, and as a result the term is applied today to that part of a theatre where the musicians play, or to the musicians themselves. The earliest dramas in Athens may have been performed in an *orchestra* in the Agora, which may have been the site of wooden seating that collapsed *c*. 500–496 BC. Performances were then probably transferred to the south slope of the Acropolis near the Theatre of Dionysos, where spectators sat on wooden benches placed on the hillside. Thespis is credited with having added a speaking actor to the original chorus by 535–533 BC; Aeschylus (525–456 BC) introduced a second actor, making dialogue more significant. Aeschylus used mechanical devices, props (such as tombs and altars) and ghostly apparitions; he also created a distinctive costume for actors, consisting of a long-sleeved robe, a high headdress, masks, and tall boots to increase their height. As a result spectacle became an important part of Greek drama, reflected in the Greek term *theatron* ('seeing place').

During the 5th century BC the chorus declined until it often provided little more than a musical interlude. The increasing importance of the actors led to the construction of temporary scene buildings, which doubled as storerooms and dressing-rooms. Sophocles (*c*. 490–406 BC) is said to have invented scene painting and placed his actors into defined settings. At the time of Lycurgus (*d* 324 BC) a *theatron* was built at Athens as well as a *skene*, both in stone. The latter probably had columns and projecting wings (*paraskenia*) like those shown on Greek vases, but there was as yet no raised stage. The *theatron* was slightly more than a semicircle, with the result that the sustaining walls converged. The Classical theatre achieved its most harmonious form at the site of EPIDAUROS (built *c*. 350 BC) with its perfectly symmetrical *theatron* divided into two sections by a horizontal curved passage. The *orchestra* is circular, and open passages divide the *theatron* from the *skene*. Greek tragedy declined in the 4th century, and comedy became increasingly popular, with the result that the *orchestra* became less significant. The rise of New Comedy, with its emphasis on individual character, resulted in the introduction of the raised stage. This development, which probably took place in the eastern Greek world in *c*. 300 BC, can be seen in the theatre at Priene which has a two-storey stone *skene* with a single-storey *proskenion* (decorative façade) roofed in wood. Most scholars believe the actors performed on this wooden planking, which was thus the stage. During the 3rd century BC this type of theatre, with its broad and narrow stage, spread to the Greek mainland, where a preference developed for ramps leading up to it instead of staircases, for example at Oropos. The next development of the Hellenistic *skene* was the creation (in the late 3rd century) of a series of large openings that gave the stage depth, as well as providing versatile spaces which could act as entrances to the stage or be closed by curtains, screens or painted scenery. Some wall-paintings at Pompeii are based upon Hellenistic stage scenery, and Vitruvius (*On Architecture* V.vi.9) describes the types suited to different kinds of drama: tragic scenes have columns, pediments, statues and the objects suited to kings; comic scenes have private dwellings with balconies and views; satyric scenes have trees, caverns, mountains and other rustic landscape objects.

See also ARCHITECTURE, §IV, 1(i)(e).

2. ROMAN. Like their Hellenistic antecedents, Roman theatres were composed of three main elements: the *cavea*, where the audience sat; the *orchestra*, which in the case of Roman theatres was approximately semicircular; and the *scaena* or stage building. The *cavea* was more or less semicircular, and the sustaining walls were parallel to the stage building. The seating abutted the wings of the *scaena*, resulting in a more organically unified building than the earlier Greek theatre. Whereas in Greek theatres the scene building and seating were separated by open passageways that led into the *orchestra*, entry to the *orchestra* in a Roman theatre was through a pair of covered passages running under the seating. The *cavea* itself could rest on a hillside or be built on substructures. An entirely flat site necessitated a fully built-up *cavea*, of which the classic example is the Theatre of Marcellus at Rome (ded. *c*. 13–11 BC). Its substructures take the form of alternately annular and radial passages, which both support and penetrate the structure, affording excellent circulation throughout the building. Even if a site was almost entirely flat, a slight depression supplemented by an earth embankment saved a lot of expense in building supporting substructures, as shown at the theatre at SABRATHA (late 2nd century AD). In general, substructures were a last resort, and whenever possible theatres were built against hillsides, although the edges of the *cavea* usually needed some artificial support. The majority of major Roman theatres, such as those at Vindobona (Vienna, Austria), Ostia (Italy) and Augusta Emerita (Mérida, Spain)—all of which date from the Augustan period—and ARAUSIO (1st century AD; Orange, France), Philadelphia (2nd century AD; Amman, Jordan) and ASPENDOS (AD 161–80; Turkey) used substructures to supplement a natural slope. Seating was usually divided into three levels—lower, middle and upper—by means of curved passages. The *cavea* was further divided by means of staircases into wedges of seats, usually in multiples of four, five and six. In some theatres a colonnade ran at the level of the upper seats of the *cavea*, its roof being the crowning feature of the *cavea* wall. The Theatre of Pompey (ded. 55 BC) had a temple at the top of the *cavea*, and this feature was adopted in many later theatres, particularly in North Africa.

The semicircular *orchestra*, which derived from the Hellenistic theatre, gradually became obsolete during the Empire when tragedy and comedy gave way to lower forms of drama such as pantomime. In most theatres the *orchestra* was surrounded by three rows of broad, shallow steps on which were placed the thrones of magistrates. In the Late Empire the *orchestra* was sometimes adapted for sports, such as the baiting of animals, or flooded for aquatic spectacles. The front of the stage (*proscaenium*) was often decorated with alternate rectangular and curved niches. The stage itself was rarely more than 1 m high, but was very broad and long. At its front was a slot into which the curtain was lowered at the beginning of a performance, and under the stage there were sometimes trap-doors, to provide for the appearances of ghosts. At the sides of the stage were large rooms (*versurae*) used either for storing props or as foyers during intervals. Behind the stage rose the richly decorated *scaenae frons*, the front of the stage building. It contained three doorways, the central *valvae regiae* ('royal' door) and flanking *hospitalia* ('guest' doors). The stage front was usually rectilinear in the eastern provinces, as at Aspendos, but a common arrangement in the western provinces was for the *valvae regiae* to be framed by a broad curved niche and the *hospitalia* by shallow rectangular ones. There were usually pairs of columns in front of each doorway, as well as a two- or three-tier screen of columns, which ran the whole width of the *scaenae frons* following the indentations of its façade. Above the columnar screen was a sloping roof, which covered only the stage, angled to deflect sound down to the audience. Behind the *scaenae frons* was a row of rooms or a single long room, the *postscaenium*, which was used by the actors or for props. Several theatres, such as those at Arausio or Aspendos, were provided with a row of brackets running along the top of the *postscaenium* and *cavea* walls for the masts that supported the awning draped over the seating to protect spectators from the sun. There was often a portico behind the *postscaenium*, as at Philadelphia, and sometimes a large porticoed square, as at Ostia and Augusta Emerita.

See also ARCHITECTURE, §VI, 1(i)(e).

M. Bieber: *The History of the Greek and Roman Theater* (Princeton, 1939, rev. 2/1961)

A. W. Picard-Cambridge: *The Theatre of Dionysus in Athens* (Oxford, 1946)

W. Beare: *The Roman Stage: A Short History of Latin Drama in the Time of the Republic* (London, 1950)

W. B. Dinsmoor: *The Architecture of Ancient Greece* (London, 1950, *R* 1978)

T. B. L. Webster: *Greek Theatre Production* (London, 1956)

A. W. Lawrence: *Greek Architecture*, Pelican Hist. A. (Harmondsworth, 1957, 2/1983), pp. 362–73

L. Crema: 'L'Architettura romana', *Enciclopedia classica* (Turin, 1959)

J. A. Hanson: *Roman Theater-Temples* (Princeton, 1959)

G. Traversari: *Gli spettacoli in acqua nel teatro tardo-antico* (Rome, 1960)

A. Neppi Modona: *Gli edifici teatrali greci e romani* (Florence, 1961)

A. Boethius: *Etruscan and Early Roman Architecture*, Pelican Hist. A. (Harmondsworth, 1978), pp. 198–206

R. Graefe: *Vela Erunt: Die Zeltdächer der römischen Theater und ähnlicher Anlagen* (Mainz, 1979)

J. B. Ward Perkins: *Roman Imperial Architecture*, Pelican Hist. A. (Harmondsworth, 1981)

E. Frézouls: 'Aspects de l'histoire architecturale du théâtre romain', *Aufstieg und Niedergang der römischen Welt*, XII/i/2 (Berlin, 1982), pp. 343–441

F. B. Sear: *Roman Architecture* (London, 1982)

R. Leacroft and H. Leacroft: *Theatre and Playhouse* (London, 1984)

C. Courtois: *Le Bâtiment de scène des théâtres d'Italie et de Sicile* (Providence, RI, 1989)

R. C. Beacham: *The Roman Theatre and its Audience* (Cambridge, MA, 1992)

A. Segal: *Theatres in Roman Palestine and Provincia Arabia* (Leiden, 1995)

P. Easterling and E. Hall: *Greek and Roman Actors: Aspects of an Ancient Profession* (Cambridge, 2002)

Theatron. Auditorium in an ancient Greek theatre.

Thebes [now Thívai] Greek city in Boiotia that flourished in the Bronze Age and Classical times. It was traditionally founded by Kadmos the Phoenician in 1313 BC; its dominance in the loose federation later known as the Boiotian League culminated in the destruction of Spartan hegemony at the Battle of Leuktra (371 BC). The city was destroyed by Alexander the Great in 336 BC, and though later rebuilt its fortunes revived only in the Middle Ages. The modern town was built on the heart of the ancient city, the oval plateau known as the Kadmeia. Here excavations (1906–21) by Keramopoulos and others have uncovered the Bronze Age palace, but most of the visible remains are medieval.

1. BRONZE AGE. A settlement of the Neolithic period was founded in the Pyri suburb on the plain north-west of the Kadmeia. During the Early Helladic (EH) period (*c*. 3600/3000–*c*. 2050 BC) Thebes became a centre of considerable importance. The EH settlement covers most of the Kadmeia, though concentrated mainly in its southern part. A large and important settlement of the same period was located and unearthed at Lithares, *c*. 10 km north of Thebes. Both settlements coexisted until the end of the EH II period (*c*. 2400 BC), when Lithares was destroyed and temporarily abandoned. Thebes continued, though with diminished power, into the EH III phase (*c*. 2400–*c*. 2050 BC). An apsidal house in the area of the Mycenaean palace (see below) is thought to have been an EH palace, and is associated with a jar containing several bronzes (Thebes Mus.). A tumulus structure containing a remarkable cist grave of the EH II period was excavated to the north of the Kadmeia on the Ampheion hill. The interior of the hill is penetrated by corridors, staircases and niches, and the surface of the hill itself is cut to form a stepped pyramidal structure with three successive terraces. It recalls the Egyptian stepped pyramids and supports the tradition of Egyptian influence on prehistoric Greece.

The existence of a megaron and well-provided graves suggests that Middle Helladic (*c*. 2050–*c*. 1600 BC) Thebes was a city of some significance. The main

Late Helladic (LH) floruit was during LH III (*c.* 1390–*c.* 1050 BC): extensive remains of a Mycenaean palatial structure have been excavated along Pindarou Street, together with high-quality finds, including fine frescoes and inscribed stirrup jars (Thebes Mus.). Founded during the LH IIIA 2 period (*c.* 1360–*c.* 1335 BC), it seems to have undergone local destructions and rebuilding before its final destruction, reliably dated to *c.* 1200 BC, during LH IIIB 2. Though it had been frequently argued that there were two successive palaces in Thebes, it is clear that there was only one complex. It is a homogeneous building, covering *c.* 20,000 sq. m, and comprises apartments and large store-magazines.

The main chamber tomb cemeteries of Thebes (dating from LH II to LH IIIC, *c.* 1500–*c.* 1050 BC) were found on the hills around the Kadmeia, but not—as it has erroneously been argued—on Ampheion. The most important tombs were found on the hill of Megalo Kastelli to the east of the city on the ancient road to Chalkis, where the graves of the Theban heroes were located, according to Pausanias, who also mentioned the graves of the sons of Oedipus. These last have been linked with the huge chamber tomb on the north slope of the hill, a spectacular monument with two dromoi (entrance passages) and a chamber measuring 7×12 m. The smaller dromos façade and most of the chamber were decorated with frescoes, representing decorative motifs as well as scenes of mourning women and a funeral palanquin accompanied by female figures. In LH IIIB (*c.* 1335–*c.* 1180 BC), when it became the royal tomb of Thebes, a deep peridromos was cut around the entire hill, and a large exedra with seats has been preserved in front of the tomb itself. The hill must have become an athletic site for the cult of the dead, where funeral games such as those described by Homer (*Iliad* XXIII) were performed.

H. Reusch: *Die zeichnerische Rekonstruktion des Frauenfrieses in böotischen Theben* (1956)
T. G. Spyropoulos: *Athens An. Archaeol.*, iv (1971)
T. G. Spyropoulos: [Egyptian colonization of Boiotia], *Athens An. Archaeol.*, v (1972), pp. 16–27
S. Symeonoglou: *Kadmeia I: Mycenaean Finds from Thebes, Greece: Excavation at 14 Oedipus St*, Stud. Medit. Archaeol., xxxv (Göteborg, 1973)
T. G. Spyropoulos and J. Chadwick: 'The Thebes Tablets II', *Salamanca* (1975), p. 9
T. G. Spyropoulos: *Ampheion* (Sparta, 1982)

2. CLASSICAL GREEK. Despite the obliteration of the ancient city by later development, excavation has uncovered the remains of fortifications and other buildings, and many small artefacts. The Classical fortifications were double; the inner ring surrounded the Kadmeia, partly following the Mycenaean wall and probably including sections of it. Traditionally it had seven gates, though it is most exceptional to find so many gates in the Mycenaean period. Little of these survives, but the site of the Elektra Gate on the south side has been excavated; it was flanked by semicircular towers. By the Archaic period the area of habitation extended outside the walls of the Kadmeia and was subsequently included in an outer ring of fortifications. This extended for 7 km and enclosed an area of over 300 ha. The walls were of mud-brick on an isodomic masonry base. Various dates have been suggested: stylistically they belong to the 5th century BC rather than the period of Theban supremacy in the 4th. Near the Elektra Gate is the Temple of Ismenian Apollo (4th century BC), built at the height of Thebes's power and prosperity to replace an earlier temple of the 6th century BC. Only foundations and scattered architectural fragments survive: it was in the Doric order (6×12 columns) and measured 46.3×22.9 m. The principal temple was that of Dionysos, on the site of the Mycenaean palace: nothing of it survives.

A. D. Keramopoulos: 'Thebaika' [Theban things], *Archaiol. Deltion*, iii (1917) [whole issue]
S. Symeonoglou: *The Topography of Thebes* (Princeton, 1985)

Theodosios I [the Great] (*b* Cauca [now Coca], Spain, *c.* AD 346; *reg* 379–95; *d* Milan, 17 Jan 395). Roman emperor and patron. His father, Count Theodosios, was executed in 376 under Valens (*reg* 364–78), but in 379 Gratian (*reg* 367–83) proclaimed Theodosios emperor of the eastern empire. In a series of campaigns he contained the invading Goths and crushed two rivals in the west: Magnus Maximus (*reg* 383–8) and Eugenius (*reg* 392–4), who was supported by leading pagans in the Roman aristocracy. He was a devout Nicene Christian and persecutor of heretics and was much influenced by St Ambrose of Milan (*c.* 339–97), who forced him to do penance for his massacre of between 7000 and 15,000 people in the Hippodrome at Thessaloniki in 390. He abolished sacrifices and confirmed the disendowment of pagan cults but gave some legal protection to statues and temples as works of art. In 384–8, however, he permitted his fanatical minister Cynegius to tour the eastern provinces destroying temples. The Empire was by then becoming firmly Christian, and the resulting flowering of Christian literature, art and architecture is known as the Theodosian Renaissance. At Rome he and his co-emperors began the construction of S Paolo fuori le Mura in 385. His commissions at Constantinople included the Forum Tauri. Imitating the Roman Forum of Trajan (*reg* 98–117), from whom Theodosius claimed descent, it incorporated a monumental column (destr. *c.* 1500) with spiral decoration similar to that on the columns of Trajan (AD 113) and Marcus Aurelius (AD 180–93) in Rome, a triumphal arch supported on columns decorated with a lopped branch design (remnants nr Hamam of Sultan Beyazit, Istanbul), a basilica (destr.) and an equestrian statue of Theodosios (destr.). The base of an obelisk, showing the imperial family presiding over scenes in the Hippodrome, stands in At Meydanı, Istanbul, supporting the Egyptian obelisk known as Dikilitaş. A splendid presentation dish, made by eastern silversmiths to celebrate his tenth anniversary, was found in 1849 near Mérida, Spain (Madrid, Real Acad. Hist.); it shows Theodosios enthroned between two co-emperors and investing an official.

J. F. Matthews: *Western Aristocracies and Imperial Court,* AD *364–425* (Oxford, 1975)

S. MacCormack: *Art and Ceremony in Late Antiquity* (Berkeley, 1981), pp. 50–61, 138–50, 205–21

B. Croke and J. Harries: *Religious Conflict in Fourth Century Rome: A Documentary Study* (Sydney, 1982)

C. Mango: *Le Développement urbain de Constantinople, IVe–VIIe siècle* (Paris, 1985), pp. 43–5

Theokosmos (*fl c.* 430–*c.* 400 BC). Greek sculptor. His most famous work was a chryselephantine (gold and ivory) cult statue of *Zeus Olympios* at his home town of Megara, left unfinished at the outbreak of the Peloponnesian War (431 BC; Pausanias: *Guide to Greece* I.xl.4). Pausanias' contention that Pheidias helped Theokosmos on this statue probably arose from the similarity of technique between it and Pheidias' *Athena Parthenos* and *Zeus*, although his description of the statue provides important clues concerning the technique of sculpting in gold and ivory. Megarian coins depicting Theokosmos' *Zeus* are too imprecise to allow us to characterize its style. Another work attributed to Theokosmos was the bronze statue of Lysander's helmsman *Hermon* that formed part of a large dedication at Delphi erected by the Spartans after the battle of Aigospotamoi (405 BC; Pausanias: X.ix.7), although its attribution may be based largely on the fact that Hermon was a native of Megara too. Although portions of the base of the dedication have been recovered, the section that supported the *Hermon* has not.

F. Imhoof-Blumer and P. Gardner: *Ancient Coins Illustrating Lost Masterpieces of Greek Art* (Chicago, 1964)

C. C. Mattusch: *Greek Bronze Statuary* (Ithaca, 1988)

Thera [Thira; Santorini]. Volcanic Greek island at the southern extremity of the Aegean Cyclades. In the Late Bronze Age (*c.* 1525 BC or earlier; *see also* CYCLADIC, §4) a violent eruption of the paroxysmal or explosive type changed the shape of the island, which was originally roughly circular, with the volcano rising to a central cone. The ejection of huge quantities of gas, pumice and ash created a void beneath the cone, which then collapsed, leaving a vast central space known as a caldera. This filled up with sea-water and, surrounded by steep-sided cliffs with a white mantle of ash, it now provides access for ships visiting the island. The outer ring left after the collapse of the centre eventually fragmented, forming the modern crescent-shaped island of Thera, the smaller Therasia and the tiny islet of Aspronisi. Excavations on Thera were begun by the French School in the mid-19th century; the current excavations at Akrotiri began in 1967 under Spiridon Marinatos and are continuing under Christos Doumas. The Bronze Age town at Akrotiri on the south-west of the island is one of the most important archaeological discoveries of the 20th century, largely because of the wonderful state of preservation of the remains, which were buried under thick layers of volcanic pumice and ash. Thus houses were preserved to a substantial height. Some of their contents were much as they were left by their inhabitants, and Akrotiri has emerged as a sort of Bronze Age Pompeii.

1. Bronze Age. 2. Greek and Roman.

1. BRONZE AGE. Excavations at Akrotiri have demonstrated that the city existed for at least 1000 years before it was destroyed in the eruption. It was a well-organized urban settlement with paved streets, multi-storey buildings and a sewerage system directly connected to the houses. The choice of site—coastal and guaranteeing safe anchorage—and the wide distribution of wealth reflected in the architecture and contents of each building suggest that trading and shipping were major economic activities of Akrotiri's citizens. Imports from distant lands (Egypt, Syria, Palestine), an abundance of lead weights (multiples of a standard unit), as well as the large quantities of stirrup jars designed for the transport of olive oil and wine, bear witness to mercantile activities. The art found in almost all the buildings explored or located also suggests a bourgeois rather than a rural mentality.

Akrotiri's town plan was articulated by various forms of thoroughfare. Cobbled streets easily wide enough for two pack animals formed the central arteries, ensuring fast circulation and distribution of goods. The impressive main entrances of buildings invariably opened on to them, or on to the squares into which they were sometimes enlarged, facilitating the delivery of supplies. Alleys, usually less than 1 m wide, formed a secondary network of communications but were designed mainly to provide light and ventilation for the houses and accommodate the sewerage system, as were narrow culs-de-sac.

All the buildings were detached structures, two or three storeys high. The principal materials were unworked stone and earth, generally reinforced by a timber framework to provide extra protection from earthquakes. Ashlar masonry was used at the corners of buildings, to frame doorways and windows, and occasionally for façades. A string course of dressed stones visible from the exterior frequently denoted the floor level of each storey. The entrance, always accompanied by a window, led into a small vestibule that gave access to the ground-floor rooms or, via the staircase, to the apartments of the upper storeys. Ground-floor rooms usually had small windows and were used as storerooms, for food preparation and as kitchens. Those in the upper storeys were mainly residential quarters, though they also accommodated such activities as weaving, which requires plenty of light, to judge from the hundreds of loom weights recovered only from the upper storeys. Although the architecture of Thera displays many local, Cycladic traits, it also incorporated elements borrowed from neighbouring Crete, such as the use of columns or pillars to support the roofs of large rooms and the use of pier-and-door partitions to unite adjoining rooms into spacious halls.

Sculpture appeared at Akrotiri in its early phase: EC II (*c.* 2800–*c.* 2300 BC) marble figurines of the folded-arm type (*see* SCULPTURE, §II, 1) have been found. The latest marble schematic figurines are associated with destruction levels in EC III (*c.* 2300–*c.* 2000 BC), while clay specimens seem to date to the Middle Cycladic (MC) period (*c.* 2000–*c.* 1600 BC).

Painting at Akrotiri had a long history: geometric linear designs were painted on the pottery of the EC III phase. The painted pottery of the MC period is characterized by pictorial as well as geometric motifs, such as plants (crocuses, lilies, papyrus, palm trees, capers and barley) and animals (goats, fish, swallows, seagulls and dolphins; *see also* POTTERY, fig. 7b). Other decorative elements include such fruits as pomegranates or bunches of grapes, or the profile of other vases, such as the breasted ewer. Linear and pictorial motifs seem to have been reserved for specific types of vases, perhaps functioning as labels for their contents or use.

The finest painting was produced during the final phase of Akrotiri's existence, when it was not restricted to pottery but was extended to wall paintings as well. Wall paintings are present in virtually every building and constitute one of the most important discoveries in Aegean archaeology since the 1960s (*see* PAINTING, §II, 1). Most were situated in upper rooms, and all date to the last 50 years before the eruption. Although scholars often refer to them as 'frescoes', they were actually executed in secco technique. The paint has often not been absorbed by the plaster and flakes off, suggesting that painting started while the plaster was wet and continued after it had dried. All the pigments used were mineral, dissolved in an unknown binder. The limited range of colours—white, red, brown, blue, black and yellow—seems to have led to the systematic substitution of one colour for another. Thus blue represents not only blue, such as for the water, but also green (e.g. palm trees, papyrus) and grey (e.g. rocks, monkeys, fish, dolphins, wild goats, duck, griffins). The blue heads of some young boys and girls most probably denote shaven hair.

All sorts of surfaces have been found bearing wall paintings: window- and doorjambs; free zones above, below and between openings, such as doors, windows and cupboards; and entire walls. Subjects appropriate to the surface were chosen. Thus lower zones were usually imitation marble dados, upper ones had friezes of either decorative patterns (e.g. horizontal bands, running spirals, ivy) or narrative scenes (e.g. riparian landscape with wildlife, sea battle, flotilla). Small panels were covered with isolated themes (e.g. plant pots, *Young Priestess, Young Fishermen, Boxing Boys;* see colour pl. 2:XIV, fig. 2), while large compositions were reserved for major wall surfaces, for example the papyruses in the House of the Ladies, the landscape with lilies in a small room, possibly a house shrine (Delta 2), the *Saffron Gatherers* or initiation scene from Xeste 3. Xeste 3 was a three-storey building that may have been intended for public assemblies and ceremonies; certainly the themes of the wall paintings there suggest that it was the setting for initiation rites marking the passage of children to adulthood. Claims that Theran wall paintings have an exclusively religious significance, however, are very difficult to prove.

S. Marinatos: *Excavations at Thera*, 7 vols (Athens, 1968–76)

C. Doumas: 'Anaskaphe Theras' [Excavations at Thera], articles in *Praktika Athen. Archaiol. Etaireias* (1975–83)

C. Doumas, ed.: *Thera and the Aegean World*, 2 vols (London, 1978–80)

P. Darcque and J.-C. Poursat, eds: *L'Iconographie minoenne: Actes de la table ronde d'Athènes, 21–22 April 1983*

C. Doumas: *Thera: Pompeii of the Ancient Aegean* (London, 1983)

L. Morgan: 'Theme in the West House Paintings at Thera', *Archaiol. Ephimeris* (1983), pp. 85–105

N. Marinatos: *Art and Religion in Thera* (Athens, 1984)

C. Televantou: 'Kosmemata apo ten proïstorike Thera' [Jewellery from prehistoric Thera], *Archaiol. Ephimeris* (1984), pp. 14–54

C. Doumas: 'E Xeste 3 kai oi kuanokephaloi sten techne tis Theras' [Xeste 3 and the blue-headed people of Thera], *Eilapine Volume in Honour of Professor Nikolaos Platon* (Herakleion, 1987), pp. 151–9

C. Doumas: *The Wall-paintings of Thera* (London, 1993)

C. A. Televantou: *Akroteri Theras: Hoi toichografies tes dytikes oikias* (Athens, 1994)

The Wall paintings of Thera: Proceedings of the First International Symposium: Petros M. Nomikos Conference Centre, Thera, 1997

P. Y. Forsyth: *Thera in the Bronze Age* (New York, 1999)

K. Palyvou: *Akroteri Thera: He oikodomike techne* (Athens, 1999)

P. I. Soterakopoulou: *Akroteri Theras: He Neolithike kai he proime epoche tou chalkou epi te vasei tes kerameikes* (Athens, 1999)

A. Michaelidou: *Akroteri Theras: He melete ton orophon sta kteria tou oikismou* (Athens, 2001)

C. Palyvou: *Akrotiri Thera: An Architecture of Affluence 3,500 Years Old* (Philadelphia, 2005)

2. GREEK AND ROMAN. After the shattering eruption of the volcano in the middle of the second millennium BC, the island of Thera seems not to have had any significant population until the time of the Dark Age migrations (11th–9th century BC), when it was resettled by people of Dorian descent. Small settlements existed in various parts of the island, but the principal town, Thera, was in the south-east, on the hill of Mesa Vouno, which is 369 m above sea-level. The approaches to the hill are covered by cemeteries dating from the Archaic period (7th–6th century BC) to the Roman (27 BC–AD 330). The remains of the town on the top of the hill are Hellenistic (323–27 BC) and later. It is possible that the Archaic settlement was elsewhere, but the town's site running along the ridge and commanding extensive views is typical of the defensive positions often chosen for Dark Age settlement. Material in the vicinity of the Temple of Apollo Karneios, at the southern end of the settlement, suggests that it already existed in the Archaic period, but evidence for buildings of this date is generally lacking.

The town itself has an unplanned layout, with a main street winding along the ridge from north-west (the approach to the town) to south-east. Important buildings of the Hellenistic period include a theatre, with curved rows of seats enclosed in a rectangular site limited by roads to either side. The Basilike Stoa in the small agora is a long enclosed hall (41.50×10.10 m), its roof supported by a central row of columns. This was built when Thera was the main Aegean naval base of the Ptolemies of Egypt (300–145 BC), whose garrison post, with a building that is presumably the residence of a governor, was near the top of the hill, accompanied by its own gymnasium. Little building work is attested in the Roman period, though the Basilike Stoa underwent repairs and a small Sanctuary of Dionysos was converted to a Kaisareion (temple for the imperial cult).

On the slopes of the hill, and elsewhere in the island, are Hellenistic and Roman tombs of heroon type, in the form of small shrines. One, near Emporio, dedicated to 'Thea Basileia' and now converted into a church of Hagios Nikolaos, is complete, with its original roof of stone slabs.

F. Hiller von Gaertringen: *Thera*, 4 vols (Berlin, 1899–1909)

J. W. Sperling: *Thera and Therasia*, Ancient Greek Cities 22 (Athens, 1973)

E. Dafi: *Late Roman–Early Byzantine Thera and the Southern Aegean Evidence from the Amphorae* (diss., U. Birmingham, 1999)

Thermon. Ancient Greek sanctuary of Apollo located in the mountains around Lake Trichonis in Aitolia, north-west Greece, which flourished in Archaic and Classical times. It was the focus of Aitolian worship of Apollo and later the meeting-place of the Aitolian League. Its remains date from the Late Bronze Age (*c.* 1600–*c.* 1050 BC) to the sacking of the site by Philip V of Macedon in 218 and 206 BC and include three successive temples of Apollo, if the mysterious edifice known as Megaron B (variously dated between *c.* 1400 and *c.* 800 BC) was indeed a temple. Initially, Megaron B was an irregular rectangular building (l. 21.5 m) with slightly curved sides and two internal cross-walls (*see* ARCHITECTURE, §IV, 1(i)(a) and fig. 5); it may have been based on an earlier hairpin-shaped structure nearby (Megaron A). It was later surrounded by a rudimentary colonnade of wooden supports on stone bases, making it, perhaps, one of the earliest peripteral Greek temples. On the other hand, the colonnade may have belonged to a different building, entirely of wood, erected after the destruction of Megaron B. These early structures were replaced *c.* 620 BC by the first securely identified temple, a larger building (38.23×12.13 m) with a peristyle of 5 by 15 wooden columns that were gradually replaced by stone ones, and a mud-brick cella with a central colonnade and opisthodomos, but no pronaos (*see* ARCHITECTURE, fig. 4). Elements of the terracotta entablature from the 7th-century BC building, including roof tiles, female-head antefixes, a sphinx acroterion and painted metopes (h. 880 mm), establish this as one of the earliest Doric temples in Greece. Analysis of the clay indicates that the metopes were imported from Corinthia, where the Doric order developed, and even before analysis confirmed their origin, comparison of the polychrome painted figures with Corinthian pottery (*see* POTTERY, §IV, 5(i)), as well as the letter forms of the inscriptions, showed them to be examples of Corinthian monumental painting; indeed, the Thermon metopes comprise the only surviving example of a cycle of monumental Greek painting.

Among the subjects on the metopes are a hunter (?Herakles or Orion) carrying a stag and a boar, *Perseus with the Head of Medusa, Chelidon, Aidon and Itys*, three seated women in lavishly decorated garments, a *Gorgoneion*, and part of a running figure. Set between borders of rosettes, the figures, rendered in shades of white, black, red, brown and yellow, display the simple, expressive outlines and loose, angular poses characteristic of Corinthian style, and their bold, flat volumes create an impression of monumentality enhanced by the absence of filler motifs. Decorative cables, rosettes and rays enrich clothing, while linear strokes and curves articulate hair and animal fur.

During the Classical and Hellenistic periods the architecture of the sanctuary was progressively enhanced. The fortified precinct of the 3rd century BC enclosed a stoa-lined avenue, a large, still-unexcavated bouleuterion for meetings of the Aitolian League, a triple-spouted fountain of polygonal masonry and numerous monument bases, including a trophy commemorating a victory over the Gauls in 279 BC, of which fragments survive. In spite of the sanctuary's architectural development, however, the final Temple of Apollo (3rd century BC) retained the plan and materials of its Archaic predecessor. Near it are the remains of two other temples: a Temple of Artemis to the north-west, and to the east a small cella dedicated to Apollo Lyseios, which bore painted metopes (?late 7th century BC).

Excavations were conducted in 1898–1932 by the Greek Archaeological Service. Major finds, including the metopes from the Archaic Temple of Apollo, are in the National Archaeological Museum in Athens; much unpublished material remains in a small museum on the site.

G. Soteriadis: 'Anaskaphai en Thermo' [Excavations at Thermon], *Archaiol. Ephimeris* (1900), pp. 161–212; (1903), pp. 71–96; (1905), pp. 55–100

G. Kawerau and G. Soteriadis: 'Der Apollotempel zu Thermos', *Ant. Dkml.*, ii (1902–8), pp. 1–8

K. A. Rhomaios: 'Ek tou Proistorikou Thermou' [From historic Thermon], *Archaiol. Deltion*, i (1915), pp. 225–84

H. G. G. Payne: 'On the Thermon Metopes', *Annu. Brit. Sch. Athens*, xxvii (1925–6), pp. 124–32

H. Drerup: 'Zu Thermos B', *Marburg.-Winckelmann Programm* (1963), pp. 1–12

I. Beyer: 'Der Triglyphenfries von Thermos C', *Archäol. Anz.*, lxxxvii (1972), pp. 197– 226

T. E. Kalpaxis: 'Zum aussergewöhnlichen Triglyphenfries vom Apollontempel C in Thermos', *Archäol. Anz.*, lxxxix (1974), pp. 105–14

B. Schmaltz: 'Bemerkungen zu Thermos B', *Archäol. Anz.*, xcv (1980), pp. 318–36
A. Mallwitz: 'Kritisches zur Architektur Griechenlands im 8. und 7. Jahrhundert', *Archäol. Anz.*, xcvi (1981), pp. 599–641
B. Wesenberg: 'Thermos B1', *Archäol. Anz.*, xcvii (1982), pp. 149–57
A. Mazarakis Ainian: 'Early Greek Temples: Their Origin and Function', *Early Greek Cult Practice. Proceedings of the 5th International Symposium at the Swedish Institute at Athens: Athens, 1986*, pp. 105–19

Thesauros. *See* TREASURY.

Thessaloniki [Salonika; Saloniki]. Greek city situated on the west slopes of Mt Chortiatis beside an inlet at the northern end of the Gulf of Thermaikos. It lies near the crossing of two important ancient routes, the Roman Via Egnatia, which traverses the city, and the River Axios (Vardar), *c.* 25 km to the west, which, with the River Morava, forms the main route from Central Europe to the Aegean.

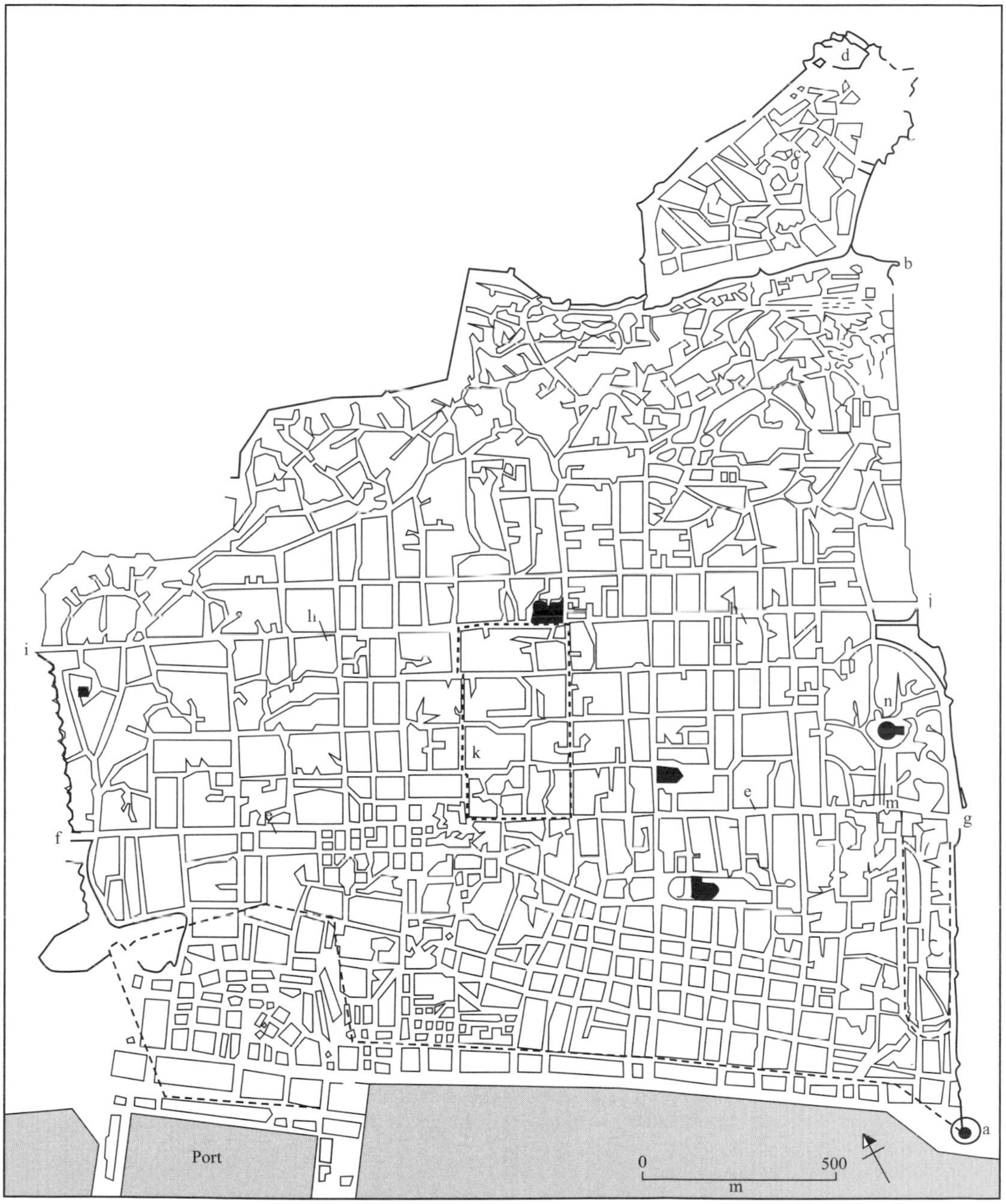

Thessaloniki, plan: (a) White Tower; (b) Chain Tower; (c) acropolis; (d) Eptapyrgion Fort; (e) Via Regia; (f) Golden (or Vardar) Gate; (g) Kassandrian Gate; (h) Hagios Demetrios Road; (i) Litea Gate; (j) New Golden Gate; (k) double agora; (l) imperial palace and adjoining circus; (m) Arch of Galerius; (n) Rotunda

1. History and urban development. Tombs of *c.* 3000 BC and Iron Age settlements of *c.* 1000 BC have been excavated in the vicinity. In 315 BC Kassander, king of Macedonia (*reg* 310–297 BC), united 26 small towns in the area, including Thermi, a little to the east, and established a new city. Thessaloniki's regular grid pattern was probably established in the following century, with six roads running east–west, set 90 m apart, intersecting with 15 roads running north–south, *c.* 50 m apart (see fig.). Few traces survive of the original fortifications, which were later incorporated into the Roman and Early Christian city walls. They were 7–8 km long, with 148 towers, and enclosed a trapezoidal area with parallel east and west walls *c.* 1.8 km apart. Two of the main wall towers remain: the White (Gr. Leuko) Tower (rebuilt *c.* 1430; a) at the south-east corner and the Chain (Gr. Alysida) Tower (b) at the north-east. Within the walls near the latter, at the highest point of the city, is the triangular acropolis (c), which contained the Eptapyrgion Fort (d).

After 168 BC Thessaloniki became the capital of the prosperous Roman province of Macedonia. Much of the evidence for the city's development until the early 4th century AD has been destroyed, although the grid layout was retained. The principal artery was the Via Regia (Egnatia; Turk. Zante Yol; e), which linked the Golden (or Vardar) Gate (f) in the west to the Kassandrian Gate (g) in the east. A parallel road (now Hagios Demetrios Road; h) ran north of this between the western Litea Gate (i) and the eastern New Golden Gate (j). Excavations in the city centre have uncovered a large agora (2nd century AD; k), comprising two squares, stoas, an odeon and a double cryptoporticus. In AD 293 Galerius (*reg* 305–1) was appointed Caesar of the East. From *c.* 300 he undertook a lavish building programme at the eastern edge of the city, including an imperial palace and an adjoining circus (l) and, to the north, a triumphal arch (m) and a Rotunda (now Hagios Georgios; n).

R. Dreyfus: 'Le Nouveau Plan de Salonique', *Architecture* [Paris], xxxvi (1923), no. 8, pp. 101–10 (1927)
M. Vickers: 'Towards Reconstruction of the Town Planning of Roman Thessaloniki', *Ancient Macedonia Symposium: Thessaloniki, 1970*, pp. 239–51
A. Vakalopoulos: *A History of Thessaloniki* (Thessaloniki, 1972)
M. Vickers: 'Hellenistic Thessaloniki', *J. Hell. Stud.*, xcii (1972), pp. 156–70
A. Vakalopoulos: *Istoria tis Thessalonikis, 316 p.ch.–1983* [History of Thessaloniki, 316 BC–1983] (Thessaloniki, 1983)
J.-M. Speiser: *Thessalonique et ses monuments du IVe au VIe siècle: Contribution à l'étude d'une ville paléochrétienne* (Thessaloniki, 1984)

2. Arch of Galerius. In the early 4th century AD Galerius built a triumphal arch, *c.* 170 m west of the Kassandrian Gate, to commemorate his victory over the Sasanians in 298. It originally comprised four piers supporting a brick dome. Only the two western piers survive, decorated with four superimposed registers of low relief depicting scenes from his campaigns and triumphal processions. Two small archways connected the triumphal arch with a rectangular chamber on the south side. The exact relationship of this complex to the palace of Galerius to the south, the Rotunda and the Via Regia has yet to be confirmed. One theory states that the arch connected the palace to the Rotunda, and that the Via Regia, flanked by colonnaded arcades, ran beneath the dome. According to this view, the arch was connected on the north side to two smaller piers that marked the beginning of a colonnaded ceremonial way leading to the Rotunda. It has been shown, however, that this pair of piers was added when the Rotunda was converted into a church and that the piers were directly related to the construction of the ceremonial way (Velenis, 1983). Originally the Via Regia would have run in front of the rectangular chamber, which, together with the triumphal arch, would have formed an imposing gateway to the sacred precinct next to the Rotunda, the southern boundary of which was marked by the colonnades on the Via Regia. The reorganization of this area when the Rotunda and its precinct were modified for Christian use may have been responsible for the diversion of the Via Regia, tentatively attributed to Theodosios I (*reg* 379–95), so that the road passed beneath the arch.

E. Dyggve: 'Recherches sur le palais impérial de Thessalonique', *Studia Orientalia Ioanni Pedersen a collegis discipulis amicis dicata* (Copenhagen, 1953), pp. 59–70
C. C. Vermeule: *Roman Imperial Art in Greece and Asia Minor* (Cambridge, MA, 1968), pp. 417–18
H. P. Laubscher: *Der Reliefschmuck des Galeriusbogens in Thessaloniki* (Berlin, 1975)
G. Velenis: 'Architektonische Probleme des Galeriusbogens in Thessaloniki', *Archäol. Anz.* (1979), pp. 249–63
H. Meyer: 'Die Frieszyklen am sogenannten Triumphbogen des Galerius in Thessaloniki', *Jb. Dt. Archäol. Inst.*, xcv (1980), pp. 374–444
G. Velenis: 'Nachträgliche Beobachtungen am Oberbau des Galeriusbogens in Thessaloniki', *Archäol. Anz.* (1983), pp. 273–5
T. Stefanidou-Tiveriou: *To mikro toxo tou Galeriou: Sto Archaiologiko Mouseio tes Thessalonikes* (Athens, 1996)

Thevestis [now Tebessa]. Algerian town at the foot of the Tebessa mountains. It was probably the site of a pre-Roman settlement that became the residence of a Roman imperial legate and his legion in the late 1st century AD, when it was raised to the rank of colony and served as the capital of an administrative and estate district.

The Roman town is known to have had a forum, a theatre, an oval amphitheatre (*c.* 86×80 m), public baths and some unidentified public works; a temple and a four-sided triumphal arch (AD 214) are perfectly preserved. In the 3rd and 4th centuries the plain surrounding the town was the location of numerous fortified farms that continued in use into the 6th century and beyond. From the time of the synod of Carthage in 256 there was a Christian community and a bishop in Thevestis. The Christian complex that was established (*c.* 400) in a pagan necropolis to the north of the town walls is the most impressive surviving example of Early Christian architecture in Algeria.

S. Gsell: *Les Monuments antiques de l'Algérie*, 2 vols (Paris, 1901)
J. Christern: *Das frühchristliche Pilgerheiligtum von Tebessa*, 2 vols (Wiesbaden, 1976)

Thira. *See* THERA.

Thívai. *See* THEBES.

Tholos. Name used by ancient Greeks for a form of circular building covered by a pyramid- or cone-shaped roof. It was constructed mainly on the Greek mainland and islands from the Archaic period (*c.* 700–480 BC) to the Roman period (27 BC–AD 330). Some tholoi have peristyles, others do not. A tholos with a peristyle is the same as a circular MONOPTEROS. The form of the tholos roof, unusual in the Greek landscape, gave some of them the name *skias* ('umbrella'). In the architecture of dressed stone, a tholos was more expensive to construct than an equivalent rectangular building, because it was more difficult to cut curved blocks than rectilinear ones and because the roof construction, its beams converging at the top and exerting centrifugal pressure on the outside edges, complicated the assembly of the structure and the production of the tiles. Tholoi are thus relatively few and tend to be elegant. Contrary to a long-accepted theory, a tholos would not necessarily have been dedicated to a chthonic cult.

Tholoi were of two types: those that served as an assembly place, built from inexpensive materials, without a peristyle, all the available area being reserved for the interior space; and those shielding a sacred place or an offering, luxuriously built and embellished with a peristyle around a smaller hall. The curious Tholos of Lathuresa in Attica (*c.* 700 BC), built of crude bricks on a base of uncut rubble (diam. 7.8 m) and covered by a thatched roof supported internally by four wooden posts, belongs to the first type. A stone bench built around the interior wall could seat some 20 people about the central altar; it marks the tholos as the local place where the magistrates of the small village nearby would meet. The earliest example of the second type was built (? by the tyrant Kleisthenes of Sikyon) of poros *c.* 580 BC (destr. 548 BC) in the Sanctuary of Apollo at DELPHI. Built of dressed stone, it was a miniature prototype (diam. 6.32 m) of the great tholoi of the 4th century BC. The 13 elegantly slender Doric columns, the 20 triglyphs and the 20 metopes of its entablature surrounded a cramped cella (diam. 3.54 m), probably a shelter for an altar or offering. The next known tholos with a peristyle in Greek architecture, again at Delphi, dates from a century later.

The Tholos of Athens (*c.* 470 BC), adjoining the Agora, was a simple cylinder of crude brick (diam. 18.32 m) mounted on a base of poros and pierced by windows. The roof, supported internally by six columns, was covered by an ingenious diamond-shaped assembly of terracotta tiles, edged by a crown of painted triangular tiles topped with palmettes, the only luxury used in the construction of this spacious *skias* (250 sq. m). In contrast, the Tholos of Athena Pronaia, built at Delphi *c.* 390–*c.* 380 BC, is, by virtue of its refinement, its elegance and its architectural and sculptural richness, the most beautiful example of a tholos treasury. Built entirely of Pentelic marble, including the roof, it was the work of an architect, Theodoros of Phokis, whom Vitruvius ranked among the greatest. The peristyle of 20 columns (diam. 14.76 m) surrounded a cella (diam. 6.80 m) with a Corinthian peristyle (the oldest known example) between the columns of which stood, on a base of dark stone 16 m long, nine statues of gods, probably chryselephantine, a sumptuous offering from an unknown donor (? the city of Delphi) that was subsequently replaced by statues of Roman emperors. The fame of this monument, about which Theodoros published a book, strongly influenced the architecture of the 4th century. It prompted Philip II of Macedon, after his victory at Chaironeia (338 BC), to consecrate at Olympia five chryselephantine statues of himself and his family within a tholos with an Ionic peristyle and a Corinthian internal peristyle of very similar dimensions (diam. 15.20 m and 7.20 m), but it was constructed in poros on a limestone base.

The tholos (also called the thymele) at EPIDAUROS, the work of the architect Polykleitos the younger, was a place of worship constructed by the city at great expense from *c.* 380 to *c.* 340 BC. The most beautiful monument of the sanctuary of Asklepios, it covered a particularly sacred place, supposedly marking the site of the god's tomb, blasted by Zeus. Its two peristyles—Doric exterior, with 26 columns of poros (diam. 21.82 m), Corinthian interior, with 14 marble columns (diam. 13.30 m)—supported impressive marble ceilings adorned with funerary symbols: white lilies, poppies, acanthus. The finial of the roof was an arrangement of perennial acanthus (2.5 m high), a promise of immortality. Here in this tholos the cult of Asklepios was celebrated under his chthonic aspect.

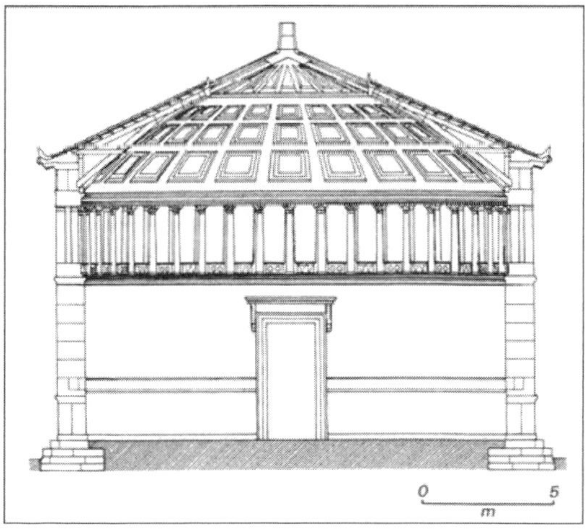

Tholos known as the Arsinoeion, Samothrace, *c.* 280 BC; reconstruction cross-section

The Arsinoeion (see fig.), the tholos dedicated to the Great Gods of SAMOTHRACE *c.* 280 BC by Arsinoe II (*reg c.* 276–270 BC), queen of Egypt, was a place both of assembly and of worship. Without a peristyle, its high marble cylinder (diam. 20.21 m—the largest circular building known in Greek architecture), surmounted by a gallery of Doric pilasters leaning against Corinthian half columns, was covered by a remarkable structure that shielded without intermediary support the 179 sq. m of the circular hall. To the same category, although their architecture is more ordinary, belong the tholos of Eretria (4th century BC; diam. 9.10 m) and the tholos with peristyle at Taman in southern Russia (3rd century BC; diam. 21.20 m). The smaller tholoi of the 4th century BC at Samothrace (diam. 4.10 m) and at Paros in the Cyclades (diam. 3.73 m), both with an interior bench, probably contained an altar.

The sculptor Praxiteles had presented his great statue of *Aphrodite* (*c.* 364–*c.* 361 BC) to Knidos under a canopy in the shape of a monopteros tholos, reduced to a colonnade. Only two tholoi of this kind are known before the end of the Hellenistic period (27 BC): the Choregic Monument of Lysikrates at Athens (334 BC; diam. 2.96 m; six columns) and the small Tholos of Hermes and Maia on the Cycladic island of Delos (2nd century BC; diam. 2.52 m; four columns). Because of its convexity, the entablature was found to overhang the columns and so threatened the balance of these graceful edifices: hence their rarity. They became more numerous during the Roman period, because the use of a cap of concrete underneath the marble slabs of the roof joined the blocks of the entablature together and held them rigid.

F. Zeiler: *Die griechische Tholos* (Mayence, 1986)

J. Borchardt: 'Ein Ptolemaion in Limyra', *Rev. Archéol.* (1991), pp. 309–22

J. R. McCredie and others: *L'Arsinoeion* (1991), vii of *Samothrace*, ed. P. Williams Lehmann (New York and Princeton, 1958–)

Tholos [Beehive] **Tomb.** Ancient form of underground built tomb, found largely in mainland Greece but also on the Greek islands and in western Asia Minor from *c.* 1600 BC to *c.* 600 BC. Pausanias (*Guide to Greece* IX. xxxvi.5, xxxvii.2 and II.xvi.6) referred to it as a treasury (*thesauros*). A tholos typically consists of a circular chamber with a corbelled vault entered through a doorway (*stomion*) that was sealed with a wall or door after burial and approached by a passageway (dromos). The term has also been applied to other structures of oval or rectangular plan: buildings at Khirokitia in Cyprus, now known to have had flat roofs, and structures of the Halaf culture in Mesopotamia, which may have had mud-brick domes; both these groups date from about the 7th millennium BC. These applications of the term 'tholos' are a modern usage; the ancient Greeks themselves applied it to a much later type of building (*see* THOLOS *and* MONOPTEROS).

In a tholos tomb, the chamber was usually constructed inside a pit cut into bedrock, and the stone vault was covered by an earthen mound. Some Iron Age tholoi (*c.* 1100–700 BC) have internal diameters of only 1 m, but their Bronze Age predecessors (*c.* 1600–*c.* 1100 BC) measure up to 14.5 m in diameter and average 5 m. Although designed for multiple inhumations, the latter were rarely used for more than a few generations. Though the construction of tholos tombs increased markedly between *c.* 1600 BC and *c.* 1400 BC, the most elaborate were built between *c.* 1400 and *c.* 1200 BC. With the decline of the Mycenaean civilization after *c.* 1200 BC, this type of burial ceased in central Greece, though smaller tholoi were still built in western Greece, Thessaly, Crete and Asia Minor. In Thessaly and Crete the type persisted until early Archaic times (7th century BC) and perhaps even influenced the Hellenistic built tombs (mainly 3rd and 2nd centuries BC). During the Bronze Age the greatest concentration of tholoi was in Messenia and in the Argolid, with a magnificent series of nine at MYCENAE.

The Mycenaean tholoi have been classified on the basis of their masonry, which ranges from rough, uncoursed stonework to ashlar, on the presence or absence of a masonry lining in the dromos, and the addition of decorative mouldings or embellishments (Wace, 1923). This suggests that the crudest structure, the Cyclopean Tomb, was the earliest (?*c.* 1500 BC) and the most carefully constructed one, the Treasury of Atreus (see fig.), among the latest

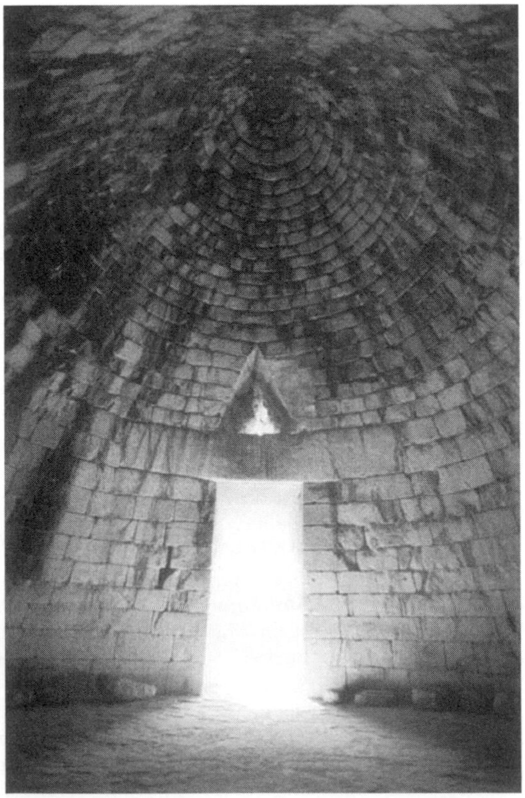

Tholos tomb, corbelled vault of the Treasury of Atreus, Mycenae, *c.* 1350–1250 BC

(*c.* 1350–1250 BC). However, though this scheme is applicable at Mycenae, the significance of the features varies regionally, and they may reflect the importance of a burial as much as its date. For example, the argument that use of a relieving triangle over the lintel of an entrance indicates a late date is refuted by the 16th-century BC oval tomb at Thorikos in Attica. Similarly, ashlar masonry occurs in both Tholos Tomb I at Peristeria and Tomb I at Tragana, both in Messenia, as early as *c.* 1500–1450 BC. A lined dromos does appear to indicate a late structure, as at Mycenae, the Argive Heraion, Dendra and Vapheio in Lakonia. The tholos tomb at Kazarma (early 16th century BC or late 15th) may, however, disprove this rule. The masonry of Cretan tholos tombs and features such as niches in their dromoi also represent regional variations. Thus the appearance of individual tombs seems ultimately to be a product of local factors, including the site, the amount of embellishment desired and the regional architectural style.

The material used in tholos tombs was generally local stone, ranging from limestone rubble, through more carefully selected schist slabs, to carefully dressed poros or conglomerate, which was prized for its tensile strength. However, carved mouldings in colourful exotic stones such as *lapis lacedaemonius, rosso antico* and gypsum adorned the Tomb of Klytemnestra (*c.* 1300–1220 BC) and the Treasury of Atreus at Mycenae, and the Treasury of Minyas at ORCHOMENOS (?13th century BC); the interior of Atreus was originally clad with bronze. The prasinite base course at Thorikos may also have been decorative. Schemes of proportion are discernible in tholos tomb architecture, especially on façades. Some 10% of extant tholos tombs remain intact. Their corbelled vaults are usually of roughly equal height and diameter, and mathematical analysis has shown that vault shape was precisely decided by structural considerations, and that tholos tombs throughout Greece follow the same essential pattern. Mycenaean expertise in corbelling remained unsurpassed.

The origins of tholos tombs have been sought in Crete, but their Minoan precursors differ in design and execution, probably exercising only an indirect influence. Earlier indigenous Helladic tomb types, such as tumuli, may also have been partial models. The skill and labour required to build tholos tombs and the rich offerings found in those that escaped plundering suggest that the finest were royal burials. Thus their appearance may reflect political developments. Though their later regional distribution cannot be used uncritically to interpret the political geography of Mycenaean Greece, the more modest tombs clearly not being royal, it supports the theory of increasing political centralization during the 14th century BC.

A. J. B. Wace: 'Excavations at Mycenae: The Tholos Tombs', *Annu. Brit. Sch. Athens*, xxv (1921–3), pp. 283–396

A. J. B. Wace: *Mycenae* (Princeton, 1949)

M. S. F. Hood: 'Tholos Tombs of the Aegean', *Antiquity*, xxxiv (1960), pp. 166–76

O. Pelon: *Tholoi, tumuli et cercles funéraires* (Paris, 1976)

R. Hope-Simpson and O. T. P. K. Dickinson: *The Mainland and the Islands*, i of *A Gazetteer of Aegean Civilization in the Bronze Age* (Göteborg, 1979)

W. G. Cavanagh and R. R. Laxton: 'The Structural Mechanics of the Mycenaean Tholos Tomb', *Annu. Brit. Sch. Athens*, lxxvi (1981), pp. 109–40

W. G. Cavanagh and R. R. Laxton: 'Corbelled Vaulting in the Late Minoan Tholos Tombs of Crete', *Annu. Brit. Sch. Athens*, lxxvii (1982), pp. 65–77

A. W. Lawrence: *Greek Architecture*, Pelican Hist. A. (Harmondsworth, 1983)

N. C. Wilkie and W. A. McDonald: 'How the Mycenaeans Buried their Dead: New Evidence from the Nichoria Tholos', *Archaeology*, xxxvii/6 (1984), pp. 40–47

Y. Papadatos: *Tholos Tomb Gamma: A Prepalatial Tholos Tomb at Phourni, Archanes* (Philadelphia, 2005)

Thracian and Dacian art. Terms applied principally to types of figural toreutic (chased and embossed) metalwork produced in south-east Europe between the 7th century BC and 1st century AD.

1. INTRODUCTION.

(i) Historical and geographical context. Thracian art dates from the 7th–1st centuries BC and is closely connected to SCYTHIAN ART. Dacian art represents the later manifestation of Thracian art (1st century BC–1st century AD), particularly in regions north of the Danube where Roman conquest came late. Information on the Thracian and Dacian peoples and their various subgroups comes from Classical texts, epigraphy, place name evidence and archaeological remains. According to Classical authors the Thracians occupied a region extending from Greek Thrace northwards to the Danube River and the Carpathian Mountains, and eastwards into Asia Minor (modern Bulgaria, part of Romania, western Turkey, Moldavia and northern Greece). To the east, the steppe extended directly to southern Siberia and the borders of China, and from it came groups of invading Scythian nomads. The Persians invaded from the east *c.* 513 BC, bringing Thrace into the Achaemenid orbit for a time. To the north-west Thrace was connected to the middle Danube basin, whence came invading Celts and Teutons. To the south and on the Aegean and Black Sea coasts the Greeks established colonies; they were followed by the Macedonians and, later, Romans, who conquered large parts of the inland areas.

The Iron Age archaeology of the Carpatho-Balkan region indicates the emergence of a complex polyethnic society, with distinct groups of sedentary agriculturalists, transhumant pastoralists, and nomadic-pastoral élites. Persian, Greek, Macedonian and Roman contact stimulated the development of social competition and hierarchy and the eventual establishment of local states. In the 5th and 4th centuries BC, the Odrysian dynasty formed a state in the Thracian plain (Bulgaria's Maritsa River valley), with a capital at Seuthopolis. The Celts established the kingdom of Tylis after the collapse of Alexander the Great's empire.

The Dacian state, centred on the southern Carpathian Mountains, came to prominence in the 1st century BC. It was probably based on a confederacy of at least four smaller groups, led by the Dacii. The state has several highly distinctive features, including the absence of cities and the rejection of literacy. It had a monumental architecture of highland temples and fortresses, a political and religious focus at Sarmizegethusa (now Gradistea Muncelului, in the Orastie range of the Transylvanian Alps, Romania). It was not until the Trajanic campaigns of the early 2nd century AD that the Dacian site was subdued by Rome and dissolved (AD 107).

(ii) Stylistic and technical background. Greek colonization from the 7th century BC onwards was important for the development of Thracian art, but the nature of the connection is disputed, and it is clear that Thracian toreutics owed as much to Scythian and Persian models as to Greek ones. Because of the apparent eclecticism of the material, much debate has been concerned with whether there is such a thing as Thracian art *per se*, and the approach taken here is that it represents a regionally distinct technical tradition of gold- and silverworking, which persisted for 500 years throughout a period of virtually constant political upheaval. Workers in the tradition were characteristically eclectic in style and produced several original syntheses. Formal derivations (e.g. from Greek art) are clearly observable, but they usually occur in new iconographic formats for which substantially altered meanings may be inferred; each iconographic and technical grouping was created in a different context for use by different élites. The archaeological record is fragmentary, but the indications are that a wide range of media was available.

Thrace was known to the Greeks as the land of Orpheus, yet few musical instruments have been excavated. A 4th-century BC repoussé silver shield boss from Panagyurishte in the Bulgarian Sredna Gora range shows a figure playing a lyre or harp (Sofia, N. Archaeol. Mus.). The *hora* dance may be represented by the sculpted women who line the 3rd-century BC grave chamber at Sveshtari, although their forms are clearly borrowed from Greek caryatids. Traces of paint have survived on the sculptures; at KAZANLUK both musical instruments and elaborate furniture are represented in detailed tomb paintings.

2. CHRONOLOGICAL DEVELOPMENT.

(i) Persian- and Greek-influenced, late 6th century BC–3rd. (ii) Thraco-Getic, mid-4th century BC. (iii) Thracian, 4th–1st century BC. (iv) Dacian, 1st century BC–1st century AD.

(i) Persian- and Greek-influenced, late 6th century BC–3rd. Towards the end of the 6th century BC, Darius I of Persia (*reg* 522–486 BC) began a programme of European conquest, ostensibly directed against the Scythians although Thracian groups such as the Getae were forcibly incorporated into Darius' army during the campaign. A Persian administrative district (the Satrapy of Skudra) may subsequently have been set up in Thrace, lasting until 480 BC in the Getic area and until the late 460s BC in the Thracian plain (Fol and Hammond). The most important group of art objects of this period come from the barrow cemetery of Douvanli (Plovdiv, Archaeol. Mus.; Sofia, N. Archaeol. Mus.) on the Upper Maritsa valley, from which it is clear that Achaemenid art had a formative effect on toreutics in Thrace. Banqueting in the Persian style required precious-metal drinking services, which occur first in Thrace, along with bronze situla-type wine jugs, at the end of the 6th century BC and represent the earliest sheet-silver repoussé work in the region. Pieces include the magnificent imported silver serving vessel found at Douvanli, which was probably a metropolitan Persian product (Taylor, 1988, no. 105a).

Techniques such as patrix-working and pattern-punching of sheet gold develop at this time (e.g. at Douvanli, Moushovitsa Mogila). The Animal style bronze from Gurchinovo, Bulgaria, may date to the early 5th century BC, along with the bronze sword 'emblem' from Medgidia, Romania. The Gurchinovo piece is often called a matrix; however, it is probably a patrix, used for pressing out a figural scene in prepared sheet metal that was then finished from the other side (a matrix indents into the intended viewing side). The Gurchinovo patrix may have been used to make a decorated strip to apply around the body of a rhyton, like that which decorates the 'Pegasos Rhyton' from Adygeya in the Kuban region to the north of the Caucasus. The piece depicts a stag with ram-headed antler tines, flanked by a lion-like predator and a hawk-like bird. Each of these large animals is partly composed of separate zoomorphic elements (the lion's penis is a bird head, as are each of the hawk's talons, etc). A narrow frieze beneath these major images shows various animals, apparently including a unicorn (possibly the earliest such image known). The late 4th century BC silver-gilt rhyton from Razgrad from northeast Bulgaria is made in the form of a one-horned Pegasos, and the winged unicorn image later occurs on one of the Sark phalerae dating to *c.* 100 BC.

In the second half of the 5th century BC Greek influence increased. The burial at Dălboki, dating to *c.* 430 BC, contained several objects of Greek manufacture, along with local versions of Greek types. These included a bronze cuirass (Taylor, 1985) and a Greek-style beaker, locally made, but from silver which may have been imported from the Athenian-controlled Laurium mines. Greeks apparently paid for grain and slaves from Thrace with silver, much of which was locally reworked into vessels of known coin weight, as at Rogozen (*see* ROGOZEN TREASURE).

(ii) Thraco-Getic, mid-4th century BC. Most silver and gold artefacts known from Thrace date to the 4th century BC. Technically, they form a tight group.

Archaeologically, they fall into two main categories: objects found in datable burials and those from hoards and stray finds. Stylistically, they can be variously divided, though the material termed Thraco-Getic represents the only well-defined group. This term was first coined by the Romanian archaeologist Dumitru Berciu (1969) to describe a few dozen objects from sites in the lower Danube basin, including those from the hoard of Craiova and the princely burial of AGIGHIOL (both Bucharest, N. Hist. Mus. Romania). Subsequent discoveries in Romania (the Peretu burial) and northeast Bulgaria (the Vratsa burial, the Rogozen hoard; both Vratsa, Hist. Mus.) have added to the corpus. Whether those for whom the art was made spoke Thracian or Scythian is still uncertain, though scholarship since 1940 has strongly favoured Thracian.

The most striking objects from the Agighiol and Peretu graves are partially gilded silver helmets, with figural repoussé decorated cheek and neck pieces and a band on the forehead on which a pair of eyes with elaborate curling eyebrows is dramatically picked out in leaf gilt. Three other 'eyed' helmets exist: a gold one from Coţofeneşti in the Wallachian sub-Carpathians; another rather fragmentary gold one from Băiceni in Romanian Moldavia; and a silver one acquired by the Detroit Institute of Arts via the Trau collection in Vienna. The latter is known as the Iron Gates Helmet, after a story that it was dredged, along with a vase and figurally-decorated bi-conical beaker, out of the Danube in the Iron Gates gorge in 1911, but proper documentation is lacking. The original context of the 'Iron Gates' material is thus uncertain; it could well have been looted from a grave. This is also true for the gold helmets from Coţofeneşti (Bucharest, N. Hist. Mus. Romania) and Băiceni (Iaşi, Moldav. Mus. Ethnog.).

Two more bi-conical beakers like that said to come from the Iron Gates (New York, Met.) come from Agighiol, and a fourth is among the 165 silver vessels that make up the Rogozen hoard. On their bases, all depict a composite, griffin-like predator attacking a wild boar, and all have an animal frieze that includes a deer, a wild goat and an eight-legged stag. The latter is given special treatment on the Agighiol beaker no. 1 and the Rogozen beaker, where its antlers join on to and metamorphose into the continuous band of decoration around the vessel's rim, its tines becoming bird heads. On all except the Agighiol beaker no. 2, a horned hawk is shown grasping a hare in its talons and a fish in its beak. This hawk also occurs on the right-hand cheek-pieces of the Peretu and Iron Gates helmets.

Two greaves from the Agighiol burial are clearly derived from a Greek type, as is that from the grave of Vratsa in Bulgaria. The Medusa head which covers the knee was considered by the Greeks to have an apotropaic function, an interpretation that has also been applied to the eyed helmets. It is possible, however, that a specifically Thracian meaning for this borrowed motif exists. On one of the Agighiol greaves a hunter is depicted, riding forward with a bow towards a ram-headed snake that coils down from above him. Below this a mail-clad man is depicted seated, a hawk on a wrist and a drinking horn in his hand. A similar scene occurs on the cheek-piece of the Băiceni Helmet, where the man drinks *à la grecque*—with rhyton and phiale—a ram-headed snake coiled beneath his chair. When such a helmet is worn, the wearer's eyes are 'doubled' by the eyes depicted above. The disturbing effect on an observer may have been coupled with a sense that the wearer—like his hawk—possessed supernaturally keen vision. Such an association is enhanced on the Agighiol, Iron Gates and Peretu helmets, which all have a decorative fringe of long flight feathers in a border around the register that depicts the eyes. The idea that the doubling of attributes indicates extended powers could also apply to the eight-legged stag, which must be supernaturally fast (indeed it flies, as suggested in the two examples where the antler tines change into birds).

The gold helmet from Coţofenesi supports the idea that qualities of predatory animals were associated with mounted hunters. The neck-guard has two registers: the lower depicts three winged, horse-headed, griffin-like predators with haunches of meat in their jaws; the upper depicts similar predators, but human-headed. A scene of domestic slaughter is depicted on the cheek-pieces, on each of which a cloaked figure is about to plunge a dagger into the neck of a kneeling ram.

The Thraco-Getic pieces, where datable, all seem to have been created *c.* 350 BC. Technically they form a tight group of repoussé figures, traced around and decorated with various pattern punches, such as dots, crescents, circles and circles-within-squares. Microscopic analysis of patterned punchmarks on the Iron Gates beaker and helmet demonstrate that one particular punch, which had a distinctively damaged corner, was used to decorate both pieces; this same tool was also used in the decoration of the Agighiol helmet and beaker no. 1.

A small horse harness appliqué (Lovech, Hist. Mus.) from the Letnitsa hoard in north-central Bulgaria depicts a hunter wearing face greaves about to spear a bear. Repairs and traces of use show that the armour found in the burials was worn in life, perhaps for hunting or as part of the ideology of the Royal Hunt, adopted by local élites sometime after the Persian occupation of Thrace. Thraco-Getic iconography may thus relate to the chase as an élite activity. Its underlying structure is that of the predator/prey dichotomy, in which the élite group identified themselves with the predators.

The motifs of the eight-legged stag, and the hawk with fish and hare, as well as the overall form of the biconical beakers and eyed-helmets, do not occur later. The sudden appearance and disappearance of such distinctive iconography, limited to a single generation but represented at widely separated sites within the lower Danube basin and Romanian Moldavia, suggests that it was instigated by a regional élite who wished to stress shared values iconographically. The result betrayed extensive borrowing from Greek and Scythian models, but reorganized such material in an original synthesis.

(iii) Thracian, 4th–1st century BC. The Persian influence in Thracian gold- and silversmithing was long-lasting and extensive. In many small pieces the typical asymmetry of the Scythian Animal style prototypes has been given greater symmetry, as in the 4th century BC silver bridle frontlet from Lukovit, northern Bulgaria. The occurrence of drinking (or symposium) sets reflects a local adoption of Persian and Greek banqueting styles. The amphora-rhyton from the Koukouva Mogila at Douvanli was probably made in the Persian empire, as was a vessel (no. 97) from Rogozen.

Hoards have preserved a great number of works of toreutic art produced during the 4th century BC. Those from Letnitsa and Rogozen contain pieces (horse-harness and vessels respectively) with elaborate figural decoration that has often been considered to indicate a development of pictorial narrative. A mounted hunter ('the Thracian rider' or 'Thracian hero') is a common motif; variations are found on the Agighiol and Coţofenesi helmets, on appliqués from Letnitsa and Lukovit (Sofia, N. Archaeol. Mus.), and on the belt plate from Lovets (Sofia, N. Archaeol. Mus.). It is considered to epitomize the noble male in Thracian cosmology.

Self-reference and 'narrative' structure broadly distinguishes the Thracian from the more hieratic Scythian Animal style (with the exception of Greco-Scythian art): greaves carry images of drinking vessels; drinking vessels carry images of mounted hunters; horse harness appliqués show hunters wearing greaves.

There are only rare examples of precious-metal objects in the Thracian Animal style dating from the period *c.* 300–100 BC. Nevertheless, the tradition must have continued, as objects clearly belonging to it appear again in 1st-century BC contexts. That these contexts are predominantly hoards may indicate the nature of the apparent depositional hiatus.

The absence of securely dated examples of precious metalwork from the 3rd and 2nd centuries BC may represent a real decrease in the amount of precious metalwork buried, perhaps because the extension of Greek-type economy in southern Thrace placed more emphasis on coinage and fiscal inheritance than on ostentatious funerary consumption, except for the very rich. Equally, it may result from extensive plundering of burials; the most important 3rd-century BC graves known—Kazanluk and Sveshtari—were both robbed. However, the absence of undisturbed graves and well-dated hoards from this period makes it difficult to make secure attributions for stray finds. One piece for which strong technical and stylistic arguments can be advanced for attribution to the 2nd century BC is the Gundestrup Cauldron (Copenhagen, Nmus.), a silver vessel of the 2nd–1st centuries BC found in 1891 in a peat bog at Gundestrup, Jutland, Denmark. The cauldron's cultural affiliation remains disputed, but it is arguably the most technically accomplished and aesthetically interesting extant example of the Thracian Animal style.

Little is known about non-funerary architecture in the 4th–1st centuries BC, beyond the fact that, as in preceding periods, there was great interregional variety. After the establishment of the Greek Black Sea colonies, many hill-fort sites in the coastal zone were abandoned as more open settlement developed in the immediate hinterland. Inland in the south, the city of Seuthopolis had a walled centre laid out following the Hippodamian grid-plan system; other cities, such as Cabyle and (probably) Philippopolis (Plovdiv), were spread more broadly around an elevated acropolis. On the northern bank of the Danube, sites such as Zimnicea serviced river trade, and beyond them to the north-west such sites as Coţofenii-din-Dos had high mud-brick bastions that emulated Greek city walls and which may have been designed as much for prestige as defence. The upland regions had their own patterns; notable are the mountain sanctuaries of the Rhodope in south-west Bulgaria, which may have influenced the development of Carpathian mountain sanctuaries in the following period.

(iv) Dacian, 1st century BC*–1st century* AD. Securely dated examples of silversmithing in southeast Europe re-occur in the 1st century BC, contemporary with the Roman advance to the Danube and the rise of the Dacian state. Hoards and rich graves may be an index of political instability at this time, and mercenaries may have buried booty. There may also have been a greater investment in 'charismatic authority' by rival groups. The most common surviving toreutics from this period are dinner-plate sized horse-harness attachments (phalerae), which occur in graves, hoards and as stray finds. The hoards and stray finds occur as far afield as Atlantic Europe, where they can plausibly be correlated with the activities of Thracian cavalry auxiliaries in the Roman army: one was found in a legionary fort at Oberaden, Germany, another in the Roman camp at Helden in the Netherlands. The largest number (13) came from a hoard found on the island of Sark in 1718, but subsequently melted down and surviving now only in the form of engravings made by George Vertue in 1725.

Excavation of a late 1st-century BC grave at Stara Zagora, central Bulgaria, uncovered two elaborately decorated phalerae (Stara Zagora, Dist. Mus. Hist.). The more complete one depicts a man stabbing a lion as it bites his thigh. The two figures are surrounded by three paired beasts (from top to bottom): bird-headed griffins, wolves or dogs, and canid-headed griffins. The background is filled with swirls of little dots that, along with large leaves and a Tree of Life motif, suggest a woodland setting. The man wears what is either a one-piece garment or knee-breeches with a short-sleeved top, the waist being covered by a broad, decorated belt; the garment is vertically banded and slightly puffed, giving the appearance of quilting or of sewn pelts. This type of costume is worn by an analogous figure, also fighting a lion (though surrounded by five rather than six beasts), who appears on a phalera found at Helden, and also by the 'shaman' figure on the Gundestrup Cauldron; a similarly banded garment is worn by a male bust on a phalera from Herăstrău in Romania (Bucharest, N. Hist. Mus. Romania). This costume may identify a new version of the 'Thracian hero' figure, who, on the evidence from the Gundestrup Cauldron, may fulfil both priestly and kingly functions.

The Hellenistic and Roman Republican portrait style is coupled with Eastern content in a typically eclectic yet original Thracian work in a piece from the 1st-century BC hoard of silver-gilt rope-and-lotus bordered phalerae from Galiche in northern Bulgaria: a high repoussé portrait-like bust of a woman with tressed hair adorned with eight neck-rings and five pairs of arm-rings flanked by a pair of birds.

Phalerae from further north also show the influence of the Roman portrait style, such as those from Herastrau in Romania. An unusual oval phalera occurs in the Surcea hoard, Transylvania, depicting a rider either with a large eagle perched on his head or wearing a bird-crested helmet. In general, however, the range of subject-matter amongst the surviving 1st-century BC material is much more restricted than before, and the quality of much of the figural silversmithing is inferior. Goldwork is extremely rare; ancient accounts stress the wealth of plate in Dacia, but its wealth was known because it was plundered. It is depicted on Trajan's Column in Rome, spilling out of panniers as it was taken away to be converted into Roman coin. The centralized nature of the Dacian economy and the Dacians' firm belief that they would not be defeated in their fastnesses, may well have meant that virtually all precious metal was called in to Sarmizegethusa before the final defeat and that very little subsequently escaped the net. Hoards tend to contain either coins or heavy costume jewellery; silver fibulae are distinctively heavy and long.

The most important architecture associated with the Dacian state is the complex of fortresses and temples centred on the site of Gradiștea Muncelului, identified with Dacian Sarmizegethusa, in Romania, where seven great fortresses with attached temple precincts are packed together. Other settlement sites of the Dacian period are known in Transylvania, Moldavia and the plain of Wallachia, but none is as striking or as well-investigated as this group. The fortresses were a focus of industrial and craft activities, including silversmithing, blacksmithing and potting. The temples seem to have had astronomical and calendrical significance.

The finest examples of Dacian blacksmithing are a round sheet-iron shield from the fortress of Piatra Roșie and an iron helmet from the princely 'Celtic' grave of Ciumești in central Transylvania (both in Cluj-Napoca, Hist. Mus. Transylvania). The former is fragmentary (original diam. 600–700 mm) and carries the relief image of an aurochs (wild bull). The latter is surmounted by a great crest in the form of a perched bird of prey, its eyes formerly of inset glass, its wings (total span *c.* 600 mm) hinged so that they flapped as the warrior rode into battle.

Dacian art is far less well understood than that of earlier Thracian times, mainly because of the wholesale Roman destruction of Dacian civilization. The sanctuaries and temples were razed and as much booty as possible was removed, so that very few intact rich graves survive from the period.

R. F. Hoddinott: *The Thracians* (London, 1981)

A. Sherratt and T. Taylor: 'Metal Vessels in Bronze Age Europe and the Context of Vulchretrun', *Thracians and Mycenaeans*, ed. J. G. P. Best and N. M. W. De Vries (Leiden, 1989)

T. Sulimirski and T. Taylor: 'The Scythians', *Cambridge Ancient History*, iv (1991), pp. 547–60

A. Ful, ed.: *Ancient Thrace* (Sofia, 2000)

N. Theodossiev: *North-western Thrace from the Fifth to First Centuries BC* (Oxford, 2000)

M. Vickers: *Scythian and Thracian Antiquities in Oxford* (Oxford, 2002)

W. S. Hanson and I.P. Haynes, eds: *Roman Dacia: The Making of a Provincial Society* (Portsmouth, RI, 2004)

Thrasymedes (*fl* early 4th century BC). Greek sculptor from Paros. The son of Arignotos, he made the gold and ivory (chryselephantine) cult statue of *Asklepios* for the Temple of Asklepios at EPIDAUROS. The god was shown seated on a throne, holding a staff in one hand, with the other hand resting above a snake. A dog lay beside the throne, which was decorated with reliefs depicting stories of Argive heroes: *Bellerophon and the Chimaera* and *Perseus with the Head of Medusa*. The *Asklepios* apparently resembled Pheidias' colossal chryselephantine *Zeus* at Olympia, because Athenagoras (*Intercession Concerning the Christians*) incorrectly attributes the *Asklepios* to Pheidias. This is further suggested by its representation on coinage from Epidauros. None of Thrasymedes' work survives, although his workshop at Epidauros has been found. A building inscription says that he received 9800 drachmas for elaborate woodwork to the ceilings and doors and other parts of the temple. This sum seems to equal approximately one tenth of the total building cost.

F. Imhoof-Blumer and P. Gardner: *Ancient Coins Illustrating Lost Masterpieces of Greek Art: A Numismatic Commentary on Pausanias* (London, 1887, rev. by A. N. Oikonomides, Chicago, 1964), G.G.7

G. Roux: *L'Architecture de l'Argolide aux IVe et IIIe siècles avant J.C.* (Paris, 1961), pp. 424–32

B. Krause: 'Zum Asklepios-Kultbild des Thrasymedes in Epidauros', *Archäol. Anz.* (1972), pp. 240–57

Throne. Ceremonial chair or seat. In ancient Greece the word *thronos* had no special royal or religious significance, merely indicating a high, raised seat or one with a back; such seats may appear in scenes of everyday life as well as in scenes showing deities. Greek thrones have been classified into four distinct types based on the type of leg. The earliest, with legs square or rectangular in section, dates from as early as the Late Geometric period (*c.* 760–*c.* 700 BC). Examples include the thrones of Zeus and Hera on the François Vase (*c.* 570 BC; Florence, Archaeol. Mus.). It has simple arms terminating in a volute and a high back ending with the head of a swan; halfway up the legs are two facing volutes, from which sprout two palmettes.

The second type, with legs in the form of animal legs—lion, griffin etc—dates to the Archaic period (*c.* 700–*c.* 480 BC) and is probably derived from Egyptian models. The back of the seat might be high or low and was often decorated with vegetal motifs (e.g. as depicted on the Nereid Monument from Xanthos; *c.* 425–*c.* 400 BC; London, BM). Thrones with legs roughly circular in section and with a variety of profiles appear to have a Near Eastern inspiration: they occur most commonly in the East Greek areas of Asia Minor. The throne of Zeus depicted on the frieze of the Ionic Siphnian Treasury at Delphi (*c.* 525 BC; Delphi, Archaeol. Mus.) has bi-concave legs with a swelling halfway up; the same form occurs on the throne of Zeus in the east frieze of the Parthenon (*c.* 435 BC; London, BM). Finally, a mixture of animal legs in front and square or rounded legs behind, with a curved back, appeared in the Hellenistic period (323–27 BC; see fig.).

The Roman throne (*solium*) was from earliest times the seat of a deity, but with the establishment of the Republic it became a more widely used symbol of authority, occupied on official occasions by high-ranking magistrates. A form of this throne was retained for

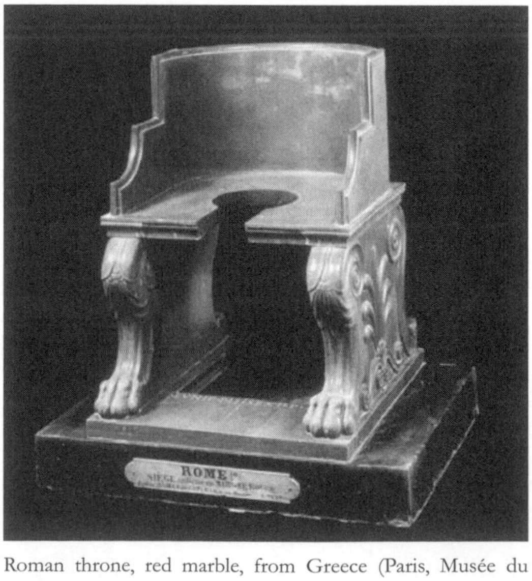

Roman throne, red marble, from Greece (Paris, Musée du Louvre)

use in private life: the *pater familias* sat on it to receive clients. The emperor's throne was distinguished for the most part merely by its rich decoration, although by the reign of Caligula (AD 37–41) the practice had arisen of isolating the imperial throne by raising it up on a podium. During the 4th century AD the throne again became the seat of high imperial officials, and in Early Christian Rome bishops gradually took over the use of the throne as a symbol of authority.

Roman thrones were made in the same varieties as earlier Greek ones, excepting the type with four animal legs. A single new form is attested in the 3rd century AD, similar to the Hellenistic Greek type: it had a round or square woven seat, with a high back and a curved profile that extended on either side to form arms.

Thugga [now Dougga]. Site of one of the best-preserved Roman towns in Africa, built on a plateau overlooking the valley of Oued Khalled in north-western Tunisia. A fine collection of archaeological material has been found there. Thugga dates back to the earliest phase of Libyan antiquity and certainly belonged to the kingdom of Numidia long before the reign of Masinissa (*d* 148 BC); writing on the invasion of Agathalus at the end of the 4th century BC, Diodorus Siculus mentioned the king Ailymas, whose domain included the territory of 'Tebagga'. During the Second Punic War between Rome and Carthage (218–201 BC), Thugga was under the Carthaginians, but it was won back by Masinissa and retained by his successors until the death of Juba I in 46 BC. Of the Numidian town there remain the megalithic wall (4th century BC), the dolmens and the Mausoleum of Atban, one of the finest Libyo-Punic monuments in North Africa; the bilingual inscription from it is now in London (BM). There are also some stelai (2nd–1st century BC), which provide evidence of the worship of Ba'al Hammon, the principal god of the Carthaginians; their inscriptions are a source of valuable information for religious beliefs and the Punic and Libyan languages.

After the battle of Thapsus in 46 BC Julius Caesar annexed the kingdom of Juba I, and Thugga became part of Africa Nova. A settlement developed at the foot of the plateau where the indigenous community lived. In the 1st century AD the forum and the market were built as tangible signs of the Roman presence at Thugga. For generations the two communities lived side by side, each keeping its own administrative organization, beliefs and customs. For this reason, and because of the uneven terrain, the plan of the town did not follow the normal grid pattern: the streets of Thugga are winding and do not form any right angles. The two communities finally merged, and in AD 195 they built a temple to Saturn over a temple to the Punic Ba'al. The process of Romanization was slow but profound; in AD 205 Thugga became a *municipium*, and in AD 261 it was declared a *colonia*.

Thugga reached the height of its territorial expansion under the Antonines and Severans (AD 138–235), when it covered more than 25 ha; its population seems to have been between 5000 and 10,000. The town profited a great deal from local benefactors; for example, P. Marcius Quadratus had the theatre built between AD 168 and 169, while the capitolium (see fig.) was constructed between AD 166 and 167 at the expense of two brothers of the Marcii family. The former building was built into the hillside at the top of the city slope and could seat over 3000 spectators; the latter is an imposing Corinthian tetrastyle building, the frieze of its portico bearing a dedication to the Capitoline triad and supporting a pediment in which is represented the imperial apotheosis. Adjoining the capitolium is a Temple of Mercury from the time of Commodus (*reg* AD 180–92); this faces the Square of the Wind Rose, which has a 3rd-century AD compass rose engraved on its pavement. The Temple of Caelestis (Severan) is set to the west of the forum in a unique crescent-shaped enclosure (w. 50 m) with a circular portico around it. There are also two arches of Severan date, the Licinian Baths of Imperial type (AD 259–68) and some magnificent houses decorated with superb mosaics depicting mythological scenes (see colour pl. 2:XV, fig. 1), as well as scenes of drinking and chariot racing (mostly in Tunis, Mus. N., Bardo).

C. Poinssot: *Les Ruines de Dougga* (Tunis, 1958)
G.-C. Picard: *La Civilisation de l'Afrique romaine* (Paris, 1959)
J. G. Février: 'La Constitution municipale de Dougga à l'époque numide', *Mél. Carthage* (1964–5), pp. 85–91

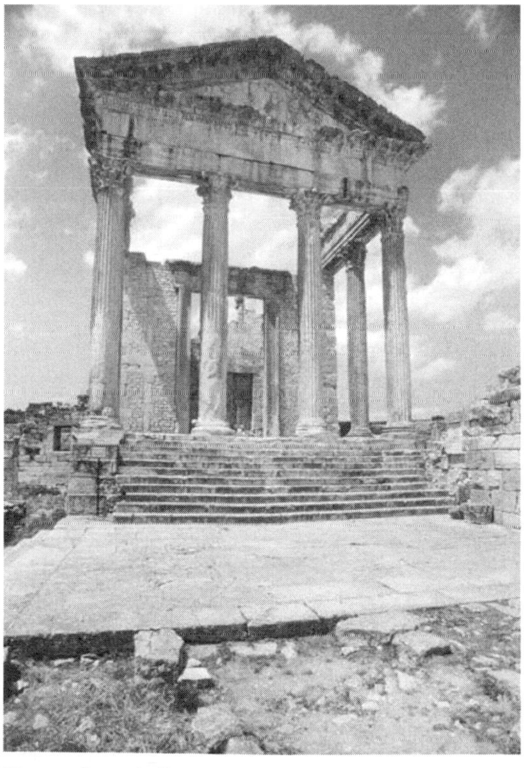

Thugga, the capitolium, AD 166–7

W. Seston: 'Des "Portes" de Thugga à la constitution de Carthage', *Rev. Hist.*, ccxxxvii (April–June 1967), pp. 277–94
M. Khanoussi and L. Maurin: *Dougga, fragments d'histoire: Choix d'inscriptions latines éditées, traduites et commentées, Ier–IVe siècles* (Bordeaux, 2000)
Rus Africum: Terra, acqua, olio nell'Africa settentrionale: Scavo e ricognizione nei dintorni di Dougga (Alto Tell tunisino) (exh. cat. by M. De Vos; Trent, Palazzo Thun, 2001)
M. Khanoussi and L. Maurin: *Mourir à Dougga: Recueil des inscriptions funéraires* ((Bordeaux, 2002)
S. Polla: 'La ricerca tedesco-tunisina a Dougga', *J. Roman Archaeol.*, xvii (2004), pp. 645–6
S. Saint-Amans: *Topographie religieuse de Thugga (Dougga): Ville romaine d'Afrique proconsulaire (Tunisie)* (Pessac, 2004)
J.-C. Golvin and M. Khanoussi: *Dougga, études d'architecture religieuse: Les sanctuaires des Victoires de Caracalla, de "Pluton" et de Caelestis* (Bordeaux, 2005)

Tiberius (Claudius Nero), Emperor (*b* Rome, 16 Nov 42 BC; *reg* AD 14–37; *d* Misenum [now Miseno], 16 March AD 37). Roman emperor and patron. In AD 23 he retired permanently to Capreae, forsaking Rome and its architectural development. However, although the reign of Tiberius was certainly modest in terms of building activity, the judgements of Suetonius (*Tiberius* xlvii.1) and Dio display the exaggerated hostility that characterizes their accounts of this emperor. In fact, apart from the various buildings he restored (including the stage-building of the Theatre of Pompey (AD 21) and the Temple of Castor in the Forum Romanum (AD 6), three elegant Corinthian columns of which are still extant), he was responsible for the Domus Tiberiana on the Palatine—the first true palace built there as a single unit by an emperor—and the Castra Praetoria, the camp of the Praetorian Guard (AD 21–23). The latter employed *opus latericium* (the use of fired clay bricks), a new system of construction that was to revive Roman architecture, as can be seen in the large stretches of its outer walls that still stand. Between 7 BC and AD 10 Tiberius rebuilt the great ruins of the Temple of Concord in the Forum Romanum. All that remain of this splendid edifice are the podium and the threshold of the cella, which measured 45×24 m. Part of the rich entablature is preserved (Rome, Tabularium), as is a capital from the cella (Rome, Antiquarium Forense). Also Tiberian is the great triumphal arch at ARAUSIO (now Orange) in Provence.

D. E. Strong and J. B. Ward-Perkins: 'The Temple of Castor in the Forum Romanum', *Pap. Brit. Sch. Rome*, xxx (1962), pp. 1–30
T. Pekary: 'Tiberius und der Tempel der Concordia in Rom', *Mitt. Dt. Archäol. Inst.: Röm Abt.*, lxxiii–lxxiv (1966–7), pp. 103–33
R. Seager: *Tiberius* (Maldon, MA, 1972/*R* 2005)
G. A. Mansuelli: *Roma e il mondo romano*, i (Turin, 1981), pp. 252–305

Tibur [now Tivoli]. Italian hill town, 37 km east of Rome, set above the cascades of the River Aniene. It was a favourite retreat of wealthy Romans escaping the summer heat. Villas were built there, the most famous being that of the Emperor Hadrian.

1. History and urban development. 2. Hadrian's Villa.

1. History and development. Because of its geographical position settlements have existed there since prehistoric times. According to one tradition Tibur was founded by Tiburnus and according to another by the Siculi. Along with the other Latins the Tiburtines were defeated by the Romans at Lake Regillus (498 BC), but the town was not fully subject to Rome until 338 BC, when it became a place of exile for important state prisoners, including Zenobia, the queen of Palmyra (AD 273). Among the leading families of Tibur were the Munatii, the most famous of whom was L. Munatius Plancus, consul in 42 BC, who founded Lugdunum (Lyon) and rebuilt the Temple of Saturn at Rome. After the Tiburtines acquired Roman citizenship (90 BC) the town became a fashionable resort for such notables as Julius Caesar, Brutus, Catullus, Horace, Augustus and Propertius. Finally Hadrian raised its position to that of an official imperial residence.

The topography of Tibur is incompletely known, although parts of the forum came to light in 1883 and 1920, when the office of public weights and measures was discovered as well as the Augusteum, a hall with a seated statue of Augustus in the apse. Two important 2nd-century BC temples survive on the acropolis: a tetrastyle pseudo-peripteral Ionic temple and a circular peripteral structure, the so-called Temple of Vesta (see fig. 1), 14.25 m in diameter, raised on a high podium, with a cella of *opus incertum* surrounded by 18 Corinthian columns. The capitals, of the Italo-Corinthian type, have two rings of lush acanthus leaves from which spring corkscrew volutes and a large flower (imitated by Sir John Soane in the Tivoli Corner of the Bank of England, London, 1805). The rectangular and circular temples have been associated with Tiburnus and Albunea (the Tiburtine Sibyl) respectively on the basis of literary sources (e.g. Horace: *Odes* I.vii.12), which record that they were worshipped near a waterfall beside the acropolis.

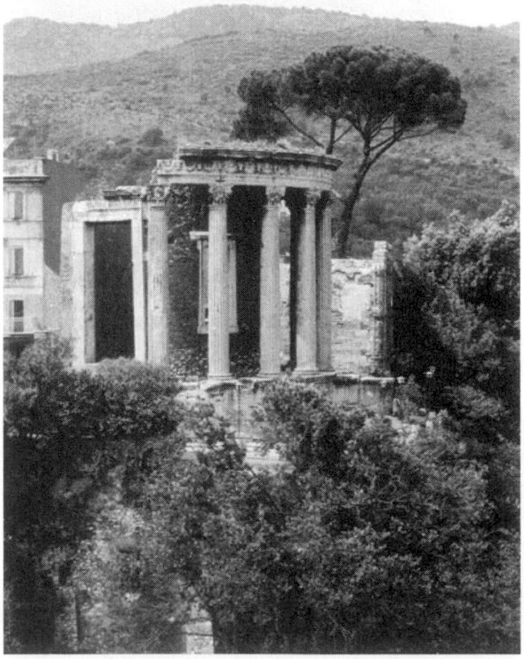

1. Tibur (Tivoli), 'Temple of Vesta', early 1st century BC

The most important cult at Tibur was that of Hercules Victor, whose large sanctuary (see fig. 2) was built just outside the walls to the west of the town. Like the Sanctuary of Fortuna at Praeneste, it has an associated theatre (2a) and temple (2b), although here the two are better integrated, since the theatrical *cavea*, 70 m wide, is situated on the lower edge of the rectangular enclosure, with the temple in the middle. The back and sides of the temple precinct are enclosed by a portico (2c) of arches framed by Doric half-columns. Underneath the temple precinct is a remarkable subterranean building complex, comprising a barrel-vaulted tunnel (2d) for the Via Tiburtina to run obliquely underneath the temple enclosure, and a row of shops (2e) accessible from the tunnel. On the Via Tiburtina just west of the sanctuary stands the so-called Tempio della Tosse, a domed rotunda built in the 4th century AD. At floor-level the drum contains four curved and two rectangular niches, as well as two entrances on opposite sides. Higher up are four semicircular and three rectangular windows. The dome, 12.75 m in diameter, has an oculus, and in its envelope are rows of brick ribs. The building, which is set within two rows of parallel walls belonging to an older building, may have been the monumental atrium of a villa.

The plains west of Tibur contain enormous beds of travertine, one of the most prized building materials used by the Romans. Its earliest known use is in the Milvian Bridge (109 BC), and it was later employed for the façade of the Colosseum. From the 2nd century

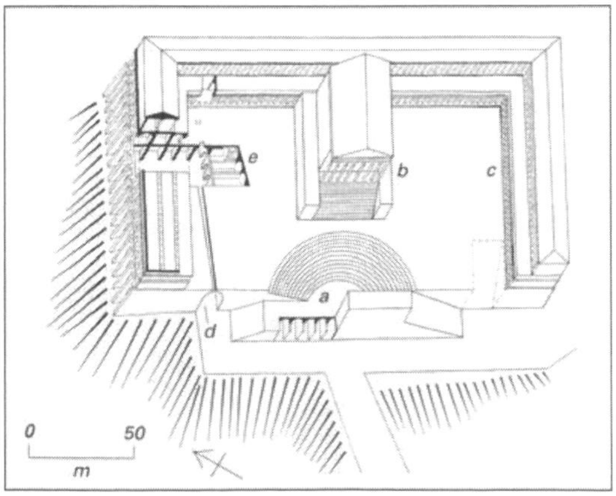

2. Tibur (Tivoli), Sanctuary of Hercules Victor, early 1st century BC, axonometric reconstruction: (a) theatre; (b) Temple of Hercules Victor; (c) portico; (d) tunnel; (e) shops

BC onwards Tibur's magnificent position attracted the villas of wealthy Romans. Just south of the town are the remains of the so-called Villa of Cassius, a large terraced complex of the late 2nd century BC with splendid views over the plains surrounding Rome. A fine series of Hadrianic sculptures (Rome, Vatican, Mus. Pio-Clementino) was found here, including *Apollo and the Muses*, a herm of *Pericles* and a series of other herms; in a nearby villa, which perhaps belonged to the Pisones, were found 16 herms of Greek philosophers and poets (Madrid, Mus. Arqueol. N.). Just north of the town in the former convent of S Antonio are the remains of a Republican villa, once called the Villa of Horace. Its large barrel-vaulted nymphaeum has walls and apse decorated with shells and chips of marble, a technique that was the forerunner of wall mosaic. Horace's Sabine villa, given to him by his patron Maecenas in 33–32 BC, is probably to be found just outside Licenza, *c.* 23 km north-east of Tibur. The villa, first excavated in 1911, has a fountain court overlooked by winter and summer dining-rooms, and a series of living-rooms and bedrooms facing on to a large garden surrounded on all sides by porticos. The situation of the villa in a shady valley accords well with Horace's own description (*Epistles* I.xvi), while the nearby spring may be the *fons Bandusiae* of *Odes* III.xiii.1.

S. Cabral and F. Del Rè: *Delle ville e de' più notabili monumenti antichi della città di Tivoli e suo territorio* (Rome, 1779)

F. Bulgarini: *Notizie storiche antiquarie statistiche ed agronomiche intorno all'antichissima città di Tivoli e suo territorio* (Rome, 1848)

T. Ashby: 'The Classical Topography of the Roman Campagna, ii: Via Nomentana, via Tiburtina', *Pap. Brit. Sch. Rome*, iii (1906), pp. 3–200 (76–197)

C. Carducci: *Tibur (Tivoli)*, Italia Romana: Municipi e Colonie (Spoleto, 1940)

C. F. Giuliani: *Tibur*, i, Forma Italiae (Rome, 1970)

F. Coarelli: *Lazio*, Guide Archeologiche Laterza (Rome, 1982), pp. 74–122

A. M.Reggiani ed. *Tivoli: Il santuario di Ercole vincitore* (Milan, 1998)

C. F. Giuliani: *Tivoli: Il santuario di Ercole vincitore* (Tivoli, 2004)

2. HADRIAN'S VILLA. The summer palace of the Emperor Hadrian, built between AD 118 and 134 and situated on an elevated plateau south-west of Tivoli. Its unusual architecture and wealth of sculpture and mosaics have fascinated artists and scholars since the Renaissance.

(i) Architecture. (ii) Sculpture. (iii) Mosaics. (iv) Rediscovery.

(i) Architecture. The buildings on the 120 ha site (see fig. 3) were named after such celebrated landmarks as the Lyceum, the Academy and the Stoa Poikile at Athens (see *Augustan History: Hadrian* xxvi.5), although they were not precise copies of these monuments, but followed a Republican tradition established by such men as Cicero, who had an Academy and a Lyceum in his villa at Tusculum. The site was fairly level, but high enough to command views of Rome. The ground fell away to the north-east to form a broad, secluded valley known as the Vale of Tempe. In typical Roman

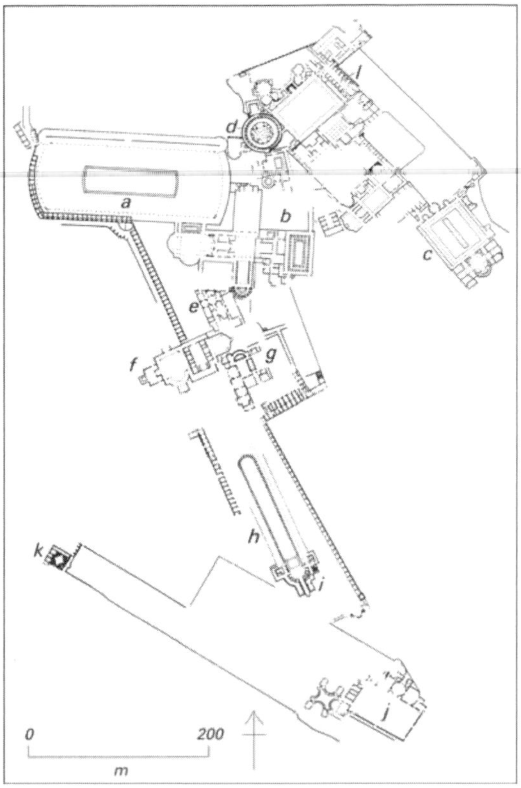

3. Tibur (Tivoli), Hadrian's Villa, AD 118–34, plan: (a) Poikile; (b) nymphaeum; (c) Piazza d'Oro; (d) Island Villa; (e) Small Baths; (f) vestibule; (g) Great Baths; (h) Canopus; (i) Serapeum; (j) Academy; (k) Roccabruna; (l) Ospitali

fashion all the elements are a blend of art and nature. Practically every group of buildings is organized around a peristyle garden, ranging from the vast, park-like enclosure of the Poikile (3a) to the small and intimate garden in the nymphaeum (3b), although little is known of their actual plantings. Apart from peripheral monuments, such as the two small theatres, the Underworld and the Temple of Aphrodite, the villa comprises six loosely related groups of buildings on different axes.

The north-east complex incorporates a Republican villa overlooking the Vale of Tempe. To the south-east of this is the Piazza d'Oro (3c), with its complex domed vestibule, elaborate nymphaeum and a peristyle court that may be based on a Hellenistic stoa. To the north-west is the Island Villa (3d), Hadrian's private retreat, and adjacent to it, but on a different axis, the Poikile. The latter is certainly a misnomer, as its vast enclosure (232×97 m) has a double running-track along one side, a large pool in the middle and a bath with sun-room nearby, which suggests that it was built in imitation of a gymnasium. Adjoining it are the main state apartments of the villa. Facing the mountains of Tibur is a secluded peristyle enclosing a large pool, while on the other side a suite of rooms with underfloor heating commands a magnificent view towards Rome. These rooms tower above a large nymphaeum in the form of a stadium and the sumptuously marbled square dining-room, on three sides of which were intimate peristyle gardens containing fountains. On a different axis following a long natural depression are the somewhat eccentrically planned Small Baths (3e), the main entrance or vestibule to the palace (3f), the more orthodox Great Baths (3g), the Canopus canal (3h) and the Serapeum (3i). The Serapeum, an enormous nymphaeum with basins in the drum of its half-dome fed by an aqueduct running around its rim, was used for summer banquets. The diners reclined under the half-dome on a vast semicircular couch, while opposite them stretched the canal (119×18 m), built in imitation of the one that linked Alexandria and Canopus, the site of the celebrated Temple of Serapis. Overlooking these, on a higher terrace with a more pronounced east–west orientation, is a complex of buildings culminating in the so-called Academy (3j). At the north-west end of the terrace is the Roccabruna (3k), an isolated square tower surmounted by a circular domed pavilion. Towers of this kind often stood in isolated parts of ancient parks to command panoramic views. They were essentially the equivalent of the follies of the 18th century.

Hadrian himself probably had a hand in the design of the villa, to judge by a remark made by the great architect APOLLODOROS OF DAMASCUS, who criticized him for drawing 'pumpkins' (Dio: *Roman History* LXIX.iv.2), perhaps a reference to the umbrella domes that constitute one of the villa's most striking architectural features. These exotic domes usually consisted of a series of concave segments, as in the vestibule of Piazza d'Oro, while the half-dome of the Serapeum comprised alternate domical and umbrella segments. The domes and most of the fabric of the villa were of concrete (the walls were faced in *opus reticulatum* or brick), since by this date the Romans had mastered the art of concrete construction and were fully aware of its potentialities. The builders of Hadrian's Villa, therefore, were able to execute designs that were as often eccentric as they were complex. For example, they seem to have had an almost obsessive interest in the curvilinear. The Island Villa is a complete miniature villa on a circular site surrounded by a moat. The four main areas of the villa—vestibule, bedroom suite, dining-room and bathing suite—are defined by four sweeping curves, with the result that the central courtyard has four concave sides. The nymphaeum of the Piazza d'Oro has a central octagonal courtyard, 10.35 m in diameter, with alternate convex and concave sides. Similarly, the walls of the domed octagonal hall of the Small Baths are alternately rectilinear and concave. Another feature of the architecture, which illustrates a developing trend, can be seen in the vestibule of the Piazza d'Oro. Previously, façade and interior, however complex the shapes involved, were given quite different architectural treatment. Here, however, the curved recesses and complex profiled dome are features of both interior and exterior. (Later interest in internal space became such that an interior could totally dictate the external appearance of a building, as in the Hunting Baths at LEPTIS MAGNA.)

H. Winnefeld: *Die Villa des Hadrian bei Tivoli* (Berlin, 1895)
G. Lugli: 'Villa Adriana', *Boll. Comm. Archeol. Com. Roma*, lv (1927), pp. 139–204
W. L. Reichardt: 'The Vestibule Group at Hadrian's Villa', *Mem. Amer. Acad. Rome*, xi (1933), pp. 127–32
H. Kaehler: *Hadrian und seine Villa bei Tivoli* (Berlin, 1950)
L. Vighi: *Villa Hadriana* (Rome, 1958)
S. Aurigemma: *Villa Adriana* (Rome, 1961)
F. L. Rakob: *Die Piazza d'Oro in der Villa Hadriana bei Tivoli* (Munich, 1967)
F. L. Rakob: 'Der Bauplan einer kaiserlichen Villa', *Festschrift K. Lankheit*, ed. K. Schauenberg (Bonn, 1973), pp. 113–25
E. Salza Prina Ricotti: 'Criptoportici e gallerie sotterranee di Villa Adriana', *Les Cryptoportiques dans l'architecture romaine* (Rome, 1973), pp. 219–59
C. Giuliani and P. Verduchi: 'Ricerche sull'architettura di Villa Adriana', *Quad. Ist. Top. Ant.*, viii (1975), pp. 3–95
A. C. G. Smith: 'The Date of the "Grandi Terme" of Hadrian's Villa at Tivoli', *Pap. Brit. Sch. Rome*, xlvi (1978), pp. 73–93
A. Hoffmann: *Das Gartenstadion in der Villa Hadriana* (Mainz, 1980)
W. L. MacDonald and J. A. Pinto: *Hadrian's Villa and its Legacy* (New Haven, 1995)
S. Aurigemma: *Villa Adriana* (Rome, 1996)
M. Falsitta: *Villa Adriana: Una questione di composizione architettonica* (Milan, 2000)
Villa Adriana: Paesaggio antico e ambiente moderno: Elementi di novità e ricerche in corso: Atti del Convegno: Rome: 2000
E. S. P. Ricotti: *Villa Adriana: Il sogno di un imperatore* (Rome, 2001)
M. Mosser and H. Lavagne, eds: *Hadrien empereur et architecte: La villa d'Hadrien, tradition et modernité d'un paysage culturel: Actes du colloque international organisé par le Centre culturel du Panthéon en collaboration avec la Mairie de Paris* (Geneva, 2002)
M. Macale: *Villa Adriana* (Rome, 2003)

(ii) Sculpture. Over 300 mythological, portrait and decorative sculptures have been actually or putatively discovered since the 16th century at Hadrian's Villa. Initially prized by antiquarian collectors and esteemed as reflections of Greek masterpieces, current understanding values them for themselves, as documents of a creative age elucidating their settings. Both attitudes are demonstrated by the various statues from Hadrian's Villa of Hercules, for example, the model hero whose fated labours imparted physical and intellectual fortitude. The 'Greek' north theatre reputedly contained a colossal version, along with herms of *Comedy* and *Tragedy* (Rome, Vatican, Mus. Pio-Clementino, inv. nos 262, 265). Another statue of *Hercules* stood in the 'Odeion', the south theatre, joined by a statue of *Minerva* and by Muses (Madrid, Prado, inv. nos 37–8, 40–41, 61–2, 68–9). The Lansdowne *Herakles* represents treasures from the villa that were removed beyond papal territory by such agents as Thomas Jenkins in the 18th century, and characterizes the creative retrospection of a classicizing age. The statue combines a Lysippically proportioned long-legged figure,

a strongly modelled Polykleitan quadratic torso, and a head and face once termed Skopadic in their pathos. These accentuations would have attracted attention in an open allée or an architectural niche, sculptural settings favoured by Hadrian.

The villa also displayed literary and political portraits, of which only marble examples have survived, including representations of Hadrian, his consort Sabina and most of their successors through the Severans. The Hadrianic examples show the typically crisp facial rendering, emulating bronze, and incipient eye definition executed by drill, which was first undertaken in this period (e.g. *Antisthenes*: Rome, Vatican, Mus. Pio-Clementino, inv. no. 2888). At least 18 statues existed of Antinous, their opposed firm and soft modelling illustrating contrasts inherent in Hadrianic art. A bust of the youth (h. 1 m; Rome, Vatican, Mus. Pio-Clementino, inv. no. 251) juxtaposes sharp delineation around the brow, and typically dreamy eyes, with soft full cheeks, between corkscrews of hair hanging from thick locks. Contradictions characterize such stylistic assimilations as an *Antinous-Osiris* (h. 2.41 m), in which an exaggerated skeletal definition conflicts with a generalized pharaonic and Greek Archaic body, and an idealized portrait head. The Greek marble statue is now in the Museo Gregoriano Egizio in the Vatican, Rome (inv. no. 22795), which also houses an Egyptian collection in dark stone from the Canopus, recalling at Hadrian's Villa a famous pleasure city linked to Alexandria by a canal. Such terms as Canopus, Tempe and Academy enhanced, in conjunction with sculpture, the illusion of distant locales and ages. Excavation of the Canopus in the 1950s revealed its sculptural adornment (replaced at the site by casts). Water flowed from a grotto into a channel, past a *Scylla* (fragments in Tivoli, Mus. N. Archeol., Villa Adriana, storeroom), to an outlet between sculptural personifications of the *Tiber* and the *Nile* (Tivoli, Mus. N. Archeol., Villa Adriana, inv. nos 2261, 2259). Along one side, backs to the water, stood two paired reproductions of the 5th-century BC caryatids from the Erechtheion, Athens (inv. nos 2230, 2233, 2238–9), once bearing an entablature, flanked by Silens supporting baskets (both inv. no. 2249). In an arcade skirting the end of the channel two other pairs of statues faced the water. *Hermes* and a *Warrior* (inv. nos 2262, 2257) derive from one 5th-century BC prototype, while *Amazons* (inv. nos 2266, 2255) stem from originals attributed to Pheidias and Kresilas. Contrasting techniques, matching contrasting placements, range from classicizing recreation to romanticized interpretation. Such groups, reproducing masterpieces of mythical content, some 650 years old, which Hadrian must have seen, engaged him and the villa in a realm of heroic, timeless myth. The settings of two statues of *Aphrodite* coordinated sculpture and architecture: an example of the Crouching Aphrodite type (Rome, Mus. N. Romano, inv. no. 108597), perched by a basin in a bath house, while a version of the *Aphrodite of Knidos* by Praxiteles (Tivoli, Mus. N. Archeol., Villa Adriana, inv. no. 2752) stood in a reconstruction of its shrine at Knidos, in the area of the villa known as the Vale of Tempe. The soft modelling of the first and summary definition of the second illustrate the variety encountered in the sculpture, apparently all Hadrianic in date.

Three works, two signed by sculptors from Aphrodisias, who maintained a workshop in Rome, wittily express the Dionysiac world. Their rich grey or red marble enhances a vivid naturalism of Hellenistic inspiration. Two centaurs, one young and joyful, the other old and pained with hands tied behind his back, both once ridden by cupids, contrast the two faces of love, while a standing smiling satyr, perhaps one of two, raises grapes (Rome, Mus. Capitolino, inv. nos 656–8). These emblems of fertility came from the Academy, where scenes of aspects of nature also appeared in mosaic. Architectural reliefs of cupids riding sea creatures decorated both the Island Villa and the Piazza d'Oro, where another frieze portrayed cupids hunting. These references to a life beyond care and of aristocratic pleasures give further definition to the villa's purpose.

(iii) Mosaics. Important examples of geometric, botanic and floral, and figural and pictorial *opus vermiculatum* mosaics have been discovered at Hadrian's Villa. The most significant mosaics *in situ* pave the ten rooms of the Ospitali, recording, in black and white over sinopia, the new preference for laying botanic over geometric shapes. In each chamber, mosaics of smaller, repeated, plant-derived forms overlie larger geometric motifs in thresholds and alcoves. A mosaic in the Piazza d'Oro illustrates how more complex geometric patterns endured, while the colouristic richness of its four-patterned sequence of coffers demonstrates the refinement of such polychromy. In the Academy was discovered, among other mosaics, that depicting a metal goblet (Rome, Mus. Capitolino), on the lip of which perch doves, one drinking and casting the shadow of its head on the water. Because Pliny the elder described such a mosaic by Sosos at Pergamon, some see the work at Hadrian's Villa as original, although the bird's shadow is distorted. Pliny failed to record the likeness of a man below the vessel's handle, an apparent allusion to the Homeric Cup of Nestor (*Iliad* XI.632ff.). While the Romans transported emblemata, Pliny's omission and the existence of other versions raises the question of the work's originality. The mosaic's discovery dates from 1737; further excavations in 1779–80 in the Academy revealed others, each giving a different area thematic focus.

The Gabinetto delle Maschere in the Vatican derives its name from three such works from Hadrian's Villa. An Apolline panel represents a griffin and Apollo's cithara, bow and quiver by a garlanded female mask on a pedestal. A Dionysiac mosaic features a cantharus, a thyrsus and a leopard with a tympanum before an ivy-wreathed mask on a hillock. A third panel displays, on a parapet, comic masks of a female, a young man and an old man above another male mask between a lyre and a broken jug, possibly recalling Menander's *Hydria*. The mosaics' original separate settings, inside garlanded frames on white fields containing twining oak tendrils, were combined into one with a non-theatrical fourth panel. This belongs thematically with another in the Sala degli Animali in the Vatican, each illustrating a deity, one seated female and one standing male, among grazing goats and sheep in spacious, idyllic landscapes. Two other visual allegories manifest divinely fated conflicts in barren, rocky settings with struggling vegetation. One, also in the Sala degli Animali, represents a lion savaging a bull, both impressively foreshortened, distressing a cow seen across a lake, her body reflected in the water. Another, in Berlin (Antikenmus.), like the dove mosaic suggested as a Hellenistic original, portrays two centaurs battling with wild beasts. A rearing centaur, who has dispatched a lion, ignores a menacing leopard and raises a boulder against a tiger who has felled his mate. All these topoi evoke antecedents in the Greek past that were beloved by Hadrian, yet their tendentious crafting characterizes the emperor's taste and time.

W. Helbig: *Führer durch die öffentlichen Sammlungen klassischer Altertümer in Rom*, 4 vols (Tübingen, 1963–72)

J. Raeder: 'Die statuarische Ausstattung der Villa Hadriana bei Tivoli', *Europäische Hochschulschriften*, XXXVIII/iv (Frankfurt am Main, 1983)

M. de Franceschini: *Villa Adriana: Mosaici, pavimenti, edifici* (Rome, 1991)

J. Charles-Gaffiot and H. Lavagne, ed.: *Hadrien: Trésors d'une villa impériale* (Milan, 1999)

(iv) Rediscovery. Hadrian's Villa ranks among the most influential monuments in the history of architecture, its resonance stemming in significant part from its association with the enigmatic personality of Hadrian himself. After the collapse of the Roman Empire, however, the villa was used as a quarry for more than a millennium, and many local structures were built from its spoils. No descriptions of it survive from this period of neglect, and the earliest account of its ruins is in 1461 by the humanist Pope Pius II (*Commentarii*), in which he meditated on the ephemeral nature of material splendour, thus introducing a topos that artists and poets have continued to explore, with the villa as a focus.

Soon afterwards, Renaissance artists and architects began to visit the villa. At the end of the 15th century Francesco di Giorgio Martini (1439–1501; Florence, Uffizi, 319A, 320, 325 and Turin, Bib. Reale, MS. Saluzzo 148) and Giuliano da Sangallo (*c.* 1445–1516; Rome, Vatican, Bib. Apostolica, Cod. Vat. Barberiniano) made measured drawings that combine accurate observation and imaginative creativity. During the early 16th century Donato Bramante (1443/4–1514), Raphael (1483–1520) and other High Renaissance architects visited the site, and though none of their drawings has been identified, the influence of the villa may be seen in their designs, notably the former's Tempietto and the latter's Villa Madama, both in Rome. By the mid-16th century references to Hadrian's Villa began to appear in guidebooks and architectural treatises, such as those of Andrea Palladio (1508–80) and Philibert de L'Orme (1514–&)), and Pirro Ligorio (*c.* 1513–83) began to excavate at the site, initiating what has been termed the first large-scale modern archaeological dig. While the primary object of his excavations was ancient statuary for his patron, Cardinal Ippolito II d'Este (1509–72), Ligorio recorded his finds in the first systematic description of the site. He assigned the grandiose names mentioned in the *Augustan History* to specific parts of the villa and added new names of his own, thereby determining the way later artists and scholars would refer to them. The villa may have influenced his own designs for the Villa d'Este at Tivoli and the Casino of Pius IV in the Vatican. Ligorio's drawings, however, were never published, so that credit for the first comprehensive survey of the site belongs to Francesco Contini (1599–1669). This was completed by 1637 and available for study by Baroque architects such as Francesco Borromini (1599–1667) and Carlo Rainaldi (1611–91) long before its publication in 1668. Attracted by the numerous departures from Vitruvian classicism embodied in the villa's design, Borromini drew inspiration for some of his greatest works, especially the Oratory dei Filippini and S Ivo alla Sapienza.

The influence of Hadrian's Villa became more diffuse during the 18th century. Artists from all over Europe came to study its remains: in 1755, for example, Charles-Louis Clérisseau (1721–1820), Robert Adam (1728–92) and Giovanni Battista Piranesi (1720–78) drew there together, while in 1760 Jean-Honoré Fragonard (1732–1806) and Hubert Robert (1733–1808) sketched on the site. Of all the artists, archaeologists and architects who have studied Hadrian's Villa, Piranesi emerges as its most inspired interpreter. At the end of his life he was planning a book on the antiquities of Tibur, for which his numerous *vedute* of the villa were intended, and his great annotated plan of the villa, issued posthumously by his son Francesco (1758–1810) in 1781, is a work of genius. In spite of errors it is still the best site plan and records a wealth of data otherwise unknown.

Since its rediscovery Hadrian's Villa has produced vast quantities of sculpture, mosaics and other works of art. During the 18th century works excavated there found their way into every major European collection; today they are scattered from Malibu to St Petersburg. Knowledge of the villa's décor was further disseminated by the publications of Charles Cameron (*The Baths of the Romans*, 1772), Nicolas Ponce and Piranesi, and its influence may be discerned in countless interiors, ranging from Cameron's Agate Rooms at Pushkin (formerly Tsarskoye Selo) to Robert Adam's Syon House. Hadrian's Villa also played a significant role in the formulation of artistic theory at a crucial juncture in the history of Western art, in the controversy over the primacy of Greek and Roman forms. The emphasis placed by JOHANN JOACHIM WINCKELMANN on the noble simplicity and quiet grandeur of Greek sculpture was grounded in no small part on works found at the villa, such as the celebrated *Antinous* relief in the Albani collection (Rome, Villa Albani, now Villa Torlonia). In contrast, Piranesi's exaltation of the richness and variety of Roman architecture was based largely on its buildings. Similarly, in the 19th century Hadrian's Villa inspired both the beaux-arts Neo-classicists and the Romantics. The acquisition of about half the site by the Italian State in 1870 paved the way for a more systematic archaeological investigation, which is still far from complete. The influence of the villa on Le Corbusier (1887–1965), Frank Lloyd Wright (1867–1959), Louis I. Kahn (1901–74) and, later still, on Charles W. Moore (1925–93) and James Stirling (1926–92) demonstrates its relevance to 20th-century architecture.

A. Palladio: *L'antichità di Roma* (Rome, 1554)

P. de L'Orme: *Le Premier Tome de l'architecture de Philibert de l'Orme, conseiller et ausmonier ordinaire du roy, abbé de Saint-Serge lez angiers* (Paris, 1567)

F. Contini: *Adriani Caesaris immanem in Tyburtino villam* (Rome, 1668)

P. Ligorio: *Descrittione della superba & magnificentissima Villa Tiburtina Hadriana*, Thesaurus Antiquitatum et Historiarum Italiae (Leiden, 1723)

F. Piranesi: *Pianta delle fabbriche esistenti nella Villa Adriana* (Rome, 1781)

N. Ponce: *Arabesques antiques des bains de Livie, et de la villa Adriana* (Paris, 1789)

P. Gusman: *La Villa impériale de Tibur* (Paris, 1904)

L. C. Gabel, ed.: *Memoirs of a Renaissance Pope: The Commentaries of Pius II*, trans. F. A. Gragg (New York, 1959 and London, 1960), pp. 328 9

E. Salza Prina Ricotti: 'Villa Adriana in Pirro Ligorio e Francesco Contini', *Atti & Mem. Accad. N. Lincei, Atti Cl. Sci. Morali*, xvii (1973–4), pp. 1–47

W. L. MacDonald and J. A. Pinto: *Hadrian's Villa and its Legacy* (New Haven and London, 1995)

Timanthes (*fl* late 5th century or early 4th century BC). Greek painter. He originated from Kythnos or Sikyon and was a contemporary and rival of Zeuxis and Parrhasios, defeating the latter in a competition on Samos (Pliny, XXXV.64, 71, 73–4). Parrhasios had painted the hero Ajax, who, in an episode recounted in the *Aethiopis* and *Little Iliad*, was defeated by Odysseus in the competition for the arms of Achilles. When the artist heard that the judges had voted in favour of Timanthes, Parrhasios said that Ajax has suffered a second indignity. It is not known what subject Timanthes painted for the competition, but Parrhasios' comment suggests it was not Ajax. None of Timanthes' works now survives. Cicero (*Brutus*, xviii.70) listed him among the painters who used a four-colour palette. Although he may occasionally have limited his palette to yellow, white, red and black, he no doubt used a wider range at other times. Timanthes was reputed to possess great skill but even greater imagination, as his most famous picture, the *Sacrifice of Iphigeneia*, illustrates. The artist varied the intensity of the emotions of the witnesses: the sorrow of Kalchas was less than that of Odysseus, which was less than that of Menelaos. The grief of Agamemnon, the father of Iphigeneia, was too great to depict, and so the artist veiled his head. It is a motif often found in later artists' work. With the *Iphigeneia*, Timanthes defeated the otherwise unknown Kolotes of Teos in a competition. Timanthes' small picture in which satyrs measure a sleeping Cyclops' thumb with a thyrsus in order to suggest his size was also praised for ingenuity of conception. He also painted the *Death of Palamedes*, which Alexander the Great admired at Ephesos; and a *Hero*, which hung in the Temple of Peace at Rome.

J. Overbeck: *Die antiken Schriftquellen zur Geschichte der bildenden Künste bei den Griechen* (Leipzig, 1868/*R* Hildesheim. 1959), nos 828, 1067, 1649, 1699, 1700, 1734–44, 2102 [full references]

Timarchides (*fl* 2nd century BC–early 1st). Name of at least two Greek sculptors, members of a family of Athenian sculptors including Polykles, Timokles and Dionysios. Pliny (*Natural History* XXXIV.xix.91) listed a Timarchides among sculptors in bronze, but his best-known work seems to have been a marble lyre-playing *Apollo* in the Temple of Apollo near the Porticus Metelli (later Octaviae) in Rome (Pliny: XXXVI.iv.35). This has been identified with a classicizing Apollo type known from several Roman copies. If it was the cult statue, the original may date to 179 BC, when the temple was rebuilt. Pliny perhaps implied that Timarchides also sculpted the cult image in the Temple of Juno Regina (ded. 179 BC) in the same porticus. He may also have been that Timarchides who worked with (?his brother) Timokles on the cult statue of Asklepios at Elateia (Pausanias: *Guide to Greece* X.xxxiv.6). They may be the 'sons of Polykles' mentioned twice by Pausanias (VI.xii.9; X.xxxiv.8), although neither name occurs with this patronymic. If so, their works suggest a connection with the Neo-Attic school of sculpture, and one may be datable to 146 BC.

A marble statue base in Athens bears the signature of a 'Timarchides the younger, son of Polykles, of Thorikos' (*Inscr. Gr./2*, ii, 4302) in lettering of the early 1st century BC. This same Timarchides, son of Polykles, and Dionysios, son of Timarchides, also signed a portrait statue of *C. Ofellius Ferus* on Delos. Its preserved body (*c.* 100 BC; Delos, Archaeol. Mus.) is a classicizing creation in Praxitelean style. Some scholars believe that it was this younger Timarchides whom Pausanias grouped with Timokles as the 'sons of Polykles', so that the latter were active at the end of the 2nd century BC, rather than in the second (Stewart) or third (Marcadé) quarter of that century.

J. Overbeck: *Die antiken Schriftquellen zur Geschichte der bildenden Künste bei den Griechen* (Leipzig, 1868/*R* Hildesheim, 1959), nos 2207, 2210–13

G. Becatti: 'Attikà: Saggio sulla scultura attica dell'ellenismo', *Riv. Reale Ist. Archeol. & Stor. A.*, vii (1940), pp. 7–116

J. Marcadé: *Recueil des signatures de sculpteurs grecs*, ii (Paris, 1957), pp. 131–3
A. Stewart: *Attika: Studies in Athenian Sculpture of the Hellenistic Age* (London, 1979), pp. 42–6
G. I. Despinis: 'Studien zur hellenistischen Plastik I: Zwei Künstlerfamilien', *Mitt. Dt. Archäol Inst.: Athen. Abt.,* cx (1995), pp. 321–72

Timgad. *See* THAMUGADI.

Timokles (*fl* mid-2nd century BC). Greek sculptor. He was presumably a member of the family of Athenian sculptors that included POLYKLES, TIMARCHIDES and DIONYSIOS. His activity is known from only two literary references. Pliny the elder (*Natural History* XXXIV.xix.52) named him with Polykles in his list of sculptors of the 156th Olympiad (156–153 BC) who revived artistic activity, which had been in decline since the 121st Olympiad (295–292 BC); Pausanias (*Guide to Greece* X.xxxiv.6) identified a statue of *Asklepios* (untraced) at Elateia as the work of Timokles and Timarchides, probably the 'sons of Polykles' who produced a portrait of *Agesarchos* at Olympia and the statue of *Athena* at Elateia (both untraced; Pausanias: VI.xii.9, X.xxxiv.8). The latter work is clearly strongly reminiscent of the so-called NEO-ATTIC sculptures of the later 2nd century BC, since the figures on its shield were apparently copied from the shield of the *Athena Parthenos* of PHEIDIAS. The portrait of *Agesarchos* may be datable to the same period, since his home city Triteia was described not as Achaian but as Arcadian, as it briefly was in 146 BC. Since Timarchides is not included in Pliny's list of sculptors of the 156th Olympiad, he may have been Timokles' younger brother, though precisely which of the two known sculptors named Timarchides he was is disputed.

G. Becatti: 'Attika: Saggio sulla scultura attica dell'ellenismo', *Riv. Ist. N. Archeol. & Stor. A.*, vii (1940), pp. 7–116
A. Stewart: *Attika: Studies in Athenian Sculpture of the Hellenistic Age* (London, 1979), pp. 42–6
G. I. Despinis: 'Studien zur hellenistischen Plastik I: Zwei Künsterfamilien aus Athen', *Mitt. Dt. Archäol Inst.: Athen. Abt.,* cx (1995), pp. 321–72

Timomachos (*fl* ?1st century BC). Greek painter. He came from Byzantium, and Pliny (XXXV.136) stated that he was a contemporary of Julius Caesar (*reg* 49–44 BC). Many scholars follow Pliny, but some suggest a date in the Classical Greek period (480–323 BC). The most celebrated picture by Timomachos was a *Medea* painted in encaustic. Its fame rested in the characterization, which combined jealous wrath and sorrowful pity. Medea's children were depicted playing, unaware that she stood near them holding a sword, intending to murder them. The picture was the last painted by Timomachos before his death. The artist also painted *Ajax in his Madness.* Cicero (II.iv.60.135) knew that the *Ajax* and the *Medea* were owned by the people of Kyzikos (Lat. Cyzicus). Pliny (XXXV.i.136; cf. XXXV.26) said that Julius Caesar paid 80 talents for them and hung them in the Temple of Venus Genetrix in Rome. A painting by Timomachos of *Orestes and Iphigeneia among the Taurians* may be reflected in Pompeian wall paintings, as may his *Medea.* Other paintings attributed to him were: a famous *Gorgon*; *Lekythion*, a master of gymnastics; an *Assembly of Notable Men*; a conversation piece of *Two Men in Cloaks.* None of his works survives.

J. Overbeck: *Die antiken Schriftquellen zur Geschichte der bildenden Künste bei den Griechen* (Leipzig, 1868), nos 1772, 2119–37
K. Jex-Blake and E. Sellers: *The Elder Pliny's Chapters on the History of Art* (London, 1896), XXXV.i.136
M. Robertson: *A History of Greek Art*, 2 vols (Cambridge, 1975), pp. 441–3, 589–90, 698, 733; pls 140b–d, 188b

Timotheos (*fl c.* 380–*c.* 350 BC). Greek sculptor. He was from Athens and was, according to Pliny (*Natural History* XXXVI.iv.30), a contemporary and rival of the sculptors Skopas, Bryaxis and Leochares. Literary sources and inscriptions record Timotheos as a sculptor on two of the major building projects of the 4th century BC, the Temple of Asklepios at EPIDAUROS and the Mausoleum at HALIKARNASSOS. Remains of the inscriptions recording payments for the erection and decoration of the Temple of Asklepios (second quarter of the 4th century BC) have survived. Timotheos was paid 900 drachmai for *typoi* in the second year of construction (*Inscr. Gr./2*, iv, 102), a term that has been interpreted in various ways. To some it means models, which would make Timotheos the master designer; to others it means any carved or modelled figure, especially relief sculpture.

Timotheos is also named as the sculptor of one set of acroteria (sculpted figures set at the corners and ridge of each of the two gables). Several of the six acroteria have survived: two *Nereids* (sea-nymphs) or *Aurai* (breezes) on horseback, a *Nike* holding a bird, the upper part of another *Nike*, and fragments of two other figures (Athens, N. Archaeol. Mus., 155, 156, 157, 162). The carving is virtuoso with skilled undercutting of the marble achieving unprecedented thinness of the stone in places. The style of the drapery is characterized by a transparent thin fabric with sharply cut folds crossing and swirling over the body underneath. Masses of fabric define the borders of the human figure. The one surviving head belonging to the acroteria has youthful and clear-cut features. The marble has been treated as if it were bronze sculpting. The 2,240 drachmai paid to Timotheos for three acroteria suggest that they were valuable sculptures. There is a tendency to ascribe the west acroteria to Timotheos: they are better preserved and more adventurous.

Several sculptures have been ascribed to Timotheos on the basis of technical and stylistic similarities to the Epidauros acroteria. Two reliefs representing a seated male figure found at Epidauros (Athens, N. Archaeol. Mus., 173, 174) have similar delicate workmanship and transparent drapery and are identified by some scholars as the *typoi* discussed above. The same contrast between the transparency of the fabric clinging to the body and massed folds between the legs and on the borders of the figure is seen in a statue of *Leda* known in 28 marble copies (most complete in Rome, Mus. Capitolino, 302). Leda is shown rising from a rock, with Zeus in the form of a swan on her lap. She is dressed in a clinging garment loose on the right shoulder, which reveals her body underneath. The Rospigliosi *Athena*, known only from copies (Florence, Uffizi, 72336 and elsewhere), is somewhat like the *Leda* in drapery, pose and features, causing some scholars to attribute its original to Timotheos as well. Also generally attributed to him on stylistic grounds is a statue identified as *Hygieia* (Athens, N. Archaeol. Mus., 299). Headless and on a slightly larger scale than the acroteria, it was dedicated in the sanctuary at Epidauros. A young girl accompanied by a snake stands, one foot raised, bending forward with drapery hanging off her body to either side.

The few works ascribed to Timotheos in the literary sources cannot be connected with these statues nor with any others in the Epidauran style. Pliny (XXXVI.iv.32) described a marble statue of *Artemis* that stood in the Temple of Apollo on the Palatine Hill at Rome. The cult statue group in the temple cella was made up of three masterpieces of the 4th century BC, reflected on an early Imperial base or altar (Sorrento, Mus. Correale Terranova, INR 6518). Pliny (XXXIV.xix.91) also listed Timotheos as a bronze sculptor of armed men, hunters and people making sacrificial offerings, and Pausanias (*Guide to Greece* II.xxxii.4) recorded a statue of *Asklepios* at Troizen by him.

According to Pliny (XXXVI.iv.30), Timotheos carved the marble sculptures on the south side of the Mausoleum (finished *c.* 350 BC) at Halikarnassos. Vitruvius (*On Architecture* VII. Preface. 12–13), however, listed Praxiteles instead of Timotheos while acknowledging that some credited Timotheos. Differences among the widely spaced figures on the reliefs (remnants in London, BM) are in carving technique, not composition, which is unified. While it seems likely that Timotheos in his later years did sculpt some of the reliefs, it has proved impossible to connect with certainty any of the surviving panels with his hand.

B. Schloerb: *Timotheos* (Berlin, 1965)
S. Karouzou: *National Archaeological Museum: Collection of Sculpture* (Athens, 1968), pp. 100, 103
A. Rieche: 'Die Kopien der "Leda des Timotheos"', *Ant. Plast.*, xvii (1978), pp. 21–55
P. Zanker: *The Power of Images in the Age of Augustus* (Ann Arbor, 1988)
A. Stewart: *Greek Sculpture: An Exploration*, i (New Haven and London, 1990), pp. 273–4
N. Yalouris: 'Die Skulpturen des Asklepiostempels in Epidauros', *Ant. Plast.*, xxi (1992)

Tiryns. Site in the Peloponnesus in southern Greece, 10 km south-south-east of Argos and 4 km north of Navplion. Tiryns flourished as a Mycenaean fortress-palace *c.* 1390–*c.* 1200 BC, occupying the summit of a rocky knoll that rises out of the coastal plain. The earliest architectural remains date to Early Helladic II (*c.* 2900/2600–*c.* 2400 BC), notably the Rundbau, a circular building (diam. 27.6 m) with stone foundations, mud-brick walls and a terracotta-tiled roof. Successive large buildings of the Middle Helladic period (*c.* 2050–*c.* 1600 BC) and some Early Mycenaean (*c.* 1600–*c.* 1390 BC) remains, including fresco fragments and column bases, also underlie the Mycenaean palace.

Tiryns was the first Mycenaean palace to be excavated. Initial investigations at the site were undertaken by Friedrich Tiersch and A. Rangabé in 1831, and by Heinrich Schliemann in 1876. Schliemann, with Wilhelm Dörpfeld, returned to Tiryns and began systematic excavation there in 1884. The Deutsches Archäologisches Institut has carried out all subsequent excavation at Tiryns, with the exception of the Greek Archaeological Service's seasons there in 1957 and 1962–3. Most of the finds are now in the Navplion Archaeological Museum and the National Archaeological Museum, Athens. An ancient robber's hoard found at Tiryns included, among other rich objects spanning the Late Helladic period (*c.* 1600–*c.* 1050 BC), a large gold ring depicting a seated goddess attended by four daemons (Athens, N. Archaeol. Mus.).

The building of the Mycenaean palace began around the start of Late Helladic (LH) IIIA: 2 (*c.* 1360 BC) and was undertaken in three main stages. During the first phase the palace, built on a rocky outcrop rising 18 m above the surrounding plain, covered an area of 67×70 m. It comprised a complex of rooms, incorporating two megara, and a circuit wall built of large, carefully cut blocks of limestone. In its second phase, in LH IIIB:1 (*c.* 1335–*c.* 1240 BC), the area of the palace roughly doubled in size and the circuit wall, strengthened and expanded to incorporate an enlargement of the site, was given a double gateway. The third and final stage dates to LH IIIB: 2 (*c.* 1240–*c.* 1180 BC). The massive Cyclopean walls of this period, built of huge blocks of roughly hewn limestone, were extended to enclose Tiryns's lower town and encompassed an area of *c.* 22,000 sq. m. Casements and galleries were built into the south and south-east sections of the wall, probably for storage (see fig.). Much building also took place within the walls, and the site as it stands today belongs largely to this final phase.

Access to the palace was by a long, steep ramp leading to the main entrance, a gap of 3 m in the walls. From there one passed along a narrow passage with a double gateway and then through the courtyards and two propylaia into the main courtyard of the palace, *c.* 18×20 m in area. On the north side of this colonnaded courtyard lay the façade of the so-called Great Megaron, the architectural focus of the palace complex. The porch, a distyle portico *in antis*, led through a Minoan-style pier and door arrangement into the vestibule, from which one entered the *domos* or main hall, a large rectangular room (*c.* 8×12 m) with a circular central hearth and a raised platform for a

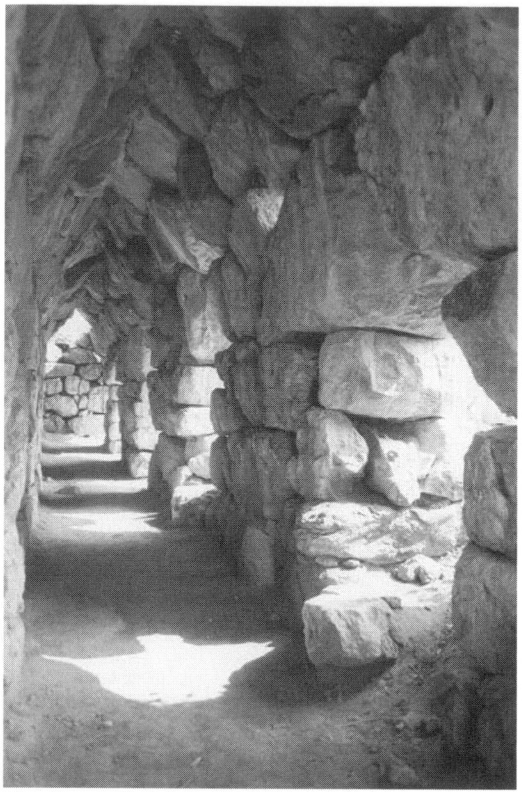

Tiryns, gallery with casements within the Cyclopean circuit wall of the citadel, Late Helladic IIIB:2 (*c*. 1240–*c*. 1180 BC)

throne. Standing around the hearth and supporting the roof were four wooden columns on stone bases. To the east of this building lay a second, smaller megaron, with two rooms and a rectangular hearth. A network of rooms and corridors surrounded these megara, and remains of staircases show that in some areas the palace reached two storeys. The walls of the palatial building had foundations of rubble, lower courses of mud and stones reaching 0.5 to 1 m above ground and a superstructure of mud-brick supported by a framework of vertical and horizontal wooden beams. The walls were then coated in mud, sometimes supplemented by lime or stucco, and decorated with frescoes in the more important rooms. The floors, some of which were also decorated, were made of cement reinforced with pebbles.

The palace at Tiryns was destroyed by fire at the end of LH IIIB: 2, but the site continued to be occupied for a further 100 years. In its Post-palatial phase Tiryns was important in pottery terms for its near continuity of LH IIIC (*c*. 1180–*c*. 1050 BC) and Protogeometric (*c*. 1050–*c*. 900 BC) styles. Around 750 BC, in the Geometric period (*c*. 900–*c*. 700 BC), a long narrow building was erected on the site of the Great Megaron. This building, which has been identified as a temple dedicated to Hera. was destroyed about 100 years later, but the site continued as a focus of religious worship well into the Classical period (*c*. 480–*c*. 323 BC).

H. Schliemann and W. Dörpfeld: *Tiryns, der prähistorische Palast der Könige von Tiryns: Ergebnisse der neuesten Ausgrabungen* (Leipzig, 1886; Eng. trans., London, 1886)
Tiryns: Die Ergebnisse der neuesten Ausgrabungen des Instituts, Bde I–IV (Leipzig, 1912; Eng. trans., 1938)
U. Jantzen: *Führer durch Tiryns* (Athens, 1975)
Tiryns: Forschungen und Berichte, Bde V–IX (Leipzig, 1971; Eng. trans., 1980)
S. Iakovidis: *Late Helladic Citadels on Mainland Greece* (Leiden, 1983)
K. Killian: 'Mycenaeans up to Date: Trends and Changes in Recent Research', *Problems in Greek Prehistory: Centenary Conference of the British School at Athens: Manchester, 1986*
W. Guntner: *Figürlich bemalte mykenische Keramik aus Tiryns* (Mainz, 2000)
H. Stülpnagel: *Mykenische Keramik der Oberburg von Tiryns: Material der Ausgrabungen 1984, 1985 im Bereich des grossen und kleinen Megarons* (diss., Freiburg im Breisgau, Albert-Ludwigs-Universität, 2000)
A. Papademetriou and D. K. Kritsela, eds: *Tiryns: A Guide to its History and Archaeology* (Athens, 2001)
W. Voigtländer: *Tiryns: Die Palastkeramik* (Mainz, 2003)
U. Polczyk [ceramics] and O. H. Krzyszkowska [ivories]: *Die archaische Keramik aus Tiryns/Mycenean Ivories from Tiryns,* xiii of *Tiryns* (Mainz, 2005)

Titus (Flavius Vespasianus), Emperor (*b* Rome, 30 Sept AD 39; *reg* AD 79–81; *d* Cutilia, 13 Sept AD 81). Roman emperor and patron. He was the eldest son of Vespasian, who entrusted him with the command of the Judean campaign (AD 69–70). Titus' building activity was considerable, despite his brief reign. In AD 80 he began to add the third and fourth orders to the Colosseum. Overlooking the Colosseum, on the slopes of the Fugutal within the grounds of the Domus Aurea, he built the Baths of Titus (AD 80), an early example of the Imperial type that was built very quickly, possibly re-adapting the private baths of Nero's palace. In the Forum Romanum, Titus began the hexastyle Corinthian Temple of the Deified Vespasian; this was later finished by Domitian (*reg* AD 81–96), who extended the dedication to include Titus. A triumphal arch for the Judean victory was built to him in the Circus Maximus, of which fragments remain (AD 71); it is possible that he began the better-known Arch of Titus at the head of the Via Sacra (AD 81, decorated with reliefs, e.g. *Triumph of Titus,* see fig.; and the *Spoils of Jerusalem*). A huge fire broke out in Rome in AD 80, raging for three days and destroying the Serapeum of the Campus Martius, the Saepta, the Poseidonion, the Baths of Agrippa, Agrippa's Pantheon, the diribitorium, the Theatre of Balbus, the stage-building of the Theatre of Pompey, the Portico of Octavia and the Temple of Jupiter Optimus Maximus on the Capitol. Many of these buildings were restored by DOMITIAN.

P. H. von Blanckenhagen: *Flavische Architektur und ihre Dekoration: Untersucht am Nervaforum* (Berlin, 1940)
M. Pfanner: *Der Titusbogen* (Mainz, 1983)

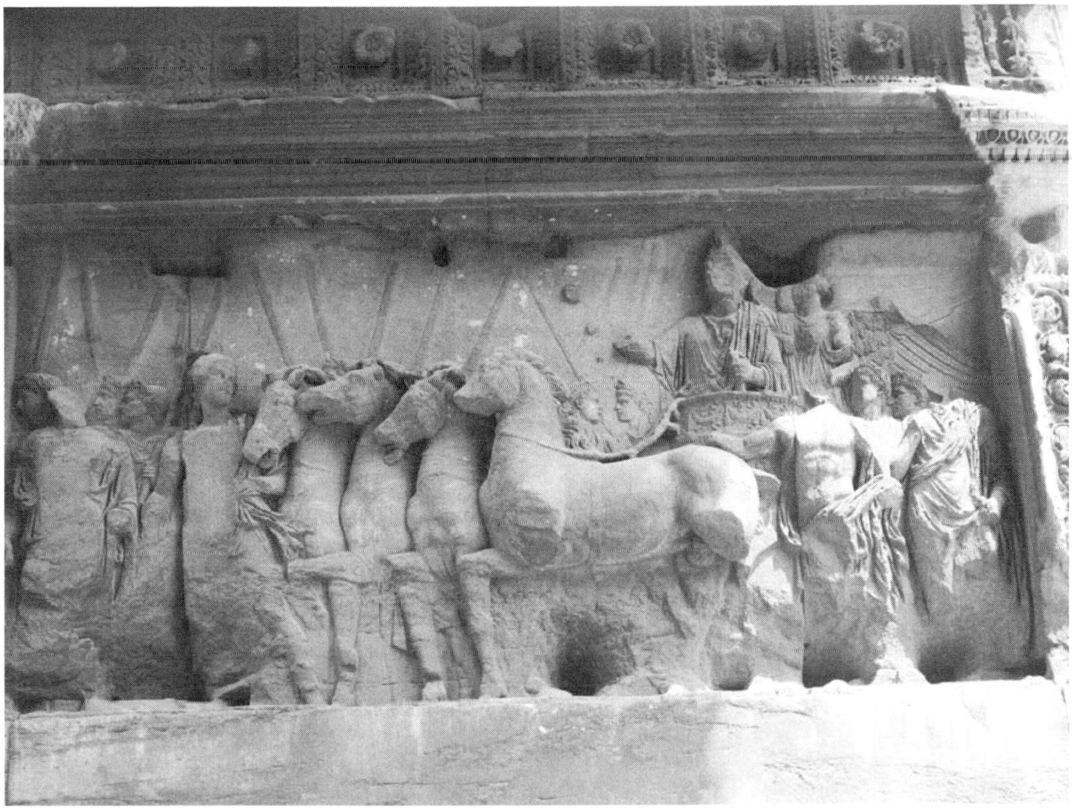

Relief from the Arch of Titus, Rome, showing the *Triumph of Titus*, marble, h. 2.39 m, AD 81

Tivoli. *See* TIBUR.

Tleson (*fl c.* 555–*c.* 535 BC). Greek vase painter. He was the son of NEARCHOS. He has been judged the 'most typical of the [Attic Black-figure] Little Masters' (Beazley, 1986), and he apparently combined potting and painting, mainly producing lip cups which he signed as potter between the handle palmettes, but also band cups. His drawing was at its most refined and accurate early in his career, when he also added abundant red and white: later his figures became more repetitive and slipshod. Tleson's lip-cup tondi usually contain birds, animals or compound creatures such as centaurs, sirens, sphinxes or Pegasus. The finest, however, have human figures (e.g. the *Returning Hunter*, London, BM, B 421; *Eris*, Berlin, Antikensamml., F 1775; *Theseus and the Minotaur*, Toledo, OH, Mus. A., 1958.70), the mythological ones being labelled. Some lip cups have no external decoration; others have the usual miniature figures at the centre of the lip on either side, generally winged compound creatures (e.g. sphinxes and sirens), poultry or quadrupeds, but in one case masturbating satyrs (London, BM, B 410). Tleson's band cups have the same animals or mythical creatures arranged in groups of three or four, the commonest scheme being two opposed cocks between two hens on one side and a stag, goat or ram between two sirens on the other. His animal decoration was carelessly imitated by several minor painters.

J. C. Hoppin: *A Handbook of Greek Black-figured Vases* (Paris, 1924), pp. 365–405

J. D. Beazley: 'Little Master Cups', *J. Hell. Stud.*, lii (1932), pp. 172–96

J. D. Beazley: *Development of Black-figure* (1951, 3/1986), pp. 50, 55

J. D. Beazley: *Black-figure* (1956), pp. 178–83

J. D. Beazley: *Paralipomena* (1971), pp. 74–6

J. Boardman: *Athenian Black Figure Vases: A Handbook* (London, 1974), p. 60

L. Burn and R. Glynn: *Beazley Addenda: Additional References to* ABV, ARV2 *and* Paralipomena (Oxford, 1982, rev. T. H. Carpenter, 2/1989), pp. 50–51

J. T. Haldenstein: *Little Master Cups: Studies in Sixth-century Attic Black-figure Vase Painting* (diss., U. Cincinnati, 1982; microfilm, Ann Arbor), pp. 70–78

Corp. Vasorum Ant., Germany, lviii, Munich 1 (1988), pp. 23–30

Corp. Vasorum Ant., Germany, lviii, Munich 2 (1989), pp. 16–18

P. Heesen: *The J. L. Theodor Collection of Attic Black-Figure Vases, Allard Pierson Series* 10 (Amsterdam, 1996), pp. 140–42

Corp. Vasorum Ant., Netherlands, Amsterdam 2 (1996), pp. 49–51, pls. 95, 96.1

Tolmeita [Tolmeta]. *See* PTOLEMAIS.

Tomb. A place of burial or the marking of a grave. As the former it can take the form of a SARCOPHAGUS, while as the latter it can take the form of a MAUSOLEUM, usually built of stone.

1. The Greek world. 2. Etruria and the Roman Empire.

1. THE GREEK WORLD. Greek tombs developed from simple burials in dug pits, stone-lined cists or large clay pots, and these forms persisted throughout antiquity, also being used by the Etruscans and the Romans. Individual graves could be grouped together under a large circular earthen tumulus, sometimes ringed by stones at its base. Tumuli probably first appeared in the Greek world on the island of Leukas in the later 3rd millennium BC, and their use spread down the western coast of Greece and beyond during the Middle Bronze Age (*c.* 2000–1550 BC). It is possible that they originated in the Kurgan culture of the Russian steppes during the 4th–3rd millennia BC and were introduced in Greece by Greek-speaking immigrants, although this is disputed. Tumuli appeared in northern Greece only towards the end of the Bronze Age (12th century BC) but persisted in Epiros and Macedonia, notably at Aigia (ii) (Vergina), into the Dark Age and even into the Hellenistic period.

Stone-built tombs occurred in Minoan Crete, especially in the Mesara plain. These small, round structures (2800–1700 BC; mostly 3rd millennium BC) contained multiple, successive burials, perhaps of family members, but the method of roofing is uncertain, and it is thus difficult to derive the distinctive corbelled Mycenaean tholos tombs from these (see below). Rich shaft tombs, grouped in two circles, occurred at Mycenae. These were, in effect, stone-lined cists at the bottom of shafts (*c.* 1–4 m deep), distinguished from earlier Greek graves by their wealth of offerings and by the practice of multiple burials, both successive and simultaneous. The shafts were filled in with earth and tumuli may once have surmounted the circles. Grave Circle B, the earlier (*c.* 1650–1550 BC), lies just outside the citadel. Grave Circle A (*c.* 1600–1500 BC) (diam. 27 m) contains six shaft tombs (the largest measures 6.4×4.5 m), and was terraced and surrounded by a circle of upright stone slabs in its final phase (13th century BC). This treatment and the rich grave-goods found there may indicate royal tombs in Circle A. Some tombs in both circles were marked by a sculpted stele (examples in Návplion, Archaeol. Mus.). Individual shaft tombs occur at a few other Bronze Age Greek sites, and they continued to be constructed until *c.* 1400 BC.

Rock-cut chamber tombs and stone tholoi (*see* THOLOS TOMB) were generally characteristic of Greece in the Mycenaean period (*c.* 1550–1100 BC). In both cases an entrance passage (dromos) led into the tomb. Both types were used for successive burials, the earlier burials and grave-goods being pushed aside. They were presumably family vaults. The tholos was usually cut into a hillside, with its lintel at surface level, and covered by an earthen tumulus. The more elaborate tholoi have stone-lined dromoi. Burials within them might be in pits or stone-lined cists. About 200 tholoi are known, and many more chamber tombs.

The origins of the tholos are uncertain; it combines the concepts of chamber tomb and tumulus with a distinctive roofing method. Its beehive-shaped vault was corbelled and buttressed by the earth mound. The earliest tholoi, in Messenia, contain Middle Helladic as well as early Mycenaean pottery. At Mycenae itself the nine tholoi (*c.* 1500–1250 BC) succeed the shaft tombs. The 'Treasury of Atreus' at Mycenae (*c.* 1250 BC) is one of the grandest examples of Greek architecture of any period. Decorated engaged columns (now in London, BM) and reliefs formed part of its façade, and its lintel block weighs 100 tons. Exceptionally, it has a side chamber, as does the 'Treasury of Minyas' at ORCHOMENOS (13th century BC). Both tholoi are unusually large (diam. 14.5 m and 14 m), but many tholoi measure less than 5 m diameter. The height of a tholos was roughly equivalent to its diameter, and large ones contain a relieving triangle (possibly derived from Egypt) above their lintel blocks. One at MARATHON has, uniquely, two facing horses buried in the dromos (*c.* 1400 BC). The unplundered Dendra tholos held a unique bronze suit of armour. By the 12th century BC tholoi had become rare. Examples occur in Dark Age Crete, Messenia and Thessaly (11th–9th centuries BC), when most of Greece had reverted to single burials, although it has been argued that in Thessaly and Thrace tholoi persisted even later.

Phrygian and Lydian tombs date from the 8th–6th centuries BC. Notable Phrygian tombs include some at 'Midas City' with rock-cut, gabled façades adorned with geometric patterns in relief, while others contain facing lions in relief. Tumuli at Gordion covered a wooden chamber, and the largest has plausibly been identified as that of Midas (diam. *c.* 300 m, h. *c.* 53 m). The only larger tumulus is the 'Tomb of Alyattes' in the Bin Tepe cemetery, near Sardis, associated with the kings of Lydia (355×69 m). The 'Tomb of Tantalus', near Smyrna, is in tumulus form although built entirely of stone (29.6×27.6 m). Rock-cut tombs occur often in Caria, while Mycenaean-type chamber tombs continued at Salamis, Cyprus. Some royal or noble tombs at Salamis had façades containing small courtyards, and in their broad dromoi vehicles and teams of horses or asses were buried (*c.* 750 BC–7th century BC).

Archaic and Classical Greek tombs are for the most part less significant architecturally than sculpturally (e.g. carved sarcophagi, stelai and other grave-markers with painted or relief decoration). Tumuli sometimes occur over individual or multiple graves, usually aristocratic. A tumulus burial at BELEVI (6th century BC or later) has a terracotta pipe leading down from the surface for the pouring of libations. Graves grouped below a rectangular enclosing wall (a peribolos) were common. The Dexileos Stele (394 BC) marking a grave belonging to a peribolos tomb is one of many from the Athenian Kerameikos cemetery, although Athenian monuments were restricted by sumptuary law at the end of the 4th century BC. Monumental Late Classical and Hellenistic tombs developed in the kingdoms of Asia Minor by combining local forms with Greek architectural elements (Macedonian tombs were essentially different; see below). The basic type was a podium supporting a chamber, which might be constructed in imitation of a Greek temple and be surmounted by a pyramid and crowning sculpture. One possible precursor is the tomb of the Persian king Cyrus at Pasargadae, a rectangular chamber built on a stepped podium (h. *c.* 11 m; 6th century BC). Another is the Lycian type of tomb, with a chamber or steep-gabled sarcophagus set on a tower-like pillar, such as the misnamed Harpy Tomb at XANTHOS (h. 8.87 m; early 5th century BC). The Nereid Monument, also at Xanthos, was the first of the type (*c.* 400 BC; reconstructed in London). It comprised a small Ionic temple (6×4 columns) on a high podium (original h. *c.* 13.5 m), with the two upper courses formed by sculpted marble friezes. Usually the podium of such tombs contained the burial. Perhaps the most famous Hellenistic tomb was the Mausoleum at HALIKARNASSOS, begun by Mausolos of Caria (*reg c.* 377–353 BC) and completed after his death. Modern reconstructions of it rely heavily on Pliny's description (*Natural History* XXXVI.iv.30–31). It was one of the Seven Wonders of the Ancient World, as much for its sculptures as for its size (h. 57.6 m). As many as 330 statues adorned it, and its 36-column Ionic peristasis was crowned by a 24-stepped pyramid surmounted by a huge four-horse chariot. The Mausoleum, like many such tombs, stood in a spacious built enclosure. Similar, smaller monuments are the Lion Tomb at Knidos (*c.* 350 BC; see fig. 1), the Lion Tomb at Amphipolis and the mausoleum at Belevi, with a partly rock-cut podium (29.65 m sq.) and a hidden vaulted chamber (h. *c.* 35 m; *c.* 300 BC). A later example is the Mylasa Tomb (2nd century AD).

The other prominent type of Hellenistic Greek tomb is the Macedonian tomb, a rectangular barrel-vaulted chamber covered by a tumulus, approached through a dromos, and often provided with a decorated façade, the best in imitation of temples. They date from the mid-4th to mid-2nd centuries BC. The architectural elements of their solid façades were applied in stucco relief and painted, and are thus purely decorative. Important, well-preserved paintings adorn the frieze of Tomb II at Aigai (*c.* 9.5×5.5×5.3 m), the interior of the neighbouring 'Tomb of Persephone' (both *c.* 340–310 BC), and the two-storey façade of the 'Great Tomb' at Leukadia (first quarter of the 3rd century BC). The tomb of Lyson and Kallikles at Leukadia (2nd century BC) has a fine, painted interior and niches for cremation urns. In other tombs the bodies were laid on stone couches. In Tomb II at Aigai were found a splendid royal burial, associated with either Philip II of Macedon (*d* 336 BC) or a successor, and perhaps the first Greek use of the technique of barrel vaulting, probably learnt from the Near East. Macedonian-style vaulted tombs exist also in other parts of Greece, for example at Eretria, Kassope and Kalydon.

Other striking eastern tombs are those with rock-cut architectural façades, especially in Lycia (e.g. at Myra and Telmessos; 4th century BC) and at Petra. The Khaznat or 'Treasury' (24.9×38.7×7 m; 1st century BC) and the 'al-Dayr tomb' (47×42 m; 1st century AD) at Petra both have elaborate two-storey baroque façades, surmounted by a canopy within a broken pediment. Tower tombs are large pillar-shaped towers on bases. Prominent at Dura Europos and Palmyra (1st century BC–3rd century AD), their use extended through North Africa and the Roman world. The influence of tower tombs and monumental tombs can be seen in the 'Tomb of Absalom' at Jerusalem, the 'Tomb of the Scipios' at Tarragona, Spain, and the canopy-topped Tomb of the Julii at Glanum (Saint-Rémy-de-Provence), France.

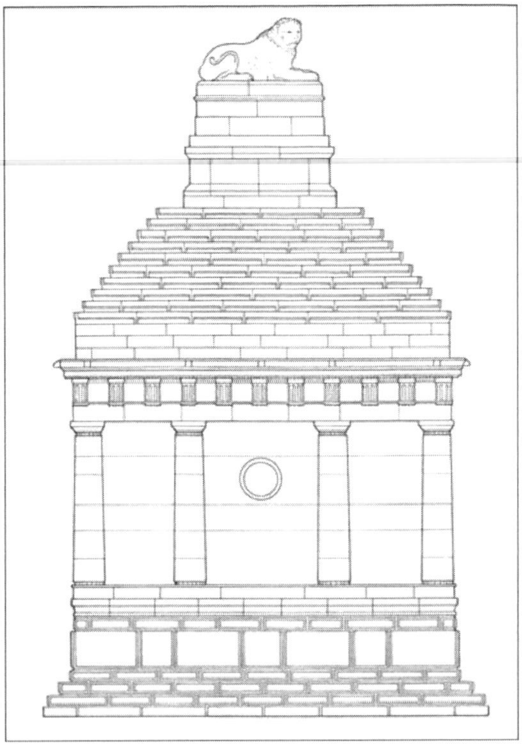

1. Lion Tomb, Knidos, h. *c.* 20 m, *c.* 350 BC; reconstruction drawing of restored elevation, from *Die Antike*, iv (Berlin and Leipzig, 1928), fig. 2

2. ETRURIA AND THE ROMAN EMPIRE. Etruscan tombs were generally grouped in necropolises, which were often laid out in regular streets, close to the particular city they served. Types of tomb show regional diversity and include rock-cut family chamber tombs and tumuli containing one or more burials. The tumuli at CAERE (Cerveteri) rest on rock-cut drums. One of the earliest burials there is the Regolini-Galassi Tomb (*c.* 700–650 BC); the Tomb of Painted Reliefs (3rd century BC) is among the last elaborate Caeretan tombs. Etruscan chamber tombs usually consist of one or more rectangular rooms, although round tholos-like tombs supported by central pillars are found at Volterra. Interior or exterior decoration often imitated that of domestic architecture. Wall

paintings in tombs reached their height at TARQUINIA around 540 BC, with the vivid interiors of, for example, the Tomb of the Bulls (*c.* 540 BC) and the Tomb of Hunting and Fishing (*c.* 510 BC).

Roman tombs typically lined streets leading from a city. Mausolea or house tombs glorifying families or individuals, sometimes grouped in contiguous blocks, stood beside the poorest graves marked by amphorae or covered by stones or roof-tiles. Typical are the tombs lining the Appian Way south of Rome, the Vatican necropolis (2nd–3rd centuries AD), the Via dei Sepolcri outside Pompeii (before AD 79) and the vast Isola Sacra cemetery north of Ostia (AD 100–250). Pompeian tombs, for example, include unroofed enclosures, exedrae, and large altar-shaped tombs. The aedicula type resembles a small shrine. Tumuli continued to be constructed in some places.

An early Roman family tomb is that of the Cornelii Scipiones, cut out of the tufa south of Rome (early 3rd century BC–*c.* 130 BC; reused during the 1st century AD). Shelf-niches (*loculi*) in its walls held sarcophagi. Later tombs, such as the marble-faced pyramid of Gaius Cestius at Rome (h. 36.4 m; late 1st century BC), reflect aristocratic display. A frieze depicting a baker's occupations adorns the large tomb of Eurysaces, also at Rome (late 1st century BC; see fig. 2). The marble relief decoration of the Tomb of the Haterii (*c.* AD 100; Rome, Vatican, Mus. Gregoriano Profano) depicts a temple-tomb on a stepped podium, like some 1st-century BC or later examples known from Ghirza, Libya (3rd and 4th centuries AD) and elsewhere. Roman circular mausolea owe something to the Etruscan stone-ringed tumuli of Caere. Possibly the first, that of Augustus by the Tiber (28 BC) contained several imperial family burials in its concentric ring-walls (h. *c.* 44.65 m; diam. *c.* 87 m) surmounted by a mound of some kind and topped by a statue of Augustus. Aristocrats adopted this type; for example the tomb of Caecilia Metella, south of Rome (late 1st century BC), consists of a large round drum on a square podium. Hadrian's tomb, the Castel Sant'Angelo, Diocletian's at Spalatum (Split), and Theodoric the Goth's at Ravenna (6th century AD) are other imperial mausolea; their circular or polygonal plan was adopted in Christian church architecture.

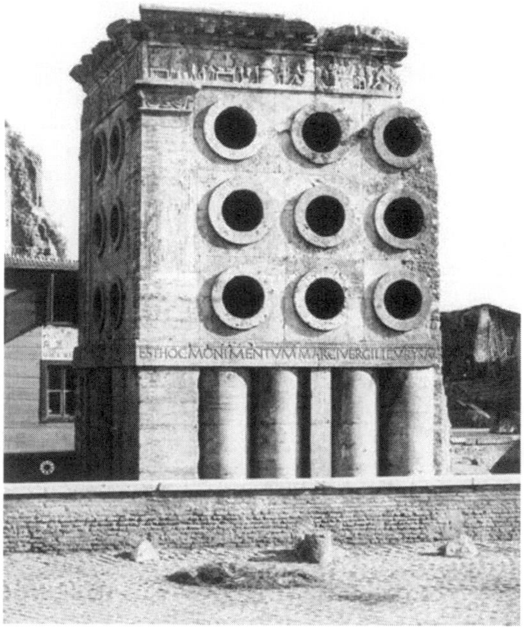

2. Tomb of Eurysaces, Rome, late 1st century BC

During the Roman Empire much use was made of underground necropolises. A HYPOGEUM is an underground tomb with *loculi* and one or more chambers for multiple burials. The best examples are found at Dura Europos and Palmyra (1st–3rd centuries AD). That of the Aurelii at Rome (early 3rd century AD) was built on several levels and contained both Christian and pagan paintings. The COLUMBARIUM was a large structure, sometimes underground, housing hundreds or thousands of niches for the cremation urns or chests of less prosperous citizens. A burial club might organize such a tomb for its members. The first known is late Republican; notable are the three 'Colombari di Vigna Codini' at Rome (1st century AD) for imperial slaves and freedmen, and two above-ground examples at Ostia.

The CATACOMB was a form of large underground necropolis, found in Hellenistic Alexandria and among the Jewish and Christian communities at Rome (from the 2nd century AD and *c.* AD 200 respectively) and elsewhere, such as at Syracuse. Burials were in niches in corridors or chambers off them. Some, such as the 4th-century AD catacomb of the Via Latina at Rome (see colour pl. 2:XV, fig. 2), contained elaborate paintings, including pagan motifs, though they were apparently not used for regular worship.

Å. Åkerström: *Studien über die etruskischen Gräber* (Lund, 1934)

V. Karageorghis: *Salamis: Recent Discoveries in Cyprus* (London, 1969)

K. Branigan: *The Tombs of Mesara* (London, 1970)

D. C. Kurtz and J. Boardman: *Greek Burial Customs* (London, 1971)

J. M. C. Toynbee: *Death and Burial in the Roman World* (London, 1971)

L. V. Grinsell: *Barrow, Pyramid and Tomb* (London, 1975)

O. Pelon: *Tholoi, tumuli et cercles funéraires* (Paris, 1976)

R. Reece, ed.: *Burial in the Roman World* (London, 1977)

J. Brinks: *Die Entwicklung der königlichen Grabanlagen des Alten Reiches* (Hildesheim, 1979)

R. Young and others: *Three Great Early Tumuli* (1981), i of *The Gordion Excavations* (Philadelphia, 1981-)

S. G. Miller: 'Macedonian Tombs: Their Architecture and Architectural Decoration', *Stud. Hist. A.*, x (Washington, 1982), pp. 152–71

M. Torelli: *Necropoli dell' Italia antica* (Milan, 1982)

I. E. S. Edwards: *The Pyramids of Egypt* (rev. Harmondsworth, 1985)
L. Manniche: *City of the Dead: Thebes in Egypt* (London, 1987)
P. J. Watson: *Egyptian Pyramids and Mastaba Tombs of the Old and Middle Kingdoms* (Aylesbury, 1987)
S. Müller: 'Les Tumuli helladiques: Où? Quand? Comment?', *Bull. Corr. Hell.*, cxiii (1989), pp. 1–42
J. Fedak: *Monumental Tombs of the Hellenistic Age* (Toronto, 1990)
S. G. Miller: *The Tomb of Lyson and Kallikles: A Painted Macedonian Tomb* (Mainz, 1993)
M. Andronicos: *Vergina: The Royal Tombs and the Ancient City* (Athens, 1997)
S. Cormack: *The Space of Death in Roman Asia Minor* (Vienna, 2004)
A. Pontrandolfo, A. Rouveret and M. Cipriani: *The Painted Tombs of Paestum* (Salerno, 2004)

Town Hall. *See* PRYTANEION.

Town Planning. *See* PLANNING.

Trabeated construction [post and lintel]. Structural system based on the use of columns or posts and beams. It contrasts with arcuated construction, involving the use of arches and vaults. In Greek architecture the use of the trabeated system was appropriate to the local limestone, as in the temples of Hera and Zeus at Olympia, or later to marble, as in the Parthenon and Erechtheion on the Acropolis at Athens. It also reflected an approach to architecture in which there was no break between structure and appearance: loads were clearly carried by carefully proportioned columns and rectangular entablature blocks, while non-structural and other architectural elements, including pilasters, were rarely introduced. The plans of buildings were usually rectangular to fit the principles of trabeated construction, and the use of arches in Greek architecture above ground was rare, although examples exist in the entrance to the stadium at Olympia and the entrance to the agora at Priene.

Roman architecture was liberated from this essentially rectangular style by its use of arches and vaulting, and trabeated construction was used only as a means of articulation for an essentially arcuated structure.

D. S. Robertson: *A Handbook of Greek and Roman Architecture* (Cambridge, 1929, rev. 2/1943); repr. as *Greek and Roman Architecture* (London, 1969)
A. W. Lawrence: *Greek Architecture*, Pelican Hist. A. (Harmondsworth, 1957, rev. 4/1983)
J. Summerson: *The Classical Language of Architecture* (London, 1963, rev. 1980)

Trajan [Marcus Ulpius Trajanus], Emperor (*b* Italica, eastern Spain, AD 53; *reg* 98–117; *d* Selinus, Turkey, 117). Roman emperor and patron. He was the adopted son of Nerva, whom he succeeded. From AD 101 to 107 he conducted the two Dacian campaigns that are depicted in the spiral reliefs on the great column that bears his name (ded. AD 113; *see* ROME, §IV, 7). It was erected as the crowning glory of the great Forum of Trajan, built between AD 107 and 113, which completed the vast urban complex of Imperial Fora. Both the arch that marked its entrance and the Basilica Ulpia at its west end—the largest ever constructed in Rome—displayed a wealth of relief sculpture: a long frieze in high relief covered the attic of the basilica for its whole length, probably on all four sides of the building. On the slopes of the Quirinal Hill, which was cut to make room for the forum, Trajan built an extensive and articulated system of shops on two levels, culminating in the great hall (*c.* AD 100–12; *see also* ARCHITECTURE, §VI, 2(i)(e)). The Markets of Trajan must have been planned together with the forum, and thus probably by the Emperor's military architect Apollodoros of Damascus. Among other major works completed were the Baths of Trajan on the Oppian Hill (ded. 109), the arch without reliefs that concluded the work on the port of Ancona (AD 115), and the arch at Beneventum (Benevento; *c.* AD 117; see fig.), with its highly decorated reliefs. Indeed, relief sculpture above all other art forms reached new heights of achievement under Trajan.

W. Gross: *Bildnisse Traianus* (Berlin, 1940)
P. Zanker: *Das Trajansforum als Monument imperialer Selbstdarstellung* (Berlin, 1970)
K. de Fine Licht: *Untersuchungen an den Trajansthermen zu Rom* (Copenhagen, 1974)
S. Settis and others: *La Colonna Traiana* (Turin, 1989)
J. E. Packer: *The Forum of Trajan in Rome: A Study of the Monuments,* 2 vols (Berkeley, 1997)
J. Bennett: *Trajan: Optimus princeps* (London, 2001)

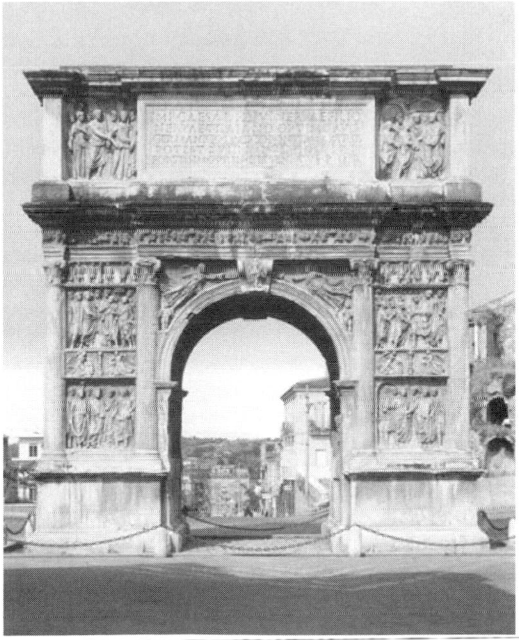

Arch of Trajan, Beneventum, *c.* AD 117

Treasury [Gr. *thesauros*]. Type of building constructed in some ancient Greek sanctuaries between the 7th and 4th centuries BC. Treasuries housed the often valuable offerings for which there was no space in the crowded temples. Among the finest examples is the Athenian treasury at DELPHI (*c*. 500–*c*. 485 BC), built of Parian marble and now completely reconstructed. These costly monuments, usually architectural showpieces and sometimes embellished with exquisite sculptures (e.g. the Athenian treasury and the Ionic treasuries at Delphi), were generally donated by cities. They commemorated victories, either in battle (e.g. the Athenian treasury, probably after the Battle of Marathon in 490 BC, that of Syracuse after the Athenian defeat in 414 BC, and that of the Thebans after Leuktra in 371 BC), or in the games (e.g. the Archaic Treasury of Myron and the Sikyonians at Olympia), or they were thank-offerings for sudden prosperity (e.g. the Siphnian treasury, *c*. 525 BC, after the discovery of gold on Siphnos). Many treasuries were, therefore, tokens of the piety, power and wealth of cities at the height of their prestige. The earliest was the treasury of the tyrant Kypselos and the Corinthians at Delphi (late 7th century BC), and the latest were those of Thebes and Cyrene at Delphi (both early 4th century BC). After the demise of the city-state in the later 4th century BC, Hellenistic rulers preferred to endow sanctuaries with large STOAS, which provided shelter for worshippers and, in some cases (e.g. the Stoa of Attalos I at Delphi, *c*. 230 BC), also functioned as treasuries.

Treasuries were markedly smaller than TEMPLES (e.g. the Sikyonian treasury at Delphi is 6.33×8.40 m). The simplest consisted merely of a rectangular chamber (e.g. the treasuries of Metapontion, Sybaris and Gela at Olympia, all earlier 6th century BC, and the Corinthian treasury at Delphi), but most comprised a chamber and a porch with two columns *in antis*, normally closed by a grille to protect the door, which was often of precious materials, and to enable visitors to see the rich offerings without entering the building. Being designed to house valuable objects, treasuries had no windows and were not accessible to the general public. The treasuries of Athens and Cyrene at Delphi and the Sikyonian treasury at Olympia (*c*. 500–*c*. 450 BC) have no steps at the front, and the only people intended to have access were the officials responsible for maintaining and guarding the contents (such as the female *neokore* at Delos who supervised the treasuries of Mykonos and Karystos), and a few important visitors.

Both treasuries and temples that doubled as treasuries were often erected for the consecration of one or more statues, usually made of precious materials such as gold and ivory. In an inscription at Delphi the Knidians recorded that they had offered their treasury and its statues to Apollo. At Olympia, Pausanias (*Guide to Greece* VI.xix.7, 10, 12) saw a colossal statue of *Zeus* in the 'Carthaginian' (actually Syracusian) treasury, a *Dionysos* with an ivory face, feet and hands in the Treasury of Selinus, and cedar-wood statues with gold inlays in the Megarian treasury (treasury buildings are dated *c*. 500–*c*. 475 BC, *c*. 540–*c*. 520 BC and *c*. 510 BC respectively). By the 2nd century AD, however, when Pausanias was writing, most of the treasuries at both Delphi and Olympia had been emptied.

The number of treasuries in a sanctuary and the diversity of their donors indicate not only how wealthy it was but also how genuinely pan-Hellenic. Delphi contained about thirty treasuries, though not all at the same time, Olympia eleven and Delos only five. Delphi's pre-eminence is explained by the fact that the town itself was only modest, forming part of the Amphiktyonic League, which shared the administration of the Sanctuary of Apollo. Other cities, therefore, had no cause to fear that their offerings would enrich a powerful rival. Similarly, Olympia was controlled by lesser cities: first Pisa, then Elis. In contrast, Delos was always subject to important powers: Naxos, Samos and, above all, Athens. The same factor accounts for the absence of treasuries at Isthmia and Nemea: although their sanctuaries were pan-Hellenic, they were controlled by the powerful cities Corinth and Argos respectively. Treasuries thus illustrate the way in which competition between ancient Greek cities stimulated the production of increasingly beautiful and elaborate architecture and sculpture. However, they also reveal the fatal political divisions that precipitated the decline of Greece.

G. Roux: 'Trésors, temples, tholos', *Temples et sanctuaires* (1984), vii of *Travaux de la Maison de l'Orient* (Lyon, 1980–), pp. 153–71

Triclinium. Dining-room in an ancient Roman house (*see* ARCHITECTURE, §VI, 1(i)(c)).

Trier. *See* AUGUSTA TREVERORUM.

Trinacria. *See* SICILY.

Triumphal arch. Monumental arch erected to commemorate national events, especially military victories. Triumphal arches were first used in ancient Rome, the term originally applying to an arch erected to commemorate a formal 'triumph' awarded at Rome to a victorious general, who led his army in procession through the Porta Triumphalis in a chariot drawn by white horses. While many such arches exist, the term is more loosely applied to other commemorative arches, which the Romans erected to mark the founding of colonies, the building of roads and bridges, the death of a member of the imperial family or the accession of a new emperor, and these became potent symbols of Roman Imperial power throughout the Empire. The arches of aqueducts at the point where they crossed an important road were sometimes decorated as if they were triumphal arches, as were important city gates.

Commemorative arches have either a single or a triple opening, or can be placed over a crossroads with arched openings on all four sides. The one-bay arch is the most widespread, and examples range from the very simple type with an opening flanked by pilasters to massive arches with elaborate sculptural decoration. The triple type has a large central aperture over the roadway flanked by lesser openings over the pavements. A commemorative arch usually stands in isolation and has no practical function but is splendidly decorated.

The openings of Roman arches are usually flanked by pilasters, half-columns or free-standing columns. 'Triumphal' arches had sculpted panels illustrating Roman victories or the triumphal procession itself, placed in the passageways, on the attic, on the pylons flanking the passageway or, in the case of a triple arch, over the side apertures. In the spandrels there were usually flying Victories carrying trophies. Dedicatory inscriptions were commonly placed on the attic, and on top of the whole structure there was sometimes a *currus triumphalis*, a bronze statue group showing the emperor in a four-horse chariot.

The forerunners of triumphal arches were *fornices* or honorific arches bearing statues, which were erected by victorious generals in public places in Rome during the later Republic. In 196 BC L. Stertinius erected a *fornix* in the Circus Maximus and another in the Forum Boarium from the spoils he brought from Spain; Scipio Africanus erected another on the Capitoline Hill in 190 BC, and Fabianus built one over the Sacred Way in the Forum Romanum in 121 BC. None of these early arches has survived. The earliest extant commemorative arch in Rome is the one that Augustus built next to the Temple of Divus Julius in the Forum Romanum in 19 BC to commemorate the recovery of the standards that the Parthians had captured from Crassus. It has a central arched opening flanked by two lesser apertures covered with horizontal lintels, and it replaced a more modest single-bay arch put up after the victory at Actium in 29 BC. Several notable single arches were erected during the reign of Augustus, such as those at Rimini (27 BC), Aosta (25 BC), Pola (27 BC), Susa (9–8 BC) and Bara (now redated to *c.* 27 BC). The column arrangements and proportions of these arches vary considerably, showing that the form was still in a developmental stage. The classic example of the single-aperture arch is the monumental Arch of Titus in the Forum Romanum (15.4×13.5 m; AD 81; see fig. 1). Relief panels in the passageways depict the *Triumph of Titus* (for illustration *see* TITUS) and *Spoils of Jerusalem*, and a rectangular panel in the soffit of the arch shows his apotheosis. The Arch of Titus seems to have inspired the similar but more richly decorated Arch of Trajan (AD 114) at Benevento, built to commemorate the opening of the Via Traiana; it has a particularly rich series of reliefs decorating its pylons and passageways. The Arch of Trajan (AD 115) at Ancona, built to mark the completion of the new harbour, is of similar design, although it is somewhat taller in proportion and less elaborately decorated.

The earliest surviving triple arch from the Imperial period is the one erected by Tiberius at ARAUSIO (Orange; AD 21), the Arch of Augustus in the Forum Romanum being technically not a triple arch because its side passageways were covered with horizontal lintels. The Arch at Arausio has many features of the classic triple arch, such as the dominant central aperture and the four columns framing the three openings. However, the unusual design of its short sides, with four engaged columns supporting an arcuated pediment, the distribution of its sculptural reliefs, the design of its attic and the fact that the columns are partly engaged all reflect its early date. One of the most celebrated triple arches is the massive Arch of Septimius Severus, built in honour of his Parthian victories and situated on a high point of the Via Sacra just below the Capitoline Hill in Rome (20.88×23.27 m; AD 203). It is entirely covered with marble, and its passageways are framed by four free-standing columns on each façade. The columns rest on high plinths that carry reliefs of Roman soldiers and Parthian prisoners. Large relief panels (3.92×4.72 m) illustrating Severus's victories are placed above the lateral arches. In the spandrels of the lateral arches are reliefs of river gods, and the spandrels of the main arch depict Victories carrying trophies. The attic bears a large dedicatory inscription that once bore the names of Septimius Severus and both his sons. Geta's name was erased after he was assassinated by his brother Caracalla, and additional illustrious titles for his murderer filled the space. Fixing holes for the bronze chariot have been found on the roof. A pair of column plinths (Florence, Boboli Gardens) probably come from an arch built by Diocletian in Rome *c.* AD 294. The high-relief figure of a Victory on one of them is carved in a self-consciously classicizing manner, reflecting hopes of a revival in Rome's fortunes under the Tetrarchy. The Arch of Constantine (AD 315), built to commemorate the victory of Constantine over Maxentius at the Milvian bridge, is similar in design to that of Septimius Severus but is even more extensively decorated with reliefs, many plundered from earlier monuments. Emperors after Constantine gen-

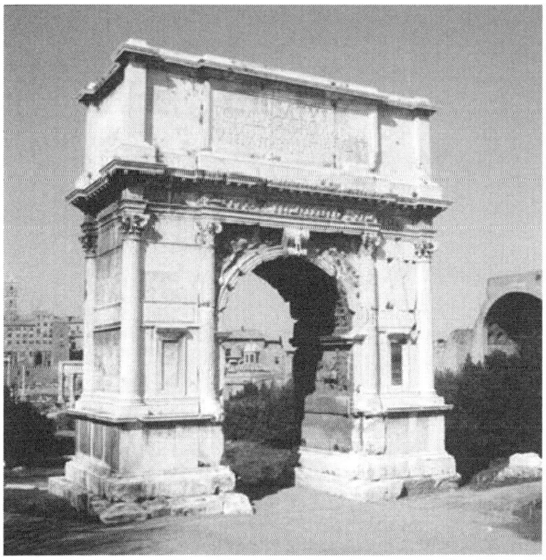

1. Arch of Titus, Forum Romanum, Rome, AD 81

erally set up their arches at or near Tiber crossings to St Peter's on heavily travelled pilgrim routes.

The *arcus quadrifrons*, erected over a crossroads and with arched openings on all four sides, was extremely popular in North Africa. The Arch of Marcus Aurelius (AD 163) at Tripoli is an exceptionally complete example of the type. Its slightly broader north and south faces have free-standing columns flanking the aperture and Victories in the spandrels. The arch is entirely sheathed in marble, and the crossing is covered in a dome of stone panels. The Arch of Caracalla (AD 214) at Thevestis is also covered with a dome, and its apertures are flanked by two tiers of paired columns. The arch of Septimius Severus (AD 203) at LEPTIS MAGNA has free-standing columns flanking all four apertures and supporting the corners of pediments with massive gaps at their centres. The sculptural decoration is rich, particularly the panels in the attic. The Arch of Galerius (AD 297–305) at THESSALONIKI is unusual in having triple openings on the Via Egnatia and single openings on the other two sides. Its pylons are elaborately decorated with bands of relief sculpture. Only late examples of the *arcus quadrifrons* survive in Rome. The arch at Malborghetto just north of Rome, probably erected to commemorate the battle *ad Saxa Rubra*, and the Janus arch in the Forum Boarium are both Constantinian. The latter is unusual in that its sides are covered with two or perhaps three tiers of round-headed niches rather than conventional reliefs. Both arches may have had pyramidal roofs.

In Rome and Italy large numbers of commemorative arches were erected up to the time of Trajan (*reg* AD 98–117), but fewer during the Hadrianic and Antonine period. In the provinces, however, the erection of arches continued unabated throughout the 2nd and 3rd centuries AD, many commemorating imperial visits. North Africa is particularly rich in triumphal arches, although in many cases their design differs somewhat from those in Italy. The Arch of Trajan (AD 116) at Mactaris in Tunisia has a single opening enclosed within a pedimented aedicula flanked by larger columns. The Arch of Caracalla (AD 216) at Cuicul (Djemila; see fig. 2) in Algeria has a pair of free-standing columns on separate plinths on each side of the aperture, echoed in the attic by smaller columns framing the inscription. The Arch of Caracalla (AD 216–17) at Volubilis is much squatter but also has pairs of free-standing columns flanking the opening. A similar arrangement occurs in the Arch of Septimius Severus (*c.* AD 200) at Ammaedara and the Arch of Diocletian (*c.* AD 284–*c.* 305) at Sufetula, although in both these cases the columns rest on a continuous podium. The Severan arch at Lambaesis in Algeria and the so-called Arch of Trajan at Thamugadi (*c.* AD 200) are triple arches with a similar column arrangement to the Arch of Septimius Severus in Rome. The outer pairs of columns at Thamugadi, however, carry large segmental pediments broken at the bottom. While the triumphal arches of the western provinces and North Africa generally followed Roman fashions, a less massive and architecturally more subtle type of arch is found in some eastern provinces. The Arch of Hadrian at Athens (*c.* AD 131) is a light, elegant structure, with an opening flanked by free-standing columns and a colonnaded upper storey rather than a solid attic. The Hadrianic arch at Gerasa (Jerash) in Jordan, however, is of the more massive type, with an extremely tall central opening flanked by two narrow side arches of the same proportions. Each face has four partly engaged columns flanking the apertures, the central pair supporting a broken pediment. Two side pavilions were later built against the arch to buttress it because its tall attic made it unstable.

B. Bartoccini: 'L'arco quadrifronte dei Severi a Lepcis (Leptis Magna)', *Africa It.*, iv (1931), pp. 32–142

R. Brilliant: 'The Arch of Septimius Severus in the Roman Forum', *Mem. Amer. Acad. Rome*, 29 (1967) [whole issue]

M. Rotili: *L'arco di Traiano a Benevento* (Rome, 1972)

G. A. Mansuelli and others: *Studi sull'arco onorario romano* (Rome, 1979)

M. Pfanner: *Der Titusbogen* (Mainz, 1983)

F. S. Kleiner: *The Arch of Nero in Rome: A Study of the Roman Honorary Arch before and under Nero* (Rome, 1985)

J. C. Anderson jr: 'The Date of the Arch at Orange', *Bonn. Jb. Rhein. Landesmus. Bonn & Ver. Altertfreund. Rheinlande*, clxxxvii (1987), pp. 159–92

S. De Maria: *Gli archi onorari di Roma e dell'Italia romano*, Bibliotheca Archaeologica (Rome, 1988)

E. Nedergaard: 'Zur Problematik der Augustusbögen auf dem Forum Romanum', *Kaiser Augustus und die verlorene Republik* (exh. cat., Berlin, Martin-Gropius-Bau, 1988), pp. 224–39

F. S. Kleiner: 'The Study of Roman Triumphal and Honorary Arches 50 Years after Kähler', *J. Roman Archaeol.*, ii (1989), pp. 195–206

C. Arnould: *Les arcs romains de Jérusalem: Architecture, décor et urbanisme* (Fribourg and Göttingen, 1997)

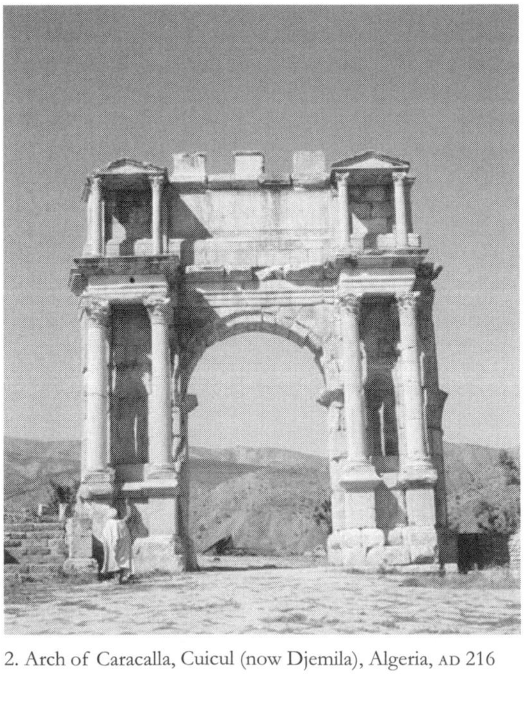

2. Arch of Caracalla, Cuicul (now Djemila), Algeria, AD 216

P. Pensabene and C. Panella, ed.: *Arco di Costantino tra archeologia e archeometria* (Rome, 1999)

B. Fornasier: *Les fragments architecturaux des arcs triomphaux en Gaule romaine* (Paris, 2003)

Troad. Region in north-west Anatolia, now part of Turkey, named after the ancient city of Troy.

1. Introduction. 2. Arts.

1. Introduction. The Troad is largely mountainous, and most of its sites are therefore situated on the coast. Stray finds of stone tools indicate the presence of palaeolithic occupation, and a neolithic site has been identified at Coşkuntepe towards the south-west tip of the Troad. The earliest traces of occupation in the region are Late Chalcolithic and were revealed by soundings at the coastal sites of Kumtepe (level Ia) and Beşik-Sivritepe, where pattern-burnished ware is characteristic. Early Bronze Age deposits of Kumtepe (level Ib), Beşik-Yassıtepe and Early Troy I, again on the coast, produced finds partly paralleled at Poliochni on Lemnos. Beşik-Yassıtepe was a fortified site with megara and apsidal structures. Clay model axes found there are paralleled at Ezero. Bronze Age Troadic culture is most fully represented at Troy (*c.* 3000–1050 BC). This site was fortified throughout most of its existence. The Early Bronze Age settlement of Late Troy II (*c.* 2465–*c.* 2150 BC) seems to have been especially wealthy, but the region apparently stagnated in the Middle Bronze Age (Troy IV–V; *c.* 2000–*c.* 1700 BC). Surveys suggest denser occupation in the Late Bronze Age (Troy VI–VII; *c.* 1700–*c.* 1050 BC), and it is tempting to relate a Mycenaean chamber tomb and cemetery on the ancient shoreline of Beşika Bay to the Achaians of the Trojan War. Continuity of occupation at some sites through the Dark Age of the late 2nd–early 1st millennium BC is suggested by grey wares similar to those of the Late Bronze Age.

In the 8th and 7th centuries BC Greek colonizers from Tenedos, Mitylene, Methymna and Miletos founded cities, mainly on the coast. During the 6th century BC the region came under Persian control, and *c.* 334–332 BC it was liberated by Alexander the Great. In the ensuing Hellenistic period (323–27 BC) smaller cities were incorporated into the larger foundations of Alexandria Troas and Ilion (Troy IX). At Assos the agora, bouleuterion, gymnasium and theatre are Hellenistic, but the fortifications and Temple of Athena originate earlier. In the late Roman times (2nd and 3rd centuries AD) there was a reversion to village life and, sometimes, to small hilltop settlements, perhaps built in response to Gothic attacks. Churches, monasteries and a few castles are of Byzantine date. The Troad passed to the Turks in AD 1306.

2. Arts.

(i) Pottery. Late Chalcolithic wares from Beşik-Sivritepe are mainly brown-red, sometimes pattern-burnished or decorated with shallow zigzag fluting. Shapes include open bowls with incurving profiles or grooved rims, fenestrated pedestals, simple jugs and vessels with horned handles. From Kumtepe (level Ia) also come white-painted wares. In Early Bronze Age (EB I) grey wares became popular, and bowl-rims were decorated with white-filled incision and with long, tubular lugs. Later pottery is best represented by finds from Troy, where grey wares still predominated in EB II (Troy I–Early Troy II). The first wheelmade articles were produced in Early Troy II, but they only became common from EB III (Middle Troy II–Troy III) onwards, when plain wares and two-handled cups were also introduced. Red wares regained their importance in the Middle Bronze Age (MB; Troy IV–V). The EB–MB repertory of shapes is fairly homogeneous. The anthropomorphic jars and lids that occur seem to be purely Troadic designs, and the tall, two-handled flaring goblet (*depas amphikypellon*) is also characteristic. The tripod jars and animal shaped jugs are typical of north-west Anatolia, as are the pedestalled pyxides that appeared in EB III. Storage jars with vertical wings are of north-east Aegean island inspiration. There are signs of Middle Helladic (MH) influence on certain shapes from Troy III–V: small cups with out-turned rims and a rising loop-handle, jars with disc-like rims, and 'hourglass' tankards. Incised decoration also recalls the patterns of MH matt-painted ware. In the Late Bronze Age (Troy VI–VII) grey wares predominated, and many shapes were borrowed directly from Greece. Mycenaean imports occur at several coastal sites and in quantity at Troy itself. The grey wares of Troy VIII appear to be descended from those of the Late Bronze Age, and there is some originality in the Troad's painted 'East Greek' wares. Thereafter Troadic pottery ceased to be distinctive.

H. Schliemann: *Ilios: The City and Country of the Trojans* (London, 1881)

C. W. Blegen and others: *Troy: Excavations Conducted by the University of Cincinnati, 1932–1938*, 4 vols (Princeton, 1950–58)

J. M. Cook: *The Troad: An Archaeological and Topographical Study* (Oxford, 1973)

J. W. Sperling: 'Kum Tepe in the Troad', *Hesperia*, xlv (1976), pp. 305–64

Archäol. Anz. (1984–8) [preliminary excav. rep. on the Beşika Bay area by M. Korfmann and others]

J. Seeher: 'Coşkuntepe-Anatolisches Neolithikum am Nordostufen der Ägäis', *Istanbul. Mitt.*, 40 (1990), pp. 9–15

G. Wagner, E. Pernicka and H.-P Ürpmann, eds: *Troia and the Troad: Scientific Approaches* (Berlin, 2003)

(ii) Jewellery. There are two principal sources for surviving Troadic jewellery, most of which dates from *c.* 2400–*c.* 2200 BC. These are Troy (level II) and a site on the island of Lemnos, known by its modern name of Poliochni. A third possible source, a collection of jewellery in the University of Pennsylvania Museum, Philadelphia, which is alleged to have come from the Troad, is best excluded as its true provenance is uncertain.

Nearly all Troadic jewellery is of gold. The source of the gold is unknown, though the geographer Strabo (64/3 BC–AD ?21) stated that there were once gold mines in the Troad, which may well have been in use in the Early Bronze Age. Troadic craftsmen, influenced by Mesopotamian and central Anatolian work, were able to exploit a number of sophisticated techniques, including repoussé, filigree, granulation and the making of ornamental chains. Their repertory consisted of diadems, earrings, beads, bracelets, dress-pins and buttons.

The jewellery known from Troy itself consists principally of 'Priam's Treasure'. Although the account of its discovery has been questioned, it still seems probable that 'Priam's Treasure' was indeed excavated by HEINRICH SCHLIEMANN as one hoard in 1873, within or just outside the walls of Troy II. The finest objects were two magnificent diadems with pendant chains that were threaded with gold beads and supported cut-outs of miniature idols. Several smaller hoards of the same date also came from Schliemann's excavations, and the American excavations of 1932–8 uncovered a few similar pieces. Nearly all Schliemann's material, which was in Berlin at the end of World War II, disappeared in 1945. All that survives are a few pieces given by Mrs Schliemann to the National Archaelogical Museum in Athens and, in Istanbul (Archaeol. Mus.), some jewellery confiscated by the Turkish authorities in about 1873 and the few pieces excavated by the Americans.

The jewellery from Lemnos was excavated by an Italian expedition in 1956 in the ruins of a house. It is now in the National Archaeological Museum in Athens. It bears a strong resemblance to the Troy material.

Troadic earrings take several forms. Among the most popular were basket-shaped earrings decorated with applied rosettes or with rows of granulation. Some have a short chain hanging from them; others have longer chains threaded with gold leaves and hung with stylized idols resembling those on the diadems from 'Priam's Treasure'. Another type of earring is in the shape of stylized cockle shells. Gold beads were abundant, over 10,000 being recorded at Troy alone. Most take simple forms: spherical, disc, cylindrical, barrel-shaped or floral. More elaborate is the quadruple-spiral. Bracelets were mostly composed of spiralled wire, but a more ornate variety consists of a gold band richly decorated with filigree spirals. Dress-pins in both gold and silver were also popular. Many have heads of two or four spirals, or heraldic arrangements of spirals and small figures of jugs. From Poliochni comes a pin with a head composed of a symmetrical arrangement of two birds.

K. R. Maxwell-Hyslop: *Western Asiatic Jewellery* (London, 1971), pp. 48–60

L. Bernabo Brea: *Poliochni: Città preistorica nell'isola di Lemnos*, ii (Rome, 1976), pp. 284–90, pls ccxl–cclii

(iii) Gold and silver plate. All the known material from the Troad is probably of EB III date (*c.* 2465–*c.* 2000 BC), and most comes from a single hoard found in Troy II. Gold, silver and electrum were used, occasionally in combination. Shapes include ovoid pedestalled flasks with vertical tubular lugs, a globular flask, two-handled tankards, a two-handled pedestalled cup, conical cups, a globular jar with flaring rim, a globular jar with cylindrical neck and stand, hemispherical bowls, a spoon comparable with much larger long-handled bronze pans of the same period, a flanged cylindrical lid with string-holes, and a two-handled sauceboat with a flaring mouth at each end. The simpler items, such as the bowls, conical cups and globular flask, were made in one piece with bases of ring, omphalos (i.e. navel) or lozenge shape, punched out as required, and rims, if present, produced by hammering. Handles were hollow, with a soldered seam along the inner edge, and attached to the vessel either by soldering or with rivets. Soldering was also used to attach the cylindrical stand to the globular jar and to reattach the foot of a golden conical cup. The commonest decoration was fluting, which could be vertical, horizontal or diagonal, though incised zigzag and fern designs also occur. One vertically fluted silver cup has electrum overlay on the rim and foot (New York, Norbert Schimmel Col.). The shapes and decoration have parallels or at least close analogies in the pottery of the Troad and the north-east Aegean islands, so that the material is probably indigenous.

H. Schmidt: *Heinrich Schliemanns Sammlung Trojanischer Altertümer* (Berlin, 1902)

O. W. Muscarella: *Ancient Art: The Norbert Schimmel Collection* (Mainz, 1974)

P. S. de Jesus: *The Development of Prehistoric Mining and Metallurgy in Anatolia*, 2 vols, Brit. Archaeol. Rep., Int. Ser. (Oxford, 1980)

Trophy. Dedication of the remains of a defeated enemy, usually on or near the battlefield. In Greece and Rome, however, the artistic commemoration of a victorious battle became very popular. The first trophy documented with certainty is Greek: the trophy of the Aiginetans in the Temple of Aphaia, celebrating their victory over Samos (520 BC). Trophies were mentioned with increasing frequency throughout the 5th century BC, but they became less popular in the 4th century BC and the Hellenistic age (323–27 BC). Among some of the Greeks, however, including the Spartans and the Macedonians, the custom of dedicating everything that remained on the battlefield to the gods remained for some time. For the rest of the Greeks the trophy was at once a symbol of victory, an ex-voto and a warning to the enemy.

Two types of trophies are known. In the first and more common type the enemy's arms were suspended from a post or cross, arranged as they had been worn by the soldier. This 'anthropomorphic trophy' was commonly connected with the figure of Victory. The second type, the 'cumulus trophy', was a stack of arms often placed on a pile of stones; the earliest form of trophy appears to have been a simple cone of stones. The array of enemy arms displayed in the two types symbolized the dedication of the defeated who had worn them to the gods who had given the victory. The first example of Victories connected with trophies was possibly the one on the balustrade of the Temple of Athena Nike on the Acropolis at Athens (late 5th century BC). In the Hellenistic period naval trophies were given a special monumentality through the display of the great bronze beaks from the prows of captured ships. Later, the cumulus trophy entered the artistic repertory.

The trophy was imported into the Roman world from Greece; there is no evidence of its existence in Etruscan art. The column in the Forum Romanum commemorating the victory of C. Duilius at Mylae in 260 BC and the trophy erected on a battlefield by Cn. Domitius and Q. Fabius Maximus in 121 BC (Florus: *Epitome* I.xxxvii.6) are the first isolated examples of a custom alien to the Latin world. It became popular as an art form in the Roman world mainly because it lent itself well to the celebratory and commemorative purposes dear to Roman art. In particular it was naturally suited to the decoration of the two main types of Roman commemorative architecture, the triumphal arch and the spiral column. The anthropomorphic trophy appeared both in reliefs and sculpture in the round, the latter form documented by numismatic evidence. A scheme often repeated in arches, early examples being those at Carpentras (1st century AD) and Glanum (?1st century BC), was the statue of the defeated barbarian; this became widespread. The so-called Dacian captive, seated on a pile of stacked arms, may have been used on a triumphal arch in the Forum of Trajan; a variant of this theme was popular during the Renaissance. The two surviving pilasters of the Armilustrium on the Aventine (where arms were consecrated) depict in low relief an impressive display of arms, armour and naval trophies amounting to more than 800 pieces. The two so-called Marius trophies, which were brought to the Piazza del Campidoglio, Rome, by Michelangelo, may also date from the Flavian age (AD 69–96).

Arms and trophies became a motif in friezes and metopes at the end of the Roman Republic. The fragments in the Museo Capitolino, Rome, which may have come from the area of the Circus Flaminius, represent naval trophies with the usual repertory of prows, anchors and rudders, together with sacrificial symbols. Innumerable types of trophies are represented on coins.

J. Durm: *Die Baukunst der Römer* (Stüttgart, 1905), pp. 733–45

K. Woelcke: 'Beiträge zur Geschichte des Tropaions', *Bonn. Jb. Rhein. Landesmus. Bonn & Ver. Altertfreund. Rheinlande*, cx (1911), pp. 127–235

E. Pottier and G. Lafaye, eds: *Dictionnaire des antiquités grecques et romaines*, v/2 (Paris, 1919), pp. 497–518

G. Picard: *Trophées d'Auguste à Saint-Bertrand-des-Comminges* (Toulouse, 1947)

G. Picard: *Les Trophées romains* (Paris, 1959)

Troy [Gk. Ilion; Turk. Hisarlık]. Bronze Age and Classical site on the Asiatic side of the south end of the Dardanelles, north-west Turkey. It was excavated by John Brunton (very briefly, 1855–6), Frank Calvert (1863 and 1865), HEINRICH SCHLIEMANN (1870–73, 1878–9, 1882, 1890), Wilhelm Dörpfeld (1893–4), and Carl Blegen for the University of Cincinnati (1932–8). In 1983 excavation of Bronze Age Troy resumed under Manfred Korfmann of Tübingen University. Brian Rose of the University of Cincinnati worked on Roman levels from 1988 to 2002; his discoveries include a large statue of the Emperor Hadrian found in 1993 and the head of a statue of Augustus found in 1997.

The prehistoric mound and later acropolis, now largely dug away, had *c.* 15 m of deposit and a diameter of *c.* 200 m; the lower town, mostly Hellenistic and Roman, covered an area *c.* 1200×800 m. The sequence of nine 'cities' distinguished by Schliemann and Dörpfeld must be understood as a sequence of 9 broad bands within a history of 50 or more building phases. Attention was focused on the site by Schliemann's contention that it was the Homeric city of Troy. He sought the remains of Priam's city in the second city of Troy (some 1000 years too early), with its megara and impressive fortifications, and discovered in 1873 a rich hoard of tools, weapons, vessels and jewellery, which he called 'Priam's Treasure'. Trojan chronology is a matter of some dispute among archaeologists; the dates used here are those established by Blegen.

See also TROAD.

1. Early and Middle Bronze Age, Troy I–V (*c.* 3000–*c.*1800 BC). 2. Late Bronze Age, Troy VI–VII (*c.* 1800–*c.* 1100 BC). 3. Classical site, Troy VIII–IX (*c.* 700 BC–*c.* AD 400).

1. EARLY AND MIDDLE BRONZE AGE, TROY I–V (*c.* 3000–*c.* 1800 BC). A promontory in a natural harbour, since silted up, provided plentiful fishing, command of the Dardanelles and the site of the citadel, which was surrounded by a stone wall 5 m thick with a mud-brick superstructure. During Troy II (*c.* 2600–*c.* 2200 BC) the wall stood on top of a stone-faced glacis. Other features of the fortifications varied in different periods: rectangular towers up to 20 m wide, sometimes enclosing gateways, projected from it during Troy I–II; in later periods gates were set further back. Outside the wall of Troy I was a broken stone stele 790 mm high with a heart-shaped human face in low relief, and beside it were two other vertical slabs with saucer-shaped indentations, all three perhaps reused. Adjoining the gate of Late Troy II was a shrine with a horned altar. Knowledge of the area within the walls is incomplete at all periods. The buildings were chiefly of mud brick and built to two traditions, dominant before and after the destruction of Middle Troy II by fire. The earlier tradition had free-standing rectangular buildings subdivided into hall and porch (megara). Some megara reached stately dimensions (up to *c.* 40×13 m) and so probably had a public use. These, with a forecourt, were enclosed within a walled colonnade broken by a formal gateway. More complex buildings lay outside the colonnade. The buildings of the later tradition had small rooms (e.g. 4×4 m), party

walls and internal courtyards, all arranged in large blocks separated by narrow streets. The pattern suggests domestic use.

The pottery was adventurous but not highly accomplished. The principal wares were red and black. Characteristic shapes included shallow wheel-made plates (from Troy II onwards), tankards with one and two handles, tall goblets with two flaring handles (wrongly identified by Schliemann as the Homeric *depas amphikypellon*), jugs with rising, even beaked, spouts sometimes cut away above the handle, and a wide range of flasks. These often had two upraised arms and three knobs representing breasts and a navel, with ears, eyes, eyebrows and nose on the neck of the flask or on the cylindrical lid. A few fanciful jugs were in animal shapes. Incised decoration on bowls and plates was common in Troy I.

Tools and weapons were of copper or bronze. Small items of jewellery, such as pins, rings and bracelets, were of copper, bronze, silver or gold. Besides tools and weapons, 'Priam's Treasure' included cups of gold and electrum, gold and silver bottles, bowls and dishes of silver and bronze, a bucket, vat and shallow pan of copper or bronze, six silver ingots, six gold bracelets, three gold headdresses (two with elaborate pendant decoration), four gold basket-earrings with pendant decoration and 56 gold shell earrings (including six with gold granulation), together with sequins, studs and, apparently, 8700 beads of gold. The authenticity of the discovery has been questioned, but excavations since 1873 at Troy and elsewhere have shown all the material to be stylistically correct for the period. The circumstances and records of the discovery tend to confirm its authenticity, although the jewellery could conceivably have been an addition. Most of the objects disappeared from the Pergamonmuseum, Berlin, in 1945, and in 1993 the Pushkin Museum of Fine Arts in Moscow admitted that it held them. Bone and stone were important materials to the ancient Trojans, but only four magnificent shaft-hole axes (one of lapis lazuli) are of artistic interest. More than 15 contemporary sites are known in the Troad, the vicinity of Troy.

2. Late Bronze Age, Troy VI–VII (*c.* 1800–*c.* 1100 BC). By the early 2nd millennium BC the citadel was twice the size of Troy II, with a finely built circuit wall. Its substructure of large blocks of masonry stood 6 m high with a mud-brick superstructure and internal parapet. Shallow offsets marked its outer face at regular intervals of 9 m, and four gates provided access to the interior. Flanking the main gate on the south side was a tower, entered from the top of the wall, containing two pillars on a stone base that probably had cultic significance; four stelae stood against the outside of the same tower. Two further towers adjoined the circuit wall; the one at the north-east corner contained a staircase leading down to a rock-cut well. Buildings within the citadel stood on concentric terraces of which the highest were removed by levelling in Roman times. All the buildings were of stone, and in level VI they were free-standing. A few were in megaron style, up to 25×17 m, but others were rectangular, with the entrance in the long side, or even L-shaped. Staircases suggest the presence of second storeys or flat roofs; one building, 13×15 m with twelve stone column bases, may have had a central nave, clerestory and two aisles. Towers and some interior buildings were trapezoidal in plan, their sides converging towards the centre of the citadel. Troy VI was destroyed *c.* 1300 BC. In the succeeding periods Troy VIIa and VIIb the citadel walls remained standing but the interior was rebuilt. The interior rebuilt in VIIa recalled its handsome predecessor, but it was destroyed *c.* 1250 BC. During VIIb the site was covered with multi-chambered houses with small rooms, thin walls and narrow, winding streets; it was abandoned *c.* 1100 BC or later.

The indigenous pottery was in two principal wares, Grey and Tan 'Minyan' ware. There was some legacy from the Early Bronze Age, but much was new. Ring bases and pedestals appeared under cups, bowls and jars. Bowls acquired a characteristic concave profile; rising spouts and beak spouts on jugs virtually disappeared. Decoration was infrequent, the most common form being incised wavy lines. Mycenaean imports appeared *c.* 1500 BC, inspiring clumsy local imitations; they became numerous during Troy VI, but sharply decreased in Troy VII. Handmade pottery with south-east European affinities appeared in VIIb: first a coarse ware with finger-impressed decoration, and later a ware ornamented with pointed, upturned knobs and fluting. Little metalwork survives from this period, although there is evidence for arrowheads, double axes, pickaxes, sickles and a small scale of armour. Luxury goods included alabaster sword-pommels, faience and ostrich egg.

The historical identification of the site with Troy and the historicity of the Trojan War remain unproven, and neither archaeology nor contemporary records provide direct confirmation. Blegen ascribed the destruction of Troy VI to an earthquake, and that of Troy VIIa to an Achaian attack; but recent work suggests that, if an earthquake occurred, it was VIIa that suffered, and that only VI, not VIIa, antedates the fall of the Mycenaean palaces. At least 16 contemporary sites are known in the Troad, including a burial ground, possibly Mycenaean, on the shore of Beşika Bay.

3. Classical Site, Troy VIII–IX (*c.* 700 BC–*c.* AD 400). The citadel walls of Troy VI–VII, still visible in VIII, were added to and repaired, but little remains of the citadel interior. The Hellenistic and Roman site, Troy IX, is better known. On the western half of the acropolis were a sanctuary, a grandstand, a possible temple on the summit and other buildings. The eastern half was redesigned in the period from Augustus to Claudius (30 BC–AD 55). A paved enclosure (110×90 m) was surrounded by a stoa and contained a Doric temple of Athena, a well with circular lantern and subterranean access, and cultic buildings now too fragmentary to be identified. To the south lay a theatre, the bouleuterion, agora, palaestra and a

built-up town area; to the east was a Roman theatre set in the hillside. The temple of Athena had been almost entirely plundered long before Schliemann's arrival, but architectural fragments show it to have had a triglyph frieze depicting scenes of combat between Greeks and barbarians, and Helios in a horse-drawn chariot. There was a rosette frieze around the doors and walls of the interior.

The pottery and metalwork are unremarkable, although the site has produced its own variety of East Greek Geometric pottery, 'G2–3 ware'. Pyramidal loomweights occur in clay, stone and lead, and discoid or lentoid weights of clay, often stamped with gem impressions, are common. There is a good series of terracotta figurines: Cybele is a frequent subject, often with a lion, but other cultic and secular subjects were also found, and detached female heads are numerous. Votive terracotta plaques show the horseman hero, a heroine, or divine symbols. Coins and inscriptions prove the site to have been Classical Ilion, believed by its inhabitants to occupy the site of ancient Troy.

At some time after AD 350 the Temple of Athena was destroyed, and some of its stones were used in later buildings. Pottery and coins show that the site was re-occupied on a modest scale in the late 12th century and the early 13th. Numerous other sites of Classical and Byzantine date are known in the Troad, of which the most important are Alexandria Troas, Abydos, Dardanos, Gergis, Scepsis, Cebren, Neandria, Assos, Lamponia, Gargara and Antandrus.

H. Schliemann: *Troy and its Remains* (London, 1874)

H. Schliemann: *Ilios: The City and Country of the Trojans* (London, 1881)

H. Schliemann: *Troja: Results of the Latest Researches and Discoveries on the Site of Homer's Troy, 1882* (London, 1884)

W. Dörpfeld: *Troja und Ilion* (Athens, 1902)

H. Schmidt: *Heinrich Schliemanns Sammlung trojanischer Altertümer* (Berlin, 1902)

C. W. Blegen and others: *Troy: Excavations Conducted by the University of Cincinnati*, 4 vols in 8 pts (Princeton, NJ, 1950–58) and 4 suppl. monographs (Princeton, 1951–82)

F. W. Goethert and H. Schleif: *Der Athenatempel von Ilion* (Berlin, 1962)

C. W. Blegen: *Troy and the Trojans* (London, 1964)

J. M. Cook: *The Troad: An Archaeological and Topographical Study* (Oxford, 1973)

D. F. Easton: 'Priam's Treasure', *Anatol. Stud.*, xxxiv (1984), pp. 141–69

D. F. Easton: 'Has the Trojan War Been Found?', *Antiquity*, lxix (1985), pp. 188–96

L. Foxhall and J. K. Davies, eds: *The Trojan War: Its Historicity and Context* (Bristol, 1985)

M. J. Mellink, ed.: *Troy and the Trojan War* (Bryn Mawr, PA, 1986)

D. Easton: 'Reconstructing Schliemann's Troy', *Heinrich Schliemann nach hundert Jahren*, ed. W. Calder III and J. Cobet (Frankfurt am Main, 1990), pp. 431–47 *Studia Troica,* 9 vols (Mainz, 1991–9) [in English and German]

D. Easton: 'Schliemanns Ausgrabungen in Troja', *Archäologie und historische Erinnerung nach 100 Jahren Heinrich Schliemann* (Essen, 1992), pp. 51–72

D. Easton: *The Quest for Troy* (London, 1997)

A Guide to Troia (Istanbul, 1999) [by the director and staff of the excavations]

D. Hertel: *Troia: Archäologie, Geschichte, Mythos* (Munich, 2001)

F. Kolb: 'Troy VI: A Trading Center and Commercial City?', *Amer. J. Archaeol.,* cviii (2004), pp. 577–614 [reply by P. Jablonka and C. B. Rose, pp. 615–30]

Tulmaythah. *See* PTOLEMAIS.

Tylissos. Site in northern Crete, 14 km south-west of Herakleion, in the foothills of the Ida massif overlooking the coastal plain, which flourished *c.* 2900–*c.* 1000 BC. It lay on routes heading both west and south and is mentioned (as tu-ri-so) in the Linear B tablets. The excavations conducted by Joseph Hazzidakis (1909–13) uncovered only a fraction of the site.

An Early Minoan (EM) II to Middle Minoan (MM) II settlement (*c.* 2900/2600–*c.* 1675 BC), represented by traces of walls and pottery but of uncertain form, was succeeded *c.* 1650 BC by free-standing, two-storey houses which differed in detail. The irregularly shaped Houses A and C have store-rooms containing pithoi, separated by corridors and stair units from living areas, including halls with pier-and-door screens and adjacent light wells, lustral basins and pillar crypts. Both have multiple access routes. House B is rectangular and only slightly less complex. All three buildings were destroyed by fire *c.* 1425 BC. Linear A tablets, sealings and a copper ingot fragment discovered in the houses attest to some form of estate management, while raw pigments, a potter's wheel, bronze chisels and precision saws/scrapers and stone tools indicate the presence of craftsmen. Linear A also occurs in graffiti on a clay figurine and on walls. Other notable finds include three massive, and one smaller, bronze cauldrons, a remarkable bronze statue representing a plump worshipper, an obsidian rhyton, and faience and ivory inlays, probably from wooden chests. Best finds are held at the Archaeological Museum in Herakleion. The houses also contained sophisticated frescoes in the Miniature style, processions and floral subjects (*see* PAINTING, §I, 2).

The only substantial later house remains on the site date from Late Minoan (LM) III to Subminoan (*c.* 1390–*c.* 1000 BC). A cistern and clay and stone channels indicate an interest in water dispersal. Burials are few: an LM III burial cave, an LM IIIB–C chamber tomb and an early cremation (?LM IIIC). There are also traces of Classical period (*c.* 475–323 BC) occupation, including an altar stone. Other religious sites in the vicinity include a peak sanctuary (EM–MM) and a sacred cave (MM–LM).

J. Hazzidakis: *Tylissos à l'époque minoenne* (Paris, 1921)

J. Hazzidakis: *Les Villas minoennes de Tylissos* (Paris, 1934)

S. G. Spanakis: *Kentriki-anatoliki* (1964), i of *I Kriti* (Herakleion, 1964–), pp. 495–503

A. Vasilakis: 'Tylissos', *The Aerial Atlas of Ancient Crete*, ed. J. W. Myers, E. E. Myers and G. Cadogan (Berkeley, 1992), pp. 270–73

Tyrant Slayers [*Tyrannicides*; Gr. *Tyrannoktonoi*]. Greek statue group originally executed in bronze by ANTENOR, which was frequently copied throughout the Greek and Roman world. Nothing from the original work survives.

In 514 BC the Athenians Harmodios and Aristogeiton assassinated the tyrant Hipparchos, son of Peisistratos, who had ruled over Athens together with his brother Hippias. Harmodios was killed on the spot; Aristogeiton briefly escaped but was put to death soon after. Hippias, the original target of the plot, remained unharmed and continued to rule for another four years. After he had finally been expelled in 510 BC and a democratic regime installed under the new leader Kleisthenes in 508/7 BC, the state commissioned a bronze monument of the 'tyrant slayers' by the sculptor Antenor. While the tyrant slayers' action did not lead to an immediate change in government, and may have been inspired by personal rather than political motives, the state nevertheless created an iconic symbol for the new democracy that all Athenians could identify with. When the exiled Hippias returned with the invading Persian army under Xerxes in 480 BC, the Antenor group was taken away to the Persian capital at Persepolis as a clear political statement. Such was the importance of the monument that, following Athens' victory in 479 BC, the Athenian state immediately commissioned a replacement group from the sculptors KRITIOS AND NESIOTES. This was set up in the Agora, the city's main public square, in 477/6 BC. More than a century later, the original group by Antenor was recovered by Alexander the Great during the sack of Persepolis and sent back to Athens.

The *Tyrant Slayers* group was a key monument of the Athenian state, and frequently reproduced in other media (vases, coins, reliefs etc). A number of Roman marble copies of the *Tyrant Slayers* have survived, together with fragments of plaster casts of the bronze originals among the BAIAE CASTS. The most complete Roman marble copy is a group now in Naples (the missing head of Aristogeiton has been replaced with a copy of a head in the Capitoline Museum in Rome; cf. Brunnsåker 1971 for a list of replicas). It shows the *Tyrant Slayers* in heroic nudity, lunging forwards side by side. The younger, beardless Harmodios attacks recklessly, with his right sword arm raised to strike a blow, while the mature and bearded Aristogeiton takes up a more defensive position with his left arm, covered by the mantle, thrust forward and the right drawn back, ready to stab. It seems that the figures of Harmodios and Aristogeiton (who, according to some sources, had a homoerotic relationship in line with the prevalent norms of Athenian society at the time) stood back to back, providing protection for each other. It is somewhat unclear whether the Roman copies show the second group by Kritios and Nesiotes or the first one by Antenor, or if copies of both may exist (in case the second simply copied the first). This is mainly because the exact date of the Antenor group, and with it the possible degree of similarity between the two monuments, is unknown. Yet it was certainly the monument by Kritios and Nesiotes that witnessed the heyday of the Athenian democracy and would therefore have been of greater significance.

S. Brunnsåker: *The Tyrant-Slayers of Kritios and Nesiotes: A Critical Study of the Sources and Restorations* (Stockholm, 2/1971)
B. Fehr: *Die Tyrannentöter, oder kann man der Demokratie ein Denkmal setzen ?* (Frankfurt am Main, 1984)
C. Landwehr: 'Statuenkopien der Tyrannenmörder-Gruppe: Die Statue des Aristogeiton in Rom', *Jb. Dt. Archäol. Inst.*, ci (1986), pp. 111–26
W. H. Schuchhardt: 'Statuenkopien der Tyrannenmörder-Gruppe: Die Gruppe der Tyrannenmörder in Neapel', *Jb. Dt. Archäol. Inst.*, ci (1986), pp. 85–110
M. W. Taylor: *The Tyrant Slayers: The Heroic Image in Fifth century BC Athenian Art and Politics* (Salem, 2/1991)

Uğura. *See* OLBA.

Underworld Painter (*fl c.* 330–*c.* 310 BC). Vase painter, active in Apulia. He is named after a famous monumental volute krater found at Canosa (Munich, Staatl. Antikensamml., 3297), with a multi-figured composition showing *Pluto and Persephone in their Palace* surrounded by figures of the Underworld (see colour pl. 2:XVI, fig. 1). This is among the most important of a group of late Apulian vases attributed to various painters that show Underworld scenes. What sets the Underworld Painter clearly apart and justifies his name is his individualistic treatment of the Underworld theme and his particular interest in the fate of Orpheus. For example, on a volute krater (Naples, Mus. Archeol. N., SA 709) he showed Orpheus not alone but standing with Eurydice before Hades, whereas other painters tended to neglect the love story. Another volute krater (Munich, Staatl. Antikensamml., 3296), the companion to his name-piece, bears an impressive representation of *Medea Slaughtering One of her Children* in the presence of the horrified ghost of her father and the demon Oistros, all the main figures being identified by inscriptions. Among the Underworld Painter's most interesting vases are unique representations of mythological twins, as on the masterful volute krater (Geneva, Mus. A. & Hist.) depicting a *Herdsman Returning Melanippe's Babies*, another scene in which the figures are identified by inscriptions. The vivid depiction of emotions expressed on the astonished faces of the family who had abandoned the babies almost equals that of the mature works of the DARIUS PAINTER. An outstanding earlier work on a tall lekythos (h. 950 mm; Richmond, VA, Mus. F.A., 80.162) represents multiple twins: the *Dioskouroi Raping the Leukippidai* (against the protest of their former bridegrooms who were also twins or at least brothers).

The Underworld Painter was evidently inspired directly or indirectly by literary sources: his rather early volute krater showing *Hector's Farewell to Andromache and his Infant Son Astyanax* (Berlin, Antikensamml., 1984.45) was probably based on the tragedy *Hector* by his contemporary, the poet Astydamas, while the story represented in the Melanippe painting may go back to Euripides. The Underworld Painter's earlier works testify more clearly to the strong influence of the Darius Painter, but his artistic temperament seems always to have been rather different: there is an element of violence in his drawing style; his lines tend to be thicker, with the physiognomies coarser, though still expressive; and subsidiary objects such as pieces of furniture are rendered with much less detail and elaboration.

A. D. Trendall and A. Cambitoglou: *The Red-figured Vases of Apulia*, ii (Oxford, 1982), pp. 531–40

A. D. Trendall and A. Cambitoglou: *The Red-figured Vases of Apulia: Supplement* 1 (London, 1983), pp. 83–6

A. D. Trendall: *Red Figure Vases of South Italy and Sicily. A Handbook* (London, 1989), pp. 90–91

A. D. Trendall and A. Cambitoglou: *The Red-figured Vases of Apulia: Supplement* 2 (London, 1992), pp. 161–5

Urban Planning. *See* PLANNING.

V

Vaison-la-Romaine. *See* Vasio Vocontiorum.

Vase painters. Ancient Greek vases can be classified by period, place of production, fabric, shape, technique and decoration. It is also possible to identify styles of individual artists when sufficient vases have been preserved from a single area of production over a significant period and when these display similar decorative figures and patterns. Most Greek vase painters so far identified were active either in Athens during the 6th to 4th centuries BC or in 4th- and 3rd-century BC South Italy. The painters have been more often identified than the potters, partly because scholars have tended to concentrate on vase decoration rather than shape.

Greek vase painting is actually line drawing on the curved surfaces of clay vases made for particular functions to which the figure scenes sometimes allude. Patterns are an integral part of the decoration and remain important even when figures occupy the major part of the painted surface. The rendering of patterns and figures on individual Athenian vases is usually so consistent that one artist must normally have been responsible for both. Since human figures dominate most scenes, it is often assumed that stylistic elements in their execution should be the primary basis for determining attribution. This is, however, incorrect: examination of the figures is only the final stage in the process of attribution. Initially the shape must be examined, then the technique of decoration, the patterns, the iconography and the overall design of the painted elements. None of these can be assessed in isolation, and attribution remains subjective, although when many features can be taken into account and many contemporary vases are available for comparison this mode of classification is greatly strengthened. Few other art forms, in effect, offer such copious material for attribution.

Greek vases are rarely signed by either painter or potter, and no artist whose signature survives is mentioned in contemporary sources. Greek vase painting is wholly undocumented, and most artists' signatures occur on Athenian 6th- and 5th-century BC Black-figure and Red-figure vases. Painters signed with the verb *egrapsen* ('painted'), potters with the verb *epoiesen* ('made'). Makers may have fashioned the vase or simply supervised its production, and they appear to have been senior to painters. Using these two types of signature, the significance of which was not then fully understood, some later 19th-century scholars began to attribute signed Athenian vases to individual artists. Results were, however, inconclusive or misleading. Then, from 1911, J. D. Beazley began to publish attributions of unsigned vases to unknown artists whom he named, often after museums housing their work (e.g. the Berlin Painter) or after a favourite subject (e.g. the Gorgon Painter). Over a period of more than 50 years he assigned more than 50,000 vases to over 1000 artists, classes and groups, publishing these attributions in what have become the standard reference works on the subject (Beazley, 1942, 1956 and 1971). Beazley left approximately the same number of vases unassigned.

Beazley's method was undoubtedly influenced by Giovanni Morelli's work on Renaissance painters, popularized in England by Bernard Berenson *c.* 1900. Morelli's system depended on detailed scrutiny of draughtsmanship, especially of the human body, and he particularly recommended the study of drawings, since these reveal use of lines more clearly than paintings. As line drawing involving human figures, Greek vase painting was admirably suited to Morellian morphological analysis. Beazley supplemented this approach with careful study of the features peculiar to Greek vases. In doing this he created his own method of attribution, which was subsequently applied to Corinthian vases by his pupil H. G. G. Payne, to Greek vases of South Italy by A. D. Trendall, and to various Archaic Greek vases by other scholars.

See also Pottery, §IV *and entries on* Acheloos painter, Achilles painter, painter of Acropolis 606, Affecter, Aison, Amasis painter, Analatos painter, Andokides painter, Antimenes painter, Arkesilaos painter, Athena painter, painter of Athens 894, Baltimore painter, Beldam painter, Berlin painter, Boreads painter, Brygos painter, C painter, Chicago painter, Darius painter, Dipylon master, Douris, Epiktetos, Eretria painter, Euphronios, Euthymides, Exekias, Ganymede painter, Gorgon painter, Group e, Group of the huge lekythoi, Group r, Heidelberg painter, Hirschfeld painter, Hunt painter, Kadmos painter, Kleitias, Kleophon painter, Kleophrades painter, Kodros painter, Kuban painter, Leagros group, Lydos, Lysippides painter, Macmillan painter, Makron, Mannerist workshop, Marsyas painter, Meidias painter,

Myson, Naukratis painter, Nearchos, Nettos painter, Nikias painter, Niobid painter, Oltos, Onesimos, Pan painter, Paseas, Phiale painter, Phintias, Polion, Polygnotos, Polyphemos painter, Priam painter, Pronomos painter, Psiax, Ram jug painter, Reed painter, Rider painter, Rycroft painter, Sophilos, Sotades painter, Swing painter, Talos painter, Tleson, Underworld painter and Villa giulia painter.

H. G. G. Payne: *Necrocorinthia: A Study of Corinthian Art in the Archaic Period* (Oxford, 1931)

J. D. Beazley: 'Citharoedus', *J. Hell. Stud.*, xxii (1942), pp. 70–98

J. D. Beazley: *Red-figure* (1942, 2/1963)

J. D. Beazley: *Black-figure* (1956)

J. D. Beazley: *Paralipomena* (1971)

C. M. Robertson: 'Beazley and After', *Münchn. Jb. Bild. Kst*, xxvii (1976), pp. 29–46

D. C. Kurtz: 'Beazley and the Connoisseurship of Greek Vases', *Greek Vases in the J. Paul Getty Museum*, iii (Malibu, 1986), pp. 237–50

D. C. Kurtz, ed.: *Lectures on Greek Vases by J. D. Beazley* (Oxford, 1989)

A. D. Trendall: *Red Figure Vases of South Italy and Sicily* (London, 1989)

T. Rasmussen and N. J. Spivey: *Looking at Greek Vases* (Cambridge and New York, 1991)

M. Robertson: *The Art of Vase-painting in Classical Athens* (Cambridge and New York, 1992/*R* 1996)

J. Boardman: *Early Greek Vase Painting: 11th–6th Centuries BC: A Handbook* (New York, 1998)

J. Boardman: *The History of Greek Vases: Potters, Painters, and Pictures* (New York, 2001)

F. Lissarrague and B. Eskenazi: *Greek Vases: The Athenians and their Images* (New York, 2001)

L. A. Buboltz: *Dance Scenes in Early Archaic Greek Vase-painting* (diss., Harvard U., 2002)

A. J. Clark, M. Elston and M. L. Hart: *Understanding Greek Vases: A Guide to Terms, Styles, and Techniques* (Los Angeles, 2002)

Vasiliki. Site in eastern Crete on low hills flanking the north-south route across the Ierapetra Isthmus, inhabited *c.* 3500–*c.* 1050 BC. First investigated by R. B. Seager (1903–6), it has been substantially reinterpreted by A. Zoïs (from 1970). Although there are traces of Early Minoan (EM) I (*c.* 3500/3000–*c.* 2900/2600 BC) pottery, the first clear signs of habitation are of early EM II (*c.* 2900/2600–*c.* 2200 BC) date. Buildings belonging to several phases had covered the main hilltop by Middle Minoan (MM) IA (*c.* 2050–*c.* 1900 BC). The main surviving structures are two buildings of early EM II date and, to their south, two of late EM II. The settlement was destroyed in a great conflagration towards the end of EM II. The southern pair (now the Red/East and West houses) were regarded by Seager as a single 'House on the Hill'. Zoïs showed that they were separate buildings, which somewhat weakens earlier theories that Vasiliki anticipated features of Minoan palatial architecture (*see* Architecture, §I). Even so, they are large and relatively complex and their layout differs from the agglutinative approach of contemporary Myrtos (Phournou Koriphi). Larger rooms, one with a well, faced on to a central space and perhaps had some communal function; smaller ones in groups and rows behind show clear differentiation of purpose. A substantial courtyard lies to the west, with other yards to the north.

Decorative features of these houses include early instances of the typical Minoan use of red-painted plaster on walls and floors. Furniture and equipment recovered are relatively meagre: a sophisticated bronze mould for double axes (Herakleion, Archaeol. Mus.) may date from this phase; otherwise there are only two broken metal axes and a few stone objects, including Cycladic-style figurines. The most important remains are of pottery. The site has given its name to a distinctive handmade ware typical of EM II. It is represented in a full range of tablewares.

MM I (*c.* 2050–*c.* 1800 BC) buildings have been found only at the periphery of the hilltop, though they are thought to extend down the east slope. Seager excavated two (his Houses A and B), Zoïs parts of three others. One contained five stone lamps (Herakleion, Archaeol. Mus.). The structures vary in quality, and though their foundations were more solidly constructed than those of their predecessors, perhaps to counter earthquakes, the site was severely damaged by a tremor in MM II (*c.* 1800–*c.* 1650 BC).

In Neo-Palatial times (MM III to Late Minoan (LM) I, *c.* 1675–*c.* 1425 BC), the whole hilltop was built over and parts of five or so structures are known. The most complete, house M, lies to the north-east, and, though not so large or well equipped as the town houses and villas of Tylissos or Amnisos, it is a substantial village dwelling that compares well with any at Gournia. Later Minoan occupation is barely represented, though a species of 'fortification' wall is broadly dated to LM III (*c.* 1390–*c.* 1050 BC). Burials in the vicinity of the settlement include a MM enclosure and cemetery of pithoi interments to the south, and, further uphill to the west, a LM IIIB–C (*c.* 1335–*c.* 1180 BC) tholos.

R. B. Seager: 'Excavations at Vasiliki, 1904', *Trans. Dept Archaeol., Free Mus. Sci. & A., U. PA*, i (1905), pp. 207–21

R. B. Seager: 'Report of Excavations at Vasiliki, Crete, in 1906', *Trans. Dept Archaeol., Free Mus. Sci. & A., U. PA*, ii (1907), pp. 111–32

A. Zoïs: 'Vasiliki, Hierapetra', *Ergon Archaiol. Etaireias* (1972), pp. 113–18; (1974), pp. 107–12; (1975), pp. 189–93; (1976), pp. 195–200; (1977), pp. 195–9; (1982), pp. 48–51

A. Zoïs: 'Excavations at Vasiliki, Hierapetra', *Praktika Athen. Archaiol. Etaireias* (1976), pp. 440–59

A. Zoïs: *Vasiliki 1*, Edition of the Archaeological Society, lxxxiii (Athens, 1976)

A. Kanta: *The Late Minoan III Period in Crete: A Survey of Sites, Pottery and their Distribution*, Stud. Medit. Archaeol., lviii (Göteborg, 1980)

A. Zoïs: 'Vasiliki', *The Aerial Atlas of Ancient Crete*, ed. J. W. Myers, E. E. Myers and G. Cadogan (Berkeley, 1992), pp. 274–9

Vasio Vocontiorum [now Vaison-la-Romaine]. Site of a Roman city (*fl* mid-1st century AD–*c.* 475). It originated as a native settlement of the Vocontii and occupied hillsides north of the River Ouvèze, southern France, over which a single-span Roman bridge still stands. The theatre (1st century AD) is the main surviving public building. Its *cavea*, cut into the north side of the Puymin Hill, has been extensively restored. The stage building was of western type with doors set in curved and rectangular exedrae. In front of it, rock-cut shafts contained the curtain mechanism. Statues of emperors and local dignitaries from the theatre are displayed in the nearby Musée Archéologique. The excavated town houses are the best-preserved in France, notable for their Hellenistic peristyle courtyards. Among those on the southern slopes of the Puymin Hill, the House of the Messii (2nd century AD) had at the east end large rooms paved in *opus sectile* facing the peristyle; the marble head of Apollo (formerly mistakenly called the Venus of Vaison; ?1st or 2nd century AD; Vaison-la-Romaine, Mus. Archaéol.) was found there. At the west end smaller rooms, including a kitchen and baths, surrounded three enclosed courtyards. In the area of La Villasse to the south-west, a street on a different alignment from those on the Puymin Hill had shops on both sides, a marble-paved and frescoed basilican hall on the east (1st century AD), and opposite, the entrance to the House of the Silver Bust, named after the bust of a man in a toga (?3rd century AD; Vaison-la-Romaine, Mus. Archéol.). This, the largest of the houses at Vaison, had three main elements: a columned vestibule leading from the street to a peristyle courtyard and a large reception room; beyond, and at right angles to that axis, a larger peristyle and two covered reception rooms with a hall or open courtyard between them; and finally a much larger trapezoidal peristyle garden with a suite of baths to the north, originally perhaps a separate establishment. To the west, the House of the Dolphins was built in the Augustan period (27 BC–AD 14) as a Hellenistic peristyle house; in the late 1st century AD the addition of an atrium beyond the tablinum gave the layout a more Roman character.

J. Sautel: *Vaison dans l'antiquité*, 3 vols (Avignon, 1941–2)

C. Goudineau: *Les Fouilles de la Maison au Dauphin: Recherches sur la romanisation de Vaison* (Paris, 1979)

Vathypetro. Large Late Minoan I (*c.* 1560–*c.* 1425 BC) country house a few kilometres south of Archanes and Knossos in northern central Crete. Excavated by Spyridon Marinatos in 1949–51, it stands on a spur overlooking fertile country, dominated by Mt Juktas to the north-west, with its shrines. The house, which measures over 20×20 m, was apparently not part of a village or hamlet. Its few outbuildings include a kiln, while in the house itself are presses for olive oil and wine. Its architecture exemplifies the high quality of building of these large villas, which probably controlled large estates. Features include ashlar masonry, column bases of different stones, pillar basements, recesses for windows and a paved west court. On the east side of the building, opposite the entrance and across a small courtyard, is a tripartite shrine, with a central recess (possibly for a seat or statue) between two square masonry structures with hollow centres. These may have held flagstaff-like masts, as depicted on the peak-sanctuary chlorite and gold rhyton from KATO ZAKROS (Herakleion, Archaeol. Mus.), or they may be the bases of platforms. Vathypetro had at least two building phases, but, as the site has not been published fully, many details that would be important for the history of Minoan architecture and society are still unclear. It nevertheless remains an excellent illustration of the tendency, particularly marked in the Neo-Palatial period, for complex buildings to be erected in rural areas, to serve not only as lavish dwellings for local dignitaries, but as centres for farming, local administration and religion.

S. Marinatos: 'Anaskaphai Vathypetrou Archanon (Kritis)' [Excavations at Vathypetro, Archanai (Crete)], *Praktika Athen. Archaiol. Etaireias* (1949), pp. 100–09

S. Marinatos: 'Megaron Vathypetrou' [The megaron of Vathypetro], *Praktika Athen. Archaiol. Etaireias* (1950), pp. 242–57

S. Marinatos: 'Anaskaphi megarou Vathypetrou (Kritis)' [Excavation of the megaron at Vathypetro (Crete)], *Praktika Athen. Archaiol. Etaireias* (1951), pp. 258–72

S. Marinatos: 'Anaskaphai en Vathypetro (Kritis)' [Excavations at Vathypetro (Crete)], *Praktika Athen. Archaiol. Etaireias* (1952), pp. 592–610

S. Marinatos and M. Hirmer: *Crete and Mycenae* (London, 1960), pp. 137, 140

C. Davaras: *Guide to Cretan Antiquities* (Park Ridge, 1976), pp. 335–7

J. W. Shaw: 'Evidence for the Minoan Tripartite Shrine', *Amer. J. Archaeol.*, lxxxii (1978), pp. 429–48 (442–6)

G. C. Gesell: *Town, Palace and House Cult in Minoan Crete*, Stud. Medit. Archaeol., lxvii (Göteborg, 1985), pp. 20, 29–30, 136–7

B. Rutkowski: *The Cult Places of the Aegean* (New Haven and London, 1986), p. 34

G. Cadogan: 'Vathypetro', *The Aerial Atlas of Ancient Crete*, ed. J. W. Myers, E. E. Myers and G. Cadogan (Berkeley, 1992), pp. 280–83

J. Driessen and I. Sakellarakis: 'The Vathypetro-Complex: Some Observations on its Architectural History and Function', *The Function of the Minoan 'Villa': Proceedings of the Eighth International Symposium at the Swedish Institute* (Athens, 1992)

Veii [Gr. Ventia; It. Veio]. Etruscan site *c.* 20 km north of Rome, set on a triangular tufa plateau bounded by two streams and accessible only from the north-west. Veii was apparently the largest city of the Etruscan twelve-city league, with an extensive territory and control of the River Tiber to the south. Excavations at Veii began in the 18th century, and the site has now been systematically explored. The earliest, small settlements on the site were Early Iron Age, and these villages later combined to form a substantial centre. The necropolises contain chamber tombs, mostly for cremation burials, but, as elsewhere in Etruria, inhumation became more common in the orientalizing period and rock-cut tombs under large tumuli were constructed. The Tomb of the Ducks (*c.* 675–*c.* 650 BC) contains probably the oldest known Etruscan wall painting, and the Campana Tomb (*c.* 600 BC) also predates any of the painted tombs at TARQUINIA. Dating from the 6th century BC there are remains of city walls (11 km in circuit) and several temple complexes. Finds from the small temple in the Piazza d'Armi include terracotta plaques from a relief frieze depicting a military parade (*c.* 600–*c.* 550 BC). The Portonaccio Temple, just south of the city, is famous for its Archaic terracotta acroterial sculptures representing Apollo and other divine figures (all *c.* 515–*c.* 490 BC; Rome, Villa Giulia; see fig.). These are among the most impressive works of Archaic Etruscan art, and may have composed a narrative group ranged along the roof-ridge of the temple. Some scholars consider the Portonaccio Group to be the work of the Veientine sculptor Vulca, mentioned in later literary sources. He may also have produced work for the Capitoline Temple at Rome (Pliny: *Natural History* XXXV.157) and is notable as the only important Etruscan artist whose name survives.

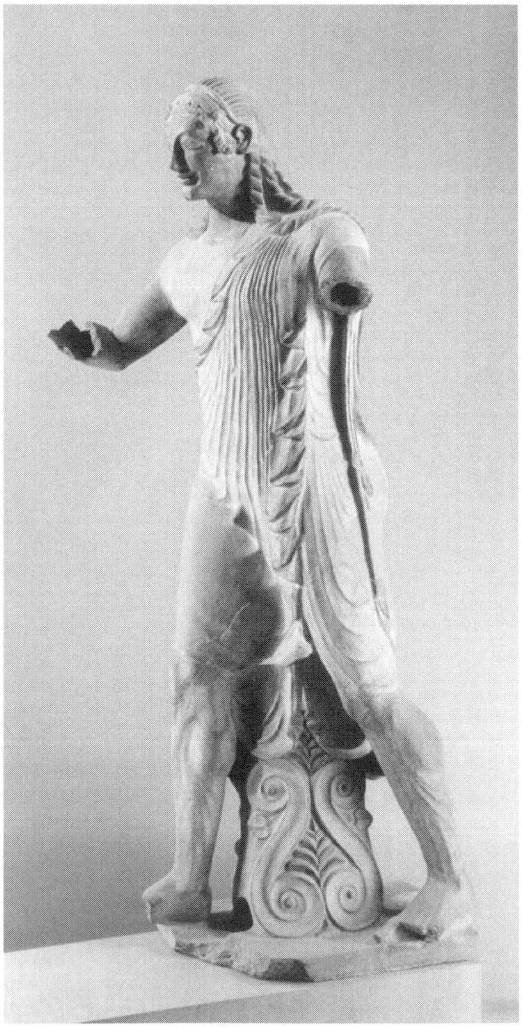

Veii, terracotta statue of *Apollo*, from the Portanaccio Temple, *c.* 515–*c.* 490 BC (Rome, Museo Nazionale di Villa Giulia e Soprintendenza alle Antichità per l'Etruria Meridionale)

There are relatively few archaeological remains of 5th-century BC date, but these may include a megaron-type house on the north side of the city. This has walls of tufa ashlar and a door with tapering jambs resembling Etruscan tomb doors. The late 5th-century BC Malavolta Head (Rome, Villa Giulia) formed part of a votive statue of a young man in the Sanctuary of Minerva and is another fine example of Veientine terracotta sculpture. During much of the 5th century BC Veii was engaged in conflict with Rome, relating to control of the River Tiber, and in 396 BC Roman forces under the dictator Furius Camillus conquered the city. Veii was destroyed and the cult of Uni (Juno) transferred to Rome. Julius Caesar later established a colony on the site, and, under Augustus, Veii became a *municipium* (free town) in 1 BC. Remains of Imperial date suggest that it was a town of respectable size, but Roman Veii did not flourish and its name continued to be used by Roman writers as a byword for decay and ruin.

J. B. Ward-Perkins: 'Veii: The Historical Topography of the Ancient City', *Pap. Brit. Sch. Rome*, xvi (1961), pp. 1–17

A. Kahane, L. M. Threipland and J. B. Ward-Perkins: 'The Ager Veientanus, North and East of Veii', *Pap. Brit. Sch. Rome*, xxiii (1968), pp. 1–28

A. Carbonara with G. Messineo and A. Pellegrino ed. *La necropoli etrusca di Volusia* (Rome, 1996)

G. Bartoloni, ed. *Le necropoli arcaiche di Veio: Giornata di studio in memoria di Massimo Pallottino* (Rome, 1997)

G. Colonna, ed. *Il santuario di Portonaccio a Veio* (Rome, 1999)

W. Regter: *Imitation and Creation: Development of Early Bucchero Design at Cerveteri in the Seventh Century BC* (Amsterdam, 2003)

Velathri [Lat. Volaterrae; now Volterra]. Etruscan city in Tuscany, *c.* 55 km south-west of Florence and *c.* 28 km east of the Tyrrhenian port of Vada. It is situated on a steep outcrop overlooking the valleys of the rivers Era and Cècina and strategically controlling the north-south routes of the Val d'Elsa. A centre of VILLANOVAN culture in the 9th–7th centuries BC, it became one of the most powerful Etruscan principalities in the 7th century BC.

Velathri was the northernmost city of the Etruscan twelve-city league; it occupied the site of modern Volterra but at its height was far more extensive. Velathri grew from Villanovan settlements, although evidence is sparse before the 7th century BC, and it did not begin to emerge as an important city until the second half of the 6th century BC. This phase was completed by the construction of city walls, enclosing an area of *c.* 10 ha, during the 5th century BC. Finds of architectural terracottas from large temples (Volterra, Mus. Etrus. Guaranacci) also date from the 5th century BC. The city's greatest period of development, however, occurred between the 4th and 2nd centuries BC, when it came to dominate an extensive territory in what is now central Tuscany. Red-figure pottery from Velathri was widely distributed

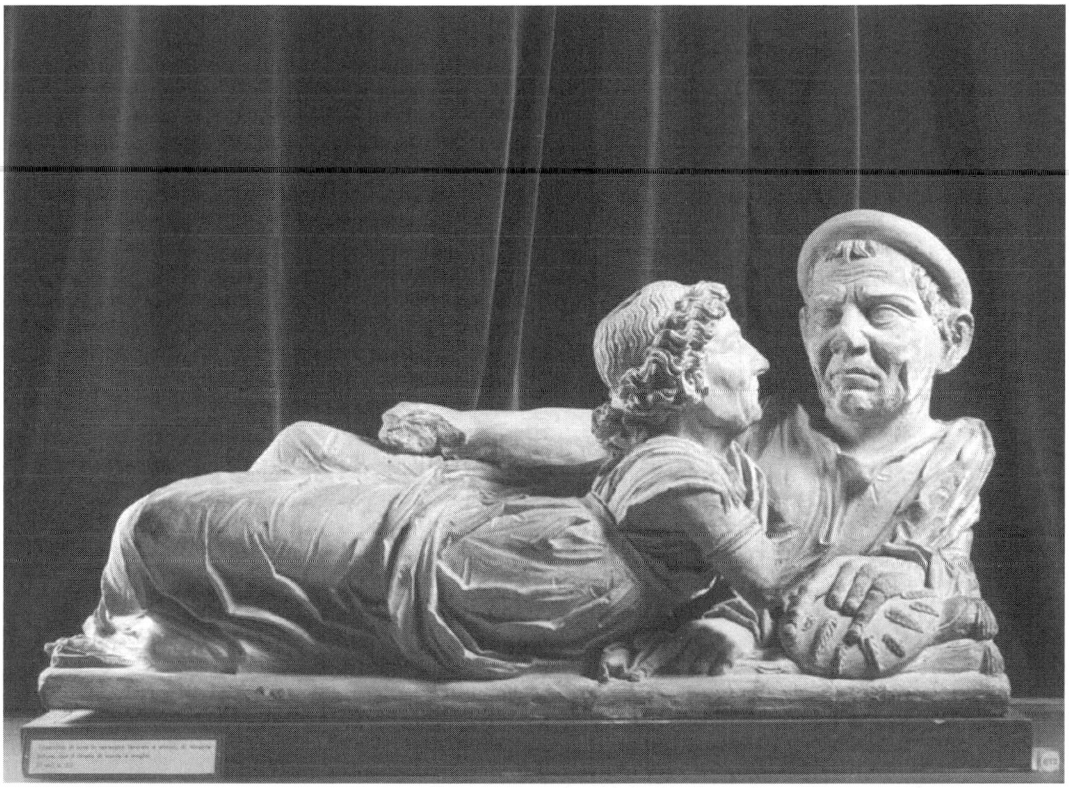

1. Velathri , terracotta urn with figures of a married couple (Volterra, Museo Etrusco Guarnacci)

in Italy, and production of alabaster funerary urns began in the mid-3rd century BC. The latter are the most characteristic artefacts from Hellenistic Velathri and reflect the practice of replacing the sarcophagi and stone beds of earlier Etruscan rock-cut tombs with numerous ash urns (see fig. 1) ranged around a single chamber (e.g. the Inghirami Tomb, early 2nd century BC; reconstructed in Florence, Mus. Archeol.). The prosperity of Hellenistic Velathri is evinced by the extended city walls (*c.* 7 km in length and enclosing 116 ha) and new gates (see fig. 2), and the issues of coinage by the city mint. Monumental buildings were constructed on the acropolis, and the necropoleis contain large family tombs from this period.

The decline of the ancient city begins to be evident from the second half of the 2nd century BC. Volaterrae sided with the consul Gaius Marius (*c.* 157–86 BC) in the Civil War that broke out in 102 BC and was besieged for two years (82–80 BC), finally capitulating to Sulla (*c.* 138–78 BC) and losing Roman citizenship. The aristocracy, however, remained sufficiently prosperous to erect several large public monuments during the 1st century BC, including the theatre dedicated by Cecina Severus, of which parts of the *cavea* and *scena* remain. From this time onwards the decline of the ancient city was gradual but continuous, counteracted only by the presence of a flourishing Christian community.

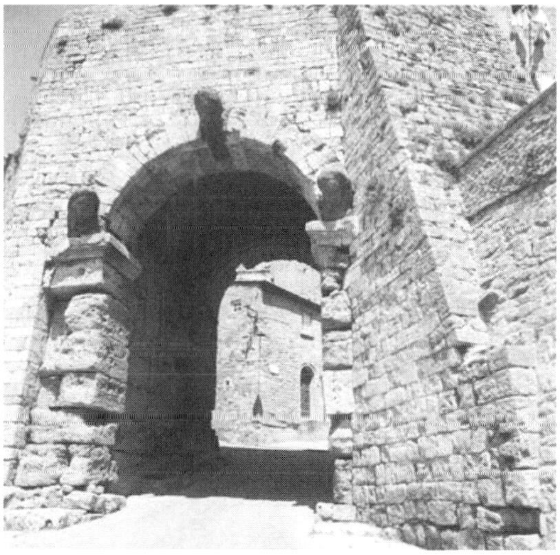

2. Velathri, city gate, 3rd–2nd century BC

E. Fiumi: 'Volterra', *Not. Scavi Ant.* (1972), pp. 52–136

M. Cristofani: 'Volterra', *Not. Scavi Ant.* (1973) [suppl. 1]

E. Fiumi: *Volterra etrusca e romana* (Pisa, 1976)

R. Ostman: *The City and Complexity: Volterra, Italy: Pottery Production during the Hellenistic Etruscan Period and the Late Roman to Late Antique Period* (Oxford, 2004)

Velc. *See* VULCI.

Velzna. *See* VOLSINII VETERES.

Ventia. *See* VEII.

Venus de' Medici. Celebrated work of antique sculpture. It depicts a nude Venus, her head turned to the left, her hands covering her breasts and genitals (h. 1.53 m; Florence, Uffizi; see fig.), and is perhaps the work of an Athenian follower of Praxiteles of the 1st century BC, probably based on a bronze original derived from the *Aphrodite of Knidos*. On the base is an inscription attributing it to Kleomenes the Athenian. The inscription is certainly spurious but, as Ennio Quirino Visconti noted, it may have been copied from an original signature. The statue, which was in the Villa Medici in Rome perhaps from the end of the 16th century, is documented there with certainty in 1638 by the three plates that François Perrier (*c.* 1594–1649) devoted to it in his survey of the most beautiful statues of Rome (*Segmenta nobilium signorum et statuarum*). In 1677 Pope Innocent XI approved its transfer to Florence, where the following year it was exhibited in the Tribune of the Uffizi. In 1800 it was loaded on a ship for Palermo in an attempt to save it from the French, but after long diplomatic negotiations they managed to obtain it, and in 1803 the *Venus* was in Paris. It was returned in 1815 and from the following year was again displayed in the Tribune. The statue has been restored in numerous places. When it arrived in Florence from Rome it was given arms made by the sculptor Ercole Ferrata (1610–86). The *Venus de' Medici* was the object of great admiration, which perhaps reached its peak during the struggle between the Florentines and the French. Luca Giordano (1634–1705) had a celebrated passion for the statue, which he copied from every angle. Jonathan Richardson was famous for standing before it for ten hours without pause, and the English writer Joseph Spence visited it almost a hundred times. It was replicated in bronze for Charles I, King of England (*reg* 1625–49), and for the Duke of Marlborough. Numerous plaster casts and marble copies were made; the lead copies made in the 18th century for English gardens are famous.

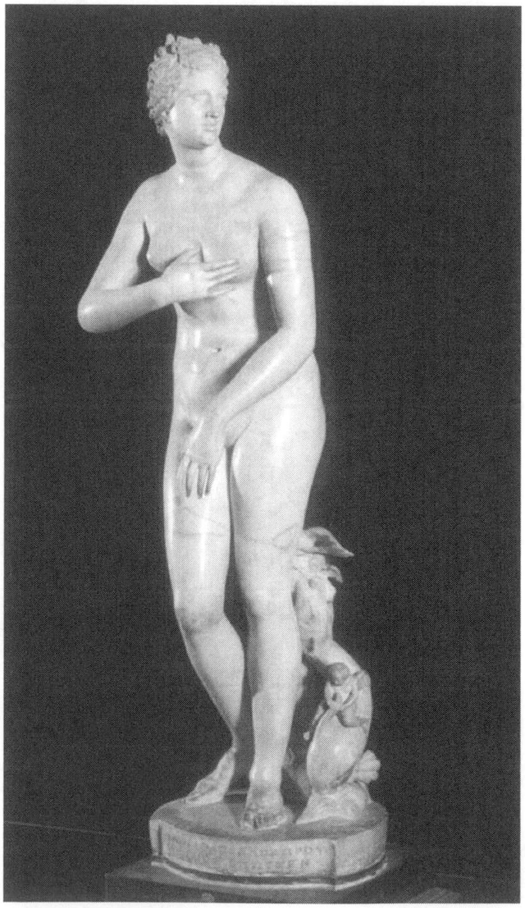

Venus de' Medici, marble, h. 1.53m, ?1st century BC (Florence, Galleria degli Uffizi)

G. A. Mansuelli: *Le sculture* (1958), i of *Galleria degli Uffizi*, 4 vols (Rome, 1958–61), pp. 71–3

M. Robertson: *A History of Greek Art* (Cambridge, 1975), p. 549

F. Haskell and N. Penny: *Taste and the Antique: The Lure of Classical Sculpture, 1500–1900* (New Haven and London, 1981), pp. 325–8

Venus de Milo. Marble statue of a semi-nude Venus (h. 2.04 m; Paris, Louvre; see fig.). Its twisting composition is probably the work of the Greek artist Alexandros of Antioch on the Maeander, active in the 2nd century BC, who in turn was inspired by a pre-Hellenistic model. The artist's name was incised on a block of stone that was found together with the *Venus* but later lost. A few scholars in the past doubted the connection between the block and the statue and hence the attribution of the work to Alexandros. Some attributed the work to Praxiteles, and the loss of the inscribed block may have been engineered to support this theory. The statue was found in 1820 by a peasant on the island of Melos. When found it was in two pieces, along with other fragments. It was bought by the Marquis de Rivière, who donated it to Louis XVIII, king of France. The latter in turn donated it to the Musée du Louvre, where the sculpture has been on display since 1821. The *Venus* was repaired in haste, evidently in order to exhibit it quickly, so that in 1875 the work had to be done again. It has never been fully restored, perhaps because of the disparity of opinions regarding its original state. Some scholars thought it should be identified as a victorious Venus, in which case she would hold the apple of Paris in her hand. Others favoured the hypothesis that the statue was a sort of guardian divinity of the island, who would also be holding a fruit, perhaps an apple, as her attribute. Others proposed that she had held a shield or a lyre, or saw her as part of a group originally including Mars.

W. Furtwängler: *Masterpieces of Greek Sculpture* (London, 1895), pp. 367–401

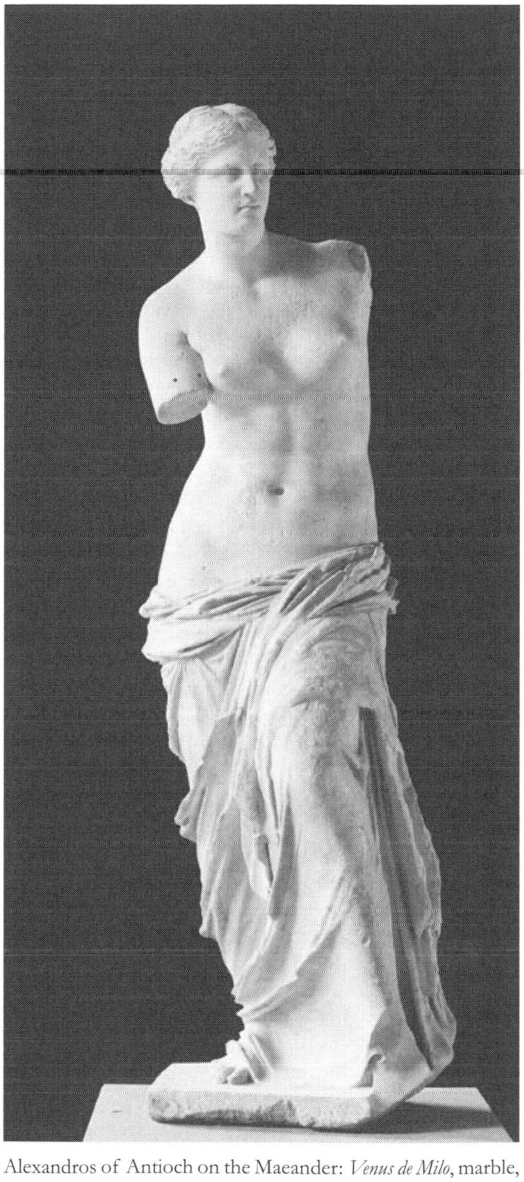

Alexandros of Antioch on the Maeander: *Venus de Milo*, marble, h. 2.04 m, *c.* 150–*c.* 120 BC (Paris, Musée du Louvre)

M. Robertson: *A History of Greek Art* (Cambridge, 1975), pp. 553–4

F. Haskell and N. Penny: *Taste and the Antique: The Lure of Classical Sculpture, 1500–1900* (New Haven and London, 1981), pp. 328–30

G. Curtis: *Disarmed: The Story of the Venus de Milo* (New York, 2005)

Vergina. *See* AIGAI (ii).

Verona. Italian city in the Veneto on the River Adige *c.* 60 km west of Venice. It has substantial Roman remains. The pre-Roman settlement, at a fording point

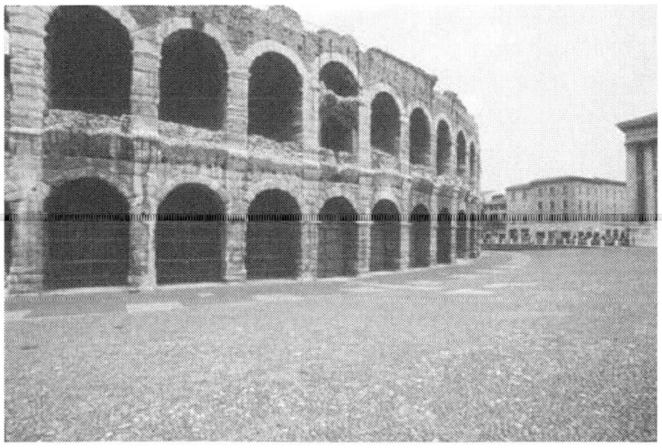

Verona, amphitheatre, 3rd century AD

on the Adige, is thought to have been situated mainly on the hill of S Pietro on the left bank of the river. The Ponte Pietra (destr. 1945; rebuilt 1957–9), which is not aligned with the Roman city layout, presumably predates the Roman settlement, although it was apparently repaired in Roman and medieval times.

The Roman city was founded on the right bank of the river in the mid-1st century BC and had reached the height of its development by *c.* AD 265. Enclosed within a loop of the Adige at the foot of the hill, it was laid out on the standard grid plan, protected to the south by a brick wall divided into two sections that met at an obtuse angle. There were two further bridges, and the Forum lay on the site of the present Piazza Erbe. Of the city gates, the only surviving trace from the Republican period is a brick and tufa facing in the ruins of the Porta Leoni, originally a square building flanked by two 16-sided towers. White stone blocks indicate later alterations to this gate. At the Porta dei Borsari, built in the 1st century AD, the whole external façade survives, incorporating an inscription recording the rebuilding of the walls in AD 265. The twin entrances with triangular pediments are surmounted by a two-storey arcaded wall, articulated with aedicules and spiral-fluted Corinthian half-columns.

The Roman theatre was built around the end of the 1st century BC (rest. 1830–1914) on the left bank of the Adige. The *cavea* was built into the slope of the hill, with, above, a series of terraces leading to a temple (destr.) on the hilltop. On the other side of the city was the other great venue for spectacles, the Amphitheatre, or Arena, which can be dated to the 3rd decade AD (restored many times since the Middle Ages). The third largest antique amphitheatre in Italy, it is surrounded by an almost intact two-tier range of superimposed arches (see fig.). Four bays of the original outer perimeter wall survive. The arena floor is large (73×44 m) and, together with the cavea, provides seating for over 20,000 spectators. It now hosts the annual outdoor opera season.

Verulamium [now St Albans]. Roman city on the River Ver in Hertfordshire, successor to a native

British settlement on the nearby hill of Prae Wood at the point where Watling Street, the Roman road north-west from London, crossed the River Ver (see fig. a). It was one of the earliest Romano-British towns to develop; Tacitus described it as a 'municipium' (*Annals* xiv.33), which implies chartered status, at the time of its destruction during the rebellion (AD 61) of Boudicca, queen of the Iceni. Excavation has shown that occupation continued well into the 5th century AD. The population subsequently shifted from the valley north-east to the present extra-mural hill-top site centred on the shrine of St Alban (*d c.* AD 209) in what was probably a Roman cemetery. Much of Verulamium, although robbed of stone, was therefore undamaged by medieval and later occupation. In the 1930s the theatre (b), adjacent temple (c), part of the forum (d) and a large residential area were excavated, and a graphic sequence of growth and decline, which greatly influenced Romano-British studies for a generation, was formulated (Wheeler and Wheeler). This interpretation, however, was much revised following excavations (1955–61) of another large residential area in the forum and on the defences (Frere).

The forum differs from the usual Romano-British type—as at CALLEVA ATREBATUM (now Silchester)—in having entrances on an axis parallel with the basilica. The latter (f), the largest in Britain apart from that in Londinium (London), was dedicated in AD 79. In the middle of the side of the forum opposite the basilica, a projecting rectangular building was probably the curia. Two further buildings, added one to each side of it after a devastating mid-2nd-century fire, are thought to have been temples.

The theatre was of north Gaulish type, combining the structural layout and perhaps the functions of the conventional Roman theatre and amphitheatre in having a broad oval arena with a stage building along one side, a simplified version of the Mediterranean stage *scaenae frons* with its proscenium of four Corinthian columns. The theatre was built after the mid-2nd-century fire and modified several times, most importantly in the early 4th century. The seating, supported on an earth bank, was then extended, almost doubling the capacity to about 6000 spectators. Its function was probably not merely entertainment but connected with celebrations at the Romano-Celtic temple immediately behind it.

Other public structures included three triumphal or commemorative arches, and another temple in a trapezoidal precinct at a road junction with Watling

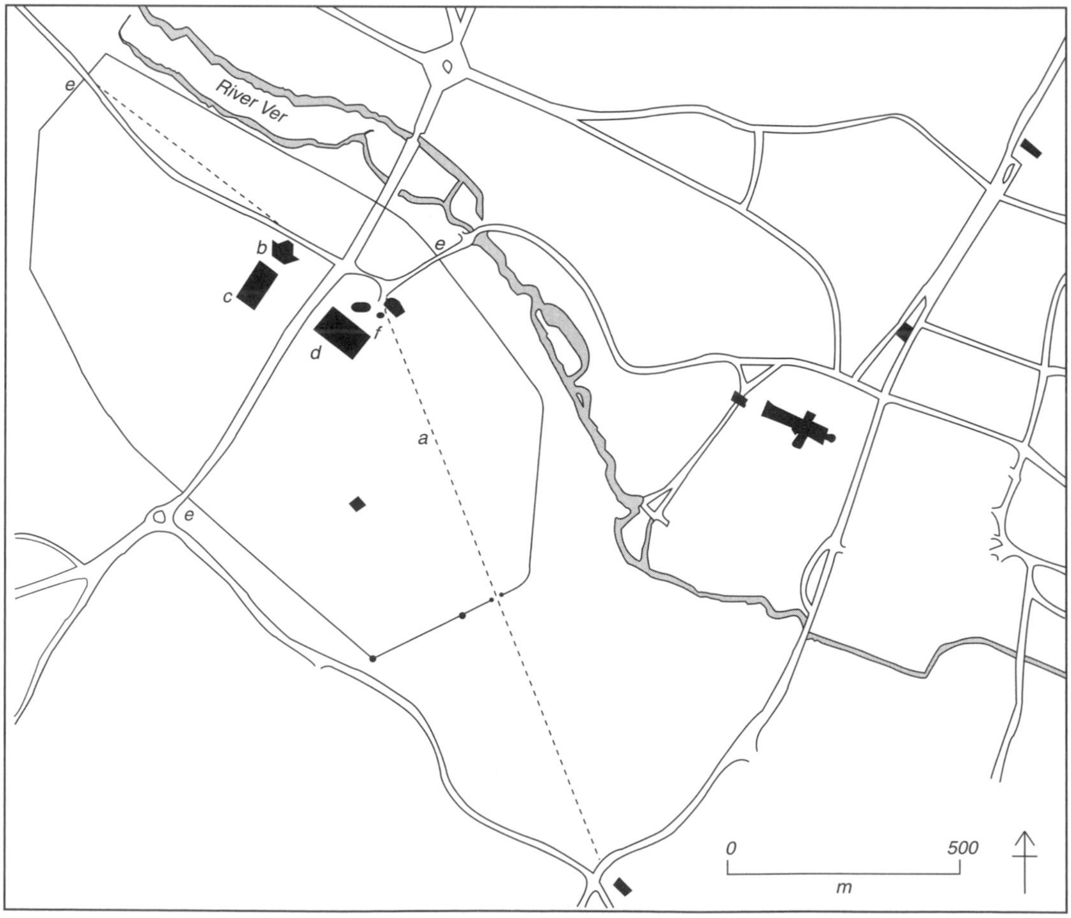

Verulamium, plan: (a) Watling Street; (b) theatre; (c) temple; (d) forum; (e) gates; (f) basilica (approx. position)

Street. The early town houses were modest, but after initial investment in public building, domestic luxury increased; 2nd- and early 3rd-century houses had mosaic floors, heated rooms and painted plaster walls and ceilings, which have been reconstructed (St Albans, Verulamium Mus.). Even in the 4th century new courtyard houses with over 30 ground-floor rooms were being built.

Verulamium's 1st-century AD earthwork defences were replaced in the late 2nd century by a new earth bank and ditch enclosing a larger area, and masonry gates with rounded gate-towers (e). A wall of mortared flint with tile courses was built in the 3rd century and inserted in front of the earth rampart except for the south-west salient, where the defended area was reduced.

R. E. M. Wheeler and T. V. Wheeler: *Verulamium: A Belgic and Two Roman Cities*, Soc. Antiqua. London Res. Rep., xi (Oxford, 1936)

S. S. Frere: *Verulamium Excavations*, Soc. Antiqua. London Res. Rep., xxviii and xli (Oxford and London, 1972–83)

I. E. Anthony: *The Roman City of Verulamium: Official Guide* (St Albans, 1983)

S. Frere and D. Charlesworth: *Verulamium Excavations* (Oxford, 1984)

D. S. Neal, A. Wardle and J. Hunn: *Excavation of the Iron Age, Roman, and Medieval Settlement at Gorhambury, St Albans* (London, 1990)

R. Niblett: *The Excavation of a Ceremonial Site at Folly Lane, Verulamium* (London, 1999)

M. Henig and P. Lindley: *Alban and St Albans: Roman and Medieval Architecture, Art and Archaeology* (Leeds, 2001)

R. Niblett: *Verulamium: The Roman City of St Albans* (Stroud, 2001)

K. K. Kenyon and S. Frere: *The Roman Theatre of Verulamium (St Albans): Official Guide* (Derby, 2002)

Vespasian [Titus Flavius Vespasianus], Emperor (*b* Reate [now Rieti], 17 Nov AD 9; *reg* AD 69–79; *d* Cutilia, 4 June AD 79). Roman ruler and patron. By the death of Nero (AD 68) he had largely subdued Judaea; he was acclaimed emperor by the troops in the civil war that followed. As Suetonius aptly expressed it (*Vespasian* viii), Vespasian wished not only to give stability to the state but also to embellish it. That aim was fully expressed in the grandiose building programme that he carried out, mainly in Rome. He enlarged the enclosure of the *pomerium* (city precinct) and made it uniform with that of the new customs barrier; he straightened the course of the Tiber and repaired roads and aqueducts; he rebuilt the Temple of the Deified Claudius (after AD 70), which had been destroyed by Nero, and that of Jupiter Optimus Maximus on the Capitol (rededicated AD 75); and he restored the stage-building of the Theatre of Marcellus. Between AD 71 and 75 the splendid Templum Pacis (*see* ROME, §IV, 2) was built on the site of the old public market to commemorate the victory in Judaea. The temple was connected to the Imperial Fora, to which it formed an appendix on the south-east side, and was surrounded by a monumental porticoed square resembling a forum, although only at the end of the Empire was it called the Forum Pacis. In the early years of his reign Vespasian also began the construction of the Colosseum, a huge amphitheatre in the valley between the Palatine, Esquiline and Caelian hills that had formerly been the centre of Nero's Domus Aurea. While still unfinished—Vespasian may have been responsible only for the first two orders of arches—the Colosseum was given its first dedication by the emperor before his death. The building was completed by Titus (*reg* AD 79–81), who inaugurated it for the second time in AD 80, and later decorated under Domitian (*reg* AD 81–96).

P. H. von Blanckenhagen: *Flavische Architektur und ihre Dekoration: Untersucht am Nervaforum* (Berlin, 1940)

G. Cozzo: *Il Colosseo* (Rome, 1971)

Vetulonia [Etrus. Vetluna]. Site of an Etruscan city, now a village, on a hilltop *c.* 18 km north-west of Grosseto, Italy. In ancient times the city overlooked Lake Prilius, as did nearby Rusellae. There are few excavated remains: a main street *c.* 3 m wide, crossed obliquely by two smaller roads, has been uncovered. The buildings were small, crowded mud-brick or stone structures, as at Veii and San Giovenale. The city walls (?6th century BC) can be traced, as can the remains of a 3rd-century BC temple. Most information about ancient Vetulonia comes, however, from its necropolises. The Early Iron Age is characterized by cremation burials and repositories containing many imported artefacts. Indigenous metalwork and small-scale three-dimensional sculpture is represented in this and the

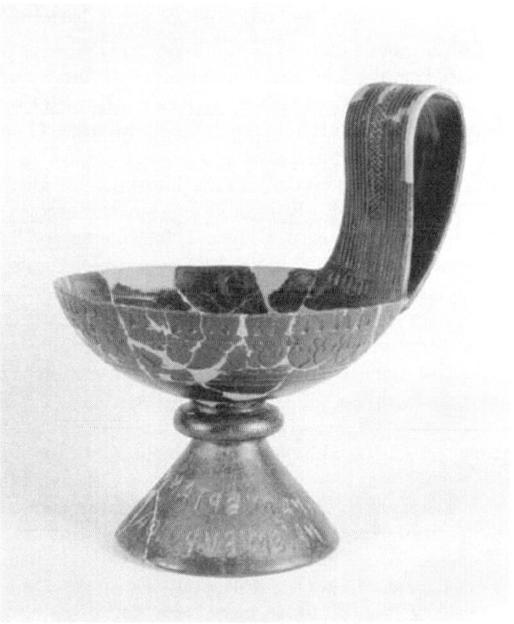

Vetulonia, kyathos, from the Tomb of the Leader (Volterra, Museo Etrusco Guarnacci)

following Orientalizing period by some fine bronze figurines, decorated vase stands and other objects (see fig.; *see also* METALWORK, §V, 2(i)). In the 7th century BC many circle-tombs were constructed: these have one or more trenches for inhumation enclosed by a circle of stone slabs (e.g. the Tomb of the Leader). From the circle-tombs have come rich finds of Oriental, Greek and Sardinian artefacts, as well as much native Etruscan work in gold and bronze. The finds of pottery are unexceptional by comparison. Towards the end of the 7th century BC these tombs were succeeded by monumental stone chamber tombs of corbelled construction. A circular tholos design with a central supporting pillar (e.g. the Pietrera Tomb; *c.* 650–*c.* 630 BC) was later replaced by tombs on a rectangular plan. All three types were surmounted by earthern tumuli. The sandstone sculpture from the Pietrera Tomb represents some of the earliest monumental sculpture discovered in Europe (*see* SCULPTURE, §V, 3). The sequence of burials at Vetulonia apparently ceased at some time during the 6th century BC, and it has been conjectured that the city was conquered or destroyed by Rusellae at this time. In Roman times it was absorbed into the tribal territory of Scaptia. Vetulonia is recorded as having assisted the Latins in overthrowing the Etruscan fifth king of Rome, Tarquinius Priscus (*reg* 616–579 BC), and may also have provided Rome with its insignia of the fasces: the axe is shown brandished by the warrior Avile Feluske on an Archaic Vetulonian stele.

A. Talocchini: 'La città e la necropoli di Vetulonia secondo i nuovi scavi, 1959–1962', *Stud. Etrus.*, xxxi (1963), pp. 435–58

G. Camporeale: *I commerci di Vetulonia in età orientalizzante* (Florence, 1969)

Vienna [now Vienne]. Roman town in Isère, France, situated on the left bank of the River Rhône, 28 km south of Lugdunum (Lyon). Before the Roman Conquest it was the chief town of the Allobroges, a Gallic tribe, but it first prospered as a *colonia* founded by Julius Caesar in the 1st century BC. The most impressive remains from Gallo-Roman Vienna are the Temple of Augustus and Livia, the Theatre, the odeion and the sites of Ste Colombe and St Romain-en-Gal, suburbs of modern Vienne on the right bank that provide evidence for its early commercial activities. Christianity was established in Vienna during the 2nd century, and in the 4th the town became the seat of an archbishopric that encompassed the entire province.

The Temple of Augustus and Livia (late 1st century BC; see fig.), dedicated originally to Rome and Augustus, is nearly intact, owing to its later adaptation as a church. Thoroughly Classical in appearance, it resembles the slightly earlier Temple of Venus Genetrix in the Forum of Caesar in Rome in being peripteral *sine postico* (i.e. with columns on three sides only), with six columns on the front, and six columns and two pilasters engaged to short spur walls along the sides. The porch is unusually deep. The main

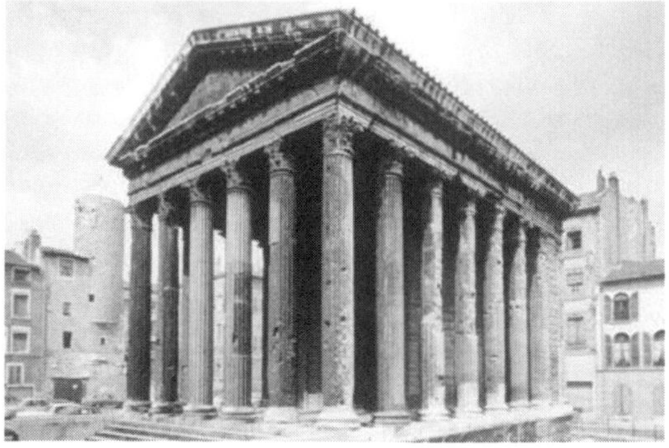

Vienna (Vienne), Temple of Augustus and Livia, late 1st century BC

theatre was also built during the period (30 BC–AD 14) and is the second largest in Gaul (that at Autun is the largest). The *cavea* (auditorium) is partly terraced into the hillside, partly vaulted, and still retains the portico round the top, with a small temple in the middle, as in the Theatre of Pompey in Rome (1st century BC). The lowest four of the forty-six tiers of seats were of white marble, and the *orchestra* had pink and yellow marble paving. The *scaenae frons* is an early example of the arrangement standard in the western provinces, of a central door projecting from a curved exedra, and doors to each side set in rectangular niches (*see* THEATRE). The facing wall of the stage had alternating curved and rectangular niches and a frieze (*in situ*; partly reconstructed) showing Dionysus and various animals.

In Hadrian's reign (AD 117–38) an odeion was built against the opposite hillside to the south, seating about 3000 spectators. The structure is poorly preserved, but remains of marble flooring and sculpture have been found. Another theatre (mid-1st century AD) was associated with a temple (first half of 1st century AD; later modified) identified from sculpture and inscriptions as that of Cybele. Adjoining underground rooms with pools and passageways presumably served for cult ritual. Near the river, 'L'Aiguille', a stone pyramid on a four-way arch, 23.35 m high, once stood on the turning-point in the circus. On the right bank of the river at St Romain-en-Gal, excavations are revealing a residential quarter with at least 12 peristyle houses, mainly dating from the 2nd century AD.

J. Formigé: *Le Théâtre romain de Vienne* (Vienne, 1950)

A. Pelletier: *Vienne antique* (Roanne, 1982)

E. de V. de Lavergne: *Le sanctuaire gallo-romain de Mazamas à Saint-Léomer (Vienne)* (Paris, 1999)

Villa. Type of house, originally built as a country retreat for a wealthy patron; the term later applied also to smaller detached suburban or urban houses in garden settings. In ancient Rome the Latin word *villa* referred to a house in the country as opposed to a town house (*aedes*); the term *villa suburbana* was commonly applied to a house close to but outside a town. Some Roman villas were luxury retreats but these were not typical; the great majority were farms (*villae rusticae*) or the centres of landed estates, where the residence was known as a *villa urbana*, and even the most palatial examples were likely to have an agricultural base.

Villas appeared in Italy from the 2nd century BC and were the product of increasing wealth as a result of Rome's recently acquired empire. In Italy the term villa implied a dwelling with at least a minimum level of comfort—a house rather than a hut—and in archaeological terms it is applied to an establishment that was an integral part of the social and economic organization of the Roman world. Ownership of land was a measure of social standing and even a determinant of political power, and the villa, along with the estate it controlled, was as much a status symbol as a financial investment. A villa owner might have been a country gentleman or a simple farmer, but he might also have been active in the political and social life of his local town, or even of Rome itself. His villa, whether his primary residence or a refuge from more public activities, would have been seen not only as a facility on which wealth could be spent but as itself a source of wealth through the working of its lands.

With the expansion of the Empire, the villa began to appear in the provinces and became one of the primary indicators of romanization, along with Roman dress and the Latin language. Like other such indicators, it was not so much imposed as eagerly adopted, being a symbol of status for the prosperous Gaulish, African and British, as it had earlier been for Italians. The frequency with which villas succeeded pre-Roman dwellings on the same sites, for example Mayen, Germany, and Lockleys, Herts, England, is a clear indication that romanized natives rather than Roman immigrants, even in the earliest stages, were mainly responsible for their construction. Even the large villas in such an area as the Somme basin of northern France appeared so early and are so obviously related to pre-Roman settlement types that they too must be seen as in this sense 'native' rather than 'Roman'. Thus, in the provinces, as in Italy, the 'origin' of the villa is to be seen primarily in economic, and only secondarily in cultural, terms: it arose at a point when the economy of a region and of individuals within it enabled it to do so. It is 'Roman' in the sense that the economic conditions that brought it into existence were the result of Roman rule, and it was defined by these conditions as much as by cultural pressures and influences. Consequently, the adoption of the villa as a building type did not everywhere involve the wholesale adoption of Italian style and design. The characteristic Italian house, looking inwards to a colonnaded courtyard, although relatively common in Spain or southern France, gave way increasingly to the equally characteristic 'corridor' house of northern regions, such as Britain, Belgium and the Rhineland. Although within an agricultural economy the role of the villa was also most commonly agricultural, this did not by any means preclude comfort and, in many cases, luxury on a lavish scale.

1. History and development. 2. Decoration. 3. Theory and archaeology.

1. History and development. Of the early Roman villas in Italy, that of San Rocco at Francolise, Campania, is a typical example. Begun *c.* 100–90 BC as a modest house with adjoining farm buildings, it was remodelled *c.* 50 BC and again *c.* 30 BC, by which time it had become an impressive residence (see fig.). Its numerous rooms, coordinated with each other and with those of earlier phases, were grouped around a central peristyle, and most were provided with mosaic pavements. Vitruvian principles of symmetry are evident in its overall design, and attention was given to its setting within the landscape and to its appearance when approached from various directions. Adjoining it, although clearly distinguished from it, was the working farm (in Vitruvian terms the *villa rustica* (b) as opposed to the *villa urbana* (a)), which included water cisterns (c), a tile kiln and olive-press, and which, like the residence, was carefully planned and constructed. Such a villa might have been owned by a wealthy farming family, the head of which perhaps had business interests or local government duties in the nearby town; alternatively, it might have served as a country retreat and source of income for someone whose primary concerns were in business or politics. Examples of the latter are common in the writings of Cicero and Pliny the younger: at Laurentum, near Ostia, was a house to which Pliny devoted an entire (and celebrated) letter (*Letters* II.17). Laurentum was more splendid than San Rocco and was not untypical of such houses: those along the

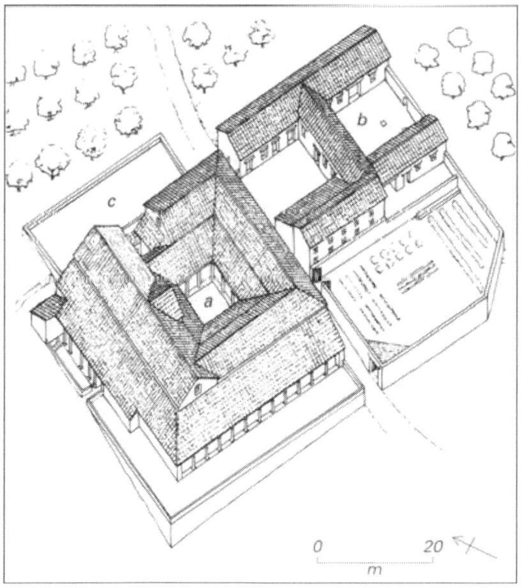

San Rocco Villa, Francolise, Campania, after final remodelling *c.* 30 BC; axonometric reconstruction drawing showing (a) *villa urbana*, (b) *villa rustica*, (c) water tank

coast, particularly around the Bay of Naples, were seized on by moralists and satirists as examples of unnecessary extravagance. What is striking, however, about Pliny's references to his many properties (and this is true also of Cicero) is that he rarely lost sight of their working aspects. Houses built solely for pleasure were the exception rather than the norm.

In the provinces of the Roman Empire the villa usually appeared within a generation or so of the imposition of Roman rule, as a product of the Roman Peace. It was partly introduced by expatriate Italians but was more commonly adopted by the local wealthy, eager to adopt the trappings (and benefits) of a romanized lifestyle. Partly for this reason and partly for reasons of climate or varying social traditions, the villa evolved differently from region to region; an examination of the many examples where reasonably complete plans are available shows that their variety and diversity are as striking as any common pattern. In size alone they range from what were little more than cottages to some that are more accurately described as palaces, for example Chiragan in south-west France, which had a residential block covering more than 2.5 ha. A number of standard types within a broadly evolving framework can nevertheless be identified, if only as a helpful and convenient means of classification and comparison with the many examples that must be regarded as exceptional.

The basic type of Roman villa, known in Britain as the 'corridor' villa and in continental Europe (more accurately) as the *Portikusvilla* or villa *à galerie-façade*, consisted of a range of rooms fronted by a portico or verandah (not a corridor) with a lean-to roof, at each end of which were symmetrical wing rooms (e.g. Mayen, Germany, and Gadebridge Park, Herts, England). This plan was developed by elongation, producing an impressive façade (e.g. Hosté, Belgium); by adding a portico at both front and rear (e.g. Hambleden, Bucks, England); or by extending the wing rooms into further ranges of rooms (e.g. Witcombe, Glos, England, and Weitersbach, Germany). This last development led logically to the full 'courtyard' villa (e.g. North Leigh, Oxon, England), and to the double courtyards common in continental Europe (e.g. Estrées-sur-Noye, France) and occurring also in Britain (e.g. Bignor, W. Sussex). These last examples are in some respects similar to San Rocco, comprising a *villa urbana* and *villa rustica*, but determined by a different evolutionary process. Not all sites went through all or part of this sequence of development, although in many cases where the plan seems initially to fall outside the sequence altogether, it is possible, by separating the building phases, to discover one or more of the familiar types. Sometimes, however, other more significant features are discovered. The early phases of the Mayen villa retained the large, central, communal room represented by the original hut, and the same is true of numerous sites both in Europe and in Britain. The persistence of pre-Roman social patterns thus implied is also suggested by other features, perhaps even by ground-plans, which occasionally suggest occupancy by extended rather than nuclear families. The extent to which, in the provinces, the villa was wholly 'Roman' has already been considered above; further detailed study of the arrangement of rooms at individual sites may reveal how much, or how little, is implied by the adoption of such Roman amenities as hypocausts, mosaic pavements and baths.

The history of Roman villas is that of the Empire itself, in the sense that they begin and end with it and reflect its rises and falls in prosperity. Houses are known to have been built or extended during periods of economic decline, however, or abandoned at times of prosperity, for reasons that are particular and unconnected with national or regional developments. Nevertheless, the broad patterns are clear. In terms of numbers, wealth and quality of design and construction, the villa reached a peak in the Severan and Antonine periods of the late 2nd century AD. In the 3rd century it fell prey to the common pressures of economic decline and barbarian invasions, and in the 4th century it was part of the partial recovery achieved under Diocletian and Constantine the Great. In some regions, notably Britain, the recovery led to even greater prosperity than before, resulting not only in a resurgence of villas, with major sites appearing for the first time, but in a decisive shift in prosperity towards the West and away from the original area of settlement. Elsewhere, however, villas were less well built and maintained than they had been at the height of the Empire and were less ostentatious. During the collapse of the Empire in the late 4th century AD and the early 5th, the majority were destroyed or abandoned, although some of the larger ones, for example that of Sidonius Apollinaris at Avitacum, near Clermont Ferrand, France, were able to survive under Gothic rule. By then, however, there were signs that their character was changing: large reception areas suggest a more public role than earlier, some were at least partially fortified, and some certainly were the property of Goths or Burgundians. The term villa, as initially defined, was by this time becoming less appropriate.

See also ARCHITECTURE, §VI, 1(i)(c).

2. DECORATION. Although rural in location and function, in residential terms the villa tended to duplicate the amenities and follow the fashions of town houses. The use of the term *villa urbana* to denote the residential as distinct from the working part of the establishment is itself an indication that it was seen as a little bit of the town in the country. Bath suites and central heating were common to both, as were mosaic pavements, painted interior walls and ornamental gardens. The use of particular architectural features and ornamental motifs was concurrent in both the town and country, and there is no evidence that in the latter they were stylistically inferior, indicating the homogeneous nature of Roman society and its economy.

In terms of decoration, MOSAICS provide the most distinctive illustration of a villa's internal appearance, as well as being a feature most likely to have survived intact. Although no figures survive to indicate their relative cost, they certainly represented a major expense and were thus indications of status as well as expressions of confidence. Their designs, whether mythical, religious or genre, were chosen with care and reveal the beliefs and attitudes of their owners. The better-quality examples are the work of skilled craftsmen, and studies in Britain, France and North Africa have gone some way towards identifying the products, if not of individuals, at least of workshops, situated presumably in the towns, their workers sent out on a journeyman basis as required. As well as such standard designs as the Orpheus mosaics favoured by the 'Corinian school' around Cirencester, Glos, England, there are recurring ornamental motifs, which suggest the use (and perhaps the exchange) of pattern books. There is also evidence of more local, amateur work, for example the pavements at Rudston, Yorks, England.

Similar to mosaic in technique and overall effect was *opus sectile*, the use of thin slabs of marble of different kinds, laid like tiles to form a decorative pattern for floors or, more frequently, walls. Examples of this work are known from houses of the wealthy in POMPEII and OSTIA, although at sites outside Italy, where buildings have tended to survive, at best, only at ground-level, remains are limited to scattered fragments. The effect, presumably, was primarily one of pattern and colour, the aim perhaps being to provide a suitable background against which to set off furniture or sculpture and to indicate, through the variety and widespread origins of the materials, something of the owner's wealth and standing.

A more common form of decoration, and certainly one more readily available, was painted plaster. The most complete examples are from town houses in Italy (e.g. the House of the Vettii and the Villa of the Mysteries, both at Pompeii), where it is possible to identify and date a whole series of styles and fashions; elsewhere it is a matter of piecing together small and badly damaged pieces. Nevertheless, some remarkable reconstructions have been achieved, and, for the western provinces of the Empire at least, the broad outlines of technique, design and dating are reasonably well established. Walls were prepared by applying layers of plaster, finishing with a fine skin on which the ground colours were painted while it was still wet. More detailed decoration, if required, was applied later, the colours being mixed with gum or another binding agent. A common practice was to divide the walls into a series of panels at eye-level and to use these as the setting for the main designs. Below them, to a height of up to a metre, was a kind of dado running round the room, decorated either with simple geometric designs or with an overall pattern; this was often flecked or mottled to imitate marble. The main panels sometimes bore simple geometric or curvilinear motifs, but they could also include leaf designs or simple patterns of flowers, birds or fishes. Human figures were less common but are found at various sites in Britain and Europe, usually within a simple rustic setting. The walls above the main panels were often left blank or painted in a single colour, but there is evidence to suggest decorated ceilings. There can be little doubt that painting in the Roman period achieved high levels of both technique and design.

Exterior decoration of Roman villas is something of which little is known, although it seems not to have been much used. Nevertheless, the external appearance of the villa was considered important: the symmetry that was so striking a feature of villa design is itself evidence of this, as is the care that was taken in the siting of houses to provide both a pleasing approach and agreeable vistas from inside. It is known from Roman writers (e.g. Varro, *De re rustica* IV.v.9) that gardens were an important part of the villa, as indeed were landscaped parks; the latter were influenced by Hellenistic *paradeisoi*, and the late Republican word for a gardener, *topiarius*, is also Greek. It is clear also from ground-plans that the provision of gardens was a major consideration. In the 'double courtyard' villa, for example, which was common in Gaul, Spain and elsewhere, the inner court adjacent to the main residential block lent itself to such treatment, and it is normally so depicted in reconstruction drawings. For the detailed design and layout of such gardens, however, surviving evidence relates to town houses, especially at Pompeii. Depictions of gardens in wall paintings suggest that they tended to be formal, with trees and flowers laid out in patterns around fountains or statues; this is further borne out by archaeological exploration, for example at the House of Diomedes or that of Loreius Tibertinus, Pompeii. The extent to which such evidence is relevant to country gardens, particularly outside Italy, is unclear. The garden at PLINY the younger's Laurentine villa contained shrubs and trees, including fruit trees, but no further detail is provided, except that it was a pleasant place in which to walk or work (*see* GARDEN). Outside Italy, information is limited to an occasional reference, indicating merely that a garden existed (e.g. Sidonius Apollinaris, *Epistles* II.2). For evidence relating to the villa garden in Britain, almost the only archaeological material is from FISHBOURNE Palace, W. Sussex, where indications again suggest a formal layout.

3. THEORY AND ARCHAEOLOGY. In early excavations of villas in the 18th century and much of the 19th, attention was directed primarily to their residential aspects and to such amenities as bath suites. What attracted the antiquary and the wider public were such indications of wealth and civilization as hypocausts and mosaics; villa sites were also seen as sources of coins, pottery and other objects for museums and private collections. Reports, when published, tended to concentrate on such findings almost exclusively, with detailed drawings and long descriptions of the most striking items. Plans were usually incomplete and were included, if at all, to indicate in which rooms particular discoveries were made. Much space was devoted to the identification of individual rooms and the day-to-day activities within them, which, like their inhabitants, were assumed to be 'Roman' rather than 'native'; the description by Pliny of Laurentum,

the technical works of Cato or Varro, or details of Pompeian town houses, were thus assumed to be wholly relevant as guides to the interpretation of a site. The 19th-century reports on Chedworth, Glos, England, are typical examples of such an approach.

In the 19th century, Roman villas tended to be studied individually; the task of the archaeologist was to describe the example, label it and, if possible, display it in the same way as he would an item in a museum. Similarities might be adduced, mosaics or hypocausts compared with others from the region or from Italy, and the dimensions of rooms recorded and similarly compared. As sites were explored in greater numbers and with greater thoroughness, attention gradually turned to the overall layout and design of villas, examples being classified according to type, consideration being given to materials and methods of construction, and attempts being made to visualize a site in its living state. Only in the early decades of the 20th century did this essentially antiquarian approach give way to one that was more historical. Questions of dating, at first mainly by coins and later by pottery and other objects, assumed greater importance, and villas were seen as having evolved and developed rather than being static entities. Excavations began to extend beyond the residential and into the working areas; occasionally, as at Köln-Müngersdorf, Germany, a whole farmyard would be explored. Scholars turned to regional studies and to questions of distribution and settlement: a striking early example is L. Joulin's study (1901) of Chiragan in south-west France, which not only related the villa to other sites in the area but attempted to determine its internal economy, with calculations of such factors as crop yields and working and residential populations. In the later 20th century the development of new survey techniques, particularly air photography, drew attention once again away from individual villas towards their economic and social context; the aerial reconnaissance by Roger Agache, carried out in the Somme basin during the 1950s and 1960s and revealing several hundred villas within a varied archaeological landscape, is one of the more impressive examples. Nevertheless, work on individual sites continues, as does the study of architectural and decorative features, notably mosaics.

See also Tibur, Capreae, Piazza armerina, Settefinestre, Sirmio *and* Spalatum.

G. E. Fox: 'The Roman Villa at Chedworth, Gloucestershire', *Archaeol. J.*, xxxxiv (1887), pp. 322–36

L. Joulin: *Les Etablissements gallo-romains de la plaise de Martres-Tolosanes* (Paris, 1901)

Receuil général des mosaïques de la Gaule (Paris, 1957–) [supplements to *Gallia*]

P. Grimal: *Les Jardins romains* (Paris, 1969)

A. L. F. Rivet: *The Roman Villa in Britain* (London, 1969)

A. Boethius and J. B. Ward-Perkins: *Etruscan and Roman Architecture*, Pelican Hist. A. (Harmondsworth, 1970)

R. Agache and B. Bréart: *Atlas d'archéologie aérienne de Picardie* (Amiens, 1975)

A. G. McKay: *Houses, Villas and Palaces in the Roman World* (London, 1975)

J. Percival: *The Roman Villa* (London, 1976, rev. 2/1988)

R. Agache: *La Somme pré-romaine et romaine* (Amiens, 1978)

D. S. Neal: *Roman Mosaics in Britain* (London, 1981)

M. A. Cotton and G. P. R. Métraux: *The San Rocco Villa at Francolise* (London, 1985)

H. Mielsch: *Die römische Villa* (Munich, 1987)

N. Purcell: 'The Roman Garden as a Domestic Building', *Roman Domestic Buildings,* ed. I. M. Barton (Exeter, 1996)

Villa Giulia Painter (*fl c.* 470–*c.* 440 BC). Greek vase painter. The Master of the Villa Giulia Calyx krater, to give him his full name, has been attributed with *c.* 120 surviving vases. Most of these are large—kraters, stamnoi, pelikai and kalpides—though he also painted smaller shapes, including alabastra, lekythoi, pyxides, rhyta and cups. The cups and the large pots are iconographically dissimilar and must be anchored in different traditions. His figures are normally tall and solemn and are frequently shown pouring a libation, as in the gathering of gods on a cylindroid (Cambridge, Fitzwilliam X13). He added a personal touch to traditional themes: a young satyr appears in the procession of adult satyrs and maenads on a calyx krater (Karlsruhe, Bad. Landesmus. 208); the infant Dionysos is shown in the lap of Hermes on a calyx krater in Moscow (Pushkin Mus. F.A. 16732); and on an alabastron (Providence, RI Sch. Des., Mus. A. 25.088) he painted a mother or nurse with two boys, one asleep on her shoulder, the other holding tight to her chiton. He must also have been fond of animals: a fawn looks up at Apollo on the replica pelikai at Malibu, CA (Getty Mus. 77. AE.12.1–2); a heron stalks through a *gynaikeion* (women's quarters) on a kalpis (Switzerland, priv. col.; sold Basle, Münzen und Medaillen AG, 19 Feb 1980, no. 105); and he frequently painted horsemen. His mythological themes include Perseus sneaking up to the Gorgon on a bell-krater in Madrid (Mus. Arqueol. N. 11010), the daughters of Pelias hatching mischief on a kalpis (Cambridge, Fitzwilliam 12.17), and, on another kalpis (Rome, Vatican, Mus. Gregoriano Etrus. 16509), the sleeping Herakles being robbed by satyrs, a scene which must have been inspired by a satyr play. More than half of his preserved stamnoi depict the Lenaia, a festival celebrating the new wine and the rebirth of Dionysos. Athenian women appear as maenads, though a parasol on one stamnos (Boston, MA, Mus. F.A. 90.155) reveals their true origins.

On his name piece (Rome, Villa Giulia 909) a dozen maidens hold each other's hands and dance to the sound of a flute. The frieze continues without interruption around the krater, though the painter normally distinguishes between front and back. One fragmentary vase is an example of a double-register krater (see Beazley, 1942, 2/1963, 619, 13); other krater fragments are covered with white slip (e.g. Reggio Calabria, Mus. N., 12939; Lausanne, Mus. Hist., 3700), a technique he also used on lekythoi and alabastra. His stamnoi and kalpides are of two distinct shapes, the latter decorated on the shoulder or belly.

Most of the cups attributed to the Villa Giulia Painter depict youths, grown men and athletes, one of whom is shown as a victor, wearing sashes all over his body (Rome, Villa Giulia 5993). On a cup in St Petersburg (Hermitage B1535) a hetaira plays with balls, and a youth is shown wearing female headgear; another has dancing maenads with winged sleeves (Basle, priv. col.; sold Basle, *Kunst und Antiquitätenmesse*, 1979, no. 93). Since Beazley's latest list of the Villa Giulia Painter's known vases in 1971, three more White-ground cups have been attributed to him; one of these, an early work, shows Apollo revealing himself to a Muse (Boston, MA, Mus. F.A. 00356). Stylistically, the Villa Giulia Painter has several roots. With his cups he follows the workshop tradition of the Brygos Painter; with some of the closed vases he might have learnt from the Berlin Painter's late school, forming—together with the Chicago and the Methyse painters—an 'academic' wing of that tradition. The period of his activity is reflected in the development of his figures from sturdy Early Classical forms to slim and elegant High Classical styles.

J. D. Beazley: 'The Master of the Villa Giulia Calyx-Krater', *Mitt. Dt. Archäol. Inst.: Röm. Abt.*, xxvii (1912), pp. 286–97
J. D. Beazley: *Red-figure* (1942, 2/1963), i, pp. 618–26; ii, 1662
J. D. Beazley: *Paralipomena* (1971), pp. 398, 514
M. J. Vickers: 'A New Cup by the Villa Giulia Painter', *J. Hell. Stud.*, xciv (1974), pp. 177–9
J. Frel: *Paintings on Vases in Ancient Greece* (Los Angeles, 1979), nos 30–31
D. von Bothmer: 'Greek and Roman Art', *Bulletin of the Metropolitan Museum of Art: Notable Acquisitions* (1979–80), pp. 14–15
L. Burn and R. Glynn: *Beazley Addenda: Additional References to* ABV, ARV2 *and* Paralipomena (Oxford, 1982, rev. T. H. Carpenter, 2/1989), pp. 270–71
D. L. Wieland: 'Achill verabschiedet sich von seinen Eltern: Ein rotfiguriger Kelchkrater des Villa Giulia-Malers', *Archäol. Samml. U. Zürich*, xv (1989), pp. 6–14
G. G. Kavvadías: 'O Theséas kai o Marathónios Taúros: Paratiríseis se éna néo attikó erythromórpho kionotó kratéra apó to Argos', *Athenian Potters and Painters: The Conference Proceedings* (Oxford, 1997), pp. 309–18

Data courtesy of the Beazley Archive, Oxford University.

Villanovan. Early culture of the European Iron Age that flourished in northern Italy, central Italy and Campania in the 8th and 9th centuries BC, continuing in northern Italy until the 6th century BC. It is named after the small town of Villanova, just east of Bologna, where the first series of finds were made, and is of particular importance for its role in the development of the ETRUSCAN civilization.

Ancient graves were discovered at Villanova in 1853 during agricultural work on the estate of Count G. Gozzadini, who immediately undertook a systematic excavation of the site. By 1855, 179 cremation urns and 14 inhumations had been uncovered. Over half the cinerary urns had been buried in pits in the ground without any special protection and were often simply covered by a stone slab. In many other cases—particularly burials with several accompanying vessels—the grave had been lined with pebbles or stone slabs. In two instances the urn was placed inside a large clay vessel (*dolium*), and in a number of cases the burial plot had been marked by stones. A few years after these excavations, extended cemeteries of similar urn graves were discovered within the town of Bologna, establishing the locality as the most important centre of 'Villanovan' culture north of the Apennines, and it was these cemeteries that proved to be the principal source for defining the nature of this culture. The fact that the burial zones dated from different periods led to a preliminary chronological categorization based on various areas of Bologna, in which the phases of S Vitale, Benacci I, Benacci II and Arnoaldi were distinguished. In the 1950s these categories were defined with greater precision as covering the period from the 9th century BC to the mid-6th and named Villanovan I–IV. These phases were followed by the Certosa period, which belonged to the fully developed Etruscan civilization of the late 6th century BC and the 5th. Other finds in the city included several clusters of round huts distributed throughout the old part of the town and a tremendous hoard of bronze objects weighing over 1.4 tonnes unearthed near the church of S Francesco. Most of the finds are in the Museo Civico Archeologico, Bologna.

Similar cemeteries were also found to the south of the Apennine region in ancient Etruria and in the area around Capua and Salerno. These, too, contained mainly urn graves, which were either hollowed out of the rock or enclosed by stones, depending on the geology of the location. Inhumation graves were also increasingly evident, the ratio between the two types of burial varying between regions. However, these necropolises essentially belong only to the 9th and 8th centuries BC; the most important collections of finds are in the Museo Archeologico in Florence and the Museo Nazionale di Villa Giulia in Rome. The grave areas are found close to settlements, most of which occupy the sites of later Etruscan towns, a continuity of location that demonstrates with particular clarity that the transition from the Villanovan culture to the orientalizing phase of the Etruscan civilization was accomplished without interruption. However, the characteristics that define Villanovan culture lasted longer around Bologna than in Etruria, and there seem to have been only loose connections with the latter. Some direct adaptations of orientalizing motifs have been found around Bologna, for example on some stone monuments. Despite this divergent cultural development, the use of the Etruscan language in the Bologna area as early as the 7th century BC is attested by finds of graffiti on vessels.

Apart from its burial practices, Villanovan culture is distinguished by finds of certain types of material. The pottery is especially notable and includes double-coned cinerary urns, covered either with a dish or with a helmet-shaped lid, and house-shaped urns (see fig.). Various other types of vessel accompanied burials in increasing quantities as time progressed. They were decorated with geometric designs, produced by scratching and stamping, or with tin pieces

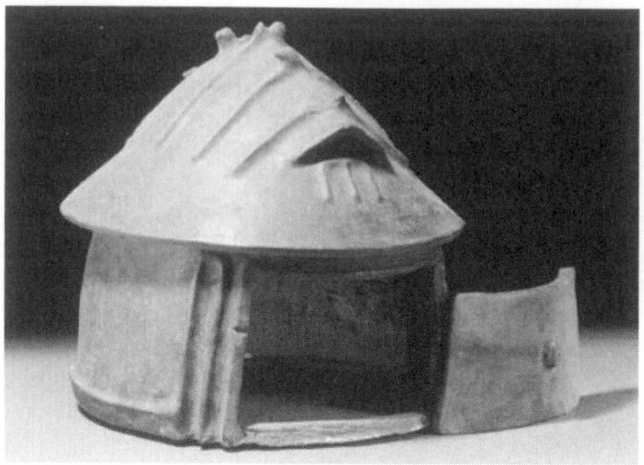

Villanovan clay hut urn, h. 330 mm, from the Alban Hills, *c.* 900–800 BC (London, British Museum)

or bronze nails. Only during the Villanovan IV phase in Bologna (7th century BC and early 6th) did painted pottery and figurative stamp-patterns become common. In richer graves the pottery was often replaced by bronze vessels, and female burials of the 9th and 8th centuries BC also contained jewellery—bronze fibulae (often decorated with glass beads), pendants and bracelets—as well as spinning whorls and distaffs. Male burials often included fibulae, needles, razors and such weapons as helmets, swords, spears and axes. Large metal belts were mainly found in women's graves, but horse trappings were common in the burials of both sexes. Some graves contained small clay models of carts and horses, perhaps intended to serve as a substitute for the real items; similar models decorate clay vessels. Rudimentary scenic depictions are found engraved on sheet-bronze objects, but symbolic signs—either engraved or modelled—are more frequent and commonly represent whole aquatic birds or parts of them, sometimes combined with sun or horse motifs.

H. Müller-Karpe: *Beiträge zur Chronologie der Urnenfelderzeit nördlich und südlich der Alpen* (Berlin, 1959)

H. Hencken: *Tarquinia, Villanovans and Early Etruscans*, 2 vols (Cambridge, MA, 1968)

K. Kilian: *Früheisenzeitliche Funde aus der Südostnekropole von Sala Consilina (Provinz Salerno): Archäologische Forschungen in Lukanien III* (Heidelberg, 1970)

M. Zuffa: 'La civiltà villanoviana', *Popoli e civiltà dell'Italia antica*, v, ed. M. Pallottino (Rome, 1976), pp. 197–363

La necropoli villanoviana di Ca' dell'Orbo a Villanova di Castenaso: Problemi del popolamento dal IX al VI secolo a.C. (exh. cat., Bologna, Mus. Civ. Archeol., 1979)

Dalla stanza delle antichità al Museo Civico: Storia della formazione del Museo Civico Archeologico di Bologna, a cura di Ch. Morigi Govi e G. Sassatelli (Bologna, 1984)

Civiltà degli Etruschi (exh. cat., ed. M. Cristofani; Florence, Mus. Archeol., 1985) [extensive bibliog.]

La formazione della città in Emilia Romagna: Prime esperienze urbane attraverso le nuove scoperte archeologiche (exh. cat., ed. G. Bermond Montanari; Bologna, Mus. Civ. Archeol., 1988)

G. Bartoloni: *La cultura villanoviana: All'inizio della storia etrusca* (Rome, 1989)

D. de Angelis: *La ceramica decorata di stile 'villanoviano' in Etruria meridionale* (Soveria Mannelli, 2001)

Villa of the Papyri. *See under* HERCULANEUM.

Villa Sileen [Silene]. *See* SILEEN VILLA.

Vitruvius (*fl* later 1st century BC). Roman architect, engineer and writer, renowned for his treatise in ten books, *On Architecture* (Lat. *De architectura*), the only text on architectural theory and practice to have survived from Classical antiquity.

1. Life and work. 2. *On Architecture*.

1. LIFE AND WORK. Vitruvius is known in the earliest manuscripts of *On Architecture* only by this name, a *nomen gentilicium* or clan name. By his own testimony (I. Preface), he was already an older man at the time he dedicated his treatise to the Emperor Augustus (?27 or 14 BC). He had earlier served Augustus' adoptive father, Julius Caesar, as a siege engineer, and at some time after Caesar's death (44 BC) he entered the service of Octavian (after 27 BC called Augustus). He enjoyed Octavian's continued patronage on the recommendation of the latter's sister, Octavia, a fact that suggests a period of service under her second husband, the triumvir Mark Antony. In addition to having sufficient education and leisure to engage in writing, Vitruvius clearly had first-hand knowledge of several areas of his subject. As might be expected, he was familiar with siege engines and made remarkable application of the study of music to the tuning of catapults. His treatment of architecture proper suggests greater experience of private, domestic building than of religious or secular public works, although Frontinus (*De aquaeductibus* XXV.1–2) indicated that Vitruvius worked under Agrippa in the construction of baths and aqueducts in the Campus Martius at Rome.

There is little external evidence concerning Vitruvius. The basilica that he allegedly built at Fano, north of Ancona (*On Architecture* V.i.6), has not been identified, and no inscription bearing his name has been discovered there. *On Architecture* is itself cited only a few times in other Classical sources. Its author is almost always named simply Vitruvius, although in the 4th century AD Faventius, who produced a condensed version of the work, gave the cognomen or family name 'Pol[l]io'. The name 'Vitruvius Pollio' has become traditional but remains unsubstantiated by contemporary documents. Vitruvius has also been identified with L. Vitruvius Mamurra, possibly the Mamurra from Formia who was Julius Caesar's chief engineer in Gaul. The name M. Vitruvius Mamurra has been found in a Roman inscription from Africa, and the *nomen gentilicium* Vitruvius occurs in Formia. Vitruvius or his literary executors may have dropped the cognomen Mamurra for good reasons: the contemporary poet Catullus had libelled Mamurra in a particularly scurrilous manner (e.g. *Poems* 29, 41,

43, 57, 94). Moreover, the same Mamurra had also acquired a reputation for extravagance by being the first person in Rome to cover whole walls of his house with marble veneer. While this theory of Vitruvius' identity has not won general acceptance, it might account for his intimate familiarity with the domestic architecture and building materials of Campania and perhaps explain his confident defence of magnificence in private architecture. It might also provide a means of connecting Vitruvius with such eminent men of letters of Julius Caesar's time as Lucretius, Cicero and Varro, each of whose ideas find resonance in his work.

2. On architecture.

(i) The text. (ii) The ten books.

(i) The text. *On Architecture* is a didactic treatise on the subject of architecture in all its branches as understood in Classical antiquity. Vitruvius' claim to represent accurately the theory and practice of ancient Greek and Roman architecture has been challenged by modern scholars, but his influence on later architects and students of Classical architectural styles, particularly in the Italian Renaissance and in northern Europe and America in early modern times, has been enormous. A revival of scholarly interest in Vitruvius' treatise, with several international colloquia during the 1980s, may also reflect renewed interest in Classical styles among architects, and an important new edition of the text, with French translation and commentary, has been undertaken.

The text of *On Architecture* presents two main obstacles. The first involves the corruptions of and lacunae in the original text that accumulated in the course of its transmission from antiquity. These are inevitably numerous, since Vitruvius' work abounds in technical terms and exotic proper names. As a consequence, there are considerable differences, even between the texts of modern printed editions. The two most popular English translations, for example (Morgan and Granger), differ significantly, being based on different Latin texts. A further problem concerns the illustrations. *On Architecture* was originally 'published' in parallel columns on papyrus scrolls, one scroll for each of its ten books, and the illustrations essential to the content of the treatise were either simple drawings inserted into the text or more elaborate figures appended to it. In most cases these illustrations did not survive the process of manuscript copying. Since the publication of the earliest printed editions, editors have needed either to reconstruct the drawings as indicated by the text or to find illustrations appropriate to otherwise obscure passages. Hence, the exact nature of Vitruvius' influence on architects from the Renaissance onwards often relates to specific printed editions.

The second obstacle stems from Vitruvius' literary style, which ranges from the laconic to the bombastic, often without full control of either. Vitruvius' stylistic shortcomings have often obscured his meaning, in terms both of detail and of broader questions. It has, for example, often been noted that the matter and the organization of the individual books vary greatly. For this reason *On Architecture* has been considered by its severest critics as nothing more than a compendium composed by an embittered, unsuccessful and unemployed architect. Perhaps anticipating such criticism, Vitruvius spoke in his own defence in the Preface to Book VII (all quoted passages are from Morgan's translation): 'From their commentaries [of earlier authors] I have gathered what I saw was useful for the present subject, and formed it into one complete treatise, and this principally because I saw that many books in this field had been published by the Greeks, but very few indeed by our countrymen.'

The overall organization of the treatise reflects the division of architecture into three parts: Books I–VIII deal with *aedificatio*, the science of building; Book IX with *gnomonice*, the art of making sundials; and Book X with *machinatio* or mechanics. The preface of each of the books is designed as a literary introduction, sometimes anecdotal, sometimes expository, to the more technical material presented in the particular book.

(ii) The ten books. The Preface to Book I dedicates *On Architecture* to the Emperor Augustus, thus indicating a date of 17 BC or later. Vitruvius avowed his thanks for Augustus' patronage and his hope of educating him concerning the discipline of architecture. Elsewhere in *On Architecture* there is evidence that Vitruvius was writing for a readership of other knowledgeable patrons and for professional architects themselves. It was Vitruvius' contemporary M. Terentius Varro (116–27 BC) who seems to have been the first Roman to raise the study of architecture to the level of the Liberal Arts, dedicating a book to it in his encyclopedic *Disciplinarum libri*. Vitruvius' work was no doubt, in addition to its other claims, intended to raise the social status of the profession (*see* Roman republic and empire, §3).

The first chapter of Book I defines a broad range of subjects appropriate to the education of the architect: he should be literate, able to draw and have a knowledge of geometry, optics, arithmetic, history, philosophy (including physics), music, medicine, law and astronomy. Though he should be educated in all the arts, the architect must not be expected to excel in each. Here Vitruvius made an important distinction between practice and theory, stating that the arts were each dualities composed of the work itself (*opus*) and its theoretical dimension (*ratiocinatio*). For the architect, the theory of architecture should suffice. However, despite the great influence that Vitruvius' treatise was to have over architectural design, it does not accord practice (*fabrica*) and theory the usual relation to one another found in dualist systems. Theory is presented not as a preparatory basis for the work in the form of design, but rather as a way of explaining or justifying the effect produced by the work. Hence, the importance of theory lies in the relation of the architect to his patron, and the treatise provides the means of appreciating the subject for those who are not professional architects.

In the second chapter the fundamental principles of both architectural practice and theory are laid out. These are: Order (*ordinatio*), Arrangement (*dispositio*), Eurhythmy (*eurythmia*), Symmetry (*symmetria*), Propriety (*decor* or *decorum*) and Economy (*distributio*). It has been noted that the six fundamental principles of architecture listed by Vitruvius actually consist of three distinct concepts, each divided into pairs according to the opposition of artistic practice and theory, or 'process' and 'product'. These are: Order/Symmetry; Arrangement/Eurhythmy; and Economy/Propriety. Certain phrases demonstrate that Vitruvius conceived of the design process as essentially synthetic, consisting of different components and their 'adjustment[s] according to quantity'. Products, on the other hand, he saw as unities subject to analysis, 'fashioned with quality'. Hence, Order is 'an adjustment according to quantity' by which the whole is constructed, whereas Symmetry, the 'proper arrangement between members of the work', is its qualitative result. Arrangement is the quantitative 'putting of things in their proper places', and Eurhythmy its qualitative result. Finally, Economy involves the architect's quantitative consideration of the appropriateness of the site and what the client can afford, and Propriety is the quality that results. Of the six principles, Propriety alone receives further analysis, being divided into three parts: religious custom or prescription (*statio*), social usage or habit (*consuetudo*) and natural causes (*natura*) (*see also* ORDERS, ARCHITECTURAL, §I, 2(ii) and II). If this passage constitutes Vitruvius' theory of architecture, his exposition leaves much to be desired. Nevertheless, the application of these principles elsewhere in his treatise is more or less consistent, indicating that, whatever the source of the theory, Vitruvius made it his own. In any case, Vitruvius' discussion is an important source for the study of ancient architectural theory (*see also* ARCHITECTURE, §IV, 3).

The remainder of Book I deals with the selection of the site for a city and its buildings. The site itself should be healthy, with a temperate balance of the four Empedoclean elements of moisture, heat, air and earth. Having ascertained that the city can be supplied by roads, rivers or sea ports, the architect should lay out encircling walls and towers. Then, setting up a gnomon in the centre of the site, he should determine from the sun's course the cardinal directions and sources of the eight winds. The text provides sufficient detail here for the illustration to be reconstructed. Having determined the cardinal directions, the architect can lay out streets and alleys. Book I ends with a discussion of the proper sites for the forum and for the temples (*see also* PLANNING, II, 2).

Book II is devoted to the materials used in construction. This book shows Vitruvius at his most original and for this reason seems to break the continuity between Book I and Book III, so that some scholars have considered it to be a later, ill-fitting addition. It presents a thorough attempt to relate materials used in building to their occurrence in nature and also views human technology as a product of man's natural inclination to learn through imitation. Like his contemporary Lucretius, Vitruvius was, therefore, inclined to discover the authority for current practices in the remote, natural origins of human culture. For example, the control of fire and the society of the hearth preceded even the development of language, a fact that lends antiquity and dignity to the profession of architecture.

In discussing the methods of building masonry walls with a concrete core, Vitruvius distinguished two types, one faced with irregular stones laid in an irregular pattern (*opus incertum*), the other employing regular wedges laid in a reticulate pattern (*opus reticulatum*). In a passage that has received much attention from archaeologists, Vitruvius preferred the more ancient *opus incertum* to the contemporary *opus reticulatum*. In declaring his allegiance to the 'Ancients' he explained the contemporary preference for *opus reticulatum* as an aesthetic rather than a structural choice. While archaeology has verified Vitruvius' relative chronology, it has also confirmed the impression that he may have been a pious antiquarian out of touch with the reasoning behind contemporary practice. Economics rather than aesthetics probably dictated the choice of *opus reticulatum*, especially since walls of both types were normally faced with stucco or marble. Furthermore, Vitruvius' misgivings about the structural properties of *opus reticulatum* do not seem to be borne out in surviving examples.

Current practices occasionally won the approval of this conservative author, however. One passage in Book II (II.viii.17) gives an invaluable glimpse of contemporary Roman multistorey city housing:

> In these tall piles reared with piers of stone, walls of burnt brick, and partitions of rubble work, and provided with floor after floor, the upper storeys can be partitioned off into rooms to very great advantage. The accommodations within the city wall being thus multiplied as a result of the many floors high in the air, the Roman people easily find excellent places in which to live.

Given Vitruvius' evident approval of this type of construction, his conservatism cannot be simply regarded as indiscriminate.

Books III and IV are both concerned with temple architecture. Book III begins with a discussion of Symmetry in temples and in the human body, and the first chapter contains the famous passage constructing the ideally proportioned 'Vitruvian Man'. In resuming the discussion of the organization of architecture according to type and returning to theory, Book III appears to continue from Book I rather than from Book II. It proceeds to a classification of temples according to plan and to a discussion of the *eustyle*, or 'well-proportioned' elevation. Vitruvius acknowledged the source for his ideas here to be the 2nd-century BC Greek architect HERMOGENES, and this has led many commentators to infer that he followed Hermogenes closely in his treatment of the

Ionic order, which in retrospect (III.v.15) he declares to have been the subject of Book III.

Accordingly, Book IV contains a discussion of material not treated by Hermogenes: the Corinthian and Doric orders, and the rules for Etruscan temples (*see also* ARCHITECTURE, §V *and* ORDERS, ARCHITECTURAL, §I, 1 and 2). Vitruvius' treatment of the Doric order (IV.iii) begins with the observation that the 'Ancients', among whom he numbers Hermogenes and PYTHEOS, considered this order unsuitable for temples because of such inherent design problems as the uneven spacing of triglyphs at the corners of a Doric building. Given Vitruvius' earlier discussion of ideal, *eustyle* proportion in the Ionic order, his treatment of Doric proportions is perfunctory, though informative. It covers the subject of such Doric refinements as curvature on the stylobate and entasis, which are considered necessary to correct optical illusions and are therefore subject to the general principle of Symmetry. Chapter seven briefly deals with the construction of an Etruscan temple using modular measurements and chapter eight is devoted to circular temples and other variations, as determined by Decorum (IV.viii.6): 'For we must not build temples according to the same rules to all gods alike, since the performance of the sacred rites varies with the various gods.'

Book V deals with the remaining public building types: fora, basilicas, theatres, baths and palaestrae. It concludes with a brief discussion of harbours, breakwaters and shipyards. The treatment of fora begins by contrasting the Greek agora with the Roman forum, the latter requiring two-storey buildings with wider intercolumniations, thanks to the custom of staging gladiatorial combats in the forum. In treating basilicas and their proportions in general, Vitruvius gave specific dimensions for his own (unlocated) building at Fano. The discussion of theatres again distinguishes between the Roman type and the Greek; both descriptions follow a treatment of harmonics based on the theories of Aristoxenos (*fl c.* 300 BC) and the amplification of the voice by means of bronze vessels. In the designs for both Roman and Greek theatres Vitruvius employed a circle containing a 12-sided polygon to determine the relation of the *orchestra* to the *cavea* (auditorium) and the stage building (*see also* THEATRE). In the Roman figure four equilateral triangles are inscribed within the circle, 'as the astrologers do in a figure of the twelve signs of the zodiac, when they are making computations from the musical harmony of the stars', and each fifth point is connected (representing the diapason). In the Greek figure three squares are inscribed: each fourth point is connected (the diatesseron). Excavation has shown that many ancient Greek theatres were designed according to the principle given by Vitruvius, but no Roman theatres have as yet been found conforming to this scheme. The passage is thus better understood as an attempt to propose new architectural principles than as evidence of Vitruvius' lack of knowledge of current practice.

Book VI is concerned with such private building types as the Roman town house (*domus*) and farm house (*villa*), and the Greek house, though a treatment of the luxury villa is noticeably absent. The material evidence from excavations at Pompeii and elsewhere in Italy has confirmed Vitruvius' account of the design of both *domus* and *villa* types, and the arrangement and proportioning of rooms of the grand houses from Pompeii conform closely to his rules. This is important evidence that he was intimately familiar with Italian domestic design as it had evolved from the 3rd–1st centuries BC. Appealing to the principle of Decorum, Vitruvius justified building on a grand scale for the houses of prominent public figures. In contrast with moralists who condemned contemporary luxury as vanity, Vitruvius noted the many public uses such houses afforded, as places for public meetings, private trials and judgements, and other functions.

Book VII addresses the interior decoration of houses, including floors, stuccoed walls and frescoes. In addition to its valuable information concerning contemporary practice, Book VII is notable for Vitruvius' historical summary of representational wall painting (VII.v.1–4) and his tirade against the decadence of the current fashion for the grotesque (VII. v.3–4). As well as providing an important document for post-Classical arguments in favour of the natural as opposed to the imaginary in art, this passage has also been important for the classification and dating of Pompeian wall painting.

Book VIII is devoted to hydrology and hydraulics and is essentially both a continuation of the study of building on certain sites and a transition to the last two books, which deal with the construction of water clocks and sundials (IX) and with mechanics (X). In addition to the ways of locating good water, Book VIII deals with aqueducts, wells and cisterns. Although Vitruvius provided technical specifications for constructing water systems with lead pipes, he strongly recommended against the use of lead for health reasons (VIII.vi.10–11). The extensive Introduction to Book IX concerns the workings of the heavens, and this book as a whole is extremely important for the history of ancient mathematics. Book X, on the subject of mechanics and ballistics, is perhaps the closest of all the books to Vitruvius' own area of expertise as a military engineer. Yet the extended treatment of mechanical advantage was also no doubt a subject of the greatest importance to contemporary civil architects and builders.

On Architecture is important both for the history of architecture and its theory, thanks to Vitruvius' conscientious habit of citing his sources; although he wrote as a historian, he had the viewpoint of a practising architect. Much has been written in criticism of Vitruvius as a historical source, but a better understanding of the biographical evidence now promises to improve his reputation.

Writings

M. H. Morgan, trans.: *The Ten Books on Architecture* (Cambridge, MA, 1914/*R* New York, 1960)

F. Granger, ed. and trans.: *On Architecture*, 2 vols (London and Cambridge, MA, 1931, 1934) [ed. from Harleian MS. 2767]
S. Ferri, ed.: *Vitruvio: Architettura, dai libri* I–VII (Rome, 1960) [with commentary]
C. Fensterbusch, ed. and trans.: *Vitruvii: De architectura libri decem* (Berlin, 1964) [with Ger. trans.]
J. Soubiran, ed. and trans.: *Vitruve: De l'architecture, Livre* IX (Paris, 1969) [with Fr. trans. and commentary]
L. Callebat, ed. and trans.: *Vitruve: De l'architecture, Livre* VIII (Paris, 1973) [with Fr. trans. and commentary]
L. Callebat and P. Fleury, eds and trans.: *Vitruve: De l'architecture, Livre* X (Paris, 1986) [with Fr. trans. and commentary]
P. Fleury, ed. and trans.: *Vitruve: De l'architecture, Livre* I (Paris, 1990) [with Fr. trans. and commentary]

Bibliography

C. Watzinger: 'Vitruvstudien', *Rhein. Mus.*, lxiv (1909), pp. 203–23
A. Boethius: 'Vitruvius and the Roman Architecture of his Age', *Dragma M. P. Nilson dedicatum* (Lund, 1939), pp. 114–43
P. Ruffel and J. Soubiran: 'Vitruve ou Mamurra?', *Pallas*, xi (1962), pp. 123–79
P. Gros: 'Vitruve: L'Architecture et sa théorie à la lumière des études récentes', *Aufstieg und Niedergang der römischen Welt*, ii (Berlin, 1982), pp. 659–95
Vitruv-Kolloquium des deutschen Archäologen-Verbandes: Darmstadt, 1982
L. Callebat and others, eds: *Vitruve, De architectura: Concordance*, 2 vols (Hildesheim, Zurich and New York, 1984)
H. Knell: *Vitruvs Architekturtheorie: Versuch einer Interpretation* (Darmstadt, 1985)
Munus non Ingratum: Proceedings of the International Symposium on Vitruvius' 'De architectura' and the Hellenistic and Republican Architecture: Leiden, 1989

Volcii. *See* VULCI.

Volos. *See* IOLKOS.

Volsinii Veteres [Etrus. Velzna; now Orvieto]. Italian city in Umbria, situated about halfway between Rome and Florence on a steep tufa spur near the confluence of the rivers Chiana, Paglia and Tiber. It was the site of Velzna, one of the major cities of the Etruscan federation, which was destroyed in 264 BC. The ancient site, which remains largely inaccessible to excavation beneath medieval and modern buildings, is generally known by its Roman name, Volsinii Veteres, although since the 19th century it has been identified as the Etruscan city of Velzna and the site of the pan-Etruscan Sanctuary of Voltumna. Parts of the ancient city walls and the foundations of the 5th-century BC Belvedere Temple (*see* ARCHITECTURE, fig. 19) can, however, still be seen.

Volsinii Veteres was an important junction in the commercial links between such coastal cities as Caere (Cerveteri), Tarquinia and Vetulonia and the settlements of the central Etruscan interior. The best evidence of the evolution of the ancient city comes from the tombs in the Cannicella and the Croce-

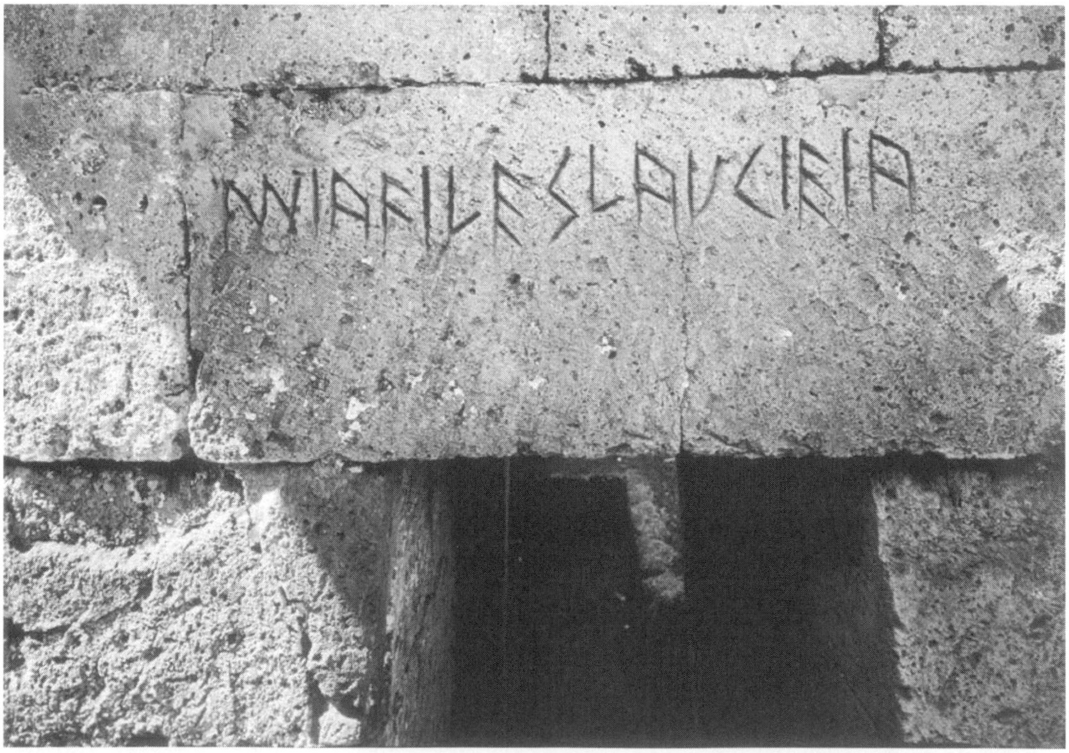

1. Volsinii Veteres (Orvieto), inscription on a lintel in the Crocefisso del Tufo necropolis, 6th century BC

fisso del Tufo necropolis. Modest Villanovan and Orientalizing burials gave way to more lavish tombs and tomb contents towards the end of the Orientalizing period (late 7th century BC). During the second half of the 6th century BC the Crocefisso del Tufo necropolis began to be laid out on a regular grid plan, which suggests the influence of Hippodamos of Miletos and Greek urban planning and can be compared with the Etruscan town excavated at MARZABOTTO. The tombs are partly rock-cut and partly built up with tufa blocks. Architraves over the entrances often bear an inscription giving the family name (see fig. 1).

The fine terracotta figures from the Belvedere Temple (Orvieto, Mus. Etrus. Faina; *see also* SCULPTURE, §V) date from the late 5th century BC to the early 4th (see fig. 2). During the Classical period there was a vigorous output of local pottery, including the Orvieto group of Black-figure vases that show a coarse but distinctive use of both figural and patterned decoration. Of the few painted tombs in this part of Etruria, several are located near Orvieto, for example the Golini I Tomb at Settecamini (*c.* 325–*c.* 300 BC), which contains a unique banqueting scene: in addition to the traditional figures of banqueters and underworld deities, there is a detailed depiction of cooks preparing the food to the accompaniment of music.

The city engaged in frequent conflicts with Rome and and was finally destroyed in 264 BC. The inhabitants fled to a new site on the north-east shore of

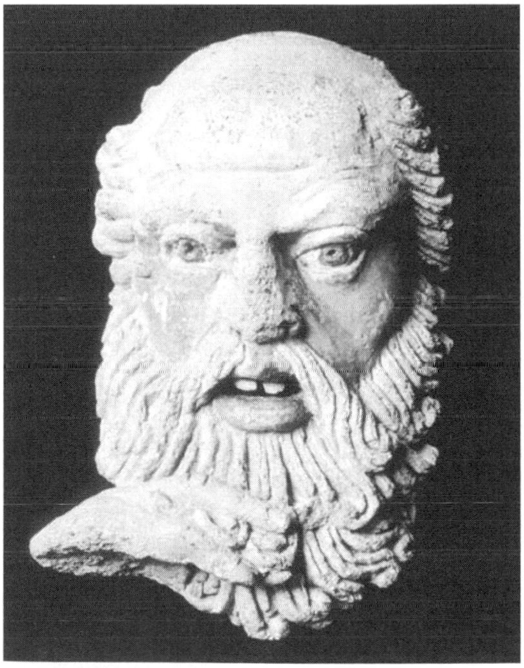

2. Volsinii Veteres (Orvieto), terracotta head of an old man, from the Belvedere Temple, late 5th century BC–early 4th (Orvieto, Museo Etrusco Faina)

Lake Bolsena, which became known as Volsinii Novi (mod. Bolsena).

M. Bizzari: *Orvieto etrusca* (Orvieto, 1972)
G. Colonna: *Santuari d'Etruria* (Milan, 1985)
F. Prayon: 'Orvieto: Tübinger Ausgrabungen in der Cannicella-Nekropole 1984–1990', *Archäol. Anz.*, i (1993), pp. 5–91
M. Bergamini and F. Roncalli: *Museo Claudio Faina di Orvieto: Monete etrusche e italiche, greche, romane repubblicane* (Perugia, 1995)
M. Bergamini and F. Roncalli: *Museo Claudio Faina di Orvieto: Monete romane imperiali da Pertinace a Valentiniano III* (Milan, 1997)

Volterra. *See* VELATHRI.

Volubilis [Arab. Walīla]. Roman site in Morocco, 20 km north of Meknès. The town was inhabited from the 3rd century BC by a Libyophoenician (mixed Berber and Carthaginian) population. It grew rapidly in the mid-1st century AD when it became a *municipium* (free town) of the Roman province of Mauretania Tingitana. Abandoned by the Romans in AD 280–85, Volubilis was briefly the capital of the Islamic Idrisid dynasty at the end of the 8th century AD. A forum was built during the reign of Nero (AD 54–68), and by the end of the 1st century AD several *insulae* (apartment blocks) had been laid out around it. In the later 2nd century AD the urban grid was extended to the north-east, and a 3–km circuit of walls was built (AD 168–9) enclosing an area of around 40 ha. The forum (see fig.) was completely reconstructed at the time of Septimius Severus (*reg* AD 193–211), and a basilica was built with twin apses and rows of two-tiered columns dividing it into nave and aisles, as at Leptis Magna. Opposite is an imposing capitolium approached by a high staircase, and nearby is the Arch of Caracalla (AD 216–17). A large number of impressive peristyle houses have been uncovered at Volubilis (2nd and 3rd centuries AD), with fountains and polychrome mosaic pavements. These include the House of Orpheus, with its circular mosaic of *Orpheus Charming the Animals with his Music*; the so-called Palace of Gordian, a huge complex with a street façade of 15 Ionic columns; and the House of the Cortège of Venus, with mosaics depicting *Diana Bathing* and *Hylas Attacked by the Nymphs*. Several fine bronzes were found on the site, notably the busts of Cato the Younger and King Juba II (both ?1st century AD; Rabat, Mus. Ant.), and smaller pieces such as a bronze barking dog (see colour pl. 2:XVI, fig. 2).

R. Thouvenot: *Volubilis* (Paris, 1949)
R. Etienne: *Le Quartier nord-est de Volubilis* (Paris, 1960)
A. Luquet: *Volubilis* (Tangier, 1972)
J.-L. Panetier and H. Limane: *Volubilis: Une cité du Maroc antique* (Paris, 2002)

Volute Krater. Ancient pottery form, used as a mixing bowl (*see* POTTERY, fig. 15(ii)e).

Vouni. Site on the north coast of Cyprus, *c.* 8 km north-east of Lefka. Here the extensive remains of a 5th-century BC palace, a complete plan of which was recovered, were excavated by the Swedish Cyprus Expedition in 1928–9. The reception rooms of the original palace (Vouni I; first half of the 5th century BC) were arranged around a central square court surrounded on three sides by a portico. On the fourth side, at the south-west, a magnificent flight of stairs led to the palace's main entrance with its flanking state apartments. The strict axiality in the arrangement of the court and the entrance block is to be noted. Service wings to the south contained living-rooms, baths, kitchens and storerooms. During a rebuilding in the later 5th century BC (Vouni II) a second court, flanked by a number of storerooms and other apartments, was added to the south-east, and the main entrance block was walled up. A new main entrance was devised, which followed a winding route into the courtyard by way of rooms in the north-west corner of the court. The palace shows the influence of contemporary Near Eastern architecture, and it is reasonable to assume that it belonged to the rulers of the nearby kingdom of Soli. The hypothesis that Vouni II represents a 'Hellenized' rebuilding scheme is based on a number of untenable assumptions. The buildings were finally destroyed in the early 4th century BC.

E. Gjerstad and others: *Finds and Results of the Excavations in Cyprus, 1927–1931* (1937), iii of *The Swedish Cyprus Expedition* (Stockholm, 1934–)

F. G. Maier: 'Factoids in Ancient History: The Case of Fifth-century Cyprus', *J. Hell. Stud.*, cv (1985), pp. 32–9

Vulci [Etrus. Velc; Gr. Olkion; Lat. Volcii]. Site of Etruscan city near Montalto di Castro, Italy. It occupies a tufa plateau overlooking the lower reaches of the River Fiora *c.* 120 km north-west of Rome and *c.* 15 km inland from its ancient port, Regisvilla, on the Tyrrhenian coast. Vulci was a member of the Etruscan 12-city league but is seldom mentioned in ancient sources, and most evidence relating to its pre-Roman history consists of finds from its surrounding necropolises. Already a substantial settlement by the Late Bronze Age, Vulci flourished during the 9th and 8th centuries BC as a metalworking centre, and the earliest imports of Near Eastern and Sardinian artefacts date from this time. From around 630 BC Vulci experienced remarkable prosperity and productivity. There were copious imports of Greek and Near Eastern artefacts which, together with the arrival of immigrant craftsmen, stimulated the establishment of local fine pottery workshops. In the 6th century BC there was prolific production of Etrusco-Corinthian and Black-figure pottery. Some of the earliest Etruscan sculpture in stone also comes from Vulci. Notable examples include the animals or monsters intended as tomb guardians (e.g. the *Centaur*; *c.* 590 BC; Rome, Villa Giulia) and the standing female figure from the Isis Tomb, all carved from nenfro, the local volcanic stone. Later, Vulci was once again primarily a metalworking centre, with workshops specializing in candelabra, rod tripods and engraved mirrors.

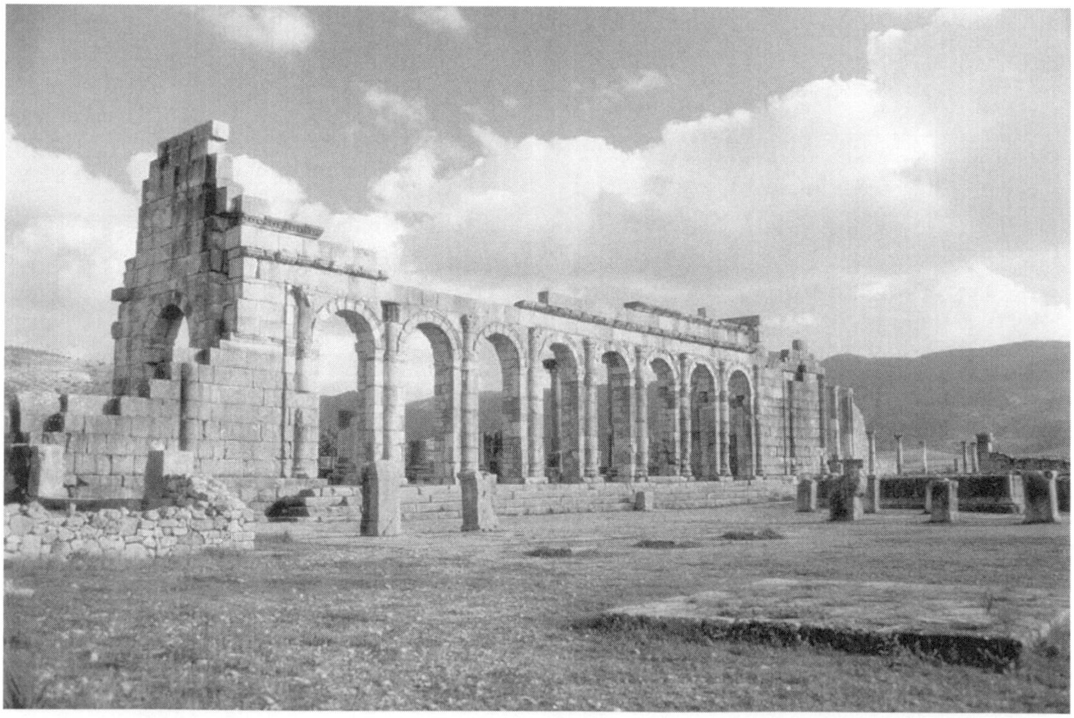

Volubilis, forum, AD 54–68

Apart from the substructure of a huge temple (36×25 m), little now remains of the Etruscan city: a few stretches of the city wall, in which there were at least four gates, are visible. The necropolises surrounding the city contain some large family chamber tombs of the Archaic period, including the Cucumella tumulus, the Isis Tomb and the Tomb of the Sun and Moon. Between *c.* 550 and *c.* 450 BC Attic Greek pottery was imported to Vulci on a scale and of a quality unparalleled elsewhere in Etruria. When modern excavations of the tombs began in the early 19th century, many thousands of examples were found. The second half of the 5th century BC was apparently a period of crisis, but elaborate later tombs (e.g. the François Tomb and the Tomb of the Inscriptions) testify to revived prosperity. The François Tomb contains some of the finest Etruscan wall paintings (*c.* 330 BC; Rome, Villa Albani), with scenes from Greek mythology and Etruscan history and daily life. A slow but marked decline began in 280 BC with the defeat of Vulci by Rome and the subsequent loss of almost all its territory. The city survived through the Republican and Imperial periods, but like other Etruscan cities near the coast Vulci was affected by the advent of malaria, and its demise came during the 8th century AD when the bishopric of the area was transferred to Montalto di Castro.

A. Hus: *Vulci étrusque et étrusco-romaine* (Paris, 1971)

Atti del X convegno di studi etruschi ed italici: Firenze, 1977

G. Riccioni: 'Vulci: A Topographical and Cultural Survey', *Italy before the Romans*, ed. D. Ridgway and F. R. Ridgway (London, 1979), pp. 241–76

P. J. Riis: *Vulcientia Vetustiora: A Study of Archaic Vulcian Bronzes* (Copenhagen, 1997)

F. R. Serra Ridgway, ed.: *Vasi greci da Vulci: Necropoli dell'Osteria scavi Ferraguti-Mengarelli, 1929–1931* (Milan, 2003)

W

Walīla. *See* Volubilis.

Wall painting. *See* Painting.

Well-head [puteal]. In its most essential form, a screen-wall or parapet, analogous to a precinct wall, surrounding a taboo place in the Greek and Roman world; also a means of enclosing a well or pit (Lat. *puteus*) in the earth. One type, a *bidental*, signified a place struck by lightning, consecrated and enclosed by the priests, where propitiatory offerings were made to the lightning. The puteal Libonis (untraced) was a *bidental* in the Forum Romanum: it appears on coins as a parapet, circular in plan, adorned with garlands, lyres and the hammer of Vulcan. It is typical of the architectural type commonly employed by both Greeks and Romans as well-heads. Larger well-heads, such as the one found at the Sanctuary of Fortuna Primigenia at Praeneste, sometimes took the form of a circular parapet supporting a monopteros. Alternatively, the well-head or parapet itself was sometimes surrounded by a monopteros or tholos (circular columnar buildings), as in the well (perhaps a *bidental*) of Numerius Trebius in the Triangular Forum at Pompeii.

Prominent religious monuments such as these undoubtedly inspired a multitude of smaller well-heads intended for both public and private use. Excavations in Sicily and Pompeii have unearthed cylindrical well-heads of terracotta, decorated on their exterior surface as altars. Well-heads sculpted in limestone and marble have been found in Delos and Pompeii. In the typical Pompeian house rainwater from the roofs collected in the *impluvium*, whence it was drained off into a cistern beneath the floor. A well-head was sometimes placed above such a cistern, located along the border of the *impluvium*. Pernice attempted to establish an evolutionary sequence for the Pompeian types, beginning with a simple fluted kind that he believed represented the Hellenistic or pre-Roman style in Pompeii. By contrast, magnificent sculpted marble well-heads were sought out by wealthy Romans of the late Republic and early Empire. Athens seems to have been the source of these, as testified by Cicero's request to Atticus (*ad Att.*, I.x) to send him two figured well-heads (*putealia sigillata*) from there. The type is represented in numerous examples taken from the luxurious villas of the Roman campagna and the Bay of Naples and now to be found in the museums of Rome and Naples (where they have traditionally been employed as statue bases). They have circular bases reminiscent of Ionic columns. Leaf patterns and cyma reversa were the mouldings most often applied. (One example (Naples, Mus. Archeol. N., 6675) has a fascia with crossed meander crowned by cyma reversa and bead and reel.) Above the base rises a sculpted frieze. The effect of an elegant sculpted altar is completed by a cyma recta moulding that answers the base moulding, but is somewhat lighter.

The sculpted friezes of such *putealia sigillata* may consist simply of garlands suspended from bucrania (bulls' skulls), emphasizing the sacred origins of the type even if employed in the decorative context of a private portico. Two examples (Naples, Mus. Archeol. N., 6676 and 120 175) show garlands of ivy and olive respectively suspended from filleted bucrania. A third example from Capreae (Naples, Mus. Archeol. N., 120 129) has branches of oak suspended from nails by means of fillets which also hold attributes of Hercules. The most elaborate plant decoration may be found in another well-head from Capreae (Naples, Mus. Archeol. N., 6671) with grapevines reminiscent of the miraculous plant depicted on the Ara Pacis. Certainly the most important *puteal sigillatum* is the Madrid Puteal which was seen by Schneider as a reflection of the central group of the east pediment of the Parthenon. Although Schneider's argument has lost much of its force through subsequent studies of the Parthenon, the connection of a Neo-Attic decorative sculpture with a famous Athenian model remains plausible. Rather similar to the Madrid Puteal is another in Naples (Mus. Archeol. N., 6670), apparently an assembly of seven male deities (Dionysus, Hercules, Mercury, Jupiter, Mars, Apollo and Aesculapius), but in reality nothing more than a simple array. The composition, if it can be called that, suggests that of contemporary Pompeian wall paintings that depict the seven planetary divinities, in which the dramatic unity characteristic of Classical prototypes gave way to a new syntax of symbols. The same obstacles to interpretation are present in another Neo-Attic puteal (Rome, Mus. Capitolino, 1019), on which 12 Olympians are depicted in archaizing style. They seem to form two processions that converge, and have been variously interpreted as the return of Hephaistos to Olympos, the birth of Athena or the apotheosis of Herakles. None of these interpretations works: the frieze is simply a Roman expression of the sacred, an array of symbols.

When interpreting the friezes on marble well-heads, whether bucrania and garlands or assemblies of the gods, the original meaning of the type must be kept in mind. Since the well-head is the wall of a sacred enclosure, it is adorned with the powerful symbols of religion. As a part of the decoration of a peristyle garden in a Roman luxury villa, the sacred well-head forms an ensemble with the CANDELABRUM and the *oscillum* (mask hung from a tree), which were also decorative forms taken from religious cult.

R. Schneider: *Die Geburt der Athena* (Vienna, 1880) [Madrid Puteal]
J. Rada y Delgado: *Catalogo del Museo arqueologico nacional . . . Madrid*, I/i (Madrid, 1883), no. 2691
J.-A. Hild: 'Puteal', *Dictionnaire des antiquités grecques et romaines*, iv, ed. E. Saglio, E. Pottier and C. Daremberg (Paris, 1903), pp. 778–9
W. Helbig: *Führer durch die öffentlichen Sammlungen klassischer Altertümer in Rom*, ii (Leipzig, 1912–13, rev. Tübingen, 4/1966), no. 1244 [Capitoline puteal]
E. Pernice: *Hellenistische Tische* (Berlin and Leipzig, 1932), pp. 14, 36
E. Nash: *Pictorial Dictionary of Ancient Rome*, ii (London, 1962, rev. 2/1968), pp. 259–61 [puteal Libonis]

Wheeler, (Robert Eric) Mortimer (*b* Glasgow, 10 Sept 1890; *d* London, 22 July 1976). English archaeologist. Educated at Bradford Grammar School and University College, London, he was made Director of the National Museum of Wales, Cardiff, in 1924, before moving to London as Keeper and Secretary of the London Museum (now the Museum of London) in 1926, where he also established the post-graduate Institute of Archaeology (1937) within the University of London. After active military service during World War II he reorganized archaeology in India as Director General of Archaeology (1944–8). On his return to London he began to reform and reshape the British Academy as Honorary Secretary. Meanwhile, he was a tireless excavator of some of the most notable sites in Britain, including the Roman temple complex at Lydney Park, Glos (1928–9; pubd 1933), the Roman city of Verulamium (now St Albans; 1930–33; pubd 1936), Maiden Castle (1934–6; pubd 1943) and Stanwick (1951–2; pubd 1954). By his actions, writings, lectures and excavations, Wheeler exercised a profound influence on the discipline of archaeology. He conceived archaeology as a synthesis of art and science, and increasingly dependent on the methodology of the natural sciences. His frequently quoted maxim was that the proper aim of the archaeologist was to 'dig up people'. Through his early grasp of the importance of the media, in particular, from the 1950s, the power of emerging television, Wheeler was to the public the most famous British archaeologist of the 20th century. This popular acclaim was matched by recognition in both academic and official circles, in Britain and abroad, of his administrative successes as well as his contribution to the study of Iron Age and Roman Britain and the archaeology of the Indian subcontinent, by his application of rigorous standards in the practice of field excavation and insistence on the importance of stratification.

ODNB
M. Wheeler: *Archaeology from the Earth* (Oxford, 1954)
M. Wheeler: *Still Digging* (London, 1955)
M. Wheeler: *Alms for Oblivion: An Antiquary's Notebook* (London, 1966)
J. Hawkes: *Mortimer Wheeler: Adventurer in Archaeology* (London, 1982)

Winckelmann, Johann Joachim (*b* Stendal, 9 Dec 1717; *d* Trieste, 8 June 1768). German art historian. His writings on the sculpture of ancient Greece and Rome redefined the history of art and provided a theoretical apologia for Neo-classicism. *Geschichte der Kunst des Alterthums* (1764) was a standard reference on the art of the ancient world until well into the 19th century. Winckelmann revolutionized archaeological studies by providing a framework for stylistic classification of antiquities by period of origin, whereas previous antiquarian scholars had concerned themselves almost exclusively with questions of subject-matter. His analysis of the aesthetics of Greek art and his account of the conditions that encouraged its flowering, which highlighted the importance of climate and the political freedom of the ancient Greek city-states, had a major impact in the art world of his time. His scholarly celebrations of masterpieces of ancient sculpture were particularly popular and were widely quoted in travel books and artistic treatises.

1. LIFE AND WRITINGS. The son of a cobbler, Winckelmann studied Greek and Latin, as well as theology, mathematics and medicine, at the universities of Halle and Jena. After five years as a Classics teacher in Seehausen, he was employed in 1748 in Count Heinrich von Bünau's library at Nöthnitz in Saxony, researching the latter's history of the early Holy Roman Empire. He moved to Dresden in 1754 and became involved with artistic circles at the court of Augustus III, Elector of Saxony, and became friends with the painter Adam Friedrich Oeser. The publication of his polemical essay *Gedanken über die Nachahmung der griechischen Werke in der Malerey und Bildhauerkunst* (1755) established his reputation. Winckelmann's intensely argued case for the pre-eminence of the ancient Greeks, his call for a return to the pure forms of a Greek art that he knew only from verbal descriptions and from engravings and casts after Greco-Roman copies and his attack on the corruption of modern art, if not entirely original, struck a strong chord among contemporaries, and it was soon translated into French, English and Italian. His phrase 'eine edle Einfalt und eine stille Grösse',

characterizing the essence of the Greek ideal, became a slogan of the 18th-century classical revival.

Winckelmann moved to Rome in 1755 after a controversial religious conversion that opened the way to patronage by the Catholic Church. In 1758 he entered the service of Cardinal Alessandro Albani, well known as a collector of antiques. On arriving in Rome, he worked on a treatise on Greek taste in collaboration with the painter Anton Raphael Mengs (1728–79), who painted his portrait (1756–61; New York, Met.) and whom he later hailed as 'a phoenix arisen from the ashes of the first Raphael'. Although unfinished, the treatise provided the basis for lyrical descriptions of Greco-Roman statuary, such as the *Apollo Belvedere*, the *Laokoon*, the Belvedere *Antinous* and the Belvedere *Torso* (all Rome, Vatican, Mus. Pio-Clementino), later incorporated in *Geschichte der Kunst des Alterthums*. A version of his description of the *Torso* was published separately in 1759. Essays on connoisseurship (1759), on grace (1759) and on beauty (1763) continued Winckelmann's polemic for a classical taste in the visual arts. He achieved public recognition as an antiquarian scholar with *Description des pierres gravées du feu Baron de Stosch* (1760), a treatise on antique engraved gems, then highly prized as exemplars of artistic taste, and the subject of learned dissertations by other connoisseurs and antiquarians such as Pierre-Joseph Mariette and the Comte de Caylus (1692–1765).

Winckelmann's central achievement was his *Geschichte der Kunst des Alterthums* (1764), which was supplemented by *Anmerkungen über die Geschichte der Kunst des Alterthums* (1767). The earliest plan for the book dates from August 1756, and the manuscript was sent to the publisher in December 1761. The book's core is an analysis of the art of ancient Greece and Rome, complemented by discussions of ancient Egyptian, Etruscan and Near Eastern art. Although Winckelmann's visual evidence was almost exclusively Greco-Roman, he was instrumental in initiating the modern view, current since the discovery of 'original' Greek sculpture such as the Parthenon marbles in the 19th century, that later Hellenistic and Roman art was an inferior imitation of earlier Classic Greek art.

Winckelmann's subsequent publications, a study of ancient allegories and emblems, *Versuch einer Allegorie, besonders für die Kunst* (1766), and an illustrated catalogue of previously unpublished or little known antiquities, *Monumenti antichi inediti* (1767), were less innovative. They remained largely within the bounds of conventional antiquarian erudition, elucidating the meanings of visual motifs through citations from ancient Greek and Roman literature. Winckelmann did, however, establish an important principle of iconographical interpretation, namely that almost all Greek and Roman art, with the exception of a few Roman public monuments, was 'ideal' in content, and featured mythological subjects, rather than representations from history. His work as an antiquarian scholar also included studies on architecture, notably his *Anmerkungen über die Baukunst der Alten* (1762), and reports on the excavations at Herculaneum (1762 and 1764).

Winckelmann's international reputation as an expert on Greek and Roman antiquities brought him official recognition as Commissioner of Antiquities to Pope Clement XIII in 1763, and he received honorary membership of various learned societies, including the Society of Antiquaries in London. His first visit to Germany since his departure for Rome, undertaken in the spring of 1768 in the company of the sculptor Bartolomeo Cavaceppi, ended in disaster. He inexplicably cut short his itinerary after attending an audience with the Empress Maria-Theresa in Vienna and on his way back to Rome was murdered in a hotel room in Trieste.

2. Influence. Winckelmann has been called the father of modern art history because *Geschichte der Kunst des Alterthums* established an important new paradigm for defining the history of an artistic tradition. The idea of elaborating a pattern of development through a logical sequence of period styles became hugely influential for the new scholarly study of the history of art that emerged in the 19th century. He set out a comprehensive history of ancient Greek art where previously there had only been vague speculation about rise and decline, or compilations of details about famous artists culled from such literary sources as Pliny. Building on the new stylistic analysis of antiquities pioneered by the Comte de Caylus in *Recueil d'antiquités égyptiennes, étrusques, grecques, romaines et gauloises* (1752–67), and drawing on the exegesis of texts on the history of Greek art of earlier Classical scholars such as Francis Junius's *De pictura veterum* (1694), Winckelmann forged a highly effective synthesis of the available visual and verbal evidence that continues to inform accounts of ancient Greek art to this day. It was the first comprehensive attempt to rethink the larger patterning of the history of art since Giorgio Vasari's *Le vite de' piu eccelenti architetti, pittori et scultori* (1550, rev. 2/1568).

Later art historians echo the models of stylistic development Winckelmann pioneered when they trace a systematic pattern of rise and decline, or, like Heinrich Wölfflin, adumbrate a less qualitative structural change in modes of visual representation, as Winckelmann did when he distinguished between an early high style and a late beautiful style in Classic Greek art. However, partly because he had almost no concrete remains of early Greek sculpture, Winckelmann was untypically selfconscious about the speculative nature of his history. He insisted that it was a conceptual 'system', not to be confused with a chronological compilation of historical detail. A disparity between the fragmentary material facts and the schema used to endow history with a coherent pattern was not disguised, as often happens in later, seemingly more objective, histories of art. Winckelmann could even countenance that his elaborate reconstruction of the Antique from its surviving traces was no more than an illusion produced by an impossible desire to recover a totality that had been irretrievably lost.

Winckelmann's account of ancient statuary is striking for its vivid evocation of the homoerotic charge of the male body in Greek art. It is this and his insistence on the darker symbolic resonances of the still marble forms of the Greek ideal that link him with such writers as Friedrich Nietzsche and Walter Pater, both of whom brought to the fore the contradictions sustaining modern interest in the art of antiquity. At the same time, Winckelmann's involvement with the minutiae of scholarly erudition and commitment to a systematic ordering of history place him at the beginning of a tradition of modern art-historical scholarship now institutionalized in museums and universities.

Unpublished sources

Paris, Bib. N. [notebooks; for listing see A. Tibal: *Inventaires des manuscrits de Winckelmann déposés à la Bibliothèque nationale* (Paris, 1911)]

Writings

Gedanken über die Nachahmung der griechischen Werke in der Malerey und Bildhauerkunst (Dresden, 1755, repr. in R, rev. 2/1756); Eng. trans. by H. Fuseli (London, 1765/*R* 1972)

'Beschreibung des Torso Belvedere zu Rom', *Bib. S. Wiss. & Frejen Kst.*, i (1759), pp. 23–41; repr. in R

'Von der Grazie in der Kunst', *Bib. S. Wiss. & Frejen Kst.*, i (1759), pp. 13–23; repr. in R; Eng. trans. by H. Fuseli (London, 1765/*R* 1972)

Description des pierres gravées du feu Baron de Stosch (Florence, 1760/*R* 1970)

Anmerkungen über die Baukunst der Alten (Leipzig, 1762/*R* 1964)

Geschichte der Kunst des Alterthums (Dresden, 1764/*R* 1966, rev. in 2 vols, Vienna, 2/1776); Eng. trans., ed. G. H. Lodge, 4 vols (London, 1849–72, rev. in 2 vols, 1881)

Versuch einer Allegorie, besonders für die Kunst (Dresden, 1766/*R* 1964)

Anmerkungen über die Geschichte der Kunst des Alterthums (Dresden, 1767/*R* 1966)

Monumenti antichi inediti, 2 vols (Rome, 1767/*R* 1967)

J. Eiselein, ed.: *Sämtliche Werke* (Donaueschingen, 1825–9)

W. Rehm, ed.: *Briefe*, 4 vols (Berlin, 1952–7)

W. Rehm, ed.: *Kleine Schriften, Vorreden, Entwürfe* (Berlin, 1968) [R]

D. Irwin, ed.: *Winckelmann: Writings on Art* (London, 1972)

Bibliography

K. Justi: *Winckelmann und seine Zeitgenossen*, 2 vols (Leipzig, 1866–72, rev. 4/1956)

W. Pater: 'Winckelmann', *Studies in the History of the Renaissance* (London, 1873), rev. as *The Renaissance: Studies in Art and Poetry* (London, 1877; rev. 4/1893; ed. D. L. Hill, Berkeley, 1980), pp. 141–85

H. R. Jauss: 'Geschichte der Kunst und Historie', *Geschichte Ereignis und Erzählung*, ed. R. Koselleck and W. D. Stempel (Munich, 1973), pp. 175–209; Eng. trans. as *Toward an Aesthetic of Reception* (Minneapolis, 1982)

H. Dilly: *Kunstgeschichte als Institution* (Frankfurt am Main, 1979)

M. Fried: 'Antiquity Now', *October*, 37 (Summer 1986), pp. 87–97

T. W. Gaehtgens, ed.: *Johann Joachim Winckelmann, 1717–1768* (Hamburg, 1986)

E. Pommier, ed.: *Winckelmann: La Naissance de l'histoire de l'art à l'époque des Lumières* (Paris, 1991)

A. Potts: *Flesh and the Ideal: Winckelmann and the Origins of Art History* (New Haven and London, 1994)

W. Leppmann: *Winckelmann: Ein Leben für Apoll* (Berlin, 1996)

W. von Wangenheim: *Der verworfene Stein: Winckelmanns Leben* (Berlin, 2005)

XYZ

Xanthos. Site in south-west Turkey, once the principal city of ancient Lycia. Xanthos flourished from the 7th century BC to Byzantine times, and its ruins occupy an impressive situation on a steep cliff above the River Xanthos near the modern village of Kınık. Inside the ancient city walls the two main areas are the Lycian acropolis and above this the later, Roman acropolis. Exploration of the site began in the mid-19th century after its rediscovery by the English traveller and archaeologist Sir Charles Fellows (1799–1860). Many of the important remains are in the British Museum, London.

1. Architecture. 2. Sculpture. 3. Nereid Monument.

1. ARCHITECTURE. Until the Macedonian conquest in 334 BC the architecture of Xanthos and the nearby Sanctuary of Leto (Letoön) demonstrated three main influences: Lycian or Anatolian, Persian and Greek. Though the first generally appeared before the others, they do not represent distinct chronological phases. From the end of the 4th century BC, however, the architecture of Xanthos and the Letoön conformed to the general evolution of the Hellenistic, Roman, then Byzantine Near East.

Funerary architecture was largely dependent on Lycian and Anatolian models. One form of monument consisted of tall monolithic pillars surmounted by a rectangular sarcophagus with either a stepped or a curved lid terminated by ogival gables. Such tombs include the Lion Tomb, which probably dates from the period of Lycian independence before the Persian invasion of the 540s BC, the Harpy Tomb (*c.* 480 BC) and the Inscribed Pillar ('Stele of Xanthos'; *c.* 425–*c.* 400 BC) carved on its four faces with two great inscriptions in Lycian and a twelve-line passage of Greek verse. The last supported a carved sarcophagus bearing the effigy of the dynast. Another form of monument is represented by the stone sarcophagi in a necropolis outside the walls. Some, such as the Sarcophagus of Merehi (4th century BC), imitate a type of wooden house with a flat roof resting on logs, examples of which can still be found. Others, such as the Tomb of Payava just inside the walls (4th century BC; base *in situ*, rest of tomb in London, BM) or the Sarcophagus of the Dancers (late 4th century BC), have a convex lid above a rectangular sarcophagus. Finally, there are numerous rock-cut tombs of Anatolian inspiration. The façades of the oldest tombs were copied from wooden structures, but 4th-century BC and later façades show the influence of the Ionic order.

Two buildings from the period of Persian occupation are particularly significant. The earlier, Building G (*c.* 460 BC), stood in the centre of a monumental terrace on the Lycian acropolis, with edges adorned by female statues. It measured 6.40×4.26 m and was modelled on a flat-roofed wooden structure with two superimposed chambers, the higher of which was decorated with external and internal friezes. This building anticipated the famous Nereid Monument (*c.* 425–*c.* 400 BC, *see* §3 below), which has been reassembled in the British Museum, London. This stood at the southern edge of a hill, again at the centre of a terrace, facing the Lycian acropolis. Its base had lower courses of limestone and upper ones of marble, crowned by two courses of ovolos. Instead of the earlier imitations of wooden houses, it was surmounted by a small Ionic temple. In the intercolumniations were female statues, possibly representing Nereids (sea nymphs), which recall the figures surrounding the terrace of Building G.

Except for a theatre, which was altered in Roman times, and large sections of the rampart, few Hellenistic remains are visible at Xanthos itself. The excavation of the Letoön, however, has revealed several Hellenistic structures, notably three temples on the rocky central platform, stoas lining the sanctuary on the north and west, and a propylon. The most important temple, dedicated to Leto, was an Ionic building measuring 30.25×15.70 m with a deep pronaos and a false opisthodomos. A small 5th-century BC Lycian temple was enclosed by its cella. A second (Doric) temple of similar dimensions stood further east and again enclosed a small Lycian edifice. The monumental nymphaeum, consisting essentially of two ranges of buildings separated by a pool, is the most remarkable Roman building at the Letoön. The east range dates from the Republican period, the west from the 2nd century AD. It comprises a slightly curved portico (27×4 m) and a large rectangular chamber (12.55×10.50 m) flanked by semicircular exedrae. The most notable Early Christian and even Middle Byzantine building at Xanthos is a large basilica with a monumental entrance leading into an atrium surrounded by three stoas. The eastern stoa took the place of a narthex and gave access to the aisled nave of the basilica via three doors. The nave communicated with the sanctuary via three further passages. The nave and aisles were decorated with geometric pavements.

2. Sculpture. The sculpture from Xanthos essentially consists of monumental funerary works, mostly associated with the main architectural tombs and nearly all now in the British Museum, London. Archaic sculpture includes the sarcophagus that surmounted the Lion Tomb. This is decorated on its north and south faces with a couchant lion and lioness in high relief, and on its east and west faces with figures of a foot soldier, a cavalryman and a man fighting a lion, all of which are of Archaic Lycian type. The later Harpy Tomb (*see* Lycia) bears four scenes in relief executed in East Greek style. On the north and south faces are audience scenes, each framed by bird-like creatures with women's heads (see fig. 1). These bear small female figures representing the souls of the dead. On the east and west faces are scenes of people bearing offerings. Building G on the Lycian acropolis crowned the terrace on which it stood with a frieze of satyrs and beasts. This too is in East Greek style. The terrace itself carried a series of female figures at intervals. At the base of the building ran a frieze of cockerels and chickens and probably placed halfway up at the level of the principal room were friezes depicting a procession of dynasts on the exterior and a banqueting scene on the interior. The Nereid Monument includes four friezes. Two of these are at the top of the podium: the lower frieze represents a series of armed encounters between Greeks and barbarians; the upper frieze depicts successive episodes from the siege of a city. On the architrave is a third frieze on which figures bearing tribute, a boar hunt and battle scenes can be identified. The fourth frieze surrounds the top of the cella walls and comprises scenes of banqueting and sacrifice. The pediment also has sculpted decoration, and the building is crowned with acroteria representing abduction scenes. The base of the Tomb of Payava carries a large battle scene on one face and an audience scene on the other. The figure of a warrior mounting or dismounting his chariot occurs twice on the convex faces of the lid. The gabled ends of the Sarcophagus of the Dancers bear figures of *kalathiskos* dancers (i.e. carrying flared baskets or crowns), a subject that often occurs in sculpture of the second half of the 5th century BC in northern and eastern Greece. The lid carries battle and hunting scenes.

At the Letoön about 14 statues (Antalya, Archaeol. Mus.), some colossal, had apparently been destroyed and buried between the faces of the rear walls of a Roman stoa. They date from the 2nd century BC and are the only Hellenistic works among the sculptures so far found in southern Anatolia, which otherwise all date from Imperial Roman times.

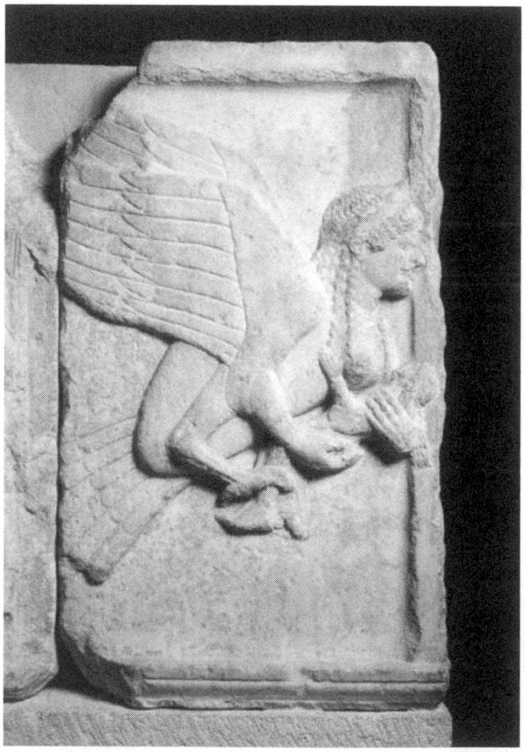

1. Xanthos, relief depicting a siren (harpy) from the Harpy Tomb, marble, h. 1.02 m, *c.* 470–460 BC (London, British Museum)

F. N. Pryce: *Prehellenic and Early Greek* (1928), I/i of *Catalogue of Sculpture in the British Museum* (London, 1928–), pp. 117–48

P. Demargne: *Les Piliers funéraires* (1958), i of *Fouilles de Xanthos* (Paris, 1958–)

H. Metzger: *L'Acropole lycienne* (1963), ii of *Fouilles de Xanthos* (Paris, 1958–)

P. Coupel and P. Demargne: *Le Monument des Néréides* (1969), iii of *Fouilles de Xanthos* (Paris, 1958–)

H. Metzger: *Anatolie*, ii (Geneva, 1969), pp. 61–78, 108–48

P. Demargne and E. Laroche: *Tombes-maisons, tombes rupestres et sarcophages* (1974), v of *Fouilles de Xanthos* (Paris, 1958–)

P. Demargne and W. P. Childs: *Le Monument des Néréides: Le Décor sculpté* (1989), viii of *Fouilles de Xanthos* (Paris, 1958–)

H. Metzger and others: *La Région nord du Letôon, les sculptures, les inscriptions gréco-lyciennes* (1992), ix of *Fouilles de Xanthos* (Paris, 1958–)

C. Rudolph: *Das Harpyien-Monument von Xanthos: Seine Bedeutung innerhalb der spätarchaischen Plastik* (Oxford, 2003)

L. Cavalier: *Architecture romaine d'Asie Mineure: Les Monuments de Xanthos et leur ornementation* (Pessac, 2005)

3. Nereid Monument Monumental tomb in the ancient Lycian city of Xanthos, probably built for Arbinas, lord of Xanthos, *c.* 400–380 BC. Located in a prominent position just outside the city walls, the Nereid Monument took the form of a small Greek-style peripteros (4×6 Ionic columns), set on a tall podium that stood in the tradition of local Lycian pillar tombs. The peripteral superstructure of the building shows a mixture of East Greek and distinctly Athenian architectural elements. The monument was

lavishly decorated with sculpture, almost certainly carved by Greek craftsmen, and was originally embellished with rich polychromy. Its iconography is characterized by a mix of Persian (or more generally Near Eastern) and Greek influences that betray Arbinas' political and cultural outlook and aspirations. The Nereid Monument was one of the grandest tombs of local dynasts in the area (cf. the heroa at Trysa and Limyra) and in many ways a precursor to the later Mausoleum at Halikarnassos. Between 1842 and 1844 Charles Fellowes removed many sculptures from the monument to the British Museum, where it is now partially reconstructed (see fig. 2); more recent French excavations have greatly advanced our understanding of the architecture of the building.

Two superimposed relief friezes (an arrangement without parallel in Greek architecture) of uneven height run along the top of the podium. The lower shows battle scenes reminiscent of Greek-style Amazonomachies, but involving only male warriors in both Greek and Oriental armour, perhaps real events draped in the language of myth that lends a more abstract, heroic air. The smaller upper frieze depicts a number of city sieges, presenting once more in the visual formulae of Greek mythological representations a standard Near Eastern motif. In one scene a leader in Oriental costume, presumably Arbinas himself, receives a delegation of city leaders; real events may be alluded to. The architrave of the peripteros bears more relief decoration with different scenes on each side, all illustrating aspects of dynastic rule and ritual (hunt, battle, procession and preparations for a banquet) and a further, smaller frieze runs along the top of the cella wall on the outside. Here the banquet continues, one isolated figure on a dining couch, complete with a Persian ceremonial beard and Persian-style rhyton (drinking horn) is again interpreted as representation of the ruler. The other sides show a sacrifice, an assembly of draped men often compared to the Parthenon east frieze, and a winged victory accompanied by other figures.

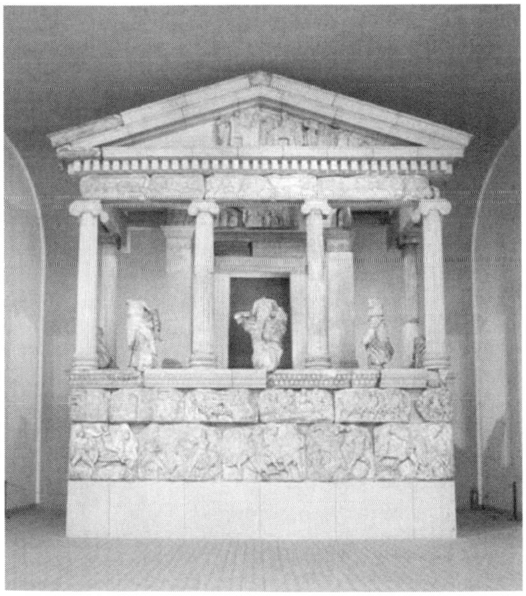
2. Xanthos, Nereid Monument, *c.* 425–*c.* 400 BC; reassembled in the British Museum, London

Yet more reliefs decorate the pediments; here the dynast recurs, enthroned in state in Greek habit surrounded by his relatives in one, and victorious in battle in the other. The central acroteria of the building were in the form of youths carrying off women, while single female figures stood at the corners. Further statues, commonly referred to as Nereids (Greek water nymphs, after whom the monument takes its name), but perhaps more likely their local Lycian counterparts, were put between the columns of the colonnade. Some of the ceiling coffers had painted figure decoration.

Commissioned by a non-Greek dynast, the sculptural decoration of the Nereid Monument elaborately celebrates various aspects of his rule. The ruthless appropriation of Greek mythological iconography for the personal self-aggrandizement of the leader foreshadows the Mausoleum and later Hellenistic royal iconography. The inherent ambiguity attached to the representation of Eastern and local themes in Greek visual terms thus ultimately proved a successful formula and was widely emulated.

P. Demargne and P. Coupel: *Fouilles de Xanthos: 3. Le monument des Néréides,* 2 vols (Paris, 1969)

W. A. P. Childs and P. Demargne: *Fouilles de Xanthos: 8. Le monument des Néréides. Le décor sculpté,* 2 vols (Paris, 1989)

T. Robinson: 'The Nereid Monument at Xanthos or the Eliyãna Monument at Arñna?' *Oxford J. Archaeol.,* xiv (1994), pp. 355–9

H. H. Nieswandt: 'Zur Herrschaftsrepräsentation am Nereiden-Monument von Xanthos anhand des Jagd-, Opfer- und Gelagefrieses.', *Lykia,* ii (1995), pp. 115–44

B. S. Ridgway: *Fourth-Century Styles in Greek Sculpture* (Madison, 1997), pp. 79–88

T. Robinson: 'Erbinna, the Nereid Monument and Xanthus', *Ancient Greeks West and East* (Leiden, 1999), pp. 361–77

S. Ebbinghaus: 'A Banquet at Xanthos: Seven Rhyta on the Northern Cella Frieze of the Nereid Monument', *Periplous: Papers on Classical Art and Archaeology Presented to Sir John Boardman,* eds G. R. Tsetskhladze and others (London 2000), pp. 98–109

Xenokrates (*fl* Athens, *c.* 280 BC). Greek sculptor and writer. Though none of his work has survived, three statue bases signed by a Xenokrates and dating from the early 3rd century BC are extant. According to Pliny (*Natural History* XXXIV.lvxxxiii) he was a pupil either of Euthykrates, the son of Lysippos, or of Teisikrates, the pupil of Euthykrates (thus closely associated with the Sikyonian school of sculpture headed by Lysippos; *see* SCULPTURE, §IV, 2(iv)), and he 'surpassed them both in the number of his statues, and wrote volumes about his art'. In the only other mention of Xenokrates in the text of the

Natural History (he is also cited in the index to book XXXIV as having written a treatise on the working of sculpture in metal) Pliny named him, along with Antigonos of Karystos, as the source for the observation that the painter Parrhasios was a master draughtsman (XXXV.lxviii). In fact, Pliny's whole discussion of the history of sculpture and painting is generally regarded as having been heavily influenced by Xenokrates. In this system, both arts gradually evolved towards perfection as each succeeding artist added something new, such as proportion or the rendering of certain details. In both cases the sequence culminated in a great master of the Sikyonian school, Lysippos in sculpture and Apelles in painting. Perhaps because he was a practising sculptor himself, Xenokrates seems to have used formal and technical criteria, rather than a work's subject-matter or moral effect, to evaluate artistic achievement. Numerous references to the history of painting and sculpture in writers other than Pliny are thought to derive from Xenokrates' accounts: he was the art critic best known to the Romans of the late Republic, whose taste he greatly influenced.

K. Jex-Blake and E. Sellers: *The Elder Pliny's Chapters on the History of Art* (London, 1896/*R* Chicago, 1976), pp. xvi–xxxvi

B. Schweitzer: 'Xenokrates von Athen', *Schr. Königsberg. Gelehrten Ges.: Geistwiss. Klasse*, ix (1932), pp. 1–52

Xenophon (*b* Athens, *c.* 428/427 BC; *d* ?Athens, *c.* 354 BC). Greek general, historian and writer. From a wealthy Athenian family, he became an enthusiastic follower of Socrates. Shortly before Socrates' death, he left Athens. He served as a general under Cyrus in Asia Minor and later accepted the patronage of Sparta, where he settled and wrote most of his major works. His writings include histories (*Hellenica, Anabasis*) and narratives of Socrates' philosophical activity (*Memorabilia, Apology, Oeconomicus, Symposium*).

Xenophon's *Memorabilia*, written some time between 370 and 354 BC, includes two dialogues (III. x.1–8) between Socrates and contemporary artists. The historical status of the two conversations is unclear, but since Xenophon's aim was to show that Socrates had made new beneficial contributions to the city, it may be assumed that the ideas expressed in the dialogues would have been found both correct and novel by Xenophon's audience. In the first, Socrates asks the painter Parrhasios how he uses colour to represent (*ekmimeisthai*) visible objects and suggests that it is not by taking a single model, but by combining features from objects of many sorts. He then asks whether Parrhasios can represent the characteristics of the soul that 'most strongly inspire longing and desire'. Parrhasios is puzzled and wonders how something that has no colour or shape can be depicted. Socrates instructs him that the soul can be represented through facial expression and bodily gesture, which are signs of it. They agree that only a good soul gives pleasure to the beholder. In the other dialogue Socrates addresses the sculptor Kleiton and asks him how he makes his statues of athletes look so alive. Kleiton does not know. Socrates tells him that it is by rendering the different parts of the body as they appear under the strain of motion. He then directs Kleiton's attention to the soul, saying that the beholder's pleasure will be heightened if careful modelling of facial features reveals the inner feelings of the type of person represented.

These conversations show three important aspects of Greek popular thought about art in this period. First, artistic *mimesis* was not understood as an exact copying of individuals; its concern was with general types, the aim being to convey the general impression of the type. Second, there was a strong and apparently new interest in the depiction of inner states through the treatment of facial expression and posture. Third, the passage displays the pervasively ethical character of Greek aesthetic thought: it was quickly agreed that only the representation of good people could yield pleasure.

Xenophon: *Memorabilia*, ed. E. Marchant, Loeb Class. Lib. (London and New York, 1923)

G. Sörbom: *Mimesis and Art* (Uppsala, 1966), pp. 78–99 [trans. and analysis of *Memorabilia* III.x.1–8]

Yerushalayim. *See* JERUSALEM.

Zagora. Site on the west coast of the Greek island of Andros in the Aegean, which was established in the 9th century BC and flourished for approximately two centuries before being abandoned. It occupies the flat top of a promontory, with sheer cliffs on all sides except the north-east, which was defended by a massive fortification wall. The settlement was clearly sited for defensive reasons rather than convenience, and this reflects the troubled period of its existence, the Greek Dark Ages. The fortification wall (9th century BC) is a most interesting and rare example of Dark Age defensive works. It is some 140 m long and varies in width from around 4 m at its northern end to about 3 m at the only gate, near its southern end. It is built of unworked local schist and marble. The gate is set back, with an outwork to the north flanking the entrance passage. Within the fortified area, part of the town has been excavated by Cambitoglou since 1976, revealing densely packed houses. These are arranged in blocks and show variations on a simple basic plan, with courtyards in front of general purpose rooms for living and storage. The walls are frequently lined with benches for standing large pithoi or smaller amphorae and are entirely of undressed stone, the most readily available building material. Roofs seem to have consisted of flat stone slabs on wooden beams, supported where necessary by internal wooden posts and presumably covered with clay waterproofing, the traditional system for roofs in the Cycladic islands. In the centre of the site, almost at the highest point, is an isolated building, constructed in the 6th century BC after the abandonment of the town. It comprises an anteroom

(2.80×6.29 m), entered by a doorway rather than a porch and leading to a cella (5.87×6.30 m). In the cella is a small trapezoidal platform, slightly off the axis of the building, which has been identified as an altar. This may antedate the building itself.

A. Cambitoglou: 'Anaskaphai Zagoras Androu' [The excavation of Zagora on Andros], *Praktika Athen. Archaiol. Etaireias* (1967), pp. 103–11; (1969), pp. 135–8; (1972), pp. 251–73

A. Cambitoglou and others: *Zagora*, i (Sydney, 1971)

P. G. Themelis: 'Zagora: Polis e necropolis?' [Zagora: city or necropolis?], *Archaiol. Ephimeris* (1975), pp. 230–66

J. N. Coldstream: *Geometric Greece* (London, 1977), pp. 210–13, 304–12

A. Cambitoglou: *Archaeological Museum of Andros: Guide to the Finds from the Excavations of the Geometric Town at Zagora* (Athens, 1981)

Zea. *See* KEA.

Zenodoros(*fl* mid-1st century AD). Greek bronze sculptor, active in Rome and Gaul. His name ('foreign gift') suggests that he may have been born in Massalia (Marseille), Asia Minor, Egypt or Syria, and according to Pliny (*Natural History* XXXIV.xviii.46) he was the foremost sculptor of colossal statues of the 1st century AD. From AD 54 to 64 Zenodoros worked in Arvernis, Gaul, making a bronze statue of *Mercury*, for which he was paid 40 million sesterces. Nero commissioned him to make a colossal imperial portrait *c.* 36 m high, which was placed in his palace, the Domus Aurea in Rome (Pliny: XXXIV.xviii.45–6; Suetonius: *Nero* xxxi). During the reign of Vespasian (AD 69–79) it was converted into a statue of the Sun god, *Sol* (Aelius Spartianicus: *Hadrian* XIX.xii; Herodian: I.xv.9; Pliny: XXXIV.xviii.45). A replica of the *Mercury* was known in Corinth in antiquity (Pausanias: *Guide to Greece* II.iii.4) and several extant copies may reflect the original appearance of the statue. The colossal statue of *Nero*, however, cannot be accurately reconstructed. According to Pliny's account, Zenodoros no longer employed the lost wax technique, and he created a polychrome effect with silver and gold additions to the bronze. He was able to imitate earlier styles, since the copies of *Mercury* resemble the work of Lysippos, while according to Pliny he copied two silver cups in the style of Kalamis.

J. Overbeck: *Die antiken Schriftquellen zur Geschichte der bildenden Künste bei den Griechen* (Leipzig, 1868/R Hildesheim, 1959), nos 2185, 2273–6

Zeuxis (*fl* late 5th century BC–early 4th). Greek painter. Zeuxis of Herakleia achieved wealth and fame as a painter in Athens around the time of the Peloponnesian Wars (431–404 BC). Pliny (*Natural History* XXXV.xxxvi.61) stated that Zeuxis began working in the fourth year of the 95th Olympiad (397 BC) and that writers who dated him to the 89th Olympiad (*c.* 424 BC) were mistaken. According to Pliny, Zeuxis was the pupil of either Demophilos of Himera or Neseus of Thasos. Both were active around 424 BC, perhaps explaining the confusion of other authors concerning Zeuxis' own date.

No paintings by Zeuxis survive, but ancient descriptions of his style suggest that he used painterly methods rather than line to create an illusion of three-dimensional form and depth. His main rival, PARRHASIOS, continued the linear tradition of APOLLODOROS by emphasizing outline and using hatching to suggest light and shade. Anecdotes record informal competitions between Zeuxis and Parrhasios in the creation of optical illusions (see Pliny: *Natural History* XXXV.xxxvi.65). These accounts may, however, be apocryphal, and the two painters seem more credibly opposed as the main practitioners of two different styles, which continued to divide artists, critics and philosophers for generations afterwards.

Using ancient literary evidence and modern painting techniques, scholars have attempted to reconstruct the essential qualities of Zeuxis' style. Pliny stated that Zeuxis painted monochromes in white (*Natural History* XXXV.xxxvi.64); although the exact meaning of this is disputed, the paintings were probably done in white on a dark background. This method would enable the painter to use impasto and opaque white highlights to suggest light: the darker, receding areas would be rendered in a thinner transparent white paint, only partly covering the background. In this way neither outline nor linear hatching would be needed to create the illusion of three-dimensional form. In polychrome painting, this method would make use of darker blues, greens and other colours to create shadows on and around a figure, replacing the hatched shadows of the linear style. Effects similar to this occur in the paintings on a Hellenistic tomb façade at Leukadia in Macedonia.

Ancient writers mentioned at least ten paintings by Zeuxis, including representations of *Herakles Strangling the Snakes, Zeus on a Throne* and *Penelope* (in which Zeuxis is said by Pliny to have represented 'morality' itself). A painting of *Helen*, which Pliny saw in the porticos of Philippus at Rome (1st century BC), reproduced the best features of five virgins from the city that had commissioned the work. Pliny (*Natural History* XXXV.xxxvi.64) stated that the painting was for the Temple of Hera Lakinia at Akragas, but Cicero (*De inventione rhetorica* II.i.1) attributed the commission to Kroton in southern Italy, where there was a famous temple of the same goddess.

The most detailed description of a painting by Zeuxis is that of the *Centaur Family* (see Lucian: *Zeuxis* iii–vii). Sulla (*c.* 138–78 BC) had apparently taken the original to Rome when he sacked Athens in 86 BC, but Lucian saw a copy in the home of a painter in Athens. It represented a female centaur reclining on the grass and nursing twin infant centaurs, one at her human breast, the other at her horse teat. Her mate was shown leaning over his family, laughing, while holding a lion cub above his head to tease or frighten the children. Lucian admired the originality of the theme, but also the contrast between the figures of the shaggy, alarming male centaur and the elegant female. He noted the subtle transition between the female's horse body and human torso. Zeuxis, on the other hand, seems to have felt that it was only the subject's novelty that was appreciated, while his artistic skill was ignored, and seems, consequently, to have withdrawn the picture from exhibition. He gave away some other works as gifts, believing that no price could reflect their true value.

Zeuxis is also said to have made terracotta statues (Pliny: *Natural History* XXXV.xxxvi.66). None has survived, but they were probably not major works, since Fulvius Nobilior left them behind in Ambrakia when he transferred some statues of Muses to Rome (189 BC). It has been claimed that Zeuxis decorated the palace of Archelaos of Macedon in the Macedonian capital.

Praised by some ancient writers (e.g. Quintilian: *Institutio oratoria* XII.x.4) as the inventor of chiaroscuro, Zeuxis was criticized by others for creating frivolous illusions. Both Aristotle (*Poetics* 1450a.27–9) and, by implication, Plato (*Republic* X.602d.1–4) condemned him for being more interested in visual tricks than in depicting character (*ethos*) or creating aesthetically pleasing compositions with simple geometric forms and a clear line. To these writers, and doubtless to many contemporary critics, Zeuxis' innovative works seemed degenerate in comparison with the linear 'character paintings' of Parrhasios and the Early Classical painter POLYGNOTOS OF THASOS. Nevertheless, he was one of the foremost painters of his time and among the most influential painters of antiquity.

J. Overbeck: *Die antiken Schriftquellen zur Geschichte der bildenden Künste bei den Griechen* (Leipzig, 1868), nos 1647–91

W. Lepik-Kopaczyńska: 'Zeuxis aus Herakleia', *Helikon*, i (1961), pp. 379–426

J. J. Pollitt: *The Art of Greece: Sources and Documents* (Englewood Cliffs, 1965/rev. Cambridge, 2/1990) [trans. of the major anc. sources; with full bibliog.]

J. J. Pollitt: *The Ancient View of Greek Art* (New Haven, 1974)

K. Gschwandtler: *Zeuxis und Parrhasios: Ein Beitrag zur antiken Künstlerbiographie* (diss., Graz, Karl-Franzens-U., 1975)

V. J. Bruno: *Form and Color in Greek Painting* (New York, 1977)

Zoophorus. Frieze with animal reliefs, such as that on the portico of the Theseion, Athens.

Zygouries [now Ayios Vasilios]. Site of an Early and Late Bronze Age town in the Corinthia of southern Greece, midway between Argos and Corinth. Excavations at the Zygouries Hill in the Kleonai Valley were conducted by Carl Blegen in 1921–2 for the American School of Classical Studies, revealing an important sequence of Bronze Age settlements. The Early Helladic (EH) phase (*c.* 3600/3000–*c.* 2050 BC) was the most abundantly represented, with at least ten houses of mud-brick on stone socle construction arranged close together on narrow streets. The rectangular, flat-roofed, two- and three-roomed structures with fixed central hearths provided one of the first definitive examples of Early Bronze Age domestic architecture. Contemporary graves yielded a broad variety of EH pottery, small gold, silver and bronze ornaments, numerous figurines and stone tools. Like its neighbours Tiryns, Asine, Lerna and Ayios Kosmas, Zygouries suffered a severe destruction at the end of EH II (*c.* 2900/2600–*c.* 2400 BC), which was followed by limited resettlement. Evidence of Middle Helladic (*c.* 2050–*c.* 1600 BC) habitation comes in the form of a few graves, mostly those of children. Modest prosperity returned to Zygouries during the Late Helladic (LH) period (*c.* 1600–*c.* 1050 BC). The most important feature of the small Mycenaean town was an LH IIIA:1–IIIB:1 (*c.* 1390–*c.* 1240 BC) house referred to by Blegen as the 'Potter's Shop', which yielded more than 1300 unused vessels of varied types. This sizeable multi-roomed structure, probably the house of the local nobleman, was equipped with a terracotta pipe drain and a second storey with painted plaster walls. Fiery destruction brought an end to the site in LH IIIB, around 1240 BC. Corinth Archaeological Museum has an important holding of finds from the site.

C. W. Blegen: *Zygouries: A Prehistoric Settlement in the Valley of Cleonae* (Cambridge, 1928)

P. M. Thomas: *LH IIIB:1 Pottery from Tsoungiza and Zygouries* (diss., Chapel Hill, U. NC, 1992)

Illustration Acknowledgements

We are grateful to those listed below for permission to reproduce copyright illustrative material and to those contributors who supplied photographs or helped us to obtain them. Every effort has been made to contact copyright holders and to credit them appropriately; we apologize to anyone who may have been omitted from the acknowledgements or cited incorrectly. Any error brought to our attention will be corrected in subsequent editions. Where illustrations have been taken from books, publication details are provided in the acknowledgements below. Line drawings, maps and plans have been obtained and/or modified from *The Dictionary of Art* (1996) © Oxford University Press.

VOLUME I

Colour Plates

pl. I, fig. 1 Erich Lessing / Art Resource, NY; fig. 2 Scala / Art Resource, NY; fig. 3 Erich Lessing / Art Resource, NY; pl. II fig. 1 Scala / Art Resource, NY; fig. 2 Vanni / Art Resource, NY; pl. III, fig. 1 Erich Lessing / Art Resource, NY; fig. 2 Nimatallah / Art Resource, NY; pl. IV, fig. 1 Gilles Mermet / Art Resource, NY; fig. 2 Erich Lessing / Art Resource, NY; fig. 3 Erich Lessing / Art Resource, NY; pl. V, fig. 1 Erich Lessing / Art Resource, NY; fig. 2 Scala / Art Resource, NY; fig. 3 Bildarchiv Preussischer Kulturbesitz / Art Resource, NY; pl. VI, fig. 1 Erich Lessing / Art Resource, NY; fig. 2 Giraudon / Art Resource, NY; fig. 3 SEF / Art Resource, NY; fig. 4 © British Museum / Art Resource, NY; pl. VII, fig. 1 Réunion des Musées Nationaux / Art Resource, NY; fig. 2 Erich Lessing / Art Resource, NY; fig. 3 Scala / Art Resource, NY; pl. VIII, fig. 1 Erich Lessing / Art Resource, NY; fig. 2 HIP / Art Resource, NY; pl. IX, fig. 1 Nimatallah / Art Resource, NY; fig. 2 Erich Lessing / Art Resource, NY; fig. 3 Erich Lessing / Art Resource, NY; pl. X, fig. 1 Réunion des Musées Nationaux / Art Resource, NY; fig. 2 © British Museum / Art Resource, NY; fig. 3 The Newark Museum / Art Resource, NY; fig. 4 Alinari / Art Resource, NY; pl. XI, fig. 1 Scala / Art Resource, NY; fig. 2 Erich Lessing / Art Resource, NY; pl. XII, fig. 1 British Museum / Art Resource, NY; fig. 2 Erich Lessing / Art Resource, NY; fig. 3 © British Museum / Art Resource, NY; fig. 4 HIP / Art Resource, NY; pl. XIII, fig. 1 Erich Lessing / Art Resource, NY; fig. 2 Scala / Art Resource, NY; fig. 3 Nimatallah / Art Resource, NY; pl. XIV, fig. 1 Bildarchiv Preussischer Kulturbesitz / Art Resource, NY; fig. 2 Scala / Art Resource, NY; fig. 3 Bildarchiv Preussischer Kulturbesitz / Art Resource, NY; fig 4 Erich Lessing / Art Resource, NY; pl. XV, fig. 1 Erich Lessing / Art Resource, NY; fig. 2 Nimatallah / Art Resource, NY; fig. 3 Scala / Art Resource, NY; fig. 4 Scala / Art Resource, NY; pl. XVI, fig. 1 Erich Lessing / Art Resource, NY; fig. 2 Nimatallah / Art Resource, NY

Black and White Images

2 Foto Marburg / Art Resource, NY; 4 Scala / Art Resource, NY; 9 Erich Lessing / Art Resource, NY; 19 Dictionary of Art; 13 (left) Vanni / Art Resource, NY; (right) Art Resource, NY; 16 Erich Lessing / Art Resource, NY; 17 Vanni / Art Resource, NY; 21 Vanni / Art Resource, NY; 23 (left) Dictionary of Art; (top right) Erich Lessing / Art Resource, NY; (bottom right) Erich Lessing / Art Resource, NY; 26 Erich Lessing / Art Resource, NY; 27 SEF / Art Resource, NY; 33 Réunion des Musées Nationaux / Art Resource, NY; 38 Erich Lessing / Art Resource, NY; 40 Réunion des Musées Nationaux / Art Resource, NY; 41 Erich Lessing / Art Resource, NY; 42 Vanni / Art Resource, NY; 45 Erich Lessing / Art Resource, NY; 50 Erich Lessing / Art Resource, NY; 54 Dictionary of Art; 56 Scala / Art Resource, NY; 58 Dictionary of Art; 59 Dictionary of Art; 60 Vanni / Art Resource, NY; 61 Vanni / Art Resource, NY; 67 Dictionary of Art; 72 Vanni / Art Resource, NY; 73 (left) Nimatallah / Art Resource, NY; (right) Dictionary of Art; 74 Dictionary of Art; 75 Dictionary of Art; 79 Dictionary of Art; 81 Dictionary of Art; 85 Dictionary of Art; 86 Dictionary of Art; 90 Dictionary of Art; 95 Dictionary of Art; 98 Dictionary of Art; 106 Dictionary of Art; 107 Dictionary

of Art; 108 Dictionary of Art; 110 Dictionary of Art; 114 Dictionary of Art; 115 Dictionary of Art; 129 Dictionary of Art; 131 Dictionary of Art; 134 Dictionary of Art; 139 Dictionary of Art; 151 Dictionary of Art; 153 Dictionary of Art; 154 (top) Dictionary of Art; (bottom) Dictionary of Art; 156 Dictionary of Art; 157 Dictionary of Art; 163 Dictionary of Art; 166 Dictionary of Art; 167 Dictionary of Art; 169 Dictionary of Art; 173 Giraudon / Art Resource, NY; 174 Dictionary of Art; 181 Erich Lessing / Art Resource, NY; 184 Vanni / Art Resource, NY; 185 Vanni / Art Resource, NY; 186 Dictionary of Art; 187 Vanni / Art Resource, NY; 189 Dictionary of Art; 191 Dictionary of Art; 192 Dictionary of Art; 194 Dictionary of Art; 195 (top) Dictionary of Art; 195 (bottom) Art Resource, NY; 196 Vanni / Art Resource, NY; 197 (left) Scala / Art Resource, NY; (right) Erich Lessing / Art Resource, NY; 199 (top) Scala / Art Resource, NY; (bottom) Erich Lessing / Art Resource, NY; 203 Dictionary of Art; 204 Dictionary of Art; 206 Dictionary of Art; 208 SEF / Art Resource, NY; 210 Vanni / Art Resource, NY; 213 Vanni / Art Resource, NY; 212 Vanni / Art Resource, NY; 214 Scala / Art Resource, NY; 218 Dictionary of Art; 219 (top) Scala / Art Resource, NY; (bottom) Dictionary of Art; 222 (top) Dictionary of Art; (bottom) Dictionary of Art; 223 Erich Lessing / Art Resource, NY; 224 Dictionary of Art; 225 © the Trustees of the British Museum; 226 Dictionary of Art; 227 Dictionary of Art; 228 Dictionary of Art; 229 Alinari / Art Resource, NY; 230 Scala / Art Resource, NY; 236 Scala / Art Resource, NY; 237 Erich Lessing / Art Resource, NY; 239 Vanni / Art Resource, NY; 240 Dictionary of Art; 242 Dictionary of Art; 244 Dictionary of Art; 246 Erich Lessing / Art Resource, NY; 249 Scala / Art Resource, NY; 252 Réunion des Musées Nationaux / Art Resource, NY; 255 Erich Lessing / Art Resource, NY; 256 Dictionary of Art; 257 Vanni / Art Resource, NY; 259 Vanni / Art Resource, NY; 261 (left) Dictionary of Art; (right) Erich Lessing / Art Resource, NY; 263 Scala / Art Resource, NY; 267 Nimatallah / Art Resource, NY; 268 Erich Lessing / Art Resource, NY; 272 Scala / Art Resource, NY; 274 Vanni / Art Resource, NY; 275 Erich Lessing / Art Resource, NY; 276 Giraudon / Art Resource, NY; 281 Bildarchiv Preussischer Kulturbesitz / Art Resource, NY; 284 Snark / Art Resource, NY; 302 Erich Lessing / Art Resource, NY; 303 Art Resource, NY; 307 Scala / Art Resource, NY; 308 Dictionary of Art; 310 Erich Lessing / Art Resource, NY; 313 Vanni / Art Resource, NY; 319 SEF / Art Resource, NY; 321 Erich Lessing / Art Resource, NY; 322 Dictionary of Art; 323 Erich Lessing / Art Resource, NY; 325 Dictionary of Art; 329 Dictionary of Art; 331 Dictionary of Art; 339 Dictionary of Art; 340 Dictionary of Art; 344 HIP / Art Resource, NY; 348 Dictionary of Art; 349 HIP / Art Resource, NY; 356 HIP / Art Resource, NY; 361 HIP / Art Resource, NY; 367 Erich Lessing / Art Resource, NY; 369 Vanni / Art Resource, NY; 370 SEF / Art Resource, NY; 373 Borromeo / Art Resource, NY; 374 Dictionary of Art; 375 Vanni / Art Resource, NY; 379 Erich Lessing / Art Resource, NY; 383 Vanni / Art Resource, NY; 384 Dictionary of Art; 389 Réunion des Musées Nationaux / Art Resource, NY; 391 Vanni / Art Resource, NY; 393 (left) Erich Lessing / Art Resource, NY; (right) Dictionary of Art; 394 HIP / Art Resource, NY; 399 Alinari / Art Resource, NY; 405 Dictionary of Art; 406 Dictionary of Art; 414 Erich Lessing / Art Resource, NY; 419 (left) Vanni / Art Resource, NY; (right) Vanni / Art Resource, NY; 421 Erich Lessing / Art Resource, NY; 424 Dictionary of Art; 425 Erich Lessing / Art Resource, NY; 427 Vanni / Art Resource, NY; 430 Dictionary of Art; 432 (left) Erich Lessing / Art Resource, NY; (right) Dictionary of Art; 434 Vanni / Art Resource, NY; 437 Erich Lessing / Art Resource, NY; 438 Réunion des Musées Nationaux / Art Resource, NY; 439 Scala / Art Resource, NY; 440 (top) Erich Lessing / Art Resource, NY; 440 (bottom) Alinari / Art Resource, NY; 442 Dictionary of Art; 447 Scala / Art Resource, NY; 449 Scala / Art Resource, NY; 455 Réunion des Musées Nationaux / Art Resource, NY; 458 Erich Lessing / Art Resource, NY; 460 Scala / Art Resource, NY; 462 HIP / Art Resource, NY; 463 Scala / Art Resource, NY; 467 Dictionary of Art; 470 Dictionary of Art; 471 Scala / Art Resource, NY; 472 (left) Bildarchiv Preussischer Kulturbesitz / Art Resource, NY; (right) Alinari / Art Resource, NY; 473 Scala / Art Resource, NY; 474 Erich Lessing / Art Resource, NY; 475 Dictionary of Art; 476 Scala / Art Resource, NY; 477 Vanni / Art Resource, NY; 480 Erich Lessing / Art Resource, NY; 482 Dictionary of Art; 483 Scala / Art Resource, NY; 487 Erich Lessing / Art Resource, NY; 490 Vanni / Art Resource, NY; 496 Bildarchiv Preussischer Kulturbesitz / Art Resource, NY; 498 (top) Erich Lessing / Art Resource, NY; (bottom) Erich Lessing / Art Resource, NY; 500 Vanni / Art Resource, NY; 505 Scala / Art Resource, NY; 507 © British Museum / Art Resource, NY; 508 Erich Lessing / Art Resource, NY; 512 Erich Lessing / Art Resource, NY; 514 Erich Lessing / Art Resource, NY; 516 Dictionary of Art; 517 Dictionary of Art; 518 Dictionary of Art; 521 Erich Lessing / Art Resource, NY; 525 Réunion des Musées Nationaux / Art Resource, NY; 526 Bildarchiv Preussischer Kulturbesitz / Art Resource, NY; 527 (top) Dictionary of Art; (bottom) Dictionary of Art; 528 Borromeo / Art Resource, NY; 530 Scala / Art Resource, NY; 531 SEF / Art Resource, NY; 532 Dictionary of Art; 534 Werner Forman / Art Resource, NY; 535 © British Museum / Art Resource, NY; 539 Erich Lessing / Art Resource, NY; 540 Réunion des Musées Nationaux / Art Resource, NY; 541 Dictionary of Art; 544 Dictionary of Art; 546 Dictionary of Art; 548 Bildarchiv Preussischer Kulturbesitz / Art Resource, NY; 549 Erich Lessing / Art Resource, NY; 550 Dictionary of Art; 552 Scala / Art Resource, NY; 554 Scala / Art Resource, NY; 557 Giraudon / Art Resource, NY; 561 Erich Lessing / Art Resource, NY; 562 Erich Lessing / Art Resource, NY; 563 Nimatallah / Art Resource, NY; 564 Dictionary of Art; 567 Nimatallah / Art Resource, NY; 568 Alinari / Art Resource, NY; 569 Scala / Art Resource, NY; 572 Scala / Art Resource, NY; 574 Vanni / Art Resource, NY; 578 Nimatallah / Art Resource, NY; 580 Dictionary of Art; 581 Erich Lessing / Art Resource, NY; 583 Réunion des Musées Nationaux / Art Resource, NY;

588 Erich Lessing / Art Resource, NY; 591 Dictionary of Art; 594 Scala / Art Resource, NY; 596 HIP / Art Resource, NY; 600 Dictionary of Art; 608 Scala / Art Resource, NY; 610 Réunion des Musées Nationaux / Art Resource, NY; 616 Dictionary of Art; 617 Erich Lessing / Art Resource, NY; 619 Bildarchiv Preussischer Kulturbesitz / Art Resource, NY; 621 Erich Lessing / Art Resource, NY; 622 (both) Nimatallah / Art Resource, NY; 625 Edgar Knobloch / Art Resource, NY; 626 Borromeo / Art Resource, NY; 628 © J. Paul Getty Museum; 629 Scala / Art Resource, NY; 634 Erich Lessing / Art Resource, NY; 635 HIP / Art Resource, NY; 636 Erich Lessing / Art Resource, NY; 639 Timothy McCarthy / Art Resource, NY; 641 HIP / Art Resource, NY; 642 Dictionary of Art; 645 SEF / Art Resource, NY; 646 Euan Wingfield / Art Resource, NY; 648 Dictionary of Art; 649 Dictionary of Art; 653 Scala / Art Resource, NY; 656 Vanni / Art Resource, NY; 657 Alinari / Art Resource, NY; 658 Vanni / Art Resource, NY; 659 © British Museum / Art Resource, NY; 662 Vanni / Art Resource, NY; 665 Scala / Art Resource, NY

VOLUME II

Colour Plates

pl. I, fig. 1 Nimatallah / Art Resource, NY; fig. 2 Vanni / Art Resource, NY; pl. II, fig. 1 Scala / Art Resource, NY, fig. 2 Nimatallah / Art Resource, NY; pl. III fig. 1 Erich Lessing / Art Resource, NY; fig. 2 Scala / Art Resource, NY; pl. IV, fig. 1 Scala / Art Resource, NY; fig. 2 Scala / Art Resource, NY; fig. 3 Scala / Art Resource, NY; pl. V, fig. 1 Michos Tzovaras / Art Resource, NY; fig. 2 Erich Lessing / Art Resource, NY; fig. 3 Alinari / Art Resource, NY; pl. VI, fig. 1 Scala / Art Resource, NY; fig. 2 Erich Lessing / Art Resource, NY; fig. 3 © British Museum / Art Resource, NY; fig. 4 Scala / Art Resource, NY; pl. VII, fig. 1 HIP / Art Resource, NY; fig. 2 Scala / Art Resource, NY; fig. 3 Erich Lessing / Art Resource, NY; fig. 4 Nimatallah / Art Resource, NY; pl. VIII Nimatallah / Art Resource, NY; IX, fig. 1 Scala / Art Resource, NY; fig. 2 Werner Forman / Art Resource, NY; pl. X, fig. 1 Erich Lessing / Art Resource, NY; fig. 2 SEF / Art Resource, NY; pl. XI, fig. 1 Erich Lessing / Art Resource, NY; fig. 2 Erich Lessing / Art Resource, NY; pl. XII, fig. 1 Erich Lessing / Art Resource, NY; fig. 2 Scala / Art Resource, NY; fig. 3 Scala / Art Resource, NY; pl. XIII, fig. 1; Vanni / Art Resource, NY; fig. 2 Erich Lessing / Art Resource, NY; fig. 3 Scala / Art Resource, NY; pl. XIV, fig. 1 Scala / Art Resource, NY; fig. 2 Scala / Art Resource, NY; pl. XV, fig. 1 Vanni / Art Resource, NY; fig. 2 Scala / Art Resource, NY; pl. XVI, fig. 1 Erich Lessing / Art Resource, NY; fig. 2 Erich Lessing / Art Resource, NY

Black and White Images

5 (top) Dictionary of Art; (bottom) © British Museum / Art Resource, NY; 7 Bildarchiv Preussischer Kulturbesitz / Art Resource, NY; 9 Bildarchiv Preussischer Kulturbesitz / Art Resource, NY; 10 Erich Lessing / Art Resource, NY; 12 Dictionary of Art; 13 (top) Dictionary of Art; 13 (bottom) Dictionary of Art; 14 SEF / Art Resource, NY; 16 Vanni / Art Resource, NY; 17 Dictionary of Art; 19 Vanni / Art Resource, NY; 20 Dictionary of Art; 21 HIP / Art Resource, NY; 23 Erich Lessing / Art Resource, NY; 24 Erich Lessing / Art Resource, NY; 25 Vanni / Art Resource, NY; 26 Erich Lessing / Art Resource, NY; 28 Erich Lessing / Art Resource, NY; 31 HIP / Art Resource, NY; 34 Erich Lessing / Art Resource, NY; 48 HIP / Art Resource, NY; 49 (left) © British Museum / Art Resource, NY; (right) © British Museum / Art Resource, NY; 59 Vanni / Art Resource, NY; 61 HIP / Art Resource, NY; 62 Dictionary of Art; 65 Dictionary of Art; 68 Dictionary of Art; 71 Dictionary of Art; 74 Dictionary of Art; 76 Dictionary of Art; 78 Dictionary of Art; 81 Dictionary of Art; 82 HIP / Art Resource, NY; 105 Dictionary of Art; 106 Erich Lessing / Art Resource, NY; 108 Scala / Art Resource, NY; 110 Réunion des Musées Nationaux / Art Resource, NY; 114 Vanni / Art Resource, NY; 117 Erich Lessing / Art Resource, NY; 118 Erich Lessing / Art Resource, NY; 119 Nimatallah / Art Resource, NY; 120 Dictionary of Art; 122 Vanni / Art Resource, NY; 123 Erich Lessing / Art Resource, NY; 124 Erich Lessing / Art Resource, NY; 127 Réunion des Musées Nationaux / Art Resource, NY; 130 (top) Vanni / Art Resource, NY; 130 (bottom) Bildarchiv Preussischer Kulturbesitz / Art Resource, NY; 131 Alinari / Art Resource, NY; 132 Réunion des Musées Nationaux / Art Resource, NY; 138 Dictionary of Art; 140 Nimatallah / Art Resource, NY; 141 Dictionary of Art; 145 Borromeo / Art Resource, NY; 146 (top) Erich Lessing / Art Resource, NY; (bottom) Erich Lessing / Art Resource, NY; 148 Dictionary of Art; 152 (left) Alinari / Art Resource, NY; (right) SEF / Art Resource, NY; 155 Dictionary of Art; 158 Vanni / Art Resource, NY; 165 (top) Erich Lessing / Art Resource, NY; (bottom) Dictionary of Art; 166 Vanni / Art Resource, NY; 172 (top) Vanni / Art Resource, NY; (bottom) SEF / Art Resource, NY; 177 Erich Lessing / Art Resource, NY; 178 Nimatallah / Art Resource, NY; 185 Scala / Art Resource, NY; 187 Erich Lessing / Art Resource, NY; 202 Scala / Art Resource, NY; 209 Erich Lessing / Art Resource, NY; 210 Scala / Art Resource, NY; 217 Scala / Art Resource, NY; 221 Dictionary of Art; 222 SEF / Art Resource, NY; 223 SEF / Art Resource, NY; 224 SEF / Art Resource, NY; 227 Réunion des Musées Nationaux / Art Resource, NY; 241 (top) Vanni / Art Resource, NY; (bottom) Scala / Art Resource, NY; 243 Nimatallah / Art Resource, NY; 244 Nimatallah / Art

Resource, NY; 250 Dictionary of Art; 251 Bildarchiv Preussischer Kulturbesitz / Art Resource, NY; 253 (left) Erich Lessing / Art Resource, NY; (right) Scala / Art Resource, NY; 255 Erich Lessing / Art Resource, NY; 257 Erich Lessing / Art Resource, NY; 260 SEF / Art Resource, NY; 262 Dictionary of Art; 264 © Ancient-Greece.org/Thomas Sakoulas; 265 Nimatallah / Art Resource, NY; 266 Erich Lessing / Art Resource, NY; 270 Réunion des Musées Nationaux / Art Resource, NY; 271 Erich Lessing / Art Resource, NY; 272 Dictionary of Art; 279 Dictionary of Art; 281 Dictionary of Art; 283 Dictionary of Art; 294 Cameraphoto Arte, Venice / Art Resource, NY; 295 Vanni / Art Resource, NY; 297 Erich Lessing / Art Resource, NY; 299 Scala / Art Resource, NY; 303 Dictionary of Art; 304 Dictionary of Art; 306 Scala / Art Resource, NY; 307 Scala / Art Resource, NY; 311 Erich Lessing / Art Resource, NY; 315 Alinari / Art Resource, NY; 316 SEF / Art Resource, NY; 317 Alinari / Art Resource, NY; 320 Dictionary of Art; 333 Dictionary of Art; 335 Dictionary of Art; 336 Dictionary of Art; 337 Nimatallah / Art Resource, NY; 340 Réunion des Musées Nationaux / Art Resource, NY; 342 Dictionary of Art; 355 Réunion des Musées Nationaux / Art Resource, NY; 367 Erich Lessing / Art Resource, NY; 382 Erich Lessing / Art Resource, NY; 403 © British Museum / Art Resource, NY; 322 Nimatallah / Art Resource, NY; 408 Erich Lessing / Art Resource, NY; 323 Dictionary of Art; 326 Dictionary of Art; 327 Erich Lessing / Art Resource, NY; 328 Dictionary of Art; 329 Dictionary of Art; 331 Dictionary of Art; 332 Dictionary of Art; 412 Scala / Art Resource, NY; 415 (left) Réunion des Musées Nationaux / Art Resource, NY; (right) Scala / Art Resource, NY; 416 Vanni / Art Resource, NY; 419 (left) Erich Lessing / Art Resource, NY; (right) Vanni / Art Resource, NY; 421 Scala / Art Resource, NY; 422 Dictionary of Art; 427 © British Museum / Art Resource, NY; 431 Erich Lessing / Art Resource, NY; 439 Dictionary of Art; 440 HIP / Art Resource, NY; 442 Metropolitan Museum of Art, Rogers Fund, 1943 (43.11.4) image © Metropolitan Museum of Art; 443 Scala / Art Resource, NY; 444 Scala / Art Resource, NY; 447 Dictionary of Art; 451 Erich Lessing / Art Resource, NY; 457 Dictionary of Art; 457 Dictionary of Art; 462 Dictionary of Art; 464 (left) Dictionary of Art; (right) Dictionary of Art; 466 Dictionary of Art; 469 (top) Scala / Art Resource, NY; (bottom) Nimatallah / Art Resource, NY; 470 Dictionary of Art; 472 Dictionary of Art; 473 Alinari / Art Resource, NY; 474 Scala / Art Resource, NY; 476 Scala / Art Resource, NY; 477 Timothy McCarthy / Art Resource, NY; 479 (left) Scala / Art Resource, NY; (right) Timothy McCarthy / Art Resource, NY; 484 Dictionary of Art; 486 Giraudon / Art Resource, NY; 487 SEF / Art Resource, NY; 489 SEF / Art Resource, NY; 490 Dictionary of Art; 491 Erich Lessing / Art Resource, NY; 492 Dictionary of Art; 494 Réunion des Musées Nationaux / Art Resource, NY; 496 Dictionary of Art; 502 Scala / Art Resource, NY; 503 Scala / Art Resource, NY; 504 Vanni / Art Resource, NY; 507 © British Museum / Art Resource, NY; 508 Dictionary of Art; 509 Erich Lessing / Art Resource, NY; 511 Dictionary of Art; 517 (top) © British Museum / Art Resource, NY; 517 (bottom) Erich Lessing / Art Resource, NY; 522 Dictionary of Art; 529 Bildarchiv Preussischer Kulturbesitz / Art Resource, NY; 534 Erich Lessing / Art Resource, NY; 536 (left) Nimatallah / Art Resource, NY; 536 (right) Réunion des Musées Nationaux / Art Resource, NY; 539 Nimatallah / Art Resource, NY; 540 Scala / Art Resource, NY; 551 Scala / Art Resource, NY; 552 Scala / Art Resource, NY; 561 HIP / Art Resource, NY; 562 Scala / Art Resource, NY; 565 Scala / Art Resource, NY; 568 Scala / Art Resource, NY; 570 Réunion des Musées Nationaux / Art Resource, NY; 579 Alinari / Art Resource, NY; 580 Erich Lessing / Art Resource, NY; 583 Scala / Art Resource, NY; 585 Erich Lessing / Art Resource, NY; 586 Scala / Art Resource, NY; 593 Bildarchiv Preussischer Kulturbesitz / Art Resource, NY; 594 (left) SEF / Art Resource, NY; (right) HIP / Art Resource, NY; 595 Scala / Art Resource, NY; 596 Scala / Art Resource, NY; 597 Scala / Art Resource, NY; 598 Erich Lessing / Art Resource, NY; 599 Scala / Art Resource, NY; 602 Scala / Art Resource, NY; 603 Scala / Art Resource, NY; 604 Scala / Art Resource, NY; 605 Alinari / Art Resource, NY; 613 Dictionary of Art; 614 Nimatallah / Art Resource, NY; 620 Erich Lessing / Art Resource, NY; 625 Bildarchiv Preussischer Kulturbesitz / Art Resource, NY; 626 (left) Dictionary of Art; 626 (right) Erich Lessing / Art Resource, NY; 627 Werner Forman / Art Resource, NY; 628 © British Museum / Art Resource, NY; 630 Vanni / Art Resource, NY; 631 Dictionary of Art; 634 Vanni / Art Resource, NY; 635 Nimatallah / Art Resource, NY; 638 Erich Lessing / Art Resource, NY; 645 Dictionary of Art; 647 Nimatallah / Art Resource, NY; 648 Erich Lessing / Art Resource, NY; 654 Erich Lessing / Art Resource, NY; 655 Vanni / Art Resource, NY; 657 Dictionary of Art; 658 Vanni / Art Resource, NY; 663 (top) Erich Lessing / Art Resource, NY; 663 (bottom) Erich Lessing / Art Resource, NY; 664 HIP / Art Resource, NY; 665 Scala / Art Resource, NY; 672 © British Museum / Art Resource, NY; 681 SEF / Art Resource, NY; 689 Dictionary of Art; 691 Dictionary of Art; 692 Vanni / Art Resource, NY; 698 Réunion des Musées Nationaux / Art Resource, NY; 699 Vanni / Art Resource, NY; 700 (left) Scala / Art Resource, NY; (right) Dictionary of Art; 701 Dictionary of Art; 708 Erich Lessing / Art Resource, NY; 709 Scala / Art Resource, NY; 711 Dictionary of Art; 712 Alinari / Art Resource, NY; 713 Scala / Art Resource, NY; 715 SEF / Art Resource, NY; 716 SEF / Art Resource, NY; 728 Scala / Art Resource, NY; 729 (top) Scala / Art Resource, NY; (bottom) SEF / Art Resource, NY; 730 Alinari / Art Resource, NY; 731 (left) Erich Lessing / Art Resource, NY; 731 (right) Vanni / Art Resource, NY; 732 Dictionary of Art; 733 Alinari / Art Resource, NY; 734 Scala / Art Resource, NY; 735 Dictionary of Art; 740 Erich Lessing / Art Resource, NY; 744 Alinari/Regione Umbria / Art Resource, NY; 745 Alinari/Regione Umbria / Art Resource, NY; 746 Erich Lessing / Art Resource, NY; 754 © British Museum / Art Resource, NY; 755 HIP / Art Resource, NY

Contributors

The contributors listed below are the authors of the original *Dictionary of Art* articles on which most of the entries in this book are based. The extent to which these articles have been altered varies very considerably: in some the revisions consist simply of updated bibliographies, but in others new excavations or new thinking has occasioned significant revision. In some cases the general editor has updated articles or written new ones, but in other instances this task has been assumed by colleagues in the profession, of whom five contributed substantially:

- Alexandra Bounia (University of the Aegean) has supplied a new article on Collection and display of art in the Ancient world.
- Diane Conlin (University of Colorado at Boulder) has written an account of the Villa of Maxentius that takes into account her current excavations.
- Eve D'Ambra (Vassar College) has contributed 4 new articles (Roman Spain, Roman private portraiture, Roman copies of Greek statuary, and Villa Sileen), and has revised articles on Faiyum and Rome (the Imperial Fora, the Oppian Hill and the Palatine Hill).
- Thorsten Opper (British Museum) has written 14 new articles (Antikythera, Antinous, Baiae casts, Balbus, Boscoreale, Delphi *Charioteer*, Loukou, Mummy portrait, Nereid Monument, Oplontis, Parthian Monument, Symposion, Tyrant Slayers, and Villa of the Papyri) and has revised 17 articles (Acrolith, Agrippa, Ara Pacis, Arms and armour, Artemision bronzes, Belvedere Torso, Brauron, Colosseum, Columbarium, Didyma, Herodes Atticus, Library, Palace (Greek), Papyrus, Polychromy, Riace bronzes and Spinario).
- Dimitris Plantzos (University of Peloponnese) has written 11 new articles (Actium Monument, Derveni, Despotikon, Dexamenos of Chios, Dion, Dioskourides, Eleutherna, Lemnos, Leukadia, Macedonian tomb and Pyrgoteles) and has revised 10 articles (Alexandria, Aphrodisias, Cycladic art, Epidauros, Kea, Kouros, Messene, Naxos, Nude and Roman Egypt)

ADAM, SHEILA
ALBANI, JENNY
ALBENDA, PAULINE
ALEXANDER-ADDA, HÉLÈNE
ANASTASSIADIS, AGHIS J.
ANDRONIKOS, MANOLIS
ANSELMI, ALESSANDRA
ANTONACCIO, C. M.
ÅSTRÖM, PAUL
AUPERT, PIERRE
AVERY, CHARLES
BAILEY, DONALD M.
BALTY, JANINE
BALTY, JEAN CH.
BAMMER, ANTON
BARBER, R. L. N.
BARBET, ALIX
BARNISH, S. J. B.
BARTMAN, ELIZABETH
BAXTER, RONALD
BERGE, L.
BERGMANN, BETTINA
BERGMANN, MARIANNE
BETANCOURT, PHILIP
BIANCHI, ROBERT S.
BINGÖL, ORHAN
BIRGE, DARICE
BLAGG, T. F. C.
BLANC, NICOLE
BLOMBERG, MARY
BONFANTE, LARISSA
BORCHHARDT, JURGEN
BOUNIA, ALEXANDRA
BOWSHER, J. M. C.
BRANIGAN, KEITH
BRAUN, THOMAS
BREWSTER, HARRY
BRIJDER, H. A. G.
BRILLIANT, RICHARD
BRINKERHOFF, DERICKSEN
BRODRICK, ANNIE
BROWNING, IAIN
BRUNEAU, PHILIPPE
BUITRON, DIANA
BURFORD, ALISON
BURN, LUCILLA
BURNETT, ANDREW
BUROW, JOHANNES
CADOGAN, GERALD
CAHILL, NICHOLAS
CALVET, YVES
CAMERON, PATRICIA
CAMP, JOHN
CAMPOREALE, GIOVANNANGELO
CARRADICE, IAN
CARTER, JANE BURR
CARTER, JOSEPH COLEMAN
CAVANAGH, W. G.
CHALKIA, EUGENIA
CHAPMAN, HUGH
CLARIDGE, A.
COHEN, BETH
COLDSTREAM, NICOLAS
COLLEDGE, MALCOLM A. R.
CONLIN, DIANA
CONNELLY, JOAN BRETON
COOK, B. F.
COOK, J. M.
COOK, R. M.
COOPER, FREDERICK
CORMACK, S.

COULTON, J. J.
COURTOIS, JACQUES-CLAUDE
CRADDOCK, P. T.
CRISTOFANI, MAURO
CROUWEL, J. H.
CURRIE, C. R. J.
D'ALBIAC, CAROLE
D'AMBRA, EVE
DASZEWSKI, WIKTOR A.
DE BERNARDI FERRERRO, DARIA
DE GRUMMOND, NANCY THOMSON
DELAINE, JANET
DELIVORRIAS, A.
DICKINSON, O. T. P. K.
DINSMOOR, ANASTASIA N.
DINSMOOR JR, WILLIAM B.
DI VITA, ANTONINO
DJURIĆ, SRDJAN
DODGE, HAZEL
DOMANSKY, YA. V.
DÖRIG, JOSÉ
DOUMAS, CHRISTOS G.
DUNBABIN, KATHERINE M. D.
DWYER, EUGENE
EASTON, DONALD F.
EDWARDS, CHARLES M.
EICHBERG, MICHAEL
EISMAN, MICHAEL M.
ELLIS, SIMON P.
ENKLAAR, A. H.
ERIM, KENAN T.
ERISTOV, HÉLÈNE
EVELY, D.
FANTAR, M'HAMED
FAVRO, DIANE
FITTON, J. LESLEY
FORTENBERRY, C. D.
FREY, O.-H.
FREYBERGER, K.
FUCHS, WERNER
FULLERTON, MARK D.
GADBERY, LAURA M.
GEBHARD, ELIZABETH R.
GIACOBBE, LUIGI
GILL, DAVID W. J.
GILL, MARGARET A. V.
GIRAUD, DEMOSTHENIS G.
GOODLETT, VIRGINIA C.
GORING, ELIZABETH
GRAEVE, V. VON
GRANGER-TAYLOR, HERO
GREENEWALT JR, CRAWFORD H.
GROSSMAN, JANET BURNETT
GUBEL, ERIC
GUTMANN, JOSEPH
HACHLILI, RACHEL
HADIDI, ADNAN
HÄGG, ROBIN
HAMMOND, PHILIP C.
HANNESTAD, N.
HARRIS, DIANE
HART, VAUGHAN
HASELBERGER, LOTHAR
HATTERSLEY-SMITH, KARA
HAYES, J. W.
HEDREEN, GUY
HELLMANN, MARIE-CHRISTINE
HELLSTRÖM, P.
HEMELRIJK, J. M.
HEMSOLL, DAVID
HENIG, MARTIN
HENNESSY, J. B.
HERMARY, A.
HIGGINS, REYNOLD
HILLER, STEFAN
HILTON, JEFFREY
HIND, JOHN
HOBEY-HAMSHER, C.
HODGE, A. TREVOR
HOEPFNER, WOLFRAM
HOFFMAN, GAIL L.
HOLLIDAY, PETER J.
HOOD, SINCLAIR
HOWE, THOMAS NOBLE
HUBER, KALINKA
HUMPHREY, J. H.
HURWIT, JEFFREY M.
IMMERWAHR, HENRY R.
JAMES, SIMON
JANNOT, J.-R.
JASHEMSKI, WILHELMINA F.
JESKE, BETTINA
JIDEJIAN, NINA
JOHNS, CATHERINE
JOHNSON, STEPHEN
JOHNSTON, ALAN
JONES, M. WILSON
KALASHNIK, YU. P.
KANE, SUSAN
KIENAST, HERMANN J.
KILIAN-DIRLMEIER, IMMA
KING, ANTHONY
KLEIN, NANCY L.
KLEINBAUER, W. EUGENE
KONSTANTINOPOULOS, GRIGORIS
KURTZ, D. C.
KUTSCHBACH, DORIS
KUTTNER, A.
KYRIELEIS, HELMUT
LANDWEHR, C.
LANGDON, SUSAN
LEBEL, A.
LEBLOND, PASCAL
LE BRUN, A.
LEFTWICH, GREGORY V.
LEHMANN, PHYLLIS WILLIAMS
LENZ, JOHN R.
LEONCINI, LUCA
LEPROHON, R. J.
LEVENTI, I.
LEZZI-HAFTER, ADRIENNE
LINANT DE BELLEFONDS, PASCALE
LITTAUER, M. A.
LLOYD-MORGAN, G.
LOVE, IRIS CORNELIA
LYTTLETON, MARGARET
MACDONALD, WILLIAM L.
MCKENZIE, JUDITH
MCPHEE, IAN
MAIER, FRANZ GEORG
MANNACK, THOMAS
MANNING, W. H.
MARCADE, JEAN
MARTELLI, MARINA
MATHESON, SUSAN B.
MATTUSCH, CAROL C.
MAXMIN, JODY
MEE, CHRISTOPHER
MELLINK, M. J.
MENICHELLA, ANNA
MERRILLEES, R. S.
METCALF, WILLIAM E.
METZGER, HENRI
MEYBOOM, P. G. P.
MICHAELIDES, DEMETRIOS
MIERSE, WILLIAM E.
MILBURN, R. L. P.
MILES, M. M.
MILLER, STEPHEN G.
MITCHELL, STEPHEN
MOIGNARD, ELIZABETH
MOMMSEN, HEIDE
MONTSERRAT, DOMINIC
MOON, WARREN G.
MOORE, MARY B.
MORENO, PAOLO
MORGAN, LYVIA
MORRIS, SARAH P.
MORRISON, KATHRYN
MÜLLER-WIENER, WOLFGANG
MURRAY, CHARLES
MUSS, ULRIKE
NOBLE, JOSEPH VEACH
NOELKE, PETER
NORMAN, NAOMI J.
NORTHEDGE, ALASTAIR
NUSSBAUM, MARTHA C.
OAKLEY, JOHN H.
O'CONNOR, JEROME MURPHY
OGDEN, JACK
OLIVER, ANDREW
ONIANS, JOHN
OPPER, THORSTEN
OSBORNE, JOHN
ØSTBY, ERIK
OUSTERHOUT, ROBERT
PALAGIA, OLGA
PEARSON, ANNE

PELTENBURG, E. J.
PENNANEN, VALERIE HUTCHINSON
PENNY, NICHOLAS
PERCIVAL, JOHN
PETERSON, SARA
PETRAKIS, S. L.
PETRUKHIN, V. YA.
PHILLIPS, DAVID
PIANU, GIAMPIERO
PINTO, JOHN
PIPLI, MARIA
PLANTZOS, DIMITRIS
POTTER, T. W.
POTTS, ALEX
POULTER, ANDREW
POURSAT, JEAN-CLAUDE
PRANGE, MATHIAS
PRICE, JENNIFER
RAMAGE, NANCY H.
RASMUSSEN, TOM
RAUTMANN, M.
RAWSON, ELIZABETH
RENDELI, MARCO
REYNOLDS, JOYCE
RICHARDSON, EMELINE
RICHARDSON, JENNY
RICHARDSON, KIM
RICKERT, FRANZ
RICKMAN, G. E.
RIDDELL, RICHARD
RIDGWAY, DAVID
ROBERTSON, MARTIN
ROGERS, J. M.
ROMANO, DAVID GILMAN
ROMANO, IRENE BALD
ROTROFF, SUSAN I.
ROUX, GEORGES
ROY, J.
RUBINSTEIN, RUTH OLITSKY
SAKELLARAKIS, J. A.
SANDERS, ELMA
SANDERSON, R. W.
SAPOUNA-SAKELLARAKIS, E.
SAREWITZ, E. B.
SCHALLES, HANS-JOACHIM
SCHMIDT, MARGOT
SCHNEIDER, PETER
SCHOFIELD, LOUISE
SCOTT, MARGARET
SEAGER, ANDREW R.
SEAR, F. B.
SERWINT, NANCY
SHEPPARD, ANNE
SHIPLEY, D. GRAHAM J.
SILBERBERG-PEIRCE, SUSAN
SIMON, CHRISTOPHER G.
SMITH, NORMAN A. F.
SMITH, R. R. R.
SNODGRASS, A. M.
SPARKES, B. A.
SPYROPOULOS, THEODORE G.
STEINGRÄBER, STEPHAN
STENTON, E. C.
STEWART, ANDREW F.
STILLMAN, DAMIE
STOPPONI, SIMONETTA
STROCKA, VOLKER MICHAEL
STUPPERICH, REINHARD
TANNER, JEREMY J.
TATTON-BROWN, VERONICA
TAYLOR, TIMOTHY
TEDESCHI GRISANTI, GIOVANNA
TIVERIOS, M. A.
TODD, IAN A.
TOMLINSON, R. A.
TRAN TAM TINH
TSAKIRGIS, BARBARA
TUBB, JONATHAN N.
TURFA, JEAN MACINTOSH
TYACK, GEOFFREY C.
UHLENBROCK, JAIMEE
VAGNETTI, LUCIA
YALOURIS, NICHOLAS
VANDERSLEYEN, CLAUDE
VAN ZANTEN, DAVID
VASSILIKA, ELENI
VERZAR, CHRISTINE
VICKERS, MICHAEL
WALKER, SUSAN
WARDLE, K. A.
WARMA, SUSANNE JULIANE
WARREN, P. M.
WATTS, CAROL MARTIN
WAYWELL, GEOFFREY
WEBB, RUTH
WEBB, VIRGINIA
WEHGARTNER, IRMA
WESCOAT, BONNA D.
WEST, JEFFREY
WHITEHOUSE, DAVID
WHITING, MARY K.
WHITTLE, ALASDAIR
WILFONG, T. G.
WILKES, J. J.
WILKINS, ANN THOMAS
WILLIAMS II, C. K.
WILLIAMS, HECTOR
WILSON, EVA
WILSON, R. J. A.
WINTER, F. E.
WINTER, NANCY A.
WISEMAN, T. P.
WOODFORD, SUSAN
WOODMAN, FRANCIS
WREDE, HENNING
WRIGHT, G. R. H.
YAĞCI, EMEL ERTEN
YEGÜL, FIKRET K.
YON, M.
ZERNER, CAROL
ZEYMAL', YE. V.

Index

Numbers in **bold** refer to volume numbers, numbers in *italics* refer to black-and-white illustrations. **Bold** volume and page numbers designate the main reference on that subject. Colour plates are introduced by the abbreviation pl. and appear after the appropriate volume number.